Literature

Reading Fiction, Poetry, Drama, and the Essay

Literature
Reading Fiction, Poetry, Drama, and the Essay

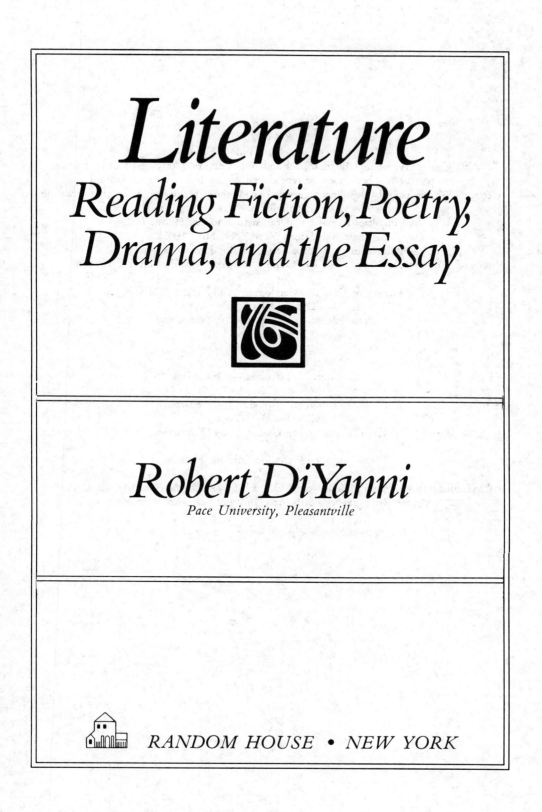

Robert DiYanni
Pace University, Pleasantville

RANDOM HOUSE · NEW YORK

Library of Congress Cataloging in Publication Data
DiYanni, Robert.
Literature: reading fiction, poetry, drama, and
the essay.

Includes index.
1. Literature. 2. Literature—Collections.
I. Title.
PN45.D59 1986   808.8   85-25678
ISBN: 0-394-33774-3
Manufactured in the United States of America

Book and Cover Design: Lorraine Hohman

Cover illustration: Pieter Breughel the Elder, *Landscape with the Fall of Icarus*, c. 1558.
Musées Royeaux des Beaux-Arts, Brussels. Scala Art Resource.

Copyrights and acknowledgments appear on pages 1533–1543.

For
Bill and Ingrid
in gratitude and love

Preface

Literature provides students with an approach to literary works that emphasizes the reading process as an active enterprise involving thought and feeling. While also introducing students to interpretation through illustrated discussions of the elements of literature, it encourages them to value their previous experience with life and with language. Students' subjective responses to texts, especially their emotional reactions to them, are seen as necessary and valuable rather than as something to be denied or discarded. Invited to consider why they respond as they do and how their responses change during subsequent readings of a work, students are asked to relate their experience in reading literature to their experience in living. They are encouraged, moreover, to see literature as a significant reflection of life and an imaginative extension of its possibilities.

Literature emphasizes the intellectual acts involved in the reading process. For each genre, one work is accompanied by an interpolated commentary that explains how readers make sense of texts *as* they read them, focusing particularly on the recursive nature of reading. Marginal annotations for an additional work in each genre are also included. These annotations show students how to become active respondents in their dialogues with texts, and encourage them to use annotation as a first step in writing about literary works (a procedure described more fully in the Appendix, Writing About Literature).

In addition to the emphases on the subjective and the intellectual aspects of the reading process, *Literature* introduces the traditional literary elements by means of discussions closely tied to works in each of the four genres: fiction, poetry, drama, and the essay. Throughout these discussions, students are asked to return to certain works to reconsider them from different perspectives. In Chapter 8, The Elements of Poetry, students are encouraged to reread particular poems as they undertake the study of a different poetic element or technique. Such repetition reinforces the recursive aspect of reading described in the opening chapters on each genre, and demonstrates the necessity of rereading literary works for the fullest possible intellectual, emotional, and aesthetic pleasure.

The poetry section of *Literature* attempts to broaden the study of the genre with two special features: a substantial number of poems in translation and a special selection of poetic transformations. In addition to more than three hundred English and American poems, *Literature* includes more than thirty-five poems translated from eight languages. Goethe and Rilke, Borges and Lorca, Pasternak and Akhmatova are among the poets represented. Included in Chapter 10, Transformations, are alternative translations of poems by Rilke, Jiminez, and Apollinaire. Also included in this chapter are ways in which poets have modified their own and other artists' work by means of revision, parody, and adaptation. Of particular interest are the artistic transformations from one genre to another: poems recast as songs and poems inspired by paintings.

Finally a word about the choice of works. The classic and contemporary selections presented reflect a wide range of styles, voices, subjects, and points of view. Complex and challenging works appear alongside more readily approachable and accessible ones. *Literature,* moreover, includes both types of works in sufficient variety for instructors to assign the more accessible ones for students to read and write about on their own, while reserving the more ambitious selections for class discussion.

Literature represents the cooperative efforts of many people. Steve Pensinger, English Editor, encouraged me to develop the book and supported my work generously and graciously. His associates at Random House brought enthusiasm and intelligence to the project. Thanks in particular to Nina Kingsdale, Ed Maluf, Elisa Turner, Cynthia Ward, Suzanne Thibodeau, Lorraine Hohman, Stacey Alexander, and Sheila Anderson. And thanks especially to Carolyn Viola-John, who as project editor orchestrated the book's production, and as copy editor improved every page she touched, strengthening the book immeasurably.

From readers of various drafts of the manuscript I received thoughtful criticism along with helpful suggestions for improvement. Thanks to the following readers: Stephen Behrendt, University of Nebraska, Lincoln; Barbara Bilson, Santa Monica College; Jon Burton, North Virginia Community College; Cornelius Cronin, Louisiana State University; Charles Crow, Bowling Green State University; Lois Cuddy, University of Rhode Island; Robert Dell, Pace University; Alan Ehmann, University of Texas, El Paso; Ruth Eisenberg, Pace University; Peter Evarts, Oakland University; Chris Farris, University of Washington; Paula Feldman, University of South Carolina; Elizabeth Flynn, Michigan Technological University; Robert Fraser, Bucks County Community College; Susan Gannon, Pace University; Frank Garratt, Tacoma Community College; Harold Gleason, Shippensburg State College; John Hanes, Duquesne University; Jacqueline Hartwich, Bellevue Community College; J. G. Janssen,

University; Jacqueline Hartwich, Bellevue Community College; J. G. Janssen, Arizona State University; Michael Johnson, University of Kansas; Leonard Leff, Oklahoma State University; Barry Maid, University of Arkansas, Little Rock; William McIntosh, United States Military Academy; George Miller, University of Delaware; Hugh Ruppersburg, University of Georgia; Robert Sayre, University of Iowa; Thomas Watson, Louisiana State University; A. K. Weatherhead, University of Oregon; Joseph Zavadil, University of New Mexico; Karl Zender, University of California, Davis.

Four reviewers deserve acknowledgment for their extensive and perceptive comments on matters of fact and interpretation: Richard F. Dietrich, University of South Florida; Kelley Griffith, University of North Carolina, Greensboro; Frank Hodgins, University of Illinois; and Richard Larson, Lehman College, City University of New York. And I take pleasure in acknowledging the expert assistance provided by Robert Lyons, Queens College, City University of New York, and Donald McQuade, University of California, Berkeley, who served as consultants. Their intelligent questions and sound advice helped me very much.

I would also like to thank my colleagues and friends at Queens College and Pace University. I have learned much from our animated conversations and spirited debates about literature. Thanks to Raymond Burns, Nancy Comley, Rosemary Deen, Frances Dell, Robert M. Dell, Douglas Doty, Ruth F. Eisenberg, Edmund Epstein, Susan Gannon, William Heyden, Robert Klaeger, Howard Livingston, Richard Marotta, Richard Podgorski, Donald Ryan, Ian Todd, and Bronislaw Wisniowski.

And finally, I would like to thank my wife, Mary, whose prompting encouraged me to undertake this project and whose assistance enabled me to complete it.

ROBERT DIYANNI

Contents

PART ONE   FICTION   1

CHAPTER ONE   *Reading Stories*   3
The Experience of Fiction   3
Luke *The Prodigal Son*   3
The Process of Reading Fiction   6
Kate Chopin *The Story of an Hour*   6
The Practice of Active Reading   10
Ernest Hemingway *Hills Like White Elephants*   10

CHAPTER TWO   *Types of Short Fiction*   16
Early Forms: Parable, Fable, and Tale   16
Aesop *The Wolf and the Mastiff*   17
Petronius *The Widow of Ephesus*   18
The Short Story   20
The Nonrealistic Story   21
The Short Novel   21

CHAPTER THREE   *Elements of Fiction*   23
Plot and Structure   23
Katherine Mansfield *The Fly*   26

xi

Character 30
 Kay Boyle *Astronomer's Wife*   32
Setting 36
 Joseph Conrad *An Outpost of Progress*   38
Point of View 53
 William Faulkner *A Rose for Emily*   56
Language and Style 62
 James Joyce *Araby*   65
Theme 69
 Guy de Maupassant *The Jewels*   70
Irony 75
 Edgar Allan Poe *The Cask of Amontillado*   77

CHAPTER *Approaching a Story: Guidelines for Reading*   83
FOUR   Luigi Pirandello *War*   84

CHAPTER *A Collection of Short Fiction*   89
FIVE   Nathaniel Hawthorne *Wakefield*   89
          Leo Tolstoy *The Death of Ivan Ilych*
            TRANSLATED BY LOUISE AND AYLMER MAUDE   94
          Sarah Orne Jewett *A White Heron*   131
          Kate Chopin *The Storm*   137
          Anton Chekhov *The Lady with the Dog*
            TRANSLATED BY CONSTANCE GARNETT   141
          Charlotte Perkins Gilman *The Yellow Wallpaper*   152
          Rudyard Kipling *The Gardener*   163
          Stephen Crane *The Bride Comes to Yellow Sky*   169
          James Joyce *The Boarding House*   177
          Franz Kafka *A Hunger Artist*
            TRANSLATED BY WILLA AND EDWIN MUIR   181
          D. H. Lawrence *The Blind Man*   187
          Katherine Mansfield *Bliss*   200
          Katherine Anne Porter *He*   208
          Jean Toomer *Theater*   215
          William Faulkner *The Bear*   218
          Ernest Hemingway *The Short Happy Life of Francis
            Macomber*   228
          Jorge Luis Borges *The Garden of the Forking Paths*
            TRANSLATED BY DONALD YATES   248
          John Steinbeck *The Snake*   254
          Frank O'Connor *Guests of the Nation*   261
          Isaac Bashevis Singer *Gimpel the Fool*
            TRANSLATED BY SAUL BELLOW   269
          Eudora Welty *A Worn Path*   278

Tillie Olsen *I Stand Here Ironing* 284
Ralph Ellison *Battle Royal* 289
Bernard Malamud *Idiots First* 299
Jean Stafford *Bad Characters* 305
Flannery O'Connor *Good Country People* 317
Gabriel Garcia Marquez *A Very Old Man with Enormous Wings*
    TRANSLATED BY GREGORY RABASSA 330
Donald Barthelme *A Shower of Gold* 335
Woody Allen *The Kugelmass Episode* 340
Raymond Carver *Cathedral* 347
Alice Walker *Everyday Use* 357
Leslie Silko *Yellow Woman* 363
Mark Helprin *North Light* 370
Bobbie Ann Mason *Drawing Names* 372

PART TWO POETRY 383

CHAPTER **Reading Poems** 385
SIX **The Experience of Poetry** 385
    Robert Hayden *Those Winter Sundays* 386
The Process of Reading Poetry 387
    Robert Frost *Stopping by Woods on a Snowy Evening* 388
The Practice of Active Reading 390
    Theodore Roethke *My Papa's Waltz* 390
Centering on Subject and Theme 392
    Emily Dickinson *Crumbling is not an instant's Act* 393

CHAPTER **Types of Poetry** 395
SEVEN **Narrative Poetry** 395
Lyric Poetry 397

CHAPTER **Elements of Poetry** 399
EIGHT **Voice: Speaker and Tone** 399
    Stephen Crane *War Is Kind* 400
    Robert Browning *My Last Duchess* 401
    Muriel Stuart *In the Orchard* 404
    Gerard Manley Hopkins *Thou art indeed just, Lord* 405
    Anonymous *Western Wind* 406
    Henry Reed *Naming of Parts* 406
    Jacques Prévert *Family Portrait* 407
Diction 408
    William Wordsworth *I wandered lonely as a cloud* 410

Edwin Arlington Robinson *Miniver Cheevy*   412

William Wordsworth *It is a beauteous evening*   414

Robert Herrick *Delight in Disorder*   414

Adrienne Rich *Rape*   415

Imagery   416

Elizabeth Bishop *First Death in Nova Scotia*   417

William Butler Yeats *The Lake Isle of Innisfree*   420

Robert Browning *Meeting at Night*   420

Hilda Doolittle *Heat*   421

Thomas Hardy *Neutral Tones*   422

Figures of Speech   422

William Shakespeare *That time of year thou may'st in me behold*   424

John Donne *Hymn to God the Father*   425

Robert Wallace *The Double-Play*   426

Louis Simpson *The Battle*   427

Judith Wright *Woman to Child*   428

Symbolism and Allegory   429

Peter Meinke *Advice to My Son*   430

Christina Rossetti *Up-Hill*   432

William Blake *A Poison Tree*   432

Robert Frost *The Road Not Taken*   433

George Herbert *Virtue*   434

Emily Dickinson *Because I could not stop for Death*   435

Syntax   436

John Donne *The Sun Rising*   437

Thomas Hardy *The Man He Killed*   439

William Butler Yeats *An Irish Airman Foresees His Death*   440

Robert Frost *The Silken Tent*   441

E. E. Cummings *"Me up at does"*   442

Stevie Smith *Mother, Among the Dustbins*   443

Sound: Rhyme, Alliteration, Assonance   443

Gerard Manley Hopkins *In the Valley of the Elwy*   446

Thomas Hardy *During Wind and Rain*   447

Alexander Pope *Sound and Sense*   448

May Swenson *The Universe*   449

Helen Chasin *The Word* Plum   450

Rhythm and Meter   451

Robert Frost *The Span of Life*   453

George Gordon, Lord Byron *The Destruction of Sennacherib*   458

Anne Sexton *Her Kind*   459

Richard Wilbur *Junk*   460

William Carlos Williams *The Red Wheelbarrow* 461
James Shirley *The Glories of Our Blood and State* 462
Structure: Closed and Open Forms 463
John Keats *On First Looking into Chapman's Homer* 464
Walt Whitman *When I heard the learn'd astronomer* 465
E. E. Cummings *l(a* 466
E. E. Cummings *[Buffalo Bill's]* 468
William Carlos Williams *The Dance* 469
Denise Levertov *O Taste and See* 470
Theodore Roethke *The Waking* 470
A. R. Ammons *Poetics* 471
C. P. Cavafy *The City* 472

CHAPTER NINE   *Approaching a Poem: Guidelines for Reading* 474
Gerard Manley Hopkins *Spring and Fall: to a Young Child* 475

CHAPTER TEN   *Transformations* 478
Revisions 478
John Keats From *The Eve of St. Agnes* 478
William Blake *London* 479
William Butler Yeats *A Dream of Death* 482
Emily Dickinson *The Wind begun to knead the Grass* 483
D. H. Lawrence *The Piano* 484
Parodies 485
William Carlos Williams *This Is Just to Say* 486
Kenneth Koch *Variations on a Theme by William Carlos Williams* 486
Anthony Brode *Breakfast with Gerard Manley Hopkins* 487
William Shakespeare *Shall I compare thee to a summer's day* 488
Howard Moss *Shall I Compare Thee to a Summer's Day?* 488
Translations 489
Rainer Maria Rilke *Der Panther*
    TRANSLATED BY STEPHEN MITCHELL AND C. F. MacINTYRE 489
Guillaume Apollinaire *Le Pont Mirabeau*
    TRANSLATED BY RICHARD WILBUR AND W. S. MERWIN 491
Juan Ramón Jiménez *Nocturno Soñado*
    TRANSLATED BY ELEANOR L. TURNBULL AND THOMAS McGREEVY 493

Adaptations   495
    Ecclesiastes *There is a Time*   495
    Pete Seeger *Turn! Turn! Turn!*   496
    Edwin Arlington Robinson *Richard Cory*   497
    Paul Simon *Richard Cory*   497
    Langston Hughes *Dream Deferred*   498
    Langston Hughes *Same in Blues*   499
Poems and Paintings   500
    Vincent Van Gogh *The Starry Night*   501
    Robert Fagles *The Starry Night*   501
    Francesco Goya y Lucientes *The Third of May*   502
    Lawrence Ferlinghetti *In Goya's greatest scenes we seem to
      see*   502
    Francesco Goya y Lucientes Two scenes from *The Disasters
      of War*   503
    Andrey Voznesensky *I Am Goya*   503
    Pieter Breughel the Elder *Landscape with the Fall of
      Icarus*   504
    William Carlos Williams *Landscape with the Fall of
      Icarus*   504
    W. H. Auden *Musée des Beaux Arts*   505
    Pieter Breughel the Elder *Hunters in the Snow*   506
    Joseph Langland *Hunters in the Snow: Breughel*   506
    John Berryman *Winter Landscape*   507
    William Blake *The Sick Rose* (engraving)   508
    William Blake *The Sick Rose* (poem)   508

CHAPTER   ***A Collection of Poems***   511
ELEVEN   Anonymous *Lord Randal*   511
    Anonymous *The Twa Corbies*   512
    Anonymous *Sir Patrick Spens*   513
    Anonymous *Edward, Edward*   515
    Anonymous *The Unquiet Grave*   517
    Anonymous *The Demon Lover*   518
    Geoffrey Chaucer *Truth*   520
    John Skelton *To Mistress Margaret Hussey*   521
    Thomas Wyatt *The long love that in my thought doth
      harbor*   522
    Thomas Wyatt *They flee from me*   522
    Henry Howard, Earl of Surrey *Love, that doth reign and
      live within my thought*   523
    Edmund Spenser *One day I wrote her name upon the
      strand*   523

Sir Walter Raleigh *The Lie* 524

Sir Walter Raleigh *The Nymph's Reply to the Shepherd* 526

Sir Philip Sidney From *Astrophel and Stella* 527

Sir Philip Sidney *Thou blind man's mark* 527

Chidiock Tichborne *Tichborne's Elegy* 528

Michael Drayton *Since there's no help, come let us kiss and part* 528

Christopher Marlowe *The Passionate Shepherd to His Love* 529

William Shakespeare *When in disgrace with fortune and men's eyes* 530

William Shakespeare *Not marble, nor the gilded monuments* 530

William Shakespeare *Let me not to the marriage of true minds* 531

William Shakespeare *Th' expense of spirit in a waste of shame* 531

William Shakespeare *My mistress' eyes are nothing like the sun* 531

Thomas Nashe *A Litany in Time of Plague* 532

John Donne *Song* 533

John Donne *The Canonization* 534

John Donne *The Anniversary* 535

John Donne *A Valediction: Forbidding Mourning* 536

John Donne *The Flea* 537

John Donne *Death, be not proud* 538

John Donne *Batter my heart, three-personed God* 538

Ben Jonson *On My First Daughter* 539

Ben Jonson *On My First Son* 539

Ben Jonson *Still to be neat, still to be dressed* 539

Ben Jonson *Come, my Celia* 540

Ben Jonson *Song: To Celia* 540

Ben Jonson *A Hymn to God the Father* 541

Robert Herrick *Upon Julia's Clothes* 542

Robert Herrick *To the Virgins, to Make Much of Time* 542

George Herbert *The Altar* 543

George Herbert *Denial* 543

George Herbert *The Pulley* 544

George Herbert *Man* 545

George Herbert *Love (III)* 546

John Milton *When I consider how my light is spent* 547

John Milton *On the Late Massacre in Piedmont* 547

Anne Bradstreet *Before the Birth of One of Her Children* 548

Anne Bradstreet *To My Dear and Loving Husband* 548

Andrew Marvell *To His Coy Mistress* 549

Andrew Marvell *A Dialogue Between the Soul and Body* 550

John Dryden *To the Memory of Mr. Oldham* 551

John Dryden *A Song for St. Cecilia's Day* 552

Jonathan Swift *A Description of the Morning* 554

Alexander Pope *Epigram Engraved on the Collar of a Dog Which I Gave to His Royal Highness* 555

Alexander Pope From *An Essay on Man* 555

Thomas Gray *Elegy Written in a Country Churchyard* 555

Johann Wolfgang von Goethe *Nature and Art* 559

William Blake *The Clod & the Pebble* 560

William Blake *The Lamb* 560

William Blake *The Tyger* 561

William Blake *The Garden of Love* 561

William Blake *Mock on, Mock on, Voltaire, Rousseau* 562

Robert Burns *A Red, Red Rose* 562

Robert Burns *Green grow the rashes* 563

William Wordsworth *The world is too much with us* 564

William Wordsworth *The Solitary Reaper* 564

William Wordsworth *She was a Phantom of delight* 565

William Wordsworth *Composed upon Westminster Bridge, September 3, 1802* 566

William Wordsworth *Lines Composed a Few Miles Above Tintern Abbey* 566

Samuel Taylor Coleridge *Kubla Khan* 570

George Gordon, Lord Byron *She walks in beauty* 572

Percy Bysshe Shelley *Ozymandias* 572

Percy Bysshe Shelley *Ode to the West Wind* 573

John Keats *When I have fears* 575

John Keats *La Belle Dame sans Merci* 576

John Keats *Ode to a Nightingale* 577

John Keats *Ode on a Grecian Urn* 579

Ralph Waldo Emerson *Concord Hymn* 581

Ralph Waldo Emerson *Hamatreya* 581

Edgar Allan Poe *To Helen* 583

Alfred, Lord Tennyson *Ulysses* 584

Alfred, Lord Tennyson *Tithonus* 585

Alfred, Lord Tennyson *The Eagle* 587

Alfred, Lord Tennyson From *In Memoriam A.H.H.*
   Dark house, by which once more I stand   587
   Thy voice is on the rolling air   588
Robert Browning *Soliloquy of the Spanish Cloister*   588
Emily Brontë *Remembrance*   591
Walt Whitman *A noiseless patient spider*   592
Walt Whitman *Vigil strange I kept on the field one
   night*   592
Walt Whitman *The Dalliance of the Eagles*   593
Walt Whitman *Crossing Brooklyn Ferry*   593
Matthew Arnold *Dover Beach*   597
Emily Dickinson *A narrow Fellow in the Grass*   599
Emily Dickinson *I like a look of Agony*   599
Emily Dickinson *Wild Nights—Wild Nights*   600
Emily Dickinson *After great pain, a formal feeling
   comes*   600
Emily Dickinson *Much Madness is divinest Sense*   601
Emily Dickinson *I died for Beauty—but was scarce*   601
Emily Dickinson *I heard a Fly buzz—when I died*   601
Emily Dickinson *The Bustle in a House*   602
Emily Dickinson *Tell all the Truth but tell it slant*   602
Emily Dickinson *Apparently with no surprise*   602
Lewis Carroll *Jabberwocky*   603
Thomas Hardy *The Darkling Thrush*   604
Thomas Hardy *The Ruined Maid*   605
Thomas Hardy *The Oxen*   605
Thomas Hardy *The Voice*   606
Thomas Hardy *Transformations*   606
Thomas Hardy *Channel Firing*   607
Thomas Hardy *Ah, are you digging on my grave*   608
Gerard Manley Hopkins *God's Grandeur*   609
Gerard Manley Hopkins *The Windhover*   609
Gerard Manley Hopkins *Pied Beauty*   610
Gerard Manley Hopkins *Binsey Poplars*   610
A. E. Housman *When I was one-and-twenty*   611
A. E. Housman *To an Athlete Dying Young*   612
A. E. Housman *With rue my heart is laden*   612
A. E. Housman *Is my team plowing*   613
William Butler Yeats *Adam's Curse*   614
William Butler Yeats *The Scholars*   615
William Butler Yeats *The Magi*   615
William Butler Yeats *Easter*   615
William Butler Yeats *The Second Coming*   617

William Butler Yeats *The Wild Swans at Coole*   618
William Butler Yeats *Leda and the Swan*   619
William Butler Yeats *Sailing to Byzantium*   619
William Butler Yeats *A Prayer for my Daughter*   620
William Butler Yeats *Crazy Jane Talks with the
    Bishop*   622
William Butler Yeats *Long-Legged Fly*   623
Edwin Arlington Robinson *Mr. Flood's Party*   624
Edwin Arlington Robinson *The Sheaves*   625
Edwin Arlington Robinson *Eros Turannos*   626
Paul Laurence Dunbar *We wear the mask*   627
Amy Lowell *Patterns*   628
Robert Frost *Mending Wall*   630
Robert Frost *Fire and Ice*   631
Robert Frost *Dust of Snow*   632
Robert Frost *Design*   632
Robert Frost *Desert Places*   632
Robert Frost *Tree at my window*   633
Robert Frost *Acquainted with the night*   633
Robert Frost *Putting in the Seed*   634
Robert Frost *To Earthward*   634
Rainer Maria Rilke *Going Blind*   635
Rainer Maria Rilke *The Swan*   636
Rainer Maria Rilke *Portrait of My Father as a
    Young Man*   636
Rainer Maria Rilke *Spanish Dancer*   637
Wallace Stevens *The Snow Man*   637
Wallace Stevens *Thirteen Ways of Looking at a
    Blackbird*   638
Wallace Stevens *The house was quiet and the world was
    calm*   640
William Carlos Williams *The Widow's Lament in
    Springtime*   640
William Carlos Williams *Spring and All*   641
William Carlos Williams *A Sort of a Song*   642
William Carlos Williams *To A Poor Old Woman*   642
William Carlos Williams *The Young Housewife*   643
William Carlos Williams *Danse Russe*   643
William Carlos Williams *Tract*   644
D. H. Lawrence *The Elephant Is Slow to Mate—*   645
D. H. Lawrence *Snake*   646
Ezra Pound *The Seafarer*   648
Ezra Pound *The Garden*   651
Ezra Pound *The River-Merchant's Wife: A Letter*   651

Marianne Moore *Poetry* 652
T. S. Eliot *Preludes* 653
T. S. Eliot *Journey of the Magi* 655
T. S. Eliot *The Love Song of J. Alfred Prufrock* 656
John Crowe Ransom *Bells for John Whiteside's
  Daughter* 659
John Crowe Ransom *Piazza Piece* 660
John Crowe Ransom *Blue Girls* 660
John Crowe Ransom *Winter Remembered* 661
Anna Akhmatova *Requiem* 662
Boris Pasternak *Winter Night* 668
Claude McKay *The Tropics in New York* 669
Claude McKay *If we must die* 670
Marina Tsvetayeva *No one has taken anything away* 670
Marina Tsvetayeva *Yesterday he still looked in my eyes* 671
Vicente Huidobro *Ars Poetica* 672
Archibald MacLeish *Ars Poetica* 673
Archibald MacLeish *You, Andrew Marvell* 674
Archibald MacLeish *"Not Marble Nor the Gilded
  Monuments"* 675
César Vallejo *Our Daily Bread* 676
César Vallejo *The Distant Footsteps* 677
Wilfred Owen *Dulce et Decorum Est* 677
E. E. Cummings *anyone lived in a pretty how town* 678
E. E. Cummings *nobody loses all the time* 679
E. E. Cummings *my father moved through dooms of love* 680
Jean Toomer *Reapers* 682
Juana de Ibarbourou *The Strong Bond* 683
Robert Graves *Symptoms of Love* 684
Eugenio Montale *The Eel* 684
Federico Garcia Lorca *Lament for Ignacio Sanchez
  Mejias* 685
Jorge Luis Borges *Chess* 690
Jorge Luis Borges *The Blind Man* 691
Robert Francis *Pitcher* 691
Countee Cullen *Incident* 692
Richard Eberhart *The Groundhog* 692
Pablo Neruda *The Word* 694
Pablo Neruda *The United Fruit Co.* 695
Robert Penn Warren *True Love* 697
Robert Penn Warren *The Corner of the Eye* 698
W. H. Auden *The Unknown Citizen* 699
W. H. Auden *Sonnets from China, XVIII* 700
W. H. Auden *In Memory of W. B. Yeats* 700

W. H. Auden *O where are you going?* 702
W. H. Auden *O what is that sound* 703
A. D. Hope *Coup de Grâce* 704
A. D. Hope *Imperial Adam* 705
Theodore Roethke *Elegy for Jane* 706
Theodore Roethke *The Premonition* 707
Elizabeth Bishop *The Fish* 707
Elizabeth Bishop *Sestina* 709
Octavio Paz *January First* 710
William Stafford *Traveling through the dark* 711
Dudley Randall *The Melting Pot* 712
Dudley Randall *George* 713
Dylan Thomas *The force that through the green fuse drives the flower* 713
Dylan Thomas *A Refusal to Mourn the Death, by Fire, of a Child in London* 714
Dylan Thomas *Fern Hill* 715
Dylan Thomas *In my craft or sullen art* 716
Dylan Thomas *Do not go gentle into that good night* 717
Margaret Walker *Lineage* 717
Robert Lowell *Skunk Hour* 718
Gwendolyn Brooks *the mother* 719
Gwendolyn Brooks *First fight. Then Fiddle* 720
Lawrence Ferlinghetti *Constantly Risking Absurdity* 721
May Swenson *Women should be pedestals* 722
May Swenson *The Watch* 722
Richard Wilbur *Mind* 723
Richard Wilbur *Juggler* 724
Marie Ponsot *Summer Sestina* 725
Philip Larkin *A Study of Reading Habits* 726
James Dickey *The Lifeguard* 727
Louis Simpson *The Heroes* 728
Louis Simpson *Walt Whitman at Bear Mountain* 729
Yves Bonnefoy *Place of the Salamander* 730
Alan Dugan *Funeral Oration for a Mouse* 731
Yehuda Amichai *The eternal mystery* 732
Yehuda Amichai *You Can Rely on Him* 733
Donald Justice *Men at forty* 733
Donald Justice *In Bertram's Garden* 734
Maxine Kumin *How It Is* 734
Philip Appleman *Ten Definitions of Lifetime* 735
A. R. Ammons *Corsons Inlet* 737
A. R. Ammons *The City Limits* 740

Robert Creeley *I Know a Man*   741
Robert Creeley *The Rain*   741
Robert Creeley *The Language*   742
Allen Ginsberg *A Supermarket in California*   743
W. D. Snodgrass *April Inventory*   743
Ruth F. Eisenberg *Jocasta*   745
Galway Kinnell *To Christ Our Lord*   754
Galway Kinnell *The Apple Tree*   755
Galway Kinnell *The Still Time*   756
Galway Kinnell *Saint Francis and the Sow*   757
James Wright *Lying in a Hammock at William Duffy's Farm
   in Pine Island, Minnesota*   757
James Wright *The Jewel*   758
James Wright *Mutterings Over the Crib of a Deaf
   Child*   758
James Wright *A Blessing*   759
W. S. Merwin *When you go away*   760
W. S. Merwin *Separation*   760
Donald Hall *My son, my executioner*   760
Donald Hall *Kicking the leaves*   761
Philip Levine *Let me begin again*   764
Anne Sexton *Two Hands*   765
Anne Sexton *Us*   765
Anne Sexton *The Starry Night*   766
Anne Sexton *Ringing the Bells*   767
Adrienne Rich *Night-pieces: For a Child*   768
Adrienne Rich *A Valediction Forbidding Mourning*   769
Adrienne Rich *Trying to Talk with a Man*   769
Adrienne Rich *Aunt Jennifer's Tigers*   770
Donald Finkel *Hunting Song*   771
X. J. Kennedy *In a prominent bar in Secaucus one day*   772
X. J. Kennedy *First Confession*   773
Thom Gunn *Innocence*   774
John Hollander *Adam's Task*   775
John Hollander *Swan and Shadow*   776
Ted Hughes *Hawk Roosting*   777
Ted Hughes *Crow's First Lesson*   777
Gregory Corso *Marriage*   778
Gary Snyder *Prayer for the Great Family*   781
Sylvia Plath *Mirror*   782
Sylvia Plath *Tulips*   783
John Updike *The Mosquito*   784
Robert Wallace *In a Spring Still Not Written Of*   784

Yevgeny Yevtushenko *People* 785
Andrey Voznesensky *Monastic Cell at Zagorsk* 787
Mark Strand *Eating Poetry* 788
Robert Mezey *My Mother* 788
Bella Akhmadulina *The Bride* 790
Seamus Heaney *Digging* 791
Seamus Heaney *The Trout* 792
Seamus Heaney *Mid-Term Break* 792
Seamus Heaney *Death of a Naturalist* 793
Margaret Atwood *This Is a Photograph of Me* 794
Raymond Carver *Photograph of My Father in His
    Twenty-second Year* 795
Nikki Giovanni *Dreams* 795
Nikki Giovanni *Ego Tripping* 796
James Tate *The Lost Pilot* 797

PART THREE DRAMA 801

CHAPTER   **Reading Plays** 803
TWELVE   **The Experience of Drama** 803
          Henrik Ibsen *A Doll House* (opening scene from Act I)
          805
          The Process of Reading Drama 810
          Bernard Shaw *Arms and the Man* (scene from Act II)
          810
          The Practice of Active Reading 815
          Sophocles *Antigonê* (excerpt from Scene II) 816

CHAPTER   **Types of Drama** 819
THIRTEEN **Tragedy** 819
          Comedy 821
          Tragicomedy 822

CHAPTER   **Elements of Drama** 823
FOUR-   **Plot** 823
TEEN   **Character** 824
          Dialogue 825
          Staging 828
          Theme 829

CHAPTER   **Approaching a Play: Guidelines for Reading** 831
FIFTEEN   Isabella Augusta Persse, Lady Gregory *The Rising of the
          Moon* 832

CHAPTER
SIXTEEN

The Greek Theater　842

Sophocles *Oedipus Rex*
TRANSLATED BY DUDLEY FITTS AND
ROBERT FITZGERALD　844
Sophocles *Antigonê*
TRANSLATED BY DUDLEY FITTS AND
ROBERT FITZGERALD　885

CHAPTER
SEVEN-
TEEN

The Elizabethan Theater　917

William Shakespeare *Othello*　919

CHAPTER
EIGHTEEN

The Neoclassical French Theater　1005

Molière (Jean Baptiste Poquelin) *Tartuffe*
TRANSLATED BY RICHARD WILBUR　1006

CHAPTER
NINETEEN

The Modern Realistic Theater　1060

Henrik Ibsen *A Doll House*
TRANSLATED BY ROLF FJELDE　1061
August Strindberg *The Father*
TRANSLATED BY MICHAEL MEYER　1113
Anton Chekhov *The Cherry Orchard*
TRANSLATED BY AVRAHM YARMOLINSKY　1148
Bernard Shaw *Arms and the Man*　1185

CHAPTER
TWENTY

The Theater of the Absurd　1232

Eugène Ionesco *The Lesson*
TRANSLATED BY DONALD M. ALLEN　1234

CHAPTER
TWENTY-
ONE

A Collection of Twentieth-Century Plays　1257

Susan Glaspell *Suppressed Desires*　1258
Arthur Miller *Death of a Salesman*　1271
Robert Bolt *A Man for All Seasons*　1342

PART FOUR　THE ESSAY　1411

CHAPTER
TWENTY-
TWO

Reading Essays　1413

The Experience of the Essay　1413
E. B. White *The Ring of Time*　1414
The Process of Reading the Essay　1418
George Orwell *Marrakech*　1418
The Practice of Active Reading　1424
Francis Bacon *Of Youth and Age*　1425

CHAPTER TWENTY-THREE **Types of Essay** 1428
Speculative Essays 1428
Argumentative Essays 1429
Narrative Essays 1429
Expository Essays 1430

CHAPTER TWENTY-FOUR **Elements of the Essay** 1431
Voice 1431
Joan Didion *Los Angeles Notebook* 1433
Style 1435
Henry David Thoreau *The Battle of the Ants* 1439
Structure 1441
Virginia Woolf *The Death of the Moth* 1442
Thought 1444
Francis Bacon *Of Revenge* 1446

CHAPTER TWENTY-FIVE **Approaching an Essay: Guidelines for Reading** 1448
Annie Dillard *Living Like Weasels* 1449

CHAPTER TWENTY-SIX **A Collection of Essays** 1454
Francis Bacon *Of Love* 1454
John Donne *Meditation XVII (For Whom the Bell Tolls)* 1455
Jonathan Swift *A Modest Proposal* 1457
Charles Lamb *A Dissertation Upon Roast Pig* 1462
Mark Twain *"Cub" Wants to Be a Pilot* 1467
E. M. Forster *Our Graves in Gallipoli* 1471
E. B. White *Once More to the Lake* 1473
George Orwell *Shooting an Elephant* 1477
Loren Eiseley *The Judgment of the Birds* 1482
James Baldwin *Notes of a Native Son* 1488
Tom Wolfe *The Right Stuff* 1501
Alice Walker *In Search of Our Mothers' Gardens* 1510

APPENDIX: WRITING ABOUT LITERATURE 1518
GLOSSARY 1528
INDEX OF AUTHORS, TITLES, AND FIRST LINES 1544

Literature
Reading Fiction, Poetry, Drama, and the Essay

Fiction

PART ONE

CHAPTER ONE

Reading Stories

THE EXPERIENCE OF FICTION

We read stories for pleasure; they entertain us. And we read them for profit; they enlighten us. Stories engage us by drawing us into their imaginative worlds and by holding us with the power of their invention. They provide us with more than the immediate interest of narrative—of something happening—more even than the pleasures of imagination: they can enlarge our understanding of ourselves and deepen our appreciation of life.

Consider this famous early story about a father and his two sons:

The Prodigal Son

A certain man had two sons: and the younger of them said to his father, "Father, give me the portion of goods that falleth to me." And he divided unto them his living. And not many days after, the younger son gathered all together, and took his journey into a far country, and there wasted his substance with riotous living. And when he had spent all, there arose a mighty famine in that land, and he began to be in want. And he went and joined himself to a citizen of that country, and he sent him into his fields to feed swine. And he would fain have filled his belly with the husks that the swine did eat: and no man gave unto him. And when he came to himself, he said, "How many hired servants of my father's have bread enough and to spare, and I perish with hunger? I will arise and go to my father, and will say unto him, 'Father, I have sinned against heaven, and before thee. And am no more worthy to be called thy son: make me as one of thy hired servants.' " And he arose, and came to his father. But when he was yet a great way off, his father saw him, and had compassion, and ran, and fell on his neck, and kissed him. And the son said unto him, "Father, I have sinned against heaven, and in thy sight, and am no more worthy to be called thy son." But the father said to his servants, "Bring forth the best robe, and put it on him, and put a ring on his hand, and shoes on his feet. And bring hither the fatted calf, and kill it, and let us eat, and be merry. For this my son was dead, and is alive again; he was lost, and is found." And they began to be merry. Now his elder son was in the field, and as he came and drew nigh to the house, he heard music and dancing. And he called one of the servants, and asked what these things meant. And he said unto him, "Thy brother is come, and thy father hath killed the fatted calf, because he hath received him safe and sound." And he was angry, and would not go in: therefore came his father out, and entreated him. And he answering said to his father, "Lo, these many years do I serve thee, neither transgressed I at any time thy commandment, and yet thou never gavest me a kid, that I might make merry with my friends: but as soon as this thy son was come, which hath devoured thy living with harlots, thou hast killed for him the fatted calf." And he said unto him, "Son, thou art ever with me, and all that I have is thine. It was meet that we should make merry, and be glad: for this thy brother was dead, and is alive again: and was lost, and is found."

What is your reaction to "The Prodigal Son"? Did the story catch and hold your interest? Did it engage your feelings? Describe your response to each character. Is the story directed toward a particular point?

Whether we are reading "The Prodigal Son" for the first, second, or the hundredth time, we do certain things mentally as we read. We first observe details: we notice elements of action and description, of language and form. We take in the story's surface details, making sense of the story by making connections among them. From these details we make inferences about the characters and their motivation. In "The Prodigal Son," for example, we notice that the father sees his younger son coming from *far off,* that he *runs* to him, falls on his *neck,* and kisses him. These details imply that the father has been watching for him, hoping for his return. Moreover, the father's actions speak eloquently of his unreserved acceptance of his son and of deep joy at his return. Reflecting on these actions, we may connect them with the father's behavior toward his elder son and wonder what is responsible for the difference.

Our experience of reading stories, however, involves something else: that we see a story as a story, even as a particular *kind* of story. We know, for example, that "The Prodigal Son" is not a factual newspaper account of the actions of a particular father and son. A journalistic account would have included their names, perhaps their ages and address, and details about the prodigal son's behavior in the foreign land, which would have been identified. But the story gives none of this information. In fact, the details included are not those we would typically expect to find in a newspaper account. It's not just that "The Prodigal Son" is short on information, but that it goes out of its way to include the kind of repetitions, for example, that would be considered unnecessary in a factual account.

Knowing that "The Prodigal Son" is a *fiction,* an imagined story that is not based on historical fact, and knowing the conventions or implicit rules of fiction is helpful to our reading. For this story is also more than a fiction to be distinguished from fact; it is a particular kind of fiction—a *parable* or brief story that teaches a lesson, often religious or spiritual in nature. As someone once cleverly put it, a parable is "an earthly story with a heavenly meaning." Parables point toward spiritual beliefs or truths and should be read symbolically, with emphasis on their spiritual meaning.

But we must go further. "The Prodigal Son" is a Christian parable—not a Hebrew or Zen parable. It was spoken by Jesus roughly two thousand years ago and recorded by the evangelist Luke in his New Testament Gospel. Aware of these facts, we look to the parable for a religious idea consistent with Jesus's teaching generally. If we have never read or heard one of Jesus's parables, or if we are unfamiliar with his teachings, then our experience and understanding of the parable will differ significantly from that of readers who have such knowledge. Each reader experiences a story differently. In the case of this parable, our response and understanding depend on our religious background, our literary sophistication, our familial situation. A woman might experience the story differently than a man; and our own experience of it at one stage of our lives (as sons or daughters, for example) will differ from our understanding and response at another (as parents).

To suggest that such differences exist, however, is not to indicate that "The Prodigal Son" has no central point, that it can mean whatever we want it to. As a parable, it has a religious meaning that may be paraphrased like this: God (the father) is willing to forgive man (the prodigal son) any sin man commits, no matter how grievous, if only he repents and asks God's forgiveness. Alternatively: God is eager to welcome the sinner back, and in fact is happier at his return than with the fidelity of those in no spiritual danger. We can read the parable, thus, as an example of God's love, as an illustration of man's need for repentance, or as a description of the relationship between God and man—or as all three.

Whatever we decide about its religious meaning, we should realize that it means, finally, more than any interpretive comments we can make about it. This is so because the full meaning of any literary text includes our experience in reading it as well as our understanding of it. It includes, that is, our emotional apprehension as well as our intellectual comprehension. It includes our thoughts and feelings both during our reading and afterwards. These thoughts and feelings include valuable precritical responses, our instinctive reactions to a story before we have had time to explain it to ourselves. Such perceptions change in subsequent readings partly because we know the work better, partly because we bring different selves to our reading.

It might be helpful at this point to share your ideas and feelings about "The Prodigal Son" with other readers. If that's not possible, you can jot in a notebook or in the margins of the text. Upon rereading the parable, keep the following questions in mind:

1. What is the function of the elder son? What would be gained or lost if he were omitted, if that is, the parable ended with the sentence, "And they began to make merry"?
2. How does the elder son react to his brother's return and to his father's response to it? Notice not only what the elder son says, but how he says it.
3. Two lines of dialogue are repeated, one by the father and one by the prodigal son. What does each reveal?
4. How does the father answer the prodigal son's request for forgiveness? What could he have said? What does his response reveal?
5. How do you feel about the characters? Did your feelings change as you read or reread it?

THE PROCESS OF READING FICTION

In our comments about reading "The Prodigal Son" we mentioned the importance of observing details and making connections among them—of making inferences based on what we notice. Another aspect of the reading process, however, concerns the way we actually move through a text, looking forwards and backwards at the same time. In reading stories we anticipate what is to come based on our memory of what has gone before. And even though we may read stories linearly, line by line, sentence by sentence, page by page, this linearity belies what happens mentally as we read. Our mental action is cyclical rather than linear. We project ahead and we glance back; we remember and we predict. By doing so, we are able to follow and understand a story in the first place, and to see more in it on subsequent readings.

To highlight this aspect of the reading process, we print Kate Chopin's "The Story of an Hour" with interpolated comments. The comments suggest the kinds of observations and connections we might make as we move back and forth through the story.

KATE CHOPIN

[1851–1904]

The Story of an Hour

Knowing that Mrs. Mallard was afflicted with a heart trouble, great care was taken to break to her as gently as possible the news of her husband's death.

It was her sister Josephine who told her, in broken sentences, veiled hints that revealed in half concealing. Her husband's friend Richards was there, too, near her. It was he who had been in the newspaper office when intelligence of the railroad disaster was received, with Brently Mallard's name leading the list of "killed." He had only taken the time to assure himself of its truth by a second telegram, and had hastened to forestall any less careful, less tender friend in bearing the sad message.

She did not hear the story as many women have heard the same, with a paralyzed inability to accept its significance. She wept at once, with sudden, wild abandonment, in her sister's arms. When the storm of grief had spent itself she went away to her room alone. She would have no one follow her.

Comment   The opening action is presented quickly and economically. We are not given Mrs. Mallard's first name. And we might wonder if there is any significance in the name "Mallard." Do we hear something odd in the expression of Mrs. Mallard's ailment as a "heart trouble"? More important than these details is the announcement of her husband's death. Mrs. Mallard is contrasted with other women who sit paralyzed by such news—women who refuse, initially at least, to accept the significance of such an announcement. Is there a difference between accepting the significance of a husband's death and accepting the simple fact of his death? We notice, finally, that Mrs. Mallard weeps with "sudden wild abandonment." The story continues:

There stood, facing the open window, a comfortable, roomy armchair. Into this she sank, pressed down by a physical exhaustion that haunted her body and seemed to reach into her soul.

She could see in the open square before her house the tops of trees that were all aquiver with the new spring life. The delicious breath of rain was in the air. In the street below a peddler was crying his wares. The notes of a distant song which some one was singing reached her faintly, and countless sparrows were twittering in the eaves.

There were patches of blue sky showing here and there through the clouds that had met and piled above the other in the west facing her window.

She sat with her head thrown back upon the cushion of the chair quite motionless, except when a sob came up into her throat and shook her, as a child who has cried itself to sleep continues to sob in its dreams.

Comment   The setting for the middle section of the story is Mrs. Mallard's room. We wonder whether the open window through which she looks is of any significance. Do the details that follow—trees, birds, rain, patches of blue sky, peddler, and song—have anything in common? We notice also that Mrs. Mallard is compared to a child who sobs in its dreams and may wonder about the implications of this comparison.

She was young, with a fair, calm face, whose lines bespoke repression and even a certain strength. But now there was a dull stare in her eyes, whose gaze was fixed away off yonder on one of those patches of blue sky. It was not a glance of reflection, but rather indicated a suspension of intelligent thought.

There was something coming to her and she was waiting for it, fearfully. What was it? She did not know; it was too subtle and elusive to name. But she felt it, creeping out of the sky, reaching toward her through the sounds, the scents, the color that filled the air.

Now her bosom rose and fell tumultuously. She was beginning to recognize this thing that was approaching to possess her, and she was striving to beat it back with her will—as powerless as her two white slender hands would have been.

Comment   These paragraphs slightly alter the tone and pace of the story. We are not told what Mrs. Mallard is waiting for. Whatever it is, however, she *feels* it; she senses it coming as she looks out the window. And we see her resisting it—powerlessly. Do we perhaps also hear sexual overtones in the description of what is "approaching to possess" her? Or do we wish to assign religious or psychological significance to this imminent possession and her ambivalent feelings about it? We notice, in addition, that Mrs. Mallard is described as not conscious of what is happening to her. Chopin says that there is "a suspension of intelligent thought." She seems to *feel* rather than think.

When she abandoned herself a little whispered word escaped her slightly parted lips. She said it over and over under her breath: "Free, free, free!" The vacant stare and the look of terror that had followed it went from her eyes. They stayed keen and bright. Her pulse beat fast, and the coursing blood warmed and relaxed every inch of her body.

Comment   In the first sentence the word "abandoned" echoes the earlier description of Mrs. Mallard's "wild abandonment." But she now seems in control of herself. Her repetition of "free" signals her excitement and perhaps convinces her of its truth. Her emotional excitement is rendered in physical imagery: her pulse beats fast, and her blood courses through her body—both signs of reawakened feeling.

She did not stop to ask if it were not a monstrous joy that held her. A clear and exalted perception enabled her to dismiss the suggestion as trivial.

She knew that she would weep again when she saw the kind, tender hands folded in death; the face that had never looked save with love upon her, fixed and gray and dead. But she saw beyond that bitter moment a long procession of years to come that would belong to her absolutely. And she opened and spread her arms out to them in welcome.

There would be no one to live for during those coming years; she would live for herself. There would be no powerful will bending her in that blind persistence with which men and women believe they have a right to impose a private will upon a fellow-creature. A kind intention or a cruel intention made the act seem no less a crime as she looked upon it in that brief moment of illumination.

And yet she had loved him—sometimes. Often she had not. What did it matter! What could love, the unsolved mystery, count for in face of this possession of self-assertion which she suddenly recognized as the strongest impulse of her being!

Comment   We pause over the words "monstrous joy." Clearly Mrs. Mallard is overjoyed. And from one perspective her joy, however honestly felt, is monstrous. She is happy—exultantly happy—that her husband is dead. But the author makes clear that the monstrousness of her joy is not something Mrs. Mallard herself feels. She does not, that is, think about what she is feeling.

The first paragraph underscores Mrs. Mallard's control and clear-sightedness. Her sense of confidence, anticipated earlier, becomes explicit and strong. We wonder if her husband treated her cruelly, but the text answers that he has been kind, which makes Mrs. Mallard's open-armed welcome of the coming years indeed monstrous. In the next paragraph Chopin does not exactly condemn Mr. Mallard but does suggest that Mrs. Mallard had to bend her will to his. Kind or not, he controlled her; loving wife or not, she resented it. Chopin here seems to move beyond the case of a particularly unhappy wife to the larger issue of the bonds of marriage, using language that strongly condemns the husband's dominance. We hear it in such words and phrases as "powerful will bending hers," "blind persistence," "impose," and "crime." This language is balanced by a lyrical evocation of Mrs. Mallard living for herself rather than for her husband in the years to come. The moment is described as "that brief moment of illumination." This description builds on the earlier description of her eyes as "keen and bright." Mrs. Mallard is possessed by a new sense of herself and a new self-confidence as she envisions her future life. This is the turning point of her life, a moment of "recognition," insight, and enlightenment, that makes her previous life with her husband pale into insignificance.

The next paragraphs could end the story:

"Free! Body and soul free!" she kept whispering.

Josephine was kneeling before the closed door with her lips to the keyhole, imploring for admission. "Louise, open the door! I beg; open the door—you will make yourself ill. What are you doing, Louise? For heaven's sake open the door."

"Go away. I am not making myself ill." No; she was drinking in a very elixir of life through that open window.

Her fancy was running riot along those days ahead of her. Spring days, and summer days, and all sorts of days that would be her own. She breathed a quick prayer that life might be long. It was only yesterday she had thought with a shudder that life might be long.

She arose at length and opened the door to her sister's importunities. There was a feverish triumph in her eyes, and she carried herself unwittingly like a goddess of Victory. She clasped her sister's waist, and together they descended the stairs. Richards stood waiting for them at the bottom.

Comment The discrepancy between what Josephine thinks is Mrs. Mallard's reason for keeping herself locked in her room and our knowledge of the real reason is ironic.* There is irony, also, in Mrs. Mallard's praying for a long life, as only the day before she had shuddered at the thought of a long life with Brently Mallard. The language of these paragraphs is charged with feeling—somewhat overcharged perhaps—but it is in keeping with extending and intensifying Mrs. Mallard's emotion. She drinks in the "elixir of life," has a "feverish triumph in her eyes," and comports herself like a "goddess of Victory." These paragraphs could end the story, but they don't. Instead Chopin has a surprise:

*Irony involves some kind of opposition, usually between what appears to be and what is or between what is said and what is meant. See page 75.

Some one was opening the front door with a latchkey. It was Brently Mallard who entered, a little travel-stained, composedly carrying his grip-sack and umbrella. He had been far from the scene of accident, and did not even know there had been one. He stood amazed at Josephine's piercing cry; at Richards's quick motion to screen him from the view of his wife.

But Richards was too late.

When the doctors came they said she had died of heart disease—of joy that kills.

Comment   The surprise, of course, is too much for Mrs. Mallard. Does she die of shock, of despair, of joy that kills? We are left with the impression that Josephine, Richards, and the doctor do not understand that Mrs. Mallard dies not of shock at seeing her husband alive, not out of joy, but out of something like despair. Why does the narrator suggest that none of them realize the truth?

Some interesting questions are left unresolved by this ending. Is Mrs. Mallard being punished for harboring a desire to be free of her husband? Or, is Mrs. Mallard a symbol of repressed womanhood yearning to be free of male bondage? In addition: does the story transcend the sexual identity of its protagonist? Could we imagine a man in Mrs. Mallard's position?

The next work, Ernest Hemingway's "Hills Like White Elephants," does not include interpolated commentary. Instead, a set of annotations that draw attention to its different facets and details accompanies the story. Like the interpolated commentary for "The Story of an Hour," the annotations for "Hills Like White Elephants" illustrate how readers actively and reflectively respond to a text.

THE PRACTICE OF ACTIVE READING

ERNEST HEMINGWAY

[1898–1961]

Hills Like White Elephants

white elephant—a possession whose trouble outweighs its value or usefulness—also something hard to get rid of

The hills across the valley of the Ebro were long and white. On this side there was no shade and no trees and the station was between two lines of rails in the sun. Close against the side of the station there was the warm shadow of the building and a curtain, made of strings of bamboo beads, hung across the open door into the bar, to keep out flies. The American and the girl with him sat at a table in the shade, outside the building. It was very hot and the express from Barcelona would come in forty minutes. It stopped at this junction for two minutes and went on to Madrid.

The story begins like the opening scene of a film —the stage is set for a dialogue.

"What should we drink?" the girl asked. She had taken off her hat and put it on the table.

"It's pretty hot," the man said.

"Let's drink beer."

"Dos cervezas," the man said into the curtain.

"Big ones?" a woman asked from the doorway.

"Yes. Two big ones."

The woman brought two glasses of beer and two felt pads. She put the felt pads and the beer glasses on the table and looked at the man and the girl. The girl was looking off at the line of hills. They were white in the sun and the country was brown and dry.

"They look like white elephants," she said.

"I've never seen one," the man drank his beer.

"No, you wouldn't have."

"I might have." the man said. "Just because you say I wouldn't have doesn't prove anything."

The girl looked at the bead curtain. "They've painted something on it," she said. "What does it say?"

"Anis del Toro. It's a drink."

"Could we try it?"

The man called "Listen" through the curtain. The woman came out from the bar.

"Four reales."

"We want two Anis del Toro."

"With water?"

"Do you want it with water?"

"I don't know," the girl said. "Is it good with water?"

"It's all right."

"You want them with water?" asked the woman.

"Yes, with water."

"It tastes like licorice," the girl said and put the glass down.

"That's the way with everything."

"Yes," said the girl. "Everything tastes of licorice. Especially all the things you've waited so long for, like absinthe."

"Oh, cut it out."

"You started it," the girl said. "I was being amused. I was having a fine time."

"Well, let's try and have a fine time."

"All right. I was trying. I said the mountains looked like white elephants. Wasn't that bright?"

"That was bright."

"I wanted to try this new drink. That's all we do, isn't it —look at things and try new drinks?"

"I guess so."

The girl looked across at the hills.

"They're lovely hills," she said. "They don't really look like

---

What is the relationship of this man and girl?

Is this imagery of the white hills and dry country important?

undertone of hostility in their conversation

She changes the subject.

The man knows things the girl doesn't.

Everything?

Started what?

Tension surfaces more strongly.

His comments are cryptic; hers are expansive.

white elephants. I just meant the coloring of their skin through
the trees."

"Should we have another drink?"

"All right."

The warm wind blew the bead curtain against the table.

"The beer's nice and cool," the man said.

"It's lovely," the girl said.

"It's really an awfully simple operation, Jig," the man said.
"It's not really an operation at all."

The girl looked at the ground the table legs rested on.

"I know you wouldn't mind it, Jig. It's really not anything.
It's just to let the air in."

The girl did not say anything.

"I'll go with you and I'll stay with you all the time. They
just let the air in and then it's all perfectly natural."

"Then what will we do afterward?"

"We'll be fine afterward. Just like we were before."

"What makes you think so?"

"That's the only thing that bothers us. It's the only thing
that's made us unhappy.

The girl looked at the bead curtain, put her hand out and
took hold of two of the strings of beads.

"And you think then we'll be all right and be happy."

"I know we will. You don't have to be afraid. I've known
lots of people that have done it."

"So have I," said the girl. "And afterward they were all so
happy."

"Well," the man said, "if you don't want to you don't have
to. I wouldn't have you do it if you didn't want to. But I
know it's perfectly simple."

"And you really want to?"

"I think it's the best thing to do. But I don't want you to
do it if you don't really want to."

"And if I do it you'll be happy and things will be like they
were and you'll love me?"

"I love you now. You know I love you."

"I know. But if I do it, then it will be nice again if I say
things are like white elephants, and you'll like it?"

"I'll love it. I love it now but I just can't think about it.
You know how I get when I worry."

"If I do it you won't ever worry?"

"I won't worry about that because it's perfectly simple."

"Then I'll do it. Because I don't care about me."

"What do you mean?"

"I don't care about me."

"Well, I care about you."

"Oh, yes. But I don't care about me. And I'll do it and then everything will be fine."

"I don't want you to do it if you feel that way."

The girl stood up and walked to the end of the station. Across, on the other side, were fields of grain and trees along the banks of the Ebro. Far away, beyond the river, were mountains. The shadow of a cloud moved across the field of grain and she saw the river through the trees.

"And we could have all this," she said. "And we could have everything and every day we make it more impossible."

"What did you say?"

"I said we could have everything."

"We can have everything."

"No, we can't."

"We could have the whole world."

"No, we can't."

"We can go everywhere."

"No, we can't. It isn't ours any more."

"It's ours."

"No, it isn't. And once they take it away, you never get it back."

"But they haven't taken it away."

"We'll wait and see."

"Come on back in the shade," he said. "You mustn't feel that way."

"I don't feel any way," the girl said. "I just know things."

"I don't want you to do anything that you don't want to do—"

"Not that isn't good for me," she said. "I know. Could we have another beer?"

"All right. But you've got to realize—"

"I realize," the girl said. "Can't we maybe stop talking?"

They sat down at the table and the girl looked across at the hills on the dry side of the valley and the man looked at her and at the table.

"You've got to realize," he said, "that I don't want you to do it if you don't want to. I'm perfectly willing to go through with it if it means anything to you."

"Doesn't it mean anything to you? We could get along."

"Of course it does. But I don't want anybody but you. I don't want any one else. And I know it's perfectly simple."

"Yes, you know it's perfectly simple."

"It's all right for you to say that, but I do know it."

"Would you do something for me now?"

"I'd do anything for you."

Marginal notes:

Will everything be "fine"?

She sees things differently now.

images of fertility in the landscape

"everything"—peace, love, happiness?

She contradicts him. She sounds strong, in control —not childlike as before.

She's brooding, pessimistic.

She "knows" things—a power shift.

She cuts him off twice— why?

Now she sees sterility in the landscape.

She is tired of him.

double meanings of "it"

"Would you please please please please please please please   Why seven pleases?
stop talking?"

He did not say anything but looked at the bags against the   Is there any significance
wall of the station. There were labels on them from all the   in the detail about the
hotels where they had spent nights.   bags?

"But I don't want you to," he said, "I don't care anything
about it."

"I'll scream," the girl said.

The woman came out through the curtains with two glasses
of beer and put them down on the damp felt pads. "The train
comes in five minutes," she said.

"What did she say?" asked the girl.

"That the train is coming in five minutes."

The girl smiled brightly at the woman, to thank her.   What kind of smile is it?

"I'd better take the bags over to the other side of the
station," the man said. She smiled at him.

"All right. Then come back and we'll finish the beer."

He picked up the two heavy bags and carried them around   Does he believe that she
the station to the other tracks. He looked up the tracks but   can feel better after this
could not see the train. Coming back, he walked through the   conversation? Does she
barroom, where people waiting for the train were drinking.   really feel "fine"? This
He drank an Anis at the bar and looked at the people. They   word has appeared
were all waiting reasonably for the train. He went out through   before.
the bead curtain. She was sitting at the table and smiled at him.

"Do you feel better?" he asked.

"I feel fine," she said. "There's nothing wrong with me. I
feel fine."

In our reading of "Hills Like White Elephants" we have noticed details that
make us question the man's honesty, decency, and sincerity. He clearly wants
the girl to have an abortion; he seems not to want the complications and
responsibilities that a child would bring to their relationship. And he misrepre-
sents how easy the abortion will be for her, how it's really "nothing." He also
insists that he loves her, cares for her, wants what is best for her. But it sounds
like he simply wants to extricate himself from an uncomfortable situation.
Moreover, he wants *her* to make the decision, presumably so that later she can't
blame *him* for what she does. After all, he implies, he doesn't want her to have
the abortion if she really doesn't want to.

We see through this as clearly as she does; and we endorse her request that
he please shut up. Why then does Jig agree to have the abortion? Or does she?
Hemingway leaves unclear just what she intends to do. Will she stay with the
man, have the abortion, and reestablish their earlier, more carefree relationship?
Or has she decided not to pursue the relationship, but instead to have the baby
and leave him? Whatever she has decided, she certainly becomes more sure of
herself, more certain of what she wants, and of what she expects from him.
Midway through the conversation, she undergoes a change: she becomes more
confident, assumes control of herself and of the conversation, and abandons her

earlier childlike questions. In fact, she stops asking questions altogether, cuts off the man's feeble attempts at reassurance, and adopts an attitude of determined resistance.

The ending is as ambiguous as the action that leads up to it. The girl smiles "brightly," and says that she feels "fine," that there's nothing wrong with her. If this is true, is it because she has decided to have the abortion? Or is she saying that she is fine in her state of pregnancy—that there's nothing physically *wrong* with her? Or does she not feel "fine" at all? Is she, instead, just saying that so she doesn't have to discuss things any further? In this case, her smiles are put on; they are false smiles that the man happily and self-deceptively accepts as the real thing. He will see and hear what he wants to; she will say and do what he expects, masking what she really feels.

Hemingway does not tell us what the characters think and feel. Instead, he lets us overhear their conversation, read between the lines, and draw our own conclusions. The closest he comes to revealing what the girl thinks is when he shows her looking across the river at the fields of grain. Their beauty and fertility is what she desires, but instead she faces the sterility of an imminent abortion and the arid lifelessness of the man's inadequate "love."

We can conclude these speculations about the story with comments about it by two prominent American critics, Lionel Trilling and Irving Howe. How do their viewpoints clarify your sense of the story? Do they enable you to make better sense of it? Does either critic open up still other windows on the story?

> Should we need a clue to where the point of the story lies, we can find it in a single word . . . *reasonably*—it is a strange adverb for the man to have alighted on. Why should he choose to remark upon the people's reasonableness? [as they wait for the train]. . . . It is because he, a reasonable man, has been having a rough time reasoning with an unreasonable woman.
>
> —LIONEL TRILLING, FROM *PREFACES TO LITERATURE*

> What we get to see—quickly as if through a few snapshots— is the spectacle of two people trapped in a relationship. . . . In a few pages, Hemingway charts the death of love. . . . The final effect of the story is one of intense pain and loss, a glimpse of human waste through the scrim of casual talk. The kind of talk that reveals the torment of two souls.
>
> —IRVING HOWE, FROM *THE EXPERIENCE OF FICTION*

CHAPTER TWO

Types of Short Fiction

In our discussion of reading stories in Chapter One, we considered three stories —a parable and two modern realistic short stories. But short fiction comes in more than these two varieties. Other popular forms we might know include fairy tales and mystery stories, science fiction stories, and popular romance. While we need not rehearse all of short fiction's various guises, it will nonetheless be useful to describe its more common and enduring types. We begin with some ancient forms.

EARLY FORMS: PARABLE, FABLE, AND TALE

In our discussion of "The Prodigal Son" (pages 4–5), we defined a parable as a brief story that teaches a lesson, often of a religious or spiritual nature. Another early story form is the fable, a relative of the parable.

Like parables, *fables* are brief stories that point to a moral. The moral of the fable is stated explicitly, whereas the moral of the parable is implied. The two forms also differ in subject and tone. Fables highlight features of human nature and character, especially human failings. They frequently include animals as characters, and their tone is satirical. As we have stated, parables are stories about common life through which a religious or spiritual point is made. Their purpose is instructive, their tone serious. Although we can distinguish conveniently between fable and parable in these ways, there are stories in which such distinctions are blurred as in George Orwell's *Animal Farm,* which includes characteristics of both. Here is a fable attributed to Aesop, whose name has become synonymous with the form.

AESOP

[*c. 620–560 B.C.*]

The Wolf and the Mastiff

A Wolf, who was almost skin and bone—so well did the dogs of the neighborhood keep guard—met, one moonshiny night, a sleek Mastiff, who was, moreover, as strong as he was fat. Bidding the Dog good-night very humbly, he praised his good looks. "It would be easy for you," replied the Mastiff, "to get as fat as I am if you liked." "What shall I have to do?" asked the Wolf. "Almost nothing," answered the Dog. They trotted off together, but, as they went along, the Wolf noticed a bare spot on the Dog's neck. "What is that mark?" said he. "Oh, the merest trifle," answered the Dog; "the collar which I wear when I am tied up is the cause of it." "Tied up!" exclaimed the Wolf, with a sudden stop; "tied up? Can you not always then run where you please?" "Well, not quite always," said the Mastiff; "but what can that matter?" "It matters much to me," rejoined the Wolf, and, leaping away, he ran once more to his native forest.

Moral: Better starve free, than be a fat slave.

Both the fable and the parable represent early forms of fiction. Another early form, one without the strong instructive intent of fable and parable, is the tale. A *tale* is a story that narrates strange or fabulous happenings in a direct manner, without detailed descriptions of character. The tale is less moralized than either fable or parable, though it is almost as generalized in its depiction of character and setting. While we may read fable and parable to understand their meaning, to get the point so to speak, our interest in tales will generally incline more toward what happens. Our interest, that is, lies in action and its outcome. Additionally, it may reside in the emotions we experience in reading tales rather than in generalizations we can make about them. The following tale, written in the first century, is from the *Satyricon* of Petronius.

PETRONIUS

[*d. A.D. 66?*]

The Widow of Ephesus

Once upon a time there was a certain married woman in the city of Ephesus whose fidelity to her husband was so famous that the women from all the neighboring towns and villages used to troop into Ephesus merely to stare at this prodigy. It happened, however, that her husband one day died. Finding the normal custom of following the cortege with hair unbound and beating her breast in public quite inadequate to express her grief, the lady insisted on following the corpse right into the tomb, an underground vault of the Greek type, and there set herself to guard the body, weeping and wailing night and day. Although in her extremes of grief she was clearly courting death from starvation, her parents were utterly unable to persuade her to leave, and even the magistrates, after one last supreme attempt, were rebuffed and driven away. In short, all Ephesus had gone into mourning for this extraordinary woman, all the more since the lady was now passing her fifth consecutive day without once tasting food. Beside the failing woman sat her devoted maid, sharing her mistress' grief and relighting the lamp whenever it flickered out. The whole city could speak, in fact, of nothing else: here at last, all classes alike agreed, was the one true example of conjugal fidelity and love.

In the meantime, however, the governor of the province gave orders that several thieves should be crucified in a spot close by the vault where the lady was mourning her dead husband's corpse. So, on the following night, the soldier who had been assigned to keep watch on the crosses so that nobody could remove the thieves' bodies for burial suddenly noticed a light blazing among the tombs and heard the sounds of groaning. And prompted by a natural human curiosity to know who or what was making those sounds, he descended into the vault.

But at the sight of a strikingly beautiful woman, he stopped short in terror, thinking he must be seeing some ghostly apparition out of hell. Then, observing the corpse and seeing the tears on the lady's face and the scratches her fingernails had gashed in her cheeks, he realized what it was: a widow, in inconsolable grief. Promptly fetching his little supper back down to the tomb, he implored the lady not to persist in her sorrow or break her heart with useless mourning. All men alike, he reminded her, have the same end; the same resting place awaits us all. He used, in short, all those platitudes we use to comfort the suffering and bring them back to life. His consolations, being unwelcome, only exasperated the widow more; more violently than ever she beat her breast, and tearing out her hair by the roots, scattered it over the dead man's body. Undismayed, the soldier repeated his arguments and pressed her to take some food, until the little maid, quite overcome by the smell of the wine, succumbed and stretched out her hand to her tempter. Then, restored by the food and wine, she began herself to assail her mistress' obstinate refusal.

"How will it help you," she asked the lady, "if you faint from hunger? Why should you bury yourself alive, and go down to death before the Fates have called you? What does Vergil say?—

Do you suppose the shades and ashes of the dead are by such sorrow touched?

No, begin your life afresh. Shake off these woman's scruples; enjoy the light while you can. Look at that corpse of your poor husband: doesn't it tell you more eloquently than any words that you should live?"

None of us, of course, really dislikes being told that we must eat, that life is to be lived. And the lady was no exception. Weakened by her long days of fasting, her resistance crumbled at last, and she ate the food the soldier offered her as hungrily as the little maid had eaten earlier.

Well, you know what temptations are normally aroused in a man on a full stomach. So the soldier, mustering all those blandishments by means of which he had persuaded the lady to live, now laid determined siege to her virtue. And chaste though she was, the lady found him singularly attractive and his arguments persuasive. As for the maid, she did all she could to help the soldier's cause, repeating like a refrain the appropriate line of Vergil:

If love is pleasing, lady, yield yourself to love.

To make the matter short, the lady's body soon gave up the struggle; she yielded and our happy warrior enjoyed a total triumph on both counts. That very night their marriage was consummated, and they slept together the second and the third night too, carefully shutting the door of the tomb so that any passing friend or stranger would have thought the lady of famous chastity had at last expired over her dead husband's body.

As you can perhaps imagine, our soldier was a very happy man, utterly delighted with his lady's ample beauty and that special charm that a secret love confers. Every night, as soon as the sun had set, he bought what few provisions his slender pay permitted and smuggled them down to the tomb. One night, however, the parents of one of the crucified thieves, noticing that the watch was being badly kept, took advantage of our hero's absence to remove their son's body and bury it. The next morning, of course, the soldier was horror-struck to discover one of the bodies missing from its cross, and ran to tell his mistress of the horrible punishment which awaited him for neglecting his duty. In the circumstances, he told her, he would not wait to be tried and sentenced, but would punish himself then and there with his own sword. All he asked of her was that she make room for another corpse and allow the same gloomy tomb to enclose husband and lover together.

Our lady's heart, however, was no less tender than pure. "God forbid," she cried, "that I should have to see at one and the same time the dead bodies of the only two men I have ever loved. No, better far, I say, to hang the dead than kill the living." With these words, she gave orders that her husband's body should be taken from its bier and strung up on the empty cross. The soldier followed this good advice, and the next morning the whole city wondered by what miracle the dead man had climbed up on the cross.

Responding to "The Widow of Ephesus" we look less to a moral than to its action. Much of the pleasure we take in a story like this is in its swift series of surprises. We may be amazed at the way the lady expresses her sorrow, surprised at her capitulation to the soldier, and amused (or appalled) at where they make love. But before we can become absorbed in these events, Petronius surprises us with another series of actions culminating in the lady's still more amazing solution to the soldier's dilemma: putting the corpse of her dead husband up on the cross.

Our admiration for the inventiveness and economy of the tale's action, however, may not eliminate our desire to look for a moral of some sort. But in such a tale, we should search cautiously. Does the story's hypothetical moral have to do with the fickleness of women? Is the story told to illustrate that all women can be tempted and seduced? Does it suggest that life is to be lived and enjoyed? Or does it imply that people are credulous, that, rather than believe the widow capable of anything but unaldered devotion to her dead husband, they believe in the miraculous ascent of a dead body onto the cross?

Whatever our sense of the tale's point and purpose, whatever meaning we finally take from it, "The Widow of Ephesus" is not as clear-cut as Aesop's fable or the parable of the Prodigal Son. And in that respect this tale more closely ressembles the modern short story whose meaning is often ambiguous or open to a variety of interpretations.

THE SHORT STORY

The *short story* as a form of short fiction developed and became popular in the nineteenth century. During this period, fiction was channeled in the direction of realism or a detailed representation of everyday life, typically the lives and experiences familiar to middle-class individuals. Besides its realistic impulse, the modern short story differed from the ancient forms of short fiction in still another way: in the ratio between summary and scene. Parables, fables, and tales tend to summarize action, to tell what happens in a general overview of the action. Short stories, on the other hand, typically reveal character in dramatic scenes, in moments of action, and in exchanges of dialogue detailed enough to represent the surface of life. In addition, the short story has traditionally been more concerned with the revelation of character through flashes of insight and shocks of recognition than the early fictional forms.

Typical features of the modern realistic short story include the following:

1. Its plot is based on probability, illustrating a sequence of causally related incidents.
2. Its characters are recognizably human, and they are motivated by identifiable social and psychological forces.
3. Its time and place are clearly established, with realistic rather than fantastic settings.
4. Its elements—plot, character, setting, style, point of view, and theme—work toward a single effect, making the story unified.

THE NONREALISTIC STORY

In an effort to break away from the dominating conventions of the realistic short story, some modern storytellers have mixed features of the early story forms—elements of the supernatural, for example—with realistic conventions. I. B. Singer's "Gimpel the Fool" (pages 269–278), Bernard Malamud's "Idiots First" (pages 299–305), and Rudyard Kipling's "The Gardener" (pages 163–169) all include supernatural elements, though they function in quite different ways in each story. Such other writers as Leslie Silko in "Yellow Woman" (pages 363–369) and Gabriel Garcia Marquez in "A Very Old Man with Enormous Wings" (pages 330–334) employ legendary materials in their stories. Shifting back and forth between the realistic and fantastic worlds, these modern storytellers have discovered and explored ways to represent human experience powerfully and incisively.

Occasionally modern writers of short fiction employ nonrealistic detail so heavily that readers are disoriented and unsettled. When we read stories like Donald Barthelme's "A Shower of Gold" (pages 335–340) and Jorge Luis Borges's "The Garden of the Forking Paths" (pages 248–254), we may be uncertain about what exactly is happening. Part of the reason for our initial confusion is attributable to the authors' use of dream logic and surrealistic action (Barthelme) or of mystery and riddle (Borges) in the development of their plots. Our confusion may also derive from our expectations: we expect the conventions of realism to operate, and when they do not we need to readjust our sense of what we are reading.

The important thing, however, about nonrealistic stories is to accept them on their own terms. In accepting their break from realistic fictional convention we increase our chances of responding fully to the pleasures they offer. We also enlarge our understanding of what a short story can be.

THE SHORT NOVEL

The short novel, sometimes called the *novella,* shares characteristics with both the novel and short story. Like the longer novel the *short novel* accumulates incidents and illustrates character over time in ways the short story cannot because of its more limited scope. Yet like the short story, the short novel relies on glimpses of understanding, flashes of insight, quick turns of action to solidify theme or reveal character. And while in the short novel such moments are both more frequent and of longer duration than in the typical short story, they are rarely rendered with the leisure or thickness of detail characteristic of most long novels.

Unlike the short story, which must make its mark quickly, the short novel can allow a slower unfolding of character, incident, idea. The quick flash of revelation, the momentary shock of recognition, the surprise twist of an ending —these are common to the short story rather than to the short novel. The short story's brevity demands a single snapshot of time rather than the collage or mosaic that can be created in a novel long or short. Moreover, what distinguishes the short novel from its longer counterpart in this respect is its greater efficiency and sharper focus. Lacking time and space to accumulate incident, develop character, and amplify theme, the short novel works within a narrow compass, disavowing the novel's amplitude and panoramic sweep. The result is a consistency of style and focus and a concentration and compression of effect that are the hallmarks of the short novel form.

Henry James, an American master of the short novel, called it a "blessed" form. And Vladimir Nabokov, a recent commentator, suggested that "by diminishing large things and enlarging small ones," the short novel is "intrinsically artistic." Finally, Irving Howe, a contemporary critic and editor of a fine collection of modern short novels, has noted that "in masterpieces of the genre, the action forms a harmonious equivalent to the motivating idea."

Our choice of a short novel that seems worthy of such high praise is Leo Tolstoy's *The Death of Iván Ilych* (pages 94–131).

CHAPTER THREE

The Elements of Fiction

In learning to read fiction well, we must understand something about its technique. One useful way to approach the techniques of fiction is to describe its basic elements or characteristics: plot and structure, character, setting, point of view, style and language, theme, and irony. We will discuss each element separately to highlight its special features. We should be aware, however, that all the elements of a story work together to convey feeling and embody meaning. Consequently, we must relate our analysis of any one fictional element —plot or character, for example—to the other elements and to the work as a whole.

PLOT AND STRUCTURE

Plot, the action element in fiction, is the arrangement of events that make up a story. A story's plot keeps us turning pages: we read to find out what will happen next. But for a plot to be effective, it must include a sequence of incidents that bear a significant causal relationship to each other. Causality is an important feature of realistic fictional plots: it simply means that one thing happens because of—as a result of—something else. The following example from E. M. Forster's *Aspects of the Novel* should clarify this point. Forster notes that "The king died and then the queen died" promises a story, but not a plot. Why? Because there is no causal connection between the two deaths. In the following alternative version, however, we have such a connection and hence a plot: "The king died and then the queen died of grief."*

Many fictional plots turn on a *conflict,* or struggle between opposing forces, that is usually resolved by the end of the story. Typical fictional plots begin with an *exposition* that provides background information we need to make sense of the action, describes the setting, and introduces the major characters; these plots develop a series of *complications* or intensifications of the conflict that lead to a *crisis* or moment of great tension. The conflict may reach a *climax* or turning point, a moment of greatest tension that fixes the outcome; then, the action falls off as the plot's complications are sorted out and resolved (the *resolution* or *denouement*). The plot of a typical realistic short story can be diagrammed in the following manner:

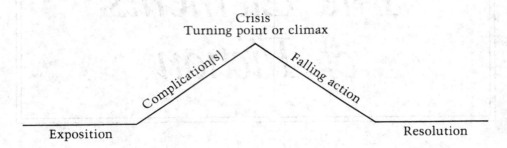

This classic diagram, however, is useful only as a point of departure for describing the plot of a particular story. Most stories do not exhibit such strict formality of design. A story's climactic moment, for example, may occur simultaneously with its ending, with little or no formal resolution. Or its action may rise and fall repeatedly in a jagged and uneven pattern rather than according to the neat symmetry of this diagram.

Whatever form the action of a realistic story assumes, it is usually composed of a sequence of causally related actions or events that are not necessarily presented in chronological order. For example, flashbacks that disrupt the linear movement of the plot to present an earlier action are employed in many stories. To distill the plot from William Faulkner's "A Rose for Emily" or Ernest Hemingway's "The Short Happy Life of Francis Macomber," we must untangle a set of events that shift between past and present. In doing so we can clarify our sense of what happened, how it happened, and why. And in searching for a plot in Hemingway's "Hills Like White Elephants," we realize that a plot is not always external, that plot can refer to internal action, to changes of mind and heart not overtly revealed.

Whatever kind of plot a story possesses, the writer has ordered the events with a view both to the overall meaning and to the responses of readers. To appreciate fictional plot, therefore, we should think about our experience in reading a story and remember what we thought and felt at different points. This subjective

*E. M. Forster, *Aspects of the Novel* (New York: Harcourt, Brace and World, Inc., 1927), p. 130.

dimension of our reading experience should prompt us to investigate why the writer has chosen one arrangement of incidents over another. And it should lead us to see how writers control our emotional responses, how they vary the tempo of the action, and how they prepare for reversals and surprises. In attending to these aspects of plot we gain an appreciation for the writer's artistry.

Consider, for example, the plot of Chopin's "The Story of an Hour," with its surprises and changes of fortune. It begins with a reference to the accident in which Brently Mallard is purportedly killed, then shows its effect on his wife. The tempo then slows down as we watch Mrs. Mallard's reactions, particularly her behavior in her room. The plot includes an ironic twist in this descriptive section as Mrs. Mallard's shock evolves into joyful self-assertion, and then produces a stronger and more abrupt and climactic ironic reversal with its final action: the arrival of a very much alive Brently Mallard and the collapse and death of Mrs. Mallard. If we return to the beginning of the story we can see how Chopin prepared for these shifts, how she shaped our expectations only to surprise us.

Hemingway's intentions in "Hills Like White Elephants" are different. Although in some ways "nothing happens" in the story, we sense that something indeed is happening. A conflict that demands a resolution spills out in the dialogue between the man and the girl, even if that resolution is only hinted at in the story. The marginal annotations (see pages 10–14) point to turns in the action, to shifts of attitude reflected in the ways the characters speak to each other and in how much or how little they say.

A story's structure can be examined in relation to its plot. If plot is the sequence of unfolding action, *structure* is the *design* or form of the completed action. In examining plot, we are concerned with causality, with how one action leads into or ties in with another. In examining structure, we look for patterns, design, the shape of content that the story as a whole possesses. Plot directs us to the story in motion, structure to the story at rest. Plot and structure together reveal aspects of the story's artistic design.

Structure is important in fiction for a number of reasons. It satisfies our need for order, for proportion, for arrangement. A story's symmetry or balance of details may please us, as may its alternation of moments of tension and relaxation. Consider the way descriptive details punctuate the dialogue of "Hills Like White Elephants." Aside from their symbolic significance, they alter the story's tempo and its form. Or consider the structure of "The Prodigal Son" with its various balances and parallels. It begins and ends with a father together with his sons, it includes repeated statements by both father and prodigal son, and it substitutes the discontent of one son for the discontent of the other. Such balances make the story's form aesthetically pleasing. But structure is important for another reason: it provides a clue to a story's meaning. The shift in control and knowledge from the man to the girl in "Hills Like White Elephants" turns the story upside down, altering the balance of power between the characters, and directing us to an important change in the girl's perceptions.

We can be alert for a story's structure even as we read it for the first time, primarily by paying attention to repeated elements and recurrent details—of action and gesture, of dialogue and description—and to shifts in direction and

changes of focus. Repetition signals important connections and relationships in
the story, relationships between characters, connections between ideas. Shifts in
direction are often signalled by such visual or aural clues as a change of scene,
a new voice, blank space in the text. They may also include changes in the time
and place of the action or alterations in characters' entrances and exits or in their
behavior, or they may appear as changes in the pace of the story, and in its
texture or language.

Keep these considerations about plot and structure in mind as you read
Katherine Mansfield's "The Fly," which follows. See how its plot, for example,
both follows and deviates from the diagram on page 24. Note especially any
shifts of emphasis and changes of tempo in the story's action. And once you have
finished reading, look back and describe your expectations about the developing
action.

KATHERINE MANSFIELD

[1888–1923]

The Fly

"Y'are very snug in here," piped old Mr. Woodifield, and he peered out of the great,
green leather arm-chair by his friend, the boss's desk, as a baby peers out of its pram.
His talk was over; it was time for him to be off. But he did not want to go. Since
he had retired, since his . . . stroke, the wife and the girls kept him boxed up in the
house every day of the week except Tuesday. On Tuesday he was dressed up and
brushed and allowed to cut back to the City for the day. Though what he did there
the wife and girls couldn't imagine. Made a nuisance of himself to his friends, they
supposed. . . . Well, perhaps so. All the same, we cling to our last pleasures as the tree
clings to its last leaves. So there sat old Woodifield, smoking a cigar and staring almost
greedily at the boss, who rolled in his office chair, stout, rosy, five years older than he,
and still going strong, still at the helm. It did one good to see him.

Wistfully, admiringly, the old voice added, "It's snug in here, upon my word!"

"Yes, it's comfortable enough," agreed the boss, and he flipped the *Financial Times*
with a paper-knife. As a matter of fact he was proud of his room; he liked to have
it admired, especially by old Woodifield. It gave him a feeling of deep, solid satisfaction
to be planted there in the midst of it in full view of that frail old figure in the muffler.

"I've had it done up lately," he explained, as he had explained for the past—how
many?—weeks. "New carpet," and he pointed to the bright red carpet with a pattern
of large white rings. "New furniture," and he nodded towards the massive bookcase
and the table with legs like twisted treacle. "Electric heating!" He waved almost
exultantly towards the five transparent, pearly sausages glowing so softly in the tilted
copper pan.

But he did not draw old Woodifield's attention to the photograph over the table of a grave-looking boy in uniform standing in one of those spectral photographers' parks with photographers' storm-clouds behind him. It was not new. It had been there for over six years.

"There was something I wanted to tell you," said old Woodifield, and his eyes grew dim remembering. "Now what was it? I had it in my mind when I started out this morning." His hands began to tremble, and patches of red showed above his beard.

Poor old chap, he's on his last pins, thought the boss. And, feeling kindly, he winked at the old man, and said jokingly, "I tell you what. I've got a little drop of something here that'll do you good before you go out into the cold again. It's beautiful stuff. It wouldn't hurt a child." He took a key off his watch-chain, unlocked a cupboard below his desk, and drew forth a dark, squat bottle. "That's the medicine," said he. "And the man from whom I got it told me on the strict Q. T. it came from the cellars at Windsor Castle."

Old Woodifield's mouth fell open at the sight. He couldn't have looked more surprised if the boss had produced a rabbit.

"It's whisky, ain't it?" he piped, feebly.

The boss turned the bottle and lovingly showed him the label. Whisky it was.

"D'you know," said he, peering up at the boss wonderingly, "they won't let me touch it at home." And he looked as though he was going to cry.

"Ah, that's where we know a bit more than the ladies," cried the boss, swooping across for two tumblers that stood on the table with the water-bottle, and pouring a generous finger into each. "Drink it down. It'll do you good. And don't put any water with it. It's sacrilege to tamper with stuff like this. Ah!" He tossed off his, pulled out his handkerchief, hastily wiped his moustaches, and cocked an eye at old Woodifield, who was rolling his in his chaps.

The old man swallowed, was silent a moment, and then said faintly, "It's nutty!"

But it warmed him; it crept into his chill old brain—he remembered.

"That was it," he said, heaving himself out of his chair. "I thought you'd like to know. The girls were in Belgium last week having a look at poor Reggie's grave, and they happened to come across your boy's. They are quite near each other, it seems."

Old Woodifield paused, but the boss made no reply. Only a quiver of his eyelids showed that he heard.

"The girls were delighted with the way the place is kept," piped the old voice. "Beautifully looked after. Couldn't be better if they were at home. You've not been across, have yer?"

"No, no!" For various reasons the boss had not been across.

"There's miles of it," quavered old Woodifield, "and it's all as neat as a garden. Flowers growing on all the graves. Nice broad paths." It was plain from his voice how much he liked a nice broad path.

The pause came again. Then the old man brightened wonderfully.

"D'you know what the hotel made the girls pay for a pot of jam?" he piped. "Ten francs! Robbery, I call it. It was a little pot, so Gertrude says, no bigger than a half-crown. And she hadn't taken more than a spoonful when they charged her ten francs. Gertrude brought the pot away with her to teach 'em a lesson. Quite right, too; it's trading on our feelings. They think because we're over there having a look around we're ready to pay anything. That's what it is." And he turned towards the door.

"Quite right, quite right!" cried the boss, though what was quite right he hadn't the least idea. He came around by his desk, followed the shuffling footsteps to the door, and saw the old fellow out. Woodifield was gone.

For a long moment the boss stayed, staring at nothing, while the grey-haired office messenger, watching him, dodged in and out of his cubbyhole like a dog that expects to be taken for a run. Then: "I'll see nobody for half an hour, Macey," said the boss. "Understand? Nobody at all."

"Very good, sir."

The door shut, the firm, heavy steps recrossed the bright carpet, the fat body plumped down in the spring chair, and leaning forward, the boss covered his face with his hands. He wanted, he intended, he had arranged to weep. . . .

It had been a terrible shock to him when old Woodifield sprang that remark upon him about the boy's grave. It was exactly as though the earth had opened and he had seen the boy lying there with Woodifield's girls staring down at him. For it was strange. Although over six years had passed away, the boss never thought of the boy except as lying unchanged, unblemished in his uniform; asleep for ever. "My son!" groaned the boss. But no tears came yet. In the past, in the first months and even years after the boy's death, he had only to say those words to be overcome by such grief that nothing short of a violent fit of weeping could relieve him. Time, he had declared then, he had told everybody, could make no difference. Other men perhaps might recover, might live their loss down, but not he. How was it possible? His boy was an only son. Ever since his birth the boss had worked at building up this business for him; it had no other meaning if it was not for the boy. Life itself had come to have no other meaning. How on earth could he have slaved, denied himself, kept going all those years without the promise for ever before him of the boy's stepping into his shoes and carrying on where he left off?

And that promise had been so near being fulfilled. The boy had been in the office learning the ropes for a year before the war. Every morning they had started off together; they had come back by the same train. And what congratulations he had received as the boy's father! No wonder; he had taken to it marvellously. As to his popularity with the staff, every man jack of them down to old Macey couldn't make enough of the boy. And he wasn't in the least spoiled. No, he was just his bright, natural self, with the right word for everybody, with that boyish look and his habit of saying, "Simply splendid!"

But all that was over and done with as though it never had been. The day had come when Macey had handed him the telegraph that brought the whole place crashing about his head. "Deeply regret to inform you . . ." And he had left the office a broken man, with his life in ruins.

Six years ago, six years . . . How quickly time passed! It might have happened yesterday. The boss took his hands from his face; he was puzzled. Something seemed to be wrong with him. He wasn't feeling as he wanted to feel. He decided to get up and have a look at the boy's photograph. But it wasn't a favorite photograph of his; the expression was unnatural. It was cold, even stern-looking. The boy had never looked like that.

At that moment the boss noticed that a fly had fallen into his broad inkpot, and was trying feebly but desperately to clamber out again. Help! help! said those struggling legs. But the sides of the inkpot were wet and slippery; it fell back again and began to swim. The boss took up a pen, picked the fly out of the ink, and shook it on to a piece of blotting-paper. For a fraction of a second it lay still on the dark patch that oozed round it. Then the front legs waved, took hold, and, pulling its small sodden body up, it began the immense task of cleaning the ink from its wings. Over and under, over and under, went a leg along a wing, as the stone goes over and under the scythe. Then there was a pause, while the fly, seeming to stand on the tips of its toes, tried to expand first one wing and then the other. It succeeded at last, and sitting down, it began, like a minute cat, to clean its face. Now one could imagine that the little front legs rubbed against each other lightly, joyfully. The horrible danger was over; it had escaped; it was ready for life again.

But just then the boss had an idea. He plunged his pen back into the ink, leaned his thick wrist on the blotting-paper, and as the fly tried its wings, down came a great, heavy blot. What would it make of that? What indeed! The little beggar seemed absolutely cowed, stunned, and afraid to move because of what would happen next. But then, as if painfully, it dragged itself forward. The front legs waved, caught hold, and, more slowly, the task began again.

He's a plucky little devil, thought the boss, and he felt a real admiration for the fly's courage. That was the way to tackle things; that was the right spirit. Never say die; it was only a question of . . . But the fly had again finished its laborious task, and the boss had just time to refill his pen, to shake fair and square on the new-cleaned body yet another drop. What about it this time? A painful moment of suspense followed. But, behold, the front legs were again waving; the boss felt a rush of relief. He leaned over the fly and said to it tenderly. "You artful little b . . ." And he actually had the brilliant notion of breathing on it to help the drying process. All the same, there was something timid and weak about its efforts now, and the boss decided that this time should be the last, as he dipped the pen into the inkpot.

It was. The last blot fell on the soaked blotting-paper, and the draggled fly lay in it and did not stir. The back legs were stuck to the body; the front legs were not to be seen.

"Come on," said the boss. "Look sharp!" And he stirred it with his pen—in vain. Nothing happened or was likely to happen. The fly was dead.

The boss lifted the corpse on the end of the paper-knife and flung it into the waste-paper basket, but such a grinding feeling of wretchedness seized him that he felt positively frightened. He started forward and pressed the bell for Macey.

"Bring me some fresh blotting-paper," he said, sternly, "and look sharp about it." And while the old dog padded away he fell to wondering what it was he had been thinking about before. What was it? It was . . . He took out his handkerchief and passed it inside his collar. For the life of him he could not remember.

QUESTION

"The Fly" is constructed in three parts, each presented as a brief scene. In the first scene we are shown the boss with old Woodifield; in the second the boss alone; in the third the boss and the fly. What do we learn from each of these scenes? How are the scenes related?

CHARACTER

As readers, we come to care about fictional *characters,* the imaginary people that writers create, sometimes identifying with them, sometimes judging them. Indeed, if one reason we read stories is to find out what happens (to see how the plot works out), an equally compelling reason is to follow the fortunes of the characters. Plot and character, in fact, are inseparable; we are often less concerned with "what happened" than with "what happened to him or her." We want to know not just "how did it work out," but "how did it work out for them?"

Well-wrought fictional characters come alive for us while we read. And they are real enough to live in our memories long after their stories have ended. We might say that fictional characters possess the kind of reality that dreams have, a reality no less intense for being imagined. Although fictional characters cannot step out of the pages of their stories, we grant them a kind of reality equivalent to if not identical with our own. In doing so we make an implied contract with the writer to suspend our disbelief that his or her story is "just a story," and instead take what happens as if it were real. When we grant fiction this kind of reality, we permit ourselves to be caught up in the life of the story and its characters, perhaps to the point of allowing our own lives to be affected by them.

In short, we can approach fictional characters with the same concerns with which we approach people. We need to be alert for how we are to take them, for what we are to make of them, and we need to see how they may reflect our own experience. We need to observe their actions, listen to *what* they say and *how* they say it, attend to how they relate to other characters and how other characters respond to them, especially to what they say about each other. To make inferences about characters, we look for connections, for links and clues to their function and significance in the story. In analyzing a character or characters' relationships (and fictional characters almost always exist in relation to one another) we relate one act, one speech, one physical detail to another until we understand the character.

Characters in fiction can be conveniently classified as major and minor, static and dynamic. A *major character* is an important figure at the center of the story's action or theme. Usually a character's status as major or minor is clear. On occasion, however, not one but two characters may dominate a story, their relationship being what matters most. In "Hills Like White Elephants" and Luigi Pirandello's "War," for example, no single character dominates the story the way Emily Grierson dominates Faulkner's "A Rose for Emily" or the narrator of "Araby" dominates James Joyce's story.

The major character is sometimes called a *protagonist* whose conflict with an *antagonist* may spark the story's conflict. Supporting the major character are one or more secondary or *minor characters* whose function is partly to illuminate the major characters. Minor characters are often *static* or unchanging: they remain the same from the beginning of a work to the end. *Dynamic characters,* on the other hand, exhibit some kind of change—of attitude, of purpose, of behavior —as the story progresses. We should be careful not to automatically equate major characters with dynamic ones or minor characters with static ones. For example, Emily Grierson, the major character in "A Rose for Emily," is as static as the minor characters Richards and Brently Mallard in Chopin's "The Story of an Hour," whose major character, Mrs. Mallard, undergoes significant changes as the story unfolds.

Characterization is the means by which writers present and reveal character. We look first at the way James Joyce characterizes Mrs. Mooney, a major character, in "The Boarding House" (pages 177–181):

> Mrs. Mooney was a butcher's daughter. She was a woman who was quite able to keep things to herself: a determined woman. She had married her father's foreman and opened a butcher's shop near Spring Gardens.

The method of characterization is narrative description with explicit judgment. We are given facts (she was a butcher's daughter) and interpretive comment (she was . . . a determined woman). From both fact and comment we derive an impression of a strong woman, one who can take care of herself. As a butcher's daughter, she does not stand high on the social ladder. This initial impression is confirmed when we later discover that after her husband had become an alcoholic, had ruined his business, and had gone after Mrs. Mooney with a meat cleaver, she left him and opened a boarding house to support herself and her two children. When the narrator informs us that "she governed the house cunningly and firmly," and when he calls her "a shrewd judge," we come to share his respect for Mrs. Mooney's abilities.

The narrator's view of Mrs. Mooney, however, is not one of unqualified admiration. We learn, for example, that "all the resident young men spoke of her as *The Madam*"—a title suggestive of authority coupled with moral disrepute. And though Mrs. Mooney does not run a house of prostitution, we can't help but be aware of the moral dubiety that this title implies, for Mrs. Mooney allows her nineteen-year-old daughter, Polly, to flirt with the male residents of the boarding house. The following comment of the narrator clearly indicates that Mrs. Mooney was serious about finding Polly a husband: "Mrs. Mooney, who was a shrewd judge, knew that the young men were only passing the time away: none of them meant business." And for Mrs. Mooney, *business* means marriage to a serious and socially suitable man such as Bob Doran, a thirty-four-year-old clerk to a wine merchant.

Throughout "The Boarding House," Joyce characterizes Mrs. Mooney by means of narrative description with explicit judgment. In introducing Polly he varies the technique:

> Polly Mooney, the Madam's daughter, would also sing. She sang:
>
> > *I'm a . . . naughty girl.*
> > *You needn't sham.*
> > *You know I am.*

Polly sings this seductive verse, presumably with her mother's approval. The implications of the song coupled with other descriptive details about Polly serve to characterize her. Unlike her mother, whose character is presented directly through narrative description with explicit judgment, Polly is characterized initially by means of narrative description with implied judgment: "Polly was a slim girl of nineteen; she had light soft hair and a small full mouth." The crucial detail is the full mouth, which suggests sensuality. Moreover, Joyce's narrator further embellishes Polly's description with the information that "her eyes ... had a habit of glancing upwards when she spoke with anyone, which made her look like a little perverse madonna," a word that sounds like *madam,* but which is quite different in connotation. Polly is associated with innocence and holiness while also being called "perverse," a contradiction of the madonna image.

Joyce uses two additional devices of characterization in this story: he reveals a character's state of mind through surface details (the fogging of Bob Doran's glasses and the shaking of his hand while he attempts unsuccessfully to shave); he also reveals characters by letting us enter their consciousness, telling us what they think and feel.

We can generalize from these techniques of characterization to list the following major methods of revealing character in fiction:

1. narrative summary without judgment;
2. narrative description with implied or explicit judgment;
3. surface details of dress and physical appearance;
4. characters' actions—what they do;
5. characters' speech—what they say (and how they say it);
6. characters' consciousness—what they think and feel.

Attend to these devices of characterization as you read Kay Boyle's "Astronomer's Wife." Examine the relationships among the three characters—the astronomer, his wife, and the plumber—noting especially details of speech, gesture, and behavior that reveal the nature of each. Account for what you think and feel about each character.

KAY BOYLE

[*b. 1903*]

Astronomer's Wife

There is an evil moment on awakening when all things seem to pause. But for women, they only falter and may be set in action by a single move: a lifted hand and the pendulum will swing, or the voice raised and through every room the pulse takes up its beating. The astronomer's wife felt the interval gaping and at once filled it to the brim. She fetched up her gentle voice and sent it warily down the stairs for coffee, swung her feet out upon the oval mat, and hailed the morning with her bare arms' quivering flesh drawn taut in rhythmic exercise: left, left, left my wife and fourteen children, right, right, right in the middle of the dusty road.

The day would proceed from this, beat by beat, without reflection, like every other day. The astronomer was still asleep, or feigning it, and she, once out of bed, had come into her own possession. Although scarcely ever out of sight of the impenetrable silence of his brow, she would be absent from him all the day in being clean, busy, kind. He was a man of other things, a dreamer. At times he lay still for hours, at others he sat upon the roof behind his telescope, or wandered down the pathway to the road and out across the mountains. This day, like any other, would go on from the removal of the spot left there from dinner on the astronomer's vest to the severe thrashing of the mayonnaise for lunch. That man might be each time the new arching wave, and woman the undertow that sucked him back, were things she had been told by his silence were so.

In spite of the earliness of the hour, the girl had heard her mistress's voice and was coming up the stairs. At the threshold of the bedroom she paused, and said: "Madame, the plumber is here."

The astronomer's wife put on her white and scarlet smock very quickly and buttoned it at the neck. Then she stepped carefully around the motionless spread of water in the hall.

"Tell him to come right up," she said. She laid her hands on the bannisters and stood looking down the wooden stairway. "Ah, I am Mrs. Ames," she said softly as she saw him mounting. "I am Mrs. Ames," she said softly, softly down the flight of stairs. "I am Mrs. Ames," spoken soft as a willow weeping. "The professor is still sleeping. Just step this way."

The plumber himself looked up and saw Mrs. Ames with her voice hushed, speaking to him. She was a youngish woman, but this she had forgotten. The mystery and silence of her husband's mind lay like a chiding finger on her lips. Her eyes were gray, for the light had been extinguished in them. The strange dim halo of her yellow hair was still uncombed and sideways on her head.

For all of his heavy boots, the plumber quieted the sound of his feet, and together they went down the hall, picking their way around the still lake of water that spread as far as the landing and lay docile there. The plumber was a tough, hardy man; but he took off his hat when he spoke to her and looked her fully, almost insolently in the eye.

"Does it come from the wash-basin," he said, "or from the other . . . ?"

"Oh, from the other," said Mrs. Ames without hesitation.

In this place the villas were scattered out few and primitive, and although beauty lay without there was no reflection of her face within. Here all was awkward and unfit; a sense of wrestling with uncouth forces gave everything an austere countenance. Even the plumber, dealing as does a woman with matters under hand, was grave and stately. The mountains round about seemed to have cast them into the shadow of great dignity.

Mrs. Ames began speaking of their arrival that summer in the little villa, mourning each event as it followed on the other.

"Then, just before going to bed last night," she said, "I noticed something was unusual."

The plumber cast down a folded square of sack-cloth on the brimming floor and laid his leather apron on it. Then he stepped boldly onto the heart of the island it shaped and looked long into the overflowing bowl.

"The water should be stopped from the meter in the garden," he said at last.

"Oh, I did that," said Mrs. Ames, "the very first thing last night. I turned it off at once, in my nightgown, as soon as I saw what was happening. But all this had already run in."

The plumber looked for a moment at her red kid slippers. She was standing just at the edge of the clear, pure-seeming tide.

"It's no doubt the soil lines," he said severely. "It may be that something has stopped them, but my opinion is that the water seals aren't working. That's the trouble often enough in such cases. If you had a valve you wouldn't be caught like this."

Mrs. Ames did not know how to meet this rebuke. She stood, swaying a little, looking into the plumber's blue relentless eye.

"I'm sorry—I'm sorry that my husband," she said, "is still—resting and cannot go into this with you. I'm sure it must be very interesting. . . ."

"You'll probably have to have the traps sealed," said the plumber grimly, and at the sound of this Mrs. Ames' hand flew in dismay to the side of her face. The plumber made no move, but the set of his mouth as he looked at her seemed to soften. "Anyway, I'll have a look from the garden end," he said.

"Oh, do," said the astronomer's wife in relief. Here was a man who spoke of action and object as simply as women did! But however hushed her voice had been, it carried clearly to Professor Ames who lay, dreaming and solitary, upon his bed. He heard their footsteps come down the hall, pause, and skip across the pool of overflow.

"Katherine!" said the astronomer in a ringing tone. "There's a problem worthy of your mettle!"

Mrs. Ames did not turn her head, but led the plumber swiftly down the stairs. When the sun in the garden struck her face, he saw there was a wave of color in it, but this may have been anything but shame.

"You see how it is," said the plumber, as if leading her mind away. "The drains run from these houses right down the hill, big enough for a man to stand upright in them, and clean as a whistle too." There they stood in the garden with the vegetation flowering in disorder all about. The plumber looked at the astronomer's wife. "They come out at the torrent on the other side of the forest beyond there," he said.

But the words the astronomer had spoken still sounded in her in despair. The mind of man, she knew, made steep and sprightly flights, pursued illusion, took foothold in the nameless things that cannot pass between the thumb and finger. But whenever the astronomer gave voice to the thoughts that soared within him, she returned in gratitude to the long expanses of his silence. Desert-like they stretched behind and before the articulation of his scorn.

Life, life is an open sea, she sought to explain it in sorrow, and to survive women cling to the floating debris on the tide. But the plumber had suddenly fallen upon his knees in the grass and had crooked his fingers through the ring of the drains' trap-door. When she looked down she saw that he was looking up into her face, and she saw too that his hair was as light as gold.

"Perhaps Mr. Ames," he said rather bitterly, "would like to come down with me and have a look around?"

"Down?" said Mrs. Ames in wonder.

"Into the drains," said the plumber brutally. "They're a study for a man who likes to know what's what."

"Oh, Mr. Ames," said Mrs. Ames in confusion. "He's still—still in bed, you see."

The plumber lifted his strong, weathered face and looked curiously at her. Surely it seemed to him strange for a man to linger in bed, with the sun pouring yellow as wine all over the place. The astronomer's wife saw his lean cheeks, his high, rugged bones, and the deep seams in his brow. His flesh was as firm and clean as wood, stained richly tan with the climate's rigor. His fingers were blunt, but comprehensible to her, gripped in the ring and holding the iron door wide. The backs of his hands were bound round and round with ripe blue veins of blood.

"At any rate," said the astronomer's wife, and the thought of it moved her lips to smile a little, "Mr. Ames would never go down there alive. He likes going up," she said. And she, in her turn, pointed, but impudently, towards the heavens. "On the roof. Or on the mountains. He's been up on the tops of them many times."

"It's a matter of habit," said the plumber, and suddenly he went down the trap. Mrs. Ames saw a bright little piece of his hair still shining, like a star, long after the rest of him had gone. Out of the depths, his voice, hollow and dark with foreboding, returned to her. "I think something has stopped the elbow," was what he said.

This was speech that touched her flesh and bone and made her wonder. When her husband spoke of height, having no sense of it, she could not picture it nor hear. Depth or magic passed her by unless a name were given. But madness in a daily shape, as elbow stopped, she saw clearly and well. She sat down on the grasses, bewildered that it should be a man who had spoken to her so.

She saw the weeds springing up, and she did not move to tear them up from life. She sat powerless, her senses veiled, with no action taking shape beneath her hands. In this way some men sat for hours on end, she knew, tracking a single thought back to its origin. The mind of man could balance and divide, weed out, destroy. She sat on the full, burdened grasses, seeking to think, and dimly waiting for the plumber to return.

Whereas her husband had always gone up, as the dead go, she knew now that there were others who went down, like the corporeal being of the dead. That men were then divided into two bodies now seemed clear to Mrs. Ames. This knowledge stunned her with its simplicity and took the uneasy motion from her limbs. She could not stir, but sat facing the mountains' rocky flanks, and harking in silence to lucidity. Her husband was the mind, this other man the meat, of all mankind.

After a little, the plumber emerged from the earth: first the light top of his head, then the burnt brow, and then the blue eyes fringed with whitest lash. He braced his thick hands flat on the pavings of the garden-path and swung himself completely from the pit.

"It's the soil lines," he said pleasantly. "The gases," he said as he looked down upon her lifted face, "are backing up the drains."

"What in the world are we going to do?" said the astronomer's wife softly. There was a young and strange delight in putting questions to which true answers would be given. Everything the astronomer had ever said to her was a continuous query to which there could be no response.

"Ah, come, now," said the plumber, looking down and smiling. "There's a remedy for every ill, you know. Sometimes it may be that," he said as if speaking to a child, "or sometimes the other thing. But there's always a help for everything amiss."

Things come out of herbs and make you young again, he might have been saying to her; or the first good rain will quench any drought; or time of itself will put a broken bone together.

"I'm going to follow the ground pipe out right to the torrent," the plumber was saying. "The trouble's between here and there and I'll find it on the way. There's nothing at all that can't be done over for the caring," he was saying, and his eyes were fastened on her face in insolence, or gentleness, or love.

The astronomer's wife stood up, fixed a pin in her hair, and turned around towards the kitchen. Even while she was calling the servant's name, the plumber began speaking again.

"I once had a cow that lost her cud," the plumber was saying. The girl came out on the kitchen-step and Mrs. Ames stood smiling at her in the sun.

"The trouble is very serious, very serious," she said across the garden. "When Mr. Ames gets up, please tell him I've gone down."

She pointed briefly to the open door in the pathway, and the plumber hoisted his kit on his arm and put out his hand to help her down.

"But I made her another in no time," he was saying, "out of flowers and things and what-not."

"Oh," said the astronomer's wife in wonder as she stepped into the heart of the earth. She took his arm, knowing that what he said was true.

QUESTIONS

1. "Astronomer's Wife" is built on two sets of character contrasts: wife versus husband; astronomer versus plumber. Explain how the characters differ. Consider physical descriptions as well as actions, words, and gestures.
2. Describe the wife's relationship with her husband.

SETTING

Writers describe the world they know, its sights and sounds, its colors, textures, and accents. Stories come to life, are imagined as occurring in a place, rooted in the soil of a writer's memories. This place or location of a story's action along with the time in which it occurs is its *setting*. For writers like James Joyce and William Faulkner, setting is essential to meaning. Functioning as more than a simple backdrop for action, it provides a historical and cultural context that reflects the characters. In Joyce's "The Boarding House," for example, Bob Doran's Irish Catholicism powerfully influences his decision to marry Polly, to make "reparation" for his sexual sin. In Faulkner's "A Rose for Emily," Emily Grierson's stubborn resistance to change is both a product of the decay of Jefferson (a fictional town in Mississippi) and the post-Civil War South and also a reflection of its shabby gentility. Moreover, Faulkner intensifies the images of decline of both Emily and the South by his careful description of the Grierson house:

> It was a big, squarish frame house that had once been white, decorated with cupolas and spires and scrolled balconies in the heavily lightsome style of the seventies, set on what had once been our most select street. But garages and cotton gins had encroached and obliterated even the august names of that neighborhood; only Miss Emily's house was left, lifting its stubborn and coquettish decay above the cotton wagons and the gasoline pumps—an eyesore among eyesores.

Later we are taken inside the house, and finally inside one very unusual room. In each case, the physical details of setting are associated with the values, ideals, and attitudes of that place in different times. Setting in "A Rose for Emily" (and in fiction in general) is an important dimension of meaning, both in reflecting character and in embodying theme.

Setting is important for an additional reason: it symbolizes the emotional state of the characters. For example, in Chopin's "The Story of an Hour," Mrs. Mallard looks out the window and sees and hears life going on—birds singing, a peddler working, trees blooming. The contrast between the enclosed space of her room and the world outside implies a tension between Mrs. Mallard's subjugation and her desire for freedom. This contrast underscores a significant difference between the natural and the human worlds: nature is free of social restrictions, of conventions, and of such obligations as marriage.

Writers know that they must root stories in a reality their readers can experience, whether it is one readers actually know or one they must imagine. They realize further that the way to universal truths is through concreteness and particularity. Both Joyce's Dublin and Faulkner's Jefferson are highly specified places. Yet both cities transcend their particular locale to become symbolic, representative places. It is a stunning paradox that works of such imaginative splendor as Chekhov's "The Lady with the Dog" and Faulkner's "A Rose for Emily" also display such careful representations of reality. Stories like these are both realistic and symbolic; they are concrete representations of actual life that illustrate universal truths about human experience, applicable not just in Yalta or Dublin or Jefferson, but anywhere human beings live.

One of our finest American storytellers, Eudora Welty, has spoken eloquently about the importance of one aspect of setting—place in fiction—suggesting no less than that "fiction depends for its life on place." Relating place to character and plot, Miss Welty writes that place is "the crossroads of circumstance, the proving ground of 'What happened? Who's here? Who's coming?'" But it is even more important than this. For as she suggests, place is the "conductor of all the currents of emotion and belief and moral conviction that charge out from the story." Moreover, when the world of experience is within reach of the world of appearance, place both makes and keeps the characters real; it animates them, so much so that, as Miss Welty observes, "every story would be another story, and unrecognizable as art, if it took up its characters and plot and happened somewhere else."*

In "An Outpost of Progress" by Joseph Conrad you will read about two English civil servants who are working at a trading station in the heart of Africa. As you read, attend to details of setting. Consider both the smaller details such as the location of the outpost house and graveyard and the larger elements of setting such as the prevalent native customs and the cultural attitudes of the Englishmen.

JOSEPH CONRAD
[1857–1924]

An Outpost of Progress

I

There were two white men in charge of the trading station. Kayerts, the chief, was short and fat; Carlier, the assistant, was tall, with a large head and a very broad trunk perched upon a long pair of thin legs. The third man on the staff was a Sierra Leone nigger, who maintained that his name was Henry Price. However, for some reason or other, the natives down the river had given him the name of Makola, and it stuck to him through all his wanderings about the country. He spoke English and French with a warbling accent, wrote a beautiful hand, understood bookkeeping, and cherished in his innermost heart the worship of evil spirits. His wife was a negress from Loanda, very large and very noisy. Three children rolled about in sunshine before the door of his low, shed-like dwelling. Makola, taciturn and impenetrable, despised the two white men. He had charge of a small clay storehouse with a dried-grass roof, and pretended to keep a correct amount of beads, cotton cloth, red kerchiefs, brass wire, and other trade goods it contained. Besides the storehouse and Makola's hut, there was only one large building in the cleared ground of the station. It was built neatly of reeds, with a verandah on all the four sides. There were three rooms in it. The one in the middle was the living-room, and had two rough tables and a few stools in it. The other two were the bedrooms for the white men. Each had a bedstead and a mosquito net for all furniture. The plank floor was littered with the belongings of the white men; open half-empty boxes, torn wearing apparel, old boots; all the things dirty, and all the things broken, that accumulate mysteriously round untidy men. There was also another dwelling-place some distance away from the buildings. In it, under a tall cross much out of the perpendicular, slept the man who had seen the beginning of all this; who had planned and had watched the construction of this outpost of progress. He had been,

*See Miss Welty's essay "Place in Fiction" in her book *The Eye of the Story* (New York: Random House, 1979), pp. 116–133.

at home, an unsuccessful painter who, weary of pursuing fame on an empty stomach, had gone out there through high protections. He had been the first chief of that station. Makola had watched the energetic artist die of fever in the just finished house with his usual kind of "I told you so" indifference. Then, for a time, he dwelt alone with his family, his account books, and the Evil Spirit that rules the lands under the equator. He got on very well with his god. Perhaps he had propitiated him by a promise of more white men to play with, by and by. At any rate the director of the Great Trading Company, coming up in a steamer that resembled an enormous sardine box with a flat-roofed shed erected on it, found the station in good order, and Makola as usual quietly diligent. The director had the cross put up over the first agent's grave, and appointed Kayerts to the post. Carlier was told off as second in charge. The director was a man ruthless and efficient, who at times, but very imperceptibly, indulged in grim humor. He made a speech to Kayerts and Carlier, pointing out to them the promising aspect of their station. The nearest trading-post was about three hundred miles away. It was an exceptional opportunity for them to distinguish themselves and to earn percentages on the trade. This appointment was a favor done to beginners. Kayerts was moved almost to tears by his director's kindness. He would, he said, by doing his best, try to justify the flattering confidence, &c., &c. Kayerts had been in the Administration of the Telegraphs, and knew how to express himself correctly. Carlier, an ex-noncommissioned officer of cavalry in an army guaranteed from harm by several European Powers, was less impressed. If there were commissions to get, so much the better; and, trailing a sulky glance over the river, the forests, the impenetrable bush that seemed to cut off the station from the rest of the world, he muttered between his teeth, "We shall see, very soon."

Next day, some bales of cotton goods and a few cases of provisions having been thrown on shore, the sardine-box steamer went off, not to return for another six months. On the deck the director touched his cap to the two agents, who stood on the bank waving their hats, and turning to an old servant of the Company on his passage to headquarters, said, "Look at those two imbeciles. They must be mad at home to send me such specimens. I told those fellows to plant a vegetable garden, build new store-houses and fences, and construct a landing-stage. I bet nothing will be done! They won't know how to begin. I always thought the station on this river useless, and they just fit the station!"

"They will form themselves there," said the old stager with a quiet smile.

"At any rate, I am rid of them for six months," retorted the director.

The two men watched the steamer round the bend, then, ascending arm in arm the slope of the bank, returned to the station. They had been in this vast and dark country only a very short time, and as yet always in the midst of other white men, under the eye and guidance of their superiors. And now, dull as they were to the subtle influences of surroundings, they felt themselves very much alone, when suddenly left unassisted to face the wilderness; a wilderness rendered more strange, more incomprehensible by the mysterious glimpses of the vigorous life it contained. They were two perfectly insignificant and incapable individuals, whose existence is only rendered possible through the high organization of civilized crowds. Few men realize that their life, the very essence of their character, their capabilities and their audacities, are only the expression of their belief in the safety of their surroundings. The courage, the composure, the confidence; the emotions and principles; every great and every insignificant thought belongs not to the individual but to the crowd: to the crowd that believes blindly in the irresistible force of its institutions and of its morals, in the power of its police and of its opinion. But the contact with pure unmitigated savagery, with primitive nature and primitive man, brings sudden and profound trouble into the heart. To the sentiment of being alone of one's kind, to the clear perception of the loneliness of one's thoughts, of one's sensations—to the negation of the habitual, which is safe, there is added the affirmation of the unusual, which is dangerous; a suggestion of things vague, uncontrollable, and repulsive, whose discomposing intrusion excites the imagination and tries the civilized nerves of the foolish and the wise alike.

Kayerts and Carlier walked arm in arm, drawing close to one another as children do in the dark; and they had the same, not altogether unpleasant, sense of danger which one half suspects to be imaginary. They chatted persistently in familiar tones. "Our station is prettily situated," said one. The other assented with enthusiasm, enlarging volubly on the beauties of the situation. Then they passed near the grave. "Poor devil!" said Kayerts. "He died of fever, didn't he?" muttered Carlier, stopping short. "Why," retorted Kayerts, with indignation, "I've been told that the fellow exposed himself recklessly to the sun. The climate here, everybody says, is not at all worse than at home, as long as you keep out of the sun. Do you hear that, Carlier? I am chief here, and my orders are that you should not expose yourself to the sun!" He assumed his superiority jocularly, but his meaning was serious. The idea that he would, perhaps, have to bury Carlier and remain alone, gave him an inward shiver. He felt suddenly that this Carlier was more precious to him here, in the center of Africa, than a brother could be anywhere else. Carlier, entering into the spirit of the thing, made a military salute and answered in a brisk tone, "Your orders shall be attended to, chief!" Then he burst out laughing, slapped Kayerts on the back and shouted, "We shall let life run easily here! Just sit still and gather in the ivory those savages will bring. This country has its good points, after all!" They both laughed loudly while Carlier thought: "That poor Kayerts; he is so fat and unhealthy. It would be awful if I had to bury him here. He is a man I respect." . . . Before they reached the verandah of their house they called one another "my dear fellow."

The first day they were very active, pottering about with hammers and nails and red calico, to put up curtains, make their house habitable and pretty; resolved to settle down comfortably to their new life. For them an impossible task. To grapple effectually with even purely material problems requires more serenity of mind and more lofty courage than people generally imagine. No two beings could have been more unfitted for such a struggle. Society, not from any tenderness, but because of its strange needs, had taken care of those two men, forbidding them all independent thought, all initiative, all departure from routine; and forbidding it under pain of death. They could only live on condition of being machines. And now, released from the fostering care of men with pens behind the ears, or of men with gold lace on the sleeves, they were like those lifelong prisoners who, liberated after many years, do not know what use to make of their freedom. They did not know what use to make of their faculties, being both, through want of practice, incapable of independent thought.

At the end of two months Kayerts often would say, "If it was not for my Melie, you wouldn't catch me here." Melie was his daughter. He had thrown up his post in the Administration of the Telegraphs, though he had been for seventeen years perfectly happy there, to earn a dowry for his girl. His wife was dead, and the child was being brought up by his sisters. He regretted the streets, the pavements, the cafés, his friends of many years; all the things he used to see, day after day; all the thoughts suggested by familiar things—the thoughts effortless, monotonous, and soothing of a Government clerk; he regretted all the gossip, the small enmities, the mild venom, and the little jokes of Government offices. "If I had had a decent brother-in-law," Carlier would remark, "a fellow with a heart, I would not be here." He had left the army and had made himself so obnoxious to his family by his laziness and impudence, that an exasperated brother-in-law had made superhuman efforts to procure him an appointment in the Company as a second-class agent. Having not a penny in the world he was compelled to accept this means of livelihood as soon as it became quite clear to him that there was nothing more to squeeze out of his relations. He, like Kayerts, regretted his old life. He regretted the clink of sabre and spurs on a fine afternoon, the barrack-room witticisms, the girls of garrison towns; but, besides, he had also a sense of grievance. He was evidently a much ill-used man. This made him moody, at times. But the two men got on well together in the fellowship of their stupidity and laziness. Together they did nothing, absolutely nothing, and enjoyed the sense of the idleness for which they were paid. And in time they came to feel something resembling affection for one another.

They lived like blind men in a large room, aware only of what came in contact with them (and of that only imperfectly), but unable to see the general aspect of things. The river, the forest, all the great land throbbing with life, were like a great emptiness. Even the brilliant sunshine disclosed nothing intelligible. Things appeared and disappeared before their eyes in an unconnected and aimless kind of way. The river seemed to come from nowhere and flow nowhither. It flowed through a void. Out of that void, at times, came canoes, and men with spears in their hands would suddenly crowd the yard of the station. They were naked, glossy black, ornamented with snowy shells and glistening brass wire, perfect of limb. They made an uncouth babbling noise when they spoke, moved in a stately manner, and sent quick, wild glances out of their startled, never-resting eyes. Those warriors would squat in long rows, four or more deep, before the verandah, while their chiefs bargained for hours with Makola over an elephant tusk. Kayerts sat on his chair and looked down on the proceedings, understanding nothing. He stared at them with his round blue eyes, called out to Carlier, "Here, look! Look at that fellow there—and that other one, to the left. Did you ever see such a face? Oh, the funny brute!"

Carlier, smoking native tobacco in a short wooden pipe, would swagger up twirling his moustaches, and surveying the warriors with haughty indulgence, would say—

"Fine animals. Brought any bone? Yes? It's not any too soon. Look at the muscles of that fellow—third from the end. I wouldn't care to get a punch on the nose from him. Fine arms, but legs no good below the knee. Couldn't make cavalry men of them." And after glancing down complacently at his own shanks, he always concluded: "Pah! Don't they stink! You, Makola! Take that herd over to the fetish" (the storehouse was in every station called the fetish, perhaps because of the spirit of civilization it contained) "and give them up some of the rubbish you keep there. I'd rather see it full of bone than full of rags."

Kayerts approved.

"Yes, yes! Go and finish that palaver over there, Mr. Makola. I will come round when you are ready, to weigh the tusk. We must be careful." Then turning to his companion: "This is the tribe that lives down the river; they are rather aromatic. I remember, they had been once before here. D'ye hear that row? What a fellow has got to put up with in this dog of a country! My head is split."

Such profitable visits were rare. For days the two pioneers of trade and progress would look on their empty courtyard in the vibrating brilliance of vertical sunshine. Below the high bank, the silent river flowed on glittering and steady. On the sands in the middle of the stream, hippos and alligators sunned themselves side by side. And stretching away in all directions, surrounding the insignificant cleared spot of the trading post, immense forests, hiding fateful complications of fantastic life, lay in the eloquent silence of mute greatness. The two men understood nothing, cared for nothing but for the passage of days that separated them from the steamer's return. Their predecessor had left some torn books. They took up these wrecks of novels, and, as they had never read anything of the kind before, they were surprised and amused. Then during long days there were interminable and silly discussions about plots and person-ages. In the center of Africa they made acquaintance of Richelieu and of d'Artagnan, of Hawk's Eye and of Father Goriot, and of many other people. All these imaginary personages became subjects for gossip as if they had been living friends. They discounted their virtues, suspected their motives, decried their successes; were scandalized at their duplicity or were doubtful about their courage. The accounts of crimes filled them with indignation, while tender or pathetic passages moved them deeply. Carlier cleared his throat and said in a soldierly voice, "What nonsense!" Kayerts, his round eyes suffused with tears, his fat cheeks quivering, rubbed his bald head, and declared, "This is a splendid book. I had no idea there were such clever fellows in the world." They also found some old copies of a home paper. That print discussed what it was pleased to call "Our Colonial Expansion" in high-flown language. It spoke much of the rights and duties of civilization, of the sacredness of the civilizing work, and extolled the merits of those who went about bringing light, and faith and commerce to the dark places of the earth. Carlier and Kayerts read, wondered, and began to think better of themselves. Carlier said one evening, waving his hand about, "In a hundred years, there will be perhaps a town here. Quays, and warehouses, and barracks, and—and—billiard-rooms. Civilization, my boy, and virtue—and all. And then, chaps will read that two good fellows, Kayerts and Carlier, were the first civilized men to live in this very spot!" Kayerts nodded, "Yes, it is a consolation to think of that." They seemed to forget their dead predecessor; but, early one day, Carlier went out and replanted the cross firmly. "It used to make me squint whenever I walked that way," he explained to Kayerts over the morning coffee. "It made me squint, leaning over so much. So I just planted it upright. And solid, I promise you! I suspended myself with both hands to the cross-piece. Not a move. Oh, I did that properly."

At times Gobila came to see them. Gobila was the chief of the neighboring villages. He was a gray-headed savage, thin and black, with a white cloth round his loins and a mangy panther skin hanging over his back. He came up with long strides of his skeleton legs, swinging a staff as tall as himself, and, entering the common room of the station, would squat on his heels to the left of the door. There he sat, watching Kayerts, and now and then making a speech which the other did not understand. Kayerts, without interrupting his occupation, would from time to time say in a friendly manner: "How goes it, you old image?" and they would smile at one another. The two whites had a liking for that old and incomprehensible creature, and called him Father Gobila. Gobila's manner was paternal, and he seemed really to love all white men. They all appeared to him very young, indistinguishably alike (except for stature), and he knew that they were all brothers, and also immortal. The death of the artist, who was the first white man whom he knew intimately, did not disturb this belief, because he was firmly convinced that the white stranger had pretended to die and got himself buried for some mysterious purpose of his own, into which it was useless to inquire. Perhaps it was his way of going home to his own country? At any rate, these were his brothers, and he transferred his absurd affection to them. They returned it in a way. Carlier slapped him on the back, and recklessly struck off matches for his amusement. Kayerts was always ready to let him have a sniff at the ammonia bottle. In short, they behaved just like that other white creature that had hidden itself in a hole in the ground. Gobila considered them attentively. Perhaps they were the same being with the other—or one of them was. He couldn't decide—clear up that mystery; but he remained always very friendly. In consequence of that friendship the women of Gobila's village walked in single file through the reedy grass, bringing every morning to the station, fowls, and sweet potatoes, and palm wine, and sometimes a goat. The Company never provisions the stations fully, and the agents required those local supplies to live. They had them through the good-will of Gobila, and lived well. Now and then one of them had a bout of fever, and the other nursed him with gentle devotion. They did not think much of it. It left them weaker, and their appearance changed for the worse. Carlier was hollow-eyed and irritable. Kayerts showed a drawn, flabby face above the rotundity of his stomach, which gave him a weird aspect. But being constantly together, they did not notice the change that took place gradually in their appearance, and also in their dispositions.

Five months passed in that way.

Then, one morning, as Kayerts and Carlier, lounging in their chairs under the verandah, talked about the approaching visit of the steamer, a knot of armed men came out of the forest and advanced towards the station. They were strangers to that part of the country. They were tall, slight, draped classically from neck to heel in blue fringed cloths, and carried percussion muskets over their bare right shoulders. Makola showed signs of excitement, and ran out of the storehouse (where he spent all his days) to meet these visitors. They came into the courtyard and looked about them with steady, scornful glances. Their leader, a powerful and determined-looking negro with blood-shot eyes, stood in front of the verandah and made a long speech. He gesticulated much, and ceased very suddenly.

There was something in his intonation, in the sounds of the long sentences he used, that startled the two whites. It was like a reminiscence of something not exactly familiar, and yet resembling the speech of civilized men. It sounded like one of those impossible languages which sometimes we hear in our dreams.

"What lingo is that?" said the amazed Carlier. "In the first moment I fancied the fellow was going to speak French. Anyway, it is a different kind of gibberish to what we ever heard."

"Yes," replied Kayerts. "Hey, Makola, what does he say? Where do they come from? Who are they?"

But Makola, who seemed to be standing on hot bricks, answered hurriedly, "I don't know. They come from very far. Perhaps Mrs. Price will understand. They are perhaps bad men."

The leader, after waiting for a while, said something sharply to Makola, who shook

his head. Then the man, after looking round, noticed Makola's hut and walked over
there. The next moment Mrs. Makola was heard speaking with great volubility. The
other strangers—they were six in all—strolled about with an air of ease, put their heads
through the door of the storeroom, congregated round the grave, pointed understand-
ingly at the cross, and generally made themselves at home.

"I don't like those chaps—and, I say, Kayerts, they must be from the coast; they've
got firearms," observed the sagacious Carlier.

Kayerts also did not like those chaps. They both, for the first time, became aware
that they lived in conditions where the unusual may be dangerous, and that there was
no power on earth outside of themselves to stand between them and the unusual. They
became uneasy, went in and loaded their revolvers. Kayerts said, "We must order
Makola to tell them to go away before dark."

The strangers left in the afternoon, after eating a meal prepared for them by Mrs.
Makola. The immense woman was excited, and talked much with the visitors. She
rattled away shrilly, pointing here and there at the forests and at the river. Makola sat
apart and watched. At times he got up and whispered to his wife. He accompanied the
strangers across the ravine at the back of the station-ground, and returned slowly
looking very thoughtful. When questioned by the white men he was very strange,
seemed not to understand, seemed to have forgotten French—seemed to have forgotten
how to speak altogether. Kayerts and Carlier agreed that the nigger had had too much
palm wine.

There was some talk about keeping a watch in turn, but in the evening everything
seemed so quiet and peaceful that they retired as usual. All night they were disturbed
by a lot of drumming in the villages. A deep, rapid roll near by would be followed
by another far off—then all ceased. Soon short appeals would rattle out here and there,
then all mingle together, increase, become vigorous and sustained, would spread out
over the forest, roll through the night, unbroken and ceaseless, near and far, as if the
whole land had been one immense drum booming out steadily an appeal to heaven.
And through the deep and tremendous noise sudden yells that resembled snatches of
songs from a madhouse darted shrill and high in discordant jets of sound which seemed
to rush far above the earth and drive all peace from under the stars.

Carlier and Kayerts slept badly. They both thought they had heard shots fired during
the night—but they could not agree as to the direction. In the morning Makola was
gone somewhere. He returned about noon with one of yesterday's strangers, and eluded
all Kayerts' attempts to close with him: had become deaf apparently. Kayerts wondered.
Carlier, who had been fishing off the bank, came back and remarked while he showed
his catch, "The niggers seem to be in a deuce of a stir; I wonder what's up. I saw about
fifteen canoes cross the river during the two hours I was there fishing." Kayerts,
worried, said, "Isn't this Makola very queer today?" Carlier advised, "Keep all our men
together in case of some trouble."

2

There were ten station men who had been left by the Director. Those fellows, having
engaged themselves to the Company for six months (without having any idea of a
month in particular and only a very faint notion of time in general), had been serving
the cause of progress for upwards of two years. Belonging to a tribe from a very distant

part of the land of darkness and sorrow, they did not run away, naturally supposing that as wandering strangers they would be killed by the inhabitants of the country; in which they were right. They lived in straw huts on the slope of a ravine overgrown with reedy grass, just behind the station buildings. They were not happy, regretting the festive incantations, the sorceries, the human sacrifices of their own land; where they also had parents, brothers, sisters, admired chiefs, respected magicians, loved friends, and other ties supposed generally to be human. Besides, the rice rations served out by the Company did not agree with them, being a food unknown to their land, and to which they could not get used. Consequently they were unhealthy and miserable. Had they been of any other tribe they would have made up their minds to die—for nothing is easier to certain savages than suicide—and so have escaped from the puzzling difficulties of existence. But belonging, as they did, to a warlike tribe with filed teeth, they had more grit, and went on stupidly living through disease and sorrow. They did very little work, and had lost their splendid physique. Carlier and Kayerts doctored them assiduously without being able to bring them back into condition again. They were mustered every morning and told off to different tasks—grass-cutting, fence-building, tree-felling, &c., &c., which no power on earth could induce them to execute efficiently. The two whites had practically very little control over them.

In the afternoon Makola came over to the big house and found Kayerts watching three heavy columns of smoke rising above the forests. "What is that?" asked Kayerts. "Some villages burn," answered Makola, who seemed to have regained his wits. Then he said abruptly: "We have got very little ivory; bad six months' trading. Do you like get a little more ivory?"

"Yes," said Kayerts, eagerly. He thought of percentages which were low.

"Those men who came yesterday are traders from Loanda who have got more ivory than they can carry home. Shall I buy? I know their camp."

"Certainly," said Kayerts. "What are those traders?"

"Bad fellows," said Makola, indifferently. "They fight with people, and catch women and children. They are bad men, and got guns. There is a great disturbance in the country. Do you want ivory?"

"Yes," said Kayerts. Makola said nothing for a while. Then: "Those workmen of ours are no good at all," he muttered, looking round. "Station in very bad order, sir. Director will growl. Better get a fine lot of ivory, then he say nothing."

"I can't help it; the men won't work," said Kayerts. "When will you get that ivory?"

"Very soon," said Makola. "Perhaps tonight. You leave it to me, and keep indoors, sir. I think you had better give some palm wine to our men to make a dance this evening. Enjoy themselves. Work better tomorrow. There's plenty palm wine—gone a little sour."

Kayerts said "yes," and Makola, with his own hands, carried big calabashes to the door of his hut. They stood there till the evening, and Mrs. Makola looked into every one. The men got them at sunset. When Kayerts and Carlier retired, a big bonfire was flaring before the men's huts. They could hear their shouts and drumming. Some men from Gobila's village had joined the station hands, and the entertainment was a great success.

In the middle of the night, Carlier waking suddenly, heard a man shout loudly; then a shot was fired. Only one. Carlier ran out and met Kayerts on the verandah. They were both startled. As they went across the yard to call Makola, they saw shadows moving in the night. One of them cried, "Don't shoot! It's me, Price." Then Makola appeared close to them. "Go back, go back, please," he urged, "you spoil all." "There are strange men about," said Carlier. "Never mind; I know," said Makola. Then he whispered, "All right. Bring ivory. Say nothing! I know my business." The two white men reluctantly went back to the house, but did not sleep. They heard footsteps, whispers, some groans. It seemed as if a lot of men came in, dumped heavy things on the ground, squabbled a long time, then went away. They lay on their hard beds and thought: "This Makola is invaluable." In the morning Carlier came out, very sleepy, and pulled at the cord of the big bell. The station hands mustered every morning to the sound of the bell. That morning nobody came. Kayerts turned out also, yawning. Across the yard they saw Makola come out of his hut, a tin basin of soapy water in his hand. Makola, a civilized nigger, was very neat in his person. He threw the soapsuds skillfully over a wretched little yellow cur he had, then turning his face to the agent's house, he shouted from the distance, "All the men gone last night!"

They heard him plainly, but in their surprise they both yelled out together: "What!" Then they stared at one another. "We are in a proper fix now," growled Carlier. "It's incredible!" muttered Kayerts. "I will go to the huts and see," said Carlier, striding off. Makola coming up found Kayerts standing alone.

"I can hardly believe it," said Kayerts, tearfully. "We took care of them as if they had been our children."

"They went with the coast people," said Makola after a moment of hesitation.

"What do I care with whom they went—the ungrateful brutes!" exclaimed the other. Then with sudden suspicion, and looking hard at Makola, he added: "What do you know about it?"

Makola moved his shoulders, looking down on the ground. "What do I know? I think only. Will you come and look at the ivory I've got there? It is a fine lot. You never saw such."

He moved towards the store. Kayerts followed him mechanically, thinking about the incredible desertion of the men. On the ground before the door of the fetish lay six splendid tusks.

"What did you give for it?" asked Kayerts, after surveying the lot with satisfaction.

"No regular trade," said Makola. "They brought the ivory and gave it to me. I told them to take what they most wanted in the station. It is a beautiful lot. No station can show such tusks. Those traders wanted carriers badly, and our men were no good here. No trade, no entry in books; all correct."

Kayerts nearly burst with indignation. "Why!" he shouted, "I believe you have sold our men for these tusks!" Makola stood impassive and silent. "I—I—will—I," stuttered Kayerts. "You fiend!" he yelled out.

"I did the best for you and the Company," said Makola, imperturbably. "Why you shout so much? Look at this tusk."

"I dismiss you! I will report you—I won't look at the tusk. I forbid you to touch them. I order you to throw them into the river. You—you!"

"You very red, Mr. Kayerts. If you are so irritable in the sun, you will get fever and die—like the first chief!" pronounced Makola impressively.

They stood still, contemplating one another with intense eyes, as if they had been looking with effort across immense distances. Kayerts shivered. Makola had meant no more than he said, but his words seemed to Kayerts full of ominous menace! He turned sharply and went away to the house. Makola retired into the bosom of his family; and the tusks, left lying before the store, looked very large and valuable in the sunshine.

Carlier came back on the verandah. "They're all gone, hey?" asked Kayerts from the far end of the common room in a muffled voice. "You did not find anybody?"

"Oh, yes," said Carlier, "I found one of Gobila's people lying dead before the huts —shot through the body. We heard that shot last night."

Kayerts came out quickly. He found his companion staring grimly over the yard at the tusks, away by the store. They both sat in silence for a while. Then Kayerts related his conversation with Makola. Carlier said nothing. At the midday meal they ate very little. They hardly exchanged a word that day. A great silence seemed to lie heavily over the station and press on their lips, Makola did not open the store; he spent the day playing with his children. He lay full-length on a mat outside his door, and the youngsters sat on his chest and clambered all over him. It was a touching picture. Mrs. Makola was busy cooking all day as usual. The white men made a somewhat better meal in the evening. Afterwards, Carlier smoking his pipe strolled over to the store; he stood for a long time over the tusks, touched one or two with his foot, even tried to lift the largest one by its small end. He came back to his chief, who had not stirred from the verandah, threw himself in the chair and said—

"I can see it! They were pounced upon while they slept heavily after drinking all that palm wine you've allowed Makola to give them. A put-up job! See? The worst is, some of Gobila's people were there, and got carried off too, no doubt. The least drunk woke up, and got shot for his sobriety. This is a funny country. What will you do now?"

"We can't touch it, of course," said Kayerts.

"Of course not," assented Carlier.

"Slavery is an awful thing," stammered out Kayerts in an unsteady voice.

"Frightful—the sufferings," grunted Carlier with conviction.

They believed their words. Everybody shows a respectful deference to certain sounds that he and his fellows can make. But about feelings people really know nothing. We talk with indignation or enthusiasm; we talk about oppression, cruelty, crime, devotion, self-sacrifice, virtue, and we know nothing real beyond the words. Nobody knows what suffering or sacrifice mean—except, perhaps the victims of the mysterious purpose of these illusions.

Next morning they saw Makola very busy setting up in the yard the big scales used for weighing ivory. By and by Carlier said: "What's that filthy scoundrel up to?" and lounged out into the yard. Kayerts followed. They stood watching. Makola took no notice. When the balance was swung true, he tried to lift a tusk into the scale. It was too heavy. He looked up helplessly without a word, and for a minute they stood round that balance as mute and still as three statues. Suddenly Carlier said: "Catch hold of the other end, Makola—you beast!" and together they swung the tusk up. Kayerts trembled in every limb. He muttered, "I say! O! I say!" and putting his hand in his pocket found there a dirty bit of paper and the stump of a pencil. He turned his back on the others, as if about to do something tricky, and noted stealthily the weights which Carlier shouted out to him with unnecessary loudness. When all was over Makola whispered to himself: "The sun's very strong here for the tusks." Carlier said to Kayerts in a careless tone: "I say, chief, I might just as well give him a lift with this lot into the store."

As they were going back to the house Kayerts observed with a sigh: "It had to be done." And Carlier said: "It's deplorable, but, the men being Company's men the ivory is Company's ivory. We must look after it." "I will report to the Director, of course," said Kayerts, "Of course; let him decide," approved Carlier.

At midday they made a hearty meal. Kayerts sighed from time to time. Whenever they mentioned Makola's name they always added to it an opprobrious epithet. It eased their conscience. Makola gave himself a half-holiday, and bathed his children in the river. No one from Gobila's villages came near the station that day. No one came the next day, and the next, nor for a whole week. Gobila's people might have been dead and buried for any sign of life they gave. But they were only mourning for those they had lost by the witchcraft of white men, who had brought wicked people into their country. The wicked people were gone, but fear remained. Fear always remains. A man may destroy everything within himself, love and hate and belief, and even doubt; but as long as he clings to life he cannot destroy fear: the fear, subtle, indestructible, and terrible, that pervades his being; that tinges his thoughts; that lurks in his heart; that watches on his lips the struggle of his last breath. In his fear, the mild old Gobila offered extra human sacrifices to all the Evil Spirits that had taken possession of his white friends. His heart was heavy. Some warriors spoke about burning and killing, but the cautious old savage dissuaded them. Who could foresee the woe those mysterious creatures, if irritated, might bring? They should be left alone. Perhaps in time they would disappear into the earth as the first one had disappeared. His people must keep away from them, and hope for the best.

Kayerts and Carlier did not disappear, but remained above on this earth, that, somehow, they fancied had become bigger and very empty. It was not the absolute and dumb solitude of the post that impressed them so much as an inarticulate feeling that something from within them was gone, something that worked for their safety, and had kept the wilderness from interfering with their hearts. The images of home; the memory of people like them, of men that thought and felt as they used to think and feel, receded into distances made indistinct by the glare of unclouded sunshine. And out of the great silence of the surrounding wilderness, its very hopelessness and savagery seemed to approach them nearer, to draw them gently, to look upon them, to envelop them with a solicitude irresistible, familiar, and disgusting.

Days lengthened into weeks, then into months. Gobila's people drummed and yelled to every new moon, as of yore, but kept away from the station. Makola and Carlier tried once in a canoe to open communications, but were received with a shower of arrows, and had to fly back to the station for dear life. That attempt set the country up and down the river into an uproar that could be very distinctly heard for days. The steamer was late. At first they spoke of delay jauntily, then anxiously, then gloomily. The matter was becoming serious. Stores were running short. Carlier cast his lines off the bank, but the river was low, and the fish kept out in the stream. They dared not stroll far away from the station to shoot. Moreover, there was no game in the impenetrable forest. Once Carlier shot a hippo in the river. They had no boat to secure it, and it sank. When it floated up it drifted away, and Gobila's people secured the carcase. It was the occasion for a national holiday, but Carlier had a fit of rage over it and talked about the necessity of exterminating all the niggers before the country could be made habitable. Kayerts mooned about silently; spent hours looking at the portrait of his Melie. It represented a little girl with long bleached tresses and a rather sour face. His legs were much swollen, and he could hardly walk. Carlier, undermined by fever, could not swagger any more, but kept tottering about, still with a devil-may-care air, as became a man who remembered his crack regiment. He had become hoarse, sarcastic, and inclined to say unpleasant things. He called it "being frank with you." They had long ago reckoned their percentages on trade, including in them that last deal of "this infamous Makola." They had also concluded not to say anything about it. Kayerts hesitated at first—was afraid of the Director.

"He has seen worse things done on the quiet," maintained Carlier, with a hoarse laugh. "Trust him! He won't thank you if you blab. He is no better than you or me. Who will talk if we hold our tongues? There is nobody here."

That was the root of the trouble! There was nobody there; and being left there alone with their weakness, they became daily more like a pair of accomplices than like a couple of devoted friends. They had heard nothing from home for eight months. Every evening they said, "Tomorrow we shall see the steamer." But one of the Company's steamers had been wrecked, and the Director was busy with the other, relieving very distant and important stations on the main river. He thought that the useless station, and the useless men, could wait. Meantime Kayerts and Carlier lived on rice boiled without salt, and cursed the Company, all Africa, and the day they were born. One must have lived on such diet to discover what ghastly trouble the necessity of swallowing one's food may become. There was literally nothing else in the station but rice and coffee; they drank the coffee without sugar. The last fifteen lumps Kayerts had solemnly locked away in his box, together with a half-bottle of Cognâc, "in case of sickness," he explained. Carlier approved. "When one is sick," he said, "any little extra like that is cheering."

They waited. Rank grass began to sprout over the courtyard. The bell never rang now. Days passed, silent, exasperating, and slow. When the two men spoke, they snarled; and their silences were bitter, as if tinged by the bitterness of their thoughts.

One day after a lunch of boiled rice, Carlier put down his cup untasted, and said: "Hang it all! Let's have a decent cup of coffee for once. Bring out that sugar, Kayerts!"

"For the sick," muttered Kayerts, without looking up.

"For the sick," mocked Carlier. "Bosh . . . Well! I am sick."

"You are no more sick than I am, and I go without," said Kayerts in a peaceful tone.

"Come! Out with that sugar, you stingy old slave-dealer."

Kayerts looked up quickly. Carlier was smiling with marked insolence. And suddenly it seemed to Kayerts that he had never seen that man before. Who was he? He knew nothing about him. What was he capable of? There was a surprising flash of violent emotion within him, as if in the presence of something undreamt-of, dangerous, and final. But he managed to pronounce with composure—

"That joke is in very bad taste. Don't repeat it."

"Joke!" said Carlier, hitching himself forward on his seat. "I am hungry—I am sick —I don't joke! I hate hypocrites. You are a hypocrite. You are a slave-dealer. I am a slave-dealer. There's nothing but slave-dealers in this cursed country. I mean to have sugar in my coffee today, anyhow!"

"I forbid you to speak to me in that way," said Kayerts with a fair show of resolution.

"You—What?" shouted Carlier, jumping up.

Kayerts stood up also. "I am your chief," he began, trying to master the shakiness of his voice.

"What?" yelled the other. "Who's chief? There's no chief here. There's nothing here: there's nothing but you and I. Fetch the sugar—you pot-bellied ass."

"Hold your tongue. Go out of this room," screamed Kayerts. "I dismiss you—you scoundrel!"

Carlier swung a stool. All at once he looked dangerously in earnest. "You flabby, good-for-nothing civilian—take that!" he howled.

Kayerts dropped under the table, and the stool struck the grass inner wall of the room. Then, as Carlier was trying to upset the table, Kayerts in desperation made a blind rush, head low, like a cornered pig would do, and overturning his friend, bolted along the verandah, and into his room. He locked the door, snatched his revolver, and stood panting. In less than a minute Carlier was kicking at the door furiously, howling, "If you don't bring out that sugar, I will shoot you at sight, like a dog. Now then —one—two—three. You won't? I will show you who's the master."

Kayerts thought the door would fall in, and scrambled through the square hole that served for a window in his room. There was then the whole breadth of the house between them. But the other was apparently not strong enough to break in the door, and Kayerts heard him running round. Then he also began to run laboriously on his swollen legs. He ran as quickly as he could, grasping the revolver, and unable yet to understand what was happening to him. He saw in succession Makola's house, the store, the river, the ravine, and the low bushes; and he saw all those things again as he ran for the second time round the house. Then again they flashed past him. That morning he could not have walked a yard without a groan.

And now he ran. He ran fast enough to keep out of sight of the other man.

Then as, weak and desperate, he thought, "Before I finish the next round I shall die," he heard the other man stumble heavily, then stop. He stopped also. He had the back and Carlier the front of the house, as before. He heard him drop into a chair cursing, and suddenly his own legs gave way, and he slid down into a sitting posture with his back to the wall. His mouth was as dry as a cinder, and his face was wet with perspiration—and tears. What was it all about? He thought it must be a horrible illusion; he thought he was dreaming; he thought he was going mad! After a while he collected his senses. What did they quarrel about? That sugar! How absurd! He would give it to him—didn't want it himself. And he began scrambling to his feet with a sudden feeling of security. But before he had fairly stood upright, a common-sense reflection occurred to him and drove him back into despair. He thought: "If I give way now to that brute of a soldier, he will begin this horror again tomorrow—and the day after—every day—raise other pretensions, trample on me, torture me, make me his slave—and I will be lost! Lost! The steamer may not come for days—may never come." He shook so that he had to sit down on the floor again. He shivered forlornly. He felt he could not, would not move any more. He was completely distracted by the sudden perception that the position was without issue—that death and life had in a moment become equally difficult and terrible.

All at once he heard the other push his chair back; and he leaped to his feet with extreme facility. He listened and got confused. Must run again! Right or left? He heard footsteps. He darted to the left, grasping his revolver, and at the very same instant, as it seemed to him, they came into violent collision. Both shouted with surprise. A loud explosion took place between them; a roar of red fire, thick smoke; and Kayerts, deafened and blinded, rushed back thinking: "I am hit—it's all over." He expected the other to come round—to gloat over his agony. He caught hold of an upright of the roof—"All over!" Then he heard a crashing fall on the other side of the house, as if somebody had tumbled headlong over a chair—then silence. Nothing more happened. He did not die. Only his shoulder felt as if it had been badly wrenched, and he had lost his revolver. He was disarmed and helpless! He waited for his fate. The other man made no sound. It was a stratagem. He was stalking him now! Along what side? Perhaps he was taking aim this very minute!

After a few moments of an agony frightful and absurd, he decided to go and meet his doom. He was prepared for every surrender. He turned the corner, steadying himself with one hand on the wall; made a few paces, and nearly swooned. He had seen on the floor, protruding past the other corner, a pair of turned-up feet. A pair of white naked feet in red slippers. He felt deadly sick, and stood for a time in profound darkness. Then Makola appeared before him, saying quietly: "Come along, Mr. Kayerts. He is dead." He burst into tears of gratitude; a loud, sobbing fit of crying. After a time he found himself sitting in a chair and looking at Carlier, who lay stretched on his back. Makola was kneeling over the body.

"Is this your revolver?" asked Makola, getting up.

"Yes," said Kayerts; then he added very quickly, "He ran after me to shoot me—you saw!"

"Yes, I saw," said Makola. "There is only one revolver; where's his?"

"Don't know," whispered Kayerts in a voice that had become suddenly very faint.

"I will go and look for it," said the other, gently. He made the round along the verandah, while Kayerts sat still and looked at the corpse. Makola came back empty-handed, stood in deep thought, then stepped quietly into the dead man's room, and came out directly with a revolver, which he held up before Kayerts. Kayerts shut his eyes. Everything was going round. He found life more terrible and difficult than death. He had shot an unarmed man.

After meditating for a while, Makola said softly, pointing at the dead man who lay there with his right eye blown out—

"He died of fever." Kayerts looked at him with a stony stare. "Yes," repeated Makola, thoughtfully, stepping over the corpse, "I think he died of fever. Bury him tomorrow."

And he went away slowly to his expectant wife, leaving the two white men alone on the verandah.

Night came, and Kayerts sat unmoving on his chair. He sat quiet as if he had taken a dose of opium. The violence of the emotions he had passed through produced a feeling of exhausted serenity. He had plumbed in one short afternoon the depths of horror and despair, and now found repose in the conviction that life had no more secrets for him: neither had death! He sat by the corpse thinking; thinking very actively, thinking very new thoughts. He seemed to have broken loose from himself altogether. His old thoughts, convictions, likes and dislikes, things he respected and things he abhorred, appeared in their true light at last! Appeared contemptible and childish, false and ridiculous. He revelled in his new wisdom while he sat by the man he had killed. He argued with himself about all things under heaven with that kind of wrong-headed lucidity which may be observed in some lunatics. Incidentally he reflected that the fellow dead there had been a noxious beast anyway; that men died every day in thousands; perhaps in hundreds of thousands—who could tell?—and that in the num-

ber, that one death could not possibly make any difference; couldn't have any importance, at least to a thinking creature. He, Kayerts, was a thinking creature. He had been
all his life, till that moment, a believer in a lot of nonsense like the rest of mankind
—who are fools; but now he thought! He knew! He was at peace; he was familiar with
the highest wisdom! Then he tried to imagine himself dead, and Carlier sitting in his
chair watching him; and his attempt met with such unexpected success, that in a very
few moments he became not at all sure who was dead and who was alive. This
extraordinary achievement of his fancy startled him, however, and by a clever and
timely effort of mind he saved himself just in time from becoming Carlier. His heart
thumped, and he felt hot all over at the thought of that danger. Carlier! What a beastly
thing! To compose his now disturbed nerves—and no wonder!—he tried to whistle
a little. Then, suddenly, he fell asleep, or thought he had slept; but at any rate there
was a fog, and somebody had whistled in the fog.

He stood up. The day had come, and a heavy mist had descended upon the land:
the mist penetrating, enveloping, and silent; the morning mist of tropical lands; the mist
that clings and kills; the mist white and deadly, immaculate and poisonous. He stood
up, saw the body, and threw his arms above his head with a cry like that of a man
who, waking from a trance, finds himself immured forever in a tomb. *"Help! . . . My
God!"*

A shriek inhuman, vibrating and sudden, pierced like a sharp dart the white shroud
of that land of sorrow. Three short, impatient screeches followed, and then, for a time,
the fog-wreaths rolled on, undisturbed, through a formidable silence. Then many more
shrieks, rapid and piercing, like the yells of some exasperated and ruthless creature, rent
the air. Progress was calling to Kayerts from the river. Progress and civilization and
all the virtues. Society was calling to its accomplished child to come, to be taken care
of, to be instructed, to be judged, to be condemned; it called him to return to that
rubbish heap from which he had wandered away, so that justice could be done.

Kayerts heard and understood. He stumbled out of the verandah, leaving the other
man quite alone for the first time since they had been thrown there together. He groped
his way through the fog, calling in his ignorance upon the invisible heaven to undo
its work. Makola flitted by in the mist, shouting as he ran—

"Steamer! Steamer! They can't see. They whistle for the station. I go ring the bell.
Go down to the landing, sir. I ring."

He disappeared. Kayerts stood still. He looked upwards; the fog rolled low over his
head. He looked round like a man who has lost his way; and he saw a dark smudge,
a cross-shaped stain, upon the shifting purity of the mist. As he began to stumble
towards it, the station bell rang in a tumultuous peal its answer to the impatient clamor
of the steamer.

The Managing Director of the Great Civilizing Company (since we know that civilization follows trade) landed first, and incontinently lost sight of the steamer. The fog
down by the river was exceedingly dense; above, at the station, the bell rang unceasing
and brazen.

The Director shouted loudly to the steamer:

"There is nobody down to meet us; there may be something wrong, though they
are ringing. You had better come, too!"

And he began to toil up the steep bank. The captain and the engine-driver of the boat followed behind. As they scrambled up the fog thinned, and they could see their Director a good way ahead. Suddenly they saw him start forward, calling to them over his shoulder:—"Run! Run to the house! I've found one of them. Run, look for the other!"

He had found one of them! And even he, the man of varied and startling experience, was somewhat discomposed by the manner of this finding. He stood and fumbled in his pockets (for a knife) while he faced Kayerts, who was hanging by a leather strap from the cross. He had evidently climbed the grave, which was high and narrow, and after tying the end of the strap to the arm, had swung himself off. His toes were only a couple of inches above the ground; his arms hung stiffly down; he seemed to be standing rigidly at attention, but with one purple cheek playfully posed on the shoulder. And, irreverently, he was putting out a swollen tongue at his Managing Director.

QUESTIONS

1. Why is it necessary for "An Outpost of Progress" to take place where it does? What effect does the setting—the location of the outpost and its environment—have on Kayerts and Carlier?
2. Is Conrad suggesting a more general relationship between a person's environment and his behavior, or even further, between environment and character?

POINT OF VIEW

An author's decisions about who is to tell the story and how it is to be told are among the most important he or she makes. Consider, for example, Hemingway's "Hills Like White Elephants," which is narrated by neither of its main characters. The narrator remains unnamed and unidentified. Such a point of view is called *objective*. In a story with an *objective point of view*, the writer shows what happens without directly stating more than can be inferred from its action and dialogue. The narrator, in short, does not tell us anything about what the characters think or feel. He remains a detached observer. The narrator of Chopin's "The Story of an Hour" also does not participate in the action as a character. Both stories employ an outside or *third-person point of view*. But there is an important difference in how much each narrator knows and reveals about the characters' inner lives. Hemingway's narrator reveals nothing directly about their thoughts and feelings. His objective point of view requires that we infer what the characters think and feel. Kate Chopin, on the other hand, employs a third-person point of view but lets us know directly what Mrs. Mallard feels. In both cases we learn about the characters from an outside source, but in the Hemingway story this source is a witness while in Chopin's it is an authority. Each of these styles of third-person point of view seems appropriate to its own story. Each is largely responsible for the kind of story it is. Consider, for example, how different Hemingway's story would be if the narrator explained what the girl or the man were thinking. Conversely, imagine Kate Chopin's story told from a detached, objective point of view in which we were not let into Mrs. Mallard's consciousness. The tone and feel of both stories as we know them would be radically altered.

Although third-person point of view may take us inside a character's consciousness or remain objective, it does not assume the perspective of any character. Stories with narrators who participate in the action are presented from a *first-person point of view.* Narrators of such fictions tell their stories in their own voices with their particular limitations of knowledge and vision. The limitations of a first-person narrator offer writers the opportunity to exploit the discrepancy between the writer's vision and the narrator's. In both Edgar Allan Poe's "The Cask of Amontillado" and Ralph Ellison's "Battle Royal," for example, we encounter narrators who perceive and present themselves one way, but whom we see in different ways. Reading stories narrated in the first person, we need to question the narrator's trustworthiness and remain alert for textual signals that either ensure or undermine it.

Whether a writer uses a first- or a third-person narrator, he or she must also decide how much to let the narrator know about the characters. If a narrator knows everything about all the characters, he or she is "omniscient" (all-knowing) as is the narrator of Joyce's "The Boarding House" who enters the minds of each of the characters and reveals what they think and feel. Stories with such narrators are written from an *omniscient point of view.* If, however, the narrator's knowledge is limited to only one character, major or minor, rather than to all, the narrator possesses *limited omniscience,* as in Chopin's "The Story of an Hour." We can readily see the difference between limited and unlimited omniscience by comparing the following passages. First the limited omniscient narration of Katherine Mansfield's "Bliss":

> Although Bertha Young was thirty she still had moments like this when she wanted to run instead of walk, to take dancing steps on and off the pavement, to bowl a hoop, to throw something up in the air and catch it again, or to stand still and laugh at— nothing—at nothing, simply.
>
> What can you do if you are thirty and, turning the corner of your own street, you are overcome, suddenly, by a feeling of bliss —absolute bliss!—as though you'd suddenly swallowed a bright piece of that late afternoon sun and it burned in your bosom, sending out a little shower of sparks into every particle, into every finger and toe? . . .
>
> Oh, is there no way you can express it without being "drunk and disorderly"? How idiotic civilization is! Why be given a body if you have to keep it shut up in a case like a rare, rare fiddle?
>
> "No, that about the fiddle is not quite what I mean," she thought, running up the steps and feeling in her bag for the key —she'd forgotten it, as usual—and rattling the letter-box. "It's not what I mean, because—Thank you, Mary"—she went into the hall. "Is nurse back?"
>
> "Yes, M'm."
>
> "And has the fruit come?"

"Yes, M'm. Everything's come."

"Bring the fruit up to the dining-room, will you? I'll arrange it before I go upstairs."

It was dusky in the dining-room and quite chilly. But all the same Bertha threw off her coat; she could not bear the tight clasp of it another moment, and the cold air fell on her arms.

But in her bosom there was still that bright glowing place— that shower of little sparks coming from it. It was almost unbearable. She hardly dared to breathe for fear of fanning it higher, and yet she breathed deeply, deeply. She hardly dared to look into the cold mirror—but she did look, and it gave her back a woman, radiant, with smiling, trembling lips, with big, dark eyes and an air of listening, waiting for something . . . divine to happen . . . that she knew must happen- . . . infallibly.

Katherine Mansfield has restricted the narrator to the consciousness of Bertha, never allowing us to see anything that Bertha herself wouldn't notice or understand. Our knowledge of the other characters is filtered through Bertha's observations and inferences about them. James Joyce imposes no such limitations on his narrator in "The Boarding House." Here is the narrator revealing the thoughts of Mrs. Mooney:

She was sure she would win. To begin with she had all the weight of social opinion on her side: she was an outraged mother. She had allowed him to live beneath her roof, assuming that he was a man of honour, and he had simply abused her hospitality. . . . youth could not be pleaded as his excuse; nor could ignorance be his excuse. . . . He had simply taken advantage of Polly's youth and inexperience: that was evident. The question was: What reparation would he make?

And here is the same narrator granting us an inside view of Mr. Doran:

He had a notion that he was being had. He could imagine his friends talking of the affair and laughing. She *was* a little vulgar; sometimes she said *I seen* and *If I had've known*. But what would grammar matter if he really loved her? He could not make up his mind whether to like her or despise her for what she had done. Of course, he had done it too. His instinct urged him to remain free, not to marry. Once you are married you are done for, it said.

Giving us an inside view of each character (Polly receives the same treatment), Joyce's omniscient narrator makes us aware of multiple perspectives. That is, he lets us see what each character experiences; he shows us their differing perceptions of the same situation. In doing so Joyce shifts our sympathies from one character to another as we come to understand their different needs and desires.

The omniscient point of view that Joyce employed in his twentieth-century story "The Boarding House" was a popular choice of eighteenth- and nineteenth-century novelists. But fashions in point of view change: the limited omniscient and first-person points of view are currently popular with contemporary writers. We have described some of the narrative points of view available to writers, but there are others. As we read stories with point of view in mind, we should remember:

1. that it is important to consider *how* point of view affects our responses to the characters and how it collaborates with the other elements of fiction to convey feeling and embody meaning;
2. that our response to a fictional narrator is influenced by the degree of the narrator's knowledge, the objectivity of a narrator's responses, and the degree of his or her participation in the action;
3. that a first-person narrator is not always a trustworthy guide: in fact a large part of our work as readers is to determine a narrator's reliability, to estimate the truth of that narrator's disclosures.

Read the story that follows, William Faulkner's "A Rose for Emily," keeping these considerations in mind. How objective is the narrator's view of Miss Emily? How does the perception we gain of her through observing her in dialogue and with other characters in action compare with the narrator's view? Where and with what effect does the narrator's focus shift from presenting Miss Emily objectively to presenting her subjectively?

WILLIAM FAULKNER

[1897–1962]

A Rose for Emily

I

When Miss Emily Grierson died, our whole town went to her funeral: the men through a sort of respectful affection for a fallen monument, the women mostly out of curiosity to see the inside of her house, which no one save an old manservant—a combined gardener and cook—had seen in at least ten years.

It was a big, squarish frame house that had once been white, decorated with cupolas and spires and scrolled balconies in the heavily lightsome style of the seventies, set on what had once been our most select street. But garages and cotton gins had encroached and obliterated even the august names of that neighborhood; only Miss Emily's house was left, lifting its stubborn and coquettish decay above the cotton wagons and the gasoline pumps—an eyesore among eyesores. And now Miss Emily had gone to join the representatives of those august names where they lay in the cedar-bemused cemetery among the ranked and anonymous graves of Union and Confederate soldiers who fell at the battle of Jefferson.

Alive, Miss Emily had been a tradition, a duty, and a care; a sort of hereditary obligation upon the town, dating from that day in 1894 when Colonel Sartoris, the mayor—he who fathered the edict that no Negro woman should appear on the streets without an apron—remitted her taxes, the dispensation dating from the death of her father on into perpetuity. Not that Miss Emily would have accepted charity. Colonel Sartoris invented an involved tale to the effect that Miss Emily's father had loaned money to the town, which the town, as a matter of business, preferred this way of repaying. Only a man of Colonel Sartoris' generation and thought could have invented it, and only a woman could have believed it.

When the next generation, with its more modern ideas, became mayors and aldermen, this arrangement created some little dissatisfaction. On the first of the year they mailed her a tax notice. February came, and there was no reply. They wrote her a formal letter, asking her to call at the sheriff's office at her convenience. A week later the mayor wrote her himself, offering to call or to send his car for her, and received in reply a note on paper of an archaic shape, in a thin, flowing calligraphy in faded ink, to the effect that she no longer went out at all. The tax notice was also enclosed, without comment.

They called a special meeting of the Board of Aldermen. A deputation waited upon her, knocked at the door through which no visitor had passed since she ceased giving china-painting lessons eight or ten years earlier. They were admitted by the old Negro into a dim hall from which a stairway mounted into still more shadow. It smelled of dust and disuse—a close, dank smell. The Negro led them into the parlor. It was furnished in heavy, leather-covered furniture. When the Negro opened the blinds of one window, they could see that the leather was cracked; and when they sat down, a faint dust rose sluggishly about their thighs, spinning with slow motes in the single sun-ray. On a tarnished gilt easel before the fireplace stood a crayon portrait of Miss Emily's father.

They rose when she entered—a small, fat woman in black, with a thin gold chain descending to her waist and vanishing into her belt, leaning on an ebony cane with a tarnished gold head. Her skeleton was small and spare; perhaps that was why what would have been merely plumpness in another was obesity in her. She looked bloated, like a body long submerged in motionless water, and of that pallid hue. Her eyes, lost in the fatty ridges of her face, looked like two small pieces of coal pressed into a lump of dough as they moved from one face to another while the visitors stated their errand.

She did not ask them to sit. She just stood in the door and listened quietly until the spokesman came to a stumbling halt. Then they could hear the invisible watch ticking at the end of the gold chain.

Her voice was dry and cold. "I have no taxes in Jefferson. Colonel Sartoris explained it to me. Perhaps one of you can gain access to the city records and satisfy yourselves."

"But we have. We are the city authorities, Miss Emily. Didn't you get a notice from the sheriff, signed by him?"

"I received a paper, yes," Miss Emily said. "Perhaps he considers himself the sheriff. . . . I have no taxes in Jefferson."

"But there is nothing on the books to show that, you see. We must go by the—"

"See Colonel Sartoris. I have no taxes in Jefferson."

"But, Miss Emily—"

"See Colonel Sartoris." (Colonel Sartoris had been dead almost ten years.) "I have no taxes in Jefferson. Tobe!" The Negro appeared. "Show these gentlemen out."

2

So she vanquished them, horse and foot, just as she had vanquished their fathers thirty years before about the smell. That was two years after her father's death and a short time after her sweetheart—the one we believed would marry her—had deserted her. After her father's death she went out very little; after her sweetheart went away, people hardly saw her at all. A few of the ladies had the temerity to call, but were not received, and the only sign of life about the place was the Negro man—a young man then—going in and out with a market basket.

"Just as if a man—any man—could keep a kitchen properly," the ladies said; so they were not surprised when the smell developed. It was another link between the gross, teeming world and the high and mighty Griersons.

A neighbor, a woman, complained to the mayor, Judge Stevens, eighty years old.

"But what will you have me do about it, madam?" he said.

"Why, send her word to stop it," the woman said. "Isn't there a law?"

"I'm sure that won't be necessary," Judge Stevens said. "It's probably just a snake or a rat that nigger of hers killed in the yard. I'll speak to him about it."

The next day he received two more complaints, one from a man who came in diffident deprecation. "We really must do something about it, Judge. I'd be the last one in the world to bother Miss Emily, but we've got to do something." That night the Board of Aldermen met—three graybeards and one younger man, a member of the rising generation.

"It's simple enough," he said. "Send her word to have her place cleaned up. Give her a certain time to do it in, and if she don't. . . ."

"Dammit, sir," Judge Stevens said, "will you accuse a lady to her face of smelling bad?"

So the next night, after midnight, four men crossed Miss Emily's lawn and slunk about the house like burglars, sniffing along the base of the brickwork and at the cellar openings while one of them performed a regular sowing motion with his hand out of a sack slung from his shoulder. They broke open the cellar door and sprinkled lime there, and in all the outbuildings. As they recrossed the lawn, a window that had been dark was lighted and Miss Emily sat in it, the light behind her, and her upright torso motionless as that of an idol. They crept quietly across the lawn and into the shadow of the locusts that lined the street. After a week or two the smell went away.

That was when people had begun to feel really sorry for her. People in our town, remembering how old lady Wyatt, her great-aunt, had gone completely crazy at last, believed that the Griersons held themselves a little too high for what they really were. None of the young men were quite good enough for Miss Emily and such. We had long thought of them as a tableau, Miss Emily a slender figure in white in the background, her father a spraddled silhouette in the foreground, his back to her and clutching a horsewhip, the two of them framed by the backflung front door. So when she got to be thirty and was still single, we were not pleased exactly, but vindicated; even with insanity in the family she wouldn't have turned down all of her chances if they had really materialized.

When her father died, it got about that the house was all that was left to her; and in a way, people were glad. At last they could pity Miss Emily. Being left alone, and a pauper, she had become humanized. Now she too would know the old thrill and the old despair of a penny more or less.

The day after his death all the ladies prepared to call at the house and offer condolence and aid, as is our custom. Miss Emily met them at the door, dressed as usual and with no trace of grief on her face. She told them that her father was not dead. She did that for three days, with the ministers calling on her, and the doctors, trying to persuade her to let them dispose of the body. Just as they were about to resort to law and force, she broke down, and they buried her father quickly.

We did not say she was crazy then. We believed she had to do that. We remembered all the young men her father had driven away, and we knew that with nothing left, she would have to cling to that which had robbed her, as people will.

3

She was sick for a long time. When we saw her again, her hair was cut short, making her look like a girl, with a vague resemblance to those angels in colored church windows—sort of tragic and serene.

The town had just let the contracts for paving the sidewalks, and in the summer after her father's death they began the work. The construction company came with niggers and mules and machinery, and a foreman named Homer Barron, a Yankee— a big, dark, ready man, with a big voice and eyes lighter than his face. The little boys would follow in groups to hear him cuss the niggers, and the niggers singing in time to the rise and fall of picks. Pretty soon he knew everybody in town. Whenever you heard a lot of laughing anywhere about the square, Homer Barron would be in the center of the group. Presently, we began to see him and Miss Emily on Sunday afternoons driving in the yellow-wheeled buggy and the matched team of bays from the livery stable.

At first we were glad that Miss Emily would have an interest, because the ladies all said, "Of course a Grierson would not think seriously of a Northerner, a day laborer." But there were still others, older people, who said that even grief could not cause a real lady to forget *noblesse oblige*—without calling it *noblesse oblige.* They just said, "Poor Emily. Her kinsfolk should come to her." She had some kin in Alabama; but years ago her father had fallen out with them over the estate of old lady Wyatt, the crazy woman, and there was no communication between the two families. They had not even been represented at the funeral.

And as soon as the old people said, "Poor Emily," the whispering began. "Do you suppose it's really so?" they said to one another. "Of course it is. What else could. . . ." This behind their hands; rustling of craned silk and satin behind jalousies closed upon the sun of Sunday afternoon as the thin, swift clop-clop-clop of the matched team passed: "Poor Emily."

She carried her head high enough—even when we believed that she was fallen. It was as if she demanded more than ever the recognition of her dignity as the last Grierson; as if it had wanted that touch of earthiness to reaffirm her imperviousness. Like when she bought the rat poison, the arsenic. That was over a year after they had begun to say "Poor Emily," and while the two female cousins were visiting her.

"I want some poison," she said to the druggist. She was over thirty then, still a slight woman, though thinner than usual, with cold, haughty black eyes in a face the flesh of which was strained across the temples and about the eyesockets as you imagine a lighthouse-keeper's face ought to look. "I want some poison," she said.

"Yes, Miss Emily. What kind? For rats and such? I'd recom——"

"I want the best you have. I don't care what kind."

The druggist named several. "They'll kill anything up to an elephant. But what you want is——"

"Arsenic," Miss Emily said. "Is that a good one?"

"Is . . . arsenic? Yes, ma'am. But what you want——"

"I want arsenic."

The druggist looked down at her. She looked back at him, erect, her face like a strained flag. "Why, of course," the druggist said. "If that's what you want. But the law requires you to tell what you are going to use it for."

Miss Emily just stared at him, her head tilted back in order to look him eye for eye, until he looked away and went and got the arsenic and wrapped it up. The Negro delivery boy brought her the package; the druggist didn't come back. When she opened the package at home there was written on the box, under the skull and bones: "For rats."

4

So the next day we all said, "She will kill herself"; and we said it would be the best thing. When she had first begun to be seen with Homer Barron, we had said, "She will marry him." Then we said, "She will persuade him yet," because Homer himself had remarked—he liked men, and it was known that he drank with the younger men in the Elks' Club—that he was not a marrying man. Later we said, "Poor Emily" behind the jalousies as they passed on Sunday afternoon in the glittering buggy, Miss Emily with her head high and Homer Barron with his hat cocked and a cigar in his teeth, reins and whip in a yellow glove.

Then some of the ladies began to say that it was a disgrace to the town and a bad example to the young people. The men did not want to interfere, but at last the ladies forced the Baptist minister—Miss Emily's people were Episcopal—to call upon her. He would never divulge what happened during that interview, but he refused to go back again. The next Sunday they again drove about the streets, and the following day the minister's wife wrote to Miss Emily's relations in Alabama.

So she had blood-kin under her roof again and we sat back to watch developments. At first nothing happened. Then we were sure that they were to be married. We learned that Miss Emily had been to the jeweler's and ordered a man's toilet set in silver, with the letters H.B. on each piece. Two days later we learned that she had bought a complete outfit of men's clothing, including a nightshirt, and we said, "They are married." We were really glad. We were glad because the two female cousins were even more Grierson than Miss Emily had ever been.

So we were not surprised when Homer Barron—the streets had been finished some time since—was gone. We were a little disappointed that there was not a public blowing-off, but we believed that he had gone on to prepare for Miss Emily's coming, or to give her a chance to get rid of the cousins. (By that time it was a cabal, and we were all Miss Emily's allies to help circumvent the cousins.) Sure enough, after another week they departed. And, as we had expected all along, within three days Homer

Barron was back in town. A neighbor saw the Negro man admit him at the kitchen door at dusk one evening.

And that was the last we saw of Homer Barron. And of Miss Emily for some time. The Negro man went in and out with the market basket, but the front door remained closed. Now and then we would see her at the window for a moment, as the men did that night when they sprinkled the lime, but for almost six months she did not appear on the streets. Then we knew that this was to be expected too; as if that quality of her father which had thwarted her woman's life so many times had been too virulent and too furious to die.

When we next saw Miss Emily, she had grown fat and her hair was turning gray. During the next few years it grew grayer and grayer until it attained an even pepper-and-salt iron-gray, when it ceased turning. Up to the day of her death at seventy-four it was still that vigorous iron-gray, like the hair of an active man.

From that time on her front door remained closed, save during a period of six or seven years, when she was about forty, during which she gave lessons in china-painting. She fitted up a studio in one of the downstairs rooms, where the daughters and granddaughters of Colonel Sartoris' contemporaries were sent to her with the same regularity and in the same spirit that they were sent to church on Sundays with a twenty-five-cent piece for the collection plate. Meanwhile her taxes had been re-mitted.

Then the newer generation became the backbone and the spirit of the town, and the painting pupils grew up and fell away and did not send their children to her with boxes of color and tedious brushes and pictures cut from the ladies' magazines. The front door closed upon the last one and remained closed for good. When the town got free postal delivery, Miss Emily alone refused to let them fasten the metal numbers above her door and attach a mailbox to it. She would not listen to them.

Daily, monthly, yearly we watched the Negro grow grayer and more stooped, going in and out with the market basket. Each December we sent her a tax notice, which would be returned by the post office a week later, unclaimed. Now and then we would see her in one of the downstairs windows—she had evidently shut up the top floor of the house—like the carven torso of an idol in a niche, looking or not looking at us, we could never tell which. Thus she passed from generation to generation—dear, inescapable, impervious, tranquil, and perverse.

And so she died. Fell ill in the house filled with dust and shadows, with only a doddering Negro man to wait on her. We did not even know she was sick; we had long since given up trying to get any information from the Negro. He talked to no one, probably not even to her, for his voice had grown harsh and rusty, as if from disuse.

She died in one of the downstairs rooms, in a heavy walnut bed with a curtain, her gray head propped on a pillow yellow and moldy with age and lack of sunlight.

5

The Negro met the first of the ladies at the front door and let them in, with their hushed, sibilant voices and their quick, curious glances, and then he disappeared. He walked right through the house and out the back and was not seen again.

The two female cousins came at once. They held the funeral on the second day, with the town coming to look at Miss Emily beneath a mass of bought flowers, with the crayon face of her father musing profoundly above the bier and the ladies sibilant and macabre; and the very old men—some in their brushed Confederate uniforms—on the porch and the lawn, talking of Miss Emily as if she had been a contemporary of theirs, believing that they had danced with her and courted her perhaps, confusing time with its mathematical progression, as the old do, to whom all the past is not a diminishing road but, instead, a huge meadow which no winter ever quite touches, divided from them now by the narrow bottleneck of the most recent decade of years.

Already we knew that there was one room in that region above stairs which no one had seen in forty years, and which would have to be forced. They waited until Miss Emily was decently in the ground before they opened it.

The violence of breaking down the door seemed to fill this room with pervading dust. A thin, acrid pall as of the tomb seemed to lie everywhere upon this room decked and furnished as for a bridal: upon the valance curtains of faded rose color, upon the rose-shaded lights, upon the dressing table, upon the delicate array of crystal and the man's toilet things backed with tarnished silver, silver so tarnished that the monogram was obscured. Among them lay a collar and tie, as if they had just been removed, which, lifted, left upon the surface a pale crescent in the dust. Upon a chair hung the suit, carefully folded; beneath it the two mute shoes and the discarded socks.

The man himself lay in the bed.

For a long while we just stood there, looking down at the profound and fleshless grin. The body had apparently once lain in the attitude of an embrace, but now the long sleep that outlasts love, that conquers even the grimace of love, had cuckolded him. What was left of him, rotted beneath what was left of the nightshirt, had become inextricable from the bed in which he lay; and upon him and upon the pillow beside him lay that even coating of the patient and biding dust.

Then we noticed that in the second pillow was the indentation of a head. One of us lifted something from it, and leaning forward, that faint and invisible dust dry and acrid in the nostrils, we saw a long strand of iron-gray hair.

QUESTION

Although "A Rose for Emily" is narrated in the first person, the narrator is not "I" but "we." The narrator thus represents a communal rather than an individual point of view. How does the narrator (and the town) view Miss Emily? Find passages that represent more than one view of her, and explain their significance.

LANGUAGE AND STYLE

The way a writer chooses words, arranges them in sentences and longer units of discourse, and exploits their significance determines his or her *style*. Style is the verbal identity of a writer, as unmistakable as his or her face or voice. Reflecting their individuality, writers' styles convey their unique ways of seeing the world.

In attending to the language and style of fiction, we will concentrate on a few central matters: *diction,* the kind of word choices a writer makes; *syntax,* the order those words assume in sentences; and the presence or absence of figurative language, especially figures of comparison (simile and metaphor).*

Let us first consider this paragraph from William Faulkner's "The Bear."

> It ran in his knowledge before he ever saw it. It loomed and towered in his dreams before he even saw the unaxed woods where it left its crooked print, shaggy, huge, red-eyed, not malevolent but just big—too big for the dogs which tried to bay it, for the horses which tried to ride it down, for the men and the bullets they fired into it, too big for the very country which was its constricting scope. He seemed to see it entire with a child's complete divination before he ever laid eyes on either—the doomed wilderness whose edges were being constantly and punily gnawed at by men with axes and plows who feared it because it was wilderness, men myriad and nameless even to one another in the land where the old bear had earned a name, through which ran not even a mortal animal but an anachronism, indomitable and invincible, out of an old dead time, a phantom, epitome and apotheosis of the old wild life at which the puny humans swarmed and hacked in a fury of abhorrence and fear, like pygmies about the ankles of a drowsing elephant: the old bear solitary, indomitable and alone, widowered, childless, and absolved of mortality—old Priam reft of his old wife and having outlived all his sons.

In this passage from the beginning of the story, Faulkner describes a ten-year-old boy's intuitive knowledge of an old bear, who has been hunted respectfully for years. In creating an impressive image of the animal, Faulkner's language ranges from the familiar ("too big for the dogs which tried to bay it") to the formal ("an anachronism indomitable and invincible . . . epitome and apotheosis of the old wild life"). Employing this highly formal language and elaborate syntax, Faulkner elevates the bear to a mythic, transcendental realm in which he seems absolved of mortality. The second and third sentences, long and convoluted, accumulate detail: "shaggy, huge, red-eyed . . . solitary, indomitable, and alone"; they surge on gathering force and momentum; they ring with the emphasis of repeated words and phrases.

Faulkner's diction and syntax create a vision of the bear's grandness, power, and majesty that is strengthened by comparisons. The bear, associated in the boy's mind with the wilderness, becomes a symbol of its vastness and grandeur. Faulkner accentuates the bear's size by comparing it to an elephant around whose ankles humans swarm like pygmies, a comparison that diminishes the men as it exalts the bear. So too does the implied comparison of men with rodents "gnawing punily" at the wilderness, which they fear, primarily because it is large and dark, wild and mysterious. And by comparing the bear with Priam, who was the last king of Troy and who survived his progeny, he associates it with the world of ancient epic, and highlights the animal's mythic timelessness.

*For an extensive discussion of figurative language see pages 422–425.

Faulkner's dense, richly textured prose contrasts with Hemingway's sparse, taut style in the following passage from "The Short Happy Life of Francis Macomber." Francis Macomber, who at an earlier point in the action had shown himself a coward by dropping his gun and running from a lion, has redeemed himself in the eyes of the professional hunter, Robert Wilson. After Macomber demonstrates courage in hunting wild buffalo (reputedly even more dangerous than hunting lion), Wilson has these thoughts:

> It had taken a strange chance of hunting, a sudden precipitation into action without opportunity for worrying beforehand, to bring this about with Macomber, but regardless of how it had happened it had most certainly happened. Look at the beggar now, Wilson thought. It's that some of them stay little boys so long, Wilson thought. Sometimes all their lives. Their figures stay boyish when they're fifty. The great American boy-men. Damned strange people. But he liked this Macomber now. Damned strange fellow. Probably meant the end of cuckoldry too. Well, that would be a damned good thing. Damned good thing. Beggar had probably been afraid all his life. Don't know what started it. But over now. Hadn't had time to be afraid with the buff. That and being angry too. Motor car too. Motor cars made it familiar. Be a damn fire eater now. He'd seen it in the war work the same way. More of a change than any loss of virginity. Fear gone like an operation. Something else grew in its place. Main thing a man had. Made him into a man. Women knew it too. No bloody fear.

Hemingway's paragraph reads and sounds differently from Faulkner's. Although both writers repeat words and phrases, Hemingway's syntax, unlike Faulkner's, creates a sense of abruptness and fragmentation, whereas Faulkner's prose flows in a stately progression and expansion of phrases, gathering force as a sentence concludes. Hemingway's emphatic tone is more like the broken, halting movement of speech. That, in fact, is what it is: the inner speech of Robert Wilson. In contrast, Faulkner's oratorical style seems suited more to public declamation than to private thought.

Hemingway's abrupt, staccato style is also reflected in his diction. Unlike Faulkner's wide curve of language with an emphasis on polysyllabic words of Latin derivation ("anachronism," "indomitable," "invincible,") Hemingway chooses short words, often monosyllables, of Anglo-Saxon rather than foreign derivation. In Robert Wilson's description of Macomber, moreover, Hemingway uses a vocabulary appropriate to the big-game hunter: words like "beggar" with its pitying affection for Macomber, and "buff" with its fond respect for the big-game adversary.

Like Faulkner, Hemingway employs comparisons to convey Wilson's assessment of Macomber. Macomber is first compared to a boy, one of many American "boy-men" Wilson has encountered. But Wilson later sees him as a "fire-eater," that is, as a man who encounters danger fearlessly, eagerly; this term conveys Wilson's admiration for Macomber's newly found courage. The most important comparisons, however, indicate the change Macomber has undergone. His fear is described as being "gone like an operation," as if a tumor were removed by surgery. This surgery of Macomber's fear makes him a man. Finally, Wilson implicitly compares Macomber's passage to manhood favorably with that of soldiers who established their manhood under fire.

Thus, the comparisons that Hemingway, Faulkner, and other writers use enrich their prose and impart a unique and personal view of the world. They are both indelible stamps of each writer's style and keys to understanding their works.

The language of the following story, "Araby" by James Joyce, is especially important in revealing both the narrator's conception of himself as a boy and his adult understanding of his boyhood. Attend carefully to the descriptions of Mangan's sister and note especially their mixture of erotic and religious details. Consider also the connotations of the first and last paragraphs and the implications of the religious imagery throughout.

J A M E S   J O Y C E

[*1882–1941*]

Araby

North Richmond Street, being blind, was a quiet street except at the hour when the Christian Brothers' School set the boys free. An uninhabited house of two storeys stood at the blind end, detached from its neighbours in a square ground. The other houses of the street, conscious of decent lives within them, gazed at one another with brown imperturbable faces.

The former tenant of our house, a priest, had died in the back drawing-room. Air, musty from having been long enclosed, hung in all the rooms, and the waste room behind the kitchen was littered with old useless papers. Among these I found a few paper-covered books, the pages of which were curled and damp: *The Abbot,* by Walter Scott, *The Devout Communicant* and *The Memoirs of Vidocq.* I liked the last best because its leaves were yellow. The wild garden behind the house contained a central apple-tree and a few straggling bushes under one of which I found the late tenant's rusty bicycle-pump. He had been a very charitable priest; in his will he had left all his money to institutions and the furniture of his house to his sister.

When the short days of winter came dusk fell before we had well eaten our dinners. When we met in the street the houses had grown sombre. The space of sky above us was the colour of ever-changing violet and towards it the lamps of the street lifted their feeble lanterns. The cold air stung us and we played till our bodies glowed. Our shouts echoed in the silent street. The career of our play brought us through the dark muddy lanes behind the houses where we ran the gantlet of the rough tribes from the cottages, to the back doors of the dark dripping gardens where odours arose from the ashpits, to the dark odorous stables where a coachman smoothed and combed the horse or shook music from the buckled harness. When we returned to the street light from the kitchen windows had filled the areas. If my uncle was seen turning the corner we hid in the shadow until we had seen him safely housed. Or if Mangan's sister came out on the doorstep to call her brother in to his tea we watched her from our shadow peer up and down the street. We waited to see whether she would remain or go in and, if she remained, we left our shadow and walked up to Mangan's steps resignedly. She was waiting for us, her figure defined by the light from the half-opened door. Her brother always teased her before he obeyed and I stood by the railings looking at her. Her dress swung as she moved her body and the soft rope of her hair tossed from side to side.

Every morning I lay on the floor in the front parlour watching her door. The blind was pulled down to within an inch of the sash so that I could not be seen. When she came out on the doorstep my heart leaped. I ran to the hall, seized my books and followed her. I kept her brown figure always in my eye and, when we came near the point at which our ways diverged, I quickened my pace and passed her. This happened morning after morning. I had never spoken to her, except for a few casual words, and yet her name was like a summons to all my foolish blood.

Her image accompanied me even in places the most hostile to romance. On Saturday evenings when my aunt went marketing I had to go to carry some of the parcels. We walked through the flaring streets, jostled by drunken men and bargaining women, amid the curses of labourers, the shrill litanies of shop-boys who stood on guard by the barrels of pigs' cheeks, the nasal chanting of street-singers, who sang a *come-all-you* about O'Donovan Rossa, or a ballad about the troubles in our native land. These noises converged in a single sensation of life for me: I imagined that I bore my chalice safely through a throng of foes. Her name sprang to my lips at moments in strange prayers and praises which I myself did not understand. My eyes were often full of tears (I could not tell why) and at times a flood from my heart seemed to pour itself out into my bosom. I thought little of the future. I did not know whether I would ever speak to her or not or, if I spoke to her, how I could tell her of my confused adoration. But my body was like a harp and her words and gestures were like fingers running upon the wires.

One evening I went into the back drawing-room in which the priest had died. It was a dark rainy evening and there was no sound in the house. Through one of the broken panes I heard the rain impinge upon the earth, the fine incessant needles of water playing in the sodden beds. Some distant lamp or lighted window gleamed below me. I was thankful that I could see so little. All my senses seemed to desire to veil themselves and, feeling that I was about to slip from them, I pressed the palms of my hands together until they trembled, murmuring: *O love! O love!* many times.

At last she spoke to me. When she addressed the first words to me I was so confused that I did not know what to answer. She asked me was I going to *Araby*. I forget whether I answered yes or no. It would be a splendid bazaar, she said; she would love to go.

—And why can't you? I asked.

While she spoke she turned a silver bracelet round and round her wrist. She could not go, she said, because there would be a retreat that week in her convent. Her brother and two other boys were fighting for their caps and I was alone at the railings. She held one of the spikes, bowing her head towards me. The light from the lamp opposite our door caught the white curve of her neck, lit up her hair that rested there and, falling, lit up the hand upon the railing. It fell over one side of her dress and caught the white border of a petticoat, just visible as she stood at ease.

—It's well for you, she said.

—If I go, I said, I will bring you something.

What innumerable follies laid waste my waking and sleeping thoughts after that evening! I wished to annihilate the tedious intervening days. I chafed against the work of school. At night in my bedroom and by day in the classroom her image came between me and the page I strove to read. The syllables of the word *Araby* were called to me through the silence in which my soul luxuriated and cast an Eastern enchantment over me. I asked for leave to go to the bazaar Saturday night. My aunt was surprised and hoped it was not some Freemason affair. I answered few questions in class. I watched my master's face pass from amiability to sternness; he hoped I was not beginning to idle. I could not call my wandering thoughts together. I had hardly any patience with the serious work of life which, now that it stood between me and my desire, seemed to me child's play, ugly monotonous child's play.

On Saturday morning I reminded my uncle that I wished to go to the bazaar in the evening. He was fussing at the hallstand, looking for the hat-brush, and answered me curtly:

—Yes, boy, I know.

As he was in the hall I could not go into the front parlour and lie at the window. I left the house in bad humour and walked slowly towards the school. The air was pitilessly raw and already my heart misgave me.

When I came home to dinner my uncle had not yet been home. Still it was early. I sat staring at the clock for some time and, when its ticking began to irritate me, I left the room. I mounted the staircase and gained the upper part of the house. The high cold empty gloomy rooms liberated me and I went from room to room singing. From the front window I saw my companions playing below in the street. Their cries reached me weakened and indistinct and, leaning my forehead against the cool glass, I looked over at the dark house where she lived. I may have stood there for an hour, seeing nothing but the brown-clad figure cast by my imagination, touched discreetly by the lamplight at the curved neck, at the hand upon the railings and at the border below the dress.

When I came downstairs again I found Mrs Mercer sitting at the fire. She was an old garrulous woman, a pawnbroker's widow, who collected used stamps for some pious purpose. I had to endure the gossip of the tea-table. The meal was prolonged beyond an hour and still my uncle did not come. Mrs Mercer stood up to go: she was sorry she couldn't wait any longer, but it was after eight o'clock and she did not like to be out late, as the night air was bad for her. When she had gone I began to walk up and down the room, clenching my fists. My aunt said:

—I'm afraid you may put off your bazaar for this night of Our Lord.

At nine o'clock I heard my uncle's latchkey in the halldoor. I heard him talking to himself and heard the hallstand rocking when it had received the weight of his overcoat. I could interpret these signs. When he was midway through his dinner I asked him to give me the money to go to the bazaar. He had forgotten.

—The people are in bed and after their first sleep now, he said.

I did not smile. My aunt said to him energetically:

—Can't you give him the money and let him go? You've kept him late enough as it is.

My uncle said he was very sorry he had forgotten. He said he believed in the old saying: *All work and no play makes Jack a dull boy.* He asked me where I was going and, when I had told him a second time he asked me did I know *The Arab's Farewell to his Steed.* When I left the kitchen he was about to recite the opening lines of the piece to my aunt.

I held a florin tightly in my hand as I strode down Buckingham Street towards the station. The sight of the streets thronged with buyers and glaring with gas recalled to me the purpose of my journey. I took my seat in a third-class carriage of a deserted train. After an intolerable delay the train moved out of the station slowly. It crept onward among ruinous houses and over the twinkling river. At Westland Row Station a crowd of people pressed to the carriage doors; but the porters moved them back, saying that it was a special train for the bazaar. I remained alone in the bare carriage. In a few minutes the train drew up beside an improvised wooden platform. I passed out on to the road and saw by the lighted dial of a clock that it was ten minutes to ten. In front of me was a large building which displayed the magical name.

I could not find any sixpenny entrance and, fearing that the bazaar would be closed, I passed in quickly through a turnstile, handing a shilling to a weary-looking man. I found myself in a big hall girdled at half its height by a gallery. Nearly all the stalls were closed and the greater part of the hall was in darkness. I recognised a silence like that which pervades a church after a service. I walked into the centre of the bazaar timidly. A few people were gathered about the stalls which were still open. Before a curtain, over which the words *Café Chantant* were written in coloured lamps, two men were counting money on a salver. I listened to the fall of the coins.

Remembering with difficulty why I had come I went over to one of the stalls and examined porcelain vases and flowered tea-sets. At the door of the stall a young lady was talking and laughing with two young gentlemen. I remarked their English accents and listened vaguely to their conversation.

—O, I never said such a thing!

—O, but you did!

—O, but I didn't!

—Didn't she say that?

—Yes. I heard her.

—O, there's a . . . fib!

Observing me the young lady came over and asked me did I wish to buy anything. The tone of her voice was not encouraging; she seemed to have spoken to me out of a sense of duty. I looked humbly at the great jars that stood like eastern guards at either side of the dark entrance to the stall and murmured:

—No, thank you.

The young lady changed the position of one of the vases and went back to the two young men. They began to talk of the same subject. Once or twice the young lady glanced at me over her shoulder.

I lingered before her stall, though I knew my stay was useless, to make my interest in her wares seem the more real. Then I turned away slowly and walked down the middle of the bazaar. I allowed the two pennies to fall against the sixpence in my pocket. I heard a voice call from one end of the gallery that the light was out. The upper part of the hall was now completely dark.

Gazing up into the darkness I saw myself as a creature driven and derided by vanity; and my eyes burned with anguish and anger.

QUESTIONS

1. Note the religious language of the fifth paragraph, especially the words "litanies," "chalice," "prayers and praises," and "confused adoration." What does this language reveal about the boy, about how he sees himself, about how he envisions what he is doing and thinking? Explain how the following sentence from this paragraph is related to the image invoked by his religious language: "But my body was like a harp and her words and gestures were like fingers running upon the wires."
2. Consider the dialogue near the end of the story. If possible, read it aloud with a friend. What do you hear? How can you characterize the conversation? What effect does it have on the boy? Why?
3. Reread the first and last paragraphs. Note repetitions and similarities in the language. Relate the use of the word "blind" for a dead-end street to the boy's situation as expressed at the end of the story. Why do the boy's "eyes" burn with "anguish" and "anger"?

THEME

In Chapter One, Reading Stories, we noted that the meaning of a literary work is more than any statement that can be made about it, that its meaning consists of both our experience in reading it and the ideas we may extract from it. With that in mind, let us clarify what we mean by the theme of a story. Simply put, a story's *theme* is its idea or point formulated as a generalization. The theme of a fable is its moral; the theme of a parable is its teaching; the theme of a short story is its implied view of life and conduct. Unlike the fable and parable, however, most fiction is not designed primarily to teach or preach. Its theme, thus, is more obliquely presented. In fact theme in fiction is rarely *presented* at all; it is abstracted from the details of character and action that compose the story.

To be clear about theme, we should distinguish it from plot, the story's sequence of action, and from *subject,* what the story is generally about. In explaining a story's theme we do more than state its subject or summarize its plot. To say, for example, that Pirandello's "War" (pages 84–88) is about parents and children is more a statement of subject than of theme. To pinpoint its theme we would have to explain what the story implies about parents and children, what it suggests about parents' love for their children, and even more specifically, what it values in the attitudes toward the loss of children expressed by the two major characters. Similarly, to say that Hemingway's "Hills Like White Elephants" is about a conversation between a man and a girl or that it is about their relationship is to point to its subject, not its theme. We get closer to its theme by noting that their relationship is troubled, that it is affected by the girl's disillusionment and the man's inadequacy, by her disillusionment with his unwillingness to be the father of the child she wants to bear.

Theme is related to the other elements of fiction more as consequence than as a parallel element that can be separately identified. A story's theme, that is, grows out of the relationship of the other elements. To formulate a story's theme, we try to explain what these elements collectively suggest. Since the theme of a story derives from its details of character, plot, setting, structure, language, and point of view, any statement of theme is valid and valuable to the extent that it accounts for these details. To explain the theme of "The Prodigal Son," for example, without accounting for the father's speech to the elder son would be to distort the meaning of the story.

Perhaps the most important thing to remember about theme is that it is an abstraction from a story's complex uses of language to describe and chart action, depict setting, and portray character. A statement of theme derives from the particulars embodied in language and action. The very concreteness and particularity of fiction should make us cautious in searching out theme. In fact, it would be more useful to avoid thinking of theme as hidden somehow beneath the surface of the story and instead to see theme as the implied significance of the story's details. Moreover, we should also be aware that not only are there a multiplicity of ways to state a story's theme, but that any such statement involves a necessary simplification of the story. In clarifying our sense of a story's idea, moreover, we also inevitably exclude some dimensions of the story and include others. We should be aware that the themes we abstract from stories are provisional understandings that never completely explain the stories.

With these considerations in mind, read Guy de Maupassant's "The Jewels," which follows, with an eye to explaining its theme.

GUY DE MAUPASSANT

[1850–1893]

The Jewels

Monsieur Lantin had met the girl at a party given one evening by his office superior and love had caught him in its net.

She was the daughter of a country tax-collector who had died a few years before. She had come to Paris then with her mother, who struck up acquaintance with a few middle-class families in her district in the hope of marrying her off. They were poor and decent, quiet and gentle. The girl seemed the perfect example of the virtuous woman to whom every sensible young man dreams of entrusting his life. Her simple beauty had a modest, angelic charm and the imperceptible smile which always hovered about her lips seemed to be a reflection of her heart.

Everybody sang her praises and people who knew her never tired of saying: "Happy the man who marries her. Nobody could find a better wife."

Monsieur Lantin, who was then a senior clerk at the Ministry of the Interior with a salary of three thousand five hundred francs a year, proposed to her and married her.

He was incredibly happy with her. She ran his household so skilfully and economically that they gave the impression of living in luxury. She lavished attention on her husband, spoiling and coddling him, and the charm of her person was so great that six years after their first meeting he loved her even more than in the early days.

He found fault with only two of her tastes: her love for the theatre and her passion for imitation jewellery.

Her friends (she knew the wives of a few petty officials) often obtained a box at the theatre for her for popular plays, and even for first nights; and she dragged her husband along willy-nilly to these entertainments, which he found terribly tiring after a day's work at the office. He therefore begged her to go to the theatre with some lady of her acquaintance who would bring her home afterwards. It was a long time before she gave in, as she thought that this arrangement was not quite respectable. But finally, just to please him, she agreed, and he was terribly grateful to her.

Now this love for the theatre soon aroused in her a desire to adorn her person. True, her dresses remained very simple, always in good taste, but unpretentious; and her gentle grace, her irresistible, humble, smiling charm seemed to be enhanced by the simplicity of her gowns. But she took to wearing two big rhinestone earrings which sparkled like diamonds, and she also wore necklaces of fake pearls, bracelets of imitation gold, and combs set with coloured glass cut to look like real stones.

Her husband, who was rather shocked by this love of show, often used to say: "My dear, when a woman can't afford to buy real jewels, she ought to appear adorned with her beauty and grace alone: those are still the rarest of gems."

But she would smile sweetly and reply: "I can't help it. I like imitation jewellery. It's my only vice. I know you're right, but people can't change their natures. I would have loved to own some real jewels."

Then she would run the pearl necklaces through her fingers and make the cut-glass gems flash in the light, saying: "Look! Aren't they beautifully made? Anyone would swear they were real."

He would smile and say: "You have the taste of a gipsy."

Sometimes, in the evening, when they were sitting together by the fireside, she would place on the tea-table the leather box in which she kept her "trash," as Monsieur Lantin called it. Then she would start examining these imitation jewels with passionate attention, as if she were enjoying some deep and secret pleasure; and she would insist on hanging a necklace around her husband's neck, laughing uproariously and crying: "How funny you look!" And then she would throw herself into his arms and kiss him passionately.

One night in winter when she had been to the Opera, she came home shivering with cold. The next morning she had a cough, and a week later she died of pneumonia.

Lantin very nearly followed her to the grave. His despair was so terrible that his hair turned white within a month. He wept from morning to night, his heart ravaged by unbearable grief, haunted by the memory, the smile, the voice, the every charm of his dead wife.

Time did nothing to assuage his grief. Often during office hours, when his colleagues came along to chat about the topics of the day, his cheeks would suddenly puff out, his nose wrinkle up, his eyes fill with tears, and with a terrible grimace he would burst out sobbing.

He had left his wife's room untouched, and every day would shut himself in it and think about her. All the furniture and even her clothes remained exactly where they had been on the day she had died.

But life soon became a struggle for him. His income, which in his wife's hands had covered all their expenses, was now no longer sufficient for him on his own; and he wondered in amazement how she had managed to provide him with excellent wines and rare delicacies which he could no longer afford on his modest salary.

He incurred a few debts and ran after money in the way people do when they are reduced to desperate shifts. Finally, one morning, finding himself without a sou a whole week before the end of the month, he decided to sell something; and immediately the idea occurred to him of disposing of his wife's "trash." He still harboured a sort of secret grudge against those false gems which had irritated him in the past, and indeed the sight of them every day somewhat spoiled the memory of his beloved.

He rummaged for a long time among the heap of gawdy trinkets she had left behind, for she had stubbornly gone on buying jewellery until the last days of her life, bringing home a new piece almost every evening. At last he decided on the large necklace which she had seemed to like best, and which, he thought, might well be worth six or seven francs, for it was beautifully made for a piece of paste.

He put it in his pocket and set off for his Ministry, following the boulevards and looking for a jeweller's shop which inspired confidence.

At last he spotted one and went in, feeling a little ashamed of exposing his poverty in this way, and of trying to sell such a worthless article.

"Monsieur," he said to the jeweller, "I would like to know what you think this piece is worth."

The man took the necklace, examined it, turned it over, weighed it, inspected it with a magnifying glass, called his assistant, made a few remarks to him in an undertone, placed the necklace on the counter and looked at it from a distance to gauge the effect.

Monsieur Lantin, embarrassed by all this ritual, was opening his mouth to say: "Oh, I know perfectly well that it isn't worth anything," when the jeweller said: "Monsieur, this necklace is worth between twelve and fifteen thousand francs; but I couldn't buy it unless you told me where it came from."

The widower opened his eyes wide and stood there gaping, unable to understand what the jeweller had said. Finally he stammered: "What was that you said? . . . Are you sure?"

The other misunderstood his astonishment and said curtly: "You can go somewhere else and see if they'll offer you more. In my opinion it's worth fifteen thousand at the most. Come back and see me if you can't find a better price."

Completely dumbfounded, Monsieur Lantin took back his necklace and left the shop, in obedience to a vague desire to be alone and to think.

Once outside, however, he felt an impulse to laugh, and he thought: "The fool! Oh, the fool! But what if I'd taken him at his word? There's a jeweller who can't tell real diamonds from paste!"

And he went into another jeweller's shop at the beginning of the Rue de la Paix. As soon as he saw the necklace, the jeweller exclaimed: "Why, I know that necklace well: it was bought here."

Monsieur Lantin asked in amazement: "How much is it worth?"

"Monsieur, I sold it for twenty-five thousand. I am prepared to buy it back for eighteen thousand once you have told me, in accordance with the legal requirements, how you came to be in possession of it."

This time Monsieur Lantin was dumbfounded. He sat down and said: "But . . . but . . . examine it carefully, Monsieur. Until now I thought it was paste."

"Will you give me your name, Monsieur?" said the jeweller.

"Certainly. My name's Lantin. I'm an official at the Ministry of the Interior, and I live at No. 16, Rue des Martyrs."

The jeweller opened his books, looked for the entry, and said: "Yes, this necklace was sent to Madame Lantin's address, No. 16, Rue des Martyrs, on the 20th of July 1876."

The two men looked into each other's eyes, the clerk speechless with astonishment, the jeweller scenting a thief. Finally the latter said: "Will you leave the necklace with me for twenty-four hours? I'll give you a receipt."

"Why, certainly," stammered Monsieur Lantin. And he went out folding the piece of paper, which he put in his pocket.

Then he crossed the street, walked up it again, noticed that he was going the wrong way, went back as far as the Tuileries, crossed the Seine, realized that he had gone wrong again, and returned to the Champs-Élysées, his mind a complete blank. He tried to think it out, to understand. His wife couldn't have afforded to buy something so valuable —that was certain. But in that case it was a present! A present! But a present from whom? And why was it given her?

He halted in his tracks and remained standing in the middle of the avenue. A horrible doubt crossed his mind. Her? But in that case all the other jewels were presents too! The earth seemed to be trembling under his feet and a tree in front of him to be falling; he threw up his arms and fell to the ground unconscious.

He came to his senses in a chemist's shop into which the passers-by had carried him. He took a cab home and shut himself up.

He wept bitterly until nightfall, biting on a handkerchief so as not to cry out. Then he went to bed worn out with grief and fatigue and slept like a log.

A ray of sunlight awoke him and he slowly got up to go to his Ministry. It was hard to think of working after such a series of shocks. It occurred to him that he could ask to be excused and he wrote a letter to his superior. Then he remembered that he had to go back to the jeweller's and he blushed with shame. He spent a long time thinking it over, but decided that he could not leave the necklace with that man. So he dressed and went out.

It was a fine day and the city seemed to be smiling under the clear blue sky. People were strolling about the streets with their hands in their pockets.

Watching them, Lantin said to himself: "How lucky rich people are! With money you can forget even the deepest of sorrows. You can go where you like, travel, enjoy yourself. Oh, if only I were rich!"

He began to feel hungry, for he had eaten nothing for two days, but his pocket was empty. Then he remembered the necklace. Eighteen thousand francs! Eighteen thousand francs! That was a tidy sum, and no mistake!

When he reached the Rue de la Paix he started walking up and down the pavement opposite the jeweller's shop. Eighteen thousand francs! A score of times he almost went in, but every time shame held him back.

He was hungry, though, very hungry, and he had no money at all. He quickly made up his mind, ran across the street so as not to have any time to think, and rushed into the shop.

As soon as he saw him the jeweller came forward and offered him a chair with smiling politeness. His assistants came into the shop, too, and glanced surreptitiously at Lantin with laughter in their eyes and on their lips.

"I have made inquiries, Monsieur," said the jeweller, "and if you still wish to sell the necklace, I am prepared to pay you the price I offered you."

"Why, certainly," stammered the clerk.

The jeweller took eighteen large banknotes out of a drawer, counted them and handed them to Lantin, who signed a little receipt and with a trembling hand put the money in his pocket.

Then, as he was about to leave the shop, he turned towards the jeweller, who was still smiling, and lowering his eyes said: "I have . . . I have some other jewels which have come to me from . . . from the same legacy. Would you care to buy them from me too?"

The jeweller bowed.

"Certainly, Monsieur."

One of the assistants went out, unable to contain his laughter; another blew his nose loudly.

Lantin, red-faced and solemn, remained unmoved.

"I will bring them to you," he said.

And he took a cab to go and fetch the jewels.

When he returned to the shop an hour later he still had had nothing to eat. The jeweller and his assistants began examining the jewels one by one, estimating the value of each piece. Almost all of them had been bought at that shop.

Lantin now began arguing about the valuations, lost his temper, insisted on seeing the sales registers, and spoke more and more loudly as the sum increased.

The large diamond earrings were worth twenty thousand francs, the bracelets thirty-five thousand, the brooches, rings and lockets sixteen thousand, a set of emeralds and sapphires fourteen thousand, and a solitaire pendant on a gold chain forty thousand—making a total sum of one hundred and ninety-six thousand francs.

The jeweller remarked jokingly: "These obviously belonged to a lady who invested all her savings in jewellery."

Lantin replied seriously: "It's as good a way as any of investing one's money."

And he went off after arranging with the jeweller to have a second expert valuation the next day.

Out in the street he looked at the Vendôme column and felt tempted to climb up it as if it were a greasy pole. He felt light enough to play leap-frog with the statue of the Emperor perched up there in the sky.

He went to Voisin's for lunch and ordered wine with his meal at twenty francs a bottle.

Then he took a cab and went for a drive in the Bois. He looked at the other carriages with a slightly contemptuous air, longing to call out to the passers-by: "I'm a rich man too! I'm worth two hundred thousand francs!"

Suddenly he remembered his Ministry. He drove there at once, strode into his superior's office, and said: "Monsieur, I have come to resign my post. I have just been left three hundred thousand francs."

He shook hands with his former colleagues and told them some of his plans for the future; then he went off to dine at the Café Anglais.

Finding himself next to a distinguished-looking gentleman, he was unable to refrain from informing him, with a certain coyness, that he had just inherited four hundred thousand francs.

For the first time in his life he was not bored at the theatre, and he spent the night with some prostitutes.

Six months later he married again. His second wife was a very virtuous woman, but extremely bad-tempered. She made him very unhappy.

QUESTIONS

1. State in a sentence or two the idea of "The Jewels." What point does the story seem to make?
2. Develop your understanding of the story's theme in a paragraph or a brief conversation. To support your views cite details of plot, character, setting, and language.

IRONY

Irony is not so much an element of fiction as a pervasive quality in it. It may appear in fiction (an in the other literary genres as well) in three ways: in the work's language, in its incidents, or in its point of view. But in whatever forms it emerges, *irony* always involves a contrast or discrepancy between one thing and another. The contrast may be between what is said and what is meant or between what happens and what is expected to happen.

In *verbal irony,* for example, we say the opposite of what we mean. When someone says "That was a brilliant remark" and we know that it was anything but brilliant, we understand the speaker's ironic intention. In such relatively simple instances there is usually no problem in perceiving irony. In more complex instances, however, the designation of an action or a remark as ironic can be much more complicated. Consider, for example, the ending of Hemingway's "Hills Like White Elephants," when the girl tells the man she feels "fine." Should we take her literally? Or is she being ironic?

Besides verbal irony—in which we understand the opposite of what a speaker says—fiction makes use of *irony of circumstance* (sometimes called *irony of situation*). Writers sometimes create discrepancies between what seems to be and what is. In Chopin's "The Story of an Hour," for example, Mrs. Mallard appears to be grieving over the news of her husband's death. At least that's how her action is perceived by other characters. But we soon realize that rather than grief, her tears celebrate the joy of her new-found freedom. Her tears are ironic because they indicate the opposite of what we expect them to. Another ironic situation prevails as Mrs. Mallard "prays" for long life, presumably so she can enjoy freedom from her husband. This action is ironic because what she is praying for and why she prays for it are out of keeping with the expected reasons for prayer on such an occasion.

Irony of circumstance or situation also refers to occasions when an individual expects one thing to occur only to discover that the opposite happens. This indeed is what Mrs. Mallard experiences when she discovers her husband had not been killed in the train crash as she had thought. The final irony, of course, is that *she* dies when she sees him walk in the door.

Although verbal irony and irony of circumstance or situation are the prevalent forms irony assumes in fiction, two others deserve mention: dramatic irony and ironic vision. More typical of plays than stories, *dramatic irony* is the discrepancy between what characters know and what readers know. Writers sometimes direct our responses by letting us see things that their characters do not. In the story that follows this discussion, Edgar Allan Poe's "Cask of Amontillado," for example, dramatic irony inheres in the difference between what Fortunato knows about Montresor's intentions and what we know. To cite another example, at the conclusion of Flannery O'Connor's "Good Country People," the reader has quite a different view of the Bible salesman's character than Mrs. Freeman or Mrs. Hopewell do (pages 317–330).

Some writers exploit the discrepancy between what readers and characters know to establish an ironic vision in a work. An *ironic vision* is established in a work as an overall tone that suggests how a writer views his or her characters and subject. It is more frequently characteristic of longer fictional works such as the novels *Pride and Prejudice* by Jane Austen or *The Adventures of Huckleberry Finn* by Mark Twain than short stories. We can find ironic visions, nonetheless, in both Conrad's "An Outpost of Progress" (pages 38–53) and O'Connor's "Good Country People" (pages 317–330). For the moment, however, consider how an ironic vision informs the opening of Jane Austen's *Pride and Prejudice:*

> It is a truth universally acknowledged, that a single man in possession of a good fortune, must be in want of a wife.
> However little known the feelings or views of such a man may be on his first entering a neighborhood, this truth is so well fixed in the minds of the surrounding families, that he is considered as the rightful property of some one or other of their daughters.

Consider the opening sentence first. Is it a truth—that is, do we accept as fact what the sentence seems to assert: that a single man of means must be looking for a wife? Do we believe that this search for a wife is a phenomenon universally acknowledged, that it is recognized around the world, not merely in nineteenth-century England or twentieth-century America? Very likely Jane Austen's sentence presents the opposite of what we believe: that single men of means more often than not are not in search of wives. The converse is probably closer to what we have seen: single women seek out single men of means as prospective husbands. This discrepancy between what the sentence says literally and what we know accounts in part for its ironic quality. We are not to take it literally; we do not accept it at face value.

We can feel more confident about the ironic quality of Austen's first sentence when we examine it in relation to the sentence that follows. We are told there that the feelings or views of the eligible bachelor mean little. But they should mean much in such an important issue. That they do not is the opposite of what we expect and hence is ironic. An additional irony is that characteristics of marriageable eligibility are limited to bachelorhood and wealth. Nothing else is mentioned as important—not character, not intelligence, not wisdom or virtue.

Portraying characters whose view of marriage is so mercenary and limited, Austen distances herself from them and from their values. This ironic distance is enforced when Austen describes their misconceptions about single men. But there is a further irony in the fact that those misconceptions finally do not matter. All that matters is the final outcome: the single man's loss of his bachelorhood and his entrance into the ranks of the family. Moreover, there is another ironic dimension to their view in that it represents a reversal of a traditional and familiar notion that a wife is a man's property. This idea is given an additional twist when Austen indicates that it hardly matters which girl of which family captures the prize.

For these reasons and for others that emerge as the novel develops, Austen's tone can be described as ironic. When such an ironic tone is established strongly from the beginning of a work and when it is sustained consistently throughout, we say that it is informed by an ironic vision. The ironic vision of *Pride and Prejudice* infuses the novel: it informs the plot, it controls the dialogue, and it surfaces everywhere in the tone of the narrator's comments.

Read the following story, Edgar Allan Poe's "The Cask of Amontillado," with an eye to its ironies. Be alert for the different types of irony described above: verbal irony, irony of situation, and dramatic irony. Consider whether the tone of the story is sufficiently ironic to characterize its vision as ironic as well.

EDGAR ALLAN POE

[1809–1849]

The Cask of Amontillado

The thousand injuries of Fortunato I had borne as I best could; but when he ventured upon insult, I vowed revenge. You, who so well know the nature of my soul, will not suppose, however, that I gave utterance to a threat. *At length* I would be avenged; this was a point definitely settled—but the very definitiveness with which it was resolved precluded the idea of risk. I must not only punish, but punish with impunity. A wrong is unredressed when retribution overtakes its redresser. It is equally unredressed when the avenger fails to make himself felt as such to him who has done the wrong.

It must be understood, that neither by word nor deed had I given Fortunato cause to doubt my good-will. I continued, as was my wont, to smile in his face, and he did not perceive that my smile *now* was at the thought of his immolation.

He had a weak point—this Fortunato—although in other regards he was a man to be respected and even feared. He prided himself on his connoisseurship in wine. Few Italians have the true virtuoso spirit. For the most part their enthusiasm is adopted to suit the time and opportunity—to practise imposture upon the British and Austrian *millionnaires.* In painting and gemmary Fortunato, like his countrymen, was a quack —but in the matter of old wines he was sincere. In this respect I did not differ from him materially: I was skilful in the Italian vintages myself, and bought largely whenever I could.

It was about dusk, one evening during the supreme madness of the carnival season, that I encountered my friend. He accosted me with excessive warmth, for he had been drinking much. The man wore motley. He had on a tight-fitting parti-striped dress, and his head was surmounted by the conical cap and bells. I was so pleased to see him, that I thought I should never have done wringing his hand.

I said to him: "My dear Fortunato, you are luckily met. How remarkably well you are looking to-day! But I have received a pipe of what passes for Amontillado, and I have my doubts."

"How?" said he. "Amontillado? A pipe? Impossible! And in the middle of the carnival!"

"I have my doubts," I replied; "and I was silly enough to pay the full Amontillado price without consulting you in the matter. You were not to be found, and I was fearful of losing a bargain."

"Amontillado!"

"I have my doubts."

"Amontillado!"

"And I must satisfy them."

"Amontillado!"

"As you are engaged, I am on my way to Luchesi. If any one has a critical turn, it is he. He will tell me—"

"Luchesi cannot tell Amontillado from Sherry."

"And yet some fools will have it that his taste is a match for your own."

"Come, let us go."

"Whither?"

"To your vaults."

"My friend, no; I will not impose upon your good nature. I perceive you have an engagement. Luchesi—"

"I have no engagement;—come."

"My friend, no. It is not the engagement, but the severe cold with which I perceive you are afflicted. The vaults are insufferably damp. They are encrusted with nitre."

"Let us go, nevertheless. The cold is merely nothing. Amontillado! You have been imposed upon. And as for Luchesi, he cannot distinguish Sherry from Amontillado."

Thus speaking, Fortunato possessed himself of my arm. Putting on a mask of black silk, and drawing a *roquelaire* closely about my person, I suffered him to hurry me to my palazzo.

There were no attendants at home; they had absconded to make merry in honor of the time. I had told them that I should not return until the morning, and had given them explicit orders not to stir from the house. These orders were sufficient, I well knew, to insure their immediate disappearance, one and all, as soon as my back was turned.

I took from their sconces two flambeaux, and giving one to Fortunato, bowed him through several suites of rooms to the archway that led into the vaults. I passed down a long and winding staircase, requesting him to be cautious as he followed. We came at length to the foot of the descent, and stood together on the damp ground of the catacombs of the Montresors.

The gait of my friend was unsteady, and the bells upon his cap jingled as he strode.

"The pipe?" said he.

"It is farther on," said I; "but observe the white web-work which gleams from these cavern walls."

He turned toward me, and looked into my eyes with two filmy orbs that distilled the rheum of intoxication.

"Nitre?" he asked, at length.

"Nitre," I replied. "How long have you had that cough?"

"Ugh! ugh! ugh!—ugh! ugh! ugh!—ugh! ugh! ugh!—ugh! ugh! ugh!—ugh! ugh! ugh!"

My poor friend found it impossible to reply for many minutes.

"It is nothing," he said, at last.

"Come," I said, with decision, "we will go back; your health is precious. You are rich, respected, admired, beloved; you are happy, as once I was. You are a man to be missed. For me it is no matter. We will go back; you will be ill, and I cannot be responsible. Besides, there is Luchesi——"

"Enough," he said; "the cough is a mere nothing; it will not kill me. I shall not die of a cough."

"True—true," I replied; "and, indeed, I had no intention of alarming you unnecessarily; but you should use all proper caution. A draught of this Medoc will defend us from the damps."

Here I knocked off the neck of a bottle which I drew from a long row of its fellows that lay upon the mould.

"Drink," I said, presenting him the wine.

He raised it to his lips with a leer. He paused and nodded to me familiarly, while his bells jingled.

"I drink," he said, "to the buried that repose around us."

"And I to your long life."

He again took my arm, and we proceeded.

"These vaults," he said, "are extensive."

"The Montresors," I replied, "were a great and numerous family."

"I forget your arms."

"A huge human foot d'or, in a field azure; the foot crushes a serpent rampant whose fangs are imbedded in the heel."

"And the motto?"

"*Nemo me impune lacessit.*"

"Good!" he said.

The wine sparkled in his eyes and the bells jingled. My own fancy grew warm with the Medoc. We had passed through walls of piled bones, with casks and puncheons intermingling, into the inmost recesses of the catacombs. I paused again, and this time I made bold to seize Fortunato by an arm above the elbow.

"The nitre!" I said; "see, it increases. It hangs like moss upon the vaults. We are below the river's bed. The drops of moisture trickle among the bones. Come, we will go back ere it is too late. Your cough——"

"It is nothing," he said; "let us go on. But first, another draught of the Medoc."

I broke and reached him a flagon of De Grâve. He emptied it at a breath. His eyes flashed with a fierce light. He laughed and threw the bottle upward with a gesticulation I did not understand.

I looked at him in surprise. He repeated the movement—a grotesque one.

"You do not comprehend?" he said.

"Not I," I replied.

"Then you are not of the brotherhood."

"How?"

"You are not of the masons."

"Yes, yes," I said; "yes, yes."

"You? Impossible! A mason?"

"A mason," I replied.

"A sign," he said.

"It is this," I answered, producing a trowel from beneath the folds of my *roquelaire*.

"You jest," he exclaimed, recoiling a few paces. "But let us proceed to the Amontillado."

"Be it so," I said, replacing the tool beneath the cloak, and again offering him my arm. He leaned upon it heavily. We continued our route in search of the Amontillado. We passed through a range of low arches, descended, passed on, and descending again, arrived at a deep crypt, in which the foulness of the air caused our flambeaux rather to glow than flame.

At the most remote end of the crypt there appeared another less spacious. Its walls had been lined with human remains, piled to the vault overhead, in the fashion of the great catacombs of Paris. Three sides of this interior crypt were still ornamented in this manner. From the fourth the bones had been thrown down, and lay promiscuously upon the earth, forming at one point a mound of some size. Within the wall thus exposed by the displacing of the bones, we perceived a still interior recess, in depth about four feet, in width three, in height six or seven. It seemed to have been constructed for no especial use within itself, but formed merely the interval between two of the colossal supports of the roof of the catacombs, and was backed by one of their circumscribing walls of solid granite.

It was in vain that Fortunato, uplifting his dull torch, endeavored to pry into the depth of the recess. Its termination the feeble light did not enable us to see.

"Proceed," I said; "herein is the Amontillado. As for Luchesi——"

"He is an ignoramus," interrupted my friend, as he stepped unsteadily forward, while I followed immediately at his heels. In an instant he had reached the extremity of the niche, and finding his progress arrested by the rock, stood stupidly bewildered. A moment more and I had fettered him to the granite. In its surface were two iron staples, distant from each other about two feet, horizontally. From one of these depended a short chain, from the other a padlock. Throwing the links about his waist, it was but the work of a few seconds to secure it. He was too much astounded to resist. Withdrawing the key I stepped back from the recess.

"Pass your hand," I said, "over the wall; you cannot help feeling the nitre. Indeed it is *very* damp. Once more let me *implore* you to return. No? Then I must positively leave you. But I must first render you all the little attentions in my power."

"The Amontillado!" ejaculated my friend, not yet recovered from his astonishment.

"True," I replied; "the Amontillado."

As I said these words I busied myself among the pile of bones of which I have before spoken. Throwing them aside, I soon uncovered a quantity of building stone and mortar. With these materials and with the aid of my trowel, I began vigorously to wall up the entrance of the niche.

I had scarcely laid the first tier of the masonry when I discovered that the intoxication of Fortunato had in a great measure worn off. The earliest indication I had of this was a low moaning cry from the depth of the recess. It was *not* the cry of a drunken man. There was then a long and obstinate silence. I laid the second tier, and the third, and the fourth; and then I heard the furious vibrations of the chain. The noise lasted for several minutes, during which, that I might hearken to it with the more satisfaction, I ceased my labors and sat down upon the bones. When at last the clanking subsided, I resumed the trowel, and finished without interruption the fifth, the sixth, and the seventh tier. The wall was now nearly upon a level with my breast. I again paused, and holding the flambeaux over the masonwork, threw a few feeble rays upon the figure within.

A succession of loud and shrill screams, bursting suddenly from the throat of the chained form, seemed to thrust me violently back. For a brief moment I hesitated— I trembled. Unsheathing my rapier, I began to grope with it about the recess; but the thought of an instant reassured me. I placed my hand upon the solid fabric of the catacombs, and felt satisfied. I reapproached the wall. I replied to the yells of him who clamored. I reechoed—I aided—I surpassed them in volume and in strength. I did this, and the clamorer grew still.

It was now midnight, and my task was drawing to a close. I had completed the eighth, the ninth, and the tenth tier. I had finished a portion of the last and the eleventh; there remained but a single stone to be fitted and plastered in. I struggled with its weight; I placed it partially in its destined position. But now there came from out the niche a low laugh that erected the hairs upon my head. It was succeeded by a sad voice, which I had difficulty in recognizing as that of the noble Fortunato. The voice said—

"Ha! ha! ha!—he! he!—a very good joke indeed—an excellent jest. We will have many a rich laugh about it at the palazzo—he! he! he!—over our wine—he! he! he!"

"The Amontillado!" I said.

"He! he! he!—he! he! he!—yes, the Amontillado. But is it not getting late? Will not they be awaiting us at the palazzo, the Lady Fortunato and the rest? Let us be gone."

"Yes," I said, "let us be gone."

"For the love of God, Montresor!"

"Yes," I said, "for the love of God!"

But to these words I hearkened in vain for a reply. I grew impatient. I called aloud: "Fortunato!"

No answer. I called again:

"Fortunato!"

No answer still. I thrust a torch through the remaining aperture and let it fall within. There came forth in return only a jingling of the bells. My heart grew sick—on account of the dampness of the catacombs. I hastened to make an end of my labor. I forced the last stone into its position; I plastered it up. Against the new masonry I re-erected the old rampart of bones. For the half of a century no mortal has disturbed them. *In pace requiescat!*

QUESTION

Identify one or two examples of verbal irony, dramatic irony, and irony of circumstance and explain how each functions in the story.

CHAPTER FOUR

Approaching a Story: Guidelines for Reading

The following guidelines to reading stories derive from our discussions of the process of reading fiction, the types of fiction, and the elements of fiction. They highlight essential approaches, offering advice about how to read stories, and suggest both a method and a context for reading fiction. Use the guidelines to direct your reading of Luigi Pirandello's "War" and the stories that follow in Chapter Five.

1. Read through the story for enjoyment. Savor its suspense, its humor, its language—whatever engages you, whatever distinguishes the work. If you have time, jot down a few responses to what you've read, perhaps a couple of questions. Think about your experience of the story, of how it affected you as you read.

2. Establish the fictional type of the story. Consider how the story's typical features guide your reading and direct your understanding.

3. Read the story a second time. During this reading concentrate on the structure of its plot and on its characters. Evaluate the characters, and examine how the writer creates whatever impression of them you have. Consider the techniques of characterization that he or she employs. During this reading also, center on the subject and tentative theme of the work, thinking about its ideas and values.

4. Consider the story from the standpoint of the elements of fiction: plot and character, structure and setting, language and style, theme, and point of view. Be aware that certain of these elements may be more noticeable and more

important in a given story. Moreover, in considering these elements, remember that the story is an integral work—that any analysis you make of its aspects should be done with a view of the whole in mind.

5. Throughout your readings, however many you do, try to be open to the work, however strange, different, or difficult it may at first seem. Relate it to your knowledge of literature and language and to your experience of life.

LUIGI PIRANDELLO

[1867–1936]

War

The passengers who had left Rome by the night express had to stop until dawn at the small station of Fabriano in order to continue their journey by the small old-fashioned local joining the main line with Sulmona.

At dawn, in a stuffy and smoky second-class carriage in which five people had already spent the night, a bulky woman in deep mourning was hoisted in—almost like a shapeless bundle. Behind her, puffing and moaning, followed her husband—a tiny man, thin and weakly, his face death-white, his eyes small and bright and looking shy and uneasy.

Having at last taken a seat he politely thanked the passengers who had helped his wife and who had made room for her; then he turned round to the woman trying to pull down the collar of her coat, and politely inquired:

"Are you all right, dear?"

The wife, instead of answering, pulled up her collar again to her eyes, so as to hide her face.

"Nasty world," muttered the husband with a sad smile.

And he felt it his duty to explain to his traveling companions that the poor woman was to be pitied, for the war was taking away from her her only son, a boy of twenty to whom both had devoted their entire life, even breaking up their home at Sulmona to follow him to Rome, where he had to go as a student, then allowing him to volunteer for war with an assurance, however, that at least for six months he would not be sent to the front and now, all of a sudden, receiving a wire saying that he was due to leave in three days' time and asking them to go and see him off.

The woman under the big coat was twisting and wriggling, at times growling like a wild animal, feeling certain that all those explanations would not have aroused even a shadow of sympathy from those people who—most likely—were in the same plight as herself. One of them, who had been listening with particular attention, said: "You should thank God that your son is only leaving now for the front. Mine has been sent there the first day of the war. He has already come back twice wounded and been sent back again to the front."

"What about me? I have two sons and three nephews at the front," said another passenger.

"Maybe, but in our case it is our *only* son," ventured the husband.

"What difference can it make? You may spoil your only son with excessive attentions, but you cannot love him more than you would all your other children if you had any. Paternal love is not like bread that can be broken into pieces and split amongst the children in equal shares. A father gives *all* his love to each one of his children without discrimination, whether it be one or ten, and if I am suffering now for my two sons, I am not suffering half for each of them but double . . ."

"True . . . true . . ." sighed the embarrassed husband, "but suppose (of course we all hope it will never be your case) a father has two sons at the front and he loses one of them, there is still one left to console him . . . while . . ."

"Yes," answered the other, getting cross, "a son left to console him but also a son left for whom he must survive, while in the case of the father of an only son if the son dies the father can die too and put an end to his distress. Which of the two positions is the worse? Don't you see how my case would be worse than yours?"

"Nonsense," interrupted another traveler, a fat, red-faced man with bloodshot eyes of the palest gray.

He was panting. From his bulging eyes seemed to spurt inner violence of an uncontrolled vitality which his weakened body could hardly contain.

"Nonsense," he repeated, trying to cover his mouth with his hand so as to hide the two missing front teeth. "Nonsense. Do we give life to our children for our own benefit?"

The other travelers stared at him in distress. The one who had his son at the front since the first day of the war sighed: "You are right. Our children do not belong to us, they belong to the Country. . . ."

"Bosh," retorted the fat traveler. "Do we think of the Country when we give life to our children? Our sons are born because . . . well, because they must be born and when they come to life they take our own life with them. This is the truth. We belong to them but they can never belong to us. And when they reach twenty they are exactly what we were at their age. We too had a father and mother, but there were so many other things as well . . . girls, cigarettes, illusions, new ties . . . and the Country, of course, whose call we would have answered—when we were twenty—even if father and mother had said no. Now at our age, the love of our Country is still great, of course, but stronger than it is the love for our children. Is there any one of us here who wouldn't gladly take his son's place at the front if he could?"

There was a silence all round, everybody nodding as to approve.

"Why then," continued the fat man, "shouldn't we consider the feelings of our children when they are twenty? Isn't it natural that at their age they should consider the love for their Country (I am speaking of decent boys, of course) even greater than the love for us? Isn't it natural that it should be so, as after all they must look upon us as upon old boys who cannot move any more and must stay at home? If Country exists, if Country is a natural necessity, like bread, of which each of us must eat in order not to die of hunger, somebody must go to defend it. And our sons go, when they are twenty, and they don't want tears, because if they die, they die inflamed and happy (I am speaking, of course, of decent boys). Now, if one dies young and happy, without having the ugly sides of life, the boredom of it, the pettiness, the bitterness of disillusion

. . . what more can we ask for him? Everyone should stop crying; everyone should laugh as I do . . . or at least thank God—as I do—because my son, before dying sent me a message saying that he was dying satisfied at having ended his life in the best way he could have wished. That is why, as you see, I do not even wear mourning. . . ."

He shook his light fawn coat as to show it; his livid lip over his missing teeth was trembling, his eyes were watery and motionless, and soon after he ended with a shrill laugh which might well have been a sob.

"Quite so . . . quite so . . ." agreed the others.

The woman who, bundled in a corner under her coat, had been sitting and listening had—for the last three months—tried to find in the words of her husband and her friends something to console her in her deep sorrow, something that might show her how a mother should resign herself to send her son not even to death but to a probably dangerous life. Yet not a word had she found amongst the many which had been said . . . and her grief had been greater in seeing that nobody—as she thought—could share her feelings.

But now the words of the traveler amazed and almost stunned her. She suddenly realized that it wasn't the others who were wrong and could not understand her but herself who could not rise up to the same height of those fathers and mothers willing to resign themselves, without crying, not only to the departure of their sons but even to their death.

She lifted her head, she bent over from her corner trying to listen with great attention to the details which the fat man was giving to his companions about the way his son had fallen as a hero, for his King and his Country, happy and without regrets. It seemed to her that she had stumbled into a world she had never dreamt of, a world so far unknown to her and she was so pleased to hear everyone joining in congratulating that brave father who could so stoically speak of his child's death.

Then suddenly, just as if she had heard nothing of what had been said and almost as if waking up from a dream, she turned to the old man, asking him:

"Then . . . is your son really dead?"

Everybody stared at her. The old man, too, turned to look at her, fixing his great, bulging, horribly watery light gray eyes, deep in her face. For some little time he tried to answer, but words failed him. He looked at her, almost as if only then—at that silly, incongruous question—he had suddenly realized at last that his son was really dead—gone for ever—for ever. His face contracted, became horribly distorted, then he snatched in haste a handkerchief from his pocket and, to the amazement of everyone, broke into harrowing, heart-rending, uncontrollable sobs.

Pirandello's "War" seems to be less about the action or experience of war than about its consequences for parents whose children have gone off to fight. That is, though the title suggests the action of battle, the story has a different focus. It is indeed about war, but from the perspective of the soldiers' parents, whose involvement is no less intense for not being directly participatory. Or we can see the story as not one about war at all, but rather about parents' love for their children. Or, to shift our attention a bit, we might think of "War" as a story about grief and the ways people come to terms with it.

The characters are not highly individualized, though they are described with brief particularity. They exist as types rather than as fully developed characters.

They seem to represent alternative ways of responding to grief, and also to typify opposing views of parents' relationship to their children. As we observe their dialogue and behavior we will come to understand them. We need especially to determine whether any one of them speaks for the author or whether one view prevails.

"War" is structured as a conversation or debate that occurs between the husband of the grief-stricken woman and the man whose two sons are at the front. A third passenger who has two sons and three nephews fighting also enters this discussion, which focuses on the question of whether a parent, particularly a father, whose only son is at the front, suffers more or less than a father who has two or more sons there. It is an argument about the quantification of love. But it is one that Pirandello does not resolve—at least not directly. Instead he uses this dialogue to prepare for the entrance of the red-faced man with blood-shot eyes, who interrupts the debate by saying: "Nonsense, do we give life to our children for our own benefit?" This man's speech is much longer than the remarks of the other characters. Following his long speech, Pirandello does not devote the next part of the story to more dialogue, but describes the state of mind of the woman who has been previously inconsolable at the thought of her son's danger. These shifts—from dialogue to description, from one character to another, from external action to internal feeling, slow the story down, inviting us to pause and reflect, as they highlight places where something important is being said.

Pirandello has set us up for the surprise that follows swiftly upon the woman's question (itself a surprise since she seemed to be burying herself in her grief when she blurts it out): "Then . . . is your son really dead?" Of interest here is that Pirandello not only shows us the effect of the woman's words—they stun everyone on the train including the red-faced man—but he also explains why the man breaks into "harrowing, heart-rending, uncontrollable sobs." It is a powerful ending. And understandable, given Pirandello's indication that the man had not really allowed the fact of his son's death to reach him fully until the woman asks her question.

"War," thus, seems to show how camouflaging or repressing grief is unnatural, and how, at the moment a person fully realizes the tragedy and confronts the loss, he or she breaks down. Yet this explanation omits an important element of the story: the woman's change of attitude, the apparent shift in her feelings. Her change is as great as the man's. Perhaps this suggests that her view of the matter, which was previously his view, is as valid as his grief, which parallels her previous grief. Perhaps, that is, Pirandello indicates that the debate is not won by the proponent of either view, recognizing instead that both views reflect deep feeling, that both experiences are valid. And perhaps he suggests further that an individual who experiences tragedy and loss can expect to oscillate between moments when one attitude gains ascendancy, only to give way to an opposite view and a counter experience. Remember also that in "War" we are not given a history of the reactions of the characters, but a close-up, a snapshot of a moment. There is nothing to deny the possibility that either the man or the woman may revert to their earlier positions and states of mind.

Thus, we might view the ending of the story as balancing the views of the man and the grief-stricken woman. But another way of taking the story's ending is to notice that the man's experience occurs last. His fall into grief is given the last word. In addition, a good deal of the story can be seen as leading up to the climactic moment when he understands the reality and depth of his loss. Structurally, then, the story seems to deny the idea that the two perspectives are equal in weight. Depending on how heavily we lean on the final details of the story, we may see "War" as an illustration of the power of grief and the inevitability of its expression. Then we might say that the man's grief at his loss prevails and his previous attempt to find something positive in his son's death is a falsification of experience.

We find additional evidence for this interpretation in the details Pirandello provides about the man. After the man's long opening speech, which ends: That is why, as you see, I do not even wear mourning," this description follows: "his livid lip over his missing teeth was trembling, his eyes were watery and motionless, and soon after he ended with a shrill laugh which might have been a sob." Pirandello places this paragraph between the man's long speech and the agreeing response of his listeners (their "Quite so . . . quite so"). But the *shrill* laugh is unnatural; it is as much a "sob" as a laugh. Moreover, there is a good deal of tension and urgency in his insistence that what had been said before was "nonsense." In fact, he says, "Nonsense" three times, not once, perhaps in an attempt to convince himself of what he is saying.

Finally, a word about point of view. The story is told in the third person by a narrator who does not participate in the action. Pirandello limits the omniscience of the narrator to the feelings of the grief-stricken woman. We enter her consciousness and are shown what she thinks and feels. Focusing on her, the story follows her perception of what is said and done. But when she says, "then . . . is your son really dead?" the narrative focus shifts. We are not told the effect of the man's sobs on the woman as we had previously been shown how his earlier speech had affected her. Instead, we are given a more objective, detached, and dramatic view. This shift in point of view at a climactic moment reinforces the idea that the story is more about the man than the woman, that only in confronting his grief does he realize the extent of his loss. This seems to be the story's central concern.

CHAPTER FIVE

A Collection of Short Fiction

NATHANIEL HAWTHORNE

[*1804–1864*]

Wakefield

In some old magazine or newspaper, I recollect a story, told as truth, of a man—let us call him Wakefield—who absented himself for a long time, from his wife. The fact, thus abstractedly stated, is not very uncommon, nor—without a proper distinction of circumstances—to be condemned either as naughty or nonsensical. Howbeit, this, though far from the most aggravated, is perhaps the strangest instance, on record, of marital delinquency; and, moreover, as remarkable a freak as may be found in the whole list of human oddities. The wedded couple lived in London. The man, under pretence of going a journey, took lodgings in the next street to his own house, and there, unheard of by his wife or friends, and without the shadow of a reason for such self-banishment, dwelt upwards of twenty years. During that period, he beheld his home every day, and frequently the forlorn Mrs. Wakefield. And after so great a gap in his matrimonial felicity—when his death was reckoned certain, his estate settled, his name dismissed from memory, and his wife, long, long ago, resigned to her autumnal widowhood—he entered the door one evening, quietly, as from a day's absence, and became a loving spouse until death.

This outline is all that I remember. But the incident, though of the purest originality, unexampled, and probably never to be repeated, is one, I think, which appeals to the general sympathies of mankind. We know, each for himself, that none of us would perpetrate such a folly, yet feel as if some other might. To my own contemplations, at least, it has often recurred, always exciting wonder, but with a sense that the story must be true, and a conception of its hero's character. Whenever any subject so forcibly affects the mind, time is well spent in thinking of it. If the reader choose, let him do his own meditation; or if he prefer to ramble with me through the twenty years of Wakefield's vagary, I bid him welcome, trusting that there will be a pervading spirit and a moral, even should we fail to find them, done up neatly, and condensed into the final sentence. Thought has always its efficacy, and every striking incident its moral.

What sort of a man was Wakefield? We are free to shape out our own idea, and call it by his name. He was now in the meridian of life; his matrimonial affections, never violent, were sobered into a calm, habitual sentiment; of all husbands, he was likely to be the most constant, because a certain sluggishness would keep his heart at rest, wherever it might be placed. He was intellectual, but not actively so; his mind occupied itself in long and lazy musings, that tended to no purpose, or had not vigor to attain it; his thoughts were seldom so energetic as to seize hold of words. Imagination, in the proper meaning of the term, made no part of Wakefield's gifts. With a cold, but not depraved nor wandering heart, and a mind never feverish with riotous thoughts, nor perplexed with originality, who could have anticipated, that our friend would entitle himself to a foremost place among the doers of eccentric deeds? Had his acquaintances been asked, who was the man in London, the surest to perform nothing to-day which should be remembered on the morrow, they would have thought of Wakefield. Only the wife of his bosom might have hesitated. She, without having analyzed his character, was partly aware of a quiet selfishness, that had rusted into his inactive mind—of a peculiar sort of vanity, the most uneasy attribute about him—of a disposition to craft, which had seldom produced more positive effects than the keeping of petty secrets, hardly worth revealing—and, lastly, of what she called a little strangeness, sometimes, in the good man. This latter quality is indefinable, and perhaps non-existent.

Let us now imagine Wakefield bidding adieu to his wife. It is the dusk of an October evening. His equipment is a drab great-coat, a hat covered with an oil-cloth, top-boots, an umbrella in one hand and a small portmanteau in the other. He has informed Mrs. Wakefield that he is to take the night-coach into the country. She would fain inquire the length of his journey, its object, and the probable time of his return; but, indulgent to his harmless love of mystery, interrogates him only by a look. He tells her not to expect him positively by the return coach, nor to look alarmed should he tarry three or four days; but, at all events, to look for him at supper on Friday evening. Wakefield himself, be it considered, has no suspicion of what is before him. He holds out his hand; she gives her own, and meets his parting kiss, in the matter-of-course way of a ten years' matrimony; and forth goes the middle-aged Mr. Wakefield, almost resolved to perplex his good lady by a whole week's absence. After the door has closed behind him, she perceives it thrust partly open, and a vision of her husband's face, through the aperture, smiling on her, and gone in a moment. For the time, this little incident is dismissed without a thought. But, long afterwards, when she has been more years a widow than a wife, that smile recurs, and flickers across all her reminiscences of Wakefield's visage. In her many musings, she surrounds the original smile with a multitude of fantasies, which make it strange and awful; as, for instance, if she imagines him in a coffin, that parting look is frozen on his pale features; or, if she dreams of him in Heaven, still his blessed spirit wears a quiet and crafty smile. Yet, for its sake, when all others have given him up for dead, she sometimes doubts whether she is a widow.

But, our business is with the husband. We must hurry after him, along the street, ere he lose his individuality, and melt into the great mass of London life. It would be vain searching for him there. Let us follow close at his heels, therefore, until, after several superfluous turns and doublings, we find him comfortably established by the fireside of a small apartment, previously bespoken. He is in the next street to his own, and at his journey's end. He can scarcely trust his good fortune, in having got thither unperceived—recollecting that, at one time, he was delayed by the throng, in the very focus of a lighted lantern; and, again, there were foot-steps, that seemed to tread behind his own, distinct from the multitudinous tramp around him; and, anon, he heard a voice shouting afar, and fancied that it called his name. Doubtless, a dozen busy-bodies had been watching him, and told his wife the whole affair. Poor Wakefield! Little knowest thou thine own insignificance in this great world! No mortal eye but mine has traced thee. Go quietly to thy bed, foolish man; and, on the morrow, if thou wilt be wise, get thee home to good Mrs. Wakefield, and tell her the truth. Remove not thyself, even for a little week, from thy place in her chaste bosom. Were she, for a single moment, to deem thee dead, or lost, or lastingly divided from her, thou wouldst be woefully conscious of a change in thy true wife, forever after. It is perilous to make a chasm in human affections; not that they gape so long and wide—but so quickly close again!

Almost repenting of his frolic, or whatever it may be termed, Wakefield lies down betimes, and starting from his first nap, spreads forth his arms into the wide and solitary waste of the unaccustomed bed. "No"—thinks he, gathering the bed-clothes about him —"I will not sleep alone another night."

In the morning, he rises earlier than usual, and sets himself to consider what he really means to do. Such are his loose and rambling modes of thought, that he has taken this very singular step, with the consciousness of a purpose, indeed, but without being able to define it sufficiently for his own contemplation. The vagueness of the project, and the convulsive effort with which he plunges into the execution of it, are equally characteristic of a feeble-minded man. Wakefield sifts his ideas, however, as minutely as he may, and finds himself curious to know the progress of matters at home—how his exemplary wife will endure her widowhood, of a week; and, briefly, how the little sphere of creatures and circumstances, in which he was a central object, will be affected by his removal. A morbid vanity, therefore, lies nearest the bottom of the affair. But, how is he to attain his ends? Not, certainly, by keeping close in this comfortable lodging, where, though he slept and awoke in the next street to his home, he is as effectually abroad, as if the stage coach had been whirling him away all night. Yet, should he reappear, the whole project is knocked in the head. His poor brains being hopelessly puzzled with this dilemma, he at length ventures out, partly resolving to cross the head of the street, and send one hasty glance towards his forsaken domicile. Habit—for he is a man of habits—takes him by the hand, and guides him, wholly unaware, to his own door, where, just at the critical moment, he is aroused by the scraping of his foot upon the step. Wakefield! whither are you going?

At that instant, his fate was turning on the pivot. Little dreaming of the doom to which his first backward step devotes him, he hurries away, breathless with agitation hitherto unfelt, and hardly dares turn his head, at the distant corner. Can it be, that

nobody caught sight of him? Will not the whole household—the decent Mrs. Wakefield, the smart maid-servant, and the dirty little footboy—raise a hue-and-cry, through
London streets, in pursuit of their fugitive lord and master? Wonderful escape! He
gathers courage to pause and look homeward, but is perplexed with a sense of change
about the familiar edifice, such as affects us all, when, after a separation of months or
years, we again see some hill or lake, or work of art, with which we were friends, of
old. In ordinary cases, this indescribable impression is caused by the comparison and
contrast between our imperfect reminiscences and the reality. In Wakefield, the magic
of a single night has wrought a similar transformation, because, in that brief period,
a great moral change has been effected. But this is a secret from himself. Before leaving
the spot, he catches a far and momentary glimpse of his wife, passing athwart the front
window, with her face turned towards the head of the street. The crafty nincompoop
takes to his heels, scared with the idea, that, among a thousand such atoms of mortality,
her eye must have detected him. Right glad is his heart, though his brain be somewhat
dizzy, when he finds himself by the coal-fire of his lodgings.

So much for the commencement of this long whim-wham. After the critical conception, and the stirring up of the man's sluggish temperament to put it in practice, the
whole matter evolves itself in a natural train. We may suppose him, as the result of
deep deliberation, buying a new wig, of reddish hair, and selecting sundry garments,
in a fashion unlike his customary suit of brown, from a Jew's old-clothes bag. It is
accomplished. Wakefield is another man. The new system being now established, a
retrograde movement to the old would be almost as difficult as the step that placed him
in his unparalleled position. Furthermore, he is rendered obstinate by a sulkiness,
occasionally incident to his temper, and brought on, at present, by the inadequate
sensation which he conceived to have been produced in the bosom of Mrs. Wakefield.
He will not go back until she be frightened half to death. Well; twice or thrice has
she passed before his sight, each time with a heavier step, a paler cheek, and more
anxious brow; and, in the third week of his nonappearance, he detects a portent of evil
entering the house, in the guise of an apothecary. Next day, the knocker is muffled.
Towards night-fall, comes the chariot of a physician, and deposits its big-wigged and
solemn burthen at Wakefield's door, whence, after a quarter of an hour's visit, he
emerges, perchance the herald of a funeral. Dear woman! Will she die? By this time,
Wakefield is excited to something like energy of feeling, but still lingers away from
his wife's bedside, pleading with his conscience, that she must not be disturbed at such
a juncture. If aught else restrains him, he does not know it. In the course of a few weeks,
she gradually recovers; the crisis is over; her heart is sad, perhaps, but quiet; and, let
him return soon or late, it will never be feverish for him again. Such ideas glimmer
through the mist of Wakefield's mind, and render him indistinctly conscious that an
almost impassible gulf divides his hired apartment from his former home. "It is but in
the next street!" he sometimes says. Fool! it is in another world. Hitherto, he has put
off his return from one particular day to another; henceforward, he leaves the precise
time undetermined. Not to-morrow—probably next week—pretty soon. Poor man!
The dead have nearly as much chance of re-visiting their earthly homes, as the self-
banished Wakefield.

Would that I had a folio to write, instead of a brief article in the New-England!
Then might I exemplify how an influence, beyond our control, lays its strong hand
on every deed which we do, and weaves its consequences into an iron tissue of necessity.
Wakefield is spell-bound. We must leave him, for ten years or so, to haunt around his

house, without once crossing the threshold, and to be faithful to his wife, with all the affection of which his heart is capable, while he is slowly fading out of hers. Long since, it must be remarked, he has lost the perception of singularity in his conduct.

Now for a scene! Amid the throng of a London street, we distinguish a man, now waxing elderly, with few characteristics to attract careless observers, yet bearing, in his whole aspect, the hand-writing of no common fate, for such as have the skill to read it. He is meagre; his low and narrow forehead is deeply wrinkled; his eyes, small and lustreless, sometimes wander apprehensively about him, but often seem to look inward. He bends his head, and moves with an indescribable obliquity of gait, as if unwilling to display his full front to the world. Watch him, long enough to see what we have described, and you will allow, that circumstances—which often produce remarkable men from nature's ordinary handiwork—have produced one such here. Next, leaving him to sidle along the footwalk, cast your eyes in the opposite direction, where a portly female, considerably in the wane of life, with a prayer-book in her hand, is proceeding to yonder church. She has the placid mien of settled widowhood. Her regrets have either died away, or have become so essential to her heart, that they would be poorly exchanged for joy. Just as the lean man and well conditioned woman are passing, a slight obstruction occurs, and brings these two figures directly in contact. Their hands touch; the pressure of the crowd forces her bosom against his shoulder; they stand, face to face, staring into each other's eyes. After a ten years' separation, thus Wakefield meets his wife!

The throng eddies away, and carries them asunder. The sober widow, resuming her former pace, proceeds to church, but pauses in the portal, and throws a perplexed glance along the street. She passes in, however, opening her prayer-book as she goes. And the man? With so wild a face, that busy and selfish London stands to gaze after him, he hurries to his lodgings, bolts the door, and throws himself upon the bed. The latent feelings of years break out; his feeble mind acquires a brief energy from their strength; all the miserable strangeness of his life is revealed to him at a glance; and he cries out, passionately—"Wakefield! Wakefield! You are mad!"

Perhaps he was so. The singularity of his situation must have so moulded him to itself, that, considered in regard to his fellow-creatures and the business of life, he could not be said to posses his right mind. He had contrived, or rather he had happened, to dissever himself from the world—to vanish—to give up his place and privileges with living men, without being admitted among the dead. The life of a hermit is nowise parallel to his. He was in the bustle of the city, as of old; but the crowd swept by, and saw him not; he was, we may figuratively say, always beside his wife, and at his hearth, yet must never feel the warmth of the one, nor the affection of the other. It was Wakefield's unprecedented fate, to retain his original share of human sympathies, and to be still involved in human interests, while he had lost his reciprocal influence on them. It would be a most curious speculation, to trace out the effect of such circumstances on his heart and intellect, separately, and in unison. Yet, changed as he was, he would seldom be conscious of it, but deem himself the same man as ever; glimpses of the truth, indeed, would come, but only for the moment; and still he would keep saying —"I shall soon go back!"—nor reflect, that he had been saying so for twenty years.

I conceive, also, that these twenty years would appear, in the retrospect, scarcely longer than the week to which Wakefield had at first limited his absence. He would look on the affair as no more than an interlude in the main business of his life. When, after a little while more, he should deem it time to re-enter his parlor, his wife would clap her hands for joy, on beholding the middle-aged Mr. Wakefield. Alas, what a mistake! Would Time but await the close of our favorite follies, we should be young men, all of us, and till Doom's Day.

One evening, in the twentieth year since he vanished, Wakefield is taking his customary walk towards the dwelling which he still calls his own. It is a gusty night of autumn, with frequent showers, that patter down upon the pavement, and are gone, before a man can put up his umbrella. Pausing near the house, Wakefield discerns, through the parlor-windows of the second floor, the red glow, and the glimmer and fitful flash, of a comfortable fire. On the ceiling, appears a grotesque shadow of good Mrs. Wakefield. The cap, the nose and chin, and the broad waist, form an admirable caricature, which dances, moreover, with the up-flickering and down-sinking blaze, almost too merrily for the shade of an elderly widow. At this instant, a shower chances to fall, and is driven, by the unmannerly gust, full into Wakefield's face and bosom. He is quite penetrated with its autumnal chill. Shall he stand, wet and shivering here, when his own hearth has a good fire to warm him, and his own wife will run to fetch the gray coat and small-clothes, which, doubtless, she has kept carefully in the closet of their bed-chamber? No! Wakefield is no such fool. He ascends the steps—heavily! —for twenty years have stiffened his legs, since he came down—but he knows it not. Stay, Wakefield! Would you go to the sole home that is left you? Then step into your grave! The door opens. As he passes in, we have a parting glimpse of his visage, and recognize the crafty smile, which was the precursor of the little joke, that he has ever since been playing off at his wife's expense. How unmercifully has he quizzed the poor woman! Well; a good night's rest to Wakefield!

This happy event—supposing it to be such—could only have occurred at an unpremeditated moment. We will not follow our friend across the threshold. He has left us much food for thought, a portion of which shall lend its wisdom to a moral, and be shaped into a figure. Amid the seeming confusion of our mysterious world, individuals are so nicely adjusted to a system, and systems to one another, and to a whole, that, by stepping aside for a moment, a man exposes himself to a fearful risk of losing his place forever. Like Wakefield, he may become, as it were, the Outcast of the Universe.

LEO NIKOLAIEVICH TOLSTOY

[1828–1910]

The Death of Iván Ilych

TRANSLATED BY LOUISE AND AYLMER MAUDE

I

During an interval in the Melvínski trial in the large building of the Law Courts the members and public prosecutor met in Iván Egórovich Shébek's private room, where the conversation turned on the celebrated Krasóvski case. Fédor Vasílievich warmly maintained that it was not subject to their jurisdiction, Iván Egórovich maintained the contrary, while Peter Ivánovich, not having entered into the discussion at the start, took no part in it but looked through the *Gazette* which had just been handed in.

"Gentlemen," he said, "Iván Ilych has died!"

"You don't say!"

"Here, read it yourself," replied Peter Ivánovich, handing Fëdor Vasílievich the paper still damp from the press. Surrounded by a black border were the words: "Praskóvya Fëdorovna Goloviná, with profound sorrow, informs relatives and friends of the demise of her beloved husband Iván Ilych Golovín, Member of the Court of Justice, which occurred on February the 4th of this year 1882. The funeral will take place on Friday at one o'clock in the afternoon."

Iván Ilych had been a colleague of the gentlemen present and was liked by them all. He had been ill for some weeks with an illness said to be incurable. His post had been kept open for him, but there had been conjectures that in case of his death Alexéev might receive his appointment, and that either Vínnikov or Shtábel would succeed Alexéev. So on receiving the news of Iván Ilych's death the first thought of each of the gentlemen in that private room was of the changes and promotions it might occasion among themselves or their acquaintances.

"I shall be sure to get Shtábel's place or Vínnikov's," thought Fëdor Vasílievich. "I was promised that long ago, and the promotion means an extra eight hundred rubles a year for me besides the allowance."

"Now I must apply for my brother-in-law's transfer from Kalúga," thought Peter Ivánovich. "My wife will be very glad, and then she won't be able to say that I never do anything for her relations."

"I thought he would never leave his bed again," said Peter Ivánovich aloud. "It's very sad."

"But what really was the matter with him?"

"The doctors couldn't say—at least they could, but each of them said something different. When last I saw him I thought he was getting better."

"And I haven't been to see him since the holidays. I always meant to go."

"Had he any property?"

"I think his wife had a little—but something quite trifling."

"We shall have to go to see her, but they live so terribly far away."

"Far away from you, you mean. Everything's far away from your place."

"You see, he never can forgive my living on the other side of the river," said Peter Ivánovich, smiling at Shébek. Then, still talking of the distances between different parts of the city, they returned to the Court.

Besides considerations as to the possible transfers and promotions likely to result from Iván Ilych's death, the mere fact of the death of a near acquaintance aroused, as usual, in all who heard of it the complacent feeling that, "it is he who is dead and not I."

Each one thought or felt, "Well, he's dead but I'm alive!" But the more intimate of Iván Ilych's acquaintances, his so-called friends, could not help thinking also that they would now have to fulfil the very tiresome demands of propriety by attending the funeral service and paying a visit of condolence to the widow.

Fëdor Vasílievich and Peter Ivánovich had been his nearest acquaintances. Peter Ivánovich had studied law with Iván Ilych and had considered himself to be under obligations to him.

Having told his wife at dinner-time of Iván Ilych's death, and of his conjecture that it might be possible to get her brother transferred to their circuit, Peter Ivánovich sacrificed his usual nap, put on his evening clothes, and drove to Iván Ilych's house.

At the entrance stood a carriage and two cabs. Leaning against the wall in the hall downstairs near the cloak-stand was a coffin-lid covered with cloth of gold, ornamented with gold cord and tassels, that had been polished up with metal powder. Two ladies in black were taking off their fur cloaks. Peter Ivánovich recognized one of them as Iván Ilych's sister, but the other was a stranger to him. His colleague Schwartz was just coming downstairs, but on seeing Peter Ivánovich enter he stopped and winked at him, as if to say: "Iván Ilych has made a mess of things—not like you and me."

Schwartz's face with his Piccadilly whiskers, and his slim figure in evening dress, had as usual an air of elegant solemnity which contrasted with the playfulness of his character and had a special piquancy here, or so it seemed to Peter Ivánovich.

Peter Ivánovich allowed the ladies to precede him and slowly followed them upstairs. Schwartz did not come down but remained where he was, and Peter Ivánovich understood that he wanted to arrange where they should play bridge that evening. The ladies went upstairs to the widow's room, and Schwartz with seriously compressed lips but a playful look in his eyes, indicated by a twist of his eyebrows the room to the right where the body lay.

Peter Ivánovich, like everyone else on such occasions, entered feeling uncertain what he would have to do. All he knew was that at such times it is always safe to cross oneself. But he was not quite sure whether one should make obeisances while doing so. He therefore adopted a middle course. On entering the room he began crossing himself and made a slight movement resembling a bow. At the same time, as far as the motion of his head and arm allowed, he surveyed the room. Two young men—apparently nephews, one of whom was a high-school pupil—were leaving the room, crossing themselves as they did so. An old woman was standing motionless, and a lady with strangely arched eyebrows was saying something to her in a whisper. A vigorous, resolute Church Reader, in a frock-coat, was reading something in a loud voice with an expression that precluded any contradiction. The butler's assistant, Gerásim, stepping lightly in front of Peter Ivánovich, was strewing something on the floor. Noticing this, Peter Ivánovich was immediately aware of a faint odour of a decomposing body.

The last time he had called on Iván Ilych, Peter Ivánovich had seen Gerásim in the study. Iván Ilych had been particularly fond of him and he was performing the duty of a sick nurse.

Peter Ivánovich continued to make the sign of the cross slightly inclining his head in an intermediate direction between the coffin, the Reader, and the icons on the table in a corner of the room. Afterwards, when it seemed to him that this movement of his arm in crossing himself had gone on too long, he stopped and began to look at the corpse.

The dead man lay, as dead men always lie, in a specially heavy way, his rigid limbs sunk in the soft cushions of the coffin, with the head forever bowed on the pillow. His yellow waxen brow with bald patches over his sunken temples was thrust up in the way peculiar to the dead, the protruding nose seeming to press on the upper lip. He was much changed and had grown even thinner since Peter Ivánovich had last seen him, but, as is always the case with the dead, his face was handsomer and above all more dignified than when he was alive. The expression on the face said that what was necessary had been accomplished, and accomplished rightly. Besides this there was in that expression a reproach and a warning to the living. This warning seemed to Peter Ivánovich out of place, or at least not applicable to him. He felt a certain discomfort and so he hurriedly crossed himself once more and turned and went out of the door —too hurriedly and too regardless of propriety, as he himself was aware.

Schwartz was waiting for him in the adjoining room with legs spread wide apart and both hands toying with his top-hat behind his back. The mere sight of that playful, well-groomed, and elegant figure refreshed Peter Ivánovich. He felt that Schwartz was above all these happenings and would not surrender to any depressing influences. His very look said that this incident of a church service for Iván Ilych could not be a sufficient reason for infringing the order of the session—in other words, that it would certainly not prevent his unwrapping a new pack of cards and shuffling them that evening while a footman placed four fresh candles on the table: in fact, that there was no reason for supposing that this incident would hinder their spending the evening agreeably. Indeed he said this in a whisper as Peter Ivánovich passed him, proposing that they should meet for a game at Fëdor Vasílievich's. But apparently Peter Ivánovich was not destined to play bridge that evening. Praskóvya Fëdorovna (a short, fat woman who despite all efforts to the contrary had continued to broaden steadily from her shoulders downwards and who had the same extraordinary arched eyebrows as the lady who had been standing by the coffin), dressed all in black, her head covered with lace, came out of her own room with some other ladies, conducted them to the room where the dead body lay, and said: "The service will begin immediately. Please go in."

Schwartz, making an indefinite bow, stood still, evidently neither accepting nor declining this invitation. Praskóvya Fëdorovna recognizing Peter Ivánovich, sighed, went close up to him, took his hand, and said: "I know you were a true friend to Iván Ilych . . ." and looked at him awaiting some suitable response. And Peter Ivánovich knew that, just as it had been the right thing to cross himself in that room, so what he had to do here was to press her hand, sigh, and say, "Believe me . . ." So he did all this and as he did it felt that the desired result had been achieved: that both he and she were touched.

"Come with me. I want to speak to you before it begins," said the widow. "Give me your arm."

Peter Ivánovich gave her his arm and they went to the inner rooms, passing Schwartz who winked at Peter Ivánovich compassionately.

"That does for our bridge! Don't object if we find another player. Perhaps you can cut in when you do escape," said his playful look.

Peter Ivánovich sighed still more deeply and despondently, and Praskóvya Fëdorovna pressed his arm gratefully. When they reached the drawing-room, upholstered in pink cretonne and lighted by a dim lamp, they sat down at the table—she on a sofa and Peter Ivánovich on a low pouffe, the springs of which yielded spasmodically under his weight. Praskóvya Fëdorovna had been on the point of warning him to take another seat, but felt that such a warning was out of keeping with her present condition and so changed her mind. As he sat down on the pouffe Peter Ivánovich recalled how Iván Ilych had arranged this room and had consulted him regarding this pink cretonne with green leaves. The whole room was full of furniture and knick-knacks, and on her way to the sofa the lace of the widow's black shawl caught on the carved edge of the table. Peter Ivánovich rose to detach it, and the springs of the pouffe, relieved of his weight, rose also and gave him a push. The widow began detaching her shawl herself, and Peter Ivánovich again sat down, suppressing the rebellious springs of the pouffe under him. But the widow had not quite freed herself and Peter Ivánovich got up again, and again the pouffe rebelled and even creaked. When this was all over she took out a clean cambric handkerchief and began to weep. The episode with the shawl and the struggle with the pouffe had cooled Peter Ivánovich's emotions and he sat there with a sullen look on his face. This awkward situation was interrupted by Sokolóv, Iván Ilych's butler, who came to report that the plot in the cemetery that Praskóvya Fëdorovna had chosen would cost two hundred rubles. She stopped weeping and, looking at Peter Ivánovich with the air of a victim, remarked in French that it was very hard for her. Peter Ivánovich made a silent gesture signifying his full conviction that it must indeed be so.

"Please smoke," she said in a magnanimous yet crushed voice, and turned to discuss with Sokolóv the price of the plot for the grave.

Peter Ivánovich while lighting his cigarette heard her inquiring very circumstantially into the prices of different plots in the cemetery and finally decide which she would take. When that was done she gave instructions about engaging the choir. Sokolóv then left the room.

"I look after everything myself," she told Peter Ivánovich, shifting the albums that lay on the table; and noticing that the table was endangered by his cigarette-ash, she immediately passed him an ash-tray, saying as she did so: "I consider it an affectation to say that my grief prevents my attending to practical affairs. On the contrary, if anything can—I won't say console me, but—distract me, it is seeing to everything concerning him." She again took out her handkerchief as if preparing to cry, but suddenly, as if mastering her feeling, she shook herself and began to speak calmly. "But there is something I want to talk to you about."

Peter Ivánovich bowed, keeping control of the springs of the pouffe, which immediately began quivering under him.

"He suffered terribly the last few days."

"Did he?" said Peter Ivánovich.

"Oh, terribly! He screamed unceasingly, not for minutes but for hours. For the last three days he screamed incessantly. It was unendurable. I cannot understand how I bore it; you could hear him three rooms off. Oh, what I have suffered!"

"Is it possible that he was conscious all that time?" asked Peter Ivánovich.

"Yes," she whispered. "To the last moment. He took leave of us a quarter of an hour before he died, and asked us to take Volódya away."

The thought of the sufferings of this man he had known so intimately, first as a merry little boy, then as a school-mate, and later as a grown-up colleague, suddenly struck Peter Ivánovich with horror, despite an unpleasant consciousness of his own and this woman's dissimulation. He again saw that brow, and that nose pressing down on the lip, and felt afraid for himself.

"Three days of frightful suffering and then death! Why, that might suddenly, at any time, happen to me," he thought, and for a moment felt terrified. But—he did not himself know how—the customary reflection at once occurred to him that this had happened to Iván Ilych and not to him, and that it should not and could not happen to him, and that to think that it could would be yielding to depression which he ought not to do, as Schwartz's expression plainly showed. After which reflection Peter

Ivánovich felt reassured, and began to ask with interest about the details of Iván Ilych's death, as though death was an accident natural to Iván Ilych but certainly not to himself.

After many details of the really dreadful physical sufferings Iván Ilych had endured (which details he learnt only from the effect those sufferings had produced on Praskóvya Fëdorovna's nerves) the widow apparently found it necessary to get to business.

"Oh, Peter Ivánovich, how hard it is! How terribly, terribly hard!" and she again began to weep.

Peter Ivánovich sighed and waited for her to finish blowing her nose. When she had done so he said, "Believe me . . ." and she again began talking and brought out what was evidently her chief concern with him—namely, to question him as to how she could obtain a grant of money from the government on the occasion of her husband's death. She made it appear that she was asking Peter Ivánovich's advice about her pension, but he soon saw that she already knew about that to the minutest detail, more even than he did himself. She knew how much could be got out of the government in consequence of her husband's death, but wanted to find out whether she could not possibly extract something more. Peter Ivánovich tried to think of some means of doing so, but after reflecting for a while and, out of propriety, condemning the government for its niggardliness, he said he thought that nothing more could be got. Then she sighed and evidently began to devise means of getting rid of her visitor. Noticing this, he put out his cigarette, rose, pressed her hand, and went out into the anteroom.

In the dining-room where the clock stood that Iván Ilych had liked so much and had bought at an antique shop, Peter Ivánovich met a priest and a few acquaintances who had come to attend the service, and he recognized Iván Ilych's daughter, a handsome young woman. She was in black and her slim figure appeared slimmer than ever. She had a gloomy, determined, almost angry expression, and bowed to Peter Ivánovich as though he were in some way to blame. Behind her, with the same offended look, stood a wealthy young man, an examining magistrate, whom Peter Ivánovich also knew and who was her fiancé, as he had heard. He bowed mournfully to them and was about to pass into the death-chamber, when from under the stairs appeared the figure of Iván Ilych's schoolboy son, who was extremely like his father. He seemed a little Iván Ilych, such as Peter Ivánovich remembered when they studied law together. His tear-stained eyes had in them the look that is seen in the eyes of boys of thirteen or fourteen who are not pure-minded. When he saw Peter Ivánovich he scowled morosely and shamefacedly. Peter Ivánovich nodded to him and entered the death-chamber. The service began: candles, groans, incense, tears, and sobs. Peter Ivánovich stood looking gloomily down at his feet. He did not look once at the dead man, did not yield to any depressing influence, and was one of the first to leave the room. There was no one in the anteroom, but Gerásim darted out of the dead man's room, rummaged with his strong hands among the fur coats to find Peter Ivánovich's and helped him on with it.

"Well, friend Gerásim," said Peter Ivánovich, so as to say something. "It's a sad affair, isn't it?"

"It's God's will. We shall all come to it some day," said Gerásim, displaying his teeth —the even, white teeth of a healthy peasant—and, like a man in the thick of urgent work, he briskly opened the front door, called the coachman, helped Peter Ivánovich into the sledge, and sprang back to the porch as if in readiness for what he had to do next.

Peter Ivánovich found the fresh air particularly pleasant after the smell of incense, the dead body, and carbolic acid.

"Where to, sir?" asked the coachman.

"It's not too late even now. . . . I'll call round on Fëdor Vasílievich."

He accordingly drove there and found them just finishing the first rubber, so that it was quite convenient for him to cut in.

2

Iván Ilych's life had been most simple and most ordinary and therefore most terrible.

He had been a member of the Court of Justice, and died at the age of forty-five. His father had been an official who after serving in various ministries and departments in Petersburg had made the sort of career which brings men to positions from which by reason of their long service they cannot be dismissed, though they are obviously unfit to hold any responsible position, and for whom therefore posts are specially created, which though fictitious carry salaries of from six to ten thousand rubles that are not fictitious and in receipt of which they live on to a great age.

Such was the Privy Councillor and superfluous member of various superfluous institutions, Ilya Epímovich Golovín.

He had three sons, of whom Iván Ilych was the second. The eldest son was following in his father's footsteps only in another department, and was already approaching that stage in the service at which a similar sinecure would be reached. The third son was a failure. He had ruined his prospects in a number of positions and was now serving in the railway department. His father and brothers, and still more their wives, not merely disliked meeting him, but avoided remembering his existence unless compelled to do so. His sister had married Baron Greff, a Petersburg official of her father's type. Iván Ilych was *le phénix de la famille*° as people said. He was neither as cold and formal as his elder brother nor as wild as the younger, but was a happy mean between them —an intelligent, polished, lively and agreeable man. He had studied with his younger brother at the School of Law, but the latter had failed to complete the course and was expelled when he was in the fifth class. Iván Ilych finished the course well. Even when he was at the School of Law he was just what he remained for the rest of his life: a capable, cheerful, good-natured, and sociable man, though strict in the fulfilment of what he considered to be his duty: and he considered his duty to be what was so considered by those in authority. Neither as a boy nor as a man was he a toady, but from early youth was by nature attracted to people of high station as a fly is drawn to the light, assimilating their ways and views of life and establishing friendly relations with them. All the enthusiasms of childhood and youth passed without leaving much trace on him; he succumbed to sensuality, to vanity, and latterly among the highest classes to liberalism, but always within limits which his instinct unfailingly indicated to him as correct.

At school he had done things which had formerly seemed to him very horrid and made him feel disgusted with himself when he did them; but when later on he saw that such actions were done by people of good position and that they did not regard them as wrong, he was able not exactly to regard them as right, but to forget about them entirely or not be at all troubled at remembering them.

le phénix de la famille   the prize of the family

Having graduated from the School of Law and qualified for the tenth rank of the civil service, and having received money from his father for his equipment, Iván Ilych ordered himself clothes at Scharmer's, the fashionable tailor, hung a medallion inscribed *respice finem*° on his watch-chain, took leave of his professor and the prince who was patron of the school, had a farewell dinner with his comrades at Donon's first-class restaurant, and with his new and fashionable portmanteau, linen, clothes, shaving and other toilet appliances, and a travelling rug, all purchased at the best shops, he set off for one of the provinces where, through his father's influence, he had been attached to the governor as an official for special service.

In the province Iván Ilych soon arranged as easy and agreeable a position for himself as he had had at the School of Law. He performed his official tasks, made his career, and at the same time amused himself pleasantly and decorously. Occasionally he paid official visits to country districts, where he behaved with dignity both to his superiors and inferiors, and performed the duties entrusted to him, which related chiefly to the sectarians,° with an exactness and incorruptible honesty of which he could not but feel proud.

In official matters, despite his youth and taste for frivolous gaiety, he was exceedingly reserved, punctilious, and even severe; but in society he was often amusing and witty, and always good-natured, correct in his manner, and *bon enfant,*° as the governor and his wife—with whom he was like one of the family—used to say of him.

In the province he had an affair with a lady who made advances to the elegant young lawyer, and there was also a milliner; and there were carousals with aides-de-camp who visited the district, and after-supper visits to a certain outlying street of doubtful reputation; and there was too some obsequiousness to his chief and even to his chief's wife, but all this was done with such a tone of good breeding that no hard names could be applied to it. It all came under the heading of the French saying: *"Il faut que jeunesse se passe."*° It was all done with clean hands, in clean linen, with French phrases, and above all among people of the best society and consequently with the approval of people of rank.

So Iván Ilych served for five years and then came a change in his official life. The new and reformed judicial institutions were introduced, and new men were needed. Iván Ilych became such a new man. He was offered the post of Examining Magistrate, and he accepted it though the post was in another province and obliged him to give up the connexions he had formed and to make new ones. His friends met to give him a send-off; they had a group-photograph taken and presented him with a silver cigarette-case, and he set off to his new post.

As examining magistrate Iván Ilych was just as *comme il faut*° and decorous a man, inspiring general respect and capable of separating his official duties from his private life, as he had been when acting as an official on special service. His duties now as examining magistrate were far more interesting and attractive than before. In his former position it had been pleasant to wear an undress uniform made by Scharmer, and to pass through the crowd of petitioners and officials who were timorously awaiting an audience with the governor, and who envied him as with free and easy gait he went straight into his chief's private room to have a cup of tea and a cigarette with him.

---

respice finem   *think of the end (of your life)*   **sectarians** *dissenters from the Orthodox Church*
bon enfant *like a well-behaved child*   ***"Il faut que jeunesse se passe."*** *"Youth doesn't last."*
comme il faut *as required, rule-abiding*

But not many people had then been directly dependent on him—only police officials and the sectarians when he went on special missions—and he liked to treat them politely, almost as comrades, as if he were letting them feel that he who had the power to crush them was treating them in this simple, friendly way. There were then but few such people. But now, as an examining magistrate, Iván Ilych felt that everyone without exception, even the most important and self-satisfied, was in his power, and that he need only write a few words on a sheet of paper with a certain heading, and this or that important, self-satisfied person would be brought before him in the role of an accused person or a witness, and if he did not choose to allow him to sit down, would have to stand before him and answer his questions. Iván Ilych never abused his power; he tried on the contrary to soften its expression, but the consciousness of it and of the possibility of softening its effect, supplied the chief interest and attraction of his office. In his work itself, especially in his examinations, he very soon acquired a method of eliminating all considerations irrelevant to the legal aspect of the case, and reducing even the most complicated case to a form in which it would be presented on paper only in its externals, completely excluding his personal opinion of the matter, while above all observing every prescribed formality. The work was new and Iván Ilych was one of the first men to apply the new Code of 1864.°

On taking up the post of examining magistrate in a new town, he made new acquaintances and connexions, placed himself on a new footing, and assumed a somewhat different tone. He took up an attitude of rather dignified aloofness towards the provincial authorities, but picked out the best circle of legal gentlemen and wealthy gentry living in the town and assumed a tone of slight dissatisfaction with the government of moderate liberalism, and of enlightened citizenship. At the same time, without at all altering the elegance of his toilet, he ceased shaving his chin and allowed his beard to grow as it pleased.

Iván Ilych settled down very pleasantly in this new town. The society there, which inclined towards opposition to the governor, was friendly, his salary was larger, and he began to play *vint*,° which he found added not a little to the pleasure of life, for he had a capacity for cards, played good-humouredly, and calculated rapidly and astutely, so that he usually won.

After living there for two years he met his future wife, Praskóvya Fëdorovna Míkhel, who was the most attractive, clever, and brilliant girl of the set in which he moved, and among other amusements and relaxations from his labours as examining magistrate, Iván Ilych established light and playful relations with her.

While he had been an official on special service he had been accustomed to dance, but now as an examining magistrate it was exceptional for him to do so. If he danced now, he did it as if to show that though he served under the reformed order of things, and had reached the fifth official rank, yet when it came to dancing he could do it better than most people. So at the end of an evening he sometimes danced with Praskóvya Fëdorovna, and it was chiefly during these dances that he captivated her. She fell in love with him. Iván Ilych had at first no definite intention of marrying, but when the girl fell in love with him he said to himself: "Really, why shouldn't I marry?"

Praskóvya Fëdorovna came of a good family, was not bad looking, and had some little property. Iván Ilych might have aspired to a more brilliant match, but even this

Code of 1864   *The emancipation of the serfs in 1861 was followed by a thorough all-round reform of judicial proceedings.* [Translators' note]   **vint**   *a form of bridge.* [Translators' note]

was good. He had his salary, and she, he hoped, would have an equal income. She was well connected, and was a sweet, pretty, and thoroughly correct young woman. To say that Iván Ilych married because he fell in love with Praskóvya Fëdorovna and found that she sympathized with his views of life would be as incorrect as to say that he married because his social circle approved of the match. He was swayed by both these considerations: the marriage gave him personal satisfaction, and at the same time it was considered the right thing by the most highly placed of his associates.

So Iván Ilych got married.

The preparations for marriage and the beginning of married life, with its conjugal caresses, the new furniture, new crockery, and new linen, were very pleasant until his wife became pregnant—so that Iván Ilych had begun to think that marriage would not impair the easy, agreeable, gay, and always decorous character of his life, approved of by society and regarded by himself as natural, but would even improve it. But from the first months of his wife's pregnancy, something new, unpleasant, depressing, and unseemly, and from which there was no way of escape, unexpectedly showed itself.

His wife, without any reason—*de gaieté de coeur*° as Iván Ilych expressed it to himself —began to disturb the pleasure and propriety of their life. She began to be jealous without any cause, expected him to devote his whole attention to her, found fault with everything, and made coarse and ill-mannered scenes.

At first Iván Ilych hoped to escape from the unpleasantness of this state of affairs by the same easy and decorous relation to life that had served him heretofore: he tried to ignore his wife's disagreeable moods, continued to live in his usual easy and pleasant way, invited friends to his house for a game of cards, and also tried going out to his club or spending his evenings with friends. But one day his wife began upbraiding him so vigorously, using such coarse words, and continued to abuse him every time he did not fulfil her demands, so resolutely and with such evident determination not to give way till he submitted—that is, till he stayed at home and was bored just as she was —that he became alarmed. He now realized that matrimony—at any rate with Praskóvya Fëdorovna—was not always conducive to the pleasures and amenities of life, but on the contrary often infringed both comfort and propriety, and that he must therefore entrench himself against such infringement. And Iván Ilych began to seek for means of doing so. His official duties were the one thing that imposed upon Praskóvya Fëdorovna, and by means of his official work and the duties attached to it he began struggling with his wife to secure his own independence.

With the birth of their child, the attempts to feed it and the various failures in doing so, and with the real and imaginary illnesses of mother and child, in which Iván Ilych's sympathy was demanded but about which he understood nothing, the need of securing for himself an existence outside his family life became still more imperative.

As his wife grew more irritable and exacting and Iván Ilych transferred the centre of gravity of his life more and more to his official work, so did he grow to like his work better and became more ambitious than before.

Very soon, within a year of his wedding, Iván Ilych had realized that marriage, though it may add some comforts to life, is in fact a very intricate and difficult affair towards which in order to perform one's duty, that is, to lead a decorous life approved of by society, one must adopt a definite attitude just as towards one's official duties.

And Iván Ilych evolved such an attitude towards married life. He only required of

de gaieté de coeur *from pure whim*

it those conveniences—dinner at home, housewife, and bed—which it could give him, and above all that propriety of external forms required by public opinion. For the rest he looked for light-hearted pleasure and propriety, and was very thankful when he found them, but if he met with antagonism and querulousness he at once retired into his separate fenced-off world of official duties, where he found satisfaction.

Iván Ilych was esteemed a good official, and after three years was made Assistant Public Prosecutor. His new duties, their importance, the possibility of indicting and imprisoning anyone he chose, the publicity his speeches received, and the success he had in all these things, made his work still more attractive.

More children came. His wife became more and more querulous and ill-tempered, but the attitude Iván Ilych had adopted towards his home life rendered him almost impervious to her grumbling.

After seven years' service in that town he was transferred to another province as Public Prosecutor. They moved, but were short of money and his wife did not like the place they moved to. Though the salary was higher the cost of living was greater, besides which two of their children died and family life became still more unpleasant for him.

Praskóvya Fëdorovna blamed her husband for every inconvenience they encountered in their new home. Most of the conversations between husband and wife, especially as to the children's education, led to topics which recalled former disputes, and those disputes were apt to flare up again at any moment. There remained only those rare periods of amorousness which still came to them at times but did not last long. These were islets at which they anchored for a while and then again set out upon that ocean of veiled hostility which showed itself in their aloofness from one another. This aloofness might have grieved Iván Ilych had he considered that it ought not to exist, but he now regarded the position as normal, and even made it the goal at which he aimed in family life. His aim was to free himself more and more from those unpleasant-nesses and to give them a semblance of harmlessness and propriety. He attained this by spending less and less time with his family, and when obliged to be at home he tried to safeguard his position by the presence of outsiders. The chief thing however was that he had his official duties. The whole interest of his life now centered in the official world and that interest absorbed him. The consciousness of his power, being able to ruin anybody he wished to ruin, the importance, even the external dignity of his entry into court, or meetings with his subordinates, his success with superiors and inferiors, and above all his masterly handling of cases, of which he was conscious—all this gave him pleasure and filled his life, together with chats with his colleagues, dinners, and bridge. So that on the whole Iván Ilych's life continued to flow as he considered it should do—pleasantly and properly.

So things continued for another seven years. His eldest daughter was already sixteen, another child had died, and only one son was left, a schoolboy and a subject of dissensions. Iván Ilych wanted to put him in the School of Law, but to spite him Praskóvya Fëdorovna entered him at the High School. The daughter had been educated at home and had turned out well: the boy did not learn badly either.

3

So Iván Ilych lived for seventeen years after his marriage. He was already a Public Prosecutor of long standing, and had declined several proposed transfers while awaiting a more desirable post, when an unanticipated and unpleasant occurrence quite upset the peaceful course of his life. He was expecting to be offered the post of presiding judge in a University town, but Happe somehow came to the front and obtained the appointment instead. Iván Ilych became irritable, reproached Happe, and quarrelled both with him and his immediate superiors—who became colder to him and again passed him over when other appointments were made.

This was in 1880, the hardest year of Iván Ilych's life. It was then that it became evident on the one hand that his salary was insufficient for them to live on, and on the other that he had been forgotten, and not only this, but that what was for him the greatest and most cruel injustice appeared to others a quite ordinary occurrence. Even his father did not consider it his duty to help him. Iván Ilych felt himself abandoned by everyone, and that they regarded his position with a salary of 3,500 rubles as quite normal and even fortunate. He alone knew that with the consciousness of the injustices done him, with his wife's incessant nagging, and with the debts he had contracted by living beyond his means, his position was far from normal.

In order to save money that summer he obtained leave of absence and went with his wife to live in the country at her brother's place.

In the country, without his work, he experienced *ennui* for the first time in his life, and not only *ennui* but intolerable depression, and he decided that it was impossible to go on living like that, and that it was necessary to take energetic measures.

Having passed a sleepless night pacing up and down the veranda, he decided to go to Petersburg and bestir himself, in order to punish those who had failed to appreciate him and to get transferred to another ministry.

Next day, despite many protests from his wife and her brother, he started for Petersburg with the sole object of obtaining a post with a salary of five thousand rubles a year. He was no longer bent on any particular department, or tendency, or kind of activity. All he now wanted was an appointment to another post with a salary of five thousand rubles, in one of the Empress Márya's Institutions,° or even in the customs —but it had to carry with it a salary of five thousand rubles and be in a ministry other than that in which they had failed to appreciate him.

And this quest of Iván Ilych's was crowned with remarkable and unexpected success. At Kursk an acquaintance of his, F. I. Ilyín, got into the first-class carriage, sat down beside Iván Ilych, and told him of a telegram just received by the governor of Kursk announcing that a change was about to take place in the ministry: Peter Ivánovich was to be superseded by Iván Semënovich.

The proposed change, apart from its significance for Russia, had a special significance for Iván Ilych, because by bringing forward a new man, Peter Petróvich, and consequently his friend Zachár Ivánovich, it was highly favourable for Iván Ilych, since Zachár Ivánovich was a friend and colleague of his.

In Moscow this news was confirmed, and on reaching Petersburg Iván Ilych found Zachár Ivánovich and received a definite promise of an appointment in his former department of Justice.

A week later he telegraphed to his wife: "Zachár in Miller's place. I shall receive appointment on presentation of report."

Thanks to this change of personnel, Iván Ilych had unexpectedly obtained an appointment in his former ministry which placed him two stages above his former

Empress Márya's Institutions   orphanages

colleagues besides giving him five thousand rubles salary and three thousand five hundred rubles for expenses connected with his removal. All his ill humour towards his former enemies and the whole department vanished, and Iván Ilych was completely happy.

He returned to the country more cheerful and contented than he had been for a long time. Praskóvya Fëdorovna also cheered up and a truce was arranged between them. Iván Ilych told of how he had been fêted by everybody in Petersburg, how all those who had been his enemies were put to shame and now fawned on him, how envious they were of his appointment, and how much everybody in Petersburg had liked him.

Praskóvya Fëdorovna listened to all this and appeared to believe it. She did not contradict anything, but only made plans for their life in the town to which they were going. Iván Ilych saw with delight that these plans were his plans, that he and his wife agreed, and that, after a stumble, his life was regaining its due and natural character of pleasant lightheartedness and decorum.

Iván Ilych had come back for a short time only, for he had to take up his new duties on the 10th of September. Moreover, he needed time to settle into the new place, to move all his belongings from the province, and to buy and order many additional things: in a word, to make such arrangements as he had resolved on, which were almost exactly what Praskóvya Fëdorovna too had decided on.

Now that everything had happened so fortunately, and that he and his wife were at one in their aims and moreover saw so little of one another they got on together better than they had done since the first years of marriage. Iván Ilych had thought of taking his family away with him at once, but the insistence of his wife's brother and her sister-in-law, who had suddenly become particularly amiable and friendly to him and his family, induced him to depart alone.

So he departed, and the cheerful state of mind induced by his success and by the harmony between his wife and himself, the one intensifying the other, did not leave him. He found a delightful house, just the thing both he and his wife had dreamt of. Spacious, lofty reception rooms in the old style, a convenient and dignified study, rooms for his wife and daughter, a study for his son—it might have been specially built for them. Iván Ilych himself superintended the arrangements, chose the wallpapers, supplemented the furniture (preferably with antiques which he considered particularly *comme il faut*), and supervised the upholstering. Everything progressed and progressed and approached the ideal he had set himself: even when things were only half completed they exceeded his expectations. He saw what a refined and elegant character, free from vulgarity, it would all have when it was ready. On falling asleep he pictured to himself how the reception-room would look. Looking at the yet unfurnished drawing-room he could see the fireplace, the screen, the what-not, the little chairs dotted here and there, the dishes and plates on the walls, and the bronzes, as they would be when everything was in place. He was pleased by the thought of how his wife and daughter, who shared his taste in this matter, would be impressed by it. They were certainly not expecting as much. He had been particularly successful in finding, and buying cheaply, antiques which gave a particularly aristocratic character to the whole place. But in his letters he intentionally understated everything in order to be able to surprise them. All this so absorbed him that his new duties—though he liked his official work—interested him less than he had expected. Sometimes he even had moments of absent-mindedness during the Court Sessions, and would consider whether he should have straight or curved cornices for his curtains. He was so interested in it all that he often did things himself, rearranging the furniture, or the curtains. Once when mounting a step-ladder to show the upholsterer, who did not understand, how he wanted the hangings draped, he made a false step and slipped, but being a strong and agile man he clung on and only knocked his side against the knob of the window frame. The bruised place was painful but the pain soon passed, and he felt particularly bright and well just then. He wrote: "I feel fifteen years younger." He thought he would have everything ready by September, but it dragged on til mid-October. But the result was charming not only in his eyes but to everyone who saw it.

In reality it was just what is usually seen in the houses of people of moderate means who want to appear rich, and therefore succeed only in resembling others like themselves: there were damasks, dark wood, plants, rugs, and dull and polished bronzes—all the things people of a certain class have in order to resemble other people of that class. His house was so like the others that it would never have been noticed, but to him it all seemed to be quite exceptional. He was very happy when he met his family at the station and brought them to the newly furnished house all lit up, where a footman in a white tie opened the door into the hall decorated with plants, and when they went on into the drawing-room and the study uttering exclamations of delight. He conducted them everywhere, drank in their praises eagerly, and beamed with pleasure. At tea that evening, when Praskóvya Fëdorovna among other things asked him about his fall, he laughed, and showed them how he had gone flying and had frightened the upholsterer.

"It's a good thing I'm a bit of an athlete. Another man might have been killed, but I merely knocked myself, just here; it hurts when it's touched, but it's passing off already —it's only a bruise."

So they began living in their new home—in which, as always happens when they got thoroughly settled in they found they were just one room short—and with the increased income, which as always was just a little (some five hundred rubles) too little, but it was all very nice.

Things went particularly well at first, before everything was finally arranged and while something had still to be done; this thing bought, that thing ordered, another thing moved, and something else adjusted. Though there were some disputes between husband and wife, they were both so well satisfied and had so much to do that it all passed off without any serious quarrels. When nothing was left to arrange it became rather dull and something seemed to be lacking, but they were then making acquaintances, forming habits, and life was growing fuller.

Iván Ilych spent his mornings at the law court and came home to dinner, and at first he was generally in a good humour, though he occasionally became irritable just on account of his house. (Every spot on the tablecloth or the upholstery, and every broken window-blind string, irritated him. He had devoted so much trouble to arranging it all that every disturbance of it distressed him.) But on the whole his life ran its course as he believed life should do: easily, pleasantly, and decorously.

He got up at nine, drank his coffee, read the paper, and then put on his undress uniform and went to the law courts. There the harness in which he worked had already been stretched to fit him and he donned it without a hitch: petitioners, inquiries at the chancery, the chancery itself, and the sittings public and administrative. In all this the thing was to exclude everything fresh and vital, which always disturbs the regular course of official business, and to admit only official relations with people, and then only on official grounds. A man would come, for instance, wanting some information. Iván Ilych, as one in whose sphere the matter did not lie, would have nothing to do with him: but if the man had some business with him in his official capacity, something that could be expressed on officially stamped paper, he would do everything, positively everything he could within the limits of such relations, and in doing so would maintain the semblance of friendly human relations, that is, would observe the courtesies of life. As soon as the official relations ended, so did everything else. Iván Ilych possessed this capacity to separate his real life from the official side of affairs and not mix the two, in the highest degree, and by long practice and natural aptitude had brought it to such a pitch that sometimes, in the manner of a virtuoso, he would even allow himself to let the human and official relations mingle. He let himself do this just because he felt that he could at any time he chose resume the strictly official attitude again and drop the human relation. And he did it all easily, pleasantly, correctly, and even artistically. In the intervals between the sessions he smoked, drank tea, chatted a little about politics, a little about general topics, a little about cards, but most of all about official appointments. Tired, but with the feelings of a virtuoso—one of the first violins who has played his part in an orchestra with precision—he would return home to find that his wife and daughter had been out paying calls, or had a visitor, and that his son had been to school, had done his homework with his tutor, and was duly learning what is taught in High Schools. Everything was as it should be. After dinner, if they had no visitors, Iván Ilych sometimes read a book that was being much discussed at the time, and in the evening settled down to work, that is, read official papers, compared the depositions of witnesses, and noted paragraphs of the Code applying to them. This was neither dull nor amusing. It was dull when he might have been playing bridge, but if no bridge was available it was at any rate better than doing nothing or sitting with his wife. Iván Ilych's chief pleasure was giving little dinners to which he invited men and women of good social position, and just as his drawing-room resembled all other drawing-rooms so did his enjoyable little parties resemble all other such parties.

Once they even gave a dance. Iván Ilych enjoyed it and everything went off well, except that it led to a violent quarrel with his wife about the cakes and sweets. Praskóvya Fëdorovna had made her own plans, but Iván Ilych insisted on getting everything from an expensive confectioner and ordered too many cakes, and the quarrel occurred because some of those cakes were left over and the confectioner's bill came to forty-five rubles. It was a great and disagreeable quarrel. Praskóvya Fëdorovna called him "a fool and an imbecile," and he clutched at his head and made angry allusions to divorce.

But the dance itself had been enjoyable. The best people were there, and Iván Ilych had danced with Princess Trúfonova, a sister of the distinguished founder of the Society "Bear my Burden."

The pleasures connected with his work were pleasures of ambition; his social pleasures were those of vanity; but Iván Ilych's greatest pleasure was playing bridge. He acknowledged that whatever disagreeable incident happened in his life, the pleasure that beamed like a ray of light above everything else was to sit down to bridge with good players, not noisy partners, and of course to four-handed bridge (with five players it was annoying to have to stand out, though one pretended not to mind), to play a clever and serious game (when the cards allowed it) and then to have supper and drink a glass of wine. After a game of bridge, especially if he had won a little (to win a large sum was unpleasant), Iván Ilych went to bed in specially good humour.

So they lived. They formed a circle of acquaintances among the best people and were visited by people of importance and by young folk. In their views as to their acquaintances, husband, wife, and daughter were entirely agreed, and tacitly and unanimously kept at arm's length and shook off the various shabby friends and relations who, with much show of affection, gushed into the drawing-room with its Japanese plates on the walls. Soon these shabby friends ceased to obtrude themselves and only the best people remained in the Golovíns' set.

Young men made up to Lisa, and Petríschhev, an examining magistrate and Dmítri Ivánovich Petríschhev's son and sole heir, began to be so attentive to her that Iván Ilych had already spoken to Praskóvya Fëdorovna about it, and considered whether they should not arrange a party for them, or get up some private theatricals.

So they lived, and all went well, without change, and life flowed pleasantly.

They were all in good health. It could not be called ill health if Iván Ilych sometimes said that he had a queer taste in his mouth and felt some discomfort in his left side.

But this discomfort increased and, though not exactly painful, grew into a sense of pressure in his side accompanied by ill humour. And his irritability became worse and worse and began to mar the agreeable, easy, and correct life that had established itself in the Golovín family. Quarrels between husband and wife became more and more frequent, and soon the ease and amenity disappeared and even the decorum was barely maintained. Scenes again became frequent, and very few of those islets remained on which husband and wife could meet without an explosion. Praskóvya Fëdorovna now had good reason to say that her husband's temper was trying. With characteristic exaggeration she said he had always had a dreadful temper, and that it had needed all her good nature to put up with it for twenty years. It was true that now the quarrels were started by him. His bursts of temper always came just before dinner, often just as he began to eat his soup. Sometimes he noticed that a plate or dish was chipped, or the food was not right, or his son put his elbow on the table, or his daughter's hair was not done as he liked it, and for all this he blamed Praskóvya Fëdorovna. At first she retorted and said disagreeable things to him, but once or twice he fell into such a rage at the beginning of dinner that she realized it was due to some physical derangement brought on by taking food, and so she restrained herself and did not answer, but only hurried to get the dinner over. She regarded this self-restraint as highly praiseworthy. Having come to the conclusion that her husband had a dreadful temper and made her life miserable, she began to feel sorry for herself, and the more she pitied herself the more she hated her husband. She began to wish he would die; yet she did not want him to die because then his salary would cease. And this irritated her against him still more. She considered herself dreadfully unhappy just because not even his death could save her, and though she concealed her exasperation, that hidden exasperation of hers increased his irritation also.

After one scene in which Iván Ilych had been particularly unfair and after which he had said in explanation that he certainly was irritable but that it was due to his not being well, she said that if he was ill it should be attended to, and insisted on his going to see a celebrated doctor.

He went. Everything took place as he had expected and as it always does. There was the usual waiting and the important air assumed by the doctor, with which he was so familiar (resembling that which he himself assumed in court), and the sounding and listening, and the questions which called for answers that were foregone conclusions and were evidently unnecessary, and the look of importance which implied that "if only you put yourself in our hands we will arrange everything—we know indubitably how it has to be done, always in the same way for everybody alike." It was all just as it was in the law courts. The doctor put on just the same air towards him as he himself put on towards an accused person.

The doctor said that so-and-so indicated that there was so-and-so inside the patient, but if the investigation of so-and-so did not confirm this, then he must assume that and that. If he assumed that and that, then . . . and so on. To Iván Ilych only one question was important: was his case serious or not? But the doctor ignored that inappropriate question. From his point of view it was not the one under consideration, the real question was to decide between a floating kidney, chronic catarrh, or appendicitis. It was not a question of Iván Ilych's life or death, but one between a floating kidney and appendicitis. And that question the doctor solved brilliantly, as it seemed to Iván Ilych, in favour of the appendix, with the reservation that should an examination of the urine give fresh indications the matter would be reconsidered. All this was just what Iván Ilych had himself brilliantly accomplished a thousand times in dealing with men on trial. The doctor summed up just as brilliantly, looking over his spectacles triumphantly and even gaily at the accused. From the doctor's summing up Iván Ilych concluded that things were bad, but that for the doctor, and perhaps for everybody else, it was a matter of indifference, though for him it was bad. And this conclusion struck him painfully, arousing in him a great feeling of pity for himself and of bitterness towards the doctor's indifference to a matter of such importance.

He said nothing of this, but rose, placed the doctor's fee on the table, and remarked with a sigh: "We sick people probably often put inappropriate questions. But tell me, in general, is this complaint dangerous, or not? . . ."

The doctor looked at him sternly over his spectacles with one eye, as if to say: "Prisoner, if you will not keep to the questions put to you, I shall be obliged to have you removed from the court."

"I have already told you what I consider necessary and proper. The analysis may show something more." And the doctor bowed.

Iván Ilych went out slowly, seated himself disconsolately in his sledge, and drove home. All the way home he was going over what the doctor had said, trying to translate those complicated, obscure, scientific phrases into plain language and find in them an answer to the question: "Is my condition bad? Is it very bad? Or is there as yet nothing much wrong?" And it seemed to him that the meaning of what the doctor had said was that it was very bad. Everything in the streets seemed depressing. The cabmen, the houses, the passers-by, and the shops, were dismal. His ache, this dull gnawing ache that never ceased for a moment, seemed to have acquired a new and more serious significance from the doctor's dubious remarks. Iván Ilych now watched it with a new and oppressive feeling.

He reached home and began to tell his wife about it. She listened, but in the middle of his account his daughter came in with her hat on, ready to go out with her mother. She sat down reluctantly to listen to this tedious story, but could not stand it long, and her mother too did not hear him to the end.

"Well, I am very glad," she said. "Mind now to take your medicine regularly. Give me the prescription and I'll send Gerásim to the chemist's." And she went to get ready to go out.

While she was in the room Iván Ilych had hardly taken time to breathe, but he sighed deeply when she left it.

"Well," he thought, "perhaps it isn't so bad after all."

He began taking his medicine and following the doctor's directions, which had been altered after the examination of the urine. But then it happened that there was a contradiction between the indications drawn from the examination of the urine and the symptoms that showed themselves. It turned out that what was happening differed from what the doctor had told him, and that he had either forgotten, or blundered, or hidden something from him. He could not, however, be blamed for that, and Iván Ilych still obeyed his orders implicitly and at first derived some comfort from doing so.

From the time of his visit to the doctor, Iván Ilych's chief occupation was the exact fulfilment of the doctor's instructions regarding hygiene and the taking of medicine, and the observation of his pain and his excretions. His chief interests came to be people's ailments and people's health. When sickness, deaths, or recoveries were mentioned in his presence, especially when the illness resembled his own, he listened with agitation which he tried to hide, asked questions, and applied what he heard to his own case.

The pain did not grow less, but Iván Ilych made efforts to force himself to think that he was better. And he could do this so long as nothing agitated him. But as soon as he had any unpleasantness with his wife, any lack of success in his official work, or held bad cards at bridge, he was at once acutely sensible of his disease. He had formerly borne such mischances, hoping soon to adjust what was wrong, to master it and attain success, or make a grand slam. But now every mischance upset him and plunged him into despair. He would say to himself: "There now, just as I was beginning to get better and the medicine had begun to take effect, comes this accursed misfortune, or unpleasantness . . ." And he was furious with the mishap, or with the people who were causing the unpleasantness and killing him, for he felt that this fury was killing him but could not restrain it. One would have thought that it should have been clear to him that this exasperation with circumstances and people aggravated his illness, and that he ought therefore to ignore unpleasant occurrences. But he drew the very opposite conclusion: he said that he needed peace, and he watched for everything that might disturb it and became irritable at the slightest infringement of it. His condition was rendered worse by the fact that he read medical books and consulted doctors. The progress of his disease was so gradual that he could deceive himself when comparing one day with another —the difference was so slight. But when he consulted the doctors it seemed to him that he was getting worse, and even very rapidly. Yet despite this he was continually consulting them.

That month he went to see another celebrity, who told him almost the same as the first had done but put his questions rather differently, and the interview with this celebrity only increased Iván Ilych's doubts and fears. A friend of a friend of his, a very good doctor, diagnosed his illness again quite differently from the others, and though he predicted recovery, his questions and suppositions bewildered Iván Ilych still more and increased his doubts. A homoeopathist diagnosed the disease in yet another way, and prescribed medicine which Iván Ilych took secretly for a week. But after a week, not feeling any improvement and having lost confidence both in the former doctor's treatment and in this one's, he became still more despondent. One day a lady acquaintance mentioned a cure effected by a wonder-working icon. Iván Ilych caught himself listening attentively and beginning to believe that it had occurred. This incident alarmed him. "Has my mind really weakened to such an extent?" he asked himself. "Nonsense! It's all rubbish. I mustn't give way to nervous fears but having chosen a doctor must keep strictly to his treatment. That is what I will do. Now it's all settled. I won't think about it, but will follow the treatment seriously till summer, and then we shall see. From now there must be no more of this wavering!" This was easy to say but impossible to carry out. The pain in his side oppressed him and seemed to grow worse and more incessant, while the taste in his mouth grew stranger and stranger. It seemed to him that his breath had a disgusting smell, and he was conscious of a loss of appetite and strength. There was no deceiving himself: something terrible, new, and more important than anything before in his life, was taking place within him of which he alone was aware. Those about him did not understand or would not understand it, but thought everything in the world was going on as usual. That tormented Iván Ilych more than anything. He saw that his household, especially his wife and daughter who were in a perfect whirl of visiting, did not understand anything of it and were annoyed that he was so depressed and so exacting, as if he were to blame for it. Though they tried to disguise it he saw that he was an obstacle in their path, and that his wife had adopted a definite line in regard to his illness and kept to it regardless of anything he said or did. Her attitude was this: "You know," she would say to her friends, "Iván Ilych can't do as other people do, and keep to the treatment prescribed for him. One day he'll take his drops and keep strictly to his diet and go to bed in good time, but the next day unless I watch him he'll suddenly forget his medicine, eat sturgeon—which is forbidden —and sit up playing cards till one o'clock in the morning."

"Oh, come, when was that?" Iván Ilych would ask in vexation. "Only once at Peter Ivánovich's."

"And yesterday with Shébek."

"Well, even if I hadn't stayed up, this pain would have kept me awake."

"Be that as it may you'll never get well like that, but will always make us wretched."

Praskóvya Fëdorovna's attitude to Iván Ilych's illness, as she expressed it both to others and to him, was that it was his own fault and was another of the annoyances he caused her. Iván Ilych felt that this opinion escaped her involuntarily—but that did not make it easier for him.

At the law courts too, Iván Ilych noticed, or thought he noticed, a strange attitude towards himself. It sometimes seemed to him that people were watching him inquisitively as a man whose place might soon be vacant. Then again, his friends would suddenly begin to chaff him in a friendly way about his low spirits, as if the awful, horrible, and unheard-of thing that was going on within him, incessantly gnawing at him and irresistibly drawing him away, was a very agreeable subject for jests. Schwartz in particular irritated him by his jocularity, vivacity, and *savoir-faire,* which reminded him of what he himself had been ten years ago.

Friends came to make up a set and they sat down to cards. They dealt, bending the new cards to soften them, and he sorted the diamonds in his hand and found he had seven. His partner said "No trumps" and supported him with two diamonds. What more could be wished for? It ought to be jolly and lively. They would make a grand slam. But suddenly Iván Ilych was conscious of that gnawing pain, that taste in his mouth, and it seemed ridiculous that in such circumstances he should be pleased to make a grand slam.

He looked at his partner Mikháil Mikháylovich, who rapped the table with his strong hand and instead of snatching up the tricks pushed the cards courteously and indulgently towards Iván Ilych that he might have the pleasure of gathering them up without the trouble of stretching out his hand for them. "Does he think I am too weak to stretch out my arm?" thought Iván Ilych, and forgetting what he was doing he over-trumped his partner, missing the grand slam by three tricks. And what was most awful of all was that he saw how upset Mikháil Mikháylovich was about it but did not himself care. And it was dreadful to realize why he did not care.

They all saw that he was suffering, and said: "We can stop if you are tired. Take a rest." Lie down? No, he was not at all tired, and he finished the rubber. All were gloomy and silent. Iván Ilych felt that he had diffused this gloom over them and could not dispel it. They had supper and went away, and Iván Ilych was left alone with the consciousness that his life was poisoned and was poisoning the lives of others, and that this poison did not weaken but penetrated more and more deeply into his whole being.

With this consciousness, and with physical pain besides the terror, he must go to bed, often to lie awake the greater part of the night. Next morning he had to get up again, dress, go to the law courts, speak, and write; or if he did not go out, spend at home those twenty-four hours a day each of which was a torture. And he had to live thus all alone on the brink of an abyss, with no one who understood or pitied him.

5

So one month passed and then another. Just before the New Year his brother-in-law came to town and stayed at their house. Iván Ilych was at the law courts and Praskóvya Fëdorovna had gone shopping. When Iván Ilych came home and entered his study he found his brother-in-law there—a healthy, florid man—unpacking his portmanteau himself. He raised his head on hearing Iván Ilych's footsteps and looked up at him for a moment without a word. That stare told Iván Ilych everything. His brother-in-law opened his mouth to utter an exclamation of surprise but checked himself, and that action confirmed it all.

"I have changed, eh?"

"Yes, there is a change."

And after that, try as he would to get his brother-in-law to return to the subject of his looks, the latter would say nothing about it. Praskóvya Fëdorovna came home and her brother went out to her. Iván Ilych locked the door and began to examine himself in the glass, first full face, then in profile. He took up a portrait of himself taken with his wife, and compared it with what he saw in the glass. The change in him was immense. Then he bared his arms to the elbow, looked at them, drew the sleeves down again, sat down on an ottoman, and grew blacker than night.

"No, no, this won't do!" he said to himself, and jumped up, went to the table, took up some law papers and began to read them, but could not continue. He unlocked the door and went into the reception-room. The door leading to the drawing-room was shut. He approached it on tiptoe and listened.

"No, you are exaggerating!" Praskóvya Fëdorovna was saying.

"Exaggerating! Don't you see it? Why, he's a dead man! Look at his eyes—there's no light in them. But what is it that is wrong with him?"

"No one knows. Niloláevich° said something, but I don't know what. And Leshchetítsky° said quite the contrary . . ."

Iván Ilych walked away, went to his own room, lay down, and began musing: "The kidney, a floating kidney." He recalled all the doctors had told him of how it detached itself and swayed about. And by an effort of imagination he tried to catch that kidney and arrest it and support it. So little was needed for this, it seemed to him. "No, I'll go to see Peter Ivánovich° again." He rang, ordered the carriage, and got ready to go.

"Where are you going, Jean?" asked his wife, with a specially sad and exceptionally kind look.

This exceptionally kind look irritated him. He looked morosely at her.

"I must go to see Peter Ivánovich."

He went to see Peter Ivánovich, and together they went to see his friend, the doctor. He was in, and Iván Ilych had a long talk with him.

Reviewing the anatomical and physiological details of what in the doctor's opinion was going on inside him, he understood it all.

There was something, a small thing, in the vermiform appendix. It might all come right. Only stimulate the energy of one organ and check the activity of another, then absorption would take place and everything would come right. He got home rather late for dinner, ate his dinner, and conversed cheerfully, but could not for a long time bring himself to go back to work in his room. At last, however, he went to his study and did what was necessary, but the consciousness that he had put something aside—an important, intimate matter which he would revert to when his work was done—never left him. When he had finished his work he remembered that this intimate matter was the thought of his vermiform appendix. But he did not give himself up to it, and went to the drawing-room for tea. There were callers there, including the examining magistrate who was a desirable match for his daughter, and they were conversing, playing the piano, and singing. Iván Ilych, as Praskóvya Fëdorovna remarked, spent that evening more cheerfully than usual, but he never for a moment forgot that he had postponed the important matter of the appendix. At eleven o'clock he said good-night and went to his bedroom. Since his illness he had slept alone in a small room next to his study. He undressed and took up a novel by Zola, but instead of reading it he fell into thought, and in his imagination that desired improvement in the vermiform appendix occurred. There was the absorption and evacuation and the re-establishment of normal activity. "Yes, that's it!" he said to himself. "One need only assist nature, that's all." He remembered his medicine, rose, took it, and lay down on his back watching for the beneficient action of the medicine and for it to lessen the pain. "I need only take it regularly and avoid all injurious influences. I am already feeling better, much better." He began touching his side: it was not painful to the touch. "There, I really don't feel it. It's much better already." He put out the light and turned on his side . . . "The appendix is getting better, absorption is occurring." Suddenly he felt the

Nikoláevich, Leshchetitsky *two doctors, the latter a celebrated specialist.* [*Translators' note*] **Peter Ivánovich** *That was the friend whose friend was a doctor.* [*Translators' note*]

old, familiar, dull, gnawing pain, stubborn and serious. There was the same familiar loathsome taste in his mouth. His heart sank and he felt dazed. "My God! My God!" he muttered. "Again, again! And it will never cease." And suddenly the matter presented itself in a quite different aspect. "Vermiform appendix! Kidney!" he said to himself. "It's not a question of appendix or kidney, but of life and . . . death. Yes, life was there and now it is going, going and I cannot stop it. Yes. Why deceive myself? Isn't it obvious to everyone but me that I'm dying, and that it's only a question of weeks, days . . . it may happen this moment. There was light and now there is darkness. I was here and now I'm going there! Where?" A chill came over him, his breathing ceased, and he felt only the throbbing of his heart.

"When I am not, what will there be? There will be nothing. Then where shall I be when I am no more? Can this be dying? No, I don't want to!" He jumped up and tried to light the candle, felt for it with trembling hands, dropped candle and candlestick on the floor, and fell back on his pillow.

"What's the use? It makes no difference," he said to himself, staring with wide-open eyes into the darkness. "Death. Yes, death. And none of them know or wish to know it, and they have no pity for me. Now they are playing." (He heard through the door the distant sound of a song and its accompaniment.) "It's all the same to them, but they will die too! Fools! I first, and they later, but it will be the same for them. And now they are merry . . . the beasts!"

Anger choked him and he was agonizingly, unbearably miserable. "It is impossible that all men have been doomed to suffer this awful horror!" He raised himself.

"Something must be wrong. I must calm myself—must think it all over from the beginning." And he again began thinking. "Yes, the beginning of my illness: I knocked my side, but I was still quite well that day and the next. It hurt a little, then rather more. I saw the doctors, then followed despondency and anguish, more doctors, and I drew nearer to the abyss. My strength grew less and I kept coming nearer and nearer, and now I have wasted away and there is no light in my eyes. I think of the appendix —but this is death! I think of mending the appendix, and all the while here is death! Can it really be death?" Again terror seized him and he gasped for breath. He leant down and began feeling for the matches, pressing with his elbow on the stand beside the bed. It was in his way and hurt him, he grew furious with it, pressed on it still harder, and upset it. Breathless and in despair he fell on his back, expecting death to come immediately.

Meanwhile the visitors were leaving. Praskóvya Fëdorovna was seeing them off. She heard something fall and came in.

"What has happened?"

"Nothing. I knocked it over accidentally."

She went out and returned with a candle. He lay there panting heavily, like a man who has run a thousand yards, and stared upwards at her with a fixed look.

"What is it, Jean?"

"No . . . o . . . thing. I upset it." ("Why speak of it? She won't understand," he thought.)

And in truth she did not understand. She picked up the stand, lit his candle, and hurried away to see another visitor off. When she came back he still lay on his back, looking upwards.

"What is it? Do you feel worse?"

"Yes."

She shook her head and sat down.

"Do you know, Jean, I think we must ask Leshchetítsky to come and see you here."

This meant calling in the famous specialist, regardless of expense. He smiled malignantly and said "No." She remained a little longer and then went up to him and kissed his forehead.

While she was kissing him he hated her from the bottom of his soul and with difficulty refrained from pushing her away.

"Good-night. Please God you'll sleep."

"Yes."

6

Iván Ilych saw that he was dying, and he was in continual despair.

In the depth of his heart he knew he was dying, but not only was he not accustomed to the thought, he simply did not and could not grasp it.

The syllogism he had learned from Kiezewetter's Logic: "Caius is a man, men are mortal, therefore Caius is mortal," had always seemed to him correct as applied to Caius, but certainly not as applied to himself. That Caius—man in the abstract—was mortal, was perfectly correct, but he was not Caius, not an abstract man, but a creature quite, quite separate from all others. He had been little Ványa, with a mamma and a papa, with Mítya and Volódya, with the toys, a coachman and a nurse, afterwards with Kátenka and with all the joys, griefs, and delights of childhood, boyhood, and youth. What did Caius know of the smell of that striped leather ball Ványa had been so fond of? Had Caius kissed his mother's hand like that, and did the silk of her dress rustle so for Caius? Had he rioted like that at school when the pastry was bad? Had Caius been in love like that? Could Caius preside at a session as he did? Caius really was mortal, and it was right for him to die; but for me, little Ványa, Iván Ilych, with all my thoughts and emotions, it's altogether a different matter. It cannot be that I ought to die. That would be too terrible.

Such was his feeling.

"If I had to die like Caius I should have known it was so. An inner voice would have told me so, but there was nothing of the sort in me and I and all my friends felt that our case was quite different from that of Caius. And now here it is!" he said to himself. "It can't be. It's impossible! But here it is. How is this? How is one to understand it?"

He could not understand it, and tried to drive this false, incorrect, morbid thought away and to replace it by other proper and healthy thoughts. But that thought, and not the thought only but the reality itself, seemed to come and confront him.

And to replace that thought he called up a succession of others, hoping to find in them some support. He tried to get back into the former current of thoughts that had once screened the thought of death from him. But strange to say, all that had formerly shut off, hidden, and destroyed, his consciousness of death, no longer had that effect. Iván Ilych now spent most of his time in attempting to re-establish that old current. He would say to himself: "I will take up my duties again—after all I used to live by them." And banishing all doubts he would go to the law courts, enter into conversation with his colleagues, and sit carelessly as was his wont, scanning the crowd with a thoughtful look and leaning both his emaciated arms on the arms of his oak chair; bending over as usual to a colleague and drawing his papers nearer he would interchange whispers with him, and then suddenly raising his eyes and sitting erect would pronounce certain words and open the proceedings. But suddenly in the midst of those proceedings the pain in his side, regardless of the stage the proceedings had reached, would begin its own gnawing work. Iván Ilych would turn his attention to it and try to drive the thought of it away, but without success. *It* would come and stand before him and look at him, and he would be petrified and the light would die out of his eyes, and he would again begin asking himself whether *It* alone was true. And his colleagues and subordinates would see with surprise and distress that he, the brilliant and subtle judge, was becoming confused and making mistakes. He would shake himself, try to pull himself together, manage somehow to bring the sitting to a close, and return home with the sorrowful consciousness that his judicial labours could not as formerly hide from him what he wanted them to hide, and could not deliver him from *It*. And what was worst of all was that *It* drew his attention to itself not in order to make him take some action but only that he should look at *It*, look it straight in the face: look at it without doing anything, suffer inexpressibly.

And to save himself from this condition Iván Ilych looked for consolations—new screens—and new screens were found and for a while seemed to save him, but then they immediately fell to pieces or rather became transparent, as if *It* penetrated them and nothing could veil *It*.

In these latter days he would go into the drawing-room he had arranged—that drawing-room where he had fallen and for the sake of which (how bitterly ridiculous it seemed) he had sacrificed his life—for he knew that his illness originated with that knock. He would enter and see that something had scratched the polished table. He would look for the cause of this and find that it was the bronze ornamentation of an album, that had got bent. He would take up the expensive album which he had lovingly arranged, and feel vexed with his daughter and her friends for their untidiness—for the album was torn here and there and some of the photographs turned upside down. He would put it carefully in order and bend the ornamentation back into position. Then it would occur to him to place all those things in another corner of the room, near the plants. He would call the footman, but his daughter or wife would come to help him. They would not agree, and his wife would contradict him, and he would dispute and grow angry. But that was all right, for then he did not think about *It*. *It* was invisible.

But then, when he was moving something himself, his wife would say: "Let the servants do it. You will hurt yourself again." And suddenly *It* would flash through the screen and he would see it. It was just a flash, and he hoped it would disappear, but he would involuntarily pay attention to his side. "It sits there as before, gnawing just the same!" And he could no longer forget *It*, but could distinctly see it looking at him from behind the flowers. "What is it all for?"

"It really is so! I lost my life over that curtain as I might have done when storming a fort. Is that possible? How terrible and how stupid. It can't be true! It can't, but it is."

He would go to his study, lie down, and again be alone with *It*: face to face with *It*. And nothing could be done with *It* except to look at it and shudder.

7

How it happened it is impossible to say because it came about step by step, unnoticed, but in the third month of Iván Ilych's illness, his wife, his daughter, his son, his acquaintances, the doctors, the servants, and above all he himself, were aware that the whole interest he had for other people was whether he would soon vacate his place, and at last release the living from the discomfort caused by his presence and be himself released from his sufferings.

He slept less and less. He was given opium and hypodermic injections of morphine, but this did not relieve him. The dull depression he experienced in a somnolent condition at first gave him a little relief, but only as something new, afterwards it became as distressing as the pain itself or even more so.

Special foods were prepared for him by the doctors' orders, but all those foods became increasingly distasteful and disgusting to him.

For his excretions also special arrangements had to be made, and this was a torment to him every time—a torment from the uncleanliness, the unseemliness, and the smell, and from knowing that another person had to take part in it.

But just through this most unpleasant matter, Iván Ilych obtained comfort. Gerásim, the butler's young assistant, always came in to carry the things out. Gerásim was a clean, fresh peasant lad, grown stout on town food and always cheerful and bright. At first the sight of him, in his clean Russian peasant costume, engaged on that disgusting task embarrassed Iván Ilych.

Once when he got up from the commode too weak to draw up his trousers, he dropped into a soft armchair and looked with horror at his bare, enfeebled thighs with the muscles so sharply marked on them.

Gerásim with a firm light tread, his heavy boots emitting a pleasant smell of tar and fresh winter air, came in wearing a clean Hessian apron, the sleeves of his print shirt tucked up over his strong bare young arms; and refraining from looking at his sick master out of consideration for his feelings, and restraining the joy of life that beamed from his face, he went up to the commode.

"Gerásim!" said Iván Ilych in a weak voice.

Gerásim started, evidently afraid he might have committed some blunder, and with a rapid movement turned his fresh, kind, simple young face which just showed the first downy signs of a beard.

"Yes, sir?"

"That must be very unpleasant for you. You must forgive me. I am helpless."

"Oh, why, sir," and Gerásim's eyes beamed and he showed his glistening white teeth, "what's a little trouble? It's a case of illness with you, sir."

And his deft strong hands did their accustomed task, and he went out of the room stepping lightly. Five minutes later he as lightly returned.

Iván Ilych was still sitting in the same position in the armchair.

"Gerásim," he said when the latter had replaced the freshly-washed utensil. "Please come here and help me." Gerásim went up to him. "Lift me up. It is hard for me to get up, and I have sent Dmítri away."

Gerásim went up to him, grasped his master with his strong arms deftly but gently, in the same way that he stepped—lifted him, supported him with one hand, and with the other drew up his trousers and would have set him down again, but Iván Ilych asked to be led to the sofa. Gerásim, without an effort and without apparent pressure, led him, almost lifting him, up to the sofa and placed him on it.

"Thank you. How easily and well you do it all!"

Gerásim smiled again and turned to leave the room. But Iván Ilych felt his presence such a comfort that he did not want to let him go.

"One thing more, please move up that chair. No, the other one—under my feet. It is easier for me when my feet are raised."

Gerásim brought the chair, set it down gently in place, and raised Iván Ilych's legs on to it. It seemed to Iván Ilych that he felt better while Gerásim was holding up his legs.

"It's better when my legs are higher," he said. "Place that cushion under them."

Gerásim did so. He again lifted the legs and placed them, and again Iván Ilych felt better while Gerásim held his legs. When he set them down Iván Ilych fancied he felt worse.

"Gerásim," he said. "Are you busy now?"

"Not at all, sir," said Gerásim, who had learnt from the townsfolk how to speak to gentlefolk.

"What have you still to do?"

"What have I to do? I've done everything except chopping the logs for to-morrow."

"Then hold my legs up a bit higher, can you?"

"Of course I can. Why not?" And Gerásim raised his master's legs higher and Iván Ilych thought that in that position he did not feel any pain at all.

"And how about the logs?"

"Don't trouble about that, sir. There's plenty of time."

Iván Ilych told Gerásim to sit down and hold his legs, and began to talk to him. And strange to say it seemed to him that he felt better while Gerásim held his legs up.

After that Iván Ilych would sometimes call Gerásim and get him to hold his legs on his shoulders, and he liked talking to him. Gerásim did it all easily, willingly, simply, and with a good nature that touched Iván Ilych. Health, strength, and vitality in other people were offensive to him, but Gerásim's strength and vitality did not mortify but soothed him.

What touched Iván Ilych most was the deception, the lie, which for some reason they all accepted, that he was not dying but was simply ill, and that he only need keep quiet and undergo a treatment and then something very good would result. He however knew that do what they would nothing would come of it, only still more agonizing suffering and death. This deception tortured him—their not wishing to admit what they all knew and what he knew, but wanting to lie to him concerning his terrible condition, and wishing and forcing him to participate in that lie. Those lies—lies enacted over him on the eve of his death and destined to degrade this awful, solemn act to the level of their visitings, their curtains, their sturgeon for dinner—were a terrible agony for Iván Ilych. And strangely enough, many times when they were going through their antics over him he had been within a hairbreadth of calling out to them: "Stop lying! You know and I know that I am dying. Then at least stop lying about it!" But he had never had the spirit to do it. The awful, terrible act of his dying was, he could see, reduced by those about him to the level of a casual, unpleasant, and almost indecorous incident (as if someone entered a drawing-room diffusing an unpleasant

odour) and this was done by that very decorum which he had served all his life long.
He saw that no one felt for him, because no one even wished to grasp his position.
Only Gerásim recognized and pitied him. And so Iván Ilych felt at ease only·with him.
He felt comforted when Gerásim supported his legs (sometimes all night long) and
refused to go to bed, saying: "Don't you worry, Iván Ilych. I'll get sleep enough later
on," or when he suddenly became familiar and exclaimed: "If you weren't sick it would
be another matter, but as it is, why should I grudge a little trouble?" Gerásim alone
did not lie; everything showed that he alone understood the facts of the case and did
not consider it necessary to disguise them, but simply felt sorry for his emaciated and
enfeebled master. Once when Iván Ilych was sending him away he even said straight
out: "We shall all of us die, so why should I grudge a little trouble?"—expressing the
fact that he did not think his work burdensome, because he was doing it for a dying
man and hoped someone would do the same for him when his time came.

Apart from this lying, or because of it, what most tormented Iván Ilych was that
no one pitied him as he wished to be pitied. At certain moments after prolonged
suffering he wished most of all (though he would have been ashamed to confess it) for
someone to pity him as a sick child is pitied. He longed to be petted and comforted.
He knew he was an important functionary, that he had a beard turning grey, and that
therefore what he longed for was impossible, but still he longed for it. And in Gerásim's
attitude towards him there was something akin to what he wished for, and so that
attitude comforted him. Iván Ilych wanted to weep, wanted to be petted and cried over,
and then his colleague Shébek would come, and instead of weeping and being petted,
Iván Ilych would assume a serious, severe, and profound air, and by force of habit
would express his opinion on a decision of the Court of Cassation and would stubbornly
insist on that view. This falsity around him and within him did more than anything
else to poison his last days.

8

It was morning. He knew it was morning because Gerásim had gone, and Peter the
footman had come and put out the candles, drawn back one of the curtains, and begun
quietly to tidy up. Whether it was morning or evening, Friday or Sunday, made no
difference, it was all just the same: the gnawing, unmitigated, agonizing pain, never
ceasing for an instant, the consciousness of life inexorably waning but not yet extinguished, the approach of that ever dreaded and hateful Death which was the only
reality, and always the same falsity. What were days, weeks, hours, in such a case?

"Will you have some tea, sir?"

"He wants things to be regular, and wishes the gentlefolk to drink tea in the
morning," thought Iván Ilych, and only said "No."

"Wouldn't you like to move onto the sofa, sir?"

"He wants to tidy up the room, and I'm in the way. I am uncleanliness and disorder,"
he thought, and said only:

"No, leave me alone."

The man went on bustling about. Iván Ilych stretched out his hand. Peter came up,
ready to help.

"What is it, sir?"

"My watch."

Peter took the watch which was close at hand and gave it to his master.

"Half-past eight. Are they up?"

"No sir, except Vladímir Ivánich" (the son) "who has gone to school. Praskóvya Fëdorovna ordered me to wake her if you asked for her. Shall I do so?"

"No, there's no need to." "Perhaps I'd better have some tea," he thought, and added aloud: "Yes, bring me some tea."

Peter went to the door, but Iván Ilych dreaded being left alone. "How can I keep him here? Oh yes, my medicine." "Peter, give me my medicine." "Why not? Perhaps it may still do me some good." He took a spoonful and swallowed it. "No, it won't help. It's all tomfoolery, all deception," he decided as soon as he became aware of the familiar, sickly, hopeless taste. "No, I can't believe in it any longer. But the pain, why this pain? If it would only cease just for a moment!" And he moaned. Peter turned towards him. "It's all right. Go and fetch me some tea."

Peter went out. Left alone Iván Ilych groaned not so much with pain, terrible though that was, as from mental anguish. Always and forever the same, always these endless days and nights. If only it would come quicker! If only *what* would come quicker? Death, darkness? . . . No, no! Anything rather than death!

When Peter returned with the tea on a tray, Iván Ilych stared at him for a time in perplexity, not realizing who and what he was. Peter was disconcerted by that look and his embarrassment brought Iván Ilych to himself.

"Oh, tea! All right, put it down. Only help me to wash and put on a clean shirt."

And Iván Ilych began to wash. With pauses for rest, he washed his hands and then his face, cleaned his teeth, brushed his hair, and looked in the glass. He was terrified by what he saw, especially by the limp way in which his hair clung to his pallid forehead.

While his shirt was being changed he knew that he would be still more frightened at the sight of his body, so he avoided looking at it. Finally he was ready. He drew on a dressing-gown, wrapped himself in a plaid, and sat down in the armchair to take his tea. For a moment he felt refreshed, but as soon as he began to drink the tea he was again aware of the same taste, and the pain also returned. He finished it with an effort, and then lay down stretching out his legs, and dismissed Peter.

Always the same. Now a spark of hope flashes up, then a sea of despair rages, and always pain; always pain, always despair, and always the same. When alone he had a dreadful and distressing desire to call someone, but he knew beforehand that with others present it would be still worse. "Another dose of morphine—to lose consciousness. I will tell him, the doctor, that he must think of something else. It's impossible, impossible, to go on like this."

An hour and another pass like that. But now there is a ring at the door bell. Perhaps it's the doctor? It is. He comes in fresh, hearty, plump, and cheerful, with that look on his face that seems to say: "There now, you're in a panic about something, but we'll arrange it all for you directly!" The doctor knows this expression is out of place here, but he has put it on once for all and can't take it off—like a man who has put on a frock-coat in the morning to pay a round of calls.

The doctor rubs his hands vigorously and reassuringly.

"Brr! How cold it is! There's such a sharp frost; just let me warm myself!" he says, as if it were only a matter of waiting till he was warm, and then he would put everything right.

"Well now, how are you?"

Iván Ilych feels that the doctor would like to say: "Well, how are our affairs?" but that even he feels that this would not do, and says instead: "What sort of a night have you had?"

Iván Ilych looks at him as much as to say: "Are you really never ashamed of lying?" But the doctor does not wish to understand this question, and Iván Ilych says: "Just as terrible as ever. The pain never leaves me and never subsides. If only something . . ."

"Yes, you sick people are always like that. . . . There, now I think I'm warm enough. Even Praskóvya Fёdorovna, who is so particular, could find no fault with my temperature. Well, now I can say good-morning," and the doctor presses his patient's hand.

Then, dropping his former playfulness, he begins with a most serious face to examine the patient, feeling his pulse and taking his temperature, and then begins the sounding and auscultation.

Iván Ilych knows quite well and definitely that all this is nonsense and pure deception, but when the doctor, getting down on his knee, leans over him, putting his ear first higher then lower, and performs various gymnastic movements over him with a significant expression on his face, Iván Ilych submits to it all as he used to submit to the speeches of the lawyers, though he knew very well that they were all lying and why they were lying.

The doctor, kneeling on the sofa, is still sounding him when Praskóvya Fёdorovna's silk dress rustles at the door and she is heard scolding Peter for not having let her know of the doctor's arrival.

She comes in, kisses her husband, and at once proceeds to prove that she has been up a long time already, and only owing to a misunderstanding failed to be there when the doctor arrived.

Iván Ilych looks at her, scans her all over, sets against her the whiteness and plumpness and cleanness of her hands and neck, the gloss of her hair, and the sparkle of her vivacious eyes. He hates her with his whole soul. And the thrill of hatred he feels for her makes him suffer from her touch.

Her attitude towards him and his disease is still the same. Just as the doctor had adopted a certain relation to his patient which he could not abandon, so had she formed one towards him—that he was not doing something he ought to do and was himself to blame, and that she reproached him lovingly for this—and she could not now change that attitude.

"You see he doesn't listen to me and doesn't take his medicine at the proper time. And above all he lies in a position that is no doubt bad for him—with his legs up."

She described how he made Gerásim hold his legs up.

The doctor smiled with a contemptuous affability that said: "What's to be done? These sick people do have foolish fancies of that kind, but we must forgive them."

When the examination was over the doctor looked at his watch, and then Praskóvya Fёdorovna announced to Iván Ilych that it was of course as he pleased, but she had sent to-day for a celebrated specialist who would examine him and have a consultation with Michael Danílovich (their regular doctor).

"Please don't raise any objections. I am doing this for my own sake," she said ironically, letting it be felt that she was doing it all for his sake and only said this to leave him no right to refuse. He remained silent, knitting his brows. He felt that he was so surrounded and involved in a mesh of falsity that it was hard to unravel anything.

Everything she did for him was entirely for her own sake, and she told him she was doing for herself what she actually was doing for herself, as if that was so incredible that he must understand the opposite.

At half-past eleven the celebrated specialist arrived. Again the sounding began and the significant conversations in his presence and in another room, about the kidneys and the appendix, and the questions and answers, with such an air of importance that again, instead of the real question of life and death which now alone confronted him, the question arose of the kidney and the appendix which were not behaving as they ought to and would now be attacked by Michael Danílovich and the specialist and forced to amend their ways.

The celebrated specialist took leave of him with a serious though not hopeless look, and in reply to the timid question Iván Ilych, with eyes glistening with fear and hope, put to him as to whether there was a chance of recovery, said that he could not vouch for it but there was a possibility. The look of hope with which Iván Ilych watched the doctor out was so pathetic that Praskóvya Fëdorovna, seeing it, even wept as she left the room to hand the doctor his fee.

The gleam of hope kindled by the doctor's encouragement did not last long. The same room, the same pictures, curtains, wall-paper, medicine bottles, were all there, and the same aching suffering body, and Iván Ilych began to moan. They gave him a subcutaneous injection and he sank into oblivion.

It was twilight when he came to. They brought him his dinner and he swallowed some beef tea with difficulty, and then everything was the same again and night was coming on.

After dinner, at seven o'clock, Praskóvya Fëdorovna came into the room in evening dress, her full bosom pushed up by her corset, and with traces of powder on her face. She had reminded him in the morning that they were going to the theatre. Sarah Bernhardt was visiting the town and they had a box, which he had insisted on their taking. Now he had forgotten about it and her toilet offended him, but he concealed his vexation when he remembered that he had himself insisted on their securing a box and going because it would be an instructive and aesthetic pleasure for the children.

Praskóvya Fëdorovna came in, self-satisfied but yet with a rather guilty air. She sat down and asked how he was, but, as he saw, only for the sake of asking and not in order to learn about it, knowing that there was nothing to learn—and then went on to what she really wanted to say: that she would not on any account have gone but that the box had been taken and Helen and their daughter were going, as well as Petríshchev (the examining magistrate, their daughter's fiancé) and that it was out of the question to let them go alone; but that she would have much preferred to sit with him for a while; and he must be sure to follow the doctor's orders while she was away.

"Oh, and Fëdor Petróvich" (the fiancé) "would like to come in. May he? And Lisa?"

"All right."

Their daughter came in in full evening dress, her fresh young flesh exposed (making a show of that very flesh which in his own case caused so much suffering), strong, healthy, evidently in love, and impatient with illness, suffering, and death, because they interfered with her happiness.

Fëdor Petróvich came in too, in evening dress, his hair curled *à la Capoul,*° a tight stiff collar round his long sinewy neck, an enormous white shirt-front and narrow black

à la Capoul   *imitating the hair-do of Victor Capoul, a contemporary French singer* trousers tightly stretched over his strong thighs. He had one white glove tightly drawn on, and was holding his opera hat in his hand.

Following him the schoolboy crept in unnoticed, in a new uniform, poor little fellow, and wearing gloves. Terribly dark shadows showed under his eyes, the meaning of which Iván Ilych knew well.

His son had always seemed pathetic to him, and now it was dreadful to see the boy's frightened look of pity. It seemed to Iván Ilych that Vásya was the only one besides Gerásim who understood and pitied him.

They sat down and again asked how he was. A silence followed. Lisa asked her mother about the opera-glasses, and there was an altercation between mother and daughter as to who had taken them and where they had been put. This occasioned some unpleasantness.

Fëdor Petróvich inquired of Iván Ilych whether he had ever seen Sarah Bernhardt. Iván Ilych did not at first catch the question, but then replied: "No, have you seen her before?"

"Yes, in *Adrienne Lecouvreur.*"

Praskóvya Fëdorovna mentioned some rôles in which Sarah Bernhardt was particularly good. Her daughter disagreed. Conversation sprang up as to the elegance and realism of her acting—the sort of conversation that is always repeated and is always the same.

In the midst of the conversation Fëdor Petróvich glanced at Iván Ilych and became silent. The others also looked at him and grew silent. Iván Ilych was staring with glittering eyes straight before him, evidently indignant with them. This had to be rectified, but it was impossible to do so. The silence had to be broken, but for a time no one dared to break it and they all became afraid that the conventional deception would suddenly become obvious and the truth become plain to all. Lisa was the first to pluck up courage and break that silence, but by trying to hide what everybody was feeling, she betrayed it.

"Well, if we are going it's time to start," she said, looking at her watch, a present from her father, and with a faint and significant smile at Fëdor Petróvich relating to something known only to them. She got up with a rustle of her dress.

They all rose, said good-night, and went away.

When they had gone it seemed to Iván Ilych that he felt better; the falsity had gone with them. But the pain remained—that same pain and that same fear that made everything monotonously alike, nothing harder and nothing easier. Everything was worse.

Again minute followed minute and hour followed hour. Everything remained the same and there was no cessation. And the inevitable end of it all became more and more terrible.

"Yes, send Gerásim here," he replied to a question Peter asked.

9

His wife returned late at night. She came in on tiptoe, but he heard her, opened his eyes, and made haste to close them again. She wished to send Gerásim away and to sit with him herself, but he opened his eyes and said: "No, go away."

"Are you in great pain?"

"Always the same."

"Take some opium."

He agreed and took some. She went away.

Till about three in the morning he was in a state of stupefied misery. It seemed to him that he and his pain were being thrust into a narrow, deep black sack, but though they were pushed further and further in they could not be pushed to the bottom. And this, terrible enough in itself, was accompanied by suffering. He was frightened yet wanted to fall through the sack, he struggled but yet co-operated. And suddenly he broke through, fell, and regained consciousness. Gerásim was sitting at the foot of the bed dozing quietly and patiently, while he himself lay with his emaciated stockinged legs resting on Gerásim's shoulders; the same shaded candle was there and the same unceasing pain.

"Go away, Gerásim," he whispered.

"It's all right, sir. I'll stay a while."

"No. Go away."

He removed his legs from Gerásim's shoulders, turned side ways onto his arm, and felt sorry for himself. He only waited till Gerásim had gone into the next room and then restrained himself no longer but wept like a child. He wept on account of his helplessness, his terrible loneliness, the cruelty of man, the cruelty of God, and the absence of God.

"Why hast Thou done all this? Why hast Thou brought me here? Why, dost Thou torment me so terribly?"

He did not expect an answer and yet wept because there was no answer and could be none. The pain again grew more acute, but he did not stir and did not call. He said to himself: "Go on! Strike me! But what is it for? What have I done to Thee? What is it for?"

Then he grew quiet and not only ceased weeping but even held his breath and became all attention. It was as though he were listening not to an audible voice but to a voice of his soul, to the current of thoughts arising within him.

"What is it you want?" was the first clear conception capable of expression in words, that he heard.

"What do you want? What do you want?" he repeated to himself.

"What do I want? To live and not to suffer," he answered.

And again he listened with such concentrated attention that even his pain did not distract him.

"To live? How?" asked his inner voice.

"Why, to live as I used to—well and pleasantly."

"As you lived before, well and pleasantly?" the voice repeated.

And in imagination he began to recall the best moments of his pleasant life. But strange to say none of those best moments of his pleasant life now seemed at all what they had then seemed—none of them except the first recollections of childhood. There, in childhood, there had been something really pleasant with which it would be possible to live if it could return. But the child who had experienced that happiness existed no longer, it was like a reminiscence of somebody else.

As soon as the period began which had produced the present Iván Ilych, all that had then seemed joys now melted before his sight and turned into something trivial and often nasty.

And the further he departed from childhood and the nearer he came to the present the more worthless and doubtful were the joys. This began with the School of Law. A little that was really good was still found there—there was light-heartedness, friendship, and hope. But in the upper classes there had already been fewer of such good moments. Then during the first years of his official career, when he was in the service of the Governor, some pleasant moments again occurred: they were the memories of love for a woman. Then all became confused and there was still less of what was good; later on again there was still less that was good, and the further he went the less there was. His marriage, a mere accident, then the disenchantment that followed it, his wife's bad breath and the sensuality and hypocrisy: then that deadly official life and those preoccupations about money, a year of it, and two, and ten, and twenty, and always the same thing. And the longer it lasted the more deadly it became. "It is as if I had been going downhill while I imagined I was going up. And that is really what it was. I was going up in public opinion, but to the same extent life was ebbing away from me. And now it is all done and there is only death."

"Then what does it mean? Why? It can't be that life is so senseless and horrible. But if it really has been so horrible and senseless, why must I die and die in agony? There is something wrong!"

"Maybe I did not live as I ought to have done," it suddenly occurred to him. "But how could that be, when I did everything properly?" he replied, and immediately dismissed from his mind this, the sole solution of all the riddles of life and death, as something quite impossible.

"Then what do you want now? To live? Live how? Live as you lived in the law courts when the usher proclaimed 'The judge is coming!' The judge is coming, the judge!" he repeated to himself. "Here he is, the judge. But I am not guilty!" he exclaimed angrily. "What is it for?" And he ceased crying, but turning his face to the wall continued to ponder on the same question: Why, and for what purpose, is there all this horror? But however much he pondered he found no answer. And whenever the thought occurred to him, as it often did, that it all resulted from his not having lived as he ought to have done, he at once recalled the correctness of his whole life, and dismissed so strange an idea.

10

Another fortnight passed. Iván Ilych now no longer left his sofa. He would not lie in bed but lay on the sofa, facing the wall nearly all the time. He suffered ever the same unceasing agonies and in his loneliness pondered always on the same insoluble question: "What is this? Can it be that it is Death?" And the inner voice answered: "Yes, it is Death."

"Why these sufferings?" And the voice answered, "For no reason—they just are so." Beyond and besides this there was nothing.

From the very beginning of his illness, ever since he had first been to see the doctor, Iván Ilych's life had been divided between two contrary and alternating moods: now it was despair and the expectation of this uncomprehended and terrible death, and now hope and an intently interested observation of the functioning of his organs. Now before his eyes there was only a kidney or an intestine that temporarily evaded its duty, and now only that incomprehensible and dreadful death from which it was impossible to escape.

These two states of mind had alternated from the very beginning of his illness, but the further it progressed the more doubtful and fantastic became the conception of the kidney, and the more real the sense of impending death.

He had but to call to mind what he had been three months before and what he was now, to call to mind with what regularity he had been going downhill, for every possibility of hope to be shattered.

Latterly during that loneliness in which he found himself as he lay facing the back of the sofa, a loneliness in the midst of a populous town and surrounded by numerous acquaintances and relations but that yet could not have been more complete anywhere —either at the bottom of the sea or under the earth—during that terrible loneliness Iván Ilych had lived only in memories of the past. Pictures of his past rose before him one after another. They always began with what was nearest in time and then went back to what was most remote—to his childhood—and rested there. If he thought of the stewed prunes that had been offered him that day, his mind went back to the raw shrivelled French plums of his childhood, their peculiar flavour and the flow of saliva when he sucked their stones, and along with the memory of that taste came a whole series of memories of those days: his nurse, his brother, and their toys. "No, I mustn't think of that. . . . It is too painful," Iván Ilych said to himself, and brought himself back to the present—to the button on the back of the sofa and the creases in its morocco. "Morocco is expensive, but it does not wear well; there had been a quarrel about it. It was a different kind of quarrel and a different kind of morocco that time when we tore father's portfolio and were punished, and mamma brought us some tarts. . . ." And again his thoughts dwelt on his childhood, and again it was painful and he tried to banish them and fix his mind on something else.

Then again together with that chain of memories another series passed through his mind—of how his illness had progressed and grown worse. There also the further back he looked the more life there had been. There had been more of what was good in life and more of life itself. The two merged together. "Just as the pain went on getting worse and worse, so my life grew worse and worse," he thought. "There is one bright spot there at the back, at the beginning of life, and afterwards all becomes blacker and blacker and proceeds more and more rapidly—in inverse ratio to the square of the distance from death," thought Iván Ilych. And the example of a stone falling downwards with increasing velocity entered his mind. Life, a series of increasing sufferings, flies further and further towards its end—the most terrible suffering. "I am flying. . . ." He shuddered, shifted himself, and tried to resist, but was already aware that resistance was impossible, and again with eyes weary of gazing but unable to cease seeing what was before them, he stared at the back of the sofa and waited—awaiting that dreadful fall and shock and destruction.

"Resistance is impossible!" he said to himself. "If I could only understand what it is all for! But that too is impossible. An explanation would be possible if it could be said that I have not lived as I ought to. But it is impossible to say that," and he remembered all the legality, correctitude, and propriety of his life. "That at any rate can certainly not be admitted," he thought, and his lips smiled ironically as if someone could see that smile and be taken in by it. "There is no explanation! Agony, death. . . . What for?"

II

Another two weeks went by in this way and during that fortnight an event occurred that Iván Ilych and his wife had desired. Petríshchev formally proposed. It happened in the evening. The next day Praskóvya Fëdorovna came into her husband's room considering how best to inform him of it, but that very night there had been a fresh change for the worse in his condition. She found him still lying on the sofa but in a different position. He lay on his back, groaning and staring fixedly straight in front of him.

She began to remind him of his medicines, but he turned his eyes towards her with such a look that she did not finish what she was saying; so great an animosity, to her in particular, did that look express.

"For Christ's sake let me die in peace!" he said.

She would have gone away, but just then their daughter came in and went up to say good morning. He looked at her as he had done at his wife, and in reply to her inquiry about his health said dryly that he would soon free them all of himself. They were both silent and after sitting with him for a while went away.

"Is it our fault?" Lisa said to her mother. "It's as if we were to blame! I am sorry for papa, but why should we be tortured?"

The doctor came at his usual time. Iván Ilych answered "Yes" and "No," never taking his angry eyes from him, and at last said: "You know you can do nothing for me, so leave me alone."

"We can ease your sufferings."

"You can't even do that. Let me be."

The doctor went into the drawing-room and told Praskóvya Fëdorovna that the case was very serious and that the only resource left was opium to allay her husband's sufferings, which must be terrible.

It was true, as the doctor said, that Iván Ilych's physical sufferings were terrible, but worse than the physical sufferings were his mental sufferings which were his chief torture.

His mental sufferings were due to the fact that that night, as he looked at Gerásim's sleepy, good-natured face with its prominent cheek-bones, the question suddenly occurred to him: "What if my whole life has really been wrong?"

It occurred to him that what had appeared perfectly impossible before, namely that he had not spent his life as he should have done, might after all be true. It occurred to him that his scarcely perceptible attempts to struggle against what was considered good by the most highly placed people, those scarcely noticeable impulses which he had immediately suppressed, might have been the real thing, and all the rest false. And his professional duties and the whole arrangement of his life and of his family, and all his social and official interests, might all have been false. He tried to defend all those things to himself and suddenly felt the weakness of what he was defending. There was nothing to defend.

"But if that is so," he said to himself, "and I am leaving this life with the consciousness that I have lost all that was given me and it is impossible to rectify it—what then?"

He lay on his back and began to pass his life in review in quite a new way. In the morning when he saw first his footman, then his wife, then his daughter, and then the doctor, their every word and movement confirmed to him the awful truth that had been revealed to him during the night. In them he saw himself—all that for which he had lived—and saw clearly that it was not real at all, but a terrible and huge deception which had hidden both life and death. This consciousness intensified his physical suffering tenfold. He groaned and tossed about, and pulled at his clothing which choked and stifled him. And he hated them on that account.

He was given a large dose of opium and became unconscious, but at noon his sufferings began again. He drove everybody away and tossed from side to side.

His wife came to him and said:

"Jean, my dear, do this for me. It can't do any harm and often helps. Healthy people often do it."

He opened his eyes wide.

"What? Take communion? Why? It's unnecessary! However . . ."

She began to cry.

"Yes, do, my dear. I'll send for our priest. He is such a nice man."

"All right. Very well," he muttered.

When the priest came and heard his confession, Iván Ilych was softened and seemed to feel a relief from his doubts and consequently from his sufferings, and for a moment there came a ray of hope. He again began to think of the vermiform appendix and the possibility of correcting it. He received the sacrament with tears in his eyes.

When they laid him down again afterwards he felt a moment's ease, and the hope that he might live awoke in him again. He began to think of the operation that had been suggested to him. "To live! I want to live!" he said to himself.

His wife came in to congratulate him after his communion, and when uttering the usual conventional words she added:

"You feel better, don't you?"

Without looking at her he said "Yes."

Her dress, her figure, the expression of her face, the tone of her voice, all revealed the same thing. "This is wrong, it is not as it should be. All you have lived for and still live for is falsehood and deception, hiding life and death from you." And as soon as he admitted that thought, his hatred and his agonizing physical suffering again sprang up, and with that suffering a consciousness of the unavoidable, approaching end. And to this was added a new sensation of grinding shooting pain and a feeling of suffocation.

The expression of his face when he uttered that "yes" was dreadful. Having uttered it, he looked her straight in the eyes, turned on his face with a rapidity extraordinary in his weak state and shouted:

"Go away! Go away! and leave me alone!"

12

From that moment the screaming began that continued for three days, and was so terrible that one could not hear it through two closed doors without horror. At the moment he answered his wife he realized that he was lost, that there was no return, that the end had come, the very end, and his doubts were still unsolved and remained doubts.

"Oh! Oh! Oh!" he cried in various intonations. He had begun by screaming "I won't!" and continued screaming on the letter "o."

For three whole days, during which time did not exist for him, he struggled in that black sack into which he was being thrust by an invisible, resistless force. He struggled as a man condemned to death struggles in the hands of the executioner, knowing that he cannot save himself. And every moment he felt that despite all his efforts he was drawing nearer and nearer to what terrified him. He felt that his agony was due to his being thrust into that black hole and still more to his not being able to get right into it. He was hindered from getting into it by his conviction that his life had been a good one. That very justification of his life held him fast and prevented his moving forward, and it caused him most torment of all.

Suddenly some force struck him in the chest and side, making it still harder to breathe, and he fell through the hole and there at the bottom was a light. What had happened to him was like the sensation one sometimes experiences in a railway carriage when one thinks one is going backwards while one is really going forwards and suddenly becomes aware of the real direction.

"Yes, it was all not the right thing," he said to himself, "but that's no matter. It can be done. But what *is* the right thing?" he asked himself, and suddenly grew quiet.

This occurred at the end of the third day, two hours before his death. Just then his schoolboy son had crept softly in and gone up to the bedside. The dying man was still screaming desperately and waving his arms. His hand fell on the boy's head, and the boy caught it, pressed it to his lips, and began to cry.

At that very moment Iván Ilych fell through and caught sight of the light, and it was revealed to him that though his life had not been what it should have been, this could still be rectified. He asked himself, "What *is* the right thing?" and grew still, listening. Then he felt that someone was kissing his hand. He opened his eyes, looked at his son, and felt sorry for him. His wife came up to him and he glanced at her. She was gazing at him open-mouthed, with undried tears on her nose and cheek and a despairing look on her face. He felt sorry for her too.

"Yes, I am making them wretched," he thought. "They are sorry, but it will be better for them when I die." He wished to say this but had not the strength to utter it. "Besides, why speak? I must act," he thought. With a look at his wife he indicated his son and said: "Take him away . . . sorry for him . . . sorry for you too. . . ." He tried to add, "forgive me," but said "forego" and waved his hand, knowing that He whose understanding mattered would understand.

And suddenly it grew clear to him that what had been oppressing him and would not leave him was all dropping away at once from two sides, from ten sides, and from all sides. He was sorry for them, he must act so as not to hurt them: release them and free himself from these sufferings. "How good and how simple!" he thought. "And the pain?" he asked himself. "What has become of it? Where are you, pain?"

He turned his attention to it.

"Yes, here it is. Well, what of it? Let the pain be."

"And death . . . where is it?"

He sought his former accustomed fear of death and did not find it. "Where is it? What death?" There was no fear because there was no death.

In place of death there was light.

"So that's what it is!" he suddenly exclaimed aloud. "What joy!"

To him all this happened in a single instant, and the meaning of that instant did not change. For those present his agony continued for another two hours. Something rattled in his throat, his emaciated body twitched, then the gasping and rattle became less and less frequent.

"It is finished!" said someone near him.

He heard these words and repeated them in his soul.

"Death is finished," he said to himself. "It is no more!"

He drew in a breath, stopped in the midst of a sigh, stretched out, and died.

SARAH ORNE JEWETT

[1849–1909]

A White Heron

I

The woods were already filled with shadows one June evening, just before eight o'clock, though a bright sunset still glimmered faintly among the trunks of the trees. A little girl was driving home her cow, a plodding, dilatory, provoking creature in her behavior, but a valued companion for all that. They were going away from the western light, and striking deep into the dark woods, but their feet were familiar with the path, and it was no matter whether their eyes could see it or not.

There was hardly a night the summer through when the old cow could be found waiting at the pasture bars; on the contrary, it was her greatest pleasure to hide herself away among the high huckleberry bushes, and though she wore a loud bell she had made the discovery that if one stood perfectly still it would not ring. So Sylvia had to hunt for her until she found her, and call Co'! Co'! with never an answering Moo, until her childish patience was quite spent. If the creature had not given good milk and plenty of it, the case would have seemed very different to her owners. Besides, Sylvia had all the time there was, and very little use to make of it. Sometimes in pleasant weather it was a consolation to look upon the cow's pranks as an intelligent attempt to play hide and seek, and as the child had no playmates she lent herself to this amusement with a good deal of zest. Though this chase had been so long that the wary animal herself had given an unusual signal of her whereabouts, Sylvia had only laughed when she came upon Mistress Moolly at the swamp-side, and urged her affectionately homeward with a twig of birch leaves. The old cow was not inclined to wander farther, she even turned in the right direction for once as they left the pasture, and stepped along the road at a good pace. She was quite ready to be milked now, and seldom stopped to browse. Sylvia wondered what her grandmother would say because they were so late. It was a great while since she had left home at half past five o'clock, but everybody knew the difficulty of making this errand a short one. Mrs. Tilley had chased the horned torment too many summer evenings herself to blame any one else for lingering, and was only thankful as she waited that she had Sylvia, nowadays, to give such valuable assistance. The good woman suspected that Sylvia loitered occasionally on her own account; there never was such a child for straying about out-of-doors since the world was made! Everybody said that it was a good change for a little maid who had tried to grow for eight years in a crowded manufacturing town, but, as for Sylvia herself, it seemed as if she never had been alive at all before she came to live at the farm. She thought often with wistful compassion of a wretched dry geranium that belonged to a town neighbor.

" 'Afraid of folks,' " old Mrs. Tilley said to herself, with a smile, after she had made the unlikely choice of Sylvia from her daughter's houseful of children, and was returning to the farm. " 'Afraid of folks,' they said! I guess she won't be troubled no great with 'em up to the old place!" When they reached the door of the lonely house and stopped to unlock it, and the cat came to purr loudly, and rub against them, a deserted pussy, indeed, but fat with young robins, Sylvia whispered that this was a beautiful place to live in, and she never should wish to go home.

The companions followed the shady wood-road, the cow taking slow steps, and the child very fast ones. The cow stopped long at the brook to drink, as if the pasture were not half a swamp, and Sylvia stood still and waited, letting her bare feet cool themselves in the shoal water, while the great twilight moths struck softly against her. She waded on through the brook as the cow moved away, and listened to the thrushes with a heart that beat fast with pleasure. There was a stirring in the great boughs overhead. They were full of little birds and beasts that seemed to be wide-awake, and going about their world, or else saying good-night to each other in sleepy twitters. Sylvia herself felt sleepy as she walked along. However, it was not much farther to the house, and the air was soft and sweet. She was not often in the woods so late as this, and it made her feel as if she were a part of the gray shadows and the moving leaves. She was just thinking how long it seemed since she first came to the farm a year ago, and wondering if everything went on in the noisy town just the same as when she was there; the thought of the great red-faced boy who used to chase and frighten her made her hurry along the path to escape from the shadow of the trees.

Suddenly this little woods-girl is horror-stricken to hear a clear whistle not very far away. Not a bird's whistle, which would have a sort of friendliness, but a boy's whistle, determined, and somewhat aggressive. Sylvia left the cow to whatever sad fate might await her, and stepped discreetly aside into the bushes, but she was just too late. The enemy had discovered her, and called out in a very cheerful and persuasive tone, "Halloa, little girl, how far is it to the road?" and trembling Sylvia answered almost inaudibly, "A good ways."

She did not dare to look boldly at the tall young man, who carried a gun over his shoulder, but she came out of her bush and again followed the cow, while he walked alongside.

"I have been hunting for some birds," the stranger said kindly, "and I have lost my way, and need a friend very much. Don't be afraid," he added gallantly. "Speak up and tell me what your name is, and whether you think I can spend the night at your house, and go out gunning early in the morning."

Sylvia was more alarmed than before. Would not her grandmother consider her much to blame? But who could have foreseen such an accident as this? It did not appear to be her fault, and she hung her head as if the stem of it were broken, but managed to answer, "Sylvy," with much effort when her companion again asked her name.

Mrs. Tilley was standing in the doorway when the trio came into view. The cow gave a loud moo by way of explanation.

"Yes, you'd better speak up for yourself, you old trial! Where'd she tucked herself away this time, Sylvy?" Sylvia kept an awed silence; she knew by instinct that her grandmother did not comprehend the gravity of the situation. She must be mistaking the stranger for one of the farmer-lads of the region.

The young man stood his gun beside the door, and dropped a heavy game-bag beside it; then he bade Mrs. Tilley good-evening, and repeated his wayfarer's story, and asked if he could have a night's lodging.

"Put me anywhere you like," he said. "I must be off early in the morning, before day; but I am very hungry, indeed. You can give me some milk at any rate, that's plain."

"Dear sakes, yes," responded the hostess, whose long slumbering hospitality seemed to be easily awakened. "You might fare better if you went out on the main road a mile or so, but you're welcome to what we've got. I'll milk right off, and you make yourself at home. You can sleep on husks or feathers," she proffered graciously. "I raised them all myself. There's good pasturing for geese just below here towards the ma'sh. Now step round and set a plate for the gentleman, Sylvy!" And Sylvia promptly stepped. She was glad to have something to do, and she was hungry herself.

It was a surprise to find so clean and comfortable a little dwelling in this New England wilderness. The young man had known the horrors of its most primitive housekeeping, and the dreary squalor of that level of society which does not rebel at the companionship of hens. This was the best thrift of an old-fashioned farmstead, though on such a small scale that it seemed like a hermitage. He listened eagerly to the old woman's quaint talk, he watched Sylvia's pale face and shining gray eyes with ever growing enthusiasm, and insisted that this was the best supper he had eaten for a month; then, afterward, the new-made friends sat down in the doorway together while the moon came up.

Soon it would be berry-time, and Sylvia was a great help at picking. The cow was a good milker, though a plaguy thing to keep track of, the hostess gossiped frankly, adding presently that she had buried four children, so that Sylvia's mother, and a son (who might be dead) in California were all the children she had left. "Dan, my boy, was a great hand to go gunning," she explained sadly. "I never wanted for pa'tridges or gray squer'ls while he was to home. He's been a great wand'rer, I expect, and he's no hand to write letters. There, I don't blame him, I'd ha' seen the world myself if it had been so I could.

"Sylvia takes after him," the grandmother continued affectionately, after a minute's pause. "There ain't a foot o' ground she don't know her way over, and the wild creatur's counts her one o' themselves. Squer'ls she'll tame to come an' feed right out o' her hands, and all sorts o' birds. Last winter she got the jay-birds to bangeing here, and I believe she'd 'a' scanted herself of her own meals to have plenty to throw out amongst 'em, if I hadn't kep' watch. Anything but crows, I tell her, I'm willin' to help support,— though Dan he went an' tamed one o' them that did seem to have reason same as folks. It was round here a good spell after he went away. Dan an' his father they didn't hitch, —but he never held up his head ag'in after Dan had dared him an' gone off."

The guest did not notice this hint of family sorrows in his eager interest in something else.

"So Sylvy knows all about birds, does she?" he exclaimed, as he looked round at the little girl who sat, very demure but increasingly sleepy, in the moonlight. "I am making a collection of birds myself. I have been at it ever since I was a boy." (Mrs. Tilley smiled.) "There are two or three very rare ones I have been hunting for these five years. I mean to get them on my own ground if they can be found."

"Do you cage 'em up?" asked Mrs. Tilley doubtfully, in response to this enthusiastic announcement.

"Oh, no, they're stuffed and preserved, dozens and dozens of them," said the ornithologist, "and I have shot or snared every one myself. I caught a glimpse of a white heron three miles from here on Saturday, and I have followed it in this direction. They have never been found in this district at all. The little white heron, it is," and he turned again to look at Sylvia with the hope of discovering that the rare bird was one of her acquaintances.

But Sylvia was watching a hop-toad in the narrow footpath.

"You would know the heron if you saw it," the stranger continued eagerly. "A queer tall white bird with soft feathers and long thin legs. And it would have a nest perhaps in the top of a high tree, made of sticks, something like a hawk's nest."

Sylvia's heart gave a wild beat; she knew that strange white bird, and had once stolen softly near where it stood in some bright green swamp grass, away over at the other side of the woods. There was an open place where the sunshine always seemed strangely yellow and hot, where tall, nodding rushes grew, and her grandmother had warned her that she might sink in the soft black mud underneath and never be heard of more. Not far beyond were the salt marshes and beyond those was the sea, the sea which Sylvia wondered and dreamed about, but never had looked upon, though its great voice could often be heard above the noise of the woods on stormy nights.

"I can't think of anything I should like so much as to find that heron's nest," the handsome stranger was saying. "I would give ten dollars to anybody who could show it to me," he added desperately, "and I mean to spend my whole vacation hunting for it if need be. Perhaps it was only migrating, or had been chased out of its own region by some bird of prey."

Mrs. Tilley gave amazed attention to all this, but Sylvia still watched the toad, not divining, as she might have done at some calmer time, that the creature wished to get to its hole under the doorstep, and was much hindered by the unusual spectators at that hour of the evening. No amount of thought, that night, could decide how many wished-for treasures the ten dollars, so lightly spoken of, would buy.

The next day the young sportsman hovered about the woods, and Sylvia kept him company, having lost her first fear of the friendly lad, who proved to be most kind and sympathetic. He told her many things about the birds and what they knew and where they lived and what they did with themselves. And he gave her a jack-knife, which she thought as great a treasure as if she were a desert-islander. All day long he did not once make her troubled or afraid except when he brought down some unsuspecting singing creature from its bough. Sylvia would have liked him vastly better without his gun; she could not understand why he killed the very birds he seemed to like so much. But as the day waned, Sylvia still watched the young man with loving admiration. She had never seen anybody so charming and delightful; the woman's heart, asleep in the child, was vaguely thrilled by a dream of love. Some premonition of that great power stirred and swayed these young foresters who traversed the solemn woodlands with soft-footed silent care. They stopped to listen to a bird's song; they pressed forward again eagerly, parting the branches—speaking to each other rarely and in whispers; the young man going first and Sylvia following, fascinated, a few steps behind, with her gray eyes dark with excitement.

She grieved because the longed-for white heron was elusive, but she did not lead the guest, she only followed, and there was no such thing as speaking first. The sound of her own unquestioned voice would have terrified her—it was hard enough to answer yes or no when there was need of that. At last evening began to fall, and they drove the cow home together, and Sylvia smiled with pleasure when they came to the place where she heard the whistle and was afraid only the night before.

2

Half a mile from home, at the farther edge of the woods, where the land was highest, a great pine-tree stood, the last of its generation. Whether it was left for a boundary mark, or for what reason, no one could say; the woodchoppers who had felled its mates were dead and gone long ago, and a whole forest of sturdy trees, pines and oaks and maples, had grown again. But the stately head of this old pine towered above them all and made a landmark for sea and shore miles and miles away. Sylvia knew it well. She had always believed that whoever climbed to the top of it could see the ocean; and the little girl had often laid her hand on the great rough trunk and looked up wistfully at those dark boughs that the wind always stirred, no matter how hot and still the air might be below. Now she thought of the tree with a new excitement, for why, if one climbed it at break of day, could not one see all the world, and easily discover whence the white heron flew, and mark the place, and find the hidden nest?

What a spirit of adventure, what wild ambition! What fancied triumph and delight and glory for the later morning when she could make known the secret! It was almost too real and too great for the childish heart to bear.

All night the door of the little house stood open, and the whippoorwills came and sang upon the very step. The young sportsman and his old hostess were sound asleep, but Sylvia's great design kept her broad awake and watching. She forgot to think of sleep. The short summer night seemed as long as the winter darkness, and at last when the whippoorwills ceased, and she was afraid the morning would after all come too soon, she stole out of the house and followed the pasture path through the woods, hastening toward the open ground beyond, listening with a sense of comfort and companionship to the drowsy twitter of a half-awakened bird, whose perch she had jarred in passing. Alas, if the great wave of human interest which flooded for the first time this dull little life should sweep away the satisfactions of an existence heart to heart with nature and the dumb life of the forest!

There was the huge tree asleep yet in the paling moonlight, and small and hopeful Sylvia began with utmost bravery to mount to the top of it, with tingling, eager blood coursing the channels of her whole frame, with her bare feet and fingers, that pinched and held like bird's claws to the monstrous ladder reaching up, up, almost to the sky itself. First she must mount the white oak tree that grew alongside, where she was almost lost among the dark branches and the green leaves heavy and wet with dew; a bird fluttered off its nest, and a red squirrel ran to and fro and scolded pettishly at the harmless housebreaker. Sylvia felt her way easily. She had often climbed there, and knew that higher still one of the oak's upper branches chafed against the pine trunk, just where its lower boughs were set close together. There, when she made the dangerous pass from one tree to the other, the great enterprise would really begin.

She crept out along the swaying oak limb at last, and took the daring step across into the old pine-tree. The way was harder than she thought; she must reach far and hold fast, the sharp dry twigs caught and held her and scratched her like angry talons, the pitch made her thin little fingers clumsy and stiff as she went round and round the tree's great stem, higher and higher upward. The sparrows and robins in the woods below were beginning to wake and twitter to the dawn, yet it seemed much lighter there aloft in the pine-tree, and the child knew that she must hurry if her project were to be of any use.

The tree seemed to lengthen itself out as she went up, and to reach farther and farther upward. It was like a great main-mast to the voyaging earth; it must truly have been amazed that morning through all its ponderous frame as it felt this determined spark of human spirit creeping and climbing from higher branch to branch. Who knows how steadily the least twigs held themselves to advantage this light, weak creature on her way! The old pine must have loved his new dependent. More than all the hawks, and bats, and moths, and even the sweet-voiced thrushes, was the brave, beating heart of the solitary gray-eyed child. And the tree stood still and held away the winds that June morning while the dawn grew bright in the east.

Sylvia's face was like a pale star, if one had seen it from the ground, when the last thorny bough was past, and she stood trembling and tired but wholly triumphant, high in the tree-top. Yes, there was the sea with the dawning sun making a golden dazzle over it, and toward that glorious east flew two hawks with slow-moving pinions. How low they looked in the air from that height when before one had only seen them far up, and dark against the blue sky. Their gray feathers were as soft as moths; they seemed only a little way from the tree, and Sylvia felt as if she too could go flying away among the clouds. Westward, the woodlands and farms reached miles and miles into the distance; here and there were church steeples, and white villages; truly it was a vast and awesome world.

The birds sang louder and louder. At last the sun came up bewilderingly bright. Sylvia could see the white sails of ships out at sea, and the clouds that were purple and rose-colored and yellow at first began to fade away. Where was the white heron's nest in the sea of green branches, and was this wonderful sight and pageant of the world the only reward for having climbed to such a giddy height? Now look down again, Sylvia, where the green marsh is set among the shining birches and dark hemlocks; there where you saw the white heron once you will see him again; look, look! a white spot of him like a single floating feather comes up from the dead hemlock and grows larger, and rises, and comes close at last, and goes by the landmark pine with steady sweep of wing and outstretched slender neck and crested head. And wait! wait! do not move a foot or a finger, little girl, do not send an arrow of light and consciousness from your two eager eyes, for the heron has perched on a pine bough not far beyond yours, and cries back to his mate on the nest, and plumes his feathers for the new day!

The child gives a long sigh a minute later when a company of shouting cat-birds comes also to the tree, and vexed by their fluttering and lawlessness the solemn heron goes away. She knows his secret now, the wild, light, slender bird that floats and wavers, and goes back like an arrow presently to his home in the green world beneath. Then Sylvia, well satisfied, makes her perilous way down again, not daring to look far below the branch she stands on, ready to cry sometimes because her fingers ache and her lamed feet slip. Wondering over and over again what the stranger would say to her, and what he would think when she told him how to find his way straight to the heron's nest.

"Sylvy, Sylvy!" called the busy old grandmother again and again, but nobody answered, and the small husk bed was empty, and Sylvia had disappeared.

The guest waked from a dream, and remembering his day's pleasure hurried to dress himself that it might sooner begin. He was sure from the way the shy little girl looked once or twice yesterday that she had at least seen the white heron, and now she must really be persuaded to tell. Here she comes now, paler than ever, and her worn old frock is torn and tattered, and smeared with pine pitch. The grandmother and the sportsman stand in the door together and question her, and the splendid moment has come to speak of the dead hemlock-tree by the green marsh.

But Sylvia does not speak after all, though the old grandmother fretfully rebukes her, and the young man's kind appealing eyes are looking straight in her own. He can make them rich with money; he has promised it, and they are poor now. He is so well worth making happy, and he waits to hear the story she can tell.

No, she must keep silence! What is it that suddenly forbids her and makes her dumb? Has she been nine years growing, and now, when the great world for the first time puts out a hand to her, must she thrust it aside for a bird's sake? The murmur of the pine's green branches is in her ears, she remembers how the white heron came flying through the golden air and how they watched the sea and the morning together, and Sylvia cannot speak; she cannot tell the heron's secret and give its life away.

Dear loyalty, that suffered a sharp pang as the guest went away disappointed later in the day, that could have served and followed him and loved him as a dog loves! Many a night Sylvia heard the echo of his whistle haunting the pasture path as she came home with the loitering cow. She forgot even her sorrow at the sharp report of his gun and the piteous sight of thrushes and sparrows dropping silent to the ground, their songs hushed and their pretty feathers stained and wet with blood. Were the birds better friends than their hunter might have been,—who can tell? Whatever treasures were lost to her, woodlands and summer-time, remember! Bring your gifts and graces and tell your secrets to this lonely country child!

KATE CHOPIN

[1851–1904]

The Storm

I

The leaves were so still that even Bibi thought it was going to rain. Bobinôt, who was accustomed to converse on terms of perfect equality with his little son, called the child's attention to certain sombre clouds that were rolling with sinister intention from the west, accompanied by a sullen, threatening roar. They were at Friedheimer's store and decided to remain there till the storm had passed. They sat within the door on two empty kegs. Bibi was four years old and looked very wise.

"Mama'll be 'fraid, yes," he suggested with blinking eyes.

"She'll shut the house. Maybe she got Sylvie helpin' her this evenin'," Bobinôt responded reassuringly.

"No; she ent got Sylvie. Sylvie was helpin' her yistiday," piped Bibi.

Bobinôt arose and going across to the counter purchased a can of shrimps, of which Calixta was very fond. Then he returned to his perch on the keg and sat stolidly holding the can of shrimps while the storm burst. It shook the wooden store and seemed to be ripping great furrows in the distant field. Bibi laid his little hand on his father's knee and was not afraid.

2

Calixta, at home, felt no uneasiness for their safety. She sat at a side window sewing furiously on a sewing machine. She was greatly occupied and did not notice the approaching storm. But she felt very warm and often stopped to mop her face on which the perspiration gathered in beads. She unfastened her white sacque at the throat. It began to grow dark, and suddenly realizing the situation she got up hurriedly and went about closing windows and doors.

Out on the small front gallery she had hung Bobinôt's Sunday clothes to air and she hastened out to gather them before the rain fell. As she stepped outside, Alcée Laballière rode in at the gate. She had not seen him very often since her marriage, and never alone. She stood there with Bobinôt's coat in her hands, and the big rain drops began to fall. Alcée rode his horse under the shelter of a side projection where the chickens had huddled and there were plows and a harrow piled up in the corner.

"May I come and wait on your gallery till the storm is over, Calixta?" he asked.

"Come 'long in, M'sieur Alcée."

His voice and her own startled her as if from a trance, and she seized Bobinôt's vest. Alcée, mounting to the porch, grabbed the trousers and snatched Bibi's braided jacket that was about to be carried away by a sudden gust of wind. He expressed an intention to remain outside, but it was soon apparent that he might as well have been out in the open: the water beat in upon the boards in driving sheets, and he went inside, closing the door after him. It was even necessary to put something beneath the door to keep the water out.

"My! what a rain! It's good two years since it rain' like that," exclaimed Calixta as she rolled up a piece of bagging and Alcée helped her to thrust it beneath the crack.

She was a little fuller of figure than five years before when she married; but she had lost nothing of her vivacity. Her blue eyes still retained their melting quality; and her yellow hair, dishevelled by the wind and rain, kinked more stubbornly than ever about her ears and temples.

The rain beat upon the low, shingled roof with a force and clatter that threatened to break an entrance and deluge them there. They were in the dining room—the sitting room—the general utility room. Adjoining was her bed room, with Bibi's couch along side her own. The door stood open, and the room with its white, monumental bed, its closed shutters, looked dim and mysterious.

Alcée flung himself into a rocker and Calixta nervously began to gather up from the floor the lengths of a cotton sheet which she had been sewing.

"If this keeps up, *Dieu sait* if the levees goin' to stan' it!" she exclaimed.

"What have you got to do with the levees?"

"I got enough to do! An' there's Bobinôt with Bibi out in that storm—if he only didn' left Friedheimer's!"

"Let us hope, Calixta, that Bobinôt's got sense enough to come in out of a cyclone."

She went and stood at the window with a greatly disturbed look on her face. She wiped the frame that was clouded with moisture. It was stiflingly hot. Alcée got up and joined her at the window, looking over her shoulder. The rain was coming down in sheets obscuring the view of far-off cabins and enveloping the distant wood in a gray mist. The playing of the lightning was incessant. A bolt struck a tall chinaberry tree at the edge of the field. It filled all visible space with a blinding glare and the crash seemed to invade the very boards they stood upon.

Calixta put her hands to her eyes, and with a cry, staggered backward. Alcée's arm encircled her, and for an instant he drew her close and spasmodically to him.

"Bonte!" she cried, releasing herself from his encircling arm and retreating from the window, "the house'll go next! If I only knew w'ere Bibi was!" She would not compose herself; she would not be seated. Alcée clasped her shoulders and looked into her face. The contact of her warm, palpitating body when he had unthinkingly drawn her into his arms, had aroused all the old-time infatuation and desire for her flesh.

"Calixta," he said, "don't be frightened. Nothing can happen. The house is too low to be struck, with so many tall trees standing about. There! aren't you going to be quiet? say, aren't you?" He pushed her hair back from her face that was warm and steaming. Her lips were as red and moist as pomegranate seed. Her white neck and a glimpse of her full, firm bosom disturbed him powerfully. As she glanced up at him the fear in her liquid blue eyes had given place to a drowsy gleam that unconsciously betrayed a sensuous desire. He looked down into her eyes and there was nothing for him to do but to gather her lips in a kiss. It reminded him of Assumption.

"Do you remember—in Assumption. Calixta?" he asked in a low voice broken by passion. Oh! she remembered; for in Assumption he had kissed her and kissed and kissed her; until his senses would well nigh fail, and to save her he would resort to a desperate flight. If she was not an immaculate dove in those days, she was still inviolate; a passionate creature whose very defenselessness had made her defense, against which his honor forbade him to prevail. Now—well, now—her lips seemed in a manner free to be tasted, as well as her round, white throat and her whiter breasts.

They did not heed the crashing torrents, and the roar of the elements made her laugh as she lay in his arms. She was a revelation in that dim, mysterious chamber; as white as the couch she lay upon. Her firm, elastic flesh that was knowing for the first time its birthright, was like a creamy lily that the sun invites to contribute its breath and perfume to the undying life of the world.

The generous abundance of her passion, without guile or trickery, was like a white flame which penetrated and found response in depths of his own sensuous nature that had never yet been reached.

When he touched her breasts they gave themselves up in quivering ecstasy, inviting his lips. Her mouth was a fountain of delight. And when he possessed her, they seemed to swoon together at the very borderland of life's mystery.

He stayed cushioned upon her, breathless, dazed, enervated, with his heart beating like a hammer upon her. With one hand she clasped his head, her lips lightly touching his forehead. The other hand stroked with a soothing rhythm his muscular shoulders.

The growl of the thunder was distant and passing away. The rain beat softly upon the shingles, inviting them to drowsiness and sleep. But they dared not yield.

The rain was over; and the sun was turning the glistening green world into a palace of gems. Calixta, on the gallery, watched Alcée ride away. He turned and smiled at her with a beaming face; and she lifted her pretty chin in the air and laughed aloud.

3

Bobinôt and Bibi, trudging home, stopped without at the cistern to make themselves presentable.

"My! Bibi, w'at will yo' mama say! You ought to be ashame'. You oughtn' put on those good pants. Look at 'em! An' that mud on yo' collar! How you got that mud on yo' collar, Bibi? I never saw such a boy!" Bibi was the picture of pathetic resignation. Bobinôt was the embodiment of serious solicitude as he strove to remove from his own person and his son's the signs of their tramp over heavy roads and through wet fields. He scraped the mud off Bibi's bare legs and feet with a stick and carefully removed all traces from his heavy brogans. Then, prepared for the worst—the meeting with an over-scrupulous housewife, they entered cautiously at the back door.

Calixta was preparing supper. She had set the table and was dripping coffee at the hearth. She sprang up as they came in.

"Oh, Bobinôt! You back! My! but I was uneasy. W'ere you been during the rain? An' Bibi? he ain't wet? he ain't hurt?" She had clasped Bibi and was kissing him effusively. Bobinôt's explanations and apologies which he had been composing all along the way, died on his lips as Calixta felt him to see if he were dry, and seemed to express nothing but satisfaction at their safe return.

"I brought you some shrimps, Calixta," offered Bobinôt, hauling the can from his ample side pocket and laying it on the table.

"Shrimps! Oh, Bobinôt! you too good fo' anything!" and she gave him a smacking kiss on the cheek that resounded. "*J'vous reponds,*° we'll have a feas' to-night! umph-umph!"

Bobinôt and Bibi began to relax and enjoy themselves, and when the three seated themselves at table they laughed much and so loud that anyone might have heard them as far away as Laballière's.

4

Alcée Laballière wrote to his wife, Clarisse, that night. It was a loving letter, full of tender solicitude. He told her not to hurry back, but if she and the babies liked it at Biloxi, to stay a month longer. He was getting on nicely; and though he missed them, he was willing to bear the separation a while longer—realizing that their health and pleasure were the first things to be considered.

J'vous reponds   Take my word for it; I assure you.

5

As for Clarisse, she was charmed upon receiving her husband's letter. She and the babies were doing well. The society was agreeable; many of her old friends and acquaintances were at the bay. And the first free breath since her marriage seemed to restore the pleasant liberty of her maiden days. Devoted as she was to her husband, their intimate conjugal life was something which she was more than willing to forego for a while.

So the storm passed and everyone was happy.

ANTON CHEKHOV

[*1860–1904*]

The Lady with the Dog

TRANSLATED BY CONSTANCE GARNETT

I

It was said that a new person had appeared on the sea-front: a lady with a little dog. Dmitri Dmitritch Gurov, who had by then been a fortnight at Yalta, and so was fairly at home there, had begun to take an interest in new arrivals. Sitting in Verney's pavilion, he saw, walking on the sea-front, a fair-haired young lady of medium height, wearing a *béret;* a white Pomeranian dog was running behind her.

And afterwards he met her in the public gardens and in the square several times a day. She was walking alone, always wearing the same *béret,* and always with the same white dog; no one knew who she was, and every one called her simply "the lady with the dog."

"If she is here alone without a husband or friends, it wouldn't be amiss to make her acquaintance," Gurov reflected.

He was under forty, but he had a daughter already twelve years old, and two sons at school. He had been married young, when he was a student in his second year, and by now his wife seemed half as old again as he. She was a tall, erect woman with dark eyebrows, staid and dignified, and, as she said of herself, intellectual. She read a great deal, used phonetic spelling, called her husband, not Dmitri, but Dimitri, and he secretly considered her unintelligent, narrow, inelegant, was afraid of her, and did not like to be at home. He had begun being unfaithful to her long ago—had been unfaithful to her often, and, probably on that account, almost always spoke ill of women, and when they were talked about in his presence, used to call them "the lower race."

It seemed to him that he had been so schooled by bitter experience that he might call them what he liked, and yet he could not get on for two days together without "the lower race." In the society of men he was bored and not himself, with them he was cold and uncommunicative; but when he was in the company of women he felt free, and knew what to say to them and how to behave; and he was at ease with them even when he was silent. In his appearance, in his character, in his whole nature, there was something attractive and elusive which allured women and disposed them in his favour; he knew that, and some force seemed to draw him, too, to them.

Experience often repeated, truly bitter experience, had taught him long ago that with decent people, especially Moscow people—always slow to move and irresolute—every intimacy, which at first so agreeably diversifies life and appears a light and charming adventure, inevitably grows into a regular problem of extreme intricacy, and in the long run the situation becomes unbearable. But at every fresh meeting with an interesting woman this experience seemed to slip out of his memory, and he was eager for life, and everything seemed simple and amusing.

One evening he was dining in the gardens, and the lady in the *béret* came up slowly to take the next table. Her expression, her gait, her dress, and the way she did her hair told him that she was a lady, that she was married, that she was in Yalta for the first time and alone, and that she was dull there. . . . The stories told of the immorality in such places as Yalta are to a great extent untrue; he despised them, and knew that such stories were for the most part made up by persons who would themselves have been glad to sin if they had been able; but when the lady sat down at the next table three paces from him, he remembered these tales of easy conquests, of trips to the mountains, and the tempting thought of a swift, fleeting love affair, a romance with an unknown woman, whose name he did not know, suddenly took possession of him.

He beckoned coaxingly to the Pomeranian, and when the dog came up to him he shook his finger at it. The Pomeranian growled: Gurov shook his finger at it again.

The lady looked at him and at once dropped her eyes.

"He doesn't bite," she said, and blushed.

"May I give him a bone?" he asked; and when she nodded he asked courteously, "Have you been long in Yalta?"

"Five days."

"And I have already dragged out a fortnight here."

There was a brief silence.

"Time goes fast, and yet it is so dull here!" she said, not looking at him.

"That's only the fashion to say it is dull here. A provincial will live in Belyov or Zhidra and not be dull, and when he comes here it's 'Oh, the dullness! Oh, the dust!' One would think he came from Grenada."

She laughed. Then both continued eating in silence, like strangers, but after dinner they walked side by side; and there sprang up between them the light jesting conversation of people who are free and satisfied, to whom it does not matter where they go or what they talk about. They walked and talked of the strange light on the sea: the water was of a soft warm lilac hue, and there was a golden streak from the moon upon it. They talked of how sultry it was after a hot day. Gurov told her that he came from Moscow, that he had taken his degree in Arts, but had a post in a bank; that he had trained as an opera-singer, but had given it up, that he owned two houses in Moscow. . . . And from her he learnt that she had grown up in Petersburg, but had lived in S——— since her marriage two years before, that she was staying another month in Yalta, and that her husband, who needed a holiday too, might perhaps come and fetch her. She was not sure whether her husband had a post in a Crown Department or under the Provincial Council—and was amused by her own ignorance. And Gurov learnt, too, that she was called Anna Sergeyevna.

Afterwards he thought about her in his room at the hotel—thought she would certainly meet him next day; it would be sure to happen. As he got into bed he thought how lately she had been a girl at school, doing lessons like his own daughter; he recalled the diffidence, the angularity, that was still manifest in her laugh and her manner of talking with a stranger. This must have been the first time in her life she had been alone in surroundings in which she was followed, looked at, and spoken to merely from a secret motive which she could hardly fail to guess. He recalled her slender, delicate neck, her lovely grey eyes.

"There's something pathetic about her, anyway," he thought, and fell asleep.

2

A week had passed since they had made acquaintance. It was a holiday. It was sultry indoors, while in the street the wind whirled the dust round and round, and blew people's hats off. It was a thirsty day, and Gurov often went into the pavilion, and pressed Anna Sergeyevna to have syrup and water or an ice. One did not know what to do with oneself.

In the evening when the wind had dropped a little, they went out on the groyne to see the steamer come in. There were a great many people walking about the harbour; they had gathered to welcome some one, bringing bouquets. And two peculiarities of a well-dressed Yalta crowd were very conspicuous: the elderly ladies were dressed like young ones, and there were great numbers of generals.

Owing to the roughness of the sea, the steamer arrived late, after the sun had set, and it was a long time turning about before it reached the groyne. Anna Sergeyevna looked through her lorgnette at the steamer and the passengers as though looking for acquaintances, and when she turned to Gurov her eyes were shining. She talked a great deal and asked disconnected questions, forgetting next moment what she had asked; then she dropped her lorgnette in the crush.

The festive crowd began to disperse; it was too dark to see people's faces. The wind had completely dropped, but Gurov and Anna Sergeyevna still stood as though waiting to see some one else come from the steamer. Anna Sergeyevna was silent now, and sniffed the flowers without looking at Gurov.

"The weather is better this evening," he said. "Where shall we go now? Shall we drive somewhere?"

She made no answer.

Then he looked at her intently, and all at once put his arm round her and kissed her on the lips, and breathed in the moisture and the fragrance of the flowers; and he immediately looked round him, anxiously wondering whether any one had seen them.

"Let us go to your hotel," he said softly. And both walked quickly.

The room was close and smelt of the scent she had bought at the Japanese shop. Gurov looked at her and thought: "What different people one meets in the world!" From the past he preserved memories of careless, good-natured women, who loved cheerfully and were grateful to him for the happiness he gave them, however brief it might be; and of women like his wife who loved without any genuine feeling, with superfluous phrases, affectedly, hysterically, with an expression that suggested that it was not love nor passion, but something more significant; and of two or three others, very beautiful, cold women, on whose faces he had caught a glimpse of a rapacious expression—an obstinate desire to snatch from life more than it could give, and these were capricious, unreflecting, domineering, unintelligent women not in their first youth, and when Gurov grew cold to them their beauty excited his hatred, and the lace on their linen seemed to him like scales.

But in this case there was still the diffidence, the angularity of inexperienced youth, an awkward feeling; and there was a sense of consternation as though some one had suddenly knocked at the door. The attitude of Anna Sergeyevna—"the lady with the dog"—to what had happened was somehow peculiar, very grave, as though it were her fall—so it seemed, and it was strange and inappropriate. Her face dropped and faded, and on both sides of it her long hair hung down mournfully; she mused in a dejected attitude like "the woman who was a sinner" in an old-fashioned picture.

"It's wrong," she said. "You will be the first to despise me now."

There was a water-melon on the table. Gurov cut himself a slice and began eating it without haste. There followed at least half an hour of silence.

Anna Sergeyevna was touching; there was about her the purity of a good, simple woman who had seen little of life. The solitary candle burning on the table threw a faint light on her face, yet it was clear that she was very unhappy.

"How could I despise you?" asked Gurov. "You don't know what you are saying."

"God forgive me," she said, and her eyes filled with tears. "It's awful."

"You seem to feel you need to be forgiven."

"Forgiven? No. I am a bad, low woman; I despise myself and don't attempt to justify myself. It's not my husband but myself I have deceived. And not only just now; I have been deceiving myself for a long time. My husband may be a good, honest man, but he is a flunkey! I don't know what he does there, what his work is, but I know he is a flunkey! I was twenty when I was married to him. I have been tormented by curiosity; I wanted something better. 'There must be a different sort of life,' I said to myself. I wanted to live! To live, to live! . . . I was fired by curiosity . . . you don't understand it, but, I swear to God, I could not control myself; something happened to me: I could not be restrained. I told my husband I was ill, and came here. . . . And here I have been walking about as though I were dazed, like a mad creature; . . . and now I have become a vulgar, contemptible woman whom any one may despise."

Gurov felt bored already, listening to her. He was irritated by the naïve tone, by this remorse, so unexpected and inopportune; but for the tears in her eyes, he might have thought she was jesting or playing a part.

"I don't understand," he said softly. "What is it you want?"

She hid her face on his breast and pressed close to him.

"Believe me, believe me, I beseech you . . . ," she said. "I love a pure, honest life, and sin is loathsome to me. I don't know what I am doing. Simple people say: 'The Evil One has beguiled me.' And I may say of myself now that the Evil One has beguiled me."

"Hush, hush! . . ." he muttered.

He looked at her fixed, scared eyes, kissed her, talked softly and affectionately, and by degrees she was comforted, and her gaiety returned; they both began laughing.

Afterwards when they went out there was not a soul on the sea-front. The town with its cypresses had quite a deathlike air, but the sea still broke noisily on the shore; a single barge was rocking on the waves, and a lantern was blinking sleepily on it.

They found a cab and drove to Oreanda.

"I found out your surname in the hall just now: it was written on the board—Von Diderits," said Gurov. "Is your husband a German?"

"No; I believe his grandfather was a German, but he is an Orthodox Russian himself."

At Oreanda they sat on a seat not far from the church, looked down at the sea, and were silent. Yalta was hardly visible through the morning mist; white clouds stood motionless on the mountain-tops. The leaves did not stir on the trees, grasshoppers chirruped, and the monotonous hollow sound of the sea rising up from below, spoke of the peace, of the eternal sleep awaiting us. So it must have sounded when there was no Yalta, no Oreanda here; so it sounds now, and it will sound as indifferently and monotonously when we are all no more. And in this constancy, in this complete indifference to the life and death of each of us, there lies hid, perhaps, a pledge of our eternal salvation, of the unceasing movement of life upon earth, of unceasing progress towards perfection. Sitting beside a young woman who in the dawn seemed so lovely, soothed and spellbound in these magical surroundings—the sea, mountains, clouds, the open sky—Gurov thought how in reality everything is beautiful in this world when one reflects: everything except what we think or do ourselves when we forget our human dignity and the higher aims of our existence.

A man walked up to them—probably a keeper—looked at them and walked away. And this detail seemed mysterious and beautiful, too. They saw a steamer come from Theodosia, with its lights out in the glow of dawn.

"There is dew on the grass," said Anna Sergeyevna, after a silence.

"Yes. It's time to go home."

They went back to the town.

Then they met every day at twelve o'clock on the sea-front, lunched and dined together, went for walks, admired the sea. She complained that she slept badly, that her heart throbbed violently; asked the same questions, troubled now by jealousy and now by the fear that he did not respect her sufficiently. And often in the square or gardens, when there was no one near them, he suddenly drew her to him and kissed her passionately. Complete idleness, these kisses in broad daylight while he looked round in dread of some one's seeing them, the heat, the smell of the sea, and the continual passing to and fro before him of idle, well-dressed, well-fed people, made a new man of him; he told Anna Sergeyevna how beautiful she was, how fascinating. He was impatiently passionate, he would not move a step away from her, while she was often pensive and continually urged him to confess that he did not respect her, did not love her in the least, and thought of her as nothing but a common woman. Rather late almost every evening they drove somewhere out of town, to Oreanda or to the waterfall; and the expedition was always a success, the scenery invariably impressed them as grand and beautiful.

They were expecting her husband to come, but a letter came from him, saying that there was something wrong with his eyes, and he entreated his wife to come home as quickly as possible. Anna Sergeyevna made haste to go.

"It's a good thing I am going away," she said to Gurov. "It's the finger of destiny!"

She went by coach and he went with her. They were driving the whole day. When she had got into a compartment of the express, and when the second bell had rung, she said:

"Let me look at you once more . . . look at you once again. That's right."

She did not shed tears, but was so sad that she seemed ill, and her face was quivering.

"I shall remember you . . . think of you," she said. "God be with you; be happy. Don't remember evil against me. We are parting forever—it must be so, for we ought never to have met. Well, God be with you."

The train moved off rapidly, its lights soon vanished from sight, and a minute later there was no sound of it, as though everything had conspired together to end as quickly as possible that sweet delirium, that madness. Left alone on the platform, and gazing into the dark distance, Gurov listened to the chirrup of the grasshoppers and the hum of the telegraph wires, feeling as though he had only just waked up. And he thought, musing, that there had been another episode or adventure in his life, and it, too, was at an end, and nothing was left of it but a memory. . . . He was moved, sad, and conscious of a slight remorse. This young woman whom he would never meet again had not been happy with him; he was genuinely warm and affectionate with her, but yet in his manner, his tone, and his caresses there had been a shade of light irony, the coarse condescension of a happy man who was, besides, almost twice her age. All the time she had called him kind, exceptional, lofty; obviously he had seemed to her different from what he really was, so he had unintentionally deceived her. . . .

Here at the station was already a scent of autumn; it was a cold evening.

"It's time for me to go north," thought Gurov as he left the platform. "High time!"

3

At home in Moscow everything was in its winter routine; the stoves were heated, and in the morning it was still dark when the children were having breakfast and getting ready for school, and the nurse would light the lamp for a short time. The frost had begun already. When the first snow has fallen, on the first day of sledge-driving it is pleasant to see the white earth, the white roofs, to draw soft, delicious breath, and the season brings back the days of one's youth. The old limes and birches, white with hoar-frost, have a good-natured expression; they are nearer to one's heart than cypresses and palms, and near them one doesn't want to be thinking of the sea and the mountains.

Gurov was Moscow born; he arrived in Moscow on a fine frosty day, and when he put on his fur coat and warm gloves, and walked along Petrovka, and when on Saturday evening he heard the ringing of the bells, his recent trip and the places he had seen lost all charm for him. Little by little he became absorbed in Moscow life, greedily read three newspapers a day, and declared he did not read the Moscow papers on principle! He already felt a longing to go to restaurants, clubs, dinner-parties, anniversary celebrations and he felt flattered at entertaining distinguished lawyers and artists, and at playing cards with a professor at the doctors' club. He could already eat a whole plateful of salt fish and cabbage. . . .

In another month, he fancied, the image of Anna Sergeyevna would be shrouded in a mist in his memory, and only from time to time would visit him in his dreams with a touching smile as others did. But more than a month passed, real winter had come, and everything was still clear in his memory as though he had parted with Anna Sergeyevna only the day before. And his memories glowed more and more vividly. When in the evening stillness he heard from his study the voices of his children, preparing their lessons, or when he listened to a song or the organ at the restaurant, or the storm howled in the chimney, suddenly everything would rise up in his memory:

what had happened on the groyne, and the early morning with the mist on the mountains, and the steamer coming from Theodosia and the kisses. He would pace a long time about his room, remembering it all and smiling; then his memories passed into dreams, and in his fancy the past was mingled with what was to come. Anne Sergeyevna did not visit him in dreams, but followed him about everywhere like a shadow and haunted him. When he shut his eyes he saw her as though she were living before him, and she seemed to him lovelier, younger, tenderer than she was; and he imagined himself finer than he had been in Yalta. In the evenings she peeped out at him from the bookcase, from the fireplace, from the corner—he heard her breathing, the caressing rustle of her dress. In the street he watched the women, looking for some one like her.

He was tormented by an intense desire to confide his memories to some one. But in his home it was impossible to talk of his love, and he had no one outside; he could not talk to his tenants nor to any one at the bank. And what had he to talk of? Had he been in love, then? Had there been anything beautiful, poetical, or edifying or simply interesting in his relations with Anna Sergeyevna? And there was nothing for him but to talk vaguely of love, of woman, and no one guessed what it meant; only his wife twitched her black eyebrows, and said: "The part of a lady-killer does not suit you at all, Dimitri."

One evening, coming out of the doctors' club with an official with whom he had been playing cards, he could not resist saying:

"If only you knew what a fascinating woman I made the acquaintance of in Yalta!"

The official got into his sledge and was driving away, but turned suddenly and shouted:

"Dmitri Dmitritch!"

"What?"

"You were right this evening: the sturgeon was a bit too strong!"

These words, so ordinary, for some reason moved Gurov to indignation, and struck him as degrading and unclean. What savage manners, what people! What senseless nights, what uninteresting, uneventful days! The rage for card-playing, the gluttony, the drunkenness, the continual talk always about the same thing. Useless pursuits and conversations always about the same things absorb the better part of one's time, the better part of one's strength, and in the end there is left a life grovelling and curtailed, worthless and trivial, and there is no escaping or getting away from it—just as though one were in a madhouse or a prison.

Gurov did not sleep all night, and was filled with indignation. And he had a headache all next day. And the next night he slept badly; he sat up in bed, thinking, or paced up and down his room. He was sick of his children, sick of the bank; he had no desire to go anywhere or to talk of anything.

In the holidays in December he prepared for a journey, and told his wife he was going to Petersburg to do something in the interests of a young friend—and he set off for S———. What for? He did not very well know himself. He wanted to see Anna Sergeyevna and to talk with her—to arrange a meeting, if possible.

He reached S——— in the morning, and took the best room at the hotel, in which the floor was covered with grey army cloth, and on the table was an inkstand, grey with dust and adorned with a figure on horseback, with its hat in its hand and its head broken off. The hotel porter gave him the necessary information; Von Diderits lived in a house of his own in Old Gontcharny Street—it was not far from the hotel: he was rich and lived in good style, and had his own horses; every one in the town knew him. The porter pronounced the name "Dridirits."

Gurov went without haste to Old Gontcharny Street and found the house. Just opposite the house stretched a long grey fence adorned with nails.

"One would run away from a fence like that," thought Gurov, looking from the fence to the windows of the house and back again.

He considered: to-day was a holiday, and the husband would probably be at home. And in any case it would be tactless to go into the house and upset her. If he were to send her a note it might fall into her husband's hands, and then it might ruin everything. The best thing was to trust to chance. And he kept walking up and down the street by the fence, waiting for the chance. He saw a beggar go in at the gate and dogs fly at him; then an hour later he heard a piano, and the sounds were faint and indistinct. Probably it was Anna Sergeyevna playing. The front door suddenly opened, and an old woman came out, followed by the familiar white Pomeranian. Gurov was on the point of calling to the dog, but his heart began beating violently, and in his excitement he could not remember the dog's name.

He walked up and down, and loathed the grey fence more and more, and by now he thought irritably that Anna Sergeyevna had forgotten him, and was perhaps already amusing herself with some one else, and that that was very natural in a young woman who had nothing to look at from morning till night but that confounded fence. He went back to his hotel room and sat for a long while on the sofa, not knowing what to do, then he had dinner and a long nap.

"How stupid and worrying it is!" he thought when he woke and looked at the dark windows: it was already evening. "Here I've had a good sleep for some reason. What shall I do in the night?"

He sat on the bed, which was covered by a cheap grey blanket, such as one sees in hospitals, and he taunted himself in his vexation:

"So much for the lady with the dog . . . so much for the adventure. . . . You're in a nice fix. . . ."

That morning at the station a poster in large letters had caught his eye. "The Geisha" was to be performed for the first time. He thought of this and went to the theatre.

"It's quite possible she may go to the first performance," he thought.

The theatre was full. As in all provincial theatres, there was a fog above the chandelier, the gallery was noisy and restless; in the front row the local dandies were standing up before the beginning of the performance, with their hands behind them; in the Governor's box the Governor's daughter, wearing a boa, was sitting in the front seat, while the Governor himself lurked modestly behind the curtain with only his hands visible; the orchestra was a long time tuning up; the stage curtain swayed. All the time the audience were coming in and taking their seats Gurov looked at them eagerly.

Anna Sergeyevna, too, came in. She sat down in the third row, and when Gurov looked at her his heart contracted, and he understood clearly that for him there was in the whole world no creature so near, so precious, and so important to him; she, this little woman, in no way remarkable, lost in a provincial crowd, with a vulgar lorgnette in her hand, filled his whole life now, was his sorrow and his joy, the one happiness that he now desired for himself, and to the sounds of the inferior orchestra, of the wretched provincial violins, he thought how lovely she was. He thought and dreamed.

A young man with small side-whiskers, tall and stooping, came in with Anna Sergeyevna, and sat down beside her; he bent his head at every step and seemed to be continually bowing. Most likely this was the husband whom at Yalta, in a rush of bitter feeling, she had called a flunkey. And there really was in his long figure, his side-whiskers, and the small bald patch on his head, something of the flunkey's obsequiousness; his smile was sugary, and in his buttonhole there was some badge of distinction like the number on a waiter.

During the first interval the husband went away to smoke; she remained alone in her stall. Gurov, who was sitting in the stalls, too, went up to her and said in a trembling voice, with a forced smile:

"Good-evening."

She glanced at him and turned pale, then glanced again with horror, unable to believe her eyes, and tightly gripped her fan and the lorgnette in her hands, evidently struggling with herself not to faint. Both were silent. She was sitting, he was standing, frightened by her confusion and not venturing to sit down beside her. The violins and the flute began tuning up. He felt suddenly frightened; it seemed as though all the people in the boxes were looking at them. She got up and went quickly to the door; he followed her, and both walked senselessly along passages, and up and down stairs, and figures in legal, scholastic, and civil service uniforms, all wearing badges, flitted before their eyes. They caught glimpses of ladies, of fur coats hanging on pegs; the draughts blew on them, bringing a smell of stale tobacco. And Gurov, whose heart was beating violently, thought:

"Oh, heavens! Why are these people here and this orchestra! . . ."

And at that instant he recalled how when he had seen Anna Sergeyevna off at the station he had thought that everything was over and they would never meet again. But how far they were still from the end!

On the narrow, gloomy staircase over which was written "To the Amphitheatre," she stopped.

"How you have frightened me!" she said, breathing hard, still pale and overwhelmed. "Oh, how you have frightened me! I am half dead. Why have you come? Why?"

"But do understand, Anna, do understand . . ." he said hastily in a low voice. "I entreat you to understand. . . ."

She looked at him with dread, with entreaty, with love; she looked at him intently, to keep his features more distinctly in her memory.

"I am so unhappy," she went on, not heeding him. "I have thought of nothing but you all the time; I live only in the thought of you. And I wanted to forget, to forget you; but why, oh, why, have you come?"

On the landing above them two schoolboys were smoking and looking down, but that was nothing to Gurov; he drew Anna Sergeyevna to him, and began kissing her face, her cheeks, and her hands.

"What are you doing, what are you doing!" she cried in horror, pushing him away. "We are mad. Go away to-day; go away at once. . . . I beseech you by all that is sacred, I implore you. . . . There are people coming this way!"

Some one was coming up the stairs.

"You must go away," Anna Sergeyevna went on in a whisper. "Do you hear, Dmitri Dmitritch? I will come and see you in Moscow. I have never been happy; I am miserable now, and I never, never shall be happy, never! Don't make me suffer still more! I swear I'll come to Moscow. But now let us part. My precious, good, dear one, we must part!"

She pressed his hand and began rapidly going downstairs, looking round at him, and from her eyes he could see that she really was unhappy. Gurov stood for a little while, listened, then, when all sound had died away, he found his coat and left the theatre.

4

And Anna Sergeyevna began coming to see him in Moscow. Once in two or three months she left S———, telling her husband that she was going to consult a doctor about an internal complaint—and her husband believed her, and did not believe her. In Moscow she stayed at the Slaviansky Bazaar hotel, and at once sent a man in a red cap to Gurov. Gurov went to see her, and no one in Moscow knew of it.

Once he was going to see her in this way on a winter morning (the messenger had come the evening before when he was out). With him walked his daughter, whom he wanted to take to school: it was on the way. Snow was falling in big wet flakes.

"It's three degrees above freezing-point, and yet it is snowing," said Gurov to his daughter. "The thaw is only on the surface of the earth; there is quite a different temperature at a greater height in the atmosphere."

"And why are there no thunderstorms in the winter, father?"

He explained that, too. He talked, thinking all the while that he was going to see *her*, and no living soul knew of it, and probably never would know. He had two lives: one, open, seen and known by all who cared to know, full of relative truth and of relative falsehood, exactly like the lives of his friends and acquaintances; and another life running its course in secret. And through some strange, perhaps accidental, conjunction of circumstances, everything that was essential, of interest and of value to him, everything in which he was sincere and did not deceive himself, everything that made the kernel of his life, was hidden from other people; and all that was false in him, the sheath in which he hid himself to conceal the truth—such, for instance, as his work in the bank, his discussions at the club, his "lower race," his presence with his wife at anniversary festivities—all that was open. And he judged of others by himself, not believing in what he saw, and always believing that every man had his real, most interesting life under the cover of secrecy and under the cover of night. All personal life rested on secrecy, and possibly it was partly on that account that civilised man was so nervously anxious that personal privacy should be respected.

After leaving his daughter at school, Gurov went on to the Slaviansky Bazaar. He took off his fur coat below, went upstairs, and softly knocked at the door. Anna Sergeyevna, wearing his favourite grey dress, exhausted by the journey and the suspense, had been expecting him since the evening before. She was pale; she looked at him, and did not smile, and he had hardly come in when she fell on his breast. Their kiss was slow and prolonged, as though they had not met for two years.

"Well, how are you getting on there?" he asked. "What news?"

"Wait; I'll tell you directly. . . . I can't talk."

She could not speak; she was crying. She turned away from him, and pressed her handkerchief to her eyes.

"Let her have her cry out. I'll sit down and wait," he thought, and he sat down in an arm-chair.

Then he rang and asked for tea to be brought him, and while he drank his tea she remained standing at the window with her back to him. She was crying from emotion, from the miserable consciousness that their life was so hard for them; they could only meet in secret, hiding themselves from people, like thieves! Was not their life shattered?

"Come, do stop!" he said.

It was evident to him that this love of theirs would not soon be over, that he could not see the end of it. Anna Sergeyevna grew more and more attached to him. She adored him, and it was unthinkable to say to her that it was bound to have an end some day; besides, she would not have believed it!

He went up to her and took her by the shoulders to say something affectionate and cheering, and at that moment he saw himself in the looking-glass.

His hair was already beginning to turn grey. And it seemed strange to him that he had grown so much older, so much plainer during the last few years. The shoulders on which his hands rested were warm and quivering. He felt compassion for this life, still so warm and lovely, but probably already not far from beginning to fade and wither like his own. Why did she love him so much? He always seemed to women different from what he was, and they loved in him not himself, but the man created by their imagination, whom they had been eagerly seeking all their lives; and afterwards, when they noticed their mistake, they loved him all the same. And not one of them had been happy with him. Time passed, he had made their acquaintance, got on with them, parted, but he had never once loved; it was anything you like, but not love.

And only now when his head was grey he had fallen properly, really in love—for the first time in his life.

Anna Sergeyevna and he loved each other like people very close and akin, like husband and wife, like tender friends; it seemed to them that fate itself had meant them for one another, and they could not understand why he had a wife and she a husband; and it was as though they were a pair of birds of passage, caught and forced to live in different cages. They forgave each other for what they were ashamed of in their past, they forgave everything in the present, and felt that this love of theirs had changed them both.

In moments of depression in the past he had comforted himself with any arguments that came into his mind, but now he no longer cared for arguments; he felt profound compassion, he wanted to be sincere and tender. . . .

"Don't cry, my darling," he said. "You've had your cry; that's enough. . . . Let us talk now, let us think of some plan."

Then they spent a long while taking counsel together, talked of how to avoid the necessity for secrecy, for deception, for living in different towns and not seeing each other for long at a time. How could they be free from this intolerable bondage?

"How? How?" he asked, clutching his head. "How?"

And it seemed as though in a little while the solution would be found, and then a new and splendid life would begin; and it was clear to both of them that they had still a long, long road before them, and that the most complicated and difficult part of it was only just beginning.

CHARLOTTE PERKINS GILMAN

[1860–1935]

The Yellow Wallpaper

It is very seldom that mere ordinary people like John and myself secure ancestral halls for the summer.

A colonial mansion, a hereditary estate, I would say a haunted house and reach the height of romantic felicity—but that would be asking too much of fate!

Still I will proudly declare that there is something queer about it.

Else, why should it be let so cheaply? And why have stood so long untenanted?

John laughs at me, of course, but one expects that.

John is practical in the extreme. He has no patience with faith, an intense horror of superstition, and he scoffs openly at any talk of things not to be felt and seen and put down in figures.

John is a physician, and *perhaps*— (I would not say it to a living soul, of course, but this is dead paper and a great relief to my mind)—*perhaps* that is one reason I do not get well faster.

You see, he does not believe I am sick! And what can one do?

If a physician of high standing, and one's own husband, assures friends and relatives that there is really nothing the matter with one but temporary nervous depression— a slight hysterical tendency—what is one to do?

My brother is also a physician, and also of high standing, and he says the same thing.

So I take phosphates or phosphites—whichever it is—and tonics, and air and exercise, and journeys, and am absolutely forbidden to "work" until I am well again.

Personally, I disagree with their ideas.

Personally, I believe that congenial work, with excitement and change, would do me good.

But what is one to do?

I did write for a while in spite of them; but it *does* exhaust me a good deal—having to be so sly about it, or else meet with heavy opposition.

I sometimes fancy that in my condition, if I had less opposition and more society and stimulus—but John says the very worst thing I can do is to think about my condition, and I confess it always makes me feel bad.

So I will let it alone and talk about the house.

The most beautiful place! It is quite alone, standing well back from the road, quite three miles from the village. It makes me think of English places that you read about, for there are hedges and walls and gates that lock, and lots of separate little houses for the gardeners and people.

There is a *delicious* garden! I never saw such a garden—large and shady, full of box-bordered paths, and lined with long grape-covered arbors with seats under them.

There were greenhouses, but they are all broken now.

There was some legal trouble, I believe, something about the heirs and co-heirs; anyhow, the place has been empty for years.

That spoils my ghostliness, I am afraid, but I don't care—there is something strange about the house—I can feel it.

I even said so to John one moonlight evening, but he said what I felt was a draught, and shut the window.

I get unreasonably angry with John sometimes. I'm sure I never used to be so sensitive. I think it is due to this nervous condition.

But John says if I feel so I shall neglect proper self-control; so I take pains to control myself—before him, at least, and that makes me very tired.

I don't like our room a bit. I wanted one downstairs that opened onto the piazza and had roses all over the window, and such pretty old-fashioned chintz hangings! But John would not hear of it.

He said there was only one window and not room for two beds, and no near room for him if he took another.

He is very careful and loving, and hardly lets me stir without special direction.

I have a schedule prescription for each hour in the day; he takes all care from me, and so I feel basely ungrateful not to value it more.

He said he came here solely on my account, that I was to have perfect rest and all the air I could get. "Your exercise depends on your strength, my dear," said he, "and your food somewhat on your appetite; but air you can absorb all the time." So we took the nursery at the top of the house.

It is a big, airy room, the whole floor nearly, with windows that look all ways, and air and sunshine galore. It was nursery first, and then playroom and gymnasium, I should judge, for the windows are barred for little children, and there are rings and things in the walls.

The paint and paper look as if a boys' school had used it. It is stripped off—the paper —in great patches all around the head of my bed, about as far as I can reach, and in a great place on the other side of the room low down. I never saw a worse paper in my life. One of those sprawling, flamboyant patterns committing every artistic sin.

It is dull enough to confuse the eye in following, pronounced enough constantly to irritate and provoke study, and when you follow the lame uncertain curves for a little distance they suddenly commit suicide—plunge off at outrageous angles, destroy themselves in unheard-of contradictions.

The color is repellent, almost revolting: a smouldering unclean yellow, strangely faded by the slow-turning sunlight. It is a dull yet lurid orange in some places, a sickly sulphur tint in others.

No wonder the children hated it! I should hate it myself if I had to live in this room long.

There comes John, and I must put this away—he hates to have me write a word.

We have been here two weeks, and I haven't felt like writing before, since that first day.

I am sitting by the window now, up in this atrocious nursery, and there is nothing to hinder my writing as much as I please, save lack of strength.

John is away all day, and even some nights when his cases are serious.

I am glad my case is not serious!

But these nervous troubles are dreadfully depressing.

John does not know how much I really suffer. He knows there is no reason to suffer, and that satisfies him.

Of course it is only nervousness. It does weigh on me so not to do my duty in any way!

I meant to be such a help to John, such a real rest and comfort, and here I am a comparative burden already!

Nobody would believe what an effort it is to do what little I am able—to dress and entertain, and order things.

It is fortunate Mary is so good with the baby. Such a dear baby!

And yet I *cannot* be with him, it makes me so nervous.

I suppose John never was nervous in his life. He laughs at me so about this wallpaper!

At first he meant to repaper the room, but afterward he said that I was letting it get the better of me, and that nothing was worse for a nervous patient than to give way to such fancies.

He said that after the wallpaper was changed it would be the heavy bedstead, and then the barred windows, and then that gate at the head of the stairs, and so on.

"You know the place is doing you good," he said, "and really, dear, I don't care to renovate the house just for a three months' rental."

"Then do let us go downstairs," I said. "There are such pretty rooms there."

Then he took me in his arms and called me a blessed little goose, and said he would go down cellar, if I wished, and have it whitewashed into the bargain.

But he is right enough about the beds and windows and things.

It is as as airy and comfortable a room as anyone need wish, and, of course, I would not be so silly as to make him uncomfortable just for a whim.

I'm really getting quite fond of the big room, all but that horrid paper.

Out of one window I can see the garden—those mysterious deep-shaded arbors, the riotous old-fashioned flowers, and bushes and gnarly trees.

Out of another I get a lovely view of the bay and a little private wharf belonging to the estate. There is a beautiful shaded lane that runs down there from the house. I always fancy I see people walking in these numerous paths and arbors, but John has cautioned me not to give way to fancy in the least. He says that with my imaginative power and habit of story-making, a nervous weakness like mine is sure to lead to all manner of excited fancies, and that I ought to use my will and good sense to check the tendency. So I try.

I think sometimes that if I were only well enough to write a little it would relieve the press of ideas and rest me.

But I find I get pretty tired when I try.

It is so discouraging not to have any advice and companionship about my work. When I get really well, John says we will ask Cousin Henry and Julia down for a long visit; but he says he would as soon put fireworks in my pillow-case as to let me have those stimulating people about now.

I wish I could get well faster.

But I must not think about that. This paper looks to me as if it *knew* what a vicious influence it had!

There is a recurrent spot where the pattern lolls like a broken neck and two bulbous eyes stare at you upside down.

I get positively angry with the impertinence of it and the everlastingness. Up and down and sideways they crawl, and those absurd unblinking eyes are everywhere. There is one place where two breadths didn't match, and the eyes go all up and down the line, one a little higher than the other.

I never saw so much expression in an inanimate thing before, and we all know how much expression they have! I used to lie awake as a child and get more entertainment and terror out of blank walls and plain furniture than most children could find in a toy-store.

I remember what a kindly wink the knobs of our big old bureau used to have, and there was one chair that always seemed like a strong friend.

I used to feel that if any of the other things looked too fierce I could always hop into that chair and be safe.

The furniture in this room is no worse than inharmonious, however, for we had to bring it all from downstairs. I suppose when this was used as a playroom they had to take the nursery things out, and no wonder! I never saw such ravages as the children have made here.

The wallpaper, as I said before, is torn off in spots, and it sticketh closer than a brother —they must have had perseverance as well as hatred.

Then the floor is scratched and gouged and splintered, the plaster itself is dug out here and there, and this great heavy bed, which is all we found in the room, looks as if it had been through the wars.

But I don't mind it a bit—only the paper.

There comes John's sister. Such a dear girl as she is, and so careful of me! I must not let her find me writing.

She is a perfect and enthusiastic housekeeper, and hopes for no better profession. I verily believe she thinks it is the writing which made me sick!

But I can write when she is out, and see her a long way off from these windows.

There is one that commands the road, a lovely shaded winding road, and one that just looks off over the country. A lovely country, too, full of great elms and velvet meadows.

This wallpaper has a kind of sub-pattern in a different shade, a particularly irritating one, for you can only see it in certain lights, and not clearly then.

But in the places where it isn't faded and where the sun is just so—I can see a strange, provoking, formless sort of figure that seems to skulk about behind that silly and conspicuous front design.

There's sister on the stairs!

Well, the Fourth of July is over! The people are all gone, and I am tired out. John thought it might do me good to see a little company, so we just had Mother and Nellie and the children down for a week.

Of course I didn't do a thing. Jennie sees to everything now.

But it tired me all the same.

John says if I don't pick up faster he shall send me to Weir Mitchell° in the fall.

But I don't want to go there at all. I had a friend who was in his hands once, and she says he is just like John and my brother, only more so!

Weir Mitchell   *Silas Weir Mitchell (1829–1914), neurologist who introduced the "rest cure" for psychoneurotics.*

Besides, it is such an undertaking to go so far.

I don't feel as if it was worthwhile to turn my hand over for anything, and I'm getting dreadfully fretful and querulous.

I cry at nothing, and cry most of the time.

Of course I don't when John is here, or anybody else, but when I am alone.

And I am alone a good deal just now. John is kept in town very often by serious cases, and Jennie is good and lets me alone when I want her to.

So I walk a little in the garden or down that lovely lane, sit on the porch under the roses, and lie down up here a good deal.

I'm getting really fond of the room in spite of the wallpaper. Perhaps *because* of the wallpaper.

It dwells in my mind so!

I lie here on this great immovable bed—it is nailed down, I believe—and follow that pattern about by the hour. It is as good as gymnastics, I assure you. I start, we'll say, at the bottom, down in the corner over there where it has not been touched, and I determine for the thousandth time that I *will* follow that pointless pattern to some sort of a conclusion.

I know a little of the principle of design, and I know this thing was not arranged on any laws of radiation, or alternation, or repetition, or symmetry, or anything else that I ever heard of.

It is repeated, of course, by the breadths, but not otherwise.

Looked at in one way, each breadth stands alone; the bloated curves and flourishes —a kind of "debased Romanesque" with delirium tremens go waddling up and down in isolated columns of fatuity.

But, on the other hand, they connect diagonally, and the sprawling outlines run off in great slanting waves of optic horror, like a lot of wallowing sea-weeds in full chase.

The whole thing goes horizontally, too, at least it seems so, and I exhaust myself trying to distinguish the order of its going in that direction.

They have used a horizontal breadth for a frieze, and that adds wonderfully to the confusion.

There is one end of the room where it is almost intact, and there, when the crosslights fade and the low sun shines directly upon it, I can almost fancy radiation after all— the interminable grotesque seems to form around a common center and rush off in headlong plunges of equal distraction.

It makes me tired to follow it. I will take a nap, I guess.

I don't know why I should write this.

I don't want to.

I don't feel able.

And I know John would think it absurd. But I *must* say what I feel and think in some way—it is such a relief!

But the effort is getting to be greater than the relief.

Half the time now I am awfully lazy, and lie down ever so much. John says I mustn't lose my strength, and has me take cod liver oil and lots of tonics and things, to say nothing of ale and wine and rare meat.

Dear John! He loves me very dearly, and hates to have me sick. I tried to have a real earnest reasonable talk with him the other day, and tell him how I wish he would let me go and make a visit to Cousin Henry and Julia.

But he said I wasn't able to go, nor able to stand it after I got there; and I did not make out a very good case for myself, for I was crying before I had finished.

It is getting to be a great effort for me to think straight. Just this nervous weakness, I suppose.

And dear John gathered me up in his arms, and just carried me upstairs and laid me on the bed, and sat by me and read to me till it tired my head.

He said I was his darling and his comfort and all he had, and that I must take care of myself for his sake, and keep well.

He says no one but myself can help me out of it, that I must use my will and self-control and not let any silly fancies run away with me.

There's one comfort—the baby is well and happy, and does not have to occupy this nursery with the horrid wallpaper.

If we had not used it, that blessed child would have! What a fortunate escape! Why, I wouldn't have a child of mine, an impressionable little thing, live in such a room for worlds.

I never thought of it before, but it is lucky that John kept me here after all; I can stand it so much easier than a baby, you see.

Of course I never mention it to them any more—I am too wise—but I keep watch for it all the same.

There are things in that wallpaper that nobody knows about but me, or ever will.

Behind that outside pattern the dim shapes get clearer every day.

It is always the same shape, only very numerous.

And it is like a woman stooping down and creeping about behind that pattern. I don't like it a bit. I wonder—I begin to think—I wish John would take me away from here!

It is so hard to talk with John about my case, because he is so wise, and because he loves me so.

But I tried it last night.

It was moonlight. The moon shines in all around just as the sun does.

I hate to see it sometimes, it creeps so slowly, and always comes in by one window or another.

John was asleep and I hated to waken him, so I kept still and watched the moonlight on that undulating wallpaper till I felt creepy.

The faint figure behind seemed to shake the pattern, just as if she wanted to get out.

I got up softly and went to feel and see if the paper *did* move, and when I came back John was awake.

"What is it, little girl?" he said. "Don't go walking about like that—you'll get cold."

I thought it was a good time to talk, so I told him that I really was not gaining here, and that I wished he would take me away.

"Why, darling!" said he. "Our lease will be up in three weeks, and I can't see how to leave before.

"The repairs are not done at home, and I cannot possibly leave town just now. Of course, if you were in any danger, I could and would, but you really are better, dear, whether you can see it or not. I am a doctor, dear, and I know. You are gaining flesh and color, your appetite is better, I feel really much easier about you."

"I don't weigh a bit more," said I, "nor as much; and my appetite may be better in the evening when you are here but it is worse in the morning when you are away!"

"Bless her little heart!" said he with a big hug. "She shall be as sick as she pleases! But now let's improve the shining hours by going to sleep, and talk about it in the morning!"

"And you won't go away?" I asked gloomily.

"Why, how can I, dear? It is only three weeks more and then we will take a nice little trip of a few days while Jennie is getting the house ready. Really, dear, you are better!"

"Better in body perhaps—" I began, and stopped short, for he sat up straight and looked at me with such a stern, reproachful look that I could not say another word.

"My darling," said he, "I beg of you, for my sake and for our child's sake, as well as for your own, that you will never for one instant let that idea enter your mind! There is nothing so dangerous, so fascinating, to a temperament like yours. It is a false and foolish fancy. Can you not trust me as a physician when I tell you so?"

So of course I said no more on that score, and we went to sleep before long. He thought I was asleep first, but I wasn't, and lay there for hours trying to decide whether that front pattern and the back pattern really did move together or separately.

On a pattern like this, by daylight, there is a lack of sequence, a defiance of law, that is a constant irritant to a normal mind.

The color is hideous enough, and unreliable enough, and infuriating enough, but the pattern is torturing.

You think you have mastered it, but just as you get well under way in following, it turns a back-somersault and there you are. It slaps you in the face, knocks you down, and tramples upon you. It is like a bad dream.

The outside pattern is a florid arabesque, reminding one of a fungus. If you can imagine a toadstool in joints, an interminable string of toadstools, budding and sprouting in endless convolutions—why, that is something like it.

That is, sometimes!

There is one marked peculiarity about this paper, a thing nobody seems to notice but myself, and that is that it changes as the light changes.

When the sun shoots in through the east window—I always watch for that first long, straight ray—it changes so quickly that I never can quite believe it.

That is why I watch it always.

By moonlight—the moon shines in all night when there is a moon—I wouldn't know it was the same paper.

At night in any kind of light, in twilight, candlelight, lamplight, and worst of all by moonlight, it becomes bars! The outside pattern, I mean, and the woman behind it is as plain as can be.

I didn't realize for a long time what the thing was that showed behind, that dim sub-pattern, but now I am quite sure it is a woman.

By daylight she is subdued, quiet. I fancy it is the pattern that keeps her so still. It is so puzzling. It keeps me quiet by the hour.

I lie down ever so much now. John says it is good for me, and to sleep all I can. Indeed he started the habit by making me lie down for an hour after each meal. It is a very bad habit, I am convinced, for you see, I don't sleep. And that cultivates deceit, for I don't tell them I'm awake—oh, no! The fact is I am getting a little afraid of John. He seems very queer sometimes, and even Jennie has an inexplicable look. It strikes me occasionally, just as a scientific hypothesis, that perhaps it is the paper! I have watched John when he did not know I was looking, and come into the room suddenly on the most innocent excuses, and I've caught him several times *looking at the paper!* And Jennie too. I caught Jennie with her hand on it once.

She didn't know I was in the room, and when I asked her in a quiet, a very quiet voice, with the most restrained manner possible, what she was doing with the paper, she turned around as if she had been caught stealing, and looked quite angry—asked me why I should frighten her so!

Then she said that the paper stained everything it touched, that she had found yellow smooches on all my clothes and John's and she wished we would be more careful!

Did not that sound innocent? But I know she was studying that pattern, and I am determined that nobody shall find it out but myself!

Life is very much more exciting now than it used to be. You see, I have something more to expect, to look forward to, to watch. I really do eat better, and am more quiet than I was.

John is so pleased to see me improve! He laughed a little the other day, and said I seemed to be flourishing in spite of my wallpaper.

I turned it off with a laugh. I had no intention of telling him it was *because* of the wallpaper—he would make fun of me. He might even want to take me away.

I don't want to leave now until I have found it out. There is a week more, and I think that will be enough.

I'm feeling so much better!

I don't sleep much at night, for it is so interesting to watch developments; but I sleep a good deal during the daytime.

In the daytime it is tiresome and perplexing.

There are always new shoots on the fungus, and new shades of yellow all over it. I cannot keep count of them, though I have tried conscientiously.

It is the strangest yellow, that wallpaper! It makes me think of all the yellow things I ever saw—not beautiful ones like buttercups, but old, foul, bad yellow things.

But there is something else about that paper—the smell! I noticed it the moment we came into the room, but with so much air and sun it was not bad. Now we have had a week of fog and rain, and whether the windows are open or not, the smell is here.

It creeps all over the house.

I find it hovering in the dining-room, skulking in the parlor, hiding in the hall, lying in wait for me on the stairs.

It gets into my hair.

Even when I go to ride, if I turn my head suddenly and surprise it—there is that smell!

Such a peculiar odor, too! I have spent hours in trying to analyze it, to find what it smelled like.

It is not bad—at first—and very gentle, but quite the subtlest, most enduring odor I ever met.

In this damp weather it is awful. I wake up in the night and find it hanging over me.

It used to disturb me at first. I thought seriously of burning the house—to reach the smell.

But now I am used to it. The only thing I can think of that it is like is the *color* of the paper! A yellow smell.

There is a very funny mark on this wall, low down, near the mopboard. A streak that runs round the room. It goes behind every piece of furniture, except the bed, a long, straight, even *smooch,* as if it had been rubbed over and over.

I wonder how it was done and who did it, and what they did it for. Round and round and round—round and round and round—it makes me dizzy!

I really have discovered something at last.

Through watching so much at night, when it changes so, I have finally found out.

The front pattern *does* move—and no wonder! The woman behind shakes it!

Sometimes I think there are a great many women behind, and sometimes only one, and she crawls around fast, and her crawling shakes it all over.

Then in the very bright spots she keeps still, and in the very shady spots she just takes hold of the bars and shakes them hard.

And she is all the time trying to climb through. But nobody could climb through that pattern—it strangles so; I think that is why it has so many heads.

They get through and then the pattern strangles them off and turns them upside down, and makes their eyes white!

If those heads were covered or taken off it would not be half so bad.

I think that woman gets out in the daytime!

And I'll tell you why—privately—I've seen her!

I can see her out of every one of my windows!

It is the same woman, I know, for she is always creeping, and most women do not creep by daylight.

I see her in that long shaded lane, creeping up and down. I see her in those dark grape arbors, creeping all around the garden.

I see her on that long road under the trees, creeping along, and when a carriage comes she hides under the blackberry vines.

I don't blame her a bit. It must be very humiliating to be caught creeping by daylight!

I always lock the door when I creep by daylight. I can't do it at night, for I know John would suspect something at once.

And John is so queer now that I don't want to irritate him. I wish he would take another room! Besides, I don't want anybody to get that woman out at night but myself.

I often wonder if I could see her out of all the windows at once.

But, turn as fast as I can, I can only see out of one at one time.

And though I always see her, she *may* be able to creep faster than I can turn! I have watched her sometimes away off in the open country, creeping as fast as a cloud shadow in a wind.

If only that top pattern could be gotten off from the under one! I mean to try it, little by little.

I have found out another funny thing, but I shan't tell it this time! It does not do to trust people too much.

There are only two more days to get this paper off, and I believe John is beginning to notice. I don't like the look in his eyes.

And I heard him ask Jennie a lot of professional questions about me. She had a very good report to give.

She said I slept a good deal in the daytime.

John knows I don't sleep very well at night, for all I'm so quiet!

He asked me all sorts of questions, too, and pretended to be very loving and kind.

As if I couldn't see through him!

Still, I don't wonder he acts so, sleeping under this paper for three months.

It only interests me, but I feel sure John and Jennie are affected by it.

Hurrah! This is the last day, but it is enough. John is to stay in town over night, and won't be out until this evening.

Jennie wanted to sleep with me—the sly thing; but I told her I should undoubtedly rest better for a night all alone.

That was clever, for really I wasn't alone a bit! As soon as it was moonlight and that poor thing began to crawl and shake the pattern, I got up and ran to help her.

I pulled and she shook. I shook and she pulled, and before morning we had peeled off yards of that paper.

A strip about as high as my head and half around the room.

And then when the sun came and that awful pattern began to laugh at me, I declared I would finish it today!

We go away tomorrow, and they are moving all my furniture down again to leave things as they were before.

Jennie looked at the wall in amazement, but I told her merrily that I did it out of pure spite at the vicious thing.

She laughed and said she wouldn't mind doing it herself, but I must not get tired.

How she betrayed herself that time!

But I am here, and no person touches this paper but Me—not *alive!*

She tried to get me out of the room—it was too patent! But I said it was so quiet and empty and clean now that I believed I would lie down again and sleep all I could, and not to wake me even for dinner—I would call when I woke.

So now she is gone, and the servants are gone, and the things are gone, and there is nothing left but that great bedstead nailed down, with the canvas mattress we found on it.

We shall sleep downstairs tonight, and take the boat home tomorrow.

I quite enjoy the room, now it is bare again.

How those children did tear about here!

This bedstead is fairly gnawed!

But I must get to work.

I have locked the door and thrown the key down into the front path.

I don't want to go out, and I don't want to have anybody come in, till John comes. I want to astonish him.

I've got a rope up here that even Jennie did not find. If that woman does get out, and tries to get away, I can tie her!

But I forgot I could not reach far without anything to stand on!

This bed will *not* move!

I tried to lift and push it until I was lame, and then I got so angry I bit off a little piece at one corner—but it hurt my teeth.

Then I peeled off all the paper I could reach standing on the floor. It sticks horribly and the pattern just enjoys it! All those strangled heads and bulbous eyes and waddling fungus growths just shriek with derision!

I am getting angry enough to do something desperate. To jump out of the window would be admirable exercise, but the bars are too strong even to try.

Besides I wouldn't do it. Of course not. I know well enough that a step like that is improper and might be misconstrued.

I don't like to *look* out of the windows even—there are so many of those creeping women, and they creep so fast.

I wonder if they all come out of that wallpaper as I did?

But I am securely fastened now by my well-hidden rope—you don't get *me* out in the road there!

I suppose I shall have to get back behind the pattern when it comes night, and that is hard!

It is so pleasant to be out in this great room and creep around as I please!

I don't want to go outside. I won't, even if Jennie asks me to.

For outside you have to creep on the ground, and everything is green instead of yellow.

But here I can creep smoothly on the floor, and my shoulder just fits in that long smooch around the wall, so I cannot lose my way.

Why, there's John at the door!

It is no use, young man, you can't open it!

How he does call and pound!

Now he's crying to Jennie for an axe.

It would be a shame to break down that beautiful door!

"John, dear!" said I in the gentlest voice. "The key is down by the front steps, under a plantain leaf!"

That silenced him for a few moments.

Then he said, very quietly indeed, "Open the door, my darling!"

"I can't," said I. "The key is down by the front door under a plantain leaf!" And then I said it again, several times, very gently and slowly, and said it so often that he had to go and see, and he got it of course, and came in. He stopped short by the door.

"What is the matter?" he cried. "For God's sake, what are you doing!"

I kept on creeping just the same, but I looked at him over my shoulder.

"I've got out at last," said I, "in spite of you and Jane. And I've pulled off most of the paper, so you can't put me back!"

Now why should that man have fainted? But he did, and right across my path by the wall, so that I had to creep over him every time!

RUDYARD KIPLING

[*1865–1936*]

The Gardener

One grave to me was given,
  One watch till Judgment Day;
And God looked down from Heaven
  And rolled the stone away.

One day in all the years,
  One hour in that one day,
His Angel saw my tears,
  And rolled the stone away!

Every one in the village knew that Helen Turrell did her duty by all her world, and by none more honourably than by her only brother's unfortunate child. The village knew, too, that George Turrell had tried his family severely since early youth, and were not surprised to be told that, after many fresh starts given and thrown away, he, an Inspector of Indian Police, had entangled himself with the daughter of a retired non-commissioned officer, and had died of a fall from a horse a few weeks before his child was born. Mercifully, George's father and mother were both dead, and though Helen, thirty-five and independent, might well have washed her hands of the whole disgraceful affair, she most nobly took charge, though she was, at the time, under threat of lung trouble which had driven her to the South of France. She arranged for the passage of the child and a nurse from Bombay, met them at Marseilles, nursed the baby through an attack of infantile dysentery due to the carelessness of the nurse, whom she had had to dismiss, and at last, thin and worn but triumphant, brought the boy late in the autumn, wholly restored, to her Hampshire home.

All these details were public property, for Helen was as open as the day, and held that scandals are only increased by hushing them up. She admitted that George had always been rather a black sheep, but things might have been much worse if the mother had insisted on her right to keep the boy. Luckily, it seemed that people of that class would do almost anything for money, and, as George had always turned to her in his scrapes, she felt herself justified—her friends agreed with her—in cutting the whole non-commissioned officer connection, and giving the child every advantage. A christening, by the Rector, under the name of Michael, was the first step. So far as she knew herself, she was not, she said, a child-lover, but, for all his faults, she had been very fond of George, and she pointed out that little Michael had his father's mouth to a line; which made something to build upon.

As a matter of fact, it was the Turrell forehead, broad, low, and well-shaped, with the widely spaced eyes beneath it, that Michael had most faithfully reproduced. His mouth was somewhat better cut than the family type. But Helen, who would concede nothing good to his mother's side, vowed he was a Turrell all over, and, there being no one to contradict, the likeness was established.

In a few years Michael took his place, as accepted as Helen had always been—fearless, philosophical, and fairly good-looking. At six, he wished to know why he could not call her "Mummy," as other boys called their mothers. She explained that she was only his auntie, and that aunties were not quite the same as mummies, but that, if it gave him pleasure, he might call her "Mummy" at bedtime, for a pet-name between themselves.

Michael kept his secret most loyally, but Helen, as usual, explained the fact to her friends; which when Michael heard, he raged.

"Why did you tell? *Why* did you tell?" came at the end of the storm.

"Because it's always best to tell the truth," Helen answered, her arm round him as he shook in his cot.

"All right, but when the troof's ugly I don't think it's nice."

"Don't you, dear?"

"No, I don't, and"—she felt the small body stiffen—"now you've told, I won't call you "Mummy" any more—not even at bedtimes."

"But isn't that rather unkind?" said Helen softly.

"I don't care! I don't care! You've hurted me in my insides and I'll hurt you back. I'll hurt you as long as I live!"

"Don't, oh, don't talk like that, dear! You don't know what—"

"I will! And when I'm dead I'll hurt you worse!"

"Thank goodness, I shall be dead long before you, darling."

"Huh! Emma says, 'Never know your luck.' (Michael had been talking to Helen's elderly, flat-faced maid.) "Lots of little boys die quite soon. So'll I. *Then* you'll see!"

Helen caught her breath and moved towards the door, but the wail of "Mummy! Mummy!" drew her back again, and the two wept together.

At ten years old, after two terms at a prep. school, something or somebody gave him the idea that his civil status was not quite regular. He attacked Helen on the subject, breaking down her stammered defences with the family directness.

"Don't believe a word of it," he said, cheerily, at the end. "People wouldn't have talked like they did if my people had been married. But don't you bother, Auntie. I've found out all about my sort in English Hist'ry and the Shakespeare bits. There was William the Conqueror to begin with, and—oh, heaps more, and they all got on first-rate. 'Twon't make any difference to you, my being *that*—will it?"

"As if anything could——" she began.

"All right. We won't talk about it any more if it makes you cry." He never mentioned the thing again of his own will, but when, two years later, he skilfully managed to have measles in the holidays, as his temperature went up to the appointed one hundred and four he muttered of nothing else, till Helen's voice, piercing at last his delirium, reached him with assurance that nothing on earth or beyond could make any difference between them.

The terms at his public school and the wonderful Christmas, Easter, and Summer holidays followed each other, variegated and glorious as jewels on a string; and as jewels Helen treasured them. In due time Michael developed his own interests, which ran their courses and gave way to others; but his interest in Helen was constant and increasing throughout. She repaid it with all that she had of affection or could command of counsel and money; and since Michael was no fool, the War took him just before what was like to have been a most promising career.

He was to have gone up to Oxford, with a scholarship, in October. At the end of August he was on the edge of joining the first holocaust of public-school boys who threw themselves into the Line; but the captain of his O.T.C., where he had been sergeant for nearly a year, headed him off and steered him directly to a commission in a battalion so new that half of it still wore the old Army red, and the other half was breeding meningitis through living overcrowdedly in damp tents. Helen had been shocked at the idea of direct enlistment.

"But it's in the family," Michael laughed.

"You don't mean to tell me that you believed that old story all this time?" said Helen. (Emma, her maid, had been dead now several years.) "I gave you my word of honour —and I give it again—that—that it's all right. It is indeed."

"Oh, *that* doesn't worry me. It never did," he replied valiantly. "What I meant was, I should have got into the show earlier if I'd enlisted—like my grandfather."

"Don't talk like that! Are you afraid of its ending so soon, then?"

"No such luck. You know what K. says."

"Yes. But my banker told me last Monday it couldn't *possibly* last beyond Christmas —for financial reasons."

"Hope he's right, but our Colonel—and he's a Regular—says it's going to be a long job."

Michael's battalion was fortunate in that, by some chance which meant several "leaves," it was used for coast-defence among shallow trenches on the Norfolk coast; thence sent north to watch the mouth of a Scotch estuary, and, lastly, held for weeks on a baseless rumour of distant service. But, the very day that Michael was to have met Helen for four whole hours at a railway-junction up the line, it was hurled out, to help make good the wastage of Loos, and he had only just time to send her a wire of farewell.

In France luck again helped the battalion. It was put down near the Salient, where it led a meritorious and unexacting life, while the Somme was being manufactured; and enjoyed the peace of the Armentières and Laventie sectors when that battle began. Finding that it had sound views on protecting its own flanks and could dig, a prudent Commander stole it out of its own Division, under pretence of helping to lay telegraphs, and used it round Ypres at large.

A month later, and just after Michael had written Helen that there was nothing special doing and therefore no need to worry, a shell-splinter dropping out of a wet dawn killed him at once. The next shell uprooted and laid down over the body what had been the foundation of a barn wall, so neatly that none but an expert would have guessed that anything unpleasant had happened.

By this time the village was old in experience of war, and, English fashion, had evolved a ritual to meet it. When the postmistress handed her seven-year-old daughter the official telegram to take to Miss Turrell, she observed to the Rector's gardener: "It's Miss Helen's turn now." He replied, thinking of his own son: "Well, he's lasted longer than some." The child herself came to the frontdoor weeping aloud, because Master Michael had often given her sweets. Helen, presently, found herself pulling down the house-blinds one after one with great care, and saying earnestly to each: "Missing *always* means dead." Then she took her place in the dreary procession that was impelled to go through an inevitable series of unprofitable emotions. The Rector, of course, preached hope and prohesied word, very soon, from a prison camp. Several friends, too, told her perfectly truthful tales, but always about other women, to whom, after months and months of silence, their missing had been miraculously restored. Other people urged her to communicate with infallible Secretaries of organisations who could communicate with benevolent neutrals, who could extract accurate information from the most secretive of Hun prison commandants. Helen did and wrote and signed everything that was suggested or put before her.

Once, on one of Michael's leaves, he had taken her over a munition factory, where she saw the progress of a shell from blank-iron to the all but finished article. It struck her at the time that the wretched thing was never left alone for a single second; and "I'm being manufactured into a bereaved next of kin," she told herself, as she prepared her documents.

In due course, when all the organisations had deeply or sincerely regretted their inability to trace, etc., something gave way within her and all sensation—save of thankfulness for the release—came to an end in blessed passivity. Michael had died and her world had stood still and she had been one with the full shock of that arrest. Now she was standing still and the world was going forward, but it did not concern her— in no way or relation did it touch her. She knew this by the ease with which she could slip Michael's name into talk and incline her head to the proper angle, at the proper murmur of sympathy.

In the blessed realisation of that relief, the Armistice with all its bells broke over her and passed unheeded. At the end of another year she had overcome her physical loathing of the living and returned young, so that she could take them by the hand and almost sincerely wish them well. She had no interest in any aftermath, national or personal, of the war, but, moving at an immense distance, she sat on various relief committees and held strong views—she heard herself delivering them—about the site of the proposed village War Memorial.

Then there came to her, as next of kin, an official intimation, backed by a page of a letter to her in indelible pencil, a silver identity-disc, and a watch, to the effect that the body of Lieutenant Michael Turrell had been found, identified, and re-interred in Hagenzeele Third Military Cemetery—the letter of the row and the grave's number in that row duly given.

So Helen found herself moved on to another process of the manufacture—to a world full of exultant or broken relatives, now strong in the certainty that there was an altar upon earth where they might lay their love. These soon told her, and by means of time-tables made clear, how easy it was and how little it interfered with life's affairs to go and see one's grave.

"*So* different," as the Rector's wife said, "if he'd been killed in Mesopotamia, or even Gallipoli."

The agony of being waked up to some sort of second life drove Helen across the Channel, where, in a new world of abbreviated titles, she learnt that Hagenzeele Third could be comfortably reached by an afternoon train which fitted in with the morning boat, and that there was a comfortable little hotel not three kilometres from Hagenzeele itself, where one could spend quite a comfortable night and see one's grave next morning. All this she had from a Central Authority who lived in a board and tar-paper shed on the skirts of a razed city full of whirling lime-dust and blown papers.

"By the way," said he, "you know your grave, of course?"

"Yes, thank you," said Helen, and showed its row and number typed on Michael's own little typewriter. The officer would have checked it, out of one of his many books; but a large Lancashire woman thrust between them and bade him tell her where she might find her son, who had been corporal in the A.S.C. His proper name, she sobbed, was Anderson, but, coming of respectable folk, he had of course enlisted under the name of Smith; and had been killed at Dickiebush, in early 'Fifteen. She had not his number nor did she know which of his two Christian names he might have used with his alias; but her Cook's tourist ticket expired at the end of Easter week, and if by then she could not find her child she should go mad. Whereupon she fell forward on Helen's breast; but the officer's wife came out quickly from a little bedroom behind the office, and the three of them lifted the woman on to the cot.

"They are often like this," said the officer's wife, loosening the tight bonnetstrings. "Yesterday she said he'd been killed at Hooge. Are you sure you know your grave? It makes such a difference."

"Yes, thank you," said Helen, and hurried out before the woman on the bed should begin to lament again.

Tea in a crowded mauve and blue striped wooden structure, with a false front, carried her still further into the nightmare. She paid her bill beside a stolid, plain-featured Englishwoman, who, hearing her inquire about the train to Hagenzeele, volunteered to come with her.

"I'm going to Hagenzeele myself," she explained. "Not to Hagenzeele Third; mine is Sugar Factory, but they call it La Rosière now. It's just south of Hagenzeele Three. Have you got your room at the hotel there?"

"Oh yes, thank you. I've wired."

"That's better. Sometimes the place is quite full, and at others there's hardly a soul. But they've put bathrooms into the old Lion d'Or—that's the hotel on the west side of Sugar Factory—and it draws off a lot of people, luckily."

"It's all new to me. This is the first time I've been over."

"Indeed! This is my ninth time since the Armistice. Not on my own account. *I* haven't lost any one, thank God—but, like every one else, I've a lot of friends at home who have. Coming over as often as I do, I find it helps them to have some one just look at the—the place and tell them about it afterwards. And one can take photos for them, too. I get quite a list of commissions to execute." She laughed nervously and tapped her slung Kodak. "There are two or three to see at Sugar Factory this time, and plenty of others in the cemeteries all about. My system is to save them up, and arrange them, you know. And when I've got enough commissions for one area to make it worth while, I pop over and execute them. It *does* comfort people."

"I suppose so," Helen answered, shivering as they entered the little train.

"Of course it does. (Isn't it lucky we've got window-seats?) It must do or they wouldn't ask one to do it, would they? I've a list of quite twelve or fifteen commissions here"—she tapped the Kodak again—"I must sort them out tonight. Oh, I forgot to ask you. What's yours?"

"My nephew," said Helen. "But I was very fond of him."

"Ah, yes! I sometimes wonder whether *they* know after death? What do you think?"

"Oh, I don't—I haven't dared to think much about that sort of thing," said Helen, almost lifting her hands to keep her off.

"Perhaps that's better," the woman answered. "The sense of loss must be enough, I expect. Well, I won't worry you any more."

Helen was grateful, but when they reached the hotel Mrs. Scarsworth (they had exchanged names) insisted on dining at the same table with her, and after the meal, in the little, hideous salon full of low-voiced relatives, took Helen through her "commissions" with biographies of the dead, where she happened to know them, and sketches of their next of kin. Helen endured till nearly half-past nine, ere she fled to her room.

Almost at once there was a knock at her door and Mrs. Scarsworth entered; her hands, holding the dreadful list, clasped before her.

"Yes—yes—*I* know," she began. "You're sick of me, but I want to tell you something. You—you aren't married, are you? Then perhaps you won't . . . But it doesn't matter. I've *got* to tell some one. I can't go on any longer like this."

"But please——"Mrs. Scarsworth had backed against the shut door, and her mouth worked dryly.

"In a minute," she said. "You—you know about these graves of mine I was telling you about downstairs, just now? They really *are* commissions. At least several of them are." Her eye wandered round the room. "What extraordinary wall-papers they have in Belgium, don't you think? . . . Yes. I swear they are commissions. But there's *one,* d'you see, and—and he was more to me than anything else in the world. Do you understand?"

Helen nodded.

"More than any one else. And, of course, he oughtn't to have been. He ought to have been nothing to me. But he *was.* He *is.* That's why I do the commissions, you see. That's all."

"But why do you tell me?" Helen asked desperately.

"Because I'm *so* tired of lying. Tired of lying—always lying—year in and year out. When I don't tell lies I've got to act 'em and I've got to think 'em, always. *You* don't know what that means. He was everything to me that he oughtn't to have been—the one real thing—the only thing that ever happened to me in all my life; and I've had to pretend he wasn't. I've had to watch every word I said, and think out what lie I'd tell next, for years and years!"

"How many years?" Helen asked.

"Six years and four months before, and two and three-quarters after. I've gone to him eight times, since. To-morrow'll make the ninth, and—and I can't—I *can't* go to him again with nobody in the world knowing. I want to be honest with some one before I go. Do you understand? It doesn't matter about *me.* I was never truthful, even as a girl. But it isn't worthy of *him.* So—so I—I had to tell you. I can't keep it up any longer. Oh, I can't!"

She lifted her joined hands almost to the level of her mouth, and brought them down sharply, still joined, to full arms' length below her waist. Helen reached forward, caught them, bowed her head over them, and murmured: "Oh, my dear! My dear!" Mrs. Scarsworth stepped back, her face all mottled.

"My God!" said she. "Is *that* how you take it?"

Helen could not speak, and the woman went out; but it was a long while before Helen was able to sleep.

Next morning Mrs. Scarsworth left early on her round of commissions, and Helen walked alone to Hagenzeele Third. The place was still in the making, and stood some five or six feet above the metalled road, which it flanked for hundreds of yards. Culverts across a deep ditch served for entrances through the unfinished boundary wall. She climbed a few wooden-faced earthen steps and then met the entire crowded level of the thing in one held breath. She did not know that Hagenzeele Third counted twenty-one thousand dead already. All she saw was a merciless sea of black crosses, bearing little strips of stamped tin at all angles across their faces. She could distinguish no order or arrangement in their mass; nothing but a waist-high wilderness as of weeds stricken dead, rushing at her. She went forward, moved to the left and the right hopelessly, wondering by what guidance she should ever come to her own. A great distance away there was a line of whiteness. It proved to be a block of some two or three hundred graves whose headstones had already been set, whose flowers were planted out, and whose new-sown grass showed green. Here she could see clear-cut letters at the ends of the rows, and, referring to her slip, realised that it was not here she must look.

A man knelt behind a line of headstones—evidently a gardener, for he was firming a young plant in the soft earth. She went towards him, her paper in her hand. He rose at her approach and without prelude or salutation asked: "Who are you looking for?"

"Lieutenant Michael Turrell—my nephew," said Helen slowly and word for word, as she had many thousands of times in her life.

The man lifted his eyes and looked at her with infinite compassion before he turned from the fresh-sown grass toward the naked black crosses.

"Come with me," he said, "and I will show you where your son lies."

When Helen left the Cemetery she turned for a last look. In the distance she saw the man bending over his young plants; and she went away, supposing him to be the gardener.

STEPHEN CRANE

[*1871–1900*]

The Bride Comes to Yellow Sky

I

The great Pullman was whirling onward with such dignity of motion that a glance from the window seemed simply to prove that the plains of Texas were pouring eastward. Vast flats of green grass, dull-hued space of mesquit and cactus, little groups of frame houses, woods of light and tender trees, all were sweeping into the east, sweeping over the horizon, a precipice.

A newly married pair had boarded this coach at San Antonio. The man's face was reddened from many days in the wind and sun, and a direct result of his new black clothes was that his brick-coloured hands were constantly performing in a most conscious fashion. From time to time he looked down respectfully at his attire. He sat with a hand on each knee, like a man waiting in a barber's shop. The glances he devoted to other passengers were furtive and shy.

The bride was not pretty, nor was she very young. She wore a dress of blue cashmere, with small reservations of velvet here and there, and with steel buttons abounding. She continually twisted her head to regard her puff sleeves, very stiff, straight, and high. They embarrassed her. It was quite apparent that she had cooked, and that she expected to cook, dutifully. The blushes caused by the careless scrutiny of some passengers as she had entered the car were strange to see upon this plain, under-class countenance, which was drawn in placid, almost emotionless lines.

They were evidently very happy. "Ever been in a parlour-car before?" he asked, smiling with delight.

"No," she answered; "I never was. It's fine, ain't it?"

"Great! And then after a while we'll go forward to the diner, and get a big lay-out. Finest meal in the world. Charge a dollar."

"Oh, do they?" cried the bride. "Charge a dollar? Why, that's too much—for us —ain't it, Jack?"

"Not this trip, anyhow," he answered bravely. "We're going to go the whole thing."

Later he explained to her about the trains. "You see, it's a thousand miles from one end of Texas to the other; and this train runs right across it, and never stops but four times." He had the pride of an owner. He pointed out to her the dazzling fittings of the coach; and in truth her eyes opened wider as she contemplated the sea-green figured velvet, the shining brass, silver, and glass, the wood that gleamed as darkly brilliant as the surface of a pool of oil. At one end a bronze figure sturdily held a support for a separated chamber, and at convenient places on the ceiling were frescos in olive and silver.

To the minds of the pair, their surroundings reflected the glory of their marriage that morning in San Antonio; this was the environment of their new estate; and the man's face in particular beamed with an elation that made him appear ridiculous to the negro porter. This individual at times surveyed them from afar with an amused and superior grin. On other occasions he bullied them with skill in ways that did not make it exactly plain to them that they were being bullied. He subtly used all the manners of the most unconquerable kind of snobbery. He oppressed them; but of this oppression they had small knowledge, and they speedily forgot that infrequently a number of travellers covered them with stares of derisive enjoyment. Historically there was supposed to be something infinitely humorous in their situation.

"We are due in Yellow Sky at 3:42," he said, looking tenderly into her eyes.

"Oh, are we?" she said, as if she had not been aware of it. To evince surprise at her husband's statement was part of her wifely amiability. She took from a pocket a little silver watch; and as she held it before her, and stared at it with a frown of attention, the new husband's face shone.

"I bought it in San Anton' from a friend of mine," he told her gleefully.

"It's seventeen minutes past twelve," she said, looking up at him with a kind of shy and clumsy coquetry. A passenger, noting this play, grew excessively sardonic, and winked at himself in one of the numerous mirrors.

At last they went to the dining-car. Two rows of negro waiters, in glowing white suits, surveyed their entrance with the interest, and also the equanimity, of men who had been forewarned. The pair fell to the lot of a waiter who happened to feel pleasure in steering them through their meal. He viewed them with the manner of a fatherly pilot, his countenance radiant with benevolence. The patronage, entwined with the ordinary deference, was not plain to them. And yet, as they returned to their coach, they showed in their faces a sense of escape.

To the left, miles down a long purple slope, was a little ribbon of mist where moved the keening Rio Grande. The train was approaching it at an angle, and the apex was Yellow Sky. Presently it was apparent that, as the distance from Yellow Sky grew shorter, the husband became commensurately restless. His brick-red hands were more insistent in their prominence. Occasionally he was even rather absent-minded and far-away when the bride leaned forward and addressed him.

As a matter of truth, Jack Potter was beginning to find the shadow of a deed weigh upon him like a leaden slab. He, the town marshal of Yellow Sky, a man known, liked, and feared in his corner, a prominent person, had gone to San Antonio to meet a girl he believed he loved, and there, after the usual prayers, had actually induced her to marry him, without consulting Yellow Sky for any part of the transaction. He was now bringing his bride before an innocent and unsuspecting community.

Of course people in Yellow Sky married as it pleased them, in accordance with a general custom; but such was Potter's thought of his duty to his friends, or of their idea of his duty, or of an unspoken form which does not control men in these matters, that he felt he was heinous. He had committed an extraordinary crime. Face to face with this girl in San Antonio, and spurred by his sharp impulse, he had gone headlong over all the social hedges. At San Antonio he was like a man hidden in the dark. A knife to sever any friendly duty, any form, was easy to his hand in that remote city. But the hour of Yellow Sky—the hour of daylight—was approaching.

He knew full well that his marriage was an important thing to his town. It could only be exceeded by the burning of the new hotel. His friends could not forgive him. Frequently he had reflected on the advisability of telling them by telegraph, but a new cowardice had been upon him. He feared to do it. And now the train was hurrying him toward a scene of amazement, glee, and reproach. He glanced out of the window at the line of haze swinging slowly in toward the train.

Yellow Sky had a kind of brass band, which played painfully, to the delight of the populace. He laughed without heart as he thought of it. If the citizens could dream of his prospective arrival with his bride, they would parade the band at the station and escort them, amid cheers and laughing congratulations, to his adobe home.

He resolved that he would use all the devices of speed and plainscraft in making the journey from the station to his house. Once within that safe citadel, he could issue some sort of vocal bulletin, and then not go among the citizens until they had time to wear off a little of their enthusiasm.

The bride looked anxiously at him. "What's worrying you, Jack?"

He laughed again. "I'm not worrying, girl; I'm only thinking of Yellow Sky."

She flushed in comprehension.

A sense of mutual guilt invaded their minds and developed a finer tenderness. They looked at each other with eyes softly aglow. But Potter often laughed the same nervous laugh; the flush upon the bride's face seemed quite permanent.

The traitor to the feelings of Yellow Sky narrowly watched the speeding landscape. "We're nearly there," he said.

Presently the porter came and announced the proximity of Potter's home. He held a brush in his hand, and, with all his airy superiority gone, he brushed Potter's new clothes as the latter slowly turned this way and that way. Potter fumbled out a coin and gave it to the porter, as he had seen others do. It was a heavy and muscle-bound business, as that of a man shoeing his first horse.

The porter took their bag, and as the train began to slow they moved forward to the hooded platform of the car. Presently the two engines and their string of coaches rushed into the station of Yellow Sky.

"They have to take water here," said Potter, from a constricted throat and in mournful cadence, as one announcing death. Before the train stopped his eye had swept the length of the platform, and he was glad and astonished to see there was none upon it but the station-agent, who, with a slightly hurried and anxious air, was walking toward the water-tanks. When the train had halted, the porter alighted first, and placed in position a little temporary step.

"Come on, girl," said Potter, hoarsely. As he helped her down they each laughed on a false note. He took the bag from the negro, and bade his wife cling to his arm. As they slunk rapidly away, his hang-dog glance perceived that they were unloading the two trunks, and also that the station-agent, far ahead near the baggage-car, had turned and was running toward him, making gestures. He laughed, and groaned as he laughed, when he noted the first effect of his marital bliss upon Yellow Sky. He gripped his wife's arm firmly to his side, and they fled. Behind them the porter stood, chuckling fatuously.

2

The California express on the Southern Railway was due at Yellow Sky in twenty-one minutes. There were six men at the bar of the Weary Gentleman saloon. One was a drummer who talked a great deal and rapidly; three were Texans who did not care to talk at that time; and two were Mexican sheepherders, who did not talk as a general practice in the Weary Gentleman saloon. The barkeeper's dog lay on the board walk that crossed in front of the door. His head was on his paws, and he glanced drowsily here and there with the constant vigilance of a dog that is kicked on occasion. Across the sandy street were some vivid green grass-plots, so wonderful in appearance, amid the sands that burned near them in a blazing sun, that they caused a doubt in the mind. They exactly resembled the grass mats used to represent lawns on the stage. At the cooler end of the railway station, a man without a coat sat in a tilted chair and smoked his pipe. The fresh-cut bank of the Rio Grande circled near the town, and there could be seen beyond it a great plum-coloured plain of mesquit.

Save for the busy drummer and his companions in the saloon, Yellow Sky was dozing. The new-comer leaned gracefully upon the bar, and recited many tales with the confidence of a bard who has come upon a new field.

"—and at the moment that the old man fell downstairs with the bureau in his arms, the old woman was coming up with two scuttles of coal, and of course—"

The drummer's tale was interrupted by a young man who suddenly appeared in the open door. He cried: "Scratchy Wilson's drunk, and has turned loose with both hands." The two Mexicans at once set down their glasses and faded out of the rear entrance of the saloon.

The drummer, innocent and jocular, answered: "All right, old man. S'pose he has? Come in and have a drink, anyhow."

But the information had made such an obvious cleft in every skull in the room that the drummer was obliged to see its importance. All had become instantly solemn. "Say," said he, mystified, "what is this?" His three companions made the introductory gesture of eloquent speech; but the young man at the door forestalled them.

"It means, my friend," he answered, as he came into the saloon, "that for the next two hours this town won't be a health resort."

The barkeeper went to the door, and locked and barred it; reaching out of the window, he pulled in heavy wooden shutters, and barred them. Immediately a solemn chapel-like gloom was upon the place. The drummer was looking from one to another.

"But say," he cried, "what is this, anyhow? You don't mean there is going to be a gun-fight?"

"Don't know whether there'll be a fight or not," answered one man, grimly; "but there'll be some shootin'—some good shootin'."

The young man who had warned them waved his hand. "Oh, there'll be a fight fast enough, if any one wants it. Anybody can get a fight out there in the street. There's a fight just waiting."

The drummer seemed to be swayed between the interest of a foreigner and a perception of personal danger.

"What did you say his name was?" he asked.

"Scratchy Wilson," they answered in chorus.

"And will he kill anybody? What are you going to do? Does this happen often? Does he rampage around like this once a week or so? Can he break in that door?"

"No; he can't break down that door," replied the barkeeper. "He's tried it three times. But when he comes you'd better lay down on the floor, stranger. He's dead sure to shoot at it, and a bullet may come through."

Thereafter the drummer kept a strict eye upon the door. The time had not yet been called for him to hug the floor, but, as a minor precaution, he sidled near to the wall. "Will he kill anybody?" he said again.

The men laughed low and scornfully at the question.

"He's out to shoot, and he's out for trouble. Don't see any good in experimentin' with him."

"But what do you do in a case like this? What do you do?"

A man responded: "Why, he and Jack Potter—"

"But," in chorus the other men interrupted, "Jack Potter's in San Anton'."

"Well, who is he? What's he got to do with it?"

"Oh, he's the town marshal. He goes out and fights Scratchy when he gets on one of these tears."

"Wow!" said the drummer, mopping his brow. "Nice job he's got."

The voices had toned away to mere whisperings. The drummer wished to ask further questions, which were born of an increasing anxiety and bewilderment; but when he attempted them, the men merely looked at him in irritation and motioned him to remain silent. A tense waiting hush was upon them. In the deep shadows of the room their eyes shone as they listened for sounds from the street. One man made three gestures at the barkeeper; and the latter, moving like a ghost, handed him a glass and a bottle. The man poured a full glass of whisky, and set down the bottle noiselessly. He gulped the whisky in a swallow, and turned again toward the door in immovable silence. The drummer saw that the barkeeper, without a sound, had taken a Winchester from beneath the bar. Later he saw this individual beckoning to him, so he tiptoed across the room.

"You better come with me back of the bar."

"No, thanks," said the drummer, perspiring; "I'd rather be where I can make a break for the back door."

Whereupon the man of bottles made a kindly but peremptory gesture. The drummer obeyed it, and, finding himself seated on a box with his head below the level of the bar, balm was laid upon his soul at sight of various zinc and copper fittings that bore a resemblance to armour-plate. The barkeeper took a seat comfortably upon an adjacent box.

"You see," he whispered, "this here Scratchy Wilson is a wonder with a gun—a perfect wonder; and when he goes on the war-trail, we hunt our holes—naturally. He's about the last one of the old gang that used to hang out along the river here. He's a terror when he's drunk. When he's sober he's all right—kind of simple—wouldn't hurt a fly—nicest fellow in town. But when he's drunk—whoo!"

There were periods of stillness. "I wish Jack Potter was back from San Anton'," said the barkeeper. "He shot Wilson up once—in the leg—and he would sail in and pull out the kinks in this thing."

Presently they heard from a distance the sound of a shot, followed by three wild yowls. It instantly removed a bond from the men in the darkened saloon. There was a shuffling of feet. They looked at each other. "Here he comes," they said.

3

A man in a maroon-coloured flannel shirt, which had been purchased for purposes of decoration, and made principally by some Jewish women on the East Side of New York, rounded a corner and walked into the middle of the main street of Yellow Sky. In either hand the man held a long, heavy, blue-black revolver. Often he yelled, and these cries rang through a semblance of a deserted village, shrilly flying over the roofs in a volume that seemed to have no relation to the ordinary vocal strength of a man. It was as if the surrounding stillness formed the arch of a tomb over him. These cries of ferocious challenge rang against walls of silence. And his boots had red tops with gilded imprints, of the kind beloved in winter by little sledding boys on the hillsides of New England.

The man's face flamed in a rage begot of whisky. His eyes, rolling, and yet keen for ambush, hunted the still doorways and windows. He walked with the creeping movement of the midnight cat. As it occurred to him, he roared menacing information. The long revolvers in his hands were as easy as straws; they were moved with an electric swiftness. The little fingers of each hand played sometimes in a musician's way. Plain from the low collar of the shirt, the cords of his neck straightened and sank, straightened and sank, as passion moved him. The only sounds were his terrible invitations. The calm adobes preserved their demeanor at the passing of this small thing in the middle of the street.

There was no offer of fight—no offer of fight. The man called to the sky. There were no attractions. He bellowed and fumed and swayed his revolvers here and everywhere.

The dog of the barkeeper of the Weary Gentleman saloon had not appreciated the advance of events. He yet lay dozing in front of his master's door. At sight of the dog, the man paused and raised his revolver humorously. At sight of the man, the dog sprang up and walked diagonally away, with a sullen head, and growling. The man yelled, and the dog broke into a gallop. As it was about to enter an alley, there was a loud noise, a whistling, and something spat the ground directly before it. The dog screamed, and, wheeling in terror, galloped headlong in a new direction. Again there was a noise, a whistling, and sand was kicked viciously before it. Fear-stricken, the dog turned and flurried like an animal in a pen. The man stood laughing, his weapons at his hips.

Ultimately the man was attracted by the closed door of the Weary Gentleman saloon. He went to it and, hammering with a revolver, demanded drink.

The door remaining imperturbable, he picked a bit of paper from the walk, and nailed it to the framework with a knife. He then turned his back contemptuously upon this popular resort and, walking to the opposite side of the street and spinning there on his heel quickly and lithely, fired at the bit of paper. He missed it by a half-inch. He swore at himself, and went away. Later he comfortably fusilladed the windows of his most intimate friend. The man was playing with this town; it was a toy for him.

But still there was no offer of fight. The name of Jack Potter, his ancient antagonist, entered his mind, and he concluded that it would be a glad thing if he should go to Potter's house and by bombardment induce him to come out and fight. He moved in the direction of his desire, chanting Apache scalp-music.

When he arrived at it, Potter's house presented the same still front as had the other adobes. Taking up a strategic position, the man howled a challenge. But this house regarded him as might a great stone god. It gave no sign. After a decent wait, the man howled further challenges, mingling with them wonderful epithets.

Presently there came the spectacle of a man churning himself into deepest rage over the immobility of a house. He fumed at it as the winter wind attacks a prairie cabin in the North. To the distance there should have gone the sound of a tumult like the fighting of two hundred Mexicans. As necessity bade him, he paused for breath or to reload his revolvers.

4

Potter and his bride walked sheepishly and with speed. Sometimes they laughed together shamefacedly and low.

"Next corner, dear," he said finally.

They put forth the efforts of a pair walking bowed against a strong wind. Potter was about to raise a finger to point the first appearance of the new home when, as they circled the corner, they came face to face with a man in a maroon-coloured shirt, who was feverishly pushing cartridges into a large revolver. Upon the instant the man dropped his revolver to the ground and, like lightning, whipped another from its holster. The second weapon was aimed at the bridegroom's chest.

There was a silence. Potter's mouth seemed to be merely a grave for his tongue. He exhibited an instinct to at once loosen his arm from the woman's grip, and he dropped the bag to the sand. As for the bride, her face had gone as yellow as old cloth. She was a slave to hideous rites, gazing at the apparitional snake.

The two men faced each other at a distance of three paces. He of the revolver smiled with a new and quiet ferocity.

"Tried to sneak up on me," he said. "Tried to sneak up on me!" His eyes grew more baleful. As Potter made a slight movement, the man thrust his revolver venomously forward. "No; don't you do it, Jack Potter. Don't you move a finger toward a gun just yet. Don't you move an eyelash. The time has come for me to settle with you, and I'm goin' to do it my own way, and loaf along with no interferin'. So if you don't want a gun bent on you, just mind what I tell you."

Potter looked at his enemy. "I ain't got a gun on me, Scratchy," he said. "Honest, I ain't." He was stiffening and steadying, but yet somewhere at the back of his mind a vision of the Pullman floated: the sea-green figured velvet, the shining brass, silver, and glass, the wood that gleamed as darkly brilliant as the surface of a pool of oil— all the glory of the marriage, the environment of the new estate. "You know I fight when it comes to fighting, Scratchy Wilson; but I ain't got a gun on me. You'll have to do all the shootin' yourself."

His enemy's face went livid. He stepped forward, and lashed his weapon to and fro before Potter's chest. "Don't you tell me you ain't got no gun on you, you whelp. Don't tell me no lie like that. There ain't a man in Texas ever seen you without no gun. Don't take me for no kid." His eyes blazed with light, and his throat worked like a pump.

"I ain't takin' you for no kid," answered Potter. His heels had not moved an inch backward. "I'm takin' you for a damn fool. I tell you I ain't got a gun, and I ain't. If you're goin' to shoot me up, you better begin now; you'll never get a chance like this again."

So much enforced reasoning had told on Wilson's rage; he was calmer. "If you ain't got a gun, why ain't you got a gun?" he sneered. "Been to Sunday-school?"

"I ain't got a gun because I've just come from San Anton' with my wife. I'm married," said Potter. "And if I'd thought there was going to be any galoots like you prowling around when I brought my wife home, I'd had a gun, and don't you forget it."

"Married!" said Scratchy, not at all comprehending.

"Yes, married. I'm married," said Potter, distinctly.

"Married?" said Scratchy. Seemingly for the first time, he saw the drooping, drowning woman at the other man's side. "No!" he said. He was like a creature allowed a glimpse of another world. He moved a pace backward, and his arm, with the revolver, dropped to his side. "Is this the lady?" he asked.

"Yes; this is the lady," answered Potter.

There was another period of silence.

"Well," said Wilson at last, slowly, "I s'pose it's all off now."

"It's all off if you say so, Scratchy. You know I didn't make the trouble." Potter lifted his valise.

"Well, I 'low it's off, Jack," said Wilson. He was looking at the ground. "Married!" He was not a student of chivalry; it was merely that in the presence of this foreign condition he was a simple child of the earlier plains. He picked up his starboard revolver, and, placing both weapons in their holsters, he went away. His feet made funnel-shaped tracks in the heavy sand.

JAMES JOYCE

[*1882–1941*]

The Boarding House

Mrs. Mooney was a butcher's daughter. She was a woman who was quite able to keep things to herself: a determined woman. She had married her father's foreman and opened a butcher's shop near Spring Gardens. But as soon as his father-in-law was dead Mr. Mooney began to go to the devil. He drank, plundered the till, ran headlong into debt. It was no use making him take the pledge: he was sure to break out again a few days after. By fighting his wife in the presence of customers and by buying bad meat he ruined his business. One night he went for his wife with the cleaver and she had to sleep in a neighbour's house.

After that they lived apart. She went to the priest and got a separation from him with care of the children. She would give him neither money nor food nor house-room; and so he was obliged to enlist himself as a sheriff's man. He was a shabby stooped little drunkard with a white face and a white moustache and white eyebrows, pencilled above his little eyes, which were pink-veined and raw; and all day long he sat in the bailiff's room, waiting to be put on a job. Mrs. Mooney, who had taken what remained of her money out of the butcher business and set up a boarding house in Hardwicke Street, was a big imposing woman. Her house had a floating population made up of tourists from Liverpool and the Isle of Man and, occasionally, *artistes* from the music halls. Its resident population was made up of clerks from the city. She governed her house cunningly and firmly, knew when to give credit, when to be stern and when to let things pass. All the resident young men spoke of her as *The Madam*.

Mrs. Mooney's young men paid fifteen shillings a week for board and lodgings (beer or stout at dinner excluded). They shared in common tastes and occupations and for this reason they were very chummy with one another. They discussed with one another the chances of favourites and outsiders. Jack Mooney, the Madam's son, who was clerk to a commission agent in Fleet Street, had the reputation of being a hard case. He was fond of using soldiers' obscenities: usually he came home in the small hours. When he met his friends he had always a good one to tell them and he was always sure to be on to a good thing—that is to say, a likely horse or a likely *artiste*. He was also handy with the mitts and sang comic songs. On Sunday nights there would often be a reunion in Mrs. Mooney's front drawing room. The music-hall *artistes* would oblige; and

Sheridan played waltzes and polkas and vamped accompaniments. Polly Mooney, the Madam's daughter, would also sing. She sang:

> *I'm a . . . naughty girl.*
> *You needn't sham:*
> *You know I am.*

Polly was a slim girl of nineteen, she had light soft hair and a small full mouth. Her eyes, which were grey with a shade of green through them, had a habit of glancing upwards when she spoke with anyone, which made her look like a little perverse madonna. Mrs. Mooney had first sent her daughter to be a typist in a corn-factor's office but, as a disreputable sheriff's man used to come every other day to the office, asking to be allowed to say a word to his daughter, she had taken her daughter home again and set her to do housework. As Polly was very lively the intention was to give her the run of the young men. Besides, young men like to feel that there is a young woman not very far away. Polly, of course, flirted with the young men but Mrs. Mooney, who was a shrewd judge, knew that the young men were only passing the time away: none of them meant business. Things went on so for a long time and Mrs. Mooney began to think of sending Polly back to typewriting when she noticed that something was going on between Polly and one of the young men. She watched the pair and kept her own counsel.

Polly knew that she was being watched, but still her mother's persistent silence could not be misunderstood. There had been no open complicity between mother and daughter, no open understanding but, though people in the house began to talk of the affair, still Mrs. Mooney did not intervene. Polly began to grow a little strange in her manner and the young man was evidently perturbed. At last, when she judged it to be the right moment, Mrs. Mooney intervened. She dealt with moral problems as a cleaver deals with meat: and in this case she had made up her mind.

It was a bright Sunday morning of early summer, promising heat, but with a fresh breeze blowing. All the windows of the boarding house were open and the lace curtains ballooned gently towards the street beneath the raised sashes. The belfry of George's Church sent out constant peals and worshippers, singly or in groups, traversed the little circus before the church, revealing their purpose by their self-contained demeanor no less than by the little volumes in their gloved hands. Breakfast was over in the boarding house and the table of the breakfast-room was covered with plates on which lay yellow streaks of eggs with morsels of bacon-fat and bacon-rind. Mrs. Mooney sat in the straw arm-chair and watched the servant Mary remove the breakfast things. She made Mary collect the crusts and pieces of broken bread to help to make Tuesday's bread-pudding. When the table was cleared, the broken bread collected, the sugar and butter safe under lock and key, she began to reconstruct the interview which she had had the night before with Polly. Things were as she had suspected: she had been frank in her questions and Polly had been frank in her answers. Both had been somewhat awkward, of course. She had been made awkward by her not wishing to receive the news in too cavalier a fashion or to seem to have connived and Polly had been made awkward not merely because allusions of that kind always made her awkward but also because she did not wish it to be thought that in her wise innocence she had divined the intention behind her mother's tolerance.

Mrs. Mooney glanced instinctively at the little gilt clock on the mantelpiece as soon as she had become aware through her revery that the bells of George's Church had stopped ringing. It was seventeen minutes past eleven: she would have lots of time to have the matter out with Mr. Doran and then catch short twelve at Marlborough Street. She was sure she would win. To begin with she had all the weight of social opinion on her side: she was an outraged mother. She had allowed him to live beneath her roof, assuming that he was a man of honour, and he had simply abused her hospitality. He was thirty-four or thirty-five years of age, so that youth could not be pleaded as his excuse; nor could ignorance be his excuse since he was a man who had seen something of the world. He had simply taken advantage of Polly's youth and inexperience: that was evident. The question was: What reparation would he make?

There must be reparation made in such cases. It is all very well for the man: he can go his ways as if nothing had happened, having had his moment of pleasure, but the girl has to bear the brunt. Some mothers would be content to patch up such an affair for a sum of money; she had known cases of it. But she would not do so. For her only one reparation could make up for the loss of her daughter's honour: marriage.

She counted all her cards again before sending Mary up to Mr. Doran's room to say that she wished to speak with him. She felt sure she would win. He was a serious young man, not rakish or loud-voiced like the others. If it had been Mr. Sheridan or Mr. Meade or Bantam Lyons her task would have been much harder. She did not think he would face publicity. All the lodgers in the house knew something of the affair; details had been invented by some. Besides, he had been employed for thirteen years in a great Catholic wine-merchant's office and publicity would mean for him, perhaps, the loss of his sit. Whereas if he agreed all might be well. She knew he had a good screw for one thing and she suspected he had a bit of stuff put by.

Nearly the half-hour! She stood up and surveyed herself in the pierglass. The decisive expression of her great florid face satisfied her and she thought of some mothers she knew who could not get their daughters off their hands.

Mr. Doran was very anxious indeed this Sunday morning. He had made two attempts to shave but his hand had been so unsteady that he had been obliged to desist. Three days' reddish beard fringed his jaws and every two or three minutes a mist gathered on his glasses so that he had to take them off and polish them with his pocket-handkerchief. The recollection of his confession of the night before was a cause of acute pain to him; the priest had drawn out every ridiculous detail of the affair and in the end had so magnified his sin that he was almost thankful at being afforded a loophole of reparation. The harm was done. What could he do now but marry her or run away? He could not brazen it out. The affair would be sure to be talked of and his employer would be certain to hear of it. Dublin is such a small city: everyone knows everyone else's business. He felt his heart leap warmly in his throat as he heard in his excited imagination old Mr. Leonard calling out in his rasping voice: *Send Mr Doran here, please.*

All his long years of service gone for nothing! All his industry and diligence thrown away! As a young man he had sown his wild oats, of course; he had boasted of his free-thinking and denied the existence of God to his companions in public-houses. But that was all passed and done with . . . nearly. He still bought a copy of *Reynold's Newspaper* every week but he attended to his religious duties and for nine-tenths of the year lived a regular life. He had money enough to settle down on; it was not that. But the family would look down on her. First of all there was her disreputable father and then her mother's boarding house was beginning to get a certain fame. He had a notion that he was being had. He could imagine his friends talking of the affair and laughing. She *was* a little vulgar; sometimes she said *I seen* and *If I had've known.* But what would grammar matter if he really loved her? He could not make up his mind whether to like her or despise her for what she had done. Of course, he had done it too. His instinct urged him to remain free, not to marry. Once you are married you are done for, it said.

While he was sitting helplessly on the side of the bed in shirt and trousers she tapped lightly at his door and entered. She told him all, that she had made a clean breast of it to her mother and that her mother would speak with him that morning. She cried and threw her arms round his neck, saying:

—O, Bob! Bob! What am I to do! What am I to do at all?

She would put an end to herself, she said.

He comforted her feebly, telling her not to cry, that it would be all right, never fear. He felt against his shirt the agitation of her bosom.

It was not altogether his fault that it had happened. He remembered well, with the curious patient memory of the celibate, the first casual caresses her dress, her breath, her fingers had given him. Then late one night as he was undressing for bed she had tapped at his door, timidly. She wanted to relight her candle at his for hers had been blown out by a gust. It was her bath night. She wore a loose open combing-jacket of printed flannel. Her white instep shone in the opening of her furry slippers and the blood glowed warmly behind her perfumed skin. From her hands and wrists too as she lit and steadied her candle a faint perfume arose.

On nights when he came in very late it was she who warmed up his dinner. He scarcely knew what he was eating, feeling her beside him alone, at night, in the sleeping house. And her thoughtfulness! If the night was anyway cold or wet or windy there was sure to be a little tumbler of punch ready for him. Perhaps they could be happy together. . . .

They used to go upstairs together on tiptoe, each with a candle, and on the third landing exchange reluctant good-nights. They used to kiss. He remembered well her eyes, the touch of her hand and his delirium. . . .

But delirium passes. He echoed her phrase, applying it to himself: *What am I to do?* The instinct of the celibate warned him to hold back. But the sin was there; even his sense of honour told him that reparation must be made for such a sin.

While he was sitting with her on the side of the bed Mary came to the door and said that the missus wanted to see him in the parlour. He stood up to put on his coat and waistcoat, more helpless than ever. When he was dressed he went over to her to comfort her. It would be all right, never fear. He left her crying on the bed and moaning softly: *O my God!*

Going down the stairs his glasses became so dimmed with moisture that he had to take them off and polish them. He longed to ascend through the roof and fly away to another country where he would never hear again of his trouble, and yet a force pushed him downstairs step by step. The implacable faces of his employer and of the Madam stared upon his discomfiture. On the last flight of stairs he passed Jack Mooney who was coming up from the pantry nursing two bottles of *Bass.* They saluted coldly; and the lover's eyes rested for a second or two on a thick bulldog face and a pair of thick short arms. When he reached the foot of the staircase he glanced up and saw Jack regarding him from the door of the return room.

Suddenly he remembered the night when one of the music-hall *artistes,* a little blond Londoner, had made a rather free allusion to Polly. The reunion had been almost broken up on account of Jack's violence. Everyone tried to quiet him. The music-hall *artiste,* a little paler than usual, kept smiling and saying that there was no harm meant: but Jack kept shouting at him that if any fellow tried that sort of a game on with *his* sister he'd bloody well put his teeth down his throat, so he would.

Polly sat for a little time on the side of the bed, crying. Then she dried her eyes and went over to the looking-glass. She dipped the end of the towel in the water-jug and refreshed her eyes with the cool water. She looked at herself in profile and readjusted a hairpin above her ear. Then she went back to the bed again and sat at the foot. She regarded the pillows for a long time and the sight of them awakened in her mind secret amiable memories. She rested the nape of her neck against the cool iron bed-rail and fell into a revery. There was no longer any perturbation visible on her face.

She waited on patiently, almost cheerfully, without alarm, her memories gradually giving place to hopes and visions of the future. Her hopes and visions were so intricate that she no longer saw the white pillows on which her gaze was fixed or remembered that she was waiting for anything.

At last she heard her mother calling. She started to her feet and ran to the banisters.

—Polly! Polly!

—Yes, mamma?

Come down, dear. Mr. Doran wants to speak to you. Then she remembered what she had been waiting for.

FRANZ KAFKA

[*1883–1924*]

A Hunger Artist

TRANSLATED BY WILLA AND EDWIN MUIR

During these last decades the interest in professional fasting has markedly diminished. It used to pay very well to stage such great performances under one's own management, but today that is quite impossible. We live in a different world now. At one time the whole town took a lively interest in the hunger artist; from day to day of his fast the excitement mounted; everybody wanted to see him at least once a day; there were people who bought season tickets for the last few days and sat from morning till night in front of his small barred cage; even in the nighttime there were visiting hours, when the whole effect was heightened by torch flares; on fine days the cage was set out in the open air, and then it was the children's special treat to see the hunger artist; for their elders he was often just a joke that happened to be in fashion, but the children stood openmouthed, holding each other's hands for greater security, marveling at him as he sat there pallid in black tights, with his ribs sticking out so prominently, not even on a seat but down among straw on the ground, sometimes giving a courteous nod, answering questions with a constrained smile, or perhaps stretching an arm through the bars so that one might feel how thin it was, and then again withdrawing deep into himself, paying no attention to anyone or anything, not even to the all-important striking of the clock that was the only piece of furniture in his cage, but merely staring into vacancy with half-shut eyes, now and then taking a sip from a tiny glass of water to moisten his lips.

Besides casual onlookers there were also relays of permanent watchers selected by the public, usually butchers, strangely enough, and it was their task to watch the hunger artist day and night, three of them at a time, in case he should have some secret recourse to nourishment. This was nothing but a formality, instituted to reassure the masses, for the initiates knew well enough that during his fast the artist would never in any circumstances, not even under forcible compulsion, swallow the smallest morsel of food; the honor of his profession forbade it. Not every watcher, of course, was capable of understanding this, there were often groups of night watchers who were very lax in carrying out their duties and deliberately huddled together in a retired corner to play cards with great absorption, obviously intending to give the hunger artist the chance of a little refreshment, which they supposed he could draw from some private hoard. Nothing annoyed the artist more than such watchers; they made him miserable; they made his fast seem unendurable; sometimes he mastered his feebleness sufficiently to sing during their watch for as long as he could keep going, to show them how unjust their suspicions were. But that was of little use; they only wondered at his cleverness in being able to fill his mouth even while singing. Much more to his taste were the watchers who sat close up to the bars, who were not content with the dim night lighting of the hall but focused him in the full glare of the electric pocket torch given them by the impresario. The harsh light did not trouble him at all, in any case he could never sleep properly, and he could always drowse a little, whatever the light, at any hour, even when the hall was thronged with noisy onlookers. He was quite happy at the prospect of spending a sleepless night with such watchers; he was ready to exchange jokes with them, to tell them stories out of his nomadic life, anything at all to keep them awake and demonstrate to them again that he had no eatables in his cage and that he was fasting as not one of them could fast. But his happiest moment was when the morning came and an enormous breakfast was brought them, at his expense, on which they flung themselves with the keen appetite of healthy men after a weary night of wakefulness. Of course there were people who argued that this breakfast was an unfair attempt to bribe the watchers, but that was going rather too far, and when they were invited to take on a night's vigil without a breakfast, merely for the sake of the cause, they made themselves scarce, although they stuck stubbornly to their suspicions.

Such suspicions, anyhow, were a necessary accompaniment to the profession of fasting. No one could possibly watch the hunger artist continuously, day and night, and so no one could produce first-hand evidence that the fast had really been rigorous and continuous; only the artist himself could know that, he was therefore bound to be the sole completely satisfied spectator of his own fast. Yet for other reasons he was never satisfied; it was not perhaps mere fasting that had brought him to such skeleton thinness that many people had regretfully to keep away from his exhibitions, because the sight of him was too much for them, perhaps it was dissatisfaction with himself that had worn him down. For he alone knew, what no other initiate knew, how easy it was to fast. It was the easiest thing in the world. He made no secret of this, yet people did not believe him, at the best they set him down as modest, most of them, however, thought he was out for publicity or else was some kind of cheat who found it easy to fast because he had discovered a way of making it easy, and then had the impudence to admit the fact, more or less. He had to put up with all that, and in the course of time had got used to it, but his inner dissatisfaction always rankled, and never yet, after any term of fasting—this must be granted to his credit—had he left the cage of his own free will. The longest period of fasting was fixed by his impresario at forty days, beyond that term he was not allowed to go, not even in great cities, and there was good reason for it, too. Experience had proved that for about forty days the interest of the public could be stimulated by a steadily increasing pressure of advertisement, but after that the town began to lose interest, sympathetic support began notably to fall off; there were of course local variations as between one town and another or one country and another, but as a general rule forty days marked the limit. So on the fortieth day the flower-bedecked cage was opened, enthusiastic spectators filled the hall, a military band played, two doctors entered the cage to measure the results of the fast, which were announced through a megaphone, and finally two young ladies appeared, blissful at having been selected for the honor, to help the hunger artist down the few steps leading to a small table on which was spread a carefully chosen invalid repast. And at this very moment the artist always turned stubborn. True, he would entrust his bony arms to the outstretched helping hands of the ladies bending over him, but stand up he would not. Why stop fasting at this particular moment, after forty days of it? He had held out for a long time, an illimitably long time, why stop now, when he was in his best fasting form, or rather, not yet quite in his best fasting form? Why should he be cheated of the fame he would get for fasting longer, for being not only the record hunger artist of all time, which presumably he was already, but for beating his own record by a performance beyond human imagination, since he felt that there were no limits to his capacity for fasting? His public pretended to admire him so much, why should it have so little patience with him; if he could endure fasting longer, why shouldn't the public endure it? Besides, he was tired, he was comfortable sitting in the straw, and now he was supposed to lift himself to his full height and go down to a meal the very thought of which gave him a nausea that only the presence of the ladies kept him from betraying, and even that with an effort. And he looked up into the eyes of the ladies who were apparently so friendly and in reality so cruel, and shook his head, which felt too heavy on its strengthless neck. But then there happened yet again what always happened. The impresario came forward, without a word—for the band made speech impossible— lifted his arms in the air above the artist, as if inviting Heaven to look down upon its creature here in the straw, this suffering martyr, which indeed he was, although in quite another sense; grasped him around the emaciated waist, with exaggerated caution, so that the frail condition he was in might be appreciated; and committed him to the care of the blenching ladies, not without secretly giving him a shaking so that his legs and body tottered and swayed. The artist now submitted completely; his head lolled on his breast as if it had landed there by chance; his body was hollowed out; his legs in a spasm of self-preservation clung close to each other at the knees, yet scraped on the ground as if it were not really solid ground, as if they were only trying to find solid ground; and the whole weight of his body, a featherweight after all, relapsed onto one of the ladies, who, looking around for help and panting a little—this post of honor was not at all what she had expected it to be—first stretched her neck as far as she could to keep her face at least free from contact with the artist, then finding this impossible, and her more fortunate companion not coming to her aid but merely holding extended in her own trembling hand the little bunch of knucklebones that was the artist's, to the great delight of the spectators burst into tears and had to be replaced by an attendant who had long been stationed in readiness. Then came the food, a little of which the impresario managed to get between the artist's lips, while he sat in a kind of half-fainting trance, to the accompaniment of cheerful patter designed to distract the public's attention from the artist's condition; after that, a toast was drunk to the public, supposedly prompted by a whisper from the artist in the impresario's ear; the band confirmed it with a mighty flourish, the spectators melted away, and no one had any cause to be dissatisfied with the proceedings, no one except the hunger artist himself, he only, as always.

So he lived for many years, with small regular intervals of recuperation, in visible glory, honored by the world, yet in spite of that troubled in spirit, and all the more troubled because no one would take his trouble seriously. What comfort could he possibly need? What more could he possibly wish for? And if some good-natured person, feeling sorry for him, tried to console him by pointing out that his melancholy was probably caused by fasting, it could happen, especially when he had been fasting for some time, that he reacted with an outburst of fury and to the general alarm began to shake the bars of his cage like a wild animal. Yet the impresario had a way of punishing these outbreaks which he rather enjoyed putting into operation. He would apologize publicly for the artist's behavior, which was only to be excused, he admitted, because of the irritability caused by fasting; a condition hardly to be understood by well-fed people; then by natural transition he went on to mention the artist's equally incomprehensible boast that he could fast for much longer than he was doing; he praised the high ambition, the good will, the great self-denial undoubtedly implicit in such a statement; and then quite simply countered it by bringing out photographs, which were also on sale to the public, showing the artist on the fortieth day of a fast lying in bed almost dead from exhaustion. This perversion of the truth, familiar to the artist though it was, always unnerved him afresh and proved too much for him. What was a consequence of the premature ending of his fast was here presented as the cause of it! To fight against this lack of understanding, against a whole world of nonunderstanding, was impossible. Time and again in good faith he stood by the bars listening to the impresario, but as soon as the photographs appeared he always let go and sank with a groan back onto his straw, and the reassured public could once more come close and gaze at him.

A few years later when the witnesses of such scenes called them to mind, they often failed to understand themselves at all. For meanwhile the aforementioned change in public interest had set in; it seemed to happen almost overnight; there may have been profound causes for it, but who was going to bother about that; at any rate the pampered hunger artist suddenly found himself deserted one fine day by the amusement-seekers, who went streaming past him to other more-favored attractions. For the last time the impresario hurried him over half Europe to discover whether the old interest might still survive here and there; all in vain; everywhere, as if by secret agreement, a positive revulsion from professional fasting was in evidence. Of course it could not really have sprung up so suddenly as all that, and many premonitory symptoms which had not been sufficiently remarked or suppressed during the rush and glitter of success now came retrospectively to mind, but it was now too late to take any countermeasures. Fasting would surely come into fashion again at some future date, yet that was no comfort for those living in the present. What, then, was the hunger artist to do? He had been applauded by thousands in his time and could hardly come down to showing himself in a street booth at village fairs, and as for adopting another profession, he was not only too old for that but too fanatically devoted to fasting. So he took leave of the impresario, his partner in an unparalleled career, and hired himself to a large circus; in order to spare his own feelings he avoided reading the conditions of his contract.

A large circus with its enormous traffic in replacing and recruiting men, animals, and apparatus can always find a use for people at any time, even for a hunger artist, provided of course that he does not ask too much, and in this particular case anyhow it was not only the artist who was taken on but his famous and long-known name as well, indeed considering the peculiar nature of his performance, which was not impaired by advancing age, it could not be objected that here was an artist past his prime, no longer at the height of his professional skill, seeking a refuge in some quiet corner of a circus; on the contrary, the hunger artist averred that he could fast as well as ever, which was entirely credible, he even alleged that if he were allowed to fast as he liked, and this was at once promised him without more ado, he could astound the world by establishing a record never yet achieved, a statement that certainly provoked a smile among the other professionals, since it left out of account the change in public opinion, which the hunger artist in his zeal conveniently forgot.

He had not, however, actually lost his sense of the real situation and took it as a matter of course that he and his cage should be stationed, not in the middle of the ring as a main attraction, but outside, near the animal cages, on a site that was after all easily accessible. Large and gaily painted placards made a frame for the cage and announced what was to be seen inside it. When the public came thronging out in the intervals to see the animals, they could hardly avoid passing the hunger artist's cage and stopping there for a moment, perhaps they might even have stayed longer had not those pressing behind them in the narrow gangway, who did not understand why they should be held up on their way toward the excitements of the menagerie, made it impossible for anyone to stand gazing quietly for any length of time. And that was the reason why the hunger artist, who had of course been looking forward to these visiting hours as the main achievement of his life, began instead to shrink from them. At first he could hardly wait for the intervals; it was exhilarating to watch the crowds come streaming his way, until only too soon—not even the most obstinate self-deception, clung to almost consciously, could hold out against the fact—the conviction was borne in upon him that these people, most of them, to judge from their actions, again and again, without exception, were all on their way to the menagerie. And the first sight of them from the distance remained the best. For when they reached his cage he was at once deafened by the storm of shouting and abuse that arose from the two contending factions, which renewed themselves continuously, of those who wanted to stop and stare at him—he soon began to dislike them more than the others—not out of real interest but only out of obstinate self-assertiveness, and those who wanted to go straight on to the animals. When the first great rush was past, the stragglers came along, and these, whom nothing could have prevented from stopping to look at him as long as they had breath, raced past with long strides, hardly even glancing at him, in their haste to get to the menagerie in time. And all too rarely did it happen that he had a stroke of luck, when some father of a family fetched up before him with his children, pointed a finger at the hunger artist, and explained at length what the phenomenon meant, telling stories of earlier years when he himself had watched similar but much more thrilling performances, and the children, still rather uncomprehending, since neither inside nor outside school had they been sufficiently prepared for this lesson—what did they care about fasting?—yet showed by the brightness of their intent eyes that new and better times might be coming. Perhaps, said the hunger artist to himself many a time, things would be a little better if his cage were set not quite so near the menagerie. That made it too easy for people to make their choice, to say nothing of what he suffered from the stench of the menagerie, the animals' restlessness by night, the carrying past of raw lumps of flesh for the beasts of prey, the roaring at feeding times, which depressed him continually. But he did not dare to lodge a complaint with the management; after all, he had the animals to thank for the troops of people who passed his cage, among whom there might always be one here and there to take an interest in him, and who could tell where they might seclude him if he called attention to his existence and thereby to the fact that, strictly speaking, he was only an impediment on the way to the menagerie.

A small impediment, to be sure, one that grew steadily less. People grew familiar with the strange idea that they could be expected, in times like these, to take an interest in a hunger artist, and with this familiarity the verdict went out against him. He might fast as much as he could, and he did so; but nothing could save him now, people passed him by. Just try to explain to anyone the art of fasting! Anyone who has no feeling for it cannot be made to understand it. The fine placards grew dirty and illegible, they were torn down; the little notice board telling the number of fast days achieved, which at first was changed carefully every day, had long stayed at the same figure, for after the first few weeks even this small task seemed pointless to the staff; and so the artist simply fasted on and on, as he had once dreamed of doing, and it was no trouble to him, just as he had always foretold, but no one counted the days, no one, not even the artist himself, knew what records he was already breaking, and his heart grew heavy. And when once in a while some leisurely passer-by stopped, made merry over the old figure on the board, and spoke of swindling, that was in its way the stupidest lie ever invented by indifference and inborn malice, since it was not the hunger artist who was cheating, he was working honestly, but the world was cheating him of his reward.

Many more days went by, however, and that too came to an end. An overseer's eye fell on the cage one day and he asked the attendants why this perfectly good cage should be left standing there unused with dirty straw inside it; nobody knew, until one man, helped out by the notice board, remembered about the hunger artist. They poked into the straw with sticks and found him in it. "Are you still fasting?" asked the overseer, "when on earth do you mean to stop?" "Forgive me, everybody," whispered the hunger artist; only the overseer, who had his ear to the bars, understood him. "Of course," said the overseer, and tapped his forehead with a finger to let the attendants know what state the man was in, "we forgive you." "I always wanted you to admire my fasting," said the hunger artist. "We do admire it," said the overseer, affably. "But you shouldn't admire it," said the hunger artist. "Well then we don't admire it," said the overseer, "but why shouldn't we admire it?" "Because I have to fast, I can't help it," said the hunger artist. "What a fellow you are," said the overseer, "and why can't you help it?" "Because," said the hunger artist, lifting his head a little and speaking, with his lips pursed, as if for a kiss, right into the overseer's ear, so that no syllable might be lost, "because I couldn't find the food I liked. If I had found it, believe me, I should have made no fuss and stuffed myself like you or anyone else." These were his last words, but in his dimming eyes remained the firm though no longer proud persuasion that he was still continuing to fast.

"Well, clear this out now!" said the overseer, and they buried the hunger artist, straw and all. Into the cage they put a young panther. Even the most insensitive felt it refreshing to see this wild creature leaping around the cage that had so long been dreary. The panther was all right. The food he liked was brought him without hesitation by the attendants; he seemed not even to miss his freedom; his noble body, furnished almost to the bursting point with all that it needed, seemed to carry freedom around with it too; somewhere in his jaws it seemed to lurk; and the joy of life streamed with such ardent passion from his throat that for the onlookers it was not easy to stand the shock of it. But they braced themselves, crowded around the cage, and did not want ever to move away.

D . H . L A W R E N C E

[*1885–1930*]

The Blind Man

Isabel Pervin was listening for two sounds—for the sound of wheels on the drive outside and for the noise of her husband's footsteps in the hall. Her dearest and oldest friend, a man who seemed almost indispensable to her living, would drive up in the rainy dusk of the closing November day. The trap had gone to fetch him from the station. And her husband, who had been blinded in Flanders, and who had a disfiguring mark on his brow, would be coming in from the outhouses.

He had been home for a year now. He was totally blind. Yet they had been very happy. The Grange was Maurice's own place. The back was a farmstead, and the Wernhams, who occupied the rear premises, acted as farmers. Isabel lived with her husband in the handsome rooms in front. She and he had been almost entirely alone together since he was wounded. They talked and sang and read together in a wonderful and unspeakable intimacy. Then she reviewed books for a Scottish newspaper, carrying on her old interest, and he occupied himself a good deal with the farm. Sightless, he could still discuss everything with Wernham, and he could also do a good deal of work about the place—menial work, it is true, but it gave him satisfaction. He milked the cows, carried in the pails, turned the separator, attended to the pigs and horses. Life was still very full and strangely serene for the blind man, peaceful with the almost incomprehensible peace of immediate contact in darkness. With his wife he had a whole world, rich and real and invisible.

They were newly and remotely happy. He did not even regret the loss of his sight in these times of dark, palpable joy. A certain exultance swelled his soul.

But as time wore on, sometimes the rich glamour would leave them. Sometimes, after months of this intensity, a sense of burden overcame Isabel, a weariness, a terrible ennui, in that silent house approached between a colonnade of tall-shafted pines. Then she felt she would go mad, for she could not bear it. And sometimes he had devastating fits of depression, which seemed to lay waste his whole being. It was worse than depression—a black misery, when his own life was a torture to him, and when his presence was unbearable to his wife. The dread went down to the roots of her soul as these black days recurred. In a kind of panic she tried to wrap herself up still further in her husband. She forced the old spontaneous cheerfulness and joy to continue. But the effort it cost her was almost too much. She knew she could not keep it up. She felt she would scream with the strain, and would give anything, anything, to escape. She longed to possess her husband utterly; it gave her inordinate joy to have him entirely to herself. And yet, when again he was gone in a black and massive misery, she could not bear him, she could not bear herself; she wished she could be snatched away off the earth altogether, anything rather than live at this cost.

Dazed, she schemed for a way out. She invited friends, she tried to give him some further connection with the outer world. But it was no good. After all their joy and suffering, after their dark, great year of blindness and solitude and unspeakable nearness, other people seemed to them both shallow, rattling, rather impertinent. Shallow prattle seemed presumptuous. He became impatient and irritated, she was wearied. And so they lapsed into their solitude again. For they preferred it.

But now, in a few weeks' time, her second baby would be born. The first had died, an infant, when her husband first went out to France. She looked with joy and relief to the coming of the second. It would be her salvation. But also she felt some anxiety. She was thirty years old, her husband was a year younger. They both wanted the child very much. Yet she could not help feeling afraid. She had her husband on her hands, a terrible joy to her, and a terrifying burden. The child would occupy her love and attention. And then, what of Maurice? What would he do? If only she could feel that he, too, would be at peace and happy when the child came! She did so want to luxuriate in a rich, physical satisfaction of maternity. But the man, what would he do? How could she provide for him, how avert those shattering black moods of his, which destroyed them both?

She sighed with fear. But at this time Bertie Reid wrote to Isabel. He was her old friend, a second or third cousin, a Scotchman, as she was a Scotchwoman. They had been brought up near to one another, and all her life he had been her friend, like a brother, but better than her own brothers. She loved him—though not in the marrying sense. There was a sort of kinship between them, an affinity. They understood one another instinctively. But Isabel would never have thought of marrying Bertie. It would have seemed like marrying in her own family.

Bertie was a barrister and a man of letters, a Scotchman of the intellectual type, quick, ironical, sentimental, and on his knees before the woman he adored but did not want to marry. Maurice Pervin was different. He came of a good old country family—the Grange was not a very great distance from Oxford. He was passionate, sensitive, perhaps over-sensitive, wincing—a big fellow with heavy limbs and a forehead that flushed painfully. For his mind was slow, as if drugged by the strong provincial blood that beat in his veins. He was very sensitive to his own mental slowness, his feelings being quick and acute. So that he was just the opposite to Bertie, whose mind was much quicker than his emotions, which were not so very fine.

From the first the two men did not like each other. Isabel felt that they ought to get on together. But they did not. She felt that if only each could have the clue to the other there would be such a rare understanding between them. It did not come off, however. Bertie adopted a slightly ironical attitude, very offensive to Maurice, who returned the Scotch irony with English resentment, a resentment which deepened sometimes into stupid hatred.

This was a little puzzling to Isabel. However, she accepted it in the course of things. Men were made freakish and unreasonable. Therefore, when Maurice was going out to France for the second time, she felt that, for her husband's sake, she must discontinue her friendship with Bertie. She wrote to the barrister to this effect. Bertram Reid simply replied that in this, as in all other matters, he must obey her wishes, if these were indeed her wishes.

For nearly two years nothing had passed between the two friends. Isabel rather gloried in the fact; she had no compunction. She had one great article of faith, which was, that husband and wife should be so important to one another, that the rest of the world simply did not count. She and Maurice were husband and wife. They loved one another. They would have children. Then let everybody and everything else fade into insignificance outside this connubial felicity. She professed herself quite happy and ready to receive Maurice's friends. She was happy and ready: the happy wife, the ready woman in possession. Without knowing why, the friends retired abashed, and came no more. Maurice, of course, took as much satisfaction in this connubial absorption as Isabel did.

He shared in Isabel's literary activities, she cultivated a real interest in agriculture and cattle-raising. For she, being at heart perhaps an emotional enthusiast, always cultivated the practical side of life and prided herself on her mastery of practical affairs. Thus the husband and wife had spent the five years of their married life. The last had been one of blindness and unspeakable intimacy. And now Isabel felt a great indifference coming over her, a sort of lethargy. She wanted to be allowed to bear her child in peace, to nod by the fire and drift vaguely, physically, from day to day. Maurice was like an ominous thunder-cloud. She had to keep waking up to remember him.

When a little note came from Bertie, asking if he were to put up a tombstone to their dead friendship, and speaking of the real pain he felt on account of her husband's loss of sight, she felt a pang, a fluttering agitation of reawakening. And she read the letter to Maurice.

"Ask him to come down," he said.

"Ask Bertie to come here!" she re-echoed.

"Yes—if he wants to."

Isabel paused for a few moments.

"I know he wants to—he'd only be too glad," she replied. "But what about you, Maurice? How should you like it?"

"I should like it."

"Well—in that case—But I thought you didn't care for him—"

"Oh, I don't know. I might think differently of him now," the blind man replied. It was rather abstruse to Isabel.

"Well, dear," she said, "if you're quite sure—"

"I'm sure enough. Let him come," said Maurice.

So Bertie was coming, coming this evening, in the November rain and darkness. Isabel was agitated, racked with her old restlessness and indecision. She had always suffered from this pain of doubt, just an agonizing sense of uncertainty. It had begun to pass off, in the lethargy of maternity. Now it returned, and she resented it. She struggled as usual to maintain her calm, composed, friendly bearing, a sort of mask she wore over all her body.

A woman had lighted a tall lamp beside the table and spread the cloth. The long dining-room was dim, with its elegant but rather severe pieces of old furniture. Only the round table glowed softly under the light. It had a rich, beautiful effect. The white cloth glistened and dropped its heavy, pointed lace corners almost to the carpet, the china was old and handsome, creamy-yellow, with a blotched pattern of harsh red and deep blue, the cups large and bell-shaped, the teapot gallant. Isabel looked at it with superficial appreciation.

Her nerves were hurting her. She looked automatically again at the high, uncurtained windows. In the last dusk she could just perceive outside a huge fir-tree swaying its boughs: it was as if she thought it rather than saw it. The rain came flying on the window panes. Ah, why had she no peace? These two men, why did they tear at her? Why did they not come—why was there this suspense?

She sat in a lassitude that was really suspense and irritation. Maurice, at least, might come in—there was nothing to keep him out. She rose to her feet. Catching sight of her reflection in a mirror, she glanced at herself with a slight smile of recognition, as if she were an old friend to herself. Her face was oval and calm, her nose a little arched. Her neck made a beautiful line down to her shoulder. With hair knotted loosely behind, she had something of a warm, maternal look. Thinking this of herself, she arched her eyebrows and her rather heavy eyelids, with a little flicker of a smile, and for a moment her gray eyes looked amused and wicked, a little sardonic, out of her transfigured Madonna face.

Then, resuming her air of womanly patience—she was really fatally self-determined —she went with a little jerk towards the door. Her eyes were slightly reddened.

She passed down the wide hall and through a door at the end. Then she was in the farm premises. The scent of dairy, and of farm-kitchen, and of farm-yard and of leather almost overcame her: but particularly the scent of dairy. They had been scalding out the pans. The flagged passage in front of her was dark, puddled, and wet. Light came out from the open kitchen door. She went forward and stood in the doorway. The farm-people were at tea, seated at a little distance from her, round a long, narrow table, in the centre of which stood a white lamp. Ruddy faces, ruddy hands holding food, red mouths working, heads bent over the tea-cups: men, landgirls, boys: it was tea-time, feeding-time. Some faces caught sight of her. Mrs. Wernham, going round behind the chairs with a large black teapot, halting slightly in her walk, was not aware of her for a moment. Then she turned suddenly.

"Oh, it is Madam!" she exclaimed. "Come in, then, come in! We're at tea." And she dragged forward a chair.

"No, I won't come in," said Isabel. "I'm afraid I interrupt your meal."

"No—no—not likely, Madam, not likely."

"Hasn't Mr. Pervin come in, do you know?"

"I'm sure I couldn't say! Missed him, have you, Madam?"

"No, I only wanted him to come in," laughed Isabel, as if shyly.

"Wanted him, did ye? Get up, boy—get up, now—"

Mrs. Wernham knocked one of the boys on the shoulder. He began to scrape to his feet, chewing largely.

"I believe he's in top stable," said another face from the table.

"Ah! No, don't get up. I'm going myself," said Isabel.

"Don't you go out on a dirty night like this. Let the lad go. Get along wi' ye, boy," said Mrs. Wernham.

"No, no," said Isabel, with a decision that was always obeyed. "Go on with your tea, Tom. I'd like to go across to the stable, Mrs. Wernham."

"Did ever you hear tell!" exclaimed the woman.

"Isn't the trap late?" asked Isabel.

"Why, no," said Mrs. Wernham, peering into the distance at the tall, dim clock. "No, Madam—we can give it another quarter or twenty minutes yet, good—yes, every bit of a quarter."

"Ah! It seems late when darkness falls so early," said Isabel.

"It do, that it do. Bother the days, that they draw in so," answered Mrs. Wernham. "Proper miserable!"

"They are," said Isabel, withdrawing.

She pulled on her overshoes, wrapped a large tartan shawl around her, put on a man's felt hat, and ventured out along the causeways of the first yard. It was very dark. The wind was roaring in the great elms behind the outhouses. When she came to the second yard the darkness seemed deeper. She was unsure of her footing. She wished she had brought a lantern. Rain blew against her. Half she liked it, half she felt unwilling to battle.

She reached at last the just visible door of the stable. There was no sign of a light anywhere. Opening the upper half, she looked in: into a simple well of darkness. The smell of horses and ammonia, and of warmth was startling to her, in that full night. She listened with all her ears but could hear nothing save the night, and the stirring of a horse.

"Maurice!" she called, softly and musically, though she was afraid. "Maurice—are you there?"

Nothing came from the darkness. She knew the rain and wind blew in upon the horses, the hot animal life. Feeling it wrong, she entered the stable and drew the lower half of the door shut, holding the upper part close. She did not stir, because she was aware of the presence of the dark hind-quarters of the horses, though she could not see them, and she was afraid. Something wild stirred in her heart.

She listened intensely. Then she heard a small noise in the distance—far away, it seemed—the chink of a pan, and a man's voice speaking a brief word. It would be Maurice, in the other part of the stable. She stood motionless, waiting for him to come through the partition door. The horses were so terrifyingly near to her, in the invisible.

The loud jarring of the inner door-latch made her start; the door was opened. She could hear and feel her husband entering and invisibly passing among the horses near to her, darkness as they were, actively intermingled. The rather low sound of his voice as he spoke to the horses came velvety to her nerves. How near he was, and how invisible! The darkness seemed to be in a strange swirl of violent life, just upon her. She turned giddy.

Her presence of mind made her call quietly and musically:

"Maurice! Maurice—dear-ar!"

"Yes," he answered. "Isabel?"

She saw nothing, and the sound of his voice seemed to touch her.

"Hello!" she answered cheerfully, straining her eyes to see him. He was still busy, attending to the horses near her, but she saw only darkness. It made her almost desperate.

"Won't you come in, dear?" she said.

"Yes, I'm coming. Just half a minute. Stand over—now! Trap's not come, has it?"

"Not yet," said Isabel.

His voice was pleasant and ordinary, but it had a slight suggestion of the stable to her. She wished he would come away. Whilst he was so utterly invisible, she was afraid of him.

"How's the time?" he asked.

"Not yet six," she replied. She disliked to answer into the dark. Presently he came very near to her, and she retreated out of doors.

"The weather blows in here," he said, coming steadily forward, feeling for the doors. She shrank away. At last she could dimly see him.

"Bertie won't have much of a drive," he said, as he closed the doors.

"He won't indeed!" said Isabel calmly, watching the dark shape at the door.

"Give me your arm, dear," she said.

She pressed his arm close to her, as she went. But she longed to see him, to look at him. She was nervous. He walked erect, with face rather lifted, but with a curious tentative movement of his powerful, muscular legs. She could feel the clever, careful, strong contact of his feet with the earth, as she balanced against him. For a moment he was a tower of darkness to her, as if he rose out of the earth.

In the house-passage he wavered and went cautiously, with a curious look of silence about him as he felt for the bench. Then he sat down heavily. He was a man with rather sloping shoulders, but with heavy limbs, powerful legs that seemed to know the earth. His head was small, usually carried high and light. As he bent down to unfasten his gaiters and boots he did not look blind. His hair was brown and crisp, his hands were large, reddish, intelligent, the veins stood out in the wrists; and his thighs and knees seemed massive. When he stood up his face and neck were surcharged with blood, the veins stood out on his temples. She did not look at his blindness.

Isabel was always glad when they had passed through the dividing door into their own regions of repose and beauty. She was a little afraid of him, out there in the animal grossness of the back. His bearings also changed, as he smelt the familiar indefinable odour that pervaded his wife's surroundings, a delicate, refined scent, very faintly spicy. Perhaps it came from the potpourri bowls.

He stood at the foot of the stairs, arrested, listening. She watched him, and her heart sickened. He seemed to be listening to fate.

"He's not here yet," he said. "I'll go up and change."

"Maurice," she said, "you're not wishing he wouldn't come, are you?"

"I couldn't quite say," he answered. "I feel myself rather on the qui vive."

"I can see you are," she answered. And she reached up and kissed his cheek. She saw his mouth relax into a slow smile.

"What are you laughing at?" she said roguishly.

"You consoling me," he answered.

"Nay," she answered. "Why should I console you? You know we love each other —you know how married we are! What does anything else matter?"

"Nothing at all, my dear."

He felt for her face and touched it, smiling.

"You're all right, aren't you?" he asked anxiously.

"I'm wonderfully all right, love," she answered. "It's you I am a little troubled about, at times."

"Why me?" he said, touching her cheeks delicately with the tips of his fingers. The touch had an almost hypnotizing effect on her.

He went away upstairs. She saw him mount into the darkness, unseeing and unchanging. He did not know that the lamps on the upper corridor were unlighted. He went on into the darkness with unchanging step. She heard him in the bath-room.

Pervin moved about almost unconsciously in his familiar surroundings, dark though everything was. He seemed to know the presence of objects before he touched them. It was a pleasure to him to rock thus through a world of things, carried on the flood in a sort of blood-prescience. He did not think much or trouble much. So long as he kept this sheer immediacy of blood-contact with the substantial world he was happy, he wanted no intervention of visual consciousness. In this state there was a certain rich positivity, bordering sometimes on rapture. Life seemed to move in him like a tide lapping, lapping, and advancing, enveloping all things darkly. It was a pleasure to stretch forth the hand and meet the unseen object, clasp it, and possess it in pure contact. He did not try to remember, to visualize. He did not want to. The new way of consciousness substituted itself in him.

The rich suffusion of this state generally kept him happy, reaching its culmination in the consuming passion for his wife. But at times the flow would seem to be checked and thrown back. Then it would beat inside him like a tangled sea, and he was tortured in the shattered chaos of his own blood. He grew to dread this arrest, this throw-back, this chaos inside himself, when he seemed merely at the mercy of his own powerful and conflicting elements. How to get some measure of control or surety, this was the question. And when the question rose maddening in him, he would clench his fists as if he would compel the whole universe to submit to him. But it was in vain. He could not even compel himself.

Tonight, however, he was still serene, though little tremors of unreasonable exasperation ran through him. He had to handle the razor very carefully, as he shaved, for it was not at one with him, he was afraid of it. His hearing also was too much sharpened. He heard the woman lighting the lamps on the corridor, and attending to the fire in the visitors' room. And then, as he went to his room, he heard the trap arrive. Then came Isabel's voice, lifted and calling, like a bell ringing:

"Is it you, Bertie? Have you come?"

And a man's voice answered out of the wind:

"Hello, Isabel! There you are."

"Have you had a miserable drive? I'm so sorry we couldn't send a closed carriage. I can't see you at all, you know."

"I'm coming. No, I liked the drive—it was like Perthshire. Well, how are you? You're looking fit as ever, as far as I can see."

"Oh, yes," said Isabel. "I'm wonderfully well. How are you? Rather thin, I think—"

"Worked to death—everybody's old cry. But I'm all right, Ciss. How's Pervin?—isn't he here?"

"Oh, yes, he's upstairs changing. Yes, he's awfully well. Take off your wet things; I'll send them to be dried."

"And how are you both, in spirits? He doesn't fret?"

"No—no, not at all. No, on the contrary, really. We've been wonderfully happy, incredibly. It's more than I can understand—so wonderful: the nearness, and the peace—"

"Ah! Well, that's awfully good news—"

They moved away. Pervin heard no more. But a childish sense of desolation had come over him, as he heard their brisk voices. He seemed shut out—like a child that is left out. He was aimless and excluded, he did not know what to do with himself. The helpless desolation came over him. He fumbled nervously as he dressed himself, in a state almost of childishness. He disliked the Scotch accent in Bertie's speech, and the slight response it found on Isabel's tongue. He disliked the slight purr of complacency in the Scottish speech. He disliked intensely the glib way in which Isabel spoke of their happiness and nearness. It made him recoil. He was fretful and beside himself like a child, he had almost a childish nostalgia to be included in the life circle. And at the same time he was a man, dark and powerful and infuriated by his own weakness. By some fatal flaw, he could not be by himself, he had to depend on the support of another. And this very dependence enraged him. He hated Bertie Reid, and at the same time he knew the hatred was nonsense, he knew it was the outcome of his own weakness.

He went downstairs. Isabel was alone in the dining-room. She watched him enter, head erect, his feet tentative. He looked so strong-blooded and healthy and, at the same time, cancelled. Cancelled—that was the word that flew across her mind. Perhaps it was his scar suggested it.

"You heard Bertie come, Maurice?" she said.

"Yes—isn't he here?"

"He's in his room. He looks very thin and worn."

"I suppose he works himself to death."

A woman came in with a tray—and after a few minutes Bertie came down. He was a little dark man, with a very big forehead, thin, wispy hair, and sad, large eyes. His expression was inordinately sad—almost funny. He had odd, short legs.

Isabel watched him hesitate under the door, and glance nervously at her husband. Pervin heard him and turned.

"Here you are, now," said Isabel. "Come, let us eat."

Bertie went across to Maurice.

"How are you, Pervin?" he said, as he advanced.

The blind man stuck his hand out into space, and Bertie took it.

"Very fit. Glad you've come," said Maurice.

Isabel glanced at them, and glanced away, as if she could not bear to see them.

"Come," she said. "Come to table. Aren't you both awfully hungry? I am, tremendously."

"I'm afraid you waited for me," said Bertie, as they sat down.

Maurice had a curious monolithic way of sitting in a chair, erect and distant. Isabel's heart always beat when she caught sight of him thus.

"No," she replied to Bertie. "We're very little later than usual. We're having a sort of high tea, not dinner. Do you mind? It gives us such a nice long evening, uninterrupted."

"I like it," said Bertie.

Maurice was feeling, with curious little movements, almost like a cat kneading her bed, for his plate, his knife and fork, his napkin. He was getting the whole geography of his cover into his consciousness. He sat erect and inscrutable, remote-seeming. Bertie watched the static figure of the blind man, the delicate tactile discernment of the large, ruddy hands, and the curious mindless silence of the brow, above the scar. With difficulty he looked away, and without knowing what he did, picked up a little crystal bowl of violets from the table, and held them to his nose.

"They are sweet-scented," he said. "Where do they come from?"

"From the garden—under the windows," said Isabel.

"So late in the year—and so fragrant! Do you remember the violets under Aunt Bell's south wall?"

The two friends looked at each other and exchanged a smile, Isabel's eyes lighting up.

"Don't I?" she replied. "Wasn't she queer!"

"A curious old girl," laughed Bertie. "There's a streak of freakishness in the family, Isabel."

"Ah—but not in you and me, Bertie," said Isabel. "Give them to Maurice, will you?" she added, as Bertie was putting down the flowers. "Have you smelled the violets, dear? Do!—they are so scented."

Maurice held out his hand, and Bertie placed the tiny bowl against his large, warm-looking fingers. Maurice's hand closed over the thin white fingers of the barrister. Bertie carefully extricated himself. Then the two watched the blind man smelling the violets. He bent his head and seemed to be thinking. Isabel waited.

"Aren't they sweet, Maurice?" she said at last, anxiously.

"Very," he said. And he held out the bowl. Bertie took it. Both he and Isabel were a little afraid, and deeply disturbed.

The meal continued. Isabel and Bertie chatted spasmodically. The blind man was silent. He touched his food repeatedly, with quick, delicate touches of his knife-point, then cut irregular bits. He could not bear to be helped. Both Isabel and Bertie suffered: Isabel wondered why. She did not suffer when she was alone with Maurice. Bertie made her conscious of a strangeness.

After the meal the three drew their chairs to the fire, and sat down to talk. The decanters were put on a table near at hand. Isabel knocked the logs on the fire, and clouds of brilliant sparks went up the chimney. Bertie noticed a slight weariness in her bearing.

"You will be glad when your child comes now, Isabel?" he said.

She looked up to him with a quick wan smile.

"Yes, I shall be glad," she answered. "It begins to seem long. Yes, I shall be very glad. So will you, Maurice, won't you?" she added.

"Yes, I shall," replied her husband.

"We are both looking forward so much to having it," she said.

"Yes, of course," said Bertie.

He was a bachelor, three or four years older than Isabel. He lived in beautiful rooms overlooking the river, guarded by a faithful Scottish manservant. And he had his friends among the fair sex—not lovers, friends. So long as he could avoid any danger of courtship or marriage, he adored a few good women with constant and unfailing homage, and he was chivalrously fond of quite a number. But if they seemed to encroach on him, he withdrew and detested them.

Isabel knew him very well, knew his beautiful constancy, and kindness, also his incurable weakness, which made him unable ever to enter into close contact of any sort. He was ashamed of himself because he could not marry, could not approach women physically. He wanted to do so. But he could not. At the centre of him he was afraid, helplessly and even brutally afraid. He had given up hope, had ceased to expect any more that he could escape his own weakness. Hence he was a brilliant and successful barrister, also a litterateur of high repute, a rich man, and a great social success. At the centre he felt himself neuter, nothing.

Isabel knew him well. She despised him even while she admired him. She looked at his sad face, his little short legs, and felt contempt of him. She looked at his dark grey eyes, with their uncanny, almost childlike, intuition, and she loved him. He understood amazingly—but she had no fear of his understanding. As a man she patronized him.

And she turned to the impassive, silent figure of her husband. He sat leaning back, with folded arms, and face a little uptilted. His knees were straight and massive. She sighed, picked up the poker, and again began to prod the fire, to rouse the clouds of soft brilliant sparks.

"Isabel tells me," Bertie began suddenly, "that you have not suffered unbearably from the loss of sight."

Maurice straightened himself to attend but kept his arms folded.

"No," he said, "not unbearably. Now and again one struggles against it, you know. But there are compensations."

"They say it is much worse to be stone deaf," said Isabel.

"I believe it is," said Bertie. "Are there compensations?" he added to Maurice.

"Yes. You cease to bother about a great many things." Again Maurice stretched his figure, stretched the strong muscles of his back, and leaned backwards, with uplifted face.

"And that is a relief," said Bertie. "But what is there in place of the bothering? What replaces the activity?"

There was a pause. At length the blind man replied, as out of a negligent, unattentive thinking:

"Oh, I don't know. There's a good deal when you're not active."

"Is there?" said Bertie. "What exactly? It always seems to me that when there is no thought and no action, there is nothing."

Again Maurice was slow in replying.

"There is something," he replied. "I couldn't tell you what it is."

And the talk lapsed once more, Isabel and Bertie chatting gossip and reminiscence, the blind man silent.

At length Maurice rose restlessly, a big obtrusive figure. He felt tight and hampered. He wanted to go away.

"Do you mind," he said, "if I go and speak to Wernham?"

"No—go along, dear," said Isabel.

And he went out. A silence came over the two friends. At length Bertie said:

"Nevertheless, it is a great deprivation, Cissie."

"It is, Bertie. I know it is."

"Something lacking all the time," said Bertie.

"Yes, I know. And yet—and yet—Maurice is right. There is something else, something there, which you never knew was there, and which you can't express."

"What is there?" asked Bertie.

"I don't know—it's awfully hard to define it—but something strong and immediate. There's something strange in Maurice's presence—indefinable—but I couldn't do without it. I agree that it seems to put one's mind to sleep. But when we're alone I miss nothing; it seems awfully rich, almost splendid, you know."

"I'm afraid I don't follow," said Bertie.

They talked desultorily. The wind blew loudly outside, rain chattered on the window-panes, making a sharp drum-sound because of the closed, mellow-golden shutters inside. The logs burned slowly, with hot, almost invisible small flames. Bertie seemed uneasy, there were dark circles round his eyes. Isabel, rich with her approaching maternity, leaned looking into the fire. Her hair curled in odd, loose strands, very pleasing to the man. But she had a curious feeling of old woe in her heart, old timeless night-woe.

"I suppose we're all deficient somewhere," said Bertie.

"I suppose so," said Isabel wearily.

"Damned, sooner or later."

"I don't know," she said, rousing herself. "I feel quite all right, you know. The child coming seems to make me indifferent to everything, just placid. I can't feel that there's anything to trouble about, you know."

"A good thing, I should say," he replied slowly.

"Well, there it is. I suppose it's just Nature. If only I felt I needn't trouble about Maurice, I should be perfectly content—"

"But you feel you must trouble about him?"

"Well—I don't know—" She even resented this much effort.

The night passed slowly. Isabel looked at the clock. "I say," she said. "It's nearly ten o'clock. Where can Maurice be? I'm sure they're all in bed at the back. Excuse me a moment."

She went out, returning almost immediately.

"It's all shut up and in darkness," she said. "I wonder where he is. He must have gone out to the farm—"

Bertie looked at her.

"I suppose he'll come in," he said.

"I suppose so," she said. "But it's unusual for him to be out now."

"Would you like me to go out and see?"

"Well—if you wouldn't mind. I'd go, but—" She did not want to make the physical effort.

Bertie put on an old overcoat and took a lantern. He went out from the side door. He shrank from the wet and roaring night. Such weather had a nervous effect on him: too much moisture everywhere made him feel almost imbecile. Unwilling, he went through it all. A dog barked violently at him. He peered in all the buildings. At last, as he opened the upper door of a sort of intermediate barn, he heard a grinding noise, and looking in, holding up his lantern, saw Maurice, in his shirtsleeves, standing listening, holding the handle of a turnip-pulper. He had been pulping sweet roots, a pile of which lay dimly heaped in a corner behind him.

"That you, Wernham?" said Maurice, listening.

"No, it's me," said Bertie.

A large, half-wild grey cat was rubbing at Maurice's leg. The blind man stooped to rub its sides. Bertie watched the scene, then unconsciously entered and shut the door behind him. He was in a high sort of barn-place, from which, right and left, ran off the corridors in front of the stalled cattle. He watched the slow, stooping motion of the other man, as he caressed the great cat.

Maurice straightened himself.

"You came to look for me?" he said.

"Isabel was a little uneasy," said Bertie.

"I'll come in. I like messing about doing these jobs."

The cat had reared her sinister, feline length against his leg, clawing at his thigh affectionately. He lifted her claws out of his flesh.

"I hope I'm not in your way at all at the Grange here," said Bertie, rather shy and stiff.

"My way? No, not a bit. I'm glad Isabel has somebody to talk to. I'm afraid it's I who am in the way. I know I'm not very lively company. Isabel's all right, don't you think? She's not unhappy, is she?"

"I don't think so."

"What does she say?"

"She says she's very content—only a little troubled about you."

"Why me?"

"Perhaps afraid that you might brood," said Bertie, cautiously.

"She needn't be afraid of that." He continued to caress the flattened grey head of the cat with his fingers. "What I am a bit afraid of," he resumed, "is that she'll find me a dead weight, always alone with me down here."

"I don't think you need think that," said Bertie, though this was what he feared himself.

"I don't know," said Maurice. "Sometimes I feel it isn't fair that she's saddled with me." Then he dropped his voice curiously. "I say," he asked, secretly struggling, "is my face much disfigured? Do you mind telling me?"

"There is the scar," said Bertie, wondering. "Yes, it is a disfigurement. But more pitiable than shocking."

"A pretty bad scar, though," said Maurice.

"Oh, yes."

There was a pause.

"Sometimes I feel I am horrible," said Maurice, in a low voice, talking as if to himself. And Bertie actually felt a quiver of horror.

"That's nonsense," he said.

Maurice again straightened himself, leaving the cat.

"There's no telling," he said. Then again, in an odd tone, he added: "I don't really know you, do I?"

"Probably not," said Bertie.

"Do you mind if I touch you?"

The lawyer shrank away instinctively. And yet, out of very philanthropy, he said, in a small voice: "Not at all."

But he suffered as the blind man stretched out a strong, naked hand to him. Maurice accidentally knocked off Bertie's hat.

"I thought you were taller," he said, starting. Then he laid his hand on Bertie Reid's head, closing the dome of the skull in a soft, firm grasp, gathering it, as it were; then, shifting his grasp and softly closing again, with a fine, close pressure, till he had covered the skull and the face of the smaller man, tracing the brows, and touching the full, closed eyes, touching the small nose and the nostrils, the rough, short moustache, the mouth, the rather strong chin. The hand of the blind man grasped the shoulder, the arm, the hand of the other man. He seemed to take him, in the soft, travelling grasp.

"You seem young," he said quietly, at last.

The lawyer stood almost annihilated, unable to answer.

"Your head seems tender, as if you were young," Maurice repeated. "So do your hands. Touch my eyes, will you?—touch my scar."

Now Bertie quivered with revulsion. Yet he was under the power of the blind man, as if hypnotized. He lifted his hand, and laid the fingers on the scar, on the scarred eyes. Maurice suddenly covered them with his own hand, pressed the fingers of the other man upon his disfigured eye-sockets, trembling in every fibre, and rocking slightly, slowly, from side to side. He remained thus for a minute or more, whilst Bertie stood as if in a swoon, unconscious, imprisoned.

Then suddenly Maurice removed the hand of the other man from his brow, and stood holding it in his own.

"Oh, my God," he said, "we shall know each other now, shan't we? We shall know each other now."

Bertie could not answer. He gazed mute and terrorstruck, overcome by his own weakness. He knew he could not answer. He had an unreasonable fear lest the other man should suddenly destroy him. Whereas Maurice was actually filled with hot, poignant love, the passion of friendship. Perhaps it was this very passion of friendship which Bertie shrank from most.

"We're all right together now, aren't we?" said Maurice. "It's all right now, as long as we live, so far as we're concerned?"

"Yes," said Bertie, trying by any means to escape.

Maurice stood with head lifted, as if listening. The new delicate fulfilment of mortal friendship had come as a revelation and surprise to him, something exquisite and unhoped-for. He seemed to be listening to hear if it were real.

Then he turned for his coat.

"Come," he said, "we'll go to Isabel."

Bertie took the lantern and opened the door. The cat disappeared. The two men went in silence along the causeways. Isabel, as they came, thought their footsteps sounded strange. She looked up pathetically and anxiously for their entrance. There seemed a curious elation about Maurice. Bertie was haggard, with sunken eyes.

"What is it?" she asked.

"We've become friends," said Maurice, standing with his feet apart, like a strange colossus.

"Friends!" re-echoed Isabel. And she looked again at Bertie. He met her eyes with a furtive, haggard look; his eyes were as if glazed with misery.

"I'm so glad," she said, in sheer perplexity.

"Yes," said Maurice.

He was indeed so glad. Isabel took his hand with both hers, and held it fast.

"You'll be happier now, dear," she said.

But she was watching Bertie. She knew that he had one desire—to escape from this intimacy, this friendship, which had been thrust upon him. He could not bear it that he had been touched by the blind man, his insane reserve broken in. He was like a mollusc whose shell is broken.

KATHERINE MANSFIELD

[1888–1923]

Bliss

Although Bertha Young was thirty she still had moments like this when she wanted to run instead of walk, to take dancing steps on and off the pavement, to bowl a hoop, to throw something up in the air and catch it again, or to stand still and laugh at— nothing—at nothing, simply.

What can you do if you are thirty and, turning the corner of your own street, you are overcome, suddenly, by a feeling of bliss—absolute bliss!—as though you'd suddenly swallowed a bright piece of that late afternoon sun and it burned in your bosom, sending out a little shower of sparks into every particle, into every finger and toe? . . .

Oh, is there no way you can express it without being "drunk and disorderly"? How idiotic civilization is! Why be given a body if you have to keep it shut up in a case like a rare, rare fiddle?

"No, that about the fiddle is not quite what I mean," she thought, running up the steps and feeling in her bag for the key—she'd forgotten it, as usual—and rattling the letter-box. "It's not what I mean, because—Thank you, Mary"—she went into the hall. "Is nurse back?"

"Yes, M'm."

"And has the fruit come?"

"Yes. M'm. Everything's come."

"Bring the fruit up to the dining-room, will you? I'll arrange it before I go upstairs."

It was dusky in the dining-room and quite chilly. But all the same Bertha threw off her coat; she could not bear the tight clasp of it another moment, and the cold air fell on her arms.

But in her bosom there was still that bright glowing place—that shower of little sparks coming from it. It was almost unbearable. She hardly dared to breathe for fear of fanning it higher, and yet she breathed deeply, deeply. She hardly dared to look into the cold mirror—but she did look, and it gave her back a woman, radiant, with smiling, trembling lips, with big, dark eyes and an air of listening, waiting for something . . . divine to happen . . . that she knew must happen . . . infallibly.

Mary brought in the fruit on a tray and with it a glass bowl, and a blue dish, very lovely, with a strange sheen on it as though it had been dipped in milk.

"Shall I turn on the light, M'm?"

"No, thank you. I can see quite well."

There were tangerines and apples stained with strawberry pink. Some yellow pears, smooth as silk, some white grapes covered with a silver bloom and a big cluster of purple ones. These last she had bought to tone in with the new dining-room carpet. Yes, that did sound rather far-fetched and absurd, but it was really why she had bought them. She had thought in the shop: "I must have some purples ones to bring the carpet up to the table." And it had seemed quite sense at the time.

When she had finished with them and had made two pyramids of these bright round shapes, she stood away from the table to get the effect—and it really was most curious. For the dark table seemed to melt into the dusky light and the glass dish and the blue bowl to float in the air. This, of course in her present mood, was so incredibly beautiful. . . . She began to laugh.

"No, no. I'm getting hysterical." And she seized her bag and coat and ran upstairs to the nursery.

Nurse sat at a low table giving Little B her supper after her bath. The baby had on a white flannel gown and a blue woollen jacket, and her dark, fine hair was brushed up into a funny little peak. She looked up when she saw her mother and began to jump.

"Now, my lovely, eat it up like a good girl," said Nurse, setting her lips in a way that Bertha knew, and that meant she had come into the nursery at another wrong moment.

"Has she been good, Nanny?"

"She's been a little sweet all the afternoon," whispered Nanny. "We went to the park and I sat down on a chair and took her out of the pram and a big dog came along and put its head on my knee and she clutched its ear, tugged it. Oh, you should have seen her."

Bertha wanted to ask if it wasn't rather dangerous to let her clutch at a strange dog's ear. But she did not dare to. She stood watching them, her hands by her side, like the poor little girl in front of the rich little girl with the doll.

The baby looked up at her again, stared, and then smiled so charmingly that Bertha couldn't help crying:

"Oh, Nanny, do let me finish giving her her supper while you put the bath things away."

"Well, M'm, she oughtn't to be changed hands while she's eating," said Nanny, still whispering. "It unsettles her; it's very likely to upset her."

How absurd it was. Why have a baby if it has to be kept—not in a case like a rare, rare fiddle—but in another woman's arms?

"Oh, I must!" said she.

Very offended, Nanny handed her over.

"Now, don't excite her after her supper. You know you do, M'm. And I have such a time with her after!"

Thank heaven! Nanny went out of the room with the bath towels.

"Now I've got you to myself, my little precious," said Bertha, as the baby leaned against her.

She ate delightfully, holding up her lips for the spoon and then waving her hands. Sometimes she wouldn't let the spoon go; and sometimes, just as Bertha had filled it, she waved it away to the four winds.

When the soup was finished Bertha turned round to the fire. "You're nice—you're very nice!" said she, kissing her warm baby. "I'm fond of you. I like you."

And, indeed, she loved Little B so much—her neck as she bent forward, her exquisite toes as they shone transparent in the firelight—that all her feeling of bliss came back again, and again she didn't know how to express it—what to do with it.

"You're wanted on the telephone," said Nanny, coming back in triumph and seizing *her* Little B.

Down she flew. It was Harry.

"Oh, is that you, Ber? Look here. I'll be late. I'll take a taxi and come along as quickly as I can, but get dinner put back ten minutes—will you? All right?"

"Yes, perfectly. Oh, Harry!"

"Yes?"

What had she to say? She'd nothing to say. She only wanted to get in touch with him for a moment. She couldn't absurdly cry: "Hasn't it been a divine day!"

"What is it?" rapped out the little voice.

"Nothing. *Entendu*," said Bertha, and hung up the receiver, thinking how more than idiotic civilization was.

They had people coming to dinner. The Norman Knights—a very sound couple—he was about to start a theatre, and she was awfully keen on interior decoration, a young man, Eddie Warren, who had just published a little book of poems and whom everybody was asking to dine, and a "find" of Bertha's called Pearl Fulton. What Miss Fulton did, Bertha didn't know. They had met at the club and Bertha had fallen in love with her, as she always did fall in love with beautiful women who had something strange about them.

The provoking thing was that, though they had been about together and met a number of times and really talked, Bertha couldn't yet make her out. Up to a certain point Miss Fulton was rarely, wonderfully frank, but the certain point was there, and beyond that she would not go.

Was there anything beyond it? Harry said "No." Voted her dullish, and "cold like all blond women, with a touch, perhaps, of anaemia of the brain." But Bertha wouldn't agree with him; not yet, at any rate.

"No, the way she has of sitting with her head a little on one side, and smiling, has something behind it, Harry, and I must find out what that something is."

"Most likely it's a good stomach," answered Harry.

He made a point of catching Bertha's heels with replies of that kind . . . "liver frozen, my dear girl," or "pure flatulence," or "kidney disease," . . . and so on. For some strange reason Bertha liked this, and almost admired it in him very much.

She went into the drawing-room and lighted the fire; then, picking up the cushions, one by one, that Mary had disposed so carefully, she threw them back on to the chairs and the couches. That made all the difference; the room came alive at once. As she was about to throw the last one she surprised herself by suddenly hugging it to her, passionately, passionately. But it did not put out the fire in her bosom. Oh, on the contrary!

The windows of the drawing-room opened on to a balcony overlooking the garden. At the far end, against the wall, there was a tall, slender pear tree in fullest, richest bloom; it stood perfect, as though becalmed against the jade-green sky. Bertha couldn't help feeling, even from this distance, that it had not a single bud or a faded petal. Down below, in the garden beds, the red and yellow tulips, heavy with flowers, seemed to lean upon the dusk. A grey cat, dragging its belly, crept across the lawn, and a black one, its shadow, trailed after. The sight of them, so intent and so quick, gave Bertha a curious shiver.

"What creepy things cats are!" she stammered, and she turned away from the window and began walking up and down. . . .

How strong the jonquils smelled in the warm room. Too strong? Oh, no. And yet, as though overcome, she flung down on a couch and pressed her hands to her eyes.

"I'm too happy—too happy!" she murmured.

And she seemed to see on her eyelids the lovely pear tree with its wide open blossoms as a symbol of her own life.

Really—really—she had everything. She was young. Harry and she were as much in love as ever, and they got on together splendidly and were really good pals. She had an adorable baby. They didn't have to worry about money. They had this absolutely satisfactory house and garden. And friends—modern, thrilling friends, writers and painters and poets or people keen on social questions—just the kind of friends they wanted. And then there were books, and there was music, and she had found a wonderful little dressmaker, and they were going abroad in the summer, and their new cook made the most superb omelettes. . . .

"I'm absurd. Absurd!" She sat up; but she felt quite dizzy, quite drunk. It must have been the spring.

Yes, it was the spring. Now she was so tired she could not drag herself upstairs to dress.

A white dress, a string of jade beads, green shoes and stockings. It wasn't intentional. She had thought of this scheme hours before she stood at the drawing-room window.

Her petals rustled softly into the hall, and she kissed Mrs. Norman Knight, who was taking off the most amusing orange coat with a procession of black monkeys round the hem and up the fronts.

". . . Why! Why! Why is the middle-class so stodgy—so utterly without a sense of humour! My dear, it's only by a fluke that I am here at all—Norman being the protective fluke. For my darling monkeys so upset the train that it rose to a man and simply ate me with its eyes. Didn't laugh—wasn't amused—that I should have loved. No, just stared—and bored me through and through."

"But the cream of it was," said Norman, pressing a large tortoiseshell-rimmed monocle into his eye, "you don't mind me telling this, Face, do you?" (In their home and among their friends they called each other Face and Mug.) "The cream of it was when she, being full fed, turned to the woman beside her and said: 'Haven't you ever seen a monkey before?'"

"Oh, yes!" Mrs. Norman Knight joined in the laughter. "Wasn't that too absolutely creamy?"

And a funnier thing still was that now her coat was off she did look like a very intelligent monkey—who had even made that yellow silk dress out of scraped banana skins. And her amber ear-rings; they were like little dangling nuts.

"This is a sad, sad fall!" said Mug, pausing in front of Little B's perambulator. "When the perambulator comes into the hall—" and he waved the rest of the quotation away.

The bell rang. It was lean, pale Eddie Warren (as usual) in a state of acute distress.

"It *is* the right house, *isn't* it?" he pleaded.

"Oh, I think so—I hope so," said Bertha brightly.

"I have had such a *dreadful* experience with a taxi-man; he was *most* sinister. I couldn't get him to *stop*. The *more* I knocked and called the *faster* he went. And *in* the moonlight this *bizarre* figure with the *flattened* head *crouching* over the *lit-tle* wheel. . . ."

He shuddered, taking off an immense white silk scarf. Bertha noticed that his socks were white, too—most charming.

"But how dreadful!" she cried.

"Yes, it really was," said Eddie, following her into the drawing-room. "I saw myself *driving* through Eternity in a *timeless* taxi."

He knew the Norman Knights. In fact, he was going to write a play for N. K. when the theatre scheme came off.

"Well, Warren, how's the play?" said Norman Knight, dropping his monocle and giving his eye a moment in which to rise to the surface before it was screwed down again.

And Mrs. Norman Knight: "Oh, Mr. Warren, what happy socks!"

"I *am* so glad you like them," said he, staring at his feet. "They seem to have got so *much* whiter since the moon rose." And he turned his lean sorrowful young face to Bertha. "There *is* a moon, you know."

She wanted to cry: "I am sure there is—often—often!"

He really was a most attractive person. But so was Face, crouched before the fire in her banana skins, and so was Mug, smoking a cigarette and saying as he flicked the ash: "Why doth the bridegroom tarry?"

"There he is, now."

Bang went the front door open and shut. Harry shouted: "Hullo, you people. Down in five minutes." And they heard him swarm up the stairs. Bertha couldn't help smiling; she knew how he loved doing things at high pressure. What, after all, did an extra five minutes matter? But he would pretend to himself that they mattered beyond measure. And then he would make a great point of coming into the drawing-room, extravagantly cool and collected.

Harry had such a zest for life. Oh, how she appreciated it in him. And his passion for fighting—for seeking in everything that came up against him another test of his power and of his courage—that, too, she understood. Even when it made him just occasionally, to other people, who didn't know him well, a little ridiculous perhaps. . . . For there were moments when he rushed into battle where no battle was. . . . She talked and laughed and positively forgot until he had come in (just as she had imagined) that Pearl Fulton had not turned up.

"I wonder if Miss Fulton has forgotten?"

"I expect so," said Harry. "Is she on the 'phone?"

"Ah! There's a taxi, now." And Bertha smiled with that little air of proprietorship that she always assumed while her women finds were new and mysterious. "She lives in taxis."

"She'll run to fat if she does," said Harry coolly, ringing the bell for dinner. "Frightful danger for blond women."

"Harry—don't," warned Bertha, laughing up at him.

Came another tiny moment, while they waited, laughing and talking, just a trifle too much at their ease, a trifle too unaware. And then Miss Fulton, all in silver, with a silver fillet binding her pale blond hair, came in smiling, her head a little on one side.

"Am I late?"

"No, not at all," said Bertha. "Come along." And she took her arm and they moved into the dining-room.

What was there in the touch of that cool arm that could fan—fan—start blazing —blazing—the fire of bliss that Bertha did not know what to do with?

Miss Fulton did not look at her; but then she seldom did look at people directly. Her heavy eyelids lay upon her eyes and the strange half smile came and went upon her lips as though she lived by listening rather than seeing. But Bertha knew, suddenly, as if the longest, most intimate look had passed between them—as if they had said to each other: "You too?"—that Pearl Fulton, stirring the beautiful red soup in the grey plate, was feeling just what she was feeling.

And the others? Face and Mug, Eddie and Harry, their spoons rising and falling— dabbing their lips with their napkins, crumbling bread, fiddling with the forks and glasses and talking.

"I met her at the Alpha show—the weirdest little person. She'd not only cut off her hair, but she seemed to have taken a dreadfully good snip off her legs and arms and her neck and her poor little nose as well."

"Isn't she very *liée* with Michael Oat?"

"The man who wrote *Love in False Teeth?*"

"He wants to write a play for me. One act. One man. Decides to commit suicide. Gives all the reasons why he should and why he shouldn't. And just as he has made up his mind either to do it or not to do it—curtain. Not half a bad idea."

"What's he going to call it—'Stomach Trouble'?"

"I *think* I've come across the *same* idea in a lit-tle French review, *quite* unknown in England."

No, they didn't share it. They were dears—dears—and she loved having them there, at her table, and giving them delicious food and wine. In fact, she longed to tell them how delightful they were, and what a decorative group they made, how they seemed to set one another off and how they reminded her of a play by Tchekof!

Harry was enjoying his dinner. It was part of his—well, not his nature, exactly, and certainly not his pose—his—something or other—to talk about food and to glory in his "shameless passion for the white flesh of the lobster" and "the green of pistachio ices—green and cold like the eyelids of Egyptian dancers."

When he looked up at her and said: "Bertha, this is a very admirable *soufflé!*" she almost could have wept with child-like pleasure.

Oh, why did she feel so tender towards the whole world tonight? Everything was good—was right. All that happened seemed to fill again her brimming cup of bliss.

And still, in the back of her mind, there was the pear tree. It would be silver now, in the light of poor dear Eddie's moon, silver as Miss Fulton, who sat there turning a tangerine in her slender fingers that were so pale a light seemed to come from them.

What she simply couldn't make out—what was miraculous—was how she should have guessed Miss Fulton's mood so exactly and so instantly. For she never doubted for a moment that she was right, and yet what had she to go on? Less than nothing.

"I believe this does happen very, very rarely between women. Never between men," thought Bertha. "But while I am making the coffee in the drawing-room perhaps she will 'give a sign.' "

What she meant by that she did not know, and what would happen after that she could not imagine.

While she thought like this she saw herself talking and laughing. She had to talk because of her desire to laugh.

"I must laugh or die."

But when she noticed Face's funny little habit of tucking something down the front of her bodice—as if she kept a tiny, secret hoard of nuts there, too—Bertha had to dig her nails into her hands—so as not to laugh too much.

It was over at last. And: "Come and see my new coffee machine," said Bertha.

"We only have a new coffee machine once a fortnight," said Harry. Face took her arm this time; Miss Fulton bent her head and followed after.

The fire had died down in the drawing-room to a red, flickering "nest of baby phoenixes," said Face.

"Don't turn up the light for a moment. It is so lovely." And down she crouched by the fire again. She was always cold . . . "without her little red flannel jacket, of course," thought Bertha.

At that moment Miss Fulton "gave the sign."

"Have you a garden?" said the cool, sleepy voice.

This was so exquisite on her part that all Bertha could do was to obey. She crossed the room, pulled the curtains apart, and opened those long windows.

"There!" she breathed.

And the two women stood side by side looking at the slender, flowering tree. Although it was so still it seemed, like the flame of a candle, to stretch up, to point, to quiver in the bright air, to grow taller and taller as they gazed—almost to touch the rim of the round, silver moon.

How long did they stand there? Both, as it were, caught in that circle of unearthly light, understanding each other perfectly, creatures of another world, and wondering what they were to do in this one with all this blissful treasure that burned in their bosoms and dropped, in silver flowers, from their hair and hands?

For ever—for a moment? And did Miss Fulton murmur: "Yes. Just *that*." Or did Bertha dream it?

Then the light was snapped on and Face made the coffee and Harry said: "My dear Mrs. Knight, don't ask me about my baby. I never see her. I shan't feel the slightest interest in her until she has a lover," and Mug took his eye out of the conservatory for a moment and then put it under glass again and Eddie Warren drank his coffee and set down the cup with a face of anguish as though he had drunk and seen the spider.

"What I want to do is to give the young men a show. I believe London is simply teeming with first-chop, unwritten plays. What I want to say to 'em is: 'Here's the theatre. Fire ahead.' "

"You know, my dear, I am going to decorate a room for the Jacob Nathans. Oh, I am so tempted to do a fried-fish scheme, with the backs of the chairs shaped like frying pans and lovely chip potatoes embroidered all over the curtains."

"The trouble with our young writing men is that they are still too romantic. You can't put out to sea without being seasick and wanting a basin. Well, why won't they have the courage of those basins?"

"A *dreadful* poem about a *girl* who was *violated* by a beggar *without* a nose in a lit-tle wood. . . ."

Miss Fulton sank into the lowest, deepest chair and Harry handed round the cigarettes.

From the way he stood in front of her shaking the silver box and saying abruptly: "Egyptian? Turkish? Virginian? They're all mixed up," Bertha realized that she not only bored him; he really disliked her. And she decided from the way Miss Fulton said: "No, thank you, I won't smoke," that she felt it, too, and was hurt.

"Oh, Harry, don't dislike her. You are quite wrong about her. She's wonderful, wonderful. And, besides, how can you feel so differently about someone who means so much to me. I shall try to tell you when we are in bed to-night what has been happening. What she and I have shared."

At those last words something strange and almost terrifying darted into Bertha's mind. And this something blind and smiling whispered to her: "Soon these people will go. The house will be quiet—quiet. The lights will be out. And you and he will be alone together in the dark room—the warm bed. . . ."

She jumped up from her chair and ran over to the piano.

"What a pity someone does not play!" she cried. "What a pity somebody does not play."

For the first time in her life Bertha Young desired her husband.

Oh, she'd loved him—she'd been in love with him, of course, in every other way, but just not in that way. And, equally, of course, she'd understood that he was different. They'd discussed it so often. It had worried her dreadfully at first to find that she was so cold, but after a time it had not seemed to matter. They were so frank with each other—such good pals. That was the best of being modern.

But now—ardently! ardently! The word ached in her ardent body! Was this what that feeling of bliss had been leading up to? But then then—

"My dear," said Mrs. Norman Knight, "you know our shame. We are the victims of time and train. We live in Hampstead. It's been so nice."

"I'll come with you into the hall," said Bertha. "I loved having you. But you must not miss the last train. That's so awful, isn't it?"

"Have a whisky, Knight, before you go?" called Harry.

"No, thanks, old chap."

Bertha squeezed his hand for that as she shook it.

"Good night, good-bye," she cried from the top step, feeling that this self of hers was taking leave of them for ever.

When she got back into the drawing-room the others were on the move.

". . . Then you can come part of the way in my taxi."

"I shall be *so* thankful *not* to have to face *another* drive *alone* after my *dreadful* experience."

"You can get a taxi at the rank just at the end of the street. You won't have to walk more than a few yards."

"That's a comfort. I'll go and put on my coat."

Miss Fulton moved towards the hall and Bertha was following when Harry almost pushed past.

"Let me help you."

Bertha knew that he was repenting his rudeness—she let him go. What a boy he was in some ways—so impulsive—so—simple.

And Eddie and she were left by the fire.

"I *wonder* if you have seen Bilks' *new* poem called *Table d'Hôte,*" said Eddie softly. "It's *so* wonderful. In the last Anthology. Have you got a copy? I'd *so* like to *show* it to you. It begins with an *incredibly* beautiful line: 'Why Must it Always be Tomato Soup?'"

"Yes," said Bertha. And she moved noiselessly to a table opposite the drawing-room door and Eddie glided noiselessly after her. She picked up the little book and gave it to him; they had not made a sound.

While he looked it up she turned her head towards the hall. And she saw . . . Harry with Miss Fulton's coat in his arms and Miss Fulton with her back turned to him and her head bent. He tossed the coat away, put his hands on her shoulders and turned her violently to him. His lips said: "I adore you," and Miss Fulton laid her moonbeam fingers on his cheeks and smiled her sleepy smile. Harry's nostrils quivered; his lips curled back in a hideous grin while he whispered: "To-morrow," and with her eyelids Miss Fulton said: "Yes."

"Here it is," said Eddie. " 'Why Must it Always be Tomato Soup?' It's so *deeply* true, don't you feel? Tomato soup is so *dreadfully* eternal."

"If you prefer," said Harry's voice, very loud, from the hall, "I can phone you a cab to come to the door."

"Oh, no. It's not necessary," said Miss Fulton, and she came up to Bertha and gave her the slender fingers to hold.

"Good-bye. Thank you so much."

"Good-bye," said Bertha.

Miss Fulton held her hand a moment longer.

"Your lovely pear tree!" she murmured.

And then she was gone, with Eddie following, like the black cat following the grey cat.

"I'll shut up shop," said Harry, extravagantly cool and collected.

"Your lovely pear tree—pear tree—pear tree!"

Bertha simply ran over to the long windows.

"Oh, what is going to happen now?" she cried.

But the pear tree was as lovely as ever and as full of flower and as still.

KATHERINE ANNE PORTER

[*1890–1980*]

He

Life was very hard for the Whipples. It was hard to feed all the hungry mouths, it was hard to keep the children in flannels during the winter, short as it was: "God knows what would become of us if we lived north," they would say: keeping them decently clean was hard. "It looks like our luck won't never let up on us," said Mr. Whipple, but Mrs. Whipple was all for taking what was sent and calling it good, anyhow when the neighbors were in earshot. "Don't ever let a soul hear us complain," she kept saying to her husband. She couldn't stand to be pitied. "No, not if it comes to it that we have to live in a wagon and pick cotton around the country," she said, "nobody's going to get a chance to look down on us."

Mrs. Whipple loved her second son, the simple-minded one, better than she loved the other two children put together. She was forever saying so, and when she talked with certain of her neighbors, she would even throw in her husband and her mother for good measure.

"You needn't keep on saying it around," said Mr. Whipple, "you'll make people think nobody else has any feelings about Him but you."

"It's natural for a mother," Mrs. Whipple would remind him. "You know yourself it's more natural for a mother to be that way. People don't expect so much of fathers, some way."

This didn't keep the neighbors from talking plainly among themselves. "A Lord's pure mercy if He should die," they said. "It's the sins of the fathers," they agreed among themselves. "There's bad blood and bad doings somewhere, you can bet on that." This behind the Whipples' backs. To their faces everybody said, "He's not so bad off. He'll be all right yet. Look how He grows!"

Mrs. Whipple hated to talk about it, she tried to keep her mind off it, but every time anybody set foot in the house, the subject always came up, and she had to talk about Him first, before she could get on to anything else. It seemed to ease her mind. "I wouldn't have anything happen to Him for all the world, but it just looks like I can't keep Him out of mischief. He's so strong and active, He's always into everything; He was like that since He could walk. It's actually funny sometimes, the way He can do anything; it's laughable to see Him up to His tricks. Emly has more accidents; I'm forever tying up her bruises, and Adna can't fall a foot without cracking a bone. But He can do anything and not get a scratch. The preacher said such a nice thing once when he was here. He said, and I'll remember it to my dying day, 'The innocent walk with God—that's why He don't get hurt.' " Whenever Mrs. Whipple repeated these words, she always felt a warm pool spread in her breast, and the tears would fill her eyes, and then she could talk about something else.

He did grow and He never got hurt. A plank blew off the chicken house and struck Him on the head and He never seemed to know it. He had learned a few words, and after this He forgot them. He didn't whine for food as the other children did, but waited until it was given Him; He ate squatting in the corner, smacking and mumbling. Rolls of fat covered Him like an overcoat, and He could carry twice as much wood and water as Adna. Emly had a cold in the head most of the time—"she takes that after me," said Mrs. Whipple—so in bad weather they gave her the extra blanket off His cot. He never seemed to mind the cold.

Just the same, Mrs. Whipple's life was a torment for fear something might happen to Him. He climbed the peach trees much better than Adna and went skittering along the branches like a monkey, just a regular monkey. "Oh, Mrs. Whipple, you hadn't ought to let Him do that. He'll lose His balance sometime. He can't rightly know what He's doing."

Mrs. Whipple almost screamed out at the neighbor. "He *does* know what He's doing! He's as able as any other child! Come down out of there, you!" When He finally reached the ground she could hardly keep her hands off Him for acting like that before people, a grin all over His face and her worried sick about Him all the time.

"It's the neighbors," said Mrs. Whipple to her husband. "Oh, I do mortally wish they would keep out of our business. I can't afford to let Him do anything for fear they'll come nosing around about it. Look at the bees, now. Adna can't handle them, they sting him up so; I haven't got time to do everything, and now I don't dare let Him. But if He gets a sting He don't really mind."

"It's just because He ain't got sense enough to be scared of anything," said Mr. Whipple.

"You ought to be ashamed of yourself," said Mrs. Whipple, "talking that way about your own child. Who's to take up for Him if we don't, I'd like to know? He sees a lot that goes on, He listens to things all the time. And anything I tell Him to do He does it. Don't never let anybody hear you say such things. They'd think you favored the other children over Him."

"Well, now I don't, and you know it, and what's the use of getting all worked up about it? You always think the worst of everything. Just let Him alone, He'll get along somehow. He gets plenty to eat and wear, don't He?" Mr. Whipple suddenly felt tired out. "Anyhow, it can't be helped now."

Mrs. Whipple felt tired too, she complained in a tired voice. "What's done can't never be undone, I know that as good as anybody; but He's my child, and I'm not going to have people say anything. I get sick of people coming around saying things all the time."

In the early fall Mrs. Whipple got a letter from her brother saying he and his wife and two children were coming over for a little visit next Sunday week. "Put the big pot in the little one," he wrote at the end. Mrs. Whipple read this part out loud twice, she was so pleased. Her brother was a great one for saying funny things. "We'll just show him that's no joke," she said, "we'll just butcher one of the sucking pigs."

"It's a waste and I don't hold with waste the way we are now," said Mr. Whipple. "That pig'll be worth money by Christmas."

"It's a shame and a pity we can't have a decent meal's vittles once in a while when my own family comes to see us," said Mrs. Whipple. "I'd hate for his wife to go back and say there wasn't a thing in the house to eat. My God, it's better than buying up a great chance of meat in town. There's where you'd spend the money!"

"All right, do it yourself then," said Mr. Whipple. "Christamighty, no wonder we can't get ahead!"

The question was how to get the little pig away from his ma, a great fighter, worse than a Jersey cow. Adna wouldn't try it: "That sow'd rip my insides out all over the pen." "All right, old fraidy," said Mrs. Whipple, "*He's* not scared. Watch *Him* do it." And she laughed as though it was all a good joke and gave Him a little push towards the pen. He sneaked up and snatched the pig right away from the teat and galloped back and was over the fence with the sow raging at His heels. The little black squirming thing was screeching like a baby in a tantrum, stiffening its back and stretching its mouth to the ears. Mrs. Whipple took the pig with her face stiff and sliced its throat with one stroke. When He saw the blood He gave a great jolting breath and ran away. "But He'll forget and eat plenty, just the same," thought Mrs. Whipple. Whenever she was thinking, her lips moved making words. "He'd eat it all if I didn't stop Him. He'd eat up every mouthful from the other two if I'd let Him."

She felt badly about it. He was ten years old now and a third again as large as Adna, who was going on fourteen. "It's a shame, a shame," she kept saying under her breath, "and Adna with so much brains!"

She kept on feeling badly about all sorts of things. In the first place it was the man's work to butcher; the sight of the pig scraped pink and naked made her sick. He was too fat and soft and pitiful-looking. It was simply a shame the way things had to happen. By the time she had finished it up, she almost wished her brother would stay at home.

Early Sunday morning Mrs. Whipple dropped everything to get Him all cleaned up. In an hour He was dirty again, with crawling under fences after a possum, and straddling along the rafters of the barn looking for eggs in the hayloft. "My Lord, look at you now after all my trying! And here's Adna and Emly staying so quiet. I get tired trying to keep you decent. Get off that shirt and put on another, people will say I don't half dress you!" And she boxed Him on the ears, hard. He blinked and blinked and rubbed His head, and His face hurt Mrs. Whipple's feelings. Her knees began to tremble, she had to sit down while she buttoned His shirt. "I'm just all gone before the day starts."

The brother came with his plump healthy wife and two great roaring hungry boys. They had a grand dinner, with the pig roasted to a crackling in the middle of the table, full of dressing, a pickled peach in his mouth and plenty of gravy for the sweet potatoes.

"This looks like prosperity all right," said the brother; "you're going to have to roll me home like I was a barrel when I'm done."

Everybody laughed out loud; it was fine to hear them laughing all at once around the table. Mrs. Whipple felt warm and good about it. "Oh, we've got six more of these; I say it's as little as we can do when you come to see us so seldom."

He wouldn't come into the dining room, and Mrs. Whipple passed it off very well. "He's timider than my other two," she said, "He'll just have to get used to you. There isn't everybody He'll make up with, you know how it is with some children, even cousins." Nobody said anything out of the way.

"Just like my Alfy here," said the brother's wife. "I sometimes got to lick him to make him shake hands with his own grandmammy."

So that was over, and Mrs. Whipple loaded up a big plate for Him first, before everybody. "I always say He ain't to be slighted, no matter who else goes without," she said, and carried it to Him herself.

"He can chin Himself on the top of the door," said Emly, helping along.

"That's fine. He's getting along fine," said the brother.

They went away after supper. Mrs. Whipple rounded up the dishes, and sent the children to bed and sat down and unlaced her shoes. "You see?" she said to Mr. Whipple. "That's the way my whole family is. Nice and considerate about everything. No out-of-the-way remarks—they *have* got refinement. I get awfully sick of people's remarks. Wasn't that pig good?"

Mr. Whipple said, "Yes, we're out three hundred pounds of pork, that's all. It's easy to be polite when you come to eat. Who knows what they had in their minds all along?"

"Yes, that's like you," said Mrs. Whipple. "I don't expect anything else from you. You'll be telling me next that my own brother will be saying around that we made Him eat in the kitchen! Oh, my God!" She rocked her head in her hands, a hard pain started in the very middle of her forehead. "Now it's all spoiled, and everything was so nice and easy. All right, you don't like them and you never did—all right, they'll not come here again soon, never you mind! But they *can't* say He wasn't dressed every lick as good as Adna—oh, honest, sometimes I wish I was dead!"

"I wish you'd let up," said Mr. Whipple. "It's bad enough as it is."

It was a hard winter. It seemed to Mrs. Whipple that they hadn't ever known anything but hard times, and now to cap it all a winter like this. The crops were about half of what they had a right to expect; after the cotton was in it didn't do much more than cover the grocery bill. They swapped off one of the plow horses, and got cheated, for the new one died of the heaves. Mrs. Whipple kept thinking all the time it was terrible to have a man you couldn't depend on not to get cheated. They cut down on everything, but Mrs. Whipple kept saying there are things you can't cut down on, and they cost money. It took a lot of warm clothes for Adna and Emly, who walked four miles to school during the three-months session. "He sets around the fire a lot, He won't need so much," said Mr. Whipple. "That's so," said Mrs. Whipple, "and when He does the outdoor chores He can wear your tarpaullion coat. I can't do no better, that's all."

In February He was taken sick, and lay curled up under His blanket looking very blue in the face and acting as if He would choke. Mr. and Mrs. Whipple did everything they could for Him for two days, and then they were scared and sent for the doctor. The doctor told them they must keep Him warm and give Him plenty of milk and eggs. "He isn't as stout as He looks, I'm afraid," said the doctor. "You've got to watch them when they're like that. You must put more cover onto Him, too."

"I just took off His big blanket to wash," said Mrs. Whipple, ashamed. "I can't stand dirt."

"Well, you'd better put it back on the minute it's dry," said the doctor, "or He'll have pneumonia."

Mr. and Mrs. Whipple took a blanket off their own bed and put His cot in by the fire. "They can't say we didn't do everything for Him," she said, "even to sleeping cold ourselves on His account."

When the winter broke He seemed to be well again, but He walked as if His feet hurt Him. He was able to run a cotton planter during the season.

"I got it all fixed up with Jim Ferguson about breeding the cow next time," said Mr. Whipple. "I'll pasture the bull this summer and give Jim some fodder in the fall. That's better than paying out money when you haven't got it."

"I hope you didn't say such a thing before Jim Ferguson," said Mrs. Whipple. "You oughtn't to let him know we're so down as all that."

"Godamighty, that ain't saying we're down. A man is got to look ahead sometimes. He can lead the bull over today. I need Adna on the place."

At first Mrs. Whipple felt easy in her mind about sending Him for the bull. Adna was too jumpy and couldn't be trusted. You've got to be steady around animals. After He was gone she started thinking, and after a while she could hardly bear it any longer. She stood in the lane and watched for Him. It was nearly three miles to go and a hot day, but He oughtn't to be so long about it. She shaded her eyes and stared until colored bubbles floated in her eyeballs. It was just like everything else in life, she must always worry and never know a moment's peace about anything. After a long time she saw

Him turn into the side lane, limping. He came on very slowly, leading the big hulk of an animal by a ring in the nose, twirling a little stick in His hand, never looking back or sideways, but coming on like a sleepwalker with His eyes half shut.

Mrs. Whipple was scared sick of bulls; she had heard awful stories about how they followed on quietly enough, and then suddenly pitched on with a bellow and pawed and gored a body to pieces. Any second now that black monster would come down on Him, my God, He'd never have sense enough to run.

She mustn't make a sound nor a move; she mustn't get the bull started. The bull heaved his head aside and horned the air at a fly. Her voice burst out of her in a shriek, and she screamed at Him to come on, for God's sake. He didn't seem to hear her clamor, but kept on twirling His switch and limping on, and the bull lumbered along behind him as gently as a calf. Mrs. Whipple stopped calling and ran towards the house, praying under her breath: "Lord, don't let anything happen to Him. Lord, you *know* people will say we oughtn't to have sent Him. You *know* they'll say we didn't take care of Him. Oh, get Him home, safe home, safe home, and I'll look out for Him better! Amen."

She watched from the window while He led the beast in, and tied him up in the barn. It was no use trying to keep up, Mrs. Whipple couldn't bear another thing. She sat down and rocked and cried with her apron over her head.

From year to year the Whipples were growing poorer and poorer. The place just seemed to run down of itself, no matter how hard they worked. "We're losing our hold," said Mrs. Whipple. "Why can't we do like other people and watch for our best chances? They'll be calling us poor white trash next."

"When I get to be sixteen I'm going to leave," said Adna. "I'm going to get a job in Powell's grocery store. There's money in that. No more farm for me."

"I'm going to be a schoolteacher," said Emly. "But I've got to finish the eighth grade, anyhow. Then I can live in town. I don't see any chances here."

"Emly takes after my family," said Mrs. Whipple. "Ambitious every last one of them, and they don't take second place for anybody."

When fall came Emly got a chance to wait on table in the railroad eating-house in the town near by, and it seemed such a shame not to take it when the wages were good and she could get her food too, that Mrs. Whipple decided to let her take it, and not bother with school until the next session. "You've got plenty of time," she said. "You're young and smart as a whip."

With Adna gone too, Mr. Whipple tried to run the farm with just Him to help. He seemed to get along fine, doing His work and part of Adna's without noticing it. They did well enough until Christmas time, when one morning He slipped on the ice coming up from the barn. Instead of getting up He thrashed round and round, and when Mr. Whipple got to Him, He was having some sort of fit.

They brought Him inside and tried to make Him sit up, but He blubbered and rolled, so they put Him to bed and Mr. Whipple rode to town for the doctor. All the way there and back he worried about where the money was to come from: it sure did look like he had about all the troubles he could carry.

From then on He stayed in bed. His legs swelled up double their size, and the fits kept coming back. After four months, the doctor said, "It's no use, I think you'd better put Him in the County Home for treatment right away. I'll see about it for you. He'll have good care there and be off your hands."

"We don't begrudge Him any care, and I won't let Him out of my sight," said Mrs. Whipple. "I won't have it said I sent my sick child off among strangers."

"I know how you feel," said the doctor. "You can't tell me anything about that, Mrs. Whipple. I've got a boy of my own. But you'd better listen to me. I can't do anything more for Him, that's the truth."

Mr. and Mrs. Whipple talked it over a long time that night after they went to bed. "It's just charity," said Mrs. Whipple, "that's what we've come to, charity! I certainly never looked for this."

"We pay taxes to help support the place just like everybody else," said Mr. Whipple, "and I don't call that taking charity. I think it would be fine to have Him where He'd get the best of everything . . . and besides, I can't keep up with these doctor bills any longer."

"Maybe that's why the doctor wants us to send Him—he's scared he won't get his money," said Mrs. Whipple.

"Don't talk like that," said Mr. Whipple, feeling pretty sick, "or we won't be able to send Him."

"Oh, but we won't keep Him there long," said Mrs. Whipple. "Soon's He's better, we'll bring Him right back home."

"The doctor has told you and told you time and again He can't ever get better, and you might as well stop talking," said Mr. Whipple.

"Doctors don't know everything," said Mrs. Whipple, feeling almost happy. "But anyhow in the summer Emly can come home for a vacation, and Adna can get down for Sundays: we'll all work together and get on our feet again, and the children will feel they've got a place to come to."

All at once she saw it full summer again, with the garden going fine, and new white roller shades up all over the house, and Adna and Emly home, so full of life, all of them happy together. Oh, it could happen, things would ease up on them.

They didn't talk before Him much, but they never knew just how much He understood. Finally the doctor set the day and a neighbor who owned a double-seated carryall offered to drive them over. The hospital would have sent an ambulance, but Mrs. Whipple couldn't stand to see Him going away looking so sick as all that. They wrapped Him in blankets, and the neighbor and Mr. Whipple lifted Him into the back seat of the carryall beside Mrs. Whipple, who had on her black shirt waist. She couldn't stand to go looking like charity.

"You'll be all right, I guess I'll stay behind," said Mr. Whipple. "It don't look like everybody ought to leave the place at once."

"Besides, it ain't as if He was going to stay forever," said Mrs. Whipple to the neighbor. "This is only for a little while."

They started away, Mrs. Whipple holding to the edges of the blankets to keep Him from sagging sideways. He sat there blinking and blinking. He worked His hands out and began rubbing His nose with His knuckles, and then with the end of the blanket. Mrs. Whipple couldn't believe what she saw; He was scrubbing away big tears that rolled out of the corners of His eyes. He sniveled and made a gulping noise. Mrs. Whipple kept saying, "Oh, honey, you don't feel so bad, do you? You don't feel so bad, do you?" for He seemed to be accusing her of something. Maybe He remembered that time she boxed His ears, maybe He had been scared that day with the bull, maybe He had slept cold and couldn't tell her about it; maybe He knew they were sending

Him away for good and all because they were too poor to keep Him. Whatever it was, Mrs. Whipple couldn't bear to think of it. She began to cry, frightfully, and wrapped her arms tight around Him. His head rolled on her shoulder: she had loved Him as much as she possibly could, there were Adna and Emly who had to be thought of too, there was nothing she could do to make up to Him for His life. Oh, what a mortal pity He was ever born.

They came in sight of the hospital, with the neighbor driving very fast, not daring to look behind him.

JEAN TOOMER
[1894–1967]

Theater

Life of nigger alleys, of pool rooms and restaurants and near-beer saloons soaks into the walls of Howard Theater and sets them throbbing jazz songs. Black-skinned, they dance and shout above the tick and trill of white-walled buildings. At night, they open doors to people who come in to stamp their feet and shout. At night, road-shows volley songs into the mass-heart of black people. Songs soak the walls and seep out to the nigger life of alleys and near-beer saloons, of the Poodle Dog and Black Bear cabarets. Afternoons, the house is dark, and the walls are sleeping singers until rehearsal begins. Or until John comes within them. Then they start throbbing to a subtle syncopation. And the space-dark air grows softly luminous.

John is the manager's brother. He is seated at the center of the theater, just before rehearsal. Light streaks down upon him from a window high above. One half his face is orange in it. One half his face is in shadow. The soft glow of the house rushes to, and compacts about, the shaft of light. John's mind coincides with the shaft of light. Thoughts rush to, and compact about it. Life of the house and of the slowly awakening stage swirls to the body of John, and thrills it. John's body is separate from the thoughts that pack his mind.

Stage-lights, soft, as if they shine through clear pink fingers. Beneath them, hid by the shadow of a set, Dorris. Other chorus girls drift in. John feels them in the mass. And as if his own body were the mass-heart of a black audience listening to them singing, he wants to stamp his feet and shout. His mind, contained above desires of his body, singles the girls out, and tries to trace origins and plot destinies.

A pianist slips into the pit and improvises jazz. The walls awake. Arms of the girls, and their limbs, which . . . jazz, jazz . . . by lifting up their tight street skirts they set free, jab the air and clog the floor in rhythm to the music. (Lift your skirts, Baby, and talk t papa!) Crude, individualized, and yet . . . monotonous. . . .

John: Soon the director will herd you, my full-lipped, distant beauties, and tame you, and blunt your sharp thrusts in loosely suggestive movements, appropriate to Broadway. (O dance!) Soon the audience will paint your dusk faces white, and call you beautiful. (O dance!) Soon I. . . . (O dance!) I'd like . . .

Girls laugh and shout. Sing discordant snatches of other jazz songs. Whirl with loose passion into the arms of passing show-men.

John: Too thick. Too easy. Too monotonous. Her whom I'd love I'd leave before she knew that I was with her. Her? Which? (O dance!) I'd like to . . .

Girls dance and sing. Men clap. The walls sing and press inward. They press the men and girls, they press John towards a center of physical ecstasy. Go to it, Baby! Fan yourself, and feed your papa! Put . . . nobody lied . . . and take . . . when they said I cried over you. No lie! The glitter and color of stacked scenes, the gilt and brass and crimson of the house, converge towards a center of physical ecstasy. John's feet and torso and his blood press in. He wills thought to rid his mind of passion.

"All right, girls. Alaska. Miss Reynolds, please."

The director wants to get the rehearsal through with.

The girls line up. John sees the front row: dancing ponies. The rest are in shadow. The leading lady fits loosely in the front. Lack-life, monotonous. "One, two, three—" Music starts. The song is somewhere where it will not strain the leading lady's throat. The dance is somewhere where it will not strain the girls. Above the staleness, one dancer throws herself into it. Dorris. John sees her. Her hair, crisp-curled, is bobbed. Bushy, black hair bobbing about her lemon-colored face. Her lips are curiously full, and very red. Her limbs in silk purple stockings are lovely. John feels them. Desires her. Holds off.

John: Stage-door johnny; chorus-girl. No, that would be all right. Dictie, educated, stuck-up; show-girl. Yep. Her suspicion would be stronger than her passion. It wouldn't work. Keep her loveliness. Let her go.

Dorris sees John and knows that he is looking at her. Her own glowing is too rich a thing to let her feel the slimness of his diluted passion.

"Who's that?" she asks her dancing partner.

"Th manager's brother. Dictie. Nothin doin, hon."

Dorris tosses her head and dances for him until she feels she has him. Then, withdrawing disdainfully, she flirts with the director.

Dorris: Nothing doin? How come? Aint I as good as him? Couldnt I have got an education if I'd wanted one? Dont I know respectable folks, lots of em, in Philadelphia and New York and Chicago? Aint I had men as good as him? Better. Doctors an lawyers. Whats a manager's brother, anyhow?

Two steps back, and two steps front.

"Say, Mame, where do you get that stuff?"

"Whatshmean, Dorris?"

"If you two girls cant listen to what I'm telling you, I know where I can get some who can. Now listen."

Mame: Go to hell, you black bastard.

Dorris: Whats eatin at him, anyway?

"Now follow me in this, you girls. Its three counts to the right, three counts to the left, and then you shimmy—"

John:—and then you shimmy. I'll bet she can. Some good cabaret, with rooms upstairs. And what in hell do you think you'd get from it? Youre going wrong. Here's right: get her to herself—(Christ, but how she'd bore you after the first five minutes)

—not if you get her right she wouldnt. Touch her, I mean. To herself—in some room perhaps. Some cheap, dingy bedroom. Hell no. Cant be done. But the point is, brother John, it can be done. Get her to herself somewhere, anywhere. Go down in yourself —and she'd be calling you all sorts of asses while you were in the process of going down. Hold em, bud. Cant be done. Let her go. (Dance and I'll love you!) And keep her loveliness.

"All right now, Chicken Chaser. Dorris and girls. Where's Dorris? I told you to stay on the stage, didnt I? Well? Now thats enough. All right. All right there, Professor? All right. One, two, three—"

Dorris swings to the front. The line of girls, four deep, blurs within the shadow of suspended scenes. Dorris wants to dance. The director feels that and steps to one side. He smiles, and picks her for a leading lady, one of these days. Odd ends of stage-men emerge from the wings, and stare and clap. A crap game in the alley suddenly ends. Black faces crowd the rear stage doors. The girls, catching joy from Dorris, whip up within the footlights' glow. They forget set steps; they find their own. The director forgets to bawl them out. Dorris dances.

John: Her head bobs to Broadway. Dance from yourself. Dance! O just a little more. Dorris' eyes burn across the space of seats to him.

Dorris: I bet he can love. Hell, he cant love. He's too skinny. His lips are too skinny. He wouldn't love me anyway, only for that. But I'd get a pair of silk stockings out of it. Red silk. I got purple. Cut it, kid. You cant win him to respect you that away. He wouldnt anyway. Maybe he would. Maybe he'd love. I've heard em say that men who look like him (what does he look like?) will marry if they love. O will you love me? And give me kids, and a home, and everything? (I'd like to make your nest, and honest, hon, I wouldnt run out on you.) You will if I make you. Just watch me.

Dorris dances. She forgets her tricks. She dances.

Glorious songs are the muscles of her limbs.

And her singing is of canebrake loves and mangrove feastings.

The walls press in, singing. Flesh of a throbbing body, they press close to John and Dorris. They close them in. John's heart beats tensely against her dancing body. Walls press his mind within his heart. And then, the shaft of light goes out the window high above him. John's mind sweeps up to follow it. Mind pulls him upward into dream. Dorris dances . . . John dreams:

> Dorris is dressed in a loose black gown, splashed with lemon ribbons. Her feet taper long and slim from trim ankles. She waits for him just inside the stage door. John, collar and tie colorful and flaring, walks towards the stage door. There are no trees in the alley. But his feet feel as though they step on autumn leaves whose rustle has been pressed out of them by the passing of a million satin slippers. The air is sweet with roasting chestnuts, sweet with bonfires of old leaves. John's melancholy is a deep thing that seals all senses but his eyes, and makes him whole.
>
> Dorris knows that he is coming. Just at the right moment she steps from the door, as if there were no door. Her face is tinted like the autumn alley. Of old flowers, or of a southern canefield, her perfume. "Glorious Dorris." So his eyes speak. And their sadness is too deep for sweet untruth. She barely touches his arm.

They glide off with footfalls softened on the leaves, the old leaves powdered by a million satin slippers.

They are in a room. John knows nothing of it. Only, that the flesh and blood of Dorris are its walls. Singing walls. Lights, soft, as if they shine through clear pink fingers. Soft lights, and warm.

John reaches for a manuscript of his, and reads. Dorris, who has no eyes, has eyes to understand him. He comes to a dancing scene. The scene is Dorris. She dances. Dorris dances. Glorious Dorris. Dorris whirls, whirls, dances. . . .

Dorris dances. The pianist crashes a bumper chord. The whole stage claps. Dorris, flushed, looks quick at John. His whole face is in shadow. She seeks for her dance in it. She finds it a dead thing in the shadow which is his dream. She rushes from the stage. Falls down the steps into her dressing-room. Pulls her hair. Her eyes, over a floor of tears, stare at the whitewashed ceiling. (Smell of dry paste, and paint, and soiled clothing.) Her pal comes in. Dorris flings herself into the old safe arms, and cries bitterly.

"I told you nothin doing," is what Mame says to comfort her.

WILLIAM FAULKNER
[1897–1962]

The Bear

He was ten. But it had already begun, long before that day when at last he wrote his age in two figures and he saw for the first time the camp where his father and Major de Spain and old General Compson and the others spent two weeks each November and two weeks again each June. He had already inherited then, without ever having seen it, the tremendous bear with one trap-ruined foot which, in an area almost a hundred miles deep, had earned itself a name, a definite designation like a living man.

He had listened to it for years: the long legend of corncribs rifled, of shotes and grown pigs and even calves carried bodily into the woods and devoured, of traps and deadfalls overthrown and dogs mangled and slain, and shotgun and even rifle charges delivered at point-blank range and with no more effect than so many peas blown through a tube by a boy—a corridor of wreckage and destruction beginning back before he was born, through which sped, not fast but rather with the ruthless and irresistible deliberation of a locomotive, the shaggy tremendous shape.

It ran in his knowledge before he ever saw it. It loomed and towered in his dreams before he even saw the unaxed woods where it left its crooked print, shaggy, huge, red-eyed, not malevolent but just big—too big for the dogs which tried to bay it, for the horses which tried to ride it down, for the men and the bullets they fired into it, too big for the very country which was its constricting scope. He seemed to see it entire with a child's complete divination before he ever laid eyes on either—the doomed wilderness whose edges were being constantly and punily gnawed at by men with axes and plows who feared it because it was wilderness, men myriad and nameless even to one another in the land where the old bear had earned a name, through which ran not even a mortal animal but an anachronism, indomitable and invincible, out of an old dead time, a phantom, epitome and apotheosis of the old wild life at which the puny humans swarmed and hacked in a fury of abhorrence and fear, like pygmies about the ankles of a drowsing elephant: the old bear solitary, indomitable and alone, widowered, childless, and absolved of mortality—old Priam reft of his old wife and having outlived all his sons.

Until he was ten, each November he would watch the wagon containing the dogs and the bedding and food and guns and his father and Tennie's Jim, the Negro, and Sam Fathers, the Indian, son of a slave woman and a Chickasaw chief, depart on the road to town, to Jefferson, where Major de Spain and the others would join them. To the boy, at seven, eight, and nine, they were not going into the Big Bottom to hunt bear and deer, but to keep yearly rendezvous with the bear which they did not even intend to kill. Two weeks later they would return, with no trophy, no head and skin. He had not expected it. He had not even been afraid it would be in the wagon. He believed that even after he was ten and his father would let him go too, for those two weeks in November, he would merely make another one, along with his father and Major de Spain and General Compson and the others, the dogs which feared to bay at it and the rifles and shotguns which failed even to bleed it, in the yearly pageant of the old bear's furious immortality.

Then he heard the dogs! It was in the second week of his first time in the camp. He stood with Sam Fathers against a big oak beside the faint crossing where they had stood each dawn for nine days now, hearing the dogs. He had heard them once before, one morning last week—a murmur, sourceless, echoing through the wet woods, swelling presently into separate voices which he could recognize and call by name. He had raised and cocked the gun as Sam told him and stood motionless again while the uproar, the invisible course, swept up and past and faded; it seemed to him that he could actually see the deer, the buck, blond, smoke-colored, elongated with speed, fleeing, vanishing, the woods, the gray solitude, still ringing even when the cries of the dogs had died away.

"Now let the hammers down," Sam said.

"You knew they were not coming here too," he said.

"Yes," Sam said. "I want you to learn how to do when you didn't shoot. It's after the chance for the bear or the deer has done already come and gone that men and dogs get killed."

"Anyway," he said, "it was just a deer."

Then on the tenth morning he heard the dogs again. And he readied the too-long, too-heavy gun as Sam had taught him, before Sam even spoke. But this time it was no deer, no ringing chorus of dogs running strong on a free scent, but a moiling yapping an octave too high, with something more than indecision and even abjectness in it, not even moving very fast, taking a long time to pass completely out of hearing, leaving then somewhere in the air that echo, thin, slightly hysterical, abject, almost grieving, with no sense of a fleeting, unseen, smoke-colored, grass-eating shape ahead of it, and Sam, who had taught him first of all to cock the gun and take position where he could see everywhere and then never move again, had himself moved up beside him; he could hear Sam breathing at his shoulder, and he could see the arched curve of the old man's inhaling nostrils.

"Hah," Sam said. "Not even running. Walking."

"Old Ben!" the boy said. "But up here!" he cried. "Way up here!"

"He do it every year," Sam said. "Once. Maybe to see who in camp this time, if he can shoot or not. Whether we got the dog yet that can bay and hold him. He'll take them to the river, then he'll send them back home. We may as well go back too; see how they look when they come back to camp."

When they reached the camp the hounds were already there, ten of them crouching back under the kitchen, the boy and Sam squatting to peer back into the obscurity where they had huddled, quiet, the eyes luminous, glowing at them and vanishing, and no sound, only that effluvium of something more than dog, stronger than dog and not just animal, just beast, because still there had been nothing in front of that abject and almost painful yapping save the solitude, the wilderness, so that when the eleventh hound came in at noon and with all the others watching—even old Uncle Ash, who called himself first a cook—Sam daubed the tattered ear and the raked shoulder with turpentine and axle grease, to the boy it was still no living creature, but the wilderness which, leaning for the moment down, had patted lightly once the hound's temerity.

"Just like a man," Sam said. "Just like folks. Put off as long as she could having to be brave, knowing all the time that sooner or later she would have to be brave to keep on living with herself, and knowing all the time beforehand what was going to happen to her when she done it."

That afternoon, himself on the one-eyed wagon mule which did not mind the smell of blood nor, as they told him, of bear, and with Sam on the other one, they rode for more than three hours through the rapid, shortening winter day. They followed no path, no trail even that he could see; almost at once they were in a country which he had never seen before. Then he knew why Sam had made him ride the mule which would not spook. The sound one stopped short and tried to whirl and bolt even as Sam got down, blowing its breath, jerking and wrenching at the rein, while Sam held it, coaxing it forward with his voice, since he could not risk tying it, drawing it forward while the boy got down from the marred one.

Then, standing beside Sam in the gloom of the dying afternoon, he looked down at the rotted over-turned log, gutted and scored with claw marks and, in the wet earth beside it, the print of the enormous warped two-toed foot. He knew now what he had smelled when he peered under the kitchen where the dogs huddled. He realized for the first time that the bear which had run in his listening and loomed in his dreams since before he could remember to the contrary, and which, therefore, must have existed in the listening and dreams of his father and Major de Spain and even old General Compson, too, before they began to remember in their turn, was a mortal animal, and that if they had departed for the camp each November without any actual hope of bringing its trophy back, it was not because it could not be slain, but because so far they had had no actual hope to.

"Tomorrow," he said.

"We'll try tomorrow," Sam said. "We ain't got the dog yet."

"We've got eleven. They ran him this morning."

"It won't need but one," Sam said. "He ain't here. Maybe he ain't nowhere. The only other way will be for him to run by accident over somebody that has a gun."

"That wouldn't be me," the boy said. "It will be Walter or Major or—"

"It might," Sam said. "You watch close in the morning. Because he's smart. That's how come he has lived this long. If he gets hemmed up and has to pick out somebody to run over, he will pick out you."

"How?" the boy said. "How will he know—" He ceased. "You mean he already knows me, that I ain't never been here before, ain't had time to find out yet whether I—" He ceased again, looking at Sam, the old man whose face revealed nothing until it smiled. He said humbly, not even amazed, "It was me he was watching. I don't reckon he did need to come but once."

The next morning they left the camp three hours before daylight. They rode this time because it was too far to walk, even the dogs in the wagon; again the first gray light found him in a place which he had never seen before, where Sam had placed him and told him to stay and then departed. With the gun which was too big for him, which did not even belong to him, but to Major de Spain, and which he had fired only once —at a stump on the first day, to learn the recoil and how to reload it—he stood against a gum tree beside a little bayou whose black still water crept without movement out of a canebrake and crossed a small clearing and into cane again, where, invisible, a bird —the big woodpecker called Lord-to-God by Negroes—clattered at a dead limb.

It was a stand like any other, dissimilar only in incidentals to the one where he had stood each morning for ten days; a territory new to him, yet no less familiar than that other one which, after almost two weeks, he had come to believe he knew a little— the same solitude, the same loneliness through which human beings had merely passed without altering it, leaving no mark, no scar, which looked exactly as it must have looked when the first ancestor of Sam Fathers' Chickasaw predecessors crept into it and looked about, club or stone ax or bone arrow drawn and poised; different only because, squatting at the edge of the kitchen, he smelled the hounds huddled and cringing beneath it and saw the raked ear and shoulder of the one who, Sam said, had had to be brave once in order to live with herself, and saw yesterday in the earth beside the gutted log the print of the living foot.

He heard no dogs at all. He never did hear them. He only heard the drumming of the woodpecker stop short off and knew that the bear was looking at him. He never saw it. He did not know whether it was in front of him or behind him. He did not move, holding the useless gun, which he had not even had warning to cock and which even now he did not cock, tasting in his saliva that taint as of brass which he knew now because he had smelled it when he peered under the kitchen at the huddled dogs.

Then it was gone. As abruptly as it had ceased, the woodpecker's dry, monotonous clatter set up again, and after a while he even believed he could hear the dogs—a murmur, scarce a sound even, which he had probably been hearing for some time before he even remarked it, drifting into hearing and then out again, dying away. They came nowhere near him. If it was a bear they ran, it was another bear. It was Sam himself who came out of the cane and crossed the bayou, followed by the injured bitch of yesterday. She was almost at heel, like a bird dog, making no sound. She came and crouched against his leg, trembling, staring off into the cane.

"I didn't see him," he said. "I didn't, Sam!"

"I know it," Sam said. "He done the looking. You didn't hear him neither, did you?"

"No," the boy said. "I——"

"He's smart," Sam said. "Too smart." He looked down at the hound, trembling faintly and steadily against the boy's knee. From the raked shoulder a few drops of fresh blood oozed and clung. "Too big. We ain't got the dog yet. But maybe someday. Maybe not next time. But someday."

So I must see him, he thought. *I must look at him.* Otherwise, it seemed to him that it would go on like this forever, as it had gone on with his father and Major de Spain, who was older than his father, and even with old General Compson, who had been old enough to be a brigade commander in 1865. Otherwise, it would go on so forever, next time and next time, after and after and after. It seemed to him that he could never see the two of them, himself and the bear, shadowy in the limbo from which time emerged, becoming time; the old bear absolved of mortality and himself partaking, sharing a little of it, enough of it. And he knew now what he had smelled in the huddled dogs and tasted in his saliva. He recognized fear. *So I will have to see him,* he thought, without dread or even hope. *I will have to look at him.*

It was in June of the next year. He was eleven. They were in camp again, celebrating Major de Spain's and General Compson's birthdays. Although the one had been born in September and the other in the depth of winter and in another decade, they had met for two weeks to fish and shoot squirrels and turkey and run coons and wildcats with the dogs at night. That is, he and Boon Hoggenbeck and the Negroes fished and shot squirrels and ran the coons and cats, because the proved hunters, not only Major de Spain and old General Compson, who spent those two weeks sitting in a rocking chair before a tremendous iron pot of Brunswick stew, stirring and tasting, with old Ash to quarrel with about how he was making it and Tennie's Jim to pour whiskey from the demijohn into the tin dipper from which he drank it, but even the boy's father and Walter Ewell, who were still young enough, scorned such, other than shooting the wild gobblers with pistols for wagers on their marksmanship.

Or, that is, his father and the others believed he was hunting squirrels. Until the third day, he thought that Sam Fathers believed that too. Each morning he would leave the camp right after breakfast. He had his own gun now, a Christmas present. He went back to the tree beside the bayou where he had stood that morning. Using the compass which old General Compson had given him, he ranged from that point; he was teaching himself to be a better-than-fair woodsman without knowing he was doing it. On the second day he even found the gutted log where he had first seen the crooked print. It was almost completely crumbled now, healing with unbelievable speed, a passionate and almost visible relinquishment, back into the earth from which the tree had grown.

He ranged the summer woods now, green with gloom; if anything, actually dimmer than in November's gray dissolution, where, even at noon, the sun fell only in intermittent dappling upon the earth, which never completely dried out and which crawled with snakes—moccasins and water snakes and rattlers, themselves the color of the dappling gloom, so that he would not always see them until they moved, returning later and later, first day, second day, passing in the twilight of the third evening the little log pen enclosing the log stable where Sam was putting up the horses for the night.

"You ain't looked right yet," Sam said.

He stopped. For a moment he didn't answer. Then he said peacefully, in a peaceful rushing burst as when a boy's miniature dam in a little brook gives way, "All right. But how? I went to the bayou. I even found that log again. I——"

"I reckon that was all right. Likely he's been watching you. You never saw his foot?"

"I," the boy said—"I didn't—I never thought——"

"It's the gun," Sam said. He stood beside the fence motionless—the old man, the Indian, in the battered faded overalls and the five-cent straw hat which in the Negro's race had been the badge of his enslavement and was now the regalia of his freedom. The camp—the clearing, the house, the barn and its tiny lot with which Major de Spain in his turn had scratched punily and evanescently at the wilderness—faded in the dusk, back into the immemorial darkness of the woods. *The gun,* the boy thought. *The gun.*

"Be scared," Sam said. "You can't help that. But don't be afraid. Ain't nothing in the woods going to hurt you unless you corner it, or it smells that you are afraid. A bear or a deer, too, has got to be scared of a coward the same as a brave man has got to be."

The gun, the boy thought.

"You will have to choose," Sam said.

He left the camp before daylight, long before Uncle Ash would wake in his quilts on the kitchen floor and start the fire for breakfast. He had only the compass and a stick for snakes. He could go almost a mile before he would begin to need the compass. He sat on a log, the invisible compass in his invisible hand, while the secret night sounds, fallen still at his movements, scurried again and then ceased for good, and the owls ceased and gave over to the waking of day birds, and he could see the compass. Then he went fast yet still quietly; he was becoming better and better as a woodsman, still without having yet realized it.

He jumped a doe and a fawn at sunrise, walked them out of the bed, close enough to see them—the crash of undergrowth, the white scut, the fawn scudding behind her faster than he had believed it could run. He was hunting right, upwind, as Sam had taught him; not that it mattered now. He had left the gun; of his own will and relinquishment he had accepted not a gambit, not a choice, but a condition in which not only the bear's heretofore inviolable anonymity but all the old rules and balances of hunter and hunted had been abrogated. He would not even be afraid, not even in the moment when the fear would take him completely—blood, skin, bowels, bones, memory from the long time before it became his memory—all save that thin, clear, immortal lucidity which alone differed him from this bear and from all the other bear and deer he would ever kill in the humility and pride of his skill and endurance, to which Sam had spoken when he leaned in the twilight on the lot fence yesterday.

By noon he was far beyond the little bayou, farther into the new and alien country than he had ever been. He was traveling now not only by the compass but by the old, heavy, biscuit-thick silver watch which had belonged to his grandfather. When he stopped at last, it was for the first time since he had risen from the log at dawn when he could see the compass. It was far enough. He had left the camp nine hours ago; nine hours from now, dark would have already been an hour old. But he didn't think that. He thought, *All right. Yes. But what?* and stood for a moment, alien and small in the green and topless solitude, answering his own question before it had formed and ceased. It was the watch, the compass, the stick—the three lifeless mechanicals with which for nine hours he had fended the wilderness off; he hung the watch and compass carefully on a bush and leaned the stick beside them and relinquished completely to it.

He had not been going very fast for the last two or three hours. He went no faster now, since distance would not matter even if he could have gone fast. And he was trying to keep a bearing on the tree where he had left the compass, trying to complete a circle which would bring him back to it or at least intersect itself, since direction would not matter now either. But the tree was not here, and he did as Sam had schooled him— made the next circle in the opposite direction, so that the two patterns would bisect somewhere, but crossing no print of his own feet, finding the tree at last, but in the wrong place—no bush, no compass, no watch—and the tree not even the tree, because there was a down log beside it and he did what Sam Fathers had told him was the next thing and the last.

As he sat down on the log he saw the crooked print—the warped, tremendous, two-toed indentation which, even as he watched it, filled with water. As he looked up, the wilderness coalesced, solidified—the glade, the tree he sought, the bush, the watch and the compass glinting where the ray of sunshine touched them. Then he saw the bear. It did not emerge, appear; it was just there, immobile, solid, fixed in the hot dappling of the green and windless noon, not as big as he had dreamed it, but as big as he had expected it, bigger, dimensionless, against the dappled obscurity, looking at him where he sat quietly on the log and looked back at it.

Then it moved. It made no sound. It did not hurry. It crossed the glade, walking for an instant into the full glare of the sun; when it reached the other side it stopped again and looked back at him across one shoulder while his quiet breathing inhaled and exhaled three times.

Then it was gone. It didn't walk into the woods, the undergrowth. It faded, sank back into the wilderness as he had watched a fish, a huge old bass, sink and vanish into the dark depths of its pool without even any movement of its fins.

He thought, *It will be next fall.* But it was not next fall, nor the next nor the next. He was fourteen then. He had killed his buck, and Sam Fathers had marked his face with the hot blood, and in the next year he killed a bear. But even before that accolade he had become as competent in the woods as many grown men with the same experience; by his fourteenth year he was a better woodsman than most grown men with more. There was no territory within thirty miles of the camp that he did not know —bayou, ridge, brake, landmark, tree and path. He could have led anyone to any point in it without deviation, and brought them out again. He knew the game trails that even Sam Fathers did not know; in his thirteenth year he found a buck's bedding place, and unbeknown to his father he borrowed Walter Ewell's rifle and lay in wait at dawn and killed the buck when it walked back to the bed, as Sam had told him how the old Chickasaw fathers did.

But not the old bear, although by now he knew its footprints better than he did his own, and not only the crooked one. He could see any one of three sound ones and distinguish it from any other, and not only by its size. There were other bears within these thirty miles which left tracks almost as large, but this was more than that. If Sam Fathers had been his mentor and the back-yard rabbits and squirrels at home his kindergarten, then the wilderness the old bear ran was his college, the old male bear itself, so long unwifed and childless as to have become its own ungendered progenitor, was his alma mater. But he never saw it.

He could find the crooked print now almost whenever he liked, fifteen or ten or five miles, or sometimes nearer the camp than that. Twice while on stand during the three years he heard the dogs strike its trail by accident; on the second time they jumped it seemingly, the voices high, abject, almost human in hysteria, as on that first morning two years ago. But not the bear itself. He would remember that noon three years ago, the glade, himself and the bear fixed during that moment in the windless and dappled blaze, and it would seem to him that it had never happened, that he had dreamed that too. But it had happened. They had looked at each other, they had emerged from the wilderness old as earth, synchronized to the instant by something more than the blood that moved the flesh and bones which bore them, and touched, pledged something, affirmed, something more lasting than the frail web of bones and flesh which any accident could obliterate.

Then he saw it again. Because of the very fact that he thought of nothing else, he had forgotten to look for it. He was still hunting with Walter Ewell's rifle. He saw it cross the end of a long blow-down, a corridor where a tornado had swept, rushing through rather than over the tangle of trunks and branches as a locomotive would have, faster than he had ever believed it could move, almost as fast as a deer even, because a deer would have spent most of that time in the air, faster than he could bring the rifle sights up with it. And now he knew what had been wrong during all the three years. He sat on a log, shaking and trembling as if he had never seen the woods before nor anything that ran them, wondering with incredulous amazement how he could have forgotten the very thing which Sam Fathers had told him and which the bear itself had proved the next day and had now returned after three years to reaffirm.

And now he knew what Sam Fathers had meant about the right dog, a dog in which size would mean less than nothing. So when he returned alone in April—school was out then, so that the sons of farmers could help with the land's planting, and at last his father had granted him permission, on his promise to be back in four days—he had the dog. It was his own, a mongrel of the sort called by Negroes a fyce, a ratter, itself not much bigger than a rat and possessing that bravery which had long since stopped being courage and had become foolhardiness.

It did not take four days. Alone again, he found the trail on the first morning. It was not a stalk; it was an ambush. He timed the meeting almost as if it were an appointment with a human being. Himself holding the fyce muffled in a feed sack and Sam Fathers with two of the hounds on a piece of a plowline rope, they lay down wind of the trail at dawn of the second morning. They were so close that the bear turned without even running, as if in surprised amazement at the shrill and frantic uproar of the released fyce, turning at bay against the trunk of a tree, on its hind feet; it seemed to the boy that it would never stop rising, taller and taller, and even the two hounds seemed to take a desperate and despairing courage from the fyce, following it as it went in.

Then he realized that the fyce was actually not going to stop. He flung, threw the gun away, and ran; when he overtook and grasped the frantically pin-wheeling little dog, it seemed to him that he was directly under the bear.

He could smell it, strong and hot and rank. Sprawling, he looked up to where it loomed and towered over him like a cloudburst and colored like a thunderclap, quite familiar, peacefully and even lucidly familiar, until he remembered: This was the way he had used to dream about it. Then it was gone. He didn't see it go. He knelt, holding the frantic fyce with both hands, hearing the abashed wailing of the hounds drawing farther and farther away, until Sam came up. He carried the gun. He laid it down quietly beside the boy and stood looking down at him.

"You've done seed him twice now with a gun in your hands," he said. "This time you couldn't have missed him."

The boy rose. He still held the fyce. Even in his arms and clear of the ground, it yapped frantically, straining and surging after the fading uproar of the two hounds like a tangle of wire springs. He was panting a little but he was neither shaking nor trembling now.

"Neither could you!" he said. "You had the gun! Neither did you!"

"And you didn't shoot," his father said. "How close were you?"

"I don't know, sir," he said. "There was a big wood tick inside his right hind leg. I saw that. But I didn't have the gun then."

"But you didn't shoot when you had the gun," his father said. "Why?"

But he didn't answer, and his father didn't wait for him to, rising and crossing the room, across the pelt of the bear which the boy had killed two years ago and the larger one which his father had killed before he was born, to the bookcase beneath the mounted head of the boy's first buck. It was the room which his father called the office, from which all the plantation business was transacted; in it for the fourteen years of his life he had heard the best of all talking. Major de Spain would be there and sometimes old General Compson, and Walter Ewell and Boon Hoggenbeck and Sam Fathers and Tennie's Jim, too, were hunters, knew the woods and what ran them.

He would hear it, not talking himself but listening—the wilderness, the big woods, bigger and older than any recorded document of white man fatuous enough to believe he had bought any fragment of it or Indian ruthless enough to pretend that any fragment of it had been his to convey. It was of the men, not white nor black nor red, but men, hunters with the will and hardihood to endure and the humility and skill to survive, and the dogs and the bear and deer juxtaposed and reliefed against it, ordered and compelled by and within the wilderness in the ancient and unremitting contest by the ancient and immitigable rules which voided all regrets and brooked no quarter, the voices quiet and weighty and deliberate for retrospection and recollection and exact remembering, while he squatted in the blazing firelight as Tennie's Jim squatted, who stirred only to put more wood on the fire and to pass the bottle from one glass to another. Because the bottle was always present, so that after a while it seemed to him that those fierce instants of heart and brain and courage and wiliness and speed were concentrated and distilled into that brown liquor which not women, not boys and children, but only hunters drank, drinking not of the blood they had spilled but some condensation of the wild immortal spirit, drinking it moderately, humbly even, not with the pagan's base hope of acquiring the virtues of cunning and strength and speed, but in salute to them.

His father returned with the book and sat down again and opened it. "Listen," he said. He read the five stanzas aloud, his voice quiet and deliberate in the room where there was no fire now because it was already spring. Then he looked up. The boy watched him. "All right," his father said. "Listen." He read again, but only the second stanza this time, to the end of it, the last two lines, and closed the book and put it on the table beside him. "She cannot fade, though thou hast not thy bliss, forever wilt thou love, and she be fair," he said.

"He's talking about a girl," the boy said.

"He had to talk about something," his father said. Then he said, "He was talking about truth. Truth doesn't change. Truth is one thing. It covers all things which touch the heart—honor and pride and pity and justice and courage and love. Do you see now?"

He didn't know. Somehow it was simpler than that. There was an old bear, fierce and ruthless, not merely just to stay alive, but with the fierce pride of liberty and freedom, proud enough of the liberty and freedom to see it threatened without fear or even alarm; nay, who at times even seemed deliberately to put that freedom and liberty in jeopardy in order to savor them, to remind his old strong bones and flesh to keep supple and quick to defend and preserve them. There was an old man, son of a Negro slave and an Indian king, inheritor on the one side of the long chronicle of a people who had learned humility through suffering, and pride through the endurance which survived the suffering and injustice, and on the other side, the chronicle of a people even longer in the land than the first, yet who no longer existed in the land at all save in the solitary brotherhood of an old Negro's alien blood and the wild and invincible spirit of an old bear. There was a boy who wished to learn humility and pride in order to become skillful and worthy in the woods, who suddenly found himself becoming so skillful so rapidly that he feared he would never become worthy because he had not learned humility and pride, although he had tried to, until one day and as suddenly he discovered that an old man who could not have defined either had led him, as though by the hand, to that point where an old bear and a little mongrel of a dog showed him that, by possessing one thing other, he would possess them both.

And a little dog, nameless and mongrel and many-fathered, grown, yet weighing less than six pounds, saying as if to itself, "I can't be dangerous, because there's nothing much smaller than I am; I can't be fierce, because they would call it just a noise; I can't be humble, because I'm already too close to the ground to genuflect; I can't be proud, because I wouldn't be near enough to it for anyone to know who was casting the shadow, and I don't even know that I'm not going to heaven, because they have already decided that I don't possess an immortal soul. So all I can be is brave. But it's all right. I can be that, even if they still call it just noise."

That was all. It was simple, much simpler than somebody talking in a book about youth and a girl he would never need to grieve over, because he could never approach any nearer her and would never have to get any farther away. He had heard about a bear, and finally got big enough to trail it, and he trailed it four years and at last met it with a gun in his hands and he didn't shoot. Because a little dog—But he could have shot long before the little dog covered the twenty yards to where the bear waited, and Sam Fathers could have shot at any time during that interminable minute while Old Ben stood on his hind feet over them. He stopped. His father was watching him gravely across the spring-rife twilight of the room; when he spoke, his words were as quiet as the twilight, too, not loud, because they did not need to be because they would last. "Courage, and honor, and pride," his father said, "and pity, and love of justice and of liberty. They all touch the heart, and what the heart holds to becomes truth, as far as we know the truth. Do you see now?"

Sam, and Old Ben, and Nip, he thought. And himself too. He had been all right too. His father had said so. "Yes, sir," he said.

ERNEST HEMINGWAY

[1898–1961]

The Short Happy Life of Francis Macomber

It was now lunch time and they were all sitting under the double green fly of the dining tent pretending that nothing had happened.

"Will you have lime juice or lemon squash?" Macomber asked.

"I'll have a gimlet," Robert Wilson told him.

"I'll have a gimlet too. I need something," Macomber's wife said.

"I suppose it's the thing to do," Macomber agreed. "Tell him to make three gimlets."

The mess boy had started them already, lifting the bottles out of the canvas cooling bags that sweated wet in the wind that blew through the trees that shaded the tents.

"What had I ought to give them?" Macomber asked.

"A quid would be plenty," Wilson told him. "You don't want to spoil them."

"Will the headman distribute it?"

"Absolutely."

Francis Macomber had, half an hour before, been carried to his tent from the edge of the camp in triumph on the arms and shoulders of the cook, the personal boys, the skinner and the porters. The gun-bearers had taken no part in the demonstration. When the native boys put him down at the door of his tent, he had shaken all their hands, received their congratulations, and then gone into the tent and sat on the bed until his wife came in. She did not speak to him when she came in and he left the tent at once to wash his face and hands in the portable wash basin outside and go over to the dining tent to sit in a comfortable canvas chair in the breeze and the shade.

"You've got your lion," Robert Wilson said to him, "and a damned fine one too."

Mrs. Macomber looked at Wilson quickly. She was an extremely handsome and well-kept woman of the beauty and social position which had, five years before, commanded five thousand dollars as the price of endorsing, with photographs, a beauty product which she had never used. She had been married to Francis Macomber for eleven years.

"He is a good lion, isn't he?" Macomber said. His wife looked at him now. She looked at both these men as though she had never seen them before.

One, Wilson, the white hunter, she knew she had never truly seen before. He was about middle height with sandy hair, a stubby mustache, a very red face and extremely cold blue eyes with faint white wrinkles at the corners that grooved merrily when he smiled. He smiled at her now and she looked away from his face at the way his shoulders sloped in the loose tunic he wore with the four big cartridges held in loops where the left breast pocket should have been, at his big brown hands, his old slacks, his very dirty boots and back to his red face again. She noticed where the baked red of his face stopped in a white line that marked the circle left by his Stetson hat that hung now from one of the pegs of the tent pole.

"Well, here's to the lion," Robert Wilson said. He smiled at her again and, not smiling, she looked curiously at her husband.

Francis Macomber was very tall, very well built if you did not mind that length of bone, dark, his hair cropped like an oarsman, rather thin-lipped, and was considered handsome. He was dressed in the same sort of safari clothes that Wilson wore except that his were new, he was thirty-five years old, kept himself very fit, was good at court games, had a number of big-game fishing records, and had just shown himself, very publicly, to be a coward.

"Here's to the lion," he said. "I can't ever thank you for what you did."

Margaret, his wife, looked away from him and back to Wilson.

"Let's not talk about the lion," she said.

Wilson looked over at her without smiling and now she smiled at him.

"It's been a very strange day," she said. "Hadn't you ought to put your hat on even under the canvas at noon? You told me that, you know."

"Might put it on," said Wilson.

"You know you have a very red face, Mr. Wilson," she told him and smiled again.

"Drink," said Wilson.

"I don't think so," she said. "Francis drinks a great deal, but his face is never red."

"It's red today," Macomber tried a joke.

"No," said Margaret. "It's mine that's red today. But Mr. Wilson's is always red."

"Must be racial," said Wilson. "I say, you wouldn't like to drop my beauty as a topic, would you?"

"I've just started on it."

"Let's chuck it," said Wilson.

"Conversation is going to be so difficult," Margaret said.

"Don't be silly, Margot," her husband said.

"No difficulty," Wilson said. "Got a damn fine lion."

Margot looked at them both and they both saw that she was going to cry. Wilson had seen it coming for a long time and he dreaded it. Macomber was past dreading it.

"I wish it hadn't happened. Oh, I wish it hadn't happened," she said and started for her tent. She made no noise of crying but they could see that her shoulders were shaking under the rose-colored, sun-proofed shirt she wore.

"Women upset," said Wilson to the tall man. "Amounts to nothing. Strain on the nerves and one thing'n another."

"No," said Macomber. "I suppose that I rate that for the rest of my life now."

"Nonsense. Let's have a spot of the giant killer," said Wilson. "Forget the whole thing. Nothing to it anyway."

"We might try," said Macomber. "I won't forget what you did for me though."

"Nothing," said Wilson. "All nonsense."

So they sat there in the shade where the camp was pitched under some wide-topped acacia trees with a boulder-strewn cliff behind them, and a stretch of grass that ran to the bank of a boulder-filled stream in front with forest beyond it, and drank their just-cool lime drinks and avoided one another's eyes while the boys set the table for lunch. Wilson could tell that the boys all knew about it now and when he saw Macomber's personal boy looking curiously at his master while he was putting dishes on the table he snapped at him in Swahili. The boy turned away with his face blank.

"What were you telling him?" Macomber asked.

"Nothing. Told him to look alive or I'd see he got about fifteen of the best."

"What's that? Lashes?"

"It's quite illegal," Wilson said. "You're supposed to fine them."

"Do you still have them whipped?"

"Oh, yes. They could raise a row if they chose to complain. But they don't. They prefer it to the fines."

"How strange!" said Macomber.

"Not strange, really," Wilson said. "Which would you rather do? Take a good birching or lose your pay?" Then he felt embarrassed at asking it and before Macomber could answer he went on, "We all take a beating every day, you know, one way or another."

This was no better. "Good God," he thought. "I am a diplomat, aren't I?"

"Yes, we take a beating," said Macomber, still not looking at him. "I'm awfully sorry about that lion business. It doesn't have to go any further, does it? I mean no one will hear about it, will they?"

"You mean will I tell it at the Mathaiga Club?" Wilson looked at him now coldly. He had not expected this. So he's a bloody four-letter man as well as a bloody coward, he thought. I rather liked him too until today. But how is one to know about an American?

"No," said Wilson. "I'm a professional hunter. We never talk about our clients. You can be quite easy on that. It's supposed to be bad form to ask us not to talk though."

He had decided now that to break would be much easier. He would eat, then, by himself and could read a book with his meals. They would eat by themselves. He would see them through the safari on a very formal basis—what was it the French called it? Distinguished consideration—and it would be a damn sight easier than having to go through this emotional trash. He'd insult him and make a good clean break. Then he could read a book with his meals and he'd still be drinking their whisky. That was the phrase for it when a safari went bad. You ran into another white hunter and you asked, "How is everything going?" and he answered, "Oh, I'm still drinking their whisky," and you knew everything had gone to pot.

"I'm sorry," Macomber said and looked at him with his American face that would stay adolescent until it became middle-aged, and Wilson noted his crew-cropped hair, fine eyes only faintly shifty, good nose, thin lips and handsome jaw. "I'm sorry I didn't realize that. There are lots of things I don't know."

So what could he do, Wilson thought. He was all ready to break it off quickly and neatly and here the beggar was apologizing after he had just insulted him. He made one more attempt. "Don't worry about me talking," he said. "I have a living to make. You know in Africa no woman ever misses her lion and no white man ever bolts."

"I bolted like a rabbit," Macomber said.

Now what in hell were you going to do about a man who talked like that, Wilson wondered.

Wilson looked at Macomber with his flat, blue, machine-gunner's eyes and the other smiled back at him. He had a pleasant smile if you did not notice how his eyes showed when he was hurt.

"Maybe I can fix it up on buffalo," he said. "We're after them next, aren't we?"

"In the morning if you like," Wilson told him. Perhaps he had been wrong. This was certainly the way to take it. You most certainly could not tell a damned thing about an American. He was all for Macomber again. If you could forget the morning. But, of course, you couldn't. The morning had been about as bad as they come.

"Here comes the Memsahib," he said. She was walking over from her tent looking refreshed and cheerful and quite lovely. She had a very perfect oval face, so perfect that you expected her to be stupid. But she wasn't stupid, Wilson thought, no, not stupid.

"How is the beautiful red-faced Mr. Wilson? Are you feeling better, Francis, my pearl?"

"Oh, much," said Macomber.

"I've dropped the whole thing," she said, sitting down at the table. "What importance is there to whether Francis is any good at killing lions? That's not his trade. That's Mr. Wilson's trade. Mr. Wilson is really very impressive killing anything. You do kill anything, don't you?"

"Oh, anything," said Wilson. "Simply anything." They are, he thought, the hardest in the world; the hardest, the cruelest, the most predatory and the most attractive and their men have softened or gone to pieces nervously as they have hardened. Or is it that they pick men they can handle? They can't know that much at the age they marry, he thought. He was grateful that he had gone through his education on American women before now because this was a very attractive one.

"We're going after buff in the morning," he told her.

"I'm coming," she said.

"No, you're not."

"Oh, yes, I am. Mayn't I, Francis?"

"Why not stay in camp?"

"Not for anything," she said. "I wouldn't miss something like today for anything."

When she left, Wilson was thinking, when she went off to cry, she seemed a hell of a fine woman. She seemed to understand, to realize, to be hurt for him and for herself and to know how things really stood. She is away for twenty minutes and now she is back, simply enamelled in that American female cruelty. They are the damnedest women. Really the damnedest.

"We'll put on another show for you tomorrow," Francis Macomber said.

"You're not coming," Wilson said.

"You're very mistaken," she told him. "And I want *so* to see you perform again. You were lovely this morning. That is if blowing things' heads off is lovely."

"Here's the lunch," said Wilson. "You're very merry, aren't you?"

"Why not? I didn't come out here to be dull."

"Well, it hasn't been dull," Wilson said. He could see the boulders in the river and the high bank beyond with the trees and he remembered the morning.

"Oh, no," she said. "It's been charming. And tomorrow. You don't know how I look forward to tomorrow."

"That's eland he's offering you," Wilson said.

"They're the big cowy things that jump like hares, aren't they?"

"I suppose that describes them," Wilson said.

"It's very good meat," Macomber said.

"Didn't you shoot it, Francis?" she asked.

"Yes."

"They're not dangerous, are they?"

"Only if they fall on you," Wilson told her.

"I'm so glad."

"Why not let up on the bitchery just a little, Margot," Macomber said, cutting the eland steak and putting some mashed potato, gravy and carrot on the down-turned fork that tined through the piece of meat.

"I suppose I could," she said, "since you put it so prettily."

"Tonight we'll have champagne for the lion," Wilson said. "It's a bit too hot at noon."

"Oh, the lion," Margot said. "I'd forgotten the lion!"

So, Robert Wilson thought to himself, she *is* giving him a ride, isn't she? Or do you suppose that's her idea of putting up a good show? How should a woman act when she discovers her husband is a bloody coward? She's damn cruel but they're all cruel. They govern, of course, and to govern one has to be cruel sometimes. Still, I've seen enough of their damn terrorism.

"Have some more eland," he said to her politely.

That afternoon, late, Wilson and Macomber went out in the motor car with the native driver and the two gun-bearers. Mrs. Macomber stayed in the camp. It was too hot to go out, she said, and she was going with them in the early morning. As they drove off Wilson saw her standing under the big tree, looking pretty rather than beautiful in her faintly rosy khaki, her dark hair drawn back off her forehead and gathered in a knot low on her neck, her face as fresh, he thought, as though she were in England. She waved to them as the car went off through the swale of high grass and curved around through the trees into the small hills of orchard bush.

In the orchard bush they found a herd of impala, and leaving the car they stalked one old ram with long, wide-spread horns and Macomber killed it with a very creditable shot that knocked the buck down at a good two hundred yards and sent the herd off bounding wildly and leaping over one another's backs in long, leg-drawn-up leaps as unbelievable and as floating as those one makes sometimes in dreams.

"That was a good shot," Wilson said. "They're a small target."

"Is it a worthwhile head?" Macomber asked.

"It's excellent," Wilson told him. "You shoot like that and you'll have no trouble."

"Do you think we'll find buffalo tomorrow?"

"There's a good chance of it. They feed out early in the morning and with luck we may catch them in the open."

"I'd like to clear away that lion business," Macomber said. "It's not very pleasant to have your wife see you do something like that."

I should think it would be even more unpleasant to do it, Wilson thought, wife or no wife, or to talk about it having done it. But he said, "I wouldn't think about that any more. Anyone could be upset by his first lion. That's all over."

But that night after dinner and a whisky and soda by the fire before going to bed, as Francis Macomber lay on his cot with his mosquito bar over him and listened to the night noises, it was not all over. It was neither all over nor was it beginning. It was there exactly as it happened with some parts of it indelibly emphasized and he was miserably ashamed at it. But more than shame he felt cold, hollow fear in him. The fear was still there like a cold slimy hollow in all the emptiness where once his confidence had been and it made him feel sick. It was still there with him now.

It had started the night before when he had wakened and heard the lion roaring somewhere up along the river. It was a deep sound and at the end there were sort of coughing grunts that made him seem just outside the tent, and when Francis Macomber woke in the night to hear it he was afraid. He could hear his wife breathing quietly, asleep. There was no one to tell he was afraid, nor to be afraid with him, and, lying alone, he did not know the Somali proverb that says a brave man is always frightened three times by a lion; when he first sees his track, when he first hears him roar and when he first confronts him. Then while they were eating breakfast by lantern light out in the dining tent, before the sun was up, the lion roared again and Francis thought he was just at the edge of camp.

"Sounds like an old-timer," Robert Wilson said, looking up from his kippers and coffee. "Listen to him cough."

"Is he very close?"

"A mile or so up the stream."

"Will we see him?"

"We'll have a look."

"Does his roaring carry that far? It sounds as though he were right in camp."

"Carries a hell of a long way," said Robert Wilson. "It's strange the way it carries. Hope he's a shootable cat. The boys said there was a very big one about here."

"If I get a shot, where should I hit him," Macomber asked, "to stop him?"

"In the shoulders," Wilson said. "In the neck if you can make it. Shoot for bone. Break him down."

"I hope I can place it properly," Macomber said.

"You shoot very well," Wilson told him. "Take your time. Make sure of him. The first one in is the one that counts."

"What range will it be?"

"Can't tell. Lion has something to say about that. Won't shoot unless it's close enough so you can make sure."

"At under a hundred yards?" Macomber asked.

Wilson looked at him quickly.

"Hundred's about right. Might have to take him a bit under. Shouldn't chance a shot at much over that. A hundred's a decent range. You can hit him wherever you want at that. Here comes the Memsahib."

"Good morning," she said. "Are we going after that lion?"

"As soon as you deal with your breakfast," Wilson said. "How are you feeling?"

"Marvellous," she said. "I'm very excited."

"I'll just go and see that everything is ready," Wilson went off. As he left the lion roared again.

"Noisy beggar," Wilson said. "We'll put a stop to that."

"What's the matter, Francis?" his wife asked him.

"Nothing," Macomber said.

"Yes, there is," she said. "What are you upset about?"

"Nothing," he said.

"Tell me," she looked at him. "Don't you feel well?"

"It's that damned roaring," he said. "It's been going on all night, you know."

"Why didn't you wake me," she said. "I'd love to have heard it."

"I've got to kill the damned thing," Macomber said, miserably.

"Well, that's what you're out here for, isn't it?"

"Yes. But I'm nervous. Hearing the thing roar gets on my nerves."

"Well then, as Wilson said, kill him and stop his roaring."

"Yes, darling," said Francis Macomber. "It sounds easy, doesn't it?"

"You're not afraid, are you?"

"Of course not. But I'm nervous from hearing him roar all night."

"You'll kill him marvellously," she said. "I know you will. I'm awfully anxious to see it."

"Finish your breakfast and we'll be starting."

"It's not light yet," she said. "This is a ridiculous hour."

Just then the lion roared in a deep-chested moaning, suddenly guttural, ascending vibration that seemed to shake the air and ended in a sigh and a heavy, deep-chested grunt.

"He sounds almost here," Macomber's wife said.

"My God," said Macomber. "I hate that damned noise."

"It's very impressive."

"Impressive. It's frightful."

Robert Wilson came up then carrying his short, ugly, shockingly big-bored .505 Gibbs and grinning.

"Come on," he said. "Your gun-bearer has your Springfield and the big gun. Everything's in the car. Have you solids?"

"Yes."

"I'm ready," Mrs. Macomber said.

"Must make him stop that racket," Wilson said. "You get in front. The Memsahib can sit back here with me."

They climbed into the motor car and, in the gray first daylight, moved off up the river through the trees. Macomber opened the breech of his rifle and saw he had metal-cased bullets, shut the bolt and put the rifle on safety. He saw his hand was trembling. He felt in his pocket for more cartridges and moved his fingers over the cartridges in the loops of his tunic front. He turned back to where Wilson sat in the rear seat of the doorless, box-bodied motor car beside his wife, them both grinning with excitement, and Wilson leaned forward and whispered,

"See the birds dropping. Means the old boy has left his kill."

On the far bank of the stream Macomber could see, above the trees, vultures circling and plummeting down.

"Chances are he'll come to drink along here," Wilson whispered. "Before he goes to lay up. Keep an eye out."

They were driving slowly along the high bank of the stream which here cut deeply to its boulder-filled bed, and they wound in and out through big trees as they drove. Macomber was watching the opposite bank when he felt Wilson take hold of his arm. The car stopped.

"There he is," he heard the whisper. "Ahead and to the right. Get out and take him. He's a marvellous lion."

Macomber saw the lion now. He was standing almost broadside, his great head up and turned toward them. The early morning breeze that blew toward them was just stirring his dark mane, and the lion looked huge, silhouetted on the rise of bank in the gray morning light, his shoulders heavy, his barrel of a body bulking smoothly.

"How far is he?" asked Macomber, raising his rifle.

"About seventy-five. Get out and take him."

"Why not shoot from where I am?"

"You don't shoot them from cars," he heard Wilson saying in his ear. "Get out. He's not going to stay there all day."

Macomber stepped out of the curved opening at the side of the front seat, onto the step and down onto the ground. The lion still stood looking majestically and coolly toward this object that his eyes only showed in silhouette, bulking like some super-rhino. There was no man smell carried toward him and he watched the object, moving his great head a little from side to side. Then watching the object, not afraid, but hesitating before going down the bank to drink with such a thing opposite him, he saw a man figure detach itself from it and he turned his heavy head and swung away toward the cover of the trees as he heard a cracking crash and felt the slam of a .30–06 220-grain solid bullet that bit his flank and ripped in sudden hot scalding nausea through his stomach. He trotted, heavy, big-footed, swinging wounded full-bellied, through the trees toward the tall grass and cover, and the crash came again to go past him ripping the air apart. Then it crashed again and he felt the blow as it hit his lower ribs and ripped on through, blood sudden hot and frothy in his mouth, and he galloped toward the high grass where he could crouch and not be seen and make them bring the crashing thing close enough so he could make a rush and get the man that held it.

Macomber had not thought how the lion felt as he got out of the car. He only knew his hands were shaking and as he walked away from the car it was almost impossible for him to make his legs move. They were stiff in the thighs, but he could feel the muscles fluttering. He raised the rifle, sighted on the junction of the lion's head and shoulders and pulled the trigger. Nothing happened though he pulled until he thought his finger would break. Then he knew he had the safety on and as he lowered the rifle to move the safety over he moved another frozen pace forward, and the lion seeing his silhouette now clear of the silhouette of the car, turned and started off at a trot, and, as Macomber fired, he heard a whunk that meant that the bullet was home; but the lion kept on going. Macomber shot again and everyone saw the bullet throw a spout of dirt beyond the trotting lion. He shot again, remembering to lower his aim, and they all heard the bullet hit, and the lion went into a gallop and was in the tall grass before he had the bolt pushed forward.

Macomber stood there feeling sick at his stomach, his hands that held the Springfield still cocked, shaking, and his wife and Robert Wilson were standing by him. Beside him too were the two gun-bearers chattering in Wakamba.

"I hit him," Macomber said. "I hit him twice."

"You gut-shot him and you hit him somewhere forward," Wilson said without enthusiasm. The gun-bearers looked very grave. They were silent now.

"You may have killed him," Wilson went on. "We'll have to wait a while before we go in to find out."

"What do you mean?"

"Let him get sick before we follow him up."

"Oh," said Macomber.

"He's a hell of a fine lion," Wilson said cheerfully. "He's gotten into a bad place though."

"Why is it bad?"

"Can't see him until you're on him."

"Oh," said Macomber.

"Come on," said Wilson. "The Memsahib can stay here in the car. We'll go to have a look at the blood spoor."

"Stay here, Margot," Macomber said to his wife. His mouth was very dry and it was hard for him to talk.

"Why?" she asked.

"Wilson says to."

"We're going to have a look," Wilson said. "You stay here. You can see even better from here."

"All right."

Wilson spoke in Swahili to the driver. He nodded and said, "Yes, Bwana."

Then they went down the steep bank and across the stream, climbing over and around the boulders and up the other bank, pulling up by some projecting roots, and along it until they found where the lion had been trotting when Macomber first shot. There was dark blood on the short grass that the gun-bearers pointed out with grass stems, and that ran away behind the river bank trees.

"What do we do?" asked Macomber.

"Not much choice," said Wilson. "We can't bring the car over. Bank's too steep. We'll let him stiffen up a bit and then you and I'll go in and have a look for him."

"Can't we set the grass on fire?" Macomber asked.

"Too green."

"Can't we send beaters?"

Wilson looked at him appraisingly. "Of course we can," he said. "But it's just a touch murderous. You see we know the lion's wounded. You can drive an unwounded lion —he'll move on ahead of a noise—but a wounded lion's going to charge. You can't see him until you're right on him. He'll make himself perfectly flat in cover you wouldn't think would hide a hare. You can't very well send boys in there to that sort of a show. Somebody bound to get mauled."

"What about the gun-bearers?"

"Oh, they'll go with us. It's their *shauri*. You see, they signed on for it. They don't look too happy though, do they?"

"I don't want to go in there," said Macomber. It was out before he knew he'd said it.

"Neither do I," said Wilson very cheerily. "Really no choice though." Then, as an afterthought, he glanced at Macomber and saw suddenly how he was trembling and the pitiful look on his face.

"You don't have to go in, of course," he said. "That's what I'm hired for, you know. That's why I'm so expensive."

"You mean you'd go in by yourself? Why not leave him there?"

Robert Wilson, whose entire occupation had been with the lion and the problem he presented, and who had not been thinking about Macomber except to note that he was rather windy, suddenly felt as though he had opened the wrong door in a hotel and seen something shameful.

"What do you mean?"

"Why not just leave him?"

"You mean pretend to ourselves he hasn't been hit?"

"No. Just drop it."

"It isn't done."

"Why not?"

"For one thing, he's certain to be suffering. For another, some one else might run onto him."

"I see."

"But you don't have to have anything to do with it."

"I'd like to," Macomber said. "I'm just scared, you know."

"I'll go ahead when we go in," Wilson said, "with Kongoni tracking. You keep behind me and a little to one side. Chances are we'll hear him growl. If we see him we'll both shoot. Don't worry about anything. I'll keep you backed up. As a matter of fact, you know, perhaps you'd better not go. It might be much better. Why don't you go over and join the Memsahib while I just get it over with?"

"No, I want to go."

"All right," said Wilson. "But don't go in if you don't want to. This is my *shauri* now, you know."

"I want to go," said Macomber.

They sat under a tree and smoked.

"Want to go back and speak to the Memsahib while we're waiting?" Wilson asked.

"No."

"I'll just step back and tell her to be patient."

"Good," said Macomber. He sat there, sweating under his arms, his mouth dry, his stomach hollow feeling, wanting to find courage to tell Wilson to go on and finish off the lion without him. He could not know that Wilson was furious because he had not noticed the state he was in earlier and sent him back to his wife. While he sat there Wilson came up. "I have your big gun," he said. "Take it. We've given him time, I think. Come on."

Macomber took the big gun and Wilson said:

"Keep behind me and about five yards to the right and do exactly as I tell you." Then he spoke in Swahili to the two gun-bearers, who looked the picture of gloom.

"Let's go," he said.

"Could I have a drink of water?" Macomber asked. Wilson spoke to the older gun-bearer, who wore a canteen on his belt, and the man unbuckled it, unscrewed the top and handed it to Macomber, who took it noticing how heavy it seemed and how hairy and shoddy the felt covering was in his hand. He raised it to drink and looked ahead at the high grass with the flat-topped trees behind it. A breeze was blowing toward them and the grass rippled gently in the wind. He looked at the gun-bearer and he could see the gun-bearer was suffering too with fear.

Thirty-five yards into the grass the big lion lay flattened out along the ground. His ears were back and his only movement was a slight twitching up and down of his long, black-tufted tail. He had turned at bay as soon as he had reached this cover and he was sick with the wound through his full belly, and weakening with the wound through his lungs that brought a thin foamy red to his mouth each time he breathed. His flanks were wet and hot and flies were on the little openings the solid bullets had made in his tawny hide, and his big yellow eyes, narrowed with hate, looked straight ahead, only blinking when the pain came as he breathed, and his claws dug in the soft baked earth. All of him, pain, sickness, hatred and all of his remaining strength, was tightening into an absolute concentration for a rush. He could hear the men talking and he waited, gathering all of himself into this preparation for a charge as soon as the men would come into the grass. As he heard their voices his tail stiffened to twitch up and down, and, as they came into the edge of the grass, he made a coughing grunt and charged.

Kongoni, the old gun-bearer, in the lead watching the blood spoor, Wilson watching the grass for any movement, his big gun ready, the second gun-bearer looking ahead and listening, Macomber close to Wilson, his rifle cocked, they had just moved into the grass when Macomber heard the blood-choked coughing grunt, and saw the swishing rush in the grass. The next thing he knew he was running; running wildly, in panic in the open, running toward the stream.

He heard the *ca-ra-wong!* of Wilson's big rifle, and again in a second crashing *carawong!* and turning saw the lion, horrible-looking now, with half his head seeming to be gone, crawling toward Wilson in the edge of the tall grass while the red-faced man worked the bolt on the short ugly rifle and aimed carefully as another blasting *carawong!* came from the muzzle, and the crawling, heavy, yellow bulk of the lion stiffened and the huge, mutilated head slid forward and Macomber, standing by himself in the clearing where he had run, holding a loaded rifle, while two black men and a white man looked back at him in contempt, knew the lion was dead. He came toward Wilson, his tallness all seeming a naked reproach, and Wilson looked at him and said:

"Want to take pictures?"

"No," he said.

That was all any one had said until they reached the motor car. Then Wilson had said:

"Hell of a fine lion. Boys will skin him out. We might as well stay here in the shade."

Macomber's wife had not looked at him nor he at her and he had sat by her in the back seat with Wilson sitting in the front seat. Once he had reached over and taken his wife's hand without looking at her and she had removed her hand from his. Looking across the stream to where the gun-bearers were skinning out the lion he could see that she had been able to see the whole thing. While they sat there his wife had reached forward and put her hand on Wilson's shoulder. He turned and she had leaned forward over the low seat and kissed him on the mouth.

"Oh, I say," said Wilson, going redder than his natural baked color.

"Mr. Robert Wilson," she said. "The beautiful red-faced Mr. Robert Wilson."

Then she sat down beside Macomber again and looked away across the stream to where the lion lay, with uplifted, white-muscled, tendon-marked naked forearms, and white bloating belly, as the black men fleshed away the skin. Finally the gun-bearers brought the skin over, wet and heavy, and climbed in behind with it, rolling it up before they got in, and the motor car started. No one had said anything more until they were back in camp.

That was the story of the lion. Macomber did not know how the lion had felt before he started his rush, nor during it when the unbelievable smash of the .505 with a muzzle velocity of two tons had hit him in the mouth, nor what kept him coming after that, when the second ripping crash had smashed his hind quarters and he had come crawling on toward the crashing, blasting thing that had destroyed him. Wilson knew something about it and only expressed it by saying, "Damned fine lion," but Macomber did not know how Wilson felt about things either. He did not know how his wife felt except that she was through with him.

His wife had been through with him before but it never lasted. He was very wealthy, and would be much wealthier, and he knew she would not leave him ever now. That was one of the few things that he really knew. He knew about that, about motorcycles —that was earliest—about motor cars, about duck-shooting, about fishing, trout, salmon and big-sea, about sex in books, many books, too many books, about all court games, about dogs, not much about horses, about hanging on to his money, about most of the other things his world dealt in, and about his wife not leaving him. His wife had been a great beauty and she was still a great beauty in Africa, but she was not a great enough beauty any more at home to be able to leave him and better herself and she knew it and he knew it. She had missed the chance to leave him and he knew it. If he had been better with women she would probably have started to worry about him getting another new, beautiful wife; but she knew too much about him to worry about him either. Also, he had always had a great tolerance which seemed the nicest thing about him if it were not the most sinister.

All in all they were known as a comparatively happily married couple, one of those whose disruption is often rumored but never occurs, and as the society columnist put it, they were adding more than a spice of *adventure* to their much envied and ever-enduring *Romance* by a *Safari* in what was known as *Darkest Africa* until the Martin Johnsons lighted it on so many silver screens where they were pursuing *Old Simba* the lion, the buffalo, *Tembo* the elephant and as well collecting specimens for the Museum of Natural History. This same columnist had reported them *on the verge* as least three times in the past and they had been. But they always made it up. They had a sound basis of union. Margot was too beautiful for Macomber to divorce her and Macomber had too much money for Margot ever to leave him.

It was now about three o'clock in the morning and Francis Macomber, who had been asleep a little while after he had stopped thinking about the lion, wakened and then slept again, woke suddenly, frightened in a dream of the bloody-headed lion standing over him, and listening while his heart pounded, he realized that his wife was not in the other cot in the tent. He lay awake with that knowledge for two hours.

At the end of that time his wife came into the tent, lifted her mosquito bar and crawled cozily into bed.

"Where have you been?" Macomber asked in the darkness.

"Hello," she said. "Are you awake?"

"Where have you been?"

"I just went out to get a breath of air."

"You did, like hell."

"What do you want me to say, darling?"

"Where have you been?"

"Out to get a breath of air."

"That's a new name for it. You *are* a bitch."

"Well, you're a coward."

"All right," he said. "What of it?"

"Nothing as far as I'm concerned. But please let's not talk, darling, because I'm very sleepy."

"You think that I'll take anything."

"I know you will, sweet."

"Well, I won't."

"Please, darling, let's not talk. I'm so very sleepy."

"There wasn't going to be any of that. You promised there wouldn't be."

"Well, there is now," she said sweetly.

"You said if we made this trip that there would be none of that. You promised."

"Yes, darling. That's the way I meant it to be. But the trip was spoiled yesterday. We don't have to talk about it, do we?"

"You don't wait long when you have an advantage, do you?"

"Please let's not talk. I'm so sleepy, darling."

"I'm going to talk."

"Don't mind me then, because I'm going to sleep." And she did.

At breakfast they were all three at the table before daylight and Francis Macomber found that, of all the many men that he had hated, he hated Robert Wilson the most.

"Sleep well?" Wilson asked in his throaty voice, filling a pipe.

"Did you?"

"Topping," the white hunter told him.

You bastard, thought Macomber, you insolent bastard.

So she woke him when she came in, Wilson thought, looking at them both with his flat, cold eyes. Well, why doesn't he keep his wife where she belongs? What does he think I am, a bloody plaster saint? Let him keep her where she belongs. It's his own fault.

"Do you think we'll find buffalo?" Margot asked, pushing away a dish of apricots.

"Chance of it," Wilson said and smiled at her. "Why don't you stay in camp?"

"Not for anything," she told him.

"Why not order her to stay in camp?" Wilson said to Macomber.

"You order her," said Macomber coldly.

"Let's not have any ordering, nor," turning to Macomber, "any silliness, Francis," Margot said quite pleasantly.

"Are you ready to start?" Macomber asked.

"Any time," Wilson told him. "Do you want the Memsahib to go?"

"Does it make any difference whether I do or not?"

The hell with it, thought Robert Wilson. The utter complete hell with it. So this is what it's going to be like. Well, this is what it's going to be like, then.

"Makes no difference," he said.

"You're sure you wouldn't like to stay in camp with her yourself and let me go out and hunt the buffalo?" Macomber asked.

"Can't do that," said Wilson. "Wouldn't talk rot if I were you."

"I'm not talking rot. I'm disgusted."

"Bad word, disgusted."

"Francis, will you please try to speak sensibly?" his wife said.

"I speak too damned sensibly," Macomber said. "Did you ever eat such filthy food?"

"Something wrong with the food?" asked Wilson quietly.

"No more than with everything else."

"I'd pull yourself together, laddybuck," Wilson said very quietly. "There's a boy waits at table that understands a little English."

"The hell with him."

Wilson stood up and puffing on his pipe strolled away, speaking a few words in Swahili to one of the gun-bearers who was standing waiting for him. Macomber and his wife sat on at the table. He was staring at his coffee cup.

"If you make a scene I'll leave you, darling," Margot said quietly.

"No, you won't."

"You can try it and see."

"You won't leave me."

"No," she said. "I won't leave you and you'll behave yourself."

"Behave myself? That's a way to talk. Behave myself."

"Yes. Behave yourself."

"Why don't *you* try behaving?"

"I've tried it so long. So very long."

"I hate that red-faced swine," Macomber said. "I loathe the sight of him."

"He's really *very* nice."

"Oh, *shut up*," Macomber almost shouted. Just then the car came up and stopped in front of the dining tent and the driver and the two gun-bearers got out. Wilson walked over and looked at the husband and wife sitting there at the table.

"Going shooting?" he asked.

"Yes," said Macomber, standing up. "Yes."

"Better bring a woolly. It will be cool in the car," Wilson said.

"I'll get my leather jacket," Margot said.

"The boy has it," Wilson told her. He climbed into the front with the driver and Francis Macomber and his wife sat, not speaking, in the back seat.

Hope the silly beggar doesn't take a notion to blow the back of my head off, Wilson thought to himself. Women *are* a nuisance on safari.

The car was grinding down to cross the river at a pebbly ford in the gray daylight and then climbed, angling up the steep bank, where Wilson had ordered a way shovelled out the day before so they could reach the parklike wooded rolling country on the far side.

It was a good morning, Wilson thought. There was a heavy dew and as the wheels went through the grass and low bushes he could smell the odor of the crushed fronds. It was an odor like verbena and he liked this early morning smell of the dew, the crushed bracken and the look of the tree trunks showing black through the early morning mist, as the car made its way through the untracked, parklike country. He had put the two in the back seat out of his mind now and was thinking about buffalo. The buffalo that he was after stayed in the daytime in a thick swamp where it was impossible to get a shot, but in the night they fed out into an open stretch of country and if he could come between them and their swamp with the car, Macomber would have a good chance at them in the open. He did not want to hunt buff with Macomber in thick cover. He did not want to hunt buff or anything else with Macomber at all, but he was a professional hunter and he had hunted with some rare ones in his time. If they got buff today there would only be rhino to come and the poor man would have gone through his dangerous game and things might pick up. He'd have nothing more to do with the woman and Macomber would get over that too. He must have gone through plenty of that before by the look of things. Poor beggar. He must have a way of getting over it. Well, it was the poor sod's own bloody fault.

He, Robert Wilson, carried a double size cot on safari to accommodate any windfalls he might receive. He had hunted for a certain clientele, the international, fast, sporting set, where the women did not feel they were getting their money's worth unless they had shared that cot with the white hunter. He despised them when he was away from them although he liked some of them well enough at the time, but he made his living by them; and their standards were his standards as long as they were hiring him.

They were his standards in all except the shooting. He had his own standards about the killing and they could live up to them or get some one else to hunt them. He knew, too, that they all respected him for this. This Macomber was an odd one though. Damned if he wasn't. Now the wife. Well, the wife. Yes, the wife. Hm, the wife. Well he'd dropped all that. He looked around at them. Macomber sat grim and furious. Margot smiled at him. She looked younger today, more innocent and fresher and not so professionally beautiful. What's in her heart God knows, Wilson thought. She hadn't talked much last night. At that it was a pleasure to see her.

The motor car climbed up a slight rise and went on through the trees and then out into a grassy prairie-like opening and kept in the shelter of the trees along the edge, the driver going slowly and Wilson looking carefully out across the prairie and all along its far side. He stopped the car and studied the opening with his field glasses. Then he motioned to the driver to go on and the car moved slowly along, the driver avoiding wart-hog holes and driving around the mud castles ants had built. Then, looking across the opening, Wilson suddenly turned and said,

"By God, there they are!"

And looking where he pointed, while the car jumped forward and Wilson spoke in rapid Swahili to the driver, Macomber saw three huge, black animals looking almost cylindrical in their long heaviness, like big black tank cars, moving at a gallop across the far edge of the open prairie. They moved at a stiff-necked, stiff bodied gallop and he could see the upswept wide black horns on their heads as they galloped heads out; the heads not moving.

"They're three old bulls," Wilson said. "We'll cut them off before they get to the swamp."

The car was going a wild forty-five miles an hour across the open and as Macomber watched, the buffalo got bigger and bigger until he could see the gray, hairless, scabby look of one huge bull and how his neck was a part of his shoulders and the shiny black of his horns as he galloped a little behind the others that were strung out in that steady plunging gait; and then, the car swaying as though it had just jumped a road, they drew up close and he could see the plunging hugeness of the bull, and the dust in his sparsely haired hide, the side boss of horn and his outstretched, wide-nostrilled muzzle, and he was raising his rifle when Wilson shouted, "Not from the car, you fool!" and he had no fear, only hatred of Wilson, while the brakes clamped on and the car skidded, plowing sideways to an almost stop and Wilson was out on one side and he on the other, stumbling as his feet hit the still speeding-by of the earth, and then he was shooting at the bull as he moved away, hearing the bullets whunk into him, emptying his rifle at him as he moved steadily away, finally remembering to get his shots forward into the shoulder, and as he fumbled to re-load, he saw the bull was down. Down on his knees, his big head tossing, and seeing the other two still galloping he shot at the leader and hit him. He shot again and missed and he heard the *carawonging* roar as Wilson shot and saw the leading bull slide forward onto his nose.

"Get that other," Wilson said. "Now you're shooting!"

But the other bull was moving steadily at the same gallop and he missed, throwing a spout of dirt, and Wilson missed and the dust rose in a cloud and Wilson shouted, "Come on. He's too far!" and grabbed his arm and they were in the car again,

Macomber and Wilson hanging on the sides and rocketing swayingly over the uneven ground, drawing up on the steady, plunging, heavy-necked, straight-moving gallop of the bull.

They were behind him and Macomber was filling his rifle, dropping shells onto the ground, jamming it, clearing the jam, then they were almost up with the bull when Wilson yelled "Stop," and the car skidded so that it almost swung over and Macomber fell forward onto his feet, slammed his bolt forward and fired as far forward as he could aim into the galloping, rounded black back, aimed and shot again, then again, then again, and the bullets, all of them hitting, had no effect on the buffalo that he could see. Then Wilson shot, the roar deafening him, and he could see the bull stagger. Macomber shot again, aiming carefully, and down he came, onto his knees.

"All right," Wilson said. "Nice work. That's the three."

Macomber felt a drunken elation.

"How many times did you shoot?" he asked.

"Just three," Wilson said. "You killed the first bull. The biggest one. I helped you finish the other two. Afraid they might have got into cover. You had them killed. I was just mopping up a little. You shot damn well."

"Let's go to the car," said Macomber. "I want a drink."

"Got to finish off that buff first," Wilson told him. The buffalo was on his knees and he jerked his head furiously and bellowed in pig-eyed, roaring rage as they came toward him.

"Watch he doesn't get up," Wilson said. Then, "Get a little broadside and take him in the neck just behind the ear."

Macomber aimed carefully at the center of the huge, jerking, rage-driven neck and shot. At the shot the head dropped forward.

"That does it," said Wilson. "Got the spine. They're a hell of a looking thing, aren't they?"

"Let's get the drink," said Macomber. In his life he had never felt so good.

In the car Macomber's wife sat very white faced. "You were marvellous, darling," she said to Macomber. "What a ride."

"Was it rough?" Wilson asked.

"It was frightful. I've never been more frightened in my life."

"Let's all have a drink," Macomber said.

"By all means," said Wilson. "Give it to the Memsahib." She drank the neat whisky from the flask and shuddered a little when she swallowed. She handed the flask to Macomber who handed it to Wilson.

"It was frightfully exciting," she said. "It's given me a dreadful headache. I didn't know you were allowed to shoot them from cars though."

"No one shot from cars," said Wilson coldly.

"I mean chase them from cars."

"Wouldn't ordinarily," Wilson said. "Seemed sporting enough to me though while we were doing it. Taking more chance driving that way across the plain full of holes and one thing and another than hunting on foot. Buffalo could have charged us each time we shot if he liked. Gave him every chance. Wouldn't mention it to any one though. It's illegal if that's what you mean."

"It seemed very unfair to me," Margot said, "chasing those big helpless things in a motor car."

"Did it?" said Wilson.

"What would happen if they heard about it in Nairobi?"

"I'd lose my license for one thing. Other unpleasantnesses," Wilson said, taking a drink from the flask. "I'd be out of business."

"Really?"

"Yes, really."

"Well," said Macomber, and he smiled for the first time all day. "Now she has something on you."

"You have such a pretty way of putting things, Francis," Margot Macomber said. Wilson looked at them both. If a four-letter man marries a five-letter woman, he was thinking, what number of letters would their children be? What he said was, "We lost a gun-bearer. Did you notice it?"

"My God, no," Macomber said.

"Here he comes," Wilson said. "He's all right. He must have fallen off when we left the first bull."

Approaching them was the middle-aged gun-bearer, limping along in his knitted cap, khaki tunic, shorts and rubber sandals, gloomy-faced and disgusted looking. As he came up he called out to Wilson in Swahili and they all saw the change in the white hunter's face.

"What does he say?" asked Margot.

"He says the first bull got up and went into the bush," Wilson said with no expression in his voice.

"Oh," said Macomber blankly.

"Then it's going to be just like the lion," said Margot, full of anticipation.

"It's not going to be a damned bit like the lion," Wilson told her. "Did you want another drink, Macomber?"

"Thanks, yes," Macomber said. He expected the feeling he had had about the lion to come back but it did not. For the first time in his life he really felt wholly without fear. Instead of fear he had a feeling of definite elation.

"We'll go and have a look at the second bull," Wilson said. "I'll tell the driver to put the car in the shade."

"What are you going to do?" asked Margaret Macomber.

"Take a look at the buff," Wilson said.

"I'll come."

"Come along."

The three of them walked over to where the second buffalo bulked blackly in the open, head forward on the grass, the massive horns swung wide.

"He's a very good head," Wilson said. "That's close to a fifty-inch spread."

Macomber was looking at him with delight.

"He's hateful looking," said Margot. "Can't we go into the shade?"

"Of course," Wilson said. "Look," he said to Macomber, and pointed. "See that patch of bush?"

"Yes."

"That's where the first bull went in. The gun-bearer said when he fell off the bull was down. He was watching us helling along and the other two buff galloping. When he looked up there was the bull up and looking at him. Gun-bearer ran like hell and the bull went off slowly into that bush."

"Can we go in after him now?" asked Macomber eagerly.

Wilson looked at him appraisingly. Damned if this isn't a strange one, he thought. Yesterday he's scared sick and today he's a ruddy fire eater.

"No, we'll give him a while."

"Let's please go into the shade," Margot said. Her face was white and she looked ill.

They made their way to the car where it stood under a single, wide-spreading tree and all climbed in.

"Chances are he's dead in there," Wilson remarked. "After a little we'll have a look."

Macomber felt a wild unreasonable happiness that he had never known before.

"By God, that was a chase," he said. "I've never felt any such feeling. Wasn't it marvellous, Margot?"

"I hated it."

"Why?"

"I hated it," she said bitterly. "I loathed it."

"You know I don't think I'd ever be afraid of anything again," Macomber said to Wilson. "Something happened in me after we first saw the buff and started after him. Like a dam bursting. It was pure excitement."

"Cleans out your liver," said Wilson. "Damn funny things happen to people."

Macomber's face was shining. "You know something did happen to me," he said. "I feel absolutely different."

His wife said nothing and eyed him strangely. She was sitting far back in the seat and Macomber was sitting forward talking to Wilson who turned sideways talking over the back of the front seat.

"You know, I'd like to try another lion," Macomber said. "I'm really not afraid of them now. After all, what can they do to you?"

"That's it," said Wilson. "Worst one can do is kill you. How does it go? Shakespeare. Damned good. See if I can remember. Oh, damned good. Used to quote it to myself at one time. Let's see. 'By my troth, I care not; a man can die but once; we owe God a death and let it go which way it will he that dies this year is quit for the next.' Damned fine, eh?"

He was very embarrassed, having brought out this thing he had lived by, but he had seen men come of age before and it always moved him. It was not a matter of their twenty-first birthday.

It had taken a strange chance of hunting, a sudden precipitation into action without opportunity for worrying beforehand, to bring this about with Macomber, but regardless of how it had happened it had most certainly happened. Look at the beggar now, Wilson thought. It's that some of them stay little boys so long, Wilson thought. Sometimes all their lives. Their figures stay boyish when they're fifty. The great American boy-men. Damned strange people. But he liked this Macomber now. Damned strange fellow. Probably meant the end of cuckoldry too. Well, that would be a damned good thing. Damned good thing. Beggar had probably been afraid all his life. Don't know what started it. But over now. Hadn't had time to be afraid with the buff. That and being angry too. Motor car too. Motor cars made it familiar. Be a damn fire eater now. He'd seen it in the war work the same way. More of a change than any loss of virginity. Fear gone like an operation. Something else grew in its place. Main thing a man had. Made him into a man. Women knew it too. No bloody fear.

From the far corner of the seat Margaret Macomber looked at the two of them. There was no change in Wilson. She saw Wilson as she had seen him the day before when she had first realized what his great talent was. But she saw the change in Francis Macomber now.

"Do you have that feeling of happiness about what's going to happen?" Macomber asked, still exploring his new wealth.

"You're not supposed to mention it," Wilson said, looking in the other's face. "Much more fashionable to say you're scared. Mind you, you'll be scared too, plenty of times."

"But you *have* a feeling of happiness about action to come?"

"Yes," said Wilson. "There's that. Doesn't do to talk too much about all this. Talk the whole thing away. No pleasure in anything if you mouth it up too much."

"You're both talking rot," said Margot. "Just because you've chased some helpless animals in a motor car you talk like heroes."

"Sorry," said Wilson. "I have been gassing too much." She's worried about it already, he thought.

"If you don't know what we're talking about why not keep out of it?" Macomber asked his wife.

"You've gotten awfully brave, awfully suddenly," his wife said contemptuously, but her contempt was not secure. She was very afraid of something.

Macomber laughed, a very natural hearty laugh. "You know I *have,*" he said. "I really have."

"Isn't it sort of late?" Margot said bitterly. Because she had done the best she could for many years back and the way they were together now was no one person's fault.

"Not for me," said Macomber.

Margot said nothing but sat back in the corner of the seat.

"Do you think we've given him time enough?" Macomber asked Wilson cheerfully.

"We might have a look," Wilson said. "Have you any solids left?"

"The gun-bearer has some."

Wilson called in Swahili and the older gun-bearer, who was skinning out one of the heads, straightened up, pulled a box of solids out of his pocket and brought them over to Macomber, who filled his magazine and put the remaining shells in his pocket.

"You might as well shoot the Springfield," Wilson said. "You're used to it. We'll leave the Mannlicher in the car with the Memsahib. Your gun-bearer can carry your heavy gun. I've this damned cannon. Now let me tell you about them." He had saved this until the last because he did not want to worry Macomber. "When a buff comes he comes with his head high and thrust straight out. The boss of the horns covers any sort of a brain shot. The only shot is straight into the nose. The only other shot is into his chest or, if you're to one side, into the neck or the shoulders. After they've been hit once they take a hell of a lot of killing. Don't try anything fancy. Take the easiest shot there is. They've finished skinning out that head now. Should we get started?"

He called to the gun-bearers, who came up wiping their hands, and the older one got into the back.

"I'll only take Kongoni," Wilson said. "The other can watch to keep the birds away."

As the car moved slowly across the open space toward the island of brushy trees that ran in a tongue of foliage along a dry water course that cut the open swale, Macomber felt his heart pounding and his mouth was dry again, but it was excitement, not fear.

"Here's where he went in," Wilson said. Then to the gun-bearer in Swahili, "Take the blood spoor."

The car was parallel to the patch of bush. Macomber, Wilson and the gun-bearer got down. Macomber, looking back, saw his wife, with the rifle by her side, looking at him. He waved to her and she did not wave back.

The brush was very thick ahead and the ground was dry. The middle-aged gun-bearer was sweating heavily and Wilson had his hat down over his eyes and his red neck showed just ahead of Macomber. Suddenly the gun-bearer said something in Swahili to Wilson and ran forward.

"He's dead in there," Wilson said. "Good work," and he turned to grip Macomber's hand and as they shook hands, grinning at each other, the gun-bearer shouted wildly and they saw him coming out of the brush sideways, fast as a crab, and the bull coming, nose out, mouth tight closed, blood dripping, massive head straight out, coming in a charge, his little pig eyes bloodshot as he looked at them. Wilson, who was ahead was kneeling shooting, and Macomber, as he fired, unhearing his shot in the roaring of Wilson's gun, saw fragments like slate burst from the huge boss of the horns, and the head jerked, he shot again at the wide nostrils and saw the horns jolt again and fragments fly, and he did not see Wilson now and, aiming carefully, shot again with the buffalo's huge bulk almost on him and his rifle almost level with the on-coming head, nose out, and he could see the little wicked eyes and the head started to lower and he felt a sudden white-hot, blinding flash explode inside his head and that was all he ever felt.

Wilson had ducked to one side to get in a shoulder shot. Macomber had stood solid and shot for the nose, shooting a touch high each time and hitting the heavy horns, splintering and chipping them like hitting a slate roof, and Mrs. Macomber, in the car, had shot at the buffalo with the 6.5 Mannlicher as it seemed about to gore Macomber and had hit her husband about two inches up and a little to one side of the base of his skull.

Francis Macomber lay now, face down, not two yards from where the buffalo lay on his side and his wife knelt over him with Wilson beside her.

"I wouldn't turn him over," Wilson said.

The woman was crying hysterically.

"I'd get back in the car," Wilson said. "Where's the rifle?"

She shook her head, her face contorted. The gun-bearer picked up the rifle.

"Leave it as it is," said Wilson. Then, "Go get Abdulla so that he may witness the manner of the accident."

He knelt down, took a handkerchief from his pocket, and spread it over Francis Macomber's crew-cropped head where it lay. The blood sank into the dry, loose earth.

Wilson stood up and saw the buffalo on his side, his legs out, his thinly-haired belly crawling with ticks. "Hell of a good bull," his brain registered automatically. "A good fifty inches, or better. Better." He called to the driver and told him to spread a blanket over the body and stay by it. Then he walked over to the motor car where the woman sat crying in the corner.

"That was a pretty thing to do," he said in a toneless voice. "He *would* have left you too."

"Stop it," she said.

"Of course it's an accident," he said. "I know that."

"Stop it," she said.

"Don't worry," he said. "There will be a certain amount of unpleasantness but I will have some photographs taken that will be very useful at the inquest. There's the testimony of the gun-bearers and the driver too. You're perfectly all right."

"Stop it," she said.

"There's a hell of a lot to be done," he said. "And I'll have to send a truck off to the lake to wireless for a plane to take the three of us into Nairobi. Why didn't you poison him? That's what they do in England."

"Stop it. Stop it. Stop it," the woman cried.

Wilson looked at her with his flat blue eyes.

"I'm through now," he said. "I was a little angry. I'd begun to like your husband."

"Oh, please stop it," she said. "Please, please stop it."

"That's better," Wilson said. "Please is much better. Now I'll stop."

JORGE LUIS BORGES

[b. 1899]

The Garden of Forking Paths

TRANSLATED BY DONALD YATES

On page 22 of Liddell Hart's *History of World War I* you will read that an attack against the Serre-Montauban line by thirteen British divisions (supported by 1,400 artillery pieces), planned for the 24th of July, 1916, had to be postponed until the morning of the 29th. The torrential rains, Captain Liddell Hart comments, caused this delay, an insignificant one, to be sure.

The following statement, dictated, reread and signed by Dr. Yu Tsun, former professor of English at the *Hochschule* at Tsingtao, throws an unsuspected light over the whole affair. The first two pages of the document are missing.

"... and I hung up the receiver. Immediately afterwards, I recognized the voice that had answered in German. It was that of Captain Richard Madden. Madden's presence in Viktor Runeberg's apartment meant the end of our anxieties and—but this seemed, *or should have seemed,* very secondary to me—also the end of our lives. It meant that Runeberg had been arrested or murdered. Before the sun set on that day, I would encounter the same fate. Madden was implacable. Or rather, he was obliged to be so. An Irishman at the service of England, a man accused of laxity and perhaps of treason, how could he fail to seize and be thankful for such a miraculous opportunity: the discovery, capture, maybe even the death of two agents of the German Reich? I went up to my room; absurdly I locked the door and threw myself on my back on the narrow iron cot. Through the window I saw the familiar roofs and the cloud-shaded six o'clock sun. It seemed incredible to me that that day without premonitions or symbols should be the one of my inexorable death. In spite of my dead father, in spite of having been a child in a symmetrical garden of Hai Feng, was I—now—going to die? Then I reflected that everything happens to a man precisely, precisely *now*. Centuries of centuries and only in the present do things happen; countless men in the air, on the face of the earth and the sea, and all that really is happening is happening to me . . . The almost intolerable recollection of Madden's horselike face banished these wanderings. In the midst of my hatred and terror (it means nothing to me now to speak of terror, now that I have mocked Richard Madden, now that my throat yearns for the noose) it occurred to me that the tumultuous and doubtless happy warrior did not suspect that I possessed the Secret. The name of the exact location of the new British artillery park on the River Ancre. A bird streaked across the gray sky and blindly I translated it into an airplane and that airplane into many (against the French sky) annihilating the artillery station with vertical bombs. If only my mouth, before a bullet shattered it, could cry out that secret name so it could be heard in Germany . . . My human voice was very weak. How might I make it carry to the ear of the Chief? To the ear of that sick and hateful man who knew nothing of Runeberg and me save that we were in Staffordshire and who was waiting in vain for our report in his arid office in Berlin, endlessly examining newspapers . . . I said out loud: *I must flee.* I sat up noiselessly, in a useless perfection of silence, as if Madden were already lying in wait for me. Something—perhaps the mere vain ostentation of proving my resources were nil—made me look through my pockets. I found what I knew I would find. The American watch, the nickel chain and the square coin, the key ring with the incriminating useless keys to Runeberg's apartment, the notebook, a letter which I resolved to destroy immediately (and which I did not destroy), a crown, two shillings and a few pence, the red and blue pencil, the handkerchief, the revolver with one bullet. Absurdly, I took it in my hand and weighed it in order to inspire courage within myself. Vaguely I thought that a pistol report can be heard at a great distance. In ten minutes my plan was perfected. The telephone book listed the name of the only person capable of transmitting the message; he lived in a suburb of Fenton, less than a half hour's train ride away.

I am a cowardly man. I say it now, now that I have carried to its end a plan whose perilous nature no one can deny. I know its execution was terrible. I didn't do it for Germany, no. I care nothing for a barbarous country which imposed upon me the abjection of being a spy. Besides, I know of a man from England—a modest man—who for me is no less great than Goethe. I talked with him for scarcely an hour, but during that hour he was Goethe . . . I did it because I sensed that the Chief somehow feared people of my race—for the innumerable ancestors who merge within me. I wanted to prove to him that a yellow man could save his armies. Besides, I had to flee from Captain Madden. His hands and his voice could call at my door at any moment. I dressed silently, bade farewell to myself in the mirror, went downstairs, scrutinized the peaceful street and went out. The station was not far from my home, but I judged it wise to take a cab. I argued that in this way I ran less risk of being recognized; the fact is that in the deserted street I felt myself visible and vulnerable, infinitely so. I remember that I told the cab driver to stop a short distance before the main entrance. I got out with voluntary, almost painful slowness; I was going to the village of Ashgrove but I bought a ticket for a more distant station. The train left within a very few minutes, at eight-fifty. I hurried; the next one would leave at nine-thirty. There was hardly a soul on the platform. I went through the coaches; I remember a few farmers, a woman dressed in mourning, a young boy who was reading with fervor the *Annals* of Tacitus, a wounded and happy soldier. The coaches jerked forward at last. A man whom I recognized ran in vain to the end of the platform. It was Captain Richard Madden. Shattered, trembling, I shrank into the far corner of the seat, away from the dreaded window.

From this broken state I passed into an almost abject felicity. I told myself that the duel had already begun and that I had won the first encounter by frustrating, even if for forty minutes, even if by a stroke of fate, the attack of my adversary. I argued that this slightest of victories foreshadowed a total victory. I argued (no less fallaciously) that my cowardly felicity proved that I was a man capable of carrying out the adventure successfully. From this weakness I took strength that did not abandon me. I foresee that man will resign himself each day to more atrocious undertakings; soon there will be no one but warriors and brigands; I give them this counsel: *The author of an atrocious undertaking ought to imagine that he has already accomplished it, ought to impose upon himself a future as irrevocable as the past.* Thus I proceeded as my eyes of a man already dead registered the elapsing of that day, which was perhaps the last, and the diffusion of the night. The train ran gently along, amid ash trees. It stopped, almost in the middle of the fields. No one announced the name of the station. "Ashgrove?" I asked a few lads on the platform. "Ashgrove," they replied. I got off.

A lamp enlightened the platform but the faces of the boys were in shadow. One questioned me, "Are you going to Dr. Stephen Albert's house?" Without waiting for my answer, another said, "The house is a long way from here, but you won't get lost if you take this road to the left and at every crossroads turn again to your left." I tossed them a coin (my last), descended a few stone steps and started down the solitary road. It went downhill, slowly. It was of elemental earth; overhead the branches were tangled; the low, full moon seemed to accompany me.

For an instant, I thought that Richard Madden in some way had penetrated my desperate plan. Very quickly, I understood that that was impossible. The instructions to turn always to the left reminded me that such was the common procedure for discovering the central point of certain labyrinths. I have some understanding of labyrinths: not for nothing am I the great grandson of that Ts'ui Pên who was governor of Yunnan and who renounced worldly power in order to write a novel that might be even more populous than the *Hung Lu Meng* and to construct a labyrinth in which all men would become lost. Thirteen years he dedicated to these heterogeneous tasks, but the hand of a stranger murdered him—and his novel was incoherent and no one found the labyrinth. Beneath English trees I meditated on that lost maze; I imagined it inviolate and perfect at the secret crest of a mountain; I imagined it erased by rice fields or beneath the water; I imagined it infinite, no longer composed of octagonal kiosks and returning paths, but of rivers and provinces and kingdoms . . . I thought of a labyrinth of labyrinths, of one sinuous spreading labyrinth that would encompass the past and the future and in some way involve the stars. Absorbed in these illusory images, I forgot my destiny of one pursued. I felt myself to be, for an unknown period of time, an abstract perceiver of the world. The vague, living countryside, the moon, the remains of the day worked on me, as well as the slope of the road which eliminated any possibility of weariness. The afternoon was intimate, infinite. The road descended and forked among the now confused meadows. A high-pitched, almost syllabic music approached and receded in the shifting of the wind, dimmed by leaves and distance.

I thought that a man can be an enemy of other men, of the moments of other men, but not of a country: not of fireflies, woods, gardens, streams of water, sunsets. Thus I arrived before a tall, rusty gate. Between the iron bars I made out a poplar grove and a pavilion. I understood suddenly two things, the first trivial, the second almost unbelievable: the music came from the pavilion, and the music was Chinese. For precisely that reason I had openly accepted it without paying it any heed. I do not remember whether there was a bell or whether I knocked with my hand. The sparkling of the music continued.

From the rear of the house within a lantern approached: a lantern that the trees sometimes striped and sometimes eclipsed, a paper lantern that had the form of a drum and the color of the moon. A tall man bore it. I didn't see his face for the light blinded me. He opened the door and said slowly, in my own language: "I see that the pious Hsi P'êng persists in correcting my solitude. You no doubt wish to see the garden?"

I recognized the name of one of our consuls and I replied, disconcerted, "The garden?"

"The garden of forking paths."

Something stirred in my memory and I uttered with incomprehensible certainty, "The garden of my ancestor Ts'ui Pên."

"Your ancestor? Your illustrious ancestor? Come in."

The damp path zigzagged like those of my childhood. We came to a library of Eastern and Western books. I recognized bound in yellow silk several volumes of the Lost Encyclopedia, edited by the Third Emperor of the Luminous Dynasty but never printed. The record on the phonograph revolved next to a bronze phoenix. I also recall a *famille rose* vase and another, many centuries older, of that shade of blue which our craftsmen copied from the potters of Persia . . .

Stephen Albert observed me with a smile. He was, as I have said, very tall, sharp-featured, with gray eyes and a gray beard. He told me that he had been a missionary in Tientsin "before aspiring to become a Sinologist."

We sat down—I on a long, low divan, he with his back to the window and a tall circular clock. I calculated that my pursuer, Richard Madden, could not arrive for at least an hour. My irrevocable determination could wait.

"An astounding fate, that of Ts'ui Pên," Stephen Albert said. "Governor of his native province, learned in astronomy, in astrology and in the tireless interpretation of the canonical books, chess player, famous poet and calligrapher—he abandoned all this in order to compose a book and a maze. He renounced the pleasures of both tyranny and justice, of his populous couch, of his banquets and even of erudition—all to close himself up for thirteen years in the Pavilion of the Limpid Solitude. When he died, his heirs found nothing save chaotic manuscripts. His family, as you may be aware, wished to condemn them to the fire; but his executor—a Taoist or Buddhist monk—insisted on their publication."

"We descendants of Ts'ui Pên," I replied, "continue to curse that monk. Their publication was senseless. The book is an indeterminate heap of contradictory drafts. I examined it once: in the third chapter the hero dies, in the fourth he is alive. As for the other undertaking of Ts'ui Pên, his labyrinth . . ."

"Here is Ts'ui Pên's labyrinth," he said, indicating a tall lacquered desk.

"An ivory labyrinth!" I exclaimed. "A minimum labyrinth."

"A labyrinth of symbols," he corrected. "An invisible labyrinth of time. To me, a barbarous Englishman, has been entrusted the revelation of this diaphanous mystery. After more than a hundred years, the details are irretrievable; but it is not hard to conjecture what happened. Ts'ui Pên must have said once: *I am withdrawing to write a book.* And another time: *I am withdrawing to construct a labyrinth.* Every one imagined two works; to no one did it occur that the book and the maze were one and the same thing. The Pavilion of the Limpid Solitude stood in the center of a garden that was perhaps intricate; that circumstance could have suggested to the heirs a physical labyrinth. Ts'ui Pên died; no one in the vast territories that were his came upon the labyrinth; the confusion of the novel suggested to me that *it* was the maze. Two circumstances gave me the correct solution of the problem. One: the curious legend that Ts'ui Pên had planned to create a labyrinth which would be strictly infinite. The other: a fragment of a letter I discovered."

Albert rose. He turned his back on me for a moment; he opened a drawer of the black and gold desk. He faced me and in his hands he held a sheet of paper that had once been crimson, but was now pink and tenuous and cross-sectioned. The fame of Ts'ui Pên as a calligrapher had been justly won. I read, uncomprehendingly and with fervor, these words written with a minute brush by a man of my blood: *I leave to the various futures (not to all) my garden of forking paths.* Wordlessly, I returned the sheet. Albert continued:

"Before unearthing this letter, I had questioned myself about the ways in which a book can be infinite. I could think of nothing other than a cyclic volume, a circular one. A book whose last page was identical with the first, a book which had the possibility of continuing indefinitely. I remembered too that night which is at the middle of the Thousand and One Nights when Scheherazade (through a magical oversight of the copyist) begins to relate word for word the story of the Thousand and One Nights, establishing the risk of coming once again to the night when she must repeat it, and thus on to infinity. I imagined as well a Platonic, hereditary work, transmitted from father to son, in which each new individual adds a chapter or corrects with pious care the pages of his elders. These conjectures diverted me; but none seemed to correspond, not even remotely, to the contradictory chapters of Ts'ui Pên. In the midst of this perplexity, I received from Oxford the manuscript you have examined. I lingered, naturally, on the sentence: *I leave to the various futures (not to all) my garden of forking paths.* Almost instantly, I understood: 'the garden of forking paths' was the chaotic novel; the phrase 'the various futures (not to all)' suggested to me the forking in time, not in space. A broad rereading of the work confirmed the theory. In all fictional works, each time a man is confronted with several alternatives, he chooses one and eliminates the others; in the fiction of Ts'ui Pên, he chooses—simultaneously—all of them. *He creates,* in this way, diverse futures, diverse times which themselves also proliferate and fork. Here, then, is the explanation of the novel's contradictions. Fang, let us say, has a secret; a stranger calls at his door; Fang resolves to kill him. Naturally, there are several possible outcomes: Fang can kill the intruder, the intruder can kill Fang, they both can escape, they both can die, and so forth. In the work of Ts'ui Pên, all possible outcomes occur; each one is the point of departure for other forkings. Sometimes, the paths of this labyrinth converge: for example, you arrive at this house, but in one of the possible pasts you are my enemy, in another, my friend. If you will resign yourself to my incurable pronunciation, we shall read a few pages."

His face, within the vivid circle of the lamplight, was unquestionably that of an old man, but with something unalterable about it, even immortal. He read with slow precision two versions of the same epic chapter. In the first, an army marches to a battle across a lonely mountain; the horror of the rocks and shadows makes the men under-value their lives and they gain an easy victory. In the second, the same army traverses a palace where a great festival is taking place; the resplendent battle seems to them a continuation of the celebration and they win the victory. I listened with proper veneration to these ancient narratives, perhaps less admirable in themselves than the fact that they had been created by my blood and were being restored to me by a man of a remote empire, in the course of a desperate adventure, on a Western isle. I remember the last words, repeated in each version like a secret commandment: *Thus fought the heroes, tranquil their admirable hearts, violent their swords, resigned to kill and to die.*

From that moment on, I felt about me and within my dark body an invisible, intangible swarming. Not the swarming of the divergent, parallel and finally coalescent armies, but a more inaccessible, more intimate agitation that they in some manner prefigured. Stephen Albert continued:

"I don't believe that your illustrious ancestor played idly with these variations. I don't consider it credible that he would sacrifice thirteen years to the infinite execution of a rhetorical experiment. In your country, the novel is a subsidiary form of literature; in Ts'ui Pên's time it was a despicable form. Ts'ui Pên was a brilliant novelist, but he was also a man of letters who doubtless did not consider himself a mere novelist. The testimony of his contemporaries proclaims—and his life fully confirms—his metaphysi-cal and mystical interests. Philosophic controversy usurps a good part of the novel. I know that of all problems, none disturbed him so greatly nor worked upon him so much as the abysmal problem of time. Now then, the latter is the only problem that does not figure in the pages of the *Garden.* He does not even use the word that signifies *time.* How do you explain this voluntary omission?"

I proposed several solutions—all unsatisfactory. We discussed them. Finally, Stephen Albert said to me:

"In a riddle whose answer is chess, what is the only prohibited word?"

I thought a moment and replied, "The word *chess.*"

"Precisely," said Albert. "*The Garden of Forking Paths* is an enormous riddle, or parable, whose theme is time; this recondite cause prohibits its mention. To omit a word always, to resort to inept metaphors and obvious periphrases, is perhaps the most emphatic way of stressing it. That is the tortuous method preferred, in each of the meanderings of his indefatigable novel, by the oblique Ts'ui Pên. I have compared hundreds of manuscripts, I have corrected the errors that the negligence of the copyists has introduced. I have guessed the plan of this chaos, I have re-established—I believe I have re-established—the primordial organization, I have translated the entire work: it is clear to me that not once does he employ the word 'time.' The explanation is obvious: *The Garden of Forking Paths* is an incomplete, but not false, image of the universe as Ts'ui Pên conceived it. In contrast to Newton and Schopenhauer, your ancestor did not believe in a uniform, absolute time. He believed in an infinite series of times, in a growing, dizzying net of divergent, convergent and parallel times. This network of times which approached one another, forked, broke off, or were unaware of one another for centuries, embraces *all* possibilities of time. We do not exist in the majority of these times; in some you exist, and not I; in others I, and not you; in others, both of us. In the present one, which a favorable fate has granted me, you have arrived at my house; in another, while crossing the garden, you found me dead; in still another, I utter these same words, but I am a mistake, a ghost."

"In every one," I pronounced, not without a tremble to my voice, "I am grateful to you and revere you for your re-creation of the garden of Ts'ui Pên."

"Not in all," he murmured with a smile. "Time forks perpetually toward innumerable futures. In one of them I am your enemy."

Once again I felt the swarming sensation of which I have spoken. It seemed to me that the humid garden that surrounded the house was infinitely saturated with invisible persons. Those persons were Albert and I, secret, busy and multiform in other dimensions of time. I raised my eyes and the tenuous nightmare dissolved. In the yellow and black garden there was only one man; but this man was as strong as a statue . . . this man was approaching along the path and he was Captain Richard Madden.

"The future already exists," I replied, "but I am your friend. Could I see the letter again?"

Albert rose. Standing tall, he opened the drawer of the tall desk; for the moment his back was to me. I had readied the revolver. I fired with extreme caution. Albert fell uncomplainingly, immediately. I swear his death was instantaneous—a lightning stroke.

The rest is unreal, insignificant. Madden broke in, arrested me. I have been condemned to the gallows. I have won out abominably; I have communicated to Berlin the secret name of the city they must attack. They bombed it yesterday; I read it in the same papers that offered to England the mystery of the learned Sinologist Stephen Albert who was murdered by a stranger, one Yu Tsun. The Chief had deciphered this mystery. He knew my problem was to indicate (through the uproar of the war) the city called Albert, and that I had found no other means to do so than to kill a man of that name. He does not know (no one can know) my innumerable contrition and weariness.

JOHN STEINBECK

[1902–1968]

The Snake

It was almost dark when young Dr. Phillips swung his sack to his shoulder and left the tide pool. He climbed up over the rocks and squashed along the street in his rubber boots. The street lights were on by the time he arrived at his little commercial laboratory on the cannery street of Monterey. It was a tight little building, standing partly on piers over the bay water and partly on the land. On both sides the big corrugated-iron sardine canneries crowded in on it.

Dr. Phillips climbed the wooden steps and opened the door. The white rats in their cages scampered up and down the wire, and the captive cats in their pens mewed for milk. Dr. Phillips turned on the glaring light over the dissection table and dumped his clammy sack on the floor. He walked to the glass cages by the window where the rattlesnakes lived, leaned over and looked in.

The snakes were bunched and resting in the corners of the cage, but every head was clear; the dusty eyes seemed to look at nothing, but as the young man leaned over the cage the forked tongues, black on the ends and pink behind, twittered out and waved slowly up and down. Then the snakes recognized the man and pulled in their tongues.

Dr. Phillips threw off his leather coat and built a fire in the tin stove; he set a kettle of water on the stove and dropped a can of beans into the water. Then he stood staring down at the sack on the floor. He was a slight young man with the mild, preoccupied eyes of one who looks through a microscope a great deal. He wore a short blond beard.

The draft ran breathily up the chimney and a glow of warmth came from the stove. The little waves washed quietly about the piles under the building. Arranged on shelves about the room were tier above tier of museum jars containing the mounted marine specimens the laboratory dealt in.

Dr. Phillips opened a side door and went into his bedroom, a book-lined cell containing an army cot, a reading light and an uncomfortable wooden chair. He pulled off his rubber boots and put on a pair of sheepskin slippers. When he went back to the other room the water in the kettle was already beginning to hum.

He lifted his sack to the table under the white light and emptied out two dozen common starfish. These he laid out side by side on the table. His preoccupied eyes turned to the busy rats in the wire cages. Taking grain from a paper sack, he poured it into the feeding troughs. Instantly the rats scrambled down from the wire and fell upon the food. A bottle of milk stood on a glass shelf between a small mounted octopus and a jellyfish. Dr. Phillips lifted down the milk and walked to the cat cage, but before he filled the containers he reached in the cage and gently picked out a big rangy alley tabby. He stroked her for a moment and then dropped her in a small black painted box, closed the lid and bolted it and then turned on a petcock which admitted gas into the killing chamber. While the short soft struggle went on in the black box he filled the saucers with milk. One of the cats arched against his hand and he smiled and petted her neck.

The box was quiet now. He turned off the petcock, for the airtight box would be full of gas.

On the stove the pan of water was bubbling furiously about the can of beans. Dr. Phillips lifted out the can with a big pair of forceps, opened it, and emptied the beans into a glass dish. While he ate he watched the starfish on the table. From between the rays little drops of milky fluid were exuding. He bolted his beans and when they were gone he put the dish in the sink and stepped to the equipment cupboard. From this he took a microscope and a pile of little glass dishes. He filled the dishes one by one with sea water from a tap and arranged them in a line beside the starfish. He took out his watch and laid it on the table under the pouring white light. The waves washed with little sighs against the piles under the floor. He took an eyedropper from a drawer and bent over the starfish.

At that moment there were quick steps on the wooden stairs and a strong knocking at the door. A slight grimace of annoyance crossed the young man's face as he went to open it. A tall, lean woman stood in the doorway. She was dressed in a severe dark suit—her straight black hair, growing low on a flat forehead, was mussed as though the wind had been blowing it. Her black eyes glittered in the strong light.

She spoke in a soft throaty voice, "May I come in? I want to talk to you."

"I'm very busy just now," he said half-heartedly. "I have to do things at times." But he stood away from the door. The tall woman slipped in.

"I'll be quiet until you can talk to me."

He closed the door and brought the uncomfortable chair from the bedroom. "You see," he apologized, "the process is started and I must get to it." So many people wandered in and asked questions. He had little routines of explanations for the commoner processes. He could say them without thinking. "Sit here. In a few minutes I'll be able to listen to you."

The tall woman leaned over the table. With the eyedropper the young man gathered fluid from between the rays of the starfish and squirted it into a bowl of water, and then he drew some milky fluid and squirted it in the same bowl and stirred the water gently with the eyedropper. He began his little patter of explanation.

"When starfish are sexually mature they release sperm and ova when they are exposed at low tide. By choosing mature specimens and taking them out of the water, I give them a condition of low tide. Now I've mixed the sperm and eggs. Now I put some of the mixture in each one of these ten watch-glasses. In ten minutes I will kill those in the first glass with menthol, twenty minutes later I will kill the second group and then a new group every twenty minutes. Then I will have arrested the process in stages, and I will mount the series on microscope slides for biologic study." He paused. "Would you like to look at this first group under the microscope?"

"No, thank you."

He turned quickly to her. People always wanted to look through the glass. She was not looking at the table at all, but at him. Her black eyes were on him, but they did not seem to see him. He realized why—the irises were as dark as the pupils, there was no color line between the two. Dr. Phillips was piqued at her answer. Although answering questions bored him, a lack of interest in what he was doing irritated him. A desire to arouse her grew in him.

"While I'm waiting the first ten minutes I have something to do. Some people don't like to see it. Maybe you'd better step into that room until I finish."

"No," she said in her soft flat tone. "Do what you wish. I will wait until you can talk to me." Her hands rested side by side on her lap. She was completely at rest. Her eyes were bright but the rest of her was almost in a state of suspended animation. He thought, "Low metabolic rate, almost as low as a frog's, from the looks." The desire to shock her out of her inanition possessed him again.

He brought a little wooden cradle to the table, laid out scalpels and scissors and rigged a big hollow needle to a pressure tube. Then from the killing chamber he brought the limp dead cat and laid it in the cradle and tied its legs to hooks in the sides. He glanced sidewise at the woman. She had not moved. She was still at rest.

The cat grinned up into the light, its pink tongue stuck out between its needle teeth. Dr. Phillips deftly snipped open the skin at the throat; with a scalpel he slit through and found an artery. With flawless technique he put the needle in the vessel and tied it in with gut. "Embalming fluid," he explained. "Later I'll inject yellow mass into the veinous system and red mass into the arterial system—for bloodstream dissection—biology classes."

He looked around at her again. Her dark eyes seemed veiled with dust. She looked without expression at the cat's open throat. Not a drop of blood had escaped. The incision was clean. Dr. Phillips looked at his watch. "Time for the first group." He shook a few crystals of menthol into the first watch-glass.

The woman was making him nervous. The rats climbed about on the wire of their cage again and squeaked softly. The waves under the building beat with little shocks on the piles.

The young man shivered. He put a few lumps of coal in the stove and sat down. "Now," he said. "I haven't anything to do for twenty minutes." He noticed how short her chin was between lower lip and point. She seemed to awaken slowly, to come up out of some deep pool of consciousness. Her head raised and her dark dusty eyes moved about the room and then came back to him.

"I was waiting," she said. Her hands remained side by side on her lap. "You have snakes?"

"Why, yes," he said rather loudly. "I have about two dozen rattlesnakes. I milk out the venom and send it to the anti-venom laboratories."

She continued to look at him but her eyes did not center on him, rather they covered him and seemed to see in a big circle all around him. "Have you a male snake, a male rattlesnake?"

"Well, it just happens I know I have. I came in one morning and found a big snake in—in coition with a smaller one. That's very rare in captivity. You see, I do know I have a male snake."

"Where is he?"

"Why, right in the glass cage by the window there."

Her head swung slowly around but her two quiet hands did not move. She turned back toward him. "May I see?"

He got up and walked to the case by the window. On the sand bottom the knot of rattlesnakes lay entwined, but their heads were clear. The tongues came out and flickered a moment and then waved up and down feeling the air for vibrations. Dr. Phillips nervously turned his head. The woman was standing beside him. He had not heard her get up from the chair. He had heard only the splash of water among the piles and the scampering of the rats on the wire screen.

She said softly, "Which is the male you spoke of?"

He pointed to a thick, dusty grey snake lying by itself in one corner of the cage. "That one. He's nearly five feet long. He comes from Texas. Our Pacific coast snakes are usually smaller. He's been taking all the rats, too. When I want the others to eat I have to take him out."

The woman stared down at the blunt dry head. The forked tongue slipped out and hung quivering for a long moment. "And you're sure he's a male."

"Rattlesnakes are funny," he said glibly. "Nearly every generalization proves wrong. I don't like to say anything definite about rattlesnakes, but—yes—I can assure you he's a male."

Her eyes did not move from the flat head. "Will you sell him to me?"

"Sell him?" he cried. "Sell him to you?"

"You do sell specimens, don't you?"

"Oh—yes. Of course I do. Of course I do."

"How much? Five dollars? Ten?"

"Oh! Not more than five. But—do you know anything about rattlesnakes? You might be bitten."

She looked at him for a moment. "I don't intend to take him. I want to leave him here, but—I want him to be mine. I want to come here and look at him and feed him and to know he's mine." She opened a little purse and took out a five-dollar bill. "Here! Now he is mine."

Dr. Phillips began to be afraid. "You could come to look at him without owning him."

"I want him to be mine."

"Oh, Lord!" he cried. "I've forgotten the time." He ran to the table. "Three minutes over. It won't matter much." He shook menthol crystals into the second watch-glass. And then he was drawn back to the cage where the woman still stared at the snake.

She asked, "What does he eat?"

"I feed them white rats, rats from the cage over there."

"Will you put him in the other cage? I want to feed him."

"But he doesn't need food. He's had a rat already this week. Sometimes they don't eat for three or four months. I had one that didn't eat for over a year."

In her low monotone she asked, "Will you sell me a rat?"

He shrugged his shoulders. "I see. You want to watch how rattlesnakes eat. All right. I'll show you. The rat will cost twenty-five cents. It's better than a bullfight if you look at it one way, and it's simply a snake eating his dinner if you look at it another." His tone had become acid. He hated people who made sport of natural processes. He was not a sportsman but a biologist. He could kill a thousand animals for knowledge, but not an insect for pleasure. He'd been over this in his mind before.

She turned her head slowly toward him and the beginning of a smile formed on her thin lips. "I want to feed my snake," she said. "I'll put him in the other cage." She had opened the top of the cage and dipped her hand in before he knew what she was doing. He leaped forward and pulled her back. The lid banged shut.

"Haven't you any sense," he asked fiercely. "Maybe he wouldn't kill you, but he'd make you damned sick in spite of what I could do for you."

"You put him in the other cage then," she said quietly.

Dr. Phillips was shaken. He found that he was avoiding the dark eyes that didn't seem to look at anything. He felt that it was profoundly wrong to put a rat into the cage, deeply sinful; and he didn't know why. Often he had put rats in the cage when someone or other had wanted to see it, but this desire tonight sickened him. He tried to explain himself out of it.

"It's a good thing to see," he said. "It shows you how a snake can work. It makes you have a respect for a rattlesnake. Then, too, lots of people have dreams about the terror of snakes making a kill. I think because it is a subjective rat. The person is the rat. Once you see it the whole matter is objective. The rat is only a rat and the terror is removed."

He took a long stick equipped with a leather noose from the wall. Opening the trap he dropped the noose over the big snake's head and tightened the thong. A piercing dry rattle filled the room. The thick body writhed and slashed about the handle of the stick as he lifted the snake out and dropped it in the feeding cage. It stood ready to strike for a time, but the buzzing gradually ceased. The snake crawled into a corner, made a big figure eight with its body and lay still.

"You see," the young man explained, "these snakes are quite tame. I've had them a long time. I suppose I could handle them if I wanted to, but everyone who does handle rattlesnakes gets bitten sooner or later. I just don't want to take the chance." He glanced at the woman. He hated to put in the rat. She had moved over in front of the new cage; her black eyes were on the stony head of the snake again.

She said, "Put in a rat."

Reluctantly he went to the rat cage. For some reason he was sorry for the rat, and such a feeling had never come to him before. His eyes went over the mass of swarming white bodies climbing up the screen toward him. "Which one?" he thought. "Which one shall it be?" Suddenly he turned angrily to the woman. "Wouldn't you rather I put in a cat? Then you'd see a real fight. The cat might even win, but if it did it might kill the snake. I'll sell you a cat if you like."

She didn't look at him. "Put in a rat," she said. "I want him to eat."

He opened the rat cage and thrust his hand in. His fingers found a tail and he lifted a plump, red-eyed rat out of the cage. It struggled up to try to bite his fingers and, failing, hung spread out and motionless from its tail. He walked quickly across the room, opened the feeding cage and dropped the rat in on the sand floor. "Now, watch it," he cried.

The woman did not answer him. Her eyes were on the snake where it lay still. Its tongue, flicking in and out rapidly, tasted the air of the cage.

The rat landed on its feet, turned around and sniffed at its pink naked tail and then unconcernedly trotted across the sand, smelling as it went. The room was silent. Dr. Phillips did not know whether the water sighed among the piles or whether the woman sighed. Out of the corner of his eye he saw her body crouch and stiffen.

The snake moved out smoothly, slowly. The tongue flicked in and out. The motion was so gradual, so smooth that it didn't seem to be motion at all. In the other end of the cage the rat perked up in a sitting position and began to lick down the fine white hair on its chest. The snake moved on, keeping always a deep S curve in its neck.

The silence beat on the young man. He felt the blood drifting up in his body. He said loudly, "See! He keeps the striking curve ready. Rattlesnakes are cautious, almost cowardly animals. The mechanism is so delicate. The snake's dinner is to be got by an operation as deft as a surgeon's job. He takes no chances with his instruments."

The snake had flowed to the middle of the cage by now. The rat looked up, saw the snake and then unconcernedly went back to licking its chest.

"It's the most beautiful thing in the world," the young man said. His veins were throbbing. "It's the most terrible thing in the world."

The snake was close now. Its head lifted a few inches from the sand. The head weaved slowly back and forth, aiming, getting distance, aiming. Dr. Phillips glanced again at the woman. He turned sick. She was weaving too, not much, just a suggestion.

The rat looked up and saw the snake. It dropped to four feet and back up, and then —the stroke. It was impossible to see, simply a flash. The rat jarred as though under an invisible blow. The snake backed hurriedly into the corner from which it had come, and settled down, its tongue working constantly.

"Perfect!" Dr. Phillips cried. "Right between the shoulder blades. The fangs must almost have reached the heart."

The rat stood still, breathing like a little white bellows. Suddenly it leaped in the air and landed on its side. Its legs kicked spasmodically for a second and it was dead.

The woman relaxed, relaxed sleepily.

"Well," the young man demanded, "it was an emotional bath, wasn't it?"

She turned her misty eyes to him. "Will he eat it now?" she asked.

"Of course he'll eat it. He didn't kill it for a thrill. He killed it because he was hungry."

The corners of the woman's mouth turned up a trifle again. She looked back at the snake. "I want to see him eat it."

Now the snake came out of its corner again. There was no striking curve in its neck, but it approached the rat gingerly, ready to jump back in case it attacked. It nudged the body gently with its blunt nose, and drew away. Satisfied that it was dead, the snake touched the body all over with its chin, from head to tail. It seemed to measure the body and to kiss it. Finally it opened its mouth and unhinged its jaws at the corners.

Dr. Phillips put his will against his head to keep it from turning toward the woman. He thought, "If she's opening her mouth, I'll be sick. I'll be afraid." He succeeded in keeping his eyes away.

The snake fitted its jaws over the rat's head and then with a slow peristaltic pulsing, began to engulf the rat. The jaws gripped and the whole throat crawled up, and the jaws gripped again.

Dr. Phillips turned away and went to his work table. "You've made me miss one of the series," he said bitterly. "The set won't be complete." He put one of the watch-glasses under a low-power microscope and looked at it, and then angrily he poured the contents of all the dishes into the sink. The waves had fallen so that only a wet whisper came up through the floor. The young man lifted a trapdoor at his feet and dropped the starfish down into the black water. He paused at the cat, crucified in the cradle and grinning comically into the light. Its body was puffed with embalming fluid. He shut off the pressure, withdrew the needle and tied the vein.

"Would you like some coffee?" he asked.

"No, thank you. I shall be going pretty soon."

He walked to her where she stood in front of the snake cage. The rat was swallowed, all except an inch of pink tail that stuck out of the snake's mouth like a sardonic tongue. The throat heaved again and the tail disappeared. The jaws snapped back into their sockets, and the big snake crawled heavily to the corner, made a big eight and dropped its head on the sand.

"He's asleep now," the woman said. "I'm going now. But I'll come back and feed my snake every little while. I'll pay for the rats. I want him to have plenty. And sometime—I'll take him away with me." Her eyes came out of their dusty dream for a moment. "Remember, he's mine. Don't take his poison. I want him to have it. Goodnight." She walked swiftly to the door and went out. He heard her footsteps on the stairs, but he could not hear her walk away on the pavement.

Dr. Phillips turned a chair around and sat down in front of the snake cage. He tried to comb out his thought as he looked at the torpid snake. "I've read so much about psychological sex symbols," he thought. "It doesn't seem to explain. Maybe I'm too much alone. Maybe I should kill the snake. If I knew—no, I can't pray to anything."

For weeks he expected her to return. "I will go out and leave her alone here when she comes," he decided. "I won't see the damned thing again."

She never came again. For months he looked for her when he walked about in the town. Several times he ran after some tall woman thinking it might be she. But he never saw her again—ever.

FRANK O'CONNOR

[*1903–1966*]

Guests of the Nation

I

At dusk the big Englishman, Belcher, would shift his long legs out of the ashes and say "Well, chums, what about it?" and Noble or me would say "All right, chum" (for we had picked up some of their curious expressions), and the little Englishman, Hawkins, would light the lamp and bring out the cards. Sometimes Jeremiah Donovan would come up and supervise the game and get excited over Hawkins's cards, which he always played badly, and shout at him as if he was one of our own, "Ah, you divil, you, why didn't you play the tray?"

But ordinarily Jeremiah was a sober and contented poor devil like the big Englishman, Belcher, and was looked up to only because he was a fair hand at documents, though he was slow enough even with them. He wore a small cloth hat and big gaiters over his long pants, and you seldom saw him with his hands out of his pockets. He reddened when you talked to him, tilting from toe to heel and back, and looking down all the time at his big farmer's feet. Noble and me used to make fun of his broad accent, because we were from the town.

I couldn't at the time see the point of me and Noble guarding Belcher and Hawkins at all, for it was my belief that you could have planted that pair down anywhere from this to Claregalway and they'd have taken root there like a native weed. I never in my short experience seen two men to take to the country as they did.

They were handed on to us by the Second Battalion when the search for them became too hot, and Noble and myself, being young, took over with a natural feeling of responsibility, but Hawkins made us look like fools when he showed that he knew the country better than we did.

"You're the bloke they calls Bonaparte," he says to me. "Mary Brigid O'Connell told me to ask you what you done with the pair of her brother's socks you borrowed."

For it seemed, as they explained it, that the Second used to have little evenings, and some of the girls of the neighborhood turned in, and, seeing they were such decent chaps, our fellows couldn't leave the two Englishmen out of them. Hawkins learned to dance "The Walls of Limerick," "The Siege of Ennis," and "The Waves of Tory" as well as any of them, though, naturally, we couldn't return the compliment, because our lads at that time did not dance foreign dances on principle.

So whatever privileges Belcher and Hawkins had with the Second they just naturally took with us, and after the first day or two we gave up all pretense of keeping a close eye on them. Not that they could have got far, for they had accents you could cut with a knife and wore khaki tunics and overcoats with civilian pants and boots. But it's my belief that they never had any idea of escaping and were quite content to be where they were.

It was a treat to see how Belcher got off with the old woman of the house where we were staying. She was a great warrant to scold, and cranky even with us, but before ever she had a chance of giving our guests, as I may call them, a lick of her tongue, Belcher had made her his friend for life. She was breaking sticks, and Belcher, who hadn't been more than ten minutes in the house, jumped up from his seat and went over to her.

"Allow me, madam," he says, smiling his queer little smile, "please allow me"; and he takes the bloody hatchet. She was struck too paralytic to speak, and after that, Belcher would be at her heels, carrying a bucket, a basket, or a load of turf, as the case might be. As Noble said, he got into looking before she leapt, and hot water, or any little thing she wanted, Belcher would have it ready for her. For such a huge man (and though I am five foot ten myself I had to look up at him) he had an uncommon shortness—or should I say lack?—of speech. It took us some time to get used to him, walking in and out, like a ghost, without a word. Especially because Hawkins talked enough for a platoon, it was strange to hear big Belcher with his toes in the ashes come out with a solitary "Excuse me, chum," or "That's right, chum." His one and only passion was cards, and I will say for him that he was a good cardplayer. He could have fleeced myself and Noble, but whatever we lost to him Hawkins lost to us, and Hawkins played with the money Belcher gave him.

Hawkins lost to us because he had too much old gab, and we probably lost to Belcher for the same reason. Hawkins and Noble would spit at one another about religion into the early hours of the morning, and Hawkins worried the soul out of Noble, whose brother was a priest, with a string of questions that would puzzle a cardinal. To make it worse, even in treating of holy subjects, Hawkins had a deplorable tongue. I never in all my career met a man who could mix such a variety of cursing and bad language into an argument. He was a terrible man, and a fright to argue. He never did a stroke of work, and when he had no one else to talk to, he got stuck in the old woman.

He met his match in her, for one day when he tried to get her to complain profanely of the drought, she gave him a great come-down by blaming it entirely on Jupiter Pluvius (a deity neither Hawkins nor I had ever heard of, though Noble said that among the pagans it was believed that he had something to do with the rain). Another day he was swearing at the capitalists for starting the German war when the old lady laid down her iron, puckered up her little crab's mouth, and said: "Mr. Hawkins, you can say what you like about the war, and think you'll deceive me because I'm only a simple poor countrywoman, but I know what started the war. It was the Italian Count that stole the heathen divinity out of the temple in Japan. Believe me, Mr. Hawkins, nothing but sorrow and want can follow the people that disturb the hidden powers."

A queer old girl, all right.

2

We had our tea one evening, and Hawkins lit the lamp and we all sat into cards. Jeremiah Donovan came in too, and sat down and watched us for a while, and it suddenly struck me that he had no great love for the two Englishmen. It came as a great surprise to me, because I hadn't noticed anything about him before.

Late in the evening a really terrible argument blew up between Hawkins and Noble, about capitalists and priests and love of your country.

"The capitalists," says Hawkins with an angry gulp, "pays the priests to tell you about the next world so as you won't notice what the bastards are up to in this."

"Nonsense, man!" says Noble, losing his temper. "Before ever a capitalist was thought of, people believed in the next world."

Hawkins stood up as though he was preaching a sermon.

"Oh, they did, did they?" he says with a sneer. "They believed all the things you believe, isn't that what you mean? And you believe that God created Adam, and Adam created Shem, and Shem created Jehoshaphat. You believe all that silly old fairytale about Eve and Eden and the apple. Well, listen to me, chum. If you're entitled to hold a silly belief like that, I'm entitled to hold my silly belief—which is that the first thing your God created was a bleeding capitalist, with morality and Rolls-Royce complete. Am I right, chum?" he says to Belcher.

"You're right, chum," says Belcher with his amused smile, and got up from the table to stretch his long legs into the fire and stroke his moustache. So, seeing that Jeremiah Donovan was going, and that there was no knowing when the argument about religion would be over, I went out with him. We strolled down to the village together, and then he stopped and started blushing and mumbling and saying I ought to be behind, keeping guard on the prisoners. I didn't like the tone he took with me, and anyway I was bored with life in the cottage, so I replied by asking him what the hell we wanted guarding them at all for. I told him I'd talked it over with Noble, and that we'd both rather be out with a fighting column.

"What use are those fellows to us?" says I.

He looked at me in surprise and said: "I thought you knew we were keeping them as hostages."

"Hostages?" I said.

"The enemy have prisoners belonging to us," he says, "and now they're talking of shooting them. If they shoot our prisoners, we'll shoot theirs."

"Shoot them?" I said.

"What else did you think we were keeping them for?" he says.

"Wasn't it very unforeseen of you not to warn Noble and myself of that in the beginning?" I said.

"How was it?" says he. "You might have known it."

"We couldn't know it, Jeremiah Donovan," says I. "How could we when they were on our hands so long?"

"The enemy have our prisoners as long and longer," says he.

"That's not the same thing at all," says I.

"What difference is there?" says he.

I couldn't tell him, because I knew he wouldn't understand. If it was only an old dog that was going to the vet's, you'd try and not get too fond of him, but Jeremiah Donovan wasn't a man that would ever be in danger of that.

"And when is this thing going to be decided?" says I.

"We might hear tonight," he says. "Or tomorrow or the next day at latest. So if it's only hanging round here that's a trouble to you, you'll be free soon enough."

It wasn't the hanging round that was a trouble to me at all by this time. I had worse things to worry about. When I got back to the cottage the argument was still on. Hawkins was holding forth in his best style, maintaining that there was no next world, and Noble was maintaining that there was; but I could see that Hawkins had had the best of it.

"Do you know what, chum?" he was saying with a saucy smile. "I think you're just as big a bleeding unbeliever as I am. You say you believe in the next world, and you know just as much about the next world as I do, which is sweet damn-all. What's heaven? You don't know. Where's heaven? You don't know. You know sweet damn-all! I ask you again, do they wear wings?"

"Very well, then," says Noble, "they do. Is that enough for you? They do wear wings."

"Where do they get them, then? Who makes them? Have they a factory for wings? Have they a sort of store where you hands in your chit and takes your bleeding wings?"

"You're an impossible man to argue with," says Noble. "Now, listen to me—" And they were off again.

It was long after midnight when we locked up and went to bed. As I blew out the candle I told Noble what Jeremiah Donovan was after telling me. Noble took it very quietly. When we'd been in bed about an hour he asked me did I think we ought to tell the Englishmen. I didn't think we should, because it was more than likely that the English wouldn't shoot our men, and even if they did, the brigade officers, who were always up and down with the Second Battalion and knew the Englishmen well, wouldn't be likely to want them plugged. "I think so too," says Noble. "It would be great cruelty to put the wind up them now."

"It was very unforeseen of Jeremiah Donovan anyhow," says I.

It was next morning that we found it so hard to face Belcher and Hawkins. We went about the house all day scarcely saying a word. Belcher didn't seem to notice; he was stretched into the ashes as usual, with his usual look of waiting in quietness for something unforeseen to happen, but Hawkins noticed and put it down to Noble's being beaten in the argument of the night before.

"Why can't you take a discussion in the proper spirit?" he says severely. "You and your Adam and Eve! I'm a Communist, that's what I am. Communist or anarchist, it all comes to much the same thing." And for hours he went round the house, muttering when the fit took him. "Adam and Eve! Adam and Eve! Nothing better to do with their time than picking bleeding apples!"

3

I don't know how we got through that day, but I was very glad when it was over, the tea things were cleared away, and Belcher said in his peaceable way: "Well, chums, what about it?" We sat round the table and Hawkins took out the cards, and just then I heard Jeremiah Donovan's footstep on the path and a dark presentiment crossed my mind. I rose from the table and caught him before he reached the door.

"What do you want?" I asked.

"I want those two soldier friends of yours," he says, getting red.

"Is that the way, Jeremiah Donovan?" I asked.

"That's the way. There were four of our lads shot this morning, one of them a boy of sixteen."

"That's bad," I said.

At that moment Noble followed me out, and the three of us walked down the path together, talking in whispers. Feeney, the local intelligence officer, was standing by the gate.

"What are you going to do about it?" I asked Jeremiah Donovan.

"I want you and Noble to get them out; tell them they're being shifted again; that'll be the quietest way."

"Leave me out of that," says Noble under his breath.

Jeremiah Donovan looks at him hard.

"All right," he says. "You and Feeney get a few tools from the shed and dig a hole by the far end of the bog. Bonaparte and myself will be after you. Don't let anyone see you with the tools. I wouldn't like it to go beyond ourselves."

We saw Feeney and Noble go round to the shed and went in ourselves. I left Jeremiah Donovan to do the explanations. He told them that he had orders to send them back to the Second Battalion. Hawkins let out a mouthful of curses, and you could see that though Belcher didn't say anything, he was a bit upset too. The old woman was for having them stay in spite of us, and she didn't stop advising them until Jeremiah Donovan lost his temper and turned on her. He had a nasty temper, I noticed. It was pitch-dark in the cottage by this time, but no one thought of lighting the lamp, and in the darkness the two Englishmen fetched their topcoats and said good-bye to the old woman.

"Just as a man makes a home of a bleeding place, some bastard at headquarters thinks you're too cushy and shunts you off," says Hawkins, shaking her hand.

"A thousand thanks, madam," says Belcher. "A thousand thanks for everything"— as though he'd made it up.

We went round to the back of the house and down towards the bog. It was only then that Jeremiah Donovan told them. He was shaking with excitement.

"There were four of our fellows shot in Cork this morning and now you're to be shot as a reprisal."

"What are you talking about?" snaps Hawkins. "It's bad enough being mucked about as we are without having to put up with your funny jokes."

"It isn't a joke," says Donovan. "I'm sorry, Hawkins, but it's true," and begins on the usual rigmarole about duty and how unpleasant it is.

I never noticed that people who talk a lot about duty find it much of a trouble to them.

"Oh, cut it out!" says Hawkins.

"Ask Bonaparte," says Donovan, seeing that Hawkins isn't taking him seriously. "Isn't it true, Bonaparte?"

"It is," I say, and Hawkins stops.

"Ah, for Christ's sake, chum."

"I mean it, chum," I say.

"You don't sound as if you meant it."

"If he doesn't mean it, I do," says Donovan, working himself up.

"What have you against me, Jeremiah Donovan?"

"I never said I had anything against you. But why did your people take out four of our prisoners and shoot them in cold blood?"

He took Hawkins by the arm and dragged him on, but it was impossible to make him understand that we were in earnest. I had the Smith and Wesson° in my pocket and I kept fingering it and wondering what I'd do if they put up a fight for it or ran, and wishing to God they'd do one or the other. I knew if they did run for it, that I'd never fire on them. Hawkins wanted to know was Noble in it, and when we said yes, he asked us why Noble wanted to plug him. Why did any of us want to plug him? What had he done to us? Weren't we all chums? Didn't we understand him and didn't he understand us? Did we imagine for an instant that he'd shoot us for all the so-and-so officers in the so-and-so British Army?

By this time we'd reached the bog, and I was so sick I couldn't even answer him. We walked along the edge of it in the darkness, and every now and then Hawkins would call a halt and begin all over again, as if he was wound up, about our being chums, and I knew that nothing but the sight of the grave would convince him that we had to do it. And all the time I was hoping that something would happen; that they'd run for it or that Noble would take over the responsibility from me. I had the feeling that it was worse on Noble than on me.

4

At last we saw the lantern in the distance and made towards it. Noble was carrying it, and Feeney was standing somewhere in the darkness behind him, and the picture of them so still and silent in the bogland brought it home to me that we were in earnest, and banished the last bit of hope I had.

Belcher, on recognizing Noble, said: "Hallo, chum," in his quiet way, but Hawkins flew at him at once, and the argument began all over again, only this time Noble had nothing to say for himself and stood with his head down, holding the lantern between his legs.

It was Jeremiah Donovan who did the answering. For the twentieth time, as though it was haunting his mind, Hawkins asked if anybody thought he'd shoot Noble.

"Yes, you would," says Jeremiah Donovan.

"No, I wouldn't, damn you!"

"You would, because you'd know you'd be shot for not doing it."

"I wouldn't, not if I was to be shot twenty times over. I wouldn't shoot a pal. And Belcher wouldn't—isn't that right, Belcher?"

"That's right, chum," Belcher said, but more by way of answering the question than of joining in the argument. Belcher sounded as though whatever unforeseen thing he'd always been waiting for had come at last.

"Anyway, who says Noble would be shot if I wasn't? What do you think I'd do if I was in his place, out in the middle of a blasted bog?"

"What would you do?" asks Donovan.

"I'd go with him wherever he was going, of course. Share my last bob with him and stick by him through thick and thin. No one can ever say of me that I let down a pal."

°**Smith and Wesson**   *pistol, like the Webley later*

"We had enough of this," says Jeremiah Donovan, cocking his revolver. "Is there any message you want to send?"

"No, there isn't."

"Do you want to say your prayers?"

Hawkins came out with a cold-blooded remark that even shocked me and turned on Noble again.

"Listen to me, Noble," he says. "You and me are chums. You can't come over to my side, so I'll come over to your side. That show you I mean what I say? Give me a rifle and I'll go along with you and the other lads."

Nobody answered him. We knew that was no way out.

"Hear what I'm saying?" he says. "I'm through with it. I'm a deserter or anything else you like. I don't believe in your stuff, but it's no worse than mine. That satisfy you?"

Noble raised his head, but Donovan began to speak and he lowered it again without replying.

"For the last time, have you any messages to send?" says Donovan in a cold, excited sort of voice.

"Shut up, Donovan! You don't understand me, but these lads do. They're not the sort to make a pal and kill a pal. They're not the tools of any capitalist."

I alone of the crowd saw Donovan raise his Webley to the back of Hawkins's neck, and as he did so I shut my eyes and tried to pray. Hawkins had begun to say something else when Donovan fired, and as I opened my eyes at the bang, I saw Hawkins stagger at the knees and lie out flat at Noble's feet, slowly and as quiet as a kid falling asleep, with the lantern-light on his lean legs and bright farmer's boots. We all stood very still, watching him settle out in the last agony.

Then Belcher took out a handkerchief and began to tie it about his own eyes (in our excitement we'd forgotten to do the same for Hawkins), and, seeing it wasn't big enough, turned and asked for the loan of mine. I gave it to him and he knotted the two together and pointed with his foot at Hawkins.

"He's not quite dead," he says. "Better give him another."

Sure enough, Hawkins's left knee is beginning to rise. I bend down and put my gun to his head; then, recollecting myself, I get up again. Belcher understands what's in my mind.

"Give him his first," he says. "I don't mind. Poor bastard, we don't know what's happening to him now."

I knelt and fired. By this time I didn't seem to know what I was doing. Belcher, who was fumbling a bit awkwardly with the handkerchiefs, came out with a laugh as he heard the shot. It was the first time I heard him laugh and it sent a shudder down my back; it sounded so unnatural.

"Poor bugger!" he said quietly. "And last night he was so curious about it all. It's very queer, chums, I always think. Now he knows as much about it as they'll ever let him know, and last night he was all in the dark."

Donovan helped him to tie the handkerchiefs about his eyes. "Thanks, chum," he said. Donovan asked if there were any messages he wanted sent.

"No, chum," he says. "Not for me. If any of you would like to write to Hawkins's mother, you'll find a letter from her in his pocket. He and his mother were great chums. But my missus left me eight years ago. Went away with another fellow and took the kid with her. I like the feeling of a home, as you may have noticed, but I couldn't start again after that."

It was an extraordinary thing, but in those few minutes Belcher said more than in all the weeks before. It was just as if the sound of the shot had started a flood of talk in him and he could go on the whole night like that, quite happily, talking about himself. We stood round like fools now that he couldn't see us any longer. Donovan looked at Noble, and Noble shook his head. Then Donovan raised his Webley, and at that moment Belcher gives his queer laugh again. He may have thought we were talking about him, or perhaps he noticed the same thing I'd noticed and couldn't understand it.

"Excuse me, chums," he says. "I feel I'm talking the hell of a lot, and so silly, about my being so handy about a house and things like that. But this thing came on me suddenly. You'll forgive me, I'm sure."

"You don't want to say a prayer?" asked Donovan.

"No, chum," he says. "I don't think it would help. I'm ready, and you boys want to get it over."

"You understand that we're only doing our duty?" says Donovan.

Belcher's head was raised like a blind man's, so that you could only see his chin and the tip of his nose in the lantern-light.

"I never could make out what duty was myself," he said. "I think you're all good lads, if that's what you mean. I'm not complaining."

Noble, just as if he couldn't bear any more of it, raised his fist at Donovan, and in a flash Donovan raised his gun and fired. The big man went over like a sack of meal, and this time there was no need of a second shot.

I don't remember much about the burying, but that it was worse than all the rest because we had to carry them to the grave. It was all mad lonely with nothing but a patch of lantern-light between ourselves and the dark, and birds hooting and screeching all round, disturbed by the guns. Noble went through Hawkins's belongings to find the letter from his mother, and then joined his hands together. He did the same with Belcher. Then, when we'd filled in the grave, we separated from Jeremiah Donovan and Feeney and took our tools back to the shed. All the way we didn't speak a word. The kitchen was dark and cold as we'd left it, and the old woman was sitting over the hearth, saying her beads. We walked past her into the room, and Noble struck a match to light the lamp. She rose quietly and came to the doorway with all her cantankerousness gone.

"What did ye do with them?" she asked in a whisper, and Noble started so that the match went out in his hand.

"What's that?" he asked without turning round.

"I heard ye," she said.

"What did you hear?" asked Noble.

"I heard ye. Do ye think I didn't hear ye, putting the spade back in the houseen?"

Noble struck another match and this time the lamp lit for him.

"Was that what ye did to them?" she asked.

Then, by God, in the very doorway, she fell on her knees and began praying, and after looking at her for a minute or two Noble did the same by the fireplace. I pushed my way out past her and left them at it. I stood at the door, watching the stars and listening to the shrieking of the birds dying out over the bogs. It is so strange what you feel at times like that you can't describe it. Noble says he saw everything ten times the size, as though there were nothing in the whole world but that little patch of bog with the two Englishmen stiffening into it, but with me it was as if the patch of bog where the Englishmen were was a million miles away, and even Noble and the old woman, mumbling behind me, and the birds and the bloody stars were all far away, and I was somehow very small and very lost and lonely like a child astray in the snow. And anything that happened me afterwards, I never felt the same about again.

ISAAC BASHEVIS SINGER

[b. 1904]

Gimpel the Fool

TRANSLATED BY SAUL BELLOW

I

I am Gimpel the fool. I don't think myself a fool. On the contrary. But that's what folks call me. They gave me the name while I was still in school. I had seven names in all: imbecile, donkey, flax-head, dope, glump, ninny, and fool. The last name stuck. What did my foolishness consist of? I was easy to take in. They said, "Gimpel, you know the rabbi's wife has been brought to childbed?" So I skipped school. Well, it turned out to be a lie. How was I supposed to know? She hadn't had a big belly. But I never looked at her belly. Was that really so foolish? The gang laughed and hee-hawed, stomped and danced and chanted a good-night prayer. And instead of the raisins they give when a woman's lying in, they stuffed my hand full of goat turds. I was no weakling. If I slapped someone he'd see all the way to Cracow. But I'm really not a slugger by nature. I think to myself: Let it pass. So they take advantage of me.

I was coming home from school and heard a dog barking. I'm not afraid of dogs, but of course I never want to start up with them. One of them may be mad, and if he bites there's not a Tartar in the world who can help you. So I made tracks. Then I looked around and saw the whole market place wild with laughter. It was no dog at all but Wolf-Leib the Thief. How was I supposed to know it was he? It sounded like a howling bitch.

When the pranksters and leg-pullers found that I was easy to fool, every one of them tried his luck with me. "Gimpel, the Czar is coming to Frampol; Gimpel, the moon fell down in Turbeen; Gimpel, little Hodel Furpiece found a treasure behind the bathhouse." And I like a golem° believed everyone. In the first place, everything is possible, as it is written in the Wisdom of the Fathers. I've forgotten just how. Second, I had to believe when the whole town came down on me! If I ever dared to say, "Ah, you're kidding!" there was trouble. People got angry. "What do you mean! You want

°**golem** *simpleton*

to call everyone a liar?" What was I to do? I believed them, and I hope at least that did them some good.

I was an orphan. My grandfather who brought me up was already bent toward the grave. So they turned me over to a baker, and what a time they gave me there! Every woman or girl who came to bake a batch of noodles had to fool me at least once. "Gimpel, there's a fair in heaven; Gimpel, the rabbi gave birth to a calf in the seventh month; Gimpel, a cow flew over the roof and laid brass eggs." A student from the yeshiva came once to buy a roll, and he said, "You, Gimpel, while you stand here scraping with your baker's shovel the Messiah has come. The dead have arisen." "What do you mean?" I said. "I heard no one blowing the ram's horn!" He said, "Are you deaf?" And all began to cry, "We heard it, we heard!" Then in came Rietze the Candle-dipper and called out in her hoarse voice, "Gimpel, your father and mother have stood up from the grave. They're looking for you."

To tell the truth, I knew very well that nothing of the sort had happened, but all the same, as folks were talking, I threw on my wool vest and went out. Maybe something had happened. What did I stand to lose by looking? Well, what a cat music went up! And then I took a vow to believe nothing more. But that was no go either. They confused me so that I didn't know the big end from the small.

I went to the rabbi to get some advice. He said, "It is written, better to be a fool all your days than for one hour to be evil. You are not a fool. They are the fools. For he who causes his neighbor to feel shame loses Paradise himself." Nevertheless the rabbi's daughter took me in. As I left the rabbinical court she said, "Have you kissed the wall yet?" I said, "No; what for?" She answered, "It's the law; you've got to do it after every visit." Well, there didn't seem to be any harm in it. And she burst out laughing. It was a fine trick. She put one over on me, all right.

I wanted to go off to another town, but then everyone got busy matchmaking, and they were after me so they nearly tore my coat tails off. They talked at me and talked until I got water on the ear. She was no chaste maiden, but they told me she was virgin pure. She had a limp, and they said it was deliberate, from coyness. She had a bastard, and they told me the child was her little brother. I cried, "You're wasting your time. I'll never marry that whore." But they said indignantly, "What a way to talk! Aren't you ashamed of yourself? We can take you to the rabbi and have you fined for giving her a bad name." I saw then that I wouldn't escape them so easily and I thought: They're set on making me their butt. But when you're married the husband's the master, and if that's all right with her it's agreeable to me too. Besides, you can't pass through life unscathed, nor expect to.

I went to her clay house, which was built on the sand, and the whole gang, hollering and chorusing, came after me. They acted like bear-baiters. When we came to the well they stopped all the same. They were afraid to start anything with Elka. Her mouth would open as if it were on a hinge, and she had a fierce tongue. I entered the house. Lines were strung from wall to wall and clothes were drying. Barefoot she stood by the tub, doing the wash. She was dressed in a worn hand-me-down gown of plush. She had her hair put up in braids and pinned across her head. It took my breath away, almost, the reek of it all.

Evidently she knew who I was. She took a look at me and said, "Look who's here! He's come, the drip. Grab a seat."

I told her all; I denied nothing. "Tell me the truth," I said, "are you really a virgin, and is that mischievous Yechiel actually your little brother? Don't be deceitful with me, for I'm an orphan."

"I'm an orphan myself," she answered, "and whoever tries to twist you up, may the end of his nose take a twist. But don't let them think they can take advantage of me. I want a dowry of fifty guilders, and let them take up a collection besides. Otherwise they can kiss my you-know-what." She was very plainspoken. I said, "It's the bride and not the groom who gives a dowry." Then she said, "Don't bargain with me. Either a flat 'yes' or a flat 'no'—Go back where you came from."

I thought: No bread will ever be baked from *this* dough. But ours is not a poor town. They consented to everything and proceeded with the wedding. It so happened that there was a dysentery epidemic at the time. The ceremony was held at the cemetery gates, near the little corpse-washing hut. The fellows got drunk. While the marriage contract was being drawn up I heard the most pious high rabbi ask, "Is the bride a widow or a divorced woman?" And the sexton's wife answered for her, "Both a widow and divorced." It was a black moment for me. But what was I to do, run away from under the marriage canopy?

There was singing and dancing. An old granny danced opposite me, hugging a braided white *chalah*. The master of revels made a "God 'a mercy" in memory of the bride's parents. The schoolboys threw burrs, as on Tishe b'Av fast day. There were a lot of gifts after the sermon: a noodle board, a kneading trough, a bucket, brooms, ladles, household articles galore. Then I took a look and saw two strapping young men carrying a crib. "What do we need this for?" I asked. So they said, "Don't rack your brains about it. It's all right, it'll come in handy." I realized I was going to be rooked. Take it another way though, what did I stand to lose? I reflected: I'll see what comes of it. A whole town can't go altogether crazy.

2

At night I came where my wife lay, but she wouldn't let me in. "Say, look here, is this what they married us for?" I said. And she said, "My monthly has come." "But yesterday they took you to the ritual bath, and that's afterward, isn't it supposed to be?" "Today isn't yesterday," said she, "and yesterday's not today. You can beat it if you don't like it." In short, I waited.

Not four months later she was in childbed. The townsfolk hid their laughter with their knuckles. But what could I do? She suffered intolerable pains and clawed at the walls. "Gimpel," she cried, "I'm going. Forgive me!" The house filled with women. They were boiling pans of water. The screams rose to the welkin.°

The thing to do was to go to the House of Prayer to repeat Psalms, and that was what I did.

The townsfolk liked that, all right. I stood in a corner saying Psalms and prayers, and they shook their heads at me. "Pray, pray!" they told me. "Prayer never made any woman pregnant." One of the congregation put a straw to my mouth and said, "Hay for the cows." There was something to that too, by God!

She gave birth to a boy. Friday at the synagogue the sexton stood up before the Ark, pounded on the reading table, and announced, "The wealthy Reb Gimpel invites the

°**welkin** *the sky*

congregation to a feast in honor of the birth of a son." The whole House of Prayer rang with laughter. My face was flaming. But there was nothing I could do. After all, I *was* the one responsible for the circumcision honors and rituals.

Half the town came running. You couldn't wedge another soul in. Women brought peppered chick-peas, and there was a keg of beer from the tavern. I ate and drank as much as anyone, and they all congratulated me. Then there was a circumcision, and I named the boy after my father, may he rest in peace. When all were gone and I was left with my wife alone, she thrust her head through the bed-curtain and called me to her.

"Gimpel," said she, "why are you silent? Has your ship gone and sunk?"

"What shall I say?" I answered. "A fine thing you've done to me! If my mother had known of it she'd have died a second time."

She said, "Are you crazy, or what?"

"How can you make such a fool," I said, "of one who should be the lord and master?"

"What's the matter with you?" she said. "What have you taken it into your head to imagine?"

I saw that I must speak bluntly and openly. "Do you think this is the way to use an orphan?" I said. "You have borne a bastard."

She answered, "Drive this foolishness out of your head. The child is yours."

"How can he be mine?" I argued. "He was born seventeen weeks after the wedding."

She told me then that he was premature. I said, "Isn't he a little too premature?" She said, she had had a grandmother who carried just as short a time and she resembled this grandmother of hers as one drop of water does another. She swore to it with such oaths that you would have believed a peasant at the fair if he had used them. To tell the plain truth, I didn't believe her; but when I talked it over next day with the schoolmaster he told me that the very same thing had happened to Adam and Eve. Two they went up to bed, and four they descended.

"There isn't a woman in the world who is not the granddaughter of Eve," he said.

That was how it was; they argued me dumb. But then, who really knows how such things are?

I began to forget my sorrow. I loved the child madly, and he loved me too. As soon as he saw me he'd wave his little hands and want me to pick him up, and when he was colicky I was the only one who could pacify him. I bought him a little bone teething ring and a little gilded cap. He was forever catching the evil eye from someone, and then I had to run to get one of those abracadabras for him that would get him out of it. I worked like an ox. You know how expenses go up when there's an infant in the house. I don't want to lie about it; I didn't dislike Elka either, for that matter. She swore at me and cursed, and I couldn't get enough of her. What strength she had! One of her looks could rob you of the power of speech. And her orations! Pitch and sulphur, that's what they were full of, and yet somehow also full of charm. I adored her every word. She gave me bloody wounds though.

In the evening I brought her a white loaf as well as a dark one, and also poppyseed rolls I baked myself. I thieved because of her and swiped everything I could lay my hands on: macaroons, raisins, almonds, cakes. I hope I may be forgiven for stealing from the Saturday pots the women left to warm in the baker's oven. I would take out scraps of meat, a chunk of pudding, a chicken leg or head, a piece of tripe, whatever I could nip quickly. She ate and became fat and handsome.

I had to sleep away from home all during the week, at the bakery. On Friday nights when I got home she always made an excuse of some sort. Either she had heartburn, or a stitch in the side, or hiccups, or headaches. You know what women's excuses are. I had a bitter time of it. It was rough. To add to it, this little brother of hers, the bastard, was growing bigger. He'd put lumps on me, and when I wanted to hit back she'd open her mouth and curse so powerfully I saw a green haze floating before my eyes. Ten times a day she threatened to divorce me. Another man in my place would have taken French leave and disappeared. But I'm the type that bears it and says nothing. What's one to do? Shoulders are from God, and burdens too.

One night there was a calamity in the bakery; the oven burst, and we almost had a fire. There was nothing to do but go home, so I went home. Let me, I thought, also taste the joy of sleeping in bed in mid-week. I didn't want to wake the sleeping mite and tiptoed into the house. Coming in, it seemed to me that I heard not the snoring of one but, as it were, a double snore, one a thin enough snore and the other like the snoring of a slaughtered ox. Oh, I didn't like that! I didn't like it at all. I went up to the bed, and things suddenly turned black. Next to Elka lay a man's form. Another in my place would have made an uproar, and enough noise to rouse the whole town, but the thought occurred to me that I might wake the child. A little thing like that —why frighten a little swallow, I thought. All right then, I went back to the bakery and stretched out on a sack of flour and till morning I never shut an eye. I shivered as if I had had malaria. "Enough of being a donkey," I said to myself. "Gimpel isn't going to be a sucker all his life. There's a limit even to the foolishness of a fool like Gimpel."

In the morning I went to the rabbi to get advice, and it made a great commotion in the town. They sent the beadle for Elka right away. She came, carrying the child. And what do you think she did? She denied it, denied everything, bone and stone! "He's out of his head," she said. "I know nothing of dreams or divinations." They yelled at her, warned her, hammered on the table, but she stuck to her guns: it was a false accusation, she said.

The butchers and the horse-traders took her part. One of the lads from the slaughter-house came by and said to me, "We've got our eye on you, you're a marked man." Meanwhile the child started to bear down and soiled itself. In the rabbinical court there was an Ark of the Covenant, and they couldn't allow that, so they sent Elka away.

I said to the rabbi, "What shall I do?"

"You must divorce her at once," said he.

"And what if she refuses?" I asked.

He said, "You must serve the divorce. That's all you'll have to do."

I said, "Well, all right, Rabbi. Let me think about it."

"There's nothing to think about," said he. "You mustn't remain under the same roof with her."

"And if I want to see the child?" I asked.

"Let her go, the harlot," said he, "and her brood of bastards with her."

The verdict he gave was that I mustn't even cross her threshold—never again, as long as I should live.

During the day it didn't bother me so much. I thought: It was bound to happen, the abscess had to burst. But at night when I stretched out upon the sacks I felt it all very bitterly. A longing took me, for her and for the child. I wanted to be angry, but that's my misfortune exactly, I don't have it in me to be really angry. In the first place

—this was how my thoughts went—there's bound to be a slip sometimes. You can't live without errors. Probably that lad who was with her led her on and gave her presents and what not, and women are often long on hair and short on sense, and so he got around her. And then since she denies it so, maybe I was only seeing things? Hallucinations do happen. You see a figure or a mannikin or something, but when you come up closer it's nothing, there's not a thing there. And if that's so, I'm doing her an injustice. And when I got so far in my thoughts I started to weep. I sobbed so that I wet the flour where I lay. In the morning I went to the rabbi and told him that I had made a mistake. The rabbi wrote on with his quill, and he said that if that were so he would have to reconsider the whole case. Until he had finished I wasn't to go near my wife, but I might send her bread and money by messenger.

3

Nine months passed before all the rabbis could come to an agreement. Letters went back and forth. I hadn't realized that there could be so much erudition about a matter like this.

Meanwhile Elka gave birth to still another child, a girl this time. On the Sabbath I went to the synagogue and invoked a blessing on her. They called me up to the Torah, and I named the child for my mother-in-law—may she rest in peace. The louts and loudmouths of the town who came into the bakery gave me a going over. All Frampol refreshed its spirits because of my trouble and grief. However, I resolved that I would always believe what I was told. What's the good of *not* believing? Today it's your wife you don't believe; tomorrow it's God Himself you won't take stock in.

By an apprentice who was her neighbor I sent her daily a corn or a wheat loaf, or a piece of pastry, rolls or bagels, or, when I got the chance, a slab of pudding, a slice of honeycake, or wedding strudel—whatever came my way. The apprentice was a goodhearted lad, and more than once he added something on his own. He had formerly annoyed me a lot, plucking my nose and digging me in the ribs, but when he started to be a visitor to my house he became kind and friendly. "Hey, you, Gimpel," he said to me, "you have a very decent little wife and two fine kids. You don't deserve them."

"But the things people say about her," I said.

"Well, they have long tongues," he said, "and nothing to do with them but babble. Ignore it as you ignore the cold of last winter."

One day the rabbi sent for me and said, "Are you certain, Gimpel, that you were wrong about your wife?"

I said, "I'm certain."

"Why, but look here! You yourself saw it."

"It must have been a shadow," I said.

"The shadow of what?"

"Just one of the beams, I think."

"You can go home then. You owe thanks to the Yanover rabbi. He found an obscure reference in Maimonides that favored you."

I seized the rabbi's hand and kissed it.

I wanted to run home immediately. It's no small thing to be separated for so long a time from wife and child. Then I reflected: I'd better go back to work now, and go home in the evening. I said nothing to anyone, although as far as my heart was concerned it was like one of the Holy Days. The women teased and twitted me as they did every day, but my thought was: Go on, with your loose talk. The truth is out, like the oil upon the water. Maimonides says it's right, and therefore it is right!

At night, when I had covered the dough to let it rise, I took my share of bread and a little sack of flour and started homeward. The moon was full and the stars were glistening, something to terrify the soul. I hurried onward, and before me darted a long shadow. It was winter, and a fresh snow had fallen. I had a mind to sing, but it was growing late and I didn't want to wake the householders. Then I felt like whistling, but I remembered that you don't whistle at night because it brings the demons out. So I was silent and walked as fast as I could.

Dogs in the Christian yards barked at me when I passed, but I thought: Bark your teeth out! What are you but mere dogs? Whereas I am a man, the husband of a fine wife, the father of promising children.

As I approached the house my heart started to pound as though it were the heart of a criminal. I felt no fear, but my heart went thump! thump! Well, no drawing back. I quietly lifted the latch and went in. Elka was asleep. I looked at the infant's cradle. The shutter was closed, but the moon forced its way through the cracks. I saw the newborn child's face and loved it as soon as I saw it—immediately—each tiny bone.

Then I came nearer to the bed. And what did I see but the apprentice lying there beside Elka. The moon went out all at once. It was utterly black, and I trembled. My teeth chattered. The bread fell from my hands, and my wife waked and said, "Who is that, ah?"

I muttered, "It's me."

"Gimpel?" she asked. "How come you're here? I thought it was forbidden."

"The rabbi said," I answered and shook as with a fever.

"Listen to me, Gimpel," she said, "go out to the shed and see if the goat's all right. It seems she's been sick." I have forgotten to say that we had a goat. When I heard she was unwell I went into the yard. The nannygoat was a good little creature. I had a nearly human feeling for her.

With hesitant steps I went up to the shed and opened the door. The goat stood there on her four feet. I felt her everywhere, drew her by the horns, examined her udders, and found nothing wrong. She had probably eaten too much bark. "Good night, little goat," I said. "Keep well." And the little beast answered with a "Maa" as though to thank me for the good will.

I went back. The apprentice had vanished.

"Where," I asked, "is the lad?"

"What lad?" my wife answered.

"What do you mean?" I said. "The apprentice. You were sleeping with him."

"The things I have dreamed this night and the night before," she said, "may they come true and lay you low, body and soul! An evil spirit has taken root in you and dazzles your sight." She screamed out, "You hateful creature! You moon calf! You spook! You uncouth man! Get out, or I'll scream all Frampol out of bed!"

Before I could move, her brother sprang out from behind the oven and struck me a blow on the back of the head. I thought he had broken my neck. I felt that something about me was deeply wrong, and I said, "Don't make a scandal. All that's needed now is that people should accuse me of raising spooks and *dybbuks*."° For that was what she had meant. "No one will touch bread of my baking."

In short, I somehow calmed her.

"Well," she said, "that's enough. Lie down, and be shattered by wheels."

Next morning I called the apprentice aside. "Listen here, brother!" I said. And so on and so forth. "What do you say?" He stared at me as though I had dropped from the roof or something.

"I swear," he said, "you'd better go to an herb doctor or some healer. I'm afraid you have a screw loose, but I'll hush it up for you." And that's how the thing stood.

To make a long story short, I lived twenty years with my wife. She bore me six children, four daughters and two sons. All kinds of things happened, but I neither saw nor heard. I believed, and that's all. The rabbi recently said to me, "Belief in itself is beneficial. It is written that a good man lives by his faith."

Suddenly my wife took sick. It began with a trifle, a little growth upon the breast. But she evidently was not destined to live long; she had no years. I spent a fortune on her. I have forgotten to say that by this time I had a bakery of my own and in Frampol was considered to be something of a rich man. Daily the healer came, and every witch doctor in the neighborhood was brought. They decided to use leeches, and after that to try cupping. They even called a doctor from Lublin, but it was too late. Before she died she called me to her bed and said, "Forgive me, Gimpel."

I said, "What is there to forgive? You have been a good and faithful wife."

"Woe, Gimpel!" she said. "It was ugly how I deceived you all these years. I want to go clean to my Maker, and so I have to tell you that the children are not yours."

If I had been clouted on the head with a piece of wood it couldn't have bewildered me more.

"Whose are they?" I asked.

"I don't know," she said. "There were a lot . . . but they're not yours." And as she spoke she tossed her head to the side, her eyes turned glassy, and it was all up with Elka. On her whitened lips there remained a smile.

I imagined that, dead as she was, she was saying, "I deceived Gimpel. That was the meaning of my brief life."

4

One night, when the period of mourning was done, as I lay dreaming on the flour sacks, there came the Spirit of Evil himself and said to me, "Gimpel, why do you sleep?"

I said, "What should I be doing? Eating *kreplach?*"

"The whole world deceives you," he said, "and you ought to deceive the world in your turn."

"How can I deceive the world?" I asked him.

He answered, "You might accumulate a bucket of urine every day and at night pour it into the dough. Let the sages of Frampol eat filth."

"What about the judgment in the world to come?" I said.

"There is no world to come," he said. "They've sold you a bill of goods and talked you into believing you carried a cat in your belly. What nonsense!"

°**dybbuks**   *demons or souls of the dead that enter the bodies of the living to take possession of them*

"Well, then," I said, "and is there a God?"

He answered, "There is no God either."

"What," I said, "*is* there, then?"

"A thick mire."

He stood before my eyes with a goatish beard and horn, long-toothed, and with a tail. Hearing such words, I wanted to snatch him by the tail, but I tumbled from the flour sacks and nearly broke a rib. Then it happened that I had to answer the call of nature, and, passing, I saw the risen dough, which seemed to say to me, "Do it!" In brief, I let myself be persuaded.

At dawn the apprentice came. We kneaded the bread, scattered caraway seeds on it, and set it to bake. Then the apprentice went away, and I was left sitting in the little trench by the oven, on a pile of rags. Well, Gimpel, I thought, you've revenged yourself on them for all the shame they've put on you. Outside the frost glittered, but it was warm beside the oven. The flames heated my face. I bent my head and fell into a doze.

I saw in a dream, at once, Elka in her shroud. She called to me, "What have you done, Gimpel?"

I said to her, "It's all your fault," and started to cry.

"You fool!" she said. "You fool! Because I was false is everything false too? I never deceived anyone but myself. I'm paying for it all, Gimpel. They spare you nothing here."

I looked at her face. It was black; I was startled and waked, and remained sitting dumb. I sensed that everything hung in the balance. A false step now and I'd lose Eternal Life. But God gave me His help. I seized the long shovel and took out the loaves, carried them into the yard, and started to dig a hole in the frozen earth.

My apprentice came back as I was doing it. "What are you doing, boss?" he said, and grew pale as a corpse.

"I know what I'm doing," I said, and I buried it all before his very eyes.

Then I went home, took my hoard from its hiding place, and divided it among the children. "I saw your mother tonight," I said. "She's turning black, poor thing."

They were so astounded they couldn't speak a word.

"Be well," I said, "and forget that such a one as Gimpel ever existed." I put on my short coat, a pair of boots, took the bag that held my prayer shawl in one hand, my stock in the other, and kissed the *mezzuzah*. When people saw me in the street they were greatly surprised.

"Where are you going?" they said.

I answered, "Into the world." And so I departed from Frampol.

I wandered over the land, and good people did not neglect me. After many years I became old and white; I heard a great deal, many lies and falsehoods, but the longer I lived the more I understood that there were really no lies. Whatever doesn't really happen is dreamed at night. It happens to one if it doesn't happen to another, tomorrow if not today, or a century hence if not next year. What difference can it make? Often I heard tales of which I said, "Now this is a thing that cannot happen." But before a year had elapsed I heard that it actually had come to pass somewhere.

Going from place to place, eating at strange tables, it often happens that I spin yarns —improbable things that could never have happened—about devils, magicians, wind-mills, and the like. The children run after me, calling, "Grandfather, tell us a story." Sometimes they ask for particular stories, and I try to please them. A fat young boy once said to me, "Grandfather, it's the same story you told us before." The little rogue, he was right.

So it is with dreams too. It is many years since I left Frampol, but as soon as I shut my eyes I am there again. And whom do you think I see? Elka. She is standing by the washtub, as at our first encounter, but her face is shining and her eyes are as radiant as the eyes of a saint, and she speaks outlandish words to me, strange things. When I wake I have forgotten it all. But while the dream lasts I am comforted. She answers all my queries, and what comes out is that all is right. I weep and implore, "Let me be with you." And she consoles me and tells me to be patient. The time is nearer than it is far. Sometimes she strokes and kisses me and weeps upon my face. When I awaken I feel her lips and taste the salt of her tears.

No doubt the world is entirely an imaginary world, but it is only once removed from the true world. At the door of the hovel where I lie, there stands the plank on which the dead are taken away. The gravedigger Jew has his spade ready. The grave waits and the worms are hungry; the shrouds are prepared—I carry them in my beggar's sack. Another *shnorrer*° is waiting to inherit my bed of straw. When the time comes I will go joyfully. Whatever may be there, it will be real, without complication, without ridicule, without deception. God be praised: there even Gimpel cannot be deceived.

EUDORA WELTY

[b. 1909]

A Worn Path

It was December—a bright frozen day in the early morning. Far out in the country there was an old Negro woman with her head tied in a red rag, coming along a path through the pinewoods. Her name was Phoenix Jackson. She was very old and small and she walked slowly in the dark pine shadows, moving a little from side to side in her steps, with the balanced heaviness and lightness of a pendulum in a grandfather clock. She carried a thin, small cane made from an umbrella, and with this she kept tapping the frozen earth in front of her. This made a grave and persistent noise in the still air, that seemed meditative like the chirping of a solitary little bird.

She wore a dark striped dress reaching down to her shoe tops, and an equally long apron of bleached sugar sacks, with a full pocket: all neat and tidy, but every time she took a step she might have fallen over her shoelaces, which dragged from her unlaced shoes. She looked straight ahead. Her eyes were blue with age. Her skin had a pattern all its own of numberless branching wrinkles and as though a whole little tree stood in the middle of her forehead, but a golden color ran underneath, and the two knobs of her cheeks were illumined by a yellow burning under the dark. Under the red rag

°*shnorrer*   a beggar; sponger

her hair came down on her neck in the frailest of ringlets, still black, and with an odor like copper.

Now and then there was a quivering in the thicket. Old Phoenix said, "Out of my way, all you foxes, owls, beetles, jack rabbits, coons and wild animals! . . . Keep out from under these feet, little bob-whites. . . . Keep the big wild hogs out of my path. Don't let none of those come running my direction. I got a long way." Under her small black-freckled hand her cane, limber as a buggy whip, would switch at the brush as if to rouse up any hiding things.

On she went. The woods were deep and still. The sun made the pine needles almost too bright to look at, up where the wind rocked. The cones dropped as light as feathers. Down in the hollow was the mourning dove—it was not too late for him.

The path ran up a hill. "Seem like there is chains about my feet, time I get this far," she said, in the voice of argument old people keep to use with themselves. "Something always take a hold of me on this hill—pleads I should stay."

After she got to the top she turned and gave a full, severe look behind her where she had come. "Up through pines," she said at length. "Now down through oaks."

Her eyes opened their widest, and she started down gently. But before she got to the bottom of the hill a bush caught her dress.

Her fingers were busy and intent, but her skirts were full and long, so that before she could pull them free in one place they were caught in another. It was not possible to allow the dress to tear. "I in the thorny bush," she said. "Thorns, you doing your appointed work. Never want to let folks pass, no sir. Old eyes thought you was a pretty little *green* bush."

Finally, trembling all over, she stood free, and after a moment dared to stoop for her cane.

"Sun so high!" she cried, leaning back and looking, while the thick tears went over her eyes. "The time getting all gone here."

At the foot of this hill was a place where a log was laid across the creek.

"Now comes the trial," said Phoenix.

Putting her right foot out, she mounted the log and shut her eyes. Lifting her skirt, leveling her cane fiercely before her, like a festival figure in some parade, she began to march across. Then she opened her eyes and she was safe on the other side.

"I wasn't as old as I thought," she said.

But she sat down to rest. She spread her skirts on the bank around her and folded her hands over her knees. Up above her was a tree in a pearly cloud of mistletoe. She did not dare to close her eyes, and when a little boy brought her a plate with a slice of marble-cake on it she spoke to him. "That would be acceptable," she said. But when she went to take it there was just her own hand in the air.

So she left that tree, and had to go through a barbed-wire fence. There she had to creep and crawl, spreading her knees and stretching her fingers like a baby trying to climb the steps. But she talked loudly to herself: she could not let her dress be torn now, so late in the day, and she could not pay for having her arm or her leg sawed off if she got caught fast where she was.

At last she was safe through the fence and risen up out in the clearing. Big dead trees, like black men with one arm, were standing in the purple stalks of the withered cotton field. There sat a buzzard.

"Who you watching?"

In the furrow she made her way along.

"Glad this not the season for bulls," she said, looking sideways, "and the good Lord made his snakes to curl up and sleep in the winter. A pleasure I don't see no two-headed snake coming around that tree, where it come once. It took a while to get by him, back in the summer."

She passed through the old cotton and went into a field of dead corn. It whispered and shook and was taller than her head. "Through the maze now," she said, for there was no path.

Then there was something tall, black, and skinny there, moving before her.

At first she took it for a man. It could have been a man dancing in the field. But she stood still and listened, and it did not make a sound. It was as silent as a ghost.

"Ghost," she said sharply, "who be you the ghost of? For I have heard of nary death close by."

But there was no answer—only the ragged dancing in the wind.

She shut her eyes, reached out her hand, and touched a sleeve. She found a coat and inside that an emptiness, cold as ice.

"You scarecrow," she said. Her face lighted. "I ought to be shut up for good," she said with laughter. "My senses is gone. I too old. I the oldest people I ever know. Dance, old scarecrow," she said, "while I dancing with you."

She kicked her foot over the furrow, and with mouth drawn down, shook her head once or twice in a little strutting way. Some husks blew down and whirled in streamers about her skirts.

Then she went on, parting her way from side to side with the cane, through the whispering field. At last she came to the end, to a wagon track where the silver grass blew between the red ruts. The quail were walking around like pullets, seeming all dainty and unseen.

"Walk pretty," she said. "This the easy place. This the easy going."

She followed the track, swaying through the quiet bare fields, through the little strings of trees silver in their dead leaves, past cabins silver from weather, with the doors and windows boarded shut, all like old women under a spell sitting there. "I walking in their sleep," she said, nodding her head vigorously.

In a ravine she went where a spring was silently flowing through a hollow log. Old Phoenix bent and drank. "Sweet-gum makes the water sweet," she said, and drank more. "Nobody know who made this well, for it was here when I was born."

The track crossed a swampy part where the moss hung as white as lace from every limb. "Sleep on, alligators, and blow your bubbles." Then the track went into the road.

Deep, deep the road went down between the high green-colored banks. Overhead the live-oaks met, and it was as dark as a cave.

A black dog with a lolling tongue came up out of the weeds by the ditch. She was meditating, and not ready, and when he came at her she only hit him a little with her cane. Over she went in the ditch, like a little puff of milkweed.

Down there, her senses drifted away. A dream visited her, and she reached her hand up, but nothing reached down and gave her a pull. So she lay there and presently went to talking. "Old woman," she said to herself, "that black dog come up out of the weeds to stall you off, and now there he sitting on his fine tail, smiling at you."

A white man finally came along and found her—a hunter, a young man, with his dog on a chain.

"Well, Granny!" he laughed. "What are you doing there?"

"Lying on my back like a June-bug waiting to be turned over, mister," she said, reaching up her hand.

He lifted her up, gave her a swing in the air, and set her down. "Anything broken, Granny?"

"No, sir, them old dead weeds is springy enough," said Phoenix, when she had got her breath. "I thank you for your trouble."

"Where do you live, Granny?" he asked, while the two dogs were growling at each other.

"Away back yonder, sir, behind the ridge. You can't even see it from here."

"On your way home?"

"No sir, I going to town."

"Why, that's too far! That's as far as I walk when I come out myself, and I get something for my trouble." He patted the stuffed bag he carried, and there hung down a little closed claw. It was one of the bob-whites, with its beak hooked bitterly to show it was dead. "Now you go home, Granny!"

"I bound to go to town, mister," said Phoenix. "The time come around."

He gave another laugh, filling the whole landscape. "I know you old colored people! Wouldn't miss going to town to see Santa Claus!"

But something held old Phoenix very still. The deep lines in her face went into a fierce and different radiation. Without warning, she had seen with her own eyes a flashing nickel fall out of the man's pocket onto the ground.

"How old are you, Granny?" he was saying.

"There is no telling, mister," she said, "no telling."

Then she gave a little cry and clapped her hands and said, "Git on away from here, dog! Look! Look at that dog!" She laughed as if in admiration. "He ain't scared of nobody. He a big black dog." She whispered, "Sic him!"

"Watch me get rid of that cur," said the man. "Sic him, Pete! Sic him!"

Phoenix heard the dogs fighting, and heard the man running and throwing sticks. She even heard a gunshot. But she was slowly bending forward by that time, further and further forward, the lids stretched down over her eyes, as if she were doing this in her sleep. Her chin was lowered almost to her knees. The yellow palm of her hand came out from the fold of her apron. Her fingers slid down and along the ground under the piece of money with the grace and care they would have in lifting an egg from under a setting hen. Then she slowly straightened up, she stood erect, and the nickel was in her apron pocket. A bird flew by. Her lips moved. "God watching me the whole time. I come to stealing."

The man came back, and his own dog panted about them. "Well, I scared him off that time," he said, and then he laughed and lifted his gun and pointed it at Phoenix.

She stood straight and faced him.

"Doesn't the gun scare you?" he said, still pointing it.

"No, sir, I seen plenty go off closer by, in my day, and for less than what I done," she said, holding utterly still.

He smiled, and shouldered the gun. "Well, Granny," he said, "you must be a hundred years old, and scared of nothing. I'd give you a dime if I had any money with me. But you take my advice and stay home, and nothing will happen to you."

"I bound to go on my way, mister," said Phoenix. She inclined her head in the red rag. Then they went in different directions, but she could hear the gun shooting again and again over the hill.

She walked on. The shadows hung from the oak trees to the road like curtains. Then she smelled wood-smoke, and smelled the river, and she saw a steeple and the cabins on their steep steps. Dozens of little black children whirled around her. There ahead was Natchez shining. Bells were ringing. She walked on.

In the paved city it was Christmas time. There were red and green electric lights strung and criss-crossed everywhere, and all turned on in the daytime. Old Phoenix would have been lost if she had not distrusted her eyesight and depended on her feet to know where to take her.

She paused quietly on the sidewalk where people were passing by. A lady came along in the crowd, carrying an armful of red-, green- and silver-wrapped presents; she gave off perfume like the red roses in hot summer, and Phoenix stopped her.

"Please, missy, will you lace up my shoe?" She held up her foot.

"What do you want, Grandma?"

"See my shoe," said Phoenix. "Do all right for out in the country, but wouldn't look right to go in a big building."

"Stand still then, Grandma," said the lady. She put her packages down on the sidewalk beside her and laced and tied both shoes tightly.

"Can't lace 'em with a cane," said Phoenix. "Thank you, missy. I doesn't mind asking a nice lady to tie up my shoe, when I gets out on the street."

Moving slowly and from side to side, she went into the big building, and into a tower of steps, where she walked up and around and around until her feet knew to stop.

She entered a door, and there she saw nailed up on the wall the document that had been stamped with the gold seal and framed in the gold frame, which matched the dream that was hung up in her head.

"Here I be," she said. There was a fixed and ceremonial stiffness over her body.

"A charity case, I suppose," said an attendant who sat at the desk before her.

But Phoenix only looked above her head. There was sweat on her face, the wrinkles in her skin shone like a bright net.

"Speak up, Grandma," the woman said. "What's your name? We must have your history, you know. Have you been here before? What seems to be the trouble with you?"

Old Phoenix only gave a twitch to her face as if a fly were bothering her.

"Are you deaf?" cried the attendant.

But then the nurse came in.

"Oh, that's just old Aunt Phoenix," she said. "She doesn't come for herself—she has a little grandson. She makes these trips just as regular as clockwork. She lives away back off the Old Natchez Trace." She bent down. "Well, Aunt Phoenix, why don't you just take a seat? We won't keep you standing after your long trip." She pointed.

The old woman sat down, bolt upright in the chair.

"Now, how is the boy?" asked the nurse.

Old Phoenix did not speak.

"I said, how is the boy?"

But Phoenix only waited and stared straight ahead, her face very solemn and withdrawn into rigidity.

"Is his throat any better?" asked the nurse. "Aunt Phoenix, don't you hear me? Is your grandson's throat any better since the last time you came for the medicine?"

With her hands on her knees, the old woman waited, silent, erect and motionless, just as if she were in armor.

"You mustn't take up our time this way, Aunt Phoenix," the nurse said. "Tell us quickly about your grandson, and get it over. He isn't dead, is he?"

At last there came a flicker and then a flame of comprehension across her face, and she spoke.

"My grandson. It was my memory had left me. There I sat and forgot why I made my long trip."

"Forgot?" The nurse frowned. "After you came so far?"

Then Phoenix was like an old woman begging a dignified forgiveness for waking up frightened in the night. "I never did go to school, I was too old at the Surrender," she said in a soft voice. "I'm an old woman without an education. It was my memory fail me. My little grandson, he is just the same, and I forgot it in the coming."

"Throat never heals, does it?" said the nurse, speaking in a loud, sure voice to old Phoenix. By now she had a card with something written on it, a little list. "Yes. Swallowed lye. When was it?—January—two-three years ago—"

Phoenix spoke unasked now. "No, missy, he not dead, he just the same. Every little while his throat begin to close up again, and he not able to swallow. He not get his breath. He not able to help himself. So the time come around, and I go on another trip for the soothing medicine."

"All right. The doctor said as long as you came to get it, you could have it," said the nurse. "But it's an obstinate case."

"My little grandson, he sit up there in the house all wrapped up, waiting by himself," Phoenix went on. "We is the only two left in the world. He suffer and it don't seem to put him back at all. He got a sweet look. He going to last. He wear a little patch quilt and peep out holding his mouth open like a little bird. I remembers so plain now. I not going to forget him again, no, the whole enduring time. I could tell him from all the others in creation."

"All right." The nurse was trying to hush her now. She brought her a bottle of medicine. "Charity," she said, making a check mark in a book.

Old Phoenix held the bottle close to her eyes, and then carefully put it into her pocket.

"I thank you," she said.

"It's Christmas time, Grandma," said the attendant. "Could I give you a few pennies out of my purse?"

"Five pennies is a nickel," said Phoenix stiffly.

"Here's a nickel," said the attendant.

Phoenix rose carefully and held out her hand. She received the nickel and then fished the other nickel out of her pocket and laid it beside the new one. She stared at her palm closely, with her head on one side.

Then she gave a tap with her cane on the floor.

"This is what come to me to do," she said. "I going to the store and buy my child a little windmill they sells, made out of paper. He going to find it hard to believe there such a thing in the world. I'll march myself back where he waiting, holding it straight up in this hand."

She lifted her free hand, gave a little nod, turned around, and walked out of the doctor's office. Then her slow step began on the stairs, going down.

TILLIE OLSEN
[b. 1913]

I Stand Here Ironing

I stand here ironing, and what you asked me moves tormented back and forth with the iron.

"I wish you would manage the time to come in and talk with me about your daughter. I'm sure you can help me understand her. She's a youngster who needs help and whom I'm deeply interested in helping."

"Who needs help." . . . Even if I came, what good would it do? You think because I am her mother I have a key, or that in some way you could use me as a key? She has lived for nineteen years. There is all that life that has happened outside of me, beyond me.

And when is there time to remember, to sift, to weigh, to estimate, to total? I will start and there will be an interruption and I will have to gather it all together again. Or I will become engulfed with all I did or did not do, with what should have been and what cannot be helped.

She was a beautiful baby. The first and only one of our five that was beautiful at birth. You do not guess how new and uneasy her tenancy in her now-loveliness. You did not know her all those years she was thought homely, or see her poring over her baby pictures, making me tell her over and over how beautiful she had been—and would be, I would tell her—and was now, to the seeing eye. But the seeing eyes were few or non-existent. Including mine.

I nursed her. They feel that's important nowadays. I nursed all the children, but with her, with all the fierce rigidity of first motherhood, I did like the books then said. Though her cries battered me to trembling and my breasts ached with swollenness, I waited till the clock decreed.

Why do I put that first? I do not even know if it matters, or if it explains anything.

She was a beautiful baby. She blew shining bubbles of sound. She loved motion, loved light, loved color and music and textures. She would lie on the floor in her blue overalls patting the surface so hard in ecstasy her hands and feet would blur. She was a miracle to me, but when she was eight months old I had to leave her daytimes with the woman downstairs to whom she was no miracle at all, for I worked or looked for work and for Emily's father, who "could no longer endure" (he wrote in his good-bye note) "sharing want with us."

I was nineteen. It was the pre-relief, pre-WPA world of the depression. I would start running as soon as I got off the streetcar, running up the stairs, the place smelling sour, and awake or asleep to startle awake, when she saw me she would break into a clogged weeping that could not be comforted, a weeping I can hear yet.

After a while I found a job hashing at night so I could be with her days, and it was better. But it came to where I had to bring her to his family and leave her.

It took a long time to raise the money for her fare back. Then she got chicken pox and I had to wait longer. When she finally came, I hardly knew her, walking quick and nervous like her father, looking like her father, thin, and dressed in a shoddy red that yellowed her skin and glared at the pockmarks. All the baby loveliness gone.

She was two. Old enough for nursery school they said, and I did not know then what I know now—the fatigue of the long day, and the lacerations of group life in the kinds of nurseries that are only parking places for children.

Except that it would have made no difference if I had known. It was the only place there was. It was the only way we could be together, the only way I could hold a job.

And even without knowing, I knew. I knew the teacher that was evil because all these years it has curdled into my memory, the little boy hunched in the corner, her rasp, "why aren't you outside, because Alvin hits you? that's no reason, go out, scaredy." I knew Emily hated it even if she did not clutch and implore "don't go Mommy" like the other children, mornings.

She always had a reason why we should stay home. Momma, you look sick, Momma. I feel sick. Momma, the teachers aren't there today, they're sick. Momma, we can't go, there was a fire there last night. Momma, it's a holiday today, no school, they told me.

But never a direct protest, never rebellion. I think of our others in their three-, four-year-oldness—the explosions, the tempers, the denunciations, the demands—and I feel suddenly ill. I put the iron down. What in me demanded that goodness in her? And what was the cost, the cost to her of such goodness?

The old man living in the back once said in his gentle way: "You should smile at Emily more when you look at her." What *was* in my face when I looked at her? I loved her. There were all the acts of love.

It was only with the others I remembered what he said, and it was the face of joy, and not of care or tightness or worry I turned to them—too late for Emily. She does not smile easily, let alone almost always as her brothers and sisters do. Her face is closed and sombre, but when she wants, how fluid. You must have seen it in her pantomimes, you spoke of her rare gift for comedy on the stage that rouses a laughter out of the audience so dear they applaud and applaud and do not want to let her go.

Where does it come from, that comedy? There was none of it in her when she came back to me that second time, after I had had to send her away again. She had a new daddy now to learn to love, and I think perhaps it was a better time.

Except when we left her alone nights, telling ourselves she was old enough.

"Can't you go some other time, Mommy, like tomorrow?" she would ask. "Will it be just a little while you'll be gone? Do you promise?"

The time we came back, the front door open, the clock on the floor in the hall. She rigid awake. "It wasn't just a little while. I didn't cry. Three times I called you, just three times, and then I ran downstairs to open the door so you could come faster. The clock talked loud. I threw it away, it scared me what it talked."

She said the clock talked loud again that night I went to the hospital to have Susan. She was delirious with the fever that comes before red measles, but she was fully conscious all the week I was gone and the week after we were home when she could not come near the new baby or me.

She did not get well. She stayed skeleton thin, not wanting to eat, and night after night she had nightmares. She would call for me, and I would rouse from exhaustion to sleepily call back: "You're all right, darling, go to sleep, it's just a dream," and if

she still called, in a sterner voice, "now go to sleep, Emily, there's nothing to hurt you."
Twice, only twice, when I had to get up for Susan anyhow, I went in to sit with her.

Now when it is too late (as if she would let me hold and comfort her like I do the
others) I get up and go to her at once at her moan or restless stirring. "Are you awake,
Emily? Can I get you something?" And the answer is always the same: "No, I'm all
right, go back to sleep, Mother."

They persuaded me at the clinic to send her away to a convalescent home in the
country where "she can have the kind of food and care you can't manage for her, and
you'll be free to concentrate on the new baby." They still send children to that place.
I see pictures on the society page of sleek young women planning affairs to raise money
for it, or dancing at the affairs, or decorating Easter eggs or filling Christmas stockings
for the children.

They never have a picture of the children so I do not know if the girls still wear
those gigantic red bows and the ravaged looks on the every other Sunday when parents
can come to visit "unless otherwise notified"—as we were notified the first six weeks.

Oh it is a handsome place, green lawns and tall trees and fluted flower beds. High
up on the balconies of each cottage the children stand, the girls in their red bows and
white dresses, the boys in white suits and giant red ties. The parents stand below
shrieking up to be heard and the children shriek down to be heard, and between them
the invisible wall "Not To Be Contaminated by Parental Germs or Physical Affection."

There was a tiny girl who always stood hand in hand with Emily. Her parents never
came. One visit she was gone. "They moved her to Rose Cottage," Emily shouted in
explanation. "They don't like you to love anybody here."

She wrote once a week, the labored writing of a seven-year-old. "I am fine. How
is the baby. If I write my letter nicly I will have a star. Love." There never was a star.
We wrote every other day, letters she could never hold or keep but only hear read
—once. "We simply do not have room for children to keep any personal possessions,"
they patiently explained when we pieced one Sunday's shrieking together to plead how
much it would mean to Emily, who loved so to keep things, to be allowed to keep
her letters and cards.

Each visit she looked frailer. "She isn't eating," they told us.

(They had runny eggs for breakfast or mush with lumps, Emily said later, I'd hold
it in my mouth and not swallow. Nothing ever tasted good, just when they had
chicken.)

It took us eight months to get her released home, and only the fact that she gained
back so little of her seven lost pounds convinced the social worker.

I used to try to hold and love her after she came back, but her body would stay
stiff, and after a while she'd push away. She ate little. Food sickened her, and I think
much of life too. Oh she had physical lightness and brightness, twinkling by on skates,
bouncing like a ball up and down up and down over the jump rope, skimming over
the hill; but these were momentary.

She fretted about her appearance, thin and dark and foreign-looking at a time when
every little girl was supposed to look or thought she should look a chubby blonde
replica of Shirley Temple. The doorbell sometimes rang for her, but no one seemed
to come and play in the house or be a best friend. Maybe because we moved so much.

There was a boy she loved painfully through two school semesters. Months later she
told me how she had taken pennies from my purse to buy him candy. "Licorice was

his favorite and I brought him some every day, but he still liked Jennifer better'n me. Why, Mommy?" The kind of question for which there is no answer.

School was a worry to her. She was not glib or quick in a world where glibness and quickness were easily confused with ability to learn. To her overworked and exasperated teachers she was an overconscientious "slow learner" who kept trying to catch up and was absent entirely too often.

I let her be absent, though sometimes the illness was imaginary. How different from my now-strictness about attendance with the others. I wasn't working. We had a new baby, I was home anyhow. Sometimes, after Susan grew old enough, I would keep her home from school, too, to have them all together.

Mostly Emily had asthma, and her breathing, harsh and labored, would fill the house with a curiously tranquil sound. I would bring the two old dresser mirrors and her boxes of collections to her bed. She would select beads and single earrings, bottle tops and shells, dried flowers and pebbles, old postcards and scraps, all sorts of oddments; then she and Susan would play Kingdom, setting up landscapes and furniture, peopling them with action.

Those were the only times of peaceful companionship between her and Susan. I have edged away from it, that poisonous feeling between them, that terrible balancing of hurts and needs I had to do between the two, and did so badly, those earlier years.

Oh there are conflicts between the others too, each one human, needing, demanding, hurting, taking—but only between Emily and Susan, no, Emily toward Susan that corroding resentment. It seems so obvious on the surface, yet it is not obvious. Susan, the second child, Susan, golden- and curly-haired and chubby, quick and articulate and assured, everything in appearance and manner Emily was not; Susan, not able to resist Emily's precious things, losing or sometimes clumsily breaking them; Susan telling jokes and riddles to company for applause while Emily sat silent (to say to me later: that was *my* riddle, Mother, I told it to Susan); Susan, who for all the five years' difference in age was just a year behind Emily in developing physically.

I am glad for that slow physical development that widened the difference between her and her contemporaries, though she suffered over it. She was too vulnerable for that terrible world of youthful competition, of preening and parading, of constant measuring of yourself against every other, of envy, "If I had that copper hair," "If I had that skin. . . ." She tormented herself enough about not looking like the others, there was enough of the unsureness, the having to be conscious of words before you speak, the constant caring—what are they thinking of me? without having it all magnified by the merciless physical drives.

Ronnie is calling. He is wet and I change him. It is rare there is such a cry now. That time of motherhood is almost behind me when the ear is not one's own but must always be racked and listening for the child cry, the child call. We sit for a while and I hold him, looking out over the city spread in charcoal with its soft aisles of light. "*Shoogily,*" he breathes and curls closer. I carry him back to bed, asleep. *Shoogily.* A funny word, a family word, inherited from Emily, invented by her to say: *comfort.*

In this and other ways she leaves her seal, I say aloud. And startle at my saying it. What do I mean? What did I start to gather together, to try and make coherent? I was at the terrible, growing years. War years. I do not remember them well. I was working, there were four smaller ones now, there was not time for her. She had to help be a mother, and housekeeper, and shopper. She had to set her seal. Mornings of crisis and near hysteria trying to get lunches packed, hair combed, coats and shoes found, everyone to school or Child Care on time, the baby ready for transportation. And always the paper scribbled on by a smaller one, the book looked at by Susan then mislaid, the homework not done. Running out to that huge school where she was one, she was lost, she was a drop; suffering over the unpreparedness, stammering and unsure in her classes.

There was so little time left at night after the kids were bedded down. She would struggle over books, always eating (it was in those years she developed her enormous appetite that is legendary in our family) and I would be ironing, or preparing food for the next day, or writing V-mail to Bill, or tending the baby. Sometimes, to make me laugh, or out of her despair, she would imitate happenings or types at school.

I think I said once: "Why don't you do something like this in the school amateur show?" One morning she phoned me at work, hardly understandable through the weeping: "Mother, I did it. I won, I won; they gave me first prize; they clapped and clapped and wouldn't let me go."

Now suddenly she was Somebody, and as imprisoned in her difference as she had been in anonymity.

She began to be asked to perform at other high schools, even in colleges, then at city and statewide affairs. The first one we went to, I only recognized her that first moment when thin, shy, she almost drowned herself into the curtains. Then: Was this Emily? The control, the command, the convulsing and deadly clowning, the spell, then the roaring, stamping audience, unwilling to let this rare and precious laughter out of their lives.

Afterwards: You ought to do something about her with a gift like that—but without money or knowing how, what does one do? We have left it all to her, and the gift has as often eddied inside, clogged and clotted, as been used and growing.

She is coming. She runs up the stairs two at a time with her light graceful step, and I know she is happy tonight. Whatever it was that occasioned your call did not happen today.

"Aren't you ever going to finish the ironing, Mother? Whistler painted his mother in a rocker. I'd have to paint mine standing over an ironing board." This is one of her communicative nights and she tells me everything and nothing as she fixes herself a plate of food out of the icebox.

She is so lovely. Why did you want me to come in at all? Why were you concerned? She will find her way.

She starts up the stairs to bed. "Don't get me up with the rest in the morning." "But I thought you were having midterms." "Oh, those," she comes back in, kisses me, and says lightly, "in a couple of years when we'll all be atom-dead they won't matter a bit."

She has said it before. She *believes* it. But because I have been dredging the past, and all that compounds a human being is so heavy and meaningful in me, I cannot endure it tonight.

I will never total it all. I will never come in to say: She was a child seldom smiled at. Her father left me before she was a year old. I had to work her first six years when there was work, or I sent her home and to his relatives. There were years she had care she hated. She was dark and thin and foreign-looking in a world where the prestige went to blondeness and curly hair and dimples, she was slow where glibness was prized.

She was a child of anxious, not proud, love. We were poor and could not afford for her the soil of easy growth. I was a young mother, I was a distracted mother. There were the other children pushing up, demanding. Her younger sister seemed all that she was not. There were years she did not want me to touch her. She kept too much in herself, her life was such she had to keep too much in herself. My wisdom came too late. She has much to her and probably little will come of it. She is a child of her age, of depression, of war, of fear.

Let her be. So all that is in her will not bloom—but in how many does it? There is still enough left to live by. Only help her to know—help make it so there is cause for her to know—that she is more than this dress on the ironing board, helpless before the iron.

RALPH ELLISON

[*b. 1914*]

Battle Royal

It goes a long way back, some twenty years. All my life I had been looking for something, and everywhere I turned someone tried to tell me what it was. I accepted their answers too, though they were often in contradiction and even self-contradictory. I was naïve. I was looking for myself and asking everyone except myself questions which I, and only I, could answer. It took me a long time and much painful boomeranging of my expectations to achieve a realization everyone else appears to have been born with: That I am nobody but myself. But first I had to discover that I am an invisible man!

And yet I am no freak of nature, nor of history. I was in the cards, other things having been equal (or unequal) eighty-five years ago. I am not ashamed of my grandparents for having been slaves. I am only ashamed of myself for having at one time been ashamed. About eighty-five years ago they were told that they were free, united with others of our country in everything pertaining to the common good, and, in everything social, separate like the fingers of the hand. And they believed it. They exulted in it. They stayed in their place, worked hard, and brought up my father to do the same. But my grandfather is the one. He was an odd old guy, my grandfather, and I am told I take after him. It was he who caused the trouble. On his deathbed he called my father to him and said, "Son, after I'm gone I want you to keep up the good fight. I never told you, but our life is a war and I have been a traitor all my born days, a spy in the enemy's country ever since I give up my gun back in the Reconstruction. Live with your head in the lion's mouth. I want you to overcome 'em with yeses, undermine 'em with grins, agree 'em to death and destruction, let 'em swoller you till they vomit or bust wide open." They thought the old man had gone out of his mind. He had been the meekest of men. The younger children were rushed from the room, the shades drawn and the flame of the lamp turned so low that it sputtered on the wick like the old man's breathing. "Learn it to the younguns," he whispered fiercely; then he died.

But my folks were more alarmed over his last words than over his dying. It was as though he had not died at all, his words caused so much anxiety. I was warned emphatically to forget what he had said and, indeed, this is the first time it has been mentioned outside the family circle. It had a tremendous effect upon me, however. I could never be sure of what he meant. Grandfather had been a quiet old man who never made any trouble, yet on his deathbed he had called himself a traitor and a spy, and he had spoken of his meekness as a dangerous activity. It became a constant puzzle which lay unanswered in the back of my mind. And whenever things went well for me I remembered my grandfather and felt guilty and uncomfortable. It was as though I was carrying out his advice in spite of myself. And to make it worse, everyone loved me for it. I was praised by the most lily-white men of the town. I was considered an example of desirable conduct—just as my grandfather had been. And what puzzled me was that the old man had defined it as *treachery*. When I was praised for my conduct I felt a guilt that in some way I was doing something that was really against the wishes of the white folks, that if they had understood they would have desired me to act just the opposite, that I should have been sulky and mean, and that that really would have been what they wanted, even though they were fooled and thought they wanted me to act as I did. It made me afraid that some day they would look upon me as a traitor and I would be lost. Still I was more afraid to act any other way because they didn't like that at all. The old man's words were like a curse. On my graduation day I delivered an oration in which I showed that humility was the secret, indeed, the very essence of progress. (Not that I believed this—how could I, remembering my grandfather?—I only believed that it worked.) It was a great success. Everyone praised me and I was invited to give the speech at a gathering of the town's leading white citizens. It was a triumph for our whole community.

It was in the main ballroom of the leading hotel. When I got there I discovered that it was on the occasion of a smoker, and I was told that since I was to be there anyway I might as well take part in the battle royal to be fought by some of my schoolmates as part of the entertainment. The battle royal came first.

All of the town's big shots were there in their tuxedoes, wolfing down the buffet foods, drinking beer and whiskey and smoking black cigars. It was a large room with a high ceiling. Chairs were arranged in neat rows around three sides of a portable boxing ring. The fourth side was clear, revealing a gleaming space of polished floor. I had some misgivings over the battle royal, by the way. Not from a distaste for fighting, but because I didn't care too much for the other fellows who were to take part. They were tough guys who seemed to have no grandfather's curse worrying their minds. No one could mistake their toughness. And besides, I suspected that fighting a battle royal might detract from the dignity of my speech. In those pre-invisible days I visualized myself as a potential Booker T. Washington. But the other fellows didn't care too much for me either, and there were nine of them. I felt superior to them in my way, and I didn't like the manner in which we were all crowded together into the servants' elevator. Nor did they like my being there. In fact, as the warmly lighted floors flashed past the elevator we had words over the fact that I, by taking part in the fight, had knocked one of their friends out of a night's work.

We were led out of the elevator through a rococo hall into an anteroom and told to get into our fighting togs. Each of us was issued a pair of boxing gloves and ushered out into the big mirrored hall, which we entered looking cautiously about us and whispering, lest we might accidentally be heard above the noise of the room. It was foggy with cigar smoke. And already the whiskey was taking effect. I was shocked to see some of the most important men of the town quite tipsy. They were all there—bankers, lawyers, judges, doctors, fire chiefs, teachers, merchants. Even one of the more fashionable pastors. Something we could not see was going on up front. A clarinet was vibrating sensuously and the men were standing up and moving eagerly forward. We were a small tight group, clustered together, our bare upper bodies touching and shining with anticipatory sweat; while up front the big shots were becoming increasingly excited over something we still could not see. Suddenly I heard the school superintendent, who had told me to come, yell, "Bring up the shines gentlemen! Bring up the little shines!"

We were rushed up to the front of the ballroom, where it smelled even more strongly of tobacco and whiskey. Then we were pushed into place. I almost wet my pants. A sea of faces, some hostile, some amused, ringed around us, and in the center, facing us, stood a magnificent blonde—stark naked. There was dead silence. I felt a blast of cold air chill me. I tried to back away, but they were behind me and around me. Some of the boys stood with lowered heads, trembling. I felt a wave of irrational guilt and fear. My teeth chattered, my skin turned to goose flesh, my knees knocked. Yet I was strongly attracted and looked in spite of myself. Had the price of looking been blindness, I would have looked. The hair was yellow like that of a circus kewpie doll, the face heavily powdered and rouged, as though to form an abstract mask, the eyes hollow and smeared a cool blue, the color of a baboon's butt. I felt a desire to spit upon her as my eyes brushed slowly over her body. Her breasts were firm and round as the domes of East Indian temples, and I stood so close as to see the fine skin texture and beads of pearly perspiration glistening like dew around the pink and erected buds of her nipples. I wanted at one and the same time to run from the room, to sink through the floor, or go to her and cover her from my eyes and the eyes of the others with my body; to feel the soft thighs, to caress her and destroy her, to love her and murder her, to hide from her, and yet to stroke where below the small American flag tattooed upon her belly her thighs formed a capital V. I had a notion that of all in the room she saw only me with her impersonal eyes.

And then she began to dance, a slow sensuous movement; the smoke of a hundred cigars clinging to her like the thinnest of veils. She seemed like a fair bird-girl girdled in veils calling to me from the angry surface of some gray and threatening sea. I was transported. Then I became aware of the clarinet playing and the big shots yelling at us. Some threatened us if we looked and others if we did not. On my right I saw one boy faint. And now a man grabbed a silver pitcher from a table and stepped close as he dashed ice water upon him and stood him up and forced two of us to support him as his head hung and moans issued from his thick bluish lips. Another boy began to plead to go home. He was the largest of the group, wearing dark red fighting trunks much too small to conceal the erection which projected from him as though in answer to the insinuating low-registered moaning of the clarinet. He tried to hide himself with his boxing gloves.

And all the while the blonde continued dancing, smiling faintly at the big shots who watched her with fascination, and faintly smiling at our fear. I noticed a certain merchant who followed her hungrily, his lips loose and drooling. He was a large man who wore diamond studs in a shirtfront which swelled with the ample paunch underneath, and each time the blonde swayed her undulating hips he ran his hand through the thin hair of his bald head and, with his arms upheld, his posture clumsy like that of an intoxicated panda, wound his belly in a slow and obscene grind. This creature was completely hypnotized. The music had quickened. As the dancer flung herself about with a detached expression on her face, the men began reaching out to touch her. I could see their beefy fingers sink into her soft flesh. Some of the others tried to stop them and she began to move around the floor in graceful circles, as they gave chase, slipping and sliding over the polished floor. It was mad. Chairs went crashing, drinks were spilt, as they ran laughing and howling after her. They caught her just as she reached a door, raised her from the floor, and tossed her as college boys are tossed at a hazing, and above her red, fixed-smiling lips I saw the terror and disgust in her eyes, almost like my own terror and that which I saw in some of the other boys. As I watched, they tossed her twice and her soft breasts seemed to flatten against the air and her legs flung wildly as she spun. Some of the more sober ones helped her to escape. And I started off the floor, heading for the anteroom with the rest of the boys.

Some were still crying and in hysteria. But as we tried to leave we were stopped and ordered to get into the ring. There was nothing to do but what we were told. All ten of us climbed under the ropes and allowed ourselves to be blindfolded with broad bands of white cloth. One of the men seemed to feel a bit sympathetic and tried to cheer us up as we stood with our backs against the ropes. Some of us tried to grin. "See that boy over there?" one of the men said. "I want you to run across at the bell and give it to him right in the belly. If you don't get him, I'm going to get you. I don't like his looks." Each of us was told the same. The blindfolds were put on. Yet even then I had been going over my speech. In my mind each word was as bright as flame. I felt the cloth pressed into place, and frowned so that it would be loosened when I relaxed.

But now I felt a sudden fit of blind terror. I was unused to darkness. It was as though I had suddenly found myself in a dark room filled with poisonous cottonmouths. I could hear the bleary voices yelling insistently for the battle royal to begin.

"Get going in there!"

"Let me at that big nigger!"

I strained to pick up the school superintendent's voice, as though to squeeze some security out of that slightly more familiar sound.

"Let me at those black sonsabitches!" someone yelled.

"No, Jackson, no!" another voice yelled. "Here, somebody, help me hold Jack."

"I want to get at that ginger-colored nigger. Tear him limb from limb," the first voice yelled.

I stood against the ropes trembling. For in those days I was what they called ginger-colored, and he sounded as though he might crunch me between his teeth like a crisp ginger cookie.

Quite a struggle was going on. Chairs were being kicked about and I could hear voices grunting as with a terrific effort. I wanted to see, to see more desperately than ever before. But the blindfold was as tight as a thick skin-puckering scab and when I raised my gloved hands to push the layers of white aside a voice yelled, "Oh, no you don't, black bastard! Leave that alone!"

"Ring the bell before Jackson kills him a coon!" someone boomed in the sudden silence. And I heard the bell clang and the sound of the feet scuffling forward.

A glove smacked against my head. I pivoted, striking out stiffly as someone went past, and felt the jar ripple along the length of my arm to my shoulder. Then it seemed as though all nine of the boys had turned upon me at once. Blows pounded me from all sides while I struck out as best I could. So many blows landed upon me that I wondered if I were not the only blindfolded fighter in the ring, or if the man called Jackson hadn't succeeded in getting me after all.

Blindfolded, I could no longer control my motions. I had no dignity. I stumbled about like a baby or a drunken man. The smoke had become thicker and with each new blow it seemed to sear and further restrict my lungs. My saliva became like hot bitter glue. A glove connected with my head, filling my mouth with warm blood. It was everywhere. I could not tell if the moisture I felt upon my body was sweat or blood. A blow landed hard against the nape of my neck. I felt myself going over, my head hitting the floor. Streaks of blue light filled the black world behind the blindfold. I lay prone, pretending that I was knocked out, but felt myself seized by hands and yanked to my feet. "Get going, black boy! Mix it up!" My arms were like lead, my head smarting from blows. I managed to feel my way to the ropes and held on, trying to catch my breath. A glove landed in my midsection and I went over again, feeling as though the smoke had become a knife jabbed into my guts. Pushed this way and that by the legs milling around me, I finally pulled erect and discovered that I could see the black, sweat-washed forms weaving in the smoky-blue atmosphere like drunken dancers weaving to the rapid drum-like thuds of blows.

Everyone fought hysterically. It was complete anarchy. Everybody fought everybody else. No group fought together for long. Two, three, four, fought one, then turned to fight each other, were themselves attacked. Blows landed below the belt and in the kidney, with the gloves open as well as closed, and with my eye partly opened now there was not so much terror. I moved carefully, avoiding blows, although not too many to attract attention, fighting from group to group. The boys groped about like blind, cautious crabs crouching to protect their mid-sections, their heads pulled in short against their shoulders, their arms stretched nervously before them, with their fists testing the smoke-filled air like the knobbed feelers of hypersensitive snails. In one corner I glimpsed a boy violently punching the air and heard him scream in pain as he smashed his hand against a ring post. For a second I saw him bent over holding his hand, then going down as a blow caught his unprotected head. I played one group against the other, slipping in and throwing a punch then stepping out of range while pushing the others into the melee to take the blows blindly aimed at me. The smoke was agonizing and there were no rounds, no bells at three minute intervals to relieve our exhaustion. The room spun round me, a swirl of lights, smoke, sweating bodies surrounded by tense white faces. I bled from both nose and mouth, the blood spattering upon my chest.

The men kept yelling, "Slug him, black boy! Knock his guts out!"

"Uppercut him! Kill him! Kill that big boy!"

Taking a fake fall, I saw a boy going down heavily beside me as though we were felled by a single blow, saw a sneaker-clad foot shoot into his groin as the two who had knocked him down stumbled upon him. I rolled out of range, feeling a twinge of nausea.

The harder we fought the more threatening the men became. And yet, I had begun to worry about my speech again. How would it go? Would they recognize my ability? What would they give me?

I was fighting automatically and suddenly I noticed that one after another of the boys was leaving the ring. I was surprised, filled with panic, as though I had been left alone with an unknown danger. Then I understood. The boys had arranged it among themselves. It was the custom for the two men left in the ring to slug it out for the winner's prize. I discovered this too late. When the bell sounded two men in tuxedoes leaped into the ring and removed the blindfold. I found myself facing Tatlock, the biggest of the gang. I felt sick at my stomach. Hardly had the bell stopped ringing in my ears than it clanged again and I saw him moving swiftly toward me. Thinking of nothing else to do I hit him smash on the nose. He kept coming, bringing the rank sharp violence of stale sweat. His face was a black blank of a face, only his eyes alive —with hate of me and aglow with a feverish terror from what had happened to us all. I became anxious. I wanted to deliver my speech and he came at me as though he meant to beat it out of me. I smashed him again and again, taking his blows as they came. Then on a sudden impulse I struck him lightly and as we clinched, I whispered, "Fake like I knocked you out, you can have the prize."

"I'll break your behind," he whispered hoarsely.

"For *them?*"

"For *me,* sonofabitch!"

They were yelling for us to break it up and Tatlock spun me half around with a blow, and as a joggled camera sweeps in a reeling scene, I saw the howling red faces crouching tense beneath the cloud of blue-gray smoke. For a moment the world wavered, unraveled, flowed, then my head cleared and Tatlock bounced before me. That fluttering shadow before my eyes was his jabbing left hand. Then falling forward, my head against his damp shoulder, I whispered,

"I'll make it five dollars more."

"Go to hell!"

But his muscles relaxed a trifle beneath my pressure and I breathed, "Seven!"

"Give it to your ma," he said, ripping me beneath the heart.

And while I still held him I butted him and moved away. I felt myself bombarded with punches. I fought back with hopeless desperation. I wanted to deliver my speech more than anything else in the world, because I felt that only these men could judge truly my ability, and now this stupid clown was ruining my chances. I began fighting carefully now, moving in to punch him and out again with my greater speed. A lucky blow to his chin and I had him going too—until I heard a loud voice yell, "I got my money on the big boy."

Hearing this, I almost dropped my guard. I was confused: Should I try to win against the voice out there? Would not this go against my speech, and was not this a moment for humility, for nonresistance? A blow to my head as I danced about sent my right eye popping like a jack-in-the-box and settled my dilemma. The room went red as I fell. It was a dream fall, my body languid and fastidious as to where to land, until the floor became impatient and smashed up to meet me. A moment later I came to. An hypnotic voice said FIVE emphatically. And I lay there, hazily watching a dark red spot of my own blood shaping itself into a butterfly, glistening and soaking into the soiled gray world of the canvas.

When the voice drawled TEN I was lifted up and dragged to a chair. I sat dazed. My eye pained and swelled with each throb of my pounding heart and I wondered if now I would be allowed to speak. I was wringing wet, my mouth still bleeding. We were grouped along the wall now. The other boys ignored me as they congratulated Tatlock and speculated as to how much they would be paid. One boy whimpered over his smashed hand. Looking up front, I saw attendants in white jackets rolling the portable ring away and placing a small square rug in the vacant space surrounded by chairs. Perhaps, I thought, I will stand on the rug to deliver my speech.

Then the M.C. called to us, "Come on up here boys and get your money."

We ran forward to where the men laughed and talked in their chairs, waiting. Everyone seemed friendly now.

"There it is on the rug," the man said. I saw the rug covered with coins of all dimensions and a few crumpled bills. But what excited me, scattered here and there, were the gold pieces.

"Boys, it's all yours," the man said. "You get all you grab."

"That's right, Sambo," a blond man said, winking at me confidentially.

I trembled with excitement, forgetting my pain. I would get the gold and the bills, I thought. I would use both hands. I would throw my body against the boys nearest me to block them from the gold.

"Get down around the rug now," the man commanded, "and don't anyone touch it until I give the signal."

"This ought to be good," I heard.

As told, we got around the square rug on our knees. Slowly the man raised his freckled hand as we followed it upward with our eyes.

I heard, "These niggers look like they're about to pray!"

Then, "Ready," the man said. "Go!"

I lunged for a yellow coin lying on the blue design of the carpet, touching it and sending a surprised shriek to join those rising around me. I tried frantically to remove my hand but could not let go. A hot, violent force tore through my body, shaking me like a wet rat. The rug was electrified. The hair bristled up on my head as I shook myself free. My muscles jumped, my nerves jangled, writhed. But I saw that this was not stopping the other boys. Laughing in fear and embarrassment, some were holding back and scooping up the coins knocked off by the painful contortions of the others. The men roared above us as we struggled.

"Pick it up, goddamnit, pick it up!" someone called like a bass-voiced parrot. "Go on, get it!"

I crawled rapidly around the floor, picking up the coins, trying to avoid the coppers and to get greenbacks and the gold. Ignoring the shock by laughing, as I brushed the coins off quickly, I discovered that I could contain the electricity—a contradiction, but it works. Then the men began to push us onto the rug. Laughing embarrassedly, we struggled out of their hands and kept after the coins. We were all wet and slippery and hard to hold. Suddenly I saw a boy lifted into the air, glistening with sweat like a circus seal, and dropped, his wet back landing flush upon the charged rug, heard him yell and saw him literally dance upon his back, his elbows beating a frenzied tattoo upon the floor, his muscles twitching like the flesh of a horse stung by many flies. When he finally rolled off, his face was gray and no one stopped him when he ran from the floor amid booming laughter.

"Get the money," the M.C. called. "That's good hard American cash!"

And we snatched and grabbed, snatched and grabbed. I was careful not to come too close to the rug now, and when I felt the hot whiskey breath descend upon me like a cloud of foul air I reached out and grabbed the leg of a chair. It was occupied and I held on desperately.

"Leggo, nigger! Leggo!"

The huge face wavered down to mine as he tried to push me free. But my body was slippery and he was too drunk. It was Mr. Colcord, who owned a chain of movie houses and "entertainment palaces." Each time he grabbed me I slipped out of his hands. It became a real struggle. I feared the rug more than I did the drunk, so I held on, surprising myself for a moment by trying to topple *him* upon the rug. It was such an enormous idea that I found myself actually carrying it out. I tried not to be obvious, yet when I grabbed his leg, trying to tumble him out of the chair, he raised up roaring with laughter, and, looking at me with soberness dead in the eye, kicked me viciously in the chest. The chair leg flew out of my hand. I felt myself going and rolled. It was as though I had rolled through a bed of hot coals. It seemed a whole century would pass before I would roll free, a century in which I was seared through the deepest levels of my body to the fearful breath within me and the breath seared and heated to the point of explosion. It'll all be over in a flash, I thought as I rolled clear. It'll all be over in a flash.

But not yet, the men on the other side were waiting, red faces swollen as though from apoplexy as they bent forward in their chairs. Seeing their fingers coming toward me I rolled away as a fumbled football rolls off the receiver's fingertips, back into the coals. That time I luckily sent the rug sliding out of place and heard the coins ringing against the floor and the boys scuffling to pick them up and the M.C. calling, "All right, boys, that's all. Go get dressed and get your money."

I was limp as a dish rag. My back felt as though it had been beaten with wires.

When we had dressed the M.C. came in and gave us each five dollars, except Tatlock, who got ten for being last in the ring. Then he told us to leave. I was not to get a chance to deliver my speech, I thought. I was going out into the dim alley in despair when I was stopped and told to go back. I returned to the ballroom, where the men were pushing back their chairs and gathering in groups to talk.

The M.C. knocked on a table for quiet. "Gentlemen," he said, "we almost forgot an important part of the program. A most serious part, gentlemen. This boy was brought here to deliver a speech which he made at his graduation yesterday. . . ."

"Bravo!"

"I'm told that he is the smartest boy we've got out there in Greenwood. I'm told that he knows more big words than a pocket-sized dictionary."

Much applause and laughter.

"So now, gentlemen, I want you to give him your attention."

There was still laughter as I faced them, my mouth dry, my eye throbbing. I began slowly, but evidently my throat was tense, because they began shouting, "Louder! Louder!"

"We of the younger generation extol the wisdom of that great leader and educator," I shouted, "who first spoke these flaming words of wisdom: 'A ship lost at sea for many days suddenly sighted a friendly vessel. From the mast of the unfortunate vessel was seen a signal: "Water, water; we die of thirst!" The answer from the friendly vessel came back: "Cast down your bucket where you are." The captain of the distressed vessel, at last heeding the injunction, cast down his bucket, and it came up full of fresh sparkling water from the mouth of the Amazon River.' And like him I say, and in his words, 'To those of my race who depend upon bettering their condition in a foreign land, or who underestimate the importance of cultivating friendly relations with the Southern white man, who is his next-door neighbor, I would say: "Cast down your bucket where you are"—cast it down in making friends in every manly way of the people of all races by whom we are surrounded. . . .' "

I spoke automatically and with such fervor that I did not realize that the men were still talking and laughing until my dry mouth, filling up with blood from the cut, almost strangled me. I coughed, wanting to stop and go to one of the tall brass, sand-filled spittoons to relieve myself, but a few of the men, especially the superintendent, were listening and I was afraid. So I gulped it down, blood, saliva and all, and continued. (What powers of endurance I had during those days! What enthusiasm! What a belief in the rightness of things!) I spoke even louder in spite of the pain. But still they talked and still they laughed, as though deaf with cotton in dirty ears. So I spoke with greater emotional emphasis. I closed my ears and swallowed blood until I was nauseated. The speech seemed a hundred times as long as before, but I could not leave out a single word. All had to be said, each memorized nuance considered, rendered. Nor was that all. Whenever I uttered a word of three or more syllables a group of voices would yell for me to repeat it. I used the phrase "social responsibility" and they yelled:

"What's the word you say, boy?"

"Social responsibility," I said.

"What?"

"Social . . ."

"Louder."

". . . responsibility."

"More!"

"Respon—"

"Repeat!"

"—sibility."

The room filled with the uproar of laughter until, no doubt, distracted by having to gulp down my blood, I made a mistake and yelled a phrase I had often seen denounced in newspaper editorials, heard debated in private.

"Social . . ."

"What?" they yelled.

". . . equality—"

The laughter hung smokelike in the sudden stillness. I opened my eyes, puzzled. Sounds of displeasure filled the room. The M.C. rushed forward. They shouted hostile phrases at me. But I did not understand.

A small dry mustached man in the front row blared out, "Say that slowly, son!"

"What sir?"

"What you just said!"

"Social responsibility, sir," I said.

"You weren't being smart, were you, boy?" he said, not unkindly.

"No, sir!"

"You sure that about 'equality' was a mistake?"

"Oh, yes, sir," I said. "I was swallowing blood."

"Well, you had better speak more slowly so we can understand. We mean to do right by you, but you've got to know your place at all times. All right, now, go on with your speech."

I was afraid. I wanted to leave but I wanted also to speak and I was afraid they'd snatch me down.

"Thank you, sir," I said, beginning where I had left off, and having them ignore me as before.

Yet when I finished there was a thunderous applause. I was surprised to see the superintendent come forth with a package wrapped in white tissue paper, and, gesturing for quiet, address the men.

"Gentlemen, you see that I did not overpraise this boy. He makes a good speech and some day he'll lead his people in the proper paths. And I don't have to tell you that that is important in these days and times. This is a good, smart boy, and so to encourage him in the right direction, in the name of the Board of Education I wish to present him a prize in the form of this . . ."

He paused, removing the tissue paper and revealing a gleaming calfskin brief case.

". . . in the form of this first-class article from Shad Whitmore's shop."

"Boy," he said, addressing me, "take this prize and keep it well. Consider it a badge of office. Prize it. Keep developing as you are and some day it will be filled with important papers that will help shape the destiny of your people."

I was so moved that I could hardly express my thanks. A rope of bloody saliva forming a shape like an undiscovered continent drooled upon the leather and I wiped it quickly away. I felt an importance that I had never dreamed.

"Open it and see what's inside," I was told.

My fingers a-tremble, I complied, smelling the fresh leather and finding an official-looking document inside. It was a scholarship to the state college for Negroes. My eyes filled with tears and I ran awkwardly off the floor.

I was overjoyed; I did not even mind when I discovered that the gold pieces I had scrambled for were brass pocket tokens advertising a certain make of automobile.

When I reached home everyone was excited. Next day the neighbors came to congratulate me. I even felt safe from grandfather, whose deathbed curse usually spoiled my triumphs. I stood beneath his photograph with my brief case in hand and smiled triumphantly into his stolid black peasant's face. It was a face that fascinated me. The eyes seemed to follow everywhere I went.

That night I dreamed I was at a circus with him and that he refused to laugh at the clowns no matter what they did. Then later he told me to open my brief case and read what was inside and I did, finding an official envelope stamped with the state seal; and inside the envelope I found another and another, endlessly, and I thought I would fall of weariness. "Them's years," he said. "Now open that one." And I did and in it I found an engraved document containing a short message in letters of gold. "Read it," my grandfather said. "Out loud."

"To Whom It May Concern," I intoned. "Keep This Nigger-Boy Running."

I awoke with the old man's laughter ringing in my ears.

(It was a dream I was to remember and dream again for many years after. But at the time I had no insight into its meaning. First I had to attend college.)

BERNARD MALAMUD

[*b. 1914*]

Idiots First

The thick ticking of the tin clock stopped. Mendel, dozing in the dark, awoke in fright. The pain returned as he listened. He drew on his cold embittered clothing, and wasted minutes sitting at the edge of the bed.

"Isaac," he ultimately sighed.

In the kitchen, Isaac, his astonished mouth open, held six peanuts in his palm. He placed each on the table. "One . . . two . . . nine."

He gathered each peanut and appeared in the doorway. Mendel, in loose hat and long overcoat, still sat on the bed. Isaac watched with small eyes and ears, thick hair graying the sides of his head.

"Schlaf," he nasally said.

"No," muttered Mendel. As if stifling he rose. "Come, Isaac."

He wound his old watch though the sight of the stopped clock nauseated him. Isaac wanted to hold it to his ear.

"No, it's late." Mendel put the watch carefully away. In the drawer he found the little paper bag of crumpled ones and fives and slipped it into his overcoat pocket. He helped Isaac on with his coat.

Isaac looked at one dark window, then at the other. Mendel stared at both blank windows.

They went slowly down the darkly lit stairs, Mendel first, Isaac watching the moving shadows on the wall. To one long shadow he offered a peanut.

"Hungrig."

In the vestibule the old man gazed through the thin glass. The November night was cold and bleak. Opening the door he cautiously thrust his head out. Though he saw nothing he quickly shut the door.

"Ginzburg, that he came to see me yesterday," he whispered in Isaac's ear.

Isaac sucked air.

"You know who I mean?"

Isaac combed his chin with his fingers.

"That's the one, with the black whiskers. Don't talk to him or go with him if he asks you."

Isaac moaned.

"Young people he don't bother so much," Mendel said in afterthought.

It was suppertime and the street was empty but the store windows dimly lit their way to the corner. They crossed the deserted street and went on. Isaac, with a happy cry, pointed to the three golden balls. Mendel smiled but was exhausted when they got to the pawnshop.

The pawnbroker, a red-bearded man with black horn-rimmed glasses, was eating a whitefish at the rear of the store. He craned his head, saw them, and settled back to sip his tea.

In five minutes he came forward, patting his shapeless lips with a large white handkerchief.

Mendel, breathing heavily, handed him the worn gold watch. The pawnbroker, raising his glasses, screwed in his eyepiece. He turned the watch over once. "Eight dollars."

The dying man wet his cracked lips. "I must have thirty-five."

"So go to Rothschild."

"Cost me myself sixty."

"In 1905." The pawnbroker handed back the watch. It had stopped ticking. Mendel wound it slowly. It ticked hollowly.

"Isaac must go to my uncle that he lives in California."

"It's a free country," said the pawnbroker.

Isaac, watching a banjo, snickered.

"What's the matter with him?" the pawnbroker asked.

"So let be eight dollars," muttered Mendel, "but where will I get the rest till tonight?"

"How much for my hat and coat?" he asked.

"No sale." The pawnbroker went behind the cage and wrote out a ticket. He locked the watch in a small drawer but Mendel still heard it ticking.

In the street he slipped the eight dollars into the paper bag, then searched in his pockets for a scrap of writing. Finding it, he strained to read the address by the light of the street lamp.

As they trudged to the subway, Mendel pointed to the sprinkled sky.

"Isaac, look how many stars are tonight."

"Eggs," said Isaac.

"First we will go to Mr. Fishbein, after we will eat."

They got off the train in upper Manhattan and had to walk several blocks before they located Fishbein's house.

"A regular palace," Mendel murmured, looking forward to a moment's warmth.

Isaac stared uneasily at the heavy door of the house.

Mendel rang. The servant, a man with long sideburns, came to the door and said Mr. and Mrs. Fishbein were dining and could see no one.

"He should eat in peace but we will wait till he finishes."

"Come back tomorrow morning. Tomorrow morning Mr. Fishbein will talk to you. He don't do business or charity at this time of the night."

"Charity I am not interested—"

"Come back tomorrow."

"Tell him it's life or death—"

"Whose life or death?"

"So if not his, then mine."

"Don't be such a big smart aleck."

"Look me in my face," said Mendel, "and tell me if I got time till tomorrow morning?"

The servant stared at him, then at Isaac, and reluctantly let them in.

The foyer was a vast high-ceilinged room with many oil paintings on the walls, voluminous silken draperies, a thick flowered rug at foot, and a marble staircase.

Mr. Fishbein, a paunchy bald-headed man with hairy nostrils and small patent leather feet, ran lightly down the stairs, a large napkin tucked under a tuxedo coat button. He stopped on the fifth step from the bottom and examined his visitors.

"Who comes on Friday night to a man that he has guests, to spoil him his supper?"

"Excuse me that I bother you, Mr. Fishbein," Mendel said. "If I didn't come now I couldn't come tomorrow."

"Without more preliminaries, please state your business. I'm a hungry man."

"Hungrig," wailed Isaac.

Fishbein adjusted his pince-nez. "What's the matter with him?"

"This is my son Isaac. He is like this all his life."

Isaac mewled.

"I am sending him to California."

"Mr. Fishbein don't contribute to personal pleasure trips."

"I am a sick man and he must go tonight on the train to my Uncle Leo."

"I never give to unorganized charity," Fishbein said, "but if you are hungry I will invite you downstairs in my kitchen. We having tonight chicken with stuffed derma."

"All I ask is thirty-five dollars for the train ticket to my uncle in California. I have already the rest."

"Who is your uncle? How old a man?"

"Eighty-one years, a long life to him."

Fishbein burst into laughter. "Eighty-one years and you are sending him this half-wit."

Mendel, flailing both arms, cried, "Please, without names."

Fishbein politely conceded.

"Where is open the door there we go in the house," the sick man said. "If you will kindly give me thirty-five dollars, God will bless you. What is thirty-five dollars to Mr. Fishbein? Nothing. To me, for my boy, is everything."

Fishbein drew himself up to his tallest height.

"Private contributions I don't make—only to institutions. This is my fixed policy."

Mendel sank to his creaking knees on the rug.

"Please, Mr. Fishbein, if not thirty-five, give maybe twenty."

"Levinson!" Fishbein angrily called.

The servant with the long sideburns appeared at the top of the stairs.

"Show this party where is the door—unless he wishes to partake food before leaving the premises."

"For what I got chicken won't cure it," Mendel said.

"This way if you please," said Levinson, descending.

Isaac assisted his father up.

"Take him to an institution," Fishbein advised over the marble balustrade. He ran quickly up the stairs and they were at once outside, buffeted by winds.

The walk to the subway was tedious. The wind blew mournfully. Mendel, breathless, glanced furtively at shadows. Isaac, clutching his peanuts in his frozen fist, clung to his father's side. They entered a small park to rest for a minute on a stone bench under a leafless two-branched tree. The thick right branch was raised, the thin left one hung down. A very pale moon rose slowly. So did a stranger as they approached the bench.

"Gut yuntif," he said hoarsely.

Mendel, drained of blood, waved his wasted arms. Isaac yowled sickly. Then a bell chimed and it was only ten. Mendel let out a piercing anguished cry as the bearded

stranger disappeared into the bushes. A policeman came running, and though he beat
the bushes with his nightstick, could turn up nothing. Mendel and Isaac hurried out
of the little park. When Mendel glanced back the dead tree had its thin arm raised,
the thick one down. He moaned.

They boarded a trolley, stopping at the home of a former friend, but he had died
years ago. On the same block they went into a cafeteria and ordered two fried eggs
for Isaac. The tables were crowded except where a heavy-set man sat eating soup with
kasha. After one look at him they left in haste, although Isaac wept.

Mendel had another address on a slip of paper but the house was too far away, in
Queens, so they stood in a doorway shivering.

What can I do, he frantically thought, in one short hour?

He remembered the furniture in the house. It was junk but might bring a few dollars.
"Come, Isaac." They went once more to the pawnbroker's to talk to him, but the shop
was dark and an iron gate—rings and gold watches glinting through it—was drawn
tight across his place of business.

They huddled behind a telephone pole, both freezing. Isaac whimpered.

"See the big moon, Isaac. The whole sky is white."

He pointed but Isaac wouldn't look.

Mendel dreamed for a minute of the sky lit up, long sheets of light in all directions.
Under the sky, in California, sat Uncle Leo drinking tea with lemon. Mendel felt warm
but woke up cold.

Across the street stood an ancient brick synagogue.

He pounded on the huge door but no one appeared. He waited till he had breath
and desperately knocked again. At last there were footsteps within, and the synagogue
door creaked open on its massive brass hinges.

A darkly dressed sexton, holding a dripping candle, glared at them.

"Who knocks this time of night with so much noise on the synagogue door?"

Mendel told the sexton his troubles. "Please, I would like to speak to the rabbi."

"The rabbi is an old man. He sleeps now. His wife won't let you see him. Go home
and come back tomorrow."

"To tomorrow I said goodbye already. I am a dying man."

Though the sexton seemed doubtful he pointed to an old wooden house next door.
"In there he lives." He disappeared into the synagogue with his lit candle casting
shadows around him.

Mendel, with Isaac clutching his sleeve, went up the wooden steps and rang the bell.
After five minutes a big-faced, gray-haired bulky woman came out on the porch with
a torn robe thrown over her nightdress. She emphatically said the rabbi was sleeping
and could not be waked.

But as she was insisting, the rabbi himself tottered to the door. He listened a minute
and said, "Who wants to see me let them come in."

They entered a cluttered room. The rabbi was an old skinny man with bent shoulders
and a wisp of white beard. He wore a flannel nightgown and black skullcap; his feet
were bare.

"Vey is mir," his wife muttered. "Put on shoes or tomorrow comes sure pneumonia."
She was a woman with a big belly, years younger than her husband. Staring at Isaac,
she turned away.

Mendel apologetically related his errand. "All I need more is thirty-five dollars."

"Thirty-five?" said the rabbi's wife. "Why not thirty-five thousand? Who has so much money? My husband is a poor rabbi. The doctors take away every penny."

"Dear friend," said the rabbi, "if I had I would give you."

"I got already seventy," Mendel said, heavy-hearted. "All I need more is thirty-five."

"God will give you," said the rabbi.

"In the grave," said Mendel. "I need tonight. Come, Isaac."

"Wait," called the rabbi.

He hurried inside, came out with a fur-lined caftan, and handed it to Mendel.

"Yascha," shrieked his wife, "not your new coat!"

"I got my old one. Who needs two coats for one body?"

"Yascha, I am screaming—"

"Who can go among poor people, tell me, in a new coat?"

"Yascha," she cried, "what can this man do with your coat? He needs tonight the money. The pawnbrokers are asleep."

"So let him wake them up."

"No." She grabbed the coat from Mendel.

He held on to a sleeve, wrestling her for the coat. Her I know, Mendel thought. "Shylock," he muttered. Her eyes glittered.

The rabbi groaned and tottered dizzily. His wife cried out as Mendel yanked the coat from her hands.

"Run," cried the rabbi.

"Run, Isaac."

They ran out of the house and down the steps.

"Stop, you thief," called the rabbi's wife. The rabbi pressed both hands to his temples and fell to the floor.

"Help!" his wife wept. "Heart attack! Help!"

But Mendel and Isaac ran through the streets with the rabbi's new fur-lined caftan. After them noiselessly ran Ginzburg.

It was very late when Mendel bought the train ticket in the only booth open.

There was no time to stop for a sandwich so Isaac ate his peanuts and they hurried to the train in the vast deserted station.

"So in the morning," Mendel gasped as they ran, "there comes a man that he sells sandwiches and coffee. Eat but get change. When reaches California the train, will be waiting for you on the station Uncle Leo. If you don't recognize him he will recognize you. Tell him I send best regards."

But when they arrived at the gate to the platform it was shut, the light out.

Mendel, groaning, beat on the gate with his fists.

"Too late," said the uniformed ticket collector, a bulky, bearded man with hairy nostrils and a fishy smell.

He pointed to the station clock. "Already past twelve."

"But I see standing there still the train," Mendel said, hopping in his grief.

"It just left—in one more minute."

"A minute is enough. Just open the gate."

"Too late I told you."

Mendel socked his bony chest with both hands. "With my whole heart I beg you this little favor."

"Favors you had enough already. For you the train is gone. You shoulda been dead already at midnight. I told you that yesterday. This is the best I can do."

"Ginzburg!" Mendel shrank from him.

"Who else?" The voice was metallic, eyes glittered, the expression amused.

"For myself," the old man begged, "I don't ask a thing. But what will happen to my boy?"

Ginzburg shrugged slightly. "What will happen happens. This isn't my responsibility. I got enough to think about without worrying about somebody on one cylinder."

"What then is your responsibility?"

"To create conditions. To make happen what happens. I ain't in the anthropomorphic business."

"Whatever business you in, where is your pity?"

"This ain't my commodity. The law is the law."

"Which law is this?"

"The cosmic universal law, goddamit, the one I got to follow myself."

"What kind of a law is it?" cried Mendel. "For God's sake, don't you understand what I went through in my life with this poor boy? Look at him. For thirty-nine years, since the day he was born, I wait for him to grow up, but he don't. Do you understand what this means in a father's heart? Why don't you let him go to his uncle?" His voice had risen and he was shouting.

Isaac mewled loudly.

"Better calm down or you'll hurt somebody's feelings," Ginzburg said with a wink toward Isaac.

"All my life," Mendel cried, his body trembling, "what did I have? I was poor. I suffered from my health. When I worked I worked too hard. When I didn't work was worse. My wife died a young woman. But I didn't ask from anybody nothing. Now I ask a small favor. Be so kind, Mr. Ginzburg."

The ticket collector was picking his teeth with a match stick.

"You ain't the only one, my friend, some got it worse than you. That's how it goes in this country."

"You dog you." Mendel lunged at Ginzburg's throat and began to choke. "You bastard, don't you understand what it means human?"

They struggled nose to nose. Ginzburg, though his astonished eyes bulged, began to laugh. "You pipsqueak nothing. I'll freeze you to pieces."

His eyes lit in rage and Mendel felt an unbearable cold like an icy dagger invading his body, all of his parts shriveling.

Now I die without helping Isaac.

A crowd gathered. Isaac yelped in fright.

Clinging to Ginzburg in his last agony, Mendel saw reflected in the ticket collector's eyes the depth of his terror. But he saw that Ginzburg, staring at himself in Mendel's eyes, saw mirrored in them the extent of his own awful wrath. He beheld a shimmering, starry, blinding light that produced darkness.

Ginzburg looked astounded. "Who me?"

His grip on the squirming old man slowly loosened, and Mendel, his heart barely beating, slumped to the ground.

"Go," Ginzburg muttered, "take him to the train."

"Let pass," he commanded a guard.

The crowd parted. Isaac helped his father up and they tottered down the steps to the platform where the train waited, lit and ready to go.

Mendel found Isaac a coach seat and hastily embraced him. "Help Uncle Leo, Isaakil. Also remember your father and mother."

"Be nice to him," he said to the conductor. "Show him where everything is."

He waited on the platform until the train began slowly to move. Isaac sat at the edge of his seat, his face strained in the direction of his journey. When the train was gone, Mendel ascended the stairs to see what had become of Ginzburg.

JEAN STAFFORD
[b. 1915]

Bad Characters

Up until I learned my lesson in a very bitter way, I never had more than one friend at a time, and my friendships, though ardent, were short. When they ended and I was sent packing in unforgetting indignation, it was always my fault; I would swear vilely in front of a girl I knew to be pious and prim (by the time I was eight, the most grandiloquent gangster could have added nothing to my vocabulary—I had an awful tongue), or I would call a Tenderfoot Scout a sissy or make fun of athletics to the daughter of the high-school coach. These outbursts came without plan; I would simply one day, in the middle of a game of Russian bank or a hike or a conversation, be possessed with a passion to be by myself, and my lips instantly and without warning would accommodate me. My friend was never more surprised than I was when this irrevocable slander, this terrible, talented invective, came boiling out of my mouth.

Afterward, when I had got the solitude I had wanted, I was dismayed, for I did not like it. Then I would sadly finish the game of cards as if someone were still across the table from me; I would sit down on the mesa and through a glaze of tears would watch my friend departing with outraged strides; mournfully, I would talk to myself. Because I had already alienated everyone I knew, I then had nowhere to turn, so a famine set in and I would have no companion but Muff, the cat, who loathed all human beings except, significantly, me—truly. She bit and scratched the hands that fed her, she arched her back like a Halloween cat if someone kindly tried to pet her, she hissed, laid her ears flat to her skull, growled, fluffed up her tail into a great bush and flailed it like a bullwhack. But she purred for me, she patted me with her paws, keeping her claws in their velvet scabbards. She was not only an ill-natured cat, she was also badly dressed. She was a calico, and the distribution of her colors was a mess; she looked as if she had been left out in the rain and her paint had run. She had a Roman nose as the result of some early injury, her tail was skinny, she had a perfectly venomous look in her eye. My family said—my family discriminated against me—that I was much closer kin to Muff than I was to any of them. To tease me into a tantrum, my brother Jack and my sister Stella often called me Kitty instead of Emily. Little Tess did not dare, because she knew I'd chloroform her if she did. Jack, the meanest boy I have ever known in my life, called me Polecat and talked about my mania for fish, which, it so happened, I despised. The name would have been far more appropriate for *him,* since he trapped skunks up in the foothills—we lived in Adams, Colorado—and quite often, because he was careless and foolhardy, his clothes had to be buried, and even when that was done, he sometimes was sent home from school on the complaint of girls sitting next to him.

Along about Christmastime when I was eleven, I was making a snowman with Virgil Meade in his backyard, and all of a sudden, just as we had got around to the right arm, I had to be alone. So I called him a son of a sea cook, said it was common knowledge that his mother had bedbugs and that his father, a dentist and the deputy marshal, was a bootlegger on the side. For a moment, Virgil was too aghast to speak—a little earlier we had agreed to marry someday and become millionaires—and then, with a bellow of fury, he knocked me down and washed my face in snow. I saw stars, and black balls bounced before my eyes. When finally he let me up, we were both crying, and he hollered that if I didn't get off his property that instant, his father would arrest me and send me to Canon City. I trudged slowly home, half frozen, critically sick at heart. So it was old Muff again for me for quite some time. Old Muff, that is, until I met Lottie Jump, although "met" is a euphemism for the way I first encountered her.

I saw Lottie for the first time one afternoon in our own kitchen, stealing a chocolate cake. Stella and Jack had not come home from school yet—not having my difficult disposition, they were popular, and they were at their friends' houses, pulling taffy, I suppose, making popcorn balls, playing casino, having fun—and my mother had taken Tess with her to visit a friend in one of the T.B. sanitariums. I was alone in the house, and making a funny-looking Christmas card, although I had no one to send it to. When I heard someone in the kitchen, I thought it was Mother home early, and I went out to ask her why the green pine tree I had pasted on a square of red paper looked as if it were falling down. And there, instead of Mother and my baby sister, was this pale, conspicuous child in the act of lifting the glass cover from the devil's-food my mother had taken out of the oven an hour before and set on the plant shelf by the window. The child had her back to me, and when she heard my footfall, she wheeled with an amazing look of fear and hatred on her pinched and pasty face. Simultaneously, she put the cover over the cake again, and then she stood motionless as if she were under a spell.

I was scared, for I was not sure what was happening, and anyhow it gives you a turn to find a stranger in the kitchen in the middle of the afternoon, even if the stranger is only a skinny child in a moldy coat and sopping-wet basketball shoes. Between us there was a lengthy silence, but there was a great deal of noise in the room: the alarm clock ticked smugly; the teakettle simmered patiently on the back of the stove; Muff, cross at having been waked up, thumped her tail against the side of the terrarium in the window where she had been sleeping—contrary to orders—among the geraniums This went on, it seemed to me, for hours and hours while that tall, sickly girl and I confronted each other. When, after a long time, she did open her mouth, it was to tell a prodigious lie. "I came to see if you'd like to play with me," she said. I think she sighed and stole a sidelong and regretful glance at the cake.

Beggars cannot be choosers, and I had been missing Virgil so sorely, as well as all those other dear friends forever lost to me, that in spite of her flagrance (she had never clapped eyes on me before, she had had no way of knowing there was a creature of my age in the house—she had come in like a hobo to steal my mother's cake), I was flattered and consoled. I asked her name and, learning it, believed my ears no better than my eyes: Lottie Jump. What on earth! What on earth—you surely will agree with me—and yet when I told her mine, Emily Vanderpool, she laughed until she coughed and gasped. "Beg pardon," she said. "Names like them always hit my funny bone. There was this towhead boy in school named Delbert Saxonfield." I saw no connection and I was insulted (what's so funny about Vanderpool, I'd like to know), but Lottie Jump was, technically, my guest and I *was* lonesome, so I asked her, since she had spoken of playing with me, if she knew how to play Andy-I-Over. She said "Naw." It turned out that she did not know how to play any games at all; she couldn't do anything and didn't want to do anything; her only recreation and her only gift was, and always had been, stealing. But this I did not know at the time.

As it happened, it was too cold and snowy to play outdoors that day anyhow, and after I had run through my list of indoor games and Lottie had shaken her head at all of them (when I spoke of Parcheesi, she went "Ugh!" and pretended to be sick), she suggested that we look through my mother's bureau drawers. This did not strike me as strange at all, for it was one of my favorite things to do, and I led the way to Mother's bedroom without a moment's hesitation. I loved the smell of the lavender she kept in gauze bags among her chamois gloves and linen handkerchiefs and filmy scarves; there was a pink fascinator knitted of something as fine as spider's thread, and it made me go quite soft—I wasn't soft as a rule, I was as hard as nails and I gave my mother a rough time—to think of her wearing it around her head as she waltzed on the ice in the bygone days. We examined stockings, nightgowns, camisoles, strings of beads, and mosaic pins, keepsake buttons from dresses worn on memorial occasions, tortoiseshell combs, and a transformation made from Aunt Joey's hair when she had racily had it bobbed. Lottie admired particularly a blue cloisonné perfume flask with ferns and peacocks on it. "Hey," she said, "this sure is cute. I like thing-daddies like this here." But very abruptly she got bored and said, "Let's talk instead. In the front room." I agreed, a little perplexed this time, because I had been about to show her a remarkable powder box that played *The Blue Danube*. We went into the parlor, where Lottie looked at her image in the pier glass for quite a while and with great absorption, as if she had never seen herself before. Then she moved over to the window seat and knelt on it, looking out at the front walk. She kept her hands in the pockets of her thin dark-red coat; once she took out one of her dirty paws to rub her nose for a minute and I saw a bulge in that pocket, like a bunch of jackstones. I know now that it wasn't jackstones, it was my mother's perfume flask; I thought at the time her hands were cold and that that was why she kept them put away, for I had noticed that she had no mittens.

Lottie did most of the talking, and while she talked, she never once looked at me but kept her eyes fixed on the approach to our house. She told me that her family had come to Adams a month before from Muskogee, Oklahoma, where her father, before he got tuberculosis, had been a brakeman on the Frisco. Now they lived down by Arapahoe Creek, on the west side of town, in one of the cottages of a wretched settlement made up of people so poor and so sick—for in nearly every ramshackle house someone was coughing himself to death—that each time I went past I blushed with guilt because my shoes were sound and my coat was warm and I was well. I wished that Lottie had not told me where she lived, but she was not aware of any pathos in her family's situation, and, indeed, it was with a certain boastfulness that she told me her mother was the short-order cook at the Comanche Café (she pronounced this word in one syllable), which I knew was the dirtiest, darkest, smelliest place in town, patronized by coal miners who never washed their faces and sometimes had such dangerous fights after drinking dago red that the sheriff had to come. Laughing, Lottie told me that her mother was half Indian, and, laughing even harder, she said that her brother didn't have any brains and had never been to school. She herself was eleven years old, but she was only in the third grade, because teachers had always had it in for her—making her go to the blackboard and all like that when she was tired. She hated school—she went to Ashton, on North Hill, and that was why I had never seen her, for I went to Carlyle Hill—and she especially hated the teacher, Miss Cudahy, who had a head shaped like a pine cone and who had killed several people with her ruler. Lottie loved the movies ("Not them Western ones or the ones with apes in," she said. "Ones about hugging and kissing. I love it when they die in that big old soft bed with the curtains up top, and he comes in and says 'Don't leave me, Marguerite de la Mar' "), and she loved to ride in cars. She loved Mr. Goodbars, and if there was one thing she despised worse than another it was tapioca. ("Pa calls it fish eyes. He calls floating island horse spit. He's a big piece of cheese. I hate him.") She did not like cats (Muff was now sitting on the mantelpiece, glaring like an owl); she kind of liked snakes—except cottonmouths and rattlers—because she found them kind of funny; she had once seen a goat eat a tin can. She said that one of these days she would take me downtown— it was a slowpoke town, she said, a one-horse burg (I had never heard such gaudy, cynical talk and was trying to memorize it all)—if I would get some money for the trolley fare; she hated to walk, and I ought to be proud that she had walked all the way from Arapahoe Creek today for the sole solitary purpose of seeing me.

Seeing our freshly baked dessert in the window was a more likely story, but I did not care, for I was deeply impressed by this bold, sassy girl from Oklahoma and greatly admired the poise with which she aired her prejudices. Lottie Jump was certainly nothing to look at. She was tall and made of skin and bones; she was evilly ugly, and her clothes were a disgrace, not just ill-fitting and old and ragged but dirty, unmention- ably so; clearly she did not wash much or brush her teeth, which were notched like a saw, and small and brown (it crossed my mind that perhaps she chewed tobacco); her long, lank hair looked as if it might have nits. But she had personality. She made me think of one of those self-contained dogs whose home is where his handout is and who travels alone but, if it suits him to, will become the leader of a pack. She was aloof, never looking at me, but amiable in the way she kept calling me "kid." I liked her enormously, and presently I told her so.

At this, she turned around and smiled at me. Her smile was the smile of a jack-o'- lantern—high, wide, and handsome. When it was over, no trace of it remained. "Well, that's keen, kid, and I like you, too," she said in her downright Muskogee accent. She gave me a long, appraising look. Her eyes were the color of mud. "Listen, kid, how much do you like me?"

"I like you loads, Lottie," I said. "Better than anybody else, and I'm not kidding."

"You want to be pals?"

"Do I!" I cried. So *there,* Virgil Meade, you big fat hootnanny, I thought.

"All right, kid, we'll be pals." And she held out her hand for me to shake. I had to go and get it, for she did not alter her position on the window seat. It was a dry, cold hand, and the grip was severe, with more feeling of bones in it than friendliness.

Lottie turned and scanned our path and scanned the sidewalk beyond, and then she said, in a lower voice, "Do you know how to lift?"

"Lift?" I wondered if she meant to lift *her*. I was sure I could do it, since she was so skinny, but I couldn't imagine why she would want me to.

"Shoplift, I mean. Like in the five-and-dime."

I did not know the term, and Lottie scowled at my stupidity.

"*Steal,* for crying in the beer!" she said impatiently. This she said so loudly that Muff jumped down from the mantel and left the room in contempt.

I was thrilled to death and shocked to pieces. "Stealing is a sin," I said. "You get put in jail for it."

"Ish ka bibble! I should worry if it's a sin or not," said Lottie, with a shrug. "And they'll never put a smart old whatsis like *me* in jail. It's fun, stealing is—it's a picnic. I'll teach you if you want to learn, kid." Shamelessly she winked at me and grinned again. (That grin! She could have taken it off her face and put it on the table.) And she added, "If you don't, we can't be pals, because lifting is the only kind of playing I like. I hate those dumb games like Statues. Kick-the-Can—phooey!"

I was torn between agitation (I went to Sunday school and knew already about morality; Judge Bay, a crabby old man who loved to punish sinners, was a friend of my father's and once had given Jack a lecture on the criminal mind when he came to call and found Jack looking up an answer in his arithmetic book) and excitement over the daring invitation to misconduct myself in so perilous a way. My life, on reflection, looked deadly prim; all I'd ever done to vary the monotony of it was to swear. I knew that Lottie Jump meant what she said—that I could have her friendship only on her terms (plainly, she had gone it alone for a long time and could go it alone for the rest of her life)—and although I trembled like an aspen and my heart went pitapat, I said, "I want to be pals with you, Lottie."

"All right, Vanderpool," said Lottie, and got off the window seat. "I wouldn't go braggin' about it if I was you. I wouldn't go telling my ma and pa and the next-door neighbor that you and Lottie Jump are going down to the five-and-dime next Saturday aft and lift us some nice rings and garters and things like that. I mean it, kid." And she drew the back of her forefinger across her throat and made a dire face.

"I won't. I promise I won't. My *gosh,* why would I?"

"That's the ticket," said Lottie, with a grin. "I'll meet you at the trolley shelter at two o'clock. You have the money. For both down and up. I ain't going to climb up that ornery hill after I've had my fun."

"Yes, Lottie," I said. Where was I going to get twenty cents? I was going to have to start stealing before she even taught me how. Lottie was facing the center of the room, but she had eyes in the back of her head, and she whirled around back to the window; my mother and Tess were turning in our front path.

"Back way," I whispered, and in a moment Lottie was gone; the swinging door that usually squeaked did not make a sound as she vanished through it. I listened and I never heard the back door open and close. Nor did I hear her, in a split second, lift the glass cover and remove that cake designed to feed six people.

I was restless and snappish between Wednesday afternoon and Saturday. When Mother found the cake was gone, she scolded me for not keeping my ears cocked. She assumed, naturally, that a tramp had taken it, for she knew I hadn't eaten it; I never ate anything if I could help it (except for raw potatoes, which I loved) and had been known as a problem feeder from the beginning of my life. At first it occurred to me to have a tantrum and bring her around to my point of view: my tantrums scared the living daylights out of her because my veins stood out and I turned blue and couldn't get my breath. But I rejected this for a more sensible plan. I said, "It just so happens I didn't hear anything. But if I had, I suppose you wish I had gone out in the kitchen and let the robber cut me up into a million little tiny pieces with his sword. You wouldn't even bury me. You'd just put me on the dump. *I* know who's wanted in this family and who isn't." Tears of sorrow, not of anger, came in powerful tides and I groped blindly to the bedroom I shared with Stella, where I lay on my bed and shook with big, silent *weltschmerzlich* sobs. Mother followed me immediately, and so did Tess, and both of them comforted me and told me how much they loved me. I said they didn't; they said they did. Presently, I got a headache, as I always did when I cried, so I got to have an aspirin and a cold cloth on my head, and when Jack and Stella came home, they had to be quiet. I heard Jack say, "Emily Vanderpool is the biggest polecat in the U.S.A. Whyn't she go in the kitchen and say, 'Hands up'? He would lit out." And Mother said, "Sh-h-h! You don't want your sister to be sick, do you?" Muff, not realizing that Lottie had replaced her, came in and curled up at my thigh, purring lustily; I found myself glad that she had left the room before Lottie Jump made her proposition to me, and in gratitude I stroked her unattractive head.

Other things happened. Mother discovered the loss of her perfume flask and talked about nothing else at meals for two whole days. Luckily, it did not occur to her that it had been stolen—she simply thought she had mislaid it—but her monomania got on my father's nerves and he lashed out at her and at the rest of us. And because I was the cause of it all and my conscience was after me with red-hot pokers, I finally *had* to have a tantrum. I slammed my fork down in the middle of supper on the second day and yelled, "If you don't stop fighting, I'm going to kill myself. Yammer, yammer, nag, nag!" And I put my fingers in my ears and squeezed my eyes tight shut and screamed so the whole county could hear, "Shut *up!*" And then I lost my breath and began to turn blue. Daddy hastily apologized to everyone, and Mother said she was sorry for carrying on so about a trinket that had nothing but sentimental value—she was just vexed with herself for being careless, that was all, and she wasn't going to say another word about it.

I never heard so many references to stealing and cake, and even to Oklahoma (ordinarily no one mentioned Oklahoma once in a month of Sundays) and the ten-cent store as I did throughout those next days. I myself once made a ghastly slip and said something to Stella about "the five-and-dime." "The five-and-*dime!*" she exclaimed. "Where'd you get *that* kind of talk? Do you by any chance have reference to the *ten-cent store?*"

The worst of all was Friday night—the very night before I was to meet Lottie Jump —when Judge Bay came to play two-handed pinochle with Daddy. The Judge, a giant in intimidating haberdashery—for some reason, the white piping on his vest bespoke, for me, handcuffs and prison bars—and with an aura of disapproval for almost every-thing on earth except what pertained directly to himself, was telling Daddy, before they began their game, about the infamous vandalism that had been going on among the college students. "I have reason to believe that there are girls in this gang as well as boys," he said. "They ransack vacant houses and take everything. In one house on

Pleasant Street, up there by the Catholic Church, there wasn't anything to take, so they took the kitchen sink. Wasn't a question of taking everything *but*—they took the kitchen sink."

"What ever would they want with a kitchen sink?" asked my mother.

"Mischief," replied the Judge. "If we ever catch them and if they come within my jurisdiction, I can tell you I will give them no quarter. A thief, in my opinion, is the lowest of the low."

Mother told about the chocolate cake. By now, the fiction was so factual in my mind that each time I thought of it I saw a funny-paper bum in baggy pants held up by rope, a hat with holes through which tufts of hair stuck up, shoes from which his toes protruded, a disreputable stubble on his face; he came up beneath the open window where the devil's food was cooling and he stole it and hotfooted it for the woods, where his companion was frying a small fish in a beat-up skillet. It never crossed my mind any longer that Lottie Jump had hooked that delicious cake.

Judge Bay was properly impressed. "If you will steal a chocolate cake, if you will steal a kitchen sink, you will steal diamonds and money. The small child who pilfers a penny from his mother's pocketbook has started down a path that may lead him to holding up a bank."

It was a good thing I had no homework that night, for I could not possibly have concentrated. We were all sent to our rooms, because the pinochle players had to have absolute quiet. I spent the evening doing cross-stitch. I was making a bureau runner for a Christmas present; as in the case of the Christmas card, I had no one to give it to, but now I decided to give it to Lottie Jump's mother. Stella was reading *Black Beauty*, crying. It was an interminable evening. Stella went to bed first; I saw to that, because I didn't want her lying there awake listening to me talking in my sleep. Besides, I didn't want her to see me tearing open the cardboard box—the one in the shape of a church, which held my Christmas Sunday-school offering. Over the door of the church was this shaming legend: "My mite for the poor widow." When Stella had begun to grind her teeth in her first deep sleep, I took twenty cents away from the poor widow, whoever she was (the owner of the kitchen sink, no doubt), for the trolley fare, and secreted it and the remaining three pennies in the pocket of my middy. I wrapped the money well in a handkerchief and buttoned the pocket and hung my skirt over the middy. And then I tore the paper church into bits—the heavens opened and Judge Bay came toward me with a double-barrelled shotgun—and hid the bits under a pile of pajamas. I did not sleep one wink. Except that I must have, because of the stupendous nightmares that kept wrenching the flesh off my skeleton and caused me to come close to perishing of thirst; once I fell out of bed and hit my head on Stella's ice skates. I would have waked her up and given her a piece of my mind for leaving them in such a lousy place, but then I remembered: I wanted *no* commotion of any kind.

I couldn't eat breakfast and I couldn't eat lunch. Old Johnny-on-the-spot Jack kept saying, "*Poor* Polecat. Polecat wants her fish for dinner." Mother made an abortive attempt to take my temperature. And when all that hullabaloo subsided, I was nearly in the soup because Mother asked me to mind Tess while she went to the sanitarium to see Mrs. Rogers, who, all of a sudden, was too sick to have anyone but grownups near her. Stella couldn't stay with the baby, because she had to go to ballet, and Jack couldn't, because he had to go up to the mesa and empty his traps. ("No, they *can't* wait. You want my skins to rot in this hot-one-day-cold-the-next weather?") I was arguing and whining when the telephone rang. Mother went to answer it and came back with a look of great sadness; Mrs. Rogers, she had learned, had had another hemorrhage. So Mother would not be going to the sanitarium after all and I needn't stay with Tess.

By the time I left the house, I was as cross as a bear. I felt awful about the widow's mite and I felt awful for being mean about staying with Tess, for Mrs. Rogers was a kind old lady, in a cozy blue hug-me-tight and an old-fangled boudoir cap, dying here all alone; she was a friend of Grandma's and had lived just down the street from her in Missouri, and all in the world Mrs. Rogers wanted to do was go back home and lie down in her own big bedroom in her own big, high-ceilinged house and have Grandma and other members of the Eastern Star come in from time to time to say hello. But they wouldn't let her go home; they were going to kill or cure her. I could not help feeling that my hardness of heart and evil of intention had had a good deal to do with her new crisis; right at the very same minute I had been saying "Does that old Mrs. Methuselah *always* have to spoil my fun?" the poor wasted thing was probably coughing up her blood and saying to the nurse, "Tell Emily Vanderpool not to mind me, she can run and play."

I had a bad character, I know that, but my badness never gave me half the enjoyment Jack and Stella thought it did. A good deal of the time I wanted to eat lye. I was certainly having no fun now, thinking of Mrs. Rogers and of depriving that poor widow of bread and milk; what if this penniless woman without a husband had a dog to feed, too? Or a baby? And besides, I didn't want to go downtown to steal anything from the ten-cent store; I didn't want to see Lottie Jump again—not really, for I knew in my bones that that girl was trouble with a capital "T." And still, in our short meeting she had mesmerized me; I would think about her style of talking and the expert way she had made off with the perfume flask and the cake (how had she carried the cake through the streets without being noticed?) and be bowled over, for the part of me that did not love God was a black-hearted villain. And apart from these considerations, I had some sort of idea that if I did not keep my appointment with Lottie Jump, she would somehow get revenge; she had seemed a girl of purpose. So, revolted and fascinated, brave and lily-livered, I plodded along through the snow in my flopping galoshes up toward the Chautauqua, where the trolley stop was. On my way, I passed Virgil Meade's house; there was not just a snowman, there was a whole snow family in the back yard, and Virgil himself was throwing a stick for his dog. I was delighted to see that he was alone.

Lottie, who was sitting on a bench in the shelter eating a Mr. Goodbar, looked the same as she had the other time except that she was wearing an amazing hat. I think I had expected her to have a black handkerchief over the lower part of her face or to be wearing a Jesse James waistcoat. But I had never thought of a hat. It was felt; it was the color of cooked meat; it had some flowers appliquéd on the front of it; it had no brim, but rose straight up to a very considerable height, like a monument. It sat so low on her forehead and it was so tight that it looked, in a way, like part of her.

"How's every little thing, bub?" she said, licking her candy wrapper.

"Fine, Lottie," I said, freshly awed.

A silence fell. I drank some water from the drinking fountain, sat down, fastened my galoshes, and unfastened them again.

"My mother's teeth grow wrong way to," said Lottie, and showed me what she meant: the lower teeth were in front of the upper ones. "That so-called trolley car takes its own sweet time. This town is blah."

To save the honor of my home town, the trolley came scraping and groaning up the hill just then, its bell clanging with an idiotic frenzy, and ground to a stop. Its broad, proud cowcatcher was filled with dirty snow, in the middle of which rested a tomato can, put there, probably, by somebody who was bored to death and couldn't think of anything else to do—I did a lot of pointless things like that on lonesome Saturday afternoons. It was the custom of this trolley car, a rather mysterious one, to pause at the shelter for five minutes while the conductor, who was either Mr. Jansen or Mr. Peck, depending on whether it was the A.M. run or the P.M., got out and stretched and smoked and spit. Sometimes the passengers got out, too, acting like sightseers whose destination was this sturdy stucco gazebo instead of, as it really was, the Piggly Wiggly or the Nelson Dry. You expected them to take snapshots of the drinking fountain or of the Chautauqua meeting house up on the hill. And when they all got back in the car, you expected them to exchange intelligent observations on the aborigines and the ruins they had seen.

Today there were no passengers, and as soon as Mr. Peck got out and began staring at the mountains as if he had never seen them before while he made himself a cigarette, Lottie, in her tall hat (was it something like the Inspector's hat in the Katzenjammer Kids?), got into the car, motioning me to follow. I put our nickels in the empty box and joined her on the very last double seat. It was only then that she mapped out the plan for the afternoon, in a low but still insouciant voice. The hat—she did not apologize for it, she simply referred to it as "my hat"—was to be the repository of whatever we stole. In the future, it would be advisable for me to have one like it. (How? Surely it was unique. The flowers, I saw on closer examination, were tulips, but they were blue, and a very unsettling shade of blue.) I was to engage a clerk on one side of the counter, asking her the price of, let's say, a tube of Daggett & Ramsdell vanishing cream, while Lottie would lift a round comb or a barrette or a hair net or whatever on the other side. Then, at a signal, I would decide against the vanishing cream and would move on to the next counter that she indicated. The signal was interesting; it was to be the raising of her hat from the rear—"like I've got the itch and gotta scratch," she said. I was relieved that I was to have no part in the actual stealing, and I was touched that Lottie, who was going to do all the work, said we would "go halvers" on the take. She asked me if there was anything in particular I wanted—she herself had nothing special in mind and was going to shop around first—and I said I would like some rubber gloves. This request was entirely spontaneous; I had never before in my life thought of rubber gloves in one way or another, but a psychologist—or Judge Bay—might have said that this was most significant and that I was planning at that moment to go on from petty larceny to bigger game, armed with a weapon on which I wished to leave no fingerprints.

On the way downtown, quite a few people got on the trolley, and they all gave us such peculiar looks that I was chickenhearted until I realized it must be Lottie's hat they were looking at. No wonder. I kept looking at it myself out of the corner of my eye; it was like a watermelon standing on end. No, it was like a tremendous test tube. On this trip—a slow one, for the trolley pottered through that part of town in a desultory, neighborly way, even going into areas where no one lived—Lottie told me some of the things she had stolen in Muskogee and here in Adams. They included a white satin prayer book (think of it!), Mr. Goodbars by the thousands (she had probably never paid for a Mr. Goodbar in her life), a dinner ring valued at two dollars, a strawberry emery, several cans of corn, some shoelaces, a set of poker chips, countless pencils, four spark plugs ("Pa had this old car, see, and it was broke, so we took 'er to get fixed; I'll build me a radio with 'em sometime—you know? Listen in on them ear muffs to Tulsa?"), a Boy Scout knife, and a Girl Scout folding cup. She made a regular practice of going through the pockets of the coats in the cloakroom every day at recess, but she had never found anything there worth a red cent and was about to give that up. Once, she had taken a gold pencil from a teacher's desk and had got caught —she was sure that this was one of the reasons she was only in the third grade. Of this unjust experience, she said, "The old hoot owl! If I was drivin' in a car on a lonesome stretch and she was settin' beside me, I'd wait till we got to a pile of gravel and then I'd stop and say, 'Git out, Miss Priss.' She'd git out, all right."

Since Lottie was so frank, I was emboldened at last to ask her what she had done with the cake. She faced me with her grin; this grin, in combination with the hat, gave me a surprise from which I have never recovered. "I ate it up," she said. "I went in your garage and sat on your daddy's old tires and ate it. It was pretty good."

There were two ten-cent stores side by side in our town, Kresge's and Woolworth's, and as we walked down the main street toward them, Lottie played with a Yo-Yo. Since the street was thronged with Christmas shoppers and farmers in for Saturday, this was no ordinary accomplishment; all in all, Lottie Jump was someone to be reckoned with. I cannot say that I was proud to be seen with her; the fact is that I hoped I would not meet anyone I knew, and I thanked my lucky stars that Jack was up in the hills with his dead skunks because if he had seen her with that lid and that Yo-Yo, I would never have heard the last of it. But in another way I *was* proud to be with her; in a smaller hemisphere, in one that included only her and me, I was swaggering—I felt like Somebody, marching along beside this lofty Somebody from Oklahoma who was going to hold up the dime store.

There is nothing like Woolworth's at Christmastime. It smells of peanut brittle and terrible chocolate candy, Djer-Kiss talcum powder and Ben Hur Perfume—smells sourly of tinsel and waxily of artificial poinsettias. The crowds are made up largely of children and women, with here and there a deliberative old man; the women are buying ribbons and wrappings and Christmas cards, and the children are buying asbestos pot holders for their mothers and, for their fathers, suède bookmarks with a burnt-in design that says "A good book is a good friend" or "Souvenir from the Garden of the Gods." It is very noisy. The salesgirls are forever ringing their bells and asking the floorwalker to bring them change for a five; babies in go-carts are screaming as parcels fall on their heads; the women, waving rolls of red tissue paper, try to attract the attention of the harried girl behind the counter. ("Miss! All I want is this one batch of the red. Can't I just give you the dime?" And the girl, beside herself, mottled with vexation, cries back, "Has to be rung up, Moddom, that's the rule.") There is pandemonium at the toy counter, where things are being tested by the customers—wound up, set off, tooted, pounded, made to say "Maaaah-Maaaah!" There is very little gaiety in the scene and, in fact, those baffled old men look as if they were walking over their own dead bodies, but there is an atmosphere of carnival, nevertheless, and as soon as Lottie and I entered the doors of Woolworth's golden-and-vermilion bedlam, I grew giddy and hot—not pleasantly so. The feeling, indeed, was distinctly disagreeable, like the beginning of a stomach upset.

Lottie gave me a nudge and said softly, "Go look at the envelopes. I want some rubber bands."

This counter was relatively uncrowded (the seasonal stationery supplies—the Christmas cards and wrapping paper and stickers—were at a separate counter), and I went around to examine some very beautiful letter paper; it was pale pink and it had a border of roses all around it. The clerk here was a cheerful middle-aged woman wearing an apron, and she was giving all her attention to a seedy old man who could not make up his mind between mucilage and paste. "Take your time, Dad," she said. "Compared to the rest of the girls, I'm on my vacation." The old man, holding a tube in one hand and a bottle in the other, looked at her vaguely and said, "I want it for stamps. Sometimes I write a letter and stamp it and then don't mail it and steam the stamp off. Must have ninety cents' worth of stamps like that." The woman laughed. "I know what you mean," she said. "I get mad and write a letter and then I tear it up." The old man gave her a condescending look and said, "That so? But I don't suppose yours are of a political nature." He bent his gaze again to the choice of adhesives.

This first undertaking was duck soup for Lottie. I did not even have to exchange a word with the woman; I saw Miss Fagin lift up *that hat* and give me the high sign, and we moved away, she down one aisle and I down the other, now and again catching a glimpse of each other through the throngs. We met at the foot of the second counter, where notions were sold.

"Fun, huh?" said Lottie, and I nodded, although I felt wholly dreary. "I want some crochet hooks," she said. "Price the rickrack."

This time the clerk was adding up her receipts and did not even look at me or at a woman who was angrily and in vain trying to buy a paper of pins. Out went Lottie's scrawny hand, up went her domed chimney. In this way for some time she bagged sitting birds: a tea strainer (there was no one at all at that counter), a box of Mrs. Carpenter's All Purpose Nails, the rubber gloves I had said I wanted, and four packages of mixed seeds. Now you have some idea of the size of Lottie Jump's hat.

I was nervous, not from being her accomplice but from being in this crowd on an empty stomach, and I was getting tired—we had been in the store for at least an hour —and the whole enterprise seemed pointless. There wasn't a thing in her hat I wanted —not even the rubber gloves. But in exact proportion as my spirits descended, Lottie's rose; clearly she had only been target-practicing and now she was moving in for the kill.

We met beside the books of paper dolls, for reconnaissance. "I'm gonna get me a pair of pearl beads," said Lottie. "You go fuss with the hairpins, hear?"

Luck, combined with her skill, would have stayed with Lottie, and her hat would have been a cornucopia by the end of the afternoon if, at the very moment her hand went out for the string of beads, that idiosyncrasy of mine had not struck me full force. I had never known it to come with so few preliminaries; probably this was so because I was oppressed by all the masses of bodies poking and pushing me, and all the open mouths breathing in my face. Anyhow, right then, at the crucial time, I *had to be alone*.

I stood staring down at the bone hairpins for a moment, and when the girl behind the counter said, "What kind does Mother want, hon? What color is Mother's hair?" I looked past her and across at Lottie and I said, "Your brother isn't the only one in your family that doesn't have any brains." The clerk, astonished, turned to look where I was looking and caught Lottie in the act of lifting up her hat to put the pearls inside. She had unwisely chosen a long strand and was having a little trouble; I had the nasty thought that it looked as if her brains were leaking out.

The clerk, not able to deal with this emergency herself, frantically punched her bell and cried, "Floorwalker! Mr. Bellamy! I've caught a thief!"

Momentarily there was a violent hush—then such a clamor as you have never heard. Bells rang, babies howled, crockery crashed to the floor as people stumbled in their rush to the arena.

Mr. Bellamy, nineteen years old but broad of shoulder and jaw, was instantly standing beside Lottie, holding her arm with one hand while with the other he removed her hat to reveal to the overjoyed audience that incredible array of merchandise. Her hair all wild, her face a mask of innocent bewilderment, Lottie Jump, the scurvy thing, pretended to be deaf and dumb. She pointed at the rubber gloves and then she pointed at me, and Mr. Bellamy, able at last to prove his mettle, said "Aha!" and, still holding Lottie, moved around the counter to me and grabbed *my* arm. He gave the hat to the clerk and asked her kindly to accompany him and his redhanded catch to the manager's office.

I don't know where Lottie is now—whether she is on the stage or in jail. If her performance after our arrest meant anything, the first is quite as likely as the second. (I never saw her again, and for all I know she lit out of town that night on a freight train. Or perhaps her whole family decamped as suddenly as they had arrived; ours was a most transient population. You can be sure I made no attempt to find her again, and for months I avoided going anywhere near Arapahoe Creek or North Hill.) She never said a word but kept making signs with her fingers, adlibbing the whole thing. They tested her hearing by shooting off a popgun right in her ear and she never batted an eyelid.

They called up my father, and he came over from the Safeway on the double. I heard very little of what he said because I was crying so hard, but one thing I did hear him say was "Well young lady, I guess you've seen to it that I'll have to part company with my good friend Judge Bay." I tried to defend myself, but it was useless. The manager, Mr. Bellamy, the clerk, and my father patted Lottie on the shoulder, and the clerk said, "Poor, afflicted child." For being a poor, afflicted child, they gave her a bag of hard candy, and she gave them the most fraudulent smile of gratitude, and slobbered a little, and shuffled out, holding her empty hat in front of her like a beggar-man. I hate Lottie Jump to this day, but I have to hand it to her—she was a genius.

The floorwalker would have liked to see me sentenced to the reform school for life, I am sure, but the manager said that considering this was my first offense, he would let my father attend to my punishment. The old-maid clerk, who looked precisely like Emmy Schmalz, clucked her tongue and shook her head at me. My father hustled me out of the office and out of the store and into the car and home, muttering the entire time; now and again I'd hear the words "morals" and "nowadays."

What's the use of telling the rest? You know what happened. Daddy on second thoughts decided not to hang his head in front of Judge Bay but to make use of his friendship in this time of need, and he took me to see the scary old curmudgeon at his house. All I remember of that long declamation, during which the Judge sat behind his desk never taking his eyes off me, was the warning "I want you to give this a great deal of thought, Miss. I want you to search and seek in the innermost corners of your conscience and root out every bit of badness." Oh, *him!* Why, listen, if I'd rooted out all the badness in me, there wouldn't have been anything left of me. My mother cried for days because she had nurtured an outlaw and was ashamed to show her face at the neighborhood store; my father was silent, and he often looked at me. Stella, who was a prig, said, "And to think you did it at *Christmas* time!" As for Jack—well, Jack a couple of times did not know how close he came to seeing glory when I had a butcher knife in my hand. It was Polecat this and Polecat that until I nearly went off my rocker. Tess, of course, didn't know what was going on, and asked so many questions that finally I told her to go to Helen Hunt Jackson in a savage tone of voice.

Good old Muff.

It is not true that you don't learn by experience. At any rate, I did that time. I began immediately to have two or three friends at a time—to be sure, because of the stigma on me, they were by no means the élite of Carlyle Hill Grade—and never again when that terrible need to be alone arose did I let fly. I would say, instead, "I've got a headache. I'll have to go home and take an aspirin," or "Gosh all hemlocks, I forgot —I've got to go to the dentist."

After the scandal died down, I got into the Campfire Girls. It was through pull, of course, since Stella had been a respected member for two years and my mother was a friend of the leader. But it turned out all right. Even Muff did not miss our periods of companionship, because about that time she grew up and started having literally millions of kittens.

FLANNERY O'CONNOR

[1925–1964]

Good Country People

Besides the neutral expression that she wore when she was alone, Mrs. Freeman had two others, forward and reverse, that she used for all her human dealings. Her forward expression was steady and driving like the advance of a heavy truck. Her eyes never swerved to left or right but turned as the story turned as if they followed a yellow line down the center of it. She seldom used the other expression because it was not often necessary for her to retract a statement, but when she did, her face came to a complete stop, there was an almost imperceptible movement of her black eyes, during which they seemed to be receding, and then the observer would see that Mrs. Freeman, though she might stand there as real as several grain sacks thrown on top of each other, was no longer there in spirit. As for getting anything across to her when this was the case, Mrs. Hopewell had given it up. She might talk her head off. Mrs. Freeman could never be brought to admit herself wrong on any point. She would stand there and if she could be brought to say anything, it was something like, "Well, I wouldn't of said it was and I wouldn't of said it wasn't," or letting her gaze range over the top kitchen shelf where there was an assortment of dusty bottles, she might remark, "I see you ain't ate many of them figs you put up last summer."

They carried on their most important business in the kitchen at breakfast. Every morning Mrs. Hopewell got up at seven o'clock and lit her gas heater and Joy's. Joy was her daughter, a large blonde girl who had an artificial leg. Mrs. Hopewell thought of her as a child though she was thirty-two years old and highly educated. Joy would get up while her mother was eating and lumber into the bathroom and slam the door, and before long, Mrs. Freeman would arrive at the back door. Joy would hear her mother call, "Come on in," and then they would talk for a while in low voices that were indistinguishable in the bathroom. By the time Joy came in, they had usually finished the weather report and were on one or the other of Mrs. Freeman's daughters, Glynese or Carramae. Joy called them Glycerin and Caramel. Glynese, a redhead, was eighteen and had many admirers; Carramae, a blonde, was only fifteen but already married and pregnant. She could not keep anything on her stomach. Every morning Mrs. Freeman told Mrs. Hopewell how many times she had vomited since the last report.

Mrs. Hopewell liked to tell people that Glynese and Carramae were two of the finest girls she knew and that Mrs. Freeman was a *lady* and that she was never ashamed to take her anywhere or introduce her to anybody they might meet. Then she would tell how she had happened to hire the Freemans in the first place and how they were a godsend to her and how she had had them four years. The reason for her keeping them so long was that they were not trash. They were good country people. She had telephoned the man whose name they had given as a reference and he had told her that Mr. Freeman was a good farmer but that his wife was the nosiest woman ever to walk the earth. "She's got to be into everything," the man said. "If she don't get there before the dust settles, you can bet she's dead, that's all. She'll want to know all your business. I can stand him real good," he had said, "but me nor my wife neither could have stood that woman one more minute on this place." That had put Mrs. Hopewell off for a few days.

She had hired them in the end because there were no other applicants but she had made up her mind beforehand exactly how she would handle the woman. Since she was the type who had to be into everything, then, Mrs. Hopewell had decided, she would not only let her be into everything, she would *see to it* that she was into everything—she would give her the responsibility of everything, she would put her in charge. Mrs. Hopewell had no bad qualities of her own but she was able to use other people's in such a constructive way that she never felt the lack. She had hired the Freemans and she had kept them four years.

Nothing is perfect. This was one of Mrs. Hopewell's favorite sayings. Another was: that is life! And still another, the most important, was: well, other people have their opinions too. She would make these statements, usually at the table, in a tone of gentle insistence as if no one held them but her, and the large hulking Joy, whose constant outrage had obliterated every expression from her face, would stare just a little to the side of her, her eyes icy blue, with the look of someone who has achieved blindness by an act of will and means to keep it.

When Mrs. Hopewell said to Mrs. Freeman that life was like that, Mrs. Freeman would say, "I always said so myself." Nothing had been arrived at by anyone that had not first been arrived at by her. She was quicker than Mr. Freeman. When Mrs. Hopewell said to her after they had been on the place a while, "You know, you're the wheel behind the wheel," and winked, Mrs. Freeman had said, "I know it. I've always been quick. It's some that are quicker than others."

"Everybody is different," Mrs. Hopewell said.

"Yes, most people is," Mrs. Freeman said.

"It takes all kinds to make the world."

"I always said it did myself."

The girl was used to this kind of dialogue for breakfast and more of it for dinner; sometimes they had it for supper too. When they had no guest they ate in the kitchen because that was easier. Mrs. Freeman always managed to arrive at some point during the meal and to watch them finish it. She would stand in the doorway if it were summer but in the winter she would stand with one elbow on top of the refrigerator and look down on them, or she would stand by the gas heater, lifting the back of her skirt slightly. Occasionally she would stand against the wall and roll her head from side to side. At no time was she in any hurry to leave. All this was very trying on Mrs. Hopewell but she was a woman of great patience. She realized that nothing is perfect and that in the Freemans she had good country people and that if, in this day and age, you get good country people, you had better hang onto them.

She had had plenty of experience with trash. Before the Freemans she had averaged one tenant family a year. The wives of these farmers were not the kind you would want to be around you for very long. Mrs. Hopewell, who had divorced her husband long ago, needed someone to walk over the fields with her; and when Joy had to be impressed for these services, her remarks were usually so ugly and her face so glum that Mrs. Hopewell would say, "If you can't come pleasantly, I don't want you at all," to which the girl, standing square and rigid-shouldered with her neck thrust slightly forward, would reply, "If you want me, here I am—LIKE I AM."

Mrs. Hopewell excused this attitude because of the leg (which had been shot off in a hunting accident when Joy was ten). It was hard for Mrs. Hopewell to realize that her child was thirty-two now and that for more than twenty years she had had only one leg. She thought of her still as a child because it tore her heart to think instead of the poor stout girl in her thirties who had never danced a step or had any *normal* good times. Her name was really Joy but as soon as she was twenty-one and away from home, she had had it legally changed. Mrs. Hopewell was certain that she had thought and thought until she had hit upon the ugliest name in any language. Then she had gone and had the beautiful name, Joy, changed without telling her mother until after she had done it. Her legal name was Hulga.

When Mrs. Hopewell thought the name, Hulga, she thought of the broad blank hull of a battleship. She would not use it. She continued to call her Joy to which the girl responded but in a purely mechanical way.

Hulga had learned to tolerate Mrs. Freeman, who saved her from taking walks with her mother. Even Glynese and Carramae were useful when they occupied attention that

might otherwise have been directed at her. At first she had thought she could not stand
Mrs. Freeman for she had found that it was not possible to be rude to her. Mrs. Freeman
would take on strange resentments and for days together she would be sullen but the
source of her displeasure was always obscure; a direct attack, a positive leer, blatant
ugliness to her face—these never touched her. And without warning one day, she began
calling her Hulga.

She did not call her that in front of Mrs. Hopewell who would have been incensed
but when she and the girl happened to be out of the house together, she would say
something and add the name Hulga to the end of it, and the big spectacled Joy-Hulga
would scowl and redden as if her privacy had been intruded upon. She considered the
name her personal affair. She had arrived at it first purely on the basis of its ugly sound
and then the full genius of its fitness had struck her. She had a vision of the name
working like the ugly sweating Vulcan who stayed in the furnace and to whom,
presumably, the goddess had to come when called. She saw it as the name of her highest
creative act. One of her major triumphs was that her mother had not been able to turn
her dust into Joy, but the greater one was that she had been able to turn it herself into
Hulga. However, Mrs. Freeman's relish for using the name only irritated her. It was
as if Mrs. Freeman's beady steel-pointed eyes had penetrated far enough behind her face
to reach some secret fact. Something about her seemed to fascinate Mrs. Freeman and
then one day Hulga realized that it was the artificial leg. Mrs. Freeman had a special
fondness for the details of secret infections, hidden deformities, assaults upon children.
Of diseases, she preferred the lingering or incurable. Hulga had heard Mrs. Hopewell
give her the details of the hunting accident, how the leg had been literally blasted off,
how she had never lost consciousness. Mrs. Freeman could listen to it any time as if
it had happened an hour ago.

When Hulga stumped into the kitchen in the morning (she could walk without
making the awful noise but she made it—Mrs. Hopewell was certain—because it was
ugly-sounding), she glanced at them and did not speak. Mrs. Hopewell would be in
her red kimono with her hair tied around her head in rags. She would be sitting at
the table, finishing her breakfast and Mrs. Freeman would be hanging by her elbow
outward from the refrigerator, looking down at the table. Hulga always put her eggs
on the stove to boil and then stood over them with her arms folded, and Mrs. Hopewell
would look at her—a kind of indirect gaze divided between her and Mrs. Freeman—
and would think that if she would only keep herself up a little, she wouldn't be so
bad looking. There was nothing wrong with her face that a pleasant expression
wouldn't help. Mrs. Hopewell said that people who looked on the bright side of things
would be beautiful even if they were not.

Whenever she looked at Joy this way, she could not help but feel that it would have
been better if the child had not taken the Ph.D. It had certainly not brought her out
any and now that she had it, there was no more excuse for her to go to school again.
Mrs. Hopewell thought it was nice for girls to go to school to have a good time but
Joy had "gone through." Anyhow, she would not have been strong enough to go again.
The doctors had told Mrs. Hopewell that with the best of care, Joy might see forty-five.
She had a weak heart. Joy had made it plain that if it had not been for this condition,
she would be far from these red hills and good country people. She would be in a
university lecturing to people who knew what she was talking about. And Mrs.
Hopewell could very well picture her there, looking like a scarecrow and lecturing to
more of the same. Here she went about all day in a six-year-old skirt and a yellow

sweat shirt with a faded cowboy on a horse embossed on it. She thought this was funny; Mrs. Hopewell thought it was idiotic and showed simply that she was still a child. She was brilliant but she didn't have a grain of sense. It seemed to Mrs. Hopewell that every year she grew less like other people and more like herself—bloated, rude, and squint-eyed. And she said such strange things! To her own mother she had said—without warning, without excuse, standing up in the middle of a meal with her face purple and her mouth half full—"Woman! do you ever look inside? Do you ever look inside and see what you are *not*? God!" she had cried sinking down again and staring at her plate, "Malebranche was right: we are not our own light. We are not our own light!" Mrs. Hopewell had no idea to this day what brought that on. She had only made the remark, hoping Joy would take it in, that a smile never hurt anyone.

The girl had taken the Ph.D. in philosophy and this left Mrs. Hopewell at a complete loss. You could say, "My daughter is a nurse," or "My daughter is a school teacher," or even, "My daughter is a chemical engineer." You could not say, "My daughter is a philosopher." That was something that had ended with the Greeks and Romans. All day Joy sat on her neck in a deep chair, reading. Sometimes she went for walks but she didn't like dogs or cats or birds or flowers or nature or nice young men. She looked at nice young men as if she could smell their stupidity.

One day Mrs. Hopewell had picked up one of the books the girl had just put down and opening it at random, she read, "Science, on the other hand, has to assert its soberness and seriousness afresh and declare that it is concerned solely with what-is. Nothing—how can it be for science anything but a horror and a phantasm? If science is right, then one thing stands firm: science wishes to know nothing of nothing. Such is after all the strictly scientific approach to Nothing. We know it by wishing to know nothing of Nothing." These words had been underlined with a blue pencil and they worked on Mrs. Hopewell like some evil incantation in gibberish. She shut the book quickly and went out of the room as if she were having a chill.

This morning when the girl came in, Mrs. Freeman was on Carramae. "She thrown up four times after supper," she said, "and was up twict in the night after three o'clock. Yesterday she didn't do nothing but ramble in the bureau drawer. All she did. Stand up there and see what she could run up on."

"She's got to eat," Mrs. Hopewell muttered, sipping her coffee, while she watched Joy's back at the stove. She was wondering what the child had said to the Bible salesman. She could not imagine what kind of a conversation she could possibly have had with him.

He was a tall gaunt hatless youth who had called yesterday to sell them a Bible. He had appeared at the door, carrying a large black suitcase that weighted him so heavily on one side that he had to brace himself against the door facing. He seemed on the point of collapse but he said in a cheerful voice, "Good morning, Mrs. Cedars!" and set the suitcase down on the mat. He was not a bad-looking young man though he had on a bright blue suit and yellow socks that were not pulled up far enough. He had prominent face bones and a streak of sticky-looking brown hair falling across his forehead.

"I'm Mrs. Hopewell," she said.

"Oh!" he said, pretending to look puzzled but with his eyes sparkling, "I saw it said 'The Cedars,' on the mailbox so I thought you was Mrs. Cedars!" and he burst out in a pleasant laugh. He picked up the satchel and under cover of a pant, he fell forward into her hall. It was rather as if the suitcase had moved first, jerking him after it. "Mrs.

Hopewell!" he said and grabbed her hand. "I hope you are well!" and he laughed again and then all at once his face sobered completely. He paused and gave her a straight earnest look and said, "Lady, I've come to speak of serious things."

"Well, come in," she muttered, none too pleased because her dinner was almost ready. He came into the parlor and sat down on the edge of a straight chair and put the suitcase between his feet and glanced around the room as if he were sizing her up by it. Her silver gleamed on the two sideboards; she decided he had never been in a room as elegant as this.

"Mrs. Hopewell," he began, using her name in a way that sounded almost intimate, "I know you believe in Chrustian service."

"Well yes," she murmured.

"I know," he said and paused, looking very wise with his head cocked on one side, "that you're a good woman. Friends have told me."

Mrs. Hopewell never liked to be taken for a fool. "What are you selling?" she asked.

"Bibles," the young man said and his eye raced around the room before he added, "I see you have no family Bible in your parlor, I see that is the one lack you got!"

Mrs. Hopewell could not say, "My daughter is an atheist and won't let me keep the Bible in the parlor." She said, stiffening slightly, "I keep my Bible by my bedside." This was not the truth. It was in the attic somewhere.

"Lady," he said, "the word of God ought to be in the parlor."

"Well, I think that's a matter of taste," she began. "I think . . ."

"Lady," he said, "for a Chrustian, the word of God ought to be in every room in the house besides in his heart. I know you're a Chrustian because I can see it in every line of your face."

She stood up and said, "Well, young man, I don't want to buy a Bible and I smell my dinner burning."

He didn't get up. He began to twist his hands and looking down at them, he said softly, "Well lady, I'll tell you the truth—not many people want to buy one nowadays and besides, I know I'm real simple. I don't know how to say a thing but to say it. I'm just a country boy." He glanced up into her unfriendly face. "People like you don't like to fool with country people like me!"

"Why!" she cried, "good country people are the salt of the earth! Besides, we all have different ways of doing, it takes all kinds to make the world go 'round. That's life!"

"You said a mouthful," he said.

"Why, I think there aren't enough good country people in the world!" she said, stirred. "I think that's what's wrong with it!"

His face had brightened. "I didn't inraduce myself," he said. "I'm Manley Pointer from out in the country around Willohobie, not even from a place, just from near a place."

"You wait a minute," she said. "I have to see about my dinner." She went out to the kitchen and found Joy standing near the door where she had been listening.

"Get rid of the salt of the earth," she said, "and let's eat."

Mrs. Hopewell gave her a pained look and turned the heat down under the vegetables. "I can't be rude to anybody," she murmured and went back into the parlor.

He had opened the suitcase and was sitting with a Bible on each knee.

"You might as well put those up," she told him. "I don't want one."

"I appreciate your honesty," he said. "You don't see any more real honest people unless you go way out in the country."

"I know," she said, "real genuine folks!" Through the crack in the door she heard a groan.

"I guess a lot of boys come telling you they're working their way through college," he said, "but I'm not going to tell you that. Somehow," he said, "I don't want to go to college. I want to devote my life to Chrustian service. See," he said, lowering his voice, "I got this heart condition. I may not live long. When you know it's something wrong with you and you may not live long, well then, lady . . ." He paused, with his mouth open, and stared at her.

He and Joy had the same condition! She knew that her eyes were filling with tears but she collected herself quickly and murmured, "Won't you stay for dinner? We'd love to have you!" and was sorry the instant she heard herself say it.

"Yes mam," he said in an abashed voice, "I would sher love to do that!"

Joy had given him one look on being introduced to him and then throughout the meal had not glanced at him again. He had addressed several remarks to her, which she had pretended not to hear. Mrs. Hopewell could not understand deliberate rudeness, although she lived with it, and she felt she had always to overflow with hospitality to make up for Joy's lack of courtesy. She urged him to talk about himself and he did. He said he was the seventh child of twelve and that his father had been crushed under a tree when he himself was eight year old. He had been crushed very badly, in fact, almost cut in two and was practically not recognizable. His mother had got along the best she could by hard working and she had always seen that her children went to Sunday School and that they read the Bible every evening. He was now nineteen year old and he had been selling Bibles for four months. In that time he had sold seventy-seven Bibles and had the promise of two more sales. He wanted to become a missionary because he thought that was the way you could do most for people. "He who losest his life shall find it," he said simply and he was so sincere, so genuine and earnest that Mrs. Hopewell would not for the world have smiled. He prevented his peas from sliding onto the table by blocking them with a piece of bread which he later cleaned his plate with. She could see Joy observing sidewise how he handled his knife and fork and she saw too that every few minutes, the boy would dart a keen appraising glance at the girl as if he were trying to attract her attention.

After dinner Joy cleared the dishes off the table and disappeared and Mrs. Hopewell was left to talk with him. He told her again about his childhood and his father's accident and about various things that had happened to him. Every five minutes or so she would stifle a yawn. He sat for two hours until finally she told him she must go because she had an appointment in town. He packed his Bibles and thanked her and prepared to leave, but in the doorway he stopped and wrung her hand and said that not on any of his trips had he met a lady as nice as her and he asked if he could come again. She had said she would always be happy to see him.

Joy had been standing in the road, apparently looking at something in the distance, when he came down the steps toward her, bent to the side with his heavy valise. He stopped where she was standing and confronted her directly. Mrs. Hopewell could not hear what he said but she trembled to think what Joy would say to him. She could see that after a minute Joy said something and that then the boy began to speak again, making an excited gesture with his free hand. After a minute Joy said something else at which the boy began to speak once more. Then to her amazement, Mrs. Hopewell saw the two of them walk off together, toward the gate. Joy had walked all the way to the gate with him and Mrs. Hopewell could not imagine what they had said to each other, and she had not yet dared to ask.

Mrs. Freeman was insisting upon her attention. She had moved from the refrigerator to the heater so that Mrs. Hopewell had to turn and face her in order to seem to be listening. "Glynese gone out with Harvey Hill again last night," she said. "She had this sty."

"Hill," Mrs. Hopewell said absently, "is that the one who works in the garage?"

"Nome, he's the one that goes to chiropracter school," Mrs. Freeman said. "She had this sty. Been had it two days. So she says when he brought her in the other night he says, 'Lemme get rid of that sty for you,' and she says, 'How?' and he says, 'You just lay yourself down acrost the seat of that car and I'll show you.' So she done it and he popped her neck. Kept on a-popping it several times until she made him quit. This morning," Mrs. Freeman said, "she ain't got no sty. She ain't got no traces of a sty."

"I never heard of that before," Mrs. Hopewell said.

"He ast her to marry him before the Ordinary," Mrs. Freeman went on, "and she told him she wasn't going to be married in no *office*."

"Well, Glynese is a fine girl," Mrs. Hopewell said, "Glynese and Carramae are both fine girls."

"Carramae said when her and Lyman was married Lyman said it sure felt sacred to him. She said he said he wouldn't take five hundred dollars for being married by a preacher."

"How much would he take?" the girl asked from the stove.

"He said he wouldn't take five hundred dollars," Mrs. Freeman repeated.

"Well we all have work to do," Mrs. Hopewell said.

"Lyman said it just felt more sacred to him," Mrs. Freeman said. "The doctor wants Carramae to eat prunes. Says instead of medicine. Says them cramps is coming from pressure. You know where I think it is?"

"She'll be better in a few weeks," Mrs. Hopewell said.

"In the tube," Mrs. Freeman said. "Else she wouldn't be as sick as she is."

Hulga had cracked her two eggs into a saucer and was bringing them to the table along with a cup of coffee that she had filled too full. She sat down carefully and began to eat, meaning to keep Mrs. Freeman there by questions if for any reason she showed an inclination to leave. She could perceive her mother's eye on her. The first roundabout question would be about the Bible salesman and she did not wish to bring it on. "How did he pop her neck?" she asked.

Mrs. Freeman went into a description of how he had popped her neck. She said he owned a '55 Mercury but that Glynese said she would rather marry a man with only a '36 Plymouth who would be married by a preacher. The girl asked what if he had a '32 Plymouth and Mrs. Freeman said what Glynese had said was a '36 Plymouth.

Mrs. Hopewell said there were not many girls with Glynese's common sense. She said what she admired in those girls was their common sense. She said that reminded her that they had a nice visitor yesterday, a young man selling Bibles. "Lord," she said, "he bored me to death but he was so sincere and genuine I couldn't be rude to him. He was just good country people, you know," she said, "—just the salt of the earth."

"I seen him walk up," Mrs. Freeman said, "and then later—I seen him walk off," and Hulga could feel the slight shift in her voice, the slight insinuation, that he had not walked off alone, had he? Her face remained expressionless but the color rose into her neck and she seemed to swallow it down with the next spoonful of egg. Mrs. Freeman was looking at her as if they had a secret together.

"Well, it takes all kinds of people to make the world go 'round," Mrs. Hopewell said. "It's very good we aren't all alike."

"Some people are more alike than others," Mrs. Freeman said.

Hulga got up and stumped, with about twice the noise that was necessary, into her room and locked the door. She was to meet the Bible salesman at ten o'clock at the gate. She had thought about it half the night. She had started thinking of it as a great joke and then she had begun to see profound implications in it. She had lain in bed imagining dialogues for them that were insane on the surface but that reached below to depths that no Bible salesman would be aware of. Their conversation yesterday had been of this kind.

He had stopped in front of her and had simply stood there. His face was bony and sweaty and bright, with a little pointed nose in the center of it, and his look was different from what it had been at the dinner table. He was gazing at her with open curiosity, with fascination, like a child watching a new fantastic animal at the zoo, and he was breathing as if he had run a great distance to reach her. His gaze seemed somehow familiar but she could not think where she had been regarded with it before. For almost a minute he didn't say anything. Then on what seemed an insuck of breath, he whispered, "You ever ate a chicken that was two days old?"

The girl looked at him stonily. He might have just put this question up for consideration at the meeting of a philosophical association. "Yes," she presently replied as if she had considered it from all angles.

"It must have been mighty small!" he said triumphantly and shook all over with little nervous giggles, getting very red in the face, and subsiding finally into his gaze of complete admiration, while the girl's expression remained exactly the same.

"How old are you?" he asked softly.

She waited some time before she answered. Then in a flat voice she said, "Seventeen."

His smiles came in succession like waves breaking on the surface of a little lake. "I see you got a wooden leg," he said. "I think you're real brave. I think you're real sweet."

The girl stood blank and solid and silent.

"Walk to the gate with me," he said. "You're a brave sweet little thing and I liked you the minute I seen you walk in the door."

Hulga began to move forward.

"What's your name?" he asked, smiling down on the top of her head.

"Hulga," she said.

"Hulga," he murmured, "Hulga. Hulga. I never heard of anybody name Hulga before. You're shy, aren't you, Hulga?" he asked.

She nodded, watching his large red hand on the handle of the giant valise.

"I like girls that wear glasses," he said. "I think a lot. I'm not like these people that a serious thought don't ever enter their heads. It's because I may die."

"I may die too," she said suddenly and looked up at him. His eyes were very small and brown, glittering feverishly.

"Listen," he said, "don't you think some people was meant to meet on account of what all they got in common and all? Like they both think serious thoughts and all?" He shifted the valise to his other hand so that the hand nearest her was free. He caught hold of her elbow and shook it a little. "I don't work on Saturday," he said. "I like to walk in the woods and see what Mother Nature is wearing. O'er the hills and far away. Pic-nics and things. Couldn't we go on a pic-nic tomorrow? Say yes, Hulga," he said and gave her a dying look as if he felt his insides about to drop out of him. He had even seemed to sway slightly toward her.

During the night she had imagined that she seduced him. She imagined that the two of them walked on the place until they came to the storage barn beyond the two back fields and there, she imagined, that things came to such a pass that she very easily seduced him and that then, of course, she had to reckon with his remorse. True genius can get an idea across even to an inferior mind. She imagined that she took his remorse in hand and changed it into a deeper understanding of life. She took all his shame away and turned it into something useful.

She set off for the gate at exactly ten o'clock, escaping without drawing Mrs. Hopewell's attention. She didn't take anything to eat, forgetting that food is usually taken on a picnic. She wore a pair of slacks and a dirty white shirt, and as an afterthought, she had put some Vapex on the collar of it since she did not own any perfume. When she reached the gate no one was there.

She looked up and down the empty highway and had the furious feeling that she had been tricked, that he had only meant to make her walk to the gate after the idea of him. Then suddenly he stood up, very tall, from behind a bush on the opposite embankment. Smiling, he lifted his hat which was new and wide-brimmed. He had not worn it yesterday and she wondered if he had bought it for the occasion. It was toast-colored with a red and white band around it and was slightly too large for him. He stepped from behind the bush still carrying the black valise. He had on the same suit and the same yellow socks sucked down in his shoes from walking. He crossed the highway and said, "I knew you'd come!"

The girl wondered acidly how he had known this. She pointed to the valise and asked, "Why did you bring your Bibles?"

He took her elbow, smiling down on her as if he could not stop. "You can never tell when you'll need the word of God, Hulga," he said. She had a moment in which she doubted that this was actually happening and then they began to climb the embankment. They went down into the pasture toward the woods. The boy walked lightly by her side, bouncing on his toes. The valise did not seem to be heavy today; he even swung it. They crossed half the pasture without saying anything and then, putting his hand easily on the small of her back, he asked softly, "Where does your wooden leg join on?"

She turned an ugly red and glared at him and for an instant the boy looked abashed. "I didn't mean you no harm," he said. "I only meant you're so brave and all. I guess God takes care of you."

"No," she said, looking forward and walking fast, "I don't even believe in God."

At this he stopped and whistled. "No!" he exclaimed as if he were too astonished to say anything else.

She walked on and in a second he was bouncing at her side, fanning with his hat. "That's very unusual for a girl," he remarked, watching her out of the corner of his eye. When they reached the edge of the wood, he put his hand on her back again and drew her against him without a word and kissed her heavily.

The kiss, which had more pressure than feeling behind it, produced that extra surge of adrenalin in the girl that enables one to carry a packed trunk out of a burning house, but in her, the power went at once to the brain. Even before he released her, her mind, clear and detached and ironic anyway, was regarding him from a great distance, with amusement but with pity. She had never been kissed before and she was pleased to discover that it was an unexceptional experience and all a matter of the mind's control. Some people might enjoy drain water if they were told it was vodka. When the boy, looking expectant but uncertain, pushed her gently away, she turned and walked on, saying nothing as if such business, for her, were common enough.

He came along panting at her side, trying to help her when he saw a root that she might trip over. He caught and held back the long swaying blades of thorn vine until she had passed beyond them. She led the way and he came breathing heavily behind her. Then they came out on a sunlit hillside, sloping softly into another one a little smaller. Beyond, they could see the rusted top of the old barn where the extra hay was stored.

The hill was sprinkled with small pink weeds. "Then you ain't saved?" he asked suddenly, stopping.

The girl smiled. It was the first time she had smiled at him at all. "In my economy," she said, "I'm saved and you are damned but I told you I didn't believe in God."

Nothing seemed to destroy the boy's look of admiration. He gazed at her now as if the fantastic animal at the zoo had put its paw through the bars and given him a loving poke. She thought he looked as if he wanted to kiss her again and she walked on before he had the chance.

"Ain't there somewheres we can sit down sometime?" he murmured, his voice softening toward the end of the sentence.

"In that barn," she said.

They made for it rapidly as if it might slide away like a train. It was a large two-story barn, cool and dark inside. The boy pointed up the ladder that led into the loft and said, "It's too bad we can't go up there."

"Why can't we?" she asked.

"Yer leg," he said reverently.

The girl gave him a contemptuous look and putting both hands on the ladder, she climbed it while he stood below, apparently awestruck. She pulled herself expertly through the opening and then looked down at him and said, "Well, come on if you're coming," and he began to climb the ladder, awkwardly bringing the suitcase with him.

"We won't need the Bible," she observed.

"You never can tell," he said, panting. After he had got into the loft, he was a few seconds catching his breath. She had sat down in a pile of straw. A wide sheath of sunlight, filled with dust particles, slanted over her. She lay back against a bale, her face turned away, looking out the front opening of the barn where hay was thrown from a wagon into the loft. The two pink-speckled hillsides lay back against a dark ridge of woods. The sky was cloudless and cold blue. The boy dropped down by her side and put one arm under her and the other over her and began methodically kissing her face, making little noises like a fish. He did not remove his hat but it was pushed far enough back not to interfere. When her glasses got in his way, he took them off of her and slipped them into his pocket.

The girl at first did not return any of the kisses but presently she began to and after she had put several on his cheek, she reached his lips and remained there, kissing him again and again as if she were trying to draw all the breath out of him. His breath was clear and sweet like a child's and the kisses were sticky like a child's. He mumbled about loving her and about knowing when he first seen her that he loved her, but the mumbling was like the sleepy fretting of a child being put to sleep by his mother. Her mind, throughout this, never stopped or lost itself for a second to her feelings. "You ain't said you love me none," he whispered finally, pulling back from her. "You got to say that."

She looked away from him off into the hollow sky and then down at a black ridge and then down farther into what appeared to be two green swelling lakes. She didn't realize he had taken her glasses but this landscape could not seem exceptional to her for she seldom paid any close attention to her surroundings.

"You got to say it," he repeated. "You got to say you love me."

She was always careful how she committed herself. "In a sense," she began, "if you use the word loosely, you might say that. But it's not a word I use. I don't have illusions. I'm one of those people who see *through* to nothing."

The boy was frowning. "You got to say it. I said it and you got to say it," he said.

The girl looked at him almost tenderly. "You poor baby," she murmured. "It's just as well you don't understand," and she pulled him by the neck, face-down, against her. "We are all damned," she said, "but some of us have taken off our blindfolds and see that there's nothing to see. It's a kind of salvation."

The boy's astonished eyes looked blankly through the ends of her hair. "Okay," he almost whined, "but do you love me or don'tcher?"

"Yes," she said and added, "in a sense. But I must tell you something. There mustn't be anything dishonest between us." She lifted his head and looked him in the eye. "I am thirty years old," she said. "I have a number of degrees."

The boy's look was irritated but dogged. "I don't care," he said. "I don't care a thing about what all you done. I just want to know if you love me or don'tcher?" and he caught her to him and wildly planted her face with kisses until she said, "Yes, yes."

"Okay then," he said, letting her go. "Prove it."

She smiled, looking dreamily out on the shifty landscape. She had seduced him without even making up her mind to try. "How?" she asked, feeling that he should be delayed a little.

He leaned over and put his lips to her ear. "Show me where your wooden leg joins on," he whispered.

The girl uttered a sharp little cry and her face instantly drained of color. The obscenity of the suggestion was not what shocked her. As a child she had sometimes been subject to feelings of shame but education had removed the last traces of that as a good surgeon scrapes for cancer; she would no more have felt it over what he was asking than she would have believed in his Bible. But she was as sensitive about the artificial leg as a peacock about his tail. No one ever touched it but her. She took care of it as someone else would his soul, in private and almost with her own eyes turned away. "No," she said.

"I known it," he muttered, sitting up. "You're just playing me for a sucker."

"Oh no no!" she cried. "It joins on at the knee. Only at the knee. Why do you want to see it?"

The boy gave her a long penetrating look. "Because," he said, "it's what makes you different. You ain't like anybody else."

She sat staring at him. There was nothing about her face or her round freezing-blue eyes to indicate that this had moved her; but she felt as if her heart had stopped and left her mind to pump her blood. She decided that for the first time in her life she was face to face with real innocence. This boy, with an instinct that came from beyond wisdom, had touched the truth about her. When after a minute, she said in a hoarse high voice, "All right," it was like surrendering to him completely. It was like losing her own life and finding it again, miraculously, in his.

Very gently he began to roll the slack leg up. The artificial limb, in a white sock and brown flat shoe, was bound in a heavy material like canvas and ended in an ugly jointure where it was attached to the stump. The boy's face and his voice were entirely reverent as he uncovered it and said, "Now show me how to take it off and on."

She took it off for him and put it back on again and then he took it off himself, handling it as tenderly as if it were a real one. "See!" he said with a delighted child's face. "Now I can do it myself!"

"Put it back on," she said. She was thinking that she would run away with him and that every night he would take the leg off and every morning put it back on again. "Put it back on," she said.

"Not yet," he murmured, setting it on its foot out of her reach. "Leave it off for a while. You got me instead."

She gave a little cry of alarm but he pushed her down and began to kiss her again. Without the leg she felt entirely dependent on him. Her brain seemed to have stopped thinking altogether and to be about some other function that it was not very good at. Different expressions raced back and forth over her face. Every now and then the boy, his eyes like two steel spikes, would glance behind him where the leg stood. Finally she pushed him off and said, "Put it back on me now."

"Wait," he said. He leaned the other way and pulled the valise toward him and opened it. It had a pale blue spotted lining and there were only two Bibles in it. He took one of these out and opened the cover of it. It was hollow and contained a pocket flask of whiskey, a pack of cards, and a small blue box with printing on it. He laid these out in front of her one at a time in an evenly spaced row, like one presenting offerings at the shrine of a goddess. He put the blue box in her hand. THIS PRODUCT TO BE USED ONLY FOR THE PREVENTION OF DISEASE, she read, and dropped it. The boy was unscrewing the top of the flask. He stopped and pointed, with a smile, to the deck of cards. It was not an ordinary deck but one with an obscene picture on the back of each card. "Take a swig," he said, offering her the bottle first. He held it in front of her, but like one mesmerized, she did not move.

Her voice when she spoke had an almost pleading sound. "Aren't you," she murmured, "aren't you just good country people?"

The boy cocked his head. He looked as if he were just beginning to understand that she might be trying to insult him. "Yeah," he said, curling his lip slightly, "but it ain't held me back none. I'm as good as you any day in the week."

"Give me my leg," she said.

He pushed it farther away with his foot. "Come on now, let's begin to have us a good time," he said coaxingly. "We ain't got to know one another good yet."

"Give me my leg!" she screamed and tried to lunge for it but he pushed her down easily.

"What's the matter with you all of a sudden?" he asked, frowning as he screwed the top on the flask and put it quickly back inside the Bible. "You just a while ago said you didn't believe in nothing. I thought you was some girl!"

Her face was almost purple. "You're a Christian!" she hissed. "You're a fine Christian! You're just like them all—say one thing and do another. You're a perfect Christian, you're . . ."

The boy's mouth was set angrily. "I hope you don't think," he said in a lofty indignant tone, "that I believe in that crap! I may sell Bibles but I know which end is up and I wasn't born yesterday and I know where I'm going!"

"Give me my leg!" she screeched. He jumped up so quickly that she barely saw him sweep the cards and the blue box back into the Bible and throw the Bible into the valise. She saw him grab the leg and then she saw it for an instant slanted forlornly across the inside of the suitcase with a Bible at either side of its opposite ends. He slammed the lid shut and snatched up the valise and swung it down the hole and then stepped through himself.

When all of him had passed but his head, he turned and regarded her with a look that no longer had any admiration in it. "I've gotten a lot of interesting things," he said. "One time I got a woman's glass eye this way. And you needn't to think you'll catch me because Pointer ain't really my name. I use a different name at every house I call at and don't stay nowhere long. And I'll tell you another thing, Hulga," he said, using the name as if he didn't think much of it, "you ain't so smart. I been believing in nothing ever since I was born!" and then the toast-colored hat disappeared down the hole and the girl was left, sitting on the straw in the dusty sunlight. When she turned her churning face toward the opening, she saw his blue figure struggling successfully over the green speckled lake.

Mrs. Hopewell and Mrs. Freeman, who were in the back pasture, digging up onions, saw him emerge a little later from the woods and head across the meadow toward the highway. "Why, that looks like that nice dull young man that tried to sell me a Bible yesterday," Mrs. Hopewell said, squinting. "He must have been selling them to the Negroes back in there. He was so simple," she said, "but I guess the world would be better off if we were all that simple."

Mrs. Freeman's gaze drove forward and just touched him before he disappeared under the hill. Then she returned her attention to the evil-smelling onion shoot she was lifting from the ground. "Some can't be that simple," she said. "I know I never could."

GABRIEL GARCIA MARQUEZ

[b. 1928]

A Very Old Man with Enormous Wings

A Tale for Children

TRANSLATED BY GREGORY RABASSA

On the third day of rain they had killed so many crabs inside the house that Pelayo had to cross his drenched courtyard and throw them into the sea, because the newborn child had a temperature all night and they thought it was due to the stench. The world had been sad since Tuesday. Sea and sky were a single ash-gray thing and the sands of the beach, which on March nights glimmered like powdered light, had become a stew of mud and rotten shellfish. The light was so weak at noon that when Pelayo was coming back to the house after throwing away the crabs, it was hard for him to see what it was that was moving and groaning in the rear of the courtyard. He had to go very close to see that it was an old man, a very old man, lying face down in the mud, who, in spite of his tremendous efforts, couldn't get up, impeded by his enormous wings.

Frightened by that nightmare, Pelayo ran to get Elisenda, his wife, who was putting compresses on the sick child, and he took her to the rear of the courtyard. They both looked at the fallen body with mute stupor. He was dressed like a rag-picker. There were only a few faded hairs left on his bald skull and very few teeth in his mouth, and his pitiful condition of a drenched great-grandfather had taken away any sense of grandeur he might have had. His huge buzzard wings, dirty and half-plucked, were forever entangled in the mud. They looked at him so long and so closely that Pelayo and Elisenda very soon overcame their surprise and in the end found him familiar. Then they dared speak to him, and he answered in an incomprehensible dialect with a strong sailor's voice. That was how they skipped over the inconvenience of the wings and quite intelligently concluded that he was a lonely castaway from some foreign ship wrecked by the storm. And yet, they called in a neighbor woman who knew everything about life and death to see him, and all she needed was one look to show them their mistake.

"He's an angel," she told them. "He must have been coming for the child, but the poor fellow is so old that the rain knocked him down."

On the following day everyone knew that a flesh-and-blood angel was held captive in Pelayo's house. Against the judgment of the wise neighbor woman, for whom angels in those times were the fugitive survivors of a celestial conspiracy, they did not have the heart to club him to death. Pelayo watched over him all afternoon from the kitchen, armed with his bailiff's club, and before going to bed he dragged him out of the mud and locked him up with the hens in the wire chicken coop. In the middle of the night, when the rain stopped, Pelayo and Elisenda were still killing crabs. A short time afterward the child woke up without a fever and with a desire to eat. Then they felt magnanimous and decided to put the angel on a raft with fresh water and provisions for three days and leave him to his fate on the high seas. But when they went out into the courtyard with the first light of dawn, they found the whole neighborhood in front of the chicken coop having fun with the angel, without the slightest reverence, tossing him things to eat through the openings in the wire as if he weren't a supernatural creature but a circus animal.

Father Gonzaga arrived before seven o'clock, alarmed at the strange news. By that time onlookers less frivolous than those at dawn had already arrived and they were making all kinds of conjectures concerning the captive's future. The simplest among them thought that he should be named mayor of the world. Others of sterner mind felt that he should be promoted to the rank of five-star general in order to win all wars. Some visionaries hoped that he could be put to stud in order to implant on earth a race of winged wise men who could take charge of the universe. But Father Gonzaga, before becoming a priest, had been a robust woodcutter. Standing by the wire, he reviewed his catechism in an instant and asked them to open the door so that he could take a close look at that pitiful man who looked more like a huge decrepit hen among the fascinated chickens. He was lying in a corner drying his open wings in the sunlight among the fruit peels and breakfast leftovers that the early risers had thrown him. Alien to the impertinences of the world, he only lifted his antiquarian eyes and murmured something in his dialect when Father Gonzaga went into the chicken coop and said good morning to him in Latin. The parish priest had his first suspicion of an imposter when he saw that he did not understand the language of God or know how to greet His ministers. Then he noticed that seen close up he was much too human: he had an unbearable smell of the outdoors, the back side of his wings was strewn with parasites and his main feathers had been mistreated by terrestrial winds, and nothing about him measured up to the proud dignity of angels. Then he came out of the chicken coop and in a brief sermon warned the curious against the risks of being ingenuous. He reminded them that the devil had the bad habit of making use of carnival tricks in order to confuse the unwary. He argued that if wings were not the essential element in determining the difference between a hawk and an airplane, they were even less so in the recognition of angels. Nevertheless, he promised to write a letter to his bishop so that the latter would write to his primate so that the latter would write to the Supreme Pontiff in order to get the final verdict from the highest courts.

His prudence fell on sterile hearts. The news of the captive angel spread with such rapidity that after a few hours the courtyard had the bustle of a marketplace and they had to call in troops with fixed bayonets to disperse the mob that was about to knock the house down. Elisenda, her spine all twisted from sweeping up so much marketplace trash, then got the idea of fencing in the yard and charging five cents admission to see the angel.

The curious came from far away. A traveling carnival arrived with a flying acrobat who buzzed over the crowd several times, but no one paid any attention to him because his wings were not those of an angel but, rather, those of a sidereal bat. The most unfortunate invalids on earth came in search of health: a poor woman who since childhood had been counting her heartbeats and had run out of numbers; a Portuguese man who couldn't sleep because the noise of the stars disturbed him; a sleepwalker who got up at night to undo the things he had done while awake; and many others with less serious ailments. In the midst of that shipwreck disorder that made the earth tremble, Pelayo and Elisenda were happy with fatigue, for in less than a week they had crammed their rooms with money and the line of pilgrims waiting their turn to enter still reached beyond the horizon.

The angel was the only one who took no part in his own act. He spent his time trying to get comfortable in his borrowed nest, befuddled by the hellish heat of the oil lamps and sacramental candles that had been placed along the wire. At first they tried to make him eat some mothballs, which, according to the wisdom of the wise neighbor woman, were the food prescribed for angels. But he turned them down, just as he turned down the papal lunches that the penitents brought him, and they never found out whether it was because he was an angel or because he was an old man that in the end he ate nothing but eggplant mush. His only supernatural virtue seemed to be patience. Especially during the first days, when the hens pecked at him, searching for the stellar parasites that proliferated in his wings, and the cripples pulled out feathers to touch their defective parts with, and even the most merciful threw stones at him, trying to get him to rise so they could see him standing. The only time they succeeded in arousing him was when they burned his side with an iron for branding steers, for he had been motionless for so many hours that they thought he was dead. He awoke with a start, ranting in his hermetic language and with tears in his eyes, and he flapped his wings a couple of times, which brought on a whirlwind of chicken dung and lunar dust and a gale of panic that did not seem to be of this world. Although many thought that his reaction had been one not of rage but of pain, from then on they were careful not to annoy him, because the majority understood that his passivity was not that of a hero taking his ease but that of a cataclysm in repose.

Father Gonzaga held back the crowd's frivolity with formulas of maidservant inspiration while awaiting the arrival of a final judgment on the nature of the captive. But the mail from Rome showed no sense of urgency. They spent their time finding out if the prisoner had a navel, if his dialect had any connection with Aramaic, how many times he could fit on the head of a pin, or whether he wasn't just a Norwegian with wings. Those meager letters might have come and gone until the end of time if a providential event had not put an end to the priest's tribulations.

It so happened that during those days, among so many other carnival attractions, there arrived in town the traveling show of the woman who had been changed into a spider for having disobeyed her parents. The admission to see her was not only less than the admission to see the angel, but people were permitted to ask her all manner of questions about her absurd state and to examine her up and down so that no one would ever doubt the truth of her horror. She was a frightful tarantula the size of a ram and with the head of a sad maiden. What was most heart-rending, however, was not her outlandish shape but the sincere affliction with which she recounted the details of her misfortune. While still practically a child she had sneaked out of her parents' house to go to a dance, and while she was coming back through the woods after having danced all night without permission, a fearful thunderclap rent the sky in two and through the crack came the lightning bolt of brimstone that changed her into a spider. Her only nourishment came from the meatballs that charitable souls chose to toss into her mouth. A spectacle like that, full of so much human truth and with such a fearful lesson, was bound to defeat without even trying that of a haughty angel who scarcely deigned to look at mortals. Besides, the few miracles attributed to the angel showed a certain mental disorder, like the blind man who didn't recover his sight but grew three new teeth, or the paralytic who didn't get to walk but almost won the lottery, and the leper whose sores sprouted sunflowers. Those consolation miracles, which were more like mocking fun, had already ruined the angel's reputation when the woman who had been changed into a spider finally crushed him completely. That was how Father Gonzaga was cured forever of his insomnia and Pelayo's courtyard went back to being as empty as during the time it had rained for three days and crabs walked through the bedrooms.

The owners of the house had no reason to lament. With the money they saved they built a two-story mansion with balconies and gardens and high netting so that crabs wouldn't get in during the winter, and with iron bars on the windows so that angels wouldn't get in. Pelayo also set up a rabbit warren close to town and gave up his job as bailiff for good, and Elisenda bought some satin pumps with high heels and many dresses of iridescent silk, the kind worn on Sunday by the most desirable women in those times. The chicken coop was the only thing that didn't receive any attention. If they washed it down with creolin and burned tears of myrrh inside it every so often, it was not in homage to the angel but to drive away the dungheap stench that still hung everywhere like a ghost and was turning the new house into an old one. At first, when the child learned to walk, they were careful that he not get too close to the chicken coop. But then they began to lose their fears and got used to the smell, and before the child got his second teeth he'd gone inside the chicken coop to play, where the wires were falling apart. The angel was no less standoffish with him than with other mortals, but he tolerated the most ingenious infamies with the patience of a dog who had no illusions. They both came down with chicken pox at the same time. The doctor who took care of the child couldn't resist the temptation to listen to the angel's heart, and he found so much whistling in the heart and so many sounds in his kidneys that it seemed impossible for him to be alive. What surprised him most, however, was the logic of his wings. They seemed so natural on that completely human organism that he couldn't understand why other men didn't have them too.

When the child began school it had been some time since the sun and rain had caused the collapse of the chicken coop. The angel went dragging himself about here and there like a stray dying man. They would drive him out of the bedroom with a broom and a moment later find him in the kitchen. He seemed to be in so many places at the same time that they grew to think that he'd been duplicated, that he was reproducing himself all through the house, and the exasperated and unhinged Elisenda shouted that it was awful living in that hell full of angels. He could scarcely eat and his antiquarian eyes had also become so foggy that he went about bumping into posts. All he had left were the bare cannulae of his last feathers. Pelayo threw a blanket over him and extended him the charity of letting him sleep in the shed, and only then did they notice that he had a temperature at night, and was delirious with the tongue twisters of an old Norwegian. That was one of the few times they became alarmed, for they thought he was going to die and not even the wise neighbor woman had been able to tell them what to do with dead angels.

And yet he not only survived his worst winter, but seemed improved with the first sunny days. He remained motionless for several days in the farthest corner of the courtyard, where no one would see him, and at the beginning of December some large, stiff feathers began to grow on his wings, the feathers of a scarecrow, which looked more like another misfortune of decrepitude. But he must have known the reason for those changes, for he was quite careful that no one should notice them, that no one should hear the sea chanteys that he sometimes sang under the stars. One morning Elisenda was cutting some bunches of onions for lunch when a wind that seemed to come from the high seas blew into the kitchen. Then she went to the window and caught the angel in his first attempts at flight. They were so clumsy that his fingernails opened a furrow in the vegetable patch and he was on the point of knocking the shed down with the ungainly flapping that slipped on the light and couldn't get a grip on the air. But he did manage to gain altitude. Elisenda let out a sigh of relief, for herself and for him, when she saw him pass over the last houses, holding himself up in some way with the risky flapping of a senile vulture. She kept watching him even when she was through cutting the onions and she kept on watching until it was no longer possible for her to see him, because then he was no longer an annoyance in her life but an imaginary dot on the horizon of the sea.

DONALD BARTHELME

[*b. 1931*]

A Shower of Gold

Because he needed the money Peterson answered an ad that said *"We'll pay you* to be on TV if your opinions are strong enough or your personal experiences have a flavor of the unusual." He called the number and was told to come to Room 1551 in the Graybar Building on Lexington. This he did and after spending twenty minutes with a Miss Arbor who asked him if he had ever been in analysis was okayed for a program called *Who Am I?* "What do you have strong opinions about?" Miss Arbor asked. "Art," Peterson said, "life, money." "For instance?" "I believe," Peterson said, "that the learning ability of mice can be lowered or increased by regulating the amount of serotonin in the brain. I believe that schizophrenics have a high incidence of unusual fingerprints, including lines that make almost complete circles. I believe that the dreamer watches his dream in sleep, by moving his eyes." *"That's very interesting!"* Miss Arbor cried. "It's all in the *World Almanac,"* Peterson replied.

"I see you're a sculptor," Miss Arbor said, "that's wonderful." "What is the nature of the program?" Peterson asked. "I've never seen it." "Let me answer your question with another question," Miss Arbor said. "Mr. Peterson, are you absurd?" Her enormous lips were smeared with a glowing white cream. "I beg your pardon?" "I mean," Miss Arbor said earnestly, "do you encounter your own existence as gratuitous? Do you feel *de trop?* Is there nausea?" "I have an enlarged liver," Peterson offered. "That's *excellent!"* Miss Arbor exclaimed. "That's a *very* good beginning! *Who Am I?* tries, Mr. Peterson, to discover what people *really are.* People today, we feel, are hidden away inside themselves, alienated, desperate, living in anguish, despair and bad faith. Why have we been thrown here, and abandoned? That's the question we try to answer, Mr. Peterson. Man stands alone in a featureless, anonymous landscape, in fear and trembling and sickness unto death. God is dead. Nothingness everywhere. Dread. Estrangement. Finitude. *Who Am I?* approaches these problems in a root radical way." "On television?" "We're interested in basics, Mr. Peterson. We don't play around." "I see," Peterson said, wondering about the amount of the fee. "What I want to know now, Mr. Peterson, is this: are you *interested* in absurdity?" "Miss Arbor," he said, "to tell you the truth, I don't know. I'm not sure I believe in it." "Oh, Mr. Peterson!" Miss Arbor said, shocked. "Don't *say* that! You'll be . . ." "Punished?" Peterson suggested. *"You* may not be interested in absurdity," she said firmly, "but absurdity is interested in *you."* "I have a lot of problems, if that helps," Peterson said. "Existence is problematic for you," Miss Arbor said, relieved. "The fee is two hundred dollars."

"I'm going to be on television," Peterson said to his dealer. "A terrible shame," Jean-Claude responded. "Is it unavoidable?" "It's unavoidable," Peterson said, "if I want to eat." "How much?" Jean-Claude asked and Peterson said: "Two hundred." He looked around the gallery to see if any of his works were on display. "A ridiculous compensation considering the infamy. Are you using your own name?" "You haven't by any chance . . ." "No one is buying," Jean-Claude said. "Undoubtedly it is the weather. People are thinking in terms of—what do you call those things?—Chris-Crafts. To boat with. You would not consider again what I spoke to you about before?" "No," Peterson said, "I wouldn't consider it." "Two little ones would move much, much faster than a single huge big one," Jean-Claude said, looking away. "To saw it across the middle would be a very simple matter." "It's supposed to be a work of art," Peterson said, as calmly as possible. "You don't go around sawing works of art across the middle, remember?" "That place where it saws," Jean-Claude said, "is not very difficult. I can put my two hands around it." He made a circle with his two hands to demonstrate. "Invariably when I look at that piece I see two pieces. Are you absolutely sure you didn't conceive it wrongly in the first instance?" "Absolutely," Peterson said. Not a single piece of his was on view, and his liver expanded in rage and hatred. "You have a very romantic impulse," Jean-Claude said. "I admire, dimly, the posture. You read too much in the history of art. It estranges you from those possibilities for authentic selfhood that inhere in the present century." "I know," Peterson said, "could you let me have twenty until the first?"

Peterson sat in his loft on lower Broadway drinking Rheingold and thinking about the President. He had always felt close to the President but felt now that he had, in agreeing to appear on the television program, done something slightly disgraceful, of which the President would not approve. But I needed the money, he told himself, the telephone is turned off and the kitten is crying for milk. And I'm running out of beer. The President feels that the arts should be encouraged, Peterson reflected, surely he doesn't want me to go without beer? He wondered if what he was feeling was simple guilt at having sold himself to television or something more elegant: nausea? His liver groaned within him and he considered a situation in which his new relationship with the President was announced. He was working in the loft. The piece in hand was to be called *Season's Greetings* and combined three auto radiators, one from a Chevrolet Tudor, one from a Ford pick-up, one from a 1932 Essex, with part of a former telephone switchboard and other items. The arrangement seemed right and he began welding. After a time the mass was freestanding. A couple of hours had passed. He put down the torch, lifted off the mask. He walked over to the refrigerator and found a sandwich left by a friendly junk dealer. It was a sandwich made hastily and without inspiration: a thin slice of ham between two pieces of bread. He ate it gratefully nevertheless. He stood looking at the work, moving from time to time so as to view it from a new angle. Then the door to the loft burst open and the President ran in, trailing a sixteen-pound sledge. His first blow cracked the principal weld in *Season's Greetings,* the two halves parting like lovers, clinging for a moment and then rushing off in opposite directions. Twelve Secret Service men held Peterson in a paralyzing combination of secret grips. He's looking good, Peterson thought, very good, healthy, mature, fit, trustworthy. I like his suit. The President's second and third blows smashed the Essex radiator and the Chevrolet radiator. Then he attacked the welding torch, the plaster sketches on the workbench, the Rodin cast and the Giacometti stickman Peterson had bought in Paris. *"But Mr. President!"* Peterson shouted. *"I thought we were friends!"* A Secret Service man bit him in the back of the neck. Then the President lifted the sledge high in the air, turned toward Peterson, and said: "Your liver is diseased? That's a good sign. You're making progress. You're thinking."

"I happen to think that guy in the White House is doing a pretty darn good job." Peterson's barber, a man named Kitchen who was also a lay analyst and the author of four books titled *The Decision To Be,* was the only person in the world to whom he had confided his former sense of community with the President. "As far as his relationship with you personally goes," the barber continued, "it's essentially a kind of I-Thou relationship, if you know what I mean. You got to handle it with full awareness of the implications. In the end one experiences only oneself, Nietzsche said. When you're angry with the President, what you experience is self-as-angry-with-the-President. When things are okay between you and him, what you experience is self-as-swinging-with-the-President. Well and good. *But,*" Kitchen said, lathering up, "you want the relationship to be such that what you experience is the-President-as-swinging-with-you. You want *his* reality, get it? So that you can break out of the hell of solipsism. How about a little more off the sides?" "Everybody knows the language but me," Peterson said irritably. "Look," Kitchen said, "when you talk about me to somebody else, you say 'my barber,' don't you? Sure you do. In the same way, I look at you as being 'my customer,' get it? But you don't regard yourself as being 'my' customer and I don't regard myself as 'your' barber. Oh, it's hell all right." The razor moved like a switchblade across the back of Peterson's neck. "Like Pascal said: 'The natural misfortune of our mortal and feeble condition is so wretched that when we consider it closely, nothing can console us.' " The razor rocketed around an ear. "Listen," Peterson said, "what do you think of this television program called *Who Am I?* Ever seen it?" "Frankly," the barber said, "it smells of the library. But they do a job on those people, I'll tell you that." "What do you mean?" Peterson said excitedly. "What kind of a job?" The cloth was whisked away and shaken with a sharp popping sound. "It's too horrible even to talk about," Kitchen said. "But it's what they deserve, those crumbs." "Which crumbs?" Peterson asked.

That night a tall foreign-looking man with a switchblade big as a butcherknife open in his hand walked into the loft without knocking and said "Good evening, Mr. Peterson, I am the cat-piano player, is there anything you'd particularly like to hear?" "Cat-piano?" Peterson said, gasping, shrinking from the knife. "What are you talking about? What do you want?" A biography of Nolde slid from his lap to the floor. "The cat-piano," said the visitor, "is an instrument of the devil, a diabolical instrument. You needn't sweat quite so much," he added, sounding aggrieved. Peterson tried to be brave. "I don't understand," he said. "Let me explain," the tall foreign-looking man said graciously. "The keyboard consists of eight cats—the octave—encased in the body of the instrument in such a way that only their heads and forepaws protrude. The player presses upon the appropriate paws, and the appropriate cats respond—with a kind of shriek. There is also provision made for pulling their tails. A tail-puller, or perhaps I should say tail *player*" (he smiled a disingenuous smile) "is stationed at the rear of the instrument, where the tails are. At the correct moment the tail-puller pulls the correct tail. The tail-note is of course quite different from the paw-note and produces sounds in the upper registers. Have you ever seen such an instrument, Mr. Peterson?" "No, and I don't believe it exists," Peterson said heroically. "There is an excellent early seventeenth-century engraving by Franz van der Wyngaert, Mr. Peterson, in which a cat-piano appears. Played, as it happens, by a man with a wooden leg. You will observe my own leg." The cat-piano player hoisted his trousers and a leglike contraption of wood, metal and plastic appeared. "And now, would you like to make a request? 'The

Martyrdom of St. Sebastian'? The 'Romeo and Juliet' overture? 'Holiday for Strings'?" "But why—" Peterson began. "The kitten cries, the cat-piano plays." "But it's not my kitten," Peterson said reasonably. "It's just a kitten that wished itself on me. I've been trying to give it away. I'm not sure it's still around. I haven't seen it since the day before yesterday." The kitten appeared, looked at Peterson reproachfully, and then rubbed itself against the cat-piano player's mechanical leg. "Wait a minute!" Peterson exclaimed. "This thing is rigged! That cat hasn't been here in two days. What do you want from me? What am I supposed to do?" "Choices, Mr. Peterson, choices. You *chose* that kitten as a way of encountering that which you are not, that is to say, kitten. An effort on the part of the *pour-soi* to—" "But it chose me!" Peterson cried, "the door was open and the first thing I knew it was lying in my bed, under the Army blanket. I didn't have anything to do with it!" The cat-piano player repeated his disingenuous smile. "Yes, Mr. Peterson, I know, I know. Things are done to you, it is all a gigantic conspiracy. I've heard the story a hundred times. But the kitten is here, is it not? The kitten is weeping, is it not?" Peterson looked at the kitten, which was crying huge tigerish tears into its empty dish. *"Listen* Mr. Peterson," the cat-piano player said, *"Listen!"* The blade of his immense knife jumped back into the handle with a thwack! and the hideous music began.

The day after the hideous music began the three girls from California arrived. Peterson opened his door, hesitantly, in response to an insistent ringing, and found himself being stared at by three girls in blue jeans and heavy sweaters, carrying suitcases. "I'm Sherry," the first girl said, "and this is Ann and this is Louise. We're from California and we need a place to stay." They were homely and extremely purposeful. "I'm sorry," Peterson said, "I can't—" "We sleep anywhere," Sherry said, looking past him into the vastness of his loft, "on the floor if we have to. We've done it before." Ann and Louise stood on their toes to get a good look. "What's that funny music?" Sherry asked, "it sounds pretty far-out. We really won't be any trouble at all and it'll just be a little while until we make a connection." "Yes," Peterson said, "but why me?" "You're an artist," Sherry said sternly, "we saw the A.I.R. sign downstairs." Peterson cursed the fire laws which made posting of the signs obligatory. "Listen," he said, "I can't even feed the cat. I can't even keep myself in beer. This is not the place. You won't be happy here. My work isn't authentic. I'm a minor artist." "The natural misfortune of our mortal and feeble condition is so wretched that when we consider it closely, nothing can console us," Sherry said. "That's Pascal." "I know," Peterson said, weakly. "Where is the john?" Louise asked. Ann marched into the kitchen and began to prepare, from supplies removed from her rucksack, something called *veal engagé*. "Kiss me," Sherry said, "I need love." Peterson flew to his friendly neighborhood bar, ordered a double brandy, and wedged himself into a telephone booth. "Miss Arbor? This is Hank Peterson. Listen, Miss Arbor, I can't do it. No, I mean really. I'm being punished horribly for even thinking about it. No, I mean it. You can't imagine what's going on around here. Please, get somebody else? I'd regard it as a great personal favor. Miss Arbor? Please?"

The other contestants were a young man in white pajamas named Arthur Pick, a karate expert, and an airline pilot in full uniform, Wallace E. Rice. "Just be natural," Miss Arbor said, "and of course be frank. We score on the basis of the validity of your answers, and of course that's measured by the polygraph." "What's this about a polygraph?" the airline pilot said. "The polygraph measures the validity of your answers," Miss Arbor said, her lips glowing whitely. "How else are we going to know if you're . . ." "Lying?" Wallace E. Rice supplied. The contestants were connected to the machine and the machine to a large illuminated tote board hanging over their heads. The master of ceremonies, Peterson noted without pleasure, resembled the President and did not look at all friendly.

The program began with Arthur Pick. Arthur Pick got up in his white pajamas and gave a karate demonstration in which he broke three half-inch pine boards with a single kick of his naked left foot. Then he told how he had disarmed a bandit, late at night at the A&P where he was an assistant manager, with a maneuver called a "rip-choong" which he demonstrated on the announcer. "How about that?" the announcer caroled. "Isn't that something? Audience?" The audience responded enthusiastically and Arthur Pick stood modestly with his hands behind his back. "Now," the announcer said, "let's play *Who Am I?* And here's your host, *Bill Lemmon!*" No, he doesn't look like the President, Peterson decided. "Arthur," Bill Lemmon said, "for twenty dollars—do you love your mother?" "Yes," Arthur Pick said. "Yes, of course." A bell rang, the tote board flashed, and the audience screamed. "He's lying!" the announcer shouted, "lying! lying! lying!" "Arthur," Bill Lemmon said, looking at his index cards, "the polygraph shows that the validity of your answer is . . . questionable. Would you like to try it again? Take another crack at it?" "You're crazy," Arthur Pick said. "Of course I love my mother." He was fishing around inside his pajamas for a handkerchief. "Is your mother watching the show tonight, Arthur?" "Yes, Bill, she is." "How long have you been studying karate?" "Two years, Bill." "And who paid for the lessons?" Arthur Pick hesitated. Then he said: "My mother, Bill." "They were pretty expensive, weren't they, Arthur?" "Yes, Bill, they were." "How expensive?" "Five dollars an hour." "Your mother doesn't make very much money, does she, Arthur?" "No, Bill, she doesn't." "Arthur, what does your mother do for a living?" "She's a garment worker, Bill. In the garment district." "And how long has she worked down there?" "All her life, I guess. Since my old man died." "And she doesn't make very much money, you said." "No. But she *wanted* to pay for the lessons. She *insisted* on it." Bill Lemmon said: "She wanted a son who could break boards with his feet?" Peterson's liver leaped and the tote board spelled out, in huge, glowing white letters, the words BAD FAITH. The airline pilot, Wallace E. Rice, was led to reveal that he had been caught, on a flight from Omaha to Miami, with a stewardess sitting on his lap and wearing his captain's cap, that the flight engineer had taken a Polaroid picture, and that he had been given involuntary retirement after nineteen years of faithful service. "It was perfectly safe," Wallace E. Rice said, "you don't understand, the automatic pilot can fly that plane better than I can." He further confessed to a lifelong and intolerable itch after stewardesses which had much to do, he said, with the way their jackets fell just on top of their hips, and his own jacket with the three gold stripes on the sleeve darkened with sweat until it was black.

I was wrong, Peterson thought, the world is absurd. The absurdity is punishing me for not believing in it. I affirm the absurdity. On the other hand, absurdity is itself absurd. Before the emcee could ask the first question, Peterson began to talk. "Yesterday," Peterson said to the television audience, "in the typewriter in front of the Olivetti showroom on Fifth Avenue, I found a recipe for Ten Ingredient Soup that included a stone from a toad's head. And while I stood there marveling a nice old lady pasted on the elbow of my best Haspel suit a little blue sticker reading THIS INDIVIDUAL IS A PART OF THE COMMUNIST CONSPIRACY FOR GLOBAL DOMINATION OF THE ENTIRE GLOBE. Coming home I passed a sign that said in ten-foot letters COWARD SHOES and heard a man singing "Golden Earrings" in a horrible voice, and last night I dreamed there was a shoot-out at our house on Meat Street and my mother shoved me in a closet to get me out of the line of fire." The emcee waved at the floor manager to turn Peterson off, but Peterson kept talking. "In this kind of a world," Peterson said, "absurd if you will, possibilities nevertheless proliferate and escalate all around us and there are opportunities for beginning again. I am a minor artist and my dealer won't even display my work if he can help it but minor is as minor does and lightning may strike even yet. Don't be reconciled. Turn off your television sets," Peterson said, "cash in your life insurance, indulge in a mindless optimism. Visit girls at dusk. Play the guitar. How can you be alienated without first having been connected? Think back and remember how it was." A man on the floor in front of Peterson was waving a piece of cardboard on which something threatening was written but Peterson ignored him and concentrated on the camera with the little red light. The little red light jumped from camera to camera in an attempt to throw him off balance but Peterson was too smart for it and followed wherever it went. "My mother was a royal virgin," Peterson said, "and my father a shower of gold. My childhood was pastoral and energetic and rich in experiences which developed my character. As a young man I was noble in reason, infinite in faculty, in form express and admirable, and in apprehension . . ." Peterson went on and on and although he was, in a sense, lying, in a sense he was not.

WOODY ALLEN

[b. 1935]

The Kugelmass Episode

Kugelmass, a professor of humanities at City College, was unhappily married for the second time. Daphne Kugelmass was an oaf. He also had two dull sons by his first wife, Flo, and was up to his neck in alimony and child support.

"Did I know it would turn out so badly?" Kugelmass whined to his analyst one day. "Daphne had promise. Who suspected she'd let herself go and swell up like a beach ball? Plus she had a few bucks, which is not in itself a healthy reason to marry a person, but it doesn't hurt, with the kind of operating nut I have. You see my point?"

Kugelmass was bald and as hairy as a bear, but he had soul.

"I need to meet a new woman," he went on. "I need to have an affair. I may not look the part, but I'm a man who needs romance. I need softness, I need flirtation. I'm not getting younger, so before it's too late I want to make love in Venice, trade quips at '21,' and exchange coy glances over red wine and candlelight. You see what I'm saying?"

Dr. Mandel shifted in his chair and said, "An affair will solve nothing. You're so unrealistic. Your problems run much deeper."

"And also this affair must be discreet," Kugelmass continued. "I can't afford a second divorce. Daphne would really sock it to me."

"Mr. Kugelmass—"

"But it can't be anyone at City College, because Daphne also works there. Not that anyone on the faculty at C.C.N.Y. is any great shakes, but some of those coeds . . ."

"Mr. Kugelmass—"

"Help me. I had a dream last night. I was skipping through a meadow holding a picnic basket and the basket was marked 'Options.' And then I saw there was a hole in the basket."

"Mr. Kugelmass, the worst thing you could do is act out. You must simply express your feelings here, and together we'll analyze them. You have been in treatment long enough to know there is no overnight cure. After all, I'm an analyst, not a magician."

"Then perhaps what I need is a magician," Kugelmass said, rising from his chair. And with that he terminated his therapy.

A couple of weeks later, while Kugelmass and Daphne were moping around in their apartment one night like two pieces of old furniture, the phone rang.

"I'll get it," Kugelmass said. "Hello."

"Kugelmass?" a voice said. "Kugelmass, this is Persky."

"Who?"

"Persky. Or should I say The Great Persky?"

"Pardon me?"

"I hear you're looking all over town for a magician to bring a little exotica into your life? Yes or no?"

"Sh-h-h," Kugelmass whispered. "Don't hang up. Where are you calling from, Persky?"

Early the following afternoon, Kugelmass climbed three flights of stairs in a broken-down apartment house in the Bushwick section of Brooklyn. Peering through the darkness of the hall, he found the door he was looking for and pressed the bell. I'm going to regret this, he thought to himself.

Seconds later, he was greeted by a short, thin, waxy-looking man.

"*You're* Persky the Great?" Kugelmass said.

"The Great Persky. You want a tea?"

"No, I want romance. I want music. I want love and beauty."

"But not tea, eh? Amazing. O.K., sit down."

Persky went to the back room, and Kugelmass heard the sounds of boxes and furniture being moved around. Persky reappeared, pushing before him a large object on squeaky roller-skate wheels. He removed some old silk handkerchiefs that were lying on its top and blew away a bit of dust. It was a cheap-looking Chinese cabinet, badly lacquered.

"Persky," Kugelmass said, "what's your scam?"

"Pay attention," Persky said. "This is some beautiful effect. I developed it for a Knights of Pythias date last year, but the booking fell through. Get into the cabinet."

"Why, so you can stick it full of swords or something?"

"You see any swords?"

Kugelmass made a face and, grunting, climbed into the cabinet. He couldn't help noticing a couple of ugly rhinestones glued onto the raw plywood just in front of his face. "If this is a joke," he said.

"Some joke. Now, here's the point. If I throw any novel into this cabinet with you, shut the doors, and tap it three times, you will find yourself projected into that book."

Kugelmass made a grimace of disbelief.

"It's the emess," Persky said. "My hand to God. Not just a novel, either. A short story, a play, a poem. You can meet any of the women created by the world's best writers. Whoever you dreamed of. You could carry on all you like with a real winner. Then when you've had enough you give a yell, and I'll see you're back here in a split second."

"Persky, are you some kind of outpatient?"

"I'm telling you it's on the level," Persky said.

Kugelmass remained skeptical. "What are you telling me—that this cheesy home-made box can take me on a ride like you're describing?"

"For a double sawbuck."

Kugelmass reached for his wallet. "I'll believe this when I see it," he said.

Persky tucked the bills in his pants pocket and turned toward his bookcase. "So who do you want to meet? Sister Carrie? Hester Prynne? Ophelia? Maybe someone by Saul Bellow? Hey, what about Temple Drake? Although for a man your age she'd be a workout."

"French. I want to have an affair with a French lover."

"Nana?"

"I don't want to have to pay for it."

"What about Natasha in 'War and Peace'?"

"I said French. I know! What about Emma Bovary? That sounds to me perfect."

"You got it, Kugelmass. Give me a holler when you've had enough." Persky tossed in a paperback copy of Flaubert's novel.

"You sure this is safe?" Kugelmass asked as Persky began shutting the cabinet doors.

"Safe. Is anything safe in this crazy world?" Persky rapped three times on the cabinet and then flung open the doors.

Kugelmass was gone. At the same moment, he appeared in the bedroom of Charles and Emma Bovary's house at Yonville. Before him was a beautiful woman, standing alone with her back turned to him as she folded some linen. I can't believe this, thought Kugelmass, staring at the doctor's ravishing wife. This is uncanny. I'm here. It's her.

Emma turned in surprise. "Goodness, you startled me," she said.

"Who are you?" She spoke in the same fine English translation as the paperback.

It's simply devastating, he thought. Then, realizing that it was he whom she had addressed, he said, "Excuse me. I'm Sidney Kugelmass. I'm from City College. A professor of humanities. C.C.N.Y.? Uptown. I—oh, boy!"

Emma Bovary smiled flirtatiously and said, "Would you like a drink? A glass of wine, perhaps?"

She is beautiful, Kugelmass thought. What a contrast with the troglodyte who shared his bed! He felt a sudden impulse to take this vision into his arms and tell her she was the kind of woman he had dreamed of all his life.

"Yes, some wine," he said hoarsely. "White. No, red. No, white. Make it white."

"Charles is out for the day," Emma said, her voice full of playful implication.

After the wine, they went for a stroll in the lovely French countryside. "I've always dreamed that some mysterious stranger would appear and rescue me from the monotony of this crass rural existence," Emma said, clasping his hand. They passed a small church. "I love what you have on," she murmured. "I've never seen anything like it around here. It's so . . . so modern."

"It's called a leisure suit," he said romantically. "It was marked down." Suddenly he kissed her. For the next hour they reclined under a tree and whispered together and told each other deeply meaningful things with their eyes. Then Kugelmass sat up. He had just remembered he had to meet Daphne at Bloomingdale's. "I must go," he told her. "But don't worry, I'll be back."

"I hope so," Emma said.

He embraced her passionately, and the two walked back to the house. He held Emma's face cupped in his palms, kissed her again, and yelled, "O.K., Persky! I got to be at Bloomingdale's by three-thirty."

There was an audible pop, and Kugelmass was back in Brooklyn.

"So? Did I lie?" Persky asked triumphantly.

"Look, Persky, I'm right now late to meet the ball and chain at Lexington Avenue, but when can I go again? Tomorrow?"

"My pleasure. Just bring a twenty. And don't mention this to anybody."

"Yeah. I'm going to call Rupert Murdoch."

Kugelmass hailed a cab and sped off to the city. His heart danced on point. I am in love, he thought, I am the possessor of a wonderful secret. What he didn't realize was that at this very moment students in various classrooms across the country were saying to their teachers, "Who is this character on page 100? A bald Jew is kissing Madame Bovary?" A teacher in Sioux Falls, South Dakota, sighed and thought, Jesus, these kids, with their pot and acid. What goes through their minds!

Daphne Kugelmass was in the bathroom-accessories department at Bloomingdale's when Kugelmass arrived breathlessly. "Where've you been?" she snapped. "It's four-thirty."

"I got held up in traffic," Kugelmass said.

Kugelmass visited Persky the next day, and in a few minutes was again passed magically to Yonville. Emma couldn't hide her excitement at seeing him. The two spent hours together, laughing and talking about their different backgrounds. Before Kugelmass left, they made love. "My God, I'm doing it with Madame Bovary!" Kugelmass whispered to himself. "Me, who failed freshman English."

As the months passed, Kugelmass saw Persky many times and developed a close and passionate relationship with Emma Bovary. "Make sure and always get me into the book before page 120," Kugelmass said to the magician one day. "I always have to meet her before she hooks up with this Rodolphe character."

"Why?" Persky asked. "You can't beat his time?"

"Beat his time. He's landed gentry. Those guys have nothing better to do than flirt and ride horses. To me, he's one of those faces you see in the pages of *Women's Wear Daily*. With the Helmut Berger hairdo. But to her he's hot stuff."

"And her husband suspects nothing?"

"He's out of his depth. He's a lackluster little paramedic who's thrown in his lot with a jitterbug. He's ready to go to sleep by ten, and she's putting on her dancing shoes. Oh, well . . . See you later."

And once again Kugelmass entered the cabinet and passed instantly to the Bovary estate at Yonville. "How you doing, cupcake?" he said to Emma.

"Oh, Kugelmass," Emma sighed. "What I have to put up with. Last night at dinner, Mr. Personality dropped off to sleep in the middle of the dessert course. I'm pouring my heart out about Maxim's and the ballet, and out of the blue I hear snoring."

"It's O.K., darling. I'm here now," Kugelmass said, embracing her. I've earned this, he thought, smelling Emma's French perfume and burying his nose in her hair. I've suffered enough. I've paid enough analysts. I've searched till I'm weary. She's young and nubile, and I'm here a few pages after Léon and just before Rodolphe. By showing up during the correct chapters, I've got the situation knocked.

Emma, to be sure, was just as happy as Kugelmass. She had been starved for excitement, and his tales of Broadway night life, of fast cars and Hollywood and TV stars, enthralled the young French beauty.

"Tell me again about O.J. Simpson," she implored that evening, as she and Kugelmass strolled past Abbé Bournisien's church.

"What can I say? The man is great. He sets all kinds of rushing records. Such moves. They can't touch him."

"And the Academy Awards?" Emma said wistfully. "I'd give anything to win one."

"First you've got to be nominated."

"I know. You explained it. But I'm convinced I can act. Of course, I'd want to take a class or two. With Strasberg maybe. Then, if I had the right agent—"

"We'll see, we'll see. I'll speak to Persky."

That night, safely returned to Persky's flat, Kugelmass brought up the idea of having Emma visit him in the big city.

"Let me think about it," Persky said. "Maybe I could work it. Stranger things have happened." Of course, neither of them could think of one.

"Where the hell do you go all the time?" Daphne Kugelmass barked at her husband as he returned home late that evening. "You got a chippie stashed somewhere?"

"Yeah, sure, I'm just the type," Kugelmass said wearily. "I was with Leonard Popkin. We were discussing Socialist agriculture in Poland. You know Popkin. He's a freak on the subject."

"Well, you've been very odd lately," Daphne said. "Distant. Just don't forget about my father's birthday. On Saturday?"

"Oh, sure, sure," Kugelmass said, heading for the bathroom.

"My whole family will be there. We can see the twins. And Cousin Hamish. You should be more polite to Cousin Hamish—he likes you."

"Right, the twins," Kugelmass said, closing the bathroom door and shutting out the sound of his wife's voice. He leaned against it and took a deep breath. In a few hours, he told himself, he would be back in Yonville again, back with his beloved. And this time, if all went well, he would bring Emma back with him.

At three-fifteen the following afternoon, Persky worked his wizardry again. Kugelmass appeared before Emma, smiling and eager. The two spent a few hours at Yonville with Binet and then remounted the Bovary carriage. Following Persky's instructions, they held each other tightly, closed their eyes, and counted to ten. When they opened them, the carriage was just drawing up at the side door of the Plaza Hotel, where Kugelmass had optimistically reserved a suite earlier in the day.

"I love it! It's everything I dreamed it would be," Emma said as she swirled joyously around the bedroom, surveying the city from their window. "There's F.A.O. Schwarz. And there's Central Park, and the Sherry is which one? Oh, there—I see. It's too divine."

On the bed there were boxes from Halston and Saint Laurent. Emma unwrapped a package and held up a pair of black velvet pants against her perfect body.

"The slacks suit is by Ralph Lauren," Kugelmass said. "You'll look like a million bucks in it. Come on, sugar, give us a kiss."

"I've never been so happy!" Emma squealed as she stood before the mirror. "Let's go out on the town. I want to see 'Chorus Line' and the Guggenheim and this Jack Nicholson character you always talk about. Are any of his flicks showing?"

"I cannot get my mind around this," a Stanford professor said. "First a strange character named Kugelmass, and now she's gone from the book. Well, I guess the mark of a classic is that you can reread it a thousand times and always find something new."

The lovers passed a blissful weekend. Kugelmass had told Daphne he would be away at a symposium in Boston and would return Monday. Savoring each moment, he and Emma went to the movies, had dinner in Chinatown, passed two hours at a discothèque, and went to bed with a TV movie. They slept till noon on Sunday, visited SoHo, and ogled celebrities at Elaine's. They had caviar and champagne in their suite on Sunday night and talked until dawn. That morning, in the cab taking them to Persky's apartment, Kugelmass thought, It was hectic, but worth it. I can't bring her here too often, but now and then it will be a charming contrast with Yonville.

At Persky's, Emma climbed into the cabinet, arranged her new boxes of clothes neatly around her, and kissed Kugelmass fondly. "My place next time," she said with a wink. Persky rapped three times on the cabinet. Nothing happened.

"Hmm," Persky said, scratching his head. He rapped again, but still no magic. "Something must be wrong," he mumbled.

"Persky, you're joking!" Kugelmass cried. "How can it not work?"

"Relax, relax. Are you still in the box, Emma?"

"Yes."

Persky rapped again—harder this time.

"I'm still here, Persky."

"I know, darling. Sit tight."

"Persky, we *have* to get her back," Kugelmass whispered. "I'm a married man, and I have a class in three hours. I'm not prepared for anything more than a cautious affair at this point."

"I can't understand it," Persky muttered. "It's such a reliable little trick."

But he could do nothing. "It's going to take a little while," he said to Kugelmass. "I'm going to have to strip it down. I'll call you later."

Kugelmass bundled Emma into a cab and took her back to the Plaza. He barely made it to his class on time. He was on the phone all day, to Persky and to his mistress. The magician told him it might be several days before he got to the bottom of the trouble.

"How was the symposium?" Daphne asked him that night.

"Fine, fine," he said, lighting the filter end of a cigarette.

"What's wrong? You're as tense as a cat."

"Me? Ha, that's a laugh. I'm as calm as a summer night. I'm just going to take a walk." He eased out the door, hailed a cab, and flew to the Plaza.

"This is no good," Emma said. "Charles will miss me."

"Bear with me, sugar," Kugelmass said. He was pale and sweaty. He kissed her again, raced to the elevators, yelled at Persky over a pay phone in the Plaza lobby, and just made it home before midnight.

"According to Popkin, barley prices in Kraków have not been this stable since 1971," he said to Daphne, and smiled wanly as he climbed into bed.

The whole week went by like that. On Friday night, Kugelmass told Daphne there was another symposium he had to catch, this one in Syracuse. He hurried back to the Plaza, but the second weekend there was nothing like the first. "Get me back into the novel or marry me," Emma told Kugelmass. "Meanwhile, I want to get a job or go to class, because watching TV all day is the pits."

"Fine. We can use the money," Kugelmass said. "You consume twice your weight in room service."

"I met an Off Broadway producer in Central Park yesterday, and he said I might be right for a project he's doing," Emma said.

"Who is this clown?" Kugelmass asked.

"He's not a clown. He's sensitive and kind and cute. His name's Jeff Something-or-Other, and he's up for a Tony."

Later that afternoon, Kugelmass showed up at Persky's drunk.

"Relax," Persky told him. "You'll get a coronary."

"Relax. The man says relax. I've got a fictional character stashed in a hotel room, and I think my wife is having me tailed by a private shamus."

"O.K., O.K. We know there's a problem." Persky crawled under the cabinet and started banging on something with a large wrench.

"I'm like a wild animal," Kugelmass went on. "I'm sneaking around town, and Emma and I have had it up to here with each other. Not to mention a hotel tab that reads like the defense budget."

"So what should I do? This is the world of magic," Persky said. "It's all nuance."

"Nuance, my foot. I'm pouring Dom Pérignon and black eggs into this little mouse, plus her wardrobe, plus she's enrolled at the Neighborhood Playhouse and suddenly needs professional photos. Also, Persky, Professor Fivish Kopkind, who teaches Comp Lit and who has always been jealous of me, has identified me as the sporadically appearing character in the Flaubert book. He's threatened to go to Daphne. I see ruin and alimony jail. For adultery with Madame Bovary, my wife will reduce me to beggary."

"What do you want me to say? I'm working on it night and day. As far as your personal anxiety goes, that I can't help you with. I'm a magician, not an analyst."

By Sunday afternoon, Emma had locked herself in the bathroom and refused to respond to Kugelmass's entreaties. Kugelmass stared out the window at the Wollman Rink and contemplated suicide. Too bad this is a low floor, he thought, or I'd do it right now. Maybe if I ran away to Europe and started life over . . . Maybe I could sell the *International Herald Tribune,* like those young girls used to.

The phone rang. Kugelmass lifted it to his ear mechanically.

"Bring her over," Persky said. "I think I got the bugs out of it."

Kugelmass's heart leaped. "You're serious?" he said. "You got it licked?"

"It was something in the transmission. Go figure."

"Persky, you're a genius. We'll be there in a minute. Less than a minute."

Again the lovers hurried to the magician's apartment, and again Emma Bovary climbed into the cabinet with her boxes. This time there was no kiss. Persky shut the doors, took a deep breath, and tapped the box three times. There was the reassuring popping noise, and when Persky peered inside, the box was empty. Madame Bovary was back in her novel. Kugelmass heaved a great sigh of relief and pumped the magician's hand.

"It's over," he said. "I learned my lesson. I'll never cheat again, I swear it." He pumped Persky's hand again and made a mental note to send him a necktie.

Three weeks later, at the end of a beautiful spring afternoon, Persky answered his doorbell. It was Kugelmass, with a sheepish expression on his face.

"O.K., Kugelmass," the magician said. "Where to this time?"

"It's just this once," Kugelmass said. "The weather is so lovely, and I'm not getting any younger. Listen, you've read 'Portnoy's Complaint'? Remember The Monkey?"

"The price is now twenty-five dollars, because the cost of living is up, but I'll start you off with one freebie, due to all the trouble I caused you."

"You're good people," Kugelmass said, combing his few remaining hairs as he climbed into the cabinet again. "This'll work all right?"

"I hope. But I haven't tried it much since all that unpleasantness."

"Sex and romance," Kugelmass said from inside the box. "What we go through for a pretty face."

Persky tossed in a copy of "Portnoy's Complaint" and rapped three times on the box. This time, instead of a popping noise there was a dull explosion, followed by a series of crackling noises and a shower of sparks. Persky leaped back, was seized by a heart attack, and dropped dead. The cabinet burst into flames, and eventually the entire house burned down.

Kugelmass, unaware of this catastrophe, had his own problems. He had not been thrust into "Portnoy's Complaint," or into any other novel, for that matter. He had been projected into an old textbook, "Remedial Spanish," and was running for his life over a barren, rocky terrain as the word *"tener"* ("to have")—a large and hairy irregular verb—raced after him on its spindly legs.

RAYMOND CARVER
[*b. 1939*]

Cathedral

This blind man, an old friend of my wife's, he was on his way to spend the night. His wife had died. So he was visiting the dead wife's relatives in Connecticut. He called my wife from his in-laws'. Arrangements were made. He would come by train, a five-hour trip, and my wife would meet him at the station. She hadn't seen him since she worked for him one summer in Seattle ten years ago. But she and the blind man had kept in touch. They made tapes and mailed them back and forth. I wasn't enthusiastic about his visit. He was no one I knew. And his being blind bothered me. My idea of blindness came from the movies. In the movies, the blind moved slowly and never laughed. Sometimes they were led by seeing-eye dogs. A blind man in my house was not something I looked forward to.

That summer in Seattle she had needed a job. She didn't have any money. The man she was going to marry at the end of the summer was in officers' training school. He didn't have any money, either. But she was in love with the guy, and he was in love with her, etc. She'd seen something in the paper: HELP WANTED—*Reading to Blind Man,* and a telephone number. She phoned and went over, was hired on the spot. She'd worked with this blind man all summer. She read stuff to him, case studies, reports, that sort of thing. She helped him organize his little office in the county social-service department. They'd become good friends, my wife and the blind man. How do I know these things? She told me. And she told me something else. On her last day in the office, the blind man asked if he could touch her face. She agreed to this. She told me he touched his fingers to every part of her face, her nose—even her neck! She never forgot it. She even tried to write a poem about it. She was always trying to write a poem. She wrote a poem or two every year, usually after something really important had happened to her.

When we first started going out together, she showed me the poem. In the poem, she recalled his fingers and the way they had moved around over her face. In the poem, she talked about what she had felt at the time, about what went through her mind when the blind man touched her nose and lips. I can remember I didn't think much of the poem. Of course, I didn't tell her that. Maybe I just don't understand poetry. I admit it's not the first thing I reach for when I pick up something to read.

Anyway, this man who'd first enjoyed her favors, the officer-to-be, he'd been her childhood sweetheart. So okay. I'm saying that at the end of the summer she let the blind man run his hands over her face, said goodbye to him, married her childhood etc., who was now a commissioned officer, and she moved away from Seattle. But they'd kept in touch, she and the blind man. She made the first contact after a year or so. She called him up one night from an Air Force base in Alabama. She wanted to talk. They talked. He asked her to send him a tape and tell him about her life. She did this. She sent the tape. On the tape, she told the blind man about her husband and about their life together in the military. She told the blind man she loved her husband but she didn't like it where they lived and she didn't like it that he was a part of the military-industrial thing. She told the blind man she'd written a poem and he was in it. She told him that she was writing a poem about what it was like to be an Air Force officer's wife. The poem wasn't finished yet. She was still writing it. The blind man made a tape. He sent her the tape. She made a tape. This went on for years. My wife's officer was posted to one base and then another. She sent tapes from Moody AFB, McGuire, McConnell, and finally Travis, near Sacramento, where one night she got to feeling lonely and cut off from people she kept losing in that moving-around life. She got to feeling she couldn't go it another step. She went in and swallowed all the pills and capsules in the medicine chest and washed them down with a bottle of gin. Then she got into a hot bath and passed out.

But instead of dying, she got sick. She threw up. Her officer—why should he have a name? he was the childhood sweetheart, and what more does he want?—came home from somewhere, found her, and called the ambulance. In time, she put it all on a tape and sent the tape to the blind man. Over the years, she put all kinds of stuff on tapes and sent the tapes off lickety-split. Next to writing a poem every year, I think it was her chief means of recreation. On one tape, she told the blind man she'd decided to live away from her officer for a time. On another tape, she told him about her divorce. She and I began going out, and of course she told her blind man about it. She told him everything, or so it seemed to me. Once she asked me if I'd like to hear the latest tape from the blind man. This was a year ago. I was on the tape, she said. So I said okay, I'd listen to it. I got us drinks and we settled down in the living room. We made ready to listen. First she inserted the tape into the player and adjusted a couple of dials. Then she pushed a lever. The tape squeaked and someone began to talk in this loud voice. She lowered the volume. After a few minutes of harmless chitchat, I heard my own name in the mouth of this stranger, this blind man I didn't even know! And then this: "From all you've said about him, I can only conclude—" But we were interrupted, a knock at the door, something, and we didn't ever get back to the tape. Maybe it was just as well. I'd heard all I wanted to.

Now this same blind man was coming to sleep in my house.

"Maybe I could take him bowling," I said to my wife. She was at the draining board doing scalloped potatoes. She put down the knife she was using and turned around.

"If you love me," she said, "you can do this for me. If you don't love me, okay. But if you had a friend, any friend, and the friend came to visit, I'd make him feel comfortable." She wiped her hands with the dish towel.

"I don't have any blind friends," I said.

"You don't have *any* friends," she said. "Period. Besides," she said, "goddamn it, his wife's just died! Don't you understand that? The man's lost his wife!"

I didn't answer. She'd told me a little about the blind man's wife. Her name was Beulah. Beulah! That's a name for a colored woman.

"Was his wife a Negro?" I asked.

"Are you crazy?" my wife said. "Have you just flipped or something?" She picked up a potato. I saw it hit the floor, then roll under the stove. "What's wrong with you?" she said. "Are you drunk?"

"I'm just asking," I said.

Right then my wife filled me in with more detail than I cared to know. I made a drink and sat at the kitchen table to listen. Pieces of the story began to fall into place.

Beulah had gone to work for the blind man the summer after my wife had stopped working for him. Pretty soon Beulah and the blind man had themselves a church wedding. It was a little wedding—who'd want to go to such a wedding in the first place?—just the two of them, plus the minister and the minister's wife. But it was a church wedding just the same. It was what Beulah had wanted, he'd said. But even then Beulah must have been carrying the cancer in her glands. After they had been inseparable for eight years—my wife's word, *inseparable*—Beulah's health went into a rapid decline. She died in a Seattle hospital room, the blind man sitting beside the bed and holding on to her hand. They'd married, lived and worked together, slept together—had sex, sure—and then the blind man had to bury her. All this without his having ever seen what the goddamned woman looked like. It was beyond my understanding. Hearing this, I felt sorry for the blind man for a little bit. And then I found myself thinking what a pitiful life this woman must have led. Imagine a woman who could never see herself as she was seen in the eyes of her loved one. A woman who could go on day after day and never receive the smallest compliment from her beloved. A woman whose husband could never read the expression on her face, be it misery or something better. Someone who could wear makeup or not—what difference to him? She could, if she wanted, wear green eye-shadow around one eye, a straight pin in her nostril, yellow slacks and purple shoes, no matter. And then to slip off into death, the blind man's hand on her hand, his blind eyes streaming tears—I'm imagining now— her last thought maybe this: that he never even knew what she looked like, and she on an express to the grave. Robert was left with a small insurance policy and half of a twenty-peso Mexican coin. The other half of the coin went into the box with her. Pathetic.

So when the time rolled around, my wife went to the depot to pick him up. With nothing to do but wait—sure, I blamed him for that—I was having a drink and watching the TV when I heard the car pull into the drive. I got up from the sofa with my drink and went to the window to have a look.

I saw my wife laughing as she parked the car. I saw her get out of the car and shut the door. She was still wearing a smile. Just amazing. She went around to the other side of the car to where the blind man was already starting to get out. This blind man, feature this, he was wearing a full beard! A beard on a blind man! Too much, I say. The blind man reached into the back seat and dragged out a suitcase. My wife took his arm, shut the car door, and, talking all the way, moved him down the drive and then up the steps to the front porch. I turned off the TV. I finished my drink, rinsed the glass, dried my hands. Then I went to the door.

My wife said, "I want you to meet Robert. Robert, this is my husband. I've told you all about him." She was beaming. She had this blind man by his coat sleeve.

The blind man let go of his suitcase and up came his hand.

I took it. He squeezed hard, held my hand, and then he let it go.

"I feel like we've already met," he boomed.

"Likewise," I said. I didn't know what else to say. Then I said, "Welcome. I've heard a lot about you." We began to move then, a little group, from the porch into the living room, my wife guiding him by the arm. The blind man was carrying his suitcase in his other hand. My wife said things like, "To your left here, Robert. That's right. Now watch it, there's a chair. That's it. Sit down right here. This is the sofa. We just bought this sofa two weeks ago."

I started to say something about the old sofa. I'd liked that old sofa. But I didn't say anything. Then I wanted to say something else, small-talk, about the scenic ride along the Hudson. How going *to* New York, you should sit on the right-hand side of the train, and coming *from* New York, the left-hand side.

"Did you have a good train ride?" I said. "Which side of the train did you sit on, by the way?"

"What a question, which side!" my wife said. "What's it matter which side?" she said.

"I just asked," I said.

"Right side," the blind man said. "I hadn't been on a train in nearly forty years. Not since I was a kid. With my folks. That's been a long time. I'd nearly forgotten the sensation. I have winter in my beard now," he said. "So I've been told, anyway. Do I look distinguished, my dear?" the blind man said to my wife.

"You look distinguished, Robert," she said. "Robert," she said. "Robert, it's just so good to see you."

My wife finally took her eyes off the blind man and looked at me. I had the feeling she didn't like what she saw. I shrugged.

I've never met, or personally known, anyone who was blind. This blind man was late forties, a heavy-set, balding man with stooped shoulders, as if he carried a great weight there. He wore brown slacks, brown shoes, a light-brown shirt, a tie, a sports coat. Spiffy. He also had this full beard. But he didn't use a cane and he didn't wear dark glasses. I'd always thought dark glasses were a must for the blind. Fact was, I wished he had a pair. At first glance, his eyes looked like anyone else's eyes. But if you looked close, there was something different about them. Too much white in the iris, for one thing, and the pupils seemed to move around in the sockets without his knowing it or being able to stop it. Creepy. As I stared at his face, I saw the left pupil turn in toward his nose while the other made an effort to keep in one place. But it was only an effort, for that eye was on the roam without his knowing it or wanting it to be.

I said, "Let me get you a drink. What's your pleasure? We have a little of everything. It's one of our pastimes."

"Bub, I'm a Scotch man myself," he said fast enough in this big voice.

"Right," I said. Bub! "Sure you are. I knew it."

He let his fingers touch his suitcase, which was sitting alongside the sofa. He was taking his bearings. I didn't blame him for that.

"I'll move that up to your room," my wife said.

"No, that's fine," the blind man said loudly. "It can go up when I go up."

"A little water with the Scotch?" I said.

"Very little," he said.

"I knew it," I said.

He said, "Just a tad. The Irish actor, Barry Fitzgerald? I'm like that fellow. When I drink water, Fitzgerald said, I drink water. When I drink whiskey, I drink whiskey." My wife laughed. The blind man brought his hand up under his beard. He lifted his beard slowly and let it drop.

I did the drinks, three big glasses of Scotch with a splash of water in each. Then we made ourselves comfortable and talked about Robert's travels. First the long flight from the West Coast to Connecticut, we covered that. Then from Connecticut up here by train. We had another drink concerning that leg of the trip.

I remembered having read somewhere that the blind didn't smoke because, as speculation had it, they couldn't see the smoke they exhaled. I thought I knew that much and that much only about blind people. But this blind man smoked his cigarette down to the nubbin and then lit another one. This blind man filled his ashtray and my wife emptied it.

When we sat down at the table for dinner, we had another drink. My wife heaped Robert's plate with cube steak, scalloped potatoes, green beans. I buttered him up two slices of bread. I said, "Here's bread and butter for you." I swallowed some of my drink. "Now let us pray," I said, and the blind man lowered his head. My wife looked at me, her mouth agape. "Pray the phone won't ring and the food doesn't get cold," I said.

We dug in. We ate everything there was to eat on the table. We ate like there was no tomorrow. We didn't talk. We ate. We scarfed. We grazed that table. We were into serious eating. The blind man had right away located his foods, he knew just where everything was on his plate. I watched with admiration as he used his knife and fork on the meat. He'd cut two pieces of meat, fork the meat into his mouth, and then go all out for the scalloped potatoes, the beans next, and then he'd tear off a hunk of buttered bread and eat that. He'd follow this up with a big drink of milk. It didn't seem to bother him to use his fingers once in a while, either.

We finished everything, including half a strawberry pie. For a few moments, we sat as if stunned. Sweat beaded on our faces. Finally, we got up from the table and left the dirty plates. We didn't look back. We took ourselves into the living room and sank into our places again. Robert and my wife sat on the sofa. I took the big chair. We had us two or three more drinks while they talked about the major things that had come to pass for them in the past ten years. For the most part, I just listened. Now and then I joined in. I didn't want him to think I'd left the room, and I didn't want her to think I was feeling left out. They talked of things that had happened to them—to them!—these past ten years. I waited in vain to hear my name on my wife's sweet lips: "And then my dear husband came into my life"—something like that. But I heard nothing of the sort. More talk of Robert. Robert had done a little of everything, it seemed, a regular blind jack-of-all-trades. But most recently he and his wife had had an Amway distributorship, from which, I gathered, they'd earned their living, such as it was. The blind man was also a ham radio operator. He talked in his loud voice about conversations he'd had with fellow operators in Guam, in the Philippines, in Alaska, and even in Tahiti. He said he'd have a lot of friends there if he ever wanted to go visit those places. From time to time, he'd turn his blind face toward me, put his hand under his beard, ask me something. How long had I been in my present position? (Three years.) Did I like my work? (I didn't.) Was I going to stay with it? (What were the options?) Finally, when I thought he was beginning to run down, I got up and turned on the TV.

My wife looked at me with irritation. She was heading toward a boil. Then she looked at the blind man and said, "Robert, do you have a TV?"

The blind man said, "My dear, I have two TVs. I have a color set and a black-and-white thing, an old relic. It's funny, but if I turn the TV on, and I'm always turning it on, I turn on the color set. It's funny, don't you think?"

I didn't know what to say to that. I had absolutely nothing to say to that. No opinion. So I watched the news program and tried to listen to what the announcer was saying.

"This is a color TV," the blind man said. "Don't ask me how, but I can tell."

"We traded up a while ago," I said.

The blind man had another taste of his drink. He lifted his beard, sniffed it, and let it fall. He leaned forward on the sofa. He positioned his ashtray on the coffee table, then put the lighter to his cigarette. He leaned back on the sofa and crossed his legs at the ankles.

My wife covered her mouth, and then she yawned. She stretched. She said, "I think I'll go upstairs and put on my robe. I think I'll change into something else. Robert, you make yourself comfortable," she said.

"I'm comfortable," the blind man said.

"I want you to feel comfortable in this house," she said.

"I am comfortable," the blind man said.

After she'd left the room, he and I listened to the weather report and then to the sports roundup. By that time, she'd been gone so long I didn't know if she was going to come back. I thought she might have gone to bed. I wished she'd come back downstairs. I didn't want to be left alone with a blind man. I asked him if he wanted another drink, and he said sure. Then I asked if he wanted to smoke some dope with me. I said I'd just rolled a number. I hadn't, but I planned to do so in about two shakes.

"I'll try some with you," he said.

"Damn right," I said. "That's the stuff."

I got our drinks and sat down on the sofa with him. Then I rolled us two fat numbers. I lit one and passed it. I brought it to his fingers. He took it and inhaled.

"Hold it as long as you can," I said. I could tell he didn't know the first thing.

My wife came back downstairs wearing her pink robe and her pink slippers.

"What do I smell?" she said.

"We thought we'd have us some cannabis," I said.

My wife gave me a savage look. Then she looked at the blind man and said, "Robert, I didn't know you smoked."

He said, "I do now, my dear. There's a first time for everything. But I don't feel anything yet."

"This stuff is pretty mellow," I said. "This stuff is mild. It's dope you can reason with," I said. "It doesn't mess you up."

"Not much it doesn't, bub," he said, and laughed.

My wife sat on the sofa between the blind man and me. I passed her the number. She took it and toked and then passed it back to me. "Which way is this going?" she said. Then she said, "I shouldn't be smoking this. I can hardly keep my eyes open as it is. That dinner did me in. I shouldn't have eaten so much."

"It was the strawberry pie," the blind man said. "That's what did it," he said, and he laughed his big laugh. Then he shook his head.

"There's more strawberry pie," I said.

"Do you want some more, Robert?" my wife said.

"Maybe in a little while," he said.

We gave our attention to the TV. My wife yawned again. She said, "Your bed is made up when you feel like going to bed, Robert. I know you must have had a long day. When you're ready to go to bed, say so." She pulled his arm. "Robert?"

He came to and said, "I've had a real nice time. This beats tapes, doesn't it?"

I said, "Coming at you," and I put the number between his fingers. He inhaled, held the smoke, and then let it go. It was like he'd been doing it since he was nine years old.

"Thanks, bub," he said. "But I think this is all for me. I think I'm beginning to feel it," he said. He held the burning roach out for my wife.

"Same here," she said. "Ditto. Me, too." She took the roach and passed it to me. "I may just sit here for a while between you two guys with my eyes closed. But don't let me bother you, okay? Either one of you. If it bothers you, say so. Otherwise, I may just sit here with my eyes closed until you're ready to go to bed," she said. "Your bed's made up, Robert, when you're ready. It's right next to our room at the top of the stairs. We'll show you up when you're ready. You wake me up now, you guys, if I fall asleep." She said that and then she closed her eyes and went to sleep.

The news program ended. I got up and changed the channel. I sat back down on the sofa. I wished my wife hadn't pooped out. Her head lay across the back of the sofa, her mouth open. She'd turned so that her robe had slipped away from her legs, exposing

a juicy thigh. I reached to draw her robe back over her, and it was then that I glanced
at the blind man. What the hell! I flipped the robe open again.

"You say when you want some strawberry pie," I said.

"I will," he said.

I said, "Are you tired? Do you want me to take you up to your bed? Are you ready
to hit the hay?"

"Not yet," he said. "No, I'll stay up with you, bub. If that's all right. I'll stay up
until you're ready to turn in. We haven't had a chance to talk. Know what I mean?
I feel like me and her monopolized the evening." He lifted his beard and he let it fall.
He picked up his cigarettes and his lighter.

"That's all right," I said. Then I said, "I'm glad for the company."

And I guess I was. Every night I smoked dope and stayed up as long as I could before
I fell asleep. My wife and I hardly ever went to bed at the same time. When I did go
to sleep, I had these dreams. Sometimes I'd wake up from one of them, my heart going
crazy.

Something about the church and the Middle Ages was on the TV. Not your
run-of-the-mill TV fare. I wanted to watch something else. I turned to the other
channels. But there was nothing on them, either. So I turned back to the first channel
and apologized.

"Bub, it's all right," the blind man said. "It's fine with me. Whatever you want to
watch is okay. I'm always learning something. Learning never ends. It won't hurt me
to learn something tonight. I got ears," he said.

We didn't say anything for a time. He was leaning forward with his head turned at
me, his right ear aimed in the direction of the set. Very disconcerting. Now and then
his eyelids drooped and then they snapped open again. Now and then he put his fingers
into his beard and tugged, like he was thinking about something he was hearing on
the television.

On the screen, a group of men wearing cowls was being set upon and tormented
by men dressed in skeleton costumes and men dressed as devils. The men dressed as devils
wore devil masks, horns, and long tails. This pageant was part of a procession. The
Englishman who was narrating the thing said it took place in Spain once a year. I tried
to explain to the blind man what was happening.

"Skeletons," he said. "I know about skeletons," he said, and he nodded.

The TV showed this one cathedral. Then there was a long, slow look at another one.
Finally, the picture switched to the famous one in Paris, with its flying buttresses and
its spires reaching up to the clouds. The camera pulled away to show the whole of the
cathedral rising above the skyline.

There were times when the Englishman who was telling the thing would shut up,
would simply let the camera move around over the cathedrals. Or else the camera would
tour the countryside, men in fields walking behind oxen. I waited as long as I could.
Then I felt I had to say something. I said, "They're showing the outside of this cathedral
now. Gargoyles. Little statues carved to look like monsters. Now I guess they're in Italy.
Yeah, they're in Italy. There's paintings on the walls of this one church."

"Are those fresco paintings, bub?" he asked, and he sipped from his drink.

I reached for my glass. But it was empty. I tried to remember what I could remember.
"You're asking me are those frescoes?" I said. "That's a good question. I don't know."

The camera moved to a cathedral outside Lisbon. The differences in the Portuguese cathedral compared with the French and Italian were not that great. But they were there. Mostly the interior stuff. Then something occurred to me, and I said, "Something has occurred to me. Do you have any idea what a cathedral is? What they look like, that is? Do you follow me? If somebody says cathedral to you, do you have any notion what they're talking about? Do you know the difference between that and a Baptist church, say?"

He let the smoke dribble from his mouth. "I know they took hundreds of workers fifty or a hundred years to build," he said. "I just heard the man say that, of course. I know generations of the same families worked on a cathedral. I heard him say that, too. The men who began their life's work on them, they never lived to see the completion of their work. In that wise, bub, they're no different from the rest of us, right?" He laughed. Then his eyelids drooped again. His head nodded. He seemed to be snoozing. Maybe he was imagining himself in Portugal. The TV was showing another cathedral now. This one was in Germany. The Englishman's voice droned on. "Cathedrals," the blind man said. He sat up and rolled his head back and forth. "If you want the truth, bub, that's about all I know. What I just said. What I heard him say. But maybe you could describe one to me? I wish you'd do it. I'd like that. If you want to know, I really don't have a good idea."

I stared hard at the shot of the cathedral on the TV. How could I even begin to describe it? But say my life depended on it. Say my life was being threatened by an insane guy who said I had to do it or else.

I stared some more at the cathedral before the picture flipped off into the countryside. There was no use. I turned to the blind man and said, "To begin with, they're very tall." I was looking around the room for clues. "They reach way up. Up and up. Toward the sky. They're so big, some of them, they have to have these supports. To help hold them up, so to speak. These supports are called buttresses. They remind me of viaducts, for some reason. But maybe you don't know viaducts, either? Sometimes the cathedrals have devils and such carved into the front. Sometimes lords and ladies. Don't ask me why this is," I said.

He was nodding. The whole upper part of his body seemed to be moving back and forth.

"I'm not doing so good, am I?" I said.

He stopped nodding and leaned forward on the edge of the sofa. As he listened to me, he was running his fingers through his beard. I wasn't getting through to him, I could see that. But he waited for me to go on just the same. He nodded, like he was trying to encourage me. I tried to think what else to say. "They're really big," I said. "They're massive. They're built of stone. Marble, too, sometimes. In those olden days, when they built cathedrals, men wanted to be close to God. In those olden days, God was an important part of everyone's life. You could tell this from their cathedral-building. I'm sorry," I said, "but it looks like that's the best I can do for you. I'm just no good at it."

"That's all right, bub," the blind man said. "Hey, listen. I hope you don't mind my asking you. Can I ask you something? Let me ask you a simple question, yes or no. I'm just curious and there's no offense. You're my host. But let me ask if you are in any way religious? You don't mind my asking?"

I shook my head. He couldn't see that, though. A wink is the same as a nod to a blind man. "I guess I don't believe in it. In anything. Sometimes it's hard. You know what I'm saying?"

"Sure, I do," he said.

"Right," I said.

The Englishman was still holding forth. My wife sighed in her sleep. She drew a long breath and went on with her sleeping.

"You'll have to forgive me," I said. "But I can't tell you what a cathedral looks like. It just isn't in me to do it. I can't do any more than I've done."

The blind man sat very still, his head down, as he listened to me.

I said, "The truth is, cathedrals don't mean anything special to me. Nothing. Cathedrals. They're something to look at on late-night TV. That's all they are."

It was then that the blind man cleared his throat. He brought something up. He took a handkerchief from his back pocket. Then he said, "I get it, bub. It's okay. It happens. Don't worry about it," he said. "Hey, listen to me. Will you do me a favor? I got an idea. Why don't you find us some heavy paper? And a pen. We'll do something. We'll draw one together. Get us a pen and some heavy paper. Go on, bub, get the stuff," he said.

So I went upstairs. My legs felt like they didn't have any strength in them. They felt like they did after I'd done some running. In my wife's room, I looked around. I found some ballpoints in a little basket on her table. And then I tried to think where to look for the kind of paper he was talking about.

Downstairs, in the kitchen, I found a shopping bag with onion skins in the bottom of the bag. I emptied the bag and shook it. I brought it into the living room and sat down with it near his legs. I moved some things, smoothed the wrinkles from the bag, spread it out on the coffee table.

The blind man got down from the sofa and sat next to me on the carpet.

He ran his fingers over the paper. He went up and down the sides of the paper. The edges, even the edges. He fingered the corners.

"All right," he said. "All right, let's do her."

He found my hand, the hand with the pen. He closed his hand over my hand. "Go ahead, bub, draw," he said. "Draw. You'll see. I'll follow along with you. It'll be okay. Just begin now like I'm telling you. You'll see. Draw," the blind man said.

So I began. First I drew a box that looked like a house. It could have been the house I lived in. Then I put a roof on it. At either end of the roof, I drew spires. Crazy.

"Swell," he said. "Terrific. You're doing fine," he said. "Never thought anything like this could happen in your lifetime, did you, bub? Well, it's a strange life, we all know that. Go on now. Keep it up."

I put in windows with arches. I drew flying buttresses. I hung great doors. I couldn't stop. The TV station went off the air. I put down the pen and closed and opened my fingers. The blind man felt around over the paper. He moved the tips of his fingers over the paper, all over what I had drawn, and he nodded.

"Doing fine," the blind man said.

I took up the pen again, and he found my hand. I kept at it. I'm no artist. But I kept drawing just the same.

My wife opened up her eyes and gazed at us. She sat up on the sofa, her robe hanging open. She said, "What are you doing? Tell me, I want to know."

I didn't answer her.

The blind man said, "We're drawing a cathedral. Me and him are working on it.

Press hard," he said to me. "That's right. That's good," he said. "Sure. You got it, bub. I can tell. You didn't think you could. But you can, can't you? You're cooking with gas now. You know what I'm saying? We're going to really have us something here in a minute. How's the old arm?" he said. "Put some people in there now. What's a cathedral without people?"

My wife said, "What's going on? Robert, what are you doing? What's going on?"

"It's all right," he said to her. "Close your eyes now," the blind man said to me.

I did it. I closed them just like he said.

"Are they closed?" he said. "Don't fudge."

"They're closed," I said.

"Keep them that way," he said. He said, "Don't stop now. Draw."

So we kept on with it. His fingers rode my fingers as my hand went over the paper. It was like nothing else in my life up to now.

Then he said, "I think that's it. I think you got it," he said. "Take a look. What do you think?"

But I had my eyes closed. I thought I'd keep them that way for a little longer. I thought it was something I ought to do.

"Well?" he said. "Are you looking?"

My eyes were still closed. I was in my house. I knew that. But I didn't feel like I was inside anything.

"It's really something," I said.

ALICE WALKER

[b. 1944]

Everyday Use

for your grandmama

I will wait for her in the yard that Maggie and I made so clean and wavy yesterday afternoon. A yard like this is more comfortable than most people know. It is not just a yard. It is like an extended living room. When the hard clay is swept clean as a floor and the fine sand around the edges lined with tiny, irregular grooves anyone can come and sit and look up into the elm tree and wait for the breezes that never come inside the house.

Maggie will be nervous until after her sister goes: she will stand hopelessly in corners homely and ashamed of the burn scars down her arms and legs, eyeing her sister with a mixture of envy and awe. She thinks her sister has held life always in the palm of one hand, that "no" is a word the world never learned to say to her.

You've no doubt seen those TV shows where the child who has "made it" is confronted, as a surprise, by her own mother and father, tottering in weakly from backstage. (A pleasant surprise, of course: What would they do if parent and child came on the show only to curse out and insult each other?) On TV mother and child embrace and smile into each other's faces. Sometimes the mother and father weep, the child wraps them in her arms and leans across the table to tell how she would not have made it without their help. I have seen these programs.

Sometimes I dream a dream in which Dee and I are suddenly brought together on a TV program of this sort. Out of a dark and soft-seated limousine I am ushered into a bright room filled with many people. There I meet a smiling, gray, sporty man like Johnny Carson who shakes my hand and tells me what a fine girl I have. Then we are on the stage and Dee is embracing me with tears in her eyes. She pins on my dress a large orchid, even though she has told me once that she thinks orchids are tacky flowers.

In real life I am a large, big-boned woman with rough, man-working hands. In the winter I wear flannel nightgowns to bed and overalls during the day. I can kill and clean a hog as mercilessly as a man. My fat keeps me hot in zero weather. I can work outside all day, breaking ice to get water for washing; I can eat pork liver cooked over the open fire minutes after it comes steaming from the hog. One winter I knocked a bull calf straight in the brain between the eyes with a sledge hammer and had the meat hung up to chill before nightfall. But of course all this does not show on television. I am the way my daughter would want me to be: a hundred pounds lighter, my skin like an uncooked barley pancake. My hair glistens in the hot bright lights. Johnny Carson has much to do to keep up with my quick and witty tongue.

But that is a mistake. I know even before I wake up. Who ever knew a Johnson with a quick tongue? Who can even imagine me looking a strange white man in the eye? It seems to me I have talked to them always with one foot raised in flight, with my head turned in whichever way is farthest from them. Dee, though. She would always look anyone in the eye. Hesitation was no part of her nature.

"How do I look, Mama?" Maggie says, showing just enough of her thin body enveloped in pink skirt and red blouse for me to know she's there, almost hidden by the door.

"Come out into the yard," I say.

Have you ever seen a lame animal, perhaps a dog run over by some careless person rich enough to own a car, sidle up to someone who is ignorant enough to be kind to him? That is the way my Maggie walks. She has been like this, chin on chest, eyes on ground, feet in shuffle, ever since the fire that burned the other house to the ground.

Dee is lighter than Maggie, with nicer hair and a fuller figure. She's a woman now, though sometimes I forget. How long ago was it that the other house burned? Ten, twelve years? Sometimes I can still hear the flames and feel Maggie's arms sticking to me, her hair smoking and her dress falling off her in little black papery flakes. Her eyes seemed stretched open, blazed open by the flames reflected in them. And Dee. I see her standing off under the sweet gum tree she used to dig gum out of; a look of concentration on her face as she watched the last dingy gray board of the house fall in toward the red-hot brick chimney. Why don't you do a dance around the ashes? I'd wanted to ask her. She had hated the house that much.

I used to think she hated Maggie, too. But that was before we raised the money, the church and me, to send her to Augusta to school. She used to read to us without pity; forcing words, lies, other folks' habits, whole lives upon us two, sitting trapped and ignorant underneath her voice. She washed us in a river of make-believe, burned us with a lot of knowledge we didn't necessarily need to know. Pressed us to her with the serious way she read, to shove us away at just the moment, like dimwits, we seemed about to understand.

Dee wanted nice things. A yellow organdy dress to wear to her graduation from high school; black pumps to match a green suit she'd made from an old suit somebody gave me. She was determined to stare down any disaster in her efforts. Her eyelids would not flicker for minutes at a time. Often I fought off the temptation to shake her. At sixteen she had a style of her own: and knew what style was.

I never had an education myself. After second grade the school was closed down. Don't ask me why: in 1927 colored asked fewer questions than they do now. Sometimes Maggie reads to me. She stumbles along good-naturedly but can't see well. She knows she is not bright. Like good looks and money, quickness passed her by. She will marry John Thomas (who has mossy teeth in an earnest face) and then I'll be free to sit here and I guess just sing church songs to myself. Although I never was a good singer. Never could carry a tune. I was always better at a man's job. I used to love to milk till I was hooked in the side in '49. Cows are soothing and slow and don't bother you, unless you try to milk them the wrong way.

I have deliberately turned my back on the house. It is three rooms, just like the one that burned, except the roof is tin; they don't make shingle roofs any more. There are no real windows, just some holes cut in the sides, like the portholes in a ship, but not round and not square, with rawhide holding the shutters up on the outside. This house is in a pasture, too, like the other one. No doubt when Dee sees it she will want to tear it down. She wrote me once that no matter where we "choose" to live, she will manage to come see us. But she will never bring her friends. Maggie and I thought about this and Maggie asked me, "Mama, when did Dee ever *have* any friends?"

She had a few. Furtive boys in pink shirts hanging about on washday after school. Nervous girls who never laughed. Impressed with her they worshiped the well-turned phrase, the cute shape, the scalding humor that erupted like bubbles in lye. She read to them.

When she was courting Jimmy T she didn't have much time to pay to us, but turned all her faultfinding power on him. He *flew* to marry a cheap gal from a family of ignorant flashy people. She hardly had time to recompose herself.

When she comes I will meet—but there they are!

Maggie attempts to make a dash for the house, in her shuffling way, but I stay her with my hand. "Come back here," I say. And she stops and tries to dig a well in the sand with her toe.

It is hard to see them clearly through the strong sun. But even the first glimpse of leg out of the car tells me it is Dee. Her feet were always neat-looking, as if God himself had shaped them with a certain style. From the other side of the car comes a short, stocky man. Hair is all over his head a foot long and hanging from his chin like a kinky mule tail. I hear Maggie suck in her breath. "Uhnnnh," is what it sounds like. Like when you see the wriggling end of a snake just in front of your foot on the road. "Uhnnnh."

Dee next. A dress down to the ground, in this hot weather. A dress so loud it hurts my eyes. There are yellows and oranges enough to throw back the light of the sun.

I feel my whole face warming from the heat waves it throws out. Earrings gold, too, and hanging down to her shoulders. Bracelets dangling and making noises when she moves her arm up to shake the folds of the dress out of her armpits. The dress is loose and flows, and as she walks closer, I like it. I hear Maggie go "Uhnnnh" again. It is her sister's hair. It stands straight up like the wool on a sheep. It is black as night and around the edges are two long pigtails that rope about like small lizards disappearing behind her ears.

"Wa-su-zo-Tean-o!" she says, coming on in that gliding way the dress makes her move. The short stocky fellow with the hair to his navel is all grinning and he follows up with "Asalamalakim, my mother and sister!" He moves to hug Maggie but she falls back, right up against the back of my chair. I feel her trembling there and when I look up I see the perspiration falling off her chin.

"Don't get up," says Dee. Since I am stout it takes something of a push. You can see me trying to move a second or two before I make it. She turns, showing white heels through her sandals, and goes back to the car. Out she peeks next with a Polaroid. She stoops down quickly and lines up picture after picture of me sitting there in front of the house with Maggie cowering behind me. She never takes a shot without making sure the house is included. When a cow comes nibbling around the edge of the yard she snaps it and me and Maggie *and* the house. Then she puts the Polaroid in the back seat of the car, and comes up and kisses me on the forehead.

Meanwhile Asalamalakim is going through the motions with Maggie's hand. Maggie's hand is as limp as a fish, and probably as cold, despite the sweat, and she keeps trying to pull it back. It looks like Asalamalakim wants to shake hands but wants to do it fancy. Or maybe he don't know how people shake hands. Anyhow, he soon gives up on Maggie.

"Well," I say. "Dee."

"No, Mama," she says. "Not 'Dee,' Wangero Leewanika Kemanjo!"

"What happened to 'Dee'?" I wanted to know.

"She's dead," Wangero said. "I couldn't bear it any longer being named after the people who oppress me."

"You know as well as me you was named after your aunt Dicie," I said. Dicie is my sister. She named Dee. We called her "Big Dee" after Dee was born.

"But who was *she* named after?" asked Wangero.

"I guess after Grandma Dee," I said.

"And who was she named after?" asked Wangero.

"Her mother," I said, and saw Wangero was getting tired. "That's about as far back as I can trace it," I said. Though, in fact, I probably could have carried it back beyond the Civil War through the branches.

"Well," said Asalamalakim, "there you are."

"Uhnnnh," I heard Maggie say.

"There I was not," I said, "before 'Dicie' cropped up in our family, so why should I try to trace it that far back?"

He just stood there grinning, looking down on me like somebody inspecting a Model A car. Every once in a while he and Wangero sent eye signals over my head.

"How do you pronounce this name?" I asked.

"You don't have to call me by it if you don't want to," said Wangero.

"Why shouldn't I?" I asked. "If that's what you want us to call you, we'll call you."

"I know it might sound awkward at first," said Wangero.

"I'll get used to it," I said. "Ream it out again."

Well, soon we got the name out of the way. Asalamalakim had a name twice as long and three times as hard. After I tripped over it two or three times he told me to just call him Hakim-a-barber. I wanted to ask him was he a barber, but I didn't really think he was, so I didn't ask.

"You must belong to those beef-cattle peoples down the road," I said. They said "Asalamalakim" when they met you, too, but they didn't shake hands. Always too busy: feeding the cattle, fixing the fences, putting up salt-lick shelters, throwing down hay. When the white folks poisoned some of the herd the men stayed up all night with rifles in their hands. I walked a mile and a half just to see the sight.

Hakim-a-barber said, "I accept some of their doctrines, but farming and raising cattle is not my style." (They didn't tell me, and I didn't ask, whether Wangero [Dee] had really gone and married him.)

We sat down to eat and right away he said he didn't eat collards and pork was unclean. Wangero, though, went on through the chitlins and corn bread, the greens and everything else. She talked a blue streak over the sweet potatoes. Everything delighted her. Even the fact that we still used the benches her daddy made for the table when we couldn't afford to buy chairs.

"Oh, Mama!" she cried. Then turned to Hakim-a-barber. "I never knew how lovely these benches are. You can feel the rump prints," she said, running her hands underneath her and along the bench. Then she gave a sigh and her hand closed over Grandma Dee's butter dish. "That's it!" she said. "I knew there was something I wanted to ask you if I could have." She jumped up from the table and went over in the corner where the churn stood, the milk in it clabber by now. She looked at the churn and looked at it.

"This churn top is what I need," she said. "Didn't Uncle Buddy whittle it out of a tree you all used to have?"

"Yes," I said.

"Uh huh," she said happily. "And I want the dasher, too."

"Uncle Buddy whittle that, too?" asked the barber.

Dee (Wangero) looked up at me.

"Aunt Dee's first husband whittled the dash," said Maggie so low you almost couldn't hear her. "His name was Henry, but they called him Stash."

"Maggie's brain is like an elephant's," Wangero said, laughing. "I can use the churn top as a centerpiece for the alcove table," she said, sliding a plate over the churn, "and I'll think of something artistic to do with the dasher."

When she finished wrapping the dasher the handle stuck out. I took it for a moment in my hands. You didn't even have to look close to see where hands pushing the dasher up and down to make butter had left a kind of sink in the wood. In fact, there were a lot of small sinks; you could see where thumbs and fingers had sunk into the wood. It was beautiful light yellow wood, from a tree that grew in the yard where Big Dee and Stash had lived.

After dinner Dee (Wangero) went to the trunk at the foot of my bed and started rifling through it. Maggie hung back in the kitchen over the dishpan. Out came Wangero with two quilts. They had been pieced by Grandma Dee and then Big Dee and me had hung them on the quilt frames on the front porch and quilted them. One was in the Lone Star pattern. The other was Walk Around the Mountain. In both of them were scraps of dresses Grandma Dee had worn fifty and more years ago. Bits and pieces of Grandpa Jarrell's Paisley shirts. And one teeny faded blue piece, about the size of a penny matchbox, that was from Great Grandpa Ezra's uniform that he wore in the Civil War.

"Mama," Wangero said sweet as a bird. "Can I have these old quilts?"

I heard something fall in the kitchen, and a minute later the kitchen door slammed.

"Why don't you take one or two of the others?" I asked. "These old things was just done by me and Big Dee from some tops your grandma pieced before she died."

"No," said Wangero. "I don't want those. They are stitched around the borders by machine."

"That'll make them last better," I said.

"That's not the point," said Wangero. "These are all pieces of dresses Grandma used to wear. She did all this stitching by hand. Imagine!" She held the quilts securely in her arms, stroking them.

"Some of the pieces, like those lavender ones, come from old clothes her mother handed down to her," I said, moving up to touch the quilts. Dee (Wangero) moved back just enough so that I couldn't reach the quilts. They already belonged to her.

"Imagine!" she breathed again, clutching them closely to her bosom.

"The truth is," I said, "I promised to give them quilts to Maggie, for when she marries John Thomas."

She gasped like a bee had stung her.

"Maggie can't appreciate these quilts!" she said. "She'd probably be backward enough to put them to everyday use."

"I reckon she would," I said. "God knows I been saving 'em for long enough with nobody using 'em. I hope she will!" I didn't want to bring up how I had offered Dee (Wangero) a quilt when she went away to college. Then she had told me they were old-fashioned, out of style.

"But they're *priceless!*" she was saying now, furiously; for she has a temper. "Maggie would put them on the bed and in five years they'd be in rags. Less than that!"

"She can always make some more," I said. "Maggie knows how to quilt."

Dee (Wangero) looked at me with hatred. "You just will not understand. The point is these quilts, *these* quilts!"

"Well," I said, stumped. "What would *you* do with them?"

"Hang them," she said. As if that was the only thing you *could* do with quilts.

Maggie by now was standing in the door. I could almost hear the sound her feet made as they scraped over each other.

"She can have them, Mama," she said, like somebody used to never winning anything, or having anything reserved for her. "I can 'member Grandma Dee without the quilts."

I looked at her hard. She had filled her bottom lip with checkerberry snuff and it gave her face a kind of dopey, hangdog look. It was Grandma Dee and Big Dee who taught her how to quilt herself. She stood there with her scarred hands hidden in the folds of her skirt. She looked at her sister with something like fear but she wasn't mad at her. This was Maggie's portion. This was the way she knew God to work.

When I looked at her like that something hit me in the top of my head and ran down to the soles of my feet. Just like when I'm in church and the spirit of God touches me and I get happy and shout. I did something I never had done before: hugged Maggie to me, then dragged her on into the room, snatched the quilts out of Miss Wangero's hands and dumped them into Maggie's lap. Maggie just sat there on my bed with her mouth open.

"Take one or two of the others," I said to Dee.

But she turned without a word and went out to Hakim-a-barber.

"You just don't understand," she said, as Maggie and I came out to the car.

"What don't I understand?" I wanted to know.

"Your heritage," she said. And then she turned to Maggie, kissed her, and said, "You ought to try to make something of yourself, too, Maggie. It's really a new day for us. But from the way you and Mama still live you'd never know it."

She put on some sunglasses that hid everything above the tip of her nose and her chin.

Maggie smiled; maybe at the sunglasses. But a real smile, not scared. After we watched the car dust settle I asked Maggie to bring me a dip of snuff. And then the two of us sat there just enjoying, until it was time to go in the house and go to bed.

LESLIE SILKO

[*b. 1948*]

Yellow Woman

I

My thigh clung to his with dampness, and I watched the sun rising up through the tamaracks and willows. The small brown water birds came to the river and hopped across the mud, leaving brown scratches in the alkali-white crust. They bathed in the river silently. I could hear the water, almost at our feet where the narrow fast channel bubbled and washed green ragged moss and fern leaves. I looked at him beside me, rolled in the red blanket on the white river sand. I cleaned the sand out of the cracks between my toes, squinting because the sun was above the willow trees. I looked at him for the last time, sleeping on the white river sand.

I felt hungry and followed the river south the way we had come the afternoon before, following our footprints that were already blurred by lizard tracks and bug trails. The horses were still lying down, and the black one whinnied when he saw me but he did not get up—maybe it was because the corral was made out of thick cedar branches and the horses had not yet felt the sun like I had. I tried to look beyond the pale red mesas to the pueblo. I knew it was there, even if I could not see it, on the sandrock hill above the river, the same river that moved past me now and had reflected the moon last night.

The horse felt warm underneath me. He shook his head and pawed the sand. The bay whinnied and leaned against the gate trying to follow, and I remembered him asleep in the red blanket beside the river. I slid off the horse and tied him close to the other horse. I walked north with the river again, and the white sand broke loose in footprints over footprints.

"Wake up."

He moved in the blanket and turned his face to me with his eyes still closed. I knelt down to touch him.

"I'm leaving."

He smiled now, eyes still closed. "You are coming with me, remember?" He sat up now with his bare dark chest and belly in the sun.

"Where?"

"To my place."

"And will I come back?"

He pulled his pants on. I walked away from him, feeling him behind me and smelling the willows.

"Yellow Woman," he said.

I turned to face him. "Who are you?" I asked.

He laughed and knelt on the low, sandy bank, washing his face in the river. "Last night you guessed my name, and you knew why I had come."

I stared past him at the shallow moving water and tried to remember the night, but I could only see the moon in the water and remember his warmth around me.

"But I only said that you were him and that I was Yellow Woman—I'm not really her—I have my own name and I come from the pueblo on the other side of the mesa. Your name is Silva and you are a stranger I met by the river yesterday afternoon."

He laughed softly. "What happened yesterday has nothing to do with what you will do today, Yellow Woman."

"I know—that's what I'm saying—the old stories about the ka'tsina spirit and Yellow Woman can't mean us."

My old grandpa liked to tell those stories best. There is one about Badger and Coyote who went hunting and were gone all day, and when the sun was going down they found a house. There was a girl living there alone, and she had light hair and eyes and she told them that they could sleep with her. Coyote wanted to be with her all night so he sent Badger into a prairie-dog hole, telling him he thought he saw something in it. As soon as Badger crawled in, Coyote blocked up the entrance with rocks and hurried back to Yellow Woman.

"Come here," he said gently.

He touched my neck and I moved close to him to feel his breathing and to hear his heart. I was wondering if Yellow Woman had known who she was—if she knew that she would become part of the stories. Maybe she'd had another name that her husband and relatives called her so that only the ka'tsina from the north and the storytellers would know her as Yellow Woman. But I didn't go on; I felt him all around me, pushing me down into the white river sand.

Yellow Woman went away with the spirit from the north and lived with him and his relatives. She was gone for a long time, but then one day she came back and she brought twin boys.

"Do you know the story?"

"What story?" He smiled and pulled me close to him as he said this. I was afraid lying there on the red blanket. All I could know was the way he felt, warm, damp, his body beside me. This is the way it happens in the stories, I was thinking, with no thought beyond the moment she meets the ka'tsina spirit and they go.

"I don't have to go. What they tell in stories was real only then, back in time immemorial, like they say."

He stood up and pointed at my clothes tangled in the blanket. "Let's go," he said.

I walked beside him, breathing hard because he walked fast, his hand around my wrist. I had stopped trying to pull away from him, because his hand felt cool and the sun was high, drying the river bed into alkali. I will see someone, eventually I will see someone, and then I will be certain that he is only a man—some man from nearby —and I will be sure that I am not Yellow Woman. Because she is from out of time past and I live now and I've been to school and there are highways and pickup trucks that Yellow Woman never saw.

It was an easy ride north on horseback. I watched the change from the cottonwood trees along the river to the junipers that brushed past us in the foothills, and finally there were only piñons, and when I looked up at the rim of the mountain plateau I could see pine trees growing on the edge. Once I stopped to look down, but the pale sandstone had disappeared and the river was gone and the dark lava hills were all around. He touched my hand, not speaking, but always singing softly a mountain song and looking into my eyes.

I felt hungry and wondered what they were doing at home now—my mother, my grandmother, my husband, and the baby. Cooking breakfast, saying, "Where did she go?—maybe kidnapped," and Al going to the tribal police with the details: "She went walking along the river."

The house was made with black lava rock and red mud. It was high above the spreading miles of arroyos and long mesas. I smelled a mountain smell of pitch and buck brush. I stood there beside the black horse, looking down on the small, dim country we had passed, and I shivered.

"Yellow Woman, come inside where it's warm."

2

He lit a fire in the stove. It was an old stove with a round belly and an enamel coffeepot on top. There was only the stove, some faded Navajo blankets, and a bedroll and cardboard box. The floor was made of smooth adobe plaster, and there was one small window facing east. He pointed at the box.

"There's some potatoes and the frying pan." He sat on the floor with his arms around his knees pulling them close to his chest and he watched me fry the potatoes. I didn't mind him watching me because he was always watching me—he had been watching me since I came upon him sitting on the river bank trimming leaves from a willow twig with his knife. We ate from the pan and he wiped the grease from his fingers on his Levis.

"Have you brought women here before?" He smiled and kept chewing, so I said, "Do you always use the same tricks?"

"What tricks?" He looked at me like he didn't understand.

"The story about being a ka'tsina from the mountains. The story about Yellow Woman."

Silva was silent; his face was calm.

"I don't believe it. Those stories couldn't happen now," I said.

He shook his head and said softly, "But someday they will talk about is, and they will say, 'Those two lived long ago when things like that happened.' "

He stood up and went out. I ate the rest of the potatoes and thought about things —about the noise the stove was making and the sound of the mountain wind outside. I remembered yesterday and the day before, and then I went outside.

I walked past the corral to the edge where the narrow trail cut through the black rim rock. I was standing in the sky with nothing around me but the wind that came down from the blue mountain peak behind me. I could see faint mountain images in the distance, miles across the vast spread of mesas and valleys and plains. I wondered who was over there to feel the mountain wind on those sheer blue edges—who walks on the pine needles in those blue mountains.

"Can you see the pueblo?" Silva was standing behind me.

I shook my head. "We're too far away."

"From here I can see the world." He stepped out on the edge. "The Navajo reservation begins over there." He pointed to the east. "The Pueblo boundaries are over here." He looked below us to the south, where the narrow trail seemed to come from. "The Texans have their ranches over there, starting with that valley, the Concho Valley. The Mexicans run some cattle over there too."

"Do you ever work for them?"

"I steal from them," Silva answered. The sun was dropping behind us and shadows were filling the land below. I turned away from the edge that dropped forever into the valleys below.

"I'm cold," I said; "I'm going inside." I started wondering about this man who could speak the Pueblo language so well but who lived on a mountain and rustled cattle. I decided that this man Silva must be Navajo, because Pueblo men didn't do things like that.

"You must be a Navajo."

Silva shook his head gently. "Little Yellow Woman," he said, "you never give up, do you? I have told you who I am. The Navajo people know me, too." He knelt down and unrolled the bedroll and spread the extra blankets out on a piece of canvas. The sun was down, and the only light in the house came from outside—the dim orange light from sundown.

I stood there and waited for him to crawl under the blankets.

"What are you waiting for?" he said, and I lay down beside him. He undressed me slowly like the night before beside the river—kissing my face gently and running his hands up and down my belly and legs. He took off my pants and then he laughed.

"Why are you laughing?"

"You are breathing so hard."

I pulled away from him and turned my back to him.

He pulled me around and pinned me down with his arms and chest. "You don't understand, do you, little Yellow Woman? You will do what I want."

And again he was all around me with his skin slippery against mine, and I was afraid because I understood that his strength could hurt me. I lay underneath him and I knew that he could destroy me. But later, while he slept beside me, I touched his face and

I had a feeling—the kind of feeling for him that overcame me that morning along the river. I kissed him on the forehead and he reached out for me.

When I woke up in the morning he was gone. It gave me a strange feeling because for a long time I sat there on the blankets and looked around the little house for some object of his—some proof that he had been there or maybe that he was coming back. Only the blankets and the cardboard box remained. The .30–30 that had been leaning in the corner was gone, and so was the knife I had used the night before. He was gone, and I had my chance to go now. But first I had to eat, because I knew it would be a long walk home.

I found some dried apricots in the cardboard box, and I sat down on a rock at the edge of the plateau rim. There was no wind and the sun warmed me. I was surrounded by silence. I drowsed with apricots in my mouth, and I didn't believe that there were highways or railroads or cattle to steal.

When I woke up, I stared down at my feet in the black mountain dirt. Little black ants were swarming over the pine needles around my foot. They must have smelled the apricots. I thought about my family far below me. They would be wondering about me, because this had never happened to me before. The tribal police would file a report. But if old Grandpa weren't dead he would tell them what happened—he would laugh and say, "Stolen by a ka'tsina, a mountain spirit. She'll come home—they usually do." There are enough of them to handle things. My mother and grandmother will raise the baby like they raised me. Al will find someone else, and they will go on like before, except that there will be a story about the day I disappeared while I was walking along the river. Silva had come for me, he said he had. I did not decide to go. I just went. Moonflowers blossom in the sand hills before dawn, just as I followed him. That's what I was thinking as I wandered along the trail through the pine trees.

It was noon when I got back. When I saw the stone house I remembered that I had meant to go home. But that didn't seem important any more, maybe because there were little blue flowers growing in the meadow behind the stone house and the gray squirrels were playing in the pines next to the house. The horses were standing in the corral, and there was a beef carcass hanging on the shady side of a big pine in front of the house. Flies buzzed around the clotted blood that hung from the carcass. Silva was washing his hands in a bucket full of water. He must have heard me coming because he spoke to me without turning to face me.

"I've been waiting for you."

"I went walking in the big pine trees."

I looked into the bucket full of bloody water with brown-and-white animal hairs floating in it. Silva stood there letting his hands drip, examining me intently.

"Are you coming with me?"

"Where?" I asked him.

"To sell the meat in Marquez."

"If you're sure it's O.K."

"I wouldn't ask you if it wasn't," he answered.

He sloshed the water around in the bucket before he dumped it out and set the bucket upside down near the door. I followed him to the corral and watched him saddle the horses. Even beside the horses he looked tall, and I asked him again if he wasn't Navajo. He didn't say anything; he just shook his head and kept cinching up the saddle.

"But Navajos are tall."

"Get on the horse," he said, "and let's go."

The last thing he did before we started down the steep trail was to grab the .30–30 from the corner. He slid the rifle into the scabbard that hung from his saddle.

"Do they ever try to catch you?" I asked.

"They don't know who I am."

"Then why did you bring the rifle?"

"Because we are going to Marquez where the Mexicans live."

3

The trail leveled out on a narrow ridge that was steep on both sides like an animal spine. On one side I could see where the trail went around the rocky gray hills and disappeared into the southeast where the pale sandrock mesas stood in the distance near my home. On the other side was a trail that went west, and as I looked far into the distance I thought I saw the little town. But Silva said no, that I was looking in the wrong place, that I just thought I saw houses. After that I quit looking off into the distance; it was hot and the wildflowers were closing up their deep-yellow petals. Only the waxy cactus flowers bloomed in the bright sun, and I saw every color that a cactus blossom can be; the white ones and the red ones were still buds, but the purple and the yellow were blossoms, open full and the most beautiful of all.

Silva saw him before I did. The white man was riding a big gray horse, coming up the trail toward us. He was traveling fast and the gray horse's feet sent rocks rolling off the trail into the dry tumbleweeds. Silva motioned for me to stop and we watched the white man. He didn't see us right away, but finally his horse whinnied at our horses and he stopped. He looked at us briefly before he loped the gray horse across the three hundred yards that separated us. He stopped his horse in front of Silva, and his young fat face was shadowed by the brim of his hat. He didn't look mad, but his small, pale eyes moved from the blood-soaked gunny sacks hanging from my saddle to Silva's face and then back to my face.

"Where did you get the fresh meat?" the white man asked.

"I've been hunting," Silva said, and when he shifted his weight in the saddle the leather creaked.

"The hell you have, Indian. You've been rustling cattle. We've been looking for the thief for a long time."

The rancher was fat, and sweat began to soak through his white cowboy shirt and the wet cloth stuck to the thick rolls of belly fat. He almost seemed to be panting from the exertion of talking, and he smelled rancid, maybe because Silva scared him.

Silva turned to me and smiled. "Go back up the mountain, Yellow Woman."

The white man got angry when he heard Silva speak in a language he couldn't understand. "Don't try anything, Indian. Just keep riding to Marquez. We'll call the state police from there."

The rancher must have been unarmed because he was very frightened and if he had a gun he would have pulled it out then. I turned my horse around and the rancher yelled, "Stop!" I looked at Silva for an instant and there was something ancient and dark—something I could feel in my stomach—in his eyes, and when I glanced at his hand I saw his finger on the trigger of the .30–30 that was still in the saddle scabbard.

I slapped my horse across the flank and the sacks of raw meat swung against my knees as the horse leaped up the trail. It was hard to keep my balance, and once I thought I felt the saddle slipping backward; it was because of this that I could not look back.

I didn't stop until I reached the ridge where the trail forked. The horse was breathing deep gasps and there was a dark film of sweat on its neck. I looked down in the direction I had come from, but I couldn't see the place. I waited. The wind came up and pushed warm air past me. I looked up at the sky, pale blue and full of thin clouds and fading vapor trails left by jets.

I think four shots were fired—I remember hearing four hollow explosions that reminded me of deer hunting. There could have been more shots after that, but I couldn't have heard them because my horse was running again and the loose rocks were making too much noise as they scattered around his feet.

Horses have a hard time running downhill, but I went that way instead of uphill to the mountain because I thought it was safer. I felt better with the horse running southeast past the round gray hills that were covered with cedar trees and black lava rock. When I got to the plain in the distance I could see the dark green patches of tamaracks that grew along the river; and beyond the river I could see the beginning of the pale sandrock mesas. I stopped the horse and looked back to see if anyone was coming; then I got off the horse and turned the horse around, wondering if it would go back to its corral under the pines on the mountain. It looked back at me for a moment and then plucked a mouthful of green tumbleweeds before it trotted back up the trail with its ears pointed forward, carrying its head daintily to one side to avoid stepping on the dragging reins. When the horse disappeared over the last hill, the gunny sacks full of meat were still swinging and bouncing.

4

I walked toward the river on a wood-hauler's road that I knew would eventually lead to the paved road. I was thinking about waiting beside the road for someone to drive by, but by the time I got to the pavement I had decided it wasn't very far to walk if I followed the river back the way Silva and I had come.

The river water tasted good, and I sat in the shade under a cluster of silvery willows. I thought about Silva, and I felt sad at leaving him; still, there was something strange about him, and I tried to figure it out all the way back home.

I came back to the place on the river bank where he had been sitting the first time I saw him. The green willow leaves that he had trimmed from the branch were still lying there, wilted in the sand. I saw the leaves and I wanted to go back to him—to kiss him and to touch him—but the mountains were too far away now. And I told myself, because I believe it, he will come back sometime and be waiting again by the river.

I followed the path up from the river into the village. The sun was getting low, and I could smell supper cooking when I got to the screen door of my house. I could hear their voices inside—my mother was telling my grandmother how to fix the Jell-O and my husband, Al, was playing with the baby. I decided to tell them that some Navajo had kidnaped me, but I was sorry that old Grandpa wasn't alive to hear my story because it was the Yellow Woman stories he liked to tell best.

MARK HELPRIN

[b. 1948]

North Light

A RECOLLECTION IN THE PRESENT TENSE

We are being held back. We are poised at a curve in the road on the southern ridge of a small valley. The sun shines from behind, illuminating with flawless light the moves and countermoves of several score tanks below us. For a long time, we have been absorbed in the mystery of matching the puffs of white smoke from tank cannon with the sounds that follow. The columns themselves move silently: only the great roar rising from the battle proves it not to be a dream.

A man next to me is deeply absorbed in sniffing his wrist. "What are you doing?" I ask.

"My wife," he says. "I can still smell her perfume on my wrist, and I taste the taste of her mouth. It's sweet."

We were called up this morning. The war is two days old. Now it is afternoon, and we are being held back—even though our forces below are greatly outnumbered. We are being held back until nightfall, when we will have a better chance on the plain; for it is packed with tanks, and we have only two old half-tracks. They are loaded with guns—it is true—but they are lightly armored, they are slow, and they present high targets. We expect to move at dusk or just before. Then we will descend on the road into the valley and fight amid the shadows. No one wants this: we all are terrified.

The young ones are frightened because, for most of them, this is the first battle. But their fear is not as strong as the blood which is rising and fills their chests with anger and strength. They have little to lose, being, as they are, only eighteen. They look no more frightened than members of a sports team before an important match: it is that kind of fear, for they are responsible only to themselves.

Married men, on the other hand, are given away by their eyes and faces. They are saying to themselves, "I must not die; I *must not die.*" They are remembering how they used to feel when they were younger; and they know that they have to fight. They may be killed, but if they don't fight they will surely be killed, because the slow self-made fear which demands constant hesitation is the most efficient of all killers. It is not the cautious who die, but the overcautious. The married men are trying to strike an exact balance between their responsibility as soldiers, their fervent desire to stay alive, and their only hope—which is to go into battle with the smooth, courageous, trancelike movements that will keep them out of trouble. Soldiers who do not know how (like dancers or mountain climbers) to let their bodies think for them are very liable to be killed. There is a flow to hard combat; it is not (as it has often been depicted) entirely chance or entirely skill. A thousand signals and signs speak to you, much as in music. And what a sad moment it is when you must, for one reason or another, ignore them.

The married men fear this moment. We should have begun hours ago. Being held back is bad luck.

"What time is it?" asks one of the young soldiers. Someone answers him.

"Fourteen hundred." No one in the Israeli Army except high-ranking officers (colonels, generals—and we have here no colonels or generals) tells time in this fashion.

"What are you, a general?" asks the young soldier. Everyone laughs, as if this were funny, because we are scared. We should not be held back like this.

Another man, a man who is close to fifty and is worrying about his two sons who are in Sinai, keeps on looking at his watch. It is expensive and Japanese, with a black dial. He looks at it every minute to see what time it is, because he has actually forgotten. If he were asked what the time was, he would not be able to respond without checking the watch, even though he has done so fifty times in the last hour. He too is very afraid. The sun glints off the crystal and explodes in our eyes.

As younger men who badly wanted to fight, we thought we knew what courage was. Now we know that courage is the forced step of going into battle when you want anything in the world but that, when there is every reason to stay out, when you have been through all the tests, and passed them, and think that it's all over. Then the war hits like an artillery shell and you are forced to be eighteen again, but you can't be eighteen again; not with the taste of your wife's mouth in your mouth, not with the smell of her perfume on your wrists. The world turns upside down in minutes.

How hard we struggle in trying to remember the easy courage we once had. But we can't. We must either be brave in a different way, or not at all. What is that way? How can we fight like seasoned soldiers when this morning we kissed our children? There is a way, hidden in the history of war. There must be, for we can see them fighting in the valley; and, high in the air, silver specks are dueling in a dream of blue silence.

Why are we merely watching? To be restrained this way is simply not fair. A quick entrance would get the fear over with, and that would help. But, then again, in the Six Day War, we waited for weeks while the Egyptian Army built up against us. And then, after that torture, we burst out and we leapt across the desert, sprinting, full of energy and fury that kept us like dancers—nimble and absorbed—and kept us alive. That is the secret: You have to be angry. When we arrived on the ridge this morning, we were anything but angry. Now we are beginning to get angry. It is our only salvation. We are angry because we are being held back.

We swear, and kick the sides of the half-tracks. We hate the voice on our radio which keeps telling us to hold to our position. We hate that man more than we hate the enemy, for now we want engagement with the enemy. We are beginning to crave battle, and we are getting angrier, and angrier, because we know that by five o'clock we will be worn out. They should let us go now.

A young soldier who has been following the battle, through binoculars, screams. "God!" he says. "Look! Look!"

The Syrians are moving up two columns of armor that will overwhelm our men on the plain below. The sergeant gets on the radio, but from it we hear a sudden waterfall of talk. Holding the microphone in his hand, he listens with us as we discover that they know. They are demanding more air support.

"What air support?" we ask. There is no air-to-ground fighting that we can see. As we watch the Syrians approach, our hearts are full of fear for those of us below. How did our soldiers know? There must be spotters or a patrol somewhere deep in, high on a hill, like us. What air support? There are planes all over the place, but not here.

Then we feel our lungs shaking like drums. The hair on our arms and on the back of our necks stands up and we shake as flights of fighters roar over the hill. They are no more than fifty feet above us. We can feel the heat from the tailpipes, and the orange flames are blinding. The noise is superb. They come three at a time; one wave, two, three, four, five, and six. These are our pilots. The mass of the machinery flying through the air is so great and graceful that we are stunned beyond the noise. We cheer in anger and in satisfaction. It seems the best thing in the world when, as they pass the ridge (How they hug the ground; what superb pilots!), they dip their wings for our sake. They are descending into a thicket of anti-aircraft missiles and radar-directed guns— and they dip their wings for us.

Now we are hot. The married men feel as if rivers are rushing through them, crossing and crashing, for they are angry and full of energy. The sergeant depresses the lever on the microphone. He identifies himself and says, "In the name of God, we want to go in *now*. Damn you if you don't let us go in."

There is hesitation and silence on the other end. "Who is this?" they ask.

"This is Shimon."

More silence, then, "Okay, Shimon. Move! Move!"

The engines start. Now we have our own thunder. It is not even three o'clock. It is the right time; they've caught us at the right time. The soldiers are not slow in mounting the half-tracks. The sound of our roaring engines has magnetized them and they *jump* in. The young drivers race the engines, as they always do.

For a magnificent half minute, we stare into the north light, smiling. The man who tasted the sweet taste of his wife kisses his wrist. The young soldiers are no longer afraid, and the married men are in a perfect sustained fury. Because they love their wives and children, they will not think of them until the battle is over. Now we are soldiers again. The engines are deafening. No longer are we held back. We are shaking; we are crying. Now we stare into the north light, and listen to the explosions below. Now we hear the levers of the gearshifts. Now our drivers exhale and begin to drive. Now we are moving.

BOBBIE ANN MASON

[*b. 1940*]

Drawing Names

On Christmas Day, Carolyn Sisson went early to her parents' house to help her mother with the dinner. Carolyn had been divorced two years before, and last Christmas, coming alone, she felt uncomfortable. This year she had invited her lover, Kent Ballard, to join the family gathering. She had even brought him a present to put under the tree, so he wouldn't feel left out. Kent was planning to drive over from Kentucky Lake by noon. He had gone there to inspect his boat because of an ice storm earlier in the week. He felt compelled to visit his boat on the holiday, Carolyn thought, as if it were a sad old relative in a retirement home.

"We're having baked ham instead of turkey," Mom said. "Your daddy never did like ham baked, but whoever heard of fried ham on Christmas? We have that all year round and I'm burnt out on it."

"I love baked ham," said Carolyn.

"Does Kent like it baked?"

"I'm sure he does." Carolyn placed her gifts under the tree. The number of packages seemed unusually small.

"It don't seem like Christmas with drawed names," said Mom.

"Your star's about to fall off." Carolyn straightened the silver ornament at the tip of the tree.

"I didn't decorate as much as I wanted to. I'm slowing down. Getting old, I guess." Mom had not combed her hair and she was wearing a workshirt and tennis shoes.

"You always try to do too much on Christmas, Mom."

Carolyn knew the agreement to draw names had bothered her mother. But the four daughters were grown, and two had children. Sixteen people were expected today. Carolyn herself could not afford to buy fifteen presents on her salary as a clerk at J. C. Penney's, and her parents' small farm had not been profitable in years.

Carolyn's father appeared in the kitchen and he hugged her so tightly she squealed in protest.

"That's all I can afford this year," he said, laughing.

As he took a piece of candy from a dish on the counter, Carolyn teased him. "You'd better watch your calories today."

"Oh, not on Christmas!"

It made Carolyn sad to see her handsome father getting older. He was a shy man, awkward with his daughters, and Carolyn knew he had been deeply disappointed over her failed marriage, although he had never said so. Now he asked, "Who bought these 'toes'?"

He would no longer say "nigger toes," the old name for the chocolate-covered creams.

"Hattie Smoot brought those over," said Mom. "I made a pants suit for her last week," she said to Carolyn. "The one that had stomach bypass?"

"When PeeWee McClain had that, it didn't work and they had to fix him back like he was," said Dad. He offered Carolyn a piece of candy, but she shook her head no.

Mom said, "I made Hattie a dress back last spring for her boy's graduation, and she couldn't even find a pattern big enough. I had to 'low a foot. But after that bypass, she's down to a size twenty."

"I think we'll all need a stomach bypass after we eat this feast you're fixing," said Carolyn.

"Where's Kent?" Dad asked abruptly.

"He went to see about his boat. He said he'd be here."

Carolyn looked at the clock. She felt uneasy about inviting Kent. Everyone would be scrutinizing him, as if he were some new character on a soap opera. Kent, who drove a truck for the Kentucky Loose-Leaf Floor, was a part-time student at Murray State.

He was majoring in accounting. When Carolyn started going with him early in the summer, they went sailing on his boat, which had "Joyce" painted on it. Later he painted over the name, insisting he didn't love Joyce anymore—she was a dietician who was always criticizing what he ate—but he had never said he loved Carolyn. She did not know if she loved him. Each seemed to be waiting for the other to say it first.

While Carolyn helped her mother in the kitchen, Dad went to get her grandfather, her mother's father. Pappy, who had been disabled by a stroke, was cared for by a live-in housekeeper who had gone home to her own family for the day. Carolyn diced apples and pears for fruit salad while her mother shaped sweet potato balls with marshmallow centers and rolled them in crushed cornflakes. On TV in the living room, *Days of Our Lives* was beginning, but the Christmas tree blocked their view of the television set.

"Whose name did you draw, Mom?" Carolyn asked, as she began seeding the grapes.

"Jim's."

"You put Jim's name in the hat?"

Mom nodded. Jim Walsh was the man Carolyn's youngest sister, Laura Jean, was living with in St. Louis. Laura Jean was going to an interior decorating school, and Jim was a textiles salesman she had met in a class. "I made him a shirt," Mom said.

"I'm surprised at you."

"Well, what was I to do?"

"I'm just surprised." Carolyn ate a grape and spit out the seeds. "Emily Post says the couple should be offered the same room when they visit."

"You know we'd never stand for that. I don't think your dad's ever got over her stacking up with that guy."

"You mean shacking up."

"Same thing." Mom dropped the potato masher, and the metal rattled on the floor. "Oh, I'm in such a tizzy," she said.

As the family began to arrive, the noise of the TV played against the greetings, the slam of the storm door, the outside wind rushing in. Carolyn's older sisters, Peggy and Iris, with their husbands and children, were arriving all at once, and suddenly the house seemed small. Peggy's children Stevie and Cheryl, without even removing their jackets, became involved in a basketball game on TV. In his lap, Stevie had a Merlin electronic toy, which beeped randomly. Iris and Ray's children, Deedee and Jonathan, went outside to look for cats.

In the living room, Peggy jiggled her baby, Lisa, on her hip and said, "You need you one of these, Carolyn."

"Where can I get one?" said Carolyn, rather sharply.

Peggy grinned. "At the gittin' place, I reckon."

Peggy's critical tone was familiar. She was the only sister who had had a real wedding. Her husband, Cecil, had a Gulf franchise, and they owned a motor cruiser, a pickup truck, a camper, a station wagon, and a new brick colonial home. Whenever Carolyn went to visit Peggy, she felt apologetic for not having a man who would buy her all these things, but she never seemed to be attracted to anyone steady or ambitious. She had been wondering how Kent would get along with the men of the family. Cecil and Ray were standing in a corner talking about gas mileage. Cecil, who was shorter than Peggy and was going bald, always worked on Dad's truck for free, and Ray usually agreed with Dad on politics to avoid an argument. Ray had an impressive government job in Frankfort. He had coordinated a ribbon-cutting ceremony when the toll road opened. What would Kent have to say to them? She could imagine him insisting that everyone go outside later to watch the sunset. Her father would think that was ridiculous. No one ever did that on a farm, but it was the sort of thing Kent would think of. Yet she knew that spontaneity was what she liked in him.

Deedee and Jonathan, who were ten and six, came inside then and immediately began shaking the presents under the tree. All the children were wearing new jeans and cowboy shirts, Carolyn noticed.

"Why are y'all so quiet?" she asked. "I thought kids whooped and hollered on Christmas."

"They've been up since *four,*" said Iris. She took a cigarette from her purse and accepted a light from Cecil. Exhaling smoke, she said to Carolyn, "We heard Kent was coming." Before Carolyn could reply, Iris scolded the children for shaking the packages. She seemed nervous.

"He's supposed to be here by noon," said Carolyn.

"There's somebody now. I hear a car."

"It might be Dad, with Pappy."

It was Laura Jean, showing off Jim Walsh as though he were a splendid Christmas gift she had just received.

"Let me kiss everybody!" she cried, as the women rushed toward her. Laura Jean had not been home in four months.

"Merry Christmas!" Jim said in a booming, official-sounding voice, something like a TV announcer, Carolyn thought. He embraced all the women and then, with a theatrical gesture, he handed Mom a bottle of Rebel Yell bourbon and a carton of boiled custard which he took from a shopping bag. The bourbon was in a decorative Christmas box.

Mom threw up her hands. "Oh, no, I'm afraid I'll be a alky-holic."

"Oh, that's ridiculous, Mom," said Laura Jean, taking Jim's coat. "A couple of drinks a day are good for your heart."

Jim insisted on getting coffee cups from a kitchen cabinet and mixing some boiled custard and bourbon. When he handed a cup to Mom, she puckered up her face.

"Law, don't let the preacher in," she said, taking a sip. "Boy, that sends my blood pressure up."

Carolyn waved away the drink Jim offered her. "I don't start this early in the day," she said, feeling confused.

Jim was a large, dark-haired man with a neat little beard, like a bird's nest cupped on his chin. He had a Northern accent. When he hugged her, Carolyn caught a whiff of cologne, something sweet, like chocolate syrup. Last summer, when Laura Jean brought him home for the first time, she had made a point of kissing and hugging him in front of everyone. Dad had virtually ignored him. Now Carolyn saw that Jim was telling Cecil that he always bought Gulf gas. Red-faced, Ray accepted a cup of boiled custard. Carolyn fled to the kitchen and began grating cheese for potatoes au gratin. She dreaded Kent's arrival.

When Dad arrived with Pappy, Cecil and Jim helped set up the wheelchair in a corner. Afterward, Dad and Jim shook hands, and Dad refused Jim's offer of bourbon. From the kitchen, Carolyn could see Dad hugging Laura Jean, not letting go. She went into the living room to greet her grandfather.

"They roll me in this buggy too fast," he said when she kissed his forehead.

Carolyn hoped he wouldn't notice the bottle of bourbon, but she knew he never missed anything. He was so deaf people had given up talking to him. Now the children tiptoed around him, looking at him with awe. Somehow, Carolyn expected the children to notice that she was alone, like Pappy.

At ten minutes of one, the telephone rang. Peggy answered and handed the receiver to Carolyn. "It's Kent," she said.

Kent had not left the lake yet. "I just got here an hour ago," he told Carolyn. "I had to take my sister over to my mother's."

"Is the boat O.K.?"

"Yeah. Just a little scraped paint. I'll be ready to go in a little while." He hesitated, as though waiting for assurance that the invitation was real.

"This whole gang's ready to eat," Carolyn said. "Can't you hurry?" She should have remembered the way he tended to get sidetracked. Once it took them three hours to get to Paducah, because he kept stopping at antique shops.

After she hung up the telephone, her mother asked, "Should I put the rolls in to brown yet?"

"Wait just a little. He's just now leaving the lake."

"When's this Kent feller coming?" asked Dad impatiently, as he peered into the kitchen. "It's time to eat."

"He's on his way," said Carolyn.

"Did you tell him we don't wait for stragglers?"

"No."

"When the plate rattles, we eat."

"I know."

"Did you tell him that?"

"No, I didn't!" cried Carolyn, irritated.

When they were alone in the kitchen, Carolyn's mother said to her, "Your dad's not his self today. He's fit to be tied about Laura Jean bringing that guy down here again. And him bringing that whiskey."

"That was uncalled for," Carolyn agreed. She had noticed that Mom had set her cup of boiled custard in the refrigerator.

"Besides, he's not too happy about that Kent Ballard you're running around with."

"What's it to him?"

"You know how he always was. He don't think anybody's good enough for one of his little girls, and he's afraid you'll get mistreated again. He don't think Kent's very dependable."

"I guess Kent's proving Dad's point."

Carolyn's sister Iris had dark brown eyes, unique in the family. When Carolyn was small, she tried to say "Iris's eyes" once and called them "Irish eyes," confusing them with a song their mother sometimes sang, "When Irish Eyes Are Smiling." Thereafter, they always teased Iris about her smiling Irish eyes. Today Iris was not smiling. Carolyn found her in a bedroom smoking, holding an ashtray in her hand.

"I drew your name," Carolyn told her. "I got you something I wanted myself."

"Well, if I don't want it, I guess I'll have to give it to you."

"What's wrong with you today?"

"Ray and me's getting a separation," said Iris.

"Really?" Carolyn was startled by the note of glee in her response. Actually, she told herself later, it was because she was glad her sister, whom she saw infrequently, had confided in her.

"The thing of it is, I had to beg him to come today, for Mom and Dad's sake. It'll kill them. Don't let on, will you?"

"I won't. What are you going to do?"

"I don't know. He's already moved out."

"Are you going to stay in Frankfort?"

"I don't know. I have to work things out."

Mom stuck her head in the door. "Well, is Kent coming or not?"

"He *said* he'd be here," said Carolyn.

"Your dad's about to have a duck with a rubber tail. He can't stand to wait on a meal."

"Well, let's go ahead, then. Kent can eat when he gets here."

When Mom left, Iris said, "Aren't you and Kent getting along?"

"I don't know. He said he'd come today, but I have a feeling he doesn't really want to."

"To hell with men." Iris laughed and stubbed out her cigarette. "Just look at us— didn't we turn out awful? First your divorce. Now me. And Laura Jean bringing that guy down. Daddy can't stand him. Did you see the look he gave him?"

"Laura Jean's got a lot more nerve than I've got," said Carolyn, nodding. "I could wring Kent's neck for being late. Well, none of us can do anything right—except Peggy."

"Daddy's precious little angel," said Iris mockingly. "Come on, we'd better get in there and help."

While Mom went to change her blouse and put on lipstick, the sisters brought the food into the dining room. Two tables had been put together. Peggy cut the ham with an electric knife, and Carolyn filled the iced tea glasses.

"Pappy gets buttermilk and Stevie gets Coke," Peggy directed her.

"I know," said Carolyn, almost snapping.

As the family sat down, Carolyn realized that no one ever asked Pappy to "turn thanks" anymore at holiday dinners. He was sitting there expectantly, as if waiting to be asked. Mom cut up his ham into small bits. Carolyn waited for a car to drive up, the phone to ring. The TV was still on.

"Y'all dig in," said Mom. "Jim? Make sure you try some of these dressed eggs like I fix."

"I thought your new boyfriend was coming," said Cecil to Carolyn.

"So did I!" said Laura Jean. "That's what you wrote me."

Everyone looked at Carolyn as she explained. She looked away.

"You're looking at that pitiful tree," Mom said to her. "I just know it don't show up good from the road."

"No, it looks fine." No one had really noticed the tree. Carolyn seemed to be seeing it for the first time in years—broken red plastic reindeer, Styrofoam snowmen with crumbling top hats, silver walnuts which she remembered painting when she was about twelve.

Dad began telling a joke about some monks who had taken a vow of silence. At each Christmas dinner, he said, one monk was allowed to speak.

"Looks like your vocal cords would rust out," said Cheryl.

"Shut up, Cheryl. Granddaddy's trying to tell something," said Cecil.

"So the first year it was the first monk's turn to talk, and you know what he said? He said, 'These taters is lumpy.' "

When several people laughed, Stevie asked, "Is that the joke?"

Carolyn was baffled. Her father had never told a joke at the table in his life. He sat at the head of the table, looking out past the family at the cornfield through the picture window.

"Pay attention now," he said. "The second year Christmas rolled around again and it was the second monk's turn to say something. He said, 'You know, I think you're right. The taters *is* lumpy.' "

Laura Jean and Jim laughed loudly.

"Reach me some light-bread," said Pappy. Mom passed the dish around the table to him.

"And so the third year," Dad continued, "the third monk got to say something. What he said"—Dad was suddenly overcome with mirth—"what he said was, 'If y'all don't shut up arguing about them taters, I'm going to leave this place!' "

After the laughter died, Mom said, "Can you imagine anybody not a-talking all year long?"

"That's the way monks are, Mom," said Laura Jean. "Monks are economical with everything. They're not wasteful, not even with words."

"The Trappist Monks are really an outstanding group," said Jim. "And they make excellent bread. No preservatives."

Cecil and Peggy stared at Jim.

"You're not eating, Dad," said Carolyn. She was sitting between him and the place set for Kent. The effort at telling the joke seemed to have taken her father's appetite.

"He ruined his dinner on nigger toes," said Mom.

"Dottie Barlow got a Barbie doll for Christmas and it's black," Cheryl said.

"Dottie Barlow ain't black, is she?" asked Cecil.

"No."

"That's funny," said Peggy. "Why would they give her a black Barbie doll?"

"She just wanted it."

Abruptly, Dad left the table, pushing back his plate. He sat down in the recliner chair in front of the TV. The Blue-Gray game was beginning, and Cecil and Ray were hurriedly finishing in order to join him. Carolyn took out second helpings of ham and jello salad, feeling as though she were eating for Kent in his absence. Jim was taking seconds of everything, complimenting Mom. Mom apologized for not having fancy napkins. Then Laura Jean described a photography course she had taken. She had been photographing close-ups of car parts—fenders, headlights, mud flaps.

"That sounds goofy," said one of the children, Deedee.

Suddenly Pappy spoke. "Use to, the menfolks would eat first, and the children separate. The womenfolks would eat last, in the kitchen."

"You know what I could do with you all, don't you?" said Mom, shaking her fist at him. "I could set up a plank out in the field for y'all to eat on." She laughed.

"Times are different now, Pappy," said Iris loudly. "We're just as good as the men."

"She gets that from television," said Ray, with an apologetic laugh.

Carolyn noticed Ray's glance at Iris. Just then Iris matter-of-factly plucked an eyelash from Ray's cheek. It was as though she had momentarily forgotten about the separation.

Later, after the gifts were opened, Jim helped clear the tables. Kent still had not come. The baby slept, and Laura Jean, Jim, Peggy, and Mom played a Star Trek board game at the dining room table, while Carolyn and Iris played Battlestar Galactica with Cheryl and Deedee. The other men were quietly engrossed in the football game, a blur of sounds. No one had mentioned Kent's absence, but after the children had distributed the gifts, Carolyn refused to tell them what was in the lone package left under the tree. It was the most extravagantly wrapped of all the presents, with an immense ribbon, not a stick-on bow. An icicle had dropped on it, and it reminded Carolyn of an abandoned float, like something from a parade.

At a quarter to three, Kent telephoned. He was still at the lake. "The gas stations are all closed," he said. "I couldn't get any gas."

"We already ate and opened the presents," said Carolyn.

"Here I am, stranded. Not a thing I can do about it."

Kent's voice was shaky and muffled, and Carolyn suspected he had been drinking. She did not know what to say, in front of the family. She chattered idly, while she played with a ribbon from a package. The baby was awake, turning dials and knobs on a Busy Box. On TV, the Blues picked up six yards on an end sweep. Carolyn fixed her eyes on the tilted star at the top of the tree. Kent was saying something about Santa Claus.

"They wanted me to play Santy at Mama's house for the littluns. I said—you know what I said? 'Bah, humbug!' Did I ever tell you what I've got against Christmas?"

"Maybe not." Carolyn's back stiffened against the wall.

"When I was little bitty, Santa Claus came to town. I was about five. I was all fired up to go see Santy, and Mama took me, but we were late, and he was about to leave. I had to run across the courthouse square to get to him. He was giving away suckers, so I ran as hard as I could. He was climbing up on the fire engine—are you listening?"

"Unh-huh." Carolyn was watching her mother, who was folding Christmas paper to save for next year.

Kent said, "I reached up and pulled at his old red pants leg, and he looked down at me, and you know what he said?"

"No—what?"

"He said, 'Piss off, kid.'"

"Really?"

"Would I lie to you?"

"I don't know."

"Do you want to hear the rest of my hard-luck story?"

"Not now."

"Oh, I forgot this was long distance. I'll call you tomorrow. Maybe I'll go paint the boat. That's what I'll do! I'll go paint it right this minute."

After Carolyn hung up the telephone, her mother said, "I think my Oriental casserole was a failure. I used the wrong kind of mushroom soup. It called for cream of mushroom and I used golden mushroom."

"Won't you *ever* learn, Mom?" cried Carolyn. "You always cook too much. You make *such* a big deal—"

Mom said, "What happened with Kent this time?"

"He couldn't get gas. He forgot the gas stations were closed."

"Jim and Laura Jean didn't have any trouble getting gas," said Peggy, looking up from the game.

"We tanked up yesterday," said Laura Jean.

"Of course you did," said Carolyn distractedly. "You always think ahead."

"It's your time," Cheryl said, handing Carolyn the Battlestar Galactica toy. "I did lousy."

"Not as lousy as I did," said Iris.

Carolyn tried to concentrate on shooting enemy missiles, raining through space. Her sisters seemed far away, like the spaceships. She was aware of the men watching football, their hands in action as they followed an exciting play. Even though Pappy had fallen asleep, with his blanket in his lap he looked like a king on a throne. Carolyn thought of the quiet accommodation her father had made to his father-in-law, just as Cecil and Ray had done with Dad, and her ex-husband had tried to do once. But Cecil had bought his way in, and now Ray was getting out. Kent had stayed away. Jim, the newcomer, was with the women, playing Star Trek as if his life depended upon it. Carolyn was glad now that Kent had not come. The story he told made her angry, and his pity for his childhood made her think of something Pappy had often said: "Christmas is for children." Earlier, she had listened in amazement while Cheryl listed on her fingers the gifts she had received that morning: a watch, a stereo, a nightgown, hot curls, perfume, candles, a sweater, a calculator, a jewelry box, a ring. Now Carolyn saw Kent's boat as his toy, more important than the family obligations of the holiday.

Mom was saying, "I wanted to make a Christmas tablecloth out of red checks with green fringe. You wouldn't think knit would do for a tablecloth, but Hattie Smoot has the prettiest one."

"You can do incredible things with knit," said Jim with sudden enthusiasm. The shirt Mom had made him was bonded knit.

"Who's Hattie Smoot?" asked Laura Jean. She was caressing the back of Jim's neck, as though soothing his nerves.

Carolyn laughed when her mother began telling Jim and Laura Jean about Hattie Smoot's operation. Jim listened attentively, leaning forward with his elbows on the table, and asked eager questions, his eyes as alert as Pappy's.

"Is she telling a joke?" Cheryl asked Carolyn.

"No. I'm not laughing at you, Mom," Carolyn said, touching her mother's hand. She felt relieved that the anticipation of Christmas had ended. Still laughing, she said, "Pour me some of that Rebel Yell, Jim. It's about time."

"I'm with you," Jim said, jumping up.

In the kitchen, Carolyn located a clean spoon while Jim washed some cups. Carolyn couldn't find the cup Mom had left in the refrigerator. As she took out the carton of boiled custard, Jim said, "It must be a very difficult day for you."

Carolyn was startled. His tone was unexpectedly kind, genuine. She was struck suddenly by what he must know about her, because of his intimacy with her sister. She knew nothing about him. When he smiled, she saw a gold cap on a molar, shining like a Christmas ornament. She managed to say, "It can't be any picnic for you either. Kent didn't want to put up with us."

"Too bad he couldn't get gas."

"I don't think he wanted to get gas."

"Then you're better off without him." When Jim looked at her, Carolyn felt that he must be examining her resemblances to Laura Jean. He said, "I think your family's great."

Carolyn laughed nervously. "We're hard on you. God, you're brave to come down here like this."

"Well, Laura Jean's worth it."

They took the boiled custard and cups into the dining room. As Carolyn sat down, her nephew Jonathan begged her to tell what was in the gift left under the tree.

"I can't tell," she said.

"Why not?"

"I'm saving it till next year, in case I draw some man's name."

"I hope it's mine," said Jonathan.

Jim stirred bourbon into three cups of boiled custard, then gave one to Carolyn and one to Laura Jean. The others had declined. Then he leaned back in his chair—more relaxed now—and squeezed Laura Jean's hand. Carolyn wondered what they said to each other when they were alone in St. Louis. She knew with certainty that they would not be economical with words, like the monks in the story. She longed to be with them, to hear what they would say. She noticed her mother picking at a hangnail, quietly ignoring the bourbon. Looking at the bottle's gift box, which showed an old-fashioned scene, children on sleds in the snow, Carolyn thought of Kent's boat again. She felt she was in that snowy scene now with Laura Jean and Jim, sailing in Kent's boat into the winter breeze, into falling snow. She thought of how silent it was out on the lake, as though the whiteness of the snow were the absence of sound.

"Cheers!" she said to Jim, lifting her cup.

Poetry

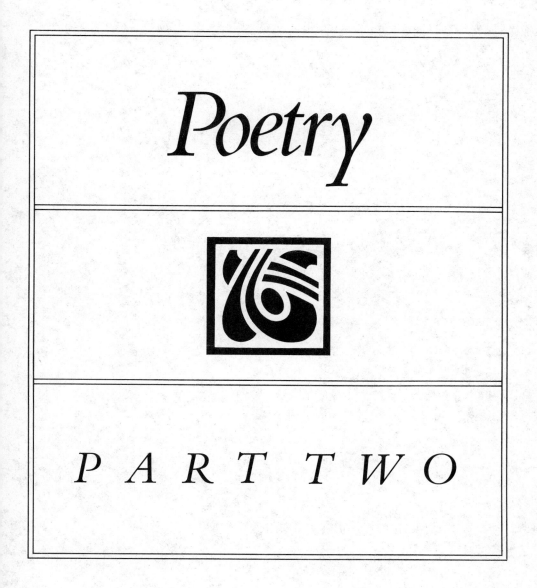

PART TWO

CHAPTER SIX

Reading Poems

THE EXPERIENCE OF READING POETRY

In some ways reading poetry is much like reading fiction, drama, and the essay: we observe details of action and language, make connections and inferences, and draw conclusions. We also bring to poetry the same intellectual and emotional dispositions, the same general experience with life and literature that we draw on in reading drama, fiction, and essay. And yet there is something different about reading poems. The difference, admittedly more one of degree than of kind, involves our being more attentive to the connotations of words, more receptive to the expressive qualities of sound and rhythm in line and stanza, more discerning about details of syntax and punctuation. This increased attention to linguistic detail is necessary because of the density and compression characteristic of poetry. Even more than fiction, drama, and essay, poetry is an art of condensation and implication; poems concentrate meaning and distill feeling.

Let us turn to a short poem and consider how our own experience and the poem's details of language collectively direct us toward what it expresses.

ROBERT HAYDEN
[1913–1980]

Those Winter Sundays

Sundays too my father got up early
and put his clothes on in the blueblack cold,
then with cracked hands that ached
from labor in the weekday weather made
banked fires blaze. No one ever thanked him.   5

I'd wake and hear the cold splintering, breaking.
When the rooms were warm, he'd call,
and slowly I would rise and dress,
fearing the chronic angers of that house,

Speaking indifferently to him,   10
who had driven out the cold
and polished my good shoes as well.
What did I know, what did I know
of love's austere and lonely offices?

Even from a single reading we see that the speaker of "Those Winter Sundays,"
now an adult, is remembering how his father used to get up on cold Sunday
mornings and light the fires that would warm the house for his sleeping family.
We sense his regret at how unappreciative of his father he was as a child. We
may wonder what prompts these memories and feelings. Our initial reading may
also call up a memory much like the one described in Hayden's poem. But even
if our experience does not echo the speaker's or if our feelings differ from his,
we may respond nonetheless to the description of waking up on a cold day in
a warm house. Such personal responses, whatever their precise nature, are
important to our reading of poetry, for in arriving at a sense of a poem's
meaning and value, we often begin with them.

Let us consider what Hayden's poem implies by returning for a second, more
deliberate reading. In this reading we might notice, for example, that the first
words, "Sundays too," indicate that the speaker's father performed his house-
warming chores every day, including Sundays. We might notice also that the
poem contrasts cold and warmth, with the cold dissipated as the warmth of the
fires the father has started suffuses the house. And we might note further that the
poem shifts from father to son, from "him" to "I." The first stanza, for example,
describes the father's act, the second the boy's awakening to a warm house, while
the third records a different kind of awakening—the speaker's understanding of
his earlier indifference and of his father's love. It is in this third and final stanza that

we feel most strongly the contrast between the speaker's past and present, between the then and the now of the poem, between the love that the speaker neither noticed nor acknowledged and now acknowledges and understands.

So far we have centered on the poem's speaker and its subject. (The *speaker* refers to the voice of the character we hear in the poem; the *subject* indicates what the poem is about.) Our first readings of a poem will usually focus on who is speaking about what, and why. In considering speaker and subject, we solidify our sense of what the poem implies, whether its implications concern, primarily, ideas or feelings. When the speaker notes that he feared "the chronic angers of that house," we may sense that he points toward something important. Presumably he feared his father's anger, which on occasion must have been directed at him. But by using the plural form of the word rather than the singular ("angers" rather than "anger") the speaker may be suggesting that there was discord between the father and other members of the family as well. Whatever the specific nature of his fear, the speaker intimates that this fear was the source of his own wariness and indifference toward his father.

The lines that convey the speaker's feeling most intensely, however, are those that end the poem:

> What did I know, what did I know
> of love's austere and lonely offices?

In these lines we sense the speaker's remorse and regret for not being aware of all his father did for him; we sense further that even though he didn't understand and feel the extent of his father's devotion, he certainly does later. Moreover, we sense the intensity of his feelings both in his repetition of the phrase "what did I know," and in the words that describe his father's actions: "love's austere and lonely offices." "Austere" suggests both the rigor and self-discipline of the father's acts and perhaps the stern severity with which he may have performed them. "Lonely" indicates that the father performed his early morning labors alone, without help from the other members of the family. It also suggests that the father was emotionally isolated from the speaker and perhaps from other members of the family.

But the word "offices" conveys other ideas as well. It implies both the duties the father fulfills and the corresponding authority he possesses. In addition, it suggests something done for another, as in the good offices of a friend. Beyond these related meanings, "offices" also refers to the daily prayers recited by clerics. Thus, the words "austere" and "offices" convey the speaker's understanding of his father's sacrifices for him. Moreover, the highly abstract language of the conclusion—so different from the concrete details of the preceding stanzas— may also indicate the speaker's inability to express affection directly (an inadequacy he intimates his father suffered from as well).

THE PROCESS OF READING POETRY

To read poetry well we need to slow down enough to observe details of language, form, and sound. By reading slowly and deliberately we give ourselves a chance to form connections among the poem's details. Read the follow-ing poem twice, both times carefully. Consider what kinds of details you notice during each reading, and how the experience of reading may differ from one reading to the next.

ROBERT FROST
[1874–1963]

Stopping by Woods on a Snowy Evening

Whose woods these are I think I know.
His house is in the village though;
He will not see me stopping here
To watch his woods fill up with snow.

My little horse must think it queer   5
To stop without a farmhouse near
Between the woods and frozen lake
The darkest evening of the year.

He gives his harness bells a shake
To ask if there is some mistake.   10
The only other sound's the sweep
Of easy wind and downy flake.

The woods are lovely, dark, and deep,
But I have promises to keep,
And miles to go before I sleep,   15
And miles to go before I sleep.

Read the poem once more, this time along with the comments that follow each stanza. Attend to the way you make sense of the poem during this third reading, particularly in light of the suggestions made in the commentary.

Whose woods these are I think I know.
His house is in the village though;
He will not see me stopping here
To watch his woods fill up with snow.

Comment   Frost's poem opens with a speaker who seems concerned momen-tarily about who owns the woods. The speaker seems reassured that the owner can't see him. We might wonder why the speaker should be concerned and why he bothers to mention it. Does he feel that he is doing something wrong? The stanza paints a picture of man, of woods, of snow. And it raises a question: Why does he stop? What attracts him? Does this first stanza indicate what might come after it, where the poem might be heading?

Here's the second stanza:

> My little horse must think it queer
> To stop without a farmhouse near
> Between the woods and frozen lake
> The darkest evening of the year.

Comment   The speaker implies that his horse is not accustomed to stopping without a practical purpose. The first line says that the horse "must" think it queer to stop this way, indicating that the horse can't really look at the man's action any other way. Accustomed to stops for food and rest, the horse couldn't possibly understand the man's nonpragmatic reason for stopping. And though the horse is said to "think," we realize that the horse's thoughts are really the speaker's—that the speaker projects his thoughts onto the horse because a part of him sees the impracticality of his action.

Stanza three:

> He gives his harness bells a shake
> To ask if there is some mistake.
> The only other sound's the sweep
> Of easy wind and downy flake.

Comment   The third stanza continues the emphasis of the second. The speaker interprets the horse's shaking of his harness bells as a signal to move on, as a sign that stopping there serves no useful purpose. We might notice that the poet here emphasizes the stillness of the night, the isolation and privacy of the moment, which is broken only by the sound of the horse's bell. Tension builds in the mind of the speaker: even though he seems to enjoy the stillness of the night and takes pleasure in the "easy wind" and the "downy flake," he also experiences some doubt about what he is doing.

Stanza four:

> The woods are lovely, dark, and deep,
> But I have promises to keep,
> And miles to go before I sleep,
> And miles to go before I sleep.

Comment   The opening line summarizes the implications of the details in the preceding stanzas. It's as if the speaker here answers the question why he stopped by the woods. The answer of course is that the speaker was attracted by their deep, dark beauty. Pulled by their lovely darkness, he nevertheless feels a pressure to move on. Not to linger but to return to the world of responsibilities and obligations ("But I have promises to keep").

The final stanza is solemn and serious: Frost slows down its pace by including more punctuational pauses and by repeating the third line, "And miles to go before I sleep," which becomes the final line of the poem. Repeating this line, Frost lifts it beyond its literal meaning, inviting us to read "sleep" as the final sleep of death. And once we make this interpretive leap, we return to the earlier details of the poem and read them in light of our sense of the ending. The "miles to go" and the "promises" then suggest perhaps the time the speaker has left to live, the obligations and responsibilities he must fulfill before he dies. His stopping to look at the snow falling in the woods might be seen as a temporary reprieve from his responsibilities; it might also be seen as a desire to escape from them, to remain beyond their weight and pressure. The point is not for us to decide now once and for all what the poem means, but to recognize that our reading involves us in a recursive process, one that rewards our repeated turns through the poem.

THE PRACTICE OF ACTIVE READING

Thus far we have read two poems, each followed by comments and questions emphasizing the experience and process of reading. Next we illustrate active reading—what we actually do when we read and reread a poem. Some of the marginal annotations record observations, others raise questions; all are abbreviated notes that reflect a reading that embodies both thought and feeling. In making notes about a poem in this manner, we become actively engaged in seeing and thinking. Our observations and questions lead us to notice details of language and to think about the poem's implications. As we formulate answers to our questions, however provisional, we find ourselves exploring both its meaning and its value.

The annotations for Theodore Roethke's "My Papa's Waltz" are unconcerned with technical matters such as the poem's form, rhyme scheme, and meter, or with what such technical features contribute to its meaning and feeling. Another set of annotations, of course, could be made specifically highlighting these features. In fact, some technical consideration of Roethke's poem appears later in discussions in Chapter 8, The Elements of Poetry (pages 409, 445). For now, however, we focus on the poem's situation and subject. Here is the poem without annotation:

THEODORE ROETHKE

[1908–1963]

My Papa's Waltz

The whiskey on your breath
Could make a small boy dizzy;

But I hung on like death:
Such waltzing was not easy.

We romped until the pans   5
Slid from the kitchen shelf;
My mother's countenance
Could not unfrown itself.

The hand that held my wrist
Was battered on one knuckle;   10
At every step you missed
My right ear scraped a buckle.

You beat time on my head
With a palm caked hard by dirt,
Then waltzed me off to bed   15
Still clinging to your shirt.

And here it is again with annotations:

My Papa's Waltz

	An affectionate term for his father—papa
The whiskey on your breath	What kind of waltzing
Could make a small boy dizzy;	and who instigated it?
But I hung on like death:	
Such waltzing was not easy.	"Waltzed" or "danced" for "romped"?
We romped until the pans	"Face" or "expression" for "countenance"?
Slid from the kitchen shelf;	
My mother's countenance	The mother—angry? disapproving? mother as audience—as non-participant—
Could not unfrown itself.	
The hand that held my wrist	
Was battered on one knuckle;	
At every step you missed	The father misses steps but he can dance—not drunk.
My right ear scraped a buckle.	
You beat time on my head	
With a palm caked hard by dirt,	
Then waltzed me off to bed	Clinging—how?
Still clinging to your shirt.	Fearfully? Joyfully? Both?

The boy's father, a manual laborer, is clearly not literally "waltzing" with his son. His "dance" is more a romp through the house with a stop in the kitchen and another at the boy's bedroom, where presumably he is unceremoniously dumped into bed. The mothers watches, her frown indicating disapproval, perhaps even anger.

The dance is somewhat rough because the boy's father has been drinking. It is also rough because he scrapes the child's ear on his belt buckle as he keeps a steady rhythm by beating time on the boy's head. The boy is described as "clinging" to his father's shirt, but the language doesn't clarify whether that clinging is purely out of terror—or whether it is part of the game father and son enjoy together. Presumably this bedtime romp is a regular ritual rather than a one-time occurrence.

The tone of the poem seems nostalgic, though not sentimentally so. The boy, now a man, remembers his father as "papa," clearly an affectionate term. The high-spirited bouncing rhythm of the poem seems to counter any indication that the father's drinking or the son's fear are its central concerns.

CENTERING ON SUBJECT AND THEME

We round out our discussion of reading poems with some further comments on the poems included above and a look at an additional poem. Our focus here will be less on either our initial experience of the poems or the process of reading them. Instead it will center on their subjects and themes.

As we have stated previously, a poem's subject is, simply, what it is about. Roethke's and Hayden's poems are about memories of their fathers, and more specifically about their responses to those memories. Robert Frost's poem is about a late-night traveler on a journey. It's also about the beauty of a dark, snow-filled, winter night. All three poems are about these specific things and more. It is the more that we sense they are about that renders these preliminary descriptions inadequate.

Hayden's "Those Winter Sundays" is also about love and sacrifice, indifference and regret; it is about how understanding sometimes comes too late. This more amplified and more abstract statement comes closer to what seems central to the poem. But it also moves beyond description of the poem's subject and into interpretation of theme, an idea about the subject. But let us be more precise about what we mean by theme.

We have previously defined theme as an abstraction or generalization drawn from the details of a literary work and stated that theme refers to an idea or intellectually apprehensible meaning inherent and implicit in a work (see pages 69–70). In determining a poem's theme we should be careful neither to oversimplify the poem nor to distort its meaning. To suggest that the theme of Hayden's "Those Winter Sundays," for example, is a father's loving concern for his family is to highlight only part of the poem's meaning, for it does not take into account the speaker's remorse about his indifference to his father. Analogously, if we see Roethke's "My Papa's Waltz" as a statement about a child's terror at his father's horseplay, we misrepresent the complexity of the speaker's response to his memories of his father and their bedtime ritual.

We should also recognize that poems can have multiple themes: poems can be interpreted from more than one perspective and there is more than one way to state or explain a poem's meaning. Let us briefly reconsider Frost's "Stopping by Woods on a Snowy Evening."

We can say, for example, that the theme of Frost's poem is the necessity to face the responsibilities inherent in adult life. We can go on to say that the poem centers on a tension in our lives between our desire for rest and peace and our need to fulfill responsibilities and meet obligations. But we shouldn't remain satisfied with this explanation. For, as we have previously stated, the speaker's "miles to go" before he "sleeps" metaphorically describes all he must accomplish before he dies. Moreover, the final stanza reveals a tension here between the speaker's desire to continue and an impulse to stay at rest, to ease himself into the peace of death. We might further interpret the seductiveness of death as an attractive way of escaping the pressures of circumstance and the weight of responsibility.

In addition to these themes, we can abstract yet another: the ability of man to appreciate beauty, particularly the beauty of nature. We might argue, for example, that Frost contrasts man's capacity for taking pleasure in watching the snow fall in a dark wood with an animal's inability to enjoy either the spectacular beauty of the scene or its serenity. Animals, unlike men, do not possess an aesthetic faculty, the ability to appreciate beauty.

Let us briefly consider the subject and theme of the following poem.

EMILY DICKINSON

[1830–1886]

Crumbling is not an instant's Act

Crumbling is not an instant's Act,
A fundamental pause
Dilapidation's processes
Are organized Decays.

'Tis first a Cobweb on the Soul,   5
A Cuticle of Dust,
A Borer in the Axis,
An Elemental Rust—

Ruin is formal—Devil's work,
Consecutive and slow—   10
Fail in an instant, no man did
Slipping—is Crash's law.

The central idea of the poem is expressed in its opening line. We might paraphrase it this way: crumbling does not happen instantaneously; it is a gradual process, occurring slowly, cumulatively over time. The remainder of the first stanza further establishes this idea by accenting how "crumbling" is a consequence of dilapidation, which is a result of "decay." The deterioration that results is progressive; it is an organized, systematic process: one stage of decay leads to the next until destruction inevitably follows.

The gradual nature of decay is further emphasized with the statement that no one ever failed in an "instant," that the catastrophe occurs after, and as a consequence of, a series of failures. We can thus read the poem as a statement about the process of ruin (personal, emotional, financial) as well as a description of the process of decay. And we can summarize its theme thus: failure and destruction can be traced to small-scale elements that precede and cause them.

This theme is further extended in the second stanza, which contains four images of decay: cobweb, rust, dust, and the borer in the axis. These images are all accompanied by bits of specifying detail. The dust is a "cuticle," an image with suggestions of something at the "edges," of something on the outside and also of something human; the "cobweb on the soul" suggests spiritual deterioration ("cobwebs" suggest neglect); the "elemental" rust puts decay at the heart of things, at the center and vital core where the "borer" is operating. We can consider each of these images of decay as applying to a person, particularly to his or her soul: the dust encircling it, the cobweb netting it, the borer eating into it, and the rust corrupting it. Such an emphasis on spiritual decay seems further warranted by the first line of the third stanza: "Ruin is formal—devil's work." Ruin is perhaps the word most strongly suggestive of human and spiritual collapse; "devil's work" speaks for itself. Thus, a statement of the poem's theme must accommodate the idea of spiritual decay.

Centering on a poem's theme then, we work toward understanding a poem's significance—what it says, what it implies, what it means. As we have suggested previously, our sense of a poem's significance may change as we reread it. Moreover, our understanding of any poem's theme depends on our experience —both our literary experience and our experience in living, and as these develop so will our understanding of poetry.

CHAPTER SEVEN

Types of Poetry

Poetry can be classified as narrative or lyric. Narrative poems stress action, and lyrics song. Each of these types has numerous subdivisions: narrative poetry includes the epic, romance, and ballad; lyric poetry includes the elegy and epigraph, sonnet and sestina, aubade and villanelle. Moreover, each major type of poetry adheres to different conventions. *Narrative poems,* for example, tell stories and describe actions; *lyric poems* combine speech and song to express feeling in varying degrees of verbal music.

NARRATIVE POETRY

The grandest of narratives is the epic. *Epics* are long narrative poems that record the adventures of a hero whose exploits are important to the history of a nation. Typically they chronicle the origins of a civilization and embody its central beliefs and values. Epics tend to be larger than life as they recount valorous deeds enacted in vast landscapes. The style of epic is as grand as the action; the conventions require that the epic be formal, complex, and serious—suitable to its important subjects.

Among the more famous epics in Western Literature are Homer's *Iliad* (about the Greek and Trojan war), Virgil's *Aeneid* (about the founding of Rome), Dante's *Divine Comedy* (a journey through hell, purgatory, and heaven), and Milton's *Paradise Lost* (about the revolt of the angels, and man's creation and

fall). For a hint of the epic's subjects and language listen to these opening lines
from *The Aeneid* and from *Paradise Lost*. First Virgil:

> I sing of warfare and a man at war.
> From the sea-coast of Troy in early days
> He came to Italy by destiny,
> To our Lavinian western shore,
> A fugitive, this captain, buffeted   5
> Cruelly on land as on the sea
> By blows from powers of the air—behind them
> Baleful Juno in her sleepless rage.
> And cruel losses were his lot in war,
> Till he could found a city and bring home   10
> His gods to Latium, land of the Latin race,
> The Alban lords, and the high walls of Rome.
> Tell me the causes now, O Muse, how galled
> In her divine pride, and how sore at heart
> From her old wound, the queen of gods compelled him—   15
> A man apart, devoted to his mission—
> To undergo so many perilous days
> And enter on so many trials.

And now Milton:

> Of man's first disobedience, and the fruit
> Of that forbidden tree whose mortal taste
> Brought death into the world, and all our woe,
> With loss of Eden, till one greater Man
> Restore us, and regain the blissful seat,   5
> Sing, Heavenly Muse, that, on the secret top
> Of Oreb, or of Sinai, didst inspire
> That shepherd who first taught the chosen seed
> In the beginning how the Heavens and Earth
> Rose out of Chaos: or, if Sion hill   10
> Delight thee more, and Siloa's brook that flowed
> Fast by the oracle of God, I thence
> Invoke thy aid to my adventurous song,
> That with no middle flight intends to soar
> Above th' Aonian mount, while it pursues   15
> Things unattempted yet in prose or rhyme.
> And chiefly thou, O Spirit, that dost prefer
> Before all temples th' upright heart and pure,
> Instruct me, for thou know'st; thou from the first
> Wast present, and, with mighty wings outspread,   20
> Dovelike sat'st brooding on the vast abyss,
> And mad'st it pregnant: what in me is dark
> Illumine; what is low, raise and support;
> That, to the height of this great argument,
> I may assert Eternal Providence,   25
> And justify the ways of God to men.

Far less ambitious than epics, *ballads* are perhaps the most popular form of narrative poetry. Originally ballads were meant to be sung or recited. Folk ballads (or popular ballads as they are sometimes called) were passed on orally, only to be written down much later. This accounts for the different versions of many ballads such as "Lord Randal" and "Edward, Edward" (pages 511 and 515).

In addition to folk ballads of unknown (and sometimes multiple) authorship, there are also literary ballads (of known authorship). One example is "La Belle Dame sans Merci" by John Keats (page 576). Literary ballads imitate the folk ballad by adhering to its basic conventions—repeated lines and stanzas in a refrain, swift action with occasional surprise endings, extraordinary events evoked in direct, simple language, and scant characterization—but are more polished stylistically and more self-conscious in their use of poetic techniques.

Another type of narrative poem is the *romance,* in which adventure is a central feature. The plots of romances tend to be complex, with surprising and even magical actions common. The chief characters are human beings, though they often confront monsters, dragons, and disguised animals in a world that does not adhere consistently to the laws of nature as we know them. Romance in short deals with the marvelous—with, for example, St. George slaying a dragon in a magical forest. Popular during the Middle Ages and Renaissance, the romance as a poetic genre has fallen from favor. Nevertheless, some of its chief characteristics have found expression in popular fictional types such as the western, the adventure story, and the romantic love story.

LYRIC POETRY

Although narrative poems, especially literary ballads, combine story with song, action with emotion, story and action predominate. In lyric poetry, however, story is subordinated to song, and action to emotion. We can define *lyrics* as subjective poems, often brief, that express the feelings and thoughts of a single speaker (who may or may not represent the poet). The lyric is more a poetic manner than a form; it is more variable and less subject to strict convention than narrative poetry.

Lyric poetry is typically characterized by brevity, melody, and emotional intensity. The music of lyrics makes them memorable, and their brevity contributes to the intensity of their emotional expression. Originally designed to be sung to a musical accompaniment (the word *lyric* derives from the Greek *lyre*), lyrics have been the predominant type of poetry in the West for several hundred years.

Forms of lyric poetry range from the *epigram,* a brief witty poem that is often satirical, such as Alexander Pope's "On the Collar of a Dog" (page 55), to the *elegy,* a lament for the dead, such as Federico Garcia Lorca's "Lament for Ignacio Sanchez Mejias" (page 685) or Thomas Gray's "Elegy in a Country Churchyard," (page 555). Lyric forms also include the *ode,* a long stately poem in stanzas of varied length, meter, and form; and the *aubade,* a love lyric expressing complaint that dawn means the speaker must part from his lover. An example of the ode is John Keats's "Ode to a Nightingale" (page 577); the aubade is represented by John Donne's "The Sun Rising" (page 437).

The tones, moods, and voices of lyric poems are as variable and as complexly intertwined as human feeling, thought, and imagination. Generally considered the most compressed poetic type, lyrics typically express much in little. The *sonnet,* for example, condenses into fourteen lines an expression of emotion or an articulation of idea according to one of two basic patterns: the *Italian* (or *Petrarchan*) and the *English* (or *Shakespearean*). An Italian sonnet is composed of an eight-line octave and a six-line sestet. A Shakespearean sonnet is composed of three four-line quatrains and a concluding two-line couplet (see pages 463–465). The thought and feeling expressed in each sonnet form typically follow the divisions suggested by their structural patterns. Thus an Italian sonnet may state a problem in the octave and present a solution in its sestet. A Shakespearean sonnet will usually introduce a subject in the first quatrain, expand and develop it in the second and third quatrains, and conclude something about it in its final couplet.

Although sonnets reached the height of their popularity during the Renaissance, later writers have continued to be attracted to the form. Some sonnet writers, in fact, like Gerard Manley Hopkins, William Butler Yeats, Robert Frost, and E.E. Cummings have combined the two basic patterns to suit their poetic needs. Occasionally these and other poets have modified the form itself. Robert Frost's "Acquainted with the Night," for example, is composed of four tercets and a couplet rather than the familiar three quatrains and a couplet. Moreover, Frost has been known to write fifteen-line sonnets as well.

Less important historically than the sonnet but no less intricate and musical are two other lyric forms, sestina and villanelle, both deriving from French poetry. The *sestina* consists of six stanzas of six lines each followed by a three-line conclusion or *envoy.* The sestina requires a strict pattern of repetition of six key words that end the lines of the first stanza. Elizabeth Bishop's "Sestina" (page 709) is an example.

The *villanelle,* which also relies heavily on repetition, is composed of five three-line tercets and a final four-line quatrain. Its singular feature is the way its first and third lines repeat throughout the poem. The entire first line reappears as the final line of the second and fourth tercets, and again as the third line of the third and fifth tercets and as the concluding line of the poem. Examples include Theodore Roethke's "The Waking" (page 470) and Dylan Thomas's "Do Not Go Gentle into That Good Night," (page 717).

CHAPTER EIGHT

Elements of Poetry

We can interpret and appreciate poems by attending to their basic elements. The elements of a poem include a *speaker* whose voice we hear in it; its *diction* or selection of words; its *syntax* or the order of those words; its *imagery* or details of sight, sound, taste, smell, and touch; its *figures of speech* or nonliteral ways of expressing one thing in terms of another, such as symbol and metaphor; its *sound effects,* especially rhyme, assonance, and alliteration; its *rhythm and meter* or the pattern of accents we hear in the poem's words, phrases, lines, and sentences; and its *structure* or formal pattern of organization. All the elements of a poem work together harmoniously to convey feeling and embody meaning. We will consider them, however, individually, to sharpen our perception of what each element contributes.

VOICE: SPEAKER AND TONE

When we read or hear a poem, we hear a speaker's voice. It is this voice that conveys the poem's *tone,* its implied attitude toward its subject. Tone is an abstraction we make from the details of a poem's language: the use of meter and rhyme (or lack of them); the inclusion of certain kinds of details and exclusion of other kinds; particular choices of words and sentence pattern, of imagery and figurative language. In listening to a poem's language, in hearing the voice of its speaker, we catch its tone and feeling and ultimately its meaning.

In listening to the speaker's voice, for example, in Roethke's "My Papa's Waltz," (page 391) we hear a tone different from that of the speaker in Hayden's "Those Winter Sundays" (page 386). Roethke's speaker remembers his father fondly and addresses him ("your breath," "you missed"). He remembers and celebrates their spirited cavorting as a "romp" and a "waltz" and includes such comic details as the mother frowning while pans slide off the kitchen shelves and the father keeping time by steadily patting the boy's head. The poem's complex tone comes from its contrasted details: the boy's hanging on "like death," his ear scraping his father's belt buckle, and his "clinging" to his father's shirt.

The speaker of Hayden's "Those Winter Sundays" admires his father and perhaps feared him as a child. His attitude is suggested by the details he remembers and by the way he meticulously describes his father's attentive labors. But his tone conveys more than admiration; it conveys also a sense of regret, disappointment, and perhaps anguish at having been indifferent toward him as a child. The tone of Hayden's poem has none of the ease and playfulness of Roethke's; it is serious in its portrayal of the speaker's father and solemn in its account of the speaker's subsequent feelings.

The range of tones we find in poems is as various and complex as the range of voices and attitudes we discern in everyday experience. One of the more important and persistent is the *ironic tone* of voice. We have previously defined irony as a way of speaking that implies a discrepancy or opposition between what is said and what is meant (see pages 75–76). The following poem by Stephen Crane illustrates this ironic tone of voice.

STEPHEN CRANE

[1871–1900]

War Is Kind

Do not weep, maiden, for war is kind.
Because your lover threw wild hands toward the sky
And the affrighted steed ran on alone,
Do not weep.
War is kind.   5

Hoarse, booming drums of the regiment,
Little souls who thirst for fight,
These men were born to drill and die.
The unexplained glory flies above them,
Great is the battle god, great, and his kingdom   10
A field where a thousand corpses lie.

Do not weep, babe, for war is kind.
Because your father tumbled in the yellow trenches,

Raged at his breast, gulped and died,
Do not weep.   15
War is kind.

      Swift blazing flag of the regiment,
      Eagle with crest of red and gold,
      These men were born to drill and die.
      Point for them the virtue of slaughter,   20
      Make plain to them the excellence of killing
      And a field where a thousand corpses lie.

Mother whose heart hung humble as a button
On the bright splendid shroud of your son,
Do not weep.   25
War is kind.

How do we know that the speaker's attitude towards war is not what his words indicate, that his words are ironic? We know because the details of death in battle are antithetical to the consoling refrain of stanzas 1, 3, and 5: "Do not weep. War is kind." Moreover the details of stanzas 2 and 4 also work toward the same ironic end, but in a different way. Instead of the ironic consoling voice of stanzas 1, 3, and 5 (which of course offers no real consolation given the brutality described), stanzas 2 and 4 sound more supportive of military glory: Crane uses a march-like rhythm along with words connoting military glory in a context that makes them sound hollow and false. The view that war is glorious and that death in battle is honorable is countered with images of slaughter. Compare Crane's poem to another treating the glory of dying for one's country ironically, Wilfred Owen's "Dulce et Decorum Est" (page 677).

    Unlike the poems we have been considering in which the speaker is alone, the next poem we will examine contains a speaker who is addressing someone present. This type of poem in which a speaker addresses a silent listener is called a *dramatic monologue*. In listening to the speaker's monologue, we usually gain a vivid sense of his character and personality. The following poem, Robert Browning's "My Last Duchess," is a striking example of the dramatic monologue.

ROBERT BROWNING

[1812–1889]

My Last Duchess

FERRARA

That's my last Duchess painted on the wall,
Looking as if she were alive. I call

That piece a wonder, now; Frà Pandolf's hands
Worked busily a day, and there she stands.
Will 't please you sit and look at her? I said   5
"Frà Pandolf" by design, for never read
Strangers like you that pictured countenance,
The depth and passion of its earnest glance,
But to myself they turned (since none puts by
The curtain I have drawn for you, but I)   10
And seemed as they would ask me, if they durst,
How such a glance came there; so, not the first
Are you to turn and ask thus. Sir, 'twas not
Her husband's presence only, called that spot
Of joy into the Duchess' cheek; perhaps   15
Frà Pandolf chanced to say, "Her mantle laps
Over my lady's wrist too much," or "Paint
Must never hope to reproduce the faint
Half-flush that dies along her throat." Such stuff
Was courtesy, she thought, and cause enough   20
For calling up that spot of joy. She had
A heart—how shall I say?—too soon made glad,
Too easily impressed; she liked whate'er
She looked on, and her looks went everywhere.
Sir, 'twas all one! My favor at her breast,   25
The dropping of the daylight in the West,
The bough of cherries some officious fool
Broke in the orchard for her, the white mule
She rode with round the terrace—all and each
Would draw from her alike the approving speech,   30
Or blush, at least. She thanked men,—good! but thanked
Somehow—I know not how—as if she ranked
My gift of a nine-hundred-years-old name
With anybody's gift. Who'd stoop to blame
This sort of trifling? Even had you skill   35
In speech—which I have not—to make your will
Quite clear to such an one, and say "Just this
Or that in you disgusts me; here you miss,
Or there exceed the mark"—and if she let
Herself be lessoned so, nor plainly set   40
Her wits to yours, forsooth, and made excuse—
E'en then would be some stooping; and I choose
Never to stoop. Oh sir, she smiled, no doubt,
Whene'er I passed her; but who passed without
Much the same smile? This grew; I gave commands;   45
Then all smiles stopped together. There she stands
As if alive. Will 't please you rise? We'll meet
The company below, then. I repeat,
The Count your master's known munificence

Is ample warrant that no just pretense   50
Of mine for dowry will be disallowed;
Though his fair daughter's self, as I avowed
At starting, is my object. Nay, we'll go
Together down, sir. Notice Neptune, though,
Taming a sea-horse, thought a rarity,   55
Which Claus of Innsbruck cast in bronze for me!

The situation of the poem is this: the Duke of Ferrara, a city-state in Renaissance Italy, is addressing an ambassador who represents a count, the father of a marriageable aristocratic daughter. Although we hear only the duke's voice, we are aware of the ambassador's presence. We probably wonder how the ambassador reacts to what the duke tells him—especially to what he says in lines 45–46. But while the poet hints at the ambassador's actions (lines 12–13; 47–48, e.g.) he doesn't reveal his thoughts. Instead he centers our attention on the duke, whose manner, language, gestures, and concerns all reveal the kind of man he is and how he conducted himself in his relations with his last duchess.

The duke reveals himself as a monumental egotist—proud, shrewd, arrogant, and murderous. He shows himself to be a man who will not allow his will to be thwarted or his honor ignored. Intolerant of his former duchess's joy in things other than those he provided, and unwilling to "stoop" to telling her how her behavior insulted him, the duke has her killed: "I gave commands," he says. "Then all smiles stopped together."

But what has the duchess done to deserve her fate? She expressed joy in compliments given her; she took pleasure in simple things—riding her white mule, watching the sun set, accepting a gift of fruit. Her crime in the duke's eyes was in not recognizing the value of his aristocratic heritage: his name, rank, and pride did not mean enough to her.

Part of our shock in realizing what the duke has done comes from his certainty that he has behaved properly. What else could I do, he seems to say. And part derives perhaps also from the matter-of-fact manner in which the duke turns the conversation from his last duchess to the business at hand, the negotiations about the marriage and the dowry. But revealing as these things are, an even stronger index of the duke's egoistic pride is the way he refers to his last duchess as an object, as a possession that has been appropriately added to his prized collection. As a portrait on the wall, the duchess is finally and fully under the duke's control. (He even keeps her portrait behind a curtain so no one can see her without his authority.) The duke's pride in his wife's portrait is equal to his pride in his prized statue of Neptune taming a sea horse.

A few poems notable for their speakers and tones of voice follow. For each identify the speaker and situation. Describe the tone(s) of voice you hear, and consider what the speaker's tone contributes to the ideas and feelings that the poems convey.

MURIEL STUART
[b. 1889]

In the Orchard

'I thought you loved me.' 'No, it was only fun.'
'When we stood there, closer than all?' 'Well, the harvest moon
Was shining and queer in your hair, and it turned my head.'
'That made you?' 'Yes.' 'Just the moon and the light it made
Under the tree?' 'Well, your mouth, too.' 'Yes, my mouth?'   5
'And the quiet there that sang like the drum in the booth.
You shouldn't have danced like that.' 'Like what?' 'So close,
With your head turned up, and the flower in your hair, a rose
That smelt all warm.' 'I loved you. I thought you knew
I wouldn't have danced like that with any but you.'   10
'I didn't know. I thought you knew it was fun.'
'I thought it was love you meant.' 'Well, it's done.' 'Yes, it's done.
I've seen boys stone a blackbird, and watched them drown
A kitten . . . it clawed at the reeds, and they pushed it down
Into the pool while it screamed. Is that fun, too?'   15
'Well, boys are like that . . . Your brothers . . .' 'Yes, I know.
But you, so lovely and strong! Not you! Not you!'
'They don't understand it's cruel. It's only a game.'
'And are girls fun, too?' 'No, still in a way it's the same.
It's queer and lovely to have a girl . . .' 'Go on.'   20
'It makes you mad for a bit to feel she's your own,
And you laugh and kiss her, and maybe you give her a ring,
But it's only in fun.' 'But I gave you everything.'
'Well, you shouldn't have done it. You know what a fellow thinks
When a girl does that.' 'Yes, he talks of her over his drinks   25
And calls her a—' 'Stop that now. I thought you knew.'
'But it wasn't with anyone else. It was only you.'
'How did I know? I thought you wanted it too.
I thought you were like the rest. Well, what's to be done?'
'To be done?' 'Is it all right?' 'Yes.' 'Sure?' 'Yes, but why?'   30
'I don't know. I thought you were going to cry.
You said you had something to tell me.' 'Yes, I know.
It wasn't anything really . . . I think I'll go.'
'Yes, it's late. There's thunder about, a drop of rain
Fell on my hand in the dark. I'll see you again   35
At the dance next week. You're sure that everything's right?'
'Yes,' 'Well, I'll be going.' 'Kiss me . . .' 'Good night.' . . . 'Good night.'

QUESTIONS

1. What differences exist in the dialogue of the two speakers? How do those differences characterize the tone of each speaker's voice?
2. What do the questions, ellipses, and repeated words contribute to the poem's tone?

GERARD MANLEY HOPKINS
[1844–1889]

Thou art indeed just, Lord

*Justus quidem tu es, Domine, si disputem tecum: verumtamen
justa loquar ad te: Quare via impiorum prosperatur?°*

Thou art indeed just, Lord, if I contend
With thee; but, sir, so what I plead is just.
Why do sinners' ways prosper? and why must
Disappointment all I endeavour end?
Wert thou my enemy, O thou my friend,   5
How wouldst thou worse, I wonder, than thou dost
Defeat, thwart me? Oh, the sots and thralls of lust
Do in spare hours more thrive than I that spend,

Sir, life upon thy cause. See, banks and brakes
Now, leavèd how thick! lacèd they are again   10
With fretty chervil, look, and fresh wind shakes

Them; birds build—but not I build; no, but strain,
Time's eunuch, and not breed one work that wakes.
Mine, O thou lord of life, send my roots rain.

QUESTIONS

1. How do the words the speaker uses to address God help establish the tone of the first four lines? What is his attitude toward God here?
2. Lines 5–7 might be paraphrased according to the familiar saying: with friends like you, who needs enemies. What tone of voice do you hear in those lines? In lines 9–13? In the final line?

THOU ART INDEED JUST, LORD   *Epigraph. The poem's opening lines (1–3) translate the Latin.*

ANONYMOUS

Western Wind

Western wind, when will thou blow,
The small rain down can rain?
Christ, if my love were in my arms
And I in my bed again!

QUESTION

What tone bursts through the final couplet? What feeling does the speaker convey? How does the tone of the following alteration compare with the poem's final two lines as written?

Oh God I wish I were in bed
With my lover again.

HENRY REED

[b. 1914]

Naming of Parts

Today we have naming of parts. Yesterday,
We had daily cleaning. And tomorrow morning,
We shall have what to do after firing. But today,
Today we have naming of parts. Japonica
Glistens like coral in all of the neighboring gardens,   5
    And today we have naming of parts.

This is the lower sling swivel. And this
Is the upper sling swivel, whose use you will see,
When you are given your slings. And this is the piling swivel,
Which in your case you have not got. The branches   10
Hold in the gardens their silent, eloquent gestures,
    Which in our case we have not got.

This is the safety-catch, which is always released
With an easy flick of the thumb. And please do not let me

See anyone using his finger. You can do it quite easy   15
If you have any strength in your thumb. The blossoms
Are fragile and motionless, never letting anyone see
    Any of them using their finger.

And this you can see is the bolt. The purpose of this
Is to open the breech, as you see. We can slide it   20
Rapidly backwards and forwards: we call this
Easing the spring. And rapidly backwards and forwards
The early bees are assaulting and fumbling the flowers:
    They call it easing the Spring.

They call it easing the Spring: it is perfectly easy   25
If you have any strength in your thumb: like the bolt,
And the breech, and the cocking-piece, and the point of balance,
Which in our case we have not got; and the almond-blossom
Silent in all of the gardens and the bees going backwards and forwards,
    For today we have naming of parts.   30

QUESTIONS

1. Each stanza of "Naming of Parts" contains two distinct voices. Where does the first voice end and the second begin? Describe and characterize each voice.
2. Pinpoint the place where the two voices converge. What is the effect of their convergence?

JACQUES PRÉVERT
[1900–1977]

Family Portrait

The mother knits
The son goes to war
She finds it all perfectly natural, Mama
And the father, what is he doing? Papa?
He is making little deals   5
His wife knits
His son goes to war
He is making little deals
He finds it all perfectly natural, Papa
And the son, the son   10

What does the son find?
The son finds absolutely nothing, the son
For the son the war his Mama the knitting his Papa little deals for him the war
When it is all over, that war
He will make little deals, he and his Papa   15
The war continues Mama continues she knits
Papa continues he carries on his activity
The son is killed he no longer carries on
Papa and Mama go to the cemetery
They find it all perfectly natural, Papa and Mama   25
Life continues life with knitting war little deals
Deals war knitting war
Deals deals activity
Life along with the cemetery.

TRANSLATED BY HARRIET ZINNES

QUESTION

Characterize the tone of the first three lines. How is this tone reinforced or altered as the poem develops? What do the repeated words and phrases contribute to the tone?

DICTION

At their most successful, poems include "the best words in the best order," as Samuel Taylor Coleridge has said. In reading any poem it is necessary to know what the words mean, but it is equally important to understand what the words imply or suggest. The *denotation* or dictionary meaning of *dictator,* for example, is "a person exercising absolute power, especially one who assumes absolute control without the free consent of the people." But *dictator* also carries additional *connotations* or associations both personal and public. Beyond its dictionary meaning, *dictator* may suggest repressive force and tyrannical oppresion; it may call up images of bloodbaths, purges, executions; it may trigger associations that prompt us to think of Hitler, for example, or Mussolini. The same kind of associative resonance occurs with a word like *vacation,* the connotations of which far outstrip its dictionary definition: "a period of suspension of work, study, or other activity."

Because poets often hint indirectly at more than their words directly state, it is necessary to develop the habit of considering the connotations of words as well as their denotations. Often for both poets and readers the "best words" are those that do the most work; they convey feelings and indirectly imply ideas rather than state them outright. Poets choose a particular word because it suggests what they want to suggest. Its appropriateness is a function of both its denotation and its connotation. Consider, for example, the second stanza of "My Papa's Waltz":

> We romped until the pans
> Slid from the kitchen shelf;
> My mother's countenance
> Could not unfrown itself.

"Romped" could be replaced by *danced* since the poet is describing a dance, specifically a waltz. Why "romped" then? For one thing, it means something different from *danced*. That is, its denotation provides a different meaning, indicating play or frolic of a boisterous nature. Although "romped" is not really a dance word at all, here it suggests a kind of rough, crude dancing, far less elegant and systematic than waltzing. But it also connotes the kind of vigorous roughhousing that fathers and sons occasionally engage in and from which many mothers are excluded—though here, of course, the romp is occasioned by the father's having had too much to drink. "Romped" then both describes more precisely the kind of dance and suggests the speaker's attitude toward the experience.

Perhaps the most unusual words in the stanza, however, are "countenance" and "unfrown." "Countenance" is less familiar and more surprising than face. This is also true of "unfrown," a word you won't find in the dictionary. What makes these words noticeable is not just their uncommonness but their strangeness in the context of the stanza. "Countenance," a formal word, contrasts with the informal language of the two lines before it, lines that describe the informal romp of a dance; it suggests the mother's formality as she watches the informal play of her husband and son. Although her frown indicates disapproval, perhaps annoyance that her pans are falling, the disapproval and annoyance may be put on, part of an act. It is possible that she is responding as she is expected to respond.

If we look up *countenance* in the *Random House College Dictionary,* here is what we find:

> noun 1. appearance, esp. the expression of the face . . .
>   2. the face; visage
>   3. calm facial expression; composure
>   4. (obsolete) bearing; behavior
> trans. verb 6. to permit or tolerate
>   7. to approve, support, or encourage. . . .

Let's consider briefly the implications of these multiple denotations. The second meaning is more general than the first. It is this first meaning to which we gave priority in the discussion above. We determined our sense of the kind of expression on the mother's face from the line, "Could not unfrown itself." But in looking at definitions 3 and 4, we encounter a problem, or at least a complication. Isn't the mother's "frown" a sign of *dis*composure rather than one of the "composure" suggested by a "calm facial expression"? Or is it possible that Roethke has used *countenance* with two meanings in mind: the meaning of "facial expression" on one hand; the meanings of "tolerate and permit, approve and encourage" on the other? This double sense of *countenance* thus parallels the double sense of the experience for the child as both pleasurable and frightening.

Let us look closely at the language of the following poem.

WILLIAM WORDSWORTH
[1770–1850]

I wandered lonely as a cloud

I wandered lonely as a cloud
That floats on high o'er vales and hills,
When all at once I saw a crowd,
A host, of golden daffodils;
Beside the lake, beneath the trees,   5
Fluttering and dancing in the breeze.

Continuous as the stars that shine
And twinkle on the milky way,
They stretched in never-ending line
Along the margin of a bay: 10
Ten thousand saw I at a glance,
Tossing their heads in sprightly dance.

The waves beside them danced; but they
Outdid the sparkling waves in glee:
A poet could not but be gay,   15
In such a jocund company:
I gazed—and gazed—but little thought
What wealth the show to me had brought:

For oft, when on my couch I lie
In vacant or in pensive mood,   20
They flash upon that inward eye
Which is the bliss of solitude;
And then my heart with pleasure fills,
And dances with the daffodils.

The words of the poem are familiar; their meanings should pose no problems. We might mention that "o'er" in line 2 is an *elision,* the omission of an unstressed vowel or syllable to preserve the meter, of *over,* and that "oft" in line 19 is an abbreviated form of *often.* The language, overall, is simple, direct, and clear.

We can assure ourselves of the rightness or appropriateness of the poem's diction by considering the connotations of a few words. We can take lines 3 and 4 as examples.

> When all at once I saw a crowd,
> A host, of golden daffodils;

Suppose they had been written this way:

> When all at once I spied a bunch,
> A group of yellow daffodils;

Consider the connotations of each version. "Spied" may indicate something secretive or even prying about the speaker's looking. It may also suggest that he was looking for them. In contrast, "saw" carries less intense and fewer connotations; it merely indicates that the speaker noticed the daffodils, and its tone is more matter-of-fact. The alternate version's "bunch" and "group" suggest, on the one hand, a smaller number than Wordsworth's corresponding "crowd" and, on the other, a less communal sense. "Crowd" and "host," moreover, carry connotations of a social gathering, of people congregated to share an experience or simply enjoy one another's company. This implicit humanizing or personifying of the daffodils (identifying them with human actions and feelings) brings the daffodils to life: they are described as dancing and as "tossing their heads" (line 12), and they are called a "jocund company" (line 16). "Company" underscores the sociality of the daffodils and "jocund" indicates the human quality of being joyful.

This emphasis on the happiness of the daffodils and their large number serves to point up sharply the isolation and disspiritedness of the speaker. Their vast number is emphasized in the second stanza where they are described as "continuous" and as stretching in a "never-ending line." (And, of course, in the count: "ten thousand.") But this important contrast between the isolation of the speaker and the solidarity of the daffodils, though continued into the second stanza, gives way in stanzas 3 and 4 as the speaker imagines himself among the daffodils rather than simply looking at them from a distance. More importantly, when he thinks about them later, he thinks about being "with" them, not literally but imaginatively.

But before we look at words describing the speaker from later stanzas, we should return to the first adjective that describes the flowers: "golden" (line 4). Wordsworth uses "golden," not "yellow," or "amber," or "tawny" because "golden" suggests more than a color; it connotes light (it shines and glitters) and wealth (money and fortune). In fact the speaker uses the word "wealth" in line 18 to indicate how important the experience of seeing the daffodils has been. And in the last two stanzas, we notice that the speaker uses in succession five words denoting *joy* ("glee," "gay," "jocund," "bliss," and "pleasure") in a crescendo that suggests the intensity of the speaker's happiness.

Although Wordsworth uses various words to indicate joy, he occasionally repeats rather than varies his diction. The repetitions of the words for seeing ("saw," "gazed") inaugurate and sustain the imagery of vision that is central to the poem's meaning; the forms of the verb *to dance* ("dancing," "danced," "dance," and "dances") suggest both that the various elements of nature are in harmony with one another and that nature is also in harmony with man. The poet conveys this by bringing the elements of nature together in pairs: daffodils and wind (stanza 1); daffodils and flowers, daffodils and stars (stanza 2); water and wind (stanza 3). Nature and man come together explicitly in stanza 4 when the speaker says that his heart dances with the daffodils.

A different kind of repetition appears in the movement from the loneliness of line one to the solitude of line 22. Both words denote an alone-ness, but they suggest a radical difference in the solitary person's attitude to his state of being alone. The poem moves from the sadly alienated separation felt by the speaker in the beginning to his joy in reimagining the natural scene, a movement framed by the words "loneliness" and "solitude." An analogous movement is suggested within the final stanza by the words "vacant" and "fills." The emptiness of the speaker's spirit is transformed into a fullness of feeling as he remembers the daffodils.

To gain practice in discerning and appreciating diction in poetry, read the following poems with special attention to their words.

EDWIN ARLINGTON ROBINSON
[1869–1935]

Miniver Cheevy

Miniver Cheevy, child of scorn,
   Grew lean while he assailed the seasons;
He wept that he was ever born,
   And he had reasons.

Miniver loved the days of old   5
   When swords were bright and steeds were prancing;
The vision of a warrior bold
   Would set him dancing.

Miniver sighed for what was not,
   And dreamed, and rested from his labors;   10
He dreamed of Thebes° and Camelot,°
   And Priam's neighbors.°

MINIVER CHEEVY   ¹¹**Thebes** *Greek city famous in history and legend.*   ¹¹**Camelot** *the seat of King Arthur's court.*   ¹²**Priam** *King of Troy during the Trojan war.*

Miniver mourned the ripe renown
    That made so many a name so fragrant;
He mourned Romance, now on the town,   15
    And Art, a vagrant.

Miniver loved the Medici,°
    Albeit he had never seen one;
He would have sinned incessantly
    Could he have been one.   20

Miniver cursed the commonplace
    And eyed a khaki suit with loathing;
He missed the mediæval grace
    Of iron clothing.

Miniver scorned the gold he sought,   25
    But sore annoyed was he without it;
Miniver thought, and thought, and thought,
    And thought about it.

Miniver Cheevy, born too late,
    Scratched his head and kept on thinking;   30
Miniver coughed, and called it fate,
    And kept on drinking.

QUESTIONS

1. List the words in the poem that illustrate what is said in line 5: that "Miniver loved the days of old." List all the verbs that describe Miniver's action or inaction. What do they reveal about him?
2. What are the connotations of "ripe"? (line 13) and "fragrant" (line 14)? What does the combination of each respectively with ideas of fame and nobility suggest about these ideas? And how do the connotations of "on the town" (to describe Romance) and "a vagrant" (to characterize Art) suggest what has happened to Art and Romance?

---

[17] **The Medici** *family of powerful merchants and bankers, rulers of Florence in the fourteenth, fifteenth, and sixteenth centuries who were known for their patronage of the arts.*

WILLIAM WORDSWORTH
[1770–1850]

It is a beauteous evening

It is a beauteous evening, calm and free,
The holy time is quiet as a Nun
Breathless with adoration; the broad sun
Is sinking down in its tranquility;
The gentleness of heaven broods o'er the Sea: 5
Listen! the mighty Being is awake,
And doth with his eternal motion make
A sound like thunder—everlastingly.
Dear Child! dear Girl! that walkest with me here,
If thou appear untouched by solemn thought,   10
Thy nature is not therefore less divine:
Thou liest in Abraham's bosom all the year,
And worship'st at the Temple's inner shrine,
God being with thee when we know it not.

QUESTION

What do the following words have in common: *holy, eternal, solemn, divine, nun, adoration, heaven, God?* What words in the last four lines are congruent with these? And how does this diction reinforce the idea and feeling of the poem?

ROBERT HERRICK
[1591–1667]

Delight in Disorder

A sweet disorder in the dress
Kindles in clothes a wantonness.
A lawn° about the shoulders thrown   fine linen
Into a fine distractiön;
An erring lace, which here and there   5
Enthralls the crimson stomacher°;

DELIGHT IN DISORDER   ⁶*stomacher*   *a garment worn under the laces of the bodice.*

A cuff neglectful, and thereby
Ribbons to flow confusedly;
A winning wave, deserving note,
In the tempestuous petticoat;   10
A careless shoestring, in whose tie
I see a wild civility;
Do more bewitch me than when art
Is too precise in every part.

QUESTIONS

1. Examine the connotations of the words suggesting disorder: *thrown, distraction, neglectful, confusedly, careless.* Consider especially the connotations and etymology (word origin) of "erring" (line 5) and "tempestuous" (line 10).
2. Consider the words that describe the speaker's reaction to the disordered dress he describes: *sweet, kindles, wantonness, fine, wild, bewitch.* What do the connotations of these words suggest about the speaker?

ADRIENNE RICH
[*b. 1929*]

Rape

There is a cop who is both prowler and father:
he comes from your block, grew up with your brothers,
had certain ideals.
You hardly know him in his boots and silver badge,
on horseback, one hand touching his gun.   5

You hardly know him but you have to get to know him:
he has access to machinery that could kill you.
He and his stallion clop like warlords among the trash,
his ideals stand in the air, a frozen cloud
from between his unsmiling lips.   10

And so, when the time comes, you have to turn to him,
the maniac's sperm still greasing your thighs,
your mind whirling like crazy. You have to confess
to him, you are guilty of the crime
of having been forced.   15

And you see his blue eyes, the blue eyes of all the family
whom you used to know, grow narrow and glisten,
his hand types out the details
and he wants them all
but the hysteria in your voice pleases him best.   20

You hardly know him but now he thinks he knows you:
he has taken down your worst moment
on a machine and filed it in a file.
He knows, or thinks he knows, how much you imagined;
he knows, or thinks he knows, what you secretly wanted.   25

He has access to machinery that could get you put away;
and if, in the sickening light of the precinct,
and if, in the sickening light of the precinct,
your details sound like a portrait of your confessor,
will you swallow, will you deny them, will you lie your way home?   30

QUESTION

The man referred to in the poem is described in line 1 as a "prowler and father," and
in line 29 as a "confessor." What are the implications of each? Explain also the
implications of line 8: "He and his stallion clop like warlords among the trash."

IMAGERY

An *image* is a concrete representation of a sense impression, a feeling, or an
idea. Images appeal to one or more of our senses or more precisely, they
trigger our imaginative reenactment of sense experience by rendering feeling
and thought in concrete details related directly to our physical apprehension of
the world. Images may be visual (something seen), aural (something heard),
tactile (something felt), olfactory (something smelled), or gustatory (something tasted).

Tactile images of heat and cold inform Hayden's "Those Winter Sundays"
(page 386), in which the speaker's father wakes up early "in the blueblack cold"
to make "banked fires blaze." Visual and tactile images appear in Frost's "Stopping by Woods" (page 388), in which the speaker has stopped "between the
woods and frozen lake" to listen to "the sweep of easy wind" and watch the
fall of "downy" flakes of snow.

Poetry, characteristically, is grounded in the concrete and the specific—in
details that appeal to our senses, for it is through our senses that we perceive
the world. We see daylight break and fade; we hear dogs bark and children
laugh; we feel the sting of a bitterly cold wind; we smell the heavy aroma of
perfume; we taste (as well as smell and feel) the ice cream or pizza we may enjoy

eating. Poetry includes such concrete details and thereby triggers our memories, stimulates our feelings, and enjoins our response.

We sometimes use the word *imagery* to refer to a pattern of related details in a poem. Shakespeare's sonnet "That time of year thou may'st in me behold," for example (page 463), includes images of darkness and light, cold and warmth, day and night. The images cluster together to describe the passing of time. When images form patterns of related details that convey an idea or feeling beyond what the images literally describe, we call them *metaphorical* or *symbolic*. Such imagistic details suggest a meaning, attitude, or idea—they suggest one thing in terms of another—as for example when images of light are indicative of knowledge or of life and images of darkness are suggestive of ignorance or death.

Poetry is rooted, anchored in the concrete and the particular. It describes specific things—daffodils, fires, and finches wings, for example. And it describes such things in specific terms: the color of the daffodils, the glare of the fire, the beating of the finches' wings. From these and other specific details we derive both meaning and feeling.

For an indication of how images work together to convey feelings and ideas, consider the images in the following poem.

ELIZABETH BISHOP
[1911–1979]

First Death in Nova Scotia

In the cold, cold parlor
my mother laid out Arthur
beneath the chromographs:
Edward, Prince of Wales,
with Princess Alexandra,   5
and King George with Queen Mary.
Below them on the table
stood a stuffed loon
shot and stuffed by Uncle
Arthur, Arthur's father.   10

Since Uncle Arthur fired
a bullet into him,
he hadn't said a word.
He kept his own counsel
on his white, frozen lake,   15
the marble-topped table.
His breast was deep and white,
cold and caressable;

his eyes were red glass,
much to be desired.   20

"Come," said my mother,
"Come and say good-bye
to your little cousin Arthur."
I was lifted up and given
one lily of the valley   25
to put in Arthur's hand.
Arthur's coffin was
a little frosted cake,
and the red-eyed loon eyed it
from his white, frozen lake.   30

Arthur was very small.
He was all white, like a doll
that hadn't been painted yet.
Jack Frost had started to paint him
the way he always painted   35
the Maple Leaf (Forever).
He had just begun on his hair,
a few red strokes, and then
Jack Frost had dropped the brush
and left him white, forever.   40

The gracious royal couples
were warm in red and ermine;
their feet were well wrapped up
in the ladies' ermine trains.
They invited Arthur to be   45
the smallest page at court.
But how could Arthur go,
clutching his tiny lily,
with his eyes shut up so tight
and the roads deep in snow?   50

The poem describes a child's view of death. It renders her incomprehension and confused feeling about her cousin Arthur's death through images, specifically through what the little girl sees and hears.

Our first sense impression is tactile: we imagine "the cold, cold parlor." Immediately after, we see two things: a picture of the British royal family and a stuffed loon, which had been shot by the dead boy's father, also named Arthur.

The second stanza describes the loon in more detail. It sits on a marble-topped table, a detail that conveys two tactile impressions, hardness and coldness. This imagery is emphasized in the description of the marble table top as the loon's "white, frozen lake."

These visual images are continued in the third stanza in which the speaker sees her dead cousin in his coffin. She holds a long-stemmed white flower which she puts in the dead boy's hand. The images of whiteness and cold (the frozen lake, marble table top, and the dead, stuffed white loon of the previous stanzas) are continued: the speaker describes Arthur's coffin as a "frosted cake." The birthday cake image also indicates the limited extent of the speaker's comprehension of the reality and finality of death.

With the repeated details about the loon's red eyes and its frozen posture and base, the child unconsciously (and the poet consciously) associate the dead boy and the dead loon. Moreover, this connection is further established by the imagery of the fourth stanza in which Arthur is described as "all white," with "a few red strokes" for his hair. Unlike the maple leaf with its complete and thorough redness, little Arthur is left "unpainted" by Jack Frost (another image of the cold) and is thus left white "forever." On the one hand, such a description clearly indicates the child's fantastic incomprehension of Arthur's death; on the other, it suggests that she intuitively senses that Arthur has been drained of color and of life. A similar combination of intuitive understanding and conscious ignorance is echoed in the speaker's comparison of Arthur with the doll. She sees how similar they look on the surface, but she does not consciously register their similar lifelessness.

The images of the final stanzas recall those of stanza 1. The royal couples of the chromograph are described as dressed in red clothes with white fur trim, details that connect directly with the dead loon. Moreover, the lily of the third stanza (white and short-lived like the boy) reappears clutched in Arthur's hand. The final image is one of whiteness and coldness: deep snow covers the cold ground where Arthur will soon lie.

The poem's concrete details, mostly visual and tactile images, strongly evoke the coldness and lifelessness of the dead child. But they suggest other things as well. The portrait of the royal family and the stuffed loon suggest something of the family's social identity—its conservatism and propriety in particular. More importantly, however, these details, along with the others noted above, reveal the limitation of the speaker's understanding. She sees the loon, for example, as quiet: "he hadn't said a word," and "he kept his own counsel." In addition, she fantasizes that the royal family (which she sees as very much alive in their warm furs) have invited little Arthur to serve as "the smallest page at court." Even though this may be the speaker's way of coping with death, the final two images of white lily and cold snow, and the tone in which she asks her final question all point toward her near acknowledgment of the truth.

It should prove useful to return at this point to a few of the poems considered in earlier sections of this introduction and examine their imagery. For further practice in responding to poetic images, read the following poems.

WILLIAM BUTLER YEATS
[1865–1939]

The Lake Isle of Innisfree

I will arise and go now, and go to Innisfree,
And a small cabin build there, of clay and wattles° made: interwoven twigs
Nine bean-rows will I have there, a hive for the honey-bee,
And live alone in the bee-loud glade.

And I shall have some peace there, for peace comes dropping slow,   5
Dropping from the veils of the morning to where the cricket sings;
There midnight's all a glimmer, and noon a purple glow,
And evening full of the linnet's wings.

I will arise and go now, for always night and day
I hear lake water lapping with low sounds by the shore;   10
While I stand on the roadway, or on the pavements gray,
I hear it in the deep heart's core.

QUESTION

Identify the images of sound and sight and explain what they contribute to the idea
and feeling of the poem.

ROBERT BROWNING
[1812–1889]

Meeting at Night

The gray sea and the long black land;
And the yellow half-moon large and low;
And the startled little waves that leap
In fiery ringlets from their sleep,
As I gain the cove with pushing prow,   5
And quench its speed i' the slushy sand.

Then a mile of warm sea-scented beach;
Three fields to cross till a farm appears;
A tap at the pane, the quick sharp scratch
And blue spurt of a lighted match,   10
And a voice less loud, through its joys and fears,
Than the two hearts beating each to each!

QUESTION

In a series of images averaging one per line, the poet describes a lover traveling to meet his beloved. Identify each image, the specific sense it stimulates, and the feelings the images evoke.

H. D.

[1886–1961]

Heat

O wind, rend open the heat,
cut apart the heat,
rend it to tatters.

Fruit cannot drop
through this thick air—   5
that presses up and blunts
the points of pears
and rounds the grapes.

Cut the heat—
plow through it,   10
turning it on either side
of your path.

QUESTION

By asking the wind to "rend open," "cut apart," and "plow through" the heat, the poet creates an image of it. Identify this image and explain what stanza 2 contributes to it.

THOMAS HARDY
[1840–1929]

Neutral Tones

We stood by a pond that winter day,
And the sun was white, as though chidden of God,
And a few leaves lay on the starving sod;
  —They had fallen from an ash, and were gray.

Your eyes on me were as eyes that rove   5
Over tedious riddles of years ago;
And some words played between us to and fro
  On which lost the more by our love.

The smile on your mouth was the deadest thing
Alive enough to have strength to die;   10
And a grin of bitterness swept thereby
  Like an ominous bird a-wing. . . .

Since then, keen lessons that love deceives,
And wrings with wrong, have shaped to me
Your face, and the God-curst sun, and a tree,   15
  And a pond edged with grayish leaves.

QUESTIONS

1. Examine the images of stanza 1. What mood do they create? How do the images
   of stanzas 2 and 3 develop and expand those of the opening stanza?
2. What do you notice about the images of the final stanza in relation to those that
   come before?

FIGURES OF SPEECH: SIMILE AND METAPHOR

Language can be conveniently classified as either literal or figurative. When we
speak literally, we mean exactly what each word conveys; when we use *figurative
language* we mean something other than the actual meaning of the words. "Go
jump in the lake," for example, if meant literally would be intended as a
command to leave (go) and jump (not dive or wade) into a lake (not a pond
or stream). Usually, however, such an expression is not literally meant. In telling

someone to go jump in the lake we are telling them something, to be sure, but what we mean is different from the literal meaning of the words. To get lost, perhaps, which is itself a figurative expression.

Rhetoricians have catalogued more than 250 different *figures of speech,* expressions or ways of using words in a nonliteral sense. They include *hyperbole* or exaggeration (I'll die if I miss that game"); *litotes* or understatement ("Being flayed alive is somewhat painful"); *synecdoche* or using a part to signify the whole ("Lend me a hand"); *metonymy* or substituting an attribute of a thing for the thing itself ("step on the gas"); *personification,* endowing inanimate objects or abstract concepts with animate characteristics or qualities ("the lettuce was lonely without tomatoes and cucumbers for company"). We will not go on to name and illustrate the others but instead will concentrate on two specially important for poetry (and for the other literary genres as well): simile and metaphor.

The heart of both these figures is comparison—the making of connections between normally unrelated things, seeing one thing in terms of another. More than 2300 years ago Aristotle defined *metaphor* as "an intuitive perception of the similarity in dissimilars." And he suggested further that to be a "master of metaphor" is the greatest of a poet's achievements. In our century, Robert Frost has echoed Aristotle by suggesting that metaphor is central to poetry, and that, essentially, poetry is a way of "saying one thing and meaning another, saying one thing in terms of another."

Although both figures involve comparisons between unlike things, *simile* establishes the comparison explicitly with the words *like* or *as. Metaphor,* on the other hand, employs no such explicit verbal clue. The comparison is *implied* in such a way that the figurative term is substituted for or identified with the literal one. "My daughter dances like an angel" is a simile; "my daughter is an angel" is a metaphor. In this example the difference involves more than the word *like:* the simile is more restricted in its comparative suggestion than is the metaphor. That is, the daughter's angelic attributes are more extensive in the unspecified and unrestricted metaphor. In the simile, however, she only dances like an angel. (There's no suggestion that she possesses other angelic qualities.)

Consider the opening line of Wordsworth's poem about the daffodils: "I wandered lonely as a cloud" (page 410). The simile suggests the speaker's isolation and his aimless wandering. But it doesn't indicate other ways in which cloud and speaker are related. Later the speaker uses another simile to compare the daffodils with stars. This simile specifically highlights one aspect of the connection between stars and flowers: number. It also contains an example of hyperbole in its suggestion that the daffodils stretch in "a never-ending line."

In these examples the poet provides explicit clues that direct us to the comparative connection. He also restricts their application, as we have noted. In an additional comparison from the poem, a metaphor, Wordsworth writes that the daffodils "flash" upon the "inward eye" of the speaker. The "flash" (an image of light) implies that he sees the flowers in his mind's eye, the inward eye of memory. Moreover, when he "sees" the daffodils in his "inward eye," he realizes the "wealth" they have brought him. This "wealth" is also figurative —Wordsworth uses "wealth" as a metaphor for joy.

These examples of simile and metaphor from Wordsworth's poem are fairly straightforward and uncomplicated. For a more complex example, consider the use of metaphor in the following sonnet by William Shakespeare.

WILLIAM SHAKESPEARE
[1564–1616]

That time of year thou may'st in me behold

That time of year thou may'st in me behold
When yellow leaves, or none, or few, do hang
Upon those boughs which shake against the cold,
Bare ruined choirs where late the sweet birds sang.
In me thou see'st the twilight of such day   5
As after sunset fadeth in the west,
Which by-and-by black night doth take away,
Death's second self that seals up all in rest.
In me thou see'st the glowing of such fire
That on the ashes of his youth doth lie,   10
As the deathbed whereon it must expire,
Consumed with that which it was nourished by.
   This thou perceiv'st, which makes thy love more strong,
   To love that well which thou must leave ere long.

Perhaps the first thing to mention about the poem's metaphorical language is that its images appeal to three senses: sight, hearing, and touch. Moreover, the images of the first four lines include appeals to each of these senses: we *see* the yellow leaves and bare branches; we *feel* the cold that shakes the boughs; we *hear* (in memory) the singing birds of summer.

But these concrete representations of sensory experience become more than images with emotional reverberations. They become metaphors, ways of talking about one thing in terms of something else. The first image extended into a metaphor is that of autumn, "that time of year" when leaves turn yellow and branches become bare. The fourth line extends the image by describing the tree branches as a choir loft that the birds have recently vacated. Because Shakespeare's speaker says that "you" (we) can behold autumn *in him* ("In me thou see'st the twilight of such day," line 5), we know that he is speaking of more than autumn. We realize that he is talking about one thing in terms of another —about ageing in terms of the seasons.

In the next four lines the metaphor of autumn gives way to another: that of twilight ending the day. The sun has set; night is coming on. The "black" night is described as taking away the sun's light (line 7); the sun's setting is seen as a dying of its light. The implied comparison of night with death is directly stated in line 8, where night is called "death's second self"; like death, night "seals up all in rest." Night's rest is, of course, temporary; death's, however, is final. The image or metaphor is both consoling (death is a kind of restful sleep) and frightening (death "seals up" life in a way that suggests there will be no unsealing).

So far we have noted two extended metaphors of autumn and of evening. Each comparison highlights the way death begins with a prelude: twilight precedes night; autumn precedes winter; illness precedes death. The speaker knows that he is in the autumn of his life, the twilight of his time. This metaphor is continued in a third image: the dying of the fire, which represents the dying out of the speaker's life. This third image emphasizes the dying out of light and the dying out of heat. Moreover, the speaker's youth is "ashes," which serve as the "deathbed" on which he will "expire" (line 11). Literally, the lines say that the fire will expire as it burns up the fuel that feeds it. As it does so, it glows with light and heat. The glowing fire is a metaphor for the speaker's life, which is presently still "glowing" but which is beginning to die out as it consumes itself. The speaker's youth, like the dying fire, has turned to ashes. We might notice that the fire will "expire," a word which means literally to "breathe out . . . to emit the last breath," an image that suggests the termination of breathing in the dying.

The final element of this image of the dying fire is given in line 12: "Consumed with that which it was nourished by." Literally the fire consumes itself by using up its fuel, burning up logs. In its very glowing it burns toward its own extinction. Analogously, the speaker's youthful vitality consumes itself in living. His very living has been and continues to be a dying.

For a few additional examples of how poets employ figurative language, read the following poems. Attend particularly to their figures of comparison and especially to how those comparisons aid your understanding.

JOHN DONNE
[1572–1631]

Hymn to God the Father

1

Wilt thou forgive that sin where I begun,
    Which was my sin though it were done before?
Wilt thou forgive that sin through which I run,
    And do run still, though still I do deplore?
        When thou hast done, thou hast not done,   5
        For I have more.

2

Wilt thou forgive that sin by which I've won
    Others to sin, and made my sin their door?
Wilt thou forgive that sin which I did shun
    A year or two, but wallowed in a score?   10
        When thou hast done, thou hast not done,
            For I have more.

3

I have a sin of fear, that when I've spun
    My last thread, I shall perish on the shore;
But swear by thyself that at my death thy son   15
    Shall shine as he shines now, and heretofore;
        And having done that, Thou hast done;
            I fear no more.

QUESTIONS

1. Explain the images in stanza 2: the door of sin and wallowing in sin. Relate these
   two images from stanza 3: spinning the last thread and perishing on the shore.
2. The final stanza contains two puns or plays on words. Identify and explain each.
   What do they contribute to the meaning and tone of the poem?

ROBERT WALLACE
[*b. 1932*]

The Double-Play

In his sea lit
distance, the pitcher winding
like a clock about to chime comes down with

the ball, hit
sharply, under the artificial   5
banks of arc-lights, bounds like a vanishing string

over the green
to the shortstop magically
scoops to his right whirling above his invisible

shadows   10
in the dust redirects
its flight to the running poised second baseman

pirouettes
leaping, above the slide, to throw
from mid-air, across the colored tightened interval,   15

to the leaning-
out first baseman ends the dance
drawing it disappearing into his long brown glove

stretches. What
is too swift for deception   20
is final, lost, among the loosened figures

jogging off the field
(the pitcher walks), casual
in the space where the poem has happened.

QUESTIONS

1. As its title suggests the poem describes a double play in baseball—getting two offensive players out on a single play. Throughout the poem the double play is compared to a dance. Pinpoint the words and phrases that establish this metaphorical connection, and explain what precisely about the double play makes it like a dance.
2. Besides the central metaphor that controls the poem, the poet has introduced other comparisons to illuminate and describe aspects or details of the double play. Identify and explain these comparisons.
3. In what way has the double play occurred "in the space where the poem has happened" (line 24)? How has a double play occurred both on the page and in the poem?

LOUIS SIMPSON

[*b. 1923*]

The Battle

Helmet and rifle, pack and overcoat
Marched through a forest. Somewhere up ahead
Guns thudded. Like the circle of a throat
The night on every side was turning red.

They halted and they dug. They sank like moles   5
Into the clammy earth between the trees.
And soon the sentries, standing in their holes,
Felt the first snow. Their feet began to freeze.

At dawn the first shell landed with a crack.
Then shells and bullets swept the icy woods.   10
This lasted many days. The snow was black.
The corpses stiffened in their scarlet hoods.

Most clearly of that battle I remember
The tiredness in eyes, how hands looked thin
Around a cigarette, and the bright ember   15
Would pulse with all the life there was within.

QUESTION

Identify and explain the figures of speech in the first two stanzas. What impression does
each create? How is the mood they establish enforced by the rest of the poem?

JUDITH WRIGHT
[b. 1915]

Woman to Child

You who were darkness warmed my flesh
where out of darkness rose the seed.
Then all a world I made in me;
all the world you hear and see
hung upon my dreaming blood.   5

There moved the multitudinous stars,
and coloured birds and fishes moved.
There swam the sliding continents.
All time lay rolled in me, and sense,
and love that knew not its beloved.   10

O node and focus of the world;
I hold you deep within that well
you shall escape and not escape—
that mirrors still your sleeping shape;
that nurtures still your crescent cell.   15

I wither and you break from me;
yet though you dance in living light
I am the earth, I am the root,
I am the stem that fed the fruit,
the link that joins you to the night.   20

QUESTION

Explain the following figurative expressions:
"All a world I made in me" (line 3)
"All time lay rolled in me" (line 9)
"I hold you deep within that well" (line 12)
"I am the earth, I am the root,
I am the stem that fed the fruit" (lines 18–19)

SYMBOLISM AND ALLEGORY

A *symbol* is any object or action that means more than itself, any object or action that represents something beyond itself. A rose, for example, can represent beauty or love or transience. A tree may represent a family's roots and branches. A soaring bird might stand for freedom. Light might symbolize hope or knowledge or life. These and other familiar symbols may represent different, even opposite things, depending on how they are deployed in a particular poem. Natural symbols like light and darkness, fire and water can stand for contradictory things. Water, for example, which typically symbolizes life (rain, fertility, food, life) can also stand for death (tempests, hurricanes, floods). And fire, which often indicates destruction, can represent purgation or purification. The meaning of any symbol, whether an object, an action, or a gesture, is controlled by its context.

How then do we know if a poetic detail is symbolic? How do we decide whether to leap beyond the poem's literal factual detail into a symbolic interpretation? There are no simple answers to these questions. Like any interpretive connections we make in reading, the decision to view something as symbolic depends partly on our skill in reading and partly on whether the poetic context invites and rewards a symbolic reading. The following questions can guide our thinking about interpreting symbols:

1. Is the object, action, gesture, or event important to the poem? Is it described in detail? Does it occur repeatedly? Does it appear at a climactic moment in the poem?
2. Does the poem seem to warrant our granting its details more significance than their immediate literal meaning?
3. Does our symbolic reading make sense? Does it account for the literal details without either ignoring or distorting them?

Even in following such guidelines, there will be occasions when we are not certain that a poem is symbolic. And there will be times when, though we are fairly confident *that* certain details are symbolic, we are not confident about *what* they symbolize. Such uncertainty is due largely to the nature of interpretation, which is an art rather than a science. But these interpretive complications are also due to the differences in complexity and variability with which poets use symbols. The most complex symbols resist definitive and final explanation. We can circle around them, but we neither exhaust their significance nor define their meaning.

As an example of how literal details assume symbolic significance observe their use in the following poem.

PETER MEINKE
[*b. 1932*]

Advice to My Son

The trick is, to live your days
as if each one may be your last
(for they go fast, and young men lose their lives
in strange and unimaginable ways)
but at the same time, plan long range   5
(for they go slow: if you survive
the shattered windshield and the bursting shell
you will arrive
at our approximation here below
of heaven or hell).   10

To be specific, between the peony and the rose
plant squash and spinach, turnips and tomatoes;
beauty is nectar
and nectar, in a desert, saves—
but the stomach craves stronger sustenance   15
than the honied vine.

Therefore, marry a pretty girl
after seeing her mother;
show your soul to one man,
work with another;   20
and always serve bread with your wine.

But, son,
always serve wine.

The concrete details that invite symbolic reading are these: peony and rose; squash, spinach, turnips and tomatoes; bread and wine. If we read the poem literally and assume the advice is meant that way, we learn something about the need to plant and enjoy these flowers and foods. But if we suspect that the speaker is advising his son about more than food and flowers, we will look toward their symbolic implications.

What then do the various plants and the bread and wine symbolize? How is the speaker's advice about them related to the more general advice about living? In the first stanza the general advice implies two contradictory courses of action: 1) live each day to the fullest as if it will be the last; 2) look to the future and plan wisely so your future will not be marred by unwise decisions. In advising his son to plant peonies and roses, the speaker urges him to see the need for beauty and luxury, implying that he needs food for the spirit as well as sustenance for the body.

The symbols of bread and wine suggest a related point. The speaker urges his son to serve both bread and wine as bread is a dietary staple, something basic and common, but wine enhances the bread, making it seem more than mere common fare. Wine symbolizes something festive; it provides a touch of celebration. Thus the speaker's advice about bread and wine parallels his earlier suggestions. In each case, he urges his son to balance and blend, to fulfill both his basic and his spiritual needs. By making his advice concrete the speaker does indeed advocate literally what he says: plant roses and peonies with your vegetables; drink wine with your bread. But by including such specific instructions in a poem that contains other more serious advice about living (live for today, live for the future) the poet invites us to see bread and wine, vegetables and flowers more than literally. If our interpretation of their symbolic dimension is congruent with other parts of the poem, and if it makes sense, then we should feel confident that we are not imposing a symbolic reading where it is not warranted.

Related to symbolism, *allegory* is a form of narrative in which people, places, and happenings have hidden or symbolic meaning; allegory is especially suitable as a vehicle for teaching. In an allegorical work there are most often two levels of meaning, the literal and the symbolic. To understand an allegorical work we must make sense of its details by interpreting their symbolic meaning.

Allegory is thus a type of symbolism. It differs from symbolism in establishing a strict system of correspondences between details of action and a pattern of meaning. Symbolic works that are not allegorical are less systematic and more open-ended in what their symbols mean.

The following allegorical poem describes a journey along an uphill road that ends with the traveler arriving at an inn. We can readily see that the uphill road represents a struggling journey through life, that day and night stand for a life-span ending in death. The question-and-answer structure of the poem and its reassuring tone suggest that it can be read as a religious allegory, specifically a Christian one.

CHRISTINA ROSSETTI
[1830–1894]

Up-Hill

Does the road wind up-hill all the way?
　　Yes, to the very end.
Will the day's journey take the whole long day?
　　From morn to night, my friend.

But is there for the night a resting-place?   5
　　A roof for when the slow dark hours begin.
May not the darkness hide it from my face?
　　You cannot miss that inn.

Shall I meet other wayfarers at night?
　　Those who have gone before.   10
Then must I knock, or call when just in sight?
　　They will not keep you standing at that door.

Shall I find comfort, travel-sore and weak?
　　Of labor you shall find the sum.
Will there be beds for me and all who seek?   15
　　Yea, beds for all who come.

For further exercise in interpreting symbol and allegory, read the following poems with attention to their symbolic and allegorical details. All the poems are symbolic, but not in the same way.

WILLIAM BLAKE
[1757–1827]

A Poison Tree

I was angry with my friend:
I told my wrath, my wrath did end.
I was angry with my foe:
I told it not, my wrath did grow.

And I waterd it in fears, 5
Night & morning with my tears;
And I sunnéd it with smiles,
And with soft deceitful wiles.

And it grew both day and night,
Till it bore an apple bright. 10
And my foe beheld it shine,
And he knew that it was mine,

And into my garden stole,
When the night had veild the pole;
In the morning glad I see 15
My foe outstretchd beneath the tree.

QUESTIONS

1. "A Poison Tree" describes a series of events—it tells a story. Explain your understanding of the story's significance.
2. What does the apple in a garden represent? What difference would it make if it were a peach in an orchard?

ROBERT FROST
[*1874–1963*]

The Road Not Taken

Two roads diverged in a yellow wood,
And sorry I could not travel both
And be one traveler, long I stood
And looked down one as far as I could
To where it bent in the undergrowth; 5

Then took the other, as just as fair,
And having perhaps the better claim,
Because it was grassy and wanted wear;
Though as for that, the passing there
Had worn them really about the same, 10

And both that morning equally lay
In leaves no step had trodden black.

Oh, I kept the first for another day!
Yet knowing how way leads on to way,
I doubted if I should ever come back.   15

I shall be telling this with a sigh
Somewhere ages and ages hence:
Two roads diverged in a wood, and I—
I took the one less traveled by,
And that has made all the difference.   20

QUESTIONS

1. On one level this is a poem about walking in the woods and choosing one of two paths to follow. What invites us to see the poem as something more? What is this something more?
2. Frost is careful not to specify what the two roads represent: he does not limit their possible symbolic meanings. And yet the nature of the experience he describes does pivot the poem on a central human problem: the inescapable necessity to make choices. Specify some of the kinds of choices we all must make that could be represented by the two roads of the poem.

GEORGE HERBERT

[1593–1633]

Virtue

Sweet day, so cool, so calm, so bright,
    The bridal of the earth and sky:
The dew shall weep thy fall tonight;
    For thou must die.

Sweet rose, whose hue, angry and brave,   5
    Bids the rash gazer wipe his eye:
Thy root is ever in its grave,
    And thou must die.

Sweet spring, full of sweet days and roses,
    A box where sweets° compacted lie;   perfumes 10
My music shows ye have your closes°,   musical cadences
    And all must die.

Only a sweet and virtuous soul,
   Like seasoned timber, never gives;
But though the whole world turn to coal,   15
   Then chiefly lives.

QUESTION

The major contrast in the poem is between things that die and the one thing that does not. Identify and comment on the aptness of Herbert's symbols for transience and mortality.

EMILY DICKINSON

[1830–1886]

Because I could not stop for Death

Because I could not stop for Death—
He kindly stopped for me—
The Carriage held but just Ourselves—
And Immortality.

We slowly drove—He knew no haste   5
And I had put away
My labor and my leisure too,
For His Civility—

We passed the School, where Children strove
At Recess—in the Ring—   10
We passed the Fields of Gazing Grain—
We passed the Setting Sun—

Or rather—He passed Us—
The Dews drew quivering and chill—
For only Gossamer, my Gown—   15
My Tippet°—only Tulle—   scarf or stole

We paused before a House that seemed
A Swelling of the Ground—
The Roof was scarcely visible—
The Cornice—in the Ground—   20

> Since then—'tis Centuries—and yet
> Feels shorter than the Day
> I first surmised the Horses' Heads
> Were toward Eternity—

QUESTION

Is this poem generally symbolic or is it allegorical? Explain the significance of the details in lines 9–13 and lines 17–20.

SYNTAX

We have previously defined *syntax* as the order of words in sentence, phrase, or clause. From a Greek word meaning "to arrange together," *syntax* refers to the grammatical structure of words in sentences and the deployment of sentences in longer units throughout the poem. Poets use syntax as they use imagery, diction, structure, sound, and rhythm—to express meaning and convey feeling. A poem's syntax is an important element of its tone and a guide to a speaker's state of mind. Speakers who repeat themselves or who break off abruptly in the midst of a thought, for example, reveal something about how they feel.

Let us briefly consider what syntax contributes to the meaning and feeling of a few poems discussed earlier. In "Those Winter Sundays" (page 386) Robert Hayden uses normal word order for each of the poem's four sentences, but he varies their lengths radically. In the first stanza, for example, Hayden follows a long sentence with a short one. The effect is to increase the emphasis on the short sentence: "No one ever thanked him." In the last stanza, Hayden uses a question rather than a statement for the speaker's remembrance of his father's acts of love. Both the question and the repetition of the phrase "What did I know" reveal the intensity of the speaker's regret at his belated understanding.

In "Stopping by Woods on a Snowy Evening" (page 388), Robert Frost achieves emphasis differently through *inversion* or the reversal of the standard order of words in a line or sentence. The word order of the first line of the poem is inverted:

> Whose woods these are I think I know.

Normal word order would be:

> I think I know whose woods these are.

In the more conversational alternative, emphasis falls on what the speaker knows or thinks he knows. In Frost's line emphasis falls on "the woods," which are more important than what the speaker thinks he knows as he looks at them. Perhaps more important still is the difference in tone between the two versions.

Frost's inverted syntax lifts the line, giving it a more even rhythm, slowing it down slightly. The alternate version lacks the rhythmic regularity of Frost's original and reads like a casual statement.

Another aspect of syntax worth noting in Frost's poem is the variations in tempo among the four stanzas. The sentences of the first and last stanzas are the most heavily stopped with punctuation and pauses. The opening stanza contains three pauses before it ends; stanza four includes three in its first line alone and five altogether. In contrast stanza three contains only one stop, halfway through. And stanza two is one long sentence without a single pause or break. Frost carefully controls the movement and speed, the pace and pause of his poem by using punctuation and grammatical form to heighten its expressiveness and to control its tone.

Unlike the inverted and varied syntax of Frost's "Stopping by Woods on a Snowy Evening," (page 388) William Wordsworth's syntax in "I wandered lonely as a cloud" (page 410) is simple and direct; it does not call attention to itself. The two little syntactic twists that it does contain highlight an important dimension of the poem—visual imagery. One is an inversion: "saw I" (line 11); the other is a repetition: "I gazed—and gazed" (line 17). And consider Walt Whitman's "When I heard the learn'd astronomer" (page 465), which is cast as a single expansive subordinate sentence that sweeps over the first four lines like a wave and then ebbs in the next four. The action of the last four lines is suspended over the first four: we are made to wait for the final simple and important act that Whitman renders in the most direct syntax of any line in the poem: the speaker "look'd up in perfect silence at the stars."

But let us consider how syntax orders thought and highlights feeling in "The Sun Rising," by John Donne.

JOHN DONNE

[1572–1631]

The Sun Rising

> Busy old fool, unruly sun,
> Why dost thou thus,
> Through windows, and through curtains call on us?
> Must to thy motions lovers' seasons run?
> Saucy pedantic wretch, go chide   5
> Late schoolboys, and sour prentices,
> Go tell court-huntsmen that the King will ride,
> Call country ants to harvest offices;
> Love, all alike, no season knows, nor clime,
> Nor hours, days, months, which are the rags of time.   10

> Thy beams, so reverend and strong
> Why shouldst thou think?
> I could eclipse and cloud them with a wink,
> But that I would not lose her sight so long;
> If her eyes have not blinded thine,   15
> Look, and tomorrow late, tell me
> Whether both the Indias of spice and mine
> Be where thou left'st them, or lie here with me.
> Ask for those kings whom thou saw'st yesterday,
> And thou shalt hear, All here in one bed lay.   20
>
> She's all states, and all princes, I,
> Nothing else is.
> Princes do but play us; compared to this,
> All's honor's mimic, all wealth alchemy.
> Thou, sun, art half as happy as we,   25
> In that the world's contracted thus;
> Thine age asks ease, and since thy duties be
> To warm the world, that's done in warming us.
> Shine here to us, and thou art everywhere;
> This bed thy center is, these walls, thy sphere.   30

Perhaps the first thing we notice is the dislocation of syntax in the two opening questions. The first question could be rewritten so as to approximate more conventional discourse:

> Unruly sun, busy old fool,
> Why dost thou thus call on us
> Through windows, and through curtains?

Besides an alteration of rhythm, we notice a different emphasis in Donne's lines. The alternate version puts the emphasis on "windows" and "curtains," far less important words than "us," the word Donne's lines emphasize, as the poem is about a pair of lovers.

After another inverted sentence ("Must to thy motions lovers' seasons run") and a short one following the longer opening sentence, we hear a series of tonal shifts. The speed and abruptness of Donne's second question convey the speaker's tone of impatient defiance. The two questions with their emphatic dislocations prepare the way for the series of imperatives that increase our sense of the speaker's authority. This tone gives way abruptly in the last two lines of the stanza to a more leisurely verse movement ("Love, all alike, no season knows, nor clime, / Nor hours, days, months, which are the rags of time"). The tone of these lines, dignified and stately, derives partly from the simple declarative sentences, partly from the monosyllabic diction, and partly from the frequent pauses marked by punctuation. The overall effect is a slower line and a more exalted tone.

In stanza two the tone shifts back to the playful exaggeration of the beginning of the poem, with similar dislocations of syntax in its opening question. The second sentence (lines 13–18), neither question, statement, nor command, is a statement of possibility. The tone remains playfully defiant ("tell me / Whether both the Indias of spice and mine / Be where thou leftst them"); the speaker continues to exaggerate. The syntax is more convoluted, the sentences more complex than in the first stanza. Again, however, as in the opening stanza, the final line of stanza two resolves into a direct authoritative assertion:

"All here in one bed lay."

Unlike the first two stanzas, the last begins with the declarative syntax and simple, direct assertiveness with which the other two stanzas end. The entire stanza is composed of a series of balanced statements, some parallel, some antithetical. (Not completely, however, since there is something of the complex argument of stanza two midway through this last stanza. And there is also a brief return to the imperative voice in line 29, "Shine here to us.") But from these deviations the speaker quickly returns to the authority of direct declaration, an authority enhanced by the parallel form of the final line, by its slight dislocation of the verbs, and by the tightness of its structure (eliminating a conjunction between the clauses and omitting the implied verb of the second half of the line):

"This bed thy center is, these walls thy sphere."

There are many syntactical possibilities available to poets. For some interesting syntactical forms and their effects see T. S. Eliot's "The Love Song of J. Alfred Prufrock" for its associative syntax (syntax that reflects the mental associations of the speaker [page 656]); Gerard Manley Hopkins's "Thou Art Indeed Just, Lord" (page 405) for its use of fractured or broken syntax; John Milton's "On the Late Massacre in Piedmont" (page 547) for its Latinate syntax; and Alexander Pope's "An Essay on Man," (page 555) for its tightly formal, balanced, and antithetical syntax.

In the poems that follow Thomas Hardy uses broken syntax in "The Man He Killed"; Robert Frost uses ambiguous syntax so that multiple meanings coexist and coincide in "The Silken Tent"; and E. E. Cummings uses mimetic syntax, which imitates what it describes, in "Me up at does."

THOMAS HARDY

[1840–1928]

The Man He Killed

"Had he and I but met
By some old ancient inn,

We should have sat us down to wet
Right many a nipperkin!

"But ranged as infantry,   5
And staring face to face,
I shot at him as he at me,
And killed him in his place.

"I shot him dead because—
Because he was my foe,   10
Just so: my foe of course he was;
That's clear enough; although

"He thought he'd 'list, perhaps,
Off-hand-like—just as I—
Was out of work—had sold his traps—   15
No other reason why.

"Yes; quaint and curious war is!
You shoot a fellow down
You'd treat if met where any bar is,
Or help to half-a-crown."   20

QUESTIONS

1. The first two stanzas are each a single sentence. Explain their logical and syntactic relationship.
2. Unlike the smooth unbroken sentences of the first two stanzas, we find breaks in the syntax (indicated by dashes) in the next two stanzas. After reading the stanzas aloud, explain what the breaks in syntax suggest about the speaker's state of mind.
3. Does the speaker's fluent syntax in the last stanza suggest that he has worked through the state of mind you found evident in stanzas three and four? Explain.

WILLIAM BUTLER YEATS

[1865–1939]

An Irish Airman Foresees His Death

I know that I shall meet my fate
Somewhere among the clouds above;
Those that I fight I do not hate,

Those that I guard I do not love;°
My country is Kiltartan Cross   5
My countrymen Kiltartan's poor,
No likely end could bring them loss
Or leave them happier than before.
Nor law, nor duty bade me fight,
Nor public men, nor cheering crowds,   10
A lonely impulse of delight
Drove to this tumult in the clouds;
I balanced all, brought all to mind,
The years to come seemed waste of breath,
A waste of breath the years behind   15
In balance with this life, this death.

QUESTIONS

1. Point out the ways the syntax of this poem is balanced and controlled. How does the poem's balanced syntax reinforce its meaning?
2. Explain the connection between its syntax and its central idea: the pilot's attitude toward his country, his enemy, his fate.

ROBERT FROST
[1874–1963]

The Silken Tent

She is as in a field a silken tent
At midday when a sunny summer breeze
Has dried the dew and all its ropes relent,
So that in guys it gently sways at ease,
And its supporting central cedar pole,   5
That is its pinnacle to heavenward
And signifies the sureness of the soul,
Seems to owe naught to any single cord,
But strictly held by none, is loosely bound
By countless silken ties of love and thought   10
To everything on earth the compass round,
And only by one's going slightly taut

AN IRISH AIRMAN FORESEES HIS DEATH   3-4 *Those that I fight . . . I do not love.* Yeats is
referring to the Germans and the English respectively; the war is World War I.

In the capriciousness of summer air
Is of the slightest bondage made aware.

QUESTION

Perhaps the most astonishing thing about this sonnet is that it is only a single sentence. Go through the poem again attending to the way the sentence develops. Account for all the conjunctions: *so* (line 4), *and* (line 5), *And* (line 7), *But* (line 9), *And* (line 12). How do those conjunctions help us follow the sentence?

E. E. C U M M I N G S

[*1894–1962*]

"Me up at does"

Me up at does

out of the floor
quietly Stare

a poisoned mouse

still who alive

is asking What
have i done that

You wouldn't have

QUESTIONS

1. Rearrange the syntax of this poem to approximate the normal word order of an English sentence. Where do you have to make the heaviest adjustment?
2. How is Cummings's word order related to the situation the poem describes? What does Cummings gain by ordering his words as he does?

STEVIE SMITH
[1902–1971]

Mother, Among the Dustbins

Mother, among the dustbins and the manure
I feel the measure of my humanity, an allure
As of the presence of God. I am sure

In the dustbins, in the manure, in the cat at play,
Is the presence of God, in a sure way   5
He moves there. Mother, what do you say?

I too have felt the presence of God in the broom
I hold, in the cobwebs in the room,
But most of all in the silence of the tomb.

Ah! but that thought that informs the hope of our kind   10
Is but an empty thing, what lies behind?—
Naught but the vanity of a protesting mind

That would not die. This is the thought that bounces
Within a conceited head and trounces
Inquiry. Man is most frivolous when he pronounces.   15

Well Mother, I shall continue to think as I do,
And I think you would be wise to do so too,
Can you question the folly of man in the creation of God?
     Who are you?

QUESTION

Examine the way the poet uses balanced phrasing, primarily repeated phrases throughout
the poem. Notice the play of long sentence against short, of question against statement.
What do these syntactic elements contribute to the tone and attitude of the poem?

SOUND: RHYME, ALLITERATION, ASSONANCE

The most familiar element of poetry is *rhyme,* which can be defined as the
matching of final vowel and consonant sounds in two or more words. When

the corresponding sounds occur at the ends of lines we have *end rhyme;* when they occur within lines we have *internal rhyme.* The opening stanza of Edgar Allan Poe's "The Raven" illustrates both:

> Once upon a midnight dreary, while I pondered weak and weary,
> Over many a quaint and curious volume of forgotten lore—
> While I nodded nearly napping, suddenly there came a tapping,
> As of some one gently rapping, rapping at my chamber door.
> "'Tis some visitor," I muttered, "tapping at my chamber door—
> Only this and nothing more."

For the reader rhyme is a pleasure, for the poet a challenge. Part of its pleasure for the reader is in anticipating and hearing a poem's echoing song. Part of its challenge for the poet is in rhyming naturally, without forcing the rhythm, the syntax, or the sense. When the challenge is met successfully, the poem is a pleasure to listen to; it sounds natural to the ear. An added bonus is that rhyme makes it easier to remember.

Robert Frost's "Stopping by Woods on a Snowy Evening" is one such rhyming success. Reread it once more, preferably aloud, and listen to its music.

> Whose woods these are I think I know.
> His house is in the village, though;
> He will not see me stopping here
> To watch his woods fill up with snow.
>
> My little horse must think it queer
> To stop without a farmhouse near
> Between the woods and frozen lake
> The darkest evening of the year.
>
> He gives his harness bells a shake
> To ask if there is some mistake.
> The only other sound's the sweep
> Of easy wind and downy flake.
>
> The woods are lovely, dark, and deep,
> But I have promises to keep,
> And miles to go before I sleep,
> And miles to go before I sleep.

Notice how in each of the first three stanzas, three of the four lines rhyme (lines 1, 2, and 4), and Frost picks up the nonrhymed sound of each stanza (the third line) and links it with the rhyming sound of the stanza that follows it, until the fourth stanza when he closes with four matching rhymes. Part of our pleasure in Frost's rhyming may derive from the pattern of departure and return it voices. Part may stem also from the way the rhyme pattern supports the poem's meaning. The speaker is caught between his desire to remain still, peacefully held by the serene beauty of the woods, and his contrasting need to leave, to return to his responsibilities. In a similar way, the poem's rhyme is caught between a surge forward toward a new sound and a return to a sound repeated earlier. The pull and counterpull of the rhyme reflect the speaker's ambivalence.

The rhymes in Frost's poem are *exact* or *perfect rhymes:* that is, the rhyming words share corresponding sounds and stresses and a similar number of syllables. While Frost's poem contains perfect rhymes ("know," "though," and "snow," for example), we sometimes hear in poems a less exact, *imperfect, approximate,* or *slant rhyme.* Emily Dickinson's "Crumbling is not an instant's Act" (page 393) includes both exact rhyme ("dust"-"rust") and slant rhyme ("slow"-"law"). Theodore Roethke's "My Papa's Waltz" (page 391) contains a slant rhyme on (*"diz* zy"-"*ea* sy"), which also exemplifies *feminine rhyme.* In feminine rhyme the final syllable of a rhymed word is unstressed; in *masculine rhyme* the final syllable is stressed—or the words rhymed are each only one syllable.

Besides rhyme, two other forms of sound play prevail in poetry: *alliteration* or the repetition of consonant sounds, especially at the beginning of words, and *assonance* or the repetition of vowel sounds. In his witty guide to poetic technique, *Rhyme's Reason,* John Hollander describes alliteration and assonance like this:

> Assonance is the spirit of a rhyme,
> A common vowel, hovering like a sigh
> After its consonantal body dies. . . .
> . . . .
> Alliteration lightly links
> Stressed syllables with common consonants.

Walt Whitman's "When I Heard the Learn'd Astronomer," (page 465) though lacking in end rhyme, possesses a high degree of assonance. The long *i*'s in lines 1, 3, and 4 accumulate and gather force as the poem glides into its last four lines: "*I,*" "*ti* red," "*ri* sing," "gl*i* ding," "*I,*" "*my* self," "*ni* ght," "*ti* me to t*i* me," and "*si* lence." This assonance sweetens the sound of the second part of the poem, highlighting its radical shift of action and feeling.

Both alliteration and assonance are clearly audible in "Stopping by Woods," particularly in the third stanza:

> He gives his harness bells a shake
> To ask if there is some mistake.
> The only other sound's the sweep
> Of easy wind and downy flake.

Notice that the long *e* of "sweep" is echoed in "*ea-*sy" and "down-*y,*" and that the *ow* of "*dow* ny" echoes the same sound in "*sou* nd's." These repetitions of sound accentuate the images the words embody, aural images (wind-blow and snow-fall), tactile images (the soft fluff of down and the feel of the gently blowing wind), and visual images (the white flakes of snow).

The alliterative *s*'s in "*s*ome," "*s*ound," and "*s*weep" are supported by the internal and terminal *s*'s: "Give*s*," "hi*s*," "harne*ss* bell*s*," and "i*s*," and also by mid-word *s*'s: "a*s*k," "mi*s*take," and "ea*s*y." There is a difference in the weight of these sounds; some are heavier than others—the two similar heavy *s*'s of "easy" and "his" contrast the lighter softer "*s*" in "harness" and "mistake."

Listen to the sound effects of rhyme, alliteration, and assonance, in the following poem. Try to determine what sound contributes to its meaning.

GERARD MANLEY HOPKINS
[1844–1889]

In the Valley of the Elwy

I remember a house where all were good
  To me, God knows, deserving no such thing:
  Comforting smell breathed at very entering,
Fetched fresh, as I suppose, off some sweet wood.
That cordial air made those kind people a hood   5
  All over, as a bevy of eggs the mothering wing
  Will, or mild nights the new morsels of Spring:
Why, it seemed of course; seemed of right it should.

Lovely the woods, waters, meadows, combes, vales,
All the air things wear that build this world of Wales;   10
  Only the inmate does not correspond:

God, lover of souls, swaying considerate scales,
Complete thy creature dear O where it fails,
  Being mighty a master, being a father and fond.

We note first that the rhyme scheme reveals a Petrarchan sonnet: *abba, abba, ccd, ccd* (see page 464). We might note too that its rhyme pattern corresponds to its sentence structure: the octave splits into two sentences, lines 1–4 and 5–8; the sestet, though only one sentence, splits into two equal parts, lines 9–11 and 12–14. Hopkins's use of the Italian rhyme scheme keeps similar sounds repeating throughout: *good, wood, hood, should; thing, entering, wing, Spring; vales, Wales, scales, fails; correspond, fond.* (The rhyme pattern of the Shakespearean or English sonnet, by contrast, as heard in "That time of year," (page 463) contains fewer rhyming repetitions, as it uses a greater number of different sounds.)

Besides extensive rhyme, Hopkins uses alliteration and assonance—lightly in the octave and more heavily in the sestet. Lines 3–6, for example, collect short *e*'s in "sm*e*ll," "v*e*ry," "*e*nt*e*ring," "f*e*tched" and "fr*e*sh," "b*e*vy" and "*e*ggs."

Lines 4–8 begin an alliterative use of *w,* which is more elaborately sounded in lines 9–10 of the sestet; in lines 4–8 we hear: "*sw*eet *w*ood," "*w*ing *W*ill," and "*w*hy." In addition, in line 7 "*mi*ld *ni*ghts" picks up the long *i* of "Why," which finds an echo in the rhyme on "*ri*ght." This seventh line also contains what we might call a reversed or crisscrossed alliteration in "*m*ild *n*ights" and "*n*ew *m*orsels."

But these sound effects are only a pale indication of what we hear in the sestet. Perhaps the most musical lines of the entire poem are the opening lines of the sestet (lines 9–10). *L*'s frame both of these lines: "*L*ove*l*y . . . va*l*es" and "*All* . . . Wa*l*es." *L*'s are further sounded in "bui*l*d this wor*l*d." The *w,* which as we noted ended the octave, is carried into the sestet in "*w*oods," "*w*aters," "meado*w*s," "*w*ear," "*w*orld," and "*W*ales." The sestet also includes a variety of vowels: lo*ve*ly, woo*ds*, wa*ter*, mea*do*ws, *co*mbes, va*les*, *a*ll, *ai*r, wea*r*, tha*t*, bui*l*d, thi*s*, wo*rld*, Wa*les*.

Hopkins sounds a similarly varied vowel music in the last line, where he also uses alliteration and repetition to call attention to important attributes of God:

> "Being mighty a master, being a father and fond."

One line, however, especially lacks music: line 11. Coming amidst such splendid sounds, it stands out even more sharply:

> "Only the inmate does not correspond."

This expressive use of sound variation supports the idea that the line conveys: that in this beautiful natural world, the "inmate," the speaker in the guise of prisoner, does not fit. He feels out of place, out of harmony with his environment. In the lines that follow (12–14), he asks God to "complete" him, to make him whole, to integrate him into the world. And he prays in language that immediately picks up the sound play of assonance and alliteration that had been momentarily suspended in line 11. The speaker's harmony and wholeness are thus restored in the poem's beauty of sound.

To further develop your ear for sound in poetry, listen to the poems that follow:

THOMAS HARDY
[*1840–1928*]

During Wind and Rain

> They sing their dearest songs—
> He, she, all of them—yea,
> Treble and tenor and bass,
> And one to play;

With the candles mooning each face. . . .   5
     Ah, no; the years O!
How the sick leaves reel down in throngs!

They clear the creeping moss—
Elders and juniors—aye,
Making the pathway neat   10
     And the garden gay;
And they build a shady seat. . . .
     Ah, no; the years, the years;
See, the white stormbirds wing across!

They are blithely breakfasting all—   15
Men and maidens—yea,
Under the summer tree,
     With a glimpse of the bay,
While pet fowl come to the knee. . . .
     Ah, no; the years O!   20
And the rotten rose is ripped from the wall.

They change to a high new house,
He, she, all of them—aye,
Clocks and carpets, and chairs
     On the lawn all day,   25
And brightest things that are theirs. . . .
     Ah, no; the years, the years;
Down their carved names the rain drop ploughs.

QUESTIONS

1. Chart the poem's rhyme scheme. Note the repetitions of lines ("Ah no: the years") and of words ("O," "aye," and "yea"). What do these repetitions contribute to the idea and feeling of the poem?
2. Identify examples of alliteration and comment on their effect.

ALEXANDER POPE
[1688–1744]

Sound and Sense

True ease in writing comes from art, not chance,
As those move easiest who have learned to dance.

'Tis not enough no harshness gives offense,
The sound must seem an echo to the sense:
Soft is the strain when Zephyr° gently blows,   5
And the smooth stream in smoother numbers flows;
But when loud surges lash the sounding shore,
The hoarse, rough verse should like the torrent roar.
When Ajax° strives, some rock's vast weight to throw,
The line too labors, and the words move slow;   10
Not so, when swift Camilla° scours the plain,
Flies o'er th' unbending corn, and skims along the main.
Hear how Timotheus'° varied lays surprise,
And bid alternate passions fall and rise!
While, at each change, the son of Libyan Jove,°   15
Now burns with glory, and then melts with love;
Now his fierce eyes with sparkling fury glow,
Now sighs steal out, and tears begin to flow;
Persians and Greeks like turns of nature found,
And the world's victor stood subdued by sound!   20
The pow'r of music all our hearts allow,
And what Timotheus was, is DRYDEN now.

QUESTIONS

1. How does the poet enact verbally what he asserts in line 4, that "the sound must seem an echo to the sense"?
2. What contrast is described and imitated in sound effects in lines 5–6 and 7–8? Between lines 9–10 and lines 11–12?

MAY SWENSON

[*b. 1919*]

The Universe

What
is it about,
the universe,
the universe about us stretching out?

SOUND AND SENSE ⁵*Zephyr* *the west wind.* ⁹*Ajax* *a strong Greek warrior in the Trojan War.*
¹¹*Camilla* *an ancient Volcian queen noted for her speed and lightness of step.* ¹³*Timotheus* *a musician in John Dryden's poem "Alexander's Feast."* ¹⁵*the son of Libyan Jove* *Alexander the Great (356–323 B.C.), king of Macedonia and military conqueror who spread Greek culture throughout the ancient world.*

We, within our brains,   5
        within it,
                think
we must unspin
the laws that spin it.
            We think *why*   10
because we think
because.
Because we think,
        we think
            the universe about us.   15

        But does it think,
            the universe?
                Then what about?
                        About us?
                If not,   20
must there be cause
            in the universe?
Must it have laws?
                And what
                if the universe   25
                        is not about us?
                Then what?
                    What
                        is it about?
                And what   30
                        about *us?*

QUESTION

Is this poem merely a witty game of repeating words or does it employ sound effects
to sound effect? Consider especially lines 10–15 and 24–31.

HELEN CHASIN

[b. 1938]

The Word *Plum*

The word *plum* is delicious

pout and push, luxury of
self-love, and savoring murmur

full in the mouth and falling
like fruit   5

taut skin
pierced, bitten, provoked into
juice, and tart flesh

question
and reply, lip and tongue   10
of pleasure.

QUESTIONS

1. How is the word *p–l–u–m* sounded and resounded in the poem? Look at and listen to lines 2–3 in particular.
2. Map out the poem's patterns of alliteration and vowel repetition.

RHYTHM AND METER

Rhythm is the pulse or beat we feel in a phrase of music or a line of poetry. Rhythm refers to the regular recurrence of the accent or stress in poem or song. We derive our sense of rhythm from everyday life and from our experience with language and music. We experience the rhythm of day and night, the seasonal rhythms of the year, the beat of our hearts, and the rise and fall of our chests as we breathe in and out.

Perhaps our earliest memories of rhythm in language are associated with nursery rhymes like

> JACK and JILL went UP the HILL*
> to FETCH a PAIL of WAter.

Later we probably learned songs like "America," whose rhythm we might indicate like this:

> MY COUN-TRY 'tis of THEE
> SWEET LAND of LIberTY
> Of THEE i SING.

Since then we have developed an ear for the rhythm of language in everyday speech:

> I THINK I'll HIT the HAY

*Capitalization indicates stressed syllables, lower case letters unstressed ones.

Did you SEE that?
Or: Did you see THAT?
or: GO and DON'T come BACK.

Poets rely heavily on rhythm to express meaning and convey feeling. In "The Sun Rising" John Donne puts words together in a pattern of stressed and unstressed syllables:

BUsy old FOOL, unRULy SUN
WHY DOST THOU THUS
Through WINdows, and through CURtains, CALL on US?

Donne uses four accents per line—even in the second more slowly paced short line. Later in the stanza, he retards the tempo further. Listen to the accents in the following lines:

LOVE, all aLIKE, no SEAson knows, nor CLIME,
Nor HOURS, DAYS, MONTHS, which ARE the RAGS of TIME.

The accents result partly from Donne's use of monosyllabic words and partly from pauses within the line (indicated by commas). Such pauses are called *caesuras* and are represented by a double slash (//). The final couplet of Donne's poem illustrates a common use of caesura—to split a line near its midpoint:

Shine here to us, // and thou art everywhere;
This bed thy center is, // these walls thy sphere.

Marking the accents as well, we get this:

SHINE HERE to US, // and THOU art EVeryWHERE;
THIS BED thy CENter IS, // THESE WALLS THY SPHERE.

Notice again how the monosyllabic diction and the balanced phrasing combine with the caesuras to slow the lines down. The stately rhythm enforces the speaker's dignified tone and serious point: "Here is everywhere; this room is a world in itself; it is all that matters to us."

In the following brief poem, you can readily hear and feel the contrasting pace and rhythms of the two lines:

ROBERT FROST

[1874–1963]

The Span of Life

The OLD DOG BARKS BACKward withOUT GETting UP.
I can reMEMber when HE was a PUP.

The first line is slower than the second. It is harder to pronounce and takes longer to say because Frost clusters the hard consonants, *d, k* and *g* sounds, in the first line, and because the first line contains seven stresses to the four accents of the second. Three of the seven stresses fall at the beginning of the line, which gets it off to a slow start, whereas the accents of the second line are evenly spaced. The contrasting rhythms of the lines reinforce their contrasting images and sound effects. More importantly, however, the differences in the sounds and rhythms in the two lines echoes the contrast of youth and age.

But we cannot proceed any further in this discussion of rhythm without introducing more precise terms to refer to the patterns of accents we hear in a poem. If rhythm is the pulse or beat we hear in the line, then we can define *meter* as the measure or patterned count of a poetic line. Meter is a count of the stresses we feel in the poem's rhythm. By convention the unit of poetic meter in English is the *foot*, a unit of measure consisting of stressed and unstressed syllables. A poetic foot may be either *iambic* or *trochaic, anapestic* or *dactylic.* An iambic line is composed primarily of *iambs,* an *iamb* being defined as an unaccented syllable followed by an accented one as in the word "preVENT" or "conTAIN." Reversing the order of accented and unaccented syllables we get a *trochee,* which is an accented syllable followed by an unaccented one, as in "FOOTball" or LIquor." We can represent an accented syllable by a ′ and an unaccented syllable by a ⌣: thus, prevént (⌣′), an iamb, and líquŏr (′⌣), a trochee. Because both iambic and trochaic feet contain two syllables per foot, they are called *duple* (or double) meters. These duple meters can be distinguished from *triple* meters (three-syllable meters) like anapestic and dactylic meters. An *anapest* (⌣⌣′) consists of two unaccented syllables followed by an accented one as in comprĕHEND or ĭntĕrVÉNE. A *dactyl* reverses the anapest, beginning with an accented syllable followed by two unaccented ones. DÁNgĕroŭs and CHÉERfŭllȳ are examples. So is the word ÁNăpĕst.

Two additional points must be noted about poetic meter. First, anapestic (⌣⌣′) and iambic (⌣′) meters move from an unstressed syllable to a stressed one. For this reason they are called *rising* meters. (They "rise" to the stressed syllable.) Lines in anapestic or iambic meter frequently end with a stressed syllable. Trochaic (′⌣) and dactylic (′⌣⌣) meters, on the other hand, are said to be *falling* meters because they begin with a stressed syllable and decline in pitch and emphasis. (Syllables at the ends of trochaic and dactylic lines are generally unstressed.)

The second point concerns the regularity of a poem's meter. In a poem predominantly in iambic meter (Shakespeare's sonnet "That time of year thou may'st in me behold," for example, or Frost's "Stopping by Woods," pages 463 and 388) every line will not usually conform exactly to the strict metrical pattern. Frost's poem is much more regular in its iambic meter than is Shakespeare's, but Frost avoids metrical monotony by subtly altering his rhythm. And in one important instance Frost departs from the pattern slightly. We can divide the last stanza of Frost's poem into metrical feet and mark the accents in this manner, separating the feet with slashes.

> The woods / are love / ly, dark, / and deep. /
> But I / have pro / mises / to keep,
> And miles / to go / before / I sleep,
> And miles / to go / before / I sleep.

If we regard the pattern of this stanza and the pattern of the poem as a whole as regularly, even insistently, iambic, then the second line of this final stanza marks a slight deviation from that norm. The second and third feet of the line can be read as two accented syllables followed by two unaccented syllables, a spondaic foot followed by a pyrrhic. That's the way I've marked them. Two accented syllables together is called a *spondee* (KNICK-KNACK); two unaccented ones, a *pyrrhic* (of the). Both spondaic and pyrrhic feet serve as substitute feet for iambic and trochaic feet. Neither can serve as the metrical norm of an English poem.

Our third point concerns the names we give to lines of poetry based on the number of feet they contain. You may have noticed in looking back at "Stopping by Woods on a Snowy Evening" that it consists of eight-syllable or *octosyllabic* lines. Since the meter is iambic (˘´) with two syllables per foot, the line contains four iambic feet and is hence called a *tetrameter* line (from the Greek word for *four*). Thus Frost's poem is written in *iambic tetrameter,* unlike Shakespeare's sonnet "That time of year thou may'st in me behold," for example, which contains ten-syllable lines, also predominantly iambic. Such five-foot lines are named *pentameters* (from the Greek "penta" for five), making the sonnet a poem in *iambic pentameter.*

Here is a chart of the various meters and poetic feet.

	Foot	Meter	Example
Rising or Ascending Feet	iamb	iambic	prevent
	anapest	anapestic	comprehend
Falling or Descending Feet	trochee	trochaic	football
	dactyl	dactylic	cheerfully
Substitute Feet	spondee	spondaic	knick-knack
	pyrrhic	pyrrhic	(light) of the (world)

Duple Meters: two syllables per foot: iambic and trochaic

Triple Meters: three syllables per foot: anapestic and dactylic

Number of feet per line

one foot	monometer
two feet	dimeter
three feet	trimeter
four feet	tetrameter
five feet	pentameter
six feet	hexameter
seven feet	heptameter
eight feet	octameter

You should now be better able to discern the meter and rhythm of a poem. You can make an instructive comparison for yourself by taking the measure of two poems in the same meter: Shakespeare's sonnet "That time of year thou may'st in me behold" (page 463) and Hopkins's "In the Valley of the Elwy," (page 446) both written in iambic pentameter. In Hopkins's sonnet, see if you account for the speed of the octave and the slower pace of the sestet: look to changes in the basic iambic pattern; look for caesuras; and watch for *enjambed* or run-on lines, whose sense and grammar runs over and into the next line. You should be alert in both poems for how parallel sentence structure and the sound play of alliteration and assonance collaborate with rhythm and meter to support each poem's feeling and meaning. Listen carefully, especially to the last line of the octave and sestet of Hopkins's sonnet and to Shakespeare's concluding couplet.

Metrical Variation

We noted earlier that Frost's "Stopping by Woods" is written in strict iambic pentameter with only one slight variation in line 14. How then does Frost manage to avoid the monotony of fifteen lines of ta TUM / ta TUM / ta TUM / ta TUM / ? One way is by varying the reader's focus on different details: woods, snow, and speaker (stanza 1); horse and darkness (stanza 2); horse and snow (stanza 3); woods and darkness and speaker (stanza 4). Another is to vary the syntax, as he does with the inversion of the opening line. A third is simply to use a familiar diction in a normal speaking voice. Fourth and perhaps most important is Frost's masterful control of tempo. Of the four stanzas none carry the same pattern of end stopping. Stanza 1 is end-stopped at the first, second, and fourth lines, with line 3 enjambed. Stanza 3 is the closest to the second stanza, with two end-stopped lines and two enjambed lines. Stanza 4 is heavily stopped with two caesuras in its initial line and with end stops at every line. (It is here that we are slowed down to feel the seductive beauty of the woods; it is here that the symbolic weight of the poem is heaviest.) But we should not overlook the contrasting second stanza, which is cast as a single flowing sentence. The iambic pattern inhabits this stanza as it beats in the others. But as a result of the variety of technical resources Frost displays in the poem, we hear the iambic beat but are not overwhelmed by it.

Frost's rhythmical variations can be compared with Whitman's expressive use of metrical variation in "When I heard the learn'd astronomer," (page 465) a poem in *free verse,* verse without a fixed metrical pattern. Whitman's poem is characteristic of much free verse in its varying line lengths and accents per line, and in its imitation of the cadences of speech. The poem's final line ("Look'd up in perfect silence at the stars"), however, differs from the others, as Paul Fussell has pointed out in *Poetic Meter and Poetic Form.* * It is written in strict iambic pentameter, a variation which carries considerable expressive power, coming after the seemingly casual metrical organization of the previous lines. Because Whitman's line must be read in the context of the whole poem for its expressive impact to be felt, you should turn to it, preferably to read it aloud. In rereading you might like to consider whether, as some readers have suggested, the poem is not really in free verse at all, but rather in *blank verse,* unrhymed iambic pentameter.

Besides this expressive use of metrical variation, Whitman's poem exhibits additional elements of rhythmic control: in its consistency of end-stopped lines; in its flexible use of caesura (lines 2, 3, and 7); in its absence of caesura from the shorter lines (1, and 4–8). We can perhaps gain a greater appreciation of Whitman's rhythmical accomplishment by recasting his lines like this:

> When I heard the learn'd astronomer,
> When the proofs, the figures
> Were ranged in columns before me,
> When I was shown the charts and diagrams
> To add, divide, and measure them,
> When I sitting heard the astronomer
> Where he lectured to much applause
> In the lecture-room. . . .

Or like this:

> When I heard
> The learn'd astronomer,
> When the proofs,
> The figures were ranged
> In columns
> Before me,
> When I was shown
> The charts and diagrams
> To add, divide and
> Measure them. . . .

Both versions destroy the poem: they eliminate the sweep of its long lines, destroying its cadences and rhythm, and ultimately inhibiting its expressiveness.

Before leaving the poem, we should note that Whitman's rhythmic effects work together with other devices of sound, structure, and diction. In the same way, for example, that the strict iambic pentameter of the last line varies the

*Paul Fussell, *Poetic Meter and Poetic Form* (New York: Random House, 1979), p. 85.

prevailing meter expressively, so too does its assonance (the long *i*'s) deviate expressively from the poem's previously established avoidance of vowel music. In addition, the meter of the final line stresses *silence* and *stars,* both of which the speaker values. Finally, the iambic rhythm of the line has us looking ÚP and ÁT the stars, an unusual metrical effect since prepositions are almost always unstressed.

Throughout these comments on the rhythm and meter of the poems by Whitman and Frost, we have been engaged in the act of *scansion,* measuring verse, identifying its prevailing meter and rhythm, and accounting for deviations from the metrical pattern. In scanning a poem, we try to determine its dominant rhythm and meter, and to account for variations from the norm. The pattern we hear as dominant will influence how we read lines that do not conform metrically, and also how we interpret and respond to those lines. Consider, for example, the words "at a glance" abstracted from their place in a line of Wordsworth's "I wandered lonely as a cloud." Do you hear them as anapestic: at ă glánce? This is a likely way to hear the words outside the context of the poem. But when we return them to the poem, we may hear them another way:

> Tĕn thóusănd sáw Ĭ at ă glánce.

In such a case we will probably hear both the rhythmic pattern of the normal speaking voice (at ă glánce) and the metrical pattern of iambic pentameter (at ă glánce). Our experience of rhythm thus will often involve a tension between the two patterns as we hear one superimposed on the other.

One last note about rhythm and meter. Without the turn of the poetic line, without the division of words into lines, we have no poem. For what distinguishes poetry from prose is the line; it is the line that creates verse (from the Latin, *versus,* to turn). And as the poet Wendell Berry has pointed out, it is the line of verse that "checks the merely impulsive flow of speech, subjects it to another pulse, to measure."* Without the measure of meter, without the turn of the line, there is no music and no poem. Meter and rhythm are not merely technical elements, no more than diction and imagery, syntax and structure and sound. All of these interrelated elements of poetry have effects on readers, do things to readers. We sense them and feel them and thereby understand a poem, not just with our minds, but also with our eyes and ears.

Here are a few additional poems for rhythmic and metrical consideration.

---

*Wendell Berry, *Standing By Words* (San Francisco: North Point Press, 1983), p. 28.

GEORGE GORDON, LORD BYRON
[1788–1824]

The Destruction of Sennacherib

The Assyrian came down like the wolf on the fold,
And his cohorts were gleaming in purple and gold;
And the sheen of their spears was like stars on the sea,
When the blue wave rolls nightly on deep Galilee.

Like the leaves of the forest when summer is green,   5
That host with their banners at sunset were seen:
Like the leaves of the forest when autumn hath blown,
That host on the morrow lay withered and strown.

For the Angel of Death spread his wings on the blast,
And breathed in the face of the foe as he passed;   10
And the eyes of the sleepers waxed deadly and chill,
And their hearts but once heaved—and for ever grew still!

And there lay the steed with his nostril all wide,
But through it there rolled not the breath of his pride;
And the foam of his gasping lay white on the turf,   15
And cold as the spray of the rock-beating surf.

And there lay the rider distorted and pale,
With the dew on his brow, and the rust on his mail;
And the tents were all silent, the banners alone,
The lances unlifted, the trumpet unblown.   20

And the widows of Ashur are loud in their wail,
And the idols are broke in the temple of Baal;
And the might of the Gentile, unsmote by the sword,
Hath melted like snow in the glance of the Lord!

QUESTIONS

1. Identify the poem's meter. What kind of movement and rhythm does the meter create?
2. How is it appropriate to the action and idea of the poem?

THE DESTRUCTION OF SENNACHERIB   *The poem is based on the biblical account (II Kings 19:35) of the Assyrian king, Sennacherib, whose army was destroyed by the angel of the Lord in an invasion of Jerusalem.*

ANNE SEXTON
[*1928–1974*]

Her Kind

I have gone out, a possessed witch,
haunting the black air, braver at night;
dreaming evil, I have done my hitch
over the plain houses, light by light:
lonely thing, twelve-fingered, out of mind.   5
A woman like that is not a woman, quite.
I have been her kind.

I have found the warm caves in the woods,
filled them with skillets, carvings, shelves,
closets, silks, innumerable goods;   10
fixed the suppers for the worms and the elves:
whining, rearranging the disaligned.
A woman like that is misunderstood.
I have been her kind.

I have ridden in your cart, driver,   15
waved my nude arms at villages going by,
learning the last bright routes, survivor
where your flames still bite my thigh
and my ribs crack where your wheels wind.
A woman like that is not ashamed to die.   20
I have been her kind.

QUESTIONS

1. Identify the prevailing meter of the poem. How does Sexton keep the poem moving?
2. Examine her uses of caesura and enjambment, and comment on their effect on the poem's rhythm.

RICHARD WILBUR
[b. *1921*]

Junk

> *Huru Welandes*
> > *worc ne geswiceð*
> *monna ænigum*
> > *ðara ðe Mimming can*
> *heardne gehealdan.*
>
> > > WALDERE

An axe angles
                from my neighbor's ashcan;
It is hell's handiwork,
                the wood not hickory,
The flow of the grain
                not faithfully followed.
The shivered shaft
                rises from a shellheap
Of plastic playthings,
                paper plates,   5
And the sheer shards
                of shattered tumblers
That were not annealed
                for the time needful.
At the same curbside,
                a cast-off cabinet
Of wavily-warped
                unseasoned wood
Waits to be trundled
                in the trash-man's truck.   10
Haul them off! Hide them!
                The heart winces
For junk and gimcrack,
                for jerrybuilt things
And the men who make them
                for a little money,
Bartering pride
                like the bought boxer
Who pulls his punches,
                or the paid-off jockey   15
Who in the home stretch
                holds in his horse.

Yet the things themselves
                in thoughtless honor
Have kept composure,
                like captives who would not
Talk under torture.
                Tossed from a tailgate
Where the dump displays
                its random dolmens,   20
Its black barrows
                and blazing valleys,
They shall waste in the weather
                and toward what they were.
The sun shall glory
                in the glitter of glass-chips,
Foreseeing the salvage
                of the prisoned sand,
And the blistering paint
                peel off in patches,   25
That the good grain
                be discovered again.
Then burnt, bulldozed,
                they shall all be buried
To the depth of diamonds,
                in the making dark
Where halt Hephaestus
                keeps his hammer
And Wayland's work
                is worn away.   30

QUESTION

How does the rhythm and meter of "Junk" differ from the meters and rhythms of the other poems in this section?

WILLIAM CARLOS WILLIAMS

[1883–1963]

The Red Wheelbarrow

so much depends
upon

a red wheel
barrow

glazed with rain
water

beside the white
chickens

QUESTIONS

1. Mark the poem's meter. Which lines match each other metrically?
2. What is the effect of the breaks between lines 3–4 and lines 5–6?

JAMES SHIRLEY
[1596–1666]

The Glories of Our Blood and State

The glories of our blood and state
Are shadows, not substantial things;
There is no armor against fate;
Death lays his icy hand on kings.
   Scepter and crown   5
   Must tumble down
And in the dust be equal made
With the poor crooked scythe and spade.

Some men with swords may reap the field
And plant fresh laurels where they kill,   10
But their strong nerves at last must yield;
They tame but one another still.
   Early or late
   They stoop to fate
And must give up their murmuring breath,   15
When they, pale captives, creep to death.

The garlands wither on your brow,
Then boast no more your mighty deeds;
Upon death's purple altar now
See where the victor-victim bleeds.   20

> Your heads must come
> To the cold tomb;
> Only the actions of the just
> Smell sweet and blossom in their dust.

QUESTIONS

1. Identify the prevailing meter of the poem.
2. What is the effect of the short lines in each stanza? Comment on the change of rhythm in line 16 and the metrical variation in lines 22 and 24.

STRUCTURE: CLOSED FORM AND OPEN FORM

When we analyze a poem's structure, we focus on its patterns of organization. *Form* exists in poems on many levels from patterns of sound and image to structures of syntax and of thought; it is as much a matter of phrase and line as of stanza and whole poem.

Among the most popular forms of poetry has been the *sonnet,* a fourteen-line poem usually written in iambic pentameter (see pages 463–465). Because the form of the sonnet is strictly constrained, it is considered a *closed* or *fixed form.* We can recognize poems in fixed forms such as the sonnet, sestina, and villanelle by their patterns of rhyme, meter, and repetition. Poems written in fixed form reveal their structural patterns both aurally and visually. We see the shapes of their stanzas and the patterns of their line lengths; we feel their metrical beat, and we hear their play of sound.

The *Shakespearean* or *English sonnet* falls into three *quatrains* or four-line sections with the rhyme pattern *abab cdcd efef* followed by a *couplet* or pair of rhymed lines with the pattern *gg.* Let us reread Shakespeare's sonnet, "That time of year thou may'st in me behold."

That time of year thou may'st in me behold	*a*	
When yellow leaves, or none, or few, do hang	*b*	
Upon those boughs which shake against the cold,	*a*	
Bare ruined choirs, where late the sweet birds sang.	*b*	
In me thou see'st the twilight of such day	*c*	5
As after sunset fadeth in the west;	*d*	
Which by-and-by black night doth take away,	*c*	
Death's second self that seals up all in rest.	*d*	
In me thou see'st the glowing of such fire	*e*	
That on the ashes of his youth doth lie,	*f*	10
As the deathbed whereon it must expire,	*e*	
Consumed with that which it was nourished by.	*f*	
This thou perceiv'st, which makes thy love more strong,	*g*	
To love that well which thou must leave ere long.	*g*	

Each of the three quatrains of the poem is a single sentence, as is the couplet. This organization of the poem's sentences corresponds to its rhyme and images, which are also arranged in three quatrains and a final couplet. The pattern is reinforced, moreover, by the use of repeated words in the three quatrains: "In me behold"; "In me thou see'st"; "In me thou see'st."

There is a progression in the imagery in the sonnet: daylight becomes twilight; twilight turns into night. And there is a countermovement from images of longer duration to those of shorter: from the dying of a season to the dying of a day to the dying of a fire. In addition, within each image there is a movement from optimism to pessimism. Each image begins more hopefully than it ends: the yellow leaves become "bare ruined choirs" (lines 1–4); the twilight gives way to "Death's second self" (lines 5–8); the "glowing . . . fire" becomes "ashes" on a "deathbed" (lines 9–12).

The couplet is both a logical and an emotional response to the three quatrains that precede it. In the couplet is an implied *therefore* or *because* that can be heard by reversing the word order of its first line: Since you perceive this, it makes your love more strong. The last line is both a plea and a command to "love that well which thou must leave ere long," with "which" carrying the force of *because*.

Not every sonnet Shakespeare wrote is structured as tightly as this one. Look at the sonnets on pages 530–532 to see how Shakespeare varies this pattern, how, for example, he uses the couplet not only to respond to the quatrains, but to summarize their point or extend their implications as well.

An alternative to the Shakespearean sonnet is the *Petrarchan* or *Italian sonnet,* which falls into two parts: an *octave* of eight lines and a *sestet* of six. The octave rhyme pattern is *abba abba* (two sets of four lines); the sestet's lines are more variable: *cde cde;* or *ced ced;* or *cd cd cd.* The following is an example of the Italian form:

JOHN KEATS
[1795–1821]

On First Looking into Chapman's Homer

Much have I traveled in the realms of gold	*a*	
And many goodly states and kingdoms seen;	*b*	
Round many western islands have I been	*b*	
Which bards in fealty° to Apollo° hold.	*a*	allegiance
Oft of one wide expanse had I been told	*a*	5
That deep-browed Homer ruled as his demesne;°	*b*	domain
Yet never did I breathe its pure serene°	*b*	atmosphere
Till I heard Chapman speak out loud and bold:	*a*	
Then felt I like some watcher of the skies	*c*	

ON FIRST LOOKING INTO CHAPMAN'S HOMER   *Title: Translation of Homer's* Odyssey *by George Chapman, a contemporary of Shakespeare.*   [4]**Apollo**   *god of the sun and poetic inspiration.*

When a new planet swims into his ken;   *d*   10
Or like stout Cortez when with eagle eyes   *c*
He stared at the Pacific—and all his men   *d*
Looked at each other with a wild surmise—   *c*
Silent, upon a peak in Darien.°   *d*

Perhaps the most notable structural feature of the Italian sonnet is the way it turns on the ninth line. The first eight lines of Keats's sonnet describe the speaker's wide reading and compare reading with traveling. Lines 9–14 dramatically convey the speaker's feelings upon first reading Chapman's translation of Homer's great epic poems, *The Iliad* and *The Odyssey*. The speaker's excitement appears in lines 12 and 13, whose broken syntax contrasts with the smooth fluency of the first part of the sonnet. In addition, the octave and sestet differ in diction as well. The diction of the octave is elevated and formal, employing archaic words like "goodly" and "bards," and roundabout expressions like "realms of gold." Such words and phrases create an impression of the remoteness of the past, of its grandeur and dignity. In the sestet the diction is simpler and more direct. Moreover, Keats's use of figures of comparison in the sestet contributes to the striking change in diction. The two major comparisons, both similes, convey the excitement of discovery. By means of descriptions of action (they "looked" and "stared") and reaction (their "wild surmise" and stunned silence) Keats conveys vividly the speaker's feeling of elation and excitement. By reserving this elation for the sestet and by employing varied diction and syntax in the octave and sestet, Keats capitalizes on the structural possibilities of the Italian sonnet.

But not all poems are written in fixed forms. Many poets have resisted the limitations inherent in using a consistent and specific metrical pattern or in rhyming lines in a prescribed manner. As an alternative to the strictness of fixed form, they developed and discovered looser, more *open* and *free forms*. *Open* or *free form* does not imply formlessness. It suggests, instead, that poets capitalize on the freedom either to create their own forms or to use the traditional fixed forms in more flexible ways. An example of a poem in open form by Walt Whitman follows.

WALT WHITMAN

[*1819–1892*]

When I heard the learn'd astronomer

When I heard the learn'd astronomer,
When the proofs, the figures, were ranged in columns before me,

---

11-14**Cortez . . . Darien**   *Spanish conqueror of Mexico. Balboa, not Cortez, however, was the first European to see the Pacific from Darien in Panama.*

When I was shown the charts and diagrams, to add, divide, and measure them,
When I sitting heard the astronomer where he lectured with much applause in the
    lecture-room,
How soon unaccountable I became tired and sick,
Till rising and gliding out I wander'd off by myself,
In the mystical moist night-air, and from time to time,
Look'd up in perfect silence at the stars.

    Although Whitman's poem is arranged as a single sentence, it can be divided into two parts, each of four lines. The two-part division accumulates a set of contrasts: the speaker with other people and the speaker alone; the speaker sitting inside and the speaker standing outside looking at the stars; the noise inside and the silence outside; the lecturer's activity and the speaker's passivity; the clutter of details in lines 1–4 and the spareness of details in lines 5–8.

    These contrasts reflect the poem's movement from one kind of learning about nature to another: from passive listening to active observation; from indirect factual knowledge to direct mystical apprehension. Whether the poet rejects the first form of knowledge for the second, or whether he suggests that both are needed is not directly stated. The emphasis, nevertheless, is on the speaker's need to be alone and to experience nature directly.

    More elaborate departures from fixed form include poems such as this unusual configuration of E. E. Cummings:

E. E. CUMMINGS

[1894–1962]

l (a

l(a

le
af
fa

ll

s)
one
l

iness

Perhaps the first things to notice are the lack of capital letters and the absence of punctuation (except for the parentheses). What we don't see is as important as what we do. We don't see any recognizable words or sentences, to say nothing of traditional stanzas or lines of poetry. The poem strikes the eye as a series of letters that stream down the page, for the most part two to a line. Rearranging the letters horizontally we find these words: *(a leaf falls) loneliness.* (The first *l* of *loneliness* appears before the parenthesis, like this: *l (a leaf falls) oneliness;* to get *loneliness* you have to move the *l* in front of *oneliness.*

A single falling leaf is a traditional symbol of loneliness; this image is not new. What is new, however, is the way Cummings has coupled the concept with the image, the way he has formed and shaped them into a nontraditional poem. But what has the poet gained by arranging his poem this way? By breaking the horizontal line of verse into a series of fragments (from the horizontal view-point), Cummings illustrates visually the separation that is the primary cause of loneliness. Both the word *loneliness* and the image described in *a leaf falls* are broken apart, separated in this way. In addition, by splitting the initial letter from *loneliness,* the poet has revealed the hidden *one* in the word. It's as if he is saying: loneliness is *one*-liness. This idea is further corroborated in the visual ambiguity of "l." Initially we are not sure whether this symbol "l" is a number —*one*— or the letter *l.* By shaping and arranging his poem this way, Cummings unites form and content, structure and idea. In addition, he invites us to play the poetry game with him by remaking the poem as we put its pieces to-gether. In doing so we step back and see in the design of the poem a leaf falling

    d

    o

    w

    n

the page. By positioning the letters as he does; Cummings pictures a leaf fall:

    le

    af

    fa

    ll

    s.

If "l(a" is a poem for the eye, the following poem, also by Cummings, is arranged for voice. From the standpoint of traditional poetic form, it too exhibits peculiarities of sound and structure, line and stanza.

E. E. CUMMINGS
[1894–1962]

[Buffalo Bill's]

Buffalo Bill's
defunct
          who used to
          ride a watersmooth-silver
                              stallion   5
and break onetwothreefourfive pigeons justlikethat
                                        Jesus
he was a handsome man
                    and what i want to know is
how do you like your blueeyed boy   10
Mister Death

Before we listen closely to the voice of the poem, let's glance at how it hits the eye. "Buffalo Bill's," "stallion," "defunct," "Jesus," and "Mister Death" are all set on separate lines *as* complete lines. "Buffalo Bill's," "Mister Death," and "Jesus" are the only words capitalized. "Buffalo Bill" and "Mister Death" frame the poem; "Jesus" is set off on its own as far to the right as the line will go. Other words also receive a visual stress. At two points in line 6, Cummings buncheswordstogetherlikethis. Both of these visual effects are translated from eye to voice to ear so that we read the poem acknowledging the stress in each case. Cummings has used typography as a formal way of laying out language on the page to direct our reading. To see and hear what he has accomplished in this respect, read aloud the following rearranged version, which deliberately flattens the special effects Cummings highlights.

Buffalo Bill's defunct,
Who used to ride
a water-smooth silver stallion
and break one, two, three, four, five
pigeons just like that
Jesus he was a handsome man
And what I would like to know is
how do you like your
blueeyed boy, Mister Death?

Let us, finally, summarize our remarks about structure and form. In discerning a poem's structure, we gain a clue to its meaning. Moreover, we can increase our ability to apprehend a poem's organization by doing the following:

1. Looking and listening for changes of diction and imagery, tone and mood, rhythm and rhyme, time and place and circumstance.
2. Watching for repeated elements: words, images, patterns of syntax, rhythm and rhyme.
3. Remembering that structure is an aspect of meaning. It is not something independent of meaning, but works with other poetic elements to embody meaning, to formulate it. A poem's structure, its form, is part of what the poem says, part of how it means what it does.

Test out these ideas by analyzing the form of the following poems.

WILLIAM CARLOS WILLIAMS
[1883–1963]

The Dance

In Breughel's° great picture, The Kermess,
the dancers go round, they go round and
around, the squeal and the blare and the
tweedle of bagpipes, a bugle and fiddles
tipping their bellies (round as the thick-   5
sided glasses whose wash they impound)
their hips and their bellies off balance
to turn them. Kicking and rolling about
the Fair Grounds, swinging their butts, those
shanks must be sound to bear up under such   10
rollicking measures, prance as they dance
in Breughel's great picture, The Kermess.

QUESTIONS

1. What kind of dance does the poem describe? What kind of action does the first long sentence imitate (lines 1–8)?
2. Comment on the relationship between the first and last lines.

THE DANCE   [1]*Breughel*   *Pieter Breughel the Elder (1525–1569), Flemish painter of peasant life.* The Kermess *is a painting of a peasant wedding dance. See pp. 504–507 for reproductions of two of Breughel's paintings and the poems they inspired.*

DENISE LEVERTOV
[b. 1923]

O Taste and See

The world is
not with us enough.
O taste and see

the subway Bible poster said,
meaning The Lord, meaning   5
if anything all that lives
to the imagination's tongue,

grief, mercy, language,
tangerine, weather, to
breathe them, bite,   10
savor, chew, swallow, transform

into our flesh our
deaths, crossing the street, plum, quince,
living in the orchard and being

hungry, and plucking   15
the fruit.

QUESTION

Imagine this poem written as a single stanza. What is the advantage of the poet's having
structured it as she has?

THEODORE ROETHKE
[1908–1963]

The Waking

I wake to sleep, and take my waking slow.
I feel my fate in what I cannot fear.
I learn by going where I have to go.

We think by feeling. What is there to know?
I hear my being dance from ear to ear. 5
I wake to sleep, and take my waking slow.

Of those so close beside me, which are you?
God bless the Ground! I shall walk softly there,
And learn by going where I have to go.

Light takes the Tree; but who can tell us how? 10
The lowly worm climbs up a winding stair;
I wake to sleep, and take my waking slow.

Great Nature has another thing to do
To you and me; so take the lively air,
And, lovely, learn by going where to go. 15

This shaking keeps me steady. I should know.
What falls away is always. And is near.
I wake to sleep, and take my waking slow.
I learn by going where I have to go.

QUESTION

Describe the patterns of repetition that prevail in the poem. Consider repeated rhyme and repeated lines. What is their effect on the poem's tone and feeling?

A. R. AMMONS

[*b. 1926*]

Poetics

I look for the way
things will turn
out spiraling from a center,
the shape
things will take to come forth in 5

so that the birch tree white
touched black at branches
will stand out
wind-glittering
totally its apparent self: 10

I look for the forms
things want to come as

from what black wells of possibility,
how a thing will
unfold: 15

not the shape on paper—though
that, too—but the
uninterfering means on paper:

not so much looking for the shape
as being available   20
to any shape that may be
summoning itself
through me
from the self not mine but ours.

QUESTIONS

1. How does the structure of "Poetics" reflect its central idea?
2. What is the poem saying about form in nature and in poems?

C. P. CAVAFY

[1863–1933]

The City

You said, "I will go to another land, I will go to another sea.
Another city will be found, a better one than this.
Every effort of mine is a condemnation of fate;
and my heart is—like a corpse—buried.
How long will my mind remain in this wasteland.   5
Wherever I turn my eyes, wherever I may look
I see black ruins of my life here,
where I spent so many years destroying and wasting."
You will find no new lands, you will find no other seas.
The city will follow you. You will roam the same   10
streets. And you will age in the same neighborhoods;
and you will grow gray in these same houses.
Always you will arrive in this city. Do not hope for any other—

There is no ship for you, there is no road.
As you have destroyed your life here 15
in this little corner, you have ruined it in the entire world.

TRANSLATED BY RAE DALVEN

QUESTION

Although this poem is not set up as a set of stanzas, it does contain an implicit division. Explain where you would divide it and why.

CHAPTER NINE

Approaching a Poem: Guidelines for Reading

The following guidelines for reading poems will help you focus on both what a poem expresses and how it expresses it. The guidelines are applied to Gerard Manley Hopkins's "Spring and Fall" and may be kept in mind as you read the poems in Chapter 11.

1. Read the poem a few times slowly and deliberately. If possible read it aloud. Identify the speaker, subject, situation, and tone.

2. Make sure you understand the grammar of each sentence so that you can follow what each sentence literally says. Note any deviations from normal syntax and consider the reasons for them.

3. Attend to the words of the poem, both their denotations and their connotations. Use a dictionary to acquaint yourself with unfamiliar words and to enrich your sense of those you already know. Look for connections among the words and images. Think about the implications of any metaphors, similes, images, or symbols you discover. Consider whether the poem is saying one thing in terms of another.

4. Listen to the poem's sound and rhythm. Identify places where music and rhythm are most expressive and try to explain why. Notice where the tempo of the poem changes or where its language is heightened or otherwise altered.

Listen for changes of rhythm and rhyme and relate the poem's sound to its meaning.

5. Consider the poem's form and how its structure shapes its thought and its emotion.

The poem:

GERARD MANLEY HOPKINS

[1844–1889]

Spring and Fall:
to a Young Child

Márgarét, áre you grieving
Over Goldengrove unleaving?
Leáves, like the things of man, you
With your fresh thoughts care for, can you?
Áh! ás the heart grows older   5
It will come to such sights colder
By and by, nor spare a sigh
Though worlds of wanwood leafmeal lie;
And yet you *will* weep and know why.
Now no matter, child, the name: 10
Sórrow's spríngs áre the same.
Nor mouth had, no nor mind, expressed
What heart heard of, ghost guessed:
It ís the blight man was born for,
It is Margaret you mourn for.   15

Speaker and Tone   An adult speaks to a child. The time: autumn; the place: a grove of trees where falling leaves have turned yellow. The child cries over the scene and also over something she is only dimly aware of. The speaker's tone mixes gentle consolation with mild reproof.

Diction   Line two stops us first with "Goldengrove," a combination of the word *grove* (a small woods) and the color of their leaves. We are confronted by another unusual word in "unleaving," a word the poet invented to describe the leaves falling from their branches. In line 8 we have "wanwood," and "leafmeal." On the order of *piecemeal, leafmeal* suggests that the fallen leaves have begun to be ground up into mealy fragments on the ground and "wanwood" suggests pale or dead wood. Together they also suggest pale woods shedding leaves little by little.

"Ghost" (line 13) means spirit or soul. Consider the connotation of "Spring and Fall" (title) and the denotation and connotations of "blight" in line 14. Try substituting *cry* or *weep* for "mourn" (line 15) Which word works best? Why?

Syntax   The poem is composed of five sentences; two are questions and three are statements. Once clear about the words in line two, the first sentence should give no trouble, but the second is a bit more difficult. Reorder the words to clarify its sense. Here is one possibility: Can you with your fresh thoughts care for leaves as you care for the things of man? Or in slightly altered form: Can you in your innocence be sad over falling leaves with the same sorrow you feel for human loss? And should you? The couplet in lines 12–13 may be paraphrased like this: "You have never said outright and have never really been consciously aware of what you have known in your heart, what your spirit has sensed." (The colon that ends line 13 tells us that what the heart and soul has sensed will follow. Lines 14–15 complete the sense of lines 12–13. In fact line 15 completes the sense of line 14 the way line 14 explains the paraphrase of lines 12–13 above.)

Other observations about syntax: The first two interrogative sentences are couplets. The third sentence (line 5) involves a change of tone introduced by "Ah!" This third sentence is expansive, covering five lines, with a break between the fourth and fifth lines. Make sure you understand the logical connection between the assertion made in line 9 and that made in lines 5–8. Consider also how the two parts of the poem's third and fourth sentences are linked.

Imagery   Visual images inhere in the following words: "goldengrove," "wan-wood," "unleaving," "leafmeal," "blight," and "springs." In addition to understanding their denotations and connotations, be alert for the sensory impression each word creates. Is "colder" (line 6) used in a tactile way? "Weep" suggests tears, of course, which are wet, thus conveying a tactile image, though more important for each is the feeling the word expresses. What implied comparisons exist in lines 5–6?

Sound   We should note that the triple rhyme on long *i* (*si* gh–*li* e–wh*y*) is framed by assonance of the same vowel sound in the lines before and after: line 6: "*si* ghts" and line 10: "chi ld." Locate the two additional rhymes in lines 6–10. Then pick up the following alliterations: *g*'s in lines 1 and 2; *l* and *v* in lines 2 and 3; *c*'s in lines 3 and 4; *s*'s in lines 6 and 7; *w*'s and *l*'s in lines eight and nine with *y*'s in line nine; *n*'s in line 10; *s*'s in line eleven; *m*'s and *n*'s in a crisscross pattern in line 12; *h*'s and *g*'s in line 13; *b*'s in line 14; *m*'s in line 15.

Line 5, the only line not alliterated, contains an assonance on long *o* ("gr*o* ws *o* lder") that introduces the rhyme in lines 5–6: "*o* lder"–"c*o* lder." This rhyme encapsulates the movement of the poem from youth to age, from caring to indifference.

And finally consider how alliteration highlights the important ideas suggested in the final lines: "*b* light . . . *b* orn"; "*M* argaret . . . *m* ourn." Notice also how the rhyme on "born"–"mourn" collaborates with that on "older"–"colder" to establish a connection between what the words literally say. The rhymes seem to suggest an inevitability, a predetermined relationship between birth and sorrow, between experience and loss.

Rhythm   Four things should be noted relating the poem's rhythm. First, the rhythm is slowed down by the displaced syntax of lines 3 and 4. It is also slowed both by the alliteration in the second half of the poem and by rhyme and assonance throughout. Second, the repeated vowels and the slower pace contribute to the solemnity of the tone. Third, the parallel syntax of the final couplet and its alliteration return to the feminine rhyme used in the first six lines; the middle section of the poem (lines 7–13) departs from this feminine rhyme. Fourth, there is skillful use of caesura and enjambment to vary the poem's tempo and tone.

Meter   The meter is basically trochaic, moving from accented to unaccented syllables. We can scan the first two lines to follow Hopkins's accentual markings:

> Már / gáret áre yŏu / gríevĭng
> Óvĕr / Góldĕn / gróve ŭn / léavĭng?

The first line poses a slight problem since it contains an odd number of syllables. Since the trochaic pattern is clear from line 2, we adapt our scansion of line 1 to correspond and hence mark the first foot of line 1 as irregular in lacking one syllable. The remainder of the line then reads easily as trochaic, which is the poem's prevailing meter. Another irregularity occurs in line length, which varies from six syllables to eight. Regardless of this variation, however, we always hear four stresses per line.

Structure   The pattern of rhyme in the poem includes six couplets with a triple rhyme (three rhymed lines in succession) splitting the couplets. The poem is divided into five sentences, two before and two after the long five-line sentence that includes the triple rhyme.

The poem *turns* on the triplet. The lines assert that as Margaret grows older she will learn not to weep over such a scene but for another reason. Margaret's grief frames the poem, with the first line containing an implied question (Margaret *why* are you grieving) and the last line answering it. Moreover, the speaker's answer corrects Margaret's sense of why she grieves.

Theme   What then can we say about the theme of "Spring and Fall"? The last couplet suggests that Margaret is mourning the loss of innocence she now possesses as a child, and the loss of life that inevitably awaits all living things. Sorrow, suffering, grief, loss—these are inevitable, inescapable. As we grow from childhood to adulthood, from innocence to experience, we experience a loss as well as a gain.

The "blight" of the last couplet is the blight of original sin, the blight of failure, weakness, death. "Blight" is linked to the "Fall" of the title, which suggests the fall into experience, into sin, the fall from grace, perfection, and happiness; the "Spring" of the title suggests youth, vitality, innocence, life. The poem suggests that the values and virtues of innocence don't last, and it suggests a sadness at the inevitable end that awaits all living things.

CHAPTER TEN

Transformations

REVISIONS

Unlike the goddess Athena, who sprang full-grown from the head of Zeus, poems rarely emerge fully formed from poets' heads. When they do, however, it is often because the poet worked on them both consciously and subconsciously before putting a word on paper. The product of labor as well as inspiration, good poems are the result of considerable care, of repeated efforts to find the right words and put them in the right order.

And yet for all the effort involved, the words and lines of a poem should seem natural, even inevitable. The great modern Irish poet William Butler Yeats put it this way:

> . . . A line will take us hours maybe;
> Yet if it does not seem a moment's thought,
> Our stitching and unstitching has been nought.

We suspect that these lines and the complete poem from which they are taken, "Adam's Curse" (page 614), took more than a few moments to compose. So too did the following lines in which John Keats describes a woman preparing for bed. Keats's notebook reveals his struggle to bring them to the point where he felt satisfied with them. Here are the lines as published in his "The Eve of St. Agnes":

> . . . her vespers done,
> Of all its wreathed pearls her hair she frees
> Unclasps her warmed jewels one by one;

Loosens her fragrant bodice; by degrees
Her rich attire creeps rustling to her knees . . .

Other less successful renderings, however, preceded this final version of the description. Previously, for example, Keats had written "her praying done" rather than "her vespers done." And before that he had written: "her prayers said." Both of these versions are less precise and less musical than the final one. "Vespers," which means evening prayers, is more precise than "prayers"; it is also more musical, echoing the *e* of "he*r*." For "frees" Keats had previously written "strips," a word with quite different connotations and sound. For "warmed" he had written "bosom," and for "rich," "sweet." Of her dress he had also written that it "falls light" instead of "creeps rustling" to her knees. In each case Keats worked toward phrases that possess greater sensuousness and that were richer in sound and imagistic effects. But it is in the fourth line that we can see Keats struggle hardest before he settles on "Loosens her fragrant bodice; by degrees." Here are the earlier attempts:

1. Loosens her bursting, her bodice from her
2. Loosens her bodice lace string
3. Loosens her bodice and her bosom bare
4. Loosens her fragrant bodice and doth bare / Her
5. Loosens her fragrant bodice: and down slips

We have only to consider the images and connotations of "bursting bodice" and "bosom bare" to see how different an effect is achieved with "fragrant bodice." Keats deliberately avoids the stronger sexual overtones of the earlier versions, replacing words suggesting physical sensuality with others of a sensuous rather than a sensual nature.

We can see the process of revision at work more fully in the following poem by William Blake, reprinted in two versions.

WILLIAM BLAKE

[1757–1827]

London

I wander thro' each dirty street,
Near where the dirty Thames does flow,
And [see] mark in every face I meet
Marks of weakness, marks of woe.

In every cry of every man   5
In [every voice of every child] every infant's cry of fear
In every voice, in every ban
The [german] mind forg'd [links I hear] manacles I hear.

[But most] How the chimney sweeper's cry
[Blackens o'er the churches' walls]
Every black'ning church appalls,   10
And the hapless soldier's sigh
Runs in blood down palace walls.

[But most the midnight harlot's curse
From every dismal street I hear,
Weaves around the marriage hearse   15
And blasts the new born infant's tear.]

[Alternate fourth stanza]
But most [from every] thro' wintry streets I hear
How the midnight harlot's curse
Blasts the new born infant's tear,   15
And [hangs] smites with plagues the marriage hearse.

London

I wander thro' each charter'd street,
Near where the charter'd Thames does flow,
And mark in every face I meet
Marks of weakness, marks of woe.

In every cry of every Man,   5
In every Infant's cry of fear,
In every voice, in every ban,
The mind-forg'd manacles I hear.

How the Chimney-sweeper's cry
Every black'ning Church appalls;   10
And the hapless Soldier's sigh
Runs in blood down Palace walls.

But most thro' midnight streets I hear
How the youthful Harlot's curse
Blasts the new born Infant's tear,   15
And blights with plagues the Marriage hearse.

Let's consider the changes in "London" stanza by stanza to determine the implications of each alteration and to estimate how the accumulated changes affect the tone and meaning of the poem as Blake published it.

Stanza 1 In line 1 "charter'd" replaces "dirty." Although both words are trochaic, the sound of "charter'd" echoes "wander." More important than this use of assonance are the meanings of "charter'd." It denotes something for lease or hire, something established by a charter (a written certificate defining the legal conditions under which a corporate body is organized). The applicable meaning seems to be "hired out." The word's connotations include something defined, planned, laid out, bounded, limited by law, perhaps fixed or determined by decree. Both the street and the river Thames are described as "charter'd," as hired out and bound.

The second alteration in this stanza is Blake's substitution of "mark" for "see." "Mark" means "to take notice of; to give attention; to consider." But it also suggests a more emotionally moving seeing, a more intense noticing than "see." This use of *mark* as a verb in line 3 is further intensified with its appearance as a noun in the next line. Two denotations of the word there seem applicable: "something appearing distinctly on a surface, as a line, spot, scar, or dent" and "something indicative of one's condition, feelings."

Stanza 2 "Man" replaces "man" and "Infant's" replaces "infant's." How important is the difference? The early version of the second line has "voice" of a "child." Why do you think Blake changed these words to the "cry" of an infant, and a "cry of fear" at that? "German" in the fourth line means "germane," suggesting something closely related or akin. This word gives way in the later version to "mind-forg'd." "Links" is replaced by "manacles." Consider the denotations and connotations of the words of the later version. How does the meaning of "manacles" support the meanings of "charter'd" and "marks"? How can "manacles" be "mind-forg'd"? And why "forg'd" and not some other word like "made"?

Stanza 3 Consider the implications of the second line in both versions. In the early version the blackening is attributed to the chimney sweeper's cry. In the revised version Blake makes "black'ning" an adjective modifying Church. How can the church's walls be blackened by the cry of a chimney sweeper? And, why does Blake use the adjective "black'ning" to modify "Church"? Reflect on the connotations of "black," "blacken," and "black'ning," and consider the denotations and connotations of "appalls."

Stanza 4 Here we have more than revisions of words or lines. Though many details from the early version are carried over to the later one, they are rearranged, recombined, and rethought. In addition, some details disappear and others emerge. The rhymes, though the same, are reversed, with "hear-tear" ending the early version and "curse-hearse" concluding the final one. In the later version "the midnight harlot" has become a "the youthful Harlot"—the word *youthful* a detail that intensifies our emotional response. The "curse" of the second line is both the curse that the harlot passes on to her infant, blinding it at birth with the effects of venereal disease, and the curse of the harlot's own life. Her position echoes the implications of "charter'd" and "wandered" of stanza one. She wanders the streets, but she is hardly free. She is bound, fixed, a body for hire. The final line of the stanza is the most heavily altered. "Blights" and "plagues" suggest not only the ruin of the harlot and her child, but also the destruction of the social order: marriage is cursed, innocent children suffer, soldiers die senselessly, and in general the London populace exhibits signs of desperate suffering.

Blake's revisions intensify his indictment of the institutions—moral, military, and legal—responsible for the human squalor and the misery suffered by innocent people. His revisions increase the emotional intensity of the poem as they darken its view of the lives of the people of London and, by extension, the lives of other urban inhabitants.

Below you will find two versions of three different poems. For each pair examine changes in diction, imagery, syntax, structure, sound, rhythm, meter, and meaning. Explain the significance of the changes and indicate which version of each pair you prefer and why.

WILLIAM BUTLER YEATS
[1865–1939]

A Dream of Death

I dreamed that one had died in a strange place
Near no accustomed hand,
And they had nailed the boards above her face
The peasants of that land,

And wondering planted by her solitude   5
A cypress and a yew.
I came and wrote upon a cross of wood—
Man had no more to do—

'She was more beautiful than thy first love,
This lady by the trees';   10
And gazed upon the mournful stars above,
And heard the mournful breeze.

A Dream of Death

I dreamed that one had died in a strange place
Near no accustomed hand;
And they had nailed the boards above her face,
The peasants of that land,
Wondering to lay her in that solitude,   5
And raised above her mound
A cross they had made out of two bits of wood,
And planted cypress round;

And left her to the indifferent stars above
Until I carved these words: 10
She was more beautiful than thy first love,
But now lies under boards.

QUESTIONS

1. Compare the tone of the last four lines of each version. Consider especially the
   difference between "mournful stars" and "indifferent stars."
2. What details have disappeared in the second version and what has been added? To
   what effect?

E M I L Y   D I C K I N S O N

[1830–1886]

The Wind begun to knead the Grass

The Wind begun to knead the Grass—
As Women do a Dough—
He flung a Hand full at the Plain—
A Hand full at the Sky—
The Leaves unhooked themselves from Trees—   5
And started all abroad—
The Dust did scoop itself like Hands—
And throw away the Road—
The Wagons quickened on the Street—
The Thunders gossiped low—   10
The Lightning showed a Yellow Head—
And then a livid Toe—
The Birds put up the Bars to Nests—
The Cattle flung to Barns—
Then came one drop of Giant Rain—   15
And then, as if the Hands
That held the Dams—had parted hold—
The Waters Wrecked the Sky—
But overlooked my Father's House—
Just Quartering a Tree—   20

The Wind begun to rock the Grass

The Wind begun to rock the Grass
With threatening Tunes and low—

He threw a Menace at the Earth—
A Menace at the Sky.

The Leaves unhooked themselves from Trees—   5
And started all abroad
The Dust did scoop itself like Hands
And threw away the Road.

The Wagons quickened on the Streets
The Thunder hurried slow—   10
The Lightning showed a Yellow Beak
And then a livid Claw.

The Birds put up the Bars to Nests—
The Cattle fled to Barns—
There came one drop of Giant Rain   15
And then as if the Hands

That held the Dams had parted hold
The Waters Wrecked the Sky,
But overlooked my Father's House—
Just quartering a Tree—   20

QUESTIONS

1. Comment on the change in the organization. Does the poem's appearance in stanzas make it easier or more difficult to read?
2. Compare the tone of the first four lines of each version.
3. In lines 11–12 of each version, which image is more consistent and more vivid?

D. H. LAWRENCE
[1885–1930]

The Piano

Somewhere beneath that piano's superb sleek black
Must hide my mother's piano, little and brown, with the back
That stood close to the wall, and the front's faded silk both torn,
And the keys with little hollows, that my mother's fingers had worn.

Softly, in the shadows, a woman is singing to me   5
Quietly, through the years I have crept back to see

A child sitting under the piano, in the boom of the shaking strings
Pressing the little poised feet of the mother who smiles as she sings.

The full throated woman has chosen a winning, living song
And surely the heart that is in me must belong   10
To the old Sunday evenings, when darkness wandered outside
And hymns gleamed on our warm lips, as we watched mother's fingers glide.

Or this is my sister at home in the old front room
Singing love's first surprised gladness, alone in the gloom.
She will start when she sees me, and blushing, spread out her hands   15
To cover my mouth's raillery, till I'm bound in her shame's heart-spun bands

A woman is singing me a wild Hungarian air
And her arms, and her bosom, and the whole of her soul is bare,
And the great black piano is clamouring as my mother's never could clamour
And my mother's tunes are devoured of this music's ravaging glamour.   20

Piano

Softly, in the dusk, a woman is singing to me;
Taking me back down the vista of years, till I see
A child sitting under the piano, in the boom of the tingling strings
And pressing the small, poised feet of a mother who smiles as she sings.

In spite of myself, the insidious mastery of song   5
Betrays me back, till the heart of me weeps to belong
To the old Sunday evenings at home, with winter outside
And hymns in the cosy parlour, the tinkling piano our guide.

So now it is vain for the singer to burst into clamour
With the great black piano appassionato. The glamour   10
Of childish days is upon me, my manhood is cast
Down in the flood of remembrance, I weep like a child for the past.

QUESTIONS

1. Which details have been eliminated from the second version? Which have been added?
2. Discuss the difference in tone and idea between the two versions of the poem.

PARODIES

A *parody* is a humorous, mocking imitation of another work. A parodic poem
ridicules by distorting and exaggerating aspects of the poem it imitates. There

may be distortions of the tone and purpose of the original poem or exaggerations of its stylistic mannerisms. The best parodists respect the works they parody, for to write parody well writers must understand and appreciate what they poke fun at. Good parodies catch the special manner and flavor of the originals. In them we hear echoes of the voice of the earlier poem. By extending the original beyond its limits, a parodist can point to the virtues of the poem he or she parodies. The following parody of William Carlos Williams's "This is Just to Say" seems to do this. First, Williams's poem.

WILLIAM CARLOS WILLIAMS
[1883–1963]

This Is Just to Say

I have eaten
the plums
that were in
the icebox

and which
you were probably   5
saving
for breakfast

Forgive me
they were delicious
so sweet   10
and so cold

Now Kenneth Koch's parody:

KENNETH KOCH
[b. 1925]

Variations on a Theme by William Carlos Williams

1

I chopped down the house that you had been saving to live in next summer.
I am sorry, but it was morning, and I had nothing to do
and its wooden beams were so inviting.

2

We laughed at the hollyhocks together
And then sprayed them with lye.   5
Forgive me. I simply do not know what I am doing.

3

I gave away the money that you had been saving to live on for the next ten years.
The man who asked for it was shabby
and the firm March wind on the porch was so juicy and cold.   10

4

Last evening we went dancing and I broke your leg.
Forgive me. I was clumsy, and
I wanted you here in the wards, where I am the doctor!

QUESTIONS

1. Explain Koch's title.
2. Would his parody be as effective if he cut it down to one or two stanzas? If the four stanzas were rearranged? How long, in comparison, is Williams's poem, and why do you think Koch made his parody four times as long?
3. What do the four variations have in common?
4. Does the parody seem fair to Williams? Is it a coherent and engaging poem in its own right?

Unlike Koch's parody of a single poem by Williams, the next poem parodies not a single poem but a style. What specific features of the style of Gerard Manley Hopkins are parodied? How, specifically, does the parodist ridicule Hopkins's poetry? Before and after reading the parody consult Hopkins's poems on pages 609–611.

ANTHONY BRODE

Breakfast with Gerard Manley Hopkins

Serious over my cereals I broke one breakfast my fast
  With something-to-read-searching retinas retained by print on a packet;
Sprung rhythm sprang, and I found (the mind fact-mining at last)
  An influence Father-Hopkins-fathered on the copy-writing racket.

Parenthesis-proud, bracket-bold, happiest with hyphens
    The writers stagger intoxicated by terms, adjective-unsteadied—
Describing in graceless phrases fizzling like soda siphons
    All things crisp, crunchy, malted, tangy, sugared and shredded.

Far too, yes, too early we are urged to be purged, to savor
    Salt, malt and phosphates in English twisted and torn,
As, sparkled and spangled with sugar for a can't-be-resisted flavor,
    Come fresh-from-the-oven flakes direct from the heart of the corn.

In the next pair of poems you hear two very different voices. Account for the difference in tone between them. Explain how Howard Moss's poem parodies Shakespeare's sonnet. Consider, finally, the sense the later poem makes on its own, unrelated to the sonnet.

WILLIAM SHAKESPEARE
[1564–1616]

Shall I compare thee to a summer's day

Shall I compare thee to a summer's day?
Thou art more lovely and more temperate:
Rough winds do shake the darling buds of May,
And summer's lease hath all too short a date;
Sometime too hot the eye of heaven shines,
And often is his gold complexion dimm'd;
And every fair from fair sometime declines,
By chance or nature's changing course untrimm'd:
But thy eternal summer shall not fade
Nor lose possession of that fair thou ow'st;
Nor shall Death brag thou wand'rest in his shade,
When in eternal lines to time thou grow'st;
So long as men can breathe or eyes can see,
So long lives this, and this gives life to thee.

HOWARD MOSS
[b. 1922]

Shall I Compare Thee to a Summer's Day?

Who says you're like one of the dog days?
You're nicer. And better.

Even in May, the weather can be gray,
And a summer sub-let doesn't last forever.
Sometimes the sun's too hot;   5
Sometimes it is not.
Who can stay young forever?
People break their necks or just drop dead!
But you? Never!
If there's just one condensed reader left   10
Who can figure out the abridged alphabet
    After you're dead and gone,
    In this poem you'll live on!

TRANSLATIONS

Robert Frost once described poetry as "what gets lost in translation." He meant, of course, that it is impossible to carry over from one language into another the special qualities of a poem—its sound and rhythm, its meter, syntax, and connotations. Some critics have felt that in translating poems, translators betray them, inevitably turning the translation into something which at best may approximate, but which invariably distorts, the original. This point of view, however, has not prevented translators from continuing their difficult but important work. (To appreciate the difficulties translators encounter, try translating a short poem such as Frost's "The Span of Life," page 453, if you know a second language.)

Read the following poems in their original languages if you know them. There are two translations for three of the poems. Compare the translations as poems in their own right. What differences do you notice in the choices translators have made in diction and imagery, in line length and rhythm, in syntax and rhyme? Which of the paired translations do you prefer as a translation? Which as a poem in itself?

RAINER MARIA RILKE

[1875–1926]

Der Panther

IM JARDIN DES PLANTES, PARIS

SEIN Blick ist vom Vorübergehn der Stäbe
so müd geworden, daß er nichts mehr hält.
Ihm ist, als ob es tausend Stäbe gäbe
und hinter tausend Stäben keine Welt.

Der weiche Gang geschmeidig starker Schritte,
der sich im allerkleinsten Kreise dreht,
ist wie ein Tanz von Kraft um eine Mitte,
in der betäubt ein großer Wille steht. 5

Nur manchmal schiebt der Vorhang der Pupille
sich lautlos auf—. Dann geht ein Bild hinein, 10
geht durch der Glieder angespannte Stille—
und hört im Herzen auf zu sein.

The Panther

IN THE JARDIN DES PLANTES, PARIS

His vision, from the constantly passing bars
has grown so weary that it cannot hold
anything else. It seems to him there are
a thousand bars; and behind the bars, no world.

As he paces in cramped circles, over and over, 5
the movement of his powerful soft strides
is like a ritual dance around a center
in which a mighty will stands paralyzed.

Only at times, the curtain of the pupils
lifts, quietly—. An image enters in, 10
rushes down through the tensed, arrested muscles,
plunges into the heart and is gone.

TRANSLATED BY STEPHEN MITCHELL

The Panther

JARDIN DES PLANTES, PARIS

His sight from ever gazing through the bars
has grown so blunt that it sees nothing more.
It seems to him that thousands of bars are
before him, and behind them nothing merely.

The easy motion of his supple stride, 5
which turns about the very smallest circle,
is like a dance of strength about a center
in which a mighty will stands stupefied.

Only sometimes when the pupil's film
soundlessly opens . . . then one image fills   10
and glides through the quiet tension of the limbs
into the heart and ceases and is still.

TRANSLATED BY C. F. MACINTYRE

GUILLAUME APOLLINAIRE

[*1880–1918*]

Le Pont Mirabeau

Sous le pont Mirabeau coule la Seine
  Et nos amours
 Faut-il qu'il m'en souvienne
La joie venait toujours après la peine

  Vienne la nuit sonne l'heure   5
  Les jours s'en vont je demeure

Les mains dans les mains restons face à face
  Tandis que sous
 Le pont de nos bras passe
Des éternels regards l'onde si lasse   10

  Vienne la nuit sonne l'heure
  Les jours s'en vont je demeure

L'amour s'en va comme cette eau courante
  L'amour s'en va
 Comme la vie est lente   15
Et comme l'Espérance est violente

  Vienne la nuit sonne l'heure
  Les jours s'en vont je demeure

Passent les jours et passent les semaines
  Ni temps passé   20
 Ni les amours reviennent
Sous le pont Mirabeau coule la Seine

  Vienne la nuit sonne l'heure
  Les jours s'en vont je demeure

Mirabeau Bridge

Under the Mirabeau Bridge there flows the Seine
  Must I recall
 Our loves recall how then
After each sorrow joy came back again

    Let night come on bells end the day   5
    The days go by me still I stay

Hands joined and face to face let's stay just so
   While underneath
  The bridge of our arms shall go
Weary of endless looks the river's flow   10

    Let night come on bells end the day
    The days go by me still I stay

All love goes by as water to the sea
   All love goes by
  How slow life seems to me   15
How violent the hope of love can be

    Let night come on bells end the day
    The days go by me still I stay

The days the weeks pass by beyond our ken
   Neither time past   20
  Nor love comes back again
Under the Mirabeau Bridge there flows the Seine

    Let night come on bells end the day
    The days go by me still I stay

TRANSLATED BY RICHARD WILBUR

The Mirabeau Bridge

LE PONT MIRABEAU

Under the Mirabeau Bridge the Seine
  Flows and our love
 Must I be reminded again
How joy came always after pain

    Night comes the hour is rung   5
    The days go I remain

Hands within hands we stand face to face
     While underneath
    The bridge of our arms passes
The loose waves of our gazing which is endless   10

    Night comes the hour is rung
    The days go I remain

Love slips away like this water flowing
     Love slips away
    How slow life is in its going   15
And hope is so violent a thing

    Night comes the hour is rung
    The days go I remain

The days pass the weeks pass and are gone
     Neither time that is gone   20
    Nor love ever returns again
Under the Mirabeau Bridge flows the Seine

    Night comes the hour is rung
    The days go I remain

TRANSLATED BY W. S. MERWIN

JUAN RAMÓN JIMÉNEZ

[1881–1958]

Nocturno Soñado

   La tierra lleva por la tierra;
mas tú, mar,
llevas por el cielo.
   ¡Con qué seguridad de luz de plata y oro,
nos marcan las estrellas   5
la ruta!—Se diría
que es la tierra el camino
del cuerpo,
que el mar es el camino
del alma—.   10
   Sí, parece
que es el alma la sola viajera
del mar, que el cuerpo, solo,
se quedó allá en las playas,

sin ella, despidiéndola,   15
pesado, frío, igual que muerto.
    ¡Qué semejante
el viaje del mar al de la muerte,
al de la eterna vida!

Dream Nocturne

The earth leads through the earth;
but you, sea,
lead through heaven.
    With what a steady light of gold and silver
do the stars show us   5
the way!—One would say
that the earth is the way
of the flesh,
that the sea is the way
of the soul—.   10
    Yes, it seems
that the soul is the only traveler
of the sea, that the flesh, alone,
remained there on the shore
without her, saying farewell,   15
heavy and cold, like unto death.
    A voyage on the ocean,
how it resembles the voyage to death,
voyage to life eternal!

TRANSLATED BY ELEANOR L. TURNBULL

Dream Nocturne

The earth leads by the earth.
But, sea,
You lead by the heavens.
With what security of gold and silver light
Do the stars mark the road for us!   5
One would think
That the earth was the road
Of the body,
That the sea was the road
Of the soul.   10
Yes. It seems
That the soul is the only traveler

Of the sea; that the body, alone,
Remains behind, on the beach,
Without her, saying goodbye,   15
Heavy, cold, as though dead.
How like
Is a journey by sea
To death,
To eternal life!

TRANSLATED BY THOMAS MCGREEVY

ADAPTATIONS

Adaptations go beyond translations; they alter literary works by bringing them into a different medium. Novels and plays, for example, are frequently adapted as films; poems are often adapted as songs and for thousands of years poetry has been closely allied with song. Below you will find three poems, one biblical and two modern. Each is paired with an adaptation which transforms the poem into song. Examine each pair and explain how the adapter has transformed the original. Consider what has been added, what deleted, and what altered.

From Ecclesiastes: 3.1–8.

To every *thing there is* a season, and a time to every
purpose under the heaven:
2 A time to be born, and a time to die; a time to plant,
and a time to pluck up *that which is* planted;
3 A time to kill, and a time to heal; a time to break
down, and a time to build up;
4 A time to weep, and a time to laugh; a time to
mourn, and a time to dance;
5 A time to cast away stones, and a time to gather
stones together; a time to embrace, and a time to refrain
from embracing;
6 A time to get, and a time to lose; a time to keep, and
a time to cast away;
7 A time to rend, and a time to sew; a time to keep
silence, and a time to speak;
8 A time to love, and a time to hate; a time of war,
and a time of peace.

PETE SEEGER
[b. 1919]

Turn! Turn! Turn!

To everything,
Turn, turn, turn,
There is a season,
Turn, turn, turn,
And a time to every purpose under heaven.

A time to be born, a time to die,
A time to plant, a time to reap,
A time to kill, a time to heal,
A time to laugh, a time to weep.

To everything,
Turn, turn, turn,
There is a season,
Turn, turn, turn,
And a time to every purpose under heaven.

A time to build up, a time to break down,
A time to get, a time to want,
A time to cast away stones, a time to gather stones together.

To everything,
Turn, turn, turn,
There is a season,
Turn, turn, turn,
And a time to every purpose under heaven.

A time of love, a time of hate,
A time of war, a time of peace,
A time you may embrace, a time to refrain from embracing.

To everything,
Turn, turn, turn,
There is a season,
Turn, turn, turn,
And a time to every purpose under heaven.

A time to gain, a time to lose,
A time to rend, a time to sew,

A time for love, a time for hate,
A time for peace, I swear it's not too late.

EDWIN ARLINGTON ROBINSON
[1869–1935]

Richard Cory

Whenever Richard Cory went down town,
We people on the pavement looked at him:
He was a gentleman from sole to crown,
Clean favored and imperially slim.

And he was always quietly arrayed,   5
And he was always human when he talked;
But still he fluttered pulses when he said,
"Good-morning," and he glittered when he walked.

And he was rich—yes, richer than a king—
And admirably schooled in every grace: 10
In fine, we thought that he was everything
To make us wish that we were in his place.

So on we worked, and waited for the light,
And went without the meat and cursed the bread;
And Richard Cory, one calm summer night,   15
Went home and put a bullet through his head.

PAUL SIMON
[b. 1942]

Richard Cory

They say that Richard Cory owns one-half of this whole town,
With political connections to spread his wealth around.
Born into society, a banker's only child,
He had everything a man could want: power, grace and style.

But I work in his factory,
And I curse the life I'm living,
And I curse my poverty

And I wish that I could be
Richard Cory.

The papers print his picture almost everywhere he goes,
Richard Cory at the opera, Richard Cory at the show,
And the rumor of his parties, and the orgies on his yacht;
Oh, he surely must be happy with everything he's got.

But I work in his factory,
And I curse the life I'm living,
And I curse my poverty
And I wish that I could be
Richard Cory.

He freely gave to charity, he had the common touch,
And they were grateful for his patronage, and they thanked him very much.
So my mind is filled with wonder, when the evening headlines read:
"Richard Cory went home last night and put a bullet through his head."

But I work in his factory,
And I curse the life I'm living,
And I curse my poverty
And I wish that I could be
Richard Cory.

LANGSTON HUGHES

[1902–1967]

Dream Deferred

What happens to a dream deferred:
Does it dry up
like a raisin in the sun?
Or fester like a sore—
And then run?   5
Does it stink like rotten meat?
Or crust and sugar over—
like a syrupy sweet?

Maybe it just sags
like a heavy load.

Or does it explode?

LANGSTON HUGHES

[*1902–1967*]

Same in Blues

I said to my baby,
Baby, take it slow.
I can't, she said, I can't!
I got to go!

There's a certain
amount of traveling
in a dream deferred.

Lulu said to Leonard,
I want a diamond ring.
Leonard said to Lulu,
You won't get a goddamn thing!

A certain
amount of nothing
in a dream deferred.

Daddy, daddy, daddy,
All I want is you.
You can have me, baby—
but my lovin' days is through.

A certain
amount of impotence
in a dream deferred.

Three parties
On my party line—
But that third party,
Lord, ain't mine!

There's liable
to be confusion
in a dream deferred.

From river to river
Uptown and down,

There's liable to be confusion
when a dream gets kicked around.

You talk like
they don't kick
dreams around
Downtown.

I expect they do—
But I'm talking about
Harlem to you!
Harlem to you!
Harlem to you!
Harlem to you!

POEMS AND PAINTINGS

In Roman times and again during the Renaissance, poems were characterized as speaking pictures and painting as silent poetry. A poem, that is, was seen as a visual image given speech, a painting as a silent visual poem. Earlier, in our discussion of structure, we noted that the shape of a poem, its arrangement on the page, is an important dimension of its effect. In this connection you might like to look at George Herbert's "The Altar" (page 543) and John Hollander's "Swan and Shadow" (page 776).

Here, however, we will consider another dimension of the relationship between words and visual images. On the pages that follow you will find poems paired with the paintings that inspired them. Three of the paintings are accompanied by more than one poem so you will have a chance to compare different interpretations and "translations," of a painting into a poem. As you consider each pairing, spend some time looking carefully at the painting. Take an inventory of its details; observe its color and texture, its organization and perspective, its line, and its form. Think about the implications of its title; examine the action or scene it depicts. Then read the poem(s) as interpretation(s) and translation(s) of the painting. Notice what the poets include, what they omit, what they alter.

Even though you will be comparing poem with painting and poem with poem, remember that each poem is a separate and individual work. Read each the way you would read any other poem, giving careful attention to its formal elements. Consider whether the poems can stand alone without their corresponding paintings. And finally, consider how each poet has transformed the painting to create a new work, one which conveys its own feelings and bears its own implications.

Vincent van Gogh, The Starry Night (1889). COLLECTION, THE MUSEUM OF MODERN ART, NEW YORK. ACQUIRED THROUGH THE LILLIE P. BLISS BEQUEST.

ROBERT FAGLES   [b. 1933]

The Starry Night

Long as I paint
I feel myself
less mad
the brush in my hand
a lightning rod to madness   5

But never ground that madness
execute it   ride the lightning up
from these benighted streets and steeple   up
with the cypress   look its black is burning green

I am that I am it cries   10
it lifts me up the nightfall   up
the cloudrack coiling like a dragon's flanks
a third of the stars of heaven wheeling in its wake
wheels in wheels around the moon that cradles round the sun

and if I can only trail these whirling eternal stars   15
with one sweep of the brush like Michael's sword if I can
cut the life out of the beast—safeguard the mother and the son
all heaven will hymn in conflagration blazing down
        the night the mountain ranges down
the claustrophobic valleys of the mad   20

                    Madness
    is what I have instead of heaven
    God deliver me—help me now deliver
    all this frenzy back into your hands
    our brushstrokes burning clearer into dawn   25

Francisco de Goya, The Third of May, 1808: The Execution of the Defenders of Madrid (1814).
PRADO MUSEUM, MADRID.

LAWRENCE FERLINGHETTI   [b. 1919]

In Goya's greatest scenes we seem to see

In Goya's greatest scenes we seem to see
        the people of the world
   exactly at the moment when
     they first attained the title of
         'suffering humanity'   5
    They writhe upon the page
       in a veritable rage
         of adversity

    Heaped up
      groaning with babies and bayonets   10
         under cement skies
   in an abstract landscape of blasted trees
    bent statues bats wings and beaks
      slippery gibbets
    cadavers and carnivorous cocks   15
   and all the final hollering monsters
     of the
        'imagination of disaster'
   they are so bloody real
      it is as if they really still existed   20
  And they do
    Only the landscape is changed

They are still ranged along the roads
    plagued by legionaires
       false windmills and demented roosters 25

They are the same people
                    only further from home
        on freeways fifty lanes wide
                    on a concrete continent
                            spaced by bland billboards   30
                    illustrating imbecile illustions of happiness
    The scene shows fewer tumbrils
                    but more maimed citizens
                                in painted cars
        and they have strange license plates   35
    and engines
                that devour America

ANDREY VOZNESENSKY   [b. 1933]

I Am Goya

I am Goya
of the bare field, by the enemy's beak gouged
till the craters of my eyes gape
I am grief

I am the tongue   5
of war, the embers of cities
on the snows of the year 1941
I am hunger

I am the gullet
of a woman hanged whose body like a bell   10
tolled over a blank square
I am Goya

O grapes of wrath!
I have hurled westward
                    the ashes of the uninvited guest!   15
and hammered stars into the unforgetting sky—like nails
I am Goya

TRANSLATED BY STANLEY KUNITZ

cisco de Goya,
Disasters of War, The Carnivorous Vulture (c. 1810).
BRITISH MUSEUM.

Francisco de Goya,
The Disasters of War, Bury and be Silent (c. 1810).
COURTESY MUSEUM OF FINE ARTS, BOSTON.

WILLIAM CARLOS WILLIAMS [1883–1963]

Landscape with the Fall of Icarus

According to Breughel
when Icarus fell
it was spring

a farmer was ploughing
his field   5
the whole pageantry

of the year was
awake tingling
with itself

sweating in the sun   10
that melted
the wings' wax

unsignificantly
off the coast
there was   15

a splash quite unnoticed
this was
Icarus drowning

W. H. AUDEN [1907–1973]

Musée des Beaux Arts

About suffering they were never wrong,
The old Masters: how well they understood
Its human position: how it takes place
While someone else is eating or opening a window or just walking dully along;
How, when the aged are reverently, passionately waiting   5
For the miraculous birth, there always must be
Children who did not specially want it to happen, skating
On a pond at the edge of the wood:
They never forgot
That even the dreadful martyrdom must run its course   10
Anyhow in a corner, some untidy spot
Where the dogs go on with their doggy life and the torturer's horse
Scratches its innocent behind on a tree.

In Breughel's *Icarus,* for instance: how everything turns away
Quite leisurely from the disaster; the ploughman may   15
Have heard the splash, the forsaken cry,
But for him it was not an important failure; the sun shone
As it had to on the white legs disappearing into the green
Water, and the expensive delicate ship that must have seen
Something amazing, a boy falling out of the sky,   20
Had somewhere to get to and sailed calmly on.

Pieter Breughel the Elder, Hunters in the Snow (1565).
KUNSTHISTORISCHES MUSEUM, VIENNA.

JOSEPH LANGLAND   [b. 1917]

Hunters in the Snow: Breughel

Quail and rabbit hunters with tawny hounds,
Shadowless, out of late afternoon
Trudge toward the neutral evening of indeterminate form.
Done with their blood-annunciated day
Public dogs and all the passionless mongrels   5
Through deep snow
Trail their deliberate masters
Descending from the upper village home in lowering light.
Sooty lamps
Glow in the stone-carved kitchens.   10

This is the fabulous hour of shape and form
When Flemish children are gray-black-olive
And green-dark-brown
Scattered and skating informal figures
On the mill ice pond.   15
Moving in stillness
A hunched dame struggles with her bundled sticks,
Letting her evening's comfort cudgel her
While she, like jug or wheel, like a wagon cart
Walked by lazy oxen along the old snowlanes,   20
Creeps and crunches down the dusky street.
High in the fire-red dooryard
Half unhitched the sign of the Inn
Hangs in wind
Tipped to the pitch of the roof.   25
Near it anonymous parents and peasant girl,
Living like proverbs carved in the alehouse walls,
Gather the country evening into their arms
And lean to the glowing flames.

506

Now in the dimming distance fades
The other village; across the valley
Imperturbable Flemish cliffs and crags
Vaguely advance, close in loom
Lost in nearness. Now   35
The night-black raven perched in branching boughs
Opens its early wing and slipping out
Above the gray-green valley
Weaves a net of slumber over the snow-capped homes.
And now the church, and then the walls and roofs
Of all the little houses are become   40
Close kin to shadow with small lantern eyes.
And now the bird of evening
With shadows streaming down from its gliding wings
Circles the neighboring hills
Of Hertogenbosch, Brabant.   45

Darkness stalks the hunters,
Slowly sliding down,
Falling in beating rings and soft diagonals.
Lodged in the vague vast valley the village sleeps.

JOHN BERRYMAN [1914–1972]

Winter Landscape

The three men coming down the winter hill
In brown, with tall poles and a pack of hounds
At heel, through the arrangement of the trees,
Past the five figures at the burning straw,
Returning cold and silent to their town,   5

Returning to the drifted snow, the rink
Lively with children, to the older men,
The long companions they can never reach,
The blue light, men with ladders, by the church
The sledge and shadow in the twilit street,   10

Are not aware that in the sandy time
To come, the evil waste of history
Outstretched, they will be seen upon the brow
Of that same hill: when all their company
Will have been irrecoverably lost,   15

These men, this particular three in brown
Witnessed by birds will keep the scene and say
By their configurations with the trees,
The small bridge, the red houses and the fire,
What place, what time, what morning occasion   20

Sent them into the wood, a pack of hounds
At heel and the tall poles upon their shoulders,
Thence to return as now we see them and
Ankle-deep in snow down the winter hill
Descend, while three birds watch and the fourth flies.   25

William Blake, The Sick Rose from *Songs of Experience* (1794).
THE HUNTINGTON LIBRARY, SAN MARINO, CALIFORNIA.

WILLIAM BLAKE [1757–1827]

The Sick Rose

O Rose, thou art sick!
The invisible worm
That flies in the night,
In the howling storm,

Has found out thy bed
Of crimson joy,
And his dark secret love
Does thy life destroy.

QUESTIONS

Vincent Van Gogh, *The Starry Night*

1. About the series of poems he wrote based on Van Gogh's paintings, Robert Fagles has written: "I wanted to try my hand at a kind of translation I hadn't done before, not from a foreign language, but from a group of paintings." What has Fagles translated from the painting into the poem?
2. Does Fagles's poem help you to see things in the painting that you had overlooked? Why or why not?
3. Does the poem seem to emphasize the painting or the painter? Does it present a neutral description of the work? Does it imply or state a judgment about it?
4. Compare Fagles's poem with Anne Sexton's "The Starry Night" (page 766).

Francesco Goya y Lucientes, *The Second of May* and *The Disasters of War*

1. Where does Ferlinghetti shift from a direct look at Goya's art to something else? To what does Ferlinghetti turn? What does his poem seem to say?
2. Compare Ferlinghetti's use of Goya with Vosnesensky's and then with Fagles's use of Van Gogh. How does each poet convey the sense of the art he describes? How does each use that art for his own purposes?
3. Is either Vosnesensky's or Ferlinghetti's poem comprehensible without the *painting* or etchings? Why or why not? Which poem helps you to see and understand Goya's art better? Why?

Pieter Breughel the Elder, *Landscape with the Fall of Icarus*

1. What is the effect, in Williams's poem, of mentioning Icarus at the end of the poem rather than earlier? Where is Icarus mentioned in Auden's poem? What does Auden end with and what is implied by that ending?
2. How does each poem offer us a clue to its intentions from the beginning? Would it matter if Williams's first stanza was omitted and the "was" of stanza 2, 5, and 6 changed to *is?*
3. "Museé des Beaux Arts" can be divided into two parts. What is the relationship between them? What is the effect of reversing the parts?
4. Which poet seems to use Breughel's painting to advance an idea? Which to describe and imitate the painting in words?
5. How does the title of each poem reflect its author's preoccupations with the painting?

Pieter Breughel the Elder, *Hunters in the Snow*

1. Which poem better helps you to see the details of the painting? Which helps you to better understand its symbolic implications?
2. Where does each poem depart from the details of the painting? In what ways and for what purposes?

3. Compare the way each poem begins. What is emphasized? How would you describe the tone of each opening stanza? Compare the endings. Which seems least like its beginning? What is implied in each ending?
4. Compare the way each poet organizes his details. Consider especially the use of the birds.
5. Neither poem rhymes, and neither uses a consistent metrical pattern, yet both poems exhibit formal organization. What devices of form, sound, and rhythm exist in each poem? What do they contribute to the meaning and feeling of the work?

William Blake, *The Sick Rose*

1. How does Blake's art help you to understand his poem? How does it enable you to see something about the poem you may have overlooked or to make connections you may have missed?
2. Does Blake's illustration channel your reading of the poem, limiting the way you interpret it? Is it possible that the poem was written to illustrate the painting, or do you think the painting was designed to parallel the poem?

CHAPTER ELEVEN

A Collection of Poems

ANONYMOUS

Lord Randal

"O where ha' you been, Lord Randal, my son?
And where ha' you been, my handsome young man?"
"I ha' been at the greenwood; mother, mak my bed soon,
For I'm wearied wi' hunting, and fain wad° lie down."   would

"An wha' met ye there, Lord Randal, my son?   5
An wha' met you there, my handsome young man?"
"O I met wi' my true-love; mother, mak my bed soon,
For I'm wearied wi' huntin', and fain wad lie down."

"And what did she give you, Lord Randal, my son?
And what did she give you, my handsome young man?"   10
"Eels fried in a pan; mother, mak my bed soon,
For I'm wearied wi' huntin', and fain wad lie down."

"And wha' gat your leavins, Lord Randal, my son?
And wha' gat your leavins, my handsome young man?"

"My hawks and my hounds; mother, mak my bed soon,   15
For I'm wearied wi' hunting, and fain wad lie down."

"And what becam of them, Lord Randal, my son?
And what becam of them, my handsome young man?"
"They stretched their legs out and died; mother, mak my bed soon,
For I'm wearied wi' huntin, and fain wad lie down."   20

"O I fear you are poisoned, Lord Randal, my son!
I fear you are poisoned, my handsome young man!"
"O yes, I am poisoned: mother, mak my bed soon,
For I'm sick at the heart, and I fain wad lie down."

"What d'ye leave to your mother, Lord Randal, my son?   25
What d'ye leave to your mother, my handsome young man?"
"Four and twenty milk kye°; mother, mak my bed soon,   kine, cattle
For I'm sick at the heart, and I fain wad lie down."

"What d'ye leave to your sister, Lord Randal, my son?
What d'ye leave to your sister, my handsome young man?"   30
"My gold and my silver; mother, mak my bed soon,
For I'm sick at the heart, an I fain wad lie down."

"What d'ye leave to your brother, Lord Randal, my son?
What d'ye leave to your brother, my handsome young man?"
"My houses and my lands; mother, mak my bed soon,   35
For I'm sick at the heart, and I fain wad lie down."

"What d'ye leave to your true-love, Lord Randal, my son?
What d'ye leave to your true-love, my handsome young man?"
"I leave her hell and fire; mother, mak my bed soon,
For I'm sick at the heart, and I fain wad lie down."   40

ANONYMOUS

The Twa Corbies

As I was walking all alane,
I heard twa corbies° making a mane°;   ravens; moan
The tane° unto the t'other say,   one
"Where sall we gang° and dine today?"   go

"In behint yon auld fail dyke°,   turf wall 5
I wot° there lies a new slain knight;   know
And naebody kens° that he lies there,   knows
But his hawk, his hound, and lady fair.

"His hound is to the hunting gane,
His hawk to fetch the wild-fowl hame,   10
His lady's ta'en another mate,
So we may mak our dinner sweet.

"Ye'll sit on his white hause-bane°,   neck bone
And I'll pike out his bonny blue een;
Wi' ae° lock o' his gowden hair   one 15
We'll theek° our nest when it grows bare.   thatch

"Mony a one for him makes mane,
But nane sall ken where he is gane;
O'er his white banes, when they are bare,
The wind sall blaw for evermair."   20

ANONYMOUS

Sir Patrick Spens

1

The king sits in Dumferling toune,
    Drinking the blude-reid° wine: blood-red
"O whar will I get guid sailor,
    To sail this schip of mine?"

2

Up and spak an eldern knicht,   5
    Sat at the kings richt kne:
"Sir Patrick Spens is the best sailor,
    That sails upon the se."

3

The king has written a braid° letter,   broad
    And signed it wi' his hand;   10
And sent it to Sir Patrick Spens,
    Was walking on the sand.

4

The first line that Sir Patrick red,
    A loud lauch° lauchèd he: laugh
The next line that Sir Patrick red,
    The teir blinded his ee.°   eye 15

5

"O wha is this has don this deid,
    This ill deid don to me;
To send me out this time o' the yeir,
    To sail upon the se?   20

6

"Mak haste, mak haste, my mirry men all,
    Our guid schip sails the morne."
"O say na sae°, my master deir,   so
    For I fear a deadlie storme.

7

"Late, late yestreen I saw the new moone   25
    Wi' the auld moone in hir arme;
And I feir, I feir, my deir master,
    That we will cum to harme."

8

O our Scots nobles wer richt laith°   loath
    To weet° their cork-heild shoone°; wet/shoes 30
Bot lang owre° a' the play wer playd,   before
    Thair hats they swam aboone.

9

O lang, lang, may thair ladies sit
    Wi' thair fans into their hand,
Or eir they se Sir Patrick Spens   35
    Cum sailing to the land.

10

O lang, lang, may the ladies stand,
    Wi' thair gold kems° in their hair,   combs
Waiting for thair ain deir lords,
    For they'll se thame na mair.   40

11

Haf owre, haf owre to Aberdour,
    It's fiftie fadom deip,
And thair lies guid Sir Patrick Spens,
    Wi' the Scots lords at his feit.

ANONYMOUS

Edward, Edward

1

"Why does your brand° sae° drap wi' bluid,   sword/so
        Edward, Edward,
Why does your brand sae drap wi' bluid,
    And why sae sad gang° ye, O?"   go
"O I ha'e killed my hawk sae guid,   5
        Mither, mither,
O I ha'e killed my hawk sae guid,
    And I had nae mair but he, O."

2

"Your hawk's bluid was never sae reid,°   red
        Edward, Edward,   10
Your hawk's bluid was never sae reid,
    My dear son, I tell thee, O."
"O I ha'e killed my reid-roan steed,
        Mither, mither,
O I ha'e killed my reid-roan steed,   15
    That erst was sae fair and free, O."

3

"Your steed was auld, and ye ha'e gat mair,
        Edward, Edward,
Your steed was auld, and ye ha'e gat mair,
    Some other dule° ye drie°, O."   grief/suffer   20
"O I ha'e killed my fader dear,
        Mither, mither,
O I ha'e killed my fader dear,
    Alas, and wae° is me, O!"   woe

4

"And whatten° penance wul ye dree for that,   what kind of 25
    Edward, Edward?
And whatten penance wul ye dree for that,
    My dear son, now tell me O?"
"I'll set my feet in yonder boat,
    Mither, mither,   30
I'll set my feet in yonder boat,
    And I'll fare over the sea, O."

5

"And what wul ye do wi' your towers and your ha',
    Edward, Edward?
And what wul ye do wi' your towers and your ha',   35
    That were sae fair to see, O?"
"I'll let them stand tul they down fa',
    Mither, mither,
I'll let them stand tul they down fa',
    For here never mair maun° I be, O."   must 40

6

"And what wul ye leave to your bairns° and your wife,   children
    Edward, Edward?
And what wul ye leave to your bairns and your wife,
    Whan ye gang over the sea, O?"
"The warlde's room, let them beg thrae° life,   through 45
    Mither, mither,
The warlde's room, let them beg thrae life,
    For them never mair wul I see, O."

7

"And what wul ye leave to your ain mither dear,
    Edward, Edward?   50
And what wul ye leave to your ain mither dear,
    My dear son, now tell me, O?"
"The curse of hell frae° me sall° ye bear,   from/shall
    Mither, mither,
The curse of hell frae me sall ye bear,
    Sic° counsels ye gave to me, O."   such 55

ANONYMOUS

The Unquiet Grave

1

"The wind doth blow today, my love,
   And a few small drops of rain;
I never had but one true-love,
   In cold grave she was lain.

2

"I'll do as much for my true love
   As any young man may;   5
I'll sit and mourn all at her grave
   For a twelvemonth, and a day."

3

The twelvemonth and a day being up,
   The dead began to speak: 10
"Oh who sits weeping on my grave,
   And will not let me sleep?"

4

" 'T is I, my love, sits on your grave,
   And will not let you sleep;
For I crave one kiss of your clay-cold lips,   15
   And that is all I seek."

5

"You crave one kiss of my clay-cold lips,
   But my breath smells earthy strong;
If you have one kiss of my clay-cold lips,
   Your time will not be long.   20

6

" 'T is down in yonder garden green,
   Love, where we used to walk,
The finest flower that e'er was seen
   Is withered to a stalk.

7

"The stalk is withered dry, my love,   25
    So will our hearts decay;
So make yourself content, my love,
    Till God calls you away."

ANONYMOUS

The Demon Lover

"O where have you been, my long, long love,
    This long seven years and more?"
"O I'm come to seek my former vows
    Ye granted me before."

"O hold your tongue of your former vows,   5
    For they will breed sad strife;
O hold your tongue of your former vows
    For I am become a wife."

He turn'd him right and round about,
    And the tear blinded his ee;   10
"I wad never hae trodden on Irish ground,
    If it had not been for thee.

"I might have had a king's daughter,
    Far, far beyond the sea;
I might have had a king's daughter,   15
    Had it not been for love o' thee."

"If ye might have had a king's daughter,
    Yersell ye had to blame;
Ye might have taken the king's daughter,
    For ye kend that I was nane.   20

"If I was to leave my husband dear,
    And my two babes also,
O what have you to take me to,
    If with you I should go?"

"I hae seven ships upon the sea,   25
    The eighth brought me to land;
With four-and-twenty bold mariners,
    And music on every hand."

She has taken up her two little babes,
    Kiss'd them baith cheek and chin;   30
"O fair ye weel, my ain two babes,
    For I'll never see you again."

She set her foot upon the ship,
    No mariners could she behold;
But the sails were o' the taffetie,   35
    And the masts o' the beaten gold.

She had not sail'd a league, a league,
    A league but barely three,
When dismal grew his countenance,
    And drumlie grew his ee.   40

They had not sailed a league, a league,
    A league but barely three,
Until she espied his cloven foot,
    And she wept right bitterlie.

"O hold your tongue of your weeping," says he,   45
    "Of your weeping now let me be;
I will show you how the lilies grow
    On the banks of Italy."

"O what hills are yon, yon pleasant hills,
    That the sun shines sweetly on?"   50
"O yon are the hills of heaven," he said,
    "Where you will never win."

"O whaten a mountain is yon," she said,
    "All so dreary wi' frost and snow?"
"O yon is the mountain of hell," he cried,   55
    "Where you and I will go."

He struck the tapmast wi' his hand,
    The foremast wi' his knee;
And he brak that gallant ship in twain,
    And sank her in the sea.   60

GEOFFREY CHAUCER
[1343–1400]

Truth

Flee fro the prees° and dwelle with soothfastnesse;   crowd
Suffise° thyn owene thing, though it be smal;   be content with
For hoord hath hate, and climbing tikelnesse°;   insecurity
Prees hath envye, and wele° blent° overal.   prosperity/blinds
Savoure° no more than thee bihoove shal;   relish   5
Rule wel thyself that other folk canst rede:°   advise
And Trouthe shal delivere, it is no drede.°   doubt

Tempest thee nought al crooked to redresse
In trust of hire that turneth as a bal;
Muche wele stant in litel bisinesse;   10
Be war therfore to spurne ayains an al.
Strive nat as dooth the crokke° with the wal.   pot
Daunte° thyself that dauntest otheres deede: master
And Trouthe shal delivere, it is no drede.

That thee is sent, receive in buxomnesse°;   obedience   15
The wrastling for the world axeth° a fal;   asks for
Here is noon hoom, here nis but wildernesse:
Forth, pilgrim, forth! Forth, beest, out of thy stal!
Know thy countree, looke up, thank God of al.
Hold the heigh way and lat thy gost° thee lede: spirit   20
And Trouthe shal delivere, it is no drede.

Therfore, thou Vache, leve thyn olde wrecchednesse
Unto the world; leve now to be thral.
Crye him mercy that of his heigh goodnesse
Made thee of nought, and in especial   25
Draw unto him, and pray in general,
For thee and eek for othere, hevenelich meede°:   reward
And Trouthe shal delivere, it is no drede.

TRUTH   *See John 8.32: "And ye shall know the truth, and the truth shall make you free."*   [3]**hoord hath**
hoarding causes.   [7]***delivere**   make you free.*   [9]**hire**   *fortune which presents different aspects to men.*
[11]***spurne . . . al***   *kick against the pricks.*

JOHN SKELTON
[1460–1529]

To Mistress Margaret Hussey

Merry Margaret,
  As midsummer flower,
Gentle as falcon
Or hawk of the tower:
With solace and gladness,   5
Much mirth and no madness,
All good and no badness;
  So joyously,
  So maidenly,
  So womanly   10
  Her demeaning
  In every thing,
  Far, far passing
  That I can indite°,   say
  Or suffice to write   15
Of Merry Margaret
  As midsummer flower,
Gentle as falcon
Or hawk of the tower.
  As patient and still   20
And as full of good will
As fair Isaphill,
Coriander,
Sweet pomander,
Good Cassander,   25
Steadfast of thought,
Well made, well wrought,
Far may be sought
Ere that ye can find
So courteous, so kind   30
As Merry Margaret,
  This midsummer flower,
Gentle as falcon
Or hawk of the tower.

TO MISTRESS MARGARET HUSSEY   22**Isaphill** *Hypsipyle, queen of an island in the Aegean Sea (Lemnos). Famed for her devotion to her father and children.*   23**coriander** *an aromatic medicinal herb.* 24**pomander** *a perfumed ball.*   25**Cassander** *Cassandra, a steadfast prophet.*

THOMAS WYATT
[1503–1542]

The long love that in my thought doth harbor

The long love that in my thought doth harbor,
And in my heart doth keep his residence,
Into my face presseth with bold pretense
And there encampeth, spreading his banner.
She that me learns° to love and suffer   teaches   5
And wills that my trust and lust's negligence
Be reined by reason, shame, and reverence
With his hardiness takes displeasure.
Wherewithal unto the heart's forest he fleeth,
Leaving his enterprise with pain and cry,   10
And there him hideth, and not appeareth.
What may I do, when my master feareth,
But in the field with him to live and die?
For good is the life ending faithfully.

They flee from me

They flee from me, that sometime did me seek,
With naked foot stalking in my chamber.
I have seen them, gentle, tame, and meek,
That now are wild, and do not remember
That sometime they put themselves in danger   5
To take bread at my hand; and now they range,
Busily seeking with a continual change.

Thanked be Fortune it hath been otherwise,
Twenty times better; but once in special,
In thin array, after a pleasant guise,   10
When her loose gown from her shoulders did fall,
And she me caught in her arms long and small,°   thin
And therewith all sweetly did me kiss
And softly said, "Dear heart, how like you this?"

It was no dream, I lay broad waking.   15
But all is turned, thorough° my gentleness,   through

THE LONG LOVE THAT IN MY THOUGHT DOTH HARBOR   *a translation from Petrarch; compare*
Surrey's "Love that doth reign . . . ," p. 523.

Into a strange fashion of forsaking;
And I have leave to go, of her goodness,
And she also to use newfangleness.
But since that I so kindely am served,   20
I fain would know what she hath deserved.

HENRY HOWARD, EARL OF SURREY
[1517–1547]

Love, that doth reign and live within my thought

Love, that doth reign and live within my thought,
And built his seat within my captive breast,
Clad in the arms wherein with me he fought,
Oft in my face he doth his banner rest.
But she that taught me love and suffer pain,   5
My doubtful hope and eke my hot desire
With shamefast° look to shadow and refrain,   *shamefaced*
Her smiling grace converteth straight to ire.
And coward Love, then, to the heart apace
Taketh his flight, where he doth lurk and plain,°   *complain* 10
His purpose lost, and dare not show his face.
For my lord's guilt thus faultless bide I pain,
Yet from my lord shall not my foot remove:
Sweet is the death that taketh end by love.

EDMUND SPENSER
[1552–1599]

One day I wrote her name upon the strand

One day I wrote her name upon the strand°,   *beach*
But came the waves and washéd it away:
Agayne I wrote it with a second hand,
But came the tyde, and made my paynes his pray.
"Vayne man," sayd she, "that doest in vaine assay,   5
A mortall thing so to immortalize,
For I my selve shall lyke to this decay,

LOVE, THAT DOTH REIGN AND LIVE WITHIN MY THOUGHT   *a translation from Petrarch;
compare Wyatt's "They flee from me," p. 522.*

And eek° my name bee wypéd out lykewize."   also
"Not so," quod° I, "let baser things devize°   said/devise
To dy in dust, but you shall live by fame: 10
My verse your vertues rare shall eternize,
And in the hevens wryte your glorious name.
Where whenas death shall all the world subdew,
Our love shall live, and later life renew."

SIR WALTER RALEIGH

[ca. 1552–1618]

The Lie

Go, soul, the body's guest,
Upon a thankless errand;
Fear not to touch the best;
The truth shall be thy warrant.
Go, since I needs must die,   5
And give the world the lie.

Say to the court, it glows
And shines like rotten wood;
Say to the church, it shows
What's good, and doth no good.   10
If church and court reply,
Then give them both the lie.

Tell potentates, they live
Acting by others' action;
Not loved unless they give,   15
Not strong but by a faction.
If potentates reply,
Give potentates the lie.

Tell men of high condition,
That manage the estate,   20
Their purpose is ambition,
Their practice only hate.
And if they once reply,
Then give them all the lie.

Tell them that brave it most,   25
They beg for more by spending,

Who, in their greatest cost,
Seek nothing but commending.
And if they make reply,
Then give them all the lie.   30

Tell zeal it wants devotion;
Tell love it is but lust;
Tell time it is but motion;
Tell flesh it is but dust.
And wish them not reply,   35
For thou must give the lie.

Tell age it daily wasteth;
Tell honor how it alters;
Tell beauty how she blasteth;
Tell favor how it falters.   40
And as they shall reply,
Give every one the lie.

Tell wit how much it wrangles
In tickle° points of niceness;   delicate
Tell wisdom she entangles   45
Herself in overwiseness.
And when they do reply,
Straight give them both the lie.

Tell physic of her boldness;
Tell skill it is pretension;   50
Tell charity of coldness;
Tell law it is contention.
And as they do reply,
So give them still the lie.

Tell fortune of her blindness;   55
Tell nature of decay;
Tell friendship of unkindness;
Tell justice of delay.
And if they will reply,
Then give them all the lie.   60

Tell arts they have no soundness,
But vary by esteeming;
Tell schools they want profoundness,
And stand too much on seeming.
If arts and schools reply,   65
Give arts and schools the lie.

Tell faith it's fled the city;
Tell how the country erreth;
Tell manhood shakes off pity;
Tell virtue least preferreth.   70
And if they do reply,
Spare not to give the lie.

So when thou hast, as I
Commanded thee, done blabbing—
Although to give the lie   75
Deserves no less than stabbing—
Stab at thee he that will,
No stab the soul can kill.

The Nymph's Reply to the Shepherd

If all the world and love were young,
And truth in every shepherd's tongue,
These pretty pleasures might me move
To live with thee and be thy love.

Time drives the flocks from field to fold   5
When rivers rage and rocks grow cold,
And Philomel becometh dumb;
The rest complains of cares to come.

The flowers do fade, and wanton fields
To wayward winter reckoning yields;   10
A honey tongue, a heart of gall,
Is fancy's spring, but sorrow's fall.

Thy gowns, thy shoes, thy beds of roses,
Thy cap, thy kirtle,° and thy posies   long dress
Soon break, soon wither, soon forgotten—   15
In folly ripe, in reason rotten.

Thy belt of straw and ivy buds,
Thy coral clasps and amber studs,
All these in me no means can move
To come to thee and be thy love.   20

THE NYMPH'S REPLY TO THE SHEPHERD   *An answer to Christopher Marlowe's "The Passionate Shepherd to His Love," p. 529.*   [7]**Philomel**   *the nightingale. According to Ovid's* Metamorphoses, *Philomel's brother-in-law Tereus had her tongue cut out to prevent her from revealing that he had raped her.*

But could youth last and love still breed,
Had joys no date° nor age no need,   end
Then these delights my mind might move
To live with thee and be thy love.

SIR PHILIP SIDNEY
[1554–1586]

From *Astrophel and Stella*

1

Loving in truth, and fain° in verse my love to show,   eager
That she dear she might take some pleasure of my pain,
Pleasure might cause her read, reading might make her know,
Knowledge might pity win, and pity grace obtain,
I sought fit words to paint the blackest face of woe: 5
Studying inventions fine, her wits to entertain,
Oft turning others' leaves, to see if thence would flow
Some fresh and fruitful showers upon my sunburned brain.
But words came halting forth, wanting Invention's stay;
Invention, Nature's child, fled stepdame Study's blows;   10
And others' feet still seemed but strangers in my way.
Thus, great with child to speak, and helpless in my throes,
Biting my truant pen, beating myself for spite:
"Fool," said my Muse to me, "look in thy heart, and write."

Thou blind man's mark

Thou blind man's mark°, thou fool's self-chosen snare,   target
Fond° fancy's scum, and dregs of scattered thought,   foolish
Bands of all evils, cradle of causeless care,
Thou web of will whose end is never wrought;

Desire, Desire, I have too dearly bought   5
With prize of mangled mind thy worthless ware!
Too long, too long asleep thou hast me brought
Who should my mind to higher things prepare.

But yet in vain thou hast my ruin sought;
In vain thou madest me to vain things aspire;   10
In vain thou kindlest all thy smoky fire.

For Virtue hath this better lesson taught:
Within myself to seek my only hire°,   payment
Desiring nought but how to kill desire.

CHIDIOCK TICHBORNE
[ca. 1558–1586]

Tichborne's Elegy

WRITTEN WITH HIS OWN HAND
IN THE TOWER BEFORE HIS EXECUTION

My prime of youth is but a frost of cares,
My feast of joy is but a dish of pain,
My crop of corn° is but a field of tares°,   wheat/weeds
And all my good is but vain hope of gain;
The day is past, and yet I saw no sun,   5
And now I live, and now my life is done.

My tale was heard and yet it was not told,
My fruit is fallen and yet my leaves are green,
My youth is spent and yet I am not old,
I saw the world and yet I was not seen;   10
My thread is cut and yet it is not spun,
And now I live, and now my life is done.

I sought my death and found it in my womb,
I looked for life and saw it was a shade,
I trod the earth and knew it was my tomb,   15
And now I die, and now I was but made;
My glass is full, and now my glass is run,
And now I live, and now my life is done.

MICHAEL DRAYTON
[1563–1631]

Since there's no help, come let us kiss and part

Since there's no help, come let us kiss and part;
Nay, I have done, you get no more of me,

TICHBORNE'S ELEGY   *Tichborne was hanged for plotting to murder Queen Elizabeth I.*   [11]**My thread
is cut . . .**   *the three fates who spun, measured, and cut the thread of men's lives.*

And I am glad, yea glad with all my heart
That thus so cleanly I myself can free;
Shake hands forever, cancel all our vows,   5
And when we meet at any time again,
Be it not seen in either of our brows
That we one jot of former love retain.
Now at the last gasp of love's latest breath,
When, his pulse failing, passion speechless lies,   10
When faith is kneeling by his bed of death,
And innocence is closing up his eyes,
    Now if thou wouldst, when all have given him over,
    From death to life thou mightst him yet recover.

CHRISTOPHER MARLOWE
[1564–1593]

The Passionate Shepherd to His Love

    Come live with me and be my love,
    And we will all the pleasures prove°   try
    That valleys, groves, hills, and fields,
    Woods, or steepy mountain yields.

    And we will sit upon the rocks,   5
    Seeing the shepherds feed their flocks,
    By shallow rivers to whose falls
    Melodious birds sing madrigals.

    And I will make thee beds of roses
    And a thousand fragrant posies,   10
    A cap of flowers, and a kirtle°   a long dress
    Embroidered all with leaves of myrtle;

    A gown made of the finest wool
    Which from our pretty lambs we pull;
    Fair lined slippers for the cold,   15
    With buckles of the purest gold;

    A belt of straw and ivy buds,
    With coral clasps and amber studs:
    And if these pleasures may thee move,
    Come live with me, and be my love.   20

THE PASSIONATE SHEPHERD TO HIS LOVE   See Ralegh's "The Nymph's Reply to the Shepherd," p. 526.

The shepherds' swains shall dance and sing
For thy delight each May morning:
If these delights thy mind may move,
Then live with me and be my love.

WILLIAM SHAKESPEARE
[1564–1616]

When in disgrace with fortune and men's eyes

When, in disgrace with fortune and men's eyes,
I all alone beweep my outcast state,
And trouble deaf heaven with my bootless° cries,   useless
And look upon myself, and curse my fate,
Wishing me like to one more rich in hope,   5
Featured like him, like him with friends possessed,
Desiring this man's art and that man's scope,
With what I most enjoy contented least;
Yet in these thoughts myself almost despising,
Haply I think on thee—and then my state,   10
Like to the lark at break of day arising
From sullen earth, sings hymns at heaven's gate;
For thy sweet love remembered such wealth brings
That then I scorn to change my state with kings.

Not marble, nor the gilded monuments

Not marble, nor the gilded monuments
Of princes, shall outlive this powerful rhyme;
But you shall shine more bright in these conténts
Than unswept stone, besmeared with sluttish time.
When wasteful war shall statues overturn,   5
And broils root out the work of masonry,
Nor Mars his sword nor war's quick fire shall burn
The living record of your memory.
'Gainst death and all-oblivious enmity
Shall you pace forth; your praise shall still find room.   10
Even in the eyes of all posterity
That wear this world out to the ending doom°.   judgment day
So, till the judgment that yourself arise,
You live in this, and dwell in lovers' eyes.

Let me not to the marriage of true minds

Let me not to the marriage of true minds
Admit impediments°. Love is not love   hindrances
Which alters when it alteration finds,
Or bends with the remover to remove:
Oh, no! it is an ever-fixéd mark,   5
That looks on tempests and is never shaken;
It is the star to every wandering bark,°   ship
Whose worth's unknown, although his height be taken.
Love's not Time's fool, though rosy lips and cheeks
Within his bending sickle's compass come;   10
Love alters not with his brief hours and weeks,
But bears° it out even to the edge of doom.°   lasts/judgment day
If this be error and upon me proved,
I never writ, nor no man ever loved.

Th' expense of spirit in a waste of shame

Th' expense of spirit in a waste of shame
Is lust in action; and till action, lust
Is perjured, murderous, bloody, full of blame,
Savage, extreme, rude, cruel, not to trust;
Enjoyed no sooner but despiséd straight: 5
Past reason hunted; and no sooner had,
Past reason hated, as a swallowed bait,
On purpose laid to make the taker mad:
Mad in pursuit, and in possession so;
Had, having, and in quest to have, extreme;   10
A bliss in proof,° and proved, a very woe;   in the experience
Before, a joy proposed; behind, a dream.
All this the world well knows; yet none knows well
To shun the heaven that leads men to this hell.

My mistress' eyes are nothing like the sun

My mistress' eyes are nothing like the sun;
Coral is far more red than her lips' red;
If snow be white, why then her breasts are dun;
If hairs be wires, black wires grow on her head.

LET ME NOT TO THE MARRIAGE OF TRUE MINDS   [8]**height be taken** *its elevation be measured.*

I have seen roses damasked,° red and white,   variegated   5
But no such roses see I in her cheeks;
And in some perfumes is there more delight
Than in the breath that from my mistress reeks.
I love to hear her speak, yet well I know
That music hath a far more pleasing sound;   10
I grant I never saw a goddess go°;   walk
My mistress, when she walks, treads on the ground.
And yet, by heaven, I think my love as rare
As any she belied with false compare.

THOMAS NASHE
[1567–1601]

A Litany in Time of Plague

Adieu, farewell, earth's bliss;
This world uncertain is;
Fond° are life's lustful joys;   foolish
Death proves them all but toys°;   trifles
None from his darts can fly;   5
I am sick, I must die.
    Lord, have mercy on us!

Rich men, trust not in wealth,
Gold cannot buy you health;
Physic himself must fade.   10
All things to end are made,
The plague full swift goes by;
I am sick, I must die.
    Lord, have mercy on us!

Beauty is but a flower   15
Which wrinkles will devour;
Brightness falls from the air;
Queens have died young and fair;
Dust hath closed Helen's eye.
I am sick, I must die.   20
    Lord, have mercy on us!

Strength stoops unto the grave,
Worms feed on Hector brave;
Swords may not fight with fate,

Earth still holds ope her gate.   25
"Come, come!" the bells do cry.
I am sick, I must die.
    Lord, have mercy on us.

Wit with his wantonness
Tasteth death's bitterness;   30
Hell's executioner
Hath no ears for to hear
What vain art can reply.
I am sick, I must die.
    Lord, have mercy on us.   35

Haste, therefore, each degree,
To welcome destiny;
Heaven is our heritage,
Earth but a player's stage;
Mount we unto the sky.   40
I am sick, I must die.
    Lord, have mercy on us.

JOHN DONNE
[1572–1631]

Song

Go, and catch a falling star,
    Get with child a mandrake root,
Tell me, where all past years are,
    Or who cleft the devil's foot,
Teach me to hear mermaids singing   5
Or to keep off envy's stinging,
      And find
      What wind
Serves to advance an honest mind.

If thou beest born to strange sights,   10
    Things invisible to see,
Ride ten thousand days and nights,
    Till age snow white hairs on thee;
Thou, when thou return'st, wilt tell me

SONG   ²**mandrake root**   *Resembling a human body, the forked root of the mandrake was used as a medicine to induce conception.*

All strange wonders that befell thee,   15
    And swear,
    No where
Lives a woman true, and fair.

If thou find'st one, let me know: 20
    Such a pilgrimage were sweet.
Yet do not, I would not go,
    Though at next door we might meet:
Though she were true when you met her,
And last till you write your letter,
    Yet she   25
    Will be
False, ere I come, to two, or three.

The Canonization

For God's sake hold your tongue, and let me love,
    Or chide my palsy, or my gout,
My five gray hairs, or ruined fortune, flout,
    With wealth your state, your mind with arts improve,
        Take you a course,° get you a place,°   direction/appointment   5
        Observe His Honor, or His Grace,
Or the King's real, or his stampéd face°   on a coin
    Contémplate; what you will, approve°,   try
    So you will let me love.

Alas, alas, who's injured by my love?   10
    What merchant's ships have my sighs drowned?
Who says my tears have overflowed his ground?
    When did my colds a forward spring remove?
        When did the heats which my veins fill
        Add one more to the plaguy bill?°   list of victims 15
Soldiers find wars, and lawyers find out still
    Litigious men, which quarrels move,
    Though she and I do love.

Call us what you will, we're made such by love;
    Call her one, me another fly,   20
We're tapers too, and at our own cost die,
    And we in us find th' eagle and the dove
        The phoenix riddle hath more wit°   sense

THE CANONIZATION   21*at our own cost die* *Death was a metaphor for sexual intercourse; each act of sexual congress supposedly shortened one's life by a day.*   23*the phoenix riddle* *a legendary, mythological bird, the only one of its kind. It is consumed in fire and then resurrected from the ashes to begin life anew.*

By us: we two being one, are it.
So, to one neutral thing both sexes fit.   25
    We die and rise the same, and prove
    Mysterious by this love.

We can die by it, if not live by love,
    And if unfit for tombs and hearse
Our legend be, it will be fit for verse;   30
    And if no piece of chronicle we prove,
        We'll build in sonnets pretty rooms;
        As well a well-wrought urn becomes
The greatest ashes, as half-acre tombs;
    And by these hymns, all shall approve   35
    Us canonized for love:

And thus invoke us: You whom reverend love
    Made one another's hermitage;
You, to whom love was peace, that now is rage;
    Who did the whole world's soul contract, and drove   40
        Into the glasses of your eyes
        (So made such mirrors, and such spies,
That they did all to you epitomize)
    Countries, towns, courts: Beg from above
    A pattern of your love!

The Anniversary

    All kings, and all their favorites,
        All glory' of honors, beauties, wits,
The sun itself, which makes times, as they pass,
Is elder by a year, now, than it was
When thou and I first one another saw: 5
All other things to their destruction draw,
    Only our love hath no decay;
This, no tomorrow hath, nor yesterday;
Running it never runs from us away,
But truly keeps his first, last, everlasting day.   10

    Two graves must hide thine and my corse;
If one might, death were no divorce:
Alas, as well as other princes, we
(Who prince enough in one another be)
Must leave at last in death, these eyes, and ears,   15
Oft fed with true oaths, and with sweet salt tears;
    But souls where nothing dwells but love

(All other thoughts being inmates) then shall prove
This, or a love increaséd there above,
When bodies to their graves, souls from their graves remove.   20

      And then we shall be throughly° blest,   thoroughly
      But we no more than all the rest;

Here upon earth, we're kings, and none but we
Can be such kings, nor of such subjects be;
Who is so safe as we, where none can do   25
Treason to us, except one of us two?
      True and false fears let us refrain,
      Let us love nobly,'and live, and add again
Years and years unto years, till we attain
To write threescore, this is the second of our reign.   30

A Valediction: Forbidding Mourning

      As virtuous men pass mildly away,
        And whisper to their souls to go,
      Whilst some of their sad friends do say,
        "The breath goes now," and some say, "No,"

      So let us melt, and make no noise,   5
        No tear-floods, nor sigh-tempests move;
      'Twere profanation of our joys
        To tell the laity our love.

      Moving of the earth° brings harms and fears,   earthquakes
        Men reckon what it did and meant;   10
      But trepidation of the spheres,
        Though greater far, is innocent.

      Dull sublunary° lovers' love   earthly
        (Whose soul is sense) cannot admit
      Absence, because it doth remove   15
        Those things which elemented° it.   composed

      But we, by a love so much refined
        That our selves know not what it is,
      Inter-assured of the mind,
        Care less, eyes, lips, and hands to miss.   20

A VALEDICTION   [11]**trepidation of the spheres**   *movement in the outermost of the heavenly spheres.*
In Ptolemy's astronomy these outer spheres caused others to vary from their orbits.

Our two souls therefore, which are one,
    Though I must go, endure not yet
A breach, but an expansion,
    Like gold to airy thinness beat.

If they be two, they are two so   25
    As stiff twin compasses are two:
Thy soul, the fixed foot, makes no show
    To move, but doth, if the other do;

And though it in the center sit,
    Yet when the other far doth roam,   30
It leans, and hearkens after it,
    And grows erect, as that comes home.

Such wilt thou be to me, who must,
    Like the other foot, obliquely run;
Thy firmness makes my circle just,   35
    And makes me end where I begun.

The Flea

Mark but this flea, and mark in this
How little that which thou deny'st me is;
It sucked me first, and now sucks thee,
And in this flea our two bloods mingled be;
Thou know'st that this cannot be said   5
A sin, nor shame, nor loss of maidenhead;
    Yet this enjoys before it woo,
    And pampered swells with one blood made of two,
    And this, alas, is more than we would do.

Oh stay, three lives in one flea spare,   10
Where we almost, yea, more than married are.
This flea is you and I, and this
Our marriage bed and marriage temple is;
Though parents grudge, and you, we are met
And cloistered in these living walls of jet.   15
    Though use° make you apt to kill me,   custom
    Let not to that, self-murder added be,
    And sacrilege, three sins in killing three.

Cruel and sudden, hast thou since
Purpled thy nail in blood of innocence?   20

---

²⁶**twin compasses** *the two feet of a mathematical compass used for drawing circles.*

Wherein could this flea guilty be,
Except in that drop which it sucked from thee?
Yet thou triumph'st and say'st that thou
Find'st not thyself, nor me the weaker now.
    'Tis true. Then learn how false fears be: 25
      Just so much honor, when thou yield'st to me,
        Will waste, as this flea's death took life from thee.

Death, be not proud

Death, be not proud, though some have calléd thee
Mighty and dreadful, for thou are not so;
For those whom thou think'st thou dost overthrow
Die not, poor Death, nor yet canst thou kill me.
From rest and sleep, which but thy pictures be,   5
Much pleasure; then from thee much more must flow,
And soonest our best men with thee do go,
Rest of their bones, and soul's delivery.
Thou art slave to fate, chance, kings, and desperate men,
And dost with poison, war, and sickness dwell,   10
And poppy or charms can make us sleep as well
And better than thy stroke; why swell'st thou then?
One short sleep past, we wake eternally
And death shall be no more; Death, thou shalt die.

Batter my heart, three-personed God

Batter my heart, three-personed God; for You
As yet but knock, breathe, shine, and seek to mend;
That I may rise and stand, o'erthrow me, and bend
Your force to break, blow, burn, and make me new.
I, like an usurped town, to another due,   5
Labor to admit You, but O, to no end;
Reason, Your viceroy in me, me should defend,
But is captíved, and proves weak or untrue.
Yet dearly I love You, and would be lovéd fain°,   gladly
But am betrothed unto Your enemy.   10
Divorce me, untie or break that knot again;
Take me to You, imprison me, for I,
Except You enthrall me, never shall be free,
Nor ever chaste, except You ravish me.

BEN JONSON

[1573–1637]

On My First Daughter

Here lies, to each her parents' ruth°,   sorrow
Mary, the daughter of their youth;
Yet all heaven's gifts being heaven's due,
It makes the father less to rue.
At six months' end she parted hence   5
With safety of her innocence;
Whose soul heaven's queen, whose name she bears,
In comfort of her mother's tears,
Hath placed amongst her virgin-train:
Where, while that severed doth remain,   10
This grave partakes the fleshly birth;
Which cover lightly, gentle earth!

On My First Son

Farewell, thou child of my right hand, and joy;
My sin was too much hope of thee, loved boy:
Seven years thou wert lent to me, and I thee pay,
Exacted by thy fate, on the just day.
O could I lose all father now! for why   5
Will man lament the state he should envý,
To have so soon 'scaped world's and flesh's rage,
And, if no other misery, yet age?
Rest in soft peace, and asked, say, "Here doth lie
Ben Jonson his best piece of poetry."   10
For whose sake henceforth all his vows be such
As what he loves may never like too much.

Still to be neat, still to be dressed

Still to be neat, still to be dressed,
As you were going to a feast;

ON MY FIRST SON   ¹*child of my right hand*   the literal meaning, in Hebrew, of Benjamin, the boy's
name.   ⁴*the just day*   Jonson's son died on his seventh birthday.
STILL TO BE NEAT   Compare with Herrick's "Delight in Disorder," p. 414.

Still to be powdered, still perfumed:
Lady, it is to be presumed,
Though art's hid causes are not found,   5
All is not sweet, all is not sound.

Give me a look, give me a face,
That makes simplicity a grace;
Robes loosely flowing, hair as free:
Such sweet neglect more taketh me   10
Than all the adulteries of art;
They strike mine eyes, but not my heart.

Come, my Celia

Come, my Celia, let us prove°,   experience
While we can, the sports of love;
Time will not be ours forever:
He at length our good will sever.
Spend not, then, his gifts in vain;   5
Suns that set may rise again,
But if once we lose this light,
'Tis with us perpetual night.
Why should we defer our joys?
Fame and rumor are but toys.   10
Cannot we delude the eyes
Of a few poor household spies?
Or his easier ears beguile,
Thus removéd by our wile?
'Tis no sin love's fruits to steal,   15
But the sweet thefts to reveal;
To be taken, to be seen,
These have crimes accounted been.

Song: To Celia

Drink to me only with thine eyes,
And I will pledge with mine;
Or leave a kiss but in the cup,
And I'll not look for wine.
The thirst that from the soul doth rise,   5
Doth ask a drink divine:

COME, MY CELIA *Compare with Marvell's "To His Coy Mistress," p. 549, and with Donne's "The Flea,"*
p. 537.

But might I of Jove's nectar sup,
I would not change for thine.

I sent thee late a rosy wreath,
Not so much honoring thee,   10
As giving it a hope, that there
It could not withered be.
But thou thereon did'st only breathe,
And sent'st it back to me;
Since when it grows and smells, I swear,   15
Not of itself, but thee.

A Hymn to God the Father

Hear me, O God!
A broken heart,
Is my best part;
Use still thy rod,
That I may prove°   experience   5
Therein thy love.

If thou hadst not
Been stern to me,
But left me free,
I had forgot   10
Myself and thee.

For sin's so sweet,
As minds ill bent
Rarely repent,
Until they meet   15
Their punishment.

Who more can crave
Than thou hast done,
That gav'st a Son,
To free a slave?   20
First made of naught,
With all since bought.

Sin, Death, and Hell,
His glorious Name
Quite overcame,
Yet I rebel,   25
And slight the same.

But I'll come in
Before my loss
Me farther toss,   30
As sure to win
Under his Cross.

ROBERT HERRICK
[1591–1667]

Upon Julia's Clothes

Whenas in silks my Julia goes,
Then, then, methinks, how sweetly flows
That liquefaction of her clothes.

Next, when I cast mine eyes and see
That brave vibration each way free,   5
O how that glittering taketh me!

To the Virgins, to Make Much of Time

Gather ye rosebuds while ye may:
    Old Time is still a-flying;
And this same flower that smiles today,
    Tomorrow will be dying.

The glorious lamp of heaven, the sun,   5
    The higher he's a-getting,
The sooner will his race be run,
    And nearer he's to setting.

That age is best which is the first,
    When youth and blood are warmer;   10
But being spent, the worse, and worst
    Times, still succeed the former.

Then be not coy, but use your time;
    And while ye may, go marry:
For, having lost but once your prime,   15
    You may for ever tarry.

GEORGE HERBERT
[1593–1633]

The Altar

A broken altar, Lord, Thy servant rears,
Made of a heart and cemented with tears;
  Whose parts are as Thy hand did frame;
  No workman's tool hath touched the same.
        A   heart   alone   5
        Is such a   stone,
        As   nothing but
        Thy power doth cut.
        Wherefore each part
        Of my hard heart   10
        Meets in this frame
        To praise Thy name,
  That if I chance to hold my peace,
  These stones to praise Thee may not cease.
Oh, let Thy blessed sacrifice be mine,   15
And sanctify this altar to be Thine.

Denial

  When my devotions could not pierce
        Thy silent ears,
Then was my heart broken, as was my verse;
    My breast was full of fears
        And disorder.   5

  My bent thoughts, like a brittle bow,
        Did fly asunder:
Each took his way; some would to pleasures go,
    Some to the wars and thunder
        Of alarms.   10

  As good go anywhere, they say,
        As to benumb
Both knees and heart, in crying night and day,
    Come, come, my God, O come!
        But no hearing.   15

O that thou shouldst give dust a tongue
To cry to thee,
And then not hear it crying! All day long
My heart was in my knee,
But no hearing.   20

Therefore my soul lay out of sight,
Untuned, unstrung:
My feeble spirit, unable to look right,
Like a nipped blossom, hung
Discontented.   25

O cheer and tune my heartless breast,
Defer no time;
That so thy favors granting my request,
They and my mind may chime,
And mend my rhyme.   30

The Pulley

When God at first made man,
Having a glass of blessings standing by,
"Let us," said he, "pour on him all we can:
Let the world's riches, which dispersèd lie,
Contract into a span."   5

So Strength first made a way;
Then Beauty flowed; then Wisdom, Honor, Pleasure.
When almost all was out, God made a stay,
Perceiving that alone of all his treasure
Rest in the bottom lay.   10

"For if I should," said he,
"Bestow this jewel also on my creature,
He would adore my gifts instead of me,
And rest in Nature, not the God of Nature;
So both should losers be.   15

"Yet let him keep the rest,
But keep them with repining restlessness:
Let him be rich and weary, that at least,
If goodness lead him not, yet weariness
May toss him to my breast."   20

Man

My God, I heard this day
That none doth build a stately habitation,
   But he that means to dwell therein.
   What house more stately hath there been,
Or can be, than is Man? to whose creation   5
   All things are in decay.

   For Man is every thing,
And more: he is a tree, yet bears more fruit;
   A beast, yet is or should be more:
   Reason and speech we only bring.   10
Parrots may thank us, if they are not mute,
   They go upon the score.

   Man is all symmetry,
Full of proportions, one limb to another,
   And all to all the world besides: 15
   Each part may call the furthest, brother;
For head with foot hath private amity,
   And both with moons and tides.

   Nothing hath got so far,
But man hath caught and kept it, as his prey.   20
   His eyes dismount the highest star:
   He is in little all the sphere.
Herbs gladly cure our flesh, because that they
   Find their acquaintance there.

   For us the winds do blow,   25
The earth doth rest, heaven move, and fountains flow.
   Nothing we see but means our good,
   As our delight or as our treasure:
The whole is either our cupboard of food,
   Or cabinet of pleasure.   30

   The stars have us to bed;
Night draws the curtain, which the sun withdraws;
   Music and light attend our head.
   All things unto our flesh are kind°   kin
In their descent and being; to our mind
     35
   In their ascent and cause.

   Each thing is full of duty:
Waters united are our navigation;

     Distinguishéd, our habitation;
    Below, our drink; above, our meat;   40
  Both are our cleanliness. Hath one such beauty?
      Then how are all things neat?

     More servants wait on Man
  Than he'll take notice of: in every path
    He treads down that which doth befriend him   45
    When sickness makes him pale and wan.
  O mighty love! Man is one world, and hath
      Another to attend him.

     Since then, my God, thou hast
  So brave a palace built, O dwell in it,   50
    That it may dwell with thee at last!
    Till then, afford us so much wit,
  That, as the world serves us, we may serve thee,
     And both thy servants be.

Love (III)

Love bade me welcome: yet my soul drew back,
     Guilty of dust and sin.
But quick-eyed Love, observing me grow slack
     From my first entrance in,
Drew nearer to me, sweetly questioning   5
     If I lacked anything.

"A guest," I answered, "worthy to be here":
     Love said, "You shall be he."
"I, the unkind, ungrateful? Ah, my dear,
     I cannot look on thee."   10
Love took my hand, and smiling did reply,
     "Who made the eyes but I?"

"Truth, Lord; but I have marred them; let my shame
     Go where it doth deserve."
"And know you not," says Love, "who bore the blame?"   15
     "My dear, then I will serve."
"You must sit down," says Love, "and taste my meat."
     So I did sit and eat.

JOHN MILTON
[1608–1674]

When I consider how my light is spent

When I consider how my light is spent
  Ere half my days, in this dark world and wide,
  And that one talent which is death to hide
  Lodged with me useless, though my soul more bent
To serve therewith my Maker, and present   5
  My true account, lest he returning chide;
  "Doth God exact day-labor, light denied?"
  I fondly° ask; but Patience to prevent   foolishly
That murmur, soon replies, "God doth not need
  Either man's work or his own gifts; who best   10
  Bear his mild yoke, they serve him best. His state
Is kingly. Thousands at his bidding speed
  And post o'er land and ocean without rest:
  They also serve who only stand and wait."

On the Late Massacre in Piedmont

Avenge, O Lord, thy slaughtered saints, whose bones
  Lie scattered on the Alpine mountains cold,
  Even them who kept thy truth so pure of old
  When all our fathers worshiped stocks° and stones   idols
Forget not: in thy book record their groans   5
  Who were thy sheep and in their ancient fold
  Slain by the bloody Piedmontese that rolled
  Mother with infant down the rocks. Their moans
The vales redoubled to the hills, and they
  To Heaven. Their martyred blood and ashes sow   10
  O'er all th' Italian fields where still doth sway
The triple tyrant: that from these may grow
  A hundredfold, who having learnt thy way
  Early may fly the Babylonian woe.

WHEN I CONSIDER HOW MY LIGHT IS SPENT   *Milton went blind in 1651.*   [3]**one talent**
*an allusion to Jesus's parable of the talents, in which the servant who buried the talent given him by his master
was cast into the darkness (Matthew 25:14–30).*
ON THE LATE MASSACRE   *The Duke of Savoy in 1655 massacred 1,700 Waldensians, members of a
Protestant sect.*   [12]**The triple tyrant**   *the pope, whose tiara contains three crowns.*

ANNE BRADSTREET
[1612–1672]

Before the Birth of One of Her Children

All things within this fading world hath end,
Adversity doth still our joys attend;
No ties so strong, no friends so dear and sweet,
But with death's parting blow is sure to meet.
The sentence past is most irrevocable,   5
A common thing, yet oh, inevitable.
How soon, my Dear, death may my steps attend,
How soon't may be thy lot to lose thy friend,
We both are ignorant, yet love bids me
These farewell lines to recommend to thee,   10
That when that knot's untied that made us one,
I may seem thine, who in effect am none.
And if I see not half my days that's due,
What nature would, God grant to yours and you;
The many faults that well you know I have   15
Let be interred in my oblivious grave;
If any worth or virtue were in me,
Let that live freshly in thy memory
And when thou feel'st no grief, as I no harms,
Yet love thy dead, who long lay in thine arms.   20
And when thy loss shall be repaid with gains
Look to my little babes, my dear remains.
And if chance to thine eyes shall bring this verse,
With some sad sighs honor my absent hearse;
And kiss this paper for thy love's dear sake,   25
Who with salt tears this last farewell did take.

To My Dear and Loving Husband

If ever two were one, then surely we.
If ever man were loved by wife, then thee;
If ever wife was happy in a man,
Compare with me, ye women, if you can.
I prize thy love more than whole mines of gold   5
Or all the riches that the East doth hold.
My love is such that rivers cannot quench,

Nor aught but love from thee give recompense.
Thy love is such I can no way repay,
The heavens reward thee manifold, I pray. 10
Then while we live, in love let's so perséver
That when we live no more, we may live ever.

ANDREW MARVELL
[1621–1678]

To His Coy Mistress

Had we but world enough, and time,
This coyness, lady, were no crime.
We would sit down, and think which way
To walk, and pass our long love's day.
Thou by the Indian Ganges' side 5
Shoudst rubies find; I by the tide
Of Humber would complain. I would
Love you ten years before the flood,
And you should, if you please, refuse
Till the conversion of the Jews. 10
My vegetable love should grow
Vaster than empires and more slow;
An hundred years should go to praise
Thine eyes, and on thy forehead gaze;
Two hundred to adore each breast, 15
But thirty thousand to the rest;
An age at least to every part,
And the last age should show your heart.
For, lady, you deserve this state,
Nor would I love at lower rate. 20
    But at my back I always hear
Time's wingéd chariot hurrying near;
And yonder all before us lie
Deserts of vast eternity.
Thy beauty shall no more be found; 25
Nor, in thy marble vault, shall sound
My echoing song; then worms shall try
That long-preserved virginity,

TO HIS COY MISTRESS   [6]*rubies* *associated with virginity.*   [7]**Humber** *the river that runs through Marvell's native town, Hull.*   [10]**the conversion of the Jews** *supposedly to occur at the end of time.* [11]**vegetable love** *a reference to the idea that vegetables have the power to grow but lack consciousness.*

And your quaint° honor turn to dust,   overscrupulous
And into ashes all my lust: 30
The grave's a fine and private place,
But none, I think, do there embrace.
   Now therefore, while the youthful hue
Sits on thy skin like morning dew
And while thy willing soul transpires°   breathes forth   35
At every pore with instant fires,
Now let us sport us while we may,
And now, like amorous birds of prey,
Rather at once our time devour
Than languish in his slow-chapped° power.   slow-jawed   40
Let us roll all our strength and all
Our sweetness up into one ball,
And tear our pleasures with rough strife
Thorough the iron gates of life:
Thus, though we cannot make our sun   45
Stand still, yet we will make him run.

A Dialogue Between the Soul and Body

Soul

Oh, who shall from this dungeon raise
A soul enslaved so many ways?
With bolts of bones that fettered stands
In feet, and manacled in hands;
Here blinded with an eye, and there   5
Deaf with the drumming of an ear;
A soul hung up, as 'twere, in chains
Of nerves and arteries and veins;
Tortured, besides each other part,
In a vain head and double heart.   10

Body

Oh, who shall me deliver whole
From bonds of this tyrannic soul?
Which stretched upright, impales me so
That mine own precipice I go,
And warms and moves this needless frame—   15
A fever could but do the same—
And, wanting where its spite to try,
Has made me live to let me die:
A body that could never rest,
Since this ill spirit it possessed.   20

Soul

What magic could me thus confine
Within another's grief to pine?
Where whatsoever it complain,
I feel, that cannot feel, the pain,
And all my care itself employs,   25
That to preserve which me destroys,
Constrained not only to endure
Diseases, but, what's worse, the cure;
And ready oft the port° to gain,   heaven
And shipwrecked into health again.   30

Body

But physic° yet could never reach   medicine
The maladies thou me dost teach:
Whom first the cramp of hope does tear,
And then the palsy shakes of fear;
The pestilence of love does heat,   35
Or hatred's hidden ulcer eat;
Joy's cheerful madness does perplex,
Or sorrow's other madness vex;
Which knowledge forces me to know,
And memory will not forgo.   40
What but a soul could have the wit
To build me up for sin so fit?
So architects do square and hew
Green trees that in the forest grew.

JOHN DRYDEN

[*1631–1700*]

To the Memory of Mr. Oldham

Farewell, too little, and too lately known,
Whom I began to think and call my own:
For sure our souls were near allied, and thine
Cast in the same poetic mold with mine.
One common note on either lyre did strike,   5
And knaves and fools we both abhorred alike.
To the same goal did both our studies° drive;   efforts
The last set out the soonest did arrive.

TO THE MEMORY OF MR. OLDHAM   *John Oldham (1653–1683), a poet whose satires Dryden admired.*

Thus Nisus fell upon the slippery place,
While his young friend performed° and won the race.   completed   10
O early ripe! to thy abundant store
What could advancing age have added more?
It might (what nature never gives the young)
Have taught the numbers° of thy native tongue.   metrics
But satire needs not those, and wit will shine   15
Through the harsh cadence of a rugged line:
A noble error, and but seldom made,
When poets are by too much force betrayed.
Thy generous fruits, though gathered ere their prime,
Still showed a quickness°, and maturing time   strength   20
But mellows what we write to the dull sweets of rhyme.
Once more, hail and farewell; farewell, thou young,
But ah too short, Marcellus of our tongue;
Thy brows with ivy, and with laurels bound;
But fate and gloomy night encompass thee around.   25

A Song for St. Cecilia's Day

1

From harmony, from heavenly harmony
This universal frame began:
When Nature underneath a heap
Of jarring atoms lay,
And could not heave her head,   5
The tuneful voice was heard from high:
"Arise, ye more than dead."
Then cold, and hot, and moist, and dry,
In order to their stations leap,
And Music's power obey.   10
From harmony, from heavenly harmony
This universal frame began:
From harmony to harmony
Through all the compass of the notes it ran,
The diapason closing full in man.   15

2

What passion cannot Music raise and quell!
When Jubal struck the corded shell°,   lyre

⁹**Nisus** *a runner in Vergil's* Aeneid *whose friend Euryalus came from behind to beat him in a race.*
²³**Marcellus** *the promising nephew of Augustus Caesar who died at 19.*   ²⁴**ivy, and with laurels**
wreaths given to poets and heroes.   ²⁵**But fate . . . around** *an echo of the* Aeneid, *Book VI, l. 866.*
A SONG FOR ST. CECILIA'S DAY *St. Cecilia was a Roman martyr and a patron saint of music.*
³**Nature** *created nature.*   ¹⁵**diapason** *an octave consonance, harmony.*   ¹⁷**Jubal** *father of the harp*
and organ (Genesis 4:21).

His listening brethren stood around,
And, wondering, on their faces fell
To worship that celestial sound.   20
Less than a god they thought there could not dwell
  Within the hollow of that shell
  That spoke so sweetly and so well.
What passion cannot Music raise and quell!

3

  The trumpet's loud clangor   25
   Excites us to arms,
  With shrill notes of anger,
   And mortal alarms.
  The double double double beat
   Of the thundering drum   30
Cries: "Hark! the foes come;
Charge, charge, 'tis too late to retreat."

4

  The soft complaining flute
  In dying notes discovers
  The woes of hopeless lovers,   35
Whose dirge is whispered by the warbling lute.

5

  Sharp violins proclaim
Their jealous pangs, and desperation,
Fury, frantic indignation,
Depth of pains, and height of passion,   40
  For the fair, disdainful dame.

6

  But O! what art can teach,
  What human voice can reach,
The sacred organ's praise?
  Notes inspiring holy love,   45
Notes that wing their heavenly ways
  To mend the choirs above.

7

Orpheus could lead the savage race;
And trees unrooted left their place,
  Sequacious° of the lyre;   *following* 50
But bright Cecilia raised the wonder higher:

48Orpheus *legendary Greek musician whose singing and playing were so irresistible the trees and rocks were said to follow him.*

When to her organ vocal breath was given,
An angel heard, and straight appeared,
    Mistaking earth for heaven.

Grand Chorus

    As from the power of sacred lays   55
        The spheres began to move,
    And sung the great Creator's praise
        To all the blest above;
    So, when the last and dreadful hour
    This crumbling pageant shall devour,   60
    The trumpet shall be heard on high,
    The dead shall live, the living die,
    And Music shall untune the sky.

JONATHAN SWIFT
[1667–1745]

A Description of the Morning

Now hardly here and there a hackney-coach°   horse-drawn carriage
Appearing, showed the ruddy morn's approach.
Now Betty from her master's bed had flown,
And softly stole to discompose her own;
The slip-shod 'prentice from his master's door   5
Had pared the dirt and sprinkled round the floor.
Now Moll had whirled her mop with dext'rous airs,
Prepared to scrub the entry and the stairs.
The youth with broomy stumps began to trace
The kennel-edge°, where wheels had worn the place.   curb   10
The small-coal man° was heard with cadence deep,   charcoal seller
Till drowned in shriller notes of chimney-sweep:
Duns at his lordship's gate began to meet;
And brickdust Moll had screamed through half the street.
The turnkey° now his flock returning sees,   jailer   15
Duly let out a-nights to steal for fees:
The watchful bailiffs° take their silent stands,   deputies
And schoolboys lag with satchels in their hands.

A DESCRIPTION OF THE MORNING   [14]*brickdust Moll*   *a woman selling powdered brick (for cleaning knives).*

ALEXANDER POPE
[*1688–1744*]

Epigram Engraved on the Collar of a Dog Which I Gave to His Royal Highness

> I am his Highness' dog at Kew;
> Pray tell me, sir, whose dog are you?

An Essay on Man
From *Epistle II*

I. Know then thyself, presume not God to scan°;   scrutinize
The proper study of mankind is Man.
Placed on this isthmus of a middle state,
A being darkly wise, and rudely° great;   crudely
With too much knowledge for the Sceptic side,   5
With too much weakness for the Stoic's pride,
He hangs between; in doubt to act, or rest,
In doubt to deem himself a god, or beast;
In doubt his mind or body to prefer,
Born but to die, and reasoning but to err;   10
Alike in ignorance, his reason such,
Whether he thinks too little, or too much:
Chaos of thought and passion, all confused;
Still by himself abused, or disabused;
Created half to rise, and half to fall;   15
Great lord of all things, yet a prey to all;
Sole judge of truth, in endless error hurled:
The glory, jest, and riddle of the world!

THOMAS GRAY
[*1716–1771*]

Elegy Written in a Country Churchyard

> The curfew tolls the knell of parting day,
> The lowing herd wind slowly o'er the lea,

The plowman homeward plods his weary way,
   And leaves the world to darkness and to me.

Now fades the glimmering landscape on the sight,   5
   And all the air a solemn stillness holds,
Save where the beetle wheels his droning flight,
   And drowsy tinklings lull the distant folds;

Save that from yonder ivy-mantled tower
   The moping owl does to the moon complain   10
Of such, as wandering near her secret bower,
   Molest her ancient solitary reign.

Beneath those rugged elms, that yew tree's shade,
   Where heaves the turf in many a moldering heap,
Each in his narrow cell forever laid,   15
   The rude° forefathers of the hamlet sleep.   rustic

The breezy call of incense-breathing morn,
   The swallow twittering from the straw-built shed,
The cock's shrill clarion, or the echoing horn°,   hunter's horn
   No more shall rouse them from their lowly bed.   20

For them no more the blazing hearth shall burn,
   Or busy housewife ply her evening care;
No children run to lisp their sire's return,
   Or climb his knees the envied kiss to share.

Oft did the harvest to their sickle yield,   25
   Their furrow oft the stubborn glebe° has broke;   soil
How jocund did they drive their team afield!
   How bowed the woods beneath their sturdy stroke!

Let not Ambition mock their useful toil,
   Their homely joys, and destiny obscure;   30
Nor Grandeur hear with a disdainful smile
   The short and simple annals of the poor.

The boast of heraldry, the pomp of power,
   And all that beauty, all that wealth e'er gave,
Awaits alike the inevitable hour.   35
   The paths of glory lead but to the grave.

Nor you, ye proud, impute to these the fault,
   If Memory o'er their tomb no trophies raise,

Where through the long-drawn aisle and fretted° vault   ornamented
    The pealing anthem swells the note of praise.   40

Can storied urn or animated° bust   lifelike
    Back to its mansion call the fleeting breath?
Can Honor's voice provoke° the silent dust,   call forth
    Or Flattery soothe the dull cold ear of Death?

Perhaps in this neglected spot is laid   45
    Some heart once pregnant with celestial fire;
Hands that the rod of empire might have swayed,
    Or waked to ecstasy the living lyre.

But Knowledge to their eyes her ample page
    Rich with the spoils of time did ne'er unroll;   50
Chill Penury repressed their noble rage°,   ardor
    And froze the genial current of the soul.

Full many a gem of purest ray serene,
    The dark unfathomed caves of ocean bear:
Full many a flower is born to blush unseen,   55
    And waste its sweetness on the desert air.

Some village Hampden, that with dauntless breast
    The little tyrant of his fields withstood;
Some mute inglorious Milton here may rest,
    Some Cromwell guiltless of his country's blood.   60

The applause of listening senates to command,
    The threats of pain and ruin to despise,
To scatter plenty o'er a smiling land,
    And read their history in a nation's eyes,

Their lot forbade: nor circumscribed alone   65
    Their growing virtues, but their crimes confined;
Forbade to wade through slaughter to a throne,
    And shut the gates of mercy on mankind,

The struggling pangs of conscious truth to hide,
    To quench the blushes of ingenuous shame,   70
Or heap the shrine of Luxury and Pride
    With incense kindled at the Muse's flame.

ELEGY WRITTEN IN A COUNTRY CHURCHYARD   [41]*storied urn*   *an urn giving a person's history in a descriptive epitaph.*   [57]*Hampden*   *John Hampden expressed opposition to a tax levied by Charles I, one of the events leading to civil war.*

Far from the madding° crowd's ignoble strife, milling
   Their sober wishes never learned to stray;
Along the cool sequestered vale of life 75
   They kept the noiseless tenor of their way.

Yet even these bones from insult to protect
   Some frail memorial still erected nigh,
With uncouth rhymes and shapeless sculpture decked,
   Implores the passing tribute of a sigh. 80

Their name, their years, spelt by the unlettered Muse,
   The place of fame and elegy supply:
And many a holy text around she strews,
   That teach the rustic moralist to die.

For who to dumb Forgetfulness a prey, 85
   This pleasing anxious being e'er resigned,
Left the warm precincts of the cheerful day,
   Nor cast one longing lingering look behind?

On some fond breast the parting soul relies,
   Some pious drops the closing eye requires; 90
Even from the tomb the voice of Nature cries,
   Even in our ashes live their wonted fires.

For thee, who mindful of the unhonored dead
   Cost in these lines their artless tale relate;
If chance, by lonely contemplation led, 95
   Some kindred spirit shall inquire thy fate,

Haply some hoary-headed swain may say,
   "Oft have we seen him at the peep of dawn
Brushing with hasty steps the dews away
   To meet the sun upon the upland lawn. 100

"There at the foot of yonder nodding beech
   That wreathes its old fantastic roots so high,
His listless length at noontide would he stretch,
   And pore upon the brook that babbles by.

"Hard by yon wood, now smiling as in scorn, 105
   Muttering his wayward fancies he would rove,
Now drooping, woeful wan, like one forlorn,
   Or crazed with care, or crossed in hopeless love.

"One morn I missed him on the customed hill,
   Along the heath and near his favorite tree; 110

Another came; nor yet beside the rill,
    Nor up the lawn, nor at the wood was he;

"The next with dirges due in sad array
    Slow through the churchway path we saw him borne.
Approach and read (for thou canst read) the lay,   115
    Graved on the stone beneath yon aged thorn."

The Epitaph

Here rests his head upon the lap of Earth
    A youth to Fortune and to Fame unknown.
Fair Science° frowned not on his humble birth,   learning
    And Melancholy marked him for her own.   120

Large was his bounty, and his soul sincere,
    Heaven did a recompense as largely send:
He gave to Misery all he had, a tear,
    He gained from Heaven ('twas all he wished) a friend.

No farther seek his merits to disclose,   125
    Or draw his frailties from their dread abode
(There they alike in trembling hope repose),
    The bosom of his Father and his God.

JOHANN WOLFGANG VON GOETHE
[1749–1832]

Nature and Art

Genius, technique—you'd swear the pair unsuited,
Yet here they stand together, hand in hand.
Nature's in love with art. Their widely bruited
Hassle's a lie, I've come to understand.

Poet, there's one thing only works: to work.   5
Hours of the sweaty effort day and night
Trying it this way, that way—going berserk.
Then you can be spontaneous. You've the right.

Habits of mind we earn. To earn's laborious.
Small chance they'll make it to a difficult goal,   10
Those do-as-you-like "free spirits," la-dee-dee!

Nose to the grindstone first, if aims are glorious.
Mastery's much in little, tight control.
Rules! They're a springboard only, and we're *free!*

TRANSLATED BY JOHN FREDERIC NIMS

WILLIAM BLAKE
[1757–1827]

The Clod & the Pebble

"Love seeketh not Itself to please,
Nor for itself hath any care;
But for another gives its ease,
And builds a Heaven in Hell's despair."

So sang a little Clod of Clay,   5
Trodden with the cattle's feet;
But a Pebble of the brook,
Warbled out these metres meet:

"Love seeketh only Self to please,
To bind another to its delight,   10
Joys in another's loss of ease,
And builds a Hell in Heaven's despite."

The Lamb

Little Lamb, who made thee?
Dost thou know who made thee?
Gave thee life & bid thee feed,
By the stream & o'er the mead;
Gave thee clothing of delight,   5
Softest clothing wooly bright;
Gave thee such a tender voice,
Making all the vales rejoice!
Little Lamb who made thee?
Dost thou know who made thee?   10

Little Lamb I'll tell thee,
Little Lamb I'll tell thee!
He is callèd by thy name,
For he calls himself a Lamb:

He is meek & he is mild, 15
He became a little child:
I a child & thou a lamb,
We are calléd by his name.
    Little Lamb God bless thee.
    Little Lamb God bless thee. 20

The Tyger

Tyger! Tyger! burning bright
In the forests of the night,
What immortal hand or eye
Could frame thy fearful symmetry?

In what distant deeps or skies 5
Burnt the fire of thine eyes?
On what wings dare he aspire?
What the hand, dare seize the fire?

And what shoulder, & what art,
Could twist the sinews of thy heart? 10
And when thy heart began to beat,
What dread hand? & what dread feet?

What the hammer? what the chain?
In what furnace was thy brain?
What the anvil? what dread grasp 15
Dare its deadly terrors clasp?

When the stars threw down their spears,
And water'd heaven with their tears,
Did he smile his work to see?
Did he who made the Lamb make thee? 20

Tyger! Tyger! burning bright
In the forests of the night,
What immortal hand or eye
Dare frame thy fearful symmetry?

The Garden of Love

I went to the Garden of Love,
And saw what I never had seen:
A Chapel was built in the midst,
Where I used to play on the green.

And the gates of this Chapel were shut,
And "Thou shalt not" writ over the door;
So I turn'd to the Garden of Love,
That so many sweet flowers bore,

And I saw it was filled with graves,
And tomb-stones where flowers should be:
And Priests in black gowns were walking their rounds,
And binding with briars my joys & desires.

Mock on, Mock on, Voltaire, Rousseau

Mock on, Mock on, Voltaire, Rousseau;
Mock on, Mock on, 'tis all in vain.
You throw the sand against the wind,
And the wind blows it back again.

And every sand becomes a Gem
Reflected in the beams divine;
Blown back, they blind the mocking Eye,
But still in Israel's paths they shine.

The Atoms of Democritus
And Newton's Particles of light
Are sands upon the Red sea shore,
Where Israel's tents do shine so bright.

ROBERT BURNS
[1759–1796]

A Red, Red Rose

O my luve's like a red, red rose,
That's newly sprung in June;
O my luve's like the melodie
That's sweetly played in tune.

MOCK ON, MOCK ON, VOLTAIRE, ROUSSEAU [1]Voltaire, Rousseau   For Blake, these critics of the established order were mockers of faith and imagination. [9]Democritus   ancient Greek philosopher who reduced nature to its smallest constituent parts—its atoms. [10]Newton's Particles of light   Sir Isaac Newton, English philosopher and scientist (1642–1727), described nature in terms of inanimate particles. [11]the Red sea shore   where God delivered the Israelites from the Egyptians (Exodus 14).

As fair art thou, my bonnie lass, 5
    So deep in luve am I;
And I will luve thee still, my dear,
    Till a' the seas gang dry.

Till a' the seas gang dry, my dear,
    And the rocks melt wi' the sun: 10
O I will love thee still, my dear,
    While the sands o' life shall run.

And fare thee weel, my only luve,
    And fare thee weel awhile!
And I will come again, my luve, 15
    Though it were ten thousand mile.

Green grow the rashes

Chorus

Green grow the rashes°, O;   rushes
    Green grow the rashes, O;
The sweetest hours that e'er I spend,
    Are spent amang the lasses, O!

There's nought but care on ev'ry han', 5
    In ev'ry hour that passes, O:
What signifies the life o' man,
    An' twere na for the lasses, O.

(Chorus)

The warly° race may riches chase,   worldly
    An' riches still may fly them, O; 10
An' though at last they catch them fast,
    Their hearts can ne'er enjoy them, O.

(Chorus)

But gie me a canny° hour at e'en,   pleasant
    My arms about my dearie, O;
An' warly cares, an' warly men, 15
    May a' gae tapsalteerie°, O!   topsy-turvy

(Chorus)

For you sae douce°, ye sneer at this,   prim
    Ye're nought but senseless asses, O:

The wisest man the warl' saw,
   He dearly loved the lasses, O.   20

   (Chorus)

Auld nature swears, the lovely dears
   Her noblest work she classes, O:
Her 'prentice han' she tried on man,
   An' then she made the lasses, O.

   (Chorus)

WILLIAM WORDSWORTH
[*1770–1850*]

The world is too much with us

The world is too much with us; late and soon,
Getting and spending, we lay waste our powers;
Little we see in Nature that is ours;
We have given our hearts away, a sordid boon°!   gift
This Sea that bares her bosom to the moon,   5
The winds that will be howling at all hours,
And are up-gathered now like sleeping flowers,
For this, for everything, we are out of tune;
It moves us not.—Great God! I'd rather be
A Pagan suckled in a creed outworn;   10
So might I, standing on this pleasant lea,
Have glimpses that would make me less forlorn;
Have sight of Proteus rising from the sea;
Or hear old Triton blow his wreathèd horn.

The Solitary Reaper

Behold her, single in the field,
   Yon solitary Highland Lass!
Reaping and singing by herself;
   Stop here, or gently pass!
Alone she cuts and binds the grain,   5
   And sings a melancholy strain;

THE WORLD IS TOO MUCH WITH US   13-14**Proteus . . . Triton**   *classical sea gods. Triton's*
conch-shell horn calmed the waves.

O listen! for the Vale profound
Is overflowing with the sound.

No Nightingale did ever chaunt
More welcome notes to weary bands   10
Of travelers in some shady haunt,
Among Arabian sands;
A voice so thrilling ne'er was heard
In springtime from the Cuckoo bird,
Breaking the silence of the seas   15
Among the farthest Hebrides.

Will no one tell me what she sings?—
Perhaps the plaintive numbers flow
For old, unhappy, far-off things,
And battles long ago;   20
Or is it some more humble lay,
Familiar matter of today?

Some natural sorrow, loss, or pain,
That has been, and may be again?
Whate'er the theme, the Maiden sang   25
As if her song could have no ending;
I saw her singing at her work,
And o'er the sickle bending—
I listened, motionless and still;
And, as I mounted up the hill,   30
The music in my heart I bore,
Long after it was heard no more.

She was a Phantom of delight

She was a Phantom of delight
When first she gleamed upon my sight;
A lovely Apparition, sent
To be a moment's ornament;
Her eyes as stars of Twilight fair;   5
Like Twilight's, too, her dusky hair;
But all things else about her drawn
From May-time and the cheerful Dawn;
A dancing Shape, an Image gay,
To haunt, to startle, and way-lay.   10

I saw her upon nearer view,
A Spirit, yet a Woman too!

Her household motions light and free,
And steps of virgin-liberty;
A countenance in which did meet   15
Sweet records, promises as sweet;
A Creature not too bright or good
For human nature's daily food;
For transient sorrows, simple wiles,
Praise, blame, love, kisses, tears, and smiles.   20

And now I see with eye serene
The very pulse of the machine;
A Being breathing thoughtful breath,
A Traveller between life and death;
The reason firm, the temperate will,   25
Endurance, foresight, strength, and skill;
A perfect Woman, nobly planned,
To warn, to comfort, and command;
And yet a Spirit still, and bright
With something of angelic light.   30

Composed upon Westminster Bridge, September 3, 1802

Earth has not anything to show more fair:
Dull would he be of soul who could pass by
A sight so touching in its majesty;
This City now doth, like a garment, wear
The beauty of the morning; silent, bare,   5
Ships, towers, domes, theaters, and temples lie
Open unto the fields, and to the sky;
All bright and glittering in the smokeless air.
Never did sun more beautifully steep
In his first splendor, valley, rock, or hill;   10
Ne'er saw I, never felt, a calm so deep!
The river glideth at his own sweet will:
Dear God! the very houses seem asleep;
And all that mighty heart is lying still!

Lines

COMPOSED A FEW MILES ABOVE TINTERN ABBEY ON REVISITING THE BANKS OF THE WYE
DURING A TOUR. JULY 13, 1798

Five years have passed; five summers, with the length
Of five long winters! and again I hear

These waters, rolling from their mountain-springs
With a soft inland murmur. Once again
Do I behold these steep and lofty cliffs,   5
That on a wild secluded scene impress
Thoughts of more deep seclusion; and connect
The landscape with the quiet of the sky.
The day is come when I again repose
Here, under this dark sycamore, and view   10
These plots of cottage ground, these orchard tufts,
Which at this season, with their unripe fruits,
Are clad in one green hue, and lose themselves
Mid groves and copses°. Once again I see   thickets
These hedgerows, hardly hedgerows, little lines   15
Of sportive wood run wild; these pastoral farms,
Green to the very door; and wreaths of smoke
Sent up, in silence, from among the trees!
With some uncertain notice, as might seem
Of vagrant dwellers in the houseless woods,   20
Or of some Hermit's cave, where by his fire
The Hermit sits alone.

                   These beauteous forms,
Through a long absence, have not been to me
As is a landscape to a blind man's eye;
But oft, in lonely rooms, and 'mid the din   25
Of towns and cities, I have owed to them,
In hours of weariness, sensations sweet,
Felt in the blood, and felt along the heart;
And passing even into my purer mind
With tranquil restoration—feelings too   30
Of unremembered pleasure; such, perhaps,
As have no slight or trivial influence
On that best portion of a good man's life,
His little, nameless, unremembered, acts
Of kindness and of love. Nor less, I trust,   35
To them I may have owed another gift,
Of aspect more sublime; that blessed mood,
In which the burthen of the mystery,
In which the heavy and the weary weight
Of all this unintelligible world,   40
Is lightened—that serene and blessed mood,
In which the affections gently lead us on—
Until, the breath of this corporeal frame
And even the motion of our human blood
Almost suspended, we are laid asleep   45
In body, and become a living soul;
While with an eye made quiet by the power

Of harmony, and the deep power of joy,
We see into the life of things.

                 If this
Be but a vain belief, yet, oh! how oft—   50
In darkness and amid the many shapes
Of joyless daylight; when the fretful stir
Unprofitable, and the fever of the world,
Have hung upon the beatings of my heart—
How oft, in spirit, have I turned to thee,   55
O sylvan Wye! thou wanderer through the woods,
How often has my spirit turned to thee!

    And now, with gleams of half-extinguished thought,
With many recognitions dim and faint,
And somewhat of a sad perplexity,   60
The picture of the mind revives again;
While here I stand, not only with the sense
Of present pleasure, but with pleasing thoughts
That in this moment there is life and food
For future years. And so I dare to hope,   65
Though changed, no doubt, from what I was when first
I came among these hills; when like a roe
I bounded o'er the mountains, by the sides
Of the deep rivers, and the lonely streams,
Wherever nature led—more like a man   70
Flying from something that he dreads than one
Who sought the thing he loved. For nature then
(The coarser pleasures of my boyish days,
And their glad animal movements all gone by)
To me was all in all.—I cannot paint   75
What then I was. The sounding cataract
Haunted me like a passion; the tall rock,
The mountain, and the deep and gloomy wood,
Their colors and their forms, were then to me
An appetite; a feeling and a love,   80
That had no need of a remoter charm,
By thought supplied, nor any interest
Unborrowed from the eye.—That time is past,
And all its aching joys are now no more,
And all its dizzy raptures. Not for this   85
Faint I, nor mourn nor murmur; other gifts
Have followed; for such loss, I would believe,
Abundant recompense. For I have learned
To look on nature, not as in the hour
Of thoughtless youth, but hearing oftentimes   90
The still, sad music of humanity,
Nor harsh nor grating, though of ample power

To chasten and subdue. And I have felt
A presence that disturbs me with the joy
Of elevated thoughts; a sense sublime   95
Of something far more deeply interfused,
Whose dwelling is the light of setting suns,
And the round ocean and the living air,
And the blue sky, and in the mind of man:
A motion and a spirit, that impels   100
All thinking things, all objects of all thought,
And rolls through all things. Therefore am I still
A lover of the meadows and the woods,
And mountains; and of all that we behold
From this green earth; of all the mighty world   105
Of eye, and ear—both what they half create,
And what perceive; well pleased to recognize
In nature and the language of the sense
The anchor of my purest thoughts, the nurse,
The guide, the guardian of my heart, and soul   110
Of all my moral being.

                             Nor perchance,
If I were not thus taught, should I the more
Suffer my genial spirits° to decay: powers
For thou art with me here upon the banks
Of this fair river; thou my dearest Friend,   115
My dear, dear Friend; and in thy voice I catch
The language of my former heart, and read
My former pleasures in the shooting lights
Of thy wild eyes. Oh! yet a little while
May I behold in thee what I was once,   120
My dear, dear Sister! and this prayer I make,
Knowing that Nature never did betray
The heart that loved her; 'tis her privilege,
Through all the years of this our life, to lead
From joy to joy: for she can so inform°   give form to   125
The mind that is within us, so impress
With quietness and beauty, and so feed
With lofty thoughts, that neither evil tongues,
Rash judgments, nor the sneers of selfish men,
Nor greetings where no kindness is, nor all   130
The dreary intercourse of daily life,
Shall e'er prevail against us, or disturb
Our cheerful faith, that all which we behold
Is full of blessings. Therefore let the moon
Shine on thee in thy solitary walk;   135

LINES COMPOSED A FEW MILES ABOVE TINTERN ABBEY   115 **Friend** Wordsworth's sister,
Dorothy.

And let the misty mountain winds be free
To blow against thee: and, in after years,
When these wild ecstasies shall be matured
Into a sober pleasure; when thy mind
Shall be a mansion for all lovely forms,   140
Thy memory be as a dwelling place
For all sweet sounds and harmonies; oh! then,
If solitude, or fear, or pain, or grief
Should be thy portion, with what healing thoughts
Of tender joy wilt thou remember me,   145
And these my exhortations! Nor, perchance—
If I should be where I no more can hear
Thy voice, nor catch from thy wild eyes these gleams
Of past existence—wilt thou then forget
That on the banks of this delightful stream   150
We stood together; and that I, so long
A worshiper of Nature, hither came
Unwearied in that service; rather say
With warmer love—oh! with far deeper zeal
Of holier love. Nor wilt thou then forget,   155
That after many wanderings, many years
Of absence, these steep woods and lofty cliffs,
And this green pastoral landscape, were to me
More dear, both for themselves and for thy sake!

SAMUEL TAYLOR COLERIDGE
[1772–1834]

Kubla Khan

OR A VISION IN A DREAM. A FRAGMENT

In Xanadu did Kubla Khan
A stately pleasure dome decree:
Where Alph, the sacred river, ran
Through caverns measureless to man
   Down to a sunless sea.   5

So twice five miles of fertile ground
With walls and towers were girdled round:
And there were gardens bright with sinuous rills,
Where blossomed many an incense-bearing tree;

KUBLA KHAN   the first ruler of the Mongol dynasty in thirteenth-century China. Coleridge's topography and
place names are imaginary.

And here were forests ancient as the hills, 10
Enfolding sunny spots of greenery.

But oh! that deep romantic chasm which slanted
Down the green hill athwart a cedarn cover!
A savage place! as holy and enchanted
As e'er beneath a waning moon was haunted 15
By woman wailing for her demon lover!
And from this chasm, with ceaseless turmoil seething,
As if this earth in fast thick pants were breathing,
A mighty fountain momently was forced:
Amid whose swift half-intermitted burst 20
Huge fragments vaulted like rebounding hail,
Or chaffy grain beneath the thresher's flail:
And 'mid these dancing rocks at once and ever
It flung up momently the sacred river.
Five miles meandering with a mazy motion 25
Through wood and dale the sacred river ran,
Then reached the caverns measureless to man,
And sank in tumult to a lifeless ocean:
And 'mid this tumult Kubla heard from far
Ancestral voices prophesying war! 30

　　The shadow of the dome of pleasure
　　Floated midway on the waves;
　　Where was heard the mingled measure
　　From the fountain and the caves.
It was a miracle of rare device, 35
A sunny pleasure dome with caves of ice!

　　A damsel with a dulcimer
　　In a vision once I saw:
　　It was an Abyssinian maid,
　　And on her dulcimer she played, 40
　　Singing of Mount Abora.
　　Could I revive within me
　　Her symphony and song,
　　To such a deep delight 'twould win me,
That with music loud and long, 45
I would build that dome in air,
That sunny dome! those caves of ice!
And all who heard should see them there,
And all should cry, Beware! Beware!
His flashing eyes, his floating hair! 50
Weave a circle round him thrice,
And close your eyes with holy dread,
For he on honey-dew hath fed,
And drunk the milk of Paradise.

GEORGE GORDON, LORD BYRON
[1788–1824]

She walks in beauty

1

She walks in beauty, like the night
  Of cloudless climes and starry skies;
And all that's best of dark and bright
  Meet in her aspect and her eyes:
Thus mellowed to that tender light   5
  Which heaven to gaudy day denies.

2

One shade the more, one ray the less,
  Had half impaired the nameless grace
Which waves in every raven tress,
  Or softly lightens o'er her face;   10
Where thoughts serenely sweet express
  How pure, how dear their dwelling place.

3

And on that cheek, and o'er that brow,
  So soft, so calm, yet eloquent,
The smiles that win, the tints that glow,   15
  But tell of days in goodness spent,
A mind at peace with all below,
  A heart whose love is innocent!

PERCY BYSSHE SHELLEY
[1792–1822]

Ozymandias

I met a traveler from an antique land
Who said: Two vast and trunkless legs of stone
Stand in the desert . . . Near them, on the sand,

OZYMANDIAS   *Greek name for the Egyptian ruler Rameses II, who erected a huge statue in his own likeness.*

Half sunk, a shattered visage lies, whose frown,
And wrinkled lip, and sneer of cold command,   5
Tell that its sculptor well those passions read
Which yet survive, stamped on these lifeless things,
The hand that mocked them, and the heart that fed:
And on the pedestal these words appear:
"My name is Ozymandias, king of kings: 10
Look on my works, ye Mighty, and despair!"
Nothing beside remains. Round the decay
Of that colossal wreck, boundless and bare
The lone and level sands stretch far away.

Ode to the West Wind

1

O wild West Wind, thou breath of Autumn's being,
Thou, from whose unseen presence the leaves dead
Are driven, like ghosts from an enchanter fleeing,

Yellow, and black, and pale, and hectic red,
Pestilence-stricken multitudes: O thou,   5
Who chariotest to their dark wintry bed

The wingéd seeds, where they lie cold and low,
Each like a corpse within its grave, until
Thine azure sister of the Spring shall blow

Her clarion° o'er the dreaming earth, and fill   trumpet call   10
(Driving sweet buds like flocks to feed in air)
With living hues and odors plain and hill:

Wild Spirit, which art moving everywhere;
Destroyer and preserver; hear, oh, hear!

2

Thou on whose stream, mid the steep sky's commotion,   15
Loose clouds like earth's decaying leaves are shed,
Shook from the tangled boughs of Heaven and Ocean,

Angels° of rain and lightning: there are spread   messengers
On the blue surface of thine aëry surge,
Like the bright hair uplifted from the head   20

Of some fierce Maenad, even from the dim verge
Of the horizon to the zenith's height,
The locks of the approaching storm. Thou dirge

Of the dying year, to which this closing night   25
Will be the dome of a vast sepulcher,
Vaulted with all thy congregated might

Of vapors, from whose solid atmosphere
Black rain, and fire, and hail will burst: oh, hear!

3

Thou who didst waken from his summer dreams
The blue Mediterranean, where he lay,   30
Lulled by the coil of his crystálline streams,

Beside a pumice isle in Baiae's bay,
And saw in sleep old palaces and towers
Quivering within the wave's intenser day,

All overgrown with azure moss and flowers   35
So sweet, the sense faints picturing them! Thou
For whose path the Atlantic's level powers

Cleave themselves into chasms, while far below
The sea-blooms and the oozy woods which wear
The sapless foliage of the ocean, know   40

Thy voice, and suddenly grow gray with fear,
And tremble and despoil themselves: oh, hear!

4

If I were a dead leaf thou mightest bear;
If I were a swift cloud to fly with thee;
A wave to pant beneath thy power, and share   45

The impulse of thy strength, only less free
Than thou, O uncontrollable! If even
I were as in my boyhood, and could be

The comrade of thy wanderings over Heaven,
As then, when to outstrip thy skyey speed   50
Scarce seemed a vision; I would ne'er have striven

ODE TO THE WEST WIND   [21]**Maenad** *frenzied female worshipper of Dionysus, god of wine and fertility.*

As thus with thee in prayer in my sore need.
Oh, lift me as a wave, a leaf, a cloud!
I fall upon the thorns of life! I bleed!

A heavy weight of hours has chained and bowed   55
One too like thee: tameless, and swift, and proud.

5

Make me thy lyre°, even as the forest is: small harp
What if my leaves are falling like its own!
The tumult of thy mighty harmonies

Will take from both a deep, autumnal tone,   60
Sweet though in sadness. Be thou, Spirit fierce,
My spirit! Be thou me, impetuous one!

Drive my dead thoughts over the universe
Like withered leaves to quicken a new birth!
And, by the incantation of this verse,   65

Scatter, as from an unextinguished hearth
Ashes and sparks, my words among mankind!
Be through my lips to unawakened earth

The trumpet of a prophecy! O Wind,
If Winter comes, can Spring be far behind?   70

JOHN KEATS
[1795–1821]

When I have fears

When I have fears that I may cease to be
  Before my pen has gleaned my teeming brain,
Before high-pilèd books, in charact'ry°,   written symbols
  Hold like rich garners the full-ripened grain;
When I behold, upon the night's starred face,   5
  Huge cloudy symbols of a high romance,
And think that I may never live to trace
  Their shadows, with the magic hand of chance;
And when I feel, fair creature of an hour,
  That I shall never look upon thee more,   10
Never have relish in the faery° power   magical

Of unreflecting love!—then on the shore
Of the wide world I stand alone, and think
Till Love and Fame to nothingness do sink.

La Belle Dame sans Merci

O what can ail thee, Knight at arms,
    Alone and palely loitering?
The sedge has withered from the Lake
    And no birds sing!

O what can ail thee, Knight at arms,   5
    So haggard, and so woebegone?
The squirrel's granary is full
    And the harvest's done.

I see a lily on thy brow
    With anguish moist and fever dew,   10
And on thy cheeks a fading rose
    Fast withereth too.

"I met a Lady in the Meads°,   meadows
    Full beautiful, a faery's child,
Her hair was long, her foot was light   15
    And her eyes were wild.

"I made a Garland for her head,
    And bracelets too, and fragrant Zone°;   girdle
She looked at me as she did love
    And made sweet moan.   20

"I set her on my pacing steed
    And nothing else saw all day long,
For sidelong would she bend and sing
    A faery's song.

"She found me roots of relish sweet,   25
    And honey wild, and manna dew,
And sure in language strange she said
    'I love thee true.'

"She took me to her elfin grot
    And there she wept and sighed full sore,   30
And there I shut her wild wild eyes
    With kisses four.

LA BELLE DAME SANS MERCI   *the beautiful lady without mercy.*

"And there she lulléd me asleep,
 And there I dreamed, Ah Woe betide!
The latest dream I ever dreamt   35
 On the cold hill side.

"I saw pale Kings, and Princes too,
 Pale warriors, death-pale were they all;
They cried, 'La belle dame sans merci
 Hath thee in thrall!'   40

"I saw their starved lips in the gloam
 With horrid warning gapéd wide,
And I awoke, and found me here
 On the cold hill's side.

"And this is why I sojourn here,   45
 Alone and palely loitering;
Though the sedge is withered from the Lake
 And no birds sing."

Ode to a Nightingale

1

My heart aches, and a drowsy numbness pains
 My sense, as though of hemlock I had drunk,
Or emptied some dull opiate to the drains°   dregs
 One minute past, and Lethe-wards had sunk:
'Tis not through envy of thy happy lot,   5
 But being too happy in thine happiness—
  That thou, light-wingéd Dryad° of the trees,   tree nymph
   In some melodious plot
 Of beechen green, and shadows numberless,
  Singest of summer in full-throated ease.   10

2

O, for a draught of vintage! that hath been
 Cooled a long age in the deep-delvéd earth,
Tasting of Flora and the country green,
 Dance, and Provençal song, and sunburnt mirth!
O for a beaker full of the warm South,   15
 Full of the true, the blushful Hippocrene,

ODE TO A NIGHTINGALE   ²*hemlock* *opiate; poisonous in large quantities.*   ⁴*Lethe-wards*
towards Lethe, the river of forgetfulness.   ¹³*Flora* *goddess of the flowers.*   ¹⁴*Provençal song*
Provence, in southern France, home of the troubadours.   ¹⁶*true . . . Hippocrene* *wine. A fountain on Mount*
Helicon in Greece, whose waters reputedly stimulated poetic imagination.

With beaded bubbles winking at the brim,
   And purple-stainéd mouth;
That I might drink, and leave the world unseen,
   And with thee fade away into the forest dim: 20

                              3

Fade far away, dissolve, and quite forget
   What thou among the leaves hast never known,
The weariness, the fever, and the fret
   Here, where men sit and hear each other groan;
Where palsy shakes a few, sad, last gray hairs,   25
   Where youth grows pale, and specter-thin, and dies,
      Where but to think is to be full of sorrow
         And leaden-eyed despairs,
   Where Beauty cannot keep her lustrous eyes,
      Or new Love pine at them beyond tomorrow.   30

                              4

Away! away! for I will fly to thee,
   Not charioted by Bacchus and his pards,
But on the viewless° wings of Poesy,   invisible
   Though the dull brain perplexes and retards:
Already with thee! tender is the night,   35
   And haply° the Queen-Moon is on her throne,   perhaps
      Clustered around by all her starry Fays°;   fairies
         But here there is no light,
   Save what from heaven is with the breezes blown
      Through verdurous glooms and winding mossy ways.   40

                              5

I cannot see what flowers are at my feet,
   Nor what soft incense hangs upon the boughs,
But, in embalméd° darkness, guess each sweet   scented
   Wherewith the seasonable month endows
The grass, the thicket, and the fruit tree wild;   45
   White hawthorn, and the pastoral eglantine°;   sweetbriar
      Fast fading violets covered up in leaves;
         And mid-May's eldest child,
   The coming musk-rose, full of dewy wine,
      The murmurous haunt of flies on summer eves.   50

                              6

Darkling° I listen; and for many a time   in darkness
   I have been half in love with easeful Death,

<hr>

³²**Bacchus . . . pards**   *the god of wine and revelry and the leopards who drew his chariot.*

Called him soft names in many a muséd rhyme,
  To take into the air my quiet breath;
Now more than ever seems it rich to die,   55
  To cease upon the midnight with no pain,
    While thou art pouring forth thy soul abroad
      In such an ecstasy!
  Still wouldst thou sing, and I have ears in vain—
    To thy high requiem become a sod.   60

7

Thou wast not born for death, immortal Bird!
  No hungry generations tread thee down;
The voice I hear this passing night was heard
  In ancient days by emperor and clown:
Perhaps the selfsame song that found a path   65
  Through the sad heart of Ruth, when, sick for home,
    She stood in tears amid the alien corn;
      The same that ofttimes hath
  Charmed magic casements, opening on the foam
    Of perilous seas, in faery lands forlorn.   70

8

Forlorn! the very word is like a bell
  To toll me back from thee to my sole self!
Adieu! the fancy cannot cheat so well
  As she is famed to do, deceiving elf.
Adieu! adieu! thy plaintive anthem fades   75
  Past the near meadows, over the still stream,
    Up the hill side; and now 'tis buried deep
      In the next valley-glades:
  Was it a vision, or a waking dream?
    Fled is that music:—Do I wake or sleep?   80

Ode on a Grecian Urn

1

Thou still unravished bride of quietness,
  Thou foster child of silence and slow time,
Sylvan° historian, who canst thus express   woodland
  A flowery tale more sweetly than our rhyme:
What leaf-fringed legend haunts about thy shape   5
  Of deities or mortals, or of both,
    In Tempe or the dales of Arcady?

---

⁶⁶⁻⁶⁷ **Ruth . . . corn** *a Biblical heroine who worked in the harvest fields in a foreign land.*
ODE ON A GRECIAN URN   ⁷ **Tempe . . . Arcady** *in Greece, beautiful rural regions.*

What men or gods are these? What maidens loath?
What mad pursuit? What struggle to escape?
    What pipes and timbrels? What wild ecstasy?   10

2

Heard melodies are sweet, but those unheard
    Are sweeter; therefore, ye soft pipes, play on;
Not to the sensual ear, but, more endeared,
    Pipe to the spirit ditties of no tone:
Fair youth, beneath the trees, thou canst not leave   15
    Thy song, nor ever can those trees be bare;
      Bold Lover, never, never canst thou kiss,
Though winning near the goal—yet, do not grieve;
      She cannot fade, though thou hast not thy bliss,
Forever wilt thou love, and she be fair!   20

3

Ah, happy, happy boughs! that cannot shed
    Your leaves, nor ever bid the Spring adieu;
And, happy melodist, unweariéd,
    Forever piping songs forever new;
More happy love! more happy, happy love!   25
    Forever warm and still to be enjoyed,
      Forever panting, and forever young;
All breathing human passion far above,
    That leaves a heart high-sorrowful and cloyed,
      A burning forehead, and a parching tongue.   30

4

Who are these coming to the sacrifice?
    To what green altar, O mysterious priest,
Lead'st thou that heifer lowing at the skies,
    And all her silken flanks with garlands dressed?
What little town by river or sea shore,   35
    Or mountain-built with peaceful citadel,
      Is emptied of this folk, this pious morn?
And, little town, thy streets forevermore
    Will silent be; and not a soul to tell
      Why thou art desolate, can e'er return.   40

5

O Attic shape! Fair attitude! with brede°   woven pattern
    Of marble men and maidens overwrought°,   ornamented
With forest branches and the trodden weed;
    Thou, silent form, dost tease us out of thought

As doth eternity: Cold Pastoral!   45
  When old age shall this generation waste,
    Thou shalt remain, in midst of other woe
  Than ours, a friend to man, to whom thou say'st,
  "Beauty is truth, truth beauty,"—that is all
    Ye know on earth, and all ye need to know.   50

RALPH WALDO EMERSON
[1803–1882]

Concord Hymn

SUNG AT THE COMPLETION OF THE BATTLE MONUMENT, JULY 4, 1837

By the rude bridge that arched the flood,
  Their flag to April's breeze unfurled,
Here once the embattled farmers stood
  And fired the shot heard round the world.

The foe long since in silence slept;   5
  Alike the conqueror silent sleeps;
And Time the ruined bridge has swept
  Down the dark stream which seaward creeps.

On this green bank, by this soft stream,
  We set to-day a votive stone;   10
That memory may their deed redeem,
  When, like our sires, our sons are gone.

Spirit, that made those heroes dare
  To die, and leave their children free,
Bid Time and Nature gently spare   15
  The shaft we raise to them and thee.

Hamatreya

Bulkeley, Hunt, Willard, Hosmer, Meriam, Flint,
Possessed the land which rendered to their toil
Hay, corn, roots, hemp, flax, apples, wool and wood.
Each of these landlords walked amidst his farm,

CONCORD HYMN   **The Battle Monument**   *commemorated the battles of Lexington and Concord in 1775.*
HAMATREYA   *a variant of the Hindu name Maitreya.*

Saying, "T is mine, my children's and my name's.   5
How sweet the west wind sounds in my own trees!
How graceful climb those shadows on my hill!
I fancy these pure waters and the flags
Know me, as does my dog: we sympathize;
And, I affirm, my actions smack of the soil.'   10

Where are these men? Asleep beneath their grounds:
And strangers, fond as they, their furrows plough.
Earth laughs in flowers, to see her boastful boys
Earth proud, proud of the earth which is not theirs;
Who steer the plough, but cannot steer their feet   15
Clear of the grave.
They added ridge to valley, brook to pond,
And sighed for all that bounded their domain;
'This suits me for a pasture, that's my park;
We must have clay, lime, gravel, granite-ledge,   20
And misty lowland, where to go for peat.
The land is well—lies fairly to the south.
'T is good, when you have crossed the sea and back,
To find the sitfast acres where you left them.'
Ah! the hot owner sees not Death, who adds   25
Him to his land, a lump of mould the more.
Hear what the Earth says:

Earth-song

Mine and yours;
Mine, not yours.
Earth endures;   30
Stars abide—
Shine down in the old sea;
Old are the shores;
But where are old men?
I who have seen much,   35
Such have I never seen.

The lawyer's deed
Ran sure,
In tail°,   entailed
To them, and to their heirs   40
Who shall succeed,
Without fail,
Forevermore.

Here is the land,
Shaggy with wood,   45
With its old valley,
Mound and flood.

But the heritors?
Fled like the flood's foam.
The lawyer, and the laws,   50
And the kingdom,
Clean swept herefrom.

They called me theirs.
Who so controlled me;
Yet every one   55
Wished to stay, and is gone,
How am I theirs,
If they cannot hold me,
But I hold them?

When I heard the Earth-song,   60
I was no longer brave;
My avarice cooled
Like lust in the chill of the grave.

E D G A R   A L L A N   P O E
[*1809–1849*]

To Helen

Helen, thy beauty is to me
  Like those Nicean barks° of yore,   ships
That gently, o'er a perfumed sea,
  The weary, way-worn wanderer bore
  To his own native shore.   5

On desperate seas long wont to roam,
  Thy hyacinth hair, thy classic face,
Thy Naiad airs have brought me home
  To the glory that was Greece
And the grandeur that was Rome.   10

Lo! in yon brilliant window-niche
  How statue-like I see thee stand!
  The agate lamp within thy hand,
Ah! Psyche from the regions which
  Are Holy Land!   15

TO HELEN   ⁷**hyacinth hair**   *allusion to the curled hair of the slain youth Hyacinthus, beloved of Apollo.*
⁸**Naiad**   *water nymph.*

ALFRED, LORD TENNYSON
[1809–1892]

Ulysses

It little profits that an idle king,
By this still hearth, among these barren crags,
Matched with an aged wife, I mete and dole
Unequal laws unto a savage race,
That hoard, and sleep, and feed, and know not me.   5
I cannot rest from travel; I will drink
Life to the lees. All times I have enjoyed
Greatly, have suffered greatly, both with those
That loved me, and alone; on shore, and when
Through scudding drifts the rainy Hyades   10
Vext the dim sea. I am become a name;
For always roaming with a hungry heart
Much have I seen and known—cities of men
And manners°, climates, councils, governments,   customs
Myself not least, but honored of them all,—   15
And drunk delight of battle with my peers,
Far on the ringing plains of windy Troy.
I am a part of all that I have met;
Yet all experience is an arch wherethrough
Gleams that untraveled world whose margin fades   20
For ever and for ever when I move.
How dull it is to pause, to make an end,
To rust unburnished, not to shine in use!
As though to breathe were life! Life piled on life
Were all too little, and of one to me   25
Little remains; but every hour is saved
From that eternal silence, something more,
A bringer of new things; and vile it were
For some three suns to store and hoard myself,
And this gray spirit yearning in desire   30
To follow knowledge like a sinking star,
Beyond the utmost bound of human thought.
    This is my son, mine own Telemachus,
To whom I leave the scepter and the isle,
Well-loved of me, discerning to fulfill   35
This labor, by slow prudence to make mild

ULYSSES   *According to Dante (in* The Inferno, *Canto 26) Ulysses, having been away for ten years during the Trojan War, is restless upon returning to his island kingdom of Ithaca, and he persuades a band of followers to accompany him on a journey.*   [10]**Hyades**   *a constellation of stars whose rising with the sun forecasts rain.*

A rugged people, and through soft degrees
Subdue them to the useful and the good.
Most blameless is he, centered in the sphere
Of common duties, decent° not to fail   proper   40
In offices° of tenderness, and pay   duties
Meet° adoration to my household gods,   appropriate
When I am gone. He works his work, I mine.
    There lies the port; the vessel puffs her sail;
There gloom the dark, broad seas. My mariners,   45
Souls that have toiled, and wrought, and thought with me,
That ever with a frolic welcome took
The thunder and the sunshine, and opposed
Free hearts, free foreheads—you and I are old;
Old age hath yet his honor and his toil.   50
Death closes all; but something ere the end,
Some work of noble note, may yet be done,
Not unbecoming men that strove with gods.
The lights begin to twinkle from the rocks;
The long day wanes; the slow moon climbs; the deep   55
Moans round with many voices. Come, my friends,
'Tis not too late to seek a newer world.
Push off, and sitting well in order smite
The sounding furrows; for my purpose holds
To sail beyond the sunset, and the baths   60
Of all the western stars, until I die.
It may be that the gulfs will wash us down;
It may be we shall touch the Happy Isles,
And see the great Achilles, whom we knew.
Though much is taken, much abides; and though   65
We are not now that strength which in old days
Moved earth and heaven, that which we are, we are,
One equal temper of heroic hearts,
Made weak by time and fate, but strong in will
To strive, to seek, to find, and not to yield.   70

Tithonus

The woods decay, the woods decay and fall,
The vapors weep their burthen to the ground,
Man comes and tills the field and lies beneath,
And after many a summer dies the swan.
Me only cruel immortality   5
Consumes; I wither slowly in thine arms,

---

[63]**Happy Isles**   *the abode after death of those favored by the gods.*
TITHONUS   *a Trojan prince loved by the dawn goddess, Eos, who asked her for immortality but not for eternal youth.*

Here at the quiet limit of the world,
A white-haired shadow roaming like a dream
The ever-silent spaces of the East,
Far-folded mists, and gleaming halls of morn.   10
    Alas! for this gray shadow, once a man—
So glorious in his beauty and thy choice,
Who madest him thy chosen, that he seemed
To his great heart none other than a God!
I asked thee, "Give me immortality."   15
Then didst thou grant mine asking with a smile,
Like wealthy men who care not how they give.
But thy strong Hours indignant worked their wills,
And beat me down and marred and wasted me,
And though they could not end me, left me maimed   20
To dwell in presence of immortal youth.
Immortal age beside immortal youth,
And all I was in ashes. Can thy love,
Thy beauty, make amends, though even now,
Close over us, the silver star° thy guide,   morning star   25
Shines in those tremulous eyes that fill with tears
To hear me? Let me go; take back thy gift.
Why should a man desire in any way
To vary from the kindly° race of men,   natural
Or pass beyond the goal of ordinance   30
Where all should pause, as is most meet° for all?   fitting
    A soft air fans the cloud apart; there comes
A glimpse of that dark world where I was born.
Once more the old mysterious glimmer steals
From thy pure brows, and from thy shoulders pure,   35
And bosom beating with a heart renewed.
Thy cheek begins to redden through the gloom,
Thy sweet eyes brighten slowly close to mine,
Ere yet they blind the stars, and the wild team
Which love thee, yearning for thy yoke, arise,   40
And shake the darkness from their loosened manes,
And beat the twilight into flakes of fire.
    Lo! ever thus thou growest beautiful
In silence, then before thine answer given
Departest, and thy tears are on my cheek.   45
    Why wilt thou ever scare me with thy tears,
And make me tremble lest a saying learnt,
In days far-off, on that dark earth, be true?
"The Gods themselves cannot recall their gifts."
    Ay me! ay me! with what another heart   50
In days far-off, and with what other eyes
I used to watch—if I be he that watched—
The lucid outline forming round thee; saw

The dim curls kindle into sunny rings;
Changed with thy mystic change, and felt my blood   55
Glow with the glow that slowly crimsoned all
Thy presence and thy portals, while I lay,
Mouth, forehead, eyelids, growing dewy-warm
With kisses balmier than half-opening buds
Of April, and could hear the lips that kissed   60
Whispering I knew not what of wild and sweet,
Like that strange song I heard Apollo sing,
While Ilion like a mist rose into towers.
  Yet hold me not for ever in thine East;
How can my nature longer mix with thine?   65
Coldly thy rosy shadows bathe me, cold
Are all thy lights, and cold my wrinkled feet
Upon thy glimmering thresholds, when the steam
Floats up from those dim fields about the homes
Of happy men that have the power to die,   70
And grassy barrows of the happier dead.
Release me, and restore me to the ground.
Thou seest all things, thou wilt see my grave;
Thou wilt renew thy beauty morn by morn,
I earth in earth forget these empty courts,   75
And thee returning on thy silver wheels.

The Eagle

FRAGMENT

He clasps the crag with crooked hands;
Close to the sun in lonely lands,
Ringed with the azure world, he stands.

The wrinkled sea beneath him crawls;
He watches from his mountain walls,   5
And like a thunderbolt he falls.

From *In Memoriam A. H. H.*

7

Dark house, by which once more I stand
Here in the long unlovely street,

62*Like that strange song . . . Apollo sing*   The walls of Troy (Ilion) rose to the music of Apollo.
IN MEMORIAM A.H.H.   *Arthur Henry Hallam (1811–1833), who had been Tennyson's close friend, died of a stroke while on a trip with his father.*

Doors, where my heart was used to beat
So quickly, waiting for a hand,

A hand that can be clasped no more—   5
   Behold me, for I cannot sleep,
   And like a guilty thing I creep
At earliest morning to the door.

He is not here; but far away
   The noise of life begins again,   10
   And ghastly through the drizzling rain
On the bald street breaks the blank day.

130

Thy voice is on the rolling air;
   I hear thee where the waters run;
   Thou standest in the rising sun,
And in the setting thou art fair.

What are thou then? I cannot guess;   5
   But though I seem in star and flower
   To feel thee some diffusive power,
I do not therefore love thee less.

My love involves the love before;
   My love is vaster passion now;   10
   Though mixed with God and Nature thou,
I seem to love thee more and more.

Far off thou art, but ever nigh;
   I have thee still, and I rejoice;
   I prosper, circled with thy voice;   15
I shall not lose thee though I die.

ROBERT BROWNING

[1812–1889]

Soliloquy of the Spanish Cloister

1

Gr-r-r—there go, my heart's abhorrence!
   Water your damned flower-pots, do!

If hate killed men, Brother Lawrence,
　　God's blood, would not mine kill you!
What? your myrtle-bush wants trimming?　　　　5
　　Oh, that rose has prior claims—
Needs its leaden vase filled brimming?
　　Hell dry you up with its flames!

2

At the meal we sit together:
　　Salve tibi! I must hear　　　　　　　　10
Wise talk of the kind of weather,
　　Sort of season, time of year:
Not a plenteous cork-crop: scarcely
　　Dare we hope oak-galls, I doubt:
What's the Latin name for "parsley"?　　　15
　　What's the Greek name for Swine's Snout?

3

Whew! We'll have our platter burnished,
　　Laid with care on our own shelf!
With a fire-new spoon we're furnished,
　　And a goblet for ourself,　　　　　　　20
Rinsed like something sacrificial
　　Ere 'tis fit to touch our chaps—
Marked with L for our initial!
　　(He-he! There his lily snaps!)

4

Saint, forsooth! While brown Dolores　　25
　　Squats outside the Convent bank
With Sanchicha, telling stories,
　　Steeping tresses in the tank,
Blue-black, lustrous, thick like horsehairs,
　　—Can't I see his dead eye glow,　　　30
Bright as 'twere a Barbary corsair's?
　　(That is, if he'd let it show!)

5

When he finishes refection°,　　　　　　　dinner
　　Knife and fork he never lays
Cross-wise, to my recollection,　　　　　　35
　　As do I, in Jesu's praise.
I the Trinity illustrate,

SOLILOQUY OF THE SPANISH CLOISTER　　⁴**God's blood**　*an oath.*　　¹⁰**Salve tibi**　*Hail to thee!*　　¹⁴**oak-galls**　*growths produced on oak leaves by gallflies.*　　³¹**Barbary corsair's**　*pirate's.*

Drinking watered orange-pulp—
In three sips the Arian frustrate;
While he drains his at one gulp.   40

6

Oh, those melons? If he's able
We're to have a feast! so nice!
One goes to the Abbot's table,
All of us get each a slice.
How go on your flowers? None double?   45
Not one fruit-sort can you spy?
Strange! And I, too, at such trouble,
Keep them close-nipped on the sly!

7

There's a great text in Galatians,
Once you trip on it, entails   50
Twenty-nine distinct damnations,
One sure, if another fails:
If I trip him just a-dying,
Sure of heaven as sure can be,
Spin him around and send him flying   55
Off to hell, a Manichee?

8

Or, my scrofulous French novel
On grey paper with blunt type!
Simply glance at it, you grovel
Hand and foot in Belial's gripe: 60
If I double down its pages
At the woeful sixteenth print,
When he gathers his greengages,
Ope a sieve and slip it in't?

9

Or, there's Satan! one might venture   65
Pledge one's soul to him, yet leave
Such a flaw in the indenture
As he'd miss till, past retrieve,
Blasted lay that rose-acacia
We're so proud of! *Hy, Zy, Hine* . . .   70

---

[39]**Arian** *Arius, a fourth-century heretic, denied the doctrine of the Trinity.* [49]**Galatians** *a New Testament epistle of St. Paul; see Chapter 5, 14–15 and 16–24.* [56]**Manichee** *The Manichean heresy divided the world into two equally powerful forces of darkness (evil) and light (good).* [60]**Belial's gripe** *in the devil's grip.* [70]**Hy, Zy, Hine** *an incantation.*

'St, there's vespers! *Plena gratiâ*
Ave, Virgo! Gr-r-r—you swine!

EMILY BRONTË

[1814–1888]

Remembrance

Cold in the earth—and the deep snow piled above thee,
Far, far removed, cold in the dreary grave!
Have I forgot, my only Love, to love thee,
Severed at last by Time's all-severing wave?

Now, when alone, do my thoughts no longer hover   5
Over the mountains, on that northern shore,
Resting their wings where heath and fern leaves cover
Thy noble heart forever, ever more?

Cold in the earth—and fifteen wild Decembers,
From those brown hills, have melted into spring;   10
Faithful, indeed, is the spirit that remembers
After such years of change and suffering!

Sweet Love of youth, forgive, if I forget thee,
While the world's tide is bearing me along;
Other desires and other hopes beset me,   15
Hopes which obscure, but cannot do thee wrong!

No later light has lightened up my heaven,
No second morn has ever shone for me;
All my life's bliss from thy dear life was given,
All my life's bliss is in the grave with thee.   20

But, when the days of golden dreams had perished,
And even Despair was powerless to destroy,
Then did I learn how existence could be cherished,
Strengthened, and fed without the aid of joy.

Then did I check the tears of useless passion—   25
Weaned my young soul from yearning after thine;
Sternly denied its burning wish to hasten
Down to that tomb already more than mine.

[71]*Plena gratiâ*   *Full of grace.*   [72]*Ave, Virgo*   *Hail Virgin (reverses the opening words of the* Ave Maria*).*

And, even yet, I dare not let it languish,
Dare not indulge in memory's rapturous pain;   30
Once drinking deep of that divinest anguish,
How could I seek the empty world again?

WALT WHITMAN
[1819–1892]

A noiseless patient spider

A noiseless patient spider,
I mark'd where on a little promontory it stood isolated,
Mark'd how to explore the vacant vast surrounding,
It launch'd forth filament, filament, filament, out of itself,
Ever unreeling them, ever tirelessly speeding them.   5

And you O my soul where you stand,
Surrounded, detached, in measureless oceans of space,
Ceaselessly musing, venturing, throwing, seeking the spheres to connect them,
Till the bridge you will need be form'd, till the ductile anchor hold,
Till the gossamer thread you fling catch somewhere, O my soul. 10

Vigil strange I kept on the field one night

Vigil strange I kept on the field one night;
When you my son and my comrade dropt at my side that day,
One look I but gave which your dear eyes return'd with a look I shall never forget,
One touch of your hand to mine O boy, reach'd up as you lay on the ground,
Then onward I sped in the battle, the even-contested battle,   5
Till late in the night reliev'd to the place at last again I made my way,
Found you in death so cold dear comrade, found your body son of responding kisses,
    (never again on earth responding,)
Bared your face in the starlight, curious the scene, cool blew the moderate night-wind,
Long there and then in vigil I stood, dimly around me the battle-field spreading,
Vigil wondrous and vigil sweet there in the fragrant silent night, 10
But not a tear fell, not even a long-drawn sigh, long I gazed,
Then on the earth partially reclining sat by your side leaning my chin in my hands,
Passing sweet hours, immortal and mystic hours with you dearest comrade—not a tear,
    not a word,
Vigil of silence, love and death, vigil for you my son and my soldier,
As onward silently stars aloft, eastward new ones upward stole,   15
Vigil final for you brave boy, (I could not save you, swift was your death,

I faithfully loved you and cared for you living, I think we shall surely meet again,)
Till at latest lingering of the night, indeed just as the dawn appear'd,
My comrade I wrapt in his blanket, envelop'd well his form,
Folded the blanket well, tucking it carefully over head and carefully under feet, 20
And there and then and bathed by the rising sun, my son in his grave, in his rude-dug
    grave I deposited,
Ending my vigil strange with that, vigil of night and battle-field dim,
Vigil for boy of responding kisses, (never again on earth responding,)
Vigil for comrade swiftly slain, vigil I never forget, how as day brighten'd,
I rose from the chill ground and folded my soldier well in his blanket, 25
And buried him where he fell.

The Dalliance of the Eagles

Skirting the river road, (my forenoon walk, my rest,)
Skyward in air a sudden muffled sound, the dalliance of the eagles,
The rushing amorous contact high in space together,
The clinching interlocking claws, a living, fierce, gyrating wheel,
Four beating wings, two beaks, a swirling mass tight grappling, 5
In tumbling turning clustering loops, straight downward falling,
Till o'er the river pois'd, the twain yet one, a moment's lull,
A motionless still balance in the air, then parting, talons loosing,
Upward again on slow-firm pinions slanting, their separate diverse flight, 10
She hers, he his, pursuing.

Crossing Brooklyn Ferry

1

Flood-tide below me! I see you face to face!
Clouds of the west—sun there half an hour high—I see you also face to face.
Crowds of men and women attired in the usual costumes, how curious you are to me!
On the ferry-boats the hundreds and hundreds that cross, returning home, are more
    curious to me than you suppose,
And you that shall cross from shore to shore years hence are more to me, and more
    in my meditations, than you might suppose. 5

2

The impalpable sustenance of me from all things at all hours of the day,
The simple, compact, well-join'd scheme, myself disintegrated, every one disintegrated
    yet part of the scheme,
The similitudes of the past and those of the future,
The glories strung like beads on my smallest sights and hearings, on the walk in the
    street and the passage over the river,

The current rushing so swiftly and swimming with me far away,   10
The others that are to follow me, the ties between me and them,
The certainty of others, the life, love, sight, hearing of others.

Others will enter the gates of the ferry and cross from shore to shore,
Others will watch the run of the flood-tide,
Others will see the shipping of Manhattan north and west, and the heights of Brooklyn
    to the south and east,   15
Others will see the islands large and small;
Fifty years hence, others will see them as they cross, the sun half an hour high,
A hundred years hence, or ever so many hundred years hence, others will see them,
Will enjoy the sunset, the pouring-in of the flood-tide, the falling-back to the sea of
    the ebb-tide.

3

It avails not, time nor place—distance avails not,   20
I am with you, you men and women of a generation, or ever so many generations hence,
Just as you feel when you look on the river and sky, so I felt,
Just as any of you is one of a living crowd, I was one of a crowd,
Just as you are refresh'd by the gladness of the river and the bright flow, I was refresh'd,
Just as you stand and lean on the rail, yet hurry with the swift current, I stood yet was
    hurried,   25
Just as you look on the numberless masts of ships and the thick-stemm'd pipes of
    steamboats, I look'd.

I too many and many a time cross'd the river of old,
Watched the Twelfth-month° sea-gulls, saw them high in the air floating   December
    with motionless wings, oscillating their bodies,
Saw how the glistening yellow lit up parts of their bodies and left the rest in strong
    shadow,
Saw the slow-wheeling circles and the gradual edging toward the south,   30
Saw the reflection of the summer sky in the water,
Had my eyes dazzled by the shimmering track of beams,
Look'd at the fine centrifugal spokes of light round the shape of my head in the sunlit
    water,
Look'd on the haze on the hills southward and south-westward,
Look'd on the vapor as it flew in fleeces tinged with violet,   35
Look'd toward the lower bay to notice the vessels arriving,
Saw their approach, saw aboard those that were near me,
Saw the white sails of schooners and sloops, saw the ships at anchor,
The sailors at work in the rigging or out astride the spars,
The round masts, the swinging motion of the hulls, the slender serpentine   40
    pennants,
The large and small steamers in motion, the pilots in their pilot-houses,
The white wake left by the passage, the quick tremulous whirl of the wheels,
The flags of all nations, the falling of them at sunset,

The scallop-edged waves in the twilight, the ladled cups, the frolicsome crests and glistening,
The stretch afar growing dimmer and dimmer, the gray walls of the granite storehouses by the docks,   45
On the river the shadowy group, the big steam-tug closely flank'd on each side by the barges, the hay-boat, the belated lighter,
On the neighboring shore the fires from the foundry chimneys burning high and glaringly into the night,
Casting their flicker of black contrasted with wild red and yellow light over the tops of houses, and down into the clefts of streets.

4

These and all else were to me the same as they are to you,
I loved well those cities, loved well the stately and rapid river,   50
The men and women I saw were all near to me,
Others the same—others who look back on me because I look'd forward to them,
(The time will come, though I stop° here to-day and to-night.)   stay

5

What is it then between us?
What is the count of the scores or hundreds of years between us?   55

Whatever it is, it avails not—distance avails not, and place avails not,
I too lived, Brooklyn of ample hills was mine,
I too walk'd the streets of Manhattan island, and bathed in the waters around it,
I too felt the curious abrupt questionings stir within me,
In the day among crowds of people sometimes they came upon me,   60
In my walks home late at night or as I lay in my bed they came upon me,
I too had been struck from the float forever held in solution,
I too had receiv'd identity by my body,
That I was I knew was of my body, and what I should be I knew I should be of my body.

6

It is not upon you alone the dark patches fall,   65
The dark threw its patches down upon me also,
The best I had done seem'd to me blank and suspicious,
My great thoughts as I supposed them, were they not in reality meager?
Nor is it you alone who know what it is to be evil,
I am he who knew what it was to be evil,   70
I too knitted the old knot of contrariety,
Blabb'd, blush'd, resented, lied, stole, grudg'd,
Had guile, anger, lust, hot wishes I dared not speak,
Was wayward, vain, greedy, shallow, sly, cowardly, malignant,
The wolf, the snake, the hog, not wanting in me,   75

The cheating look, the frivolous word, the adulterous wish, not wanting,
Refusals, hates, postponements, meanness, laziness, none of these wanting,
Was one with the rest, the days and haps of the rest,
Was call'd by my nighest name by clear loud voices of young men as they saw me
    approaching or passing,
Felt their arms on my neck as I stood, or the negligent leaning of their flesh against
    me as I sat,   80
Saw many I loved in the street or ferry-boat or public assembly, yet never told them
    a word,
Lived the same life with the rest, the same old laughing, gnawing, sleeping,
Play'd the part that still looks back on the actor or actress,
The same old role, the role that is what we make it, as great as we like,
Or as small as we like, or both great and small.   85

7

Closer yet I approach you,
What thought you have of me now, I had as much of you—I laid in my stores in
    advance,
I consider'd long and seriously of you before you were born.

Who was to know what should come home to me?
Who knows but I am enjoying this?   90
Who knows, for all the distance, but I am as good as looking at you now, for all you
    cannot see me?

8

Ah, what can ever be more stately and admirable to me than mast-hemm'd Manhattan?
River and sunset and scallop-edg'd waves of flood-tide?
The sea-gulls oscillating their bodies, the hay-boat in the twilight, and the belated
    lighter?
What gods can exceed these that clasp me by the hand, and with voices I love call me
    promptly and loudly by my nighest name as I approach?   95
What is more subtle than this which ties me to the woman or man that looks in my
    face?
Which fuses me into you now, and pours my meaning into you?

We understand then do we not?
What I promis'd without mentioning it, have you not accepted?
What the study could not teach—what the preaching could not accomplish is accom-
    plish'd, is it not?   100

9

Flow on, river! flow with the flood-tide, and ebb with the ebb-tide!
Frolic on, crested and scallop-edg'd waves!
Gorgeous clouds of the sunset! drench with your splendor me, or the men and women
    generations after me!
Cross from shore to shore, countless crowds of passengers!

Stand up, tall masts of Mannahatta! stand up, beautiful hills of Brooklyn!   105
Throb, baffled and curious brain! throw out questions and answers!
Suspend here and everywhere, eternal float of solution!
Gaze, loving and thirsting eyes, in the house or street or public assembly!
Sound out, voices of young men! loudly and musically call me by my nighest name!
Live, old life! play the part that looks back on the actor or actress!   110
Play the old role, the role that is great or small according as one makes it!
Consider, you who peruse me, whether I may not in unknown ways be looking upon
     you;
Be firm, rail over the river, to support those who lean idly, yet haste with the hasting
     current;
Fly on, sea birds! fly sideways, or wheel in large circles high in the air;
Receive the summer sky, you water, and faithfully hold it till all downcast eyes have
     time to take it from you!   115
Diverge, fine spokes of light, from the shape of my head, or any one's head, in the sunlit
     water!
Come on, ships from the lower bay! pass up or down, white-sail'd schooners, sloops,
     lighters!
Flaunt away, flags of all nations! be duly lower'd at sunset!
Burn high your fires, foundry chimneys! cast black shadows at nightfall! cast red and
     yellow light over the tops of the houses!
Appearances, now or henceforth, indicate what you are,   120
You necessary film, continue to envelop the soul,
About my body for me, and your body for you, be hung our divinest aromas,
Thrive, cities—bring your freight, bring your shows, ample and sufficient rivers,
Expand, being than which none else is perhaps more spiritual,
Keep your places, objects than which none else is more lasting.   125

You have waited, you always wait, you dumb, beautiful ministers,
We receive you with free sense at last, and are insatiate henceforward,
Not you any more shall be able to foil us, or withhold yourselves from us,
We use you, and do not cast you aside—we plant you permanently within us,
We fathom you not—we love you—there is perfection in you also,   130
You furnish your parts toward eternity,
Great or small, you furnish your parts toward the soul.

MATTHEW ARNOLD

[*1822–1888*]

Dover Beach

       The sea is calm tonight.
       The tide is full, the moon lies fair

DOVER BEACH   See Sophocles, Antigone, *ll. 583–591.*

Upon the straits; on the French coast the light
Gleams and is gone; the cliffs of England stand,
Glimmering and vast, out in the tranquil bay.   5
Come to the window, sweet is the night-air!
Only, from the long line of spray
Where the sea meets the moon-blanched land,
Listen! you hear the grating roar
Of pebbles which the waves draw back, and fling,   10
At their return, up the high strand,
Begin, and cease, and then again begin,
With tremulous cadence slow, and bring
The eternal note of sadness in.

Sophocles long ago   15
Heard it on the Aegean, and it brought
Into his mind the turbid ebb and flow
Of human misery; we
Find also in the sound a thought,
Hearing it by this distant northern sea.   20

The Sea of Faith
Was once, too, at the full, and round earth's shore
Lay like the folds of a bright girdle furled.
But now I only hear
Its melancholy, long, withdrawing roar,   25
Retreating, to the breath
Of the night-wind, down the vast edges drear
And naked shingles of the world.

Ah, love, let us be true
To one another! for the world, which seems   30
To lie before us like a land of dreams,
So various, so beautiful, so new,
Hath really neither joy, nor love, nor light,
Nor certitude, nor peace, nor help for pain;
And we are here as on a darkling plain   35
Swept with confused alarms of struggle and flight,
Where ignorant armies clash by night.

EMILY DICKINSON
[1830–1886]

A narrow Fellow in the Grass

A narrow Fellow in the Grass
Occasionally rides—
You may have met Him—did you not
His notice sudden is—

The Grass divides as with a Comb—   5
A spotted shaft is seen—
And then it closes at your feet
And opens further on—

He likes a Boggy Acre
A Floor too cool for Corn—   10
Yet when a Boy, and Barefoot—
I more than once at Noon

Have passed, I thought, a Whip lash
Unbraiding in the Sun
When stopping to secure it   15
It wrinkled, and was gone—

Several of Nature's People
I know, and they know me—
I feel for them a transport
Of cordiality—   20

But never met this Fellow
Attended, or alone
Without a tighter breathing
And Zero at the Bone—

I like a look of Agony

I like a look of Agony,
Because I know it's true—
Men do not sham Convulsion,
Nor simulate, a Throe—

The Eyes glaze once—and that is Death—
Impossible to feign
The Beads upon the Forehead
By homely Anguish strung.   5

Wild Nights—Wild Nights

Wild Nights—Wild Nights!
Were I with thee
Wild Nights should be
Our luxury!

Futile—the Winds—   5
To a Heart in port—
Done with the Compass—
Done with the Chart!

Rowing in Eden—
Ah, the Sea!   10
Might I but moor—Tonight—
In Thee!

After great pain, a formal feeling comes

After great pain, a formal feeling comes—
The Nerves sit ceremonious, like Tombs—
The stiff Heart questions was it He, that bore,
And Yesterday, or Centuries before?

The Feet, mechanical, go round—   5
Of Ground, or Air, or Ought—
A Wooden way
Regardless grown,
A Quartz contentment, like a stone—

This is the Hour of Lead—   10
Remembered, if outlived,
As Freezing persons, recollect the Snow—
First—Chill—then Stupor—then the letting go—

Much Madness is divinest Sense

Much Madness is divinest Sense—
To a discerning Eye—
Much Sense—the starkest Madness—
'Tis the Majority
In this, as All, prevail—   5
Assent—and you are sane—
Demur—you're straightway dangerous—
And handled with a Chain—

I died for Beauty—but was scarce

I died for Beauty—but was scarce
Adjusted in the Tomb
When One who died for Truth, was lain
In an adjoining Room—

He questioned softly "Why I failed?"   5
"For Beauty," I replied—
"And I—for Truth—Themself are One—
We Brethren, are," He said—

And so, as Kinsmen, met a Night—
We talked between the Rooms—   10
Until the Moss had reached our lips—
And covered up—our names—

I heard a Fly buzz—when I died

I heard a Fly buzz—when I died—
The Stillness in the Room
Was like the Stillness in the Air—
Between the Heaves of Storm—

The Eyes around—had wrung them dry—   5
And Breaths were gathering firm
For that last Onset—when the King
Be witnessed—in the Room—

I willed my Keepsakes—Signed away
What portion of me be   10

Assignable—and then it was
There interposed a Fly—

With Blue—uncertain stumbling Buzz—
Between the light—and me—
And then the Windows failed—and then   15
I could not see to see—

The Bustle in a House

The Bustle in a House
The Morning after Death
Is solemnest of industries
Enacted upon Earth—

The Sweeping up the Heart   5
And putting Love away
We shall not want to use again
Until Eternity.

Tell all the Truth but tell it slant

Tell all the Truth but tell it slant—
Success in Circuit lies
Too bright for our infirm Delight
The Truth's superb surprise

As Lightning to the Children eased   5
With explanation kind
The Truth must dazzle gradually
Or every man be blind—

Apparently with no surprise

Apparently with no surprise
To any happy Flower
The Frost beheads it at its play—
In accidental power—
The blonde Assassin passes on—   5
The Sun proceeds unmoved
To measure off another Day
For an Approving God.

LEWIS CARROLL (CHARLES LUTWIDGE DODGSON)

[1832–1898]

Jabberwocky

'Twas brillig, and the slithy toves
    Did gyre and gimble in the wabe:
All mimsy were the borogoves,
    And the mome raths outgrabe.

"Beware the Jabberwock, my son!   5
    The jaws that bite, the claws that catch!
Beware the Jubjub bird, and shun
    The frumious Bandersnatch!"

He took his vorpal sword in hand:
    Long time the manxome foe he sought—   10
So rested he by the Tumtum tree,
    And stood awhile in thought.

And, as in uffish thought he stood,
    The Jabberwock, with eyes of flame,
Came whiffling through the tulgey wood,   15
    And burbled as it came!

One, two! One, two! And through and through
    The vorpal blade went snicker-snack!
He left it dead, and with its head
    He went galumphing back.   20

"And hast thou slain the Jabberwock?
    Come to my arms, my beamish boy!
O frabjous day! Callooh! Callay!"
    He chortled in his joy.

'Twas brillig, and the slithy toves   25
    Did gyre and gimble in the wabe:
All mimsy were the borogoves,
    And the mome raths outgrabe.

THOMAS HARDY
[1840–1928]

The Darkling Thrush

I leant upon a coppice gate
    When Frost was specter-gray,
And Winter's dregs made desolate
    The weakening eye of day.
The tangled bine-stems scored the sky   5
    Like strings of broken lyres,
And all mankind that haunted nigh
    Had sought their household fires.

The land's sharp features seemed to be
    The Century's corpse outleant°,   stretched out   10
His crypt the cloudy canopy,
    The wind his death-lament.
The ancient pulse of germ and birth
    Was shrunken hard and dry,
And every spirit upon earth   15
    Seemed fervorless as I.

At once a voice arose among
    The bleak twigs overhead
In a full-hearted evensong
    Of joy illimited;   20
An aged thrush, frail, gaunt, and small,
    In blast-beruffled plume,
Had chosen thus to fling his soul
    Upon the growing gloom.

So little cause for carolings   25
    Of such ecstatic sound
Was written on terrestrial things
    Afar or night around,
That I could think there trembled through
    His happy good-night air   30
Some blessed Hope, whereof he knew
    And I was unaware.

THE DARKLING THRUSH   ¹coppice thicket or small woods.   ⁵bine-stems shoots of a climbing
plant or vine.

The Ruined Maid

"O'Melia, my dear, this does everything crown!
Who could have supposed I should meet you in Town?
And whence such fair garments, such prosperi–ty?"
"O didn't you know I'd been ruined?" said she.

"You left us in tatters, without shoes or socks,   5
Tired of digging potatoes, and spudding up docks;
And now you've gay bracelets and bright feathers three!"
"Yes: that's how we dress when we're ruined," said she.

"At home in the barton° you said 'thee' and 'thou,'   farm
And 'thik oon,' and 'theäs oon,' and 't'other'; but now   10
Your talking quite fits 'ee for high compa–ny!"
"Some polish is gained with one's ruin," said she.

"Your hands were like paws then, your face blue and bleak
But now I'm bewitched by your delicate cheek,
And your little gloves fit as on any la–dy!"   15
"We never do work when we're ruined," said she.

"You used to call home-life a hag-ridden dream,
And you'd sigh, and you'd sock; but at present you seem
To know not of megrims° or melancho–ly!"   low spirits
"True. One's pretty lively when ruined," said she.   20

"I wish I had feathers, a fine sweeping gown,
And a delicate face, and could strut about Town!"
"My dear—a raw country girl, such as you be,
Cannot quite expect that. You ain't ruined," said she.

The Oxen

Christmas Eve, and twelve of the clock.
   "Now they are all on their knees,"
An elder said as we sat in a flock
   By the embers in hearthside ease.

We pictured the meek mild creatures where   5
   They dwelt in their strawy pen,

THE OXEN   ¹⁻²*Christmas . . . knees*   *Legend has it that at midnight on Christmas Eve all creatures
knelt in prayer and adoration.*

    Nor did it occur to one of us there
      To doubt they were kneeling then.

So fair a fancy few would weave
    In these years! Yet, I feel,   10
If someone said on Christmas Eve,
    "Come; see the oxen kneel,

"In the lonely barton° by yonder coomb   farm/valley
    Our childhood used to know,"
I should go with him in the gloom,   15
    Hoping it might be so.

The Voice

Woman much missed, how you call to me, call to me,
Saying that now you are not as you were
When you had changed from the one who was all to me,
But as at first, when our day was fair.

Can it be you that I hear? Let me view you, then,   5
Standing as when I drew near to the town
Where you would wait for me: yes, as I knew you then,
Even to the original air-blue gown!

Or is it only the breeze, in its listlessness
Traveling across the wet mead to me here,   10
You being ever dissolved to wan wistlessness,
Heard no more again far or near?

    Thus I; faltering forward,
    Leaves around me falling,
Wind oozing thin through the thorn from norward.   15
    And the woman calling.

Transformations

    Portion of this yew
    Is a man my grandsire knew,
    Bosomed here at its foot:
    This branch may be his wife,
    A ruddy human life   5
    Now turned to a green shoot.

These grasses must be made
Of her who often prayed,
Last century, for repose;
And the fair girl long ago   10
Whom I often tried to know
May be entering this rose.

So, they are not underground,
But as nerves and veins abound
In the growths of upper air,   15
And they feel the sun and rain,
And the energy again
That made them what they were!

Channel Firing

That night your great guns, unawares,
Shook all our coffins as we lay,
And broke the chancel window-squares,
We thought it was the Judgment-day

And sat upright. While drearisome   5
Arose the howl of wakened hounds:
The mouse let fall the altar-crumb,
The worms drew back into the mounds,

The glebe° cow drooled. Till God called, "No;   small field
It's gunnery practice out at sea   10
Just as before you went below;
The world is as it used to be:

"All nations striving strong to make
Red war yet redder. Mad as hatters
They do no more for Christés sake   15
Than you who are helpless in such matters.

"That this is not the judgment-hour
For some of them's a blessed thing,
For if it were they'd have to scour
Hell's floor for so much threatening. . . .   20

"Ha, ha. It will be warmer when
I blow the trumpet (if indeed
I ever do; for you are men,
And rest eternal sorely need)."

So down we lay again. "I wonder,
Will the world ever saner be,"
Said one, "than when He sent us under
In our indifferent century!"　　　　　　　　　　25

And many a skeleton shook his head.
"Instead of preaching forty year,"　　　　　　30
My neighbor Parson Thirdly said,
"I wish I had stuck to pipes and beer."

Again the guns disturbed the hour,
Roaring their readiness to avenge,
As far inland as Stourton Tower,　　　　　　　35
And Camelot, and starlit Stonehenge.

Ah, are you digging on my grave

"Ah, are you digging on my grave,
　　My loved one?—planting rue?"
—"No: yesterday he went to wed
One of the brightest wealth has bred.
'It cannot hurt her now,' he said,　　　　　　5
　　'That I should not be true.' "

"Then who is digging on my grave?
　　My nearest dearest kin?"
—"Ah, no: they sit and think, 'What use!
What good will planting flowers produce?　　　10
No tendance of her mound can loose
　　Her spirit from Death's gin.' "

"But some one digs upon my grave?
　　My enemy?—prodding sly?"
—"Nay: When she heard you had passed the Gate　　15
That shuts on all flesh soon or late,
She thought you no more worth her hate,
　　And cares not where you lie."

"Then, who is digging on my grave?
　　Say—since I have not guessed!"　　　　　　20
—"O it is I, my mistress dear,
Your little dog, who still lives near,
And much I hope my movements here
　　Have not disturbed your rest?"

CHANNEL FIRING　　[36]**Stonehenge**　*a circular grouping of stone monuments near Salisbury, England,
dating back to the Bronze Age.*

"Ah, yes! *You* dig upon my grave . . .   25
    Why flashed it not on me
That one true heart was left behind!
What feeling do we ever find
To equal among human kind
    A dog's fidelity!"   30

"Mistress, I dug upon your grave
    To bury a bone, in case
I should be hungry near this spot
When passing on my daily trot.
I am sorry, but I quite forgot   35
    It was your resting-place."

GERARD MANLEY HOPKINS
[1844–1889]

God's Grandeur

The world is charged with the grandeur of God.
    It will flame out, like shining from shook foil;
    It gathers to a greatness, like the ooze of oil
Crushed. Why do men then now not reck his rod?
Generations have trod, have trod, have trod;   5
    And all is seared with trade; bleared, smeared with toil;
    And wears man's smudge and shares man's smell: the soil
Is bare now, nor can foot feel, being shod.

And for all this, nature is never spent;
    There lives the dearest freshness deep down things;   10
And though the last lights off the black West went
    Oh, morning, at the brown brink eastward, springs—
Because the Holy Ghost over the bent
    World broods with warm breast and with ah! bright wings.

The Windhover

TO CHRIST OUR LORD

I caught this morning morning's minion°, king-   darling
    dom of daylight's dauphin°, dapple-dawn-drawn Falcon, in his   prince
        riding

GOD'S GRANDEUR   ²*foil* *gold or tinsel foil.*   ⁴**Crushed** *as when olives are crushed for their oil.*
THE WINDHOVER *a kestrel, a kind of falcon.*

Of the rolling level underneath him steady air, and striding
High there, how he rung upon the rein of a wimpling° wing   rippling
In his ecstasy! then off, off forth on swing,   5
    As a skate's heel sweeps smooth on a bow-bend: the hurl and gliding
    Rebuffed the big wind. My heart in hiding
Stirred for a bird,—the achieve of, the mastery of the thing!

Brute beauty and valour and act, oh, air, pride, plume, here
    Buckle! AND the fire that breaks from thee then, a billion
Times told lovelier, more dangerous, O my chevalier°!   knight   10

No wonder of it: shéer plód makes plough down sillion°   furrow
Shine, and blue-bleak embers, ah my dear,
    Fall, gall themselves, and gash gold-vermilion.

Pied° Beauty   *variegated*

Glory be to God for dappled things—
    For skies of couple-colour as a brinded° cow;   brindled, streaked
        For rose-moles all in stipple upon trout that swim;
Fresh-firecoal chestnut-falls; finches' wings;
    Landscape plotted and pieced—fold, fallow, and plough;   5
        And áll trádes, their gear and tackle and trim°.   equipment
All things counter, original, spare°, strange;   unusual
    Whatever is fickle, freckled (who knows how?)
        With swift, slow; sweet, sour; adazzle, dim;
He fathers-forth whose beauty is past change: 10
                    Praise him.

Binsey Poplars

FELLED 1879

        My aspens dear, whose airy cages quelled°,   subdued
        Quelled or quenched in leaves the leaping sun,
        All felled, felled, are all felled;
            Of a fresh and following folded rank
                Not spared, not one   5
                That dandled and sandalled
                Shadow that swam or sank

PIED BEAUTY   [4]*chestnut-falls*   *roasted chestnuts stripped of their husks.*

On meadow and river and wind-wandering
　weed-winding bank.

O if we but knew what we do   10
　　When we delve or hew—
　Hack and rack the growing green!
　　Since country is so tender
　To touch, her being só slender,
　That, like this sleek and seeing ball   15
　But a prick will make no eye at all,
　Where we, even where we mean
　　　To mend her we end her,
　When we hew or delve:
After-comers cannot guess the beauty been.   20
Ten or twelve, only ten or twelve
　Strokes of havoc únselve
　　The sweet especial scene,
　Rural scene, a rural scene,
　Sweet especial rural scene.

A. E. HOUSMAN

[1859–1936]

When I was one-and-twenty

When I was one-and-twenty
　I heard a wise man say,
'Give crowns and pounds and guineas
　But not your heart away;
Give pearls away and rubies   5
　But keep your fancy free.'
But I was one-and-twenty,
　No use to talk to me.

When I was one-and-twenty
　I heard him say again,   10
'The heart out of the bosom
　Was never given in vain;
'Tis paid with sighs a plenty
　And sold for endless rue.'
And I am two-and-twenty,   15
　And oh, 'tis true, 'tis true.

To an Athlete Dying Young

The time you won your town the race
We chaired you through the market-place;
Man and boy stood cheering by,
And home we brought you shoulder-high.

To-day, the road all runners come,   5
Shoulder-high we bring you home,
And set you at your threshold down,
Townsman of a stiller town.

Smart lad, to slip betimes away
From fields where glory does not stay   10
And early though the laurel grows
It withers quicker than the rose.

Eyes the shady night has shut
Cannot see the record cut,
And silence sounds no worse than cheers   15
After earth has stopped the ears:

Now you will not swell the rout
Of lads that wore their honours out,
Runners whom renown outran
And the name died before the man.   20

So set, before its echoes fade,
The fleet foot on the sill of shade,
And hold to the low lintel up
The still-defended challenge-cup.

And round that early-laurelled head   25
Will flock to gaze the strengthless dead
And find unwithered on its curls
The garland briefer than a girl's.

With rue my heart is laden

With rue my heart is laden
For golden friends I had,
For many a rose-lipt maiden
And many a lightfoot lad.

By brooks too broad for leaping
  The lightfoot boys are laid;
The rose-lipt girls are sleeping
  In fields where roses fade.

Is my team plowing

"Is my team plowing,
  That I was used to drive
And hear the harness jingle
  When I was man alive?"

Ay, the horses trample,
  The harness jingles now;
No change though you lie under
  The land you used to plow.

"Is football playing
  Along the river shore,
With lads to chase the leather,
  Now I stand up no more?"

Ay, the ball is flying,
  The lads play heart and soul;
The goal stands, up, the keeper
  Stands up to keep the goal.

"Is my girl happy,
  That I thought hard to leave,
And has she tired of weeping
  As she lies down at eve?"

Ay, she lies down lightly,
  She lies not down to weep:
Your girl is well contented.
  Be still, my lad, and sleep.

"Is my friend hearty,
  Now I am thin and pine,
And has he found to sleep in
  A better bed than mine?"

Yes, lad, I lie easy,
  I lie as lads would choose;
I cheer a dead man's sweetheart,
  Never ask me whose.

WILLIAM BUTLER YEATS
[1865–1939]

Adam's Curse

We sat together at one summer's end,
That beautiful mild woman, your close friend,
And you and I, and talked of poetry.
I said, "A line will take us hours maybe;
Yet if it does not seem a moment's thought,   5
Our stitching and unstitching has been naught.
Better go down upon your marrow-bones
And scrub a kitchen pavement, or break stones
Like an old pauper, in all kinds of weather;
For to articulate sweet sounds together   10
Is to work harder than all these, and yet
Be thought an idler by the noisy set
Of bankers, schoolmasters, and clergymen
The martyrs call the world."

                       And thereupon
That beautiful mild woman for whose sake   15
There's many a one shall find out all heartache
On finding that her voice is sweet and low
Replied, "To be born woman is to know—
Although they do not talk of it at school—
That we must labor to be beautiful."   20

I said, "It's certain there is no fine thing
Since Adam's fall but needs much laboring.
There have been lovers who thought love should be
So much compounded of high courtesy
That they would sigh and quote with learned looks   25
Precedents out of beautiful old books;
Yet now it seems an idle trade enough."

We sat grown quiet at the name of love;
We saw the last embers of daylight die,
And in the trembling blue-green of the sky   30
A moon, worn as if it had been a shell
Washed by time's waters as they rose and fell
About the stars and broke in days and years.

ADAM'S CURSE   *See Genesis 3:17–19. Evicted from Eden, Adam was cursed with pain and hard labor.*

I had a thought for no one's but your ears:
That you were beautiful, and that I strove   35
To love you in the old high way of love;
That it had all seemed happy, and yet we'd grown
As weary-hearted as that hollow moon.

The Scholars

Bald heads forgetful of their sins,
Old, learned, respectable bald heads
Edit and annotate the lines
That young men, tossing on their beds,
Rhymed out in love's despair   5
To flatter beauty's ignorant ear.

All shuffle there; all cough in ink;
All wear the carpet with their shoes;
All think what other people think;
All know the man their neighbor knows.   10
Lord, what would they say
Did their Catullus walk that way?

The Magi

Now as at all times I can see in the mind's eye,
In their stiff, painted clothes, the pale unsatisfied ones
Appear and disappear in the blue depth of the sky
With all their ancient faces like rain-beaten stones,
And all their helms of silver hovering side by side,   5
And all their eyes still fixed, hoping to find once more,
Being by Calvary's turbulence unsatisfied,
The uncontrollable mystery on the bestial floor.

Easter 1916

I have met them at close of day
Coming with vivid faces
From counter or desk among gray
Eighteenth-century houses.

THE MAGI   *Compare Eliot's "Journey of the Magi," p. 655.*
EASTER 1916   *The title refers to an insurrection of Irish nationalists on Easter Monday, 1916; the four leaders mentioned were executed by the English.*

I have passed with a nod of the head   5
Or polite meaningless words,
Or have lingered awhile and said
Polite meaningless words,
And thought before I had done
Of a mocking tale or a gibe   10
To please a companion
Around the fire at the club,
Being certain that they and I
But lived where motley is worn:
All changed, changed utterly: 15
A terrible beauty is born.

That woman's days were spent
In ignorant good will,
Her nights in argument
Until her voice grew shrill.   20
What voice more sweet than hers
When, young and beautiful,
She rode to harriers°?   hounds
This man had kept a school
And rode our wingéd horse;   25
This other his helper and friend
Was coming into his force;
He might have won fame in the end,
So sensitive his nature seemed,
So daring and sweet his thought.   30
This other man I had dreamed
A drunken, vainglorious lout.
He had done most bitter wrong
To some who are near my heart,
Yet I number him in the song;   35
He, too, has resigned his part
In the casual comedy;
He, too, has been changed in his turn,
Transformed utterly:
A terrible beauty is born.   40

Hearts with one purpose alone
Through summer and winter seem
Enchanted to a stone
To trouble the living stream.
The horse that comes from the road,   45
The rider, the birds that range
From cloud to tumbling cloud,

14*motley* fool's costume.

Minute by minute they change;
A shadow of cloud on the stream
Changes minute by minute;   50
A horse-hoof slides on the brim,
And a horse plashes within it;
The long-legged moor-hens dive,
And hens to moor-cocks call;
Minute by minute they live: 55
The stone's in the midst of all.
Too long a sacrifice
Can make a stone of the heart.
O when may it suffice?
That is Heaven's part, our part   60
To murmur name upon name,
As a mother names her child
When sleep at last has come
On limbs that had run wild.
What is it but nightfall?   65
No, no, not night but death;
Was it needless death after all?
For England may keep faith
For all that is done and said.
We know their dream; enough   70
To know they dreamed and are dead;
And what if excess of love
Bewildered them till they died?
I write it out in a verse—
MacDonagh and MacBride   75
And Connolly and Pearse
Now and in time to be,
Wherever green is worn,
Are changed, changed utterly:
A terrible beauty is born.   80

The Second Coming

Turning and turning in the widening gyre°   spiral
The falcon cannot hear the falconer;
Things fall apart; the center cannot hold;
Mere anarchy is loosed upon the world,
The blood-dimmed tide is loosed, and everywhere   5
The ceremony of innocence is drowned;

THE SECOND COMING   *The title alludes to the prophesied return of Jesus Christ and also to the beast of the Apocalypse. See Matthew 24 and Revelation.*

The best lack all conviction, while the worst
Are full of passionate intensity.

Surely some revelation is at hand;
Surely the Second Coming is at hand;   10
The Second Coming! Hardly are those words out
When a vast image out of *Spiritus Mundi*
Troubles my sight: somewhere in sands of the desert
A shape with lion body and the head of a man,
A gaze blank and pitiless as the sun,   15
Is moving its slow thighs, while all about it
Reel shadows of the indignant desert birds.
The darkness drops again; but now I know
That twenty centuries of stony sleep
Were vexed to nightmare by a rocking cradle,   20
And what rough beast, its hour come round at last,
Slouches towards Bethlehem to be born?

The Wild Swans at Coole

The trees are in their autumn beauty,
The woodland paths are dry,
Under the October twilight the water
Mirrors a still sky;
Upon the brimming water among the stones   5
Are nine-and-fifty swans.

The nineteenth autumn has come upon me
Since I first made my count;
I saw, before I had well finished,
All suddenly mount   10
And scatter wheeling in great broken rings
Upon their clamorous wings.

I have looked upon those brilliant creatures,
And now my heart is sore.
All's changed since I, hearing at twilight,   15
The first time on this shore,
The bell-beat of their wings above my head,
Trod with a lighter tread.

Unwearied still, lover by lover,
They paddle in the cold   20
Companionable streams or climb the air;

---

[12]**Spiritus Mundi**   *for Yeats, a common storehouse of images, a communal human memory.*

Their hearts have not grown old;
Passion or conquest, wander where they will,
Attend upon them still.

But now they drift on the still water,   25
Mysterious, beautiful;
Among what rushes will they build,
By what lake's edge or pool
Delight men's eyes when I awake some day
To find they have flown away?   30

Leda and the Swan

A sudden blow: the great wings beating still
Above the staggering girl, her thighs caressed
By the dark webs, her nape caught in his bill,
He holds her helpless breast upon his breast.

How can those terrified vague fingers push   5
The feathered glory from her loosening thighs?
And how can body, laid in that white rush,
But feel the strange heart beating where it lies?

A shudder in the loins engenders there
The broken wall, the burning roof and tower   10
And Agamemnon dead.
                              Being so caught up,
So mastered by the brute blood of the air,
Did she put on his knowledge with his power
Before the indifferent beak could let her drop?   15

Sailing to Byzantium

1

That is no country for old men. The young
In one another's arms, birds in the trees
—Those dying generations—at their song,
The salmon-falls, the mackerel-crowded seas,

LEDA AND THE SWAN   *Zeus, in the guise of a swan, raped Leda, Queen of Sparta. Helen, their daughter, married Menelaus, King of Sparta, but ran off with Paris, son of Priam, King of Troy. A ten-year siege of Troy by the Greeks ensued to bring Helen back.*
SAILING TO BYZANTIUM   *Byzantium was the capital of the eastern Roman Empire and an important center of art and architecture.*

Fish, flesh, or fowl, commend all summer long 5
Whatever is begotten, born, and dies.
Caught in that sensual music all neglect
Monuments of unaging intellect.

2

An aged man is but a paltry thing,
A tattered coat upon a stick, unless 10
Soul clap its hands and sing, and louder sing
For every tatter in its mortal dress,
Nor is there singing school but studying
Monuments of its own magnificence;
And therefore I have sailed the seas and come 15
To the holy city of Byzantium.

3

O sages standing in God's holy fire
As in the gold mosaic of a wall,
Come from the holy fire, perne° in a gyre°, descend/spiral
And be the singing-masters of my soul. 20
Consume my heart away; sick with desire
And fastened to a dying animal
It knows not what it is; and gather me
Into the artifice of eternity.

4

Once out of nature I shall never take 25
My bodily form from any natural thing,
But such a form as Grecian goldsmiths make
Of hammered gold and gold enameling
To keep a drowsy Emperor awake;
Or set upon a golden bough to sing 30
To lords and ladies of Byzantium
Of what is past, or passing, or to come.

A Prayer for My Daughter

Once more the storm is howling, and half hid
Under this cradle-hood and coverlid
My child sleeps on. There is no obstacle
But Gregory's wood and one bare hill
Whereby the haystack- and roof-leveling wind, 5
Bred on the Atlantic, can be stayed;

And for an hour I have walked and prayed
Because of the great gloom that is in my mind.

I have walked and prayed for this young child an hour
And heard the sea-wind scream upon the tower,   10
And under the arches of the bridge, and scream
In the elms above the flooded stream;
Imagining in excited reverie
That the future years had come,
Dancing to a frenzied drum,   15
Out of the murderous innocence of the sea.

May she be granted beauty and yet not
Beauty to make a stranger's eye distraught,
Or hers before a looking glass, for such,
Being made beautiful overmuch,   20
Consider beauty a sufficient end,
Lose natural kindness and maybe
The heart-revealing intimacy
That chooses right, and never find a friend.

Helen being chosen found life flat and dull   25
And later had much trouble from a fool,
While that great Queen, that rose out of the spray,
Being fatherless could have her way
Yet chose a bandy-leggèd smith for man.
It's certain that fine women eat   30
A crazy salad with their meat,
Whereby the Horn of Plenty is undone.

In courtesy I'd have her chiefly learned;
Hearts are not had as a gift but hearts are earned
By those that are not entirely beautiful;   35
Yet many, that have played the fool
For beauty's very self, has charm made wise,
And many a poor man that has roved,
Loved and thought himself beloved,
From a glad kindness cannot take his eyes.   40

May she become a flourishing hidden tree
That all her thoughts may like the linnet° be,   small bird
And have no business but dispensing round
Their magnanimities of sound,
Nor but in merriment begin a chase,   45

A PRAYER FOR MY DAUGHTER   [25]**Helen**   Helen of Troy, whose beauty was legendary.
[27]**Queen**   Aphrodite, Greek goddess of love.

Nor but in merriment a quarrel.
Oh, may she live like some green laurel
Rooted in one dear perpetual place.

My mind, because the minds that I have loved,
The sort of beauty that I have approved,   50
Prosper but little, has dried up of late,
Yet knows that to be choked with hate
May well be of all evil chances chief.
If there's no hatred in a mind
Assault and battery of the wind   55
Can never tear the linnet from the leaf.

An intellectual hatred is the worst,
So let her think opinions are accursed.
Have I not seen the loveliest woman born
Out of the mouth of Plenty's horn,   60
Because of her opinionated mind
Barter that horn and every good
By quiet natures understood
For an old bellows full of angry wind?

Considering that, all hatred driven hence,   65
The soul recovers radical innocence
And learns at last that it is self-delighting,
Self-appeasing, self-affrighting,
And that its own sweet will is Heaven's will;
She can, though every face should scowl   70
And every windy quarter howl
Or every bellows burst, be happy still.

And may her bridegroom bring her to a house
Where all's accustomed, ceremonious;
For arrogance and hatred are the wares   75
Peddled in the thoroughfares.
How but in custom and in ceremony
Are innocence and beauty born?
Ceremony's a name for the rich horn,
And custom for the spreading laurel tree.   80

Crazy Jane Talks with the Bishop

I met the Bishop on the road
And much said he and I.
'Those breasts are flat and fallen now,

Those veins must soon be dry;
Live in a heavenly mansion,   5
Not in some foul sty.'

'Fair and foul are near of kin,
And fair needs foul,' I cried.
'My friends are gone, but that's a truth
Nor grave nor bed denied,   10
Learned in bodily lowliness
And in the heart's pride.

'A woman can be proud and stiff
When on love intent;
But Love has pitched his mansion in   15
The place of excrement;
For nothing can be sole or whole
That has not been rent.'

Long-Legged Fly

That civilization may not sink,
Its great battle lost,
Quiet the dog, tether the pony
To a distant post;
Our master Caesar is in the tent   5
Where the maps are spread,
His eyes fixed upon nothing,
A hand under his head.
Like a long-legged fly upon the stream
His mind moves upon silence.   10

That the topless towers be burnt
And men recall that face,
Move most gently if move you must
In this lonely place.
She thinks, part woman, three parts a child,   15
That nobody looks; her feet
Practice a tinker shuffle
Picked up on a street.
Like a long-legged fly upon the stream
Her mind moves upon silence.   20

That girls at puberty may find
The first Adam in their thought,
Shut the door of the Pope's chapel,

Keep those children out.
There on that scaffolding reclines   25
Michael Angelo.
With no more sound than the mice make
His hand moves to and fro.
Like a long-legged fly upon the stream
His mind moves upon silence.   30

EDWIN ARLINGTON ROBINSON
[1869–1935]

Mr. Flood's Party

Old Eben Flood, climbing alone one night
Over the hill between the town below
And the forsaken upland hermitage
That held as much as he should ever know
On earth again of home, paused warily.   5
The road was his with not a native near;
And Eben, having leisure, said aloud,
For no man else in Tilbury Town to hear:

"Well, Mr. Flood, we have the harvest moon
Again, and we may not have many more;   10
The bird is on the wing, the poet says,
And you and I have said it here before.
Drink to the bird." He raised up to the light
The jug that he had gone so far to fill,
And answered huskily: "Well, Mr. Flood,   15
Since you propose it, I believe I will."

Alone, as if enduring to the end
A valiant armor of scarred hopes outworn,
He stood there in the middle of the road
Like Roland's ghost winding a silent horn.   20
Below him, in the town among the trees,
Where friends of other days had honored him,
A phantom salutation of the dead
Rang thinly till old Eben's eyes were dim.

MR. FLOOD'S PARTY   [11]*the poet* Edward FitzGerald.   [20]*Roland's ghost . . . silent horn*
In The Song of Roland, *a medieval French epic, Roland sounds his horn before he dies to warn his emperor,*
Charlemagne.

Then, as a mother lays her sleeping child 25
Down tenderly, fearing it may awake,
He set the jug down slowly at his feet
With trembling care, knowing that most things break;
And only when assured that on firm earth
It stood, as the uncertain lives of men 30
Assuredly did not, he paced away,
And with his hand extended paused again:

"Well, Mr. Flood, we have not met like this
In a long time; and many a change has come
To both of us, I fear, since last it was 35
We had a drop together. Welcome home!"
Convivially returning with himself,
Again he raised the jug up to the light;
And with an acquiescent quaver said:
"Well, Mr. Flood, if you insist, I might. 40

"Only a very little, Mr. Flood—
For auld lang syne. No more, sir; that will do."
So, for the time, apparently it did,
And Eben evidently thought so too;
For soon amid the silver loneliness 45
Of night he lifted up his voice and sang,
Secure, with only two moons listening,
Until the whole harmonious landscape rang—

"For auld lang syne." The weary throat gave out,
The last word wavered; and the song being done, 50
He raised again the jug regretfully
And shook his head, and was again alone.
There was not much that was ahead of him,
And there was nothing in the town below—
Where strangers would have shut the many doors 55
That many friends had opened long ago.

The Sheaves

Where long the shadows of the wind had rolled,
Green wheat was yielding to the change assigned;
And as by some vast magic undivined
The world was turning slowly into gold.
Like nothing that was ever bought or sold 5
It waited there, the body and the mind;

And with a mighty meaning of a kind
That tells the more the more it is not told.

So in a land where all days are not fair,   10
Fair days went on till on another day
A thousand golden sheaves were lying there,
Shining and still, but not for long to stay—
As if a thousand girls with golden hair
Might rise from where they slept and go away.

Eros Turannos

She fears him, and will always ask
    What fated her to choose him;
She meets in his engaging mask
    All reasons to refuse him;
But what she meets and what she fears   5
Are less than are the downward years,
Drawn slowly to the foamless weirs
    Of age, were she to lose him.

Between a blurred sagacity
    That once had power to sound him,   10
And Love, that will not let him be
    The Judas that she found him,
Her pride assuages her almost,
As if it were alone the cost.
He sees that he will not be lost,   15
    And waits and looks around him.

A sense of ocean and old trees
    Envelopes and allures him;
Tradition, touching all he sees,
    Beguiles and reassures him;   20
And all her doubts of what he says
Are dimmed with what she knows of days—
Till even prejudice delays
    And fades, and she secures him.

The falling leaf inaugurates   25
    The reign of her confusion;
The pounding wave reverberates
    The dirge of her illusion;
And home, where passion lived and died,
Becomes a place where she can hide,   30

EROS TURANNOS   Love the tyrant.

    While all the town and harbor side
      Vibrate with her seclusion.

    We tell you, tapping on our brows,
      The story as it should be,
    As if the story of a house   35
      Were told, or ever could be;
    We'll have no kindly veil between
    Her visions and those we have seen,
    As if we guessed what hers have been,
      Or what they are or would be.   40

    Meanwhile we do no harm; for they
      That with a god have striven,
    Not hearing much of what we say,
      Take what the god has given;
    Though like waves breaking it may be,   45
    Or like a changed familiar tree,
    Or like a stairway to the sea
      Where down the blind are driven.

PAUL LAURENCE DUNBAR

[1872–1906]

We wear the mask

    We wear the mask that grins and lies,
    It hides our cheeks and shades our eyes—
    This debt we pay to human guile;
    With torn and bleeding hearts we smile,
    And mouth with myriad subtleties.   5

    Why should the world be over-wise,
    In counting all our tears and sighs?
    Nay, let them only see us, while
      We wear the mask.

    We smile, but, O great Christ, our cries
    To thee from tortured souls arise.   10
    We sing, but oh the clay is vile
    Beneath our feet, and long the mile;
    But let the world dream otherwise,
      We wear the mask!

AMY LOWELL
[1874–1925]

Patterns

I walk down the garden-paths,
And all the daffodils
Are blowing, and the bright blue squills.
I walk down the patterned garden-paths
In my stiff, brocaded gown.   5
With my powdered hair and jeweled fan,
I too am a rare
Pattern. As I wander down
The garden-paths.

My dress is richly figured,   10
And the train
Makes a pink and silver stain
On the gravel, and the thrift
Of the borders.
Just a plate of current fashion,   15
Tripping by in high-heeled, ribboned shoes.
Not a softness anywhere about me,
Only whalebone and brocade.
And I sink on a seat in the shade
Of a lime tree. For my passion   20
Wars against the stiff brocade.
The daffodils and squills
Flutter in the breeze
As they please.
And I weep;   25
For the lime-tree is in blossom
And one small flower has dropped upon my bosom.

And the plashing of waterdrops
In the marble fountain
Comes down the garden-paths.   30
The dripping never stops.
Underneath my stiffened gown
Is the softness of a woman bathing in a marble basin,
A basin in the midst of hedges grown
So thick, she cannot see her lover hiding,   35
But she guesses he is near,
And the sliding of the water

Seems the stroking of a dear
Hand upon her.
What is Summer in a fine brocaded gown!   40
I should like to see it lying in a heap upon the ground.
All the pink and silver crumpled up on the ground.
I would be the pink and silver as I ran along the paths,
And he would stumble after,
Bewildered by my laughter.   45
I should see the sun flashing from his sword-hilt and the buckles on his shoes.
I would choose
To lead him in a maze along the patterned paths,
A bright and laughing maze for my heavy-booted lover.
Till he caught me in the shade,   50
And the buttons of his waistcoat bruised my body as he clasped me,
Aching, melting, unafraid.
With the shadows of the leaves and the sundrops,
And the plopping of the waterdrops,
All about us in the open afternoon—   55
I am very like to swoon
With the weight of this brocade,
For the sun sifts through the shade.

Underneath the fallen blossom
In my bosom   60
Is a letter I have hid.
It was brought to me this morning by a rider from the Duke.
"Madam, we regret to inform you that Lord Hartwell
Died in action Thursday se'ennight."
As I read it in the white, morning sunlight,   65
The letters squirmed like snakes.
"Any answer, Madam," said my footman.
"No," I told him.
"See that the messenger takes some refreshment.
No, no answer."   70
And I walked into the garden,
Up and down the patterned paths,
In my stiff, correct brocade.
The blue and yellow flowers stood up proudly in the sun,
Each one.   75
I stood upright too,
Held rigid to the pattern
By the stiffness of my gown;
Up and down I walked,
Up and down: 80

In a month he would have been my husband.
In a month, here, underneath this lime,
We would have broke the pattern;

He for me, and I for him,
He as Colonel, I as Lady,   85
On this shady seat.
He had a whim
That sunlight carried blessing.
And I answered, "It shall be as you have said."
Now he is dead.   90

In Summer and in Winter I shall walk
Up and down
The patterned garden-paths.
The squills and daffodils
Will give place to pillared roses, and to asters, and to snow. 95
I shall go
Up and down
In my gown.
Gorgeously arrayed,
Boned and stayed.   100
And the softness of my body will be guarded from embrace
By each button, hook, and lace.
For the man who should loose me is dead,
Fighting with the Duke in Flanders,
In a pattern called a war.   105
Christ! What are patterns for?

ROBERT FROST

[1874–1963]

Mending Wall

Something there is that doesn't love a wall,
That sends the frozen-ground-swell under it,
And spills the upper boulders in the sun;
And makes gaps even two can pass abreast.
The work of hunters is another thing: 5
I have come after them and made repair
Where they have left not one stone on a stone,
But they would have the rabbit out of hiding,
To please the yelping dogs. The gaps I mean,
No one has seen them made or heard them made, 10
But at spring mending-time we find them there.
I let my neighbor know beyond the hill;

And on a day we meet to walk the line
And set the wall between us once again.
We keep the wall between us as we go.   15
To each the boulders that have fallen to each.
And some are loaves and some so nearly balls
We have to use a spell to make them balance:
'Stay where you are until our backs are turned!'
We wear our fingers rough with handling them.   20
Oh, just another kind of outdoor game,
One on a side. It comes to little more:
There where it is we do not need the wall:
He is all pine and I am apple orchard.
My apple trees will never get across   25
And eat the cones under his pines, I tell him.
He only says, 'Good fences make good neighbors.'
Spring is the mischief in me, and I wonder
If I could put a notion in his head:
'*Why* do they make good neighbors? Isn't it   30
Where there are cows? But here there are no cows.
Before I built a wall I'd ask to know
What I was walling in or walling out,
And to whom I was like to give offense.
Something there is that doesn't love a wall,   35
That wants it down.' I could say 'Elves' to him,
But it's not elves exactly, and I'd rather
He said it for himself. I see him there
Bringing a stone grasped firmly by the top
In each hand, like an old-stone savage armed.   40
He moves in darkness as it seems to me,
Not of woods only and the shade of trees.
He will not go behind his father's saying,
And he likes having thought of it so well
He says again, 'Good fences make good neighbors.'   45

Fire and Ice

Some say the world will end in fire,
Some say in ice.
From what I've tasted of desire
I hold with those who favor fire.
But if it had to perish twice,   5
I think I know enough of hate
To say that for destruction ice
Is also great
And would suffice.

Dust of Snow

The way a crow
Shook down on me
The dust of snow
From a hemlock tree

Has given my heart   5
A change of mood
And saved some part
Of a day I had rued.

Design

I found a dimpled spider, fat and white,
On a white heal-all, holding up a moth
Like a white piece of rigid satin cloth—
Assorted characters of death and blight
Mixed ready to begin the morning right,   5
Like the ingredients of a witches' broth—
A snow-drop spider, a flower like a froth,
And dead wings carried like a paper kite.

What had that flower to do with being white,
The wayside blue and innocent heal-all?   10
What brought the kindred spider to that height,
Then steered the white moth thither in the night?
What but design of darkness to appall?—
If design govern in a thing so small.

Desert Places

Snow falling and night falling fast, oh, fast
In a field I looked into going past,
And the ground almost covered smooth in snow,
But a few weeds and stubble showing last.

The woods around it have it—it is theirs.   5
All animals are smothered in their lairs.
I am too absent-spirited to count;
The loneliness includes me unawares.

And lonely as it is, that loneliness
Will be more lonely ere it will be less—   10

A blanker whiteness of benighted snow
With no expression, nothing to express.

They cannot scare me with their empty spaces
Between stars—on stars where no human race is.
I have it in me so much nearer home   15
To scare myself with my own desert places.

Tree at my window

Tree at my window, window tree,
My sash is lowered when night comes on;
But let there never be curtain drawn
Between you and me.

Vague dream-head lifted out of the ground,   5
And thing next most diffuse to cloud,
Not all your light tongues talking aloud
Could be profound.

But, tree, I have seen you taken and tossed,
And if you have seen me when I slept,   10
You have seen me when I was taken and swept
And all but lost.

That day she put our heads together,
Fate had her imagination about her,
Your head so much concerned with outer,   15
Mine with inner, weather.

Acquainted with the night

I have been one acquainted with the night.
I have walked out in rain—and back in rain.
I have outwalked the furthest city light.

I have looked down the saddest city lane.
I have passed by the watchman on his beat   5
And dropped my eyes, unwilling to explain.

I have stood still and stopped the sound of feet
When far away an interrupted cry
Came over houses from another street,

But not to call me back or say good-by;   10
And further still at an unearthly height
One luminary clock against the sky

Proclaimed the time was neither wrong nor right.
I have been one acquainted with the night.

Putting in the Seed

You come to fetch me from my work tonight
When supper's on the table, and we'll see
If I can leave off burying the white
Soft petals fallen from the apple tree
(Soft petals, yes, but not so barren quite,   5
Mingled with these, smooth bean and wrinkled pea),
And go along with you ere you lose sight
Of what you came for and become like me,
Slave to a springtime passion for the earth.
How Love burns through the Putting in the Seed   10
On through the watching for that early birth
When, just as the soil tarnishes with weed,
The sturdy seedling with arched body comes
Shouldering its way and shedding the earth crumbs.

To Earthward

Love at the lips was touch
As sweet as I could bear;
And once that seemed too much;
I lived on air

That crossed me from sweet things,   5
The flow of—was it musk
From hidden grapevine springs
Downhill at dusk?

I had the swirl and ache
From sprays of honeysuckle   10
That when they're gathered shake
Dew on the knuckle.

I craved strong sweets, but those
Seemed strong when I was young;

The petal of the rose 15
It was that stung.

Now no joy but lacks salt,
That is not dashed with pain
And weariness and fault;
I crave the stain 20

Of tears, the aftermark
Of almost too much love,
The sweet of bitter bark
And burning clove.

When stiff and sore and scarred 25
I take away my hand
From leaning on it hard
In grass and sand,

The hurt is not enough:
I long for weight and strength 30
To feel the earth as rough
To all my length.

RAINER MARIA RILKE

[1875–1926]

Going Blind

She sat just like the others at the table.
But on second glance, she seemed to hold her cup
a little differently as she picked it up.
She smiled once. It was almost painful.

And when they finished and it was time to stand 5
and slowly, as chance selected them, they left
and moved through many rooms (they talked and laughed),
I saw her. She was moving far behind

the others, absorbed, like someone who will soon
have to sing before a large assembly; 10
upon her eyes, which were radiant with joy,
light played as on the surface of a pool.

She followed slowly, taking a long time,
as though there were some obstacle in the way;
and yet: as though, once it was overcome,
she would be beyond all walking, and would fly.

TRANSLATED BY STEPHEN MITCHELL

The Swan

This laboring through what is still undone,
as though, legs bound, we hobbled along the way,
is like the awkward walking of the swan.

And dying—to let go, no longer feel
the solid ground we stand on every day—
is like his anxious letting himself fall

into the water, which receives him gently
and which, as though with reverence and joy,
draws back past him in streams on either side;
while, infinitely silent and aware,
in his full majesty and ever more
indifferent, he condescends to glide.

TRANSLATED BY STEPHEN MITCHELL

Portrait of My Father as a Young Man

In the eyes: dream. The brow as if it could feel
something far off. Around the lips, a great
freshness—seductive, though there is no smile.
Under the rows of ornamental braid
on the slim Imperial officer's uniform:
the saber's basket-hilt. Both hands stay
folded upon it, going nowhere, calm
and now almost invisible, as if they
were the first to grasp the distance and dissolve.
And all the rest so curtained with itself,
so cloudy, that I cannot understand
this figure as it fades into the background—.

Oh quickly disappearing photograph
in my more slowly disappearing hand.

TRANSLATED BY STEPHEN MITCHELL

Spanish Dancer

As on all its sides a kitchen-match darts white
flickering tongues before it bursts into flame:
with the audience around her, quickened, hot,
her dance begins to flicker in the dark room.

And all at once it is completely fire. 5

One upward glance and she ignites her hair
and, whirling faster and faster, fans her dress
into passionate flames, till it becomes a furnace
from which, like startled rattlesnakes, the long
naked arms uncoil, aroused and clicking. 10

And then: as if the fire were too tight
around her body, she takes and flings it out
haughtily, with an imperious gesture,
and watches: it lies raging on the floor,
still blazing up, and the flames refuse to die—. 15
Till, moving with total confidence and a sweet
exultant smile, she looks up finally
and stamps it out with powerful small feet.

TRANSLATED BY STEPHEN MITCHELL

WALLACE STEVENS
[1879–1955]

The Snow Man

One must have a mind of winter
To regard the frost and the boughs
Of the pine-trees crusted with snow;

And have been cold a long time
To behold the junipers shagged with ice, 5
The spruces rough in the distant glitter

Of the January sun; and not to think
Of any misery in the sound of the wind,
In the sound of a few leaves,

Which is the sound of the land
Full of the same wind
That is blowing in the same bare place
For the listener, who listens in the snow,
And, nothing himself, beholds
Nothing that is not there and the nothing that is. 15

Thirteen Ways of Looking at a Blackbird

1

Among twenty snowy mountains,
The only moving thing
Was the eye of the blackbird.

2

I was of three minds,
Like a tree 5
In which there are three blackbirds.

3

The blackbird whirled in the autumn winds.
It was a small part of the pantomime.

4

A man and a woman
Are one. 10
A man and a woman and a blackbird
Are one.

5

I do not know which to prefer,
The beauty of inflections
Or the beauty of innuendoes, 15
The blackbird whistling
Or just after.

6

Icicles filled the long window
With barbaric glass.
The shadow of the blackbird 20
Crossed it to and fro.
The mood

Traced in the shadow
An indecipherable cause.

7

O thin men of Haddam, 25
Why do you imagine golden birds?
Do you not see how the blackbird
Walks around the feet
Of the women about you?

8

I know noble accents 30
And lucid, inescapable rhythms;
But I know, too,
That the blackbird is involved
In what I know.

9

When the blackbird flew out of sight, 35
It marked the edge
Of one of many circles.

10

At the sight of blackbirds
Flying in a green light,
Even the bawds of euphony 40
Would cry out sharply.

11

He rode over Connecticut
In a glass coach.
Once, a fear pierced him,
In that he mistook 45
The shadow of his equipage
For blackbirds.

12

The river is moving.
The blackbird must be flying.

13

It was evening all afternoon. 50
It was snowing
And it was going to snow.

The blackbird sat
In the cedar-limbs.

The house was quiet and the world was calm

The house was quiet and the world was calm.
The reader became the book; and summer night

Was like the conscious being of the book.
The house was quiet and the world was calm.

The words were spoken as if there was no book,   5
Except that the reader leaned above the page,

Wanted to lean, wanted much most to be
The scholar to whom his book is true, to whom

The summer night is like a perfection of thought.   10
The house was quiet because it had to be.

The quiet was part of the meaning, part of the mind:
The access of perfection to the page.

And the world was calm. The truth in a calm world,
In which there is no other meaning, itself

Is calm, itself is summer and night, itself   15
Is the reader leaning late and reading there.

WILLIAM CARLOS WILLIAMS
[1883–1963]

The Widow's Lament in Springtime

Sorrow is my own yard
where the new grass
flames as it has flamed
often before but not
with the cold fire   5
that closes round me this year.
Thirtyfive years
I lived with my husband.

The plumtree is white today
with masses of flowers.   10
Masses of flowers
loaded the cherry branches
and color some bushes
yellow and some red
but the grief in my heart   15
is stronger than they
for though they were my joy
formerly, today I notice them
and turned away forgetting.
Today my son told me   20
that in the meadows,
at the edge of the heavy woods
in the distance, he saw
trees of white flowers.
I feel that I would like   25
to go there
and fall into those flowers
and sink into the marsh near them.

Spring and All

By the road to the contagious hospital
under the surge of the blue
mottled clouds driven from the
northeast—a cold wind. Beyond, the
waste of broad, muddy fields   5
brown with dried weeds, standing and fallen

patches of standing water
the scattering of tall trees

All along the road the reddish
purplish, forked, upstanding, twiggy   10
stuff of bushes and small trees
with dead, brown leaves under them
leafless vines—

Lifeless in appearance, sluggish
dazed spring approaches—   15

They enter the new world naked,
cold, uncertain of all
save that they enter. All about them
the cold, familiar wind—

Now the grass, tomorrow   20
the stiff curl of wildcarrot leaf
One by one objects are defined—
It quickens: clarity, outline of leaf

But now the stark dignity of
entrance—Still, the profound change   25
has come upon them: rooted, they
grip down and begin to awaken

A Sort of a Song

Let the snake wait under
his weed
and the writing
be of words, slow and quick, sharp
to strike, quiet to wait,   5
sleepless.

—through metaphor to reconcile
the people and the stones.
Compose. (No ideas
but in things) Invent!   10
Saxifrage is my flower that splits
the rocks.

To a Poor Old Woman

munching a plum on
the street a paper bag
of them in her hand

They taste good to her
They taste good   5
to her. They taste
good to her

You can see it by
the way she gives herself
to the one half   10
sucked out in her hand

Comforted
a solace of ripe plums

seeming to fill the air
They taste good to her   15

The Young Housewife

At ten A.M. the young housewife
moves about in negligee behind
the wooden walls of her husband's house.
I pass solitary in my car.

Then again she comes to the curb   5
to call the ice-man, fish-man, and stands
shy, uncorseted, tucking in
stray ends of hair, and I compare her
to a fallen leaf.

The noiseless wheels of my car   10
rush with a crackling sound over
dried leaves as I bow and pass smiling.

Danse Russe

If when my wife is sleeping
and the baby and Kathleen
are sleeping
and the sun is a flame-white disc
in silken mists   5
above shining trees,—
if I in my north room
dance naked, grotesquely
before my mirror
waving my shirt round my head   10
and singing softly to myself:
"I am lonely, lonely.
I was born to be lonely,
I am best so!"
If I admire my arms, my face,   15
my shoulders, flanks, buttocks
against the yellow drawn shades,—

Who shall say I am not
the happy genius of my household?

Tract

I will teach you my townspeople
how to perform a funeral
for you have it over a troop
of artists—
unless one should scour the world—   5
you have the ground sense necessary.

See! the hearse leads.
I begin with a design for a hearse.
For Christ's sake not black—
nor white either—and not polished!   10
Let it be weathered—like a farm wagon—
with gilt wheels (this could be
applied fresh at small expense)
or no wheels at all:
a rough dray to drag over the ground.   15

Knock the glass out!
My God—glass, my townspeople!
For what purpose? Is it for the dead
to look out or for us to see
how well he is housed or to see   20
the flowers or the lack of them—
or what?
To keep the rain and snow from him?
He will have a heavier rain soon:
pebbles and dirt and what not.   25
Let there be no glass—
and no upholstery, phew!
and no little brass rollers
and small easy wheels on the bottom—
my townspeople what are you thinking of?   30

A rough plain hearse then
with gilt wheels and no top at all.
On this the coffin lies
by its own weight.

                    No wreaths please—   35
especially no hot house flowers.
Some common memento is better,
something he prized and is known by:
his old clothes—a few books perhaps—
God knows what! You realize   40
how we are about these things

my townspeople—
something will be found—anything
even flowers if he had come to that.
So much for the hearse.   45

For heaven's sake though see to the driver!
Take off the silk hat! In fact
that's no place at all for him—
up there unceremoniously
dragging our friend out to his own dignity!   50
Bring him down—bring him down!
Low and inconspicuous! I'd not have him ride
on the wagon at all—damn him—
the undertaker's understrapper!
Let him hold the reins   55
and walk at the side
and inconspicuously too!

Then briefly as to yourselves:
Walk behind—as they do in France,
seventh class, or if you ride   60
Hell take curtains! Go with some show
of inconvenience; sit openly—
to the weather as to grief.
Or do you think you can shut grief in?
What—from us? We who have perhaps   65
nothing to lose? Share with us
share with us—it will be money
in your pockets.
                         Go now
I think you are ready.   70

D . H . L A W R E N C E
[*1885–1930*]

The Elephant Is Slow to Mate—

The elephant, the huge old beast,
          is slow to mate;
he finds a female, they show no haste
          they wait

for the sympathy in their vast shy hearts   5
          slowly, slowly to rouse

    as they loiter along the river-beds
        and drink and browse

    and dash in panic through the brake
        of forest with the herd,   10
    and sleep in massive silence, and wake
        together, without a word.

    So slowly the great hot elephant hearts
        grow full of desire,
    and the great beasts mate in secret at last,   15
        hiding their fire.

    Oldest they are and the wisest of beasts
        so they know at last
    how to wait for the loneliest of feasts
        for the full repast.   20

    They do not snatch, they do not tear;
        their massive blood
    moves as the moon-tides, near, more near,
        till they touch in flood.

Snake

A snake came to my water-trough
On a hot, hot day, and I in pajamas for the heat,
To drink there.

In the deep, strange-scented shade of the great dark carob-tree
I came down the steps with my pitcher   5
And must wait, must stand and wait, for there he was at the trough before me.

He reached down from a fissure in the earth-wall in the gloom
And trailed his yellow-brown slackness soft-bellied down, over the edge of the
   stone trough
And rested his throat upon the stone bottom,
And where the water had dripped from the tap, in a small clearness,   10
He sipped with his straight mouth,
Softly drank through his straight gums, into his slack long body,
Silently.

Someone was before me at my water-trough,
And I, like a second comer, waiting.   15

He lifted his head from his drinking, as cattle do,
And looked at me vaguely, as drinking cattle do,
And flickered his two-forked tongue from his lips, and mused a moment,
And stooped and drank a little more,
Being earth-brown, earth-golden from the burning bowels of the earth   20
On the day of Sicilian July, with Etna smoking.

The voice of my education said to me
He must be killed,
For in Sicily the black, black snakes are innocent, the gold are venomous.

And voices in me said, If you were a man   25
You would take a stick and break him now, and finish him off.

But must I confess how I liked him,
How glad I was he had come like a guest in quiet, to drink at my water-trough

And depart peaceful, pacified, and thankless,
Into the burning bowels of this earth?   30

Was it cowardice, that I dared not kill him?
Was it perversity, that I longed to talk to him?
Was it humility, to feel so honored?
I felt so honored.

And yet those voices:
If you were not afraid, you would kill him!   35

And truly I was afraid, I was most afraid,
But even so, honored still more
That he should seek my hospitality
From out the dark door of the secret earth.

He drank enough   40
And lifted his head, dreamily, as one who has drunken,
And flickered his tongue like a forked night on the air, so black,
Seeming to lick his lips,
And looked around like a god, unseeing, into the air,
And slowly turned his head,   45
And slowly, very slowly, as if thrice adream,
Proceeded to draw his slow length curving round
And climb again the broken bank of my wall-face.

And as he put his head into that dreadful hole,
And as he slowly drew up, snake-easing his shoulders, and entered farther,   50
A sort of horror, a sort of protest against his withdrawing into that horrid black hole,

Deliberately going into the blackness, and slowly drawing himself after,
Overcame me now his back was turned.

I looked round, I put down my pitcher,
I picked up a clumsy log   55
And threw it at the water-trough with a clatter.

I think it did not hit him,
But suddenly that part of him that was left behind convulsed in undignified haste.
Writhed like lightning, and was gone
Into the black hole, the earth-lipped fissure in the wall-front,   60
At which, in the intense still noon, I stared with fascination.

And immediately I regretted it.
I thought how paltry, how vulgar, what a mean act!
I despised myself and the voices of my accursed human education.

And I thought of the albatross   65
And I wished he would come back, my snake.

For he seemed to me again like a king,
Like a king in exile, uncrowned in the underworld,
Now due to be crowned again.

And so, I missed my chance with one of the lords   70
Of life.
And I have something to expiate;
A pettiness.

EZRA POUND

[1885–1972]

The Seafarer

FROM THE ANGLO-SAXON

May I for my own self song's truth reckon,
Journey's jargon, how I in harsh days
Hardship endured oft.
Bitter breast-cares have I abided,
Known on my keel many a care's hold,   5

THE SEAFARER   *Pound's poem is a translation of the first 99 lines of an Old English poem 124 lines long.*

And dire sea-surge, and there I oft spent
Narrow nightwatch nigh the ship's head
While she tossed close to cliffs. Coldly afflicted,
My feet were by frost benumbed.
Chill its chains are; chafing sighs   10
Hew my heart round and hunger begot
Mere-weary° mood. Lest man know not   sea-weary
That he on dry land loveliest liveth,
List how I, care-wretched, on ice-cold sea,
Weathered the winter, wretched outcast   15
Deprived of my kinsmen;
Hung with hard ice-flakes, where hail-scur° flew,   hail-storms
There I heard naught save the harsh sea
And ice-cold wave, at whiles the swan cries,
Did for my games the gannet's clamor,   20
Sea-fowls' loudness was for me laughter,
The mews' singing all my mead-drink.
Storms, on the stone-cliffs beaten, fell on the stern
In icy feathers; full oft the eagle screamed
With spray on his pinion.
                              Not any protector   25
May make merry man faring needy.
This he little believes, who aye in winsome life
Abides 'mid burghers some heavy business,
Wealthy and wine-flushed, how I weary oft
Must bide above brine.   30
Neareth nightshade, snoweth from north,
Frost froze the land, hail fell on earth then,
Corn of the coldest. Nathless° there knocketh now   Nonetheless
The heart's thought that I on high streams
The salt-wavy tumult traverse alone.   35
Moaneth alway my mind's lust
That I fare forth, that I afar hence
Seek out a foreign fastness.
For this there's no mood-lofty man over earth's midst,
Not though he be given his good, but will have in his youth greed; 40
Nor his deed to the daring, nor his king to the faithful
But shall have his sorrow for sea-fare
Whatever his lord will.
He hath not heart for harping, nor in ring-having
Nor winsomeness to wife, nor world's delight   45
Nor any whit else save the wave's slash,
Yet longing comes upon him to fare forth on the water.
Bosque° taketh blossom, cometh beauty of berries,   grove
Fields to fairness, land fares brisker,
All this admonisheth man eager of mood,   50
The heart turns to travel so that he then thinks

On flood-ways to be far departing.
Cuckoo calleth with gloomy crying,
He singeth summerward, bodeth sorrow,
The bitter heart's blood. Burgher knows not—   55
He the prosperous man—what some perform
Where wandering them widest draweth.
So that but now my heart burst from my breastlock,
My mood 'mid the mere-flood°,   sea-flood
Over the whale's acre, would wander wide.   60
On earth's shelter cometh oft to me,
Eager and ready, the crying lone-flyer,
Whets for the whale-path the heart irresistibly,
O'er tracks of ocean; seeing that anyhow
My lord deems to me this dead life   65
On loan and on land, I believe not
That any earth-weal eternal standeth
Save there be somewhat calamitous
That, ere a man's tide go, turn it to twain.
Disease or oldness or sword-hate   70
Beats out the breath from doom-gripped body.
And for this, every earl whatever, for those speaking after—
Laud of the living, boasteth some last word,
That he will work ere he pass onward,
Frame on the fair earth 'gainst foes his malice,   75
Daring ado°, . . .   brave deeds
So that all men shall honor him after
And his laud beyond them remain 'mid the English
Aye, for ever, a lasting life's-blast,
Delight 'mid the doughty.
                        Days little durable,   80
And all arrogance of earthen riches,
There come now no kings nor Caesars
Nor gold-giving lords like those gone.
Howe'er in mirth most magnified,
Whoe'er lived in life most lordliest,   85
Drear all this excellence, delights undurable!
Waneth the watch, but the world holdeth.
Tomb hideth trouble. The blade is layed low.
Earthly glory ageth and seareth.
No man at all going the earth's gait,   90
But age fares against him, his face paleth,
Gray-haired he groaneth, knows gone companions,
Lordly men, are to earth o'ergiven,
Nor may he then the flesh-cover, whose life ceaseth,
Nor eat the sweet nor feel the sorry,   95
Nor stir hand nor think in mid heart,
And though he strew the grave with gold,

His born brothers, their buried bodies
Be an unlikely treasure hoard.

The Garden

En robe de parade.
—SAMAIN

Like a skein of loose silk blown against a wall
She walks by the railing of a path in Kensington Gardens,
And she is dying piecemeal
    of a sort of emotional anemia.

And round about there is a rabble   5
Of the filthy, sturdy, unkillable infants of the very poor.
They shall inherit the earth.

In her is the end of breeding.
Her boredom is exquisite and excessive.
She would like some one to speak to her,   10
And is almost afraid that I
    will commit that indiscretion.

The River-Merchant's Wife: A Letter

While my hair was still cut straight across my forehead
Played I about the front gate, pulling flowers.
You came by on bamboo stilts, playing horse,
You walked about my seat, playing with blue plums.
And we went on living in the village of Chōkan: 5
Two small people, without dislike or suspicion.

At fourteen I married My Lord you.
I never laughed, being bashful.
Lowering my head, I looked at the wall.
Called to, a thousand times, I never looked back.   10

At fifteen I stopped scowling,
I desired my dust to be mingled with yours

THE GARDEN **En . . . parade** *dressed as for a state occasion. The phrase is from a poem by the French poet Albert Samain (1858–1900).* [7]**They . . . earth** *See Matthew 5:5, "Blessed are the meek, for they shall inherit the earth."*
THE RIVER-MERCHANT'S WIFE *Pound translated this poem from the Chinese.*

Forever and forever and forever.
Why should I climb the look out?

At sixteen you departed,   15
You went into far Ku-tō-en, by the river of swirling eddies,
And you have been gone five months.
The monkeys make sorrowful noise overhead.

You dragged your feet when you went out.
By the gate now, the moss is grown, the different mosses,   20
Too deep to clear them away!
The leaves fall early this autumn, in wind.
The paired butterflies are already yellow with August
Over the grass in the West garden;
They hurt me. I grow older.   25
If you are coming down through the narrows of the river Kiang,
Please let me know before hand,
And I will come out to meet you
                        As far as Chō-fū-Sa.   30

BY RIHAKU (LI T'AI PO)

MARIANNE MOORE

[1887–1972]

Poetry

I, too, dislike it: there are things that are important beyond all this fiddle.
   Reading it, however, with a perfect contempt for it, one discovers in
   it after all, a place for the genuine.
      Hands that can grasp, eyes
      that can dilate, hair that can rise   5
         if it must, these things are important not because a

high-sounding interpretation can be put upon them but because they are
   useful. When they become so derivative as to become unintelligible,
   the same thing may be said for all of us, that we
      do not admire what   10
      we cannot understand: the bat
        holding on upside down or in quest of something to

eat, elephants pushing, a wild horse taking a roll, a tireless wolf under
   a tree, the immovable critic twitching his skin like a horse that feels
      a flea, the base-

ball fan, the statistician—   15
     nor is it valid
        to discriminate against "business documents and

school-books"; all these phenomena are important. One must make a distinction
    however: when dragged into prominence by half poets, the result is not poetry,
    nor till the poets among us can be   20
       "literalists of
       the imagination"—above
        insolence and triviality and can present

for inspection, "imaginary gardens with real toads in them," shall we have
    it. In the meantime, if you demand on the one hand,   25
    the raw material of poetry in
       all its rawness and
       that which is on the other hand
        genuine, you are interested in poetry.

T. S. ELIOT

[1888–1965]

Preludes

1

The winter evening settles down
With smell of steaks in passageways.
Six o'clock.
The burnt-out ends of smoky days.
And now a gusty shower wraps   5
The grimy scraps
Of withered leaves about your feet
And newspapers from vacant lots;
The showers beat
On broken blinds and chimney-pots,   10
And at the corner of the street
A lonely cab-horse steams and stamps.
And then the lighting of the lamps.

2

The morning comes to consciousness
Of faint stale smells of beer   15
From the sawdust-trampled street

With all its muddy feet that press
To early coffee-stands.
With the other masquerades
That time resumes, 20
One thinks of all the hands
That are raising dingy shades
In a thousand furnished rooms.

3

You tossed a blanket from the bed,
You lay upon your back, and waited; 25
You dozed, and watched the night revealing
The thousand sordid images
Of which your soul was constituted;
They flickered against the ceiling.
And when all the world came back 30
And the light crept up between the shutters
And you heard the sparrows in the gutters,
You had such a vision of the street
As the street hardly understands;
Sitting along the bed's edge, where 35
You curled the papers from your hair,
Or clasped the yellow soles of feet
In the palms of both soiled hands.

4

His soul stretched tight across the skies
That fade behind a city block, 40
Or trampled by insistent feet
At four and five and six o'clock;
And short square fingers stuffing pipes,
And evening newspapers, and eyes
Assured of certain certainties, 45
The conscience of a blackened street
Impatient to assume the world.

I am moved by fancies that are curled
Around these images, and cling:
The notion of some infinitely gentle 50
Infinitely suffering thing.

Wipe your hand across your mouth, and laugh;
The worlds revolve like ancient women
Gathering fuel in vacant lots.

Journey of the Magi

'A cold coming we had of it,
Just the worst time of the year
For a journey, and such a long journey:
The ways deep and the weather sharp,
The very dead of winter.'   5
And the camels galled, sore-footed, refractory,
Lying down in the melting snow.
There were times we regretted
The summer palaces on slopes, the terraces,
And the silken girls bringing sherbet.   10
Then the camel men cursing and grumbling
And running away, and wanting their liquor and women,
And the night-fires going out, and the lack of shelters,
And the cities hostile and the towns unfriendly
And the villages dirty and charging high prices: 15
A hard time we had of it.
At the end we preferred to travel all night,
Sleeping in snatches,
With the voices singing in our ears, saying
That this was all folly.   20

Then at dawn we came down to a temperate valley,
Wet, below the snow line, smelling of vegetation;
With a running stream and a water-mill beating the darkness,
And three trees on the low sky,
And an old white horse galloped away in the meadow.   25
Then we came to a tavern with vine-leaves over the lintel,
Six hands at an open door dicing for pieces of silver,
And feet kicking the empty wine-skins.
But there was no information, and so we continued
And arrived at evening, not a moment too soon   30
Finding the place; it was (you may say) satisfactory.

All this was a long time ago, I remember,
And I would do it again, but set down
This set down
This: were we led all that way for   35
Birth or Death? There was a Birth, certainly,
We had evidence and no doubt. I had seen birth and death,
But had thought they were different; this Birth was
Hard and bitter agony for us, like Death, our death.
We returned to our places, these Kingdoms,   40
But no longer at ease here, in the old dispensation,

With an alien people clutching their gods.
I should be glad of another death.

The Love Song of J. Alfred Prufrock

S'io credesse che mia risposta fosse
A persona che mai tornasse al mondo,
Questa fiamma staria senza più scosse.
Ma perciocche giammai di questo fondo
Non tornò vivo alcun, s'i'odo il vero,
Senza tema d'infamia ti rispondo.

Let us go then, you and I,
When the evening is spread out against the sky
Like a patient etherized upon a table;
Let us go, through certain half-deserted streets,
The muttering retreats   5
Of restless nights in one-night cheap hotels
And sawdust restaurants with oyster-shells:
Streets that follow like a tedious argument
Of insidious intent
To lead you to an overwhelming question . . .   10
Oh, do not ask, "What is it?"
Let us go and make our visit.

In the room the women come and go
Talking of Michelangelo.

The yellow fog that rubs its back upon the window-panes   15
The yellow smoke that rubs its muzzle on the window-panes
Licked its tongue into the corners of the evening,
Lingered upon the pools that stand in drains,
Let fall upon its back the soot that falls from chimneys,
Slipped by the terrace, made a sudden leap,   20
And seeing that it was a soft October night,
Curled once about the house, and fell asleep.

And indeed there will be time
For the yellow smoke that slides along the street,
Rubbing its back upon the window-panes;   25
There will be time, there will be time
To prepare a face to meet the faces that you meet;

THE LOVE SONG OF J. ALFRED PRUFROCK   *Epigraph from Dante's* Inferno, *canto XXVII, 61–66.*
The words are spoken by Guido da Montefeltro when asked to identify himself: "If I thought my answer were given
to anyone who could ever return to the world, this flame would shake no more; but since none ever did return above
from this depth, if what I hear is true, without fear of infamy I answer thee."

There will be time to murder and create,
And time for all the works and days of hands
That lift and drop a question on your plate;　　　　　30
Time for you and time for me,
And time yet for a hundred indecisions,
And for a hundred visions and revisions,
Before the taking of a toast and tea.

In the room the women come and go　　　　　35
Talking of Michelangelo.

And indeed there will be time
To wonder, "Do I dare?" and, "Do I dare?"
Time to turn back and descend the stair,
With a bald spot in the middle of my hair——　　　　　40
[They will say: "How his hair is growing thin!"]
My morning coat, my collar mounting firmly to the chin,
My necktie rich and modest, but asserted by a simple pin——
[They will say: "But how his arms and legs are thin!"]
Do I dare　　　　　45
Disturb the universe?
In a minute there is time
For decisions and revisions which a minute will reverse.

For I have known them all already, known them all:
Have known the evenings, mornings, afternoons,　　　　　50
I have measured out my life with coffee spoons;
I know the voices dying with a dying fall
Beneath the music from a farther room.
　　So how should I presume?

And I have known the eyes already, known them all——　　　　　55
The eyes that fix you in a formulated phrase,
And when I am formulated, sprawling on a pin,
When I am pinned and wriggling on the wall,
Then how should I begin
To spit out all the butt-ends of my days and ways?　　　　　60
　　And how should I presume?

And I have known the arms already, known them all——
Arms that are braceleted and white and bare
[But in the lamplight, downed with light brown hair!]
Is it perfume from a dress　　　　　65
That makes me so digress?
Arms that lie along a table, or wrap about a shawl.
　　And should I then presume?
　　And how should I begin?

Shall I say, I have gone at dusk through narrow streets   70
And watched the smoke that rises from the pipes
Of lonely men in shirt-sleeves, leaning out of windows? . . .

I should have been a pair of ragged claws
Scuttling across the floors of silent seas.

And the afternoon, the evening, sleeps so peacefully!   75
Smoothed by long fingers,
Asleep . . . tired . . . or it malingers,
Stretched on the floor, here beside you and me.
Should I, after tea and cakes and ices,
Have the strength to force the moment to its crisis?   80
But though I have wept and fasted, wept and prayed,
Though I have seen my head [grown slightly bald] brought in upon a platter,
I am no prophet—and here's no great matter;
I have seen the moment of my greatness flicker,
And I have seen the eternal Footman hold my coat, and snicker,   85
And in short, I was afraid.

And would it have been worth it, after all,
After the cups, the marmalade, the tea,
Among the porcelain, among some talk of you and me,
Would it have been worth while,   90
To have bitten off the matter with a smile,
To have squeezed the universe into a ball
To roll it toward some overwhelming question,
To say: "I am Lazarus, come from the dead,
Come back to tell you all, I shall tell you all"—   95
If one, settling a pillow by her head,
     Should say: "That is not what I meant at all.
     That is not it, at all."

And would it have been worth it, after all,
Would it have been worth while,   100
After the sunsets and the dooryards and the sprinkled streets,
After the novels, after the teacups, after the skirts that trail along the floor—
And this, and so much more?—
It is impossible to say just what I mean!
But as if a magic lantern threw the nerves in patterns on a screen: 105
Would it have been worth while
If one, settling a pillow or throwing off a shawl,
And turning toward the window, should say:

[82]**head . . . platter**   *John the Baptist was beheaded at the order of King Herod to please his wife and daughter.
See Matthew 14:1–11.*   [94]**Lazarus**   *Jesus raised him from the dead. See John 11:1–44.*

"That is not it at all,
That is not what I meant, at all." 110

. . . . .

No! I am not Prince Hamlet, nor was meant to be;
Am an attendant lord, one that will do
To swell a progress, start a scene or two,
Advise the prince; no doubt, an easy tool,
Deferential, glad to be of use, 115
Politic, cautious, and meticulous;
Full of high sentence°, but a bit obtuse; *sententiousness*
At times, indeed, almost ridiculous—
Almost, at times, the Fool.

I grow old . . . I grow old . . . 120
I shall wear the bottoms of my trousers rolled.

Shall I part my hair behind? Do I dare to eat a peach?
I shall wear white flannel trousers, and walk upon the beach.
I have heard the mermaids singing, each to each.

I do not think that they will sing to me. 125

I have seen them riding seaward on the waves
Combing the white hair of the waves blown back
When the wind blows the water white and black.

We have lingered in the chambers of the sea
By sea-girls wreathed with seaweed red and brown 130
Till human voices wake us, and we drown.

JOHN CROWE RANSOM
[*1888–1974*]

Bells for John Whiteside's Daughter

There was such speed in her little body,
And such lightness in her footfall,
It is no wonder her brown study° *reverie*
Astonishes us all.

Her wars were bruited° in our high window. *sounded* 5
We looked among orchard trees and beyond

Where she took arms against her shadow,
Or harried unto the pond

The lazy geese, like a snow cloud
Dripping their snow on the green grass,   10
Tricking and stopping, sleepy and proud,
Who cried in goose, Alas,

For the tireless heart within the little
Lady with rod that made them rise
From their noon apple-dreams and scuttle   15
Goose-fashion under the skies!

But now go the bells, and we are ready,
In one house we are sternly stopped
To say we are vexed at her brown study,
Lying so primly propped.   20

Piazza Piece

—I am a gentleman in a dustcoat trying
To make you hear. Your ears are soft and small
And listen to an old man not at all,
They want the young men's whispering and sighing.
But see the roses on your trellis dying   5
And hear the spectral singing of the moon;
For I must have my lovely lady soon,
I am a gentleman in a dustcoat trying.

—I am a lady young in beauty waiting
Until my truelove comes, and then we kiss.   10
But what grey man among the vines is this
Whose words are dry and faint as in a dream?
Back from my trellis, Sir, before I scream!
I am a lady young in beauty waiting.

Blue Girls

Twirling your blue skirts, travelling the sward
Under the towers of your seminary,
Go listen to your teachers old and contrary
Without believing a word.

Tie the white fillets then about your hair 5
And think no more of what will come to pass
Than bluebirds that go walking on the grass
And chattering on the air.

Practise your beauty, blue girls, before it fail;
And I will cry with my loud lips and publish 10
Beauty which all our power shall never establish,
It is so frail.

For I could tell you a story which is true;
I know a woman with a terrible tongue,
Blear eyes fallen from blue, 15
All her perfections tarnished—yet it is not long
Since she was lovelier than any of you.

Winter Remembered

Two evils, monstrous either one apart,
Possessed me, and were long and loath at going:
A cry of Absence, Absence, in the heart,
And in the wood the furious winter blowing.

Think not, when fire was bright upon my bricks, 5
And past the tight boards hardly a wind could enter,
I glowed like them, the simple burning sticks,
Far from my cause, my proper heat and center.

Better to walk forth in the frozen air
And wash my wound in the snows; that would be healing; 10
Because my heart would throb less painful there,
Being caked with cold, and past the smart of feeling.

And where I walked, the murderous winter blast
Would have this body bowed, these eyeballs streaming,
And though I think this heart's blood froze not fast 15
It ran too small to spare one drop for dreaming.

Dear love, these fingers that had known your touch,
And tied our separate forces first together,
Were ten poor idiot fingers not worth much,
Ten frozen parsnips hanging in the weather. 20

ANNA AKHMATOVA
[b. 1889]

Requiem

No, not far beneath some foreign sky then,
Not with foreign wings to shelter me,—
I was with my people then, close by them
Where my luckless people chanced to be.

By Way of a Preface

In the terrible years of the Yezhovshchina, I spent seventeen months in the prison queues in Leningrad. Somehow, one day, someone "identified" me. Then a woman standing behind me, whose lips were blue with cold, and who, naturally enough, had never even heard of my name, emerged from that state of torpor common to us all and, putting her lips close to my ear (there, everyone spoke in whispers), asked me:

—And could you describe *this?*

And I answered her:

—I can.

Then something vaguely like a smile flashed across what once had been her face.

1 April 1957
Leningrad

Dedication

Mountains bow beneath that boundless sorrow,
And the mighty river stops its flow.
But those prison bolts are tried and thorough,
And beyond them, every "convict's burrow"
Tells a tale of mortal woe.   5
Someone, somewhere, feels the cool wind, bracing,
Sees the sun go nestling down to rest—
We know nothing, we, together facing
Still the sickening clank of keys, the pacing
Of the sentries with their heavy steps.   10
We'd rise, as for early Mass, each morning,
Cross the callous city, wend our way,
Meet, more lifeless than the dead, half mourning,
Watch the sun sink, the Neva mist forming,
But with hope still singing far away.   15

REQUIEM *Preface* **Yezhovshchina** *roughly, "the reign of Yezhov." Yezhov was head of the Soviet secret police in the late 1930's until he himself became a victim of one of Stalin's purges.*

Sentenced . . . And at once the tears come rolling,
Cut off from the world, quite on her own,
Heart reduced to shreds, and almost falling,
Just as if some lout had sent her sprawling,
Still . . . She staggers on her way . . . Alone . . .   20
Where are now the friends of my misfortune,
Those that shared my own two years of hell?
What do the Siberian snow-winds caution,
What bodes the moon circle for their fortunes?
Theirs be this, my greeting and farewell.   25

Prelude

It was when no one smiled any longer
Save the dead, who were glad of release.
And when Leningrad dangled, incongruous,
By its prisons—a needless caprice.
And when, out of their minds with sheer suffering,   30
The long lines of the newly condemned
Heard the engines' shrill whistles go sputtering
A brief song of farewell to their friends.
Stars of death stood above us, and Russia,
In her innocence, twisted in pain   35
Under blood-spattered boots, and the shudder
Of the Black Marias in their train.

1

It was dawn when they took you. I followed,
As a widow walks after the bier.
By the icons—a candle, burnt hollow;   40
In the bed-room—the children, in tears.
Your lips—cool from the kiss of the icon,
Still to think—the cold sweat on your brow . . .
Like the wives of the Streltsy, now I come
To wail under the Kremlin's gaunt towers.   45

2

Silent flows the silent Don,
Yellow moon looks quietly on,

Cap askew, looks in the room,
Sees a shadow in the gloom.

Sees this woman, sick, at home,   50
Sees this woman, all alone,

[37] **Black Marias**   *black automobiles used to carry off prisoners abducted during the night during the time of Stalin's purges.*

Husband buried, then to see
Son arrested . . . Pray for me.

3

No, this is not me, this is somebody else that suffers.
I could never face that, and all that has happened: 55
Let sackcloth and ashes enshroud it,
And see all the lamps are removed . . .
            Night.

4

You, my mocking one, pet of society,
And gay sinner of Tsarskoe Selo: 60
Had you dreamt, in your sweet notoriety,
Of the future that lay in store—
How you'd stand at the Crosses, three-hundredth
In the queue, each bleak New Year,
Hug your precious parcel of comforts, 65
Melt the ice with your hot bright tears.
There the poplar, used to imprisonment,
Sways aloft. Not a sound. But think
Of the numbers rotting there, innocent . . .

5

For seventeen long months my pleas, 70
My cries have called you home.
I've begged the hangman on my knees,
My son, my dread, my own.
My mind's mixed up for good, and I'm
No longer even clear 75
Who's man, who's beast, nor how much time
Before the end draws near.
And only flowers decked with dust,
And censers ringing, footprints thrust
Somewhere-nowhere, afar. 80
And, staring me straight in the eye
And warning me that death is nigh—
One monumental star.

6

Weeks fly past in light profusion,
How to fathom what's been done: 85
How those long white nights, dear son,

[60]**Tsarskoe Selo** *The poet spent her youth here.* [63]**The Crosses** *a prison in Leningrad whose buildings form a cross.*

Watched you in your cell's seclusion.
How once more they watch you there,
Eyes like hawks' that burn right through you,
Speak to you of death, speak to you   90
Of the lofty cross you bear.

7

Sentence

And the word in stone has fallen heavy
On my breast, which was alive till now.
Never mind—for, mark you, I was ready,
I shall get along somehow.   95

So much to be done before tomorrow:
Crush the memory till no thoughts remain,
Carve a heart in stone, immune to sorrow,
Teach myself to face life once again,—

And if not . . . The rustling heat of summer   100
Fills my window with its festive tone.
I long since foresensed that there would come a
Sunny day like this—and empty home.

8

To Death

You'll come in any case—then why not right away?
I'm waiting—life has dragged me under.   105
I've put the lamp out, left the door to show the way
When you come in your simple wonder.
For that, choose any guise you like: Burst in on me,
A shell with poison-gas container,
Or, bandit with a heavy weight, creep up on me,   110
Or poison me with typhus vapour.
Or be a fable, known *ad nauseam*
To everyone denounced in error,
So I may see the top of that blue cap, and scan
The face of the house-porter, white with terror.   115
But nothing matters now. The Yenisey° swirls by,   a river
The Pole star shines above the torrent.
And the glint of those beloved eyes
Conceals the last, the final horror.

---

[114]*blue cap*   *refers to the uniform worn by the secret police (NKVD).*

9

So madness now has wrapped its wings   120
Round half my soul and plies me, heartless,
With draughts of fiery wine, begins
To lure me towards the vale of darkness.

And I can see that I must now
Concede the victory—as I listen,   125
The dream that dogged my fevered brow
Already seems an outside vision.

And though I go on bended knee
To plead, implore its intercession,
There's nothing I may take with me,   130
It countenances no concession:

Nor yet my son's distracted eyes—
The rock-like suffering rooted in them,
The day the storm broke from clear skies,
The hour spent visiting the prison,   135

Nor yet the kind, cool clasp of hands,
The lime-tree shadows' fitful darting,
The far light call across the land—
The soothing words exchanged on parting.

10

Crucifixion

Weep not for Me, Mother,
that I am in the grave.

I

The angels hailed that solemn hour and stately,   140
The heavens dissolved in tongues of fire. And He
Said to the Father: "Why didst Thou forsake Me!"
And to His Mother: "Weep thou not for Me . . ."

II

Magdalena sobbed, and the disciple,
He whom Jesus loved, stood petrified.   145
But there, where His Mother stood in silence,
No one durst so much as lift their eyes.

Epilogue

I

I've learned how faces droop and then grow hollow,
How fear looks out from underneath the lids,
How cheeks, carved out of suffering and of sorrow, 150
Take on the lines of rough cuneiform scripts.
How heads of curls, but lately black or ashen,
Turn suddenly to silver overnight,
Smiles fade on lips reduced to dread submission,
A hoarse dry laugh stands in for trembling fright. 155
I pray, not for myself alone, my cry
Goes up for all those with me there—for all,
In heart of winter, heat-wave of July,
Who stood beneath that blind, deep-crimson wall.

II

The hour of remembrance is with us again. 160
I see you, I hear you, I feel you as then:

There's one they scarce dragged to the window, and one
Whose days in the land of her forebears are done,

And one tossed her beautiful head back when shown
Her corner, and said: "It's like being back home!" 165

I'd like to remember each one by her name,
But they took the list, and there's no more remain.

I've worked them a funeral shroud from each word
Of pain that escaped them, and I overheard.

I'll think of them everywhere, always, each one. 170
I shall not forget them in dark days to come.

And should they once silence my mortified lips,
Let one hundred millions for whom my voice speaks—

Let *them* take my place, and remember each year
Whenever my day of remembrance draws near. 175

And should they one day, in this country, agree
To raise a memorial somewhere to me,

I'd willingly give my consent to their plan,
But on one condition, which is—that it stand,

Not down by the sea, where I entered this world
(I've cut the last links that once bound us of old),

Nor yet by the tree-stump in old Tsarsky Sad,
Whose shade seeks me still with disconsolate love,

But here, where they let me stand three hundred hours,   185
And never so much as unbolted the doors.

For even in death I still fear to forget
The grim Black Marias, their thundering tread,

The sickening slam of that loathsome cell-door,
The old woman's howl, like a wounded beast's roar.

And may the snow, melting, well forth clear and strong,   190
Like tears from my eye-lids, unmoving, like bronze,

And may the lone prison-dove coo from afar,
And boats travel silently down the Neva.

TRANSLATED BY ROBIN KEMBALL

BORIS PASTERNAK
[1890–1960]

Winter Night

Snow, snow over the whole land
across all boundaries.
The candle burned on the table,
the candle burned.

As in summer swarms   5
of midges fly to a flame,
snowflakes fluttered
around the windowframe.

Blown snow stuck   10
rings and arrows on the glass.
The candle burned on the table,
the candle burned.

Shadows were lying
on the lighted ceiling,
of crossed arms, crossed legs,   15
crossed destinies.

Two shoes fell
noisily on the floor.
The night light wept
wax drops on a dress.   20

Everything was lost in the
greying white snow haze.
The candle burned on the table,
the candle burned.

Draught at the candle from the corner,   25
the heat of temptation
angel-like raised two wings
in the form of a cross.

Snow fell all February
and now and then   30
the candle burned on the table,
the candle burned.

TRANSLATED BY RICHARD MCKANE

CLAUDE MCKAY

[1890–1948]

The Tropics in New York

Bananas ripe and green, and ginger-root,
   Cocoa in pods and alligator pears,
And tangerines and mangoes and grape fruit,
   Fit for the highest prize at parish fairs,

Set in the window, bringing memories   5
   Of fruit-trees laden by low-singing rills,
And dewy dawns, and mystical blue skies
   In benediction over nun-like hills.

My eyes grew dim, and I could no more gaze;
   A wave of longing through my body swept,   10

And, hungry for the old, familiar ways,
    I turned aside and bowed my head and wept.

If we must die

If we must die, let it not be like hogs
Hunted and penned in an inglorious spot,
While round us bark the mad and hungry dogs,
Making their mock at our accursed lot.
If we must die, O let us nobly die,   5
So that our precious blood may not be shed
In vain; then even the monsters we defy
Shall be constrained to honor us though dead!
O kinsmen! we must meet the common foe!
Though far outnumbered let us show us brave,   10
And for their thousand blows deal one deathblow!
What though before us lies the open grave?
Like men we'll face the murderous, cowardly pack,
Pressed to the wall, dying, but fighting back!

MARINA TSVETAYEVA

[1892–1941]

No one has taken anything away

No one has taken anything away—
    there is even a sweetness for me in being apart.
I kiss you now across the many
    hundreds of miles that separate us.

I know: our gifts are unequal, which is   5
    why my voice is—quiet, for the first time.
What can my untutored verse
    matter to you, a young Derzhavin?

For your terrible flight I give you blessing.
    Fly, then, young eagle! You   10
have stared into the sun without blinking.
    Can my young gaze be too heavy for you?

No one has ever stared more
    tenderly or more fixedly after you . . .

I kiss you—across hundreds of
    separating years.   15

TRANSLATED BY ELAINE FEINSTEIN

Yesterday he still looked in my eyes

Yesterday he still looked in my eyes, yet
    today   his looks are bent aside.   Yesterday
he sat here until the birds began, but
    today   all those larks are   ravens.

Stupid creature! And you are wise, you   5
    live while I am stunned.
Now for the lament of women in all times:
    —My love, what was it I did to you?

And tears are   water, blood is   water,
    a woman always washes in blood and tears.   10
Love is a step-mother, and no mother:
    then expect no justice or mercy from her.

Ships carry away the ones we love.
    Along the white road they are taken away.
And one cry stretches across the earth: 15
    —My love, what was it I did to you?

Yesterday he lay at my feet. He even
    compared me with the Chinese empire! Then
suddenly he let his hands fall open, and
    my life fell out like   a rusty kopeck.   20

A child-murderer, before some court
    I stand   loathsome and timid I am.
And yet even in Hell I shall demand:
    —My love, what was it I did to you?

I ask this chair, I ask the bed: Why?   25
    Why do I suffer and live in penury?
His kisses stopped. He wanted to break you.
    To kiss another girl is their reply.

He taught me to live in fire, he threw me there,
    and then abandoned me on steppes of ice.   30
My love, I know what you have done to me.
    —My love, what was it I did to you?

I know everything, don't argue with me!
   I can see now, I'm a lover no longer.
And now I know wherever love holds power   35
   Death approaches soon   like a gardener.

It is almost like shaking a tree, in time
   some ripe apple comes falling down. So
for everything, for everything   forgive me,
   —my love   whatever it was I did to you.   40

TRANSLATED BY ELAINE FEINSTEIN

VICENTE HUIDOBRO

[1892–1948]

Ars Poetica

Let poetry be like a key
Opening a thousand doors.
A leaf falls; something flies by;
Let all the eye sees be created
And the soul of the listener tremble.   5

Invent new worlds and watch your word;
The adjective, when it doesn't give life, kills it.

We are in the age of nerves.
The muscle hangs,
Like a memory, in museums;   10
But we are not the weaker for it:
True vigor
Resides in the head.

Oh Poets, why sing of roses!
Let them flower in your poems;   15

For us alone
Do all things live beneath the Sun.

The poet is a little God.

TRANSLATED BY DAVID M. GUSS

ARS POETICA   *the art of poetry.*

ARCHIBALD MACLEISH
[1892–1982]

Ars Poetica

A poem should be palpable and mute
As a globed fruit,

Dumb
As old medallions to the thumb,

Silent as the sleeve-worn stone
Of casement ledges where the moss has grown—

A poem should be wordless
As the flight of birds.

A poem should be motionless in time
As the moon climbs,

Leaving, as the moon releases
Twig by twig the night-entangled trees,

Leaving, as the moon behind the winter leaves,
Memory by memory the mind—

A poem should be motionless in time
As the moon climbs.

A poem should be equal to:
Not true.

For all the history of grief
An empty doorway and a maple leaf.

For love
The leaning grasses and two lights above the sea—

A poem should not mean
But be.

You, Andrew Marvell

And here face down beneath the sun
And here upon earth's noonward height
To feel the always coming on
The always rising of the night

To feel creep up the curving east   5
The earthy chill of dusk and slow
Upon those under lands the vast
And ever climbing shadow grow

And strange at Ecbatan the trees
Take leaf by leaf the evening strange   10
The flooding dark about their knees
The mountains over Persia change

And now at Kermanshah the gate
Dark empty and the withered grass
And through the twilight now the late   15
Few travelers in the westward pass

And Baghdad darken and the bridge
Across the silent river gone
And through Arabia the edge
Of evening widen and steal on   20

And deepen on Palmyra's street
The wheel rut in the ruined stone
And Lebanon fade out and Crete
High through the clouds and overblown

And over Sicily the air   25
Still flashing with the landward gulls
And loom and slowly disappear
The sails above the shadowy hulls

And Spain go under and the shore
Of Africa the gilded sand   30
And evening vanish and no more
The low pale light across that land

YOU, ANDREW MARVELL   *See Marvell's "To His Coy Mistress," p. 549, especially the last two lines.*
[9]**Ecbatan** *the ancient capital of Media (now part of Iran).*   [13]**Kermanshah** *west of Ecbatan, also a city in Iran.*   [17]**Baghdad** *capital of Iraq, west of Kermanshah.*   [21]**Palmyra's** *The movement west continues to Palmyra, Lebanon, Crete, Sicily, Spain, and the United States ("here," l. 34).*

Nor now the long light on the sea
And here face downward in the sun
To feel how swift how secretly   35
The shadow of the night comes on. . . .

"Not Marble Nor the Gilded Monuments"

The praisers of women in their proud and beautiful poems
Naming the grave mouth and the hair and the eyes
Boasted those they loved should be forever remembered
These were lies

The words sound but the face in the Istrian sun is forgotten   5
The poet speaks but to her dead ears no more
The sleek throat is gone—and the breast that was troubled to listen
Shadow from door

Therefore I will not praise your knees nor your fine walking
Telling you men shall remember your name as long   10
As lips move or breath is spent or the iron of English
Rings from a tongue

I shall say you were young and your arms straight and your mouth scarlet
I shall say you will die and none will remember you
Your arms change and none remember the swish of your garments   15
Nor the click of your shoe

Not with my hand's strength not with difficult labor
Springing the obstinate words to the bones of your breast
And the stubborn line to your young stride and the breath to your breathing
And the beat to your haste   20
Shall I prevail on the hearts of unborn men to remember

(What is a dead girl but a shadowy ghost
Or a dead man's voice but a distant and vain affirmation
Like dream words most)

Therefore I will not speak of the undying glory of women   25
I will say you were young and straight and your skin fair
And you stood in the door and the sun was a shadow of leaves on your shoulders
And a leaf on your hair

I will not speak of the famous beauty of dead women
I will say the shape of a leaf lay once on your hair   30

"NOT MARBLE NOR THE GILDED MONUMENTS" *See Shakespeare's Sonnet, p. 530.*   [5]*Istrian*
referring to Istria, a peninsula on the Adriatic Sea.

Till the world ends and the eyes are out and the mouths broken
Look! It is there!

CÉSAR VALLEJO
[1892–1938]

Our Daily Bread

(FOR ALEJANDRO GAMBOA)

Breakfast is drunk down . . . Damp earth
of the cemetery gives off the fragrance of the precious blood.
City of winter . . . the mordant crusade
of a cart that seems to pull behind it
an emotion of fasting that cannot get free!   5

I wish I could beat on all the doors,
and ask for somebody; and then
look at the poor, and, while they wept softly,
give bits of fresh bread to them.
And plunder the rich of their vineyards   10
with those two blessed hands
which blasted the nails with one blow of light,
and flew away from the Cross!

Eyelash of morning, you cannot lift yourselves!
Give us our daily bread,   15
Lord . . . !

Every bone in me belongs to others;
and maybe I robbed them.
I came to take something for myself that maybe
was meant for some other man;   20
and I start thinking that, if I had not been born,
another poor man could have drunk this coffee.
I feel like a dirty thief . . . Where will I end?

And in this frigid hour, when the earth
has the odor of human dust and is so sad,   25
I wish I could beat on all the doors
and beg pardon from someone,
and make bits of fresh bread for him
here, in the oven of my heart . . . !

TRANSLATED BY JAMES WRIGHT

The Distant Footsteps

My father is sleeping. His noble face
suggests a mild heart;
he is so sweet now . . .
if anything bitter is in him, I must be the bitterness.

There is loneliness in the parlor; they are praying;   5
and there is no news of the children today.
My father wakes, he listens
for the flight into Egypt, the good-bye that dresses wounds.
Now he is so near;
if anything distant is in him, I must be the distance.   10

And my mother walks past in the orchard,
savoring a taste already without savor.
Now she is so gentle,
so much wing, so much farewell, so much love.

There is loneliness in the parlor with no sound,   15
no news, no greenness, no childhood.
And if something is broken this afternoon,
and if something descends or creaks,
it is two old roads, curving and white.
Down them my heart is walking on foot.   20

TRANSLATED BY JAMES WRIGHT AND JOHN KNOEPFLE

WILFRED OWEN

[1893–1918]

Dulce et Decorum Est

Bent double, like old beggars under sacks,
Knock-kneed, coughing like hags, we cursed through sludge,
Till on the haunting flares we turned our backs
And towards our distant rest began to trudge.
Men marched asleep. Many had lost their boots   5
But limped on, blood-shod. All went lame; all blind;
Drunk with fatigue; deaf even to the hoots
Of tired, outstripped Five-Nines that dropped behind.

DULCE ET DECORUM EST   *"It is sweet and fitting to die for one's country."* The title and last two lines
are from Horace, Odes, III, ii.13.

Gas! GAS! Quick, boys!—An ecstasy of fumbling,   10
Fitting the clumsy helmets just in time;
But someone still was yelling out and stumbling
And flound'ring like a man in fire or lime . . .
Dim, through the misty panes and thick green light,
As under a green sea, I saw him drowning.

In all my dreams, before my helpless sight,   15
He plunges at me, guttering, choking, drowning.

If in some smothering dreams you too could pace
Behind the wagon that we flung him in,
And watch the white eyes writhing in his face,
His hanging face, like a devil's sick of sin;   20
If you could hear, at every jolt, the blood
Come gargling from the froth-corrupted lungs,
Obscene as cancer, bitter as the cud
Of vile, incurable sores on innocent tongues,—
My friend, you would not tell with such high zest   25
To children ardent for some desperate glory,
The old Lie: *Dulce et decorum est*
Pro patria mori.

E. E. CUMMINGS

[*1894–1962*]

anyone lived in a pretty how town

anyone lived in a pretty how town
(with up so floating many bells down)
spring summer autumn winter
he sang his didn't he danced his did.

Women and men (both little and small)   5
cared for anyone not at all
they sowed their isn't they reaped their same
sun moon stars rain

children guessed (but only a few
and down they forgot as up they grew   10
autumn winter spring summer)
that noone loved him more by more

when by now and tree by leaf
she laughed his joy she cried his grief
bird by snow and stir by still   15
anyone's any was all to her

someones married their everyones
laughed their cryings and did their dance
(sleep wake hope and then)they
said their nevers they slept their dream   20

stars rain sun moon
(and only the snow can begin to explain
how children are apt to forget to remember
with up so floating many bells down)

one day anyone died i guess   25
(and noone stooped to kiss his face)
busy folk buried them side by side
little by little and was by was

all by all and deep by deep
and more by more they dream their sleep   30
noone and anyone earth by april
wish by spirit and if by yes.

Women and men (both dong and ding)
summer autumn winter spring
reaped their sowing and went their came   35
sun moon stars rain

nobody loses all the time

nobody loses all the time

i had an uncle named
Sol who was a born failure and
nearly everybody said he should have gone
into vaudeville perhaps because my Uncle Sol could   5
sing McCann He Was A Diver on Xmas Eve like Hell Itself which
may or may not account for the fact that my Uncle

Sol indulged in that possibly most inexcusable
of all to use a highfalootin phrase
luxuries that is or to   10
wit farming and be

it needlessly
added

my Uncle Sol's farm
failed because the chickens   15
ate the vegetables so
my Uncle Sol had a
chicken farm till the
skunks ate the chickens when

my Uncle Sol   20
had a skunk farm but
the skunks caught cold and
died and so
my Uncle Sol imitated the
skunks in a subtle manner   25

or by drowning himself in the watertank
but somebody who'd given my Uncle Sol a Victor
Victrola and records while he lived presented to
him upon the auspicious occasion of his decease a
scrumptious not to mention splendiferous funeral with   30
tall boys in black gloves and flowers and everything and

i remember we all cried like the Missouri
when my Uncle Sol's coffin lurched because
somebody pressed a button
(and down went   35
my Uncle
Sol

and started a worm farm)

my father moved through dooms of love

my father moved through dooms of love
through sames of am through haves of give,
singing each morning out of each night
my father moved through depths of height

this motionless forgetful where   5
turned at his glance to shining here;
that if (so timid air is firm)
under his eyes would stir and squirm

newly as from unburied which
floats the first who,his april touch   10
drove sleeping selves to swarm their fates
woke dreamers to their ghostly roots

and should some why completely weep
my father's fingers brought her sleep:
vainly no smallest voice might cry   15
for he could feel the mountains grow.

Lifting the valleys of the sea
my father moved through griefs of joy;
praising a forehead called the moon
singing desire into begin   20

joy was his song and joy so pure
a heart of star by him could steer
and pure so now and now so yes
the wrists of twilight would rejoice

keen as midsummer's keen beyond   25
conceiving mind of sun will stand,
so strictly (over utmost him
so hugely) stood my father's dream

his flesh was flesh his blood was blood:
no hungry man but wished him food;   30
no cripple wouldn't creep one mile
uphill to only see him smile.

Scorning the pomp of must and shall
my father moved through dooms of feel;
his anger was as right as rain   35
his pity was as green as grain

septembering arms of year extend
less humbly wealth to foe and friend
than he to foolish and to wise
offered immeasurable is   40

proudly and (by octobering flame
beckoned) as earth will downward climb,
so naked for immortal work
his shoulders marched against the dark

his sorrow was as true as bread: 45
no liar looked him in the head;

if every friend became his foe
he'd laugh and build a world with snow.

My father moved through theys of we,
singing each new leaf out of each tree   50
(and every child was sure that spring
danced when she heard my father sing)

then let men kill which cannot share,
let blood and flesh be mud and mire,
scheming imagine,passion willed,   55
freedom a drug that's bought and sold

giving to steal and cruel kind,
a heart to fear,to doubt a mind,
to differ a disease of same,
conform the pinnacle of am   60

though dull were all we taste as bright,
bitter all utterly things sweet,
maggoty minus and dumb death
all we inherit,all bequeath

and nothing quite so least as truth   65
—i say though hate were why men breathe—
because my father lived his soul
love is the whole and more than all

JEAN TOOMER

[1894–1967]

Reapers

Black reapers with the sound of steel on stones
Arc sharpening scythes. I see them place the hones
In their hip-pockets as a thing that's done,
And start their silent swinging, one by one.
Black horses drive a mower through the weeds,   5
And there, a field rat, startled, squealing bleeds,
His belly close to ground. I see the blade,
Blood-stained, continue cutting weeds and shade.

JUANA DE IBARBOUROU
[*b. 1895*]

The Strong Bond

I grew
for you.
Lay waste to me. My acacia
implores its finishing touch from your hands.

I flowered   5
for you.
Cut me. When born
my lily doubted being flower or candle.

I flowed
for you.   10
Drink me. Crystal
envies the clarity of my spring.

I gave wings
for you.
Hunt me. Butterfly of night   15
I encircle your impatient flame.

For you I will suffer.
Blessed the pain that your love gives me!
Blessed the axe, the net
and praised the scissors and thirst!   20

My side will ooze blood,
my love.
What lovelier brooch, what handsomer jewel
than a scarlet thorn for you?

Instead of glass beads for my hair   25
seven long thorns,
and instead of earrings
two hot coals for two rubies.

You will see me laugh
watching me suffer.   30

And you will cry
and then . . . you will be mine as never before!

TRANSLATED BY LINDA SCHEER

ROBERT GRAVES
[b. 1895]

Symptoms of Love

Love is a universal migraine,
A bright stain on the vision
Blotting out reason.

Symptoms of true love
Are leanness, jealousy,   5
Laggard dawns;

Are omens and nightmares—
Listening for a knock,
Waiting for a sign:

For a touch of her fingers   10
In a darkened room,
For a searching look.

Take courage, lover!
Could you endure such pain
At any hand but hers?   15

EUGENE MONTALE
[b. 1896]

The Eel

The eel, the
siren of sleety seas, abandoning
the Baltic for our waters,
our estuaries, our
freshets—to thresh upcurrent under the brunt   5
of the flood, sunk deep, from brook to brook, and then

trickle to trickle dwindling,
more inner always, always more in the heart
of the living rock,
needling in ruts of the mud, until, one day,   10
explosion of splendor from the chestnut groves
kindles a flicker in deadwater sumps,
in ditches pitched
from ramparts of the Apennine to Romagna;
eel: torch and whip;   15
arrow of love on earth,
which nothing but our gorges or bone-dry
gutters of the Pyrenees usher back
to edens of fertility;
green soul that probes   20
for life where only
fevering heat or devastation preys,
spark that says
the whole commences when the whole would seem
charred black, an old stick buried;   25
brief rainbow, twin
to that within your lashes' dazzle, that
you keep alive, inviolate, among
the sons of men, steeped in your mire—in this
not recognize a sister?   30

TRANSLATED BY JOHN FREDERICK NIMS

FEDERICO GARCIA LORCA

[1899–1936]

Lament for Ignacio Sanchez Mejias

1. Cogida and Death

At five in the afternoon.
It was exactly five in the afternoon.
A boy brought the white sheet
at five in the afternoon.
A frail of lime ready prepared   5
at five in the afternoon.
The rest was death, and death alone
at five in the afternoon.

The wind carried away the cottonwool
at five in the afternoon.   10

And the oxide scattered crystal and nickel
at five in the afternoon.
Now the dove and the leopard wrestle
at five in the afternoon.
And a thigh with a desolate horn
at five in the afternoon.
The bass-string struck up
at five in the afternoon.
Arsenic bells and smoke
at five in the afternoon.
Groups of silence in the corners
at five in the afternoon.
And the bull alone with a high heart!
At five in the afternoon.
When the sweat of snow was coming
at five in the afternoon,
when the bull ring was covered in iodine
at five in the afternoon.
Death laid eggs in the wound
at five in the afternoon.
At five in the afternoon.
Exactly at five o'clock in the afternoon.

A coffin on wheels is his bed
at five in the afternoon.
Bones and flutes resound in his ears
at five in the afternoon.
Now the bull was bellowing through his forehead
at five in the afternoon.
The room was iridescent with agony
at five in the afternoon.
In the distance the gangrene now comes
at five in the afternoon.
Horn of the lily through green groins
at five in the afternoon.
The wounds were burning like suns
at five in the afternoon,
and the crowd was breaking the windows
at five in the afternoon.
At five in the afternoon.
Ah, that fatal five in the afternoon!
It was five by all the clocks!
It was five in the shade of the afternoon!

2. The Spilled Blood

I will not see it!

Tell the moon to come
for I do not want to see the blood   55
of Ignacio on the sand.

I will not see it!

The moon wide open.
Horse of still clouds,
and the grey bull ring of dreams   60
with willows in the barreras.
The tiers of seats, and spills
over the corduroy and the leather
of a thirsty multitude.
Who shouts that I should come near!   65
Do not ask me to see it!

His eyes did not close
when he saw the horns near,
but the terrible mothers
lifted their heads.   70
And across the ranches,
an air of secret voices rose,
shouting to celestial bulls,
herdsmen of pale mist.
There was no prince in Seville   75
who could compare with him,
nor sword like his sword
nor heart so true.
Like a river of lions
was his marvellous strength,   80
and like a marble torso
his firm drawn moderation.
The air of Andalusian Rome
gilded his head
where his smile was a spikenard   85
of wit and intelligence.
What a great torero in the ring!
What a good peasant in the sierra!
How gentle with the sheaves!
How hard with the spurs!   90
How tender with the dew!
How dazzling in the fiesta!
How tremendous with the final
banderillas of darkness!

But now he sleeps without end.   95
Now the moss and the grass

open with sure fingers
the flower of his skull.
And now his blood comes out singing;
singing along marshes and meadows,   100
sliding on frozen horns,
faltering soulless in the mist,
stumbling over a thousand hoofs
like a long, dark, sad tongue,
to form a pool of agony   105
close to the starry Guadalquivir.
Oh, white wall of Spain!
Oh, black bull of sorrow!
Oh, hard blood of Ignacio!
Oh, nightingale of his veins!   110
No.
I will not see it!
No chalice can contain it,
no swallows can drink it,
no frost of light can cool it,   115
nor song nor deluge of white lilies,
no glass can cover it with silver.
No.
I will not see it!

3. The Laid Out Body

Stone is a forehead where dreams grieve   120
without curving waters and frozen cypresses.
Stone is a shoulder on which to bear Time
with trees formed of tears and ribbons and planets.

I have seen grey showers move towards the waves
raising their tender riddled arms,   125
to avoid being caught by the lying stone
which loosens their limbs without soaking the blood.

For stone gathers seed and clouds,
skeleton larks and wolves of penumbra:
but yields not sounds nor crystals nor fire,   130
only bull rings and bull rings and more bull rings without walls.

Now, Ignacio the well born lies on the stone.
All is finished. What is happening? Contemplate his face:
death has covered him with pale sulphur
and has placed on him the head of a dark minotaur.   135

All is finished. The rain penetrates his mouth.
The air, as if mad, leaves his sunken chest,

and Love, soaked through with tears of snow,
warms itself on the peak of the herd.

What are they saying? A stenching silence settles down.   140
We are here with a body laid out which fades away,
Go, Ignacio; feel not the hot bellowing.
Sleep, fly, rest: even the sea dies!

4. Absent Soul

The bull does not know you, nor the fig tree,
nor the horses, nor the ants in your own house.   145
The child and the afternoon do not know you
because you have died for ever.

The back of the stone does not know you,
nor the black satin in which you crumble.
Your silent memory does not know you   150
because you have died for ever.

The autumn will come with small white snails,
misty grapes and with clustered hills,
but no one will look into your eyes
because you have died for ever.   155

Because you have died for ever,
like all the dead of the Earth,
like all the dead who are forgotten
in a heap of lifeless dogs.

Nobody knows you. No. But I sing of you.   160
For posterity I sing of your profile and grace.
Of the signal maturity of your understanding.
Of your appetite for death and the taste of its mouth.
Of the sadness of your once valiant gaiety.

It will be a long time, if ever, before there is born   165
an Andalusian so true, so rich in adventure.
I sing of his elegance with words that groan,
and I remember a sad breeze through the olive trees.

TRANSLATED BY STEPHEN SPENDER AND J. L. GILI

JORGE LUIS BORGES
[b. 1899]

Chess

I

Set in their studious corners, the players
move the gradual pieces. Until dawn
the chessboard keeps them in its strict confinement
with its two colors set at daggers drawn.

Within the game itself the forms give off   5
their magic rules: Homeric castle, knight
swift to attack, queen warlike, king decisive,
slanted bishop, and attacking pawns.

Eventually, when the players have withdrawn,
when time itself has finally consumed them,   10
the ritual certainly will not be done.

It was in the East, this war took fire.
Today the whole earth is its theatre.
Like the game of love, this game goes on forever.

II

Faint-hearted king, sly bishop, ruthless queen,   15
straightforward castle, and deceitful pawn—
over the checkered black and white terrain
they seek out and begin their armed campaign.

They do not know it is the player's hand
that dominates and guides their destiny.   20
They do not know an adamantine fate
controls their will and lays the battle plan.

The player too is captive of caprice
(the words are Omar's) on another ground
where black nights alternate with white of days.   25

God moves the player, he in turn, the piece.
But what god beyond God begins the round
of dust and time and sleep and agonies?

TRANSLATED BY ALASTAIR REID

The Blind Man

1

He is divested of the diverse world,
of faces, which still stay as once they were,
of the adjoining streets, now far away,
and of the concave sky, once infinite.
Of books, he keeps no more than what is left him   5
by memory, that brother of forgetting,
which keeps the formula but not the feeling
and which reflects no more than tag and name.
Traps lie in wait for me. My every step
might be a fall. I am a prisoner   10
shuffling through a time which feels like dream,
taking no note of mornings or of sunsets.
It is night. I am alone. In verse like this,
I must create my insipid universe.

2

Since I was born, in 1899,   15
beside the concave vine and the deep cistern,
frittering time, so brief in memory,
kept taking from me all my eye-shaped world.
Both days and nights would wear away the profiles
of human letters and of well-loved faces.   20
My wasted eyes would ask their useless questions
of pointless libraries and lecterns.
Blue and vermilion both are now a fog,
both useless sounds. The mirror I look into
is gray. I breathe a rose across the garden,   25
a wistful rose, my friends, out of the twilight.
Only the shades of yellow stay with me
and I can see only to look on nightmares.

TRANSLATED BY ALASTAIR REID

ROBERT FRANCIS

[*b. 1901*]

Pitcher

His art is eccentricity, his aim
How not to hit the mark he seems to aim at,

His passion how to avoid the obvious,
His technique how to vary the avoidance.

The others throw to be comprehended. He
Throws to be a moment misunderstood.

Yet not too much. Not errant, arrant, wild,
But every seeming aberration willed.

Not to, yet still, still to communicate
Making the batter understand too late.

COUNTEE CULLEN
[1903–1946]

Incident

Once riding in old Baltimore,
    Heart-filled, head-filled with glee,
I saw a Baltimorean
    Keep looking straight at me.

Now I was eight and very small,
    And he was no whit bigger,
And so I smiled, but he poked out
    His tongue and called me, "Nigger."

I saw the whole of Baltimore
    From May until December:
Of all the things that happened there
    That's all that I remember.

RICHARD EBERHART
[b. 1904]

The Groundhog

In June, amid the golden fields,
I saw a groundhog lying dead.
Dead lay he; my senses shook,
And mind outshot our naked frailty.

There lowly in the vigorous summer 5
His form began its senseless change,
And made my senses waver dim
Seeing nature ferocious in him.
Inspecting close his maggots' might
And seething cauldron of his being, 10
Half with loathing, half with a strange love,
I poked him with an angry stick.
The fever arose, became a flame
And Vigour circumscribed the skies,
Immense energy in the sun, 15
And through my frame a sunless trembling.
My stick had done nor good nor harm.
Then stood I silent in the day
Watching the object, as before;
And kept my reverence for knowledge 20
Trying for control, to be still,
To quell the passion of the blood;
Until I had bent down on my knees
Praying for joy in the sight of decay.
And so I left; and I returned 25
In Autumn strict of eye, to see
The sap gone out of the groundhog,
But the bony sodden hulk remained.
But the year had lost its meaning,
And in intellectual chains 30
I lost both love and loathing,
Mured up in the wall of wisdom.
Another summer took the fields again
Massive and burning, full of life,
But when I chanced upon the spot 35
There was only a little hair left,
And bones bleaching in the sunlight
Beautiful as architecture;
I watched them like a geometer,
And cut a walking stick from a birch. 40
It has been three years, now.
There is no sign of the groundhog.
I stood there in the whirling summer,
My hand capped a withered heart,
And thought of China and of Greece, 45
Of Alexander° in his tent;
Of Montaigne° in his tower,
Of Saint Theresa° in her wild lament.

THE GROUNDHOG   46**Alexander**   *The Great, Greek military leader (4th century B.C.).*   47**Montaigne**   *French essayist (1533–1592) whose study was in a small tower.*   48**Saint Theresa**   *Catholic saint and Spanish mystic (1515–1582), often portrayed experiencing an ecstatic combination of love and pain.*

PABLO NERUDA
[*b. 1904*]

The Word

The word
was born in the blood,
grew in the dark body, beating,
and took flight through the lips and the mouth.

Farther away and nearer   5
still, still it came
from dead fathers and from wandering races,
from lands which had turned to stone,
lands weary of their poor tribes,
for when grief took to the roads   10
the people set out and arrived
and married new land and water
to grow their words again.
And so this is the inheritance;
this is the wavelength which connects us   15
with dead men and the dawning
of new beings not yet come to light.

Still the atmosphere quivers
with the first word uttered
dressed up   20
in terror and sighing.
It emerged
from the darkness
and until now there is no thunder
that ever rumbles with the iron voice   25
of that word,
the first
word uttered—
perhaps it was only a ripple, a single drop,
and yet its great cataract falls and falls.   30

Later on, the word fills with meaning.
Always with child, it filled up with lives.
Everything was births and sounds—
affirmation, clarity, strength,
negation, destruction, death—   35

the verb took over all the power
and blended existence with essence
in the electricity of its grace.

Human word, syllable, flank
of extending light and solid silverwork, 40
hereditary goblet which receives
the communications of the blood—
here is where silence came together with
the wholeness of the human word,
and, for human beings, not to speak is to die— 45
language extends even to the hair,
the mouth speaks without the lips moving,
all of a sudden, the eyes are words.

I take the word and pass it through my senses
as though it were no more than a human shape; 50
its arrangements awe me and I find my way
through each resonance of the spoken word—
I utter and I am and, speechless, I approach
across the edge of words silence itself.

I drink to the word, raising 55
a word or a shining cup;
in it I drink

the pure wine of language
or inexhaustible water,
maternal source of words, 60
and cup and water and wine
give rise to my song
because the verb is the source
and vivid life—it is blood,
blood which expresses its substance 65
and so ordains its own unwinding.
Words give glass quality to glass, blood to blood,
and life to life itself.

TRANSLATED BY ALASTAIR REID

The United Fruit Co.

When the trumpet sounded, it was
all prepared on the earth,
and Jehovah parceled out the earth
to Coca-Cola, Inc., Anaconda,

Ford Motors, and other entities:
The Fruit Company, Inc.
reserved for itself the most succulent,
the central coast of my own land,
the delicate waist of America.
It rechristened its territories
as the "Banana Republics"
and over the sleeping dead,
over the restless heroes
who brought about the greatness,
the liberty and the flags,
it established the comic opera:
abolished the independencies,
presented crowns of Caesar,
unsheathed envy, attracted
the dictatorship of the flies,
Trujillo flies, Tacho flies,
Carias flies, Martinez flies,
Ubico flies, damp flies
of modest blood and marmalade,
drunken flies who zoom
over the ordinary graves,
circus flies, wise flies
well trained in tryanny.

Among the bloodthirsty flies
the Fruit Company lands its ships,
taking off the coffee and the fruit;
the treasure of our submerged
territories flows as though
on plates into the ships.

Meanwhile Indians are falling
into the sugared chasms
of the harbors, wrapped
for burial in the mist of the dawn:
a body rolls, a thing
that has no name, a fallen cipher,
a cluster of dead fruit
thrown down on the dump.

TRANSLATED BY ROBERT BLY

ROBERT PENN WARREN
[*b. 1905*]

True Love

In silence the heart raves. It utters words
Meaningless, that never had
A meaning. I was ten, skinny, red-headed,

Freckled. In a big black Buick,
Driven by a big grown boy, with a necktie, she sat   5
In front of the drugstore, sipping something

Through a straw. There is nothing like
Beauty. It stops your heart. It
Thickens your blood. It stops your breath. It

Makes you feel dirty. You need a hot bath.   10
I leaned against a telephone pole, and watched.
I thought I would die if she saw me.

How could I exist in the same world with that brightness?
Two years later she smiled at me. She
Named my name. I thought I would wake up dead.   15

Her grown brothers walked with the bent-knee
Swagger of horsemen. They were slick-faced.
Told jokes in the barbershop. Did no work.

Their father was what is called a drunkard.
Whatever he was he stayed on the third floor   20
Of the big white farmhouse under the maples for twenty-five years.

He never came down. They brought everything up to him.
I did not know what a mortgage was.
His wife was a good, Christian woman, and prayed.

When the daughter got married, the old man came down wearing   25
An old tail coat, the pleated shirt yellowing.
The sons propped him. I saw the wedding. There were

Engraved invitations, it was so fashionable. I thought
I would cry. I lay in bed that night
And wondered if she would cry when something was done to her. 30

The mortgage was foreclosed. That last word was whispered.
She never came back. The family
Sort of drifted off. Nobody wears shiny boots like that now.

But I know she is beautiful forever, and lives
In a beautiful house, far away.   35
She called my name once. I didn't even know she knew it.

The Corner of the Eye

The poem is just beyond the corner of the eye.
You cannot see it—not yet—but sense the faint gleam,

Or stir. It may be like a poor little shivering fieldmouse,
One tiny paw lifted from snow while, far off, the owl

Utters. Or like breakers, far off, almost as soundless as dream.   5
Or the rhythmic rasp of your father's last breath, harsh

As the grind of a great file the blacksmith sets to hoof.
Or the whispering slither the torn morning newspaper makes,

Blown down an empty slum street in New York, at midnight,
Past dog shit and garbage cans, while the full moon,   10

Phthisic and wan, above the East River, presides
Over that last fragment of history which is

Our lives. Or the foggy glint of old eyes of
The sleepless patient who no longer wonders

If he will once more see in that window the dun-   15
Bleached dawn that promises what. Or the street corner

Where always, for years, in passing you felt, unexplained, a pang
Of despair, like nausea, till one night, late, late on that spot

You were struck stock-still and again remembered—felt
Her head thrust to your shoulder, she clinging, while you   20

Mechanically pat the fur coat, hear sobs, and stare up
Where tall buildings, frailer than reed-stalks, reel among stars.

Yes, something there at eye-edge lurks, hears ball creak in socket,
Knows, before you do, tension of muscle, change

Of blood pressure, heart-heave of sadness, foot's falter, for   25
It has stalked you all day, or years, breath rarely heard, fangs dripping.

And now, any moment, great hindquarters may hunch, ready—
Or is it merely a poem, after all?

W . H . A U D E N

[1907–1973]

The Unknown Citizen

(To JS/07/M/378 This Marble Monument Is Erected by the State)

He was found by the Bureau of Statistics to be
One against whom there was no official complaint,
And all the reports on his conduct agree
That, in the modern sense of an old-fashioned word, he was a saint,
For in everything he did he served the Greater Community.   5
Except for the War till the day he retired
He worked in a factory and never got fired
But satisfied his employers, Fudge Motors Inc.
Yet he wasn't a scab or odd in his views,
For his Union reports that he paid his dues,   10
(Our report on his Union shows it was sound)
And our Social Psychology workers found
That he was popular with his mates and liked a drink.
The Press are convinced that he bought a paper every day
And that his reactions to advertisements were normal in every way.   15
Policies taken out in his name prove that he was fully insured,
And his Health-card shows he was once in hospital but left it cured.
Both Producers Research and High-Grade Living declare
He was fully sensible to the advantages of the Installment Plan
And had everything necessary to the Modern Man,   20
A phonograph, a radio, a car and a frigidaire.
Our researchers into Public Opinion are content
That he held the proper opinions for the time of year;
When there was peace, he was for peace; when there was war, he went.
He was married and added five children to the population,   25
Which our Eugenist says was the right number for a parent of his generation.
And our teachers report that he never interfered with their education.

Was he free? Was he happy? The question is absurd:
Had anything been wrong, we should certainly have heard.

Sonnets from China, XVIII

Chilled by the Present, its gloom and its noise,
On waking we sigh for an ancient South,
A warm nude age of instinctive poise,
A taste of joy in an innocent mouth.

At night in our huts we dream of a part   5
In the balls of the Future: each ritual maze
Has a musical plan, and a musical heart
Can faultlessly follow its faultless ways.

We envy streams and houses that are sure,
But, doubtful, articled to error, we   10
Were never nude and calm as a great door,

And never will be faultless like our fountains:
We live in freedom by necessity,
A mountain people dwelling among mountains.

In Memory of W. B. Yeats

[d. January 1939]

1

He disappeared in the dead of winter:
The brooks were frozen, the air-ports almost deserted,
And snow disfigured the public statues;
The mercury sank in the mouth of the dying day.
O all the instruments agree   5
The day of his death was a dark cold day.

Far from his illness
The wolves ran on through the evergreen forests,
The peasant river was untempted by the fashionable quays;
By mourning tongues   10
The death of the poet was kept from his poems.

But for him it was his last afternoon as himself,
An afternoon of nurses and rumours;
The provinces of his body revolted,
The squares of his mind were empty,   15
Silence invaded the suburbs,
The current of his feeling failed: he became his admirers.

Now he is scattered among a hundred cities
And wholly given over to unfamiliar affections;
To find his happiness in another kind of wood   20
And be punished under a foreign code of conscience.
The words of a dead man
Are modified in the guts of the living.

But in the importance and noise of to-morrow
When the brokers are roaring like beasts on the floor of
    the Bourse°,   stock exchange   25
And the poor have the sufferings to which they are fairly accustomed,
And each in the cell of himself is almost convinced of his freedom;
A few thousand will think of this day
As one thinks of a day when one did something slightly unusual.

O all the instruments agree   30
The day of his death was a dark cold day.

2

You were silly like us: your gift survived it all;
The parish of rich women, physical decay,
Yourself; mad Ireland hurt you into poetry.
Now Ireland has her madness and her weather still,   35
For poetry makes nothing happen: it survives
In the valley of its saying where executives
Would never want to tamper; it flows south
From ranches of isolation and the busy griefs,
Raw towns that we believe and die in; it survives,   40
A way of happening, a mouth.

3

Earth, receive an honoured guest;
William Yeats is laid to rest:
Let the Irish vessel lie
Emptied of its poetry.   45

Time that is intolerant
Of the brave and innocent,
And indifferent in a week
To a beautiful physique,

Worships language and forgives   50
Everyone by whom it lives;
Pardons cowardice, conceit,
Lays its honours at their feet.

Time that with this strange excuse
Pardoned Kipling and his views,   55
And will pardon Paul Claudel,
Pardons him for writing well.

In the nightmare of the dark
All the dogs of Europe bark,
And the living nations wait,   60
Each sequestered in its hate;

Intellectual disgrace
Stares from every human face,
And the seas of pity lie
Locked and frozen in each eye.   65

Follow, poet, follow right
To the bottom of the night,
With your unconstraining Voice
Still persuade us to rejoice;

With the farming of a verse   70
Make a vineyard of the curse,
Sing of human unsuccess
In a rapture of distress;

In the deserts of the heart
Let the healing fountain start,   75
In the prison of his days
Teach the free man how to praise.

O *where are you going?*

"O where are you going?" said reader to rider,
"That valley is fatal when furnaces burn,
Yonder's the midden whose odors will madden,
That gap is the grave where the tall return."

"O do you imagine," said fearer to farer,   5
"That dusk will delay on your path to the pass,
Your diligent looking discover the lacking
Your footsteps feel from granite to grass?"

IN MEMORY OF W. B. YEATS   55*Kipling*   Rudyard Kipling (1865–1936), English writer with
imperialistic views.   56*Paul Claudel*   French Catholic writer (1868–1955) of extreme political conservatism.
58*the dark*   World War II broke out a few months after Auden wrote this poem.

"O what was that bird," said horror to hearer,
"Did you see that shape in the twisted trees?   10
Behind you swiftly the figure comes softly,
The spot on your skin is a shocking disease."

"Out of this house"—said rider to reader,
"Yours never will"—said farer to fearer,
"They're looking for you"—said hearer to horror,   15
As he left them there, as he left them there.

O what is that sound

O what is that sound which so thrills the ear
   Down in the valley drumming, drumming?
Only the scarlet soldiers, dear,
   The soldiers coming.

O what is that light I see flashing so clear   5
   Over the distance brightly, brightly?
Only the sun on their weapons, dear,
   As they step lightly.

O what are they doing with all that gear,
   What are they doing this morning, this morning?   10
Only their usual manoeuvres, dear,
   Or perhaps a warning.

O why have they left the road down there,
   Why are they suddenly wheeling, wheeling?
Perhaps a change in their orders, dear.   15
   Why are you kneeling?

O haven't they stopped for the doctor's care,
   Haven't they reined their horses, their horses?
Why, they are none of them wounded, dear,
   None of these forces.   20

O is it the parson they want, with white hair,
   Is it the parson, is it, is it?
No, they are passing his gateway, dear,
   Without a visit.

O it must be the farmer who lives so near.   25
   It must be the farmer so cunning, so cunning?
They have passed the farmyard already, dear,
   And now they are running.

O where are you going? Stay with me here!
    Were the vows you swore deceiving, deceiving?   30
No, I promised to love you, dear,
    But I must be leaving.

O it's broken the lock and splintered the door,
    O it's the gate where they're turning, turning;
Their boots are heavy on the floor   35
    And their eyes are burning.

A . D . H O P E

[b. 1907]

Coup de Grâce

Just at that moment the Wolf,
Shag jaws and slavering grin,
Steps from the property wood.
O, what a gorge, what a gulf
Opens to gobble her in,   5
Little Red Riding Hood!

O, what a face full of fangs!
Eyes like saucers at least

Roll to seduce and beguile.
Miss, with her dimples and bangs,   10
Thinks him a handsome beast;
Flashes the Riding Hood Smile;

Stands her ground like a queen,
Velvet red of the rose
Framing each little milk-tooth,   15
Pink tongue peeping between.
Then, wider than anyone knows,
Opens her minikin mouth,

Swallows up Wolf in a trice;
Tail going down gives a flick,   20
Caught as she closes her jaws.
Bows, all sugar and spice.
O, what a lady-like trick!
O, what a round of applause!

Imperial° Adam   emperor

Imperial Adam, naked in the dew,
Felt his brown flanks and found the rib was gone.
Puzzled he turned and saw where, two and two,
The mighty spoor° of Jahweh° marked the lawn.   tracks/God

Then he remembered through mysterious sleep   5
The surgeon fingers probing at the bone,
The voice so far away, so rich and deep:
"It is not good for him to live alone."

Turning once more he found Man's counterpart
In tender parody breathing at his side.   10
He knew her at first sight, he knew by heart
Her allegory of sense unsatisfied.

The pawpaw drooped its golden breasts above
Less generous than the honey of her flesh;
The innocent sunlight showed the place of love;   15
The dew on its dark hairs winked crisp and fresh.

This plump gourd severed from his virile root,
She promised on the turf of Paradise
Delicious pulp of the forbidden fruit;
Sly as the snake she loosed her sinuous thighs,   20

And waking, smiled up at him from the grass;
Her breasts rose softly and he heard her sigh—
From all the beasts whose pleasant task it was
In Eden to increase and multiply

Adam had learned the jolly deed of kind: 25
He took her in his arms and there and then,
Like the clean beasts, embracing from behind,
Began in joy to found the breed of men.

Then from the spurt of seed within her broke
Her terrible and triumphant female cry,   30
Split upward by the sexual lightning stroke.
It was the beasts now who stood watching by:

The gravid elephant, the calving hind,
The breeding bitch, the she-ape big with young

IMPERIAL ADAM   [8]*It is not good . . .*   see Genesis 2.18:   *"And the Lord said, It is not good that
the man should be alone."*

Were the first gentle midwives of mankind;   35
The teeming lioness rasped her with her tongue;

The proud vicuña nuzzled her as she slept
Lax on the grass; and Adam watching too
Saw how her dumb breasts at their ripening wept,
The great pod of her belly swelled and grew,   40

And saw its water break, and saw, in fear,
Its quaking muscles in the act of birth,
Between her legs a pigmy face appear,
And the first murderer° lay upon the earth.   Cain

THEODORE ROETHKE

[1908–1963]

Elegy for Jane

MY STUDENT, THROWN BY A HORSE

I remember the neckcurls, limp and damp as tendrils;
And her quick look, a sidelong pickerel smile;
And how, once startled into talk, the light syllables leaped for her,
And she balanced in the delight of her thought,
A wren, happy, tail into the wind,   5
Her song trembling the twigs and small branches.
The shade sang with her;
The leaves, their whispers turned to kissing;
And the mold sang in the bleached valleys under the rose.

Oh, when she was sad, she cast herself down into such a pure depth,   10
Even a father could not find her:
Scraping her cheek against straw;
Stirring the clearest water.

My sparrow, you are not here,
Waiting like a fern, making a spiny shadow.   15
The sides of wet stones cannot console me,
Nor the moss, wound with the last light.

If only I could nudge you from this sleep,
My maimed darling, my skittery pigeon.
Over this damp grave I speak the words of my love: 20

I, with no rights in this matter,
Neither father nor lover.

The Premonition

Walking this field I remember
Days of another summer.
Oh that was long ago! I kept
Close to the heels of my father,
Matching his stride with half-steps   5
Until we came to a river.
He dipped his hand in the shallow:
Water ran over and under
Hair on a narrow wrist bone;
His image kept following after,—   10
Flashed with the sun in the ripple.
But when he stood up, that face
Was lost in a maze of water.

ELIZABETH BISHOP
[1911–1979]

The Fish

I caught a tremendous fish
and held him beside the boat
half out of water, with my hook
fast in a corner of his mouth.
He didn't fight.   5
He hadn't fought at all.
He hung a grunting weight,
battered and venerable
and homely. Here and there
his brown skin hung in strips   10
like ancient wallpaper,
and its pattern of darker brown
was like wallpaper:
shapes like full-blown roses
stained and lost through age.   15
He was speckled with barnacles,
fine rosettes of lime,
and infested

with tiny white sea-lice,
and underneath two or three   20
rags of green weed hung down.
While his gills were breathing in
the terrible oxygen
—the frightening gills,
fresh and crisp with blood,   25
that can cut so badly—
I thought of the coarse white flesh
packed in like feathers,
the big bones and the little bones,
the dramatic reds and blacks   30
of his shiny entrails,
and the pink swim-bladder
like a big peony.
I looked into his eyes
which were far larger than mine   35
but shallower, and yellowed,
the irises backed and packed
with tarnished tinfoil
seen through the lenses
of old scratched isinglass°.   mica   40
They shifted a little, but not
to return my stare.
—It was more like the tipping
of an object toward the light.
I admired his sullen face,   45
the mechanism of his jaw,
and then I saw
that from his lower lip
—if you could call it a lip—
grim, wet, and weaponlike,   50
hung five old pieces of fish-line,
or four and a wire leader
with the swivel still attached,
with all their five big hooks
grown firmly in his mouth.   55
A green line, frayed at the end
where he broke it, two heavier lines,
and a fine black thread
still crimped from the strain and snap
when it broke and he got away.   60
Like medals with their ribbons
frayed and wavering,
a five-haired beard of wisdom
trailing from his aching jaw.
I stared and stared   65

and victory filled up
the little rented boat,
from the pool of bilge
where oil had spread a rainbow
around the rusted engine   70
to the bailer rusted orange,
the sun-cracked thwarts,
the oarlocks on their strings,
the gunnels—until everything
was rainbow, rainbow, rainbow!   75
And I let the fish go.

Sestina

September rain falls on the house.
In the failing light, the old grandmother
sits in the kitchen with the child
beside the Little Marvel Stove,
reading the jokes from the almanac,   5
laughing and talking to hide her tears.

She thinks that her equinoctial tears
and the rain that beats on the roof of the house
were both foretold by the almanac,
but only known to a grandmother.   10
The iron kettle sings on the stove.
She cuts some bread and says to the child,

It's time for tea now; but the child
is watching the teakettle's small hard tears
dance like mad on the hot black stove,   15
the way the rain must dance on the house.
Tidying up, the old grandmother
hangs up the clever almanac

on its string. Birdlike, the almanac
hovers half open above the child,   20
hovers above the old grandmother
and her teacup full of dark brown tears.
She shivers and says she thinks the house
feels chilly, and puts more wood in the stove.

It was to be, says the Marvel Stove.   25
I know what I know, says the almanac.
With crayons the child draws a rigid house
and a winding pathway. Then the child

puts in a man with buttons like tears
and shows it proudly to the grandmother.   30

But secretly, while the grandmother
busies herself about the stove,
the little moons fall down like tears
from between the pages of the almanac
into the flower bed the child   35
has carefully placed in the front of the house.

Time to plant tears, says the almanac.
The grandmother sings to the marvelous stove
and the child draws another inscrutable house.

OCTAVIO PAZ
[b. 1914]

January First

The year's doors open
like those of language,
toward the unknown.
Last night you told me:
                              tomorrow   5
we shall have to think up signs,
sketch a landscape, fabricate a plan
on the double page
of day and paper.
Tomorrow, we shall have to invent,   10
once more,
the reality of this world.

I opened my eyes late.
For a second of a second
I felt what the Aztec felt,   15
on the crest of the promontory,
lying in wait
for time's uncertain return
through cracks in the horizon.

But no, the year had returned.   20
It filled all the room
and my look almost touched it.

Time, with no help from us,
had placed
in exactly the same order as yesterday   25
houses in the empty street,
snow on the houses,
silence on the snow.

You were beside me,
still asleep.   30
The day had invented you
but you hadn't yet accepted
being invented by the day.
—Nor possibly my being invented, either.
You were in another day.   35

You were beside me
and I saw you, like the snow,
asleep among appearances.
Time, with no help from us,
invents houses, streets, trees   40
and sleeping women.

When you open your eyes
we'll walk, once more,
among the hours and their inventions.
We'll walk among appearances   45
and bear witness to time and its conjugations.
Perhaps we'll open the day's doors.
And then we shall enter the unknown.

TRANSLATED BY ELIZABETH BISHOP

WILLIAM STAFFORD

[*b. 1914*]

Traveling through the dark

Traveling through the dark I found a deer
dead on the edge of the Wilson River road.
It is usually best to roll them into the canyon:
that road is narrow; to swerve might make more dead.

By glow of the tail-light I stumbled back of the car   5
and stood by the heap, a doe, a recent killing;

she had stiffened already, almost cold.
I dragged her off; she was large in the belly.

My fingers touching her side brought me the reason—
her side was warm; her fawn lay there waiting,   10
alive, still, never to be born.
Beside that mountain road I hesitated.

The car aimed ahead its lowered parking lights;
under the hood purred the steady engine.
I stood in the glare of the warm exhaust turning red;   15
around our group I could hear the wilderness listen.

I thought hard for us all—my only swerving—,
then pushed her over the edge into the river.

DUDLEY RANDALL

[b. 1914]

The Melting Pot

There is a magic melting pot
where any girl or man
can step in Czech or Greek or Scot,
step out American.

Johann and *Jan* and *Jean* and *Juan,*   5
Giovanni and *Ivan*
step in and then step out again
all freshly christened *John.*

Sam, watching, said, "Why, I was here
even before they came,"   10
and stepped in too, but was tossed out
before he passed the brim.

And every time Sam tried that pot
they threw him out again.
"Keep out. This is our private pot.   15
We don't want your black stain."

At last, thrown out a thousand times,
Sam said, "I don't give a damn.
Shove your old pot. You can like it or not,
but I'll be just what I am."   20

George

When I was a boy desiring the title of man
And toiling to earn it
In the inferno of the foundry knockout,
I watched and admired you working by my side,
As, goggled, with mask on your mouth and shoulders bright with sweat,   5
You mastered the monstrous, lumpish cylinder blocks,
And when they clotted the line and plunged to the floor
With force enough to tear your foot in two,
You calmly stepped aside.

One day when the line broke down and the blocks reared up   10
Groaning, grinding, and mounted like an ocean wave
And then rushed thundering down like an avalanche,
And we frantically dodged, then braced our heads together
To form an arch to lift and stack them,
You gave me your highest accolade: 15
You said: "You not afraid of sweat. You strong as a mule."

Now, here, in the hospital,
In a ward where old men wait to die,
You sit, and watch time go by.
You cannot read the books I bring, not even   20
Those that are only picture books,
As you sit among the senile wrecks,
The psychopaths, the incontinent.

One day when you fell from your chair and stared at the air
With the look of fright which sight of death inspires,   25
I lifted you like a cylinder block, and said,
"Don't be afraid
Of a little fall, for you'll be here
A long time yet, because you're strong as a mule."

DYLAN THOMAS
[1914–1953]

The force that through the green fuse drives the flower

The force that through the green fuse drives the flower
Drives my green age; that blasts the roots of trees
Is my destroyer.

And I am dumb to tell the crooked rose
My youth is bent by the same wintry fever.   5

The force that drives the water through the rocks
Drives my red blood; that dries the mouthing streams
Turns mine to wax.
And I am dumb to mouth unto my veins
How at the mountain spring the same mouth sucks.   10

The hand that whirls the water in the pool
Stirs the quicksand; that ropes the blowing wind
Hauls my shroud sail.
And I am dumb to tell the hanging man
How of my clay is made the hangman's lime.   15

The lips of time leech to the fountain head;
Love drips and gathers, but the fallen blood
Shall calm her sores.
And I am dumb to tell a weather's wind
How time has ticked a heaven round the stars.   20

And I am dumb to tell the lover's tomb
How at my sheet goes the same crooked worm.

A Refusal to Mourn the Death, by Fire, of a Child in London

Never until the mankind making
Bird beast and flower
Fathering and all humbling darkness
Tells with silence the last light breaking
And the still hour   5
Is come of the sea tumbling in harness

And I must enter again the round
Zion of the water bead
And the synagogue of the ear of corn
Shall I let pray the shadow of a sound   10
Or sow my salt seed
In the least valley of sackcloth to mourn

The majesty and burning of the child's death.
I shall not murder
The mankind of her going with a grave truth   15
Nor blaspheme down the stations of the breath

With any further
Elegy of innocence and youth.

Deep with the first dead lies London's daughter,
Robed in the long friends,   20
The grains beyond age, the dark veins of her mother,
Secret by the unmourning water
Of the riding Thames.
After the first death, there is no other.

Fern Hill

Now as I was young and easy under the apple boughs
About the lilting house and happy as the grass was green,
    The night above the dingle starry,
       Time let me hail and climb
    Golden in the heydays of his eyes,   5
And honored among wagons I was prince of the apple towns
And once below a time I lordly had the trees and leaves
       Trail with daisies and barley
    Down the rivers of the windfall light.

And as I was green and carefree, famous among the barns   10
About the happy yard and singing as the farm was home,
    In the sun that is young once only,
       Time let me play and be
    Golden in the mercy of his means,
And green and golden I was huntsman and herdsman, the calves   15
Sang to my horn, the foxes on the hills barked clear and cold,
       And the sabbath rang slowly
    In the pebbles of the holy streams.

All the sun long it was running, it was lovely, the hay
Fields high as the house, the tunes from the chimneys, it was air   20
    And playing, lovely and watery
       And fire green as grass.
    And nightly under the simple stars
As I rode to sleep the owls were bearing the farm away,
All the moon long I heard, blessed among stables, the night-jars   25
    Flying with the ricks, and the horses
       Flashing into the dark.

And then to awake, and the farm, like a wanderer white
With the dew, come back, the cock on his shoulder: it was all
    Shining, it was Adam and maiden,   30

The sky gathered again
And the sun grew round that very day.
So it must have been after the birth of the simple light
In the first, spinning place, the spellbound horses walking warm
    Out of the whinnying green stable
        On to the fields of praise.

35

And honored among foxes and pheasants by the gay house
Under the new made clouds and happy as the heart was long,
    In the sun born over and over,
        I ran my heedless ways,
    My wishes raced through the house high hay
And nothing I cared, at my sky blue trades, that time allows
In all his tuneful turning so few and such morning songs
    Before the children green and golden
        Follow him out of grace,

40

45

Nothing I cared, in the lamb white days, that time would take me
Up to the swallow thronged loft by the shadow of my hand,
    In the moon that is always rising,
        Nor that riding to sleep
    I should hear him fly with the high fields
And wake to the farm forever fled from the childless land.
Oh as I was young and easy in the mercy of his means,
    Time held me green and dying
    Though I sang in my chains like the sea.

50

In my craft or sullen art

In my craft or sullen art
Exercised in the still night
When only the moon rages
And the lovers lie abed
With all their griefs in their arms,
I labor by singing light
Not for ambition or bread
Or the strut and trade of charms
On the ivory stages
But for the common wages
Of their most secret heart.

5

10

Not for the proud man apart
From the raging moon I write
On these spindrift pages
Nor for the towering dead

15

With their nightingales and psalms
But for the lovers, their arms
Round the griefs of the ages,
Who pay no praise or wages
Nor heed my craft or art.   20

Do not go gentle into that good night

Do not go gentle into that good night,
Old age should burn and rave at close of day;
Rage, rage against the dying of the light.

Though wise men at their end know dark is right,
Because their words had forked no lightning they   5
Do not go gentle into that good night.

Good men, the last wave by, crying how bright
Their frail deeds might have danced in a green bay,
Rage, rage against the dying of the light.

Wild men who caught and sang the sun in flight,   10
And learn, too late, they grieved it on its way,
Do not go gentle into that good night.

Grave men, near death, who see with blinding sight
Blind eyes could blaze like meteors and be gay,
Rage, rage against the dying of the light.   15

And you, my father, there on the sad height,
Curse, bless, me now with your fierce tears, I pray.
Do not go gentle into that good night.
Rage, rage against the dying of the light.

MARGARET WALKER

[*b. 1915*]

Lineage

My grandmothers were strong.
They followed plows and bent to toil.
They moved through fields sowing seed.

They touched earth and grain grew.
They were full of sturdiness and singing.   5
My grandmothers were strong.

My grandmothers are full of memories.
Smelling of soap and onions and wet clay
With veins rolling roughly over quick hands
They have many clean words to say.   10
My grandmothers were strong.
Why am I not as they?

ROBERT LOWELL

[1917–1977]

Skunk Hour

(For Elizabeth Bishop)

Nautilus Island's hermit
heiress still lives through winter in her Spartan cottage;
her sheep still graze above the sea.
Her son's a bishop. Her farmer
is first selectman in our village;   5
she's in her dotage.

Thirsting for
the hierarchic privacy
of Queen Victoria's century,
she buys up all   10
the eyesores facing her shore,
and lets them fall.

The season's ill—
we've lost our summer millionaire,
who seemed to leap from an L. L. Bean   15
catalogue. His nine-knot yawl
was auctioned off to lobstermen.
A red fox stain covers Blue Hill.

And now our fairy
decorator brightens his shop for fall;   20

SKUNK HOUR   5*selectman* *senior town official.*   15*L. L. Bean*   *mail-order store in Maine specializing in camping and sports clothing and equipment.*   18*A . . . Hill*   *Lowell meant to suggest, he wrote, "the rusty, reddish color of autumn on Blue Hill, a Maine mountain."*

his fishnet's filled with orange cork,
orange, his cobbler's bench and awl;
there is no money in his work,
he'd rather marry.

One dark night,   25
my Tudor Ford climbed the hill's skull;
I watched for love-cars. Lights turned down,
they lay together, hull to hull,
where the graveyard shelves on the town. . . .
My mind's not right.   30

A car radio bleats,
"Love, O careless Love. . . ." I hear
my ill-spirit sob in each blood cell,
as if my hand were at its throat. . . .
I myself am hell;   35
nobody's here—

only skunks, that search
in the moonlight for a bite to eat.
They march on their soles up Main Street:
white stripes, moonstruck eyes' red fire   40
under the chalk-dry and spar spire
of the Trinitarian Church.

I stand on top
of our back steps and breathe the rich air—
a mother skunk with her column of kittens swills the garbage pail.   45
She jabs her wedge-head in a cup
of sour cream, drops her ostrich tail,
and will not scare.

GWENDOLYN BROOKS

[b. 1917]

the mother

Abortions will not let you forget.
You remember the children you got that you did not get,
The damp small pulps with a little or with no hair,
The singers and workers that never handled the air.

---

[35]*I . . . hell* echoes Milton's Satan in Paradise Lost *IV, 75: "Which way I fly is Hell; my self am Hell."*

You will never neglect or beat
Them, or silence or buy with a sweet.
You will never wind up the sucking-thumb
Or scuttle off ghosts that come.
You will never leave them, controlling your luscious sigh,
Return for a snack of them, with gobbling mother-eye.   10

I have heard in the voices of the wind the voices of my dim killed children.
I have contracted. I have eased
My dim dears at the breasts they could never suck.
I have said, Sweets, if I sinned, if I seized
Your luck   15
And your lives from your unfinished reach,
If I stole your births and your names,
Your straight baby tears and your games,
Your stilted or lovely loves, your tumults, your marriages, aches, and your deaths,
If I poisoned the beginnings of your breaths,
Believe that even in my deliberateness I was not deliberate.   20
Though why should I whine,
Whine that the crime was other than mine?—
Since anyhow you are dead.
Or rather, or instead,
You were never made.   25

But that too, I am afraid,
Is faulty: oh, what shall I say, how is the truth to be said?
You were born, you had body, you died.
It is just that you never giggled or planned or cried.

Believe me, I loved you all.   30
Believe me, I knew you, though faintly, and I loved, I loved you
All.

First fight. Then fiddle

First fight. Then fiddle. Ply the slipping string
With feathery sorcery; muzzle the note
With hurting love; the music that they wrote
Bewitch, bewilder. Qualify to sing
Threadwise. Devise no salt, no hempen thing   5
For the dear instrument to bear. Devote
The bow to silks and honey. Be remote
A while from malice and from murdering.
But first to arms, to armor. Carry hate
In front of you and harmony behind.   10

Be deaf to music and to beauty blind.
Win war. Rise bloody, maybe not too late
For having first to civilize a space
Wherein to play your violin with grace.

LAWRENCE FERLINGHETTI

[*b. 1919*]

Constantly Risking Absurdity

Constantly risking absurdity
       and death
   whenever he performs
      above the heads
         of his audience   5

 the poet like an acrobat
     climbs on rime
       to a high wire of his own making
and balancing on eyebeams
      above a sea of faces   10
  paces his way
     to the other side of day
 performing entrechats

       and sleight-of-foot tricks
and other high theatrics   15
      and all without mistaking
   any thing
     for what it may not be

 For he's the super realist
       who must perforce perceive 20
    taut truth
      before the taking of each stance or step
in his supposed advance
      toward that still higher perch
where Beauty stands and waits   25
     with gravity
      to start her death-defying leap

 And he
    a little charleychaplin man

30

who may or may not catch
her fair eternal form
         spreadeagled in the empty air
of existence

MAY SWENSON
[b. 1919]

Women should be pedestals

Women should be pedestals
moving pedestals
moving to the motions of men
Or they should be little horses
those wooden sweet oldfashioned painted rocking horses   5
the gladdest things in the toyroom
The pegs of their ears so familiar and dear
to the trusting fists
To be chafed feelingly
and then unfeelingly   10
To be joyfully ridden
until the restored egos dismount and the legs stride away
Immobile sweetlipped sturdy and smiling
women should always be waiting
willing to be set into motion   15
Women should be pedestals to men

The Watch

When I
took my
watch to the watchfixer I
felt privileged but also pained to watch the operation. He
had long fingernails and a voluntary squint. He   5
fixed a magnifying cup over his
squint eye. He
undressed my
watch. I
watched him   10
split her
in three layers and lay her
middle—a quivering viscera—in a circle on a little plinth. He
shoved shirtsleeves up and leaned like an ogre over my

naked watch. With critical pincers he
poked and stirred. He
lifted out little private things with a magnet too tiny for me
to watch almost. "Watch out!" I
almost said. His
eye watched, enlarged, the secrets of my
watch, and I
watched anxiously. Because what if he
touched her
ticker too rough, and she
gave up the ghost out of pure fright? Or put her
things back backwards so she'd
run backwards after this? Or he
might lose a minuscule part, connected to her
exquisite heart, and mix her
up, instead of fix her.
And all the time,
all the time-
pieces on the walls, on the shelves, told the time,
told the time
in swishes and ticks,
swishes and ticks,
and seemed to be gloating, as they watched and told. I
felt faint, I
was about to lose my
breath—my
ticker going lickety-split—when watchfixer clipped her
three slices together with a gleam and two flicks of his
tools like chopsticks. He
spat out his
eye, lifted her
high, gave her
a twist, set her
hands right, and laid her
little face, quite as usual, in its place on my
wrist.

15

20

25

30

35

40

45

50

RICHARD WILBUR

[*b. 1921*]

Mind

Mind in the purest play is like some bat
That beats about in caverns all alone,

Contriving by a kind of senseless wit
Not to conclude against a wall of stone.

It has no need to falter or explore;   5
Darkly it knows what obstacles are there,
And so may weave and flitter, dip and soar
In perfect courses through the blackest air.

And has this simile a like perfection?
The mind is like a bat. Precisely. Save   10
That in the very happiest intellection
A graceful error may correct the cave.

Juggler

A ball will bounce, but less and less. It's not
A light-hearted thing, resents its own resilience.
Falling is what it loves, and the earth falls
So in our hearts from brilliance,
Settles and is forgot.   5
It takes a skyblue juggler with five red balls

To shake our gravity up. Whee, in the air
The balls roll round, wheel on his wheeling hands,
Learning the ways of lightness, alter to spheres
Grazing his finger ends,   10
Cling to their courses there,
Swinging a small heaven about his ears.

But a heaven is easier made of nothing at all
Than the earth regained, and still and sole within
The spin of worlds, with a gesture sure and noble   15
He reels that heaven in,
Landing it ball by ball,
And trades it all for a broom, a plate, a table.

Oh, on his toe the table is turning, the broom's
Balancing up on his nose, and the plate whirls   20
On the tip of the broom! Damn, what a show, we cry:
The boys stamp, and the girls
Shriek, and the drum booms
And all comes down, and he bows and says good-bye.

If the juggler is tired now, if the broom stands   25
In the dust again, if the table starts to drop

Through the daily dark again, and though the plate
Lies flat on the table top,
For him we batter our hands
Who has won for once over the world's weight.   30

MARIE PONSOT
[*b. 1922*]

Summer Sestina
FOR ROSEMARY

Her daylilies are afloat on evening
As their petals, lemon- or melon-colored,
Dim and lift in the loosening grip of light
Until their leaves lie like their shadows, there
Where she had hid dry corms of them, in earth   5
She freed of stones, weeded, and has kept rich.

With dusk, the dense air rises unmixed, rich,
Around our bodies dim with evening;
Creek air pours up the cliff to her tilled earth
And we swim in cool, our thoughts so colored   10
They can haunt each other, speechless, there
Where bubbles of birdsong burst like mental light,

Among the isles of lilies soaked with light.
We wait for moonrise that may make us rich
With the outsight of insight, spilling there   15
On her meadow when the moon ends evening
And brings back known shapes, strangely uncolored,
To this earthly garden, this gardened earth.

Deep deep go these dug fertile beds of earth
Where mystery prepares the thrust for light.   20
Years of leaffall, raked wet and discolored
With winter kitchen scraps, make the mix rich;
The odds against such loam are evening,
Worked on by her intentions buried there.

Why she does it is neither here nor there—   25
Why would anyone choose to nurture earth,
Kneel to its dayneeds, dream it at evening,

Plan and plant according to soil and light,
Apple, basil, snowpea, each season rich—
What counts isn't that her world is colored   30

Or that by it our vision is colored,
But that the gardener who gardens there
Has been so gardened by her garden: grown rich,
Grown fruitful, grown to stand upon the earth
In answer to the ordering of light   35
She lends to us this August evening.

By her teaching there we are changed, colored,
Made ready for evening, reconciled to earth,
Gardened to richness by her spendthrift light.

PHILIP LARKIN
[b. 1922]

A Study of Reading Habits

When getting my nose in a book
Cured most things short of school,
It was worth ruining my eyes
To know I could still keep cool,
And deal out the old right hook   5
To dirty dogs twice my size.

Later, with inch-thick specs,
Evil was just my lark:
Me and my cloak and fangs
Had ripping times in the dark.   10
The women I clubbed with sex!
I broke them up like meringues.

Don't read much now: the dude
Who lets the girl down before
The hero arrives, the chap   15
Who's yellow and keeps the store,
Seem far too familiar. Get stewed:
Books are a load of crap.

JAMES DICKEY
[*b. 1923*]

The Lifeguard

In a stable of boats I lie still,
From all sleeping children hidden.
The leap of a fish from its shadow
Makes the whole lake instantly tremble.
With my foot on the water, I feel   5
The moon outside

Take on the utmost of its power.
I rise and go out through the boats.
I set my broad sole upon silver,
On the skin of the sky, on the moonlight,   10
Stepping outward from earth onto water
In quest of the miracle

This village of children believed
That I could perform as I dived
For one who had sunk from my sight.   15
I saw his cropped haircut go under.
I leapt, and my steep body flashed
Once, in the sun.

Dark drew all the light from my eyes.
Like a man who explores his death   20
By the pull of his slow-moving shoulders,
I hung head down in the cold,
Wide-eyed, contained, and alone
Among the weeds,

And my fingertips turned into stone   25
From clutching immovable blackness.
Time after time I leapt upward
Exploding in breath, and fell back
From the change in the children's faces
At my defeat.   30

Beneath them I swam to the boathouse
With only my life in my arms
To wait for the lake to shine back

At the risen moon with such power
That my steps on the light of the ripples   35
Might be sustained.

Beneath me is nothing but brightness
Like the ghost of a snowfield in summer.
As I move toward the center of the lake,
Which is also the center of the moon,   40
I am thinking of how I may be
The savior of one

Who has already died in my care.
The dark trees fade from around me.
The moon's dust hovers together.   45
I call softly out, and the child's
Voice answers through blinding water.
Patiently, slowly,

He rises, dilating to break
The surface of stone with his forehead.   50
He is one I do not remember
Having ever seen in his life.
The ground I stand on is trembling
Upon his smile.

I wash the black mud from my hands.   55
On a light given off by the grave
I kneel in the quick of the moon
At the heart of a distant forest
And hold in my arms a child
Of water, water, water.   60

LOUIS SIMPSON

[b. 1923]

The Heroes

I dreamed of war-heroes, of wounded war-heroes
With just enough of their charms shot away
To make them more handsome. The women moved nearer
To touch their brave wounds and their hair streaked with gray.

I saw them in long ranks ascending the gang-planks;   5
The girls with the doughnuts were cheerful and gay.

They minded their manners and muttered their thanks;
The Chaplain advised them to watch and to pray.

They shipped these rapscallions, these sea-sick battalions
To a patriotic and picturesque spot;   10
They gave them new bibles and marksmen's medallions,
Compasses, maps, and committed the lot.

A fine dust has settled on all that scrap metal.
The heroes were packaged and sent home in parts
To pluck at a poppy and sew on a petal   15
And count the long night by the stroke of their hearts.

Walt Whitman at Bear Mountain

. . . life which does not give the preference to any other life,
of any previous period, which therefore prefers its own existence . . .

—ORTEGA Y GASSET

Neither on horseback nor seated,
But like himself, squarely on two feet,
The poet of death and lilacs
Loafs by the footpath. Even the bronze looks alive
Where it is folded like cloth. And he seems friendly.   5

"Where is the Mississippi panorama
And the girl who played the piano?
What are you, Walt?
The Open Road goes to the used-car lot.

"Where is the nation you promised?   10
These houses built of wood sustain
Colossal snows,
And the light above the street is sick to death.

"As for the people—see how they neglect you!
Only a poet pauses to read the inscription."   15

"I am here," he answered.
"It seems you have found me out.
Yet, did I not warn you that it was Myself
I advertised? Were my words not sufficiently plain?

"I gave no prescriptions,   20
And those who have taken my moods for prophecies

WALT WHITMAN AT BEAR MOUNTAIN Quotation *José Ortega y Gasset was a Spanish philosopher,*
writer, and statesman (1883–1955).

Mistake the matter."
Then, vastly amused—"Why do you reproach me?
I freely confess I am wholly disreputable.
Yet I am happy, because you have found me out."   25

A crocodile in wrinkled metal loafing . . .

Then all the realtors,
Pickpockets, salesmen, and the actors performing
Official scenarios,
Turned a deaf ear, for they had contracted   30
American dreams.

But the man who keeps a store on a lonely road,
And the housewife who knows she's dumb,
And the earth, are relieved.

All that grave weight of America   35
Cancelled! Like Greece and Rome.
The future in ruins!
The castles, the prisons, the cathedrals
Unbuilding, and roses
Blossoming from the stones that are not there . . .   40

The clouds are lifting from the high Sierras.
The Bay mists clearing;
And the angel in the gate, the flowering plum,
Dances like Italy, imagining red.

YVES BONNEFOY

[b. 1923]

Place of the Salamander

The startled salamander freezes
And feigns death.
This is the first step of consciousness among the stones,
The purest myth,
A great fire passed through, which is spirit.   5

The salamander was halfway up
The wall, in the light from our windows.

Its gaze was merely a stone,
But I saw its heart beat eternal.

O my accomplice and my thought, allegory   10
Of all that is pure,
How I love that which clasps to its silence thus
The single force of joy.

How I love that which gives itself to the stars by the inert
Mass of its whole body,   15
How I love that which awaits the hour of its victory
And holds its breath and clings to the ground.

TRANSLATED BY GALWAY KINNELL

ALAN DUGAN

[*b. 1923*]

Funeral Oration for a Mouse

This, Lord, was an anxious brother and
a living diagram of fear: full of health himself,
he brought diseases like a gift
to give his hosts. Masked in a cat's moustache
but sounding like a bird, he was a ghost   5
of lesser noises and a kitchen pest
for whom some ladies stand on chairs. So,
Lord, accept our felt though minor guilt
for an ignoble foe and ancient sin:
the murder of a guest   10
who shared our board: just once he ate
too slowly, dying in our trap
from necessary hunger and a broken back.

Humors of love aside, the mousetrap was our own
opinion of the mouse, but for the mouse   15
it was the tree of knowledge with
its consequential fruit, the true cross
and the gate of hell. Even to approach
it makes him like or better than
its maker: his courage as a spoiler never once   20

FUNERAL ORATION FOR A MOUSE   16*the tree of knowledge*   See *Genesis 2:16–17, in which
God commands man not to eat of the tree of the knowledge of good and evil under pain of death.*

impressed us, but to go out cautiously at night,
into the dining room;—what bravery, what
hunger! Younger by far, in dying he
was older than us all: his mobile tail and nose
spasmed in the pinch of our annoyance. Why,   25
then, at that snapping sound, did we, victorious,
begin to laugh without delight?

Our stomachs, deep in an analysis
of their own stolen baits
(and asking, "Lord, Host, to whom are we the pests?"),   30
contracted and demanded a retreat
from our machine and its effect of death,
as if the mouse's fingers, skinnier
than hairpins and as breakable as cheese,
could grasp our grasping lives, and in   35
their drowning movement pull us under too,
into the common death beyond the mousetrap.

YEHUDA AMICHAI

[b. 1924]

The eternal mystery

The eternal mystery of oars
that strike back while the boat floats forward,
thus actions and words strike back the past
so the body can move on with the man inside.

Once I was sitting in a barber's chair by the street   5
and in the large mirror I saw people coming toward me
and suddenly they were cut off and swallowed up in the abyss
beyond the large mirror.

And the eternal mystery of the sun setting in the sea:
even a professor of physics says: 10
Look the sun is setting in the sea, red and lovely.

Or the mystery of phrases like
"I could be your father,"
"What was I doing a year ago today?"
and other such words.   15

TRANSLATED BY GLENDA ABRAMSON AND TUDOR PARFITT

You Can Rely on Him

Happiness has no father. No happiness ever
Learns from the one before, and it dies, without heirs.
But sadness has a long tradition,
Passes from eye to eye, from heart to heart.

And what did I learn from my father: to weep full and   5
       to laugh loud
And to pray three times a day.
And what did I learn from my mother: to close my lips, collar,
Cupboard, dream and suitcase, and to put everything back
In its place and to pray three times a day.   10

Now I have recovered from the lesson. The hair of my head
Is cropped, like a soldier from the Second World War,
Round and round, and my ears not only hold up my skull but
       the whole sky.

Now they say about me: "You can rely on him."   15
I've come to this! I've sunk this low!
Only those who really love me
Know you cannot.

TRANSLATED BY GLENDA ABRAMSON AND TUDOR PARFITT

DONALD JUSTICE
[b. 1925]

Men at forty

Men at forty
Learn to close softly
The doors to rooms they will not be
Coming back to.

At rest on a stair landing,   5
They feel it moving
Beneath them now like the deck of a ship,
Though the swell is gentle.

And deep in mirrors
They rediscover   10

The face of the boy as he practices tying
His father's tie there in secret

And the face of that father,
Still warm with the mystery of lather.
They are more fathers than sons themselves now.   15
Something is filling them, something

That is like the twilight sound
Of the crickets, immense,
Filling the woods at the foot of the slope
Behind their mortgaged houses.   20

In Bertram's Garden

Jane looks down at her organdy skirt
As if *it* somehow were the thing disgraced,
For being there, on the floor, in the dirt,
And she catches it up about her waist,
Smooths it out along one hip,   5
And pulls it over the crumpled slip.

On the porch, green-shuttered, cool,
Asleep is Bertram, that bronze boy,
Who, having wound her around a spool,
Sends her spinning like a toy   10
Out to the garden, all alone,
To sit and weep on a bench of stone.

Soon the purple dark will bruise
Lily and bleeding-heart and rose,
And the little Cupid lose   15
Eyes and ears and chin and nose,
And Jane lie down with others soon
Naked to the naked moon.

MAXINE KUMIN

[*b. 1925*]

How It Is

Shall I say how it is in your clothes?
A month after your death I wear your blue jacket.
The dog at the center of my life recognizes

you've come to visit, he's ecstatic.
In the left pocket, a hole.   5
In the right, a parking ticket
delivered up last August on Bay State Road.
In my heart, a scatter like milkweed,
a flinging from the pods of the soul.
My skin presses your old outline.   10
It is hot and dry inside.

I think of the last day of your life,
old friend, how I would unwind it, paste
it together in a different collage,
back from the death car idling in the garage,   15
back up the stairs, your praying hands unlaced,
reassembling the bites of bread and tuna fish
into a ceremony of sandwich,
running the home movie backward to a space
we could be easy in, a kitchen place   20
with vodka and ice, our words like living meat.

Dear friend, you have excited crowds
with your example. They swell
like wine bags, straining at your seams.
I will be years gathering up our words,   25
fishing out letters, snapshots, stains,
leaning my ribs against this durable cloth
to put on the dumb blue blazer of your death.

PHILIP APPLEMAN

[b. 1926]

Ten Definitions of Lifetime

1

Slush, my brother said, it's
slush—the first word
I ever knew I was learning. Ankle-deep,
I shivered with cold
understanding.   5

2

Scout's Honor: it was another boy scout
who betrayed me—one way of finding out
what honor means.

3

At graduation, bold with endings,
I kissed her at last.   10
Twelve years, she said,
erasing the difference
between delay and loss.

4

When the bomb dissolved Hiroshima
every man in my company   15
got bombed on PX°   military post exchange
patriotism.

5

I told the bosun:
a ship defines the ocean.
He said: horse   20
shit.

6

The many words for love
come easily; we would not learn the sounds
of separation.

7

In that single moment   25
I wanted to be immortal.
She whispered: a man who was immortal
would be as ugly
as a plastic flower.

8

All I learned in grad school   30
was the meaning of humility;
all I have ever forgotten
is what I learned in grad school.

9

Universe
ity: those who can, teach;   35
those who cannot
are the servants of teachers.

10

The poet is the unacknowledged
lexicographer of mankind.

A. R. AMMONS
[b. 1926]

Corsons Inlet

I went for a walk over the dunes again this morning
to the sea,
then turned right along
    the surf

        rounded a naked headland   5
        and returned

  along the inlet shore:

it was muggy sunny, the wind from the sea steady and high,
crisp in the running sand,
    some breakthroughs of sun   10
  but after a bit

continuous overcast:

the walk liberating, I was released from forms,
from the perpendiculars,
    straight lines, blocks, boxes, binds   15
of thought
into the hues, shadings, rises, flowing bends and blends
    of sight:

        I allow myself eddies of meaning:
yield to a direction of significance   20
running
like a stream through the geography of my work:
  you can find
in my sayings
    swerves of action   25
      like the inlet's cutting edge:
  there are dunes of motion,
organizations of grass, white sandy paths of remembrance
in the overall wandering of mirroring mind:

but Overall is beyond me: is the sum of these events   30
I cannot draw, the ledger I cannot keep, the accounting
beyond the account:

in nature there are few sharp lines: there are areas of
primrose
          more or less dispersed;   35
disorderly orders of bayberry; between the rows
of dunes,
irregular swamps of reeds,
though not reeds alone, but grass, bayberry, yarrow, all . . .
predominantly reeds: 40

I have reached no conclusions, have erected no boundaries,
shutting out and shutting in, separating inside
          from outside: I have
          drawn no lines:
          as   45

manifold events of sand
change the dune's shape that will not be the same shape
tomorrow,

so I am willing to go along, to accept
the becoming   50
thought, to stake off no beginnings or ends, establish
          no walls:

by transitions the land falls from grassy dunes to creek
to undercreek: but there are no lines, though
          change in that transition is clear   55
          as any sharpness: but "sharpness" spread out,
allowed to occur over a wider range
than mental lines can keep:

the moon was full last night: today, low tide was low:
black shoals of mussels exposed to the risk   60
of air
and, earlier, of sun,
waved in and out with the waterline, waterline inexact,
caught always in the event of change:
          a young mottled gull stood free on the shoals   65
          and ate
to vomiting: another gull, squawking possession, cracked a crab,
picked out the entrails, swallowed the soft-shelled legs, a ruddy
turnstone running in to snatch leftover bits:

risk is full: every living thing in 70
siege: the demand is life, to keep life: the small
white blacklegged egret, how beautiful, quietly stalks and spears
          the shallows, darts to shore
                  to stab—what? I couldn't
      see against the black mudflats—a frightened 75
      fiddler crab?

        the news to my left over the dunes and
reeds and bayberry clumps was
          fall: thousands of tree swallows 80
          gathering for flight:
          an order held
          in constant change: a congregation
rich with entropy: nevertheless, separable, noticeable
      as one event,
              not chaos: preparations for 85
flight from winter,
cheet, cheet, cheet, cheet, wings rifling the green clumps,
beaks
at the bayberries
     a perception full of wind, flight, curve, 90
     sound:
     the possibility of rule as the sum of rulelessness:
the "field" of action
with moving, incalculable center:

in the smaller view, order tight with shape: 95
blue tiny flowers on a leafless weed: carapace of crab:
snail shell:
      pulsations of order
      in the bellies of minnows: orders swallowed,
broken down, transferred through membranes 100
to strengthen larger orders: but in the large view, no
lines or changeless shapes: the working in and out, together
      and against, of millions of events: this,
         so that I make
         no form 105
         formlessness:

orders as summaries, as outcomes of actions override
or in some way result, not predictably (seeing me gain
the top of a dune,
the swallows 110
could take flight—some other fields of bayberry
     could enter fall
      berryless) and there is serenity:

no arranged terror: no forcing of image, plan,
or thought: 115
no propaganda, no humbling of reality to precept:

terror pervades but is not arranged, all possibilities
of escape open: no route shut, except in
   the sudden loss of all routes:

      I see narrow orders, limited tightness, but will   120
not run to that easy victory:
      still around the looser, wider forces work:
      I will try
     to fasten into order enlarging grasps of disorder, widening
scope, but enjoying the freedom that   125
Scope eludes my grasp, that there is no finality of vision,
that I have perceived nothing completely,
     that tomorrow a new walk is a new walk.

The City Limits

When you consider the radiance, that it does not withhold
itself but pours its abundance without selection into every
nook and cranny not overhung or hidden; when you consider

that birds' bones make no awful noise against the light but
lie low in the light as in a high testimony; when you consider   5
the radiance, that it will look into the guiltiest

swervings of the weaving heart and bear itself upon them,
not flinching into disguise or darkening; when you consider
the abundance of such resource as illuminates the glow-blue

bodies and gold-skeined wings of flies swarming the dumped   10
guts of a natural slaughter or the coil of shit and in no
way winces from its storms of generosity; when you consider

that air or vacuum, snow or shale, squid or wolf, rose or lichen,
each is accepted into as much light as it will take, then
the heart moves roomier, the man stands and looks about, the   15

leaf does not increase itself above the grass, and the dark
work of the deepest cells is of a tune with May bushes
and fear lit by the breadth of such calmly turns to praise.

ROBERT CREELEY
[*b. 1926*]

I Know a Man

As I sd to my
friend, because I am
always talking,—John, I

sd, which was not his
name, the darkness sur-   5
rounds us, what

can we do against
it, or else, shall we &
why not, buy a goddamn big car,

drive, he sd, for   10
christ's sake, look
out where yr going.

The Rain

All night the sound had
come back again,
and again falls
this quiet, persistent rain.

What am I to myself   5
that must be remembered,
insisted upon
so often? Is it

that never the ease,
even the hardness,   10
of rain falling
will have for me

something other than this,
something not so insistent—
am I to be locked in this   15
final uneasiness?

Love, if you love me,
lie next to me.
Be for me, like rain,
the getting out   20

of the tiredness, the fatuousness, the semi-
lust of intentional indifference.
Be wet
with a decent happiness.

The Language

Locate *I*
love you some-
where in

teeth and
eyes, bite   5
it but

take care not
to hurt, you
want so

much so   10
little. Words
say everything,

I
love you
again,   15

then what
is emptiness
for. To

fill, fill.
I heard words   20
and words full

of holes
aching. Speech
is a mouth.

ALLEN GINSBERG

[*b. 1926*]

A Supermarket in California

What thoughts I have of you tonight, Walt Whitman, for I walked down the sidestreets under the trees with a headache self-conscious looking at the full moon.

In my hungry fatigue, and shopping for images, I went into the neon fruit supermarket, dreaming of your enumerations!

What peaches and what penumbras! Whole families shopping at night! Aisles full of husbands! Wives in the avocados, babies in the tomatoes!—and you, Garcia Lorca, what were you doing down by the watermelons?

I saw you, Walt Whitman, childless, lonely old grubber, poking among the meats in the refrigerator and eyeing the grocery boys.

I heard you asking questions of each: Who killed the pork chops? What price bananas? Are you my Angel? 5

I wandered in and out of the brilliant stacks of cans following you, and followed in my imagination by the store detective.

We strode down the open corridors together in our solitary fancy tasting artichokes, possessing every frozen delicacy, and never passing the cashier.

Where are we going, Walt Whitman? The doors close in an hour. Which way does your beard point tonight?

(I touch your book and dream of our odyssey in the supermarket and feel absurd.)

Will we walk all night through solitary streets? The trees add shade to shade, lights out in the houses, we'll both be lonely. 10

Will we stroll dreaming of the lost America of love past blue automobiles in driveways, home to our silent cottage?

Ah, dear father, graybeard, lonely old courage-teacher, what America did you have when Charon quit poling his ferry and you got out on a smoking bank and stood watching the boat disappear on the black waters of Lethe?

W. D. SNODGRASS

[*b. 1926*]

April Inventory

The green catalpa tree has turned
All white; the cherry blooms once more.

In one whole year I haven't learned
A blessed thing they pay you for.
The blossoms snow down in my hair;   5
The trees and I will soon be bare.

The trees have more than I to spare.
The sleek, expensive girls I teach,
Younger and pinker every year,
Bloom gradually out of reach.   10
The pear tree lets its petals drop
Like dandruff on a tabletop.

The girls have grown so young by now
I have to nudge myself to stare.
This year they smile and mind me how   15
My teeth are falling with my hair.
In thirty years I may not get
Younger, shrewder, or out of debt.

The tenth time, just a year ago,
I made myself a little list   20
Of all the things I'd ought to know,
Then told my parents, analyst,
And everyone who's trusted me
I'd be substantial, presently.

I haven't read one book about   25
A book or memorized one plot.
Or found a mind I did not doubt.
I learned one date. And then forgot.
And one by one the solid scholars
Get the degrees, the jobs, the dollars.   30

And smile above their starchy collars.
I taught my classes Whitehead's notions;
One lovely girl, a song of Mahler's.
Lacking a source-book or promotions,
I showed one child the colors of   35
A luna moth and how to love.

I taught myself to name my name,
To bark back, loosen love and crying;
To ease my woman so she came,
To ease an old man who was dying.   40
I have not learned how often I
Can win, can love, but choose to die.

I have not learned there is a lie
Love shall be blonder, slimmer, younger;
That my equivocating eye   45
Loves only by my body's hunger;
That I have forces, true to feel,
Or that the lovely world is real.

While scholars speak authority
And wear their ulcers on their sleeves,   50
My eyes in spectacles shall see
These trees procure and spend their leaves.
There is a value underneath
The gold and silver in my teeth.

Though trees turn bare and girls turn wives,   55
We shall afford our costly seasons;
There is a gentleness survives
That will outspeak and has its reasons.
There is a loveliness exists,
Preserves us, not for specialists.   60

RUTH F. EISENBERG

[b. 1927]

Jocasta

1

When she learned the king's power,
Jocasta lost delight in being queen.
Laius was a cold, dry man. Looking at him
brought the image of her baby, his feet
pierced and bound, her baby left to die   5
on the mountain slope. They would
have no other children.

I remember Laius drunk that night, crying
for Chrysippus, the source of his curse.
Wanting his boy, he took me instead   10
and threw me on my back to have his way.
I am fifteen and afraid to resist

JOCASTA   wife and mother of Oedipus. See Sophocles' play Oedipus Rex, pp. 844–885.   [3]*Laius*
father of Oedipus.   [9]*Chrysippus   Laius's male lover.*

and tell myself it is my husband's right;
the gods decree a wife obey her spouse.

Sober, Laius recalls Apollo's threat: 15
our son will kill him, beget upon me.
Nine months drag like oxen ploughing.
With icy eyes Laius watches me swell.
I fear the gods and beg Hera, for a girl,
but as foretold, I give birth to a son.   20
Laius takes the child to bind its feet.
The baby cries, and Laius turns away.
He summons a servant and orders me to hand
my baby over, threatening me when I cry.
The king will keep his own hands clean.   25

At the public altar, Laius
offered bulls and lambs in ritual
slaughter. The everburning fire raged
so the offerings charred, and Jocasta
trembled at the gods' displeasure.   30

Upon the gates this dawn, a strange creature
appeared and woke all Thebes. In raucous voice
she cried, "A riddle. Who'll solve my riddle?"
At first our people came to gawk, then marvel.
Some trembled, children hid their heads and cried.   35
I've heard old tales the minstrels sing of her,
but never did expect to really see
a Sphinx—part woman, bird, and lion too . . .
And what she asks is strange as well: four legs,
then two, then three. What can it be? No one   40
knows the answer. No one.

The Sphinx brought pestilence and
drought. Rivers and streams ran dry, vines
shriveled. But until her riddle was solved,
the creature would not leave. On the gates   45
she stayed, her destructive song echoing
from empty wells.

My life is a toad. All day and all night
the Sphinx. We cannot escape her song.
Song! More like wail or whine or scream.   50
Laius is useless as always. Deceitful
man, I hate him, hate his touch.

[15]*Apollo*   The sun god.   [19]*Hera*   *wife of Zeus, leader of the gods.*

The land is parched; flocks die. Our people
haggard, starving, plead to ease their distress.
What can we do? Mortals cannot make the rain.   55
I suggest Laius seek Apollo's help.
To get away, he welcomes the idea to go
to Delphi and proclaims a pilgrimage.

On the sunswept road to Delphi,
Laius was killed. The servant reporting   60
the death begged Jocasta to let him tend
flocks in the hills. Sending him on his way,
she shut herself in the palace.

The prophesy was false. How can that be
if gods control all things? For surely chance   65
does not . . . No, no. Yet Laius killed our son
and not the other way. That sin diseased
his soul. I bless the gods that I,
at last, am free.

I dream of my baby night after night.   70
He is dancing for the gods with bound feet.
I do not understand how he can dance so.
When he jumps, he trips, falling in a heap.
The gods just laugh and turn away to drink.
I sit ravelling knots. The knots become rope.   75
I wake shaking and muffle my tears in the sheets.

2

"Man" answered the young stranger
whose red hair caught the sun's rays,
and the riddle was solved. True to her
promise, the Sphinx dashed herself to   80
death. Thebes was free.

Hailing their hero, the people
elected Oedipus king. Gratefully,
he accepted the rule and with it the hand
of Thebes' queen, Jocasta.   85

I see young Oedipus in radiant
sunlight, Apollo blinding me to all
but young and vital strength. Deep in myself
I feel a pulsebeat, something asleep
begins to wake, as though a dormant seed   90
sends up a shoot, opens a leaf. That's how

Aphrodite touches me. I love this youth.
My sun, I rise to him and rise with him.

From a land of rock and misery, Thebes
became a bower. Brilliant poppies   95
dotted the land. The wells filled, crops
flourished, and the flocks grew fat again.

Before the people's eyes, Jocasta
became young. Her dark hair gleamed, her
eye was bright and her laughter cheered   100
the halls of the palace.

Oedipus has become my Apollo warming
my days and nights. I am eighteen again
with poppies in my hair. I am the poppies,
bright little blooms with milk in them.   105
Like them, I seem to spring from rocky ground.
Like their color and his hair, our love flames.

Sweet Aphrodite, you rush through me, a stream
until you burst like foam that crests the sea.
Your blessing washes what was once a barren   110
ground. I walk among the roses, feel
your blush upon my cheeks. Oh lovely goddess,
I send you swans and doves.

Thebes prospered these years:
the gnarled olive bent lower with fruit.   115
Lambs frisked in the fields and pipers'
songs rang through the hills. Jocasta had
four children. Psalms of joy were sung
and danced for the gods.

With four children, the hours run away.   120
Their hunger, games and tears take all my time.
In bed, with Oedipus, I sleep in peace.
He was at first my headstrong bull, but now
he is what a man, a king, should be.
I like to see him walking in the yard,   125
his funny stiff gait, his hair burnished
by Apollo's brilliant rays.

Mine turns grey but he doesn't seem to mind.
Our love has brought to me the joy I missed
when I was young and thought I'd never know.   130

At last, I lay to rest my little boy,
his shadow vanished now from all my dreams.

3

Years of plenty at an end, Thebes
was inflicted with drought. The earth
burned as crops withered, cattle and   135
sheep sickened.

While days were once too short, now each one drags
a slow furrow, the earth heavy with heat,
lament and prayer. When I go to the fields
the women clutch my gown and plead my help.   140
Too many children sicken. The healthy droop.
At home, the girls sit listless, my sons tangle
while Oedipus complains his ankles twinge.
He limps and growls just like a wounded pup.

Jocasta, very grey now, walked   145
with a more measured step. More than
a loving wife, she was also counsellor
to Oedipus.

Blaming himself because the land is parched,
Oedipus frets alarmed he's failed the gods   150
in some unknown way, searching within himself.
In turn, I pray, lighting fire after fire,
but none burn true. I call on Aphrodite
and offer her doves, but they flap their wings
and peck each others' eyes. When I ask Apollo   155
to dim his eye, his answer scalds.

No relief at hand, Oedipus sought
aid from Delphi. The report came back
a confusing riddle about Laius' death.
Suspecting treason, Oedipus feared   160
conspiracy against his own throne.

Oedipus needs someone to blame. He calls
Creon traiter, Tiresias false seer.
I take him in my arms and stroke his hair.
He tells me what Tiresias has foreseen.   165
I laugh and tell him I too once believed
that prophesy controlled our lives, that seers
had magic vision the rest of us did not.
I tell the story of Laius, how it

was foretold he would die at his son's hand   170
and how that baby died when one week old.

As I speak I feel so strange, as though my tale
came from another life about someone else.

My words do not comfort, they flame new fears.
He relates what drove him from home, tales that he   175
would kill his father and bring rank fruit
from his mother's womb. He fears he has
been cursed. Dear gods, how can I comfort him?

4

From Corinth, a messenger
brought news of Polybus' death,   180
the king whom Oedipus called father.

You say that Polybus is dead. Dare I
greet death with joy? Can that be blasphemy?
My heart flies into song: His father's dead—
my Oedipus lives safe. His prophesy   185
is false. Is false as Laius' was. Oh bless
your fate, dear love, you need no longer fear.

Corinth wished Oedipus to return
and rule. Fearing he would sleep with
his mother, Oedipus refused. Nothing   190
to fear, the messenger assured. Merope
was a barren woman.

Jocasta began to tremble. Her hands
rose to cover her mouth.

What's this? What's this? What words do I hear?   195
How can I shut his silly mouth, tell him
Go. Leave. We will not heed your words.
My tongue stops, rooted in my mouth.

I look at Oedipus. He does not see
me watching him. His face is strained, his eyes   200
are glaring blue. I try to stop the questions.
"Oedipus, I beg, you, do not hear this out."

When Oedipus insisted, the
messenger told the story of the king's
infancy,—how he, a shepherd then,   205

had helped to save the king's life
when a baby, a baby with bound feet.

> Oh God. Oh cold, gold God. Apollo,
> you chill me. My mind is ice, and I hear
> my mouth say freezing words to Oedipus.   210
> To my husband. My son. "God keep you from
> the knowledge of who you are. Unhappy,
> Oedipus, my poor, damned Oedipus,
> that is all I can call you, and the last thing
> I shall ever call you."   215

5

Her face ashen, Jocasta rushed
into the palace, her hands showing her
the way to her own quarters. She
ordered the guards to let no one in.
Ignoring all offers of help, she commanded   220
her women to leave her alone.

> I can't believe. I can't believe. Oh God.
> He is my son. I've loved my son but not
> as mothers should, but in my bed, in me.
> All that I loved the most, his youth that made   225
> our love the summer sun, wrong, all wrong.
> Vile. He caressed me here and here. And I
> returend his touch. Odious hands. My flesh
> crawls with worms.

> My God, we've had four children.   230

In her chamber, she looked at her
bed, sat on it, then jumped up as though
stung. Covering her eyes with her hands,
she shook her head back and forth, again
and again, her body rocking.   235

> Oh, Oedipus, what good was our love if
> it comes only to shame? To children whom
> all Thebes can curse? Such children, even ours,
> are rightly damned.

> Although we could not know who we were   240
> and loved in innocence, still we are monsters
> in the eyes of god and man. Our names will mean
> disgrace and guilt forever.

Walking to her dressing table,
she stood before it picking up small   245
objects: combs, a gold box, a pair of
brooches. Noticing a bracelet given her
by her father when she was a bride,
she let forth a dreadful groan.

Oh Laius, Laius, you brought this on me.   250
My fate was sealed my wedding day. Chrysippus
was innocent as I; for you this curse
was uttered, a curse that falls on me. Oh,
that I must bear the shame, that I must be
destroyed by your corruption. And our son,   255
because you sinned, is ruined, damned.

My marriage day . . . what choices did I have?
As many as the night you came to me.
The only choice a woman has is that she wed
accepting what the gods and men decree.   260
It is not just. It never can be right.

Moving decisively, she walked to the
doors and bolted them, straining against
their heavy weight. The women on the other
side called to her, but again she bade them   265
go away.

Falling on her knees, she pummeled
her stomach as though to punish her
womb. As she did, she called her child-
ren's names, one name, Oedipus, again   270
and again.

I thought him buried, forgotten. But no,
for countless days and nights these many years
he's thrust himself on me instead. My bed
once stained with birthing blood is now forever   275
stained; what once was love become a rank
corruption.

Rising painfully, sore, she turned
to the small altar in her chamber.
Smashing a jar which held incense, she   280
began in a voice of char to call on
Apollo and Aphrodite.

As she raised her eyes, she raised
her fist and shook it against
the silent air.   285

    Apollo, you blinded me to his scars,
his age, any resemblance to Laius.
And you, Aphrodite, cruel sister of the sun,
set my woman's body afire, matching my
ripe years and hungers with his youth and strength.   290
Paralyzing my mind, you inflamed my heart.

    The years I prayed to you and praised you
were all charade. You so enjoyed my dance.
We are your fools to trifle with, your joke.

    We tremble to question what the future holds.   295
As though it matters, we think asking will spoil
our luck, but your injustice mocks all hope.

    I hear a chant pounding inside my head.
Five babies. Five abominations.
As though a chorus raises call to prayer.   300
Five babies. Five abominations.

    No call to prayer. It is a call to curse
the gods. No longer will I be their fool.

From her robe, she removed her
braided belt. As she looped its strands,   305
she heard, from the courtyard, a man's
voice scream in anguish. Undeflected, she
tied the necessary knots, slipping the loop
back and forth. Satisfied, she settled
the noose around her neck.   310

    Five babies cursed by heavenly whim,
cursed in their lives without chance or hope.
Mothers ought not love their children so.

Gathering her skirts, she climbed
up on the stool.   315

    And wives be more than merely bedside pawns.
Those who cannot shape their lives are better
dead.

She stepped onto the air.

GALWAY KINNELL

[b. 1927]

To Christ Our Lord

The legs of the elk punctured the snow's crust
And wolves floated lightfooted on the land
Hunting Christmas elk living and frozen;
Inside snow melted in a basin, and a woman basted
A bird spread over coals by its wings and head.   5

Snow had sealed the windows; candles lit
The Christmas meal. The Christmas grace chilled
The cooked bird, being long-winded and the room cold.
During the words a boy thought, it is fitting
To eat this creature killed on the wing?   10

He had killed it himself, climbing out
Alone on snowshoes in the Christmas dawn,
The fallen snow swirling and the snowfall gone,
Heard its throat scream as the rifle shouted,
Watched it drop, and fished from the snow the dead.   15

He had not wanted to shoot. The sound
Of wings beating into the hushed air
Had stirred his love, and his fingers
Froze in his gloves, and he wondered,
Famishing, could he fire? Then he fired.   20

Now the grace praised his wicked act. At its end
The bird on the plate
Stared at his stricken appetite.
There had been nothing to do but surrender,
To kill and to eat; he ate as he had killed, with wonder.   25

At night on snowshoes on the drifting field
He wondered again, for whom had love stirred?
The stars glittered on the snow and nothing answered.
Then the Swan spread her wings, cross of the cold north,
The pattern and mirror of the acts of earth.   30

The Apple Tree

I remember this tree,
its white flowers all unfallen.
It's the fall, the unfallen apples
hold their brightness
a little longer into the blue air, hold the dream   5
they can be brighter.

We create without turning,
without looking back, without ever
really knowing we create.
Having tasted   10
the first flower of the first spring
we go on,
we don't turn again
until we touch the last flower of the last spring.

And that day, fondling   15
each grain one more time, like the overturned hourglass,
we die
of the return-streaming of everything we have lived.

When the fallen apple rolls
into the grass, the apple worm   20
stops, then goes
all the way through and looks out
at the creation unopposed, the world
made entirely of lovers.

Or else there is no such thing as memory,   25
or else there are only the empty branches,
only the blossoms upon them,
only the apples,
that still grow full,
that still fail into brightness,   30
that still invent past their own decay the dream
they can be brighter,

that still
that still

The one who holds still and looks out,   35
alone
of all of us, that one may die mostly of happiness.

The Still Time

I know there is still time—
time for the hands
to open, for the bones of them
to be filled
by those failed harvests of want,   5
the bread imagined of the days of not having.

Now that the fear
has been rummaged down to its husk,
and the wind blowing
the flesh away translates itself   10
into flesh and the flesh
gives itself in its reveries to the wind.

I remember those summer nights
when I was young and empty,
when I lay through the darkness   15
wanting, wanting,
knowing
I would have nothing of anything I wanted—
that total craving
that hollows the heart out irreversibly.   20

So it surprises me now to hear
the steps of my life following me—
so much of it gone
it returns, everything that drove me crazy
comes back, blessing the misery   25
of each step it took me into the world;
as though a prayer had ended
and the bit of changed air
between the palms goes free
to become the glitter   30
on some common thing that inexplicably shines.

And the old voice,
which once made its broken-off, choked, parrot-incoherences,
speaks again,
this time on the palatum cordis,   35
this time saying there is time, still time,
for one who can groan
to sing,
for one who can sing to be healed.

Saint Francis and the Sow

The bud
stands for all things,
even for those things that don't flower,
for everything flowers, from within, of self-blessing;
though sometimes it is necessary   5
to reteach a thing its loveliness,
to put a hand on its brow
of the flower
and retell it in words and in touch
it is lovely   10
until it flowers again from within, of self-blessing;
as Saint Francis
put his hand on the creased forehead
of the sow, and told her in words and in touch
blessings of earth on the sow, and the sow   15
began remembering all down her thick length,
from the earthen snout all the way
through the fodder and slops to the spiritual curl of the tail,
from the hard spininess spiked out from the spine
down through the great broken heart   20
to the sheer blue milken dreaminess spurting and shuddering
from the fourteen teats into the fourteen mouths sucking and
     blowing beneath them:
the long, perfect loveliness of sow.

JAMES WRIGHT
[b. 1927]

Lying in a Hammock at William Duffy's Farm in Pine Island, Minnesota

Over my head, I see the bronze butterfly,
Asleep on the black trunk,
Blowing like a leaf in green shadow.
Down the ravine behind the empty house,
The cowbells follow one another   5
Into the distances of the afternoon.

SAINT FRANCIS AND THE SOW   [12]**Saint Francis**   *Saint Francis of Assisi (1182–1226) was famed
for his love of all creation, especially animals.*

To my right,
In a field of sunlight between two pines,
The droppings of last year's horses
Blaze up into golden stones.　　　　　　　　　　10
I lean back, as the evening darkens and comes on.
A chicken hawk floats over, looking for home.
I have wasted my life.

The Jewel

There is this cave
In the air behind my body
That nobody is going to touch:
A cloister, a silence
Closing around a blossom of fire.　　　　　　5
When I stand upright in the wind,
My bones turn to dark emeralds.

Mutterings Over the Crib of a Deaf Child

"How will he hear the bell at school
Arrange the broken afternoon,
And know to run across the cool
Grasses where the starlings cry,
Or understand the day is gone?"　　　　　5

Well, someone lifting cautious brows
Will take the measure of the clock.
And he will see the birchen boughs
Outside the sagging dark from the sky,
And the shade crawling upon the rock.　　　10

"And how will he know to rise at morning?
His mother has other sons to waken,
She has the stove she must build to burning
Before the coals of the night-time die,
And he never stirs when he is shaken."　　　15

I take it the air affects the skin,
And you remember, when you were young,
Sometimes you could feel the dawn begin,
And the fire would call you, by and by,
Out of the bed and bring you along.　　　20

"Well, good enough. To serve his needs
All kinds of arrangements can be made.
But what will you do if his finger bleeds?
Or a bobwhite whistles invisibly
And flutes like an angel off in the shade?"   25

He will learn pain. And, as for the bird,
It is always darkening when that comes out.
I will putter as though I had not heard,
And lift him into my arms and sing
Whether he hears my song or not.   30

A Blessing

Just off the highway to Rochester, Minnesota,
Twilight bounds softly forth on the grass.
And the eyes of those two Indian ponies
Darken with kindness.
They have come gladly out of the willows   5
To welcome my friend and me.
We step over the barbed wire into the pasture
Where they have been grazing all day, alone.
They ripple tensely, they can hardly contain their happiness
That we have come.   10
They bow shyly as wet swans. They love each other.
There is no loneliness like theirs.
At home once more,

They begin munching the young tufts of spring in the darkness.
I would like to hold the slenderer one in my arms,   15
For she has walked over to me
And nuzzled my left hand.
She is black and white,
Her mane falls wild on her forehead,
And the light breeze moves me to caress her long ear   20
That is delicate as the skin over a girl's wrist.
Suddenly I realize
That if I stepped out of my body I would break
Into blossom.

W. S. MERWIN
[b. 1927]

When you go away

When you go away the wind clicks around to the north
The painters work all day but at sundown the paint falls
Showing the black walls
The clock goes back to striking the same hour
That has no place in the years   5

And at night wrapped in the bed of ashes
In one breath I wake
It is the time when the beards of the dead get their growth
I remember that I am falling
That I am the reason   10
And that my words are the garment of what I shall never be
Like the tucked sleeve of a one-armed boy

Separation

Your absence has gone through me
Like thread through a needle.
Everything I do is stitched with its color.

DONALD HALL
[b. 1928]

My son, my executioner

My son, my executioner,
    I take you in my arms,
Quiet and small and just astir,
    And whom my body warms.

Sweet death, small son, our instrument   5
    Of immortality,

Your cries and hungers document
Our bodily decay.

We twenty-five and twenty-two,
Who seemed to live forever,   10
Observe enduring life in you
And start to die together.

Kicking the leaves

1

Kicking the leaves, October, as we walk home together
from the game, in Ann Arbor,
on a day the color of soot, rain in the air;
I kick at the leaves of maples,
reds of seventy different shades, yellow   5
like old paper; and poplar leaves, fragile and pale;
and elm leaves, flags of a doomed race.
I kick at the leaves, making a sound I remember
as the leaves swirl upward from my boot,
and flutter; and I remember   10
Octobers walking to school in Connecticut,
wearing corduroy knickers that swished
with a sound like leaves; and a Sunday buying
a cup of cider at a roadside stand
on a dirt road in New Hampshire; and kicking the leaves,   15
autumn 1955 in Massachusetts, knowing
my father would die when the leaves were gone.

2

Each fall in New Hampshire, on the farm
where my mother grew up, a girl in the country,
my grandfather and grandmother   20
finished the autumn work, taking the last vegetables in
from the cold fields, canning, storing roots and apples
in the cellar under the kitchen. Then my grandfather
raked leaves against the house
as the final chore of autumn.   25
One November I drove up from college to see them.
We pulled big rakes, as we did when we hayed in summer,
pulling the leaves against the granite foundations
around the house, on every side of the house,
and then, to keep them in place, we cut spruce boughs   30

and laid them across the leaves,
green on red, until the house
was tucked up, ready for snow
that would freeze the leaves in tight, like a stiff skirt.
Then we puffed through the shed door,   35
taking off boots and overcoats, slapping our hands,
and sat in the kitchen, rocking, and drank
black coffee my grandmother made,
three of us sitting together, silent, in gray November.

3

One Saturday when I was little, before the war,   40
my father came home at noon from his half day at the office
and wore his Bates sweater, black on red,
with the crossed hockey sticks on it, and raked beside me
in the back yard, and tumbled in the leaves with me,
laughing, and carried me, laughing, my hair full of leaves,   45
to the kitchen window
where my mother could see us, and smile, and motion
to set me down, afraid I would fall and be hurt.

4

Kicking the leaves today, as we walk home together
from the game, among crowds of people   50
with their bright pennants, as many and bright as leaves,
my daughter's hair is the red-yellow color
of birch leaves, and she is tall like a birch,
growing up, fifteen, growing older; and my son
flamboyant as maple, twenty,   55
visits from college, and walks ahead of us, his step
springing, impatient to travel
the woods of the earth. Now I watch them
from a pile of leaves beside this clapboard house
in Ann Arbor, across from the school   60
where they learned to read,
as their shapes grow small with distance, waving,
and I know that I
diminish, not them, as I go first
into the leaves, taking   65
the step they will follow, Octobers and years from now.

5

This year the poems came back, when the leaves fell.
Kicking the leaves, I heard the leaves tell stories,
remembering, and therefore looking ahead, and building

the house of dying. I looked up into the maples 70
and found them, the vowels of bright desire.
I thought they had gone forever
while the bird sang *I love you, I love you*
and shook its black head
from side to side, and its red eye with no lid, 75
through years of winter, cold
as the taste of chicken wire, the music of cinder block.

6

Kicking the leaves, I uncover the lids of graves.
My grandfather died at seventy-seven, in March
when the sap was running; and I remember my father 80
twenty years ago,
coughing himself to death at fifty-two in the house
in the suburbs. Oh, how we flung
leaves in the air! How they tumbled and fluttered around us,
like slowly cascading water, when we walked together 85
in Hamden, before the war, when Johnson's Pond
had not surrendered to houses, the two of us
hand in hand, and in the wet air the smell of leaves
burning;
and in six years I will be fifty-two. 90

7

Now I fall, now I leap and fall
to feel the leaves crush under my body, to feel my body
buoyant in the ocean of leaves, the night of them,
night heaving with death and leaves, rocking like the ocean.
Oh, this delicious falling into the arms of leaves, 95
into the soft laps of leaves!
Face down, I swim into the leaves, feathery,
breathing the acrid odor of maple, swooping
in long glides to the bottom of October—
where the farm lies curled against winter, and soup steams 100
its breath of onion and carrot
onto damp curtains and windows; and past the windows
I see the tall bare maple trunks and branches, the oak
with its few brown weathery remnant leaves,
and the spruce trees, holding their green. 105
Now I leap and fall, exultant, recovering
from death, on account of death, in accord with the dead,
the smell and taste of leaves again,
and the pleasure, the only long pleasure, of taking a place
in the story of leaves. 110

PHILIP LEVINE

[b. 1928]

Let me begin again

Let me begin again as a speck
of dust caught in the night winds
sweeping out to sea. Let me begin
this time knowing the world is
salt water and dark clouds, the world   5
is grinding and sighing all night, and dawn
comes slowly and changes nothing. Let
me go back to land after a lifetime
of going nowhere. This time lodged
in the feathers of some scavenging gull   10
white above the black ship that docks
and broods upon the oily waters of
your harbor. This leaking freighter
has brought a hold full of hayforks
from Spain, great jeroboams of dark   15
Algerian wine and quill pens that can't
write English. The sailors have stumbled
off toward the bars or the bright houses.
The captain closes his log and falls asleep.
1/10'28. Tonight I shall enter my life   20
after being at sea for ages, quietly,
in a hospital named for an automobile.
The one child of millions of children
who has flown alone by the stars
above the black wastes of moonless waters   25
that stretched forever, who has turned
golden in the full sun of a new day.
A tiny wise child who this time will love
his life because it is like no other.

ANNE SEXTON
[1928–1975]

Two Hands

From the sea came a hand,
ignorant as a penny,
troubled with the salt of its mother,
mute with the silence of the fishes,
quick with the altars of the tides,   5
and God reached out of His mouth
and called it man.
Up came the other hand
and God called it woman.
The hands applauded.   10
And this was no sin.
It was as it was meant to be.

I see them roaming the streets:
Levi complaining about his mattress,
Sarah studying a beetle,   15
Mandrake holding his coffee mug,
Sally playing the drum at a football game,
John closing the eyes of the dying woman,
and some who are in prison,
even the prison of their bodies,   20
as Christ was prisoned in His body
until the triumph came.

Unwind, hands,
you angel webs,
unwind like the coil of a jumping jack,   25
cup together and let yourselves fill up with sun
and applaud, world,
applaud.

Us

I was wrapped in black
fur and white fur and
you undid me and then
you placed me in gold light

and then you crowned me,
while snow fell outside
the door in diagonal darts.
While a ten-inch snow
came down like stars
in small calcium fragments,
we were in our own bodies
(that room that will bury us)

and you were in my body
(that room that will outlive us)
and at first I rubbed your
feet dry with a towel
because I was your slave
and then you called me princess.
Princess!

Oh then
I stood up in my gold skin
and I beat down the psalms
and I beat down the clothes
and you undid the bridle
and you undid the reins
and I undid the buttons,
the bones, the confusions,
the New England postcards,
the January ten o'clock night,
and we rose up like wheat,
acre after acre of gold,
and we harvested,
we harvested.

The Starry Night

That does not keep me from having a terrible need of—shall I say the word—religion.
Then I go out at night to paint the stars.

VINCENT VAN GOGH in a letter to his brother

The town does not exist
except where one black-haired tree slips
up like a drowned woman into the hot sky.
The town is silent. The night boils with eleven stars
Oh starry starry night! This is how
I want to die.

THE STARRY NIGHT Epigraph **Vincent Van Gogh** *Dutch painter (1853–1890) whose famous work*
The Starry Night *inspired a number of poems, including this one. See page 501.*

It moves. They are all alive.
Even the moon bulges in its orange irons
to push children, like a god, from its eye.
The old unseen serpent swallows up the stars.   10
Oh starry starry night! This is how
I want to die:

into that rushing beast of the night,
sucked up by that great dragon, to split
from my life with no flag,   15
no belly,
no cry.

Ringing the Bells

And this is the way they ring
the bells in Bedlam
and this is the bell-lady
who comes each Tuesday morning
to give us a music lesson   5
and because the attendants make you go
and because we mind by instinct,
like bees caught in the wrong hive,
we are the circle of the crazy ladies
who sit in the lounge of the mental house   10
and smile at the smiling woman
who passes us each a bell,
who points at my hand
that holds my bell, E flat,
and this is the gray dress next to me   15
who grumbles as if it were special
to be old, to be old,
and this is the small hunched squirrel girl
on the other side of me
who picks at the hairs over her lip,   20
who picks at the hairs over her lip all day,
and this is how the bells really sound,
as untroubled and clean
as a workable kitchen,
and this is always my bell responding   25
to my hand that responds to the lady
who points at me, E flat;
and although we are no better for it,
they tell you to go. And you do.

ADRIENNE RICH
[b. 1929]

Night-Pieces: For a Child

1. The Crib

You sleeping I bend to cover.
Your eyelids work. I see
your dream, cloudy as a negative,
swimming underneath.
You blurt a cry. Your eyes   5
spring open, still filmed in dream.
Wider, they fix me—
—death's head, sphinx, medusa?
You scream.
Tears lick my cheeks, my knees   10
droop at your fear.
Mother I no more am,
but woman, and nightmare.

2. Her Waking

Tonight I jerk astart in a dark
hourless as Hiroshima,   15
almost hearing you breathe
in a cot three doors away.

You still breathe, yes—
and my dream with its gift of knives,
its murderous hider and seeker,   20
ebbs away, recoils

back into the egg of dreams,
the vanishing point of mind.
All gone.

But you and I—   25
swaddled in a dumb dark
old as sickheartedness,
modern as pure annihilation—

we drift in ignorance.
If I could hear you now   30

mutter some gentle animal sound!
If milk flowed from my breast again. . . .

A Valediction Forbidding Mourning

My swirling wants. Your frozen lips.
The grammar turned and attacked me.
Themes, written under duress.
Emptiness of the notations.

They gave me a drug that slowed the healing of wounds.   5

I want you to see this before I leave:
the experience of repetition as death
the failure of criticism to locate the pain
the poster in the bus that said:
my bleeding is under control.   10

A red plant in a cemetery of plastic wreaths.

A last attempt: the language is a dialect called metaphor.
These images go unglossed: hair, glacier, flashlight.
When I think of a landscape I am thinking of a time.
When I talk of taking a trip I mean forever.   15
I could say: those mountains have a meaning
but further than that I could not say.

To do something very common, in my own way.

Trying to Talk with a Man

Out in this desert we are testing bombs,

that's why we came here.

Sometimes I feel an underground river
forcing its way between deformed cliffs
an acute angle of understanding   5
moving itself like a locus of the sun
into this condemned scenery.

What we've had to give up to get here—
whole LP collections, films we starred in

A VALEDICTION FORBIDDING MOURNING See John Donne's poem of the same title, p. 536.

playing in the neighborhoods, bakery windows   10
full of dry, chocolate-filled Jewish cookies,
the language of love-letters, of suicide notes,
afternoons on the riverbank
pretending to be children

Coming out to this desert   15
we meant to change the face of
driving among dull green succulents
walking at noon in the ghost town
surrounded by a silence

that sounds like the silence of the place   20
except that it came with us
and is familiar
and everything we were saying until now
was an effort to blot it out—
coming out here we are up against it   25

Out here I feel more helpless
with you than without you.

You mention the danger
and list the equipment
we talk of people caring for each other   30
in emergencies—laceration, thirst—
but you look at me like an emergency

Your dry heat feels like power
your eyes are stars of a different magnitude
they reflect lights that spell out: EXIT   35
when you get up and pace the floor

talking of the danger
as if it were not ourselves
as if we were testing anything else.

Aunt Jennifer's Tigers

Aunt Jennifer's tigers prance across a screen,
Bright topaz denizens of a world of green.
They do not fear the men beneath the tree;
They pace in sleek chivalric certainty.

Aunt Jennifer's fingers fluttering through her wool   5
Find even the ivory needle hard to pull.

The massive weight of Uncle's wedding band
Sits heavily upon Aunt Jennifer's hand.

When Aunt is dead, her terrified hands will lie
Still ringed with ordeals she was mastered by.   10
The tigers in the panel that she made
Will go on prancing, proud and unafraid.

DONALD FINKEL
[*b. 1929*]

Hunting Song

The fox came lolloping, lolloping,
Lolloping. His tongue hung out
And his ears were high.
He was like death at the end of a string
When he came to the hollow   5
Log. Ran in one side
And out of the other. O
He was sly.

The hounds came tumbling, tumbling,
Tumbling. Their heads were low   10
And their eyes were red.

The sound of their breath was louder than death
When they came to the hollow
Log. They held at one end
But a bitch found the scent. O   15
They were mad.

The hunter came galloping, galloping,
Galloping. All damp was his mare
From her hooves to her mane.
His coat and his mouth were redder than death   20
When he came to the hollow
Log. He took in the rein
And over he went. O
He was fine.

The log, he just lay there, alone in   25
The clearing. No fox nor hound

Nor mounted man
Saw his black round eyes in their perfect disguise
(As the ends of a hollow
Log). He watched death go through him,   30
Around him and over him. O
He was wise.

X. J. KENNEDY

[b. 1929]

In a prominent bar in Secaucus one day

TO THE TUNE OF "THE OLD ORANGE FLUTE" OR
THE TUNE OF "SWEET BETSY FROM PIKE"

In a prominent bar in Secaucus one day
Rose a lady in skunk with a topheavy sway,
Raised a knobby red finger—all turned from their beer—
While with eyes bright as snowcrust she sang high and clear:

"Now who of you'd think from an eyeload of me   5
That I once was a lady as proud as could be?
Oh I'd never sit down by a tumbledown drunk
If it wasn't, my dears, for the high cost of junk.

"All the gents used to swear that the white of my calf
Beat the down of the swan by a length and a half.   10
In the kerchief of linen I caught to my nose
Ah, there never fell snot, but a little gold rose.

"I had seven gold teeth and a toothpick of gold,
My Virginia cheroot° was a leaf of it rolled   cigar
And I'd light it each time with a thousand in cash—   15
Why the bums used to fight if I flicked them an ash.

"Once the toast of the Biltmore, the belle of the Taft,
I would drink bottle beer at the Drake, never draft,
And dine at the Astor on Salisbury steak
With a clean tablecloth for each bite I did take.   20

"In a car like the Roxy I'd roll to the track,
A steel-guitar trio, a bar in the back,

IN A PROMINENT BAR IN SECAUCUS ONE DAY   17-19*Biltmore . . . Astor*   *once-fine hotels*
in New York City.   21*Roxy   a large, garish movie theater.*

And the wheels made no noise, they turned over so fast,
Still it took you ten minutes to see me go past.

"When the horses bowed down to me that I might choose,   25
I bet on them all, for I hated to lose.
Now I'm saddled each night for my butter and eggs
And the broken threads race down the backs of my legs.

"Let you hold in mind, girls, that your beauty must pass
Like a lovely white clover that rusts with its grass.   30
Keep your bottoms off barstools and marry you young
Or be left—an old barrel with many a bung.

"For when time takes you out for a spin in his car
You'll be hard-pressed to stop him from going too far
And be left by the roadside, for all your good deeds,   35
Two toadstools for tits and a face full of weeds."

All the house raised a cheer, but the man at the bar
Made a phonecall and up pulled a red patrol car
And she blew us a kiss as they copped her away
From that prominent bar in Secaucus, N.J.

First Confession

Blood thudded in my ears. I scuffed
   Steps stubborn, to the telltale booth
Beyond whose curtained portal coughed
   The robed repositor of truth.

The slat shot back. The universe   5
   Bowed down his cratered dome to hear
Enumerated my each curse,
   The sip snitched from my old man's beer,

My sloth pride envy lechery,
   The dime held back from Peter's Pence   10
With which I'd bribed my girl to pee
   That I might spy her instruments.

Hovering scale-pans when I'd done
   Settled their balance slow as silt
While in the restless dark I burned   15
   Bright as a brimstone in my guilt

FIRST CONFESSION   [10]**Peter's Pence** *a collection contribution, specifically for the Vatican's expenses.*

Until as one feeds birds he doled
  Seven Our Fathers and a Hail
Which I to double-scrub my soul
  Intoned twice at the altar rail   20

Where Sunday in seraphic light
  I knelt, as full of grace as most,
And stuck my tongue out at the priest:
  A fresh roost for the Holy Ghost.

THOM GUNN
[b. 1929]

Innocence

He ran the course and as he ran he grew,
And smelt his fragrance in the field. Already,
Running he knew the most he ever knew,
The egotism of a healthy body.

Ran into manhood, ignorant of the past: 5
Culture of guilt and guilt's vague heritage,
Self-pity and the soul; what he possessed
Was rich, potential, like the bud's tipped rage.

The Corps developed, it was plain to see,
Courage, endurance, loyalty and skill   10
To a morale firm as morality,
Hardening him to an instrument, until

The finitude of virtues that were there
Bodied within the swarthy uniform
A compact innocence, child-like and clear,   15
No doubt could penetrate, no act could harm.

When he stood near the Russian partisan
Being burned alive, he therefore could behold
The ribs wear gently through the darkening skin
And sicken only at the Northern cold,   20

Could watch the fat burn with a violet flame
And feel disgusted only at the smell,

---

[18]**Seven . . . Hail**   *seven repetitions of the Lord's Prayer and a "Hail Mary," recited as penance.*

And judge that all pain finishes the same
As melting quietly by his boots it fell.

JOHN HOLLANDER
[*b. 1929*]

Adam's Task

"And Adam gave names to all cattle, and to the fowl of the air, and to every beast of the field . . ."

GEN. 2:20

Thou, paw-paw-paw; thou, glurd; thou, spotted
   Glurd; thou, whitestap, lurching through
The high-grown brush; thou, pliant-footed,
   Implex; thou, awagabu.

Every burrower, each flier   5
   Came for the name he had to give:
Gay, first work, ever to be prior,
   Not yet sunk to primitive.

Thou, verdle; thou, McFleery's pomma;
   Thou; thou; thou—three types of grawl;   10
Thou, flisket; thou, kabasch; thou, comma-
   Eared mashawk; thou, all; thou, all.

Were, in a fire of becoming,
   Laboring to be burned away,
Then work, half-measuring, half-humming,   15
   Would be as serious as play.

Thou, pambler; thou, rivarn; thou, greater
   Wherret, and thou, lesser one;
Thou, sproal; thou, zant; thou, lily-eater.
   Naming's over. Day is done.   20

Swan and Shadow

                    Dusk
                 Above the
            water hang the
                  loud
                  flies
                  Here
                  O so
                  gray
                  then
          What   A pale signal will appear   5
          When   Soon before its shadow fades
          Where   Here in this pool of opened eye
      In us   No Upon us As at the very edges
      of where we take shape in the dark air
          this object bares its image awakening
              ripples of recognition that will
                  brush darkness up into light
even after this bird this hour both drift by atop the perfect sad instant now
              already passing out of sight
              toward yet-untroubled reflection
          this image bears its object darkening
      into memorial shades Scattered bits of
      light   No of water Or something across
      water   Breaking up No Being regathered
      soon   Yet by then a swan will have
          gone   Yes out of mind into what
              vast
              pale
              hush
              of a
              place
              past
      sudden dark as
      if a swan
          sang

TED HUGHES
[*b. 1930*]

Hawk Roosting

I sit in the top of the wood, my eyes closed.
Inaction, no falsifying dream
Between my hooked head and hooked feet:
Or in sleep rehearse perfect kills and eat.

The convenience of the high trees!　　　　　　　　　5
The air's buoyancy and the sun's ray
Are of advantage to me;
And the earth's face upward for my inspection.

My feet are locked upon the rough bark.
It took the whole of Creation　　　　　　　　　10
To produce my foot, my each feather:
Now I hold Creation in my foot

Or fly up, and revolve it all slowly—
I kill where I please because it is all mine.
There is no sophistry in my body:　　　　　　　　15
My manners are tearing off heads—

The allotment of death.
For the one path of my flight is direct
Through the bones of the living.
No arguments assert my right:　　　　　　　　20

The sun is behind me.
Nothing has changed since I began.
My eye has permitted no change.
I am going to keep things like this.

Crow's First Lesson

God tried to teach Crow how to talk.
"Love," said God. "Say, Love."
Crow gaped, and the white shark crashed into the sea
And went rolling downwards, discovering its own depth.

"No, no," said God, "Say Love. Now try it. LOVE."   5
Crow gaped, and a bluefly, a tsetse, a mosquito
Zoomed out and down
To their sundry flesh-pots.

"A final try," said God. "Now, LOVE."
Crow convulsed, gaped, retched and   10
Man's bodiless prodigious head
Bulbed out onto the earth, with swivelling eyes,
Jabbering protest—

And Crow retched again, before God could stop him.
And woman's vulva dropped over man's neck and tightened.   15
The two struggled together on the grass.
God struggled to part them, cursed, wept—

Crow flew guiltily off.

GREGORY CORSO

[b. 1930]

Marriage

Should I get married? Should I be good?
Astound the girl next door with my velvet suit and faustus hood?
Don't take her to movies but to cemeteries
tell all about werewolf bathtubs and forked clarinets
then desire her and kiss her and all the preliminaries   5
and she going just so far and I understanding why
not getting angry saying You must feel! It's beautiful to feel!
Instead take her in my arms lean against an old crooked tombstone
and woo her the entire night the constellations in the sky—

When she introduces me to her parents   10
back straightened, hair finally combed, strangled by a tie,
should I sit knees together on their 3rd degree sofa
and not ask Where's the bathroom?
How else to feel other than I am,
often thinking Flash Gordon soap—   15
O how terrible it must be for a young man
seated before a family and the family thinking

MARRIAGE   ²*faustus hood* *Dr. Faustus, the central figure of Christopher Marlowe's play, sold his soul*
to the devil.

We never saw him before! He wants our Mary Lou!
After tea and homemade cookies they ask What do you do for a living?

Should I tell them? Would they like me then? 20
Say All right get married, we're losing a daughter
but we're gaining a son—
And should I then ask Where's the bathroom?

O God, and the wedding! All her family and her friends
and only a handful of mine all scroungy and bearded 25
just wait to get at the drinks and food—
And the priest! he looking at me as if I masturbated
asking me Do you take this woman for your lawful wedded wife?
And I trembling what to say say Pie Glue!
I kiss the bride all those corny men slapping me on the back 30
She's all yours, boy! Ha-ha-ha!
And in their eyes you could see some obscene honeymoon going on—
Then all that absurd rice and clanky cans and shoes
Niagara Falls! Hordes of us! Husbands! Wives! Flowers! Chocolates!
All streaming into cozy hotels 35
All going to do the same thing tonight

The indifferent clerk he knowing what was going to happen
The lobby zombies they knowing what
The whistling elevator man he knowing
The winking bellboy knowing 40
Everybody knowing! I'd be almost inclined not to do anything!
Stay up all night! Stare that hotel clerk in the eye!
Screaming: I deny honeymoon! I deny honeymoon!
running rampant into those almost climactic suites
yelling Radio belly! Cat shovel! 45
O I'd live in Niagara forever! in a dark cave beneath the Falls
I'd sit there the Mad Honeymooner
devising ways to break marriages, a scourge of bigamy
a saint of divorce—

But I should get married I should be good 50
How nice it'd be to come home to her
and sit by the fireplace and she in the kitchen
aproned young and lovely wanting my baby
and so happy about me she burns the roast beef
and comes crying to me and I get up from my big papa chair 55
saying Christmas teeth! Radiant brains! Apple deaf!
God what a husband I'd make! Yes, I should get married!
So much to do! like sneaking into Mr Jones' house late at night
and cover his golf clubs with 1920 Norwegian books

Like hanging a picture of Rimbaud on the lawnmower   60
like pasting Tannu Tuva postage stamps all over the picket fence
like when Mrs Kindhead comes to collect for the Community Chest
grab her and tell her There are unfavorable omens in the sky!
And when the mayor comes to get my vote tell him
When are you going to stop people killing whales!   65
And when the milkman comes leave him a note in the bottle
Penguin dust, bring me penguin dust, I want penguin dust—

Yet if I should get married and it's Connecticut and snow
and she gives birth to a child and I am sleepless, worn,
up for nights, head bowed against a quiet window, the past behind me,   70
finding myself in the most common of situations a trembling man
knowledged with responsibility not twig-smear nor Roman coin soup—
O what would that be like!
Surely I'd give it for a nipple a rubber Tacitus
For a rattle a bag of broken Bach records   75
Tack Della Francesca all over its crib
Sew the Greek alphabet on its bib
And build for its playpen a roofless Parthenon

No, I doubt I'd be that kind of father
Not rural not snow no quiet window   80
but hot smelly tight New York City
seven flights up, roaches and rats in the walls
a fat Reichian wife screeching over potatoes Get a job!
And five nose running brats in love with Batman
And the neighbors all toothless and dry haired   85
like those hag masses of the 18th century
all wanting to come in and watch TV

The landlord wants his rent
Grocery store Blue Cross Gas & Electric Knights of Columbus
Impossible to lie back and dream Telephone snow, ghost parking—   90
No! I should not get married I should never get married!
But—imagine if I were married to a beautiful sophisticated woman
tall and pale wearing an elegant black dress and long black gloves
holding a cigarette holder in one hand and a highball in the other
and we lived high up in a penthouse with a huge window   95
from which we could see all of New York and ever farther on clearer days
No, can't imagine myself married to that pleasant prison dream—

O but what about love? I forget love
not that I am incapable of love

[60]*Rimbaud*   Arthur Rimbaud (1854–1891), French poet.   [61]*Tannu Tuva*   a republic in Siberia, part
of the USSR.   [74]*Tacitus*   Roman historian (A.D. 55–117).   [76]*Della Francesca*   Italian Renaissance
painter (1420–1492).   [83]*Reichian*   follower of psychoanalyst Wilhelm Reich (1897–1957).

it's just that I see love as odd as wearing shoes—   100
I never wanted to marry a girl who was like my mother
And Ingrid Bergman was always impossible
And there's maybe a girl now but she's already married
And I don't like men and—
but there's got to be somebody!   105
Because what if I'm 60 years old and not married,
all alone in a furnished room with pee stains on my underwear
and everybody else is married! All the universe married but me!

Ah, yet well I know that were a woman possible as I am possible
then marriage would be possible—   110
Like SHE in her lonely alien gaud waiting her Egyptian lover
so I wait—bereft of 2,000 years and the bath of life.

GARY SNYDER

[b. 1930]

Prayer for the Great Family

Gratitude to Mother Earth, sailing through night and day—
    and to her soil: rich, rare, and sweet
        in our minds so be it.

Gratitude to Plants, the sun-facing light-changing leaf
    and fine root-hairs; standing still through wind   5
    and rain; their dance is in the flowing spiral grain
        in our minds so be it.

Gratitude to Air, bearing the soaring Swift and the silent
    Owl at dawn. Breath of our song
    clear spirit breeze   10
        in our minds so be it.

Gratitude to Wild Beings, our brothers, teaching secrets,
    freedoms, and ways; who share with us their milk;
    self-complete, brave, and aware
        in our minds so be it.   15

Gratitude to Water: clouds, lakes, rivers, glaciers;
    holding or releasing; streaming through all

---

[111]**SHE**   the heroine of H. Rider Haggard's novel She *(1887) who gains eternal youth by bathing in fire and who waits thousands of years for her lover's return.*

our bodies salty seas
in our minds so be it.

Gratitude to the Sun: blinding pulsing light through   20
trunks of trees, through mists, warming caves where
bears and snakes sleep—he who wakes us—
in our minds so be it.

Gratitude to the Great Sky
who holds billions of stars—and goes yet beyond that—   25
beyond all powers, and thoughts
and yet is within us—
Grandfather Space.
The Mind is his Wife.

so be it.   30

after a Mohawk prayer

SYLVIA PLATH
[1932–1963]

Mirror

I am silver and exact. I have no preconceptions.
Whatever I see I swallow immediately
Just as it is, unmisted by love or dislike.
I am not cruel, only truthful—
The eye of a little god, four-cornered.   5
Most of the time I meditate on the opposite wall.
It is pink, with speckles. I have looked at it so long
I think it is a part of my heart. But it flickers.
Faces and darkness separate us over and over.

Now I am a lake. A woman bends over me,   10
Searching my reaches for what she really is.
Then she turns to those liars, the candles or the moon.
I see her back, and reflect it faithfully.
She rewards me with tears and an agitation of hands.
I am important to her. She comes and goes.   15
Each morning it is her face that replaces the darkness.
In me she has drowned a young girl, and in me an old woman
Rises toward her day after day, like a terrible fish.

Tulips

The tulips are too excitable, it is winter here.
Look how white everything is, how quiet, how snowed-in.
I am learning peacefulness, lying by myself quietly
As the light lies on these white walls, this bed, these hands.
I am nobody; I have nothing to do with explosions. 5
I have given my name and my day-clothes up to the nurses
And my history to the anaesthetist and my body to surgeons.

They have propped my head between the pillow and the sheet-cuff
Like an eye between two white lids that will not shut.
Stupid pupil, it has to take everything in. 10
The nurses pass and pass, they are no trouble,
They pass the way gulls pass inland in their white caps,
Doing things with their hands, one just the same as another,
So it is impossible to tell how many there are.

My body is a pebble to them, they tend it as water 15
Tends to the pebbles it must run over, smoothing them gently.
They bring me numbness in their bright needles, they bring me sleep.
Now I have lost myself I am sick of baggage—
My patent leather overnight case like a black pillbox,
My husband and child smiling out of the family photo; 20
Their smiles catch onto my skin, little smiling hooks.

I have let things slip, a thirty-year-old cargo boat
Stubbornly hanging on to my name and address.
They have swabbed me clear of my loving associations.
Scared and bare on the green plastic-pillowed trolley 25
I watched my tea-set, my bureaus of linen, my books
Sink out of sight, and the water went over my head.
I am a nun now, I have never been so pure.

I didn't want any flowers, I only wanted
To lie with my hands turned up and be utterly empty. 30
How free it is, you have no idea how free—
The peacefulness is so big it dazes you,
And it asks nothing, a name tag, a few trinkets.
It is what the dead close on, finally; I imagine them
Shutting their mouths on it, like a Communion tablet. 35

The tulips are too red in the first place, they hurt me.
Even through the gift paper I could hear them breathe
Lightly, through their white swaddlings, like an awful baby.
Their redness talks to my wound, it corresponds.

They are subtle: they seem to float, though they weigh me down,   40
Upsetting me with their sudden tongues and their colour,
A dozen red lead sinkers round my neck.

JOHN UPDIKE
[b. 1932]

The Mosquito

On the fine wire of her whine she walked,
Unseen in the ominous bedroom dark.
A traitor to her camouflage, she talked
A thirsty blue streak distinct as a spark.

I was to her a fragrant lake of blood   5
From which she had to sip a drop or die.
A reservoir, a lavish field of food,
I lay awake, unconscious of my size.

We seemed fair-matched opponents. Soft she dropped
Down like an anchor on her thread of song.   10
Her nose sank thankfully in; then I slapped
At the sting on my arm, cunning and strong.

A cunning, strong Gargantua, I struck
This lover pinned in the feast of my flesh,
Lulled by my blood, relaxed, half-sated, stuck   15
Engrossed in the gross rivers of myself.

Success! Without a cry the creature died,
Became a fleck of fluff upon the sheet.
The small welt of remorse subsides as side
By side we, murderer and murdered, sleep.   20

ROBERT WALLACE
[b. 1932]

In a Spring Still Not Written Of

This morning
with a class of girls outdoors, I saw

how frail poems are
in a world burning up with flowers,
in which, overhead, 5
the great elms
—green, and tall—
stood carrying leaves in their arms.

The girls listened equally
to my drone, reading, and to the bees' 10
ricocheting
among them for the blossom on the bone,
or gazed off at a distant mower's
astronomies of green
and clover, flashing, 15
threshing in the new, untarnished sunlight.

And all the while, dwindling,
tinier, the voices—Yeats, Marvell, Donne—
sank drowning
in a spring still not written of, 20
as only the sky
clear above the brick bell-tower
—blue, and white—
was shifting toward the hour.

Calm, indifferent, cross-legged 25
or on elbows half-lying in the grass—
how should the great dead
tell them of dying?
They will come to time for poems at last,
when they have found they are no more 30
the beautiful and young
all poems are for.

YEVGENY YEVTUSHENKO

[b. 1933]

People

No people are uninteresting.
Their fate is like the chronicle of planets.

Nothing in them is not particular,
and planet is dissimilar from planet.

And if a man lived in obscurity
making his friends in that obscurity
obscurity is not uninteresting.

To each his world is private,
and in that world one excellent minute.

And in that world one tragic minute.
These are private.

In any man who dies there dies with him
his first snow and kiss and fight.
It goes with him.

They are left books and bridges
and painted canvas and machinery.

Whose fate is to survive.
But what has gone is also not nothing:

by the rule of the game something has gone.
Not people die but worlds die in them.

Whom we knew as faulty, the earth's creatures.
Of whom, essentially, what did we know?

Brother of a brother? Friend of friends?
Lover of lover?

We who knew our fathers
in everything, in nothing.

They perish. They cannot be brought back.
The secret worlds are not regenerated.

And every time again and again
I make my lament against destruction.

TRANSLATED BY ROBIN MILNER-GULAND AND PETER LEVI

ANDREY VOZNESENSKY

[b. 1933]

Monastic Cell at Zagorsk

Sniffing through grey ascetic noses,
Cassocks half undone,
They gossip, watching television,
(Mild ecclesiastic fun).

I sit with a pallid acolyte   5
And hear a drab mish-mash
Of aunts who live in the provinces,
Religious goods and petty cash.

I tell him: "Seize the moment:
Drop the marian beads.   10
Get on the motorbike
And find what a woman needs.

Abandon plainsong:
Learn the guitar:
Leave the gregorian   15
Chants where they are.

Learn to jive, to shuffle,
Do the somersault dance:
The girls would fall in cataracts
If you gave them a chance."   20

He answers "I suppose you're right"
But furtively he tries
to hide the irresistible
Blue Nestorian eyes,

And hurries behind the grille.   25
He's safe inside cell walls:
(A friend's a friend
But a calling calls).

TRANSLATED BY MILES BURROWS

MARK STRAND

[*b. 1934*]

Eating Poetry

Ink runs from the corners of my mouth.
There is no happiness like mine.
I have been eating poetry.

The librarian does not believe what she sees.
Her eyes are sad   5
and she walks with her hands in her dress.

The poems are gone.
The light is dim.
The dogs are on the basement stairs and coming up.

Their eyeballs roll,   10
their blond legs burn like brush.
The poor librarian begins to stamp her feet and weep.

She does not understand.
When I get on my knees and lick her hand,
she screams.   15

I am a new man.
I snarl at her and bark.
I romp with joy in the bookish dark.

ROBERT MEZEY

[*b. 1935*]

My Mother

My mother writes from Trenton,
a comedian to the bone
but underneath, serious
and all heart. "Honey," she says,
"be a mensch° and Mary too,   a person   5

its no good to worry, you
are doing the best you can
your Dad and everyone
thinks you turned out very well
as long as you pay your bills   10
nobody can say a word
you can tell them to drop dead
so save a dollar it can't
hurt—remember Frank you went
to highschool with? he still lives   15
with his wife's mother, his wife
works while he writes his books and
did he ever sell a one
the four kids run around naked
36 and he's never had,   20
you'll forgive my expression
even a pot to piss in
or a window to throw it,
such a smart boy he couldn't
read the footprints on the wall   25
honey you think you know all
the answers you don't, please try
to put some money away
believe me it wouldn't hurt
artist shmartist life's too short   30
for that kind of, forgive me,
horsehit, I know what you want
better than you, all that counts
is to make a good living
and the best of everything,   35
as Sholem Aleichem said
he was a great writer did
you ever read his books dear,
you should make what he makes a year
anyway he says some place   40
Poverty is no disgrace
but its no honor either
that's what I say,
               love,
                  Mother"   45

BELLA AKHMADULINA
[b. 1937]

The Bride

Oh to be a bride
Brilliant in my curls
Under the white canopy
Of a modest veil!

How my hands tremble,   5
Bound by my icy rings!
The glasses gather, brimming
With red compliments.

At last the world says yes;
It wishes me roses and sons.   10
My friends stand shyly at the door,
Carrying love gifts.

Chemises in cellophane,
Plates, flowers, lace . . .
They kiss my cheeks, they marvel   15
I'm to be a wife.

Soon my white gown
Is stained with wine like blood;
I feel both lucky and poor
As I sit, listening, at the table.   20

Terror and desire
Loom in the forward hours.
My mother, the darling, weeps—
Mama is like the weather.

. . . My rich, royal attire   25
I lay aside on the bed.
I find I am afraid
To look at you, to kiss you.

Loudly the chairs are set
Against the wall, eternity . . .   30

My love, what more can happen
To you and to me?

TRANSLATED BY STEPHAN STEPANCHEV

SEAMUS HEANEY
[*b. 1939*]

Digging

Between my finger and my thumb
The squat pen rests; snug as a gun.

Under my window, a clean rasping sound
When the spade sinks into gravelly ground:
My father, digging. I look down   5

Till his straining rump among the flowerbeds
Bends low, comes up twenty years away
Stooping in rhythm through potato drills
Where he was digging.

The coarse boot nestled on the lug, the shaft   10
Against the inside knee was levered firmly.
He rooted out tall tops, buried the bright edge deep
To scatter new potatoes that we picked
Loving their cool hardness in our hands.

By God, the old man could handle a spade.   15
Just like his old man.

My grandfather cut more turf in a day
Than any other man on Toner's bog.
Once I carried him milk in a bottle
Corked sloppily with paper. He straightened up   20
To drink it, then fell to right away

Nicking and slicing neatly, heaving sods
Over his shoulder, going down and down
For the good turf. Digging.

The cold smell of potato mould, the squelch and slap   25
Of soggy peat, the curt cuts of an edge

Through living roots awaken in my head.
But I've no spade to follow men like them.

Between my finger and my thumb
The squat pen rests.   30
I'll dig with it.

The Trout

Hangs, a fat gun-barrel,
deep under arched bridges
or slips like butter down
the throat of the river.

From depths smooth-skinned as plums   5
his muzzle gets bull's eye;
picks off grass-seed and moths
that vanish, torpedoed.

Where water unravels
over gravel-beds he   10
is fired from the shallows
white belly reporting

flat; darts like a tracer-
bullet back between stones
and is never burnt out.   15
A volley of cold blood

ramrodding the current.

Mid-Term Break

I sat all morning in the college sick bay
Counting bells knelling classes to a close.
At two o'clock our neighbors drove me home.

In the porch I met my father crying—
He had always taken funerals in his stride—   5
And Big Jim Evans saying it was a hard blow.

The baby cooed and laughed and rocked the pram
When I came in, and I was embarrassed
By old men standing up to shake my hand

And tell me they were "sorry for my trouble,"
Whispers informed strangers I was the eldest,
Away at school, as my mother held my hand

In hers and coughed out angry tearless sighs.
At ten o'clock the ambulance arrived
With the corpse, stanched and bandaged by the nurses.

Next morning I went up into the room. Snowdrops
And candles soothed the bedside; I saw him
For the first time in six weeks. Paler now,

Wearing a poppy bruise on his left temple,
He lay in the four foot box as in his cot.
No gaudy scars, the bumper knocked him clear.

A four foot box, a foot for every year.

Death of a Naturalist

All year the flax-dam festered in the heart
Of the townland; green and heavy headed
Flax had rotted there, weighted down by huge sods.
Daily it sweltered in the punishing sun.
Bubbles gargled delicately, bluebottles
Wove a strong gauze of sound around the smell.
There were dragon-flies, spotted butterflies,
But best of all was the warm thick slobber
Of frogspawn that grew like clotted water
In the shade of the banks. Here, every spring
I would fill jampotfuls of the jellied
Specks to range on window-sills at home,
On shelves at school, and wait and watch until
The fattening dots burst into nimble-
Swimming tadpoles. Miss Walls would tell us how
The daddy frog was called a bullfrog
And how he croaked and how the mammy frog
Laid hundreds of little eggs and this was
Frogspawn. You could tell the weather by frogs too
For they were yellow in the sun and brown
In rain.

Then one hot day when fields were rank
With cowdung in the grass the angry frogs
Invaded the flax-dam; I ducked through hedges

To a coarse croaking that I had not heard
Before. The air was thick with a bass chorus. 25
Right down the dam gross-bellied frogs were cocked
On sods; their loose necks pulsed like sails. Some hopped:
The slap and plop were obscene threats. Some sat
Poised like mud grenades, their blunt heads farting.
I sickened, turned, and ran. The great slime kings 30
Were gathered there for vengeance and I knew
That if I dipped my hand the spawn would clutch it.

MARGARET ATWOOD
[b. 1939]

This Is a Photograph of Me

It was taken some time ago.
At first it seems to be
a smeared
print: blurred lines and gray flecks
blended with the paper; 5

then, as you scan
it, you see in the left-hand corner
a thing that is like a branch: part of a tree
(balsam or spruce) emerging
and, to the right, halfway up 10
what ought to be a gentle
slope, a small frame house.

In the background there is a lake,
and beyond that, some low hills.

(The photograph was taken 15
the day after I drowned.

I am in the lake, in the center
of the picture, just under the surface.

It is difficult to say where
precisely, or to say 20
how large or small I am:

the effect of water
on light is a distortion

but if you look long enough,
eventually
you will be able to see me.)

25

RAYMOND CARVER
[b. 1939]

Photograph of My Father in His Twenty-second Year

October. Here in this dank, unfamiliar kitchen
I study my father's embarrassed young man's face.
Sheepish grin, he holds in one hand a string
of spiny yellow perch, in the other
a bottle of Carlsbad beer.

5

In jeans and denim shirt, he leans
against the front fender of a 1934 Ford.
He would like to pose bluff and hearty for his posterity,
wear his old hat cocked over his ear.
All his life my father wanted to be bold.

10

But the eyes give him away, and the hands
that limply offer the string of dead perch
and the bottle of beer. Father, I love you,
yet how can I say thank you, I who can't hold my liquor either,
and don't even know the places to fish?

15

NIKKI GIOVANNI
[b. 1943]

Dreams

i used to dream militant
dreams of taking
over america to show
these white folks how it should be
done
i used to dream radical dreams

5

of blowing everyone away with my perceptive powers
of correct analysis
i even used to think i'd be the one
to stop the riot and negotiate the peace   10
then i awoke and dug
that if i dreamed natural
dreams of being a natural
woman doing what a woman
does when she's natural   15
i would have a revolution

Ego Tripping

(THERE MAY BE A REASON WHY)

I was born in the congo
I walked to the fertile crescent and built
        the sphinx
I designed a pyramid so tough that a star
        that only glows every one hundred years falls   5
        into the center giving divine perfect light
I am bad

I sat on the throne
        drinking nectar with allah
I got hot and sent an ice age to europe   10
        to cool my thirst
My oldest daughter is nefertiti
        the tears from my birth pains
        created the nile
I am a beautiful woman   15

I gazed on the forest and burned
        out the sahara desert
        with a packet of goat's meat
        and a change of clothes
I crossed it in two hours   20
I am a gazelle so swift
        so swift you can't catch me

For a birthday present when he was three
I gave my son hannibal an elephant
        He gave me rome for mother's day   25
My strength flows ever on

My son noah built new/ark and
I stood proudly at the helm
    as we sailed on a soft summer day
I turned myself into myself and was
    jesus
    men intone my loving name
    All praises All praises
I am the one who would save

I sowed diamonds in my back yard
My bowels deliver uranium
    the filings from my fingernails are
    semi-precious jewels
    On a trip north
I caught a cold and blew
My nose giving oil to the arab world
I am so hip even my errors are correct
I sailed west to reach east and had to round off
    the earth as I went
    The hair from my head thinned and gold was laid
    across three continents
I am so perfect so divine so ethereal so surreal
I cannot be comprehended
    except by my permission

I mean . . . I . . . can fly
    like a bird in the sky . . .

30

35

40

45

50

JAMES TATE

[b. 1943]

The Lost Pilot

FOR MY FATHER, 1922–1944

Your face did not rot
like the others—the co-pilot,
for example, I saw him

yesterday. His face is corn-
mush: his wife and daughter,
the poor ignorant people, stare

5

as if he will compose soon.
He was more wronged than Job.
But your face did not rot

like the others—it grew dark,   10
and hard like ebony;
the features progressed in their

distinction. If I could cajole
you to come back for an evening,
down from your compulsive   15

orbiting, I would touch you,
read your face as Dallas,
your hoodlum gunner, now,

with the blistered eyes, reads
his braille editions. I would   20
touch your face as a disinterested

scholar touches an original page.
However frightening, I would
discover you, and I would not

turn you in; I would not make   25
you face your wife, or Dallas,
or the co-pilot, Jim. You

could return to your crazy
orbiting, and I would not try
to fully understand what   30

it means to you. All I know
is this: when I see you,
as I have seen you at least

once every year of my life,
spin across the wilds of the sky   35
like a tiny, African god,

I feel dead. I feel as if I were
the residue of a stranger's life,
that I should pursue you.

My head cocked toward the sky,   40
I cannot get off the ground,
and, you, passing over again,

fast, perfect, and unwilling
to tell me that you are doing
well, or that it was mistake   45

that placed you in that world,
and me in this; or that misfortune
placed these worlds in us.

Drama

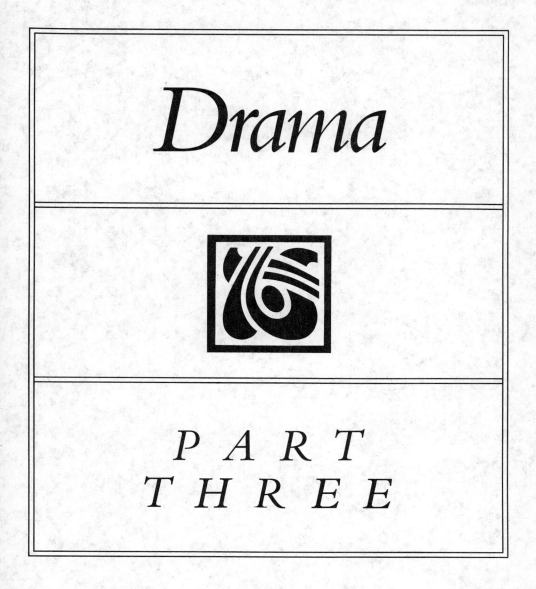

PART
THREE

CHAPTER TWELVE

Reading Plays

THE EXPERIENCE OF DRAMA

Drama differs from the other literary genres in being a staged art. Plays are written to be performed by actors before an audience. Yet even though drama is realized primarily through performance, the availability of performances is beyond our control. We might have to wait years, for example, to see a production of Sophocles' *Antigone* or Arthur Miller's *Death of a Salesman*. Other plays we simply might never have an opportunity to see. A reasonable alternative is to read them with attention to both their theatrical and literary dimensions. We will touch on characteristics of each.

As a literary genre drama has affinities with fiction, poetry, and the essay. Like fiction, drama possesses a narrative dimension. A play, that is, often narrates a story in the form of a plot. Like fiction, drama relies on dialogue and description, which takes the form of *stage directions,* lines describing characters, scenes, or actions with clues to production. Unlike fiction, however, in which a narrator often mediates between us and the story, there is no such authorial presence in drama. Instead, we hear the words of the characters directly.

Although drama is most like fiction, it shares features with poetry as well. Plays may, in fact, be written in verse: Shakespeare wrote in *blank verse* (unrhymed iambic pentameter), Molière in rhymed couplets. Plays, like lyric poems, are also overheard: we listen to characters expressing their concerns as if there were no audience present. To consider the connection between drama and poetry from the other side, poems can contain dramatic elements. The dramatic lyrics and monologues of Robert Browning and some of the poems of John Donne, for example, portray characters speaking and listening to one another.

The essay can also be linked with drama. Like essays, plays may be vehicles of persuasion. Playwrights like Henrik Ibsen and Bernard Shaw frequently used the stage to dramatize ideas and issues. And for most of his plays Shaw wrote essay prefaces in which he discussed their dominant ideas. In both essay and drama, ideas possess more of a primacy than they do in poetry and fiction, something to which critics of the genre testify. Aristotle, for example, made *thought* one of his six elements of drama; Eric Bentley, a modern critic, entitled one of his books *The Playwright as Thinker.*

But in looking exclusively to the literary aspects of drama, to its poetic and fictional elements, and to its dramatization of ideas, we may fail to appreciate its uniquely theatrical idiom. How then should we read drama to accomplish this? By attending to its performance elements. We can read with our mind's eye and ear, imagining sights and sounds created on our mental stage. We can try to hear the voices of characters, and imagine tones and inflections. We can try to see mentally how characters look, where they stand in relation to one another, how they move and gesture. We can read, in short, as armchair directors and as aspiring actors and actresses considering the physical and practical realities of performance.

As active readers of drama we will bring a special awareness of the ways the written text of a play (its *script*) suggests possibilities for performance. To suggest how we might do this, we include excerpts from three plays, each accompanied by notes and comments. As you read the first excerpt, the opening scene of Henrik Ibsen's *A Doll House,* consider what the stage directions and cast of characters reveal about the world of the play. Consider the function of the stage props and how language and gesture reveal character.

CHARACTERS

TORVALD HELMER, *a lawyer*

NORA, *his wife*

DR. RANK

MRS. LINDE

NILS KROGSTAD, *a bank clerk*

THE HELMERS' THREE SMALL CHILDREN

ANNE-MARIE, *their nurse*

HELENE, *a maid*

A DELIVERY BOY

The action takes place in HELMER'S *residence.*

ACT I

A comfortable room, tastefully but not expensively furnished. A door to the right in the back wall leads to the entryway, another to the left leads to HELMER's *study. Between these doors, a piano. Midway in the left-hand wall a door, and further back a window. Near the window a round table with an armchair and a small sofa. In the right-hand wall, toward the rear a door, and nearer the foreground a porcelain stove with two armchairs and a rocking chair beside it. Between the stove and the side door, a small table. Engravings on the walls. An etagère with china figures and other small art objects; a small bookcase with richly bound books; the floor carpeted; a fire burning in the stove. It is a winter day.*

A bell rings in the entryway; shortly after we hear the door being unlocked. NORA *comes into the room, humming happily to herself; she is wearing street clothes and carries an armload of packages, which she puts down on the table to the right. She has left the hall door open; and through it a* DELIVERY BOY *is seen, holding a Christmas tree and a basket which he gives to the* MAID *who let them in.*

NORA   Hide the tree well, Helene. The children mustn't get a glimpse of it till this evening, after it's trimmed. *(To the* DELIVERY BOY, *taking out her purse)* How much?

DELIVERY BOY   Fifty, ma'am.

NORA   There's a crown. No, keep the change. *(The* BOY *thanks her and leaves.* NORA *shuts the door. She laughs softly to herself while taking off her street things. Drawing a bag of macaroons from her pocket, she eats a couple, then steals over and listens at her husband's study door.)* Yes, he's home. *(Hums again as she moves to the table, right.)*

HELMER   *(from the study)* Is that my little lark twittering out there?

NORA   *(busy opening some packages)* Yes, it is.

HELMER   Is that my squirrel rummaging around?

NORA   Yes!

HELMER   When did my squirrel get in?

NORA   Just now. *(Putting the macaroon bag in her pocket and wiping her mouth)* Do come in, Torvald, and see what I've bought.

HELMER   Can't be disturbed. *(After a moment he opens the door and peers in, pen in hand.)* Bought, you say? All that there? Has the little spendthrift been out throwing money around again?

NORA   Oh, but Torvald, this year we really should let ourselves go a bit. It's the first Christmas we haven't had to economize.

HELMER   But you know we can't go squandering.

NORA   Oh yes, Torvald, we can squander a little now. Can't we? Just a tiny, wee bit. Now that you've got a big salary and are going to make piles and piles of money.

HELMER   Yes—starting New Year's. But then it's a full three months till the raise comes through.

NORA   Pooh! We can borrow that long.

HELMER   Nora! *(Goes over and playfully takes her by the ear)* Are your scatter-brains off again? What if today I borrowed a thousand crowns, and you squandered them over Christmas week, and then on New Year's Eve a roof tile fell on my head, and I lay there—

NORA *(putting her hand on his mouth)* Oh! Don't say such things!

HELMER   Yes, but what if it happened—then what?

NORA   If anything so awful happened, then it just wouldn't matter if I had debts or not.

HELMER   Well, but the people I'd borrowed from?

NORA   Them? Who cares about them! They're strangers.

HELMER   Nora, Nora, how like a woman! No, but seriously, Nora, you know what I think about that. No debts! Never borrow! Something of freedom's lost—and something of beauty, too—from a home that's founded on borrowing and debt. We've made a brave stand up to now, the two of us; and we'll go right on like that the little while we have to.

NORA *(going toward the stove)* Yes, whatever you say, Torvald.

HELMER *(following her)* Now, now, the little lark's wings mustn't droop. Come on, don't be a sulky squirrel. *(Taking out his wallet)* Nora, guess what I have here.

NORA *(turning quickly)* Money!

HELMER   There, see. *(Hands her some notes)* Good grief, I know how costs go up in a house at Christmastime.

NORA   Ten—twenty—thirty—forty. Oh, thank you, Torvald; I can manage no end on this.

HELMER   You really will have to.

NORA   Oh yes, I promise I will! But come here so I can show you everything I bought. And so cheap! Look, new clothes for Ivar here—and a sword. Here a horse and a trumpet for Bob. And a doll and a doll's bed here for Emmy; they're nothing much, but she'll tear them to bits in no time anyway. And here I have dress material and handkerchiefs for the maids. Old Anne-Marie really deserves something more.

HELMER   And what's in that package there?

NORA *(with a cry)* Torvald, no! You can't see that till tonight!

HELMER   I see. But tell me now, you little prodigal, what have you thought of for yourself?

NORA   For myself? Oh, I don't want anything at all.

HELMER   Of course you do. Tell me just what—within reason—you'd most like to have.

NORA   I honestly don't know. Oh, listen, Torvald—

HELMER   Well?

NORA *(fumbling at his coat buttons, without looking at him)* If you want to give me something, then maybe you could—you could—

HELMER   Come on, out with it.

NORA *(hurriedly)* You could give me money, Torvald. No more than you think you can spare, then one of these days I'll buy something with it.

HELMER   But Nora—

NORA   Oh, please, Torvald darling, do that! I beg you, please. Then I could hang the bills in pretty gilt paper on the Christmas tree. Wouldn't that be fun?

HELMER   What are those little birds called that always fly through their fortunes?

NORA   Oh yes, spendthrifts; I know all that. But let's do as I say, Torvald; then I'll have time to decide what I really need most. That's very sensible, isn't it?

HELMER   *(smiling)* Yes, very—that is, if you actually hung onto the money I give you, and you actually used it to buy yourself something. But it goes for the house and for all sorts of foolish things, and then I only have to lay out some more.

NORA   Oh, but Torvald—

HELMER   Don't deny it, my dear little Nora. *(Putting his arm around her waist)* Spendthrifts are sweet, but they use up a frightful amount of money. It's incredible what it costs a man to feed such birds.

NORA   Oh, how can you say that! Really, I save everything I can.

HELMER   *(laughing)* Yes, that's the truth. Everything you can. But that's nothing at all.

NORA   *(humming, with a smile of quiet satisfaction)* Hm, if you only knew what expenses we larks and squirrels have, Torvald.

HELMER   You're an odd little one. Exactly the way your father was. You're never at a loss for scaring up money; but the moment you have it, it runs right out through your fingers; you never know what you've done with it. Well, one takes you as you are. It's deep in your blood. Yes, these things are hereditary, Nora.

NORA   Ah, I could wish I'd inherited many of Papa's qualities.

HELMER   And I couldn't wish you anything but just what you are, my sweet little lark. But wait; it seems to me you have a very—what should I call it?— a very suspicious look today—

NORA   I do?

HELMER   You certainly do. Look me straight in the eye.

NORA   *(looking at him)* Well?

HELMER   *(shaking an admonitory finger)* Surely my sweet tooth hasn't been running riot in town today, has she?

NORA   No. Why do you imagine that?

HELMER   My sweet tooth really didn't make a little detour through the confectioner's?

NORA   No, I assure you, Torvald—

HELMER   Hasn't nibbled some pastry?

NORA   No, not at all.

HELMER   Not even munched a macaroon or two?

NORA   No, Torvald, I assure you, really—

HELMER   There, there now. Of course I'm only joking.

NORA   *(going to the table, right)* You know I could never think of going against you.

HELMER   No, I understand that; and you *have* given me your word. *(Going over to her)* Well, you keep your little Christmas secrets to yourself, Nora darling. I expect they'll come to light this evening, when the tree is lit.

NORA   Did you remember to ask Dr. Rank?

HELMER   No. But there's no need for that; it's assumed he'll be dining with us. All the same, I'll ask him when he stops by here this morning. I've ordered some fine wine. Nora, you can't imagine how I'm looking forward to this evening.

NORA   So am I. And what fun for the children, Torvald!

HELMER   Ah, it's so gratifying to know that one's gotten a safe, secure job, and with a comfortable salary. It's a great satisfaction, isn't it?

NORA   Oh, its wonderful!

HELMER   Remember last Christmas? Three whole weeks before, you shut yourself in every evening till long after midnight, making flowers for the Christmas tree, and all the other decorations to surprise us. Ugh, that was the dullest time I've ever lived through.

NORA   It wasn't at all dull for me.

HELMER   *(smiling)* But the outcome *was* pretty sorry, Nora.

NORA   Oh, don't tease me with that again. How could I help it that the cat came in and tore everything to shreds.

HELMER   No, poor thing, you certainly couldn't. You wanted so much to please us all, and that's what counts. But it's just as well that the hard times are past.

NORA   Yes, it's really wonderful.

HELMER   Now I don't have to sit here alone, boring myself, and you don't have to tire your precious eyes and your fair little delicate hands—

NORA   *(clapping her hands)* No, is it really true, Torvald, I don't have to? Oh, how wonderfully lovely to hear! *(Taking his arm)* Now I'll tell you just how I've thought we should plan things. Right after Christmas—*(The doorbell rings.)* Oh, the bell. *(Straightening the room up a bit)* Somebody would have to come. What a bore!

HELMER   I'm not at home to visitors, don't forget.

MAID   *(from the hall doorway)* Ma'am, a lady to see you—

NORA   All right, let her come in.

MAID   *(to HELMER)* And the doctor's just come too.

HELMER   Did he go right to my study?

MAID   Yes, he did.

The first thing we notice is the title: *A Doll House.* Does Ibsen alert us to a central concern of the play with this provocative title? Is it literal or symbolic? As we read the opening scene we test our preliminary sense of the title's implications. As we watch the relationship between Nora and Torvald unfold, we consider what the title suggests about their marriage.

Beneath the title is a list of characters. It's worth pausing over, for a playwright may signal important relationships there. Although only the husband-and-wife relationship of Torvald and Nora is signaled in Ibsen's list, we gain a sense of the play's social milieu from it. We notice that Torvald Helmer is a lawyer and Nils Krogstad a bank clerk, and that another woman and a doctor appear (in addition to minor figures such as a nurse and delivery boy).

We may pass quickly over these details before getting to the script. The first sentences set the scene we must keep in our mind's eye. The italicized words are stage directions (notes to the reader that establish the play's social context). Ibsen's opening stage directions describe the living room of a middle-class family with its piano, books, and pictures. The room represents a familiar world for many readers both in its realistic detail and its bourgeois domesticity.

The manner of Nora's arrival with her packages, the Christmas tree, and basket create an impression of the gaiety typically associated with the Christmas season. The playful quality of Nora's first words—about hiding the Christmas tree—reinforce our sense of this lightheartedness.

As we watch the inital incidents unfold, we begin making inferences and drawing tentative conclusions about the characters. We may wonder, for example, about the large tip Nora gives the delivery boy. Is it a sign of generosity or of extravagance? Does it reflect her state of mind? Does it reveal an inadequate attentiveness to money? Such questions occur almost unconsciously as we read, and the provisional answers we arrive at will be modified, strengthened, or abandoned as we read further.

After the exchange with the delivery boy, Nora hums softly to herself. Eating a few macaroons, she tiptoes stealthily to the closed door of her husband's study. Whatever our sense of these opening moments, the brief series of actions forms a prologue to the first major action of the play, Nora's conversation with Torvald. It is here that we gain our sense of Torvald, particularly of his concern for Nora's spending habits, which may unsettle our previous expectations about Nora's tip as an instance of generosity. We become alert.

Perhaps even stronger is our response to Torvald's pet names for Nora. He calls her "little lark" and "my squirrel," and repeatedly uses diminutives and possessives in addressing her. He also teases her, calling her "the little spendthrift," then gives her the money she wants. In a few swift strokes of dialogue and action, Ibsen shows us how seriously Torvald takes himself and how patronizingly he treats his wife.

Nora seems to accept the role Torvald assigns her. She submits to his teasing, accepts his explanations, and responds with childlike enthusiasm. Their gestures bear out the implications of the dialogue: Torvald pulls her ear, Nora clamps her hand over his mouth, plays flirtatiously with Torvald's coat buttons, claps her hands, and twice walks away from him—presumably knowing that he will follow. Torvald seems to enjoy the game as much as Nora. He follows her, probably not realizing that she is leading him and that he is responding as she wants him to.

When we see Torvald wag his finger at Nora and accuse her of eating sweets, we may sense that he doesn't really believe his accusation; he says as much almost immediately. But we, of course, know something that he does not: that Nora has indeed been eating macaroons. And we may suspect that there are other things about her that Torvald does not know from her previous remark, "Hm. If you only knew what expenses we larks and squirrels have, Torvald."

This dialogue is worth considering a bit further. Essentially, Ibsen has Torvald repeat his suspicious question and Nora deny that she has eaten sweets four times. The game that they make of this suggests that it is a familiar ritual. The action seems humorous partly because Torvald's accusations become increasingly accurate while he seems to remain unaware of their truth. Ibsen treats him ironically, revealing a discrepancy between his view of himself and our view of him. How do we respond to his presumption and complacency? How do we evaluate his position as master of his house? And how might we sum up Torvald's attitude toward women as revealed in his dialogue and behavior?

As we read the opening scene of *A Doll House,* observing the action and listening in on the dialogue, we have been drawing tentative conclusions about the characters and their relationship. Our curiosity has been aroused by dialogue, by action, and by the arrival of additional characters. Subsequent dialogue and action will either confirm our initial impressions or dispel them. We are left at the end of this first scene with a sense of uncertainty. While we don't know that this is not a happy household, neither do we know that it is. We have become alerted to possible problems involving matters of money and of secrecy. And we have been prepared to attend to the developing action as the scene changes and new characters appear. When we read the entire play (pages 1061–1112), we will discover if our inferences are accurate and our suspicions justified.

THE PROCESS OF READING DRAMA

Now that we have examined a scene from Ibsen's *A Doll House* with particular attention to both its visual detail and the gestures and actions of the characters, we will observe how dialogue orients us to a play. Reading the opening scene of *A Doll House,* we considered how we make our way through a dramatic text. Here we will attend more consciously to the process of reading a play, focusing on its language—though without losing sight of gesture and action.

The language we hear in this next excerpt, a scene from Act II of Bernard Shaw's *Arms and the Man,* differs from the language we heard in *A Doll House.* In Shaw's play we move away from the realistic bourgeois patterns of speech of Ibsen's play toward a more oratorical and theatrical language. The scene presents Raina, the fiancé of Sergius, alone with him for the first time since his return from a successful military battle. The scene is accompanied by commentary which is meant to suggest the kinds of thinking we do in the process of reading drama.

RAINA   *(placing her hands on his shoulders as she looks up at him with admiration and worship)* My hero! My king!

SERGIUS   My queen! *(He kisses her on the forehead.)*

RAINA   How I have envied you, Sergius! You have been out in the world, on the field of battle, able to prove yourself there worthy of any woman in the world; whilst I have had to sit at home inactive—dreaming—useless—doing nothing that could give me the right to call myself worthy of any man.

SERGIUS   Dearest: all my deeds have been yours. You inspired me. I have gone through the war like a knight in a tournament with his lady looking down at him!

RAINA   And you have never been absent from my thoughts for a moment. *(Very solemnly)* Sergius: I think we two have found the higher love. When I think of you, I feel that I could never do a base deed, or think an ignoble thought.

SERGIUS   My lady and my saint! *(He clasps her reverently.)*

RAINA   *(returning his embrace)* My lord and my—

SERGIUS   Sh—sh! Let me be the worshipper, dear. You little know how unworthy even the best man is of a girl's pure passion!

Comment   What are we to make of such grand language and such royal gestures? Do we see them as heroic and the characters as impressive? Or do we take the characters with less seriousness than they take themselves? Their style of speech and their manner are suitable for a certain kind of play, heroic melodrama, a type of play Shaw's nineteenth-century audience was familiar with. But it doesn't take us long to discover that the scene is comical because the actions of Raina and Sergius and the language of the other characters fail to support the seemingly heroic dialogue.

Consider Raina's elevation of Sergius to royal heights ("My hero! My king!") and Sergius's reciprocal coronation of Raina ("My queen!"). This language is exaggerated and their behavior stilted, for Shaw was satirizing the attitudes toward romantic love and military glory they represent. We also hear Raina's speech as a set of clichés: the valiant hero fights at war while the helpless female waits uselessly behind; she is the lady who inspires her knight to heights of valor. We hear Sergius's speech as a bit of heroic posturing, which we quickly come to see through.

Their talk of the "higher" love extends their idealization of each other. The exaggeration continues to the point of absurdity with their reverential language —"My lady and my saint!" . . . "My lord and my——." Poking fun at their romanticizing deification of one another, Shaw suggests that their devotion is part of an act, a game they play with and for each other. Sergius comes close to honesty, however, in his remark that a man is not worthy of his fiancée's pure passion. Sergius's remark is comical because it can be understood in two ways: 1) as passion divested of its erotic and physical elements, as spiritualized passion; 2) as pure or unadulterated passionate desire in the erotic and physical sense. And even if we ignore this ambiguity and take Sergius's remark to mean simply that he is unworthy of Raina's devoted love, we sense that he is implying something about himself and about men generally that makes them incapable of the "higher," spiritual love he and Raina have been talking about.

RAINA   I trust you. I love you. You will never disappoint me, Sergius. *(*LOUKA *is heard singing within the house. They quickly release each other.)* I can't pretend to talk indifferently before her: my heart is too full. *(*LOUKA *comes from the house with her tray. She goes to the table, and begins to clear it, with her back turned to them.)* I will get my hat; and then we can go out until lunch time. Wouldn't you like that?

SERGIUS   Be quick. If you are away five minutes, it will seem five hours. *(*RAINA *runs to the top of the steps, and turns there to exchange looks with him and wave him a kiss with both hands. He looks after her with emotion for a moment; then turns slowly away, his face radiant with the loftiest exaltation. The movement shifts* *his field of vision, into the corner of which there now comes the tail of* LOUKA'S *double apron. His attention is arrested at once. He takes a stealthy look at her, and begins to twirl his moustache mischievously, with his left hand akimbo on his hip. Finally, striking the ground with his heels in something of a cavalry swagger, he strolls over to the other side of the table, opposite her, and says*) Louka: do you know what the higher love is?

LOUKA   *(astonished)* No, sir.

SERGIUS   Very fatiguing thing to keep up for any length of time, Louka. One feels the need of some relief after it.

LOUKA   *(innocently)* Perhaps you would like some coffee, sir? *(She stretches her hand across the table for the coffee pot.)*

SERGIUS   *(taking her hand)* Thank you, Louka.

LOUKA   *(pretending to pull)* Oh, sir, you know I didn't mean that. I'm surprised at you!

SERGIUS   *(coming clear of the table and drawing her with him)* I am surprised at myself, Louka. What would Sergius, the hero of Slivnitza, say if he saw me now? What would Sergius, the apostle of the higher love, say if he saw me now? What would the half dozen Sergiuses who keep popping in and out of this handsome figure of mine say if they caught us here? *(Letting go her hand and slipping his arm dexterously round her waist)* Do you consider my figure handsome, Louka?

LOUKA   Let me go, sir. I shall be disgraced. *(She struggles: he holds her inexorably.)* Oh, will you let go?

SERGIUS   *(looking straight into her eyes)* No.

LOUKA   Then stand back where we can't be seen. Have you no common sense?

SERGIUS   Ah! that's reasonable. *(He takes her into the stable yard gateway, where they are hidden from the house.)*

Comment   Ironies emerge in Raina's comment that she can't pretend in front of the servant girl, Louka. She means, of course, that she won't be able to conceal her emotion, that the effort to engage in polite conversation with Sergius in her presence will be unbearable. And Sergius's pretense is made apparent as he approaches Louka. It is additionally ironic that neither can pretend in front of Louka, partly because Louka is too smart to be taken in by their act, and partly because her view of romance and reality differs from theirs. Notice, by the way, that Louka sings as she works, which is her way of warning the lovers that she is coming. She also keeps her back to them as she cleans the table, not wanting to embarrass them and presumably not wanting to let them see she is aware of anything going on.

The crux of this part of the scene, however, is Sergius's abrupt change of behavior. His mischievous, swaggering gestures and his dialogue with Louka quickly puncture the bubble of the "higher" love he had been blowing up moments before. Notice also Louka's gestures. She too is playing a part, especially by feigning surprise at the turn of events. Her acquiescence after a brief and cursory struggle parallels the change in Sergius's behavior.

LOUKA   *(plaintively)* I may have been seen from the windows: Miss Raina is sure to be spying about after you.

SERGIUS   *(stung: letting her go)* Take care, Louka. I may be worthless enough to betray the higher love; but do not you insult it.

LOUKA   *(demurely)* Not for the world, sir, I'm sure. May I go on with my work, please, now?

SERGIUS   *(again putting his arm round her)* You are a provoking little witch, Louka. If you were in love with me, would you spy out of windows on me?

LOUKA   Well, you see, sir, since you say you are half a dozen different gentlemen all at once, I should have a great deal to look after.

SERGIUS   *(charmed)* Witty as well as pretty. *(He tries to kiss her.)*

LOUKA   *(avoiding him)* No: I don't want your kisses. Gentlefolk are all alike: you making love to me behind Miss Raina's back; and she doing the same behind yours.

SERGIUS   *(recoiling a step)* Louka!

LOUKA   It shews how little you really care.

SERGIUS   *(dropping his familiarity, and speaking with freezing politeness)* If our conversation is to continue, Louka, you will please remember that a gentleman does not discuss the conduct of the lady he is engaged to with her maid.

LOUKA   It's so hard to know what a gentleman considers right. I thought from your trying to kiss me that you had given up being so particular.

SERGIUS   *(turning from her and striking his forehead as he comes back into the garden from the gateway)* Devil! devil!

LOUKA   Ha! ha! I expect one of the six of you is very like me, sir; though I am only Miss Raina's maid. *(She goes back to her work at the table, taking no further notice of him.)*

SERGIUS   *(speaking to himself)* Which of the six is the real man? that's the question that torments me. One of them is a hero, another a buffoon, another a humbug, another perhaps a bit of a blackguard. *(He pauses, and looks furtively at* LOUKA *as he adds, with deep bitterness)* And one, at least, is a coward: jealous, like all cowards. *(He goes to the table.)* Louka.

LOUKA   Yes?

SERGIUS   Who is my rival?

LOUKA   You shall never get that out of me, for love or money.

SERGIUS   Why?

LOUKA   Never mind why. Besides, you would tell that I told you; and I should lose my place.

SERGIUS   *(holding out his right hand in affirmation)* No! on the honor of a— *(He checks himself; and his hand drops, nerveless, as he concludes sardonically)*— of a man capable of behaving as I have been behaving for the last five minutes. Who is he?

LOUKA   I don't know. I never saw him. I only heard his voice through the door of her room.

SERGIUS   Damnation! How dare you?

LOUKA   *(retreating)* Oh, I mean no harm: you've no right to take up my words like that. The mistress knows all about it. And I tell you that if that gentleman ever comes here again, Miss Raina will marry him, whether he likes it or not. I know the difference between the sort of manner you and she put on before one another and the real manner.

Comment   Shaw keeps the surprises coming. Just as we have adjusted to amorous play between Louka and Sergius, Sergius shifts ground to defend the honor of his insulted lady when Louka suggests that Raina is spying on him. (We subsequently discover that she really was spying on him, a fact that affects our response to her remark that she trusts Sergius.) Shaw continues the back and forth movement in action and dialogue as Sergius advances on Louka and then retreats, feigning offended pride. Louka comes across as shrewd, quick-witted, and capable of taking care of herself. She knows the difference between real passion and counterfeit coin, and in her suspicion of Sergius's mannered artifice, she gives voice to a realistic rather than a romantic view of love. She uses Sergius's words against him, making him look a fool, which he acknowledges by calling himself a buffoon and a humbug. Moreover, in accepting Louka's accusation so readily, he assents to a view of Raina, of himself, and of the nature of love radically at variance with what he and Raina had declared earlier.

(SERGIUS *shivers as if she had stabbed him. Then, setting his face like iron, he strides grimly to her, and grips her above the elbows with both hands.*)

SERGIUS   Now listen you to me.

LOUKA   *(wincing)* Not so tight: you're hurting me.

SERGIUS   That doesn't matter. You have stained my honor by making me a party to your eavesdropping. And you have betrayed your mistress.

LOUKA   *(writhing)* Please—

SERGIUS   That shews that you are an abominable little clod of common clay, with the soul of a servant. *(He lets her go as if she were an unclean thing, and turns away, dusting his hands of her, to the bench by the wall, where he sits down with averted head, meditating gloomily.)*

LOUKA   *(whimpering angrily with her hands up her sleeves, feeling her bruised arms)* You know how to hurt with your tongue as well as with your hands. But I don't care, now I've found out that whatever clay I'm made of, you're made of the same. As for her, she's a liar; and her fine airs are a cheat; and I'm worth six of her. *(She shakes the pain off hardily; tosses her head; and sets to work to put the things on the tray.)*

(*He looks doubtfully at her. She finishes packing the tray, and laps the cloth over the edges, so as to carry all out together. As she stoops to lift it, he rises.*)

SERGIUS   Louka! *(She stops and looks defiantly at him.)* A gentleman has no right to hurt a woman under any circumstances. *(With profound humility, uncovering his head)* I beg your pardon.

LOUKA   That sort of apology may satisfy a lady. Of what use is it to a servant?

SERGIUS   *(rudely crossed in his chivalry, throws it off with a bitter laugh, and says slightingly)* Oh! you wish to be paid for the hurt! *(He puts on his shako, and takes some money from his pocket.)*

LOUKA   *(her eyes filling with tears in spite of herself)* No: I want my hurt made well.

SERGIUS   *(sobered by her tone)* How?

(She rolls up her left sleeve; clasps her arm with the thumb and fingers of her right hand; and looks down at the bruise. Then she raises her head and looks straight at him. Finally, with a superb gesture, she presents her arm to be kissed. Amazed, he looks at her; at the arm; at her again; hesitates; and then, with shuddering intensity, exclaims Never! *and gets away as far as possible from her.*

Her arm drops. Without a word, and with unaffected dignity, she takes her tray, and is approaching the house when RAINA *returns, wearing a hat and jacket in the height of the Vienna fashion of the previous year, 1885.* LOUKA *makes way proudly for her, and then goes into the house.)*

RAINA   I'm ready. What's the matter? *(Gaily)* Have you been flirting with Louka?

SERGIUS   *(hastily)* No, no. How can you think such a thing?

RAINA   *(ashamed of herself)* Forgive me, dear: it was only a jest. I am so happy today.

Comment   Louka's forthright declaration angers Sergius to the point of hurting her. But Louka insists that although she may be "clay," so is Sergius, that he and Raina are no better and no "higher" than she. The scene ends with Sergius frustrated, Louka resentful, and Raina lighthearted as she teases Sergius about his flirtation. At this point, we wonder where Shaw will take Sergius, Raina, and Louka.

THE PRACTICE OF ACTIVE READING

So far we have read scenes from two plays, one followed by an informal commentary stressing visual details and gestures, the other accompanied by interpolated comments focusing largely on dialogue. The scene that follows from Sophocles' *Antigonê* has been annotated. As with the earlier commentaries, these annotations suggest some of the kinds of observations we make and questions we raise as we read. They illustrate one way we can get involved with a text even during our first reading.

Scene II of *Antigonê* begins at the point in the play where Antigonê, the daughter of Oedipus, has been taken into custody for violating an edict of Creon, King of Thebes. Creon's edict concerns Antigonê's brother, Polyneicês, who was killed in a battle while fighting against Thebes. Creon has forbidden Polyneicês' burial; Antigonê has buried him. We pick up the scene with Creon confronting Antigonê over her disobedience of his orders:

CREON [*to Sentry*]. You may go.

[*To Antigonê.*] Tell me, tell me briefly:

Had you heard my proclamation touching this matter?

ANTIGONÊ. It was public. Could I help hearing it?

CREON. And yet you dared defy the law.

ANTIGONÊ.   I dared.

It was not God's proclamation. That final Justice
That rules the world below makes no such laws.

Your edict, King, was strong,
But all your strength is weakness itself against
The immortal unrecorded laws of God.
They are not merely now: they were, and shall be,
Operative for ever, beyond man utterly.

I knew I must die, even without your decree:
I am only mortal. And if I must die
Now, before it is my time to die,
Surely this is no hardship: can anyone
Living, as I live, with evil all about me,
Think Death less than a friend? This death of mine
Is of no importance; but if I had left my brother
Lying in death unburied, I should have suffered.
Now I do not.
                    You smile at me. Ah Creon,
Think me a fool, if you like; but it may well be
That a fool convicts me of folly.

CHORAGOS. Like father, like daughter: both headstrong,
deaf to reason!

She has never learned to yield.

CREON.   She has much to learn.
The inflexible heart breaks first, the toughest iron
Cracks first, and the wildest horses bend their necks
At the pull of the smallest curb.
                                        Pride? In a slave?
This girl is guilty of a double insolence,
Breaking the given laws and boasting of it.
Who is the man here,
She or I, if this crime goes unpunished?
Sister's child, or more than sister's child,
Or closer yet in blood—she and her sister
Win bitter death for this!
[*To servants.*]   Go, some of you,
Arrest Ismenê. I accuse her equally.
Bring her: you will find her sniffling in the house
there.

Creon uses formal, self-important language. Creon's conception of daring differs from Antigonê's—as does his view of her action. God's law versus man's law: Antigonê implies that Creon's law was a bad one.

Antigonê puts Creon in his place, reminding him that he is not almighty.

She suggests that it is better to die rather than to live in a corrupt society.

Her burial of her brother was necessary for her own peace of mind.

She turns the tables on him—her folly is not really folly—he is the fool.

Creon's speech balances and answers Antigonê's.

Creon's manhood is on the line. Is he insecure in position and power?

Her mind's a traitor: crimes kept in the dark
Cry for light, and the guardian brain shudders;
But how much worse than this
Is brazen boasting of barefaced anarchy!

ANTIGONÊ. Creon, what more do you want than my death?

CREON. Nothing.
That gives me everything.

ANTIGONÊ.   Then I beg you: kill me.
This talking is a great weariness: your words
Are distasteful to me, and I am sure that mine
Seem so to you. And yet they should not seem so:
I should have praise and honor for what I have done.
All these men here would praise me
Were their lips not frozen shut with fear of you.
[*Bitterly.*] Ah the good fortune of kings,
Licensed to say and do whatever they please!

CREON. You are alone here in that opinion.

ANTIGONÊ. No, they are with me. But they keep their tongues in leash.

CREON. Maybe. But you are guilty, and they are not.

ANTIGONÊ. There is no guilt in reverence for the dead.

CREON. But Eteoclês—was he not your brother too?

ANTIGONÊ. My brother too.

CREON.   And you insult his memory?

ANTIGONÊ [*softly*]. The dead man would not say that I insult it.

CREON. He would: for you honor a traitor as much as him.

ANTIGONÊ. His own brother, traitor or not, and equal in blood.

CREON. He made war on his country. Eteoclês defended it.

ANTIGONÊ. Nevertheless, there are honors due all the dead.

CREON. But not the same for the wicked as for the just.

ANTIGONÊ. Ah Creon, Creon,
Which of us can say what the gods hold wicked?

CREON. An enemy is an enemy, even dead.

ANTIGONÊ. It is my nature to join in love, not hate.

CREON [*finally losing patience*]. Go join them, then; if you must have your love,
Find it in hell!

To Creon, Antigonê's trumpeting of her deed is worse than Ismenê's alleged hiding of it.

Creon sees Antigonê's act as a step toward political chaos.

Should she have praise and honor?

Creon concedes with his "maybe."

Antigonê's tone changes here.

The pace and tempo of this dialogue speed up in this stylized exchange.

Once we have annotated a text we can ask ourselves what considerations about the play emerge from our notes. In the excerpt above we see a conflict developing between Creon and Antigonê, one that is more than a clash of two stubborn wills. Conflicting views of propriety emerge along with contrasting moral values and attitudes toward political authority. What are we to make of their attitudes, their arguments, their behavior—of their tone and manner as well as the substance of their speech and action?

This scene outlines the conflict that is developed as the play proceeds. As we continue reading we will be alert for additional arguments Creon and Antigonê marshal in their support. We will note how other characters respond to their quarrel and how Sophocles resolves their conflict. But what is perhaps most important is simply that we actively read and annotate the text.

CHAPTER THIRTEEN

Types of Drama

Some plays elicit laughter, others evoke tears. Some are comic, others tragic, still others a mixture of both. The two major dramatic modes, *tragedy* and *comedy,* have been represented traditionally by contrasting masks, one sorrowful, the other joyful. The two masks represent more than different types of plays: they also stand for contrasting ways of looking at the world, aptly summarized in Horace Walpole's remark that "the world is a comedy to those who think and a tragedy to those who feel."

The comic view celebrates life and affirms it; it is typically joyous and festive. The tragic view highlights life's sorrows; it is typically brooding and solemn. Tragic plays end unhappily, often with the death of the hero; comedies usually end happily, often with a celebration such as a marriage. Both comedy and tragedy contain changes of fortune, with the fortunes of comic characters turning from bad to good and those of tragic characters from good to bad.

TRAGEDY

In the *Poetics,* Aristotle described *tragedy* as "an imitation of an action that is serious, complete in itself, and of a certain magnitude." This definition suggests that tragedies are dignified plays concerned with consequential actions and further indicates that the action of a tragedy is complete—that it possesses a beginning, a middle, and an end. Elsewhere in the *Poetics,* Aristotle notes that the incidents of a tragedy must be causally connected. The events, that is, have to be logically related, one growing naturally out of another, each leading to the inevitable catastrophe, usually the downfall of the hero.

Some readers of tragedy have suggested that, according to Aristotle, the catastrophe results from a flaw in the character of the hero. Others have contended that the hero's tragic flaw results from fate or coincidence, from circumstances beyond the hero's control. A third view proposes that tragedy results from an error of judgment committed by the hero, one that may or may not have as its source a weakness in character. Typically, tragic protagonists make mistakes: they misjudge other characters, they misinterpret events, and they confuse appearance with reality. Shakespeare's Othello, for example, mistakes Iago for an honest, loving friend; and he mistakes his faithful wife, Desdemona, for an adultress. Sophocles' Oedipus mistakes his own identity and misconstrues his destiny. The misfortune and catastrophes of tragedy are frequently precipitated by errors of judgment; mistaken perceptions lead to misdirected actions that eventually result in catastrophe.

Tragic heroes such as Oedipus and Othello are grand, noble characters. They are men, as Aristotle says, "of high estate," who enjoy "great reputation and prosperity." Tragic heroes, in short, are privileged, exalted personages whose high repute and status have been earned by heroic exploit (Othello), by intelligence (Oedipus), or by their inherent nobility (Othello and Oedipus). Their tragedy resides in a fall from glory that crushes not only the tragic hero himself but other related characters as well. Othello's tragedy includes his wife and his faithful lieutenant, Cassio. Oedipus' tragedy extends to his entire family, including his wife-mother, his two sons, his daughters, and even his brother-in-law, Creon, and his family. Greek tragedy, typically, involves the destruction and downfall of a house or family, reaching across generations. The catastrophe of Shakespearean tragedy is usually not as extensive.

An essential element of the tragic hero's experience is a *recognition* of what has happened to him. Frequently this takes the form of the hero discovering something previously unknown or something he knew but misconstrued. According to Aristotle, the tragic hero's recognition (or discovery) is allied with a reversal of his expectations. Such an ironic reversal occurs in *Oedipus Rex* when the messenger's speech unsettles rather than reassures Oedipus about who he is and what he has done. Once the reversal and discovery occur, tragic plots move swiftly to their conclusions.

Another consideration raised by Aristotle in his discussion of tragedy is why, amidst such suffering and catastrophe, tragedies are not depressing. Perhaps, because as he himself suggested, the pity and fear aroused in the audience are purged or released so that the audience experiences a cleansing of those emotions and a sense of relief that the action is over. Or, because we recognize that tragedy represents the ultimate downfall we will all experience in death: we watch in fascination and awe a dramatic reminder of our own inevitable mortality. Or perhaps for still another reason: we are somehow exalted in witnessing the high human aspiration and the noble conception of human character embodied in tragic heroes like Oedipus and Othello.

COMEDY

Some of the same dramatic elements we find in tragedy occur in comedy as well. Discovery scenes and consequent reversals of fortune, for example, occur in both. So too do misperceptions and errors of judgment, exhibitions of human weakness and failure. But in comedy the reversals and errors lead not to calamity as in tragedy, but to prosperity and happiness. And although comic heroes may parallel tragic heroes in their domination of their respective plays, comic heroes are ordinary people; they are less grand, less noble than tragic protagonists. Moreover, comic characters are frequently one-dimensional to the extent that many are stereotypes: the braggart, for example, or the hypocrite, the unfaithful wife, the cuckold, the ardent young lovers.

If comic characters are frequently predictable in their behavior, comic plots are not: they thrive on the surprise of the unexpected, and on improbability. Cinderella stories like these are the staples of comedy: an impoverished student inherits a fortune; a beggar turns out to be a prince; a wife (or husband or child) presumed dead turns up alive and well; the war (between nations, classes, families, the sexes) ends, the two sides are reconciled and everybody lives happily ever after. To these large-scale improbabilities we can add smaller-scale incongruities: for example, in Shaw's *Arms and the Man,* Bluntschli carries chocolate creams rather than bullets in his cartridge belt; Sergius professes devoted love to Raina then tries to seduce the housemaid; the Petkoffs' *library* about which we hear so much is a mere shelf of a few odd books. But whether the incongruities of comedy exist between a character's speech and actions, between what we expect the characters to be and what they show themselves to be, between how they think of themselves and how we see them, things work out in the end.

The happy endings of comedies are not always happy for all the characters involved. This marks one of the significant differences between the two major types of comedy: *satiric* and *romantic* comedy. Though much of what we have said so far about comedy applies to both types, it applies more extensively to romantic than to satiric comedy, or satire. *Satire* exposes human folly and aims to correct it. Ridiculing the weaknesses of human nature, satiric comedy exposes it for what it is, showing us in the process the low level to which human behavior can sink. Molière's *Tartuffe* is such a satiric comedy; it exposes religious hypocrisy, castigates folly, and ultimately celebrates virtue. Although things work out well in the end for most of the characters, the play contains some harsh moments and a bitter ending for at least one character.

Whatever adversities the heroes and heroines of romantic comedy must overcome, the tone of romantic comedy is typically devoid of rancor and bitterness. The world of satire with its criticism of human conduct and indictment of human failings is darker, harsher than the romantic one. Romantic comedy portrays characters gently, even generously; its spirit is more tolerant and its tone more genial. The humor of romantic comedy is more sympathetic than corrective, and it intends more to entertain than instruct, to delight than ridicule.

Because of such differences our approach to reading satire and romance should be different. When we read satiric comedies such as Shaw's *Arms and the Man,* we should identify the object of the dramatist's criticism and determine why the behavior of certain characters is objectionable. In reading romantic comedies, such as Shakespeare's *A Midsummer Night's Dream,* we are invited less to discern a satiric focus than to enjoy the raveling and unraveling of plot as the protagonists are led to the inevitable happy ending. These distinctions, however, are useful only as they help us gauge a play's prevailing characteristics. They should serve as guidelines to prevailing tendencies rather than as rigid descriptions of dramatic types. Frequently romantic comedies may contain elements of satire and satiric comedies elements of romance. *Tartuffe,* for example, is unmistakably a satire. But it contains, nevertheless, a staple of romantic comedy in its pair of young lovers. And *Arms and the Man* mixes romance and satire in about equal measure.

TRAGICOMEDY

Many modern plays mix not just modes of comedy, but elements of comedy and tragedy as well. Ibsen's *A Doll House,* for example, begins like a comedy but ends more like a tragedy, and Eugene Ionesco's *The Lesson,* which ends with a brutal murder, has some uproariously funny moments. These and other works are not so easy to classify. In fact, it's often less important to decide whether a play is predominantly comic or tragic, romantic or satiric, than to acknowledge its mixture of modes and to respond fully to the characters or situations it dramatizes. Such plays as Anton Chekhov's *The Cherry Orchard* and Samuel Beckett's *Endgame* do not adhere strictly to tragic or comic conventions, and are often designated *tragicomedies* to identify their mode. Moreover, some twentieth-century dramatists have found that tragicomedy is more suitable for representing a complex, uncertain, and often irrational world than tragedy or comedy alone.

CHAPTER FOURTEEN

Elements of Drama

The elements that constitute drama include plot, character, dialogue, staging, and theme. Our discussions of each of these elements individually allows us to highlight the characteristic features of drama in a convenient way. We should remember, however, that analysis of any single element of drama (plot, for example) should not blind us to its function with such other elements as character. Ultimately any analysis we engage in must be followed by an act of synthesis in which we bring a number of elements of the play into relationship with one another.

PLOT

Plot is the structure of a play's action. Although it encompasses what happens in a play, plot is more than a sum of its incidents. Plot is the order of the incidents, their arrangement and form. Following Aristotle, we can distinguish between all the little actions or incidents that make up a play and the single *action* that unifies them. It is this unified structure of incidents (or little actions) Aristotle calls *action* and we call *plot*.

Traditional plot structure has been described according to the following formula: *exposition,* presentation of background information necessary for the development of the plot; *rising action,* a set of conflicts and crises; *climax,* the play's most decisive crisis; *falling action,* a follow-up that moves toward the play's resolution or *denouement* (French for the untying of a knot).

Whether playwrights use a traditional plot structure or vary the formula, they control our expectations about what is happening through plot. They decide when to present action and information, what to reveal and what to conceal. By the arrangement of incidents, a dramatist may create suspense, evoke laughter, cause anxiety, or elicit surprise. One of our main sources of pleasure in plot is surprise, whether we are shown something we didn't expect or whether we see *how* something will happen even when we may know *what* will happen. Frequently surprise follows suspense—fulfilling our need to find out what will happen as we wait for a resolution of a play's action.

Suspense is created by conflict. Drama is essentially the development and resolution of conflicts. Each of the scenes excerpted in Chapter 13, Reading Plays, contains conflict. The conflict in Sophocles' *Antigonê* is overt and explicit. It occurs relentlessly in the play's dialogue and action. In the opening scene of Ibsen's *A Doll House* the conflict is implicit, at least initially. As the play develops, we see that Nora's conflict is less an opposition to Torvald than a conflict within herself. And in Shaw's *Arms and the Man* the conflict is a collision of different attitudes toward romantic love and military glory.

Besides looking at how instances of conflict are structured into plot in these scenes, we must also consider what each contributes to the plot of the play overall. What, for example, does Antigonê's debate with Creon lead up to? How does the behavior of Raina and Sergius relate to their behavior in previous and successive scenes in *Arms and the Man*? How is the opening scene of *A Doll House* related to its developing action, its thematic preoccupations, its concluding scene?

When we examine the plot of any play, we should concern ourselves with its developing action, the play in motion, and its completed action, the play at rest. By remaining attentive to what happens to us as we read and by highlighting the arrangement of scenes, we alert ourselves to the play as a performance. As we detach ourselves from the play to study its construction, the relationship among its parts, we study and appreciate the play as literature. Drama, as we have insisted, is both performance and literature. Study of plot can enrich our experience of each.

CHARACTER

If plot is the skeletal framework of a play, character is its vital center. Characters bring plays to life. First and last we attend to characters: to how they look and what their appearance tells us about them; to what they say and what their manner of saying expresses; to what they do and how their actions reveal who they are and what they represent. We may come to know them and respond to them in ways we come to know and respond to actual people, all the while realizing that characters are literary imitations of human beings.

But even though the characters in plays are not real people, their human dimension is impossible to ignore since actors portray them, and their human qualities are perhaps their most engaging feature. It is, indeed, their *human* aspect that attracts us to the characters of drama, not their symbolic significance. When we see characters engaged in significant human action, we examine their words and deeds. We make sense of them by relying on models of human behavior and by applying standards of conduct derived from our everyday experience; we assess their motives and evaluate their behavior in accordance with psychological probability. It is nearly impossible not to.

Nonetheless, it is helpful to remain mindful of the distinction between dramatic characters and actual people so that we do not always expect them to behave realistically. Nor should we expect playwrights to tell us everything about them. They will tell us only what we need to know. If it is not important for us to know Nora's age or Raina's height, the playwrights won't bother us with such information. Dramatists like Ibsen and Shaw reveal only what is relevant to their dramatic purposes.

Drama lives in the encounter of characters, for its action is interaction. Its essence is human relationships, the things men and women say and do to each other. Dramatic characters come together and affect each other, making things happen by coming into conflict. It is in conflict that characters reveal themselves and advance the plot.

DIALOGUE

Ezra Pound, the modern American poet, once described drama as "persons moving about on a stage using words"—in short, people talking. Listening to their talk we hear identifiable, individual voices. In their presence we encounter persons, for dialogue inevitably brings us back to character, drama's human center. And though dialogue in plays typically has three major functions—to advance the plot, to establish setting (the time and place of the action), and to reveal character, its most important and consistent function is the revelation of character.

Our examples come from Act IV, Scene III of Shakespeare's *Othello*. Consider first the following conversation between Desdemona (wife of the military hero Othello) and Emilia (maid to Desdemona and wife of Othello's lieutenant, Iago). They are talking about adultery:

DESDEMONA. Dost thou in conscience think, tell me, Emilia,
        That there be women do abuse their husbands
        In such gross kind?
EMILIA.   There be some such, no question.
DESDEMONA. Wouldst thou do such a deed for all the world?
EMILIA. Why, would not you?
DESDEMONA.   No, by this heavenly light!
EMILIA. Nor I either by this heavenly light.
        I might do't as well i'the dark.
DESDEMONA. Wouldst thou do such a deed for all the world?
EMILIA. The world's a huge thing; it is a great price for a small vice.
DESDEMONA.   In troth, I think thou
    wouldst not.
EMILIA. In troth, I think I should; and undo't when I had done. Marry, I would not do such

a thing for a joint-ring, nor for measures of lawn, nor gowns, petticoats, nor caps, nor any petty exhibition, but for all the whole world? Why, who would not make her husband a cuckold to make a monarch? I should venture purgatory for't.

DESDEMONA. Beshrew me if I would do such a wrong for the whole world.

EMILIA. Why, the wrong is but a wrong i' th'world; and having the world for your labor, 'tis a wrong in your own world, and you might quickly make it right.

DESDEMONA. I do not think there is any such woman.

In this dialogue we not only see and hear evidence of a radical difference of values, but we observe a striking difference of character. Desdemona's innocence is underscored by her unwillingness to be unfaithful to her husband; her naiveté, by her inability to believe in any woman's infidelity. Emilia is willing to compromise her virtue and finds enough practical reasons to assure herself of its correctness. Her joking tone and bluntness also contrast with Desdemona's solemnity and inability to name directly what she is referring to: adultery.

And now listen to Iago working on Desdemona's father, Brabantio, to tell him about his daughter's elopement with Othello (Act I, Scene I):

> Zounds, sir y'are robbed! For shame. Put on your gown.
> Your heart is burst, you have lost half your soul.
> Even now, now, very now, an old black ram
> Is tupping your white ewe. Arise, arise!
> Awake the snorting citizens with the bell,
> Or else the devil will make a grandsire of you.
> . . . .
> I am one sir, that comes to tell you your daughter
> and the Moor are making the beast with two backs.

Iago's language reveals his coarseness; he crudely reduces sexual love to animal copulation. It also shows his ability to make things happen: he has infuriated Brabantio. The remainder of the scene shows the consequences of his speech, its power to inspire action. Iago is thus revealed as both an instigator and a man of crude sensibilities.

His language is cast in a similar mold in Act II, Scene I, when he tries to convince Roderigo, a rejected suitor of Desdemona, that Desdemona will tire of Othello and turn to someone else for sexual satisfaction. Notice how Iago's words stress the carnality of sex and reveal his violent imagination:

> Her eye must be fed. And what delight
> shall she have to look on the devil? When the
> blood is made dull with the act of sport, there
> should be a game to inflame it and to give
> satiety a fresh appetite, loveliness in favor,
> sympathy in years, manners, and beauties; all
> which the Moor is defective in. Now for want of
> these required conveniences, her delicate tenderness will find
> itself abused, begin to heave the gorge, disrelish and
> abhor the Moor. Very nature will instruct her in it
> and compel her to some second choice. . . .

Othello's language, like Iago's, reveals his character and his decline from a courageous and confident leader to a jealous lover distracted to madness by Iago's insinuations about his wife's infidelity. The elegance and control, even the exaltation of his early speeches, give way to the crude degradation of his later remarks. Here is Othello in Act I, Scene II, responding to a search party out to find him:

> Hold your hands,
> Both you of my inclining and the rest,
> Were it my cue to fight, I should have known it
> Without a prompter. Whither will you that I go
> To answer this your charge?

The language of this speech is formal, stately, and controlled. It bespeaks a man in command of himself, one who assumes authority naturally and easily.

In Act I, Scene III, Othello speaks to the political authorities and to Brabantio, Desdemona's enraged father:

> Most potent, grave, and reverend signiors,
> My very noble and approved good masters,
> That I have ta'en away this old man's daughter,
> It is most true; true I have married her.
> The very head and front of my offending
> Hath this extent, no more. . . .

From these few lines alone we can sense Othello's stature, his dignity, his self-confidence, and his courtesy. Coupled with other passages from the first two acts of the play, we come away impressed with Othello's gravity and grandeur. His language in large part accounts for our sympathetic response to him, for our admiration, not only for his military exploits, but for his measure of control, poise, and equanimity.

By the middle of Act III, however, this view of Othello is no longer tenable. Othello is reduced by Iago to an incoherent babbler, to a man at odds with himself, one who has lost his equilibrium. In Act IV, Scene I, we see the Othello Iago has created by suggesting that Desdemona has been unchaste with Othello's lieutenant, Michael Cassio:

OTHELLO.   Lie with her? Lie on her?—We say lie on her when they belie her—Lie with her! Zounds, that's fulsome. Handkerchief—confession—handkerchief—To confess, and be hanged for his labor—first to be hanged, and then to confess! I tremble at it. . . . It is not words that shake me thus.—Pish! Noses, ears, and lips? Is't possible?—Confess?—Handkerchief?—O devil.

In the language of both Iago and Othello we see meaning enacted as well as expressed. The verbal dimension of their dialogue is reinforced by action, gesture, movement. We can observe in these brief excerpts and throughout the play not only how language reveals character, advances the action, and establishes the setting, but how it also makes things happen and in effect itself becomes action.

STAGING

By *staging* we have in mind the spectacle a play presents in performance, its visual detail. This includes such things as the positions of actors onstage (sometimes referred to as *blocking*), their nonverbal gestures and movements (also called *stage business*), the scenic background, the props and costumes, lighting, and sound effects.

Though often taken for granted, costumes can reveal the characters beneath them. It is true that costume emerges partly from historical circumstances, particularly fashion. The soldiers' costumes in Shaw's *Arms and the Man,* for example, reflect the military attire of nineteenth-century Europe. But costume also emerges from the characters themselves. Sergius's full-dress uniform, weighted with decorations, testifies to his importance—at least to his self-importance and dubious heroism. Bluntschli's simple attire contrasts dramatically with Sergius's ornate costume; it suggests his naturalness, bluntness, and lack of pretension. It is important to notice, also, that Bluntschli's change of costume during the play indicates his changing fortunes.

Like Bluntschli, whose costume change signals changing circumstances (but not, however, a change in character), Ibsen's Nora changes costumes more than once. She appears by turns in ordinary clothing, in a multicolored shawl, in a dancing costume, and in a black shawl. Each costume change expresses a change in Nora's feelings.

Besides costume, any physical object that appears in a play has the potential to become an important dramatic symbol. The Christmas tree, which stands throughout Ibsen's *A Doll House,* is an ironic visual counterpart to the play's unfolding action. In Robert Bolt's *A Man for All Seasons* the goblet offered as a bribe to Sir Thomas More and the medallion he wears as a sign of his Chancellor's office become emblems of bribery and office respectively. While not exactly symbols, they evoke the political aura of the play, serving as forms of visual shorthand for political realities. More dramatic perhaps and more central to plot is the handkerchief in *Othello.* Having its own history, which we learn when Desdemona wipes Othello's brow, the handkerchief becomes a crucial dramatic object, one that offers Othello the "ocular proof" he requires to condemn Desdemona as an adulterer.

Visual tokens need not be physical objects. In *Arms and the Man* Raina's and Sergius's exaggerated gestures of loving adoration speak to us of their excessive and false sentiments. So too does Raina's superbly comic gesture of holding up Sergius's framed picture in what seems like a parody of religious devotion. With a rather different action, Sir Thomas More, in *A Man for All Seasons,* cups his hands to highlight visually his explanation of why he must live according to his principles. Here are More's words with the playwrights's accompanying stage direction:

> When a man takes an oath, Meg, he's holding his own self in
> his own hands. Like water. *(He cups his hands.)* And if he opens
> his fingers *then*—he needn't hope to find himself again. Some
> men aren't capable of this, but I'd be loath to think your father
> one of them.

In this brief speech, visual gesture coincides with language to dramatize More's character and illustrate his belief.

From costumes, objects, and gestures we turn to sound. At the end of *A Man for All Seasons,* as Sir Thomas More is about to be executed, the playwright, Robert Bolt, calls for a harsh roar of kettledrums—and then quiet, followed by the executioner banging down the instrument used for beheading. (Bolt accentuates these sound effects by a dramatic visual maneuver—blacking out the stage.) Ibsen also uses sound effectively in *A Doll House* when he asks for music to accompany Nora's frenzied dancing as she attempts to delay Torvald's discovery of Krogstad's letter. In this same scene Ibsen also uses sound to heighten suspense as he has Torvald open the mailbox off-stage: we hear but don't see the mailbox click open. We can also note Chekhov's use of sound in Act IV of *The Cherry Orchard.* The finality of Madame Ranavskaya's loss of her property is emphasized by the sounds of footsteps echoing through empty rooms, of doors being closed and locked, of carriages driving away, and perhaps most dramatically, with the off-stage sounds of the mysteriously snapping string and of axes striking the trunks of the cherry trees.

A playwright's stage directions will sometimes help us see and hear things like these as we read. But with or without stage directions, we have to use our aural as well as our visual imagination. An increased imaginative alertness to the sights and sounds of a play, while no substitute for direct physical apprehension, can nonetheless help us approximate the experience of a dramatic performance. It can also enhance our appreciation of the dramatist's craftsmanship and increase our understanding of the play.

THEME

From plot, character, dialogue, and staging we derive a sense of the play's meaning or significance. An abstraction of this meaning is its central idea or *theme.* It is often helpful to try to express the theme of a play in a carefully worded sentence or two, but we should be aware, however, that any summary statement of a complex work of art is bound to be limited and limiting.

Nonetheless as readers we reach for theme as a way of organizing our responses to a play. At the same time we also let the work modify and alter our notion of its theme. We work back and forth between its details (of dialogue, gesture, and movement, for example) and our conception of their significance. As we notice details and connect them, as we discover and remember, our sense of the play's theme changes. It may change in such a way that we end up, provisionally at least, seeing the play's theme as ambiguous (suggesting contradictory or opposite ideas simultaneously with a resulting uncertainty and indefiniteness about its meaning). And of course there is the very good chance that a play will include more than one theme.

Perhaps we can best approach consideration of a play's theme by noting the dialogue of its characters, who frequently represent conflicting ideals and viewpoints. Some plays, for example, Sophocles' *Antigonê,* can certainly be approached this way. Antigonê herself, for example, represents a commitment to a religious ideal ineluctably in conflict with the political idea that Creon stands for. In her debate with Creon, Antigonê appeals to higher laws, religious and spiritual principles that require burial of the dead, especially if the dead are relatives. Because Antigonê acts in violation of Creon's edict, and since Creon as king represents the supreme authority of the state, she can be seen to pit God's law against man's. Another way of saying this is to note that she values a religious obligation more than a legal code. Still another is to see it as a conflict between two kinds of duty: duty to the state and duty to one's family. Legal obligation conflicts with moral responsibility; public duty collides with private conscience.

We have stated that Antigonê and Creon represent two different positions, two conflicting ideals. We make such a generalization, confident that we are not violating the play because the speeches of both characters refer directly to the ideals that motivate them. If we elaborate, however, we will have to qualify the view of their conflict suggested so far for two reasons. This paradigm is too neat: it ignores aspects of Antigonê's and Creon's motivation and character, and it also reduces the play as a whole to this conflict of values.

Because Greek tragedy typically enacts a reconciliation of the human and divine orders, Antigonê's appeal must be seen as an attempt to make that reconciliation and Creon's refusal as a denial of it. Thus, her appeal is not only personal—based on family honor—but is much more inclusive, far more so than Creon's reasons of state. To express this as a theme we might say that in the conflict between two goods, one divinely based (Antigonê's) and one humanly based (Creon's) the higher good should prevail.

We have been using Sophocles' drama to suggest that it is both natural and necessary to generalize from a play's action and dialogue to an idea it embodies. But we have also noted that to reduce the play's thought to a satisfactorily inclusive statement of theme is no easy matter. At best such a statement offers an approximation of a play's meaning, one that clarifies and illuminates our experience. At worst it oversimplifies the play, distorting its significance and impoverishing our experience of it.

CHAPTER FIFTEEN

Approaching a Play: Guidelines for Reading

The following guidelines summarize the main ideas about reading plays in the preceding chapters. These guidelines are then followed by a one-act play, Lady Gregory's *The Rising of the Moon,* and a commentary that applies them.

1. Read the opening stage directions carefully. Try to set the scene mentally. If a cast of characters is listed, spend a few minutes ascertaining the characters' relationships.

2. Read the opening scene slowly, referring back to the cast of characters if you become confused about who is who. Read slowly and deliberately, noting details which may assume prominence later.

3. Note places in the action where conflicts develop most intensely. Satisfy yourself that you understand the nature of the conflict—what causes it and how it might be resolved. Pinpoint the play's crisis and consider its implications.

4. Decide what values the characters embody and believe in. Consider what they may represent. Examine their relationships with one another, attending especially to their effects on each other.

5. Listen carefully to the play's dialogue. Notice what the characters say and *how* they say things. Try to hear their tones of voice; try to imagine the pace and tempo of the dialogue. Consider what the characters' speech reveals about them.

6. Try staging parts of the play in your mind. Imagine where the actors would stand, how they would be dressed, how they would deliver their lines, and what nonverbal gestures they might make. Try to visualize the play's setting by attending to dialogue and stage directions. Notice the visual details of the play. Consider their dramatic function and their possible symbolic significance.

7. Consider whether the play is a tragedy, comedy, or tragicomedy. If it is a comedy, is it satiric or romantic? Also consider the play's mood and tone.

8. Try to sum up your sense of the play's central ideas. What point does it seem to make? What values emerge, what attitudes are taken toward these values, and where does the playwright seem to stand on the issues, attitudes, and ideas the play embodies?

ISABELLA AUGUSTA PERSSE, LADY GREGORY

[1859–1932]

The Rising of the Moon

Scene: Side of a quay in a seaport town. Some posts and chains. A large barrel. Enter three policemen. Moonlight.

SERGEANT, who is older than the others, crosses the stage to right and looks down steps. The others put down a pastepot and unroll a bundle of placards.

POLICEMAN B.   I think this would be a good place to put up a notice. *(He points to barrel.)*

POLICEMAN X.   Better ask him. *(Calls to* SERGEANT*)* Will this be a good place for a placard? *(No answer.)*

POLICEMAN B.   Will we put up a notice here on the barrel? *(No answer.)*

SERGEANT.   There's a flight of steps here that leads to the water. This is a place that should be minded well. If he got down here, his friends might have a boat to meet him; they might send it in here from outside.

POLICEMAN B.   Would the barrel be a good place to put a notice up?

SERGEANT.   It might; you can put it there.
                    (They paste the notice up.)

SERGEANT   *(reading it).* Dark hair—dark eyes, smooth face, height five feet five—there's not much to take hold of in that—It's a pity I had no chance of seeing him before he broke out of gaol. They say he's a wonder, that it's he makes all the plans for the whole organization. There isn't another man in Ireland would have broken gaol the way he did. He must have some friends among the gaolers.

POLICEMAN B.   A hundred pounds is little enough for the Government to offer for him. You may be sure any man in the force that takes him will get promotion.

SERGEANT.   I'll mind this place myself. I wouldn't wonder at all if he came this way. He might come slipping along there *(points to side of quay),* and his friends might be waiting for him there *(points down steps),* and once he got away it's little chance we'd have of finding him; it's maybe under a load of kelp he'd be in a fishing boat, and not one to help a married man that wants it to the reward.

POLICEMAN X.   And if we get him itself, nothing but abuse on our heads for it from the people, and maybe from our own relations.

SERGEANT.   Well, we have to do our duty in the force. Haven't we the whole country depending on us to keep law and order? It's those that are down would be up and those that are up would be down, if it wasn't for us. Well, hurry on, you have plenty of other places to placard yet, and come back here then to me. You can take the lantern. Don't be too long now. It's very lonesome here with nothing but the moon.

POLICEMAN B.   It's a pity we can't stop with you. The Government should have brought more police into the town, with *him* in gaol, and at assize time too. Well, good luck to your watch. *(They go out.)*

SERGEANT   *(walks up and down once or twice and looks at placard).* A hundred pounds and promotion sure. There must be a great deal of spending in a hundred pounds. It's a pity some honest man not to be the better of that.

(A ragged man appears at left and tries to slip past. SERGEANT *suddenly turns.)*

SERGEANT.   Where are you going?

MAN.   I'm a poor ballad-singer, your honor. I thought to sell some of these *(holds out bundle of ballads)* to the sailors. *(He goes on.)*

SERGEANT.   Stop! Didn't I tell you to stop? You can't go on there.

MAN.   Oh, very well. It's a hard thing to be poor. All the world's against the poor!

SERGEANT.   Who are you?

MAN.   You'd be as wise as myself if I told you, but I don't mind. I'm one Jimmy Walsh, a ballad-singer.

SERGEANT.   Jimmy Walsh? I don't know that name.

MAN.   Ah, sure, they know it well enough in Ennis. Were you ever in Ennis, Sergeant?

SERGEANT.   What brought you here?

MAN.   Sure, it's to the assizes I came, thinking I might make a few shillings here or there. It's in the one train with the judges I came.

SERGEANT.   Well, if you came so far, you may as well go farther, for you'll walk out of this.

MAN.   I will, I will; I'll just go on where I was going. *(Goes toward steps.)*

SERGEANT.   Come back from those steps; no one has leave to pass down them tonight.

MAN.   I'll just sit on the top of the steps till I see will some sailor buy a ballad off me that would give me my supper. They do be late going back to the ship. It's often I saw them in Cork carried down the quay in a hand-cart.

SERGEANT.   Move on, I tell you. I won't have any one lingering about the quay tonight.

MAN. Well, I'll go. It's the poor have the hard life! Maybe yourself might like one, Sergeant. Here's a good sheet now. *(Turns one over)* "Content and a pipe"—that's not much. "The Peeler and the Goat"—you wouldn't like that. "Johnny Hart"—that's a lovely song.

SERGEANT. Move on.

MAN. Ah, wait till you hear it.

(Sings.)

There was a rich farmer's daughter lived near the town of Ross;
She courted a Highland soldier, his name was Johnny Hart;
Says the mother to her daughter, "I'll go distracted mad
If you marry that Highland soldier dressed up in Highland plaid."

SERGEANT. Stop that noise.

(MAN *wraps up his ballads and shuffles toward the steps.*)

SERGEANT. Where are you going?

MAN. Sure you told me to be going, and I am going.

SERGEANT. Don't be a fool. I didn't tell you to go that way; I told you to go back to the town.

MAN. Back to the town, is it?

SERGEANT *(taking him by the shoulder and shoving him before him)*. Here, I'll show you the way. Be off with you. What are you stopping for?

MAN *(who has been keeping his eye on the notice, points to it)*. I think I know what you're waiting for, Sergeant.

SERGEANT. What's that to you?

MAN. And I know well the man you're waiting for—I know him well— I'll be going. *(He shuffles on.)*

SERGEANT. You know him? Come back here. What sort is he?

MAN. Come back is it, Sergeant? Do you want to have me killed?

SERGEANT. Why do you say that?

MAN. Never mind. I'm going. I wouldn't be in your shoes if the reward was ten times as much. *(Goes on off stage to left)* Not if it was ten times as much.

SERGEANT *(rushing after him)*. Come back here, come back. *(Drags him back)* What sort is he? Where did you see him?

MAN. I saw him in my own place, in the County Clare. I tell you you wouldn't like to be looking at him. You'd be afraid to be in the one place with him. There isn't a weapon he doesn't know the use of, and as to strength, his muscles are as hard as that board. *(Slaps barrel.)*

SERGEANT. Is he as bad as that?

MAN. He is then.

SERGEANT. Do you tell me so?

MAN. There was a poor man in our place, a sergeant from Ballyvaughan. —It was with a lump of stone he did it.

SERGEANT. I never heard of that.

MAN. And you wouldn't, Sergeant. It's not everything that happens gets into the papers. And there was a policeman in plain clothes, too . . . It is in Limerick he was. . . . It was after the time of the attack on the police barrack at Kilmallock. . . . Moonlight . . . just like this . . . waterside. . . . Nothing was known for certain.

SERGEANT.   Do you say so? It's a terrible county to belong to.

MAN.   That's so, indeed! You might be standing there, looking out that way, thinking you saw him coming up this side of the quay *(points)*, and he might be coming up this other side *(points)*, and he'd be on you before you knew where you were.

SERGEANT.   It's a whole troop of police they ought to put here to stop a man like that.

MAN.   But if you'd like me to stop with you, I could be looking down this side. I could be sitting up here on this barrel.

SERGEANT.   And you know him well, too?

MAN.   I'd know him a mile off, Sergeant.

SERGEANT.   But you wouldn't want to share the reward?

MAN.   Is it a poor man like me, that has to be going the roads and singing in fairs, to have the name on him that he took a reward? But you don't want me. I'll be safer in the town.

SERGEANT.   Well, you can stop.

MAN *(getting up on barrel)*.   All right, Sergeant. I wonder, now, you're not tired out, Sergeant, walking up and down the way you are.

SERGEANT.   If I'm tired I'm used to it.

MAN.   You might have hard work before you tonight yet. Take it easy while you can. There's plenty of room up here on the barrel, and you see farther when you're higher up.

SERGEANT.   Maybe so. *(Gets up beside him on barrel, facing right. They sit back to back, looking different ways)* You made me feel a bit queer with the way you talked.

MAN.   Give me a match, Sergeant *(he gives it and* MAN *lights pipe)*; take a draw yourself? It'll quiet you. Wait now till I give you a light, but you needn't turn round. Don't take your eye off the quay for the life of you.

SERGEANT.   Never fear, I won't. *(Lights pipe. They both smoke)* Indeed it's a hard thing to be in the force, out at night and no thanks for it, for all the danger we're in. And it's little we get but abuse from the people, and no choice but to obey our orders, and never asked when a man is sent into danger, if you are a married man with a family.

MAN *(sings)*.

> As through the hills I walked to view the hills and shamrock plain,
> I stood awhile where nature smiles to view the rocks and streams,
> On a matron fair I fixed my eyes beneath a fertile vale,
> As she sang her song it was on the wrong of poor old Granuaile.

SERGEANT.   Stop that; that's no song to be singing in these times.

MAN.   Ah, Sergeant, I was only singing to keep my heart up. It sinks when I think of him. To think of us two sitting here, and he creeping up the quay, maybe, to get to us.

SERGEANT.   Are you keeping a good lookout?

MAN   I am; and for no reward too. Amn't I the foolish man? But when I saw a man in trouble, I never could help trying to get him out of it. What's that? Did something hit me? *(Rubs his heart.)*

SERGEANT *(patting him on the shoulder)*.   You will get your reward in heaven.

MAN.   I know that, I know that, Sergeant, but life is precious.

SERGEANT.   Well, you can sing if it gives you more courage.

MAN (sings).

> Her head was bare, her hands and feet with iron bands were bound,
> Her pensive strain and plaintive wail mingles with the evening gale,
> And the song she sang with mournful air, I am old Granuaile.
> Her lips so sweet that monarchs kissed . . .

SERGEANT.   That's not it. . . . "Her gown she wore was stained with gore."
. . . That's it—you missed that.

MAN.   You're right, Sergeant, so it is; I missed it. (Repeats line) But to think
of a man like you knowing a song like that.

SERGEANT.   There's many a thing a man might know and might not have
any wish for.

MAN.   Now, I daresay, Sergeant, in your youth, you used to be sitting up
on a wall, the way you are sitting up on this barrel now, and the other lads beside
you, and you singing "Granuaile"? . . .

SERGEANT.   I did then.

MAN.   And the "Shan Bhean Bhocht"? . . .

SERGEANT.   I did then.

MAN.   And the "Green on the Cape"?

SERGEANT.   That was one of them.

MAN.   And maybe the man you are watching for tonight used to be sitting
on the wall, when he was young, and singing those same songs. . . . It's a queer
world.

SERGEANT.   Whisht! . . . I think I see something coming. . . . It's only a dog.

MAN.   And isn't it a queer world? . . . Maybe it's one of the boys you used
to be singing with that time you will be arresting today or tomorrow, and
sending into the dock.

SERGEANT.   That's true indeed.

MAN.   And maybe one night, after you had been singing, if the other boys
had told you some plan they had, some plan to free the country, you might have
joined with them . . . and maybe it is you might be in trouble now.

SERGEANT.   Well, who knows but I might? I had a great spirit in those days.

MAN.   It's a queer world, Sergeant, and it's little any mother knows when
she sees her child creeping on the floor what might happen to it before it has
gone through its life, or who will be who in the end.

SERGEANT.   That's a queer thought now, and a true thought. Wait now till
I think it out. . . . If it wasn't for the sense I have, and for my wife and family,
and for me joining the force the time I did, it might be myself now would be
after breaking gaol and hiding in the dark, and it might be him that's hiding
in the dark and that got out of gaol would be sitting up where I am on this
barrel. . . . And it might be myself would be creeping up trying to make my
escape from himself, and it might be himself would be keeping the law, and
myself would be breaking it, and myself would be trying maybe to put a bullet
in his head, or to take up a lump of a stone the way you said he did . . . no,
that myself did. . . . Oh! (Gasps. After a pause) What's that? (Grasps MAN's arm.)

MAN (jumps off barrel and listens, looking out over water). It's nothing, Sergeant.

SERGEANT.   I thought it might be a boat. I had a notion there might be friends of his coming about the quays with a boat.

MAN.   Sergeant, I am thinking it was with the people you were, and not with the law you were, when you were a young man.

SERGEANT.   Well, if I was foolish then, that time's gone.

MAN.   Maybe, Sergeant, it comes into your head sometimes, in spite of your belt and your tunic, that it might have been as well for you to have followed Granuaile.

SERGEANT.   It's no business of yours what I think.

MAN.   Maybe, Sergeant, you'll be on the side of the country yet.

SERGEANT   *(gets off barrel).* Don't talk to me like that. I have my duties and I know them. *(Looks round)* That was a boat; I hear the oars. *(Goes to the steps and looks down.)*

MAN   *(sings).*

O, then, tell me, Shawn O'Farrell,
    Where the gathering is to be.
In the old spot by the river
    Right well known to you and me!

SERGEANT.   Stop that! Stop that, I tell you!

MAN   *(sings louder).*

One word more, for signal token,
    Whistle up the marching tune,
With your pike upon your shoulder,
    At the Rising of the Moon.

SERGEANT.   If you don't stop that, I'll arrest you.

(A whistle from below answers, repeating the air.)

SERGEANT.   That's a signal. *(Stands between him and steps)* You must not pass this way. . . . Step farther back. . . . Who are you? You are no ballad-singer.

MAN.   You needn't ask who I am; that placard will tell you. *(Points to placard.)*

SERGEANT.   You are the man I am looking for.

MAN   *(takes off hat and wig.* SERGEANT *seizes them).* I am. There's a hundred pounds on my head. There is a friend of mine below in a boat. He knows a safe place to bring me to.

SERGEANT   *(looking still at hat and wig).* It's a pity! It's a pity. You deceived me. You deceived me well.

MAN.   I am a friend of Granuaile. There is a hundred pounds on my head.

SERGEANT.   It's a pity, it's a pity!

MAN.   Will you let me pass, or must I make you let me?

SERGEANT.   I am in the force. I will not let you pass.

MAN.   I thought to do it with my tongue. *(Puts hand in breast)* What is that?

(Voice of POLICEMAN X *outside.)* Here, this is where we left him.

SERGEANT.   It's my comrades coming.

MAN.   You won't betray me . . . the friend of Granuaile. *(Slips behind barrel.)*

(Voice of POLICEMAN B.) That was the last of the placards.

POLICEMAN X   *(as they come in).* If he makes his escape it won't be unknown he'll make it.

(SERGEANT puts hat and wig behind his back.)

POLICEMAN B.   Did any one come this way?

SERGEANT   *(after a pause).* No one.

POLICEMAN B.   No one at all?

SERGEANT.   No one at all.

POLICEMAN B.   We had no orders to go back to the station; we can stop along with you.

SERGEANT.   I don't want you. There is nothing for you to do here.

POLICEMAN B.   You bade us to come back here and keep watch with you.

SERGEANT.   I'd sooner be alone. Would any man come this way and you making all that talk? It is better the place to be quiet.

POLICEMAN B.   Well, we'll leave you the lantern anyhow. *(Hands it to him.)*

SERGEANT.   I don't want it. Bring it with you.

POLICEMAN B.   You might want it. There are clouds coming up and you have the darkness of the night before you yet. I'll leave it over here on the barrel. *(Goes to barrel.)*

SERGEANT.   Bring it with you I tell you. No more talk.

POLICEMAN B.   Well, I thought it might be a comfort to you. I often think when I have it in my hand and can be flashing it about into every dark corner *(doing so)* that it's the same as being beside the fire at home, and the bits of bogwood blazing up now and again. *(Flashes it about, now on the barrel, now on* SERGEANT.*)*

SERGEANT   *(furious).* Be off the two of you, yourselves and your lantern! *(They go out.* MAN *comes from behind barrel. He and* SERGEANT *stand looking at one another.)*

SERGEANT.   What are you waiting for?

MAN.   For my hat, of course, and my wig. You wouldn't wish me to get my death of cold?

(SERGEANT gives them.)

MAN   *(going toward steps).* Well, good night, comrade, and thank you. You did me a good turn tonight, and I'm obliged to you. Maybe I'll be able to do as much for you when the small rise up and the big fall down . . . when we all change places at the Rising *(waves his hand and disappears)* of the Moon.

SERGEANT   *(turning his back to audience and reading placard).* A hundred pounds reward! A hundred pounds! *(Turns toward audience)* I wonder, now, am I as great a fool as I think I am?

Plot   The play is tightly structured; the plot is unified, the action centering overtly on the appearance and disappearance of the wanted man and covertly on the Sergeant's crisis of conscience. The larger action of the play can be broken down into a series of incidents. The first comprises the discussion between the Sergeant and the police officers about putting up placards and finding the criminal. This segment ending with the appearance of "the ragged man" is the play's exposition.

A second incident begins with the conversation between the sergeant and the ragged man. A conflict develops as the sergeant tries to move the man on and he, while pretending to acquiesce, remains where he is. This initial complication begins the play's rising action, which continues with an additional conflict, the sergeant's internal one. The sergeant's conflict occurs when the ballad singer tells him that he knows the wanted man. The dramatist complicates the action here as we discover that the escaped man has a reputation for being dangerous. Tension and suspense build as we watch the Sergeant become increasingly anxious about his situation. The next incident complicates the action further by introducing questions about how the Sergeant's life might have been different. These questions lead to a moment of crisis as the Sergeant realizes who the man is. At this point we wonder what the Sergeant will do. The playwright stretches this section of the play out to retain suspense, then takes the play up to and through the climax when the other policemen return and the Sergeant makes his decision. The play's falling action begins when the Sergeant reveals his decision and sends the other two policemen off. The denouement occurs with the play's final conversation.

In addition to noting the unity and economy of this plot, we should also acknowledge its reliance upon irony. The action reverses itself, with the Sergeant doing the very thing he least expects to do—the opposite, in fact, of what he expected to do. Moreover this ironic action follows upon the additional ironic reversal of his sitting, smoking, and talking with the very man he seeks to capture and imprison. These and other small-scale ironies are revealed further in the playwright's presentation of character.

Character   Policemen B and X are clearly minor characters, necessary primarily to the functioning of the plot. They also serve to reveal the character of the Sergeant. In the first scene, we note how differently the Sergeant responds to the state of affairs than they do. Policemen B and X are quite matter-of-fact about their job. They seem more concerned with details like finding a place for the placards than with the nature of their job—to capture a dangerous criminal. The Sergeant, by contrast, is visibly uneasy. His anxiety surfaces when, intent on scanning the water for signs of the criminal, he does not hear his subordinates' questions about the placards. He's also shown to be a more seasoned veteran of police work and more aware of the dangers involved than the two younger policemen.

But the most important relationship is the one that develops between the Sergeant and the man. Their relationship is fundamentally ironic because neither is what he seems to be. The Sergeant does not uphold the law and arrest the man; the man does not live up to his reputation as a dangerous killer. Both have ample opportunity to act within their respective roles, but neither does. Each surprises the other; both surprise us and probably themselves as well.

The most significant moment of character revelation occurs as the Sergeant muses about fate. He can imagine his life having turned out differently, with himself as a hunted criminal. And in a corresponding leap of imagination, he envisions the hunted criminal as an officer of the law hunting him. At this moment the Sergeant realizes the essential similarity, the connection between seemingly different and opposing individuals. It's an important moment of understanding, an illumination that leads him to a radically altered perception of his responsibility as a man. Perceiving the essential brotherhood he shares with the other man, the Sergeant realizes the injustice of the escaped man's predicament and the justness of his cause.

Dialogue   The connections between protagonist and antagonist (Sergeant and man) are underscored in the play's action and dialogue. Notice, for example, how their first verbal exchange shows a radical difference in their speech: the Sergeant's curt, firm tone contrasts with the man's relaxed familiarity. And notice too how by the end of the play they converse naturally, casually, familiarly—like friends rather than adversaries, like brothers rather than strangers. Consider, also, how the simple natural eloquence of the man helps turn the Sergeant's thoughts to his past, to his youthful idealism, which, presumably, has been buried under the pressures of responsibility and circumstance. The man's eloquence, in short, brings about their spiritual companionship by triggering the Sergeant's memories and reminding him of what he once believed in. In addition, the Sergeant himself turns eloquent at the man's instigation as he imagines the reversal of their fortunes.

We should note also the ambivalence of the Sergeant's final remark about what he has done. He seems to lament the loss of the one-hundred-pound reward. At the same time, however, though he sees himself as a fool, he is also happy with his decision to let the man go. His tone reveals a contented and easy mind, one radically different from the state of mind he exhibited at the beginning of the play. Yet, while he clearly is at peace with himself (his conscience is clear), he can't help thinking how close he came to the reward.

A similar ambivalence is revealed in his language at the beginning of the play. As he reads the man's description from the placard, he seems to regret not having seen the man personally, presumably because he would then know who he was looking for. At the same time, however, there's more than a note of admiration in his voice as he recounts what people say about the escapee: "They say he's a wonder, that it's he makes all the plans for the whole organization. There isn't another man in Ireland would have broken gaol the way he did."

Staging   Let us first consider sound. How do we hear the characters' voices? How much admiration, for example, might an actor convey in reading the Sergeant's speech in the preceding paragraph? None? Some? A lot? And in what tone of voice and with how much strength and feeling should the man sing his ballads? Even in reading the ballad stanzas we can imagine, if not their tune, at least their tone—the way their sentiments could be expressed. We should note here, too, how the playwright has integrated the ballads into the dialogue, making them echo the play's thematic concerns while simultaneously advancing the action.

Besides effective use of sound, the play contains simple but significant uses of visual details and of gesture. For example, toward the end of the play as the two policemen return and the Sergeant allows the man to hide behind the barrel, he holds behind his back the man's hat and wig. The hat and wig, of course, are a disguise. By hiding them, the Sergeant effectually hides the man and protects him. Thus, the visual details underscore their collaboration. Their connection also is established by yet another set of visual details. The image created by the two of them sitting on the barrel like friends expresses simply but eloquently their fundamental brotherhood. At the same time, however, their act of sharing the barrel occurs at a moment when the Sergeant is unaware of who sits there with him. By having them sit back to back, Lady Gregory underscores the danger the Sergeant is in and increases our suspense.

The other detail suggesting their connection involves a similar gesture. Both the Sergeant and the man point to the side of the quay as they imagine, in similar language, where the man or his friends might appear.

> SERGEANT. [*to* POLICEMEN] I wouldn't wonder at all if he came this way. He might come slipping along there *(points to side of quay),* and his friends might be waiting for him there *(points down steps),* and once he got away it's little chance we'd have of finding him.
>
> MAN. [*to* SERGEANT] That's so, indeed! You might be standing there, looking out that way, thinking you saw him coming up this side of the quay *(points),* and he might be coming up this other side *(points),* and he'd be on you before you knew where you were.

Theme What, finally, does the play add up to? Without insisting upon a message, we can point to a few of its central issues and speculate about what it implies about them.

First, it is a political play, taking as its context the political turmoil of a beleaguered Irish populace. The historical details of the political situation are not explicitly rendered (because they would be familiar to Lady Gregory's audience) but they are alluded to in references to "Granuaile." Clearly, we are meant to side with the man who fights for the cause of Granuaile.

Another aspect of the play's political impulse is the way it suggests that the rich and poor will change places. A revolution is in order: there's a spirit of optimism and idealism, and a sense that things won't always remain as they are, with injustice and inequity prevailing. There's an implication and a belief that the common people eventually will triumph and that the country will be free.

This political context is closely associated with the crisis of conscience that the Sergeant undergoes. His decision to trust his instinctive sympathy for the man and his cause, and his impulse to act in accordance with his reawakened idealism rather than to capture the criminal are dramatized powerfully and economically. And though the play ends with a question, it is clearly rhetorical. When the Sergeant asks, "Am I as great a fool as I think I am," we answer "No, you're not a fool, but a decent man, and you're at one with the people from whom you sprang."

CHAPTER SIXTEEN

The Greek Theater

Greek drama developed from celebrations honoring Dionysus, the Greek god of wine and fertility. These celebrations included choric dancing as part of the religious ritual. It is possible that the leader of the chorus (the *choragos*) may have engaged the rest of the chorus in responsive chanting. Legend suggests that the poet Thespis introduced a speaker who, detached from the chorus, engaged in dialogue with it. At that point drama was born. A second actor was added by Aeschylus (524–456 B.C.) and a third by Sophocles (496?–406 B.C.). In Greek drama no more than three characters appeared onstage together at one time, although it was common for actors to double and triple parts, changing masks for their multiple roles.

Greek plays were performed in huge outdoor amphitheaters capable of seating upwards of fourteen thousand people. Members of the audience were seated in tiers that sloped up hillsides where the theaters were built; the hills echoed the sound of the actors' voices. The actors wore masks that amplified their voices in the manner of megaphones. The masks were large, and with the elevated shoes sometimes worn by the actors, they projected the characters as larger-than-life figures. The masks and elevated shoes restricted what the actors could do and what the dramatist could expect of them. Subtle nuances of voice, of facial expression, and of gesture were impossible. The playwright's language rather than his stage business conveyed nuances of meaning and feeling.

The plays were performed on an elevated platform. Behind the acting area was a scene building *(skene)* that functioned both as dressing room and as scenic background, and below the stage was the *orchestra* or dancing place for the chorus. Standing between the actors and the audience, the chorus represented the common or communal viewpoint. Its leader, the choragos, sometimes engaged the chorus in dialogue with the other characters, and sometimes the choragos engaged in dialogue with the chorus itself.

An important function of the chorus was to mark the divisions between the scenes of a play, when the chorus would dance and chant poetry. Lyric rather than dramatic in form, these choral interludes sometimes commented on the action, sometimes generalized from it. They remained in Greek drama as vestiges of its origins in religious ritual. For modern readers these choric interludes pace the play, affording respite from the gradually intensifying action, and allowing time to ponder its implications.

The scenes of Greek plays usually consist of two, sometimes three characters with the third usually acting as an observer who occasionally comments on the debate occurring between the other two characters. Sometimes most of a scene is given over to a debate between two characters, as, for example, in Scene III of *Antigonê* with Haimon challenging Creon, his father, or Scene I of *Oedipus Rex* in which Oedipus argues with Teiresias. Some scenes, such as Scene II of *Antigonê,* include debates between Creon-Antigonê, Antigonê-Ismenê, Ismenê-Creon, and Creon-Choragos. The debates typically begin with leisurely speeches in which each character sets forth a position. The speeches are followed by rapid-fire dialogue *(stichomythia)* that brings the characters' antagonisms to a climax. This pattern is repeated throughout the play in something like a theme with variations, each scene usually developing a conflict. The accumulation of conflicts advances the action, leading to the inevitable tragic catastrophe.

Brevity is a characteristic of Greek tragedy: the plays are short with most having a playing time of roughly ninety minutes. Greek dramatists based their plays on myths that were familiar to the audience, which reduced the amount of time allotted for exposition. The plays also have a musical dimension, which, combined with the dancing and chanting of the chorus, increased the emotional impact of the ancient performances.

Of the three great Greek tragic dramatists, Sophocles is perhaps the most widely read today. Unlike his forebear Aeschylus, Sophocles focused his plays on human rather than religious concerns. As theater historian Peter Arnott has noted, he wrote "for a generation whose religious faith was waning."* His most famous plays center on a crisis and portray characters under duress. *Antigonê,* which takes place in Thebes, a city prostrated by war, turns on the difficult decisions both Antigonê and Creon must make. In *Oedipus Rex,* set against a background of the plague-stricken city of Thebes, Sophocles examines the behavior of Oedipus, who has been destined to murder his father and marry his mother. Though the two tragedies differ in the way their calamities ensue, both raise questions about inescapable human problems and portray characters confronting them with dignity and courage.

---

*Peter Arnott, *The Theatre in Its Time* (Boston: Little, Brown, 1981), page 51.

The following chart clarifies the relationships among the Theban royal families:

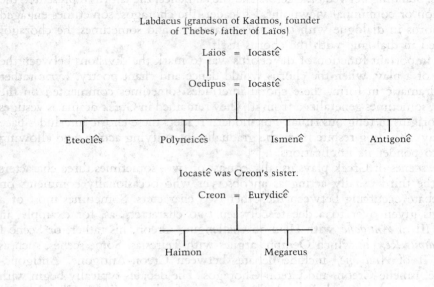

Labdacus (grandson of Kadmos, founder
of Thebes, father of Laïos)

Laïos = Iocastê

Oedipus = Iocastê

Eteoclês   Polyneicês   Ismenê   Antigonê

Iocastê was Creon's sister.

Creon = Eurydicê

Haimon   Megareus

SOPHOCLES

[496?–406 B.C.]

Oedipus Rex

AN ENGLISH VERSION BY DUDLEY FITTS AND ROBERT FITZGERALD

CHARACTERS

OEDIPUS
A PRIEST
CREON
TEIRESIAS
IOCASTÊ
MESSENGER
SHEPHERD OF LAÏOS
SECOND MESSENGER
CHORUS OF THEBAN ELDERS

Scene. *Before the palace of* OEDIPUS, *King of Thebes. A central door and two lateral doors open onto a platform which runs the length of the façade. On the platform, right and left, are altars; and three steps lead down into the "orchestra," or chorus-ground. At the beginning of the action these steps are crowded by* SUPPLIANTS *who have brought branches and chaplets of olive leaves and who lie in various attitudes of despair.* OEDIPUS *enters.*

PROLOGUE

OEDIPUS. My children, generations of the living
   In the line of Kadmos,° nursed at his ancient hearth:
   Why have you strewn yourselves before these altars
   In supplication, with your boughs and garlands?
   The breath of incense rises from the city   5
   With a sound of prayer and lamentation.
                            Children,
   I would not have you speak through messengers,
   And therefore I have come myself to hear you—
   I, Oedipus, who bear the famous name.
   (To a PRIEST.*)* You, there, since you are eldest in the company,   10
   Speak for them all, tell me what preys upon you,
   Whether you come in dread, or crave some blessing:
   Tell me, and never doubt that I will help you
   In every way I can; I should be heartless
   Were I not moved to find you suppliant here.   15
PRIEST. Great Oedipus, O powerful King of Thebes!
   You see how all the ages of our people
   Cling to your altar steps: here are boys
   Who can barely stand alone, and here are priests
   By weight of age, as I am a priest of God,   20
   And young men chosen from those yet unmarried;
   As for the others, all that multitude,
   They wait with olive chaplets in the squares,
   At the two shrines of Pallas,° and where Apollo°
   Speaks in the glowing embers.
                      Your own eyes   25
   Must tell you: Thebes is in her extremity
   And cannot lift her head from the surge of death.
   A rust consumes the buds and fruits of the earth;
   The herds are sick; children die unborn,
   And labor is vain. The god of plague and pyre   30
   Raids like detestable lightning through the city,
   And all the house of Kadmos is laid waste,
   All emptied, and all darkened: Death alone
   Battens upon the misery of Thebes.
   You are not one of the immortal gods, we know;   35

---

²**Kadmos** *legendary founder of Thebes.*   ²⁴**Pallas** *Athena, goddess of wisdom.*   ²⁴**Apollo** *god of poetry and prophecy.*

Yet we have come to you to make our prayer
As to the man of all men best in adversity
And wisest in the ways of God. You saved us
From the Sphinx,° that flinty singer, and the tribute
We paid to her so long; yet you were never   40
Better informed than we, nor could we teach you:
It was some god breathed in you to set us free.

Therefore, O mighty King, we turn to you:
Find us our safety, find us a remedy,
Whether by counsel of the gods or the men.   45
A king of wisdom tested in the past
Can act in a time of troubles, and act well.
Noblest of men, restore
Life to your city! Think how all men call you
Liberator for your triumph long ago;   50
Ah, when your years of kingship are remembered,
Let them not say *We rose, but later fell*—
Keep the State from going down in the storm!
Once, years ago, with happy augury,
You brought us fortune; be the same again!   55
No man questions your power to rule the land:
But rule over men, not over a dead city!
Ships are only hulls, citadels are nothing,
When no life moves in the empty passageways.
OEDIPUS. Poor children! You may be sure I know   60
All that you longed for in your coming here.
I know that you are deathly sick; and yet,
Sick as you are, not one is as sick as I.
Each of you suffers in himself alone
His anguish, not another's; but my spirit   65
Groans for the city, for myself, for you.

I was not sleeping, you are not waking me.
No, I have been in tears for a long while
And in my restless thought walked many ways.
In all my search, I found one helpful course,   70
And that I have taken: I have sent Creon,
Son of Menoikeus, brother of the Queen,
To Delphi, Apollo's place of revelation,
To learn there, if he can,
What act or pledge of mine may save the city.   75
I have counted the days, and now, this very day,
I am troubled, for he has overstayed his time.

---

[39] **The Sphinx**   *a monster with a lion's body, birds' wings, and woman's face. It terrorized Thebes by devouring all who passed and could not answer its riddle: What walks on four legs in the morning, two legs in the afternoon, and three in the evening? Oedipus saved Thebes by answering, "Man," and was made king.*

What is he doing? He has been gone too long.
Yet whenever he comes back, I should do ill
To scant whatever hint the god may give.   80
PRIEST. It is a timely promise. At this instant
They tell me Creon is here.
OEDIPUS.   O Lord Apollo!
May his news be fair as his face is radiant!
PRIEST. It could not be otherwise: he is crowned with bay,
The chaplet is thick with berries.
OEDIPUS.   We shall soon know;   85
He is near enough to hear us now.

Enter CREON.

O Prince:
Brother: son of Menoikeus:
What answer do you bring us from the god?
CREON. It is favorable. I can tell you, great afflictions
Will turn out well, if they are taken well.   90
OEDIPUS. What was the oracle? These vague words
Leave me still hanging between hope and fear.
CREON. Is it your pleasure to hear me with all these
Gathered around us? I am prepared to speak,
But should we not go in?
OEDIPUS.   Let them all hear it.   95
It is for them I suffer, more than myself.
CREON. Then I will tell you what I heard at Delphi.

In plain words
The god commands us to expel from the land of Thebes
An old defilement that it seems we shelter.   100
It is a deathly thing, beyond expiation.
We must not let it feed upon us longer.
OEDIPUS. What defilement? How shall we rid ourselves of it?
CREON. By exile or death, blood for blood. It was
Murder that brought the plague-wind on the city.   105
OEDIPUS. Murder of whom? Surely the god has named him?
CREON. My lord: long ago Laïos was our king,
Before you came to govern us.
OEDIPUS.   I know;
I learned of him from others; I never saw him.
CREON. He was murdered; and Apollo commands us now   110
To take revenge upon whoever killed him.
OEDIPUS. Upon whom? Where are they? Where shall we find a clue
To solve that crime, after so many years?
CREON. Here in this land, he said.
                              If we make enquiry,
We may touch things that otherwise escape us.   115

OEDIPUS. Tell me: Was Laïos murdered in his house,
 Or in the fields, or in some foreign country?
CREON. He said he planned to make a pilgrimage.
 He did not come home again.
OEDIPUS.   And was there no one,
 No witness, no companion, to tell what happened?   120
CREON. They were all killed but one, and he got away
 So frightened that he could remember one thing only.
OEDIPUS. What was that one thing? One may be the key
 To everything, if we resolve to use it.
CREON. He said that a band of highwaymen attacked them,   125
 Outnumbered them, and overwhelmed the King.
OEDIPUS. Strange, that a highwayman should be so daring—
 Unless some faction here bribed him to do it.
CREON. We thought of that. But after Laïos' death
 New troubles arose and we had no avenger.   130
OEDIPUS. What troubles could prevent your hunting down the killers?
CREON. The riddling Sphinx's song
 Made us deaf to all mysteries but her own.
OEDIPUS. Then once more I must bring what is dark to light.
 It is most fitting that Apollo shows,   135
 As you do, this compunction for the dead.
 You shall see how I stand by you, as I should,
 To avenge the city and the city's god,
 And not as though it were for some distant friend,
 But for my own sake, to be rid of evil.   140
 Whoever killed King Laïos might—who knows?—
 Decide at any moment to kill me as well.
 By avenging the murdered king I protect myself.
 Come, then, my children: leave the altar steps,
 Lift up your olive boughs!
        One of you go   145
 And summon the people of Kadmos to gather here.
 I will do all that I can; you may tell them that.

      (Exit a PAGE.*)*

 So, with the help of God,
 We shall be saved—or else indeed we are lost.
PRIEST. Let us rise, children. It was for this we came,   150
 And now the King has promised it himself.
 Phoibos° has sent us an oracle; may he descend
 Himself to save us and drive out the plague.

Exeunt OEDIPUS *and* CREON *into the palace by the central door. The* PRIEST *and the*
SUPPLIANTS *disperse right and left. After a short pause the* CHORUS *enters the orchestra.*

¹⁵²**Phoibos** *Phoebus Apollo, the sun god.*

PÁRODOS°

Strophe 1

CHORUS. What is God singing in his profound
    Delphi of gold and shadow?
    What oracle for Thebes, the sunwhipped city?
    Fear unjoints me, the roots of my heart tremble.
    Now I remember, O Healer, your power, and wonder;   5
    Will you send doom like a sudden cloud, or weave it
    Like nightfall of the past?
    Speak, speak to us, issue of holy sound:
    Dearest to our expectancy: be tender!

Antistrophe 1

    Let me pray to Athenê, the immortal daughter of Zeus,   10
    And to Artemis her sister
    Who keeps her famous throne in the market ring,
    And to Apollo, bowman at the far butts of heaven—

    O gods, descend! Like three streams leap against
    The fires of our grief, the fires of darkness;   15
    Be swift to bring us rest!

    As in the old time from the brilliant house
    Of air you stepped to save us, come again!

Strophe 2

    Now our afflictions have no end,
    Now all our stricken host lies down   20
    And no man fights off death with his mind;

    The noble plowland bears no grain,
    And groaning mothers cannot bear—

    See, how our lives like birds take wing.
    Like sparks that fly when a fire soars,   25
    To the shore of the god of evening.

Antistrophe 2

    The plague burns on, it is pitiless,
    Though pallid children laden with death
    Lie unwept in the stony ways,

°*Párodos*   *sung as the chorus enters the stage area. Presumbly they sang the* strophe *while dancing from right to left and the antistrophe as they reversed direction.*

And old gray women by every path
Flock to the strand about the altars

There to strike their breasts and cry
Worship of Phoibos in wailing prayers:
Be kind, God's golden child!

Strophe 3

There are no swords in this attack by fire, 35
No shields, but we are ringed with cries.
Send the besieger plunging from our homes
Into the vast sea-room of the Atlantic
Or into the waves that foam eastward of Thrace—
For the day ravages what the night spares— 40

Destroy our enemy, lord of the thunder!
Let him be riven by lightning from heaven!

Antistrophe 3

Phoibos Apollo, stretch the sun's bowstring,
That golden cord, until it sing for us,
Flashing arrows in heaven!
                    Artemis,° Huntress, 45
Race with flaring lights upon our mountains!
O scarlet god, O golden-banded brow,
O Theban Bacchos° in a storm of Maenads,°

        Enter OEDIPUS, *center.*

Whirl upon Death, that all the Undying hate!
Come with blinding cressets, come in joy! 50

SCENE I

OEDIPUS. Is this your prayer? It may be answered. Come,
Listen to me, act as the crisis demands,
And you shall have relief from all these evils.

Until now I was a stranger to this tale,
As I had been a stranger to the crime. 5
Could I track down the murderer without a clue?
But now, friends,

---

⁴⁵*Artemis* *goddess of hunting and chastity.*   ⁴⁸*Bacchos . . . Maenads* *god of wine and revelry with his attendants.*

As one who became a citizen after the murder,
I make this proclamation to all Thebans:
If any man knows by whose hand Laïos, son of Labdakos,   10
Met his death, I direct that man to tell me everything,
No matter what he fears for having so long withheld it.
Let it stand as promised that no further trouble
Will come to him, but he may leave the land in safety.

Moreover: If anyone knows the murderer to be foreign,   15
Let him not keep silent: he shall have his reward from me.
However, if he does conceal it; if any man
Fearing for his friend or for himself disobeys this edict,
Hear what I propose to do:

I solemnly forbid the people of this country,   20
Where power and throne are mine, ever to receive that man
Or speak to him, no matter who he is, or let him
Join in sacrifice, lustration, or in prayer.
I decree that he be driven from every house,

Being, as he is, corruption itself to us: the Delphic   25
Voice of Zeus has pronounced this revelation.
Thus I associate myself with the oracle
And take the side of the murdered king.

As for the criminal, I pray to God—
Whether it be a lurking thief, or one of a number—   30
I pray that that man's life be consumed in evil and
     wretchedness.
And as for me, this curse applies no less
If it should turn out that the culprit is my guest here,
Sharing my hearth.
                    You have heard the penalty.
I lay it on you now to attend to this   35
For my sake, for Apollo's, for the sick
Sterile city that heaven has abandoned.
Suppose the oracle had given you no command:
Should this defilement go uncleansed for ever?
You should have found the murderer: your king,   40
A noble king, had been destroyed!
                              Now I,
Having the power that he held before me,
Having his bed, begetting children there
Upon his wife, as he would have, had he lived—
Their son would have been my children's brother,   45
If Laïos had had luck in fatherhood!
(But surely ill luck rushed upon his reign)—

I say I take the son's part, just as though
I were his son, to press the fight for him
And see it won! I'll find the hand that brought   50
Death to Labdakos' and Polydoros' child,
Heir of Kadmos' and Agenor's line.
And as for those who fail me,
May the gods deny them the fruit of the earth,
Fruit of the womb, and may they rot utterly!   55
Let them be wretched as we are wretched, and worse!

For you, for loyal Thebans, and for all
Who find my actions right, I pray the favor
Of justice, and of all the immortal gods.
CHORAGOS. Since I am under oath, my lord, I swear   60
I did not do the murder, I cannot name
The murderer. Might not the oracle
That has ordained the search tell where to find him?
OEDIPUS. An honest question. But no man in the world
Can make the gods do more than the gods will.   65
CHORAGOS. There is one last expedient—
OEDIPUS.   Tell me what it is.
Though it seem slight, you must not hold it back.
CHORAGOS. A lord clairvoyant to the lord Apollo,
As we all know, is the skilled Teiresias.
One might learn much about this from him, Oedipus.   70
OEDIPUS. I am not wasting time:
Creon spoke of this, and I have sent for him—
Twice, in fact; it is strange that he is not here.
CHORAGOS. The other matter—that old report—seems useless.
OEDIPUS. Tell me. I am interested in all reports.   75
CHORAGOS. The King was said to have been killed by highwaymen.
OEDIPUS. I know. But we have no witnesses to that.
CHORAGOS. If the killer can feel a particle of dread,
Your curse will bring him out of hiding!
OEDIPUS.   No.
The man who dared that act will fear no curse.   80

Enter the blind seer TEIRESIAS, *led by a* PAGE.

CHORAGOS. But there is one man who may detect the criminal.
This is Teiresias, this is the holy prophet
In whom, alone of all men, truth was born.
OEDIPUS. Teiresias: seer: student of mysteries,
Of all that's taught and all that no man tells,   85
Secrets of Heaven and secrets of the earth:
Blind though you are, you know the city lies
Sick with plague; and from this plague, my lord,
We find that you alone can guard or save us.

Possibly you did not hear the messengers? 90
Apollo, when we sent to him,
Sent us back word that this great pestilence
Would lift, but only if we established clearly
The identity of those who murdered Laïos.
They must be killed or exiled. 95

                    Can you use
Birdflight or any art of divination
To purify yourself, and Thebes, and me
From this contagion? We are in your hands.
There is no fairer duty
Than that of helping others in distress. 100

TEIRESIAS. How dreadful knowledge of the truth can be
  When there's no help in truth! I knew this well,
  But did not act on it: else I should not have come.
OEDIPUS. What is troubling you? Why are your eyes so cold?
TEIRESIAS. Let me go home. Bear your own fate, and I'll 105
  Bear mine. It is better so: trust what I say.
OEDIPUS. What you say is ungracious and unhelpful
  To your native country. Do not refuse to speak.
TEIRESIAS. When it comes to speech, your own is neither temperate
  Nor opportune. I wish to be more prudent. 110
OEDIPUS. In God's name, we all beg you—
TEIRESIAS.   You are all ignorant.
  No; I will never tell you what I know.
  Now it is my misery; then, it would be yours.
OEDIPUS. What! You do know something, and will not tell us?
  You would betray us all and wreck the State? 115
TEIRESIAS. I do not intend to torture myself, or you.
  Why persist in asking? You will not persuade me.
OEDIPUS. What a wicked old man you are! You'd try a stone's
  Patience! Out with it! Have you no feeling at all?
TEIRESIAS. You call me unfeeling. If you could only see 120
  The nature of your own feelings . . .
OEDIPUS.   Why,
  Who would not feel as I do? Who could endure
  Your arrogance toward the city?
TEIRESIAS.   What does it matter!
  Whether I speak or not, it is bound to come.
OEDIPUS. Then, if "it" is bound to come, you are bound
  to tell me. 125
TEIRESIAS. No, I will not go on. Rage as you please.
OEDIPUS. Rage? Why not!
               And I'll tell you what I think:
  You planned it, you had it done, you all but
  Killed him with your own hands: if you had eyes,
  I'd say the crime was yours, and yours alone. 130

TEIRESIAS. So? I charge you, then,
    Abide by the proclamation you have made:
    From this day forth
    Never speak again to these men or to me;
    You yourself are the pollution of this country.   135

OEDIPUS. You dare say that! Can you possibly think you have
    Some way of going free, after such insolence?

TEIRESIAS. I have gone free. It is the truth sustains me.

OEDIPUS. Who taught you shamelessness? It was not your craft.

TEIRESIAS. You did. You made me speak. I did not want to.   140

OEDIPUS. Speak what? Let me hear it again more clearly.

TEIRESIAS. Was it not clear before? Are you tempting me?

OEDIPUS. I did not understand it. Say it again.

TEIRESIAS. I say that you are the murderer whom you seek.

OEDIPUS. Now twice you have spat out infamy. You'll
    pay for it!   145

TEIRESIAS. Would you care for more? Do you wish to be really angry?

OEDIPUS. Say what you will. Whatever you say is worthless.

TEIRESIAS. I say you live in hideous shame with those
    Most dear to you. You cannot see the evil.

OEDIPUS. It seems you can go on mouthing like this for ever.   150

TEIRESIAS. I can, if there is power in truth.

OEDIPUS.   There is:
    But not for you, not for you,
    You sightless, witless, senseless, mad old man!

TEIRESIAS. You are the madman. There is no one here
    Who will not curse you soon, as you curse me.   155

OEDIPUS. You child of endless night! You cannot hurt me
    Or any other man who sees the sun.

TEIRESIAS. True: it is not from me your fate will come.
    That lies within Apollo's competence,
    As it is his concern.

OEDIPUS.   Tell me: 160
    Are you speaking for Creon, or for yourself?

TEIRESIAS. Creon is no threat. You weave your own doom.

OEDIPUS. Wealth, power, craft of statesmanship!
    Kingly position, everywhere admired!
    What savage envy is stored up against these,   165
    If Creon, whom I trusted, Creon my friend,
    For this great office which the city once
    Put in my hands unsought—if for this power
    Creon desires in secret to destroy me!

    He has brought this decrepit fortune-teller, this   170
    Collector of dirty pennies, this prophet fraud—
    Why, he is no more clairvoyant than I am!
                                Tell us:

Has your mystic mummery ever approached the truth?
When that hellcat the Sphinx was performing here,
What help were you to these people?   175
Her magic was not for the first man who came along:
It demanded a real exorcist. Your birds—
What good were they? or the gods, for the matter of that?
But I came by,
Oedipus, the simple man, who knows nothing—   180
I thought it out for myself, no birds helped me!
And this is the man you think you can destroy,
That you may be close to Creon when he's king!
Well, you and your friend Creon, it seems to me,
Will suffer most. If you were not an old man,   185
You would have paid already for your plot.
CHORAGOS. We cannot see that his words or yours
  Have been spoken except in anger, Oedipus,
  And of anger we have no need. How can God's will
  Be accomplished best? That is what most concerns us.   190
TEIRESIAS. You are a king. But where argument's concerned
  I am your man, as much a king as you.
  I am not your servant, but Apollo's.
  I have no need of Creon to speak for me.

  Listen to me. You mock my blindness, do you?   195
  But I say that you, with both your eyes, are blind:
  You cannot see the wretchedness of your life,
  Nor in whose house you live, no, nor with whom.
  Who are your father and mother? Can you tell me?
  You do not even know the blind wrongs   200
  That you have done them, on earth and in the world below.
  But the double lash of your parents' curse will whip you
  Out of this land some day, with only night
  Upon your precious eyes.
  Your cries then—where will they not be heard?   205
  What fastness of Kithairon will not echo them?
  And that bridal-descant of yours—you'll know it then,
  The song they sang when you came here to Thebes
  And found your misguided berthing.
  All this, and more, that you cannot guess at now,   210
  Will bring you to yourself among your children.
  Be angry, then. Curse Creon. Curse my words.
  I tell you, no man that walks upon the earth
  Shall be rooted out more horribly than you.
OEDIPUS. Am I to bear this from him?—Damnation   215
  Take you! Out of this place! Out of my sight!
TEIRESIAS. I would not have come at all if you had not asked me.
OEDIPUS. Could I have told that you'd talk nonsense, that

You'd come here to make a fool of yourself, and of me?

TEIRESIAS. A fool? Your parents thought me sane enough.   220

OEDIPUS. My parents again!—Wait: who were my parents?

TEIRESIAS. This day will give you a father, and break your heart.

OEDIPUS. Your infantile riddles! Your damned abracadabra!

TEIRESIAS. You were a great man once at solving riddles.

OEDIPUS. Mock me with that if you like; you will find it true.   225

TEIRESIAS. It was true enough. It brought about your ruin.

OEDIPUS. But if it saved this town?

TEIRESIAS *(to the* PAGE*)*. Boy, give me your hand.

OEDIPUS. Yes, boy; lead him away.

                               —While you are here

We can do nothing. Go; leave us in peace.

TEIRESIAS. I will go when I have said what I have to say.   230

How can you hurt me? And I tell you again:

The man you have been looking for all this time,

The damned man, the murderer of Laïos,

That man is in Thebes. To your mind he is foreignborn,

But it will soon be shown that he is a Theban,   235

A revelation that will fail to please.

                                A blind man,

Who has his eyes now; a penniless man, who is rich now;

And he will go tapping the strange earth with his staff;

To the children with whom he lives now he will be

Brother and father—the very same; to her   240

Who bore him, son and husband—the very same

Who came to his father's bed, wet with his father's blood.

Enough. Go think that over.

If later you find error in what I have said,

You may say that I have no skill in prophecy.   245

       Exit TEIRESIAS, *led by his* PAGE. OEDIPUS *goes into the palace.*

ODE I°

Strophe 1

CHORUS. The Delphic stone of prophecies

     Remembers ancient regicide

     And a still bloody hand.

     That killer's hour of flight has come.

     He must be stronger than riderless   5

     Coursers of untiring wind,

°**Ode**   *a poetic song sung by the chorus.*

For the son of Zeus° armed with his father's thunder
Leaps in lightning after him;
And the Furies° follow him, the sad Furies.

Antistrophe 1

Holy Parnossos' peak of snow   10
Flashes and blinds that secret man,
That all shall hunt him down:
Though he may roam the forest shade
Like a bull gone wild from pasture
To rage through glooms of stone.   15
Doom comes down on him; flight will not avail him;
For the world's heart calls him desolate,
And the immortal Furies follow, for ever follow.

Strophe 2

But now a wilder thing is heard
From the old man skilled at hearing Fate in the
    wingbeat of a bird.   20
Bewildered as a blown bird, my soul hovers and cannot find
Foothold in this debate, or any reason or rest of mind.
But no man ever brought—none can bring
Proof of strife between Thebes' royal house,
Labdakos' line,° and the son of Polybos;°   25
And never until now has any man brought word
Of Laïos' dark death staining Oedipus the King.

Antistrophe 2

Divine Zeus and Apollo hold
Perfect intelligence alone of all tales ever told;
And well though this diviner works, he works in his own night;   30
No man can judge that rough unknown or trust in second sight,
For wisdom changes hands among the wise.
Shall I believe my great lord criminal
At a raging word that a blind old man let fall?
I saw him, when the carrion woman faced him of old,   35
Prove his heroic mind! These evil words are lies.

---

[7] *son of Zeus* Apollo.   [9] *the Furies* *three women spirits who punished evildoers.*   [25] *Labdakos' line*
his descendants.   [25] *Polybos* *King of Corinth who adopted Oedipus as an infant.*

SCENE II

CREON. Men of Thebes:
　I am told that heavy accusations
　Have been brought against me by King Oedipus.
　I am not the kind of man to bear this tamely.

　If in these present difficulties   5
　He holds me accountable for any harm to him
　Through anything I have said or done—why, then,
　I do not value life in this dishonor.
　It is not as though this rumor touched upon
　Some private indiscretion. The matter is grave.   10
　The fact is that I am being called disloyal
　To the State, to my fellow citizens, to my friends.
CHORAGOS. He may have spoken in anger, not from his mind.
CREON. But did you not hear him say I was the one
　Who seduced the old prophet into lying?   15
CHORAGOS. The thing was said; I do not know how seriously.
CREON. But you were watching him! Were his eyes steady?
　Did he look like a man in his right mind?
CHORAGOS.　　　　　　　　　　　　　　I do not know.
　I cannot judge the behavior of great men.
　But here is the King himself.

Enter OEDIPUS.

OEDIPUS.　　　　　　　　　　So you dared come back.   20
　Why? How brazen of you to come to my house,
　You murderer!
　　　　　　　Do you think I do not know
　That you plotted to kill me, plotted to steal my throne?
　Tell me, in God's name: am I coward, a fool,
　That you should dream you could accomplish this?   25
　A fool who could not see your slippery game?
　A coward, not to fight back when I saw it?
　You are the fool, Creon, are you not? hoping
　Without support or friends to get a throne?
　Thrones may be won or bought: you could do neither.   30
CREON. Now listen to me. You have talked; let me talk, too.
　You cannot judge unless you know the facts.
OEDIPUS. You speak well: there is one fact; but I find it hard
　To learn from the deadliest enemy I have.
CREON. That above all I must dispute with you.   35
OEDIPUS. That above all I will not hear you deny.
CREON. If you think there is anything good in being stubborn
　Against all reason, then I say you are wrong.

OEDIPUS. If you think a man can sin against his own kind
  And not be punished for it, I say you are mad. 40
CREON. I agree. But tell me: what have I done to you?
OEDIPUS. You advised me to send for that wizard, did you not?
CREON. I did. I should do it again.
OEDIPUS.   Very well. Now tell me:
  How long has it been since Laïos—
CREON.   What of Laïos?
OEDIPUS. Since he vanished in that onset by the road? 45
CREON. It was long ago, a long time.
OEDIPUS.   And this prophet,
  Was he practicing here then?
CREON.   He was; and with honor, as now.
OEDIPUS. Did he speak of me at that time?
CREON.   He never did;
  At least, not when I was present.
OEDIPUS.   But . . . the enquiry?
  I suppose you held one?
CREON.   We did, but we learned nothing. 50
OEDIPUS. Why did the prophet not speak against me then?
CREON. I do not know; and I am the kind of man
  Who holds his tongue when he has no facts to go on.
OEDIPUS. There's one fact that you know, and you could tell it.
CREON. What fact is that? If I know it, you shall have it. 55
OEDIPUS. If he were not involved with you, he could not say
  That it was I who murdered Laïos.
CREON. If he says that, you are the one that knows it!—
  But now it is my turn to question you.
OEDIPUS. Put your questions. I am no murderer. 60
CREON. First, then: You married my sister?
OEDIPUS.   I married your sister.
CREON. And you rule the kingdom equally with her?
OEDIPUS. Everything that she wants she has from me.
CREON. And I am the third, equal to both of you?
OEDIPUS. That is why I call you a bad friend. 65
CREON. No. Reason it out, as I have done.
  Think of this first. Would any sane man prefer
  Power, with all a king's anxieties,
  To that same power and the grace of sleep?
  Certainly not I. 70
  I have never longed for the king's power—only his rights.
  Would any wise man differ from me in this?
  As matters stand, I have my way in everything
  With your consent, and no responsibilities.
  If I were king, I should be a slave to policy. 75
  How could I desire a scepter more
  Than what is now mine—untroubled influence?

No, I have not gone mad; I need no honors,
Except those with the perquisites I have now.
I am welcome everywhere; every man salutes me,   80
And those who want your favor seek my ear,
Since I know how to manage what they ask.
Should I exchange this ease for that anxiety?
Besides, no sober mind is treasonable.
I hate anarchy   85
And never would deal with any man who likes it.

Test what I have said. Go to the priestess
At Delphi, ask if I quoted her correctly.
And as for this other thing: if I am found
Guilty of treason with Teiresias,   90
Then sentence me to death! You have my word
It is a sentence I should cast my vote for—
But not without evidence!
                              You do wrong
When you take good men for bad, bad men for good.
A true friend thrown aside—why, life itself   95
Is not more precious!
                          In time you will know this well:
For time, and time alone, will show the just man,
Though scoundrels are discovered in a day.
CHORAGOS. This is well said, and a prudent man would ponder it.
Judgments too quickly formed are dangerous.   100
OEDIPUS. But is he not quick in his duplicity?
And shall I not be quick to parry him?
Would you have me stand still, hold my peace, and let
This man win everything, through my inaction?
CREON. And you want—what is it, then? To banish me? 105
OEDIPUS. No, not exile. It is your death I want,
So that all the world may see what treason means.
CREON. You will persist, then? You will not believe me?
OEDIPUS. How can I believe you?
CREON.   Then you are a fool.
OEDIPUS. To save myself?
CREON.   In justice, think of me.   110
OEDIPUS. You are evil incarnate.
CREON.   But suppose that you are wrong?
OEDIPUS. Still I must rule.
CREON.   But not if you rule badly.
OEDIPUS. O city, city!
CREON.   It is my city, too!
CHORAGOS. Now, my lords, be still. I see the Queen,
Iocastê, coming from her palace chambers;   115

And it is time she came, for the sake of you both.
This dreadful quarrel can be resolved through her.

Enter IOCASTÊ.

IOCASTÊ. Poor foolish men, what wicked din is this?
With Thebes sick to death, is it not shameful
That you should rake some private quarrel up?　　　　　120

(To OEDIPUS.*)*

Come into the house.
　　　　　　　—And you, Creon, go now:
Let us have no more of this tumult over nothing.
CREON. Nothing? No, sister: what your husband plans for me
Is one of two great evils: exile or death.
OEDIPUS. He is right.
　　　　　　Why, woman, I have caught him squarely　　　　125
Plotting against my life.
CREON. 　　　　　　No! Let me die
Accurst if ever I have wished you harm!
IOCASTÊ. Ah, believe it, Oedipus!
In the name of the gods, respect this oath of his
For my sake, for the sake of these people here!　　　　　130

Strophe 1

CHORAGOS. Open your mind to her, my lord. Be ruled by her, I beg you!
OEDIPUS. What would you have me do?
CHORAGOS. Respect Creon's word. He has never spoken like a fool,
And now he has sworn an oath.
OEDIPUS. You know what you ask?
CHORAGOS. 　　　　　　　　I do.
OEDIPUS. 　　　　　　　　　　Speak on, then.
CHORAGOS. A friend so sworn should not be baited so,　　　　135
In blind malice, and without final proof.
OEDIPUS. You are aware, I hope, that what you say
Means death for me, or exile at the least.

Strophe 2

CHORAGOS. No, I swear by Helios, first in Heaven!
May I die friendless and accurst,　　　　　140
The worst of deaths, if ever I meant that!
　　　It is the withering fields
　　　　　That hurt my sick heart:
　　　Must we bear all these ills,
　　　　　And now your bad blood as well?　　　　145
OEDIPUS. Then let him go. And let me die, if I must,

Or be driven by him in shame from the land of Thebes.
It is your unhappiness, and not his talk,
That touches me.
        As for him—
Wherever he is, I will hate him as long as I live.   150
CREON. Ugly in yielding, as you were ugly in rage!
   Natures like yours chiefly torment themselves.
OEDIPUS. Can you not go? Can you not leave me?
CREON.   I can.
   You do not know me; but the city knows me,
   And in its eyes I am just, if not in yours.   155

(Exit CREON.*)*

Antistrophe 1

CHORAGOS. Lady Iocastê, did you not ask the King
   to go to his chambers?
IOCASTÊ. First tell me what has happened.
CHORAGOS. There was suspicion without evidence; yet it rankled
   As even false charges will.
IOCASTÊ.   On both sides?
CHORAGOS.   On both.
IOCASTÊ.   But what was said?
CHORAGOS. Oh let it rest, let it be done with!   160
   Have we not suffered enough?
OEDIPUS. You see to what your decency has brought you:
   You have made difficulties where my heart saw none.

Antistrophe 2

CHORAGOS. Oedipus, it is not once only I have told you—
   You must know I should count myself unwise   165
   To the point of madness, should I now forsake you—
       You, under whose hand,
          In the storm of another time,
      Our dear land sailed out free.
         But now stand fast at the helm!   170
IOCASTÊ. In God's name, Oedipus, inform your wife as well:
   Why are you so set in this hard anger?
OEDIPUS. I will tell you, for none of these men deserves
   My confidence as you do. It is Creon's work,
   His treachery, his plotting against me.   175
IOCASTÊ. Go on, if you can make this clear to me.
OEDIPUS. He charges me with the murder of Laïos.
IOCASTÊ. Has he some knowledge? Or does he speak from hearsay?
OEDIPUS. He would not commit himself to such a charge,

But he has brought in that damnable soothsayer 180
To tell his story.

IOCASTÊ.   Set your mind at rest.
If it is a question of soothsayers, I tell you
That you will find no man whose craft gives knowledge
Of the unknowable.

          Here is my proof:

An oracle was reported to Laïos once 185
(I will not say from Phoibos himself, but from
His appointed ministers, at any rate)
That his doom would be death at the hands of his own son—
His son, born of his flesh and of mine!

Now, you remember the story: Laïos was killed 190
By marauding strangers where three highways meet;
But his child had not been three days in this world
Before the King had pierced the baby's ankles
And left him to die on a lonely mountainside.

Thus, Apollo never caused that child 195
To kill his father, and it was not Laïos' fate
To die at the hands of his son, as he had feared.
This is what prophets and prophecies are worth!
Have no dread of them.
               It is God himself
Who can show us what he wills, in his own way. 200

OEDIPUS. How strange a shadowy memory crossed my mind,
    Just now while you were speaking; it chilled my heart.

IOCASTÊ. What do you mean? What memory do you speak of?

OEDIPUS. If I understand you, Laïos was killed
    At a place where three roads meet.

IOCASTÊ.   So it was said; 205
    We have no later story.

OEDIPUS.   Where did it happen?

IOCASTÊ. Phokis, it is called: at a place where the Theban Way
    Divides into the roads towards Delphi and Daulia.

OEDIPUS. When?

IOCASTÊ.   We had the news not long before you came
    And proved the right to your succession here. 210

OEDIPUS. Ah, what net has God been weaving for me?

IOCASTÊ. Oedipus! Why does this trouble you?

OEDIPUS.   Do not ask me yet.
    First, tell me how Laïos looked, and tell me
    How old he was.

IOCASTÊ.   He was tall, his hair just touched
    With white; his form was not unlike your own. 215

OEDIPUS. I think that I myself may be accurst
   By my own ignorant edict.
IOCASTÊ.   You speak strangely.
   It makes me tremble to look at you, my King.
OEDIPUS. I am not sure that the blind man cannot see.
   But I should know better if you were to tell me—   220
IOCASTÊ. Anything—though I dread to hear you ask it.
OEDIPUS. Was the King lightly escorted, or did he ride
   With a large company, as a ruler should?
IOCASTÊ. There were five men with him in all: one was a herald;
   And a single chariot, which he was driving.   225
OEDIPUS. Alas, that makes it plain enough!
                                But who—
   Who told you how it happened?
IOCASTÊ.   A household servant,
   The only one to escape.
OEDIPUS.   And is he still
   A servant of ours?
IOCASTÊ.   No; for when he came back at last
   And found you enthroned in the place of the dead king,   230
   He came to me, touched my hand with his, and begged
   That I would send him away to the frontier district
   Where only the shepherds go—
   As far away from the city as I could send him.
   I granted his prayer; for although the man was a slave,   235
   He had earned more than this favor at my hands.
OEDIPUS. Can he be called back quickly?
IOCASTÊ.   Easily.
   But why?
OEDIPUS.   I have taken too much upon myself
   Without enquiry; therefore I wish to consult him.
IOCASTÊ. Then he shall come.
                    But am I not one also   240
   To whom you might confide these fears of yours!
OEDIPUS. That is your right; it will not be denied you,
   Now least of all; for I have reached a pitch
   Of wild foreboding. Is there anyone
   To whom I should sooner speak?   245
   Polybos of Corinth is my father.
   My mother is a Dorian: Meropê.
   I grew up chief among the men of Corinth
   Until a strange thing happened—
   Not worth my passion, it may be, but strange.   250

   At a feast, a drunken man maundering in his cups
   Cries out that I am not my father's son!

I contained myself that night, though I felt anger
And a sinking heart. The next day I visited
My father and mother, and questioned them. They stormed,   255
Calling it all the slanderous rant of a fool;
And this relieved me. Yet the suspicion
Remained always aching in my mind;
I knew there was talk; I could not rest;
And finally, saying nothing to my parents,   260
I went to the shrine at Delphi.
The god dismissed my question without reply;
He spoke of other things.

                      Some were clear,
Full of wretchedness, dreadful, unbearable:
As, that I should lie with my own mother, breed   265
Children from whom all men would turn their eyes;
And that I should be my father's murderer.

I heard all this, and fled. And from that day
Corinth to me was only in the stars
Descending in that quarter of the sky,   270
As I wandered farther and farther on my way
To a land where I should never see the evil
Sung by the oracle. And I came to this country
Where, so you say, King Laïos was killed.
I will tell you all that happened there, my lady.   275

There were three highways
Coming together at a place I passed;
And there a herald came towards me, and a chariot
Drawn by horses, with a man such as you describe
Seated in it. The groom leading the horses   280
Forced me off the road at his lord's command;
But as this charioteer lurched over towards me
I struck him in my rage. The old man saw me
And brought his double goad down upon my head
As I came abreast.

                He was paid back, and more!   285
Swinging my club in this right hand I knocked him
Out of his car, and he rolled on the ground.

                          I killed him.

I killed them all.
Now if that stranger and Laïos were—kin,
Where is a man more miserable than I?   290
More hated by the gods? Citizen and alien alike
Must never shelter me or speak to me—
I must be shunned by all.

                     And I myself
Pronounced this malediction upon myself!

Think of it: I have touched you with these hands,   295
These hands that killed your husband. What defilement!

Am I all evil, then? It must be so,
Since I must flee from Thebes, yet never again
See my own countrymen, my own country,
For fear of joining my mother in marriage   300
And killing Polybos, my father.
                       Ah,
If I was created so, born to this fate,
Who could deny the savagery of God?

O holy majesty of heavenly powers!
May I never see that day! Never!   305
Rather let me vanish from the race of men
Than know the abomination destined me!
CHORAGOS. We too, my lord, have felt dismay at this.
     But there is hope: you have yet to hear the shepherd.
OEDIPUS. Indeed, I fear no other hope is left me.   310
IOCASTÊ. What do you hope from him when he comes?
OEDIPUS.   This much:
     If his account of the murder tallies with yours,
     Then I am cleared.
IOCASTÊ.   What was it that I said
     Of such importance?
OEDIPUS.   Why, "marauders," you said,
     Killed the King, according to this man's story.   315
     If he maintains that still, if there were several,
     Clearly the guilt is not mine: I was alone.
     But if he says one man, singlehanded, did it,
     Then the evidence all points to me.
IOCASTÊ. You may be sure that he said there were several;   320
     And can he call back that story now? He cannot.
     The whole city heard it as plainly as I.
     But suppose he alters some detail of it:
     He cannot ever show that Laïos' death
     Fulfilled the oracle: for Apollo said   325
     My child was doomed to kill him; and my child—
     Poor baby!—it was my child that died first.

No. From now on, where oracles are concerned,
     I would not waste a second thought on any.
OEDIPUS. You may be right.
                 But come: let someone go   330

For the shepherd at once. This matter must be settled.
IOCASTÊ. I will send for him.
I would not wish to cross you in anything,
And surely not in this.—Let us go in.

Exeunt into the palace.

ODE II

Strophe 1

CHORUS. Let me be reverent in the ways of right,
   Lowly the paths I journey on;
   Let all my words and actions keep
   The laws of the pure universe
   From highest Heaven handed down.   5
   For Heaven is their bright nurse,
   Those generations of the realms of light;
   Ah, never of mortal kind were they begot,
   Nor are they slaves of memory, lost in sleep:
   Their Father is greater than Time, and ages not.   10

Antistrophe 1

   The tyrant is a child of Pride
   Who drinks from his great sickening cup
   Recklessness and vanity,
   Until from his high crest headlong
   He plummets to the dust of hope.   15
   That strong man is not strong.
   But let no fair ambition be denied;
   May God protect the wrestler for the State
   In government, in comely policy,
   Who will fear God, and on His ordinance wait.   20

Strophe 2

   Haughtiness and the high hand of disdain
   Tempt and outrage God's holy law;
   And any mortal who dares hold
   No immortal Power in awe
   Will be caught up in a net of pain: 25
   The price for which his levity is sold.
   Let each man take due earnings, then,
   And keep his hands from holy things,
   And from blasphemy stand apart—

Else the crackling blast of heaven
Blows on his head, and on his desperate heart;   30
Though fools will honor impious men,
In their cities no tragic poet sings.

Antistrophe 2

Shall we lose faith in Delphi's obscurities,
We who have heard the world's core   35
Discredited, and the sacred wood
Of Zeus at Elis praised no more?
The deeds and the strange prophecies
Must make a pattern yet to be understood.
Zeus, if indeed you are lord of all,   40
Throned in light over night and day,
Mirror this in your endless mind:
Our masters call the oracle
Words on the wind, and the Delphic vision blind!
Their hearts no longer know Apollo,   45
And reverence for the gods has died away.

SCENE III

Enter IOCASTÊ.

IOCASTÊ. Princes of Thebes, it has occurred to me
To visit the altars of the gods, bearing
These branches as a suppliant, and this incense.
Our King is not himself: his noble soul
Is overwrought with fantasies of dread,   5
Else he would consider
The new prophecies in the light of the old.
He will listen to any voice that speaks disaster,
And my advice goes for nothing.
          She approaches the altar, right.
               To you, then, Apollo,
Lycean lord, since you are nearest, I turn in prayer.   10
Receive these offerings, and grant us deliverance
From defilement. Our hearts are heavy with fear
When we see our leader distracted, as helpless sailors
Are terrified by the confusion of their helmsman.

Enter MESSENGER.

MESSENGER. Friends, no doubt you can direct me: 15
　Where shall I find the house of Oedipus,
　Or, better still, where is the King himself?
CHORAGOS. It is this very place, stranger; he is inside.
　This is his wife and mother of his children.
MESSENGER. I wish her happiness in a happy house,   20
　Blest in all the fulfillment of her marriage.
IOCASTÊ. I wish as much for you: your courtesy
　Deserves a like good fortune. But now, tell me:
　Why have you come? What have you to say to us?
MESSENGER. Good news, my lady, for your house and your husband.
IOCASTÊ. What news? Who sent you here?
MESSENGER.   I am from Corinth.
　The news I bring ought to mean joy for you,
　Though it may be you will find some grief in it.
IOCASTÊ. What is it? How can it touch us in both ways?
MESSENGER. The people of Corinth, they say,   30
　Intend to call Oedipus to be their king.
IOCASTÊ. But old Polybos—is he not reigning still?
MESSENGER. No. Death holds him in his sepulchre.
IOCASTÊ. What are you saying? Polybos is dead?
MESSENGER. If I am not telling the truth, may I die myself.   35
IOCASTÊ (*to a* MAIDSERVANT). Go in, go quickly; tell this to your master.

　O riddlers of God's will, where are you now!
　This was the man whom Oedipus, long ago,
　Feared so, fled so, in dread of destroying him—
　But it was another fate by which he died.   40

Enter OEDIPUS, *center.*

OEDIPUS. Dearest Iocastê, why have you sent for me?
IOCASTÊ. Listen to what this man says, and then tell me
　What has become of the solemn prophecies.
OEDIPUS. Who is this man? What is his news for me?
IOCASTÊ. He has come from Corinth to announce your father's death!   45
OEDIPUS. Is it true, stranger? Tell me in your own words.
MESSENGER. I cannot say it more clearly: the King is dead.
OEDIPUS. Was it by treason? Or by an attack of illness?
MESSENGER. A little thing brings old men to their rest.
OEDIPUS. It was sickness, then?
MESSENGER.   Yes, and his many years.   50
OEDIPUS. Ah!
　Why should a man respect the Pythian hearth,° or
　Give heed to the birds that jangle above his head?

---

[52] **Pythian hearth** *Delphi, also called Pytho because a large dragon, the Python, had guarded the chasm at Delphi until Apollo killed it and established his oracle on the site.*

They prophesied that I should kill Polybos,
Kill my own father; but he is dead and buried,   55
And I am here—I never touched him, never,
Unless he died in grief for my departure,
And thus, in a sense, through me. No. Polybos
Has packed the oracles off with him underground.
They are empty words.

IOCASTÊ.   Had I not told you so?   60

OEDIPUS. You had; it was my faint heart that betrayed me.

IOCASTÊ. From now on never think of those things again.

OEDIPUS. And yet—must I not fear my mother's bed?

IOCASTÊ. Why should anyone in this world be afraid,
Since Fate rules us and nothing can be foreseen?   65
A man should live only for the present day.
Have no more fear of sleeping with your mother:
How many men, in dreams, have lain with their mothers!
No reasonable man is troubled by such things.

OEDIPUS. That is true; only—   70
If only my mother were not still alive!
But she is alive. I cannot help my dread.

IOCASTÊ. Yet this news of your father's death is wonderful.

OEDIPUS. Wonderful. But I fear the living woman.

MESSENGER. Tell me, who is this woman that you fear?   75

OEDIPUS. It is Meropê, man; the wife of King Polybos.

MESSENGER. Meropê? Why should you be afraid of her?

OEDIPUS. An oracle of the gods, a dreadful saying.

MESSENGER. Can you tell me about it or are you sworn to silence?

OEDIPUS. I can tell you, and I will.   80
Apollo said through his prophet that I was the man
Who should marry his own mother, shed his father's blood
With his own hands. And so, for all these years
I have kept clear of Corinth, and no harm has come—
Though it would have been sweet to see my parents again.   85

MESSENGER. And is this the fear that drove you out of Corinth?

OEDIPUS. Would you have me kill my father?

MESSENGER.   As for that
You must be reassured by the news I gave you.

OEDIPUS. If you could reassure me, I would reward you.

MESSENGER. I had that in mind, I will confess: I thought   90
I could count on you when you returned to Corinth.

OEDIPUS. No: I will never go near my parents again.

MESSENGER. Ah, son, you still do not know what you are doing—

OEDIPUS. What do you mean? In the name of God tell me!

MESSENGER.—If these are your reasons for not going home.   95

OEDIPUS. I tell you, I fear the oracle may come true.

MESSENGER. And guilt may come upon you through your parents?

OEDIPUS. That is the dread that is always in my heart.

MESSENGER. Can you not see that all your fears are groundless?
OEDIPUS. How can you say that? They are my parents, surely? 100
MESSENGER. Polybos was not your father.
OEDIPUS.   Not my father?
MESSENGER. No more your father than the man speaking to you.
OEDIPUS. But you are nothing to me!
MESSENGER.   Neither was he.
OEDIPUS. Then why did he call me son?
MESSENGER.   I will tell you:
  Long ago he had you from my hands, as a gift. 105
OEDIPUS. Then how could he love me so, if I was not his?
MESSENGER. He had no children, and his heart turned to you.
OEDIPUS. What of you? Did you buy me? Did you find me by chance?
MESSENGER. I came upon you in the crooked pass of Kithairon.
OEDIPUS. And what were you doing there?
MESSENGER.   Tending my flocks. 110
OEDIPUS. A wandering shepherd?
MESSENGER.   But your savior, son, that day.
OEDIPUS. From what did you save me?
MESSENGER.   Your ankles should tell you that.
OEDIPUS. Ah, stranger, why do you speak of that childhood pain?
MESSENGER. I cut the bonds that tied your ankles together.
OEDIPUS. I have had the mark as long as I can remember. 115
MESSENGER. That was why you were given the name you bear.°
OEDIPUS. God! Was it my father or my mother who did it?
  Tell me!
MESSENGER. I do not know. The man who gave you to me
  Can tell you better than I. 120
OEDIPUS. It was not you that found me, but another?
MESSENGER. It was another shepherd gave you to me.
OEDIPUS. Who was he? Can you tell me who he was?
MESSENGER. I think he was said to be one of Laïos' people.
OEDIPUS. You mean the Laïos who was king here years ago? 125
MESSENGER. Yes; King Laïos; and the man was one of his herdsmen.
OEDIPUS. Is he still alive? Can I see him?
MESSENGER.   These men here
  Know best about such things.
OEDIPUS.   Does anyone here
  Know this shepherd that he is talking about?
  Have you seen him in the fields, or in the town? 130
  If you have, tell me. It is time things were made plain.
CHORAGOS. I think the man he means is that same shepherd
  You have already asked to see. Iocastê perhaps
  Could tell you something.
OEDIPUS.   Do you know anything

---

[116]*name you bear*   *"Oedipus" means "swollen-foot."*

About him, Lady? Is he the man we have summoned?   135
Is that the man this shepherd means?
IOCASTÊ.   Why think of him?
Forget this herdsman. Forget it all.
This talk is a waste of time.
OEDIPUS.   How can you say that,
When the clues to my true birth are in my hands?
IOCASTÊ. For God's love, let us have no more questioning!   140
Is your life nothing to you?
My own is pain enough for me to bear.
OEDIPUS. You need not worry. Suppose my mother a slave,
And born of slaves: no baseness can touch you.
IOCASTÊ. Listen to me, I beg you: do not do this thing!   145
OEDIPUS. I will not listen; the truth must be made known.
IOCASTÊ. Everything that I say is for your own good!
OEDIPUS.   My own good
Snaps my patience, then: I want none of it.
IOCASTÊ. You are fatally wrong! May you never learn who you are!
OEDIPUS. Go, one of you, and bring the shepherd here.   150
Let us leave this woman to brag of her royal name.
IOCASTÊ. Ah, miserable!
That is the only word I have for you now.
That is the only word I can ever have.

Exit into the palace.

CHORAGOS. Why has she left us, Oedipus? Why has she gone   155
In such a passion of sorrow? I fear this silence:
Something dreadful may come of it.
OEDIPUS.   Let it come!
However base my birth, I must know about it.
The Queen, like a woman, is perhaps ashamed
To think of my low origin. But I   160
Am a child of luck; I cannot be dishonored.
Luck is my mother; the passing months, my brothers,
Have seen me rich and poor.
                          If this is so,
How could I wish that I were someone else?
How could I not be glad to know my birth?   165

ODE III

Strophe

CHORUS. If ever the coming time were known
To my heart's pondering,

Kithairon, now by Heaven I see the torches
At the festival of the next full moon,
And see the dance, and hear the choir sing   5
A grace to your gentle shade:
Mountain where Oedipus was found,
O mountain guard of a noble race!
May the god who heals us lend his aid,
And let that glory come to pass   10
For our king's cradling-ground.

Antistrophe

Of the nymphs that flower beyond the years,
Who bore you, royal child,
To Pan of the hills or the timberline Apollo,
Cold in delight where the upland clears,   15
Or Hermês for whom Kyllenê's heights° are piled?
Or flushed as evening cloud,
Great Dionysos, roamer of mountains,
He—was it he who found you there,
And caught you up in his own proud   20
Arms from the sweet god-ravisher
Who laughed by the Muses' fountains?

SCENE IV

OEDIPUS. Sirs: though I do not know the man,
I think I see him coming, this shepherd we want:
He is old, like our friend here, and the men
Bringing him seem to be servants of my house.
But you can tell, if you have ever seen him.   5

Enter SHEPHERD *escorted by servants.*

CHORAGOS. I know him, he was Laïos' man. You can trust him.
OEDIPUS. Tell me first, you from Corinth: is this the shepherd
We were discussing?
MESSENGER.   This is the very man.
OEDIPUS *(to* SHEPHERD*).* Come here. No, look at me. You must answer
Everything I ask.—You belonged to Laïos?   10
SHEPHERD. Yes: born his slave, brought up in his house.
OEDIPUS. Tell me: what kind of work did you do for him?
SHEPHERD. I was a shepherd of his, most of my life.
OEDIPUS. Where mainly did you go for pasturage?

[16] *Kyllenê's heights   holy mountain, birthplace of Hermes, messenger of the gods.*

SHEPHERD. Sometimes Kithairon, sometimes the hills near-by.   15
OEDIPUS. Do you remember ever seeing this man out there?
SHEPHERD. What would he be doing there? This man?
OEDIPUS. This man standing here. Have you ever seen him before?
SHEPHERD. No. At least, not to my recollection.
MESSENGER. And that is not strange, my lord. But I'll refresh   20
    His memory: he must remember when we two
    Spent three whole seasons together, March to September,
    On Kithairon or thereabouts. He had two flocks;
    I had one. Each autumn I'd drive mine home
    And he would go back with his to Laïos' sheepfold.—   25
    Is this not true, just as I have described it?
SHEPHERD. True, yes; but it was all so long ago.
MESSENGER. Well, then: do you remember, back in those days
    That you gave me a baby boy to bring up as my own?
SHEPHERD. What if I did? What are you trying to say?   30
MESSENGER. King Oedipus was once that little child.
SHEPHERD. Damn you, hold your tongue!
OEDIPUS.   No more of that!
    It is your tongue needs watching, not this man's.
SHEPHERD. My King, my Master, what is it I have done wrong?
OEDIPUS. You have not answered his question about the boy.   35
SHEPHERD. He does not know . . . He is only making trouble . . .
OEDIPUS. Come, speak plainly, or it will go hard with you.
SHEPHERD. In God's name, do not torture an old man!
OEDIPUS. Come here, one of you; bind his arms behind him.
SHEPHERD. Unhappy king! What more do you wish to learn?   40
OEDIPUS. Did you give this man the child he speaks of?
SHEPHERD.   I did.
    And I would to God I had died that very day.
OEDIPUS. You will die now unless you speak the truth.
SHEPHERD. Yet if I speak the truth, I am worse than dead.
OEDIPUS. Very well; since you insist upon delaying—   45
SHEPHERD. No! I have told you already that I gave him the boy.
OEDIPUS. Where did you get him? From your house? From somewhere else?
    From somewhere else?
SHEPHERD. Not from mine, no. A man gave him to me.
OEDIPUS. Is that man here? Do you know whose slave he was?
SHEPHERD. For God's love, my King, do not ask me any more!   50
OEDIPUS. You are a dead man if I have to ask you again.
SHEPHERD. Then . . . Then the child was from the palace of Laïos.
OEDIPUS. A slave child? or a child of his own line?
SHEPHERD. Ah, I am on the brink of dreadful speech!
OEDIPUS. And I of dreadful hearing. Yet I must hear.   55
SHEPHERD. If you must be told, then . . .
                             They said it was Laïos' child,
    But it is your wife who can tell you about that.

OEDIPUS. My wife!—Did she give it to you?
SHEPHERD.   My lord, she did.
OEDIPUS. Do you know why?
SHEPHERD.   I was told to get rid of it.
OEDIPUS. An unspeakable mother!
SHEPHERD.   There had been prophecies . . .   60
OEDIPUS. Tell me.
SHEPHERD.   It was said that the boy would kill his own father.
OEDIPUS. Then why did you give him over to this old man?
SHEPHERD. I pitied the baby, my King.
   And I thought that this man would take him far away
   To his own country.
                    He saved him—but for what a fate!   65
   For if you are what this man says you are,
   No man living is more wretched than Oedipus.
OEDIPUS. Ah God!
   It was true!
            All the prophecies!
                         —Now,
   O Light, may I look on you for the last time!   70
   I, Oedipus,
   Oedipus, damned in his birth, in his marriage damned,
   Damned in the blood he shed with his own hand!

                    He rushes into the palace.

                         ODE IV

Strophe 1

CHORUS. Alas for the seed of men.
   What measure shall I give these generations
   That breathe on the void and are void
   And exist and do not exist?

   Who bears more weight of joy   5
   Than mass of sunlight shifting in images,
   Or who shall make his thought stay on
   That down time drifts away?

   Your splendor is all fallen.

   O naked brow of wrath and tears,   10
   O change of Oedipus!
   I who saw your days call no man blest—
   Your great days like ghósts góne.

Antistrophe 1

> That mind was a strong bow.
> Deep, how deep you drew it then, hard archer,   15
> At a dim fearful range,
> And brought dear glory down!
>
> You overcame the stranger—
> The virgin with her hooking lion claws—
> And though death sang, stood like a tower   20
> To make pale Thebes take heart.
>
> Fortress against our sorrow!
>
> Divine king, giver of laws,
> Majestic Oedipus!
> No prince in Thebes had ever such renown,   25
> No prince won such grace of power.

Strophe 2

> And now of all men ever known
> Most pitiful is this man's story:
> His fortunes are most changed, his state
> Fallen to a low slave's   30
> Ground under bitter fate.
>
> O Oedipus, most royal one!
> The great door that expelled you to the light
> Gave at night—ah, gave night to your glory:
> As to the father, to the fathering son.   35
>
> All understood too late.
>
> How could that queen whom Laïos won,
> The garden that he harrowed at his height,
> Be silent when that act was done?

Antistrophe 2

> But all eyes fail before time's eye,   40
> All actions come to justice there.
> Though never willed, though far down the deep past,
> Your bed, your dread sirings,
> Are brought to book at last.
> Child by Laïos doomed to die,   45
> Then doomed to lose that fortunate little death,

Would God you never took breath in this air
That with my wailing lips I take to cry:

For I weep the world's outcast.

I was blind, and now I can tell why: 50
Asleep, for you had given ease of breath
To Thebes, while the false years went by.

EXODOS

Enter, from the palace, SECOND MESSENGER.

SECOND MESSENGER. Elders of Thebes, most honored in this land,
  What horrors are yours to see and hear, what weight
  Of sorrow to be endured, if, true to your birth,
  You venerate the line of Labdakos!
  I think neither Istros nor Phasis, those great rivers,   5
  Could purify this place of the corruption
  It shelters now, or soon must bring to light—
  Evil not done unconsciously, but willed.

The greatest griefs are those we cause ourselves.
CHORAGOS. Surely, friend, we have grief enough already;   10
  What new sorrow do you mean?
SECOND MESSENGER.   The Queen is dead.
CHORAGOS. Iocastê? Dead? But at whose hand?
SECOND MESSENGER.   Her own.
  The full horror of what happened you cannot know,
  For you did not see it; but I, who did, will tell you
  As clearly as I can how she met her death.   15

When she had left us,
  In passionate silence, passing through the court,
  She ran to her apartment in the house,
  Her hair clutched by the fingers of both hands.
  She closed the doors behind her; then, by that bed   20
  Where long ago the fatal son was conceived—
  That son who should bring about his father's death—
  We heard her call upon Laïos, dead so many years,
  And heard her wail for the double fruit of her marriage,
  A husband by her husband, children by her child.   25

Exactly how she died I do not know:
  For Oedipus burst in moaning and would not let us

Keep vigil to the end: it was by him
As he stormed about the room that our eyes were caught.
From one to another of us he went, begging a sword,   30
Cursing the wife who was not his wife, the mother
Whose womb had carried his own children and himself.
I do not know: it was none of us aided him,
But surely one of the gods was in control!
For with a dreadful cry   35
He hurled his weight, as though wrenched out of himself,
At the twin doors: the bolts gave, and he rushed in.
And there we saw her hanging, her body swaying
From the cruel cord she had noosed about her neck.
A great sob broke from him heartbreaking to hear,   40
As he loosed the rope and lowered her to the ground.

I would blot out from my mind what happened next!
For the King ripped from her gown the golden brooches
That were her ornament, and raised them, and plunged them down
Straight into his own eyeballs, crying, "No more,   45
No more shall you look on the misery about me,
The horrors of my own doing! Too long you have known
The faces of those whom I should never have seen,
Too long been blind to those for whom I was searching!
From this hour, go in darkness!" And as he spoke,   50
He struck at his eyes—not once, but many times;
And the blood spattered his beard,
Bursting from his ruined sockets like red hail.

So from the unhappiness of two this evil has sprung,
A curse on the man and woman alike. The old   55
Happiness of the house of Labdakos
Was happiness enough: where is it today?
It is all wailing and ruin, disgrace, death—all
The misery of mankind that has a name—
And it is wholly and for ever theirs.   60
CHORAGOS. Is he in agony still? Is there no rest for him?
SECOND MESSENGER. He is calling for someone to lead him to the gates
So that all the children of Kadmos may look upon
His father's murderer, his mother's—no,
I cannot say it!
              And then he will leave Thebes,   65
Self-exiled, in order that the curse
Which he himself pronounced may depart from the house.
He is weak, and there is none to lead him,
So terrible is his suffering.
              But you will see:

Look, the doors are opening; in a moment 70
You will see a thing that would crush a heart of stone.

The central door is opened; OEDIPUS, *blinded, is led in.*

CHORAGOS. Dreadful indeed for men to see.
Never have my own eyes
Looked on a sight so full of fear.

Oedipus! 75
What madness came upon you, what daemon
Leaped on your life with heavier
Punishment than a mortal man can bear?
No: I cannot even
Look at you, poor ruined one. 80
And I would speak, question, ponder,
If I were able. No.
You make me shudder.
OEDIPUS. God. God.
Is there a sorrow greater? 85
Where shall I find harbor in this world?
My voice is hurled far on a dark wind.
What has God done to me?
CHORAGOS. Too terrible to think of, or to see.

Strophe 1

OEDIPUS. O cloud of night, 90
Never to be turned away: night coming on,
I cannot tell how: night like a shroud!
My fair winds brought me here.
                          Oh God. Again
The pain of the spikes where I had sight,
The flooding pain 95
Of memory, never to be gouged out.
CHORAGOS. This is not strange.
You suffer it all twice over, remorse in pain,
Pain in remorse.

Antistrophe 1

OEDIPUS. Ah dear friend 100
Are you faithful even yet, you alone?
Are you still standing near me, will you stay here,
Patient, to care for the blind?
                          The blind man!
Yet even blind I know who it is attends me,

By the voice's tone—   105
Though my new darkness hide the comforter.
CHORAGOS. Oh fearful act!
   What god was it drove you to rake black
   Night across your eyes?

Strophe 2

OEDIPUS. Apollo. Apollo. Dear   110
   Children, the god was Apollo.
   He brought my sick, sick fate upon me.
   But the blinding hand was my own!
   How could I bear to see
   When all my sight was horror everywhere?   115
CHORAGOS. Everywhere; that is true.
OEDIPUS. And now what is left?
   Images? Love? A greeting even,
   Sweet to the senses? Is there anything?
   Ah, no, friends: lead me away.   120
   Lead me away from Thebes.
                              Lead the great wreck
   And hell of Oedipus, whom the gods hate.
CHORAGOS. Your fate is clear, you are not blind to that.
   Would God you had never found it out!

Antistrophe 2

OEDIPUS. Death take the man who unbound   125
   My feet on that hillside
   And delivered me from death to life! What life?
   If only I had died,
   This weight of monstrous doom
   Could not have dragged me and my darlings down.   130
CHORAGOS. I would have wished the same.
OEDIPUS. Oh never to have come here
   With my father's blood upon me! Never
   To have been the man they call his mother's husband!
   Oh accurst! Oh child of evil,   135
   To have entered that wretched bed—
                              the selfsame one!
   More primal than sin itself, this fell to me.
CHORAGOS. I do not know how I can answer you.
   You were better dead than alive and blind.
OEDIPUS. Do not counsel me any more. This punishment   140
   That I have laid upon myself is just.
   If I had eyes,
   I do not know how I could bear the sight

Of my father, when I came to the house of Death,
Or my mother: for I have sinned against them both   145
So vilely that I could not make my peace
By strangling my own life.
                              Or do you think my children,
Born as they were born, would be sweet to my eyes?
Ah never, never! Nor this town with its high walls,
Nor the holy images of the gods.
                              For I,   150
Thrice miserable—Oedipus, noblest of all the line
Of Kadmos, have condemned myself to enjoy
These things no more, by my own malediction
Expelling that man whom the gods declared
To be a defilement in the house of Laïos.   155
After exposing the rankness of my own guilt,
How could I look men frankly in the eyes?
No, I swear it,
If I could have stifled my hearing at its source,
I would have done it and made all this body   160
A tight cell of misery, blank to light and sound:
So I should have been safe in a dark agony
Beyond all recollection.
                              Ah Kithairon!
Why did you shelter me? When I was cast upon you,
Why did I not die? Then I should never   165
Have shown the world my execrable birth.

Ah Polybos! Corinth, city that I believed
The ancient seat of my ancestors: how fair
I seemed, your child! And all the while this evil
Was cancerous within me!
                              For I am sick   170
In my daily life, sick in my origin.

O three roads, dark ravine, woodland and way
Where three roads met you, drinking my father's blood,
My own blood, spilled by my own hand: can you remember
The unspeakable things I did there, and the things   175
I went on from there to do?
                              O marriage, marriage!
The act that engendered me, and again the act
Performed by the son in the same bed—
                              Ah, the net
Of incest, mingling fathers, brothers, sons,
With brides, wives, mothers: the last evil   180
That can be known by men: no tongue can say
How evil!

No. For the love of God, conceal me
Somewhere far from Thebes; or kill me; or hurl me
Into the sea, away from men's eyes for ever.
Come, lead me. You need not fear to touch me.   185
Of all men, I alone can bear this guilt.

Enter CREON.

CHORAGOS. We are not the ones to decide; but Creon here
    May fitly judge of what you ask. He only
    Is left to protect the city in your place.
OEDIPUS. Alas, how can I speak to him? What right have I   190
    To beg his courtesy whom I have deeply wronged?
CREON. I have not come to mock you, Oedipus,
    Or to reproach you, either.
                    (To ATTENDANTS.*)*
                —You, standing there:
    If you have lost all respect for man's dignity,
    At least respect the flame of Lord Helios: 195
    Do not allow this pollution to show itself
    Openly here, an affront to the earth
    And Heaven's rain and the light of day. No, take him
    Into the house as quickly as you can.
    For it is proper   200
    That only the close kindred see his grief.
OEDIPUS. I pray you in God's name, since your courtesy
    Ignores my dark expectation, visiting
    With mercy this man of all men most execrable:
    Give me what I ask—for your good, not for mine.   205
CREON. And what is it that you would have me do?
OEDIPUS. Drive me out of this country as quickly as may be
    To a place where no human voice can ever greet me.
CREON. I should have done that before now—only,
    God's will had not been wholly revealed to me.   210
OEDIPUS. But his command is plain: the parricide
    Must be destroyed. I am that evil man.
CREON. That is the sense of it, yes; but as things are,
    We had best discover clearly what is to be done.
OEDIPUS. You would learn more about a man like me?   215
CREON. You are ready now to listen to the god.
OEDIPUS. I will listen. But it is to you
    That I must turn for help. I beg you, hear me.

The woman in there—
Give her whatever funeral you think proper: 220
She is your sister.
                —But let me go, Creon!
Let me purge my father's Thebes of the pollution

Of my living here, and go out to the wild hills,
To Kithairon, that has won such fame with me,
The tomb my mother and father appointed for me,   225
And let me die there, as they willed I should.
And yet I know
Death will not ever come to me through sickness
Or in any natural way: I have been preserved
For some unthinkable fate. But let that be.   230
As for my sons, you need not care for them.
They are men, they will find some way to live.
But my poor daughters, who have shared my table,
Who never before have been parted from their father—
Take care of them, Creon; do this for me.   235
And will you let me touch them with my hands
A last time, and let us weep together?
Be kind, my lord,
Great prince, be kind!

            Could I but touch them,
They would be mine again, as when I had my eyes.   240

       Enter ANTIGONÊ *and* ISMENÊ, *attended.*

Ah, God!
Is it my dearest children I hear weeping?
Has Creon pitied me and sent my daughters?
CREON. Yes, Oedipus: I knew that they were dear to you
    In the old days, and know you must love them still.   245
OEDIPUS. May God bless you for this—and be a friendlier
    Guardian to you than he has been to me!

Children, where are you?
Come quickly to my hands: they are your brother's—
Hands that have brought your father's once clear eyes   250
To this way of seeing—
              Ah dearest ones,
I had neither sight nor knowledge then, your father
By the woman who was the source of his own life!
And I weep for you—having no strength to see you—,
I weep for you when I think of the bitterness   255
That men will visit upon you all your lives.
What homes, what festivals can you attend
Without being forced to depart again in tears?
And when you come to marriageable age,
Where is the man, my daughters, who would dare   260
Risk the bane that lies on all my children?
Is there any evil wanting? Your father killed
His father; sowed the womb of her who bore him;
Engendered you at the fount of his own existence!

That is what they will say of you.

                     Then, whom   265
Can you ever marry? There are no bridegrooms for you,
And your lives must wither away in sterile dreaming.
O Creon, son of Menoikeus!
You are the only father my daughters have,
Since we, their parents, are both of us gone for ever.   270
They are your own blood: you will not let them
Fall into beggary and loneliness;
You will keep them from the miseries that are mine!
Take pity on them; see, they are only children,
Friendless except for you. Promise me this,   275
Great Prince, and give me your hand in token of it.

                CREON *clasps his right hand.*

Children:
I could say much, if you could understand me,
But as it is, I have only this prayer for you:
Live where you can, be as happy as you can—   280
Happier, please God, than God has made your father!

CREON. Enough. You have wept enough. Now go within.

OEDIPUS. I must; but it is hard.

CREON.   Time eases all things.

OEDIPUS. But you must promise—

CREON.   Say what you desire.

OEDIPUS. Send me from Thebes!

CREON.   God grant that I may!   285

OEDIPUS. But since God hates me . . .

CREON.   No, he will grant your wish.

OEDIPUS. You promise?

CREON.   I cannot speak beyond my knowledge.

OEDIPUS. Then lead me in.

CREON.   Come now, and leave your children.

OEDIPUS. No! Do not take them from me!

CREON.   Think no longer
That you are in command here, but rather think   290
How, when you were, you served your own destruction.

Exeunt into the house all but the CHORUS; *the* CHORAGOS *chants directly to the audience.*

CHORAGOS. Men of Thebes: look upon Oedipus.
This is the king who solved the famous riddle
And towered up, most powerful of men
No mortal eyes but looked on him with envy.   295
Yet in the end ruin swept over him.
Let every man in mankind's frailty
Consider his last day; and let none

Presume on his good fortune until he find
Life, at his death, a memory without pain. 300

QUESTIONS

1. What makes Oedipus a tragic hero? What makes his predicament fascinating rather than merely horrifying? Account for the continued appeal of the play.
2. Evaluate Oedipus' actions. Is he to blame for what happens? Account for his change of attitude and manner by comparing his speech and behavior in the opening and closing scenes. What is your impression of Oedipus at these points?
3. Identify and explain the different types of irony in *Oedipus Rex*. (For a discussion of irony see pages 75–77.)
4. How is the imagery of light and darkness employed throughout the play? How is it related to Oedipus' blindness?
5. What roles do the chorus and choragos assume? Compare their functions in the beginning, middle, and end of the play.
6. Rather than dramatize on stage the shocking and horrible events in which the play culminates, Sophocles has them occur offstage, and we learn about them through a messenger's report. What are the limitations and advantages of such a method?
7. Iocastê appears a number of times, but she has little to say. What is she like? How much do we know about her—especially her thoughts and feelings? Read Ruth Eisenberg's poem "Jocasta" (pages 364–372) and compare Eisenberg's characterization of Iocastê with Sophocles' in *Oedipus Rex*.

SOPHOCLES

[*496?–406 B.C.*]

Antigonê

AN ENGLISH VERSION BY DUDLEY FITTS AND ROBERT FITZGERALD

CHARACTERS

ANTIGONÊ
ISMENÊ
EURYDICÊ
CREON

HAIMON
TEIRESIAS
A SENTRY
A MESSENGER
CHORUS

Scene. *Before the palace of* CREON, *King of Thebes. A central double door, and two lateral doors. A platform extends the length of the façade, and from this platform three steps lead down into the "orchestra," or chorus-ground.*

Time. *Dawn of the day after the repulse of the Argive army from the assault on Thebes.*

PROLOGUE

ANTIGONÊ *and* ISMENÊ *enter from the central door of the palace.*

ANTIGONÊ. Ismenê, dear sister,
  You would think that we had already suffered enough
  For the curse on Oedipus.°
  I cannot imagine any grief
  That you and I have not gone through. And now—   5
  Have they told you of the new decree of our King Creon?
ISMENÊ. I have heard nothing: I know
  That two sisters lost two brothers, a double death
  In a single hour; and I know that the Argive army
  Fled in the night; but beyond this, nothing.   10
ANTIGONÊ. I thought so. And that is why I wanted you
  To come out here with me. There is something we must do.
ISMENÊ. Why do you speak so strangely?
ANTIGONÊ. Listen, Ismenê:
  Creon buried our brother Eteoclês   15
  With military honors, gave him a soldier's funeral,
  And it was right that he should; but Polyneicês,
  Who fought as bravely and died as miserably,—
  They say that Creon has sworn
  No one shall bury him, no one mourn for him,   20
  But his body must lie in the fields, a sweet treasure
  For carrion birds to find as they search for food.
  That is what they say, and our good Creon is coming here

³**Oedipus,** *former King of Thebes, father of Antigonê and Ismenê, and of Polyneicês and Eteoclês, their brothers. Oedipus unwittingly killed his father, Laïos, and married his mother, Iocastê. When he learned what he had done, he blinded himself and left Thebes. Eteoclês and Polyneicês quarreled; Polyneicês was defeated but returned to assault Thebes. Both brothers were killed in the battle; Creon ordered that Polyneicês remain unburied.*

To announce it publicly; and the penalty—
Stoning to death in the public square!

There it is,

And now you can prove what you are:
A true sister, or a traitor to your family.

ISMENÊ. Antigonê, you are mad! What could I possibly do?

ANTIGONÊ. You must decide whether you will help me or not.

ISMENÊ. I do not understand you. Help you in what?

ANTIGONÊ. Ismenê, I am going to bury him. Will you come?

ISMENÊ. Bury him! You have just said the new law forbids it.

ANTIGONÊ. He is my brother. And he is your brother, too.

ISMENÊ. But think of the danger! Think what Creon will do!

ANTIGONÊ. Creon is not strong enough to stand in my way.

ISMENÊ. Ah sister!
Oedipus died, everyone hating him
For what his own search brought to light, his eyes
Ripped out by his own hand; and Iocastê died,
His mother and wife at once: she twisted the cords
That strangled her life; and our two brothers died,
Each killed by the other's sword. And we are left:
But oh, Antigonê,
Think how much more terrible than these
Our own death would be if we should go against Creon
And do what he has forbidden! We are only women,
We cannot fight with men, Antigonê!
The law is strong, we must give in to the law
In this thing, and in worse. I beg the Dead
To forgive me, but I am helpless: I must yield
To those in authority. And I think it is dangerous business
To be always meddling.

ANTIGONÊ.   If that is what you think,
I should not want you, even if you asked to come.
You have made your choice, you can be what you want to be.
But I will bury him; and if I must die,
I say that this crime is holy: I shall lie down
With him in death, and I shall be as dear
To him as he to me.

It is the dead,

Not the living, who make the longest demands:
We die for ever . . .

You may do as you like,

Since apparently the laws of the gods mean nothing to you.

ISMENÊ. They mean a great deal to me; but I have no strength
To break laws that were made for the public good.

ANTIGONÊ. That must be your excuse, I suppose. But as for me,
I will bury the brother I love.

ISMENÊ.   Antigonê,
  I am so afraid for you!
ANTIGONÊ.   You need not be:
  You have yourself to consider, after all.
ISMENÊ. But no one must hear of this, you must tell no one!
  I will keep it a secret, I promise!
ANTIGONÊ.   O tell it! Tell everyone!
  Think how they'll hate you when it all comes out   70
  If they learn that you knew about it all the time!
ISMENÊ. So fiery! You should be cold with fear.
ANTIGONÊ. Perhaps. But I am doing only what I must.
ISMENÊ. But can you do it? I say that you cannot.
ANTIGONÊ. Very well: when my strength gives out,
  I shall do no more.   75
ISMENÊ. Impossible things should not be tried at all.
ANTIGONÊ. Go away, Ismenê:
  I shall be hating you soon, and the dead will too,
  For your words are hateful. Leave me my foolish plan:
  I am not afraid of the danger; if it means death,   80
  It will not be the worst of deaths—death without honor.
ISMENÊ. Go then, if you feel that you must.
  You are unwise,
  But a loyal friend indeed to those who love you.

> *Exit into the palace.* ANTIGONÊ *goes off, left. Enter the* CHORUS.

PÁRODOS

Strophe 1

CHORUS. Now the long blade of the sun, lying
  Level east to west, touches with glory
  Thebes of the Seven Gates. Open, unlidded
  Eye of golden day! O marching light
  Across the eddy and rush of Dircê's stream,°   5
  Striking the white shields of the enemy
  Thrown headlong backward from the blaze of morning!
CHORAGOS.° Polyneicês their commander
  Roused them with windy phrases,
  He the wild eagle screaming   10
  Insults above our land,
  His wings their shields of snow,
  His crest their marshalled helms.

5*Dircê's stream*   *river near Thebes.*   8*Choragos*   *leader of the chorus.*

Antistrophe 1

CHORUS. Against our seven gates in a yawning ring
    The famished spears came onward in the night;   15
    But before his jaws were sated with our blood,
    Or pinefire took the garland of our towers,
    He was thrown back; and as he turned, great Thebes—
    No tender victim for his noisy power—
    Rose like a dragon behind him, shouting war.   20
CHORAGOS. For God hates utterly
    The bray of bragging tongues;
    And when he beheld their smiling,
    Their swagger of golden helms,
    The frown of his thunder blasted   25
    Their first man from our walls.

Strophe 2

CHORUS. We heard his shout of triumph high in the air
    Turn to a scream; far out in a flaming arc
    He fell with his windy torch, and the earth struck him.
    And others storming in fury no less than his   30
    Found shock of death in the dusty joy of battle.
CHORAGOS. Seven captains at seven gates
    Yielded their clanging arms to the god
    That bends the battle-line and breaks it.
    These two only, brothers in blood,   35
    Face to face in matchless rage,
    Mirroring each the other's death,
    Clashed in long combat.

Antistrophe 2

CHORUS. But now in the beautiful morning of victory
    Let Thebes of the many chariots sing for joy!   40
    With hearts for dancing we'll take leave of war:
    Our temples shall be sweet with hymns of praise,
    And the long nights shall echo with our chorus.

SCENE I

CHORAGOS. But now at last our new King is coming:
    Creon of Thebes, Menoikeus' son.
    In this auspicious dawn of his reign
    What are the new complexities

That shifting Fate has woven for him?   5
What is his counsel? Why has he summoned
The old men to hear him?

Enter CREON *from the palace, center. He addresses the* CHORUS *from the top step.*

CREON. Gentlemen: I have the honor to inform you that our Ship of State, which recent storms have threatened to destroy, has come safely to harbor at last, guided by the merciful wisdom of Heaven. I have summoned you 10 here this morning because I know that I can depend upon you: your devotion to King Laïos was absolute; you never hesitated in your duty to our late ruler Oedipus; and when Oedipus died, your loyalty was transferred to his children. Unfortunately, as you know, his two sons, the princes Eteoclês and Polyneicês, have killed each other in battle; and I, as 15 the next in blood, have succeeded to the full power of the throne.

I am aware, of course, that no Ruler can expect complete loyalty from his subjects until he has been tested in office. Nevertheless, I say to you at the very outset that I have nothing but contempt for the kind of Governor who is afraid, for whatever reason, to follow the course that he knows is 20 best for the State; and as for the man who sets private friendship above the public welfare,—I have no use for him, either. I call God to witness that if I saw my country headed for ruin, I should not be afraid to speak out plainly; and I need hardly remind you that I would never have any dealings with an enemy of the people. No one values friendship more 25 highly than I; but we must remember that friends made at the risk of wrecking our Ship are not real friends at all.

These are my principles, at any rate, and that is why I have made the following decision concerning the sons of Oedipus: Eteoclês, who died as a man should die, fighting for his country, is to be buried with full 30 military honors, with all the ceremony that is usual when the greatest heroes die; but his brother Polyneicês, who broke his exile to come back with fire and sword against his native city and the shrines of his fathers' gods, whose one idea was to spill the blood of his blood and sell his own people into slavery—Polyneicês, I say, is to have no burial: no man is to 35 touch him or say the least prayer for him; he shall lie on the plain, unburied; and the birds and the scavenging dogs can do with him whatever they like.

This is my command, and you can see the wisdom behind it. As long as I am King, no traitor is going to be honored with the loyal man. But 40 whoever shows by word and deed that he is on the side of the State,— he shall have my respect while he is living and my reverence when he is dead.

CHORAGOS. If that is your will, Creon son of Menoikeus,
You have the right to enforce it: we are yours.   45
CREON. That is my will. Take care that you do your part.
CHORAGOS. We are old men: let the younger ones carry it out.
CREON. I do not mean that: the sentries have been appointed.
CHORAGOS. Then what is it that you would have us do?

CREON. You will give no support to whoever breaks this law. 50
CHORAGOS. Only a crazy man is in love with death!
CREON. And death it is; yet money talks, and the wisest
　Have sometimes been known to count a few coins too many.

Enter SENTRY *from left.*

SENTRY. I'll not say that I'm out of breath from running, King, because every
time I stopped to think about what I have to tell you, I felt like going 55
　back. And all the time a voice kept saying, "You fool, don't you know
　you're walking straight into trouble?"; and then another voice: "Yes, but
　if you let somebody else get the news to Creon first, it will be even worse
　than that for you!" But good sense won out, at least I hope it was good
　sense, and here I am with a story that makes no sense at all; but I'll tell 60
　it anyhow, because, as they say, what's going to happen's going to happen
　and—
CREON. Come to the point. What have you to say?
SENTRY. I did not do it. I did not see who did it. You must not punish me
　for what someone else has done. 65
CREON. A comprehensive defense! More effective, perhaps,
　If I knew its purpose. Come: what is it?
SENTRY: A dreadful thing . . . I don't know how to put it—
CREON. Out with it!
SENTRY. 　　　　　　Well, then;
　The dead man—
　　　　Polyneicês—

Pause. The SENTRY *is overcome, fumbles for words.* CREON *waits impassively.*

　　　　　　　out there—
　　　　　　　　　　someone,— 70
New dust on the slimy flesh!

Pause. No sign from CREON.

Someone has given it burial that way, and
Gone . . .

Long pause. CREON *finally speaks with deadly control.*

CREON. And the man who dared do this?
SENTRY. 　　　　　　　　　　I swear I
Do not know! You must believe me! 75
　Listen:
The ground was dry, not a sign of digging, no,
Not a wheeltrack in the dust, no trace of anyone.
It was when they relieved us this morning: and one of them,
The corporal, pointed to it.
　　　　　　There it was,
The strangest—
　　　　Look: 80

The body, just mounded over with light dust: you see?
Not buried really, but as if they'd covered it
Just enough for the ghost's peace. And no sign
Of dogs or any wild animal that had been there.
And then what a scene there was! Every man of us   85
Accusing the other: we all proved the other man did it,
We all had proof that we could not have done it.
We were ready to take hot iron in our hands,
Walk through fire, swear by all the gods,
It was not I!   90
I do not know who it was, but it was not I!

CREON's *rage has been mounting steadily, but the* SENTRY *is too intent upon his story to notice it.*

And then, when this came to nothing, someone said
A thing that silenced us and made us stare
Down at the ground: you had to be told the news,
And one of us had to do it! We threw the dice,   95
And the bad luck fell to me. So here I am,
No happier to be here than you are to have me:
Nobody likes the man who brings bad news.
CHORAGOS. I have been wondering, King: can it be that the gods have
     done this?
CREON (*furiously*). Stop!   100
Must you doddering wrecks
Go out of your heads entirely? "The gods"!
Intolerable!
The gods favor this corpse? Why? How had he served them?
Tried to loot their temples, burn their images,   105
Yes, and the whole State, and its laws with it!
Is it your senile opinion that the gods love to honor bad men?
A pious thought!—
                    No, from the very beginning
There have been those who have whispered together,
Stiff-necked anarchists, putting their heads together,   110
Scheming against me in alleys. These are the men,
And they have bribed my own guard to do this thing.
(*Sententiously.*) Money!
There's nothing in the world so demoralizing as money.
Down go your cities,   115
Homes gone, men gone, honest hearts corrupted,
Crookedness of all kinds, and all for money!
                    (*To* SENTRY.)
                                   But you—!
I swear by God and by the throne of God,
The man who has done this thing shall pay for it!

Find that man, bring him here to me, or your death 120
Will be the least of your problems: I'll string you up
Alive, and there will be certain ways to make you
Discover your employer before you die;
And the process may teach you a lesson you seem to have missed:
The dearest profit is sometimes all too dear: 125
That depends on the source. Do you understand me?
A fortune won is often misfortune.
SENTRY. King, may I speak?
CREON.   Your very voice distresses me.
SENTRY. Are you sure that it is my voice, and not your conscience?
CREON. By God, he wants to analyze me now! 130
SENTRY. It is not what I say, but what has been done, that hurts you.
CREON. You talk too much.
SENTRY.   Maybe; but I've done nothing.
CREON. Sold your soul for some silver: that's all you've done.
SENTRY. How dreadful it is when the right judge judges wrong!
CREON. Your figures of speech 135
May entertain you now; but unless you bring me the man,
You will get little profit from them in the end.

Exit CREON *into the palace.*

SENTRY. "Bring me the man"—!
I'd like nothing better than bringing him the man!
But bring him or not, you have seen the last of me here. 140
At any rate, I am safe!

(Exit SENTRY.*)*

ODE I

Strophe 1

CHORUS. Numberless are the world's wonders, but none
More wonderful than man; the stormgray sea
Yields to his prows, the huge crests bear him high;
Earth, holy and inexhaustible, is graven
With shining furrows where his plows have gone 5
Year after year, the timeless labor of stallions.

Antistrophe 1

The lightboned birds and beasts that cling to cover,
The lithe fish lighting their reaches of dim water,
All are taken, tamed in the net of his mind;

The lion on the hill, the wild horse windy-maned,   10
Resign to him; and his blunt yoke has broken
The sultry shoulders of the mountain bull.

Strophe 2

Words also, and thought as rapid as air,
He fashions to his good use; statecraft is his,
And his the skill that deflects the arrows of snow,   15
The spears of winter rain: from every wind
He has made himself secure—from all but one:
In the late wind of death he cannot stand.

Antistrophe 2

O clear intelligence, force beyond all measure!
O fate of man, working both good and evil!   20
When the laws are kept, how proudly his city stands!
When the laws are broken, what of his city then?
Never may the anárchic man find rest at my hearth,
Never be it said that my thoughts are his thoughts.

SCENE II

Reenter SENTRY *leading* ANTIGONÊ.

CHORAGOS. What does this mean? Surely this captive woman
   Is the Princess, Antigonê. Why should she be taken?
SENTRY. Here is the one who did it! We caught her
   In the very act of burying him.—Where is Creon?
CHORAGOS. Just coming from the house.

Enter CREON, *center.*

CREON.   What has happened?   5
   Why have you come back so soon?
SENTRY *(expansively).*   O King,
A man should never be too sure of anything:
I would have sworn
That you'd not see me here again: your anger
Frightened me so, and the things you threatened me with;   10
But how could I tell then
That I'd be able to solve the case so soon?
No dice-throwing this time: I was only too glad to come!
Here is this woman. She is the guilty one:
We found her trying to bury him.   15

Take her, then; question her; judge her as you will.
I am through with the whole thing now, and glad of it.
CREON. But this is Antigonê! Why have you brought her here?
SENTRY. She was burying him, I tell you!
CREON *(severely)*.   Is this the truth?
SENTRY. I saw her with my own eyes. Can I say more?   20
CREON. The details: come, tell me quickly!
SENTRY.   It was like this:
After those terrible threats of yours, King,
We went back and brushed the dust away from the body.
The flesh was soft by now, and stinking,
So we sat on a hill to windward and kept guard.   25
No napping this time! We kept each other awake.
But nothing happened until the white round sun
Whirled in the center of the round sky over us:
Then, suddenly,
A storm of dust roared up from the earth, and the sky   30
Went out, the plain vanished with all its trees
In the stinging dark. We closed our eyes and endured it.
The whirlwind lasted a long time, but it passed;
And then we looked, and there was Antigonê!
I have seen   35
A mother bird come back to a stripped nest, heard
Her crying bitterly a broken note or two
For the young ones stolen. Just so, when this girl
Found the bare corpse, and all her love's work wasted,
She wept, and cried on heaven to damn the hands   40
That had done this thing.
                         And then she brought more dust
And sprinkled wine three times for her brother's ghost.

We ran and took her at once. She was not afraid,
Not even when we charged her with what she had done.
She denied nothing.
                   And this was a comfort to me,   45
And some uneasiness: for it is a good thing
To escape from death, but it is no great pleasure
To bring death to a friend.
                           Yet I always say
There is nothing so comfortable as your own safe skin!
CREON *(slowly, dangerously)*. And you, Antigonê,   50
You with your head hanging,—do you confess this thing?
ANTIGONÊ. I do. I deny nothing.
CREON *(to* SENTRY*)*.   You may go.
                         (Exit SENTRY.*)*
(To ANTIGONÊ*)* Tell me, tell me briefly:
Had you heard my proclamation touching this matter?
ANTIGONÊ. It was public. Could I help hearing it?   55

CREON. And yet you dared defy the law.

ANTIGONÊ.   I dared.
   It was not God's proclamation. That final Justice
   That rules the world below makes no such laws.

   Your edict, King, was strong,
   But all your strength is weakness itself against   60
   The immortal unrecorded laws of God.
   They are not merely now: they were, and shall be,
   Operative for ever, beyond man utterly.

   I knew I must die, even without your decree:
   I am only mortal. And if I must die   65
   Now, before it is my time to die,
   Surely this is no hardship: can anyone
   Living, as I live, with evil all about me,
   Think Death less than a friend? This death of mine
   Is of no importance; but if I had left my brother   70
   Lying in death unburied, I should have suffered.
   Now I do not.
               You smile at me. Ah Creon,
   Think me a fool, if you like; but it may well be
   That a fool convicts me of folly.

CHORAGOS. Like father, like daughter: both headstrong, deaf to reason!   75
   She has never learned to yield:

CREON.   She has much to learn.
   The inflexible heart breaks first, the toughest iron
   Cracks first, and the wildest horses bend their necks
   At the pull of the smallest curb.
                    Pride? In a slave?
   This girl is guilty of a double insolence,   80
   Breaking the given laws and boasting of it.
   Who is the man here,
   She or I, if this crime goes unpunished?
   Sister's child, or more than sister's child,
   Or closer yet in blood—she and her sister   85
   Win bitter death for this!

           (To SERVANTS.*)*
           Go, some of you,
   Arrest Ismenê. I accuse her equally.
   Bring her: you will find her sniffling in the house there.

   Her mind's a traitor: crimes kept in the dark
   Cry for light, and the guardian brain shudders;   90
   But how much worse than this
   Is brazen boasting of barefaced anarchy!

ANTIGONÊ. Creon, what more do you want than my death?

CREON. Nothing.
That gives me everything.
ANTIGONÊ. Then I beg you: kill me.
This talking is a great weariness: your words   95
Are distasteful to me, and I am sure that mine
Seem so to you. And yet they should not seem so:
I should have praise and honor for what I have done.
All these men here would praise me
Were their lips not frozen shut with fear of you.   100
(*Bitterly.*) Ah the good fortune of kings,
Licensed to say and do whatever they please!
CREON. You are alone here in that opinion.
ANTIGONÊ. No, they are with me. But they keep their tongues in leash.
CREON. Maybe. But you are guilty, and they are not.   105
ANTIGONÊ. There is no guilt in reverence for the dead.
CREON. But Eteoclês—was he not your brother too?
ANTIGONÊ. My brother too.
CREON. And you insult his memory?
ANTIGONÊ (*softly*). The dead man would not say that I insult it.
CREON. He would: for you honor a traitor as much as him.   110
ANTIGONÊ. His own brother, traitor or not, and equal in blood.
CREON. He made war on his country. Eteoclês defended it.
ANTIGONÊ. Nevertheless, there are honors due all the dead.
CREON. But not the same for the wicked as for the just.
ANTIGONÊ. Ah Creon, Creon,   115
Which of us can say what the gods hold wicked?
CREON. An enemy is an enemy, even dead.
ANTIGONÊ. It is my nature to join in love, not hate.
CREON (*finally losing patience*). Go join them then; if you must have your love,
Find it in hell!   120
CHORAGOS. But see, Ismenê comes:

Enter ISMENÊ, *guarded*.

Those tears are sisterly, the cloud
That shadows her eyes rains down gentle sorrow.
CREON. You too, Ismenê,
Snake in my ordered house, sucking my blood   125
Stealthily—and all the time I never knew
That these two sisters were aiming at my throne!
Ismenê,
Do you confess your share in this crime, or deny it?
Answer me.
ISMENÊ. Yes, if she will let me say so. I am guilty.   130
ANTIGONÊ (*coldly*). No, Ismenê. You have no right to say so.
You would not help me, and I will not have you help me.
ISMENÊ. But now I know what you meant; and I am here
To join you, to take my share of punishment.

ANTIGONÊ. The dead man and the gods who rule the dead   135
    Know whose act this was. Words are not friends.

ISMENÊ. Do you refuse me, Antigonê? I want to die with you:
    I too have a duty that I must discharge to the dead.

ANTIGONÊ. You shall not lessen my death by sharing it.

ISMENÊ. What do I care for life when you are dead?   140

ANTIGONÊ. Ask Creon. You're always hanging on his opinions.

ISMENÊ. You are laughing at me. Why, Antigonê?

ANTIGONÊ. It's a joyless laughter, Ismenê.

ISMENÊ.   But can I do nothing?

ANTIGONÊ. Yes. Save yourself. I shall not envy you.
    There are those who will praise you; I shall have honor, too.   145

ISMENÊ. But we are equally guilty!

ANTIGONÊ.   No more, Ismenê.
    You are alive, but I belong to Death.

CREON (to the CHORUS). Gentlemen, I beg you to observe these girls:
    One has just now lost her mind; the other,
    It seems, has never had a mind at all.   150

ISMENÊ. Grief teaches the steadiest minds to waver, King.

CREON. Yours certainly did, when you assumed guilt with the guilty!

ISMENÊ. But how could I go on living without her?

CREON.   You are.
    She is already dead.

ISMENÊ.   But your own son's bride!

CREON. There are places enough for him to push his plow.   155
    I want no wicked women for my sons!

ISMENÊ. O dearest Haimon, how your father wrongs you!

CREON. I've had enough of your childish talk of marriage!

CHORAGOS. Do you really intend to steal this girl from your son?

CREON. No; Death will do that for me.

CHORAGOS.   Then she must die?   160

CREON (ironically). You dazzle me.

                    —But enough of this talk!

(To GUARDS.) You, there, take them away and guard them well:
    For they are but women, and even brave men run
    When they see Death coming.

            Exeunt ISMENÊ, ANTIGONÊ, *and* GUARDS.

ODE II

Strophe 1

CHORUS. Fortunate is the man who has never tasted God's vengeance!
    Where once the anger of heaven has struck, that house is shaken
    For ever: damnation rises behind each child

Like a wave cresting out of the black northeast,
When the long darkness under sea roars up
And bursts drumming death upon the windwhipped sand.

Antistrophe 1

I have seen this gathering sorrow from time long past
Loom upon Oedipus' children: generation from generation
Takes the compulsive rage of the enemy god.
So lately this last flower of Oedipus' line
Drank the sunlight! but now a passionate word
And a handful of dust have closed up all its beauty.

Strophe 2

What mortal arrogance
Transcends the wrath of Zeus?
Sleep cannot lull him nor the effortless long months
Of the timeless gods: but he is young for ever,
And his house is the shining day of high Olympos.
All that is and shall be,
And all the past, is his.
No pride on earth is free of the curse of heaven.

Antistrophe 2

The straying dreams of men
May bring them ghosts of joy:
But as they drowse, the waking embers burn them;
Or they walk with fixed eyes, as blind men walk.
But the ancient wisdom speaks for our own time:
Fate works most for woe
With Folly's fairest show.
Man's little pleasure is the spring of sorrow.

SCENE III

CHORAGOS. But here is Haimon, King, the last of all your sons.
Is it grief for Antigonê that brings him here,
And bitterness at being robbed of his bride?

Enter HAIMON.

CREON. We shall soon see, and no need of diviners.
—Son,

You have heard my final judgment on that girl:

Have you come here hating me, or have you come
With deference and with love, whatever I do?
HAIMON. I am your son, father. You are my guide.
You make things clear for me, and I obey you.
No marriage means more to me than your continuing wisdom.   10
CREON. Good. That is the way to behave: subordinate
Everything else, my son, to your father's will.
This is what a man prays for, that he may get
Sons attentive and dutiful in his house,
Each one hating his father's enemies,   15
Honoring his father's friends. But if his sons
Fail him, if they turn out unprofitably,
What has he fathered but trouble for himself
And amusement for the malicious?
                              So you are right
Not to lose your head over this woman.   20
Your pleasure with her would soon grow cold, Haimon,
And then you'd have a hellcat in bed and elsewhere.
Let her find her husband in Hell!
Of all the people in this city, only she
Has had contempt for my law and broken it.   25

Do you want me to show myself weak before the people?
Or to break my sworn word? No, and I will not.
The woman dies.
I suppose she'll plead "family ties." Well, let her.
If I permit my own family to rebel,   30
How shall I earn the world's obedience?
Show me the man who keeps his house in hand,
He's fit for public authority.
                              I'll have no dealings
With lawbreakers, critics of the government:
Whoever is chosen to govern should be obeyed—   35
Must be obeyed, in all things, great and small,
Just and unjust! O Haimon,
The man who knows how to obey, and that man only,
Knows how to give commands when the time comes.
You can depend on him, no matter how fast   40
The spears come: he's a good soldier, he'll stick it out.

Anarchy, anarchy! Show me a greater evil!
This is why cities tumble and the great houses rain down,
This is what scatters armies!
No, no: good lives are made so by discipline.   45
We keep the laws then, and the lawmakers,
And no woman shall seduce us. If we must lose,
Let's lose to a man, at least! Is a woman stronger than we?

CHORAGOS. Unless time has rusted my wits,
    What you say, King, is said with point and dignity.   50
HAIMON *(boyishly earnest).* Father:
    Reason is God's crowning gift to man, and you are right
    To warn me against losing mine. I cannot say—
    I hope that I shall never want to say!—that you
    Have reasoned badly. Yet there are other men   55
    Who can reason, too; and their opinions might be helpful.
    You are not in a position to know everything
    That people say or do, or what they feel:
    Your temper terrifies—everyone
    Will tell you only what you like to hear.   60
    But I, at any rate, can listen; and I have heard them
    Muttering and whispering in the dark about this girl.
    They say no woman has ever, so unreasonably,
    Died so shameful a death for a generous act:
    "She covered her brother's body. Is this indecent?   65
    She kept him from dogs and vultures. Is this a crime?
    Death?—She should have all the honor that we can give her!"

    This is the way they talk out there in the city.

    You must believe me:
    Nothing is closer to me than your happiness.   70
    What could be closer? Must not any son
    Value his father's fortune as his father does his?
    I beg you, do not be unchangeable:
    Do not believe that you alone can be right.
    The man who thinks that,   75
    The man who maintains that only he has the power
    To reason correctly, the gift to speak, the soul—
    A man like that, when you know him, turns out empty.

    It is not reason never to yield to reason!

    In flood time you can see how some trees bend,   80
    And because they bend, even their twigs are safe,
    While stubborn trees are torn up, roots and all.
    And the same thing happens in sailing:
    Make your sheet fast, never slacken,—and over you go,
    Head over heels and under: and there's your voyage.   85
    Forget you are angry! Let yourself be moved!
    I know I am young; but please let me say this:
    The ideal condition
    Would be, I admit, that men should be right by instinct;
    But since we are all too likely to go astray,   90
    The reasonable thing is to learn from those who can teach.

CHORAGOS. You will do well to listen to him, King,
  If what he says is sensible. And you, Haimon,
  Must listen to your father.—Both speak well.
CREON. You consider it right for a man of my years and experience   95
  To go to school to a boy?
HAIMON.   It is not right
  If I am wrong. But if I am young, and right,
  What does my age matter?
CREON. You think it right to stand up for an anarchist?
HAIMON. Not at all. I pay no respect to criminals.   100
CREON. Then she is not a criminal?
HAIMON. The City would deny it, to a man.
CREON. And the City proposes to teach me how to rule?
HAIMON. Ah. Who is it that's talking like a boy now?
CREON. My voice is the one voice giving orders in this City!   105
HAIMON. It is no City if it takes orders from one voice.
CREON. The State is the King!
HAIMON.   Yes, if the State is a desert.

Pause.

CREON. This boy, it seems, has sold out to a woman.
HAIMON. If you are a woman: my concern is only for you.
CREON. So? Your "concern"! In a public brawl with your father!   110
HAIMON. How about you, in a public brawl with justice?
CREON. With justice, when all that I do is within my rights?
HAIMON. You have no right to trample on God's right.
CREON *(completely out of control).* Fool, adolescent fool! Taken in
  by a woman!
HAIMON. You'll never see me taken in by anything vile.   115
CREON. Every word you say is for her!
HAIMON *(quietly, darkly).*   And for you.
  And for me. And for the gods under the earth.
CREON. You'll never marry her while she lives.
HAIMON. Then she must die.—But her death will cause another.
CREON. Another?   120
  Have you lost your senses? Is this an open threat?
HAIMON. There is no threat in speaking to emptiness.
CREON. I swear you'll regret this superior tone of yours!
  You are the empty one!
HAIMON.   If you were not my father, I'd say you were
  perverse.   125
CREON. You girlstruck fool, don't play at words with me!
HAIMON. I am sorry. You prefer silence.
CREON.   Now, by God—!
  I swear, by all the gods in heaven above us,
  You'll watch it, I swear you shall!
                    (To the SERVANTS.*)*
                              Bring her out!

Bring the woman out! Let her die before his eyes!   130
Here, this instant, with her bridegroom beside her!
HAIMON. Not here, no; she will not die here, King.
And you will never see my face again.
Go on raving as long as you've a friend to endure you.

(Exit HAIMON.*)*

CHORAGOS. Gone, gone.
Creon, a young man in a rage is dangerous!   135
CREON. Let him do, or dream to do, more than a man can.
He shall not save these girls from death.
CHORAGOS.   These girls?
You have sentenced them both?
CREON.   No, you are right.
I will not kill the one whose hands are clean.   140
CHORAGOS. But Antigonê?
CREON *(somberly).*   I will carry her far away
Out there in the wilderness, and lock her
Living in a vault of stone. She shall have food,
As the custom is, to absolve the State of her death.
And there let her pray to the gods of hell: 145
They are her only gods:
Perhaps they will show her an escape from death,
Or she may learn,
                though late,
That piety shown the dead is pity in vain.

(Exit CREON.*)*

ODE III

Strophe

CHORUS. Love, unconquerable
Waster of rich men, keeper
Of warm lights and all-night vigil
In the soft face of a girl:
Sea-wanderer, forest-visitor!   5
Even the pure Immortals cannot escape you,
And mortal man, in his one day's dusk,
Trembles before your glory.

Antistrophe

Surely you swerve upon ruin
The just man's consenting heart,   10
As here you have made bright anger

Strike between father and son—
And none has conquered but Love!
A girl's glánce wórking the will of heaven:
Pleasure to her alone who mocks us,   15
Merciless Aphroditê.°

SCENE IV

CHORAGOS *(as* ANTIGONÊ *enters guarded).* But I can no longer stand
      in awe of this,
   Nor, seeing what I see, keep back my tears.
   Here is Antigonê, passing to that chamber
   Where all find sleep at last.

Strophe 1

ANTIGONÊ. Look upon me, friends, and pity me   5
   Turning back at the night's edge to say
   Good-by to the sun that shines for me no longer;
   Now sleepy Death
   Summons me down to Acheron,° that cold shore:
   There is no bridesong there, nor any music.   10
CHORUS. Yet not unpraised, not without a kind of honor,
   You walk at last into the underworld;
   Untouched by sickness, broken by no sword.
   What woman has ever found your way to death?

Antistrophe 1

ANTIGONÊ. How often I have heard the story of Niobê,   15
   Tantalos' wretched daughter, how the stone
   Clung fast about her, ivy-close: and they say
   The rain falls endlessly
   And sifting soft snow; her tears are never done.
   I feel the loneliness of her death in mine.   20
CHORUS. But she was born of heaven, and you
   Are woman, woman-born. If her death is yours,
   A mortal woman's, is this not for you
   Glory in our world and in the world beyond?

Strophe 2

ANTIGONÊ. You laugh at me. Ah, friends, friends,   25
   Can you not wait until I am dead? O Thebes,

---

[16] *Aphroditê* *goddess of love.*   [9] *Acheron* *a river of the underworld.*

O men many-charioted, in love with Fortune,
Dear springs of Dircê, sacred Theban grove,
Be witnesses for me, denied all pity,
Unjustly judged! and think a word of love   30
For her whose path turns
Under dark earth, where there are no more tears.
CHORUS. You have passed beyond human daring and come at last
Into a place of stone where Justice sits.
I cannot tell   35
What shape of your father's guilt appears in this.

Antistrophe 2

ANTIGONÊ. You have touched it at last: that bridal bed
Unspeakable, horror of son and mother mingling:
Their crime, infection of all our family!
O Oedipus, father and brother!   40
Your marriage strikes from the grave to murder mine.
I have been a stranger here in my own land:
All my life
The blasphemy of my birth has followed me.
CHORUS. Reverence is a virtue, but strength   45
Lives in established law: that must prevail.
You have made your choice,
Your death is the doing of your conscious hand.

Epode

ANTIGONÊ. Then let me go, since all your words are bitter,
And the very light of the sun is cold to me.   50
Lead me to my vigil, where I must have
Neither love nor lamentation; no song, but silence.

CREON *interrupts impatiently.*

CREON. If dirges and planned lamentations could put off death,
Men would be singing for ever.
(To the SERVANTS.*)*
Take her, go!
You know your orders: take her to the vault   55
And leave her alone there. And if she lives or dies,
That's her affair, not ours: our hands are clean.

ANTIGONÊ. O tomb, vaulted bride-bed in eternal rock,
Soon I shall be with my own again
Where Persephonê° welcomes the thin ghosts underground: 60
And I shall see my father again, and you, mother,

---

⁶⁰**Persephonê**   *queen of the underworld.*

And dearest Polyneicês—
                    dearest indeed
To me, since it was my hand
That washed him clean and poured the ritual wine:
And my reward is death before my time!   65

And yet, as men's hearts know, I have done no wrong,
I have not sinned before God. Or if I have,
I shall know the truth in death. But if the guilt
Lies upon Creon who judged me, then, I pray,
May his punishment equal my own.
CHORAGOS.   O passionate heart,   70
Unyielding, tormented still by the same winds!
CREON. Her guards shall have good cause to regret their delaying.
ANTIGONÊ. Ah! That voice is like the voice of death!
CREON. I can give you no reason to think you are mistaken.
ANTIGONÊ. Thebes, and you my fathers' gods,   75
And rulers of Thebes, you see me now, the last
Unhappy daughter of a line of kings,
Your kings, led away to death. You will remember
What things I suffer, and at what men's hands,
Because I would not transgress the laws of heaven.   80
(To the GUARDS, *simply.)* Come: let us wait no longer.

(Exit ANTIGONÊ, *left, guarded.)*

ODE IV

Strophe 1

CHORUS. All Danaê's beauty was locked away
In a brazen cell where the sunlight could not come:
A small room still as any grave, enclosed her.
Yet she was a princess too,
And Zeus in a rain of gold poured love upon her.   5
O child, child,
No power in wealth or war
Or tough sea-blackened ships
Can prevail against untiring Destiny!

Antistrophe 1

And Dryas' son° also, that furious king,   10
Bore the god's prisoning anger for his pride:

¹⁰*Dryas' son   Lycurgus, King of Thrace.*

Sealed up by Dionysos in deaf stone,
His madness died among echoes.
So at the last he learned what dreadful power
His tongue had mocked: 15
For he had profaned the revels,
And fired the wrath of the nine
Implacable Sisters° that love the sound of the flute.

Strophe 2

And old men tell a half-remembered tale
Of horror where a dark ledge splits the sea   20
And a double surf beats on the gráy shóres:
How a king's new woman°, sick
With hatred for the queen he had imprisoned,
Ripped out his two sons' eyes with her bloody hands
While grinning Arês° watched the shuttle plunge   25
Four times: four blind wounds crying for revenge,

Antistrophe 2

Crying, tears and blood mingled.—Piteously born,
Those sons whose mother was of heavenly birth!
Her father was the god of the North Wind
And she was cradled by gales,   30
She raced with young colts on the glittering hills
And walked untrammeled in the open light:
But in her marriage deathless Fate found means
To build a tomb like yours for all her joy.

SCENE V

Enter blind TEIRESIAS, *led by a boy. The opening speeches of* TEIRESIAS *should be in singsong contrast to the realistic lines of* CREON.

TEIRESIAS. This is the way the blind man comes, Princes, Princes,
    Lock-step, two heads lit by the eyes of one.
CREON. What new thing have you to tell us, old Teiresias?
TEIRESIAS. I have much to tell you: listen to the prophet, Creon.
CREON. I am not aware that I have ever failed to listen.   5
TEIRESIAS. Then you have done wisely, King, and ruled well.
CREON. I admit my debt to you. But what have you to say?

---

[18]*Implacable Sisters* The Muses.   [23]*King's new woman* Eidothea, second wife of King Phineas, blinded her stepsons after the King had imprisoned their mother in a cave.   [25]*Arês* god of war.

TEIRESIAS. This, Creon: you stand once more on the edge of fate.
CREON. What do you mean? Your words are a kind of dread.
TEIRESIAS. Listen, Creon: 10
    I was sitting in my chair of augury, at the place
    Where the birds gather about me. They were all a-chatter,
    As is their habit, when suddenly I heard
    A strange note in their jangling, a scream, a
    Whirring fury; I knew that they were fighting,   15
    Tearing each other, dying
    In a whirlwind of wings clashing. And I was afraid.
    I began the rites of burnt-offering at the altar,
    But Hephaistos° failed me: instead of bright flame,
    There was only the sputtering slime of the fat thigh-flesh   20
    Melting: the entrails dissolved in gray smoke,
    The bare bone burst from the welter. And no blaze!

    This was a sign from heaven. My boy described it,
    Seeing for me as I see for others.

    I tell you, Creon, yourself have brought   25
    This new calamity upon us. Our hearths and altars
    Are stained with the corruption of dogs and carrion birds
    That glut themselves on the corpse of Oedipus' son.
    The gods are deaf when we pray to them, their fire
    Recoils from our offering, their birds of omen   30
    Have no cry of comfort, for they are gorged
    With the thick blood of the dead.
                                     O my son,
    These are no trifles! Think: all men make mistakes,
    But a good man yields when he knows his course is wrong,
    And repairs the evil. The only crime is pride.   35

    Give in to the dead man, then: do not fight with a corpse—
    What glory is it to kill a man who is dead?
    Think, I beg you:
    It is for your own good that I speak as I do.
    You should be able to yield for your own good.   40
CREON. It seems that prophets have made me their especial province.
    All my life long
    I have been a kind of butt for the dull arrows
    Of doddering fortune-tellers!
                                  No, Teiresias:
    If your birds—if the great eagles of God himself   45
    Should carry him stinking bit by bit to heaven,
    I would not yield. I am not afraid of pollution:
    No man can defile the gods.

---

¹⁹**Hephaistos** *god of fire.*

Do what you will,
Go into business, make money, speculate
In India gold or that synthetic gold from Sardis,   50
Get rich otherwise than by my consent to bury him.
Teiresias, it is a sorry thing when a wise man
Sells his wisdom, lets out his words for hire!
TEIRESIAS. Ah Creon! Is there no man left in the world—
CREON. To do what?—Come, let's have the aphorism!   55
TEIRESIAS. No man who knows that wisdom outweighs any wealth?
CREON. As surely as bribes are baser than any baseness.
TEIRESIAS. You are sick, Creon! You are deathly sick!
CREON. As you say: it is not my place to challenge a prophet.
TEIRESIAS. Yet you have said my prophecy is for sale.   60
CREON. The generation of prophets has always loved gold.
TEIRESIAS. The generation of kings has always loved brass.
CREON. You forget yourself! You are speaking to your King.
TEIRESIAS. I know it. You are a king because of me.
CREON. You have a certain skill; but you have sold out.   65
TEIRESIAS. King, you will drive me to words that—
CREON.   Say them, say them!
Only remember: I will not pay you for them.
TEIRESIAS. No, you will find them too costly.
CREON.   No doubt. Speak:
Whatever you say, you will not change my will.
TEIRESIAS. Then take this, and take it to heart!   70
The time is not far off when you shall pay back
Corpse for corpse, flesh of your own flesh.
You have thrust the child of this world into living night,
You have kept from the gods below the child that is theirs:
The one in a grave before her death, the other,   75
Dead, denied the grave. This is your crime:
And the Furies and the dark gods of Hell
Are swift with terrible punishment for you.

Do you want to buy me now, Creon?
Not many days,
And your house will be full of men and women weeping,   80
And curses will be hurled at you from far
Cities grieving for sons unburied, left to rot
Before the walls of Thebes.

These are my arrows, Creon: they are all for you.

(*To* BOY.) But come, child: lead me home.   85
Let him waste his fine anger upon younger men.
Maybe he will learn at last
To control a wiser tongue in a better head.
(*Exit* TEIRESIAS.)

CHORAGOS. The old man has gone, King, but his words
　　Remain to plague us. I am old, too,
　　But I cannot remember that he was ever false.
CREON. That is true. . . . It troubles me.
　　Oh it is hard to give in! but it is worse
　　To risk everything for stubborn pride.
CHORAGOS. Creon: take my advice.
CREON.　　　　　　　　　　　　What shall I do?　　　　　　95
CHORAGOS. Go quickly: free Antigonê from her vault
　　And build a tomb for the body of Polyneicês.
CREON. You would have me do this!
CHORAGOS.　　　　　　　　　　Creon, yes!
　　And it must be done at once: God moves
　　Swiftly to cancel the folly of stubborn men.　　　　　100
CREON. It is hard to deny the heart! But I
　　Will do it: I will not fight with destiny.
CHORAGOS. You must go yourself, you cannot leave it to others.
CREON. I will go.
　　　　　　　　—Bring axes, servants:
　　Come with me to the tomb. I buried her. I　　　　　105
　　Will set her free.
　　　　　　　　Oh quickly!
　　My mind misgives—
　　The laws of the gods are mighty, and a man must serve them
　　To the last day of his life!

(Exit CREON.*)*

PAEAN°

Strophe 1

CHORAGOS. God of many names
CHORUS.　　　　　　　　　O Iacchos°
　　　　　　　　　　　　　　　son
　　of Kadmeian Sémelê°
　　　　　　　　　　O born of the Thunder!
　　Guardian of the West
　　　　　　　　　　Regent
　　of Eleusis' plain
　　　　　　　　O Prince of maenad° Thebes
　　and the Dragon Field by rippling Ismenós.°　　　　5

Paean *a hymn.* ¹**Iacchos** *Bacchos or Dionysos, god of wine and revelry.* ²**Sémelê** *mother of Iacchos, consort of Zeus.* ⁴**maenad** *female worshipper, attendant of Iacchos.* ⁵**Ismenós** *a river near Thebes where, according to legend, dragon's teeth were sown from which sprang the ancestors of Thebes.*

Antistrophe 1

CHORAGOS. God of many names
CHORUS.   the flame of torches
   flares on our hills
                    the nymphs of Iacchos
   dance at the spring of Castalia.°
   from the vine-close mountain
                          come ah come in ivy:
   Evohé evohé! sings through the streets of Thebes   10

Strophe 2

CHORAGOS. God of many names
CHORUS.   Iacchos of Thebes
   heavenly Child
                 of Sémelê bride of the Thunderer!
   The shadow of plague is upon us:
                                come
   with clement feet
                  oh come from Parnasos
   down the long slopes
                   across the lamenting water   15

Antistrophe 2

CHORAGOS. Iô Fire! Chorister of the throbbing stars!
   O purest among the voices of the night!
   Thou son of God, blaze for us!
CHORUS. Come with choric rapture of circling Maenads
   Who cry *Iô Iacche!*
                 God of many names!   20

EXODOS

Enter MESSENGER *from left.*

MESSENGER. Men of the line of Kadmos,° you who live
   Near Amphion's citadel,°
                   I cannot say
   Of any condition of human life "This is fixed,

---

⁸**Castalia** *a spring on Mount Parnasos.*   ¹**Kadmos** *sowed the dragon's teeth; founded Thebes.*
²**Amphion's citadel** *Amphion's lyre playing charmed stones to form a wall around Thebes.*

This is clearly good, or bad." Fate raises up,
And Fate casts down the happy and unhappy alike: 5
No man can foretell his Fate.
                            Take the case of Creon:
Creon was happy once, as I count happiness:
Victorious in battle, sole governor of the land,
Fortunate father of children nobly born.
And now it has all gone from him! Who can say   10
That a man is still alive when his life's joy fails?
He is a walking dead man. Grant him rich,
Let him live like a king in his great house:
If his pleasure is gone, I would not give
So much as the shadow of smoke for all he owns.   15
CHORAGOS. Your words hint at sorrow: what is your news for us?
MESSENGER. They are dead. The living are guilty of their death.
CHORAGOS. Who is guilty? Who is dead? Speak!
MESSENGER.   Haimon.
Haimon is dead; and the hand that killed him
Is his own hand.
CHORAGOS. His father's? or his own?   20
MESSENGER. His own, driven mad by the murder his father had done.
CHORAGOS. Teiresias, Teiresias, how clearly you saw it all!
MESSENGER. This is my news: you must draw what conclusions you can
    from it.
CHORAGOS. But look: Eurydicê, our Queen:
Has she overheard us?   25

Enter EURYDICÊ *from the palace, center.*

EURYDICÊ. I have heard something, friends:
As I was unlocking the gate of Pallas' shrine,
For I needed her help today, I heard a voice
Telling of some new sorrow. And I fainted
There at the temple with all my maidens about me.   30
But speak again: whatever it is, I can bear it:
Grief and I are no strangers.
MESSENGER.   Dearest Lady,
I will tell you plainly all that I have seen.
I shall not try to comfort you: what is the use,
Since comfort could lie only in what is not true?   35
The truth is always best.
                       I went with Creon
To the outer plain where Polyneicês was lying,
No friend to pity him, his body shredded by dogs.
We made our prayers in that place to Hecatê
And Pluto, that they would be merciful. And we bathed   40
The corpse with holy water, and we brought

Fresh-broken branches to burn what was left of it,
And upon the urn we heaped up a towering barrow
Of the earth of his own land.
                              When we were done, we ran
To the vault where Antigonê lay on her couch of stone.   45
One of the servants had gone ahead,
And while he was yet far off he heard a voice
Grieving within the chamber, and he came back
And told Creon. And as the King went closer,
The air was full of wailing, the words lost,   50
And he begged us to make all haste. "Am I a prophet?"
He said, weeping, "And must I walk this road,
The saddest of all that I have gone before?
My son's voice calls me on. Oh quickly, quickly!
Look through the crevice there, and tell me   55
If it is Haimon, or some deception of the gods!"

We obeyed; and in the cavern's farthest corner
We saw her lying:
She had made a noose of her fine linen veil
And hanged herself. Haimon lay beside her,   60
His arms about her waist, lamenting her,
His love lost under ground, crying out
That his father had stolen her away from him.

When Creon saw him the tears rushed to his eyes
And he called to him: "What have you done, child?
     Speak to me.   65
What are you thinking that makes your eyes so strange?
O my son, my son, I come to you on my knees!"
But Haimon spat in his face. He said not a word,
Staring—
          And suddenly drew his sword
And lunged. Creon shrank back, the blade missed; and the boy,   70
Desperate against himself, drove it half its length
Into his own side, and fell. And as he died
He gathered Antigonê close in his arms again,
Choking, his blood bright red on her white cheek.
And now he lies dead with the dead, and she is his   75
At last, his bride in the house of the dead.

                    Exit EURYDICÊ *into the palace.*

CHORAGOS. She has left us without a word. What can this mean?
MESSENGER. It troubles me, too; yet she knows what is best,
     Her grief is too great for public lamentation,

And doubtless she has gone to her chamber to weep   80
For her dead son, leading her maidens in his dirge.

Pause.

CHORAGOS. It may be so: but I fear this deep silence.
MESSENGER. I will see what she is doing. I will go in.

Exit MESSENGER *into the palace.*

Enter CREON *with attendants, bearing* HAIMON'S *body.*

CHORAGOS. But here is the king himself: oh look at him,
    Bearing his own damnation in his arms.   85
CREON. Nothing you say can touch me any more.
    My own blind heart has brought me
    From darkness to final darkness. Here you see
    The father murdering, the murdered son—
    And all my civic wisdom!   90

    Haimon my son, so young, so young to die,
    I was the fool, not you; and you died for me.
CHORAGOS. That is the truth; but you were late in learning it.
CREON. This truth is hard to bear. Surely a god
    Has crushed me beneath the hugest weight of heaven,   95
    And driven me headlong a barbaric way
    To trample out the thing I held most dear.

    The pains that men will take to come to pain!

Enter MESSENGER *from the palace.*

MESSENGER. The burden you carry in your hands is heavy,
    But it is not all: you will find more in your house.   100
CREON. What burden worse than this shall I find there?
MESSENGER. The Queen is dead.
CREON. O port of death, deaf world,
    Is there no pity for me? And you, Angel of evil,
    I was dead, and your words are death again.   105
    Is it true, boy? Can it be true?
    Is my wife dead? Has death bred death?
MESSENGER. You can see for yourself.

The doors are opened and the body of EURYDICÊ *is disclosed within.*

CREON. Oh pity!
    All true, all true, and more than I can bear!   110
    O my wife, my son!
MESSENGER. She stood before the altar, and her heart
    Welcomed the knife her own hand guided,

And a great cry burst from her lips for Megareus dead,
And for Haimon dead, her sons; and her last breath   115
Was a curse for their father, the murderer of her sons.
And she fell, and the dark flowed in through her closing eyes.
CREON. O God, I am sick with fear.
Are there no swords here? Has no one a blow for me?
MESSENGER. Her curse is upon you for the deaths of both.   120
CREON. It is right that it should be. I alone am guilty.
I know it, and I say it. Lead me in,
Quickly, friends.
I have neither life nor substance. Lead me in.
CHORAGOS. You are right, if there can be right in so much wrong.   125
The briefest way is best in a world of sorrow.
CREON. Let it come,
Let death come quickly, and be kind to me.
I would not ever see the sun again.
CHORAGOS. All that will come when it will; but we, meanwhile,   130
Have much to do. Leave the future to itself.
CREON. All my heart was in that prayer!
CHORAGOS. Then do not pray any more: the sky is deaf.
CREON. Lead me away. I have been rash and foolish.
I have killed my son and my wife.   135
I look for comfort; my comfort lies here dead.
Whatever my hands have touched has come to nothing.
Fate has brought all my pride to a thought of dust.

As CREON *is being led into the house, the* CHORAGOS *advances and speaks directly to
the audience.*

CHORAGOS. There is no happiness where there is no wisdom;
No wisdom but in submission to the gods.   140
Big words are always punished,
And proud men in old age learn to be wise.

QUESTIONS

1. Describe the central problem of the play. Whose rights should assume priority—
   Creon's to legislate and punish, or Antigonê's to bury her brother? Is there any way
   to resolve the competing claims of Creon and Antigonê?
2. How does Sophocles characterize Creon and Antigonê? Consider their speeches,
   actions, and gestures.
3. What is Haimon's role in the play? What does Haimon's dialogue with his father
   reveal about the two characters?
4. What do Ismenê and Euridycê contribute to the play? How would *Antigonê* differ
   if either or both were absent?

5. Describe the structure of the play. How is its plot constructed and developed? Explain the focus of each scene. What is the purpose of the poetic odes that punctuate the dramatic action of the play?

6. What is the chorus's role? Single out two important comments made by the chorus and explain their significance.

7. Compare Antigonê's tragedy with Creon's suffering. Which character do you sympathize with most? Why?

8. Compare Creon's actions at the beginning and end of the play. How does he change?

CHAPTER SEVENTEEN

The Elizabethan Theater

The drama of Shakespeare's time, the Elizabethan Age (1558–1603), shares some features with Greek drama. Like Greek dramatists, Elizabethan playwrights wrote both comedies and tragedies, but the Elizabethans extended the possibilities of each genre. They wrote, for example, domestic tragedies, tragedies of character, and revenge tragedies; they contributed comedies of manners and comedies of humors to the earlier romantic and satiric comedies. As in the Greek theater, props were few, scenery was simple, and dialogue often indicated changes of locale and time. Also, Elizabethan plays, like Greek dramas, were written in verse rather than prose.

Unlike the large Greek amphitheaters, which could seat thousands (fifteen thousand at Epidaurus), an Elizabethan playhouse such as the Globe, where many of Shakespeare's plays were staged, had a much smaller seating capacity. The Globe, for example, could accommodate about twenty-three hundred people, including roughly eight hundred groundlings who, exposed to the elements, stood around the stage. The stage itself projected from an inside wall into their midst. More prosperous spectators sat in one of the three stories that nearly encircled the stage. The vastly smaller size and seating capacity of the Elizabethan theater and the projection of its stage made for a greater intimacy between actors and audience. Though actors still had to project their voices and exaggerate their gestures, they could be heard and seen without the aid of large megaphonic masks and elevated shoes. Elizabethan actors could modulate their voices and vary their pitch, stress, and intonation in ways not suited to the Greek stage. They could also make greater and more subtle use of facial expression and of gesture to enforce their greater verbal and vocal flexibility.

In addition to greater intimacy, the Elizabethan stage also offered more versatility than its Greek counterpart. Although the Greek *skene* building could be used for scenes occuring above the ground, such as a god descending in a machine (*deus ex machina*),* the Greek stage was really a single-level acting area. Not so the Elizabethan stage, which contained a second-level balcony (from which Brabantio looks out in Act I, scene ii of *Othello*). Besides its balcony, Shakespeare's stage had doors at the back for entrances and exits, a curtained alcove (useful for scenes of intrigue), and a stage floor trapdoor, from which the Ghost ascends in Shakespeare's *Hamlet*. Such a stage was suitable for rapidly shifting scenes and continuous action. Thus, Elizabethan stage conventions did not include divisions between scenes as in Greek drama. The act and scene divisions that appear in *Othello* were devised by modern editors.

Shakespeare's plays generally, and *Othello* in particular, appealed to an audience ranging from the illiterate to the educated: bawdy jokes exist alongside sublime poetry; subtle introspective moments coexist with violence and passion. Shakespeare's language is among the richest and most resourceful ever written (and spoken), and *Othello* testifies to its vitality and exuberance. Written predominantly in blank verse, *Othello* also includes prose passages (many spoken by Iago) and rhymed couplets (which punctuate the ends of some scenes). The play's language is rich in metaphor and images, puns, and other forms of wordplay.

Deriving the story of Othello from a sixteenth-century tale by Giraldi Cinthio, Shakespeare improved the plot, enriched the language, and deepened the characters. *Othello* has been among the most admired of the thirty-seven plays Shakespeare wrote. Part of its attraction is its language, but its characters are perhaps even more immediately compelling: the noble Othello; his gentle and naive Venetian wife, Desdemona; the brilliant, magnetic, and inexplicable Iago; his crude and manipulated wife, Emilia. The play's central concerns—love and trust, good and evil, nobility and debasement—are also engaging.

---

*A god who resolves the entanglements of a play by his supernatural intervention (literally, a god from the machine) or any artificial device used to resolve a plot.

WILLIAM SHAKESPEARE
[*1564–1616*]

The Tragedy of Othello
THE MOOR OF VENICE

EDITED BY ALVIN KERNAN

CHARACTERS

OTHELLO, *the Moor*
BRABANTIO, *father to Desdemona*
CASSIO, *an honorable lieutenant*
IAGO, *a villain*
RODERIGO, *a gulled gentleman*
DUKE OF VENICE
SENATORS
MONTANO, *Governor of Cyprus*
GENTLEMEN OF CYPRUS
LODOVICO AND GRATIANO, *two noble Venetians*
SAILORS
CLOWN
DESDEMONA, wife to Othello
EMILIA, wife to Iago
BIANCA, a courtesan
(MESSENGER, HERALD, OFFICERS, GENTLEMEN, MUSICIANS, ATTENDANTS)

Scene. *Venice and Cyprus.*

ACT I

Scene I [*Venice. A street.*]

RODERIGO: Tush! Never tell me? I take it much unkindly
  That thou, Iago, who hast had my purse
  As if the strings were thine, shouldst know of this.
IAGO: 'Sblood°, but you'll not hear me! If ever I did dream
  Of such a matter, abhor me.

I.i.   4 *'Sblood* *by God's blood.*

RODERIGO: Thou told'st me   5
Thou didst hold him in thy hate.
IAGO: Despise me
If I do not. Three great ones of the city,
In personal suit to make me his lieutenant,
Off-capped° to him; and, by the faith of man,
I know my price; I am worth no worse a place.   10
But he, as loving his own pride and purposes,
Evades them with a bombast circumstance°,
Horribly stuffed with epithets of war;
Nonsuits° my mediators. For, "Certes," says he,
"I have already chose my officer." And what was he?   15
Forsooth, a great arithmetician°,
One Michael Cassio, a Florentine,
(A fellow almost damned in a fair wife)°
That never set a squadron in the field,
Nor the division of a battle knows   20
More than a spinster; unless the bookish theoric,
Wherein the tonguèd° consuls can propose
As masterly as he. Mere prattle without practice
Is all his soldiership. But he, sir, had th' election;
And I, of whom his eyes had seen the proof   25
At Rhodes, at Cyprus, and on other grounds
Christian and heathen, must be belee'd and calmed
By debitor and creditor. This counter-caster°,
He, in good time, must his lieutenant be,
And I—God bless the mark!—his Moorship's ancient°.   30
RODERIGO: By heaven, I rather would have been his hangman.
IAGO: Why, there's no remedy. 'Tis the curse of service:
Preferment goes by letter and affection°,
And not by old gradation°, where each second
Stood heir to th' first. Now, sir, be judge yourself,   35
Whether I in any just term am affined°
To love the Moor.
RODERIGO: I would not follow him then.
IAGO: O, sir, content you.
I follow him to serve my turn upon him.
We cannot all be masters, nor all masters   40
Cannot be truly followed. You shall mark

---

⁹**Off-capped** *doffed their caps—as a mark of respect.* ¹²**bombast circumstance** *stuffed, roundabout speech.* ¹⁴**Nonsuits** *rejects.* ¹⁶**arithmetician** *theorist (rather than practical).* ¹⁸**A . . . wife** *(a much-disputed passage, probably best taken as a general sneer at Cassio as a dandy and a ladies' man. But in the story from which Shakespeare took his plot the counterpart of Cassio is married, and it may be that at the beginning of the play Shakespeare had decided to keep him married but later changed his mind).* ²²**tonguèd** *eloquent.* ²⁸**counter-caster** *i.e., a bookkeeper who casts (reckons up) figures on a counter (abacus).* ³⁰**ancient** *standard-bearer; an under-officer.* ³³**letter and affection** *recommendations (from men of power) and personal preference.* ³⁴**old gradation** *seniority.* ³⁶**affined** *bound.*

Many a duteous and knee-crooking° knave
That, doting on his own obsequious bondage,
Wears out his time, much like his master's ass,
For naught but provender; and when he's old, cashiered. 45
Whip me such honest knaves! Others there are
Who, trimmed in forms and visages of duty,
Keep yet their hearts attending on themselves,
And, throwing but shows of service on their lords,
Do well thrive by them, and when they have lined their coats, 50
Do themselves homage. These fellows have some soul;
And such a one do I profess myself. For, sir,
It is as sure as you are Roderigo,
Were I the Moor, I would not be Iago.
In following him, I follow but myself. 55
Heaven is my judge, not I for love and duty,
But seeming so, for my peculiar° end;
For when my outward action doth demonstrate
The native° act and figure of my heart
In complement extern°, 'tis not long after 60
But I will wear my heart upon my sleeve
For daws to peck at; I am not what I am.
RODERIGO: What a full fortune does the thick-lips owe°
If he can carry't thus!
IAGO: Call up her father,
Rouse him. Make after him, poison his delight, 65
Proclaim him in the streets, incense her kinsmen,
And though he in a fertile climate dwell,
Plague him with flies; though that his joy be joy,
Yet throw such chances of vexation on't
As it may lose some color. 70
RODERIGO: Here is her father's house. I'll call aloud.
IAGO: Do, with like timorous° accent and dire yell
As when, by night and negligence, the fire
Is spied in populous cities.
RODERIGO: What, ho, Brabantio! Signior Brabantio, ho! 75
IAGO: Awake! What, ho, Brabantio! Thieves! Thieves!
Look to your house, your daughter, and your bags!
Thieves! Thieves!

BRABANTIO *above*° [*at a window*].

BRABANTIO: What is the reason of this terrible summons?
What is the matter there? 80

---

⁴²**knee-crooking** *bowing.*   ⁵⁷**peculiar** *personal.*   ⁵⁹**native** *natural, innate.*   ⁶⁰**complement
extern** *outward appearance.*   ⁶³**owe** *own.*   ⁷²**timorous** *frightening.*   ⁷⁸**s.d. above** *(i.e., on
the small upper stage above and to the rear of the main platform stage, which resembled the projecting upper story
of an Elizabethan house).*

RODERIGO: Signior, is all your family within?

IAGO: Are your doors locked?

BRABANTIO: Why, wherefore ask you this?

IAGO: Zounds, sir, y'are robbed! For shame. Put on your gown!
  Your heart is burst, you have lost half your soul.
  Even now, now, very now, an old black ram   85
  Is tupping your white ewe. Arise, arise!
  Awake the snorting citizens with the bell,
  Or else the devil will make a grandsire of you.
  Arise, I say!

BRABANTIO: What, have you lost your wits?

RODERIGO: Most reverend signior, do you know my voice?   90

BRABANTIO: Not I. What are you?

RODERIGO: My name is Roderigo.

BRABANTIO: The worser welcome!
  I have charged thee not to haunt about my doors.
  In honest plainness thou hast heard me say
  My daughter is not for thee; and now, in madness,   95
  Being full of supper and distemp'ring draughts°,
  Upon malicious knavery dost thou come
  To start° my quiet.

RODERIGO: Sir, sir, sir—

BRABANTIO: But thou must needs be sure
  My spirits and my place° have in their power   100
  To make this bitter to thee.

RODERIGO: Patience, good sir.

BRABANTIO: What tell'st thou me of robbing? This is Venice,
  My house is not a grange°.

RODERIGO: Most grave Brabantio,
  In simple and pure soul I come to you.

IAGO: Zounds, sir, you are one of those that will not serve God if the devil   105
  bid you. Because we come to do you service and you think we are ruffians,
  you'll have your daughter covered with a Barbary° horse, you'll have your
  nephews° neigh to you, you'll have coursers for cousins°, and gennets for
  germans°.

BRABANTIO: What profane wretch art thou?   110

IAGO: I am one, sir, that comes to tell you your daughter and the Moor
  are making the beast with two backs.

BRABANTIO: Thou art a villain.

IAGO: You are—a senator.

BRABANTIO: This thou shalt answer. I know thee, Roderigo.

RODERIGO: Sir, I will answer anything. But I beseech you,   115
  If't be your pleasure and most wise consent,
  As partly I find it is, that your fair daughter,

---

⁹⁶*distemp'ring draughts*   unsettling drinks.   ⁹⁸*start* disrupt.   ¹⁰⁰*place*   rank, i.e., of senator.
¹⁰³*grange*   isolated house.   ¹⁰⁷*Barbary*   Arabian, i.e., Moorish.   ¹⁰⁸*nephews*   i.e., grandsons.
¹⁰⁹*cousins*   relations.   ¹⁰⁹*gennets for germans*   Spanish horses for blood relatives.

At this odd-even° and dull watch o' th' night,
Transported, with no worse nor better guard
But with a knave of common hire, a gondolier,   120
To the gross clasps of a lascivious Moor—
If this be known to you, and your allowance,
We then have done you bold and saucy wrongs;
But if you know not this, my manners tell me
We have your wrong rebuke. Do not believe   125
That from the sense of all civility°
I thus would play and trifle with your reverence.
Your daughter, if you have not given her leave,
I say again, hath made a gross revolt,
Tying her duty, beauty, wit, and fortunes   130
In an extravagant° and wheeling stranger
Of here and everywhere. Straight satisfy yourself.
If she be in her chamber, or your house,
Let loose on me the justice of the state
For thus deluding you.
BRABANTIO: Strike on the tinder, ho!   135
Give me a taper! Call up all my people!
This accident° is not unlike my dream.
Belief of it oppresses me already.
Light, I say! Light!   *Exit* [*above*].
IAGO: Farewell, for I must leave you.
It seems not meet, nor wholesome to my place,   140
To be produced—as, if I stay, I shall—
Against the Moor. For I do know the State,
However this may gall him with some check°,
Cannot with safety cast° him; for he's embarked
With such loud reason to the Cyprus wars,   145
Which even now stands in act°, that for their souls
Another of his fathom° they have none
To lead their business; in which regard,
Though I do hate him as I do hell-pains,
Yet, for necessity of present life,   150
I must show out a flag and sign of love,
Which is indeed but sign. That you shall surely find him,
Lead to the Sagittary° that raisèd search:
And there will I be with him. So farewell.   [*Exit.*]

    Enter BRABANTIO [*in his nightgown*], *with* SERVANTS *and torches.*

BRABANTIO: It is too true an evil. Gone she is;   155
And what's to come of my despisèd time
Is naught but bitterness. Now, Roderigo,

---

¹¹⁸*odd-even* *between night and morning.*   ¹²⁶*sense of all civility* *feeling of what is proper.*
¹³¹*extravagant* *vagrant, wandering (Othello is not Venetian and thus may be considered a wandering soldier of fortune).*   ¹³⁷*accident* *happening.*   ¹⁴³*check* *restraint.*   ¹⁴⁴*cast* *dismiss.*   ¹⁴⁶*stands in act* *takes place.*   ¹⁴⁷*fathom* *ability.*   ¹⁵³*Sagittary* *(probably the name of an inn).*

Where didst thou see her?—O unhappy girl!—
With the Moor, say'st thou?—Who would be a father?—
How didst thou know 'twas she?—O, she deceives me   160
Past thought!—What said she to you? Get moe° tapers!
Raise all my kindred!—Are they married, think you?

RODERIGO: Truly I think they are.

BRABANTIO: O heaven! How got she out? O treason of the blood!
Fathers, from hence trust not your daughters' minds   165
By what you see them act°. Is there not charms
By which the property° of youth and maidhood
May be abused? Have you not read, Roderigo,
Of some such thing?

RODERIGO: Yes, sir, I have indeed.

BRABANTIO: Call up my brother.—O, would you had had her!—   170
Some one way, some another.—Do you know
Where we may apprehend her and the Moor?

RODERIGO: I think I can discover him, if you please
To get good guard and go along with me.

BRABANTIO: Pray you lead on. At every house I'll call;   175
I may command at most.—Get weapons, ho!
And raise some special officers of night.—
On, good Roderigo; I will deserve your pains°.   [*Exeunt.*]

Scene II [*A street.*]

Enter OTHELLO, IAGO, ATTENDANTS *with torches.*

IAGO: Though in the trade of war I have slain men,
Yet do I hold it very stuff° o' th' conscience
To do no contrived murder. I lack iniquity
Sometime to do me service. Nine or ten times
I had thought t' have yerked° him here, under the ribs.   5

OTHELLO: 'Tis better as it is.

IAGO: Nay, but he prated,
And spoke such scurvy and provoking terms
Against your honor, that with the little godliness I have
I did full hard forbear him. But I pray you, sir,
Are you fast married? Be assured of this,   10
That the magnifico° is much beloved,
And hath in his effect a voice potential
As double as the Duke's°. He will divorce you,
Or put upon you what restraint or grievance
The law, with all his might to enforce it on,   15

161*moe* more.   166*act* do.   167*property* true nature.   178*deserve your pains* be worthy of
(and reward) your efforts.   **I.ii.**   2*stuff* essence.   5*yerked* stabbed.   11*magnifico* nobleman.
12–13*hath . . . Duke's* i.e., can be as effective as the Duke.

Will give him cable°.

OTHELLO: Let him do his spite.
My services which I have done the Signiory°
Shall out-tongue his complaints. 'Tis yet to know°—
Which when I know that boasting is an honor
I shall promulgate—I fetch my life and being   20
From men of royal siege°, and my demerits°
May speak unbonneted to as proud a fortune
As this that I have reached°. For know, Iago,
But that I love the gentle Desdemona,
I would not my unhousèd° free condition   25
Put into circumscription and confine
For the seas' worth. But look, what lights come yond?

Enter CASSIO, *with* [OFFICERS *and*] *torches.*

IAGO: Those are the raisèd father and his friends.
You were best go in.

OTHELLO: Not I. I must be found.
My parts, my title, and my perfect soul°   30
Shall manifest me rightly. Is it they?

IAGO: By Janus, I think no.

OTHELLO: The servants of the Duke? And my lieutenant?
The goodness of the night upon you, friends.
What is the news?

CASSIO: The Duke does greet you, general;   35
And he requires your haste-posthaste appearance
Even on the instant.

OTHELLO: What is the matter, think you?

CASSIO: Something from Cyprus, as I may divine.
It is a business of some heat. The galleys
Have sent a dozen sequent° messengers   40
This very night at one another's heels,
And many of the consuls, raised and met,
Are at the Duke's already. You have been hotly called for.
When, being not at your lodging to be found,
The Senate hath sent about three several° quests   45
To search you out.

OTHELLO: 'Tis well I am found by you.
I will but spend a word here in the house,
And go with you.   [*Exit.*]

CASSIO: Ancient, what makes he here?

IAGO: Faith, he tonight hath boarded a land carack°.
If it prove lawful prize, he's made forever.   50

---

[16]*cable:* range, scope.   [17]*Signiory*   the rulers of Venice.   [18]*yet to know*   unknown as yet.   [21]*siege*   rank.   [21]*demerits*   deserts.   [22-23]*May . . . reached*   i.e., are the equal of the family I have married into.   [25]*unhousèd*   unconfined.   [30]*perfect soul*   clear, unflawed conscience.   [40]*sequent* successive.   [45]*several*   separate.   [49]*carack*   treasure ship.

CASSIO: I do not understand.
IAGO: He's married.
CASSIO: To who?

[*Enter* OTHELLO.]

IAGO: Marry°, to—Come captain, will you go?
OTHELLO: Have with you.
CASSIO: Here comes another troop to seek for you.

Enter BRABANTIO, RODERIGO, *with* OFFICERS *and torches.*

IAGO: It is Brabantio. General, be advised.
    He comes to bad intent.
OTHELLO: Holla! Stand there!   55
RODERIGO: Signior, it is the Moor.
BRABANTIO: Down with him, thief! [*They draw swords.*]
IAGO: You, Roderigo? Come, sir, I am for you.
OTHELLO: Keep up your bright swords, for the dew will rust them.
    Good signior, you shall more command with years
    Than with your weapons.   60
BRABANTIO: O thou foul thief, where hast thou stowed my daughter?
    Damned as thou art, thou hast enchanted her!
    For I'll refer me to all things of sense°,
    If she in chains of magic were not bound,
    Whether a maid so tender, fair, and happy,   65
    So opposite to marriage that she shunned
    The wealthy, curlèd darlings of our nation,
    Would ever have, t'incur a general mock°,
    Run from her guardage to the sooty bosom
    Of such a thing as thou—to fear, not to delight.   70
    Judge me the world if'tis not gross in sense°
    That thou hast practiced° on her with foul charms,
    Abused her delicate youth with drugs or minerals
    That weaken motion°. I'll have't disputed on;
    'Tis probable, and palpable to thinking.   75
    I therefore apprehend and do attach° thee
    For an abuser of the world, a practicer
    Of arts inhibited and out of warrant°.
    Lay hold upon him. If he do resist,
    Subdue him at his peril.
OTHELLO: Hold your hands,   80
    Both you of my inclining and the rest.
    Were it my cue to fight, I should have known it

---

⁵²*Marry: By Mary (an interjection).*   ⁶³*refer . . . sense   i.e., base (my argument) on all ordinary understanding of nature.*   ⁶⁸*general mock   public shame.*   ⁷¹*gross in sense   obvious.*   ⁷²*practiced   used tricks.*   ⁷⁴*motion   thought, i.e., reason.*   ⁷⁶*attach   arrest.*   ⁷⁸*inhibited . . . warrant   prohibited and illegal (black magic).*

Without a prompter. Whither will you that I go
To answer this your charge?

BRABANTIO: To prison, till fit time
Of law and course of direct session   85
Call thee to answer.

OTHELLO: What if I do obey?
How may the Duke be therewith satisfied,
Whose messengers are here about my side
Upon some present° business of the state
To bring me to him?

OFFICER: 'Tis true, most worthy signior.   90
The Duke's in council, and your noble self
I am sure is sent for.

BRABANTIO: How? The Duke in council?
In this time of the night? Bring him away.
Mine's not an idle cause. The Duke himself,
Or any of my brothers° of the state,   95
Cannot but feel this wrong as 'twere their own;
For if such actions may have passage free,
Bondslaves and pagans shall our statesmen be.   *Exeunt.*

Scene III [*A council chamber.*]

Enter DUKE, SENATORS, *and* OFFICERS [*set at a table, with lights and* ATTENDANTS].

DUKE: There's no composition° in this news
That gives them credit°.

FIRST SENATOR: Indeed, they are disproportioned.
My letters say a hundred and seven galleys.

DUKE: And mine a hundred forty.

SECOND SENATOR: And mine two hundred.
But though they jump° not on a just accompt°—   5
As in these cases where the aim° reports
'Tis oft with difference—yet do they all confirm
A Turkish fleet, and bearing up to Cyprus.

DUKE: Nay, it is possible enough to judgment°.
I do not so secure me in the error,   10
But the main article I do approve
In fearful sense°.

SAILOR *(Within):*   What, ho! What, ho! What, ho!

Enter SAILOR.

---

[89]*present* immediate.   [95]*brothers* i.e., the other senators.   **I.iii.** [1]*composition* agreement.
[2]*gives them credit* makes them believable.   [5]*jump* agree.   [5]*just accompt* exact counting.
[6]*aim* approximation.   [9]*to judgment* when carefully considered.   [10-12]*I do . . . sense* i.e., just
because the numbers disagree in the reports, I do not doubt that the principal information (that the Turkish fleet
is out) is fearfully true.

OFFICER: A messenger from the galleys.

DUKE: Now? What's the business?

SAILOR: The Turkish preparation makes for Rhodes.
So was I bid report here to the State   15
By Signior Angelo.

DUKE: How say you by this change?

FIRST SENATOR: This cannot be
By no assay of reason. 'Tis a pageant°
To keep us in false gaze°. When we consider
Th' importancy of Cyprus to the Turk,   20
And let ourselves again but understand
That, as it more concerns the Turk than Rhodes,
So may he with more facile question° bear it,
For that it stands not in such warlike brace°,
But altogether lacks th' abilities   25
That Rhodes is dressed in. If we make thought of this,
We must not think the Turk is so unskillful
To leave that latest which concerns him first,
Neglecting an attempt of ease and gain
To wake and wage a danger profitless.   30

DUKE: Nay, in all confidence he's not for Rhodes.

OFFICER: Here is more news.

Enter a MESSENGER.

MESSENGER: The Ottomites, reverend and gracious,
Steering with due course toward the isle of Rhodes,
Have there injointed them with an after° fleet.   35

FIRST SENATOR: Ay, so I thought. How many, as you guess?

MESSENGER: Of thirty sail; and now they do restem
Their backward course, bearing with frank appearance
Their purposes toward Cyprus. Signior Montano,
Your trusty and most valiant servitor,   40
With his free duty° recommends° you thus,
And prays you to believe him.

DUKE: 'Tis certain then for Cyprus.
Marcus Luccicos, is not he in town?

FIRST SENATOR: He's now in Florence.   45

DUKE: Write from us to him; post-posthaste dispatch.

FIRST SENATOR: Here comes Brabantio and the valiant Moor.

Enter BRABANTIO, OTHELLO, CASSIO, IAGO, RODERIGO, *and* OFFICERS.

DUKE: Valiant Othello, we must straight° employ you
Against the general° enemy Ottoman.
[*To* BRABANTIO] I did not see you. Welcome, gentle signior.   50

---

[18] *pageant*   show, pretense.   [19] *in false gaze*   looking the wrong way.   [23] *facile question*   easy
struggle.   [24] *warlike brace*   "military posture."   [35] *after*   following.   [41] *free duty*   unlimited respect.   [41] *recommends*   informs.   [48] *straight*   at once.   [49] *general*   universal.

We lacked your counsel and your help tonight.
BRABANTIO: So did I yours. Good your grace, pardon me.
Neither my place, nor aught I heard of business,
Hath raised me from my bed; nor doth the general care
Take hold on me; for my particular grief   55
Is of so floodgate and o'erbearing nature
That it engluts and swallows other sorrows,
And it is still itself.
DUKE: Why, what's the matter?
BRABANTIO: My daughter! O, my daughter!
SENATORS: Dead?
BRABANTIO: Ay, to me.
She is abused, stol'n from me, and corrupted   60
By spells and medicines bought of mountebanks;
For nature so prepost'rously to err,
Being not deficient, blind, or lame of sense,
Sans° witchcraft could not.
DUKE: Whoe'er he be that in this foul proceeding   65
Hath thus beguiled your daughter of herself,
And you of her, the bloody book of law
You shall yourself read in the bitter letter
After your own sense; yea, though our proper° son
Stood in your action°.
BRABANTIO: Humbly I thank your Grace.   70
Here is the man—this Moor, whom now, it seems,
Your special mandate for the state affairs
Hath hither brought.
ALL: We are very sorry for't.
DUKE [*To* OTHELLO]: What in your own part can you say to this?
BRABANTIO: Nothing, but this is so.   75
OTHELLO: Most potent, grave, and reverend signiors,
My very noble and approved° good masters,
That I have ta'en away this old man's daughter,
It is most true; true I have married her.
The very head and front° of my offending   80
Hath this extent, no more. Rude am I in my speech,
And little blessed with the soft phrase of peace.
For since these arms of mine had seven years' pith°
Till now some nine moons wasted°, they have used
Their dearest° action in the tented field;   85
And little of this great world can I speak
More than pertains to feats of broils and battle;
And therefore little shall I grace my cause
In speaking for myself. Yet, by your gracious patience,

---

[64]*Sans* *without.*   [69]*proper* *own.*   [70]*Stood in your action* *were the accused in your suit.*
[77]*approved* *tested, proven by past performance.*   [80]*head and front* *extreme form (front = forehead).*
[83]*pith* *strength.*   [84]*wasted* *past.*   [85]*dearest* *most important.*

I will a round° unvarnished tale deliver   90
Of my whole course of love—what drugs, what charms,
What conjuration, and what mighty magic,
For such proceeding I am charged withal,
I won his daughter—
BRABANTIO: A maiden never bold,
Of spirit so still and quiet that her motion   95
Blushed at herself°, and she, in spite of nature,
Of years, of country, credit, everything,
To fall in love with what she feared to look on!
It is a judgment maimed and most imperfect
That will confess perfection so could err   100
Against all rules of nature, and must be driven
To find out practices of cunning hell
Why this should be. I therefore vouch again
That with some mixtures pow'rful o'er the blood,
Or with some dram, conjured to this effect,   105
He wrought upon her.
DUKE: To vouch this is no proof,
Without more wider and more overt test
Than these thin habits° and poor likelihoods
Of modern° seeming do prefer against him.
FIRST SENATOR: But, Othello, speak.   110
Did you by indirect and forcèd courses
Subdue and poison this young maid's affections?
Or came it by request, and such fair question°
As soul to soul affordeth?
OTHELLO: I do beseech you,
Send for the lady to the Sagittary   115
And let her speak of me before her father.
If you do find me foul in her report,
The trust, the office, I do hold of you
Not only take away, but let your sentence
Even fall upon my life.
DUKE: Fetch Desdemona hither.   120
OTHELLO: Ancient, conduct them; you best know the place.

[*Exit* IAGO, *with two or three* ATTENDANTS.]

And till she come, as truly as to heaven
I do confess the vices of my blood,
So justly to your grave ears I'll present
How I did thrive in this fair lady's love,   125
And she in mine.
DUKE: Say it, Othello.

---

⁹⁰**round** blunt.   ⁹⁵⁻⁹⁶**her motion/Blushed at herself** i.e., she was so modest that she blushed at every thought (and movement).   ¹⁰⁸**habits** clothing.   ¹⁰⁹**modern** trivial.   ¹¹³**question** discussion.

OTHELLO: Her father loved me; oft invited me;
   Still° questioned me the story of my life
   From year to year, the battle, sieges, fortune
   That I have passed.   130
   I ran it through, even from my boyish days
   To th' very moment that he bade me tell it.
   Wherein I spoke of most disastrous chances,
   Of moving accidents by flood and field,
   Of hairbreadth scapes i' th' imminent° deadly breach,   135
   Of being taken by the insolent foe
   And sold to slavery, of my redemption thence
   And portance° in my travel's history,
   Wherein of anters° vast and deserts idle°,
   Rough quarries, rocks, and hills whose heads touch heaven,   140
   It was my hint to speak. Such was my process.
   And of the Cannibals that each other eat,
   The Anthropophagi°, and men whose heads
   Grew beneath their shoulders. These things to hear
   Would Desdemona seriously incline;   145
   But still the house affairs would draw her thence;
   Which ever as she could with haste dispatch,
   She'd come again, and with a greedy ear
   Devour up my discourse. Which I observing,
   Took once a pliant hour, and found good means   150
   To draw from her a prayer of earnest heart
   That I would all my pilgrimage dilate°,
   Whereof by parcels she had something heard,
   But not intentively°. I did consent,
   And often did beguile her of her tears   155
   When I did speak of some distressful stroke
   That my youth suffered. My story being done,
   She gave me for my pains a world of kisses.
   She swore in faith 'twas strange, 'twas passing° strange;
   'Twas pitiful, 'twas wondrous pitiful.   160
   She wished she had not heard it; yet she wished
   That heaven had made her such a man. She thanked me,
   And bade me, if I had a friend that loved her,
   I should but teach him how to tell my story,
   And that would woo her. Upon this hint I spake.   165
   She loved me for the dangers I had passed,
   And I loved her that she did pity them.
   This only is the witchcraft I have used.
   Here comes the lady. Let her witness it.

---

[128]*Still* *regularly.*   [135]*imminent* *threatening.*   [138]*portance* *manner of acting.*   [139]*anters*
caves.   [139]*idle* *empty, sterile.*   [143]*Anthropophagi* *maneaters.*   [152]*dilate* *relate in full.*
[154]*intentively* *at length and in sequence.*   [159]*passing* *surpassing.*

Enter DESDEMONA, IAGO, ATTENDANTS.

DUKE: I think this tale would win my daughter too.   170
    Good Brabantio, take up this mangled matter at the best°.
    Men do their broken weapons rather use
    Than their bare hands.
BRABANTIO: I pray you hear her speak.
    If she confess that she was half the wooer,
    Destruction on my head if my bad blame   175
    Light on the man. Come hither, gentle mistress.
    Do you perceive in all this noble company
    Where most you owe obedience?
DESDEMONA: My noble father,
    I do perceive here a divided duty.
    To you I am bound for life and education;   180
    My life and education both do learn me
    How to respect you. You are the lord of duty,
    I am hitherto your daughter. But here's my husband,
    And so much duty as my mother showed
    To you, preferring you before her father,   185
    So much I challenge° that I may profess
    Due to the Moor my lord.
BRABANTIO: God be with you. I have done.
    Please it your Grace, on to the state affairs.
    I had rather to adopt a child than get° it.
    Come hither, Moor.   190
    I here do give thee that with all my heart
    Which, but thou hast already, with all my heart
    I would keep from thee. For your sake°, jewel,
    I am glad at soul I have no other child,
    For thy escape would teach me tyranny,   195
    To hang clogs on them. I have done, my lord.
DUKE: Let me speak like yourself and lay a sentence°
    Which, as a grise° or step, may help these lovers.
    When remedies are past, the griefs are ended
    By seeing the worst, which late on hopes depended°.   200
    To mourn a mischief that is past and gone
    Is the next° way to draw new mischief on.
    What cannot be preserved when fortune takes,
    Patience her injury a mock'ry makes.
    The robbed that smiles, steals something from the thief;   205
    He robs himself that spends a bootless° grief.
BRABANTIO: So let the Turk of Cyprus us beguile:

171*take . . . best* *i.e., make the best of this disaster.*   186*challenge* *claim as right.*   189*get* *beget.*
193*For your sake* *because of you.*   197*lay a sentence* *provide a maxim.*   198*grise* *step.*
200*late on hopes depended* *was supported by hope (of a better outcome) until lately.*   202*next* *closest,*
surest.   206*bootless* *valueless.*

We lose it not so long as we can smile.
He bears the sentence well that nothing bears
But the free comfort which from thence he hears;   210
But he bears both the sentence and the sorrow
That to pay grief must of poor patience borrow.
These sentences, to sugar, or to gall,
Being strong on both sides, are equivocal.
But words are words. I never yet did hear   215
That the bruisèd heart was piercèd° through the ear.
I humbly beseech you, proceed to th' affairs of state.

DUKE: The Turk with a most mighty preparation makes for Cyprus. Othello,
the fortitude° of the place is best known to you; and though we have there
a substitute° of most allowed sufficiency°, yet opinion, a more sovereign²²⁰
mistress of effects, throws a more safer voice on you°. You must therefore
be content to slubber° the gloss of your new fortunes with this more
stubborn and boisterous° expedition.

OTHELLO: The tyrant Custom, most grave senators,
Hath made the flinty and steel couch of war   225
My thrice-driven° bed of down. I do agnize°
A natural and prompt alacrity
I find in hardness and do undertake
These present wars against the Ottomites.
Most humbly, therefore, bending to your state,   230
I crave fit disposition for my wife,
Due reference of place, and exhibition°,
With such accommodation and besort
As levels with° her breeding.

DUKE: Why, at her father's.

BRABANTIO: I will not have it so.

OTHELLO: Nor I.   235

DESDEMONA: Nor would I there reside,
To put my father in impatient thoughts
By being in his eye. Most gracious Duke,
To my unfolding° lend your prosperous° ear,
And let me find a charter° in your voice,   240
T' assist my simpleness.

DUKE: What would you, Desdemona?

DESDEMONA: That I love the Moor to live with him,

---

²¹⁶*piercèd* (some editors emend to piecèd, i.e., "healed." But piercèd *makes good sense: Brabantio is saying in effect that his heart cannot be further hurt [pierced] by the indignity of the useless, conventional advice the Duke offers him. Pierced can also mean, however, "lanced" in the medical sense, and would then mean "treated").* ²¹⁹*fortitude* fortification. ²²⁰*substitute* viceroy. ²²⁰*most allowed sufficiency* generally acknowledged capability. ²²⁰⁻²²¹*opinion . . . you* i.e., the general opinion, which finally controls affairs, is that you would be the best man in this situation. ²²²*slubber* besmear. ²²³*stubborn and boisterous* rough and violent. ²²⁶*thrice-driven* i.e., softest. ²²⁶*agnize* know in myself. ²³²*exhibition* grant of funds. ²³⁴*levels with* is suitable to. ²³⁹*unfolding* explanation. ²³⁹*prosperous* favoring. ²⁴⁰*charter* permission.

My downright violence, and storm of fortunes,
May trumpet to the world. My heart's subdued
Even to the very quality of my lord.°   245
I saw Othello's visage in his mind,
And to his honors and his valiant parts
Did I my soul and fortunes consecrate.
So that, dear lords, if I be left behind,
A moth of peace, and he go to the war,   250
The rites° for why I love him are bereft me,
And I a heavy interim shall support
By his dear absence. Let me go with him.

OTHELLO: Let her have your voice°.
Vouch with me, heaven, I therefore beg it not   255
To please the palate of my appetite,
Nor to comply with heat°—the young affects°
In me defunct—and proper satisfaction°;
But to be free and bounteous to her mind;
And heaven defend° your good souls that you think   260
I will your serious and great business scant
When she is with me. No, when light-winged toys
Of feathered Cupid seel° with wanton° dullness
My speculative and officed instrument°,
That my disports corrupt and taint my business,   265
Let housewives make a skillet of my helm,
And all indign° and base adversities
Make head° against my estimation°!—

DUKE: Be it as you shall privately determine,
Either for her stay or going. Th' affair cries haste,   270
And speed must answer it.

FIRST SENATOR: You must away tonight.

OTHELLO: With all my heart.

DUKE: At nine i' th' morning here we'll meet again.
Othello, leave some officer behind,
And he shall our commission bring to you,   275
And such things else of quality and respect
As doth import you.

OTHELLO: So please your grace, my ancient;
A man he is of honesty and trust.
To his conveyance I assign my wife,
With what else needful your good grace shall think   280
to be sent after me.

DUKE: Let it be so.

---

²⁴⁴⁻²⁴⁵*My . . . lord* i.e., I have become one in nature and being with the man I married (therefore, I too would go to the wars like a soldier). ²⁵¹*rites* (may refer either to the marriage rites or to the rites, formalities, of war). ²⁵⁴*voice* consent. ²⁵⁷*heat* lust. ²⁵⁷*affects* passions. ²⁵⁸*proper satisfaction* i.e., consummation of the marriage. ²⁶⁰*defend* forbid. ²⁶³*seel* sew up. ²⁶³*wanton* lascivious. ²⁶⁴*speculative . . . instrument* i.e., sight (and, by extension, the mind). ²⁶⁷*indign* unworthy. ²⁶⁸*Make head* form an army, i.e., attack. ²⁶⁸*estimation* reputation.

Good night to every one. [*To* BRABANTIO] And, noble signior,
If virtue no delighted° beauty lack,
Your son-in-law is far more fair than black.
FIRST SENATOR: Adieu, brave Moor. Use Desdemona well.   285
BRABANTIO: Look to her, Moor, if thou hast eyes to see:
She has deceived her father, and may thee.

[*Exeunt* DUKE, SENATORS, OFFICERS, *& c.*]

OTHELLO: My life upon her faith! Honest Iago,
My Desdemona must I leave to thee.
I prithee let thy wife attend on her,   290
And bring them after in the best advantage°.
Come, Desdemona. I have but an hour
Of love, of worldly matter, and direction
To spend with thee. We must obey the time.

Exit [MOOR *with* DESDEMONA].

RODERIGO: Iago?   295
IAGO: What say'st thou, noble heart?
RODERIGO: What will I do, think'st thou?
IAGO: Why, go to bed and sleep.
RODERIGO: I will incontinently° drown myself.
IAGO: If thou dost, I shall never love thee after. Why, thou silly gentleman?300
RODERIGO: It is silliness to live when to live is torment; and then have we a
    prescription to die when death is our physician.
IAGO: O villainous! I have looked upon the world for four times seven years,
    and since I could distinguish betwixt a benefit and an injury, I never found
    man that knew how to love himself. Ere I would say I would drown305
    myself for the love of a guinea hen, I would change my humanity with
    a baboon.
RODERIGO: What should I do? I confess it is my shame to be so fond, but it
    is not in my virtue° to amend it.
IAGO: Virtue? A fig! 'Tis in ourselves that we are thus, or thus. Our bodies310
    are our gardens, to the which our wills are gardeners; so that if we will
    plant nettles or sow lettuce, set hyssop and weed up thyme, supply it with
    one gender of herbs or distract° it with many—either to have it sterile with
    idleness or manured with industry—why, the power and corrigible° au-
    thority of this lies in our wills. If the balance of our lives had not one scale315
    of reason to poise another of sensuality, the blood and baseness of our
    natures would conduct us to most prepost'rous conclusions°. But we have
    reason to cool our raging motions, our carnal sting or unbitted° lusts,
    whereof I take this that you call love to be a sect or scion°.
RODERIGO: It cannot be.   320

---

²⁸³*delighted* *delightful.*   ²⁹¹*advantage* *opportunity.*   ²⁹⁹*incontinently* *at once.*   ³⁰⁹*vir-*
tue *strength (Roderigo is saying that his nature controls him).*   ³¹³*distract* *vary.*   ³¹⁴*corrigible*
corrective.   ³¹⁷*conclusions* *ends.*   ³¹⁸*unbitted* *i.e., uncontrolled.*   ³¹⁹*sect or scion* *off-*
shoot.

IAGO: It is merely a lust of the blood and a permission of the will. Come, be a man! Drown thyself? Drown cats and blind puppies! I have professed me thy friend, and I confess me knit to thy deserving with cables of perdurable toughness. I could never better stead° thee than now. Put money in thy purse. Follow thou the wars; defeat thy favor° with an usurped° 325 beard. I say, put money in thy purse. It cannot be long that Desdemona should continue her love to the Moor. Put money in thy purse. Nor he his to her. It was a violent commencement in her and thou shalt see an answerable° sequestration—put but money in thy purse. These Moors are changeable in their wills—fill thy purse with money. The food that to him 330 now is as luscious as locusts° shall be to him shortly as bitter as coloquintida°. She must change for youth; when she is sated with his body, she will find the errors of her choice. Therefore, put money in thy purse. If thou wilt needs damn thyself, do it a more delicate way than drowning. Make all the money thou canst. If sanctimony° and a frail vow betwixt an err- 335 ing° barbarian and supersubtle Venetian be not too hard for my wits, and all the tribe of hell, thou shalt enjoy her. Therefore, make money. A pox of drowning thyself, it is clean out of the way. Seek thou rather to be hanged in compassing° thy joy than to be drowned and go without her.   340

RODERIGO: Wilt thou be fast to my hopes, if I depend on the issue?

IAGO: Thou art sure of me. Go, make money. I have told thee often, and I retell thee again and again, I hate the Moor. My cause is hearted°; thine hath no less reason. Let us be conjunctive° in our revenge against him. If thou canst cuckold him, thou dost thyself a pleasure, me a sport. There are 345 many events in the womb of time, which will be delivered. Traverse, go, provide thy money! We will have more of this tomorrow. Adieu.

RODERIGO: Where shall we meet i' th' morning?

IAGO: At my lodging.

RODERIGO: I'll be with thee betimes.   350

IAGO: Go to, farewell. Do you hear, Roderigo?

RODERIGO: I'll sell all my land.   *Exit.*

IAGO: Thus do I ever make my fool my purse;
For I mine own gained knowledge° should profane
If I would time expend with such snipe   355
But for my sport and profit. I hate the Moor,
And it is thought abroad that 'twixt my sheets
H'as done my office. I know not if't be true,
But I, for mere suspicion in that kind,
Will do, as if for surety°. He holds me well;   360
The better shall my purpose work on him.

---

³²⁴**stead** *serve.*   ³²⁵**defeat thy favor** *disguise your face.*   ³²⁵**usurped** *assumed.*   ³²⁹**answerable** *similar.*   ³³¹**locusts** *(a sweet fruit).*   ³³²**coloquintida** *a purgative derived from a bitter apple.*   ³³⁵**sanctimony** *sacred bond (of marriage).*   ³³⁶**erring** *wandering.*   ³³⁹**compassing** *encompassing, achieving.*   ³⁴³**hearted** *deepseated in the heart.*   ³⁴⁴**conjunctive** *joined.*   ³⁵⁴**gained knowledge** *i.e., practical, worldly wisdom.*   ³⁶⁰**surety** *certainty.*

Cassio's a proper° man. Let me see now:
To get his place, and to plume up my will°
In double knavery. How? How? Let's see.
After some time, to abuse Othello's ears   365
That he is too familiar with his wife.
He hath a person and a smooth dispose°
To be suspected—framed° to make women false.
The Moor is of a free and open nature
That thinks men honest that but seem to be so;   370
And will as tenderly be led by th' nose
As asses are.
I have't! It is engendered! Hell and night
Must bring this monstrous birth to the world's light.   [*Exit.*]

ACT II

Scene I [*Cyprus.*]

Enter MONTANO *and two* GENTLEMEN [*one above*]°.

MONTANO: What from the cape can you discern at sea?
FIRST GENTLEMAN: Nothing at all, it is a high-wrought flood.
I cannot 'twixt the heaven and the main
Descry a sail.
MONTANO: Methinks the wind hath spoke aloud at land;   5
A fuller blast ne'er shook our battlements.
If it hath ruffianed so upon the sea,
What ribs of oak, when mountains melt on them,
Can hold the mortise? What shall we hear of this?
SECOND GENTLEMAN: A segregation° of the Turkish fleet.   10
For do but stand upon the foaming shore,
The chidden billow seems to pelt the clouds;
The wind-shaked surge, with high and monstrous main°,
Seems to cast water on the burning Bear
And quench the guards of th' ever-fixèd pole.°   15
I never did like molestation view
On the enchafèd flood.
MONTANO: If that the Turkish fleet
Be not ensheltered and embayed, they are drowned;
It is impossible to bear it out.

---

³⁶²*proper* handsome.   ³⁶³*plume up my will* (many explanations have been offered for this crucial line, which in Q₁ reads "make up my will." The general sense is something like "to make more proud and gratify my ego").   ³⁶⁷*dispose* manner.   ³⁶⁸*framed* designed.   **II.i. s.d.** (the Folio arrangement of this scene requires that the First Gentleman stand above—on the upper stage—and act as a lookout reporting sights which cannot be seen by Montano standing below on the main stage).   ¹⁰*segregation* separation.   ¹³*main* (both "ocean" and "strength").   ¹⁴⁻¹⁵*Seems . . . pole* (the constellation Ursa Minor contains two stars which are the guards, or companions, of the pole, or North Star).

Enter a [third] GENTLEMAN.

THIRD GENTLEMAN: News, lads! Our wars are done.   20
  The desperate tempest hath so banged the Turks
  That their designment halts. A noble ship of Venice
  Hath seen a grievous wrack and sufferance°
  On most part of their fleet.
MONTANO: How? Is this true?
THIRD GENTLEMAN: The ship is here put in,   25
  A Veronesa; Michael Cassio,
  Lieutenant to the warlike Moor Othello,
  Is come on shore; the Moor himself at sea,
  And is in full commission here for Cyprus.
MONTANO: I am glad on't. 'Tis a worthy governor.   30
THIRD GENTLEMAN: But this same Cassio, though he speak of comfort
  Touching the Turkish loss, yet he looks sadly
  And prays the Moor be safe, for they were parted
  With foul and violent tempest.
MONTANO: Pray heavens he be;
  For I have served him, and the man commands   35
  Like a full soldier. Let's to the seaside, ho!
  As well to see the vessel that's come in
  As to throw out our eyes for brave Othello,
  Even till we make the main and th' aerial blue
  An indistinct regard°.
THIRD GENTLEMAN: Come, let's do so;   40
  For every minute is expectancy
  Of more arrivancie°.

Enter CASSIO.

CASSIO: Thanks, you the valiant of the warlike isle,
  That so approve° the Moor. O, let the heavens
  Give him defense against the elements,   45
  For I have lost him on a dangerous sea.
MONTANO: Is he well shipped?
CASSIO: His bark is stoutly timbered, and his pilot
  Of very expert and approved allowance°;
  Therefore my hopes, not surfeited to death°,   50
  Stand in bold cure°. (*Within:* A sail, a sail, a sail!)
CASSIO: What noise?
FIRST GENTLEMAN: The town is empty; on the brow o' th' sea
  Stand ranks of people, and they cry, "A sail!"
CASSIO: My hopes do shape him for the governor.   [*A shot.*] 55

23*sufferance* damage.   39-40*the main . . . regard* i.e., the sea and sky become indistinguishable.
42*arrivancie* arrivals.   44*approve* ("honor" or, perhaps, "are as warlike and valiant as your governor").
49*approved allowance* known and tested.   50*not surfeited to death* i.e., not so great as to be in danger.
51*Stand in bold cure* i.e., are likely to be restored.

SECOND GENTLEMAN: They do discharge their shot of courtesy:
Our friends at least.

CASSIO: I pray you, sir, go forth
And give us truth who 'tis that is arrived.

SECOND GENTLEMAN: I shall.   [*Exit.*]

MONTANO: But, good lieutenant, is your general wived?   60

CASSIO: Most fortunately. He hath achieved a maid
That paragons° description and wild fame°;
One that excels the quirks of blazoning pens°,
And in th' essential vesture of creation°
Does tire the ingener°.

Enter [Second] GENTLEMAN.

                    How now? Who has put in?   65

SECOND GENTLEMAN: 'Tis one Iago, ancient to the general.

CASSIO: H'as had most favorable and happy speed:
Tempests themselves, high seas, and howling winds,
The guttered° rocks and congregated° sands,
Traitors ensteeped° to enclog the guiltless keel,   70
As having sense° of beauty, do omit
Their mortal° natures, letting go safely by
The divine Desdemona.

MONTANO: What is she?

CASSIO: She that I spake of, our great captain's captain,
Left in the conduct of the bold Iago,   75
Whose footing° here anticipates our thoughts
A se'nnight's° speed. Great Jove, Othello guard,
And swell his sail with thine own pow'rful breath,
That he may bless this bay with his tall° ship,
Make love's quick pants in Desdemona's arms,   80
Give renewed fire to our extinct spirits.

Enter DESDEMONA, IAGO, RODERIGO, *and* EMILIA.

O, behold! The riches of the ship is come on shore!
You men of Cyprus, let her have your knees.   [*Kneeling.*]
Hail to thee, lady! and the grace of heaven,
Before, behind thee, and on every hand,   85
Enwheel thee round.

DESDEMONA: I thank you, valiant Cassio.
What tidings can you tell of my lord?

CASSIO: He is not yet arrived, nor know I aught
But that he's well and will be shortly here.

---

⁶²*paragons* exceeds.   ⁶²*wild fame* extravagant report.   ⁶³*quirks of blazoning pens* ingenuities
of praising pens.   ⁶⁴*essential vesture of creation* essential human nature as given by the Creator.
⁶⁵*tire the ingener* a difficult line that probably means something like "outdo the human ability to imagine and
picture."   ⁶⁹*guttered* jagged.   ⁶⁹*congregated* gathered.   ⁷⁰*ensteeped* submerged.
⁷¹*sense* awareness.   ⁷²*mortal* deadly.   ⁷⁶*footing* landing.   ⁷⁷*se'nnight's* week's.
⁷⁹*tall* brave.

DESDEMONA: O but I fear. How lost you company? 90

CASSIO: The great contention of sea and skies

    Parted our fellowship. (*Within:* A sail, a sail!)   [*A shot.*]

    But hark. A sail!

SECOND GENTLEMAN: They give this greeting to the citadel;

    This likewise is a friend.

CASSIO: See for the news.   [*Exit* GENTLEMAN.] 95

    Good ancient, you are welcome. [*To* EMILIA] Welcome, mistress.

    Let it not gall your patience, good Iago,

    That I extend° my manners. 'Tis my breeding°

    That gives me this bold show of courtesy.   [*Kisses* EMILIA.]

IAGO: Sir, would she give you so much of her lips 100

    As of her tongue she oft bestows on me,

    You would have enough.

DESDEMONA: Alas, she has no speech.

IAGO: In faith, too much.

    I find it still when I have leave to sleep°.

    Marry, before your ladyship°, I grant, 105

    She puts her tongue a little in her heart

    And chides with thinking.

EMILIA: You have little cause to say so.

IAGO: Come on, come on! You are pictures° out of door,

    Bells in your parlors, wildcats in your kitchens,

    Saints in your injuries°, devils being offended, 110

    Players in your housewifery°, and housewives in your beds.

DESDEMONA: O, fie upon thee, slanderer!

IAGO: Nay, it is true, or else I am a Turk:

    You rise to play, and go to bed to work.

EMILIA: You shall not write my praise.

IAGO: No, let me not. 115

DESDEMONA: What wouldst write of me, if thou shouldst praise me?

IAGO: O gentle lady, do not put me to't.

    For I am nothing if not critical.

DESDEMONA: Come on, assay. There's one gone to the harbor?

IAGO: Ay, madam.

DESDEMONA [*Aside*]: I am not merry; but I do beguile 120

    The thing I am by seeming otherwise.—

    Come, how wouldst thou praise me?

IAGO: I am about it; but indeed my invention

    Comes from my pate as birdlime° does from frieze°—

    It plucks out brains and all. But my Muse labors, 125

---

⁹⁸*extend* stretch.   ⁹⁸*breeding* *careful training in manners (Cassio is considerably more the polished gentleman than Iago, and aware of it).*   ¹⁰⁴*still ... sleep* *i.e., even when she allows me to sleep she continues to scold.*   ¹⁰⁵*before your ladyship* *in your presence.*   ¹⁰⁸*pictures* *models (of virtue).*   ¹¹⁰*in your injuries* *when you injure others.*   ¹¹¹*housewifery* *this word can mean "careful, economical household management," and Iago would then be accusing women of only pretending to be good housekeepers, while in bed they are either [1] economical of their favors, or more likely [2] serious and dedicated workers.*   ¹²⁴*birdlime* *a sticky substance put on branches to catch birds.*   ¹²⁴*frieze* *rough cloth.*

And thus she is delivered:
If she be fair° and wise: fairness and wit,
The one's for use, the other useth it.

DESDEMONA: Well praised. How if she be black° and witty?

IAGO: If she be black, and thereto have a wit, 130
She'll find a white that shall her blackness fit.

DESDEMONA: Worse and worse!

EMILIA: How if fair and foolish?

IAGO: She never yet was foolish that was fair,
For even her folly helped her to an heir. 135

DESDEMONA: Those are old fond° paradoxes to make fools laugh i' th' alehouse.
What miserable praise hast thou for her that's foul and foolish?

IAGO: There's none so foul, and foolish thereunto,
But does foul pranks which fair and wise ones do.

DESDEMONA: O heavy ignorance. Thou praisest the worst best. But what praise 140
couldst thou bestow on a deserving woman indeed—one that in the
authority of her merit did justly put on the vouch of very malice it-
self°?

IAGO: She that was ever fair, and never proud;
Had tongue at will, and yet was never loud; 145
Never lacked gold, and yet went never gay;
Fled from her wish, and yet said "Now I may";
She that being angered, her revenge being nigh,
Bade her wrong stay, and her displeasure fly;
She that in wisdom never was so frail 150
To change the cod's head for the salmon's tail°;
She that could think, and nev'r disclose her mind;
See suitors following, and not look behind:
She was a wight° (if ever such wights were)—

DESDEMONA: To do what? 155

IAGO: To suckle fools and chronicle small beer°.

DESDEMONA: O most lame and impotent conclusion. Do not learn of him,
Emilia, though he be thy husband. How say you, Cassio? Is he not a most
profane and liberal° counselor?

CASSIO: He speaks home°, madam. You may relish him more in° the soldier 160
than in the scholar. [*Takes* DESDEMONA's *hand.*]

IAGO [*Aside*]: He takes her by the palm. Ay, well said, whisper! With as little
a web as this will I ensnare as great a fly as Cassio. Ay, smile upon her,
do! I willgyve° thee in thine own courtship.—You say true; 'tis so, indeed!
—If such tricks as these strip you out of your lieutenantry, it had been 165
better you had not kissed your three fingers so oft—which now again you

---

¹²⁷***fair*** light-complexioned.   ¹²⁹***black*** brunette.   ¹³⁶***fond*** foolish.   ^{141–43}***one . . . itself***
i.e., a woman so honest and deserving that even malice would be forced to approve of her.   ¹⁵¹***To . . . tail***
i.e., to exchange something valuable for something useless.   ¹⁵⁴***wight*** *person.*   ¹⁵⁶***chronicle small***
beer *i.e., keep household accounts (the most trivial of occupations in Iago's opinion).*   ¹⁵⁹***liberal*** *licentious.*
¹⁶⁰***speaks home*** *thrusts deeply with his speech.*   ¹⁶⁰***relish him more in*** *enjoy him more as.*
¹⁶⁴***gyve*** *bind.*

are most apt to play the sir° in. Very good! Well kissed! An excellent
curtsy°! 'Tis so, indeed. Yet again your fingers to your lips? Would they
were clyster pipes° for your sake! [*Trumpets within.*] The Moor! I know
his trumpet°.   170

CASSIO: 'Tis truly so.

DESDEMONA: Let's meet him and receive him.

CASSIO: Lo, where he comes.

Enter OTHELLO *and* ATTENDANTS.

OTHELLO: O my fair warrior!

DESDEMONA: My dear Othello.

OTHELLO: It gives me wonder great as my content   175
  To see you here before me. O my soul's joy!
  If after every tempest come such calms,
  May the winds blow till they have wakened death.
  And let the laboring bark climb hills of seas
  Olympus-high, and duck again as low   180
  As hell's from heaven. If it were now to die,
  'Twere now to be most happy; for I fear
  My soul hath her content so absolute
  That not another comfort like to this
  Succeeds in unknown fate.

DESDEMONA: The heavens forbid   185
  But that our loves and comforts should increase
  Even as our days do grow.

OTHELLO: Amen to that, sweet powers!
  I cannot speak enough of this content:
  It stops me here [*touches his heart*]; it is too much of joy.
  And this, and this, the greatest discords be   [*They kiss.*]190
  That e'er our hearts shall make!

IAGO [*Aside*]:   O, you are well tuned now!
  But I'll set down the pegs° that make this music,
  As honest as I am.

OTHELLO: Come, let us to the castle.
  News, friends! Our wars are done; the Turks are drowned.
  How does my old acquaintance of this isle?   195
  Honey, you shall be well desired in Cyprus;
  I have found great love amongst them. O my sweet,
  I prattle out of fashion, and I dote
  In mine own comforts. I prithee, good Iago,
  Go to the bay and disembark my coffers.   200
  Bring thou the master to the citadel;
  He is a good one and his worthiness

---

¹⁶⁷*the sir* *the fashionable gentleman.*   ¹⁶⁸*curtsy* *courtesy, i.e., bow.*   ¹⁶⁹*clyster pipes* *enema
tubes.*   ¹⁷⁰*his trumpet* *(great men had their own distinctive calls).*   ¹⁹²*set down the pegs* *loosen
the strings (to produce discord).*

Does challenge° much respect. Come, Desdemona,
Once more well met at Cyprus.

Exit OTHELLO *and* DESDEMONA [*and all but* IAGO *and* RODERIGO].

IAGO [*To an Attendant*]: Do thou meet me presently at the harbor. [*To* 205
RODERIGO] Come hither. If thou be'st valiant (as they say base men being
in love have then a nobility in their natures more than is native to them),
list me. The lieutenant tonight watches on the court of guard°. First, I must
tell thee this: Desdemona is directly in love with him.

RODERIGO: With him? Why, 'tis not possible.   210

IAGO: Lay thy finger thus [*puts his finger to his lips*], and let thy soul be
instructed. Mark me with what violence she first loved the Moor but for
bragging and telling her fantastical lies. To love him still for prating? Let
not thy discreet heart think it. Her eye must be fed. And what delight shall
she have to look on the devil? When the blood is made dull with the act 215
of sport, there should be a game° to inflame it and to give satiety a fresh
appetite, loveliness in favor°, sympathy in years°, manners, and beauties;
all which the Moor is defective in. Now for want of these required
conveniences°, her delicate tenderness will find itself abused, begin to heave
the gorge°, disrelish and abhor the Moor. Very nature will instruct her in 220
it and compel her to some second choice. Now sir, this granted—as it is
a most pregnant° and unforced position—who stands so eminent in the
degree of this fortune as Cassio does? A knave very voluble; no further
conscionable° than in putting on the mere form of civil and humane°
seeming for the better compass of his salt° and most hidden loose° affection. 225
Why, none! Why, none! A slipper° and subtle knave, a finder of occasion,
that has an eye can stamp and counterfeit advantages, though true advantage never present itself. A devilish knave. Besides, the knave is handsome,
young, and hath all those requisites in him that folly and green minds look
after. A pestilent complete knave, and the woman hath found him already. 230

RODERIGO: I cannot believe that in her; she's full of most blessed condition.

IAGO: Blessed fig's-end! The wine she drinks is made of grapes. If she had been
blessed, she would never have loved the Moor. Blessed pudding! Didst
thou not see her paddle with the palm of his hand? Didst not mark that? 235

RODERIGO: Yes, that I did; but that was but courtesy.

IAGO: Lechery, by this hand! [*Extends his index finger.*] An index° and obscure
prologue to the history of lust and foul thoughts. They met so near with
their lips that their breaths embraced together. Villainous thoughts,
Roderigo. When these mutualities so marshal the way, hard at hand comes 240
the master and main exercise, th' incorporate° conclusion: Pish! But, sir,

---

203*challenge* *require, exact.* 208*court of guard* *guardhouse.* 216*game* *sport (with the added
sense of "gamey," "rank").* 217*favor* *countenance, appearance.* 217*sympathy in years* *sameness of
age.* 219*conveniences* *advantages.* 220*heave the gorge* *vomit.* 222*pregnant* *likely.*
223-24*no further conscionable* *having no more conscience.* 224*humane* *polite.* 225*salt* *lecher-
ous.* 225*loose* *immoral.* 226*slipper* *slippery.* 237*index* *pointer.* 241*incorporate* *car-
nal.*

be you ruled by me. I have brought you from Venice. Watch you tonight; for the command, I'll lay't upon you. Cassio knows you not. I'll not be far from you. Do you find some occasion to anger Cassio, either by speaking too loud, or tainting° his discipline, or from what other course[245] you please which the time shall more favorably minister.

RODERIGO: Well.

IAGO: Sir, he's rash and very sudden in choler°, and haply may strike at you. Provoke him that he may; for even out of that will I cause these of Cyprus to mutiny, whose qualification shall come into no true taste° again but by[250] the displanting of Cassio. So shall you have a shorter journey to your desires by the means I shall then have to prefer them; and the impediment most profitably removed without the which there were no expectation of our prosperity.

RODERIGO: I will do this if you can bring it to any opportunity.   255

IAGO: I warrant thee. Meet me by and by at the citadel. I must fetch his necessaries ashore. Farewell.

RODERIGO: Adieu.   *Exit.*

IAGO: That Cassio loves her, I do well believe't;
That she loves him, 'tis apt and of great credit.   260
The Moor, howbeit that I endure him not,
Is of a constant, loving, noble nature,
And I dare think he'll prove to Desdemona
A most dear° husband. Now I do love her too;
Not out of absolute° lust, though peradventure°   265
I stand accountant for as great a sin,
But partly led to diet° my revenge,
For that I do suspect the lusty Moor
Hath leaped into my seat; the thought whereof
Doth, like a poisonous mineral, gnaw my inwards;   270
And nothing can or shall content my soul
Till I am evened with him, wife for wife.
Or failing so, yet that I put the Moor
At least into a jealousy so strong
That judgment cannot cure. Which thing to do,   275
If this poor trash of Venice, whom I trace°
For his quick hunting, stand the putting on,
I'll have our Michael Cassio on the hip,
Abuse him to the Moor in the right garb°
(For I fear Cassio with my nightcap too),   280
Make the Moor thank me, love me, and reward me
For making him egregiously an ass

---

[245]*tainting* discrediting.   [248]*choler* anger.   [250]*qualification . . . taste* i.e., appeasement will not be brought about (wine was "qualified" by adding water).   [264]*dear* expensive.   [264]*out of absolute* absolutely out of.   [264]*peradventure* perchance.   [267]*diet* feed.   [276]*trace* (most editors emend to "trash," meaning to hang weights on a dog to slow his hunting: but "trace" clearly means something like "put on the trace" or "set on the track").   [279]*right garb* i.e., "proper fashion."

And practicing upon° his peace and quiet,
Even to madness. 'Tis here, but yet confused:
Knavery's plain face is never seen till used.   *Exit.* 285

Scene II [*A street.*]

Enter OTHELLO'S HERALD, *with a proclamation.*

HERALD: It is Othello's pleasure, our noble and valiant general, that upon
certain tidings now arrived importing the mere perdition° of the Turkish
fleet, every man put himself into triumph. Some to dance, some to make
bonfires, each man to what sport and revels his addition° leads him. For,
besides these beneficial news, it is the celebration of his nuptial. So much   5
was his pleasure should be proclaimed. All offices° are open, and there is
full liberty of feasting from this present hour of five till the bell have told
eleven. Bless the isle of Cyprus and our noble general Othello!   *Exit.*

Scene III [*The citadel of Cyprus.*]

Enter OTHELLO, DESDEMONA, CASSIO, *and* ATTENDANTS.

OTHELLO: Good Michael, look you to the guard tonight.
Let's teach ourselves that honorable stop,
Not to outsport direction.
CASSIO: Iago hath discretion what to do;
But notwithstanding, with my personal eye   5
Will I look to't.
OTHELLO: Iago is most honest.
Michael, good night. Tomorrow with your earliest
Let me have speech with you. [*To* DESDEMONA] Come, my dear love,
The purchase made, the fruits are to ensue.
That profit's yet to come 'tween me and you.   10
Good night.   *Exit* [OTHELLO *with* DESDEMONA *and* ATTENDANTS].

Enter IAGO.

CASSIO: Welcome, Iago. We must to the watch.
IAGO: Not this hour, lieutenant; 'tis not yet ten o' th' clock. Our general cast°
us thus early for the love of his Desdemona; who let us not therefore blame.
He hath not yet made wanton the night with her, and she is sport for Jove.   15
CASSIO: She's a most exquisite lady.
IAGO: And, I'll warrant her, full of game.
CASSIO: Indeed, she's a most fresh and delicate creature.
IAGO: What an eye she has! Methinks it sounds a parley to provocation.   20
CASSIO: An inviting eye; and yet methinks right modest.
IAGO: And when she speaks, is it not an alarum° to love?

---

²⁸³*practicing upon* *scheming to destroy.*   **II.ii.**   ²*mere perdition* *absolute destruction.*   ⁴*addition* *rank.*   ⁶*offices* *kitchens and storerooms of food.*   **II.iii.**   ¹³*cast* *dismissed.*   ²²*alarum*
the call to action, "general quarters."

CASSIO: She is indeed perfection.

IAGO: Well, happiness to their sheets! Come, lieutenant, I have a stoup° of
wine, and here without are a brace of Cyprus gallants that would fain have 25
a measure to the health of black Othello.

CASSIO: Not tonight, good Iago. I have very poor and unhappy brains for
drinking; I could well wish courtesy would invent some other custom of
entertainment.

IAGO: O, they are our friends. But one cup! I'll drink for you.   30

CASSIO: I have drunk but one tonight, and that was craftily qualified° too; and
behold what innovation it makes here. I am unfortunate in the infirmity
and dare not task my weakness with any more.

IAGO: What, man! 'Tis a night of revels, the gallants desire it.

CASSIO: Where are they?   35

IAGO: Here, at the door. I pray you call them in.

CASSIO: I'll do't, but it dislikes me.   *Exit.*

IAGO: If I can fasten but one cup upon him
With that which he hath drunk tonight already,
He'll be as full of quarrel and offense   40
As my young mistress' dog. Now, my sick fool Roderigo,
Whom love hath turned almost the wrong side out,
To Desdemona hath tonight caroused
Potations pottle-deep°; and he's to watch.
Three else° of Cyprus, noble swelling spirits,   45
That hold their honors in a wary distance°,
The very elements of this warlike isle,
Have I tonight flustered with flowing cups,
And they watch too. Now, 'mongst this flock of drunkards
Am I to put our Cassio in some action   50
That may offend the isle. But here they come.

Enter CASSIO, MONTANO, *and* GENTLEMEN.

If consequence do but approve my dream,
My boat sails freely, both with wind and stream.

CASSIO: 'Fore God, they have given me a rouse° already.

MONTANO: Good faith, a little one; not past a pint, as I am a soldier.   55

IAGO: Some wine, ho!

[*Sings*] And let me the canakin clink, clink;
            And let me the canakin clink.
        A soldier's a man;
        O man's life's but a span;   60
        Why then, let a soldier drink.

Some wine, boys!

CASSIO: 'Fore God, an excellent song!

---

²⁴**stoup** *two-quart tankard.*   ³¹**qualified** *diluted.*   ⁴⁴**pottle-deep** *to the bottom of the cup.*
⁴⁵**else** *others.*   ⁴⁶**hold . . . distance** *are scrupulous in maintaining their honor.*   ⁵⁴**rouse** *drink.*

IAGO: I learned it in England, where indeed they are most potent in potting. Your Dane, your German, and your swag-bellied° Hollander—Drink, ho!— 65 are nothing to your English.

CASSIO: Is your Englishman so exquisite° in his drinking?

IAGO: Why, he drinks you with facility your Dane dead drunk; he sweats not to overthrow your Almain; he gives your Hollander a vomit ere the next pottle can be filled. 70

CASSIO: To the health of our general!

MONTANO: I am for it, lieutenant, and I'll do you justice.

IAGO: O sweet England!

[*Sings*] King Stephen was and a worthy peer;
His breeches cost him but a crown; 75
He held them sixpence all too dear,
With that he called the tailor lown°.
He was a wight of high renown,
And thou art but of low degree:
'Tis pride that pulls the country down; 80
And take thine auld cloak about thee.

Some wine, ho!

CASSIO: 'Fore God, this is a more exquisite song than the other.

IAGO: Will you hear't again?

CASSIO: No, for I hold him to be unworthy of his place that does those things. 85 Well, God's above all; and there be souls must be saved, and there be souls must not be saved.

IAGO: It's true, good lieutenant.

CASSIO: For mine own part—no offense to the general, nor any man of quality —I hope to be saved. 90

IAGO: And so do I too, lieutenant.

CASSIO: Ay, but, by your leave, not before me. The lieutenant is to be saved before the ancient. Let's have no more of this; let's to our affairs.—God forgive us our sins!—Gentlemen, let's look to our business. Do not think, gentlemen, I am drunk. This is my ancient; this is my right hand, and this 95 is my left. I am not drunk now. I can stand well enough, and I speak well enough.

GENTLEMEN: Excellent well!

CASSIO: Why, very well then. You must not think then that I am drunk.

Exit.

MONTANO: To th' platform, masters. Come, let's set the watch. 100

IAGO: You see this fellow that is gone before.
He's a soldier fit to stand by Caesar
And give direction; and do but see his vice.
'Tis to his virtue a just equinox°,
The one as long as th' other. 'Tis pity of him. 105

---

⁶⁵**swag-bellied** *pendulous-bellied.*   ⁶⁷**exquisite** *superb.*   ⁷⁷**lown** *lout.*   ¹⁰⁴**just equinox** *exact balance (of dark and light).*

I fear the trust Othello puts him in,
On some odd time of his infirmity,
Will shake this island.
MONTANO: But is he often thus?
IAGO: 'Tis evermore his prologue to his sleep:
He'll watch the horologe a double set°   110
If drink rock not his cradle.
MONTANO: It were well
The general were put in mind of it.
Perhaps he sees it not, or his good nature
Prizes the virtue that appears in Cassio
And looks not on his evils. Is not this true?   115

Enter RODERIGO.

IAGO [*Aside*]: How now, Roderigo?
I pray you after the lieutenant, go!   [*Exit* RODERIGO.]
MONTANO: And 'tis great pity that the noble Moor
Should hazard such a place as his own second
With one of an ingraft° infirmity.   120
It were an honest action to say so
To the Moor.
IAGO: Not I, for this fair island!
I do love Cassio well and would do much
To cure him of this evil.   (Help! Help! *Within*.)
But hark! What noise?   125

Enter CASSIO, *pursuing* RODERIGO.

CASSIO: Zounds, you rogue! You rascal!
MONTANO: What's the matter, lieutenant?
CASSIO: A knave teach me my duty? I'll beat the knave into a twiggen°
     bottle.
RODERIGO: Beat me?   130
CASSIO: Dost thou prate, rogue?   [*Strikes him.*]
MONTANO: Nay, good lieutenant! I pray you, sir, hold your hand.

[*Stays him.*]

CASSIO: Let me go, sir, or I'll knock you o'er the mazzard°.
MONTANO: Come, come, you're drunk!
CASSIO: Drunk?   [*They fight.*]135
IAGO [*Aside to* RODERIGO]: Away, I say! Go out and cry a mutiny!

[*Exit* RODERIGO.]

Nay, good lieutenant. God's will, gentlemen!
Help, ho! Lieutenant. Sir. Montano.
Help, masters! Here's a goodly watch indeed!   [*A bell rung.*]

---

[110] **watch ... set** *stay awake twice around the clock.*   [120]**ingraft** *ingrained.*   [128]**twiggen** *wicker-*
covered.   [133]**mazzard** *head.*

Who's that which rings the bell? Diablo, ho!   140
The two will rise. God's will, lieutenant,
You'll be ashamed forever.

Enter OTHELLO *and* ATTENDANTS.

OTHELLO: What is the matter here?
MONTANO: Zounds, I bleed still. I am hurt to the death.
  He dies.   [*He and* CASSIO *fight again.*]
OTHELLO: Hold for your lives!   145
IAGO: Hold, ho! Lieutenant. Sir. Montano. Gentlemen!
  Have you forgot all place of sense and duty?
  Hold! The general speaks to you. Hold, for shame!
OTHELLO: Why, how now, ho? From whence ariseth this?
  Are we turned Turks, and to ourselves do that   150
  Which heaven hath forbid the Ottomites°?
  For Christian shame put by this barbarous brawl!
  He that stirs next to carve for his own rage
  Holds his soul light°; he dies upon his motion.
  Silence that dreadful bell! It frights the isle   155
  From her propriety°. What is the matter, masters?
  Honest Iago, that looks dead with grieving,
  Speak. Who began this? On thy love, I charge thee.
IAGO: I do not know. Friends all, but now, even now,
  In quarter° and in terms like bride and groom   160
  Devesting them for bed; and then, but now—
  As if some planet had unwitted men—
  Swords out, and tilting one at other's breasts
  In opposition bloody. I cannot speak
  Any beginning to this peevish odds°,   165
  And would in action glorious I had lost
  Those legs that brought me to a part of it!
OTHELLO: How comes it, Michael, you are thus forgot?
CASSIO: I pray you pardon me; I cannot speak.
OTHELLO: Worthy Montano, you were wont to be civil;   170
  Thy gravity and stillness of your youth
  The world hath noted, and your name is great
  In mouths of wisest censure°. What's the matter
  That you unlace° your reputation thus
  And spend your rich opinion° for the name   175
  Of a night-brawler? Give me answer to it.
MONTANO: Worthy Othello, I am hurt to danger.
  Your officer, Iago, can inform you.
  While I spare speech, which something now offends° me,

---

[151]*heaven . . . Ottomites* *i.e., by sending the storm which dispersed the Turks.*   [154]*Holds his soul light* *values his soul lightly.*   [156]*propriety* *proper order.*   [160]*In quarter* *on duty.*   [165]*odds* *quar-rel.*   [173]*censure* *judgment.*   [174]*unlace* *undo (the term refers specifically to the dressing of a wild boar killed in the hunt).*   [175]*opinion* *reputation.*   [179]*offends* *harms, hurts.*

Of all that I do know; nor know I aught   180
By me that's said or done amiss this night,
Unless self-charity be sometimes a vice,
And to defend ourselves it be a sin
When violence assails us.

OTHELLO: Now, by heaven,
My blood begins my safer guides to rule,   185
And passion, having my best judgment collied°,
Assays to lead the way. If I once stir
Or do but lift this arm, the best of you
Shall sink in my rebuke. Give me to know
How this foul rout began, who set it on;   190
And he that is approved in this offense,
Though he had twinned with me, both at a birth,
Shall lose me. What? In a town of war
Yet wild, the people's hearts brimful of fear,
To manage° private and domestic quarrel?   195
In night, and on the court and guard of safety?
'Tis monstrous. Iago, who began't?

MONTANO: If partially affined, or leagued in office°,
Thou dost deliver more or less than truth,
Thou art no soldier.

IAGO: Touch me not so near.   200
I had rather have this tongue cut from my mouth
Than it should do offense to Michael Cassio.
Yet I persuade myself to speak the truth
Shall nothing wrong him. This it is, general.
Montano and myself being in speech,   205
There comes a fellow crying out for help,
And Cassio following him with determined sword
To execute upon him. Sir, this gentleman
Steps in to Cassio and entreats his pause.
Myself the crying fellow did pursue,   210
Lest by his clamor—as it so fell out—
The town might fall in fright. He, swift of foot,
Outran my purpose; and I returned then rather
For that I heard the clink and fall of swords,
And Cassio high in oath; which till tonight   215
I ne'er might say before. When I came back—
For this was brief—I found them close together
At blow and thrust, even as again they were
When you yourself did part them.
More of this matter cannot I report;   220
But men are men; the best sometimes forget.

---

¹⁸⁶*collied* darkened.   ¹⁹⁵*manage* conduct.   ¹⁹⁸*If . . . office* if you are partial because you are related ("affined") or the brother officer (of Cassio).

Though Cassio did some little wrong to him,
As men in rage strike those that wish them best,
Yet surely Cassio I believe received
From him that fled some strange indignity,   225
Which patience could not pass°.

OTHELLO: I know, Iago,
Thy honesty and love doth mince° this matter,
Making it light to Cassio. Cassio, I love thee;
But never more be officer of mine.

Enter DESDEMONA, *attended.*

Look if my gentle love be not raised up.   230
I'll make thee an example.

DESDEMONA: What is the matter, dear?

OTHELLO: All's well, sweeting; come away to bed.
[*To* MONTANO] Sir, for your hurts, myself will be your surgeon.
Lead him off.   [MONTANO *led off.*]
Iago, look with care about the town   235
And silence those whom this vile brawl distracted.
Come, Desdemona: 'tis the soldiers' life
To have their balmy slumbers waked with strife.

Exit [*with all but* IAGO *and* CASSIO].

IAGO: What, are you hurt, lieutenant?

CASSIO: Ay, past all surgery.   240

IAGO: Marry, God forbid!

CASSIO: Reputation, reputation, reputation! O, I have lost my reputation! I
have lost the immortal part of myself, and what remains is bestial. My
reputation, Iago, my reputation.

IAGO: As I am an honest man, I had thought you had received some bodily 245
wound. There is more sense° in that than in reputation. Reputation is an
idle and most false imposition°, oft got without merit and lost without
deserving. You have lost no reputation at all unless you repute yourself
such a loser. What, man, there are more ways to recover the general again.
You are but now cast in his mood°—a punishment more in policy° than 250
in malice—even so as one would beat his offenseless dog to affright an
imperious lion. Sue to him again, and he's yours.

CASSIO: I will rather sue to be despised than to deceive so good a commander
with so slight, so drunken, and so indiscreet an officer. Drunk! And speak
parrot°! And squabble! Swagger! Swear! and discourse fustian° with one's 255
own shadow! O thou invisible spirit of wine, if thou hast no name to be
known by, let us call thee devil!

---

²²⁶*pass* allow to pass.   ²²⁷*mince* cut up (i.e., tell only part of).   ²⁴⁶*sense* physical feeling.
²⁴⁷*imposition* external thing.   ²⁵⁰*cast in his mood* dismissed because of his anger.   ²⁵⁰*in policy*
politically necessary.   ²⁵⁴⁻⁵⁵*speak parrot* gabble without sense.   ²⁵⁵*discourse fustian* speak nonsense ("fustian" was a coarse cotton cloth used for stuffing).

IAGO: What was he that you followed with your sword?
  What had he done to you?

CASSIO: I know not.   260

IAGO: Is't possible?

CASSIO: I remember a mass of things, but nothing distinctly: a quarrel, but
  nothing wherefore. O God, that men should put an enemy in their mouths
  to steal away their brains! that we should with joy, pleasance, revel, and
  applause transform ourselves into beasts!   265

IAGO: Why, but you are now well enough. How came you thus recovered?

CASSIO: It hath pleased the devil drunkenness to give place to the devil wrath.
  One unperfectness shows me another, to make me frankly despise myself.

IAGO: Come, you are too severe a moraler. As the time, the place, and the
  condition of this country stands, I could heartily wish this had not befall'n; 270
  but since it is as it is, mend it for your own good.

CASSIO: I will ask him for my place again: he shall tell me I am a drunkard.
  Had I as many mouths as Hydra, such an answer would stop them all. To
  be now a sensible man, by and by a fool, and presently a beast! O strange!
  Every inordinate cup is unblest, and the ingredient is a devil.   275

IAGO: Come, come, good wine is a good familiar creature if it be well used.
  Exclaim no more against it. And, good lieutenant, I think you think I love
  you.

CASSIO: I have well approved it, sir. I drunk?

IAGO: You or any man living may be drunk at a time, man. I tell you what   280
  you shall do. Our general's wife is now the general. I may say so in this
  respect, for all he hath devoted and given up himself to the contemplation,
  mark, and devotement of her parts° and graces. Confess yourself freely to
  her; importune her help to put you in your place again. She is of so free,
  so kind, so apt, so blessed a disposition she holds it a vice in her goodness 285
  not to do more than she is requested. This broken joint between you and
  her husband entreat her to splinter°; and my fortunes against any lay° worth
  naming, this crack of your love shall grow stronger than it was before.

CASSIO: You advise me well.

IAGO: I protest, in the sincerity of love and honest kindness.   290

CASSIO: I think it freely; and betimes in the morning I will beseech the virtuous
  Desdemona to undertake for me. I am desperate of my fortunes if they
  check° me.

IAGO: You are in the right. Good night, lieutenant; I must to the watch.

CASSIO: Good night, honest Iago.   *Exit* CASSIO. 295

IAGO: And what's he then that says I play the villain,
  When this advice is free° I give, and honest,
  Probal to° thinking, and indeed the course
  To win the Moor again? For 'tis most easy
  Th' inclining° Desdemona to subdue   300

283*devotement of her parts* devotion to her qualities.   287*splinter* splint.   287*lay* wager.
293*check* repulse.   297*free* generous and open.   298*Probal to* provable by.   300*inclining*
inclined (to be helpful).

In any honest suit; she's framed as fruitful°
As the free elements°. And then for her
To win the Moor—were't to renounce his baptism,
All seals and symbols of redeemèd sin—
His soul is so enfettered to her love   305
That she may make, unmake, do what she list,
Even as her appetite° shall play the god
With his weak function°. How am I then a villain
To counsel Cassio to this parallel course,
Directly to his good? Divinity of hell!   310
When devils will the blackest sins put on°,
They do suggest at first with heavenly shows°,
As I do now. For whiles this honest fool
Plies Desdemona to repair his fortune,
And she for him pleads strongly to the Moor,   315
I'll pour this pestilence into his ear:
That she repeals him° for her body's lust;
And by how much she strives to do him good,
She shall undo her credit with the Moor.
So will I turn her virtue into pitch,   320
And out of her own goodness make the net
That shall enmesh them all. How now, Roderigo?

Enter RODERIGO.

RODERIGO: I do not follow here in the chase, not like a hound that hunts, but
one that fills up the cry°. My money is almost spent; I have been tonight
exceedingly well cudgeled; and I think the issue will be, I shall have so   325
much experience for my pains; and so, with no money at all, and a little
more wit, return again to Venice.
IAGO: How poor are they that have not patience!
What wound did ever heal but by degrees?
Thou know'st we work by wit, and not by witchcraft;   330
And wit depends on dilatory time.
Does't not go well? Cassio hath beaten thee,
And thou by that small hurt hath cashiered Cassio.
Though other things grow fair against the sun,
Yet fruits that blossom first will first be ripe.   335
Content thyself awhile. By the mass, 'tis morning!
Pleasure and action make the hours seem short.
Retire thee, go where thou art billeted.
Away, I say! Thou shalt know more hereafter.
Nay, get thee gone!   *Exit* RODERIGO.
Two things are to be done: 340

---

³⁰¹*framed as fruitful*   *made as generous.*   ³⁰²*elements*   *i.e., basic nature.*   ³⁰⁷*appetite*   *liking.*
³⁰⁸*function*   *thought.*   ³¹¹*put on*   *advance, further.*   ³¹²*shows*   *appearances.*   ³¹⁷*repeals him*
asks for (Cassio's reinstatement).   ³²⁴*fills up the cry*   *makes up one of the hunting pack, adding to the noise*
but not actually tracking.

My wife must move° for Cassio to her mistress;
I'll set her on;
Myself awhile° to draw the Moor apart
And bring him jump° when he may Cassio find
Soliciting his wife. Ay, that's the way!   345
Dull not device by coldness and delay.   *Exit.*

ACT III

Scene I [*A street.*]

Enter CASSIO [*and*] MUSICIANS.

CASSIO: Masters, play here. I will content your pains°.
    Something that's brief; and bid "Good morrow, general." [*They play.*]

[*Enter* CLOWN°.]

CLOWN: Why, masters, have your instruments been in Naples° that they speak
    i' th' nose thus?
MUSICIAN: How, sir, how?   5
CLOWN: Are these, I pray you, wind instruments?
MUSICIAN: Ay, marry, are they, sir.
CLOWN: O, thereby hangs a tale.
MUSICIAN: Whereby hangs a tale, sir?
CLOWN: Marry, sir, by many a wind instrument that I know. But, masters,   10
    here's money for you; and the general so likes your music that he desires
    you, for love's sake, to make no more noise with it.
MUSICIAN: Well, sir, we will not.
CLOWN: If you have any music that may not be heard, to't again. But, as they
    say, to hear music the general does not greatly care.   15
MUSICIAN: We have none such, sir.
CLOWN: Then put up your pipes in your bag, for I'll away. Go, vanish into
    air, away!   *Exit* MUSICIANS.
CASSIO: Dost thou hear me, mine honest friend?
CLOWN: No. I hear not your honest friend. I hear you.   20
CASSIO: Prithee keep up thy quillets°. There's a poor piece of gold for thee.
    If the gentlewoman that attends the general's wife be stirring, tell
    her there's one Cassio entreats her a little favor of speech. Wilt thou do
    this?
CLOWN: She is stirring, sir. If she will stir hither, I shall seem to notify unto   25
    her°.   *Exit* CLOWN.

---

³⁴¹*move* petition.   ³⁴³*awhile* at the same time.   ³⁴⁴*jump* at the precise moment and place.
III.i.   ¹*content your pains* reward your efforts.   s.d.*Clown* fool.   ³*Naples* this may refer either
to the Neapolitan nasal tone, or to syphilis—rife in Naples—which breaks down the nose.   ²¹*quillets* puns.
²⁵⁻²⁶*seem . . . her* (the Clown is mocking Cassio's overly elegant manner of speaking).

Enter IAGO.

CASSIO: In happy time, Iago.
IAGO: You have not been abed then?
CASSIO: Why no, the day had broke before we parted.
  I have made bold, Iago, to send in to your wife;
  My suit to her is that she will to virtuous Desdemona   30
  Procure me some access.
IAGO: I'll send her to you presently,
  And I'll devise a mean to draw the Moor
  Out of the way, that your converse and business
  May be more free.
CASSIO: I humbly thank you for't.   *Exit* [IAGO]. 35
                              I never knew
  A Florentine° more kind and honest.

Enter EMILIA.

EMILIA: Good morrow, good lieutenant. I am sorry
  For your displeasure°; but all will sure be well.
  The general and his wife are talking of it,   40
  And she speaks for you stoutly. The Moor replies
  That he you hurt is of great fame in Cyprus
  And great affinity°, and that in wholesome wisdom
  He might not but refuse you. But he protests he loves you.
  And needs no other suitor but his likings   45
  To bring you in again.
CASSIO: Yet I beseech you,
  If you think fit, or that it may be done,
  Give me advantage of some brief discourse
  With Desdemona alone.
EMILIA: Pray you come in.
  I will bestow you where you shall have time   50
  To speak your bosom° freely.
CASSIO: I am much bound to you.   [*Exeunt.*]

Scene II [*The citadel.*]

Enter OTHELLO, IAGO, *and* GENTLEMEN.

OTHELLO: These letters give, Iago, to the pilot
  And by him do my duties to the Senate.
  That done, I will be walking on the works;
  Repair° there to me.
IAGO: Well, my good lord, I'll do't.
OTHELLO: This fortification, gentlemen, shall we see't?   5
GENTLEMEN: We'll wait upon your lordship.   *Exeunt.*

---

³⁷**Florentine** *i.e., Iago is as kind as if he were from Cassio's home town, Florence.* ³⁹**displeasure**
discomforting. ⁴³**affinity** *family.* ⁵¹**bosom** *inmost thoughts.* **III.ii.** ⁴**Repair** *go.*

Scene III [*The citadel.*]

Enter DESDEMONA, CASSIO, *and* EMILIA.

DESDEMONA: Be thou assured, good Cassio, I will do
    All my abilities in thy behalf.
EMILIA: Good madam, do. I warrant it grieves my husband
    As if the cause were his.
DESDEMONA: O, that's an honest fellow. Do not doubt, Cassio,   5
    But I will have my lord and you again
    As friendly as you were.
CASSIO: Bounteous madam,
    Whatever shall become of Michael Cassio,
    He's never anything but your true servant.
DESDEMONA: I know't; I thank you. You do love my lord.   10
    You have known him long, and be you well assured
    He shall in strangeness stand no farther off
    Than in a politic distance.°
CASSIO: Ay, but, lady,
    That policy may either last so long,
    Or feed upon such nice° and waterish diet,   15
    Or breed itself so out of circumstances°,
    That, I being absent, and my place supplied°,
    My general will forget my love and service.
DESDEMONA: Do not doubt° that; before Emilia here
    I give thee warrant of thy place. Assure thee,   20
    If I do vow a friendship, I'll perform it
    To the last article. My lord shall never rest;
    I'll watch him tame° and talk him out of patience;
    His bed shall seem a school, his board a shrift°;
    I'll intermingle everything he does   25
    With Cassio's suit. Therefore be merry, Cassio,
    For thy solicitor shall rather die
    Than give thy cause away.

Enter OTHELLO *and* IAGO [*at a distance*].

EMILIA: Madam, here comes my lord.
CASSIO: Madam, I'll take my leave.   30
DESDEMONA: Why, stay, and hear me speak.
CASSIO: Madam, not now. I am very ill at ease,
    Unfit for mine own purposes.
DESDEMONA: Well, do your discretion.   *Exit* CASSIO.
IAGO: Ha! I like not that.

III.iii. ¹²⁻¹³*He . . . distance* i.e., he shall act no more distant to you than is necessary for political reasons. ¹⁵*nice* trivial. ¹⁶*Or . . . circumstances* i.e., or grow so on the basis of accidental happenings and political needs. ¹⁷*supplied* filled. ¹⁹*doubt* imagine. ²³*watch him tame* (animals were tamed by being kept awake) ²⁴*board a shrift* table (seem) a confessional.

OTHELLO: What dost thou say?   35
IAGO: Nothing, my lord; or if—I know not what.
OTHELLO: Was not that Cassio parted from my wife?
IAGO: Cassio, my lord? No, sure, I cannot think it
  That he would steal away so guilty-like,
  Seeing you coming.
OTHELLO: I do believe 'twas he.   40
DESDEMONA [*Coming to them*]: How now, my lord?
  I have been talking with a suitor here,
  A man that languishes in your displeasure.
OTHELLO: Who is't you mean?
DESDEMONA: Why, your lieutenant, Cassio. Good my lord,   45
  If I have any grace or power to move you,
  His present° reconciliation take.
  For if he be not one that truly loves you,
  That errs in ignorance, and not in cunning,
  I have no judgment in an honest face.   50
  I prithee call him back.
OTHELLO: Went he hence now?
DESDEMONA: I' sooth so humbled
  That he hath left part of his grief with me
  To suffer with him. Good love, call him back.
OTHELLO: Not now, sweet Desdemon; some other time.   55
DESDEMONA: But shall't be shortly?
OTHELLO: The sooner, sweet, for you.
DESDEMONA: Shall't be tonight at supper?
OTHELLO: No, not tonight.
DESDEMONA: Tomorrow dinner then?
OTHELLO: I shall not dine at home;
  I meet the captains at the citadel.
DESDEMONA: Why then, tomorrow night, on Tuesday morn,   60
  On Tuesday noon, or night, on Wednesday morn.
  I prithee name the time, but let it not
  Exceed three days. In faith, he's penitent;
  And yet his trespass, in our common reason
  (Save that, they say, the wars must make example   65
  Out of her best), is not almost a fault
  T' incur a private check.° When shall he come?
  Tell me, Othello. I wonder in my soul
  What you would ask me that I should deny
  Or stand so mamm'ring° on. What? Michael Cassio,   70
  That came awooing with you, and so many a time,
  When I have spoke of you dispraisingly,
  Hath ta'en your part—to have so much to do

---

⁴⁷**present** *immediate.*   ⁶⁶⁻⁶⁷**is . . . check** *is almost not serious enough for a private rebuke (let alone a public disgrace).*   ⁷⁰**mamm'ring** *hesitating.*

To bring him in? By'r Lady, I could do much—
OTHELLO: Prithee no more. Let him come when he will!   75
   I will deny thee nothing.
DESDEMONA: Why, this is not a boon;
   'Tis as I should entreat you wear your gloves,
   Or feed on nourishing dishes, or keep you warm,
   Or sue to you to do a peculiar profit°
   To your own person. Nay, when I have a suit   80
   Wherein I mean to touch your love indeed,
   It shall be full of poise° and difficult weight,
   And fearful to be granted.
OTHELLO: I will deny thee nothing!
   Whereon I do beseech thee grant me this,
   To leave me but a little to myself.   85
DESDEMONA: Shall I deny you? No. Farewell, my lord.
OTHELLO: Farewell, my Desdemona: I'll come to thee straight°.
DESDEMONA: Emilia, come. Be as your fancies teach you;
   Whate'er you be, I am obedient.   *Exit [with* EMILIA].
OTHELLO: Excellent wretch! Perdition catch my soul   90
   But I do love thee! And when I love thee not,
   Chaos is come again.
IAGO: My noble lord—
OTHELLO: What dost thou say, Iago?
IAGO: Did Michael Cassio, when you wooed my lady,
   Know of your love?   95
OTHELLO: He did, from first to last. Why dost thou ask?
IAGO: But for a satisfaction of my thought,
   No further harm.
OTHELLO: Why of thy thought, Iago?
IAGO: I did not think he had been acquainted with her.
OTHELLO: O, yes, and went between us° very oft.   100
IAGO: Indeed?
OTHELLO: Indeed? Ay, indeed! Discern'st thou aught in that?
   Is he not honest?
IAGO: Honest, my lord?
OTHELLO: Honest? Ay, honest.
IAGO: My lord, for aught I know.
OTHELLO: What dost thou think?
IAGO: Think, my lord?
OTHELLO: Think, my lord?   105
   By heaven, thou echoest me,
   As if there were some monster in thy thought
   Too hideous to be shown. Thou dost mean something.
   I heard thee say even now, thou lik'st not that,

79*peculiar profit*   *particularly personal good.*   82*poise*   *weight.*   87*straight*   *at once.*   100*be-*
tween us   *i.e., as messenger.*

When Cassio left my wife. What didst not like? 110
And when I told thee he was of my counsel°
Of my whole course of wooing, thou cried'st "Indeed?"
And didst contract and purse thy brow together,
As if thou then hadst shut up in thy brain
Some horrible conceit°. If thou dost love me, 115
Show me thy thought.

IAGO: My lord, you know I love you.

OTHELLO: I think thou dost;
And, for I know thou'rt full of love and honesty
And weigh'st thy words before thou giv'st them breath,
Therefore these stops° of thine fright me the more; 120
For such things in a false disloyal knave
Are tricks of custom°; but in a man that's just
They're close dilations°, working from the heart
That passion cannot rule.

IAGO: For Michael Cassio,
I dare be sworn, I think that he is honest. 125

OTHELLO: I think so too.

IAGO: Men should be what they seem;
Or those that be not, would they might seem none!

OTHELLO: Certain, men should be what they seem.

IAGO: Why then, I think Cassio's an honest man.

OTHELLO: Nay, yet there's more in this? 130
I prithee speak to me as to thy thinkings,
As thou dost ruminate, and give thy worst of thoughts
The worst of words.

IAGO: Good my lord, pardon me:
Though I am bound to every act of duty,
I am not bound to that all slaves are free to. 135
Utter my thoughts? Why, say they are vile and false,
As where's that palace whereinto foul things
Sometimes intrude not? Who has that breast so pure
But some uncleanly apprehensions
Keep leets and law days°, and in sessions sit 140
With meditations lawful?

OTHELLO: Thou dost conspire against thy friend, Iago,
If thou but think'st him wronged, and mak'st his ear
A stranger to thy thoughts.

IAGO: I do beseech you—
Though I perchance am vicious in my guess 145
(As I confess it is my nature's plague
To spy into abuses, and of my jealousy

---

[111]*of my counsel* *in my confidence.*   [115]*conceit* *thought.*   [120]*stops* *interruptions.*
[122]*of custom* *customary.*   [123]*close dilations* *expressions of hidden thoughts.*   [140]*leets and law*
days *meetings of local courts.*

Shape faults that are not), that your wisdom
From one that so imperfectly conceits
Would take no notice, nor build yourself a trouble   150
Out of his scattering and unsure observance.
It were not for your quiet nor your good,
Nor for my manhood, honesty, and wisdom,
To let you know my thoughts.

OTHELLO: What dost thou mean?

IAGO: Good name in man and woman, dear my lord,   155
Is the immediate jewel of their souls.
Who steals my purse steals trash; 'tis something, nothing;
'Twas mine, 'tis his, and has been slave to thousands;
But he that filches from me my good name
Robs me of that which not enriches him   160
And makes me poor indeed.

OTHELLO: By heaven, I'll know thy thoughts!

IAGO: You cannot, if my heart were in your hand;
Nor shall not whilst 'tis in my custody.

OTHELLO: Ha!

IAGO: O, beware, my lord, of jealousy!   165
It is the green-eyed monster, which doth mock
The meat it feeds on. That cuckold lives in bliss
Who, certain of his fate, loves not his wronger;
But O, what damnèd minutes tells° he o'er
Who dotes, yet doubts—suspects, yet fondly° loves!   170

OTHELLO: O misery.

IAGO: Poor and content is rich, and rich enough;
But riches fineless° is as poor as winter
To him that ever fears he shall be poor.
Good God the souls of all my tribe defend   175
From jealousy!

OTHELLO: Why? Why is this?
Think'st thou I'd make a life of jealousy,
To follow still° the changes of the moon
With fresh suspicions? No! To be once in doubt
Is to be resolved. Exchange me for a goat   180
When I shall turn the business of my soul
To such exsufflicate and blown° surmises,
Matching thy inference. 'Tis not to make me jealous
To say my wife is fair, feeds well, loves company,
Is free of speech, sings, plays, and dances;   185
Where virtue is, these are more virtuous.
Nor from mine own weak merits will I draw
The smallest fear or doubt of her revolt,

---

¹⁶⁹*tells* counts.   ¹⁷⁰*fondly* foolishly.   ¹⁷³*fineless* infinite.   ¹⁷⁸*To follow still* to change always (as the phases of the moon).   ¹⁸²*exsufflicate and blown* inflated and flyblown.

For she had eyes, and chose me. No, Iago;
I'll see before I doubt; when I doubt, prove;   190
And on the proof there is no more but this:
Away at once with love or jealousy!

IAGO: I am glad of this; for now I shall have reason
To show the love and duty that I bear you
With franker spirit. Therefore, as I am bound,   195
Receive it from me. I speak not yet of proof.
Look to your wife; observe her well with Cassio;
Wear your eyes thus: not jealous nor secure.
I would not have your free and noble nature
Out of self-bounty° be abused. Look to't.   200
I know our country disposition well:
In Venice they do let heaven see the pranks
They dare not show their husbands; their best conscience
Is not to leave't undone, but kept unknown.°

OTHELLO: Dost thou say so?   205

IAGO: She did deceive her father, marrying you;
And when she seemed to shake and fear your looks,
She loved them most.

OTHELLO: And so she did.

IAGO: Why, go to then!
She that so young could give out such a seeming
To seel° her father's eyes up close as oak°—   210
He thought 'twas witchcraft. But I am much to blame.
I humbly do beseech you of your pardon
For too much loving you.

OTHELLO: I am bound to thee forever.

IAGO: I see this hath a little dashed your spirits.

OTHELLO: Not a jot, not a jot.

IAGO: Trust me, I fear it has.   215
I hope you will consider what is spoke
Comes from my love. But I do see y' are moved.
I am to pray you not to strain° my speech
To grosser issues nor to larger reach°
Than to suspicion.   220

OTHELLO: I will not.

IAGO: Should you do so, my lord,
My speech should fall into such vile success
Which my thoughts aimed not. Cassio's my worthy friend—
My lord, I see y' are moved.

OTHELLO: No, not much moved.
I do not think but Desdemona's honest.   225

200**self-bounty**   *innate kindness (which attributes his own motives to others).*   203-4**their . . . unknown**
i.e., their morality does not forbid adultery, but it does forbid being found out.   210**seel**   *hoodwink.*
210**oak**   *(a close-grained wood).*   218**strain**   *enlarge the meaning.*   219**reach**   *meaning.*

IAGO: Long live she so. And long live you to think so.

OTHELLO: And yet, how nature erring from itself—

IAGO: Ay, there's the point, as (to be bold with you)
    Not to affect many proposèd matches
    Of her own clime, complexion, and degree°,   230
    Whereto we see in all things nature tends°—
    Foh! one may smell in such a will most rank,
    Foul disproportions, thoughts unnatural.
    But, pardon me, I do not in position°
    Distinctly° speak of her; though I may fear   235
    Her will, recoiling to her better judgment,
    May fall to match° you with her country forms°,
    And happily° repent.

OTHELLO: Farewell, farewell!
    If more thou dost perceive, let me know more.
    Set on thy wife to observe. Leave me, Iago.   240

IAGO: My lord, I take my leave.   [*Going.*]

OTHELLO: Why did I marry? This honest creature doubtless
    Sees and knows more, much more, than he unfolds.

IAGO [*Returns*]: My lord, I would I might entreat your honor
    To scan this thing no farther. Leave it to time.   245
    Although 'tis fit that Cassio have his place,
    For sure he fills it up with great ability,
    Yet, if you please to hold him off awhile,
    You shall by that perceive him and his means.
    Note if your lady strains his entertainment°   250
    With any strong or vehement importunity;
    Much will be seen in that. In the meantime
    Let me be thought too busy in my fears
    (As worthy cause I have to fear I am)
    And hold her free, I do beseech your honor.   255

OTHELLO: Fear not my government°.

IAGO: I once more take my leave.   *Exit.*

OTHELLO: This fellow's of exceeding honesty,
    And knows all qualities°, with a learnèd spirit
    Of human dealings. If I do prove her haggard°,
    Though that her jesses° were my dear heartstrings,   260
    I'd whistle her off and let her down the wind°
    To prey at fortune. Haply for° I am black
    And have not those soft parts° of conversation

---

²³⁰*degree* social station.   ²³¹*in . . . tends* i.e., all things in nature seek out their own kind.
²³⁴*position* general argument.   ²³⁵*Distinctly* specifically.   ²³⁷*fall to match* happen to compare.
²³⁷*country forms* i.e., the familiar appearance of her countrymen.   ²³⁸*happily* by chance.
²⁵⁰*strains his entertainment* urge strongly that he be reinstated.   ²⁵⁶*government* self-control.
²⁵⁸*qualities* natures, types of people.   ²⁵⁹*haggard* a partly trained hawk which has gone wild again.
²⁶⁰*jesses* straps which held the hawk's legs to the trainer's wrist.   ²⁶¹*I'd . . . wind* I would release her
(like an untamable hawk) and let her fly free.   ²⁶²*Haply for* it may be because.   ²⁶³*soft parts* gentle
qualities and manners.

That chamberers° have, or for I am declined
Into the vale of years—yet that's not much—   265
She's gone. I am abused, and my relief
Must be to loathe her. O curse of marriage,
That we can call these delicate creatures ours,
And not their appetites! I had rather be a toad
And live upon the vapor of a dungeon   270
Than keep a corner in the thing I love
For others' uses. Yet 'tis the plague to great ones;
Prerogatived are they less than the base.
'Tis destiny unshunnable, like death.
Even then this forkèd° plague is fated to us   275
When we do quicken°. Look where she comes.

Enter DESDEMONA *and* EMILIA.

If she be false, heaven mocked itself!
I'll not believe't.
DESDEMONA: How now, my dear Othello?
Your dinner, and the generous islanders
By you invited, do attend° your presence.   280
OTHELLO: I am to blame.
DESDEMONA: Why do you speak so faintly?
Are you not well?
OTHELLO: I have a pain upon my forehead, here°.
DESDEMONA: Why, that's with watching; 'twill away again,
Let me but bind it hard, within this hour   285
It will be well.
OTHELLO: Your napkin° is too little;

[*He pushes the handkerchief away, and it falls.*]

Let it° alone. Come, I'll go in with you.
DESDEMONA: I am very sorry that you are not well.   *Exit* [*with* OTHELLO].
EMILIA: I am glad I have found this napkin;
This was her first remembrance from the Moor.   290
My wayward husband hath a hundred times
Wooed me to steal it; but she so loves the token
(For he conjured her she should ever keep it)
That she reserves it evermore about her
To kiss and talk to. I'll have the work ta'en out°   295
And give't Iago. What he will do with it,
Heaven knows, not I; I nothing° but to please his fantasy°.

---

²⁶⁴*chamberers* *courtiers—or, perhaps, accomplished seducers.*   ²⁷⁵*forkèd* *horned (the sign of the cuckold
was horns).*   ²⁷⁶*do quicken* *are born.*   ²⁸⁰*attend* *wait.*   ²⁸³*here* *(he points to his imaginary
horns).*   ²⁸⁶*napkin* *elaborately worked handkerchief.*   ²⁸⁷*it* *(it makes a considerable difference in the
interpretation of later events whether this "it" refers to Othello's forehead or to the handkerchief; nothing in the
text makes the reference clear).*   ²⁹⁵*work ta'en out* *needlework copied.*   ²⁹⁷I nothing I wish nothing.*   ²⁹⁷*fantasy* *fancy, whim.*

Enter IAGO.

IAGO: How now? What do you here alone?

EMILIA: Do not you chide; I have a thing for you.

IAGO: You have a thing for me? It is a common thing— 300

EMILIA: Ha?

IAGO: To have a foolish wife.

EMILIA: O, is that all? What will you give me now
    For that same handkerchief?

IAGO: What handkerchief?

EMILIA: What handkerchief! 305
    Why, that the Moor first gave to Desdemona,
    That which so often you did bid me steal.

IAGO: Hast stol'n it from her?

EMILIA: No, but she let it drop by negligence,
    And to th' advantage°, I, being here, took't up. 310
    Look, here 't is.

IAGO: A good wench. Give it me.

EMILIA: What will you do with't, that you have been so earnest
    To have me filch it?

IAGO: Why, what is that to you?   *[Takes it.]*

EMILIA: If it be not for some purpose of import°,
    Give't me again. Poor lady, she'll run mad 315
    When she shall lack° it.

IAGO: Be not acknown on't°.
    I have use for it. Go, leave me.   *Exit* EMILIA.
    I will in Cassio's lodging lose this napkin
    And let him find it. Trifles light as air
    Are to the jealous confirmations strong 320
    As proofs of Holy Writ. This may do something.
    The Moor already changes with my poison:
    Dangerous conceits are in their natures poisons,
    Which at the first are scarce found to distaste°,
    But with a little°, act upon the blood, 325
    Burn like the mines of sulfur. I did say so.

Enter OTHELLO.

    Look where he comes! Not poppy nor mandragora°,
    Nor all the drowsy syrups of the world,
    Shall ever medicine thee to that sweet sleep
    Which thou owedst° yesterday.

OTHELLO: Ha! ha! False to me? 330

IAGO: Why, how now, general? No more of that.

---

³¹⁰*to th' advantage* *being lucky.*   ³¹⁴*import* *importance.*   ³¹⁶*lack* *miss.*   ³¹⁶*Be not acknown on't* *forget you ever saw it.*   ³²⁴*are scarce found to distaste* *scarcely can be tasted.* ³²⁵*with a little* *in a short time.*   ³²⁷*poppy nor mandragora* *soporifics.*   ³³⁰*owedst* *possessed.*

OTHELLO: Avaunt! be gone! Thou hast set me on the rack.
  I swear 'tis better to be much abused
  Than but to know't a little.

IAGO: How now, my lord?

OTHELLO: What sense had I of her stol'n hours of lust?   335
  I saw't not, thought it not, it harmed not me;
  I slept the next night well, fed well, was free and merry;
  I found not Cassio's kisses on her lips.
  He that is robbed, not wanting° what is stol'n,
  Let him not know't, and he's not robbed at all.   340

IAGO: I am sorry to hear this.

OTHELLO: I had been happy if the general camp,
  Pioners° and all, had tasted her sweet body,
  So I had nothing known. O now, forever
  Farewell the tranquil mind! Farewell content!   345
  Farewell the plumèd troops, and the big wars
  That make ambition virtue! O, farewell!
  Farewell the neighing steed and the shrill trump,
  The spirit-stirring drum, th' ear-piercing fife,
  The royal banner, and all quality,   350
  Pride, pomp, and circumstance° of glorious war!
  And O you mortal engines° whose rude throats
  Th' immortal Jove's dread clamors° counterfeit,
  Farewell! Othello's occupation's gone!

IAGO: Is't possible, my lord?   355

OTHELLO: Villain, be sure thou prove my love a whore!
  Be sure of it; give me the ocular proof;
  Or, by the worth of mine eternal soul,
  Thou hadst been better have been born a dog
  Than answer my waked wrath!

IAGO: Is't come to this?   360

OTHELLO: Make me to see't; or at the least so prove it
  That the probation° bear no hinge nor loop
  To hang a doubt on—or woe upon thy life!

IAGO: My noble lord—

OTHELLO: If thou dost slander her and torture me,   365
  Never pray more; abandon all remorse;
  On horror's head horrors accumulate;
  Do deeds to make heaven weep, all earth amazed;
  For nothing canst thou to damnation add
  Greater than that.

IAGO: O grace! O heaven forgive me!   370
  Are you a man? Have you a soul or sense?

---

³³⁹**wanting** *missing.*   ³⁴³**Pioners** *the basest manual laborers in the army, who dug trenches and mines.*
³⁵¹**circumstance** *pageantry.*   ³⁵²**mortal engines** *lethal weapons, i.e., cannon.*   ³⁵³**clamors** *i.e.,*
thunder.   ³⁶²**probation** *proof.*

God b' wi' you! Take mine office. O wretched fool,
That lov'st to make thine honesty a vice!
O monstrous world! Take note, take note, O world,   375
To be direct and honest is not safe.
I thank you for this profit, and from hence
I'll love no friend, sith° love breeds such offense.
OTHELLO: Nay, stay. Thou shouldst be honest.
IAGO: I should be wise; for honesty's a fool
And loses that it works for.
OTHELLO: By the world,   380
I think my wife be honest, and think she is not;
I think that thou art just, and think thou are not.
I'll have some proof. My name, that was as fresh
As Dian's° visage, is now begrimed and black
As mine own face. If there be cords, or knives,   385
Poison, or fire, or suffocating streams,
I'll not endure it. Would I were satisfied!
IAGO: I see you are eaten up with passion.
I do repent me that I put it to you.
You would be satisfied?
OTHELLO: Would? Nay, and I will.   390
IAGO: And may; but how? How satisfied, my lord?
Would you, the supervisor°, grossly gape on?
Behold her topped?
OTHELLO: Death and damnation! O!
IAGO: It were a tedious° difficulty, I think,
To bring them to that prospect°. Damn them then,   395
If ever mortal eyes do see them bolster°
More than their own! What then? How then?
What shall I say? Where's satisfaction?
It is impossible you should see this,
Were they as prime° as goats, as hot as monkeys,   400
As salt as wolves in pride°, and fools as gross
As ignorance made drunk. But yet, I say,
If imputation and strong circumstances
Which lead directly to the door of truth
Will give you satisfaction, you might hav't.   405
OTHELLO: Give me a living reason she's disloyal.
IAGO: I do not like the office°.
But sith I am entered in this cause so far,
Pricked° to't by foolish honesty and love,
I will go on. I lay with Cassio lately,   410

377*sith* since.   384*Dian's* Diana's (goddess of the moon and of chastity).   392*supervisor* on-
looker.   394*tedious* hard to arrange.   395*prospect* sight (where they can be seen).   396*bolster*
go to bed with.   400-01*prime, salt* lustful.   401*pride* heat.   407*office* duty.   409*Pricked*
spurred.

And being troubled with a raging tooth,
I could not sleep.
There are a kind of men so loose of soul
That in their sleeps will mutter their affairs.
One of this kind is Cassio.   415
In sleep I heard him say, "Sweet Desdemona,
Let us be wary, let us hide our loves!"
And then, sir, would he gripe° and wring my hand,
Cry "O sweet creature!" Then kiss me hard,
As if he plucked up kisses by the roots   420
That grew upon my lips; laid his leg o'er my thigh,
And sigh, and kiss, and then cry, "Cursèd fate
That gave thee to the Moor!"
OTHELLO: O monstrous! monstrous!
IAGO: Nay, this was but his dream.
OTHELLO: But this denoted a foregone conclusion°,   425
'Tis a shrewd doubt°, though it be but a dream.
IAGO: And this may help to thicken other proofs
That do demonstrate° thinly.
OTHELLO: I'll tear her all to pieces!
IAGO: Nay, yet be wise. Yet we see nothing done;
She may be honest yet. Tell me but this: 430
Have you not sometimes seen a handkerchief
Spotted with strawberries in your wife's hand?
OTHELLO: I gave her such a one; 'twas my first gift.
IAGO: I know not that; but such a handkerchief—
I am sure it was your wife's—did I today   435
See Cassio wipe his beard with.
OTHELLO: If it be that—
IAGO: If it be that or any that was hers,
It speaks against her with the other proofs.
OTHELLO: O, that the slave had forty thousand lives!
One is too poor, too weak for my revenge.   440
Now do I see 'tis true. Look here, Iago:
All my fond love thus do I blow to heaven.
'Tis gone.
Arise, black vengeance, from the hollow hell!
Yield up, O love, thy crown and hearted° throne   445
To tyrannous hate! Swell, bosom, with thy fraught°,
For 'tis of aspics'° tongues.
IAGO: Yet be content°.
OTHELLO: O, blood, blood, blood!
IAGO: Patience, I say. Your mind may change.

---

[418]*gripe* *seize.* [425]*foregone conclusion* *consummated fact.* [426]*shrewd doubt* *penetrating guess.* [428]*demonstrate* *show, appear.* [445]*hearted* *seated in the heart.* [446]*fraught* *burden.* [447]*aspics'* *asps'.* [447]*content* *patient, quiet.*

OTHELLO: Never, Iago. Like to the Pontic Sea°,   450
  Whose icy current and compulsive course
  Nev'r keeps retiring ebb, but keeps due on
  To the Propontic and the Hellespont,
  Even so my bloody thoughts, with violent pace,
  Shall nev'r look back, nev'r ebb to humble love,   455
  Till that a capable and wide° revenge
  Swallow them up. [*He kneels.*] Now, by yond marble heaven,
  In the due reverence of a sacred vow
  I here engage my words.
IAGO: Do not rise yet.   [IAGO *kneels.*]
  Witness, you ever-burning lights above,   460
  You elements that clip° us round about,
  Witness that here Iago doth give up
  The execution° of his wit, hands, heart
  To wronged Othello's service! Let him command,
  And to obey shall be in me remorse°,   465
  What bloody business ever°.   [*They rise.*]
OTHELLO: I greet thy love,
  Not with vain thanks but with acceptance bounteous°,
  And will upon the instant put thee to 't°
  Within these three days let me hear thee say
  That Cassio's not alive.   470
IAGO: My friend is dead. 'Tis done at your request.
  But let her live.
OTHELLO: Damn her, lewd minx! O, damn her! Damn her!
  Come, go with me apart. I will withdraw
  To furnish me with some swift means of death
  For the fair devil. Now art thou my lieutenant.   475
IAGO: I am your own forever.   *Exeunt.*

Scene IV [*A street.*]

Enter DESDEMONA, EMILIA, *and* CLOWN.

DESDEMONA: Do you know, sirrah, where Lieutenant Cassio lies°?
CLOWN: I dare not say he lies anywhere.
DESDEMONA: Why, man?
CLOWN: He's a soldier, and for me to say a soldier lies, 'tis stabbing.
DESDEMONA: Go to. Where lodges he?   5
CLOWN: To tell you where he lodges is to tell you where I lie.
DESDEMONA: Can anything be made of this?

450*Pontic Sea*   the Black Sea (famous for the strong and constant current with which it flows through the Bosporus
into the Mediterranean, where the water level is lower).   456*capable and wide*   sufficient and far-reaching
461*clip*   enfold.   463*execution*   workings,   action.   465*remorse*   pity.   466*ever*   soever.
467*bounteous*   absolute.   468*to't*   i.e., to the work you have said you are prepared to do.   **III.iv.**
1*lies*   lodges.

CLOWN: I know not where he lodges, and for me to devise a lodging, and say he lies here or he lies there, were to lie in mine own throat°.

DESDEMONA: Can you enquire him out, and be edified° by report?   10

CLOWN: I will catechize the world for him; that is, make questions, and by them answer.

DESDEMONA: Seek him, bid him come hither. Tell him I have moved° my lord on his behalf and hope all will be well.

CLOWN: To do this is within the compass° of man's wit, and therefore I will   15
attempt the doing it.   *Exit* CLOWN.

DESDEMONA: Where should° I lose the handkerchief, Emilia?

EMILIA: I know not, madam.

DESDEMONA: Believe me, I had rather have lost my purse
Full of crusadoes°. And but my noble Moor   20
Is true of mind, and made of no such baseness
As jealous creatures are, it were enough
To put him to ill thinking.

EMILIA: Is he not jealous?

DESDEMONA: Who? He? I think the sun where he was born
Drew all such humors° from him.

EMILIA: Look where he comes.   25

Enter OTHELLO.

DESDEMONA: I will not leave him now till Cassio
Be called to him. How is't with you, my lord?

OTHELLO: Well, my good lady. [*Aside*] O, hardness to dissemble°!—
How do you, Desdemona?

DESDEMONA: Well, my good lord.

OTHELLO: Give me your hand. This hand is moist°, my lady.   30

DESDEMONA: It hath felt no age nor known no sorrow.

OTHELLO: This argues° fruitfulness and liberal° heart.
Hot, hot, and moist. This hand of yours requires
A sequester° from liberty; fasting and prayer;
Much castigation; exercise devout;   35
For here's a young and sweating devil here
That commonly rebels. 'Tis a good hand,
A frank one.

DESDEMONA: You may, indeed, say so;
For 'twas that hand that gave away my heart.

OTHELLO: A liberal hand! The hearts of old gave hands,   40

---

⁹**lie in mine own throat** (to lie in the throat is to lie absolutely and completely).   ¹⁰**edified** enlightened
(Desdemona mocks the Clown's overly elaborate diction).   ¹³**moved** pleaded with.   ¹⁵**compass** reach.
¹⁷**should** might.   ²⁰**crusadoes** Portuguese gold coins.   ²⁵**humors** characteristics.   ²⁸**hardness to dissemble** (Othello may refer here either to the difficulty he has in maintaining his appearance of
composure, or to what he believes to be Desdemona's hardened hypocrisy).   ³⁰**moist** (a moist, hot hand was
taken as a sign of a lustful nature).   ³²**argues** suggests.   ³²**liberal** free, open (but also with a
suggestion of "licentious"; from here on in this scene Othello's words bear a double meaning, seeming to be normal
but accusing Desdemona of being unfaithful).   ³⁴**sequester** separation.

But our new heraldry° is hands, not hearts.
DESDEMONA: I cannot speak of this. Come now, your promise!
OTHELLO: What promise, chuck?
DESDEMONA: I have sent to bid Cassio come speak with you.
OTHELLO: I have a salt and sorry rheum° offends me.   45
   Lend me thy handkerchief.
DESDEMONA: Here, my lord.
OTHELLO: That which I gave you.
DESDEMONA: I have it not about me.
OTHELLO: Not?
DESDEMONA: No, indeed, my lord.
OTHELLO: That's a fault.   50
   That handkerchief
   Did an Egyptian to my mother give.
   She was a charmer°, and could almost read
   The thoughts of people. She told her, while she kept it
   'Twould make her amiable° and subdue my father
   Entirely to her love; but if she lost it   55
   Or made a gift of it, my father's eye
   Should hold her loathèd, and his spirits should hunt
   After new fancies. She, dying, gave it me,
   And bid me, when my fate would have me wived,
   To give it her. I did so; and take heed on't;   60
   Make it a darling like your precious eye.
   To lose't or give't away were such perdition
   As nothing else could match.
DESDEMONA: Is't possible?
OTHELLO: 'Tis true. There's magic in the web° of it.
   A sibyl that had numbered in the world   65
   The sun to course two hundred compasses,
   In her prophetic fury° sewed the work;
   The worms were hallowed that did breed the silk,
   And it was dyed in mummy° which the skillful
   Conserved of maidens' hearts.
DESDEMONA: Indeed? Is't true?   70
OTHELLO: Most veritable. Therefore look to't well.
DESDEMONA: Then would to God that I had never seen't!
OTHELLO: Ha! Wherefore?
DESDEMONA: Why do you speak so startingly and rash?
OTHELLO: Is't lost? Is't gone? Speak, is it out o' th' way?   75
DESDEMONA: Heaven bless us!
OTHELLO: Say you?
DESDEMONA: It is not lost. But what an if it were?

---

[41]**heraldry** *heraldic symbolism.*   [45]**a salt and sorry rheum** *a heavy, running head cold.*
[52]**charmer** *magician.* [54]**amiable** *desirable.* [64]**web** *weaving.* [67]**prophetic fury** *seized by the spirit and able to prophesy.* [69]**mummy** *liquid drained from embalmed bodies.*

OTHELLO: How?

DESDEMONA: I say it is not lost. 80

OTHELLO: Fetch't, let me see't!

DESDEMONA: Why, so I can; but I will not now.
  This is a trick to put me from my suit:
  Pray you let Cassio be received again.

OTHELLO: Fetch me the handkerchief! My mind misgives. 85

DESDEMONA: Come, come!
  You'll never meet a more sufficient° man—

OTHELLO: The handkerchief!

DESDEMONA: A man that all his time
  Hath founded his good fortunes on your love,
  Shared dangers with you— 90

OTHELLO: The handkerchief!

DESDEMONA: I'faith, you are to blame.

OTHELLO: Away!   *Exit* OTHELLO.

EMILIA: Is not this man jealous?

DESDEMONA: I nev'r saw this before. 95
  Sure there's some wonder in this handkerchief;
  I am most unhappy in the loss of it.

EMILIA: 'Tis not a year or two shows us a man.
  They are all but stomachs, and we all but food;
  They eat us hungerly, and when they are full, 100
  They belch us.

Enter IAGO *and* CASSIO.

  Look you, Cassio and my husband.

IAGO: There is no other way; 'tis she must do't.
  And lo the happiness! Go and importune her.

DESDEMONA: How now, good Cassio? What's the news with you?

CASSIO: Madam, my former suit. I do beseech you 105
  That by your virtuous means I may again
  Exist, and be a member of his love
  Whom I with all the office° of my heart
  Entirely honor. I would not be delayed.
  If my offense be of such mortal kind 110
  That nor my service past, nor present sorrows,
  Nor purposed merit in futurity,
  Can ransom me into his love again,
  But to know so must be my benefit°.
  So shall I clothe me in a forced content, 115
  And shut myself up in some other course
  To fortune's alms.

DESDEMONA: Alas, thrice-gentle Cassio,
  My advocation° is not now in tune.

---

[87]*sufficient* *complete, with all proper qualities.* [108]*office* *duty.* [114]*benefit* *good.* [118]*advocation* *advocacy.*

My lord is not my lord; nor should I know him
Were he in favor° as in humor altered.   120
So help me every spirit sanctified
As I have spoken for you all my best
And stood within the blank° of his displeasure
For my free speech. You must awhile be patient.
What I can do I will; and more I will   125
Than for myself I dare. Let that suffice you.

IAGO: Is my lord angry?

EMILIA: He went hence but now,
And certainly in strange unquietness.

IAGO: Can he be angry? I have seen the cannon
When it hath blown his ranks into the air   130
And, like the devil, from his very arm
Puffed his own brother. And is he angry?
Something of moment° then. I will go meet him.
There's matter in't indeed if he be angry.

DESDEMONA: I prithee do so.   *Exit* [IAGO.]
                                 Something sure of state°,   135
Either from Venice or some unhatched practice°
Made demonstrable here in Cyprus to him,
Hath puddled° his clear spirit; and in such cases
Men's natures wrangle with inferior things,
though great ones are their object. 'Tis even so.   140
For let our finger ache, and it endues°
Our other, healthful members even to a sense
Of pain. Nay, we must think men are not gods,
Nor of them look for such observancy
As fits the bridal. Beshrew me much, Emilia,   145
I was, unhandsome warrior as I am,
Arraigning his unkindness with my soul;
But now I find I had suborned the witness,
And he's indicted falsely.

EMILIA: Pray heaven it be
State matters, as you think, and no conception   150
Nor no jealous toy° concerning you.

DESDEMONA: Alas the day! I never gave him cause.

EMILIA: But jealous souls will not be answered so;
They are not ever jealous for the cause,
But jealous for they're jealous. It is a monster   155
Begot upon itself, born on itself.

DESDEMONA: Heaven keep the monster from Othello's mind!

EMILIA: Lady, amen.

---

¹²⁰*favor* countenance.   ¹²³*blank* bull's-eye of a target.   ¹³³*moment* importance.   ¹³⁵*of state* state affairs.   ¹³⁶*unhatched practice* undisclosed plot.   ¹³⁸*puddled* muddied.   ¹⁴¹*endues* leads.   ¹⁵¹*toy* trifle.

DESDEMONA: I will go seek him. Cassio, walk here about.
 If I do find him fit°, I'll move your suit   160
 And seek to effect it to my uttermost.
CASSIO: I humbly thank your ladyship.   *Exit* [DESDEMONA *with* EMILIA].

Enter BIANCA.

BIANCA: Save you, friend Cassio!
CASSIO: What make you from home?
 How is't with you, my most fair Bianca?
 I' faith, sweet love, I was coming to your house.   165
BIANCA: And I was going to your lodging, Cassio.
 What, keep a week away? Seven days and nights?
 Eightscore eight hours? And lovers' absent hours
 More tedious than the dial eightscore times?
 O weary reck'ning°.
CASSIO: Pardon me, Bianca.   170
 I have this while with leaden thoughts been pressed,
 But I shall in a more continuate° time
 Strike off this score° of absence. Sweet Bianca,

[*Gives her* DESDEMONA'S *handkerchief.*]

Take me this work out.
BIANCA: O Cassio, whence came this?
 This is some token from a newer friend.   175
 To the felt absence now I feel a cause.
 Is't come to this? Well, well.
CASSIO: Go to, woman!
 Throw your vile guesses in the devil's teeth,
 From whence you have them. You are jealous now
 That this is from some mistress, some remembrance.   180
 No, by my faith, Bianca.
BIANCA: Why, whose is it?
CASSIO: I know not neither; I found it in my chamber.
 I like the work well; ere it be demanded°,
 As like enough it will, I would have it copied.
 Take it and do't, and leave me for this time.   185
BIANCA: Leave you? Wherefore?
CASSIO: I do attend here on the general
 And think it no addition, nor my wish,
 To have him see me womaned.
BIANCA: Why, I pray you?
CASSIO: Not that I love you not.
BIANCA: But that you do not love me!   190

---

¹⁶⁰*fit* receptive.   ¹⁷⁰*reck'ning* addition.   ¹⁷²*continuate* uninterrupted.   ¹⁷³***Strike off this***
score *i.e., pay this bill (the* score *being the account of drinks kept in a tavern).*   ¹⁸³*demanded* asked for
(by the person who lost it).

I pray you bring° me on the way a little,
And say if I shall see you soon at night.
CASSIO: 'Tis but a little way that I can bring you,
For I attend here; but I'll see you soon.
BIANCA: 'Tis very good. I must be circumstanced°.   *Exeunt omnes.* 195

ACT IV

Scene I [A street.]

Enter OTHELLO *and* IAGO.

IAGO: Will you think so?
OTHELLO: Think so, Iago?
IAGO: What,
  To kiss in private?
OTHELLO: An unauthorized° kiss?
IAGO: Or to be naked with her friend in bed
  An hour or more, not meaning any harm?
OTHELLO: Naked in bed, Iago, and not mean harm?   5
  It is hypocrisy against the devil.
  They that mean virtuously, and yet do so,
  The devil their virtue tempts, and they tempt heaven.
IAGO: If they do nothing, 'tis a venial slip.
  But if I give my wife a handkerchief—   10
OTHELLO: What then?
IAGO: Why, then 'tis hers, my lord; and being hers,
  She may, I think, bestow't on any man.
OTHELLO: She is protectress of her honor too.
  May she give that?   15
IAGO: Her honor is an essence that's not seen;
  They have it very oft that have it not.
  But for the handkerchief—
OTHELLO: By heaven, I would most gladly have forgot it!
  Thou said'st—O, it comes o'er my memory   20
  As doth the raven° o'er the infected house,
  Boding to all—he had my handkerchief.
IAGO: Ay, what of that?
OTHELLO: That's not so good now.
IAGO: What if I had said I had seen him do you wrong?
  Or heard him say—as knaves be such abroad°   25
  Who having, by their own importunate suit,
  Or voluntary dotage° of some mistress,

---

¹⁹¹**bring** *accompany.*   ¹⁹⁵**be circumstanced** *accept things as they are.*   **IV.i.**   ²**unauthorized**
illicit.   ²¹**raven** *(a harbinger of death).*   ²⁵**abroad** *i.e., in the world.*   ²⁷**voluntary dotage**
weakness of the will.

Convincèd or supplied° them, cannot choose
But they must blab—
OTHELLO: Hath he said anything?
IAGO: He hath, my lord; but be you well assured,   30
No more than he'll unswear.
OTHELLO: What hath he said?
IAGO: Why, that he did—I know not what he did.
OTHELLO: What? what?
IAGO: Lie—
OTHELLO: With her?
IAGO: With her, on her; what you will.   35
OTHELLO: Lie with her? Lie on her?—We say lie on her when they belie her.
—Lie with her! Zounds, that's fulsome°.—Handkerchief—confessions—
handkerchief!—To confess, and be hanged for his labor—first to be
hanged, and then to confess! I tremble at it. Nature would not invest herself
in such shadowing passion without some instruction°. It is not words that 40
shakes me thus.—Pish! Noses, ears, and lips? Is't possible?—Confess?—
Handkerchief?—O devil!   *Falls in a trance.*
IAGO: Work on.
My med'cine works! Thus credulous fools are caught,
And many worthy and chaste dames even thus,   45
All guiltless, meet reproach°. What, ho! My lord!
My lord, I say! Othello!

Enter CASSIO.

How now, Cassio?
CASSIO: What's the matter?
IAGO: My lord is fall'n into an epilepsy.
This is his second fit; he had one yesterday.   50
CASSIO: Rub him about the temples.
IAGO: The lethargy° must have his quiet course.
If not, he foams at mouth, and by and by
Breaks out to savage madness. Look, he stirs.
Do you withdraw yourself a little while.   55
He will recover straight. When he is gone,
I would on great occasion° speak with you.   [*Exit* CASSIO.]
How is it, general? Have you not hurt your head?
OTHELLO: Dost thou mock° me?
IAGO: I mock you not, by heaven.
Would you would bear your fortune like a man.   60
OTHELLO: A hornèd man's a monster and a beast.

---

²⁸**Convincèd or supplied** *persuaded or gratified (the mistress).*   ³⁷**fulsome** *foul, repulsive.*
³⁹⁻⁴⁰**Nature . . . instruction** *i.e., my mind would not become so darkened (with anger) unless there were something in this (accusation); (it should be remembered that Othello believes in the workings of magic and supernatural forces).*   ⁴⁶**reproach** *shame.*   ⁵²**lethargy** *coma.*   ⁵⁷**great occasion** *very important matter.*   ⁵⁹**mock** *(Othello takes Iago's comment as a reference to his horns—which it is).*

IAGO: There's many a beast then in a populous city,
  And many a civil° monster.
OTHELLO: Did he confess it?
IAGO: Good, sir, be a man.
  Think every bearded fellow that's but yoked   65
  May draw° with you. There's millions now alive
  That nightly lie in those unproper° beds
  Which they dare swear peculiar.° Your case is better.
  O, 'tis the spite of hell, the fiend's arch-mock,
  To lip a wanton in a secure couch,   70
  And to suppose her chaste. No, let me know;
  And knowing what I am, I know what she shall be.
OTHELLO: O, thou art wise! 'Tis certain.
IAGO: Stand you awhile apart;
  Confine yourself but in a patient list.°
  Whilst you were here, o'erwhelmèd with your grief—   75
  A passion most unsuiting such a man—
  Cassio came hither. I shifted him away°
  And laid good 'scuses upon your ecstasy°,
  Bade him anon return, and here speak with me;
  The which he promised. Do but encave° yourself   80
  And mark the fleers°, the gibes, and notable° scorns
  That dwell in every region of his face.
  For I will make him tell the tale anew:
  Where, how, how oft, how long ago, and when
  He hath, and is again to cope your wife.   85
  I say, but mark his gesture. Marry patience,
  Or I shall say you're all in all in spleen°,
  And nothing of a man.
OTHELLO: Dost thou hear, Iago?
  I will be found most cunning in my patience;
  But—dost thou hear?—most bloody.
IAGO: That's not amiss;   90
  But yet keep time in all. Will you withdraw?

[OTHELLO *moves to one side, where his remarks are not audible to* CASSIO *and* IAGO.]

  Now will I question Cassio of Bianca,
  A huswife° that by selling her desires
  Buys herself bread and cloth. It is a creature
  That dotes on Cassio, as 'tis the strumpet's plague   95
  To beguile many and be beguiled by one.

---

⁶³*civil* city-dwelling.   ⁶⁶*draw* i.e., like the horned ox.   ⁶⁷*unproper* i.e., not exclusively the hus-
band's.   ⁶⁸*peculiar* their own alone.   ⁷⁴*a patient list* the bounds of patience.   ⁷⁷*shifted him*
away got rid of him by a strategem.   ⁷⁸*ecstasy* trance (the literal meaning, "outside oneself," bears on
the meaning of the change Othello is undergoing).   ⁸⁰*encave* hide.   ⁸¹*fleers* mocking looks or
speeches.   ⁸¹*notable* obvious.   ⁸⁷*spleen* passion, particularly anger.   ⁹³*huswife* housewife
(but with the special meaning here of "prostitute").

He, when he hears of her, cannot restrain
From the excess of laughter. Here he comes.

Enter CASSIO.

As he shall smile, Othello shall go mad:
And his unbookish° jealousy must conster°   100
Poor Cassio's smiles, gestures, and light behaviors
Quite in the wrong. How do you, lieutenant?
CASSIO: The worser that you give me the addition°
Whose want even kills me.
IAGO: Ply Desdemona well, and you are sure on't.   105
Now, if this suit lay in Bianca's power,
How quickly should you speed!
CASSIO: Alas, poor caitiff!°
OTHELLO: Look how he laughs already!
IAGO: I never knew woman love man so.
CASSIO: Alas, poor rogue! I think, i' faith, she loves me.   110
OTHELLO: Now he denies it faintly, and laughs it out.
IAGO: Do you hear, Cassio?
OTHELLO: Now he importunes him
To tell it o'er. Go to! Well said, well said!
IAGO: She gives it out that you shall marry her.
Do you intend it?   115
CASSIO: Ha, ha, ha!
OTHELLO: Do ye triumph, Roman? Do you triumph?
CASSIO: I marry? What, a customer°? Prithee bear some charity to my wit;
do not think it so unwholesome. Ha, ha, ha!
OTHELLO: So, so, so, so. They laugh that win.   120
IAGO: Why, the cry goes that you marry her.
CASSIO: Prithee, say true.
IAGO: I am a very villain else.
OTHELLO: Have you scored° me? Well.
CASSIO: This is the monkey's own giving out. She is persuaded I will marry 125
her out of her own love and flattery, not out of my promise.
OTHELLO: Iago beckons me; now he begins the story.

[OTHELLO *moves close enough to hear.*]

CASSIO: She was here even now; she haunts me in every place. I was the other
day talking on the sea bank with certain Venetians, and thither comes the
bauble°, and falls me thus about my neck—   130
OTHELLO: Crying "O dear Cassio!" as it were. His gesture imports it.
CASSIO: So hangs, and lolls, and weeps upon me; so shakes and pulls me! Ha,
ha, ha!

---

¹⁰⁰**unbookish** *ignorant.*   ¹⁰⁰**conster** *construe.*   ¹⁰³**addition** *title.*   ¹⁰⁷**caitiff** *wretch.*
¹¹⁸**customer** *one who sells, a merchant (here, a prostitute).*   ¹²⁴**scored** *marked, defaced.*   ¹³⁰**bauble**
plaything.

OTHELLO: Now he tells how she plucked him to my chamber. O, I see that nose of yours, but not that dog I shall throw it to. 135

CASSIO: Well, I must leave her company.

IAGO: Before me!° Look where she comes.

Enter BIANCA.

CASSIO: 'Tis such another fitchew!° Marry a perfumed one? What do you mean by this haunting of me?

BIANCA: Let the devil and his dam haunt you! What did you mean by that 140 same handkerchief you gave me even now? I was a fine fool to take it. I must take out the work? A likely piece of work that you should find it in your chamber and know not who left it there! This is some minx's token, and I must take out the work? There! [*She throws down the handkerchief.*] Give it your hobbyhorse°. Wheresoever you had it, I'll take 145 out no work on't.

CASSIO: How now, my sweet Bianca? How now? how now?

OTHELLO: By heaven, that should be my handkerchief!

BIANCA: If you'll come to supper tonight, you may; if you will not, come when you are next prepared for°.   *Exit.* 150

IAGO: After her, after her!

CASSIO: Faith, I must; she'll rail in the streets else.

IAGO: Will you sup there?

CASSIO: Yes, I intend so.

IAGO: Well, I may chance to see you, for I would very fain speak with you. 155

CASSIO: Prithee come. Will you?

IAGO: Go to, say no more.   [*Exit* CASSIO.]

OTHELLO [*Comes forward*]: How shall I murder him, Iago?

IAGO: Did you perceive how he laughed at his vice?

OTHELLO: O Iago!   160

IAGO: And did you see the handkerchief?

OTHELLO: Was that mine?

IAGO: Yours, by this hand! And to see how he prizes the foolish woman your wife! She gave it him, and he hath giv'n it his whore.

OTHELLO: I would have him nine years a-killing!——A fine woman, a fair 165 woman, a sweet woman?

IAGO: Nay, you must forget that.

OTHELLO: Ay, let her rot, and perish, and be damned tonight; for she shall not live. No, my heart is turned to stone; I strike it, and it hurts my hand. O, the world hath not a sweeter creature! She might lie by an emperor's side 170 and command him tasks.

IAGO: Nay, that's not your way°.

OTHELLO: Hang her! I do but say what she is. So delicate with her needle.

137*Before me!* *(an exclamation of surprise).*   138*fitchew* polecat, i.e., strong-smelling creature. 145*hobbyhorse* prostitute.   150*next prepared for* next expected—i.e., never.   172*way* proper course.

An admirable musician. O, she will sing the savageness out of a bear! Of
so high and plenteous wit and invention°—   175
IAGO: She's the worse for all this.
OTHELLO: O, a thousand, a thousand times. And then, of so gentle a condi-
tion°?
IAGO: Ay, too gentle.
OTHELLO: Nay, that's certain. But yet the pity of it, Iago. O Iago, the pity[180]
of it, Iago.
IAGO: If you are so fond over her iniquity, give her patent to offend; for if
it touch° not you, it comes near nobody.
OTHELLO: I will chop her into messes°! Cuckold me!
IAGO: O, 'tis foul in her.   185
OTHELLO: With mine officer!
IAGO: That's fouler.
OTHELLO: Get me some poison, Iago, this night. I'll not expostulate with her,
lest her body and beauty unprovide my mind° again. This night, Iago!
IAGO: Do it not with poison. Strangle her in her bed, even the bed she hath[190]
contaminated.
OTHELLO: Good, good! The justice of it pleases. Very good!
IAGO: And for Cassio, let me be his undertaker°. You shall hear more by
midnight.
OTHELLO: Excellent good!   [*A trumpet.*]
                        What trumpet is that same?   195
IAGO: I warrant something from Venice.
                Enter LODOVICO, DESDEMONA, *and* ATTENDANTS.

                        'Tis Lodovico.
This comes from the Duke. See, your wife's with him.
LODOVICO: God save you, worthy general.
OTHELLO: With° all my heart, sir.
LODOVICO: The Duke and the senators of Venice greet you.

                                                        [*Gives him a letter.*]

OTHELLO: I kiss the instrument of their pleasures.   200

                                                        [*Opens the letter and reads.*]

DESDEMONA: And what's the news, good cousin Lodovico?
IAGO: I am very glad to see you, signior.
        Welcome to Cyprus.
LODOVICO: I thank you. How does Lieutenant Cassio?
IAGO: Lives, sir.
DESDEMONA: Cousin, there's fall'n between him and my lord   205
        An unkind° breach; but you shall make all well.

---

¹⁷⁵*invention* imagination.   ^{177–78}*gentle a condition* (1) well born (2) of a gentle nature.
¹⁸³*touch* affects.   ¹⁸⁴*messes* bits.   ¹⁸⁷*unprovide my mind* undo my resolution.   ¹⁹³*un-*
dertaker (not "burier" but "one who undertakes to do something").   ¹⁹⁸*With* i.e., I greet you with.
²⁰⁶*unkind* unnatural.

OTHELLO: Are you sure of that?

DESDEMONA: My lord?

OTHELLO [*Reads*]: "This fail you not to do, as you will—"

LODOVICO: He did not call; he's busy in the paper.   210
    Is there division 'twixt my lord and Cassio?

DESDEMONA: A most unhappy one. I would do much
    T' atone° them, for the love I bear to Cassio.

OTHELLO: Fire and brimstone!

DESDEMONA: My lord?

OTHELLO: Are you wise?

DESDEMONA: What, is he angry?

LODOVICO: May be th' letter moved him;   215
    For, as I think, they do command him home,
    Deputing Cassio in his government°.

DESDEMONA: Trust me, I am glad on't.

OTHELLO: Indeed?

DESDEMONA: My lord?

OTHELLO: I am glad to see you mad.

DESDEMONA: Why, sweet Othello—

OTHELLO: Devil!   [*Strikes her.*]220

DESDEMONA: I have not deserved this.

LODOVICO: My lord, this would not be believed in Venice,
    Though I should swear I saw't. 'Tis very much.
    Make her amends; she weeps.

OTHELLO: O devil, devil!
    If that the earth could teem° with woman's tears,   225
    Each drop she falls° would prove a crocodile°.
    Out of my sight!

DESDEMONA: I will not stay to offend you.   [*Going.*]

LODOVICO: Truly, an obedient lady.
    I do beseech your lordship call her back.

OTHELLO: Mistress!

DESDEMONA: My lord?

OTHELLO: What would you with her, sir?   230

LODOVICO: Who? I, my lord?

OTHELLO: Ay! You did wish that I would make her turn.
    Sir, she can turn, and turn, and yet go on
    And turn again; and she can weep, sir, weep;
    And she's obedient; as you say, obedient.   235
    Very obedient. Proceed you in your tears.
    Concerning this, sir—O well-painted passion!
    I am commanded home.—Get you away;
    I'll send for you anon.—Sir, I obey the mandate
    And will return to Venice.—Hence, avaunt!   [*Exit* DESDEMONA.]240
    Cassio shall have my place. And, sir, tonight

---

²¹³*atone* reconcile.   ²¹⁷*government* office.   ²²⁵*teem* conceive.   ²²⁶*falls* drops.
²²⁶*crocodile* (*the crocodile was supposed to shed false tears to lure its victims*).

I do entreat that we may sup together.
You are welcome, sir, to Cyprus.——Goats and monkeys! *Exit.*
LODOVICO: Is this the noble Moor whom our full Senate
Call all in all sufficient? Is this the nature   245
Whom passion could not shake? whose solid virtue
The shot of accident nor dart of chance
Could neither graze nor pierce?
IAGO: He is much changed.
LODOVICO: Are his wits safe? Is he not light of brain?
IAGO: He's that he is; I may not breathe my censure.   250
What he might be (if, what he might, he is not)
I would to heaven he were!
LODOVICO: What, strike his wife?
IAGO: Faith, that was not so well; yet would I knew
That stroke would prove the worst.
LODOVICO: Is it his use?°
Or did the letters work upon his blood°   255
And new-create his fault?
IAGO: Alas, alas!
It is not honesty in me to speak
What I have seen and known. You shall observe him,
And his own courses° will denote him so
That I may save my speech. Do but go after   260
And mark how he continues.
LODOVICO: I am sorry that I am deceived in him. *Exeunt.*

Scene II [*The citadel.*]

Enter OTHELLO *and* EMILIA.

OTHELLO: You have seen nothing then?
EMILIA: Nor ever heard, nor ever did suspect.
OTHELLO: Yes, you have seen Cassio and she together.
EMILIA: But then I saw no harm, and then I heard
Each syllable that breath made up° between them.   5
OTHELLO: What, did they never whisper?
EMILIA: Never, my lord.
OTHELLO: Nor send you out o' th' way?
EMILIA: Never.
OTHELLO: To fetch her fan, her gloves, her mask, nor nothing?
EMILIA: Never, my lord.   10
OTHELLO: That's strange.
EMILIA: I durst, my lord, to wager she is honest,
Lay down my soul at stake°. If you think other,
Remove your thought. It doth abuse your bosom.
If any wretch have put this in your head,   15

---

²⁵⁴*use* habit.   ²⁵⁵*blood* passion.   ²⁵⁹*courses* actions.   **IV.ii.**   ⁵*that breath made up*
spoken.   ¹³*at stake* as the wager.

Let heaven requite it with the serpent's curse°,
For if she be not honest°, chaste, and true,
There's no man happy. The purest of their wives
Is foul as slander.
OTHELLO: Bid her come hither. Go.   *Exit* EMILIA.
She says enough; yet she's a simple bawd°   20
That cannot say as much. This is a subtle whore,
A closet lock and key of villainous secrets,
And yet she'll kneel and pray; I have seen her do't.

Enter DESDEMONA *and* EMILIA.

DESDEMONA: My lord, what is your will?
OTHELLO: Pray you, chuck, come hither.
DESDEMONA: What is your pleasure?
OTHELLO: Let me see your eyes.   25
Look in my face.
DESDEMONA: What horrible fancy's this?
OTHELLO [*To* EMILIA]: Some of your function°, mistress:
Leave procreants alone and shut the door;
Cough or cry hem if anybody come.
Your mystery°, your mystery! Nay, dispatch!   *Exit* EMILIA. 30
DESDEMONA: Upon my knee, what doth your speech import?
I understand a fury in your words°.
OTHELLO: Why, what art thou?
DESDEMONA: Your wife, my lord; your true
And loyal wife.
OTHELLO: Come, swear it, damn thyself;
Lest, being like one of heaven, the devils themselves   35
Should fear to seize thee. Therefore be doubledamned:
Swear thou art honest.
DESDEMONA: Heaven doth truly know it.
OTHELLO: Heaven truly knows that thou art false as hell.
DESDEMONA: To whom, my lord? With whom? How am I false?
OTHELLO: Ah, Desdemon! Away! Away! Away!   40
DESDEMONA: Alas the heavy day! Why do you weep?
Am I the motive° of these tears, my lord?
If haply° you my father do suspect
An instrument of this your calling back,
Lay not your blame on me. If you have lost him,   45
I have lost him too.
OTHELLO: Had it pleased heaven
To try me with affliction, had they rained

---

[16]*serpent's curse* (*God's curse on the serpent after the fall in Eden*).   [17]*honest   chaste.*   [20]*bawd*
procuress.   [27]*Some of your function   do your proper work (as the operator of a brothel).*   [30]*mystery*
trade.   [32]*words   (Q1 adds to this line, "But not the words").*   [42]*motive   cause.*   [43]*haply   by*
chance.

All kinds of sores and shames on my bare head,
Steeped° me in poverty to the very lips,
Given to captivity me and my utmost hopes, 50
I should have found in some place of my soul
A drop of patience. But alas, to make me
The fixèd figure for the time of scorn°
To point his slow and moving finger at.
Yet could I bear that too, well, very well. 55
But there where I have garnered up my heart,
Where either I must live or bear no life,
The fountain from the which my current runs
Or else dries up—to be discarded thence,
Or keep it as a cistern for foul toads 60
To knot and gender° in—turn thy complexion there,
Patience, thou young and rose-lipped cherubin!
I here look grim as hell!°

DESDEMONA: I hope my noble lord esteems me honest.

OTHELLO: O, ay, as summer flies are in the shambles°, 65
That quicken even with blowing°. O thou weed,
Who art so lovely fair, and smell'st so sweet,
That the sense aches at thee, would thou hadst never been born!

DESDEMONA: Alas, what ignorant° sin have I committed?

OTHELLO: Was this fair paper, this most goodly book, 70
Made to write "whore" upon? What committed?
Committed? O thou public commoner°,
I should make very forges of my cheeks
That would to cinders burn up modesty,
Did I but speak thy deeds. What committed? 75
Heaven stops the nose at it, and the moon winks°;
The bawdy wind that kisses all it meets
Is hushed within the hollow mine of earth
And will not hear't. What committed?

DESDEMONA: By heaven, you do me wrong! 80

OTHELLO: Are not you a strumpet?

DESDEMONA: No, as I am a Christian!
If to preserve this vessel for my lord
From any other foul unlawful touch
Be not to be a strumpet, I am none.

OTHELLO: What, not a whore?

DESDEMONA: No, as I shall be saved! 85

OTHELLO: Is't possible?

---

⁴⁹*Steeped* submerged.   ⁵³*The . . . scorn*   the very image of scorn in our time.   ⁶¹*knot and gender*
twist in bunches and procreate.   ⁶¹⁻⁶³*turn . . . hell*   (the rough sense would seem to be "even Patience would
grow pale, turn complexion, at Desdemona's perfidy, but that Othello looks grimly on").   ⁶⁵*shambles*
abattoirs.   ⁶⁶*quicken even with blowing*   become impregnated as soon as they lay their eggs.
⁶⁹*ignorant* unknowing.   ⁷²*commoner* prostitute.   ⁷⁶*winks*   closes its eyes (the moon was the symbol of chastity).

DESDEMONA: O, heaven forgive us!

OTHELLO: I cry you mercy° then.
　I took you for that cunning whore of Venice
　That married with Othello. [*Calling*] You, mistress,

Enter EMILIA.

　That have the office opposite to Saint Peter   90
　And keep the gate of hell! You, you, ay, you!
　We have done our course; there's money for your pains.

　　　　　　[*Throws her some coins.*]

　I pray you turn the key and keep our counsel.   *Exit.*

EMILIA: Alas, what does this gentleman conceive?
　How do you, madam? How do you, my good lady?   95

DESDEMONA: Faith, half asleep.

EMILIA: Good madam, what's the matter with my lord?

DESDEMONA: With who?

EMILIA: Why, with my lord, madam.

DESDEMONA: Who is thy lord?

EMILIA: He that is yours, sweet lady.   100

DESDEMONA: I have none. Do not talk to me, Emilia.
　I cannot weep, nor answers have I none
　But what should go by water°. Prithee tonight
　Lay on my bed my wedding sheets, remember;
　And call thy husband hither.

EMILIA: Here's a change indeed!   *Exit.* 105

DESDEMONA: 'Tis meet I should be used so, very meet.
　How have I been behaved, that he might stick
　The small'st opinion on my least misuse°?

Enter IAGO *and* EMILIA.

IAGO: What is your pleasure, madam? How is't with you?

DESDEMONA: I cannot tell. Those that do teach young babes   110
　Do it with gentle means and easy tasks.
　He might have chid me so; for, in good faith,
　I am a child to chiding.

IAGO: What is the matter, lady?

EMILIA: Alas, Iago, my lord hath so bewhored her,
　Thrown such despite° and heavy terms upon her   115
　That true hearts cannot bear it.

DESDEMONA: Am I that name, Iago?

IAGO   What name, fair lady?

DESDEMONA: Such as she said my lord did say I was.

EMILIA: He called her whore. A beggar in his drink
　Could not have laid such terms upon his callet°.   120

IAGO: Why did he so?

---

[87]***cry you mercy*** *ask your pardon.*　[103]***water*** *tears.*　[107–08]***stick ... misuse*** *base any doubt on my smallest fault.*　[115]***despite*** *abuse.*　[120]***callet*** *slut.*

DESDEMONA: I do not know; I am sure I am none such.

IAGO: Do not weep, do not weep. Alas the day.

EMILIA: Hath she forsook so many noble matches,
 Her father and her country, and her friends,   125
 To be called whore? Would it not make one weep?

DESDEMONA: It is my wretched fortune.

IAGO: Beshrew° him for't!
 How comes this trick upon him?

DESDEMONA: Nay, heaven doth know.

EMILIA: I will be hanged if some eternal villain,
 Some busy and insinuating rogue,   130
 Some cogging°, cozening slave, to get some office,
 Have not devised this slander. I will be hanged else.

IAGO: Fie, there is no such man! It is impossible.

DESDEMONA: If any such there be, heaven pardon him.

EMILIA: A halter pardon him! And hell gnaw his bones!   135
 Why should he call her whore? Who keeps her company?
 What place? What time? What form? What likelihood?
 The Moor's abused by some most villainous knave,
 Some base notorious knave, some scurvy fellow.
 O heavens, that such companions° thou'dst unfold°,   140
 And put in every honest hand a whip
 To lash the rascals naked through the world
 Even from the east to th' west!

IAGO: Speak within door°.

EMILIA: O, fie upon them! Some such squire° he was
 That turned your wit the seamy side without   145
 And made you to suspect me with the Moor.

IAGO: You are a fool. Go to.

DESDEMONA: Alas, Iago,
 What shall I do to win my lord again?
 Good friend, go to him, for, by this light of heaven,
 I know not how I lost him. Here I kneel: 150
 If e'er my will did trespass 'gainst his love
 Either in discourse of thought° or actual deed,
 Or that mine eyes, mine ears, or any sense
 Delighted them in any other form;
 Or that I do not yet, and ever did,   155
 And ever will (though he do shake me off
 To beggarly divorcement) love him dearly,
 Comfort forswear me. Unkindness may do much,
 And his unkindness may defeat° my life,
 But never taint my love. I cannot say "whore."   160
 It does abhor me now I speak the word;

---

[127]*Beshrew* curse.   [131]*cogging* cheating.   [40]*companions* fellows, rogues.   [140]*unfold* disclose.   [143]*within door* more quietly and moderately.   [144]*squire* (a term of contempt). [152]*discourse of thought* thinking.   [159]*defeat* destroy.

To do the act that might the addition earn
Not the world's mass of vanity could make me.

IAGO: I pray you be content. 'Tis but his humor°.   165
The business of the state does him offense.

DESDEMONA: If 'twere no other.

IAGO: It is but so, I warrant.   [*Trumpets within.*]
Hark how these instruments summon to supper.
The messengers of Venice stay the meat°.
Go in, and weep not. All things shall be well.

[*Exeunt* DESDEMONA *and* EMILIA. *Enter* RODERIGO.]

How now, Roderigo?   170

RODERIGO: I do not find that thou deal'st justly with me.

IAGO: What in the contrary?

RODERIGO: Every day thou daff'st° me with some device°, Iago, and rather,
as it seems to me now, keep'st from me all conveniency° than suppliest me
with the least advantage of hope. I will indeed no longer endure it; nor   175
am I yet persuaded to put up° in peace what already I have foolishly
suffered.

IAGO: Will you hear me, Roderigo?

RODERIGO: I have heard too much, and your words and performances are no
kin together.   180

IAGO: You charge me most unjustly.

RODERIGO: With naught but truth. I have wasted myself out of my means.
The jewels you have had from me to deliver Desdemona would half have
corrupted a votarist°. You have told me she hath received them, and
returned me expectations and comforts of sudden respect° and acquaint-   185
ance; but I find none.

IAGO: Well, go to; very well.

RODERIGO: Very well? Go to? I cannot go to, man; nor 'tis not very well. Nay,
I think it is scurvy, and begin to find myself fopped° in it.

IAGO: Very well.   190

RODERIGO: I tell you 'tis not very well. I will make myself known to
Desdemona. If she will return me my jewels, I will give over my suit and
repent my unlawful solicitation. If not, assure yourself I will seek satisfaction of you.

IAGO: You have said now?   195

RODERIGO: Ay, and said nothing but what I protest° intendment of doing.

IAGO: Why, now I see there's mettle° in thee, and even from this instant do
build on thee a better opinion than ever before. Give me thy hand,
Roderigo. Thou hast taken against me a most just exception°, but yet I
protest I have dealt most directly° in thy affair.   200

RODERIGO: It hath not appeared.

164*humor* mood.   168*stay the meat* await the meal.   173*daff'st* put off.   173*device* scheme.
174*conveniency* what is needful.   176*put up* accept.   184*votarist* nun.   185*sudden respect*
immediate consideration.   189*fopped* duped.   196*protest* aver.   197*mettle* spirit.   199*exception* objection.   200*directly* straightforwardly.

IAGO: I grant indeed it hath not appeared, and your suspicion is not without wit and judgment. But, Roderigo, if thou hast that in thee indeed which I have greater reason to believe now than ever—I mean purpose, courage, and valor—this night show it. If thou the next night following enjoy not[205] Desdemona, take me from this world with treachery and devise engines for° my life.

RODERIGO: Well, what is it? Is it within reason and compass°?

IAGO: Sir, there is especial commission come from Venice to depute Cassio in Othello's place. [210]

RODERIGO: Is that true? Why, then Othello and Desdemona return again to Venice.

IAGO: O, no; he goes into Mauritania and taketh away with him the fair Desdemona, unless his abode be lingered here by some accident; wherein none can be so determinate° as the removing of Cassio. [215]

RODERIGO: How do you mean, removing him?

IAGO: Why, by making him uncapable of Othello's place—knocking out his brains.

RODERIGO: And that you would have me to do?

IAGO: Ay, if you dare do yourself a profit and a right. He sups tonight with[220] a harlotry°, and thither will I go to him. He knows not yet of his honorable fortune. If you will watch his going thence, which I will fashion to fall out° between twelve and one, you may take him at your pleasure. I will be near to second° your attempt, and he shall fall between us. Come, stand not amazed at it, but go along with me. I will show you such a necessity[225] in his death that you shall think yourself bound to put it on him. It is now high supper time, and the night grows to waste. About it.

RODERIGO: I will hear further reason for this.

IAGO: And you shall be satisfied. *Exeunt.*

Scene III [*The citadel.*]

Enter OTHELLO, LODOVICO, DESDEMONA, EMILIA, *and* ATTENDANTS.

LODOVICO: I do beseech you, sir, trouble yourself no further.

OTHELLO: O, pardon me; 'twill do me good to walk.

LODOVICO: Madam, good night. I humbly thank your ladyship.

DESDEMONA: Your honor is most welcome.

OTHELLO: Will you walk, sir? O, Desdemona. [5]

DESDEMONA: My lord?

OTHELLO: Get you to bed on th' instant; I will be returned forthwith. Dismiss your attendant there. Look't be done.

DESDEMONA: I will, my lord. *Exit* [OTHELLO, *with* LODOVICO *and* ATTENDANTS].

EMILIA: How goes it now? He looks gentler than he did. [10]

DESDEMONA: He says he will return incontinent°,

206–207*engines   for   schemes   against.*   208*compass   possibility.*   215*determinate   effective.*
221*harlotry   female.*   222–223*fall   out   occur.*   224*second   support.*   **IV.iii.**   11*incontinent
at once.*

And hath commanded me to go to bed.
And bade me to dismiss you.
EMILIA: Dismiss me?
DESDEMONA: It was his bidding; therefore, good Emilia,
  Give me my nightly wearing, and adieu.   15
  We must not now displease him.
EMILIA: I would you had never seen him!
DESDEMONA: So would not I. My love doth so approve him
  That even his stubbornness, his checks°, his frowns—
  Prithee unpin me—have grace and favor.   20
EMILIA: I have laid these sheets you bade me on the bed.
DESDEMONA: All's one°. Good Father, how foolish are our minds!
  If I do die before, prithee shroud me
  In one of these same sheets.
EMILIA: Come, come! You talk.
DESDEMONA: My mother had a maid called Barbary.   25
  She was in love; and he she loved proved mad
  And did forsake her. She had a song of "Willow";
  An old thing 'twas, but it expressed her fortune,
  And she died singing it. That song tonight
  Will not go from my mind; I have much to do   30
  But to go hang my head all at one side
  And sing it like poor Barbary. Prithee dispatch.
EMILIA: Shall I go fetch your nightgown?
DESDEMONA: No, unpin me here.
  This Lodovico is a proper man.   35
EMILIA: A very handsome man.
DESDEMONA: He speaks well.
EMILIA: I know a lady in Venice would have walked barefoot to Palestine
  for a touch of his nether lip.
DESDEMONA [*Sings*]:
  "The poor soul sat singing by a sycamore tree,   40
    Sing all a green willow;
  Her hand on her bosom, her head on her knee,
    Sing willow, willow, willow.
  The fresh streams ran by her and murmured her moans;
    Sing willow, willow, willow;   45
  Her salt tears fell from her, and soft'ned the stones—
    Sing willow, willow, willow—"
  Lay by these.   [*Gives* EMILIA *her clothes.*]
  "Willow, Willow"—
  Prithee hie° thee; he'll come anon°.   50
  "Sing all a green willow must be my garland
  Let nobody blame him; his scorn I approve"—
  Nay, that's not next. Hark! Who is't that knocks?

---

¹⁹*checks* *rebukes.*   ²²*All's one* *no matter.*   ⁵⁰*hie* *hurry.*   ⁵⁰*anon* *at once.*

EMILIA: It is the wind.
DESDEMONA [*Sings*]:
　"I called my love false love; but what said he then?   55
　　Sing willow, willow, willow:
　If I court moe° women, you'll couch with moe men."
　So, get thee gone; good night. Mine eyes do itch.
　Doth that bode weeping?
EMILIA:　　　　　　　　　　　　'Tis neither here nor there.
DESDEMONA: I have heard it said so. O, these men, these men.   60
　Dost thou in conscience think, tell me, Emilia,
　That there be women do abuse their husbands
　In such gross kind?
EMILIA:　　　　　　　　There be some such, no question.
DESDEMONA: Wouldst thou do such a deed for all the world?
EMILIA: Why, would not you?
DESDEMONA:　　　　　No, by this heavenly light!   65
EMILIA: Nor I neither by this heavenly light.
　I might do't as well i' th' dark.
DESDEMONA: Wouldst thou do such a deed for all the world?
EMILIA: The world's a huge thing; it is a great price for a small vice.
DESDEMONA: In troth, I think thou wouldst not.   70
EMILIA: In troth, I think I should; and undo't when I had done. Marry, I would
　not do such a thing for a joint-ring°, nor for measures of lawn°, nor for
　gowns, petticoats, nor caps, nor any petty exhibition°, but for all the whole
　world? Why, who would not make her husband a cuckold to make him
　a monarch? I should venture purgatory for't.   75
DESDEMONA: Beshrew me if I would do such a wrong for the whole world.
EMILIA: Why, the wrong is but a wrong i' th' world; and having the world
　for your labor, 'tis a wrong in your own world, and you might quickly
　make it right.
DESDEMONA: I do not think there is any such woman.   80
EMILIA: Yes, a dozen; and as many to th' vantage as would store° the world
　they played for.
　But I do think it is their husbands' faults
　If wives do fall. Say that they slack their duties
　And pour our treasures into foreign° laps;   85
　Or else break out in peevish jealousies,
　Throwing restraint upon us; or say they strike us,
　Or scant our former having in despite°—
　Why, we have galls; and though we have some grace,
　Yet have we some revenge. Let husbands know   90
　Their wives have sense like them. They see, and smell,
　And have their palates both for sweet and sour,

---

⁵⁷*moe*　more.　　⁷²*joint-ring*　*(a ring with two interlocking halves).*　　⁷²*lawn*　*fine linen.*
⁷³*exhibition*　*payment.*　　⁸¹*to . . . store*　*in addition as would fill.*　　⁸⁵*foreign*　*alien, i.e., other than*
the wife.　　⁸⁸*scant . . . despite*　*reduce, in spite, our household allowance (?).*

As husbands have. What is it that they do
When they change° us for others? Is it sport?
I think it is. And doth affection° breed it?   95
I think it doth. Is't frailty that thus errs?
It is so too. And have not we affections?
Desires for sport? and frailty? as men have?
Then let them use us well; else let them know,
The ills we do, their ills instruct us so°.   100

DESDEMONA: Good night, good night. Heaven me such uses° send,
Not to pick bad from bad, but by bad mend.   *Exeunt.*

ACT V

Scene I [*A street.*]

Enter IAGO *and* RODERIGO.

IAGO: Here, stand behind this bulk°; straight will he come.
Wear thy good rapier bare, and put it home.
Quick, quick! Fear nothing; I'll be at thy elbow.
It makes us, or it mars us, think on that,
And fix most firm thy resolution.   5

RODERIGO: Be near at hand; I may miscarry in't.

IAGO: Here, at thy hand. Be bold, and take thy stand.   [*Moves to one side.*]

RODERIGO: I have no great devotion to the deed,
And yet he hath given me satisfying reasons.
'Tis but a man gone. Forth my sword! He dies!   10

IAGO: I have rubbed this young quat° almost to the sense°,
And he grows angry. Now, whether he kill Cassio,
Or Cassio him, or each do kill the other,
Every way makes my gain. Live Roderigo,
He calls me to a restitution large   15
Of gold and jewels that I bobbed° from him
As gifts to Desdemona.
It must not be. If Cassio do remain,
He hath a daily beauty in his life
That makes me ugly; and besides, the Moor   20
May unfold me to him; there stand I in much peril.
No, he must die. But so, I hear him coming.

Enter CASSIO.

RODERIGO: I know his gait. 'Tis he. Villain, thou diest!   [*Thrusts at* CASSIO.]

CASSIO: That thrust had been mine enemy indeed

---

⁹⁴*change* exchange.   ⁹⁵*affection* strong feeling, desire.   ¹⁰⁰*instruct us so* teach us to do likewise.
¹⁰¹*uses* practices.   **V.i.** ¹*bulk* projecting stall of a shop.   ¹¹*quat* pimple.   ¹¹*to the sense*
raw.   ¹⁶*bobbed* swindled.

But that my coat° is better than thou know'st.   25
I will make proof of thine.   *[Fights with* RODERIGO.]
RODERIGO: O, I am slain!°
CASSIO: I am maimed forever. Help, ho! Murder! Murder!

Enter OTHELLO *[to one side]*.

OTHELLO: The voice of Cassio. Iago keeps his word.
RODERIGO: O, villain that I am!
OTHELLO: It is even so.
CASSIO: O help, ho! Light! A surgeon!   30
OTHELLO: 'Tis he. O brave Iago, honest and just,
That hast such noble sense of thy friend's wrong!
Thou teachest me. Minion°, your dear lies dead,
And your unblest° fate hies°. Strumpet, I come.
Forth of my heart those charms, thine eyes, are blotted.   35
Thy bed, lust-stained, shall with lust's blood be spotted.

Exit OTHELLO. *Enter* LODOVICO *and* GRATIANO.

CASSIO: What, ho? No watch? No passage°? Murder! Murder!
GRATIANO: 'Tis some mischance. The voice is very direful.
CASSIO: O, help!
LODOVICO: Hark!   40
RODERIGO: O wretched villain!
LODOVICO: Two or three groan. 'Tis heavy night.
These may be counterfeits. Let's think't unsafe
To come into the cry without more help.
RODERIGO: Nobody come? Then shall I bleed to death.   45
LODOVICO: Hark!

Enter IAGO *[with a light]*.

GRATIANO: Here's one comes in his shirt, with light and weapons.
IAGO: Who's there? Whose noise is this that cries on murder?
LODOVICO: We do not know.
IAGO: Do not you hear a cry?
CASSIO: Here, here! For heaven's sake, help me!
IAGO: What's the matter?   50
GRATIANO: This is Othello's ancient, as I take it.
LODOVICO: The same indeed, a very valiant fellow.
IAGO: What are you here that cry so grievously?
CASSIO: Iago? O, I am spoiled, undone by villains.
Give me some help.   55

---

²⁵**coat**   *i.e., a mail shirt or bulletproof vest.*   ²⁶**slain**   *most editors add here a stage direction that has Iago wounding Cassio in the leg from behind, but remaining unseen. However, nothing in the text requires this, and Cassio's wound can be given him in the fight with Roderigo, for presumably when Cassio attacks Roderigo the latter would not simply accept the thrust but would parry. Since Iago enters again at line 46, he must exit at some point after line 22.*   ³³**Minion**   *hussy, i.e., Desdemona.*   ³⁴**unblest**   *unsanctified.*   ³⁴**hies**   *approaches swiftly.*   ³⁷**passage**   *passers-by.*

IAGO: O me, lieutenant! What villains have done this?
CASSIO: I think that one of them is hereabout
  And cannot make away.
IAGO: O treacherous villains!
  [*To* LODOVICO *and* GRATIANO] What are you there?
  Come in, and give some help.   60
RODERIGO: O, help me here!
CASSIO: That's one of them.
IAGO: O murd'rous slave! O villain! [*Stabs* RODERIGO.]
RODERIGO: O damned Iago! O inhuman dog!
IAGO: Kill men i' th' dark?—Where be these bloody thieves?—
  How silent is this town!—Ho! Murder! Murder!—   65
  What may you be? Are you of good or evil?
LODOVICO: As you shall prove us, praise us.
IAGO: Signior Lodovico?
LODOVICO: He, sir.
IAGO: I cry you mercy. Here's Cassio hurt by villains.   70
GRATIANO: Cassio?
IAGO: How is't, brother?
CASSIO: My leg is cut in two.
IAGO: Marry, heaven forbid!
  Light, gentlemen. I'll bind it with my shirt.

Enter BIANCA.

BIANCA: What is the matter, ho? Who is't that cried?   75
IAGO: Who is't that cried?
BIANCA: O my dear Cassio! My sweet Cassio!
  O Cassio, Cassio, Cassio!
IAGO: O notable strumpet!—Cassio, may you suspect
  Who they should be that have thus mangled you?   80
CASSIO: No.
GRATIANO: I am sorry to find you thus. I have been to seek you.
IAGO: Lend me a garter. So. O for a chair
  To bear him easily hence.
BIANCA: Alas, he faints! O Cassio, Cassio, Cassio!   85
IAGO: Gentlemen all, I do suspect this trash
  To be a party in this injury.—
  Patience awhile, good Cassio.—Come, come.
  Lend me a light. Know we this face or no?
  Alas, my friend and my dear countryman   90
  Roderigo? No.—Yes, sure.—Yes, 'tis Roderigo!
GRATIANO: What, of Venice?
IAGO: Even he, sir. Did you know him?
GRATIANO: Know him? Ay.
IAGO: Signior Gratiano? I cry your gentle pardon.
  These bloody accidents must excuse my manners   95
  That so neglected you.

GRATIANO: I am glad to see you.
IAGO: How do you, Cassio?—O, a chair, a chair!
GRATIANO: Roderigo?
IAGO: He, he, 'tis he! [*A chair brought in.*] O, that's well said°; the chair.
Some good man bear him carefully from hence.   100
I'll fetch the general's surgeon. [*To* BIANCA] For you, mistress,
Save you your labor. [*To* CASSIO] He that lies slain here, Cassio,
Was my dear friend. What malice was between you?
CASSIO: None in the world; nor do I know the man.
IAGO: What, look you pale?—O, bear him out o' th' air.   105

[CASSIO *is carried off.*]

Stay you, good gentlemen.—Look you pale, mistress?
Do you perceive the gastness° of her eye?
Nay, if you stare, we shall hear more anon.
Behold her well; I pray you look upon her.
Do you see, gentlemen? Nay, guiltiness will speak,   110
Though tongues were out of use°.

[*Enter* EMILIA.]

EMILIA: Alas, what is the matter? What is the matter, husband?
IAGO: Cassio hath here been set on in the dark
By Roderigo and fellows that are scaped.
He's almost slain, and Roderigo quite dead.   115
EMILIA: Alas, good gentleman! Alas, good Cassio!
IAGO: This is the fruits of whoring. Prithee, Emilia,
Go know of Cassio where he supped tonight.
[*To* BIANCA] What, do you shake at that?
BIANCA: He supped at my house; but I therefore shake not.   120
IAGO: O, did he so? I charge° you go with me.
EMILIA: Oh fie upon thee, strumpet!
BIANCA: I am no strumpet, but of life as honest
As you that thus abuse me.
EMILIA: As I? Fie upon thee!
IAGO: Kind gentlemen, let's go see poor Cassio dressed°.   125
[*To* BIANCA] Come, mistress, you must tell's another tale.
Emilia, run you to the citadel
And tell my lord and lady what hath happed   [*Exit* EMILIA.]
Will you go on afore?   *Exeunt* [*all but* IAGO].
This is the night
That either makes me or fordoes me quite°.   [*Exit.*]130

Scene II. [DESDEMONA'S *chamber.*]

Enter OTHELLO [*with a light*]; *and* DESDEMONA *in her bed.*

⁹⁹*well said* well done.   ¹⁰⁷*gastness* terror.   ¹¹¹*tongues were out of use* men no longer spoke.
¹²¹*charge* command.   ¹²⁵*dressed* bandaged.   ¹³⁰*fordoes me quite* completely ruins me.

OTHELLO: It is the cause, it is the cause, my soul.
Let me not name it to you, you chaste stars.
It is the cause. Yet I'll not shed her blood,
Nor scar that whiter skin of hers than snow
And smooth as monumental alabaster.   5
Yet she must die, else she'll betray more men.
Put out the light, and then put out the light.
If I quench thee, thou flaming minister°,
I can again thy former light restore,
Should I repent me; but once put out thy light,   10
Thou cunning'st° pattern of excelling nature,
I know not where is that Promethean heat°
That can thy light relume°. When I have plucked the rose,
I cannot give it vital° growth again;
It needs must wither. I'll smell thee on the tree.   [*He kisses her.*] 15
O balmy breath, that dost almost persuade
Justice to break her sword. One more, one more!
Be thus when thou art dead, and I will kill thee,
And love thee after. One more, and that's the last!
So sweet was ne'er so fatal. I must weep,   20
But they are cruel tears. This sorrow's heavenly;
It strikes where it doth love. She wakes.
DESDEMONA: Who's there? Othello?
OTHELLO: Ay, Desdemona.
DESDEMONA: Will you come to bed, my lord?
OTHELLO: Have you prayed tonight, Desdemon?
DESDEMONA: Ay, my lord.   25
OTHELLO: If you bethink yourself of any crime
Unreconciled as yet to heaven and grace,
Solicit for it straight.
DESDEMONA: Alack, my lord, what may you mean by that?
OTHELLO: Well, do it, and be brief; I will walk by°.   30
I would not kill thy unpreparèd spirit.
No, heavens forfend! I would not kill thy soul.
DESDEMONA: Talk you of killing?
OTHELLO: Ay, I do.
DESDEMONA: Then heaven
Have mercy on me!
OTHELLO: Amen, with all my heart.
DESDEMONA: If you say so, I hope you will not kill me.   35
OTHELLO: Humh.
DESDEMONA: And yet I fear you; for you're fatal then
When your eyes roll so. Why I should fear I know not,

V.ii.   [8]*minister* *worker, servant.*   [11]*cunning'st*   *most intricate and skillfully wrought (by nature excell-*
ing itself).   [12]*Promethean heat*   *divine fire (Prometheus is the Titan who stole fire from heaven and gave*
it to man).   [13]*relume*   *relight.*   [14]*vital*   *living.*   [30]*by*   *nearby.*

Since guiltiness I know not; but yet I feel I fear.
OTHELLO: Think on thy sins.
DESDEMONA: They are loves I bear to you.   40
OTHELLO: Ay, and for that thou diest.
DESDEMONA: That death's unnatural that kills for loving.
   Alas, why gnaw you so your nether lip?
   Some bloody passion shakes your very frame.
   These are portents; but yet I hope, I hope,   45
   They do not point on me.
OTHELLO: Peace and be still.
DESDEMONA: I will so. What's the matter?
OTHELLO: That handkerchief which I so loved and gave thee,
   Thou gav'st to Cassio.
DESDEMONA: No, by my life and soul!
   Send for the man and ask him.
OTHELLO: Sweet soul, take heed,   50
   Take heed of perjury; thou art on thy deathbed.
DESDEMONA: Ay, but not yet to die.
OTHELLO: Presently°.
   Therefore confess thee freely of thy sin,
   For to deny each article° with oath
   Cannot remove nor choke the strong conception   55
   That I do groan withal. Thou art to die.
DESDEMONA: Then Lord have mercy on me.
OTHELLO: I say, amen.
DESDEMONA: And have you mercy too. I never did
   Offend you in my life; never loved Cassio
   But with such general warranty° of heaven   60
   As I might love. I never gave him token.
OTHELLO: By heaven, I saw my handkerchief in's hand!
   O perjured woman! thou dost stone° my heart,
   And mak'st me call what I intend to do
   A murder, which I thought a sacrifice.   65
   I saw the handkerchief.
DESDEMONA: He found it then.
   I never gave it him. Send for him hither.
   Let him confess a truth.
OTHELLO: He hath confessed.
DESDEMONA: What, my lord?
OTHELLO: That he hath used thee.
DESDEMONA: How? Unlawfully?
OTHELLO: Ay.   70
DESDEMONA: He will not say so.
OTHELLO: No, his mouth is stopped.

---

⁵²**Presently** *immediately.*   ⁵⁴**article** *item (of the charge of adultery. Othello makes heavy use of legal terms in this scene).*   ⁶⁰**warranty** *allowance.*   ⁶³**stone** *turn to stone.*

Honest Iago hath ta'en order for't°.
DESDEMONA: O, my fear interprets. What, is he dead?
OTHELLO: Had all his hairs been lives, my great revenge   75
  Had stomach° for them all.
DESDEMONA: Alas, he is betrayed, and I undone!
OTHELLO: Out, strumpet! Weep'st thou for him to my face?
DESDEMONA: O, banish me, my lord, but kill me not!
OTHELLO: Down, strumpet!
DESDEMONA: Kill me tomorrow; let me live tonight!   80
OTHELLO: Nay, if you strive—
DESDEMONA: But half an hour!
OTHELLO: Being done, there is no pause.
DESDEMONA: But while I say one prayer!
OTHELLO: It is too late.   *Smothers her.*

EMILIA *at the door.*

EMILIA [*Calls within*]: My lord, my lord! What, ho, my lord, my lord!
OTHELLO: What noise is this? Not dead? Not yet quite dead?   85
  I that am cruel am yet merciful;
  I would not have thee linger in thy pain.
EMILIA [*Within*]: What, ho! My lord, my lord!
OTHELLO: So, so. Who's there?
EMILIA [*Within*]: O, good my lord, I would speak a word with you.
OTHELLO: Yes, 'tis Emilia.—By and by.—She's dead.—   90
  'Tis like she comes to speak of Cassio's death.
  The noise was high°. Ha! No more moving?
  Still as the grave.—Shall she come in? Were't good?—
  I think she stirs again. No.—What's best to do?
  If she come in, she'll sure speak to my wife.   95
  My wife! My wife! What wife? I have no wife.
  O, insupportable! O heavy hour!
  Methinks it should be now a huge eclipse
  Of sun and moon, and that th' affrighted globe
  Should yawn° at alteration.
EMILIA [*Within*]:   I do beseech you   100
  That I may speak with you, O good my lord!
OTHELLO: I had forgot thee. O, come in, Emilia.
  Soft, by and by.—Let me the curtains draw.—

[*Draws the bed hangings and then opens the door.*]

Where art thou?

Enter EMILIA.

What's the matter with thee now?

---

⁷²**ta'en order for't** *made sure of it.*   ⁷⁵**stomach** *appetite.*   ⁹²**high** *loud (Q1 reads "here").*
⁹⁸⁻¹⁰⁰**Methinks . . . alteration** *(the Elizabethans believed that great changes in human affairs were reflected by disorders in nature).*   ¹⁰⁰**yawn** *gape open (as in an earthquake).*

EMILIA: O my good lord, yonder's foul murders done!   105
OTHELLO: What? Now?
EMILIA: But now, my lord.
OTHELLO: It is the very error° of the moon.
   She comes more nearer earth than she was wont
   And makes men mad.   110
EMILIA: Cassio, my lord, hath killed a young Venetian
   Called Roderigo.
OTHELLO: Roderigo killed?
   And Cassio killed?
EMILIA: No, Cassio is not killed.
OTHELLO: Not Cassio killed? Then murder's out of tune,
   And sweet revenge grows harsh.   115
DESDEMONA: O, falsely, falsely murdered!
EMILIA: O Lord! What cry is that?
OTHELLO: That? What?
EMILIA: Out and alas! that was my lady's voice.
   Help! Help, ho! Help! O lady, speak again!
   Sweet Desdemona! O sweet mistress, speak!   120
DESDEMONA: A guiltless death I die.
EMILIA: O, who hath done this deed?
DESDEMONA: Nobody—I myself. Farewell.
   Commend me to my kind lord. O, farewell!   [*She dies.*]
OTHELLO: Why, how should she be murd'red?
EMILIA: Alas, who knows?   125
OTHELLO: You heard her say herself, it was not I.
EMILIA: She said so. I must needs report the truth.
OTHELLO: She's like a liar gone to burning hell!
   'Twas I that killed her.
EMILIA: O, the more angel she,
   And you the blacker devil!   130
OTHELLO: She turned to folly, and she was a whore.
EMILIA: Thou dost belie her, and thou art a devil.
OTHELLO: She was false as water.
EMILIA: Thou art rash as fire to say
   That she was false. O, she was heavenly true!
OTHELLO: Cassio did top her. Ask thy husband else.   135
   O, I were damned beneath all depth in hell
   But that I did proceed upon just grounds
   To this extremity. Thy husband knew it all.
EMILIA: My husband?
OTHELLO: Thy husband.
EMILIA: That she was false to wedlock?
OTHELLO: Ay, with Cassio. Had she been true,   140

---

[108] *error*   *wandering out of regular course (disorders in the heavens were believed by some to cause disorders on earth, as well as vice versa).*

If heaven would make me such another world
Of one entire and perfect chrysolite°,
I'd not have sold her for it.

EMILIA: My husband?

OTHELLO: Ay, 'twas he that told me on her first.   145
An honest man he is, and hates the slime
That sticks on filthy deeds.

EMILIA: My husband?

OTHELLO: What needs this iterance? Woman, I say thy husband.

EMILIA: O mistress, villainy hath made mocks with love!
My husband say she was false?

OTHELLO: He, woman.
I say, thy husband. Dost understand the word?   150
My friend, thy husband; honest, honest Iago.

EMILIA: If he say so, may his pernicious soul
Rot half a grain a day! He lies to th' heart.
She was too fond of her most filthy bargain.

OTHELLO: Hah?   155

EMILIA: Do thy worst.
This deed of thine is no more worthy heaven
Than thou wast worthy her.

OTHELLO: Peace, you were best°.

EMILIA: Thou hast not half that pow'r to do me harm
As I have to be hurt. O gull! O dolt!   160
As ignorant as dirt! Thou hast done a deed—

[OTHELLO *moves to draw his sword.*]

I care not for thy sword; I'll make thee known,
Though I lost twenty lives. Help! Help! Ho! Help!
The Moor hath killed my mistress! Murder! murder!

Enter MONTANO, GRATIANO, *and* IAGO [*and Others*].

MONTANO: What is the matter? How now, general?   165

EMILIA: O, are you come, Iago? You have done well,
That men must lay their murders on your neck.

GRATIANO: What is the matter?

EMILIA: Disprove this villain, if thou be'st a man.
He says thou told'st him that his wife was false.   170
I know thou didst not; thou'rt not such a villain.
Speak, for my heart is full.

IAGO: I told him what I thought, and told no more
Than what he found himself was apt and true.

EMILIA: But did you ever tell him she was false?   175

IAGO: I did.

EMILIA: You told a lie, an odious damnèd lie!

---

¹⁴²*chrysolite* *topaz.*   ¹⁵⁸*Peace, you were best* *i.e., you had better be silent.*

Upon my soul, a lie! A wicked lie!
She false with Cassio? Did you say with Cassio?
IAGO: With Cassio, mistress. Go to, charm° your tongue.   180
EMILIA: I will not charm my tongue; I am bound to speak:
  My mistress here lies murdered in her bed.
ALL: O heavens forfend!
EMILIA: And your reports have set the murder on.
OTHELLO: Nay, stare not, masters. It is true indeed.   185
GRATIANO: 'Tis a strange truth.
MONTANO: O monstrous act!
EMILIA: Villainy, villainy, villainy!
  I think upon't—I think I smell't!—O villainy!
  I thought so then.—I'll kill myself for grief.—
  O villainy, villainy!   190
IAGO: What, are you mad? I charge you get you home.
EMILIA: Good gentlemen, let me have leave to speak.
  'Tis proper I obey him, but not now.
  Perchance, Iago, I will ne'er go home.
OTHELLO: O! O! O!   *[Falls on the bed.]*   195
EMILIA: Nay, lay thee down and roar,
  For thou hast killed the sweetest innocent
  That e'er did lift up eye.
OTHELLO: O, she was foul!   *[Rises.]*
  I scarce did know you, uncle. There lies your niece,
  Whose breath, indeed, these hands have newly stopped.
  I know this act shows horrible and grim.   200
GRATIANO: Poor Desdemona! I am glad thy father's dead.
  Thy match was mortal to him, and pure grief
  Shore his old thread in twain. Did he live now,
  This sight would make him do a desperate turn;
  Yea, curse his better angel from his side,   205
  And fall to reprobation°.
OTHELLO: 'Tis pitiful; but yet Iago knows
  That she with Cassio hath the act of shame
  A thousand times committed. Cassio confessed it;
  And she did gratify his amorous works   210
  With that recognizance and pledge of love,
  Which I first gave her. I saw it in his hand.
  It was a handkerchief, an antique token
  My father gave my mother.
EMILIA: O God! O heavenly God!   215
IAGO: Zounds, hold your peace!
EMILIA: 'Twill out, 'twill out! I peace?
  No, I will speak as liberal as the north°.

---

¹⁸⁰**charm** *control.*   ²⁰⁶**reprobation** *damnation.*   ²¹⁷**liberal as the north** *freely (and bitingly) as the north wind blows.*

Let heaven and men and devils, let them all,
All, all, cry shame against me, yet I'll speak.
IAGO: Be wise, and get you home.
EMILIA: I will not.   220

[IAGO *draws and threatens* EMILIA.]

GRATIANO: Fie! Your sword upon a woman?
EMILIA: O thou dull Moor, that handkerchief thou speak'st of
I found by fortune, and did give my husband;
For often with a solemn earnestness—
More than indeed belonged to such a trifle—   225
He begged of me to steal't.
IAGO: Villainous whore!
EMILIA: She give it Cassio? No, alas, I found it,
And I did give't my husband.
IAGO: Filth, thou liest!
EMILIA: By heaven, I do not, I do not, gentlemen.
O murd'rous coxcomb! What should such a fool   230
Do with so good a wife?
OTHELLO: Are there no stones° in heaven
But what serves for the thunder? Precious villain!

[*The* MOOR *runs at* IAGO, *but is disarmed by* MONTANO. IAGO *kills his wife*.]

GRATIANO: The woman falls. Sure he hath killed his wife.
EMILIA: Ay, ay. O, lay me by my mistress' side.   [*Exit* IAGO.]
GRATIANO: He's gone, but his wife's killed.   235
MONTANO: 'Tis a notorious° villain. Take you this weapon,
Which I have recovered from the Moor.
Come, guard the door without. Let him not pass,
But kill him rather. I'll after that same villain,
For 'tis a damnèd slave.   *Exit* [*with all but* OTHELLO *and* EMILIA].
OTHELLO: I am not valiant neither;   240
But every puny whipster° gets my sword.
But why should honor outlive honesty?
Let it go all.
EMILIA: What did thy song bode, lady?
Hark, canst thou hear me? I will play the swan,
And die in music. [*Sings*] "Willow, willow, willow."   245
Moor, she was chaste. She loved thee, cruel Moor,
So come my soul to bliss as I speak true.
So speaking as I think, alas, I die.   [*She dies*.]
OTHELLO: I have another weapon in this chamber;
It was a sword of Spain, the ice-brook's temper.   250
O, here it is.—Uncle, I must come forth.

231**stones**   *thunderbolts.*   236**notorious**   *out-and-out.*   241**puny   whipster**   *small   top-whipping
boy (?).*

GRATIANO [*Within*]: If thou attempt it, it will cost thee dear.
  Thou hast no weapon, and perforce must suffer.
OTHELLO: Look in upon me then and speak with me,
  Or, naked as I am, I will assault thee.   255

[*Enter* GRATIANO.]

GRATIANO: What is the matter?
OTHELLO: Behold, I have a weapon;
  A better never did itself sustain
  Upon a soldier's thigh. I have seen the day
  That with this little arm and this good sword
  I have made my way through more impediments   260
  Than twenty times your stop. But O vain boast!
  Who can control his fate? 'Tis not so now.
  Be not afraid, though you do see me weaponed.
  Here is my journey's end, here is my butt°,
  And very seamark of my utmost sail°.   265
  Do you go back dismayed? 'Tis a lost fear.
  Man but a rush° against Othello's breast.
  And he retires. Where should Othello go?
  Now, how dost thou look now? O ill-starred wench!
  Pale as thy smock! When we shall meet at compt°,   270
  This look of thine will hurl my soul from heaven,
  And fiends will snatch at it. Cold, cold, my girl?
  Even like thy chastity.
  O cursèd, cursèd slave! Whip me, ye devils,
  From the possession of° this heavenly sight!   275
  Blow me about in winds! roast me in sulfur!
  Wash me in steep-down gulfs of liquid fire!
  O Desdemon! Dead Desdemon; dead. O! O!

Enter LODOVICO, CASSIO, MONTANO, *and* IAGO [*as prisoner,*] *with Officers.*

LODOVICO: Where is this rash and most unfortunate man?
OTHELLO: That's he that was Othello? Here I am.   280
LODOVICO: Where is that viper? Bring the villain forth.
OTHELLO: I look down towards his feet°—but that's a fable.
  If that thou be'st a devil, I cannot kill thee.   [*Wounds* IAGO.]
LODOVICO: Wrench his sword from him.   [OTHELLO *is disarmed.*]
IAGO: I bleed, sir, but not killed.
OTHELLO: I am not sorry neither. I'd have thee live;   285
  For in my sense, 'tis happiness to die.
LODOVICO: O thou Othello that was once so good,

---

²⁶⁴*butt* target, stopping place.   ²⁶⁵*seamark of my utmost sail* maker of my furthest journey.
²⁶⁷*Man but a rush* attack with only a reed.   ²⁷⁰*compt* Judgment Day.   ²⁷⁵*the possession of*
being possessed by.   ²⁸²*towards his feet* i.e., for his cloven hoofs.

　　　Fall'n in the practice° of a cursèd slave,
　　　What shall be said to thee?
OTHELLO:　　　　　　　　Why, anything:
　　　An honorable murderer, if you will;
　　　For naught I did in hate, but all in honor.　　　　　　　　290
LODOVICO: This wretch hath part confessed his villainy.
　　　Did you and he consent in Cassio's death?
OTHELLO: Ay.
CASSIO: Dear general, I never gave you cause.　　　　　　　　295
OTHELLO: I do believe it, and I ask your pardon.
　　　Will you, I pray, demand that demi-devil
　　　Why he hath thus ensnared my soul and body?
IAGO: Demand me nothing. What you know, you know.
　　　From this time forth I never will speak word.　　　　　　　300
LODOVICO: What, not to pray?
GRATIANO:　　　　　　　　Torments will ope your lips.
OTHELLO: Well, thou dost best.
LODOVICO: Sir, you shall understand what hath befall'n,
　　　Which, as I think, you know not. Here is a letter
　　　Found in the pocket of the slain Roderigo;　　　　　　　305
　　　And here another. The one of them imports
　　　The death of Cassio to be undertook
　　　By Roderigo.
OTHELLO: O villain!
CASSIO:　　　　　　　　Most heathenish and most gross!
LODOVICO: Now here's another discontented paper　　　　　　310
　　　Found in his pocket too; and this, it seems,
　　　Roderigo meant t' have sent this damnèd villain;
　　　But that, belike, Iago in the interim
　　　Came in and satisfied him.
OTHELLO:　　　　　　　　O thou pernicious caitiff!
　　　How came you, Cassio, by that handkerchief　　　　　　315
　　　That was my wife's?
CASSIO:　　　　　　　　I found it in my chamber;
　　　And he himself confessed it but even now
　　　That there he dropped it for a special purpose
　　　Which wrought to his desire.
OTHELLO:　　　　　　　　O fool! Fool! Fool!
CASSIO: There is besides in Roderigo's letter,　　　　　　　320
　　　How he upbraids Iago that he made him
　　　Brave me upon the watch; whereon it came
　　　That I was cast; and even but now he spake,
　　　After long seeming dead—Iago hurt him,
　　　Iago set him on.　　　　　　　325
LODOVICO: You must forsake this room and go with us.

---

²⁸⁸*practice*　plotting.

Your power and your command is taken off,
And Cassio rules in Cyprus. For this slave,
If there be any cunning cruelty
That can torment him much and hold him long,   330
It shall be his. You shall close prisoner rest
Till that the nature of your fault be known
To the Venetian state. Come, bring away.

OTHELLO: Soft you, a word or two before you go.
I have done the state some service and they know't.   335
No more of that. I pray you, in your letters,
When you shall these unlucky deeds relate,
Speak of me as I am. Nothing extenuate,
Nor set down aught in malice. Then must you speak
Of one that loved not wisely, but too well;   340
Of one not easily jealous, but, being wrought,
Perplexed in the extreme; of one whose hand,
Like the base Judean°, threw a pearl away
Richer than all his tribe; of one whose subdued eyes,
Albeit unusèd to the melting mood,   345
Drops tears as fast as the Arabian trees
Their med'cinable gum. Set you down this.
And say besides that in Aleppo once,
Where a malignant and a turbaned Turk
Beat a Venetian and traduced the state,   350
I took by th' throat the circumcisèd dog
And smote him—thus.   [*He stabs himself.*]

LODOVICO: O bloody period!°

GRATIANO: All that is spoke is marred.

OTHELLO: I kissed thee ere I killed thee. No way but this,
Killing myself, to die upon a kiss.   [*He falls over* DESDEMONA *and dies.*] 355

CASSIO: This did I fear, but thought he had no weapon;
For he was great of heart.

LODOVICO [*To* IAGO]:   O Spartan dog,
More fell° than anguish, hunger, or the sea!
Look on the tragic loading of this bed.
This is thy work. The object poisons sight;   360
Let it be hid.   [*Bed curtains drawn.*]
                Gratiano, keep° the house,
And seize upon the fortunes of the Moor,
For they succeed on you. To you, lord governor,
Remains the censure of this hellish villain,
The time, the place, the torture. O, enforce it!   365
Myself will straight aboard, and to the state
This heavy act with heavy heart relate.   *Exeunt.*

---

³⁴³**Judean**   *(most editors use the Q1 reading, "Indian," here, but F is clear: both readings point toward the infidel,*
the unbeliever.   ³⁵³**period**   *end.*   ³⁵⁸**fell**   *cruel.*   ³⁶¹**keep**   *remain in.*

QUESTIONS

1. What makes Othello a tragic figure? Is his tragedy self-inflicted or is it beyond his control? What is his tragic flaw?
2. Compare Othello's speeches from the beginning, middle, and end of the play (Acts I, III, and V). Explain the significance of their differences in style and tone.
3. Iago is a resourceful and clever character who knows how to manipulate people. Explain how he manipulates Roderigo, Cassio, and Othello.
4. What reason does Iago give for seeking Othello's destruction? Does this seem an adequate or a credible motive?
5. How does Emilia's role help us to better understand Iago? In what ways is she a *foil* (a contrasting character) to Desdemona? What other characters serve to balance each other?
6. Of what significance is Bianca's role in the play? Brabantio's?
7. *Othello* has a dual setting—Venice and Cyprus. With what values and ideas is each place associated and how are these related to the action and themes of the play?
8. What ideas about love are expressed by Othello and Desdemona? What images of the sexual bond emerge in the speech and actions of Roderigo, Iago, and Emilia?
9. How does Shakespeare use Desdemona's handkerchief dramatically and symbolically? In which scenes is it most important? With what is it associated?
10. Examine the scene in which Othello kills Desdemona (Act V, Scene II). Read his speech beginning, "It is the cause" (lines 1–22). Explain how Othello sees himself at this point and describe his state of mind.
11. Examine the scene in which Othello secretly watches Cassio talking to Bianca (Act IV, Scene I). Explain how Iago controls Othello's perception, leading him to misinterpret what he sees. In what other scenes does Iago direct other characters to misinterpret one another's actions and speech?
12. Any staging of *Othello* requires careful attention to lighting. Single out two scenes in which lighting is especially important and explain how you would stage them.
13. Look carefully at the beginning and ending of any two acts. Consider how Shakespeare guides the audience's responses at these points. Consider also the effectiveness of each beginning and ending in relation to the development of the plot.
14. Locate two scenes in which the characters' speeches shift between prose and verse. Explain the significance of these shifts.

CHAPTER EIGHTEEN

The Neoclassical French Theater

Perhaps the first thing to say about the neoclassical French theater of Molière (1622–1673, born Jean-Baptiste Poquelin) is that its conventions were inspired by the classical drama of Greece and Rome. Hence the term *neoclassical* to describe it. Like its ancient antecedents, the seventeenth-century French theater observed what Aristotle described as the *unities:* the unity of time, a stipulation that a play's action be confined to a twenty-four-hour period; the unity of place, a single setting; and the unity of action, a single plot. Molière's *Tartuffe* honors all three. Plays that violated the unities were thought to be crude and inelegant by Molière's educated audience, which consisted largely of courtiers and aristocrats (*Tartuffe* was performed for the court of Louis XIV) and well-to-do merchants. His plays sometimes reflected the ideas and upheld the values popular among these classes; sometimes they satirized them. In either case, the good manners, wit, and common sense of Molière's comedy mirrored his world and suited his audience.

The neoclassical stage differed from those of Shakespeare and Sophocles. Molière's was an indoor theater with a picture-frame stage. The proscenium arch with its curtain separated audience from actors. Molière's plays were enacted on a box stage, which represented a room with a missing fourth wall, allowing the audience to look in on the action. Though the scenery was not elaborate, it was painted and it served as a backdrop for the action. Candles and lanterns illuminated both the actors and the audience. Costume tended toward the elaborate and ornate as in Elizabethan drama. On both the Elizabethan and neoclassical stages actors were ordinarily costumed in contemporary dress that was appropriate to the social status of the characters. A major difference between neoclassical and earlier drama was that female actresses assumed women's roles, enabling playwrights to include more extensive, more frequent, and more realistic love scenes than had been possible previously (since boys had assumed women's roles in Shakespeare's time). As in the earlier eras of drama, however, language still did much of the work, so that even though the intimacy of the French neoclassical playhouse—with a capacity to seat perhaps four hundred spectators—allowed for refinements of facial and physical gesture, action remained subordinate to dialogue.

Molière, like Shakespeare and Sophocles before him, was a poet and an actor as well as a playwright. Like Shakespeare, Molière also performed in his own plays, playing Orgon in *Tartuffe*. Molière's genius, unlike Shakespeare's however, was limited to comedy. And his comedies, again unlike Shakespeare's, were satiric rather than romantic. *Tartuffe* satirizes both religious hypocrisy and fraudulence. It also pokes fun at the obsessive fanaticism and the blind gullibility of those who allow themselves to be victimized by the greedy and the self-serving.

When *Tartuffe* was first staged in 1664, it stirred up those who considered it an attack on religion. Even though Molière retitled it *The Impostor* to indicate that Tartuffe's piety is fraudulent, the original version of the play was censored and banned. To defend himself and the play against charges that *Tartuffe* attacked religion, Molière wrote three prefaces and later changed his original ending. The publicity enhanced the play's popularity, and the work was returned to the stage under the protection of the King. Its three-hundred-year-plus life span, however, is due neither to royal protection nor to notoriety, but rather to the ingenuity and vitality of its plot, the profundity of its characterization, and the brilliance of its language, unerringly translated by Richard Wilbur into rhymed couplets in iambic pentameter.

MOLIÈRE (JEAN-BAPTISTE POQUELIN)

[1622–1673]

Tartuffe

TRANSLATED BY RICHARD WILBUR

CHARACTERS

MADAME PERNELLE, *Orgon's mother*
ORGON, *Elmire's husband*
ELMIRE, *Orgon's wife*

DAMIS, *Orgon's son, Elmire's stepson*

MARIANE, *Orgon's daughter, Elmire's stepdaughter, in love with Valère*

VALÈRE, *in love with Mariane*

CLÉANTE, *Orgon's brother-in-law*

TARTUFFE, *a hypocrite*

DORINE, *Mariane's lady's-maid*

MONSIEUR LOYAL, *a bailiff*

A POLICE OFFICER

FLIPOTE, *Madame Pernelle's maid*

The Scene throughout: ORGON's *house in Paris.*

ACT I

Scene I

MADAME PERNELLE *and* FLIPOTE, *her maid,* ELMIRE, MARIANE, DORINE, DAMIS, CLÉANTE

MADAME PERNELLE: Come, come, Flipote; it's time I left this place.

ELMIRE: I can't keep up, you walk at such a pace.

MADAME PERNELLE: Don't trouble, child; no need to show me out.
It's not your manners I'm concerned about.

ELMIRE: We merely pay you the respect we owe.   5
But Mother, why this hurry? Must you go?

MADAME PERNELLE: I must. This house appalls me. No one in it
Will pay attention for a single minute.
Children, I take my leave much vexed in spirit.
I offer good advice, but you won't hear it.   10
You all break in and chatter on and on.
It's like a madhouse with the keeper gone.

DORINE: If . . .

MADAME PERNELLE:
                    Girl, you talk too much, and I'm afraid
You're far too saucy for a lady's-maid.
You push in everywhere and have your say.   15

DAMIS: But . . .

MADAME PERNELLE:
                    You, boy, grow more foolish every day.
To think my grandson should be such a dunce!
I've said a hundred times, if I've said it once,
That if you keep the course on which you've started,
You'll leave your worthy father broken-hearted.   20

MARIANE: I think . . .

MADAME PERNELLE: And you, his sister, seem so pure,

So shy, so innocent, and so demure.
But you know what they say about still waters.
I pity parents with secretive daughters.

ELMIRE: Now, Mother . . .

MADAME PERNELLE: And as for you, child, let me add   25
That your behavior is extremely bad,
And a poor example for these children, too.
Their dear, dead mother did far better than you.
You're much too free with money, and I'm distressed
To see you so elaborately dressed.   30
When it's one's husband that one aims to please,
One has no need of costly fripperies.

CLÉANTE: Oh, Madam, really . . .

MADAME PERNELLE: You are her brother, Sir,
And I respect and love you; yet if I were
My son, this lady's good and pious spouse,   35
I wouldn't make you welcome in my house.
You're full of worldly counsels which, I fear,
Aren't suitable for decent folk to hear.
I've spoken bluntly, Sir; but it behooves us
Not to mince words when righteous fervor moves us.   40

DAMIS: Your man Tartuffe is full of holy speeches . . .

MADAME PERNELLE: And practices precisely what he preaches.
He's a fine man, and should be listened to.
I will not hear him mocked by fools like you.

DAMIS: Good God! Do you expect me to submit   45
To the tyranny of that carping hypocrite?
Must we forgo all joys and satisfactions
Because that bigot censures all our actions?

DORINE: To hear him talk—and he talks all the time—
There's nothing one can do that's not a crime.   50
He rails at everything, your dear Tartuffe.

MADAME PERNELLE: Whatever he reproves deserves reproof.
He's out to save your souls, and all of you
Must love him, as my son would have you do.

DAMIS: Ah no, Grandmother, I could never take   55
To such a rascal, even for my father's sake.
That's how I feel, and I shall not dissemble.
His every action makes me seethe and tremble
With helpless anger, and I have no doubt
That he and I will shortly have it out.   60

DORINE: Surely it is a shame and a disgrace
To see this man usurp the master's place—
To see this beggar who, when first he came,
Had not a shoe or shoestring to his name
So far forget himself that he behaves   65
As if the house were his, and we his slaves.

MADAME PERNELLE: Well, mark my words, your souls would fare far better
  If you obeyed his precepts to the letter.

DORINE: You see him as a saint. I'm far less awed;
  In fact, I see right through him. He's a fraud.   70

MADAME PERNELLE: Nonsense!

DORINE: His man Laurent's the same, or worse;
  I'd not trust either with a penny purse.

MADAME PERNELLE: I can't say what his servant's morals may be;
  His own great goodness I can guarantee.
  You all regard him with distaste and fear   75
  Because he tells you what you're loath to hear,
  Condemns your sins, points out your moral flaws,
  And humbly strives to further Heaven's cause.

DORINE: If sin is all that bothers him, why is it
  He's so upset when folk drop in to visit?   80
  Is Heaven so outraged by a social call
  That he must prophesy against us all?
  I'll tell you what I think: if you ask me,
  He's jealous of my mistress' company.

MADAME PERNELLE:
  Rubbish! *(To* ELMIRE:*)* He's not alone, child, in complaining   85
  Of all of your promiscuous entertaining.
  Why, the whole neighborhood's upset, I know,
  By all these carriages that come and go,
  With crowds of guests parading in and out
  And noisy servants loitering about.   90
  In all of this, I'm sure there's nothing vicious;
  But why give people cause to be suspicious?

CLÉANTE: They need no cause; they'll talk in any case.
  Madam, this world would be a joyless place
  If, fearing what malicious tongues might say,   95
  We locked our doors and turned our friends away.
  And even if one did so dreary a thing,
  D'you think those tongues would cease their chattering?
  One can't fight slander; it's a losing battle;
  Let us instead ignore their tittle-tattle.   100
  Let's strive to live by conscience' clear decrees,
  And let the gossips gossip as they please.

DORINE: If there is talk against us, I know the source:
  It's Daphne and her little husband, of course.
  Those who have greatest cause for guilt and shame   105
  Are quickest to besmirch a neighbor's name.
  When there's a chance for libel, they never miss it;
  When something can be made to seem illicit
  They're off at once to spread the joyous news,
  Adding to fact what fantasies they choose.   110
  By talking up their neighbor's indiscretions

They seek to camouflage their own transgressions,
Hoping that others' innocent affairs
Will lend a hue of innocence to theirs,
Or that their own black guilt will come to seem   115
Part of a general shady color-scheme.

MADAME PERNELLE: All that is quite irrelevant. I doubt
That anyone's more virtuous and devout
Than dear Orante; and I'm informed that she
Condemns your mode of life most vehemently.   120

DORINE: Oh, yes, she's strict, devout, and has no taint
Of worldliness; in short, she seems a saint.
But it was time which taught her that disguise;
She's thus because she can't be otherwise.
So long as her attractions could enthrall,   125
She flounced and flirted and enjoyed it all,
But now that they're no longer what they were
She quits a world which fast is quitting her,
And wears a veil of virtue to conceal
Her bankrupt beauty and her lost appeal.   130
That's what becomes of old coquettes today:
Distressed when all their lovers fall away,
They see no recourse but to play the prude,
And so confer a style on solitude.
Thereafter, they're severe with everyone,   135
Condemning all our actions, pardoning none,
And claiming to be pure, austere, and zealous
When, if the truth were known, they're merely jealous,
And cannot bear to see another know
The pleasures time has forced them to forgo.   140

MADAME PERNELLE *(initially to* ELMIRE*):*
That sort of talk is what you like to hear;
Therefore you'd have us all keep still, my dear,
While Madam rattles on the livelong day.
Nevertheless, I mean to have my say.
I tell you that you're blest to have Tartuffe   145
Dwelling, as my son's guest, beneath this roof;
That Heaven has sent him to forestall its wrath
By leading you, once more, to the true path;
That all he reprehends is reprehensible,
And that you'd better heed him, and be sensible.   150
These visits, balls, and parties in which you revel
Are nothing but inventions of the Devil.
One never hears a word that's edifying:
Nothing but chaff and foolishness and lying,
As well as vicious gossip in which one's neighbor   155
Is cut to bits with epee, foil, and saber.
People of sense are driven half-insane

At such affairs, where noise and folly reign
And reputations perish thick and fast.
As a wise preacher said on Sunday last, 160
Parties are Towers of Babylon, because
The guests all babble on with never a pause;
And then he told a story which, I think . . .

(To CLÉANTE:*)*

I heard that laugh, Sir, and I saw that wink!
Go find your silly friends and laugh some more! 165
Enough; I'm going; don't show me to the door.
I leave this household much dismayed and vexed;
I cannot say when I shall see you next.

(Slapping FLIPOTE:*)*

Wake up, don't stand there gaping into space!
I'll slap some sense into that stupid face. 170
Move, move, you slut.

Scene II

CLÉANTE, DORINE

CLÉANTE: I think I'll stay behind;
I want no further pieces of her mind.
How that old lady . . .
DORINE: Oh, what wouldn't she say
If she could hear you speak of her that way!
She'd thank you for the *lady,* but I'm sure 5
She'd find the *old* a little premature.
CLÉANTE: My, what a scene she made, and what a din!
And how this man Tartuffe has taken her in!
DORINE: Yes, but her son is even worse deceived;
His folly must be seen to be believed. 10
In the late troubles, he played an able part
And served his king with wise and loyal heart,
But he's quite lost his senses since he fell
Beneath Tartuffe's infatuating spell.
He calls him brother, and loves him as his life, 15
Preferring him to mother, child, or wife.
In him and him alone will he confide;
He's made him his confessor and his guide;
He pets and pampers him with love more tender
Than any pretty maiden could engender, 20
Gives him the place of honor when they dine,
Delights to see him gorging like a swine,

Stuffs him with dainties till his guts distend,
And when he belches, cries "God bless you, friend!"
In short, he's mad; he worships him; he dotes;   25
His deeds he marvels at, his words he quotes,
Thinking each act a miracle, each word
Oracular as those that Moses heard.
Tartuffe, much pleased to find so easy a victim,
Has in a hundred ways beguiled and tricked him,   30
Milked him of money, and with his permission
Established here a sort of Inquisition.
Even Laurent, his lackey, dares to give
Us arrogant advice on how to live;
He sermonizes us in thundering tones   35
And confiscates our ribbons and colognes.
Last week he tore a kerchief into pieces
Because he found it pressed in a *Life of Jesus:*
He said it was a sin to juxtapose
Unholy vanities and holy prose.   40

Scene III

ELMIRE, MARIANE, DAMIS, CLÉANTE, DORINE

ELMIRE *(to* CLÉANTE*):* You did well not to follow; she stood in the door
    And said *verbatim* all she'd said before.
    I saw my husband coming. I think I'd best
    Go upstairs now, and take a little rest.
CLÉANTE: I'll wait and greet him here; then I must go.   5
    I've really only time to say hello.
DAMIS: Sound him about my sister's wedding, please.
    I think Tartuffe's against it, and that he's
    Been urging Father to withdraw his blessing.
    As you well know, I'd find that most distressing.   10
    Unless my sister and Valère can marry,
    My hopes to wed *his* sister will miscarry,
    And I'm determined . . .
DORINE: He's coming.

Scene IV

ORGON, CLÉANTE, DORINE

ORGON: Ah, Brother, good-day.
CLÉANTE: Well, welcome back. I'm sorry I can't stay.
    How was the country? Blooming, I trust, and green?
ORGON: Excuse me, Brother; just one moment.

(*To* DORINE:)

> Dorine . . .

(*To* CLÉANTE:)

To put my mind at rest, I always learn   5
The household news the moment I return.

(*To* DORINE:)

Has all been well, these two days I've been gone?
How are the family? What's been going on?
DORINE: Your wife, two days ago, had a bad fever,
And a fierce headache which refused to leave her.   10
ORGON: Ah. And Tartuffe?
DORINE: Tartuffe? Why, he's round and red,
Bursting with health, and excellently fed.
ORGON: Poor fellow!
DORINE: That night, the mistress was unable
To take a single bite at the dinner-table.
Her headache-pains, she said, were simply hellish.   15
ORGON: Ah. And Tartuffe?
DORINE: He ate his meal with relish,
And zealously devoured in her presence
A leg of mutton and a brace of pheasants.
ORGON: Poor fellow!
DORINE: Well, the pains continued strong,
And so she tossed and tossed the whole night long,   20
Now icy-cold, now burning like a flame.
We sat beside her bed till morning came.
ORGON: Ah. And Tartuffe?
DORINE: Why, having eaten, he rose
And sought his room, already in a doze,
Got into his warm bed, and snored away   25
In perfect peace until the break of day.
ORGON: Poor fellow!
DORINE: After much ado, we talked her
Into dispatching someone for the doctor.
He bled her, and the fever quickly fell.
ORGON: Ah. And Tartuffe?
DORINE: He bore it very well.   30
To keep his cheerfulness at any cost,
And make up for the blood *Madame* had lost,
He drank, at lunch, four beakers full of port.
ORGON: Poor fellow!
DORINE: Both are doing well, in short.
I'll go and tell *Madame* that you've expressed   35
Keen sympathy and anxious interest.

Scene V

ORGON, CLÉANTE

CLÉANTE: That girl was laughing in your face, and though
  I've no wish to offend you, even so
  I'm bound to say that she had some excuse.
  How can you possibly be such a goose?
  Are you so dazed by this man's hocus-pocus   5
  That all the world, save him, is out of focus?
  You've given him clothing, shelter, food, and care;
  Why must you also . . .
ORGON: Brother, stop right there.
  You do not know the man of whom you speak.
CLÉANTE: I grant you that. But my judgment's not so weak   10
  That I can't tell, by his effect on others . . .
ORGON: Ah, when you meet him, you two will be like brothers!
  There's been no loftier soul since time began.
  He is a man who . . . a man who . . . an excellent man.
  To keep his precepts is to be reborn,   15
  And view this dunghill of a world with scorn.
  Yes, thanks to him I'm a changed man indeed.
  Under his tutelage my soul's been freed
  From earthly loves, and every human tie:
  My mother, children, brother, and wife could die,   20
  And I'd not feel a single moment's pain.
CLÉANTE: That's a fine sentiment, Brother; most humane.
ORGON: Oh, had you seen Tartuffe as I first knew him,
  Your heart, like mine, would have surrendered to him.
  He used to come into our church each day   25
  And humbly kneel nearby, and start to pray.
  He'd draw the eyes of everybody there
  By the deep fervor of his heartfelt prayer;
  He'd sigh and weep, and sometimes with a sound
  Of rapture he would bend and kiss the ground;   30
  And when I rose to go, he'd run before
  To offer me holy-water at the door.
  His serving-man, no less devout than he,
  Informed me of his master's poverty;
  I gave him gifts, but in his humbleness   35
  He'd beg me every time to give him less.
  "Oh, that's too much," he'd cry, "too much by twice!
  I don't deserve it. The half, Sir, would suffice."
  And when I wouldn't take it back, he'd share
  Half of it with the poor, right then and there.   40
  At length, Heaven prompted me to take him in

To dwell with us, and free our souls from sin.
He guides our lives, and to protect my honor
Stays by my wife, and keeps an eye upon her;
He tells me whom she sees, and all she does,   45
And seems more jealous than I ever was!
And how austere he is! Why, he can detect
A mortal sin where you would least suspect;
In smallest trifles, he's extremely strict.
Last week, his conscience was severely pricked   50
Because, while praying, he had caught a flea
And killed it, so he felt, too wrathfully.
CLÉANTE: Good God, man! Have you lost your common sense—
Or is this all some joke at my expense?
How can you stand there and in all sobriety . . .   55
ORGON: Brother, your language savors of impiety.
Too much free-thinking's made your faith unsteady,
And as I've warned you many times already,
'Twill get you into trouble before you're through.
CLÉANTE: So I've been told before by dupes like you: 60
Being blind, you'd have all others blind as well;
The clear-eyed man you call an infidel,
And he who sees through humbug and pretense
Is charged, by you, with want of reverence.
Spare me your warnings, Brother; I have no fear   65
Of speaking out, for you and Heaven to hear,
Against affected zeal and pious knavery.
There's true and false in piety, as in bravery,
And just as those whose courage shines the most
In battle, are the least inclined to boast,   70
So those whose hearts are truly pure and lowly
Don't make a flashy show of being holy.
There's a vast difference, so it seems to me,
Between true piety and hypocrisy:
How do you fail to see it, may I ask?   75
Is not a face quite different from a mask?
Cannot sincerity and cunning art,
Reality and semblance, be told apart?
Are scarecrows just like men, and do you hold
That a false coin is just as good as gold?   80
Ah, Brother, man's a strangely fashioned creature
Who seldom is content to follow Nature,
But recklessly pursues his inclination
Beyond the narrow bounds of moderation,
And often, by transgressing Reason's laws,   85
Perverts a lofty aim or noble cause.
A passing observation, but it applies.
ORGON: I see, dear Brother, that you're profoundly wise;

You harbor all the insight of the age.
You are our one clear mind, our only sage,   90
The era's oracle, its Cato too,
And all mankind are fools compared to you.
CLÉANTE: Brother, I don't pretend to be a sage,
Nor have I all the wisdom of the age.
There's just one insight I would dare to claim: 95
I know that true and false are not the same;
And just as there is nothing I more revere
Than a soul whose faith is steadfast and sincere,
Nothing that I more cherish and admire
Than honest zeal and true religious fire,   100
So there is nothing that I find more base
Than specious piety's dishonest face—
Than these bold mountebanks, these histrios
Whose impious mummeries and hollow shows
Exploit our love of Heaven, and make a jest   105
Of all that men think holiest and best;
These calculating souls who offer prayers
Not to their Maker, but as public wares,
And seek to buy respect and reputation
With lifted eyes and sighs of exaltation;   110
These charlatans, I say, whose pilgrim souls
Proceed, by way of Heaven, toward earthly goals,
Who weep and pray and swindle and extort,
Who preach the monkish life, but haunt the court,
Who make their zeal the partner of their vice—   115
Such men are vengeful, sly, and cold as ice,
And when there is an enemy to defame
They cloak their spite in fair religion's name,
Their private spleen and malice being made
To seem a high and virtuous crusade,   120
Until, to mankind's reverent applause,
They crucify their foe in Heaven's cause.
Such knaves are all too common; yet, for the wise,
True piety isn't hard to recognize,
And, happily, these present times provide us   125
With bright examples to instruct and guide us.
Consider Ariston and Périandre;
Look at Oronte, Alcidamas, Clitandre;
Their virtue is acknowledged; who could doubt it?
But you won't hear them beat the drum about it.   130
They're never ostentatious, never vain,
And their religion's moderate and humane;
It's not their way to criticize and chide:
They think censoriousness a mark of pride,
And therefore, letting others preach and rave,   135

They show, by deeds, how Christians should behave.
They think no evil of their fellow man,
But judge of him as kindly as they can.
They don't intrigue and wangle and conspire;
To lead a good life is their one desire;   140
The sinner wakes no rancorous hate in them;
It is the sin alone which they condemn;
Nor do they try to show a fiercer zeal
For Heaven's cause than Heaven itself could feel.
These men I honor, these men I advocate   145
As models for us all to emulate.
Your man is not their sort at all, I fear:
And, while your praise of him is quite sincere,
I think that you've been dreadfully deluded.
ORGON: Now then, dear Brother, is your speech concluded?   150
CLÉANTE: Why, yes.
ORGON: Your servant, Sir. *(He turns to go.)*
CLÉANTE: No, Brother; wait.
  There's one more matter. You agreed of late
  That young Valère might have your daughter's hand.
ORGON: I did.
CLÉANTE: And set the date, I understand.
ORGON: Quite so.
CLÉANTE: You've now postponed it; is that true?   155
ORGON: No doubt.
CLÉANTE: The match no longer pleases you?
ORGON: Who knows?
CLÉANTE: D'you mean to go back on your word?
ORGON: I won't say that.
CLÉANTE: Has anything occurred
  Which might entitle you to break your pledge?
ORGON: Perhaps.
CLÉANTE: Why must you hem, and haw, and hedge?   160
  The boy asked me to sound you in this affair . . .
ORGON: It's been a pleasure.
CLÉANTE: But what shall I tell Valère?
ORGON: Whatever you like.
CLÉANTE: But what have you decided?
  What are your plans?
ORGON: I plan, Sir, to be guided
  By Heaven's will.
CLÉANTE: Come, Brother, don't talk rot.   165
  You've given Valère your word; will you keep it, or not?
ORGON: Good day.
CLÉANTE: This looks like poor Valère's undoing;
  I'll go and warn him that there's trouble brewing.

ACT II

Scene I

ORGON, MARIANE

ORGON: Mariane.
MARIANE: Yes, Father?
ORGON: A word with you; come here.
MARIANE: What are you looking for?
ORGON *(peering into a small closet):* Eavesdroppers, dear.
  I'm making sure we shan't be overheard.
  Someone in there could catch our every word.
  Ah, good, we're safe. Now, Mariane, my child,   5
  You're a sweet girl who's tractable and mild,
  Whom I hold dear, and think most highly of.
MARIANE: I'm deeply grateful, Father, for your love.
ORGON: That's well said, Daughter; and you can repay me
  If, in all things, you'll cheerfully obey me.   10
MARIANE: To please you, Sir, is what delights me best.
ORGON: Good, good. Now, what d'you think of Tartuffe, our guest?
MARIANE: I, Sir?
ORGON: Yes. Weigh your answer; think it through.
MARIANE: Oh, dear. I'll say whatever you wish me to.
ORGON: That's wisely said, my Daughter. Say of him, then,   15
  That he's the very worthiest of men,
  And that you're fond of him, and would rejoice
  In being his wife, if that should be my choice.
  Well?
MARIANE: What?
ORGON: What's that?
MARIANE: I . . .
ORGON: Well?
MARIANE: Forgive me, pray.
ORGON: Did you not hear me?
MARIANE: Of *whom*, Sir, must I say   20
  That I am fond of him, and would rejoice
  In being his wife, if that should be your choice?
ORGON: Why, of Tartuffe.
MARIANE: But, Father, that's false, you know.
  Why would you have me say what isn't so?
ORGON: Because I am resolved it shall be true.   25
  That it's my wish should be enough for you.
MARIANE: You can't mean, Father . . .
ORGON: Yes, Tartuffe shall be
  Allied by marriage to this family,

And he's to be your husband, is that clear?
It's a father's privilege . . .   30

Scene II

DORINE, ORGON, MARIANE

ORGON *(to Dorine):*   What are you doing in here?
  Is curiosity so fierce a passion
  With you, that you must eavesdrop in this fashion?
DORINE: There's lately been a rumor going about—
  Based on some hunch or chance remark, no doubt—   5
  That you mean Mariane to wed Tartuffe.
  I've laughed it off, of course, as just a spoof.
ORGON: You find it so incredible?
DORINE: Yes, I do.
  I won't accept that story, even from you.
ORGON: Well, you'll believe it when the thing is done.   10
DORINE: Yes, yes, of course. Go on and have your fun.
ORGON: I've never been more serious in my life.
DORINE: Ha!
ORGON: Daughter, I mean it; you're to be his wife.
DORINE: No, don't believe your father; it's all a hoax.
ORGON: See here, young woman . . .
DORINE: Come, Sir, no more jokes;   15
  You can't fool us.
ORGON: How dare you talk that way?
DORINE: All right, then; we believe you, sad to say.
  But how a man like you, who looks so wise
  And wears a moustache of such splendid size,
  Can be so foolish as to . . .
ORGON: Silence, please!   20
  My girl, you take too many liberties.
  I'm master here, as you must not forget.
DORINE: Do let's discuss this calmly; don't be upset.
  You can't be serious, Sir, about this plan.
  What should that bigot want with Mariane?   25
  Praying and fasting ought to keep him busy.
  And then, in terms of wealth and rank, what is he?
  Why should a man of property like you
  Pick out a beggar son-in-law?
ORGON: That will do.
  Speak of his poverty with reverence.   30
  His is a pure and saintly indigence
  Which far transcends all worldly pride and pelf.
  He lost his fortune, as he says himself,

Because he cared for Heaven alone, and so
Was careless of his interests here below.   35
I mean to get him out of his present straits
And help him to recover his estates—
Which, in his part of the world, have no small fame.
Poor though he is, he's a gentleman just the same.
DORINE: Yes, so he tells us; and, Sir, it seems to me   40
Such pride goes very ill with piety.
A man whose spirit spurns this dungy earth
Ought not to brag of lands and noble birth;
Such worldly arrogance will hardly square
With meek devotion and the life of prayer.   45
. . . But this approach, I see, has drawn a blank;
Let's speak, then, of his person, not his rank.
Doesn't it seem to you a trifle grim
To give a girl like her to a man like him?
When two are so ill-suited, can't you see   50
What the sad consequence is bound to be?
A young girl's virtue is imperiled, Sir,
When such a marriage is imposed on her;
For if one's bridegroom isn't to one's taste,
It's hardly an inducement to be chaste,   55
And many a man with horns upon his brow
Has made his wife the thing that she is now.
It's hard to be a faithful wife, in short,
To certain husbands of a certain sort,
And he who gives his daughter to a man she hates   60
Must answer for her sins at Heaven's gates.
Think, Sir, before you play so risky a role.
ORGON: This servant-girl presumes to save my soul!
DORINE: You would do well to ponder what I've said.
ORGON: Daughter, we'll disregard this dunderhead.   65
Just trust your father's judgment. Oh, I'm aware
That I once promised you to young Valère;
But now I hear he gambles, which greatly shocks me;
What's more, I've doubts about his orthodoxy.
His visits to church, I note, are very few.   70
DORINE: Would you have him go at the same hours as you,
And kneel nearby, to be sure of being seen?
ORGON: I can dispense with such remarks, Dorine.

(*To* MARIANE:)

Tartuffe, however, is sure of Heaven's blessing,
And that's the only treasure worth possessing.   75
This match will bring you joys beyond all measure;
Your cup will overflow with every pleasure;
You two will interchange your faithful loves
Like two sweet cherubs, or two turtle-doves.

No harsh word shall be heard, no frown be seen,   80
  And he shall make you happy as a queen.
DORINE: And she'll make him a cuckold, just wait and see.
ORGON: What language!
DORINE: Oh, he's a man of destiny;
  He's *made* for horns, and what the stars demand
  Your daughter's virtue surely can't withstand.   85
ORGON: Don't interrupt me further. Why can't you learn
  That certain things are none of your concern?
DORINE: It's for your own sake that I interfere.

(She repeatedly interrupts ORGON *just as he is turning to speak to his daughter:)*

ORGON: Most kind of you. Now, hold your tongue, d'you hear?
DORINE: If I didn't love you . . .
ORGON: Spare me your affection.   90
DORINE: I'll love you, Sir, in spite of your objection.
ORGON: Blast!
DORINE: I can't bear, Sir, for your honor's sake,
  To let you make this ludicrous mistake.
ORGON: You mean to go on talking?
DORINE: If I didn't protest
  This sinful marriage, my conscience couldn't rest.   95
ORGON: If you don't hold your tongue, you little shrew . . .
DORINE: What, lost your temper? A pious man like you?
ORGON: Yes! Yes! You talk and talk. I'm maddened by it.
  Once and for all, I tell you to be quiet.
DORINE: Well, I'll be quiet. But I'll be thinking hard.   100
ORGON: Think all you like, but you had better guard
  That saucy tongue of yours, or I'll . . .
              (Turning back to MARIANE:*)*

                    Now, child,
  I've weighed this matter fully.
DORINE *(aside):*   It drives me wild
  That I can't speak.
              *(*ORGON *turns his head, and she is silent.)*
ORGON: Tartuffe is no young dandy,
  But, still, his person . . .
DORINE *(aside):*   Is as sweet as candy.   105
ORGON: Is such that, even if you shouldn't care
  For his other merits . . .
              (He turns and stands facing DORINE, *arms crossed.)*
DORINE *(aside):*   They'll make a lovely pair.
  If I were she, no man would marry me
  Against my inclination, and go scot-free.
  He'd learn, before the wedding-day was over,   110
  How readily a wife can find a lover.
ORGON *(to* DORINE*):* It seems you treat my orders as a joke.

DORINE: Why, what's the matter? 'Twas not to you I spoke.
ORGON: What *were* you doing?
DORINE: Talking to myself, that's all.
ORGON: Ah! *(aside:)* One more bit of impudence and gall,   115
    And I shall give her a good slap in the face.

(He puts himself in position to slap her; DORINE, *whenever he glances at her, stands
    immobile and silent:)*

Daughter, you shall accept, and with good grace,
The husband I've selected . . . Your wedding day . . .

(To DORINE:*)*

Why don't you talk to yourself?
DORINE: I've nothing to say.
ORGON: Come, just one word.
DORINE: No thank you, Sir. I pass.   120
ORGON: Come, speak; I'm waiting.
DORINE: I'd not be such an ass.
ORGON *(turning to Mariane):* In short, dear Daughter, I mean to be obeyed,
    And you must bow to the sound choice I've made.
DORINE *(moving away):* I'd not wed such a monster, even in jest.

*(*ORGON *attempts to slap her, but misses.)*

ORGON: Daughter, that maid of yours is a thorough pest;   125
    She makes me sinfully annoyed and nettled.
    I can't speak further; my nerves are too unsettled.
    She's so upset me by her insolent talk,
    I'll calm myself by going for a walk.

Scene III

DORINE, MARIANE

DORINE *(returning):* Well, have you lost your tongue, girl? Must I play
    Your part, and say the lines you ought to say?
    Faced with a fate so hideous and absurd,
    Can you not utter one dissenting word?
MARIANE: What good would it do? A father's power is great.   5
DORINE: Resist him now, or it will be too late.
MARIANE: But . . .
DORINE: Tell him one cannot love at a father's whim;
    That you shall marry for yourself, not him;
    That since it's you who are to be the bride,
    It's you, not he, who must be satisfied;   10
    And that if his Tartuffe is so sublime,
    He's free to marry him at any time.

MARIANE: I've bowed so long to Father's strict control,
    I couldn't oppose him now, to save my soul.
DORINE: Come, come, Mariane. Do listen to reason, won't you?   15
    Valère has asked your hand. Do you love him, or don't you?
MARIANE: Oh, how unjust of you! What can you mean
    By asking such a question, dear Dorine?
    You know the depth of my affection for him;
    I've told you a hundred times how I adore him.   20
DORINE: I don't believe in everything I hear;
    Who knows if your professions were sincere?
MARIANE: They were, Dorine, and you do me wrong to doubt it;
    Heaven knows that I've been all too frank about it.
DORINE: You love him, then?
MARIANE: Oh, more than I can express.   25
DORINE: And he, I take it, cares for you no less?
MARIANE: I think so.
DORINE: And you both, with equal fire,
    Burn to be married?
MARIANE: That is our one desire.
DORINE: What of Tartuffe, then? What of your father's plan?
MARIANE: I'll kill myself, if I'm forced to wed that man.   30
DORINE: I hadn't thought of that recourse. How splendid!
    Just die, and all your troubles will be ended!
    A fine solution. Oh, it maddens me
    To hear you talk in that self-pitying key.
MARIANE: Dorine, how harsh you are! It's most unfair.   35
    You have no sympathy for my despair.
DORINE: I've none at all for people who talk drivel
    And, faced with difficulties, whine and snivel.
MARIANE: No doubt I'm timid, but it would be wrong . . .
DORINE: True love requires a heart that's firm and strong.   40
MARIANE: I'm strong in my affection for Valère,
    But coping with my father is his affair.
DORINE: But if your father's brain has grown so cracked
    Over his dear Tartuffe that he can retract
    His blessing, though your wedding day was named,   45
    It's surely not Valère who's to be blamed.
MARIANE: If I defied my father, as you suggest,
    Would it not seem unmaidenly, at best?
    Shall I defend my love at the expense
    Of brazenness and disobedience?   50
    Shall I parade my heart's desires, and flaunt . . .
DORINE: No, I ask nothing of you. Clearly you want
    To be Madame Tartuffe, and I feel bound
    Not to oppose a wish so very sound.
    What right have I to criticize the match?   55
    Indeed, my dear, the man's a brilliant catch.

Monsieur Tartuffe! Now, there's a man of weight!
Yes, yes, Monsieur Tartuffe, I'm bound to state,
Is quite a person; that's not to be denied;
'Twill be no little thing to be his bride.   60
The world already rings with his renown;
He's a great noble—in his native town;
His ears are red, he has a pink complexion,
And all in all, he'll suit you to perfection.

MARIANE: Dear God!

DORINE: Oh, how triumphant you will feel   65
At having caught a husband so ideal!

MARIANE: Oh, do stop teasing, and use your cleverness
To get me out of this appalling mess.
Advise me, and I'll do whatever you say.

DORINE: Ah no, a dutiful daughter must obey   70
Her father, even if he weds her to an ape.
You've a bright future; why struggle to escape?
Tartuffe will take you back where his family lives,
To a small town aswarm with relatives—
Uncles and cousins whom you'll be charmed to meet.   75
You'll be received at once by the elite,
Calling upon the bailiff's wife, no less—
Even, perhaps, upon the mayoress,
Who'll sit you down in the *best* kitchen chair.
Then, once a year, you'll dance at the village fair   80
To the drone of bagpipes—two of them, in fact—
And see a puppet-show, or an animal act.
Your husband . . .

MARIANE: Oh, you turn my blood to ice!
Stop torturing me, and give me your advice.

DORINE *(threatening to go):* Your servant, Madam.

MARIANE: Dorine, I beg of you . . . 85

DORINE: No, you deserve it; this marriage must go through.

MARIANE: Dorine!

DORINE: No.

MARIANE: Not Tartuffe! You know I think him . . .

DORINE: Tartuffe's your cup of tea, and you shall drink him.

MARIANE: I've always told you everything, and relied . . .

DORINE: No. You deserve to be tartuffified.   90

MARIANE: Well, since you mock me and refuse to care,
I'll henceforth seek my solace in despair:
Despair shall be my counsellor and friend,
And help me bring my sorrows to an end.

(She starts to leave.)

DORINE: There, now, come back; my anger has subsided.   95
You do deserve some pity, I've decided.

MARIANE: Dorine, if Father makes me undergo
　　This dreadful martyrdom, I'll die, I know.
DORINE: Don't fret; it won't be difficult to discover
　　Some plan of action . . . But here's Valère, your lover.   100

Scene IV

VALÈRE, MARIANE, DORINE

VALÈRE: Madam, I've just received some wondrous news
　　Regarding which I'd like to hear your views.
MARIANE: What news?
VALÈRE: 　　　　　　You're marrying Tartuffe.
MARIANE: 　　　　　　　　　　　　　　　　　I find
　　That Father does have such a match in mind.
VALÈRE: Your father, Madam . . .
MARIANE: 　　　　　　　　　　. . . has just this minute said   5
　　That it's Tartuffe he wishes me to wed.
VALÈRE: Can he be serious?
MARIANE: 　　　　　　　　Oh, indeed he can;
　　He's clearly set his heart upon the plan.
VALÈRE: And what position do you propose to take,
　　Madam?
MARIANE: 　Why—I don't know.
VALÈRE: 　　　　　　　　　　For heaven's sake—   10
　　You don't know?
MARIANE: 　　　　　　No.
VALÈRE: 　　　　　　　　Well, well!
MARIANE: 　　　　　　　　　　　　Advise me, do.
VAÈRE: Marry the man. That's my advice to you.
MARIANE: That's your advice?
VALÈRE: 　　　　　　　　　Yes.
MARIANE: 　　　　　　　　　　Truly?
VALÈRE: 　　　　　　　　　　　　Oh, absolutely.
　　You couldn't choose more wisely, more astutely.
MARIANE: Thanks for this counsel; I'll follow it, of course.   15
VALÈRE: Do, do; I'm sure 'twill cost you no remorse.
MARIANE: To give it didn't cause your heart to break.
VALÈRE: I gave it, Madam, only for your sake.
MARIANE: And it's for your sake that I take it, Sir.
DORINE (*withdrawing to the rear of the stage*):
　　Let's see which fool will prove the stubborner.   20
VALÈRE: So! I am nothing to you, and it was flat
　　Deception when you . . .
MARIANE: 　　　　　　　　Please, enough of that.
　　You've told me plainly that I should agree

To wed the man my father's chosen for me, 25
And since you've deigned to counsel me so wisely,
I promise, Sir, to do as you advise me.
VALÈRE: Ah, no, 'twas not by me that you were swayed.
No, your decision was already made;
Though now, to save appearances, you protest 30
That you're betraying me at my behest.
MARIANE: Just as you say.
VALÈRE: Quite so. And I now see
That you were never truly in love with me.
MARIANE: Alas, you're free to think so if you choose.
VALÈRE: I choose to think so, and here's a bit of news: 35
You've spurned my hand, but I know where to turn
For kinder treatment, as you shall quickly learn.
MARIANE: I'm sure you do. Your noble qualities
Inspire affection . . .
VALÈRE: Forget my qualities, please.
They don't inspire you overmuch, I find.
But there's another lady I have in mind 40
Whose sweet and generous nature will not scorn
To compensate me for the loss I've borne.
MARIANE: I'm no great loss, and I'm sure that you'll transfer
Your heart quite painlessly from me to her.
VALÈRE: I'll do my best to take it in my stride. 45
The pain I feel at being cast aside
Time and forgetfulness may put an end to.
Or if I can't forget, I shall pretend to.
No self-respecting person is expected
To go on loving once he's been rejected. 50
MARIANE: Now, that's a fine, high-minded sentiment.
VALÈRE: One to which any sane man would assent.
Would you prefer it if I pined away
In hopeless passion till my dying day?
Am I to yield you to a rival's arms 55
And not console myself with other charms?
MARIANE: Go then; console yourself; don't hesitate.
I wish you to; indeed, I cannot wait.
VALÈRE: You wish me to?
MARIANE: Yes.
VALÈRE: That's the final straw.
Madam, farewell. Your wish shall be my law. 60

(He starts to leave, and then returns: this repeatedly:)

MARIANE: Splendid.
VALÈRE *(coming back again)*:
                          This breach, remember, is of your making;
It's you who've driven me to the step I'm taking.

MARIANE: Of course.

VALÈRE *(coming back again):*

Remember, too, that I am merely
Following your example.

MARIANE: I see that clearly.

VALÈRE: Enough. I'll go and do your bidding, then. 65

MARIANE: Good.

VALÈRE *(coming back again):*

You shall never see my face again.

MARIANE: Excellent.

VALÈRE *(walking to the door, then turning about):*

Yes?

MARIANE: What?

VALÈRE: What's that? What did you say?

MARIANE: Nothing. You're dreaming.

VALÈRE: Ah. Well, I'm on my way.
Farewell, *Madame.*

(He moves slowly away.)

MARIANE: Farewell.

DORINE *(to* MARIANE*):* If you ask me,
Both of you are as mad as mad can be. 70
Do stop this nonsense, now. I've only let you
Squabble so long to see where it would get you.
Whoa there, Monsieur Valère!

(She goes and seizes VALÈRE *by the arm; he makes a great show of resistance.)*

VALÈRE: What's this, Dorine?

DORINE: Come here.

VALÈRE: No, no, my heart's too full of spleen.
Don't hold me back; her wish must be obeyed. 75

DORINE: Stop!

VALÈRE: It's too late now; my decision's made.

DORINE: Oh, pooh!

MARIANE *(aside):* He hates the sight of me, that's plain.
I'll go, and so deliver him from pain.

DORINE *(leaving* VALÈRE, *running after* MARIANE*):*
And now *you* run away! Come back.

MARIANE: No, no.
Nothing you say will keep me here. Let go! 80

VALÈRE *(aside):* She cannot bear my presence, I perceive.
To spare her further torment, I shall leave.

DORINE *(leaving* MARIANE, *running after* VALÈRE*):*
Again! You'll not escape, Sir; don't you try it.
Come here, you two. Stop fussing, and be quiet.

(She takes VALÈRE *by the hand, then* MARIANE, *and draws them together.)*

VALÈRE *(to* DORINE*):* What do you want of me?
MARIANE *(to* DORINE*):*   What is the point of this? 85
DORINE: We're going to have a little armistice.

(To VALÈRE*:)*

Now, weren't you silly to get so overheated?
VALÈRE: Didn't you see how badly I was treated?
DORINE *(to* MARIANE*):* Aren't you a simpleton, to have lost your head?
MARIANE: Didn't you hear the hateful things he said?   90
DORINE *(to* VALÈRE*):* You're both great fools. Her sole desire, Valère,
    Is to be yours in marriage. To that I'll swear.

(To MARIANE*:)*

He loves you only, and he wants no wife
    But you, Mariane. On that I'll stake my life.
MARIANE *(to* VALÈRE*):* Then why you advised me so, I cannot see.   95
VALÈRE *(to* MARIANE*):* On such a question, why ask advice of *me?*
DORINE: Oh, you're impossible. Give me your hands, you two.

(To VALÈRE*:)*

Yours first.
VALÈRE *(giving* DORINE *his hand):*
          But why?
DORINE *(to* MARIANE*):*   And now a hand from you.
MARIANE *(also giving* DORINE *her hand):*
What are you doing?
DORINE: There: a perfect fit.
    You suit each other better than you'll admit.   100

*(*VALÈRE *and* MARIANE *hold hands for some time without looking at each other.)*

VALÈRE *(turning toward* MARIANE*):*
    Ah, come, don't be so haughty. Give a man
    A look of kindness, won't you, Mariane?

*(*MARIANE *turns toward* VALÈRE *and smiles.)*

DORINE: I tell you, lovers are completely mad!
VALÈRE *(to* MARIANE*):* Now come, confess that you were very bad
    To hurt my feelings as you did just now.   105
    I have a just complaint, you must allow.
MARIANE: *You* must allow that you were most unpleasant . . .
DORINE: Let's table that discussion for the present;
    Your father has a plan which must be stopped.
MARIANE: Advise us, then; what means must we adopt?   110
DORINE: We'll use all manner of means, and all at once.

(To MARIANE*:)*

Your father's addled; he's acting like a dunce.
Therefore you'd better humor the old fossil.

Pretend to yield to him, be sweet and docile, 115
And then postpone, as often as necessary,
The day on which you have agreed to marry.
You'll thus gain time, and time will turn the trick.
Sometimes, for instance, you'll be taken sick,
And that will seem good reason for delay; 120
Or some bad omen will make you change the day—
You'll dream of muddy water, or you'll pass
A dead man's hearse, or break a looking-glass.
If all else fails, no man can marry you
Unless you take his ring and say "I do." 125
But now, let's separate. If they should find
Us talking here, our plot might be divined.

(To VALÈRE:*)*

Go to your friends, and tell them what's occurred,
And have them urge her father to keep his word.
Meanwhile, we'll stir her brother into action,
And get Elmire, as well, to join our faction. 130
Good-bye.
VALÈRE *(to* MARIANE*):*
      Though each of us will do his best,
It's your true heart on which my hopes shall rest.
MARIANE *(to* VALÈRE*):* Regardless of what Father may decide,
None but Valère shall claim me as his bride.
VALÈRE: Oh, how those words content me! Come what will . . . 135
DORINE: Oh, lovers, lovers! Their tongues are never still.
Be off, now.
VALÈRE *(turning to go, then turning back):*
      One last word . . .
DORINE: No time to chat:
You leave by this door; and *you* leave by that.

(Dorine pushes them, by the shoulders, toward opposing doors.)

ACT III

Scene I

DAMIS, DORINE

DAMIS: May lightning strike me even as I speak,
May all men call me cowardly and weak,
If any fear or scruple holds me back
From settling things, at once, with that great quack!
DORINE: Now, don't give way to violent emotion. 5

Your father's merely talked about this notion,
And words and deeds are far from being one.
Much that is talked about is never done.

DAMIS: No, I must stop that scoundrel's machinations;   10
   I'll go and tell him off; I'm out of patience.

DORINE: Do calm down and be practical. I had rather
   My mistress dealt with him—and with your father.
   She has some influence with Tartuffe, I've noted.
   He hangs upon her words, seems most devoted,
   And may, indeed, be smitten by her charm.   15
   Pray Heaven it's true! 'Twould do our cause no harm.
   She sent for him, just now, to sound him out
   On this affair you're so incensed about;
   She'll find out where he stands, and tell him too,
   What dreadful strife and trouble will ensue   20
   If he lends countenance to your father's plan.
   I couldn't get in to see him, but his man
   Says that he's almost finished with his prayers.
   Go, now. I'll catch him when he comes downstairs.

DAMIS: I want to hear this conference, and I will.   25

DORINE: No, they must be alone.

DAMIS: Oh, I'll keep still.

DORINE: Not you. I know your temper. You'd start a brawl,
   And shout and stamp your foot and spoil it all.
   Go on.

DAMIS: I won't; I have a perfect right . . .

DORINE: Lord, you're a nuisance! He's coming; get out of sight.   30

(DAMIS *conceals himself in a closet at the rear of the stage.*)

Scene II

TARTUFFE, DORINE

TARTUFFE *(observing* DORINE, *and calling to his manservant offstage):*
   Hang up my hair-shirt, put my scourge in place,
   And pray, Laurent, for Heaven's perpetual grace.
   I'm going to the prison now, to share
   My last few coins with the poor wretches there.

DORINE *(aside):* Dear God, what affectation! What a fake!   5

TARTUFFE: You wished to see me?

DORINE: Yes . . .

TARTUFFE *(taking a handkerchief from his pocket):*
                                    For mercy's sake,
   Please take this handkerchief, before you speak.

DORINE: What?

TARTUFFE: Cover that bosom, girl. The flesh is weak,

And unclean thoughts are difficult to control.
Such sights as that can undermine the soul.   10
DORINE: Your soul, it seems, has very poor defenses,
And flesh makes quite an impact on your senses.
It's strange that you're so easily excited;
My own desires are not so soon ignited,
And if I saw you naked as a beast,   15
Not all your hide would tempt me in the least.
TARTUFFE: Girl, speak more modestly; unless you do,
I shall be forced to take my leave of you.
DORINE: Oh, no, it's I who must be on my way;
I've just one little message to convey.   20
Madame is coming down, and begs you, Sir,
To wait and have a word or two with her.
TARTUFFE: Gladly.
DORINE *(aside):*   *That* had a softening effect!
I think my guess about him was correct.
TARTUFFE: Will she be long?
DORINE: No: that's her step I hear.   25
Ah, here she is, and I shall disappear.

Scene III

ELMIRE, TARTUFFE

TARTUFFE: May Heaven, whose infinite goodness we adore,
Preserve your body and soul forevermore,
And bless your days, and answer thus the plea
Of one who is its humblest votary.
ELMIRE: I thank you for that pious wish, but please,   5
Do take a chair and let's be more at ease.

(They sit down.)

TARTUFFE: I trust that you are once more well and strong?
ELMIRE: Oh, yes: the fever didn't last for long.
TARTUFFE: My prayers are too unworthy, I am sure,
To have gained from Heaven this most gracious cure;   10
But lately, Madam, my every supplication
Has had for object your recuperation.
ELMIRE: You shouldn't have troubled so. I don't deserve it.
TARTUFFE: Your health is priceless, Madam, and to preserve it
I'd gladly give my own, in all sincerity.   15
ELMIRE: Sir, you outdo us all in Christian charity.
You've been most kind. I count myself your debtor.
TARTUFFE: 'Twas nothing, Madam. I long to serve you better.
ELMIRE: There's a private matter I'm anxious to discuss.
I'm glad there's no one here to hinder us.   20

TARTUFFE: I too am glad; it floods my heart with bliss
    To find myself alone with you like this.
    For just this chance I've prayed with all my power—
    But prayed in vain, until this happy hour.
ELMIRE: This won't take long, Sir, and I hope you'll be   25
    Entirely frank and unconstrained with me.
TARTUFFE: Indeed, there's nothing I had rather do
    Than bare my inmost heart and soul to you.
    First, let me say that what remarks I've made
    About the constant visits you are paid   30
    Were prompted not by any mean emotion,
    But rather by a pure and deep devotion,
    A fervent zeal . . .
ELMIRE: No need for explanation.
    Your sole concern, I'm sure, was my salvation.
TARTUFFE (*taking* ELMIRE'S *hand and pressing her fingertips*):
    Quite so; and such great fervor do I feel . . .   35
ELMIRE: Ooh! Please! You're pinching!
TARTUFFE: 'Twas from excess of zeal.
    I never meant to cause you pain, I swear.
    I'd rather . . .
                    (*He places his hand on* ELMIRE'S *knee*.)
ELMIRE: What can your hand be doing there?
TARTUFFE: Feeling your gown: what soft, fine-woven stuff!
ELMIRE: Please, I'm extremely ticklish. That's enough.   40

    (*She draws her chair away;* TARTUFFE *pulls his after her*.)

TARTUFFE (*fondling the lace collar of her gown*):
    My, my, what lovely lacework on your dress!
    The workmanship's miraculous, no less.
    I've not seen anything to equal it.
ELMIRE: Yes, quite. But let's talk business for a bit.
    They say my husband means to break his word   45
    And give his daughter to you, Sir. Had you heard?
TARTUFFE: He did once mention it. But I confess
    I dream of quite a different happiness.
    It's elsewhere, Madam, that my eyes discern
    The promise of that bliss for which I yearn.   50
ELMIRE: I see: you care for nothing here below.
TARTUFFE: Ah, well—my heart's not made of stone, you know.
ELMIRE: All your desires mount heavenward, I'm sure,
    In scorn of all that's earthly and impure.
TARTUFFE: A love of heavenly beauty does not preclude   55
    A proper love for earthly pulchritude;
    Our senses are quite rightly captivated
    By perfect works our Maker has created.
    Some glory clings to all that Heaven has made;

In you, all Heaven's marvels are displayed. 60
On that fair face, such beauties have been lavished,
The eyes are dazzled and the heart is ravished;
How could I look on you, O flawless creature,
And not adore the Author of all Nature,
Feeling a love both passionate and pure
For you, his triumph of self-portraiture? 65
At first, I trembled lest that love should be
A subtle snare that Hell had laid for me;
I vowed to flee the sight of you, eschewing
A rapture that might prove my soul's undoing;
But soon, fair being, I became aware 70
That my deep passion could be made to square
With rectitude, and with my bounden duty.
I thereupon surrendered to your beauty.
It is, I know, presumptuous on my part
To bring you this poor offering of my heart, 75
And it is not my merit, Heaven knows,
But your compassion on which my hopes repose.
You are my peace, my solace, my salvation;
On you depends my bliss—or desolation;
I bide your judgment and, as you think best, 80
I shall be either miserable or blest.

ELMIRE: Your declaration is most gallant, Sir,
But don't you think it's out of character?
You'd have done better to restrain your passion
And think before you spoke in such a fashion. 85
It ill becomes a pious man like you . . .

TARTUFFE: I may be pious, but I'm human too:
With your celestial charms before his eyes,
A man has not the power to be wise.
I know such words sound strangely, coming from me, 90
But I'm no angel, nor was meant to be,
And if you blame my passion, you must needs
Reproach as well the charms on which it feeds.
Your loveliness I had no sooner seen
Than you became my soul's unrivalled queen; 95
Before your seraph glance, divinely sweet,
My heart's defenses crumbled in defeat,
And nothing fasting, prayer, or tears might do
Could stay my spirit from adoring you.
My eyes, my sighs have told you in the past 100
What now my lips make bold to say at last,
And if, in your great goodness, you will deign
To look upon your slave, and ease his pain,—
If, in compassion for my soul's distress,
You'll stoop to comfort my unworthiness, 105

I'll raise to you, in thanks for that sweet manna,
An endless hymn, an infinite hosanna.
With me, of course, there need be no anxiety,
No fear of scandal or of notoriety.
These young court gallants, whom all the ladies fancy,   110
Are vain in speech, in action rash and chancy;
When they succeed in love, the world soon knows it;
No favor's granted them but they disclose it
And by the looseness of their tongues profane
The very altar where their hearts have lain.   115
Men of my sort, however, love discreetly,
And one may trust our reticence completely.
My keen concern for my good name insures
The absolute security of yours;
In short, I offer you, my dear Elmire,   120
Love without scandal, pleasure without fear.

ELMIRE: I've heard your well-turned speeches to the end,
And what you urge I clearly apprehend.
Aren't you afraid that I may take a notion
To tell my husband of your warm devotion,   125
And that, supposing he were duly told,
His feelings toward you might grow rather cold?

TARTUFFE: I know, dear lady, that your exceeding charity
Will lead your heart to pardon my temerity;
That you'll excuse my violent affection   130
As human weakness, human imperfection;
And that—O fairest!—you will bear in mind
That I'm but flesh and blood, and am not blind.

ELMIRE: Some women might do otherwise, perhaps,
But I shall be discreet about your lapse;   135
I'll tell my husband nothing of what's occurred
If, in return, you'll give your solemn word
To advocate as forcefully as you can
The marriage of Valère and Mariane,
Renouncing all desire to dispossess   140
Another of his rightful happiness,
And . . .

Scene IV

DAMIS, ELMIRE, TARTUFFE

DAMIS *(emerging from the closet where he has been hiding):*
        No! We'll not hush up this vile affair;
I heard it all inside that closet there,
Where Heaven, in order to confound the pride

Of this great rascal, prompted me to hide.
Ah, now I have my long-awaited chance   5
To punish his deceit and arrogance,
And give my father clear and shocking proof
Of the black character of his dear Tartuffe.

ELMIRE: Ah no, Damis! I'll be content if he
  Will study to deserve my leniency.   10
I've promised silence—don't make me break my word;
To make a scandal would be too absurd.
Good wives laugh off such trifles, and forget them;
Why should they tell their husbands, and upset them?

DAMIS: You have your reasons for taking such a course,   15
  And I have reasons, too, of equal force.
To spare him now would be insanely wrong.
I've swallowed my just wrath for far too long
And watched this insolent bigot bringing strife
And bitterness into our family life.   20
Too long he's meddled in my father's affairs,
Thwarting my marriage-hopes, and poor Valère's.
It's high time that my father was undeceived,
And now I've proof that can't be disbelieved—
Proof that was furnished me by Heaven above.   25
It's too good not to take advantage of.
This is my chance, and I deserve to lose it
If, for one moment, I hesitate to use it.

ELMIRE: Damis . . .

DAMIS: No, I must do what I think right.
  Madam, my heart is bursting with delight,   30
And, say whatever you will, I'll not consent
To lose the sweet revenge on which I'm bent.
I'll settle matters without more ado;
And here, most opportunely, is my cue.

Scene V

ORGON, DAMIS, TARTUFFE, ELMIRE

DAMIS: Father, I'm glad you've joined us. Let us advise you
  Of some fresh news which doubtless will surprise you.
You've just now been repaid with interest
For all your loving-kindness to our guest.
He's proved his warm and grateful feelings toward you;   5
It's with a pair of horns he would reward you.
Yes, I surprised him with your wife, and heard
His whole adulterous offer, every word.
She, with her all too gentle disposition,

Would not have told you of his proposition;   10
But I shall not make terms with brazen lechery,
And feel that not to tell you would be treachery.

ELMIRE: And I hold that one's husband's peace of mind
Should not be spoilt by tattle of this kind.
One's honor doesn't require it: to be proficient   15
In keeping men at bay is quite sufficient.
These are my sentiments, and I wish, Damis,
That you had heeded me and held your peace.

Scene VI

ORGON, DAMIS, TARTUFFE

ORGON: Can it be true, this dreadful thing I hear?
TARTUFFE: Yes, Brother, I'm a wicked man, I fear:
A wretched sinner, all depraved and twisted,
The greatest villain that has ever existed.
My life's one heap of crimes, which grows each minute;   5
There's naught but foulness and corruption in it;
And I perceive that Heaven, outraged by me,
Has chosen this occasion to mortify me.
Charge me with any deed you wish to name;
I'll not defend myself, but take the blame.   10
Believe what you are told, and drive Tartuffe
Like some base criminal from beneath your roof;
Yes, drive me hence, and with a parting curse:
I shan't protest, for I deserve far worse.
ORGON (to DAMIS): Ah, you deceitful boy, how dare you try   15
To stain his purity with so foul a lie?
DAMIS: What! Are you taken in by such a bluff?
Did you not hear . . . ?
ORGON: Enough, you rogue, enough!
TARTUFFE: Ah, Brother, let him speak: you're being unjust.
Believe his story; the boy deserves your trust.   20
Why, after all, should you have faith in me?
How can you know what I might do, or be?
Is it on my good actions that you base
Your favor? Do you trust my pious face?
Ah, no, don't be deceived by hollow shows;   25
I'm far, alas, from being what men suppose;
Though the world takes me for a man of worth,
I'm truly the most worthless man on earth.

(To DAMIS:*)*

Yes, my dear son, speak out now: call me the chief
Of sinners, a wretch, a murderer, a thief;   30

Load me with all the names men most abhor;
I'll not complain; I've earned them all, and more;
I'll kneel here while you pour them on my head
As a just punishment for the life I've led.

ORGON *(to* TARTUFFE*):* This is too much, dear Brother.

(To DAMIS:*)*

Have you no heart? 35

DAMIS: Are you so hoodwinked by this rascal's art . . . ?

ORGON: Be still, you monster.

(To TARTUFFE:*)*

Brother, I pray you, rise.

(To DAMIS:*)*

Villain!

DAMIS: But . . .

ORGON: Silence!

DAMIS: Can't you realize . . . ?

ORGON: Just one word more, and I'll tear you limb from limb.

TARTUFFE: In God's name, Brother, don't be harsh with him. 40
I'd rather far be tortured at the stake
Than see him bear one scratch for my poor sake.

ORGON *(to* DAMIS*):* Ingrate!

TARTUFFE: If I must beg you, on bended knee,
To pardon him . . .

ORGON *(falling to his knees, addressing* TARTUFFE*):*
Such goodness cannot be!

(To DAMIS:*)*

Now, *there's* true charity!

DAMIS: What, you . . . ?

ORGON: Villain, be still! 45
I know your motives; I know you wish him ill:
Yes, all of you—wife, children, servants, all—
Conspire against him and desire his fall,
Employing every shameful trick you can
To alienate me from this saintly man. 50
Ah, but the more you seek to drive him away,
The more I'll do to keep him. Without delay,
I'll spite this household and confound its pride
By giving him my daughter as his bride.

DAMIS: You're going to force her to accept his hand? 55

ORGON: Yes, and this very night, d'you understand?
I shall defy you all, and make it clear
That I'm the one who gives the orders here.
Come, wretch, kneel down and clasp his blessed feet,
And ask his pardon for your black deceit. 60

DAMIS: I ask that swindler's pardon? Why, I'd rather . . .

ORGON: So! You insult him, and defy your father!
A stick! A stick! *(To* TARTUFFE:*)* No, no—release me, do.

(To DAMIS:)

Out of my house this minute! Be off with you,
And never dare set foot in it again.   65
DAMIS: Well, I shall go, but . . .
ORGON: Well, go quickly, then.
I disinherit you; an empty purse
Is all you'll get from me—except my curse!

Scene VII

ORGON, TARTUFFE

ORGON: How he blasphemed your goodness! What a son!
TARTUFFE: Forgive him, Lord, as I've already done.

(To ORGON:)

You can't know how it hurts when someone tries
To blacken me in my dear Brother's eyes.
ORGON: Ahh!
TARTUFFE: The mere thought of such ingratitude   5
Plunges my soul into so dark a mood . . .
Such horror grips my heart . . . I gasp for breath,
And cannot speak, and feel myself near death.
ORGON: *(He runs, in tears, to the door through which he has just driven his son.)*
You blackguard! Why did I spare you? Why did I not
Break you in little pieces on the spot?   10
Compose yourself, and don't be hurt, dear friend.
TARTUFFE: These scenes, these dreadful quarrels, have got to end.
I've much upset your household, and I perceive
That the best thing will be for me to leave.
ORGON: What are you saying!
TARTUFFE: They're all against me here;   15
They'd have you think me false and insincere.
ORGON: Ah, what of that? Have I ceased believing in you?
TARTUFFE: Their adverse talk will certainly continue,
And charges which you now repudiate
You may find credible at a later date.   20
ORGON: No, Brother, never.
TARTUFFE: Brother, a wife can sway
Her husband's mind in many a subtle way.
ORGON: No, no.
TARTUFFE: To leave at once is the solution;
Thus only can I end their persecution.

ORGON: No, no, I'll not allow it; you shall remain. 25
TARTUFFE: Ah, well; 'twill mean much martyrdom and pain,
  But if you wish it . . .
ORGON: Ah!
TARTUFFE: Enough; so be it.
  But one thing must be settled, as I see it.
  For your dear honor, and for our friendship's sake,
  There's one precaution I feel bound to take. 30
  I shall avoid your wife, and keep away . . .
ORGON: No, you shall not, whatever they may say.
  It pleases me to vex them, and for spite
  I'd have them see you with her day and night.
  What's more, I'm going to drive them to despair 35
  By making you my only son and heir;
  This very day, I'll give to you alone
  Clear deed and title to everything I own.
  A dear, good friend and son-in-law-to-be
  Is more than wife, or child, or kin to me. 40
  Will you accept my offer, dearest son?
TARTUFFE: In all things, let the will of Heaven be done.
ORGON: Poor fellow! Come, we'll go draw up the deed.
  Then let them burst with disappointed greed!

ACT IV

Scene I

CLÉANTE, TARTUFFE

CLÉANTE: Yes, all the town's discussing it, and truly,
  Their comments do not flatter you unduly.
  I'm glad we've met, Sir, and I'll give my view
  Of this sad matter in a word or two.
  As for who's guilty, that I shan't discuss; 5
  Let's say it was Damis who caused the fuss;
  Assuming, then, that you have been ill-used
  By young Damis, and groundlessly accused,
  Ought not a Christian to forgive, and ought
  He not to stifle every vengeful thought? 10
  Should you stand by and watch a father make
  His only son an exile for your sake?
  Again I tell you frankly, be advised:
  The whole town, high and low, is scandalized;
  This quarrel must be mended, and my advice is 15
  Not to push matters to a further crisis.

No, sacrifice your wrath to God above,
And help Damis regain his father's love.

TARTUFFE: Alas, for my part I should take great joy
In doing so. I've nothing against the boy.   20
I pardon all, I harbor no resentment;
To serve him would afford me much contentment.
But Heaven's interest will not have it so:
If he comes back, then I shall have to go.
After his conduct—so extreme, so vicious—   25
Our further intercourse would look suspicious.
God knows what people would think! Why, they'd describe
My goodness to him as a sort of bribe;
They'd say that out of guilt I made pretense
Of loving-kindness and benevolence—   30
That, fearing my accuser's tongue, I strove
To buy his silence with a show of love.

CLÉANTE: Your reasoning is badly warped and stretched,
And these excuses, Sir, are most far-fetched.
Why put yourself in charge of Heaven's cause?   35
Does Heaven need our help to enforce its laws?
Leave vengeance to the Lord, Sir; while we live,
Our duty's not to punish, but forgive;
And what the Lord commands, we should obey
Without regard to what the world may say.   40
What! Shall the fear of being misunderstood
Prevent our doing what is right and good?
No, no: let's simply do what Heaven ordains,
And let no other thoughts perplex our brains.

TARTUFFE: Again, Sir, let me say that I've forgiven   45
Damis, and thus obeyed the laws of Heaven;
But I am not commanded by the Bible
To live with one who smears my name with libel.

CLÉANTE: Were you commanded, Sir, to indulge the whim
Of poor Orgon, and to encourage him   50
In suddenly transferring to your name
A large estate to which you have no claim?

TARTUFFE: 'Twould never occur to those who know me best
To think I acted from self-interest.
The treasures of this world I quite despise;   55
Their specious glitter does not charm my eyes;
And if I have resigned myself to taking
The gift which my dear Brother insists on making,
I do so only, as he well understands,
Lest so much wealth fall into wicked hands,   60
Lest those to whom it might descend in time
Turn it to purposes of sin and crime,
And not, as I shall do, make use of it
For Heaven's glory and mankind's benefit.

CLÉANTE: Forget these trumped-up fears. Your argument   65
　　Is one the rightful heir might well resent;
　　It *is* a moral burden to inherit
　　Such wealth, but give Damis a chance to bear it.
　　And would it not be worse to be accused
　　Of swindling, than to see that wealth misused?   70
　　I'm shocked that you allowed Orgon to broach
　　This matter, and that you feel no self-reproach:
　　Does true religion teach that lawful heirs
　　May freely be deprived of what is theirs?
　　And if the Lord has told you in your heart   75
　　That you and young Damis must dwell apart,
　　Would it not be the decent thing to beat
　　A generous and honorable retreat,
　　Rather than let the son of the house be sent,
　　For your convenience, into banishment?   80
　　Sir, if you wish to prove the honesty
　　Of your intentions . . .
TARTUFFE:　　　　　　　Sir, it is half-past three.
　　I've certain pious duties to attend to,
　　And hope my prompt departure won't offend you.
CLÉANTE *(alone):* Damn.

Scene II

ELMIRE, MARIANE, CLÉANTE, DORINE

DORINE: Stay, Sir, and help Mariane, for Heaven's sake!
　　She's suffering so, I fear her heart will break.
　　Her father's plan to marry her off tonight
　　Has put the poor child in a desperate plight.
　　I hear him coming. Let's stand together, now,   5
　　And see if we can't change his mind, somehow,
　　About this match we all deplore and fear.

Scene III

ORGON, ELMIRE, MARIANE, CLÉANTE, DORINE

ORGON: Hah! Glad to find you all assembled here.

(*To* MARIANE:)

　　This contract, child, contains your happiness,
　　And what it says I think your heart can guess.
MARIANE *(falling to her knees):*
　　Sir, by that Heaven which sees me here distressed,
　　And by whatever else can move your breast,   5

Do not employ a father's power, I pray you,
To crush my heart and force it to obey you,
Nor by your harsh commands oppress me so
That I'll begrudge the duty which I owe—
And do not so embitter and enslave me   10
That I shall hate the very life you gave me.
If my sweet hopes must perish, if you refuse
To give me to the one I've dared to choose,
Spare me at least—I beg you, I implore—
The pain of wedding one whom I abhor;   15
And do not, by a heartless use of force,
Drive me to contemplate some desperate course.

ORGON (*feeling himself touched by her:*)
Be firm, my soul. No human weakness, now.

MARIANE: I don't resent your love for him. Allow
Your heart free rein, Sir; give him your property,   20
And if that's not enough, take mine from me;
He's welcome to my money; take it, do,
But don't, I pray, include my person too.
Spare me, I beg you; and let me end the tale
Of my sad days behind a convent veil.   25

ORGON: A convent! Hah! When crossed in their amours,
All lovesick girls have the same thought as yours.
Get up! The more you loathe the man, and dread him,
The more ennobling it will be to wed him.
Marry Tartuffe, and mortify your flesh!   30
Enough; don't start that whimpering afresh.

DORINE: But why . . . ?

ORGON: Be still, there. Speak when you're spoken to.
Not one more bit of impudence out of you.

CLÉANTE: If I may offer a word of counsel here . . .

ORGON: Brother, in counselling you have no peer;   35
All your advice is forceful, sound, and clever;
I don't propose to follow it, however.

ELMIRE (*to Orgon*): I am amazed, and don't know what to say;
Your blindness simply takes my breath away.
You are indeed bewitched, to take no warning   40
From our account of what occurred this morning.

ORGON: Madam, I know a few plain facts, and one
Is that you're partial to my rascal son;
Hence, when he sought to make Tartuffe the victim
Of a base lie, you dared not contradict him.   45
Ah, but you underplayed your part, my pet;
You should have looked more angry, more upset.

ELMIRE: When men make overtures, must we reply
With righteous anger and a battle-cry?
Must we turn back their amorous advances   50
With sharp reproaches and with fiery glances?

Myself, I find such offers merely amusing,
And make no scenes and fusses in refusing;
My taste is for good-natured rectitude,
And I dislike the savage sort of prude   55
Who guards her virtue with her teeth and claws,
And tears men's eyes out for the slightest cause:
The Lord preserve me from such honor as that,
Which bites and scratches like an alley-cat!
I've found that a polite and cool rebuff   60
Discourages a lover quite enough.

ORGON: I know the facts, and I shall not be shaken.

ELMIRE: I marvel at your power to be mistaken.
Would it, I wonder, carry weight with you
If I could *show* you that our tale was true?   65

ORGON: Show me?

ELMIRE: Yes.

ORGON: Rot.

ELMIRE: Come, what if I found a way
To make you see the facts as plain as day?

ORGON: Nonsense.

ELMIRE: Do answer me; don't be absurd.
I'm not now asking you to trust our word.
Suppose that from some hiding-place in here   70
You learned the whole sad truth by eye and ear—
What would you say of your good friend, after that?

ORGON: Why, I'd say . . . nothing, by Jehoshaphat!
It can't be true.

ELMIRE: You've been too long deceived,
And I'm quite tired of being disbelieved.   75
Come now: let's put my statements to the test,
And you shall see the truth made manifest.

ORGON: I'll take that challenge. Now do your uttermost.
We'll see how you make good your empty boast.

ELMIRE *(to* DORINE*):* Send him to me.

DORINE: He's crafty; it may be hard   80
To catch the cunning scoundrel off his guard.

ELMIRE: No, amorous men are gullible. Their conceit
So blinds them that they're never hard to cheat.
Have him come down
                    (To CLÉANTE *and* MARIANE*:)*
                    Please leave us, for a bit.

Scene IV

ELMIRE, ORGON

ELMIRE: Pull up this table, and get under it.

ORGON: What?

ELMIRE: It's essential that you be well-hidden.
ORGON: Why there?
ELMIRE: Oh, Heavens! Just do as you are bidden.
   I have my plans; we'll soon see how they fare.
   Under the table, now; and once you're there,   5
   Take care that you are neither seen nor heard.
ORGON: Well, I'll indulge you, since I gave my word
   To see you through this infantile charade.
ELMIRE: Once it is over, you'll be glad we played.

(To her husband, who is now under the table:)

I'm going to act quite strangely, now, and you   10
Must not be shocked at anything I do.
Whatever I may say, you must excuse
As part of that deceit I'm forced to use.
I shall employ sweet speeches in the task
Of making that imposter drop his mask;   15
I'll give encouragement to his bold desires,
And furnish fuel to his amorous fires.
Since it's for your sake, and for his destruction,
That I shall seem to yield to his seduction,
I'll gladly stop whenever you decide   20
That all your doubts are fully satisfied.
I'll count on you, as soon as you have seen
What sort of man he is, to intervene,
And not expose me to his odious lust
One moment longer than you feel you must.   25
Remember: you're to save me from my plight
Whenever . . . He's coming! Hush! Keep out of sight!

Scene V

TARTUFFE, ELMIRE, ORGON

TARTUFFE: You wish to have a word with me, I'm told.
ELMIRE: Yes. I've a little secret to unfold.
   Before I speak, however, it would be wise
   To close that door, and look about for spies.

(TARTUFFE goes to the door, closes it, and returns.)

The very last thing that must happen now   5
Is a repetition of this morning's row.
I've never been so badly caught off guard.
Oh, how I feared for you! You saw how hard
I tried to make that troublesome Damis
Control his dreadful temper, and hold his peace.   10

In my confusion, I didn't have the sense
Simply to contradict his evidence;
But as it happened, that was for the best,
And all has worked out in our interest.
This storm has only bettered your position;   15
My husband doesn't have the least suspicion,
And now, in mockery of those who do,
He bids me be continually with you.
And that is why, quite fearless of reproof,
I now can be alone with my Tartuffe,   20
And why my heart—perhaps too quick to yield—
Feels free to let its passion be revealed.

TARTUFFE: Madam, your words confuse me. Not long ago,
   You spoke in quite a different style, you know.

ELMIRE: Ah, Sir, if that refusal made you smart,   25
   It's little that you know of woman's heart,
   Or what that heart is trying to convey
   When it resists in such a feeble way!
   Always, at first, our modesty prevents
   The frank avowal of tender sentiments;   30
   However high the passion which inflames us,
   Still, to confess its power somehow shames us.
   Thus we reluct, at first, yet in a tone
   Which tells you that our heart is overthrown,
   That what our lips deny, our pulse confesses,   35
   And that, in time, all noes will turn to yesses.
   I fear my words are all too frank and free,
   And a poor proof of woman's modesty;
   But since I'm started, tell me, if you will—
   Would I have tried to make Damis be still,   40
   Would I have listened, calm and unoffended,
   Until your lengthy offer of love was ended,
   And been so very mild in my reaction,
   Had your sweet words not given me satisfaction?
   And when I tried to force you to undo   45
   The marriage-plans my husband has in view,
   What did my urgent pleading signify
   If not that I admired you, and that I
   Deplored the thought that someone else might own
   Part of a heart I wished for mine alone?   50

TARTUFFE: Madam, no happiness is so complete
   As when, from lips we love, come words so sweet;
   Their nectar floods my every sense, and drains
   In honeyed rivulets through all my veins.
   To please you is my joy, my only goal;   55
   Your love is the restorer of my soul;
   And yet I must beg leave, now, to confess

Some lingering doubts as to my happiness.
Might not this be a trick? Might not the catch
Be that you wish me to break off the match   60
With Mariane, and so have feigned to love me?
I shan't quite trust your fond opinion of me
Until the feelings you've expressed so sweetly
Are demonstrated somewhat more concretely,
And you have shown, by certain kind concessions,   65
That I may put my faith in your professions.

ELMIRE *(She coughs, to warn her husband.)*
Why be in such a hurry? Must my heart
Exhaust its bounty at the very start?
To make that sweet admission cost me dear,
But you'll not be content, it would appear,   70
Unless my store of favors is disbursed
To the last farthing, and at the very first.

TARTUFFE: The less we merit, the less we dare to hope,
And with our doubts, mere words can never cope.
We trust no promised bliss till we receive it;   75
Not till a joy is ours can we believe it.
I, who so little merit your esteem,
Can't credit this fulfillment of my dream,
And shan't believe it, Madam, until I savor
Some palpable assurance of your favor.   80

ELMIRE: My, how tyrannical your love can be,
And how it flusters and perplexes me!
How furiously you take one's heart in hand,
And make your every wish a fierce command!
Come, must you hound and harry me to death?   85
Will you not give me time to catch my breath?
Can it be right to press me with such force,
Give me no quarter, show me no remorse,
And take advantage, by your stern insistence,
Of the fond feelings which weaken my resistance?   90

TARTUFFE: Well, if you look with favor upon my love,
Why, then, begrudge me some clear proof thereof?

ELMIRE: But how can I consent without offense
To Heaven, toward which you feel such reverence?

TARTUFFE: If Heaven is all that holds you back, don't worry. 95
I can remove that hindrance in a hurry.
Nothing of that sort need obstruct our path.

ELMIRE: Must one not be afraid of Heaven's wrath?

TARTUFFE: Madam, forget such fears, and be my pupil,
And I shall teach you how to conquer scruple.   100
Some joys, it's true, are wrong in Heaven's eyes;
Yet Heaven is not averse to compromise;
There is a science, lately formulated,

Whereby one's conscience may be liberated,
And any wrongful act you care to mention   105
May be redeemed by purity of intention.
I'll teach you, Madam, the secrets of that science;
Meanwhile, just place on me your full reliance.
Assuage my keen desires, and feel no dread:
The sin, if any, shall be on my head.   110

(ELMIRE *coughs, this time more loudly.*)

You've a bad cough.
ELMIRE: Yes, yes. It's bad indeed.
TARTUFFE *(producing a little paper bag):*
  A bit of licorice may be what you need.
ELMIRE: No, I've a stubborn cold, it seems. I'm sure it
  Will take much more than licorice to cure it.
TARTUFFE: How aggravating.
ELMIRE: Oh, more than I can say.   115
TARTUFFE: If you're still troubled, think of things this way:
  No one shall know our joys, save us alone,
  And there's no evil till the act is known;
  It's scandal, Madam, which makes it an offense,
  And it's no sin to sin in confidence.   120
ELMIRE *(having coughed once more):* Well, clearly I must do as
      you require,
  And yield to your importunate desire.
  It is apparent, now, that nothing less
  Will satisfy you, and so I acquiesce.
  To go so far is much against my will;   125
  I'm vexed that it should come to this; but still,
  Since you are so determined on it, since you
  Will not allow mere language to convince you,
  And since you ask for concrete evidence, I
  See nothing for it, now, but to comply.   130
  If this is sinful, if I'm wrong to do it,
  So much the worse for him who drove me to it.
  The fault can surely not be charged to me.
TARTUFFE: Madam, the fault is mine, if fault there be,
  And . . .
ELMIRE: Open the door a little, and peek out;   135
  I wouldn't want my husband poking about.
TARTUFFE: Why worry about the man? Each day he grows
  More gullible; one can lead him by the nose.
  To find us here would fill him with delight,
  And if he saw the worst, he'd doubt his sight.   140
ELMIRE: Nevertheless, do step out for a minute
  Into the hall, and see that no one's in it.

Scene VI

ORGON, ELMIRE

ORGON *(coming out from under the table):*
  That man's a perfect monster, I must admit!
  I'm simply stunned. I can't get over it.
ELMIRE: What, coming out so soon? How premature!
  Get back in hiding, and wait until you're sure.
  Stay till the end, and be convinced completely;   5
  We mustn't stop till things are proved concretely.
ORGON: Hell never harbored anything so vicious!
ELMIRE: Tut, don't be hasty. Try to be judicious.
  Wait, and be certain that there's no mistake.
  No jumping to conclusions, for Heaven's sake!   10

         (She places ORGON *behind her, as* TARTUFFE *re-enters.)*

Scene VII

TARTUFFE, ELMIRE, ORGON

TARTUFFE *(not seeing* ORGON*):*
  Madam, all things have worked out to perfection;
  I've given the neighboring rooms a full inspection;
  No one's about; and now I may at last . . .
ORGON *(intercepting him):* Hold on, my passionate fellow, not so fast!
  I should advise a little more restraint.   5
  Well, so you thought you'd fool me, my dear saint!
  How soon you wearied of the saintly life—
  Wedding my daughter, and coveting my wife!
  I've long suspected you, and had a feeling
  That soon I'd catch you at your double-dealing.   10
  Just now, you've given me evidence galore;
  It's quite enough; I have no wish for more.
ELMIRE *(to* TARTUFFE*):* I'm sorry to have treated you so slyly,
  But circumstances forced me to be wily.
TARTUFFE: Brother, you can't think . . .
ORGON: No more talk from you;   15
  Just leave this household, without more ado.
TARTUFFE: What I intended . . .
ORGON: That seems fairly clear.
  Spare me your falsehoods and get out of here.
TARTUFFE: No, I'm the master, and you're the one to go!
  This house belongs to me, I'll have you know,   20
  And I shall show you that you can't hurt *me*
  By this contemptible conspiracy,

That those who cross me know not what they do,
And that I've means to expose and punish you,
Avenge offended Heaven, and make you grieve 25
That ever you dared order me to leave.

Scene VIII

ELMIRE, ORGON

ELMIRE: What was the point of all that angry chatter?
ORGON: Dear God, I'm worried. This is no laughing matter.
ELMIRE: How so?
ORGON: I fear I understood his drift.
  I'm much disturbed about that deed of gift.
ELMIRE: You gave him . . . ?
ORGON: Yes, it's all been drawn and signed. 5
  But one thing more is weighing on my mind.
ELMIRE: What's that?
ORGON: I'll tell you; but first let's see if there's
  A certain strong-box in his room upstairs.

ACT V

Scene I

ORGON, CLÉANTE

CLÉANTE: Where are you going so fast?
ORGON: God knows!
CLÉANTE: Then wait;
  Let's have a conference, and deliberate
  On how this situation's to be met.
ORGON: That strong-box has me utterly upset;
  This is the worst of many, many shocks. 5
CLÉANTE: Is there some fearful mystery in that box?
ORGON: My poor friend Argas brought that box to me
  With his own hands, in utmost secrecy;
  'Twas on the very morning of his flight.
  It's full of papers which, if they came to light, 10
  Would ruin him—or such is my impression.
CLÉANTE: Then why did you let it out of your possession?
ORGON: Those papers vexed my conscience, and it seemed best
  To ask the counsel of my pious guest.
  The cunning scoundrel got me to agree 15
  To leave the strong-box in his custody,

So that, in case of an investigation,
I could employ a slight equivocation
And swear I didn't have it, and thereby,
At no expense to conscience, tell a lie.   20

CLÉANTE: It looks to me as if you're out on a limb.
Trusting him with that box, and offering him
That deed of gift, were actions of a kind
Which scarcely indicate a prudent mind.
With two such weapons, he has the upper hand,   25
And since you're vulnerable, as matters stand,
You erred once more in bringing him to bay.
You should have acted in some subtler way.

ORGON: Just think of it: behind that fervent face,
A heart so wicked, and a soul so base!   30
I took him in, a hungry beggar, and then . . .
Enough, by God! I'm through with pious men:
Henceforth I'll hate the whole false brotherhood,
And persecute them worse than Satan could.

CLÉANTE: Ah, there you go—extravagant as ever!   35
Why can you not be rational? You never
Manage to take the middle course, it seems,
But jump, instead, between absurd extremes.
You've recognized your recent grave mistake
In falling victim to a pious fake;   40
Now, to correct that error, must you embrace
An even greater error in its place,
And judge our worthy neighbors as a whole
By what you've learned of one corrupted soul?
Come, just because one rascal made you swallow   45
A show of zeal which turned out to be hollow,
Shall you conclude that all men are deceivers,
And that, today, there are no true believers?
Let atheists make that foolish inference;
Learn to distinguish virtue from pretense,   50
Be cautious in bestowing admiration,
And cultivate a sober moderation.
Don't humor fraud, but also don't asperse
True piety; the latter fault is worse,
And it is best to err, if err one must,   55
As you have done, upon the side of trust.

Scene II

DAMIS, ORGON, CLÉANTE

DAMIS: Father, I hear that scoundrel's uttered threats
Against you; that he pridefully forgets

How, in his need, he was befriended by you,
And means to use your gifts to crucify you.
ORGON: It's true, my boy. I'm too distressed for tears.   5
DAMIS: Leave it to me, Sir; let me trim his ears.
Faced with such insolence, we must not waver.
I shall rejoice in doing you the favor
Of cutting short his life, and your distress.
CLÉANTE: What a display of young hotheadedness!   10
Do learn to moderate your fits of rage.
In this just kingdom, this enlightened age,
One does not settle things by violence.

Scene III

MADAME PERNELLE, MARIANE, ELMIRE, DORINE, DAMIS, ORGON, CLÉANTE

MADAME PERNELLE: I hear strange tales of very strange events.
ORGON: Yes, strange events which these two eyes beheld.
The man's ingratitude is unparalleled.
I save a wretched pauper from starvation,
House him, and treat him like a blood relation,   5
Shower him every day with my largesse,
Give him my daughter, and all that I possess;
And meanwhile the unconscionable knave
Tries to induce my wife to misbehave;
And not content with such extreme rascality,   10
Now threatens me with my own liberality,
And aims, by taking base advantage of
The gifts I gave him out of Christian love,
To drive me from my house, a ruined man,
And make me end a pauper, as he began.   15
DORINE: Poor fellow!
MADAME PERNELLE: No, my son, I'll never bring
Myself to think him guilty of such a thing.
ORGON: How's that?
MADAME PERNELLE: The righteous always were maligned.
ORGON: Speak clearly, Mother. Say what's on your mind.
MADAME PERNELLE: I mean that I can smell a rat, my dear.   20
You know how everybody hates him, here.
ORGON: That has no bearing on the case at all.
MADAME PERNELLE: I told you a hundred times, when you were small,
That virtue in this world is hated ever;
Malicious men may die, but malice never.   25
ORGON: No doubt that's true, but how does it apply?
MADAME PERNELLE: They've turned you against him by a clever lie.
ORGON: I've told you, I was there and saw it done.

MADAME PERNELLE: Ah, slanderers will stop at nothing, Son.

ORGON: Mother, I'll lose my temper . . . For the last time,   30
    I tell you I was witness to the crime.

MADAME PERNELLE: The tongues of spite are busy night and noon,
    And to their venom no man is immune.

ORGON: You're talking nonsense. Can't you realize
    I saw it; saw it; saw it with my eyes?   35
    Saw, do you understand me? Must I shout it
    Into your ears before you'll cease to doubt it?

MADAME PERNELLE: Appearances can deceive, my son. Dear me,
    We cannot always judge by what we see.

ORGON: Drat! Drat!

MADAME PERNELLE: One often interprets things awry;   40
    Good can seem evil to a suspicious eye.

ORGON: Was I to see his pawing at Elmire
    As an act of charity?

MADAME PERNELLE: Till his guilt is clear,
    A man deserves the benefit of the doubt.
    You should have waited, to see how things turned out.   45

ORGON: Great God in Heaven, what more proof did I need?
    Was I to sit there, watching, until he'd . . .
    You drive me to the brink of impropriety.

MADAME PERNELLE: No, no, a man of such surpassing piety
    Could not do such a thing. You cannot shake me.   50
    I don't believe it, and you shall not make me.

ORGON: You vex me so that, if you weren't my mother,
    I'd say to you . . . some dreadful thing or other.

DORINE: It's your turn now, Sir, not to be listened to;
    You'd not trust us, and now she won't trust you.   55

CLÉANTE: My friends, we're wasting time which should be spent
    In facing up to our predicament.
    I fear that scoundrel's threats weren't made in sport.

DAMIS: Do you think he'd have the nerve to go to court?

ELMIRE: I'm sure he won't; they'd find it all too crude   60
    A case of swindling and ingratitude.

CLÉANTE: Don't be too sure. He won't be at a loss
    To give his claims a high and righteous gloss;
    And clever rogues with far less valid cause
    Have trapped their victims in a web of laws.   65
    I say again that to antagonize
    A man so strongly armed was most unwise.

ORGON: I know it; but the man's appalling cheek
    Outraged me so, I couldn't control my pique.

CLÉANTE: I wish to Heaven that we could devise   70
    Some truce between you, or some compromise.

ELMIRE: If I had known what cards he held, I'd not
    Have roused his anger by my little plot.

ORGON *(to* DORINE, *as* M. LOYAL *enters):*
  What is that fellow looking for? Who is he?
  Go talk to him—and tell him that I'm busy.   75

Scene IV

MONSIEUR LOYAL, MADAME PERNELLE, ORGON, DAMIS, MARIANE, DORINE, ELMIRE, CLÉANTE

MONSIEUR LOYAL: Good day, dear sister. Kindly let me see
  Your master.
DORINE: He's involved with company,
  And cannot be disturbed just now, I fear.
MONSIEUR LOYAL: I hate to intrude; but what has brought me here
  Will not disturb your master, in any event.   5
  Indeed, my news will make him most content.
DORINE: Your name?
MONSIEUR LOYAL: Just say that I bring greetings from
  Monsieur Tartuffe, on whose behalf I've come.
DORINE *(to* ORGON*):* Sir, he's a very gracious man, and bears
  A message from Tartuffe, which, he declares,   10
  Will make you most content.
CLÉANTE: Upon my word,
  I think this man had best be seen, and heard.
ORGON: Perhaps he has some settlement to suggest.
  How shall I treat him? What manner would be best?
CLÉANTE: Control your anger, and if he should mention   15
  Some fair adjustment, give him your full attention.
MONSIEUR LOYAL: Good health to you, good Sir. May Heaven confound
  Your enemies, and may your joys abound.
ORGON *(aside, to* CLÉANTE*):* A gentle salutation: it confirms
  My guess that he is here to offer terms.   20
MONSIEUR LOYAL: I've always held your family most dear;
  I served your father, Sir, for many a year.
ORGON: Sir, I must ask your pardon; to my shame,
  I cannot now recall your face or name.
MONSIEUR LOYAL: Loyal's my name; I come from Normandy,   25
  And I'm a bailiff, in all modesty.
  For forty years, praise God, it's been my boast
  To serve with honor in that vital post,
  And I am here, Sir, if you will permit
  The liberty, to serve you with this writ . . .   30
ORGON: To—*what?*
MONSIEUR LOYAL: Now, please, Sir, let us have no friction:
  It's nothing but an order of eviction.
  You are to move your goods and family out
  And make way for new occupants, without
  Deferment or delay, and give the keys . . .   35

ORGON: I? Leave this house?

MONSIEUR LOYAL: Why yes, Sir, if you please.
　This house, Sir, from the cellar to the roof,
　Belongs now to the good Monsieur Tartuffe,
　And he is lord and master of your estate
　By virtue of a deed of present date,   40
　Drawn in due form, with clearest legal phrasing . . .

DAMIS: Your insolence is utterly amazing!

MONSIEUR LOYAL: Young man, my business here is not with you,
　But with your wise and temperate father, who,
　Like every worthy citizen, stands in awe   45
　Of justice, and would never obstruct the law.

ORGON: But . . .

MONSIEUR LOYAL:
　　　　　　　　Not for a million, Sir, would you rebel
　Against authority; I know that well.
　You'll not make trouble, Sir, or interfere
　With the execution of my duties here.   50

DAMIS: Someone may execute a smart tattoo
　On that black jacket of yours, before you're through.

MONSIEUR LOYAL: Sir, bid your son be silent. I'd much regret
　Having to mention such a nasty threat
　Of violence, in writing my report.   55

DORINE *(aside):* This man Loyal's a most disloyal sort!

MONSIEUR LOYAL: I love all men of upright character,
　And when I agreed to serve these papers, Sir,
　It was your feelings that I had in mind.
　I couldn't bear to see the case assigned   60
　To someone else, who might esteem you less
　And so subject you to unpleasantness.

ORGON: What's more unpleasant than telling a man to leave
　His house and home?

MONSIEUR LOYAL: You'd like a short reprieve?
　If you desire it, Sir, I shall not press you,   65
　But wait until tomorrow to dispossess you.
　Splendid. I'll come and spend the night here, then,
　Most quietly, with half a score of men.
　For form's sake, you might bring me, just before
　You go to bed, the keys to the front door.   70
　My men, I promise, will be on their best
　Behavior, and will not disturb your rest.
　But bright and early, Sir, you must be quick
　And move out all your furniture, every stick:
　The men I've chosen are both young and strong,   75
　And with their help it shouldn't take you long.
　In short, I'll make things pleasant and convenient,
　And since I'm being so extremely lenient,

Please show me, Sir, a like consideration,
And give me your entire cooperation.   80
ORGON (*aside*): I may be all but bankrupt, but I vow
    I'd give a hundred louis, here and now,
    Just for the pleasure of landing one good clout
    Right on the end of that complacent snout.
CLÉANTE: Careful; don't make things worse.
DAMIS: My bootsole itches   85
    To give that beggar a good kick in the breeches.
DORINE: Monsieur Loyal, I'd love to hear the whack
    Of a stout stick across your fine broad back.
MONSIEUR LOYAL: Take care: a woman too may go to jail if
    She uses threatening language to a bailiff.   90
CLÉANTE: Enough, enough, Sir. This must not go on.
    Give me that paper, please, and then begone.
MONSIEUR LOYAL: Well, *au revoir*. God give you all good cheer!
ORGON: May God confound you, and him who sent you here!

Scene V

> ORGON, CLÉANTE, MARIANE, ELMIRE, MADAME PERNELLE, DORINE, DAMIS

ORGON: Now, Mother, was I right or not? This writ
    Should change your notion of Tartuffe a bit.
    Do you perceive his villainy at last?
MADAME PERNELLE: I'm thunderstruck. I'm utterly aghast.
DORINE: Oh, come, be fair. You mustn't take offense   5
    At this new proof of his benevolence.
    He's acting out of selfless love, I know.
    Material things enslave the soul, and so
    He kindly has arranged your liberation
    From all that might endanger your salvation.   10
ORGON: Will you not ever hold your tongue, you dunce?
CLÉANTE: Come, you must take some action, and at once.
ELMIRE: Go tell the world of the low trick he's tried.
    The deed of gift is surely nullified
    By such behavior, and public rage will not   15
    Permit the wretch to carry out his plot.

Scene VI

> VALÈRE, ORGON, CLÉANTE, ELMIRE, MARIANE, MADAME PERNELLE, DAMIS, DORINE

VALÈRE: Sir, though I hate to bring you more bad news,
    Such is the danger that I cannot choose.
    A friend who is extremely close to me

And knows my interest in your family
Has, for my sake, presumed to violate   5
The secrecy that's due to things of state,
And sends me word that you are in a plight
From which your one salvation lies in flight.
That scoundrel who's imposed upon you so
Denounced you to the King an hour ago   10
And, as supporting evidence, displayed
The strong-box of a certain renegade
Whose secret papers, so he testified,
You had disloyally agreed to hide.
I don't know just what charges may be pressed,   15
But there's a warrant out for your arrest;
Tartuffe has been instructed, furthermore,
To guide the arresting officer to your door.
CLÉANTE: He's clearly done this to facilitate
His seizure of your house and your estate.   20
ORGON: That man, I must say, is a vicious beast!
VALÈRE: You can't afford to delay, Sir, in the least.
My carriage is outside, to take you hence;
This thousand louis should cover all expense.
Let's lose no time, or you shall be undone;   25
The sole defense, in this case, is to run.
I shall go with you all the way, and place you
In a safe refuge to which they'll never trace you.
ORGON: Alas, dear boy, I wish that I could show you
My gratitude for everything I owe you.   30
But now is not the time; I pray the Lord
That I may live to give you your reward.
Farewell, my dears; be careful . . .
CLÉANTE: Brother, hurry.
We shall take care of things; you needn't worry.

Scene VII

THE OFFICER, TARTUFFE, VALÈRE, ORGON, ELMIRE, MARIANE, MADAME PERNELLE,
DORINE, CLÉANTE, DAMIS

TARTUFFE: Gently, Sir, gently; stay right where you are.
No need for haste; your lodging isn't far.
You're off to prison, by order of the Prince.
ORGON: This is the crowning blow, you wretch; and since
It means my total ruin and defeat,   5
Your villainy is now at last complete.
TARTUFFE: You needn't try to provoke me; it's no use.
Those who serve Heaven must expect abuse.

CLÉANTE: You are indeed most patient, sweet, and blameless.

DORINE: How he exploits the name of Heaven! It's shameless. 10

TARTUFFE: Your taunts and mockeries are all for naught;
    To do my duty is my only thought.

MARIANE: Your love of duty is most meritorious,
    And what you've done is little short of glorious.

TARTUFFE: All deeds are glorious, Madam, which obey 15
    The sovereign prince who sent me here today.

ORGON: I rescued you when you were destitute;
    Have you forgotten that, you thankless brute?

TARTUFFE: No, no, I well remember everything;
    But my first duty is to serve my King. 20
    That obligation is so paramount
    That other claims, beside it, do not count;
    And for it I would sacrifice my wife,
    My family, my friend, or my own life.

ELMIRE: Hypocrite!

DORINE: All that we most revere, he uses 25
    To cloak his plots and camouflage his ruses.

CLÉANTE: If it is true that you are animated
    By pure and loyal zeal, as you have stated,
    Why was this zeal not roused until you'd sought
    To make Orgon a cuckold, and been caught? 30
    Why weren't you moved to give your evidence
    Until your outraged host had driven you hence?
    I shan't say that the gift of all his treasure
    Ought to have damped your zeal in any measure;
    But if he is a traitor, as you declare, 35
    How could you condescend to be his heir?

TARTUFFE (to the OFFICER):
    Sir, spare me all this clamor; it's growing shrill.
    Please carry out your orders, if you will.

OFFICER: Yes, I've delayed too long, Sir. Thank you kindly.
    You're just the proper person to remind me. 40
    Come, you are off to join the other boarders
    In the King's prison, according to his orders.

TARTUFFE: Who? I, Sir?

OFFICER: Yes.

TARTUFFE: To prison? This can't be true!

OFFICER: I owe an explanation, but not to you.

(To ORGON:)

    Sir, all is well; rest easy, and be grateful. 45
    We serve a Prince to whom all sham is hateful,
    A Prince who sees into our inmost hearts,
    And can't be fooled by any trickster's arts.
    His royal soul, though generous and human,

Views all things with discernment and acumen;   50
His sovereign reason is not lightly swayed,
And all his judgments are discreetly weighed.
He honors righteous men of every kind,
And yet his zeal for virtue is not blind,
Nor does his love of piety numb his wits   55
And make him tolerant of hypocrites.
'Twas hardly likely that this man could cozen
A King who's foiled such liars by the dozen.
With one keen glance, the King perceived the whole
Perverseness and corruption of his soul,   60
And thus high Heaven's justice was displayed:
Betraying you, the rogue stood self-betrayed.
The King soon recognized Tartuffe as one
Notorious by another name, who'd done
So many vicious crimes that one could fill   65
Ten volumes with them, and be writing still.
But to be brief: our sovereign was appalled
By this man's treachery toward you, which he called
The last, worst villainy of a vile career,
And bade me follow the imposter here   70
To see how gross his impudence could be,
And force him to restore your property.
Your private papers, by the King's command,
I hereby seize and give into your hand.
The King, by royal order, invalidates   75
The deed which gave this rascal your estates,
And pardons, furthermore, your grave offense
In harboring an exile's documents.
By these decrees, our Prince rewards you for
Your loyal deeds in the late civil war,   80
And shows how heartfelt is his satisfaction
In recompensing any worthy action,
How much he prizes merit, and how he makes
More of men's virtues than of their mistakes.

DORINE: Heaven be praised!

MADAME PERNELLE: I breathe again, at last.   85

ELMIRE: We're safe.

MARIANE: I can't believe the danger's past.

ORGON (*to* TARTUFFE):
    Well, traitor, now you see . . .

CLÉANTE: Ah, Brother, please,
    Let's not descend to such indignities.
    Leave the poor wretch to his unhappy fate,
    And don't say anything to aggravate   90
    His present woes; but rather hope that he
    Will soon embrace an honest piety,

And mend his ways, and by a true repentance
Move our just King to moderate his sentence.
Meanwhile, go kneel before your sovereign's throne   95
And thank him for the mercies he has shown.
ORGON: Well said: let's go at once and, gladly kneeling,
Express the gratitude which all are feeling.
Then, when that first great duty has been done,
We'll turn with pleasure to a second one,   100
And give Valère, whose love has proven so true,
The wedded happiness which is his due.

QUESTIONS

1. Do you find Tartuffe an appealing or an appalling character? Is it possible to condemn his behavior while simultaneously admiring his shrewdness? What makes him engaging, even entertaining?
2. Tartuffe does not make his appearance until Act III, Scene 1. What effect does this delay have? What do we know about him by the time he enters? How well does Tartuffe fulfill the expectations we have about him?
3. Describe briefly the central role of the following characters: Orgon, Elmire, Cléante, and Dorine. Who is the most complex character? Who is the most entertaining? Can any be seen as a spokesman for Molière himself?
4. What makes *Tartuffe* a satiric rather than a romantic comedy? What elements of romance exist in the play? How would you characterize its prevailing tone?
5. Examine any scene you find particularly effective as comedy. Discuss how this scene should be staged, considering such details as the location of the characters, their relative positions, their physical gestures and facial expressions, and their tones of voice.
6. *Tartuffe* has been criticized as a play that ridicules religion and piety. Agree or disagree with this assessment.

CHAPTER NINETEEN

The Modern Realistic Theater

Realism can be defined as the representation of everyday life in literature. Concerned with the average, the commonplace, the ordinary, realism employs theatrical conventions to create the illusion of everyday life. With realistic drama came the depiction of subjects close to the lives of middle-class people: work, marriage, and family life. From this standpoint, Arthur Miller's *Death of a Salesman* and Henrik Ibsen's *A Doll House* are more realistic than Shakespeare's *Othello,* which in turn, is more realistic than Sophocles' *Oedipus the King.* Though each of these plays possesses a true-to-life quality, each operates according to different theatrical conventions. Royal personages, gods, military heroes, and exalted language are absent from Miller's and Ibsen's plays as modern dramatists turned to an approximation of the daily life of the lower and middle classes.

One means by which realistic drama creates the illusion of everyday life is through setting. Whereas settings consist primarily of painted backdrops in Molière's plays and are often established by dialogue in Shakespeare's plays, the settings of modern realistic plays are designed to look authentic. Moreover, setting in plays such as Ibsen's *A Doll House* and Chekhov's *The Cherry Orchard* often functions symbolically. In *Elements of Literature 3,* Robert Scholes has noted that the elaborately detailed setting of *A Doll House* symbolizes both "the impact of the Helmers' environment on their marriage" and the "very nature of their marriage"; it also embodies "the profound pressures placed on Helmer and Nora by the material and social conditions of their world."*

*Robert Scholes, *et al., Elements of Literature 3* (New York: Oxford University Press, 1982), page 966.

Other conventions designed to create and sustain the illusion that the audience was watching a slice of domestic life include the following: the use of a three-walled room with an open fourth wall into which the audience peers to view and overhear the action; dialogue that approximates the idiom of everyday discourse, polished to be sure, but designed especially to sound like speech rather than poetry; plots that, though highly contrived, seem to turn on a series of causally related actions; subjects not from mythology or history, but from the concerns of ordinary life.

Henrik Ibsen

Besides accommodating himself to the conventions of realism in *A Doll House,* Ibsen also made the play a *cause célèbre* by raising questions in it about the rights of women, a subject that was beginning to receive attention in the late nineteenth century. *A Doll House,* written in 1879, performed in London (1889) and Paris (1894), attracted attention wherever it played. Nonetheless, Ibsen insisted that the play was less about the rights of women than about human rights generally, less about the particular social conditions responsible for the position of women in nineteenth-century Norway than about the need for individuals of both sexes to treat each other with mutual respect.

HENRIK IBSEN

[*1828–1906*]

A Doll House

TRANSLATED BY ROLF FJELDE

CHARACTERS

TORVALD HELMER, *a lawyer*
NORA, *his wife*
DR. RANK
MRS. LINDE
NILS KROGSTAD, *a bank clerk*
THE HELMERS' THREE SMALL CHILDREN
ANNE-MARIE, *their nurse*
HELENE, *a maid*
A DELIVERY BOY

The action takes place in HELMER'S *residence.*

ACT I

A comfortable room, tastefully but not expensively furnished. A door to the right in the back wall leads to the entryway, another to the left leads to HELMER'S *study. Between these doors, a piano. Midway in the left-hand wall a door, and further back a window. Near the window a round table with an armchair and a small sofa. In the right-hand wall, toward the rear a door, and nearer the foreground a porcelain stove with two armchairs and a rocking chair beside it. Between the stove and the side door, a small table. Engravings on the walls. An etagére with china figures and other small art objects; a small bookcase with richly bound books; the floor carpeted; a fire burning in the stove. It is a winter day.*

A bell rings in the entryway; shortly after we hear the door being unlocked. NORA *comes into the room, humming happily to herself; she is wearing street clothes and carries an armload of packages, which she puts down on the table to the right. She has left the hall door open; and through it a* DELIVERY BOY *is seen, holding a Christmas tree and a basket which he gives to the* MAID *who let them in.*

NORA   Hide the tree well, Helene. The children mustn't get a glimpse of it till this evening, after it's trimmed. (*To the* DELIVERY BOY, *taking out her purse*) How much?

DELIVERY BOY   Fifty, ma'am.

NORA   There's a crown. No, keep the change. (*The* BOY *thanks her and leaves.* NORA *shuts the door. She laughs softly to herself while taking off her street things. Drawing a bag of macaroons from her pocket, she eats a couple, then steals over and listens at her husband's study door.*) Yes, he's home. (*Hums again as she moves to the table, right.*)

HELMER   (*from the study*) Is that my little lark twittering out there?

NORA   (*busy opening some packages*) Yes, it is.

HELMER   Is that my squirrel rummaging around?

NORA   Yes!

HELMER   When did my squirrel get in?

NORA   Just now. (*Putting the macaroon bag in her pocket and wiping her mouth*) Do come in, Torvald, and see what I've bought.

HELMER   Can't be disturbed. (*After a moment he opens the door and peers in, pen in hand.*) Bought, you say? All that there? Has the little spendthrift been out throwing money around again?

NORA   Oh, but Torvald, this year we really should let ourselves go a bit. It's the first Christmas we haven't had to economize.

HELMER   But you know we can't go squandering.

NORA   Oh yes, Torvald, we can squander a little now. Can't we? Just a tiny, wee bit. Now that you've got a big salary and are going to make piles and piles of money.

HELMER   Yes—starting New Year's. But then it's a full three months till the raise comes through.

NORA   Pooh! We can borrow that long.

HELMER   Nora! (*Goes over and playfully takes her by the ear*) Are your scatter-brains off again? What if today I borrowed a thousand crowns, and you squandered them over Christmas week, and then on New Year's Eve a roof tile fell on my head, and I lay there—

NORA   (*putting her hand on his mouth*) Oh! Don't say such things!

HELMER   Yes, but what if it happened—then what?

NORA   If anything so awful happened, then it just wouldn't matter if I had debts or not.

HELMER   Well, but the people I'd borrowed from?

NORA   Them? Who cares about them! They're strangers.

HELMER   Nora, Nora, how like a woman! No, but seriously, Nora, you know what I think about that. No debts! Never borrow! Something of freedom's lost—and something of beauty, too—from a home that's founded on borrowing and debt. We've made a brave stand up to now, the two of us; and we'll go right on like that the little while we have to.

NORA   (*going toward the stove*) Yes, whatever you say, Torvald.

HELMER   (*following her*) Now, now, the little lark's wings mustn't droop. Come on, don't be a sulky squirrel. (*Taking out his wallet*) Nora, guess what I have here.

NORA   (*turning quickly*) Money!

HELMER   There, see. (*Hands her some notes*) Good grief, I know how costs go up in a house at Christmastime.

NORA   Ten—twenty—thirty—forty. Oh, thank you. Torvald; I can manage no end on this.

HELMER   You really will have to.

NORA   Oh yes, I promise I will! But come here so I can show you everything I bought. And so cheap! Look, new clothes for Ivar here—and a sword. Here a horse and a trumpet for Bob. And a doll and a doll's bed here for Emmy; they're nothing much, but she'll tear them to bits in no time anyway. And here I have dress material and handkerchiefs for the maids. Old Anne-Marie really deserves something more.

HELMER   And what's in that package there?

NORA   (*with a cry*) Torvald, no! You can't see that till tonight!

HELMER   I see. But tell me now, you little prodigal, what have you thought of for yourself?

NORA   For myself? Oh, I don't want anything at all.

HELMER   Of course you do. Tell me just what—within reason—you'd most like to have.

NORA   I honestly don't know. Oh, listen, Torvald—

HELMER   Well?

NORA   (*fumbling at his coat buttons, without looking at him*) If you want to give me something, then maybe you could—you could—

HELMER   Come on, out with it.

NORA   (*hurriedly*) You could give me money, Torvald. No more than you think you can spare, then one of these days I'll buy something with it.

HELMER   But Nora—

NORA   Oh, please, Torvald darling, do that! I beg you, please. Then I could hang the bills in pretty gilt paper on the Christmas tree. Wouldn't that be fun?

HELMER   What are those little birds called that always fly through their fortunes?

NORA   Oh yes, spendthrifts; I know all that. But let's do as I say, Torvald; then I'll have time to decide what I really need most. That's very sensible, isn't it?

HELMER   (*smiling*) Yes, very—that is, if you actually hung onto the money I give you, and you actually used it to buy yourself something. But it goes for the house and for all sorts of foolish things, and then I only have to lay out some more.

NORA   Oh, but Torvald—

HELMER   Don't deny it, my dear little Nora. (*Putting his arm around her waist*) Spendthrifts are sweet, but they use up a frightful amount of money. It's incredible what it costs a man to feed such birds.

NORA   Oh, how can you say that! Really, I save everything I can.

HELMER   (*laughing*) Yes, that's the truth. Everything you can. But that's nothing at all.

NORA   (*humming, with a smile of quiet satisfaction*) Hm, if you only knew what expenses we larks and squirrels have, Torvald.

HELMER   You're an odd little one. Exactly the way your father was. You're never at a loss for scaring up money; but the moment you have it, it runs right out through your fingers; you never know what you've done with it. Well, one takes you as you are. It's deep in your blood. Yes, these things are hereditary, Nora.

NORA   Ah, I could wish I'd inherited many of Papa's qualities.

HELMER   And I couldn't wish you anything but just what you are, my sweet little lark. But wait; it seems to me you have a very—what should I call it?—a very suspicious look today—

NORA   I do?

HELMER   You certainly do. Look me straight in the eye.

NORA   (*looking at him*) Well?

HELMER   (*shaking an admonitory finger*) Surely my sweet tooth hasn't been running riot in town today, has she?

NORA   No. Why do you imagine that?

HELMER   My sweet tooth really didn't make a little detour through the confectioner's?

NORA   No, I assure you, Torvald—

HELMER   Hasn't nibbled some pastry?

NORA   No, not at all.

HELMER   Nor even munched a macaroon or two?

NORA   No, Torvald, I assure you, really—

HELMER   There, there now. Of course I'm only joking.

NORA   (*going to the table, right*) You know I could never think of going against you.

HELMER   No, I understand that; and you *have* given me your word. (*Going over to her.*) Well, you keep your little Christmas secrets to yourself, Nora darling. I expect they'll come to light this evening, when the tree is lit.

NORA Did you remember to ask Dr. Rank?

HELMER No. But there's no need for that; it's assumed he'll be dining with us. All the same, I'll ask him when he stops by here this morning. I've ordered some fine wine. Nora, you can't imagine how I'm looking forward to this evening.

NORA So am I. And what fun for the children, Torvald!

HELMER Ah, it's so gratifying to know that one's gotten a safe, secure job, and with a comfortable salary. It's a great satisfaction, isn't it?

NORA Oh, it's wonderful!

HELMER Remember last Christmas? Three whole weeks before, you shut yourself in every evening till long after midnight, making flowers for the Christmas tree, and all the other decorations to surprise us. Ugh, that was the dullest time I've ever lived through.

NORA It wasn't at all dull for me.

HELMER (*smiling*) But the outcome *was* pretty sorry, Nora.

NORA Oh, don't tease me with that again. How could I help it that the cat came in and tore everything to shreds.

HELMER No, poor thing, you certainly couldn't. You wanted so much to please us all, and that's what counts. But it's just as well that the hard times are past.

NORA Yes, it's really wonderful.

HELMER Now I don't have to sit here alone, boring myself, and you don't have to tire your precious eyes and your fair little delicate hands—

NORA (*clapping her hands*) No, is it really true, Torvald, I don't have to? Oh, how wonderfully lovely to hear! (*Taking his arm.*) Now I'll tell you just how I've thought we should plan things. Right after Christmas—(*The doorbell rings.*) Oh, the bell. (*Straightening the room up a bit.*) Somebody would have to come. What a bore!

HELMER I'm not at home to visitors, don't forget.

MAID (*from the hall doorway*) Ma'am, a lady to see you—

NORA All right, let her come in.

MAID (*to Helmer*) And the doctor's just come too.

HELMER Did he go right to my study?

MAID Yes, he did.

HELMER *goes into his room. The* MAID *shows in* MRS. LINDE, *dressed in traveling clothes, and shuts the door after her.*

MRS. LINDE (*in a dispirited and somewhat hesitant voice*) Hello, Nora.

NORA (*uncertain*) Hello—

MRS. LINDE You don't recognize me.

NORA No, I don't know—but wait, I think—(*Exclaiming.*) What! Kristine! Is it really you?

MRS. LINDE Yes, it's me.

NORA Kristine! To think I didn't recognize you. But then, how could I? (*More quietly.*) How you've changed, Kristine!

MRS. LINDE Yes, no doubt I have. In nine—ten long years.

NORA Is it so long since we met! Yes, it's all of that. Oh, these last eight years have been a happy time, believe me. And so now you've come in to town, too. Made the long trip in the winter. That took courage.

MRS. LINDE   I just got here by ship this morning.

NORA   To enjoy yourself over Christmas, of course. Oh, how lovely! Yes, enjoy ourselves, we'll do that. But take your coat off. You're not still cold? (*Helping her.*) There now, let's get cozy here by the stove. No, the easy chair there! I'll take the rocker here. (*Seizing her hands.*) Yes, now you have your old look again; it was only in that first moment. You're a bit more pale, Kristine —and maybe a bit thinner.

MRS. LINDE   And much, much older, Nora.

NORA   Yes, perhaps, a bit older; a tiny, tiny bit; not much at all. (*Stopping short; suddenly serious*) Oh, but thoughtless me, to sit here, chattering away. Sweet, good Kristine, can you forgive me?

MRS. LINDE   What do you mean, Nora?

NORA   (*softly*) Poor Kristine, you've become a widow.

MRS. LINDE   Yes, three years ago.

NORA   Oh, I knew it, of course; I read it in the papers. Oh Kristine, you must believe me; I often thought of writing you then, but I kept postponing it, and something always interfered.

MRS. LINDE   Nora dear, I understand completely.

NORA   No, it was awful of me, Kristine. You poor thing, how much you must have gone through. And he left you nothing?

MRS. LINDE   No.

NORA   And no children?

MRS. LINDE   No.

NORA   Nothing at all, then?

MRS. LINDE   Not even a sense of loss to feed on.

NORA   (*looking incredulously at her*) But Kristine, how could that be?

MRS. LINDE   (*smiling wearily and smoothing her hair*) Oh, sometimes it happens, Nora.

NORA   So completely alone. How terribly hard that must be for you. I have three lovely children. You can't see them now; they're out with the maid. But now you must tell me everything—

MRS. LINDE   No, no, no, tell me about yourself.

NORA   No, you begin. Today I don't want to be selfish. I want to think only of you today. But there *is* something I must tell you. Did you hear of the wonderful luck we had recently?

MRS. LINDE   No, what's that?

NORA   My husband's been made manager in the bank, just think!

MRS. LINDE   Your husband? How marvelous!

NORA   Isn't it? Being a lawyer is such an uncertain living, you know, especially if one won't touch any cases that aren't clean and decent. And of course Torvald would never do that, and I'm with him completely there. Oh, we're simply delighted, believe me! He'll join the bank right after New Year's and start getting a huge salary and lots of commissions. From now on we can live quite differently—jus as we want. Oh, Kristine, I feel so light and happy! Won't it be lovely to have stacks of money and not a care in the world?

MRS. LINDE   Well, anyway, it would be lovely to have enough for necessities.

NORA   No, not just for necessities, but stacks and stacks of money!

MRS. LINDE   (*smiling*) Nora, Nora, aren't you sensible yet? Back in school you were such a free spender.

NORA   (*with a quiet laugh*) Yes, that's what Torvald still says. (*Shaking her finger*) But "Nora, Nora" isn't as silly as you all think. Really, we've been in no position for me to go squandering. We've had to work, both of us.

MRS. LINDE   You too?

NORA   Yes, at odd jobs—needlework, crocheting, embroidery, and such— (*Casually*) and other things too. You remember that Torvald left the department when we were married? There was no chance of promotion in his office, and of course he needed to earn more money. But that first year he drove himself terribly. He took on all kinds of extra work that kept him going morning and night. It wore him down, and then he fell deathly ill. The doctors said it was essential for him to travel south.

MRS. LINDE   Yes, didn't you spend a whole year in Italy?

NORA   That's right. It wasn't easy to get away, you know. Ivar had just been born. But of course we had to go. Oh, that was a beautiful trip, and it saved Torvald's life. But it cost a frightful sum, Kristine.

MRS. LINDE   I can well imagine.

NORA   Four thousand, eight hundred crowns it cost. That's really a lot of money.

MRS. LINDE   But it's lucky you had it when you needed it.

NORA   Well, as it was, we got it from Papa.

MRS. LINDE   I see. It was just about the time your father died.

NORA   Yes, just about then. And, you know, I couldn't make the trip out to nurse him. I had to stay here, expecting Ivar any moment, and with my poor sick Torvald to care for. Dearest Papa, I never saw him again, Kristine. Oh, that was the worst time I've known in all my marriage.

MRS. LINDE   I know how you loved him. And then you went off to Italy?

NORA   Yes. We had the means now, and the doctors urged us. So we left a month after.

MRS. LINDE   And your husband came back completely cured?

NORA   Sound as a drum!

MRS. LINDE   But—the doctor?

NORA   Who?

MRS. LINDE   I thought the maid said he was a doctor, the man who came in with me.

NORA   Yes, that was Dr. Rank—but he's not making a sick call. He's our closest friend, and he stops by at least once a day. No, Torvald hasn't had a sick moment since, and the children are fit and strong, and I am, too. (*Jumping up and clapping her hands*) Oh, dear God, Kristine, what a lovely thing to live and be happy! But how disgusting of me—I'm talking of nothing but my own affairs. (*Sits on a stool close by* KRISTINE, *arms resting across her knees*) Oh, don't be angry with me! Tell me, is it really true that you weren't in love with your husband? Why did you marry him, then?

MRS. LINDE   My mother was still alive, but bedridden and helpless—and I had two younger brothers to look after. In all conscience, I didn't think I could turn him down.

NORA   No, you were right there. But was he rich at the time?

MRS. LINDE   He was very well off, I'd say. But the business was shaky, Nora. When he died, it all fell apart, and nothing was left.

NORA   And then—?

MRS. LINDE   Yes, so I had to scrape up a living with a little shop and a little teaching and whatever else I could find. The last three years have been like one endless workday without a rest for me. Now it's over, Nora. My poor mother doesn't need me, for she's passed on. Nor the boys, either; they're working now and can take care of themselves.

NORA   How free you must feel—

MRS. LINDE   No—only unspeakably empty. Nothing to live for now. (*Standing up anxiously*) That's why I couldn't take it any longer out in that desolate hole. Maybe here it'll be easier to find something to do and keep my mind occupied. If I could only be lucky enough to get a steady job, some office work—

NORA   Oh, but Kristine, that's so dreadfully tiring, and you already look so tired. It would be much better for you if you could go off to a bathing resort.

MRS. LINDE   (*going toward the window*) I have no father to give me travel money, Nora.

NORA   (*rising*) Oh, don't be angry with me.

MRS. LINDE   (*going to her*) Nora dear, don't you be angry with me. The worst of my kind of situation is all the bitterness that's stored away. No one to work for, and yet you're always having to snap up your opportunities. You have to live; and so you grow selfish. When you told me the happy change in your lot, do you know I was delighted less for your sakes than for mine?

NORA   How so? Oh, I see. You think maybe Torvald could do something for you.

MRS. LINDE   Yes, that's what I thought.

NORA   And he will, Kristine! Just leave it to me; I'll bring it up so delicately —find something attractive to humor him with. Oh, I'm so eager to help you.

MRS. LINDE   How very kind of you, Nora, to be so concerned over me— doubly kind, considering you really know so little of life's burdens yourself.

NORA   I—? I know so little—?

MRS. LINDE   (*smiling*) Well, my heavens—a little needlework and such— Nora, you're just a child.

NORA   (*tossing her head and pacing the floor*) You don't have to act so superior.

MRS. LINDE   Oh?

NORA   You're just like the others. You all think I'm incapable of anything serious—

MRS. LINDE   Come now—

NORA   That I've never had to face the raw world.

MRS. LINDE   Nora dear, you've just been telling me all your troubles.

NORA   Hm! Trivia! (*Quietly*) I haven't told you the big thing.

MRS. LINDE   Big thing? What do you mean?

NORA   You look down on me so, Kristine, but you shouldn't. You're proud that you worked so long and hard for your mother.

MRS. LINDE   I don't look down on a soul. But it is true; I'm proud—and happy, too—to think it was given to me to make my mother's last days almost free of care.

NORA   And you're also proud thinking of what you've done for your brothers.

MRS. LINDE   I feel I've a right to be.

NORA   I agree. But listen to this, Kristine—I've also got something to be proud and happy for.

MRS. LINDE   I don't doubt it. But whatever do you mean?

NORA   Not so loud. What if Torvald heard! He mustn't, not for anything in the world. Nobody must know, Kristine. No one but you.

MRS. LINDE   But what is it, then?

NORA   Come here. (*Drawing her down beside her on the sofa*) It's true—I've also got something to be proud and happy for. I'm the one who saved Torvald's life.

MRS. LINDE   Saved—? Saved how?

NORA   I told you about the trip to Italy. Torvald never would have lived if he hadn't gone south—

MRS. LINDE   Of course, your father gave you the means—

NORA   (*smiling*) That's what Torvald and all the rest think, but—

MRS. LINDE   But—?

NORA   Papa didn't give us a pin. I was the one who raised the money.

MRS. LINDE   You? The whole amount?

NORA   Four thousand, eight hundred crowns. What do you say to that?

MRS. LINDE   But Nora, how was it possible? Did you win the lottery?

NORA   (*disdainfully*) The lottery? Pooh! No art to that.

MRS. LINDE   But where did you get it from then?

NORA   (*humming, with a mysterious smile*) Hmm, tra-la-la-la.

MRS. LINDE   Because you couldn't have borrowed it.

NORA   No? Why not?

MRS. LINDE   A wife can't borrow without her husband's consent.

NORA   (*tossing her head*) Oh, but a wife with a little business sense, a wife who knows how to manage—

MRS. LINDE   Nora, I simply don't understand—

NORA   You don't have to. Whoever said I *borrowed* the money? I could have gotten it other ways. (*Throwing herself back on the sofa*) I could have gotten it from some admirer or other. After all, a girl with my ravishing appeal—

MRS. LINDE   You lunatic.

NORA   I'll bet you're eaten up with curiosity, Kristine.

MRS. LINDE   Now listen here, Nora—you haven't done something indiscreet?

NORA   (*sitting up again*) Is it indiscreet to save your husband's life?

MRS. LINDE   I think it's indiscreet that without his knowledge you—

NORA   But that's the point: he mustn't know! My Lord, can't you understand? He mustn't ever know the close call he had. It was to *me* the doctors came to say his life was in danger—that nothing could save him but a stay in the south. Didn't I try strategy then! I began talking about how lovely it would be for me to travel abroad like other young wives; I begged and I cried; I told him please to remember my condition, to be kind and indulge me; and then I dropped a hint that he could easily take out a loan. But at that, Kristine, he nearly exploded. He said I was frivolous, and it was his duty as man of the house not to indulge me in whims and fancies—as I think he called them. Aha, I thought, now you'll just have to be saved—and that's when I saw my chance.

MRS. LINDE   And your father never told Torvald the money wasn't from him?

NORA   No, never. Papa died right about then. I'd considered bringing him into my secret and begging him never to tell. But he was too sick at the time —and then, sadly, it didn't matter.

MRS. LINDE   And you've never confided in your husband since?

NORA   For heaven's sake, no! Are you serious? He's so strict on that subject. Besides—Torvald, with all his masculine pride—how painfully humiliating for him if he ever found out he was in debt to me. That would just ruin our relationship. Our beautiful happy home would never be the same.

MRS. LINDE   Won't you ever tell him?

NORA   *(thoughtfully, half smiling)* Yes—maybe sometime, years from now, when I'm no longer so attractive. Don't laugh! I only mean when Torvald loves me less than now, when he stops enjoying my dancing and dressing up and reciting for him. Then it might be wise to have something in reserve—*(Breaking off)* How ridiculous! That'll never happen—Well, Kristine, what do you think of my big secret? I'm capable of something too, hm? You can imagine, of course, how this thing hangs over me. It really hasn't been easy meeting the payments on time. In the business world there's what they call quarterly interest and what they call amortization, and these are always so terribly hard to manage. I've had to skimp a little here and there, wherever I could, you know. I could hardly spare anything from my house allowance, because Torvald has to live well. I couldn't let the children go poorly dressed; whatever I got for them, I felt I had to use up completely—the darlings!

MRS. LINDE   Poor Nora, so it had to come out of your own budget, then?

NORA   Yes, of course. But I was the one most responsible, too. Every time Torvald gave me money for new clothes and such, I never used more than half; always bought the simplest, cheapest outfits. It was a godsend that everything looks so well on me that Torvald never noticed. But it did weigh me down at times, Kristine. It *is* such a joy to wear fine things. You understand.

MRS. LINDE   Oh, of course.

NORA   And then I found other ways of making money. Last winter I was lucky enough to get a lot of copying to do. I locked myself in and sat writing every evening till late in the night. Ah, I was tired so often, dead tired. But still it was wonderful fun, sitting and working like that, earning money. It was almost like being a man.

MRS. LINDE   But how much have you paid off this way so far?

NORA   That's hard to say, exactly. These accounts, you know, aren't easy to figure. I only know that I've paid out all I could scrape together. Time and again I haven't known where to turn. *(Smiling)* Then I'd sit here dreaming of a rich old gentleman who had fallen in love with me—

MRS. LINDE   What! Who is he?

NORA   Oh, really! And that he'd died, and when his will was opened, there in big letters it said, "All my fortune shall be paid over in cash, immediately, to that enchanting Mrs. Nora Helmer."

MRS. LINDE But Nora dear—who *was* this gentleman?

NORA Good grief, can't you understand? The old man never existed; that was only something I'd dream up time and again whenever I was at my wits' end for money. But it makes no difference now; the old fossil can go where he pleases for all I care; I don't need him or his will—because now I'm free. (*Jumping up*) Oh, how lovely to think of that, Kristine! Carefree! To know you're carefree, utterly carefree, to be able to romp and play with the children, and to keep up a beautiful, charming home—everything just the way Torvald likes it! And think, spring is coming, with big blue skies. Maybe we can travel a little then. Maybe I'll see the ocean again. Oh yes, it *is* so marvelous to live and be happy!

(*The front doorbell rings.*)

MRS. LINDE (*rising*) There's the bell. It's probably best that I go.

NORA No, stay. No one's expected. It must be for Torvald.

MAID (*from the hall doorway*) Excuse me, ma'am—there's a gentleman here to see Mr. Helmer, but I didn't know—since the doctor's with him—

NORA Who is the gentleman?

KROGSTAD (*from the doorway*) It's me, Mrs. Helmer.

(MRS. LINDE *starts and turns away toward the window.*)

NORA (*stepping toward him, tense, her voice a whisper*) You? What is it? Why do you want to speak to my husband?

KROGSTAD Bank business—after a fashion. I have a small job in the investment bank, and I hear now your husband is going to be our chief—

NORA In other words, it's—

KROGSTAD Just dry business, Mrs. Helmer. Nothing but that.

NORA Yes, then please be good enough to step into the study. (*She nods indifferently, as she sees him out by the hall door, then returns and begins stirring up the stove.*)

MRS. LINDE Nora—who was that man?

NORA That was a Mr. Krogstad—a lawyer.

MRS. LINDE Then it really was him.

NORA Do you know that person?

MRS. LINDE I did once—many years ago. For a time he was a law clerk in our town.

NORA Yes, he's been that.

MRS. LINDE How he's changed.

NORA I understand he had a very unhappy marriage.

MRS. LINDE He's a widower now.

NORA With a number of children. There now, it's burning. (*She closes the stove door and moves the rocker a bit to one side.*)

MRS. LINDE They say he has a hand in all kinds of business.

NORA Oh? That may be true; I wouldn't know. But let's not think about business. It's so dull.

(DR. RANK *enters from* HELMER'S *study.*)

RANK   (*still in the doorway*) No, no, really—I don't want to intrude, I'd just as soon talk a little while with your wife. (*Shuts the door, then notices* MRS. LINDE) Oh, beg pardon, I'm intruding here too.

NORA   No, not at all. (*Introducing him*) Dr. Rank, Mrs. Linde.

RANK   Well now, that's a name much heard in this house. I believe I passed the lady on the stairs as I came.

MRS. LINDE   Yes, I take the stairs very slowly. They're rather hard on me.

RANK   Uh-hm, some touch of internal weakness?

MRS. LINDE   More overexertion, I'd say.

RANK   Nothing else? Then you're probably here in town to rest up in a round of parties?

MRS. LINDE   I'm here to look for work.

RANK   Is that the best cure for overexertion?

MRS. LINDE   One has to live, Doctor.

RANK   Yes, there's a common prejudice to that effect.

NORA   Oh, come on, Dr. Rank—you really do want to live yourself.

RANK   Yes, I really do. Wretched as I am, I'll gladly prolong my torment indefinitely. All my patients feel like that. And it's quite the same, too, with the morally sick. Right at this moment there's one of those moral invalids in there with Helmer—

MRS. LINDE   (*softly*) Ah!

NORA   Who do you mean?

RANK   Oh, it's a lawyer, Krogstad, a type you wouldn't know. His character is rotten to the root—but even he began chattering all-importantly about how he had to *live.*

NORA   Oh? What did he want to talk to Torvald about?

RANK   I really don't know. I only heard something about the bank.

NORA   I didn't know that Krog—that this man Krogstad had anything to do with the bank.

RANK   Yes, he's gotten some kind of berth down there. (*To* MRS. LINDE) I don't know if you also have, in your neck of the woods, a type of person who scuttles about breathlessly, sniffing out hints of moral corruption, and then maneuvers his victim into some sort of key position where he can keep an eye on him. It's the healthy these days that are out in the cold.

MRS. LINDE   All the same, it's the sick who most need to be taken in.

RANK   (*with a shrug*) Yes, there we have it. That's the concept that's turning society into a sanatorium.

(NORA, *lost in her thoughts, breaks out into quiet laughter and claps her hands.*)

RANK   Why do you laugh at that? Do you have any real idea of what society is?

NORA   What do I care about dreary old society? I was laughing at something quite different—something terribly funny. Tell me, Doctor—is everyone who works in the bank dependent now on Torvald?

RANK   Is that what you find so terribly funny?

NORA (*smiling and humming*) Never mind, never mind! (*Pacing the floor*)
Yes, that's really immensely amusing: that we—that Torvald has so much power
now over all those people. (*Taking the bag out of her pocket*) Dr. Rank, a little
macaroon on that?

RANK See here, macaroons! I thought they were contraband here.

NORA Yes, but these are some that Kristine gave me.

MRS. LINDE What? I—?

NORA Now, now, don't be afraid. You couldn't possibly know that Torvald
had forbidden them. You see, he's worried they'll ruin my teeth. But hmp! Just
this once! Isn't that so, Dr. Rank? Help yourself! (*Puts a macaroon in his mouth*)
And you too, Kristine. And I'll also have one, only a little one—or two, at the
most. (*Walking about again*) Now I'm really tremendously happy. Now there's
just one last thing in the world that I have an enormous desire to do.

RANK Well! And what's that?

NORA It's something I have such a consuming desire to say so Torvald could
hear.

RANK And why can't you say it?

NORA I don't dare. It's quite shocking.

MRS. LINDE Shocking?

RANK Well, then it isn't advisable. But in front of us you certainly can.
What do you have such a desire to say so Torvald could hear?

NORA I have such a huge desire to say—to hell and be damned!

RANK Are you crazy?

MRS. LINDE My goodness, Nora!

RANK Go on, say it. Here he is.

NORA (*hiding the macaroon bag*) Shh, shh, shh!

(HELMER *comes in from his study, hat in hand, overcoat over his arm.*)

NORA (*going toward him*) Well, Torvald dear, are you through with him?

HELMER Yes, he just left.

NORA Let me introduce you—this is Kristine, who's arrived here in town.

HELMER Kristine—? I'm sorry, but I don't know—

NORA Mrs. Linde, Torvald dear. Mrs. Kristine Linde.

HELMER Of course. A childhood friend of my wife's, no doubt?

MRS. LINDE Yes, we knew each other in those days.

NORA And just think, she made the long trip down here in order to talk
with you.

HELMER What's this?

MRS. LINDE Well, not exactly—

NORA You see, Kristine is remarkably clever in office work, and so she's
terribly eager to come under a capable man's supervision and add more to what
she already knows—

HELMER Very wise, Mrs. Linde.

NORA And then when she heard that you'd become a bank manager—the
story was wired out to the papers—then she came in as fast as she could and
—Really, Torvald, for my sake you can do a little something for Kristine, can't
you?

HELMER   Yes, it's not at all impossible. Mrs. Linde, I suppose you're a widow?

MRS. LINDE   Yes.

HELMER   Any experience in office work?

MRS. LINDE   Yes, a good deal.

HELMER   Well, it's quite likely that I can make an opening for you—

NORA   (*clapping her hands*) You see, you see!

HELMER   You've come at a lucky moment, Mrs. Linde.

MRS. LINDE   Oh, how can I thank you?

HELMER   Not necessary. (*Putting his overcoat on*) But today you'll have to excuse me—

RANK   Wait, I'll go with you. (*He fetches his coat from the hall and warms it at the stove.*)

NORA   Don't stay out long, dear.

HELMER   An hour; no more.

NORA   Are you going too, Kristine?

MRS. LINDE   (*putting on her winter garments*) Yes, I have to see about a room now.

HELMER   Then perhaps we can all walk together.

NORA   (*helping her*) What a shame we're so cramped here, but it's quite impossible for us to—

MRS. LINDE   Oh, don't even think of it! Good-bye, Nora dear, and thanks for everything.

NORA   Good-bye for now. Of course you'll be back again this evening. And you too, Dr. Rank. What? If you're well enough? Oh, you've got to be! Wrap up tight now.

(*In a ripple of small talk the company moves out into the hall; children's voices are heard outside on the steps.*)

NORA   There they are! There they are! (*She runs to open the door. The children come in with their nurse,* ANNE-MARIE.) Come in, come in! (*Bends down and kisses them*) Oh, you darlings—! Look at them, Kristine. Aren't they lovely!

RANK   No loitering in the draft here.

HELMER   Come, Mrs. Linde—this place is unbearable now for anyone but mothers.

(DR. RANK, HELMER, *and* MRS. LINDE *go down the stairs.* ANNE-MARIE *goes into the living room with the children.* NORA *follows, after closing the hall door.*)

NORA   How fresh and strong you look. Oh, such red cheeks you have! Like apples and roses. (*The children interrupt her throughout the following.*) And it was so much fun? That's wonderful. Really? You pulled both Emmy and Bob on the sled? Imagine, all together! Yes, you're a clever boy, Ivar. Oh, let me hold her a bit, Anne-Marie. My sweet little doll baby! (*Takes the smallest from the nurse and dances with her*) Yes, yes, Mama will dance with Bob as well. What? Did you throw snowballs? Oh, if I'd only been there! No, don't bother, Anne-Marie—I'll undress them myself. Oh yes, let me. It's such fun. Go in and rest; you look half frozen. There's hot coffee waiting for you on the stove.

(*The nurse goes into the room to the left. Nora takes the children's winter things off, throwing them about, while the children talk to her all at once.*) Is that so? A big dog chased you? But it didn't bite? No, dogs never bite little, lovely doll babies. Don't peek in the packages, Ivar! What is it? Yes, wouldn't you like to know. No, no, it's an ugly something. Well? Shall we play? What shall we play? Hide-and-seek? Yes, let's play hide-and-seek. Bob must hide first. I must? Yes, let me hide first. (*Laughing and shouting, she and the children play in and out of the living room and the adjoining room to the right. At last* NORA *hides under the table. The children come storming in, search, but cannot find her, then hear her muffled laughter, dash over to the table, lift the cloth and find her. Wild shouting. She creeps forward as if to scare them. More shouts. Meanwhile, a knock at the hall door; no one has noticed it. Now the door half opens, and* KROGSTAD *appears. He waits a moment; the game goes on.*)

KROGSTAD   Beg pardon, Mrs. Helmer—

NORA   (*with a strangled cry, turning and scrambling to her knees*) Oh! what do you want?

KROGSTAD   Excuse me. The outer door was ajar; it must be someone forgot to shut it—

NORA   (*rising*) My husband isn't home, Mr. Krogstad.

KROGSTAD   I know that.

NORA   Yes—then what do you want here?

KROGSTAD   A word with you.

NORA   With—? (*To the children, quietly*) Go in to Anne-Marie. What? No, the strange man won't hurt Mama. When he's gone, we'll play some more. (*She leads the children into the room to the left and shuts the door after them. Then, tense and nervous*) You want to speak to me?

KROGSTAD   Yes, I want to.

NORA   Today? But it's not yet the first of the month—

KROGSTAD   No, it's Christmas Eve. It's going to be up to you how merry a Christmas you have.

NORA   What is it you want? Today I absolutely can't—

KROGSTAD   We won't talk about that till later. This is something else. You do have a moment to spare, I suppose?

NORA   Oh yes, of course—I do, except—

KROGSTAD   Good. I was sitting over at Olsen's Restaurant when I saw your husband go down the street—

NORA   Yes?

KROGSTAD   With a lady.

NORA   Yes. So?

KROGSTAD   If you'll pardon my asking: wasn't that lady a Mrs. Linde?

NORA   Yes.

KROGSTAD   Just now come into town?

NORA   Yes, today.

KROGSTAD   She's a good friend of yours?

NORA   Yes, she is. But I don't see—

KROGSTAD   I also knew her once.

NORA   I'm aware of that.

KROGSTAD   Oh? You know all about it. I thought so, Well, then let me ask you short and sweet: is Mrs. Linde getting a job in the bank?

NORA   What makes you think you can cross-examine me, Mr. Krogstad—you, one of my husband's employees? But since you ask, you might as well know—yes, Mrs. Linde's going to be taken on at the bank. And I'm the one who spoke for her, Mr. Krogstad. Now you know.

KROGSTAD   So I guessed right.

NORA   (*pacing up and down*) Oh, one does have a tiny bit of influence, I should hope. Just because I am a woman, don't think it means that—When one has a subordinate position, Mr. Krogstad, one really ought to be careful about pushing somebody who—hm—

KROGSTAD   Who has influence?

NORA   That's right.

KROGSTAD   (*in a different tone*) Mrs. Helmer, would you be good enough to use your influence on my behalf?

NORA   What? What do you mean?

KROGSTAD   Would you please make sure that I keep my subordinate position in the bank?

NORA   What does that mean? Who's thinking of taking away your position?

KROGSTAD   Oh, don't play the innocent with me. I'm quite aware that your friend would hardly relish the chance of running into me again; and I'm also aware now whom I can thank for being turned out.

NORA   But I promise you—

KROGSTAD   Yes, yes, yes, to the point: there's still time, and I'm advising you to use your influence to prevent it.

NORA   But Mr. Krogstad, I have absolutely no influence.

KROGSTAD   You haven't? I thought you were just saying—

NORA   You shouldn't take me so literally. I! How can you believe that I have any such influence over my husband?

KROGSTAD   Oh, I've known your husband from our student days. I don't think the great bank manager's more steadfast than any other married man.

NORA   You speak insolently about my husband, and I'll show you the door.

KROGSTAD   The lady has spirit.

NORA   I'm not afraid of you any longer. After New Year's, I'll soon be done with the whole business.

KROGSTAD   (*restraining himself*) Now listen to me, Mrs. Helmer. If necessary, I'll fight for my little job in the bank as if it were life itself.

NORA   Yes, so it seems.

KROGSTAD   It's not just a matter of income; that's the least of it. It's something else—All right, out with it! Look, this is the thing. You know, just like all the others, of course, that once, a good many years ago, I did something rather rash.

NORA   I've heard rumors to that effect.

KROGSTAD   The case never got into court; but all the same, every door was closed in my face from then on. So I took up those various activities you know about. I had to grab hold somewhere; and I dare say I haven't been among the worst. But now I want to drop all that. My boys are growing up. For their sakes, I'll have to win back as much respect as possible here in town. That job in the bank was like the first rung in my ladder. And now your husband wants to kick me right back down in the mud again.

NORA   But for heaven's sake, Mr. Krogstad, it's simply not in my power to help you.

KROGSTAD   That's because you haven't the will to—but I have the means to make you.

NORA   You certainly won't tell my husband that I owe you money?

KROGSTAD   Hm—what if I told him that?

NORA   That would be shameful of you. (*Nearly in tears*) This secret—my joy and my pride—that he should learn it in such a crude and disgusting way —learn it from you. You'd expose me to the most horrible unpleasantness—

KROGSTAD   Only unpleasantness?

NORA   (*vehemently*) But go on and try. It'll turn out the worst for you, because then my husband will really see what a crook you are, and then you'll *never* be able to hold your job.

KROGSTAD   I asked if it was just domestic unpleasantness you were afraid of?

NORA   If my husband finds out, then of course he'll pay what I owe at once, and then we'd be through with you for good.

KROGSTAD   (*a step closer*) Listen, Mrs. Helmer—you've either got a very bad memory, or else no head at all for business. I'd better put you a little more in touch with the facts.

NORA   What do you mean?

KROGSTAD   When your husband was sick, you came to me for a loan of four thousand, eight hundred crowns.

NORA   Where else could I go?

KROGSTAD   I promised to get you that sum—

NORA   And you got it.

KROGSTAD   I promised to get you that sum, on certain conditions. You were so involved in your husband's illness, and so eager to finance your trip, that I guess you didn't think out all the details. It might just be a good idea to remind you. I promised you the money on the strength of a note I drew up.

NORA   Yes, and that I signed.

KROGSTAD   Right. But at the bottom I added some lines for your father to guarantee the loan. He was supposed to sign down there.

NORA   Supposed to? He did sign.

KROGSTAD   I left the date blank. In other words, your father would have dated his signature himself. Do you remember that?

NORA   Yes, I think—

KROGSTAD   Then I gave you the note for you to mail to your father. Isn't that so?

NORA   Yes.

KROGSTAD   And naturally you sent it at once—because only some five, six days later you brought me the note, properly signed. And with that, the money was yours.

NORA   Well, then; I've made my payments regularly, haven't I?

KROGSTAD   More or less. But—getting back to the point—those were hard times for you then, Mrs. Helmer.

NORA   Yes, they were.

KROGSTAD   Your father was very ill, I believe.

NORA   He was near the end.

KROGSTAD   He died soon after?

NORA   Yes.

KROGSTAD   Tell me, Mrs. Helmer, do you happen to recall the date of your father's death? The day of the month, I mean.

NORA   Papa died the twenty-ninth of September.

KROGSTAD   That's quite correct; I've already looked into that. And now we come to a curious thing—*(Taking out a paper)* which I simply cannot comprehend.

NORA   Curious thing? I don't know—

KROGSTAD   This is the curious thing: that your father co-signed the note for your loan three days after his death.

NORA   How—? I don't understand.

KROGSTAD   Your father died the twenty-ninth of September. But look. Here your father dated his signature October second. Isn't that curious, Mrs. Helmer? (NORA *is silent.*) Can you explain it to me? (NORA *remains silent.*) It's also remarkable that the words "October second" and the year aren't written in your father's hand, but rather in one that I think I know. Well, it's easy to understand. Your father forgot perhaps to date his signature, and then someone or other added it, a bit sloppily, before anyone knew of his death. There's nothing wrong in that. It all comes down to the signature. And there's no question about *that,* Mrs. Helmer. It really *was* your father who signed his own name here, wasn't it?

NORA   *(after a short silence, throwing her head back and looking squarely at him)* No, it wasn't. I signed Papa's name.

KROGSTAD   Wait, now—are you fully aware that this is a dangerous confession?

NORA   Why? You'll soon get your money.

KROGSTAD   Let me ask you a question—why didn't you send the paper to your father?

NORA   That was impossible. Papa was so sick. If I'd asked him for his signature, I also would have had to tell him what the money was for. But I couldn't tell him, sick as he was, that my husband's life was in danger. That was just impossible.

KROGSTAD   Then it would have been better if you'd given up the trip abroad.

NORA   I couldn't possibly. The trip was to save my husband's life. I couldn't give that up.

KROGSTAD   But didn't you ever consider that this was a fraud against me?

NORA   I couldn't let myself be bothered by that. You weren't any concern of mine. I couldn't stand you, with all those cold complications you made, even though you knew how badly off my husband was.

KROGSTAD   Mrs. Helmer, obviously you haven't the vaguest idea of what you've involved yourself in. But I can tell you this: it was nothing more and nothing worse than I once did—and it wrecked my whole reputation.

NORA   You? Do you expect me to believe that you ever acted bravely to save your wife's life?

KROGSTAD   Laws don't inquire into motives.

NORA   Then they must be very poor laws.

KROGSTAD   Poor or not—if I introduce this paper in court, you'll be judged according to law.

NORA   This I refuse to believe. A daughter hasn't a right to protect her dying father from anxiety and care? A wife hasn't a right to save her husband's life? I don't know much about laws, but I'm sure that somewhere in the books these things are allowed. And you don't know anything about it—you who practice the law? You must be an awful lawyer, Mr. Krogstad.

KROGSTAD   Could be. But business—the kind of business we two are mixed up in—don't you think I know about that? All right. Do what you want now. But I'm telling you *this:* if I get shoved down a second time, you're going to keep me company.   (*He bows and goes out through the hall.*)

NORA   (*pensive for a moment, then tossing her head*) Oh, really! Trying to frighten me! I'm not so silly as all that. (*Begins gathering up the children's clothes, but soon stops*) But—? No, but that's impossible! I did it out of love.

THE CHILDREN   (*in the doorway, left*) Mama, that strange man's gone out the door.

NORA   Yes, yes, I know it. But don't tell anyone about the strange man. Do you hear. Not even Papa!

THE CHILDREN   No, Mama. But now will you play again?

NORA   No, not now.

THE CHILDREN   Oh, but Mama, you promised.

NORA   Yes, but I can't now. Go inside; I have too much to do. Go in, go in, my sweet darlings. (*She herds them gently back in the room and shuts the door after them. Settling on the sofa, she takes up a piece of embroidery and makes some stitches, but soon stops abruptly.*) No! (*Throws the work aside, rises, goes to the hall door and calls out*) Helene! Let me have the tree in here. (*Goes to the table, left, opens the table drawer, and stops again*) No, but that's utterly impossible!

MAID   (*with the Christmas tree*) Where should I put it, Ma'am?

NORA   There. The middle of the floor.

MAID   Should I bring anything else?

NORA   No, thanks. I have what I need.

(*The* MAID, *who has set the tree down, goes out.*)

NORA   (*absorbed in trimming the tree*) Candles here—and flowers here. That terrible creature! Talk, talk, talk! There's nothing to it at all. The tree's going to be lovely. I'll do anything to please you, Torvald. I'll sing for you, dance for you—

(HELMER *comes in from the hall, with a sheaf of papers under his arm.*)

NORA   Oh! You're back so soon?

HELMER   Yes. Has anyone been here?

NORA   Here? No.

HELMER   That's odd. I saw Krogstad leaving the front door.

NORA   So? Oh yes, that's true. Krogstad was here a moment.

HELMER   Nora, I can see by your face that he's been here, begging you to put in a good word for him.

NORA   Yes.

HELMER   And it was supposed to seem like your own idea? You were to hide it from me that he'd been here. He asked you that, too, didn't he?

NORA   Yes, Torvald, but—

HELMER   Nora, Nora, and you could fall for that? Talk with that sort of person and promise him anything? And then in the bargain, tell me an untruth.

NORA   An untruth—?

HELMER   Didn't you say that no one had been here? (*Wagging his finger*) My little songbird must never do that again. A songbird needs a clean beak to warble with. No false notes. (*Putting his arm about her waist*) That's the way it should be, isn't it? Yes, I'm sure of it. (*Releasing her*) And so, enough of that. (*Sitting by the stove*) Ah, how snug and cozy it is here. (*Leafing among his papers*)

NORA   (*busy with the tree, after a short pause*) Torvald!

HELMER   Yes.

NORA   I'm so much looking forward to the Stenborg's costume party, day after tomorrow.

HELMER   And I can't wait to see what you'll surprise me with.

NORA   Oh, that stupid business.

HELMER   What?

NORA   I can't find anything that's right. Everything seems so ridiculous, so inane.

HELMER   So my little Nora's come to *that* recognition?

NORA   (*going behind his chair, her arms resting on its back*) Are you very busy, Torvald?

HELMER   Oh—

NORA   What papers are those?

HELMER   Bank matters.

NORA   Already?

HELMER   I've gotten full authority from the retiring management to make all necessary changes in personnel and procedure. I'll need Christmas week for that. I want to have everything in order by New Year's.

NORA   So that was the reason this poor Krogstad—

HELMER   Hm.

NORA   (*still leaning on the chair and slowly stroking the nape of his neck*) If you weren't so very busy, I would have asked you an enormous favor, Torvald.

HELMER   Let's hear. What is it?

NORA   You know, there isn't anyone who has your good taste—and I want so much to look well at the costume party. Torvald, couldn't you take over and decide what I should be and plan my costume?

HELMER   Ah, is my stubborn little creature calling for a lifeguard?

NORA   Yes, Torvald, I can't get anywhere without your help.

HELMER   All right—I'll think it over. We'll hit on something.

NORA   Oh, how sweet of you. (*Goes to the tree again. Pause.*) Aren't the red flowers pretty—? But tell me, was it really such a crime that this Krogstad committed?

HELMER   Forgery. Do you have any idea what that means?

NORA   Couldn't he have done it out of need?

HELMER   Yes, or thoughtlessness, like so many others. I'm not so heartless that I'd condemn a man categorically for just one mistake.

NORA   No, of course not, Torvald!

HELMER   Plenty of men have redeemed themselves by openly confessing their crimes and taking their punishments.

NORA   Punishment—?

HELMER   But now Krogstad didn't go that way. He got himself out by sharp practices, and that's the real cause of his moral breakdown.

NORA   Do you really think that would—?

HELMER   Just imagine how a man with that sort of guilt in him has to lie and cheat and deceive on all sides, has to wear a mask even with the nearest and dearest he has, even with his own wife and children. And with the children, Nora —that's where it's most horrible.

NORA   Why?

HELMER   Because that kind of atmosphere of lies infects the whole life of a home. Every breath the children take in is filled with the terms of something degenerate.

NORA   (*coming closer behind him*) Are you sure of that?

HELMER   Oh, I've seen it often enough as a lawyer. Almost everyone who goes bad early in life has a mother who's a chronic liar.

NORA   Why just—the mother?

HELMER   It's usually the mother's influence that's dominant, but the father's works in the same way, of course. Every lawyer is quite familiar with it. And still this Krogstad's been going home year in, year out, poisoning his own children with lies and pretense; that's why I call him morally lost. (*Reaching his hands out toward her*) So my sweet little Nora must promise me never to plead his cause. Your hand on it. Come, come, what's this? Give me your hand. There, now. All settled. I can tell you it'd be impossible for me to work alongside of him. I literally feel physically revolted when I'm anywhere near such a person.

NORA   (*withdraws her hand and goes to the other side of the Christmas tree*) How hot it is here! And I've got so much to do.

HELMER   (*getting up and gathering his papers*) Yes, and I have to think about getting some of these read through before dinner. I'll think about your costume, too. And something to hang on the tree in gilt paper, I may even see about that. (*Putting his hand on her head*) Oh you, my darling little songbird.

(*He goes into his study and closes the door after him.*)

NORA   (*softly, after a silence*) Oh, really! it isn't so. It's impossible. It must be impossible.

ANNE-MARIE   (*in the doorway, left*) The children are begging so hard to come in to Mama.

NORA   No, no, no, don't let them in to me! You stay with them, Anne-Marie.

ANNE-MARIE   Of course, Ma'am. (*Closes the door*)

NORA   (*pale with terror*) Hurt my children—! Poison my home? (*A moment's pause; then she tosses her head.*) That's not true. Never. Never in all the world.

ACT II

Same room. Beside the piano the Christmas tree now stands stripped of ornament, burned-down candle stubs on its ragged branches. NORA's *street clothes lie on the sofa.* NORA, *alone in the room, moves restlessly about; at last she stops at the sofa and picks up her coat.*

NORA   (*dropping the coat again*) Someone's coming! (*Goes toward the door, listens*) No—there's no one. Of course—nobody's coming today, Christmas Day—or tomorrow, either. But maybe—(*Opens the door and looks out*) No, nothing in the mailbox. Quite empty. (*Coming forward*) What nonsense! He won't do anything serious. Nothing terrible could happen. It's impossible. Why, I have three small children.

(ANNE-MARIE, *with a large carton, comes in from the room to the left.*)

ANNE-MARIE   Well, at last I found the box with the masquerade clothes.
NORA   Thanks. Put it on the table.
ANNE-MARIE   (*does so*) But they're all pretty much of a mess.
NORA   Ahh! I'd love to rip them in a million pieces!
ANNE-MARIE   Oh, mercy, they can be fixed right up. Just a little patience.
NORA   Yes, I'll go get Mrs. Linde to help me.
ANNE-MARIE   Out again now? In this nasty weather? Miss Nora will catch cold—get sick.
NORA   Oh, worse things could happen—How are the children?
ANNE-MARIE   The poor mites are playing with their Christmas presents, but—
NORA   Do they ask for me much?
ANNE-MARIE   They're so used to having Mama around, you know.
NORA   Yes, but Anne-Marie, I *can't* be together with them as much as I was.
ANNE-MARIE   Well, small children get used to anything.
NORA   You think so? Do you think they'd forget their mother if she was gone for good?
ANNE-MARIE   Oh, mercy—gone for good!
NORA   Wait, tell me, Anne-Marie—I've wondered so often—how could you ever have the heart to give your child over to strangers?
ANNE-MARIE   But I had to, you know, to become little Nora's nurse.
NORA   Yes, but how could you *do* it?
ANNE-MARIE   When I could get such a good place? A girl who's poor and who's gotten in trouble is glad enough for that. Because that slippery fish, he didn't do a thing for me, you know.
NORA   But your daughter's surely forgotten you.
ANNE-MARIE   Oh, she certainly has not. She's written to me, both when she was confirmed and when she was married.
NORA   (*clasping her about the neck*) You old Anne-Marie, you were a good mother for me when I was little.
ANNE-MARIE   Poor little Nora, with no other mother but me.

NORA   And if the babies didn't have one, then I know that you'd—What silly talk! (*Opening the carton*) Go in to them. Now I'll have to—Tomorrow you can see how lovely I'll look.

ANNE-MARIE   Oh, there won't be anyone at the party as lovely as Miss Nora.
(*She goes off into the room, left.*)

NORA   (*begins unpacking the box, but soon throws it aside*) Oh, if I dared to go out. If only nobody would come. If only nothing would happen here while I'm out. What craziness—nobody's coming. Just don't think. This muff—needs a brushing. Beautiful gloves, beautiful gloves. Let it go. Let it go! One, two, three, four, five, six—(*With a cry*) Oh, there they are! (*Poises to move toward the door, but remains irresolutely standing.* MRS. LINDE *enters from the hall, where she has removed her street clothes.*)

NORA   Oh, it's you, Kristine. There's no one else out there? How good that you've come.

MRS. LINDE   I hear you were up asking for me.

NORA   Yes, I just stopped by. There's something you really can help me with. Let's get settled on the sofa. Look, there's going to be a costume party tomorrow evening at the Stenborgs' right above us, and now Torvald wants me to go as a Neapolitan peasant girl and dance the tarantella that I learned in Capri.

MRS. LINDE   Really, you are giving a whole performance?

NORA   Torvald says yes, I should. See, here's the dress. Torvald had it made for me down there; but now it's all so tattered that I just don't know—

MRS. LINDE   Oh, we'll fix that up in no time. It's nothing more than the trimmings—they're a bit loose here and there. Needle and thread? Good, now we have what we need.

NORA   Oh, how sweet of you!

MRS. LINDE   (*sewing*) So you'll be in disguise tomorrow, Nora. You know what? I'll stop by then for a moment and have a look at you all dressed up. But listen, I've absolutely forgotten to thank you for that pleasant evening yesterday.

NORA   (*getting up and walking about*) I don't think it was as pleasant as usual yesterday. You should have come to town a bit sooner, Kristine—Yes, Torvald really knows how to give a home elegance and charm.

MRS. LINDE   And you do, too, if you ask me. You're not your father's daughter for nothing. But tell me, is Dr. Rank always so down in the mouth as yesterday?

NORA   No, that was quite an exception. But he goes around critically ill all the time—tuberculosis of the spine, poor man. You know, his father was a disgusting thing who kept mistresses and so on—and that's why the son's been sickly from birth.

MRS. LINDE   (*lets her sewing fall to her lap*) But my dearest Nora, how do you know about such things?

NORA   (*walking more jauntily*) Hmp! When you've had three children, then you've had a few visits from—women who know something of medicine, and they tell you this and that.

MRS. LINDE   (*resumes sewing; a short pause*) Does Dr. Rank come here every day?

NORA   Every blessed day. He's Torvald's best friend from childhood, and *my* good friend, too. Dr. Rank almost belongs to this house.

MRS. LINDE   But tell me—is he quite sincere? I mean, doesn't he rather enjoy flattering people?

NORA   Just the opposite. Why do you think that?

MRS. LINDE   When you introduced us yesterday, he was proclaiming that he'd often heard my name in this house; but later I noticed that your husband hadn't the slightest idea who I really was. So how could Dr. Rank—?

NORA   But it's all true, Kristine. You see, Torvald loves me beyond words, and, as he puts it, he'd like to keep me all to himself. For a long time he'd almost be jealous if I even mentioned any of my old friends back home. So of course I dropped that. But with Dr. Rank I talk a lot about such things, because he likes hearing about them.

MRS. LINDE   Now listen, Nora; in many ways you're still like a child. I'm a good deal older than you, with a little more experience. I'll tell you something; you ought to put an end to all this with Dr. Rank.

NORA   What should I put an end to?

MRS. LINDE   Both parts of it, I think. Yesterday you said something about a rich admirer who'd provide you with money—

NORA   Yes, one who doesn't exist—worse luck. So?

MRS. LINDE   Is Dr. Rank well off?

NORA   Yes, he is.

MRS. LINDE   With no dependents?

NORA   No, no one. But—

MRS. LINDE   And he's over here every day?

NORA   Yes, I told you that.

MRS. LINDE   How can a man of such refinement be so grasping?

NORA   I don't follow you at all.

MRS. LINDE   Now don't try to hide it, Nora. You think I can't guess who loaned you the forty-eight hundred crowns?

NORA   Are you out of your mind? How could you think of such a thing! A friend of ours, who comes here every single day. What an intolerable situation that would have been!

MRS. LINDE   Then it really wasn't him.

NORA   No, absolutely not. It never even crossed my mind for a moment— And he had nothing to lend in those days; his inheritance came later.

MRS. LINDE   Well, I think that was a stroke of luck for you, Nora dear.

NORA   No, it never would have occurred to me to ask Dr. Rank—Still, I'm quite sure that if I had asked him—

MRS. LINDE   Which you won't, of course.

NORA   No, of course not. I can't see that I'd ever need to. But I'm quite positive that if I talked to Dr. Rank—

MRS. LINDE   Behind your husband's back?

NORA   I've got to clear up this other thing; *that's* also behind his back. I've *got* to clear it all up.

MRS. LINDE   Yes, I was saying that yesterday, but—

NORA   (*pacing up and down*) A man handles these problems so much better than a woman—

MRS. LINDE One's husband does, yes.

NORA Nonsense. (*Stopping*) When you pay everything you owe, then you get your note back, right?

MRS. LINDE Yes, naturally.

NORA And can rip it into a million pieces and burn it up—that filthy scrap of paper!

MRS. LINDE (*looking hard at her, laying her sewing aside, and rising slowly*) Nora, you're hiding something from me.

NORA You can see it in my face?

MRS. LINDE Something's happened to you since yesterday morning. Nora, what is it?

NORA (*hurrying toward her*) Kristine! (*Listening*) Shh! Torvald's home. Look, go in with the children a while. Torvald can't bear all this snipping and stitching. Let Anne-Marie help you.

MRS. LINDE (*gathering up some of the things*) All right, but I'm not leaving here until we've talked this out. (*She disappears into the room, left, as* TORVALD *enters from the hall.*)

NORA Oh, how I've been waiting for you, Torvald dear.

HELMER Was that the dressmaker?

NORA No, that was Kristine. She's helping me fix up my costume. You know, it's going to be quite attractive.

HELMER Yes, wasn't that a bright idea I had?

NORA Brilliant! But then wasn't I good as well to give in to you?

HELMER Good—because you give in to your husband's judgment? All right, you little goose, I know you didn't mean it like that. But I won't disturb you. You'll want to have a fitting, I suppose.

NORA And you'll be working?

HELMER Yes. (*Indicating a bundle of papers*) See. I've been down to the bank. (*Starts toward his study*)

NORA Torvald.

HELMER (*stops*) Yes.

NORA If your little squirrel begged you, with all her heart and soul, for something—?

HELMER What's that?

NORA Then would you do it?

HELMER First, naturally, I'd have to know what it was.

NORA Your squirrel would scamper about and do tricks, if you'd only be sweet and give in.

HELMER Out with it.

NORA Your lark would be singing high and low in every room—

HELMER Come on, she does that anyway.

NORA I'd be a wood nymph and dance for you in the moonlight.

HELMER Nora—don't tell me it's that same business from this morning?

NORA (*coming closer*) Yes, Torvald, I beg you, please!

HELMER And you actually have the nerve to drag that up again?

NORA Yes, yes, you've got to give in to me; you have to let Krogstad keep his job in the bank.

HELMER My dear Nora, I've slated his job for Mrs. Linde.

NORA   That's awfully kind of you. But you could just fire another clerk instead of Krogstad.

HELMER   This is the most incredible stubbornness! Because you go and give an impulsive promise to speak up for him, I'm expected to—

NORA   That's not the reason, Torvald. It's for your own sake. That man does writing for the worst papers; you said it yourself. He could do you any amount of harm. I'm scared to death of him—

HELMER   Ah, I understand. It's the old memories haunting you.

NORA   What do you mean by that?

HELMER   Of course, you're thinking about your father.

NORA   Yes, all right. Just remember how those nasty gossips wrote in the papers about Papa and slandered him so cruelly. I think they'd have had him dismissed if the department hadn't sent you up to investigate, and if you hadn't been so kind and open-minded toward him.

HELMER   My dear Nora, there's a notable difference between your father and me. Your father's official career was hardly above reproach. But mine is; and I hope it'll stay that way as long as I hold my position.

NORA   Oh, who can ever tell what vicious minds can invent? We could be so snug and happy now in our quiet, carefree home—you and I and the children, Torvald! That's why I'm pleading with you so—

HELMER   And just by pleading for him you make it impossible for me to keep him on. It's already known at the bank that I'm firing Krogstad. What if it's rumored around now that the new bank manager was vetoed by his wife—

NORA   Yes, what then—?

HELMER   Oh yes—as long as your little bundle of stubbornness gets her way—! I should go and make myself ridiculous in front of the whole office —give people the idea I can be swayed by all kinds of outside pressure. Oh, you can bet I'd feel the effects of that soon enough! Besides—there's something that rules Krogstad right out at the bank as long as I'm the manager.

NORA   What's that?

HELMER   His moral failings I could maybe overlook if I had to—

NORA   Yes, Torvald, why not?

HELMER   And I hear he's quite efficient on the job. But he was a crony of mine back in my teens—one of those rash friendships that crop up again and again to embarrass you later in life. Well, I might as well say it straight out: we're on a first-name basis. And that tactless fool makes no effort at all to hide it in front of others. Quite the contrary—he thinks that entitles him to take a familiar air around me, and so every other second he comes booming out with his "Yes, Torvald!" and "Sure thing, Torvald!" I tell you, it's been excruciating for me. He's out to make my place in the bank unbearable.

NORA   Torvald, you can't be serious about all this.

HELMER   Oh no? Why not?

NORA   Because these are such petty considerations.

HELMER   What are you saying? Petty? You think I'm petty!

NORA   No, just the opposite, Torvald dear. That's exactly why—

HELMER   Never mind. You call my motives petty; then I might as well be just that. Petty! All right! We'll put a stop to this for good. (*Goes to the hall door and calls*) Helene!

NORA   What do you want?

HELMER   (*searching among his papers*) A decision. (*The* MAID *comes in.*) Look here; take this letter; go out with it at once. Get hold of a messenger and have him deliver it. Quick now. It's already addressed. Wait, here's some money.

MAID   Yes, sir. (*She leaves with the letter.*)

HELMER   (*straightening his papers*) There, now, little Miss Willful.

NORA   (*breathlessly*) Torvald, what was that letter?

HELMER   Krogstad's notice.

NORA   Call it back, Torvald! There's still time. Oh, Torvald, call it back! Do it for my sake—for your sake, for the children's sake! Do you hear, Torvald; do it! You don't know how this can harm us.

HELMER   Too late.

NORA   Yes, too late.

HELMER   Nora dear, I can forgive you this panic, even though basically you're insulting me. Yes, you are! Or isn't it an insult to think that I should be afraid of a courtroom hack's revenge? But I forgive you anyway, because this shows so beautifully how much you love me. (*Takes her in his arms*) This is the way it should be, my darling Nora. Whatever comes, you'll see: when it really counts, I have strength and courage enough as a man to take on the whole weight myself.

NORA   (*terrified*) What do you mean by that?

HELMER   The whole weight, I said.

NORA   (*resolutely*) No, never in all the world.

HELMER   Good. So we'll share it, Nora, as man and wife. That's as it should be. (*Fondling her*) Are you happy now? There, there, there—not these frightened dove's eyes. It's nothing at all but empty fantasies—Now you should run through your tarantella and practice your tambourine. I'll go to the inner office and shut both doors, so I won't hear a thing; you can make all the noise you like. (*Turning in the doorway*) And when Rank comes, just tell him where he can find me. (*He nods to her and goes with his papers into the study, closing the door.*)

NORA   (*standing as though rooted, dazed with fright, in a whisper*) He really could do it. He will do it. He'll do it in spite of everything. No, not that, never, never! Anything but that! Escape! A way out—(*The doorbell rings.*) Dr. Rank! Anything but that! Anything, whatever it is! (*Her hands pass over her face, smoothing it; she pulls herself together, goes over and opens the hall door.* DR. RANK *stands outside, hanging his fur coat up. During the following scene, it begins getting dark.*)

NORA   Hello, Dr. Rank. I recognized your ring. But you mustn't go in to Torvald yet; I believe he's working.

RANK   And you?

NORA   For you, I always have an hour to spare—you know that. (*He has entered, and she shuts the door after him.*)

RANK   Many thanks. I'll make use of these hours while I can.

NORA   What do you mean by that? While you can?

RANK   Does that disturb you?

NORA   Well, it's such an odd phrase. Is anything going to happen?

RANK   What's going to happen is what I've been expecting so long—but I honestly didn't think it would come so soon.

NORA   (*gripping his arm*) What is it you've found out? Dr. Rank, you have to tell me!

RANK   (*sitting by the stove*) It's all over with me. There's nothing to be done about it.

NORA   (*breathing easier*) Is it you—then—?

RANK   Who else? There's no point in lying to one's self. I'm the most miserable of all my patients, Mrs. Helmer. These past few days I've been auditing my internal accounts. Bankrupt! Within a month I'll probably be laid out and rotting in the churchyard.

NORA   Oh, what a horrible thing to say.

RANK   The thing itself is horrible. But the worst of it is all the other horror before it's over. There's only one final examination left; when I'm finished with that, I'll know about when my disintegration will begin. There's something I want to say. Helmer with his sensitivity has such a sharp distaste for anything ugly. I don't want him near my sickroom.

NORA   Oh, but Dr. Rank—

RANK   I won't have him in there. Under no condition. I'll lock my door to him—As soon as I'm completely sure of the worst, I'll send you my calling card marked with a black cross, and you'll know then the wreck has started to come apart.

NORA   No, today you're completely unreasonable. And I wanted you so much to be in a really good humor.

RANK   With death up my sleeve? And then to suffer this way for somebody else's sins. Is there any justice in that? And in every single family, in some way or another, this inevitable retribution of nature goes on—

NORA   (*her hands pressed over her ears*) Oh, stuff! Cheer up! Please—be gay!

RANK   Yes, I'd just as soon laugh at it all. My poor, innocent spine, serving time for my father's gay army days.

NORA   (*by the table, left*) He was so infatuated with asparagus tips and *pâté de foie gras,* wasn't that it?

RANK   Yes—and with truffles.

NORA   Truffles, yes. And then with oysters, I suppose?

RANK   Yes, tons of oysters, naturally.

NORA   And then the port and champagne to go with it. It's so sad that all these delectable things have to strike at our bones.

RANK   Especially when they strike at the unhappy bones that never shared in the fun.

NORA   Ah, that's the saddest of all.

RANK   (*looks searchingly at her*) Hm.

NORA   (*after a moment*) Why did you smile?

RANK   No, it was you who laughed.

NORA   No, it was you who smiled, Dr. Rank!

RANK   (*getting up*) You're even a bigger tease than I'd thought.

NORA   I'm full of wild ideas today.

RANK   That's obvious.

NORA   (*putting both hands on his shoulders*) Dear, dear Dr. Rank, you'll never die for Torvald and me.

RANK   Oh, that loss you'll easily get over. Those who go away are soon forgotten.

NORA   (*looks fearfully at him*) You believe that?

RANK   One makes new connections, and then——

NORA   Who makes new connections?

RANK   Both you and Torvald will when I'm gone. I'd say you're well under way already. What was that Mrs. Linde doing here last evening?

NORA   Oh, come—you can't be jealous of poor Kristine?

RANK   Oh yes, I am. She'll be my successor here in the house. When I'm down under, that woman will probably——

NORA   Shh! Not so loud. She's right in there.

RANK   Today as well. So you see.

NORA   Only to sew on my dress. Good gracious, how unreasonable you are. (*Sitting on the sofa*) Be nice now, Dr. Rank. Tomorrow you'll see how beautifully I'll dance, and you can imagine then that I'm dancing only for you—yes, and of course for Torvald, too—that's understood. (*Takes various items out of the carton*) Dr. Rank, sit over here and I'll show you something.

RANK   (*sitting*) What's that?

NORA   Look here. Look.

RANK   Silk stockings.

NORA   Flesh-colored. Aren't they lovely? Now it's so dark here, but tomorrow—No, no, no, just look at the feet. Oh well, you might as well look at the rest.

RANK   Hm——

NORA   Why do you look so critical? Don't you believe they'll fit?

RANK   I've never had any chance to form an opinion on that.

NORA   (*glancing at him a moment*) Shame on you. (*Hits him lightly on the ear with the stockings*) That's for you. (*Puts them away again*)

RANK   And what other splendors am I going to see now?

NORA   Not the least bit more, because you've been naughty. (*She hums a little and rummages among her things.*)

RANK   (*after a short silence*) When I sit here together with you like this, completely easy and open, then I don't know—I simply can't imagine—whatever would have become of me if I'd never come into this house.

NORA   (*smiling*) Yes, I really think you feel completely at ease with us.

RANK   (*more quietly, staring straight ahead*) And then to have to go away from it all——

NORA   Nonsense, you're not going away.

RANK   (*his voice unchanged*)——and not even be able to leave some poor show of gratitude behind, scarcely a fleeting regret—no more than a vacant place that anyone can fill.

NORA   And if I asked you now for——? No——

RANK   For what?

NORA   For a great proof of your friendship——

RANK   Yes, yes?

NORA   No, I mean—for an exceptionally big favor——

RANK   Would you really, for once, make me so happy?

NORA   Oh, you haven't the vaguest idea what it is.

RANK   All right, then tell me.

NORA   No, but I can't, Dr. Rank—it's all out of reason. It's advice and help, too—and a favor—

RANK   So much the better. I can't fathom what you're hinting at. Just speak out. Don't you trust me?

NORA   Of course. More than anyone else. You're my best and truest friend, I'm sure. That's why I want to talk to you. All right, then, Dr. Rank: there's something you can help me prevent. You know how deeply, how inexpressibly dearly Torvald loves me; he'd never hesitate a second to give up his life for me.

RANK   *(leaning close to her)* Nora—do you think he's the only one—

NORA   *(with a slight start)* Who—?

RANK   Who'd gladly give up his life for you.

NORA   *(heavily)* I see.

RANK   I swore to myself you should know this before I'm gone. I'll never find a better chance. Yes, Nora, now you know. And also you know now that you can trust me beyond anyone else.

NORA   *(rising, natural and calm)* Let me by.

RANK   *(making room for her, but still sitting)* Nora—

NORA   *(in the hall doorway)* Helene, bring the lamp in. *(Goes over to the stove)* Ah, dear Dr. Rank, that was really mean of you.

RANK   *(getting up)* That I've loved you just as deeply as somebody else? Was *that* mean?

NORA   No, but that you came out and told me. That was quite unnecessary—

RANK   What do you mean? Have you known—?

(The MAID *comes in with the lamp, sets it on the table, and goes out again.)*

RANK   Nora—Mrs. Helmer—I'm asking you: have you known about it?

NORA   Oh, how can I tell what I know or don't know? Really, I don't know what to say—Why did you have to be so clumsy, Dr. Rank! Everything was so good.

RANK   Well, in any case, you now have the knowledge that my body and soul are at your command. So won't you speak out?

NORA   *(Looking at him)* After that?

RANK   Please, just let me know what it is.

NORA   You can't know anything now.

RANK   I have to. You mustn't punish me like this. Give me the chance to do whatever is humanly possible for you.

NORA   Now there's nothing you can do for me. Besides, actually, I don't need any help. You'll see—it's only my fantasies. That's what it is. Of course! *(Sits in the rocker, looks at him, and smiles)* What a nice one you are, Dr. Rank. Aren't you a little bit ashamed, now that the lamp is here?

RANK   No, not exactly. But perhaps I'd better go—for good?

NORA   No, you certainly can't do that. You must come here just as you always have. You know Torvald can't do without you.

RANK   Yes, but *you?*

NORA   You know how much I enjoy it when you're here.

RANK   That's precisely what threw me off. You're a mystery to me. So many times I've felt you'd almost rather be with me than with Helmer.

NORA   Yes—you see, there are some people that one loves most and other people that one would almost prefer being with.

RANK   Yes, there's something to that.

NORA   When I was back home, of course I loved Papa most. But I always thought it was so much fun when I could sneak down to the maids' quarters, because they never tried to improve me, and it was always so amusing, the way they talked to each other.

RANK   Aha, so it's *their* place that I've filled.

NORA   (*jumping up and going to him*) Oh, dear sweet Dr. Rank, that's not what I meant at all. But you can understand that with Torvald it's just the same as with Papa—

(*The* MAID *enters from the hall.*)

MAID   Ma'am—please! (*She whispers to* NORA *and hands her a calling card.*)

NORA   (*glancing at the card*) Ah! (*Slips in into her pocket*)

RANK   Anything wrong?

NORA   No, no, not at all. It's only some—it's my new dress—

RANK   Really? But—there's your dress.

NORA   Oh, that. But this is another one—I ordered it—Torvald mustn't know—

RANK   Ah, now we have the big secret.

NORA   That's right. Just go in with him—he's back in the inner study. Keep him there as long as—

RANK   Don't worry. He won't get away.   (*Goes into the study.*)

NORA   (*to the* MAID) And he's standing waiting in the kitchen.

MAID   Yes, he came up by the back stairs.

NORA   But didn't you tell him somebody was here?

MAID   Yes, but that didn't do any good.

NORA   He won't leave?

MAID   No, he won't go till he's talked with you, ma'am.

NORA   Let him come in, then—but quietly. Helene, don't breathe a word about this. It's a surprise for my husband.

MAID   Yes, yes, I understand—   (*Goes out.*)

NORA   This horror—it's going to happen. No, no, no, it can't happen, it mustn't. (*She goes and bolts* HELMER'S *door. The* MAID *opens the hall door for* KROGSTAD *and shuts it behind him. He is dressed for travel in a fur coat, boots and a fur cap.*)

NORA   (*going toward him*) Talk softly. My husband's home.

KROGSTAD   Well, good for him.

NORA   What do you want?

KROGSTAD   Some information.

NORA   Hurry up, then. What is it?

KROGSTAD   You know, of course, that I got my notice.

NORA   I couldn't prevent it, Mr. Krogstad. I fought for you to the bitter end, but nothing worked.

KROGSTAD   Does your husband's love for you run so thin? He knows everything I can expose you too, and all the same he dares to——

NORA   How can you imagine he knows anything about this?

KROGSTAD   Ah, no——I can't imagine it either, now. It's not at all like my fine Torvald Helmer to have so much guts——

NORA   Mr. Krogstad, I demand respect for my husband!

KROGSTAD   Why, of course——all due respect. But since the lady's keeping it so carefully hidden, may I presume to ask if you're also a bit better informed than yesterday about what you've actually done?

NORA   More than you ever could teach me.

KROGSTAD   Yes, I *am* such an awful lawyer.

NORA   What is it you want from me?

KROGSTAD   Just a glimpse of how you are, Mrs. Helmer. I've been thinking about you all day long. A cashier, a night-court scribbler, a——well, a type like me also has a little of what they call a heart, you know.

NORA   Then show it. Think of my children.

KROGSTAD   Did you or your husband ever think of mine? But never mind. I simply wanted to tell you that you don't need to take this thing too seriously. For the present, I'm not proceeding with any action.

NORA   Oh no, really! Well——I knew that.

KROGSTAD   Everything can be settled in a friendly spirit. It doesn't have to get around town at all; it can stay just among us three.

NORA   My husband may never know anything of this.

KROGSTAD   How can you manage that? Perhaps you can pay me the balance?

NORA   No, not right now.

KROGSTAD   Or you know some way of raising the money in a day or two?

NORA   No way that I'm willing to use.

KROGSTAD   Well, it wouldn't have done you any good, anyway. If you stood in front of me with a fistful of bills, you still couldn't buy your signature back.

NORA   Then tell me what you're going to do with it.

KROGSTAD   I'll just hold onto it——keep it on file. There's no outsider who'll even get wind of it. So if you've been thinking of taking some desperate step——

NORA   I have.

KROGSTAD   Been thinking of running away from home——

NORA   I have!

KROGSTAD   Or even of something worse——

NORA   How could you guess that?

KROGSTAD   You can drop those thoughts.

NORA   How could you guess I was thinking of *that?*

KROGSTAD   Most of us think about *that* at first. I thought about it too, but I discovered I hadn't the courage——

NORA   (*lifelessly*) I don't either.

KROGSTAD   (*relieved*) That's true, you haven't the courage? You too?

NORA   I don't have it——I don't have it.

KROGSTAD   It would be terribly stupid, anyway. After that first storm at home blows out, why, then——I have here in my pocket a letter for your husband——

NORA   Telling everything?

KROGSTAD   As charitably as possible.

NORA   (*quickly*) He mustn't ever get that letter. Tear it up. I'll find some way to get money.

KROGSTAD   Beg pardon, Mrs. Helmer, but I think I just told you—

NORA   Oh, I don't mean the money I owe you. Let me know how much you want from my husband, and I'll manage it.

KROGSTAD   I don't want any money from your husband.

NORA   What do you want, then?

KROGSTAD   I'll tell you what. I want to recoup, Mrs. Helmer; I want to get on in the world—and there's where your husband can help me. For a year and a half I've kept myself clean of anything disreputable—all that time struggling with the worst conditions; but I was satisfied, working my way up step by step. Now I've been written right off, and I'm just not in the mood to come crawling back. I tell you, I want to move on. I want to get back in the bank—in a better position. Your husband can set up a job for me—

NORA   He'll never do that!

KROGSTAD   He'll do it. I know him. He won't dare breathe a word of protest. And once I'm in there together with him, you just wait and see! Inside of a year, I'll be the manager's right-hand man. It'll be Nils Krogstad, not Torvald Helmer, who runs the bank.

NORA   You'll never see the day!

KROGSTAD   Maybe you think you can—

NORA   I have the courage now—for *that*.

KROGSTAD   Oh, you don't scare me. A smart, spoiled lady like you—

NORA   You'll see; you'll see!

KROGSTAD   Under the ice, maybe? Down in the freezing, coal-black water? There, till you float up in the spring, ugly, unrecognizable, with your hair falling out—

NORA   You don't frighten me.

KROGSTAD   Nor do you frighten me. One doesn't do these things, Mrs. Helmer. Besides, what good would it be? I'd still have him safe in my pocket.

NORA   Afterwards? When I'm no longer—?

KROGSTAD   Are you forgetting that *I'll* be in control then over your final reputation? (NORA *stands speechless, staring at him.*) Good; now I've warned you. Don't do anything stupid. When Helmer's read my letter, I'll be waiting for his reply. And bear in mind that it's your husband himself who's forced me back to my old ways. I'll never forgive him for that. Good-bye, Mrs. Helmer.

(*He goes out through the hall.*)

NORA   (*goes to the hall door, opens it a crack, and listens*) He's gone. Didn't leave the letter. Oh no, no, that's impossible too! (*Opening the door more and more*) What's that? He's standing outside—not going downstairs. He's thinking it over? Maybe he'll—? (*A letter falls in the mailbox; then* KROGSTAD'S *footsteps are heard, dying away down a flight of stairs.* NORA *gives a muffled cry and runs over toward the sofa table. A short pause.*) In the mailbox. (*Slips warily over to the hall door*) It's lying there. Torvald, Torvald—now we're lost!

MRS. LINDE   (*entering with the costume from the room, left*) There now, I can't see anything else to mend. Perhaps you'd like to try—

NORA   (*in a hoarse whisper*) Kristine, come here.

MRS. LINDE   (*tossing the dress on the sofa*) What's wrong? You look upset.

NORA   Come here. See that letter? *There!* Look—through the glass in the mailbox.

MRS. LINDE   Yes, yes, I see it.

NORA   That letter's from Krogstad—

MRS. LINDE   Nora—it's Krogstad who loaned you the money!

NORA   Yes, and now Torvald will find out everything.

MRS. LINDE   Believe me, Nora, it's best for both of you.

NORA   There's more you don't know. I forged a name.

MRS. LINDE   But for heaven's sake—?

NORA   I only want to tell you that, Kristine, so that you can be my witness.

MRS. LINDE   Witness? Why should I—?

NORA   If I should go out of my mind—it could easily happen—

MRS. LINDE   Nora!

NORA   Or anything else occurred—so I couldn't be present here—

MRS. LINDE   Nora, Nora, you aren't yourself at all!

NORA   And someone should try to take on the whole weight, all of the guilt, you follow me—

MRS. LINDE   Yes, of course, but why do you think—?

NORA   Then you're the witness that it isn't true, Kristine. I'm very much myself; my mind right now is perfectly clear; and I'm telling you: nobody else has known about this; I alone did everything. Remember that.

MRS. LINDE   I will. But I don't understand all this.

NORA   Oh, how could you ever understand it? It's the miracle now that's going to take place.

MRS. LINDE   The miracle?

NORA   Yes, the miracle. But it's so awful, Kristine. It mustn't take place, not for anything in the world.

MRS. LINDE   I'm going right over and talk with Krogstad.

NORA   Don't go near him; he'll do you some terrible harm!

MRS. LINDE   There was a time once when he'd gladly have done anything for me.

NORA   He?

MRS. LINDE   Where does he live?

NORA   Oh, how do I know? Yes. (*Searches in her pocket*) Here's his card. But the letter, the letter—!

HELMER   (*from the study, knocking on the door*) Nora!

NORA   (*with a cry of fear*) Oh! What is it? What do you want?

HELMER   Now, now, don't be so frightened. We're not coming in. You locked the door—are you trying on the dress?

NORA   Yes, I'm trying it. I'll look just beautiful, Torvald.

MRS. LINDE   (*who has read the card*) He's living right around the corner.

NORA   Yes, but what's the use? We're lost. The letter's in the box.

MRS. LINDE   And your husband has the key?

NORA   Yes, always.

MRS. LINDE   Krogstad can ask for his letter back unread; he can find some excuse—

NORA   But it's just this time that Torvald usually—

MRS. LINDE   Stall him. Keep him in there. I'll be back as quick as I can. (*She hurries out through the hall entrance.*)

NORA   (*goes to* HELMER's *door, opens it, and peers in*) Torvald!

HELMER   (*from the inner study*) Well—does one dare set foot in one's own living room at last? Come on, Rank, now we'll get a look—(*In the doorway*) But what's this?

NORA   What, Torvald dear?

HELMER   Rank had me expecting some grand masquerade.

RANK   (*in the doorway*) That was my impression, but I must have been wrong.

NORA   No one can admire me in my splendor—not until tomorrow.

HELMER   But Nora dear, you look so exhausted. Have you practiced too hard?

NORA   No, I haven't practiced at all yet.

HELMER   You know, it's necessary—

NORA   Oh, it's absolutely necessary, Torvald. But I can't get anywhere without your help. I've forgotten the whole thing completely.

HELMER   Ah, we'll soon take care of that.

NORA   Yes, take care of me, Torvald, please! Promise me that? Oh, I'm so nervous. That big party—You must give up everything this evening for me. No business—don't even touch your pen. Yes? Dear Torvald, promise?

HELMER   It's a promise. Tonight I'm totally at your service—you little helpless thing. Hm—but first there's one thing I want to—(*Goes toward the hall door*)

NORA   What are you looking for?

HELMER   Just to see if there's any mail.

NORA   No, no, don't do that, Torvald!

HELMER   Now what?

NORA   Torvald, please. There isn't any.

HELMER   Let me look, though. (*Starts out.* NORA, *at the piano, strikes the first notes of the tarantella.* HELMER, *at the door, stops.*) Aha!

NORA   I can't dance tomorrow if I don't practice with you.

HELMER   (*going over to her*) Nora dear, are you really so frightened?

NORA   Yes, so terribly frightened. Let me practice right now; there's still time before dinner. Oh, sit down and play for me, Torvald. Direct me. Teach me, the way you always have.

HELMER   Gladly, if it's what you want. (*Sits at the piano*)

NORA   (*snatches the tambourine up from the box, then a long, varicolored shawl, which she throws around herself, whereupon she springs forward and cries out*) Play for me now! Now I'll dance!

(HELMER *plays and* NORA *dances.* RANK *stands behind* HELMER *at the piano and looks on.*)

HELMER   (*as he plays*) Slower. Slow down.

NORA   Can't change it.

HELMER   Not so violent, Nora!

NORA   Has to be just like this.

HELMER   (*stopping*) No, no, that won't do at all.

NORA   (*laughing and swinging her tambourine*) Isn't that what I told you?

RANK   Let me play for her.

HELMER   (*getting up*) Yes, go on. I can teach her more easily then.

(RANK *sits at the piano and plays;* NORA *dances more and more wildly.* HELMER *has stationed himself by the stove and repeatedly gives her directions; she seems not to hear them; her hair loosens and falls over her shoulders; she does not notice, but goes on dancing.* MRS. LINDE *enters.*)

MRS. LINDE   (*standing dumbfounded at the door*) Ah——!

NORA   (*still dancing*) See what fun, Kristine!

HELMER   But Nora darling, you dance as if your life were at stake.

NORA   And it is.

HELMER   Rank, stop! This is pure madness. Stop it, I say!

(RANK *breaks off playing, and* NORA *halts abruptly.*)

HELMER   (*going over to hear*) I never would have believed it. You've forgotten everything I taught you.

NORA   (*throwing away the tambourine*) You see for yourself.

HELMER   Well, there's certainly room for instruction here.

NORA   Yes, you see how important it is. You've got to teach me to the very last minute. Promise me that, Torvald?

HELMER   You can bet on it.

NORA   You mustn't, either today or tomorrow, think about anything else but me; you mustn't open any letters—or the mailbox—

HELMER   Ah, it's still the fear of that man—

NORA   Oh yes, yes, that too.

HELMER   Nora, it's written all over you—there's already a letter from him out there.

NORA   I don't know. I guess so. But you mustn't read such things now; there mustn't be anything ugly between us before it's all over.

RANK   (*quietly to* HELMER) You shouldn't deny her.

HELMER   (*putting his arm around her*) The child can have her way. But tomorrow night, after you've danced—

NORA   Then you'll be free.

MAID   (*in the doorway, right*) Ma'am, dinner is served.

NORA   We'll be wanting champagne, Helene.

MAID   Very good, ma'am.   (*Goes out*)

HELMER   So—a regular banquet, hm?

NORA   Yes, a banquet—champagne till daybreak! (*Calling out*) And some macaroons, Helene. Heaps of them—just this once.

HELMER   (*taking her hands*) Now, now, now—no hysterics. Be my own little lark again.

NORA   Oh, I will soon enough. But go on in—and you, Dr. Rank. Kristine, help me put up my hair.

RANK   (*whispering, as they go*) There's nothing wrong—really wrong, is there?

HELMER   Oh, of course not. It's nothing more than this childish anxiety I was telling you about. *(They go out, right.)*

NORA   Well?

MRS. LINDE   Left town.

NORA   I could see by your face.

MRS. LINDE   He'll be home tomorrow evening. I wrote him a note.

NORA   You shouldn't have. Don't try to stop anything now. After all, it's a wonderful joy, this waiting here for the miracle.

MRS. LINDE   What is it you're waiting for?

NORA   Oh, you can't understand that. Go in to them, I'll be along in a moment.

(MRS. LINDE goes into the dining room. NORA stands a short while as if composing herself; then she looks at her watch.)

NORA   Five. Seven hours to midnight. Twenty-four hours to the midnight after, and then the tarantella's done. Seven and twenty-four? Thirty-one hours to live.

HELMER   *(in the doorway, right)* What's become of the little lark?

NORA   *(going toward him with open arms)* Here's your lark!

ACT III

Same scene. The table, with chairs around it, has been moved to the center of the room. A lamp on the table is lit. The hall door stands open. Dance music drifts down from the floor above. MRS. LINDE sits at the table, absently paging through a book, trying to read, but apparently unable to focus her thoughts. Once or twice she pauses, tensely listening for a sound at the outer entrance.

MRS. LINDE   *(glancing at her watch)* Not yet—and there's hardly any time left. If only he's not—*(Listening again)* Ah, there he is. *(She goes out in the hall and cautiously opens the outer door. Quiet footsteps are heard on the stairs. She whispers.)* Come in. Nobody's here.

KROGSTAD   *(in the doorway)* I found a note from you at home. What's back of all this?

MRS. LINDE   I just *had* to talk to you.

KROGSTAD   Oh? And it just *had* to be here in this house?

MRS. LINDE   At my place it was impossible; my room hasn't a private entrance. Come in; we're all alone. The maid's asleep, and the Helmers are at the dance upstairs.

KROGSTAD   *(entering the room)* Well, well, the Helmers are dancing tonight? Really?

MRS. LINDE   Yes, why not?

KROGSTAD   How true—why not?

MRS. LINDE   All right, Krogstad, let's talk.

KROGSTAD   Do we two have anything more to talk about?

MRS. LINDE   We have a great deal to talk about.

KROGSTAD   I wouldn't have thought so.

MRS. LINDE   No, because you've never understood me, really.

KROGSTAD   Was there anything more to understand—except what's all too common in life? A calculating woman throws over a man the moment a better catch comes by.

MRS. LINDE   You think I'm so thoroughly calculating? You think I broke it off lightly?

KROGSTAD   Didn't you?

MRS. LINDE   Nils—is that what you really thought?

KROGSTAD   If you cared, then why did you write me the way you did?

MRS. LINDE   What else could I do? If I had to break off with you, then it was my job as well to root out everything you felt for me.

KROGSTAD   (*wringing his hands*) So that was it. And this—all this, simply for money!

MRS. LINDE   Don't forget I had a helpless mother and two small brothers. We couldn't wait for you, Nils; you had such a long road ahead of you then.

KROGSTAD   That may be; but you still hadn't the right to abandon me for somebody else's sake.

MRS. LINDE   Yes—I don't know. So many, many times I've asked myself if I did have that right.

KROGSTAD   (*more softly*) When I lost you, it was as if all the solid ground dissolved from under my feet. Look at me; I'm a half-drowned man now, hanging onto a wreck.

MRS. LINDE   Help may be near.

KROGSTAD   It was near—but then you came and blocked it off.

MRS. LINDE   Without my knowing it, Nils. Today for the first time I learned that it's you I'm replacing at the bank.

KROGSTAD   All right—I believe you. But now that you know, will you step aside?

MRS. LINDE   No, because that wouldn't benefit you in the slightest.

KROGSTAD   Not "benefit" me, hm! I'd step aside anyway.

MRS. LINDE   I've learned to be realistic. Life and hard, bitter necessity have taught me that.

KROGSTAD   And life's taught me never to trust fine phrases.

MRS. LINDE   Then life's taught you a very sound thing. But you do have to trust in actions, don't you?

KROGSTAD   What does that mean?

MRS. LINDE   You said you were hanging on like a half-drowned man to a wreck.

KROGSTAD   I've good reason to say that.

MRS. LINDE   I'm also like a half-drowned woman on a wreck. No one to suffer with; no one to care for.

KROGSTAD   You made your choice.

MRS. LINDE   There wasn't any choice then.

KROGSTAD   So—what of it?

MRS. LINDE   Nils, if only we two shipwrecked people could reach across to each other.

KROGSTAD   What are you saying?

MRS. LINDE   Two on one wreck are at least better off than each on his own.

KROGSTAD   Kristine!

MRS. LINDE   Why do you think I came into town?

KROGSTAD   Did you really have some thought of me?

MRS. LINDE   I have to work to go on living. All my born days, as long as I can remember, I've worked, and it's been my best and my only joy. But now I'm completely alone in the world; it frightens me to be so empty and lost. To work for yourself—there's no joy in that. Nils, give me something—someone to work for.

KROGSTAD   I don't believe all this. It's just some hysterical feminine urge to go out and make a noble sacrifice.

MRS. LINDE   Have you ever found me to be hysterical?

KROGSTAD   Can you honestly mean this? Tell me—do you know everything about my past?

MRS. LINDE   Yes.

KROGSTAD   And you know what they think I'm worth around here.

MRS. LINDE   From what you were saying before, it would seem that with me you could have been another person.

KROGSTAD   I'm positive of that.

MRS. LINDE   Couldn't it happen still?

KROGSTAD   Kristine—you're saying this in all seriousness? Yes, you are! I can see it in you. And do you really have the courage, then—?

MRS. LINDE   I need to have someone to care for; and your children need a mother. We both need each other. Nils, I have faith that you're good at heart —I'll risk everything together with you.

KROGSTAD   (*gripping her hands*) Kristine, thank you, thank you—Now I know I can win back a place in their eyes. Yes—but I forgot—

MRS. LINDE   (*listening*) Shh! The tarantella. Go now! Go on!

KROGSTAD   Why? What is it?

MRS. LINDE   Hear the dance up there? When that's over, they'll be coming down.

KROGSTAD   Oh, then I'll go. But—it's all pointless. Of course, you don't know the move I made against the Helmers.

MRS. LINDE   Yes, Nils, I know.

KROGSTAD   And all the same, you have the courage to—?

MRS. LINDE   I know how far despair can drive a man like you.

KROGSTAD   Oh, if I only could take it all back.

MRS. LINDE   You easily could—your letter's still lying in the mailbox.

KROGSTAD   Are you sure of that?

MRS. LINDE   Positive. But—

KROGSTAD   (*looks at her searchingly*) Is that the meaning of it, then? You'll have your friend at any price. Tell me straight out. Is that it?

MRS. LINDE   Nils—anyone who's sold herself for somebody else once isn't going to do it again.

KROGSTAD   I'll demand my letter back.

MRS. LINDE   No, no.

KROGSTAD   Yes, of course. I'll stay here till Helmer comes down; I'll tell him to give me my letter again—that it only involves my dismissal—that he shouldn't read it—

MRS. LINDE   No, Nils, don't call the letter back.

KROGSTAD   But wasn't that exactly why you wrote me to come here?

MRS. LINDE   Yes, in that first panic. But it's been a whole day and night since then, and in that time I've seen such incredible things in this house. Helmer's got to learn everything; this dreadful secret has to be aired; those two have to come to a full understanding; all these lies and evasions can't go on.

KROGSTAD   Well, then, if you want to chance it. But at least there's one thing I can do, and do right away—

MRS. LINDE   (*listening*) Go now, go quick! The dance is over. We're not safe another second.

KROGSTAD   I'll wait for you downstairs.

MRS. LINDE   Yes, please do; take me home.

KROGSTAD   I can't believe it; I've never been so happy. (*He leaves by way of the outer door; the door between the room and the hall stays open.*)

MRS. LINDE   (*straightening up a bit and getting together her street clothes*) How different now! How different! Someone to work for, to live for—a home to build. Well, it is worth the try! Oh, if they'd only come! (*Listening*) Ah, there they are. Bundle up. (*She picks up her hat and coat.* NORA's *and* HELMER's *voices can be heard outside; a key turns in the lock, and* HELMER *brings* NORA *into the hall almost by force. She is wearing the Italian costume with a large black shawl about her; he has on evening dress, with a black domino open over it.*)

NORA   (*struggling in the doorway*) No, no, no, not inside! I'm going up again. I don't want to leave so soon.

HELMER   But Nora dear—

NORA   Oh, I beg you, please, Torvald. From the bottom of my heart, *please* —only an hour more!

HELMER   Not a single minute, Nora darling. You know our agreement. Come on, in we go; you'll catch cold out here. (*In spite of her resistance, he gently draws her into the room.*)

MRS. LINDE   Good evening.

NORA   Kristine!

HELMER   Why, Mrs. Linde—are you here so late?

MRS. LINDE   Yes, I'm sorry, but I did want to see Nora in costume.

NORA   Have you been sitting here, waiting for me?

MRS. LINDE   Yes. I didn't come early enough; you were all upstairs; and then I thought I really couldn't leave without seeing you.

HELMER   (*removing* NORA's *shawl*) Yes, take a good look. She's worth looking at, I can tell you that, Mrs. Linde. Isn't she lovely?

MRS. LINDE   Yes, I should say—

HELMER   A dream of loveliness, isn't she? That's what everyone thought at the party, too. But she's horribly stubborn—this sweet little thing. What's to be done with her? Can you imagine, I almost had to use force to pry her away.

NORA   Oh, Torvald, you're going to regret you didn't indulge me, even for just a half hour more.

HELMER   There, you see. She danced her tarantella and got a tumultuous hand —which was well earned, although the performance may have been a bit too naturalistic—I mean it rather overstepped the proprieties of art. But never mind —what's important is, she made a success, an overwhelming success. You think I could let her stay on after that and spoil the effect? Oh no; I took my lovely little Capri girl—my capricious little Capri girl, I should say—took her under my arm; one quick tour of the ballroom, a curtsy to every side, and then—as they say in novels—the beautiful vision disappeared. An exit should always be effective, Mrs. Linde, but that's what I can't get Nora to grasp. Phew, it's hot in here. (*Flings the domino on a chair and opens the door to his room*) Why's it dark in here? Oh yes, of course. Excuse me. (*He goes in and lights a couple of candles.*)

NORA   (*in a sharp, breathless whisper*) So?

MRS. LINDE   (*quietly*) I talked with him.

NORA   And—?

MRS. LINDE   Nora—you must tell your husband everything.

NORA   (*dully*) I knew it.

MRS. LINDE   You've got nothing to fear from Krogstad, but you have to speak out.

NORA   I won't tell.

MRS. LINDE   Then the letter will.

NORA   Thanks, Kristine. I know now what's to be done. Shh!

HELMER   (*reentering*) Well, then, Mrs. Linde—have you admired her?

MRS. LINDE   Yes, and now I'll say good night.

HELMER   Oh, come, so soon? Is this yours, this knitting?

MRS. LINDE   Yes, thanks. I nearly forgot it.

HELMER   Do you knit, then?

MRS. LINDE   Oh yes.

HELMER   You know what? You should embroider instead.

MRS. LINDE   Really? Why?

HELMER   Yes, because it's a lot prettier. See here, one holds the embroidery so, in the left hand, and then one guides the needle with the right—so—in an easy, sweeping curve—right?

MRS. LINDE   Yes, I guess that's—

HELMER   But, on the other hand, knitting—it can never be anything but ugly. Look, see here, the arms tucked in, the knitting needles going up and down —there's something Chinese about it. Ah, that was really a glorious champagne they served.

MRS. LINDE   Yes, good night, Nora, and don't be stubborn anymore.

HELMER   Well put, Mrs. Linde!

MRS. LINDE   Good night, Mr. Helmer.

HELMER   (*accompanying her to the door*) Good night, good night. I hope you get home all right. I'd be very happy to—but you don't have far to go. Good night, good night. (*She leaves. He shuts the door after her and returns.*) There, now, at last we got her out the door. She's a deadly bore, that creature.

NORA   Aren't you pretty tired, Torvald?

HELMER   No, not a bit.

NORA   You're not sleepy?

HELMER   Not at all. On the contrary, I'm feeling quite exhilarated. But you? Yes, you really look tired and sleepy.

NORA   Yes, I'm very tired. Soon now I'll sleep.

HELMER   See! You see! I was right all along that we shouldn't stay longer.

NORA   Whatever you do is always right.

HELMER   (*kissing her brow*) Now my little lark talks sense. Say, did you notice what a time Rank was having tonight?

NORA   Oh, was he? I didn't get to speak with him.

HELMER   I scarcely did either, but it's a long time since I've seen him in such high spirits. (*Gazes at her a moment, then comes nearer her*) Hm—it's marvelous, though, to be back home again—to be completely alone with you. Oh, you bewitchingly lovely young woman!

NORA   Torvald, don't look at me like that!

HELMER   Can't I look at my richest treasure? At all that beauty that's mine, mine alone—completely and utterly.

NORA   (*moving around to the other side of the table*) You mustn't talk to me that way tonight.

HELMER   (*following her*) The tarantella is still in your blood, I can see—and it makes you even more enticing. Listen. The guests are beginning to go. (*Dropping his voice*) Nora—it'll soon be quiet through this whole house.

NORA   Yes, I hope so.

HELMER   You do, don't you, my love? Do you realize—when I'm out at a party like this with you—do you know why I talk to you so little, and keep such a distance away; just send you a stolen look now and then—you know why I do it? It's because I'm imagining then that you're my secret darling, my secret young bride-to-be, and that no one suspects there's anything between us.

NORA   Yes, yes; oh, yes, I know you're always thinking of me.

HELMER   And then when we leave and I place the shawl over those fine young rounded shoulders—over that wonderful curving neck—then I pretend that you're my young bride, that we're just coming from the wedding, that for the first time I'm bringing you into my house—that for the first time I'm alone with you—completely alone with you, your trembling young beauty! All this evening I've longed for nothing but you. When I saw you turn and sway in the tarantella—my blood was pounding till I couldn't stand it—that's why I brought you down here so early—

NORA   Go away, Torvald! Leave me alone. I don't want all this.

HELMER   What do you mean? Nora, you're teasing me. You will, won't you? Aren't I your husband—?

(*A knock at the outside door*)

NORA   (*startled*) What's that?

HELMER   (*going toward the hall*) Who is it?

RANK   (*outside*) It's me. May I come in a moment?

HELMER   (*with quiet irritation*) Oh, what does he want now? (*Aloud*) Hold on. (*Goes and opens the door*) Oh, how nice that you didn't just pass us by!

RANK   I thought I heard your voice, and then I wanted so badly to have a look in. (*Lightly glancing about*) Ah, me, these old familiar haunts. You have it snug and cozy in here, you two.

HELMER   You seemed to be having it pretty cozy upstairs, too.

RANK   Absolutely. Why shouldn't I? Why not take in everything in life? As much as you can, anyway, and as long as you can. The wine was superb—

HELMER   The champagne especially.

RANK   You noticed that too? It's amazing how much I could guzzle down.

NORA   Torvald also drank a lot of champagne this evening.

RANK   Oh?

NORA   Yes, and that always makes him so entertaining.

RANK   Well, why shouldn't one have a pleasant evening after a well-spent day?

HELMER   Well spent? I'm afraid I can't claim that.

RANK   (*slapping him on the back*) But I can, you see!

NORA   Dr. Rank, you must have done some scientific research today.

RANK   Quite so.

HELMER   Come now—little Nora talking about scientific research!

NORA   And can I congratulate you on the results?

RANK   Indeed you may.

NORA   Then they were good?

RANK   The best possible for both doctor and patient—certainty.

NORA   (*quickly and searchingly*) Certainty?

RANK   Complete certainty. So don't I owe myself a gay evening afterwards?

NORA   Yes, you're right, Dr. Rank.

HELMER   I'm with you—just so long as you don't have to suffer for it in the morning.

RANK   Well, one never gets something for nothing in life.

NORA   Dr. Rank—are you very fond of masquerade parties?

RANK   Yes, if there's a good array of odd disguises—

NORA   Tell me, what should we two go as at the next masquerade?

HELMER   You little feather head—already thinking of the next!

RANK   We two? I'll tell you what: you must go as Charmed Life—

HELMER   Yes, but find a costume for *that!*

RANK   Your wife can appear just as she looks every day.

HELMER   That was nicely put. But don't you know what you're going to be?

RANK   Yes, Helmer, I've made up my mind.

HELMER   Well?

RANK   At the next masquerade I'm going to be invisible.

HELMER   That's a funny idea.

RANK   They say there's a hat—black, huge—have you never heard of the hat that makes you invisible? You put it on, and then no one on earth can see you.

HELMER   (*suppressing a smile*) Ah, of course.

RANK   But I'm quite forgetting what I came for. Helmer, give me a cigar, one of the dark Havanas.

HELMER   With the greatest pleasure. (*Holds out his case*)

RANK   Thanks. (*Takes one and cuts off the tip*)

NORA   (*striking a match*) Let me give you a light.

RANK   Thank you. (*She holds the match for him; he lights the cigar.*) And now good-bye.

HELMER   Good-bye, good-bye, old friend.

NORA   Sleep well, Doctor.

RANK   Thanks for that wish.

NORA   Wish me the same.

RANK   You? All right, if you like—Sleep well. And thanks for the light.
(*He nods to them both and leaves.*)

HELMER   (*his voice subdued*) He's been drinking heavily.

NORA   (*absently*) Could be. (HELMER *takes his keys from his pocket and goes out in the hall.*) Torvald—what are you after?

HELMER   Got to empty the mailbox; it's nearly full. There won't be room for the morning papers.

NORA   Are you working tonight?

HELMER   You know I'm not. Why—what's this? Someone's been at the lock.

NORA   At the lock—?

HELMER   Yes, I'm positive. What do you suppose—? I can't imagine one of the maids—? Here's a broken hairpin. Nora, it's yours—

NORA   (*quickly*) Then it must be the children—

HELMER   You'd better break them of that. Hm, hm—well, opened it after all. (*Takes the contents out and calls into the kitchen*) Helene! Helene, would you put out the lamp in the hall. (*He returns to the room, shutting the hall door, then displays the handful of mail.*) Look how it's piled up. (*Sorting through them*) Now what's this?

NORA   (*at the window*) The letter! Oh, Torvald, no!

HELMER   Two calling cards—from Rank.

NORA   From Dr. Rank?

HELMER   (*examining them*) "Dr. Rank, Consulting Physician." They were on top. He must have dropped them in as he left.

NORA   Is there anything on them?

HELMER   There's a black cross over the name. See? That's a gruesome notion. He could almost be announcing his own death.

NORA   That's just what he's doing.

HELMER   What! You've heard something? Something he's told you?

NORA   Yes. That when those cards came, he'd be taking his leave of us. He'll shut himself in now and die.

HELMER   Ah, my poor friend! Of course I knew he wouldn't be here much longer. But so soon—And then to hide himself away like a wounded animal.

NORA   If it has to happen, then it's best it happens in silence—don't you think so, Torvald?

HELMER   (*pacing up and down*) He's grown right into our lives. I simply can't imagine him gone. He with his suffering and loneliness—like a dark cloud setting off our sunlit happiness. Well, maybe it's best this way. For him, at least. (*Standing still*) Any maybe for us too, Nora. Now we're thrown back on each other, completely. (*Embracing her*) Oh you, my darling wife, how can I hold you close enough? You know what, Nora—time and again I've wished you were in some terrible danger, just so I could stake my life and soul and everything, for your sake.

NORA (*tearing herself away, her voice firm and decisive*) Now you must read your mail, Torvald.

HELMER No, no, not tonight. I want to stay with you, dearest.

NORA With a dying friend on your mind?

HELMER You're right. We've both had a shock. There's ugliness between us —these thoughts of death and corruption. We'll have to get free of them first. Until then—we'll stay apart.

NORA (*clinging about his neck*) Torvald—good night! Good night!

HELMER (*kissing her on the cheek*) Good night, little songbird. Sleep well, Nora. I'll be reading my mail now.

(*He takes the letters into his room and shuts the door after him.*)

NORA (*with bewildered glances, groping about, seizing* HELMER's *domino, throwing it around her, and speaking in short, hoarse, broken whispers*) Never see him again. Never, never. (*Putting her shawl over her head*) Never see the children either—them, too. Never, never. Oh, the freezing black water! The depths— down—Oh, I wish it were over—He has it now; he's reading it—now. Oh no, no, not yet. Torvald, good-bye, you and the children— (*She starts for the hall; as she does,* HELMER *throws open his door and stands with an open letter in his hand.*)

HELMER Nora!

NORA (*screams*) Oh—!

HELMER What is this? You know what's in this letter?

NORA Yes, I know. Let me go! Let me out!

HELMER (*holding her back*) Where are you going?

NORA (*struggling to break loose*) You can't save me, Torvald!

HELMER (*slumping back*) True! Then it's true what he writes? How horrible! No, no, it's impossible—it can't be true.

NORA It *is* true. I've loved you more than all this world.

HELMER Ah, none of your slippery tricks.

NORA (*taking one step toward him*) Torvald—!

HELMER What *is* this you've blundered into!

NORA Just let me loose. You're not going to suffer for my sake. You're not going to take on my guilt.

HELMER No more playacting. (*Locks the hall door*) You stay right here and give me a reckoning. You understand what you've done? Answer! You understand?

NORA (*looking squarely at him, her face hardening*) Yes. I'm beginning to understand everything now.

HELMER (*striding about*) Oh, what an awful awakening! In all these eight years—she who was my pride and joy—a hypocrite, a liar—worse, worse— a criminal! How infinitely disgusting it all is! The shame! (NORA *says nothing and goes on looking straight at him. He stops in front of her.*) I should have suspected something of the kind. I should have known. All your father's flimsy values— Be still! All your father's flimsy values have come out in you. No religion, no morals, no sense of duty—Oh, how I'm punished for letting him off! I did it for your sake, and you repay me like this.

NORA   Yes, like this.

HELMER   Now you've wrecked all my happiness—ruined my whole future. Oh, it's awful to think of. I'm in a cheap little grafter's hands; he can do anything he wants with me, ask for anything, play with me like a puppet—and I can't breathe a word. I'll be swept down miserably into the depths on account of a featherbrained woman.

NORA   When I'm gone from this world, you'll be free.

HELMER   Oh, quit posing. Your father had a mess of those speeches too. What good would that ever do me if you were gone from this world, as you say? Not the slightest. He can still make the whole thing known; and if he does, I could be falsely suspected as your accomplice. They might even think that I was behind it—that I put you up to it. And all that I can thank you for—you that I've coddled the whole of our marriage. Can you see now what you've done to me?

NORA   (*icily calm*) Yes.

HELMER   It's so incredible, I just can't grasp it. But we'll have to patch up whatever we can. Take off the shawl. I said, take it off! I've got to appease him somehow or other. The thing has to be hushed up at any cost. And as for you and me, it's got to seem like everything between us is just as it was—to the outside world, that is. You'll go right on living in this house, of course. But you can't be allowed to bring up the children; I don't dare trust you with them —Oh, to have to say this to someone I've loved so much! Well, that's done with. From now on happiness doesn't matter; all that matters is saving the bits and pieces, the appearance—(*The doorbell rings.* HELMER *starts.*) What's that? And so late. Maybe the worst—? You think he'd—? Hide, Nora! Say you're sick. (NORA *remains standing motionless.* HELMER *goes and opens the door.*)

MAID   (*half dressed, in the hall*) A letter for Mrs. Helmer.

HELMER   I'll take it. (*Snatches the letter and shuts the door*) Yes, it's from him. You don't get it; I'm reading it myself.

NORA   Then read it.

HELMER   (*by the lamp*) I hardly dare. We may be ruined, you and I. But— I've got to know. (*Rips open the letter, skims through a few lines, glances at an enclosure, then cries out joyfully*) Nora! (NORA *looks inquiringly at him.*) Nora! Wait—better check it again—Yes, yes, it's true. I'm saved. Nora, I'm saved!

NORA   And I?

HELMER   You too, of course. We're both saved, both of us. Look. He's sent back your note. He says he's sorry and ashamed—that a happy development in his life—oh, who cares what he says! Nora, we're saved! No one can hurt you. Oh, Nora, Nora—but first, this ugliness all has to go. Let me see— (*Takes a look at the note*) No, I don't want to see it; I want the whole thing to fade like a dream. (*Tears the note and both letters to pieces, throws them into the stove and watches them burn*) There—now there's nothing left—He wrote that since Christmas Eve you—Oh, they must have been three terrible days for you, Nora.

NORA   I fought a hard fight.

HELMER   And suffered pain and saw no escape but—No, we're not going to dwell on anything unpleasant. We'll just be grateful and keep on repeating; it's over now, it's over! You hear me, Nora? You don't seem to realize—it's over. What's it mean—that frozen look? Oh, poor little Nora, I understand. You can't believe I've forgiven you. But I have, Nora; I swear I have. I know that what you did, you did out of love for me.

NORA   That's true.

HELMER   You loved me the way a wife ought to love her husband. It's simply the means that you couldn't judge. But you think I love you any the less for not knowing how to handle your affairs? No, no—just lean on me: I'll guide you and teach you. I wouldn't be a man if this feminine helplessness didn't make you twice as attractive to me. You mustn't mind those sharp words I said—that was all in the first confusion of thinking my world had collapsed. I've forgiven you, Nora; I swear I've forgiven you.

NORA   My thanks for your forgiveness. (*She goes out through the door, right.*)

HELMER   No, wait—(*Peers in*) What are you doing in there?

NORA   (*inside*) Getting out of my costume.

HELMER   (*by the open door*) Yes, do that. Try to calm yourself and collect your thoughts again, my frightened little songbird. You can rest easy now; I've got wide wings to shelter you with. (*Walking about close by the door*) How snug and nice our home is, Nora. You're safe here; I'll keep you like a hunted dove I've rescued out of a hawk's claws. I'll bring peace to your poor, shuddering heart. Gradually it'll happen, Nora; you'll see. Tomorrow all this will look different to you; then everything will be as it was. I won't have to go on repeating I forgive you; you'll feel it for yourself. How can you imagine I'd ever conceivably want to disown you—or even blame you in any way? Ah, you don't know a man's heart, Nora. For a man there's something indescribably sweet and satisfying in knowing he's forgiven his wife—and forgiven her out of a full and open heart. It's as if she belongs to him in two ways now: in a sense he's given her fresh into the world again, and she's become his wife and his child as well. From now on that's what you'll be to me—you little, bewildered, helpless thing. Don't be afraid of anything, Nora; just open your heart to me, and I'll be conscience and will to you both—(NORA *enters in her regular clothes.*) What's this? Not in bed? You've changed your dress?

NORA   Yes, Torvald, I've changed my dress.

HELMER   But why now, so late?

NORA   Tonight I'm not sleeping.

HELMER   But Nora dear—

NORA   (*looking at her watch*) It's still not so very late. Sit down, Torvald; we have a lot to talk over. (*She sits at one side of the table.*)

HELMER   Nora—what is this? That hard expression—

NORA   Sit down. This'll take some time. I have a lot to say.

HELMER   (*sitting at the table directly opposite her*) You worry me, Nora. And I don't understand you.

NORA   No, that's exactly it. You don't understand me. And I've never understood you either—until tonight. No, don't interrupt. You can just listen to what I say. We're closing out accounts, Torvald.

HELMER   How do you mean that?

NORA   (*after a short pause*) Doesn't anything strike you about our sitting here like this?

HELMER   What's that?

NORA   We've been married now eight years. Doesn't it occur to you that this is the first time we two, you and I, man and wife, have ever talked seriously together?

HELMER   What do you mean—seriously?

NORA   In eight whole years—longer even—right from our first acquaintance, we've never exchanged a serious word on any serious thing.

HELMER   You mean I should constantly go and involve you in problems you couldn't possibly help me with?

NORA   I'm not talking of problems, I'm saying that we've never sat down seriously together and tried to get to the bottom of anything.

HELMER   But dearest, what good would that ever do you?

NORA   That's the point right there: you've never understood me. I've been wronged greatly, Torvald—first by Papa, and then by you.

HELMER   What! By us—the two people who've loved you more than anyone else?

NORA   (*shaking her head*) You never loved me. You've thought it fun to be in love with me, that's all.

HELMER   Nora, what a thing to say!

NORA   Yes, it's true now, Torvald. When I lived at home with Papa, he told me all his opinions, so I had the same ones too; or if they were different I hid them, since he wouldn't have cared for that. He used to call me his doll-child, and he played with me the way I played with my dolls. Then I came into your house—

HELMER   How can you speak of our marriage like that?

NORA   (*unperturbed*) I mean, then I went from Papa's hands into yours. You arranged everything to your own taste, and so I got the same taste as you— or I pretended to; I can't remember. I guess a little of both, first one, then the other. Now when I look back, it seems as if I'd lived here like a beggar—just from hand to mouth. I've lived by doing tricks for you, Torvald. But that's the way you wanted it. It's a great sin what you and Papa did to me. You're to blame that nothing's become of me.

HELMER   Nora, how unfair and ungrateful you are! Haven't you been happy here?

NORA   No, never. I thought so—but I never have.

HELMER   Not—not happy!

NORA   No, only lighthearted. And you've always been so kind to me. But our home's been nothing but a playpen. I've been your doll-wife here, just as at home I was Papa's doll-child. And in turn the children have been my dolls. I thought it was fun when you played with me, just as they thought it fun when I played with them. That's been our marriage, Torvald.

HELMER   There's some truth in what you're saying—under all the raving exaggeration. But it'll all be different after this. Playtime's over; now for the schooling.

NORA   Whose schooling—mine or the children's?

HELMER   Both yours and the children's, dearest.

NORA   Oh, Torvald, you're not the man to teach me to be a good wife to you.

HELMER   And you can say that?

NORA   And I—how am I equipped to bring up children?

HELMER   Nora!

NORA   Didn't you say a moment ago that that was no job to trust me with?

HELMER   In a flare of temper! Why fasten on that?

NORA   Yes, but you were so very right. I'm not up to the job. There's another job I have to do first. I have to try to educate myself. You can't help me with that. I've got to do it alone. And that's why I'm leaving you now.

HELMER   (*jumping up*) What's that?

NORA   I have to stand completely alone, if I'm ever going to discover myself and the world out there. So I can't go on living with you.

HELMER   Nora, Nora!

NORA   I want to leave right away. Kristine should put me up for the night—

HELMER   You're insane! You've no right! I forbid you!

NORA   From here on, there's no use forbidding me anything. I'll take with me whatever is mine. I don't want a thing from you, either now or later.

HELMER   What kind of madness is this!

NORA   Tomorrow I'm going home—I mean, home where I came from. It'll be easier up there to find something to do.

HELMER   Oh, you blind, incompetent child!

NORA   I must learn to be competent, Torvald.

HELMER   Abandon your home, your husband, your children! And you're not even thinking what people will say.

NORA   I can't be concerned about that. I only know how essential this is.

HELMER   Oh, it's outrageous. So you'll run out like this on your most sacred vows.

NORA   What do you think are my most sacred vows?

HELMER   And I have to tell you that! Aren't they your duties to your husband and children?

NORA   I have other duties equally sacred.

HELMER   That isn't true. What duties are they?

NORA   Duties to myself.

HELMER   Before all else, you're a wife and a mother.

NORA   I don't believe in that anymore. I believe that, before all else, I'm a human being, no less than you—or anyway, I ought to try to become one. I know the majority thinks you're right, Torvald, and plenty of books agree with you, too. But I can't go on believing what the majority says, or what's written in books. I have to think over these things myself and try to understand them.

HELMER   Why can't you understand your place in your own home? On a point like that, isn't there one everlasting guide you can turn to? Where's your religion?

NORA   Oh, Torvald, I'm really not sure what religion is.

HELMER   What—?

NORA   I only know what the minister said when I was confirmed. He told me religion was this thing and that. When I get clear and away by myself, I'll go into that problem too. I'll see if what the minister said was right, or, in any case, if it's right for me.

HELMER   A young woman your age shouldn't talk like that. If religion can't move you, I can try to rouse your conscience. You do have some moral feeling? Or, tell me—has that gone too?

NORA   It's not easy to answer that, Torvald. I simply don't know. I'm all confused about these things. I just know I see them so differently from you. I find out, for one thing, that the law's not at all what I'd thought—but I can't get it through my head that the law is fair. A woman hasn't a right to protect her dying father or save her husband's life! I can't believe that.

HELMER   You talk like a child. You don't know anything of the world you live in.

NORA   No, I don't. But now I'll begin to learn for myself. I'll try to discover who's right, the world or I.

HELMER   Nora, you're sick; you've got a fever. I almost think you're out of your head.

NORA   I've never felt more clearheaded and sure in my life.

HELMER   And—clearheaded and sure—you're leaving your husband and children?

NORA   Yes.

HELMER   Then there's only one possible reason.

NORA   What?

HELMER   You no longer love me.

NORA   No. That's exactly it.

HELMER   Nora! You can't be serious!

NORA   Oh, this is so hard, Torvald—you've been so kind to me always. But I can't help it. I don't love you anymore.

HELMER   (*struggling for composure*) Are you also clearheaded and sure about that?

NORA   Yes, completely. That's why I can't go on staying here.

HELMER   Can you tell me what I did to lose your love?

NORA   Yes, I can tell you. It was this evening when the miraculous thing didn't come—then I knew you weren't the man I'd imagined.

HELMER   Be more explicit; I don't follow you.

NORA   I've waited now so patiently eight long years—for, my Lord, I know miracles don't come every day. Then this crisis broke over me, and such a certainty filled me: *now* the miraculous event would occur. While Krogstad's letter was lying out there, I never for an instant dreamed that you could give in to his terms. I was so utterly sure you'd say to him: go on, tell your tale to the whole wide world. And when he'd done that—

HELMER   Yes, what then? When I'd delivered my own wife into shame and disgrace—!

NORA   When he'd done that, I was so utterly sure that you'd step forward, take the blame on yourself and say: I am the guilty one.

HELMER   Nora—!

NORA   You're thinking I'd never accept such a sacrifice from you? No, of course not. But what good would my protests be against you? That was the miracle I was waiting for, in terror and hope. And to stave that off, I would have taken my life.

HELMER   I'd gladly work for you day and night, Nora—and take on pain and deprivation. But there's no one who gives up honor for love.

NORA   Millions of women have done just that.

HELMER   Oh, you think and talk like a silly child.

NORA   Perhaps. But you neither think nor talk like the man I could join myself to. When your big fright was over—and it wasn't from any threat against me, only for what might damage you—when all the danger was past, for you it was just as if nothing had happened. I was exactly the same, your little lark, your doll, that you'd have to handle with double care now that I'd turned out so brittle and frail. (*Gets up*) Torvald—in that instant it dawned on me that for eight years I've been living here with a stranger, and that I'd even conceived three children—oh, I can't stand the thought of it! I could tear myself to bits.

HELMER   (*heavily*) I see. There's a gulf that's opened between us—that's clear. Oh, but Nora, can't we bridge it somehow?

NORA   The way I am now, I'm no wife for you.

HELMER   I have the strength to make myself over.

NORA   Maybe—if your doll gets taken away.

HELMER   But to part! To part from you! No, Nora, no—I can't imagine it.

NORA   (*going out, right*) All the more reason why it has to be. (*She reenters with her coat and a small overnight bag, which she puts on a chair by the table.*)

HELMER   Nora, Nora, not now! Wait till tomorrow.

NORA   I can't spend the night in a strange man's room.

HELMER   But couldn't we live here like brother and sister—

NORA   You know very well how long that would last. (*Throws her shawl about her*) Good-bye, Torvald. I won't look in on the children. I know they're in better hands than mine. The way I am now, I'm no use to them.

HELMER   But someday, Nora—someday—?

NORA   How can I tell? I haven't the least idea what'll become of me.

HELMER   But you're my wife, now and wherever you go.

NORA   Listen, Torvald—I've heard that when a wife deserts her husband's house just as I'm doing, then the law frees him from all responsibility. In any case, I'm freeing you from being responsible. Don't feel yourself bound, any more than I will. There has to be absolute freedom for us both. Here, take your ring back. Give me mine.

HELMER   That too?

NORA   That too.

HELMER   There it is.

NORA   Good. Well, now it's all over. I'm putting the keys here. The maids know all about keeping up the house—better than I do. Tomorrow, after I've left town, Kristine will stop by to pack up everything that's mine from home. I'd like those things shipped to me.

HELMER   Over! All over! Nora, won't you ever think about me?

NORA   I'm sure I'll think of you often, and about the children and the house here.

HELMER   May I write you?

NORA   No—never. You're not to do that.

HELMER   Oh, but let me send you—

NORA   Nothing. Nothing.

HELMER   Or help you if you need it.

NORA   No. I accept nothing from strangers.

HELMER   Nora—can I never be more than a stranger to you?

NORA   (*picking up the overnight bag*) Ah, Torvald—it would take the greatest miracle of all—

HELMER   Tell me the greatest miracle!

NORA   You and I both would have to transform ourselves to the point that —Oh, Torvald, I've stopped believing in miracles.

HELMER   But I'll believe. Tell me! Transform ourselves to the point that—?

NORA   That our living together could be a true marriage.

(*She goes out down the hall.*)

HELMER   (*sinks down on a chair by the door, face buried in his hands*) Nora! Nora! (*Looking about and rising*) Empty. She's gone. (*A sudden hope leaps in him*) The greatest miracle—?

(*From below, the sound of a door slamming shut*)

QUESTIONS

1. Describe Torvald Helmer. What aspects of his character are most evident in the early scenes? Does he give any evidence of having changed by the end of the play? Do you think he is capable of sharing the kind of marriage Nora describes at the end of the play?

2. Evaluate Nora's behavior. Does she make the right decision in leaving her family? Why or why not?

3. Ibsen has remarked that *A Doll House* is more about human rights than women's rights. What kind of rights do you think he had in mind?

4. *A Doll House* has been performed with an alternative ending in which Nora and Torvald are reconciled, and Nora remains with her family. Is this an artistically appropriate and theatrically effective ending? Why or why not?

5. Consider the function of the following characters: Nils Krogstad, Dr. Rank, and Kristine Linde.

6. Examine the play's plot. How does Ibsen control our responses and arouse our curiosity? Point out places where the tempo or pace of the play changes. What effects do these changes have?

7. Identify two or three visual details or objects that function as symbols, and explain their significance.

8. Choose one scene important for its revelation of character and explain how you would dramatize it.

August Strindberg

Like *A Doll House*, Strindberg's *The Father* is a realistic drama. Its action, characters, language, and setting all suggest a middle-class world. But the tone of the play is different. It is far more feverish and obsessive than the tone of Ibsen's play. The language of *The Father* is more tempestuous and its situation more extreme than the language and situation of *A Doll House*. The realism of Strindberg's play takes on a darker coloration and a more sombre tone.

An additional feature distinguishing Strindberg's realism from Ibsen's is an emphasis on subconscious, irrational forces within the characters. The psychological realism of *The Father* separates it from the more socially conscious domestic drama of *A Doll House*. Moreover, Strindberg's play is informed by the kind of intensity and inevitability we have come to associate with Greek tragedy.

The Father was published in 1887 and produced in 1888 in Stockholm, Sweden. It became almost immediately notorious and successful, winning praise from the French naturalistic novelist Emile Zola, who found the play profoundly moving. It also won the favor of the German philosopher Friedrich Nietzsche, who found its mingling of war and hate with love splendidly and powerfully effective.

AUGUST STRINDBERG

[1849–1912]

The Father

TRANSLATED BY MICHAEL MEYER

THE CAPTAIN
LAURA
BERTHA
DR. ÖSTERMARK
THE PASTOR
THE NURSE
NÖJD
THE CAPTAIN'S BATMAN

ACT I

A room in the CAPTAIN'S *house. Upstage right, a door. In the centre of the room is a large round table, with newspapers and magazines. On the right, a leather sofa and* a table. In the right-hand corner, a concealed door. On the left, a secretaire, with an ornamental clock on it, and a door which leads to the rest of the house. There are weapons on the wall; rifles and game-bags. By the door, clothes-hangers with military tunics on them. On the large table a lamp is burning.

Scene I

The CAPTAIN *and the* PASTOR *on the leather sofa. The* CAPTAIN *is in undress uniform, with riding-boots and spurs. The* PASTOR *is in black, with a white stock, but without his clerical bands. He is smoking a pipe.*

The CAPTAIN *rings. The* BATMAN *enters.*

BATMAN: Sir?
CAPTAIN: Is Nöjd out there?
BATMAN: He's waiting for orders in the kitchen, sir.
CAPTAIN: In the kitchen again! Send him here at once!
BATMAN: Sir! (*Goes*)
PASTOR: What's the matter now?
CAPTAIN: Oh, the blackguard's been mucking about with one of the girls again. Damned nuisance, that fellow!
PASTOR: Nöjd? Why, you had trouble with him last year too!
CAPTAIN: You remember? Perhaps you'd give him a friendly talking-to—that might have some effect. I've sworn at him, and given him a tanning, but it doesn't do any good.
PASTOR: So you want me to read him a sermon! Do you think the Word of God will have any effect on a cavalryman?
CAPTAIN: Well, brother-in-law, it doesn't have much effect on me, as you know—
PASTOR: Yes, I know!
CAPTAIN: But on him—? Try, anyway.

Scene II

The CAPTAIN. *The* PASTOR. NÖJD.

CAPTAIN: Well, Nöjd, what have you been up to now?
NÖJD: God bless you, Captain, I couldn't tell you before his Reverence.
PASTOR: Come, come, don't be bashful, my lad!
CAPTAIN: Own up, or you know what'll happen!
NÖJD: Well, sir, it was like this, you see. We was dancing up at Gabriel's, and then, yes, well, Louis said—
CAPTAIN: What's Louis got to do with it? Stick to the facts!
NÖJD: Well, Emma suggested we should go to the barn.
CAPTAIN: I see! So it was Emma who seduced you!
NÖJD: Not far off. And I'll say this—if a girl ain't willing, she don't run no danger.

CAPTAIN: Out with it! Are you the child's father or not?

NÖJD: How should I know?

CAPTAIN: What! You don't know!

NÖJD: Well, you can never be sure.

CAPTAIN: Weren't you the only one, then?

NÖJD: I was that time, but that don't mean to say I was the only one.

CAPTAIN: Are you saying Louis's to blame? Is that it?

NÖJD: It ain't easy to say who's to blame.

CAPTAIN: But you've told Emma you want to marry her.

NÖJD: Yes, well, you have to tell them that.

CAPTAIN (*to* PASTOR): This is monstrous!

PASTOR: It's the old story. Now, look here, Nöjd, surely you're man enough to know whether you're the father!

NÖJD: Well, I did go with her, but, as your Reverence knows, that don't necessarily mean anything need happen.

PASTOR: Come, come, my lad, don't start trying to evade the issue! You surely don't want to leave the girl alone with the child! Of course we can't force you to marry her, but you must accept responsibility for the child. You must!

NÖJD: All right, but Louis must pay his share.

CAPTAIN: Oh, very well, it'll have to go to court. I can't unravel the rights and wrongs of this, and I don't feel inclined to try. Right, get out!

PASTOR: Nöjd! One moment. Hm! Don't you regard it as dishonourable to leave a girl high and dry like that with a child? Eh? Well? Don't you feel such behaviour would be—hm—?

NÖJD: Oh, yes, if I knew I was the child's father. But that's something a man can never be sure of, your Reverence. And it's no joke spending your whole life sweating for other men's children. I'm sure you and the Captain'll both appreciate that.

CAPTAIN: Get out!

NÖJD: Sir! (*Goes.*)

CAPTAIN: And keep out of the kitchen, damn you!

Scene III

CAPTAIN: Well, why didn't you lay into him?

PASTOR: What? I thought I spoke very strictly.

CAPTAIN: Oh, you just sat there mumbling to yourself.

PASTOR: To be honest, I don't know what one ought to say. It's bad luck on the girl, yes. But it's bad luck on the boy, too. Suppose he isn't the father? The girl can suckle the child for four months at the orphanage, and then she'll be shot of him, but the boy can't dodge his responsibility like that. She'll get a good job afterwards in some decent home, but if he gets thrown out of his regiment, he's finished.

CAPTAIN: Yes, I wouldn't like to be the magistrate who has to judge this case. I don't suppose the lad's completely innocent—one can't be sure. But one thing you can be sure of. The girl's guilty—if you can say anyone's guilty.

PASTOR: Yes, yes! I'm not condemning anyone! But what were we speaking about when this blessed business intervened? Bertha's confirmation, wasn't it?

CAPTAIN: It's not just her confirmation. It's the whole question of her upbringing. This house is stuffed with women every one of whom wants to bring up my child. My mother-in-law wants to make her a spiritualist, Laura wants her to be a painter, her governess wants her to be a Methodist, old Margaret wants her to be a Baptist, and the maids are trying to get her into the Salvation Army. Well, you can't patch a soul together like a damned quilt. I have the chief right to decide her future, and I'm obstructed whichever way I turn. I've got to get her out of this house.

PASTOR: You've too many women running your home.

CAPTAIN: You needn't tell me that. It's like a cage full of tigers—if I didn't keep a red-hot iron in front of their noses, they'd claw me to the ground the first chance they got. Yes, you can laugh, you old fox! It wasn't enough that I married your sister, you had to palm your old stepmother off on me too!

PASTOR: Well, good heavens, one can't have one's stepmother living under one's roof.

CAPTAIN: But one's mother-in-law is all right! Yes, under someone else's roof.

PASTOR: Well, well. We all have our cross to bear.

CAPTAIN: Yes, but I've a damned sight too many. I've got my old nurse too, and she treats me as though I was still in a bib! Oh, she's a dear old soul, heaven knows, but she doesn't belong here!

PASTOR: You should keep your women in their place, Adolf. You let them rule you.

CAPTAIN: My dear brother-in-law, will you kindly tell me how one keeps women in their place?

PASTOR: To speak frankly, Laura—I know she's my sister, but—well, she was always a little difficult.

CAPTAIN: Oh, Laura has her moods, but she's not too bad.

PASTOR: Ah, come on! I know her!

CAPTAIN: Well, she's had a romantic upbringing, and has a little difficulty in accepting life, but, after all, she is my wife—

PASTOR: And is therefore the best of women. No, Adolf, she's the biggest stone round your neck.

CAPTAIN: Yes, well, anyway, now the whole house has become impossible. Laura doesn't want to let Bertha out of her sight. But I can't let her stay in this asylum.

PASTOR: So? Laura won't—? Hm, then I'm afraid things aren't going to be easy. When she was a child, she used to lie absolutely still like a corpse until she'd got what she wanted. And when she'd got it, she'd give it back, explaining that it wasn't the *thing* she wanted, simply the fact of having her will.

CAPTAIN: I see, she was like that already, was she? Hm! She gets so emotional sometimes that I become frightened, and wonder if she isn't—well—sick.

PASTOR: But what is it you want for Bertha that she finds so unacceptable? Can't you meet each other halfway?

CAPTAIN: You mustn't imagine I want to build the child into a prodigy, or a copy of myself. But I don't want to play the pimp and educate her just simply for marriage—if I do that and she stays single, she'll become one of these embittered spinsters. On the other hand, I don't want to train her for some masculine vocation that'll need years of study and be completely wasted if she does get married.

PASTOR: What do you want, then?

CAPTAIN: I'd like her to become a teacher. Then, if she stays single she'll be able to look after herself, and won't be worse off than these wretched schoolmasters who have to support a family. And if she does marry, she can use the knowledge she's gained in bringing up her own children. That's logical, isn't it?

PASTOR: Perfectly. But hasn't she shown a great talent for painting? Wouldn't it be bad for her to repress that?

CAPTAIN: No, no. I've shown her efforts to a prominent artist, and he says it's only the kind of thing people learn to do at schools. But then some young ass came here last summer who knew more about such matters, and said she was a genius—and as far as Laura was concerned, that settled it.

PASTOR: Was he in love with the girl?

CAPTAIN: I presume so.

PASTOR: Then God help you, my dear fellow, for there'll be nothing you can do about that! But this is a sad business, and of course Laura has allies—in there.

CAPTAIN: Oh, yes, never you fear! The whole household is up in arms—and, between you and me, they're not fighting strictly according to the rules of chivalry.

PASTOR (*gets up*): Do you think I haven't been through all this?

CAPTAIN: You too?

PASTOR: Are you surprised?

CAPTAIN: But the worst is, it seems to me Bertha's future is being decided in there from motives of hatred. They keep dropping hints that men will see that women can do this and do that. Man versus woman, that's their theme, all day long. Must you go now? No, stay for supper. I can't offer you much, but, did I tell you, I'm expecting the new doctor to pay a call? Have you seen him?

PASTOR: I caught a glimpse of him on my way here. He looks a pleasant, straightforward chap.

CAPTAIN: Does he? Good! Think he might be on my side?

PASTOR: Who knows? It depends how much he's had to do with women.

CAPTAIN: Oh, come on, do stay!

PASTOR: No thanks, my dear fellow. I've promised to be home for supper, and my old lady gets so worried if I'm late.

CAPTAIN: Worried? Angry, you mean! Well, as you wish. Let me give you a hand with your coat.

PASTOR: It's certainly very cold tonight. Thank you. You want to look after yourself, Adolf. You look nervy.

CAPTAIN: Do I?

PASTOR: You're not quite yourself, are you?

CAPTAIN: Has Laura given you that idea? She's been treating me like a budding corpse for twenty years.

PASTOR: Laura? No, no, I just wondered—Take care of yourself! That's my advice. Well, goodbye, old chap. But didn't you want to talk to me about confirmation?

CAPTAIN: No, that'll have to take its course. Chalk that one up to society's conscience. I don't intend to be a martyr for the sake of truth. I'm past all that. Goodbye! Give my regards to your wife!

PASTOR: Goodbye, brother! Give mine to Laura!

Scene IV

The CAPTAIN. *Then* LAURA.

CAPTAIN   (*opens the secretaire, sits down at it and starts counting*): Thirty-four —nine—forty-three—seven, eight—fifty-six.

LAURA   (*enters from the main part of the house*): Would you mind—

CAPTAIN: In a moment. Sixty-six, seventy-one, eighty-four, eighty-nine, ninety-two, one hundred. What is it?

LAURA: Perhaps I'm disturbing you.

CAPTAIN: Not at all. The housekeeping money, I suppose?

LAURA: Yes. The housekeeping money.

CAPTAIN: Leave the bills there, and I'll go through them.

LAURA: Bills?

CAPTAIN: Yes.

LAURA: Oh, you want bills now?

CAPTAIN: Of course I want bills. We are financially embarrassed, and if things come to a head I've got to be able to produce accounts. Otherwise I can be punished as a negligent debtor.

LAURA: It isn't my fault if we're financially embarrassed.

CAPTAIN: That's just what the bills will establish.

LAURA: I'm not to blame if our tenant won't pay the lease of his farm.

CAPTAIN: Who recommended him? You. Why did you recommend such a—what shall we call him? Drone?

LAURA: If he's such a drone, why did you take him?

CAPTAIN: Because you wouldn't let me eat in peace, sleep in peace or work in peace until you'd got him here. You wanted to have him because your brother wanted to be rid of him, your mother wanted to have him because I didn't want to have him, the governess wanted to have him because he was a Methodist, and old Margaret wanted to have him because she'd known his grandmother since they were children. So we took him, and if I hadn't I should now be either sitting in an asylum or lying in the family vault. However, here is your household allowance, and some pin money. You can give me the bills later.

LAURA   (*curtseys*): Thank you, sir. Do you keep bills for your private expenses?

CAPTAIN: That's none of your business.

LAURA: True; no more than my child's upbringing. Have you gentlemen reached a decision now, after your evening session?

CAPTAIN: I had already made my decision. I merely wished to impart it to the only friend whom I and my family have in common. Bertha is to live in town. She will leave in a fortnight.

LAURA: And where is she to live, if I may be allowed to ask?

CAPTAIN: I have arranged for her to lodge with my lawyer, Mr. Saevberg.

LAURA: That freethinker!

CAPTAIN: The law states that a child is to be brought up in her father's faith.

LAURA: And the mother has no say in the matter?

CAPTAIN: None. She has sold her birthright by legal contract, and has surrendered all her claims. In return, the husband supports her and her children.

LAURA: So she has no rights over her own child?

CAPTAIN: None whatever. Once you have sold something, you can't get it back and keep the money.

LAURA: But if the father and mother should agree on a compromise—?

CAPTAIN: How is that possible? I want her to live in town, you want her to stay at home. The arithmetical mean would be that she should live at the railway station, halfway between. This is a situation which cannot be resolved by compromise.

LAURA: Then it must be resolved by force. What did Nöjd want here?

CAPTAIN: That is my professional secret.

LAURA: The whole kitchen knows.

CAPTAIN: Then you should.

LAURA: I do.

CAPTAIN: And have passed judgment?

LAURA: The law is quite explicit on the matter.

CAPTAIN: The law is not explicit as to who is the child's father.

LAURA: No. But one usually knows.

CAPTAIN: Wise men say one can never be sure about such things.

LAURA: Not be sure who is a child's father?

CAPTAIN: They say not.

LAURA: How extraordinary! Then how can the father have all these rights over her child?

CAPTAIN: He only has them if he accepts responsibility for the child—or has the responsibility forced upon him. And in marriage, of course, the question of paternity does not arise.

LAURA: Never?

CAPTAIN: I should hope not.

LAURA: But if the wife has been unfaithful?

CAPTAIN: That is not relevant to our discussion. Are there any other questions you want to ask me?

LAURA: None whatever.

CAPTAIN: Then I shall go to my room. Please be so good as to inform me when the Doctor comes. (*Shuts the secretaire and rises.*)

LAURA: Very well.

CAPTAIN   (*going through concealed door right*): The moment he arrives! I don't wish to insult him. You understand? (*Goes.*)

LAURA: I understand.

Scene V

LAURA *alone. She looks at the banknotes she is holding in her hand.*

GRANDMOTHER   (*offstage*): Laura!

LAURA: Yes?

GRANDMOTHER: Is my tea ready?

LAURA   (*in the doorway left*): I'll bring it in a moment.

Goes towards the door upstage. Just before she reaches it, the BATMAN *opens it.*

BATMAN: Dr. Östermark!

DOCTOR   (*enters*): Mrs. Lassen?

LAURA   (*goes to greet him, and stretches out her hand*): How do you do, Doctor! Welcome to our home. The Captain is out, but he will be back shortly.

DOCTOR: Please forgive me for coming so late. I've already had to visit some patients.

LAURA: Won't you sit down?

DOCTOR: Thank you, Mrs. Lassen, thank you.

LAURA: Yes, there's a lot of illness around here just now. However, I do hope you'll be happy here. We lead such a lonely life out here in the country, so it's important for us to have a doctor who takes an interest in his patients. And I've heard many flattering reports of you, so I hope we shall see a good deal of each other.

DOCTOR: You are too kind, Mrs. Lassen. But I trust, for your sake, that my visits will not always have to be professional! Your family enjoys good health—?

LAURA: We've never had any serious illnesses, I am glad to say. But things aren't quite as they should be—

DOCTOR: Indeed?

LAURA: I'm afraid they are not at all as we could wish.

DOCTOR: Really? You alarm me!

LAURA: There are certain domestic matters which a woman's honour and conscience require her to conceal from the world—

DOCTOR: But not from her doctor.

LAURA: Precisely. So I feel it is my painful duty to be quite open with you from the start.

DOCTOR: Could we not postpone this conversation until I have had the pleasure of making the Captain's acquaintance?

LAURA: No. You must hear what I have to say before you see him.

DOCTOR: It concerns him, then?

LAURA: Yes—my poor, beloved husband!

DOCTOR: You alarm me, Mrs. Lassen. Believe me, I am deeply touched by your distress.

LAURA   (*takes out her handkerchief*): My husband is mentally unbalanced. Now you know. You will be able to judge for yourself later.

DOCTOR: What! But I have read with admiration the Captain's excellent dissertations on mineralogy, and have always received the impression of a powerful and lucid intelligence.

LAURA: Indeed? I should be most happy if it could be proved that we have all been mistaken.

DOCTOR: It is of course possible that his mind may be unhinged where other matters are concerned. Pray proceed.

LAURA: That is what we fear. You see, sometimes he has the most extraordinary ideas, which we would gladly indulge if they didn't threaten the existence of his whole family. For example, he has a mania for buying things.

DOCTOR: That is unfortunate. But what does he buy?

LAURA: Whole crates of books, which he never reads.

DOCTOR: Well, it isn't so unusual for a scholar to buy books.

LAURA: You don't believe me?

DOCTOR: Yes, Mrs. Lassen, I am sure that what you say is true.

LAURA: But is it reasonable for a man to claim that he can see in a microscope what is happening on another planet?

DOCTOR: Does he say that?

LAURA: Yes.

DOCTOR: In a microscope?

LAURA: Yes, in a microscope.

DOCTOR: If that is so, it is serious—

LAURA: *If* it is so! You don't believe me, Doctor. And I sit here telling you all our family secrets—

DOCTOR: Now listen, Mrs. Lassen. I am honoured that you should confide in me. But as a doctor, I must investigate the matter thoroughly before I can make a diagnosis. Has the Captain shown any symptoms of capriciousness or vacillation?

LAURA: Any symptoms! We've been married for twenty years, and he has never yet taken a decision without reversing it.

DOCTOR: Is he stubborn?

LAURA: He always insists on having his own way, but once he has got it he loses interest and begs me to decide.

DOCTOR: This is serious. I must observe him closely. You see, my dear Mrs. Lassen, will is the backbone of the mind. If the will is impaired, the mind crumples.

LAURA: God knows I've done my best to meet his wishes during all these long years of trial. Oh, if you knew the things I have had to put up with! If you knew!

DOCTOR: Mrs. Lassen, your distress moves me deeply, and I promise you I will see what can be done. But after what you have told me, I must ask you one thing. Avoid touching on any subject that might excite your husband. In a sick brain, fancies grow like weeds, and can easily develop into obsessions or even monomania. You understand?

LAURA: You mean I must take care not to make him suspicious?

DOCTOR: Exactly. A sick man is receptive to the slightest impression, and can therefore be made to imagine anything.

LAURA: Really? I understand. Yes. Yes. (*A bell rings within the house.*) Excuse me, my mother wishes to speak with me. Wait a moment—this must be Adolf!

Scene VI

The DOCTOR. *The* CAPTAIN *enters through the concealed door.*

CAPTAIN: Ah, you here already, Doctor? Delighted to meet you!

DOCTOR: Good evening, Captain. It is a great honour for me to make the acquaintance of so distinguished a scientist.

CAPTAIN: Oh, nonsense. My military duties don't allow me much time for research. All the same, I think I'm on to a new discovery.

DOCTOR: Indeed?

CAPTAIN: You see, I've been submitting meteorites to spectral analysis, and I've discovered carbon! Evidence of organic life! What do you say to that?

DOCTOR: You can see that in the microscope?

CAPTAIN: Microscope? Good God, no—spectroscope!

DOCTOR: Spectroscope? Ah—yes, of course, I mean spectroscope. Well, then, you'll soon be able to tell us what is happening on Jupiter.

CAPTAIN: Not what *is* happening, but what *has* happened. If only that damned shop in Paris would send those books! I really believe all the booksellers in the world have entered into a conspiracy against me. Would you believe it, for two months I haven't had a reply to a single order, letter or even telegram! It's driving me mad. I just don't understand it.

DOCTOR: Oh, that's just common laziness. You mustn't take it too seriously.

CAPTAIN: Yes, but, damn it, I won't be able to get my thesis ready in time —I know there's a fellow in Berlin working on the same lines. Still, we haven't met to talk about that, but about you. If you'd care to live here, we have a small apartment in the wing—or would you rather take over your predecessor's lodgings?

DOCTOR: Just as you please.

CAPTAIN: No, as *you* please. Say, now.

DOCTOR: You must decide, Captain.

CAPTAIN: No, no, I can't decide. You must say what you want. I've no feelings in the matter, no feelings at all.

DOCTOR: Yes, but I can't decide—

CAPTAIN: For God's sake, man, say what you want! I've no inclinations in the matter, I couldn't care less what you do! Are you such a nitwit that you don't know what you want? Answer, or I'll get angry!

DOCTOR: If I must decide, then I'll live here!

CAPTAIN: Good! Thank you. Oh—! Forgive me, Doctor, but nothing annoys me so much as to hear people say it's all the same to them!

He rings. The NURSE *enters.*

CAPTAIN: Oh, is it you, Margaret? Tell me, old dear, do you know if the wing is ready for the doctor?

NURSE: Yes, sir, it's all ready.

CAPTAIN: Good. Then I won't keep you, Doctor—I expect you're tired. Good night. I'll look forward to seeing you again tomorrow.

DOCTOR: Good night, Captain.

CAPTAIN: I suppose my wife told you a few things about conditions here, to put you in the picture?

DOCTOR: She did mention one or two details she thought it might be useful for a stranger to know. Good night, Captain.

Scene VII

The CAPTAIN. *The* NURSE.

CAPTAIN: What do you want, old darling? Is something the matter?

NURSE: Now, listen, Mr. Adolf, pet.

CAPTAIN: What is it, Margaret? Speak out, my dear. You're the only one I can listen to without getting spasms.

NURSE: Now, listen, Mr. Adolf. Why don't you go halfway to meet madam about the child? Remember, she's a mother.

CAPTAIN: Remember I'm a father, Margaret.

NURSE: Now, now, now! A father has other things beside his child, but a mother has nothing. She's only got her child.

CAPTAIN: Exactly. She has only one burden, but I have three, including hers. Do you think I'd have stayed a soldier all my life if I hadn't been saddled with her and her child?

NURSE: Oh, I didn't mean that.

CAPTAIN: No, I'm sure you didn't. You're trying to put me in the wrong.

NURSE: Surely you think I want what's best for you, Mr. Adolf?

CAPTAIN: Yes, yes, my dear, I'm sure you do. But you don't know what's best for me. You see, it isn't enough for me to have given the child life. I want to give it my soul too.

NURSE: Well, I don't understand that. But I still think you ought to be able to come to some agreement.

CAPTAIN: You are not my friend, Margaret.

NURSE: I? Why, Mr. Adolf, how can you say such a thing? Do you think I can forget you were my baby when you were little?

CAPTAIN: Have *I* ever forgotten it, my dear? You've been like a mother to me—you've supported me, up to now, when everyone's been against me—but now, when I need you most, now you betray me and go over to the enemy.

NURSE: Enemy!

CAPTAIN: Yes, enemy! You know how things are in this house. You've seen it all, from beginning to end.

NURSE: Yes, I've seen enough. Blessed Jesus, why must two human beings torment the life out of each other? You're both so good and kind—madam's never like that to me or anyone else.

CAPTAIN: Only to me. Yes, I know. But I'm telling you, Margaret—if you betray me now, you are committing a sin. A web is being spun around me here, and that doctor is not my friend.

NURSE: Oh, Mr. Adolf, you think bad of everyone. But that's because you don't follow the true faith. That's the cause of it.

CAPTAIN. And you've found the only true faith, you and your Baptists. Aren't you lucky!

NURSE: Well, I'm luckier than you, Mr. Adolf. And happier. Humble your heart, and you'll see. God will make you happy, and you'll love your neighbour.

CAPTAIN: It's extraordinary—as soon as you start talking about God and love, your voice becomes hard and your eyes fill with hatred. No, Margaret, you haven't found the true faith.

NURSE: Ah, you're proud. All your learning won't get you far at the Day of Judgment.

CAPTAIN: How arrogantly thou speakest, O humble heart! Yes, I know learning means nothing to animals like you.

NURSE: Shame on you! Never mind. Old Margaret loves her big, big boy best of all, and when the storm comes he'll creep back to her like the good little child he is.

CAPTAIN: Margaret! Forgive me, but—believe me, there's no one here who loves me except you. Help me. I feel something is going to happen here—I don't know what, but there's something evil threatening———(*There is a scream from within the house.*) What's that? Who's screaming?

Scene VIII

The CAPTAIN. *The* NURSE. BERTHA *enters.*

BERTHA: Father, father! Help me! Save me!

CAPTAIN: What is it, my beloved child? Tell me.

BERTHA: Help me! I think she wants to hurt me!

CAPTAIN: Who wants to hurt you? Tell me. Tell me.

BERTHA: Grandmamma. But it was my fault. I played a trick on her.

CAPTAIN: Tell me about it.

BERTHA: But you mustn't say anything! Promise you won't!

CAPTAIN: Very well. But tell me what it is.

The NURSE *goes.*

BERTHA: Well—in the evenings, she turns down the lamp and sits me down at the table with a pen and paper. And then she says that the spirits are going to write.

CAPTAIN: What! Why haven't you told me about this before?

BERTHA: Forgive me—I didn't dare. Grandmamma says the spirits take their revenge if anyone talks about them. And then the pen writes, but I don't know if it's me. And sometimes it goes all right, but sometimes it won't move at all. And when I'm tired, nothing comes—but it's *got* to come! And tonight I thought I was writing well, but then grandmamma said I was copying from some old poem and playing a trick on her—and then she became so horribly angry!

CAPTAIN: Do you believe that spirits exist?

BERTHA: I don't know.

CAPTAIN: But I know they do not!

BERTHA: But grandmamma says you don't understand, and that you have much worse things, that can see what's happening on other planets.

CAPTAIN: She says that, does she? What else does she say?

BERTHA: She says you can't work magic.

CAPTAIN: I haven't said I can. You know what meteors are? Yes, stones that fall from other heavenly bodies. I can study them and say whether they contain the same elements as our earth. That's all I can see.

BERTHA: But grandmamma says there are things that she can see but you can't.

CAPTAIN: Well, she's lying.

BERTHA: Grandmamma doesn't tell lies.

CAPTAIN: How do you know?

BERTHA: Then mother would be lying too.

CAPTAIN: Hm!

BERTHA: If you say mother's lying, I'll never believe you again!

CAPTAIN: I haven't said that, and you must believe me when I tell you that your happiness and your whole future depend on your leaving this house. Would you like that? Would you like to go and live in town, and learn something new?

BERTHA: Oh, I'd so love to live in town and get away from here! As long as I can see you sometimes—often! In there everything's so gloomy, so horrible, like a winter night—but when you come, father, it's like throwing open the window on a spring morning!

CAPTAIN: My child! My child!

BERTHA: But, father, you must be nice to mother, do you hear? She cries so often.

CAPTAIN: Hm! So you want to go and live in town?

BERTHA: Yes! Yes!

CAPTAIN: But if your mother doesn't want you to?

BERTHA: But she must!

CAPTAIN: But if she doesn't?

BERTHA: Well, then—I don't know. But she must! She must!

CAPTAIN: Will you ask her?

BERTHA: You must ask her, nicely. She doesn't pay any attention to me.

CAPTAIN: Hm! Well, if you want it and I want it, and she doesn't want it, what shall we do then?

BERTHA: Oh, then everything'll be difficult again. Why can't you both—?

Scene IX

The CAPTAIN. BERTHA. LAURA.

LAURA: Oh, she's here. Now perhaps we can hear her opinion. Since her fate is about to be decided.

CAPTAIN: The child can hardly be expected to hold an informed opinion on what a young girl ought to do with her life. We are at least partly qualified to judge, since we have seen a good many young girls grow up.

LAURA: But since we differ, let Bertha decide.

CAPTAIN: No! I permit no one to usurp my rights—neither woman nor child. Bertha, leave us.

BERTHA *goes.*

LAURA: You were afraid to let her speak, because you knew she'd agree with me.

CAPTAIN: I happen to know she wants to leave home. But I also know that you have the power to alter her will at your pleasure.

LAURA: Oh, am I so powerful?

CAPTAIN: Yes. You have a satanic genius for getting what you want. But that's always the way with people who aren't scrupulous about what means they use. How, for example, did you get rid of Dr. Norling, and find this new man?

LAURA: Well, how did I?

CAPTAIN: You insulted Norling, so that he went, and got your brother to fix this fellow's appointment.

LAURA: Well, that was very simple, wasn't it? And quite legal. Is Bertha to leave at once?

CAPTAIN: In a fortnight.

LAURA: Is that final?

CAPTAIN: Yes.

LAURA: Have you spoken to Bertha?

CAPTAIN: Yes.

LAURA: Then I shall have to stop it.

CAPTAIN: You can't.

LAURA: Can't? You think I'm prepared to let my daughter live with people who'll tell her that everything I taught her is nonsense, so that she'll despise her mother for the rest of her life?

CAPTAIN: Do you think I am prepared to allow ignorant and conceited women to teach my daughter that her father is a charlatan?

LAURA: That should matter less to you.

CAPTAIN: Why?

LAURA: Because a mother is closer to her child. It has recently been proved that no one can be sure who is a child's father.

CAPTAIN: What has that to do with us?

LAURA: You can't be sure that you are Bertha's father.

CAPTAIN: I—can't be sure—!

LAURA: No. No one can be sure, so you can't.

CAPTAIN: Are you trying to be funny?

LAURA: I'm only repeating what you've said to me. Anyway, how do you know I haven't been unfaithful to you?

CAPTAIN: I could believe almost anything of you, but not that. Besides, if it were true you wouldn't talk about it.

LAURA: Suppose I were prepared for anything—to be driven out, despised, anything—rather than lose my child? Suppose I am telling you the truth now, when I say to you: "Bertha is my child, but not yours!" Suppose—!

CAPTAIN: Stop!

LAURA: Just suppose. Your power over her would be ended.

CAPTAIN: If you could prove I was not the father.

LAURA: That wouldn't be difficult. Would you like me to?

CAPTAIN: Stop it! At once!

LAURA: I'd only need to name the true father, and tell you the time and place. When was Bertha born? Three years after our marriage—

CAPTAIN: Stop it, or—!

LAURA: Or what? All right, I'll stop. But think carefully before you take any decision. And, above all, don't make yourself ridiculous.

CAPTAIN: God—I could almost weep—!

LAURA: Then you *will* be ridiculous.

CAPTAIN: But not you!

LAURA: No. Our relationship to our children is not in question.

CAPTAIN: That is why one cannot fight with you.

LAURA: Why try to fight with an enemy who is so much stronger?

CAPTAIN: Stronger?

LAURA: Yes. It's strange, but I've never been able to look at a man without feeling that I am stronger than him.

CAPTAIN: Well, for once you're going to meet your match. And I'll see you never forget it.

LAURA: That'll be interesting.

NURSE   (*enters*): Dinner's ready. Will you come and eat?

LAURA: Thank you.

The CAPTAIN *hesitates, then sits in a chair by the table, next to the sofa.*

LAURA: Aren't you going to eat?

CAPTAIN: No, thank you. I don't want anything.

LAURA: Are you sulking?

CAPTAIN: No. I'm not hungry.

LAURA: Come along, or there'll be questions asked. Be sensible, now. Oh, very well. If you won't, you'd better go on sitting there. (*Goes.*)

NURSE: Mr. Adolf! What is all this?

CAPTAIN: I don't know. Can you explain to me how it is that you women can treat an old man as though he was a child?

NURSE: Don't ask me. I suppose it's because, whether you're little boys or grown men, you're all born of woman.

CAPTAIN: But no woman is born of man. Yes, but I *am* Bertha's father! Tell me, Margaret! You do believe that? Don't you?

NURSE: Lord, what a child you are! Of course you're your own daughter's father. Come and eat now, and don't sit there sulking. There! There now, come along!

CAPTAIN (*gets up*): Get out, woman! Back to hell, you witches! (*Goes to the door leading to the hall.*) Svaerd! Svaerd!

BATMAN   (*enters*): Sir?

CAPTAIN: Harness the sleigh! At once!

NURSE: Captain! Now, listen—!

CAPTAIN: Out, woman! At once!

NURSE: Lord help us, what's going to happen now?

CAPTAIN   (*puts on his hat and makes ready to go out*): Don't expect me home before midnight! (*Goes.*)

NURSE: Blessed Jesus preserve us, how's all this going to end?

ACT II

As in Act One. The lamp is burning on the table. It is night.

Scene I

The DOCTOR. LAURA.

DOCTOR: After my conversation with your husband, I am by no means convinced that your fears are justified. You made a mistake when you told me he had reached these surprising conclusions about other heavenly bodies by the use of a microscope. Now that I hear it was a spectroscope, he must not only be acquitted of any suspicion of derangement, but appears to have made a genuine contribution to science.

LAURA: But I never said that.

DOCTOR: Madam, I took notes of our conversation, and I remember I questioned you on this very point, because I thought I must have misheard you. One must be most meticulous in such accusations, for they could result in a man being certified as incapable of managing his affairs.

LAURA: Certified as incapable—?

DOCTOR: Yes. Surely you know that a person who is *non compos* loses all his civic and family rights?

LAURA: No, I didn't know that.

DOCTOR: There is one further point on which I feel uneasy. He told me that his letters to booksellers had remained unanswered. Permit me to ask whether you, no doubt from the best of motives, perhaps intercepted them?

LAURA: Yes, I did. I had to protect my family. I couldn't let him ruin us all without doing something.

DOCTOR: Forgive me, but I don't think you can have realised the consequences of such an action. If he finds that you have been secretly interfering in his affairs, his suspicions will be confirmed, and they will grow like an avalanche. Besides, by doing this you have fettered his will and further inflamed his impatience. You must have felt yourself how agonising it is when one's most fervent wishes are obstructed, and one's wings are clipped.

LAURA: Yes, I have felt it.

DOCTOR: Well, then, judge how he must feel.

LAURA   (*rises*): It's midnight, and he hasn't come home. We must be ready for the worst.

DOCTOR: But, tell me, Mrs. Lassen, what happened this evening after I left? I must know everything.

LAURA: Oh, he raved and said the most extraordinary things. Can you imagine—he asked if he really was the father of his child!

DOCTOR: How very strange! Where did he get that idea?

LAURA: I can't imagine. Unless—well, he'd been questioning one of the servants about who was the father to some baby, and when I took the girl's side he became furious and said no one could know for sure who was any child's father. God knows I tried my best to calm him, but now I don't see that there's anything more we can do. (*Weeps.*)

DOCTOR: This mustn't be allowed to continue. Something must be done. But we mustn't arouse his suspicions. Tell me, has the Captain had such hallucinations before?

LAURA: It was the same six years ago. Then he actually admitted in a letter to the doctor that he feared for his own sanity.

DOCTOR: Dear me! This obviously springs from something very deep-rooted. I mustn't enquire into the sacred secrets of family life, etcetera; I must confine myself to visible symptoms. What is done cannot, alas, be undone; but some steps should have been taken earlier. Where do you suppose he is now?

LAURA: I can't imagine. He gets such crazy ideas nowadays.

DOCTOR: Would you like me to wait till he comes back? I could say that your mother has been feeling poorly, and that I have been attending her. That would lull his suspicions.

LAURA: Yes, do that. Oh, please don't leave us! If you knew how worried I am! But wouldn't it be better to tell him straight out what you think about his condition?

DOCTOR: No, one must never do that with people who are mentally sick. Certainly not until they raise the subject themselves, and then only under certain circumstances. It all depends how things develop. But we mustn't sit in here. Perhaps I should go next door? Then he won't suspect anything.

LAURA: Yes, that's a good idea. Margaret can sit in here. She always stays up when he goes out, and she's the only one who can do anything with him. (*Goes to the door, left.*) Margaret! Margaret!

NURSE: What is it, madam? Is the master home?

LAURA: No, but I want you to sit here and wait for him. When he comes, tell him that my mother is ill and the doctor has come to visit her.

NURSE: Very well. You leave it to me.

LAURA (*opens the door, left*): Will you come in here, Doctor?

DOCTOR: Thank you.

Scene II

NURSE (*at the table; picks up a prayerbook and her spectacles*): Yes, yes! Yes, yes!

(*Reads half to herself.*)

A wretched and a grievous thing
Is life, this vale of suffering.
Death's angel hovers ever near,
And whispers into each man's ear:
"All's vanity! All's vanity!"
    Yes, yes! Yes, yes!

All things that live upon the earth
Fall to the ground before his wrath;

And only sorrow's ghost survives
To carve above the green-dug grave:
"All's vanity! All's vanity!"
Yes, yes! Yes, yes!

BERTHA   (*enters with a tray of coffee and a piece of embroidery. She whispers*):
Margaret, can I sit with you? It's so horrid up there.

NURSE: Heaven preserve us! Are you still up?

BERTHA: I've got to finish father's Christmas present, you see. And, look!
I've something for you!

NURSE: But, my dear Miss Bertha, you can't do this. You've got to get up
in the morning, and it's past midnight.

BERTHA: Well, what of it? I daren't sit up there alone. I'm sure there are
ghosts about.

NURSE: You see! What did I say? Yes, mark my word, there's no good spirit
guarding this house. What kind of thing did you hear?

BERTHA: Oh, do you know—I heard someone singing in the attic!

NURSE: In the attic! At this time of night!

BERTHA: Yes. It was a sad song—so sad—I've never heard anything like it
before. And it sounded as if it came from the cupboard where the cradle is—
you know, on the left—

NURSE: Oi, oi, oi! And with such a storm blowing tonight! I'm frightened
it'll bring the chimney-pots down. "What is this life but toil and care? A
moment's hope, then long despair!" Well, my dear child, may God grant us a
happy Christmas!

BERTHA: Margaret, is it true father is ill?

NURSE: I'm afraid so.

BERTHA: Then we won't be able to *have* Christmas. But how can he be up,
if he's ill?

NURSE: Well, my child, with his kind of illness you can stay up. Ssh! There's
someone on the steps. Go to bed, now, and hide this (*indicates the coffee tray*),
or the master'll be angry.

BERTHA   (*goes out with the tray*): Good night, Margaret.

NURSE: Good night, my child. God bless you.

Scene III

The NURSE. The CAPTAIN.

CAPTAIN   (*takes off his greatcoat*): Are you still up? Go to bed!

NURSE: I only wanted to wait till you—

The CAPTAIN *lights a candle, opens the secretaire, sits down at it immediately and takes from
his pocket letters and newspapers.*

NURSE: Mr. Adolf!

CAPTAIN: What do you want?

NURSE: The old lady's sick. And the doctor's here.

CAPTAIN: Is it dangerous?

NURSE: No, I don't think so. Just a chill.

CAPTAIN (*gets up*): Who was the father of your child, Margaret?

NURSE: Oh, I've told you so many times. That good-for-nothing Johansson.

CAPTAIN: Are you sure it was he?

NURSE: Don't be silly. Of course I'm sure. He was the only one.

CAPTAIN: Yes, but was *he* sure he was the only one? No, he couldn't be. But you could be. There's a difference, you see.

NURSE: I can't see the difference.

CAPTAIN: No, you can't see it, but the difference is there. (*Turns the pages of a photograph album on the table.*) Do you think Bertha is like me? (*Looks at a portrait in the album.*)

NURSE: You're as alike as two berries on a bough.

CAPTAIN: Did Johansson admit he was the father?

NURSE: He had to.

CAPTAIN: It's horrible—! There's the doctor.

Scene IV

The CAPTAIN. *The* NURSE. *The* DOCTOR.

CAPTAIN: Good evening, Doctor. How is my mother-in-law?

DOCTOR: Oh, it's nothing serious. She's just sprained her left foot slightly.

CAPTAIN: I thought Margaret said she had a chill. There seem to be two rival diagnoses. Go to bed, Margaret.

(*The* NURSE *goes. Pause.*)

CAPTAIN: Please sit down, Doctor.

DOCTOR (*sits*): Thank you.

CAPTAIN: Is it true that if you cross a zebra with a horse, you get striped foals?

DOCTOR (*surprised*): That is perfectly correct.

CAPTAIN: Is it also true that if you cross the same mare with an ordinary stallion, the foals may continue to be striped?

DOCTOR: Yes, that is also true.

CAPTAIN: Then, in certain circumstances a brown stallion can sire a striped foal, and vice versa?

DOCTOR: Apparently.

CAPTAIN: *Ergo,* the resemblance that a child bears to its father means nothing?

DOCTOR: Oh——

CAPTAIN: *Ergo,* it can never be proved who is a child's father?

DOCTOR: Er—hm——!

CAPTAIN: You are a widower and have had children?

DOCTOR: Er—yes——

CAPTAIN: Didn't you sometimes feel that your position was ridiculous? I know nothing so ludicrous as to see a father walking with his child on the street, or hear a father talking about his children. "My wife's children," he should say.

Did you never feel the falseness of your position, had you never any pinpricks of doubt? I don't use the word suspicion, for as a gentleman I assume that your wife was above suspicion.

DOCTOR: Indeed I did not! Has not Goethe written: "A man must take his children on trust"?

CAPTAIN: Trust, where a woman's concerned? That's risky!

DOCTOR: But there are so many kinds of women.

CAPTAIN: Recent research has proved that there is only one kind. When I was young, I was strong and, I flatter myself, handsome. Let me quote you just two incidents which subsequently caused me to ponder. Once I was travelling on a steamer. I was sitting with some friends in the lounge. The young waitress came and sat herself opposite me in tears, and told me that her fiancé had been drowned. We pitied her, and I ordered some champagne. After the second glass, I touched her foot; after the fourth, her knee; and before morning, I had consoled her.

DOCTOR: That was just a fly in winter.

CAPTAIN: Now to my second; and this was a fly in summer. I was at Lysekil. There was a young wife there, with her children—but her husband was in town. She was religious, had very strict principles, read me moral lectures, preached sermons at me——was completely honourable, I still believe. I lent her a book, two books. When the time came for her to leave, strange to relate, she returned them. Three months later, I found in one of these books a visiting card bearing a pretty explicit declaration of love. It was innocent, as innocent as a declaration of love can be from a married woman to a stranger who has never made an advance to her. The moral? Never trust anyone too much!

DOCTOR: Or too little!

CAPTAIN: Exactly; just so far and no further. But, you see, Doctor, that woman was so unconsciously mischievous that she told her husband she had developed a passion for me. That's just the danger, they don't realise their instinctive capacity for creating mischief. It's an extenuating circumstance, but it doesn't nullify their guilt, it merely lessens it.

DOCTOR: Captain, these are unhealthy thoughts. You should keep a watch on yourself——

CAPTAIN: You mustn't use that word, unhealthy. You see, all boilers explode when the manometer reaches breaking-point; but they don't all have the same breaking-point—you understand? Still, you're here to keep an eye on me. If I were not a man I would have the right to accuse—or, as the polite phrase is, to lay a complaint. Then I might perhaps be able to give you a complete diagnosis of my illness, and, what is more, its history. But unfortunately, I am a man, and so I can only, like a Roman, fold my arms across my breast and hold my breath until I die. Good night.

DOCTOR: Captain! If you are ill, it cannot be any reflection on your honour as a man to tell me the truth. I must hear both sides.

CAPTAIN: I should have thought you'd had enough listening to one.

DOCTOR: No, Captain. Do you know, when I sat in the theatre the other evening and heard Mrs. Alving orating over her dead husband, I thought to myself: "What a damned shame the fellow's dead and can't defend himself!"

CAPTAIN: If he'd been alive, do you think he'd have dared to open his mouth? If any dead man rose from his grave, do you think he'd be believed? Good night, Doctor. As you can hear, I am perfectly calm, so you can sleep in peace.

DOCTOR: Good night, then, Captain. I cannot take any further part in this matter.

CAPTAIN: Are we enemies?

DOCTOR: By no means. The pity is that we cannot be friends. Good night. (*Goes.*)

CAPTAIN (*accompanies the* DOCTOR *to the door upstage. Then he goes to the door left, and opens it slightly*): Come in, and let's talk. I heard you listening.

Scene V

LAURA *enters embarrassed. The* CAPTAIN *sits down at the secretaire.*

CAPTAIN: It's late, but we must talk this matter out. Sit down! [*Pause.*] This evening I went to the post office and collected my letters. It is evident from them that you have been intercepting both my outgoing and my incoming correspondence. The resultant waste of time has virtually destroyed the value of my researches.

LAURA: I was acting from kindness. You were neglecting your duties for this work.

CAPTAIN: You were not acting from kindness. You feared that some day I might win more honour through these researches than through my military career, and you were determined that I should not win any honour, because that would throw into relief your insignificance. Now I have confiscated some letters addressed to you.

LAURA: How noble of you.

CAPTAIN: I'm glad you appreciate my qualities. It is clear from these letters that for some time you have been turning all my former friends against me by spreading a rumour concerning my sanity. And you've succeeded, for now hardly one of them, from my commanding officer to my cook, regards me as sane. The situation regarding my mental condition is as follows. My brain is, as you know, unaffected, since I can perform both my professional duties and my duties as a father. I still have my emotions more or less under control, and my will is, to date, fairly unimpaired, but you have been chipping and chafing at it so that soon the cogs will disengage and the wheels will start whirling backwards. I shall not appeal to your feelings, for you have none—that is your strength. But I appeal to your self-interest.

LAURA: Go on.

CAPTAIN: By your behaviour you have succeeded in filling my mind with doubt, so that soon my judgment will be clouded and my thoughts begin to wander. This is the approaching dementia for which you have been waiting, and which may come at any time. Now you must ask yourself the question: is it not more to your interest that I should be well rather than ill? Think carefully? If I break down, I shall lose my job, and you will be without support. If I die, you will receive the insurance on my life; but if I kill myself, you will get nothing. So it is to your own interest that I should go on living.

LAURA: Is this a trap?

CAPTAIN: Yes. It is up to you whether you go round it or stick your neck in it.

LAURA: You say you'll kill yourself. You won't!

CAPTAIN: Are you sure? Do you think a man can live when he has nothing and no one to live for?

LAURA: Then you capitulate?

CAPTAIN: No. I propose an armistice.

LAURA: And your conditions?

CAPTAIN: That I retain my sanity. Free me from my doubts, and I will abandon the battle.

LAURA: What doubts?

CAPTAIN: About Bertha's parentage.

LAURA: Are there any doubts about that?

CAPTAIN: In my mind there are. You have awoken them.

LAURA: I?

CAPTAIN: Yes. You have dripped them into my ear like poison, and events have fostered their growth. Free me from my uncertainty, tell me straight out: "It is so!" and already I forgive you.

LAURA: How can I confess to a crime I have not committed?

CAPTAIN: What does it matter? You know I shan't reveal it. Do you think a man goes around trumpeting his shame?

LAURA: If I say it isn't true, you won't be sure; but if I say it is, you will be. So you would rather it was true.

CAPTAIN: Yes. It's strange, but I suppose it's because the one cannnot be proved, whereas the other can.

LAURA: Have you any grounds for your suspicions?

CAPTAIN: Yes and no.

LAURA: I suppose you'd like me to be guilty so that you could throw me out and keep the child to yourself. But you won't catch me with a trick like that.

CAPTAIN: Do you think I'd want to keep some other man's child if I knew you were guilty?

LAURA: I'm sure you wouldn't. And that's why I realise you were lying just now when you said you already forgave me.

CAPTAIN   (*gets up*): Laura, save me and my sanity. You don't understand what I'm saying. If the child is not mine, I have no rights over her, and want none—and that is all that *you* want. Isn't it? Or do you want something else too? Do you want to retain your power over the child, but to keep me here as the breadwinner?

LAURA: Power? Yes. What has this life-and-death struggle been for if not for power?

CAPTAIN: I do not believe in resurrection, and to me this child was my life hereafter. She was my idea of immortality—perhaps the only one that has any roots in reality. If you take her away, you cut short my life.

LAURA: Why didn't we part while there was still time?

CAPTAIN: Because the child bound us together. But the bond became a chain. How did it become that? How? I've never thought about it, but now memories return, accusing, condemning. We had been married for two years, and had no children, you best know why. I fell ill, and lay near to death. In a lucid moment I heard voices from the drawing-room. It was you and the lawyer, talking about my money—I still had some then. He is explaining that you cannot inherit anything because we have no children, and he asks if you are pregnant. I didn't hear your reply. I got better, and we had a child. Who is the father?

LAURA: You!

CAPTAIN: No, it is not I! A crime lies buried here, and it's beginning to come to light. And what a fiendish crime! You women were soft-hearted enough to free your black slaves, but you keep your white ones! I have worked and slaved for you, for your child, your mother, your servants. I have sacrificed my life and my career, I have undergone torture, scourging, sleeplessness, every kind of torment for you, my hair has turned grey, all so that you might live free from care and, when you grow old, enjoy new life through your child. All this I have borne without complaint, because I believed I was the father to this child. This is the most arrant form of theft, the most brutal slavery. I have served seventeen years of hard labour for a crime I did not commit. What can you give me in return?

LAURA: Now you really *are* mad.

CAPTAIN   (*sits*): So you hope. And I have seen how you worked to hide your crime. I pitied you, because I didn't understand why you were sad. I often calmed your evil conscience, supposing that I was driving away some sick thought. I heard you cry aloud in your sleep, though I didn't want to listen. Now I remember—the night before last! It was Bertha's birthday. It was between two and three o'clock in the morning, and I was sitting up, reading. You screamed as though someone was trying to strangle you: "Don't come, don't come!" I banged on the wall because—because I didn't want to hear any more. I have had my suspicions for a long time, but I didn't dare to hear them confirmed. I have suffered all this for you. What will you do for me?

LAURA: What can I do? I will swear by God and all that is sacred that you are Bertha's father.

CAPTAIN: What good will that do, when you have already said that a mother can and should commit any crime for the sake of her child? I entreat you, by the memory of the past—I beg you, as a wounded man begs for mercy —tell me everything! Don't you see that I am as helpless as a child, can't you hear me crying for pity like a child crying to its mother, can't you forget that I am a man, a soldier who with a word can tame men and beasts? I ask only for the pity you would extend to a sick man, I lay down the insignia of my power and cry for mercy—for my life.

LAURA   (*has approached him and lays her hand on his forehead*): What! Man, you're crying!

CAPTAIN: Yes, I am crying, although I am a man. But has not a man eyes? Has not a man hands, limbs, heart, thoughts, passions? Does he not live by the same food, is he not wounded by the same weapons, warmed and cooled by the same summer and winter as a woman? If you prick us, do we not bleed? If you tickle us, do we not laugh? If you poison us, do we not die? Why should a man be forbidden to complain, or a soldier to weep? Because it is unmanly? Why is it unmanly?

LAURA: Weep, my child. Your mother is here to comfort you. Do you remember, it was as your second mother that I first entered into your life? Your big, strong body was afraid. You were a great child who had come too late into the world, or had come unwanted.

CAPTAIN: Yes, I suppose it was that. Father and mother had me against their will, and so I was born without a will. When you and I became one, I thought I was making myself whole; so I let you rule; and I who, in the barracks, among the soldiers, issued commands, was, with you, the one who obeyed. I grew up at your side, looked up to you as though to a superior being, listened to you as though I was your innocent child.

LAURA: Yes. That's how it was, and I loved you as my child. But, do you know—I suppose you noticed it—every time your feelings towards me changed, and you approached me as my lover, I felt bashful, and your embrace was an ecstasy followed by pangs of conscience, as though my blood was ashamed. The mother became the mistress—ugh!

CAPTAIN: Yes. I saw it, but I didn't understand. I thought you despised my lack of masculinity, and I wanted to win you as a woman by being a man.

LAURA: That was where you made your mistake. The mother was your friend, you see, but the woman was your enemy. Love between man and woman is war. And don't think I gave myself. I didn't give, I took—what I wanted to have. But you had the upper hand. I felt it, and I wanted to make you feel it.

CAPTAIN: No, you were always the one who had the upper hand. You could hypnotise me so that I neither saw nor heard, but only obeyed. You could give me a raw potato and make me think it was a peach, you could force me to admire your stupid ideas as strokes of genius, you could have driven me to crime, yes, even to vice. For you lacked intelligence, and instead of following my advice you did as *you* wanted. But when, later, I awoke and looked about me and saw that my honour had been sullied, I wanted to wipe out the stain through a noble action, a brave deed, a discovery, or an honourable suicide. I wanted to go to war, but I couldn't. It was then that I turned to science. Now, when I should stretch out my hand to receive the fruits of my labour, you chop off my arm. Now I am without honour, and I cannot go on living, for a man cannot live without honour.

LAURA: But a woman——

CAPTAIN: She has her children, but he has none. Yet you and I and all the other men and women in the world have gone on living, as innocently as children, living on fancies, ideals and illusions. And then we awoke. Yes, we awoke, but with our feet on the pillow, and He Who woke us was Himself a sleepwalker. When women grow old and cease to be women, they get beards on their chins. I wonder what men get when they grow old and cease to be men? We who greeted the dawn were no longer cocks but capons, and the hens answered our false call, so that when the sun should have risen we found ourselves sitting in moonlight among ruins, just like in the good old days. It had only been a fretful slumber, a wild dream. It was no awakening.

LAURA: You know, you ought to have been a poet.

CAPTAIN: Perhaps I ought.

LAURA: Well, I'm sleepy. If you've any more fantasies, keep them until morning.

CAPTAIN: One word more—and this isn't a fantasy. Do you hate me?

LAURA: Sometimes. When you are a man.

CAPTAIN: This is like racial hatred. If it is true that we are descended from the ape, it must have been from two different species. We aren't of the same blood, are we?

LAURA: What do you mean by all that?

CAPTAIN: I feel that, in this war, one of us must go under.

LAURA: Which one?

CAPTAIN: The weaker, of course.

LAURA: And the stronger is in the right?

CAPTAIN: Always. Because he is the one with power.

LAURA: Then I am in the right.

CAPTAIN: You think you have the power?

LAURA: Yes. And tomorrow I shall have it legally, when I have you certified.

CAPTAIN: Certified——?

LAURA: Yes. And then I shall bring up the child myself, without having to listen to your visions.

CAPTAIN: And who will pay for the child's upbringing, when I am gone?

LAURA: Your pension.

CAPTAIN (*goes towards her threateningly*): How can you have me certified?

LAURA (*takes out a letter*): By this letter, an attested copy of which I have deposited with the authorities.

CAPTAIN: What letter?

LAURA (*moves backwards towards the door*): Yours! The one you wrote to the doctor telling him you were mad. (*The* CAPTAIN *looks at her dumbly.*) You have done your job as a father and a breadwinner. Now you are no longer needed, and you can go. You realize that my intelligence is equal to my will, and since you are not prepared to stay and admit it, you can go!

The CAPTAIN *goes to the table, takes the burning lamp and throws it at* LAURA, *who has retreated through the door.*

ACT III

As in Act Two. But another lamp. The concealed door is barricaded with a chair.

Scene I

LAURA. *The* NURSE.

LAURA: Did he give you the keys?

NURSE: Give them to me? No, God forgive me, I took them out of his pocket. He'd left them in the coat he'd given Nöjd to brush.

LAURA: So Nöjd's on duty today, is he?

NURSE: Yes.

LAURA: Give them to me.

NURSE: But that's like stealing! Very well. Oh, listen to him up there, madam! To and fro, to and fro.

LAURA: Is the door safely locked?

NURSE: Yes. It's locked all right.

LAURA   (*opens the secretaire and sits down to it*): You must try to control your feelings, Margaret. Our only hope is to remain calm. (*There is a knock on the door.*) Who's that?

NURSE   (*opens the door to the hall*): It's Nöjd.

LAURA: Tell him to come in.

NÖJD   (*enters*): A despatch from the Colonel!

LAURA: Give it to me. (*Reads.*) Nöjd, have you removed all the cartridges from the rifles and pouches?

NÖJD: As you ordered, ma'am.

LAURA: Then wait outside, while I answer the Colonel's letter.

NÖJD *goes.* LAURA *writes.*

NURSE: Madam, listen! Whatever can he be doing up there?

LAURA: Be quiet while I'm writing.

The sound of sawing is heard.

NURSE   (*half to herself*): Merciful Jesus preserve us all! Where's this going to end?

LAURA: There. Give this to Nöjd. My mother must know nothing of this. You hear!

The NURSE *goes to the door.* LAURA *opens the drawers of the secretaire and takes out some papers.*

Scene II

LAURA. *The* PASTOR *takes a chair and sits beside* LAURA *at the secretaire.*

PASTOR: Good evening, sister. I've been away all day, as you know, so I couldn't come before. Well, this is a sad story.

LAURA: Yes, brother. It's the worst twenty-four hours I have ever experienced.

PASTOR: At all events I see no harm has come to you.

LAURA: No, thank God. But think what could have happened.

PASTOR: But tell me one thing. How did it begin? I've heard so many different versions.

LAURA: Well, it started with him talking some nonsense about not being Bertha's father, and ended with him throwing the burning lamp in my face.

PASTOR: But this is terrible! This is real madness. What are we to do?

LAURA: Try to prevent any further violence. The doctor has sent to the asylum for a straitjacket. I've written to the Colonel, and am trying to get these accounts into some kind of order. It's really disgraceful the way he's neglected them.

PASTOR: What a tragedy! Mind you, I've always feared something like this might happen! Fire and water, you know—they're bound to end in an explosion. What have you got in that drawer?

LAURA *(has pulled a drawer out of the desk)*: Look. This is where he's been hiding everything.

PASTOR *(looks in the drawer)*: Great heavens! Why, there's your doll! And your christening-cap—and Bertha's rattle—and your letters—and that locket—! *(Touches his eyes with his handkerchief.)* He must have loved you very much, Laura, in spite of everything. I haven't kept things like that.

LAURA: I think he used to love me once. But time—time changes so many things.

PASTOR: What's that big paper? Why, it's a receipt for—for a grave! Well, better a grave than the asylum. Laura! Tell me—have you no share of the blame for all this?

LAURA: I? How could I be to blame for a man going mad?

PASTOR: Well, well. I shan't say anything. After all, blood is thicker than water.

LAURA: What do you mean by that?

PASTOR *(looks at her)*: Now, listen, Laura.

LAURA: Yes?

PASTOR: Listen to me. You cannot deny that this fits in very nicely with your wish that you should bring up the child yourself.

LAURA: I don't understand.

PASTOR: I can't help but admire you!

LAURA: Me! Hm!

PASTOR: And I am to become the guardian of that freethinker! Do you know, I have always regarded him as a tare among our wheat.

LAURA *(gives a short, stifled laugh. Then, suddenly serious)*: And you dare say that to me—his wife?

PASTOR: You are too strong for me, Laura. Incredibly strong! Like a fox in a trap; you'd rather bite off your own leg than let yourself be caught. Like a master-thief; you scorn any accomplice, even your own conscience. Look at yourself in the mirror! You daren't!

LAURA: I never use mirrors.

PASTOR: No, you daren't. May I look at your hand? Not one spot of blood to betray you, no trace of the poison that lies hidden there! One small, innocent murder, that the law cannot touch; an unconscious crime—unconscious? Brilliant, my dear, brilliant! But do you hear how he's working away up there? Take care? If that man gets free, he'll cut you to pieces!

LAURA: You talk too much. Have you a bad conscience? Accuse me; if you can.

PASTOR: I cannot.

LAURA: You see! You can't; I am innocent. You do your duty, and I'll do mine. Here comes the Doctor.

Scene III

LAURA. *The* PASTOR. *The* DOCTOR.

LAURA [*rises*]: Good evening, Doctor. At least you'll help me, won't you? Though I'm afraid there's not much anyone can do. You hear how he's carrying on up there? Are you convinced now?

DOCTOR: I am convinced that an act of violence has been committed. The question is whether it was an outbreak of anger or of madness.

PASTOR: Even if one ignores the actual assault, you must surely admit that he suffers from fixed ideas.

DOCTOR: I think your ideas are even more fixed, Pastor.

PASTOR: If you are referring to my spiritual convictions——

DOCTOR: I wasn't. Madam, it is up to you whether you choose to condemn your husband to imprisonment and a fine, or the asylum. How would you describe the Captain's conduct?

LAURA: I can't answer that now.

DOCTOR: You mean you are not certain which course would best serve the interests of your family? Well, Pastor, what do you say?

PASTOR: There'll be a terrible scandal either way. I really don't know——

LAURA: If he only has to pay a fine, he may commit violence again.

DOCTOR: And if he goes to prison he will soon be released. Then I suppose we must regard it as best for all concerned that he be treated as insane. Where is the nurse?

LAURA: Why do you ask?

DOCTOR: She must put the straitjacket on him, after I have talked with him and given her the signal. But not before! I have the thing outside. (*Goes into the hall and returns with a large package.*) Please ask the nurse to come in.

LAURA *rings.*

PASTOR: Dreadful, dreadful!

The NURSE *enters.*

DOCTOR (*unpacks the straitjacket*): You see this? When I decide that the moment has come, you must approach the Captain from behind and put this coat on him, to prevent any further outbreaks. As you see, it has unusually long sleeves, to limit his movements. You must fasten these behind his back. These two straps go through these buckles here, and you can then tie them to the back of the chair, or the sofa, whichever is more convenient. Will you do this?

NURSE: No, Doctor, I can't. I can't!

LAURA: Why don't you do it yourself, Doctor?

DOCTOR: Because the patient mistrusts me. You, madam, would be the most proper person to do it; but perhaps he mistrusts you too? (LAURA *does not reply.*) Perhaps you, Pastor——?

PASTOR: No, no! I couldn't possibly!

Scene IV

LAURA. *The* PASTOR. *The* DOCTOR. *The* NURSE. NÖJD.

LAURA: Have you delivered the letter already?

NÖJD: Yes, madam.

DOCTOR: Ah, it's you, Nöjd. Now you know what's happened, don't you? The Captain is—ill. You must help us to take care of him.

NÖJD: If there's anything I can do for the Captain, he knows I'll do it.

DOCTOR: Good. Now you must put this coat on him——

NURSE: No, he mustn't touch him! He'd hurt him. No, I'll do it myself—so gently, gently. Let him wait outside, to help me if need be. He can do that.

There is a banging on the concealed door.

DOCTOR: There he is! Hide this under the shawl—yes, on that chair—and go outside, all of you. The Pastor and I will wait in here. That door won't hold for long. Get outside, now, all of you!

NURSE (*goes out left*): Blessed Jesus, help us!

LAURA *closes the secretaire and goes out.* NÖJD *exits upstage.*

Scene V

The lock snaps, the chair crashes to the floor and the concealed door is flung open. The CAPTAIN *enters with a pile of books under his arm. The* DOCTOR. *The* PASTOR.

CAPTAIN (*puts the books on the table*): It's all here. I wasn't mad, you see. For example—*The Odyssey,* Book I, line 215, page 6 in the Upsala translation. Telemachus speaking to Athene. "Truly my mother asserts that he whom men call Odysseus is my father. But of this I cannot be sure, for no man knows for sure from whom he springs." And he says this of Penelope, the chastest of women! Pretty, eh? And here we have the prophet Ezekiel. "The fool saith: 'See, here is my father!' But who can tell whose loins have begotten him?" That's clear enough. Now, what have we here? Mersläkow's *History of Russian Literature.* "Alexander Pushkin, Russia's greatest poet, died more of grief at the widespread rumours of his wife's infidelity than of the bullet he received in the breast in a duel. On his deathbed, he swore that she was innocent." Idiot! Idiot! How could he swear to *that?* You see! I read my books! Hullo, Jonas, you here? And the Doctor—yes, of course! Have they told you what I once said to an Englishwoman who complained that the Irish throw burning lamps in their wives' faces? "God, what women!" I said. "Women?" she lisped. "Yes!" I replied. "When things have reached the pitch that a man who has loved and worshipped a woman takes a burning lamp and throws it in her face, then you know——!"

PASTOR: Then you know what?

CAPTAIN: Nothing! One never knows—one only believes—eh, Jonas? One believes, and is saved. Yes, saved! But I know that belief can damn a man! I know that.

DOCTOR: Captain!

CAPTAIN: Oh, shut up. I don't want to talk to you. I don't want to hear you echoing everything they say in there like one of these damned telephones! Yes, you know what I mean! Tell me, Jonas, do you believe that you are your children's father? I remember you used to have a tutor living with you whom people talked about. Such beautiful eyes, they said he had.

PASTOR: Adolf! Take care, now———!

CAPTAIN: Put your hand under your hair and see if you can't feel a couple of bumps there! I'm blessed if he hasn't gone pale! Yes, yes, it was only talk —but, my God, how they talked! But we're all objects of ridicule, we husbands. Isn't that true, Doctor? How about your marriage couch? Didn't you have a lieutenant billeted on you? Wait, now, let me guess—wasn't he called———? (*Whispers in the* DOCTOR's *ear.*) You see, he's gone pale too! Don't cry, now. She's dead and buried, and what's done can't be done again! I knew him, though —now he's a—look at me, Doctor!—no, in the eyes!—a major in the Dragoons. By God, I believe he's grown horns too!

DOCTOR: Captain, can we please discuss something else?

CAPTAIN: You see! As soon as I mention the word horns, he wants to talk about something else!

PASTOR: My poor brother, don't you realise you are mad?

CAPTAIN: Yes, I know. But if I had the care of your antlered heads for a week or two, I'd have you all behind bars too! I am mad, but how did I become mad? You don't care. Nobody cares. Let's talk about something else. (*Takes the photograph album from the table.*) Dear God—there is my child! Mine? How can we tell? Do you know what we have to do to be sure? First, marry to become socially respectable; then, soon afterwards, get divorced; and become lovers; and adopt the child. Then at least you can be sure it's your own adopted child. That's right, isn't it? But what good is all this to me? What good is anything to me now that you have taken away my hope of immortality, what good is my science and my philosophy now that I have nothing to live for, what use is my life to me now that I have no honour left? I grafted my right arm, half my brain, half my spinal cord on to another stem, because I believed they would unite into a single, more perfect tree, and then someone comes with a knife and cuts beneath the graft, so that now I am only half a tree—but the other tree goes on growing with my arm and half my brain, while I wither and die, for I gave the best parts of myself. Now I want to die! Do what you will with me! I no longer exist!

The DOCTOR *whispers to the* PASTOR. *They go into the room on the left. A few moments later,* BERTHA *enters.*

Scene VI

The CAPTAIN. BERTHA.

The CAPTAIN *sits huddled at the table.* BERTHA *goes over to him.*

BERTHA: Are you ill, father?

CAPTAIN   (*looks up dully*): I?

BERTHA: Do you know what you've done? Do you know you threw a burning lamp at mother?

CAPTAIN: Did I?

BERTHA: Yes, you did! Think if you'd hurt her!

CAPTAIN: What would that have mattered?

BERTHA: You aren't my father if you can talk like that!

CAPTAIN: What's that you say? I'm not your father? How do you know? Who has told you that? Who is your father, then? Who?

BERTHA: Well, not you, anyway.

CAPTAIN: Still not me! Who, then? Who? You seem well informed. Who's been priming you? Must I endure this, that my child comes and tells me to my face that I am not her father? But do you realise you're insulting your mother by saying that? Don't you understand that, if this is true, she is the one who has sinned?

BERTHA: Don't say anything against Mother, do you hear?

CAPTAIN: No, you stick together, you're all against me! And you've done so all the time!

BERTHA: Father!

CAPTAIN: Don't use that word again!

BERTHA: Father, father!

CAPTAIN (*draws her to him*): Bertha, my darling, my beloved child, of course you are my child! Yes, yes—it must be so—it *is* so. Those were just sick thoughts that came with the wind like pestilence and fever. Look at me, let me see my soul in your eyes! But I see her soul too! You have two souls, and you love me with one and hate me with the other! You must only love me! You must only have one soul, or you will never find peace, nor shall I. You must have only one thought, the child of my thought, and you shall have only one will, mine.

BERTHA: I don't want that! I want to be myself!

CAPTAIN: You mustn't do that! You see, I'm a cannibal, and I want to eat you. Your mother wanted to eat me, but she couldn't. I am Saturn, who ate his children because it had been prophesied that otherwise they would eat him. To eat or be eaten! That is the question. If I don't eat you, you will eat me, and you have already shown me your teeth. But don't be afraid, my beloved child. I won't hurt you. (*Goes to where the guns are on the wall and takes a revolver.*)

BERTHA (*tries to escape*): Help, mother, help! He wants to murder me!

NURSE (*enters*): Mr. Adolf, what is it?

CAPTAIN (*looks at the revolver*): Have you taken the cartridges?

NURSE: Yes, I've hidden them away. But sit down and calm yourself, and I'll bring them back to you.

She takes the CAPTAIN *by the arm and coaxes him down into the chair, where he remains sitting dully. Then she takes the straitjacket and goes behind his chair.* BERTHA *tiptoes out left.*

NURSE: Do you remember, Mr. Adolf, when you were my dear little baby, how I used to tuck you up at night and say your prayers with you? And do you remember how I used to get up in the night to fetch you a drink? Do you remember how I lit the candle and told you pretty stories when you had bad dreams and couldn't sleep? Do you remember?

CAPTAIN: Go on talking, Margaret. It soothes my head so. Go on talking.

NURSE: All right, but you must listen, then. Do you remember how once you took the carving knife and wanted to make boats, and how I came in and had to get the knife away from you by telling you a story? You were such a silly baby, so we had to tell you stories, because you thought we all wanted to hurt you. Give me that snake, I said, otherwise he'll bite you. And you let go of the knife. (*Takes the gun from the* CAPTAIN's *hand.*) And then, when you had to get dressed and you didn't want to. Then I had to coax you and say I'd give you a gold coat and dress you like a prince. And I took your little body-garment, which was only of green wool, and held it in front of you and said: "Put your arms in," and then I said: "Sit still, now, and be a good boy while I button up the back!" (*She has got the straitjacket on him.*) And then I said: "Stand up now, and walk nicely, so I can see how you look." (*She leads him to the sofa.*) And then I said: "Now it's time to go to bed."

CAPTAIN: What's that, Nanny? Must I go to bed when I'm dressed? Damnation! What have you done to me? (*Tries to free himself.*) Oh, you damned cunning woman! Who would have believed you were so crafty? (*Lies down on the sofa.*) Caught, cropped, and cozened! And not to be allowed to die!

NURSE: Forgive me, Mr. Adolf, forgive me! But I wanted to stop you from killing the child!

CAPTAIN: Why didn't you let me kill the child? Life is a hell, and death a heaven, and the child belongs to heaven.

NURSE: What do you know about what comes after death?

CAPTAIN: That is all one does know. About life, one knows nothing. Oh, if one had only known from the beginning!

NURSE: Mr. Adolf! Humble your proud heart and pray to God to forgive you. It still isn't too late. It wasn't too late for the robber on the cross, when our Saviour said to him: "Today shalt thou be with me in Paradise."

CAPTAIN: Are you croaking for carrion already, you old crow? (*The* NURSE *takes a prayer-book from her pocket. The* CAPTAIN *roars.*) Nöjd! Is Nöjd there?

NÖJD enters.

CAPTAIN: Throw this woman out! She wants to choke me to death with her prayer-book! Throw her out through the window, or up the chimney! Anywhere!

NÖJD   (*looks at the* NURSE.) God bless you, Captain, I can't do that! I just can't! If there were six men, yes, but a woman——

CAPTAIN: Aren't you stronger than a woman?

NÖJD: Of course I'm stronger, but there's something special about a woman that stops a man raising his hand against her.

CAPTAIN: What's special about them? Haven't they raised their hands against me?

NÖJD: Yes, but I can't, Captain! It's just as though you was to ask me to strike the Pastor. It's something that's in a man's blood, like religion. I can't!

Scene VII

As before. LAURA *gestures to* NÖJD *to go.*

CAPTAIN: Omphale! Omphale! Now you play with the club while Hercules winds your wool!

LAURA (*comes over to the sofa*): Adolf! Look at me! Do you think I am your enemy?

CAPTAIN: Yes, I do. I think you are all my enemies. My mother was my enemy. She didn't want to bring me into the world because my birth would cause her pain. She robbed my first embryo of its nourishment, so that I was born half-crippled. My sister was my enemy, when she taught me that I was her inferior. The first woman I kissed was my enemy—she gave me ten years of sickness in return for the love I gave her. My daughter became my enemy, when you forced her to choose between you and me. And you, my wife, you were my mortal enemy, for you didn't let go of me until you had throttled the life out of me.

LAURA: I don't know that I ever planned, or intended, what you think I have done. I may have felt a vague desire to be rid of you, because you were an obstacle in my path; but if you see a plan in the way I have acted, then perhaps there was one, though I wasn't aware of it. I didn't plot any of this—it just glided forward on rails which you laid yourself—and before God and my conscience, I feel that I am innocent, even if I am not. Your presence has been like a stone on my heart, pressing and pressing until my heart rebelled against its suffocating weight. This is the truth, and if I have unintentionally hurt you, I ask your forgiveness.

CAPTAIN: That all sounds plausible. But how does it help me? And who is to blame? Perhaps the idea of marriage is to blame. In the old days, one married a wife; now one forms a company with a woman who goes out to work, or moves in to live with a friend. And then one seduces the partner, or defiles the friend. What became of love—healthy, sensuous love? It died, starved. And what is the offspring of this broker's-love, a blank cheque drawn on a bankrupt account? Who will honour it when the crash comes? Who is the bodily father to the spiritual child?

LAURA: Those suspicions of yours about the child are completely unfounded.

CAPTAIN: That's just what's so horrible. If they were real, at least one would have something to grip on, something to cling to. Now there are only shadows, hiding in the bushes and poking out their heads to laugh—it's like fighting with air, a mock battle with blank cartridges. A real betrayal would have acted as a challenge, roused my soul to action. But now my thoughts dissolve in twilight, my brain grinds emptiness until it catches fire! Give me a pillow under my head! And put something over me, I'm cold. I'm so terribly cold!

LAURA *takes her shawl and spreads it over him. The* NURSE *goes out to fetch a pillow.*

LAURA: Give me your hand, friend.

CAPTAIN: My hand! Which you have tied behind my back? Omphale!

Omphale! But I feel your soft shawl against my mouth. It's warm and smooth like your arm, and it smells of vanilla, as your hair did when you were young. Laura—when you were young—and we walked in the birch woods among the primroses—and thrushes sang! Beautiful, beautiful! How beautiful life was! And now it has become like this. You didn't want it to be like this, I didn't want it, and yet it happened. Who rules our lives?

LAURA: God alone rules—

CAPTAIN: The God of battle, then! Or the goddess, nowadays! Take away this cat that's lying on me! Take it away! (*The* NURSE *enters with the pillow and removes the shawl.*) Give me my tunic. Put it over me! (*The* NURSE *takes his military tunic from the clothes-hanger and drapes it over him.*) Ah, my brave lion's skin, that you would take from me! Omphale! Omphale! O cunning woman, who so loved peace that you discovered the art of disarming men! Awake, Hercules, before they take your club from you! You would rob us of our armour and have us believe that it is only tinsel. No, it was iron before it became tinsel. In the old days it was the smith who forged the soldier's tunic; now it is the seamstress. Omphale! Omphale! Strength has been vanquished by craft and weakness! Curse you, damned woman, and all your sex! [*Rises himself to spit, but falls back on the couch.*] What kind of a pillow have you given me, Margaret? It's so hard, and so cold, so cold! Come and sit beside me here, on the chair. That's right. May I rest my head in your lap? So. That's warm! Bend over so that I can feel your breast. Oh, it is sweet to sleep at a woman's breast, whether a mother's or a mistress's, but sweetest at a mother's!

LAURA: Do you want to see your child, Adolf? Speak!

CAPTAIN: My child? A man has no children. Only women have children, and so the future belongs to them, while we die childless. Gentle Jesus, meek and mild, look upon this little child—!

NURSE: Listen! He's praying to God!

CAPTAIN: No, to you, to send me to sleep. I'm so tired, so tired. Good night, Margaret. Blessed be thou amongst women——

> *He raises himself, but falls with a cry in the* NURSE's *lap.*

Scene VIII

LAURA *goes left, and calls the* DOCTOR, *who enters with the* PASTOR.

LAURA: Help us, Doctor, if it isn't too late. Look, he's stopped breathing!

DOCTOR   (*takes the* CAPTAIN's *pulse*): He has had a stroke.

PASTOR: Is he dead?

DOCTOR: No. He may still awake, and live. But to what he will awake, we do not know.

PASTOR: "Once to die, but after this the judgment——"

DOCTOR: We must not judge or accuse him. You, who believe that there is a God who rules men's destinies, must plead this man's cause before the bar of Heaven.

NURSE: Oh, Pastor, he prayed to God in his last moment!

PASTOR   (*to* LAURA): Is this true?

LAURA: It is true.

DOCTOR: Then my art is useless. Now you must try yours, Pastor.

LAURA: Is that all you have to say at this death-bed, Doctor?

DOCTOR: That is all. My knowledge ends here. He who knows more, let him speak.

BERTHA *(enters left and runs to her mother)*: Mother, mother!

LAURA: My child! *My* child!

PASTOR: Amen!

QUESTIONS

1. How would you describe the atmosphere or mood of *The Father?* What details of action, setting, and dialogue contribute most to its tone?
2. What ideas motivate and what impulses animate the Captain and his wife, Laura? What is Bertha's response to their battle of wills?
3. Strindberg structures *The Father* as a series of short scenes. What is the effect of such an arrangement? Would it make much difference if there were fewer, but longer scenes?
4. Choose one scene and describe how you would stage it. Consider how the actors would be costumed, where they would be positioned, how they would use gesture and facial expression, and in what tones of voice they would speak their lines.
5. What is the function of the Pastor? Of the Nurse? Of the Doctor?
6. What is the play's theme?

Anton Chekhov

Although Chekhov, like Ibsen and Strindberg, is a realistic dramatist, the stamp of his realism differs from theirs. *The Cherry Orchard,* for example, lacks the intensity and ferocity of Strindberg's *The Father,* particularly its embittered dialogue. Chekhov's drama also lacks the tight resolution of a play whose plot presents a series of gradual revelations and complications that come to a final tidy conclusion.

Chekhov's dramas lack plot in the traditional sense. His plays don't tell stories the way many of Ibsen's do. Very little actually happens in *The Cherry Orchard.* Nor do his characters seem to accomplish much. Unsure what to do, how to find happiness, they do nothing, consoling themselves with illusory thoughts of the future.

The characters of *The Cherry Orchard,* like those in other of Chekhov's plays, are neither heroic nor villainous. None is a mouthpiece for the author's views. Most, if not all of them, seem to mean more than they can say, to express more than they can actually articulate. We must pay attention to their fractured conversations, broken sentences, random remarks, and incompleted actions to discover the heart of Chekhov's drama. And it is to his balanced sympathy and judgment of his characters that we should attend to gauge the essence of his tone.

The Cherry Orchard was written at a time when an old social order was dying in Russia: the landed aristocracy was losing its power and a new middle class was emerging. That Chekhov scrupulously avoids making a political issue out of this historical circumstance, condemning neither one side nor the other, testifies to his dispassionate attempt to present life rather than to comment on it. Unlike Ibsen and Strindberg, Chekhov predicates nothing, advertising no theses, advancing no arguments, engaging in no polemics. Instead as drama critic Francis Fergusson has noted, *The Cherry Orchard* is a "theatre-poem" about "the suffering of change," representing in alternation "his characters' perceptions of their situations."*

Konstantin Stanislavsky, the play's first producer, staged it as a tragedy, but Chekhov himself repeatedly insisted it was a comedy. Moreover, contrary to the views of some readers and theatergoers who see his characters as gloomy and lifeless, Chekhov saw them as alive, steadfast, hopeful. In the play there is both humor and sadness, gaiety, and suffering. Its combination of pathos with comedy and its apparent randomness of dialogue and action contribute to its life-like, authentic and elusive realism.

ANTON CHEKHOV

[1860–1904]

The Cherry Orchard

A COMEDY IN FOUR ACTS

TRANSLATED BY AVRAHM YARMOLINSKY

CHARACTERS

LUBOV ANDREYEVNA RANEVSKAYA, a landowner.
ANYA, her seventeen-year-old daughter.
VARYA, her adopted daughter, twenty-two years old.
LEONID ANDREYEVICH GAYEV, MME. RANEVSKAYA's brother.
YERMOLAY ALEXEYEVICH LOPAHIN, a merchant.
PYOTR SERGEYEVICH TROFIMOV, a student.
SIMEONOV-PISHCHIK, a landowner.
CHARLOTTA IVANOVNA, a governess.
SEMYON YEPIHODOV, a clerk.

*Francis Fergusson, *The Idea of a Theatre* (Princeton, N.J.: Princeton University Press, 1954) 176.

DUNYASHA, a maid.

FIRS (pronounced *fierce*), a man-servant, aged eighty-seven.

YASHA, a young valet.

A TRAMP.

STATIONMASTER, POST OFFICE CLERK, GUESTS, SERVANTS.

The action takes place on MME. RANEVSKAYA'S *estate.*

ACT I

A room that is still called the nursery. One of the doors leads into Anya's room. Dawn, the sun will soon rise. It is May, the cherry trees are in blossom, but it is cold in the orchard; there is a morning frost. The windows are shut. Enter DUNYASHA *with a candle, and* LOPAHIN *with a book in his hand.*

LOPAHIN: The train is in, thank God. What time is it?

DUNYASHA: Nearly two. (*Puts out the candle*) It's light already.

LOPAHIN: How late is the train, anyway? Two hours at least. (*Yawns and stretches*) I'm a fine one! What a fool I've made of myself! I came here on purpose to meet them at the station, and then I went and overslept. I fell asleep in my chair. How annoying! You might have waked me . . .

DUNYASHA: I thought you'd left. (*Listens.*) I think they're coming!

LOPAHIN (*listens*): No, they've got to get the luggage, and one thing and another . . . (*Pause*) Lubov Andreyevna spent five years abroad, I don't know what she's like now . . . She's a fine person—lighthearted, simple. I remember when I was a boy of fifteen, my poor father—he had a shop here in the village then—punched me in the face with his fist and made my nose bleed. We'd come into the yard, I don't know what for, and he'd had a drop too much. Lubov Andreyevna, I remember her as if it were yesterday—she was still young and so slim—led me to the wash-basin, in this very room . . . in the nursery. "Don't cry, little peasant," she said, "it'll heal in time for your wedding. . . ." (*Pause*) Little peasant . . . my father was a peasant, it's true, and here I am in a white waistcoat and yellow shoes. A pig in a pastry shop, you might say. It's true I'm rich, I've got a lot of money. . . . But when you look at it closely, I'm a peasant through and through. (*Pages the book*) Here I've been reading this book and I didn't understand a word of it. . . . was reading it and fell asleep. . . . (*Pause*)

DUNYASHA: And the dogs were awake all night, they feel that their masters are coming.

LOPAHIN: Dunyasha, why are you so—

DUNYASHA: My hands are trembling. I'm going to faint.

LOPAHIN: You're too soft, Dunyasha. You dress like a lady, and look at the way you do your hair. That's not right. One should remember one's place.

(*Enter* YEPIHODOV *with a bouquet; he wears a jacket and highly polished boots that squeak badly. He drops the bouquet as he comes in.*)

YEPIHODOV (*picking up the bouquet*): Here, the gardener sent these, said you're to put them in the dining room. (*Hands the bouquet to* DUNYASHA)

LOPAHIN: And bring me some *kvass.*

DUNYASHA: Yes, sir. (*Exits*)

YEPIHODOV: There's a frost this morning—three degrees below—and yet the cherries are all in blossom. I cannot approve of our climate. (*Sighs*) I cannot. Our climate does not activate properly. And, Yermolay Alexeyevich, allow me to make a further remark. The other day I bought myself a pair of boots, and I make bold to assure you, they squeak so that it is really intolerable. What should I grease them with?

LOPAHIN: Oh, get out! I'm fed up with you.

YEPIHODOV: Every day I meet with misfortune. And I don't complain, I've got used to it, I even smile.

(DUNYASHA *enters, hands* LOPAHIN *the kvass*)

YEPIHODOV: I am leaving. (*Stumbles against a chair, which falls over*) There! (*Triumphantly, as it were*) There again, you see what sort of circumstance, pardon the expression. . . . It is absolutely phenomenal! (*Exits*)

DUNYASHA: You know, Yermolay Alexeyevich, I must tell you, Yepihodov has proposed to me.

LOPAHIN: Ah!

DUNYASHA: I simply don't know . . . he's a quiet man, but sometimes when he starts talking, you can't make out what he means. He speaks nicely—and it's touching—but you can't understand it. I sort of like him though, and he is crazy about me. He's an unlucky man . . . every day something happens to him. They tease him about it here . . . they call him, Two-and-Twenty Troubles.

LOPAHIN (*listening*): There! I think they're coming.

DUNYASHA: They *are* coming! What's the matter with me? I feel cold all over.

LOPAHIN: They really are coming. Let's go and meet them. Will she recognize me? We haven't seen each other for five years.

DUNYASHA (*in a flutter*): I'm going to faint this minute. . . . Oh, I'm going to faint!

(*Two carriages are heard driving up to the house.* LOPAHIN *and* DUNYASHA *go out quickly. The stage is left empty. There is a noise in the adjoining rooms.* FIRS, *who had driven to the station to meet Lubov Andreyevna Ranevskaya, crosses the stage hurriedly, leaning on a stick. He is wearing an old-fashioned livery and a tall hat. He mutters to himself indistinctly. The hubbub off-stage increases. A voice: "Come, let's go this way." Enter* LUBOV ANDREYEVNA, ANYA *and* CHARLOTTA IVANOVNA, *with a pet dog on a leash, all in traveling dresses;* VARYA, *wearing a coat and kerchief;* GAYEV, SIMEONOV, PISHCHIK, LOPAHIN, DUNYASHA *with a bag and an umbrella, servants with luggage. All walk across the room.*)

ANYA: Let's go this way. Do you remember what room this is, mamma?

MME. RANEVSKAYA (*joyfully, through her tears*): The nursery!

VARYA: How cold it is! My hands are numb. (*To* MME. RANEVSKAYA) Your rooms are just the same as they were mamma, the white one and the violet.

MME. RANEVSKAYA: The nursery! My darling, lovely room! I slept here when I was a child . . . (*Cries*) And here I am, like a child again! (*Kisses her brother and* VARYA, *and then her brother again*) Varya's just the same as ever, like a nun. And I recognized Dunyasha. (*Kisses* DUNYASHA)

GAYEV: The train was two hours late. What do you think of that? What a way to manage things!

CHARLOTTA   (*to* PISHCHIK): My dog eats nuts, too.

PISHCHIK   (*in amazement*): You don't say so! (*All go out, except* ANYA *and* DUNYASHA)

DUNYASHA: We've been waiting for you for hours. (*Takes Anya's hat and coat*)

ANYA: I didn't sleep on the train for four nights and now I'm frozen . . .

DUNYASHA: It was Lent when you left; there was snow and frost, and now . . . My darling! (*Laughs and kisses her*) I have been waiting for you, my sweet, my darling! But I must tell you something . . . I can't put it off another minute . . .

ANYA   (*listlessly*): What now?

DUNYASHA: The clerk, Yepihodov, proposed to me, just after Easter.

ANYA: There you are, at it again . . . (*Straightening her hair*) I've lost all my hair-pins . . . (*She is staggering with exhaustion*)

DUNYASHA: Really, I don't know what to think. He loves me—he loves me so!

ANYA   (*looking towards the door of her room, tenderly*): My own room, my windows, just as though I'd never been away. I'm home! Tomorrow morning I'll get up and run into the orchard. Oh, if I could only get some sleep. I didn't close my eyes during the whole journey—I was so anxious.

DUNYASHA: Pyotr Sergeyevich came the day before yesterday.

ANYA   (*joyfully*): Petra!

DUNYASHA: He's asleep in the bath-house. He has settled there. He said he was afraid of being in the way. (*Looks at her watch*) I should wake him, but Miss Varya told me not to. "Don't you wake him," she said.

(*Enter* VARYA *with a bunch of keys at her belt*)

VARYA: Dunyasha, coffee, and be quick . . . Mamma's asking for coffee.

DUNYASHA: In a minute. (*Exits*)

VARYA: Well, thank God, you've come. You're home again. (*Fondling* ANYA) My darling is here again. My pretty one is back.

ANYA: Oh, what I've been through!

VARYA: I can imagine.

ANYA: When we left, it was Holy Week, it was cold then, and all the way Charlotta chattered and did her tricks. Why did you have to saddle me with Charlotta?

VARYA: You couldn't have traveled all alone, darling—at seventeen!

ANYA: We got to Paris, it was cold there, snowing. My French is dreadful. Mamma lived on the fifth floor; I went up there, and found all kinds of Frenchmen, ladies, an old priest with a book. The place was full of tobacco smoke, and so bleak. Suddenly I felt sorry for mamma, so sorry, I took her head in my arms and hugged her and couldn't let go of her. Afterwards mamma kept fondling me and crying . . .

VARYA   (*through tears*): Don't speak of it . . . don't.

ANYA: She had already sold her villa at Mentone, she had nothing left, nothing. I hadn't a kopeck left either, we had only just enough to get home. And mamma wouldn't understand! When we had dinner at the stations, she always ordered the most expensive dishes, and tipped the waiters a whole ruble. Charlotta, too. And Yasha kept ordering, too—it was simply awful. You know Yasha's mamma's footman now, we brought him here with us.

VARYA: Yes, I've seen the blackguard.

ANYA: Well, tell me—have you paid the interest?

VARYA: How could we?

ANYA: Good heavens, good heavens!

VARYA: In August the estate will be put up for sale.

ANYA: My God!

LOPAHIN   (*peeps in at the door and bleats*): Meh-h-h. (*Disappears*)

VARYA   (*through tears*): What I couldn't do to him! (*Shakes her fist threateningly*)

ANYA   (*embracing* VARYA, *gently*): Varya, has he proposed to you? (VARYA *shakes her head*) But he loves you. Why don't you come to an understanding? What are you waiting for?

VARYA: Oh, I don't think anything will ever come of it. He's too busy, he has no time for me . . . pays no attention to me. I've washed my hands of him —I can't bear the sight of him. They all talk about our getting married, they all congratulate me—and all the time there's really nothing to it—it's all like a dream. (*In another tone*) You have a new brooch—like a bee.

ANYA   (*sadly*): Mamma bought it. (*She goes into her own room and speaks gaily like a child*) And you know, in Paris I went up in a balloon.

VARYA: My darling's home, my pretty one is back! (DUNYASHA *returns with the coffee-pot and prepares coffee.* VARYA *stands at the door of Anya's room.*) All day long, darling, as I go about the house, I keep dreaming. If only we could marry you off to a rich man, I should feel at ease. Then I would go into a convent, and afterwards to Kiev, to Moscow . . . I would spend my life going from one holy place to another . . . I'd go on and on . . . What a blessing that would be!

ANYA: The birds are singing in the orchard. What time is it?

VARYA: It must be after two. Time you were asleep, darling. (*Goes into Anya's room*) What a blessing that would be!

(YASHA *enters with a plaid and a traveling bag, crosses the stage*)

YASHA   (*finally*): May I pass this way, please?

DUNYASHA: A person could hardly recognize you, Yasha. Your stay abroad has certainly done wonders for you.

YASHA: Hm-m . . . and who are you?

DUNYASHA: When you went away I was that high—(*Indicating with her hand*) I'm Dunyasha—Fyodor Kozoyedev's daughter. Don't you remember?

YASHA: Hm! What a peach!

(*He looks round and embraces her. She cries out and drops a saucer.* YASHA *leaves quickly*)

VARYA (*in the doorway, in a tone of annoyance*): What's going on here?

DUNYASHA (*through tears*): I've broken a saucer.

VARYA: Well, that's good luck.

ANYA (*coming out of her room*): We ought to warn mamma that Petya's here.

VARYA: I left orders not to wake him.

ANYA (*musingly*): Six years ago father died. A month later brother Grisha was drowned in the river. . . . Such a pretty little boy he was—only seven. It was more than mamma could bear, so she went away, went away without looking back . . . (*Shudders*) How well I understand her, if she only knew! (*Pauses*) And Petya Trofimov was Grisha's tutor, he may remind her of it all. . . .

(*Enter* FIRS, *wearing a jacket and a white waistcoat. He goes up to the coffee-pot.*)

FIRS (*anxiously*): The mistress will have her coffee here. (*Puts on white gloves*) Is the coffee ready? (*Sternly; to* DUNYASHA) Here, you! And where's the cream?

DUNYASHA: Oh, my God! (*Exits quickly*)

FIRS (*fussing over the coffee-pot*): Hah! the addlehead! (*Mutters to himself*) Home from Paris. And the old master used to go to Paris too . . . by carriage. (*Laughs*)

VARYA: What is it, Firs?

FIRS: What is your pleasure, Miss? (*Joyfully*) My mistress has come home, and I've seen her at last! Now I can die. (*Weeps with joy*)

(*Enter* MME. RANEVSKAYA, GAYEV, *and* SIMEONOV-PISHCHIK. *The latter is wearing a tight-waisted, pleated coat of fine cloth, and full trousers.* GAYEV, *as he comes in, goes through the motions of a billiard player with his arms and body.*)

MME. RANEVSKAYA: Let's see, how does it go? Yellow ball in the corner! Bank shot in the side pocket!

GAYEV: I'll tip it in the corner! There was a time, sister, when you and I used to sleep in this very room, and now I'm fifty-one, strange as it may seem.

LOPAHIN: Yes, time flies.

GAYEV: Who?

LOPAHIN: I say, time flies.

GAYEV: It smells of patchouli here.

ANYA: I'm going to bed. Good night, mamma. (*Kisses her mother*)

MME. RANEVSKAYA: My darling child! (*Kisses her hands*) Are you happy to be home? I can't come to my senses.

ANYA: Good night, uncle.

GAYEV (*kissing her face and hands*): God bless you, how like your mother you are! (*To his sister*) At her age, Luba, you were just like her.

(ANYA *shakes hands with* LOPAHIN *and* PISHCHIK, *then goes out, shutting the door behind her*)

MME. RANEVSKAYA: She's very tired.

PISHCHIK: Well, it was a long journey.

VARYA (*to* LOPAHIN *and* PISHCHIK): How about it, gentlemen? It's past two o'clock—isn't it time for you to go?

MME. RANEVSKAYA (*laughs*): You're just the same as ever, Varya. (*Draws her close and kisses her*) I'll have my coffee and then we'll all go. (*Firs puts a small cushion under her feet*) Thank you, my dear. I've got used to coffee. I drink it day and night. Thanks, my dear old man. (*Kisses him*)

VARYA: I'd better see if all the luggage has been brought in. (*Exits*)

MME. RANEVSKAYA: Can it really be I sitting here? (*Laughs*) I feel like dancing, waving my arms about. (*Covers her face with her hands*) But maybe I am dreaming! God knows I love my country, I love it tenderly; I couldn't look out of the window in the train, I kept crying so. (*Through tears*) But I must have my coffee. Thank you, Firs, thank you, dear old man. I'm so happy that you're still alive.

FIRS: Day before yesterday.

GAYEV: He's hard of hearing.

LOPAHIN: I must go soon, I'm leaving for Kharkov about five o'clock. How annoying! I'd like to have a good look at you, talk to you . . . You're just as splendid as ever.

PISHCHIK   (*breathing heavily*): She's even better-looking . . . Dressed in the latest Paris fashion . . . Perish my carriage and all its four wheels . . .

LOPAHIN: Your brother, Leonid Andreyevich, says I'm a vulgarian and an exploiter. But it's all the same to me—let him talk. I only want you to trust me as you used to. I want you to look at me with your touching, wonderful eyes, as you used to. Dear God! My father was a serf of your father's and grandfather's, but you, you yourself, did so much for me once . . . so much . . . that I've forgotten all about that; I love you as though you were my sister —even more.

MME. RANEVSKAYA: I can't sit still, I simply can't. (*Jumps up and walks about in violent agitation*) This joy is too much for me . . . Laugh at me, I'm silly! My own darling bookcase! My darling table! (*Kisses it*)

GAYEV: While you were away, nurse died.

MME. RANEVSKAYA   (*sits down and takes her coffee*): Yes, God rest her soul; they wrote me about it.

GAYEV: And Anastasy is dead. Petrushka Kossoy has left me and has gone into town to work for the police inspector. (*Takes a box of sweets out of his pocket and begins to suck one*)

PISHCHIK: My daughter Dashenka sends her regards.

LOPAHIN: I'd like to tell you something very pleasant—cheering. (*Glancing at his watch*) I am leaving directly. There isn't much time to talk. But I will put it in a few words. As you know, your cherry orchard is to be sold to pay your debts. The sale is to be on the twenty-second of August; but don't you worry, my dear, you may sleep in peace; there is a way out. Here is my plan. Give me your attention! Your estate is only fifteen miles from the town; the railway runs close by it; and if the cherry orchard and the land along the river bank were cut up into lots and these leased for summer cottages, you would have an income of at least 25,000 rubles a year out of it.

GAYEV: Excuse me . . . What nonsense.

MME. RANEVSKAYA: I don't quite understand you, Yermolay Alexeyevich.

LOPAHIN: You will get an annual rent of at least ten rubles per acre, and if you advertise at once, I'll give you any guarantee you like that you won't have a square foot of ground left by autumn, all the lots will be snapped up. In short, congratulations, you're saved. The location is splendid—by that deep river. . . . Only, of course the ground must be cleared . . . all the old buildings, for instance, must be torn down, and this house, too, which is useless, and of course, the old cherry orchard must be cut down.

MME. RANEVSKAYA: Cut down? My dear, forgive me, but you don't know what you're talking about. If there's one thing that's interesting—indeed, re-markable—in the whole province, it's precisely our cherry orchard.

LOPAHIN: The only remarkable thing about this orchard is that it's a very large one. There's a crop of cherries every other year, and you can't do anything with them; no one buys them.

GAYEV: This orchard is even mentioned in the Encyclopedia.

LOPAHIN   (*glancing at his watch*): If we can't think of a way out, if we don't come to a decision, on the twenty-second of August the cherry orchard and the whole estate will be sold at auction. Make up your minds! There's no other way out—I swear. None, none.

FIRS: In the old days, forty or fifty years ago, the cherries were dried, soaked, pickled, and made into jam, and we used to—

GAYEV: Keep still, Firs.

FIRS: And the dried cherries would be shipped by the cartload. It meant a lot of money! And in those days the dried cherries were soft and juicy, sweet, fragrant . . . They knew the way to do it, then.

MME. RANEVSKAYA: And why don't they do it that way now?

FIRS: They've forgotten. Nobody remembers it.

PISHCHIK   (*to* MME. RANEVSKAYA): What's doing in Paris? Eh? Did you eat frogs there?

MME. RANEVSKAYA: I ate crocodiles.

PISHCHIK: Just imagine!

LOPAHIN: There used to be only landowners and peasants in the country, but now these summer people have appeared on the scene . . . All the towns, even the small ones, are surrounded by these summer cottages; and in another twenty years, no doubt, the summer population will have grown enormously. Now the summer resident only drinks tea on his porch, but maybe he'll take to working his acre, too, and then your cherry orchard will be a rich, happy, luxuriant place.

GAYEV   (*indignantly*): Poppycock!

(*Enter* VARYA *and* YASHA)

VARYA: There are two telegrams for you, mamma dear. (*Picks a key from the bunch at her belt and noisily opens an old-fashioned bookcase*) Here they are.

MME. RANEVSKAYA: They're from Paris. (*Tears them up without reading them*) I'm through with Paris.

GAYEV: Do you know, Luba, how old this bookcase is? Last week I pulled out the bottom drawer and there I found the date burnt in it. It was made exactly a hundred years ago. Think of that! We could celebrate its centenary. True, it's an inanimate object, but nevertheless, a bookcase . . .

PISHCHIK   (*amazed*): A hundred years! Just imagine!

GAYEV: Yes. (*Tapping it*) That's something. . . . Dear, honored bookcase, hail to you who for more than a century have served the glorious ideals of goodness and justice! Your silent summons to fruitful toil has never weakened in all those hundred years (*through tears*) sustaining, through successive generations of our family, courage and faith in a better future, and fostering in us ideals of goodness and social consciousness . . . (*Pauses*)

LOPAHIN: Yes . . .

MME. RANEVSKAYA: You haven't changed a bit, Leonid.

GAYEV (*somewhat embarrassed*): I'll play it off the red in the corner! Tip it in the side pocket!

LOPAHIN (*looking at his watch*): Well it's time for me to go . . .

YASHA (*handing a pill box to* MME. RANEVSKAYA): Perhaps you'll take your pills now.

PISHCHIK: One shouldn't take medicines, dearest lady, they do neither harm nor good. . . . Give them here, my valued friend. (*Takes the pill box, pours the pills into his palm, blows on them, puts them in his mouth, and washes them down with some kvass*) There!

MME. RANEVSKAYA (*frightened*): You must be mad!

PISHCHIK: I've taken all the pills.

LOPAHIN: What a glutton!

(*All laugh*)

FIRS: The gentleman visited us in Easter week, ate half a bucket of pickles, he did . . . (*Mumbles*)

MME. RANEVSKAYA: What's he saying?

VARYA: He's been mumbling like that for the last three years—we're used to it.

YASHA: His declining years!

(CHARLOTTA IVANOVNA, *very thin, tightly laced, dressed in white, a lorgnette at her waist, crosses the stage*)

LOPAHIN: Forgive me, Charlotta Ivanovna, I've not had time to greet you. (*Tries to kiss her hand*)

CHARLOTTA (*pulling away her hand*): If I let you kiss my hand, you'll be wanting to kiss my elbow next, and then my shoulder.

LOPAHIN: I've no luck today. (*All laugh*) Charlotta Ivanovna, show us a trick.

MME. RANEVSKAYA: Yes, Charlotta, do a trick for us.

CHARLOTTA: I don't see the need. I want to sleep.

(*Exits*)

LOPAHIN: In three weeks we'll meet again. (*Kisses* MME. RANEVSKAYA's *hand*) Goodby till then. Time's up. (*To* GAYEV) Bye-bye. (*Kisses* PISHCHIK) Bye-bye. (*Shakes hands with* VARYA, *then with* FIRS *and* YASHA) I hate to leave. (*To* MME. RANEVSKAYA) If you make up your mind about the cottages, let me know; I'll get you a loan of 50,000 rubles. Think it over seriously.

VARYA (*crossly*): Will you never go!

LOPAHIN: I'm going, I'm going. (*Exits*)

GAYEV: The vulgarian. But, excuse me . . . Varya's going to marry him, he's Varya's fiancé.

VARYA: You talk too much, uncle dear.

MME. RANEVSKAYA: Well, Varya, it would make me happy. He's a good man.

PISHCHIK: Yes, one must admit, he's a most estimable man. And my Dashenka . . . she too says that . . . she says . . . lots of things. (*Snores; but wakes up at once*) All the same, my valued friend, could you oblige me . . . with a loan of 240 rubles? I must pay the interest on the mortgage tomorrow.

VARYA   (*alarmed*): We can't, we can't!

MME. RANEVSKAYA: I really haven't any money.

PISHCHIK: It'll turn up. (*Laughs*) I never lose hope, I thought everything was lost, that I was done for, when lo and behold, the railway ran through my land . . . and I was paid for it . . . And something else will turn up again, if not today, then tomorrow . . . Dashenka will win two hundred thousand . . . she's got a lottery ticket.

MME. RANEVSKAYA: I've had my coffee, now let's go to bed.

FIRS   (*brushes off* GAYEV; *admonishingly*): You've got the wrong trousers on again. What am I to do with you?

VARYA   (*softly*): Anya's asleep. (*Gently opens the window*) The sun's up now, it's not a bit cold. Look, mamma dear, what wonderful trees. And heavens, what air! The starlings are singing!

GAYEV   (*opens the other window*): The orchard is all white. You've not forgotten it? Luba? That's the long alley that runs straight, straight as an arrow; how it shines on moonlight nights, do you remember? You've not forgotten?

MME. RANEVSKAYA   (*looking out of the window into the orchard*): Oh, my childhood, my innocent childhood. I used to sleep in this nursery—I used to look out into the orchard, happiness waked with me every morning, the orchard was just the same then . . . nothing has changed. (*Laughs with joy*) All, all white! Oh, my orchard! After the dark, rainy autumn and the cold winter, you are young again, and full of happiness, the heavenly angels have not left you . . . If I could free my chest and my shoulders from this rock that weighs on me, if I could only forget the past!

GAYEV: Yes, and the orchard will be sold to pay our debts, strange as it may seem. . . .

MME. RANEVSKAYA: Look! There is our poor mother walking in the orchard . . . all in white . . . (*Laughs with joy*) It is she!

GAYEV: Where?

VARYA: What are you saying, mamma dear!

MME. RANEVSKAYA: There's no one there, I just imagined it. To the right, where the path turns towards the arbor, there's a little white tree, leaning over, that looks like a woman . . .

(TROFIMOV *enters, wearing a shabby student's uniform and spectacles*)

MME. RANEVSKAYA: What an amazing orchard! White masses of blossom, the blue sky . . .

TROFIMOV: Lubov Andreyevna! (*She looks round at him*) I just want to pay my respects to you, then I'll leave at once. (*Kisses her hand ardently*) I was told to wait until morning, but I hadn't the patience . . . (MME. RANEVSKAYA *looks at him, perplexed*)

VARYA   (*through tears*): This is Petya Trofimov.

TROFIMOV: Petya Trofimov, formerly your Grisha's tutor. . . . Can I have changed so much? (MME. RANEVSKAYA *embraces him and weeps quietly*)

GAYEV   (*embarrassed*): Don't, don't, Luba.

VARYA   (*crying*): I told you, Petya, to wait until tomorrow.

MME. RANEVSKAYA: My Grisha . . . my little boy . . . Grisha . . . my son.

VARYA: What can one do, mamma dear, it's God's will.

TROFIMOV   (*softly, through tears*): There . . . there.

MME. RANEVSKAYA   (*weeping quietly*): My little boy was lost . . . drowned. Why? Why, my friend? (*More quietly*) Anya's asleep in there, and here I am talking so loudly . . . making all this noise. . . . But tell me, Petya, why do you look so badly? Why have you aged so?

TROFIMOV: A mangy master, a peasant woman in the train called me.

MME. RANEVSKAYA: You were just a boy then, a dear little student, and now your hair's thin—and you're wearing glasses! Is it possible you're still a student? (*Goes towards the door*)

TROFIMOV: I suppose I'm a perpetual student.

MME. RANEVSKAYA   (*kisses her brother, then* VARYA): Now, go to bed . . . You have aged, too, Leonid.

PISHCHIK   (*follows her*): So now we turn in. Oh, my gout! I'm staying the night here . . . Lubov Andreyevna, my angel, tomorrow morning. . . . I do need 240 rubles.

GAYEV: He keeps at it.

PISHCHIK: I'll pay it back, dear . . . it's a trifling sum.

MME. RANEVSKAYA: All right, Leonid will give it to you. Give it to him, Leonid.

GAYEV: Me give it to him! That's a good one!

MME. RANEVSKAYA: It can't be helped. Give it to him! He needs it. He'll pay it back.

(MME. RANEVSKAYA, TROFIMOV, PISHCHIK, *and* FIRS *go out;* GAYEV, VARYA, *and* YASHA *remain*)

GAYEV: Sister hasn't got out of the habit of throwing money around. (*To* YASHA) Go away, my good fellow, you smell of the barnyard.

YASHA   (*with a grin*): And you, Leonid Andreyevich, are just the same as ever.

GAYEV: Who? (*To* VARYA) What did he say?

VARYA   (*to* YASHA): Your mother's come from the village; she's been sitting in the servants' room since yesterday, waiting to see you.

YASHA: Botheration!

VARYA: You should be ashamed of yourself!

YASHA: She's all I needed! She could have come tomorrow. (*Exit*)

VARYA: Mamma is just the same as ever; she hasn't changed a bit. If she had her own way, she'd keep nothing for herself.

GAYEV: Yes . . . (*Pauses*) If a great many remedies are offered for some disease, it means it is incurable; I keep thinking and racking my brains; I have many remedies, ever so many, and that really means none. It would be fine if we came in for a legacy; it would be fine if we married off our Anya to a very rich man; or we might go to Yaroslavl and try our luck with our aunt, the Countess. She's very, very rich, you know . . .

VARYA   (*weeping*): If only God would help us!

GAYEV: Stop bawling. Aunt's very rich, but she doesn't like us. In the first place, sister married a lawyer who was no nobleman . . . (ANYA *appears in the doorway*) She married beneath her, and it can't be said that her behavior has been very exemplary. She's good, kind, sweet, and I love her, but no matter what extenuating circumstances you may adduce, there's no denying that she has no morals. You sense it in her least gesture.

VARYA   (*in a whisper*): Anya's in the doorway.

GAYEV: Who? (*Pauses*) It's queer, something got into my right eye—my eyes are going back on me. . . . And on Thursday, when I was in the circuit court—

(*Enter Anya*)

VARYA: Why aren't you asleep, Anya?

ANYA: I can't get to sleep, I just can't.

GAYEV: My little pet! (*Kisses* ANYA's *face and hands*) My child! (*Weeps*) You are not my niece, you're my angel! You're everything to me. Believe me, believe—

ANYA: I believe you, uncle. Everyone loves you and respects you . . . but, uncle dear, you must keep still. . . . You must. What were you saying just now about my mother? Your own sister? What made you say that?

GAYEV: Yes, yes . . . (*Covers his face with her hand*) Really, that was awful! Good God! Heaven help me! Just now I made a speech to the bookcase . . . so stupid! And only after I was through, I saw how stupid it was.

VARYA: It's true, uncle dear, you ought to keep still. Just don't talk, that's all.

ANYA: If you could only keep still, it would make things easier for you too.

GAYEV: I'll keep still. (*Kisses* ANYA's *and* VARYA's *hands*) I will. But now about business. On Thursday I was in court; well, there were a number of us there, and we began talking of one thing and another, and this and that, and do you know, I believe it will be possible to raise a loan on a promissory note, to pay the interest at the bank.

VARYA: If only God would help us!

GAYEV: On Tuesday I'll go and see about it again. (*To* VARYA) Stop bawling. (*To* ANYA) Your mamma will talk to Lopahin, and he, of course, will not refuse her . . . and as soon as you're rested, you'll go to Yaroslavl to the Countess, your great-aunt. So we'll be working in three directions at once, and the thing is in the bag. We'll pay the interest—I'm sure of it. (*Puts a candy in his mouth*) I swear on my honor, I swear by anything you like, the estate shan't be sold. (*Excitedly*) I swear by my own happiness! Here's my hand on it, you can call me a swindler and a scoundrel if I let it come to an auction! I swear by my whole being.

ANYA   (*relieved and quite happy again*): How good you are, uncle, and how clever! (*Embraces him*) Now I'm at peace, quite at peace, I'm happy.

FIRS   (*reproachfully*): Leonid Andreyevich, have you no fear of God? When are you going to bed?

GAYEV: Directly, directly. Go away. Firs, I'll . . . yes, I will undress myself. Now, children, 'nightie-'nightie. We'll consider details tomorrow, but now go to sleep. (*Kisses* ANYA *and* VARYA) I am a man of the 'Eighties; they have nothing good to say of that period nowadays. Nevertheless, in the course of my life I have suffered not a little for my convictions. It's not for nothing that the peasant loves me; one should know the peasant; one should know from which—

ANYA: There you go again, uncle.

VARYA: Uncle dear, be quiet.

FIRS   (*angrily*): Leonid Andreyevich!

GAYEV: I'm coming, I'm coming! Go to bed! Double bank shot in the side pocket! Here goes a clean shot . . .

(*Exits,* FIRS *hobbling after him*)

ANYA: I am at peace now. I don't want to go to Yaroslavl—I don't like my great-aunt, but still, I am at peace, thanks to uncle. (*Sits down*)

VARYA: We must get some sleep. I'm going now. While you were away something unpleasant happened. In the old servants' quarters there are only the old people, as you know; Yefim, Polya, Yevstigney, and Karp, too. They began letting all sorts of rascals in to spend the night. . . . I didn't say anything. Then I heard they'd been spreading a report that I gave them nothing but dried peas to eat—out of stinginess, you know . . . and it was all Yevstigney's doing. . . . All right, I thought, if that's how it is, I thought, just wait. I sent for Yevstigney. . . . (*Yawns*) He comes. . . . "How's this, Yevstigney?" I say, "You fool . . ." (*Looking at* ANYA) Anichka! (*Pauses*) She's asleep. (*Puts her arm around Anya*) Come to your little bed. . . . Come . . . (*Leads her*) My darling has fallen asleep. . . . Come.

(*They go out. Far away beyond the orchard a shepherd is piping.* TROFIMOV *crosses the stage and, seeing* VARYA *and* ANYA, *stands still.*)

VARYA: Sh! She's asleep . . . asleep . . . Come, darling.

ANYA   (*softly, half-asleep*): I'm so tired. Those bells . . . uncle . . . dear. . . . Mamma and uncle . . .

VARYA: Come, my precious, come along. (*They go into* ANYA'S *room*)

TROFIMOV   (*with emotion*): My sunshine, my spring!

ACT II

A meadow. An old, long-abandoned, lopsided little chapel; near it, a well, large slabs, which had apparently once served as tombstones, and an old bench. In the background, the road to the Gayev estate. To one side poplars loom darkly, where the cherry orchard begins. In the distance a row of telegraph poles, and far off, on the horizon, the faint outline of a large city which is seen only in fine, clear weather. The sun will soon be setting. CHARLOTTA, YASHA, *and* DUNYASHA *are seated on the bench.* YEPIHODOV *stands near and plays a guitar. All are pensive.* CHARLOTTA *wears an old peaked cap. She has taken a gun from her shoulder and is straightening the buckle on the strap.*

CHARLOTTA (*musingly*): I haven't a real passport, I don't know how old I am, and I always feel that I am very young. When I was a little girl, my father and mother used to go from fair to fair and give performances, very good ones. And I used to do the *salto mortale,* and all sorts of other tricks. And when papa and mamma died, a German lady adopted me and began to educate me. Very good. I grew up and became a governess. But where I come from and who I am, I don't know. . . . Who were my parents? Perhaps they weren't even married. . . . I don't know. . . . (*Takes a cucumber out of her pocket and eats it*) I don't know a thing. (*Pause*) One wants so much to talk, and there isn't anyone to talk to. . . . I haven't anybody.

YEPIHODOV (*plays the guitar and sings*): "What care I for the jarring world? What's friend or foe to me? . . ." How agreeable it is to play the mandolin.

DUNYASHA: That's a guitar, not a mandolin. (*Looks in a hand mirror and powders her face*)

YEPIHODOV: To a madman in love it's a mandolin. (*Sings*) "Would that the heart were warmed by the fire of mutual love!" (YASHA *joins in*)

CHARLOTTA: How abominably these people sing. Pfui! Like jackals!

DUNYASHA, to *Yasha*: How wonderful it must be though to have stayed abroad!

YASHA: Ah, yes, of course, I cannot but agree with you there. (*Yawns and lights a cigar*)

YEPIHODOV: Naturally. Abroad, everything has long since achieved full perplexion.

YASHA: That goes without saying.

YEPIHODOV: I'm a cultivated man, I read all kinds of remarkable books. And yet I can never make out what direction I should take, what is it that I want, properly speaking. Should I live, or should I shoot myself, properly speaking? Nevertheless, I always carry a revolver about me. . . . Here it is . . . (*Shows revolver*)

CHARLOTTA: I've finished. I'm going. (*Puts the gun over her shoulder*) You are a very clever man, Yepihodov, and a very terrible one; women must be crazy about you. Br-r-r! (*Starts to go*) These clever men are all so stupid; there's no one for me to talk to . . . always alone, alone, I haven't a soul . . . and who I am, and why I am, nobody knows. (*Exits unhurriedly*)

YEPIHODOV: Properly speaking and letting other subjects alone, I must say regarding myself, among other things, that fate treats me mercilessly, like a storm treats a small boat. If I am mistaken, let us say, why then do I wake up this morning, and there on my chest is a spider of enormous dimensions . . . like this . . . (*indicates with both hands*) Again, I take up a pitcher of kvass to have a drink, and in it there is something unseemly to the highest degree, something like a cockroach. (*Pause*) Have you read Buckle? (*Pause*) I wish to have a word with you, Avdotya Fyodorovna, if I may trouble you.

DUNYASHA: Well, go ahead.

YEPIHODOV: I wish to speak with you alone. (*Sighs*)

DUNYASHA,   (*embarrassed*): Very well. Only first bring me my little cape. You'll find it near the wardrobe. It's rather damp here.

YEPIHODOV: Certainly, ma'am; I will fetch it, ma'am. Now I know what to do with my revolver. (*Takes the guitar and goes off playing it*)

YASHA: Two-and-Twenty Troubles! An awful fool, between you and me. (*Yawns*)

DUNYASHA: I hope to God he doesn't shoot himself! (*Pause*) I've become so nervous, I'm always fretting. I was still a little girl when I was taken into the big house. I am quite unused to the simple life now, and my hands are white, as white as a lady's. I've become so soft, so delicate, so refined, I'm afraid of everything. It's so terrifying; and if you deceive me, Yasha, I don't know what will happen to my nerves. (YASHA *kisses her*)

YASHA: You're a peach! Of course, a girl should never forget herself; and what I dislike more than anything is when a girl don't behave properly.

DUNYASHA: I've fallen passionately in love with you; you're educated—you have something to say about everything (*Pause*)

YASHA   (*yawns*): Yes, ma'am. Now the way I look at it, if a girl loves someone, it means she is immoral. (*Pause*) It's agreeable smoking a cigar in the fresh air. (*Listens*) Someone's coming this way . . . It's our madam and the others. (DUNYASHA *embraces him impulsively*) You go home, as though you'd been to the river to bathe; go by the little path, or else they'll run into you and suspect me of having arranged to meet you here. I can't stand that sort of thing.

DUNYASHA   (*coughing softly*): Your cigar's made my head ache.

(*Exits. Yasha standing near the chapel. Enter* MME. RANEVSKAYA, GAYEV, *and* LOPAHIN.)

LOPAHIN: You must make up your mind once and for all—there's no time to lose. It's quite a simple question, you know. Do you agree to lease your land for summer cottages or not? Answer in one word, yes or no; only one word!

MME. RANEVSKAYA: Who's been smoking such abominable cigars here? (*Sits down*)

GAYEV: Now that the railway line is so near, it's made things very convenient. (*Sits down*) Here we've been able to have lunch in town. Yellow ball in the side pocket! I feel like going into the house and playing just one game.

MME. RANEVSKAYA: You can do that later.

LOPAHIN: Only one word! (*Imploringly*) Do give me an answer!

GAYEV   (*yawning*): Who?

MME. RANEVSKAYA   (*looks into her purse*): Yesterday I had a lot of money and now my purse is almost empty. My poor Varya tries to economize by feeding us just milk soup; in the kitchen the old people get nothing but dried peas to eat, while I squander money thoughtlessly (*Drops the purse, scattering gold pieces*) You see there they go . . . (*Shows vexation*)

YASHA: Allow me—I'll pick them up. (*Picks up the money*)

MME. RANEVSKAYA: Be so kind, Yasha. And why did I go to lunch in town?

That nasty restaurant, with its music and the tablecloth smelling of soap . . . Why drink so much, Leonid? Why eat so much? Why talk so much? Today again you talked a lot, and all so inappropriately about the 'Seventies, about the decadents. And to whom? Talking to waiters about decadents!

LOPAHIN: Yes.

GAYEV (*Waving his hand*): I'm incorrigible; that's obvious. (*Irritably, to* YASHA) Why do you keep dancing about in front of me?

YASHA (*laughs*): I can't hear your voice without laughing—

GAYEV: Either he or I—

MME. RANEVSKAYA: Go away, Yasha; run along.

YASHA (*handing* MME. RANEVSKAYA *her purse*): I'm going, at once. (*Hardly able to suppress his laughter*) This minute. (*Exits*)

LOPAHIN: That rich man, Deriganov, wants to buy your estate. They say he's coming to the auction himself.

MME. RANEVSKAYA: Where did you hear that?

LOPAHIN: That's what they are saying in town.

GAYEV: Our aunt in Yaroslavl has promised to help; but when she will send the money, and how much, no one knows.

LOPAHIN: How much will she send? A hundred thousand? Two hundred?

MME. RANEVSKAYA: Oh, well, ten or fifteen thousand; and we'll have to be grateful for that.

LOPAHIN: Forgive me, but such frivolous people as you are, so queer and unbusinesslike—I never met in my life. One tells you in plain language that your estate is up for sale, and you don't seem to take it in.

MME. RANEVSKAYA: What are we to do? Tell us what to do.

LOPAHIN: I do tell you, every day; every day I say the same thing! You must lease the cherry orchard and the land for summer cottages, you must do it and as soon as possible—right away. The auction is close at hand. Please understand! Once you've decided to have the cottages, you can raise as much money as you like, and you're saved.

MME. RANEVSKAYA: Cottages—summer people—forgive me, but it's all so vulgar.

GAYEV: I agree with you absolutely.

LOPAHIN: I shall either burst into tears or scream or faint! I can't stand it! You've worn me out! (*To* GAYEV) You're an old woman!

GAYEV: Who?

LOPAHIN: An old woman! (*Gets up to go*)

MME. RANEVSKAYA (*alarmed*): No, don't go! Please stay, I beg you, my dear. Perhaps we shall think of something.

LOPAHIN: What is there to think of?

MME. RANEVSKAYA: Don't go, I beg you. With you here it's more cheerful anyway. (*Pause*) I keep expecting something to happen, it's as though the house were going to crash about our ears.

GAYEV (*in deep thought*): Bank shot in the corner. . . . Three cushions in the side pocket. . . .

MME. RANEVSKAYA: We have been great sinners . . .

LOPAHIN: What sins could you have committed?

GAYEV (*putting a candy in his mouth*): They say I've eaten up my fortune in candy! (*Laughs*)

MME. RANEVSKAYA: Oh, my sins! I've squandered money away recklessly, like a lunatic, and I married a man who made nothing but debts. My husband drank himself to death on champagne, he was a terrific drinker. And then, to my sorrow, I fell in love with another man, and I lived with him. And just then —that was my first punishment—a blow on the head: my little boy was drowned here in the river. And I went abroad, went away forever . . . never to come back, never to see this river again . . . I closed my eyes and ran, out of my mind. . . . But he followed me, pitiless, brutal. I bought a villa near Mentone, because he fell ill there; and for three years, day and night, I knew no peace, no rest. The sick man wore me out, he sucked my soul dry. Then last year, when the villa was sold to pay my debts, I went to Paris, and there he robbed me, abandoned me, took up with another woman, I tried to poison myself—it was stupid, so shameful—and then suddenly I felt drawn back to Russia, back to my own country, to my little girl. (*Wipes her tears away*) Lord, Lord! Be merciful, forgive me my sins—don't punish me any more! (*Takes a telegram out of her pocket*) This came today from Paris—he begs me to forgive him, implores me to go back . . . (*Tears up the telegram*) Do I hear music? (*Listens*)

GAYEV: That's our famous Jewish band, you remember? Four violins, a flute, and a double bass.

MME. RANEVSKAYA: Does it still exist? We ought to send for them some evening and have a party.

LOPAHIN (*listens*): I don't hear anything. (*Hums softly*) "The Germans for a fee will Frenchify a Russian." (*Laughs*) I saw a play at the theater yesterday —awfully funny.

MME. RANEVSKAYA: There was probably nothing funny about it. You shouldn't go to see plays, you should look at yourselves more often. How drab your lives are—how full of unnecessary talk.

LOPAHIN: That's true; come to think of it, we do live like fools. (*Pause*) My pop was a peasant, an idiot; he understood nothing, never taught me anything, all he did was beat me when he was drunk, and always with a stick. Fundamentally, I'm just the same kind of blockhead and idiot. I was never taught anything —I have a terrible handwriting. I write so that I feel ashamed before people, like a pig.

MME. RANEVSKAYA: You should get married, my friend.

LOPAHIN: Yes . . . that's true.

MME. RANEVSKAYA: She's a girl who comes of simple people, she works all day long; and above all, she loves you. Besides, you've liked her for a long time now.

LOPAHIN: Well, I've nothing against it. She's a good girl. (*Pause*)

GAYEV: I've been offered a place in the bank—6,000 a year. Have you heard?

MME. RANEVSKAYA: You're not up to it. Stay where you are.

(FIRS *enters, carrying an overcoat*)

FIRS (*to* GAYEV): Please put this on, sir, it's damp.

GAYEV (*putting it on*): I'm fed up with you, brother.

FIRS: Never mind. This morning you drove off without saying a word. (*Looks him over*)

MME. RANEVSKAYA: How you've aged, Firs.

FIRS: I beg your pardon?

LOPAHIN: The lady says you've aged.

FIRS: I've lived a long time; they were arranging my wedding and your papa wasn't born yet. (*Laughs*) When freedom came I was already head footman. I wouldn't consent to be set free then; I stayed on with the master . . . (*Pause*) I remember they were all very happy, but why they were happy, they didn't know themselves.

LOPAHIN: It was fine in the old days! At least there was flogging!

FIRS   (*not hearing*): Of course. The peasants kept to the masters, the masters kept to the peasants; but now they've all gone their own ways, and there's no making out anything.

GAYEV: Be quiet, Firs. I must go to town tomorrow. They've promised to introduce me to a general who might let us have a loan.

LOPAHIN: Nothing will come of that. You won't even be able to pay the interest, you can be certain of that.

MME. RANEVSKAYA: He's raving, there isn't any general. (*Enter* TROFIMOV, ANYA, *and* VARYA)

GAYEV: Here come our young people.

ANYA: There's mamma, on the bench.

MME. RANEVSKAYA   (*tenderly*): Come here, come along, my darlings. (*Embraces* ANYA *and* VARYA) If you only knew how I love you both! Sit beside me —there, like that. (*All sit down*)

LOPAHIN: Our perpetual student is always with the young ladies.

TROFIMOV: That's not any of your business.

LOPAHIN: He'll soon be fifty, and he's still a student!

TROFIMOV: Stop your silly jokes.

LOPAHIN: What are you so cross about, you queer bird?

TROFIMOV: Oh, leave me alone.

LOPAHIN   (*laughs*): Allow me to ask you, what do you think of me?

TROFIMOV: What I think of you, Yermolay Alexeyevich, is this: you are a rich man who will soon be a millionaire. Well, just as a beast of prey, which devours everything that comes in its way, is necessary for the process of metabolism to go on, so you too are necessary. (*All laugh*)

VARYA: Better tell us something about the planets, Petya.

MME. RANEVSKAYA: No, let's go on with yesterday's conversation.

TROFIMOV: What was it about?

GAYEV: About man's pride.

TROFIMOV: Yesterday we talked a long time, but we came to no conclusion. There is something mystical about man's pride in your sense of the word. Perhaps you're right, from your own point of view. But if you reason simply, without going into subtleties, then what call is there for pride? Is there any sense in it, if man is so poor a thing physiologically, and if, in the great majority of cases, he is coarse, stupid, and profoundly unhappy? We should stop admiring ourselves. We should work, and that's all.

GAYEV: You die, anyway.

TROFIMOV: Who knows? And what does it mean—to die? Perhaps man has a hundred senses, and at his death only the five we know perish, while the other ninety-five remain alive.

MME. RANEVSKAYA: How clever you are, Petya!

LOPAHIN   (*ironically*): Awfully clever!

TROFIMOV: Mankind goes forward, developing its powers. Everything that is now unattainable for it will one day come within man's reach and be clear to him; only we must work, helping with all our might those who seek the truth. Here among us in Russia only the very few work as yet. The great majority of the intelligentsia, as far as I can see, seek nothing, do nothing, are totally unfit for work of any kind. They call themselves the intelligentsia, yet they are uncivil to their servants, treat the peasants like animals, are poor students, never read anything serious, do absolutely nothing at all, only talk about science, and have little appreciation of the arts. They are all solemn, have grim faces, they all philosophize and talk of weighty matters. And meanwhile the vast majority of us, ninety-nine out of a hundred, live like savages. At the least provocation— a punch in the jaw, and curses. They eat disgustingly, sleep in filth and stuffiness, bedbugs everywhere, stench and damp and moral slovenliness. And obviously, the only purpose of all our fine talk is to hoodwink ourselves and others. Show me where the public nurseries are that we've heard so much about, and the libraries. We read about them in novels, but in reality they don't exist, there is nothing but dirt, vulgarity, and Asiatic backwardness. I don't like very solemn faces, I'm afraid of them, I'm afraid of serious conversations. We'd do better to keep quiet for a while.

LOPAHIN: Do you know, I get up at five o'clock in the morning, and I work from morning till night; and I'm always handling money, my own and other people's, and I see what people around me are really like. You've only to start doing anything to see how few honest, decent people there are. Sometimes when I lie awake at night, I think: "Oh, Lord, thou hast given us immense forests, boundless fields, the widest horizons, and living in their midst, we ourselves ought really to be giants."

MME. RANEVSKAYA: Now you want giants! They're only good in fairy tales; otherwise they're frightening.

(YEPIHODOV *crosses the stage at the rear, playing the guitar*)

MME. RANEVSKAYA   (*pensively*): There goes Yepihodov.

ANYA   (*pensively*): There goes Yepihodov.

GAYEV: Ladies and gentlemen, the sun has set.

TROFIMOV: Yes.

GAYEV   (*in a low voice, declaiming as it were*): Oh, Nature, wondrous Nature, you shine with eternal radiance, beautiful and indifferent! You, whom we call our mother, unite within yourself life and death! You animate and destroy!

VARYA   (*pleadingly*): Uncle dear!

ANYA: Uncle, again!

TROFIMOV: You'd better bank the yellow ball in the side pocket.

GAYEV: I'm silent, I'm silent . . .

(*All sit plunged in thought. Stillness reigns. Only* FIRS's *muttering is audible. Suddenly a distant sound is heard, coming from the sky as it were, the sound of a snapping string, mournfully dying away.*)

MME. RANEVSKAYA: What was that?

LOPAHIN: I don't know. Somewhere far away, in the pits, a bucket's broken loose; but somewhere very far away.

GAYEV: Or it might be some sort of bird, perhaps a heron.

TROFIMOV: Or an owl . . .

MME. RANEVSKAYA   (*shudders*): It's weird, somehow. (*Pause*)

FIRS: Before the calamity the same thing happened—the owl screeched, and the samovar hummed all the time.

GAYEV: Before what calamity?

FIRS: Before the Freedom. (*Pause*)

MME. RANEVSKAYA: Come, my friends, let's be going. It's getting dark. (*To* ANYA) You have tears in your eyes. What is it, my little one? (*Embraces her*)

ANYA: I don't know, mamma; it's nothing.

TROFIMOV: Somebody's coming.

(*A tramp appears, wearing a shabby white cap and an overcoat. He is slightly drunk.*)

TRAMP: Allow me to inquire, will this short-cut take me to the station?

GAYEV: It will. Just follow that road.

TRAMP: My heartfelt thanks. (*Coughing*) The weather is glorious. (*Recites*) "My brother, my suffering brother . . . Go down to the Volga! Whose groans . . . ?" (*To* VARYA) Mademoiselle, won't you spare 30 kopecks for a hungry Russian?

(VARYA, *frightened, cries out*)

LOPAHIN   (*angrily*): Even panhandling has its proprieties.

MME. RANEVSKAYA   (*scared*): Here, take this. (*Fumbles in her purse*) I haven't any silver . . . never mind, here's a gold piece.

TRAMP: My heartfelt thanks. (*Exits. Laughter*)

VARYA   (*frightened*): I'm leaving. I'm leaving . . . Oh, mamma dear, at home the servants have nothing to eat, and you gave him a gold piece!

MME. RANEVSKAYA: What are you going to do with me? I'm such a fool. When we get home, I'll give you everything I have. Yermolay Alexeyevich, you'll lend me some more . . .

LOPAHIN: Yes, ma'am.

MME. RANEVSKAYA: Come, ladies and gentlemen, it's time to be going. Oh! Varya, we've settled all about your marriage. Congratulations!

VARYA   (*through tears*): Really, mamma, that's not a joking matter.

LOPAHIN: "Aurelia, get thee to a nunnery, go . . ."

GAYEV: And do you know, my hands are trembling: I haven't played billiards in a long time.

LOPAHIN: "Aurelia, nymph, in your orisons, remember me!"

MME. RANEVSKAYA: Let's go, it's almost suppertime.

VARYA: He frightened me! My heart's pounding.

LOPAHIN: Let me remind you, ladies and gentlemen, on the 22nd of August the cherry orchard will be up for sale. Think about that! Think!

(*All except* TROFIMOV *and* ANYA *go out*)

ANYA   (*laughs*): I'm grateful to that tramp, he frightened Varya and so we're alone.

TROFIMOV: Varya's afraid we'll fall in love with each other all of a sudden. She hasn't left us alone for days. Her narrow mind can't grasp that we're above love. To avoid the petty and illusory, everything that prevents us from being free and happy—that is the goal and meaning of our life. Forward! Do not fall behind, friends!

ANYA   (*strikes her hands together*): How well you speak! (*Pause*) It's wonderful here today.

TROFIMOV: Yes, the weather's glorious.

ANYA: What have you done to me, Petya? Why don't I love the cherry orchard as I used to? I loved it so tenderly. It seemed to me there was no spot on earth lovelier than our orchard.

TROFIMOV: All Russia is our orchard. Our land is vast and beautiful, there are many wonderful places in it. (*Pause*) Think of it, Anya, your grandfather, your great-grandfather and all your ancestors were serf-owners, owners of living souls, and aren't human beings looking at you from every tree in the orchard, from every leaf, from every trunk? Don't you hear voices? Oh, it's terrifying! Your orchard is a fearful place, and when you pass through it in the evening or at night, the old bark on the trees gleams faintly, and the cherry trees seem to be dreaming of things that happened a hundred, two hundred years ago and to be tormented by painful visions. What is there to say? We're at least two hundred years behind, we've really achieved nothing yet, we have no definite attitude to the past, we only philosophize, complain of the blues, or drink vodka. It's all so clear: in order to live in the present, we should first redeem our past, finish with it, and we can expiate it only by suffering, only by extraordinary, unceasing labor. Realize that, Anya.

ANYA: The house in which we live has long ceased to be our own, and I will leave it, I give you my word.

TROFIMOV: If you have the keys, fling them into the well and go away. Be free as the wind.

ANYA   (*in ecstasy*): How well you put that!

TROFIMOV: Believe me, Anya, believe me! I'm not yet thirty, I'm young, I'm still a student—but I've already suffered so much. In winter I'm hungry, sick, harassed, poor as a beggar, and where hasn't Fate driven me? Where haven't I been? And yet always, every moment of the day and night, my soul is filled with inexplicable premonitions. . . . I have a premonition of happiness, Anya. . . . I see it already!

ANYA   (*pensively*): The moon is rising.

(YEPIHODOV *is heard playing the same mournful tune on the guitar. The moon rises. Somewhere near the poplars* VARYA *is looking for* ANYA *and calling* "Anya, where are you.")

TROFIMOV: Yes, the moon is rising. (*Pause*) There it is, happiness, it's approaching, it's coming nearer and nearer, I can already hear its footsteps. And if we don't see it, if we don't know it, what does it matter? Others will!

VARYA'S (*voice*): "Anya! Where are you?"

TROFIMOV: That Varya again! (*Angrily*) It's revolting!

ANYA: Never mind, let's go down to the river. It's lovely there.

TROFIMOV: Come on. (*They go*)

VARYA'S (*voice*): "Anya! Anya!"

ACT III

A drawing-room separated by an arch from a ballroom. Evening. Chandelier burning. The Jewish band is heard playing in the anteroom. In the ballroom they are dancing the Grand Rond. PISHCHIK *is heard calling, "Promenade à une paire."* PISHCHIK *and* CHARLOTTA, TROFIMOV *and* MME. RANEVSKAYA, ANYA *and the* POST OFFICE CLERK, VARYA *and the* STATION-MASTER, *and others, enter the drawing-room in couples.* DUNYASHA *is in the last couple.* VARYA *weeps quietly, wiping her tears as she dances. All parade through drawing-room.* PISHCHIK *calling "Grand rond, balancez!" and "Les cavaliers à genoux et remerciez vos dames!"* FIRS, *wearing a dress-coat, brings in soda-water on a tray.* PISHCHIK *and* TROFIMOV *enter the drawing-room.*

PISHCHIK: I'm a full-blooded man; I've already had two strokes. Dancing's hard work for me; but as they say, "If you run with the pack, you can bark or not, but at least wag your tail." Still, I'm as strong as a horse. My late lamented father, who would have his joke, God rest his soul, used to say, talking about our origin, that the ancient line of the Simeonov-Pishchiks was descended from the very horse that Caligula had made a senator. (*Sits down*) But the trouble is, I have no money. A hungry dog believes in nothing but meat. (*Snores and wakes up at once*) It's the same with me—I can think of nothing but money.

TROFIMOV: You know, there *is* something equine about your figure.

PISHCHIK: Well, a horse is a fine animal—one can sell a horse.

(*Sound of billiards being played in an adjoining room.* VARYA *appears in the archway.*)

TROFIMOV (*teasing her*): Madam Lopahina! Madam Lopahina!

VARYA (*angrily*): Mangy master!

TROFIMOV: Yes, I am a mangy master and I'm proud of it.

VARYA (*reflecting bitterly*): Here we've hired musicians, and what shall we pay them with? (*Exits*)

TROFIMOV (*to Pishchik*): If the energy you have spent during your lifetime looking for money to pay interest had gone into something else, in the end you could have turned the world upside down.

PISHCHIK: Nietzsche, the philosopher, the greatest, most famous of men, that colossal intellect, says in his works, that it is permissible to forge banknotes.

TROFIMOV: Have you read Nietzsche?

PISHCHIK: Well . . . Dashenka told me . . . And now I've got to the point where forging banknotes is about the only way out for me. . . . The day after tomorrow I have to pay 310 rubles—I already have 130 (. . . *Feels in his pockets. In alarm*) The money's gone! I've lost my money! (*Through tears*) Where's my money? (*Joyfully*) Here it is! Inside the lining . . . I'm all in a sweat . . .

(*Enter* MME. RANEVSKAYA *and* CHARLOTTA)

MME. RANEVSKAYA   (*hums the "Lezginka"*): Why isn't Leonid back yet? What is he doing in town? (*To* DUNYASHA) Dunyasha, offer the musicians tea.

TROFIMOV: The auction hasn't taken place, most likely.

MME. RANEVSKAYA: It's the wrong time to have the band, and the wrong time to give a dance. Well, never mind. (*Sits down and hums softly*)

CHARLOTTA   (*hands* PISHCHIK *a pack of cards*): Here is a pack of cards. Think of any card you like.

PISHCHIK: I've thought of one.

CHARLOTTA: Shuffle the pack now. That's right. Give it here, my dear Mr. Pishchik. (*Ein, zwei, drei!*) Now look for it—it's in your side pocket.

PISHCHIK   (*taking the card out of his pocket*): The eight of spades! Perfectly right! Just imagine!

CHARLOTTA   (*holding pack of cards in her hands. To* TROFIMOV): Quickly, name the top card.

TROFIMOV: Well, let's see—the queen of spades.

CHARLOTTA: Right! (*To* PISHCHIK) Now name the top card.

PISHCHIK: The ace of hearts.

CHARLOTTA: Right! (*Claps her hands and the pack of cards disappears*) Ah, what lovely weather it is today! (*A mysterious feminine voice which seems to come from under the floor, answers her*) "Oh, yes, it's magnificent weather, madam."

CHARLOTTA: You are my best ideal.

VOICE: "And I find you pleasing too, madam."

STATIONMASTER   (*applauding*): The lady ventriloquist, bravo!

PISHCHIK   (*amazed*): Just imagine! Enchanting Charlotta Ivanovna, I'm simply in love with you.

CHARLOTTA: In love? (*Shrugs her shoulders*) Are you capable of love? *Guter Mensch, aber schlechter Musikant.*

TROFIMOV   (*claps* PISHCHIK *on the shoulder*): You old horse, you!

CHARLOTTA: Attention please! One more trick! (*Takes a plaid from a chair*) Here is a very good plaid; I want to sell it. (*Shaking it out*) Does anyone want to buy it?

PISHCHIK   (*in amazement*): Just imagine!

CHARLOTTA: Ein, zwei, drei!

(*Raises the plaid quickly, behind it stands* ANYA. *She curtsies, runs to her mother, embraces her, and runs back into the ballroom, amidst general enthusiasm.*)

MME. RANEVSKAYA   (*applauds*): Bravo! Bravo!

CHARLOTTA: Now again! Ein, zwei, drei! (*Lifts the plaid; behind it stands* VARYA *bowing*)

PISHCHIK   (*running after her*): The rascal! What a woman, what a woman! (*Exits*)

MME. RANEVSKAYA: And Leonid still isn't here. What is he doing in town so long? I don't understand. It must be all over by now. Either the estate has been sold, or the auction hasn't taken place. Why keep us in suspense so long?

VARYA   (*trying to console her*): Uncle's bought it, I feel sure of that.

TROFIMOV   (*mockingly*): Oh, yes!

VARYA: Great-aunt sent him an authorization to buy it in her name, and to transfer the debt. She's doing it for Anya's sake. And I'm sure that God will help us, and uncle will buy it.

MME. RANEVSKAYA: Great-aunt sent fifteen thousand to buy the estate in her name, she doesn't trust us, but that's not even enough to pay the interest. (*Covers her face with her hands*) Today my fate will be decided, my fate—

TROFIMOV   (*teasing* VARYA): Madam Lopahina!

VARYA   (*angrily*): Perpetual student! Twice already you've been expelled from the university.

MME. RANEVSKAYA: Why are you so cross, Varya? He's teasing you about Lopahin. Well, what of it? If you want to marry Lopahin, go ahead. He's a good man, and interesting; if you don't want to, don't. Nobody's compelling you, my pet!

VARYA: Frankly, mamma dear, I take this thing seriously; he's a good man and I like him.

MME. RANEVSKAYA: All right then, marry him. I don't know what you're waiting for.

VARYA: But, mamma, I can't propose to him myself. For the last two years everyone's been talking to me about him—talking. But he either keeps silent, or else cracks jokes. I understand; he's growing rich, he's absorbed in business —he has no time for me. If I had money, even a little, say, 100 rubles, I'd throw everything up and go far away—I'd go into a nunnery.

TROFIMOV: What a blessing . . .

VARYA: A student ought to be intelligent (*Softly, with tears in her voice*) How homely you've grown, Petya! How old you look! (*To* MME. RANEVSKAYA, *with dry eyes*) But I can't live without work, mamma dear; I must keep busy every minute.

(*Enter* YASHA)

YASHA   (*hardly restraining his laughter*): Yepihodov has broken a billiard cue! (*Exits*)

VARYA: Why is Yepihodov here? Who allowed him to play billiards? I don't understand these people! (*Exits*)

MME. RANEVSKAYA: Don't tease her, Petya. She's unhappy enough without that.

TROFIMOV: She bustles so—and meddles in other people's business. All summer long she's given Anya and me no peace. She's afraid of a love-affair between us. What business is it of hers? Besides, I've given no grounds for it, and I'm far from such vulgarity. We are above love.

MME. RANEVSKAYA: And I suppose I'm beneath love? (*Anxiously*) What can be keeping Leonid. If I only knew whether the estate has been sold or not. Such a calamity seems so incredible to me that I don't know what to think—I feel lost. . . . I could scream. . . . I could do something stupid. . . . Save me, Petya, tell me something, talk to me!

TROFIMOV: Whether the estate is sold today or not, isn't it all one? That's all done with long ago—there's no turning back, the path is overgrown. Calm yourself, my dear. You mustn't deceive yourself. For once in your life you must face the truth.

MME. RANEVSKAYA: What truth? You can see the truth, you can tell it from falsehood, but I seem to have lost my eyesight, I see nothing. You settle every great problem so boldly, but tell me, my dear boy, isn't it because you're young, because you don't yet know what one of your problems means in terms of suffering? You look ahead fearlessly, but isn't it because you don't see and don't expect anything dreadful, because life is still hidden from your young eyes? You're bolder, more honest, more profound than we are, but think hard, show just a bit of magnanimity, spare me. After all, I was born here, my father and mother lived here, and my grandfather; I love this house. Without the cherry orchard, my life has no meaning for me, and if it really must be sold, then sell me with the orchard. (*Embraces* TROFIMOV, *kisses him on the forehead*) My son was drowned here. (*Weeps*) Pity me, you good, kind fellow!

TROFIMOV: You know, I feel for you with all my heart.

MME. RANEVSKAYA: But that should have been said differently, so differently! (*Takes out her handkerchief—a telegram falls on the floor*) My heart is so heavy today—you can't imagine! The noise here upsets me—my inmost being trembles at every sound—I'm shaking all over. But I can't go into my own room; I'm afraid to be alone. Don't condemn me, Petya. . . . I love you as though you were one of us, I would gladly let you marry Anya—I swear I would— only, my dear boy, you must study—you must take your degree—you do nothing, you let yourself be tossed by Fate from place to place—it's so strange. It's true, isn't it? And you should do something about your beard, to make it grow somehow! (*Laughs*) You're so funny!

TROFIMOV   (*picks up the telegram*): I've no wish to be a dandy.

MME. RANEVSKAYA: That's a telegram from Paris. I get one every day. One yesterday and one today. That savage is ill again—he's in trouble again. He begs forgiveness, implores me to go to him, and really I ought to go to Paris to be near him. Your face is stern, Petya; but what is there to do, my dear boy? What am I to do? He's ill, he's alone and unhappy, and who is to look after him, who is to keep him from doing the wrong thing, who is to give him his medicine on time? And why hide it or keep still about it—I love him! That's clear. I love him, love him! He's a millstone round my neck, he'll drag me to the bottom, but I love that stone. I can't live without it. (*Presses* TROFIMOV's *hand*) Don't think badly of me, Petya, and don't say anything, don't say . . .

TROFIMOV   (*through tears*): Forgive me my frankness in heaven's name; but, you know, he robbed you!

MME. RANEVSKAYA: No, no, no, you mustn't say such things! (*Covers her ears*)

TROFIMOV: But he's a scoundrel! You're the only one who doesn't know it. He's a petty scoundrel—a nonentity!

MME. RANEVSKAYA (*controlling her anger*): You are twenty-six or twenty-seven years old, but you're still a schoolboy.

TROFIMOV: That may be.

MME. RANEVSKAYA: You should be a man at your age. You should understand people who love—and ought to be in love yourself. You ought to fall in love! (*Angrily*) Yes, yes! And it's not purity in you, it's prudishness, you're simply a queer fish, a comical freak!

TROFIMOV (*horrified*): What is she saying!

MME. RANEVSKAYA: "I am above love!" You're not above love, but simply, as our Firs says, you're an addlehead. At your age not to have a mistress!

TROFIMOV (*horrified*): This is frightful! What is she saying! (*Goes rapidly into the ballroom, clutching his head*) It's frightful—I can't stand it, I won't stay! (*Exits, but returns at once*) All is over between us! (*Exits into anteroom*)

MME. RANEVSKAYA (*shouts after him*): Petya! Wait! You absurd fellow, I was joking. Petya!

(*Sound of somebody running quickly downstairs and suddenly falling down with a crash.* ANYA *and* VARYA *scream. Sound of laughter a moment later.*)

MME. RANEVSKAYA: What's happened? (*Anya runs in*)

ANYA (*laughing*): Petya's fallen downstairs! (*Runs out*)

MME. RANEVSKAYA: What a queer bird that Petya is!

(*Stationmaster, standing in the middle of the ballroom, recites Alexey Tolstoy's "Magdalene," to which all listen, but after a few lines, the sound of a waltz is heard from the anteroom and the reading breaks off. All dance.* TROFIMOV, ANYA, VARYA, *and* MME. RANEVSKAYA *enter from the anteroom.*)

MME. RANEVSKAYA: Petya, you pure soul, please forgive me. . . . Let's dance.

(*Dances with* PETYA. ANYA *and* VARYA *dance. Firs enters, puts his stick down by the side door.* YASHA *enters from the drawing-room and watches the dancers.*)

YASHA: Well, grandfather?

FIRS: I'm not feeling well. In the old days it was generals, barons, and admirals that were dancing at our balls, and now we have to send for the Post Office clerk and the Stationmaster, and even they aren't too glad to come. I feel kind of shaky. The old master that's gone, their grandfather, dosed everyone with sealing-wax, whatever ailed 'em. I've been taking sealing-wax every day for twenty years or more. Perhaps that's what's kept me alive.

YASHA: I'm fed up with you, grandpop. (*Yawns*) It's time you croaked.

FIRS: Oh, you addlehead! (*Mumbles*)

(TROFIMOV *and* MME. RANEVSKAYA *dance from the ballroom into the drawing-room*)

MME. RANEVSKAYA: *Merci.* I'll sit down a while. (*Sits down*) I'm tired.

(*Enter* ANYA)

ANYA (*excitedly*): There was a man in the kitchen just now who said the cherry orchard was sold today.

MME. RANEVSKAYA: Sold to whom?

ANYA: He didn't say. He's gone. (*Dances off with* TROFIMOV)

YASHA: It was some old man gabbing, a stranger.

FIRS: And Leonid Andreyevich isn't back yet, he hasn't come. And he's wearing his lightweight between-season overcoat; like enough, he'll catch cold. Ah, when they're young they're green.

MME. RANEVSKAYA: This is killing me. Go, Yasha, find out to whom it has been sold.

YASHA: But the old man left long ago. (*Laughs*)

MME. RANEVSKAYA: What are you laughing at? What are you pleased about?

YASHA: That Yepihodov is such a funny one. A funny fellow, Two-and-Twenty Troubles!

MME. RANEVSKAYA: Firs, if the estate is sold, where will you go?

FIRS: I'll go where you tell me.

MME. RANEVSKAYA: Why do you look like that? Are you ill? You ought to go to bed.

FIRS: Yes! (*With a snigger*) Me go to bed, and who's to hand things round? Who's to see to things? I'm the only one in the whole house.

YASHA   (*to* MME. RANEVSKAYA): Lubov Andreyevna, allow me to ask a favor of you, be so kind! If you go back to Paris, take me with you, I beg you. It's positively impossible for me to stay here. (*Looking around; sotto voce*) What's the use of talking? You see for yourself, it's an uncivilized country, the people have no morals, and then the boredom! The food in the kitchen's revolting, and besides there's this Firs wanders about mumbling all sorts of inappropriate words. Take me with you, be so kind!

(*Enter* PISHCHIK)

PISHCHIK: May I have the pleasure of a waltz with you, charming lady? (MME. RANEVSKAYA *accepts*) All the same, enchanting lady, you must let me have 180 rubles . . . You must let me have (*dancing*) just one hundred and eighty rubles. (*They pass into the ballroom*)

YASHA   (*hums softly*): "Oh, wilt thou understand the tumult in my soul?"

(*In the ballroom a figure in a gray top hat and checked trousers is jumping about and waving its arms; shouts: "Bravo, Charlotta Ivanovna!"*)

DUNYASHA   (*stopping to powder her face; to Firs*) The young miss has ordered me to dance. There are so many gentlemen and not enough ladies. But dancing makes me dizzy, my heart begins to beat fast, Firs Nikolayevich. The Post Office clerk said something to me just now that quite took my breath away. (*Music stops*)

FIRS: What did he say?

DUNYASHA: "You're like a flower," he said.

YASHA   (*yawns*): What ignorance. (*Exits*)

DUNYASHA: "Like a flower!" I'm such a delicate girl. I simply adore pretty speeches.

FIRS: You'll come to a bad end.

(*Enter* YEPIHODOV)

YEPIHODOV   (*to* DUNYASHA): You have no wish to see me, Avdotya Fyodorovna . . . as though I was some sort of insect. (*Sighs*) Ah, life!

DUNYASHA: What is it you want?

YEPIHODOV: Indubitably you may be right. (*Sighs*) But of course, if one looks at it from the point of view, if I may be allowed to say so, and apologizing for my frankness, you have completely reduced me to a state of mind. I know my fate. Every day some calamity befalls me, and I grew used to it long ago, so that I look upon my fate with a smile. You gave me your word, and though I—

DUNYASHA: Let's talk about it later, please. But just now leave me alone, I am daydreaming. (*Plays with a fan*)

YEPIHODOV: A misfortune befalls me every day; and if I may be allowed to say so, I merely smile, I even laugh.

(*Enter* VARYA)

VARYA   (*to* YEPIHODOV): Are you still here? What an impertinent fellow you are really! Run along, Dunyasha. (*To* YEPIHODOV) Either you're playing billiards and breaking a cue, or you're wandering about the drawing-room as though you were a guest.

YEPIHODOV: You cannot, permit me to remark, penalize me.

VARYA: I'm not penalizing you. I'm just telling you. You merely wander from place to place, and don't do your work. We keep you as a clerk, but Heaven knows what for.

YEPIHODOV   (*offended*): Whether I work or whether I walk, whether I eat or whether I play billiards, is a matter to be discussed only by persons of understanding and of mature years.

VARYA   (*enraged*): You dare say that to me—you dare? You mean to say I've no understanding? Get out of here at once! This minute!

YEPIHODOV   (*scared*): I beg you to express yourself delicately.

VARYA   (*beside herself*): Clear out this minute! Out with you!

(YEPIHODOV *goes towards the door,* VARYA *following*)

VARYA: Two-and-Twenty Troubles! Get out—don't let me set eyes on you! (*Exit* YEPIHODOV. *His voice is heard behind the door*): "I shall lodge a complaint against you!"

VARYA: Oh, you're coming back? (*She seizes the stick left near door by* FIRS) Well, come then . . . come . . . I'll show you . . . Ah, you're coming? You're coming? . . . Come . . . (*Swings the stick just as Lopahin enters*)

LOPAHIN: Thank you kindly.

VARYA   (*angrily and mockingly*): I'm sorry.

LOPAHIN: It's nothing. Thank you kindly for your charming reception.

VARYA: Don't mention it. (*Walks away, looks back and asks softly*) I didn't hurt you, did I?

LOPAHIN: Oh, no, not at all. I shall have a large bump, though. (*Voices from the ballroom*): "Lopahin is here! Lopahin!"

(*Enter* PISHCHIK)

PISHCHIK: My eyes do see, my ears do hear! (*Kisses* LOPAHIN)

LOPAHIN: You smell of cognac, my dear friends. And we've been celebrating here, too. (*Enter* MME. RANEVSKAYA)

MME. RANEVSKAYA: Is that you, Yermolay Alexeyevich? What kept you so long? Where's Leonid?

LOPAHIN: Leonid Andreyevich arrived with me. He's coming.

MME. RANEVSKAYA: Well, what happened? Did the sale take place? Speak!

LOPAHIN   (*embarrassed, fearful of revealing his joy*): The sale was over at four o'clock. We missed the train—had to wait till half past nine. (*Sighing heavily*) Ugh. I'm a little dizzy.

(*Enter* GAYEV. *In his right hand he holds parcels, with his left he is wiping away his tears*)

MME. RANEVSKAYA: Well, Leonid? What news? (*Impatiently, through tears*) Be quick, for God's sake!

GAYEV   (*not answering, simply waves his hand. Weeping, to* FIRS): Here, take these; anchovies, Kerch herrings . . . I haven't eaten all day. What I've been through! (*The click of billiard balls comes through the open door of the billiard room and* YASHA'S *voice is heard*) "Seven and eighteen!" (GAYEV'S *expression changes, he no longer weeps*) I'm terribly tired. Firs, help me change. (*Exits, followed by* FIRS)

PISHCHIK: How about the sale? Tell us what happened.

MME. RANEVSKAYA: Is the cherry orchard sold?

LOPAHIN: Sold.

MME. RANEVSKAYA: Who bought it?

LOPAHIN: I bought it.

(*Pause.* MME. RANEVSKAYA *is overcome. She would fall to the floor, were it not for the chair and table near which she stands.* VARYA *takes the keys from her belt, flings them on the floor in the middle of the drawing-room and goes out.*)

LOPAHIN: I bought it. Wait a bit, ladies and gentlemen, please, my head is swimming. I can't talk. (*Laughs*) We got to the auction and Deriganov was there already. Leonid Andreyevich had only 15,000 and straight off Deriganov bid 30,000 over and above the mortgage. I saw how the land lay, got into the fight, bid 40,000. He bid 45,000. I bid fifty-five. He kept adding five thousands, I ten. Well . . . it came to an end. I bid ninety above the mortgage and the estate was knocked down to me. Now the cherry orchard's mine! Mine! (*Laughs uproari-ously*) Lord! God in Heaven! The cherry orchard's mine! Tell me that I'm drunk —out of my mind—that it's all a dream. (*Stamps his feet*) Don't laugh at me! If my father and my grandfather could rise from their graves and see all that has happened—how their Yermolay, who used to be flogged, their half-literate Yermolay, who used to run about barefoot in winter, how that very Yermolay has bought the most magnificent estate in the world. I bought the estate where my father and grandfather were slaves, where they weren't even allowed to enter the kitchen. I'm asleep—it's only a dream—I only imagine it . . . It's the fruit of your imagination, wrapped in the darkness of the unknown! (*Picks up the keys, smiling genially*) She threw down the keys, wants to show she's no longer mistress here. (*Jingles keys*) Well, no matter. (*The band is heard tuning up*) Hey, musicians! Strike up! I want to hear you! Come, everybody, and see how Yermolay Lopahin will lay the ax to the cherry orchard and how the trees will fall to the ground. We will build summer cottages there, and our grandsons and great-grandsons will see a new life here. Music! Strike up!

(*The band starts to play.* MME. RANEVSKAYA *has sunk into a chair and is weeping bitterly.*)

LOPAHIN (*reproachfully*): Why, why didn't you listen to me? My dear friend, my poor friend, you can't bring it back now. (*Tearfully*) Oh, if only this were over quickly! Oh, if only our wretched, disordered life were changed!

PISHCHIK (*takes him by the arm; sotto voce*): She's crying. Let's go into the ballroom. Let her be alone. Come. (*Takes his arm and leads him into the ballroom*)

LOPAHIN: What's the matter? Musicians, play so I can hear you! Let me have things the way I want them. (*Ironically*) Here comes the new master, the owner of the cherry orchard. (*Accidentally he trips over a little table, almost upsetting the candelabra*) I can pay for everything. (*Exits with* PISHCHIK. MME. RANEVSKAYA, *alone, sits huddled up, weeping bitterly. Music plays softly. Enter* ANYA *and* TROFIMOV *quickly.* ANYA *goes to her mother and falls on her knees before her.* TROFIMOV *stands in the doorway.*)

ANYA: Mamma, mamma, you're crying! Dear, kind, good mamma, my precious, I love you. I bless you! The cherry orchard is sold, it's gone, that's true, quite true. But don't cry, mamma, life is still before you, you still have your kind, pure heart. Let us go, let us go away from here, darling. We will plant a new orchard, even more luxuriant than this one. You will see it, you will understand, and like the sun at evening, joy—deep, tranquil joy—will sink into your soul, and you will smile, mamma. Come, darling, let us go.

ACT IV

Scene as in Act I. No window curtains or pictures, only a little furniture, piled up in a corner, as if for sale. A sense of emptiness. Near the outer door and at the back, suitcases, bundles, etc., are piled up. A door open on the left and the voices of VARYA *and* ANYA *are heard.* LOPAHIN *stands waiting.* YASHA *holds a tray with glasses full of champagne.* YEPIHODOV *in the anteroom is typing up a box. Behind the scene a hum of voices: peasants have come to say good-by. Voice of* GAYEV: *"Thanks, brothers, thank you."*

YASHA: The country folk have come to say good-by. In my opinion, Yermolay Alexeyevich, they are kindly souls, but there's nothing in their heads.

(*The hum dies away. Enter* MME. RANEVSKAYA *and* GAYEV. *She is not crying, but is pale, her face twitches and she cannot speak.*)

GAYEV: You gave them your purse, Luba. That won't do! That won't do!

MME. RANEVSKAYA: I couldn't help it! I couldn't! (*They go out*)

LOPAHIN (*calls after them*): Please, I beg you, have a glass at parting. I didn't think of bringing any champagne from town and at the station I could find only one bottle. Please, won't you? (*Pause*) What's the matter, ladies and gentlemen, don't you want any? (*Moves away from the door*) If I'd known, I wouldn't have bought it. Well, then I won't drink any, either. (*Yasha carefully sets the tray down on a chair*) At least you have a glass, Yasha.

YASHA: Here's to the travelers! And good luck to those that stay! (*Drinks*) This champagne isn't the real stuff, I can assure you.

LOPAHIN: Eight rubles a bottle. (*Pause*) It's devilishly cold here.

YASHA: They didn't light the stoves today—it wasn't worth it, since we're leaving. (*Laughs*)

LOPAHIN: Why are you laughing?

YASHA: It's just that I'm pleased.

LOPAHIN: It's October, yet it's as still and sunny as though it were summer. Good weather for building. (*Looks at his watch, and speaks off*) Bear in mind, ladies and gentlemen, the train goes in forty-seven minutes, so you ought to start for the station in twenty minutes. Better hurry up!

(*Enter* TROFIMOV *wearing an overcoat*)

TROFIMOV: I think it's time to start. The carriages are at the door. The devil only knows what's become of my rubbers; they've disappeared. (*Calling off*) Anya! My rubbers are gone. I can't find them.

LOPAHIN: I've got to go to Kharkov. I'll take the same train you do. I'll spend the winter in Kharkov. I've been hanging round here with you, till I'm worn out with loafing. I can't live without work—I don't know what to do with my hands, they dangle as if they didn't belong to me.

TROFIMOV: Well, we'll soon be gone, then you can go on with your useful labors again.

LOPAHIN: Have a glass.

TROFIMOV: No, I won't.

LOPAHIN: So you're going to Moscow now?

TROFIMOV: Yes. I'll see them into town, and tomorrow I'll go on to Moscow.

LOPAHIN: Well, I'll wager the professors aren't giving any lectures, they're waiting for you to come.

TROFIMOV: That's none of your business.

LOPAHIN: Just how many years have you been at the university?

TROFIMOV: Can't you think of something new? Your joke's stale and flat. (*Looking for his rubbers*) We'll probably never see each other again, so allow me to give you a piece of advice at parting: don't wave your hands about! Get out of the habit. And another thing: building bungalows, figuring that summer residents will eventually become small farmers, figuring like that is just another form of waving your hands about. . . . Never mind, I love you anyway; you have fine, delicate fingers, like an artist; you have a fine, delicate soul.

LOPAHIN   (*embracing him*): Good-by, my dear fellow. Thank you for everything. Let me give you some money for the journey, if you need it.

TROFIMOV: What for? I don't need it.

LOPAHIN: But you haven't any.

TROFIMOV: Yes, I have, thank you. I got some money for a translation—here it is in my pocket. (*Anxiously*) But where are my rubbers?

VARYA (*from the next room*): Here! Take the nasty things. (*Flings a pair of rubbers onto the stage*)

TROFIMOV: What are you so cross about, Varya? Hm . . . and these are not my rubbers.

LOPAHIN: I sowed three thousand acres of poppies in the spring, and now I've made 40,000 on them, clear profit; and when my poppies were in bloom, what a picture it was! So, as I say, I made 40,000; and I am offering you a loan because I can afford it. Why turn up your nose at it? I'm a peasant—I speak bluntly.

TROFIMOV: Your father was a peasant, mine was a druggist—that proves absolutely nothing whatever. (LOPAHIN *takes out his wallet*) Don't, put that away! If you were to offer me two hundred thousand I wouldn't take it. I'm a free man. And everything that all of you, rich and poor alike, value so highly and hold so dear, hasn't the slightest power over me. It's like so much fluff floating in the air. I can get on without you, I can pass you by, I'm strong and proud. Mankind is moving towards the highest truth, towards the highest happiness possible on earth, and I am in the front ranks.

LOPAHIN: Will you get there?

TROFIMOV: I will. (*Pause*) I will get there, or I will show others the way to get there.

(*The sound of axes chopping down trees is heard in the distance*)

LOPAHIN: Well, good-by, my dear fellow. It's time to leave. We turn up our noses at one another, but life goes on just the same. When I'm working hard, without resting, my mind is easier, and it seems to me that I too know why I exist. But how many people are there in Russia, brother, who exist nobody knows why? Well, it doesn't matter. That's not what makes the wheels go round. They say Leonid Andreyevich has taken a position in the bank, 6,000 rubles a year. Only, of course, he won't stick to it, he's too lazy. . . .

ANYA (*in the doorway*): Mamma begs you not to start cutting down the cherry-trees until she's gone.

TROFIMOV: Really, you should have more tact! (*Exits*)

LOPAHIN: Right away—right away! Those men . . . (*Exits*)

ANYA: Has Firs been taken to the hospital?

YASHA: I told them this morning. They must have taken him.

ANYA (*to* YEPIHODOV *who crosses the room*): Yepihodov, please find out if Firs has been taken to the hospital.

YASHA (*offended*): I told Yegor this morning. Why ask a dozen times?

YEPIHODOV: The aged Firs, in my definitive opinion, is beyond mending. It's time he was gathered to his fathers. And I can only envy him. (*Puts a suitcase down on a hat-box and crushes it*) There now, of course. I knew it! (*Exits*)

YASHA (*mockingly*): Two-and-Twenty Troubles!

VARYA (*through the door*): Has Firs been taken to the hospital?

ANYA: Yes.

VARYA: Then why wasn't the note for the doctor taken too?

ANYA: Oh! Then someone must take it to him. (*Exits*)

VARYA (*from adjoining room*): Where's Yasha? Tell him his mother's come and wants to say good-by.

YASHA (*waves his hand*): She tries my patience.

(DUNYASHA *has been occupied with the luggage. Seeing* YASHA *alone, she goes up to him.*)

DUNYASHA: You might just give me one little look, Yasha. You're going away . . . You're leaving me . . . (*weeps and throws herself on his neck*)

YASHA: What's there to cry about? (*Drinks champagne*) In six days I shall be in Paris again. Tomorrow we get into an express train and off we go, that's the last you'll see of us. . . . I can scarcely believe it. *Vive la France!* It don't suit me here, I just can't live here. That's all there is to it. I'm fed up with the ignorance here. I've had enough of it. (*Drinks champagne*) What's there to cry about? Behave yourself properly, and you'll have no cause to cry.

DUNYASHA   (*powders her face, looking in pocket mirror*): Do send me a letter from Paris. You know I loved you, Yasha, how I loved you! I'm a delicate creature, Yasha.

YASHA: Somebody's coming! (*Busies himself with the luggage, hums softly*)

(*Enter* MME. RANEVSKAYA, GAYEV, ANYA, *and* CHARLOTTA)

GAYEV: We ought to be leaving. We haven't much time. (*Looks at* YASHA) Who smells of herring?

MME. RANEVSKAYA: In about ten minutes we should be getting into the carriages. (*Looks around the room*) Good-by, dear old home, good-by, grandfather. Winter will pass, spring will come, you will no longer be here, they will have torn you down. How much these walls have seen! (*Kisses* ANYA *warmly*) My treasure, how radiant you look! Your eyes are sparkling like diamonds. Are you glad? Very?

ANYA   (*gaily*): Very glad. A new life is beginning, mamma.

GAYEV: Well, really, everything is all right now. Before the cherry orchard was sold, we all fretted and suffered; but afterwards, when the question was settled finally and irrevocably, we all calmed down, and even felt quite cheerful. I'm a bank employee now, a financier. The yellow ball in the side pocket! And anyhow, you are looking better Luba, there's no doubt of that.

MME. RANEVSKAYA: Yes, my nerves are better, that's true. (*She is handed her hat and coat*) I sleep well. Carry out my things, Yasha. It's time. (*To* ANYA) We shall soon see each other again, my little girl. I'm going to Paris, I'll live there on the money your great-aunt sent us to buy the estate with—long live Auntie! But that money won't last long.

ANYA: You'll come back soon, soon, mamma, won't you? Meanwhile I'll study, I'll pass my high school examination, and then I'll go to work and help you. We'll read all kinds of books together, mamma, won't we? (*Kisses her mother's hands*) We'll read in the autumn evenings, we'll read lots of books, and a new wonderful world will open up before us. (*Falls into a revery*) Mamma, do come back.

MME. RANEVSKAYA: I will come back, my precious.

(*Embraces her daughter. Enter* LOPAHIN *and* CHARLOTTA *who is humming softly.*)

GAYEV: Charlotta's happy: she's singing.

CHARLOTTA   (*picks up a bundle and holds it like a baby in swaddling-clothes*): Bye, baby, bye. (*A baby is heard crying*) "Wah! Wah!" Hush, hush, my pet, my little one. "Wah! Wah!" I'm so sorry for you! (*Throws the bundle down*) You will find me a position, won't you? I can't go on like this.

LOPAHIN: We'll find one for you, Charlotta Ivanovna, don't worry.

GAYEV: Everyone's leaving us. Varya's going away. We've suddenly become of no use.

CHARLOTTA: There's no place for me to live in town, I must go away. (*Hums*)

(*Enter* PISHCHIK)

LOPAHIN: There's nature's masterpiece!

PISHCHIK (*gasping*): Oh . . . let me get my breath . . . I'm in agony. . . . Esteemed friends . . . Give me a drink of water. . . .

GAYEV: Wants some money, I suppose. No, thank you. . . . I'll keep out of harm's way. (*Exits*)

PISHCHIK: It's a long while since I've been to see you, most charming lady. (*To* LOPAHIN) So you are here . . . glad to see you, you intellectual giant. . . . There . . . (*Gives* LOPAHIN *money*) Here's 400 rubles, and I still owe you 840.

LOPAHIN (*shrugging his shoulders in bewilderment*): I must be dreaming . . . Where did you get it?

PISHCHIK: Wait a minute . . . It's hot . . . A most extraordinary event! Some Englishmen came to my place and found some sort of white clay on my land . . . (*To* MME. RANEVSKAYA) And 400 for you . . . most lovely . . . most wonderful . . . (*Hands her the money*) The rest later. (*Drinks water*) A young man in the train was telling me just now that a great philosopher recommends jumping off roofs. "Jump!" says he; "that's the long and the short of it!" (*In amazement*) Just imagine! Some more water!

LOPAHIN: What Englishmen?

PISHCHIK: I leased them the tract with the clay on it for twenty-four hours. . . . And now, forgive me, I can't stay. . . . I must be dashing on. . . . I'm going over to Znoikov . . . to Kardamanov . . . I owe them all money . . . (*Drinks water*) Good-by, everybody . . . I'll look in on Thursday . . .

MME. RANEVSKAYA: We're just moving into town; and tomorrow I go abroad.

PISHCHIK (*upset*): What? Why into town? That's why the furniture is like that . . . and the suitcases . . . Well, never mind! (*Through tears*) Never mind . . . Men of colossal intellect, these Englishmen . . . Never mind . . . Be happy. God will come to your help. . . . Never mind. . . . Everything in this world comes to an end. (*Kisses* MME. RANEVSKAYA's *hand*) If the rumor reaches you that it's all up with me, remember this old . . . horse, and say: Once there lived a certain . . . Simeonov-Pishchik . . . the kingdom of Heaven be his . . . Glorious weather . . . Yes . . . (*Exits, in great confusion, but at once returns and says in the doorway*) My daughter Dashenka sends her regards. (*Exit*)

MME. RANEVSKAYA: Now we can go. I leave with two cares weighing on me. The first is poor old Firs. (*Glancing at her watch*) We still have about five minutes.

ANYA: Mamma, Firs has already been taken to the hospital. Yasha sent him there this morning.

MME. RANEVSKAYA: My other worry is Varya. She's used to getting up early and working; and now, with no work to do, she is like a fish out of water. She has grown thin and pale, and keeps crying, poor soul. (*Pause*) You know this very well, Yermolay Alexeyevich; I dreamed of seeing her married to you, and it looked as though that's how it would be. (*Whispers to* ANYA, *who nods to* CHARLOTTA *and both go out*) She loves you. You find her attractive. I don't know, I don't know why it is you seem to avoid each other; I can't understand it.

LOPAHIN: To tell you the truth, I don't understand it myself. It's all a puzzle. If there's still time, I'm ready now, at once. Let's settle it straight off, and have done with it! Without you, I feel I'll never be able to propose.

MME. RANEVSKAYA: That's splendid. After all, it will only take a minute. I'll call her at once. . . .

LOPAHIN: And luckily, here's champagne too. (*Looks at the glasses*) Empty! Somebody's drunk it all. (*Yasha coughs*) That's what you might call guzzling. . . .

MME. RANEVSKAYA   (*animatedly*): Excellent! We'll go and leave you alone. Yasha, *allez!* I'll call her. (*At the door*) Varya, leave everything and come here. Come! (*Exits with Yasha*)

LOPAHIN   (*looking at his watch*): Yes . . .

(*Pause behind the door, smothered laughter and whispering; at last, enter* VARYA)

VARYA   (*looking over the luggage in leisurely fashion*): Strange, I can't find it . . .

LOPAHIN: What are you looking for?

VARYA: Packed it myself, and I don't remember . . . (*Pause*)

LOPAHIN: Where are you going now, Varya?

VARYA: I? To the Ragulins'. I've arranged to take charge there—as housekeeper, if you like.

LOPAHIN: At Yashnevo? About fifty miles from here. (*Pause*) Well, life in this house is ended!

VARYA   (*examining luggage*): Where is it? Perhaps I put it in the chest. Yes, life in this house is ended. . . . There will be no more of it.

LOPAHIN: And I'm just off to Kharkov—by this next train. I've a lot to do there. I'm leaving Yepihodov here . . . I've taken him on.

VARYA: Oh!

LOPAHIN: Last year at this time it was snowing, if you remember, but now it's sunny and there's no wind. It's cold, though. . . . It must be three below.

VARYA: I didn't look. (*Pause*) And besides, our thermometer's broken. (*Pause. Voice from the yard*) "Yermolay Alexeyevich!"

LOPAHIN   (*as if he had been waiting for the call*): This minute!

(*Exit quickly.* VARYA *sits on the floor and sobs quietly, her head on a bundle of clothes. Enter* MME. RANEVSKAYA *cautiously.*)

MME. RANEVSKAYA: Well? (*Pause*) We must be going.

VARYA   (*wiping her eyes*): Yes, it's time, mamma dear. I'll be able to get to the Ragulins' today, if only we don't miss the train.

MME. RANEVSKAYA   (*at the door*): Anya, put your things on.

(*Enter* ANYA, GAYEV, CHARLOTTA. GAYEV *wears a heavy overcoat with a hood. Enter servants and coachmen.* YEPIHODOV *bustles about the luggage.*)

MME. RANEVSKAYA: Now we can start on our journey.

ANYA   (*joyfully*): On our journey!

GAYEV: My friends, my dear, cherished friends, leaving this house forever, can I be silent? Can I at leave-taking refrain from giving utterance to those emotions that now fill my being?

ANYA   (*imploringly*): Uncle!

VARYA: Uncle, uncle dear, don't.

GAYEV   (*Forlornly*): I'll bank the yellow in the side pocket . . . I'll be silent . . .

(*Enter* TROFIMOV, *then* LOPAHIN)

TROFIMOV: Well, ladies and gentlemen, it's time to leave.

LOPAHIN: Yepihodov, my coat.

MME. RANEVSKAYA: I'll sit down just a minute. It seems as though I'd never before seen what the walls of this house were like, the ceilings, and now I look at them hungrily, with such tender affection.

GAYEV: I remember when I was six years old sitting on that window sill on Whitsunday, watching my father going to church.

MME. RANEVSKAYA: Has everything been taken?

LOPAHIN: I think so. (*Putting on his overcoat*) Yepihodov, see that everything's in order.

YEPIHODOV   (*in a husky voice*): You needn't worry, Yermolay Alexeyevich.

LOPAHIN: What's the matter with your voice?

YEPIHODOV: I just had a drink of water. I must have swallowed something.

YASHA   (*contemptuously*): What ignorance!

MME. RANEVSKAYA: When we're gone, not a soul will be left here.

LOPAHIN: Until the spring.

(VARYA *pulls an umbrella out of a bundle, as though about to hit someone with it.* LOPAHIN *pretends to be frightened.*)

VARYA: Come, come, I had no such idea!

TROFIMOV: Ladies and gentlemen, let's get into the carriages—it's time. The train will be in directly.

VARYA: Petya, there they are, your rubbers, by that trunk. (*Tearfully*) And what dirty old things they are!

TROFIMOV   (*puts on rubbers*): Let's go, ladies and gentlemen.

GAYEV   (*greatly upset, afraid of breaking down*): The train . . . the station . . . Three cushions in the side pocket, I'll bank this one in the corner . . .

MME. RANEVSKAYA: Let's go.

LOPAHIN: Are we all here? No one in there? (*Locks the side door on the left*) There are some things stored here, better lock up. Let us go!

ANYA: Good-by, old house! Good-by, old life!

TROFIMOV: Hail to you, new life!

(*Exit with* ANYA, VARYA *looks round the room and goes out slowly.* YASHA *and* CHARLOTTA *with her dog go out.*)

LOPAHIN: And so, until the spring. Go along, friends . . . 'Bye-'bye! (*Exits*)

(MME. RANEVSKAYA *and* GAYEV *remain alone. As though they had been waiting for this, they throw themselves on each other's necks, and break into subdued, restrained sobs, afraid of being overheard.*)

GAYEV   (*in despair*): My sister! My sister!

MME. RANEVSKAYA: Oh, my orchard—my dear, sweet, beautiful orchard! My life, my youth, my happiness—good-by! Good-by! (*Voice of* ANYA, *gay and summoning*) "Mamma!" (*Voice of* TROFIMOV, *gay and excited*) "Halloo!"

MME. RANEVSKAYA: One last look at the walls, at the windows . . . Our poor mother loved to walk about this room . . .

GAYEV: My sister, my sister! (*Voice of* ANYA) "Mamma!" (*Voice of* TROFIMOV) "Halloo!"

MME. RANEVSKAYA: We're coming.

(*They go out. The stage is empty. The sound of doors being locked, of carriages driving away. Then silence. In the stillness is heard the muffled sound of the ax striking a tree, a mournful, lonely sound.*

Footsteps are heard. FIRS *appears in the doorway on the right. He is dressed as usual in a jacket and white waistcoat and wears slippers. He is ill.*)

FIRS   (*goes to the door, tries the handle*): Locked! They've gone . . . (*Sits down on the sofa*) They've forgotten me . . . Never mind . . . I'll sit here a bit . . . I'll wager Leonid Andreyevich hasn't put his fur coat on, he's gone off in his light overcoat . . . (*Sighs anxiously*) I didn't keep an eye on him . . . Ah, when they're young, they're green . . . (*Mumbles something indistinguishable*) Life has gone by as if I had never lived. (*Lies down*) I'll lie down a while . . . There's no strength left in you, old fellow; nothing is left, nothing. Ah, you addlehead!

(*Lies motionless. A distant sound is heard coming from the sky as it were, the sound of a snapping string mournfully dying away. All is still again, and nothing is heard but the strokes of the ax against a tree far away in the orchard.*)

QUESTIONS

1. Discuss the genre of *The Cherry Orchard*. Explain why some readers might see the play as tragic and others might see it as comic. How did you respond to the play?
2. Describe the tone of the play. What is Chekhov's attitude toward his characters and their situations?
3. On occasion the dialogue seems fragmented and disjointed—more a series of disconnected remarks than a real dialogue. Find one such passage and consider its purpose and point.
4. Some readers feel that little or nothing happens in Chekhov's plays. Can this criticism be leveled against *The Cherry Orchard*? Why or why not?

5. Examine the scene near the end of the play (Act IV) when Lopahin is alone with Varya. What did you expect to happen? Why? Why does Lopahin leave without proposing marriage?
6. Explain how Chekhov uses sound effectively throughout *The Cherry Orchard*, especially at the end.
7. How does Chekhov make the cherry orchard a central presence in the play? What does it stand for? Identify and explain the symbols in the play.

Bernard Shaw

Another comic realist who, like Chekhov, straddles the nineteenth and twentieth centuries is Bernard Shaw. Shaw lived considerably longer than Chekhov and wrote much more. His more than sixty plays have been collected with his letters, novels, and criticism in over thirty volumes. In whatever genre he worked, Shaw's comedy turned not just on characters and situations, but on ideas. Ideas permeate his work the way they do Ibsen's. But Shaw's use of ideas is much more various than Ibsen's and considerably more comical. Frequently, as in *Arms and the Man,* Shaw turns to satire as a mode of dramatizing ideas.

Produced in 1894 and published in 1898, *Arms and the Man* was Shaw's first "pleasant" play, as he called a group of them, and his first to be commercially staged. In his preface to *Plays Pleasant,* Shaw explained his antipathy to "idealism, which is only a flattering name for romance in politics and morals." With such idealistic, romanticized notions of love and war in mind, Shaw wrote *Arms and the Man,* a witty satire that expresses a more realistic view of each.

Unlike Chekhov, whose realism included a studious avoidance of witty repartee, of curtain clinching acts, and of convoluted, melodramatic plots, Shaw took full advantage of such devices. His realism and his comedy thus differ radically from Chekhov's as does his desire to use his plays like Ibsen did for didactic purposes. As we have stated previously, Shaw's didactic and polemical impulses found expression in a series of long prefaces he wrote to many of his plays, prefaces in which he discoursed on issues the plays dramatized. Nor was Shaw above replying to critics of his plays as he does to critics of *Arms* in his essay "A Dramatic Realist to His Critics." From that essay we gain a sense of Shaw as a realist dramatist whose business is to get outside systems that classify characters ethically or morally.

Basically Shaw was an iconoclast who encouraged his audience to look more critically at ideas and ideals that they had previously accepted without question. Beneath the witty surface of his comedies lie serious questions. *Arms and the Man,* whose title announces its dual subjects, love and war, and whose first line echoes Vergil's *Aeneid* (page 396) ends with a question: "Is he a man!" Sergius asks this about Bluntschli, the antiheroic hero of the play. And we wonder as we read the play, "just what is a man anyway?"

BERNARD SHAW
[*1856–1950*]

Arms and the Man

A PLEASANT PLAY

CHARACTERS

RAINA PETKOFF, *a young Bulgarian lady.*
CATHERINE PETKOFF, *her mother.*
LOUKA, *the Petkoffs' maid.*
CAPTAIN BLUNTSCHLI, *a Swiss officer in the Serbian army.*
A RUSSIAN OFFICER *in the Bulgarian army.*
NICOLA, *the Petkoffs' butler.*
PETKOFF, *Raina's father, a major in the Bulgarian army.*
SERGIUS SARANOFF, *Raina's fiancé, a major in the Bulgarian army.*

ACT I

(*Night: A lady's bedchamber in Bulgaria, in a small town near the Dragoman Pass, late in November in the year 1885. Through an open window with a little balcony a peak of the Balkans, wonderfully white and beautiful in the starlit snow, seems quite close at hand, though it is really miles away. The interior of the room is not like anything to be seen in the west of Europe. It is half rich Bulgarian, half cheap Viennese. Above the head of the bed, which stands against a little wall cutting off the left hand corner of the room, is a painted wooden shrine, blue and gold, with an ivory image of Christ, and a light hanging before it in a pierced metal ball suspended by three chains. The principal seat, placed towards the other side of the room and opposite the window, is a Turkish ottoman. The counterpane and hangings of the bed, the window curtains, the little carpet, and all the ornamental textile fabrics in the room are oriental and gorgeous; the paper on the walls is occidental and paltry. The washstand, against the wall on the side nearest the ottoman and window, consists of an enamelled iron basin with a pail beneath it in a painted metal frame, and a single towel on the rail at the side. The dressing table, between the bed and the window, is a common pine table, covered with a cloth of many colours, with an expensive toilet mirror on it. The door is on the side nearest the bed; and there is a chest of drawers between. This chest of drawers is also covered by a variegated native cloth; and on it there is a pile of paper backed novels, a box of chocolate creams, and a miniature easel with a large photograph of an extremely handsome officer, whose lofty bearing and magnetic glance can be felt even from the portrait. The room is lighted by a candle on the chest of drawers, and another on the dressing table with a box of matches beside it.*

The window is hinged doorwise and stands wide open. Outside, a pair of wooden shutters, opening outwards, also stand open. On the balcony a young lady, intensely conscious of the romantic beauty of the night, and of the fact that her own youth and beauty are part of it, is gazing at the snowy Balkans. She is in her nightgown, well covered by a long mantle of furs, worth, on a moderate estimate, about three times the furniture of the room.

Her reverie is interrupted by her mother, CATHERINE PETKOFF, *a woman over forty, imperiously energetic, with magnificent black hair and eyes, who might be a very splendid specimen of the wife of a mountain farmer, but is determined to be a Viennese lady, and to that end wears a fashionable tea gown on all occasions.*)

CATHERINE (*entering hastily, full of good news*): Raina! (*She pronounces it Rah-eena, with the stress on the ee.*) Raina! (*She goes to the bed, expecting to find* RAINA *there.*) Why, where——? (RAINA *looks into the room.*) Heavens, child! are you out in the night air instead of in your bed? You'll catch your death. Louka told me you were asleep.

RAINA (*dreamily*): I sent her away. I wanted to be alone. The stars are so beautiful! What is the matter?

CATHERINE: Such news! There has been a battle.

RAINA (*her eyes dilating*): Ah! (*She comes eagerly to* CATHERINE.)

CATHERINE: A great battle at Slivnitza! A victory! And it was won by Sergius.

RAINA (*with a cry of delight*): Ah! (*They embrace rapturously.*) Oh, mother! (*Then, with sudden anxiety*) is father safe?

CATHERINE: Of course: he sends me the news. Sergius is the hero of the hour, the idol of the regiment.

RAINA: Tell me, tell me. How was it? (*Ecstatically*) Oh, mother! mother! mother! (*She pulls her mother down on the ottoman; and they kiss one another frantically.*)

CATHERINE (*with surging enthusiasm*): You can't guess how splendid it is. A cavalry charge! think of that! He defied our Russian commanders—acted without orders—led a charge on his own responsibility—headed it himself— was the first man to sweep through their guns. Can't you see it, Raina: our gallant splendid Bulgarians with their swords and eyes flashing, thundering down like an avalanche and scattering the wretched Serbs and their dandified Austrian officers like chaff. And you! you kept Sergius waiting a year before you would be betrothed to him. Oh, if you have a drop of Bulgarian blood in your veins, you will worship him when he comes back.

RAINA: What will he care for my poor little worship after the acclamations of a whole army of heroes? But no matter: I am so happy! so proud! (*She rises and walks about excitedly.*) It proves that all our ideas were real after all.

CATHERINE (*indignantly*): Our ideas real! What do you mean?

RAINA: Our ideas of what Sergius would do. Our patriotism. Our heroic ideals. I sometimes used to doubt whether they were anything but dreams. Oh, what faithless little creatures girls are! When I buckled on Sergius's sword he looked so noble: it was treason to think of disillusion or humiliation or failure. And yet—and yet—(*She sits down again suddenly.*) Promise me you'll never tell him.

CATHERINE: Don't ask me for promises until I know what I'm promising.

RAINA: Well, it came into my head just as he was holding me in his arms and looking into my eyes, that perhaps we only had our heroic ideas because we are so fond of reading Byron and Pushkin, and because we were so delighted with the opera that season at Bucharest. Real life is so seldom like that! indeed never, as far as I knew it then. (*Remorsefully*) Only think, mother: I doubted him: I wondered whether all his heroic qualities and his soldiership might not prove mere imagination when he went into a real battle. I had an uneasy fear that he might cut a poor figure there beside all those clever officers from the Tsar's court.

CATHERINE: A poor figure! Shame on you! The Serbs have Austrian officers who are just as clever as the Russians; but we have beaten them in every battle for all that.

RAINA (*laughing and snuggling against her mother*): Yes: I was only a prosaic little coward. Oh, to think that it was all true! that Sergius is just as splendid and noble as he looks! that the world is really a glorious world for women who can see its glory and men who can act its romance! What happiness! what unspeakable fulfillment!

(*They are interrupted by the entry of* LOUKA, *a handsome proud girl in a pretty Bulgarian peasant's dress with double apron, so defiant that her servility to* RAINA *is almost insolent. She is afraid of* CATHERINE, *but even with her goes as far as she dares.*)

LOUKA: If you please, madam, all the windows are to be closed and the shutters made fast. They say there may be shooting in the streets. (RAINA *and* CATHERINE *rise together, alarmed.*) The Serbs are being chased right back through the pass; and they say they may run into the town. Our cavalry will be after them; and our people will be ready for them, you may be sure, now they're running away. (*She goes out on the balcony, and pulls the outside shutters to; then steps back into the room.*)

CATHERINE (*businesslike, housekeeping instincts aroused*): I must see that everything is made safe downstairs.

RAINA: I wish our people were not so cruel. What glory is there in killing wretched fugitives?

CATHERINE: Cruel! Do you suppose they would hesitate to kill you—or worse?

RAINA (*to* LOUKA): Leave the shutters so that I can just close them if I hear any noise.

CATHERINE (*authoritatively, turning on her way to the door*): Oh no, dear: you must keep them fastened. You would be sure to drop off to sleep and leave them open. Make them fast, Louka.

LOUKA: Yes, madam. (*She fastens them.*)

RAINA: Don't be anxious about me. The moment I hear a shot, I shall blow out the candles and roll myself up in bed with my ears well covered.

CATHERINE: Quite the wisest thing you can do, my love. Goodnight.

RAINA: Goodnight. (*Her emotion comes back for a moment.*) Wish me joy. (*They kiss.*) This is the happiest night of my life—if only there are no fugitives.

CATHERINE: Go to bed, dear; and don't think of them. (*She goes out.*)

LOUKA (*secretly to* RAINA): If you would like the shutters open, just give them a push like this (*she pushes them: they open: she pulls them to again.*) One of them ought to be bolted at the bottom; but the bolt's gone.

RAINA (*with dignity, reproving her*): Thanks, Louka; but we must do what we are told. (LOUKA *makes a grimace.*) Goodnight.

LOUKA (*carelessly*): Goodnight. (*She goes out, swaggering.*)

(RAINA, *left alone, takes off her fur cloak and throws it on the ottoman. Then she goes to the chest of drawers, and adores the portrait there with feelings that are beyond all expression. She does not kiss it or press it to her breast, or shew it any mark of bodily affection; but she takes it in her hands and elevates it, like a priestess.*)

RAINA (*looking up at the picture*): Oh, I shall never be unworthy of you any more, my soul's hero: never, never, never. (*She replaces it reverently. Then she selects a novel from the little pile of books. She turns over the leaves dreamily; finds her page; turns the book inside out at it; and, with a happy sigh, gets into bed and prepares to read herself to sleep. But before abandoning herself to fiction, she raises her eyes once more, thinking of the blessed reality, and murmurs.*) My hero! my hero!

(*A distant shot breaks the quiet of the night. She starts, listening; and two more shots, much nearer, follow, startling her so that she scrambles out of bed, and hastily blows out the candle on the chest of drawers. Then, putting her fingers in her ears, she runs to the dressing table, blows out the light there, and hurries back to bed in the dark, nothing being visible but the glimmer of the light in the pierced ball before the image, and the starlight seen through the slits at the top of the shutters. The firing breaks out again: there is a startling fusillade quite close at hand. Whilst it is still echoing, the shutters disappear, pulled open from without; and for an instant the rectangle of snowy starlight flashes out with the figure of a man silhouetted in black upon it. The shutters close immediately; and the room is dark again. But the silence is now broken by the sound of panting. Then there is a scratch; and the flame of a match is seen in the middle of the room.*)

RAINA (*crouching on the bed*): Who's there? (*The match is out instantly.*) Who's there? Who is that?

A MAN'S VOICE (*in the darkness, subduedly, but threateningly*): Sh—sh! Don't call out; or you'll be shot. Be good; and no harm will happen to you. (*She is heard leaving her bed, and making for the door.*) Take care: it's no use trying to run away.

RAINA: But who—

THE VOICE (*warning*): Remember: if you raise your voice my revolver will go off. (*Commandingly*) Strike a light and let me see you. Do you hear. (*Another moment of silence and darkness as she retreats to the chest of drawers. Then she lights a candle; and the mystery is at an end. He is a man of about 35, in a deplorable plight, bespattered with mud and blood and snow, his belt and the strap of his revolver case keeping together the torn ruins of the blue tunic of a Serbian artillery officer. All that the candlelight and his unwashed unkempt condition make it possible to discern is that he is of middling stature and undistinguished appearance, with strong neck and shoul-*

ders, *roundish obstinate looking head covered with short crisp bronze curls, clear quick eyes and good brows and mouth, hopelessly prosaic nose like that of a strong minded baby, trim soldierlike carriage and energetic manner, and with all his wits about him in spite of his desperate predicament: even with a sense of the humor of it, without, however, the least intention of trifling with it or throwing away a chance. Reckoning up what he can guess about* RAINA: *her age, her social position, her character, and the extent to which she is frightened, he continues, more politely but still most determinedly*) Excuse my disturbing you; but you recognize my uniform? Serb! If I'm caught I shall be killed. (*Menacingly*) Do you understand that?

RAINA: Yes.

THE MAN: Well, I don't intend to get killed if I can help it. (*Still more formidably*) Do you understand that? (*He locks the door quickly but quietly.*)

RAINA   (*disdainfully*): I suppose not. (*She draws herself up superbly, and looks him straight in the face, adding, with cutting emphasis*) Some soldiers, I know, are afraid to die.

THE MAN   (*with grim goodhumor*): All of them, dear lady, all of them, believe me. It is our duty to live as long as we can. Now, if you raise an alarm—

RAINA   (*cutting him short*): You will shoot me. How do you know that *I* am afraid to die?

THE MAN   (*cunningly*): Ah; but suppose I don't shoot you, what will happen then? A lot of your cavalry will burst into this pretty room of yours and slaughter me here like a pig; for I'll fight like a demon: they shan't get me into the street to amuse themselves with: I know what they are. Are you prepared to receive that sort of company in your present undress? (RAINA, *suddenly conscious of her nightgown, instinctively shrinks and gathers it more closely about her neck. He watches her and adds pitilessly*) Hardly presentable, eh? (*She turns to the ottoman. He raises his pistol instantly, and cries*) Stop! (*She stops.*) Where are you going?

RAINA   (*with dignified patience*): Only to get my cloak.

THE MAN   (*passing swiftly to the ottoman and snatching the cloak*): A good idea! I'll keep the cloak; and you'll take care that nobody comes in and sees you without it. This is a better weapon than the revolver: eh? (*He throws the pistol down on the ottoman.*)

RAINA   (*revolted*): It is not the weapon of a gentleman!

THE MAN: It's good enough for a man with only you to stand between him and death. (*As they look at one another for a moment,* RAINA *hardly able to believe that even a Serbian officer can be so cynically and selfishly unchivalrous, they are startled by a sharp fusillade in the street. The chill of imminent death hushes the man's voice as he adds*) Do you hear? If you are going to bring those blackguards in on me you shall receive them as you are.

(*Clamor and disturbance. The pursuers in the street batter at the house door, shouting,* Open the door! Open the door! Wake up, will you! *A man servant's voice calls to them angrily from within,* This is Major Petkoff's house: you can't come in here; *but a renewal of the clamor, and a torrent of blows on the door, end with his letting a chain down with a clank, followed by a rush of heavy footsteps and a din of triumphant yells, dominated at last by the voice of* CATHERINE, *indignantly addressing an officer with* What does this mean, sir? Do you know where you are? *The noise subsides suddenly.*)

LOUKA (*outside, knocking at the bedroom door*): My lady! my lady! get up quick and open the door. If you don't they will break it down.

(*The fugitive throws up his head with the gesture of a man who sees that it is all over with him, and drops the manner he has been assuming to intimidate* RAINA.)

THE MAN (*sincerely and kindly*): No use, dear: I'm done for. (*Flinging the cloak to her*) Quick! wrap yourself up: they're coming.
RAINA: Oh, thank you. (*She wraps herself up with intense relief.*)
THE MAN (*between his teeth*): Don't mention it.
RAINA (*anxiously*): What will you do?
THE MAN (*grimly*): The first man in will find out. Keep out of the way; and don't look. It won't last long; but it will not be nice. (*He draws his sabre and faces the door, waiting.*)
RAINA (*impulsively*): I'll help you. I'll save you.
THE MAN: You can't.
RAINA: I can. I'll hide you. (*She drags him towards the window.*) Here! behind the curtains.
THE MAN (*yielding to her*): There's just half a chance, if you keep your head.
RAINA (*drawing the curtain before him*): S-sh! (*She makes for the ottoman.*)
THE MAN (*putting out his head*): Remember—
RAINA (*running back to him*): Yes?
THE MAN:—nine soldiers out of ten are born fools.
RAINA: Oh! (*She draws the curtain angrily before him.*)
THE MAN (*looking out at the other side*): If they find me, I promise you a fight: a devil of a fight.

(*She stamps at him. He disappears hastily. She takes off her cloak, and throws it across the foot of the bed. Then, with a sleepy, disturbed air, she opens the door.* LOUKA *enters excitedly.*)

LOUKA: One of those beasts of Serbs has been seen climbing up the waterpipe to your balcony. Our men want to search for him; and they are so wild and drunk and furious. (*She makes for the other side of the room to get as far from the door as possible.*) My lady says you are to dress at once and to—(*She sees the revolver lying on the ottoman, and stops, petrified.*)
RAINA (*as if annoyed at being disturbed*): They shall not search here. Why have they been let in?
CATHERINE (*coming in hastily*): Raina, darling, are you safe? Have you seen anyone or heard anything?
RAINA: I heard the shooting. Surely the soldiers will not dare come in here?
CATHERINE: I have found a Russian officer, thank Heaven: he knows Sergius. (*Speaking through the door to someone outside*) Sir: will you come in now. My daughter will receive you.

(*A young Russian officer, in Bulgarian uniform, enters, sword in hand.*)

OFFICER (*with soft feline politeness and stiff military carriage*): Good evening, gracious lady. I am sorry to intrude; but there is a Serb hiding on the balcony. Will you and the gracious lady your mother please to withdraw whilst we search?
RAINA (*petulantly*): Nonsense, sir: you can see that there is no one on the

balcony. (*She throws the shutters wide open and stands with her back to the curtain where the man is hidden, pointing to the moonlit balcony. A couple of shots are fired right under the window; and a bullet shatters the glass opposite* RAINA, *who winks and gasps, but stands her ground; whilst* CATHERINE *screams, and* THE OFFICER, *with a cry of* Take care! *rushes to the balcony.*)

THE OFFICER   (*on the balcony, shouting savagely down to the street*): Cease firing there, you fools: do you hear? Cease firing, damn you! (*He glares down for a moment; then turns to* RAINA, *trying to resume his polite manner.*) Could anyone have got in without your knowledge? Were you asleep?

RAINA: No: I have not been to bed.

THE OFFICER   (*impatiently, coming back into the room*): Your neighbors have their heads so full of runaway Serbs that they see them everywhere. (*Politely*) Gracious lady: a thousand pardons. Goodnight. (*Military bow, which* RAINA *returns coldly. Another to* CATHERINE, *who follows him out.*)

(RAINA *closes the shutters. She turns and sees* LOUKA, *who has been watching the scene curiously.*)

RAINA: Don't leave my mother, Louka, until the soldiers go away.

(LOUKA *glances at* RAINA, *at the ottoman, at the curtain; then purses her lips secretively, laughs insolently, and goes out.* RAINA, *highly offended by this demonstration, follows her to the door, and shuts it behind her with a slam, locking it violently. The man immediately steps out from behind the curtain, sheathing his sabre. Then, dismissing the danger from his mind in a businesslike way, he comes affably to* RAINA.)

THE MAN: A narrow shave; but a miss is as good as a mile. Dear young lady: your servant to the death. I wish for your sake I had joined the Bulgarian army instead of the other one. I am not a native Serb.

RAINA   (*haughtily*): No: you are one of the Austrians who set the Serbs on to rob us of our national liberty, and who officer their army for them. We hate them!

THE MAN: Austrian! not I. Don't hate me, dear young lady. I am a Swiss, fighting merely as a professional soldier. I joined the Serbs because they came first on the road from Switzerland. Be generous: you've beaten us hollow.

RAINA: Have I not been generous?

THE MAN: Noble! Heroic! But I'm not saved yet. This particular rush will soon pass through; but the pursuit will go on all night by fits and starts. I must take my chance to get off in a quiet interval. (*Pleasantly*) You don't mind my waiting just a minute or two, do you?

RAINA   (*putting on her most genteel society manner*): Oh, not at all. Won't you sit down?

THE MAN: Thanks. (*He sits on the foot of the bed.*)

(RAINA *walks with studied elegance to the ottoman and sits down. Unfortunately she sits on the pistol, and jumps up with a shriek. The man, all nerves, shies like a frightened horse to the other side of the room.*)

THE MAN   (*irritably*): Don't frighten me like that. What is it?

RAINA: Your revolver! It was staring that officer in the face all the time. What an escape!

THE MAN   (*vexed at being unnecessarily terrified*): Oh, is that all?

RAINA   (*staring at him rather superciliously as she conceives a poorer and poorer opinion of him, and feels proportionately more and more at her ease*): I am sorry I frightened you. (*She takes up the pistol and hands it to him.*) Pray take it to protect yourself against me.

THE MAN   (*grinning wearily at the sarcasm as he takes the pistol*): No use, dear young lady; there's nothing in it. It's not loaded. (*He makes a grimace at it, and drops it despairingly into his revolver case.*)

RAINA: Load it by all means.

THE MAN: I've no ammunition. What use are cartridges in battle? I always carry chocolate instead; and I finished the last cake of that hours ago.

RAINA   (*outraged in her most cherished ideals of manhood*): Chocolate! Do you stuff your pockets with sweets—like a schoolboy—even in the field?

THE MAN   (*grinning*): Yes: isn't it contemptible? (*Hungrily*) I wish I had some now.

RAINA: Allow me. (*She sails away scornfully to the chest of drawers, and returns with the box of confectionery in her hand.*) I am sorry I have eaten them all except these. (*She offers him the box.*)

THE MAN   (*ravenously*): You're an angel! (*He gobbles the contents.*) Creams! Delicious! (*He looks anxiously to see whether there are any more. There are none: he can only scrape the box with his fingers and suck them. When that nourishment is exhausted he accepts the inevitable with pathetic goodhumor, and says, with grateful emotion*) Bless you, dear lady! You can always tell an old soldier by the inside of his holsters and cartridge boxes. The young ones carry pistols and cartridges: the old ones, grub. Thank you. (*He hands back the box. She snatches it contemptuously from him and throws it away. He shies again, as if she had meant to strike him.*) Ugh! Don't do things so suddenly, gracious lady. It's mean to revenge yourself because I frightened you just now.

RAINA   (*loftily*): Frighten me! Do you know, sir, that though I am only a woman, I think I am at heart as brave as you.

THE MAN: I should think so. You haven't been under fire for three days as I have. I can stand two days without shewing it much; but no man can stand three days: I'm as nervous as a mouse. (*He sits down on the ottoman, and takes his head in his hands.*) Would you like to see me cry?

RAINA   (*alarmed*): No.

THE MAN: If you would, all you have to do is to scold me just as if I were a little boy and you my nurse. If I were in camp now, they'd play all sorts of tricks on me.

RAINA   (*a little moved*): I'm sorry. I won't scold you. (*Touched by the sympathy in her tone, he raises his head and looks gratefully at her: she immediately draws back and says stiffly*): You must excuse me: our soldiers are not like that. (*She moves away from the ottoman.*)

THE MAN: Oh yes they are. There are only two sorts of soldiers: old ones and young ones. I've served fourteen years: half of your fellows never smelt powder before. Why, how is it that you've just beaten us? Sheer ignorance of the art of war, nothing else. (*Indignantly*) I never saw anything so unprofessional.

RAINA   (*ironically*): Oh! was it unprofessional to beat you?

THE MAN: Well, come! is it professional to throw a regiment of cavalry on a battery of machine guns, with the dead certainty that if the guns go off not a horse or man will ever get within fifty yards of the fire? I couldn't believe my eyes when I saw it.

RAINA   (*eagerly turning to him, as all her enthusiasm and her dreams of glory rush back on her*): Did you see the great cavalry charge? Oh, tell me about it. Describe it to me.

THE MAN: You never saw a cavalry charge, did you?

RAINA: How could I?

THE MAN: Ah, perhaps not. No: of course not! Well, it's a funny sight. It's like slinging a handful of peas against a window pane: first one comes; then two or three close behind him; and then all the rest in a lump.

RAINA   (*her eyes dilating as she raises her clasped hands ecstatically*): Yes, first One! the bravest of the brave!

THE MAN   (*prosaically*): Hm! you should see the poor devil pulling at his horse.

RAINA: Why should he pull at his horse?

THE MAN   (*impatient of so stupid a question*): It's running away with him, of course: do you suppose the fellow wants to get there before the others and be killed? Then they all come. You can tell the young ones by their wildness and their slashing. The old ones come bunched up under the number one guard: they know that they're mere projectiles, and that it's no use trying to fight. The wounds are mostly broken knees, from the horses cannoning together.

RAINA: Ugh! But I don't believe the first man is a coward. I know he is a hero!

THE MAN   (*goodhumoredly*): That's what you'd have said if you'd seen the first man in the charge today.

RAINA   (*breathless, forgiving him everything*): Ah, I knew it! Tell me. Tell me about him.

THE MAN: He did it like an operatic tenor. A regular handsome fellow, with flashing eyes and lovely moustache, shouting his war-cry and charging like Don Quixote at the windmills. We did laugh.

RAINA: You dared to laugh!

THE MAN: Yes; but when the sergeant ran up as white as a sheet, and told us they'd sent us the wrong ammunition, and that we couldn't fire a round for the next ten minutes, we laughed at the other side of our mouths. I never felt so sick in my life; though I've been in one or two very tight places. And I hadn't even a revolver cartridge: only chocolate. We'd no bayonets: nothing. Of course, they just cut us to bits. And there was Don Quixote flourishing like a drum major, thinking he'd done the cleverest thing ever known, whereas he ought to be courtmartialled for it. Of all the fools ever let loose on a field of battle, that man must be the very maddest. He and his regiment simply committed suicide; only the pistol missed fire: that's all.

RAINA   (*deeply wounded, but steadfastly loyal to her ideals*): Indeed! Would you know him again if you saw him?

THE MAN: Shall I ever forget him!

(*She again goes to the chest of drawers. He watches her with a vague hope that she may have something more for him to eat. She takes the portrait from its stand and brings it to him.*)

RAINA: That is a photograph of the gentleman—the patriot and hero—to whom I am betrothed.

THE MAN (*recognizing it with a shock*): I'm really very sorry. (*Looking at her*) Was it fair to lead me on? (*He looks at the portrait again.*) Yes: that's Don Quixote: not a doubt of it. (*He stifles a laugh.*)

RAINA (*quickly*): Why do you laugh?

THE MAN (*apologetic, but still greatly tickled*): I didn't laugh, I assure you. At least I didn't mean to. But when I think of him charging the windmills and imagining he was doing the finest thing—(*He chokes with suppressed laughter.*)

RAINA (*sternly*): Give me back the portrait, sir.

THE MAN (*with sincere remorse*): Of course. Certainly. I'm really very sorry. (*He hands her the picture. She deliberately kisses it and looks him straight in the face before returning to the chest of drawers to replace it. He follows her, apologizing.*) Perhaps I'm quite wrong, you know: no doubt I am. Most likely he had got wind of the cartridge business somehow, and knew it was a safe job.

RAINA: That is to say, he was a pretender and a coward! You did not dare say that before.

THE MAN (*with a comic gesture of despair*): It's no use, dear lady: I can't make you see it from the professional point of view. (*As he turns away to get back to the ottoman, a couple of distant shots threaten renewed trouble.*)

RAINA (*sternly, as she sees him listening to the shots*): So much the better for you!

THE MAN (*turning*): How?

RAINA: You are my enemy; and you are at my mercy. What would I do if I were a professional soldier?

THE MAN: Ah, true, dear young lady: you're always right. I know how good you've been to me: to my last hour I shall remember those three chocolate creams. It was unsoldierly; but it was angelic.

RAINA (*coldly*): Thank you. And now I will do a soldierly thing. You cannot stay here after what you have just said about my future husband; but I will go out on the balcony and see whether it is safe for you to climb down into the street. (*She turns to the window.*)

THE MAN (*changing countenance*): Down that waterpipe! Stop! Wait! I can't! I daren't! The very thought of it makes me giddy. I came up it fast enough with death behind me. But to face it now in cold blood—! (*He sinks on the ottoman.*) It's no use: I give up: I'm beaten. Give the alarm. (*He drops his head on his hands in the deepest dejection.*)

RAINA (*disarmed by pity*): Come: don't be disheartened. (*She stoops over him almost maternally: he shakes his head.*) Oh, you are a very poor soldier: a chocolate cream soldier! Come, cheer up! it takes less courage to climb down than to face capture: remember that.

THE MAN (*dreamily, lulled by her voice*): No: capture only means death; and death is sleep: oh, sleep, sleep, sleep, undisturbed sleep! Climbing down the pipe means doing something—exerting myself—thinking! Death ten times over first.

RAINA (*softly and wonderingly, catching the rhythm of his weariness*): Are you as sleepy as that?

THE MAN: I've not had two hours undisturbed sleep since I joined. I haven't closed my eyes for forty-eight hours.

RAINA   (*at her wit's end*): But what am I to do with you?

THE MAN   (*staggering up, roused by her desperation*): Of course. I must do something. (*He shakes himself; pulls himself together; and speaks with rallied vigor and courage.*) You see, sleep or no sleep, hunger or no hunger, tired or not tired, you can always do a thing when you know it must be done. Well, that pipe must be got down: (*he hits himself on the chest*) do you hear that, you chocolate cream soldier? (*He turns to the window.*)

RAINA   (*anxiously*): But if you fall?

THE MAN: I shall sleep as if the stones were a feather bed. Goodbye. (*He makes boldly for the window; and his hand is on the shutter when there is a terrible burst of firing in the street beneath.*)

RAINA   (*rushing to him*): Stop! (*She seizes him recklessly, and pulls him quite round.*) They'll kill you.

THE MAN   (*coolly, but attentively*): Never mind: this sort of thing is all in my day's work. I'm bound to take my chance. (*Decisively*) Now do what I tell you. Put out the candle; so that they shan't see the light when I open the shutters. And keep away from the window, whatever you do. If they see me they're sure to have a shot at me.

RAINA   (*clinging to him*): They're sure to see you: it's bright moonlight. I'll save you. Oh, how can you be so indifferent! You want me to save you, don't you?

THE MAN: I really don't want to be troublesome. (*She shakes him in her impatience.*) I am not indifferent, dear young lady, I assure you. But how is it to be done?

RAINA: Come away from the window. (*She takes him firmly back to the middle of the room. The moment she releases him he turns mechanically towards the window again. She seizes him and turns him back, exclaiming*) Please! (*He becomes motionless, like a hypnotized rabbit, his fatigue gaining fast on him. She releases him, and addresses him patronizingly.*) Now listen. You must trust to our hospitality. You do not yet know in whose house you are. I am a Petkoff.

THE MAN: A pet what?

RAINA   (*rather indignantly*): I mean that I belong to the family of the Petkoffs, the richest and best known in our country.

THE MAN: Oh, yes, of course. I beg your pardon. The Petkoffs, to be sure. How stupid of me!

RAINA: You know you never heard of them until this moment. How can you stoop to pretend!

THE MAN: Forgive me: I'm too tired to think; and the change of subject was too much for me. Don't scold me.

RAINA: I forgot. It might make you cry. (*He nods, quite seriously. She pouts and then resumes her patronizing tone.*) I must tell you that my father holds the highest command of any Bulgarian in our army. He is (*proudly*) a Major.

THE MAN   (*pretending to be deeply impressed*): A Major! Bless me! Think of that!

RAINA: You shewed great ignorance in thinking that it was necessary to climb up to the balcony because ours is the only private house that has two rows of windows. There is a flight of stairs inside to get up and down by.

THE MAN: Stairs! How grand! You live in great luxury indeed, dear young lady.

RAINA: Do you know what a library is?

THE MAN: A library? A roomful of books?

RAINA: Yes. We have one, the only one in Bulgaria.

THE MAN: Actually a real library! I should like to see that.

RAINA (*affectedly*): I tell you these things to shew you that you are not in the house of ignorant country folk who would kill you the moment they saw your Serbian uniform, but among civilized people. We go to Bucharest every year for the opera season; and I have spent a whole month in Vienna.

THE MAN: I saw that, dear young lady. I saw at once that you knew the world.

RAINA: Have you ever seen the opera of Ernani?

THE MAN: Is that the one with the devil in it in red velvet, and a soldiers' chorus?

RAINA (*contemptuously*): No!

THE MAN (*stifling a heavy sigh of weariness*): Then I don't know it.

RAINA: I thought you might have remembered the great scene where Ernani, flying from his foes just as you are tonight, takes refuge in the castle of his bitterest enemy, an old Castilian noble. The noble refuses to give him up. His guest is sacred to him.

THE MAN (*quickly, waking up a little*): Have your people got that notion?

RAINA (*with dignity*): My mother and I can understand that notion, as you call it. And if instead of threatening me with your pistol as you did you had simply thrown yourself as a fugitive on our hospitality, you would have been as safe as in your father's house.

THE MAN: Quite sure?

RAINA (*turning her back on him in disgust*): Oh, it is useless to try to make you understand.

THE MAN: Don't be angry: you see how awkward it would be for me if there was any mistake. My father is a very hospitable man: he keeps six hotels; but I couldn't trust him as far as that. What about your father?

RAINA: He is away at Slivnitza fighting for his country. I answer for your safety. There is my hand in pledge of it. Will that reassure you? (*She offers him her hand.*)

THE MAN (*looking dubiously at his own hand*): Better not touch my hand, dear young lady. I must have a wash first.

RAINA (*touched*): That is very nice of you. I see that you are a gentleman.

THE MAN (*puzzled*): Eh?

RAINA: You must not think I am surprised. Bulgarians of really good standing—people in our position—wash their hands nearly every day. So you see I can appreciate your delicacy. You may take my hand. (*She offers it again.*)

THE MAN (*kissing it with his hands behind his back*): Thanks, gracious young lady: I feel safe at last. And now would you mind breaking the news to your mother? I had better not stay here secretly longer than is necessary.

RAINA: If you will be so good as to keep perfectly still whilst I am away.

THE MAN: Certainly. (*He sits down on the ottoman.*)

(RAINA *goes to the bed and wraps herself in the fur cloak. His eyes close. She goes to the door. Turning for a last look at him, she sees that he is dropping off to sleep.*)

RAINA   (*at the door*): You are not going asleep, are you?

(*He murmurs inarticulately: she runs to him and shakes him.*) Do you hear? Wake up: you are falling asleep.

THE MAN: Eh? Falling aslee—? Oh no: not the least in the world: I was only thinking. It's all right: I'm wide awake.

RAINA   (*severely*): Will you please stand up while I am away. (*He rises reluctantly.*) All the time, mind.

THE MAN   (*standing unsteadily*): Certainly. Certainly: you may depend on me.

(RAINA *looks doubtfully at him. He smiles weakly. She goes reluctantly, turning again at the door, and almost catching him in the act of yawning. She goes out.*)

THE MAN   (*drowsily*): Sleep, sleep, sleep, sleep, slee—(*The words trail off into a murmur. He wakes again with a shock on the point of falling.*) Where am I? That's what I want to know: where am I? Must keep awake. Nothing keeps me awake except danger: remember that: (*intently*) danger, danger, danger, dan—(*trailing off again: another shock*) Where's danger? Mus' find it. (*He starts off vaguely round the room in search of it.*) What am I looking for? Sleep—danger—don't know. (*He stumbles against the bed.*) Ah yes: now I know. All right now. I'm to go to bed, but not to sleep. Be sure not to sleep, because of danger. Not to lie down either, only sit down. (*He sits on the bed. A blissful expression comes into his face.*) Ah! (*With a happy sigh he sinks back at full length; lifts his boots into the bed with a final effort; and falls fast asleep instantly.*)

(CATHERINE *comes in, followed by* RAINA.)

RAINA   (*looking at the ottoman*): He's gone! I left him here.
CATHERINE: Here! Then he must have climbed down from the—
RAINA   (*seeing him*): Oh! (*She points.*)
CATHERINE   (*scandalized*): Well! (*She strides to the bed,* RAINA *following until she is opposite her on the other side.*) He's fast asleep. The brute!
RAINA   (*anxiously*): Sh!
CATHERINE   (*shaking him*): Sir! (*Shaking him again, harder*) Sir!! (*Vehemently, shaking very hard*) Sir!!!
RAINA   (*catching her arm*): Don't, mamma; the poor darling is worn out. Let him sleep.
CATHERINE   (*letting him go, and turning amazed to* RAINA): The poor darling! Raina!!! (*She looks sternly at her daughter.*)

(*The man sleeps profoundly.*)

ACT II

(*The sixth of March, 1886. In the garden of* MAJOR PETKOFF's *house. It is a fine spring morning: the garden looks fresh and pretty. Beyond the paling the tops of a couple of minarets can be seen, shewing that there is a valley there, with the little town in it. A few miles further the Balkan mountains rise and shut in the landscape. Looking towards them from within the garden, the side of the house is seen on the left, with a garden door reached by a little flight of steps. On the right the stable yard, with its gateway, encroaches on the garden. There are fruit bushes along the paling and house, covered with washing spread out to dry. A path runs by the house, and rises by two steps at the corner, where it turns out of sight. In the middle, a small table, with two bent wood chairs at it, is laid for breakfast with Turkish coffee pot, cups, rolls, etc.; but the cups have been used and the bread broken. There is a wooden garden seat against the wall on the right.*

LOUKA, *smoking a cigaret, is standing between the table and the house, turning her back with angry disdain on a man servant who is lecturing her. He is a middle-aged man of cool temperament and low but clear and keen intelligence, with the complacency of the servant who values himself on his rank in servitude, and the imperturbability of the accurate calculator who has no illusions. He wears a white Bulgarian costume: jacket with embroidered border, sash, wide knickerbockers, and decorated gaiters. His head is shaved up to the crown, giving him a high Japanese forehead. His name is* NICOLA.)

NICOLA: Be warned in time, Louka: mend your manners. I know the mistress. She is so grand that she never dreams that any servant could dare be disrespectful to her; but if she once suspects that you are defying her, out you go.

LOUKA: I do defy her. I will defy her. What do I care for her?

NICOLA: If you quarrel with the family, I never can marry you. It's the same as if you quarrelled with me!

LOUKA: You take her part against me, do you?

NICOLA (*sedately*): I shall always be dependent on the good will of the family. When I leave their service and start a shop in Sofia, their custom will be half my capital: their bad word would ruin me.

LOUKA: You have no spirit. I should like to catch them saying a word against me!

NICOLA (*pityingly*): I should have expected more sense from you, Louka. But you're young: you're young!

LOUKA: Yes; and you like me the better for it, don't you? But I know some family secrets they wouldn't care to have told, young as I am. Let them quarrel with me if they dare!

NICOLA (*with compassionate superiority*): Do you know what they would do if they heard you talk like that?

LOUKA: What could they do?

NICOLA: Discharge you for untruthfulness. Who would believe any stories you told after that? Who would give you another situation? Who in this house would dare be seen speaking to you ever again? How long would your father be left on his little farm? (*She impatiently throws away the end of her cigaret, and stamps on it.*) Child: you don't know the power such high people have over the like of you and me when we try to rise out of our poverty against them. (*He goes close to her and lowers his voice.*) Look at me, ten years in their service. Do you think I know no secrets? I know things about the mistress that she wouldn't have the master know for a thousand levas. I know things about him that she wouldn't let him hear the last of for six months if

I blabbed them to her. I know things about Raina that would break off her match with Sergius if—

LOUKA   (*turning on him quickly*): How do you know? I never told you!

NICOLA   (*opening his eyes cunningly*): So that's your little secret, is it? I thought it might be something like that. Well, you take my advice and be respectful; and make the mistress feel that no matter what you know or don't know, she can depend on you to hold your tongue and serve the family faithfully. That's what they like; and that's how you'll make most out of them.

LOUKA   (*with searching scorn*): You have the soul of a servant, Nicola.

NICOLA   (*complacently*): Yes: that's the secret of success in service.

(*A loud knocking with a whip handle on a wooden door is heard from the stable yard.*)

MALE VOICE OUTSIDE: Hollo! Hollo there! Nicola!

LOUKA: Master! back from the war!

NICOLA   (*quickly*): My word for it, Louka, the war's over. Off with you and get some fresh coffee. (*He runs out into the stable yard.*)

LOUKA   (*as she collects the coffee pot and cups on the tray, and carries it into the house*): You'll never put the soul of a servant into me.

(MAJOR PETKOFF *comes from the stable yard, followed by* NICOLA. *He is a cheerful, excitable, insignificant, unpolished man of about fifty, naturally unambitious except as to his income and his importance in local society, but just now greatly pleased with the military rank which the war has thrust on him as a man of consequence in his town. The fever of plucky patriotism which the Serbian attack roused in all the Bulgarians has pulled him through the war; but he is obviously glad to be home again.*)

PETKOFF   (*pointing to the table with his whip*): Breakfast out here, eh?

NICOLA: Yes, sir. The mistress and Miss Raina have just gone in.

PETKOFF   (*sitting down and taking a roll*): Go in and say I've come; and get me some fresh coffee.

NICOLA: It's coming, sir. (*He goes to the house door.* LOUKA, *with fresh coffee, a clean cup, and a brandy bottle on her tray, meets him.*) Have you told the mistress?

LOUKA: Yes: she's coming.

(NICOLA *goes into the house.* LOUKA *brings the coffee to the table.*)

PETKOFF: Well: the Serbs haven't run away with you, have they?

LOUKA: No, sir.

PETKOFF: That's right. Have you brought me some cognac?

LOUKA   (*putting the bottle on the table*): Here, sir.

PETKOFF: That's right. (*He pours some into his coffee.*)

(CATHERINE, *who, having at this early hour made only a very perfunctory toilet, wears a Bulgarian apron over a once brilliant but now half worn-out dressing gown, and a colored handkerchief tied over her thick black hair, comes from the house with Turkish slippers on her bare feet, looking astonishingly handsome and stately under all the circumstances.* LOUKA *goes into the house.*)

CATHERINE: My dear Paul: what a surprise for us! (*She stoops over the back of his chair to kiss him.*) Have they brought you fresh coffee?

PETKOFF: Yes: Louka's been looking after me. The war's over. The treaty was signed three days ago at Bucharest; and the decree for our army to demobilize was issued yesterday.

CATHERINE   (*springing erect, with flashing eyes*): Paul: have you let the Austrians force you to make peace?

PETKOFF   (*submissively*): My dear: they didn't consult me. What could *I* do? (*She sits down and turns away from him.*) But of course we saw to it that the treaty was an honorable one. It declares peace—

CATHERINE   (*outraged*): Peace!

PETKOFF   (*appeasing her*):—but not friendly relations: remember that. They wanted to put that in; but I insisted on its being struck out. What more could I do?

CATHERINE: You could have annexed Serbia and made Prince Alexander Emperor of the Balkans. That's what I would have done.

PETKOFF: I don't doubt it in the least, my dear. But I should have had to subdue the whole Austrian Empire first; and that would have kept me too long away from you. I missed you greatly.

CATHERINE   (*relenting*): Ah! (*She stretches her hand affectionately across the table to squeeze his.*)

PETKOFF: And how have you been, my dear?

CATHERINE: Oh, my usual sore throats: that's all.

PETKOFF   (*with conviction*): That comes from washing your neck every day. I've often told you so.

CATHERINE: Nonsense, Paul!

PETKOFF   (*over his coffee and cigaret*): I don't believe in going too far with these modern customs. All this washing can't be good for the health; it's not natural. There was an Englishman at Philippopolis who used to wet himself all over with cold water every morning when he got up. Disgusting! It all comes from the English: their climate makes them so dirty that they have to be perpetually washing themselves. Look at my father! he never had a bath in his life; and he lived to be ninety-eight, the healthiest man in Bulgaria. I don't mind a good wash once a week to keep up my position; but once a day is carrying the thing to a ridiculous extreme.

CATHERINE: You are a barbarian at heart still, Paul. I hope you behaved yourself before all those Russian officers.

PETKOFF: I did my best. I took care to let them know that we have a library.

CATHERINE: Ah; but you didn't tell them that we have an electric bell in it? I have had one put up.

PETKOFF: What's an electric bell?

CATHERINE: You touch a button; something tinkles in the kitchen; and then Nicola comes up.

PETKOFF: Why not shout for him?

CATHERINE: Civilized people never shout for their servants. I've learnt that while you were away.

PETKOFF: Well, I'll tell you something I've learnt too. Civilized people don't hang out their washing to dry where visitors can see it: so you'd better have all that (*indicating the clothes on the bushes*) put somewhere else.

CATHERINE: Oh, that's absurd, Paul: I don't believe really refined people notice such things.

SERGIUS   (*knocking at the stable gates*): Gate, Nicola!

PETKOFF: There's Sergius. (*Shouting*) Hollo, Nicola!

CATHERINE: Oh, don't shout, Paul: it really isn't nice.

PETKOFF: Bosh! (*He shouts louder than before*): Nicola!

NICOLA   (*appearing at the house door*): Yes, sir.

PETKOFF: Are you deaf? Don't you hear Major Saranoff knocking? Bring him round this way. (*He pronounces the name with the stress on the second syllable: Sarahnoff.*)

NICOLA: Yes, Major. (*He goes into the stable yard.*)

PETKOFF: You must talk to him, my dear, until Raina takes him off our hands. He bores my life out about our not promoting him. Over my head, if you please.

CATHERINE: He certainly ought to be promoted when he marries Raina. Besides, the country should insist on having at least one native general.

PETKOFF: Yes; so that he could throw away whole brigades instead of regiments. It's no use, my dear: he hasn't the slightest chance of promotion until we're quite sure that the peace will be a lasting one.

NICOLA   (*at the gate, announcing*): Major Sergius Saranoff! (*He goes into the house and returns presently with a third chair, which he places at the table. He then withdraws.*)

MAJOR SERGIUS SARANOFF, *the original of the portrait in* RAINA'S *room, is a tall romantically handsome man, with the physical hardihood, the high spirit, and the susceptible imagination of an untamed mountaineer chieftain. But his remarkable personal distinction is of a characteristically civilized type. The ridges of his eyebrows, curving with an interrogative twist round the projections at the outer corners; his jealously observant eye; his nose, thin, keen, and apprehensive in spite of the pugnacious high bridge and large nostril; his assertive chin would not be out of place in a Parisian salon, shewing that the clever imaginative barbarian has an acute critical faculty which has been thrown into intense activity by the arrival of western civilization in the Balkans. The result is precisely what the advent of nineteenth century thought first produced in England: to wit, Byronism. By his brooding on the perpetual failure, not only of others, but of himself, to live up to his ideals; by his consequent cynical scorn for humanity; by his jejune credulity as to the absolute validity of his concepts and the unworthiness of the world in disregarding them; by his wincings and mockeries under the sting of the petty disillusions which every hour spent among men brings to his sensitive observation, he has acquired the half tragic, half ironic air, the mysterious moodiness, the suggestion of a strange and terrible history that has left nothing but undying remorse, by which Childe Harold fascinated the grandmothers of his English contemporaries. It is clear that here or nowhere is* RAINA'S *ideal hero.* CATHERINE *is hardly less enthusiastic about him than her daughter, and much less reserved in shewing her enthusiasm. As he enters from the stable gate, she rises effusively to greet him.* PETKOFF *is distinctly less disposed to make a fuss about him.*)

PETKOFF: Here already, Sergius! Glad to see you.

CATHERINE: My dear Sergius! (*She holds out both her hands.*)

SERGIUS   (*kissing them with scrupulous gallantry*): My dear mother, if I may call you so.

PETKOFF (*drily*): Mother-in-law, Sergius: mother-in-law! Sit down; and have some coffee.

SERGIUS: Thank you: none for me. (*He gets away from the table with a certain distaste for* PETKOFF'S *enjoyment of it, and posts himself with conscious dignity against the rail of the steps leading to the house.*)

CATHERINE: You look superb. The campaign has improved you, Sergius. Everybody here is mad about you. We were all wild with enthusiasm about that magnificant cavalry charge.

SERGIUS (*with grave irony*): Madam: it was the cradle and the grave of my military reputation.

CATHERINE: How so?

SERGIUS: I won the battle the wrong way when our worthy Russian generals were losing it the right way. In short, I upset their plans, and wounded their self-esteem. Two Cossack colonels had their regiments routed on the most correct principles of scientific warfare. Two major-generals got killed strictly according to military etiquette. The two colonels are now major-generals; and I am still a simple major.

CATHERINE: You shall not remain so, Sergius. The women are on your side; and they will see that justice is done you.

SERGIUS: It is too late. I have only waited for the peace to send in my resignation.

PETKOFF (*dropping his cup in his amazement*): Your resignation!

CATHERINE: Oh, you must withdraw it!

SERGIUS (*with resolute measured emphasis, folding his arms*): I never withdraw.

PETKOFF (*vexed*): Now who could have supposed you were going to do such a thing?

SERGIUS (*with fire*): Everyone that knew me. But enough of myself and my affairs. How is Raina; and where is Raina?

RAINA (*suddenly coming round the corner of the house and standing at the top of the steps in the path*): Raina is here.

(*She makes a charming picture as they turn to look at her. She wears an underdress of pale green silk, draped with an overdress of thin ecru canvas embroidered with gold. She is crowned with a dainty eastern cap of gold tinsel. Sergius goes impulsively to meet her. Posing regally, she presents her hand: he drops chivalrously on one knee and kisses it.*)

PETKOFF (*aside to* CATHERINE, *beaming with parental pride*): Pretty, isn't it? She always appears at the right moment.

CATHERINE (*impatiently*): Yes; she listens for it. It is an abominable habit.

(SERGIUS *leads* RAINA *forward with splendid gallantry. When they arrive at the table, she turns to him with a bend of the head: he bows; and thus they separate, he coming to his place and she going behind her father's chair.*)

RAINA (*stooping and kissing her father*): Dear father! Welcome home!

PETKOFF (*patting her cheek*): My little pet girl. (*He kisses her. She goes to the chair left by* NICOLA *for* SERGIUS, *and sits down.*)

CATHERINE: And so you're no longer a soldier, Sergius.

SERGIUS: I am no longer a soldier. Soldiering, my dear madam, is the coward's art of attacking mercilessly when you are strong, and keeping out of harm's way when you are weak. That is the whole secret of successful fighting. Get your enemy at a disadvantage; and never, on any account, fight him on equal terms.

PETKOFF: They wouldn't let us make a fair stand-up fight of it. However, I suppose soldiering has to be a trade like any other trade.

SERGIUS: Precisely. But I have no ambition to shine as a tradesman; so I have taken the advice of that bagman of a captain that settled the exchange of prisoners with us at Pirot, and given it up.

PETKOFF: What! that Swiss fellow? Sergius: I've often thought of that exchange since. He over-reached us about those horses.

SERGIUS: Of course he over-reached us. His father was a hotel and livery stable keeper; and he owed his first step to his knowledge of horse-dealing. (*With mock enthusiasm*) Ah, he was a soldier: every inch a soldier! If only I had bought the horses for my regiment instead of foolishly leading it into danger, I should have been a field-marshal now!

CATHERINE: A Swiss? What was he doing in the Serbian army?

PETKOFF: A volunteer, of course: keen on picking up his profession. (*Chuckling*) We shouldn't have been able to begin fighting if these foreigners hadn't shewn us how to do it: we knew nothing about it; and neither did the Serbs. Egad, there'd have been no war without them!

RAINA: Are there many Swiss officers in the Serbian Army?

PETKOFF: No. All Austrians, just as our officers were all Russians. This was the only Swiss I came across. I'll never trust a Swiss again. He humbugged us into giving him fifty ablebodied men for two hundred worn out chargers. They weren't even eatable!

SERGIUS: We were two children in the hands of that consummate soldier, Major: simply two innocent little children.

RAINA: What was he like?

CATHERINE: Oh, Raina, what a silly question!

SERGIUS: He was like a commercial traveller in uniform. Bourgeois to his boots!

PETKOFF   (*grinning*): Sergius: tell Catherine that queer story his friend told us about how he escaped after Slivnitza. You remember. About his being hid by two women.

SERGIUS   (*with bitter irony*): Oh yes: quite a romance! He was serving in the very battery I so unprofessionally charged. Being a thorough soldier, he ran away like the rest of them, with our cavalry at his heels. To escape their sabres he climbed a waterpipe and made his way into the bedroom of a young Bulgarian lady. The young lady was enchanted by his persuasive commercial traveller's manners. She very modestly entertained him for an hour or so, and then called in her mother lest her conduct should appear unmaidenly. The old lady was equally fascinated; and the fugitive was sent on his way in the morning, disguised in an old coat belonging to the master of the house, who was away at the war.

RAINA   (*rising with marked stateliness*): Your life in the camp has made you coarse, Sergius. I did not think you would have repeated such a story before me. (*She turns away coldly.*)

CATHERINE *(also rising)*: She is right, Sergius. If such women exist, we should be spared the knowledge of them.

PETKOFF: Pooh! nonsense! what does it matter?

SERGIUS *(ashamed)*: No, Petkoff: I was wrong. *(To* RAINA, *with earnest humility)*: I beg your pardon. I have behaved abominably. Forgive me, Raina. *(She bows reservedly.)* And you too, madam. *(CATHERINE bows graciously and sits down. He proceeds solemnly, again addressing RAINA.)* The glimpses I have had of the seamy side of life during the last few months have made me cynical; but I should not have brought my cynicism here: least of all into your presence, Raina. I— *(Here, turning to the others, he is evidently going to begin a long speech when the Major interrupts him.)*

PETKOFF: Stuff and nonsense, Sergius! That's quite enough fuss about nothing: a soldier's daughter should be able to stand up without flinching to a little strong conversation. *(He rises.)* Come: it's time for us to get to business. We have to make up our minds how those three regiments are to get back to Philippopolis: there's no forage for them on the Sofia route. *(He goes towards the house.)* Come along. *(SERGIUS is about to follow him when CATHERINE rises and intervenes.)*

CATHERINE: Oh, Paul, can't you spare Sergius for a few moments? Raina has hardly seen him yet. Perhaps I can help you to settle about the regiments.

SERGIUS *(protesting)*: My dear madam, impossible: you—

CATHERINE *(stopping him playfully)*: You stay here, my dear Sergius: there's no hurry. I have a word or two to say to Paul. *(SERGIUS instantly bows and steps back.)* Now, dear *(taking PETKOFF's arm)*: come and see the electric bell.

PETKOFF: Oh, very well, very well.

(They go into the house together affectionately. SERGIUS, *left alone with* RAINA, *looks anxiously at her, fearing that she is still offended. She smiles, and stretches out her arms to him.)*

SERGIUS *(hastening to her)*: Am I forgiven?

RAINA *(placing her hands on his shoulders as she looks up at him with admiration and worship)*: My hero! My king!

SERGIUS: My queen! *(He kisses her on the forehead.)*

RAINA: How I have envied you, Sergius! You have been out in the world, on the field of battle, able to prove yourself there worthy of any woman in the world; whilst I have had to sit at home inactive—dreaming—useless—doing nothing that could give me the right to call myself worthy of any man.

SERGIUS: Dearest: all my deeds have been yours. You inspired me. I have gone through the war like a knight in a tournament with his lady looking down at him!

RAINA: And you have never been absent from my thoughts for a moment. *(Very solemnly)* Sergius: I think we two have found the higher love. When I think of you, I feel that I could never do a base deed, or think an ignoble thought.

SERGIUS: My lady and my saint! *(He clasps her reverently.)*

RAINA *(returning his embrace)*: My lord and my—

SERGIUS: Sh—sh! Let me be the worshipper, dear. You little know how unworthy even the best man is of a girl's pure passion!

RAINA: I trust you. I love you. You will never disappoint me, Sergius. (LOUKA *is heard singing within the house. They quickly release each other.*) I can't pretend to talk indifferently before her: my heart is too full. (LOUKA *comes from the house with her tray. She goes to the table, and begins to clear it, with her back turned to them.*) I will get my hat; and then we can go out until lunch time. Wouldn't you like that?

SERGIUS: Be quick. If you are away five minutes, it will seem five hours. (RAINA *runs to the top of the steps, and turns there to exchange looks with him and wave him a kiss with both hands. He looks after her with emotion for a moment; then turns slowly away, his face radiant with the loftiest exaltation. The movement shifts his field of vision, into the corner of which there now comes the tail of* LOUKA's *double apron. His attention is arrested at once. He takes a stealthy look at her, and begins to twirl his moustache mischievously, with his left hand akimbo on his hip. Finally, striking the ground with his heels in something of a cavalry swagger, he strolls over to the other side of the table, opposite her, and says*) Louka: do you know what the higher love is?

LOUKA   (*astonished*): No, sir.

SERGIUS: Very fatiguing thing to keep up for any length of time, Louka. One feels the need of some relief after it.

LOUKA   (*innocently*): Perhaps you would like some coffee, sir? (*She stretches her hand across the table for the coffee pot.*)

SERGIUS   (*taking her hand*): Thank you, Louka.

LOUKA   (*pretending to pull*): Oh, sir, you know I didn't mean that. I'm surprised at you!

SERGIUS   (*coming clear of the table and drawing her with him*): I am surprised at myself, Louka. What would Sergius, the hero of Slivnitza, say if he saw me now? What would Sergius, the apostle of the higher love, say if he saw me now? What would the half dozen Sergiuses who keep popping in and out of this handsome figure of mine say if they caught us here? (*Letting go her hand and slipping his arm dexterously round her waist*) Do you consider my figure handsome, Louka?

LOUKA: Let me go, sir. I shall be disgraced. (*She struggles: he holds her inexorably.*) Oh, will you let go?

SERGIUS   (*looking straight into her eyes*): No.

LOUKA: Then stand back where we can't be seen. Have you no common sense?

SERGIUS: Ah! that's reasonable. (*He takes her into the stable yard gateway, where they are hidden from the house.*)

LOUKA   (*plaintively*): I may have been seen from the windows: Miss Raina is sure to be spying about after you.

SERGIUS   (*stung: letting her go*): Take care, Louka. I may be worthless enough to betray the higher love; but do not you insult it.

LOUKA   (*demurely*): Not for the world, sir, I'm sure. May I go on with my work, please, now?

SERGIUS   (*again putting his arm round her*): You are a provoking little witch, Louka. If you were in love with me, would you spy out of windows on me?

LOUKA: Well, you see, sir, since you say you are half a dozen different gentlemen all at once, I should have a great deal to look after.

SERGIUS   (*charmed*): Witty as well as pretty. (*He tries to kiss her.*)

LOUKA   (*avoiding him*): No: I don't want your kisses. Gentlefolk are all alike: you making love to me behind Miss Raina's back; and she doing the same behind yours.

SERGIUS   (*recoiling a step*): Louka!

LOUKA: It shews how little you really care.

SERGIUS   (*dropping his familiarity, and speaking with freezing politeness*): If our conversation is to continue, Louka, you will please remember that a gentleman does not discuss the conduct of the lady he is engaged to with her maid.

LOUKA: It's so hard to know what a gentleman considers right. I thought from your trying to kiss me that you had given up being so particular.

SERGIUS   (*turning from her and striking his forehead as he comes back into the garden from the gateway*): Devil! devil!

LOUKA: Ha! ha! I expect one of the six of you is very like me, sir; though I am only Miss Raina's maid. (*She goes back to her work at the table, taking no further notice of him.*)

SERGIUS   (*speaking to himself*): Which of the six is the real man? that's the question that torments me. One of them is a hero, another a buffoon, another a humbug, another perhaps a bit of a blackguard. (*He pauses, and looks furtively at* LOUKA *as he adds, with deep bitterness*) And one, at least, is a coward: jealous, like all cowards. (*He goes to the table.*) Louka.

LOUKA: Yes?

SERGIUS: Who is my rival?

LOUKA: You shall never get that out of me, for love or money.

SERGIUS: Why?

LOUKA: Never mind why. Besides, you would tell that I told you; and I should lose my place.

SERGIUS   (*holding out his right hand in affirmation*): No! on the honor of a— (*He checks himself; and his hand drops, nerveless, as he concludes sardonically*)—of a man capable of behaving as I have been behaving for the last five minutes. Who is he?

LOUKA: I don't know. I never saw him. I only heard his voice through the door of her room.

SERGIUS: Damnation! How dare you?

LOUKA   (*retreating*): Oh, I mean no harm: you've no right to take up my words like that. The mistress knows all about it. And I tell you that if that gentleman ever comes here again, Miss Raina will marry him, whether he likes it or not. I know the difference between the sort of manner you and she put on before one another and the real manner.

(SERGIUS *shivers as if she had stabbed him. Then, setting his face like iron, he strides grimly to her, and grips her above the elbows with both hands.*)

SERGIUS: Now listen you to me.

LOUKA   (*wincing*): Not so tight: you're hurting me.

SERGIUS: That doesn't matter. You have stained my honor by making me a party to your eavesdropping. And you have betrayed your mistress.

LOUKA   (*writhing*): Please—

SERGIUS: That shews that you are an abominable little clod of common clay, with the soul of a servant. (*He lets her go as if she were an unclean thing, and turns away, dusting his hands of her, to the bench by the wall, where he sits down with averted head, meditating gloomily.*)

LOUKA (*whimpering angrily with her hands up her sleeves, feeling her bruised arms*): You know how to hurt with your tongue as well as with your hands. But I don't care, now I've found out that whatever clay I'm made of, you're made of the same. As for her, she's a liar; and her fine airs are a cheat; and I'm worth six of her. (*She shakes the pain off hardily; tosses her head; and sets to work to put the things on the tray.*)

(*He looks doubtfully at her. She finishes packing the tray, and laps the cloth over the edges, so as to carry all out together. As she stoops to lift it, he rises.*)

SERGIUS: Louka! (*She stops and looks defiantly at him.*) A gentleman has no right to hurt a woman under any circumstances. (*With profound humility, uncovering his head*) I beg your pardon.

LOUKA: That sort of apology may satisfy a lady. Of what use is it to a servant?

SERGIUS (*rudely crossed in his chivalry, throws it off with a bitter laugh, and says slightingly*): Oh! you wish to be paid for the hurt! (*He puts on his shako, and takes some money from his pocket.*)

LOUKA (*her eyes filling with tears in spite of herself*): No: I want my hurt made well.

SERGIUS (*sobered by her tone*): How?

(*She rolls up her left sleeve; clasps her arm with the thumb and fingers of her right hand; and looks down at the bruise. Then she raises her head and looks straight at him. Finally, with a superb gesture, she presents her arm to be kissed. Amazed, he looks at her; at the arm; at her again; hesitates; and then, with shuddering intensity, exclaims* Never! *and gets away as far as possible from her.*

Her arm drops. Without a word, and with unaffected dignity, she takes her tray, and is approaching the house when RAINA *returns, wearing a hat and jacket in the height of the Vienna fashion of the previous year, 1885.* LOUKA *makes way proudly for her, and then goes into the house.*)

RAINA: I'm ready. What's the matter? (*Gaily*) Have you been flirting with Louka?

SERGIUS (*hastily*): No, no. How can you think such a thing?

RAINA (*ashamed of herself*): Forgive me, dear: it was only a jest. I am so happy today.

(*He goes quickly to her, and kisses her hand remorsefully.* CATHERINE *comes out and calls to them from the top of the steps.*)

CATHERINE (*coming down to them*): I am sorry to disturb you, children; but Paul is distracted over those three regiments. He doesnt know how to send them to Philippopolis; and he objects to every suggestion of mine. You must go and help him, Sergius. He is in the library.

RAINA (*disappointed*): But we are just going out for a walk.

SERGIUS: I shall not be long. Wait for me just five minutes. (*He runs up the steps to the door.*)

RAINA   (*following him to the foot of the steps and looking up at him with timid coquetry*): I shall go round and wait in full view of the library windows. Be sure you draw father's attention to me. If you are a moment longer than five minutes, I shall go in and fetch you, regiments or no regiments.

SERGIUS   (*laughing*): Very well. (*He goes in.*)

(RAINA *watches him until he is out of her sight. Then, with a perceptible relaxation of manner, she begins to pace up and down the garden in a brown study.*)

CATHERINE: Imagine their meeting that Swiss and hearing the whole story! The very first thing your father asked for was the old coat we sent him off in. A nice mess you have got us into!

RAINA   (*gazing thoughtfully at the gravel as she walks*): The little beast!

CATHERINE: Little beast! What little beast?

RAINA: To go and tell! Oh, if I had him here, I'd cram him with chocolate creams til he couldn't ever speak again!

CATHERINE: Don't talk such stuff. Tell me the truth, Raina. How long was he in your room before you came to me?

RAINA   (*whisking round and recommencing her march in the opposite direction*): Oh, I forget.

CATHERINE: You cannot forget! Did he really climb up after the soldiers were gone: or was he there when that officer searched the room?

RAINA: No. Yes: I think he must have been there then.

CATHERINE: You think! Oh, Raina! Raina! Will anything ever make you straightforward? If Sergius finds out, it will be all over between you.

RAINA   (*with cool impertinence*): Oh, I know Sergius is your pet. I sometimes wish you could marry him instead of me. You would just suit him. You would pet him, and spoil him, and mother him to perfection.

CATHERINE   (*opening her eyes very widely indeed*): Well, upon my word!

RAINA   (*capriciously: half to herself*): I always feel a longing to do or say something dreadful to him—to shock his propriety—to scandalize the five senses out of him. (*To* CATHERINE, *perversely*) I don't care whether he finds out about the chocolate cream soldier or not. I half hope he may. (*She again turns and strolls flippantly away up the path to the corner of the house.*)

CATHERINE: And what should I be able to say to your father, pray?

RAINA   (*over her shoulder, from the top of the two steps*): Oh, poor father! As if he could help himself! (*She turns the corner and passes out of sight.*)

CATHERINE   (*looking after her, her fingers itching*): Oh, if you were only ten years younger! (LOUKA *comes from the house with a salver, which she carries hanging down by her side.*) Well?

LOUKA: There's a gentleman just called, madam. A Serbian officer.

CATHERINE   (*flaming*): A Serb! And how dare he—(*checking herself bitterly*): Oh, I forgot. We are at peace now. I suppose we shall have them calling every day to pay their compliments. Well: if he is an officer why don't you tell your master? He is in the library with Major Saranoff. Why do you come to me?

LOUKA: But he asks for you, madam. And I don't think he knows who you are: he said the lady of the house. He gave me this little ticket for you. (*She takes a card out of her bosom; puts it on the salver; and offers it to* CATHERINE).

CATHERINE   (*reading*): "Captain Bluntschli"? That's a German name.

LOUKA: Swiss, madam, I think.

CATHERINE   (*with a bound that makes* LOUKA *jump back*): Swiss! What is he like?

LOUKA   (*timidly*): He has a big carpet bag, madam.

CATHERINE: Oh Heavens! he's come to return the coat. Send him away: say we're not at home: ask him to leave his address and I'll write to him. Oh stop: that will never do. Wait! (*She throws herself into a chair to think it out.* LOUKA *waits.*) The master and Major Saranoff are busy in the library, aren't they?

LOUKA: Yes, madam.

CATHERINE   (*decisively*): Bring the gentleman out here at once. (*Peremptorily*): And be very polite to him. Don't delay. Here (*impatiently snatching the salver from her*): leave that here; and go straight back to him.

LOUKA: Yes, madam (*going.*)

CATHERINE: Louka!

LOUKA   (*stopping*): Yes, madam.

CATHERINE: Is the library door shut?

LOUKA: I think so, madam.

CATHERINE: If not, shut it as you pass through.

LOUKA: Yes, madam (*going*).

CATHERINE: Stop (LOUKA *stops.*) He will have to go that way (*indicating the gate of the stable yard.*) Tell Nicola to bring his bag here after him. Don't forget.

LOUKA   (*surprised*): His bag?

CATHERINE: Yes: here: as soon as possible. (*Vehemently*) Be quick! (LOUKA *runs into the house.* CATHERINE *snatches her apron off and throws it behind a bush. She then takes up the salver and uses it as a mirror, with the result that the handkerchief tied round her head follows the apron. A touch to her hair and a shake to her dressing gown make her presentable.*) Oh, how? how? how can a man be such a fool! Such a moment to select! (LOUKA *appears at the door of the house, announcing* Captain Bluntschli. *She stands aside at the top of the steps to let him pass before she goes in again. He is the man of the midnight adventure in* RAINA'S *room, clean, well brushed, smartly uniformed, and out of trouble, but still unmistakably the same man. The moment* LOUKA'S *back is turned,* CATHERINE *swoops on him with impetuous, urgent, coaxing appeal.*) Captain Bluntschli: I am very glad to see you; but you must leave this house at once. (*He raises his eyebrows.*) My husband has just returned with my future son-in-law; and they know nothing. If they did, the consequences would be terrible. You are a foreigner: you do not feel our national animosities as we do. We still hate the Serbs: the effect of the peace on my husband has been to make him feel like a lion baulked of his prey. If he discovers our secret, he will never forgive me; and my daughter's life will hardly be safe. Will you, like the chivalrous gentleman and soldier you are, leave at once before he finds you here?

BLUNTSCHLI   (*disappointed, but philosophical*): At once, gracious lady. I only came to thank you and return the coat you lent me. If you will allow me to take it out of my bag and leave it with your servant as I pass out, I need detain you no further. (*He turns to go into the house.*)

CATHERINE   (*catching him by the sleeve*): Oh, you must not think of going back that way. (*Coaxing him across to the stable gates*) This is the shortest way out. Many thanks. So glad to have been of service to you. Goodbye.

BLUNTSCHLI: But my bag?

CATHERINE: It shall be sent on. You will leave me your address.

BLUNTSCHLI: True. Allow me. (*He takes out his cardcase, and stops to write his address, keeping* CATHERINE *in an agony of impatience. As he hands her the card,* PETKOFF, *hatless, rushes from the house in a fluster of hospitality, followed by* SERGIUS.)

PETKOFF (*as he hurries down the steps*): My dear Captain Bluntschli—

CATHERINE: Oh Heavens! (*She sinks on the seat against the wall.*)

PETKOFF (*too preoccupied to notice her as he shakes* BLUNTSCHLI's *hand heartily*): Those stupid people of mine thought I was out here, instead of in the—haw! —library (*he cannot mention the library without betraying how proud he is of it*). I saw you through the window. I was wondering why you didn't come in. Saranoff is with me: you remember him, don't you?

SERGIUS (*saluting humorously, and then offering his hand with great charm of manner*): Welcome, our friend the enemy!

PETKOFF: No longer the enemy, happily. (*Rather anxiously*) I hope you've called as a friend, and not about horses or prisoners.

CATHERINE: Oh, quite as a friend, Paul. I was just asking Captain Bluntschli to stay to lunch; but he declares he must go at once.

SERGIUS (*sardonically*): Impossible, Bluntschli. We want you here badly. We have to send on three cavalry regiments to Philippopolis; and we don't in the least know how to do it.

BLUNTSCHLI (*suddenly attentive and businesslike*): Philippopolis? The forage is the trouble, I suppose.

PETKOFF (*eagerly*): Yes: that's it. (*To* SERGIUS) He sees the whole thing at once.

BLUNTSCHLI: I think I can shew you how to manage that.

SERGIUS: Invaluable man! Come along! (*Towering over* BLUNTSCHLI, *he puts his hand on his shoulder and takes him to the steps,* PETKOFF *following.*)

(RAINA *comes from the house as* BLUNTSCHLI *puts his foot on the first step.*)

RAINA: Oh! The chocolate cream soldier!

(BLUNTSCHLI *stands rigid.* SERGIUS, *amazed, looks at* RAINA, *then at* PETKOFF, *who looks back at him and then at his wife.*)

CATHERINE (*with commanding presence of mind*): My dear Raina, don't you see that we have a guest here? Captain Bluntschli: one of our new Serbian friends.

(RAINA *bows:* BLUNTSCHLI *bows.*)

RAINA: How silly of me! (*She comes down into the centre of the group, between* BLUNTSCHLI *and* PETKOFF.) I made a beautiful ornament this morning for the ice pudding; and that stupid Nicola has just put down a pile of plates on it and spoilt it. (*To* BLUNTSCHLI, *winningly*) I hope you didn't think that you were the chocolate cream soldier, Captain Bluntschli.

BLUNTSCHLI (*laughing*): I assure you I did. (*Stealing a whimsical glance at her*) Your explanation was a relief.

PETKOFF   (*suspiciously, to* RAINA): And since when, pray, have you taken to cooking?

CATHERINE: Oh, whilst you were away. It is her latest fancy.

PETKOFF   (*testily*): And has Nicola taken to drinking? He used to be careful enough. First he shews Captain Bluntschli out here when he knew quite well I was in the library; and then he goes downstairs and breaks Raina's chocolate soldier. He must—(NICOLA *appears at the top of the steps with the bag. He descends; places it respectfully before* BLUNTSCHLI; *and waits for further orders. General amazement.* NICOLA, *unconscious of the effect he is producing, looks perfectly satisfied with himself. When* PETKOFF *recovers his power of speech, he breaks out at him with*) Are you mad, Nicola?

NICOLA   (*taken aback*): Sir?

PETKOFF: What have you brought that for?

NICOLA: My lady's orders, major. Louka told me that—

CATHERINE   (*interrupting him*): My orders! Why should I order you to bring Captain Bluntschli's luggage out here? What are you thinking of, Nicola?

NICOLA   (*after a moment's bewilderment, picking up the bag as he addresses* BLUNTSCHLI *with the very perfection of servile discretion*): I beg your pardon, captain, I am sure. (*To* CATHERINE): My fault, madame: I hope you'll overlook it. (*He bows, and is going to the steps with the bag, when* PETKOFF *addresses him angrily.*)

PETKOFF: You'd better go and slam that bag, too, down on Miss Raina's ice pudding! (*This is too much for* NICOLA. *The bag drops from his hand almost on his master's toes, eliciting a roar of*) Begone, you butter-fingered donkey.

NICOLA   (*snatching up the bag, and escaping into the house*): Yes, Major.

CATHERINE: Oh, never mind. Paul: don't be angry.

PETKOFF   (*blustering*): Scoundrel! He's got out of hand while I was away. I'll teach him. Infernal blackguard! The sack next Saturday! I'll clear out the whole establishment—(*He is stifled by the caresses of his wife and daughter, who hang round his neck, petting him.*)

CATHERINE   Now, now, now, it

                                        (*together*):

RAINA   Wow, wow, wow:

                        mustn't be angry. He meant
                        not on your first day at home.

                        no harm. Be good to please
                        I'll make another ice pudding.

                        me, dear. Sh-sh-sh-sh!
                        Tch-ch-ch!

PETKOFF   (*yielding*): Oh well, never mind. Come, Bluntschli: let's have no more nonsense about going away. You know very well you're not going back to Switzerland yet. Until you do go back you'll stay with us.

RAINA: Oh, do, Captain Bluntschli.

PETKOFF   (*to* CATHERINE): Now, Catherine: it's of you he's afraid. Press him: and he'll stay.

CATHERINE: Of course I shall be only too delighted if (*appealingly*) Captain Bluntschli really wishes to stay. He knows my wishes.

BLUNTSCHLI   (*in his driest military manner*): I am at madam's orders.

SERGIUS   (*cordially*): That settles it!

PETKOFF   (*heartily*): Of course!

RAINA: You see you must stay.

BLUNTSCHLI   (*smiling*): Well, if I must, I must. (*Gesture of despair from* CATHERINE.)

ACT III

(*In the library after lunch. It is not much of a library. Its literary equipment consists of a single fixed shelf stocked with old paper covered novels, broken backed, coffee stained, torn and thumbed; and a couple of little hanging shelves with a few gift books on them: the rest of the wall space being occupied by trophies of war and the chase. But it is a most comfortable sitting room. A row of three large windows shews a mountain panorama, just now seen in one of its friendliest aspects in the mellowing afternoon light. In the corner next the right hand window a square earthenware stove, a perfect tower of glistening pottery, rises nearly to the ceiling and guarantees plenty of warmth. The ottoman is like that in* RAINA's *room, and similarly placed; and the window seats are luxurious with decorated cushions. There is one object, however, hopelessly out of keeping with its surroundings. This is a small kitchen table, much the worse for wear, fitted as a writing table with an old canister full of pens, an eggcup filled with ink, and a deplorable scrap of heavily used pink blotting paper.*

At the side of this table, which stands to the left of anyone facing the window, BLUNTSCHLI *is hard at work with a couple of maps before him, writing orders. At the head of it sits* SERGIUS, *who is supposed to be also at work, but is actually gnawing the feather of a pen, and contemplating* BLUNTSCHLI's *quick, sure, businesslike progress with a mixture of envious irritation at his own incapacity and awestruck wonder at an ability which seems to him almost miraculous, though its prosaic character forbids him to esteem it.* THE MAJOR *is comfortably established on the ottoman, with a newspaper in his hand and the tube of his hookah within easy reach.* CATHERINE *sits at the stove, with her back to them, embroidering.* RAINA, *reclining on the divan, is gazing in a daydream out at the Balkan landscape, with a neglected novel in her lap.*

The door is on the same side as the stove, farther from the window. The button of the electric bell is at the opposite side, behind BLUNTSCHLI.)

PETKOFF   (*looking up from his paper to watch how they are getting on at the table*): Are you sure I can't help in any way, Bluntschli?

BLUNTSCHLI   (*without interrupting his writing or looking up*): Quite sure, thank you. Saranoff and I will manage it.

SERGIUS   (*grimly*): Yes: we'll manage it. He finds out what to do; draws up the orders; and I sign 'em. Division of labor! (BLUNTSCHLI *passes him a paper.*)

Another one? Thank you. (*He plants the paper squarely before him; sets his chair carefully parallel to it; and signs with his cheek on his elbow and his protruded tongue following the movements of his pen.*) This hand is more accustomed to the sword than to the pen.

PETKOFF: It's very good of you, Bluntschli: it is indeed, to let yourself be put upon in this way. Now are you quite sure I can do nothing?

CATHERINE   (*in a low warning tone*): You can stop interrupting, Paul.

PETKOFF   (*starting and looking round at her*): Eh? Oh! Quite right, my love: Quite right. (*He takes his newspaper up again, but presently lets it drop.*) Ah, you haven't been campaigning, Catherine: you don't know how pleasant it is for us to sit here, after a good lunch, with nothing to do but enjoy ourselves. There's only one thing I want to make me thoroughly comfortable.

CATHERINE: What is that?

PETKOFF: My old coat. I'm not at home in this one: I feel as if I were on parade.

CATHERINE: My dear Paul, how absurd you are about that old coat! It must be hanging in the blue closet where you left it.

PETKOFF: My dear Catherine, I tell you I've looked there. Am I to believe my own eyes or not? (CATHERINE *rises and crosses the room to press the button of the electric bell.*) What are you shewing off that bell for? (*She looks at him majestically, and silently resumes her chair and her needlework.*) My dear: if you think the obstinacy of your sex can make a coat out of two old dressing gowns of Raina's, your waterproof, and my mackintosh, you're mistaken. That's exactly what the blue closet contains at present.

(NICOLA *presents himself.*)

CATHERINE: Nicola: go to the blue closet and bring your master's old coat here: the braided one he wears in the house.

NICOLA: Yes, madame. (*He goes out.*)

PETKOFF: Catherine.

CATHERINE: Yes, Paul.

PETKOFF: I bet you any piece of jewellery you like to order from Sofia against a week's housekeeping money that the coat isn't there.

CATHERINE: Done, Paul!

PETKOFF   (*excited by the prospect of a gamble*): Come: here's an opportunity for some sport. Who'll bet on it? Bluntschli: I'll give you six to one.

BLUNTSCHLI   (*imperturbably*): It would be robbing you, Major. Madame is sure to be right. (*Without looking up, he passes another batch of papers to* SERGIUS.)

SERGIUS   (*also excited*): Bravo, Switzerland! Major: I bet my best charger against an Arab mare for Raina that Nicola finds the coat in the blue closet.

PETKOFF   (*eagerly*): Your best char—

CATHERINE   (*hastily interrupting him*): Don't be foolish, Paul. An Arabian mare will cost you 50,000 levas.

RAINA   (*suddenly coming out of her picturesque revery*): Really, mother, if you are going to take the jewellery, I don't see why you should grudge me my Arab.

(NICOLA *comes back with the coat, and brings it to* PETKOFF, *who can hardly believe his eyes.*)

CATHERINE: Where was it, Nicola?

NICOLA: Hanging in the blue closet, madame.

PETKOFF: Well, I am d—

CATHERINE (*stopping him*): Paul!

PETKOFF: I could have sworn it wasn't there. Age is beginning to tell on me. I'm getting hallucinations. (*To* NICOLA) Here: help me to change. Excuse me, Bluntschli. (*He begins changing coats,* NICOLA *acting as valet.*) Remember: I didn't take that bet of yours, Sergius. You'd better give Raina that Arab steed yourself, since you've roused her expectations. Eh, Raina? (*He looks round at her; but she is again rapt in the landscape. With a little gush of parental affection and pride, he points her out to them, and says*) She's dreaming, as usual.

SERGIUS: Assuredly she shall not be the loser.

PETKOFF: So much the better for her. *I* shan't come off so cheaply, I expect. (*The change is now complete.* NICOLA *goes out with the discarded coat.*) Ah, now I feel at home at last. (*He sits down and takes his newspaper with a grunt of relief.*)

BLUNTSCHLI (*to* SERGIUS, *handing a paper*): That's the last order.

PETKOFF (*jumping up*): What! Finished?

BLUNTSCHLI: Finished.

PETKOFF (*with childlike envy*): Haven't you anything for me to sign?

BLUNTSCHLI: Not necessary. His signature will do.

PETKOFF (*inflating his chest and thumping it*): Ah well, I think we've done a thundering good day's work. Can I do anything more?

BLUNTSCHLI: You had better both see the fellows that are to take these. (SERGIUS *rises.*) Pack them off at once; and shew them that I've marked on the orders the time they should hand them in by. Tell them that if they stop to drink or tell stories—if they're five minutes late, they'll have the skin taken off their backs.

SERGIUS (*stiffening indignantly*): I'll say so. (*He strides to the door.*) And if one of them is man enough to spit in my face for insulting him, I'll buy his discharge and give him a pension. (*He goes out.*)

BLUNTSCHLI (*confidentially*): Just see that he talks to them properly, Major, will you?

PETKOFF (*officiously*): Quite right, Bluntschli, quite right. I'll see to it. (*He goes to the door importantly, but hesitates on the threshold.*) By the bye, Catherine, you may as well come too. They'll be far more frightened of you than of me.

CATHERINE (*putting down her embroidery*): I daresay I had better. You would only splutter at them. (*She goes out,* PETKOFF *holding the door for her and following her.*)

BLUNTSCHLI: What an army! They make cannons out of cherry trees; and the officers send for their wives to keep discipline! (*He begins to fold and docket the papers.*)

(RAINA, *who has risen from the divan, marches slowly down the room with her hands clasped behind her, and looks mischievously at him.*)

RAINA: You look ever so much nicer than when we last met. (*He looks up, surprised.*) What have you done to yourself?

BLUNTSCHLI: Washed; brushed; good night's sleep and breakfast. That's all.

RAINA: Did you get back safely that morning?

BLUNTSCHLI: Quite, thanks.

RAINA: Were they angry with you for running away from Sergius's charge?

BLUNTSCHLI *(grinning)*: No: they were glad; because they'd all just run away themselves.

RAINA *(going to the table, and leaning over it towards him)*: It must have made a lovely story for them: all that about me and my room.

BLUNTSCHLI: Capital story. But I only told it to one of them: a particular friend.

RAINA: On whose discretion you could absolutely rely?

BLUNTSCHLI: Absolutely.

RAINA: Hm! He told it all to my father and Sergius the day you exchanged the prisoners. *(She turns away and strolls carelessly across to the other side of the room.)*

BLUNTSCHLI *(deeply concerned, and half incredulous)*: No! You don't mean that, do you?

RAINA *(turning, with sudden earnestness)*: I do indeed. But they don't know that it was in this house you took refuge. If Sergius knew, he would challenge you and kill you in a duel.

BLUNTSCHLI: Bless me! then don't tell him.

RAINA: Please be serious, Captain Bluntschli. Can you not realize what it is to me to deceive him? I want to be quite perfect with Sergius: no meanness, no smallness, no deceit. My relation to him is the one really beautiful and noble part of my life. I hope you can understand that.

BLUNTSCHLI *(sceptically)*: You mean that you wouldn't like him to find out that the story about the ice pudding was a—a—a—You know.

RAINA *(wincing)*: Ah, don't talk of it in that flippant way. I lied: I know it. But I did it to save your life. He would have killed you. That was the second time I ever uttered a falsehood. (BLUNTSCHLI *rises quickly and looks doubtfully and somewhat severely at her.*) Do you remember the first time?

BLUNTSCHLI: I! No. Was I present?

RAINA: Yes; and I told the officer who was searching for you that you were not present.

BLUNTSCHLI: True. I should have remembered it.

RAINA *(greatly encouraged)*: Ah, it is natural that you should forget it first. It cost you nothing: it cost me a lie! A lie!

(She sits down on the ottoman, looking straight before her with her hands clasped round her knee. BLUNTSCHLI, *quite touched, goes to the ottoman with a particularly reassuring and considerate air, and sits down beside her.)*

BLUNTSCHLI: My dear young lady, don't let this worry you. Remember: I'm a soldier. Now what are the two things that happen to a soldier so often that he comes to think nothing of them? One is hearing people tell lies (RAINA *recoils*): the other is getting his life saved in all sorts of ways by all sorts of people.

RAINA *(rising in indignant protest)*: And so he becomes a creature incapable of faith and of gratitude.

BLUNTSCHLI *(making a wry face)*: Do you like gratitude? I don't. If pity is akin to love, gratitude is akin to the other thing.

RAINA: Gratitude! (*Turning on him*) If you are incapable of gratitude you are incapable of any noble sentiment. Even animals are grateful. Oh, I see now exactly what you think of me! You were not surprised to hear me lie. To you it was something I probably did every day! every hour! That is how men think of women. (*She paces the room tragically.*)

BLUNTSCHLI (*dubiously*): There's reason in everything. You said you'd told only two lies in your whole life. Dear young lady: isn't that rather a short allowance? I'm quite a straightforward man myself; but it wouldn't last me a whole morning.

RAINA (*staring haughtily at him*): Do you know, sir, that you are insulting me?

BLUNTSCHLI: I can't help it. When you strike that noble attitude and speak in that thrilling voice, I admire you; but I find it impossible to believe a single word you say.

RAINA (*superbly*): Captain Bluntschli!

BLUNTSCHLI (*unmoved*): Yes?

RAINA (*standing over him, as if she could not believe her senses*): Do you mean what you said just now? Do you know what you said just now?

BLUNTSCHLI: I do.

RAINA (*gasping*): I! I!!! (*She points to herself incredulously, meaning "I, Raina Petkoff tell lies!" He meets her gaze unflinchingly. She suddenly sits down beside him, and adds, with a complete change of manner from the heroic to a babyish familiarity*) How did you find me out?

BLUNTSCHLI (*promptly*): Instinct, dear young lady. Instinct, and experience of the world.

RAINA (*wonderingly*): Do you know, you are the first man I ever met who did not take me seriously?

BLUNTSCHLI: You mean, don't you, that I am the first man that has ever taken you quite seriously?

RAINA: Yes: I suppose I do mean that. (*Cosily, quite at her ease with him*) How strange it is to be talked to in such a way! You know, I've always gone on like that.

BLUNTSCHLI: You mean the—?

RAINA: I mean the noble attitude and the thrilling voice. (*They laugh together.*) I did it when I was a tiny child to my nurse. She believed in it. I do it before my parents. They believe in it. I do it before Sergius. He believes in it.

BLUNTSCHLI: Yes: he's a little in that line himself, isn't he?

RAINA (*startled*): Oh! Do you think so?

BLUNTSCHLI: You know him better than I do.

RAINA: I wonder—I wonder is he? If I thought that—! (*Discouraged*) Ah, well; what does it matter? I suppose, now you've found me out, you despise me.

BLUNTSCHLI (*warmly, rising*): No, my dear young lady, no, no, no a thousand times. It's part of your youth: part of your charm. I'm like all the rest of them: the nurse, your parents, Sergius: I'm your infatuated admirer.

RAINA (*pleased*): Really?

BLUNTSCHLI   (*slapping his breast smartly with his hand, German fashion*): Hand aufs Herz! Really and truly.

RAINA   (*very happy*): But what did you think of me for giving you my portrait?

BLUNTSCHLI   (*astonished*): Your portrait! You never gave me your portrait.

RAINA   (*quickly*): Do you mean to say you never got it?

BLUNTSCHLI: No. (*He sits down beside her, with renewed interest, and says, with some complacency*) When did you send it to me?

RAINA   (*indignantly*): I did not send it to you. (*She turns her head away, and adds, reluctantly*) It was in the pocket of that coat.

BLUNTSCHLI   (*pursing his lips and rounding his eyes*): Oh-o-oh! I never found it. It must be there still.

RAINA   (*springing up*): There still! for my father to find the first time he puts his hand in his pocket! Oh, how could you be so stupid?

BLUNTSCHLI   (*rising also*): It doesn't matter: I suppose it's only a photograph: how can he tell who it was intended for? Tell him he put it there himself.

RAINA   (*bitterly*): Yes: that is so clever! isn't it? (*Distractedly*) Oh! what shall I do?

BLUNTSCHLI: Ah, I see. You wrote something on it. That was rash.

RAINA   (*vexed almost to tears*): Oh, to have done such a thing for you, who care no more—except to laugh at me—oh! Are you sure nobody has touched it?

BLUNTSCHLI: Well, I can't be quite sure. You see, I couldn't carry it about with me all the time: one can't take much luggage on active service.

RAINA: What did you do with it?

BLUNTSCHLI: When I got through to Pirot I had to put it in safe keeping somehow. I thought of the railway cloak room; but that's the surest place to get looted in modern warfare. So I pawned it.

RAINA: Pawned it!!!

BLUNTSCHLI: I know it doesn't sound nice: but it was much the safest plan. I redeemed it the day before yesterday. Heaven only knows whether the pawnbroker cleared out the pockets or not.

RAINA   (*furious: throwing the words right into his face*): You have a low shopkeeping mind. You think of things that would never come into a gentleman's head.

BLUNTSCHLI   (*phlegmatically*): That's the Swiss national character, dear lady. (*He returns to the table.*)

RAINA: Oh, I wish I had never met you. (*She flounces away, and sits at the window fuming.*)

(LOUKA *comes in with a heap of letters and telegrams on her salver, and crosses, with her bold free gait, to the table. Her left sleeve is looped up to the shoulder with a brooch, shewing her naked arm, with a broad gilt bracelet covering the bruise.*)

LOUKA   (*to* BLUNTSCHLI): For you. (*She empties the salver with a fling on to the table.*) The messenger is waiting. (*She is determined not to be civil to an enemy, even if she must bring him his letters.*)

BLUNTSCHLI   (*to* RAINA): Will you excuse me: the last postal delivery that reached me was three weeks ago. These are the subsequent accumulations. Four telegrams: a week old. (*He opens one.*) Oho! Bad news!

RAINA (*rising and advancing a little remorsefully*): Bad news?

BLUNTSCHLI: My father's dead. (*He looks at the telegram with his lips pursed, musing on the unexpected change in his arrangements.* LOUKA *crosses herself hastily.*)

RAINA: Oh, how very sad!

BLUNTSCHLI: Yes: I shall have to start for home in an hour. He has left a lot of big hotels behind him to be looked after. (*He takes up a fat letter in a long blue envelope.*) Here's a whacking letter from the family solicitor. (*He puts out the enclosures and glances over them.*) Great Heavens! Seventy! Two hundred! (*In a crescendo of dismay*) Four hundred! Four thousand!! Nine thousand six hundred!!! What on earth am I to do with them all?

RAINA (*timidly*): Nine thousand hotels?

BLUNTSCHLI: Hotels nonsense. If you only knew! Oh, it's too ridiculous! Excuse me: I must give my fellow orders about starting. (*He leaves the room hastily, with the documents in his hand.*)

LOUKA (*knowing instinctively that she can annoy* RAINA *by disparaging* BLUNTS-CHLI): He has not much heart, that Swiss. He has not a word of grief for his poor father.

RAINA (*bitterly*): Grief! A man who has been doing nothing but killing people for years! What does he care? What does any soldier care? (*She goes to the door, restraining her tears with difficulty.*)

LOUKA: Major Saranoff has been fighting too; and he has plenty of heart left. (RAINA, *at the door, draws herself up haughtily and goes out.*) Aha! I thought you wouldn't get much feeling out of your soldier. (*She is following* RAINA *when* NICOLA *enters with an armful of logs for the stove.*)

NICOLA (*grinning amorously at her*): I've been trying all the afternoon to get a minute alone with you, my girl. (*His countenance changes as he notices her arm.*) Why, what fashion is that of wearing your sleeve, child?

LOUKA (*proudly*): My own fashion.

NICOLA: Indeed! If the mistress catches you, she'll talk to you. (*He puts the logs down, and seats himself comfortably on the ottoman.*)

LOUKA: Is that any reason why you should take it on yourself to talk to me?

NICOLA: Come! don't be contrary with me. I've some good news for you. (*She sits down beside him. He takes out some paper money.* LOUKA, *with an eager gleam in her eyes, tries to snatch it; but he shifts it quickly to his left hand, out of her reach.*) See! a twenty leva bill! Sergius gave me that, out of pure swagger. A fool and his money are soon parted. There's ten levas more. The Swiss gave me that for backing up the mistress' and Raina's lies about him. He's no fool, he isn't. You should have heard old Catherine downstairs as polite as you please to me, telling me not to mind the Major being a little impatient; for they knew what a good servant I was—after making a fool and a liar of me before them all! The twenty will go to our savings; and you shall have the ten to spend if you'll only talk to me so as to remind me I'm a human being. I get tired of being a servant occasionally.

LOUKA: Yes: sell your manhood for 30 levas, and buy me for 10! (*Rising scornfully*) Keep your money. You were born to be a servant. I was not. When you set up your shop you will only be everybody's servant instead of somebody's servant. (*She goes moodily to the table and seats herself regally in* SERGIUS'S *chair.*)

NICOLA   (*picking up his logs, and going to the stove*): Ah, wait til you see. We shall have our evenings to ourselves; and I shall be master in my own house, I promise you. (*He throws the logs down and kneels at the stove.*)

LOUKA: You shall never be master in mine.

NICOLA   (*turning, still on his knees, and squatting down rather forlornly on his calves, daunted by her implacable disdain*): You have a great ambition in you, Louka. Remember: if any luck comes to you, it was I that made a woman of you.

LOUKA: You!

NICOLA   (*scrambling up and going to her*): Yes, me. Who was it made you give up wearing a couple of pounds of false black hair on your head and reddening your lips and cheeks like any other Bulgarian girl! I did. Who taught you to trim your nails, and keep your hands clean, and be dainty about yourself, like a fine Russian lady! Me: do you hear that? me! (*She tosses her head defiantly; and he turns away, adding more coolly*) I've often thought that if Raina were out of the way, and you just a little less of a fool and Sergius just a little more of one, you might come to be one of my grandest customers, instead of only being my wife and costing me money.

LOUKA: I believe you would rather be my servant than my husband. You would make more out of me. Oh, I know that soul of yours.

NICOLA   (*going closer to her for greater emphasis*): Never you mind my soul; but just listen to my advice. If you want to be a lady, your present behaviour to me won't do at all, unless when we're alone. It's too sharp and impudent; and impudence is a sort of familiarity: it shews affection for me. And don't you try being high and mighty with me, either. You're like all country girls: you think it's genteel to treat a servant the way I treat a stableboy. That's only your ignorance; and don't you forget it. And don't be so ready to defy everybody. Act as if you expected to have your own way, not as if you expected to be ordered about. The way to get on as a lady is the same as the way to get on as a servant: you've got to know your place: that's the secret of it. And you may depend on me to know my place if you get promoted. Think over it, my girl. I'll stand by you: one servant should always stand by another.

LOUKA   (*rising impatiently*): Oh, I must behave in my own way. You take all the courage out of me with your cold-blooded wisdom. Go and put those logs in the fire: that's the sort of thing you understand.

(*Before* NICOLA *can retort,* SERGIUS *comes in. He checks himself a moment on seeing* LOUKA; *then goes to the stove.*)

SERGIUS   (*to* NICOLA): I am not in the way of your work, I hope.

NICOLA   (*in a smooth, elderly manner*): Oh no, sir: thank you kindly. I was only speaking to this foolish girl about her habit of running up here to the library whenever she gets a chance, to look at the books. That's the worst of her education, sir: it gives her habits above her station. (*To* LOUKA) Make that table tidy, Louka, for the Major. (*He goes out sedately.*)

(LOUKA, *without looking at* SERGIUS, *pretends to arrange the papers on the table. He crosses slowly to her, and studies the arrangement of her sleeve reflectively.*)

SERGIUS: Let me see: is there a mark there? (*He turns up the bracelet and sees the bruise made by his grasp. She stands motionless, not looking at him: fascinated, but on her guard*): Ffff! Does it hurt?

LOUKA: Yes.

SERGIUS: Shall I cure it?

LOUKA   (*instantly withdrawing herself proudly, but still not looking at him*): No. You cannot cure it now.

SERGIUS   (*masterfully*): Quite sure? (*He makes a movement as if to take her in his arms.*)

LOUKA: Don't trifle with me, please. An officer should not trifle with a servant.

SERGIUS   (*indicating the bruise with a merciless stroke of his forefinger*): That was no trifle, Louka.

LOUKA   (*flinching; then looking at him for the first time*): Are you sorry?

SERGIUS   (*with measured emphasis, folding his arms*): I am never sorry.

LOUKA   (*wistfully*): I wish I could believe a man could be as unlike a woman as that. I wonder are you really a brave man?

SERGIUS   (*unaffectedly, relaxing his attitude*): Yes: I am a brave man. My heart jumped like a woman's at the first shot; but in the charge I found that I was brave. Yes: that at least is real about me.

LOUKA: Did you find in the charge that the men whose fathers are poor like mine were any less brave than the men who are rich like you?

SERGIUS   (*with bitter levity*): Not a bit. They all slashed and cursed and yelled like heroes. Psha! the courage to rage and kill is cheap. I have an English bull terrier who has as much of that sort of courage as the whole Bulgarian nation, and the whole Russian nation at its back. But he lets my groom thrash him, all the same. That's your soldier all over! No, Louka: your poor men can cut throats; but they are afraid of their officers; they put up with insults and blows; they stand by and see one another punished like children: aye, and help to do it when they are ordered. And the officers!!! Well (*with a short harsh laugh*) *I* am an officer. Oh, (*fervently*) give me the man who will defy to the death any power on earth or in heaven that sets itself up against his own will and conscience: he alone is the brave man.

LOUKA: How easy it is to talk! Men never seem to me to grow up: they all have schoolboy's ideas. You don't know what true courage is.

SERGIUS   (*ironically*): Indeed! I am willing to be instructed. (*He sits on the ottoman, sprawling magnificently.*)

LOUKA: Look at me! How much am I allowed to have my own will? I have to get your room ready for you: to sweep and dust, to fetch and carry. How could that degrade me if it did not degrade you to have it done for you? But (*with subdued passion*) if I were Empress of Russia, above everyone in the world, then!! Ah then, though according to you I could shew no courage at all, you should see, you should see.

SERGIUS: What would you do, most noble Empress?

LOUKA: I would marry the man I loved, which no other queen in Europe has the courage to do. If I loved you, though you would be as far beneath me as I am beneath you, I would dare to be the equal of my inferior. Would you dare as much if you loved me? No: if you felt the beginnings of love for me you would not let it grow. You would not dare: you would marry a rich man's daughter because you would be afraid of what other people would say of you.

SERGIUS   (*bounding up*): You lie: it is not so, by all the stars! If I loved you, and I were the Tsar himself, I would set you on the throne by my side. You know that I love another woman, a woman as high above you as heaven is above earth. And you are jealous of her.

LOUKA: I have no reason to be. She will never marry you now. The man I told you of has come back. She will marry the Swiss.

SERGIUS   (*recoiling*): The Swiss!

LOUKA: A man worth ten of you. Then you can come to me; and I will refuse you. You are not good enough for me. (*She turns to the door.*)

SERGIUS   (*springing after her and catching her fiercely in his arms*): I will kill the Swiss; and afterwards I will do as I please with you.

LOUKA   (*in his arms, passive and steadfast*): The Swiss will kill you, perhaps. He has beaten you in love. He may beat you in war.

SERGIUS   (*tormentedly*): Do you think I believe that she—she! whose worst thoughts are higher than your best ones, is capable of trifling with another man behind my back?

LOUKA: Do you think she would believe the Swiss if he told her now that I am in your arms?

SERGIUS   (*releasing her in despair*): Damnation! Oh, damnation! Mockery! mockery everywhere! everything I think is mocked by everything I do! (*He strikes himself frantically on the breast.*) Coward! liar! fool! Shall I kill myself like a man, or live and pretend to laugh at myself? (*She again turns to go.*) Louka! (*She stops near the door.*) Remember: you belong to me.

LOUKA   (*turning*): What does that mean? An insult?

SERGIUS   (*commandingly*): It means that you love me, and that I have had you here in my arms, and will perhaps have you there again. Whether that is an insult I neither know nor care: take it as you please. But (*vehemently*) I will not be a coward and a trifler. If I choose to love you, I dare marry you, in spite of all Bulgaria. If these hands ever touch you again, they shall touch my affianced bride.

LOUKA: We shall see whether you dare keep your word. And take care. I will not wait long.

SERGIUS   (*again folding his arms and standing motionless in the middle of the room*): Yes: we shall see. And you shall wait my pleasure.

(BLUNTSCHLI, *much preoccupied, with his papers still in his hand, enters, leaving the door open for* LOUKA *to go out. He goes across to the table, glancing at her as he passes.* SERGIUS, *without altering his resolute attitude, watches him steadily.* LOUKA *goes out, leaving the door open.*)

BLUNTSCHLI   (*absently, sitting at the table as before, and putting down his papers*): Thats a remarkable-looking young woman.

SERGIUS   (*gravely, without moving*): Captain Bluntschli.

BLUNTSCHLI: Eh?

SERGIUS: You have deceived me. You are my rival. I brook no rivals. At six o'clock I shall be in the drilling-ground on the Klissoura road, alone, on horseback, with my sabre. Do you understand?

BLUNTSCHLI   (*staring, but sitting quite at his ease*): Oh, thank you: that's a cavalry man's proposal. I'm in the artillery; and I have the choice of weapons. If I go, I shall take a machine gun. And there shall be no mistake about the cartridges this time.

SERGIUS   (*flushing, but with deadly coldness*): Take care, sir. It is not our custom in Bulgaria to allow invitations of that kind to be trifled with.

BLUNTSCHLI   (*warmly*): Pooh! don't talk to me about Bulgaria. You don't know what fighting is. But have it your own way. Bring your sabre along. I'll meet you.

SERGIUS   (*fiercely delighted to find his opponent a man of spirit*): Well said, Switzer. Shall I lend you my best horse?

BLUNTSCHLI: No: damn your horse! thank you all the same, my dear fellow. (RAINA *comes in, and hears the next sentence.*) I shall fight you on foot. Horseback's too dangerous; I don't want to kill you if I can help it.

RAINA   (*hurrying forward anxiously*): I have heard what Captain Bluntschli said, Sergius. You are going to fight. Why? (SERGIUS *turns away in silence, and goes to the stove, where he stands watching her as she continues, to* BLUNTSCHLI) What about?

BLUNTSCHLI: I don't know: he hasn't told me. Better not interfere, dear young lady. No harm will be done: I've often acted as sword instructor. He won't be able to touch me; and I'll not hurt him. It will save explanations. In the morning I shall be off home; and you'll never see me or hear of me again. You and he will then make it up and live happily ever after.

RAINA   (*turning away deeply hurt, almost with a sob in her voice*): I never said I wanted to see you again.

SERGIUS   (*striding forward*): Ha! That is a confession.

RAINA   (*haughtily*): What do you mean?

SERGIUS: You love that man!

RAINA   (*scandalized*): Sergius!

SERGIUS: You allow him to make love to you behind my back, just as you treat me as your affianced husband behind his. Bluntschli: you knew our relations; and you deceived me. It is for that that I call you to account, not for having received favors *I* never enjoyed.

BLUNTSCHLI   (*jumping up indignantly*): Stuff! Rubbish! I have received no favors. Why, the young lady doesn't even know whether I'm married or not.

RAINA   (*forgetting herself*): Oh! (*Collapsing on the ottoman*) Are you?

SERGIUS: You see the young lady's concern, Captain Bluntschli. Denial is useless. You have enjoyed the privilege of being received in her own room, late at night—

BLUNTSCHLI   (*interrupting him pepperily*): Yes, you blockhead! she received me with a pistol at her head. Your cavalry were at my heels. I'd have blown out her brains if she'd uttered a cry.

SERGIUS   (*taken aback*): Bluntschli! Raina: is this true?

RAINA   (*rising in wrathful majesty*): Oh, how dare you, how dare you?

BLUNTSCHLI: Apologize, man: apologize. (*He resumes his seat at the table.*)

SERGIUS   (*with the old measured emphasis, folding his arms*): I never apologize!

RAINA   (*passionately*): This is the doing of that friend of yours, Captain Bluntschli. It is he who is spreading this horrible story about me. (*She walks about excitedly.*)

BLUNTSCHLI: No: he's dead. Burnt alive.

RAINA   (*stopping, shocked*): Burnt alive!

BLUNTSCHLI: Shot in the hip in a woodyard. Couldn't drag himself out. Your fellows' shells set the timber on fire and burnt him, with a half a dozen other poor devils in the same predicament.

RAINA: How horrible!

SERGIUS: And how ridiculous! Oh, war! war! the dream of patriots and heroes! A fraud, Bluntschli. A hollow sham, like love.

RAINA   (*outraged*): Like love! You say that before me!

BLUNTSCHLI: Come, Saranoff: that matter is explained.

SERGIUS: A hollow sham, I say. Would you have come back here if nothing had passed between you except at the muzzle of your pistol? Raina is mistaken about your friend who was burnt. He was not my informant.

RAINA: Who then? (*Suddenly guessing the truth*) Ah, Louka! my maid! my servant! You were with her this morning all that time after—after—Oh, what sort of god is this I have been worshipping! (*He meets her gaze with sardonic enjoyment of her disenchantment. Angered all the more, she goes closer to him, and says, in a lower, intenser tone*) Do you know that I looked out of the window as I went upstairs, to have another sight of my hero; and I saw something I did not understand then. I know now that you were making love to her.

SERGIUS   (*with grim humor*): You saw that?

RAINA: Only too well. (*She turns away, and throws herself on the divan under the centre window, quite overcome.*)

SERGIUS   (*cynically*): Raina: our romance is shattered. Life's a farce.

BLUNTSCHLI   (*to* RAINA, *whimsically*): You see: he's found himself out now.

SERGIUS   (*going to him*): Bluntschli: I have allowed you to call me a blockhead. You may now call me a coward as well. I refuse to fight you. Do you know why?

BLUNTSCHLI: No; but it doesn't matter. I didn't ask the reason when you cried on; and I don't ask the reason now that you cry off. I'm a professional soldier! I fight when I have to, and am very glad to get out of it when I haven't to. You're only an amateur: you think fighting's an amusement.

SERGIUS   (*sitting down at the table, nose to nose with him*): You shall hear the reason all the same, my professional. The reason is that it takes two men—real men—men of heart, blood and honor—to make a genuine combat. I could no more fight with you than I could make love to an ugly woman. You've no magnetism: you're not a man: you're a machine.

BLUNTSCHLI   (*apologetically*): Quite true, quite true. I always was that sort of chap. I'm very sorry.

SERGIUS: Psha!

BLUNTSCHLI: But now that you've found that life isn't a farce, but something quite sensible and serious, what further obstacle is there to your happiness?

RAINA   (*rising*): You are very solicitous about my happiness and his. Do you forget his new love—Louka? It is not you that he must fight now, but his rival, Nicola.

SERGIUS: Rival!! (*Bouncing half across the room.*)

RAINA: Don't you know that they're engaged?

SERGIUS: Nicola! Are fresh abysses opening? Nicola!

RAINA   (*sarcastically*): A shocking sacrifice, isn't it? Such beauty! such intellect! such modesty! wasted on a middle-aged servant man. Really, Sergius, you cannot stand by and allow such a thing. It would be unworthy of your chivalry.

SERGIUS   (*losing all self-control*): Viper! Viper! (*He rushes to and fro, raging.*)

BLUNTSCHLI: Look here, Saranoff: you're getting the worst of this.

RAINA   (*getting angrier*): Do you realize what he has done, Captain Bluntschli? He has set this girl as a spy on us; and her reward is that he makes love to her.

SERGIUS: False! Monstrous!

RAINA: Monstrous! (*Confronting him*) Do you deny that she told you about Captain Bluntschli being in my room?

SERGIUS: No; but—

RAINA   (*interrupting*): Do you deny that you were making love to her when she told you?

SERGIUS: No; but I tell you—

RAINA   (*cutting him short contemptuously*): It is unnecessary to tell us anything more. That is quite enough for us. (*She turns away from him and sweeps majestically back to the window.*)

BLUNTSCHLI   (*quietly, as* SERGIUS, *in an agony of mortification, sinks on the ottoman, clutching his averted head between his fists*): I told you you were getting the worst of it, Saranoff.

SERGIUS: Tiger cat!

RAINA   (*running excitedly to* BLUNTSCHLI): You hear this man calling me names, Captain Bluntschli?

BLUNTSCHLI: What else can he do, dear lady? He must defend himself somehow. Come (*very persuasively*): don't quarrel. What good does it do?

(RAINA, *with a gasp, sits down on the ottoman, and after a vain effort to look vexedly at* BLUNTSCHLI, *falls a victim to her sense of humor, and actually leans back babyishly against the writhing shoulder of* SERGIUS.)

SERGIUS: Engaged to Nicola! Ha! ha! Ah well, Bluntschli, you are right to take this huge imposture of a world coolly.

RAINA   (*quaintly to* BLUNTSCHLI, *with an intuitive guess at his state of mind*): I daresay you think us a couple of grownup babies, don't you?

SERGIUS   (*grinning savagely*): He does: he does. Swiss civilization nursetending Bulgarian barbarism, eh?

BLUNTSCHLI   (*blushing*): Not at all, I assure you. I'm only very glad to get you two quieted. There! there! let's be pleasant and talk it over in a friendly way. Where is this other young lady?

RAINA: Listening at the door, probably.

SERGIUS   (*shivering as if a bullet had struck him, and speaking with quiet but deep indignation*): I will prove that that, at least, is a calumny. (*He goes with dignity to the door and opens it. A yell of fury bursts from him as he looks out. He darts into the passage, and returns dragging in* LOUKA, *whom he flings violently against the table, exclaiming*) Judge her, Bluntschli. You, the cool impartial one: judge the eavesdropper.

(LOUKA *stands her ground, proud and silent.*)

BLUNTSCHLI   (*shaking his head*): I mustn't judge her. I once listened myself outside a tent when there was a mutiny brewing. It's all a question of the degree of provocation. My life was at stake.

LOUKA: My love was at stake. I am not ashamed.

RAINA   (*contemptuously*): Your love! Your curiosity, you mean.

LOUKA   (*facing her and returning her contempt with interest*): My love, stronger than anything you can feel, even for your chocolate cream soldier.

SERGIUS   (*with quick suspicion, to* LOUKA): What does that mean?

LOUKA   (*fiercely*): It means—

SERGIUS   (*interrupting her slightingly*): Oh, I remember: the ice pudding. A paltry taunt, girl!

(MAJOR PETKOFF *enters, in his shirtsleeves.*)

PETKOFF: Excuse my shirtsleeves, gentlemen. Raina: somebody has been wearing that coat of mine: I'll swear it. Somebody with a differently shaped back. It's all burst open at the sleeve. Your mother is mending it. I wish she'd make haste: I shall catch cold. (*He looks more attentively at them.*) Is anything the matter?

RAINA: No. (*She sits down at the stove, with a tranquil air.*)

SERGIUS: Oh no. (*He sits down at the end of the table, as at first.*)

BLUNTSCHLI   (*who is already seated*): Nothing. Nothing.

PETKOFF   (*sitting down on the ottoman in his old place*): That's all right. (*He notices* LOUKA.) Anything the matter, Louka?

LOUKA: No, sir.

PETKOFF   (*genially*): That's all right. (*He sneezes*): Go and ask your mistress for my coat, like a good girl, will you?

(NICOLA *enters with the coat.* LOUKA *makes a pretence of having business in the room by taking the little table with the hookah away to the wall near the windows.*)

RAINA   (*rising quickly as she sees the coat on* NICOLA'S *arm*): Here it is papa. Give it to me Nicola; and do you put some more wood on the fire. (*She takes the coat, and brings it to* THE MAJOR, *who stands up to put it on.* NICOLA *attends to the fire.*)

PETKOFF   (*to* RAINA, *teasing her affectionately*): Aha! Going to be very good to poor old papa just for one day after his return from the wars, eh?

RAINA   (*with solemn reproach*): Ah, how can you say that to me, father?

PETKOFF: Well, well, only a joke, little one. Come: give me a kiss. (*She kisses him.*) Now give me the coat.

RAINA: No: I am going to put it on for you. Turn your back. (*He turns his back and feels behind him with his arms for the sleeves. She dexterously takes the photograph from the pocket and throws it on the table before* BLUNTSCHLI, *who covers it with a sheet of paper under the very nose of* SERGIUS, *who looks on amazed, with his suspicions roused in the highest degree. She then helps* PETKOFF *on with his coat.*) There, dear! Now are you comfortable?

PETKOFF: Quite, little love. Thanks. (*He sits down; and* RAINA *returns to her seat near the stove.*) Oh, by the bye, I've found something funny. What's the meaning of this? (*He puts his hand into the picked pocket.*) Eh? Hallo! (*He tries the other pocket.*) Well, I could have sworn—! (*Much puzzled, he tries the breast pocket.*) I wonder—(*trying the original pocket.*) Where can it—? (*He rises, exclaiming*) Your mother's taken it!

RAINA   (*very red*): Taken what?

PETKOFF: Your photograph, with the inscription: "Raina, to her Chocolate Cream Soldier: a Souvenir." Now you know there's something more in this than meets the eye; and I'm going to find it out. (*Shouting*) Nicola!

NICOLA   (*coming to him*): Sir!

PETKOFF: Did you spoil any pastry of Miss Raina's this morning?

NICOLA: You heard Miss Raina say that I did, sir.

PETKOFF: I know that, you idiot. Was it true?

NICOLA: I am sure Miss Raina is incapable of saying anything that is not true, sir.

PETKOFF: Are you? Then I'm not. (*Turning to the others*) Come: do you think I don't see it all? (*He goes to* SERGIUS, *and slaps him on the shoulder.*) Sergius: you're the chocolate cream soldier, aren't you?

SERGIUS   (*starting up*): I! A chocolate cream soldier! Certainly not.

PETKOFF: Not! (*He looks at them. They are all very serious and very conscious.*) Do you mean to tell me that Raina sends things like that to other men?

SERGIUS   (*enigmatically*): The world is not such an innocent place as we used to think, Petkoff.

BLUNTSCHLI   (*rising*): It's all right, Major. I'm the chocolate cream soldier. (PETKOFF *and* SERGIUS *are equally astonished.*) The gracious young lady saved my life by giving me chocolate creams when I was starving: shall I ever forget their flavour! My late friend Stolz told you the story at Pirot. I was the fugitive.

PETKOFF: You! (*He gasps.*) Sergius: do you remember how those two women went on this morning when we mentioned it? (SERGIUS *smiles cynically.* PETKOFF *confronts* RAINA *severely.*) You're a nice young woman, aren't you?

RAINA   (*bitterly*): Major Saranoff has changed his mind. And when I wrote that on the photograph, I did not know that Captain Bluntschli was married.

BLUNTSCHLI   (*startled into vehement protest*): I'm not married.

RAINA   (*with deep reproach*): You said you were.

BLUNTSCHLI: I did not. I positively did not. I never was married in my life.

PETKOFF   (*exasperated*): Raina: will you kindly inform me, if I am not asking too much, which of these gentlemen you are engaged to?

RAINA: To neither of them. This young lady (*introducing* LOUKA, *who faces them all proudly*) is the object of Major Saranoff's affections at present.

PETKOFF: Louka! Are you mad, Sergius? Why, this girl's engaged to Nicola.

NICOLA: I beg your pardon, sir. There is a mistake. Louka is not engaged to me.

PETKOFF: Not engaged to you, you scoundrel! Why, you had twenty-five levas from me on the day of your betrothal; and she had that gilt bracelet from Miss Raina.

NICOLA   (*with cool unction*): We gave it out so, sir. But it was only to give Louka protection. She had a soul above her station; and I have been no more than her confidential servant. I intend, as you know, sir, to set up a shop later on in Sofia; and I look forward to her custom and recommendation should she marry into the nobility. (*He goes out with impressive discretion, leaving them all staring after him.*)

PETKOFF   (*breaking the silence*): Well, I am—hm!

SERGIUS: This is either the finest heroism or the most crawling baseness. Which is it, Bluntschli?

BLUNTSCHLI: Never mind whether it's heroism or baseness. Nicola's the ablest man I've met in Bulgaria. I'll make him manager of a hotel if he can speak French and German.

LOUKA   (*suddenly breaking out at* SERGIUS): I have been insulted by everyone here. You set them the example. You owe me an apology.

(SERGIUS, *like a repeating clock of which the spring has been touched, immediately begins to fold his arms.*)

BLUNTSCHLI   (*before he can speak*): It's no use. He never apologizes.

LOUKA: Not to you, his equal and his enemy. To me, his poor servant, he will not refuse to apologize.

SERGIUS   (*approvingly*): You are right. (*He bends his knee in his grandest manner.*) Forgive me.

LOUKA: I forgive you. (*She timidly gives him her hand, which he kisses.*) That touch makes me your affianced wife.

SERGIUS   (*springing up*): Ah! I forgot that.

LOUKA   (*coldly*): You can withdraw if you like.

SERGIUS: Withdraw! Never! You belong to me. (*He puts his arm about her.*)

(CATHERINE *comes in and finds* LOUKA *in* SERGIUS' *arms, with all the rest gazing at them in bewildered astonishment.*)

CATHERINE: What does this mean?

(SERGIUS *releases* LOUKA.)

PETKOFF: Well, my dear, it appears that Sergius is going to marry Louka instead of Raina. (*She is about to break out indignantly at him: he stops her by exclaiming testily*): Don't blame me: I've nothing to do with it. (*He retreats to the stove.*)

CATHERINE: Marry Louka! Sergius: you are bound by your word to us!

SERGIUS   (*folding his arms*) Nothing binds me.

BLUNTSCHLI   (*much pleased by this piece of common sense*): Saranoff: your hand. My congratulations. These heroics of yours have their practical side after all. (*To* LOUKA): Gracious young lady: the best wishes of a good Republican! (*He kisses her hand, to* RAINA'S *great disgust, and returns to his seat.*)

CATHERINE: Louka: you have been telling stories.

LOUKA: I have done Raina no harm.

CATHERINE   (*haughtily*): Raina!

(RAINA, *equally indignant, almost snorts at the liberty.*)

LOUKA: I have a right to call her Raina: she calls me Louka. I told Major Saranoff she would never marry him if the Swiss gentleman came back.

BLUNTSCHLI   (*rising, much surprised*): Hallo!

LOUKA   (*turning to* RAINA): I thought you were fonder of him than of Sergius. You know best whether I was right.

BLUNTSCHLI: What nonsense! I assure you, my dear Major, my dear Madame, the gracious young lady simply saved my life, nothing else. She never cared two straws for me. Why, bless my heart and soul, look at the young lady and look at me. She, rich, young, beautiful, with her imagination full of fairy princes and noble natures and cavalry charges and goodness knows what! And I, a commonplace Swiss soldier who hardly knows what a decent life is after fifteen years of barracks and battles: a vagabond, a man who has spoiled all his chances in life through an incurably romantic disposition, a man—

SERGIUS   (*starting as if a needle had pricked him and interrupting* BLUNTSCHLI *in incredulous amazement*): Excuse me, Bluntschli: what did you say had spoiled your chances in life?

BLUNTSCHLI   (*promptly*): An incurably romantic disposition. I ran away from home twice when I was a boy. I went into the army instead of into my father's business. I climbed the balcony of this house when a man of sense would have dived into the nearest cellar. I came sneaking back here to have another look at the young lady when any other man of my age would have sent the coat back—

PETKOFF: My coat!

BLUNTSCHLI:—yes: that's the coat I mean—would have sent it back and gone quietly home. Do you suppose I am the sort of fellow a young girl falls in love with? Why, look at our ages! I'm thirty-four: I don't suppose the young lady is much over seventeen. (*This estimate produces a marked sensation, all the rest turning and staring at one another. He proceeds innocently*): All that adventure which was life or death to me, was only a schoolgirl's game to her—chocolate creams and hide and seek. Here's the proof! (*He takes the photograph from the table.*) Now, I ask you, would a woman who took the affair seriously have sent me this and written on it "Raina, to her Chocolate Cream Soldier: a Souvenir"? (*He exhibits the photograph triumphantly, as if it settled the matter beyond all possibility of refutation.*)

PETKOFF: That's what I was looking for. How the deuce did it get there? (*He comes from the stove to look at it, and sits down on the ottoman.*)

BLUNTSCHLI   (*to* RAINA, *complacently*): I have put everything right, I hope, gracious young lady.

RAINA   (*going to the table to face him*): I quite agree with your account of yourself. You are a romantic idiot. (BLUNTSCHLI *is unspeakably taken back.*) Next time, I hope you will know the difference between a schoolgirl of seventeen and a woman of twenty-three.

BLUNTSCHLI   (*stupefied*): Twenty-three!

(RAINA *snaps the photograph contemptuously from his hand; tears it up; throws the pieces in his face; and sweeps back to her former place.*)

SERGIUS   (*with grim enjoyment of his rival's discomfiture*): Bluntschli: my one last belief is gone. Your sagacity is a fraud, like everything else. You have less sense than even I!

BLUNTSCHLI   (*overwhelmed*): Twenty-three! Twenty-three!! (*He considers.*) Hm! (*Swiftly making up his mind and coming to his host*) In that case, Major Petkoff, I beg to propose formally to become a suitor for your daughter's hand, in place of Major Saranoff retired.

RAINA: You dare!

BLUNTSCHLI: If you were twenty-three when you said those things to me this afternoon, I shall take them seriously.

CATHERINE   (*loftily polite*): I doubt, sir, whether you quite realize either my daughter's position or that of Major Sergius Saranoff, whose place you propose to take. The Petkoffs and the Saranoffs are known as the richest and most important families in the country. Our position is almost historical: we can go back for twenty years.

PETKOFF: Oh, never mind that, Catherine. (*To* BLUNTSCHLI) We should be most happy, Bluntschli, if it were only a question of your position; but hang it, you know, Raina is accustomed to a very comfortable establishment. Sergius keeps twenty horses.

BLUNTSCHLI: But who wants twenty horses? We're not going to keep a circus.

CATHERINE   (*severely*): My daughter, sir, is accustomed to a first-rate stable.

RAINA: Hush, mother: you're making me ridiculous.

BLUNTSCHLI: Oh well, if it comes to a question of an establishment, here goes! (*He darts impetuously to the table; seizes the papers in the blue envelope; and turns to* SERGIUS.) How many horses did you say?

SERGIUS: Twenty, noble Switzer.

BLUNTSCHLI: I have two hundred horses. (*They are amazed.*) How many carriages?

SERGIUS: Three.

BLUNTSCHLI: I have seventy. Twenty-four of them will hold twelve inside, besides two on the box, without counting the driver and conductor. How many tablecloths have you?

SERGIUS: How the deuce do I know?

BLUNTSCHLI: Have you four thousand?

SERGIUS: No.

BLUNTSCHLI: I have. I have nine thousand six hundred pairs of sheets and blankets, with two thousand four hundred eider-down quilts. I have ten thousand knives and forks, and the same quantity of dessert spoons. I have three hundred servants. I have six palatial establishments, besides two livery stables, a tea garden, and a private house. I have four medals for distinguished services; I have the rank of an officer and the standing of a gentleman; and I have three native languages. Shew me any man in Bulgaria that can offer as much!

PETKOFF   (*with childish awe*): Are you Emperor of Switzerland?

BLUNTSCHLI: My rank is the highest known in Switzerland: I am a free citizen.

CATHERINE: Then, Captain Bluntschli, since you are my daughter's choice—

RAINA *(mutinously)*: He's not.

CATHERINE *(ignoring her)*:—I shall not stand in the way of her happiness. (PETKOFF *is about to speak.*) That is Major Petkoff's feeling also.

PETKOFF: Oh, I shall be only too glad. Two hundred horses! Whew!

SERGIUS: What says the lady?

RAINA *(pretending to sulk)*: The lady says that he can keep his tablecloths and his omnibuses. I am not here to be sold to the highest bidder. (*She turns her back on him.*)

BLUNTSCHLI: I won't take that answer. I appealed to you as a fugitive, a beggar, and a starving man. You accepted me. You gave me your hand to kiss, your bed to sleep in, and your roof to shelter me.

RAINA: I did not give them to the Emperor of Switzerland.

BLUNTSCHLI: That's just what I say. (*He catches her by the shoulders and turns her face-to-face with him.*) Now tell us whom you did give them to.

RAINA *(succumbing with a shy smile)*: To my chocolate cream soldier.

BLUNTSCHLI *(with a boyish laugh of delight)*: That'll do. Thank you. (*He looks at his watch and suddenly becomes businesslike.*) Time's up, Major. You've managed those regiments so well that you're sure to be asked to get rid of some of the infantry of the Timok division. Send them home by way of Lom Palanka. Saranoff: don't get married until I come back: I shall be here punctually at five in the evening on Tuesday fortnight. Gracious ladies (*his heels click*) good evening. (*He makes them a military bow, and goes.*)

SERGIUS: What a man! Is he a man!

QUESTIONS

1. Which elements of *Arms and the Man* make it a romantic play and which make it a satiric one?
2. How important are Shaw's stage directions? What functions do they serve?
3. How does the play's title reflect its subjects? What are the meanings of *arms*? What are the connotations of *man*?
4. Of what importance are Louka and Nicola to the play? What does each contribute individually and what is their function as a couple?
5. Compare and contrast the characters of Sergius and Bluntschli. Consider how each role should be acted.
6. What do you make of the ending? How seriously are we to take Raina's and Bluntschli's changes of attitude?

CHAPTER TWENTY

The Theater of the Absurd

One of the most noteworthy developments in theater following the rise of realism has been the emergence of the Theater of the Absurd in the second half of the twentieth century. Absurdist drama, as it is called, is nonrealistic, even antirealistic. Rejecting the conventions of realism, absurdist playwrights substitute storyless action for well-contrived plots; they replace believable characters of psychological complexity with barely recognizable figures; and for witty repartee and grand speeches they offer incoherent ramblings and disconnected dialogue.

Why such an about-face, why such a rejection of realistic theatrical conventions? Primarily because ways of perceiving reality had changed so radically that realistic dramatic conventions were inadequate to the task of representing reality as dramatists of the absurd envisioned it. Absurdist dramatists reject the implications that lie behind realistic conventions; they object, for example, to the idea that characters can be understood or that plot should be ordered. For them people are not understandable, and life is disorderly and chaotic. Absurdist writers attempt to dramatize these and other conceptions in plays that depict experience as meaningless and existence as purposeless; they portray human beings as irrational, pathetic figures, helpless against life's chaos. For the absurdist, man is deracinated, cut off from his historical context, dispossessed of religious certainty, alienated from his social and physical environment, and unable to communicate with others.

Martin Esslin, a leading drama critic and expert on absurdist drama, has noted that the word *absurd* when used with reference to the Theater of the Absurd does not mean "ridiculous," but "out of harmony."* Modern man is out of synch with his world—with nature, with other men, and ultimately with himself. This sense of being out of harmony, of being at odds with life, is both cause and consequence of the desperate loneliness and alienation that thwart his happiness and rob his life of meaning.

Esslin has also recognized that dramatists of the absurd, like Ionesco, have moved beyond arguing about the absurdity of the human condition to present it "in terms of concrete stage images." When dramatists of the absurd violate the rules of conventional dramaturgy, they do so because they see that strategy as the most effective way to dramatize the conditions they experience. Their intention is to make us experience the condition of absurdity. Hence the outrageousness that characterizes many of their plays.

Absurdist plays can be comic and horrifying simultaneously. Eugène Ionesco's *The Lesson* includes comic dialogue that rivals Molière's in *Tartuffe* or Shaw's in *Arms and the Man*. But unlike those plays, *The Lesson* serves up violence along with its humor, and its farce gives way to nightmare. Such rapid shifts in action and tone can disturb our sense of comfort and our certainty about what we are reading (or viewing) and perhaps shake us up enough to question our perceptions of reality.

Absurdist plays rely on more than abrupt changes of direction and tone to create their effects. Since a dominant theme of much absurdist drama is the inadequacy of language to serve the ends of human communication, many absurdist plays illustrate the breakdown of language as an instrument of communication. Dialogue, for example, may be riddled with nonsequiturs and disconnected remarks by different characters, or it may be absent altogether as characters mime and gesture rather than talk. In *The Lesson* Ionesco illustrates the inability of teacher and student to understand each other. Although their conversational exchanges are funny, they also frighteningly portray their inability to communicate. Language, as the dialogue of *The Lesson* suggests, is closely allied with power and dominance. As nightmarish as the action of the play becomes, perhaps it is not as illogical and random as it may at first seem. Perhaps it has something to do with the way some absurdist writers see all human communication: as a contest for control, as a conflict to determine mastery rather than an attempt to establish human connections.

*Martin Esslin, *The Theatre of the Absurd* (New York: Doubleday, 1969) 5–7.

EUGÈNE IONESCO
[b. 1912]

The Lesson

TRANSLATED BY DONALD M. ALLEN

THE CHARACTERS

THE PROFESSOR, *aged 50 to 60*
THE YOUNG PUPIL, *aged 18*
THE MAID, *aged 45 to 50*

Scene: *The office of the old professor, which also serves as a dining room. To the left, a door opens onto the apartment stairs; upstage, to the right, another door opens onto a corridor of the apartment. Upstage, a little left of center, a window, not very large, with plain curtains; on the outside sill of the window are ordinary potted plants. The low buildings with red roofs of a small town can be seen in the distance. The sky is grayish-blue. On the right stands a provincial buffet. The table doubles as a desk, it stands at stage center. There are three chairs around the table, and two more stand on each side of the window. Light-colored wallpaper, some shelves with books.*

[*When the curtain rises the stage is empty, and it remains so for a few moments. Then we hear the doorbell ring.*]

VOICE OF THE MAID   [*from the corridor*]: Yes. I'm coming.

[*The* MAID *comes in, after having run down the stairs. She is stout, aged 45 to 50, red-faced, and wears a peasant woman's cap. She rushes in, slamming the door to the right behind her, and dries her hands on her apron as she runs towards the door on the left. Meanwhile we hear the doorbell ring again.*]

MAID: Just a moment, I'm coming.

[*She opens the door. A young* PUPIL, *aged 18, enters. She is wearing a gray student's smock, a small white collar, and carries a student's satchel under her arm.*]

MAID: Good morning, miss.
PUPIL: Good morning, madam. Is the Professor at home?
MAID: Have you come for the lesson?

PUPIL: Yes, I have.

MAID: He's expecting you. Sit down for a moment. I'll tell him you're here.

PUPIL: Thank you.

[*She seats herself near the table, facing the audience; the hall door is to her left; her back is to the other door, through which the* MAID *hurriedly exits, calling:*]

MAID: Professor, come down please, your pupil is here.

VOICE OF THE PROFESSOR   [*rather reedy*]: Thank you. I'm coming . . . in just a moment . . .

[*The* MAID *exits; the* PUPIL *draws in her legs, holds her satchel on her lap, and waits demurely. She casts a glance or two around the room, at the furniture, at the ceiling too. Then she takes a notebook out of her satchel, leafs through it, and stops to look at a page for a moment as though reviewing a lesson, as though taking a last look at her homework. She seems to be a well-brought-up girl, polite, but lively, gay, dynamic; a fresh smile is on her lips. During the course of the play she progressively loses the lively rhythm of her movement and her carriage, she becomes withdrawn. From gay and smiling she becomes progressively sad and morose; from very lively at the beginning, she becomes more and more fatigued and somnolent. Towards the end of the play her face must clearly express a nervous depression; her way of speaking shows the effects of this, her tongue becomes thick, words come to her memory with difficulty and emerge from her mouth with as much difficulty; she comes to have a manner vaguely paralyzed, the beginning of aphasia. Firm and determined at the beginning, so much so as to appear to be almost aggressive, she becomes more and more passive, until she is almost a mute and inert object, seemingly inanimate in the* PROFESSOR'S *hands, to such an extent that when he makes his final gesture, she no longer reacts. Insensible, her reflexes deadened, only her eyes in an expressionless face will show inexpressible astonishment and fear. The transition from one manner to the other must of course be made imperceptibly.*

The PROFESSOR *enters. He is a little old man with a little white beard. He wears pince-nez, a black skullcap, a long black schoolmaster's coat, trousers and shoes of black, detachable white collar, a black tie. Excessively polite, very timid, his voice deadened by his timidity, very proper, very much the teacher. He rubs his hands together constantly; occasionally a lewd gleam comes into his eyes and is quickly repressed.*

During the course of the play his timidity will disappear progressively, imperceptibly; and the lewd gleams in his eyes will become a steady devouring flame in the end. From a manner that is inoffensive at the start, the PROFESSOR *becomes more and more sure of himself, more and more nervous, aggressive, dominating, until he is able to do as he pleases with the* PUPIL, *who has become, in his hands, a pitiful creature. Of course, the voice of the* PROFESSOR *must change too, from thin and reedy, to stronger and stronger, until at the end it is extremely powerful, ringing, sonorous, while the* PUPIL'S *voice changes from the very clear and ringing tones that she has at the beginning of the play until it is almost inaudible. In these first scenes the* PROFESSOR *might stammer very slightly.*]

PROFESSOR: Good morning, young lady. You . . . I expect that you . . . that you are the new pupil?

PUPIL   [*turns quickly with a lively and self-assured manner; she gets up, goes toward the* PROFESSOR, *and gives him her hand*]: Yes, Professor. Good morning, Professor. As you see, I'm on time. I didn't want to be late.

PROFESSOR: That's fine, miss. Thank you, you didn't really need to hurry. I am very sorry to have kept you waiting . . . I was just finishing up . . . well . . . I'm sorry . . . You will excuse me, won't you? . . .

PUPIL: Oh, certainly, Professor. It doesn't matter at all, Professor.

PROFESSOR: Please excuse me . . . Did you have any trouble finding the house?

PUPIL: No . . . Not at all. I just asked the way. Everybody knows you around here.

PROFESSOR: For thirty years I've lived in this town. You've not been here for long? How do you find it?

PUPIL: It's all right. The town is attractive and even agreeable, there's a nice park, a boarding school, a bishop, nice shops and streets . . .

PROFESSOR: That's very true, young lady. And yet, I'd just as soon live somewhere else. In Paris, or at least Bordeaux.

PUPIL: Do you like Bordeaux?

PROFESSOR: I don't know. I've never seen it.

PUPIL: But you know Paris?

PROFESSOR: No, I don't know it either, young lady, but if you'll permit me, can you tell me, Paris is the capital city of . . . miss?

PUPIL [*searching her memory for a moment, then, happily guessing*]: Paris is the capital city of . . . France?

PROFESSOR: Yes, young lady, bravo, that's very good, that's perfect. My congratulations. You have your French geography at your finger tips. You know your chief cities.

PUPIL: Oh! I don't know them all yet, Professor, it's not quite that easy, I have trouble learning them.

PROFESSOR: Oh! it will come . . . you mustn't give up . . . young lady . . . I beg your pardon . . . have patience . . . little by little . . . You will see, it will come in time . . . What a nice day it is today . . . or rather, not so nice . . . Oh! but then yes it is nice. In short, it's not too bad a day, that's the main thing . . . ahem . . . ahem . . . it's not raining and it's not snowing either.

PUPIL: That would be most unusual, for it's summer now.

PROFESSOR: Excuse me, miss, I was just going to say so . . . but as you will learn, one must be ready for anything.

PUPIL: I guess so, Professor.

PROFESSOR: We can't be sure of anything, young lady, in this world.

PUPIL: The snow falls in the winter. Winter is one of the four seasons. The other three are . . . uh . . . spr . . .

PROFESSOR: Yes?

PUPIL: . . . ing, and then summer . . . and . . . uh . . .

PROFESSOR: It begins like "automobile," miss.

PUPIL: Ah, yes, autumn . . .

PROFESSOR: That's right, miss. That's a good answer, that's perfect. I am convinced that you will be a good pupil. You will make real progress. You are intelligent, you seem to me to be well informed, and you've a good memory.

PUPIL: I know my seasons, don't I, Professor?

PROFESSOR: Yes, indeed, miss . . . or almost. But it will come in time. In any case, you're coming along. Soon you'll know all the seasons, even with your eyes closed. Just as I do.

PUPIL: It's hard.

PROFESSOR: Oh, no. All it takes is a little effort, a little good will, miss. You will see. It will come, you may be sure of that.

PUPIL: Oh, I do hope so, Professor. I have a great thirst for knowledge. My parents also want me to get an education. They want me to specialize. They consider a little general culture, even if it is solid, is no longer enough, in these times.

PROFESSOR: Your parents, miss, are perfectly right. You must go on with your studies. Forgive me for saying so, but it is very necessary. Our contemporary life has become most complex.

PUPIL: And so very complicated too . . . My parents are fairly rich, I'm lucky. They can help me in my work, help me in my very advanced studies.

PROFESSOR: And you wish to qualify for . . . ?

PUPIL: Just as soon as possible, for the first doctor's orals. They're in three weeks' time.

PROFESSOR: You already have your high school diploma, if you'll pardon the question?

PUPIL: Yes, Professor, I have my science diploma and my arts diploma, too.

PROFESSOR: Ah, you're very far advanced, even perhaps too advanced for your age. And which doctorate do you wish to qualify for? In the physical sciences or in moral philosophy?

PUPIL: My parents are very much hoping—if you think it will be possible in such a short time—they very much hope that I can qualify for the total doctorate.

PROFESSOR: The total doctorate? . . . You have great courage, young lady, I congratulate you sincerely. We will try, miss, to do our best. In any case, you already know quite a bit, and at so young an age too.

PUPIL: Oh, Professor.

PROFESSOR: Then, if you'll permit me, pardon me, please, I do think that we ought to get to work. We have scarcely any time to lose.

PUPIL: Oh, but certainly, Professor, I want to. I beg you to.

PROFESSOR: Then, may I ask you to sit down . . . there . . . Will you permit me, miss, that is if you have no objections, to sit down opposite you?

PUPIL: Oh, of course, Professor, please do.

PROFESSOR: Thank you very much, miss. [*They sit down facing each other at the table, their profiles to the audience.*] There we are. Now have you brought your books and notebooks?

PUPIL [*taking notebooks and books out of her satchel*]: Yes, Professor. Certainly, I have brought all that we'll need.

PROFESSOR: Perfect, miss. This is perfect. Now, if this doesn't bore you . . . shall we begin?

PUPIL: Yes, indeed, Professor, I am at your disposal.

PROFESSOR: At my disposal? [*A gleam comes into his eyes and is quickly extinguished; he begins to make a gesture that he suppresses at once.*] Oh, miss, it is I who am at *your* disposal. I am only your humble servant.

PUPIL: Oh, Professor . . .

PROFESSOR: If you will . . . now . . . we . . . we . . . I . . . I will begin by making a brief examination of your knowledge, past and present, so that we may chart our future course . . . Good. How is your perception of plurality?

PUPIL: It's rather vague . . . confused.

PROFESSOR: Good. We shall see.

[*He rubs his hands together. The* MAID *enters, and this appears to irritate the* PROFESSOR. *She goes to the buffet and looks for something, lingering.*]

PROFESSOR: Now, miss, would you like to do a little arithmetic, that is if you want to . . .

PUPIL: Oh, yes, Professor. Certainly, I ask nothing better.

PROFESSOR: It is rather a new science, a modern science, properly speaking, it is more a method than a science . . . And it is also a therapy. [*To the* MAID:] Have you finished, Marie?

MAID: Yes, Professor, I've found the plate. I'm just going . . .

PROFESSOR: Hurry up then. Please go along to the kitchen, if you will.

MAID: Yes, Professor, I'm going. [*She starts to go out.*] Excuse me, Professor, but take care, I urge you to remain calm.

PROFESSOR: You're being ridiculous, Marie. Now, don't worry.

MAID: That's what you always say.

PROFESSOR: I will not stand for your insinuations. I know perfectly well how to comport myself. I am old enough for that.

MAID: Precisely, Professor. You will do better not to start the young lady on arithmetic. Arithmetic is tiring, exhausting.

PROFESSOR: Not at my age. And anyhow, what business is it of yours? This is my concern. And I know what I'm doing. This is not your department.

MAID: Very well, Professor. But you can't say that I didn't warn you.

PROFESSOR: Marie, I can get along without your advice.

MAID: As you wish, Professor. [*She exits.*]

PROFESSOR: Miss, I hope you'll pardon this absurd interruption . . . Excuse this woman . . . She is always afraid that I'll tire myself. She fusses over my health.

PUPIL: Oh, that's quite all right, Professor. It shows that she's very devoted. She loves you very much. Good servants are rare.

PROFESSOR: She exaggerates. Her fears are stupid. But let's return to our arithmetical knitting.

PUPIL: I'm following you, Professor.

PROFESSOR   [*wittily*]: Without leaving your seat!

PUPIL   [*appreciating his joke*]: Like you, Professor.

PROFESSOR: Good. Let us arithmetize a little now.

PUPIL: Yes, gladly, Professor.

PROFESSOR: It wouldn't be too tiresome for you to tell me . . .

PUPIL: Not at all, Professor, go on.

PROFESSOR: How much are one and one?

PUPIL: One and one make two.

PROFESSOR   [*marveling at the* PUPIL's *knowledge*]: Oh, but that's very good.

You appear to me to be well along in your studies. You should easily achieve the total doctorate, miss.

PUPIL: I'm so glad. Especially to have someone like you tell me this.

PROFESSOR: Let's push on: how much are two and one?

PUPIL: Three.

PROFESSOR: Three and one?

PUPIL: Four.

PROFESSOR: Four and one?

PUPIL: Five.

PROFESSOR: Five and one?

PUPIL: Six.

PROFESSOR: Six and one?

PUPIL: Seven.

PROFESSOR: Seven and one?

PUPIL: Eight.

PROFESSOR: Seven and one?

PUPIL: Eight again.

PROFESSOR: Very well answered. Seven and one?

PUPIL: Eight once more.

PROFESSOR: Perfect. Excellent. Seven and one?

PUPIL: Eight again. And sometimes nine.

PROFESSOR: Magnificent. You are magnificent. You are exquisite. I congratulate you warmly, miss. There's scarcely any point in going on. At addition you are a past master. Now, let's look at subtraction. Tell me, if you are not exhausted, how many are four minus three?

PUPIL: Four minus three? . . . Four minus three?

PROFESSOR: Yes. I mean to say: subtract three from four.

PUPIL: That makes . . . seven?

PROFESSOR: I am sorry but I'm obliged to contradict you. Four minus three does not make seven. You are confused: four plus three makes seven, four minus three does not make seven . . . This is not addition anymore, we must subtract now.

PUPIL   [*trying to understand*]: Yes . . . yes . . .

PROFESSOR: Four minus three makes . . . How many? . . . How many?

PUPIL: Four?

PROFESSOR: No, miss, that's not it.

PUPIL: Three, then.

PROFESSOR: Not that either, miss . . . Pardon, I'm sorry . . . I ought to say, that's not it . . . excuse me.

PUPIL: Four minus three . . . Four minus three . . . Four minus three? . . . But now doesn't that make ten?

PROFESSOR: Oh, certainly not, miss. It's not a matter of guessing, you've got to think it out. Let's try to deduce it together. Would you like to count?

PUPIL: Yes, Professor. One . . . two . . . uh . . .

PROFESSOR: You know how to count? How far can you count up to?

PUPIL: I can count to . . . to infinity.

PROFESSOR: That's not possible, miss.

PUPIL: Well then, let's say to sixteen.

PROFESSOR: That is enough. One must know one's limits. Count then, if you will, please.

PUPIL: One . . . two . . . and after two, comes three . . . then four . . .

PROFESSOR: Stop there, miss. Which number is larger? Three or four?

PUPIL: Uh . . . three or four? Which is the larger? The larger of three or four? In what sense larger?

PROFESSOR: Some numbers are smaller and others are larger. In the larger numbers there are more units than in the small . . .

PUPIL: Than in the small numbers?

PROFESSOR: Unless the small ones have smaller units. If they are very small, then there might be more units in the small numbers than in the large . . . if it is a question of other units . . .

PUPIL: In that case, the small numbers can be larger than the large numbers?

PROFESSOR: Let's not go into that. That would take us much too far. You must realize simply that more than numbers are involved here . . . there are also magnitudes, totals, there are groups, there are heaps, heaps of such things as plums, trucks, geese, prune pits, etc. To facilitate our work, let's merely suppose that we have only equal numbers, then the bigger numbers will be those that have the most units.

PUPIL: The one that has the most is the biggest? Ah, I understand, Professor, you are identifying quality with quantity.

PROFESSOR: That is too theoretical, miss, too theoretical. You needn't concern yourself with that. Let us take an example and reason from a definite case. Let's leave the general conclusions for later. We have the number four and the number three, and each has always the same number of units. Which number will be larger, the smaller or the larger?

PUPIL: Excuse me, Professor . . . What do you mean by the larger number? Is it the one that is not so small as the other?

PROFESSOR: That's it, miss, perfect. You have understood me very well.

PUPIL: Then, it is four.

PROFESSOR: What is four—larger or smaller than three?

PUPIL: Smaller . . . no, larger.

PROFESSOR: Excellent answer. How many units are there between three and four? . . . Or between four and three, if you prefer?

PUPIL: There aren't any units, Professor, between three and four. Four comes immediately after three; there is nothing at all between three and four!

PROFESSOR: I haven't made myself very well understood. No doubt, it is my fault. I've not been sufficiently clear.

PUPIL: No, Professor, it's my fault.

PROFESSOR: Look here. Here are three matches. And here is another one, that makes four. Now watch carefully—we have four matches. I take one away, now how many are left?

[*We don't see the matches, nor any of the objects that are mentioned. The* PROFESSOR *gets up from the table, writes on the imaginary blackboard with an imaginary piece of chalk, etc.*]

PUPIL: Five. If three and one make four, four and one make five.

PROFESSOR: That's not it. That's not it at all. You always have a tendency to add. But one must be able to subtract too. It's not enough to integrate, you must also disintegrate. That's the way life is. That's philosophy. That's science. That's progress, civilization.

PUPIL: Yes, Professor.

PROFESSOR: Let's return to our matches. I have four of them. You see, there are really four. I take one away, and there remain only . . .

PUPIL: I don't know, Professor.

PROFESSOR: Come now, think. It's not easy, I admit. Nevertheless, you've had enough training to make the intellectual effort required to arrive at an understanding. So?

PUPIL: I can't get it, Professor. I don't know, Professor.

PROFESSOR: Let us take a simpler example. If you had two noses, and I pulled one of them off . . . how many would you have left?

PUPIL: None.

PROFESSOR: What do you mean, none?

PUPIL: Yes, it's because you haven't pulled off any, that's why I have one now. If you had pulled it off, I wouldn't have it anymore.

PROFESSOR: You've not understood my example. Suppose that you have only one ear.

PUPIL: Yes, and then?

PROFESSOR: If I gave you another one, how many would you have then?

PUPIL: Two.

PROFESSOR: Good. And if I gave you still another ear. How many would you have then?

PUPIL: Three ears.

PROFESSOR: Now, I take one away . . . and there remain . . . how many ears?

PUPIL: Two.

PROFESSOR: Good. I take away still another one, how many do you have left?

PUPIL: Two.

PROFESSOR: No. You have two, I take one away, I eat one up, then how many do you have left?

PUPIL: Two.

PROFESSOR: I eat one of them . . . one.

PUPIL: Two.

PROFESSOR: One.

PUPIL: Two.

PROFESSOR: One!

PUPIL: Two!

PROFESSOR: One!!!

PUPIL: Two!!!

PROFESSOR: One!!!

PUPIL: Two!!!

PROFESSOR: One!!!

PUPIL: Two!!!

PROFESSOR: No. No. That's not right. The example is not . . . it's not convincing. Listen to me.

PUPIL: Yes, Professor.

PROFESSOR: You've got . . . you've got . . . you've got . . .

PUPIL: Ten fingers!

PROFESSOR: If you wish. Perfect. Good. You have then ten fingers.

PUPIL: Yes, Professor.

PROFESSOR: How many would you have if you had only five of them?

PUPIL: Ten, Professor.

PROFESSOR: That's not right!

PUPIL: But it is, Professor.

PROFESSOR: I tell you it's not!

PUPIL: You just told me that I had ten . . .

PROFESSOR: I also said, immediately afterwards, that you had five!

PUPIL: I don't have five, I've got ten!

PROFESSOR: Let's try another approach . . . for purposes of subtraction let's limit ourselves to the numbers from one to five . . . Wait now, miss, you'll soon see. I'm going to make you understand.

[*The* PROFESSOR *begins to write on the imaginary blackboard. He moves it closer to the* PUPIL, *who turns around in order to see it.*]

PROFESSOR: Look here, miss . . . [*He pretends to draw a stick on the blackboard and the number 1 below the stick; then two sticks and the number 2 below, then three sticks and the number 3 below, then four sticks with the number 4 below.*] You see . . .

PUPIL: Yes, Professor.

PROFESSOR: These are sticks, miss, sticks. This is one stick, these are two sticks, and three sticks, then four sticks, then five sticks. One stick, two sticks, three sticks, four and five sticks, these are numbers. When we count the sticks, each stick is a unit, miss . . . What have I just said?

PUPIL: "A unit, miss! What have I just said?"

PROFESSOR: Or a figure! Or a number! One, two, three, four, five, these are the elements of numeration, miss.

PUPIL [*hesitant*]: Yes, Professor. The elements, figures, which are sticks, units and numbers . . .

PROFESSOR: At the same time . . . that's to say, in short—the whole of arithmetic is there.

PUPIL: Yes, Professor. Good, Professor. Thanks, Professor.

PROFESSOR: Now, count, if you will please, using these elements . . . add and subtract . . .

PUPIL [*as though trying to impress them on her memory*]: Sticks are really figures and numbers are units?

PROFESSOR: Hmm . . . so to speak. And then?

PUPIL: One could subtract two units from three units, but can one subtract two twos from three threes? And two figures from four numbers? And three numbers from one unit?

PROFESSOR: No, miss.

PUPIL: Why, Professor?

PROFESSOR: Because, miss.

PUPIL: Because why, Professor? Since one is the same as the other?

PROFESSOR: That's the way it is, miss. It can't be explained. This is only comprehensible through internal mathematical reasoning. Either you have it or you don't.

PUPIL: So much the worse for me.

PROFESSOR: Listen to me, miss, if you don't achieve a profound understanding of these principles, these arithmetical archetypes, you will never be able to perform correctly the functions of a polytechnician. Still less will you be able to teach a course in a polytechnical school . . . or the primary grades. I realize that this is not easy, it is very, very abstract . . . obviously . . . but unless you can comprehend the primary elements, how do you expect to be able to calculate mentally—and this is the least of the things that even an ordinary engineer must be able to do—how much, for example, are three billion seven hundred fifty-five million nine hundred ninety-eight thousand two hundred fifty-one, multiplied by five billion one hundred sixty-two million three hundred and three thousand five hundred and eight?

PUPIL [*very quickly*]: That makes nineteen quintillion three hundred ninety quadrillion two trillion eight hundred forty-four billion two hundred nineteen million one hundred sixty-four thousand five hundred and eight . . .

PROFESSOR [*astonished*]: No. I don't think so. That must make nineteen quintillion three hundred ninety quadrillion two trillion eight hundred forty-four billion two hundred nineteen million one hundred sixty-four thousand five hundred and nine . . .

PUPIL: . . . No . . . five hundred and eight . . .

PROFESSOR [*more and more astonished, calculating mentally*]: Yes . . . you are right . . . the result is indeed . . . [*He mumbles unintelligibly:*] . . . quintillion, quadrillion, trillion, billion, million . . . [*Clearly:*] one hundred sixty-four thousand five hundred and eight . . . [*Stupefied:*] But how did you know that, if you don't know the principles of arithmetical reasoning?

PUPIL: It's easy. Not being able to rely on my reasoning, I've memorized all the products of all possible multiplications.

PROFESSOR: That's pretty good . . . However, permit me to confess to you that that doesn't satisfy me, miss, and I do not congratulate you: in mathematics and in arithmetic especially, the thing that counts—for in arithmetic it is always necessary to count—the thing that counts is, above all, understanding . . . It is by mathematical reasoning, simultaneously inductive and deductive, that you ought to arrive at this result—as well as at any other result. Mathematics is the sworn enemy of memory, which is excellent otherwise, but disastrous, arithmetically speaking! . . . That's why I'm not happy with this . . . this won't do, not at all . . .

PUPIL [*desolated*]: No, Professor.

PROFESSOR: Let's leave it for the moment. Let's go on to another exercise . . .

PUPIL: Yes, Professor.

MAID   [*entering*]: Hmm, hmm, Professor . . .

PROFESSOR   [*who doesn't hear her*]: It is unfortunate, miss, that you aren't further along in specialized mathematics . . .

MAID   [*taking him by the sleeve*]: Professor! Professor!

PROFESSOR: I hear that you will not be able to qualify for the total doctor's orals . . .

PUPIL: Yes, Professor, it's too bad!

PROFESSOR: Unless you . . . [*To the* MAID:] Let me be, Marie . . . Look here, why are you bothering me? Go back to the kitchen! To your pots and pans! Go away! Go away! [*To the* PUPIL:] We will try to prepare you at least for the partial doctorate . . .

MAID: Professor! . . . Professor! . . . [*She pulls his sleeve.*]

PROFESSOR   [*to the* MAID]: Now leave me alone! Let me be! What's the meaning of this? . . . [*To the* PUPIL:] I must therefore teach you, if you really do insist on attempting the partial doctorate . . .

PUPIL: Yes, Professor.

PROFESSOR: . . . The elements of linguistics and of comparative philology . . .

MAID: No, Professor, no! . . . You mustn't do that! . . .

PROFESSOR: Marie, you're going too far!

MAID: Professor, especially not philology, philology leads to calamity . . .

PUPIL   [*astonished*]: To calamity? [*Smiling, a little stupidly:*] That's hard to believe.

PROFESSOR   [*to the* MAID]: That's enough now! Get out of here!

MAID: All right, Professor, all right. But you can't say that I didn't warn you! Philology leads to calamity!

PROFESSOR: I'm an adult, Marie!

PUPIL: Yes, Professor.

MAID: As you wish.

[*She exits.*]

PROFESSOR: Let's continue, miss.

PUPIL: Yes, Professor.

PROFESSOR: I want you to listen now with the greatest possible attention to a lecture I have prepared . . .

PUPIL: Yes, Professor!

PROFESSOR: . . . Thanks to which, in fifteen minutes' time, you will be able to acquire the fundamental principles of the linguistic and comparative philology of the neo-Spanish languages.

PUPIL: Yes, Professor, oh good!

[*She claps her hands.*]

PROFESSOR   [*with authority*]: Quiet! What do you mean by that?

PUPIL: I'm sorry, Professor.

[*Slowly, she replaces her hands on the table.*]

PROFESSOR: Quiet! [*He gets up, walks up and down the room, his hands behind his back; from time to time he stops at stage center or near the* PUPIL, *and underlines his words with a gesture of his hand; he orates, but without being too emotional. The* PUPIL *follows him with her eyes, occasionally with some difficulty, for she has to turn her head far around; once or twice, not more, she turns around completely.*] And now, miss, Spanish is truly the mother tongue which gave birth to all the neo-Spanish languages, of which Spanish, Latin, Italian, our own French, Portuguese, Romanian, Sardinian or Sardanapalian, Spanish and neo-Spanish—and also, in certain of its aspects, Turkish which is otherwise very close to Greek, which is only logical, since it is a fact that Turkey is a neighbor of Greece and Greece is even closer to Turkey than you are to me—this is only one more illustration of the very important linguistic law which states that geography and philology are twin sisters . . . You may take notes, miss.

PUPIL   [*in a dull voice*]: Yes, Professor!

PROFESSOR: That which distinguishes the neo-Spanish languages from each other and their idioms from the other linguistic groups, such as the group of languages called Austrian and neo-Austrian or Hapsburgian, as well as the Esperanto, Helvetian, Monacan, Swiss, Andorran, Basque, and jai alai groups, and also the groups of diplomatic and technical languages—that which distinguishes them, I repeat, is their striking resemblance which makes it so hard to distinguish them from each other—I'm speaking of the neo-Spanish languages which one is able to distinguish from each other, however, only thanks to their distinctive characteristics, absolutely indisputable proofs of their extraordinary resemblance, which renders indisputable their common origin, and which, at the same time, differentiates them profoundly—through the continuation of the distinctive traits which I've just cited.

PUPIL: Ooooh! Ye-e-e-s-s-s, Professor!

PROFESSOR: But let's not linger over generalities . . .

PUPIL   [*regretfully, but won over*]: Oh, Professor . . .

PROFESSOR: This appears to interest you. All the better, all the better.

PUPIL: Oh, yes, Professor . . .

PROFESSOR: Don't worry, miss. We will come back to it later . . . That is if we come back to it at all. Who can say?

PUPIL   [*enchanted in spite of everything*]: Oh, yes, Professor.

PROFESSOR: Every tongue—you must know this, miss, and remember it *until the hour of your death* . . .

PUPIL: Oh! yes, Professor, until the hour of my death . . . Yes, Professor . . .

PROFESSOR: . . . And this, too, is a fundamental principle, every tongue is at bottom nothing but language, which necessarily implies that it is composed of sounds, or . . .

PUPIL: Phonemes . . .

PROFESSOR: Just what I was going to say. Don't parade your knowledge. You'd do better to listen.

PUPIL: All right, Professor. Yes, Professor.

PROFESSOR: The sounds, miss, must be seized on the wing as they fly so that they'll not fall on deaf ears. As a result, when you set out to articulate, it is recommended, insofar as possible, that you lift up your neck and chin very high, and rise up on the tips of your toes, you see, this way . . .

PUPIL: Yes, Professor.

PROFESSOR: Keep quiet. Remain seated, don't interrupt me . . . And project
the sounds very loudly with all the force of your lungs in conjunction with that
of your vocal cords. Like this, look: "Butterfly," "Eureka," "Trafalgar," "Pa-
paya." This way, the sounds become filled with a warm air that is lighter than
the surrounding air so that they can fly without danger of falling on deaf ears,
which are veritable voids, tombs of sonorities. If you utter several sounds at an
accelerated speed, they will automatically cling to each other, constituting thus
syllables, words, even sentences, that is to say groupings of various importance,
purely irrational assemblages of sounds, denuded of all sense, but for that very
reason the more capable of maintaining themselves without danger at a high
altitude in the air. By themselves, words charged with significance will fall,
weighted down by their meaning, and in the end they always collapse,
fall . . .

PUPIL: . . . On deaf ears.

PROFESSOR: That's it, but don't interrupt . . . and into the worst confusion
. . . Or else burst like balloons. Therefore, miss . . . [*The* PUPIL *suddenly appears
to be unwell.*] What's the matter?

PUPIL: I've got a toothache, Professor.

PROFESSOR: That's not important. We're not going to stop for anything so
trivial. Let us go on . . .

PUPIL [*appearing to be in more and more pain*]: Yes, Professor.

PROFESSOR: I draw your attention in passing to the consonants that change
their nature in combinations. In this case *f* becomes *v, d* becomes *t, g* becomes
k, and vice versa, as in these examples that I will cite for you: "That's all right,"
"hens and chickens," "Welsh rabbit," "lots of nothing," "not at all."*

PUPIL: I've got a toothache.

PROFESSOR: Let's continue.

PUPIL: Yes.

PROFESSOR: To resume: it takes years and years to learn to pronounce.
Thanks to science, we can achieve this in a few minutes. In order to project
words, sounds and all the rest, you must realize that it is necessary to pitilessly
expel air from the lungs, and make it pass delicately, caressingly, over the vocal
cords, which, like harps or leaves in the wind, will suddenly shake, agitate,
vibrate, vibrate, vibrate or uvulate, or fricate or jostle against each other, or
sibilate, sibilate, placing everything in movement, the uvula, the tongue, the
palate, the teeth . . .

PUPIL: I have a toothache.

PROFESSOR: . . . And the lips . . . Finally the words come out through the
nose, the mouth, the ears, the pores, drawing along with them all the organs
that we have named, torn up by the roots, in a powerful, majestic flight, which
is none other than what is called, improperly, the voice, whether modulated in
singing or transformed into a terrible symphonic storm with a whole procession
. . . of garlands of all kinds of flowers, of sonorous artifices: labials, dentals,
occlusives, palatals, and others, some caressing, some bitter or violent.

PUPIL: Yes, Professor, I've got a toothache.

PROFESSOR: Let's go on, go on. As for the neo-Spanish languages, they are

*All to be heavily elided.—Translator's note.

closely related, so closely to each other, that they can be considered as true second cousins. Moreover, they have the same mother: Spanishe, with a mute *e*. That is why it is so difficult to distinguish them from one another. That is why it is so useful to pronounce carefully, and to avoid errors in pronunciation. Pronunciation itself is worth a whole language. A bad pronunciation can get you into trouble. In this connection, permit me, parenthetically, to share a personal experience with you. [*Slight pause. The* PROFESSOR *goes over his memories for a moment; his features mellow, but he recovers at once.*] I was very young, little more than a child. It was during my military service. I had a friend in the regiment, a vicomte, who suffered from a rather serious defect in his pronunciation: he could not pronounce the letter *f*. Instead of *f*, he said *f*. Thus, instead of "Birds of a feather flock together," he said: "Birds of a feather flock together." He pronounced filly instead of filly, Firmin instead of Firmin, French bean instead of French bean, go frig yourself instead of go frig yourself, farrago instead of farrago, fee fi fo fum instead of fee fi fo fum, Philip instead of Philip, fictory instead of fictory, February instead of February, March-April instead of March-April, Gerard de Nerval and not as is correct—Gerard de Nerval, Mirabeau instead of Mirabeau, etc., instead of etc., and thus instead of etc., instead of etc., and thus and so forth. However, he managed to conceal his fault so effectively that, thanks to the hats he wore, no one ever noticed it.

PUPIL: Yes, I've got a toothache.

PROFESSOR   [*abruptly changing his tone, his voice hardening*]: Let's go on. We'll first consider the points of similarity in order the better to apprehend, later on, that which distinguishes all these languages from each other. The differences can scarcely be recognized by people who are not aware of them. Thus, all the words of all the languages . . .

PUPIL: Uh, yes? . . . I've got a toothache.

PROFESSOR: Let's continue . . . are always the same, just as all the suffixes, all the prefixes, all the terminations, all the roots . . .

PUPIL: Are the roots of words square?

PROFESSOR: Square or cube. That depends.

PUPIL: I've got a toothache.

PROFESSOR: Let's go on. Thus, to give you an example which is little more than an illustration, take the word "front" . . .

PUPIL: How do you want me to take it?

PROFESSOR: However you wish, so long as you take it, but above all do not interrupt.

PUPIL: I've got a toothache.

PROFESSOR: Let's continue . . . I said: Let's continue. Take now the word "front." Have you taken it?

PUPIL: Yes, yes, I've got it. My teeth, my teeth . . .

PROFESSOR: The word "front" is the root of "frontispiece." It is also to be found in "affronted." "Ispiece" is the suffix, and "af" the prefix. They are so called because they do not change. They don't want to.

PUPIL: I've got a toothache.

PROFESSOR: Let's go on. [*Rapidly:*] These prefixes are of Spanish origin. I hope you noticed that, did you?

PUPIL: Oh, how my tooth aches.

PROFESSOR: Let's continue. You've surely also noticed that they've not changed in French. And now, young lady, nothing has succeeded in changing them in Latin either, nor in Italian, nor in Portuguese, nor in Sardanapalian, nor in Sardanapali, nor in Romanian, nor in neo-Spanish, nor in Spanish, nor even in the Oriental: front, frontispiece, affronted, always the same word, invariably with the same root, the same suffix, the same prefix, in all the languages I have named. And it is always the same for all words.

PUPIL: In all languages, these words mean the same thing? I've got a toothache.

PROFESSOR: Absolutely. Moreover, it's more a notion than a word. In any case, you have always the same signification, the same composition, the same sound structure, not only for this word, but for all conceivable words, in all languages. For one single notion is expressed by one and the same word, and its synonyms, in all countries. Forget about your teeth.

PUPIL: I've got a toothache. Yes, yes, yes.

PROFESSOR: Good, let's go on. I tell you, let's go on . . . How would you say, for example, in French: the roses of my grandmother are as yellow as my grandfather who was Asiatic?

PUPIL: My teeth ache, ache, ache.

PROFESSOR: Let's go on, let's go on, go ahead and answer, anyway.

PUPIL: In French?

PROFESSOR: In French.

PUPIL: Uhh . . . I should say in French: the roses of my grandmother are . . . ?

PROFESSOR: As yellow as my grandfather who was Asiatic . . .

PUPIL: Oh well, one would say, in French, I believe, the roses . . . of my . . . how do you say "grandmother" in French?

PROFESSOR: In French? Grandmother.

PUPIL: The roses of my grandmother are as yellow—in French, is it "yellow"?

PROFESSOR: Yes, of course!

PUPIL: Are as yellow as my grandfather when he got angry.

PROFESSOR: No . . . who was A . . .

PUPIL: . . . siatic . . . I've got a toothache.

PROFESSOR: That's it.

PUPIL: I've got a tooth . . .

PROFESSOR: Ache . . . so what . . . let's continue! And now translate the same sentence into Spanish, then into neo-Spanish . . .

PUPIL: In Spanish . . . this would be: the roses of my grandmother are as yellow as my grandfather who was Asiatic.

PROFESSOR: No. That's wrong.

PUPIL: And in neo-Spanish: the roses of my grandmother are as yellow as my grandfather who was Asiatic.

PROFESSOR: That's wrong. That's wrong. That's wrong. You have inverted it, you've confused Spanish with neo-Spanish, and neo-Spanish with Spanish . . . Oh . . . no . . . it's the other way around . . .

PUPIL: I've got a toothache. You're getting mixed up.

PROFESSOR: You're the one who is mixing me up. Pay attention and take notes. I will say the sentence to you in Spanish, then in neo-Spanish, and finally, in Latin. You will repeat after me. Pay attention, for the resemblances are great. In fact, they are identical resemblances. Listen, follow carefully . . .

PUPIL: I've got a tooth . . .

PROFESSOR: . . . Ache.

PUPIL: Let us go on . . . Ah! . . .

PROFESSOR: . . . In Spanish: the roses of my grandmother are as yellow as my grandfather who was Asiatic; in Latin: the roses of my grandmother are as yellow as my grandfather who was Asiatic. Do you detect the differences? Translate this into . . . Romanian.

PUPIL: The . . . how do you say "roses" in Romanian?

PROFESSOR: But "roses," what else?

PUPIL: It's not "roses"? Oh, how my tooth aches!

PROFESSOR: Certainly not, certainly not, since "roses" is a translation in Oriental of the French word "roses," in Spanish "roses," do you get it? In Sardanapali, "roses" . . .

PUPIL: Excuse me, Professor, but . . . Oh, my toothache! . . . I don't get the difference.

PROFESSOR: But it's so simple! So simple! It's a matter of having a certain experience, a technical experience and practice in these diverse languages, which are so diverse in spite of the fact that they present wholly identical characteristics. I'm going to try to give you a key . . .

PUPIL: Toothache . . .

PROFESSOR: That which differentiates these languages, is neither the words, which are absolutely the same, nor the structure of the sentence which is everywhere the same, nor the intonation, which does not offer any differences, nor the rhythm of the language . . . that which differentiates them . . . are you listening?

PUPIL: I've got a toothache.

PROFESSOR: Are you listening to me, young lady? Aah! We're going to lose our temper.

PUPIL: You're bothering me, Professor. I've got a toothache.

PROFESSOR: Son of a cocker spaniel! Listen to me!

PUPIL: Oh well . . . yes . . . yes . . . go on . . .

PROFESSOR: That which distinguishes them from each other, on the one hand, and from their mother, Spanishe with its mute *e,* on the other hand . . . is . . .

PUPIL   [*grimacing*]: Is what?

PROFESSOR: Is an intangible thing. Something intangible that one is able to perceive only after very long study, with a great deal of trouble and after the broadest experience . . .

PUPIL: Ah?

PROFESSOR: Yes, young lady. I cannot give you any rule. One must have a feeling for it, and well, that's it. But in order to have it, one must study, study, and then study some more.

PUPIL: Toothache.

PROFESSOR: All the same, there are some specific cases where words differ from one language to another . . . but we cannot base our knowledge on these cases, which are, so to speak, exceptional.

PUPIL: Oh, yes? . . . Oh, Professor, I've got a toothache.

PROFESSOR: Don't interrupt! Don't make me lose my temper! I can't answer for what I'll do. I was saying, then . . . Ah, yes, the exceptional cases, the so-called easily distinguished . . . or facilely distinguished . . . or conveniently . . . if you prefer . . . I repeat, if you prefer, for I see that you're not listening to me . . .

PUPIL: I've got a toothache.

PROFESSOR: I say then: in certain expressions in current usage, certain words differ totally from one language to another, so much so that the language employed is, in this case, considerably easier to identify. I'll give you an example: the neo-Spanish expression, famous in Madrid: "My country is the new Spain," becomes in Italian: "My country is . . .

PUPIL: The new Spain.

PROFESSOR: No! "My country is Italy." Tell me now, by simple deduction, how do you say "Italy" in French?

PUPIL: I've got a toothache.

PROFESSOR: But it's so easy: for the word "Italy," in French we have the word "France," which is an exact translation of it. My country is France. And "France" in Oriental: "Orient!" My country is the Orient. And "Orient" in Portuguese: "Portugal!" The Oriental expression: My country is the Orient is translated then in the same fashion into Portuguese: My country is Portugal! And so on . . .

PUPIL: Oh, no more, no more. My teeth . . .

PROFESSOR: Ache! ache! ache! . . . I'm going to pull them out, I will! One more example. The word "capital"—it takes on, according to the language one speaks, a different meaning. That is to say that when a Spaniard says: "I reside in the capital," the word "capital" does not mean at all the same thing that a Portuguese means when he says: "I reside in the capital." All the more so in the case of a Frenchman, a neo-Spaniard, a Romanian, a Latin, a Sardanapali . . . Whenever you hear it, young lady—young lady, I'm saying this for you! Pooh! Whenever you hear the expression: "I reside in the capital," you will immediately and easily know whether this is Spanish or Spanish, neo-Spanish, French, Oriental, Romanian, or Latin, for it is enough to know which metropolis is referred to by the person who pronounces the sentence . . . at the very moment he pronounces it . . . But these are almost the only precise examples that I can give you . . .

PUPIL: Oh dear! My teeth . . .

PROFESSOR: Silence! Or I'll bash in your skull!

PUPIL: Just try to! Skulldugger!

[*The* PROFESSOR *seizes her wrist and twists it.*]

PUPIL: Oww!

PROFESSOR: Keep quiet now! Not a word!

PUPIL [*whimpering*]: Toothache . . .

PROFESSOR: One thing that is the most . . . how shall I say it? . . . the most paradoxical . . . yes . . . that's the word . . . the most paradoxical thing, is that a lot of people who are completely illiterate speak these different languages . . . do you understand? What did I just say?

PUPIL: . . . "Speak these different languages! What did I just say?"

PROFESSOR: You were lucky that time! . . . The common people speak a Spanish full of neo-Spanish words that they are entirely unaware of, all the while believing that they are speaking Latin . . . or they speak Latin, full of Oriental words, all the while believing that they're speaking Romanian . . . or Spanish, full of neo-Spanish, all the while believing that they're speaking Sardanapali, or Spanish . . . Do you understand?

PUPIL: Yes! yes! yes! yes! What more do you want . . . ?

PROFESSOR: No insolence, my pet, or you'll be sorry . . . [*In a rage:*] But the worst of all, young lady, is that certain people, for example, in a Latin that they suppose is Spanish, say: "Both my kidneys are of the same kidney," in addressing themselves to a Frenchman who does not know a word of Spanish, but the latter understands it as if it were his own language. For that matter he thinks it is his own language. And the Frenchman will reply, in French: "Me too, sir, mine are too," and this will be perfectly comprehensible to a Spaniard, who will feel certain that the reply is in pure Spanish and that Spanish is being spoken . . . when, in reality, it was neither Spanish nor French, but Latin in the neo-Spanish dialect . . . Sit still, young lady, don't fidget, stop tapping your feet . . .

PUPIL: I've got a toothache.

PROFESSOR: How do you account for the fact that, in speaking without knowing which language they speak, or even while each of them believes that he is speaking another, the common people understand each other at all?

PUPIL: I wonder.

PROFESSOR: It is simply one of the inexplicable curiosities of the vulgar empiricism of the common people—not to be confused with experience!—a paradox, a non-sense, one of the aberrations of human nature, it is purely and simply instinct—to put it in a nutshell . . . That's what is involved here.

PUPIL: Hah! hah!

PROFESSOR: Instead of staring at the flies while I'm going to all this trouble . . . you would do much better to try to be more attentive . . . it is not I who is going to qualify for the partial doctor's orals . . . I passed mine a long time ago . . . and I've won my total doctorate, too . . . and my supertotal diploma . . . Don't you realize that what I'm saying is for your own good?

PUPIL: Toothache!

PROFESSOR: Ill-mannered . . . It can't go on like this, it won't do, it won't do, it won't do . . .

PUPIL: I'm . . . listening . . . to you . . .

PROFESSOR: Ahah! In order to learn to distinguish all the different languages, as I've told you, there is nothing better than practice . . . Let's take them up in order. I am going to try to teach you all the translations of the word "knife."

PUPIL: Well, all right . . . if you want . . .

PROFESSOR [*calling the* MAID]: Marie! Marie! She's not there . . . Marie!

Marie! . . . Marie, where are you? [*He opens the door on the right.*]
Marie! . . .

[*He exits. The* PUPIL *remains alone several minutes, staring into space, wearing a stupefied expression.*]

PROFESSOR [*offstage, in a shrill voice*]: Marie! What are you up to? Why
don't you come! When I call you, you must come! [*He re-enters, followed by
Marie.*] It is I who gives the orders, do you hear? [*He points at the* PUPIL:] She
doesn't understand anything, that girl. She doesn't understand!

MAID: Don't get into such a state, sir, you know where it'll end! You're
going to go too far, you're going to go too far.

PROFESSOR: I'll be able to stop in time.

MAID: That's what you always say. I only wish I could see it.

PUPIL: I've got a toothache.

MAID: You see, it's starting, that's the symptom!

PROFESSOR: What symptom? Explain yourself? What do you mean?

PUPIL [*in a spiritless voice*]: Yes, what do you mean? I've got a toothache.

MAID: The final symptom! The chief symptom!

PROFESSOR: Stupid! stupid! stupid! [*The* MAID *starts to exit.*] Don't go away
like that! I called you to help me find the Spanish, neo-Spanish, Portuguese,
French, Oriental, Romanian, Sardanapali, Latin and Spanish knives.

MAID [*severely*]: Don't ask me. [*She exits.*]

PROFESSOR [*makes a gesture as though to protest, then refrains, a little helpless.
Suddenly, he remembers*]: Ah! [*He goes quickly to the drawer where he finds a big
knife, invisible or real according to the preference of the director. He seizes it and
brandishes it happily.*] Here is one, young lady, here is a knife. It's too bad that
we only have this one, but we're going to try to make it serve for all the
languages, anyway! It will be enough if you will pronounce the word "knife"
in all the languages, while looking at the object, very closely, fixedly, and
imagining that it is in the language that you are speaking.

PUPIL: I've got a toothache.

PROFESSOR [*almost singing, chanting*]: Now, say "kni," like "kni," "fe," like
"fe" . . . And look, look, look at it, watch it . . .

PUPIL: What is this one in? French, Italian or Spanish?

PROFESSOR: That doesn't matter now . . . That's not your concern. Say:
"kni."

PUPIL: "Kni."

PROFESSOR: . . . "fe" . . . Look.

[*He brandishes the knife under the* PUPIL'S *eyes.*]

PUPIL: "fe" . . .

PROFESSOR: Again . . . Look at it.

PUPIL: Oh, no! My God! I've had enough. And besides, I've got a toothache,
my feet hurt me, I've got a headache.

PROFESSOR [*abruptly*]: Knife . . . look . . . knife . . . look . . . knife . . .
look . . .

PUPIL: You're giving me an earache, too. Oh, your voice! It's so piercing!

PROFESSOR: Say: knife . . . kni . . . fe . . .

PUPIL: No! My ears hurt, I hurt all over . . .

PROFESSOR: I'm going to tear them off, your ears, that's what I'm going to do to you, and then they won't hurt you anymore, my pet.

PUPIL: Oh . . . you're hurting me, oh, you're hurting me . . .

PROFESSOR: Look, come on, quickly, repeat after me: "kni" . . .

PUPIL: Oh, since you insist . . . knife . . . knife . . . [*In a lucid moment, ironically:*] Is that neo-Spanish . . . ?

PROFESSOR: If you like, yes, it's neo-Spanish, but hurry up . . . we haven't got time . . . And then, what do you mean by that insidious question? What are you up to?

PUPIL [*becoming more and more exhausted, weeping, desperate, at the same time both exasperated and in a trance*]: Ah!

PROFESSOR: Repeat, watch. [*He imitates a cuckoo:*] Knife, knife . . . knife, knife . . . knife, knife . . . knife, knife . . .

PUPIL: Oh, my head . . . aches . . . [*With her hand she caressingly touches the parts of her body as she names them:*] . . . My eyes . . .

PROFESSOR [*like a cuckoo*]: Knife, knife . . . knife, knife . . .

[*They are both standing. The* PROFESSOR *still brandishes his invisible knife, nearly beside himself, as he circles around her in a sort of scalp dance, but it is important that this not be exaggerated and that his dance steps be only suggested. The* PUPIL *stands facing the audience, then recoils in the direction of the window, sickly, languid, victimized.*]

PROFESSOR: Repeat, repeat: knife . . . knife . . . knife . . .

PUPIL: I've got a pain . . . my throat, neck . . . oh, my shoulders . . . my breast . . . knife . . .

PROFESSOR: Knife . . . knife . . . knife . . .

PUPIL: My hips . . . knife . . . my thighs . . . kni . . .

PROFESSOR: Pronounce it carefully . . . knife . . . knife . . .

PUPIL: Knife . . . my throat . . .

PROFESSOR: Knife . . . knife . . .

PUPIL: Knife . . . my shoulders . . . my arms, my breast, my hips . . . knife . . . knife . . .

PROFESSOR: That's right . . . Now, you're pronouncing it well . . .

PUPIL: Knife . . . my breast . . . my stomach . . .

PROFESSOR [*changing his voice*]: Pay attention . . . don't break my window . . . the knife kills . . .

PUPIL [*in a weak voice*]: Yes, yes . . . the knife kills?

PROFESSOR [*striking the* PUPIL *with a very spectacular blow of the knife*]: Aaah! That'll teach you!

[PUPIL *also cries "Aah!" then falls, flopping in an immodest position onto a chair which, as though by chance, is near the window. The murderer and his victim shout "Aaah!" at the same moment. After the first blow of the knife, the* PUPIL *flops onto the chair, her legs spread wide and hanging over both sides of the chair. The* PROFESSOR *remains standing in front of her, his back to the audience. After the first blow, he strikes her dead with a second slash of the knife, from bottom to top. After that blow a noticeable convulsion shakes his whole body.*]

PROFESSOR   [*winded, mumbling*]: Bitch . . . Oh, that's good, that does me good
. . . Ah! Ah! I'm exhausted . . . I can scarcely breathe . . . Aah! [*He breathes
with difficulty; he falls—fortunately a chair is there; he mops his brow, mumbles some
incomprehensible words; his breathing becomes normal. He gets up, looks at the knife
in his hand, looks at the young girl, then as though he were waking up, in a panic:*]
What have I done! What's going to happen to me now! What's going to
happen! Oh! dear! Oh dear, I'm in trouble! Young lady, young lady, get up!
[*He is agitated, still holding onto the invisible knife, which he doesn't know what to
do with.*] Come now, young lady, the lesson is over . . . you may go . . . you
can pay another time . . . Oh! she is dead . . . dea-ead . . . And by my knife
. . . She is dea-ead . . . It's terrible. [*He calls the* MAID:] Marie! Marie! My good
Marie, come here! Ah! ah! [*The door on the right opens a little and* MARIE *appears.*]
No . . . don't come in . . . I made a mistake . . . I don't need you, Marie
. . . I don't need you anymore . . . do you understand? . . .

[MAID *enters wearing a stern expression, without saying a word. She sees the corpse.*]

PROFESSOR   [*in a voice less and less assured*]: I don't need you, Marie . . .
MAID   [*sarcastic*]: Then, you're satisfied with your pupil, she's profited by
your lesson?
PROFESSOR   [*holding the knife behind his back*]: Yes, the lesson is finished
. . . but . . . she . . . she's still there . . . she doesn't want to leave . . .
MAID   [*very harshly*]: Is that a fact? . . .
PROFESSOR   [*trembling*]: It wasn't I . . . it wasn't I . . . Marie . . . No
. . . I assure you . . . it wasn't I, my little Marie . . .
MAID: And who was it? Who was it then? Me?
PROFESSOR: I don't know . . . maybe . . .
MAID: Or the cat?
PROFESSOR: That's possible . . . I don't know . . .
MAID: And today makes it the fortieth time! . . . And every day it's the same
thing! Every day! You should be ashamed, at your age . . . and you're going
to make yourself sick! You won't have any pupils left. That will serve you right.
PROFESSOR   [*irritated*]: It wasn't my fault! She didn't want to learn! She was
disobedient! She was a bad pupil! She didn't want to learn!
MAID: Liar! . . .
PROFESSOR   [*craftily approaching the* MAID, *holding the knife behind his back*]:
It's none of your business! [*He tries to strike her with a great blow of the knife; the*
MAID *seizes his wrist in mid-gesture and twists it; the* PROFESSOR *lets the knife fall
to the floor*]: . . . I'm sorry!
MAID   [*gives him two loud, strong slaps; the* PROFESSOR *falls onto the floor, on
his prat; he sobs*]: Little murderer! bastard! You're disgusting! You wanted to
do that to me? I'm not one of your pupils, not me! [*She pulls him up by the collar,
picks up his skullcap and puts it on his head; he's afraid she'll slap him again and holds
his arm up to protect his face, like a child.*] Put the knife back where it belongs,
go on! [*The* PROFESSOR *goes and puts it back in the drawer of the buffet, then comes
back to her.*] Now didn't I warn you, just a little while ago: arithmetic leads to
philology, and philology leads to crime . . .
PROFESSOR: You said "to calamity"!
MAID: It's the same thing.

PROFESSOR: I didn't understand you. I thought that "calamity" was a city and that you meant that philology leads to the city of Calamity . . .

MAID: Liar! Old fox! An intellectual like you is not going to make a mistake in the meanings of words. Don't try to pull the wool over my eyes.

PROFESSOR   [*sobbing*]: I didn't kill her on purpose!

MAID: Are you sorry at least?

PROFESSOR: Oh, yes, Marie, I swear it to you!

MAID: I can't help feeling sorry for you! Ah! you're a good boy in spite of everything! I'll try to fix this. But don't start it again . . . It could give you a heart attack . . .

PROFESSOR: Yes, Marie! What are we going to do, now?

MAID: We're going to bury her . . . along with the thirty-nine others . . . that will make forty coffins . . . I'll call the undertakers and my lover, Father Auguste . . . I'll order the wreaths . . .

PROFESSOR: Yes, Marie, thank you very much.

MAID: Well, that's that. And perhaps it won't be necessary to call Auguste, since you yourself are something of a priest at times, if one can believe the gossip.

PROFESSOR: In any case, don't spend too much on the wreaths. She didn't pay for her lesson.

MAID: Don't worry . . . The least you can do is cover her up with her smock, she's not decent that way. And then we'll carry her out . . .

PROFESSOR: Yes, Marie, yes. [*He covers up the body.*] There's a chance that we'll get pinched . . . with forty coffins . . . Don't you think . . . people will be surprised . . . Suppose they ask us what's inside them?

MAID: Don't worry so much. We'll say that they're empty. And besides, people won't ask questions, they're used to it.

PROFESSOR: Even so . . .

MAID   [*she takes out an armband with an insignia, perhaps the Nazi swastika*]: Wait, if you're afraid, wear this, then you won't have anything more to be afraid of. [*She puts the armband around his arm.*] . . . That's good politics.

PROFESSOR: Thanks, my little Marie. With this, I won't need to worry . . . You're a good girl, Marie . . . very loyal . . .

MAID: That's enough. Come on, sir. Are you all right?

PROFESSOR: Yes, my little Marie. [*The* MAID *and the* PROFESSOR *take the body of the young girl, one by the shoulders, the other by the legs, and move towards the door on the right.*] Be careful. We don't want to hurt her.

[*They exit. The stage remains empty for several moments. We hear the doorbell ring at the left.*]

VOICE OF THE MAID: Just a moment, I'm coming!

[*She appears as she was at the beginning of the play, and goes towards the door. The doorbell rings again.*]

MAID   [*aside*]: She's certainly in a hurry, this one! [*Aloud:*] Just a moment! [*She goes to the door on the left, and opens it.*] Good morning, miss! You are the new pupil? You have come for the lesson? The Professor is expecting you. I'll go tell him that you've come. He'll be right down. Come in, miss, come in!

QUESTIONS

1. Describe your emotional response to the play. Did you find yourself responding with different feelings at different places in the action? How did you respond to the ending?
2. What comic ingredients does the play include? Single out an especially funny segment and account for its comic effects. How would you characterize the nature and purpose of the play's comedy?
3. Consider *The Lesson* as a satire. What does it ridicule? By what means?
4. What is the function of the housekeeper? Would it make any difference if her role were deleted?
5. What lesson(s) does the play teach, either directly or indirectly?
6. How would you cast and direct the play? What advice would you give the performers?

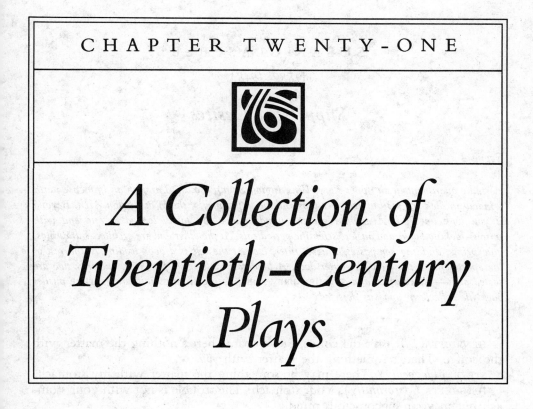

CHAPTER TWENTY-ONE

A Collection of Twentieth-Century Plays

Susan Glaspell

Susan Glaspell, American novelist and playwright, was one of the founders of the Provincetown Players. She collaborated with her husband, George Cram Cook, on a number of plays, including *Suppressed Desires,* which was produced in 1915 and published in 1916. The play, clearly meant as light entertainment, satirizes psychoanalysis, which in the early part of the century was just beginning to achieve notoriety. Like Chekhov's one-act comic sketches (*The Boor* and *A Marriage Proposal* most notably), *Suppressed Desires* offers aspiring actors and actresses a chance to test their comic skills. It affords readers an opportunity to enjoy Glaspell's genial humor and her sharp wit.

SUSAN GLASPELL

[1882–1948]

Suppressed Desires

Scene I

*A studio apartment in an upper story, Washington Square South. Through an immense north window in the back wall appear tree tops and the upper part of the Washington Arch. Beyond it you look up Fifth Avenue. Near the window is a big table, loaded at one end with serious-looking books and austere scientific periodicals. At the other end are architect's drawings, blue prints, dividing compasses, square, ruler, etc. At the left is a door leading to the rest of the apartment; at the right the outer door. A breakfast table is set for three, but only two are seated at it—*HENRIETTA *and* STEPHEN BREWSTER. *As the curtains withdraw* STEVE *pushes back his coffee cup and sits dejected.*

HENRIETTA.   It isn't the coffee, Steve dear. There's nothing the matter with the coffee. There's something the matter with *you.*

STEVE   (*doggedly*). There may be something the matter with my stomach.

HENRIETTA   (*scornfully*). Your stomach! The trouble is not with your stomach but in your subconscious mind.

STEVE.   Subconscious piffle! (*Takes morning paper and tries to read.*)

HENRIETTA.   Steve, you never used to be so disagreeable. You certainly have got some sort of a complex. You're all inhibited. You're no longer open to new ideas. You won't listen to a word about psychoanalysis.

STEVE.   A word! I've listened to volumes!

HENRIETTA.   You've ceased to be creative in architecture—your work isn't going well. You're not sleeping well—

STEVE.   How can I sleep, Henrietta, when you're always waking me up to find out what I'm dreaming?

HENRIETTA.   But dreams are so important, Steve. If you'd tell yours to Dr. Russell he'd find out exactly what's wrong with you.

STEVE.   There's nothing wrong with me.

HENRIETTA.   You don't even talk as well as you used to.

STEVE.   Talk? I can't say a thing without you looking at me in that dark fashion you have when you're on the trail of a complex.

HENRIETTA.   This very irritability indicates that you're suffering from some suppressed desire.

STEVE.   I'm suffering from a suppressed desire for a little peace.

HENRIETTA.   Dr. Russell is doing simply wonderful things with nervous cases. Won't you go to him, Steve?

STEVE   (*slamming down his newspaper*). No, Henrietta, I won't!

HENRIETTA.   But Stephen—!

STEVE.   Tst! I hear Mabel coming. Let's not be at each other's throats the first day of her visit. (*He takes out cigarettes.* MABEL *comes in from door left, the side opposite* STEVE, *so that he is facing her. She is wearing a rather fussy negligee in contrast to* HENRIETTA, *who wears "radical" clothes.* MABEL *is what is called plump.*)

MABEL.   Good morning.

HENRIETTA.   Oh, here you are, little sister.

STEVE.   Good morning, Mabel.

(MABEL *nods to him and turns, her face lighting up, to* HENRIETTA.)

HENRIETTA (*giving* MABEL *a hug as she leans against her*). It's so good to have you here. I was going to let you sleep, thinking you'd be tired after the long trip. Sit down. There'll be fresh toast in a minute and (*rising*) will you have—

MABEL.   Oh, I ought to have told you, Henrietta. Don't get anything for me. I'm not eating breakfast.

HENRIETTA (*at first in mere surprise*). Not eating breakfast? (*She sits down, then leans toward* MABEL *who is seated now, and scrutinizes her.*)

STEVE (*half to himself*). The psychoanalytical look!

HENRIETTA.   Mabel, why are you not eating breakfast?

MABEL (*a little startled*). Why, no particular reason. I just don't care much for breakfast, and they say it keeps down—(*A hand on her hip—the gesture of one who is "reducing"*) that is, it's a good thing to go without it.

HENRIETTA.   Don't you sleep well? Did you sleep well last night?

MABEL.   Oh, yes, I slept all right. Yes, I slept fine last night, only (*laughing*) I did have the funniest dream!

STEVE.   S-h! S-t!

HENRIETTA (*moving closer*). And what did you dream, Mabel?

STEVE.   Look-a-here, Mabel, I feel it's my duty to put you on. Don't tell Henrietta your dreams. If you do she'll find out that you have an underground desire to kill your father and marry your mother—

HENRIETTA.   Don't be absurd, Stephen Brewster. (*Sweetly to* MABEL) What was your dream, dear?

MABEL (*laughing*). Well, I dreamed I was a hen.

HENRIETTA.   A hen?

MABEL.   Yes; and I was pushing along through a crowd as fast as I could, but being a hen I couldn't walk very fast—it was like having a tight skirt, you know; and there was some sort of creature in a blue cap—you know how mixed up dreams are—and it kept shouting after me, "Step, Hen! Step, Hen!" until I got all excited and just couldn't move at all.

HENRIETTA (*resting chin in palm and peering*). You say you became much excited?

MABEL (*laughing*). Oh, yes; I was in a terrible state.

HENRIETTA (*leaning back, murmurs*). This is significant.

STEVE.   She dreams she's a hen. She is told to step lively. She becomes violently agitated. What can it mean?

HENRIETTA (*turning impatiently from him*). Mabel, do you know anything about psychoanalysis?

MABEL   (*feebly*). Oh—not much. No—I— (*Brightening*) It's something about the war, isn't it?

STEVE.   Not that kind of war.

MABEL   (*abashed*). I thought it might be the name of a new explosive.

STEVE.   It *is*.

MABEL   (*apologetically to* HENRIETTA, *who is frowning*). You see, Henrietta, I—we do not live in touch with intellectual things, as you do. Bob being a dentist—somehow our friends—

STEVE   (*softly*). Oh, to be a dentist! (*Goes to window and stands looking out.*)

HENRIETTA.   Don't you see anything more of that editorial writer—what was his name?

MABEL.   Lyman Eggleston?

HENRIETTA.   Yes, Eggleston. He was in touch with things. Don't you see him?

MABEL.   Yes, I see him once in a while. Bob doesn't like him very well.

HENRIETTA.   Your husband does not like Lyman Eggleston? (*Mysteriously*) Mabel, are you perfectly happy with your husband?

STEVE   (*sharply*). Oh, come now, Henrietta—that's going a little strong!

HENRIETTA.   Are you perfectly happy with him, Mabel?

(STEVE *goes to work-table.*)

MABEL.   Why—yes—I guess so. Why—of course I am!

HENRIETTA.   Are you happy? Or do you only think you are? Or do you only think you *ought* to be?

MABEL.   Why, Henrietta, I don't know what you mean!

STEVE   (*seizes stack of books and magazines and dumps them on the breakfast table*). This is what she means, Mabel. Psychoanalysis. My work-table groans with it. Books by Freud, the new Messiah; books by Jung, the new St. Paul; the Psychoanalytical Review—back numbers two-fifty per.

MABEL.   But what's it all about?

STEVE.   All about your sub-un-nonconscious mind and desires you know not of. They may be doing you a great deal of harm. You may go crazy with them. Oh, yes! People are doing it right and left. Your dreaming you're a hen— (*Shakes his head darkly.*)

HENRIETTA.   Any fool can ridicule anything.

MABEL   (*hastily, to avert a quarrel*). But what do you say it is, Henrietta?

STEVE   (*looking at his watch*). Oh, if Henrietta's going to start that! (*During* HENRIETTA'S *next speech settles himself at work-table and sharpens a lead pencil.*)

HENRIETTA.   It's like this, Mabel. You want something. You think you can't have it. You think it's wrong. So you try to think you don't want it. Your mind protects you—avoids pain—by refusing to think the forbidden thing. But it's there just the same. It stays there shut up in your unconscious mind, and it festers.

STEVE.   Sort of an ingrowing mental toenail.

HENRIETTA.   Precisely. The forbidden impulse is there full of energy which has simply got to do something. It breaks into your consciousness in disguise, masks itself in dreams, makes all sorts of trouble. In extreme cases it drives you insane.

MABEL *(with a gesture of horror)*. Oh!

HENRIETTA *(reassuring)*. But psychoanalysis has found out how to save us from that. It brings into consciousness the suppressed desire that was making all the trouble. Psychoanalysis is simply the latest scientific method of preventing and curing insanity.

STEVE *(from his table)*. It is also the latest scientific method of separating families.

HENRIETTA *(mildly)*. Families that ought to be separated.

STEVE. The Dwights, for instance. You must have met them, Mabel, when you were here before. Helen was living, apparently, in peace and happiness with good old Joe. Well—she went to this psychoanalyzer—she was "psyched," and biff!—bang!—home she comes with an unsuppressed desire to leave her husband. *(He starts work, drawing lines on a drawing board with a T-square.)*

MABEL. How terrible! Yes, I remember Helen Dwight. But—but did she have such a desire?

STEVE. First she'd known of it.

MABEL. And she *left* him?

HENRIETTA *(coolly)*. Yes, she did.

MABEL. Wasn't he good to her?

HENRIETTA. Why, yes, good enough.

MABEL. Wasn't he kind to her?

HENRIETTA. Oh, yes—kind to her.

MABEL. And she left her good, kind husband—!

HENRIETTA. Oh, Mabel! "Left her good, kind husband!" How naïve— forgive me, dear, but how bourgeois you are! She came to know herself. And she had the courage!

MABEL. I may be very naïve and—bourgeois—but I don't see the good of a new science that breaks up homes.

(STEVE *applauds.*)

STEVE. In enlightening Mabel, we mustn't neglect to mention the case of Art Holden's private secretary, Mary Snow, who has just been informed of her suppressed desire for her employer.

MABEL. Why, I think it is terrible, Henrietta! It would be better if we didn't know such things about ourselves.

HENRIETTA. No, Mabel, that is the old way.

MABEL. But—but her employer? Is he married?

STEVE *(grunts)*. Wife and four children.

MABEL. Well, then, what good does it do the girl to be told she has a desire for him? There's nothing can be done about it.

HENRIETTA. Old institutions will have to be reshaped so that something can be done in such cases. It happens, Mabel, that this suppressed desire was on the point of landing Mary Snow in the insane asylum. Are you so tight-minded that you'd rather have her in the insane asylum than break the conventions?

MABEL. But—but have people always had these awful suppressed desires?

HENRIETTA. Always.

STEVE. But they've just been discovered.

HENRIETTA.   The harm they do has just been discovered. And free, sane people must face the fact that they have to be dealt with.

MABEL   (*stoutly*). I don't believe they have them in Chicago.

HENRIETTA   (*business of giving* MABEL *up*). People "have them" wherever the living Libido—the center of the soul's energy—is in conflict with petrified moral codes. That means everywhere in civilization. Psychoanalysis—

STEVE.   Good God! I've got the roof in the cellar!

HENRIETTA.   The roof in the cellar!

STEVE   (*holding plan at arm's length*). That's what psychoanalysis does!

HENRIETTA.   That's what psychoanalysis could *un*-do. Is it any wonder I'm concerned about Steve? He dreamed the other night that the walls of his room melted away and he found himself alone in a forest. Don't you see how significant it is for an architect to have *walls* slip away from him? It symbolizes his loss of grip in his work. There's some suppressed desire—

STEVE   (*hurling his ruined plan viciously to the floor*). Suppressed hell!

HENRIETTA.   You speak more truly than you know. It is through suppressions that hells are formed in us.

MABEL   (*looking at* STEVE, *who is tearing his hair*). Don't you think it would be a good thing, Henrietta, if we went somewhere else? (*They rise and begin to pick up the dishes.* MABEL *drops a plate which breaks.* HENRIETTA *draws up short and looks at her—the psychoanalytic look.*) I'm sorry, Henrietta. One of the Spode plates, too. (*Surprised and resentful as* HENRIETTA *continues to peer at her*) Don't take it so to heart, Henrietta.

HENRIETTA.   I can't help taking it to heart.

MABEL.   I'll get you another. (*Pause. More sharply as* HENRIETTA *does not answer*) I said I'll get you another plate, Henrietta.

HENRIETTA.   It's not the plate.

MABEL.   For heaven's sake, what is it then?

HENRIETTA.   It's the significant little false movement that made you drop it.

MABEL.   Well, I suppose everyone makes a false movement once in a while.

HENRIETTA.   Yes, Mabel, but these false movements all mean something.

MABEL   (*about to cry*). I don't think that's very nice! It was just because I happened to think of that Mabel Snow you were talking about—

HENRIETTA.   *Mabel* Snow!

MABEL.   Snow—Snow—well, what was her name, then?

HENRIETTA.   Her name is Mary. You substituted *your own* name for hers.

MABEL.   Well, *Mary* Snow, then; *Mary* Snow. I never heard her name but once. I don't see anything to make such a fuss about.

HENRIETTA   (*gently*). Mabel dear—mistakes like that in names—

MABEL   (*desperately*). They don't mean something, too, do they?

HENRIETTA   (*gently*). I am sorry, dear, but they do.

MABEL.   But I'm always doing that!

HENRIETTA   (*after a start of horror*). My poor little sister, tell me about it.

MABEL.   About what?

HENRIETTA.   About your not being happy. About your longing for another sort of life.

MABEL.   But I *don't*.

HENRIETTA. Ah, I understand these things, dear. You feel Bob is limiting you to a life in which you do not feel free—

MABEL. Henrietta! When did I ever say such a thing?

HENRIETTA. You said you are not in touch with things intellectual. You showed your feeling that it is Bob's profession—that has engendered a resentment which has colored your whole life with him.

MABEL. Why—Henrietta!

HENRIETTA. Don't be afraid of me, little sister. There's nothing can shock me or turn me from you. I am not like that. I wanted you to come for this visit because I had a feeling that you needed more from life than you were getting. No one of these things I have seen would excite my suspicion. It's the combination. You don't eat breakfast (*enumerating on her fingers*); you make false moves; you substitute your own name for the name of another *whose love is misdirected.* You're nervous; you *look* queer; in your eyes there's a frightened look that is most unlike you. And this dream. A *hen.* Come with me this afternoon to Dr. Russell! Your whole life may be at stake, Mabel.

MABEL (*gasping*). Henrietta, I—you—you always were the smartest in the family, and all that, but—this is terrible! I don't think we *ought* to think such things. (*Brightening*) Why, I'll tell you why I dreamed I was a hen. It was because last night, telling about that time in Chicago, you said I was as mad as a wet hen.

HENRIETTA (*superior*). Did you dream you were a *wet* hen?

MABEL (*forced to admit it*). No.

HENRIETTA. No. You dreamed you were a *dry* hen. And why, being a hen, were you urged to step?

MABEL. Maybe it's because when I am getting on a street car it always irritates me to have them call "Step lively."

HENRIETTA. No, Mabel, that is only a child's view of it—if you will forgive me. You see merely the elements used in the dream. You do not see into the dream; you do not see its meaning. This dream of the hen—

STEVE. Hen—hen—wet hen—dry hen—mad hen! (*Jumps up in a rage*) Let me out of this!

HENRIETTA (*hastily picking up dishes, speaks soothingly*). Just a minute, dear, and we'll have things so you can work in quiet. Mabel and I are going to sit in my room. (*She goes out left, carrying dishes.*)

STEVE (*seizing hat and coat from an alcove near the outside door*). I'm going to be psychoanalyzed. I'm going now! I'm going straight to that infallible doctor of hers—that priest of this new religion. If he's got honesty enough to tell Henrietta there's nothing the matter with my unconscious mind, perhaps I can be let alone about it, and then I *will* be all right. (*From the door in a low voice*) Don't tell Henrietta I'm going. It might take weeks, and I couldn't stand all the talk. (*He hurries out.*)

HENRIETTA (*returning*). Where's Steve? Gone? (*With a hopeless gesture*) You see how impatient he is—how unlike himself! I tell you, Mabel, I'm nearly distracted about Steve.

MABEL. I think he's a little distracted, too.

HENRIETTA. Well, if he's gone—you might as well stay here. I have a committee meeting at the bookshop, and will have to leave you to yourself for an hour or two. (*As she puts her hat on, taking it from the alcove where* STEVE *found his, her eye, lighting up almost carnivorously, falls on an enormous volume on the floor beside the work-table. The book has been half hidden by the wastebasket. She picks it up and carries it around the table toward* MABEL.) Here, dear, is one of the simplest statements of psychoanalysis. You just read this and then we can talk more intelligently. (MABEL *takes volume and staggers back under its weight to chair rear center,* HENRIETTA *goes to outer door, stops and asks abruptly*) How old is Lyman Eggleston?

MABEL   (*promptly*). He isn't forty yet. Why, what made you ask that, Henrietta? (*As she turns her head to look at* HENRIETTA *her hands move toward the upper corners of the book balanced on her knees.*)

HENRIETTA.   Oh, nothing. Au revoir.

(*She goes out.* MABEL *stares at the ceiling. The book slides to the floor. She starts; looks at the book, then at the broken plate on the table.*)

MABEL.   The plate! The book! (*She lifts her eyes, leans forward, elbow on knee, chin on knuckles and plaintively queries*) Am I unhappy?

Curtain

Scene II

Two weeks later. The stage is as in Scene I, except that the breakfast table has been removed. During the first few minutes the dusk of a winter afternoon deepens. Out of the darkness spring rows of double street-lights almost meeting in the distance. HENRIETTA *is at the psychoanalytical end of* STEVE'S *work-table, surrounded by open books and periodicals, writing.* STEVE *enters briskly.*

STEVE.   What are you doing, my dear?

HENRIETTA.   My paper for the Liberal Club.

STEVE.   Your paper on——?

HENRIETTA.   On a subject which does not have your sympathy.

STEVE.   Oh, I'm not sure I'm wholly out of sympathy with psychoanalysis, Henrietta. You worked it so hard. I couldn't even take a bath without its meaning something.

HENRIETTA   (*loftily*). I talked it because I knew you needed it.

STEVE.   You haven't said much about it these last two weeks. Uh—your faith in it hasn't weakened any?

HENRIETTA.   Weakened? It's grown stronger with each new thing I've come to know. And Mabel. She is with Dr. Russell now. Dr. Russell is wonderful! From what Mabel tells me I believe his analysis is going to prove that I was right. Today I discovered a remarkable confirmation of my theory in the hen-dream.

STEVE.   What is your theory?

HENRIETTA.   Well, you know about Lyman Eggleston. I've wondered about him. I've never seen him, but I know he's less bourgeois than Mabel's other friends—more intellectual—and (*significantly*) she doesn't see much of him because Bob doesn't like him.

STEVE.   But what's the confirmation?

HENRIETTA.   Today I noticed the first syllable of his name.

STEVE.   Ly?

HENRIETTA.   No—egg.

STEVE.   Egg?

HENRIETTA   (*patiently*). Mabel dreamed she was a *hen*. (STEVE *laughs*.) You wouldn't laugh if you knew how important names are in interpreting dreams. Freud is full of just such cases in which a whole hidden complex is revealed by a single significant syllable—like this egg.

STEVE.   Doesn't the traditional relation of hen and egg suggest rather a maternal feeling?

HENRIETTA.   There is something maternal in Mabel's love, of course, but that's only one element.

STEVE.   Well, suppose Mabel hasn't a suppressed desire to be this gentleman's mother, but his beloved. What's to be done about it? What about Bob? Don't you think it's going to be a little rough on him?

HENRIETTA.   That can't be helped. Bob, like everyone else, must face the facts of life. If Dr. Russell should arrive independently at this same interpretation I shall not hesitate to advise Mabel to leave her present husband.

STEVE.   Um—hum! (*The lights go up on Fifth Avenue*. STEVE *goes to the window and looks out*) How long is it we've lived here, Henrietta?

HENRIETTA.   Why, this is the third year, Steve.

STEVE.   I—we—one would miss this view if one went away, wouldn't one?

HENRIETTA.   How strangely you speak! Oh, Stephen, I *wish* you'd go to Dr. Russell. Don't think my fears have abated because I've been able to restrain myself. I had to on account of Mabel. But now, dear—won't you go?

STEVE.   I— (*He breaks off, turns on the light, then comes and sits beside* HEN-RIETTA) How long have we been married, Henrietta?

HENRIETTA.   Stephen, I don't understand you! You *must* go to Dr. Russell.

STEVE.   I have gone.

HENRIETTA.   You—what?

STEVE   (*jauntily*). Yes, Henrietta, I've been psyched.

HENRIETTA.   You went to Dr. Russell?

STEVE.   The same.

HENRIETTA.   And what did he say?

STEVE.   He said—I—I was a little surprised by what he said, Henrietta.

HENRIETTA   (*breathlessly*). Of course—one can so seldom anticipate. But tell me—your dream, Stephen? It means—?

STEVE.   It means—I was considerably surprised by what it means.

HENRIETTA.   *Don't* be so exasperating!

STEVE.   It means—you really want to know, Henrietta?

HENRIETTA.   Stephen, you'll drive me mad!

STEVE.   He said—of course he may be wrong in what he said.

HENRIETTA.   He *isn't* wrong. *Tell* me!

STEVE.   He said my dream of the walls receding and leaving me alone in a forest indicates a suppressed desire—

HENRIETTA.   Yes—yes!

STEVE.   To be freed from—

HENRIETTA.   Yes—freed from—?

STEVE.   Marriage.

HENRIETTA   (*crumples. Stares*). Marriage!

STEVE.   He—he may be mistaken, you know.

HENRIETTA.   *May* be mistaken?

STEVE.   I—well, of course, I hadn't taken any stock in it myself. It was only your great confidence—

HENRIETTA.   Stephen, are you telling me that Dr. Russell—Dr. A. E. Russell —told you this? (STEVE *nods*) Told you you have a suppressed desire to separate from *me?*

STEVE.   That's what he said.

HENRIETTA.   Did he know who you were?

STEVE.   Yes.

HENRIETTA.   That you were married to me?

STEVE.   Yes, he knew that.

HENRIETTA.   And he told you to leave me?

STEVE.   It seems he must be wrong, Henrietta.

HENRIETTA   (*rising*). And I've sent him more patients—! (*Catches herself and resumes coldly*) What reason did he give for this analysis?

STEVE.   He says the confining walls are a symbol of my feeling about marriage and that their fading away is a wish-fulfillment.

HENRIETTA   (*gulping*). Well, is it? Do you want our marriage to end?

STEVE.   It was a great surprise to me that I did. You see I hadn't known what was in my unconscious mind.

HENRIETTA   (*flaming*). What did you tell Dr. Russell about me to make him think you weren't happy?

STEVE.   I never told him a thing, Henrietta. He got it all from his confounded clever inferences. I—I tried to refute them, but he said that was only part of my self-protective lying.

HENRIETTA.   And that's why you were so—happy—when you came in just now!

STEVE.   Why, Henrietta, how can you say such a thing? I was *sad*. Didn't I speak sadly of—of the view? Didn't I ask how long we had been married?

HENRIETTA   (*rising*). Stephen Brewster, have you no sense of the seriousness of this? Dr. Russell doesn't know what our marriage has been. You do. You should have laughed him down! Confined—in life with me? Did you tell him that I *believe* in freedom?

STEVE.   I very emphatically told him that his results were a great surprise to me.

HENRIETTA.   But you accepted them.

STEVE.   Oh, not at all. I merely couldn't refute his arguments. I'm not a psychologist. I came home to talk it over with you. You being a disciple of psychoanalysis—

HENRIETTA.   If you are going, I wish you would go tonight!

STEVE. Oh, my dear! I—surely I couldn't do that! Think of my feelings. And my laundry hasn't come home.

HENRIETTA. I ask you to go tonight. Some women would falter at this, Steve, but I am not such a woman. I leave you free. I do not repudiate psychoanalysis; I say again that it has done great things. It has also made mistakes, of course. But since you accept this analysis— (*She sits down and pretends to begin work*) I have to finish this paper. I wish you would leave me.

STEVE (*scratches his head, goes to the inner door*). I'm sorry, Henrietta, about my unconscious mind.

(*Alone,* HENRIETTA's *face betrays her outraged state of mind—disconcerted, resentful, trying to pull herself together. She attains an air of bravely bearing an outrageous thing.—The outer door opens and* MABEL *enters in great excitement.*)

MABEL (*breathless*). Henrietta, I'm so glad you're here. And alone? (*Looks toward the inner door*) Are you alone, Henrietta?

HENRIETTA (*with reproving dignity*). Very much so.

MABEL (*rushing to her*). Henrietta, he's found it!

HENRIETTA (*aloof*). Who has found what?

MABEL. Who has found what? Dr. Russell has found my suppressed desire!

HENRIETTA. That is interesting.

MABEL. He finished with me today—he got hold of my complex—in the most amazing way! But, oh, Henrietta—it is so terrible!

HENRIETTA. Do calm yourself, Mabel. Surely there's no occasion for all this agitation.

MABEL. But there is! And when you think of the lives that are affected— the readjustments that must be made in order to bring the suppressed hell out of me and save me from the insane asylum—!

HENRIETTA. The insane asylum!

MABEL. You said that's where these complexes brought people!

HENRIETTA. What did the doctor tell you, Mabel?

MABEL. Oh, I don't know how I can tell you—it is so awful—so unbelievable.

HENRIETTA. I rather have my hand in at hearing the unbelievable.

MABEL. Henrietta, who would ever have thought it? How can it be true? But the doctor is perfectly certain that I have a suppressed desire for— (*Looks at* HENRIETTA, *is unable to continue.*)

HENRIETTA. Oh, go on, Mabel. I'm not unprepared for what you have to say.

MABEL. Not unprepared? You mean you have suspected it?

HENRIETTA. From the first. It's been my theory all along.

MABEL. But, Henrietta, I didn't know myself that I had this secret desire for Stephen.

HENRIETTA (*jumps up*). Stephen!

MABEL. My brother-in-law! My own sister's husband!

HENRIETTA. *You* have a suppressed desire for *Stephen!*

MABEL. Oh, Henrietta, aren't these unconscious selves terrible? They seem so unlike *us!*

HENRIETTA. What insane thing are you driving at?

MABEL (*blubbering*). Henrietta, don't you use that word to me. I don't *want* to go to the insane asylum.

HENRIETTA. What did Dr. Russell say?

MABEL. Well, you see—oh, it's the strangest thing! But you know the voice in my dream that called "Step, Hen!" Dr. Russell found out today that when I was a little girl I had a story-book in words of one syllable and I read the name Stephen wrong. I used to read it S-t-e-p, step, h-e-n, hen. (*Dramatically*) Step Hen is Stephen. (*Enter* STEPHEN, *his head bent over a time-table*) Stephen is Step Hen!

STEVE. I? Step Hen?

MABEL (*triumphantly*). S-t-e-p, step, H-e-n, hen, Stephen!

HENRIETTA (*exploding*). Well, what if Stephen is Step Hen? (*Scornfully*) Step Hen! Step Hen! For that ridiculous coincidence—

MABEL. Coincidence! But it's childish to look at the mere elements of a dream. You have to look *into* it—you have to see what it *means!*

HENRIETTA. On account of that trivial, meaningless play on syllables—on that flimsy basis—you are ready— (*Wails*) O-h!

STEVE. What on earth's the matter? What has happened? Suppose I *am* Step Hen? What about it? What does it mean?

MABEL (*crying*). It means—that I—have a suppressed desire for *you!*

STEVE. For me! The douce you have! (*Feebly*) What—er—makes you think so?

MABEL. Dr. Russell has worked it out scientifically.

HENRIETTA. Yes. Through the amazing discovery that Step Hen equals Stephen!

MABEL (*tearfully*). Oh, that isn't all—that isn't near all. Henrietta won't give me a chance to tell it. She'd rather I'd go to the insane asylum than be unconventional.

HENRIETTA. We'll all go there if you can't control yourself. We are still waiting for some rational report.

MABEL (*drying her eyes*). Oh, there's such a lot about names. (*With some pride*) I don't see how I ever did it. It all works in together. I dreamed I was a hen because that's the first syllable of *Hen*rietta's name, and when I dreamed I was a hen, I was putting myself in Henrietta's place.

HENRIETTA. With Stephen?

MABEL. With Stephen.

HENRIETTA (*outraged*). Oh! (*Turns in rage upon* STEPHEN, *who is fanning himself with the time-table*) What are you doing with that time-table?

STEVE. Why—I thought—you were so keen to have me go tonight—I thought I'd just take a run up to Canada, and join Billy—a little shooting—but—

MABEL. But there's more about the names.

HENRIETTA. Mabel, have you thought of Bob—dear old Bob—your good, kind husband?

MABEL. Oh, Henrietta, "my good, kind husband!"

HENRIETTA. Think of him, Mabel, out there alone in Chicago, working his head off, fixing people's *teeth*—for you!

MABEL.   Yes, but think of the living Libido—in conflict with petrified moral codes! And think of the perfectly wonderful way the names all prove it. Dr. Russell said he's never seen anything more convincing. Just look at Stephen's last name—Brewster. I dream I'm a hen, and the name Brewster—you have to say its first letter by itself—and then the hen, that's me, she says to him: "Stephen, Be Rooster!"

(HENRIETTA *and* STEPHEN *collapse into the nearest chairs.*)

MABEL.   I think it's perfectly wonderful! Why, if it wasn't for psychoanalysis you'd never find out how wonderful your own mind is!

STEVE   (*begins to chuckle*). Be Rooster! Stephen, Be Rooster!

HENRIETTA.   You think it's funny, do you?

STEVE.   Well, what's to be done about it? Does Mabel have to go away with me?

HENRIETTA.   Do you want Mabel to go away with you?

STEVE.   Well, but Mabel herself—her complex, her suppressed desire—!

HENRIETTA   (*going to her*). Mabel, are you going to insist on going away with Stephen?

MABEL.   I'd rather go with Stephen than go to the insane asylum!

HENRIETTA.   For heaven's sake, Mabel, drop that insane asylum! If you *did* have a suppressed desire for Stephen hidden away in you—God knows it isn't hidden now. Dr. Russell has brought it into your consciousness—with a vengeance. That's all that's necessary to break up a complex. Psychoanalysis doesn't say you have to *gratify* every suppressed desire.

STEVE   (*softly*). Unless it's for Lyman Eggleston.

HENRIETTA   (*turning on him*). Well, if it comes to that, Stephen Brewster, I'd like to know why that interpretation of mine isn't as good as this one? Step, Hen!

STEVE.   But Be Rooster! (*He pauses, chuckling to himself*) Step-Hen B-rooster. And *Hen*rietta. Pshaw, my dear, Doc Russell's got you beat a mile! (*He turns away and chuckles*) Be rooster!

MABEL.   What has Lyman Eggleston got to do with it?

STEVE.   According to Henrietta, you, the hen, have a suppressed desire for *Egg*leston, the egg.

MABEL.   Henrietta, I think that's indecent of you! He is bald as an egg and little and fat—the idea of you thinking such a thing of me!

HENRIETTA.   Well, Bob isn't little and bald and fat! Why don't you stick to your own husband? (*To* STEPHEN) What if Dr. Russell's interpretation has got mine "beat a mile"? (*Resentful look at him*) It would only mean that Mabel doesn't want Eggleston and does want you. Does that mean she has to have you?

MABEL.   But you said Mabel Snow—

HENRIETTA.   *Mary* Snow! You're not as much like her as you think—substituting your name for hers! The cases are entirely different. Oh, I wouldn't have *believed* this of you, Mabel. (*Beginning to cry*) I brought you here for a pleasant visit—thought you needed brightening *up*—wanted to be *nice* to you—and now you—my husband—you insist— (*In fumbling her way to her chair she brushes to the floor some sheets from the psychoanalytical table.*)

STEVE   (*with solicitude*). Careful, dear. Your paper on psychoanalysis! (*Gathers up sheets and offers them to her.*)

HENRIETTA.   I don't want my paper on psychoanalysis! I'm sick of psychoanalysis!

STEVE   (*eagerly*). Do you mean that, Henrietta?

HENRIETTA.   Why shouldn't I mean it? Look at all I've done for psychoanalysis—and— (*Raising a tear-stained face*) what has psychoanalysis done for me?

STEVE.   Do you mean, Henrietta, that you're going to stop *talking* psychoanalysis?

HENRIETTA.   Why shouldn't I stop talking it? Haven't I seen what it does to people? Mabel has gone crazy about psychoanalysis!

(*At the word "crazy" with a moan* MABEL *sinks to chair and buries her face in her hands.*)

STEVE   (*solemnly*). Do you swear never to wake me up in the night to find out what I'm dreaming?

HENRIETTA.   Dream what you please—I don't care what you're dreaming.

STEVE.   Will you clear off my work-table so the Journal of Morbid Psychology doesn't stare me in the face when I'm trying to plan a house?

HENRIETTA   (*pushing a stack of periodicals off the table*). I'll *burn* the Journal of Morbid Psychology!

STEVE.   My dear Henrietta, if you're going to separate from psychoanalysis, there's no reason why I should separate from *you.*

(*They embrace ardently.* MABEL *lifts her head and looks at them woefully.*)

MABEL   (*jumping up and going toward them*). But what about me? What am I to do with my suppressed desire?

STEVE   (*with one arm still around* HENRIETTA, *gives* MABEL *a brotherly hug*). Mabel, you just keep right on suppressing it!

CURTAIN

Arthur Miller

Death of a Salesman is Arthur Miller's most famous and notable play. Produced and published in 1949, it had a long original Broadway run and has been frequently revived, most recently in 1984 with noted film actor Dustin Hoffman as the salesman Willy Loman. The play is in the tradition of social realism inaugurated by Ibsen and continued by Chekhov, Strindberg, and Shaw, among others. The dialogue of the characters, their financial and emotional problems, and their behavior are all indicative of a typically realistic drama. Moreover, like Ibsen's *A Doll House,* Miller's *Salesman* raises questions about social values and attitudes—in this case, the pursuit of success and the American dream. Like Chekhov's in *The Cherry Orchard,* Miller's tone mixes sympathy and judgment, criticism and compassion. And as Shaw did in *Arms and the Man,* Miller provides extensive and detailed stage directions. Miller's directions differ, however, from

Shaw's in one important way: Shaw provides elaborate descriptions of scene and setting, whereas Miller furnishes information about the lives his characters lead, giving us a greater sense of their past.

These realistic touches blend, however, with other dramatic elements that are less realistic and that we will call *expressionistic*. Expressionistic playwrights attempt to dramatize a subjective picture of reality as seen by an individual consciousness. They attempt to show the inner life of a character, portraying external reality as he or she sees it. *Death of a Salesman* is expressionistic in that it dramatizes Willy Loman's subjective sense of things, rather than exhibiting a concern for a strict and exact representation of external detail. The play is particularly expressionistic in its memory scenes in which Willy recalls events from the past in such a way that he reenacts rather than merely remembers them. In these scenes different times, places, and states of mind fluctuate and merge as Miller reveals Willy's thoughts, attitudes, and beliefs, his inflated hopes and deflated dreams. The expressionistic quality of the play is enhanced by lighting and music that contribute to its mood and that signal flashbacks.

One issue readers, audiences, and critics have consistently raised about *Death of a Salesman* concerns its status as tragedy. The main question turns on whether Willy Loman is a tragic figure. Is he grand and noble enough to be a tragic hero? Is his failure tragic or merely pathetic? Over the years Miller has written about these and related questions in essays such as "On Social Drama" and "Tragedy and the Common Man." He has suggested that "the common man is as apt a subject for tragedy as kings"; and also that "the tragic feeling is evoked in us when we are in the presence of a character who is ready to lay down his life" to secure his dignity. How far these observations apply to Willy Loman is a matter for discussion.

ARTHUR MILLER

[*b. 1915*]

Death of a Salesman

CERTAIN PRIVATE CONVERSATIONS IN TWO ACTS
AND A REQUIEM

CHARACTERS

WILLY LOMAN

LINDA

BIFF

HAPPY

BERNARD

THE WOMAN

CHARLEY

UNCLE BEN

HOWARD WAGNER

JENNY

STANLEY

MISS FORSYTHE

LETTA

The action takes place in WILLY LOMAN'S *house and yard and in various places he visits in the New York and Boston of today.*

Throughout the play, in the stage directions, left and right mean stage left and stage right.

ACT I

A melody is heard, played upon a flute. It is small and fine, telling of grass and trees and the horizon. The curtain rises.

Before us is the Salesman's house. We are aware of towering, angular shapes behind it, surrounding it on all sides. Only the blue light of the sky falls upon the house and forestage; the surrounding area shows an angry glow of orange. As more light appears, we see a solid vault of apartment houses around the small, fragile-seeming home. An air of the dream clings to the place, a dream rising out of reality. The kitchen at center seems actual enough, for there is a kitchen table with three chairs, and a refrigerator. But no other fixtures are seen. At the back of the kitchen there is a draped entrance, which leads to the livingroom. To the right of the kitchen, on a level raised two feet, is a bedroom furnished only with a brass bedstead and a straight chair. On a shelf over the bed a silver athletic trophy stands. A window opens onto the apartment house at the side.

Behind the kitchen, on a level raised six and a half feet, is the boys' bedroom, at present barely visible. Two beds are dimly seen, and at the back of the room a dormer window. (This bedroom is above the unseen livingroom.) At the left a stairway curves up to it from the kitchen.

The entire setting is wholly or, in some places, partially transparent. The roof-line of the house is one-dimensional; under and over it we see the apartment buildings. Before the house lies an apron, curving beyond the forestage into the orchestra. This forward area serves as the back yard as well as the locale of all WILLY'S *imaginings and of his city scenes. Whenever the action is in the present the actors observe the imaginary wall-lines, entering the house only through the door at the left. But in the scenes of the past these boundaries are broken, and characters enter or leave a room by stepping "through" a wall onto the forestage.*

From the right, WILLY LOMAN, *the Salesman, enters, carrying two large sample cases. The flute plays on. He hears but is not aware of it. He is past sixty years of age, dressed quietly. Even as he crosses the stage to the doorway of the house, his exhaustion is apparent. He unlocks the door, comes into the kitchen, and thankfully lets his burden down, feeling the soreness of his palms. A word-sigh escapes his lips—it might be "Oh, boy, oh, boy." He closes the door, then carries his cases out into the livingroom, through the draped kitchen doorway.*

LINDA, *his wife, has stirred in her bed at the right. She gets out and puts on a robe, listening. Most often jovial, she has developed an iron repression of her exceptions to* WILLY's *behavior —she more than loves him, she admires him, as though his mercurial nature, his temper, his massive dreams and little cruelties, served her only as sharp reminders of the turbulent longings within him, longings which she shares but lacks the temperament to utter and follow to their end.*

LINDA   (*hearing* WILLY *outside the bedroom, calls with some trepidation*): Willy!

WILLY: It's all right. I came back.

LINDA: Why? What happened? (*Slight pause.*) Did something happen, Willy?

WILLY: No, nothing happened.

LINDA: You didn't smash the car, did you?

WILLY   (*with casual irritation*): I said nothing happened. Didn't you hear me?

LINDA: Don't you feel well?

WILLY: I am tired to the death. (*The flute has faded away. He sits on the bed beside her, a little numb.*) I couldn't make it. I just couldn't make it, Linda.

LINDA   (*very carefully, delicately*): Where were you all day? You look terrible.

WILLY: I got as far as a little above Yonkers. I stopped for a cup of coffee. Maybe it was the coffee.

LINDA: What?

WILLY   (*after a pause*): I suddenly couldn't drive any more. The car kept going onto the shoulder, y'know?

LINDA   (*helpfully*): Oh. Maybe it was the steering again. I don't think Angelo knows the Studebaker.

WILLY: No, it's me, it's me. Suddenly I realize I'm goin' sixty miles an hour and I don't remember the last five minutes. I'm—I can't seem to—keep my mind to it.

LINDA: Maybe it's your glasses. You never went for your new glasses.

WILLY: No, I see everything. I came back ten miles an hour. It took me nearly four hours from Yonkers.

LINDA   (*resigned*): Well, you'll just have to take a rest, Willy, you can't continue this way.

WILLY: I just got back from Florida.

LINDA: But you didn't rest your mind. Your mind is overactive, and the mind is what counts, dear.

WILLY: I'll start out in the morning. Maybe I'll feel better in the morning. (*She is taking off his shoes.*) These goddam arch supports are killing me.

LINDA: Take an aspirin. Should I get you an aspirin? It'll soothe you.

WILLY   (*with wonder*): I was driving along, you understand? And I was fine. I was even observing the scenery. You can imagine, me looking at scenery, on the road every week of my life. But it's so beautiful up there, Linda, the trees are so thick, and the sun is warm. I opened the windshield and just let the warm air bathe over me. And then all of a sudden I'm goin' off the road! I'm tellin' ya, I absolutely forgot I was driving. If I'd've gone the other way over the white line I might've killed somebody. So I went on again—and five minutes later

I'm dreamin' again, and I nearly— (*He presses two fingers against his eyes.*) I have such thoughts, I have such strange thoughts.

LINDA: Willy, dear. Talk to them again. There's no reason why you can't work in New York.

WILLY: They don't need me in New York. I'm the New England man. I'm vital in New England.

LINDA: But you're sixty years old. They can't expect you to keep traveling every week.

WILLY: I'll have to send a wire to Portland. I'm supposed to see Brown and Morrison tomorrow morning at ten o'clock to show the line. Goddammit, I could sell them! (*He starts putting on his jacket.*)

LINDA   (*taking the jacket from him*): Why don't you go down to the place tomorrow and tell Howard you've simply got to work in New York? You're too accommodating, dear.

WILLY: If old man Wagner was alive I'd a been in charge of New York now! That man was a prince, he was a masterful man. But that boy of his, that Howard, he don't appreciate. When I went north the first time, the Wagner Company didn't know where New England was!

LINDA: Why don't you tell those things to Howard, dear?

WILLY   (*encouraged*): I will, I definitely will. Is there any cheese?

LINDA: I'll make you a sandwich.

WILLY: No, go to sleep. I'll take some milk. I'll be up right away. The boys in?

LINDA: They're sleeping. Happy took Biff on a date tonight.

WILLY   (*interested*): That so?

LINDA: It was so nice to see them shaving together, one behind the other, in the bathroom. And going out together. You notice? The whole house smells of shaving lotion.

WILLY: Figure it out. Work a lifetime to pay off a house. You finally own it, and there's nobody to live in it.

LINDA: Well, dear, life is a casting off. It's always that way.

WILLY: No, no, some people—some people accomplish something. Did Biff say anything after I went this morning?

LINDA: You shouldn't have criticized him, Willy, especially after he just got off the train. You mustn't lose your temper with him.

WILLY: When the hell did I lose my temper? I simply asked him if he was making any money. Is that a criticism?

LINDA: But, dear, how could he make any money?

WILLY   (*worried and angered*): There's such an undercurrent in him. He became a moody man. Did he apologize when I left this morning?

LINDA: He was crestfallen, Willy. You know how he admires you. I think if he finds himself, then you'll both be happier and not fight any more.

WILLY: How can he find himself on a farm? Is that a life? A farmhand? In the beginning, when he was young, I thought, well, a young man, it's good for him to tramp around, take a lot of different jobs. But it's more than ten years now and he has yet to make thirty-five dollars a week!

LINDA: He's finding himself, Willy.

WILLY: Not finding yourself at the age of thirty-four is a disgrace!

LINDA: Shh!

WILLY: The trouble is he's lazy, goddammit!

LINDA: Willy, please!

WILLY: Biff is a lazy bum!

LINDA: They're sleeping. Get something to eat. Go on down.

WILLY: Why did he come home? I would like to know what brought him home.

LINDA: I don't know. I think he's still lost, Willy. I think he's very lost.

WILLY: Biff Loman is lost. In the greatest country in the world a young man with such—personal attractiveness, gets lost. And such a hard worker. There's one thing about Biff—he's not lazy.

LINDA: Never.

WILLY (*with pity and resolve*): I'll see him in the morning; I'll have a nice talk with him. I'll get him a job selling. He could be big in no time. My God! Remember how they used to follow him around in high school? When he smiled at one of them their faces lit up. When he walked down the street . . . (*He loses himself in reminiscences.*)

LINDA (*trying to bring him out of it*): Willy, dear, I got a new kind of American-type cheese today. It's whipped.

WILLY: Why do you get American when I like Swiss?

LINDA: I just thought you'd like a change—

WILLY: I don't want a change! I want Swiss cheese. Why am I always being contradicted?

LINDA (*with a covering laugh*): I thought it would be a surprise.

WILLY: Why don't you open a window in here, for God's sake?

LINDA (*with infinite patience*): They're all open, dear.

WILLY: The way they boxed us in here. Bricks and windows, windows and bricks.

LINDA: We should've bought the land next door.

WILLY: The street is lined with cars. There's not a breath of fresh air in the neighborhood. The grass don't grow any more, you can't raise a carrot in the back yard. They should've had a law against apartment houses. Remember those two beautiful elm trees out there? When I and Biff hung the swing between them?

LINDA: Yeah, like being a million miles from the city.

WILLY: They should've arrested the builder for cutting those down. They massacred the neighborhood. (*Lost.*) More and more I think of those days, Linda. This time of year it was lilac and wisteria. And then the peonies would come out, and the daffodils. What fragrance in this room!

LINDA: Well, after all, people had to move somewhere.

WILLY: No, there's more people now.

LINDA: I don't think there's more people. I think—

WILLY: There's more people! That's what's ruining this country! Population is getting out of control. The competition is maddening! Smell the stink from that apartment house! And another on the other side . . . How can they whip cheese?

On WILLY'S *last line,* BIFF *and* HAPPY *raise themselves up in their beds, listening.*

LINDA: Go down, try it. And be quiet.

WILLY   (*turning to* LINDA, *guiltily*): You're not worried about me, are you, sweetheart?

BIFF: What's the matter?

HAPPY: Listen!

LINDA: You've got too much on the ball to worry about.

WILLY: You're my foundation and my support, Linda.

LINDA: Just try to relax, dear. You make mountains out of molehills.

WILLY: I won't fight with him any more. If he wants to go back to Texas, let him go.

LINDA: He'll find his way.

WILLY: Sure. Certain men just don't get started till later in life. Like Thomas Edison, I think. Or B. F. Goodrich. One of them was deaf. (*He starts for the bedroom doorway.*) I'll put my money on Biff.

LINDA: And Willy—if it's warm Sunday we'll drive in the country. And we'll open the windshield, and take lunch.

WILLY: No, the windshields don't open on the new cars.

LINDA: But you opened it today.

WILLY: Me? I didn't. (*He stops.*) Now isn't that peculiar! Isn't that a remarkable— (*He breaks off in amazement and fright as the flute is heard distantly.*)

LINDA: What, darling?

WILLY: That is the most remarkable thing.

LINDA: What, dear?

WILLY: I was thinking of the Chevvy. (*Slight pause.*) Nineteen twenty-eight . . . when I had that red Chevvy— (*Breaks off.*) That funny? I coulda sworn I was driving that Chevvy today.

LINDA: Well, that's nothing. Something must've reminded you.

WILLY: Remarkable. Ts. Remember those days? The way Biff used to simonize that car? The dealer refused to believe there was eighty thousand miles on it. (*He shakes his head.*) Heh! (*To* LINDA.) Close your eyes, I'll be right up. (*He walks out of the bedroom.*)

HAPPY   (*to Biff*): Jesus, maybe he smashed up the car again!

LINDA   (*calling after* WILLY): Be careful on the stairs, dear! The cheese is on the middle shelf! (*She turns, goes over to the bed, takes his jacket, and goes out of the bedroom.*)

Light has risen on the boys' room. Unseen, WILLY *is heard talking to himself, "Eighty thousand miles," and a little laugh.* BIFF *gets out of bed, comes downstage a bit, and stands attentively.* BIFF *is two years older than his brother* HAPPY, *well built, but in these days bears a worn air and seems less self-assured. He has succeeded less, and his dreams are stronger and less acceptable than* HAPPY'S. HAPPY *is tall, powerfully made. Sexuality is like a visible color on him, or a scent that many women have discovered. He, like his brother, is lost, but in a different way, for he has never allowed himself to turn his face toward defeat and is thus more confused and hard-skinned, although seemingly more content.*

HAPPY   (*getting out of bed*): He's going to get his license taken away if he keeps that up. I'm getting nervous about him, y'know, Biff?

BIFF: His eyes are going.

HAPPY: No, I've driven with him. He sees all right. He just doesn't keep his mind on it. I drove into the city with him last week. He stops at a green light and then it turns red and he goes. (*He laughs.*)

BIFF: Maybe he's color-blind.

HAPPY: Pop? Why he's got the finest eye for color in the business. You know that.

BIFF   (*sitting down on his bed*): I'm going to sleep.

HAPPY: You're not still sour on Dad, are you, Biff?

BIFF: He's all right, I guess.

WILLY   (*underneath them, in the livingroom*): Yes, sir, eighty thousand miles —eighty-two thousand!

BIFF: You smoking?

HAPPY   (*holding out a pack of cigarettes*): Want one?

BIFF   (*taking a cigarette*): I can never sleep when I smell it.

WILLY: What a simonizing job, heh!

HAPPY   (*with deep sentiment*): Funny, Biff, y'know? Us sleeping in here again? The old beds. (*He pats his bed affectionately.*) All the talk that went across those two beds, huh? Our whole lives.

BIFF: Yeah. Lotta dreams and plans.

HAPPY   (*with a deep and masculine laugh*): About five hundred women would like to know what was said in this room.

They share a soft laugh.

BIFF: Remember that big Betsy something—what the hell was her name— over on Bushwick Avenue?

HAPPY   (*combing his hair*): With the collie dog!

BIFF: That's the one. I got you in there, remember?

HAPPY: Yeah, that was my first time—I think. Boy, there was a pig! (*They laugh, almost crudely.*) You taught me everything I know about women. Don't forget that.

BIFF: I bet you forgot how bashful you used to be. Especially with girls.

HAPPY: Oh, I still am, Biff.

BIFF: Oh, go on.

HAPPY: I just control it, that's all. I think I got less bashful and you got more so. What happened, Biff? Where's the old humor, the old confidence? (*He shakes* BIFF'S *knee.* BIFF *gets up and moves restlessly about the room.*) What's the matter?

BIFF: Why does Dad mock me all the time?

HAPPY: He's not mocking you, he—

BIFF: Everything I say there's a twist of mockery on his face. I can't get near him.

HAPPY: He just wants you to make good, that's all. I wanted to talk to you about Dad for a long time, Biff. Something's—happening to him. He—talks to himself.

BIFF: I noticed that this morning. But he always mumbled.

HAPPY: But not so noticeable. It got so embarrassing I sent him to Florida. And you know something? Most of the time he's talking to you.

BIFF: What's he say about me?

HAPPY: I can't make it out.

BIFF: What's he say about me?

HAPPY: I think the fact that you're not settled, that you're still kind of up in the air . . .

BIFF: There's one or two other things depressing him, Happy.

HAPPY: What do you mean?

BIFF: Never mind. Just don't lay it all to me.

HAPPY: But I think if you just got started—I mean—is there any future for you out there?

BIFF: I tell ya, Hap, I don't know what the future is. I don't know—what I'm supposed to want.

HAPPY: What do you mean?

BIFF: Well, I spent six or seven years after high school trying to work myself up. Shipping clerk, salesman, business of one kind or another. And it's a measly manner of existence. To get on that subway on the hot mornings in summer. To devote your whole life to keeping stock, or making phone calls, or selling or buying. To suffer fifty weeks of the year for the sake of a two-week vacation, when all you really desire is to be outdoors, with your shirt off. And always to have to get ahead of the next fella. And still—that's how you build a future.

HAPPY: Well, you really enjoy it on a farm? Are you content out there?

BIFF   (*with rising agitation*): Hap, I've had twenty or thirty different kinds of jobs since I left home before the war, and it always turns out the same. I just realized it lately. In Nebraska when I herded cattle, and the Dakotas, and Arizona, and now in Texas. It's why I came home now, I guess, because I realized it. This farm I work on, it's spring there now, see? And they've got about fifteen new colts. There's nothing more inspiring or—beautiful than the sight of a mare and a new colt. And it's cool there now, see? Texas is cool now, and it's spring. And whenever spring comes to where I am, I suddenly get the feeling, my God, I'm not gettin' anywhere! What the hell am I doing, playing around with horses, twenty-eight dollars a week! I'm thirty-four years old, I oughta be makin' my future. That's when I come running home. And now, I get here, and I don't know what to do with myself. (*After a pause.*) I've always made a point of not wasting my life, and everytime I come back here I know that all I've done is to waste my life.

HAPPY: You're a poet, you know that, Biff? You're a—you're an idealist!

BIFF: No, I'm mixed up very bad. Maybe I oughta get married. Maybe I oughta get stuck into something. Maybe that's my trouble. I'm like a boy. I'm not married, I'm not in business, I just—I'm like a boy. Are you content, Hap? You're a success, aren't you? Are you content?

HAPPY: Hell, no!

BIFF: Why? You're making money, aren't you?

HAPPY   (*moving about with energy, expressiveness*): All I can do now is wait for the merchandise manager to die. And suppose I get to be merchandise manager? He's a good friend of mine, and he just built a terrific estate on Long Island. And he lived there about two months and sold it, and now he's building another one. He can't enjoy it once it's finished. And I know that's just what I would do. I don't know what the hell I'm workin' for. Sometimes I sit in my apartment—all alone. And I think of the rent I'm paying. And it's crazy. But then, it's what I always wanted. My own apartment, a car, and plenty of women. And still, goddammit, I'm lonely.

BIFF *(with enthusiasm)*: Listen, why don't you come out West with me?

HAPPY: You and I, heh?

BIFF: Sure, maybe we could buy a ranch. Raise cattle, use our muscles. Men built like we are should be working out in the open.

HAPPY *(avidly)*: The Loman Brothers, heh?

BIFF *(with vast affection)*: Sure, we'd be known all over the counties!

HAPPY *(enthralled)*: That's what I dream about, Biff. Sometimes I want to just rip my clothes off in the middle of the store and outbox that goddam merchandise manager. I mean I can outbox, outrun, and outlift anybody in that store, and I have to take orders from those common, petty, sons-of-bitches till I can't stand it any more.

BIFF: I'm tellin' you, kid, if you were with me I'd be happy out there.

HAPPY *(enthused)*: See, Biff, everybody around me is so false that I'm constantly lowering my ideals . . .

BIFF: Baby, together we'd stand up for one another, we'd have someone to trust.

HAPPY: If I were around you—

BIFF: Hap, the trouble is we weren't brought up to grub for money. I don't know how to do it.

HAPPY: Neither can I!

BIFF: Then let's go!

HAPPY: The only thing is—what can you make out there?

BIFF: But look at your friend. Builds an estate and then hasn't the peace of mind to live in it.

HAPPY: Yeah, but when he walks into the store the waves part in front of him. That's fifty-two thousand dollars a year coming through the revolving door, and I got more in my pinky finger than he's got in his head.

BIFF: Yeah, but you just said—

HAPPY: I gotta show some of those pompous, self-important executives over there that Hap Loman can make the grade. I want to walk into the store the way he walks in. Then I'll go with you, Biff. We'll be together yet, I swear. But take those two we had tonight. Now weren't they gorgeous creatures?

BIFF: Yeah, yeah, most gorgeous I've had in years.

HAPPY: I get that any time I want, Biff. Whenever I feel disgusted. The only trouble is, it gets like bowling or something. I just keep knockin' them over and it doesn't mean anything. You still run around a lot?

BIFF: Naa. I'd like to find a girl—steady, somebody with substance.

HAPPY: That's what I long for.

BIFF: Go on! You'd never come home.

HAPPY: I would! Somebody with character, with resistance! Like Mom, y'know? You're gonna call me a bastard when I tell you this. That girl Charlotte I was with tonight is engaged to be married in five weeks. *(He tries on his new hat.)*

BIFF: No kiddin'!

HAPPY: Sure, the guy's in line for the vice-presidency of the store. I don't know what gets into me, maybe I just have an overdeveloped sense of competition or something, but I went and ruined her, and furthermore I can't get rid of her. And he's the third executive I've done that to. Isn't that a crummy characteristic? And to top it all, I go to their weddings! (*Indignantly, but laughing.*) Like I'm not supposed to take bribes. Manufacturers offer me a hundred-dollar bill now and then to throw an order their way. You know how honest I am, but it's like this girl, see. I hate myself for it. Because I don't want the girl, and, still, I take it and—I love it!

BIFF: Let's go to sleep.

HAPPY: I guess we didn't settle anything, heh?

BIFF: I just got one idea that I think I'm going to try.

HAPPY: What's that?

BIFF: Remember Bill Oliver?

HAPPY: Sure, Oliver is very big now. You want to work for him again?

BIFF: No, but when I quit he said something to me. He put his arm on my shoulder, and he said, "Biff, if you ever need anything, come to me."

HAPPY: I remember that. That sounds good.

BIFF: I think I'll go to see him. If I could get ten thousand or even seven or eight thousand dollars I could buy a beautiful ranch.

HAPPY: I bet he'd back you. 'Cause he thought highly of you, Biff, I mean, they all do. You're well liked, Biff. That's why I say to come back here, and we both have the apartment. And I'm tellin' you, Biff, any babe you want . . .

BIFF: No, with a ranch I could do the work I like and still be something. I just wonder though. I wonder if Oliver still thinks I stole that carton of basketballs.

HAPPY: Oh, he probably forgot that long ago. It's almost ten years. You're too sensitive. Anyway, he didn't really fire you.

BIFF: Well, I think he was going to. I think that's why I quit. I was never sure whether he knew or not. I know he thought the world of me, though. I was the only one he'd let lock up the place.

WILLY   (*below*): You gonna wash the engine, Biff?

HAPPY: Shh!

BIFF *looks at* HAPPY, *who is gazing down, listening.* WILLY *is mumbling in the parlor.*

HAPPY: You hear that?

They listen. WILLY *laughs warmly.*

BIFF   (*growing angry*): Doesn't he know Mom can hear that?

WILLY: Don't get your sweater dirty, Biff!

A look of pain crosses BIFF'S *face.*

HAPPY: Isn't that terrible? Don't leave again, will you? You'll find a job here. You gotta stick around. I don't know what to do about him, it's getting embarrassing.

WILLY: What a simonizing job!

BIFF: Mom's hearing that!

WILLY: No kiddin', Biff, you got a date? Wonderful!

HAPPY: Go on to sleep. But talk to him in the morning, will you?

BIFF (*reluctantly getting into bed*): With her in the house. Brother!

HAPPY (*getting into bed*): I wish you'd have a good talk with him.

The light on their room begins to fade.

BIFF (*to himself in bed*): That selfish, stupid . . .

HAPPY: Sh . . . Sleep, Biff.

Their light is out. Well before they have finished speaking, WILLY's *form is dimly seen below in the darkened kitchen. He opens the refrigerator, searches in there, and takes out a bottle of milk. The apartment houses are fading out, and the entire house and surroundings become covered with leaves. Music insinuates itself as the leaves appear.*

WILLY: Just wanna be careful with those girls, Biff, that's all. Don't make any promises. No promises of any kind. Because a girl, y'know, they always believe what you tell 'em, and you're very young, Biff, you're too young to be talking seriously to girls.

Light rises on the kitchen. WILLY, *talking, shuts the refrigerator door and comes downstage to the kitchen table. He pours milk into a glass. He is totally immersed in himself, smiling faintly.*

WILLY: Too young entirely, Biff. You want to watch your schooling first. Then when you're all set, there'll be plenty of girls for a boy like you. (*He smiles broadly at a kitchen chair.*) That so? The girls pay for you? (*He laughs.*) Boy, you must really be makin' a hit.

WILLY *is gradually addressing—physically—a point offstage, speaking through the wall of the kitchen, and his voice has been rising in volume to that of a normal conversation.*

WILLY: I been wondering why you polish the car so careful. Ha! Don't leave the hubcaps, boys. Get the chamois to the hubcaps. Happy, use newspaper on the windows, it's the easiest thing. Show him how to do it, Biff! You see, Happy? Pad it up, use it like a pad. That's it, that's it, good work. You're doin' all right, Hap. (*He pauses, then nods in approbation for a few seconds, then looks upward.*) Biff, first thing we gotta do when we get time is clip that big branch over the house. Afraid it's gonna fall in a storm and hit the roof. Tell you what. We get a rope and sling her around, and then we climb up there with a couple of saws and take her down. Soon as you finish the car, boys, I wanna see ya. I got a surprise for you, boys.

BIFF (*offstage*): Whatta ya got, Dad?

WILLY: No, you finish first. Never leave a job till you're finished—remember that. (*Looking toward the "big trees."*) Biff, up in Albany I saw a beautiful hammock. I think I'll buy it next trip, and we'll hang it right between those two elms. Wouldn't that be something? Just swingin' there under those branches. Boy, that would be . . .

YOUNG BIFF *and* YOUNG HAPPY *appear from the direction* WILLY *was addressing.* HAPPY *carries rags and a pail of water.* BIFF, *wearing a sweater with a block "S," carries a football.*

BIFF   (*pointing in the direction of the car offstage*): How's that, Pop, professional?

WILLY: Terrific. Terrific job, boys. Good work, Biff.

HAPPY: Where's the surprise, Pop?

WILLY: In the back seat of the car.

HAPPY: Boy! (*He runs off.*)

BIFF: What is it, Dad? Tell me, what'd you buy?

WILLY   (*laughing, cuffs him*): Never mind, something I want you to have.

BIFF   (*turns and starts off*): What is it, Hap?

HAPPY   (*offstage*): It's a punching bag!

BIFF: Oh, Pop!

WILLY: It's got Gene Tunney's signature on it!

HAPPY *runs onstage with a punching bag.*

BIFF: Gee, how'd you know we wanted a punching bag?

WILLY: Well, it's the finest thing for the timing.

HAPPY   (*lies down on his back and pedals with his feet*): I'm losing weight, you notice, Pop?

WILLY   (*to* HAPPY): Jumping rope is good too.

BIFF: Did you see the new football I got?

WILLY   (*examining the ball*): Where'd you get a new ball?

BIFF: The coach told me to practice my passing.

WILLY: That so? And he gave you the ball, heh?

BIFF: Well, I borrowed it from the locker room. (*He laughs confidentially.*)

WILLY   (*laughing with him at the theft*): I want you to return that.

HAPPY: I told you he wouldn't like it!

BIFF   (*angrily*): Well, I'm bringing it back!

WILLY   (*stopping the incipient argument, to* HAPPY): Sure, he's gotta practice with a regulation ball, doesn't he? (*To* BIFF.) Coach'll probably congratulate you on your initiative!

BIFF: Oh, he keeps congratulating my initiative all the time, Pop.

WILLY: That's because he likes you. If somebody else took that ball there'd be an uproar. So what's the report, boys, what's the report?

BIFF: Where'd you go this time, Dad? Gee we were lonesome for you.

WILLY   (*pleased, puts an arm around each boy and they come down to the apron*): Lonesome, heh?

BIFF: Missed you every minute.

WILLY: Don't say? Tell you a secret, boys. Don't breathe it to a soul. Someday I'll have my own business, and I'll never have to leave home any more.

HAPPY: Like Uncle Charley, heh?

WILLY: Bigger than Uncle Charley! Because Charley is not—liked. He's liked, but he's not—well liked.

BIFF: Where'd you go this time, Dad?

WILLY: Well, I got on the road, and I went north to Providence. Met the Mayor.

BIFF: The Mayor of Providence!

WILLY: He was sitting in the hotel lobby.

BIFF: What'd he say?

WILLY: He said, "Morning!" And I said, "You've got a fine city here, Mayor." And then he had coffee with me. And then I went to Waterbury. Waterbury is a fine city. Big clock city, the famous Waterbury clock. Sold a nice bill there. And then Boston—Boston is the cradle of the Revolution. A fine city. And a couple of other towns in Mass., and on to Portland and Bangor and straight home!

BIFF: Gee, I'd love to go with you sometime, Dad.

WILLY: Soon as summer comes.

HAPPY: Promise?

WILLY: You and Hap and I, and I'll show you all the towns. America is full of beautiful towns and fine, upstanding people. And they know me, boys, they know me up and down New England. The finest people. And when I bring you fellas up, there'll be open sesame for all of us, 'cause one thing, boys: I have friends. I can park my car in any street in New England, and the cops protect it like their own. This summer, heh?

BIFF AND HAPPY (*together*): Yeah! You bet!

WILLY: We'll take our bathing suits.

HAPPY: We'll carry your bags, Pop!

WILLY: Oh, won't that be something! Me comin' into the Boston stores with you boys carryin' my bags. What a sensation!

       BIFF *is prancing around, practicing passing the ball.*

WILLY: You nervous, Biff, about the game?

BIFF: Not if you're gonna be there.

WILLY: What do they say about you in school, now that they made you captain?

HAPPY: There's a crowd of girls behind him everytime the classes change.

BIFF (*taking* WILLY'S *hand*): This Saturday, Pop, this Saturday—just for you, I'm going to break through for a touchdown.

HAPPY: You're supposed to pass.

BIFF: I'm takin' one play for Pop. You watch me, Pop, and when I take off my helmet, that means I'm breakin' out. Then you watch me crash through that line!

WILLY (*kisses* BIFF): Oh, wait'll I tell this in Boston!

BERNARD *enters in knickers. He is younger than* BIFF, *earnest and loyal, a worried boy.*

BERNARD: Biff, where are you? You're supposed to study with me today.

WILLY: Hey, looka Bernard. What're you lookin' so anemic about, Bernard?

BERNARD: He's gotta study, Uncle Willy. He's got Regents next week.

HAPPY (*tauntingly, spinning* BERNARD *around*): Let's box, Bernard!

BERNARD: Biff! (*He gets away from* HAPPY.) Listen, Biff, I heard Mr. Birnbaum say that if you don't start studyin' math he's gonna flunk you, and you won't graduate. I heard him!

WILLY: You better study with him, Biff. Go ahead now.

BERNARD: I heard him!

BIFF: Oh, Pop, you didn't see my sneakers! (*He holds up a foot for* WILLY *to look at.*)

WILLY: Hey, that's a beautiful job of printing!

BERNARD (*wiping his glasses*): Just because he printed University of Virginia on his sneakers doesn't mean they've got to graduate him, Uncle Willy!

WILLY (*angrily*): What're you talking about? With scholarships to three universities they're gonna flunk him?

BERNARD: But I heard Mr. Birnbaum say—

WILLY: Don't be a pest, Bernard! (*To his boys.*) What an anemic!

BERNARD: Okay, I'm waiting for you in my house, Biff.

BERNARD *goes off. The* LOMANS *laugh.*

WILLY: Bernard is not well liked, is he?

BIFF: He's liked, but he's not well liked.

HAPPY: That's right, Pop.

WILLY: That's just what I mean. Bernard can get the best marks in school, y'understand, but when he gets out in the business world, y'understand, you are going to be five times ahead of him. That's why I thank Almighty God you're both built like Adonises. Because the man who makes an appearance in the business world, the man who creates personal interest, is the man who gets ahead. Be liked and you will never want. You take me, for instance. I never have to wait in line to see a buyer. "Willy Loman is here!" That's all they have to know, and I go right through.

BIFF: Did you knock them dead, Pop?

WILLY: Knocked 'em cold in Providence, slaughtered 'em in Boston.

HAPPY (*on his back, pedaling again*): I'm losing weight, you notice, Pop?

LINDA *enters, as of old, a ribbon in her hair, carrying a basket of washing.*

LINDA (*with youthful energy*): Hello, dear!

WILLY: Sweetheart!

LINDA: How'd the Chevvy run?

WILLY: Chevrolet, Linda, is the greatest car ever built. (*To the boys.*) Since when do you let your mother carry wash up the stairs?

BIFF: Grab hold there, boy!

HAPPY: Where to, Mom?

LINDA: Hang them up on the line. And you better go down to your friends, Biff. The cellar is full of boys. They don't know what to do with themselves.

BIFF: Ah, when Pop comes home they can wait!

WILLY (*laughs appreciatively*): You better go down and tell them what to do, Biff.

BIFF: I think I'll have them sweep out the furnace room.

WILLY: Good work, Biff.

BIFF (*goes through wall-line of kitchen to doorway at back and calls down*): Fellas! Everybody sweep out the furnace room! I'll be right down!

VOICES: All right! Okay, Biff.

BIFF: George and Sam and Frank, come out back! We're hangin' up the wash! Come on, Hap, on the double! (*He and* HAPPY *carry out the basket.*)

LINDA: The way they obey him!

WILLY: Well, that's training, the training. I'm tellin' you, I was sellin' thousands and thousands, but I had to come home.

LINDA: Oh, the whole block'll be at that game. Did you sell anything?

WILLY: I did five hundred gross in Providence and seven hundred gross in Boston.

LINDA: No! Wait a minute, I've got a pencil. (*She pulls pencil and paper out of her apron pocket.*) That makes your commission . . . Two hundred—my God! Two hundred and twelve dollars!

WILLY: Well, I didn't figure it yet, but . . .

LINDA: How much did you do?

WILLY: Well, I—I did—about a hundred and eighty gross in Providence. Well, no—it came to—roughly two hundred gross on the whole trip.

LINDA (*without hesitation*); Two hundred gross. That's . . . (*She figures.*)

WILLY: The trouble was that three of the stores were half closed for inventory in Boston. Otherwise I woulda broke records.

LINDA: Well, it makes seventy dollars and some pennies. That's very good.

WILLY: What do we owe?

LINDA: Well, on the first there's sixteen dollars on the refrigerator—

WILLY: Why sixteen?

LINDA: Well, the fan belt broke, so it was a dollar eighty.

WILLY: But it's brand new.

LINDA: Well, the man said that's the way it is. Till they work themselves in, y'know.

They move through the wall-line into the kitchen.

WILLY: I hope we didn't get stuck on that machine.

LINDA: They got the biggest ads of any of them!

WILLY: I know, it's a fine machine. What else?

LINDA: Well, there's nine-sixty for the washing machine. And for the vacuum cleaner there's three and a half due on the fifteenth. Then the roof, you got twenty-one dollars remaining.

WILLY: It don't leak, does it?

LINDA: No, they did a wonderful job. Then you owe Frank for the carburetor.

WILLY: I'm not going to pay that man! That goddam Chevrolet, they ought to prohibit the manufacture of that car!

LINDA: Well, you owe him three and a half. And odds and ends, comes to around a hundred and twenty dollars by the fifteenth.

WILLY: A hundred and twenty dollars! My God, if business don't pick up I don't know what I'm gonna do!

LINDA: Well, next week you'll do better.

WILLY: Oh, I'll knock them dead next week. I'll go to Hartford. I'm very well liked in Hartford. You know, the trouble is, Linda, people don't seem to take to me.

They move onto the forestage.

LINDA: Oh, don't be foolish.

WILLY: I know it when I walk in. They seem to laugh at me.

LINDA: Why? Why would they laugh at you? Don't talk that way, Willy.

WILLY moves to the edge of the stage. LINDA *goes into the kitchen and starts to darn stockings.*

WILLY: I don't know the reason for it, but they just pass me by. I'm not noticed.

LINDA: But you're doing wonderful, dear. You're making seventy to a hundred dollars a week.

WILLY: But I gotta be at it ten, twelve hours a day. Other men—I don't know—they do it easier. I don't know why—I can't stop myself—I talk too much. A man oughta come in with a few words. One thing about Charley. He's a man of few words, and they respect him.

LINDA: You don't talk too much, you're just lively.

WILLY   *(smiling)*: Well, I figure, what the hell, life is short, a couple of jokes. *(To himself.)* I joke too much! *(The smile goes.)*

LINDA: Why? You're—

WILLY: I'm fat. I'm very—foolish to look at, Linda. I didn't tell you, but Christmas time I happened to be calling on F. H. Stewarts, and a salesman I know, as I was going in to see the buyer I heard him say something about—walrus. And I—I cracked him right across the face. I won't take that. I simply will not take that. But they do laugh at me. I know that.

LINDA: Darling . . .

WILLY: I gotta overcome it. I know I gotta overcome it. I'm not dressing to advantage, maybe.

LINDA: Willy, darling, you're the handsomest man in the world—

WILLY: Oh, no, Linda.

LINDA: To me you are. *(Slight pause.)* The handsomest.

From the darkness is heard the laughter of a woman. WILLY *doesn't turn to it, but it continues through* LINDA's *lines.*

LINDA: And the boys, Willy. Few men are idolized by their children the way you are.

Music is heard as behind a scrim, to the left of the house, THE WOMAN, *dimly seen, is dressing.*

WILLY   *(with great feeling)*: You're the best there is, Linda, you're a pal, you know that? On the road—on the road I want to grab you sometimes and just kiss the life outa you.

The laughter is loud now, and he moves into a brightening area at the left, where THE WOMAN *has come from behind the scrim and is standing, putting on her hat, looking into a "mirror" and laughing.*

WILLY: 'Cause I get so lonely—especially when business is bad and there's nobody to talk to. I get the feeling that I'll never sell anything again, that I won't make a living for you, or a business, a business for the boys. *(He talks through* THE WOMAN's *subsiding laughter;* THE WOMAN *primps at the "mirror.")* There's so much I want to make for—

THE WOMAN: Me? You didn't make me, Willy. I picked you.

WILLY   *(pleased)*: You picked me?

THE WOMAN   *(who is quite proper-looking,* WILLY's *age)*: I did. I've been sitting at that desk watching all the salesmen go by, day in, day out. But you've got such a sense of humor, and we do have such a good time together, don't we?

WILLY: Sure, sure. (*He takes her in his arms.*) Why do you have to go now?

THE WOMAN: It's two o'clock . . .

WILLY: No, come on in! (*He pulls her.*)

THE WOMAN: . . . my sisters'll be scandalized. When'll you be back?

WILLY: Oh, two weeks about. Will you come up again?

THE WOMAN: Sure thing. You do make me laugh. It's good for me. (*She squeezes his arm, kisses him.*) And I think you're a wonderful man.

WILLY: You picked me, heh?

THE WOMAN: Sure. Because you're so sweet. And such a kidder.

WILLY: Well, I'll see you next time I'm in Boston.

THE WOMAN: I'll put you right through to the buyers.

WILLY (*slapping her bottom*): Right. Well, bottoms up!

THE WOMAN (*slaps him gently and laughs*): You just kill me, Willy. (*He suddenly grabs her and kisses her roughly.*) You kill me. And thanks for the stockings. I love a lot of stockings. Well, good night.

WILLY: Good night. And keep your pores open!

THE WOMAN: Oh, Willy!

THE WOMAN *bursts out laughing, and* LINDA's *laughter blends in.* THE WOMAN *disappears into the dark. Now the area at the kitchen table brightens.* LINDA *is sitting where she was at the kitchen table, but now is mending a pair of silk stockings.*

LINDA: You are, Willy. The handsomest man. You've got no reason to feel that—

WILLY (*coming out of* THE WOMAN's *dimming area and going over to* LINDA): I'll make it all up to you, Linda, I'll—

LINDA: There's nothing to make up, dear. You're doing fine, better than—

WILLY (*noticing her mending*): What's that?

LINDA: Just mending my stockings. They're so expensive—

WILLY (*angrily, taking them from her*): I won't have you mending stockings in this house! Now throw them out!

LINDA *puts the stockings in her pocket.*

BERNARD (*entering on the run*): Where is he? If he doesn't study!

WILLY (*moving to the forestage, with great agitation*): You'll give him the answers!

BERNARD: I do, but I can't on a Regents! That's a state exam! They're liable to arrest me!

WILLY: Where is he? I'll whip him, I'll whip him!

LINDA: And he'd better give back that football, Willy, it's not nice.

WILLY: Biff! Where is he? Why is he taking everything?

LINDA: He's too tough with the girls, Willy. All the mothers are afraid of him!

WILLY: I'll whip him!

BERNARD: He's driving the car without a license!

THE WOMAN's *laugh is heard.*

WILLY: Shut up!

LINDA: All the mothers—

WILLY: Shut up!

BERNARD   (*backing quietly away and out*): Mr. Birnbaum says he's stuck up.

WILLY: Get outa here!

BERNARD: If he doesn't buckle down he'll flunk math! (*He goes off.*)

LINDA: He's right, Willy, you've gotta—

WILLY   (*exploding at her*): There's nothing the matter with him! You want him to be a worm like Bernard? He's got spirit, personality . . .

As he speaks, LINDA, *almost in tears, exits into the livingroom.* WILLY *is alone in the kitchen, wilting and staring. The leaves are gone. It is night again, and the apartment houses look down from behind.*

WILLY: Loaded with it. Loaded! What is he stealing? He's giving it back, isn't he? Why is he stealing? What did I tell him? I never in my life told him anything but decent things.

HAPPY *in pajamas has come down the stairs;* WILLY *suddenly becomes aware of* HAPPY's *presence.*

HAPPY: Let's go now, come on.

WILLY   (*sitting down at the kitchen table*): Huh! Why did she have to wax the floors herself? Everytime she waxes the floors she keels over. She knows that!

HAPPY: Shh! Take it easy. What brought you back tonight?

WILLY: I got an awful scare. Nearly hit a kid in Yonkers. God! Why didn't I go to Alaska with my brother Ben that time! Ben! That man was a genius, that man was success incarnate! What a mistake! He begged me to go.

HAPPY: Well, there's no use in—

WILLY: You guys! There was a man started with the clothes on his back and ended up with diamond mines!

HAPPY: Boy, someday I'd like to know how he did it.

WILLY: What's the mystery? The man knew what he wanted and went out and got it! Walked into a jungle, and comes out, the age of twenty-one, and he's rich! The world is an oyster, but you don't crack it open on a mattress!

HAPPY: Pop, I told you I'm gonna retire you for life.

WILLY: You'll retire me for life on seventy goddam dollars a week? And your women and your car and your apartment, and you'll retire me for life! Christ's sake, I couldn't get past Yonkers today! Where are you guys, where are you? The woods are burning! I can't drive a car!

CHARLEY *has appeared in the doorway. He is a large man, slow of speech, laconic, immovable. In all he says, despite what he says, there is pity, and, now, trepidation. He has a robe over his pajamas, slippers on his feet. He enters the kitchen.*

CHARLEY: Everything all right?

HAPPY: Yeah, Charley, everything's . . .

WILLY: What's the matter?

CHARLEY: I heard some noise. I thought something happened. Can't we do something about the walls? You sneeze in here, and in my house hats blow off.

HAPPY: Let's go to bed, Dad. Come on.

CHARLEY signals to HAPPY to go.

WILLY: You go ahead, I'm not tired at the moment.

HAPPY (*to* WILLY): Take it easy, huh? (*He exits.*)

WILLY: What're you doin' up?

CHARLEY (*sitting down at the kitchen table opposite* WILLY): Couldn't sleep good. I had a heartburn.

WILLY: Well, you don't know how to eat.

CHARLEY: I eat with my mouth.

WILLY: No, you're ignorant. You gotta know about vitamins and things like that.

CHARLEY: Come on, let's shoot. Tire you out a little.

WILLY (*hesitantly*): All right. You got cards?

CHARLEY (*taking a deck from his pocket*): Yeah, I got them. Someplace. What is it with those vitamins?

WILLY (*dealing*): They build up your bones. Chemistry.

CHARLEY: Yeah, but there's no bones in a heartburn.

WILLY: What are you talkin' about? Do you know the first thing about it?

CHARLEY: Don't get insulted.

WILLY: Don't talk about something you don't know anything about.

They are playing. Pause.

CHARLEY: What're you doin' home?

WILLY: A little trouble with the car.

CHARLEY: Oh. (*Pause.*) I'd like to take a trip to California.

WILLY: Don't say.

CHARLEY: You want a job?

WILLY: I got a job, I told you that. (*After a slight pause.*) What the hell are you offering me a job for?

CHARLEY: Don't get insulted.

WILLY: Don't insult me.

CHARLEY: I don't see no sense in it. You don't have to go on this way.

WILLY: I got a good job. (*Slight pause.*) What do you keep comin' in here for?

CHARLEY: You want me to go?

WILLY (*after a pause, withering*): I can't understand it. He's going back to Texas again. What the hell is that?

CHARLEY: Let him go.

WILLY: I got nothin' to give him, Charley, I'm clean, I'm clean.

CHARLEY: He won't starve. None a them starve. Forget about him.

WILLY: Then what have I got to remember?

CHARLEY: You take it too hard. To hell with it. When a deposit bottle is broken you don't get your nickel back.

WILLY: That's easy enough for you to say.

CHARLEY: That ain't easy for me to say.

WILLY: Did you see the ceiling I put up in the livingroom?

CHARLEY: Yeah, that's a piece of work. To put up a ceiling is a mystery to me. How do you do it?

WILLY: What's the difference?

CHARLEY: Well, talk about it.

WILLY: You gonna put up a ceiling?

CHARLEY: How could I put up a ceiling?

WILLY: Then what the hell are you bothering me for?

CHARLEY: You're insulted again.

WILLY: A man who can't handle tools is not a man. You're disgusting.

CHARLEY: Don't call me disgusting, Willy.

UNCLE BEN, *carrying a valise and an umbrella, enters the forestage from around the right corner of the house. He is a stolid man, in his sixties, with a mustache and an authoritative air. He is utterly certain of his destiny, and there is an aura of far places about him. He enters exactly as* WILLY *speaks.*

WILLY: I'm getting awfully tired, Ben.

BEN's *music is heard.* BEN *looks around at everything.*

CHARLEY: Good, keep playing; you'll sleep better. Did you call me Ben?

BEN *looks at his watch.*

WILLY: That's funny. For a second there you reminded me of my brother Ben.

BEN: I have only a few minutes. (*He strolls, inspecting the place.* WILLY *and* CHARLEY *continue playing.*)

CHARLEY: You never heard from him again, heh? Since that time?

WILLY: Didn't Linda tell you? Couple of weeks ago we got a letter from his wife in Africa. He died.

CHARLEY: That so.

BEN   (*chuckling*): So this is Brooklyn, eh?

CHARLEY: Maybe you're in for some of his money.

WILLY: Naa, he had seven sons. There's just one opportunity I had with that man . . .

BEN: I must make a train, William. There are several properties I'm looking at in Alaska.

WILLY: Sure, sure! If I'd gone with him to Alaska that time, everything would've been totally different.

CHARLEY: Go on, you'd froze to death up there.

WILLY: What're you talking about?

BEN: Opportunity is tremendous in Alaska, William. Surprised you're not up there.

WILLY: Sure, tremendous.

CHARLEY: Heh?

WILLY: There was the only man I ever met who knew the answers.

CHARLEY: Who?

BEN: How are you all?

WILLY (*taking a pot, smiling*): Fine, fine.

CHARLEY: Pretty sharp tonight.

BEN: Is Mother living with you?

WILLY: No, she died a long time ago.

CHARLEY: Who?

BEN: That's too bad. Fine specimen of a lady, Mother.

WILLY (*to* CHARLEY): Heh?

BEN: I'd hoped to see the old girl.

CHARLEY: Who died?

BEN: Heard anything from Father, have you?

WILLY (*unnerved*): What do you mean, who died?

CHARLEY (*taking a pot*): What're you talkin' about?

BEN (*looking at his watch*): William, it's half-past eight!

WILLY (*as though to dispel his confusion he angrily stops* CHARLEY'S *hand*): That's my build!

CHARLEY: I put the ace—

WILLY: If you don't know how to play the game I'm not gonna throw my money away on you!

CHARLEY (*rising*): It was my ace, for God's sake!

WILLY: I'm through, I'm through!

BEN: When did Mother die?

WILLY: Long ago. Since the beginning you never knew how to play cards.

CHARLEY (*picks up the cards and goes to the door*): All right! Next time I'll bring a deck with five aces.

WILLY: I don't play that kind of game!

CHARLEY (*turning to him*): You should be ashamed of yourself!

WILLY: Yeah?

CHARLEY: Yeah! (*He goes out.*)

WILLY (*slamming the door after him*): Ignoramus!

BEN (*as* WILLY *comes toward him through the wall-line of the kitchen*): So you're William.

WILLY (*shaking* BEN'S *hand*): Ben! I've been waiting for you so long! What's the answer? How did you do it?

BEN: Oh, there's a story in that.

LINDA *enters the forestage, as of old, carrying the wash basket.*

LINDA: Is this Ben?

BEN (*gallantly*): How do you do, my dear.

LINDA: Where've you been all these years? Willy's always wondered why you—

WILLY (*pulling* BEN *away from her impatiently*): Where is Dad? Didn't you follow him? How did you get started?

BEN: Well, I don't know how much you remember.

WILLY: Well, I was just a baby, of course, only three or four years old—

BEN: Three years and eleven months.

WILLY: What a memory, Ben!

BEN: I have many enterprises, William, and I have never kept books.

WILLY: I remember I was sitting under the wagon in—was it Nebraska?

BEN: It was South Dakota, and I gave you a bunch of wild flowers.

WILLY: I remember you walking away down some open road.

BEN (*laughing*): I was going to find Father in Alaska.

WILLY: Where is he?

BEN: At that age I had a very faulty view of geography, William. I discovered after a few days that I was heading due south, so instead of Alaska, I ended up in Africa.

LINDA: Africa!

WILLY: The Gold Coast!

BEN: Principally, diamond mines.

LINDA: Diamond mines!

BEN: Yes, my dear. But I've only a few minutes—

WILLY: No! Boys! Boys! (YOUNG BIFF *and* HAPPY *appear.*) Listen to this. This is your Uncle Ben, a great man! Tell my boys, Ben!

BEN: Why, boys, when I was seventeen I walked into the jungle, and when I was twenty-one I walked out. (*He laughs.*) And by God I was rich.

WILLY (*to the boys*): You see what I been talking about? The greatest things can happen!

BEN (*glancing at his watch*): I have an appointment in Ketchikan Tuesday week.

WILLY: No, Ben! Please tell about Dad. I want my boys to hear. I want them to know the kind of stock they spring from. All I remember is a man with a big beard, and I was in Mamma's lap, sitting around a fire, and some kind of high music.

BEN: His flute. He played the flute.

WILLY: Sure, the flute, that's right!

New music is heard, a high, rollicking tune.

BEN: Father was a very great and a very wild-hearted man. We would start in Boston, and he'd toss the whole family into the wagon, and then he'd drive the team right across the country; through Ohio, and Indiana, Michigan, Illinois, and all the Western states. And we'd stop in the towns and sell the flutes that he'd made on the way. Great inventor, Father. With one gadget he made more in a week than a man like you could make in a lifetime.

WILLY: That's just the way I'm bringing them up, Ben—rugged, well liked, all-around.

BEN: Yeah? (*To* BIFF.) Hit that, boy—hard as you can. (*He pounds his stomach.*)

BIFF: Oh, no, sir!

BEN (*taking boxing stance*): Come on, get to me! (*He laughs.*)

WILLY: Go to it, Biff! Go ahead, show him!

BIFF: Okay! (*He cocks his fist and starts in.*)

LINDA (*to* WILLY): Why must he fight, dear?

BEN (*sparring with* BIFF): Good boy! Good boy!

WILLY: How's that, Ben, heh?

HAPPY: Give him the left, Biff!

LINDA: Why are you fighting?

BEN: Good boy! (*Suddenly comes in, trips* BIFF, *and stands over him, the point of his umbrella poised over* BIFF'S *eye.*)

LINDA: Look out, Biff!

BIFF: Gee!

BEN (*patting* BIFF'S *knee*): Never fight fair with a stranger, boy. You'll never get out of the jungle that way. (*Taking* LINDA'S *hand and bowing.*) It was an honor and a pleasure to meet you, Linda.

LINDA (*withdrawing her hand coldly, frightened*): Have a nice—trip.

BEN (*to* WILLY): And good luck with your—what do you do?

WILLY: Selling.

BEN: Yes. Well . . . (*He raises his hand in farewell to all.*)

WILLY: No, Ben, I don't want you to think . . . (*He takes* BEN'S *arm to show him.*) It's Brooklyn, I know, but we hunt too.

BEN: Really, now.

WILLY: Oh, sure, there's snakes and rabbits and—that's why I moved out here. Why, Biff can fell any one of these trees in no time! Boys! Go right over to where they're building the apartment house and get some sand. We're gonna rebuild the entire front stoop right now! Watch this, Ben!

BIFF: Yes, sir! On the double, Hap!

HAPPY (*as he and* BIFF *run off*): I lost weight, Pop, you notice?

> CHARLEY *enters in knickers, even before the boys are gone.*

CHARLEY: Listen, if they steal any more from that building the watchman'll put the cops on them!

LINDA (*to* WILLY): Don't let Biff . . .

> BEN *laughs lustily.*

WILLY: You shoulda seen the lumber they brought home last week. At least a dozen six-by-tens worth all kinds a money.

CHARLEY: Listen, if that watchman—

WILLY: I gave them hell, understand. But I got a couple of fearless characters there.

CHARLEY: Willy, the jails are full of fearless characters.

BEN (*clapping* WILLY *on the back, with a laugh at* CHARLEY): And the stock exchange, friend!

WILLY (*joining in* BEN'S *laughter*): Where are the rest of your pants?

CHARLEY: My wife bought them.

WILLY: Now all you need is a golf club and you can go upstairs and go to sleep. (*To* BEN.) Great athlete! Between him and his son Bernard they can't hammer a nail!

BERNARD (*rushing in*): The watchman's chasing Biff!

WILLY (*angrily*): Shut up! He's not stealing anything!

LINDA (*alarmed, hurrying off left*): Where is he? Biff, dear! (*She exits.*)

WILLY (*moving toward the left, away from* BEN): There's nothing wrong. What's the matter with you?

BEN: Nervy boy. Good!

WILLY   (*laughing*): Oh, nerves of iron, that Biff!

CHARLEY: Don't know what it is. My New England man comes back and he's bleedin', they murdered him up there.

WILLY: It's contacts, Charley, I got important contacts!

CHARLEY   (*sarcastically*): Glad to hear it, Willy. Come in later, we'll shoot a little casino. I'll take some of your Portland money. (*He laughs at* WILLY *and exits.*)

WILLY   (*turning to* BEN): Business is bad, it's murderous. But not for me, of course.

BEN: I'll stop by on my way back to Africa.

WILLY   (*longingly*): Can't you stay a few days? You're just what I need, Ben, because I—I have a fine position here, but I—well, Dad left when I was such a baby and I never had a chance to talk to him and I still feel—kind of temporary about myself.

BEN: I'll be late for my train.

They are at opposite ends of the stage.

WILLY: Ben, my boys—can't we talk? They'd go into the jaws of hell for me, see, but I—

BEN: William, you're being first-rate with your boys. Outstanding, manly chaps!

WILLY   (*hanging on to his words*): Oh, Ben, that's good to hear! Because sometimes I'm afraid that I'm not teaching them the right kind of— Ben, how should I teach them?

BEN   (*giving great weight to each word, and with a certain vicious audacity*): William, when I walked into the jungle, I was seventeen. When I walked out I was twenty-one. And, by God, I was rich! (*He goes off into darkness around the right corner of the house.*)

WILLY: . . . was rich! That's just the spirit I want to imbue them with! To walk into a jungle! I was right! I was right! I was right!

BEN *is gone, but* WILLY *is still speaking to him as* LINDA, *in nightgown and robe, enters the kitchen, glances around for* WILLY, *then goes to the door of the house, looks out and sees him. Comes down to his left. He looks at her.*

LINDA: Willy, dear? Willy?

WILLY: I was right!

LINDA: Did you have some cheese? (*He can't answer.*) It's very late, darling. Come to bed, heh?

WILLY   (*looking straight up*): Gotta break your neck to see a star in this yard.

LINDA: You coming in?

WILLY: What ever happened to that diamond watch fob? Remember? When Ben came from Africa that time? Didn't he give me a watch fob with a diamond in it?

LINDA: You pawned it, dear. Twelve, thirteen years ago. For Biff's radio correspondence course.

WILLY: Gee, that was a beautiful thing. I'll take a walk.

LINDA: But you're in your slippers.

WILLY (*starting to go around the house at the left*): I was right! I was! (*Half to* LINDA, *as he goes, shaking his head.*) What a man! There was a man worth talking to. I was right!

LINDA (*calling after* WILLY): But in your slippers, Willy!

WILLY *is almost gone when* BIFF, *in his pajamas, comes down the stairs and enters the kitchen.*

BIFF: What is he doing out there?

LINDA: Sh!

BIFF: God Almighty, Mom, how long has he been doing this?

LINDA: Don't, he'll hear you.

BIFF: What the hell is the matter with him?

LINDA: It'll pass by morning.

BIFF: Shouldn't we do anything?

LINDA: Oh, my dear, you should do a lot of things, but there's nothing to do, so go to sleep.

HAPPY *comes down the stairs and sits on the steps.*

HAPPY: I never heard him so loud, Mom.

LINDA: Well, come around more often; you'll hear him. (*She sits down at the table and mends the lining of* WILLY'S *jacket.*)

BIFF: Why didn't you ever write me about this, Mom?

LINDA: How would I write to you? For over three months you had no address.

BIFF: I was on the move. But you know I thought of you all the time. You know that, don't you, pal?

LINDA: I know, dear, I know. But he likes to have a letter. Just to know that there's still a possibility for better things.

BIFF: He's not like this all the time, is he?

LINDA: It's when you come home he's always the worst.

BIFF: When I come home?

LINDA: When you write you're coming, he's all smiles, and talks about the future, and—he's just wonderful. And then the closer you seem to come, the more shaky he gets, and then, by the time you get here, he's arguing, and he seems angry at you. I think it's just that maybe he can't bring himself to—to open up to you. Why are you so hateful to each other? Why is that?

BIFF (*evasively*): I'm not hateful, Mom.

LINDA: But you no sooner come in the door than you're fighting!

BIFF: I don't know why. I mean to change. I'm tryin', Mom, you understand?

LINDA: Are you home to stay now?

BIFF: I don't know. I want to look around, see what's doin'.

LINDA: Biff, you can't look around all your life, can you?

BIFF: I just can't take hold, Mom. I can't take hold of some kind of a life.

LINDA: Biff, a man is not a bird, to come and go with the springtime.

BIFF: Your hair . . . (*He touches her hair.*) Your hair got so gray.

LINDA: Oh, it's been gray since you were in high school. I just stopped dyeing it, that's all.

BIFF: Dye it again, will ya? I don't want my pal looking old. (*He smiles.*)

LINDA: You're such a boy! You think you can go away for a year and
. . . You've got to get it into your head now that one day you'll knock on this
door and there'll be strange people here—

BIFF: What are you talking about? You're not even sixty, Mom.

LINDA: But what about your father?

BIFF   (*lamely*): Well, I meant him too.

HAPPY: He admires Pop.

LINDA: Biff, dear, if you don't have any feeling for him, then you can't have
any feeling for me.

BIFF: Sure I can, Mom.

LINDA: No. You can't just come to see me, because I love him. (*With a threat,
but only a threat, of tears.*) He's the dearest man in the world to me, and I won't
have anyone making him feel unwanted and low and blue. You've got to make
up your mind now, darling, there's no leeway any more. Either he's your father
and you pay him that respect, or else you're not to come here. I know he's not
easy to get along with—nobody knows that better than me—but . . .

WILLY   (*from the left, with a laugh*): Hey, hey, Biffo!

BIFF   (*starting to go out after* WILLY): What the hell is the matter with him?
(HAPPY *stops him.*)

LINDA: Don't—don't go near him!

BIFF: Stop making excuses for him! He always, always wiped the floor with
you. Never had an ounce of respect for you.

HAPPY: He's always had respect for—

BIFF: What the hell do you know about it?

HAPPY   (*surlily*): Just don't call him crazy!

BIFF: He's got no character—Charley wouldn't do this. Not in his own
house—spewing out that vomit from his mind.

HAPPY: Charley never had to cope with what he's got to.

BIFF: People are worse off than Willy Loman. Believe me, I've seen them!

LINDA: Then make Charley your father, Biff. You can't do that, can you?
I don't say he's a great man. Willy Loman never made a lot of money. His name
was never in the paper. He's not the finest character that ever lived. But he's
a human being, and a terrible thing is happening to him. So attention must be
paid. He's not to be allowed to fall into his grave like an old dog. Attention,
attention must be finally paid to such a person. You called him crazy—

BIFF: I didn't mean—

LINDA: No, a lot of people think he's lost his—balance. But you don't have
to be very smart to know what his trouble is. The man is exhausted.

HAPPY: Sure!

LINDA: A small man can be just as exhausted as a great man. He works for
a company thirty-six years this March, opens up unheard-of territories to their
trademark, and now in his old age they take his salary away.

HAPPY   (*indignantly*): I didn't know that, Mom.

LINDA: You never asked, my dear! Now that you get your spending money
someplace else you don't trouble your mind with him.

HAPPY: But I gave you money last—

LINDA: Christmas time, fifty dollars! To fix the hot water it cost ninety-seven fifty! For five weeks he's been on straight commission, like a beginner, an unknown!

BIFF: Those ungrateful bastards!

LINDA: Are they any worse than his sons? When he brought them business, when he was young, they were glad to see him. But now his old friends, the old buyers that loved him so and always found some order to hand him in a pinch—they're all dead, retired. He used to be able to make six, seven calls a day in Boston. Now he takes his valises out of the car and puts them back and takes them out again and he's exhausted. Instead of walking he talks now. He drives seven hundred miles, and when he gets there no one knows him any more, no one welcomes him. And what goes through a man's mind, driving seven hundred miles home without having earned a cent? Why shouldn't he talk to himself? Why? When he has to go to Charley and borrow fifty dollars a week and pretend to me that it's his pay? How long can that go on? How long? You see what I'm sitting here and waiting for? And you tell me he has no character? The man who never worked a day but for your benefit? When does he get the medal for that? Is this his reward—to turn around at the age of sixty-three and find his sons, who he loved better than his life, one a philandering bum—

HAPPY: Mom!

LINDA: That's all you are, my baby! (*To* BIFF.) And you! What happened to the love you had for him? You were such pals! How you used to talk to him on the phone every night! How lonely he was till he could come home to you!

BIFF: All right, Mom. I'll live here in my room, and I'll get a job. I'll keep away from him, that's all.

LINDA: No, Biff. You can't stay here and fight all the time.

BIFF: He threw me out of this house, remember that.

LINDA: Why did he do that? I never knew why.

BIFF: Because I know he's a fake and he doesn't like anybody around who knows!

LINDA: Why a fake? In what way? What do you mean?

BIFF: Just don't lay it all at my feet. It's between me and him—that's all I have to say. I'll chip in from now on. He'll settle for half my pay check. He'll be all right. I'm going to bed. (*He starts for the stairs.*)

LINDA: He won't be all right.

BIFF (*turning on the stairs, furiously*): I hate this city and I'll stay here. Now what do you want?

LINDA: He's dying, Biff.

HAPPY *turns quickly to her, shocked.*

BIFF (*after a pause.*): Why is he dying?

LINDA: He's been trying to kill himself.

BIFF (*with great horror*): How?

LINDA: I live from day to day.

BIFF: What're you talking about?

LINDA: Remember I wrote you that he smashed up the car again? In February?

BIFF: Well?

LINDA: The insurance inspector came. He said that they have evidence. That all these accidents in the last year—weren't—weren't—accidents.

HAPPY: How can they tell that? That's a lie.

LINDA: It seems there's a woman . . . (*She takes a breath as—*)

BIFF   (*sharply but contained*): What woman?

LINDA   (*simultaneously*): . . . and this woman . . .

LINDA: What?

BIFF: Nothing. Go ahead.

LINDA: What did you say?

BIFF: Nothing. I just said what woman?

HAPPY: What about her?

LINDA: Well, it seems she was walking down the road and saw his car. She says that he wasn't driving fast at all, and that he didn't skid. She says he came to that little bridge, and then deliberately smashed into the railing, and it was only the shallowness of the water that saved him.

BIFF: Oh, no, he probably just fell asleep again.

LINDA: I don't think he fell asleep.

BIFF: Why not?

LINDA: Last month . . . (*With great difficulty.*) Oh, boys, it's so hard to say a thing like this! He's just a big stupid man to you, but I tell you there's more good in him than in many other people. (*She chokes, wipes her eyes.*) I was looking for a fuse. The lights blew out, and I went down the cellar. And behind the fuse box—it happened to fall out—was a length of rubber pipe—just short.

HAPPY: No kidding?

LINDA: There's a little attachment on the end of it. I knew right away. And sure enough, on the bottom of the water heater there's a new little nipple on the gas pipe.

HAPPY   (*angrily*): That—jerk.

BIFF: Did you have it taken off?

LINDA: I'm—I'm ashamed to. How can I mention it to him? Every day I go down and take away that little rubber pipe. But, when he comes home, I put it back where it was. How can I insult him that way? I don't know what to do. I live from day to day, boys. I tell you, I know every thought in his mind. It sounds so old-fashioned and silly, but I tell you he put his whole life into you and you've turned your backs on him. (*She is bent over in the chair, weeping, her face in her hands.*) Biff, I swear to God! Biff, his life is in your hands!

HAPPY   (*to* BIFF): How do you like that damned fool!

BIFF   (*kissing her*): All right, pal, all right. It's all settled now. I've been remiss. I know that, Mom. But now I'll stay, and I swear to you, I'll apply myself. (*Kneeling in front of her, in a fever of self-reproach.*) It's just—you see, Mom, I don't fit in business. Not that I won't try. I'll try, and I'll make good.

HAPPY: Sure you will. The trouble with you in business was you never tried to please people.

BIFF: I know, I—

HAPPY: Like when you worked for Harrison's. Bob Harrison said you were tops, and then you go and do some damn fool thing like whistling whole songs in the elevator like a comedian.

BIFF   (*against* HAPPY): So what? I like to whistle sometimes.

HAPPY: You don't raise a guy to a responsible job who whistles in the elevator!

LINDA: Well, don't argue about it now.

HAPPY: Like when you'd go off and swim in the middle of the day instead of taking the line around.

BIFF   (*his resentment rising*): Well, don't you run off? You take off sometimes, don't you? On a nice summer day?

HAPPY: Yeah, but I cover myself!

LINDA: Boys!

HAPPY: If I'm going to take a fade the boss can call any number where I'm supposed to be and they'll swear to him that I just left. I'll tell you something that I hate to say, Biff, but in the business world some of them think you're crazy.

BIFF   (*angered*): Screw the business world!

HAPPY: All right, screw it! Great, but cover yourself!

LINDA: Hap, Hap!

BIFF: I don't care what they think! They've laughed at Dad for years, and you know why? Because we don't belong in this nut-house of a city! We should be mixing cement on some open plain, or—or carpenters. A carpenter is allowed to whistle!

WILLY *walks in from the entrance of the house, at left.*

WILLY: Even your grandfather was better than a carpenter. (*Pause. They watch him.*) You never grew up. Bernard does not whistle in the elevator, I assure you.

BIFF   (*as though to laugh* WILLY *out of it*): Yeah, but you do, Pop.

WILLY: I never in my life whistled in an elevator! And who in the business world thinks I'm crazy?

BIFF: I didn't mean it like that, Pop. Now don't make a whole thing out of it, will ya?

WILLY: Go back to the West! Be a carpenter, a cowboy, enjoy yourself!

LINDA: Willy, he was just saying—

WILLY: I heard what he said!

HAPPY   (*trying to quiet* WILLY): Hey, Pop, come on now . . .

WILLY   (*continuing over* HAPPY's *line*): They laugh at me, heh? Go to Filene's, go to the Hub, go to Slattery's, Boston. Call out the name Willy Loman and see what happens! Big shot!

BIFF: All right, Pop.

WILLY: Big!

BIFF: All right!

WILLY: Why do you always insult me?

BIFF: I didn't say a word. (*To* LINDA.) Did I say a word?

LINDA: He didn't say anything, Willy.

WILLY   (*going to the doorway of the livingroom*): All right, good night, good night.

LINDA: Willy, dear, he just decided . . .

WILLY   (*to* BIFF): If you get tired hanging around tomorrow, paint the ceiling I put up in the livingroom.

BIFF: I'm leaving early tomorrow.

HAPPY: He's going to see Bill Oliver, Pop.

WILLY   (*interestedly*): Oliver? For what?

BIFF   (*with reserve, but trying, trying*): He always said he'd stake me. I'd like to go into business, so maybe I can take him up on it.

LINDA: Isn't that wonderful?

WILLY: Don't interrupt. What's wonderful about it? There's fifty men in the City of New York who'd stake him. (*To* BIFF.) Sporting goods?

BIFF: I guess so. I know something about it and—

WILLY: He knows something about it! You know sporting goods better than Spalding, for God's sake! How much is he giving you?

BIFF: I don't know, I didn't even see him yet, but—

WILLY: Then what're you talkin' about?

BIFF   (*getting angry*): Well, all I said was I'm gonna see him, that's all!

WILLY   (*turning away*): Ah, you're counting your chickens again.

BIFF   (*starting left for the stairs*): Oh, Jesus, I'm going to sleep!

WILLY   (*calling after him*): Don't curse in this house!

BIFF   (*turning*): Since when did you get so clean!

HAPPY   (*trying to stop them*): Wait a . . .

WILLY: Don't use that language to me! I won't have it!

HAPPY   (*grabbing* BIFF, *shouts*): Wait a minute! I got an idea. I got a feasible idea. Come here, Biff, let's talk this over now, let's talk some sense here. When I was down in Florida last time, I thought of a great idea to sell sporting goods. It just came back to me. You and I, Biff—we have a line, the Loman Line. We train a couple of weeks, and put on a couple of exhibitions, see?

WILLY: That's an idea!

HAPPY: Wait! We form two basketball teams, see? Two water-polo teams. We play each other. It's a million dollars' worth of publicity. Two brothers, see? The Loman Brothers. Displays in the Royal Palms—all the hotels. And banners over the ring and the basketball court: "Loman Brothers." Baby, we could sell sporting goods!

WILLY: That is a one-million-dollar idea.

LINDA: Marvelous!

BIFF: I'm in great shape as far as that's concerned.

HAPPY: And the beauty of it is, Biff, it wouldn't be like a business. We'd be out playin' ball again . . .

BIFF   (*enthused*): Yeah, that's . . .

WILLY: Million-dollar . . .

HAPPY: And you wouldn't get fed up with it, Biff. It'd be the family again. There'd be the old honor, and comradeship, and if you wanted to go off for a swim or somethin'—well, you'd do it! Without some smart cooky gettin' up ahead of you!

WILLY: Lick the world! You guys together could absolutely lick the civilized world.

BIFF: I'll see Oliver tomorrow. Hap, if we could work that out . . .

LINDA: Maybe things are beginning to—

WILLY (*wildly enthused, to* LINDA): Stop interrupting! (*To* BIFF.) But don't wear sport jacket and slacks when you see Oliver.

BIFF: No, I'll—

WILLY: A business suit, and talk as little as possible, and don't crack any jokes.

BIFF: He did like me. Always liked me.

LINDA: He loved you!

WILLY (*to* LINDA): Will you stop! (*To* BIFF.) Walk in very serious. You are not applying for a boy's job. Money is to pass. Be quiet, fine, and serious. Everybody likes a kidder, but nobody lends him money.

HAPPY: I'll try to get some myself, Biff. I'm sure I can.

WILLY: I can see great things for you, kids, I think your troubles are over. But remember, start big and you'll end big. Ask for fifteen. How much you gonna ask for?

BIFF: Gee, I don't know—

WILLY: And don't say "Gee." "Gee" is a boy's word. A man walking in for fifteen thousand dollars does not say "Gee!"

BIFF: Ten, I think, would be top though.

WILLY: Don't be so modest. You always started too low. Walk in with a big laugh. Don't look worried. Start off with a couple of your good stories to lighten things up. It's not what you say, it's how you say it—because personality always wins the day.

LINDA: Oliver always thought the highest of him—

WILLY: Will you let me talk?

BIFF: Don't yell at her, Pop, will ya?

WILLY (*angrily*): I was talking, wasn't I?

BIFF: I don't like you yelling at her all the time, and I'm tellin' you, that's all.

WILLY: What're you, takin' over this house?

LINDA: Willy—

WILLY (*turning on her*): Don't take his side all the time, goddammit!

BIFF (*furiously*): Stop yelling at her!

WILLY (*suddenly pulling on his cheek, beaten down, guilt ridden*): Give my best to Bill Oliver—he may remember me. (*He exits through the livingroom doorway.*)

LINDA (*her voice subdued*): What'd you have to start that for? (BIFF *turns away.*) You see how sweet he was as soon as you talked hopefully? (*She goes over to* BIFF.) Come up and say good night to him. Don't let him go to bed that way.

HAPPY: Come on, Biff, let's buck him up.

LINDA: Please, dear. Just say good night. It takes so little to make him happy. Come. (*She goes through the livingroom doorway, calling upstairs from within the livingroom.*) Your pajamas are hanging in the bathroom. Willy!

HAPPY   (*looking toward where* LINDA *went out*): What a woman! They broke the mold when they made her. You know that, Biff?

BIFF: He's off salary. My God, working on commission!

HAPPY: Well, let's face it: he's no hot-shot selling man. Except that sometimes, you have to admit, he's a sweet personality.

BIFF   (*deciding*): Lend me ten bucks, will ya? I want to buy some new ties.

HAPPY: I'll take you to a place I know. Beautiful stuff. Wear one of my striped shirts tomorrow.

BIFF: She got gray. Mom got awful old. Gee, I'm gonna go in to Oliver tomorrow and knock him for a—

HAPPY: Come on up. Tell that to Dad. Let's give him a whirl. Come on.

BIFF   (*steamed up*): You know, with ten thousand bucks, boy!

HAPPY   (*as they go into the livingroom*): That's the talk, Biff, that's the first time I've heard the old confidence out of you! (*From within the livingroom, fading off.*) You're gonna live with me, kid, and any babe you want just say the word . . . (*The last lines are hardly heard. They are mounting the stairs to their parents' bedroom.*)

LINDA   (*entering her bedroom and addressing* WILLY, *who is in the bathroom. She is straightening the bed for him*): Can you do anything about the shower? It drips.

WILLY   (*from the bathroom*): All of a sudden everything falls to pieces! Goddam plumbing, oughta be sued, those people. I hardly finished putting it in and the thing . . . (*His words rumble off.*)

LINDA: I'm just wondering if Oliver will remember him. You think he might?

WILLY   (*coming out of the bathroom in his pajamas*): Remember him? What's the matter with you, you crazy? If he'd've stayed with Oliver he'd be on top by now! Wait'll Oliver gets a look at him. You don't know the average caliber any more. The average young man today—(*he is getting into bed*)—is got a caliber of zero. Greatest thing in the world for him was to bum around.

BIFF *and* HAPPY *enter the bedroom. Slight pause.*

WILLY   (*stops short, looking at* BIFF): Glad to hear it, boy.

HAPPY: He wanted to say good night to you, sport.

WILLY   (*to* BIFF): Yeah. Knock him dead, boy. What'd you want to tell me?

BIFF: Just take it easy, Pop. Good night. (*He turns to go.*)

WILLY   (*unable to resist*): And if anything falls off the desk while you're talking to him—like a package or something—don't you pick it up. They have office boys for that.

LINDA: I'll make a big breakfast—

WILLY: Will you let me finish? (*To* BIFF.) Tell him you were in the business in the West. Not farm work.

BIFF: All right, Dad.

LINDA: I think everything—

WILLY   (*going right through her speech*): And don't undersell yourself. No less than fifteen thousand dollars.

BIFF   (*unable to bear him*): Okay. Good night, Mom. (*He starts moving.*)

WILLY: Because you got a greatness in you, Biff, remember that. You got all kinds a greatness . . . (*He lies back, exhausted.* BIFF *walks out.*)

LINDA   (*calling after* BIFF): Sleep well, darling!

HAPPY: I'm gonna get married, Mom. I wanted to tell you.

LINDA: Go to sleep, dear.

HAPPY   (*going*): I just wanted to tell you.

WILLY: Keep up the good work. (HAPPY *exits*.) God . . . remember that Ebbets Field game? The championship of the city?

LINDA: Just rest. Should I sing to you?

WILLY: Yeah. Sing to me. (LINDA *hums a soft lullaby*.) When that team came out—he was the tallest, remember?

LINDA: Oh, yes. And in gold.

BIFF *enters the darkened kitchen, takes a cigarette, and leaves the house. He comes downstage into a golden pool of light. He smokes, staring at the night.*

WILLY: Like a young god. Hercules—something like that. And the sun, the sun all around him. Remember how he waved to me? Right up from the field, with the representatives of three colleges standing by? And the buyers I brought, and the cheers when he came out—Loman, Loman, Loman! God Almighty, he'll be great yet. A star like that, magnificent, can never really fade away!

The light on WILLY *is fading. The gas heater begins to glow through the kitchen wall, near the stairs, a blue flame beneath red coils.*

LINDA   (*timidly*): Willy, dear, what has he got against you?

WILLY: I'm so tired. Don't talk any more.

BIFF *slowly returns to the kitchen. He stops, stares toward the heater.*

LINDA: Will you ask Howard to let you work in New York?

WILLY: First thing in the morning. Everything'll be all right.

BIFF *reaches behind the heater and draws out a length of rubber tubing. He is horrified and turns his head toward* WILLY'S *room, still dimly lit, from which the strains of* LINDA'S *desperate but monotonous humming rise.*

WILLY   (*staring through the window into the moonlight*): Gee, look at the moon moving between the buildings!

BIFF *wraps the tubing around his hand and quickly goes up the stairs. Curtain.*

ACT II

Music is heard, gay and bright. The curtain rises as the music fades away. WILLY, *in shirt sleeves, is sitting at the kitchen table, sipping coffee, his hat in his lap.* LINDA *is filling his cup when she can.*

WILLY: Wonderful coffee. Meal in itself.

LINDA: Can I make you some eggs?

WILLY: No. Take a breath.

LINDA: You look so rested, dear.

WILLY: I slept like a dead one. First time in months. Imagine, sleeping till ten on a Tuesday morning. Boys left nice and early, heh?

LINDA: They were out of here by eight o'clock.

WILLY: Good work!

LINDA: It was so thrilling to see them leaving together. I can't get over the shaving lotion in this house.

WILLY   (*smiling*): Mmm—

LINDA: Biff was very changed this morning. His whole attitude seemed to be hopeful. He couldn't wait to get downtown to see Oliver.

WILLY: He's heading for a change. There's no question, there simply are certain men that take longer to get—solidified. How did he dress?

LINDA: His blue suit. He's so handsome in that suit. He could be a—anything in that suit!

> WILLY *gets up from the table.* LINDA *holds his jacket for him.*

WILLY: There's no question, no question at all. Gee, on the way home tonight I'd like to buy some seeds.

LINDA   (*laughing*): That'd be wonderful. But not enough sun gets back there. Nothing'll grow any more.

WILLY: You wait, kid, before it's all over we're gonna get a little place out in the country, and I'll raise some vegetables, a couple of chickens . . .

LINDA: You'll do it yet, dear.

> WILLY *walks out of his jacket.* LINDA *follows him.*

WILLY: And they'll get married, and come for a weekend. I'd build a little guest house. 'Cause I got so many fine tools, all I'd need would be a little lumber and some peace of mind.

LINDA   (*joyfully*): I sewed the lining . . .

WILLY: I could build two guest houses, so they'd both come. Did he decide how much he's going to ask Oliver for?

LINDA   (*getting him into the jacket*): He didn't mention it, but I imagine ten or fifteen thousand. You going to talk to Howard today?

WILLY: Yeah. I'll put it to him straight and simple. He'll just have to take me off the road.

LINDA: And Willy, don't forget to ask for a little advance, because we've got the insurance premium. It's the grace period now.

WILLY: That's a hundred . . . ?

LINDA: A hundred and eight, sixty-eight. Because we're a little short again.

WILLY: Why are we short?

LINDA: Well, you had the motor job on the car . . .

WILLY: That goddam Studebaker!

LINDA: And you got one more payment on the refrigerator . . .

WILLY: But it just broke again!

LINDA: Well, it's old, dear.

WILLY: I told you we should've bought a well-advertised machine. Charley bought a General Electric and it's twenty years old and it's still good, that son-of-a-bitch.

LINDA: But, Willy—

WILLY: Whoever heard of a Hastings refrigerator? Once in my life I would like to own something outright before it's broken! I'm always in a race with the junkyard! I just finished paying for the car and it's on its last legs. The refrigerator consumes belts like a goddam maniac. They time those things. They time them so when you finally paid for them, they're used up.

LINDA   (*buttoning up his jacket as he unbuttons it*): All told, about two hundred dollars would carry us, dear. But that includes the last payment on the mortgage. After this payment, Willy, the house belongs to us.

WILLY: It's twenty-five years!

LINDA: Biff was nine years old when we bought it.

WILLY: Well, that's a great thing. To weather a twenty-five year mortgage is—

LINDA: It's an accomplishment.

WILLY: All the cement, the lumber, the reconstruction I put in this house! There ain't a crack to be found in it any more.

LINDA: Well, it served its purpose.

WILLY: What purpose? Some stranger'll come along, move in, and that's that. If only Biff would take this house, and raise a family . . . (*He starts to go.*) Good-by, I'm late.

LINDA   (*suddenly remembering*): Oh, I forgot! You're supposed to meet them for dinner.

WILLY: Me?

LINDA: At Frank's Chop House on Forty-eighth near Sixth Avenue.

WILLY: Is that so! How about you?

LINDA: No, just the three of you. They're gonna blow you to a big meal!

WILLY: Don't say! Who thought of that?

LINDA: Biff came to me this morning, Willy, and he said, "Tell Dad, we want to blow him to a big meal." Be there six o'clock. You and your two boys are going to have dinner.

WILLY: Gee whiz! That's really somethin'. I'm gonna knock Howard for a loop, kid. I'll get an advance, and I'll come home with a New York job. Goddammit, now I'm gonna do it!

LINDA: Oh, that's the spirit, Willy!

WILLY: I will never get behind a wheel the rest of my life!

LINDA: It's changing, Willy, I can feel it changing!

WILLY: Beyond a question. G'by, I'm late. (*He starts to go again.*)

LINDA   (*calling after him as she runs to the kitchen table for a handkerchief*): You got your glasses?

WILLY   (*feels for them, then comes back in*): Yeah, yeah, got my glasses.

LINDA   (*giving him the handkerchief*): And a handkerchief.

WILLY: Yeah, handkerchief.

LINDA: And your saccharine?

WILLY: Yeah, my saccharine.

LINDA: Be careful on the subway stairs.

She kisses him, and a silk stocking is seen hanging from her hand. WILLY *notices it.*

WILLY: Will you stop mending stockings? At least while I'm in the house. It gets me nervous. I can't tell you. Please.

LINDA *hides the stocking in her hand as she follows* WILLY *across the forestage in front of the house.*

LINDA: Remember, Frank's Chop House.

WILLY   (*passing the apron*): Maybe beets would grow out there.

LINDA   (*laughing*): But you tried so many times.

WILLY: Yeah. Well, don't work hard today. (*He disappears around the right corner of the house.*)

LINDA: Be careful!

As WILLY *vanishes,* LINDA *waves to him. Suddenly the phone rings. She runs across the stage and into the kitchen and lifts it.*

LINDA: Hello? Oh, Biff! I'm so glad you called, I just . . . Yes, sure, I just told him. Yes, he'll be there for dinner at six o'clock, I didn't forget. Listen, I was just dying to tell you. You know that little rubber pipe I told you about? That he connected to the gas heater? I finally decided to go down the cellar this morning and take it away and destroy it. But it's gone! Imagine? He took it away himself, it isn't there! (*She listens.*) When? Oh, then you took it. Oh— nothing, it's just that I'd hoped he'd taken it away himself. Oh, I'm not worried, darling, because this morning he left in such high spirits, it was like the old days! I'm not afraid any more. Did Mr. Oliver see you? . . . Well, you wait there then. And make a nice impression on him, darling. Just don't perspire too much before you see him. And have a nice time with Dad. He may have big news too! . . . That's right, a New York job. And be sweet to him tonight, dear. Be loving to him. Because he's only a little boat looking for a harbor. (*She is trembling with sorrow and joy.*) Oh, that's wonderful, Biff, you'll save his life. Thanks, darling. Just put your arm around him when he comes into the restaurant. Give him a smile. That's the boy . . . Good-by, dear. . . . You got your comb? . . . That's fine. Good-by, Biff dear.

In the middle of her speech, HOWARD WAGNER, *thirty-six, wheels in a small typewriter table on which is a wire-recording machine and proceeds to plug it in. This is on the left forestage. Light slowly fades on* LINDA *as it rises on* HOWARD. HOWARD *is intent on threading the machine and only glances over his shoulder as* WILLY *appears.*

WILLY: Pst! Pst!

HOWARD: Hello, Willy, come in.

WILLY: Like to have a little talk with you, Howard.

HOWARD: Sorry to keep you waiting. I'll be with you in a minute.

WILLY: What's that, Howard?

HOWARD: Didn't you ever see one of these? Wire recorder.

WILLY: Oh. Can we talk a minute?

HOWARD: Records things. Just got delivery yesterday. Been driving me crazy, the most terrific machine I ever saw in my life. I was up all night with it.

WILLY: What do you do with it?

HOWARD: I bought it for dictation, but you can do anything with it. Listen to this. I had it home last night. Listen to what I picked up. The first one is my daughter. Get this. (*He flicks the switch and "Roll out the Barrel" is heard being whistled.*) Listen to that kid whistle.

WILLY: That is lifelike, isn't it?

HOWARD: Seven years old. Get that tone.

WILLY: Ts, ts. Like to ask a little favor if you . . .

The whistling breaks off, and the voice of HOWARD'S DAUGHTER *is heard.*

HIS DAUGHTER: "Now you, Daddy."

HOWARD: She's crazy for me! (*Again the same song is whistled.*) That's me! Ha! (*He winks.*)

WILLY: You're very good!

The whistling breaks off again. The machine runs silent for a moment.

HOWARD: Sh! Get this now, this is my son.

HIS SON: "The capital of Alabama is Montgomery; the capital of Arizona is Phoenix; the capital of Arkansas is Little Rock; the capital of California is Sacramento . . ." (*And on, and on.*)

HOWARD (*holding up five fingers*): Five years old, Willy!

WILLY: He'll make an announcer some day!

HIS SON (*continuing*): "The capital . . ."

HOWARD: Get that—alphabetical order! (*The machine breaks off suddenly.*) Wait a minute. The maid kicked the plug out.

WILLY: It certainly is a—

HOWARD: Sh, for God's sake!

HIS SON: "It's nine o'clock, Bulova watch time. So I have to go to sleep."

WILLY: That really is—

HOWARD: Wait a minute! The next is my wife.

They wait.

HOWARD'S VOICE: "Go on, say something." (*Pause.*) "Well, you gonna talk?"

HIS WIFE: "I can't think of anything."

HOWARD'S VOICE: "Well, talk—it's turning."

HIS WIFE (*shyly, beaten*): "Hello." (*Silence.*) "Oh, Howard, I can't talk into this . . ."

HOWARD (*snapping the machine off*): That was my wife.

WILLY: That is a wonderful machine. Can we—

HOWARD: I tell you, Willy, I'm gonna take my camera, and my bandsaw, and all my hobbies, and out they go. This is the most fascinating relaxation I ever found.

WILLY: I think I'll get one myself.

HOWARD: Sure, they're only a hundred and a half. You can't do without it. Supposing you wanna hear Jack Benny, see? But you can't be at home at that hour. So you tell the maid to turn the radio on when Jack Benny comes on, and this automatically goes on with the radio . . .

WILLY: And when you come home you . . .

HOWARD: You can come home twelve o'clock, one o'clock, any time you like, and you get yourself a Coke and sit yourself down, throw the switch, and there's Jack Benny's program in the middle of the night!

WILLY: I'm definitely going to get one. Because lots of time I'm on the road, and I think to myself, what I must be missing on the radio!

HOWARD: Don't you have a radio in the car?

WILLY: Well, yeah, but who ever thinks of turning it on?

HOWARD: Say, aren't you supposed to be in Boston?

WILLY: That's what I want to talk to you about, Howard. You got a minute?

He draws a chair in from the wing.

HOWARD: What happened? What're you doing here?

WILLY: Well . . .

HOWARD: You didn't crack up again, did you?

WILLY: Oh, no. No . . .

HOWARD: Geez, you had me worried there for a minute. What's the trouble?

WILLY: Well, to tell you the truth, Howard, I've come to the decision that I'd rather not travel any more.

HOWARD: Not travel! Well, what'll you do?

WILLY: Remember, Christmas time, when you had the party here? You said you'd try to think of some spot for me here in town.

HOWARD: With us?

WILLY: Well, sure.

HOWARD: Oh, yeah, yeah. I remember. Well, I couldn't think of anything for you, Willy.

WILLY: I tell ya, Howard. The kids are all grown up, y'know. I don't need much any more. If I could take home—well, sixty-five dollars a week, I could swing it.

HOWARD: Yeah, but Willy, see I—

WILLY: I tell ya why, Howard. Speaking frankly and between the two of us, y'know—I'm just a little tired.

HOWARD: Oh, I could understand that, Willy. But you're a road man, Willy, and we do a road business. We've only got a half-dozen salesmen on the floor here.

WILLY: God knows, Howard, I never asked a favor of any man. But I was with the firm when your father used to carry you in here in his arms.

HOWARD: I know that, Willy, but—

WILLY: Your father came to me the day you were born and asked me what I thought of the name of Howard, may he rest in peace.

HOWARD: I appreciate that, Willy, but there just is no spot here for you. If I had a spot I'd slam you right in, but I just don't have a single, solitary spot.

He looks for his lighter. WILLY *has picked it up and gives it to him. Pause.*

WILLY   (*with increasing anger*): Howard, all I need to set my table is fifty dollars a week.

HOWARD: But where am I going to put you, kid?

WILLY: Look, it isn't a question of whether I can sell merchandise, is it?

HOWARD: No, but it's a business, kid, and everybody's gotta pull his own weight.

WILLY (*desperately*): Just let me tell you a story, Howard—

HOWARD: 'Cause you gotta admit, business is business.

WILLY (*angrily*): Business is definitely business, but just listen for a minute. You don't understand this. When I was a boy—eighteen, nineteen—I was already on the road. And there was a question in my mind as to whether selling had a future for me. Because in those days I had a yearning to go to Alaska. See, there were three gold strikes in one month in Alaska, and I felt like going out. Just for the ride, you might say.

HOWARD (*barely interested*): Don't say.

WILLY: Oh, yeah, my father lived many years in Alaska. He was an adventurous man. We've got quite a little streak of self-reliance in our family. I thought I'd go out with my older brother and try to locate him, and maybe settle in the North with the old man. And I was almost decided to go, when I met a salesman in the Parker House. His name was Dave Singleman. And he was eighty-four years old, and he'd drummed merchandise in thirty-one states. And old Dave, he'd go up to his room, y'understand, put on his green velvet slippers—I'll never forget—and pick up his phone and call the buyers, and without ever leaving his room, at the age of eighty-four, he made his living. And when I saw that, I realized that selling was the greatest career a man could want. 'Cause what could be more satisfying than to be able to go, at the age of eighty-four, into twenty or thirty different cities, and pick up a phone, and be remembered and loved and helped by so many different people? Do you know? when he died—and by the way he died the death of a salesman, in his green velvet slippers in the smoker of the New York, New Haven and Hartford, going into Boston—when he died, hundreds of salesmen and buyers were at his funeral. Things were sad on a lotta trains for months after that. (*He stands up. HOWARD has not looked at him.*) In those days there was personality in it, Howard. There was respect, and comradeship, and gratitude in it. Today, it's all cut and dried, and there's no chance for bringing friendship to bear—or personality. You see what I mean? They don't know me any more.

HOWARD (*moving away, to the right*): That's just the thing, Willy.

WILLY: If I had forty dollars a week—that's all I'd need. Forty dollars, Howard.

HOWARD: Kid, I can't take blood from a stone, I—

WILLY (*desperation is on him now*): Howard, the year Al Smith was nominated, your father came to me and—

HOWARD (*starting to go off*): I've got to see some people, kid.

WILLY (*stopping him*): I'm talking about your father! There were promises made across this desk! You mustn't tell me you've got people to see—I put thirty-four years into this firm, Howard, and now I can't pay my insurance! You can't eat the orange and throw the peel away—a man is not a piece of fruit! (*After a pause.*) Now pay attention. Your father—in 1928 I had a big year. I averaged a hundred and seventy dollars a week in commissions.

HOWARD (*impatiently*): Now, Willy, you never averaged—

WILLY   (*banging his hand on the desk*): I averaged a hundred and seventy dollars a week in the year of 1928! And your father came to me—or rather, I was in the office here—it was right over this desk—and he put his hand on my shoulder—

HOWARD   (*getting up*): You'll have to excuse me, Willy, I gotta see some people. Pull yourself together. (*Going out.*) I'll be back in a little while.

On HOWARD's *exit, the light on his chair grows very bright and strange.*

WILLY: Pull myself together! What the hell did I say to him? My God, I was yelling at him! How could I! (WILLY *breaks off, staring at the light, which occupies the chair, animating it. He approaches this chair, standing across the desk from it.*) Frank, Frank, don't you remember what you told me that time? How you put your hand on my shoulder, and Frank . . . (*He leans on the desk and as he speaks the dead man's name he accidentally switches on the recorder, and instantly—*)

HOWARD'S SON: ". . . of New York is Albany. The capital of Ohio is Cincinnati, the capital of Rhode Island is . . ." (*The recitation continues.*)

WILLY   (*leaping away with fright, shouting*): Ha! Howard! Howard! Howard!

HOWARD   (*rushing in*): What happened?

WILLY   (*pointing at the machine, which continues nasally, childishly, with the capital cities*): Shut it off! Shut it off!

HOWARD   (*pulling the plug out*): Look, Willy . . .

WILLY   (*pressing his hands to his eyes*): I gotta get myself some coffee. I'll get some coffee . . .

WILLY *starts to walk out.* HOWARD *stops him.*

HOWARD   (*rolling up the cord*): Willy, look . . .

WILLY: I'll go to Boston.

HOWARD: Willy, you can't go to Boston for us.

WILLY: Why can't I go?

HOWARD: I don't want you to represent us. I've been meaning to tell you for a long time now.

WILLY: Howard, are you firing me?

HOWARD: I think you need a good long rest, Willy.

WILLY: Howard—

HOWARD: And when you feel better, come back, and we'll see if we can work something out.

WILLY: But I gotta earn money, Howard. I'm in no position—

HOWARD: Where are your sons? Why don't your sons give you a hand?

WILLY: They're working on a very big deal.

HOWARD: This is no time for false pride, Willy. You go to your sons and tell them that you're tired. You've got two great boys, haven't you?

WILLY: Oh, no question, no question, but in the meantime . . .

HOWARD: Then that's that, heh?

WILLY: All right, I'll go to Boston tomorrow.

HOWARD: No, no.

WILLY: I can't throw myself on my sons. I'm not a cripple!

HOWARD: Look, kid, I'm busy this morning.

WILLY (*grasping* HOWARD'S *arm*): Howard, you've got to let me go to Boston!

HOWARD (*hard, keeping himself under control*): I've got a line of people to see this morning. Sit down, take five minutes, and pull yourself together, and then go home, will ya? I need the office, Willy. (*He starts to go, turns, remembering the recorder, starts to push off the table holding the recorder.*) Oh, yeah. Whenever you can this week, stop by and drop off the samples. You'll feel better, Willy, and then come back and we'll talk. Pull yourself together, kid, there's people outside.

HOWARD *exits, pushing the table off left.* WILLY *stares into space, exhausted. Now the music is heard—*BEN'S *music—first distantly, then closer, closer. As* WILLY *speaks,* BEN *enters from the right. He carries valise and umbrella.*

WILLY: Oh, Ben, how did you do it? What is the answer? Did you wind up the Alaska deal already?

BEN: Doesn't take much time if you know what you're doing. Just a short business trip. Boarding ship in an hour. Wanted to say good-by.

WILLY: Ben, I've got to talk to you.

BEN (*glancing at his watch*): Haven't the time, William.

WILLY (*crossing the apron to* BEN): Ben, nothing's working out. I don't know what to do.

BEN: Now, look here, William. I've bought timberland in Alaska and I need a man to look after things for me.

WILLY: God, timberland! Me and my boys in those grand outdoors!

BEN: You've a new continent at your doorstep, William. Get out of these cities, they're full of talk and time payments and courts of law. Screw on your fists and you can fight for a fortune up there.

WILLY: Yes, yes! Linda! Linda!

LINDA *enters as of old, with the wash.*

LINDA: Oh, you're back?

BEN: I haven't much time.

WILLY: No, wait! Linda, he's got a proposition for me in Alaska.

LINDA: But you've got— (*To* BEN.) He's got a beautiful job here.

WILLY: But in Alaska, kid, I could—

LINDA: You're doing well enough, Willy!

BEN (*to* LINDA): Enough for what, my dear?

LINDA (*frightened of* BEN *and angry at him*): Don't say those things to him! Enough to be happy right here, right now. (*To* WILLY, *while* BEN *laughs.*) Why must everybody conquer the world? You're well liked, and the boys love you, and someday—(*to* BEN)—why, old man Wagner told him just the other day that if he keeps it up he'll be a member of the firm, didn't he, Willy?

WILLY: Sure, sure. I am building something with this firm, Ben, and if a man is building something he must be on the right track, mustn't he?

BEN: What are you building? Lay your hand on it. Where is it?

WILLY (*hesitantly*): That's true, Linda, there's nothing.

LINDA: Why? (*To* BEN.) There's a man eighty-four years old—

WILLY: That's right, Ben, that's right. When I look at that man I say, what is there to worry about?

BEN: Bah!

WILLY: It's true, Ben. All he has to do is go into any city, pick up the phone, and he's making his living and you know why?

BEN   (*picking up his valise*): I've got to go.

WILLY   (*holding* BEN *back*): Look at this boy!

BIFF, *in his high school sweater, enters carrying suitcase.* HAPPY *carries* BIFF'S *shoulder guards, gold helmet, and football pants.*

WILLY: Without a penny to his name, three great universities are begging for him, and from there the sky's the limit, because it's not what you do, Ben. It's who you know and the smile on your face! It's contacts, Ben, contacts! The whole wealth of Alaska passes over the lunch table at the Commodore Hotel, and that's the wonder, the wonder of this country, that a man can end with diamonds here on the basis of being liked! (*He turns to* BIFF.) And that's why when you get out on that field today it's important. Because thousands of people will be rooting for you and loving you. (*To* BEN, *who has again begun to leave.*) And Ben! when he walks into a business office his name will sound out like a bell and all the doors will open to him! I've seen it, Ben, I've seen it a thousand times! You can't feel it with your hand like timber, but it's there!

BEN: Good-by, William.

WILLY: Ben, am I right? Don't you think I'm right? I value your advice.

BEN: There's a new continent at your doorstep, William. You could walk out rich. Rich. (*He is gone.*)

WILLY: We'll do it here, Ben! You hear me? We're gonna do it here!

Young BERNARD *rushes in. The gay music of the boys is heard.*

BERNARD: Oh, gee, I was afraid you left already!

WILLY: Why? What time is it?

BERNARD: It's half-past one!

WILLY: Well, come on, everybody! Ebbets Field next stop! Where's the pennants? (*He rushes through the wall-line of the kitchen and out into the livingroom.*)

LINDA   (*to* BIFF): Did you pack fresh underwear?

BIFF   (*who has been limbering up*): I want to go!

BERNARD: Biff, I'm carrying your helmet, ain't I?

HAPPY: No, I'm carrying the helmet.

BERNARD: Oh, Biff, you promised me.

HAPPY: I'm carrying the helmet.

BERNARD: How am I going to get in the locker room?

LINDA: Let him carry the shoulder guards. (*She puts her coat and hat on in the kitchen.*)

BERNARD: Can I, Biff? 'Cause I told everybody I'm going to be in the locker room.

HAPPY: In Ebbets Field it's the clubhouse.

BERNARD: I meant the clubhouse. Biff!

HAPPY: Biff!

BIFF (*grandly, after a slight pause*): Let him carry the shoulder guards.

HAPPY (*as he gives* BERNARD *the shoulder guards*): Stay close to us now.

WILLY *rushes in with the pennants.*

WILLY (*handing them out*): Everybody wave when Biff comes out on the field. (HAPPY *and* BERNARD *run off.*) You set now, boy?

The music has died away.

BIFF: Ready to go, Pop. Every muscle is ready.

WILLY (*at the edge of the apron*): You realize what this means?

BIFF: That's right, Pop.

WILLY (*feeling* BIFF's *muscles*): You're comin' home this afternoon captain of the All-Scholastic Championship Team of the City of New York.

BIFF: I got it, Pop. And remember, pal, when I take off my helmet, that touchdown is for you.

WILLY: Let's go! (*He is starting out, with his arm around* BIFF, *when* CHARLEY *enters, as of old, in knickers.*) I got no room for you, Charley.

CHARLEY: Room? For what?

WILLY: In the car.

CHARLEY: You goin' for a ride? I wanted to shoot some casino.

WILLY (*furiously*): Casino! (*Incredulously*): Don't you realize what today is?

LINDA: Oh, he knows, Willy. He's just kidding you.

WILLY: That's nothing to kid about!

CHARLEY: No, Linda, what's goin' on?

LINDA: He's playing in Ebbets Field.

CHARLEY: Baseball in this weather?

WILLY: Don't talk to him. Come on, come on! (*He is pushing them out.*)

CHARLEY: Wait a minute, didn't you hear the news?

WILLY: What?

CHARLEY: Don't you listen to the radio? Ebbets Field just blew up.

WILLY: You go to hell! (CHARLEY *laughs. Pushing them out.*) Come on, come on! We're late.

CHARLEY (*as they go*): Knock a homer, Biff, knock a homer!

WILLY (*the last to leave, turning to* CHARLEY): I don't think that was funny, Charley. This is the greatest day of his life.

CHARLEY: Willy, when are you going to grow up?

WILLY: Yeah, heh? When this game is over, Charley, you'll be laughing out of the other side of your face. They'll be calling him another Red Grange. Twenty-five thousand a year.

CHARLEY (*kidding*): Is that so?

WILLY: Yeah, that's so.

CHARLEY: Well, then, I'm sorry, Willy. But tell me something.

WILLY: What?

CHARLEY: Who is Red Grange?

WILLY: Put up your hands. Goddam you, put up your hands!

CHARLEY, *chuckling, shakes his head and walks away, around the left corner of the stage.* WILLY *follows him. The music rises to a mocking frenzy.*

WILLY: Who the hell do you think you are, better than everybody else? You don't know everything, you big, ignorant, stupid . . . Put up your hands!

Light rises, on the right side of the forestage, on a small table in the reception room of CHARLEY'S *office. Traffic sounds are heard.* BERNARD, *now mature, sits whistling to himself. A pair of tennis rackets and an overnight bag are on the floor beside him.*

WILLY   (*offstage*): What are you walking away for? Don't walk away! If you're going to say something say it to my face! I know you laugh at me behind my back. You'll laugh out of the other side of your goddam face after this game. Touchdown! Touchdown! Eighty thousand people! Touchdown! Right between the goal posts.

BERNARD *is a quiet, earnest, but self-assured young man.* WILLY'S *voice is coming from right upstage now.* BERNARD *lowers his feet off the table and listens.* JENNY, *his father's secretary, enters.*

JENNY   (*distressed*): Say, Bernard, will you go out in the hall?
BERNARD: What is that noise? Who is it?
JENNY: Mr. Loman. He just got off the elevator.
BERNARD   (*getting up*): Who's he arguing with?
JENNY: Nobody. There's nobody with him. I can't deal with him any more, and your father gets all upset everytime he comes. I've got a lot of typing to do, and your father's waiting to sign it. Will you see him?
WILLY   (*entering*): Touchdown! Touch— (*He sees* JENNY.) Jenny, Jenny, good to see you. How're ya? Workin'? Or still honest?
JENNY: Fine. How've you been feeling?
WILLY: Not much any more, Jenny. Ha, ha! (*He is surprised to see the rackets.*)
BERNARD: Hello, Uncle Willy.
WILLY   (*almost shocked*): Bernard! Well, look who's here! (*He comes quickly, guiltily, to* BERNARD *and warmly shakes his hand.*)
BERNARD: How are you? Good to see you.
WILLY: What are you doing here?
BERNARD: Oh, just stopped by to see Pop. Get off my feet till my train leaves. I'm going to Washington in a few minutes.
WILLY: Is he in?
BERNARD: Yes, he's in his office with the accountant. Sit down.
WILLY   (*sitting down*): What're you going to do in Washington?
BERNARD: Oh, just a case I've got there, Willy.
WILLY: That so? (*indicating the rackets.*) You going to play tennis there?
BERNARD: I'm staying with a friend who's got a court.
WILLY: Don't say. His own tennis court. Must be fine people, I bet.
BERNARD: They are, very nice. Dad tells me Biff's in town.
WILLY   (*with a big smile*): Yeah, Biff's in. Working on a very big deal, Bernard.
BERNARD: What's Biff doing?

WILLY: Well, he's been doing very big things in the West. But he decided to establish himself here. Very big. We're having dinner. Did I hear your wife had a boy?

BERNARD: That's right. Our second.

WILLY: Two boys! What do you know!

BERNARD: What kind of a deal has Biff got?

WILLY: Well, Bill Oliver—very big sporting-goods man—he wants Biff very badly. Called him in from the West. Long distance, carte blanche, special deliveries. Your friends have their own private tennis court?

BERNARD: You still with the old firm, Willy?

WILLY   (*after a pause*): I'm—I'm overjoyed to see how you made the grade, Bernard, overjoyed. It's an encouraging thing to see a young man really—really — Looks very good for Biff—very— (*He breaks off, then.*) Bernard— (*He is so full of emotion, he breaks off again.*)

BERNARD: What is it, Willy?

WILLY   (*small and alone*): What—what's the secret?

BERNARD: What secret?

WILLY: How—how did you? Why didn't he ever catch on?

BERNARD: I wouldn't know that, Willy.

WILLY   (*confidentially, desperately*): You were his friend, his boyhood friend. There's something I don't understand about it. His life ended after that Ebbets Field game. From the age of seventeen nothing good ever happened to him.

BERNARD: He never trained himself for anything.

WILLY: But he did, he did. After high school he took so many correspondence courses. Radio mechanics; television; God knows what, and never made the slightest mark.

BERNARD   (*taking off his glasses*): Willy, do you want to talk candidly?

WILLY   (*rising, faces* BERNARD): I regard you as a very brilliant man, Bernard. I value your advice.

BERNARD: Oh, the hell with the advice, Willy. I couldn't advise you. There's just one thing I've always wanted to ask you. When he was supposed to graduate, and the math teacher flunked him—

WILLY: Oh, that son-of-a-bitch ruined his life.

BERNARD: Yeah, but, Willy, all he had to do was go to summer school and make up that subject.

WILLY: That's right, that's right.

BERNARD: Did you tell him not to go to summer school?

WILLY: Me? I begged him to go. I ordered him to go!

BERNARD: Then why wouldn't he go?

WILLY: Why? Why! Bernard, that question has been trailing me like a ghost for the last fifteen years. He flunked the subject, and laid down and died like a hammer hit him!

BERNARD: Take it easy, kid.

WILLY: Let me talk to you—I got nobody to talk to. Bernard, Bernard, was it my fault? Y'see? It keeps going around in my mind, maybe I did something to him. I got nothing to give him.

BERNARD: Don't take it so hard.

WILLY: Why did he lay down? What is the story there? You were his friend!

BERNARD: Willy, I remember, it was June, and our grades came out. And he'd flunked math.

WILLY: That son-of-a-bitch!

BERNARD: No, it wasn't right then. Biff just got very angry, I remember, and he was ready to enroll in summer school.

WILLY *(surprised)*: He was?

BERNARD: He wasn't beaten by it at all. But then, Willy, he disappeared from the block for almost a month. And I got the idea that he'd gone up to New England to see you. Did he have a talk with you then?

WILLY *stares in silence.*

BERNARD: Willy?

WILLY *(with a strong edge of resentment in his voice)*: Yeah, he came to Boston. What about it?

BERNARD: Well, just that when he came back—I'll never forget this, it always mystifies me. Because I'd thought so well of Biff, even though he'd always taken advantage of me. I loved him, Willy, y'know? And he came back after that month and took his sneakers—remember those sneakers with "University of Virginia" printed on them? He was so proud of those, wore them every day. And he took them down in the cellar, and burned them up in the furnace. We had a fist fight. It lasted at least half an hour. Just the two of us, punching each other down the cellar, and crying right through it. I've often thought of how strange it was that I knew he'd given up his life. What happened in Boston, Willy?

WILLY *looks at him as at an intruder.*

BERNARD: I just bring it up because you asked me.

WILLY *(angrily)*: Nothing. What do you mean, "What happened?" What's that got to do with anything?

BERNARD: Well, don't get sore.

WILLY: What are you trying to do, blame it on me? If a boy lays down is that my fault?

BERNARD: Now, Willy, don't get—

WILLY: Well, don't—don't talk to me that way! What does that mean, "What happened?"

CHARLEY *enters. He is in his vest, and he carries a bottle of bourbon.*

CHARLEY: Hey, you're going to miss that train. *(He waves the bottle.)*

BERNARD: Yeah, I'm going. *(He takes the bottle.)* Thanks, Pop. *(He picks up his rackets and bag.)* Good-by, Willy, and don't worry about it. You know, "If at first you don't succeed . . ."

WILLY: Yes, I believe in that.

BERNARD: But sometimes, Willy, it's better for a man just to walk away.

WILLY: Walk away?

BERNARD: That's right.

WILLY: But if you can't walk away?

BERNARD   (*after a slight pause*): I guess that's when it's tough. (*Extending his hand.*) Good-by, Willy.

WILLY   (*shaking* BERNARD's *hand*): Good-by, boy.

CHARLEY   (*an arm on* BERNARD's *shoulder*): How do you like this kid? Gonna argue a case in front of the Supreme Court.

BERNARD   (*protesting*): Pop!

WILLY   (*genuinely shocked, pained, and happy*): No! The Supreme Court!

BERNARD: I gotta run. 'By, Dad!

CHARLEY: Knock 'em dead, Bernard!

BERNARD *goes off.*

WILLY   (*as* CHARLEY *takes out his wallet*): The Supreme Court! And he didn't even mention it!

CHARLEY   (*counting out money on the desk*): He don't have to—he's gonna do it.

WILLY: And you never told him what to do, did you? You never took any interest in him.

CHARLEY: My salvation is that I never took any interest in anything. There's some money—fifty dollars. I got an accountant inside.

WILLY: Charley, look . . . (*With difficulty.*) I got my insurance to pay. If you can manage it—I need a hundred and ten dollars.

CHARLEY *doesn't reply for a moment; merely stops moving.*

WILLY: I'd draw it from my bank but Linda would know, and I . . .

CHARLEY: Sit down, Willy.

WILLY   (*moving toward the chair*): I'm keeping an account of everything, remember. I'll pay every penny back. (*He sits.*)

CHARLEY: Now listen to me, Willy.

WILLY: I want you to know I appreciate . . .

CHARLEY   (*sitting down on the table*): Willy, what're you doin'? What the hell is goin' on in your head?

WILLY: Why? I'm simply . . .

CHARLEY: I offered you a job. You can make fifty dollars a week. And I won't send you on the road.

WILLY: I've got a job.

CHARLEY: Without pay? What kind of a job is a job without pay? (*He rises.*) Now, look, kid, enough is enough. I'm no genius but I know when I'm being insulted.

WILLY: Insulted!

CHARLEY: Why don't you want to work for me?

WILLY: What's the matter with you? I've got a job.

CHARLEY: Then what're you walkin' in here every week for?

WILLY   (*getting up*): Well, if you don't want me to walk in here—

CHARLEY: I am offering you a job.

WILLY: I don't want your goddam job!

CHARLEY: When the hell are you going to grow up?

WILLY   (*furiously*): You big ignoramus, if you say that to me again I'll rap you one! I don't care how big you are! (*He's ready to fight.*)

Pause.

CHARLEY   (*kindly, going to him*): How much do you need, Willy?

WILLY: Charley, I'm strapped. I'm strapped. I don't know what to do. I was just fired.

CHARLEY: Howard fired you?

WILLY: That snotnose. Imagine that? I named him. I named him Howard.

CHARLEY: Willy, when're you gonna realize that them things don't mean anything? You named him Howard, but you can't sell that. The only thing you got in this world is what you can sell. And the funny thing is that you're a salesman, and you don't know that.

WILLY: I've always tried to think otherwise, I guess. I always felt that if a man was impressive, and well liked, that nothing—

CHARLEY: Why must everybody like you? Who liked J. P. Morgan? Was he impressive? In a Turkish bath he'd look like a butcher. But with his pockets on he was very well liked. Now listen, Willy, I know you don't like me, and nobody can say I'm in love with you, but I'll give you a job because—just for the hell of it, put it that way. Now what do you say?

WILLY: I—I just can't work for you, Charley.

CHARLEY: What're you, jealous of me?

WILLY: I can't work for you, that's all, don't ask me why.

CHARLEY   (*angered, takes out more bills*): You been jealous of me all your life, you damned fool! Here, pay your insurance. (*He puts the money in* WILLY's *hand.*)

WILLY: I'm keeping strict accounts.

CHARLEY: I've got some work to do. Take care of yourself. And pay your insurance.

WILLY   (*moving to the right*): Funny, y'know? After all the highways, and the trains, and the appointments, and the years, you end up worth more dead than alive.

CHARLEY: Willy, nobody's worth nothin' dead. (*After a slight pause.*) Did you hear what I said?

WILLY *stands still, dreaming.*

CHARLEY: Willy!

WILLY: Apologize to Bernard for me when you see him. I didn't mean to argue with him. He's a fine boy. They're all fine boys, and they'll end up big —all of them. Someday they'll all play tennis together. Wish me luck, Charley. He saw Bill Oliver today.

CHARLEY: Good luck.

WILLY   (*on the verge of tears*): Charley, you're the only friend I got. Isn't that a remarkable thing? (*He goes out.*)

CHARLEY: Jesus!

CHARLEY *stares after him a moment and follows. All light blacks out. Suddenly raucous music is heard, and a red glow rises behind the screen at right.* STANLEY, *a young waiter, appears, carrying a table, followed by* HAPPY, *who is carrying two chairs.*

STANLEY (*putting the table down*): That's all right, Mr. Loman, I can handle it myself. (*He turns and takes the chairs from* HAPPY *and places them at the table.*)

HAPPY (*glancing around*): Oh, this is better.

STANLEY: Sure, in the front there you're in the middle of all kinds a noise. Whenever you got a party, Mr. Loman, you just tell me and I'll put you back here. Y'know, there's a lotta people they don't like it private, because when they go out they like to see a lotta action around them because they're sick and tired to stay in the house by theirself. But I know you, you ain't from Hackensack. You know what I mean?

HAPPY (*sitting down*): So how's it coming, Stanley?

STANLEY: Ah, it's a dog's life. I only wish during the war they'd a took me in the Army. I coulda been dead by now.

HAPPY: My brother's back, Stanley.

STANLEY: Oh, he come back, heh? From the Far West.

HAPPY: Yeah, big cattle man, my brother, so treat him right. And my father's coming too.

STANLEY: Oh, your father too!

HAPPY: You got a couple of nice lobsters?

STANLEY: Hundred per cent, big.

HAPPY: I want them with the claws.

STANLEY: Don't worry, I don't give you no mice. (HAPPY *laughs.*) How about some wine? It'll put a head on the meal.

HAPPY: No. You remember, Stanley, that recipe I brought you from overseas? With the champagne in it?

STANLEY: Oh, yeah, sure. I still got it tacked up yet in the kitchen. But that'll have to cost a buck apiece anyways.

HAPPY: That's all right.

STANLEY: What'd you, hit a number or somethin'?

HAPPY: No, it's a little celebration. My brother is—I think he pulled off a big deal today. I think we're going into business together.

STANLEY: Great! That's the best for you. Because a family business, you know what I mean?—that's the best.

HAPPY: That's what I think.

STANLEY: 'Cause what's the difference? Somebody steals? It's in the family. Know what I mean? (*Sotto voce.*) Like this bartender here. The boss is goin' crazy what kinda leak he's got in the cash register. You put it in but it don't come out.

HAPPY (*raising his head*): Sh!

STANLEY: What?

HAPPY: You notice I wasn't lookin' right or left, was I!

STANLEY: No.

HAPPY: And my eyes are closed.

STANLEY: So what's the—?

HAPPY: Strudel's comin'.

STANLEY   (*catching on, looks around*): Ah, no, there's no—

He breaks off as a furred, lavishly dressed GIRL *enters and sits at the next table. Both follow her with their eyes.*

STANLEY: Geez, how'd ya know?

HAPPY: I got radar or something. (*Staring directly at her profile.*) Ooooooooo . . . Stanley.

STANLEY: I think that's for you, Mr. Loman.

HAPPY: Look at that mouth. Oh, God. And the binoculars.

STANLEY: Geez, you got a life, Mr. Loman.

HAPPY: Wait on her.

STANLEY   (*going to* THE GIRL's *table*): Would you like a menu, ma'am?

GIRL: I'm expecting someone, but I'd like a—

HAPPY: Why don't you bring her—excuse me, miss, do you mind? I sell champagne, and I'd like you to try my brand. Bring her a champagne, Stanley.

GIRL: That's awfully nice of you.

HAPPY: Don't mention it. It's all company money. (*He laughs.*)

GIRL: That's a charming product to be selling, isn't it?

HAPPY: Oh, gets to be like everything else. Selling is selling, y'know.

GIRL: I suppose.

HAPPY: You don't happen to sell, do you?

GIRL: No, I don't sell.

HAPPY: Would you object to a compliment from a stranger? You ought to be on a magazine cover.

GIRL   (*looking at him a little archly*): I have been.

STANLEY *comes in with a glass of champagne.*

HAPPY: What'd I say before, Stanley? You see? She's a cover girl.

STANLEY: Oh, I could see, I could see.

HAPPY   (*to* THE GIRL): What magazine?

GIRL: Oh, a lot of them. (*She takes the drink.*) Thank you.

HAPPY: You know what they say in France, don't you? "Champagne is the drink of the complexion"—Hya, Biff!

BIFF *has entered and sits with* HAPPY.

BIFF: Hello, kid. Sorry I'm late.

HAPPY: I just got here. Uh, Miss—?

GIRL: Forsythe.

HAPPY: Miss Forsythe, this is my brother.

BIFF: Is Dad here?

HAPPY: His name is Biff. You might've heard of him. Great football player.

GIRL: Really? What team?

HAPPY: Are you familiar with football?

GIRL: No, I'm afraid I'm not.

HAPPY: Biff is quarterback with the New York Giants.

GIRL: Well, that is nice, isn't it? (*She drinks.*)

HAPPY: Good health.

GIRL: I'm happy to meet you.

HAPPY: That's my name. Hap. It's really Harold, but at West Point they called me Happy.

GIRL (*now really impressed*): Oh, I see. How do you do? (*She turns her profile.*)

BIFF: Isn't Dad coming?

HAPPY: You want her?

BIFF: Oh, I could never make that.

HAPPY: I remember the time that idea would never come into your head. Where's the old confidence, Biff?

BIFF: I just saw Oliver—

HAPPY: Wait a minute. I've got to see that old confidence again. Do you want her? She's on call.

BIFF: Oh, no. (*He turns to look at* THE GIRL.)

HAPPY: I'm telling you. Watch this. (*Turning to* THE GIRL.) Honey? (*She turns to him.*) Are you busy?

GIRL: Well, I am . . . but I could make a phone call.

HAPPY: Do that, will you, honey? And see if you can get a friend. We'll be here for a while. Biff is one of the greatest football players in the country.

GIRL (*standing up*): Well, I'm certainly happy to meet you.

HAPPY: Come back soon.

GIRL: I'll try.

HAPPY: Don't try, honey, try hard.

THE GIRL *exits.* STANLEY *follows, shaking his head in bewildered admiration.*

HAPPY: Isn't that a shame now? A beautiful girl like that? That's why I can't get married. There's not a good woman in a thousand. New York is loaded with them, kid!

BIFF: Hap, look—

HAPPY: I told you she was on call!

BIFF (*strangely unnerved*): Cut it out, will ya? I want to say something to you.

HAPPY: Did you see Oliver?

BIFF: I saw him all right. Now look, I want to tell Dad a couple of things and I want you to help me.

HAPPY: What? Is he going to back you?

BIFF: Are you crazy? You're out of your goddam head, you know that?

HAPPY: Why? What happened?

BIFF (*breathlessly*): I did a terrible thing today, Hap. It's been the strangest day I ever went through. I'm all numb, I swear.

HAPPY: You mean he wouldn't see you?

BIFF: Well, I waited six hours for him, see? All day. Kept sending my name in. Even tried to date his secretary so she'd get me to him, but no soap.

HAPPY: Because you're not showin' the old confidence, Biff. He remembered you, didn't he?

BIFF (*stopping* HAPPY *with a gesture*): Finally, about five o'clock, he comes out. Didn't remember who I was or anything. I felt like such an idiot, Hap.

HAPPY: Did you tell him my Florida idea?

BIFF: He walked away. I saw him for one minute. I got so mad I could've torn the walls down! How the hell did I ever get the idea I was a salesman there? I even believed myself that I'd been a salesman for him! And then he gave me one look and—I realized what a ridiculous lie my whole life has been! We've been talking in a dream for fifteen years. I was a shipping clerk.

HAPPY: What'd you do?

BIFF   (*with great tension and wonder*): Well, he left, see. And the secretary went out. I was all alone in the waiting-room. I don't know what came over me, Hap. The next thing I know I'm in his office—paneled walls, everything. I can't explain it. I—Hap, I took his fountain pen.

HAPPY: Geez, did he catch you?

BIFF: I ran out. I ran down all eleven flights. I ran and ran and ran.

HAPPY: That was an awful dumb—what'd you do that for?

BIFF   (*agonized*): I don't know, I just—wanted to take something, I don't know. You gotta help me, Hap. I'm gonna tell Pop.

HAPPY: You crazy? What for?

BIFF: Hap, he's got to understand that I'm not the man somebody lends that kind of money to. He thinks I've been spiting him all these years and it's eating him up.

HAPPY: That's just it. You tell him something nice.

BIFF: I can't.

HAPPY: Say you got a lunch date with Oliver tomorrow.

BIFF: So what do I do tomorrow?

HAPPY: You leave the house tomorrow and come back at night and say Oliver is thinking it over. And he thinks it over for a couple of weeks, and gradually it fades away and nobody's the worse.

BIFF: But it'll go on forever!

HAPPY: Dad is never so happy as when he's looking forward to something!

WILLY enters.

HAPPY: Hello, scout!

WILLY: Gee, I haven't been here in years!

STANLEY has followed WILLY in and sets a chair for him. STANLEY starts off but HAPPY stops him.

HAPPY: Stanley!

STANLEY stands by, waiting for an order.

BIFF   (*going to* WILLY *with guilt, as to an invalid*): Sit down, Pop. You want a drink?

WILLY: Sure, I don't mind.

BIFF: Let's get a load on.

WILLY: You look worried.

BIFF: N-no. (*To* STANLEY.) Scotch all around. Make it doubles.

STANLEY: Doubles, right. (*He goes.*)

WILLY: You had a couple already, didn't you?

BIFF: Just a couple, yeah.

WILLY: Well, what happened, boy? (*Nodding affirmatively, with a smile.*) Everything go all right?

BIFF   (*takes a breath, then reaches out and grasps* WILLY's *hand*): Pal . . . (*He is smiling bravely, and* WILLY *is smiling too.*) I had an experience today.

HAPPY: Terrific, Pop.

WILLY: That so? What happened?

BIFF   (*high, slightly alcoholic, above the earth*): I'm going to tell you everything from first to last. It's been a strange day. (*Silence. He looks around, composes himself as best he can, but his breath keeps breaking the rhythm of his voice.*) I had to wait quite a while for him, and—

WILLY: Oliver?

BIFF: Yeah, Oliver. All day, as a matter of cold fact. And a lot of—instances —facts, Pop, facts about my life came back to me. Who was it, Pop? Who ever said I was a salesman with Oliver?

WILLY: Well, you were.

BIFF: No, Dad, I was a shipping clerk.

WILLY: But you were practically—

BIFF   (*with determination*): Dad, I don't know who said it first, but I was never a salesman for Bill Oliver.

WILLY: What're you talking about?

BIFF: Let's hold on to the facts tonight, Pop. We're not going to get anywhere bullin' around. I was a shipping clerk.

WILLY   (*angrily*): All right, now listen to me—

BIFF: Why don't you let me finish?

WILLY: I'm not interested in stories about the past or any crap of that kind because the woods are burning, boys, you understand? There's a big blaze going on all around. I was fired today.

BIFF   (*shocked*): How could you be?

WILLY: I was fired, and I'm looking for a little good news to tell your mother, because the woman has waited and the woman has suffered. The gist of it is that I haven't got a story left in my head, Biff. So don't give me a lecture about facts and aspects. I am not interested. Now what've you got to say to me?

STANLEY *enters with three drinks. They wait until he leaves.*

WILLY: Did you see Oliver?

BIFF: Jesus, Dad!

WILLY: You mean you didn't go up there?

HAPPY: Sure he went up there.

BIFF: I did. I—saw him. How could they fire you?

WILLY   (*on the edge of his chair*): What kind of a welcome did he give you?

BIFF: He won't even let you work on commission?

WILLY: I'm out! (*Driving.*) So tell me, he gave you a warm welcome?

HAPPY: Sure, Pop, sure!

BIFF   (*driven*): Well, it was kind of—

WILLY: I was wondering if he'd remember you. (*To* HAPPY.) Imagine, man doesn't see him for ten, twelve years and gives him that kind of a welcome!

HAPPY: Damn right!

BIFF (*trying to return to the offensive*): Pop, look—

WILLY: You know why he remembered you, don't you? Because you impressed him in those days.

BIFF: Let's talk quietly and get this down to the facts, huh?

WILLY (*as though* BIFF *had been interrupting*): Well, what happened? It's great news, Biff. Did he take you into his office or'd you talk in the waiting-room?

BIFF: Well, he came in, see, and—

WILLY: (*with a big smile*): What'd he say? Betcha he threw his arm around you.

BIFF: Well, he kinda—

WILLY: He's a fine man. (*To* HAPPY.) Very hard man to see, y'know.

HAPPY (*agreeing*): Oh, I know.

WILLY (*to* BIFF): Is that where you had the drinks?

BIFF: Yeah, he gave me a couple of—no, no!

HAPPY (*cutting in*): He told him my Florida idea.

WILLY: Don't interrupt. (*To* BIFF.) How'd he react to the Florida idea?

BIFF: Dad, will you give me a minute to explain?

WILLY: I've been waiting for you to explain since I sat down here! What happened? He took you into his office and what?

BIFF: Well—I talked. And—and he listened, see.

WILLY: Famous for the way he listens, y'know. What was his answer?

BIFF: His answer was— (*He breaks off, suddenly angry.*) Dad, you're not letting me tell you what I want to tell you!

WILLY (*accusing, angered*): You didn't see him, did you?

BIFF: I did see him!

WILLY: What'd you insult him or something? You insulted him, didn't you?

BIFF: Listen, will you let me out of it, will you just let me out of it!

HAPPY: What the hell!

WILLY: Tell me what happened!

BIFF (*to* HAPPY): I can't talk to him!

A single trumpet note jars the ear. The light of green leaves stains the house, which holds the air of night and a dream. YOUNG BERNARD *enters and knocks on the door of the house.*

YOUNG BERNARD (*frantically*): Mrs. Loman, Mrs. Loman!

HAPPY: Tell him what happened!

BIFF (*to* HAPPY): Shut up and leave me alone!

WILLY: No, no! You had to go and flunk math!

BIFF: What math? What're you talking about?

YOUNG BERNARD: Mrs. Loman, Mrs. Loman!

LINDA *appears in the house, as of old.*

WILLY (*wildly*): Math, math, math!

BIFF: Take it easy, Pop!

YOUNG BERNARD: Mrs. Loman!

WILLY (*furiously*): If you hadn't flunked you'd've been set by now!

BIFF: Now, look, I'm gonna tell you what happened, and you're going to listen to me.

YOUNG BERNARD: Mrs. Loman!

BIFF: I waited six hours—

HAPPY: What the hell are you saying?

BIFF: I kept sending in my name but he wouldn't see me. So finally he . . . (*He continues unheard as light fades low on the restaurant.*)

YOUNG BERNARD: Biff flunked math!

LINDA: No!

YOUNG BERNARD: Birnbaum flunked him! They won't graduate him!

LINDA: But they have to. He's gotta go to the university. Where is he? Biff! Biff!

YOUNG BERNARD: No, he left. He went to Grand Central.

LINDA: Grand— You mean he went to Boston!

YOUNG BERNARD: Is Uncle Willy in Boston?

LINDA: Oh, maybe Willy can talk to the teacher. Oh, the poor, poor boy!

Light on house area snaps out.

BIFF (*at the table, now audible, holding up a gold fountain pen*): . . . so I'm washed up with Oliver, you understand? Are you listening to me?

WILLY (*at a loss*): Yeah, sure. If you hadn't flunked—

BIFF: Flunked what? What're you talking about?

WILLY: Don't blame everything on me! I didn't flunk math—you did! What pen?

HAPPY: That was awful dumb, Biff, a pen like that is worth—

WILLY (*seeing the pen for the first time*): You took Oliver's pen?

BIFF (*weakening*): Dad, I just explained it to you.

WILLY: You stole Bill Oliver's fountain pen!

BIFF: I didn't exactly steal it! That's just what I've been explaining to you!

HAPPY: He had it in his hand and just then Oliver walked in, so he got nervous and stuck it in his pocket!

WILLY: My God, Biff!

BIFF: I never intended to do it, Dad!

OPERATOR'S VOICE: Standish Arms, good evening!

WILLY (*shouting*): I'm not in my room!

BIFF (*frightened*): Dad, what's the matter? (*He and* HAPPY *stand up.*)

OPERATOR: Ringing Mr. Loman for you!

WILLY: I'm not there, stop it!

BIFF (*horrified, gets down on one knee before* WILLY): Dad, I'll make good, I'll make good. (WILLY *tries to get to his feet.* BIFF *holds him down.*) Sit down now.

WILLY: No, you're no good, you're no good for anything.

BIFF: I am, Dad, I'll find something else, you understand? Now don't worry about anything. (*He holds up* WILLY's *face.*) Talk to me, Dad.

OPERATOR: Mr. Loman does not answer. Shall I page him?

WILLY (*attempting to stand, as though to rush and silence the* OPERATOR): No, no, no!

HAPPY: He'll strike something, Pop.

WILLY: No, no . . .

BIFF (*desperately, standing over* WILLY): Pop, listen! Listen to me! I'm telling you something good. Oliver talked to his partner about the Florida idea. You listening? He—he talked to his partner, and he came to me . . . I'm going to be all right, you hear? Dad, listen to me, he said it was just a question of the amount!

WILLY: Then you . . . got it?

HAPPY: He's gonna be terrific, Pop!

WILLY   (*trying to stand*): Then you got it, haven't you? You got it! You got it!

BIFF   (*agonized, holds* WILLY *down*): No, no. Look, Pop. I'm supposed to have lunch with them tomorrow. I'm just telling you this so you'll know that I can still make an impression, Pop. And I'll make good somewhere, but I can't go tomorrow, see?

WILLY: Why not? You simply—

BIFF: But the pen, Pop!

WILLY: You give it to him and tell him it was an oversight!

HAPPY: Sure, have lunch tomorrow!

BIFF: I can't say that—

WILLY: You were doing a crossword puzzle and accidentally used his pen!

BIFF: Listen, kid, I took those balls years ago, now I walk in with his fountain pen? That clinches it, don't you see? I can't face him like that! I'll try elsewhere.

PAGE'S VOICE: Paging Mr. Loman!

WILLY: Don't you want to be anything?

BIFF: Pop, how can I go back?

WILLY: You don't want to be anything, is that what's behind it?

BIFF   (*now angry at* WILLY *for not crediting his sympathy*): Don't take it that way! You think it was easy walking into that office after what I'd done to him? A team of horses couldn't have dragged me back to Bill Oliver!

WILLY: Then why'd you go?

BIFF: Why did I go? Why did I go? Look at you! Look at what's become of you!

Off left, THE WOMAN *laughs.*

WILLY: Biff, you're going to go to that lunch tomorrow, or—

BIFF: I can't go. I've got no appointment!

HAPPY: Biff, for . . . !

WILLY: Are you spiting me?

BIFF: Don't take it that way! Goddammit!

WILLY   (*strikes* BIFF *and falters away from the table*): You rotten little louse! Are you spiting me?

THE WOMAN: Someone's at the door, Willy!

BIFF: I'm no good, can't you see what I am?

HAPPY   (*separating them*): Hey, you're in a restaurant! Now cut it out, both of you! (THE GIRLS *enter.*) Hello, girls, sit down.

THE WOMAN *laughs, off left.*

MISS FORSYTHE: I guess we might as well. This is Letta.

THE WOMAN: Willy, are you going to wake up?

BIFF   (*ignoring* WILLY): How're ya, miss, sit down. What do you drink?

MISS FORSYTHE: Letta might not be able to stay long.

LETTA: I gotta get up very early tomorrow. I got jury duty. I'm so excited! Were you fellows ever on a jury?

BIFF: No, but I been in front of them! (THE GIRLS *laugh.*) This is my father.

LETTA: Isn't he cute? Sit down with us, Pop.

HAPPY: Sit him down, Biff!

BIFF   (*going to him*): Come on, slugger, drink us under the table. To hell with it! Come on, sit down, pal.

On BIFF's *last insistence,* WILLY *is about to sit.*

THE WOMAN   (*now urgently*): Willy, are you going to answer the door!

THE WOMAN's *call pulls* WILLY *back. He starts right, befuddled.*

BIFF: Hey, where are you going?

WILLY: Open the door.

BIFF: The door?

WILLY: The washroom . . . the door . . . where's the door?

BIFF   (*leading* WILLY *to the left*): Just go straight down.

WILLY *moves left.*

THE WOMAN: Willy, Willy, are you going to get up, get up, get up, get up?

WILLY *exits left.*

LETTA: I think it's sweet you bring your daddy along.

MISS FORSYTHE: Oh, he isn't really your father!

BIFF   (*at left, turning to her resentfully*): Miss Forsythe, you've just seen a prince walk by. A fine, troubled prince. A hard-working, unappreciated prince. A pal, you understand? A good companion. Always for his boys.

LETTA: That's so sweet.

HAPPY: Well, girls, what's the program? We're wasting time. Come on, Biff. Gather round. Where would you like to go?

BIFF: Why don't you do something for him?

HAPPY: Me!

BIFF: Don't you give a damn for him, Hap?

HAPPY: What're you talking about? I'm the one who—

BIFF: I sense it, you don't give a good goddam about him. (*He takes the rolled-up hose from his pocket and puts it on the table in front of* HAPPY.) Look what I found in the cellar, for Christ's sake. How can you bear to let it go on?

HAPPY: Me? Who goes away? Who runs off and—

BIFF: Yeah, but he doesn't mean anything to you. You could help him— I can't! Don't you understand what I'm talking about? He's going to kill himself, don't you know that?

HAPPY: Don't I know it! Me!

BIFF: Hap, help him! Jesus . . . help him . . . Help me, help me, I can't bear to look at his face! (*Ready to weep, he hurries out, up right.*)

HAPPY   (*starting after him*): Where are you going?

MISS FORSYTHE: What's he so mad about?

HAPPY: Come on, girls, we'll catch up with him.

MISS FORSYTHE   (*as* HAPPY *pushes her out*): Say, I don't like that temper of his!

HAPPY: He's just a little overstrung, he'll be all right!

WILLY   (*off left, as* THE WOMAN *laughs*): Don't answer! Don't answer!

LETTA: Don't you want to tell your father—

HAPPY: No, that's not my father. He's just a guy. Come on, we'll catch Biff, and, honey, we're going to paint this town! Stanley, where's the check! Hey, Stanley!

> They exit. STANLEY *looks toward left.*

STANLEY   (*calling to* HAPPY *indignantly*): Mr. Loman! Mr. Loman!

STANLEY picks up a chair and follows them off. Knocking is heard off left. THE WOMAN *enters, laughing.* WILLY *follows her. She is in a black slip; he is buttoning his shirt. Raw, sensuous music accompanies their speech.*

WILLY: Will you stop laughing? Will you stop?

THE WOMAN: Aren't you going to answer the door? He'll wake the whole hotel.

WILLY: I'm not expecting anybody.

THE WOMAN: Whyn't you have another drink, honey, and stop being so damn self-centered?

WILLY: I'm so lonely.

THE WOMAN: You know you ruined me, Willy? From now on, whenever you come to the office, I'll see that you go right through to the buyers. No waiting at my desk any more, Willy. You ruined me.

WILLY: That's nice of you to say that.

THE WOMAN: Gee, you are self-centered! Why so sad? You are the saddest self-centeredest soul I ever did see-saw. (*She laughs. He kisses her.*) Come on inside, drummer boy. It's silly to be dressing in the middle of the night. (*As knocking is heard.*) Aren't you going to answer the door?

WILLY: They're knocking on the wrong door.

THE WOMAN: But I felt the knocking. And he heard us talking in here. Maybe the hotel's on fire!

WILLY   (*his terror rising*): It's a mistake.

THE WOMAN: Then tell him to go away!

WILLY: There's nobody there.

THE WOMAN: It's getting on my nerves, Willy. There's somebody standing out there and it's getting on my nerves!

WILLY   (*pushing her away from him*): All right, stay in the bathroom here, and don't come out. I think there's a law in Massachusetts about it, so don't come out. It may be that new room clerk. He looked very mean. So don't come out. It's a mistake, there's no fire.

The knocking is heard again. He takes a few steps away from her, and she vanishes into the wing. The light follows him, and now he is facing YOUNG BIFF, *who carries a suitcase.* BIFF *steps toward him. The music is gone.*

BIFF: Why didn't you answer?

WILLY: Biff! What are you doing in Boston?

BIFF: Why didn't you answer? I've been knocking for five minutes, I called you on the phone—

WILLY: I just heard you. I was in the bathroom and had the door shut. Did anything happen home?

BIFF: Dad—I let you down.

WILLY: What do you mean?

BIFF: Dad . . .

WILLY: Biffo, what's this about? (*Putting his arm around* BIFF.) Come on, let's go downstairs and get you a malted.

BIFF: Dad, I flunked math.

WILLY: Not for the term?

BIFF: The term. I haven't got enough credits to graduate.

WILLY: You mean to say Bernard wouldn't give you the answers?

BIFF: He did, he tried, but I only got a sixty-one.

WILLY: And they wouldn't give you four points?

BIFF: Birnbaum refused absolutely. I begged him, Pop, but he won't give me those points. You gotta talk to him before they close the school. Because if he saw the kind of man you are, and you just talked to him in your way, I'm sure he'd come through for me. The class came right before practice, see, and I didn't go enough. Would you talk to him? He'd like you, Pop. You know the way you could talk.

WILLY: You're on. We'll drive right back.

BIFF: Oh, Dad, good work! I'm sure he'll change it for you!

WILLY: Go downstairs and tell the clerk I'm checkin' out. Go right down.

BIFF: Yes, Sir! See, the reason he hates me, Pop—one day he was late for class so I got up at the blackboard and imitated him. I crossed my eyes and talked with a lithp.

WILLY (*laughing*): You did? The kids like it?

BIFF: They nearly died laughing!

WILLY: Yeah? What'd you do?

BIFF: The thquare root of thixthy twee is . . . (WILLY *bursts out laughing;* BIFF *joins him.*) And in the middle of it he walked in!

WILLY *laughs and* THE WOMAN *joins in offstage.*

WILLY (*without hesitating*): Hurry downstairs and—

BIFF: Somebody in there?

WILLY: No, that was next door.

THE WOMAN *laughs offstage.*

BIFF: Somebody got in your bathroom!

WILLY: No, it's the next room, there's a party—

THE WOMAN (*enters, laughing. She lisps this*): Can I come in? There's something in the bathtub, Willy, and it's moving!

WILLY *looks at* BIFF, *who is staring open-mouthed and horrified at* THE WOMAN.

WILLY: Ah—you better go back to your room. They must be finished painting by now. They're painting her room so I let her take a shower here. Go back, go back . . . (*He pushes her.*)

THE WOMAN   (*resisting*): But I've got to get dressed, Willy, I can't—

WILLY: Get out of here! Go back, go back . . . (*Suddenly striving for the ordinary.*) This is Miss Francis, Biff, she's a buyer. They're painting her room. Go back, Miss Francis, go back . . .

THE WOMAN: But my clothes, I can't go out naked in the hall!

WILLY   (*pushing her offstage*): Get outa here! Go back, go back!

BIFF *slowly sits down on his suitcase as the argument continues offstage.*

THE WOMAN: Where's my stockings? You promised me stockings, Willy!

WILLY: I have no stockings here!

THE WOMAN: You had two boxes of size nine sheers for me, and I want them!

WILLY: Here, for God's sake, will you get outa here!

THE WOMAN   (*enters holding a box of stockings*): I just hope there's nobody in the hall. That's all I hope. (*To* BIFF.) Are you football or baseball?

BIFF: Football.

THE WOMAN   (*angry, humiliated*): That's me too. G'night. (*She snatches her clothes from* WILLY, *and walks out.*)

WILLY   (*after a pause*): Well, better get going. I want to get to the school first thing in the morning. Get my suits out of the closet. I'll get my valise. (BIFF *doesn't move.*) What's the matter? (BIFF *remains motionless, tears falling.*) She's a buyer. Buys for J. H. Simmons. She lives down the hall—they're painting. You don't imagine— (*He breaks off. After a pause.*) Now listen, pal, she's just a buyer. She sees merchandise in her room and they have to keep it looking just so . . . (*Pause. Assuming command.*) All right, get my suits. (BIFF *doesn't move.*) Now stop crying and do as I say. I gave you an order. Biff, I gave you an order! Is that what you do when I give you an order? How dare you cry! (*Putting his arm around* BIFF.) Now look, Biff, when you grow up you'll understand about these things. You mustn't—you mustn't overemphasize a thing like this. I'll see Birnbaum first thing in the morning.

BIFF: Never mind.

WILLY   (*getting down beside* BIFF): Never mind! He's going to give you those points. I'll see to it.

BIFF: He wouldn't listen to you.

WILLY: He certainly will listen to me. You need those points for the U. of Virginia.

BIFF: I'm not going there.

WILLY: Heh? If I can't get him to change that mark you'll make it up in summer school. You've got all summer to—

BIFF   (*his weeping breaking from him*): Dad . . .

WILLY   (*infected by it*): Oh, my boy . . .

BIFF: Dad . . .

WILLY: She's nothing to me, Biff. I was lonely, I was terribly lonely.

BIFF: You—you gave her Mama's stockings! (*His tears break through and he rises to go.*)

WILLY (*grabbing for* BIFF): I gave you an order!

BIFF: Don't touch me, you—liar!

WILLY: Apologize for that!

BIFF: You fake! You phony little fake! You fake! (*Overcome, he turns quickly and weeping fully goes out with his suitcase.* WILLY *is left on the floor on his knees.*)

WILLY: I gave you an order! Biff, come back here or I'll beat you! Come back here! I'll whip you!

STANLEY *comes quickly in from the right and stands in front of* WILLY.

WILLY (*shouts at* STANLEY): I gave you an order . . .

STANLEY: Hey, let's pick it up, pick it up, Mr. Loman. (*He helps* WILLY *to his feet.*) Your boys left with the chippies. They said they'll see you home.

A second waiter watches some distance away.

WILLY: But we were supposed to have dinner together.

Music is heard, WILLY'S *theme.*

STANLEY: Can you make it?

WILLY: I'll—sure, I can make it. (*Suddenly concerned about his clothes.*) Do I—I look all right?

STANLEY: Sure, you look all right. (*He flicks a speck off* WILLY'S *lapel.*)

WILLY: Here—here's a dollar.

STANLEY: Oh, your son paid me. It's all right.

WILLY (*putting it in* STANLEY'S *hand*): No, take it. You're a good boy.

STANLEY: Oh, no, you don't have to . . .

WILLY: Here—here's some more, I don't need it any more. (*After a slight pause.*) Tell me—is there a seed store in the neighborhood?

STANLEY: Seeds? You mean like to plant?

As WILLY *turns,* STANLEY *slips the money back into his jacket pocket.*

WILLY: Yes. Carrots, peas . . .

STANLEY: Well, there's hardware stores on Sixth Avenue, but it may be too late now.

WILLY (*anxiously*): Oh, I'd better hurry. I've got to get some seeds. (*He starts off to the right.*) I've got to get some seeds, right away. Nothing's planted. I don't have a thing in the ground.

WILLY *hurries out as the light goes down.* STANLEY *moves over to the right after him, watches him off. The other waiter has been staring at* WILLY.

STANLEY (*to the waiter*): Well, whatta you looking at?

The waiter picks up the chairs and moves off right. STANLEY *takes the table and follows him. The light fades on this area. There is a long pause, the sound of the flute coming over. The light gradually rises on the kitchen, which is empty.* HAPPY *appears at the door of the house, followed by* BIFF. HAPPY *is carrying a large bunch of long-stemmed roses. He enters the kitchen, looks around for* LINDA. *Not seeing her, he turns to* BIFF, *who is just outside the house door, and makes a gesture with his hands, indicating "Not here, I guess." He looks into the livingroom and freezes. Inside,* LINDA, *unseen, is seated,* WILLY's *coat on her lap. She rises ominously and quietly and moves toward* HAPPY, *who backs up into the kitchen, afraid.*

HAPPY: Hey, what're you doing up? (LINDA *says nothing but moves toward him implacably.*) Where's Pop? (*He keeps backing to the right, and now* LINDA *is in full view in the doorway to the livingroom.*) Is he sleeping?

LINDA: Where were you?

HAPPY   (*trying to laugh it off*): We met two girls, Mom, very fine types. Here, we brought you some flowers. (*Offering them to her.*) Put them in your room, Ma.

She knocks them to the floor at BIFF's *feet. He has now come inside and closed the door behind him. She stares at* BIFF, *silent.*

HAPPY: Now what'd you do that for? Mom, I want you to have some flowers—

LINDA   (*cutting* HAPPY *off, violently to* BIFF): Don't you care whether he lives or dies?

HAPPY   (*going to the stairs*): Come upstairs, Biff.

BIFF   (*with a flare of disgust, to* HAPPY): Go away from me! (*To* LINDA.) What do you mean, lives or dies? Nobody's dying around here, pal.

LINDA: Get out of my sight! Get out of here!

BIFF: I wanna see the boss.

LINDA: You're not going near him!

BIFF: Where is he? (*He moves into the livingroom and* LINDA *follows.*)

LINDA   (*shouting after* BIFF): You invite him for dinner. He looks forward to it all day—(BIFF *appears in his parents' bedroom, looks around, and exits*)—and then you desert him there. There's no stranger you'd do that to!

HAPPY: Why? He had a swell time with us. Listen, when I—(LINDA *comes back into the kitchen*)—desert him I hope I don't outlive the day!

LINDA: Get out of here!

HAPPY: Now look, Mom . . .

LINDA: Did you have to go to women tonight? You and your lousy rotten whores!

BIFF *re-enters the kitchen.*

HAPPY: Mom, all we did was follow Biff around trying to cheer him up! (*To* BIFF.) Boy, what a night you gave me!

LINDA: Get out of here, both of you, and don't come back! I don't want you tormenting him any more. Go on now, get your things together! (*To* BIFF.) You can sleep in his apartment. (*She starts to pick up the flowers and stops herself.*) Pick up this stuff, I'm not your maid any more. Pick it up, you bum, you!

HAPPY *turns his back to her in refusal.* BIFF *slowly moves over and gets down on his knees, picking up the flowers.*

LINDA: You're a pair of animals! Not one, not another living soul would have had the cruelty to walk out on that man in a restaurant!

BIFF   (*not looking at her*): Is that what he said?

LINDA: He didn't have to say anything. He was so humiliated he nearly limped when he came in.

HAPPY: But, Mom, he had a great time with us—

BIFF   (*cutting him off violently*): Shut up!

Without another word, HAPPY *goes upstairs.*

LINDA: You! You didn't even go in to see if he was all right!

BIFF   (*still on the floor in front of* LINDA, *the flowers in his hand; with self-loathing*): No. Didn't. Didn't do a damned thing. How do you like that, heh? Left him babbling in a toilet.

LINDA: You louse. You . . .

BIFF: Now you hit it on the nose! (*He gets up, throws the flowers in the wastebasket.*) The scum of the earth, and you're looking at him!

LINDA: Get out of here!

BIFF: I gotta talk to the boss, Mom. Where is he?

LINDA: You're not going near him. Get out of this house!

BIFF   (*with absolute assurance, determination*): No. We're gonna have an abrupt conversation, him and me.

LINDA: You're not talking to him!

Hammering is heard from outside the house, off right. BIFF *turns toward the noise.*

LINDA   (*suddenly pleading*): Will you please leave him alone?

BIFF: What's he doing out there?

LINDA: He's planting the garden!

BIFF   (*quietly*): Now? Oh, my God!

BIFF *moves outside,* LINDA *following. The light dies down on them and comes up on the center of the apron as* WILLY *walks into it. He is carrying a flashlight, a hoe and a handful of seed packets. He raps the top of the hoe sharply to fix it firmly, and then moves to the left, measuring off the distance with his foot. He holds the flashlight to look at the seed packets, reading off the instructions. He is in the blue of night.*

WILLY: Carrots . . . quarter-inch apart. Rows . . . one-foot rows. (*He measures it off.*) One foot. (*He puts down a package and measures off.*) Beets. (*He puts down another package and measures again.*) Lettuce. (*He reads the package, puts it down.*) One foot— (*He breaks off as* BEN *appears at the right and moves slowly down to him.*) What a proposition, ts, ts. Terrific, terrific. 'Cause she's suffered, Ben, the woman has suffered. You understand me? A man can't go out the way he came in, Ben, a man has got to add up to something. You can't, you can't — (BEN *moves toward him as though to interrupt.*) You gotta consider, now. Don't answer so quick. Remember, it's a guaranteed twenty-thousand-dollar proposition. Now look, Ben, I want you to go through the ins and outs of this thing with me. I've got nobody to talk to, Ben, and the woman has suffered, you hear me?

BEN   (*standing still, considering*): What's the proposition?

WILLY: It's twenty thousand dollars on the barrelhead. Guaranteed, gilt-edged, you understand?

BEN: You don't want to make a fool of yourself. They might not honor the policy.

WILLY: How can they dare refuse? Didn't I work like a coolie to meet every premium on the nose? And now they don't pay off? Impossible!

BEN: It's called a cowardly thing, William.

WILLY: Why? Does it take more guts to stand here the rest of my life ringing up a zero?

BEN   (*yielding*): That's a point, William. (*He moves, thinking, turns.*) And twenty thousand—that is something one can feel with the hand, it is there.

WILLY   (*now assured, with rising power*): Oh, Ben, that's the whole beauty of it! I see it like a diamond, shining in the dark, hard and rough, that I can pick up and touch in my hand. Not like—like an appointment! This would not be another damned-fool appointment, Ben, and it changes all the aspects. Because he thinks I'm nothing, see, and so he spites me. But the funeral— (*Straightening up.*) Ben, that funeral will be massive! They'll come from Maine, Massachusetts, Vermont, New Hampshire! All the old-timers with the strange license plates—that boy will be thunder-struck, Ben, because he never realized—I am known! Rhode Island, New York, New Jersey—I am known, Ben, and he'll see it with his eyes once and for all. He'll see what I am, Ben! He's in for a shock, that boy!

BEN   (*coming down to the edge of the garden*): He'll call you a coward.

WILLY   (*suddenly fearful*): No, that would be terrible.

BEN: Yes. And a damned fool.

WILLY: No, no, he mustn't, I won't have that! (*He is broken and desperate.*)

BEN: He'll hate you, William.

The gay music of the boys is heard.

WILLY: Oh, Ben, how do we get back to all the great times? Used to be so full of light, and comradeship, the sleigh-riding in winter, and the ruddiness on his cheeks. And always some kind of good news coming up, always something nice coming up ahead. And never even let me carry the valises in the house, and simonizing, simonizing that little red car! Why, why can't I give him something and not have him hate me?

BEN: Let me think about it. (*He glances at his watch.*) I still have a little time. Remarkable proposition, but you've got to be sure you're not making a fool of yourself.

BEN *drifts off upstage and goes out of sight.* BIFF *comes down from the left.*

WILLY   (*suddenly conscious of* BIFF, *turns and looks up at him, then begins picking up the packages of seeds in confusion*): Where the hell is that seed? (*Indignantly.*) You can't see nothing out here! They boxed in the whole goddam neighborhood!

BIFF: There are people all around here. Don't you realize that?

WILLY: I'm busy. Don't bother me.

BIFF (*taking the hoe from* WILLY): I'm saying good-by to you, Pop. (WILLY *looks at him, silent, unable to move.*) I'm not coming back any more.

WILLY: You're not going to see Oliver tomorrow?

BIFF: I've got no appointment, Dad.

WILLY: He put his arm around you, and you've got no appointment?

BIFF: Pop, get this now, will you? Everytime I've left it's been a fight that sent me out of here. Today I realized something about myself and I tried to explain it to you and I—I think I'm just not smart enough to make any sense out of it for you. To hell with whose fault it is or anything like that. (*He takes* WILLY's *arm.*) Let's just wrap it up, heh? Come on in, we'll tell Mom. (*He gently tries to pull* WILLY *to the left.*)

WILLY (*frozen, immobile, with guilt in his voice*): No, I don't want to see her.

BIFF: Come on! (*He pulls again, and* WILLY *tries to pull away.*)

WILLY (*highly nervous*): No, no, I don't want to see her.

BIFF (*tries to look into* WILLY's *face, as if to find the answer there*): Why don't you want to see her?

WILLY (*more harshly now*): Don't bother me, will you?

BIFF: What do you mean, you don't want to see her? You don't want them calling you yellow, do you? This isn't your fault; it's me, I'm a bum. Now come inside! (WILLY *strains to get away.*) Did you hear what I said to you?

WILLY *pulls away and quickly goes by himself into the house.* BIFF *follows.*

LINDA (*to* WILLY): Did you plant, dear?

BIFF (*at the door, to* LINDA): All right, we had it out. I'm going and I'm not writing any more.

LINDA (*going to* WILLY *in the kitchen*): I think that's the best way, dear. 'Cause there's no use drawing it out, you'll just never get along.

WILLY *doesn't respond.*

BIFF: People ask where I am and what I'm doing, you don't know, and you don't care. That way it'll be off your mind and you can start brightening up again. All right? That clears it, doesn't it? (WILLY *is silent, and* BIFF *goes to him.*) You gonna wish me luck, scout? (*He extends his hand.*) What do you say?

LINDA: Shake his hand, Willy.

WILLY (*turning to her, seething with hurt*): There's no necessity to mention the pen at all, y'know.

BIFF (*gently*): I've got no appointment, Dad.

WILLY (*erupting fiercely*): He put his arm around . . . ?

BIFF: Dad, you're never going to see what I am, so what's the use of arguing? If I strike oil I'll send you a check. Meantime forget I'm alive.

WILLY (*to* LINDA): Spite, see?

BIFF: Shake hands, Dad.

WILLY: Not my hand.

BIFF: I was hoping not to go this way.

WILLY: Well, this is the way you're going. Good-by.

BIFF *looks at him a moment, then turns sharply and goes to the stairs.*

WILLY   *(stops him with)*: May you rot in hell if you leave this house!

BIFF   *(turning)*: Exactly what is it that you want from me?

WILLY   I want you to know, on the train, in the mountains, in the valleys, wherever you go, that you cut down your life for spite!

BIFF: No, no.

WILLY: Spite, spite, is the word of your undoing! And when you're down and out, remember what did it. When you're rotting somewhere beside the railroad tracks, remember, and don't you dare blame it on me!

BIFF: I'm not blaming it on you!

WILLY: I won't take the rap for this, you hear?

HAPPY *comes down the stairs and stands on the bottom step, watching.*

BIFF: That's just what I'm telling you!

WILLY   *(sinking into a chair at the table, with full accusation)*: You're trying to put a knife in me—don't think I don't know what you're doing!

BIFF: All right, phony! Then let's lay it on the line. *(He whips the rubber tube out of his pocket and puts it on the table.)*

HAPPY: You crazy—

LINDA: Biff! *(She moves to grab the hose, but BIFF holds it down with his hand.)*

BIFF: Leave it there! Don't move it!

WILLY   *(not looking at it)*: What is that?

BIFF: You know goddam well what that is.

WILLY   *(caged, wanting to escape)*: I never saw that.

BIFF: You saw it. The mice didn't bring it into the cellar! What is this supposed to do, make a hero out of you? This supposed to make me sorry for you?

WILLY: Never heard of it.

BIFF: There'll be no pity for you, you hear it? No pity!

WILLY   *(to LINDA)*: You hear the spite!

BIFF: No, you're going to hear the truth—what you are and what I am!

LINDA: Stop it!

WILLY: Spite!

HAPPY   *(coming down toward BIFF)*: You cut it now!

BIFF   *(to HAPPY)*: The man don't know who we are! The man is gonna know! *(To WILLY.)* We never told the truth for ten minutes in this house!

HAPPY: We always told the truth!

BIFF   *(turning on him)*: You big blow, are you the assistant buyer? You're one of the two assistants to the assistant, aren't you?

HAPPY: Well, I'm practically—

BIFF: You're practically full of it! We all are! And I'm through with it. *(To WILLY.)* Now hear this, Willy, this is me.

WILLY: I know you!

BIFF: You know why I had no address for three months? I stole a suit in Kansas City and I was in jail. *(To LINDA, who is sobbing.)* Stop crying. I'm through with it.

LINDA *turns away from them, her hands covering her face.*

WILLY: I suppose that's my fault!

BIFF: I stole myself out of every good job since high school!

WILLY: And whose fault is that?

BIFF: And I never got anywhere because you blew me so full of hot air I could never stand taking orders from anybody! That's whose fault it is!

WILLY: I hear that!

LINDA: Don't, Biff!

BIFF: It's goddam time you heard that! I had to be boss big shot in two weeks, and I'm through with it!

WILLY: Then hang yourself! For spite, hang yourself!

BIFF: No! Nobody's hanging himself, Willy! I ran down eleven flights with a pen in my hand today. And suddenly I stopped, you hear me? And in the middle of that office building, do you hear this? I stopped in the middle of that building and I saw—the sky. I saw the things that I love in this world. The work and the food and time to sit and smoke. And I looked at the pen and said to myself, what the hell am I grabbing this for? Why am I trying to become what I don't want to be? What am I doing in an office, making a contemptuous, begging fool of myself, when all I want is out there, waiting for me the minute I say I know who I am! Why can't I say that, Willy? (*He tries to make* WILLY *face him, but* WILLY *pulls away and moves to the left.*)

WILLY   (*with hatred, threateningly*): The door of your life is wide open!

BIFF: Pop! I'm a dime a dozen, and so are you!

WILLY   (*turning on him now in an uncontrolled outburst*): I am not a dime a dozen! I am Willy Loman, and you are Biff Loman!

BIFF *starts for* WILLY, *but is blocked by* HAPPY. *In his fury,* BIFF *seems on the verge of attacking his father.*

BIFF: I am not a leader of men, Willy, and neither are you. You were never anything but a hard-working drummer who landed in the ash can like all the rest of them! I'm one dollar an hour, Willy! I tried seven states and couldn't raise it. A buck an hour! Do you gather my meaning? I'm not bringing home any prizes any more, and you're going to stop waiting for me to bring them home!

WILLY   (*directly to* BIFF): You vengeful, spiteful mutt!

BIFF *breaks from* HAPPY. WILLY, *in fright, starts up the stairs.* BIFF *grabs him.*

BIFF   (*at the peak of his fury*): Pop, I'm nothing! I'm nothing, Pop. Can't you understand that? There's no spite in it any more. I'm just what I am, that's all.

BIFF'S *fury has spent itself, and he breaks down, sobbing, holding on to* WILLY, *who dumbly fumbles for* BIFF'S *face.*

WILLY   (*astonished*): What're you doing? What're you doing? (*To* LINDA.) Why is he crying?

BIFF   (*crying, broken*): Will you let me go, for Christ's sake? Will you take that phony dream and burn it before something happens? (*Struggling to contain himself, he pulls away and moves to the stairs.*) I'll go in the morning. Put him —put him to bed. (*Exhausted,* BIFF *moves up the stairs to his room.*)

WILLY (*after a long pause, astonished, elevated*): Isn't that remarkable? Biff—he likes me!

LINDA: He loves you, Willy!

HAPPY (*deeply moved*): Always did, Pop.

WILLY: Oh, Biff! (*Staring wildly.*) He cried! Cried to me. (*He is choking with his love, and now cries out his promise.*) That boy—that boy is going to be magnificent!

BEN *appears in the light just outside the kitchen.*

BEN: Yes, outstanding, with twenty thousand behind him.

LINDA (*sensing the racing of his mind, fearfully, carefully*): Now come to bed, Willy. It's all settled now.

WILLY (*finding it difficult not to rush out of the house*): Yes, we'll sleep. Come on. Go to sleep, Hap.

BEN: And it does take a great kind of man to crack the jungle.

In accents of dread, BEN's *idyllic music starts up.*

HAPPY (*his arm around* LINDA): I'm getting married, Pop, don't forget it. I'm changing everything. I'm gonna run that department before the year is up. You'll see, Mom. (*He kisses her.*)

BEN: The jungle is dark but full of diamonds, Willy.

WILLY *turns, moves, listening to* BEN.

LINDA: Be good. You're both good boys, just act that way, that's all.

HAPPY: 'Night, Pop. (*He goes upstairs.*)

LINDA (*to* WILLY): Come, dear.

BEN (*with greater force*): One must go in to fetch a diamond out.

WILLY (*to* LINDA, *as he moves slowly along the edge of the kitchen, toward the door*): I just want to get settled down, Linda. Let me sit alone for a little.

LINDA (*almost uttering her fear*): I want you upstairs.

WILLY (*taking her in his arms*): In a few minutes, Linda. I couldn't sleep right now. Go on, you look awful tired. (*He kisses her.*)

BEN: Not like an appointment at all. A diamond is rough and hard to the touch.

WILLY: Go on now. I'll be right up.

LINDA: I think this is the only way, Willy.

WILLY: Sure, it's the best thing.

BEN: Best thing!

WILLY: The only way. Everything is gonna be—go on, kid, get to bed. You look so tired.

LINDA: Come right up.

WILLY: Two minutes.

LINDA *goes into the livingroom, then reappears in her bedroom.* WILLY *moves just outside the kitchen door.*

WILLY: Loves me. (*Wonderingly.*) Always loved me. Isn't that a remarkable thing? Ben, he'll worship me for it!

BEN   (*with promise*): It's dark there, but full of diamonds.

WILLY: Can you imagine that magnificence with twenty thousand dollars in his pocket?

LINDA   (*calling from her room*): Willy! Come up!

WILLY   (*calling from the kitchen*): Yes! Yes. Coming! It's very smart, you realize that, don't you, sweetheart? Even Ben sees it. I gotta go, baby. 'By! By! (*Going over to* BEN, *almost dancing.*) Imagine? When the mail comes he'll be ahead of Bernard again!

BEN: A perfect proposition all around.

WILLY: Did you see how he cried to me? Oh, if I could kiss him, Ben!

BEN: Time, William, time!

WILLY: Oh, Ben, I always knew one way or another we were gonna make it, Biff and I!

BEN   (*looking at his watch*): The boat. We'll be late. (*He moves slowly off into the darkness.*)

WILLY   (*elegiacally, turning to the house*): Now when you kick off, boy, I want a seventy-yard boot, and get right down the field under the ball, and when you hit, hit low and hit hard, because it's important, boy. (*He swings around and faces the audience.*) There's all kinds of important people in the stands, and the first thing you know . . . (*Suddenly realizing he is alone.*) Ben! Ben, where do I . . . ? (*He makes a sudden movement of search.*) Ben, how do I . . . ?

LINDA   (*calling*): Willy, you coming up?

WILLY   (*uttering a gasp of fear, whirling about as if to quiet her*): Sh! (*He turns around as if to find his way; sounds, faces, voices, seem to be swarming in upon him and he flicks at them, crying.*) Sh! Sh! (*Suddenly music, faint and high, stops him. It rises in intensity, almost to an unbearable scream. He goes up and down on his toes, and rushes off around the house.*) Shhh!

LINDA: Willy?

There is no answer. LINDA *waits.* BIFF *gets up off his bed. He is still in his clothes.* HAPPY *sits up.* BIFF *stands listening.*

LINDA   (*with real fear*): Willy, answer me! Willy!

There is the sound of a car starting and moving away at full speed.

LINDA: No!

BIFF   (*rushing down the stairs*): Pop!

As the car speeds off, the music crashes down in a frenzy of sound, which becomes the soft pulsation of a single cello string. BIFF *slowly returns to his bedroom. He and* HAPPY *gravely don their jackets.* LINDA *slowly walks out of her room. The music has developed into a dead march. The leaves of day are appearing over everything.* CHARLEY *and* BERNARD, *somberly dressed, appear and knock on the kitchen door.* BIFF *and* HAPPY *slowly descend the stairs to the kitchen as* CHARLEY *and* BERNARD *enter. All stop a moment when* LINDA, *in clothes of mourning, bearing a little bunch of roses, comes through the draped doorway into the kitchen. She goes to* CHARLEY *and takes his arm. Now all move toward the audience, through the wall-line of the kitchen. At the limit of the apron,* LINDA *lays down the flowers, kneels, and sits back on her heels. All stare down at the grave.*

REQUIEM

CHARLEY: It's getting dark, Linda.

LINDA *doesn't react. She stares at the grave.*

BIFF: How about it, Mom? Better get some rest, heh? They'll be closing the gate soon.

LINDA *makes no move. Pause.*

HAPPY   (*deeply angered*): He had no right to do that! There was no necessity for it. We would've helped him.

CHARLEY   (*grunting*): Hmmm.

BIFF: Come along, Mom.

LINDA: Why didn't anybody come?

CHARLEY: It was a very nice funeral.

LINDA: But where are all the people he knew? Maybe they blame him.

CHARLEY: Naa. It's a rough world, Linda. They wouldn't blame him.

LINDA: I can't understand it. At this time especially. First time in thirty-five years we were just about free and clear. He only needed a little salary. He was even finished with the dentist.

CHARLEY: No man only needs a little salary.

LINDA: I can't understand it.

BIFF: There were a lot of nice days. When he'd come home from a trip; or on Sundays, making the stoop; finishing the cellar; putting on the new porch; when he built the extra bathroom; and put up the garage. You know something, Charley, there's more of him in that front stoop than in all the sales he ever made.

CHARLEY: Yeah. He was a happy man with a batch of cement.

LINDA: He was so wonderful with his hands.

BIFF: He had the wrong dreams. All, all, wrong.

HAPPY   (*almost ready to fight* BIFF): Don't say that!

BIFF: He never knew who he was.

CHARLEY   (*stopping* HAPPY's *movement and reply. To* BIFF.) Nobody dast blame this man. You don't understand: Willy was a salesman. And for a salesman, there is no rock bottom to the life. He don't put a bolt to a nut, he don't tell you the law or give you medicine. He's a man out there in the blue, riding on a smile and a shoeshine. And when they start not smiling back—that's an earthquake. And then you get yourself a couple of spots on your hat, and you're finished. Nobody dast blame this man. A salesman is got to dream, boy. It comes with the territory.

BIFF: Charley, the man didn't know who he was.

HAPPY   (*infuriated*): Don't say that!

BIFF: Why don't you come with me, Happy?

HAPPY: I'm not licked that easily. I'm staying right in this city, and I'm gonna beat this racket! (*He looks at* BIFF, *his chin set.*) The Loman Brothers!

BIFF: I know who I am, kid.

HAPPY: All right, boy. I'm gonna show you and everybody else that Willy Loman did not die in vain. He had a good dream. It's the only dream you can have—to come out number-one man. He fought it out here, and this is where I'm gonna win it for him.

BIFF (*with a hopeless glance at* HAPPY, *bends toward his mother*): Let's go, Mom.

LINDA: I'll be with you in a minute. Go on, Charley. (*He hesitates.*) I want to, just for a minute. I never had a chance to say good-by.

CHARLEY *moves away, followed by* HAPPY. BIFF *remains a slight distance up and left of* LINDA. *She sits there, summoning herself. The flute begins, not far away, playing behind her speech.*

LINDA: Forgive me, dear. I can't cry. I don't know what it is, but I can't cry. I don't understand it. Why did you ever do that? Help me, Willy, I can't cry. It seems to me that you're just on another trip. I keep expecting you. Willy, dear, I can't cry. Why did you do it? I search and search and I search, and I can't understand it, Willy. I made the last payment on the house today. Today, dear. And there'll be nobody home. (*A sob rises in her throat.*) We're free and clear. (*Sobbing more fully, released.*) We're free. (BIFF *comes slowly toward her.*) We're free . . . We're free . . .

BIFF *lifts her to her feet and moves out up right with her in his arms.* LINDA *sobs quietly.* BERNARD *and* CHARLEY *come together and follow them, followed by* HAPPY. *Only the music of the flute is left on the darkening stage as over the house the hard towers of the apartment buildings rise into sharp focus, and—*

CURTAIN

Robert Bolt

A Man for All Seasons deals with the life of the English sixteenth-century writer, statesman, and saint, Sir Thomas More. Like any fine historical play, it illuminates issues of the present while describing the past. More's individualism, spirituality, geniality, and wit help him preserve his sense of self as he contends with political forces that ultimately kill him. The crux of the play is More's refusal to take an oath of allegiance to King Henry VIII as head of the Church in England. To understand the issues and More's response to them, it is necessary to be familiar with a few historical details.

When the wife of Henry VIII, Catherine of Aragon, did not bear him a son, the king wanted their marriage annulled so he could marry the presumably more fertile Anne Boleyn, and ensure a male successor to his throne. Because Sir Thomas More was a prominent statesman respected for his high moral standards, Henry asked him to swear an oath alleging that the king's intended action was beyond reproach. When More refused, he was executed, ostensibly for treason after being charged with false testimony. When the Pope refused to declare Henry's marriage to Catherine invalid, the king declared the Pope's authority to be limited to that of any other bishop. Henry then appointed Thomas Cranmer archbishop of Canterbury since Cranmer would declare Henry's marriage annulled. Henry then divorced Catherine, married Anne Boleyn (who never did provide the heir he so desperately desired and who was later beheaded), and established what soon became the official Church of England. More, who by taking the oath could have made things easier for Henry, had made them considerably more complicated. And though his refusal to compromise cost him his life, it also established him as a man of character, integrity, and ultimately, of saintliness.

In a preface to the play Bolt has written that he tried for a "bold and beautiful verbal architecture" in the dialogue and speeches. He strove to write a play that would read and act well. In his preface he also wondered how successful was his device of using the Common Man to address the audience and comment on the action. Both of these aspects of the play deserve our consideration, as does Bolt's comment (also from his preface) that More was "a man with an adamantine sense of his own self," a man who "knew where he began and left off."

ROBERT BOLT

[b. 1924]

A Man for All Seasons

CHARACTERS

THE COMMON MAN: *Late middle age. He wears from head to foot black tights which delineate his pot-bellied figure. His face is crafty, loosely benevolent, its best expression that of base humor.*

SIR THOMAS MORE: *Late forties. Pale, middle-sized, not robust. But the life of the mind in him is so abundant and debonair that it illuminates the body. His movements are open and swift but never wild, having a natural moderation. The face is intellectual and quickly delighted, the norm to which it returns serious and compassionate. Only in moments of high crisis does it become ascetic— though then freezingly.*

RICHARD RICH: *Early thirties. A good body unexercised. A studious unhappy face lit by the fire of banked-down appetite. He is an academic hounded by self-doubt to be in the world of affairs and longing to be rescued from himself.*

DUKE OF NORFOLK: *Late forties. Heavy, active, a sportsman and soldier held together by rigid adherence to the minimal code of conventional duty. Attractively aware of his moral and intellectual insignificance, but also a great nobleman, untouchably convinced that his acts and ideas are important because they are his.*

ALICE MORE: *Late forties. Born into the merchant class, now a great lady; she is absurd at a distance, impressive close to. Overdressed, coarsely fashioned, she worships society; brave, hot-hearted, she worships her husband. In consequence, troubled by and defiant towards both.*

MARGARET MORE: *Middle twenties. A beautiful girl of ardent moral fineness; she both suffers and shelters behind a reserved stillness which it is her father's care to mitigate.*

CARDINAL WOLSEY: *Old. A big decayed body in scarlet. An almost megalomaniac ambition unhappily matched by an excelling intellect, he now inhabits a lonely den of self-indulgence and contempt.*

THOMAS CROMWELL: *Late thirties. Subtle and serious; the face expressing not inner tension but the tremendous outgoing will of the renaissance. A self-conceit that can cradle gross crimes in the name of effective action. In short, an intellectual bully.*

CHAPUYS: *Sixties. A professional diplomat and lay ecclesiastic dressed in black. Much on his dignity as a man of the world, he in fact trots happily along a mental footpath as narrow as a peasant's.*

CHAPUYS' ATTENDANT: *An apprentice diplomat of good family.*

WILLIAM ROPER: *Early thirties; a stiff body and an immobile face. Little imagination, moderate brain, but an all-consuming rectitude which is his cross, his solace, and his hobby.*

THE KING: *Not the Holbein Henry, but a much younger man, clean-shaven, bright-eyed, graceful and athletic. The Golden Hope of the New Learning throughout Europe. Only the levity with which he handles his absolute power foreshadows his future corruption.*

A WOMAN: *Middle fifties. Self-opinionated, self-righteous, selfish, indignant.*

CRANMER: *Late forties. Sharp-minded, sharp-faced. He treats the Church as a job of administration, and theology as a set of devices, for he lacks personal religiosity.*

THE SET is the same throughout but capable of varied lightings, as indicated. Its form is finally a matter for the designer, but to some extent is dictated by the action of the play. I have visualized two galleries of flattened Tudor arches, one above the other, able to be entered from off-stage. A flight of stairs leading from the upper gallery to the stage. A projection which can suggest an alcove or closet, with a tapestry curtain to be drawn across it. A table and some chairs, sufficiently heavy to be congruous indoors or out.

THE COSTUMES are also a matter for the designer, but I have visualized no exact reproductions of the elaborate style of the period. I think plain colors should be used, thus scarlet for the Cardinal, gray for More, gold for the King, green for the Duke, blue for Margaret, black and pinstripe for the administrators Rich and Cromwell, and so on.

ACT I

When the curtain rises, the set is in darkness but for a single spot upon the COMMON MAN, *who sits on a big property basket.*

COMMON MAN   (*Rises*) It is perverse! To start a play made up of Kings and Cardinals in speaking costumes and intellectuals with embroidered mouths, with me.

If a King or a Cardinal had done the prologue he'd have had the right materials. And an intellectual would have shown enough majestic meanings, colored propositions, and closely woven liturgical stuff to dress the House of Lords! But this!

Is this a costume? Does this say anything? It barely covers one man's nakedness! A bit of black material to reduce Old Adam to the Common Man.

Oh, if they'd let me come on naked, I could have shown you something of my own. Which would have told you without words—! Something I've forgotten . . . Old Adam's muffled up. (*Backing towards the basket*) Well, for a proposition of my own, I need a costume. (*Takes out and puts on the coat and hat of* STEWARD) Matthew! The Household Steward of Sir Thomas More! (*Lights come up swiftly on set. He takes from the basket five silver goblets, one larger than the others, and a jug with a lid, with which he furnishes the table. A burst of conversational merriment off; he pauses and indicates head of stairs*) There's company to dinner. (*He pours a cup of wine*) All right! A Common Man! A Sixteenth-Century Butler! (*He drinks from the cup*) All right—the Six—(*He breaks off, agreeably surprised by the quality of the liquor, regards the jug respectfully and drinks again from jug*) The Sixteenth Century is the Century of the Common Man. (*He puts down the jug*) Like all the other centuries. And that's my proposition. (*During the last part of the speech, voices are heard off. Now, enter, at the head of the stairs,* SIR THOMAS MORE)

STEWARD   That's Sir Thomas More.

MORE   The wine please, Matthew?

STEWARD   It's there, Sir Thomas.

MORE   (*Looking into the jug*) Is it good?

STEWARD   Bless you, sir! I don't know.

MORE   (*Mildly*) Bless you too, Matthew. (*Enter* RICH *at the head of the stairs*)

RICH   (*Enthusiastically pursuing an argument*) But every man has his price!

MORE   No-no-no—

STEWARD   (*Contemptuously*) Master Richard Rich.

RICH   But yes! In money too.

MORE   (*With gentle impatience*) No no no.

RICH   Or pleasure. Titles, women, bricks-and-mortar, there's always something.

MORE   Childish.

RICH   Well, in suffering, certainly.

MORE   (*Interested*) Buy a man with suffering?

RICH   Impose suffering, and offer him—escape.

MORE   Oh. For a moment I thought you were being profound.

(*He gives a cup to* RICH)

RICH (*To* STEWARD) Good evening, Matthew.

STEWARD (*Snubbing*) 'Evening, sir.

RICH No, not a bit profound; it then becomes a purely practical question of how to make him suffer sufficiently.

MORE Mm . . . (*He takes him by the arm and walks with him*) And . . . who recommended you to read Signor Machiavelli? (RICH *breaks away laughing—a fraction too long.* MORE *smiles*) No, who? (*More laughter*) . . . Mm?

RICH Master Cromwell.

MORE Oh . . . (*He goes back to the wine jug and cups*) He's a very able man.

RICH And so he is!

MORE Yes, I say he is. He's very able.

RICH And he will do something for me, he says.

MORE I didn't know you knew him.

RICH Pardon me, Sir Thomas, but how much do you know about me?

MORE Whatever you've let me know.

RICH I've let you know everything!

MORE Richard, you should go back to Cambridge, you're deteriorating.

RICH Well, I'm not used! . . . D'you know how much I have to show for seven months' work—

MORE Work?

RICH Work! Waiting's work when you wait as I wait, hard! . . . For seven months, that's two hundred days, I have to show: the acquaintance of the Cardinal's outer doorman, the indifference of the Cardinal's inner doorman, and the Cardinal's chamberlain's hand in my chest! . . . Oh—also one half of a Good Morning delivered at fifty paces by the Duke of Norfolk. Doubtless he mistook me for someone.

MORE He was very affable at dinner.

RICH Oh, everyone's affable *here* . . . (MORE *is pleased*) Also, of course, the friendship of Sir Thomas More. Or should I say acquaintance?

MORE Say friendship.

RICH Well, there! "A friend of Sir Thomas and still no office? There must be something wrong with him."

MORE I thought we said friendship . . . (*He considers; then*) The Dean of St. Paul's offers you a post; with a house, a servant and fifty pounds a year.

RICH What? What post?

MORE At the new school.

RICH (*Bitterly disappointed*) A teacher!

MORE A man should go where he won't be tempted. Look, Richard, see this. (*He hands him a silver cup*) Look . . . Look . . .

RICH Beautiful.

MORE Italian . . . Do you want it?

RICH Why?

MORE No joke; keep it; or sell it.

RICH Well—Thank you, of course. Thank you! Thank you! But—

MORE You'll sell it, won't you?

RICH Well—I—Yes, I will.

MORE   And buy, what?

RICH   (*With sudden ferocity*) Some decent clothes!

MORE   (*With sympathy*) Ah.

RICH   I want a gown like yours.

MORE   You'll get several gowns for that I should think. It was sent to me a little while ago by some woman. Now she's put a lawsuit into the Court of Requests. It's a bribe, Richard.

RICH   Oh . . . (*Chagrined*) So you give it away, of course.

MORE   Yes!

RICH   To me?

MORE   Well, I'm not going to keep it, and you need it. Of course—if you feel it's contaminated . . .

RICH   No, No. I'll risk it.

(*They both smile*)

MORE   But, Richard, in office they offer you all sorts of things. I was once offered a whole village, with a mill, and a manor house, and heaven knows what else—a coat of arms, I shouldn't be surprised. Why not be a teacher? You'd be a fine teacher. Perhaps even a great one.

RICH   And if I was, who would know it?

MORE   You, your pupils, your friends, God. Not a bad public, that . . . Oh, and a *quiet* life.

RICH   (*Laughing*) *You* say that!

MORE   Richard, I was commanded into office; it was inflicted on me . . . (RICH *regards him*) Can't you believe that?

RICH   It's hard.

MORE   (*Grimly*) Be a teacher.

NORFOLK   (*Enters at the head of the stairs*) It was magnificent!

STEWARD   (*To audience*) The Duke of Norfolk. Earl Marshal of England.

NORFOLK   I tell you he stooped from the clouds! (*Breaks off; irritably*) Alice!

(ALICE *enters instantly at the head of the stairs*)

ALICE   (*Irritably*) Here!

STEWARD   (*To audience*) Lady Alice. My master's wife.

NORFOLK   I tell you he stooped—

ALICE   He didn't—

NORFOLK   Goddammit, he did—

ALICE   Couldn't—

NORFOLK   He *does*—

ALICE   Not possible—

NORFOLK   But *often*—

ALICE   Never.

NORFOLK   Well, damn my soul.

MORE   (*To* MARGARET, *who has appeared on the gallery*) Come down, Meg.

STEWARD   (*Soapy; to audience*) Lady Margaret, my master's daughter; lovely, really lovely.

ALICE   (*Glances suspiciously at* STEWARD) Matthew, get about your business.

(STEWARD *exits*) We'll settle this, my lord, we'll put it to Thomas. Thomas, no falcon could stoop from a cloud, could it?

MORE   I don't know, my dear; it sounds unlikely. I have seen falcons do some very splendid things.

ALICE   But how could he stoop from a cloud? He couldn't see where he was going.

NORFOLK   You see, Alice—you're ignorant of the subject; a real falcon don't care where he's going! (*He takes some wine*) Thank you, Thomas. Anyway, I'm talking to Meg. (*A sportsman's story*) 'Twas the very first cast of the day, Meg; the sun was behind us. And from side to side of the valley like the roof of a tent was solid mist—

ALICE   Oh, mist.

NORFOLK   Well, mist is cloud, isn't it?

ALICE   No.

RICH   The opinion of Aristotle is that mists are an exhalation of the earth whereas clouds—

NORFOLK   He stooped five hundred feet! Like that! Like an Act of God, isn't he, Thomas?

MORE   He's tremendous.

NORFOLK   (*To* ALICE) Tremendous.

MARGARET   Did he kill the heron?

NORFOLK   Oh, the *heron* was *clever*. (*Very evidently discreditable*) It was a royal stoop though. (*Slyly*) If you could ride, Alice, I'd show you.

ALICE   (*Hotly*) I can ride, my lord!

MORE   No, no, you'll make yourself ill.

ALICE   And I'll bet—twenty-five—no, thirty shillings I see no falcon stoop from no cloud!

NORFOLK   Done.

MORE   Alice—you can't ride with *them*.

ALICE   God's body, Thomas, remember who you are. Am I a city wife?

MORE   No indeed, you've just lost thirty shillings, I think; there *are* such birds. And the heron got home to his chicks, Meg, so everything was satisfactory.

MARGARET   (*Smiling*) Yes.

MORE   What was that of Aristotle's, Richard?

RICHARD   Nothing, Sir Thomas—'twas out of place.

NORFOLK   (*To* RICH) I've never found much use in Aristotle myself, not practically. Great philosopher, of course. Wonderful mind.

RICH   Exactly, Your Grace!

NORFOLK   (*Suspicious*) Eh?

MORE   Master Rich is newly converted to the doctrines of Machiavelli.

RICH   Oh *no* . . . !

NORFOLK   Oh, the Italian. Nasty book, from what I hear.

MARGARET   Very practical, Your Grace.

NORFOLK   You read it? Amazing girl, Thomas, but where are you going to find a husband for her?

MORE   (MORE *and* MEG *exchange a glance*) Where indeed?

RICH   The doctrines of Machiavelli have been largely mistaken, I think;

indeed, properly apprehended, he has no doctrine. Master Cromwell has the sense of it I think when he says—

NORFOLK   You know Cromwell?

RICH   . . . Slightly, Your Grace . . .

NORFOLK   The Cardinal's Secretary.

(*Exclamations of shock from* MORE, MARGARET *and* ALICE)

ALICE   Never—it can't be.

MARGARET   The Cardinal's—it's impossible.

MORE   Not possible!

NORFOLK   It's a fact.

MORE   When, Howard?

NORFOLK   Two, three days.

(*They move about uneasily*)

ALICE   A *farrier's* son?

NORFOLK   Well, the Cardinal's a butcher's son, isn't he?

ALICE   It'll be up quick and down quick with Master Cromwell.

(NORFOLK *grunts*)

MORE   (*Quietly*) Did you know this?

RICH   No!

MARGARET   Do you *like* Master Cromwell, Master Rich?

ALICE   He's the only man in London if he does!

RICH   I think I do, Lady Alice!

MORE   (*Pleased*) Good . . . Well, you don't need *my* help now.

RICH   Sir Thomas, if only you knew how much, much rather I'd yours than his!

(*Enter* STEWARD, *who gives a letter to* MORE, *who opens it and reads*)

MORE   Talk of the Cardinal's Secretary and the Cardinal appears. He wants me. Now.

ALICE   At this time of the night?

MORE   (*Mildly*) The King's business.

ALICE   The Queen's business.

NORFOLK   More than likely, Alice, more than likely.

MORE   (*Cuts in sharply*) What's the time?

STEWARD   Eleven o'clock, sir.

MORE   Is there a boat?

STEWARD   Waiting, sir.

MORE   (*To* ALICE *and* MARGARET) Go to bed. You'll excuse me, Your Grace? Richard? Now you'll go to bed . . . (*The* MORE *family, as a matter of routine, put their hands together*)

MORE, ALICE, MARGARET   Dear Lord, give us rest tonight, or if we must be wakeful, cheerful. Careful only for our soul's salvation. For Christ's sake. Amen.

MORE   And bless our Lord the King.

ALICE *and* MARGARET   And bless our Lord the King.

ALL   Amen.

(*And then immediately a brisk leave-taking:* MORE *moving off below, the others mounting the stairs*)

MORE   Howard, are *you* at Richmond?
NORFOLK   No, down the river.
MORE   Then good night! (*He sees* RICH *disconsolate*) Oh, Your Grace, here's a young man desperate for employment. Something in the clerical line.
NORFOLK   Well, if you recommend him.
MORE   No. I don't recommend him; but I point him out. (*Moving off*) He's at the New Inn. Can you take him there?
NORFOLK   (*To* RICH; *mounting the stairs*) All right, come on.
RICH   My Lord.
NORFOLK   We'll hawk at Hounslow, Alice.
ALICE   Wherever you like.

(ALICE *and* MARGARET *follow* NORFOLK)

RICH   (*At foot of the stairs*) Sir Thomas! . . . (MORE *turns*) Thank you.
MORE   Be a teacher. (*Moving off again*) Alice! The ground's hard at Hounslow!
NORFOLK   Eh? (*Delighted roar*) That's where the Cardinal crushed his bum!
MORE, NORFOLK, ALICE, RICH   Good night. Good night! (*They process off along the gallery*)
MORE   (*Softly*) Margaret!
MARGARET   Yes?
MORE   Go to bed.

(MARGARET *exits above,* MORE *exits below. After a moment* RICH *walks swiftly back, picks up the goblet and is going off with it*)

STEWARD   (*Takes goblet*) Eh!
RICH   What— Oh . . . It's a gift, Matthew. Sir Thomas gave it to me. (STEWARD *regards it silently*) He gave it to me.
STEWARD   (*Returns it*) Very nice present, sir.
RICH   (*Beginning to leave with it*) Yes. Good night, Matthew.
STEWARD   Sir Thomas has taken quite a fancy to you, sir.
RICH   Er, here—

(*Gives him some money and goes*)

STEWARD   Thank you, sir . . . (*To audience*) That one'll come to nothing. (*Begins packing props into basket. Pauses with a cup in hand*) My master Thomas More would give anything to anyone. Some say that's good and some say that's bad, but I say he can't help it—and that's bad . . . because some day someone's going to ask him for something that he wants to keep; and he'll be out of practice. (*Puts a cloth, papers, pen and ink, and candles on the table*) There must be something that he wants to keep. That's only common sense.

(*Enter* WOLSEY. *He sits at the table and immediately commences writing, watched by* COMMON MAN, *who then exits. Enter* MORE)

WOLSEY   (*Writing*) It's half-past one. Where've you been? (*A bell strikes one*)

MORE   One o'clock, Your Grace. I've been on the river. (WOLSEY *writes in silence while* MORE *waits standing*)

WOLSEY   (*Still writing, pushes paper across the table*) Since you seemed so violently opposed to the dispatch for Rome, I thought you'd like to look it over.

MORE   (*Touched*) Thank you, Your Grace.

WOLSEY   Before it goes.

MORE   (*Smiles*) Your Grace is very kind. (*He takes it and reads*) Thank you.

WOLSEY   Well, what d'you think of it? (*He is still writing*)

MORE   It seems very well phrased, Your Grace.

WOLSEY   (*Permits himself a chuckle*) The devil it does! (*He sits back*) And apart from the style, Sir Thomas?

MORE   (*Crisply*) It's addressed to Cardinal Campeggio.

WOLSEY   Yes?

MORE   Not to our ambassador.

WOLSEY   Our ambassador's a ninny.

MORE   (*A smile*) Your Grace appointed him.

WOLSEY   (*Treats it at the level of humor, mock exasperation*) Yes I need a *ninny* in Rome! So that I can write to Cardinal Campeggio!

MORE   (*Won't respond; with aesthetic distaste—not moral disapproval*) It's devious.

WOLSEY   It's a devious situation!

MORE   There must be something simple in the middle of it. (*Again this is not a moral dictum; it is said rather wistfully, as of something he is beginning to doubt*)

WOLSEY   (*After a pause, rather gently*) I believe you believe that. (*Briskly*) You're a constant regret to me, Thomas. If you could just see facts flat on, without that horrible moral squint; with just a little common sense, you could have been a statesman.

MORE   (*After a little pause*) Oh, Your Grace flatters me.

WOLSEY   Don't frivol . . . Thomas, are you going to help me?

MORE   (*Hesitates, looks away*) If Your Grace will be specific.

WOLSEY   Ach, you're a plodder! Take you altogether, Thomas, your scholarship, your experience, what are you? (*A single trumpet calls, distant, frosty and clear.* WOLSEY *gets up and goes and looks from the window*) Come here. (MORE *joins him*) The King.

MORE   Yes.

WOLSEY   Where has he been? D'you know?

MORE   I, Your Grace?

WOLSEY   Oh, spare me your discretion. He's been to play in the mud again.

MORE   (*Coldly*) Indeed.

WOLSEY   Indeed! Indeed! Are you going to oppose me? (*Trumpet sounds again.* WOLSEY *visibly relaxes*) He's gone in . . . (*He leaves the window*) All right, we'll plod. The King wants a son; what are you going to do about it?

MORE   (*Dry murmur*) I'm very sure the King needs no advice from me on what to do about it.

WOLSEY   (*From behind, grips his shoulder fiercely*) Thomas, we're alone. I give you my word. There's no one here.

MORE I didn't suppose there was, Your Grace.

WOLSEY Oh. Sit down! (*He goes to the table, sits, signals* MORE *to sit.* MORE *unsuspectingly obeys. Then, deliberately loud*) Do you favor a change of dynasty, Sir Thomas? Thomas? D'you think two Tudors is sufficient?

MORE (*Starting up in horrified alarm*) For God's sake, Your Grace—

WOLSEY Then the King needs a son; I repeat, what are you going to do about it?

MORE (*Steadily*) I pray for it daily.

WOLSEY (*Softly*) God's death, he means it . . . That thing out there's at least fertile, Thomas.

MORE But she's not his wife.

WOLSEY No, Catherine's his wife and she's as barren as a brick. Are you going to pray for a miracle?

MORE There *are* precedents.

WOLSEY Yes. All right. Good. Pray. Pray by all means. But in addition to prayer there is effort. My effort's to secure a divorce. Have I your support or have I not?

MORE (*Sits*) A dispensation was granted so that the King might marry Queen Catherine, for state reasons. Now we are to ask the Pope to—dispense with his dispensation, also for state reasons?

WOLSEY I don't *like* plodding, Thomas, don't make me plod longer than I have to— Well?

MORE Then clearly all we have to do is approach His Holiness and ask him.

(*The pace becomes rapid*)

WOLSEY I think we might influence His Holiness' answer—

MORE Like this?

(*Indicating the dispatch*)

WOLSEY Like that and in other ways—

MORE I've already expressed my opinion on this—

WOLSEY Then, good night! Oh, your conscience is your own affair; but you're a statesman! Do you *remember* the Yorkist Wars?

MORE Very clearly.

WOLSEY Let him die without an heir and we'll have them back again. Let him die without an heir and this "peace" you think so much of will go out like that! (*He extinguishes the candle*) Very well then . . . England needs an heir; certain measures, perhaps regrettable, perhaps not— (*Pompous*) there is much in the Church that *needs* reformation, Thomas— (MORE *smiles*) All right, regrettable! But necessary, to get us an heir! Now explain how you as Councilor of England can obstruct those measures for the sake of your own, private, conscience.

MORE Well . . . I believe, when statesmen forsake their own private conscience for the sake of their public duties . . . they lead their country by a short route to chaos. (*During this speech he relights the candle with another*) And we shall have my prayers to fall back on.

WOLSEY You'd like that, wouldn't you? To govern the country by prayers?

MORE   Yes, I should.

WOLSEY   I'd like to be there when you try. Who *will?* (*He half lifts the chain from his shoulders*) Who will put his neck in this—after me? You? Tunstall? Suffolk?

MORE   Tunstall for me.

WOLSEY   Aye, but for the King. What about my Secretary, Master Cromwell?

MORE   Cromwell!

WOLSEY   You'd rather do it yourself?

MORE   Me rather than Cromwell?

WOLSEY   Then come down to earth, Thomas. (*He looks away*) And until you do, bear in mind you have an enemy!

MORE   (*Wishing to make sure, quietly*) Where, Your Grace?

WOLSEY   (*Looks back at him, hard-faced, harsh; for the first time we see this is a carnivore*) Here, Thomas.

MORE   As Your Grace pleases.

WOLSEY   As God wills!

MORE   Perhaps, Your Grace.

(*Mounting stairs*)

WOLSEY   More! You should have been a cleric!!

MORE   (*Amused, looking down from gallery*) Like yourself, Your Grace?

(*Exit* MORE. WOLSEY *is left staring, then exits through the lower arches with candle, taking most of the light from the stage as he does so. But the whole rear of the stage is now patterned with webbed reflections thrown from brightly moonlit water, so that the structure is thrown into black relief, while a strip of light descends along the front of the stage, which is to be the acting area for the next scene. An oar and a bundle of clothing are lowered into this area from above. Enter* COMMON MAN; *he unties the bundle and begins to don the coat and hat of* BOATMAN)

MORE   (*Off*) Boat! Boat! (*Approaching*) Boat!

BOATMAN   (*Donning coat and hat*) Here, sir!

MORE   (*Off*) A boatman please!

BOATMAN   Boat here, sir!

(*He seizes the oar. Enter* MORE)

MORE   (*Peering*) Boatman?

BOATMAN   Yes, sir. (*To audience, indicating oar*) A boatman.

MORE   Take me home.

BOATMAN   (*Pleasantly*) I was just going home myself, sir.

MORE   Then find me another boat.

BOATMAN   Bless you, sir—that's all right. (*Comfortably*) I expect you'll make it worth my while, sir.

CROMWELL   (*Stepping from behind an arch*) Boatman, have you a license?

BOATMAN   Eh? Bless you, sir, yes; I've got a license.

CROMWELL   Then you know that the fares are fixed—(*Turns to* MORE. *Exaggerated pleasure*) Why, it's Sir Thomas!

MORE   Good morning, Master Cromwell. You work very late.

CROMWELL   I'm on my way to the Cardinal.

MORE   (*Recollecting*) Ah yes, you are to be felicitated. Good morning, Master Secretary.

(He smiles politely)

CROMWELL   (*Smiling*) Yes.

MORE   If it *is* felicity to be busy in the night.

CROMWELL   It is.

MORE   Felicitations then.

(They exchange a dry little bow)

CROMWELL   You have just left him, I think.

MORE   Yes, I have.

CROMWELL   You left him . . . in his laughing mood, I hope?

MORE   On the whole I would say not. No, not laughing.

CROMWELL   Oh, I'm sorry. (*Backing to exit*) I am one of your *multitudinous* admirers, Sir Thomas. A penny ha'penny to Chelsea, Boatman.

(Exit CROMWELL*)*

BOATMAN   The coming man they say, sir.

MORE   Do they? Well, where's your boat?

BOATMAN   Just along the wharf, sir.

(They are going when CHAPUYS *and his* ATTENDANT *enter)*

CHAPUYS   Sir Thomas More!

MORE   Signor Chapuys? You're up very late, Your Excellency.

CHAPUYS   (*Significantly*). So is the Cardinal, Sir Thomas.

MORE   (*Closing up*) He sleeps very little.

CHAPUYS   You have just left him, I think.

MORE   You are correctly informed. As always.

CHAPUYS   I will not ask you the subject of your conversation . . .

(He waits)

MORE   No, of course not.

CHAPUYS   Sir Thomas, I will be plain with you . . . plain, that is, so far as the diplomatic decencies permit. (*Loudly*) My master Charles, the King of Spain! (*Pulls* MORE *aside; discreetly*) My master Charles, the King of Spain, feels himself concerned in anything concerning his blood relations. He would feel himself insulted by any insult offered to his mother's sister! I refer, of course, to Queen Catherine. (*He regards* MORE *keenly*) The King of Spain would feel himself insulted by any insult offered to Queen Catherine.

MORE   His feeling would be natural.

CHAPUYS   (*Consciously shy*) Sir Thomas, may I ask if you and the Cardinal parted, how shall I say, amicably?

MORE   Amicably . . . Yes.

CHAPUYS   (*A shade indignant*) In agreement?

MORE   Amicably.

CHAPUYS   (*Warmly*) Say no more, Sir Thomas; I understand.

MORE   (*A bit worried*) I hope you do, Your Excellency.

CHAPUYS   You are a good man.

MORE   I don't see how you deduce that from what I told you.

CHAPUYS   (*Holds up a hand*) A nod is as good as a wink to a blind horse. I understand. You are a good man. (*He turns to exit*) Dominus vobiscum.

(CHAPUYS *exits.* MORE *looks after him*)

MORE   (*Abstracted*) . . . spiritu tuo . . .

BOATMAN   (*Mournful; he is squatting on the ground*) Some people think boats stay afloat on their own, sir, but they don't; they cost money. (MORE *is abstractedly gazing over the audience*) Take anchor rope, sir, you may not believe me, for a little skiff like mine, but it's a penny a fathom. (MORE *is still abstracted*) And with a young wife, sir, as you know . . .

MORE   (*Abstracted*) I'll pay what I always pay you . . . The river looks very black tonight. They say it's silting up, is that so?

BOATMAN   (*Joining him*) Not in the middle, sir. There's a channel there getting deeper all the time.

MORE   How is your wife?

BOATMAN   She's losing her shape, sir, losing it fast.

MORE   Well, so are we all.

BOATMAN   Oh yes, sir; it's common.

MORE   (*Going*) Well, take me home.

(*Exit* MORE)

BOATMAN   That I will, sir! (*Crossing to the basket and pulling it out*) From Richmond to Chelsea, a penny halfpenny . . . (*He goes for the tablecloth*) from Chelsea to Richmond, a penny halfpenny. From Richmond to Chelsea, it's a quiet float downstream, from Chelsea to Richmond, it's a hard pull upstream. And it's a penny halfpenny either way. Whoever makes the regulations doesn't row a boat. (*Puts the cloth into the basket, takes out slippers*) Home again.

(*Lighting changes to* MORE'S *house.* MORE *enters, sits wearily. He takes off hat, half takes off coat but is too tired. A bell chimes three.* STEWARD *kneels to put on his slippers for him*)

MORE   Ah, Matthew . . . Is Lady Alice in bed?

STEWARD   Yes, sir.

MORE   Lady Margaret?

STEWARD   No, sir. Master Roper's here.

MORE   (*Surprised*) At this hour? . . . Who let him in?

STEWARD   He's a hard man to keep out, sir.

MORE   Where are they?

(MARGARET *and* ROPER *enter*)

MARGARET   Here, Father.

MORE   Thank you, Matthew. (STEWARD *exits.* MORE, *regarding them; resignedly*) Good morning, William. It's a little early for breakfast.

ROPER (*Stolidly*) I haven't come for breakfast, sir. (MORE *looks at him and sighs*)

MARGARET Will wants to marry me, Father.

MORE Well, he can't marry you.

ROPER Sir Thomas, I'm to be called to the Bar.

MORE (*Warmly*) Oh, congratulations, Robert!

ROPER My family may not be at the palace, sir, but in the City—

MORE The Ropers were advocates when the Mores were selling pewter; there's nothing wrong with your family. There's nothing wrong with your fortune—there's nothing wrong with you— (*Sourly*) except you need a clock—

ROPER I can buy a clock, sir.

MORE Roper, the answer's "no." (*Firmly*) And will be "no" so long as you're a heretic.

ROPER (*Firing*) That's a word I don't like, Sir Thomas!

MORE It's not a likable word. (*Coming to life*) It's not a likable thing!

(MARGARET *is alarmed, and from behind* MORE *tries to silence* ROPER)

ROPER The Church is heretical! Doctor Luther's proved that to my satisfaction!

MORE Luther's an excommunicate.

ROPER From a heretic Church! Church? It's a shop—Forgiveness by the florin! Job lots now in Germany! . . . Mmmm, and divorces.

MORE (*Expressionless*) Divorces?

ROPER Oh, half England's buzzing with that.

MORE "Half England." The Inns of Court may be buzzing, England doesn't buzz so easily.

ROPER It will. And is that a Church? Is that a Cardinal? Is that a Pope? Or Antichrist! (MORE *looks up angrily.* MARGARET *signals frantically*) Look, what I know I'll say!

MARGARET You've no sense of the *place*!

MORE (*Rueful*) He's no sense of the time.

ROPER I—

(But MORE *gently holds up his hand and he stops*)

MORE Listen, Roper. Two years ago you were a passionate Churchman; now you're a passionate—Lutheran. We must just pray that when your head's finished turning, your face is to the front again.

ROPER Don't lengthen your prayers with *me*, sir!

MORE Oh, one more or less . . . Is your horse here?

ROPER No, I walked.

MORE Well, take a horse from the stables and get back home. (ROPER *hesitates*) Go along.

ROPER May I come again?

(MORE *indicates* MARGARET)

MARGARET   Yes. Soon.

ROPER   Good night, sir.

(ROPER *exits*)

MARGARET   Is that final, Father?

MORE   As long as he's a heretic, Meg, that's absolute. (*Warmly*) Nice boy . . . Terribly strong principles though. I thought I told you to go to bed.

MARGARET   Yes, why?

MORE   (*Lightly*) Because I intended you to *go* to bed. You're very pensive?

MARGARET   You're very gay. Did the Cardinal talk about the divorce?

MORE   Mm? You know I think we've been on the wrong track with Will — It's no good arguing with a Roper—

MARGARET   Father, did he?

MORE   *Old* Roper was just the same. Now let him think he's going *with* the current and he'll turn round and start swimming in the opposite direction. What we want is a really substantial attack on the Church.

MARGARET   We're going to get it, aren't we?

MORE   Margaret, I'll not have you talk treason . . . And I'll not have you repeat lawyer's gossip. I'm a lawyer myself and I know what it's worth.

ALICE   (*Off. Indignant and excited*) Thomas!

MORE   Now look what you've done.

(ALICE *enters at the head of the stairs in her nightgown*)

ALICE   Young Roper! I've just seen young Roper! On *my* horse.

MORE   He'll bring it back, dear. He's been to see Margaret.

ALICE   Oh—why you don't beat that girl!

MORE   No, no, she's full of education—and it's a delicate commodity.

ALICE   Mm! And more's the pity!

MORE   Yes, but it's there now and think what it cost. (*He sneezes*)

ALICE   (*Pouncing*) Ah! Margaret—hot water.

(*Exit* MARGARET)

MORE   I'm sorry you were awakened, chick.

ALICE   I wasn't sleeping very deeply. Thomas—what did Wolsey want?

MORE   (*Innocently*) Young Roper asked me for Margaret.

ALICE   What! Impudence!

MORE   Yes, wasn't it?

ALICE   Old fox! What did he want, Thomas?

MORE   He wanted me to read a dispatch.

ALICE   Was that all?

MORE   A Latin dispatch.

ALICE   Oh! You don't want to talk about it?

MORE   (*Gently*) No.

(*Enter* MARGARET *with a cup, which she takes to* MORE)

ALICE   Norfolk was speaking for you as Chancellor before he left.

MORE   He's a dangerous friend then. Wolsey's Chancellor, God help him.

We don't want another. (MARGARET *takes the cup to him; he sniffs it*) I don't want this.

ALICE   Drink it. Great men get colds in the head just the same as commoners.

MORE   That's dangerous, leveling talk, Alice. Beware of the Tower.

ALICE   Drink it!

MORE   (*Rises*) I will, I'll drink it in bed.

(*They move to the stairs and ascend, talking*)

MARGARET   Would you want to be Chancellor?

MORE   No.

MARGARET   That's what I said. But Norfolk said if Wolsey fell—

MORE   (*No longer flippant*) If Wolsey fell, the splash would swamp a few small boats like ours. There will be no new Chancellors while Wolsey lives.

(*They exit above. The light is dimmed there and a bright spot descends below. Into this bright circle is thrown a great red robe and the Cardinal's hat. The COMMON MAN enters and roughly piles them into his basket. He then takes from his pocket a pair of spectacles and from the basket a book*)

COMMON MAN   (*Reading*) "Whether we follow tradition in ascribing Wolsey's death to a broken heart, or accept Professor Larcomb's less feeling diagnosis of pulmonary pneumonia, its effective cause was the King's displeasure. He died at Leicester on 29 November, 1530, while on his way to the Tower under charge of High Treason.

"England's next Lord Chancellor was Sir Thomas More, a scholar and, by popular repute, a saint. His scholarship is supported by his writings; saintliness is a quality less easy to establish. But from his willful indifference to realities which were obvious to quite ordinary contemporaries, it seems all too probable that he had it."

(*Exit COMMON MAN. As he goes, lights come up and a screen is lowered depicting Hampton Court. CROMWELL is sitting halfway up the stairs. RICH enters*)

CROMWELL   Rich! (*RICH stops, sees him, and smiles willingly*) What brings you to Hampton?

RICH   I came with the Duke last night, Master Cromwell. They're hunting again.

CROMWELL   It's a kingly pastime, Master Rich. (*Both smile*) I'm glad you found employment. You're the Duke's Secretary, are you not?

RICH   (*Flustered*) My work is mostly secretarial.

CROMWELL   (*As if making an effort of memory*) Or is it his librarian you are?

RICH   I do look after His Grace's library, yes.

CROMWELL   Oh. Well, that's something. And I don't suppose you're bothered much by His Grace—in the library? (*RICH smiles uncertainly*) It's odd how differently men's fortunes flow. My late master, Wolsey, died in disgrace, and here I am in the King's own service. There you are in a *comparative* backwater —yet the new Lord Chancellor's an old friend of yours.

(*He looks at RICH directly*)

RICH　(*Uncertain*) He isn't really my *friend*. . . .

CROMWELL　Oh, I thought he was.

(*He gets up, prepares to go*)

RICH　In a sense he is.

CROMWELL　(*Reproachful*) Well, I always understood he set you up in life.

RICH　He recommended me to the Duke.

CROMWELL　Ah yes. Are you very attached to His Grace's library, or would you be free to accept an office?

RICH　(*Suspicious*) Have you offices in gift?

CROMWELL　(*Deprecating*) I am listened to by those who have.

RICH　Master Cromwell—what *is* it that you do for the King?

(*Enter* CHAPUYS)

CHAPUYS　(*Roguish*) Yes, *I* should like to know that, Master Cromwell.

CROMWELL　Ah, Signor Chapuys. You've met His Excellency Rich? (*He indicates* CHAPUYS) The Spanish Ambassador. (*He indicates* RICH) The Duke of Norfolk's librarian.

CHAPUYS　But how should we introduce *you*, Master Cromwell, if we had the happiness?

CROMWELL　Oh, sly! Do you notice how sly he is, Rich? Well, I suppose you would call me (*He suddenly turns*) "The King's Ear" . . . (*A deprecating shrug*) It's a useful organ, the ear. But in fact it's even simpler than that. When the King wants something done, I do it.

CHAPUYS　Ah. (*Mock interest*) But then why these Justices, Chancellors, Admirals?

CROMWELL　Oh, *they* are the constitution. Our ancient, English constitution. I merely do things.

CHAPUYS　For example, Master Cromwell. . . .

CROMWELL　(*Admiring*) O-ho—beware these professional diplomats. Well now, for example; next week at Deptford we are launching the *Great Harry*—one thousand tons, four masts, sixty-six guns, an overall length of one hundred and seventy-five feet; it's expected to be very effective—all this you probably know. However, you may not know that the King himself will guide her down the river; yes, the King himself will be her pilot. He will have assistance, of course, but he himself will be her pilot. He will have the pilot's whistle upon which he will blow, and he will wear in every respect a common pilot's uniform. Except for the material, which will be cloth of gold. These innocent fancies require more preparation than you might suppose and someone has to do it. (*He spreads his hands*) Meanwhile, I do prepare myself for higher things. I stock my mind.

CHAPUYS　Alas, Master Cromwell, don't we all? This ship for instance—it has fifty-six guns by the way, not sixty-six, and only forty of them heavy. After the launching, I understand, the King will take his barge to Chelsea.

(CROMWELL's *face darkens during this speech*)

CROMWELL   (*Sharply*) Yes—
CHAPUYS   To—
CROMWELL   Sir Thomas More's.
CHAPUYS   (*Sweetly*) Will you be there?
CROMWELL   Oh no—they'll talk about the divorce. (*It is* CHAPUYS' *turn to be shocked.* RICH *draws away uneasily*) The King will ask him for an answer.
CHAPUYS   (*Ruffled*) He has given his answer!
CROMWELL   The King will ask him for another.
CHAPUYS   Sir Thomas is a good son of the Church!
CROMWELL   Sir Thomas is a man.

(*Enter* STEWARD. *Both* CROMWELL *and* CHAPUYS *look towards him sharply, then back at one another*)

CHAPUYS   (*Innocently*) Isn't that his Steward now?
CROMWELL   I believe it is. Well, good day, Your Excellency.
CHAPUYS   (*Eagerly*) Good day, Master Cromwell.

(*He expects him to go*)

CROMWELL   (*Standing firm*) Good day.

(*And* CHAPUYS *has to go.* CROMWELL *walks aside with furtive and urgent beckonings to* STEWARD *to follow.* RICH *follows but hangs off. Meanwhile* CHAPUYS *and his* ATTENDANT *have gone behind screen, beneath which their legs protrude clearly*)

STEWARD   (*Conspiratorially*) Sir, Sir Thomas doesn't talk about it. (*He waits but* CROMWELL *remains stony*) He doesn't talk about it to his wife, sir.

(*He waits again*)

CROMWELL   This is worth nothing.
STEWARD   (*Significantly*) But he doesn't talk about it to Lady Margaret—that's his daughter, sir.
CROMWELL   So?
STEWARD   So he's worried, sir . . . (CROMWELL *is interested*) Frightened . . . (CROMWELL *takes out a coin but pauses suspiciously*) Sir, he goes *white* when it's mentioned!
CROMWELL   (*Hands him the coin*) All right.
STEWARD   (*Looks at the coin; reproachfully*) Oh, *sir*!
CROMWELL   (*Waves him away*) Are you coming in my direction, Rich?
RICH   (*Still hanging off*) No no.
CROMWELL   I think you should, you know.
RICH   *I* can't tell you anything!

(*Exit* CROMWELL *and* RICH *in separate directions.* CHAPUYS *and* ATTENDANT *come from behind screen*)

CHAPUYS   (*Beckons* STEWARD) Well?
STEWARD   Sir Thomas rises at six, sir, and prays for an hour and a half.
CHAPUYS   Yes?
STEWARD   During Lent, sir, he lived entirely on bread and water.

CHAPUYS Yes?

STEWARD He goes to confession twice a week, sir. Parish priest. Dominican.

CHAPUYS Ah. He is a true son of the Church.

STEWARD (*Soapy*) That he is, sir.

CHAPUYS What did Master Cromwell want?

STEWARD Same as you, sir.

CHAPUYS No man can serve two masters, Steward.

STEWARD No indeed, sir; I serve *one*.

(*He pulls to the front an enormous cross until then hanging at his back on a length of string —a caricature of the ebony cross worn by* CHAPUYS)

CHAPUYS Good, simple man. Here. (*Gives him a coin. Going*) Peace be with you.

STEWARD And with you, sir.

CHAPUYS Our Lord watch you.

STEWARD You too, sir. (*Exit* CHAPUYS *and* ATTENDANT) That's a very religious man.

(*Enter* RICH)

RICH Matthew! What does Signor Chapuys want?

STEWARD I've no idea, sir.

RICH (*Gives him a coin*) What did you tell him?

STEWARD I told him that Sir Thomas says his prayers and goes to confession.

RICH Why that?

STEWARD That's what he wanted to know, sir. I mean I could have told him any number of things about Sir Thomas—that he has rheumatism, prefers red wine to white, is easily seasick, fond of kippers, afraid of drowning. But that's what he wanted to know, sir.

RICH What did he say?

STEWARD He said that Sir Thomas is a good churchman, sir.

RICH (*Going*) Well, that's true, isn't it?

STEWARD I'm just telling you what he said, sir. Oh, uh, Master Cromwell went that way, sir.

RICH (*Furious*) Did I ask you which way Master Cromwell went?

(RICH *exits in opposite direction*)

STEWARD (*To audience, thoughtfully*) The great thing's not to get out of your depth . . . What I can tell them's common knowledge! But now they've given money for it and everyone wants value for his money. They'll make a secret of it now to prove they've not been bilked . . . They'll make it a secret by making it dangerous . . . Mm . . . Oh, when I can't touch the bottom I'll go deaf, blind and dumb. (*He holds out coins*) And that's more than I *earn* in a fortnight!

(*A fanfare of trumpets; the rear of the stage becomes a source of glittering blue light; Hampton Court is hoisted out of sight, and a rosebay is lowered. As the fanfare ceases,* NORFOLK, ALICE, MARGARET *erupt onto the stage*)

ALICE   (*With chain of office which she puts on table. Distressed*) No sign of him, my lord!

NORFOLK   God's body, Alice, he must be found!

ALICE   (*To* MEG) He *must* be in the house!

MARGARET   He's *not* in the house, Mother!

ALICE   Then he must be here in the garden!

(*They "search" among the screens*)

NORFOLK   He takes things too far, Alice.

ALICE   Do I not know it?

NORFOLK   It will end badly for him!

ALICE   I know that too!

(*They "notice" the* STEWARD)

NORFOLK   Where's your master?

MARGARET   Matthew! Where's my father? }(*Together*)

ALICE   Where is Sir Thomas?

(*Fanfare, shorter but nearer*)

NORFOLK   (*Despairing*) Oh, my God.

ALICE   Oh, Jesus!

STEWARD   My lady—the King?

NORFOLK   Yes, fool! (*Threatening*) And if the King arrives and the Chancellor's not here—

STEWARD   Sir, my lady, it's not *my* fault!

NORFOLK   (*Quietly displeased*) Lady Alice, Thomas'll get no good of it. This is not how Wolsey made himself great.

ALICE   (*Stiffly*) Thomas has his own way of doing things, my lord!

NORFOLK   (*Testily*) Yes yes, Thomas is unique; but where *is* Thomas?

(STEWARD *swings onstage a small Gothic door. Plainsong is heard. All run to the door.* NORFOLK *opens it*)

ALICE   Thomas!

STEWARD   Sir!

MARGARET   Father!

NORFOLK   (*Indignantly*) My Lord Chancellor! (MORE *enters through the doorway. He blinks in the light. He is wearing a cassock; he shuts the door behind him*) What sort of fooling is this? Does the King visit you every day?

MORE   No, but I go to vespers most days.

NORFOLK   He's here!

MORE   But isn't this visit *meant* to be a surprise?

NORFOLK   (*Grimly*) For you, yes, not for him.

MARGARET   Father . . .

(*She indicates his cassock*)

NORFOLK   Yes—d'you propose to meet the King disguised as a parish clerk? (*They fall upon him to drag the cassock over his head*) A parish clerk, my Lord Chancellor! You dishonor the King and his office!

MORE   (*Appearing momentarily from the folds of the cassock*) The service of God is not a dishonor to any office. (*The cassock is pulled off*) Believe me, my friend, I do not belittle the honor His Majesty is doing me. (*Briskly*) Well! That's a lovely dress, Alice; so's that, Margaret. (*He looks at* NORFOLK) I'm a dowdy bird, aren't I? (*Looks at* ALICE) Calm yourself. (STEWARD *swings the door offstage*) Alice, we're all ready now.

(*He turns about and we see that his gown is caught up behind him revealing his spindly legs in long hose laced up at the thighs*)

ALICE   Thomas!

(MARGARET *laughs*)

MORE   What's the matter?

(*He turns around again and his womenfolk pursue him to pull down the gown while* NORFOLK *throws his hands in the air. Expostulation, explanation, exclamation overlap in a babble*)

NORFOLK   By God, you can be harebrained!
MARGARET   Be still!
ALICE   Oh, Thomas! Thomas!

(MARGARET *spies chain of office, brings it to* MORE)

NORFOLK   What whim possessed you—
MORE   'Twas not a whim!
ALICE   Your second-best stockings!
MARGARET   (*Offering the chain*) Father—
MORE   (*Refusing*) No, no, no, no—
NORFOLK   Oh, enough's enough!
MORE   Haven't you done—

(*Fanfare—at the end of which* HENRY, *in cloth of gold, runs out of the sunlight halfway down the steps and blows a blast on his pilot's whistle. All kneel. In the silence he descends slowly to their level, blowing softly*)

MORE   Your Majesty does my house more honor than I fear my household can bear.
HENRY   No ceremony, Thomas! No ceremony! (*They rise*) A passing fancy —I happened to be on the river. (*Holds out a shoe, proudly*) Look, mud.
MORE   We do it in better style, Your Grace, when we come by the road.
HENRY   Oh, the road! There's the road for me, Thomas, the river; *my* river . . . By heaven, what an evening! Lady Alice, I fear we come upon you unexpectedly.
ALICE   (*Shocked*) Oh no, Your Grace— (*Remembering*) that is yes, but we are ready for you—ready to entertain Your Grace, that is.
MORE   This is my daughter Margaret, sir. She has not had the honor to meet Your Grace.

(*She curtsies low*)

HENRY   (*Looking her over*) Why, Margaret, they told me you were a scholar.

(MARGARET *is confused*)

MORE   Answer, Margaret.

MARGARET   Among women I pass for one, Your Grace. (NORFOLK *and* ALICE *exchange approving glances*)

HENRY   Antiquone modo Latine loqueris, an Oxoniensi?
[Is your Latin the old Latin, or Oxford Latin?]

MARGARET   Quem me docuit pater, Domine.
[My father's Latin, Sire.]

HENRY   Bene. Optimus est. Graecamne linguam quoque te docuit?
[Good. That is the best. And has he taught you Greek too?]

MARGARET   Graecam me docuit non pater meus sed mei patris amicus, Johannes Coletus, Sancti Pauli Decanus. In litteris Graecis tamen, non minus quam Latinis, ars magistri minuitur discipuli stultitia.
[Not my father, Sire, but my father's friend, John Colet, Dean of St. Paul's. But it is with the Greek as it is with the Latin; the skill of the master is lost in the pupil's lack of it.]

(*Her Latin is better than his; he is not altogether pleased*)

HENRY   Ho! (*He walks away from her, talking; she begins to rise from her curtsy;* MORE *gently presses her down again before* KING HENRY *turns*) Take care, Thomas: "too much learning is a weariness of the flesh, and there is no end to the making of books." (*Back to* MARGARET) Can you dance, too?

MARGARET   Not well, Your Grace.

HENRY   Well, *I* dance superlatively! (*He plants his leg before her face*) That's a dancer's leg. Margaret! (*She has the wit to look straight up and smile at him. All good humor, he pulls her to her feet, sees* NORFOLK *grinning the grin of a comrade*) Hey, Norfolk? (*Indicates* NORFOLK'S *leg with much distaste*) Now *that's* a wrestler's leg. But I can throw him. (*Seizes* NORFOLK) Shall I show them, Howard? (NORFOLK *is alarmed for his dignity. To* MARGARET) Shall I?

MARGARET   (*Looking at* NORFOLK; *gently*) No, Your Grace.

HENRY   (*Releases* NORFOLK; *seriously*) You are gentle. (*To* MORE, *approvingly*) That's good. (*To* MARGARET) You shall read to me. (MARGARET *is about to demur*) No no, you shall read to me. Lady Alice, the river's given me an appetite.

ALICE   If Your Grace would share a very simple supper.

HENRY   It would please me to. (*Preparing to lead off, sees* MARGARET *again*) I'm something of a scholar too, Margaret, did you know?

MARGARET   All the world knows Your Grace's book, asserting the seven sacraments of the Church.

HENRY   Ah yes. Between ourselves, your father had a hand in that; eh, Thomas?

MORE   Here and there, Your Grace. In a minor capacity.

HENRY   (*Looking at him*) He seeks to shame me with his modesty . . . (*Turns to* ALICE) On second thought we'll follow, Lady Alice, Thomas and I will follow. (*He waves them off. They bow, withdraw to the steps and start up*) Wait! (*Raises whistle to lips*) Margaret, are you fond of music?

MARGARET   Yes, Your Grace.

HENRY   (*Beckons her to him; holds out whistle*) Blow. (*She is uncertain*) Blow. (*She does*) Louder! (*She does and at once music is heard without, stately and oversweet. Expressions of pleasure all round*) I brought them with me, Lady Alice; take them in! (*Exit all but* MORE *and* HENRY. *The music begins to recede*) Listen to this, Thomas. (*He walks about, the auditor, beating time*) Do you know it?

MORE   No, Your Grace, I—

HENRY   Sh! (MORE *is silent;* HENRY *goes on with his listening*) . . . I launched a ship today, Thomas.

MORE   Yes, Your Grace, I—

HENRY   *Listen,* man, *listen* . . . (*A pause*) . . . The *Great Harry* . . . I steered her, Thomas, under sail.

MORE   You have many accomplishments, Your Grace.

HENRY   (*Holds up a finger for silence. A pause*) A great experience. (MORE *keeps silent*) . . . A great experience, Thomas.

MORE   Yes, Your Grace.

(*The music is growing fainter*)

HENRY   I am a fool.

MORE   How so, Your Grace?

HENRY   (*A pause, during which the music fades to silence*) What else but a fool to live in a Court, in a licentious mob—when I have friends, with gardens.

MORE   Your Grace—

HENRY   No courtship, no ceremony, Thomas. Be seated. You *are* my friend, are you not?

(MORE *sits*)

MORE   Your Majesty.

HENRY   (*Eyes lighting on the chain on the table by* MORE) And thank God I have a friend for my Chancellor. (*Laughingly, but implacably, he takes up the chain and lowers it over* MORE's *head*) Readier to be friends, I trust, than he was to be Chancellor.

MORE   My own knowledge of my poor abilities—

HENRY   I will judge your abilities, Thomas . . . Did you know that Wolsey named you for Chancellor?

MORE   Wolsey!

HENRY   Aye, before he died. Wolsey named you and Wolsey was no fool.

MORE   He was a statesman of incomparable ability, Your Grace.

HENRY   Was he? Was he so? (*He rises*) Then why did he fail me? Be seated —it was villainy then! Yes, villainy. I was right to break him; he was all pride, Thomas; a proud man; pride right through. And he failed me! (MORE *opens his mouth*) He failed me in the one thing that mattered! The one thing that matters, Thomas, then or now. And why? He wanted to be Pope! Yes, he wanted to be the Bishop of Rome. I'll tell you something, Thomas, and you can check this for yourself—it was never merry in England while we had Cardinals amongst us. (*He nods significantly at* MORE, *who lowers his eyes*) But look now —(*Walking away*)—I shall not forget the feel of that . . . great tiller under my hands . . . I took her down to Dogget's Bank, went about and brought her up in Tilbury Roads. A man could sail clean round the world in that ship.

MORE   (*With affectionate admiration*) Some men could, Your Grace.

HENRY   (*Offhand*) Touching this matter of my divorce, Thomas; have you thought of it since we last talked?

MORE   Of little else.

HENRY   Then you see your way clear to me?

MORE   That you should put away Queen Catherine, Sire? Oh, alas. (*He thumps the chair in distress*) As I think of it I see so clearly that I can *not* come with Your Grace, that my endeavor is not to think of it at all.

HENRY   Then you have not thought enough! . . . (*With real appeal*) Great God, Thomas, why do you hold out against me in the desire of my heart—the very wick of my heart?

MORE   (*Draws up his sleeve, baring his arm*) There is my right arm. (*A practical proposition*) Take your dagger and saw it from my shoulder, and I will laugh and be thankful, if by that means I can come with Your Grace with a clear conscience.

HENRY   (*Uncomfortably pulls at the sleeve*) I know it, Thomas I know . . .

MORE   (*Rises, formally*) I crave pardon if I offend.

HENRY   (*Suspiciously*) Speak then.

MORE   When I took the Great Seal, Your Majesty promised not to pursue me on this matter.

HENRY   Ha! So I break my word, Master More! No no, I'm joking . . . I joke roughly . . . (*He wanders away*) I often think I'm a rough fellow . . . Yes, a rough young fellow. (*He shakes his head indulgently*) Be seated . . . That's a rosebay. We have one like it at Hampton—not so red as that though. Ha— I'm in an excellent frame of mind. (*Glances at the rosebay*) Beautiful. (*Reasonable, pleasant*) You must consider, Thomas, that I stand in peril of my soul. It was no marriage; she was my brother's widow. Leviticus: "Thou shalt not uncover the nakedness of thy brother's wife." Leviticus, Chapter eighteen, Verse sixteen.

MORE   Yes, Your Grace. But Deuteronomy—

HENRY   (*Triumphant*) Deuteronomy's ambiguous!

MORE   (*Bursting out*) Your Grace, I'm not fit to meddle in these matters— to me it seems a matter for the Holy See—

HENRY   (*Reprovingly*) Thomas, Thomas, does a man need a Pope to tell him when he's sinned? It was a sin, Thomas; I admit it; I repent. And God has punished me; I have no son . . . Son after son she's borne me, Thomas, all dead at birth, or dead within the month; I never saw the hand of God so clear in anything . . . I have a daughter, she's a good child, a well-set child— But I have no son. (*He flares up*) It is my bounden *duty* to put away the Queen, and all the Popes back to St. Peter shall not come between me and my duty! How is it that you cannot see? Everyone else does.

MORE   (*Eagerly*) Then why does Your Grace need my poor support?

HENRY   Because you are honest. What's more to the purpose, you're known to be honest . . . There are those like Norfolk who follow me because I wear the crown, and there are those like Master Cromwell who follow me because they are jackals with sharp teeth and I am their lion, and there is a mass that follow me because it follows anything that moves—and there is you.

MORE   I am sick to think how much I must displease Your Grace.

HENRY   No, Thomas, I respect your sincerity. Respect? Oh, man, it's water in the desert . . . How did you like our music? That air they played, it had a certain—well, tell me what you thought of it.

MORE   (*Relieved at this turn; smiling*) Could it have been Your Grace's own?

HENRY   (*Smiles back*) Discovered! Now I'll never know your true opinion. And that's irksome, Thomas, for we artists, though we love praise, yet we love truth better.

MORE   (*Mildly*) Then I will tell Your Grace truly what I thought of it.

HENRY   (*A little disconcerted*) Speak then.

MORE   To me it seemed—delightful.

HENRY   Thomas—I chose the right man for Chancellor.

MORE   I must in fairness add that my taste in music is reputedly deplorable.

HENRY   Your taste in music is excellent. It exactly coincides with my own. Ah music! Music! Send them back without me, Thomas; I will live here in Chelsea and make music.

MORE   My house is at Your Grace's disposal.

HENRY   Thomas, you understand me; we will stay here together and make music.

MORE   Will Your Grace honor my roof after dinner?

HENRY   (*Walking away, blowing moodily on his whistle*) Mm? Yes, I expect I'll bellow for you . . .

MORE   My wife will be more—

HENRY   Yes, yes. (*He turns, his face set*) Touching this other business, mark you, Thomas, I'll have no opposition.

MORE   (*Sadly*) Your Grace?

HENRY   No opposition, I say! No opposition! Your conscience is your own affair; but you are my Chancellor! There, you have my word—I'll leave you out of it. But I don't take it kindly, Thomas, and I'll have no opposition! I see how it will be; the bishops will oppose me. The full-fed, hypocritical "Princes of the *Church*"! Ha! As for the Pope! Am I to burn in Hell because the Bishop of Rome, with the King of Spain's knife to his throat, mouths me Deuteronomy? Hypocrites! They're all hypocrites! Mind they do not take you in, Thomas! Lie low if you will, but I'll brook no opposition—no noise! No words, no signs, no letters, no pamphlets—Mind that, Thomas—no writings against me!

MORE   Your Grace is unjust. I am Your Grace's loyal minister. If I cannot serve Your Grace in this great matter of the Queen—

HENRY   I have no Queen! Catherine is not my wife and no priest can make her so, and they that say she is my wife are not only liars . . . but traitors! Mind it, Thomas!

MORE   Am I a babbler, Your Grace?

(*But his voice is unsteady*)

HENRY   You are stubborn . . . (*Wooingly*) If you could come with me, you are the man I would soonest raise—yes, with my own hand.

MORE   (*Covers his face*) Oh, Your Grace overwhelms me!

(*A complicated chiming of little bells is heard*)

HENRY   What's that?

MORE   Eight o'clock, Your Grace.

HENRY   (*Uneasily eying* MORE) Oh, lift yourself up, man—have I not promised? (MORE *braces*) Shall we eat?

MORE   If Your Grace pleases. (*Recovering*) What will Your Grace sing for us?

HENRY   Eight o'clock you said? Thomas, the tide will be changing. I was forgetting the tide. I'd better go.

MORE   (*Gravely*) I'm sorry, Your Grace.

HENRY   I must catch the tide or I'll not get back to Richmond till . . . No, don't come. Tell Norfolk. (*He has his foot on the stairs when* ALICE *enters above*) Oh, Lady Alice, I must go. (ALICE *descends, her face serious*) I want to catch the tide. To tell the truth, Lady Alice, I have forgotten in your haven here how time flows past outside. Affairs call me to court and so I give you my thanks and say good night. (*He mounts*)

MORE and ALICE   (*Bowing*) Good night, Your Grace.

(*Exit* HENRY, *above*)

ALICE   What's this? You crossed him.

MORE   Somewhat.

ALICE   Why?

MORE   (*Apologetic*) I couldn't find the other way.

ALICE   (*Angrily*) You're too nice altogether, Thomas!

MORE   Woman, mind your house.

ALICE   I *am* minding my house!

MORE   (*Taking in her anxiety*) Well, Alice. What would you *want* me to do?

ALICE   Be ruled! If you won't rule him, be ruled!

MORE   (*Quietly*) I neither could nor would rule my King. (*Pleasantly*) But there's a little . . . little, area . . . where I must rule myself. It's very little— less to him than a tennis court. (*Her face is still full of foreboding; he sighs*) Look; it was eight o'clock. At eight o'clock, Lady Anne likes to dance.

ALICE   (*Relieved*) Oh?

MORE   I think so.

ALICE   (*With irritation*) And *you* stand between them!

MORE   I? What stands between them is a sacrament of the Church. I'm less important than you think, Alice.

ALICE   (*Appealing*) Thomas, stay friends with him.

MORE   Whatever can be done by smiling, you may rely on me to do.

ALICE   You don't know *how* to flatter.

MORE   I flatter very well! My recipe's beginning to be widely copied. It's the basic syrup with just a soupçon of discreet impudence . . .

ALICE   (*Still uneasy*) I wish he'd eaten here . . .

MORE   Yes—we shall be living on that "simple supper" of yours for a fortnight. (*She won't laugh*) Alice . . . (*She won't turn*) Alice . . . (*She turns*) Set your mind at rest—this (*Tapping himself*) is not the stuff of which martyrs are made.

(*Enter above, quickly,* ROPER)

ROPER   Sir Thomas!

MORE   (*Winces*) Oh, no . . .

(*Enter after* ROPER, MARGARET)

ALICE   Will Roper—what do you want?

MARGARET   William, I told you not to!

ROPER   I'm not easily "told," Meg.

MARGARET   I *asked* you not to.

ROPER   Meg, I'm full to here!

(*Indicates his throat*)

MARGARET   It's not convenient!

ROPER   Must everything be made convenient? I'm not a convenient man, Meg—I've got an inconvenient conscience! (MARGARET *gestures helplessly to* MORE)

MORE   (*Laughs*) Joshua's trumpet. One note on that brass conscience of yours and my daughter's walls are down.

ROPER   (*Descending*) You raised her, sir.

MORE   (*A bit puzzled*) How long have you been here? Are you in the King's party?

ROPER   No, sir, I am *not* in the King's party! (*Advancing*) It's of that I wish to speak to you. My spirit is perturbed.

MORE   (*Suppressing a grin*) It is, Will? Why?

ROPER   I've been offered a seat in the next Parliament. (MORE *looks up sharply*) Ought I to take it?

MORE   No . . . Well that depends. With your views on Church Reform I should have thought you could do yourself a lot of good in the next Parliament.

ROPER   My views on the Church, I must confess—Since last we met my views have somewhat modified. (MORE *and* MARGARET *exchange a smile*) I modify nothing concerning the *body* of the Church—the money-changers in the temple must be scourged from thence—with a scourge of fire if that is needed! But an attack on the Church herself! No, I see behind that an attack on God—

MORE   Roper—

ROPER   The Devil's work!

MORE   Roper!

ROPER   To be done by the Devil's ministers!

MORE   For heaven's sake remember my office!

ROPER   Oh, if you stand on your office—

MORE   I don't stand on it, but there are certain things I may not hear!

ROPER   Sophistication. It is what I was told. The Court has corrupted you,

Sir Thomas; you are not the man you were; you have learned to study your "convenience"; you have learned to flatter!

MORE   There, Alice, you see? I have a reputation for it.

ALICE   God's Body, young man, if I was the Chancellor I'd have you whipped!

(Enter STEWARD*)*

STEWARD   Master Rich is here, Sir Thomas.

*(*RICH *follows him closely)*

RICH   Good evening, sir.

MORE   Ah, Richard?

RICH   Good evening, Lady Alice. (ALICE *nods, noncommittally)* Lady Margaret.

MARGARET   *(Quite friendly but very clear)* Good evening, Master Rich.

(A pause)

MORE   Do you know—*(Indicates* ROPER*)* William Roper, the younger?

RICH   By reputation, of course.

ROPER   Good evening, Master . . .

RICH   Rich.

ROPER   Oh. *(Recollecting something)* Oh.

RICH   *(Quickly and hostilely)* You have heard of me?

ROPER   *(Shortly)* Yes.

RICH   *(Excitedly)* In what connection? I don't know what you can have heard—*(He looks about; hotly)* I sense that I'm not welcome here!

(He has jumped the gun; they are startled)

MORE   *(Gently)* Why, Richard, have you done something that should make you not welcome?

RICH   Why, do you suspect me of it?

MORE   I shall begin to.

RICH   *(Drawing closer to him and speaking hurriedly)* Cromwell is asking questions. About you. About you particularly. (MORE *is unmoved)* He is continually collecting information about you!

MORE   I know it. (STEWARD *begins to slide out)* Stay a minute, Matthew.

RICH   *(Pointing) That's* one of his sources!

MORE   Of course; that's one of my servants.

RICH   *(Hurriedly, in a low voice again)* Signor Chapuys, the Spanish Ambassador—

MORE   —collects information too. That's one of his functions. *(He looks at* RICH *very gravely)*

RICH   *(Voice cracking)* You look at me as though I were an enemy!

MORE   *(Putting out a hand to steady him)* Why, Richard, you're shaking.

RICH   I'm adrift. Help me.

MORE   How?

RICH   Employ me.

MORE   No.

RICH   (*Desperately*) Employ me!

MORE   No!

RICH   (*Moves swiftly to exit; turns*) I would be steadfast!

MORE   Richard, you couldn't answer for yourself even so far as tonight.

(RICH *exits. All watch him; the others turn to* MORE, *their faces alert*)

ROPER   Arrest him.

ALICE   Yes!

MORE   For what?

ALICE   He's dangerous!

ROPER   For libel; he's a spy.

ALICE   He is! Arrest him!

MARGARET   Father, that man's bad.

MORE   There is no law against that.

ROPER   There is! God's law!

MORE   Then God can arrest him.

ROPER   Sophistication upon sophistication!

MORE   No, sheer simplicity. The law, Roper, the law. I know what's legal not what's right. And I'll stick to what's legal.

ROPER   Then you set man's law above God's!

MORE   No, far below; but let me draw your attention to a fact—I'm *not* God. The currents and eddies of right and wrong, which you find such plain sailing, I can't navigate. I'm no voyager. But in the thickets of the law, oh, there I'm a forester. I doubt if there's a man alive who could follow me there, thank God . . .

(*He says this last to himself*)

ALICE   (*Exasperated, pointing after* RICH) While you talk, he's gone!

MORE   And go he should, if he was the Devil himself, until he broke the law!

ROPER   So now you'd give the Devil benefit of law!

MORE   Yes. What would you do? Cut a great road through the law to get after the Devil?

ROPER   I'd cut down every law in England to do that!

MORE   (*Roused and excited*) Oh? (*Advances on* ROPER) And when the last law was down, and the Devil turned round on you—where would you hide, Roper, the laws all being flat? (*He leaves him*) This country's planted thick with laws from coast to coast—man's laws, not God's—and if you cut them down—and you're just the man to do it—d'you really think you could stand upright in the winds that would blow then? (*Quietly*) Yes, I'd give the Devil benefit of law, for my own safety's sake.

ROPER   I have long suspected this; this is the golden calf; the law's your god.

MORE   (*Wearily*) Oh, Roper, you're a fool, God's my god. . . . (*Rather bitterly*) But I find him rather too (*Very bitterly*) subtle . . . I don't know where he is nor what he wants.

ROPER   My god wants service, to the end and unremitting; nothing else!

MORE   (*Dryly*) Are you sure that's God? He sounds like Moloch. But indeed it may be God—And whoever hunts for me, Roper, God or Devil, will find me hiding in the thickets of the law! And I'll hide my daughter with me! Not hoist her up the mainmast of your seagoing principles! They put about too nimbly!

(*Exit* MORE. *They all look after him.* MARGARET *touches* ROPER'S *hand*)

MARGARET   Oh, that was harsh.

ROPER   (*Turning to her; seriously*) What's happened here?

ALICE   (*Still with her back to them, her voice strained*) He can't abide a fool, that's all! Be off!

ROPER   (*To* MARGARET) Hide you. Hide you from what?

ALICE   (*Turning, near to tears*) He said nothing about hiding me, you noticed! I've got too fat to hide, I suppose!

MARGARET   You know he meant us both.

ROPER   But from what?

ALICE   I don't know. I don't know if he knows. He's not said one simple, direct word to me since this divorce came up. It's not God who's gone subtle! It's him!

(*Enter* MORE, *a little sheepish. He goes to* ROPER)

MORE   (*Kindly*) Roper, that was harsh: your principles are—(*He can't resist sending him up*) excellent—the very best quality. (ROPER *bridles. Contritely*) No, truly now, your principles are fine. (*Indicating the stairs, to all*) Look, we must make a start on all that food.

MARGARET   Father, can't you be plain with us?

MORE   (*Looks quickly from daughter to wife. Takes* ALICE's *hand*) I stand on the wrong side of no statute, and no common law. (*Takes* MEG's *hand too*) I have not disobeyed my sovereign. I truly believe no man in England is safer than myself. And I want my supper. (*He starts them up the stairs and goes to* ROPER) We shall need your assistance, Will. There's an excellent Burgundy—if your principles permit.

ROPER   They don't, sir.

MORE   Well, have some water in it.

ROPER   Just the water, sir.

MORE   My poor boy.

ALICE   (*Stopping at the head of the stairs, as if she will be answered*) Why does Cromwell collect information about you?

MORE   I'm a prominent figure. Someone somewhere's collecting information about Cromwell. Now no more shirking; we must make a start. (*Shepherding* ROPER *up the stairs*) There's a stuffed swan if you please. (ALICE *and* MARGARET *exit above*) Will, I'd trust *you* with my life. But not your principles. (*They mount the stairs*) You see, we speak of being anchored to our principles. But if the weather turns nasty you up with an anchor and let it down where there's less wind, and the fishing's better. And "Look," we say, "look, I'm anchored!"

(*Laughing, inviting* ROPER *to laugh with him*) "To my principles!" (*Exit above,* MORE *and* ROPER. *Enter* COMMON MAN *pulling the basket. From it he takes an inn sign, which he hangs in the alcove. He inspects it*)

COMMON MAN   "The Loyal Subject" . . . (*To audience*) A pub. (*Takes from the basket and puts on a jacket, cap and napkin*) A publican. (*Places two stools at the table, and on it mugs and a candle, which he lights*) Oh, he's a deep one, that Sir Thomas More . . . Deep . . . It takes a lot of education to get a man as deep as that . . . (*Straight to audience*) And a deep nature to begin with too. (*Deadpan*) The likes of me can hardly be expected to follow the process of a man like that. . . . (*Slyly*) Can we? (*He inspects the pub*) Right, ready. (*He goes right*) Ready, sir! (CROMWELL *enters, carrying a bottle*)

CROMWELL   Is this a *good* place for a conspiracy, innkeeper?

PUBLICAN   (*Woodenly*) You asked for a private room, sir.

CROMWELL   (*Looking round*) Yes, I want one without too many little dark corners.

PUBLICAN   I don't understand you, sir. Just the four corners as you see.

CROMWELL   (*Sardonically*) You don't understand me.

PUBLICAN   That's right, sir.

CROMWELL   Do you know who I am?

PUBLICAN   (*Promptly*) No, sir.

CROMWELL   Don't be too tactful, innkeeper.

PUBLICAN   I don't understand, sir.

CROMWELL   When the likes of you *are* too tactful, the likes of me begin to wonder who's the fool.

PUBLICAN   I just don't understand you, sir.

CROMWELL   (*Puts back his head and laughs silently*) The master statesman of us all. "I don't understand." (*Looks at* PUBLICAN *almost with hatred*) All right. Get out. (*Exit* PUBLICAN. CROMWELL *goes to the exit. Calling*) Come on. (*Enter* RICH. *He glances at the bottle in* CROMWELL'S *hand and remains cautiously by the exit*) Yes, it may be that I am a little intoxicated. (*Leaves* RICH *standing*) But not with alcohol, I've a strong head for that. With success! And who has a strong head for success? None of us gets enough of it. Except Kings. And they're born drunk.

RICH   Success? What success?

CROMWELL   Guess.

RICH   Collector of Revenues for York.

CROMWELL   (*Amused*) You do keep your ear to the ground, don't you? No.

RICH   What then?

CROMWELL   Sir Thomas Paget is—retiring.

RICH   Secretary to the Council!

CROMWELL   'Tis astonishing, isn't it?

RICH   (*Hastily*) Oh no—I mean—one sees, it's logical.

CROMWELL   No ceremony, no courtship. Be seated. (RICH *starts to sit*) As His Majesty would say. (RICH *jumps up—is pulled down, laughs nervously and involuntarily glances round*) Yes; see how I trust you.

RICH   Oh, I would never repeat or report a thing like that—

CROMWELL   (*Pouring the wine*) What kind of thing would you repeat or report?

RICH   Well, nothing said in friendship—may I say "friendship"?

CROMWELL   If you like. D'you believe that—that you would never repeat or report anything et cetera?

RICH   Yes!

CROMWELL   No, but seriously.

RICH   Why, yes!

CROMWELL   (*Puts down the bottle. Not sinister, but rather as a kindly teacher with a promising pupil*) Rich; seriously.

RICH   (*Pauses, then bitterly*) It would depend what I was offered.

CROMWELL   Don't say it just to please me.

RICH   It's true. It would depend what I was offered.

CROMWELL   (*Patting his arm*) Everyone knows it; not many people can say it.

RICH   There are *some* things one wouldn't do for anything. Surely.

CROMWELL   Mm—that idea's like these life lines they have on the embankment: comforting, but you don't expect to have to use them. (*Briskly*) Well, congratulations!

RICH   (*Suspiciously*) On what?

CROMWELL   I think you'd make a good Collector of Revenues for York Diocese.

RICH   (*Gripping himself*) Is it in your gift?

CROMWELL   It will be.

RICH   (*With conscious cynicism*) What do I have to do for it?

CROMWELL   Nothing. (*He lectures*) It isn't like that, Rich. There are no rules. With rewards and penalties—so much wickedness purchases so much worldly prospering—(*Rises. He breaks off and stops, suddenly struck*) Are you sure you're not religious?

RICH   Almost sure.

CROMWELL   Get sure. (*Resumes pacing up steps*) No, it's not like that, it's much more a matter of convenience, administrative convenience. The normal aim of administration is to keep steady this factor of convenience—and Sir Thomas would agree. Now normally when a man wants to change his woman, you let him if it's convenient and prevent him if it's not—normally indeed it's of so little importance that you leave it to the priests. But the constant factor is this element of convenience.

RICH   Whose convenience?

(CROMWELL *stops*)

CROMWELL   (*Sits*) Oh, ours. But everybody's too. However, in the present instance the man who wants to change his woman is our Sovereign Lord, Harry, by the Grace of God, the Eighth of that name. Which is a quaint way of saying that if he wants to change his woman he will. (*He rises and walks back towards* RICH) So *that* becomes the constant factor. And our job as administrators is to make it as convenient as we can. I say "our" job, on the assumption that you'll take this post at York I've offered you? (*Makes* RICH *move over*)

RICH   Yes . . . yes, yes.

(*But he seems gloomy*)

CROMWELL   (*Sits. Sharply*) It's a bad sign when people are depressed by their own good fortune.

RICH   (*Defensively*) I'm not depressed!

CROMWELL   You look depressed.

RICH   (*Hastily buffooning*) I'm lamenting. I've lost my innocence.

CROMWELL   You lost that some time ago. If you've only just noticed, it can't have been very important to you.

RICH   (*Much struck*) That's true! Why that's true, it can't!

CROMWELL   We experience a sense of release, do we, Master Rich? An unfamiliar freshness in the head, as of open air?

RICH   (*Takes the wine*) Collector of Revenues isn't bad!

CROMWELL   Not bad for a start. (*He watches* RICH *drink*) Now our present Lord Chancellor—*there's* an innocent man.

RICH   (*Indulgently*) The odd thing is—he *is*.

CROMWELL   (*Looks at him with dislike*) Yes, I say he is. (*With the light tone again*) The trouble is, his innocence is tangled in this proposition that you can't change your woman without a divorce, and can't have a divorce unless the Pope says so. And although his present Holiness is—judged even by the most liberal standards—a strikingly corrupt old person, yet he still has this word "Pope" attached to him. And from this quite meaningless circumstance I fear some degree of . . .

RICH   (*Pleased, waving his cup*) . . . Administrative inconvenience.

CROMWELL   (*Nodding as to a word-perfect pupil*) Just so. (*Deadpan*) This goblet that he gave you, how much was it worth? (RICH *looks down. Quite gently*) Come along, Rich, he gave you a silver goblet. How much did you get for it?

RICH   Fifty shillings.

CROMWELL   Could you take me to the shop?

RICH   Yes.

CROMWELL   Where did he get it? (*No reply.* RICH *puts the cup down*) It was a gift from a litigant, a woman, wasn't it?

RICH   Yes.

CROMWELL   Which court? Chancery? (*Takes the bottle; restrains* RICH *from filling his glass*) No, don't get drunk. In which court was this litigant's case?

RICH   Court of Requests.

CROMWELL   (*Grunts, his face abstracted. Becoming aware of* RICH's *regard, he smiles*) There, that wasn't too painful, was it?

RICH   (*Laughing a little and a little rueful*) No!

CROMWELL   (*Spreading his hands*) That's all there is. And you'll find it easier next time.

RICH   (*Looks up briefly, unhappily*) What application do they have, these tidbits of information you collect?

CROMWELL   None at all, usually.

RICH   (*Stubbornly, not looking up*) But sometimes.

CROMWELL   Well, there are these men—you know—"upright," "steadfast," men who want themselves to be the constant factor in the situation; which, of course, they can't be. The situation rolls forward in any case.

RICH   (*Still stubbornly*) So what happens?

CROMWELL   (*Not liking his tone, coldly*) If they've any sense they get out of its way.

RICH   What if they haven't any sense?

CROMWELL   (*Still coldly*) What, none at all? Well, then they're only fit for Heaven. But Sir Thomas has plenty of sense; he could be frightened.

RICH   (*Looks up, his face nasty*) Don't forget he's an innocent, Master Cromwell.

CROMWELL   I think we'll finish there for tonight. After all, he *is* the Lord Chancellor.

(*Going*)

RICH   You wouldn't find him easy to frighten! (CROMWELL *exits. He calls after him*) You've mistaken your man this time! He doesn't know how to be frightened!

CROMWELL   (*Returning.* RICH *rises at his approach*) Doesn't know how to be frightened? Why, then he never put his hand in a candle . . . Did he?

(*And seizing* RICH *by the wrist he holds his hand in the candle flame*)

RICH   (*Screeches and darts back, hugging his hand in his armpit, regarding* CROMWELL *with horror*) You enjoyed that! (CROMWELL's *downturned face is amazed. Triumphantly*) You enjoyed it!

Curtain

ACT II

The scene is as for start of Act One. When the curtain rises the stage is in darkness save for a spot, in which stands the COMMON MAN. *He carries the book, a place marked by his finger, and wears his spectacles.*

COMMON MAN   The interval started early in the year 1530 and it's now the middle of May, 1532. (*Explanatory*) Two years. During that time a lot of water's flowed under the bridge, and one of the things that have come floating along on it is . . . (*Reads*) "The Church of England, that finest flower of our Island genius for compromise; that system, peculiar to these shores, the despair of foreign observers, which deflects the torrents of religious passion down the canals of moderation." That's very well put. (*Returns to the book, approvingly*) "Typically, this great effect was achieved not by bloodshed but by simple Act of Parliament. Only an unhappy few were found to set themselves against the current of their times, and in so doing to court disaster. For we are dealing with an age less fastidious than our own. Imprisonment without trial, and even examination under torture, were common practice."

(*Lights rise to show* MORE, *seated, and* ROPER, *standing. Exit* COMMON MAN. ROPER *is dressed in black and wears a cross. He commences to walk up and down, watched by* MORE. *A pause*)

MORE   Must you wear those clothes, Will?

ROPER   Yes, I must.

MORE   Why?

ROPER   The time has come for decent men to declare their allegiance!

MORE   And what allegiance are those designed to express?

ROPER   My allegiance to the Church.

MORE   Well, you *look* like a Spaniard.

ROPER   All credit to Spain then!

MORE   You wouldn't last six months in Spain. You'd have been burned alive in Spain, during your heretic period.

ROPER   I suppose you have the right to remind me of it. (*Points accusingly*) That chain of office that *you* wear is a degradation!

MORE   (*Glances down at it*) I've told you. If the bishops in Convocation submitted this morning, I'll take it off . . . It's no degradation. Great men have worn this.

ROPER   When d'you expect to hear from the bishops?

MORE   About now. I was promised an immediate message.

ROPER   (*Recommences pacing*) I don't see what difference Convocation can make. The Church is already a wing of the Palace, is it not? The King is already its "Supreme Head"! Is he not?

MORE   No.

ROPER   (*Startled*) You are denying the Act of Supremacy!

MORE   No, I'm not; the Act states that the King—

ROPER   —is Supreme Head of the Church in England.

MORE   Supreme Head of the Church in England—(*Underlining the words*) "so far as the law of God allows." How far the law of God does allow it remains a matter of opinion, since the Act doesn't state it.

ROPER   A legal quibble.

MORE   Call it what you like, it's there, thank God.

ROPER   Very well; in your opinion how far does the law of God allow this?

MORE   I'll keep my opinion to myself, Will.

ROPER   Yes? I'll tell you mine—

MORE   Don't! If your opinion's what I think it is, it's High Treason, Roper! (*Enter* MARGARET *above, unseen*) Will you remember you've a wife now! And may have children!

MARGARET   Why must he remember that?

ROPER   To keep myself "discreet."

MARGARET   (*Smiling*) Then I'd rather you forgot it.

MORE   (*Unsmiling*) You are either idiots, or children. (*Enter* CHAPUYS, *above*)

CHAPUYS   (*Very sonorously*) Or saints, my lord!

MARGARET   Oh, Father, Signor Chapuys has come to see you.

MORE   (*Rising*) Your Excellency.

CHAPUYS   (*Strikes pose with* MARGARET *and* ROPER) Or saints, my lord; or saints.

MORE   (*Grins maliciously at* ROPER) That's it of course—saints! Roper—turn your head a bit—yes, I think I do detect a faint radiance. (*Reproachfully*) You should have told us, Will.

CHAPUYS   Come come, my lord; you too at this time are not free from some suspicion of saintliness.

MORE   (*Quietly*) I don't like the sound of that, Your Excellency. What do you require of me? What, Your Excellency?

CHAPUYS   (*Awkward beneath his sudden keen regard*) May I not come simply to pay my respects to the English Socrates—as I see your angelic friend Erasmus calls you.

MORE   (*Wrinkles nose*) Yes, I'll think of something presently to call Erasmus. (*Checks*) Socrates! I've no taste for hemlock, Your Excellency, if that's what you require.

CHAPUYS   (*With a display of horror*) Heaven forbid!

MORE   (*Dryly*) Amen.

CHAPUYS   (*Spreads hands*) Must I require anything? (*Sonorously*) After all, we are brothers in Christ, you and I!

MORE   A characteristic we share with the rest of humanity. You live in Cheapside, Signor? To make contact with a brother in Christ you have only to open your window and empty a chamberpot. There was no need to come to Chelsea. (CHAPUYS *titters nervously.* *Coldly*) William. The Spanish Ambassador is here on business. Would you mind?

(ROPER *and* MARGARET *begin to go*)

CHAPUYS   (*Rising, unreal protestations*) Oh no! I protest!

MORE   He is clearly here on business.

CHAPUYS   No; but really, I protest! (*It is no more than token; when* ROPER *and* MARGARET *reach head of stairs he calls*) Dominus vobiscum filli mei!

ROPER   (*Pompously*) Et cum spiritu tuo, excellencies!

(*Exit* ROPER *and* MARGARET)

CHAPUYS   (*Approaching* MORE, *thrillingly*) And how much longer shall we hear that holy language in these shores?

MORE   (*Alert, poker-faced*) 'Tisn't "holy," Your Excellency; just old.

(CHAPUYS *sits with the air of one getting down to brass tacks*)

CHAPUYS   My lord, I cannot believe you will allow yourself to be associated with the recent actions of King Henry! In respect of Queen Catherine.

MORE   Subjects are associated with the actions of Kings willy-nilly.

CHAPUYS   The Lord Chancellor is not an ordinary subject. He bears responsibility (*He lets the word sink in;* MORE *shifts*) for what is done.

MORE   (*Agitation begins to show through*) Have you considered that what has been done badly, might have been done worse, with a different Chancellor.

CHAPUYS   (*Mounting confidence, as* MORE'S *attention is caught*) Believe me, Sir

Thomas, your influence in these policies has been much searched for, and where it has been found it has been praised—*but* . . . There comes a point, does there not? . . .

MORE   Yes. (*Agitated*) There does come such a point.

CHAPUYS   When the sufferings of one unfortunate lady swell to an open attack on the religion of an entire country that point has been passed. Beyond that point, Sir Thomas, one is not merely "compromised," one is in truth corrupted.

MORE   (*Stares at him*) What do you want?

CHAPUYS   Rumor has it that if the Church in Convocation has submitted to the King, you will resign.

MORE   (*Looks down and regains composure*) I see. (*Suavely*) Supposing rumor to be right. Would you approve of that?

CHAPUYS   Approve, applaud, admire.

MORE   (*Still looking down*) Why?

CHAPUYS   Because it would show one man—and that man known to be temperate—unable to go further with this wickedness.

MORE   And that man known to be Chancellor of England too.

CHAPUYS   Believe me, my lord, such a signal would be seen—

MORE   "Signal"?

CHAPUYS   Yes, my lord; it would be seen and understood.

MORE   (*Now positively silky*) By whom?

CHAPUYS   By half of your fellow countrymen! (*Now* MORE *looks up sharply*) Sir Thomas, I have just returned from Yorkshire and Northumberland, where I have made a tour.

MORE   (*Softly*) Have you indeed?

CHAPUYS   Things are very different there, my lord. There they are ready.

MORE   For what?

CHAPUYS   Resistance!

MORE   (*Softly, as before*) Resistance by what means? (*Suddenly his agitation must find expression, if only physical. He is galvanized from his seat and as he suddenly stops, with his back to* CHAPUYS, MORE's *face is electrically alert.* CHAPUYS *hears the excitement in:*) By force of arms?

CHAPUYS   (*Almost sure the fish is hooked, leaning forward but playing it cool*) We are adjured by St. Paul to don the arms of God when the occasion warrants.

MORE   Metaphorical arms. The breastplate of righteousness and the helmet of salvation. Do you mean a metaphorical resistance?

(*Indignation and fear make his voice vibrate with the excitement of enthusiasm*)

CHAPUYS   (*Intones*) "He shall flee the *iron* weapons, and the bow of steel shall strike him through."

MORE   (*There is a pause while his agile mind scans the full frightening implications of this for himself; it is almost with a start of recollection that he remembers to answer* CHAPUYS *at all*) I see.

(*Enter* ROPER, *above, excited*)

ROPER Sir Thomas! (MORE *looks up angrily*) Excuse me, sir—(*Indicates off*) His Grace the Duke of Norfolk—(MORE *and* CHAPUYS *rise.* ROPER *excitedly descends*) It's all over, sir, they've—

(*Enter* NORFOLK *above,* ALICE *and* MARGARET, *below*)

NORFOLK One moment, Roper, I'll do this! Thomas—(*Sees* CHAPUYS) Oh.

(*He stares at* CHAPUYS *hostilely*)

CHAPUYS I was on the point of leaving, Your Grace. Just a personal call. I have been trying . . . er, to borrow a book . . . but without success—you're sure you have no copy, my lord? Then I'll leave you. (*Bowing*) Gentlemen, ladies.

(*Going up the stairs, he stops unnoticed as* ROPER *speaks*)

ROPER Sir Thomas—

NORFOLK I'll do it, Roper! Convocation's knuckled under, Thomas. They're to pay a fine of a hundred thousand pounds. And . . . we've severed the connection with Rome.

MORE (*Smiling bitterly*) "The connection with Rome" is nice. (*Bitterly*) "The connection with Rome."

ROPER (*Addressing* NORFOLK, *but looking at* MORE) Your Grace, this is quite certain, is it?

NORFOLK Yes. (MORE *puts his hand to his chin.* CHAPUYS *exits. All turn*) Funny company, Thomas?

MORE It's quite unintentional. He doesn't mean to be funny. (*He fumbles with the chain*) Help me with this.

NORFOLK Not I.

ROPER (*Takes a step forward. Then, subdued*) Shall I, sir?

MORE No thank you, Will. Alice?

ALICE Hell's fire—God's Blood and Body, *no!* Sun and moon, Master More, you're taken for a wise man! Is this wisdom—to betray your ability, abandon practice, forget your station and your duty to your kin and behave like a printed book!

MORE (*Listens gravely; then*) Margaret, will you?

MARGARET If you want.

MORE There's my clever girl. (*She takes it from his neck*)

NORFOLK Well, Thomas, why? Make me understand—because I'll tell you now, from where I stand, this looks like cowardice!

MORE (*Excited and angry*) All right I will—this isn't "Reformation," this is war against the Church! . . . (*Indignant*) Our King, Norfolk, has declared war on the Pope—because the Pope will not declare that our Queen is not his wife.

NORFOLK And is she?

MORE (*With cunning*) I'll answer that question for one person only, the King. Aye, and that in private too.

NORFOLK (*Contemptuously*) Man, you're cautious.

MORE Yes, cautious. I'm not one of your hawks.

NORFOLK   (*Walks away and turns*) All right—we're at war with the Pope! The Pope's a Prince, isn't he?

MORE   He is.

NORFOLK   And a bad one?

MORE   Bad enough. But the theory is that he's also the Vicar of God, the descendant of St. Peter, our only link with Christ.

NORFOLK   (*Sneering*) A tenuous link.

MORE   Oh, tenuous indeed.

NORFOLK   (*To the others*) Does this make sense? (*No reply; they look at* MORE) You'll forfeit all you've got—which includes the respect of your country—for a theory?

MORE   (*Hotly*) The Apostolic Succession of the Pope is—(*Stops; interested*) . . . Why, it's a theory, yes; you can't see it; can't touch it; it's a theory. (*To* NORFOLK, *very rapidly but calmly*) But what matters to me is not whether it's true or not but that I believe it to be true, or rather, not that I *believe* it, but that *I* believe it . . . I trust I make myself obscure?

NORFOLK   Perfectly.

MORE   That's good. Obscurity's what I have need of now.

NORFOLK   Thomas. This isn't Spain, you know.

MORE   (*Looks at him, takes him aside; in a lowered voice*) Have I your word that what we say here is between us and has no existence beyond these walls?

NORFOLK   (*Impatient*) Very well.

MORE   (*Almost whispering*) And if the King should command you to repeat what I have said?

NORFOLK   I should keep my word to you!

MORE   Then what has become of your oath of obedience to the King?

NORFOLK   (*Indignant*) You lay traps for me!

MORE   (*Now grown calm*) No, I show you the times.

NORFOLK   Why do you insult me with these lawyer's tricks?

MORE   Because I am afraid.

NORFOLK   And here's your answer. The King accepts your resignation very sadly; he is mindful of your goodness and past loyalty, and in any matter concerning your honor and welfare he will be your good lord. So much for your fear.

MORE   (*Flatly*) You will convey my humble gratitude.

NORFOLK   I will. Good day, Alice. (*Going*) I'd rather deal with you than your husband.

MORE   (*Complete change of tone; briskly professional*) Oh, Howard! (*He stops him*) Signor Chapuys tells me he's just made a "tour" of the North Country. He thinks we shall have trouble there. So do I.

NORFOLK   (*Stolid*) Yes? What kind of trouble?

MORE   The Church—the old Church, not the new Church—is very strong up there. I'm serious, Howard, keep an eye on the border this next spring; and bear in mind the Old Alliance.

NORFOLK   (*Looks at him*) We will. We do . . . As for the Spaniard, Thomas, it'll perhaps relieve your mind to know that one of Secretary Cromwell's agents made the tour with him.

MORE   Oh. (*A flash of jealousy*) Of course if Master Cromwell has matters in hand—

NORFOLK   He has.

MORE   Yes, I can imagine.

NORFOLK   But thanks for the information. (*Going upstairs*) It's good to know you still have . . . some vestige of patriotism.

MORE   (*Angrily*) That's a remarkably stupid observation, Norfolk!

(NORFOLK *exits*)

ALICE   So there's an end of you. What will you do now—sit by the fire and make goslings in the ash?

MORE   Not at all, Alice, I expect I'll write a bit. (*He woos them with unhappy cheerfulness*) I'll write, I'll read, I'll think. I think I'll learn to fish! I'll play with my grandchildren—when son Roper's done his duty. (*Eagerly*) Alice, shall I teach you to read?

ALICE   No, by God!

MORE   Son Roper, you're pleased with me I hope?

ROPER   (*Goes to him; moved*) Sir, you've made a noble gesture.

MORE   (*Blankly*) A gesture? (*Eagerly*) It wasn't possible to continue, Will. I was not *able* to continue. I would have if I could! I make no gesture! (*Apprehensive, looks after* NORFOLK) My God, I hope it's understood I make no gesture! (*He turns back to them*) Alice, you don't think I would do this to you for a gesture! *That's* a gesture! (*Thumbs his nose*) That's a gesture! (*Jerks up two fingers*) I'm no street acrobat to make gestures! I'm practical!

ROPER   You belittle yourself, sir, this was not practical; (*Resonantly*) this was moral!

MORE   Oh, now I understand you, Will. Morality's *not* practical. Morality's a gesture. A complicated gesture learned from books—that's what you say, Alice, isn't it? . . . and you, Meg?

MARGARET   It *is,* for most of us, Father.

MORE   Oh no, if you're going to plead humility! Oh, you're cruel. I have a cruel family.

ALICE   Yes, you can fit the cap on anyone you want, I know that well enough. If there's cruelty in this house, I know where to look for it.

MARGARET   No, Mother!

ALICE   Oh, you'd walk on the bottom of the sea and think yourself a crab if he suggested it! (*To* ROPER) And you! You'd dance him to the Tower—You'd dance him to the block! Like David with a harp! Scattering hymn books in his path! (*To* MORE) Poor silly man, d'you think they'll *leave* you here to learn to fish?

MORE   (*Straight at her*) If we govern our tongues they will! Now listen, I have a word to say about that. I have made no statement. I've resigned, that's *all.* On the King's Supremacy, the King's divorce which he'll now grant himself, the marriage he'll then make—have you heard me make a statement?

ALICE   No—and if I'm to lose my rank and fall to housekeeping I want to know the reason; so make a statement now.

MORE   No— (ALICE *exhibits indignation*) Alice, it's a point of law! Accept it from me, Alice, that in silence is my safety under the law, but my silence must be absolute, it must extend to you.

ALICE   In short you don't trust us!

MORE   A man would need to be half-witted not to trust you—but— (*Impatiently*) Look—(*He advances on her*) I'm the Lord Chief Justice, I'm Cromwell, I'm the King's Head Jailer—and I take your hand (*He does so*) and I clamp it on the Bible, on the Blessed Cross (*Clamps her hand to his closed fist*) and I say: "Woman, has your husband made a statement on these matters?" Now—on peril of your soul remember—what's your answer?

ALICE   No.

MORE   And so it must remain. (*He looks around at their grave faces*) Oh, it's only a life line, we shan't have to use it but it's comforting to have. No, no, when they find I'm silent they'll ask nothing better than to leave me silent; you'll see.

(*Enter* STEWARD)

STEWARD   Sir, the household's in the kitchen. They want to know what's happened.

MORE   Oh. Yes. We must speak to them. Alice, they'll mostly have to go, my dear. (*To* STEWARD) But not before we've found them places.

ALICE   We can't find places for them all!

MORE   Yes, we can; yes, we can. Tell them so.

ALICE   God's death, it comes on us quickly . . .

(*Exit* ALICE, MARGARET *with the chain, and* ROPER)

MORE   What about you, Matthew? It'll be a smaller household now, and for you I'm afraid, a smaller wage. Will you stay?

STEWARD   Don't see how I could then, sir.

MORE   You're a single man.

STEWARD   (*Awkwardly*) Well, yes, sir, but I mean I've got my own—

MORE   (*Quickly*) Quite right, why should you? . . . I shall miss you, Matthew.

STEWARD   (*With man-to-man jocosity*) No-o-o. You never had much time for me, sir. You see through *me*, sir, I know that. (*He almost winks*)

MORE   (*Gently insists*) I shall miss you, Matthew; I shall miss you.

(*Exit* MORE. STEWARD *snatches off his hat and hurls it to the floor*)

STEWARD   Now, damn me, isn't that them all over! (*He broods, face down-turned*) Miss? . . . He . . . Miss? . . . Miss me? . . . What's *in* me for *him* to miss? . . . (*Suddenly he cries out like one who sees a danger at his very feet*) Wo-AH! (*Chuckling*) We-e-eyup! (*To audience*) I nearly fell for it. (*He walks away*) "Matthew, will you kindly take a cut in your wages?" "No, Sir Thomas, I will not." That's it and (*Fiercely*) that's all of it! (*Falls to thought again. Resentfully*) All right, so he's down on his luck! I'm sorry. I don't mind saying that: I'm sorry! Bad luck! If I'd any good luck to spare he could have some. I wish we could *all* have good luck, *all* the time! I wish we had wings! I wish rain water was beer! But it isn't! . . . And what with not having wings but walking—on two flat feet; and good luck and bad luck being just exactly even stevens; and rain being water—don't you complicate the job by putting things in me for me to miss! (*He takes off his steward's coat, picks up his hat; draws the curtain to the alcove. Chuckling*) I did, you know. I nearly fell for it.

(*Exit* COMMON MAN. NORFOLK *and* CROMWELL *enter to alcove*)

NORFOLK   But he makes no noise, Mr. Secretary; he's silent, why not leave him silent?

CROMWELL   (*Patiently*) Not being a man of letters, Your Grace, you perhaps don't realize the extent of his reputation. This "silence" of his is bellowing up and down Europe! Now may I recapitulate: He reported the Spaniard's conversation to you, informed on the Spaniard's tour of the North Country, warned against a possible rebellion there.

NORFOLK   He did!

CROMWELL   We may say, then, that he showed himself hostile to the hopes of Spain.

NORFOLK   That's what I say!

CROMWELL   (*Patiently*) Bear with me, Your Grace. Now if he opposes Spain, he supports us. Well, surely that follows? (*Sarcastically*) Or do you see some third alternative?

NORFOLK   No no, that's the line-up all right. And I may say Thomas More—

CROMWELL   Thomas More will line up on the right side.

NORFOLK   Yes! Crank he may be, traitor he is not.

CROMWELL   (*Spreading his hands*) And with a little pressure, he can be got to say so. And that's all we need—a brief declaration of his loyalty to the present administration.

NORFOLK   I still say let sleeping dogs lie.

CROMWELL   (*Heavily*) The King does not agree with you.

NORFOLK   (*Glances at him, flickers, but then rallies*) What kind of "pressure" d'you think you can bring to bear?

CROMWELL   I have evidence that Sir Thomas, during the period of his judicature, accepted bribes.

NORFOLK   (*Incredulous*) What! Goddammit, he was the only judge since Cato who *didn't* accept bribes! When was there last a Chancellor whose possessions after three years in office totaled one hundred pounds and a gold chain.

CROMWELL   (*Rings hand bell and calls*) Richard! It is, as you imply, common practice, but a practice may be common and remain an offense; this offense could send a man to the Tower.

NORFOLK   (*Contemptuously*) I don't believe it.

(*Enter a* WOMAN *and* RICH, *who motions her to remain and approaches the table, where* CROMWELL *indicates a seat.* RICH *has acquired self-importance*)

CROMWELL   Ah, Richard. You know His Grace, of course.

RICH   (*Respectful affability*) Indeed yes, we're *old* friends.

NORFOLK   (*Savage snub*) Used to look after my books or something, didn't you?

CROMWELL (*Clicks his fingers at* WOMAN) Come here. This woman's name is Catherine Anger; she comes from Lincoln. And she put a case in the Court of Requests in—(*Consults a paper*)

WOMAN A property case, it was.

CROMWELL Be quiet. A property case in the Court of Requests in April, 1526.

WOMAN And got a wicked false judgment!

CROMWEEL And got an impeccably correct judgment from our friend Sir Thomas.

WOMAN No, sir, it was not!

CROMWELL We're not concerned with the judgment but the gift you gave the judge. Tell this gentleman about that. The judgment, for what it's worth, was the right one.

WOMAN No, sir! (CROMWELL *looks at her; she hastily addresses* NORFOLK) I sent him a cup, sir, an Italian silver cup I bought in Lincoln for a hundred shillings.

NORFOLK Did Sir Thomas accept this cup?

WOMAN I sent it.

CROMWELL He did accept it, we can corroborate that. You can go. (*She opens her mouth*) Go!

(*Exit* WOMAN)

NORFOLK (*Scornfully*) Is that your witness?

CROMWELL No; by an odd coincidence this cup later came into the hands of Master Rich here.

NORFOLK How?

RICH He gave it to me.

NORFOLK (*Brutally*) Can you corroborate that?

CROMWELL I have a fellow outside who can; he was More's steward at that time. Shall I call him?

NORFOLK Don't bother, I know him. When did Thomas give you this thing?

RICH I don't exactly remember.

NORFOLK Well, make an effort. Wait! I can tell you! I can tell you—it was that spring—it was that night we were there together. You had a cup with you when we left; was that it? (RICH *looks to* CROMWELL *for guidance but gets none*)

RICH It may have been.

NORFOLK Did he often give you cups?

RICH I don't suppose so, Your Grace.

NORFOLK That was it then. (*New realization*) And it was April! The April of twenty-six. The very month that cow first put her case before him! (*Triumphantly*) In other words, the moment he knew it was a bribe, he got rid of it.

CROMWELL (*Nodding judicially*) The facts will bear that interpretation, I suppose.

NORFOLK Oh, this is a horse that won't run, Master Secretary.

CROMWELL Just a trial canter, Your Grace. We'll find something better.

NORFOLK (*Between bullying and pleading*) Look here, Cromwell, I want no part of this.

CROMWELL You have no choice.

NORFOLK What's that you say?

CROMWELL The King particularly wishes you to be active in the matter.

NORFOLK (*Winded*) He has not told me that.

CROMWELL (*Politely*) Indeed? He told me.

NORFOLK But *why*?

CROMWELL We felt that, since you are known to have been a friend of More's, your participation will show that there is nothing in the nature of a "persecution," but only the strict processes of law. As indeed you've just demonstrated. I'll tell the King of your loyalty to your friend. If you like, I'll tell him that you "want no part of it," too.

NORFOLK (*Furious*) Are you threatening me, Cromwell?

CROMWELL My *dear* Norfolk . . . This isn't Spain.

(NORFOLK *stares, turns abruptly and exits.* CROMWELL *turns a look of glacial coldness upon* RICH)

RICH I'm sorry, Secretary, I'd forgotten he was there that night.

CROMWELL (*Scrutinizes him dispassionately; then*) You must try to remember these things.

RICH Secretary, I'm sincerely—

CROMWELL (*Dismisses the topic with a wave and turns to look after* NORFOLK) Not such a fool as he looks, the Duke.

RICH (*Civil Service simper*) That would hardly be possible, Secretary.

CROMWELL (*Straightening his papers, briskly*) Sir Thomas is going to be a slippery fish, Richard; we need a net with a finer mesh.

RICH Yes, Secretary?

CROMWELL We'll weave one for him, shall we, you and I?

RICH (*Uncertainly*) I'm only anxious to do what is correct, Secretary.

CROMWELL (*Smiling at him*) Yes, Richard, I know. (*Straight-faced*) You're absolutely right, it must be done by law. It's just a matter of finding the right law. Or making one. Bring my papers, will you?

(*Exit* CROMWELL. *Enter* STEWARD)

STEWARD Could we have a word now, sir?

RICH We don't require you after all, Matthew.

STEWARD No, sir, but about . . .

RICH Oh yes. . . . Well, I begin to need a steward, certainly; my household is expanding . . . (*Sharply*) But as I remember, Matthew, your attitude to me was sometimes—disrespectful!

(*The last word is shrill*)

STEWARD (*With humble dignity*) Oh. Oh, I must contradict you there, sir; that's your imagination. In those days, sir, you still had your way to make. And a gentleman in that position often imagines these things. Then when he's reached his proper level, sir, he stops thinking about them. (*As if offering tangible proof*) Well—I don't think you find people "disrespectful" nowadays, do you, sir?

RICH   There may be something in that. Bring my papers. (*Going, he turns at the exit and anxiously scans* STEWARD'S *face for signs of impudence*) I'll permit no breath of insolence!

STEWARD   (*The very idea is shocking*) I should hope not, sir. (*Exit* RICH) Oh, I can manage this one! He's just my size! (*Lighting changes so that the set looks drab and chilly*) Sir Thomas More's again. Gone down a bit.

(*Exit* COMMON MAN. *Enter* CHAPUYS *and* ATTENDANT, *cloaked.* ALICE *enters above wearing a big coarse apron over her dress*)

ALICE   My husband is coming down, Your Excellency.

CHAPUYS   Thank you, madam.

ALICE   And I beg you to be gone before he does!

CHAPUYS   (*Patiently*) Madam, I have a Royal Commission to perform.

ALICE   Aye. You said so.

(ALICE *exits*)

CHAPUYS   For sheer barbarity, commend me to a good-hearted English-woman of a certain class. . . .

(*Wraps cloak about him*)

ATTENDANT   It's very cold, Excellency.

CHAPUYS   I remember when these rooms were warm enough.

ATTENDANT   (*Looking about*) "Thus it is to incur the enmity of a King."

CHAPUYS   A heretic King. (*Looking about*) Yes, Sir Thomas is a good man.

ATTENDANT   Yes, Excellency, I like Sir Thomas very much.

CHAPUYS   Carefully, carefully.

ATTENDANT   It *is* uncomfortable dealing with him, isn't it?

CHAPUYS   (*Smiling patronizing*) Goodness can be a difficulty.

ATTENDANT   (*Somewhat shocked*) Excellency?

CHAPUYS   (*Recovers instantly his official gravity*) In the long run, of course, all good men everywhere are allies of Spain. No good man cannot be, and no man who is not can be good . . .

ATTENDANT   Then he is really for us.

CHAPUYS   (*Still graciously instructing*) He is opposed to Cromwell, is he not?

ATTENDANT   (*Smiling back*) Oh, yes, Excellency.

CHAPUYS   (*As a genteel card player, primly triumphant, produces the ace of trumps*) If he's opposed to Cromwell, he's for us. (*No answer; a little more sharply*) There's no third alternative?

ATTENDANT   I suppose not, Excellency.

CHAPUYS   (*Rides him down, tried beyond all bearing*) Oh—I wish your mother had chosen some other career for you. You've no political sense whatever! (*Enter* MORE) Sir Thomas! (*Goes to him, solemnly and affectionately places hands on his shoulders, gazing into his eyes*) Ah, Sir Thomas, in a better state this threadbare stuff will metamorphose into shining garments, these dank walls to walls of pearl, this cold light to perpetual sunshine.

(*He bends upon* MORE *a melancholy look of admiration*)

MORE   (*As yet quite friendly, smiles quizzically*) It sounds not unlike Madrid . . . ?

CHAPUYS   (*Throws up his hands delightedly*) Even in times like this, even now, a pleasure to converse with you.

MORE   (*Chuckles a little, takes* CHAPUYS *by the wrist, waggles it a little and then releases it as though to indicate that pleasantries must now end*) Is this another "personal" visit, Chapuys, or is it official?

CHAPUYS   It falls between the two, Sir Thomas.

MORE   (*Reaching the bottom of stairs*) Official then.

CHAPUYS   No, I have a personal letter for you.

MORE   From whom?

CHAPUYS   My master, the King of Spain. (MORE *puts his hands behind his back*) You will take it?

MORE   I will not lay a finger on it.

CHAPUYS   It is in no way an affair of State. It expresses my master's admiration for the stand which you and Bishop Fisher of Rochester have taken over the so-called divorce of Queen Catherine.

MORE   I have taken no stand!

CHAPUYS   But your views, Sir Thomas, are well known—

MORE   My views are much guessed at. (*Irritably*) Oh come, sir, could you understand to convince (*Grimly*) King Harry that this letter is "in no way an affair of State?"

CHAPUYS   My dear Sir Thomas, I have taken extreme precautions. I came here very much incognito. (*A self-indulgent chuckle*) Very nearly in disguise.

MORE   You misunderstand me. It is not a matter of your precautions but my duty, which would be to take this letter immediately to the King.

CHAPUYS   (*Flabbergasted*) But, Sir Thomas, your views—

MORE   (*With the heat of fear behind it*) Are well known you say. It seems my loyalty to my King is less so!

CHAPUYS   (*Glibly*) "Render unto Caesar the things which *are* Caesar's—(*He raises a reproving finger*) But unto God—"

MORE   Stop! (*He walks about, suppressing his agitation, and then as one who excuses a display of bad manners*) Holy writ is holy, Excellency.

(*Enter* MARGARET *bearing before her a huge bundle of bracken. The entry of the bracken affords him a further opportunity to collect himself*)

MARGARET   Look, Father! (*She dumps it*) Will's getting more.

MORE   Oh, well done! (*This is not whimsy; they're cold and their interest in fuel is serious*) Is it dry? (*He feels it expertly*) Oh it *is.* (*Sees* CHAPUYS *staring; laughs*) It's bracken, Your Excellency. We burn it. (*Enter* ALICE) Alice, look at this.

ALICE   (*Eying* CHAPUYS) Aye.

MORE   (*Crossing to* CHAPUYS) May I? (*Takes the letter to* ALICE *and* MARGARET) This is a letter from the King of Spain; I want you to see it's not been opened. I have declined it. You see the seal has not been broken? (*Returning it to* CHAPUYS) I wish I could ask you to stay, Your Excellency—the bracken fire is a luxury.

CHAPUYS   (*With a cold smile*) One I must forgo. (*Aside to* ATTENDANT) Come.
(*Crosses to exit, pauses*) May I say I am sure my master's admiration will not
be diminished. (*Bows, noncommittally*) Ladies.

MORE   I'm gratified.

CHAPUYS   (*Bows to them, the ladies curtsy*) The man's utterly unreliable.

(*Exit* CHAPUYS *and* ATTENDANT)

ALICE   (*After a little silence kicks the bracken*) "Luxury"!

(*She sits wearily on the bundle*)

MORE   Well, it's a luxury while it lasts . . . There's not much sport in it for
you, is there? (*She neither answers nor looks at him from the depths of her fatigue.
After a moment's hesitation he braces himself*) Alice, the money from the bishops.
I can't take it. I wish—oh, heaven, how I wish I could! But I can't.

ALICE   (*As one who has ceased to expect anything*) I didn't think you would.

MORE   (*Reproachfully*) Alice, there are reasons.

ALICE   We couldn't come so deep into your confidence as to *know* these
reasons why a man in poverty can't take four thousand pounds?

MORE   (*Gently but very firmly*) Alice, this isn't poverty.

ALICE   D'you know what we shall eat tonight?

MORE   (*Trying for a smile*) Yes, parsnips.

ALICE   Yes, parsnips and stinking mutton! (*Straight at him*) For a knight's
lady!

MORE   (*Pleading*) But at the worst, we could be beggars, and still keep
company, and be merry together!

ALICE   (*Bitterly*) Merry!

MORE   (*Sternly*) Aye, merry!

MARGARET   (*Her arm about her mother's waist*) I think you should take that
money.

MORE   Oh, don't you see? (*He sits by them*) If I'm paid by the Church for
my writings—

ALICE   This had nothing to do with your writings! This was charity pure
and simple! Collected from the clergy high and low!

MORE   It would *appear* as payment.

ALICE   You're not a man who deals in appearances!

MORE   (*Fervently*) Oh, am I not though. . . . (*Calmly*) If the King takes this
matter any further, with me or with the Church, it will be very bad, if I even
appear to have been in the pay of the Church.

ALICE   (*Sharply*) Bad?

MORE   If you will have it, dangerous.

MARGARET   But you don't write against the King.

MORE   (*Rises*) I write! And that's enough in times like these!

ALICE   You said there *was* no danger!

MORE   I don't think there is! And I don't want there to be!

(*Enter* ROPER *carrying a sickle*)

ROPER   (*Steadily*) There's a gentleman here from Hampton Court. You are to go before Secretary Cromwell. To answer certain charges.

(ALICE *rises and* MARGARET, *appalled, turns to* MORE)

MORE   (*After a silence, rubs his nose*) Well, that's all right. We expected that. (*He is not very convincing*) When?

ROPER   Now.

ALICE   (*Exhibits distress*) Ah—

MORE   Alice, that means nothing; that's just technique . . . Well, I suppose "now" means now.

(*Lighting changes, darkness gathering on the others, leaving* MORE *isolated in the light*)

MARGARET   Can I come with you?

MORE   Why? No. I'll be back for dinner. I'll bring Cromwell to dinner, shall I? It'd serve him right.

MARGARET   Oh, Father, don't be witty!

MORE   Why not? Wit's what's in question.

ROPER   (*Quietly*) While we are witty, the Devil may enter us unawares.

MORE   He's not the Devil, son Roper, he's a lawyer! And my case is watertight!

ALICE   They say he's a very penetrating lawyer.

MORE   What, Cromwell? Pooh, he's a pragmatist—and that's the only resemblance he has to the Devil, son Roper; a pragmatist, the merest plumber.

(EXIT ALICE, MARGARET, ROPER, *in darkness. Lights come up. Enter* CROMWELL, *bustling, carrying a file of papers*)

CROMWELL   I'm sorry to invite you here at such short notice, Sir Thomas; good of you to come. (*Draws back curtain from alcove, revealing* RICH *seated at a table, with writing materials*) Will you take a seat? I think you know Master Rich?

MORE   Indeed yes, we're old friends. That's a nice gown you have, Richard.

CROMWELL   Master Rich will make a record of our conversation.

MORE   Good of you to tell me, Master Secretary.

CROMWELL   (*Laughs appreciatively; then*) Believe me, Sir Thomas—no, that's asking too much—but let me tell you all the same, you have no more sincere admirer than myself. (RICH *begins to scribble*) Not yet, Rich, not yet.

(*Invites* MORE *to join him in laughing at* RICH)

MORE   If I might hear the charges?

CROMWELL   Charges?

MORE   I understand there are certain charges.

CROMWELL   Some ambiguities of behavior I should like to clarify—hardly "charges."

MORE   Make a note of that will you, Master Rich? There are no charges.

CROMWELL   (*Laughing and shaking head*) Sir Thomas, Sir Thomas . . . You know it amazes me that you, who were once so effective *in* the world and are

now so *much* retired from it, should be opposing yourself to the whole movement of the times?

(*He ends on a note of interrogation*)

MORE   (*Nods*) It amazes me too.

CROMWELL   (*Picks up and drops a paper; sadly*) The King is not pleased with
you.

MORE   I am grieved.

CROMWELL   Yet do you know that even now, if you could bring yourself
to agree with the Universities, the Bishops and the Parliament of this realm,
there is no honor which the King would be likely to deny you?

MORE   (*Stonily*) I am well acquainted with His Grace's generosity.

CROMWELL   (*Coldly*) Very well. (*Consults the paper*) You have heard of the
so-called Holy Maid of Kent—who was executed for prophesying against the
King?

MORE   Yes, I knew the poor woman.

CROMWELL   (*Quickly*) You sympathize with her?

MORE   She was ignorant and misguided; she was a bit mad, I think. And she
has paid for her folly. Naturally I sympathize with her.

CROMWELL   (*Grunts*) You admit meeting her. You met her—and yet you
did not warn His Majesty of her treason. How was that?

MORE   She spoke no treason. Our conversation was not political.

CROMWELL   My dear More, the woman was notorious! Do you expect me
to believe that?

MORE   Happily there are witnesses.

CROMWELL   You wrote a letter to her?

MORE   Yes, I wrote advising her to abstain from meddling with the affairs
of Princes and the State. I have a copy of this letter—also witnessed.

CROMWELL   You have been cautious.

MORE   I like to keep my affairs regular.

CROMWELL   Sir Thomas, there is a more serious charge—

MORE   Charge?

CROMWELL   For want of a better word. In the May of 1526 the King
published a book. (*He permits himself a little smile*) A theological work. It was
called *A Defence of the Seven Sacraments.*

MORE   Yes. (*Bitterly*) For which he was named "Defender of the Faith," by
His Holiness the Pope.

CROMWELL   By the Bishop of Rome. Or do you insist on "Pope"?

MORE   No, "Bishop of Rome" if you like. It doesn't alter his authority.

CROMWELL   Thank you, you come to the point very readily; what *is* that
authority? As regards the Church in Europe; (*Approaching*) for example, the
Church in England. What exactly *is* the Bishop of Rome's authority?

MORE   You will find it very ably set out and defended, Master Secretary,
in the King's book.

CROMWELL   The book published under the King's name would be more
accurate. You wrote that book.

MORE   I wrote no part of it.

CROMWELL   I do not mean you actually held the pen.

MORE   I merely answered to the best of my ability certain questions on canon law which His Majesty put to me. As I was bound to do.

CROMWELL   Do you deny that you *instigated* it?

MORE   It was from first to last the King's own project. This is trivial, Master Cromwell.

CROMWELL   I should not think so if I were in your place.

MORE   Only two people know the truth of the matter. Myself and the King. And, whatever he may have said to you, he will not give evidence to support this accusation.

CROMWELL   Why not?

MORE   Because evidence is given on oath, and he will not perjure himself. If you don't know that, you don't yet know him.

(CROMWELL *looks at him viciously*)

CROMWELL   (*Goes apart; formally*) Sir Thomas More, is there anything you wish to say to me concerning the King's marriage with Queen Anne?

MORE   (*Very still*) I understood I was not to be asked that again.

CROMWELL   Evidently you understood wrongly. These charges—

MORE   (*With a sudden, contemptuous sweep of his arm*) They are terrors for children, Master Secretary—an empty cupboard! To frighten children in the dark, not me.

CROMWELL   (*It is some time now since anybody treated him like this, and it costs him some effort to control his anger, but he does and even manages a little smile as one who sportingly admits defeat*) True . . . true, Sir Thomas, very apt. (*Then coldly*) To frighten a man, there must be something *in* the cupboard, must there not?

MORE   (*Made wary again by the tone*) Yes, and there is nothing in it.

CROMWELL   For the moment there is this: (*Picks up a paper and reads*) "I charge you with great ingratitude. I remind you of many benefits graciously given and ill received. I tell you that no King of England ever had nor could have so villainous a servant nor so traitorous a subject as yourself." (*During this,* MORE's *face goes ashen and his hand creeps up to his throat in an unconscious gesture of fear and protection.* CROMWELL *puts down the paper and says*) The words are not mine, Sir Thomas, but the King's. Believe that.

MORE   I do. (*He lowers his hands, looks up again, and with just a spark of his old impudence*) I recognize the style. So I am brought here at last.

CROMWELL   Brought? You brought yourself to where you stand now.

MORE   Yes—Still, in another sense—I was brought.

CROMWELL   Oh, yes. You may go home now. (*After a fractional hesitation,* MORE *goes, his face fearful and his step thoughtful, and he pauses uncertainly as* CROMWELL *calls after him*) For the present. (MORE *carries on, and exits*) I don't like him so well as I did. There's a man who raises the gale and won't come out of the harbor.

RICH   (*A covert jeer*) Do you still think you can frighten him?

CROMWELL   Oh, yes.

RICH   (*Given pause*) What will you do?

CROMWELL   We'll put something in the cupboard.

RICH   (*Now definitely uneasy*) What?

CROMWELL   (*As to an importunate child*) Whatever's necessary. The King's a man of conscience and he wants either Sir Thomas More to bless his marriage or Sir Thomas More destroyed.

RICH   (*Shakily*) They seem odd alternatives, Secretary.

CROMWELL   Do they? That's because you're not a man of conscience. If the King destroys a man, that's proof to the King that it must have been a bad man, the kind of man a man of conscience *ought* to destroy—and of course a bad man's blessing's not worth having. So either will do.

RICH   (*Subdued*) I see.

CROMWELL   Oh, there's no going back, Rich. I find we've made ourselves the keepers of this conscience. And it's ravenous. (*Exit* CROMWELL *and* RICH. *Enter* MORE. COMMON MAN *enters, removes a cloth, hears* MORE, *shakes head, exits*)

MORE   (*Calling*) Boat! . . . Boat! . . . (*To himself*) Oh, come along, it's not as bad as that. . . . (*Calls*) Boat! (*Enter* NORFOLK. *He stops. Turning, pleased*) Howard! . . . I can't get home. They won't bring me a boat.

NORFOLK   Do you blame them?

MORE   Is it as bad as that?

NORFOLK   It's every bit as bad as that!

MORE   (*Gravely*) Then it's good of you to be seen with me.

NORFOLK   (*Looking back, off*) I followed you.

MORE   (*Surprised*) Were *you* followed?

NORFOLK   Probably. (*Facing him*) So listen to what I have to say: You're behaving like a fool. You're behaving like a crank. You're not behaving like a gentleman—All right, that means nothing to you; but what about your friends?

MORE   What about them?

NORFOLK   Goddammit, you're dangerous to know!

MORE   Then don't know me.

NORFOLK   There's something further . . . You must have realized by now there's a . . . policy, with regards to you. (MORE *nods*) The King is using me in it.

MORE   That's clever. That's Cromwell . . . You're between the upper and the nether millstones then.

NORFOLK   I am!

MORE   Howard, you must cease to know me.

NORFOLK   I do know you! I wish I didn't but I do!

MORE   I mean as a friend.

NORFOLK   You *are* my friend!

MORE   I can't relieve you of your obedience to the King, Howard. You must relieve yourself of our friendship. No one's safe now, and you have a son.

NORFOLK   You might as well advise a man to change the color of his hair! I'm fond of you, and there it is! You're fond of me, and there it is!

MORE   What's to be done then?

NORFOLK   (*With deep appeal*) Give in.

MORE   (*Gently*) I can't give in, Howard—(*A smile*) You might as well advise a man to change the color of his eyes. I can't. Our friendship's more mutable than *that*.

NORFOLK   Oh, that's immutable, is it? The one fixed point in a world of changing friendships is that Thomas More will not give in!

MORE   (*Urgent to explain*) To me it *has* to be, for that's myself! Affection goes as deep in me as you think, but only God is love right through, Howard; and *that's* my *self*.

NORFOLK   And who are you? Goddammit, man, it's disproportionate! *We*'re supposed to be the arrogant ones, the proud, splenetic ones—and we've all given in! Why must you stand out? (*Quietly and quickly*) You'll break my heart.

MORE   (*Moved*) We'll do it now, Howard: part, as friends, and meet as strangers. (*He attempts to take* NORFOLK's *hand*)

NORFOLK   (*Throwing it off*) Daft, Thomas! Why d'you want to take your friendship from me? For friendship's sake! You say we'll meet as strangers and every word you've said confirms our friendship!

MORE   (*Takes a last affectionate look at him*) Oh, that can be remedied. (*Walks away, turns; in a tone of deliberate insult*) Norfolk, you're a fool.

NORFOLK   (*Starts; then smiles and folds his arms*) You can't place a quarrel; you haven't the style.

MORE   Hear me out. You and your class have "given in"—as you rightly call it—because the religion of this country means nothing to you one way or the other.

NORFOLK   Well, that's a foolish saying for a start; the nobility of England has always been—

MORE   The nobility of England, my lord, would have snored through the Sermon on the Mount. But you'll labor like Thomas Aquinas over a rat-dog's pedigree. Now what's the name of those distorted creatures you're all breeding at the moment?

NORFOLK   (*Steadily, but roused towards anger by* MORE's *tone*) An artificial quarrel's not a quarrel.

MORE   Don't deceive yourself, my lord, we've had a quarrel since the day we met, our friendship was but sloth.

NORFOLK   You can be cruel when you've a mind to be; but I've always known that.

MORE   What's the name of those dogs? Marsh mastiffs? Bog beagles?

NORFOLK   Water spaniels!

MORE   And what would you do with a water spaniel that was afraid of water? You'd hang it! Well, as a spaniel is to water, so is a man to his own self. I will not give in because I oppose it—*I* do—not my pride, not my spleen, nor any other of my appetites but *I* do—*I!* (MORE *goes up to him and feels him up and down like an animal.* MARGARET's *voice is heard, well off, calling her father.* MORE's *attention is irresistibly caught by this; but he turns back determinedly to* NORFOLK) Is there no single sinew in the midst of this that serves no appetite of Norfolk's but is just Norfolk? There is! Give *that* some exercise, my lord!

MARGARET   (*Off, nearer*) Father?

NORFOLK   (*Breathing hard*) Thomas . . .

MORE Because as you stand, you'll go before your Maker in a very ill condition!

(Enter MARGARET, *below; she stops; amazed at them)*

NORFOLK Now steady, Thomas. . . .

MORE And he'll have to think that somewhere back along your pedigree— a bitch got over the wall!

*(*NORFOLK *lashes out at him; he ducks and winces. Exit* NORFOLK*)*

MARGARET Father! *(As he straightens up)* Father, what was that?

MORE That was Norfolk.

(He looks after him wistfully. ROPER *enters)*

ROPER *(Excited, almost gleeful)* Do you know, sir? Have you heard? *(*MORE *is still looking off, not answering. To* MARGARET*)* Have you told him?

MARGARET *(Gently)* We've been looking for you, Father.

*(*MORE *is still looking off)*

ROPER There's to be a new Act through Parliament, sir!

MORE *(Half-turning, half-attending)* Act?

ROPER Yes, sir—about the marriage!

MORE *(Indifferently)* Oh.

(Turning back again. ROPER *and* MARGARET *look at one another)*

MARGARET *(Puts a hand on his arm)* Father, by this Act, they're going to administer an oath.

MORE *(With instantaneous attention)* An oath! *(He looks from one to the other)* On what compulsion?

ROPER It's expected to be treason!

MORE *(Very still)* What is the oath?

ROPER *(Puzzled)* It's about the marriage, sir.

MORE But what is the wording?

ROPER We don't need to know the *(Contemptuously)* wording—we know what it will mean!

MORE It will mean what the words say! An oath is made of words! It may be possible to take it. Or avoid it. *(To* MARGARET*)* Have we a copy of the Bill?

MARGARET There's one coming out from the City.

MORE Then let's get home and look at it. Oh, I've no boat.

(He looks off again after NORFOLK*)*

MARGARET *(Gently)* Father, he tried to hit you.

MORE Yes—I spoke, slightingly, of water spaniels. Let's get home.

(He turns and sees ROPER *excited and truculent)*

ROPER But sir—

MORE Now listen, Will. And, Meg, you listen, too, you know I know you well. God made the *angels* to show him splendor—as he made animals for innocence and plants for their simplicity. But Man he made to serve him wittingly, in the tangle of his mind! If he suffers us to fall to such a case that there is no escaping, then we may stand to our tackle as best we can, and yes, Will, then we may clamor like champions . . . if we have the spittle for it. And no doubt it delights God to see splendor where He only looked for complexity. But it's God's part, not our own, to bring ourselves to that extremity! Our natural business lies in escaping—so let's get home and study this Bill.

(Exit MORE, ROPER *and* MARGARET. *Enter* COMMON MAN, *dragging a cage. The rear of the stage remains in moonlight. Now descends a rack, which remains suspended)*

COMMON MAN *(Aggrieved. Brings the basket on)* Now look! . . . I don't suppose anyone enjoyed it any more than he did. Well, not much more. *(Takes from the basket and dons a coat and hat)* Jailer! *(Shrugs. Pushes basket off and arranges three chairs behind the table)* The pay scale being what it is they have to take a rather common type of man into the prison service. But it's a job. *(Admits* MORE *to jail, turns keys)* Bit nearer the knuckle than most perhaps, but it's a job like any other job—*(Sits on steps. Enter* CROMWELL, NORFOLK, CRANMER, *who sit, and* RICH, *who stands behind them.* MORE *enters the cage and lies down)* They'd let him out if they could, but for various reasons they can't. *(Twirling keys)* I'd let him out if I could but I can't. Not without taking up residence in there myself. And he's in there already, so what'd be the point? You know the old adage? "Better a live rat than a dead lion," and that's about it. *(An envelope descends swiftly before him. He opens it and reads)* "With reference to the old adage: Thomas Cromwell was found guilty of High Treason and executed on 28 July, 1540. Norfolk was found guilty of High Treason and should have been executed on 27 January, 1547, but on the night of 26 January, the King died of syphilis and wasn't able to sign the warrant. Thomas Cranmer"—Archbishop of Canterbury *(Jerking thumb)*, that's the other one—"was burned alive on 21 March, 1556." *(He is about to conclude but sees a postscript)* Oh. "Richard Rich became a Knight and Solicitor-General, a Baron and Lord Chancellor, and died in his bed." So did I. And so, I hope, will all of you. *(He goes to* MORE *and rouses him)* Wake up, Sir Thomas.

MORE *(Rousing)* What, again?
JAILER Sorry, sir.
MORE *(Flops back)* What time is it?
JAILER One o'clock sir.
MORE Oh, this is iniquitous!
JAILER *(Anxiously)* Sir.
MORE *(Sitting up)* All right, *(Putting on slippers)* Who's there?
JAILER The Secretary, the Duke, and the Archbishop.
MORE I'm flattered. *(He stands, claps hand to hip)* Ooh! *(Preceded by* JAILER *he limps across the stage; he has aged and is pale, but his manner, though wary, is relaxed; while that of the Commission is bored, tense, and jumpy)*
NORFOLK *(Looks at him)* A seat for the prisoner. *(While* JAILER *brings a stool from under the stairs and* MORE *sits on it,* NORFOLK *rattles off)* This is the Seventh Commission to inquire into the case of Sir Thomas More, appointed by His Majesty's Council. Have you anything to say?

MORE   No. (*To* JAILER) Thank you.

NORFOLK   (*Sitting back*) Master Secretary.

CROMWELL   Sir Thomas—(*He breaks off*) Do the witnesses attend?

RICH   Secretary.

JAILER   Sir.

CROMWELL   (*To* JAILER) Nearer! (*He advances a bit*) Come where you can hear! (JAILER *takes up stance by* RICH. *To* MORE) Sir Thomas, you have seen this document before?

MORE   Many times.

CROMWELL   It is the Act of Succession. These are the names of those who have sworn to it.

MORE   I have, as you say, seen it before.

CROMWELL   Will you swear to it?

MORE   No.

NORFOLK   Thomas, we must know plainly—

CROMWELL   (*Throws down document*) Your Grace, *please!*

NORFOLK   Master Cromwell!

(*They regard one another in hatred*)

CROMWELL   I beg Your Grace's pardon.

(*Sighing, rests his head in his hands*)

NORFOLK   Thomas, we must know plainly whether you recognize the off-spring of Queen Anne as heirs to His Majesty.

MORE   The King in Parliament tells me that they are. Of course I recognize them.

NORFOLK   Will you swear that you do?

MORE   Yes.

NORFOLK   Then why won't you swear to the Act?

CROMWELL   (*Impatiently*) Because there is more than that *in* the Act.

NORFOLK   Is that it?

MORE   (*After a pause*) Yes.

NORFOLK   Then we must find out what it is in the Act that he objects to!

CROMWELL   Brilliant. (NORFOLK *rounds on him*) God's wounds!

CRANMER   (*Hastily*) Your Grace—May I try?

NORFOLK   Certainly. I've no pretension to be an expert in police work.

(*During the next speech* CROMWELL *straightens up and folds arms resignedly*)

CRANMER   (*Clears his throat fussily*) Sir Thomas, it states in the preamble that the King's former marriage, to the Lady Catherine, was unlawful, she being previously his brother's wife and the—er—"Pope" having no authority to sanction it. (*Gently*) Is that what you deny? (*No reply*) Is that what you dispute? (*No reply*) Is that what you are not sure of? (*No reply*)

NORFOLK   Thomas, you insult the King and His Council in the person of the Lord Archbishop!

MORE   I insult no one. I will not take the oath. I will not tell you why I will not.

NORFOLK   Then your reasons must be treasonable!

MORE   Not "must be"; may be.

NORFOLK   It's a fair assumption!

MORE   The law requires more than an assumption; the law requires a fact.

(CROMWELL *looks at him and away again*)

CRANMER   I cannot judge your legal standing in the case; but until I know the *ground* of your objections, I can only guess your spiritual standing too.

MORE   (*For a second furiously affronted; then humor overtakes him*) If you're willing to guess at that, Your Grace, it should be a small matter to guess my objections.

CROMWELL   (*Quickly*) You do have objections to the Act?

NORFOLK   (*Happily*) Well, we know *that,* Cromwell!

MORE   You don't, my lord. You may suppose I have objections. All you *know* is that I will not swear to it. From sheer delight to give you trouble it might be.

NORFOLK   Is it material why you won't?

MORE   It's most material. For refusing to swear, my goods are forfeit and I am condemned to life imprisonment. You cannot lawfully harm me further. But if you were right in supposing I had reasons for refusing and right again in supposing my reasons to be treasonable, the law would let you cut my head off.

NORFOLK   (*He has followed with some difficulty*) Oh yes.

CROMWELL   (*An admiring murmur*) Oh, well done, Sir Thomas. I've been trying to make that clear to His Grace for some time.

NORFOLK   (*Hardly responds to the insult; his face is gloomy and disgusted*) Oh, confound all this . . . (*With real dignity*) I'm not a scholar, as Master Cromwell never tires of pointing out, and frankly I don't know whether the marriage was lawful or not. But damn it, Thomas, look at those names . . . You know those men! Can't you do what I did, and come with us, for fellowship?

MORE   (*Moved*) And when we stand before God, and you are sent to Paradise for doing according to your conscience, and I am damned for not doing according to mine, will you come with me, for fellowship?

CRANMER   So those of us whose names are there are damned, Sir Thomas?

MORE   I don't know, Your Grace. I have no window to look into another man's conscience. I condemn no one.

CRANMER   Then the matter is capable of question?

MORE   Certainly.

CRANMER   But that you owe obedience to your King is not capable of question. So weigh a doubt against a certainty—and sign.

MORE   Some men think the Earth is round, others think it flat; it is a matter capable of question. But if it is flat, will the King's command make it round? And if it is round, will the King's command flatten it? No, I will not sign.

CROMWELL   (*Leaping up, with ceremonial indignation*) Then you have more regard to your own doubt than you have to his command!

MORE   For myself, I have no doubt.

CROMWELL   No doubt of what?

MORE   No doubt of my grounds for refusing this oath. Grounds I will tell to the King alone, and which you, Master Secretary, will not trick out of me.

NORFOLK   Thomas—

MORE   Oh, gentlemen, can't I go to bed?

CROMWELL   You don't seem to appreciate the seriousness of your position.

MORE   I defy anyone to live in that cell for a year and not appreciate the seriousness of his position.

CROMWELL   Yet the State has harsher punishments.

MORE   You threaten like a dockside bully.

CROMWELL   How should I threaten?

MORE   Like a Minister of State, with justice!

CROMWELL   Oh, justice is what you're threatened with.

MORE   Then I'm not threatened.

NORFOLK   Master Secretary, I think the prisoner may retire as he requests. Unless you, my lord—

CRANMER   (*Pettishly*) No, I see no purpose in prolonging the interview.

NORFOLK   Then good night, Thomas.

MORE   (*Hesitates*) Might I have one or two more books?

CROMWELL   You have books?

MORE   Yes.

CROMWELL   I didn't know; you shouldn't have.

MORE   (*Turns to go, pauses. Desperately*) May I see my family?

CROMWELL   No! (MORE *returns to cell*) Jailer!

JAILER   Sir!

CROMWELL   Have you ever heard the prisoner speak of the King's divorce, or the King's Supremacy of the Church, or the King's marriage?

JAILER   No, sir, not a word.

CROMWELL   If he does, you will of course report it to the Lieutenant.

JAILER   Of course, sir.

CROMWELL   You will swear an oath to that effect.

JAILER   (*Cheerfully*) Certainly, sir!

CROMWELL   Archbishop?

CRANMER   (*Laying the cross of his vestment on the table*) Place your left hand on this and raise your right hand—take your hat off—Now say after me: I swear by my immortal soul—(JAILER, *overlapping, repeats the oath with him*)—that I will report truly anything said by Sir Thomas More against the King, the Council or the State of the Realm. So help me God. Amen.

JAILER   (*Overlapping*) So help me God. Amen.

CROMWELL   And there's fifty guineas in it if you do.

JAILER   (*Looks at him gravely*) Yes, sir.

(*He goes*)

CRANMER   (*Hastily*) That's not to tempt you into perjury, my man!

JAILER   No, sir! (*At exit he pauses; to audience*) Fifty guineas isn't tempting; fifty guineas is alarming. If he'd left it at swearing . . . But fifty—That's serious money. If it's worth that much now it's worth my neck presently. (*With deci-*

sion) I want no part of it. They can sort it out between them. I feel my deafness coming on.

(*Exit* JAILER. *The Commission rises*)

CROMWELL   Rich!

RICH   Secretary?

CROMWELL   Tomorrow morning, remove the prisoner's books.

NORFOLK   Is that necessary?

CROMWELL   (*Suppressed exasperation*) Norfolk. With regards this case, the King is becoming impatient.

NORFOLK   Aye, with you.

CROMWELL   With all of us. (*He walks over to the rack*) You know the King's impatience, how commodious it is!

(NORFOLK *and* CRANMER *exit.* CROMWELL *is brooding over the instrument of torture*)

RICH   Secretary!

CROMWELL   (*Abstracted*) Yes . . .

RICH   Sir Redvers Llewellyn has retired.

CROMWELL   (*Not listening*) Mm . . .

RICH   (*Goes to the other end of the rack and faces him. With some indignation*) The Attorney-General for Wales. His post is vacant. You said I might approach you.

CROMWELL   (*Contemptuous impatience*) Oh, not *now* . . . (*Broods*) He must submit, the alternatives are bad. While More's alive the King's conscience breaks into fresh stinking flowers every time he gets from bed. And if I bring about More's death—I plant my own, I think. There's no other good solution! He must submit! (*He whirls the windlass of the rack, producing a startling clatter from the ratchet. They look at each other. He turns it again slowly, shakes his head and lets go*) No; the King will not permit it. (*He walks away*) We have to find some gentler way.

(*The scene change commences as he says this, and exit* RICH *and* CROMWELL. *From night it becomes morning, cold gray light from off the gray water. Enter* JAILER *and* MARGARET)

JAILER   Wake up, Sir Thomas! Your family's here!

MORE   (*Starting up. A great cry*) Margaret! What's this? You can visit me? (*Thrusts his arms through the cage*) Meg. Meg. (*She goes to him. Then horrified*) For God's sake, Meg, they've not put you in here?

JAILER   (*Reassuringly*) No-o-o, sir. Just a visit; a short one.

MORE   (*Excited*) Jailer, jailer, let me out of this.

JAILER   Yes, sir. I'm allowed to let you out.

MORE   Thank you. (*Goes to the door of the cage, gabbling while* JAILER *unlocks it*) Thank you, thank you. (*He comes out. He and she regard each other; then she drops into a curtsy*)

MARGARET   Good morning, Father.

MORE   (*Ecstatic, wraps her to him*) Oh, good morning—Good morning. (*Enter* ALICE, *supported by* ROPER. *She, like* MORE, *has aged and is poorly dressed*) Good morning, Alice. Good morning, Will.

(ROPER *is staring at the rack in horror.* ALICE *approaches* MORE *and peers at him technically*)

ALICE   (*Almost accusatory*) Husband, how do you do?

MORE   (*Smiling over* MARGARET) As well as need be, Alice. Very happy now. Will?

ROPER   This is an awful place!

MORE   Except it's keeping me from you, my dears, it's not so bad. Remarkably like any other place.

ALICE   (*Looks up critically*) It drips!

MORE   Yes. Too near the river.

(ALICE *goes apart and sits, her face bitter*)

MARGARET   (*Disengages from him, takes basket from her mother*) We've brought you some things. (*Shows him. There is constraint between them*) Some cheese . . .

MORE   Cheese.

MARGARET   And a custard . . .

MORE   A custard!

MARGARET   And, these other things . . .

(*She doesn't look at him*)

ROPER   And a bottle of wine.

(*Offering it*)

MORE   Oh. (*Mischievously*) Is it good, son Roper?

ROPER   I don't know, sir.

MORE   (*Looks at them, puzzled*) Well.

ROPER   Sir, come out! Swear to the Act! Take the oath and come out!

MORE   Is this why they let you come?

ROPER   Yes . . . Meg's under oath to persuade you.

MORE   (*Coldly*) That was silly, Meg. How did you come to do that?

MARGARET   I wanted to!

MORE   You want me to swear to the Act of Succession?

MARGARET   "God more regards the thoughts of the heart than the words of the mouth." Or so you've always told me.

MORE   Yes.

MARGARET   Then say the words of the oath and in your heart think otherwise.

MORE   What is an oath then but words we say to God?

MARGARET   That's very neat.

MORE   Do you mean it isn't true?

MARGARET   No, it's true.

MORE   Then it's a poor argument to call it "neat," Meg. When a man takes an oath, Meg, he's holding his own self in his own hands. Like water. (*He cups his hands*) And if he opens his fingers *then*—he needn't hope to find himself again. Some men aren't capable of this, but I'd be loath to think your father one of them.

MARGARET   In any State that was half good, you would be raised up high, not here, for what you've done already. It's not your fault the State's three-quarters bad. Then if you elect to suffer for it, you elect yourself a hero.

MORE   That's very neat. But look now . . . If we lived in a State where virtue was profitable, common sense would make us good, and greed would make us saintly. And we'd live like animals or angels in the happy land that *needs* no heroes. But since in fact we see that avarice, anger, envy, pride, sloth, lust and stupidity commonly profit far beyond humility, chastity, fortitude, justice and thought, and have to choose, to be human at all . . . why then perhaps we *must* stand fast a little—even at the risk of being heroes.

MARGARET   (*Emotionally*) But in reason! Haven't you done as much as God can reasonably *want*?

MORE   Well . . . finally . . . it isn't a matter of reason; finally it's a matter of love.

ALICE   (*Hostile*) You're content, then, to be shut up here with mice and rats when you might be home with us!

MORE   (*Flinching*) Content? If they'd open a crack that wide (*Between finger and thumb*) I'd be through it. (*To* MARGARET) Well, has Eve run out of apples?

MARGARET   I've not yet told you what the house is like, without you.

MORE   Don't, Meg.

MARGARET   What we do in the evenings, now that you're not there.

MORE   Meg, have done!

MARGARET   We sit in the dark because we've no candles. And we've no talk because we're wondering what they're doing to you here.

MORE   The King's more merciful than you. He doesn't use the rack.

(*Enter* JAILER)

JAILER   Two minutes to go, sir. I thought you'd like to know.

MORE   Two minutes!

JAILER   Till seven o'clock, sir. Sorry. Two minutes.

(*Exit* JAILER)

MORE   Jailer! (*Seizes* ROPER *by the arm*) Will—go to him, talk to him, keep him occupied—

(*Propelling him after* JAILER)

ROPER   How, sir?

MORE   Anyhow! Have you got any money?

ROPER   (*Eagerly*) Yes!

MORE   No, don't try and bribe him! Let him play for it; he's got a pair of dice. And talk to him, you understand! And take this—(*He hands him the wine*) and mind you share it—do it properly, Will! (ROPER *nods vigorously and exits*) Now listen, you must leave the country. All of you must leave the country.

MARGARET   And leave you here?

MORE   It makes no difference, Meg; they won't let you see me again. (*Breathlessly, a prepared speech under pressure*) You must all go on the same day, but not on the same boat; different boats from different ports—

MARGARET   After the trial, then.

MORE   There'll be no trial, they have no case. Do this for me, I beseech you?

MARGARET   Yes.

MORE   Alice? (*She turns her back*) Alice, I command you!

ALICE   (*Harshly*) Right!

MORE   (*Looks into the basket*) Oh, this is splendid; I know who packed this.

ALICE   (*Harshly*) I packed it.

MORE   Yes. (*He eats a morsel*) You still make superlative custard, Alice.

ALICE   Do I?

MORE   That's a nice dress you have on.

ALICE   It's my cooking dress.

MORE   It's very nice anyway. Nice color.

ALICE   (*Turns. Quietly*) By God, you think very little of me. (*Mounting bitterness*) I know I'm a fool. But I'm no such fool as at this time to be lamenting for my dresses! Or to relish complimenting on my custard!

MORE   (*Regarding her with frozen attention. He nods once or twice*) I am well rebuked. (*He holds out his hands*) Al—

ALICE   No!

(She remains where she is, glaring at him)

MORE   (*He is in great fear of her*) I am faint when I think of the worst that they may do to me. But worse than that would be to go with you not understanding why I go.

ALICE   I don't!

MORE   (*Just hanging on to his self-possession*) Alice, if you can tell me that you understand, I think I can make a good death, if I have to.

ALICE   Your death's no "good" to me!

MORE   Alice, you must tell me that you understand!

ALICE   I don't (*She throws it straight at his head*) I don't believe this had to happen.

MORE   (*His face is drawn*) If you say that, Alice, I don't see how I'm to face it.

ALICE   It's the truth!

MORE   (*Gasping*) You're an honest woman.

ALICE   Much good may it do me! I'll tell you what I'm afraid of: that when you've gone, I shall hate you for it.

MORE   (*Turns from her, his face working*) Well, you mustn't, Alice, that's all. (*Swiftly she crosses the stage to him; he turns and they clasp each other fiercely*) You mustn't, you—

ALICE   (*Covers his mouth with her hand*) S-s-sh . . . As for understanding, I understand you're the best man that I ever met or am likely to; and if you go —well, God knows why I suppose—though as God's my witness God's kept deadly quiet about it! And if anyone wants my opinion of the King and his Council they've only to ask for it!

MORE   Why, it's a lion I married! A lion! A lion! (*He breaks away from her, his face shining*) Say what you may—this custard's very good. It's very, very good.

(*He puts his face in his hands;* ALICE *and* MARGARET *comfort him;* ROPER *and* JAILER *erupt onto the stage above, wrangling fiercely*)

JAILER   It's no good, sir! I know what you're up to! And it can't be done!
ROPER   Another minute, man!
JAILER   (*Descending; to* MORE) Sorry, sir, time's up!
ROPER   (*Gripping his shoulder from behind*) For pity's sake!
JAILER   (*Shaking him off*) Now don't do that, sir! Sir Thomas, the ladies will have to go now!
MORE   You said seven o'clock!
JAILER   It's seven now. You must understand my position, sir.
MORE   But one more minute!
MARGARET   Only a little while—give us a little while!
JAILER   (*Reprovingly*) Now, miss, you don't want to get me into trouble.
ALICE   Do as you're told. Be off at once!

(*The first stroke of seven is heard on a heavy, deliberate bell, which continues, reducing what follows to a babble*)

JAILER   (*Taking* MARGARET *firmly by the upper arm*) Now come along, miss; you'll get your father into trouble as well as me. (ROPER *descends and grabs him*) Are you obstructing me, sir? (MARGARET *embraces* MORE *and dashes up the stairs and exits, followed by* ROPER. *Taking* ALICE *gingerly by the arm*) Now, my lady, no trouble!
ALICE   (*Throwing him off as she rises*) *Don't* put your muddy hand on me!
JAILER   Am I to call the guard then? Then come on!

(ALICE, *facing him, puts foot on bottom stair and so retreats before him, backwards*)

MORE   For God's sake, man, we're saying goodbye!
JAILER   You don't know what you're asking, sir. You don't know how you're watched.
ALICE   Filthy, stinking, gutter-bred turnkey!
JAILER   Call me what you like, ma'am; you've got to go.
ALICE   I'll see you suffer for this!
JAILER   You're doing your husband no good!
MORE   Alice, goodbye, my love!

(*On this, the last stroke of the seven sounds,* ALICE *raises her hand, turns, and with considerable dignity, exits.* JAILER *stops at the head of the stairs and addresses* MORE, *who, still crouching, turns from him, facing audience*)

JAILER   (*Reasonably*) You understand my position, sir, there's nothing I can do! I'm a plain, simple man and just want to keep out of trouble.
MORE   (*Cries out passionately*) Oh, Sweet Jesus! These plain, simple men!

(*Immediately music, portentous and heraldic, is heard. Bars, rack and cage are flown swiftly upwards. The lighting changes from cold gray to warm yellow, re-creating a warm interior. Small coat of arms comes down and hangs, followed by large coat of arms above stairs, then two medium coats of arms. Then the largest coat of arms appears. During this the* JAILER *takes off jailer's coat, throws it off, takes off the small chair and moves armchair to the center. Moves the table under the stairs. He brings on the jury bench, takes hats from the basket and puts them on poles with a juryman's hat, takes jailer's hat off head and puts it on a pole. Seven are plain gray hats, four are those worn by the* STEWARD, BOATMAN, INNKEEPER *and* JAILER. *And the last is another of the plain gray ones. He takes a portfolio from the basket and puts it on the table, and pushes basket into a corner. He then brings on two throne chairs. While he is still doing this, and just before coats of arms have finished their descent, enter* CROMWELL. *He ringingly addresses the audience as soon as the music ends*)

    CROMWELL   (*Indicating descending props*)

        What Englishman can behold without Awe
        The Canvas and the Rigging of the Law!

        (*Brief fanfare*)

        Forbidden here the galley-master's whip—
        Hearts of Oak, in the Law's Great Ship!

(*Brief fanfare. To* COMMON MAN *who is tiptoeing discreetly off stage*) Where are you going?
    COMMON MAN   I've finished here, sir.
    CROMWELL   You're the Foreman of the Jury.
    COMMON MAN   Oh no, sir.
    CROMWELL   You are John Dauncey. A general dealer?
    COMMON MAN   (*Gloomily*) Yes, sir?
    CROMWELL   (*Resuming his rhetorical stance*) Foreman of the Jury. Does the cap fit?
    COMMON MAN   (*Puts on the gray hat. It fits*) Yes, sir.
    CROMWELL

        So, now we'll apply the good, plain sailor's art,
        And fix these quicksands on the Law's plain chart!

(*Several narrow panels, orange and bearing the monogram "HR VIII" in gold letters, are lowered. Renewed, more prolonged fanfare; during which enter* CRANMER *and* NORFOLK, *who sit on throne chairs. On their entry* MORE *and* FOREMAN *rise. As soon as the fanfare is finished* NORFOLK *speaks*)

    NORFOLK   (*Takes refuge behind a rigorously official manner*) Sir Thomas More, you are called before us here at the Hall of Westminster to answer charge of High Treason. Nevertheless, and though you have heinously offended the King's Majesty, we hope if you will even now forthink and repent of your obstinate opinions, you may still taste his gracious pardon.
    MORE   My lords, I thank you. Howbeit I make my petition to Almighty God that He will keep me in this, my honest mind, to the last hour that I shall live . . . As for the matters you may charge me with, I fear, from my present weakness, that neither my wit nor my memory will serve to make sufficient answers . . . I should be glad to sit down.

NORFOLK   Be seated. Master Secretary Cromwell, have you the charge?

CROMWELL   I have, my lord.

NORFOLK   Then read the charge.

CROMWELL   (*Formally*) That you did conspire traitorously and maliciously to deny and deprive our liege lord Henry of his undoubted certain title, Supreme Head of the Church in England.

MORE   (*With surprise, shock, and indignation*) But I have never denied this title!

CROMWELL   You refused the oath tendered to you at the Tower and elsewhere—

MORE   (*Again shocked and indignant*) Silence is not denial. And for my silence I am punished, with imprisonment. Why have I been called again?

(*At this point he is sensing that the trial has been in some way rigged*)

NORFOLK   On a charge of High Treason, Sir Thomas.

CROMWELL   For which the punishment is *not* imprisonment.

MORE   Death . . . comes for us all, my lords. Yes, even for Kings he comes, to whom amidst all their Royalty and brute strength he will neither kneel nor make them any reverence nor pleasantly desire them to come forth, but roughly grasp them by the very breast and rattle them until they be stark dead! So causing their bodies to be buried in a pit and sending *them* to a judgment . . . whereof at their death their success is uncertain.

CROMWELL   Treason enough here!

NORFOLK   The death of Kings is not in question, Sir Thomas.

MORE   Nor mine, I trust, until I'm proven guilty.

NORFOLK   (*Leaning forward urgently*) Your life lies in your own hand, Thomas, as it always has.

MORE   (*Absorbs this*) For our own deaths, my lord, yours and mine, dare we for shame enter the Kingdom with ease, when Our Lord Himself entered with so much pain? (*And now he faces* CROMWELL, *his eyes sparkling with suspicion*)

CROMWELL   Now, Sir Thomas, you stand upon your silence.

MORE   I do.

CROMWELL   But, Gentlemen of the Jury, there are many kinds of silence. Consider first the silence of a man when he is dead. Let us say we go into the room where he is lying; and let us say it is in the dead of night—there's nothing like darkness for sharpening the ear; and we listen. What do we hear? Silence. What does it betoken, this silence? Nothing. This is silence, pure and simple. But consider another case. Suppose I were to draw a dagger from my sleeve and make to kill the prisoner with it, and suppose their lordships there, instead of crying out for me to stop or crying out for help to stop me, maintained their silence. That *would* betoken! It would betoken a willingness that I should do it, and under the law they would be guilty with me. So silence can, according to circumstances, speak. Consider, now, the circumstances of the prisoner's silence. The oath was put to good and faithful subjects up and down the country and they had declared His Grace's title to be just and good. And when it came to the prisoner he refused. He calls this silence. Yet is there a man in this court, is there a man in this country, who does not *know* Sir Thomas More's opinion of the King's title? Of course not! But how can that be? Because this silence betokened—nay, this silence was not silence at all but most eloquent denial.

MORE (*With some of the academic's impatience for a shoddy line of reasoning*) Not so, Master Secretary, the maxim is "qui tacet consentire." (*Turns to* COMMON MAN) The maxim of the law is (*Very carefully*) "Silence gives consent." If, therefore, you wish to construe what my silence "betokened," you must construe that I consented, not that I denied.

CROMWELL Is that what the world in fact construes from it? Do you pretend that is what you *wish* the world to construe from it?

MORE The world must construe according to its wits. This Court must construe according to the law.

CROMWELL I put it to the Court that the prisoner is perverting the law— making smoky what should be a clear light to discover to the Court his own wrongdoing!

(CROMWELL's *official indignation is slipping into genuine anger and* MORE *responds*)

MORE The law is not a "light" for you or any man to see by; the law is not an instrument of any kind. (*To the* FOREMAN) The law is a causeway upon which, so long as he keeps to it, a citizen may walk safely. (*Earnestly addressing him*) In matters of conscience—

CROMWELL (*Smiling bitterly*) The conscience, the conscience . . .

MORE (*Turning*) The word is not familiar to you?

CROMWELL By God, too familiar! I am very used to hear it in the mouths of criminals!

MORE I am used to hear bad men misuse the name of God, yet God exists. (*Turning back*) In matters of conscience, the loyal subject is more bounden to be loyal to his conscience than to any other thing.

CROMWELL (*Breathing hard; straight at* MORE) And so provide a noble motive for his frivolous self-conceit!

MORE (*Earnestly*) It is not so, Master Cromwell—very and pure necessity for respect of my own soul.

CROMWELL Your own self, you mean!

MORE Yes, a man's soul is his self!

CROMWELL (*Thrusts his face into* MORE's. *They hate each other and each other's standpoint*) A miserable thing, whatever you call it, that lives like a bat in a Sunday School! A shrill incessant pedagogue about its own salvation—but nothing to say of your place in the State! Under the King! In a great native country!

MORE (*Not untouched*) Is it my place to say "good" to the State's sickness? Can I help my King by giving him lies when he asks for truth? Will you help England by populating her with liars?

CROMWELL (*Backs away. His face stiff with malevolence*) My lords, I wish to call (*He raises his voice*) Sir Richard Rich! (*Enter* RICH. *He is now splendidly official, in dress and bearing; even* NORFOLK *is a bit impressed*) Sir Richard. (*Indicating* CRANMER)

CRANMER (*Proffering Bible*) I do solemnly swear . . .

RICH　I do solemnly swear that the evidence I shall give before the Court shall be the truth, the whole truth, and nothing but the truth.

CRANMER　(*Discreetly*) So help me God, Sir Richard.

RICH　So help me God.

NORFOLK　Take your stand there, Sir Richard.

CROMWELL　Now, Rich, on 12 March, you were at the Tower?

RICH　I was.

CROMWELL　With what purpose?

RICH　I was sent to carry away the prisoner's books.

CROMWELL　Did you talk with the prisoner?

RICH　Yes.

CROMWELL　Did you talk about the King's Supremacy of the Church?

RICH　Yes.

CROMWELL　What did you say?

RICH　I said to him: "Supposing there was an Act of Parliament to say that I, Richard Rich, were to be King, would not you, Master More, take me for King?" "That I would," he said, "for then you would be King."

CROMWELL　Yes?

RICHARD　Then he said—

NORFOLK　(*Sharply*) The prisoner?

RICH　Yes, my lord. "But I will put you a higher case," he said. "How if there were an Act of Parliament to say that God should not be God?"

MORE　This is true; and then you said—

NORFOLK　Silence! Continue.

RICH　I said, "Ah, but I will put you a middle case. Parliament has made our King Head of the Church. Why will you not accept him?"

NORFOLK　(*Strung up*) Well?

RICH　Then he said Parliament had no power to do it.

NORFOLK　Repeat the prisoner's words!

RICH　He said, "Parliament has not the competence." Or words to that effect.

CROMWELL　He denied the title?

RICH　He did.

(*All look to* MORE, *but he looks to* RICH)

MORE　In good faith, Rich, I am sorrier for your perjury than my peril.

NORFOLK　Do you deny this?

MORE　Yes! My lords, if I were a man who heeded not the taking of an oath, you know well I need not to be here. Now I will take an oath! If what Master Rich has said is true, then I pray I may never see God in the face! Which I would not say were it otherwise for anything on earth.

CROMWELL　(*To* FOREMAN, *calmly, technically*) That is not evidence.

MORE　Is it probable—is it probable—that after so long a silence on this, the very point so urgently sought of me, I should open my mind to such a man as that?

CROMWELL　(*To* RICH) Do you wish to modify your testimony?

RICH　No, Secretary.

MORE　There were two other men! Southwell and Palmer!

CROMWELL   Unhappily, Sir Richard Southwell and Master Palmer are both in Ireland on the King's business. (MORE *gestures helplessly*) It has no bearing. I have their deposition here in which the Court will see they state that being busy with the prisoner's books they did not hear what was said.

(*Hands deposition to* FOREMAN, *who examines it with much seriousness*)

MORE   If I had really said this is it not obvious he would instantly have called these men to witness?

CROMWELL   Sir Richard, have you anything to add?

RICH   Nothing, Mr. Secretary.

NORFOLK   Sir Thomas?

MORE   (*Looking at* FOREMAN) To what purpose? I am a dead man. (*To* CROMWELL) You have your desire of me. What you have hunted me for is not my actions, but the thoughts of my heart. It is a long road you have opened. For first men will disclaim their hearts and presently they will have no hearts. God help the people whose Statesmen walk your road.

NORFOLK   Then the witness may withdraw.

(RICH *crosses the stage, watched by* MORE)

MORE   I *have* one question to ask the witness. (RICH *stops*) That's a chain of office you are wearing. (*Reluctantly* RICH *faces him*) May I see it? (NORFOLK *motions him to approach.* MORE *examines the medallion*) The red dragon. (*To* CROMWELL) What's this?

CROMWELL   Sir Richard is appointed Attorney-General for Wales.

MORE   (*Looking into* RICH's *face, with pain and amusement*) For Wales? Why, Richard, it profits a man nothing to give his soul for the whole world . . . But for Wales! (*Exit* RICH, *stiff-faced, but infrangibly dignified*)

CROMWELL   Now I must ask the Court's indulgence! I have a message for the prisoner from the King. (*Urgently*) Sir Thomas, I am empowered to tell you that even now—

MORE   No no, it cannot be.

CROMWELL   The case rests! (NORFOLK *is staring at* MORE) My lord!

NORFOLK   The jury will retire and consider the evidence.

CROMWELL   Considering the evidence it shouldn't be necessary for them to retire. (*Standing over* FOREMAN) Is it necessary?

FOREMAN   (*Shakes his head*) No, sir!

NORFOLK   Then is the prisoner guilty or not guilty?

FOREMAN   Guilty, my lord!

NORFOLK   (*Leaping to his feet; all rise save* MORE) Prisoner at the bar, you have been found guilty of High Treason. The sentence of the Court—

MORE   My lord! (NORFOLK *breaks off.* MORE *has a sly smile. From this point to end of play his manner is of one who has fulfilled all his obligations and will now consult no interests but his own*) My lord, when I was practicing the law, the manner was to ask the prisoner *before* pronouncing sentence, if he had anything to say.

NORFOLK   (*Flummoxed*) Have you anything to say?

MORE   Yes. (*He rises; all others sit*) To avoid this I have taken every path my winding wits would find. Now that the Court has determined to condemn me, God knoweth how, I will discharge my mind . . . concerning my indictment and the King's title. The indictment is grounded in an Act of Parliament which is directly repugnant to the Law of God. The King in Parliament cannot bestow the Supremacy of the Church because it is a Spiritual Supremacy! And more to this the immunity of the Church is promised both in Magna Carta and the King's own Coronation Oath!

CROMWELL   Now, we plainly see that you *are* malicious!

MORE   Not so, Master Secretary! (*He pauses, and launches, very quietly, ruminatively, into his final stock-taking*) I am the King's true subject, and pray for him and all the realm . . . I do none harm, I say none harm, I think none harm. And if this be not enough to keep a man alive, in good faith I long not to live . . . I have, since I came into prison, been several times in such a case that I thought to die within the hour, and I thank Our Lord I was never sorry for it, but rather sorry when it passed. And therefore, my poor body is at the King's pleasure. Would God my death might do him some good . . . (*With a great flash of scorn and anger*) Nevertheless, it is not for the Supremacy that you have sought my blood—but because I would not bend to the marriage!

(*Immediately the scene change commences, while* NORFOLK *reads the sentence*)

NORFOLK   Prisoner at the bar, you have been found guilty of the charge of High Treason. The sentence of the Court is that you shall be taken from this Court to the Tower, thence to the place of execution, and there your head shall be stricken from your body, and may God have mercy on your soul!

(*The trappings of justice are flown upwards.* NORFOLK *and* CRANMER *exit with chairs. The lights are dimmed save for three areas: spots, left, center, and right front, and a black arch cutout is lowered. Through this arch—where the ax and the block are silhouetted against a light of steadily increasing brilliance—comes the murmur of a large crowd, formalized almost into a chant. The* FOREMAN *doffs cap, and as* COMMON MAN *he removes the prisoner's chair and the two benches.* CROMWELL *pushes the table off, takes a small black mask from basket and puts it on* COMMON MAN. *The* COMMON MAN *thus becomes the traditional Headsman. He ascends the stairs, sets up the block from its trap, gets the ax and then straddles his legs. At once the crowd falls silent. Exit* CROMWELL, *dragging basket.* NORFOLK *joins* MORE *in the center spot.* CRANMER *takes his position on the rostrum. The* WOMAN *goes under the stairs*) I can come no further, Thomas. (*Proferring a goblet*) Here, drink this.

MORE   My Master had easel and gall, not wine, given him to drink. Let me be going.

MARGARET   Father! (*She runs to him in the center spot and flings herself upon him*) Father! Father, Father, Father, Father!

MORE   Have patience, Margaret, and trouble not thyself. Death comes for us all; even at our birth—(*He holds her head and looks down at it for a moment in recollection*)—even at our birth, death does but stand aside a little. And every day he looks towards us and muses somewhat to himself whether that day or the next he will draw nigh. It is the law of nature, and the will of God. (*He disengages from her. Dispassionately*) You have long known the secrets of my heart.

(MARGARET *exits with* NORFOLK)

WOMAN   Sir Thomas! (*He stops*) Remember me, Sir Thomas? When you were Chancellor, you gave a false judgment against me. Remember that now.

MORE   Woman, you see how I am occupied. (*With sudden decision goes to her in the left spot. Crisply*) I remember your matter well, and if I had to give sentence now I assure you I should not alter it. You have no injury; so go your way; and content yourself; and trouble me not! (*She exits. He walks swiftly to the stairs, then stops, realizing that* CRANMER, *carrying his Bible, has followed him. Quite kindly*) I beseech Your Grace, go back. (*Offended,* CRANMER *does so. The lighting is now complete, i.e., darkness save for three areas of light, the one at cutout arch now dazzlingly brilliant. When* MORE *gets to head of stairs by the Headsman, he turns to Headsman*) Friend, be not afraid of your office. You send me to God.

CRANMER   (*Envious rather than waspish*) You're very sure of that, Sir Thomas.

(*He exits*)

MORE   (*Takes off his hat, revealing the gray disordered hair*) He will not refuse one who is so blithe to go to him.

(*Kneeling. Immediately is heard a harsh roar of kettledrums. There is total blackout at head of the stairs, while the drums roar. Then the drums cease*)

HEADSMAN   (*Bangs the trap down, in the darkness*) Behold—the head—of a traitor!

(*The lights come up*)

COMMON MAN   (*Comes to the center of the stage, having taken off his mask*) I'm breathing . . . Are you breathing too? . . . It's nice, isn't it? It isn't difficult to keep alive, friends—just don't *make* trouble—or if you must make trouble, make the sort of trouble that's expected. Well, I don't need to tell you that. Good night. If we should bump into one another, recognize me.

(*He exits*)

The Essay

PART FOUR

CHAPTER TWENTY-TWO

Reading Essays

THE EXPERIENCE OF THE ESSAY

Essays have long had an uncertain status as literature. In contrast to the imaginative representations of reality that we expect in fiction, poetry, and drama, the essay is typically factual. Its usual purpose is to explain a set of circumstances and to persuade us of a particular view of them. We therefore often respond differently to the essay than we do to other literary genres. Instead of the suggestiveness of language and concern with symbolic form that we associate with fiction, poetry, and drama, we expect the essay to be direct and explicit. We also expect it to subordinate narrative incident and figurative language to the exposition of ideas. We read an essay in part to acquire information about a subject, but our first purpose is to encounter the writer's ideas about some aspect of public concern or private experience.

To emphasize the primacy of idea in the essay is not to deny that essays can be imaginative and visionary. In fact, reading essays with attention only to their ideas and information while ignoring their styles and voices is to miss the experience of this unique literary form. The essays in this book are literature —as much so as the stories, poems, and plays. They invite and gratify the considered, deliberative, active reading necessary for reading any literary genre.

With this idea in mind, we now turn to a short essay, "The Ring of Time," by E. B. White. As you read, keep track of your responses. Consider, for example, whether White engages you, provokes your thinking, stirs your feelings, triggers your memories. If you become confused, notice where, and think about why.

E. B. WHITE

[1889–1985]

The Ring of Time

After the lions had returned to their cages, creeping angrily through the chutes, a little bunch of us drifted away and into an open doorway nearby, where we stood for a while in semidarkness, watching a big brown circus horse go harumphing around the practice ring. His trainer was a woman of about forty, and the two of them, horse and woman, seemed caught up in one of those desultory treadmills of afternoon from which there is no apparent escape. The day was hot, and we kibitzers were grateful to be briefly out of the sun's glare. The long rein, or tape, by which the woman guided her charge counterclockwise in his dull career formed the radius of their private circle, of which she was the revolving center; and she, too, stepped a tiny circumference of her own, in order to accommodate the horse and allow him his maximum scope. She had on a short-skirted costume and a conical straw hat. Her legs were bare and she wore high heels, which probed deep into the loose tanbark and kept her ankles in a state of constant turmoil. The great size and meekness of the horse, the repetitious exercise, the heat of the afternoon, all exerted a hypnotic charm that invited boredom; we spectators were experiencing a languor—we neither expected relief nor felt entitled to any. We had paid a dollar to get into the grounds, to be sure, but we had got our dollar's worth a few minutes before, when the lion trainer's whiplash had got caught around a toe of one of the lions. What more did we want for a dollar?

Behind me I heard someone say, "Excuse me, please," in a low voice. She was halfway into the building when I turned and saw her—a girl of sixteen or seventeen, politely threading her way through us onlookers who blocked the entrance. As she emerged in front of us, I saw that she was barefoot, her dirty little feet fighting the uneven ground. In most respects she was like any of two or three dozen showgirls you encounter if you wander about the winter quarters of Mr. John Ringling North's circus, in Sarasota—cleverly proportioned, deeply browned by the sun, dusty, eager, and almost naked. But her grave face and the naturalness of her manner gave her a sort of quick distinction and brought a new note into the gloomy octagonal building where we had all cast our lot for a few moments. As soon as she had squeezed through the crowd, she spoke a word or two to the older woman, whom I took to be her mother, stepped to the ring, and waited while the horse coasted to a stop in front of her. She gave the animal a couple of affectionate swipes on his enormous neck and then swung herself aboard. The horse immediately resumed his rocking canter, the woman goading him on, chanting something that sounded like "Hop! Hop!"

In attempting to recapture this mild spectacle, I am merely acting as recording secretary for one of the oldest of societies—the society of those who, at one time or another, have surrendered, without even a show of resistance, to the bedazzlement of a circus rider. As a writing man, or secretary, I have always felt charged with the safekeeping of all unexpected items of worldly or unworldly enchantment, as though I might be held personally responsible if even a small one were to be lost. But it is not easy to communicate anything of this nature. The circus comes as close to being the world in microcosm as anything I know; in a way, it puts all the rest of show business in the shade. Its magic is universal and complex. Out of its wild disorder comes order; from its rank smell rises the good aroma of courage and daring; out of its preliminary shabbiness comes the final splendor. And buried in the familiar boasts of its advance agents lies the modesty of most of its people. For me the circus is at its best before it has been put together. It is at its best at certain moments when it comes to a point, as through a burning glass, in the activity and destiny of a single performer out of so many. One ring is always bigger than three. One rider, one aerialist, is always greater than six. In short, a man has to catch the circus unawares to experience its full impact and share its gaudy dream.

The ten-minute ride the girl took achieved—as far as I was concerned, who wasn't looking for it, and quite unbeknownst to her, who wasn't even striving for it—the thing that is sought by performers everywhere, on whatever stage, whether struggling in the tidal currents of Shakespeare or bucking the difficult motion of a horse. I somehow got the idea she was just cadging a ride, improving a shining ten minutes in the diligent way all serious artists seize free moments to hone the blade of their talent and keep themselves in trim. Her brief tour included only elementary postures and tricks, perhaps because they were all she was capable of, perhaps because her warmup at this hour was unscheduled and the ring was not rigged for a real practice session. She swung herself off and on the horse several times, gripping his mane. She did a few knee-stands—or whatever they are called—dropping to her knees and quickly bouncing back up on her feet again. Most of the time she simply rode in a standing position, well aft on the beast, her hands hanging easily at her sides, her head erect, her straw-colored ponytail lightly brushing her shoulders, the blood of exertion showing faintly through the tan of her skin. Twice she managed a one-foot stance—a sort of ballet pose, with arms outstretched. At one point the neck strap of her bathing suit broke and she went twice around the ring in the classic attitude of a woman making minor repairs to a garment. The fact that she was standing on the back of a moving horse while doing this invested the matter with a clownish significance that perfectly fitted the spirit of the circus—jocund, yet charming. She just rolled the strap into a neat ball and stowed it inside her bodice while the horse rocked and rolled beneath her in dutiful innocence. The bathing suit proved as self-reliant as its owner and stood up well enough without benefit of strap.

The richness of the scene was in its plainness, its natural condition—of horse, of ring, of girl, even to the girl's bare feet that gripped the bare back of her proud and ridiculous mount. The enchantment grew not out of anything that happened or was performed but out of something that seemed to go round and around and around with the girl, attending her, a steady gleam in the shape of a circle—a ring of ambition, of happiness, of youth. (And the positive pleasures of equilibrium under difficulties.) In a week or two, all would be changed, all (or almost all) lost: the girl would wear makeup, the horse would wear gold, the ring would be painted, the bark would be clean for the feet of the horse, the girl's feet would be clean for the slippers that she'd wear. All, all would be lost.

As I watched with the others, our jaws adroop, our eyes alight, I became painfully conscious of the element of time. Everything in the hideous old building seemed to take the shape of a circle, conforming to the course of the horse. The rider's gaze, as she peered straight ahead, seemed to be circular, as though bent by force of circumstance; then time itself began running in circles, and so the beginning was where the end was, and the two were the same, and one thing ran into the next and time went round and around and got nowhere. The girl wasn't so young that she did not know the delicious satisfaction of having a perfectly behaved body and the fun of using it to do a trick most people can't do, but she was too young to know that time does not really move in a circle at all. I thought: "She will never be as beautiful as this again"—a thought that made me acutely unhappy—and in a flash my mind (which is too much of a busybody to suit me) had projected her twenty-five years ahead, and she was now in the center of the ring, on foot, wearing a conical hat and high-heeled shoes, the image of the older woman, holding the long rein, caught in the treadmill of an afternoon long in the future. "She is at that enviable moment in life [I thought] when she believes she can go once around the ring, make one complete circuit, and at the end be exactly the same age as at the start." Everything in her movements, her expression, told you that for her the ring of time was perfectly formed, changeless, predictable, without beginning or end, like the ring in which she was traveling at this moment with the horse that wallowed under her. And then I slipped back into my trance, and time was circular again—time, pausing quietly with the rest of us, so as not to disturb the balance of a performer.

Her ride ended as casually as it had begun. The older woman stopped the horse, and the girl slid to the ground. As she walked toward us to leave, there was a quick, small burst of applause. She smiled broadly, in surprise and pleasure; then her face suddenly regained its gravity and she disappeared through the door.

It has been ambitious and plucky of me to attempt to describe what is indescribable, and I have failed, as I knew I would. But I have discharged my duty to my society; and besides, a writer, like an acrobat, must occasionally try a stunt that is too much for him. At any rate, it is worth reporting that long before the circus comes to town, its most notable performances have already been given. Under the bright lights of the finished show, a performer need only reflect the electric candle power that is directed upon him; but in the dark and dirty old training rings and in the makeshift cages, whatever light is generated, whatever excitement, whatever beauty, must come from original sources—from internal fires of professional hunger and delight, from the exuberance and gravity of youth. It is the difference between planetary light and the combustion of stars.

When we read such an essay as "The Ring of Time," we do more than look for the writer's point, though we do that as well. Before we consider what the writer is saying we can consider our responses to what he describes. Did some parts of the essay engage you more than others? Did you relate E. B. White's experience and feelings to your own? Did you find yourself agreeing or disagreeing with something he said?

As with any work of literature, we often derive more from reading an essay after sharing our responses with others. If possible, talk about "The Ring of Time" with your classmates and teacher. See how their responses amplify your own. Most literary works trigger different associations and provoke divergent reactions in their readers. Gaining a sense of the variety of readers' responses and seeing also what is common among them can provide both assurance that others see the work as we do and alternative perspectives from which to understand it.

Such discussions prepare us to reread the essay. This second reading differs from the first because our knowledge of the work is greater and our sense of how it might be approached is augmented. Now we can turn from the subjectivity of our first responses to a more objective consideration of the writer's point. We may, in fact, often begin doing this during our first reading, but we do it more consciously and thoroughly during the second.

What is the subject of "The Ring of Time"? What does White seem most concerned with—the circus, performance, practice, writing, time? Something else? What ideas about these subjects surface in the essay? What is the author's attitude toward them? Once we determine what the writer's subject is and what he says about it, we can return to a consideration of how our experience bears out what he says.

Let's consider just one of the subjects of White's essay—his reflections on time. One thing White suggests is that time is circular—a ring—that it goes around and around, seeming endlessly to repeat itself. The image of the ring of time, called to our attention by the title, suggests that things don't change, that they remain essentially the same. Details supporting this cyclical view of time include the description of the mother holding the rein as her feet make small circles on the ground while she leads the horse around the ring. (Notice the many words that describe *circle* in the first paragraph.)

The circularity of time is further accented and clarified in this sentence from the sixth paragraph: "The rider's gaze, as she peered straight ahead, seemed to be circular, as though bent by force of circumstance; then time itself began running in circles, and so the beginning was where the end was, and the two were the same, and one thing ran into the next and time went round and around and got nowhere." But almost as soon as White says this, he contradicts himself by saying that although the girl "believes she can go once around the ring . . . and at the end be exactly the same age as at the start," she was really "too young to know that time does not really move in a circle at all." With this counterview, White provokes us to think about time, to decide whether it is circular or linear, to consider, in part, whether things change or remain the same. Of course, we may conclude that time can be experienced both ways, that the two views White presents are complementary rather than contradictory. We can make such a compromise if we think of the seventeen-year-old girl growing up and losing her beauty and agility—if we recognize time's linearity, its inevitable sequence of changes. We can recognize that on the other hand, even though the girl moves through time in a linear fashion, she is also part of a larger family unit, which itself is part of a still larger social context—the circus and its performers. And these larger units don't change. One day she will replace her mother at the center of the practice ring. One day she will hold the reins for another young performer, her daughter perhaps, who will practice and perform as she does now. Time, White seems to say, forms both a line and a circle.

When we reflect on the implications of these and other ideas in White's essay, about the performer's discipline and dedication, for example, we relate them to our own perceptions and experience. We engage, that is, in a series of double actions—at once subjective and objective, intellectual and emotional, interpretive and evaluative. In the process, our own experience and knowledge increase as we gain added perspectives on what we already know. Our reading then is essentially a process of making connections between what we read and what we know and between what we know intellectually and what we feel emotionally.

THE PROCESS OF READING THE ESSAY

Having considered our experience in reading an essay, we now turn to the actual process we engage in as we read. George Orwell's "Marrakech" is printed in segments with intervening commentary. Our intention in this stop-and-go reading is to make observations and raise questions, to think about the implications of these observations and the resolutions of our questions. Our slow reading will emphasize the way we make inferences about what we don't know based on what we do (the essay's details and direct statements) and about where the essay is headed.

GEORGE ORWELL
[*1903–1950*]

Marrakech

As the corpse went past the flies left the restaurant table in a cloud and rushed after it, but they came back a few minutes later.

The little crowd of mourners—all men and boys, no women—threaded their way across the market-place between the piles of pomegranates and the taxis and the camels, wailing a short chant over and over again. What really appeals to the flies is that the corpses here are never put into coffins, they are merely wrapped in a piece of rag and carried on a rough wooden bier on the shoulders of four friends. When the friends get to the burying-ground they hack an oblong hole a foot or two deep, dump the body in it and fling over it a little of the dried-up, lumpy earth, which is like broken brick. No gravestone, no name, no identifying mark of any kind. The burying-ground is merely a huge waste of hummocky earth, like a derelict building-lot. After a month or two no one can even be certain where his own relatives are buried.

When you walk through a town like this—two hundred thousand inhabitants, of whom at least twenty thousand own literally nothing except the rags they stand up in —when you see how the people live, and still more how easily they die, it is always difficult to believe that you are walking among human beings. All colonial empires are in reality founded upon that fact. The people have brown faces—besides, there are so many of them! Are they really the same flesh as yourself? Do they even have names? Or are they merely a kind of undifferentiated brown stuff, about as individual as bees or coral insects? They rise out of the earth, they sweat and starve for a few years, and then they sink back into the nameless mounds of the graveyard and nobody notices that they are gone. And even the graves themselves soon fade back into the soil. Sometimes, out for a walk, as you break your way through the prickly pear, you notice that it is rather bumpy underfoot, and only a certain regularity in the bumps tells you that you are walking over skeletons.

Comment   Orwell's description accentuates the extreme poverty of Marrakech and the little regard in which human life is held. The gravediggers, for example, "hack" and "fling" the dirt, then "dump" the body in the ground. Moreover the dead individual is seen not as a person (is it man, woman, or child?) but as a "corpse," an inert object. Additional details reinforce the lack of dignity in death and the lack of value accorded human life. Orwell compares the burial ground to an abandoned building lot, run down and neglected. The grave plots are unmarked, which suggests that the people of Marrakech are as anonymous in death as they were in life.

The third paragraph reinforces the poverty of Marrakech's people. Many have only the rags that they will buried in. Besides accentuating their poverty and anonymity, Orwell goes further by questioning whether they are really human beings at all. They live in squalor; they die easily, readily, more like insects than people. Orwell compares them to insects by highlighting their vast number and lack of individuality. Our question here may be: Does Orwell not value them as human beings? Or is he pointing out how they live in hopelessness, poverty, and futility to awaken his readers to these facts? Indeed, how do we feel as we read this description?

Notice too that Orwell slips in a sentence of generalization, suggesting that colonial empires are built on the kinds of attitudes and conditions he describes. This comment can be taken as an indictment of colonialism or as a simple assertion of fact, of how things are, with such suffering a necessary evil that colonialism nust accommodate. This political question is crucial: our sense of Orwell's point and purpose in "Marrakech" hinge on our response to it.

The first part of the essay ends with a description of the makeshift cemetery. What do we expect to follow? Where do we think Orwell might be heading? Here is the second section:

I was feeding one of the gazelles in the public gardens.

Gazelles are almost the only animals that look good to eat when they are still alive, in fact, one can hardly look at their hindquarters without thinking of mint sauce. The gazelle I was feeding seemed to know that this thought was in my mind, for though it took the piece of bread I was holding out it obviously did not like me. It nibbled rapidly at the bread, then lowered its head and tried to butt me, then took another nibble and then butted again. Probably its idea was that if it could drive me away the bread would somehow remain hanging in mid-air.

An Arab navvy working on the path nearby lowered his heavy hoe and sidled slowly towards us. He looked from the gazelle to the bread and from the bread to the gazelle, with a sort of quiet amazement, as though he had never seen anything quite like this before. Finally he said shyly in French:

"*I* could eat some of that bread."

I tore off a piece and he stowed it gratefully in some secret place under his rags. This man is an employee of the Municipality.

Comment   As we read this vignette about the gazelle, we look for some connection to what went before. Not until the Arab navvy (a manual laborer who excavates roads, canals) makes his appearance does the connection become apparent: he's hungry and poor. His shy, indirect request for food suggests that he wants to preserve his self-respect and dignity. There seems to be some tension between this desire and the urgency of his need. What makes the situation more poignant is that the man does not devour the bread but instead hides it under his rags. Presumably he is saving it, which implies that for him bread is a precious commodity. The final detail of the section is important: this man has a job. With this detail Orwell implies how extreme the poverty of Marrakech is.

Having read the two sections, what connections do you see? How does your sense of the first two parts prepare you to read the third?

When you go through the Jewish quarters you gather some idea of what the medieval ghettoes were probably like. Under their Moorish rulers the Jews were only allowed to own land in certain restricted areas, and after centuries of this kind of treatment they have ceased to bother about overcrowding. Many of the streets are a good deal less than six feet wide, the houses are completely windowless, and sore-eyed children cluster everywhere in unbelievable numbers, like clouds of flies. Down the centre of the street there is generally running a little river of urine.

In the bazaar huge families of Jews, all dressed in the long black robe and little black skull-cap, are working in dark fly-infested booths that look like caves. A carpenter sits crosslegged at a prehistoric lathe, turning chair-legs at lightning speed. He works the lathe with a bow in his right hand and guides the chisel with his left foot, and thanks to a lifetime of sitting in this position his left leg is warped out of shape. At his side his grandson, aged six, is already starting on the simpler parts of the job.

I was just passing the coppersmiths' booths when somebody noticed that I was lighting a cigarette. Instantly, from the dark holes all around, there was a frenzied rush of Jews, many of them old grandfathers with flowing grey beards, all clamouring for a cigarette. Even a blind man somewhere at the back of one of the booths heard a rumour of cigarettes and came crawling out, groping in the air with his hand. In about a minute I had used up the whole packet. None of these people, I suppose, works less than twelve hours a day, and every one of them looks on a cigarette as a more or less impossible luxury.

As the Jews live in self-contained communities they follow the same trades as the Arabs, except for agriculture. Fruitsellers, potters, silversmiths, blacksmiths, butchers, leatherworkers, tailors, water-carriers, beggars, porters—whichever way you look you see nothing but Jews. As a matter of fact there are thirteen thousand of them, all living in the space of a few acres. A good job Hitler wasn't here. Perhaps he was on his way, however. You hear the usual dark rumours about the Jews, not only from the Arabs but from the poorer Europeans.

"Yes, mon vieux, they took my job away from me and gave it to a Jew. The Jews! They're the real rulers of this country, you know. They've got all the money. They control the banks, finance—everything."

"But," I said, "isn't it a fact that the average Jew is a labourer working for about a penny an hour?"

"Ah, that's only for show! They're all moneylenders really. They're cunning, the Jews."

In just the same way, a couple of hundred years ago, poor old women used to be burned for witchcraft when they could not even work enough magic to get themselves a square meal.

Comment In the third section Orwell takes us into the Jewish ghetto. By now we realize that the essay is largely descriptive and that its descriptive details are tied together by two issues: poverty and anonymity.

We can divide this vignette into two parts. First, Orwell indicates the crowded and filthy conditions in which the Jews live. He compares the children to clouds of flies, primarily to indicate their vast numbers and insignificance. Details about the working conditions reveal their destructive consequences. Orwell doesn't spell out what the future of the six-year-old grandson who works beside his physically deformed grandfather will be. Instead, he accentuates the injustice by describing the fracas over a few cigarettes, which are beyond the purchasing power of people who work "only" twelve hours a day.

The second section of the this vignette depicts the severe prejudice Jews suffer from. The dialogue reveals Orwell's attempt to undermine the unfair caricature of the Jews as rich moneylenders. Prejudice, fear, and hatred run so deep, however, that the Jewish poverty and powerlessness described by Orwell are explained away by a poor European as a "trick." Against this kind of closed-mindedness what can be said? The analogy Orwell draws with witch hunters of an earlier time testifies to the power of prejudice, and it evokes our sympathy for those who suffer unjustly. Orwell's implied criticism of such attitudes transcends the Jewish quarter of Marrakech to all places where human dignity is violated by hatred and prejudice.

Will Orwell provide additional evidence for his argument? Will he turn to still another dimension of his experience in Marrakech? This next section is the longest of the essay.

All people who work with their hands are partly invisible, and the more important the work they do, the less visible they are. Still, a white skin is always fairly conspicuous. In northern Europe, when you see a labourer ploughing a field, you probably give him a second glance. In a hot country, anywhere south of Gibraltar or east of Suez, the chances are that you don't even see him. I have noticed this again and again. In a tropical landscape one's eye takes in everything except the human beings. It takes in the dried-up soil, the prickly pear, the palm tree and the distant mountain, but it always misses the peasant hoeing at his patch. He is the same colour as the earth, and a great deal less interesting to look at.

It is only because of this that the starved countries of Asia and Africa are accepted as tourist resorts. No one would think of running cheap trips to the Distressed Areas. But where the human beings have brown skins their poverty is simply not noticed. What does Morocco mean to a Frenchman? An orange-grove or a job in Government service. Or to an Englishman? Camels, castles, palm trees, Foreign Legionnaires, brass trays, and bandits. One could probably live there for years without noticing that for nine-tenths of the people the reality of life is an endless, back-breaking struggle to wring a little food out of an eroded soil.

Most of Morocco is so desolate that no wild animal bigger than a hare can live on it. Huge areas which were once covered with forest have turned into a treeless waste where the soil is exactly like broken-up brick. Nevertheless a good deal of it is cultivated, with frightful labour. Everything is done by hand. Long lines of women, bent double like inverted capital L's, work their way slowly across the fields, tearing up the prickly weeds with their hands, and the peasant gathering lucerne for fodder pulls it up stalk by stalk instead of reaping it, thus saving an inch or two on each stalk. The plough is a wretched wooden thing, so frail that one can easily carry it on one's shoulder, and fitted underneath with a rough iron spike which stirs the soil to a depth of about four inches. This is as much as the strength of the animals is equal to. It is usual to plough with a cow and a donkey yoked together. Two donkeys would not be quite strong enough, but on the other hand two cows would cost a little more to feed. The peasants possess no harrows, they merely plough the soil several times over in different directions, finally leaving it in rough furrows, after which the whole field has to be shaped with hoes into small oblong patches to conserve water. Except for a day or two after the rare rainstorms there is never enough water. Along the edges of the fields channels are hacked out to a depth of thirty or forty feet to get at the tiny trickles which run through the subsoil.

Every afternoon a file of very old women passes down the road outside my house, each carrying a load of firewood. All of them are mummified with age and the sun, and all of them are tiny. It seems to be generally the case in primitive communities that the women, when they get beyond a certain age, shrink to the size of children. One day a poor old creature who could not have been more than four feet tall crept past me under a vast load of wood. I stopped her and put a five-sou piece (a little more than a farthing) into her hand. She answered with a shrill wail, almost a scream, which was partly gratitude but mainly surprise. I suppose that from her point of view, by taking any notice of her, I seemed almost to be violating a law of nature. She accepted her status as an old woman, that is to say as a beast of burden. When a family is travelling it is quite usual to see a father and a grown-up son riding ahead on donkeys, and an old woman following on foot, carrying the baggage.

But what is strange about these people is their invisibility. For several weeks, always at about the same time of day, the file of old women had hobbled past the house with their firewood, and though they had registered themselves on my eyeballs I cannot truly say that I had seen them. Firewood was passing—that was how I saw it. It was only that one day I happened to be walking behind them, and the curious up-and-down motion of a load of wood drew my attention to the human being beneath it. Then for the first time I noticed the poor old earth-coloured bodies, bodies reduced to bones and leathery skin, bent double under the crushing weight. Yet I suppose I had not been five minutes on Moroccan soil before I noticed the overloading of the donkeys and was infuriated by it. There is no question that the donkeys are damnably treated. The Moroccan donkey is hardly bigger than a St. Bernard dog, it carries a load which in the British Army would be considered too much for a fifteen-hands mule, and very often its pack-saddle is not taken off its back for weeks together. But what is peculiarly pitiful is that it is the most willing creature on earth, it follows its master like a dog and does not need either bridle or halter. After a dozen years of devoted work it suddenly drops dead, whereupon its master tips it into the ditch and the village dogs have torn its guts out before it is cold.

This kind of thing makes one's blood boil, whereas—on the whole—the plight of the human beings does not. I am not commenting, merely pointing to a fact. People with brown skins are next door to invisible. Anyone can be sorry for the donkey with its galled back, but it is generally owing to some kind of accident if one even notices the old woman under her load of sticks.

Comment This section centers on the invisibility of the natives. They are not noticed, presumably because they are not important. They become part of the landscape, a fact which further suggests their lack of distinction, and which also recalls the burial scene of section one. Their dark skins render them invisible.

The information Orwell provides about the land's aridity and the primitive farming tools and methods shows the futility and harshness of their lives. People, especially old women, are reduced to the status of beasts of burden. Orwell acknowledges his acquiescence in the *status quo:* he admits to seeing "firewood" passing rather than the human beings carrying that firewood. It is the abusive treatment of the donkeys, however, not the wretchedness of the women, that initially angers him. Perhaps Orwell suggests here how easy it is to become accustomed to such conditions—as long as one is not subject to them oneself. Perhaps he confesses his guilt, recognizing his deficiencies of perception and sensitivity.

We might note also that the language Orwell uses to describe the dead donkey echoes his description of the human burial in the first vignette. In both instances, the burial reveals a complete disregard for life. Both man and beast serve their purposes, and when they are no longer useful, are unceremoniously disposed of.

The essay concludes with a shift of focus:

As the storks flew northward the Negroes were marching southward—a long, dusty column, infantry, screw-gun batteries, and then more infantry, four or five thousand men in all, winding up the road with a clumping of boots and a clatter of iron wheels.

They were Senegalese, the blackest Negroes in Africa, so black that sometimes it is difficult to see whereabouts on their necks the hair begins. Their splendid bodies were hidden in reach-me-down khaki uniforms, their feet squashed into boots that looked like blocks of wood, and every tin hat seemed to be a couple of sizes too small. It was very hot and the men had marched a long way. They slumped under the weight of their packs and the curiously sensitive black faces were glistening with sweat.

As they went past a tall, very young Negro turned and caught my eye. But the look he gave me was not in the least the kind of look you might expect. Not hostile, not contemptuous, not sullen, not even inquisitive. It was the shy, wide-eyed Negro look, which actually is a look of profound respect. I saw how it was. This wretched boy, who is a French citizen and has therefore been dragged from the forest to scrub floors and catch syphilis in garrison towns, actually has feelings of reverence before a white skin. He has been taught that the white race are his masters, and he still believes it.

But there is one thought which every white man (and in this connection it doesn't matter twopence if he calls himself a socialist) thinks when he sees a black army marching past. "How much longer can we go on kidding these people? How long before they turn their guns in the other direction?"

It was curious, really. Every white man there had this thought stowed somewhere or other in his mind. I had it, so had the other onlookers, so had the officers on their sweating chargers and the white N.C.O.'s marching in the ranks. It was a kind of secret which we all knew and were too clever to tell; only the Negroes didn't know it. And really it was like watching a flock of cattle to see the long column, a mile or two miles of armed men, flowing peacefully up the road, while the great white birds drifted over them in the opposite direction, glittering like scraps of paper.

Comment   The description of the Senegalese troops is charged with tension. With his description of the blackness of the troops and their servility, Orwell calls attention to a racial inequality he had implied earlier. Orwell's imagery in the final paragraphs suggests that colonial oppression cannot last forever, that when the oppressed realize their strength and numbers, they will overthrow their imperialist subjugators.

THE PRACTICE OF ACTIVE READING

Although we found some explicitly stated ideas in George Orwell's "Marrakech," for the most part we arrived at our sense of the essay by repeatedly generalizing from its details. Orwell's method in "Marrakech" is indirect and oblique rather than direct. The following essay by Francis Bacon is different. It is primarily explanatory rather than descriptive. And although it advances ideas and arguments, its point is less insistent and consistent than Orwell's. Bacon advances ideas about youth and age, setting them off against each other. The essay is printed with marginal annotation to illustrate in another way the process of active reading. The annotations suggest some ways we can respond to nonfictional prose as we read; they provide one way to get involved with a text. As with the previous essay, you may prefer to read it through once completely before turning to the observations and questions in the margins.

FRANCIS BACON
[1533–1592]

Of Youth and Age

Title implies comparison and contrast.

A man that is young in years may be old in hours, if he have lost no time. But that happeneth rarely. Generally youth is like the first cogitations, not so wise as the second. For there is a youth in thoughts, as well as in ages. And yet the invention of young men is more lively than that of old, and imaginations stream into their minds better, and as it were more divinely. Natures that have much heat and great and violent desires and perturbations are not ripe for action till they have passed the meridian of their years, as it was with Julius Cæsar and Septimius Severus. Of the latter of whom it is said, *Juventutem egit erroribus, imo furoribus, plenam.*° And yet he was the ablest emperor, almost, of all the list. But reposed natures may do well in youth. As it is seen in Augustus Cæsar, Cosmus, Duke of Florence, Gaston de Fois and others. On the other side, heat and vivacity in age is an excellent composition for business. Young men are fitter to invent than to judge, fitter for execution than for counsel, and fitter for new projects than for settled business. For the experience of age, in things that fall within the compass of it, directeth them, but in new things abuseth them. The errors of young men are the ruin of business; but the errors of aged men amount but to this, that more might have been done, or sooner. Young men in the conduct and manage of actions embrace more than they can hold; stir more than they can quiet; fly to the end, without consideration of the means and degrees; pursue some few principles which they have chanced upon absurdly; care not to innovate which draws unknown inconveniences; use extreme remedies at first; and that which doubleth all errors, will not acknowledge or retract them, like an unready horse that will neither stop nor turn. Men of age object too much, consult too long, adventure too little, repent too soon, and seldom drive business home to the full period, but content themselves with a mediocrity of success. Certainly it is good to compound employments of both: for that will be good for the present, because the virtues of either age may correct the defects of both; and good for

Bacon talks of mind, of thought more than about age and youth.

Youth and age are not strictly matters of time, of chronology.

Is he suggesting that youth refrain from action till middle age?

"But," "yet," "if," "on the other side"—lots of shifts of viewpoint, much consideration of the "other" side.

He makes qualifications—avoids oversimplification.

He suggests young men are better suited to some things, old men to others.

A catalogue of youth's faults.

Youth imaged as horse—compare earlier image of ripeness.

A shorter list of age's shortcomings.

Juventutem . . . plenam *He spent a youth full of errors and madness.*

succession, that young men may be learners, while men in age are actors; and, lastly, good for extern accidents, because authority followeth old men, and favour and popularity youth. But for the mortal part, perhaps youth will have the preeminence, as age hath for the politic. A certain rabbin, upon the text, *Your young men shall see visions, and your old men shall dream dreams,* inferreth that young men are admitted nearer to God than old, because vision is a clearer revelation than a dream. And certainly the more a man drinketh of the world, the more it intoxicateth, and age doth profit rather in the powers of understanding than in the virtues of the will and affections. There be some have an over-early ripeness in their years, which fadeth betimes. These are, first, such as have brittle wits the edge whereof is soon turned, such as was Hermogenes the rhetorician, whose books are exceeding subtle, who afterwards waxed stupid. A second sort is of those that have some natural dispositions which have better grace in youth than in age, such as is a fluent and luxuriant speech, which becomes youth well, but not age; so Tully saith of Hortensius, *Idem manebat, neque idem decebat.*° The third is of such as take too high a strain at the first, and are magnanimous more than tract of years can uphold. As was Scipio Africanus, of whom Livy saith in effect, *Ultima primis cedebant.*°

An old man's understanding of the world does not necessarily lead to virtue.

Biblical reference—Is this distinction valid—or just clever?

He ends with examples of youthful success none of which carries into age.

The three types of youth fading into age imply a judgment of some sort, but exactly what kind isn't made clear.

The essay stops rather than concludes. Can we say that Bacon celebrates age over youth or youth over age?

Bacon's essay is more than a straightforward comparison and contrast. Though it does point to specific advantages of age over youth and of youth over age, it does not have a clearly articulated thesis as many expository essays do. In addition, Bacon's essay does not conform to a clear-cut pattern of organization, something which would probably make it easier to follow. Instead Bacon oscillates rapidly and repeatedly between observations on youth and age, without providing transitions from one aspect of his discussion to another. Our experience in reading the essay, consequently, is quite different from what it would be had the essay been organized in a more conventional way.

Bacon makes our experience in reading "Of Youth and Age" an exercise in uncertainty, in qualification, in thinking. Before he allows us to rest in certainty about the advantages of either youth or age, Bacon qualifies his praise or criticism with its opposite. As we read, we frequently have to adjust our sense of what Bacon thinks. And when we finish we may wonder if we have arrived at any definitive understanding of the advantages of either age or youth. Perhaps Bacon's point, if we can call it that, is less a proposition about age and youth than an attempt to disturb our search for comfortable certainties about them. Perhaps Bacon's purpose is to undermine our desire for a final answer about the subject. His inconclusive ending and his unsettling organization suggest that, yes,

Idem . . . decebat   *He remained the same when the same was not suitable.*   **Ultima . . . cedebant**   *His last actions fell short of his first.*

there are specific assets and liabilities to both youth and age, but each time we say something positive or negative about one it can be countered with the opposite view. The young will see the argument one way; the aged will see it another. There is no way to settle it.

CHAPTER TWENTY-THREE

Types of Essays

We can classify essays in a rough way as speculative, argumentative, narrative, and expository. Narrative essays tell stories and chronicle events; expository essays explain ideas and attitudes; speculative essays explore ideas and feelings; argumentative essays make claims and present evidence to support them. Nearly all essays are persuasive to one degree or another. Whatever their dominant mode and form, most essays attempt to convince readers about something.

SPECULATIVE ESSAYS

Let us glance first at what we have called the *speculative essay*. *To speculate* means to contemplate, conjecture, or surmise. A *speculative essay* is concerned less with making a point overtly and decisively than with exploring an idea, perception, or feeling. The tone of a speculative essay is typically less authoritative and less insistent than the tone of expository or argumentative essays. Speculative essays frequently take their form from the way thought flows in the mind of the writer. Rather than employing a conventional pattern of organization such as comparison and contrast, a speculative essayist will find a looser, less immediately recognizable organization. Charles Lamb's "A Dissertation Upon Roast Pig" (page 1462) and John Donne's "Meditation XVII: For Whom the Bell Tolls" (page 1455), for example, are primarily associative in structure. As Donne's title indicates, his essay is more a meditation than an argument.

Writers of speculative (or meditative) essays seem less interested in advancing arguments than in exploring them. They prefer thinking around ideas rather than thinking through them. Rather than take readers on a clearly marked journey from point A through point B to point C, they often invite readers to accompany them on an excursion into thought. This is not to suggest that a speculative essay makes no point. In fact it may make multiple points as the essayist plays with ideas and explores them. E. B. White's "The Ring of Time" (page 1414) is one speculative essay that makes any number of points. But it does not have a single, clear-cut thesis as narrative and expository essays often do.

ARGUMENTATIVE ESSAYS

Unlike speculative essays, which are loose in structure and informal in tone, *argumentative essays* make their claims directly and explicitly. Though argumentative essays assume various patterns of organization, they share a basic concern: to establish a point by providing evidence to support it. The support may take the form of examples, analogies, facts, statistics, anecdote, and evidence. In addition, argumentative essayists may present counterviews and counterarguments either to dismiss or demolish them. Counter positions in an essay may include the competing claims of a pro and con structure such as the one Francis Bacon employs in "Of Youth and Age" (page 1425) and "Of Love" (page 1454). Or it may take the form of debate as in E. M. Forster's "Our Graves in Gallipoli" (page 1471). But whatever structure argumentative essayists employ and whatever methods they use to discredit opposing viewpoints, their intentions are clearly and consistently persuasive.

NARRATIVE ESSAYS

Midway between the formality of the argumentative essay and the informality of the speculative essay are narrative and expository essays. *Narrative essays* include stories, sometimes a single incident, as in George Orwell's "Shooting an Elephant" (page 1477), or sometimes multiple events, as in Loren Eiseley's "The Judgment of the Birds" (page 1482). The stories in narrative essays are almost always autobiographical: they form a part of the writer's experience. But even in cases where the story in such an essay is fictional rather than factual, it is used to make a point—the idea is primary. This distinguishes a narrative essay from a short story in which an idea may be inherent in the work, but where the fictional story *per se* takes precedence over any idea we may derive from it. Orwell's "Shooting an Elephant," for example, consists largely of the story of how Orwell (or a fictional narrator) shot an elephant. Although the incident possesses considerable interest as a story, its primary purpose is to advance an idea about imperialism, which is presented explicitly midway through the essay and is referred to again at the end.

EXPOSITORY ESSAYS

Expository essays also advance ideas, but with less insistence than argumentative essays. Although expository writing may contain narrative elements (anecdote for instance), these elements are usually less developed and less central than in narrative writing. The purpose of most expository essays is explanation, to make something clear for readers. They attempt to lay out for consideration some idea or insight, some fact or experience so readers can better understand it. And although it is important to remember that nearly all essays contain some element of persuasion, their argumentative edge may be dull or sharp. In some expository prose, moreover, the persuasive dimension nearly disappears.

We have suggested that essays can be categorized with respect to their differing purposes, tones, and patterns of organization. But we should also note that essays rarely appear in such pure forms. More often than not, essayists mix modes, combining narration with exposition, or using exposition and narration in the service of argument. Being aware of the options essayists have at their disposal and being alert for their deployment in amalgamated forms will help us read essays more confidently, particularly when we confront experiments in nonfictional prose.

One such recent development has been the marriage of fact and fiction pioneered by writers dubbed "new journalists." One of the most widely read of the new journalists is Tom Wolfe, who has experimented more fully perhaps than anyone else with the possibilities of the form. Wolfe himself singled out four techniques that have special importance for the new essay style. These include scene-by-scene construction, with a consequent reduction of straight narrative and explanation; a heavy reliance on dialogue, for as Wolfe has noted, "realistic dialogue involves the reader more completely than any other single device"; a manipulation of point of view to "give the reader the feeling of being inside a character's mind and experiencing the emotional reality of the scene as he experiences it"; and the use of symbolic details derived from everyday experience such as gestures, habits, manners, glances, poses, and styles of dress.*

This brief overview of different types of essays is not meant to be an exhaustive catalogue of essay forms. Essayists don't choose a form from a menu. Rather, they design their essays and discover their form, making use of whatever strategies of organization suit their various purposes, audiences, and occasions. Moreover, it is the sense the essay makes, the ideas it advances that matter in the end. For, whatever our experience of an essay, and whatever its purpose, ultimately an essay attempts to formulate a thought, explore it, work out its implications, and communicate them to readers.

*Tom Wolfe, ed., *The New Journalism* (New York: Harper and Row, 1973), 31–32.

CHAPTER TWENTY-FOUR

Elements of the Essay

An essay, like a poem, play, or story, can be studied from a number of perspectives. In analyzing essays, we can consider voice, style, structure, and thought—the elements of the essay as a literary form. To clarify our understanding of how essayists say what they mean, we begin by analyzing the essay's voice.

VOICE

When we read an essay we hear a writer's voice, someone speaking to us person to person. The essayist's voice may be commanding or cajoling, intimate or reserved, urgent and insistent, witty and charming—to suggest a few possibilities. The writer's voice is our key to his *tone,* his attitude toward his subject. Consider George Orwell's voice in the third paragraph of "Marrakech," reprinted here for convenience:

When you walk through a town like this—two hundred thousand inhabitants, of whom at least twenty thousand own literally nothing except the rags they stand up in —when you see how the people live, and still more how easily they die, it is always difficult to believe that you are walking among human beings. All colonial empires are in reality founded upon that fact. The people have brown faces—besides, there are so many of them! Are they really the same flesh as yourself? Do they even have names? Or are they merely a kind of undifferentiated brown stuff, about as individual as bees or coral insects? They rise out of the earth, they sweat and starve for a few years, and then they sink back into the nameless mounds of the graveyard and nobody notices that they are gone. And even the graves themselves soon fade back into the soil. Sometimes, out for a walk, as you break your way through the prickly pear, you notice that it is rather bumpy underfoot, and only a certain regularity in the bumps tells you that you are walking over skeletons.

Perhaps the first thing we hear is the writer speaking directly to us, calling us "you." As our eyes and ears, the narrator shares with us what he sees, hears, and more importantly, what he thinks and feels about these things. He also invites our response. When he asks, for example, whether the Moroccans even have names, our response is complex. On the one hand, "no," for they are unknown, obscure, anonymous; on the other hand, we might answer "yes, of course they have names." And when he asks "are they merely an undifferentiated brown stuff, about as individual as bees or coral insects," our answer is more complex still. From one perspective the implied argument is that they are no more individual than bees or "brown stuff." But clearly this is not Orwell's view. In fact, it is this inhuman, exploitative view that his essay criticizes. Orwell attacks a viewpoint that many of his readers would subscribe to. They, of course, would not see imperialism as responsible for causing or even contributing to the problems he describes. Orwell, however, aims to make clear that colonialism, founded on a view of human beings as material to be exploited, perpetuates the misery he describes.

Another thing to note about the voice of this passage is its tone at the end and how it is achieved. The final sentence of this paragraph is a statement rather than a question. Like the first sentence, it conveys a sense of the starkness of life for the poor. They "rise" and "sink," "sweat" and "starve." That's it; it can hardly be called *living* in the sense that Orwell's readers would think of life. Balancing the phrases to create a rising and falling rhythm, Orwell communicates the heaviness of life for these people. The tone is compassionate rather than angry. The voice is quiet and controlled with emotion held in check.

Francis Bacon's voice in "Of Youth and Age" differs from Orwell's in "Marrakech" primarily in its formality. Bacon's voice is authoritative and impersonal. Absent is Orwell's direct address, his talk with us as "you." Moreover, Bacon's voice seems more annunciatory than Orwell's: he simply announces what he thinks without describing incidents and without providing supporting evidence. The few details and examples Bacon does include are references to literature rather than to life. He uses other books as his authorities, a habit which detaches his voice and self further from direct experience. His voice, as a result, is less familiar and intimate, more reserved and distant than the voice we hear in "Marrakech."

To develop your ability to hear an essayist's voice, read the following essay by Joan Didion.

JOAN DIDION
[*b. 1934*]
Los Angeles Notebook

There is something uneasy in the Los Angeles air this afternoon, some unnatural stillness, some tension. What it means is that tonight a Santa Ana will begin to blow, a hot wind from the northeast whining down through the Cajon and San Gorgonio Passes, blowing up sandstorms out along Route 66, drying the hills and the nerves to the flash point. For a few days now we will see smoke back in the canyons, and hear sirens in the night. I have neither heard nor read that a Santa Ana is due, but I know it, and almost everyone I have seen today knows it too. We know it because we feel it. The baby frets. The maid sulks. I rekindle a waning argument with the telephone company, then cut my losses and lie down, given over to whatever it is in the air. To live with the Santa Ana is to accept, consciously or unconsciously, a deeply mechanistic view of human behavior.

I recall being told, when I first moved to Los Angeles and was living on an isolated beach, that the Indians would throw themselves into the sea when the bad wind blew. I could see why. The Pacific turned ominously glossy during a Santa Ana period, and one woke in the night troubled not only by the peacocks screaming in the olive trees but by the eerie absence of surf. The heat was surreal. The sky had a yellow cast, the kind of light sometimes called "earthquake weather." My only neighbor would not come out of her house for days, and there were no lights at night, and her husband roamed the place with a machete. One day he would tell me that he had heard a trespasser, the next a rattlesnake.

"On nights like that," Raymond Chandler once wrote about the Santa Ana, "every booze party ends in a fight. Meek little wives feel the edge of the carving knife and study their husbands' necks. Anything can happen." That was the kind of wind it was. I did not know then that there was any basis for the effect it had on all of us, but it turns out to be another of those cases in which science bears out folk wisdom. The Santa Ana, which is named for one of the canyons it rushes through, is a *foehn* wind, like the *foehn* of Austria and Switzerland and the *hamsin* of Israel. There are a number of persistent malevolent winds, perhaps the best known of which are the mistral of France and the Mediterranean sirocco, but a *foehn* wind has distinct characteristics: it occurs on the leeward slope of a mountain range and, although the air begins as a cold mass, it is warmed as it comes down the mountain and appears finally as a hot dry wind. Whenever and wherever a *foehn* blows, doctors hear about headaches and nausea and allergies, about "nervousness," about "depression." In Los Angeles some teachers do not attempt to conduct formal classes during a Santa Ana, because the children become unmanageable. In Switzerland the suicide rate goes up during the *foehn,* and in the courts of some Swiss cantons the wind is considered a mitigating circumstance for crime. Surgeons are said to watch the wind, because blood does not clot normally during a *foehn*. A few years ago an Israeli physicist discovered that not only during such winds, but for the ten or twelve hours which precede them, the air carries an unusually high ratio of positive to negative ions. No one seems to know exactly why that should be; some talk about friction and others suggest solar disturbances. In any case the positive ions are there, and what an excess of positive ions does, in the simplest terms, is make people unhappy. One cannot get much more mechanistic than that.

Easterners commonly complain that there is no "weather" at all in Southern California, that the days and the seasons slip by relentlessly, numbingly bland. That is quite misleading. In fact the climate is characterized by infrequent but violent extremes: two periods of torrential subtropical rains which continue for weeks and wash out the hills and send subdivisions sliding toward the sea; about twenty scattered days a year of the Santa Ana, which, with its incendiary dryness, invariably means fire. At the first prediction of a Santa Ana, the Forest Service flies men and equipment from northern California into the southern forests, and the Los Angeles Fire Department cancels its ordinary non-firefighting routines. The Santa Ana caused Malibu to burn the way it did in 1956, and Bel Air in 1961, and Santa Barbara in 1964. In the winter of 1966–67 eleven men were killed fighting a Santa Ana fire that spread through the San Gabriel Mountains.

Just to watch the front-page news out of Los Angeles during a Santa Ana is to get very close to what it is about the place. The longest single Santa Ana period in recent years was in 1957, and it lasted not the usual three or four days but fourteen days, from November 21 until December 4. On the first day 25,000 acres of the San Gabriel Mountains were burning, with gusts reaching 100 miles an hour. In town, the wind reached Force 12, or hurricane force, on the Beaufort Scale; oil derricks were toppled and people ordered off the downtown streets to avoid injury from flying objects. On November 22 the fire in the San Gabriels was out of control. On November 24 six people were killed in automobile accidents, and by the end of the week the Los Angeles *Times* was keeping a box score of traffic deaths. On November 26 a prominent Pasadena attorney, depressed about money, shot and killed his wife, their two sons, and himself. On November 27 a South Gate divorcée, twenty-two, was murdered and thrown from a moving car. On November 30 the San Gabriel fire was still out of control, and the wind in town was blowing eighty miles an hour. On the first day of December four people died violently, and on the third the wind began to break.

It is hard for people who have not lived in Los Angeles to realize how radically the Santa Ana figures in the local imagination. The city burning is Los Angeles's deepest image of itself: Nathanael West perceived that, in *The Day of the Locust;* and at the time of the 1965 Watts riots what struck the imagination most indelibly were the fires. For days one could drive the Harbor Freeway and see the city on fire, just as we had always known it would be in the end. Los Angeles weather is the weather of catastrophe, of apocalypse, and, just as the reliably long and bitter winters of New England determine the way life is lived there, so the violence and the unpredictability of the Santa Ana affect the entire quality of life in Los Angeles, accentuate its impermanence, its unreliability. The wind shows us how close to the edge we are.

QUESTIONS

1. How urgent is Didion's tone? How insistent is she about what she is saying? How personal is her voice?
2. What does her relentless accumulation of facts contribute to the essay's tone?

STYLE

A writer's style in an essay derives from choices he or she makes in diction, syntax, and figurative language. Notice how James Baldwin uses these aspects of style in this passage from "Notes of a Native Son" (page 1488) in which he describes his father:

He was, I think, very handsome. I gather this from photographs and from my own memories of him, dressed in his Sunday best and on his way to preach a sermon somewhere, when I was little. Handsome, proud, and ingrown, "like a toe-nail," somebody said. But he looked to me, as I grew older, like pictures I had seen of African tribal chieftains: he really should have been naked, with war-paint on and barbaric mementos, standing among spears. He could be chilling in the pulpit and indescribably cruel in his personal life and he was certainly the most bitter man I have ever met; yet it must be said that there was something else in him, buried in him, which lent him his tremendous power and, even, a rather crushing charm. It had something to do with his blackness, I think—he was very black—with his blackness and his beauty, and with the fact that he knew that he was black but did not know that he was beautiful. He claimed to be proud of his blackness but it had also been the cause of much humiliation and it had fixed bleak boundaries to his life. He was not a young man when we were growing up and he had already suffered many kinds of ruin; in his outrageously demanding and protective way he loved his children, who were black like him and menaced, like him; and all these things sometimes showed in his face when he tried, never to my knowledge with any success, to establish contact with any of us. When he took one of his children on his knee to play, the child always became fretful and began to cry; when he tried to help one of us with our homework the absolutely unabating tension which emanated from him caused our minds and our tongues to become paralyzed, so that he, scarcely knowing why, flew into a rage and the child, not knowing why, was punished. If it ever entered his head to bring a surprise home for his children, it was, almost unfailingly, the wrong surprise and even the big watermelons he often brought home on his back in the summertime led to the most appalling scenes. I do not remember, in all those years, that one of his children was ever glad to see him come home. From what I was able to gather of his early life, it seemed that this inability to establish contact with other people had always marked him and had been one of the things which had driven him out of New Orleans. There was something in him, therefore, groping and tentative, which was never expressed and which was buried with him. One saw it most clearly when he was facing new people and hoping to impress them. But he never did, not for long.

The style here is formal, dignified, elegant, allusive. Baldwin writes about his father, about their relationship, and about the environment in which they lived. He writes personally but not informally. Even though he writes in the first person, using *I* and *we, me* and *mine,* he treats his subject with a solemnity achieved by careful control of diction. Baldwin consistently elevates his diction: "contemptuous," "apprehensive," "unabating," "emanated," and he includes abstractions: "injustice," "hatred," "bitterness," "pride." Such elevated diction contributes to the serious tone of the essay.

Another element that contributes to the solemnity of Baldwin's style is its rhythm. Baldwin tends to interrupt the linear movement of his sentences by embedding or interpolating words and phrases that create a stop-and-go movement, a rising and falling sound. The rise and fall of the rhythm adds to the dignity of Baldwin's style. Consider the following pair of sentences and the alternative versions.

> He was, I think, very handsome. (Baldwin)
> I think he was very handsome. (alternate)

> I do not remember, in all those years, that one of his children
> was ever glad to see him come home. (Baldwin)
> In all those years, I do not remember that one of his children
> was ever glad to see him come home. (alternate)

Baldwin's repeated use of balance and parallelism contributes to his formal style: "He loved his children, who were black like him and menaced like him. . . . When he took one of his children on his knee to play, the child always became fretful and began to cry; when he tried to help one of us with our homework the absolutely unabating tension which emanated from him caused our minds and our tongues to become paralyzed, so that he, scarcely knowing why, flew into a rage and the child, not knowing why, was punished." Baldwin also employs parallel sentences: "It seemed to me that. . . . And it seemed to me, too, that. . . ." Again: "When he was dead I. . . . When he had been dead a long time I. . . ." Such repetitions of sentence structure and repetitions of words ("black," "blackness," and "beauty"; "bitter," "bitterness," and "pride") reinforce Baldwin's formal and solemn tone.

We hear a different tone as Alice Walker describes her mother in this passage from her essay "In Search of Our Mothers' Gardens" (page 1510).

Five children later, I was born. And this is how I came to know my mother: she seemed a large, soft, loving-eyed woman who was rarely impatient in our home. Her quick, violent temper was on view only a few times a year, when she battled with the white landlord who had the misfortune to suggest to her that her children did not need to go to school.

She made all the clothes we wore, even my brothers' overalls. She made all the towels and sheets we used. She spent the summers canning vegetables and fruits. She spent the winter evenings making quilts enough to cover all our beds.

During the "working" day, she labored beside—not behind—my father in the fields. Her day began before sunup, and did not end until late at night. There was never a moment for her to sit down, undisturbed, to unravel her own private thoughts; never a time free from interruption—by work or the noisy inquiries of her many children. And yet, it is to my mother—and all our mothers who were not famous—that I went in search of the secret of what has fed that muzzled and often mutilated, but vibrant, creative spirit that the black woman has inherited, and that pops out in wild and unlikely places to this day.

Like Mem, a character in *The Third Life of Grange Copeland,* my mother adorned with flowers whatever shabby house we were forced to live in. And not just your typical straggly country stand of zinnias, either. She planted ambitious gardens—and still does—with over fifty different varieties of plants that bloom profusely from early March until late November. Before she left home for the fields, she watered her flowers, chopped up the grass, and laid out new beds. When she returned from the fields she might divide clumps of bulbs, dig a cold pit, uproot and replant roses, or prune branches from her taller bushes or trees—until night came and it was too dark to see.

Whatever she planted grew as if by magic, and her fame as a grower of flowers spread over three counties. Because of her creativity with her flowers, even my memories of poverty are seen through a screen of blooms—sunflowers, petunias, roses, dahlias, forsythia, spirea, delphiniums, verbena . . . and on and on.

And I remember people coming to my mother's yard to be given cuttings from her flowers; I hear again the praise showered on her because whatever rocky soil she landed on, she turned into a garden. A garden so brilliant with colors, so original in its design, so magnificent with life and creativity, that to this day people drive by our house in Georgia—perfect strangers and imperfect strangers—and ask to stand or walk among my mother's art.

I notice that it is only when my mother is working in her flowers that she is radiant, almost to the point of being invisible—except as Creator: hand and eye. She is involved in work her soul must have. Ordering the universe in the image of her personal conception of Beauty.

Walker, like Baldwin, writes in the first person and about a parent. Her tone differs from his largely because her subject and attitude differ. Walker's appreciation of her mother shines through her prose and is evident in her selection of details. (Compare the details Baldwin includes to describe his father.) Walker's style is lighter, more informal than Baldwin's. Describing her mother's temper as being "on view" and saying that she "battled" with the landlord, Walker uses everyday speech rather than formal diction. Her sentences are simple and short as in the second paragraph, which begins "She made all the clothes we wore, even my brothers' overalls." . . . Walker comments on her mother's skill with flowers in an informal and directly personal way: "and not just your typical straggly country stand of zinnias either." Further accentuating her informal tone is the way she breaks into sentences with off-hand interruptions, highlighting their casualness by punctuating them with dashes: "—and still does"; "—and all our mothers who were not farmers." She even trails off at one point: ". . . and on and on."

One additional stylistic feature distinguishes Walker's style from Baldwin's and contributes to her informal tone: her sentence fragments. Twice in the passage quoted above Walker employs sentence fragments, both times at the end of a paragraph: "A garden so brilliant . . . my mother's art"; "Ordering the universe . . . conception of beauty." As a rhetorical strategy for achieving emphasis, the fragment can drive a fact or feeling across with intensity and power. Such features of Walker's prose make her writing more casual and intimate than Baldwin's. Although Walker, like Baldwin, is capable of writing long, intricate sentences, her eloquence is achieved with different stylistic techniques.

Like poets, dramatists, and fiction writers, essayists use language in literal and nonliteral ways. The kinds of figurative language most prevalent in essays are those that involve comparison, particularly in the forms of *simile* and *metaphor*. Essayists employ simile and metaphor to clarify their thought and their feeling. They use these forms of comparison to make one thing clear in terms of another. Sometimes the writer's intention in using the comparison is clear and explicit, as in the following examples. In pointing out young men's faults, Bacon notes that they "will not acknowledge or retract them, like an unready horse that will neither stop nor turn." Orwell compares the Marrakech burial ground to a derelict building lot and its lumpy earth to broken brick. Orwell's comparisons communicate an image and impression of the place that is sharper and clearer with the comparison. Bacon communicates the idea that young men can be stubborn and recalcitrant by illustrating their stubbornness with an example.

These examples, all similes, are relatively simple. Both Bacon and Orwell use other less explicit and more complex comparisons when they speak metaphorically of one thing in terms of another. Bacon does this when he suggests that some men are not "ripe for action" until they reach middle age. The implicit comparison is between men and plants, specifically fruit. Like fruit, men come to maturity over time. In the same way that not all fruit ripens at the same time, men do not all become ready for action based on mature decisions at the same time. Some men, like some fruit, ripen faster than others.

Another example of an implicit comparison occurs in Joan Didion's "Los Angeles Notebook" when she talks about *rekindling* an argument with the telephone company. The comparison is carried in her verb, "rekindle," an image of conflagration appropriate to an essay that describes the fiery consequences of the Santa Ana. Moreover, Didion develops the fire imagery much more fully in the final paragraph where she alludes to Nathanael West's novel *The Day of the Locust,* which ends with a vivid depiction of Los Angeles burning. Throughout her essay Didion refers both literally and figuratively to fire.

We can note also in this brief discussion of comparative images that the passages quoted above from Baldwin and Walker also employ comparison in various ways. Walker uses the garden as an image or symbol of her mother's creativity. Elsewhere in her essay, Walker extends the symbolic implications of the garden image to include the creativity of all women, particularly those whose creativity could not find expression in ways available to women today.

In using figurative language, expecially images of comparison, essayists ally themselves with literary artists working in other genres. In fact we might say that the essay's use of figurative language is one element that invites our consideration of it as literature rather than simply as information. Stripped of its comparative figures, of its imagery, the essay becomes less engaging as literature and more strictly a matter of factual reporting. And even though literary essayists like Orwell and Didion do a good deal of reporting in their essays, they do it by means of linguistic and rhetorical strategies and of formal patterns common to the other literary genres. By designing their essays to move us as well as instruct us, writers like Orwell, Didion, Walker, and Baldwin elevate the factuality of their essays to the status of imaginative literature.

As an exercise in examining aspects of an essayist's style, consider the following selection from Henry David Thoreau's *Walden*.

HENRY DAVID THOREAU
[1817–1862]

The Battle of the Ants

One day when I went out to my wood-pile, or rather my pile of stumps, I observed two large ants, the one red, the other much larger, nearly half an inch long, and black, fiercely contending with one another. Having once got hold they never let go, but struggled and wrestled and rolled on the chips incessantly. Looking farther, I was surprised to find that the chips were covered with such combatants, that it was not a *duellum,* but a *bellum,*° a war between two races of ants, the red always pitted against the black, and frequently two red ones to one black. The legions of these Myrmidons° covered all the hills and vales in my woodyard, and the ground was already strewn with the dead and dying, both red and black. It was the only battle which I have ever witnessed, the only battle-field I ever trod while the battle was raging; internecine war; the red republicans on the one hand, the black imperialists on the other. On every side they were engaged in deadly combat, yet without any noise that I could hear, and human soldiers never fought so resolutely. I watched a couple that were fast locked in each other's embraces, in a little sunny valley amid the chips, now at noonday prepared to fight till the sun went down, or life went out. The smaller red champion had fastened himself like a vise to his adversary's front, and through all the tumblings on that field never for an instant ceased to gnaw at one of his feelers near the root, having already caused the other to go by the board; while the stronger black one dashed him from side to side, and, as I saw on looking nearer, had already divested him of several of his members. They fought with more pertinacity than bulldogs. Neither manifested the least disposition to retreat. It was evident that their battle-cry was "Conquer or die." In the meanwhile there came along a single red ant on the hillside of this valley, evidently full of excitement, who either had dispatched his foe, or had not yet taken part in the battle; probably the latter, for he had lost none of his limbs;

---

not a duellum . . . bellum *not a duel but a war.*   **Myrmidons** *soldiers who followed the Greek warrior Achilles.* Myrmes *is the Greek word for* ant.

whose mother had charged him to return with his shield or upon it.° Or perchance he was some Achilles, who had nourished his wrath apart, and had now come to avenge or rescue his Patroclus.° He saw this unequal combat from afar,—for the blacks were nearly twice the size of the red,—he drew near with rapid pace till he stood on his guard within half an inch of the combatants; then, watching his opportunity, he sprang upon the black warrior, and commenced his operations near the root of his right fore leg, leaving the foe to select among his own members; and so there were three united for life, as if a new kind of attraction had been invented which put all other locks and cements to shame. I should not have wondered by this time to find that they had their respective musical bands stationed on some eminent chip, and playing their national airs the while, to excite the slow and cheer the dying combatants. I was myself excited somewhat even as if they had been men. The more you think of it, the less the difference. And certainly there is not the fight recorded in Concord history, at least, if in the history of America, that will bear a moment's comparison with this, whether for the numbers engaged in it, or for the patriotism and heroism displayed. For numbers and for carnage it was an Austerlitz or Dresden.° Concord fight! Two killed on the patriot's side, and Luther Blanchard wounded! Why here every ant was a Buttrick,—"Fire, for God's sake fire!"—and thousands shared the fate of Davis and Hosmer.° There was not one hireling there. I have no doubt that it was a principle they fought for, as much as our ancestors, and not to avoid a three-penny tax on their tea; and the results of this battle will be as important and memorable to those whom it concerns as those of the battle of Bunker Hill, at least.

I took up the chip on which the three I have particularly described were struggling, carried it into my house, and placed it under a tumbler on my window-sill, in order to see the issue. Holding a microscope to the first-mentioned red ant, I saw that, though he was assiduously gnawing at the near fore leg of his enemy, having severed his remaining feeler, his own breast was all torn away, exposing what vitals he had there to the jaws of the black warrior, whose breastplate was apparently too thick for him to pierce; and the dark carbuncles of the sufferer's eyes shone with ferocity such as war only could excite. They struggled half an hour longer under the tumbler, and when I looked again the black soldier had severed the heads of his foes from their bodies, and the still living heads were hanging on either side of him like ghastly trophies at his saddle-bow, still apparently as firmly fastened as ever, and he was endeavoring with feeble struggles, being without feelers and with only the remnant of a leg, and I know not how many other wounds, to divest himself of them; which at length, after half an hour more, he accomplished. I raised the glass, and he went off over the window-sill in that crippled state. Whether he finally survived that combat, and spent the remainder of his days in some Hôtel des Invalides,° I do not know; but I thought that his industry would not be worth much thereafter. I never learned which party was victorious, nor

---

to return with his shield . . . upon it   *Spartan mothers told their sons this as they departed for war.*
Patroclus   *Achilles' close friend. When Patroclus was killed, Achilles, who had not been fighting because of wounded pride, returned to battle the Trojans, especially to avenge the death of his friend by killing the Trojan hero Hector.*   **Austerlitz or Dresden**   *two fierce battles of the Napoleonic wars.*   **Concord fight . . . Hosmer**   *The first battle of the American Revolution was fought at Concord Bridge. In that famous fight, Major John Buttrick and his militiamen repelled the British regular army and hired soldiers. Davis and Hosmer were Americans killed, Blanchard an American wounded.*   **Hôtel des Invalides**   *a veteran's hospital in Paris.*

the cause of the war; but I felt for the rest of that day as if I had had my feelings excited and harrowed by witnessing the struggle, the ferocity and carnage of a human battle before my door.

QUESTIONS

1. Identify and comment on the effectiveness of Thoreau's comparisons. Consider the small-scale brief similes and the overall analogy between the ant war and the Trojan War.
2. What does Thoreau gain by including the quoted phrases "Conquer or die" and "Fire, for God's sake fire!"
3. What does Thoreau's Latinate diction contribute to the effects of his prose? Consider especially the following words: *incessantly, internecine, resolutely, divested, pertinacity, dispatched, eminent, carnage, assiduously, industry,* and *ferocity.*

STRUCTURE

The structural features of an essay are not as visible as the stanzas of poems or the acts and scenes of plays. We can gain some sense of the essay's structural variety by considering a few of the essays in this book.

George Orwell's "Shooting an Elephant" (page 1477) is largely a chronological account that describes the shooting of an elephant. The sequence of actions, however, is preceded by a two-paragraph introduction, which sets the scene, establishes the tone, and announces the subject. The chronological narrative is then followed by a coda in which Orwell comments on what happened. The narrative portion is thus framed by brief explanations, each of which helps us understand its significance. Moreover, Orwell breaks into the narrative section with an important explanatory paragraph, in which he comments extensively on the meaning the event had for him and on its larger, more generalized political significance.

E. B. White uses an alternating structure in "The Ring of Time" (page 1414). He presents a picture of what he sees and then raises questions about it; then he presents more description and again speculates about it. This pattern continues throughout the essay until the final paragraph, which echoes the essay's opening. This gives the essay an alternating structure and a circular one. And that, in part, is an aspect of the the essay's theme—the circular, repetitive ring of time itself.

Some clues for relating the structure of an essay to its meaning include being alert for shifts of focus such as Orwell's shifting scenes in "Marrakech," Bacon's oscillation between aspects of age and youth in "Of Youth and Age," and Didion's shifts from one type of information to another in "Los Angeles Notebook." In addition, we can look for connections between one part of an essay and another, once we decide what those parts are. Orwell helps us see the parts of "Marrakech" by dividing the five parts with blank space. Bacon signals his shifts of focus and emphasis with verbal signals such as *but, and yet,* and *on the other side.* Didion gives us neither such visual nor such explicit verbal markers; she does, however, shift attention to different kinds of information—historical, literary, scientific, and personal.

Perhaps the most important thing to remember about the structure of essays is this: structure reflects thought and is inextricably connected with it. The form of an essay, its structure of thought, is a clue to how we should read it; its form is an aspect of its meaning. When writers alter the structure of essays, they alter both the meaning of their works and their readers' experience of them. Rearranging the paragraphs of E. B. White's "The Ring of Time," for example, to cluster descriptive paragraphs together and separate them from speculative ones alters our experience of the essay. Rewriting Orwell's "Shooting an Elephant" to keep the entire story together without the intrusion of narrative comment alters the effects the essay now creates. In short, if we change the form of a literary work, we change its meaning and effect.

Consider the structure of the following brief essay by Virginia Woolf.

VIRGINIA WOOLF

[1882–1941]

The Death of the Moth

Moths that fly by day are not properly to be called moths; they do not excite that pleasant sense of dark autumn nights and ivy-blossom which the commonest yellow-underwing asleep in the shadow of the curtain never fails to rouse in us. They are hybrid creatures, neither gay like butterflies nor sombre like their own species. Nevertheless the present specimen, with his narrow hay-coloured wings, fringed with a tassel of the same colour, seemed to be content with life. It was a pleasant morning, mid-September, mild, benignant, yet with a keener breath than that of the summer months. The plough was already scoring the field opposite the window, and where the share had been, the earth was pressed flat and gleamed with moisture. Such vigour came rolling in from the fields and the down beyond that it was difficult to keep the eyes strictly turned upon the book. The rooks too were keeping one of their annual festivities; soaring round the tree tops until it looked as if a vast net with thousands of black knots in it had been cast up into the air; which, after a few moments, sank slowly down upon the trees until every twig seemed to have a knot at the end of it. Then, suddenly, the net would be thrown into the air again in a wider circle this time, with the utmost clamour and vociferation, as though to be thrown into the air and settle slowly down upon the tree tops were a tremendously exciting experience.

The same energy which inspired the rooks, the ploughmen, the horses, and even, it seemed, the lean bare-backed downs, sent the moth fluttering from side to side of his square of the window-pane. One could not help watching him. One was, indeed, conscious of a queer feeling of pity for him. The possibilities of pleasure seemed that morning so enormous and so various that to have only a moth's part in life, and a day moth's at that, appeared a hard fate, and his zest in enjoying his meagre opportunities to the full, pathetic. He flew vigorously to one corner of his compartment, and, after waiting there a second, flew across to the other. What remained for him but to fly to a third corner and then to a fourth? That was all he could do, in spite of the size of the downs, the width of the sky, the far-off smoke of houses, and the romantic voice, now and then, of a steamer out at sea. What he could do he did. Watching him, it seemed as if a fibre, very thin but pure, of the enormous energy of the world had been thrust into his frail and diminutive body. As often as he crossed the pane, I could fancy that a thread of vital light became visible. He was little or nothing but life.

Yet, because he was so small, and so simple a form of the energy that was rolling in at the open window and driving its way through so many narrow and intricate corridors in my own brain and in those of other human beings, there was something marvelous as well as pathetic about him. It was as if someone had taken a tiny bead of pure life and decking it as lightly as possible with down and feathers, had set it dancing and zigzagging to show us the true nature of life. Thus displayed one could not get over the strangeness of it. One is apt to forget all about life, seeing it humped and bossed and garnished and cumbered so that it has to move with the greatest circumspection and dignity. Again, the thought of all that life might have been had he been born in any other shape caused one to view his simple activities with a kind of pity.

After a time, tired by his dancing apparently, he settled on the window ledge in the sun, and, the queer spectacle being at an end, I forgot about him. Then, looking up, my eye was caught by him. He was trying to resume his dancing, but seemed either so stiff or so awkward that he could only flutter to the bottom of the window-pane; and when he tried to fly across it he failed. Being intent on other matters I watched these futile attempts for a time without thinking, unconsciously waiting for him to resume his flight, as one waits for a machine, that has stopped momentarily, to start again without considering the reason of its failure. After perhaps a seventh attempt he slipped from the wooden ledge and fell, fluttering his wings, onto his back on the window sill. The helplessness of his attitude roused me. It flashed upon me he was in difficulties; he could no longer raise himself; his legs struggled vainly. But, as I stretched out a pencil, meaning to help him to right himself, it came over me that the failure and awkwardness were the approach of death. I laid the pencil down again.

The legs agitated themselves once more. I looked as if for the enemy against which he struggled. I looked out of doors. What had happened there? Presumably it was midday, and work in the fields had stopped. Stillness and quiet had replaced the previous animation. The birds had taken themselves off to feed in the brooks. The horses stood still. Yet the power was there all the same, massed outside indifferent, impersonal, not attending to anything in particular. Somehow it was opposed to the little hay-coloured moth. It was useless to try to do anything. One could only watch the extraordinary efforts made by those tiny legs against an oncoming doom which could, had it chosen, have submerged an entire city, not merely a city, but masses of human beings; nothing, I knew, had any chance against death. Nevertheless after a pause of exhaustion the legs fluttered again. It was superb this last protest, and so frantic that he succeeded at last in righting himself. One's sympathies, of course, were all on the side of life. Also, when there was nobody to care or to know, this gigantic effort on the part of an insignificant little moth, against a power of such magnitude, to retain what no one else valued or desired to keep, moved one strangely. Again, somehow, one saw life a pure bead. I lifted the pencil again, useless though I knew it to be. But even as I did so, the unmistakable tokens of death showed themselves. The body relaxed, and instantly grew stiff. The struggle was over. The insignificant little creature now knew death. As I looked at the dead moth, this minute wayside triumph of so great a force over so mean an antagonist filled me with wonder. Just as life had been strange a few minutes before, so death was now as strange. The moth having righted himself now lay most decently and uncomplainingly composed. O yes, he seemed to say, death is stronger than I am.

QUESTIONS

1. The essay is divided into five paragraphs. What is the focus of each? How is each paragraph related to the one that precedes and follows it?
2. Woolf gives the essay a narrative structure: it recounts an incident—the death of the moth. How, where, and why does she modify the linear chronology of the narrative?
3. What details recur in the essay? What does Woolf accomplish by including them?

THOUGHT

Edward Hoagland, a contemporary American essayist, has described the essay as a work that "hangs somewhere on a line between two sturdy poles: this is what I think, and this is what I am."* The sense of self and selves provided by essayists is manifested in their styles and voices—Hoagland's "what I am." This we have discussed in the sections on *Voice* and *Style* above. Here we will consider the essayist's "what I think," the way he or she speaks to us, as Hoagland says, "mind to mind."

When writers choose to write an essay rather than a poem, play, or story, it is because, presumably, they have something on their minds. The very choice of factual rather than fictional discourse testifies to the essayist's concern for expressing an idea. Even when essayists rely heavily on narrative to tell stories or description to convey feelings and attitudes, their emphasis ultimately is most often on an idea. It is this primacy of idea, in fact, that makes an essay what it is.

Let us consider the way idea is explored and illustrated in Joan Didion's "Los Angeles Notebook." Although Didion uses many concrete details in building up an impression of Los Angeles, her primary concern is to clarify the nature and effects of the Santa Ana wind. Allied with this is a persuasive intention: to argue for a causal connection between climate and human behavior. Didion

The Tugman's Passage (New York: Random House, 1982), 25.

enforces a proposition—that climate strongly influences people's behavior, that it determines how they act and react. How far she pushes this idea is a matter for discussion; so is our own sense of how far the idea should be taken. But propose it Didion certainly does. In fact, everything about her six-paragraph discourse is directed toward this single idea.

In a similar way we can see that George Orwell has an idea to advance in "Shooting an Elephant" (page 1477). Like the descriptive details of "Marrakech," those of "Shooting an Elephant" illustrate a point. That point surfaces most clearly in the following paragraph—the seventh of the essay.

> But at that moment I glanced round at the crowd that had followed me. It was an immense crowd, two thousand at the least and growing every minute. It blocked the road for a long distance on either side. I looked at the sea of yellow faces above the garish clothes—faces all happy and excited over this bit of fun, all certain that the elephant was going to be shot. They were watching me as they would watch a conjurer about to perform a trick. They did not like me, but with the magical rifle in my hands I was momentarily worth watching. And suddenly I realized that I should have to shoot the elephant after all. The people expected it of me and I had got to do it; I could feel their two thousand wills pressing me forward, irresistibly. And it was at this moment, as I stood there with the rifle in my hands, that I first grasped the hollowness, the futility of the white man's dominion in the East. Here was I, the white man with his gun, standing in front of the unarmed native crowd—seemingly the leading actor of the piece; but in reality I was only an absurd puppet pushed to and fro by the will of those yellow faces behind. I perceived in this moment that when the white man turns tyrant it is his own freedom that he destroys. He becomes a sort of hollow, posing dummy, the conventionalized figure of a sahib. For it is the condition of his rule that he shall spend his life in trying to impress the "natives," and so in every crisis he has got to do what the "natives" expect of him. He wears a mask, and his face grows to fit it. I had got to shoot the elephant. I had committed myself to doing it when I sent for the rifle. A sahib has got to act like a sahib; he has got to appear resolute, to know his own mind and do definite things. To come all that way, rifle in hand, with two thousand people marching at my heels, and then to trail feebly away, having done nothing—no, that was impossible. The crowd would laugh at me. And my whole life, every white man's life in the East, was one long struggle not to be laughed at.

In this paragraph, Orwell interrupts his story about the elephant to specify the significance of the experience. His political point is clear: imperialism is evil; it is destructive of both the oppressed and the oppressors. Orwell does not make this point abstractly or generally. Instead, he presents it within a specific context of time, place, and action: the shooting of an elephant in Burma in the 1930s by a British colonial. To increase the impact of his idea, Orwell uses irony and imagery. Irony inheres in the discrepancy between what seems to be the case (that the narrator, an authority figure, is in charge) and what is really the case (that he is at the mercy of the unarmed natives, whose will he is following). The ironic contrast is underscored by the contrasting image of the narrator as the "leading actor" and as an "absurd puppet," with *actor* indicating his role playing and *puppet* his lack of control. Orwell further establishes his point with the image of the mask, which extends the theatrical imagery prevalent in this passage and in the essay overall. This image suggests that although a person may originally keep himself distinct from a role he performs, at some point he may actually become what he initially pretends to be. Orwell suggests that what was initially a part in a drama can become an aspect of an identity.

This complex idea leads forcefully into his statement that "when the white man turns tyrant it is his own freedom that he destroys." The last section of the paragraph explains this point. It is, of course, ironic that in gaining control over others, in assuming power, one loses one's freedom. That paradoxical idea is the heart of both this central explanatory paragraph and the essay overall. Moreover, it is emphasized in the last paragraph where Orwell confesses that he shot the elephant "to avoid looking the fool."

A final point about idea in essays: thought does not exist independently of feeling. The ideas we discover in essays are felt, not merely thought out. They derive from the writer's emotions; they have their basis in feeling. Feeling, in fact, is mixed with all thought given expression in language. So much so, perhaps, that we might say that there is no thinking without feeling. In essays like Alice Walker's and James Baldwin's, especially, we can discover powerful examples of thought felt with passion, of feeling conveyed with incisive intelligence.

The essay that follows expresses some thoughts about revenge. Consider both what these thoughts are and how strongly they are felt.

FRANCIS BACON

[1533–1592]

Of Revenge

Revenge is a kind of wild justice, which the more man's nature runs to, the more ought law to weed it out. For as for the first wrong, it doth but offend the law, but the revenge of that wrong putteth the law out of office. Certainly in taking revenge, a man is but even with his enemy, but in passing it over, he is superior, for it is a prince's part to pardon. And Solomon, I am sure, saith, "It is the glory of a man to pass by an offense." That which is past is gone and irrevocable, and wise men have enough to do with things present and to come; therefore they do but trifle with themselves that labor in past matters. There is no man doth a wrong for the wrong's sake, but thereby to purchase himself profit, or pleasure, or honor, or the like. Therefore why should I be angry with a man for loving himself better than me? And if any man should do wrong merely out of ill nature, why, yet it is but like the thorn or briar, which prick and scratch because they can do no other. The most tolerable sort of revenge is for those wrongs which there is no law to remedy, but then let a man take heed the revenge be such as there is no law to punish; else a man's enemy is still beforehand, and it is two for one. Some, when they take revenge, are desirous the party should know whence it cometh. This the more generous. For the delight seemeth to not be so much in doing the hurt as in making the party repent. But base and crafty cowards are like the arrow that flieth in the dark. Cosmus, duke of Florence, had a desperate saying against perfidious or neglecting friends, as if those wrongs were unpardonable: "You shall read," saith he, "that we are commanded to forgive our enemies; but you never read that we are commanded to forgive our friends." But yet the spirit of Job was in better tune: "Shall we," saith he, "take good at God's hands, and not be content to take evil also?" And so of friends in a proportion. This is certain, that a man that studieth revenge keeps his own wounds green, which otherwise would heal and do well. Public revenges are for the most part fortunate, as that for the death of Caesar, for the death of Pertinax, for the death of Henry the Third of France, and many more. But in private revenges it is not so. Nay rather, vindictive persons live the life of witches, who, as they are mischievous, so end they unfortunate.

QUESTIONS

1. Why can revenge be defined as "a kind of wild justice"? What is wild about revenge? What about it is just?
2. What arguments does Bacon make against revenge? Are his objections primarily moral or practical?
3. What do Bacon's historical and biblical allusions contribute to his ideas about revenge? Why do you think he includes these allusions?

CHAPTER TWENTY-FIVE

Approaching an Essay: Guidelines for Reading

The guidelines that follow summarize our discussion of reading essays; we will use them to guide our analysis of a contemporary essay by Annie Dillard.

1. Read through the entire essay to get a feel for what it is about. Center on subject and idea. During this initial reading, be alert to your responses to the work. Jot down your thoughts and feelings in the margins or at the end of the piece.

2. Make your second reading more analytical. Key in on the essay's structure and on the development of its argument. Consider how the structure orders its ideas. Be alert for shifts of direction, for changes of language and tone, example and image, scene and point of view. Determine your sense of the writer's tone.

3. During your second reading—or possibly during a third—attend to language and style. Consider diction and syntax; be alert for imagery and figurative language. Consider what the style reveals about the writer's purpose and the audience for whom the essay seems intended.

4. Be alert for connections both within the essay and beyond it. Single out passages that highlight the central idea. Consider, in addition, whether the essay shares features with one or more of the other literary genres, and what use the essay makes of techniques associated with those genres.

ANNIE DILLARD

[b. 1945]

Living Like Weasels

A weasel is wild. Who knows what he thinks? He sleeps in his underground den, his tail draped over his nose. Sometimes he lives in his den for two days without leaving. Outside, he stalks rabbits, mice, muskrats, and birds, killing more bodies than he can eat warm, and often dragging the carcasses home. Obedient to instinct, he bites his prey at the neck, either splitting the jugular vein at the throat or crunching the brain at the base of the skull, and he does not let go. One naturalist refused to kill a weasel who was socketed into his hand deeply as a rattlesnake. The man could in no way pry the tiny weasel off, and he had to walk half a mile to water, the weasel dangling from his palm, and soak him off like a stubborn label.

And once, says Ernest Thompson Seton—once, a man shot an eagle out of the sky. He examined the eagle and found the dry skull of a weasel fixed by the jaws to his throat. The supposition is that the eagle had pounced on the weasel and the weasel swiveled and bit as instinct taught him, tooth to neck, and nearly won. I would like to have seen that eagle from the air a few weeks or months before he was shot: was the whole weasel still attached to his feathered throat, a fur pendant? Or did the eagle eat what he could reach, gutting the living weasel with his talons before his breast, bending his beak, cleaning the beautiful airborne bones?

I have been reading about weasels because I saw one last week. I startled a weasel who startled me, and we exchanged a long glance.

Twenty minutes from my house, through the woods by the quarry and across the highway, is Hollins Pond, a remarkable piece of shallowness, where I like to go at sunset and sit on a tree trunk. Hollins Pond is also called Murray's Pond; it covers two acres of bottomland near Tinker Creek with six inches of water and six thousand lily pads. In winter, brown-and-white steers stand in the middle of it, merely dampening their hooves; from the distant shore they look like miracle itself, complete with miracle's nonchalance. Now, in summer, the steers are gone. The water lilies have blossomed and spread to a green horizontal plane that is terra firma to plodding blackbirds, and tremulous ceiling to black leeches, crayfish, and carp.

This is, mind you, suburbia. It is a five-minute walk in three directions to rows of houses, though none is visible here. There's a 55 mph highway at one end of the pond, and a nesting pair of wood ducks at the other. Under every bush is a muskrat hole or a beer can. The far end is an alternating series of fields and woods, fields and woods, threaded everywhere with motorcycle tracks—in whose bare clay wild turtles lay eggs.

So. I had crossed the highway, stepped over two low barbed-wire fences, and traced the motorcycle path in all gratitude through the wild rose and poison ivy of the pond's shoreline up into high grassy fields. Then I cut down through the woods to the mossy fallen tree where I sit. This tree is excellent. It makes a dry, upholstered bench at the upper, marshy end of the pond, a plush jetty raised from the thorny shore between a shallow blue body of water and a deep blue body of sky.

The sun had just set. I was relaxed on the tree trunk, ensconced in the lap of lichen, watching the lily pads at my feet tremble and part dreamily over the thrusting path of a carp. A yellow bird appeared to my right and flew behind me. It caught my eye; I swiveled around—and the next instant, inexplicably, I was looking down at a weasel, who was looking up at me.

Weasel! I'd never seen one wild before. He was ten inches long, thin as a curve, a muscled ribbon, brown as fruitwood, soft-furred, alert. His face was fierce, small and pointed as a lizard's; he would have made a good arrowhead. There was just a dot of chin, maybe two brown hairs' worth, and then the pure white fur began that spread down his underside. He had two black eyes I didn't see, any more than you see a window.

The weasel was stunned into stillness as he was emerging from beneath an enormous shaggy wild rose bush four feet away. I was stunned into stillness twisted backward on the tree trunk. Our eyes locked, and someone threw away the key.

Our look was as if two lovers, or deadly enemies, met unexpectedly on an overgrown path when each had been thinking of something else: a clearing blow to the gut. It was also a bright blow to the brain, or a sudden beating of brains, with all the charge and intimate grate of rubbed balloons. It emptied our lungs. It felled the forest, moved the fields, and drained the pond; the world dismantled and tumbled into that black hole of eyes. If you and I looked at each other that way, our skulls would split and drop to our shoulders. But we don't. We keep our skulls. So.

He disappeared. This was only last week, and already I don't remember what shattered the enchantment. I think I blinked, I think I retrieved my brain from the weasel's brain, and tried to memorize what I was seeing, and the weasel felt the yank of separation, the careening splashdown into real life and the urgent current of instinct. He vanished under the wild rose. I waited motionless, my mind suddenly full of data and my spirit with pleadings, but he didn't return.

Please do not tell me about "approach-avoidance conflicts." I tell you I've been in that weasel's brain for sixty seconds, and he was in mine. Brains are private places, muttering through unique and secret tapes—but the weasel and I both plugged into another tape simultaneously, for a sweet and shocking time. Can I help it if it was a blank?

What goes on in his brain the rest of the time? What does a weasel think about? He won't say. His journal is tracks in clay, a spray of feathers, mouse blood and bone: uncollected, unconnected, loose-leaf, and blown.

I would like to learn, or remember, how to live. I come to Hollins Pond not so much to learn how to live as, frankly, to forget about it. That is, I don't think I can learn from a wild animal how to live in particular—shall I suck warm blood, hold my tail high, walk with my footprints precisely over the prints of my hands?—but I might learn something of mindlessness, something of the purity of living in the physical senses and the dignity of living without bias or motive. The weasel lives in necessity and we live in choice, hating necessity and dying at the last ignobly in its talons. I would like to live as I should, as the weasel lives as he should. And I suspect that for me the way is like the weasel's: open to time and death painlessly, noticing everything, remembering nothing, choosing the given with a fierce and pointed will.

I missed my chance. I should have gone for the throat. I should have lunged for that streak of white under the weasel's chin and held on, held on through mud and into the wild rose, held on for a dearer life. We could live under the wild rose wild as weasels, mute and uncomprehending. I could very calmly go wild. I could live two days in the den, curled, leaning on mouse fur, sniffing bird bones, blinking, licking, breathing musk, my hair tangled in the roots of grasses. Down is a good place to go, where the mind is single. Down is out, out of your ever-loving mind and back to your careless senses. I remember muteness as a prolonged and giddy fast, where every moment is a feast of utterance received. Time and events are merely poured, unremarked, and ingested directly, like blood pulsed into my gut through a jugular vein. Could two live that way? Could two live under the wild rose, and explore by the pond, so that the smooth mind of each is as everywhere present to the other, and as received and as unchallenged, as falling snow?

We could, you know. We can live any way we want. People take vows of poverty, chastity, and obedience—even of silence—by choice. The thing is to stalk your calling in a certain skilled and supple way, to locate the most tender and live spot and plug into that pulse. This is yielding, not fighting. A weasel doesn't "attack" anything; a weasel lives as he's meant to, yielding at every moment to the perfect freedom of single necessity.

I think it would be well, and proper, and obedient, and pure, to grasp your one necessity and not let it go, to dangle from it limp wherever it takes you. Then even death, where you're going no matter how you live, cannot you part. Seize it and let it seize you up aloft even, till your eyes burn out and drop; let your musky flesh fall off in shreds, and let your very bones unhinge and scatter, loosened over fields, over fields and woods, lightly, thoughtless, from any height at all, from as high as eagles.

Voice   Dillard's voice is informal. She speaks to us in the first person, casually, directly: "I tell you I've been in that weasel's brain for sixty seconds. . . ." In advancing the proposition that we live like weasels, Dillard reassures us with "we could, you know." She is thus both confident and authoritative while being personal, even informal. As a result we feel obliged to hear her out, to respond to her passionate insistence; we feel obliged to try to understand even when her explanation grazes mystery.

Style   Dillard's voice is part of her style. Her sentences are short—they speak to the point whether that point is factual or mystical. There are few connectives, almost no coordinative *ands, buts,* and *fors;* and there is no subordination through the use of *because, although, if,* and *whenever.* The lack of formal syntactic links contributes to the force and authority of Dillard's style. "A weasel is wild," she tells us, announcing her theme. Before long we learn just how wild. Later she notes that "a weasel lives as he's meant to," concisely summing up both the weasel and the essay.

Dillard seems fond of questions. Her questions engage us, stimulate our responses, spur our thinking: "What goes on in his brain the rest of the time? What does a weasel think about?" Like her assertions, Dillard's questions are clear, direct, cryptic. Some of her questions are simultaneously speculative and provocative as when she writes, "Could two live that way? Could two live under the wild rose, and explore by the pond?" These questions she answers: "We could, you know," a somewhat frightening kind of assurance. Beyond her authoritative declarations and her frequent startling questions is a single exclamation: "Weasel!" which catches us by surprise and captures Dillard's surprise in encountering it. We shouldn't miss the imperative of her final sentence, which startles as much by its commanding tone as by its startling advice.

A further stylistic observation: Dillard leans heavily on verbs, especially verbs of action, often violent action. She stacks verbs up, which results in a driving, relentless prose. Here are two examples:

> Obedient to instinct, he bites his prey at the neck, either splitting the jugular vein at the throat or crunching the brain at the base of the skull, and he does not let go.

> It emptied our lungs. It felled the forest, moved the fields, and drained the pond; the world dismantled and tumbled into that black hole of eyes.

We should also note her fondness for and skill in using figures of comparison. Describing the weasel, Dillard compares him to "a muscled ribbon," and an "arrowhead" with a color "brown as fruitwood." Describing the impact of her encounter she reaches even further into analogy: "Our look was as if two lovers, or deadly enemies, met unexpectedly." The effect of this look, which she describes in another place as eyes locked together, is "a clearing blow to the gut." Moreover, the energy of her style is captured in the physical imagery and the taut syntax of this phrase.

Structure   The structure of the essay can be mapped like this:

1. Paragraphs 1–2: facts about weasels, especially their wildness and their ability to hang on and not let go; two stunning examples (the naturalist and the eagle) one for each of the first two paragraphs.

2. Paragraphs 3–7: This second, longer chunk of the essay depicts Dillard encountering the weasel, exchanging glances with it. The middle paragraphs (4–6) set the scene, with paragraphs 3 and 7 framing the section with the repeated mention of Dillard and the weasel's locked glances. Paragraph 5 mixes details as it contrasts wilderness and civilization. The two exist side-by-side, one within the other: beer cans coexist with muskrat holes; turtle eggs sit in motorcycle tracks; a highway runs alongside a duck pond.

3. Paragraphs 8–13: The crescendo and climax of the essay. Here Dillard describes in detail the weasel (paragraph 8); the shock of their locked looks (9

and 10); and the shattering of the spell (11). She also laments her unsuccessful attempt to reforge the link with the weasel after it had been snapped. The section ends with Dillard (and us) pondering the mystery she has experienced.

4. Paragraphs 14–17: Dillard speculates about the meaning of the encounter with the weasel. She contemplates living like a weasel—what it means, why it appeals (to her) and perhaps appalls (us). She explores the implications of what a weasel's life is like—how it relates to human life, especially her own. She concludes with an image from the opening: an eagle carrying something that is clinging fiercely to it, not letting go, holding on into and beyond death. The image brings the essay full circle—but with one significant difference: we have taken the weasel's place.

Thought What begins as an expository essay detailing facts about weasels, especially their wildness and tenacity, turns into a meditation on the value and necessity of wildness, instinct, and tenacity in human life. By the end of the essay Dillard has made the weasel a symbol, a model of how we should live. Her tone changes from the factual declaration of the opening first into speculative wonder, and then into admonition.

But what does she mean? How can we live like weasels? How can we imitate and appropriate the weasel's wildness and tenacity? Dillard doesn't say, exactly. She only exhorts us to seize necessity, to lock on to what is essential and not let go for anything. She seems to invite us to decide for ourselves what our necessity is and then relentlessly catch and hold it.

Another idea surfaces in the essay: that man and animal can indeed communicate and understand one another. Dillard opts for a mystical communion between man and beast, by necessity a brief communion, one beyond the power of words to describe (though Dillard seems to have pulled it off). The experience for woman and weasel "stuns into stillness," stops time, empties one consciousness into another. In linking her mind even momentarily with the weasel, Dillard undergoes an extraordinary experience, a transforming one. It's something she would like to repeat, to get more of, find out more about. The experience prompts her to read up on weasels, reading she turns to good account in using memorable details to launch her essay. She wants not just to learn more about weasels but to know a weasel in this mystical way again. But she can't because her own consciousness, the distinctive human quality of her thinking mind, prevents her from being at one and staying at one with an animal.

There seems to be, thus, in Dillard's essay, a pull in two directions. On one hand, there is the suggestion that we can link ourselves with the weasel and like him live in necessity instinctively, opening ourselves to time and death, noticing everything and remembering nothing. On the other hand sits a counter idea: that we cannot stay linked with the weasel or with any animal, primarily because our minds prohibit it. We are creatures for whom remembering is necessary, vital. Dillard, in fact, could never have savored her experience and shared it with us without the capacity of remembering. The weasel's mindlessness, its purity of living, cannot be wholly hers or ours, for we are mindful creatures, not mindless ones. Our living as we should is necessarily different from the weasel's living as it should. Although we can learn from the weasel's instinct, its pure living, its tenacity, we can follow it only so far on the way to wildness.

CHAPTER TWENTY-SIX

A Collection of Essays

FRANCIS BACON

[*1533–1592*]

Of Love

The stage is more beholding to Love than the life of man. For as to the stage, love is ever matter of comedies, and now and then of tragedies, but in life it doth much mischief, sometimes like a syren, sometimes like a fury. You may observe that amongst all the great and worthy persons (whereof the memory remaineth, either ancient or recent) there is not one that hath been transported to the mad degree of love, which shows that great spirits and great business do keep out this weak passion. You must except nevertheless Marcus Antonius, the half partner of the empire of Rome, and Appius Claudius, the decemvir and lawgiver; whereof the former was indeed a voluptuous man, and inordinate, but the latter was an austere and wise man; and therefore it seems (though rarely) that love can find entrance not only into an open heart, but also into a heart well fortified, if watch be not well kept. It is a poor saying of Epicurus, *Satis magnum alter alteri theatrum sumus,* as if man, made for the contemplation of heaven and all noble objects, should do nothing but kneel before a little idol, and make himself a subject, though not of the mouth (as beasts are), yet of the eye, which was given him for higher purposes. It is a strange thing to note the excess of this passion, and how it braves the nature and value of things, by this: that the speaking in a perpetual hyperbole is comely in nothing but in love. Neither is it merely in the phrase, for whereas it hath been well said that the arch-flatterer, with whom all the petty flatterers have intelligence, is a man's self, certainly the lover is more. For there was never proud man thought so absurdly well of himself as the lover doth of the person loved; and therefore it was well said, *That it is impossible to love and to be wise.* Neither doth this weakness appear to others only, and not to the party loved, but to the loved most of all, except the love be reciproque. For it is a true rule that love is ever rewarded either with the reciproque or with an inward and secret contempt. By how much the more men ought to beware of this passion, which loseth not only other things but itself. As for the other losses, the poet's relation doth well figure them: that he that preferred Helena quitted the gifts of Juno and Pallas. For whosoever esteemeth too much of amorous affection quitteth both riches and wisdom. This passion hath his floods in the very times of weakness, which are great prosperity and great adversity, though this latter hath been less observed, both which times kindle love, and make it more fervent, and therefore show it to be the child of folly. They do best who, if they cannot but admit love, yet make it keep quarter and sever it wholly from their serious affairs and actions of life, for if it check once with business, it troubleth men's fortunes, and maketh men that they can no ways be true to their own ends. I know not how, but martial men are given to love; I think it is but as they are given to wine, for perils commonly ask to be paid in pleasures. There is in man's nature a secret inclination and motion towards love of others, which if it be not spent upon some one or a few, doth naturally spread itself towards many, and maketh men become humane and charitable, as it is seen sometime in friars. Nuptial love maketh mankind; friendly love perfecteth it; but wanton love corrupteth and embaseth it.

JOHN DONNE

[1572–1631]

Meditation XVII: For Whom the Bell Tolls

Perchance he for whom this bell tolls may be so ill, as that he knows not it tolls for him; and perchance I may think myself so much better than I am, as that they who are about me, and see my state, may have caused it to toll for me, and I know not that. The church is Catholic, universal, so are all her actions; all that she does belongs to all. When she baptizes a child, that action concerns me; for that child is thereby connected to that body which is my head too, and ingrafted into that body whereof I am a member. And when she buries a man, that action concerns me: all mankind is of one author, and is one volume; when one man dies, one chapter is not torn out of the book, but translated into a better language; and every chapter must be so translated;

God employs several translators; some pieces are translated by age, some by sickness, some by war, some by justice; but God's hand is in every translation, and his hand shall bind up all our scattered leaves again for that library where every book shall lie open to one another. As therefore the bell that rings to a sermon calls not upon the preacher only, but upon the congregation to come, so this bell calls us all; but how much more me, who am brought so near the door by this sickness. There was a contention as far as a suit (in which both piety and dignity, religion and estimation, were mingled), which of the religious orders should ring to prayers first in the morning; and it was determined, that they should ring first that rose earliest. If we understand aright the dignity of this bell that tolls for our evening prayer, we would be glad to make it ours by rising early, in that application, that it might be ours as well as his, whose indeed it is. The bell doth toll for him that thinks it doth; and though it intermit again, yet from that minute that that occasion wrought upon him, he is united to God. Who casts not up his eye to the sun when it rises? but who takes off his eye from a comet when that breaks out? Who bends not his ear to any bell which upon any occasion rings? but who can remove it from that bell which is passing a piece of himself out of this world? No man is an island, entire of itself; every man is a piece of the continent, a part of the main. If a clod be washed away by the sea, Europe is the less, as well as if a promontory were, as well as if a manor of thy friend's or of thine own were: any man's death diminishes me, because I am involved in mankind, and therefore never send to know for whom the bells tolls; it tolls for thee. Neither can we call this a begging of misery, or a borrowing of misery, as though we were not miserable enough of ourselves, but must fetch in more from the next house, in taking upon us the misery of our neighbours. Truly it were an excusable covetousness if we did, for affliction is a treasure, and scarce any man hath enough of it. No man hath affliction enough that is not matured and ripened by it, and made fit for God by that affliction. If a man carry treasure in bullion, or in a wedge of gold, and have none coined into current money, his treasure will not defray him as he travels. Tribulation is treasure in the nature of it, but it is not current money in the use of it, except we get nearer and nearer our home, heaven, by it. Another man may be sick too, and sick to death, and this affliction may lie in his bowels, as gold in a mine, and be of no use to him; but this bell, that tells me of his affliction, digs out and applies that gold to me: if by this consideration of another's danger I take mine own into contemplation, and so secure myself, by making my recourse to my God, who is our only security.

JONATHAN SWIFT

[1667–1745]

A Modest Proposal

FOR PREVENTING THE CHILDREN OF POOR PEOPLE IN IRELAND FROM BEING A BURDEN TO THEIR PARENTS OR COUNTRY, AND FOR MAKING THEM BENEFICIAL TO THE PUBLIC

It is a melancholy object to those who walk through this great town or travel in the country, when they see the streets, the roads, and cabin doors crowded with beggars of the female sex, followed by three, four, or six children, all in rags and importuning every passenger for an alms. These mothers, instead of being able to work for their honest livelihood, are forced to employ all their time in strolling to beg sustenance for their helpless infants, who, as they grow up, either turn thieves for want of work, or leave their dear native country to fight for the Pretender in Spain, or sell themselves to the Barbadoes.

I think it is agreed by all parties that this prodigious number of children in the arms, or on the backs, or at the heels of their mothers, and frequently of their fathers, is in the present deplorable state of the kingdom a very great additional grievance; and therefore whoever could find out a fair, cheap, and easy method of making these children sound and useful members of the commonwealth would deserve so well of the public as to have his statue set up for a preserver of the nation.

But my intention is very far from being confined to provide only for the children of professed beggars; it is of a much greater extent, and shall take in the whole number of infants at a certain age who are born of parents in effect as little able to support them as those who demand our charity in the streets.

As to my own part, having turned my thoughts for many years upon this important subject, and maturely weighed the several schemes of other projectors, I have always found them grossly mistaken in their computation. It is true a child just dropped from its dam may be supported by her milk for a solar year with little other nourishment, at most not above the value of two shillings, which the mother may certainly get, or the value in scraps, by her lawful occupation of begging; and it is exactly at one year old that I propose to provide for them in such a manner as instead of being a charge upon their parents or the parish, or wanting food and raiment for the rest of their lives, they shall, on the contrary, contribute to the feeding and partly to the clothing of many thousands.

There is likewise another great advantage in my scheme, that it will prevent those voluntary abortions, and that horrid practice of women murdering their bastard children, alas! too frequent among us, sacrificing the poor innocent babes, I doubt, more to avoid the expense than the shame, which would move tears and pity in the most savage and inhuman breast.

The number of souls in this kingdom being usually reckoned one million and a half, of these I calculate there may be about two hundred thousand couples whose wives are breeders; from which number I subtract thirty thousand couples who are able to maintain their own children, although I apprehend there cannot be so many, under the present distress of the kingdom; but this being granted, there will remain an hundred and seventy thousand breeders. I again subtract fifty thousand for those women who miscarry, or whose children die by accident or disease within the year. There only remain an hundred and twenty thousand children of poor parents annually born. The question therefore is, how this number shall be reared and provided for, which, as I have already said, under the present situation of affairs is utterly impossible by all the methods hitherto proposed. For we can neither employ them in handicraft or agriculture; we neither build houses (I mean in the country) nor cultivate land: they can very seldom pick up a livelihood by stealing till they arrive at six years old, except where they are of towardly parts; although I confess they learn the rudiments much earlier, during which time they can, however, be properly looked upon only as probationers, as I have been informed by a principal gentleman in the county of Cavan, who protested to me that he never knew above one or two instances under the age of six, even in a part of the kingdom so renowned for the quickest proficiency in that art.

I am assured by our merchants that a boy or girl before twelve years old is no salable commodity; and even when they come to this age they will not yield above three pounds or three pounds and half-a-crown at most on the Exchange; which cannot turn to account either to the parents or the kingdom, the charge of nutriment and rags having been at least four times that value.

I shall now therefore humbly propose my own thoughts, which I hope will not be liable to the least objection.

I have been assured by a very knowing American of my acquaintance in London that a young healthy child well nursed is at a year old a most delicious, nourishing, and wholesome food, whether stewed, roasted, baked, or boiled; and I make no doubt that it will equally serve in a fricassee or a ragout.

I do therefore humbly offer it to public consideration that of the hundred and twenty thousand children already computed, twenty thousand may be reserved for breed, whereof only one-fourth part to be males, which is more than we allow to sheep, black cattle or swine; and my reason is that these children are seldom the fruits of marriage, a circumstance not much regarded by our savages; therefore one male will be sufficient to serve four females. That the remaining hundred thousand may at a year old be offered in sale to the persons of quality and fortune through the kingdom, always advising the mother to let them suck plentifully in the last month, so as to render them plump and fat for a good table. A child will make two dishes at an entertainment for friends; and when the family dines alone, the fore or hind quarter will make a reasonable dish, and seasoned with a little pepper or salt will be very good boiled on the fourth day, especially in winter.

I have reckoned upon a medium that a child just born will weigh twelve pounds, and in a solar year if tolerably nursed increaseth to twenty-eight pounds.

I grant this food will be somewhat dear, and therefore very proper for landlords, who, as they have already devoured most of the parents, seem to have the best title to the children.

Infants' flesh will be in season throughout the year, but more plentiful in March, and a little before and after; for we are told by a grave author, an eminent French physician, that fish being a prolific diet, there are more children born in Roman Catholic countries about nine months after Lent than at any other season; therefore reckoning a year after Lent, the markets will be more glutted than usual, because the number of popish infants is at least three to one in this kingdom; and therefore it will have one other collateral advantage, by lessening the number of Papists among us.

I have already computed the charge of nursing a beggar's child (in which list I reckon all cottagers, laborers, and four-fifths of the farmers) to be about two shillings per annum, rags included; and I believe no gentleman would repine to give ten shillings for the carcass of a good fat child, which, as I have said, will make four dishes of excellent nutritive meat, when he hath only some particular friend or his own family to dine with him. Thus the squire will learn to be a good landlord, and grow popular among his tenants; the mother will have eight shillings net profit, and be fit for work till she produces another child.

Those who are more thrifty (as I must confess the times require) may flay the carcass; the skin of which artificially dressed will make admirable gloves for ladies, and summer boots for fine gentlemen.

As to our city of Dublin, shambles may be appointed for this purpose in the most convenient parts of it, and butchers we may be assured will not be wanting; although I rather recommend buying the children alive, and dressing them hot from the knife, as we do roasting pigs.

A very worthy person, a true lover of his country, and whose virtues I highly esteem, was lately pleased, in discoursing on this matter, to offer a refinement upon my scheme. He said that many gentlemen of this kingdom, having of late destroyed their deer, he conceived that the want of venison might be well supplied by the bodies of young lads and maidens, not exceeding fourteen years of age nor under twelve, so great a number of both sexes in every country being now ready to starve for want of work and service: and these to be disposed of by their parents, if alive, or otherwise by their nearest relations. But with due deference to so excellent a friend and so deserving a patriot, I cannot be altogether in his sentiments. For as to the males, my American acquaintance assured me from frequent experience that their flesh was generally tough and lean, like that of our schoolboys, by continual exercise, and their taste disagreeable; and to fatten them would not answer the charge. Then as to the females, it would, I think, with humble submission, be a loss to the public, because they soon would become breeders themselves: and besides, it is not improbable that some scrupulous people might be apt to censure such a practice (although indeed very unjustly) as a little bordering upon cruelty; which, I confess, hath always been with me the strongest objection against any project, how well soever intended.

But in order to justify my friend, he confessed that this expedient was put into his head by the famous Psalmanazar, a native of the island Formosa, who came from thence to London above twenty years ago, and in conversation told my friend that in his country when any young person happened to be put to death, the executioner sold the carcass to persons of quality as a prime dainty, and that in his time the body of a plump girl of fifteen, who was crucified for an attempt to poison the emperor, was sold to his Imperial Majesty's prime minister of state, and other great mandarins of the court, in joints from the gibbet, at four hundred crowns. Neither indeed can I deny that if the same use were made of several plump young girls in this town, who, without one single groat to their fortunes, cannot stir abroad without a chair, and appear at the playhouse and assemblies in foreign fineries, which they never will pay for, the kingdom would not be the worse.

Some persons of a desponding spirit are in great concern about that vast number of poor people, who are aged, diseased, or maimed, and I have been desired to employ my thoughts what course may be taken to ease the nation of so grievous an encumbrance. But I am not in the least pain upon that matter, because it is very well known that they are every day dying and rotting, by cold and famine, and filth and vermin, as fast as can be reasonably expected. And as to the younger laborers, they are now in almost as hopeful a condition. They cannot get work, and consequently pine away for want of nourishment, to a degree that if at any time they are accidentally hired to common labor, they have not strength to perform it; and thus the country and themselves are happily delivered from the evils to come.

I have too long digressed, and therefore shall return to my subject. I think the advantages by the proposal which I have made are obvious and many, as well as of the highest importance.

For first, as I have already observed, it would greatly lessen the number of Papists, with whom we are yearly overrun, being the principal breeders of the nation as well as our most dangerous enemies; and who stay at home on purpose with a design to deliver the kingdom to the Pretender, hoping to take their advantage by the absence of so many good Protestants, who have chosen rather to leave their country than stay at home and pay tithes against their conscience to an Episcopal curate.

Secondly, the poorer tenants will have something valuable of their own, which by law may be made liable to distress, and help to pay their landlord's rent; their corn and cattle being already seized, and money a thing unknown.

Thirdly, whereas the maintenance of an hundred thousand children, from two years old and upwards, cannot be computed at less than ten shillings apiece per annum, the nation's stock will be thereby increased fifty thousand pounds per annum, besides the profit of a new dish introduced to the tables of all gentlemen of fortune in the kingdom who have any refinement in taste. And the money will circulate among ourselves, the goods being entirely of our own growth and manufacture.

Fourthly, the constant breeders, besides the gain of eight shillings sterling per annum by the sale of their children, will be rid of the charge of maintaining them after the first year.

Fifthly, this food would likewise bring great custom to taverns, where the vintners will certainly be so prudent as to procure the best receipts for dressing it to perfection, and consequently have their houses frequented by all the fine gentlemen, who justly value themselves upon their knowledge in good eating; and a skillful cook, who understands how to oblige his guests, will contrive to make it as expensive as they please.

Sixthly, this would be a great inducement to marriage, which all wise nations have either encouraged by rewards or enforced by laws and penalties. It would increase the care and tenderness of mothers toward their children, when they were sure of a settlement for life to the poor babes, provided in some sort by the public, to their annual profit instead of expense. We should see an honest emulation among the married women, which of them could bring the fattest child to the market. Men would become as fond of their wives during the time of their pregnancy as they are now of their mares in foal, their cows in calf, or sows when they are ready to farrow; nor offer to beat or kick them (as is too frequent a practice) for fear of miscarriage.

Many other advantages might be enumerated. For instance, the addition of some thousand carcasses in our exportation of barreled beef, the propagation of swine's flesh, and improvement in the art of making good bacon, so much wanted among us by the great destruction of pigs, too frequent at our tables, and are no way comparable in taste or magnificence to a well-grown, fat yearling child, which roasted whole will make a considerable figure at a lord mayor's feast, or any other public entertainment. But this and many others I omit, being studious of brevity.

Supposing that one thousand families in this city would be constant customers for infants' flesh, besides others who might have it at merry meetings, particularly weddings and christenings, I compute that Dublin would take off annually about twenty thousand carcasses, and the rest of the kingdom (where probably they will be sold somewhat cheaper) the remaining eighty thousand.

I can think of no one objection that will possibly be raised against this proposal, unless it should be urged that the number of people will be thereby much lessened in the kingdom. This I freely own, and it was indeed one principal design in offering it to the world. I desire the reader will observe that I calculate my remedy for this one individual kingdom of Ireland, and for no other that ever was, is, or, I think, ever can be upon earth. Therefore let no man talk to me of other expedients: of taxing our absentees at five shillings a pound; of using neither clothes nor household furniture except what is of our own growth and manufacture; of utterly rejecting the materials and instruments that promote foreign luxury; of curing the expensiveness of pride, vanity, idleness, and gaming in our women; of introducing a vein of parsimony, prudence, and temperance; of learning to love our country, in the want of which we differ even from Laplanders and the inhabitants of Topinamboo; of quitting our animosities and factions, nor act any longer like the Jews, who were murdering one another at the very moment their city was taken; of being a little cautious not to sell our country and consciences for nothing; of teaching landlords to have at least one degree of mercy toward their tenants; lastly, of putting a spirit of honesty, industry, and skill into our shopkeepers, who, if a resolution could now be taken to buy only our native goods, would immediately unite to cheat and exact upon us in the price, the measure, and the goodness, nor could ever yet be brought to make one fair proposal of just dealing, though often and earnestly invited to it.

Therefore I repeat, let no man talk to me of these and the like expedients, till he has at least some glimpse of hope that there will be ever some hearty and sincere attempt to put them in practice.

But as to myself, having been wearied out for many years with offering vain, idle, visionary thoughts, and at length utterly despairing of success, I fortunately fell upon this proposal, which, as it is wholly new, so it has something solid and real, of no expense and little trouble, full in our own power, and whereby we can incur no danger in disobliging England. For this kind of commodity will not bear exportation, the flesh being of too tender a consistence to admit a long continuance in salt, although perhaps I could name a country which would be glad to eat up our whole nation without it.

After all, I am not so violently bent upon my own opinion as to reject any offer proposed by wise men, which shall be found equally innocent, cheap, easy, and effectual. But before something of that kind shall be advanced in contradiction to my scheme, and offering a better, I desire the author or authors will be pleased maturely to consider two points. First, as things now stand, how they will be able to find food and raiment for an hundred thousand useless mouths and backs. And secondly, there being a round million of creatures in human figure throughout this kingdom, whose whole subsistence put into a common stock would leave them in debt two millions of pounds sterling, adding those who are beggars by profession to the bulk of farmers, cottagers, and laborers, with their wives and children, who are beggars in effect; I desire those politicians who dislike my overture, and may perhaps be so bold as to attempt an answer, that they will first ask the parents of these mortals whether they would not at this day think it a great happiness to have been sold for food at a year old in the manner I prescribe, and thereby have avoided such a perpetual scene of misfortunes as they have since gone through by the oppression of landlords, the impossibility of paying rent without money or trade, the want of common sustenance, with neither house nor clothes to cover them from the inclemencies of the weather, and the most inevitable prospect of entailing the like or greater miseries upon their breed for ever.

I profess, in the sincerity of my heart, that I have not the least personal interest in endeavoring to promote this necessary work, having no other motive than the public good of my country, by advancing our trade, providing for infants, relieving the poor, and giving some pleasure to the rich. I have no children by which I can propose to get a single penny; the youngest being nine years old, and my wife past child-bearing.

CHARLES LAMB

[1775–1847]

A Dissertation Upon Roast Pig

Mankind, says a Chinese manuscript, which my friend M. was obliging enough to read and explain to me, for the first seventy thousand ages ate their meat raw, clawing or biting it from the living animal, just as they do in Abyssinia to this day. This period is not obscurely hinted at by their great Confucius in the second chapter of his Mundane Mutations, where he designates a kind of golden age by the term Chofang, literally the Cook's Holiday.

The manuscript goes on to say, that the art of roasting, or rather broiling (which I take to be the elder brother) was accidentally discovered in the manner following. The swineherd, Ho-ti, having gone out into the woods one morning, as his manner was, to collect mast for his hogs, left his cottage in the care of his eldest son Bo-bo, a great lubberly boy, who being fond of playing with fire, as younkers of his age commonly are, let some sparks escape into a bundle of straw, which kindling quickly, spread the conflagration over every part of their poor mansion, till it was reduced to ashes.

Together with the cottage (a sorry antediluvian makeshift of a building, you may think it), what was of much more importance, a fine litter of new-farrowed pigs, no less than nine in number, perished. China pigs have been esteemed a luxury all over the East, from the remotest periods that we read of. Bo-bo was in the utmost consternation, as you may think, not so much for the sake of the tenement, which his father and he could easily build up again with a few dry branches, and the labour of an hour or two, at any time, as for the loss of the pigs.

While he was thinking what he should say to his father, and wringing his hands over the smoking remnants of one of those untimely sufferers, an odour assailed his nostrils, unlike any scent which he had before experienced. What could it proceed from?—not from the burnt cottage—he had smelt that smell before—indeed this was by no means the first accident of the kind which had occurred through the negligence of this unlucky young fire-brand. Much less did it resemble that of any known herb, weed, or flower. A premonitory moistening at the same time overflowed his nether lip. He knew not what to think.

He next stooped down to feel the pig, if there were any signs of life in it. He burnt his fingers, and to cool them he applied them in his booby fashion to his mouth. Some of the crumbs of the scorched skin had come away with his fingers, and for the first time in his life (in the world's life indeed, for before him no man had known it) he tasted—*crackling!* Again he felt and fumbled at the pig. It did not burn him so much now, still he licked his fingers from a sort of habit.

The truth at length broke into his slow understanding, that it was the pig that smelt so, and the pig that tasted so delicious; and surrendering himself up to the newborn pleasure, he fell to tearing up whole handfuls of the scorched skin with the flesh next it, and was cramming it down his throat in his beastly fashion, when his sire entered amid the smoking rafters, armed with retributory cudgel, and finding how affairs stood, began to rain blows upon the young rogue's shoulders, as thick as hailstones, which Bo-bo heeded not any more than if they had been flies. The tickling pleasure, which he experienced in his lower regions, had rendered him quite callous to any inconveniences he might feel in those remote quarters. His father might lay on, but he could not beat him from his pig, till he had fairly made an end of it, when, becoming a little more sensible of his situation, something like the following dialogue ensued.

"You graceless whelp, what have you got there devouring? Is it not enough that you have burnt me down three houses with your dog's tricks, and be hanged to you! but you must be eating fire, and I know not what—what have you got there, I say?"

"O father, the pig, the pig! do come and taste how nice the burnt pig eats."

The ears of Ho-ti tingled with horror. He cursed his son, and he cursed himself that ever he should beget a son that should eat burnt pig.

Bo-bo, whose scent was wonderfully sharpened since morning, soon raked out another pig, and fairly rending it asunder, thrust the lesser half by main force into the fists of Ho-ti, still shouting out, "Eat, eat, eat the burnt pig, father, only taste—O Lord!"—with suchlike barbarous ejaculations, cramming all the while as if he would choke.

Ho-ti trembled every joint while he grasped the abominable thing, wavering whether he should not put his son to death for an unnatural young monster, when the crackling scorching his fingers, as it had done his son's, and applying the same remedy to them, he in his turn tasted some of its flavour, which, make what sour mouths he would for a pretense, proved not altogether displeasing to him. In conclusion (for the manuscript here is a little tedious), both father and son fairly set down to the mess, and never left off till they had despatched all that remained of the litter.

Bo-bo was strictly enjoined not to let the secret escape, for the neighbours would certainly have stoned them for a couple of abominable wretches, who could think of improving upon the good meat which God had sent them. Nevertheless, strange stories got about. It was observed that Ho-ti's cottage was burnt down now more frequently than ever. Nothing but fires from this time forward. Some would break out in broad day, others in the night-time. As often as the sow farrowed, so sure was the house of Ho-ti to be in a blaze; and Ho-ti himself, which was the more remarkable, instead of chastizing his son, seemed to grow more indulgent to him than ever.

At length they were watched, the terrible mystery discovered, and father and son summoned to take their trial at Pekin, then an inconsiderable assize town. Evidence was given, the obnoxious food itself produced in court, and verdict about to be pronounced, when the foreman of the jury begged that some of the burnt pig, of which the culprits stood accused, might be handed into the box. He handled it, and they all handled it; and burning their fingers, as Bo-bo and his father had done before them, and nature prompting to each of them the same remedy, against the face of all the facts, and the clearest charge which judge had ever given—to the surprise of the whole court, townsfolk, strangers, reporters, and all present—without leaving the box, or any manner of consultation whatever, they brought in a simultaneous verdict of Not Guilty.

The judge, who was a shrewd fellow, winked at the manifest iniquity of the decision: and when the court was dismissed, went privily and bought up all the pigs that could be had for love or money. In a few days his lordship's town-house was observed to be on fire. The thing took wing, and now there was nothing to be seen but fire in every direction. Fuel and pigs grew enormously dear all over the district. The insurance-offices one and all shut up shop. People built slighter and slighter every day, until it was feared that the very science of architecture would in no long time be lost to the world.

Thus this custom of firing houses continued, till in process of time, says my manuscript, a sage arose, like our Locke, who made a discovery that the flesh of swine, or indeed of any other animal, might be cooked (*burnt,* as they called it) without the necessity of consuming a whole house to dress it. Then first began the rude form of a gridiron. Roasting by the string or spit came in a century or two later, I forget in whose dynasty. By such slow degrees, concludes the manuscript, do the most useful, and seemingly the most obvious, arts make their way among mankind. . . .

Without placing too implicit faith in the account above given, it must be agreed that if a worthy pretext for so dangerous an experiment as setting houses on fire (especially in these days) could be assigned in favour of any culinary object, that pretext and excuse might be found in ROAST PIG.

Of all the delicacies in the whole *mundus edibilis,* I will maintain it to be the most delicate—*princeps obsoniorum.*

I speak not of your grown porkers—things between pig and pork—those hobbydehoys—but a young and tender suckling—under a moon old—guiltless as yet of the sty—with no original speck of the *amor immunditæ,* the hereditary failing of the first parent, yet manifest—his voice as yet not broken, but something between a childish treble and a grumble—the mild forerunner or *præludium* of a grunt.

He must be roasted. I am not ignorant that our ancestors ate them seethed, or boiled —but what a sacrifice to the exterior tegument!

There is no flavour comparable, I will contend, to that of the crisp, tawny, well-watched, not over-roasted, *crackling,* as it is well called—the very teeth are invited to their share of the pleasure at this banquet in overcoming the coy, brittle resistance— with the adhesive oleaginous—O call it not fat! but an indefinable sweetness growing up to it—the tender blossoming of fat—fat cropped in the bud—taken in the shoot —in the first innocence—the cream and quintessence of the child-pig's yet pure food —the lean, no lean, but a kind of animal manna—or, rather, fat and lean (if it must be so) so blended and running into each other, that both together make but one ambrosian result or common substance.

Behold him, while he is "doing"—it seemeth rather a refreshing warmth, than a scorching heat, that he is so passive to. How equably he twirleth round the string! Now he is just done. To see the extreme sensibility of that tender age! he hath wept out his pretty eyes—radiant jellies—shooting stars.

See him in the dish, his second cradle, how meek he lieth!—wouldst thou have had this innocent grow up to the grossness and indocility which too often accompany maturer swinehood? Ten to one he would have proved a glutton, a sloven, an obstinate, disagreeable animal—wallowing in all manner of filthy conversation—from these sins he is happily snatched away—

> Ere sin could blight or sorrow fade,
> Death came with timely care—

his memory is odoriferous—no clown curseth, while his stomach half rejecteth, the rank bacon—no coalheaver bolteth him in reeking sausages—he hath a fair sepulchre in the grateful stomach of the judicious epicure—and for such a tomb might be content to die.

He is the best of sapors. Pineapple is great. She is indeed almost too transcendent —a delight, if not sinful, yet so like to sinning that really a tender-conscienced person would do well to pause—too ravishing for mortal taste, she woundeth and excoriateth the lips that approach her—like lovers' kisses, she biteth—she is a pleasure bordering on pain from the fierceness and insanity of her relish—but she stoppeth at the palate —she meddleth not with the appetite—and the coarsest hunger might barter her consistently for a mutton-chop.

Pig—let me speak his praise—is no less provocative of the appetite, than he is satisfactory to the criticalness of the censorious palate. The strong man may batten on him, and the weakling refuseth not his mild juices.

Unlike to mankind's mixed characters, a bundle of virtues and vices, inexplicably intertwisted, and not to be unravelled without hazard, he is—good throughout. No part of him is better or worse than another. He helpeth, as far as his little means extend, all around. He is the least envious of banquets. He is all neighbours' fare.

I am one of those, who freely and ungrudgingly impart a share of the good things of this life which fall to their lot (few as mine are in this kind) to a friend. I protest

I take as great an interest in my friend's pleasures, his relishes, and proper satisfactions, as in mine own. "Presents," I often say, "endear Absents." Hares, pheasants, partridges, snipes, barndoor chickens (those "tame villatic fowl"), capons, plovers, brawn, barrels of oysters, I dispense as freely as I receive them. I love to taste them, as it were, upon the tongue of my friend. But a stop must be put somewhere. One would not, like Lear, "give everything." I make my stand upon pig. Methinks it is an ingratitude to the Giver of all good flavours to extra-domiciliate, or send out of the house slightingly (under pretext of friendship, or I know not what) a blessing so particularly adapted, predestined, I may say, to my individual palate. It argues an insensibility.

I remember a touch of conscience in this kind at school. My good old aunt, who never parted from me at the end of a holiday without stuffing a sweetmeat, or some nice thing into my pocket, had dismissed me one evening with a smoking plum-cake, fresh from the oven. In my way to school (it was over London Bridge) a grey-headed old beggar saluted me (I have no doubt, at this time of day, that he was a counterfeit). I had no pence to console him with, and in the vanity of self-denial and the very coxcombry of charity, schoolboylike, I made him a present of—the whole cake! I walked on a little, buoyed up, as one is on such occasions, with a sweet soothing of self-satisfaction; but before I had got to the end of the bridge, my better feelings returned, and I burst into tears, thinking how ungrateful I had been to my good aunt, to go and give her good gift away to a stranger that I had never seen before, and who might be a bad man for aught I knew; and then I thought of the pleasure my aunt would be taking in thinking that I—I myself, and not another—would eat her nice cake—and what should I say to her the next time I saw her—how naughty I was to part with her pretty present!—and the odour of that spicy cake came back upon my recollection, and the pleasure and the curiosity I had taken in seeing her make it, and her joy when she sent it to the oven, and how disappointed she would feel that I had never had a bit of it in my mouth at last—and I blamed my impertinent spirit of alms-giving, and out-of-place hypocrisy of goodness; and above all I wished never to see the face again of that insidious, good-for-nothing, old grey impostor.

Our ancestors were nice in their method of sacrificing these tender victims. We read of pigs whipt to death with something of a shock, as we hear of any other obsolete custom. The age of discipline is gone by, or it would be curious to inquire (in a philosophical light merely) what effect this process might have towards intenerating and dulcifying a substance, naturally so mild and dulcet as the flesh of young pigs. It looks like refining a violet. Yet we should be cautious, while we condemn the inhumanity, how we censure the wisdom of the practice. It might impart a gusto.

I remember an hypothesis, argued upon by the young students, when I was at St. Omer's, and maintained with much learning and pleasantry on both sides, "Whether, supposing that the flavour of a pig who obtained his death by whipping (*per flagellationem extremam*) superadded a pleasure upon the palate of a man more intense than any possible suffering we can conceive in the animal, is man justified in using that method of putting the animal to death?" I forget the decision.

His sauce should be considered. Decidedly, a few bread crumbs, done up with his liver and brains, and a dash of mild sage. But banish, dear Mrs. Cook, I beseech you, the whole onion tribe. Barbecue your whole hogs to your palate, steep them in shalots, stuff them out with plantations of the rank and guilty garlic; you cannot poison them, or make them stronger than they are—but consider, he is a weakling—a flower.

MARK TWAIN

[*1835–1910*]

"*Cub*" *Wants to Be a Pilot*

When I was a boy there was but one permanent ambition among my comrades in our village on the west bank of the Mississippi River. That was to be a steamboatman. We had transient ambitions of other sorts but they were only transient. When a circus came and went, it left us all burning to become clowns; the first Negro minstrel show that ever came to our section left us all suffering to try that kind of life; now and then we had a hope that, if we lived and were good, God would permit us to be pirates. These ambitions faded out, each in its turn; but the ambition to be a steamboatman always remained.

Once a day a cheap, gaudy packet arrived upward from St. Louis, and another downward from Keokuk. Before these events, the day was glorious with expectancy; after them, the day was a dead and empty thing. Not only the boys but the whole village felt this. After all these years I can picture that old time to myself now, just as it was then: the white town drowsing in the sunshine of a summer's morning; the streets empty or pretty nearly so; one or two clerks sitting in front of the Water Street stores, with their splint-bottomed chairs tilted back against the walls, chins on breasts, hats slouched over their faces, asleep—with shingle-shavings enough around to show what broke them down; a sow and a litter of pigs loafing along the sidewalk, doing a good business in watermelon rinds and seeds; two or three lonely little freight piles scattered about the "levee"; a pile of "skids" on the slope of the stone-paved wharf, and the fragrant town drunkard asleep in the shadow of them; two or three wood flats at the head of the wharf but nobody to listen to the peaceful lapping of the wavelets against them; the great Mississippi, the majestic, the magnificent Mississippi, rolling its mile-wide tide along, shining in the sun; the dense forest away on the other side; the "point" above the town, and the "point" below, bounding the river-glimpse and turning it into a sort of sea, and withal a very still and brilliant and lonely one. Presently a film of dark smoke appears above one of those remote "points"; instantly a Negro drayman, famous for his quick eye and prodigious voice, lifts up the cry, "S-t-e-a-m-boat a-comin'!" and the scene changes! The town drunkard stirs, the clerks wake up, a furious clatter of drays follows, every house and store pours out a human contribution, and all in a twinkling the dead town is alive and moving. Drays, carts, men, boys, all go hurrying from many quarters to a common center, the wharf. Assembled there, the people fasten their eyes upon the coming boat as upon a wonder they are seeing for the first time. And the boat *is* rather a handsome sight, too. She is long and sharp and trim and pretty; she has two tall, fancy-topped chimneys, with a gilded device of some kind swung between them; a fanciful pilot-house, all glass and "gingerbread," perched on top of the "texas" deck behind them; the paddle-boxes are gorgeous with a picture or with gilded rays above the boat's name; the boiler-deck, the hurricane-deck, and the texas deck are fenced and ornamented with clean white railings; there is a flag gallantly flying from the jack-staff; the furnace doors are open and the fires glaring bravely; the upper decks are black with passengers; the captain stands by the big bell, calm, imposing, the envy of all; great volumes of the blackest smoke are rolling and tumbling out of the chimneys —a husbanded grandeur created with a bit of pitch-pine just before arriving at a town; the crew are grouped on the forecastle; the broad stage is run far out over the port bow and an envied deck-hand stands picturesquely on the end of it with a coil of rope in his hand; the pent steam is screaming through the gauge-cocks; the captain lifts his hand, a bell rings, the wheels stop; then they turn back, churning the water to foam, and the steamer is at rest. Then such a scramble as there is to get aboard and to get ashore, and to take in freight and to discharge freight, all at one and the same time; and such a yelling and cursing as the mates facilitate it all with! Ten minutes later the steamer is under way again, with no flag on the jack-staff and no black smoke issuing from the chimneys. After ten more minutes the town is dead again and the town drunkard asleep by the skids once more.

My father was a justice of the peace and I supposed he possessed the power of life and death over all men and could hang anybody that offended him. This was distinction enough for me as a general thing, but the desire to be a steamboatman kept intruding nevertheless. I first wanted to be a cabin-boy, so that I could come out with a white apron on and shake a table-cloth over the side, where all my old comrades could see me; later I thought I would rather be the deck-hand who stood on the end of the stage-plank with the coil of rope in his hand, because he was particularly conspicuous. But these were only day-dreams—they were too heavenly to be contemplated as real possibilities. By and by one of our boys went away. He was not heard of for a long time. At last he turned up as apprentice engineer or "striker" on a steamboat. This thing shook the bottom out of all my Sunday-school teachings. That boy had been notoriously worldly and I just the reverse; yet he was exalted to this eminence and I left in obscurity and misery. There was nothing generous about this fellow in his greatness. He would always manage to have a rusty bolt to scrub while his boat tarried at our town, and he would sit on the inside guard and scrub it, where we all could see him and envy him and loathe him. And whenever his boat was laid up he would come home and swell around the town in his blackest and greasiest clothes, so that nobody could help remembering that he was a steamboatman; and he used all sorts of steamboat technicalities in his talk, as if he were so used to them that he forgot common people could not understand them. He would speak of the "labboard" side of a horse in an easy, natural way that would make one wish he was dead. And he was always talking about "St. Looy" like an old citizen; he would refer casually to occasions when he was "coming down Fourth Street," or when he was "passing by the Planter's House," or when there was a fire and he took a turn on the brakes of "the old Big Missouri"; and then he would go on and lie about how many towns the size of ours were burned down there that day. Two or three of the boys had long been persons of consideration among us because they had been to St. Louis once and had a vague general knowledge of its wonders, but the day of their glory was over now. They lapsed into a humble silence and learned to disappear when the ruthless "cub"-engineer approached. This fellow had money, too, and hair-oil. Also an ignorant silver watch and a showy brass watch-chain. He wore a leather belt and used no suspenders. If ever a youth was cordially admired and hated by his comrades, this one was. No girl could withstand his charms. He "cut out" every boy in the village. When his boat blew up at last, it diffused a tranquil contentment among us such as we had not known for months. But when he came home the next week, alive, renowned, and appeared in church all battered up and bandaged, a shining hero, stared at and wondered over by everybody, it seemed to us that the partiality of Providence for an undeserving reptile had reached a point where it was open to criticism.

This creature's career could produce but one result, and it speedily followed. Boy after boy managed to get on the river. The minister's son became an engineer. The doctor's and the postmaster's sons became "mud clerks"; the wholesale liquor dealer's son became a barkeeper on a boat; four sons of the chief merchant and two sons of the county judge became pilots. Pilot was the grandest position of all. The pilot, even in those days of trivial wages, had a princely salary—from a hundred and fifty to two hundred and fifty dollars a month, and no board to pay. Two months of his wages would pay a preacher's salary for a year. Now some of us were left disconsolate. We could not get on the river—at least our parents would not let us.

So, by and by, I ran away. I said I would never come home again till I was a pilot and could come in glory. But somehow I could not manage it. I went meekly aboard a few of the boats that lay packed together like sardines at the long St. Louis wharf, and humbly inquired for the pilots, but got only a cold shoulder and short words from mates and clerks. I had to make the best of this sort of treatment for the time being, but I had comforting day-dreams of a future when I should be a great and honored pilot, with plenty of money, and could kill some of these mates and clerks and pay for them.

Months afterward the hope within me struggled to a reluctant death, and I found myself without an ambition. But I was ashamed to go home. I was in Cincinnati, and I set to work to map out a new career. I had been reading about the recent exploration of the river Amazon by an expedition sent out by our government. It was said that the expedition, owing to difficulties, had not thoroughly explored a part of the country lying about the headwaters, some four thousand miles from the mouth of the river. It was only about fifteen hundred miles from Cincinnati to New Orleans, where I could doubtless get a ship. I had thirty dollars left; I would go and complete the exploration of the Amazon. This was all the thought I gave to the subject. I never was great in matters of detail. I packed my valise, and took passage on an ancient tub called the *Paul Jones,* for New Orleans. For the sum of sixteen dollars I had the scarred and tarnished splendors of "her" main saloon principally to myself, for she was not a creature to attract the eye of wiser travelers.

When we presently got under way and went poking down the broad Ohio, I became a new being and the subject of my own admiration. I was a traveler! A word never had tasted so good in my mouth before. I had an exultant sense of being bound for mysterious lands and distant climes which I never have felt in so uplifting a degree since. I was in such a glorified condition that all ignoble feelings departed out of me, and I was able to look down and pity the untraveled with a compassion that had hardly a trace of contempt in it. Still, when we stopped at villages and wood-yards, I could not help lolling carelessly upon the railings of the boiler-deck to enjoy the envy of the country boys on the bank. If they did not seem to discover me, I presently sneezed to attract their attention, or moved to a position where they could not help seeing me. And as soon as I knew they saw me I gaped and stretched, and gave other signs of being mightily bored with traveling.

I kept my hat off all the time, and stayed where the wind and the sun could strike me, because I wanted to get the bronzed and weather-beaten look of an old traveler. Before the second day was half gone I experienced a joy which filled me with the purest gratitude, for I saw that the skin had begun to blister and peel off my face and neck. I wished that the boys and girls at home could see me now.

We reached Louisville in time—at least the neighborhood of it. We stuck hard and fast on the rocks in the middle of the river and lay there four days. I was now beginning to feel a strong sense of being a part of the boat's family, a sort of infant son to the captain and younger brother to the officers. There is no estimating the pride I took in this grandeur or the affection that began to swell and grow in me for those people. I could not know how the lordly steamboatman scorns that sort of presumption in a mere landsman. I particularly longed to acquire the least trifle of notice from the big stormy mate, and I was on the alert for an opportunity to do him a service to that end. It came at last. The riotous pow-wow of setting a spar was going on down on the forecastle, and I went down there and stood around in the way—or mostly skipping out of it—till the mate suddenly roared a general order for somebody to bring him a capstan bar. I sprang to his side and said: "Tell me where it is—I'll fetch it!"

If a rag-picker had offered to do a diplomatic service for the Emperor of Russia, the monarch could not have been more astounded than the mate was. He even stopped swearing. He stood and stared down at me. It took him ten seconds to scrape his disjointed remains together again. Then he said impressively, "Well, if this don't beat h——l!," and turned to his work with the air of a man who had been confronted with a problem too abstruse for solution.

I crept away and courted solitude for the rest of the day. I did not go to dinner, I stayed away from supper until everybody else had finished. I did not feel so much like a member of the boat's family now as before. However, my spirits returned, in instalments, as we pursued our way down the river. I was sorry I hated the mate so, because it was not in (young) human nature not to admire him. He was huge and muscular, his face was bearded and whiskered all over, he had a red woman and a blue woman tattooed on his right arm—one on each side of a blue anchor with a red rope to it—and in the matter of profanity he was sublime. When he was getting out cargo at a landing, I was always where I could see and hear. He felt all the majesty of his great position and made the world feel it too. When he gave even the simplest order, he discharged it like a blast of lightning and sent a long, reverberating peal of profanity thundering after it. I could not help contrasting the way in which the average landsman would give an order with the mate's way of doing it. If the landsman should wish the gang-plank moved a foot farther forward, he would probably say, "James, or William, one of you push that plank forward, please," but put the mate in his place, and he would roar out, "Here, now, start that gang-plank for'ard! Lively, now! *What*'re you about! Snatch it! *snatch* it! There! there! aft again! aft again! Don't you hear me? Dash it to dash! are you going to *sleep* over it! 'Vast heaving. 'Vast heaving, I tell you! Going to heave it clear astern? WHERE're you going with that barrel! *for'ard* with it 'fore I make you swallow it, you dash-dash-dash-*dashed* split between a tired mud-turtle and a crippled hearse-horse!"

I wished I could talk like that.

When the soreness of my adventure with the mate had somewhat worn off, I began timidly to make up to the humblest official connected with the boat—the night watchman. He snubbed my advances at first, but I presently ventured to offer him a new chalk pipe, and that softened him. So he allowed me to sit with him by the big bell on the hurricane-deck, and in time he melted into conversation. He could not well have helped it, I hung with such homage on his words and so plainly showed that I felt honored by his notice. He told me the names of dim capes and shadowy islands as we glided by them in the solemnity of the night under the winking stars, and by and by got to talking about himself. He seemed over-sentimental for a man whose salary was six dollars a week—or rather he might have seemed so to an older person than I. But I drank in his words hungrily and with a faith that might have moved mountains if it had been applied judiciously. What was it to me that he was soiled and seedy and fragrant with gin? What was it to me that his grammar was bad, his construction worse, and his profanity so void of art that it was an element of weakness rather than strength in his conversation? He was a wronged man, a man who had seen trouble, and that was enough for me. As he mellowed into his plaintive history his tears dripped upon the lantern in his lap, and I cried too from sympathy. He said he was the son of an English nobleman, either an earl or an alderman, he could not remember which, but believed was both; his father, the nobleman, loved him but his mother hated him from the cradle; and so while he was still a little boy he was sent to "one of them old, ancient colleges," he couldn't remember which; and by and by his father died and his mother seized the property and "shook" him, as he phrased it. After his mother shook him, members of the nobility with whom he was acquainted used their influence to get him the position of "loblolly-boy in a ship," and from that point my watchman threw off all trammels of date and locality and branched out into a narrative that bristled all along with incredible adventures, a narrative that was so reeking with bloodshed and so crammed with hair-breadth escapes and the most engaging and unconscious personal villainies that I sat speechless, enjoying, shuddering, wondering, worshiping.

It was a sore blight to find out afterward that he was a low, vulgar, ignorant, sentimental, half-witted humbug, an untraveled native of the wilds of Illinois, who had absorbed wildcat literature and appropriated its marvels, until in time he had woven odds and ends of the mess into this yarn and then gone on telling it to fledglings like me until he had come to believe it himself.

E. M. FORSTER

[1879–1970]

Our Graves in Gallipoli

FIRST GRAVE   We are important again upon earth. Each morning men mention us.

SECOND GRAVE   Yes, after seven years' silence.

FIRST GRAVE   Every day some eminent public man now refers to the "sanctity of our graves in Gallipoli."

SECOND GRAVE   Why do the eminent men speak of "our" graves, as if they were themselves dead? It is we, not they, who lie on Achi Baba.

FIRST GRAVE   They say "our" out of geniality and in order to touch the great heart of the nation more quickly. *Punch,* the great-hearted jester, showed a picture lately in which the Prime Minister of England, Lloyd George, fertile in counsels, is urged to go to war to protect "the sanctity of our graves in Gallipoli." The elderly artist who designed that picture is not dead and does not mean to die. He hopes to illustrate this war as he did the last, for a sufficient salary. Nevertheless he writes "our" graves, as if he was inside one, and all persons of position now say the same.

SECOND GRAVE   If they go to war, there will be more graves.

FIRST GRAVE   That is what they desire. That is what Lloyd George, prudent in counsels, and lion-hearted Churchill, intend.

SECOND GRAVE   But where will they dig them?

FIRST GRAVE   There is still room over in Chanak. Also, it is well for a nation that would be great to scatter its graves all over the world. Graves in Ireland, graves in Irak, Russia, Persia, India, each with its inscription from the Bible or Rupert Brooke. When England thinks fit, she can launch an expedition to protect the sanctity of her graves, and can follow that by another expedition to protect the sanctity of the additional graves. That is what Lloyd George, prudent in counsels, and lion-hearted Churchill, have planned. Churchill planned this expedition to Gallipoli, where I was killed. He planned the expedition to Antwerp, where my brother was killed. Then he said that Labour is not fit to govern. Rolling his eyes for fresh worlds, he saw Egypt, and fearing that peace might be established there, he intervened and prevented it. Whatever he undertakes is a success. He is Churchill the Fortunate, ever in office, and clouds of dead heroes attend him. Nothing for schools, nothing for houses, nothing for the life of the body, nothing for the spirit. England cannot spare a penny for anything except for her heroes' graves.

SECOND GRAVE   Is she really putting herself to so much expense on our account?

FIRST GRAVE   For us, and for the Freedom of the Straits. That water flowing below us now—it must be thoroughly free. What freedom is, great men are uncertain, but all agree that the water must be free for all nations; if in peace, then for all nations in peace; if in war, then for all nations in war.

SECOND GRAVE   So all nations now support England.

FIRST GRAVE   It is almost inexplicable. England stands alone. Of the dozens of nations into which the globe is divided, not a single one follows her banner, and even her own colonies hang back.

SECOND GRAVE   Yes . . . inexplicable. Perhaps she fights for some other reason.

FIRST GRAVE   Ah, the true reason of a war is never known until all who have fought in it are dead. In a hundred years' time we shall be told. Meanwhile seek not to inquire. There are rumours that rich men desire to be richer, but we cannot know.

SECOND GRAVE   If rich men desire more riches, let them fight. It is reasonable to fight for our desires.

FIRST GRAVE   But they cannot fight. They must not fight. There are too few of them. They would be killed. If a rich man went into the interior of Asia and tried to take more gold or more oil, he might be seriously injured at once. He must persuade poor men, who are numerous, to go there for him. And perhaps this is what Lloyd George, fertile in counsels, has decreed. He has tried to enter Asia by means of the Greeks. It was the Greeks who, seven years ago, failed to join England after they had promised to do so, and our graves in Gallipoli are the result of this. But Churchill the Fortunate, ever in office, ever magnanimous, bore the Greeks no grudge, and he and Lloyd George persuaded their young men to enter Asia. They have mostly been killed there, so English young men must be persuaded instead. A phrase must be thought of, and "the Gallipoli graves" is the handiest. The clergy must wave their Bibles, the old men their newspapers, the old women their knitting, the unmarried girls must wave white feathers, and all must shout, "Gallipoli graves, Gallipoli graves, Gallipoli, Gally Polly, Gally Polly," until the young men are ashamed and think, What sound can that be but my country's call? and Chanak receives them.

SECOND GRAVE   Chanak is to sanctify Gallipoli.

FIRST GRAVE   It will make our heap of stones for ever England, apparently.

SECOND GRAVE   It can scarcely do that to my portion of it. I was a Turk.

FIRST GRAVE   What! a Turk! You a Turk? And I have lain beside you for seven years and never known!

SECOND GRAVE   How should you have known? What is there to know except that I am your brother?

FIRST GRAVE   I am yours . . .

SECOND GRAVE   All is dead except that. All graves are one. It is their unity that sanctifies them, and some day even the living will learn this.

FIRST GRAVE   Ah, but why can they not learn it while they are still alive?

E. B. WHITE

[1899–1985]

Once More to the Lake

One summer, along about 1904, my father rented a camp on a lake in Maine and took us all there for the month of August. We all got ringworm from some kittens and had to rub Pond's Extract on our arms and legs night and morning, and my father rolled over in a canoe with all his clothes on; but outside of that the vacation was a success and from then on none of us ever thought there was any place in the world like that lake in Maine. We returned summer after summer—always on August 1 for one month. I have since become a salt-water man, but sometimes in summer there are days when the restlessness of the tides and the fearful cold of the sea water and the incessant wind that blows across the afternoon and into the evening make me wish for the placidity of a lake in the woods. A few weeks ago this feeling got so strong I bought myself a couple of bass hooks and a spinner and returned to the lake where we used to go, for a week's fishing and to revisit old haunts.

I took along my son, who had never had any fresh water up his nose and who had seen lily pads only from train windows. On the journey over to the lake I began to wonder what it would be like. I wondered how time would have marred this unique, this holy spot—the coves and streams, the hills that the sun set behind, the camps and the paths behind the camps. I was sure that the tarred road would have found it out, and I wondered in what other ways it would be desolated. It is strange how much you can remember about places like that once you allow your mind to return into the grooves that lead back. You remember one thing, and that suddenly reminds you of another thing. I guess I remembered clearest of all the early mornings, when the lake was cool and motionless, remembered how the bedroom smelled of the lumber it was made of and of the wet woods whose scent entered through the screen. The partitions in the camp were thin and did not extend clear to the top of the rooms, and as I was always the first up I would dress softly so as not to wake the others, and sneak out into the sweet outdoors and start out in the canoe, keeping close along the shore in the long shadows of the pines. I remembered being very careful never to rub my paddle against the gunwale for fear of disturbing the stillness of the cathedral.

The lake had never been what you would call a wild lake. There were cottages sprinkled around the shores, and it was in farming country although the shores of the lake were quite heavily wooded. Some of the cottages were owned by nearby farmers, and you would live at the shore and eat your meals at the farmhouse. That's what our family did. But although it wasn't wild, it was a fairly large and undisturbed lake and there were places in it that, to a child at least, seemed infinitely remote and primeval.

I was right about the tar: it led to within half a mile of the shore. But when I got back there, with my boy, and we settled into a camp near a farmhouse and into the kind of summertime I had known, I could tell that it was going to be pretty much the same as it had been before—I knew it, lying in bed the first morning, smelling the bedroom and hearing the boy sneak quietly out and go off along the shore in a boat. I began to sustain the illusion that he was I, and therefore, by simple transposition, that I was my father. This sensation persisted, kept cropping up all the time we were there. It was not an entirely new feeling, but in this setting it grew much stronger. I seemed to be living a dual existence. I would be in the middle of some simple act, I would be picking up a bait box or laying down a table fork, or I would be saying something, and suddenly it would be not I but my father who was saying the words or making the gesture. It gave me a creepy sensation.

We went fishing the first morning. I felt the same damp moss covering the worms in the bait can, and saw the dragonfly alight on the the tip of my rod as it hovered a few inches from the surface of the water. It was the arrival of this fly that convinced me beyond any doubt that everything was as it always had been, that the years were a mirage and that there had been no years. The small waves were the same, chucking the rowboat under the chin as we fished at anchor, and the boat was the same boat, the same color green and the ribs broken in the same places, and under the floorboards the same fresh-water leavings and débris—the dead helgramite, the wisps of moss, the rusty discarded fishhook, the dried blood from yesterday's catch. We stared silently at the tips of our rods, at the dragonflies that came and went. I lowered the tip of mine into the water, tentatively, pensively dislodging the fly, which darted two feet away, poised, darted two feet back, and came to rest again a little farther up the rod. There had been no years between the ducking of this dragonfly and the other one—the one that was part of memory. I looked at the boy, who was silently watching his fly, and it was my hands that held his rod, my eyes watching. I felt dizzy and didn't know which rod I was at the end of.

We caught two bass, hauling them in briskly as though they were mackerel, pulling them over the side of the boat in a businesslike manner without any landing net, and stunning them with a blow on the back of the head. When we got back for a swim before lunch, the lake was exactly where we had left it, the same number of inches from the dock, and there was only the merest suggestion of a breeze. This seemed an utterly enchanted sea, this lake you could leave to its own devices for a few hours and come back to, and find that it had not stirred, this constant and trustworthy body of water. In the shallows, the dark, water-soaked sticks and twigs, smooth and old, were undulating in clusters on the bottom against the clean ribbed sand, and the track of the mussel was plain. A school of minnows swam by, each minnow with its small individual shadow, doubling the attendance, so clear and sharp in the sunlight. Some of the other campers were in swimming, along the shore, one of them with a cake of soap, and the water felt thin and clear and unsubstantial. Over the years there had been this person with the cake of soap, this cultist, and here he was. There had been no years.

Up to the farmhouse to dinner through the teeming, dusty field, the road under our sneakers was only a two-track road. The middle track was missing, the one with the marks of the hooves and the splotches of dried, flaky manure. There had always been three tracks to choose from in choosing which track to walk in; now the choice was narrowed down to two. For a moment I missed terribly the middle alternative. But the way led past the tennis court, and something about the way it lay there in the sun reassured me; the tape had loosened along the backline, the alleys were green with plantains and other weeds, and the net (installed in June and removed in September) sagged in the dry noon, and the whole place steamed with midday heat and hunger and emptiness. There was a choice of pie for dessert, and one was blueberry and one was apple, and the waitresses were the same country girls, there having been no passage of time, only the illusion of it as in a dropped curtain—the waitresses were still fifteen; their hair had been washed, that was the only difference—they had been to the movies and seen the pretty girls with the clean hair.

Summertime, oh, summertime, pattern of life indelible, the fadeproof lake, the woods unshatterable, the pasture with the sweetfern and the juniper forever and ever, summer without end; this was the background, and the life along the shore was the design, the cottagers with their innocent and tranquil design, their tiny docks with the flagpole and the American flag floating against the white clouds in the blue sky, the little paths over the roots of the trees leading from camp to camp and the paths leading back to the outhouses and the can of lime for sprinkling, and at the souvenir counters at the store the miniature birchbark canoes and the postcards that showed things looking a little better than they looked. This was the American family at play, escaping the city heat, wondering whether the newcomers in the camp at the head of the cove were "common" or "nice," wondering whether it was true that the people who drove up for Sunday dinner at the farmhouse were turned away because there wasn't enough chicken.

It seemed to me, as I kept remembering all this, that those times and those summers had been infinitely precious and worth saving. There had been jollity and peace and goodness. The arriving (at the beginning of August) had been so big a business in itself, at the railway station the farm wagon drawn up, the first smell of the pine-laden air, the first glimpse of the smiling farmer, and the great importance of the trunks and your father's enormous authority in such matters, and the feel of the wagon under you for the long ten-mile haul, and at the top of the last long hill catching the first view of the lake after eleven months of not seeing this cherished body of water. The shouts and cries of the other campers when they saw you, and the trunks to be unpacked, to give up their rich burden. (Arriving was less exciting nowadays, when you sneaked up in your car and parked it under a tree near the camp and took out the bags and in five minutes it was all over, no fuss, no loud wonderful fuss about trunks.)

Peace and goodness and jollity. The only thing that was wrong now, really, was the sound of the place, an unfamiliar nervous sound of the outboard motors. This was the note that jarred, the one thing that would sometimes break the illusion and set the years moving. In those other summertimes all motors were inboard; and when they were at a little distance, the noise they made was a sedative, an ingredient of summer sleep. They were one-cylinder and two-cylinder engines, and some were make-and-break and some were jump-spark, but they all made a sleepy sound across the lake. The one-lungers throbbed and fluttered, and the twin-cylinder ones purred and purred, and that was a quiet sound, too. But now the campers all had outboards. In the daytime, in the hot mornings, these motors made a petulant, irritable sound; at night, in the still evening when the afterglow lit the water, they whined about one's ears like mosquitoes. My boy loved our rented outboard, and his great desire was to achieve single-handed mastery over it, and authority, and he soon learned the trick of choking it a little (but not too much), and the adjustment of the needle valve. Watching him I would remember the things you could do with the old one-cylinder engine with the heavy flywheel, how you could have it eating out of your hand if you got really close to it spiritually. Motorboats in those days didn't have clutches, and you would make a landing by shutting off the motor at the proper time and coasting in with a dead rudder. But there was a way of reversing them, if you learned the trick, by cutting the switch and putting it on again exactly on the final dying revolution of the flywheel, so that it would kick back against compression and begin reversing. Approaching a dock in a strong following breeze, it was difficult to slow up sufficiently by the ordinary coasting method, and if a boy felt he had complete mastery over his motor, he was tempted to keep it running beyond its time and then reverse it a few feet from the dock. It took a cool nerve, because if you threw the switch a twentieth of a second too soon you would catch the flywheel when it still had speed enough to go up past center, and the boat would leap ahead, charging bull-fashion at the dock.

We had a good week at the camp. The bass were biting well and the sun shone endlessly, day after day. We would be tired at night and lie down in the accumulated heat of the little bedrooms after the long hot day and the breeze would stir almost imperceptibly outside and the smell of the swamp drift in through the rusty screens. Sleep would come easily and in the morning the red squirrel would be on the roof, tapping out his gay routine. I kept remembering everything, lying in bed in the mornings—the small steamboat that had a long rounded stern like the lip of a Ubangi, and how quietly she ran on the moonlight sails, when the older boys played their mandolins and the girls sang and we ate doughnuts dipped in sugar, and how sweet the music was on the water in the shining night, and what it had felt like to think about girls then. After breakfast we would go up to the store and the things were in the same place—the minnows in a bottle, the plugs and spinners disarranged and pawed over by the youngsters from the boys' camp, the Fig Newtons and the Beeman's gum. Outside, the road was tarred and cars stood in front of the store. Inside, all was just as it had always been, except there was more Coca-Cola and not so much Moxie and root beer and birch beer and sarsaparilla. We would walk out with the bottle of pop apiece and sometimes the pop would backfire up our noses and hurt. We explored the streams, quietly, where the turtles slid off the sunny logs and dug their way into the soft bottom; and we lay on the town wharf and fed worms to the tame bass. Everywhere we went I had trouble making out which was I, the one walking at my side, the one walking in my pants.

One afternoon while we were there at that lake a thunderstorm came up. It was like the revival of an old melodrama that I had seen long ago with childish awe. The second-act climax of the drama of the electrical disturbance over a lake in America had not changed in any important respect. This was the big scene, still the big scene. The whole thing was so familiar, the first feeling of oppression and heat and a general air around camp of not wanting to go very far away. In mid-afternoon (it was all the same) a curious darkening of the sky, and a lull in everything that had made life tick; and then the way the boats suddenly swung the other way at their moorings with the coming of a breeze out of the new quarter, and the premonitory rumble. Then the kettle drum, then the snare, then the bass drum and cymbals, then crackling light against the dark, and the gods grinning and licking their chops in the hills. Afterward the calm, the rain steadily rustling in the calm lake, the return of light and hope and spirits, and the campers running out in joy and relief to go swimming in the rain, their bright cries perpetuating the deathless joke about how they were getting simply drenched, and the children screaming with delight at the new sensation of bathing in the rain, and the joke about getting drenched linking the generations in a strong indestructible chain. And the comedian who waded in carrying an umbrella.

When the others went swimming, my son said he was going in, too. He pulled his dripping trunks from the line where they had hung all through the shower and wrung them out. Languidly, and with no thought of going in, I watched him, his hard little body, skinny and bare, saw him wince slightly as he pulled up around his vitals the small, soggy, icy garment. As he buckled the swollen belt, suddenly my groin felt the chill of death.

GEORGE ORWELL

[1903–1950]

Shooting an Elephant

In Moulmein, in lower Burma, I was hated by large numbers of people—the only time in my life that I have been important enough for this to happen to me. I was sub-divisional police officer of the town, and in an aimless, petty kind of way anti-European feeling was very bitter. No one had the guts to raise a riot, but if a European woman went through the bazaars alone somebody would probably spit betel juice over her dress. As a police officer I was an obvious target and was baited whenever it seemed safe to do so. When a nimble Burman tripped me up on the football field and the referee (another Burman) looked the other way, the crowd yelled with hideous laughter. This happened more than once. In the end the sneering yellow faces of young men that met me everywhere, the insults hooted after me when I was at a safe distance, got badly on my nerves. The young Buddhist priests were the worst of all. There were several thousands of them in the town and none of them seemed to have anything to do except stand on street corners and jeer at Europeans.

All this was perplexing and upsetting. For at that time I had already made up my mind that imperialism was an evil thing and the sooner I chucked up my job and got out of it the better. Theoretically—and secretly, of course—I was all for the Burmese and all against their oppressors, the British. As for the job I was doing, I hated it more bitterly than I can perhaps make clear. In a job like that you see the dirty work of Empire at close quarters. The wretched prisoners huddling in the stinking cages of the lock-ups, the gray, cowed faces of the long-term convicts, the scarred buttocks of the men who had been flogged with bamboos—all these oppressed me with an intolerable sense of guilt. But I could get nothing into perspective. I was young and ill educated and I had had to think out my problems in the utter silence that is imposed on every Englishman in the East. I did not even know that the British Empire is dying, still less did I know that it is a great deal better than the younger empires that are going to supplant it. All I knew was that I was stuck between my hatred of the empire I served and my rage against the evil-spirited little beasts who tried to make my job impossible. With one part of my mind I thought of the British Raj as an unbreakable tyranny, as something clamped down, in *saecula saeculorum,* upon the will of prostrate peoples; with another part I thought that the greatest joy in the world would be to drive a bayonet into a Buddhist priest's guts. Feelings like these are the normal by-products of imperialism; ask any Anglo-Indian official, if you can catch him off duty.

One day something happened which in a roundabout way was enlightening. It was a tiny incident in itself, but it gave me a better glimpse than I had had before of the real nature of imperialism—the real motives for which despotic governments act. Early one morning the sub-inspector at a police station the other end of the town rang me up on the 'phone and said that an elephant was ravaging the bazaar. Would I please come and do something about it? I did not know what I could do, but I wanted to see what was happening and I got on to a pony and started out. I took my rifle, an old .44 Winchester and much too small to kill an elephant, but I thought the noise might be useful *in terrorem.* Various Burmans stopped me on the way and told me about the elephant's doings. It was not, of course, a wild elephant, but a tame one which had gone "must." It had been chained up, as tame elephants always are when their attack of "must" is due, but on the previous night it had broken its chain and escaped. Its mahout, the only person who could manage it when it was in that state, had set out in pursuit, but had taken the wrong direction and was now twelve hours' journey away, and in the morning the elephant had suddenly reappeared in the town. The Burmese population had no weapons and were quite helpless against it. It had already destroyed somebody's bamboo hut, killed a cow and raided some fruit-stalls and devoured the stock; also it had met the municipal rubbish van and, when the driver jumped out and took to his heels, had turned the van over and inflicted violences upon it.

The Burmese sub-inspector and some Indian constables were waiting for me in the quarter where the elephant had been seen. It was a very poor quarter, a labyrinth of squalid bamboo huts, thatched with palm-leaf, winding all over a steep hillside. I remember that it was a cloudy, stuffy morning at the beginning of the rains. We began questioning the people as to where the elephant had gone and, as usual, failed to get any definite information. That is invariably the case in the East; a story always sounds clear enough at a distance, but the nearer you get to the scene of events the vaguer it becomes. Some of the people said that the elephant had gone in one direction, some said that he had gone in another, some professed not even to have heard of any elephant. I had almost made up my mind that the whole story was a pack of lies, when we heard yells a little distance away. There was a loud, scandalized cry of "Go away, child! Go away this instant!" and an old woman with a switch in her hand came round the corner of a hut, violently shooing away a crowd of naked children. Some more women followed, clicking their tongues and exclaiming; evidently there was something that the children ought not to have seen. I rounded the hut and saw a man's dead body sprawling in the mud. He was an Indian, a black Dravidian coolie, almost naked, and he could not have been dead many minutes. The people said that the elephant had come suddenly upon him round the corner of the hut, caught him with its trunk, put its foot on his back and ground him into the earth. This was the rainy season and the ground was soft, and his face had scored a trench a foot deep and a couple of yards long. He was lying on his belly with arms crucified and head sharply twisted to one side. His face was coated with mud, the eyes wide open, the teeth bared and grinning with an expression of unendurable agony. (Never tell me, by the way, that the dead look peaceful. Most of the corpses I have seen looked devilish.) The friction of the great beast's foot had stripped the skin from his back as neatly as one skins a rabbit. As soon as I saw the dead man I sent an orderly to a friend's house nearby to borrow an elephant rifle. I had already sent back the pony, not wanting it to go mad with fright and throw me if it smelt the elephant.

The orderly came back in a few minutes with a rifle and five cartridges, and meanwhile some Burmans had arrived and told us that the elephant was in the paddy fields below, only a few hundred yards away. As I started forward practically the whole population of the quarter flocked out of the houses and followed me. They had seen the rifle and were all shouting excitedly that I was going to shoot the elephant. They had not shown much interest in the elephant when he was merely ravaging their homes, but it was different now that he was going to be shot. It was a bit of fun to them, as it would be to an English crowd; besides they wanted the meat. It made me vaguely uneasy. I had no intention of shooting the elephant—I had merely sent for the rifle to defend myself if necessary—and it is always unnerving to have a crowd following you. I marched down the hill, looking and feeling a fool, with the rifle over my shoulder and an ever-growing army of people jostling at my heels. At the bottom, when you got away from the huts, there was a metalled road and beyond that a miry waste of paddy fields a thousand yards across, not yet ploughed but soggy from the first rains and dotted with coarse grass. The elephant was standing eight yards from the road, his left side toward us. He took not the slightest notice of the crowd's approach. He was tearing up bunches of grass, beating them against his knees to clean them, and stuffing them into his mouth.

I had halted on the road. As soon as I saw the elephant I knew with perfect certainty that I ought not to shoot him. It is a serious matter to shoot a working elephant—it is comparable to destroying a huge and costly piece of machinery—and obviously one ought not to do it if it can possibly be avoided. And at that distance, peacefully eating, the elephant looked no more dangerous than a cow. I thought then and I think now that his attack of "must" was already passing off; in which case he would merely wander harmlessly about until the mahout came back and caught him. Moreover, I did not in the least want to shoot him. I decided that I would watch him for a little while to make sure that he did not turn savage again, and then go home.

But at that moment I glanced round at the crowd that had followed me. It was an immense crowd, two thousand at the least and growing every minute. It blocked the road for a long distance on either side. I looked at the sea of yellow faces above the garish clothes—faces all happy and excited over this bit of fun, all certain that the elephant was going to be shot. They were watching me as they would watch a conjurer about to perform a trick. They did not like me, but with the magical rifle in my hands I was momentarily worth watching. And suddenly I realized that I should have to shoot the elephant after all. The people expected it of me and I had got to do it; I could feel their two thousand wills pressing me forward, irresistibly. And it was at this moment, as I stood there with the rifle in my hands, that I first grasped the hollowness, the futility of the white man's dominion in the East. Here was I, the white man with his gun, standing in front of the unarmed native crowd—seemingly the leading actor of the piece; but in reality I was only an absurd puppet pushed to and fro by the will of those yellow faces behind. I perceived in this moment that when the white man turns tyrant it is his own freedom that he destroys. He becomes a sort of hollow, posing dummy, the conventionalized figure of a sahib. For it is the condition of his rule that he shall spend his life in trying to impress the "natives," and so in every crisis he has got to do what the "natives" expect of him. He wears a mask, and his face grows to fit it. I had got to shoot the elephant. I had committed myself to doing it when I sent for the rifle. A sahib has got to act like a sahib; he has got to appear resolute, to know his own mind and do definite things. To come all that way, rifle in hand, with two thousand people marching at my heels, and then to trail feebly away, having done nothing—no, that was impossible. The crowd would laugh at me. And my whole life, every white man's life in the East, was one long struggle not to be laughed at.

But I did not want to shoot the elephant. I watched him beating his bunch of grass against his knees with that preoccupied grandmotherly air that elephants have. It seemed to me that it would be murder to shoot him. At that age I was not squeamish about killing animals, but I had never shot an elephant and never wanted to. (Somehow it always seems worse to kill a *large* animal.) Besides, there was the beast's owner to be considered. Alive, the elephant was worth at least a hundred pounds; dead, he would only be worth the value of his tusks, five pounds, possibly. But I had got to act quickly. I turned to some experienced-looking Burmans who had been there when we arrived, and asked them how the elephant had been behaving. They all said the same thing: he took no notice of you if you left him alone, but he might charge if you went too close to him.

It was perfectly clear to me what I ought to do. I ought to walk up to within, say, twenty-five yards of the elephant and test his behavior. If he charged, I could shoot; if he took no notice of me, it would be safe to leave him until the mahout came back. But also I knew that I was going to do no such thing. I was a poor shot with a rifle and the ground was soft mud into which one would sink at every step. If the elephant charged and I missed him, I should have about as much chance as a toad under a steam-roller. But even then I was not thinking particularly of my own skin, only of the watchful yellow faces behind. For at that moment, with the crowd watching me, I was not afraid in the ordinary sense, as I would have been if I had been alone. A white man mustn't be frightened in front of "natives"; and so, in general, he isn't frightened. The sole thought in my mind was that if anything went wrong those two thousand Burmans would see me pursued, caught, trampled on, and reduced to a grinning corpse like that Indian up the hill. And if that happened it was quite probable that some of them would laugh. That would never do. There was only one alternative. I shoved the cartridges into the magazine and lay down on the road to get a better aim.

The crowd grew very still, and a deep, low, happy sigh, as of people who see the theater curtain go up at last, breathed from innumerable throats. They were going to have their bit of fun after all. The rifle was a beautiful German thing with cross-hair sights. I did not then know that in shooting an elephant one would shoot to cut an imaginary bar running from ear-hole to ear-hole. I ought, therefore, as the elephant was sideways on, to have aimed straight at his ear-hole; actually I aimed several inches in front of this, thinking the brain would be further forward.

When I pulled the trigger I did not hear the bang or feel the kick—one never does when a shot goes home—but I heard the devilish roar of glee that went up from the crowd. In that instant, in too short a time, one would have thought, even for the bullet to get there, a mysterious, terrible change had come over the elephant. He neither stirred nor fell, but every line of his body had altered. He looked suddenly stricken, shrunken, immensely old, as though the frightful impact of the bullet had paralyzed him without knocking him down. At last, after what seemed a long time —it might have been five seconds, I dare say—he sagged flabbily to his knees. His mouth slobbered. An enormous senility seemed to have settled upon him. One could have imagined him thousands of years old. I fired again into the same spot. At the second shot he did not collapse but climbed with desperate slowness to his feet and stood weakly upright, with legs sagging and head drooping. I fired a third time. That was the shot that did for him. You could see the agony of it jolt his whole body and knock the last remnant of strength from his legs. But in falling he seemed for a moment to rise, for as his hind legs collapsed beneath him he seemed to tower upward like a huge rock toppling, his trunk reaching skyward like a tree. He trumpeted, for the first and only time. And then down he came, his belly toward me, with a crash that seemed to shake the ground even where I lay.

I got up. The Burmans were already racing past me across the mud. It was obvious that the elephant would never rise again, but he was not dead. He was breathing very rhythmically with long rattling gasps, his great mound of a side painfully rising and falling. His mouth was wide open—I could see far down into caverns of pale pink throat. I waited a long time for him to die, but his breathing did not weaken. Finally I fired my two remaining shots into the spot where I thought his heart must be. The thick blood welled out of him like red velvet, but still he did not die. His body did not even jerk when the shots hit him, the tortured breathing continued without a pause. He was dying, very slowly and in great agony, but in some world remote from me where not even a bullet could damage him further. I felt that I had got to put an end to that dreadful noise. It seemed dreadful to see the great beast lying there, powerless to move and yet powerless to die, and not even to be able to finish him. I sent back for my small rifle and poured shot after shot into his heart and down his throat. They seemed to make no impression. The tortured gasps continued as steadily as the ticking of a clock.

In the end I could not stand it any longer and went away. I heard later that it took him half an hour to die. Burmans were bringing dahs and baskets even before I left, and I was told they had stripped his body almost to the bones by the afternoon.

Afterward, of course, there were endless discussions about the shooting of the elephant. The owner was furious, but he was only an Indian and could do nothing. Besides, legally I had done the right thing, for a mad elephant has to be killed, like a mad dog, if its owner fails to control it. Among the Europeans opinion was divided. The older men said I was right, the younger men said it was a damn shame to shoot an elephant for killing a coolie, because an elephant was worth more than any damn Coringhee coolie. And afterward I was very glad that the coolie had been killed; it put me legally in the right and it gave me a sufficient pretext for shooting the elephant. I often wondered whether any of the others grasped that I had done it solely to avoid looking a fool.

LOREN EISELEY

[1907–1977]

The Judgment of the Birds

It is a commonplace of all religious thought, even the most primitive, that the man seeking visions and insight must go apart from his fellows and live for a time in the wilderness. If he is of the proper sort, he will return with a message. It may not be a message from the god he set out to seek, but even if he has failed in that particular, he will have had a vision or seen a marvel, and these are always worth listening to and thinking about.

The world, I have come to believe, is a very queer place, but we have been part of this queerness for so long that we tend to take it for granted. We rush to and fro like Mad Hatters upon our peculiar errands, all the time imagining our surroundings to be dull and ourselves quite ordinary creatures. Actually, there is nothing in the world to encourage this idea, but such is the mind of man, and this is why he finds it necessary from time to time to send emissaries into the wilderness in the hope of learning of great events, or plans in store for him, that will resuscitate his waning taste for life. His great news services, his worldwide radio network, he knows with a last remnant of healthy distrust will be of no use to him in this matter. No miracle can withstand a radio broadcast, and it is certain that it would be no miracle if it could. One must seek, then, what only the solitary approach can give—a natural revelation.

Let it be understood that I am not the sort of man to whom is entrusted direct knowledge of great events or prophecies. A naturalist, however, spends much of his life alone, and my life is no exception. Even in New York City there are patches of wilderness, and a man by himself is bound to undergo certain experiences falling into the class of which I speak. I set mine down, therefore: a matter of pigeons, a flight of chemicals, and a judgment of birds, in the hope that they will come to the eye of those who have retained a true taste for the marvelous, and who are capable of discerning in the flow of ordinary events the point at which the mundane world gives way to quite another dimension.

New York is not, on the whole, the best place to enjoy the downright miraculous nature of the planet. There are, I do not doubt, many remarkable stories to be heard there and many strange sights to be seen, but to grasp a marvel fully it must be savored from all aspects. This cannot be done while one is being jostled and hustled along a crowded street. Nevertheless, in any city there are true wildernesses where a man can be alone. It can happen in a hotel room, or on the high roofs at dawn.

One night on the twentieth floor of a midtown hotel I awoke in the dark and grew restless. On an impulse I climbed upon the broad old-fashioned window sill, opened the curtains, and peered out. It was the hour just before dawn, the hour when men sigh in their sleep or, if awake, strive to focus their wavering eyesight upon a world emerging from the shadows. I leaned out sleepily through the open window. I had expected depths, but not the sight I saw.

I found I was looking down from that great height into a series of curious cupolas or lofts that I could just barely make out in the darkness. As I looked, the outlines of these lofts became more distinct because the light was being reflected from the wings of pigeons who, in utter silence, were beginning to float outward upon the city. In and out through the open slits in the cupolas passed the white-winged birds on their mysterious errands. At this hour the city was theirs, and quietly, without the brush of a single wing tip against stone in that high, eerie place, they were taking over the spires of Manhattan. They were pouring upward in a light that was not yet perceptible to human eyes, while far down in the black darkness of the alleys it was still midnight.

As I crouched half-asleep across the sill, I had a moment's illusion that the world had changed in the night, as in some immense snowfall, and that, if I were to leave, it would have to be as these other inhabitants were doing, by the window. I should have to launch out into that great bottomless void with the simple confidence of young birds reared high up there among the familiar chimney pots and interposed horrors of the abyss.

I leaned farther out. To and fro went the white wings, to and fro. There were no sounds from any of them. They knew man was asleep and this light for a little while was theirs. Or perhaps I had only dreamed about man in this city of wings—which he could surely never have built. Perhaps I, myself, was one of these birds dreaming unpleasantly a moment of old dangers far below as I teetered on a window ledge.

Around and around went the wings. It needed only a little courage, only a little shove from the window ledge, to enter that city of light. The muscles of my hands were already making little premonitory lunges. I wanted to enter that city and go away over the roofs in the first dawn. I wanted to enter it so badly that I drew back carefully into the room and opened the hall door. I found my coat on the chair, and it slowly became clear to me that there was a way down through the floors, that I was, after all, only a man.

I dressed then and went back to my own kind, and I have been rather more than usually careful ever since not to look into the city of light. I had seen, just once, man's greatest creation from a strange inverted angle, and it was not really his at all. I will never forget how those wings went round and round, and how, by the merest pressure of the fingers and a feeling for air, one might go away over the roofs. It is a knowledge, however, that is better kept to oneself. I think of it sometimes in such a way that the wings, beginning far down in the black depths of the mind, begin to rise and whirl till all the mind is lit by their spinning, and there is a sense of things passing away, but lightly, as a wing might veer over an obstacle.

To see from an inverted angle, however, is not a gift allotted merely to the human imagination. I have come to suspect that within their degree it is sensed by animals, though perhaps as rarely as among men. The time has to be right; one has to be, by chance or intention, upon the border of two worlds. And sometimes these two borders may shift or interpenetrate and one sees the miraculous.

I once saw this happen to a crow.

This crow lives near my house, and though I have never injured him, he takes good care to stay up in the very highest trees and, in general, to avoid humanity. His world begins at about the limit of my eyesight.

On the particular morning when this episode occurred, the whole countryside was buried in one of the thickest fogs in years. The ceiling was absolutely zero. All planes were grounded, and even a pedestrian could hardly see his outstretched hand before him.

I was groping across a field in the general direction of the railroad station, following a dimly outlined path. Suddenly out of the fog, at about the level of my eyes, and so closely that I flinched, there flashed a pair of immense black wings and a huge beak. The whole bird rushed over my head with a frantic cawing outcry of such hideous terror as I have never heard in a crow's voice before and never expect to hear again.

He was lost and startled, I thought, as I recovered my poise. He ought not to have flown out in this fog. He'd knock his silly brains out.

All afternoon that great awkward cry rang in my head. Merely being lost in a fog seemed scarcely to account for it—especially in a tough, intelligent old bandit such as I knew that particular crow to be. I even looked once in the mirror to see what it might be about me that had so revolted him that he had cried out in protest to the very stones.

Finally, as I worked my way homeward along the path, the solution came to me. It should have been clear before. The borders of our worlds had shifted. It was the fog that had done it. That crow, and I knew him well, never under normal circumstances flew low near men. He had been lost all right, but it was more than that. He had thought he was high up, and when he encountered me looming gigantically through the fog, he had perceived a ghastly and, to the crow mind, unnatural sight. He had seen a man walking on air, desecrating the very heart of the crow kingdom, a harbinger of the most profound evil a crow mind could conceive of—air-walking men. The encounter, he must have thought, had taken place a hundred feet over the roofs.

He caws now when he sees me leaving for the station in the morning, and I fancy that in that note I catch the uncertainty of a mind that has come to know things are not always what they seem. He has seen a marvel in his heights of air and is no longer as other crows. He has experienced the human world from an unlikely perspective. He and I share a viewpoint in common: our worlds have interpenetrated, and we both have faith in the miraculous.

It is a faith that in my own case has been augmented by two remarkable sights. I once saw some very odd chemicals fly across a waste so dead it might have been upon the moon, and once, by an even more fantastic piece of luck, I was present when a group of birds passed a judgment upon life.

On the maps of the old voyageurs it is called *Mauvaises Terres,* the evil lands, and, slurred a little with the passage through many minds, it has come down to us anglicized as the badlands. The soft shuffle of moccasins has passed through its canyons on the grim business of war and flight, but the last of those slight disturbances of immemorial silences died out almost a century ago. The land, if one can call it a land, is a waste as lifeless as that valley in which lie the kings of Egypt. Like the Valley of the Kings, it is a mausoleum, a place of dry bones in what once was a place of life. Now it has silences as deep as those in the moon's airless chasms.

Nothing grows among its pinnacles; there is no shade except under great toadstools of sandstone whose bases have been eaten to the shape of wine glasses by the wind. Everything is flaking, cracking, disintegrating, wearing away in the long, imperceptible weather of time. The ash of ancient volcanic outbursts still sterilizes its soil, and its colors in that waste are the colors that flame in the lonely sunsets on dead planets. Men come there but rarely, and for one purpose only, the collection of bones.

It was a late hour on a cold, wind-bitten autumn day when I climbed a great hill spined like a dinosaur's back and tried to take my bearings. The tumbled waste fell away in waves in all directions. Blue air was darkening into purple along the bases of the hills. I shifted my knapsack, heavy with the petrified bones of long-vanished creatures, and studied my compass. I wanted to be out of there by nightfall, and already the sun was going sullenly down in the west.

It was then that I saw the flight coming on. It was moving like a little close-knit body of black specks that danced and darted and closed again. It was pouring from the north and heading toward me with the undeviating relentlessness of a compass needle. It streamed through the shadows rising out of monstrous gorges. It rushed over towering pinnacles in the red light of the sun or momentarily sank from sight within their shade. Across that desert of eroding clay and wind-worn stone they came with a faint wild twittering that filled all the air about me as those tiny living bullets hurtled past into the night.

It may not strike you as a marvel. It would not, perhaps, unless you stood in the middle of a dead world at sunset, but that was where I stood. Fifty million years lay under my feet, fifty million years of bellowing monsters moving in a green world now gone so utterly that its very light was traveling on the farther edge of space. The chemicals of all that vanished age lay about me in the ground. Around me still lay the shearing molars of dead titanotheres, the delicate sabers of soft-stepping cats, the hollow sockets that had held the eyes of many a strange, outmoded beast. Those eyes had looked out upon a world as real as ours; dark, savage brains had roamed and roared their challenges into the steaming night.

Now they were still here, or, put it as you will, the chemicals that made them were here about me in the ground. The carbon that had driven them ran blackly in the eroding stone. The stain of iron was in the clays. The iron did not remember the blood it had once moved within, the phosphorus had forgot the savage brain. The little individual moment had ebbed from all those strange combinations of chemicals as it would ebb from our living bodies into the sinks and runnels of oncoming time.

I had lifted up a fistful of that ground. I held it while that wild flight of south-bound warblers hurtled over me into the oncoming dark. There went phosphorus, there went iron, there went carbon, there beat the calcium in those hurrying wings. Alone on a dead planet I watched that incredible miracle speeding past. It ran by some true compass over field and waste land. It cried its individual ecstasies into the air until the gullies rang. It swerved like a single body, it knew itself, and, lonely, it bunched close in the racing darkness, its individual entities feeling about them the rising night. And so, crying to each other their identity, they passed away out of my view.

I dropped my fistful of earth. I heard it roll inanimate back into the gully at the base of the hill: iron, carbon, the chemicals of life. Like men from those wild tribes who had haunted these hills before me seeking visions, I made my sign to the great darkness. It was not a mocking sign, and I was not mocked. As I walked into my camp late that night, one man, rousing from his blankets beside the fire, asked sleepily, "What did you see?"

"I think, a miracle," I said softly, but I said it to myself. Behind me that vast waste began to glow under the rising moon.

I have said that I saw a judgment upon life, and that it was not passed by men. Those who stare at birds in cages or who test minds by their closeness to our own may not care for it. It comes from far away out of my past, in a place of pouring waters and green leaves. I shall never see an episode like it again if I live to be a hundred, nor do I think that one man in a million has ever seen it, because man is an intruder into such silences. The light must be right, and the observer must remain unseen. No man sets up such an experiment. What he sees, he sees by chance.

You may put it that I had come over a mountain, that I had slogged through fern and pine needles for half a long day, and that on the edge of a little glade with one long, crooked branch extending across it, I had sat down to rest with my back against a stump. Through accident I was concealed from the glade, although I could see into it perfectly.

The sun was warm there, and the murmurs of forest life blurred softly away into my sleep. When I awoke, dimly aware of some commotion and outcry in the clearing, the light was slanting down through the pines in such a way that the glade was lit like some vast cathedral. I could see the dust motes of wood pollen in the long shaft of light, and there on the extended branch sat an enormous raven with a red and squirming nestling in his beak.

The sound that awoke me was the outraged cries of the nestling's parents, who flew helplessly in circles about the clearing. The sleek black monster was indifferent to them. He gulped, whetted his beak on the dead branch a moment, and sat still. Up to that point the little tragedy had followed the usual pattern. But suddenly, out of all that area of woodland, a soft sound of complaint began to rise. Into the glade fluttered small birds of half a dozen varieties drawn by the anguished outcries of the tiny parents.

No one dared to attack the raven. But they cried there in some instinctive common misery, the bereaved and the unbereaved. The glade filled with their soft rustling and their cries. They fluttered as though to point their wings at the murderer. There was a dim intangible ethic he had violated, that they knew. He was a bird of death.

And he, the murderer, the black bird at the heart of life, sat on there glistening in the common light, formidable, unmoving, unperturbed, untouchable.

The sighing died. It was then I saw the judgment. It was the judgment of life against death. I will never see it again so forcefully presented. I will never hear it again in notes so tragically prolonged. For in the midst of protest, they forgot the violence. There, in that clearing, the crystal note of a song sparrow lifted hesitantly in the hush. And finally, after painful fluttering, another took the song, and then another, the song passing from one bird to another, doubtfully at first, as though some evil thing were being slowly forgotten. Till suddenly they took heart and sang from many throats joyously together as birds are known to sing. They sang because life is sweet and sunlight beautiful. They sang under the brooding shadow of the raven. In simple truth they had forgotten the raven, for they were the singers of life, and not of death.

I was not of that airy company. My limbs were the heavy limbs of an earthbound creature who could climb mountains, even the mountains of the mind, only by a great effort of will. I knew I had seen a marvel and observed a judgment, but the mind which was my human endowment was sure to question it and to be at me day by day with its heresies until I grew to doubt the meaning of what I had seen. Eventually darkness and subtleties would ring me round once more.

And so it proved until, on the top of a stepladder, I made one more observation upon life. It was cold that autumn evening, and, standing under a suburban street light in a spate of leaves and beginning snow, I was suddenly conscious of some huge and hairy shadows dancing over the pavement. They seemed attached to an odd, globular shape that was magnified above me. There was no mistaking it. I was standing under the shadow of an orb-weaving spider. Gigantically projected against the street, she was about her spinning when everything was going underground. Even her cables were magnified upon the sidewalk and already I was half-entangled in their shadows.

"Good Lord," I thought, "she has found herself a kind of minor sun and is going to upset the course of nature."

I procured a ladder from my yard and climbed up to inspect the situation. There she was, the universe running down around her, warmly arranged among her guy ropes attached to the lamp supports—a great black and yellow embodiment of the life force, not giving up to either frost or stepladders. She ignored me and went on tightening and improving her web.

I stood over her on the ladder, a faint snow touching my cheeks, and surveyed her universe. There were a couple of iridescent green beetle cases turning slowly on a loose strand of web, a fragment of luminescent eye from a moth's wing and a large indeterminable object, perhaps a cicada, that had struggled and been wrapped in silk. There were also little bits and slivers, little red and blue flashes from the scales of anonymous wings that had crashed there.

Some days, I thought, they will be dull and gray and the shine will be out of them; then the dew will polish them again and drops hang on the silk until everything is gleaming and turning in the light. It is like a mind, really, where everything changes but remains, and in the end you have these eaten-out bits of experience like beetle wings.

I stood over her a moment longer, comprehending somewhat reluctantly that her adventure against the great blind forces of winter, her seizure of this warming globe of light, would come to nothing and was hopeless. Nevertheless it brought the birds back into my mind, and that faraway song which had traveled with growing strength around a forest clearing years ago—a kind of heroism, a world where even a spider refuses to lie down and die if a rope can still be spun on to a star. Maybe man himself will fight like this in the end, I thought, slowly realizing that the web and its threatening yellow occupant had been added to some luminous store of experience, shining for a moment in the fogbound reaches of my brain.

The mind, it came to me as I slowly descended the ladder, is a very remarkable thing; it has gotten itself a kind of courage by looking at a spider in a street lamp. Here was something that ought to be passed on to those who will fight our final freezing battle with the void. I thought of setting it down carefully as a message to the future: *In the days of the frost seek a minor sun.*

But as I hesitated, it became plain that something was wrong. The marvel was escaping—a sense of bigness beyond man's power to grasp, the essence of life in its great dealings with the universe. It was better, I decided, for the emissaries returning from the wilderness, even if they were merely descending from a stepladder, to record their marvel, not to define its meaning. In that way it would go echoing on through the minds of men, each grasping at that beyond out of which the miracles emerge, and which, once defined, ceases to satisfy the human need for symbols.

In the end I merely made a mental note: One specimen of Epeira observed building a web in a street light. Late autumn and cold for spiders. Cold for men, too. I shivered and left the lamp glowing there in my mind. The last I saw of Epeira she was hauling steadily on a cable. I stepped carefully over her shadow as I walked away.

JAMES BALDWIN

[*b. 1924*]

Notes of a Native Son

I

On the 29th of July, in 1943, my father died. On the same day, a few hours later, his last child was born. Over a month before this, while all our energies were concentrated in waiting for these events, there had been, in Detroit, one of the bloodiest race riots of the century. A few hours after my father's funeral, while he lay in state in the undertaker's chapel, a race riot broke out in Harlem. On the morning of the 3rd of August, we drove my father to the graveyard through a wilderness of smashed plate glass.

The day of my father's funeral had also been my nineteenth birthday. As we drove him to the graveyard, the spoils of injustice, anarchy, discontent, and hatred were all around us. It seemed to me that God himself had devised, to mark my father's end, the most sustained and brutally dissonant of codas. And it seemed to me, too, that the violence which rose all about us as my father left the world had been devised as a corrective for the pride of his eldest son. I had declined to believe in that apocalypse which had been central to my father's vision; very well, life seemed to be saying, here is something that will certainly pass for an apocalypse until the real thing comes along. I had inclined to be contemptuous of my father for the conditions of his life, for the conditions of our lives. When his life had ended I began to wonder about that life and also, in a new way, to be apprehensive about my own.

I had not known my father very well. We had got on badly, partly because we shared, in our different fashions, the vice of stubborn pride. When he was dead I realized that I had hardly ever spoken to him. When he had been dead a long time I began to wish I had. It seems to be typical of life in America, where opportunities, real and fancied, are thicker than anywhere else on the globe, that the second generation has no time to talk to the first. No one, including my father, seems to have known exactly how old he was, but his mother had been born during slavery. He was of the first generation of free men. He, along with thousands of other Negroes, came North after 1919 and I was part of that generation which had never seen the landscape of what Negroes sometimes call the Old Country.

He had been born in New Orleans and had been a quite young man there during the time that Louis Armstrong, a boy, was running errands for the dives and honky-tonks of what was always presented to me as one of the most wicked of cities—to this day, whenever I think of New Orleans, I also helplessly think of Sodom and Gomorrah. My father never mentioned Louis Armstrong, except to forbid us to play his records; but there was a picture of him on our wall for a long time. One of my father's strong-willed female relatives had placed it there and forbade my father to take it down. He never did, but he eventually maneuvered her out of the house and when, some years later, she was in trouble and near death, he refused to do anything to help her.

He was, I think, very handsome. I gather this from photographs and from my own memories of him, dressed in his Sunday best and on his way to preach a sermon somewhere, when I was little. Handsome, proud, and ingrown, "like a toe-nail," somebody said. But he looked to me, as I grew older, like pictures I had seen of African tribal chieftains: he really should have been naked, with war-paint on and barbaric mementos, standing among spears. He could be chilling in the pulpit and indescribably cruel in his personal life and he was certainly the most bitter man I have ever met; yet it must be said that there was something else in him, buried in him, which lent him his tremendous power and, even, a rather crushing charm. It had something to do with his blackness, I think—he was very black—with his blackness and his beauty, and with the fact that he knew that he was black but did not know that he was beautiful. He claimed to be proud of his blackness but it had also been the cause of much humiliation and it had fixed bleak boundaries to his life. He was not a young man when we were growing up and he had already suffered many kinds of ruin; in his outrageously demanding and protective way he loved his children, who were black like him and menaced, like him; and all these things sometimes showed in his face when he tried, never to my knowledge with any success, to establish contact with any of us. When he took one of his children on his knee to play, the child always became fretful and began to cry; when he tried to help one of us with our homework the absolutely unabating tension which emanated from him caused our minds and our tongues to become paralyzed, so that he, scarcely knowing why, flew into a rage and the child, not knowing why, was punished. If it ever entered his head to bring a surprise home for his children, it was, almost unfailingly, the wrong surprise and even the big watermelons he often brought home on his back in the summertime led to the most appalling scenes. I do not remember, in all those years, that one of his children was ever glad to see him come home. From what I was able to gather of his early life, it seemed that this inability to establish contact with other people had always marked him and had been one of the things which had driven him out of New Orleans. There was something in him, therefore, groping and tentative, which was never expressed and which was buried with him. One saw it most clearly when he was facing new people and hoping to impress them. But he never did, not for long. We went from church to smaller and more improbable church, he found himself in less and less demand as a minister, and by the time he died none of his friends had come to see him for a long time. He had lived and died in an intolerable bitterness of spirit and it frightened me, as we drove him to the graveyard through those unquiet, ruined streets, to see how powerful and overflowing this bitterness could be and to realize that this bitterness now was mine.

When he died I had been away from home for a little over a year. In that year I had had time to become aware of the meaning of all my father's bitter warnings, had discovered the secret of his proudly pursed lips and rigid carriage: I had discovered the weight of white people in the world. I saw that this had been for my ancestors and now would be for me an awful thing to live with and that the bitterness which had helped to kill my father could also kill me.

He had been ill a long time—in the mind, as we now realized, reliving instances of his fantastic intransigence in the new light of his affliction and endeavoring to feel a sorrow for him which never, quite, came true. We had not known that he was being eaten up by paranoia, and the discovery that his cruelty, to our bodies and our minds, had been one of the symptoms of his illness was not, then, enough to enable us to forgive him. The younger children felt, quite simply, relief that he would not be coming home anymore. My mother's observation that it was he, after all, who had kept them alive all these years meant nothing because the problems of keeping children alive are not real for children. The older children felt, with my father gone, that they could invite their friends to the house without fear that their friends would be insulted or, as had sometimes happened with me, being told that their friends were in league with the devil and intended to rob our family of everything we owned. (I didn't fail to wonder, and it made me hate him, what on earth we owned that anybody else would want.)

His illness was beyond all hope of healing before anyone realized that he was ill. He had always been so strange and had lived, like a prophet, in such unimaginably close communion with the Lord that his long silences which were punctuated by moans and hallelujahs and snatches of old songs while he sat at the living-room window never seemed odd to us. It was not until he refused to eat because, he said, his family was trying to poison him that my mother was forced to accept as a fact what had, until then, been only an unwilling suspicion. When he was committed, it was discovered that he had tuberculosis and, as it turned out, the disease of his mind allowed the disease of his body to destroy him. For the doctors could not force him to eat, either, and, though he was fed intravenously, it was clear from the beginning that there was no hope for him.

In my mind's eye I could see him, sitting at the window, locked up in his terrors; hating and fearing every living soul including his children who had betrayed him, too, by reaching towards the world which had despised him. There were nine of us. I began to wonder what it could have felt like for such a man to have had nine children whom he could barely feed. He used to make little jokes about our poverty, which never, of course, seemed very funny to us; they could not have seemed very funny to him, either, or else our all too feeble response to them would never have caused such rages. He spent great energy and achieved, to our chagrin, no small amount of success in keeping us away from the people who surrounded us, people who had all-night rent parties to which we listened when we should have been sleeping, people who cursed and drank and flashed razor blades on Lenox Avenue. He could not understand why, if they had so much energy to spare, they could not use it to make their lives better. He treated almost everybody on our block with a most uncharitable asperity and neither they, nor, of course, their children were slow to reciprocate.

The only white people who came to our house were welfare workers and bill collectors. It was almost always my mother who dealt with them, for my father's temper, which was at the mercy of his pride, was never to be trusted. It was clear that he felt their very presence in his home to be a violation: this was conveyed by his carriage, almost ludicrously stiff, and by his voice, harsh and vindictively polite. When I was around nine or ten I wrote a play which was directed by a young, white schoolteacher, a woman, who then took an interest in me, and gave me books to read and, in order to corroborate my theatrical bent, decided to take me to see what she somewhat tactlessly referred to as "real" plays. Theatergoing was forbidden in our house, but, with the really cruel intuitiveness of a child, I suspected that the color of this woman's skin would carry the day for me. When, at school, she suggested taking me to the theater, I did not, as I might have done if she had been a Negro, find a way of discouraging her, but agreed that she should pick me up at my house one evening. I then, very cleverly, left all the rest to my mother, who suggested to my father, as I knew she would, that it would not be very nice to let such a kind woman make the trip for nothing. Also, since it was a schoolteacher, I imagine that my mother countered the idea of sin with the idea of "education," which word, even with my father, carried a kind of bitter weight.

Before the teacher came my father took me aside to ask *why* she was coming, what *interest* she could possibly have in our house, in a boy like me. I said I didn't know but I, too, suggested that it had something to do with education. And I understood that my father was waiting for me to say something—I didn't quite know what; perhaps that I wanted his protection against this teacher and her "education." I said none of these things and the teacher came and we went out. It was clear, during the brief interview in our living room, that my father was agreeing very much against his will and that he would have refused permission if he had dared. The fact that he did not dare caused me to despise him: I had no way of knowing that he was facing in that living room a wholly unprecedented and frightening situation.

Later, when my father had been laid off from his job, this woman became very important to us. She was really a very sweet and generous woman and went to a great deal of trouble to be of help to us, particularly during one awful winter. My mother called her by the highest name she knew. She said she was a "christian." My father could scarcely disagree but during the four or five years of our relatively close association he never trusted her and was always trying to surprise in her open, Midwestern face the genuine, cunningly hidden, and hideous motivation. In later years, particularly when it began to be clear that this "education" of mine was going to lead me to perdition, he became more explicit and warned me that my white friends in high school were not really my friends and that I would see, when I was older, how white people would do anything to keep a Negro down. Some of them could be nice, he admitted, but none of them were to be trusted and most of them were not even nice. The best thing was to have as little to do with them as possible. I did not feel this way and I was certain, in my innocence, that I never would.

But the year which preceded my father's death had made a great change in my life. I had been living in New Jersey, working in defense plants, working and living among southerners, white and black. I knew about the south, of course, and about how southerners treated Negroes and how they expected them to behave, but it had never entered my mind that anyone would look at me and expect *me* to behave that way. I learned in New Jersey that to be a Negro meant, precisely, that one was never looked at but was simply at the mercy of the reflexes the color of one's skin caused in other people. I acted in New Jersey as I had always acted, that is as though I thought a great deal of myself—I had to *act* that way—with results that were, simply, unbelievable. I had scarcely arrived before I had earned the enmity, which was extraordinarily ingenious, of all my superiors and nearly all my co-workers. In the beginning, to make matters worse, I simply did not know what was happening. I did not know what I had done, and I shortly began to wonder what *anyone* could possibly do, to bring about such unanimous, active, and unbearably vocal hostility. I knew about jim-crow but I had never experienced it. I went to the same self-service restaurant three times and stood with all the Princeton boys before the counter, waiting for a hamburger and coffee; it was always an extraordinarily long time before anything was set before me; but it was not until the fourth visit that I learned that, in fact, nothing had ever been set before me: I had simply picked something up. Negroes were not served there, I was told, and they had been waiting for me to realize that I was always the only Negro present. Once I was told this, I determined to go there all the time. But now they were ready for me and, though some dreadful scenes were subsequently enacted in that restaurant, I never ate there again.

It was the same story all over New Jersey, in bars, bowling alleys, diners, places to live. I was always being forced to leave, silently, or with mutual imprecations. I very shortly became notorious and children giggled behind me when I passed and their elders whispered or shouted—they really believed that I was mad. And it did begin to work on my mind, of course; I began to be afraid to go anywhere and to compensate for this I went places to which I really should not have gone and where, God knows, I had no desire to be. My reputation in town naturally enhanced my reputation at work and my working day became one long series of acrobatics designed to keep me out of trouble. I cannot say that these acrobatics succeeded. It began to seem that the machinery of the organization I worked for was turning over, day and night, with but one aim: to eject me. I was fired once, and contrived, with the aid of a friend from New York, to get back on the payroll; was fired again, and bounced back again. It took a while to fire me for the third time, but the third time took. There were no loopholes anywhere. There was not even any way of getting back inside the gates.

That year in New Jersey lives in my mind as though it were the year during which, having an unsuspected predilection for it, I first contracted some dread, chronic disease, the unfailing symptom of which is a kind of blind fever, a pounding in the skull and fire in the bowels. Once this disease is contracted, one can never be really carefree again, for the fever, without an instant's warning, can recur at any moment. It can wreck more important things than race relations. There is not a Negro alive who does not have this rage in his blood—one has the choice, merely, of living with it consciously or surrendering to it. As for me, this fever has recurred in me, and does, and will until the day I die.

My last night in New Jersey, a white friend from New York took me to the nearest big town, Trenton, to go to the movies and have a few drinks. As it turned out, he also saved me from, at the very least, a violent whipping. Almost every detail of that night stands out very clearly in my memory. I even remember the name of the movie we saw because its title impressed me as being so patly ironical. It was a movie about the German occupation of France, starring Maureen O'Hara and Charles Laughton and called *This Land Is Mine*. I remember the name of the diner we walked into when the movie ended: it was the "American Diner." When we walked in the counterman asked what we wanted and I remember answering with the casual sharpness which had become my habit: "We want a hamburger and a cup of coffee, what do you think we want?" I do not know why, after a year of such rebuffs, I so completely failed to anticipate his answer, which was, of course, "We don't serve Negroes here." This reply failed to discompose me, at least for the moment. I made some sardonic comment about the name of the diner and we walked out into the streets.

This was the time of what was called the "brown-out," when the lights in all American cities were very dim. When we re-entered the streets something happened to me which had the force of an optical illusion, or a nightmare. The streets were very crowded and I was facing north. People were moving in every direction but it seemed to me, in that instant, that all of the people I could see, and many more than that, were moving toward me, against me, and that everyone was white. I remember how their faces gleamed. And I felt, like a physical sensation, a *click* at the nape of my neck as though some interior string connecting my head to my body had been cut. I began to walk. I heard my friend call after me, but I ignored him. Heaven only knows what was going on in his mind, but he had the good sense not to touch me—I don't know what would have happened if he had—and to keep me in sight. I don't know what was going on in my mind, either; I certainly had no conscious plan. I wanted to do something to crush these white faces, which were crushing me. I walked for perhaps a block or two until I came to an enormous, glittering, and fashionable restaurant in which I knew not even the intercession of the Virgin would cause me to be served. I pushed through the doors and took the first vacant seat I saw, at a table for two, and waited.

I do not know how long I waited and I rather wonder, until today, what I could possibly have looked like. Whatever I looked like, I frightened the waitress who shortly appeared, and the moment she appeared all of my fury flowed towards her. I hated her for her white face, and for her great, astounded, frightened eyes. I felt that if she found a black man so frightening I would make her fright worth-while.

She did not ask me what I wanted, but repeated, as though she had learned it somewhere, "We don't serve Negroes here." She did not say it with the blunt, decisive hostility to which I had grown so accustomed, but, rather, with a note of apology in her voice, and fear. This made me colder and more murderous than ever. I felt I had to do something with my hands. I wanted her to come close enough for me to get her neck between my hands.

So I pretended not to have understood her, hoping to draw her closer. And she did step a very short step closer, with her pencil poised incongruously over her pad, and repeated the formula: ". . . don't serve Negroes here."

Somehow, with the repetition of that phrase, which was already ringing in my head like a thousand bells of a nightmare, I realized that she would never come any closer and that I would have to strike from a distance. There was nothing on the table but an ordinary water-mug half full of water, and I picked this up and hurled it with all my strength at her. She ducked and it missed her and shattered against the mirror behind the bar. And, with that sound, my frozen blood abruptly thawed, I returned from wherever I had been, I *saw,* for the first time, the restaurant, the people with their mouths open, already, as it seemed to me, rising as one man, and I realized what I had done, and where I was, and I was frightened. I rose and began running for the door. A round, potbellied man grabbed me by the nape of the neck just as I reached the doors and began to beat me about the face. I kicked him and got loose and ran into the streets. My friend whispered, *"Run!"* and I ran.

My friend stayed outside the restaurant long enough to misdirect my pursuers and the police, who arrived, he told me, at once. I do not know what I said to him when he came to my room that night. I could not have said much. I felt, in the oddest, most awful way, that I had somehow betrayed him. I lived it over and over and over again, the way one relives an automobile accident after it has happened and one finds oneself alone and safe. I could not get over two facts, both equally difficult for the imagination to grasp, and one was that I could have been murdered. But the other was that I had been ready to commit murder. I saw nothing very clearly but I did see this: that my life, my *real* life, was in danger, and not from anything other people might do but from the hatred I carried in my own heart.

2

I had returned home around the second week in June—in great haste because it seemed that my father's death and my mother's confinement were both but a matter of hours. In the case of my mother, it soon became clear that she had simply made a miscalculation. This had always been her tendency and I don't believe that a single one of us arrived in the world, or has since arrived anywhere else, on time. But none of us dawdled so intolerably about the business of being born as did my baby sister. We sometimes amused ourselves, during those endless, stifling weeks, by picturing the baby sitting within in the safe, warm dark, bitterly regretting the necessity of becoming a part of our chaos and stubbornly putting it off as long as possible. I understood her perfectly and congratulated her on showing such good sense so soon. Death, however, sat as purposefully at my father's bedside as life stirred within my mother's womb and it was harder to understand why he so lingered in that long shadow. It seemed that he had bent, and for a long time, too, all of his energies towards dying. Now death was ready for him but my father held back.

All of Harlem, indeed, seemed to be infected by waiting. I had never before known it to be so violently still. Racial tensions throughout this country were exacerbated during the early years of the war, partly because the labor market brought together hundreds of thousands of ill-prepared people and partly because Negro soldiers, regardless of where they were born, received their military training in the south. What happened in defense plants and army camps had repercussions, naturally, in every Negro ghetto. The situation in Harlem had grown bad enough for clergymen, policemen, educators, politicians, and social workers to assert in one breath that there was no "crime wave" and to offer, in the very next breath, suggestions as to how to combat it. These suggestions always seemed to involve playgrounds, too. Playground or not, crime wave or not, the Harlem police force had been augmented in March, and the unrest grew —perhaps, in fact, partly as a result of the ghetto's instinctive hatred of policemen. Perhaps the most revealing news item, out of the steady parade of reports of muggings, stabbings, shootings, assaults, gang wars, and accusations of police brutality is the item concerning six Negro girls who set upon a white girl in the subway because, as they all too accurately put it, she was stepping on their toes. Indeed she was, all over the nation.

I had never before been so aware of policemen, on foot, on horseback, on corners, everywhere, always two by two. Nor had I ever been so aware of small knots of people. They were on stoops and on corners and in doorways, and what was striking about them, I think, was that they did not seem to be talking. Never, when I passed these groups, did the usual sound of a curse or a laugh ring out and neither did there seem to be any hum of gossip. There was certainly, on the other hand, occurring between them communication extraordinarily intense. Another thing that was striking was the unexpected diversity of the people who made up these groups. Usually, for example, one would see a group of sharpies standing on the street corner, jiving the passing chicks; or a group of older men, usually, for some reason, in the vicinity of a barber shop, discussing baseball scores, or the numbers, or making rather chilling observations about women they had known. Women, in a general way, tended to be seen less often together—unless they were church women, or very young girls, or prostitutes met together for an unprofessional instant. But that summer I saw the strangest combinations: large, respectable, churchly matrons standing on the stoops or the corners with their hair tied up, together with a girl in sleazy satin whose face bore the marks of gin and the razor, or heavyset, abrupt, no-nonsense older men, in company with the most disreputable and fanatical "race" men, or these same "race" men with the sharpies, or these sharpies with the churchly women. Seventh Day Adventists and Methodists and Spiritualists seemed to be hobnobbing with Holyrollers and they were all, alike, entangled with the most flagrant disbelievers; something heavy in their stance seemed to indicate that they had all, incredibly, seen a common vision, and on each face there seemed to be the same strange, bitter shadow.

The churchly women and the matter-of-fact, no-nonsense men had children in the Army. The sleazy girls they talked to had lovers there, the sharpies and the "race" men had friends and brothers there. It would have demanded an unquestioning patriotism, happily as uncommon in this country as it is undesirable, for these people not to have been disturbed by the bitter letters they received, by the newspaper stories they read, not to have been enraged by the posters, then to be found all over New York, which described the Japanese as "yellowbellied Japs." It was only the "race" men, to be sure, who spoke ceaselessly of being revenged—how this vengeance was to be exacted was not clear—for the indignities and dangers suffered by Negro boys in uniform; but everybody felt a directionless, hopeless bitterness, as well as that panic which can scarcely be suppressed when one knows that a human being one loves is beyond one's reach, and in danger. This helplessness and this gnawing uneasiness does something, at length, to even the toughest mind. Perhaps the best way to sum all this up is to say that the people I knew felt, mainly, a peculiar kind of relief when they knew that their boys were being shipped out of the south, to do battle overseas. It was, perhaps, like feeling that the most dangerous part of a dangerous journey had been passed and that now, even if death should come, it would come with honor and without the complicity of their countrymen. Such a death would be, in short, a fact with which one could hope to live.

It was on the 28th of July, which I believe was a Wednesday, that I visited my father for the first time during his illness and for the last time in his life. The moment I saw him I knew why I had put off this visit so long. I had told my mother that I did not want to see him because I hated him. But this was not true. It was only that I *had* hated him and I wanted to hold on to this hatred. I did not want to look on him as a ruin: it was not a ruin I had hated. I imagine that one of the reasons people cling to their hates so stubbornly is because they sense, once hate is gone, that they will be forced to deal with pain.

We traveled out to him, his older sister and myself, to what seemed to be the very end of a very Long Island. It was hot and dusty and we wrangled, my aunt and I, all the way out, over the fact that I had recently begun to smoke and, as she said, to give myself airs. But I knew that she wrangled with me because she could not bear to face the fact of her brother's dying. Neither could I endure the reality of her despair, her unstated bafflement as to what had happened to her brother's life, and her own. So we wrangled and I smoked and from time to time she fell into a heavy reverie. Covertly, I watched her face, which was the face of an old woman; it had fallen in, the eyes were sunken and lightless; soon she would be dying, too.

In my childhood—it had not been so long ago—I had thought her beautiful. She had been quick-witted and quick-moving and very generous with all the children and each of her visits had been an event. At one time one of my brothers and myself had thought of running away to live with her. Now she could no longer produce out of her handbag some unexpected and yet familiar delight. She made me feel pity and revulsion and fear. It was awful to realize that she no longer caused me to feel affection. The closer we came to the hospital the more querulous she became and at the same time, naturally, grew more dependent on me. Between pity and guilt and fear I began to feel that there was another me trapped in my skull like a jack-in-the-box who might escape my control at any moment and fill the air with screaming.

She began to cry the moment we entered the room and she saw him lying there, all shriveled and still, like a little black monkey. The great, gleaming apparatus which fed him and would have compelled him to be still even if he had been able to move brought to mind, not beneficence, but torture; the tubes entering his arm made me think of pictures I had seen when a child, of Gulliver, tied down by the pygmies on that island. My aunt wept and wept, there was a whistling sound in my father's throat; nothing was said; he could not speak. I wanted to take his hand, to say something. But I do not know what I could have said, even if he could have heard me. He was not really in that room with us, he had at last really embarked on his journey; and though my aunt told me that he said he was going to meet Jesus, I did not hear anything except that whistling in his throat. The doctor came back and we left, into that unbearable train again, and home. In the morning came the telegram saying that he was dead. Then the house was suddenly full of relatives, friends, hysteria, and confusion and I quickly left my mother and the children to the care of those impressive women, who, in Negro communities at least, automatically appear at times of bereavement armed with lotions, proverbs, and patience, and an ability to cook. I went downtown. By the time I returned, later the same day, my mother had been carried to the hospital and the baby had been born.

3

For my father's funeral I had nothing black to wear and this posed a nagging problem all day long. It was one of those problems, simple, or impossible of solution, to which the mind insanely clings in order to avoid the mind's real trouble. I spent most of that day at the downtown apartment of a girl I knew, celebrating my birthday with whiskey and wondering what to wear that night. When planning a birthday celebration one naturally does not expect that it will be up against competition from a funeral and this girl had anticipated taking me out that night, for a big dinner and a night club afterwards. Sometime during the course of that long day we decided that we would go out anyway, when my father's funeral service was over. I imagine I decided it, since, as the funeral hour approached, it became clearer and clearer to me that I would not know what to do with myself when it was over. The girl, stifling her very lively concern as to the possible effects of the whiskey on one of my father's chief mourners, concentrated on being conciliatory and practically helpful. She found a black shirt for me somewhere and ironed it and, dressed in the darkest pants and jacket I owned, and slightly drunk, I made my way to my father's funeral.

The chapel was full, but not packed, and very quiet. There were, mainly, my father's relatives, and his children, and here and there I saw faces I had not seen since childhood, the faces of my father's one-time friends. They were very dark and solemn now, seeming somehow to suggest that they had known all along that something like this would happen. Chief among the mourners was my aunt, who had quarreled with my father all his life; by which I do not mean to suggest that her mourning was insincere or that she had not loved him. I suppose that she was one of the few people in the world who had, and their incessant quarreling proved precisely the strength of the tie that bound them. The only other person in the world, as far as I knew, whose relationship to my father rivaled my aunt's in depth was my mother, who was not there.

It seemed to me, of course, that it was a very long funeral. But it was, if anything, a rather shorter funeral than most, nor, since there were no overwhelming, uncontrollable expressions of grief, could it be called—if I dare to use the word—successful. The minister who preached my father's funeral sermon was one of the few my father had still been seeing as he neared his end. He presented to us in his sermon a man whom none of us had ever seen—a man thoughtful, patient, and forbearing, a Christian inspiration to all who knew him, and a model for his children. And no doubt the children, in their disturbed and guilty state, were almost ready to believe this; he had been remote enough to be anything and, anyway, the shock of the incontrovertible, that it was really our father lying up there in that casket, prepared the mind for anything. His sister moaned and this grief-stricken moaning was taken as corroboration. The other faces held a dark, non-committal thoughtfulness. This was not the man they had known, but they had scarcely expected to be confronted with *him;* this was, in a sense deeper than questions of fact, the man they had not known, and the man they had not known may have been the real one. The real man, whoever he had been, had suffered and now he was dead: this was all that was sure and all that mattered now. Every man in the chapel hoped that when his hour came he, too, would be eulogized,

which is to say forgiven, and that all of his lapses, greeds, errors, and strayings from
the truth would be invested with coherence and looked upon with charity. This was
perhaps the last thing human beings could give each other and it was what they
demanded, after all, of the Lord. Only the Lord saw the midnight tears, only He was
present when one of His children, moaning and wringing hands, paced up and down
the room. When one slapped one's child in anger the recoil in the heart reverberated
through heaven and became part of the pain of the universe. And when the children
were hungry and sullen and distrustful and one watched them, daily, growing wilder,
and further away, and running headlong into danger, it was the Lord who knew what
the charged heart endured as the strap was laid to the backside; the Lord alone who
knew what one *would* have said if one had had, like the Lord, the gift of the living
word. It was the Lord who knew of the impossibility every parent in that room faced:
how to prepare the child for the day when the child would be despised and how to
create in the child—by what means?—a stronger antidote to this poison than one had
found for oneself. The avenues, side streets, bars, billiard halls, hospitals, police stations,
and even the playgrounds of Harlem—not to mention the houses of correction, the jails,
and the morgue—testified to the potency of the poison while remaining silent as to
the efficacy of whatever antidote, irresistibly raising the question of whether or not such
an antidote existed; raising, which was worse, the question of whether or not an antidote
was desirable; perhaps poison should be fought with poison. With these several schisms
in the mind and with more terrors in the heart than could be named, it was better not
to judge the man who had gone down under an impossible burden. It was better to
remember: *Thou knowest this man's fall; but thou knowest not his wrassling.*

While the preacher talked and I watched the children—years of changing their
diapers, scrubbing them, slapping them, taking them to school, and scolding them had
had the perhaps inevitable result of making me love them, though I am not sure I knew
this then—my mind was busily breaking out with a rash of disconnected impressions.
Snatches of popular songs, indecent jokes, bits of books I had read, movie sequences,
faces, voices, political issues—I thought I was going mad; all these impressions suspended, as it were, in the solution of the faint nausea produced in me by the heat and
liquor. For a moment I had the impression that my alcoholic breath, inefficiently
disguised with chewing gum, filled the entire chapel. Then someone began singing one
of my father's favorite songs and, abruptly, I was with him, sitting on his knee, in the
hot, enormous, crowded church which was the first church we attended. It was the
Abyssinia Baptist Church on 138th Street. We had not gone there long. With this
image, a host of others came. I had forgotten, in the rage of my growing up, how proud
my father had been of me when I was little. Apparently, I had had a voice and my
father had liked to show me off before the members of the church. I had forgotten what
he had looked like when he was pleased but now I remembered that he had always
been grinning with pleasure when my solos ended. I even remembered certain expressions on his face when he teased my mother—had he loved her? I would never know.
And when had it all begun to change? For now it seemed that he had not always been
cruel. I remembered being taken for a haircut and scraping my knee on the footrest
of the barber's chair and I remembered my father's face as he soothed my crying and
applied the stinging iodine. Then I remembered our fights, fights which had been of
the worst possible kind because my technique had been silence.

I remembered the one time in all our life together when we had really spoken to
each other.

It was on a Sunday and it must have been shortly before I left home. We were walking, just the two of us, in our usual silence, to or from church. I was in high school and had been doing a lot of writing and I was, at about this time, the editor of the high school magazine. But I had also been a Young Minister and had been preaching from the pulpit. Lately, I had been taking fewer engagements and preached as rarely as possible. It was said in the church, quite truthfully, that I was "cooling off."

My father asked me abruptly, "You'd rather write than preach, wouldn't you?"

I was astonished at his question—because it was a real question. I answered, "Yes."

That was all we said. It was awful to remember that that was all we had *ever* said.

The casket now was opened and the mourners were being led up the aisle to look for the last time on the deceased. The assumption was that the family was too overcome with grief to be allowed to make this journey alone and I watched while my aunt was led to the casket and, muffled in black, and shaking, led back to her seat. I disapproved of forcing the children to look on their dead father, considering that the shock of his death, or, more truthfully, the shock of death as a reality, was already a little more than a child could bear, but my judgment in this matter had been overruled and there they were, bewildered and frightened and very small, being led, one by one, to the casket. But there is also something very gallant about children at such moments. It has something to do with their silence and gravity and with the fact that one cannot help them. Their legs, somehow, seem *exposed,* so that it is at once incredible and terribly clear that their legs are all they have to hold them up.

I had not wanted to go to the casket myself and I certainly had not wished to be led there, but there was no way of avoiding either of these forms. One of the deacons led me up and I looked on my father's face. I cannot say that it looked like him at all. His blackness had been equivocated by powder and there was no suggestion in that casket of what his power had or could have been. He was simply an old man dead, and it was hard to believe that he had ever given anyone either joy or pain. Yet, his life filled that room. Further up the avenue his wife was holding his newborn child. Life and death so close together, and love and hatred, and right and wrong, said something to me which I did not want to hear concerning man, concerning the life of man.

After the funeral, while I was downtown desperately celebrating my birthday, a Negro soldier, in the lobby of the Hotel Braddock, got into a fight with a white policeman over a Negro girl. Negro girls, white policemen, in or out of uniform, and Negro males—in or out of uniform—were part of the furniture of the lobby of the Hotel Braddock and this was certainly not the first time such an incident had occurred. It was destined, however, to receive an unprecedented publicity, for the fight between the policeman and the soldier ended with the shooting of the soldier. Rumor, flowing immediately to the streets outside, stated that the soldier had been shot in the back, an instantaneous and revealing invention, and that the soldier had died protecting a Negro woman. The facts were somewhat different—for example, the soldier had not been shot in the back, and was not dead, and the girl seems to have been as dubious a symbol of womanhood as her white counterpart in Georgia usually is, but no one was interested in the facts. They preferred the invention because this invention expressed and cor-roborated their hates and fears so perfectly. It is just as well to remember that people are always doing this. Perhaps many of those legends, including Christianity, to which the world clings began their conquest of the world with just some such concerted surrender to distortion. The effect, in Harlem, of this particular legend was like the effect of a lit match in a tin of gasoline. The mob gathered before the doors of the Hotel Braddock simply began to swell and to spread in every direction, and Harlem exploded.

The mob did not cross the ghetto lines. It would have been easy, for example, to have gone over to Morningside Park on the west side or to have crossed the Grand Central railroad tracks at 125th Street on the east side, to wreak havoc in white neighborhoods. The mob seems to have been mainly interested in something more potent and real than the white face, that is, in white power, and the principal damage done during the riot of the summer of 1943 was to white business establishments in Harlem. It might have been a far bloodier story, of course, if, at the hour the riot began, these establishments had still been open. From the Hotel Braddock the mob fanned out, east and west along 125th Street, and for the entire length of Lenox, Seventh, and Eighth avenues. Along each of these avenues, and along each major side street—116th, 125th, 135th, and so on—bars, stores, pawnshops, restaurants, even little luncheonettes had been smashed open and entered and looted—looted, it might be added, with more haste than efficiency. The shelves really looked as though a bomb had struck them. Cans of beans and soup and dog food, along with toilet paper, corn flakes, sardines and milk tumbled every which way, and abandoned cash registers and cases of beer leaned crazily out of the splintered windows and were strewn along the avenues. Sheets, blankets, and clothing of every description formed a kind of path, as though people had dropped them while running. I truly had not realized that Harlem *had* so many stores until I saw them all smashed open; the first time the word *wealth* ever entered my mind in relation to Harlem was when I saw it scattered in the streets. But one's first, incongruous impression of plenty was countered immediately by an impression of waste. None of this was doing anybody any good. It would have been better to have left the plate glass as it had been and the goods lying in the stores.

It would have been better, but it would also have been intolerable, for Harlem had needed something to smash. To smash something is the ghetto's chronic need. Most of the time it is the members of the ghetto who smash each other, and themselves. But as long as the ghetto walls are standing there will always come a moment when these outlets do not work. That summer, for example, it was not enough to get into a fight on Lenox Avenue, or curse out one's cronies in the barber shops. If ever, indeed, the violence which fills Harlem's churches, pool halls, and bars erupts outward in a more direct fashion, Harlem and its citizens are likely to vanish in an apocalyptic flood. That this is not likely to happen is due to a great many reasons, most hidden and powerful among them the Negro's real relation to the white American. This relation prohibits, simply, anything as uncomplicated and satisfactory as pure hatred. In order really to hate white people, one has to blot so much out of the mind—and the heart—that this hatred itself becomes an exhausting and self-destructive pose. But this does not mean, on the other hand, that love comes easily: the white world is too powerful, too complacent, too ready with gratuitous humiliation, and, above all, too ignorant and too innocent for that. One is absolutely forced to make perpetual qualifications and one's own reactions are always canceling each other out. It is this, really, which has driven so many people mad, both white and black. One is always in the position of having to decide between amputation and gangrene. Amputation is swift but time may prove that the amputation was not necessary—or one may delay the amputation too long. Gangrene is slow, but it is impossible to be sure that one is reading one's symptoms right. The idea of going through life as a cripple is more than one can bear, and equally unbearable is the risk of swelling up slowly, in agony, with poison. And the trouble, finally, is that the risks are real even if the choices do not exist.

"But as for me and my house," my father had said, "we will serve the Lord." I wondered, as we drove him to a resting place, what this line had meant for him. I had heard him preach it many times. I had preached it once myself, proudly giving it an interpretation different from my father's. Now the whole thing came back to me, as though my father and I were on our way to Sunday school and I were memorizing the golden text: *And if it seem evil unto you to serve the Lord, choose you this day whom you will serve; whether the gods which your fathers served that were on the other side of the flood, or the gods of the Amorites, in whose land ye dwell: but as for me and my house, we will serve the Lord.* I suspected in these familiar lines a meaning which had never been there for me before. All of my father's texts and songs, which I had decided were meaningless, were arranged before me at his death like empty bottles, waiting to hold the meaning which life would give them for me. This was his legacy: nothing is ever escaped. That bleakly memorable morning I hated the unbelievable streets and the Negroes and whites who had, equally, made them that way. But I knew that it was folly, as my father would have said, this bitterness was folly. It was necessary to hold on to the things that mattered. The dead man mattered, the new life mattered; blackness and whiteness did not matter; to believe that they did was to acquiesce in one's own destruction. Hatred, which could destroy so much, never failed to destroy the man who hated and this was an immutable law.

It began to seem that one would have to hold in the mind forever two ideas which seemed to be in opposition. The first idea was acceptance, the acceptance, totally without rancor, of life as it is, and men as they are: in the light of this idea, it goes without saying that injustice is a commonplace. But this did not mean that one could be complacent, for the second idea was of equal power: that one must never, in one's own life, accept these injustices as commonplace but must fight them with all one's strength. This fight begins, however, in the heart and it now had been laid to my charge to keep my own heart free of hatred and despair. This intimation made my heart heavy and, now that my father was irrecoverable, I wished that he had been beside me so that I could have searched his face for the answers which only the future would give me now.

TOM WOLFE

[*b. 1931*]

The Right Stuff

A young man might go into military flight training believing that he was entering some sort of technical school in which he was simply going to acquire a certain set of skills. Instead, he found himself all at once enclosed in a fraternity. And in this fraternity, even though it was military, men were not rated by their outward rank as ensigns, lieutenants, commanders, or whatever. No, herein the world was divided into those who had it and those who did not. This quality, that *it,* was never named, however, nor was it talked about in any way.

As to just what this ineffable quality was . . . well, it obviously involved bravery. But it was not bravery in the simple sense of being willing to risk your life. The idea seemed to be that any fool could do that, if that was all that was required, just as any fool could throw away his life in the process. No, the idea here (in the all-enclosing fraternity) seemed to be that a man should have the ability to go up in a hurtling piece of machinery and put his hide on the line and then have the moxie, the reflexes, the experience, the coolness, to pull it back in the last yawning moment—and then to go up again *the next day,* and the next day, and every next day, even if the series should prove infinite—and, ultimately, in its best expression, do so in a cause that means something to thousands, to a people, a nation, to humanity, to God. Nor was there *a test* to show whether or not a pilot had this righteous quality. There was, instead, a seemingly infinite series of tests. A career in flying was like climbing one of those ancient Babylonian pyramids made up of a dizzy progression of steps and ledges, a ziggurat, a pyramid extraordinarily high and steep; and the idea was to prove at every foot of the way up that pyramid that you were one of the elected and anointed ones who had *the right stuff* and could move higher and higher and even—ultimately, God willing, one day—that you might be able to join that special few at the very top, that elite who had the capacity to bring tears to men's eyes, the very Brotherhood of the Right Stuff itself.

None of this was to be mentioned, and yet it was acted out in a way that a young man could not fail to understand. When a new flight (i.e., a class) of trainees arrived at Pensacola, they were brought into an auditorium for a little lecture. An officer would tell them: "Take a look at the man on either side of you." Quite a few actually swiveled their heads this way and that, in the interest of appearing diligent. Then the officer would say: "One of the three of you is not going to make it!"—meaning, not get his wings. That was the opening theme, the *motif* of primary training. We already know that one-third of you do not have the right stuff—it only remains to find out who.

Furthermore, that was the way it turned out. At every level in one's progress up that staggeringly high pyramid, the world was once more divided into those men who had the right stuff to continue the climb and those who had to be *left behind* in the most obvious way. Some were eliminated in the course of the opening classroom work, as either not smart enough or not hardworking enough, and were left behind. Then came the basic flight instruction, in single-engine, propeller-driven trainers, and a few more—even though the military tried to make this stage easy—were washed out and left behind. Then came more demanding levels, one after the other, formation flying, instrument flying, jet training, all-weather flying, gunnery, and at each level more were washed out and left behind. By this point easily a third of the original candidates had been, indeed, eliminated . . . from the ranks of those who might prove to have the right stuff.

In the Navy, in addition to the stages that Air Force trainees went through, the neophyte always had waiting for him, out in the ocean, a certain grim gray slab; namely, the deck of an aircraft carrier; and with it perhaps the most difficult routine in military flying, carrier landings. He was shown films about it, he heard lectures about it, and he knew that carrier landings were hazardous. He first practiced touching down on the shape of a flight deck painted on an airfield. He was instructed to touch down and gun right off. This was safe enough—the shape didn't move, at least—but it could do terrible things to, let us say, the gyroscope of the soul. *That shape!—it's so damned small!* And more candidates were washed out and left behind. Then came the day, without warning, when those who remained were sent out over the ocean for the first of many days of reckoning with the slab. The first day was always a clear day with little wind and a calm sea. The carrier was so steady that it seemed, from up there in the air, to be resting on pilings, and the candidate usually made his first carrier landing successfully, with relief and even *élan.* Many young candidates looked like terrific aviators up to that very point—and it was not until they were actually standing on the carrier deck that they first began to wonder if they had the proper stuff, after all. In the training film the flight deck was a grand piece of gray geometry, perilous, to be sure, but an amazing abstract shape as one looks down upon it on the screen. And yet once the newcomer's two feet were on it . . . *Geometry*—my God, man, this is a . . . skillet! It *heaved,* it moved up and down underneath his feet, it pitched up, it pitched down, it rolled to port (this great beast *rolled!*) and it rolled to starboard, as the ship moved into the wind and, therefore, into the waves, and the wind kept sweeping across, sixty feet up in the air out in the open sea, and there were no railings whatsoever. This was a *skillet!*—a frying pan!—a short-order grill!—not gray but black, smeared with skid marks from one end to the other and glistening with pools of hydraulic fluid and the occasional jet-fuel slick, all of it still hot, sticky, greasy, runny, virulent from God knows what traumas—still ablaze!—consumed in detonations, explosions, flames, combustion, roars, shrieks, whines, blasts, horrible shudders, fracturing impacts, as little men in screaming red and yellow and purple and green shirts with black Mickey Mouse helmets over their ears skittered about on the surface as if for their very lives (you've said it now!), hooking fighter planes onto the catapult shuttles so that they can explode their afterburners and be slung off the deck in a red-mad fury with a *kaboom!* that pounds through the entire deck—a procedure that seems absolutely controlled, orderly, sublime, however, compared to what he is about to watch as aircraft return to the ship for what is known in the engineering stoicisms of the military as "recovery and arrest." To say that an F-4 was coming back onto this heaving barbecue from out of the sky at a speed of 135 knots . . . that might have been the truth in the training lecture, but it did not begin to get across the idea of what the newcomer saw from the deck itself, because it created the notion that perhaps the plane was gliding in. On the deck one knew differently! As the aircraft came closer and the carrier heaved on into the waves and the plane's speed did not diminish and the deck did not grow steady—indeed, it pitched up and down five or ten feet per greasy heave—one experienced a neural alarm that no lecture could have prepared him for: This is not an *airplane* coming toward me, it is a brick with some poor sonofabitch riding it *(someone much like myself!),* and it is not *gliding,* it is *falling,* a fifty-thousand-pound brick, headed not for a stripe on the deck but for *me*—and with a horrible *smash!* it hits the skillet, and with a blur of momentum as big as a freight train's it hurtles toward the far end of the deck—another blinding storm!—another roar as the pilot pushes the throttle up to full military power and another smear of rubber screams out over the skillet—and this is nominal! —quite okay!—for a wire stretched across the deck has grabbed the hook on the end of the plane as it hit the deck tail down, and the smash was the rest of the fifteen-ton brute slamming onto the deck, as it tripped up, so that it is now straining against the wire at full throttle, in case it hadn't held and the plane had "boltered" off the end of the deck and had to struggle up into the air again. And already the Mickey Mouse helmets are running toward the fiery monster . . .

And the candidate, looking on, begins to *feel* that great heaving sun-blazing death-board of a deck wallowing in his own vestibular system—and suddenly he finds himself backed up against his own limits. He ends up going to the flight surgeon with so-called conversion symptoms. Overnight he develops blurred vision or numbness in his hands and feet or sinusitis so severe that he cannot tolerate changes in altitude. On one level the symptom is real. He really cannot see too well or use his fingers or stand the pain. But somewhere in his subconscious he knows it is a plea and a beg-off; he shows not the slightest concern (the flight surgeon notes) that the condition might be permanent and affect him in whatever life awaits him outside the arena of the right stuff.

Those who remained, those who qualified for carrier duty—and even more so those who later on qualified for *night* carrier duty—began to feel a bit like Gideon's warriors. *So many have been left behind!* The young warriors were now treated to a deathly sweet and quite unmentionable sight. They could gaze at length upon the crushed and wilted pariahs who had washed out. They could inspect those who did not have that righteous stuff.

The military did not have very merciful instincts. Rather than packing up these poor souls and sending them home, the Navy, like the Air Force and the Marines, would try to make use of them in some other role, such as flight controller. So the washout has to keep taking classes with the rest of his group, even though he can no longer touch an airplane. He sits there in the classes staring at sheets of paper with cataracts of sheer human mortification over his eyes while the rest steal looks at him . . . this man reduced to an ant, this untouchable, this poor sonofabitch. And in what test had he been found wanting? Why, it seemed to be nothing less than *manhood* itself. Naturally, this was never mentioned, either. Yet there it was. *Manliness, manhood, manly courage* . . . there was something ancient, primordial, irresistible about the challenge of this stuff, no matter what a sophisticated and rational age one might think he lived in.

Perhaps because it could not be talked about, the subject began to take on superstitious and even mystical outlines. A man either had it or he didn't! There was no such thing as having *most* of it. Moreover, it could blow at any seam. One day a man would be ascending the pyramid at a terrific clip, and the next—bingo!—he would reach his own limits in the most unexpected way. Conrad and Schirra met an Air Force pilot who had had a great pal at Tyndall Air Force Base in Florida. This man had been the budding ace of the training class; he had flown the hottest fighter-style trainer, the T-38, like a dream; and then he began the routine step of being checked out in the T-33. The T-33 was not nearly as hot an aircraft as the T-38; it was essentially the old P-80 jet fighter. It had an exceedingly small cockpit. The pilot could barely move his shoulders. It was the sort of airplane of which everybody said, "You don't get into it, you *wear* it." Once inside a T-33 cockpit this man, this budding ace, developed claustrophobia of the most paralyzing sort. He tried everything to overcome it. He even went to a psychiatrist, which was a serious mistake for a military officer if his superiors learned of it. But nothing worked. He was shifted over to flying jet transports, such as the C-135. Very demanding and necessary aircraft they were, too, and he was still spoken of as an excellent pilot. But as everyone knew—and, again, it was never explained in so many words—only those who were assigned to fighter squadrons, the "fighter jocks," as they called each other with a self-satisfied irony, remained in the true fraternity. Those assigned to transports were not humiliated like washouts—*somebody* had to fly those planes—nevertheless, they, too, had been *left behind* for lack of the right stuff.

Or a man could go for a routine physical one fine day, feeling like a million dollars, and be grounded for *fallen arches*. It happened!—just like that! (And try raising them.) Or for breaking his wrist and losing only *part* of its mobility. Or for a minor deterioration of eyesight, or for any of hundreds of reasons that would make no difference to a man in an ordinary occupation. As a result all fighter jocks began looking upon doctors as their natural enemies. Going to see a flight surgeon was a no-gain proposition; a pilot could only hold his own or lose in the doctor's office. To be grounded for a medical reason was no humiliation, looked at objectively. But it was a humiliation, nonetheless!—for it meant you no longer had that indefinable, unutterable, integral stuff. (It could blow at *any* seam.)

All the hot young fighter jocks began trying to test the limits themselves in a superstitious way. They were like believing Presbyterians of a century before who used to probe their own experience to see if they were truly among *the elect*. When a fighter pilot was in training, whether in the Navy or the Air Force, his superiors were continually spelling out strict rules for him, about the use of the aircraft and conduct in the sky. They repeatedly forbade so-called hot-dog stunts, such as outside loops, buzzing, flat-hatting, hedgehopping and flying under bridges. But somehow one got the message that the man who truly *had* it could ignore those rules—not that he should make a point of it, but that he *could*—and that after all there was only one way to find out—and that in some strange unofficial way, peeking through his fingers, his instructor halfway expected him to challenge all the limits. They would give a lecture about how a pilot should never fly without a good solid breakfast—eggs, bacon, toast, and so forth—because if he tried to fly with his blood-sugar level too low, it could impair his alertness. Naturally, the next day every hot dog in the unit would get up and have a breakfast consisting of one cup of black coffee and take off and go up into a vertical climb until the weight of the ship exactly canceled out the upward pull of the engine and his air speed was zero, and he would hang there for one thick adrenal instant—and then fall like a rock, until one of three things happened: he keeled over nose first and regained his aerodynamics and all was well, he went into a spin and fought his way out of it, or he went into a spin and had to eject or crunch it, which was always supremely possible.

Likewise, "hassling"—mock dogfighting—was strictly forbidden, and so naturally young fighter jocks could hardly wait to go up in, say, a pair of F-100s and start the duel by making a pass at each other at 800 miles an hour, the winner being the pilot who could slip in behind the other one and get locked in on his tail ("wax his tail"), and it was not uncommon for some eager jock to try too tight an outside turn and have his engine flame out, whereupon, unable to restart it, he has to eject . . . and he shakes his fist at the victor as he floats down by parachute and his half-a-million-dollar aircraft goes *kaboom!* on the palmetto grass or the desert floor, and he starts thinking about how he can get together with the other guy back at the base in time for the two of them to get their stories straight before the investigation: "I don't know what happened, sir. I was pulling up after a target run, and it just flamed out on me." Hassling was forbidden, and hassling that led to the destruction of an aircraft was a serious court-martial offense, and the man's superiors knew that the engine hadn't *just flamed out,* but every unofficial impulse on the base seemed to be saying: "Hell, we wouldn't give you a nickel for a pilot who hasn't done some crazy rat-racing like that. It's all part of the right stuff."

The other side of this impulse showed up in the reluctance of the young jocks to admit it when they had maneuvered themselves into a bad corner they couldn't get out of. There were two reasons why a fighter pilot hated to declare an emergency. First, it triggered a complex and very public chain of events at the field: all other incoming flights were held up, including many of one's comrades who were probably low on fuel; the fire trucks came trundling out to the runway like yellow toys (as seen from way up there), the better to illustrate one's hapless state; and the bureaucracy began to crank up the paper monster for the investigation that always followed. And second, to declare an emergency, one first had to reach that conclusion in his own mind, which to the young pilot was the same as saying: "A minute ago I still *had it*—now I need your help!" To have a bunch of young fighter pilots up in the air thinking this way used to drive flight controllers crazy. They would see a ship beginning to drift off the radar, and they couldn't rouse the pilot on the microphone for anything other than a few meaningless mumbles, and they would know he was probably out there with engine failure at a low altitude, trying to reignite by lowering his auxiliary generator rig, which had a little propeller that was supposed to spin in the slipstream like a child's pinwheel.

"Whiskey Kilo Two Eight, do you want to declare an emergency?"

This would rouse him!—to say: "Negative, negative, Whiskey Kilo Two Eight is not declaring an emergency."

Kaboom. Believers in the right stuff would rather crash and burn.

One fine day, after he had joined a fighter squadron, it would dawn on the young pilot exactly how the losers in the great fraternal competition were now being left behind. Which is to say, not by instructors or other superiors or by failures at prescribed levels of competence, but by death. At this point the essence of the enterprise would begin to dawn on him. Slowly, step by step, the ante had been raised until he was now involved in what was surely the grimmest and grandest gamble of manhood. Being a fighter pilot—for that matter, simply taking off in a single-engine jet fighter of the Century series, such as an F-102, or any of the military's other marvelous bricks with fins on them—presented a man, on a perfectly sunny day, with more ways to get himself killed than his wife and children could imagine in their wildest fears. If he was barreling down the runway at two hundred miles an hour, completing the takeoff run, and the board started lighting up red, should he (a) abort the takeoff (and try to wrestle with the monster, which was gorged with jet fuel, out in the sand beyond the end of the runway) or (b) eject (and hope that the goddamned human cannonball trick works at zero altitude and he doesn't shatter an elbow or a kneecap on the way out) or (c) continue the takeoff and deal with the problem aloft (knowing full well that the ship may be on fire and therefore seconds away from exploding)? He would have one second to sort out the options and act, and this kind of little workaday decision came up all the time. Occasionally a man would look coldly at the binary problem he was now confronting every day—Right Stuff/Death—and decide it wasn't worth it and voluntarily shift over to transports or reconnaissance or whatever. And his comrades would wonder, for a day or so, what evil virus had invaded his soul . . . as they left him behind. More often, however, the reverse would happen. Some college graduate would enter Navy aviation through the Reserves, simply as an alternative to the Army draft, fully intending to return to civilian life, to some waiting profession or family business; would become involved in the obsessive business of ascending the ziggurat pyramid of flying; and, at the end of his enlistment, would astound everyone back home and very likely himself as well by signing up for another one. What on earth got into him? He couldn't explain it. After all, the very words for it had been amputated. A Navy study showed that two-thirds of the fighter pilots who were rated in the top rungs of their groups —i.e., the hottest young pilots—reenlisted when the time came, and practically all were college graduates. By this point, a young fighter jock was like the preacher in *Moby Dick* who climbs up into the pulpit on a rope ladder and then pulls the ladder up behind him; except the pilot could not use the words necessary to express the vital lessons. Civilian life, and even home and hearth, now seemed not only far away but far *below*, back down many levels of the pyramid of the right stuff.

A fighter pilot soon found he wanted to associate only with other fighter pilots. Who else could understand the nature of the little proposition (right stuff/death) they were all dealing with? And what other subject could compare with it? It was riveting! To talk about it in so many words was forbidden, of course. The very words *death, danger, bravery, fear* were not to be uttered except in the occasional specific instance or for ironic effect. Nevertheless, the subject could be adumbrated in *code* or *by example*. Hence the endless evenings of pilots huddled together talking about flying. On these long and drunken evenings (the band of their family life) certain theorems would be propounded and demonstrated—and all by *code* and *example*. One theorem was: There are no *accidents* and no fatal flaws in the machines; there are only pilots with the wrong stuff. (I.e., blind Fate can't kill me.) When Bud Jennings crashed and burned in the swamps at Jacksonville, the other pilots in Pete Conrad's squadron said: *How could he have been so stupid?* It turned out that Jennings had gone up in the SNJ with his cockpit canopy opened in a way that was expressly forbidden in the manual, and carbon monoxide had been sucked in from the exhaust, and he passed out and crashed. All agreed that Bud Jennings was a good guy and a good pilot, but his epitaph on the ziggurat was: *How could he have been so stupid?* This seemed shocking at first, but by the time Conrad had reached the end of that bad string at Pax River, he was capable of his own corollary to the theorem: viz., no single factor ever killed a pilot; there was always a chain of mistakes. But what about Ted Whelan, who fell like a rock from 8,100 feet when his parachute failed? Well, the parachute was merely part of the chain: first, someone should have caught the structural defect that resulted in the hydraulic leak that triggered the emergency; second, Whelan did not check out his seat-parachute rig, and the drogue failed to separate the main parachute from the seat; but even after those two mistakes, Whelan had fifteen or twenty seconds, as he fell, to disengage himself from the seat and open the parachute manually. Why just stare at the scenery coming up to smack you in the face! And everyone nodded. (He failed—but I wouldn't have!) Once the theorem and the corollary were understood, the Navy's statistics about one in every four Navy aviators dying meant nothing. The figures were averages, and averages applied to those with average stuff.

A riveting subject, especially if it were one's own hide that was on the line. Every evening at bases all over America, there were military pilots huddled in officers clubs eagerly cutting the right stuff up in coded slices so they could talk about it. What more compelling topic of conversation was there in the world? In the Air Force there were even pilots who would ask the tower for priority landing clearance so that they could make the beer call on time, at 4 p.m. sharp, at the Officers Club. They would come right out and state the reason. The drunken rambles began at four and sometimes went on for ten or twelve hours. Such conversations! They diced that righteous stuff up into little bits, bowed ironically to it, stumbled blindfolded around it, groped, lurched, belched, staggered, bawled, sang, roared, and feinted at it with self-deprecating humor. Nevertheless!—they never mentioned it by name. No, they used the approved codes, such as: "Like a jerk I got myself into a hell of a corner today." They told of how they "lucked out of it." To get across the extreme peril of his exploit, one would use certain oblique cues. He would say, "I looked over at Robinson"—who would be known to the listeners as a non-com who sometimes rode backseat to read radar—"and he wasn't talking any more, he was just staring at the radar, like this, giving it that *zombie* look. Then I *knew* I was in trouble!" Beautiful! Just right! For it would also be known to the listeners that the non-coms advised one another: "*Never* fly with a lieutenant. *Avoid* captains and majors. Hell, man, do yourself a favor: don't fly with anybody below colonel." Which in turn said: "Those young bucks shoot dice with death!" And yet once in the air the non-com had his own standards. He was determined to remain as outwardly cool as the pilot, so that when the pilot did something that truly petrified him, he would say nothing; instead, he would turn silent, catatonic, like a zombie. Perfect! *Zombie.* There you had it, compressed into a single word all of the foregoing. I'm a hell of a pilot! I shoot dice with death! And now all you fellows know it! And I haven't spoken of that unspoken stuff even once!

The talking and drinking began at the beer call, and then the boys would break for dinner and come back afterward and get more wasted and more garrulous or else more quietly fried, drinking good cheap PX booze until 2 A.M. The night was young! Why not get the cars and go out for a little proficiency run? It seemed that every fighter jock thought himself an ace driver, and he would do anything to obtain a hot car, especially a sports car, and the drunker he was, the more convinced he would be about his driving skills, as if the right stuff, being indivisible, carried over into any enterprise whatsoever, under any conditions. A little proficiency run, boys! (There's only one way to find out!) And they would roar off in close formation from, say, Nellis Air Force Base, down Route 15, into Las Vegas, barreling down the highway, rat-racing, sometimes four abreast, jockeying for position, piling into the most listless curve in the desert flats as if they were trying to root each other out of the groove at the Rebel 500— and then bursting into downtown Las Vegas with a rude fraternal roar like the Hell's Angels—and the natives chalked it up to youth and drink and the bad element that the Air Force attracted. They knew nothing about the right stuff, of course.

More fighter pilots died in automobiles than in airplanes. Fortunately, there was always some kindly soul up the chain to certify the papers "line of duty," so that the widow could get a better break on the insurance. That was okay and only proper because somehow the system itself had long ago said *Skol!* and *Quite right!* to the military cycle of Flying & Drinking and Drinking & Driving, as if there were no other way. Every young fighter jock knew the feeling of getting two or three hours' sleep and then waking up at 5:30 A.M. and having a few cups of coffee, a few cigarettes, and then carting his poor quivering liver out to the field for another day of flying. There were those who arrived not merely hungover but still drunk, slapping oxygen tank cones over their faces and trying to burn the alcohol out of their systems, and then going up, remarking later: "I don't *advise* it, you understand, but it *can* be done." (Provided you have the right stuff, you miserable pudknocker.)

Air Force and Navy airfields were usually on barren or marginal stretches of land

and would have looked especially bleak and Low Rent to an ordinary individual in the chilly light of dawn. But to a young pilot there was an inexplicable bliss to coming out to the flight line while the sun was just beginning to cook up behind the rim of the horizon, so that the whole field was still in shadow and the ridges in the distance were in silhouette and the flight line was a monochrome of Exhaust Fume Blue, and every little red light on top of the water towers or power stanchions looked dull, shriveled, congealed, and the runway lights, which were still on, looked faded, and even the landing lights on a fighter that had just landed and was taxiing in were no longer dazzling, as they would be at night, and looked instead like shriveled gobs of candle-power out there—and yet it was beautiful, exhilarating!—for he was revved up with adrenalin, anxious to take off before the day broke, to burst up into the sunlight over the ridges before all those thousands of comatose souls down there, still dead to the world, snug in home and hearth, even came to their senses. To take off in an F-100F at dawn and cut on the afterburner and hurtle twenty-five thousand feet up into the sky in thirty seconds, so suddenly that you felt not like a bird but like a trajectory, yet with full control, full control of *four tons* of thrust, all of which flowed from your will and through your fingertips, with the huge engine right beneath you, so close that it was as if you were riding it bareback, until all at once you were supersonic, an event registered on earth by a tremendous cracking boom that shook windows, but up here only by the fact that you now felt utterly free of the earth—to describe it, even to wife, child, near ones and dear ones, seemed impossible. So the pilot kept it to himself, along with an even more indescribable . . . an even more sinfully inconfessable . . . feeling of superiority, appropriate to him and to his kind, lone bearers of the right stuff.

From *up here* at dawn the pilot looked down upon poor hopeless Las Vegas (or Yuma, Corpus Christi, Meridian, San Bernardino, or Dayton) and began to wonder: How can all of them down there, those poor souls who will soon be waking up and trudging out of their minute rectangles and inching along their little noodle highways toward whatever slots and grooves make up their everyday lives—how could they live like that, with such earnestness, if they had the faintest idea of what it was like up here in this righteous zone?

But of course! Not only the washed-out, grounded, and dead pilots had been left behind—but also all of those millions of sleepwalking souls who never even attempted the great gamble. The entire world below . . . *left behind.* Only at this point can one begin to understand just how big, how titanic, the ego of the military pilot could be. The world was used to enormous egos in artists, actors, entertainers of all sorts, in politicians, sports figures, and even journalists, because they had such familiar and convenient ways to show them off. But that slim young man over there in uniform, with the enormous watch on his wrist and the withdrawn look on his face, that young officer who is so shy that he can't even open his mouth unless the subject is flying— that young pilot—well, my friends, his ego is even *bigger!*—so big, it's *breathtaking!* Even in the 1950's it was difficult for civilians to comprehend such a thing, but *all* military officers and many enlisted men tended to feel superior to civilians. It was really quite ironic, given the fact that for a good thirty years the rising business classes in the cities had been steering their sons away from the military, as if from a bad smell, and the officer corps had never been held in lower esteem. Well, career officers returned the contempt in trumps. They looked upon themselves as men who lived by higher standards of behavior than civilians, as men who were the bearers and protectors of the most important values of American life, who maintained a sense of discipline while civilians abandoned themselves to hedonism, who maintained a sense of honor while civilians lived by opportunism and greed. Opportunism and greed: there you had your much-vaunted corporate business world. Khrushchev was right about one thing: when it came time to hang the capitalist West, an American businessman would sell him the rope. When the showdown came—and the showdowns always came—not all the wealth in the world or all the sophisticated nuclear weapons and radar and missile systems it could buy would take the place of those who had the uncritical willingness to face danger, those who, in short, had the right stuff.

In fact, the feeling was so righteous, so exalted, it could become religious. Civilians seldom understood this, either. There was no one to teach them. It was no longer the fashion for serious writers to describe the glories of war. Instead, they dwelt upon its horrors, often with cynicism or disgust. It was left to the occasional pilot with a literary flair to provide a glimpse of the pilot's self-conception in its heavenly or spiritual aspect. When a pilot named Robert Scott flew his P-43 over Mount Everest, quite a feat at the time, he brought his hand up and snapped a salute to his fallen adversary. He thought he had *defeated* the mountain, surmounting all the forces of nature that had made it formidable. And why not? "God is my co-pilot," he said—that became the title of his book—and he meant it. So did the most gifted of all the pilot authors, the Frenchman Antoine de Saint-Exupéry. As he gazed down upon the world . . . from up there . . . during transcontinental flights, the good Saint-Ex saw civilization as a series of tiny fragile patches clinging to the otherwise barren rock of Earth. He felt like a lonely sentinel, a protector of those vulnerable little oases, ready to lay down his life in their behalf, if necessary; a saint, in short, true to his name, flying up here at the right hand of God. The good Saint-Ex! And he was not the only one. He was merely the one who put it into words most beautifully and anointed himself before the altar of the right stuff.

ALICE WALKER

[b. 1944]

In Search of Our Mothers' Gardens

I described her own nature and temperament. Told how they needed a larger life for their expression. . . . I pointed out that in lieu of proper channels, her emotions had overflowed into paths that dissipated them. I talked, beautifully I thought, about an art that would be born, an art that would open the way for women the likes of her. I asked her to hope, and build up an inner life against the coming of that day. . . . I sang, with a strange quiver in my voice, a promise song.

—"AVEY," JEAN TOOMER, *CANE*
The poet speaking to a prostitute who falls asleep while he's talking

When the poet Jean Toomer walked through the South in the early twenties, he discovered a curious thing: black women whose spirituality was so intense, so deep, so *unconscious,* they were themselves unaware of the richness they held. They stumbled blindly through their lives: creatures so abused and mutilated in body, so dimmed and confused by pain, that they considered themselves unworthy even of hope. In the selfless abstractions their bodies became to the men who used them, they became more than "sexual objects," more even than mere women: they became "Saints." Instead of being perceived as whole persons, their bodies became shrines: what was thought to be their minds became temples suitable for worship. These crazy Saints stared out at the world, wildly, like lunatics—or quietly, like suicides; and the "God" that was in their gaze was as mute as a great stone.

Who were these Saints? These crazy, loony, pitiful women?

Some of them, without a doubt, were our mothers and grandmothers.

In the still heat of the post-Reconstruction South, this is how they seemed to Jean Toomer: exquisite butterflies trapped in an evil honey, toiling away their lives in an era, a century, that did not acknowledge them, except as "the *mule* of the world." They dreamed dreams that no one knew—not even themselves, in any coherent fashion—and saw visions no one could understand. They wandered or sat about the countryside crooning lullabies to ghosts, and drawing the mother of Christ in charcoal on court-house walls.

They forced their minds to desert their bodies and their striving spirits sought to rise, like frail whirlwinds from the hard red clay. And when those frail whirlwinds fell, in scattered particles, upon the ground, no one mourned. Instead, men lit candles to celebrate the emptiness that remained, as people do who enter a beautiful but vacant space to resurrect a God.

Our mothers and grandmothers, some of them: moving to music not yet written. And they waited.

They waited for a day when the unknown thing that was in them would be made known; but guessed, somehow in their darkness, that on the day of their revelation they would be long dead. Therefore to Toomer they walked, and even ran, in slow motion. For they were going nowhere immediate, and the future was not yet within their grasp. And men took our mothers and grandmothers, "but got no pleasure from it." So complex was their passion and their calm.

To Toomer, they lay vacant and fallow as autumn fields, with harvest time never in sight: and he saw them enter loveless marriages, without joy; and become prostitutes, without resistance; and become mothers of children, without fulfillment.

For these grandmothers and mothers of ours were not Saints, but Artists; driven to a numb and bleeding madness by the springs of creativity in them for which there was no release. They were Creators, who lived lives of spiritual waste, because they were so rich in spirituality—which is the basis of Art—that the strain of enduring their unused and unwanted talent drove them insane. Throwing away this spirituality was their pathetic attempt to lighten the soul to a weight their work-worn, sexually abused bodies could bear.

What did it mean for a black woman to be an artist in our grandmothers' time? In our great-grandmothers' day? It is a question with an answer cruel enough to stop the blood.

Did you have a genius of a great-great-grandmother who died under some ignorant and depraved white overseer's lash? Or was she required to bake biscuits for a lazy backwater tramp, when she cried out in her soul to paint watercolors of sunsets, or the rain falling on the green and peaceful pasturelands? Or was her body broken and forced to bear children (who were more often than not sold away from her)—eight, ten, fifteen, twenty children—when her one joy was the thought of modeling heroic figures of rebellion, in stone or clay?

How was the creativity of the black woman kept alive, year after year and century after century, when for most of the years black people have been in America, it was a punishable crime for a black person to read or write? And the freedom to paint, to sculpt, to expand the mind with action did not exist. Consider, if you can bear to imagine it, what might have been the result if singing, too, had been forbidden by law. Listen to the voices of Bessie Smith, Billie Holiday, Nina Simone, Roberta Flack, and Aretha Franklin, among others, and imagine those voices muzzled for life. Then you may begin to comprehend the lives of our "crazy," "Sainted" mothers and grandmothers. The agony of the lives of women who might have been Poets, Novelists, Essayists, and Short-Story Writers (over a period of centuries), who died with their real gifts stifled within them.

And, if this were the end of the story, we would have cause to cry out in my paraphrase of Okot p'Bitek's great poem:

> O, my clanswomen
> Let us all cry together!
> Come,
> Let us mourn the death of our mother,
> The death of a Queen
> The ash that was produced
> By a great fire!
> O, this homestead is utterly dead
> Close the gates
> With *lacari* thorns,
> For our mother
> The creator of the Stool is lost!
> And all the young men
> Have perished in the wilderness!

But this is not the end of the story, for all the young women—our mothers and grandmothers, *ourselves*—have not perished in the wilderness. And if we ask ourselves why, and search for and find the answer, we will know beyond all efforts to erase it from our minds, just exactly who, and of what, we black American women are.

One example, perhaps the most pathetic, most misunderstood one, can provide a backdrop for our mothers' work: Phillis Wheatley, a slave in the 1700s.

Virginia Woolf, in her book *A Room of One's Own,* wrote that in order for a woman to write fiction she must have two things, certainly: a room of her own (with key and lock) and enough money to support herself.

What then are we to make of Phillis Wheatley, a slave, who owned not even herself? This sickly, frail black girl who required a servant of her own at times—her health was so precarious—and who, had she been white, would have been easily considered the intellectual superior of all the women and most of the men in the society of her day.

Virginia Woolf wrote further, speaking of course not of our Phillis, that "any woman born with a great gift in the sixteenth century [insert "eighteenth century," insert "black woman," insert "born or made a slave"] would certainly have gone crazed, shot herself, or ended her days in some lonely cottage outside the village, half witch, half wizard [insert "Saint"], feared and mocked at. For it needs little skill and psychology to be sure that a highly gifted girl who had tried to use her gift of poetry would have been so thwarted and hindered by contrary instincts [add "chains, guns, the lash, the ownership of one's body by someone else, submission to an alien religion"], that she must have lost her health and sanity to a certainty."

The key words, as they relate to Phillis, are "contrary instincts." For when we read the poetry of Phillis Wheatley—as when we read the novels of Nella Larsen or the oddly false-sounding autobiography of that freest of all black women writers, Zora Hurston—evidence of "contrary instincts" is everywhere. Her loyalties were completely divided, as was, without question, her mind.

But how could this be otherwise? Captured at seven, a slave of wealthy, doting whites who instilled in her the "savagery" of the Africa they "rescued" her from . . . one wonders if she was even able to remember her homeland as she had known it, or as it really was.

Yet, because she did try to use her gift for poetry in a world that made her a slave, she was "so thwarted and hindered by . . . contrary instincts, that she . . . lost her health. . . ." In the last years of her brief life, burdened not only with the need to express her gift but also with a penniless, friendless "freedom" and several small children for whom she was forced to do strenuous work to feed, she lost her health, certainly. Suffering from malnutrition and neglect and who knows what mental agonies, Phillis Wheatley died.

So torn by "contrary instincts" was black, kidnapped, enslaved Phillis that her description of "the Goddess"—as she poetically called the Liberty she did not have—is ironically, cruelly humorous. And, in fact, has held Phillis up to ridicule for more than a century. It is usually read prior to hanging Phillis's memory as that of a fool. She wrote:

> The Goddess comes, she moves divinely fair,
> Olive and laurel binds her *golden* hair.
> Wherever shines this native of the skies,
> Unnumber'd charms and recent graces rise. [My italics]

It is obvious that Phillis, the slave, combed the "Goddess's" hair every morning; prior, perhaps, to bringing in the milk, or fixing her mistress's lunch. She took her imagery from the one thing she saw elevated above all others.

With the benefit of hindsight we ask, "How could she?"

But at last, Phillis, we understand. No more snickering when your stiff, struggling, ambivalent lines are forced on us. We know now that you were not an idiot or a traitor; only a sickly little black girl, snatched from your home and country and made a slave; a woman who still struggled to sing the song that was your gift, although in a land of barbarians who praised you for your bewildered tongue. It is not so much what you sang, as that you kept alive, in so many of our ancestors, *the notion of song.*

Black women are called, in the folklore that so aptly identifies one's status in society, "the *mule* of the world," because we have been handed the burdens that everyone else —*everyone* else—refused to carry. We have also been called "Matriarchs," "Super-women," and "Mean and Evil Bitches." Not to mention "Castraters" and "Sapphire's Mama." When we have pleaded for understanding, our character has been distorted; when we have asked for simple caring, we have been handed empty inspirational appellations, then stuck in the farthest corner. When we have asked for love, we have been given children. In short, even our plainer gifts, our labors of fidelity and love, have been knocked down our throats. To be an artist and a black woman, even today, lowers our status in many respects, rather than raises it: and yet, artists we will be.

Therefore we must fearlessly pull out of ourselves and look at and identify with our lives the living creativity some of our great-grandmothers were not allowed to know. I stress *some* of them because it is well known that the majority of our great-grandmothers knew, even without "knowing" it, the reality of their spirituality, even if they didn't recognize it beyond what happened in the singing at church—and they never had any intention of giving it up.

How they did it—those millions of black women who were not Phillis Wheatley, or Lucy Terry or Frances Harper or Zora Hurston or Nella Larsen or Bessie Smith; or Elizabeth Catlett, or Katherine Dunham, either—brings me to the title of this essay, "In Search of Our Mothers' Gardens," which is a personal account that is yet shared, in its theme and its meaning, by all of us. I found, while thinking about the far-reaching world of the creative black woman, that often the truest answer to a question that really matters can be found very close.

In the late 1920s my mother ran away from home to marry my father. Marriage, if not running away, was expected of seventeen-year-old girls. By the time she was twenty, she had two children and was pregnant with a third. Five children later, I was born. And this is how I came to know my mother: she seemed a large, soft, loving-eyed woman who was rarely impatient in our home. Her quick, violent temper was on view only a few times a year, when she battled with the white landlord who had the misfortune to suggest to her that her children did not need to go to school.

She made all the clothes we wore, even my brothers' overalls. She made all the towels and sheets we used. She spent the summers canning vegetables and fruits. She spent the winter evenings making quilts enough to cover all our beds.

During the "working" day, she labored beside—not behind—my father in the fields. Her day began before sunup, and did not end until late at night. There was never a moment for her to sit down, undisturbed, to unravel her own private thoughts; never a time free from interruption—by work or the noisy inquiries of her many children. And yet, it is to my mother—and all our mothers who were not famous—that I went in search of the secret of what has fed that muzzled and often mutilated, but vibrant, creative spirit that the black woman has inherited, and that pops out in wild and unlikely places to this day.

But when, you will ask, did my overworked mother have time to know or care about feeding the creative spirit?

The answer is so simple that many of us have spent years discovering it. We have constantly looked high, when we should have looked high—and low.

For example: in the Smithsonian Institution in Washington, D.C., there hangs a quilt unlike any other in the world. In fanciful, inspired, and yet simple and identifiable figures, it portrays the story of the Crucifixion. It is considered rare, beyond price. Though it follows no known pattern of quiltmaking, and though it is made of bits and pieces of worthless rags, it is obviously the work of a person of powerful imagination and deep spiritual feeling. Below this quilt I saw a note that says it was made by "an anonymous Black woman in Alabama, a hundred years ago."

If we could locate this "anonymous" black woman from Alabama, she would turn out to be one of our grandmothers—an artist who left her mark in the only materials she could afford, and in the only medium her position in society allowed her to use.

As Virginia Woolf wrote further, in *A Room of One's Own:*

> Yet genius of a sort must have existed among women as it must have existed among the working class. [Change this to "slaves" and "the wives and daughters of sharecroppers."] Now and again an Emily Brontë or a Robert Burns [change this to "a Zora Hurston or a Richard Wright"] blazes out and proves its presence. But certainly it never got itself on to paper. When, however, one reads of a witch being ducked, of a woman possessed by devils [or "Sainthood"], of a wise woman selling herbs [our root workers], or even a very remarkable man who had a mother, then I think we are on the track of a lost novelist, a suppressed poet, or some mute and inglorious Jane Austen. . . . Indeed, I would venture to guess that Anon, who wrote so many poems without signing them, was often a woman. . . .

And so our mothers and grandmothers have, more often than not anonymously, handed on the creative spark, the seed of the flower they themselves never hoped to see: or like a sealed letter they could not plainly read.

And so it is, certainly, with my own mother. Unlike "Ma" Rainey's songs, which retained their creator's name even while blasting forth from Bessie Smith's mouth, no song or poem will bear my mother's name. Yet so many of the stories that I write, that we all write, are my mother's stories. Only recently did I fully realize this: that through years of listening to my mother's stories of her life, I have absorbed not only the stories themselves, but something of the manner in which she spoke, something of the urgency that involves the knowledge that her stories—like her life—must be recorded. It is probably for this reason that so much of what I have written is about characters whose counterparts in real life are so much older than I am.

But the telling of these stories, which came from my mother's lips as naturally as breathing, was not the only way my mother showed herself as an artist. For stories, too, were subject to being distracted, to dying without conclusion. Dinners must be started, and cotton must be gathered before the big rains. The artist that was and is my mother showed itself to me only after many years. This is what I finally noticed:

Like Mem, a character in *The Third Life of Grange Copeland,* my mother adorned with flowers whatever shabby house we were forced to live in. And not just your typical straggly country stand of zinnias, either. She planted ambitious gardens—and still does—with over fifty different varieties of plants that bloom profusely from early March until late November. Before she left home for the fields, she watered her flowers, chopped up the grass, and laid out new beds. When she returned from the fields she might divide clumps of bulbs, dig a cold pit, uproot and replant roses, or prune branches from her taller bushes or trees—until night came and it was too dark to see.

Whatever she planted grew as if by magic, and her fame as a grower of flowers spread over three counties. Because of her creativity with her flowers, even my memories of poverty are seen through a screen of blooms—sunflowers, petunias, roses, dahlias, forsythia, spirea, delphiniums, verbena . . . and on and on.

And I remember people coming to my mother's yard to be given cuttings from her flowers; I hear again the praise showered on her because whatever rocky soil she landed on, she turned into a garden. A garden so brilliant with colors, so original in its design, so magnificent with life and creativity, that to this day people drive by our house in Georgia—perfect strangers and imperfect strangers—and ask to stand or walk among my mother's art.

I notice that it is only when my mother is working in her flowers that she is radiant, almost to the point of being invisible—except as Creator: hand and eye. She is involved in work her soul must have. Ordering the universe in the image of her personal conception of Beauty.

Her face, as she prepares the Art that is her gift, is a legacy of respect she leaves to me, for all that illuminates and cherishes life. She has handed down respect for the possibilities—and the will to grasp them.

For her, so hindered and intruded upon in so many ways, being an artist has still been a daily part of her life. This ability to hold on, even in very simple ways, is work black women have done for a very long time.

This poem is not enough, but it is something, for the woman who literally covered the holes in our walls with sunflowers:

> They were women then
> My mama's generation
> Husky of voice—Stout of
> Step
> With fists as well as
> Hands
> How they battered down
> Doors
> And ironed
> Starched white
> Shirts
> How they led
> Armies

Headragged Generals
Across mined
Fields
Booby-trapped
Kitchens
To discover books
Desks
A place for us
How they knew what we
Must know
Without knowing a page
Of it
Themselves.

Guided by my heritage of a love of beauty and a respect for strength—in search of my mother's garden, I found my own.

And perhaps in Africa over two hundred years ago, there was just such a mother; perhaps she painted vivid and daring decorations in oranges and yellows and greens on the walls of her hut; perhaps she sang—in a voice like Roberta Flack's—*sweetly* over the compounds of her village; perhaps she wove the most stunning mats or told the most ingenious stories of all the village storytellers. Perhaps she was herself a poet—though only her daughter's name is signed to the poems that we know.

Perhaps Phillis Wheatley's mother was also an artist.

Perhaps in more than Phillis Wheatley's biological life is her mother's signature made clear.

Appendix
Writing About Literature

Why write about literature? For one reason certainly: writing about a literary work requires you to read it more attentively and to notice details you might overlook in a more casual reading. Writing about literature also stimulates your thinking about it. Through written discourse you come to a better understanding of what you think about literary works, how you feel about them, and why. You may also write about literary works for an additional reason: to increase your understanding of their artistic and aesthetic achievement.

THE WRITING PROCESS

Choosing a Topic—Getting Started

The first problem you face in writing about any literary work is to decide on a topic. Sometimes this is settled for you when an instructor provides a topic or a series of choices. When you must discover your own topic, however, you should keep a few things in mind. First, make sure it is suited to the required length of the paper. If your essay is going to be five hundred to one thousand words, such a subject as "*Othello* as Tragedy" will be too broad. By narrowing your subject to consider a single aspect of the play's tragic action, for example, "Othello's Tragic Flaw," you are more likely to avoid superficial generalization and write a paper of greater depth and specificity.

Additional considerations about your choice of topic include how powerfully the topic engages your interest and how quickly you can clarify it for your readers. Choose a topic you are willing to invest time and effort in exploring. And once you decide on a topic, make it clear to your readers from the start. One way to do this is to include a title that reflects the nature and focus of your subject. A topic such as "Types of Love in *Othello*" directs your readers to the central concerns of your paper. In addition, a clearly focused topic can serve as a point of reference when you later write and revise your paper, a reminder of your intention should you wander off the track.

To increase your chances of finding a topic that meets the criteria of suitability, specificity, and interest, it pays to read the work you plan to write about carefully at least twice. Mark up the text as you read, underlining words and sentences, checking off significant passages of dialogue and description, and writing brief marginal notes. Examples of marginal annotations that can lead to the discovery of a *subject,* or a focused aspect of a work worth exploring in writing, can be found on pages 10–14, 391, 816–817, and 1425–1426 of this text. These general annotations concern various features of four literary works—a story, a poem, a scene from a play, and an essay. You can also focus on one aspect of a work and annotate it. You might decide, for example, to analyze the imagery of William Shakespeare's sonnet, "That time of year, thou may'st in me behold," or the ironic dimensions of Kate Chopin's "The Story of an Hour." In such instances, annotating a single feature of a work can be an excellent preparation for the later stages of the writing process—developing your ideas in a draft, organizing your thinking, and revising.

Another technique useful in finding a topic can be used in conjunction with annotation: listing and relating details. An efficient way to get started when you write, listing can prod you to notice details you might otherwise overlook. More importantly, listing can also help you discover connections and relationships that are more difficult to discern when the details are scattered throughout the work. For example, you can list and link the images in Shakespeare's "That time of year," like this:

Grouping related details will help you see the connections among the poem's images:

yellow leaves	twilight	cold	sunset
few leaves	sunset	ashes	glowing fire
none (no leaves)	night	death (bed)	nourished
(bare boughs)		consumed	

Such lists of related details coupled with annotations and questions can lead to a focused analysis of the poem's imagery like the one found on pages 424–425.

Drafting the Paper—Developing Your Ideas

Once you have a tentative subject and an angle of approach to the text, you can write a rough draft. Your purpose in this draft is simply to get your ideas down and to see how you can develop and support them. Think of the rough draft as an exploratory occasion to discover what you think about your subject and to test and refine your ideas. You shouldn't worry about having a clearly defined thesis or main idea before you begin writing the rough draft. Instead, you can use this draft to find a thesis and sharpen it so that eventually it becomes clear.

In drafting your paper, consider your purpose. Are you writing to provide information and make observations about the work? Are you writing to argue for a particular way to interpret it? Ultimately, of course, all explanations of literary works are interpretations, and all interpretations are forms of argument. That is, they are persuasive attempts to see the literary text one way rather than in other ways. When you write about a literary work you will often be attempting to convince others that what you see and say about it makes sense. You will be arguing for the validity of your way of seeing, not necessarily to the exclusion of all other ways, but to demonstrate that your understanding of the work is reasonable and valuable. Moreover, since your readers will respond as much to how you support your arguments as to what your ideas are, you will need to concentrate on providing evidence for your ideas carefully and thoroughly. Most often this evidence will come in the form of textual support—details of action, dialogue, imagery, description, language, and structure. Additional evidence may come from secondary sources, from the comments of experienced readers whose observations and interpretations may influence and support your own thinking. In marshalling evidence for your ideas from the work itself and from secondary sources, however, keep the following guidelines in mind:

1. Be fairminded. Avoid oversimplifying or distorting either the work or what others have written about it.
2. Be cautious. Qualify your claims. Limit your discussion to what you feel confident you can reasonably demonstrate.
3. Be logical. See that the various elements of your argument fit together and that one part of your approach doesn't contradict another.
4. Be accurate. If you present facts, details, or quotations, present them accurately.
5. Be confident. You should believe in your ideas and present them with conviction.

APPROACHES TO A TEXT

Analysis and Explication   In drafting a paper on a literary work you will often find yourself analyzing it. *Analysis* involves breaking a subject down into its constituent parts and examining the relationships among them. When you analyze literary works you study their elements to see what each reveals about the work overall. You might analyze a short story's point of view, characterization, plot, or setting, for example, and discuss what the element contributes to its meaning and effect.

Analysis is not an end in itself. We analyze works to better understand both *what* they mean and *how* they come to mean what they do. We take works apart to reconstruct or put them back together with an enriched sense of their significance and artistry. The many analyses contained in *Literature* (see especially Chapters 3, 4, 8, 9, 14, 15, 24, and 25) illustrate how analysis of the elements of literature enlarges our understanding of it.

One form your analysis may take is an *explication,* the unfolding of the layers of meaning in a text. Explication provides a close-up view of the language of a passage in the course of explaining its meaning. To explicate is to interpret. Most often explication is reserved for sections of works—for an important descriptive passage in a short story, for example, or for a segment of dialogue in a play, or a crucial paragraph in an essay—perhaps its introduction or conclusion. Brief lyric poems, however, are sometimes explicated in their entirety.

Throughout Chapter 8, Elements of Poetry (pages 399–473), you will find many explications. We can illustrate the process here briefly with a look at the concluding lines of Gerard Manley Hopkins's "Spring and Fall: to a Young Child" (page 475):

> It is the blight man was born for.
> It is Margaret you mourn for.

Coming at the end, these lines announce what has been implicit in the poem from the beginning: that Margaret is weeping not over the leaves of autumn, but over her own mortality. The older speaker clarifies what the child had subconsciously intuited: that beauty fades and life ends. Margaret, though weeping for her own mortality, is also weeping over the mortality of all men and of nature, which mirrors man's end in its own decay. Moreover, by saying that man was "born for" death and by calling man's birth a "blight," the speaker suggests that man brings disease with him into the world—not only physical decay and death, but also sin, which "blights" man's soul.

Though focused on two lines, this explication picks up the implications of earlier lines (see the discussion in Chapter 8). Keep in mind that even though you may be examining a small part of a literary work, your explication must make sense in light of the central meaning of the entire work, and provide evidence for your interpretation.

Comparison and Contrast   Another approach you can employ in drafting a paper is *comparison* and *contrast* of elements of a single work or of an aspect of different works. You might compare and contrast the speech and actions of the two male characters in Kay Boyle's "Astronomer's Wife," for example. Or you could compare the central character in that story with the protagonist of another such as Leslie Silko's "Yellow Woman."

Comparative analysis can sharpen your perception of the works you are considering. Looking at two works together or at two aspects of a single work, you see what each lacks as well as what it possesses. Comparing two short stories, you might notice, for example, that one includes much dialogue and the other little; that in one the action is external while in the other it is internal; or that the settings, tone, or point of view of the stories differ in significant and interesting ways. Such comparative observations will lead you to ask why those differences exist and why the writers developed the stories as they did.

For some examples of how comparison and contrast serve to elucidate literary works, see pages 16–17; 21–22; 53–54; 64–65; 803–804; 821–822; 1437–1438. And in writing comparative papers, keep the following guidelines in mind:

1. Compare two things that seem worth the trouble, that will reward your effort. By attending carefully to a work's details you will often find significant parallels and contrasts. Follow the leads the work provides.
2. Compare works that have a significant feature in common, such as authorship, style, genre, historical period, subject, situation, or an aspect of technique like meter or point of view.
3. Make a point. Use comparison and contrast in the service of an idea, an argument, an interpretation. Your comparative analysis should lead you to a conclusion, perhaps to an evaluation, not merely to a set of parallels.
4. Decide whether to organize your comparative discussion according to the "block" method in which you discuss each subject separately; or according to the "alternating" method in which you discuss the two central subjects in point-by-point comparisons of specific characteristics. If you are comparing two characters, according to the block method, for example, you would devote the first half of your paper to one and the second half to the other character. If you followed the alternating structure, you would consider each side-by-side as you focused on such characteristics as their physical appearance, their interactions with other characters, their behavior at critical moments of the action, and so on.

Redrafting Your Paper—Organizing Your Thinking

Once you have written the draft, let it sit overnight, longer if possible, before returning to consider what you have. Try to assess whether what you are saying makes sense and whether you have provided enough examples to make your ideas clear and sufficient evidence to make them convincing. Read your draft critically, asking yourself what holds up and what doesn't, what makes sense and what doesn't. Consider whether it centers on a single idea, whether it stays on track. If your first draft does these things you can begin thinking about how to tighten its organization and polish its style. If, on the other hand, it contains frequent changes of direction and a number of different ideas, you will need to decide what ideas to salvage and redraft the paper to focus more exclusively and specifically on them.

When you have written a draft that centers on an idea, you are ready to view it with an eye to its organization. Consider whether you have arranged your ideas and examples in a coherent and logical manner. Consider also whether you have allotted sufficient space (or perhaps too much space) to clarifying and supporting your views. You should be clear in your own mind about how your paper is structured, how it progresses from one part or one paragraph to another.

In discussing the ironic action of Chopin's "The Story of an Hour," for example, you might focus on three or four details notable for their ironic character. But you will also need to decide on a particular order in which to discuss them. You will need to ask yourself how the ironic aspects of the story's action can be related to one another. You will very probably see some actions and details as more important than others; you may be able to subdivide and pair your examples, perhaps contrasting some with others. Or you may elect to consider them in an order of increasing complexity or importance. It is necessary, though, that you devise an organization that makes sense to you and that will seem natural to your readers.

Besides deciding on the order of ideas in your essay and the amount of space you alot each, you must consider how to get from one idea to another. You will need to link the sections of your discussion so that your writing flows smoothly. Generally, you can create transitions with phrases and sentences at the beginnings of paragraphs. Sometimes, however, you will not need an explicit mark of transition from one point to another. In such instances, the context of your developing argument will make clear your shift to a different facet of your discussion.

Revising Your Paper

Revision is not something that occurs once, at the end of the writing process. Redrafting your paper with an eye to organization is a significant act of revision. So too is your rereading of the literary text and your thinking about it. Revision is a process that goes on through the entire span of reading and writing and essentially involves reconsidering both your writing and your thinking. You make this reconsideration on three levels: conceptual, organizational, and stylistic.

Conceptual revision involves reconsidering your ideas. As you write a first or second draft of a paper about a literary work, your understanding of the work and of what you might say about it may change. Accumulating textual evidence in support of one interpretation of the work, you may discover stronger evidence for a contrasting position. When this happens you will need to recast your developing paper to accommodate your revised vision of the work. This will mean, of course, that you will make major changes in your original draft. You may very well end up scrapping much of it and beginning again with a stronger conviction about a different approach or a revised idea.

Structural or organizational revision involves reconsidering the shape your paper takes. You will need to ask yourself whether the arrangement of its parts best presents your line of reasoning. Is the organizational framework of your paper readily discernible? A general organizational framework for your paper would include an introduction that clarifies your purpose and intention; a set of internal paragraphs that explore, develop, and explain your ideas; and a conclusion that rounds off the discussion, leaving readers convinced of the value and validity of your perspective.

Stylistic revision concerns smaller-scale details such as matters of syntax or word order, diction or word choice, tone, imagery, and rhythm. Even though you may have such considerations in mind in early drafts, it is wise to defer strict attention to them until you have written a final draft (largely because such details will undergo significant alteration as you rethink and reorganize your ideas).

To help you focus on aspects of style that may require revision, use the following questions as a guide.

1. Are your sentences concise and clear?
2. Can you eliminate words that are not doing their job?
3. Is the tone consistent?
4. Is the level of language appropriate for your audience?
5. Do your words and sentences say what you want to say?

6. Are there any distracting grammatical errors: inconsistencies in verb tenses, problems with subject-verb agreement, run-on sentences, and the like?

7. Are there any errors in spelling and punctuation?

Finally, proofread the paper, making sure it conforms to your instructor's guidelines on manuscript form.

DOCUMENTING SOURCES

You may want to refer to outside sources when writing a literature paper—to get additional information and ideas and to see how a work has been received by critics over time. If you incorporate the work of others into your paper, it will be necessary to credit your sources through documentation. You should always provide source credit when quoting directly, paraphrasing (rewriting a passage in your own words), borrowing ideas, or picking up facts that aren't general knowledge.

In crediting your sources, you are participating honestly and correctly in shared intellectual activity. You are showing your reader that your knowledge of a text includes some insights into what others have thought and said about it. And you are assisting your reader, who may want to consult the sources that you found valuable.

In literary study most writers follow the documentation style recommended by the Modern Language Association of America (MLA). The MLA guidelines have changed recently, so that the association now endorses a parenthetical citation and reference list form over its earlier raised number and footnote-or-endnote form. Since both forms are still in use, they are both illustrated on the following pages. You can find a complete guide to the new MLA style in Joseph Gibaldi and Walter S. Achtert's *MLA Handbook for Writers of Research Papers,* Second Edition.

New MLA Style and Alternate MLA Style

In the new MLA style, parenthetical citations within the text indicate that a source has been used. These citations refer the reader to a reference list, which should start on a new page at the end of the paper. In the "alternate" or "old" MLA style, references are marked by raised numbers in the text that correspond to numbered notes either at the foot of the page (footnotes) or the end of the paper (endnotes). Both the reference list and the endnotes and footnotes contain bibliographic information about the sources; however, the arrangement, punctuation, and capitalization of the sources differs between the two reference styles.

NEW MLA STYLE: PARENTHETICAL CITATIONS PAIRED WITH A REFERENCE LIST

When you refer to a specific section of a work in the body of your paper, provide your reader with the author and page numbers of your source. Place the page numbers in parentheses, and add the author's name if it isn't contained in your sentence.

According to Lawrence Lipking (30–39), a poet's life involves much more than his or her literal biography.

A recent critic argues that a poet's life involves much more than his or her literal biography (Lipking 30–39).

If your paper includes two or more works by the same author, add the title of the work before the page number(s). The following are examples of other kinds of citations commonly found in literature papers.

A work in an anthology:

Bacon's "On Revenge" affords us a glimpse at his view of human nature: "There is no man doth a wrong for the wrong's sake, but thereby to purchase himself profit, or pleasure, or honor, or the like" (DiYanni 1447).

(The editor's name and the page number of the quotation appear in parentheses.)

A classic verse play or poem:

"She loved me for the dangers I had passed," recounts Othello, "And I loved her that she did pity them" (I.iii.166–167).

(Act, scene, and line numbers are used instead of page numbers. Arabic numbers may also be used for the act and scene.)

Tennyson's Ulysses compares a dull existence to a dull sword when he says: "How dull it is to pause, to make an end,/ To rust unburnished, not to shine in use!" (22–23).

(Line numbers are used instead of page numbers. Note the use of a slash [/] to indicate the end of a line.)

STYLING A REFERENCE LIST

The items in a reference list should be alphabetically arranged. The following are typical kinds of entries for a literature paper.

A book by a single author:

Lipking, Lawrence. *The Life of the Poet: Beginning and Ending Poetic Careers.* Chicago: U of Chicago P, 1981.

(The second line is indented five spaces.)

An article in a book:

Williams, Sherley Anne. "The Black Musician: The Black Hero as Light Bearer." *James Baldwin: A Collection of Critical Essays.* Ed. Kenneth Kinnamon. Englewood Cliffs, NJ: Prentice-Hall, 1974. 147–154.

(The page numbers "147–154" refer to the entire article. References to specific pages would appear in parenthetical citations.)

A journal article:

Walker, Janet. "Hardy's Somber Lyrics." *Poetry* 17 (1976): 25–39.

(The article appeared in issue 17 of the journal *Poetry.* The page numbers refer to the entire article.)

A work in an anthology:

Bacon, Francis. "On Revenge." *Literature: Reading Fiction, Poetry, Drama, and the Essay.* Ed. Robert DiYanni. New York: Random House, 1986. 1446–1447.

(The page numbers refer to the entire essay.)

Cite the anthology itself if you are using more than one selection from it. The selections can simply be cited without repeating the anthology title and publication data.

>DiYanni, Robert, ed. *Literature: Reading Fiction, Poetry, Drama, and the Essay.* New York: Random House, 1986.

>Tennyson, Alfred, Lord. "Ulysses." DiYanni. 584–585.

A multivolume work; a second edition:

>Daiches, David. *A Critical History of English Literature.* 2nd ed. 2 vols. New York: Ronald, 1970.

A translation:

>Auerbach, Erich. *Mimesis: The Represeutation of Reality in Western Literature.* Trans. Willard Trask. Princeton: Princeton UP, 1953.

Alternate MLA Style: Note Numbers Paired with Endnotes/Footnotes

USING NOTE NUMBERS

Raised note numbers, in consecutive order, follow the quotation or information being cited. They belong *after* all punctuation, except a dash.

>"She loved me for the dangers I had passed," recounts Othello, "And I loved her that she did pity them."[1]

If you include several quotations from the same text in your paper, you may switch to parenthetical citations after the first note. This will reduce the number of footnotes or endnotes.

>Emilia tells Desdemona that jealousy is "a monster begot upon itself, born on itself" (III.iv.155–156).

USING ENDNOTES/FOOTNOTES

Each raised note number corresponds to a footnote or endnote. The only difference between footnotes and endnotes is their placement in the paper. Footnotes appear at the bottom of the page on which the reference occurs: quadruple-space between the last line of text and the first note. Endnotes are grouped together on a separate page immediately following the last page of text.

The following are the same sources given on pages 1525–1526, now in endnote form. Note that specific page references are given for each entry; these page references would be contained in parentheses in new MLA style.

[1]Lawrence Lipking, *The Life of the Poet: Beginning and Ending Poetic Careers* (Chicago: U of Chicago P, 1981) 30–39.

[2]Sherley Anne Williams, "The Black Musician: The Black Hero as Light Bearer," in *James Baldwin: A Collection of Critical Essays,* ed. Kenneth Kinnamon (Englewood Cliffs, N.J.: Prentice-Hall, 1974) 147.

[3]Janet Walker, "Hardy's Somber Lyrics," *Poetry* 17 (1976): 35.

[4]Francis Bacon, "On Revenge," *Literature: Reading Fiction, Poetry, Drama, and the Essay,* ed. Robert DiYanni (New York: Random House, 1986) 1447.

[5]David Daiches, *A Critical History of English Literature,* 2nd ed., 2 vols. (New York: Ronald, 1970) 2:530.

[6]Erich Auerbach, *Mimesis: The Representation of Reality in Western Literature,* trans. Willard Trask (Princeton: Princeton UP, 1953) 77.

NOTING SUBSEQUENT REFERENCES

It is usually enough simply to list the author's name and the appropriate page(s) in subsequent references to a source.

[7]Lipking 98.

Glossary

Allegory   A symbolic narrative in which the surface details imply a secondary meaning. Allegory often takes the form of a story in which the characters represent moral qualities.

Alliteration   The repetition of consonant sounds, especially at the beginning of words.

Anapest   Two unaccented syllables followed by an accented one as in cŏmprĕhénd or ĭntĕrvéne.

Antagonist   A character or force against which a main character struggles.

Argumentative essay   An essay that puts forth a claim directly and explicitly supports it with evidence.

Assonance   The repetition of similar vowel sounds in a sentence or a line of poetry as in "I rose and told him of my woe."

Aubade   A love lyric in which the speaker complains about the arrival of the dawn, when he must part from his lover.

Ballad   A narrative poem written in four-line stanzas, characterized by swift action and narrated in a direct style.

Blank verse   A line of poetry or prose in unrhymed iambic pentameter.

Caesura   A strong pause within a line of verse.

Character   An imaginary person that lives in a literary work. Literary characters may be major or minor, static or dynamic.

Characterization   The means by which writers present and reveal character.

Chorus A group of characters in Greek tragedy who comment on the action of a play without participating in it. Their leader is the choragos.

Climax The turning point of the action in the plot of a play or story. The climax represents the point of greatest tension in the work.

Closed form A type of form or structure in poetry characterized by regularity and consistency in such elements as rhyme, line length, and metrical pattern.

Comedy A type of drama in which the characters experience reversals of fortune, usually for the better. In comedy things work out happily in the end. Comic drama may be either romantic—characterized by a tone of tolerance and geniality—or satiric. Satiric plays offer a darker vision of human nature, one that ridicules human folly.

Complication An intensification of the conflict in a story or play.

Conflict A struggle between opposing forces in a story or play, usually resolved by the end of the work.

Connotation The personal and emotional associations called up by a word that go beyond its dictionary meaning.

Convention A customary feature of a literary work such as the use of a chorus in Greek tragedy or an explicit moral in a fable.

Couplet A pair of rhymed lines that may or may not constitute a separate stanza in a poem.

Dactyl A stressed syllable followed by two unstressed ones as in flút-tĕr-ĭng or blúe-bĕr-r̆y.

Denotation The dictionary meaning of a word.

Denouement The resolution of the plot of a literary work.

Deus ex machina A god who resolves the entanglements of a play by his supernatural intervention (literally, a god from the machine) or any artificial device used to resolve a plot.

Dialogue The conversation of characters in a literary work.

Diction The selection of words in a literary work.

Dramatic monologue A type of poem in which a speaker addresses a silent listener.

Elegy A lyric poem that laments the dead.

Elision The omission of an unstressed vowel or syllable to preserve the meter of a line of poetry.

Enjambment A run-on line of poetry in which logical and grammatical sense carries over from one line into the next. An enjambed line differs from an end-stopped line in which the grammatical and logical sense is completed within the line. In the opening lines of Robert Browning's "My Last Duchess," for example, the first line is end-stopped and the second enjambed:

> That's my last Duchess painted on the wall,
> Looking as if she were alive. I call
> That piece a wonder, now. . . .

Epic A long narrative poem that records the adventures of a hero. Epics typically chronicle the origins of a civilization and embody its central values.

Epigram A brief witty poem, often satirical.

Exposition The first stage of a fictional or dramatic plot in which necessary background information is provided.

Expository essay   An essay that advances an idea in a direct manner. Its primary purpose is to provide information.

Fable   A brief story with an explicit moral, often including animals as characters.

Falling action   In the plot of a story or play the action following the climax of the work that moves it towards resolution.

Falling meter   Poetic meters such as trochaic and dactylic that move or fall from a stressed to an unstressed syllable.

Fiction   An imagined story.

Figurative language   A form of language use in which writers and speakers mean something other than the literal meaning of their words. See *hyperbole, metaphor, metonymy, simile, synecdoche,* and *understatement.*

Flashback   An interruption of a work's chronology to describe or present an incident that occurred prior to the main time frame of the action.

Foil   A character who contrasts and parallels the main character in a play or story.

Foot   A metrical unit composed of stressed and unstressed syllables. For example, an *iamb* or *iambic foot* is represented by ˘ ´, that is, an unaccented syllable followed by an accented one. See the chart on p. 454.

Free verse   Poetry without a regular pattern of meter or rhyme.

Gesture   The physical movement of a character during a play.

Hyperbole   A figure of speech involving exaggeration.

Iamb   An unstressed syllable followed by a stressed one, as in tŏdáy.

Image   A concrete representation of a sense impression, a feeling, or an idea. Imagery refers to the pattern of related details in a work.

Irony   A contrast or discrepancy between what is said and what is meant or between what happens and what is expected to happen. In verbal irony characters say the opposite of what they mean. In irony of circumstance or situation the opposite of what is expected happens. In dramatic irony a character speaks in ignorance of a situation or event known to the audience or to other characters.

Literal language   A form of language in which writers and speakers mean exactly what their words denote.

Lyric poem   A type of poem characterized by brevity, compression, and the expression of feeling.

Metaphor   A comparison between essentially unlike things without a word such as *like* or *as.* An example: "My love is a red, red rose."

Meter   The measured pattern of rhythmic accents in poems.

Metonymy   A figure of speech in which a closely related term is substituted for an object or idea. An example: "We have always remained loyal to the crown."

Narrative essay   A type of essay in which an idea is illustrated by means of a story or a series of incidents.

Narrative poem   A poem that tells a story.
Narrator   The voice and implied speaker of a fictional work, to be distinguished from the actual living author.

Octave   An eight-line unit, which may constitute a stanza or a section of a poem, as in the octave of a sonnet.
Ode   A long, stately poem in stanzas of varied length, meter, and form. Usually a serious poem on an exalted subject.
Onomatopoeia   The use of words to imitate the sounds they describe. Words such as *buzz* and *crack* are onomatopoetic.
Open form   A type of structure or form in poetry characterized by freedom from regularity and consistency in such elements as rhyme, line length, and metrical pattern.

Parable   A brief story that teaches a lesson often ethical or spiritual.
Parody   A humorous, mocking imitation of a literary work.
Personification   The endowment of inanimate objects or abstract concepts with animate or living qualities. An example: "The yellow leaves flaunted their color gaily in the wind."
Plot   The unified structure of incidents in a literary work.
Point of view   The angle of vision from which a story is narrated. See pp. 53–56.
Protagonist   The main character of a literary work.

Quatrain   A four-line stanza in a poem.

Resolution   The sorting out or unraveling of a plot at the end of a drama or narrative.
Rhetorical question   A question to which an overt answer is not expected. Writers use rhetorical questions to set up an explanation they are about to provide and to trigger a reader's mental response.
Rising action   A set of conflicts and crises that constitute that part of a play's plot leading up to the climax.
Rising meter   Poetic meters such as iambic and anapestic that move or ascend from an unstressed to a stressed syllable.
Rhyme   The matching of final vowel or consonant sounds in two or more words.
Rhythm   The recurrence of accent or stress in lines of verse.
Romance   A type of narrative fiction or poem in which adventure is a central feature and in which an idealized vision of reality is presented.

Satire   A literary work that criticizes human misconduct and ridicules vices, stupidities, and follies.
Sestet   A six-line unit of verse constituting a stanza or section of a poem; the last six lines of an Italian sonnet.
Sestina   A poem of thirty-nine lines written in iambic pentameter. Its six-line stanzas repeat in an intricate and prescribed order the six last words of each line in the opening stanza. After the sixth stanza there is a three-line *envoi* (or envoy) which uses the six repeating words, two to a line.
Setting   The time and place of a literary work that establish its context.
Simile   A figure of speech involving a comparison between unlike things using *like, as,* or *as though.* An example: "My love is like a red, red rose."

Soliloquy   A speech in a play which is meant to be heard by the audience but not by other characters on the stage. If there are no other characters present the soliloquy represents the character's thinking aloud.

Sonnet   A fourteen-line poem in iambic pentameter. The *Shakespearean* or *English sonnet* is arranged as three quatrains and a couplet, rhyming *abab cdcd efef gg*. The *Petrarchan* or *Italian sonnet* divides into two parts: an eight-line octave and a six-line sestet, rhyming *abba abba cde cde* or *cd cd cd*.

Speculative essay   A meditative essay generally loose in structure concerned with exploring an idea, a perception, or a feeling.

Spondee   A metrical foot represented by two stressed syllables such as kníck-knáck.

Stage direction   A playwright's descriptive or interpretive comments that provide readers (and actors) with information about the dialogue, setting, and action of a play.

Staging   The spectacle a play presents in performance, including the positions of actors on stage, the scenic background, the props and costumes, and the lighting and sound effects.

Stanza   A division or unit of a poem that is repeated in the same form—with similar or identical patterns of rhyme and meter.

Structure   The design or form of a literary work.

Style   The way an author chooses words, arranges them in sentences or in lines of dialogue or verse, and develops ideas and actions *with* description, imagery, and other literary techniques.

Subject   What a story or play is about; to be distinguished from plot and theme.

Symbol   An object or action in a literary work that means more than itself, that stands for something beyond itself.

Synecdoche   A figure of speech in which a part is substituted for the whole. An example: "Lend me a hand."

Syntax   The grammatical order of words in a sentence or line of verse or dialogue.

Tale   A story that narrates strange happenings in a direct manner, without detailed descriptions of character.

Tercet   A three-line stanza.

Theme   The idea of a literary work abstracted from its details of language, character, and action, and cast in the form of a generalization.

Tone   The implied attitude of a writer toward the subject and characters of a work.

Tragedy   A type of drama in which the characters experience reversals of fortune, usually for the worse. In tragedy catastrophe and suffering await many of the characters, especially the hero.

Tragic flaw   A weakness or limitation of character resulting in the fall of the tragic hero.

Tragic hero   a privileged exalted character of high repute, who by virtue of a tragic flaw and fate suffers a fall from glory into suffering.

tragicomedy   a type of play that contains elements of both tragedy and comedy.

Understatement   a figure of speech in which a writer or speaker says less than what he or she means; the converse of exaggeration.

Villanelle   A nineteen-line lyric poem that relies heavily on repetition. The first and third lines alternate throughout the poem, which is structured in six stanzas—five tercets and a final quatrain.

Poetry

Index

of Authors, Titles, and First Lines

Selection titles appear in italics, and first lines of poems appear in roman type. Numbers in roman type indicate the page of a selection, and italic numbers indicate discussion of the selection.

A ball will bounce, but less and less. It's not 724

A broken altar, Lord, Thy servant rears *500*, 543

'A cold coming we had of it 655

A narrow Fellow in the Grass 599

A noiseless patient spider 592

A poem should be palpable and mute 673

A snake came to my water-trough 646

A sudden blow: the great wings beating still 619

A sweet disorder in the dress 414

Abortions will not let you forget 719

About suffering they were never wrong 505

According to Breughel 504

Acquainted with the night 398, 633

Adam's Curse 478, 614

Adam's Task 775

Adieu, farewell, earth's bliss 532

Advice to My Son 430, *431*

Aesop
  The Wolf and the Mastiff 17, *17*

After great pain, a formal feeling comes 600

Ah, are you digging on my grave 608

Akhmadulina, Bella
  The Bride 790

Akhmatova, Anna
  Requiem 662

All kings, and all their favorites 535

All night the sound had 741

All things within this fading world hath end 548

All year the flax-dam festered in the heart, 793

Allen, Woody
  The Kugelmass Episode 340

Altar, The 500, 543

Amichai, Yehuda
  The eternal mystery 732
  You Can Rely On Him 733
Ammons, A. R.
  Corsons Inlet 737
  Poetics 471
  The City Limits 740
Among twenty snowy mountains 638
An axe angles 460
And here face down beneath the sun 674
And this is the way they ring 767
Anniversary, The 535
Anonymous
  Edward, Edward 397, 515
  Lord Randal 397, 511
  Sir Patrick Spens 513
  The Demon Lover 518
  The Twa Corbies 512
  The Unquiet Grave 517
  Western Wind 406
Antigonê 803, 815–18, 824, 830, 843, 885
anyone lived in a pretty how town 678
Apollinaire, Guillaume
  Le Pont Mirabeau 491
  Mirabeau Bridge 492
  The Mirabeau Bridge 492
Apparently with no surprise 602
Apple Tree, The 755
Appleman, Philip
  Ten Definitions of Lifetime 735
April Inventory 743
Araby 30, 65, 65, 69
*Arms and the Man 810–12, 814–15, 821–22,
    824–25, 828, 1185,* 1186, *1233,
    1270–71*
Arnold, Matthew
  Dover Beach 597
Ars Poetica (Huidobro) 672
Ars Poetica (MacLeish) 673
As I sd to my 741
As I was walking all alane 512
As on all its sides a kitchen-match darts
    white 637
As virtuous men pass mildly away 536
Astronomer's Wife 32, 32
Astrophel and Stella 527
At five in the afternoon *397,* 685
At ten A.M. the young housewife 643

Atwood, Margaret
  This Is a Photograph of Me 794
Auden, W. H.
  In Memory of W. B. Yeats 700
  Musée des Beaux Arts 505
  O what is that sound 703
  "O where are you going?" 702
  Sonnets from China, XVIII 700
  The Unknown Citizen 699
Aunt Jennifer's Tigers 770
Aunt Jennifer's tigers prance across a screen
    770
Avenge, O Lord, thy slaughtered saints,
    whose bones *439,* 547

Bacon, Francis
  Of Love 1429, 1454
  Of Revenge 1446
  *Of Youth and Age 1424–27, 1425, 1429,
    1432, 1438–39*
Bad Characters 305
Bald heads forgetful of their sins 615
Baldwin, James
  Notes of a Native Son 1435–39, 1446, 1488
Bananas ripe and green, and ginger-root 669
Barthelme, Donald
  A Shower of Gold 21, 335
Batter my heart, three-personed God 538
Battle of the Ants, The 1439
Battle Royal 54, 289
Battle, The 427
Bear, The 63–65, 218
Because I could not stop for Death 435
Before the Birth of One of Her Children 548
Behold her, single in the field 564
Belle Dame sans Merci, La 397, 576
Bells for John Whiteside's Daughter 659
Bent double, like old beggars under sacks
    401, 677
Berryman, John
  Winter Landscape 507
Between my finger and my thumb 791
Binsey Poplars 610
Bishop, Elizabeth
  *First Death in Nova Scotia 417, 417,
    418–19*
  Sestina 398, 709
  The Fish 707

Black reapers with the sound of steel on stones 682

Blake, William
A Poison Tree 432
London 479, 479–82, 480
Mock on, Mock on, Voltaire, Rousseau, 562
The Clod & the Pebble 560
The Garden of Love 561
The Lamb 560
The Sick Rose 508
The Tyger 561

Blessing, A 759
Blind Man, The (Borges) 691
Blind Man, The (Lawrence) 187
Bliss 54–55, 200
Blood thudded in my ears. I scuffed 773
Blue Girls 660
Boarding House, The 31–32, 36–37, 54–56, 177

Bolt, Robert
A Man for All Seasons 828–29, 1341–42, 1342

Bonnefoy, Yves
Place of the Salamander 730

Borges, Jorge Luis
Chess 690
The Blind Man 691
The Garden of Forking Paths 248

Boyle, Kay
Astronomer's Wife 32, 32

Bradstreet, Anne
Before the Birth of One of Her Children 548
To My Dear and Loving Husband 548

Breakfast is drunk down . . . Damp earth 676
Breakfast with Gerard Manley Hopkins 487, 487
Bride, The 790
Bride Comes to Yellow Sky, The 169

Brode, Anthony
Breakfast with Gerard Manley Hopkins 487, 487

Brontë, Emily
Remembrance 591

Brooks, Gwendolyn
First fight. Then fiddle 720
the mother 719

Browning, Robert
Meeting at Night 420
My Last Duchess 401, 401, 403
Soliloquy of the Spanish Cloister 588

[Buffalo Bill's] 468, 468

Bulkeley, Hunt, Willard, Hosmer, Meriam, Flint 581

Burns, Robert
A Red, Red Rose 562
Green grow the rashes 563

Busy old fool, unruly sun 398, 437, 438–39, 452

By the road to the contagious hospital 641
By the rude bridge that arched the flood 581

Byron, George Gordon, Lord
She walks in beauty 572
The Destruction of Sennacherib 458

Canonization, The 534

Carroll, Lewis (Charles Lutwidge Dodgson)
Jabberwocky 603

Carver, Raymond
Cathedral 347
Photograph of My Father in His Twenty-second Year 795

Cask of Amontillado, The 54, 76–77, 77
Cathedral 347

Cavafy, C. P.
The City 472

Channel Firing 607

Chasin, Helen
The Word Plum 450

Chaucer, Geoffrey
Truth 520

Chekhov, Anton
The Cherry Orchard 822, 829, 1060–61, 1147–48, 1148, 1185, 1270–71
The Lady with the Dog 37, 141

Cherry Orchard, The 822, 829, 1060–61, 1147–48, 1148, 1185, 1270–71

Chess 690

Chilled by the Present, its gloom and its noise 700

Chopin, Kate

The Storm 137

The Story of an Hour 6, *6, 7–10, 25, 31,
37, 53–54, 75–76*

Christmas Eve, and twelve of the clock 605

City, The 472

City Limits, The 740

Clod & the Pebble, The 560

Cold in the earth—and the deep snow piled
above thee 591

Coleridge, Samuel Taylor
Kubla Khan 570

Come live with me and be my love 529

Come, my Celia 540

*Composed upon Westminster Bridge, September
3, 1802* 566

Concord Hymn 581

Conrad, Joseph
An Outpost of Progress 38, *38, 76*

Constantly Risking Absurdity 721

Corner of the Eye, The 698

Corso, Gregory
Marriage 778

Corsons Inlet 737

Coup de Grâce 704

Crane, Stephen
The Bride Comes to Yellow Sky 169
War Is Kind 400–401, *400*

Crazy Jane Talks with the Bishop 622

Creeley, Robert
I Know a Man 741
The Language 742
The Rain 741

Crossing Brooklyn Ferry 593

Crow's First Lesson 777

Crumbling is not an instant's Act 393,
393–94, 445

"Cub" Wants to Be a Pilot 1467

Cullen, Countee
Incident 692

Cummings, E. E.
anyone lived in a pretty how town 678
[Buffalo Bill's] 468, *468*
l(a 466, *466, 467*
Me up at does *439,* 442
my father moved through dooms of love
680
nobody loses all the time 679

Dalliance of the Eagles, The 593

Dance, The 469

Danse Russe 643

Dark house, by which once more I stand
587

Darkling Thrush, The 604

De Ibarbourou, Juana
The Strong Bond 683

Death, be not proud 538

Death of a Naturalist 793

Death of a Salesman 803, *1060–61, 1270–71,
1271*

Death of Iván Ilych, The 22, *94*

Death of the Moth, The 1442, *1444*

Delight in Disorder 414

Demon Lover, The 518

Denial 543

Description of the Morning, A 554

Desert Places 632

Design 632

Destruction of Sennacherib, The 458

Dialogue Between the Soul and Body, A 550

Dickey, James
The Lifeguard 727

Dickinson, Emily
A narrow Fellow in the Grass 599
After great pain, a formal feeling comes
600
Apparently with no surprise 602
Because I could not stop for Death 435
Crumbling is not an instant's Act 393,
393–94, 445
I died for Beauty—but was scarce 601
I heard a Fly buzz—when I died 601
I like a look of Agony 599
Much Madness is divinest Sense 601
Tell all the Truth but tell it slant 602
The Bustle in a House 602
The Wind begun to knead the Grass 483
The Wind begun to rock the Grass 483
Wild Nights—Wild Nights! 600

Didion, Joan
Los Angeles Notebook 1432, *1433,
1438–39, 1441–42, 1444–45*

Digging 791

Dillard, Annie
Living Like Weasels 1448, *1449, 1451–53*

Dissertation Upon Roast Pig, A 1428–29, 1462

Distant Footsteps, The 677

Do not go gentle into that good night *398*, 717

Do not weep, maiden, for war is kind 400, *400–401*

Does the road wind up-hill all the way? *431*, 432

Doll House, A 804, 808–10, 822, 824–25, 828–29, 1060–61, 1061, 1112, 1113, 1270–71

Donne, John
    A Valediction: Forbidding Mourning 536
    Batter my heart, three-personed God 538
    Death, be not proud 538
    Hymn to God the Father 425, 426
    Meditation XVII: For Whom the Bell Tolls 1428–29, 1455
    Song 533
    The Anniversary 535
    The Canonization 534
    The Flea 537
    The Sun Rising 398, 437, 438–39, 452

Double-Play, The 426, 427

Dover Beach 597

Drawing Names 372

Drayton, Michael
    Since there's no help, come let us kiss and part 528

Dream Deferred 498

Dream Nocturne 494

Dream of Death, A 482

Dreams 795

Drink to me only with thine eyes 540

Dryden, John
    A Song for St. Cecilia's Day 552
    To the Memory of Mr. Oldham 551

Dugan, Alan
    Funeral Oration for a Mouse 731

Dulce et Decorum Est 401, 677

Dunbar, Paul Laurence
    We wear the mask 627

During Wind and Rain 447

Dusk *500*, 776

Dust of Snow 632

Eagle, The 587

Earth has not anything to show more fair 566

Easter 1916 615

Eating Poetry 788

Eberhart, Richard
    The Groundhog 692

Ecclesiastes: 3.1–8 495

Edward, Edward 397, 515

Eel, The 684

Ego Tripping 796

Eiseley, Loren
    The Judgment of the Birds 1429, 1482

Eisenberg, Ruth F.
    Jocasta 745

Elegy for Jane 706

Elegy Written in a Country Churchyard 397, 555

Elephant Is Slow to Mate—, The 645

Eliot, T. S.
    Journey of the Magi 655
    Preludes 653
    The Love Song of J. Alfred Prufrock 439, 656

Ellison, Ralph
    Battle Royal 54, 289

Emerson, Ralph Waldo
    Concord Hymn 581
    Hamatreya 581

Epigram Engraved on the Collar of a Dog Which I Gave to His Royal Highness 397, 555

Eros Turannos 626

Essay on Man, An 555

eternal mystery, The 732

Everyday Use 357

Fagles, Robert
    The Starry Night 501

Family Portrait 407

Farewell, thou child of my right hand, and joy 539

Farewell, too little, and too lately known 551

Father, The 1113, *1113, 1147–48*

Faulkner, William

A Rose for Emily 24, 30–31, 36–37, 56, 56, 62

The Bear 63–65, 218

Ferlinghetti, Lawrence
  Constantly Risking Absurdity 721
  In Goya's greatest scenes we seem to see 502

Fern Hill 715

Finkel, Donald
  Hunting Song 771

Fire and Ice 631

First Confession 773

First Death in Nova Scotia 417, 417, 418–19

First fight. Then fiddle 720

Fish, The 707

Five years have passed; five summers, with the length 566

Flea, The 537

Flee fro the prees and dwelle with soothfastnesse 520

Flood-tide below me! I see you face to face! 593

Fly, The 26, 26, 29

For God's sake hold your tongue, and let me love 534

Forster, E. M.
  Our Graves in Gallipoli 1429, 1471

Francis, Robert
  Pitcher 691

From harmony, from heavenly harmony 552

From the sea came a hand 765

Frost, Robert
  Acquainted with the Night 398, 633
  Desert Places 632
  Design 632
  Dust of Snow 632
  Fire and Ice 631
  Mending Wall 630
  Putting in the Seed 634
  Stopping by Woods on a Snowy Evening 388, *388–90, 392–93, 416, 436–37, 444–46, 454–57*
  The Road Not Taken 433, *434*
  The Silken Tent 439, 441, *442*

The Span of Life 453, *453–57*

To Earthward 634

Tree at my window 633

Funeral Oration for a Mouse 731

Garcia Lorca, Federico
  Lament for Ignacio Sanchez Mejias 397, 685

Garcia Marquez, Gabriel
  A Very Old Man with Enormous Wings 21, 330

Garden, The 651

Garden of Forking Paths, The 21, 248

Garden of Love, The 561

Gardener, The 21 163

Gather Ye rosebuds while ye may 542

Genius, technique—you'd swear the pair unsuited 559

George, 713

Gilman, Charlotte Perkins
  The Yellow Wallpaper 152

Gimpel the Fool 21, 269

Ginsberg, Allen
  A Supermarket in California 743

Giovanni, Nikki
  Dreams 795
  Ego Tripping 796

Glaspell, Susan
  Suppressed Desires, 1257, 1258

Glory be to God for dappled things 610

Go, and catch a falling star 533

Go, soul, the body's guest, 524

God tried to teach Crow how to talk 777

God's Grandeur 609

Goethe, Johann Wolfgang von
  Nature and Art 559

Going Blind 635

Good Country People 76, 317

Gratitude to Mother Earth, sailing through night and day 781

Graves, Robert
  Symptoms of Love 684

Gray, Thomas
  Elegy Written in a Country Churchyard 397, 555

Green grow the rashes 563

Gregory, Isabella Augusta Persse, Lady
  The Rising of the Moon 831–32, *832,*
    838–41
Groundhog, The 692
Gr-r-r—There go, my heart's abhorrence!
  588
Guests of the Nation 261
Gunn, Thom
  Innocence 774

"Had he and I but met 439, *439, 440*
Had we but world enough, and time 549
Hall, Donald
  Kicking the leaves 761
  My son, my executioner 760
Hamatreya 581
Hangs, a fat gun-barrel 792
Happiness has no father. No happiness ever
  733
Hardy, Thomas
  Ah, are you digging on my grave 608
  Channel Firing 607
  During Wind and Rain 447
  Neutral Tones 422
  The Darkling Thrush 604
  The Man He Killed 439, *439, 440*
  The Oxen 605
  The Ruined Maid 605
  The Voice 606
  Transformations 606
Hawk Roosting 777
Hawthorne, Nathaniel
  Wakefield 89
Hayden, Robert
  Those Winter Sundays 386, *386–87, 392,*
    400, 416, 436
H. D.
  Heat 421
He 208
He clasps the crag with crooked hands 587
He disappeared in the dead of winter 700
He is divested of the diverse world 691
He ran the course and as he ran he grew
  774
He was found by the Bureau of Statistics to
  be 699
Heaney, Seamus

Death of a Naturalist 793
Digging 791
Mid-Term Break 792
Trout 792
Hear me, O God! 451
Heat 421
Helen, thy beauty is to me 583
Helmet and rifle, pack and overcoat 427
Helprin, Mark
  North Light 370
Hemingway, Ernest
  Hills Like White Elephants 10, *10–15,*
    24–25, 30, 53, 69–70, 75
  The Short Happy Life of Francis Macomber
    24, *64–65, 228*
Her daylilies are afloat on evening 725
Her Kind 459
Herbert, George
  Denial 543
  Love (III) 546
  Man 545
  The Altar 500, *543*
  The Pulley 544
  Virtue 434, *435*
Here lies, to each her parents' ruth 539
Heroes, The 728
Herrick, Robert
  Delight in Disorder 414
  To the Virgins, to Make Much of Time 542
  Upon Julia's Clothes 542
Hills Like White Elephants 10, *10–15, 24–25,*
  30, 53, 69–70, 75
His art is eccentricity, his aim 691
His sight from ever gazing through the bars
  490
His vision, from the constantly passing bars
  490
Hollander, John
  Adam's Task 775
  Swan and Shadow 500, *776*
Hope, A. D.
  Coup de Grâce 704
  Imperial Adam 705
Hopkins, Gerard Manley
  Binsey Poplars 610
  God's Grandeur 609
  In the Valley of the Elwy 446, *446–47, 455*

Pied Beauty 610

Spring and Fall: to a Young Child 474,
    475, 475–77

The Windhover 609

Thou art indeed just, Lord 405, *439*

Housman, A. E.
    "Is my team plowing 613
    To an Athlete Dying Young 612
    When I was one-and-twenty 611
    With rue my heart is laden 612

How It Is 734

"How will he hear the bell at school 758

Hughes, Langston
    Dream Deferred 498
    Same in Blues 499

Hughes, Ted
    Crow's First Lesson 777
    Hawk Roosting 777

Huidobro, Vicente
    Ars Poetica 672

Hunger, Artist, A 181

Hunters in the Snow: Breughel 506

Hunting Song 771

Hymn to God the Father (Donne) 425, *426*

Hymn to God the Father, A (Jonson) 541

—I am a gentleman in a dustcoat trying 660

I Am Goya 503

I am his Highness' dog at Kew 397, 555

I am silver and exact. I have no
    preconceptions 782

I caught a tremendous fish 707

I caught this morning morning's minion
    king 609

I chopped down the house that you had
    been saving to live in next summer
    486, *487*

I died for Beauty—but was scarce 601

I dreamed of war-heroes, of wounded
    war-heroes 728

I dreamed that one had died in a strange
    place 482

I found a dimpled spider, fat and white 632

I grew 683

I have been one acquainted with the night
    398, 633

I have eaten 486, *486*

I have gone out, a possessed witch 459

I have met them at close of day 615

I heard a Fly buzz—when I died 601

I Know a Man 741

I know that I shall meet my fate 440

I know there is still time 756

I leant upon a coppice gate 604

I like a look of Agony 599

I look for the way 471

I met a traveler from an antique land 572

I met the Bishop on the road 622

I remember a house where all were good
    446, *446–47, 455*

I remember the neckcurls, limp and damp as
    tendrils 706

I remember this tree 755

I said to my baby 499

I sat all morning in the college sick bay 792

I sit in the top of the wood, my eyes closed
    777

I Stand Here Ironing 284

'I thought you loved me.' 'No, it was only
    fun' 404

I, too, dislike it: there are things that are
    important beyond all this fiddle 652

i used to dream militant 795

I wake to sleep, and take my waking slow
    470

I walk down the garden-paths 628

I wander thro' each charter'd street *479–82,*
    480

I wander thro' each dirty street 479, *479–82*

I wandered lonely as a cloud 410, *410–12,*
    423–24, 437, 457

I was angry with my friend 432

I was born in the congo 796

I was wrapped in black 765

I went for a walk over dunes again this
    morning 737

I went to the Garden of Love 561

I will arise and go now, and go to Innisfree
    420

I will teach you my townspeople 644

Ibsen, Henrik
    A Doll House 804, *808–10, 822, 824–25,*
    828–29, 1060–61, 1061, *1112, 1113,*
    1270–71

Idiots First 21, 299
If all the world and love were young 526
If ever two were one, then surely we 548
If we must die 670
If when my wife is sleeping 643
Imperial Adam 705
Imperial Adam, naked in the dew 705
In a prominent bar in Secaucus one day 772
In a Spring Still Not Written Of 784
In a stable of boats I lie still 727
In Bertram's Garden 734
In Breughel's great picture, The Kermess 469
In Goya's greatest scenes we seem to see 502
In his sea lit 426, *427*
In June, amid the golden fields 692
In Memoriam A. H. H. 587
In Memory of W. B. Yeats 700
In my craft or sullen art 716
In Search of Our Mothers' Gardens 1436–39,
    1510
In silence the heart raves. It utters words 697
In the cold, cold parlor 417, *417, 418–19*
In the eyes: dream. The brow as if it could
    feel 636
In the Orchard 404
In the Valley of the Elwy 446, *446–47, 455*
In Xanadu did Kubla Khan 570
Incident 692
Ink runs from the corners of my mouth 788
Innocence 774
Ionesco, Eugene
    The Lesson 822, 1233, 1234
Irish Airman Foresees His Death, An 440
"Is my team plowing 613
It is a beauteous evening 414
It little profits that an idle king 584
It was taken some time ago 794

Jabberwocky 603
Jane looks down at her organdy skirt 734
January First 710
Jewel, The 758
Jewels, The 70
Jewett, Sarah Orne
    A White Heron 131
Jiménez, Juan Ramón

Dream Nocturne 494
Nocturno Soñado 493
Jocasta 745
Jonson, Ben
    A Hymn to God the Father 541
    Come, my Celia 540
    On My First Daughter 539
    On My First Son 539
    Song: To Celia 540
    Still to be neat, still to be dressed 539
Journey of the Magi 655
Joyce, James
    Araby 30, 65, *65,* 69
    The Boarding House 31–32, 36–37, 54–56,
        177
Judgment of the Birds, The 1429, 1482
Juggler 724
Junk 460
Just at the moment the Wolf 704
Just off the highway to Rochester,
    Minnesota 759
Justice, Donald
    In Bertram's Garden 734
    Men at forty 733

Kafka, Franz
    A Hunger Artist 181
Keats, John
    La Belle Dame sans Merci 397, 576
    Ode on a Grecian Urn 579
    Ode to a Nightingale 398, 577
    On First Looking into Chapman's Homer
        464, *464, 465*
    When I have fears 575
Kennedy, X. J.
    First Confession 773
    In a prominent bar in Secaucus one day
        772
Kicking the leaves 761
Kinnell, Galway
    Saint Francis and the Sow 756
    The Apple Tree 755
    The Still Time 756
    To Christ Our Lord 754
Kipling, Rudyard
    The Gardener 21, 163

Know then thyself, presume not God to scan
555

Koch, Kenneth
*Variations on a Theme by William Carlos
Williams* 416, *417*

Kubla Khan 570

Kugelmass Episode, The 340

Kumin, Maxine
How It Is 734

l(a 466, *466*, 467

La tierra lleva por la tierra 493

Lady with the Dog, The 37, 141

Lake Isle of Innisfree, The 420

Lamb, Charles
A Dissertation Upon Roast Pig 1428–29,
1462

Lamb, The 560

Lament for Ignacio Sanchez Mejias 397, 685

Landscape with the Fall of Icarus 504

Langland, Joseph
Hunters in the Snow: Breughel 506

Language, The 742

Larkin, Philip
A Study of Reading Habits 726

Lawrence, D. H.
Snake 645
The Blind Man 187
The Elephant Is Slow to Mate 645
The Piano 484, 485

Leda and the Swan 619

Lesson, The 822, *1233*, 1234

Let me begin again 764

Let me not to the marriage of true minds
531

Let poetry be like a key 672

Let the snake wait under 642

Let us go then, you and I 656

Levertov, Denise
O Taste and See 470

Levine, Philip
Let me begin again 764

Lie, The 524

Lifeguard, The 727

Like a skein of loose silk blown against a
wall 651

Lineage 717

Lines 566

Litany in Time of Plague, A 532

Little Lamb, who made thee? 560

Living Like Weasels 1448, 1449, *1451–53*

Locate *I* 742

London 479, *479–82*, 480

Long as I paint 501

Long-Legged Fly 623

Lorca, Federico Garcia
Lament for Ignacio Sanchez Mejias 397,
685

Lord Randal 397, 511

Los Angeles Notebook 1432, 1433, *1438–39*,
1441–42, 1444–45

Lost Pilot, The 797

Love at the lips was touch 634

Love bade me welcome: yet my soul drew
back 546

Love is a universal migraine 684

"Love seeketh not Itself to please 560

Love Song of J. Alfred Prufrock, The 439 656

Love, that doth reign and live within my
thought 523

Love (III) 546

Loving in truth, and fain in verse my love
to show 527

Lowell, Amy
Patterns 628

Lowell, Robert
Skunk Hour 718

*Lying in a Hammock at William Duffy's Farm
in Pine Island, Minnesota* 757

MacLeish, Archibald
Ars Poetica 673
"Not Marble Nor the Gilded Monuments"
675
You, Andrew Marvell 674

Magi, The 615

Malamud, Bernard
Idiots First 21, 299

Man 545

Man for All Seasons, A 828–29, 1341–42,
1342

Man He Killed, The 439, *439*, 440

Mansfield, Katherine
  Bliss 54–55, 200
  The Fly 26, 26, 29
Margaret, are you grieving *474–75,* 475,
  475–77
Mark but this flea, and mark in this 537
Marlowe, Christopher
  The Passionate Shepherd to His Love 529
Marquez, Gabriel Garcia
  A Very Old Man with Enormous Wings
  21, 330
Marrakech 1418, *1419–24, 1431–32, 1438–39,*
  1441–42
Marriage 778
Marvell, Andrew
  A Dialogue Between the Soul and Body 550
  To His Coy Mistress 549
Mason, Bobbie Ann
  Drawing Names 372
Maupassant, Guy de
  The Jewels 70
May I for my own self son's truth reckon
  648
McKay, Claude
  If we must die 670
  The Tropics in New York 669
Me up at does *439,* 442
Meditation XVII: For Whom the Bell Tolls
  1428–29, 1455
Meeting at Night 420
Meinke, Peter
  Advice to My Son 430, *431*
Melting Pot, The 712
Men at forty 733
Mending Wall 630
Merry Margaret 521
Merwin, W. S.
  Separation 760
  When you go away 760
Mezey, Robert
  My Mother 788
Mid-Term Break 792
Miller, Arthur
  Death of a Salesman 803, *1060–61,*
  1270–71, 1271
Milton, John
  On the Late Massacre in Piedmont 439, 547

When I consider how my light is spent
  547
Mind 723
Mind in the purest play is like some bat 723
Miniver Cheevy 412
Miniver Cheevy, child of scorn 412
Mirabeau Bridge 492
Mirabeau Bridge, The 492
Mirror 782
Mock on, Mock on, Voltaire, Rousseau
  562
Modest Proposal, A 1457
Molière (Jean-Baptiste Poquelin)
  Tartuffe 821–22, 1005–6, 1006, *1233*
Monastic Cell at Zagorsk 787
Montale, Eugene
  The Eel 684
Moore, Marianne
  Poetry 652
Mosquito, The 784
Moss, Howard
  Shall I Compare Thee to a Summer's Day?
  488, *488*
Mother, among the dustbins 443, *443*
mother, the 719
Mr. Flood's Party 624
Much have I traveled in the realms of gold
  464, *464,* 465
Much Madness is divinest Sense 601
munching a plum on 642
Musée des Beaux Arts 505
Mutterings Over the Crib of a Deaf Child
  758
My aspens dear, whose airy cages quelled
  610
My father is sleeping. His noble face 677
my father moved through dooms of love
  680
My God, I heard this day 545
My grandmothers were strong 717
My heart aches, and a drowsy numbness
  pains *398,* 577
My Last Duchess 401, *401, 403*
My mistress's eyes are nothing like the sun
  531
My Mother 788
My mother writes from Trenton 788

My Papa's Waltz 390, *390–92*, *400, 409*,
445
My prime of youth is but a frost of cares
528
My son, my executioner 760
My swirling wants. Your frozen lips 769

Naming of Parts 406
Nashe, Thomas
    A Litany in Time of Plague 532
Nature and Art 559
Nautilus Island's hermit 718
Neither on horseback nor seated 729
Neruda, Pablo
    The United Fruit Co. 695
    The word 694
Neutral Tones 422
Never until the mankind making 714
Night-Pieces: For a Child 768
No, not far beneath some foreign sky then
662
No one has taken anything away 670
No people are uninteresting 785
nobody loses all the time 679
Nocturno Soñado 493
noiseless patient spider, A 592
North Light 370
"Not Marble Nor the Gilded Monuments"
    (MacLeish) 675
Not marble, nor the gilded monuments
    (Shakespeare) 530
Notes of a Native Son 1435–39, 1488
Now as at all times I can see in the mind's
    eye 615
Now as I was young and easy under the
    apple boughs 715
Now hardly here and there a hackney-coach
554
Nymph's Reply to the Shepherd, The 526

O my luve's like a red, red rose 562
O Rose, thou art sick 508
O Taste and See 470
O what can ail thee, Knight at arms *397*,
576
O what is that sound 703
"O where are you going?" 702

"O where ha' you been, Lord Randal, my
    son? *397,* 511
"O where have you been, my long, long
    love 518
O wild West Wind, thou breath of
    Autumn's being 573
O wind, rend open the heat 421
O'Connor, Flannery
    Good Country People 76, 317
O'Connor, Frank
    Guests of the Nation 261
October. Here in this dank, unfamiliar
    kitchen 795
Ode on a Grecian Urn 579
Ode to a Nightingale 398, 577
Ode to the West Wind 573
Oedipus Rex 820, 843–44, 844, 1060–61
Of Love 1429, 1454
Of Revenge 1446
Of Youth and Age 1424–27, 1425, *1429,*
    1432, 1438–39
Oh to be a bride 790
Oh, who shall from this dungeon raise
550
Old Eben Flood, climbing alone one night
624
Olsen, Tillie
    I Stand Here Ironing 284
"O'Melia, my dear, this does everything
    crown! 605
On First Looking Into Chapman's Homer 464,
    464, 465
On My First Daughter 539
On My First Son 539
On the fine wire of her whine she walked
784
On the Late Massacre in Piedmont 439, 547
Once more the storm is howling, and half
    hid 620
Once More to the Lake 1473
Once riding in old Baltimore 692
One day I wrote her name upon the strand
523
One must have a mind of winter 637
Orwell, George
    Marrakech 1418, *1419–24, 1431–32,*
    1438–39, 1441–42

Shooting an Elephant 1429, 1441–42, 1445–46, 1477
Our Daily Bread 676
Our Graves in Gallipoli 1429, 1471
Out in this desert we are testing bombs 769
Outpost of Progress, An 38, 38, 76
Over my head, I see the bronze butterfly 757
Owen, Wilfred
    Dulce et Decorum Est 401, 677
Oxen, The 605
Ozymandias 572

Panther, Der 489
Panther, The 490
Passionate Shepherd to His Love, The 529
Pasternak, Boris
    Winter Night 668
Patterns 628
Paz, Octavio
    January First 710
People 785
Petronius
    Satyricon 17, 17
    The Widow of Ephesus 18, 20
Piano, The 484, 485
Piazza Piece 660
Pied Beauty 610
Pirandello, Luigi
    War 30, 69, 83–84, 84
Pitcher 691
Place of the Salamander 730
Plath, Sylvia
    Mirror 782
    Tulips 783
Poe, Edgar Allan
    The Cask of Amontillado 54, 76–77, 77
    To Helen 583
Poetics 471
Poetry 652
Poison Tree, A 432
Ponsot, Marie
    Summer Sestina 725
Pont Mirabeau, Le 491
Pope, Alexander
    An Essay on Man 555

Epigram Engraved on the Collar of a Dog Which I Gave to His Royal Highness 397, 555
    Sound and Sense 448
Porter, Katherine Anne
    He 208
Portion of this yew 606
Portrait of My Father as a Young Man 636
Pound, Ezra
    The Garden 651
    The River-Merchant's Wife: A Letter 651
    The Seafarer 648
Prayer for My Daughter, A 620
Prayer for the Great Family 781
Preludes 603
Premonition, The 707
Prévert, Jacques
    Family Portrait 407
Prodigal Son, The 3, 4–5, 6, 25, 70
Pulley, The 544
Putting in the Seed 634

Quail and rabbit hunters, with tawny hounds 506

Rain, The 741
Raleigh, Sir Walter
    The Lie 524
    The Nymph's Reply to the Shepherd 526
Randall, Dudley
    George 713
    The Melting Pot 712
Ransom, John Crowe
    Bells for John Whiteside's Daughter 659
    Blue Girls 660
    Piazza Piece 660
    Winter Remembered 661
Rape 415
Reapers 682
Red, Red, Rose, A 562
Red Wheelbarrow, The 461
Reed, Henry
    Naming of Parts 406
Refusal to Mourn the Death, by Fire, of a Child in London, A 714
Remembrance 591
Requiem 662

Rich, Adrienne
  A Valediction Forbidding Mourning 769
  Aunt Jennifer's Tigers 770
  Night-Pieces: For a Child 768
  Rape 415
  Trying to Talk with a Man 769
Richard Cory (Robinson) 497
Richard Cory (Simon) 497
Right Stuff, The 1501
Rilke, Rainer Maria
  Der Panther 489
  Going Blind 635
  Portrait of My Father as a Young Man 636
  Spanish Dancer 637
  The Panther 490
  The Swan 636
Ring of Time, The 1413, 1414, *1416–18*,
  1429, *1441–42*
Ringing the Bells 767
Rising of the Moon, The 831–32, 832, *838–*
  41
River-Merchant's Wife: A Letter, The 651
Road Not Taken, The 433, *434*
Robinson, Edwin Arlington
  Eros Turannos 626
  Miniver Cheevy 412
  Mr. Flood's Party 624
  Richard Cory 497
  The Sheaves 625
Roethke, Theodore
  Elegy for Jane 706
  My Papa's Waltz 390, *390–92*, *400*, *409*,
  445
  The Premonition 707
  The Waking 398, 470
Rose for Emily, A 24, *30–31*, *36–37*, 56, *56*,
  62
Rossetti, Christina
  Up-Hill 431, 432
Ruined Maid, The 605

Sailing to Byzantium 619
Saint Francis and the Sow 756
Same in Blues 499
Satyricon 17, *17*
Scholars, The 615

Seafarer, The 648
Second Coming, The 617
Seeger, Pete
  Turn! Turn! Turn! 496
Sein Blick ist vom Vorübergehn der Stäbe
  489
Separation 760
September rains falls on the house *398*, 709
Serious over my cereals I broke one
  breakfast my fast 487, *487*
Sestina 398, 709
Set in their studious corners, the players
  690
Sexton, Anne
  Her Kind 459
  Ringing the Bells 767
  The Starry Night 766
  Two Hands 765
  Us 765
Shakespeare, William
  Let me not to the marriage of true minds
    531
  My mistress' eyes are nothing like the sun
    531
  Not marble, nor the gilded monuments
    530
  Shall I compare thee to a summer's day?
    488, *488*
  Th' expense of spirit in a waste of shame
    531
  That time of year thou may'st in me
    behold *417*, 424, *424–25*, *454–57*,
    463–64
  The Tragedy of Othello, 820, *825–28*, *918*,
    919, *1060–61*
  When in disgrace with fortune and men's
    eyes 530
Shall I Compare Thee to a Summer's Day?
  (Moss), 488, *488*
Shall I compare thee to a summer's day?
  (Shakespeare), 488, *488*
Shall I say how it is in your clothes? 734
Shaw, Bernard
  Arms and the Man, 810–12, ·814–15,
    821–22, *824–25*, *828*, *1185*, 1186, *1233*,
    1270–71
She fears him, and will always ask 626

She is in a field a silken tent *439*, 441, *442*
She sat just like the others at the table 635
She walks in beauty 572
She was a Phantom of delight 565
Sheaves, The 625
Shelley, Percy Bysshe
  Ode to the West Wind 573
  Ozymandias 572
Shirley, James
  The glories of our blood and state 462
Shooting an Elephant 1429, 1441–42,
  1445–46, 1477
Short Happy Life of Francis Macomber, The
  24, 64–65, 228
Should I get married? Should I be good?
  778
Shower of Gold, A 21, 335
Sick Rose, The 508
Sidney, Sir Philip
  Astrophel and Stella 527
  Thou blind man's mark 527
Silken Tent, The 439, 441, *442*
Silko, Leslie
  Yellow Woman 21, 363
Simon, Paul
  Richard Cory 497
Simpson, Louis
  The Battle 427
  The Heroes 728
  Walt Whitman at Bear Mountain 729
Since there's no help, come let us kiss and
  part 528
Singer, Isaac Bashevis
  Gimpel the Fool 21, 269
Sir Patrick Spens 513
Skelton, John
  To Mistress Margaret Hussey 521
Skirting the river road, (my forenoon walk,
  my rest,) 593
Skunk Hour 718
Slush, my brother said, it's 735
Smith, Stevie
  Mother, among the dustbins 443, *443*
Snake 645
Snake, The 254
Sniffing through grey ascetic noses 787

Snodgrass, W. D.
  April Inventory 743
Snow falling and night falling fast, oh, fast
  632
Snow Man, The 637
Snow, snow over the whole land 668
Snyder, Gary
  Prayer for the Great Family 781
so much depends 461
Softly, in the dusk, a woman is singing to
  me 485
Soliloquy of the Spanish Cloister 588
Solitary Reaper, The 564
Some say the world will end in fire 631
Something there is that doesn't love a wall
  630
Somewhere beneath that piano's superb sleek
  black 484
Song 533
Song for St. Cecilia's Day, A 552
Song: To Celia 540
Sonnets from China, XVIII 700
Sophocles
  Antigonê 803, 815–18, 824, 830, 843,
    885
  Oedipus Rex 820, 843–44, 844, 1060–61
Sorrow is my own yard 640
Sort of a Song, A 642
Sound and Sense 448
Sous le pont Mirabeau coule la Seine 491
Span of Life, The 453, 453–57
Spanish Dancer 637
Spenser, Edmund
  One day I wrote her name upon the
    strand 523
Spring and All 641
Spring and Fall: to a Young Child 474–75,
  475, 475–77
Stafford, Jean
  Bad Characters 305
Stafford, William
  Traveling through the dark 711
Starry Night, The (Fagles) 501
Starry Night, The (Sexton) 766
Steinbeck, John
  The Snake 254

Stevens, Wallace
    The house was quiet and the world was calm 640
    The Snow Man 637
    Thirteen Ways of Looking at a Blackbird 638
Still Time, The 756
Still to be neat, still to be dressed 539
Stopping by Woods on a Snowy Evening 388, *388–90, 392–93, 416, 436–37, 444–46, 454–57*
Storm, The 137
Story of an Hour, The 6, *6, 7–10, 25, 31, 37, 53–54, 75–76*
Strand, Mark
    Eating Poetry 788
Strindberg, August
    The Father 1113, *1113, 1147–48*
Strong Bond, The 683
Stuart, Muriel
    In the Orchard 404
Study of Reading Habits, A 726
Summer Sestina 725
Sun Rising, The 398, *437, 438–39, 452*
Sundays too my father got up early 386, *386–87, 392, 400, 416, 436*
Supermarket in California, A 743
Suppressed Desires 1257, 1258
Surrey, Henry Howard, Earl of
    Love, that doth reign and live within my thought, 523
Swan, The 636
Swan and Shadow 500, 776
Sweet day, so cool, so calm, so bright 434, *434*
Swenson, May
    The Universe 449
    The Watch 722
    Women should be pedestals 722
Swift, Jonathan
    A Description of the Morning 554
    A Modest Proposal 1457
Symptoms of Love 684

Tartuffe 821–22, 1005–6, 1006, *1233*
Tate, James
    The Lost Pilot 797

Tell all the Truth but tell it slant 602
Ten Definitions of Lifetime 735
Tennyson, Alfred, Lord
    In Memoriam A. H. H. 587
    The Eagle 587
    Tithonus 585
    Ulysses 584
Th' expense of spirit in a waste of shame 531
That civilization may not sink 623
That is no country for old men. The young 619
That night your great guns, unawares 607
That time of year thou may'st in me behold 417, 424, *424–25, 454–57, 463–64*
That's my last Duchess painted on the wall 401, *401, 403*
The Assyrian came down like the wolf on the fold 458
The bud 756
The Bustle in a House 602
The curfew tolls the knell of parting day *397, 555*
The earth leads by the earth 494
The earth leads through the earth 494
The eel, the 684
The elephant, the huge old beast 645
The eternal mystery of ours 732
The force that through the green fuse drives the flower 713
The fox came lolloping, lolloping 771
The glories of our blood and state 467
The gray sea and the long black land 420
The green catalpa tree has turned 743
The house was quiet and the world was calm 640
The king sits in Dumferling toune 513
The legs of the elk punctured the snow's crust 754
The long love that in my thought doth harbor 522
The mother knits 407
The old dog barks backward without getting up 453, *453–57*
The poem is just beyond the corner of the eye 698

The praisers of women in their proud and beautiful poems 675

The sea is calm tonight 597

The startled salamander freezes 730

The three men coming down the winter hill 507

The time you won your town the race 612

The town does not exist 766

The trees are in their autumn beauty 618

The trick is, to live your days 430, *431*

The tulips are too excitable, it is winter here 783

The way a crow 632

The whiskey on your breath 390, *390–92, 400, 409, 445*

The Wind begun to knead the Grass 483

The Wind begun to rock the Grass 483

"The wind doth blow today, my love 517

The winter evening settles down 653

The woods decay, the woods decay and fall 585

The word 694

The word *plum* is delicious 450

The world is 470

The world is charged with the grandeur of God 609

The world is too much with us 564

The year's doors open 710

Theater 215

There is a cop who is both prowler and father 415

There is a magic melting pot 712

There is this cave 758

There was such speed in her little body 659

They flee from me 522

They say that Richard Cory owns one-half of this whole town 497

They sing their dearest songs 447

Thirteen Ways of Looking at a Blackbird 638

This Is a Photograph of Me 794

This is Just to Say 486, *486*

This laboring through what is still undone 636

This, Lord, was an anxious brother and 731

This morning 784

Thomas, Dylan
  A Refusal to Mourn the Death, by Fire, of a Child in London 714
  Do not go gentle into that good night *398*, 717
  Fern Hill 715
  In my craft or sullen art 716
  The force that through the green fuse drives the flower 713

Thoreau, Henry David
  The Battle of the Ants 1439

Those Winter Sundays 386, *386–87, 392, 400, 416, 436*

Thou art indeed just, Lord 405, *439*

Thou blind man's mark 527

Thou, paw-paw-paw; thou, glurd; thou, spotted 775

Thou still unravished bride of quietness 579

Tichborne, Chidiock
  Tichborne's Elegy 528

Tithonus 585

To a Poor Old Woman 642

To an Athlete Dying Young 612

To Christ Our Lord 754

To Earthward 634

To every thing there is a season, and a time to every 495

To everything 496

To Helen 583

To His Coy Mistress 549

To Mistress Margaret Hussey 521

To My Dear and Loving Husband 548

To the Memory of Mr. Oldham 551

To the Virgins, to Make Much of Time 542

Today we have naming of parts. Yesterday 406

Tolstoy, Leo Nikolaievich
  The Death of Iván Ilych 22, 94

Toomer, Jean
  Reapers 682
  Theater 215

Tract 644

Tragedy of Othello, The 820, *825–28, 918, 919, 1060–61*

Transformations 606

Traveling through the dark 711

Tree at my window 633

Tropics in New York, The 669

Trout 792

True ease in writing comes from art, not chance 448

True Love 697

Truth 520

Trying to Talk with a Man 769

Tsvetayeva, Marina
  No one has taken anything away 670
  Yesterday he still looked in my eyes 671

Tulips 783

Turn! Turn! Turn! 496

Turning and turning in the widening gyre 617

Twa Corbies, The 512

Twain, Mark
  "Cub" Wants to Be a Pilot 1467

'Twas brillig, and the slithy toves 603

Twirling your blue skirts, travelling the sward 660

Two evils, monstrous either one apart 661

Two Hands 765

Two roads diverged in a yellow wood 433, *434*

Tyger, The 561

Tyger! Tyger! burning bright 561

Ulysses 584

Under the Mirabeau Bridge the Seine 492

Under the Mirabeau Bridge there flows the Seine 492

United Fruit Co., The 695

Universe, The 449

Unknown Citizen, The 699

Unquiet Grave, The 517

Updike, John
  The Mosquito 784

Up-Hill 431, 432

Upon Julia's Clothes 542

Us 765

Valediction: Forbidding Mourning, A (Donne) 536

Valediction Forbidding Mourning, A (Rich) 769

Vallejo, César
  Our Daily Bread 676
  The Distant Footsteps 677

Variations on a Theme by William Carlos Williams 486, *487*

Very Old Man with Enormous Wings, A 21, 330

Vigil strange I kept on the field one night 592

Virtue 434, *435*

Voice, The 606

Voznesensky, Andrey
  I Am Goya 503
  Monastic Cell at Zagorsk 787

Wakefield 89

Waking The 398, *470*

Walker, Alice
  Everyday Use 357
  In Search of Our Mothers' Gardens *1436–39, 1446,* 1510

Walker, Margaret
  Lineage 717

Walking this field I remember 707

Wallace, Robert
  In a Spring Still Not Written Of 784
  The Double-Play 426, *427*

Walt Whitman at Bear Mountain 729

War 30, 69, *83–84,* 84

War Is Kind 400, *400–401*

Warren, Robert Penn
  The Corner of the Eye 698
  True Love 697

Watch, The 722

We sat together at one summer's end *478,* 614

We stood by a pond that winter day 422

We wear the mask 627

Welty, Eudora
  A Worn Path 278

Western Wind 406

Western wind, when will thou blow 406

What 449

What happens to a dream deferred 498

What thoughts I have of you tonight, Walt Whitman, for I walked down the 743

When getting my nose in a book 726

When God at first made man 544
When I 722
When I consider how my light is spent
    547
When I have fears 575
When I heard the learn'd astronomer *437,
    445, 455–57, 465, 465, 466*
When I was a boy desiring the title of man
    713
When I was one-and-twenty 611
When in disgrace with fortune and men's
    eyes 530
When my devotions could not pierce 543
When she learned the king's power 745
When the trumpet sounded, it was 695
When you consider the radiance, that it does
    not withhold 740
When you go away 760
Whenas in silks my Julia goes 542
Whenever Richard Cory went down town
    497
Where long the shadows of the wind had
    rolled 625
While my hair was still cut straight across
    my forehead 651
White, E. B.
    Once More to the Lake 1473
    The Ring of Time 1413, 1414, *1416–18,
        1429, 1441–42*
White Heron, A 131
Whitman, Walt
    A noiseless patient spider 592
    Crossing Brooklyn Ferry 593
    The Dalliance of the Eagles 593
    Vigil strange I kept on the field one night
        592
    When I heard the learn'd astronomer *437,
        445, 455–57, 465, 465, 466*
Who says you're like one of the dog days?
    488, *488*
Whose woods these are I think I know 388,
    *388–90, 392–93, 416, 436–37, 444–46,
    454–57*
"Why does your brand sae drap wi' bluid
    397, 515
Widow of Ephesus, The 18, *20*
Widow's Lament in Springtime, The 640

Wilbur, Richard
    Juggler 724
    Junk 460
    Mind 723
Wild Nights—Wild Nights! 600
Wild Swans at Coole, The 618
Williams, William Carlos
    A Sort of a Song 642
    Danse Russe 643
    Landscape with the Fall of Icarus 504
    Spring and All 641
    The Dance 469
    The Red Wheelbarrow 461
    The Widow's Lament in Springtime 640
    The Young Housewife 643
    This is Just to Say 486, *486*
    To a Poor Old Woman 642
    Tract 644
Wilt thou forgive that sin where I begun
    425, *426*
Windhover, The 609
Winter Landscape 507
Winter Night 668
Winter Remembered 661
With rue my heart is laden 612
Wolf and the Mastiff, The 17, *17*
Wolfe, Tom
    The Right Stuff 1501
Woman much missed, how you call to me,
    call to me 606
Woman to Child 428
Women should be pedestals 722
Woolf, Virginia
    The Death of the Moth 1442, *1444*
Word Plum, The 450
Wordsworth, William
    *Composed upon Westminster Bridge,
        September 3, 1802* 566
    I wandered lonely as a cloud 410, *410–12,
        423–24, 437, 457*
    It is a beauteous evening 414
    Lines 566
    She was a Phantom of delight 565
    The Solitary Reaper 564
    The world is too much with us 564
Worn Path, A 278
Wright, James

A Blessing 759
Lying in a Hammock at William Duffy's Farm in Pine Island, Minnesota 757
Mutterings Over the Crib of a Deaf Child 758
The Jewel 758
Wright, Judith
   Woman to Child 428
Wyatt, Thomas
   The long love that in my thought doth harbor 522
   They flee from me 522

Yeats, William Butler
   A Dream of Death 482
   A Prayer for My Daughter 620
   Adam's Curse 478, 614
   An Irish Airman Foresees His Death 440
   Crazy Jane Talks with the Bishop 622
   Easter 1916 615
   Leda and the Swan 619
   Long-Legged Fly 623

Sailing to Byzantium 619
The Lake Isle of Innisfree 420
The Magi 615
The Scholars 615
The Second Coming 617
The Wild Swans at Coole 618
Yellow Wallpaper, The 152
Yellow Woman 21, 363
Yesterday he still looked in my eyes 671
Yevtushenko, Yevgeny
   People 785
You, Andrew Marvell 674
You Can Rely on Him 733
You come to fetch me from my work tonight 634
You said, "I will go to another land, I will go to another sea 472
You sleeping I bend to cover 768
You who were darkness warmed my flesh 428
Young Housewife, The 643
Your absence has gone through me 760
Your face did not rot 797

About the Author

Robert DiYanni is an Associate Professor of English at Pace University, Pleasantville, where he directs the Writing Program and teaches British and American Literature and Composition. He received his B.A. from Rutgers and his Ph.D. from the City University of New York. His publications include articles and reviews on various aspects of English and American literature and on rhetoric and composition. Included also are a number of textbooks: *Connections: Reading, Writing, and Thinking* (Boynton/Cook, 1985); *Modern American Prose* with John Clifford (Random House, 1986); and a pair of collaborations with Eric Gould and Bill Smith: *The Art of Reading* and *The Craft of Writing,* both forthcoming from Random House. He is currently writing a book on George Orwell.